Health Information Management

Concepts, Principles, and Practice

Fourth Edition

Kathleen M. LaTour, MA, RHIA, FAHIMA
Shirley Eichenwald Maki, MBA, RHIA, FAHIMA
Pamela Oachs, MA, RHIA

Editors

AHIMA PRESS

ii

ISBN: 978-1-58426-359-3
AHIMA Product No.: AB103312

AHIMA Staff:
Claire Blondeau, MBA, Managing Editor
Jason O. Malley, Director Content Creation and Development
Jessica Block, MA, Assistant Editor
Katie Greenock, MS, Editorial and Production Coordinator
Ashley Sullivan, Project Editor

The websites listed in this book were current and valid as of the date of publication. However, webpage addresses and the information on them may change at any time. The user is encouraged to perform his or her own general web searches to locate any site addresses listed here that are no longer valid.

CPT® is a registered trademark of the American Medical Association. All other copyrights and trademarks mentioned in this book are the possession of their respective owners. AHIMA makes no claim of ownership by mentioning products that contain such marks.

For more information, including updates, about AHIMA Press publications, visit http://www.ahima.org/publications/press.aspx.

American Health Information Management Association
233 North Michigan Avenue, 21st Floor
Chicago, Illinois 60601-5809
ahima.org

Table of Contents

About the Editors and Contributors   vii
Foreword   xvii
Acknowledgments   xix

Part I   Health Information Management

Chapter 1   **Introduction** **3**
Shirley Eichenwald Maki, MBA, RHIA, FAHIMA, Kathleen M. LaTour, MA, RHIA, FAHIMA, and Pamela K. Oachs, MA, RHIA

Chapter 2   **The US Healthcare Delivery System** **7**
Sandra R. Fuller, MA, RHIA, FAHIMA

Chapter 3   **The Health Information Management Profession** **49**
Susan Parker, MEd, RHIA

Chapter 4   **Health Information Systems: Supporting Technologies and Systems Development** **81**
Ryan H. Sandefer, MA, CPHIT, and Patricia B. Seidl, RHIA

Chapter 5   **Electronic Health Records: Conceptual Framework** **113**
Margret K. Amatayakul, MBA, RHIA, CHPS, CPEHR, FHIMSS

Part II   Healthcare Data Management

Chapter 6   **Healthcare Data Life Cycle: Governance and Stewardship** **157**
Linda L. Kloss, RHIA, CAE, FAHIMA

Chapter 7   **Data Capture, Maintenance, and Quality** **169**
Valerie J.M. Watzlaf, PhD, RHIA, FAHIMA

Chapter 8   **Health Informatics Standards** **193**
Kathy Giannangelo, MA, RHIA, CCS, CPHIMS, FAHIMA

Chapter 9   **Health Information Exchange and the Nationwide Health Information Network** **217**
Cheryl Stephens, MBA, PhD

PART III   Development of the Patient Health Record

Chapter 10   **Content and Structure of Paper and Hybrid Records** **237**
Elizabeth D. Bowman, MPA, RHIA, FAHIMA, and
Rebecca B. Reynolds, EdD, RHIA

Chapter 11 **Electronic Health Records: Application in Practice**..**281**
Danika Brinda, MA, RHIA, CHPS, and Janelle Wapola, MA, RHIA

Chapter 12 **Legal Issues in Health Information Management**.......................................**299**
Lynda A. Russell, EdD, JD, RHIA, CHP, and Rita K. Bowen, MA, RHIA, CHPS

Chapter 13 **Ethical Issues in Health Information Management**.................................**341**
Laurinda B. Harman, PhD, RHIA, FAHIMA

PART IV Aggregate Healthcare Data

Chapter 14 **Secondary Records and Healthcare Databases**...**367**
Marcia Y. Sharp, EdD, MBA, RHIA

Chapter 15 **Clinical Classifications and Terminologies**..**387**
Brooke Palkie, MA, RHIA

Chapter 16 **Reimbursement Methodologies**..**411**
Anita C. Hazelwood, MLS, RHIA, FAHIMA, and Carol A. Venable, MPH, RHIA, FAHIMA

Chapter 17 **Revenue Cycle Management**..**459**
Colleen Malmgren, MS, RHIA, and C. Jeanne Solberg, MA, RHIA

PART V Comparative Healthcare Data

Chapter 18 **Healthcare Statistics**..**481**
Loretta A. Horton, MEd, RHIA

Chapter 19 **Healthcare Data Analytics**...**525**
Susan White, PhD, CHDA

Chapter 20 **Research Methods**..**545**
Elizabeth Forrestal, PhD, RHIA, CCS, FAHIMA

Chapter 21 **Biomedical and Research Support**...**607**
Valerie J.M. Watzlaf, PhD, RHIA, FAHIMA

Chapter 22 **Clinical Quality Management**...**649**
Chris R. Elliott, MS, RHIA

PART VI Management of Health Information Services

Chapter 23 **Managing and Leading During Organization Change**...............................**683**
David X. Swenson, PhD

Chapter 24 **Human Resources Management and Employee Training and Development**...........**717**
Karen R. Patena, MBA, RHIA, and Madonna M. LeBlanc, MA, RHIA

Chapter 25 **Financial Management**...**761**
Rick Revoir, EdD, MBA, CPA

Chapter 26 **Work Design and Process Improvement**...**795**
Pamela K. Oachs, MA, RHIA

Chapter 27   **Project Management** **835**
Patricia B. Seidl, RHIA

Chapter 28   **Managing Organizational Compliance and Risk** **851**
Carol Ann Quinsey, MS, RHIA, CHPS

Chapter 29   **Strategic Thinking: Strategic Management and Leading Change** **865**
Susan E. McClernon, MHA, FACHE

Chapter 30   **Envisioning the Future of the Health Information Management Profession**..........**885**
Bonnie S. Cassidy, MPA, RHIA, FAHIMA, FHIMSS, 2011 President of AHIMA

Glossary, Index, and Appendices

Glossary **893**

Index **959**

Appendix A   **Sample Documentation Forms**..*(Online Resource)*

Appendix B   **AHIMA Code of Ethics, Standards of Ethical Coding, and Ethical Standards
for Clinical Documentation Improvement Professionals**....................................*(Online Resource)*

Appendix C   **Answers to Check Your Understanding Exercises** ....*(Online Resource)*

Appendix D   **Web Resources**..*(Online Resource)*

Kathleen M. LaTour, MA, RHIA, FAHIMA, is an assistant professor and former chair of the department of healthcare informatics and information management (HIIM) at the College of St. Scholastica in Duluth, Minnesota. She is an active member of the Minnesota Health Information Management Association, where she was selected as the Distinguished Member in 1992. She has served as chair and member of many AHIMA councils and as a member of AHIMA's Board of Directors from 1993 to 1997. She participated in the development of the AHIMA Model Curricula for both bachelor's- and master's-level programs. She is currently a member of the Edictorial Review Board for Perspectives on Health Information Management (PHIM) and is a CAHIIM accreditation reviewer. She has authored several articles and contributed a chapter to *Health Information Management Technology: An Applied Approach,* second edition, a textbook published by AHIMA in 2006. She was awarded fellowship in AHIMA in recognition of sustained contributions to the field of HIM and, in 2004, was corecipient of AHIMA's Legacy Award. She currently serves on the board of the Community Health Information Collaborative (CHIC) in Duluth and on the board of directors of the Benedictine Health System in Duluth and Cambridge, MN.

Shirley Eichenwald Maki, MBA, RHIA, FAHIMA, is an assistant professor in the department of healthcare informatics and information management at the College of St. Scholastica in Duluth. From 2002 to 2008, she served as project director for The ATHENS Project, a health sciences EHR curriculum project funded by a grant from the US Department of Education, Title III program. She is the 2001 recipient of the College of St. Scholastica's Max H. Lavine Award for Teaching Excellence. A former AHIMA board member and former president of AHIMA, she was awarded the association's Distinguished Member Award in 1998. She has held the position of director of education and accreditation at AHIMA. She was awarded fellowship in AHIMA in recognition of sustained contributions to the field of HIM and, in 2004, was corecipient of

AHIMA's Legacy Award. Shirley is a coauthor of the text *Using the Electronic Health Record in the Health Care Provider Practice*, second edition, published in 2012 by Delmar Cengage Learning.

Pamela K. Oachs, MA, RHIA, is an assistant professor in the College of St. Scholastica's Health Informatics and Information Management Department. She teaches courses related to health information technology, system development and implementation, workflow redesign, healthcare management, and applied research. She has more than 15 years of healthcare experience. Her career has included a variety of positions, both managerial and professional, in the areas of utilization management, quality improvement, medical staff credentialing, Joint Commission coordination, information technology, project management, and patient access. She has been involved in system implementations, both small and large, in a variety of healthcare settings. She has served on the Board of Directors of the Minnesota Health Information Management Association and is currently president of the Northeastern Minnesota Health Information Management Association.

Amy L. Watters, MA, RHIA, FAHIMA, is the editor of the Instructor Manual for the 4th edition of this textbook. She is an assistant professor and director of the HIM graduate program at the College of St. Scholastica. She has more than 15 years of HIM experience. Her career has included a variety of positions, including release of information experience, HIM and admitting management experience in acute-care settings, product management experience at a software and consulting firm, and HIPAA security experience at a multispecialty physician group. She has served on the board of the Minnesota Health Information Management Association and the Minnesota Healthcare Information and Management Systems Society, and is past president of the Northeastern Minnesota Health Information Management Association. She coauthored a chapter in the third edition of this textbook, and was awarded Fellowship in AHIMA in 2011.

Margret K. Amatayakul, MBA, RHIA, CHPS, FHIMSS, is president of Margret\A Consulting, LLC, in Schaumburg, Illinois, a consulting firm specializing in electronic health records, HIPAA and HITECH, and associated HIM standards and regulations. She has more than 40 years of experience in national and international HIM. A leading authority on electronic health record (EHR) strategies for healthcare organizations, she has extensive experience in EHR selection and project management, and she formed and served as executive director of the Computer-based Patient Record Institute (CPRI). Other positions held include associate executive director of AHIMA, associate professor at the University of Illinois, and director of medical record services at the Illinois Eye and Ear Infirmary. She is a much-sought-after speaker, has published extensively, and has earned several professional service awards. Amatayakul also serves as an adjunct faculty member of the College of St. Scholastica.

Rita K. Bowen, MA, RHIA, CHPS, has nearly 30 years of experience in healthcare information management. She is currently the senior vice president of HIM Best Practices and privacy officer for HealthPort Corporation in Alpharetta, Georgia. She previously served as the enterprise director of Health Information Services and served as their first privacy officer for Erlanger Health System in Chattanooga, Tennessee for thirteen years. She has held positions as director of health information services, marketing director, and medical records consultant at various hospitals and medical services companies throughout the United States. Bowen has an MA in health information management technology from the College of St. Scholastica and earned her bachelor's degree in medical science from Emory University in Atlanta. She has a continuous history of activities with AHIMA and the Tennessee HIMA. She served on AHIMA's Board of Directors from 2006 to 2011 and as president in 2010. Rita received AHIMA's Triumph Mentor award and is proud to continue service as an adjunct faculty for UT Memphis's Master of HIIM program and the Associate program at Chattanooga State Technical Community College.

Elizabeth D. Bowman, MPA, RHIA, FAHIMA, has served as a professor in the HIIM program at the University of Tennessee Health Science Center in Memphis for more than 30 years. She received a bachelor's degree from Millsaps College and a master's degree in public administration with a concentration in healthcare administration from the University of Memphis. Elizabeth is a fellow of the American Health Information Management Association. She has served as chair of the AHIMA Professional Development Committee as well as the AHIMA Assembly on Education. She received the AHIMA Educator Award in 1999 and the University of Tennessee Alumni Association Outstanding Teacher Award in 2009. She is a recipient of the Tennessee Health Information Management Association's Distinguished Member Award as well as its Educator/Mentor Award. In addition, she has served as a commissioner on the Commission on Accreditation for Health Informatics and Information Management Education and as chair of the commission in 2007. Currently she is a member of the CAHIIM Board of Surveyors.

Danika E. Brinda, MA, RHIA, CHPS, is an assistant professor in the Health Information and Informatics Department at the College of St. Scholastica in Duluth, Minnesota. She teaches HIM concepts, HIM Technologies, Medicolegal Issues, and Clinical Data Management. She also works as a HIT consultant for REACH, the regional extension center for Minnesota and North Dakota. She also is the privacy and security subject matter expert for REACH. Danika is the 2010 recipient of the AHIMA Rising Star Triumph Award. Danika is current pursuing her PhD in information technology with a focus in information assurance and security from Capella University. She has received both her undergraduate and graduate degrees from the College of St. Scholastica.

Bonnie S. Cassidy, MPA, RHIA, FAHIMA, FHIMSS, was the 2011 President of AHIMA serving as the Chairman of the AHIMA Board. She continues to serve on the Board as the 2012 Past President Director. Bonnie previously served on the AHIMA Board as a Director from 2006 to 2008. Bonnie is the Vice President of HIM Innovation for QuadraMed, having previously served as the Vice President of HIM Product Management. Bonnie is an AHIMA Academy ICD-10-CM/PCS Certificate Holder and Ambassador. Prior to joining QuadraMed, Bonnie served as an executive with the Certification Commission for Healthcare Information Technology (CCHIT). Bonnie is an experienced healthcare consultant and advisor, having worked for the national management consulting firms of Price Waterhouse (now PwC) and Ernst & Young, and was an HIM Administrator at two major teaching hospitals including the Cleveland Clinic Foundation. Bonnie was the President of the Ohio Health Information Management Association and was honored to receive the OHIMA Distinguished Member Award. Ms. Cassidy is the recipient of three AHIMA awards: Legacy Award, Volunteer Excellence Award, and Professional Achievement Award.

Chris Elliott, MS, RHIA, holds a master's degree in information systems and has pursued significant graduate study in medical informatics at the University of Utah. He recently retired as director of Health Information Services and privacy officer designee at San Francisco General Hospital Medical Center after 40 years of public service in hospitals and health professions education settings.

Sandra R. Fuller, MA, RHIA, FAHIMA, is an independent consultant serving healthcare and association clients. She was the Executive Vice President and Chief Operating Officer at AHIMA, where she lead the professional and membership facing services of the association. Prior to joining AHIMA, she was the Director of Patient Data Services at the University of Washington Medical Center. She served on the Board of Directors of AHIMA and was the President of the Washington State Health Information Management Association. She was awarded the WSHIMA Professional Achievement Award in 1996. She authored the book *Secure and Access Guidelines for Managing Patient Information*, published in 1997 by AHIMA.

Kathy Giannangelo, MA, RHIA, CCS, CPHIMS, FAHIMA, has a comprehensive background in the field of clinical terminologies, classification, and data standards with more than 30 years of experience in the health information management (HIM) field. In her current position as a health information and informatics management (HIIM) consultant, she utilizes her clinical, information technology, and HIM experience in work involving vocabulary and data standards, including SNOMED-CT and ICD-10-CM/PCS. Examples of current and past projects include conducting new product research and development; serving as editor of the AHIMA textbook *Healthcare Code Sets, Clinical Terminologies, and Classification Systems*; authoring books such as AHIMA's *Transitioning to ICD-10-CM/ PCS: The Essential Guide to General Equivalence Mappings* and distance education courses such as ICD-10-CM/PCS: Fundamentals of General Equivalence Mappings; and consulting, teaching, and training on a global basis. Giannangelo serves as adjunct faculty at the College of St. Scholastica, where she teaches the graduate-level course Clinical Vocabularies and Classification Systems. In addition, she is actively involved as a volunteer in the HIM profession at the international, national, state, and local levels. Giannangelo has served on the AHIMA Board of Directors from 2011 to 2013. Previously, she was director of content management for Apelon, where she oversaw the terminologies found within the Core Content suite and helped clients define terminology requirements, create or extend structured terminologies, or integrate terminology components into their products. As a medical informaticist with Language and Computing (L&C), her role was to support the ontology, modeling, sales, and product development activities related to the creation and implementation of natural language processing applications in which clinical terminology and classification systems are utilized. Prior to L&C, she was a director of practice leadership with AHIMA. Giannangelo also has served as senior nosologist for a health information services company and worked in various HIM roles, including vice president of product development, education specialist, director of medical records, quality assurance coordinator, and Centers for Disease Control and Prevention research team manager.

Laurinda B. Harman, PhD, RHIA, FAHIMA, Associate Professor Emeritus, Department of Health Information Management in the College of Health Professions and Social Work at Temple University in Philadelphia, has been an HIM professional and educator for over 40 years. She has directed HIM baccalaureate programs at Temple University,

George Washington University in Washington, DC, and The Ohio State University in Columbus. Dr. Harman was a faculty member in the health information technology program at Northern Virginia Community College and served as Director of Education and Human Resource Development for the Department of Health Care Sciences at George Washington University. She edited *Ethical Challenges in the Management of Health Information* in 2001; the second edition was published in 2006, and the third edition is in progress. She contributed chapters to *Health Informatics Research: Practices and Innovative Approaches*; *Health Information Management: Concepts, Principles, and Practice;* and *Health Information Technology: An Applied Approach* for the American Health Information Management Association. Dr. Harman is on the editorial board of *Perspectives in Health Information Management,* has contributed articles to the *Journal of American Health Information Management Association,* and has delivered presentations at international, national, state, and local association meetings on topics related to HIM and ethics. She received a Bachelor of Science degree in biology with a concentration in medical record administration from Daemen College in Buffalo, New York, a Master of Science degree in education at Virginia Polytechnic and State University in Blacksburg, Virginia, and a PhD in human and organizational systems at Fielding Graduate University in Santa Barbara, California. Dr. Harman received the AHIMA 2001 Triumph Legacy Award for *Ethical Challenges in the Management of Health Information*, the 2011 Triumph Legacy Educator Award, and the 2011 Dorland Peoples Ethicist Award for her textbook and its contribution to helping healthcare professionals deal with ever-increasing health information ethics issues.

Anita C. Hazelwood, MLS, RHIA, FAHIMA, is a Professor in the Health Information Management Department at the University of Louisiana at Lafayette and has been a credentialed Registered Health Information Administrator (RHIA) for more than 34 years. Anita has actively consulted in hospitals, nursing homes, physician's offices, clinics, facilities for the developmentally challenged, and other educational institutions. She acts as the health information management consultant to the Louisiana Mental Health Advocacy Service. She has conducted numerous ICD-9-CM and CPT coding workshop throughout the state for hospitals and physicians' offices and has written numerous articles and coauthored chapters in several HIM textbooks. Anita has coauthored and edited several

AHIMA publications including *ICD-9-CM and ICD-10-CM Coding and Reimbursement for Physician Services*, *Certified Coding Specialist—Physician-Based Exam Preparation*, *Clinical Coding Workout: Practice Exercises for Skill Development,* and *ICD-10-CM Preview,* for which she won AHIMA's Legacy Award in 2003. She has coauthored a chapter in AHIMA's *Effective Management of Coding Services*. Anita has been a member of the American Health Information Management Association (AHIMA) for over 34 years and has served on various committees and boards. Anita is a member of the Louisiana Health Information Management Association (LHIMA) and was selected as its 1997 Distinguished Member. She has served throughout the years as president, president-elect, treasurer, strategy manager, and board member and has directed numerous committees and projects.

Loretta A. Horton, MEd, RHIA, FAHIMA, received a medical record technician certificate from Research Hospital and Medical Center and a bachelor's degree in psychology from Rockhurst College, both in Kansas City, Missouri; a health information administration certificate from Stephens College in Columbia, Missouri; and a master's degree in education, with an emphasis in curriculum and instruction, from Wichita State University in Wichita, Kansas. She also has completed graduate work in sociology at the University of Nebraska in Omaha. Currently, Loretta is Co-Chair of the Allied Health Department and Coordinator of the health information technology program at Hutchinson Community College in Hutchinson, Kansas. Previously, she worked in a variety of health information settings, including acute-care and mental health, and has consulted with long-term care, mental retardation, home health, hospice, and prison systems. Loretta has been active in component state organizations as well as the American Health Information Management Association having served on national and state committees.

Linda L. Kloss, MA, RHIA, FAHIMA, is founder and President of Kloss Strategic Advisors, Ltd. providing thought leadership and advisory services to health information business leaders, provider organizations, and healthcare associations on health information asset management, strategy and organization development, governance, and change leadership. In 2011, Kloss was appointed to a four-year term on the National Committee on Vital and Health Statistics (NCVHS) and co-chairs its Privacy, Confidentiality, and Security Subcommittee. NCVHS advises the

Secretary of Health and Human Services on national health information policy. Previously, Ms. Kloss served as CEO of AHIMA from 1995 to 2010, leading a period of unprecedented growth and expanded influence. Linda was recognized for expanding the influence of AHIMA through extensive collaboration and an expanded role in setting standards and shaping national policy for health information reform. In 2007 *Modern Healthcare* named her as one of the top 25 women in healthcare and from 2002 to 2007 to the list of the top 100 most influential people in healthcare. She earned a master's degree in organization development with a concentration on nonprofit change leadership from DePaul University and a baccalaureate degree in health information management from the College of St. Scholastica. She was awarded an honorary doctoral degree from the College of St. Scholastica in recognition of her leadership to her profession and to the College. She is also a Certified Association Executive (CAE) by the American Society of Association Executives.

Elizabeth Forrestal, PhD, RHIA, CCS, FAHIMA, is a professor in the Department of Health Services and Information Management at East Carolina University, Greenville, North Carolina. She previously worked at Hennepin County Medical Center and the University of Minnesota Hospitals, both in Minneapolis, from 1974 through 1990. Dr. Layman worked in several departments, such as third-party reimbursement, credit and collections, account auditing, outpatient registration, inpatient admissions, research studies, and quality management. In 1990, Dr. Layman joined the faculty of the Medical College of Georgia in Augusta. While on the faculty, she also consulted for the Physicians' Practice Group. Dr. Layman successfully sat for the first CCS examination in 1992. In 2001, she was awarded the designation of Fellow of the American Health Information Management Association, one of the first two individuals in the country to receive this award. She is the coauthor of *Principles of Healthcare Reimbursement*, published by AHIMA in 2006 and revised in 2011, for which she and her coauthor were recipients of AHIMA's Legacy Award in 2007. She contributed chapters to the third edition of *Health Information Management: Concepts, Principles, and Practice* and coauthored *Health Informatics Research Methods: Principles and Practice*, both AHIMA publications. She was the first editor of *Perspectives in Health Information Management* and has delivered presentations at numerous AHIMA events. She earned her baccalaureate degree from the

University of Minnesota. While working, she returned to school to earn her associate's degree in medical record technology. She completed St. Scholastica's progression program to earn her postbaccalaureate certificate in health information administration. She earned her master's degree in organizational leadership from the College of St. Catherine's and her doctorate in higher education from Georgia State University.

Madonna M. LeBlanc, MA, RHIA, is an assistant professor in the health informatics and information management program (HIIM) in the School of Health Science (SHS) at the College of St. Scholastica (CSS) in Duluth, Minnesota, and a graduate of CSS's MA in HIM program. Prior to her teaching role, she managed HIM services at St. Mary's/Duluth Clinic Health System in Superior, Wisconsin. Her responsibilities included a broad spectrum of acute-care HIM functions, from physician education to Joint Commission survey coordination. Madonna's field experience also includes cancer registry and physician peer administration. At CSS, she served as the HIIM faculty lead for the ATHENS Project (currently known as the Academic Electronic Health Record [AEHR])—an SHS effort to integrate an electronic health record system into professional curricula as a teaching or learning tool. Madonna served six years on Minnesota Health Information Management Association's (MHIMA) BoD as Director Delegate, President, CSA Community Education Coordinator for AHIMA's myPHR campaign, and currently as an AHIMA Council for Excellence in Education (CEE) Community Workgroup volunteer member.

Colleen Malmgren, MS, RHIA, is the Corporate Director of Pricing and Charge Description Master for Fairview Health Services in Minneapolis Minnesota. She is also an adjunct professor for the College of St. Scholastica in Duluth, where she teaches an online course in healthcare revenue cycle improvement. Previously, she served as Director of HIM for Fairview Lakes Hospital in Wyoming, Minnesota, and was the HIM and Quality Management Director at a California-based healthcare facility. She is an alumnus of the College of St. Scholastica's health information management program and earned her master's in healthcare administration at Central Michigan University. She has served in several board positions for the Minnesota Health Information Management Association and presented at the local and state levels on revenue cycle improvement efforts.

Susan E. McClernon, MHA, FACHE, currently serves as the CEO and President of Innovative Healthcare Leadership, a healthcare consulting firm based in Duluth, Minnesota. She also serves as adjunct faculty for the College of St. Scholastica, University of Minnesota–Duluth, University of Minnesota–Twin Cities, and as faculty director for the UMN College of Continuing Education (CCE). Sue previously served as a chief operating officer and administrator for large tertiary hospitals, including St. Mary's Medical Center in Duluth, Minnesota, and Brackenridge Hospital in Austin, Texas. Brackenridge Hospital was named a top 100 hospital in 2001, 2002, and 2003 by *Modern Healthcare's* Solucient Benchmarking process during Sue's tenure as administrator. She is an active fellow in the American College of Healthcare Executives and was named Hospital Administrator of the Year in 2007 by HCAAM and MHA. She received her bachelor's degree in healthcare management from the College of St. Scholastica and her master's degree in healthcare administration from the University of Minnesota. She is currently completing her dissertation as a doctoral candidate in health research, policy, and administration through the University of Minnesota, School of Public Health. Sue has also been active in the American Hospital Association and Catholic Healthcare Association.

Brooke N. Palkie, MA, RHIA, is an assistant professor in the department of healthcare informatics and information management (HIIM) at the College of St. Scholastica. She teaches courses related to the foundations of HIM, clinical quality management, and clinical classification systems. She has most recently participated as the quality metrics and HIIM subject matter expert for a HRSA Grant–funded research project focused on preparing critical access hospitals to meet selected CMS meaningful use direct quality reporting criteria. She has presented on and authored several articles on the topics of reporting quality metrics from the EHR, the transition of ICD-9 to ICD-10, and the crossroads of ICD-10 and meaningful use. She is an active member of AHIMA and has served in elected positions as a member in the Minnesota Health Information Management Association and the Northeastern Minnesota Health Information Management Association. Brooke is also an AHIMA ICD-10-CM/PCS Approved Trainer and AHIMA ICD-10 Ambassador.

Susan L. Parker, MEd, RHIA, is president of Seagate Consultants, an HIM recruiting firm. For the past 22 years, she has been actively involved in workforce issues impacting the health information community through recruitment, career counseling, and professional service. Susan also volunteered as AHIMA's Career Counselor, providing individual assistance related to career decisions and academic training. Previously Susan was a tenured associate professor and director of a bachelor's degree program in HIM. Susan serves on the AHIMA Board of Directors as the very first Speaker of the House for the 2012 AHIMA House of Delegates, helping establish a new foundation for house governance. Susan previously served on the AHIMA Board from 2000 to 2003. She has been president of the North Carolina Health Information Management Association as well as Arkansas HIMA and was awarded the State's Distinguished Member award. Susan has contributed numerous articles, online updates, and public speaking engagements regarding the profession and career management.

Karen R. Patena, MBA, RHIA, FAHIMA, is a clinical associate professor and undergraduate program coordinator in the HIM program, Department of Biomedical and Health Information Sciences, College of Applied Health Sciences, at the University of Illinois at Chicago (UIC). She earned an MBA from DePaul University and is currently pursuing a doctorate degree at UIC. She is an alumnus of the University of Illinois health information management program. Previously, Patena was director of the independent study division of AHIMA and a faculty member at Indiana University and Prairie State College. She also has extensive experience in hospital medical record department management, including computer systems planning and implementation. Her areas of expertise include management, quality improvement and TQM, and the use of computers in healthcare and systems analysis. She has presented numerous tutorials at local, state, and national levels on the use of the Internet in HIM. She currently serves on the board of accreditation surveyors for the Commission on Accreditation for Health Informatics and Information Management Education (CAHIIM) and is a commissioner on the Commission on Certification for Health Informatics and Information Mangement.

Carol Ann Quinsey, MS, RHIA, CHPS, has spent more than 30 years working in the HIM profession. She has worked as a manager or interim manager in community hospitals and ambulatory facilities. Quinsey has worked extensively in acute and corporate care settings as the organizational leader for medical records, medical transcription, quality improvement, utilization management, and medical staff services. She also has held training and leadership positions for the implementation of clinical information systems in a number of organizations. She worked as an HIM Practice Manager for AHIMA from 2003 to 2006. She is currently working as an ICD-10 implementation project manager for Group Health, based in Seattle. Quinsey is an active volunteer in HIM professional activities at both state and national levels. In May 2011, she was recognized as a distinguished member of the Washington State Health Information Management Association (WSHIMA). In June 2012, she completed a term as Past-President of WSHIMA and has served previously on many WSHIMA Committees. Quinsey holds a Bachelor of Science degree in Health Information Management from Seattle University. She was awarded a Certificate in Healthcare Informatics in 2005 and completed a Master of Science degree in Health Information Management in 2011 from the College of St. Scholastica in Duluth, Minnesota.

Rick Revoir, EdD, MBA, CPA, is an assistant professor in the School of Business and Technology at the College of St. Scholastica, teaching both healthcare finance and accounting courses. He created an online healthcare finance course for HIM students that he teaches on a regular basis. He has 11 years of healthcare finance experience in a variety of positions including Director of Financial Analysis, Senior Financial Analyst, and Cost Accountant. He serves as Commissioner of the Duluth Seaway Port Authority and has served on several not-for-profit boards. He is a member of the Healthcare Financial Management Association and the American Institute of Certified Public Accountants.

Rebecca B. Reynolds, EdD, RHIA, is an associate professor and department chair in health informatics and information management. She is past-president of the Tennessee Health Information Management Association and has served on the AHIMA Nominating Committee. She is a recipient of the Tennessee Health Information Management Association's Distinguished Member Award and the Outstanding New Professional Award. Reynolds was a 2006 recipient of AHIMA's Faculty Development Stipend Award and is a member of the inaugural class of AHIMA's HIM Research Training Institute. She received a master's degree in healthcare administration and her EdD in higher education leadership from the University of Memphis. She is currently on the Editorial Review Board for *Perspectives*

in Health Information Management and most recently coedited and coauthored the *Fundamentals of Law for Health Informatics and Information Management* textbook published by AHIMA. She, along with the other book editors, received the 2010 AHIMA Legacy Award for the textbook.

Lynda A. Russell, EdD, JD, RHIA, CHP, is an adjunct instructor with the College of St. Scholastica Masters in Health Informatics and Information Program and the Santa Barbara City College HIT Program. She previously served as the privacy manager at Cedars-Sinai Medical Center in Los Angeles. Russell holds a baccalaureate degree in medical record science from the Georgia Health Sciences University, formerly the Medical College of Georgia; a master's and doctorate in educational administration and supervision from the University of Central Florida; and a JD from the University of Florida. A member of the California Bar, she is licensed to practice before the Superior Court of California and the Federal Court of the Central District of California. Russell has been an HIM professional for more than 40 years and has been active professionally on the national, state, and local levels. She served as president of the Florida HIMA and of the California Health Information Association (CHIA). She has held numerous local, state, and national committee appointments, including chair of AHIMA's Education Strategy Committee and AHIMA's Component State Association Advisory Committee as well as chair of CHIA's Editorial Board.

Ryan H. Sandefer, MA, CPHIT, is chair and assistant professor in the Health Informatics and Information Management Department at the College of St. Scholastica. He teaches research methods, program evaluation, and technology applications. He is currently engaged in multiple research projects, including projects related to electronic clinical quality measure reporting in rural hospitals and usability of mobile technologies. He is also serving as a regional HIT extension center consultant for Minnesota and North Dakota. Sandefer regularly presents at national and local meetings of HIM and HIT professionals and has published articles in the areas of health policy and health workforce. He is a member of the American Health Information Management Association, the American Medical Informatics Association, and the Health Information Management Systems Society. He is currently pursuing a PhD in Health Informatics from the University of Minnesota–Twin Cities. He received both his undergraduate and graduate degrees in political science from the University of Wyoming.

Patricia B. Seidl, RHIA, has a varied career in health information management, information technology, and clinical research. Her experience includes project management, methodology development, information system implementations, and clinical research data management. Seidl previously was an adjunct professor teaching project management in the HIM graduate program at the College of St. Scholastica and was a contributing author to *Special Edition: Using Microsoft Project 2000.* She served on the AHIMA Quality Initiatives and Secondary Data Practices Council and has contributed several articles to the *Journal of AHIMA.* She received a bachelor's degree from the College of St. Scholastica and an associate of applied science degree in computer science from the University of Southern Colorado.

Marcia Y. Sharp, EdD, MBA, RHIA, is an assistant professor in the Department of Health Informatics and Information Management at the University of Tennessee Health Sciences Center. She has had an outstanding career in Health Information Management and in Human Resource Management. She is an active member of the Memphis Health Information Management Association, serving as former treasurer, and the Tennessee Health Information Management Association, serving as TN delegate to the AHIMA House of Delegates and former member of the TN Nominating Committee. She is currently a member of the Editorial Review Board for *Perspectives on Health Information Management (PHIM).* She has contributed chapters to several AHIMA publications, *Health Information Management Technology: An Applied Approach* and *Fundamentals of Law for Health Informatics and Information Management.*

C. Jeanne Solberg, MA, RHIA, is President and Owner of Solberg Solutions, Inc., a health information management consulting firm. She is an adjunct faculty member with the College of St. Scholastica and teaches Healthcare Data Analytics at the graduate level. Solberg's work experience includes roles as Director of Business Processes at a large healthcare insurer; EHR Manager of Patient Access at a multihospital and clinic organization; Senior Implementation Consultant for a large publicly traded healthcare services company; Manager of Decision Support Services and Clinical Decision Support at large tertiary care hospitals in the East and Midwest; and Director of HIM, Quality Assessment and Utilization Management in acute-care hospitals with large ambulatory care practices. She is currently a second-year director on the AHIMA Board; served as Chair of the Commission on Accreditation of Health Informatics and Information Management Education (CAHIIM), and chaired AHIMA's Program Committee. Jeanne has a strong interest in clinical and financial decision support, data governance and management, business management and leadership, and revenue cycle management.

Cheryl Stephens, MBA, PhD, is the President and CEO of Community Health Information Collaborative. Dr. Stephens has over 27 years of senior-level healthcare administration experience with an emphasis on expanding rural capacity. Much of her time has been devoted to the development of new healthcare networks in the areas of health information exchange, emergency preparedness, and managed care. She is a member of the Minnesota eHealth Advisory Committee as HIE Representative and is on the HIE Workgroup, Adoption and Meaningful Use Workgroup, and Standards and Interoperability Workgroup of this committee. She is also a member of the Nationwide Health Information Network Exchange's Coordinating Committee. Previous work done in partnership with the Office of the National Coordinator includes participating in the writing of the Data Use and Reciprocal Support Agreement (DURSA), piloting the electronic exchange of medical records for use in disability determinations by the Social Security Administration and the Veteran's Administration Virtual Lifetime Electronic Record (VLER) project, designed to pull all medical information into a single record from both private and public healthcare providers. She serves on the Board of the Healthier Minnesota Community Clinic Fund, formed to provide funding to safety net providers in the state of Minnesota. She formerly served on the Board of the American Immunization Registry Association and as co-chair of its Education Committee. Cheryl has a BS in Medical Technology, an MBA, and has earned a PhD in business administration—her dissertation topic was in the area of Public and Private Partnerships in Healthcare.

David X. Swenson, PhD, is a professor of management in the School of Business and Technology at the College of St. Scholastica, where he teaches strategic management, organization development, leadership, and marketing. He is also the program coordinator of a new online MBA program for health professionals.

He has a part-time consulting practice in organization development and forensic psychology, also holding a post-doctoral diplomate in the latter field. He has worked in the field of psychology for more than 40 years and has served as director of student development at the College of St. Scholastica and director of clinical services at the Human Resource Center of Douglas County, Wisconsin. He has authored more than 100 publications, including *Stress Management for Law Enforcement*. A doctoral graduate of the University of Missouri at Columbia in counseling and personnel services, David also has master's degrees in management, school counseling, and educational media and technology and is currently completing another master's in information technology leadership.

Carol A. Venable, MPH, RHIA, FAHIMA, is a professor and department head of HIM at the University of Louisiana at Lafayette and has been an HIM professional for over 30 years. She is actively involved with AHIMA's Board of Accreditation Surveyors and several other committees as well as the Louisiana Health Information Management Association, where she has held many leadership positions and was selected s Distinguished Member in 1991. She has served throughout the years as president, president-elect, treasurer, strategy manager, and board member and has also directed numerous projects and committees. Previously, she was director of medical records at Lafayette General Medical Center, has consulted in a variety of healthcare facilities and educational institutions, and conducts coding workshops for hospitals and physician offices. Venable has written, coauthored, and edited numerous publications, including AHIMA's *ICD-9-CM Diagnostic Coding and Reimbursement for Physician Services, Certified Coding Specialist—Physician-Based (CCS-P) Exam Preparation, Clinical Coding Workout,* and *ICD-10-CM Preview*, for which she was awarded AHIMA's Legacy Award in 2003. She frequently serves as a reviewer for publishers of HIM-related textbooks, certification exams, and electronic materials.

Janelle Wapola, MA, RHIA, is an assistant professor in the Health Informatics and Information Management Department at the College of St. Scholastica, teaching both online and traditional courses. She has 17 years of health information management experience in a variety of positions including HIM Department Assistant Director, HIM Consultant and ROI Specialist. She is currently serving as a Minnesota Health Information Management Association Delegate Director and a regional HIT Extension Center (REACH) HIT Consultant for Minnesota and North Dakota and serves on several campus committees in the Duluth community. She is a contributor to the text *Using the Electronic Health Record in the Healthcare Provider Practice*, published by Cengage Delmar Learning. She served as the Technology Lead on the US Department of Education, Title III grant, which brought an electronic health record into the academic setting as a teaching/learning tool. She has given several presentations about a 2011 international, study-abroad trip to India where she guided several HIM students on different field research topics, including a project involving the development of a personal health record for international travelers. She received both her undergraduate and graduate degrees in health information management from the College of St. Scholastica.

Valerie J.M. Watzlaf, PhD, RHIA, FAHIMA, is an Associate Professor within the Department of HIM at the University of Pittsburgh. She also holds a secondary faculty appointment in the Graduate School of Public Health. She has been chair of AHIMA's Coding, Policy, and Strategy Committee, the Research Committee, and the Council on Accreditation. She served on the board of directors of AHIMA and the AHIMA Foundation. She is also on the Editorial Advisory Board for the *Journal of AHIMA* and for *PHIM*. Valerie has published extensively in the field of health information management and is the recipient of numerous awards and professional accolades including AHIMA's Research Award.

Susan E. White, PhD, CHDA, is a Clinical Associate Professor in the Health Information Management and Systems Division at The Ohio State University. She teaches statistics, healthcare finance, and database design and development courses. Prior to that appointment, she was the Vice President of Research and Development for Cleverley + Associates and the Vice President of Data Operations for CHIPS/Ingenix. Dr. White has written numerous books and articles regarding the benchmarking of healthcare facilities, healthcare financial management, and the application of statistical techniques in analyzing healthcare data. She is the author AHIMA's *Healthcare Financial Management for Health Information and Informatics* text. Susan received her PhD in Statistics from The Ohio State University. She is a member of AHIMA, the American Statistical Association, and the Heathcare Financial Management Association. She has presented to both national and local meetings of healthcare executives and HIM professionals.

What drives us, inspires us, and motivates us to do our best? As health information managers, we believe that the heart of our profession is providing information that is trustworthy, confidential, secure, timely, accurate, and reliable. By providing this information to others, the best decisions can be made for patient care and the healthcare system as a whole. Whether information is used to care for a loved one being treated for disease or illness, for research, public policy health initiatives, future planning, value-based purchasing, or reimbursement, we want to make sure that the information we provide empowers others to make educated and informed decisions.

In order to provide this trusted information, we must be educated and highly trained in how to collect and store patient information, as well as how to analyze and apply the data for decision making. It is with that in mind that this fourth edition of *Health Information Management: Concepts, Principles, and Practice* was revised and published.

Today, more than ever, our healthcare world is changing and in order to make informed decisions about these changes, one must rely on information. The *Atlanta Journal Constitution* has published a report where industry experts addressed challenges facing our country. One of the top two recommendations for improving our healthcare system was emphasizing the advancement and importance of healthcare technology. This increase in healthcare technology impacts our role as health information management professionals. We must deal with data breaches, patient privacy concerns, and medical identity theft. Also, the increase in social media and the use of mobile devices to access EHR information needs to be considered. (B. Foster, Dec. 5, 2011).

Health information management professionals will also lead the way in providing information for performance measurements, value-based purchasing, population health management, care management, decision support, privacy and security, mobile health, and personalized medicine.

Health Information Management: Concepts, Principles, and Practice shares content that provides guidance to HIM professionals and provides knowledge on how to succeed in our current and future world of healthcare information.

Volume editors Kathleen M. LaTour, MA, RHIA, FAHIMA; Shirley Eichenwald-Maki, MBA, RHIA, FAHIMA; and Pamela Oachs, MA, RHIA, provide an overview of healthcare information management from the capture of data to the use of information. They have carefully selected an authoritative group of distinguished authors who are leaders in our field—educators, practitioners, and consultants. Their backgrounds and expertise assist the reader in understanding our current roles in HIM and help us think strategically in order to address the information needs of our future healthcare industry.

A background in health information management is covered by contributors Sandra R. Fuller, MA, RHIA, FAHIMA; Susan Parker, MEd, RHIA; Ryan H. Sandefer, MA, CPHIT; Patricia B. Seidl, RHIA; and Margret K. Amatayakul, MBA, RHIA, CHPS, CPEHR, FHIMSS.

Linda L. Kloss, RHIA, CAE, FAHIMA; Valerie J.M. Watzlaf, PhD, RHIA, FAHIMA; Kathy Giannangelo, MA, RHIA, CCS, CPHIMS, FAHIMA; and Cheryl Stephens, PhD, MBA, discuss healthcare data management.

The development of the patient health record is authored by Elizabeth D. Bowman, MPA, RHIA, FAHIMA; Rebecca B. Reynolds, EdD, RHIA; Danika Brinda, MA, RHIA, CHPS; Janelle Wapola, MA, RHIA; Lynda A. Russell, EdD, JD, RHIA, CHP; Rita Bowen, MA, RHIA, CHPS; and Laurinda B. Harman, PhD, RHIA, FAHIMA.

Contributors to aggregate healthcare data are Marcia Y. Sharp, EdD, MBA, RHIA; Brooke N. Palkie, MA, RHIA; Anita C. Hazelwood, MLS, RHIA, FAHIMA; Carol A. Venable, MPH, RHIA, FAHIMA; Colleen Malmgren, MS, RHIA; and Jeanne Solberg, MA, RHIA.

Loretta A. Horton, MEd, RHIA; Susan White, PhD, CHDA; Elizabeth Forrestal, PhD, RHIA, CCS, FAHIMA; Valarie J.M. Watzlaf, PhD, RHIA, FAHIMA; and Chris Elliott, MS, RHIA, discuss comparative health data.

Management of health information services is covered by David X. Swenson, PhD; Karen R. Patena, MBA, RHIA, FAHIMA; Madonna M. LeBlanc, MA, RHIA; Rick Revoir, EdD, MBA, CPA; Pamela K. Oachs, MA, RHIA; Patricia B. Seidl, RHIA; Carol Ann Quinsey, MS, RHIA, CHPS; and Susan E. McClernon, MHA, FACHE.

Bonnie S. Cassidy, MPA, RHIA, FAHIMA, FHIMSS, authors the final chapter on envisioning the future of the health information management profession.

With an aging population, there is no doubt that work in our field will always be available, with the number of job titles increasing as new specialties develop and to accommodate new technology (for example, electronic health records, new legislation, and the inevitable implementation of ICD-10 in the United States). The variety and range of positions and other opportunities available to the HIM professional will be expanded.

Our future is now. The decisions we make every day will impact the quality of our work, the care that patients receive, and our healthcare delivery systems. This book is a resource that provides the key to understanding our current realities and expanded vision for the future. We need to ensure that our profession will be able to lead in a dynamic and rapidly changing healthcare environment. In addition to preparing you for the future, AHIMA's goal is to create leaders with increased influence and respect. Most importantly, we need to be confident that the right information is available for patient care at the right time. Our job is to make sure there is healthcare information we can *trust* available for decision makers.

To the editors, contributors, and AHIMA staff who contributed to this publication, I extend my gratitude and appreciation for your knowledge. Also, I am thankful for the time each of you took to share your wisdom and expertise with current and emerging leaders in the health information management profession.

Lynne Thomas Gordon, MBA, RHIA, FACHE
Chief Executive Officer
American Health Information Management
Association

Acknowledgments

The editors and publications staff would like to express appreciation to the many authors who contributed chapters to this textbook. They willingly shared their expertise, met tight deadlines, accepted feedback, and contributed to building the body of knowledge related to health information management. Writing a chapter is a time-consuming and demanding task, and we are grateful for the authors' contributions.

We would also like to thank authors who contributed to previous editions of this textbook:

- Bonnie S. Cassidy, MPA, RHIA, FAHIMA, FHIMSS
- Nadinia Davis, MBA, CIA, CPA, RHIA, FAHIMA
- Mehnaz Farishta, MS
- Susan H. Fenton, MBA, RHIA
- Margaret M. (Maggie) Foley, PhD, RHIA, CCS
- Michelle A. Green, MPS, RHIA, CMA
- Matthew J. Greene, RHIA, CSS
- J. Michael Hardin, PhD
- Diana Lynn Johnson, PhD
- Deborah Kohn, MPH, RHIA, CPHIMS, FHIMSS
- Mary Cole McCain, MPA, RHIA
- Carol E. Osborn, PhD, RHIA
- Uzma Raja, PhD
- Rita Scichilone, MHSA, RHIA, CCS, CCS-P, CHC-F
- Kam Shams, MA
- Carol Marie Spielman, MA, RHIA
- Karen Wager, DBA
- Andrea Weatherby White, PhD, RHIA
- Frances Wickham Lee, DBA, RHIA
- Vicki Zeman, MA, RHIA

We also would like to thank the following reviewers who lent a critical eye to this endeavor.
Current edition reviewers:

- Janie L. Batres, RHIT, CCS
- Jill S. Clark, MBA, RHIA
- Kathryn DeVault, RHIA, CCS, CCS-P
- Julie A. Dooling, RHIT
- Melanie A. Endicott, MBA/HCM, RHIA, CCS, CCS-P
- Karen Kostick, RHIT, CCS, CCS-P
- Theresa Rihanek, MHA, RHIA, CCS
- Angela Dinh Rose, MHA, RHIA, CHPS
- Diana M. Warner, MS, RHIA, CHPS, FAHIMA
- Lou Ann Wiedemann, MS, FAHIMA, RHIA, CPEHR

Previous edition reviewers also include

- Donna Bowers, JD, RHIA, CHP
- June E. Bronnert, RHIA, CCS, CCS-P
- Jill Burrington-Brown, MS, RHIA
- Christopher G. Chute, MD, DrPH
- Claire Dixon-Lee, PhD, RHIA, FAHIMA
- Michelle L. Dougherty, RHIA, CHP
- Susan H. Fenton, MBA, RHIA
- Leslie A. Fox, MA, RHIA, FAHIMA
- Jennifer Garvin, PhD, RHIA, CPHQ, CCS, FAHIMA
- Kathy Giannangelo, RHIA, CCS
- Barry S. Herrin, Esq.
- Beth Hjort, RHIA, CHPS

- Susan Hull, MPH, RHIA, CCS, CCS-P
- Lolita M. Jones, RHIA, CCS
- Donald T. Mon, PhD, FHIMSS
- Carol Ann Quinsey, RHIA, CHPS
- Harry Rhodes, MBA, RHIA, CHPS
- Dan Rode, MBA, FHFMA
- Rita A. Scichilone, MHSA, RHIA, CCS, CCS-P, CHC
- Stephen A. Sivo, PhD
- Mary H. Stanfill, RHIA, CCS, CCS-P
- Valerie J.M. Watzlaf, PhD, RHIA, FAHIMA
- Maggie Williams, MA
- Ann Zeisset, RHIT, CCS-P, CCS

We would also like to acknowledge students from the College of St. Scholastica who reviewed the Check Your Understanding exercises in each of the fourth edition chapters. Their help is greatly appreciated.

- Meaghan Baldwin
- Brandi Bierbrauer
- Allison Bristol
- Sara Dahl

- Rachel Hagel
- Lori Hurin
- Chasity Joarnt
- Kierstin Johnson
- Cole Karsky
- Chris Lambach
- Rachel R. Mach
- Molly McBride
- Darcee J. Roeschlein
- Bryanna Schoeffel
- Cara Sobolik
- Antonia Susnik
- Andrew "Drew" Torres
- Tanner M. Viola
- Ellie J. Whiteman
- Kayla M. Zirbes

Finally the editors wish to acknowledge the guidance, patience, and expertise of Ashley Sullivan, project editor, and managing editor Claire Blondeau, MBA. From the beginning to the end of this project, they are the glue that held the entire project together.

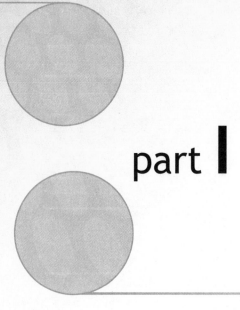

part I

Health Information Management

Introduction

Shirley Eichenwald Maki, MBA, RHIA, FAHIMA, Pam Oachs, MA, RHIA,
and Kathleen M. LaTour, MA, RHIA, FAHIMA

The field of health information management (HIM) has been a recognized field of professional study for 85 years. It was originally called medical record science and members of the profession were originally called medical record librarians. From its inception, the profession's mission was to elevate the standards of clinical recordkeeping in hospitals, dispensaries, and other healthcare facilities. Since its founding, the professional association, now known as the American Health Information Management Association (AHIMA), and the professionals affiliated with it have been advocates for the effective management of clinical data and health records to ensure their confidentiality, integrity, and availability in every type of healthcare setting.

"Health information management (HIM) professionals work in a variety of different settings and job titles. They often serve in bridge roles, connecting clinical, operational, and administrative functions. In short, AHIMA members affect the quality of patient information and patient care at every touchpoint in the healthcare delivery cycle. Having skilled HIM professionals on staff ensures an organization has the right information on hand when and where it is needed while maintaining the highest standards of data integrity, confidentiality, and security. AHIMA members perform diverse roles in healthcare and are employed in a variety of work settings, including hospitals, physician offices, ambulatory care facilities, managed care facilities, long-term care facilities, consulting firms, information system vendors, colleges and universities, insurance providers, pharmaceutical companies, rehabilitation centers, and other venues" (AHIMA 2012a).

Beginning with the managed care movement in the 1980s, information management began to emerge as a top priority for healthcare institutions. Currently, there are significant government and industry initiatives focused on the goal of using health information technologies in meaningful ways to inform clinical decision making at the point of care, improve the quality of heathcare, reduce the cost of healthcare, and improve the coordination of care among healthcare organizations (HHS 2012). These initiatives are being supported through a series of publicly and privately funded programs, most notably programs funded under the Health Information Technology for Economical and Clinical Health Act (HITECH Act) and provisions of the American Recovery and Reinvestment Act (ARRA) of 2009 (AHIMA 2012b). Included among the programs are education and training programs aimed at increasing preparation of a workforce that is prepared to function in the electronic healthcare environment of the future.

This chapter provides a brief introduction to the HIM profession and focuses on the changing nature of its core domain of practice as the health information infrastructure transitions to a fully electronic environment. It sets the stage for the remaining chapters by providing a context for the broad range of topics that must be addressed in a textbook whose purpose is to describe the concepts, principles, and practices associated with the HIM profession in its current state of transformation. (A full discussion of the HIM profession and related professional associations is presented in chapter 3.)

The Modern Healthcare Environment

In the 1990s, competition among healthcare providers was stimulated by major changes in the reimbursement system used by Medicare and Medicaid (two federally mandated healthcare programs). Integrated healthcare delivery systems began to emerge as significant organizational models, and managed care delivery systems continued to expand. As a result of these developments, the availability of timely and accurate clinical information has become critical to the viability of healthcare organizations. Medical and administrative staffs recognize that the information gathered from clinical records is an invaluable organizational asset. They also understand that this information represents an important quality indicator and a vital tool for efficiently managing the business of healthcare in a tight financial environment.

In the 2000s, the efficient and effective application of sophisticated computer technologies also has received increased attention among healthcare professionals and organizations. Information handling technologies are the obvious solution to the healthcare industry's need for greater efficiency in managing the ever-increasing volume of healthcare data. In addition, as diverse healthcare decision makers look for flexibility in how to access and analyze vast electronic repositories of clinical data, advanced decision support applications are critical to meeting that demand.

Today, these trends continue to affect the practice of health information management and healthcare in general as:

- The federal government strategic vision includes every American having an interoperable electronic health record (EHR) by the year 2014.
- State governments and regional public and private partnerships work to establish health information exchange (HIE) systems that facilitate the transfer of health information among authorized parties to enhance the coordination of care and reduce the cost of healthcare services.
- Payers pilot reimbursement systems (for example, Accountable Care Organizations, patient-centered medical homes) that provide incentives for healthcare organizations to implement health information technologies (HIT) to support quality-of-care programs.
- Regulators and accreditation agencies focus on the use of computer-based information technologies to improve patient safety and reduce the number of medical errors.
- Healthcare consumers are creating and maintaining personal health records (PHRs) with the support of many employers, healthcare providers, third-party payers, and independent HIT vendors to facilitate access to more complete and accurate information for continuing care.
- Workforce shortages place greater emphasis on technological systems for improving productivity of the healthcare workforce.
- Integrated information system (IS) solutions as well as more clinician-friendly hardware and applications are continuing to evolve.
- The Internet and its derived technologies make access to web-based information systems and connectivity across otherwise disparate information systems available and affordable for all sizes and types of healthcare organizations.

Contemporary Health Information Management

The HIM profession is the only profession that has as its core professional mission the collection and maintenance of high-quality data gathered as a direct by-product of the delivery of healthcare services and preferably at the point-of-service. Although clinical and allied healthcare professionals depend on the availability of high-quality data to support their clinical decision making, their primary concern is providing diagnostic and therapeutic services, not managing clinical information. The administrators and managers of healthcare organizations also need high-quality clinical data to support their planning and administration of healthcare operations and services; however, managing the quality of the data is not their major concern. Similarly, computer scientists and technicians are concerned primarily with the performance of software and hardware configurations; researchers are concerned primarily with the development of scientific solutions to important questions; third-party payers are concerned primarily with the control of financial resources; and policy makers are concerned primarily with incentives for cost-effectiveness, social justice, and ethical practice. While all of these stakeholders rely on high-quality clinical data, only the HIM profession is focused primarily on ensuring the availability of high-quality data for a variety of uses and users.

Today the HIM profession remains committed to its original mission to elevate health record standards and practices. It does so, however, in a healthcare environment that is becoming more and more technology driven in both its work processes and its information flow, as well as more and more dependent on the quality and accessibility of the information contained within clinical records. HIM professionals work to ensure that their communities and customers are provided high-quality and cost-effective healthcare information services.

Within the healthcare industry's information-intensive environment increasingly embedded within a technology-supported infrastructure, HIM professionals must continuously build and market their unique knowledge base and competencies in the following areas:

- Practice standards, laws, and regulations related to ensuring the accuracy, completeness, integrity, privacy, and security of healthcare information
- The legal health record, as the business record for each healthcare organization
- Healthcare data and informatics standards
- Healthcare data analytics and reporting methods
- Clinical coding, classification, and reimbursement systems, especially related to the anticipated transition from ICD-9-CM to ICD-10-CM/PCS classification system
- Health record and information systems design, functions, and maintenance
- Organizational and cross-disciplinary modes of functioning to achieve quality and productivity goals

Once applied in a world of paper-based records and manual systems, the HIM professionals' knowledge base and competencies are now needed to effectively transition vital clinical data resources into electronic clinical repositories and EHR systems. "HIM professionals now serve in a broad range of roles that involve planning, organizing, and managing clinical content, integrity, accessibility, use, and protection in the transition from paper to electronic records and the management of electronic content, that is, a transition from HIM to e-HIM®" (AHIMA 2012c). (Chapter 3 discusses the roles for HIM professionals.)

Working in strong collaborative partnerships with specialists in information technologies and with specialized healthcare data and information users (physicians, nurses, pharmacists, therapists, administrators, researchers, policy makers, and others), health information managers have become key players within the emerging discipline of healthcare informatics. Healthcare informatics focuses on designing and implementing technology-based information systems of many types to support the specialized activities associated with each type of healthcare worker. For example, nursing informatics focuses on systems that support the work of nurses, and medical informatics focuses on systems that support the work of physicians. Similarly, consumer informatics systems support the activities of patients, long-term care residents, and healthcare clients (Shortliff et al. 2000).

Thus, to carry on the important legacy of their predecessors, today's HIM professionals support an adapted vision of their unique contribution. They envision how the concepts, principles, and practices at the core of the HIM knowledge base and competencies continue to apply in their changing work environment and settings. In addition, they assess their adaptive strengths and weaknesses relative to that vision and, most important, they take action to position themselves appropriately to contribute their unique expertise to the organizations they serve. The new Core Model of HIM practice developed by AHIMA identifies and supports new skill sets, roles, and functions. The Core Model is addressed in Chapter 3.

legacy by elevating the standards for collecting, maintaining, and analyzing clinical data within a healthcare environment that demands integrated, computer-based, user-focused data repositories and warehouses. The viability and vitality of the HIM profession in the future depends on the commitment of current and future professionals to think and act strategically in order to address the legitimate data and information needs of an evolving healthcare industry. To meet that challenge, HIM professionals must continually update their knowledge base and competencies through self-assessment and commitment to lifelong learning, and they must actively take part in their professional organizations' activities at the local, regional, state, and national levels.

References

American Health Information Management Association. 2012a. Vision. http://www.ahima.org/about/mission.aspx.

American Health Information Management Association. 2012b. Health Care Reform and Health IT Stimulus: ARRA and HITECH. http://www.ahima.org/advocacy/arrahitech.aspx.

American Health Information Management Association. 2012c. e-HIM®. http://www.ahima.org/ehim/.

Department of Health and Human Services. 2012. Office of the National Coordinator for Health Information Technology. Electronic Health Records and Meaningful Use. http://healthit.hhs.gov/portal/server.pt/community/healthit_hhs_gov__meaningful_use_announcement/2996.

Shortliffe, E.H., L.E. Perreault, G. Wiederhold, and L.M. Fagan, eds. 2000. *Medical Informatics: Computer Applications in Health Care and Biomedicine.* New York: Springer-Verlag.

Summary

The HIM profession began with the founding of the Association of Record Librarians of North America in 1928. The association's original goal was to improve clinical record-keeping in healthcare facilities. The association, now known as the American Health Information Management Association, and a new generation of HIM professionals have inherited a powerful legacy from those original medical record pioneers. Today, HIM professionals have an extraordinary opportunity and obligation to build on their professional

chapter 2

The US Healthcare Delivery System

Sandra R. Fuller, MA, RHIA, FAHIMA

Learning Objectives

- Understand the history of the healthcare delivery system from ancient times to the present
- Know the basic organization of the various types of hospitals and healthcare organizations
- Recognize the impact of external forces on the healthcare industry
- Identify the various functional components of an integrated delivery system
- Describe the systems used for reimbursement of healthcare services
- Recognize the role of government in healthcare services
- Recognize the impact of regulatory change on the healthcare delivery system

Key Terms

Accountable care organization (ACO)
Accreditation
Acute care
Ambulatory care
Ambulatory care center (ACC)
American Association of Medical Colleges (AAMC)
American College of Healthcare Executives (ACHE)
American College of Surgeons
American Health Information Management Association (AHIMA)
American Hospital Association (AHA)
American Medical Association (AMA)
American Nurses Association (ANA)
Average length of stay (ALOS)
Behavioral healthcare
Biotechnology
Blue Cross and Blue Shield Association
Case management
Centers for Medicare and Medicaid Services (CMS)
Chief executive officer (CEO)
Chief financial officer (CFO)
Chief information officer (CIO)
Chief nursing officer (CNO)

Chief operating officer (COO)
Clinical privileges
Commission on Accreditation of Health Informatics and Information Management Education (CAHIIM)
Conditions of Participation
Continuous quality improvement (CQI)
Continuum of care
Deemed status
Evidence-based medicine
Extended care facility
Health Insurance Portability and Accountability Act (HIPAA)
Health savings account (HSA)
Health systems agency
Home healthcare
Hospice care
Hospital Survey and Construction Act (Hill-Burton Act)
Integrated delivery network (IDN)
Integrated delivery system (IDS)
Investor-owned hospital chain
Joint Commission
Long-term care
Malpractice

Managed care
Managed care organization (MCO)
Meaningful use
Medicaid
Medical device
Medical staff bylaws
Medical staff classification
Medical tourism
Medicare
National Institutes of Health (NIH)
National Practitioner Data Bank (NPDB)
Patient-centered medical home (PCMH)
Patient Protection and Affordable Care Act (ACA)
Peer review
Peer review organization (PRO)

Physician assistant (PA)
Post-acute care
Prospective payment system (PPS)
Public Health Service (PHS)
Quality improvement organization (QIO)
Reengineering
Rehabilitation services
Retail clinics
Skilled nursing facility (SNF)
Tax Equity and Fiscal Responsibility Act (TEFRA)
Telehealth
TRICARE
Utilization Review Act
Value-Based Purchasing
Workers' compensation

A broad array of healthcare services is available in the United States today, ranging from simple preventive measures such as vaccinations to complex lifesaving procedures such as heart transplants. An individual's contact with the healthcare delivery system often begins with family planning and prenatal care before he or she is born and continues through end-of-life planning and hospice care.

Healthcare services are provided by physicians, nurses, and other clinical providers who work in ambulatory care, acute care, rehabilitative and psychiatric care, and long-term care facilities. Healthcare services also are provided in the homes of hospice and home care patients. Assisted living centers, industrial medical clinics, and public health department clinics also provide services to many Americans.

While most healthcare is experienced locally and individually, healthcare is the single largest part of the US economy, consuming 17.6 percent of the gross domestic product (GDP) in 2009 (Wilson 2011). It is delivered by an ever-expanding variety of providers from large multi-institutional integrated delivery networks (IDNs) to nurse practitioners within the neighborhood drug store. Although the growth in healthcare spending has been slowing since 2003 it continues to outpace the overall growth in the US economy and US healthcare spending rose to $2.5 trillion in 2009.

In the first quarter of 2011, 46.5 million Americans remained uninsured despite the fact that the United States spends more on healthcare than other industrialized nations, and those countries provide health insurance to all their citizens (Cohen and Martinez 2011). Healthcare reform remains a significant political issue and information management and technology are increasingly seen as important elements of a solution.

In 2010, there were 5,754 registered hospitals in the United States according to the American Hospital Association (AHA 2012). Almost 5,000 of those were community hospitals, which include nonfederal, short-term general hospitals and other specialty hospitals. They also include academic medical centers and teaching hospitals that were not owned by the federal government. About 20 percent of the community

hospitals were for-profit and investor-owned, and almost 3,000 were part of a system. Multihospital systems include two or more hospitals owned, leased, sponsored, or contract managed by a central organization. Hospitals can also be part of a network, which is a group of hospitals, physicians, and other providers and payers that collaborate to coordinate and deliver services to their community.

In addition to hospital systems and networks there are other forms of organized healthcare delivery. Jonas and Kovner define organized healthcare delivery to mean "that care providers have established relationships and mechanisms for communicating and working to coordinate patient care across health conditions, services, and care settings over time" (Jonas and Kovner 2011, 206). A multispecialty physician group practice that includes a health insurer is another example of organized care. Recent healthcare reform legislation, economic pressure, and the opportunity to provide better care through coordination and improved access to information continue to move healthcare away from the traditional free-standing solo practice of the past.

This chapter discusses the origin of the healthcare industry in the United States and examines the history from the 1800s to the 21st century. Included in this history is the impact of external forces that have shaped the healthcare system of today.

History of Western Medicine

Modern Western medicine is rooted in antiquity. The ancient Greeks developed surgical procedures, documented clinical cases, and created medical books. Before modern times, European, African, and Native American cultures all had traditions of folk medicine based on spiritual healing and herbal cures. The first hospitals were created by religious orders in medieval Europe to provide care and respite to religious pilgrims traveling back and forth from the Holy Land. However, it was not until the late 1800s that medicine became a scientific discipline. More progress and change occurred during the 20th century than over the preceding 2,000 years. The past few decades have seen dramatic developments in the way diseases are diagnosed and treated as well as the way healthcare is delivered.

Before the advent of modern Western medicine, epidemics and plagues were common. Epidemics of smallpox, measles, yellow fever, influenza, scarlet fever, and diphtheria killed millions of people. Bubonic plague spread periodically through Europe and killed millions more. Disease was carried by rodents and insects as well as by the travelers who moved along intercontinental trade routes.

The medical knowledge that had been gained by ancient Greek scholars such as Hippocrates was lost during the Middle Ages. The European Renaissance, a historical period beginning in the 14th century, revived interest in the classical arts, literature, and philosophy as well as in the scientific study of nature. This period also was characterized by economic growth and concern for the welfare of workers at all levels of society. With this concept came a growing awareness that a healthy population promoted economic growth.

North America's First Hospitals

Early settlers in the British colonies of North America appointed commissions to care for the sick, to provide for orphans, and to bury the dead. During the mid-1700s, the citizens of Philadelphia recognized the need for a place to provide relief to the sick and injured. They also recognized the need to isolate newly arrived immigrants who had caught communicable diseases on the long voyage from Europe.

In Philadelphia, Benjamin Franklin and other colonists persuaded the legislature to develop a hospital for the community. It was the first hospital in the British colonies of North America. The Pennsylvania Hospital was established in Philadelphia in 1752. (Almost 200 years earlier, Hernando Cortez established the first hospital in Mexico, and it still serves patients today.)

Over its first 150 years, the Pennsylvania Hospital served as a model for the organization of hospitals in other communities. The New York Hospital opened in 1771 and started its first register of patients in 1791. Boston's Massachusetts General Hospital opened in 1821.

Standardization of Medical Practice

Human anatomy and physiology and the causes of disease were not well understood before the 20th century. At one time, it was believed that four basic fluids, called humors, determined a person's temperament and health and that the imbalances in the proportion of humors in the body caused disease. The therapeutic bleeding of patients was practiced until the early 20th century. Early physicians also treated patients by administering a variety of substances with no scientific basis for their effectiveness.

An individual's early medical education consisted of serving as an apprentice to an established practitioner. The medical profession recognized that some of its members achieved better results than others, and leaders in the profession attempted to regulate the practice of medicine in the late 1700s. The first attempts at regulation took the form of licensure. The first licenses to practice medicine were issued in New York in 1760. As the population of the United States grew and settlers moved westward, the demand for medical practitioners far exceeded the supply. To staff new hospitals and serve a growing population, many private medical schools appeared almost overnight. By 1869, there were 72 medical schools in the United States. However, these schools did not follow an established course of study, and some graduated students with as little as six months of training. The result was an oversupply of poorly trained physicians. The American Medical Association (AMA) was established in 1847 to represent the interests of physicians across the United States. In 1876, the **American Association of Medical Colleges (AAMC)** was established. The AAMC was dedicated to standardizing the curriculum for US medical schools and to developing the public's understanding of the need to license physicians.

By the early 20th century, it had become apparent that improving the quality of American medicine required regulation through curriculum reform as well as licensure. The situation attracted the attention of the Carnegie Foundation for the Advancement of Teaching. The president of the foundation offered to sponsor and fund an independent review of the medical colleges then operating in the United States. Abraham Flexner, an educator from Louisville, Kentucky, undertook the review in 1906.

Over the following four years, Flexner visited every medical college in the country and carefully documented his findings. In his 1910 report to the Carnegie Foundation, the AMA, and the AAMC, he described the poor quality of the training provided in the colleges. He noted that medical school applicants often lacked knowledge of the basic sciences. Flexner also reported how the absence of hospital-based training limited the clinical skills of medical school graduates. Perhaps most important, he reported that huge numbers of graduates were being produced every year and that most of them had unacceptable levels of medical skill. He recommended closing most of the existing medical schools to address the problem of oversupply.

Several reform initiatives grew out of Flexner's report and from recommendations made by the AMA's Committee on Medical Education. One of the reforms required medical school applicants to hold a college degree. Another required that medical training be founded in the basic sciences. Reforms also required that medical students receive practical, hospital-based training in addition to classroom work. These reforms were carried out in the decade following Flexner's report, but only about half of the medical schools actually closed. By 1920, most of the medical colleges in the United States had met rigorous academic standards and were approved by the AAMC (Cooke et al. 2006).

Today, medical school graduates must pass a test before they can obtain a license to practice medicine. The licensure tests are administered by state medical boards. Many states now use a standardized licensure test developed in 1968 by the Federation of State Medical Boards of the United States. However, passing scores for the test vary by state. Most physicians also complete several years of residency training in addition to medical school.

Specialty physicians also complete extensive postgraduate medical education. Board certification for the various specialties requires the completion of postgraduate training as well as a passing score on a standardized examination. The most common medical specialties include the following:

- Internal medicine
- Pediatrics
- Family practice
- Cardiology
- Psychiatry
- Neurology
- Oncology
- Radiology

The most common surgical specialties include:

- Anesthesiology
- Cardiovascular surgery
- Obstetrics and gynecology
- Orthopedics
- Urology
- Ophthalmology
- Otorhinolaryngology
- Plastic and reconstructive surgery
- Neurosurgery

Some medical and surgical specialists undergo further graduate training to qualify to practice subspecialties. For example, the subspecialties of internal medicine include endocrinology, pulmonary medicine, rheumatology, geriatrics, and hematology. Physicians also may limit their practices to the treatment of specific illnesses such as an endocrinologist limiting his or her practice to the treatment of diabetes. Surgeons can work as general surgeons or as specialists or subspecialists. For example, an orthopedic surgeon may limit his practice to surgery of the hand, surgery of the knee, surgery of the ankle, or surgery of the spine.

Some physicians and healthcare organizations employ **physician assistants (PAs)** and surgeon assistants (SAs) to help them carry out their clinical responsibilities. Such assistants may perform routine clinical assessments, provide patient education and counseling, and perform simple therapeutic procedures. Most PAs work in primary care settings, and most SAs work in hospitals and ambulatory surgery clinics. PAs and SAs always work under the supervision of licensed physicians and surgeons.

Standardization of Nursing Practice

Until the late 1800s, nurses received no formal education and little training. Nursing staff for the hospitals was often recruited from the surrounding community, and many poor women who had no other skills became nurses. The nature of nursing care at that time was unsophisticated. Indeed, the lack of basic hygiene often promoted disease. Many patients died from infections contracted while hospitalized for surgery, maternity care, and other illnesses.

In 1868, the AMA called the medical profession's attention to the need for trained nurses. During the years that followed, the public also began to call for better nursing care in hospitals.

The first general training school for nurses was opened at the New England Hospital for Women and Children in 1872. It became a model for other institutions throughout the country. As hospital after hospital struggled to find competent nursing staff, many institutions and their medical staffs developed their own nurse training programs.

In 1897, a group of nurses attending the annual meeting of the American Society of Superintendents of Training Schools for Nursing founded the Nurses Associated Alumnae of the United States and Canada. In 1911, the organization was renamed the **American Nurses Association (ANA)**. During the early meetings of the association, members established a nursing code of ethics and discussed the need for nursing licensure and for publications devoted to the practice of nursing. Today, all 50 states have laws that spell out the requirements for the registration and licensure of nursing professionals.

Modern registered nurses (RNs) must have either a two-year associate's degree or a four-year bachelor's degree from a state-approved nursing school. Nurse practitioners, researchers, educators, and administrators generally have a four-year degree in nursing and additional postgraduate education in nursing. The postgraduate degree may be a master's of science or a doctorate in nursing. Nurses who graduate from nonacademic training programs are called licensed practical nurses (LPNs) or licensed vocational nurses (LVNs). Nondegreed nursing personnel work under the direct supervision of registered nurses. Nurses in all 50 states must pass an exam to obtain a license to practice.

Today's RNs are highly trained clinical professionals. Many specialize in specific areas of practice such as surgery, psychiatry, and intensive care. Nurse-midwives complete advanced training and are certified by the American College of Nurse-Midwives. Similarly, nurse-anesthetists are certified by the Council on Certification and Council on Recertification of Nurse Anesthetists. Nurse practitioners also receive advanced training at the master's level that qualifies them to provide primary care services to patients. They are certified by several organizations (for example, the National Board of Pediatric Nurse Practitioners) to practice in the area of their specialty.

Standardization of Hospital Care

In 1910, Dr. Franklin H. Martin suggested that the surgical area of medical practice needed to become more concerned with patient outcomes. He had been introduced to this concept in discussions with Dr. Ernest Codman. Codman was a British physician who believed that hospital practitioners should track their patients for a significant amount of time after treatment so that they could determine whether the end result had been positive or negative. Codman also supported the use of outcome information to identify the practices that led to the best results for patients (Hazelwood et al. 2005)

At that time, Martin and other American physicians were concerned about the conditions in US hospitals. Many observers felt that part of the problem was related to the lack of organization in medical staffs and lax professional standards. In the early 20th century, before the development of antibiotics and other pharmaceuticals, hospitals were used mainly by physicians who needed facilities in which to perform surgery. Most nonsurgical medical care was still provided in the home. It was natural, then, for the force behind improved hospital care to come from surgeons.

The push for hospital reforms eventually led to the formation of the **American College of Surgeons** in 1913. The organization faced a difficult task. In 1917, the leaders of the college asked the Carnegie Foundation for funding to plan and develop a hospital standardization program. The college then formed a committee to develop a set of minimum standards for hospital care. It published the formal standards under the title of the Minimum Standards.

During 1918 and part of 1919, the college examined the hospitals in the United States and Canada just as Flexner had reviewed the medical colleges a decade earlier. The performance of 692 hospitals was compared to the college's Minimum Standards. Only 89 of the hospitals fully met the college's standards; some of the best-known hospitals in the country failed to meet them.

Adoption of the Minimum Standards was the basis of the Hospital Standardization Program and marked the beginning of the modern **accreditation** process for healthcare organizations. Basically, accreditation standards are developed to reflect reasonable quality standards. The performance of each participating organization is evaluated annually against the standards. The accreditation process is voluntary. Healthcare organizations choose to participate in order to improve the care they provide to their patients.

The American College of Surgeons continued to sponsor the hospital accreditation program until the early 1950s. At that time, four professional associations from the United States and Canada decided to join forces with the college to create a new accreditation organization. This organization was called the Joint Commission on Accreditation of Hospitals. The associations were the American College of Physicians, the AMA, the American Hospital Association (AHA), and the Canadian Medical Association. The new organization was formally incorporated in 1952 and began to perform accreditation surveys in 1953.

The Joint Commission continues to survey several different types of healthcare organizations today, including:

- Acute-care hospitals
- Long-term care facilities
- Ambulatory care facilities
- Psychiatric facilities
- Home health agencies

Several other organizations also perform accreditation of healthcare organizations. These include the American Osteopathic Association (AOA), the Commission on Accreditation of Rehabilitation Facilities (CARF), and the Accreditation Association for Ambulatory Health Care (AAAHC).

Professionalism of the Allied Health Professions

After the First World War, many of the roles previously played by nurses and nonclinical personnel began to change. With the advent of modern diagnostic and therapeutic technology in the middle of the 20th century, the complex skills needed by ancillary medical personnel fostered the growth of specialized training programs and professional accreditation and licensure.

According to the AMA's definition, *allied health* incorporates the healthcare-related professions that function to assist, facilitate, and complement the work of physicians and other clinical specialists. The Health Professions Education Amendment of 1991 describes allied health professionals as health professionals (other than RNs, physicians, and PAs) who have received a certificate, an associate's degree, a bachelor's degree, a master's degree, a doctorate, or postdoctoral training in a healthcare-related science. Such individuals share responsibility for the delivery of healthcare services with clinicians (physicians, nurses, and PAs).

Allied health occupations are among the fastest growing in healthcare. The number of allied health professionals is difficult to estimate and depends on the definition of allied health. Unlike medicine, women dominate most of the allied health professions, representing between 75 and 95 percent in most of the occupations. All 50 states require licensure for some allied health professions (physical therapy, for example). Practitioners in other allied health professions (occupational therapy, for example) may be licensed in some states, but not in others.

The following list briefly describes some of the major occupations usually considered to be allied health professions (Jonas and Kovner 2005, 446–448):

- *Clinical laboratory science:* Originally referred to as medical laboratory technology, this field is now referred to more appropriately as clinical laboratory science. Clinical laboratory technicians perform a wide array of tests on body fluids, tissues, and cells to assist in the detection, diagnosis, and treatment of diseases and illnesses.

Diagnostic imaging technology: Originally referred to as x-ray technology and then radiologic technology, this field is now more appropriately referred to as diagnostic imaging. The field continues to expand to include nuclear medicine technologists, radiation therapists, sonographers (ultrasound technologists), and magnetic resonance technologists.

Dietetics: Registered dietitians (RDs), sometimes called clinical nutritionists, are trained in nutrition. They are responsible for providing nutritional care to individuals and for overseeing nutrition and food services in a variety of settings, ranging from hospitals to schools.

Emergency medical technology: Emergency medical technicians (EMTs) are responsible for providing a wide range of services on an emergency basis for cases of traumatic injury and other emergency situations and in the transport of emergency patients.

Health information management: Health information management (HIM) professionals (formerly called medical record managers) oversee health record systems and manage health-related information to ensure that it meets relevant medical, administrative, and legal requirements. Health records are the responsibility of registered health information administrators (RHIAs) and registered health information technicians (RHITs).

Occupational therapy: Occupational therapists (OTs) evaluate and treat patients whose illnesses or injuries have resulted in significant psychological, physical, or work-related impairment.

Physical therapy: Physical therapists (PTs) evaluate and treat patients to improve functional mobility, reduce pain, maintain cardiopulmonary function, and limit disability. PTs treat movement dysfunction resulting from accidents, trauma, stroke, fractures, multiple sclerosis, cerebral palsy, arthritis, and heart and respiratory illness. Physical therapy assistants work under the direction of PTs and help carry out the treatment plans developed by PTs.

Respiratory therapy: Respiratory therapists evaluate, treat, and care for patients with breathing disorders. They work under the direction of qualified physicians and provide services such as emergency care for stroke, heart failure, and shock as well as treat patients with emphysema and asthma.

Speech-language pathology and audiology: Speech-language pathologists and audiologists identify, assess, and provide treatment for individuals with speech, language, or hearing problems.

Check Your Understanding 2.1

Instructions: On a separate piece of paper, write down the word or term that correctly completes each of the sentences.

1. The ancient ___ developed surgical procedures, documented clinical cases, and created medical books.

   A. Egyptians
   B. Greeks
   C. Phoenicians
   D. Chinese

2. The ___ was established in 1847 to represent the interests of physicians across the United States.

   A. American Association of Medical Colleges
   B. American College of Surgeons
   C. Committee on Medical Education
   D. American Medical Association

3. Today, medical school students must pass a test before they can obtain a ___ to practice medicine.

   A. degree
   B. residency
   C. specialty
   D. license

4. The first general training school for ___ was opened at the New England Hospital for Women and Children in 1872.

   A. nurses
   B. physician assistants
   C. surgical specialists
   D. surgeons

5. Modern ___ must have either a two-year associate's degree or a four-year bachelor's degree from a state-approved nursing school.

   A. nurse practitioners
   B. licensed vocational nurses
   C. registered nurses
   D. licensed practical nurses

6. In 1910, Dr. Franklin H. Martin suggested that the surgical area of medical practice needed to become more concerned with ___.

   A. patient care
   B. professional standards
   C. patient outcomes
   D. nonsurgical medical care

7. Adoption of the Minimum Standards marked the beginning of the modern ___ process for healthcare organizations.

   A. accreditation
   B. licensing
   C. reform
   D. educational

8. According to the AMA's definition, ___ incorporates the healthcare-related professions that function to assist, facilitate, and complement the work of physicians and other clinical specialists.

   A. home health
   B. nursing care
   C. ambulatory care
   D. allied health

Modern Healthcare Delivery in the United States

Until the Second World War, most healthcare was provided in the home. Quality in healthcare services was considered a product of appropriate medical practice and oversight by physicians and surgeons. Even the Minimum Standards used to evaluate the performance of hospitals were based on factors directly related to the composition and skills of the hospital medical staff.

The 20th century was a period of tremendous change in American society. Advances in medical science promised better outcomes and increased the demand for healthcare services. But medical care has never been free. Even in the best economic times, many Americans have been unable to take full advantage of what medicine has to offer because they cannot afford it.

Concern over access to healthcare was especially evident during the Great Depression of the 1930s. During the Depression, America's leaders were forced to consider how the poor and disadvantaged could receive the care they needed. Before the Depression, medical care for the poor and elderly had been handled as a function of social welfare agencies. During the 1930s, however, few people were able to pay for medical care. The problem of how to pay for the healthcare needs of millions of Americans became a public and governmental concern. Working Americans turned to prepaid health plans to help them pay for healthcare, but the unemployed and the unemployable needed help from a different source.

Effects of the Great Depression

The concept of prepaid healthcare, or health insurance, began with the financial problems of one hospital, Baylor University Hospital in Dallas, Texas (AHA 1999, 14). In 1929, the administrator of the hospital arranged to provide hospital services to Dallas's schoolteachers for 50 cents per person per month. Before that time, a few large employers had set up company clinics and hired company physicians to care for their workers, but the idea of a prepaid health plan that could be purchased by individuals had never been tried before.

The idea of public funding for healthcare services also goes back to the Great Depression. The decline in family income during the 1930s curtailed the use of medical services by the poor. In 10 working-class communities studied between 1929 and 1933, the proportion of families with incomes under $150 per capita had increased from 10 to 43 percent. A 1938 Gallup poll asked people whether they had put off seeing a physician because of the cost. The results showed that 68 percent of lower-income respondents had put off medical care, compared with 24 percent of respondents in upper-income brackets (Starr 1982, 271).

The decreased use of medical services and the inability of many patients to pay meant lower incomes for physicians. Hospitals were in similar trouble. Beds were empty, bills went unpaid, and contributions to hospital fundraising efforts tumbled. As a result, private physicians and charities could no longer meet the demand for free services. For the first time, physicians and hospitals asked state welfare departments to pay for the treatment of people on relief.

The push for government-sponsored health insurance continued in the late 1930s during the administration of President Franklin D. Roosevelt. However, compulsory health insurance stood on the margins of national politics throughout the New Deal era. It was not made part of the new Social Security program, and it was never fully supported by President Roosevelt.

Postwar Efforts toward Improving Healthcare Access

After World War II, the issue of healthcare access finally moved to the center of national politics. In the late 1940s, President Harry Truman expressed unreserved support for a national health insurance program. However, the issue of compulsory health insurance became entangled with America's fear of communism. Opponents of Truman's healthcare program labeled it "socialized medicine," and the program failed to win legislative support.

The idea of national health insurance did not resurface until the administration of Lyndon Johnson and the Great Society legislation of the 1960s. The Medicare and Medicaid programs were legislated in 1965 to pay the cost of providing healthcare services to the elderly and the poor, respectively. The issues of healthcare reform and national health insurance were again given priority during the first four years of President Bill Clinton's administration in the 1990s. However, the complexity of American healthcare issues at the end of the 20th century doomed reform efforts. Healthcare continues to be a major political issue; significant healthcare reform legislation was proposed by President Barack Obama and passed in 2010. The **Patient Protection and Affordable Care Act** (ACA) addresses healthcare costs, coverage, and quality, but it remains highly controversial and is scheduled to take years to be fully enacted.

Influence of Federal Legislation

During the 20th century, Congress passed many pieces of legislation that had a significant impact on the delivery of healthcare services in the United States. Many of these legislative efforts are described in the following subsections.

Biologics Control Act of 1902

Direct federal sponsorship of medical research began with early research on methods for controlling epidemics of infectious disease. The Marine Hospital Service performed the first research. In 1887, a young physician named Joseph Kinyoun set up a bacteriological laboratory in the Marine Hospital at Staten Island, New York. Four years later, the Hygienic Laboratory was moved to Washington, D.C. It was given authority to test and improve biological products in 1902 when Congress passed the Biologics Control Act. This act regulated the vaccines and sera sold via interstate commerce. That same year, the Hygienic Laboratory added divisions in chemistry, pharmacology, and zoology.

In 1912, the service, by then called the US Public Health Service, was authorized to study chronic as well as infectious diseases. In 1930, reorganized under the Randsdell Act, the Hygienic Laboratory became the **National Institutes of Health (NIH)**. In 1938, the NIH moved to a large, privately donated estate in Bethesda, Maryland (Starr 1982, 340).

Today, the mission of the NIH is to uncover new medical knowledge that can lead to health improvements for everyone. The NIH accomplishes its mission by conducting and supporting medical research, fostering communication of up-to-date medical information, and training research investigators. The organization has played a vital role in recent clinical research on treatment of the following diseases:

- Heart disease and stroke
- Cancer
- Depression and schizophrenia
- Spinal cord injuries

Social Security Act of 1935

The Great Depression revived the dormant social reform movement in the United States as well as more radical currents in American politics. Even before Roosevelt took office in 1933, a steady movement toward some sort of social insurance program had been growing. By 1931, nine states had passed legislation creating old-age pension programs. As governor of New York, Roosevelt had endorsed unemployment insurance in 1930. Wisconsin became the first state to adopt such a measure early in 1932.

Although old-age pension and unemployment insurance bills were introduced into Congress soon after his election, Roosevelt refused to give them his strong support. Instead, he created a program of his own. In June 1934, he announced that he would appoint the Committee on Economic Security to study the issue comprehensively and report to Congress in January 1935. The committee consisted of four members of the cabinet and the federal relief administrator and was headed by the secretary of labor, Frances Perkins.

Sentiment in favor of health insurance was strong among members of the Committee on Economic Security. However, many members of the committee were convinced that adding a health insurance amendment would spell defeat for the entire Social Security legislation. Ultimately, the Social Security bill included only one reference to health insurance as a subject that the new Social Security Board might study. The Social Security Act was passed in 1935.

The omission of health insurance from the legislation was by no means the act's only conservative feature. It relied on a regressive tax and gave no coverage to some of the nation's poorest people, such as farmers and domestic workers. However, the act did extend the federal government's role in public health through several provisions unrelated to social insurance. It gave the states funds on a matching basis for maternal and infant care, rehabilitation of crippled children, general public health work, and aid for dependent children under the age of 16.

Hospital Survey and Construction Act of 1946

Passage of the **Hill-Burton Act** was another important development in American healthcare delivery. Enacted in 1946 as the **Hospital Survey and Construction Act**, this legislation authorized grants for states to construct new hospitals and, later, to modernize old ones. The funded expansion of the hospital system was to achieve a goal of 4.5 beds per 1,000 persons. The availability of federal financing created a boom in hospital construction during the 1950s. The hospital system grew from 6,000 hospitals in 1946 to a high of approximately 7,200 acute-care hospitals.

Growth in Number of Hospitals

The number of hospitals in the United States increased from 178 in 1873 to 4,300 in 1909. In 1946, at the close of World War II, there were 6,000 American hospitals, with 3.2 beds available for every 1,000 persons.

In 2012, there are 5,754 hospitals in the United States, with a total of 941,995 beds. Hospital costs total $751 billion or 30 percent of the total spent on healthcare. The majority of the hospitals in the United States are nonprofit or owned by local, state, or federal governments (AHA 2012).

Decline in Number of Hospitals

During the 1980s, medical advances and cost-containment measures caused many procedures that once required inpatient hospitalization to be performed on an outpatient basis. Outpatient hospital visits increased by 40 percent with a resultant decrease in hospital admissions. Fewer patient admissions and shortened lengths of stay (LOS) resulted in a significant reduction in the number of hospitals and hospital beds. Healthcare reform efforts and the acceptance of managed care as the major medical practice style of US healthcare resulted in enough hospital closings and mergers to reduce the number of government and community-based hospitals in the United States to approximately 5,000 (Sultz and Young 2004, 68).

Public Law 89-97 of 1965

In 1965, passage of a number of amendments to the Social Security Act brought Medicare and Medicaid into existence. These two programs have greatly changed how healthcare organizations are reimbursed. Recent attempts to curtail Medicare and Medicaid spending continue to affect healthcare organizations.

Medicare (Title XVIII of the Social Security Act) is a federal program that provides healthcare benefits for people 65 years old and older who are covered by Social Security. The program was inaugurated in 1966. Over the years, amendments have extended coverage to individuals who are not covered by Social Security but who are willing to pay a premium for coverage, to the disabled, and to those suffering from chronic kidney disease.

The companion program, **Medicaid** (Title XIX of the Social Security Act), was established at the same time to support medical and hospital care for persons classified as medically indigent. Originally targeted to recipients of public assistance (primarily single-parent families and the aged, blind, and disabled), Medicaid has expanded to additional groups so that it now targets poor children, disabled, pregnant women, and very poor adults (including those 65 years of age and over). The only exception to these expansions was passage of the Personal Responsibility and Work Opportunity Reconciliation Act of 1996 (PRWORA, P.L. 104-193, 1996), which changed eligibility for legal and illegal immigrants (Cohen 2007). Medicaid today is a federally mandated program that provides healthcare benefits to low-income people and their children. Medicaid programs are administered and partially paid for by individual states. Medicaid is an umbrella for 50 different state programs designed specifically to serve the poor. Beginning in January 1967, Medicaid provided federal funds to states on a cost-sharing basis to ensure that welfare recipients would be guaranteed medical services. Coverage of four types of care was required: inpatient and outpatient services, other laboratory and x-ray services, physician services, and nursing facility care for persons over 21 years of age.

Many enhancements have been made in the years since Medicaid was enacted. Services now include family planning and 31 other optional services such as prescription drugs and dental services. With few exceptions, recipients of cash assistance are automatically eligible for Medicaid. Medicaid also pays the Medicare premium, deductible, and coinsurance costs for some low-income Medicare beneficiaries.

Four million individuals were enrolled in Medicaid during 1966, its first year of implementation. By 2008, 59.5 million people were enrolled in Medicaid programs. In 2009, the states and the federal government expended $366.4 billion on Medicaid, most of which was directed toward the elderly, the blind, or the disabled. Elderly and disabled participants comprised about one-quarter of the Medicaid rolls, yet the program expends almost three-quarters of all funds on this group (Kaiser 2009).

Public Law 92-603 of 1972

Utilization review (UR) was a mandatory component of the original Medicare legislation. Medicare required hospitals and **extended care facilities** to establish a plan for UR as well as a permanent UR committee. The goal of the UR process was to ensure that the services provided to Medicare beneficiaries were medically necessary.

In an effort to curtail Medicare and Medicaid spending, additional amendments to the Social Security Act were instituted in 1972. Public Law 92-603 required concurrent review for Medicare and Medicaid patients. It also established the professional standards review organization (PSRO) program to implement concurrent review. PSROs performed professional review and evaluated patient care services for necessity, quality, and cost-effectiveness.

Four major eras occurred in healthcare policy from 1975 through 2000. Like an archeological site, these eras have mostly accumulated on top of one another, rather than fully replacing that which precedes them. The health policy eras can be identified as the following (Etheredge 2001; Siegel and Channin 2001):

- *Age of traditional insurance* (1965–1982), which began with the enactment of Medicare and Medicaid and which was based on open-ended, fee-for-service health insurance
- *Age of regulated prices for government programs* (1983–1992), which was launched with the enactment of the Medicare diagnosis-related group (DRG) system
- *Age of markets, purchasing, and managed care* (1993–2000), the era that has seen the population move to managed care plans in both the private and public coverage programs
- *Information age* (2000–present), the arrival of the new millennium has thrust the healthcare delivery system into the "information age"; improving the delivery of healthcare both in a quantitative and qualitative sense will depend on improving management of digital information within and among healthcare institutions (Siegel and Channin 2001)

Health Systems Agency (HSA)

The Health Planning and Resources Development Act of 1974 called for a new local organization, the **health systems agency** or nationwide system of local health planning agencies, to have broad representation of healthcare providers and consumers on governing boards and committees. Although the governance structure required participation by consumers, interested parties from the provider groups dominated the discussions. Health systems agencies were fundamentally unsuccessful in materially influencing decisions about service or technology expansion. Their decisions became undeniably political, and attempts to achieve consensus based on real service needs were counterbalanced by community interests in economic and employment expansions. Concurrent with attempts to slow cost increases through a planning approach, a number of other legislative initiatives took shape that were directly related to concerns over Medicare costs and service quality (Sultz and Young 2004, 39, 242). The legislation that created the HSAs, or nationwide system of local health planning agencies, was repealed in 1986.

Utilization Review Act of 1977

In 1977, the **Utilization Review Act** of 1977 made it a requirement that hospitals conduct continued-stay reviews for Medicare and Medicaid patients. Continued-stay reviews determine whether it is medically necessary for a patient to remain hospitalized. This legislation also included fraud and abuse regulations.

Peer Review Improvement Act of 1982

The Peer Review Improvement Act of 1982 redesigned the PSRO program and renamed the agencies **peer review organizations (PROs)**. At this time, hospitals began to review the medical necessity and appropriateness of certain admissions even before patients were admitted. PROs were given a new name in 2002 and are now called **quality improvement organizations (QIOs)**. They currently emphasize quality improvement processes. Every state and territory, as well as the District of Columbia, now has its own QIO. The mission of the QIO is to ensure the quality, efficiency, and cost-effectiveness of the healthcare services provided to Medicare beneficiaries in its locale.

Tax Equity and Fiscal Responsibility Act of 1982

In 1982, Congress passed the **Tax Equity and Fiscal Responsibility Act (TEFRA)**. TEFRA required extensive changes in the Medicare program. Its purpose was to control the rising cost of providing healthcare services to Medicare beneficiaries. Before this legislation was passed, healthcare services provided to Medicare beneficiaries were reimbursed on a retrospective, or fee-based, payment system. TEFRA required the gradual implementation of a **prospective payment system** (PPS) for Medicare reimbursement.

In a retrospective payment system, a service is provided, a claim for payment for the service is made, and the healthcare provider is reimbursed for the cost of delivering the service. In a PPS, a predetermined level of reimbursement is established before the service is provided.

Prospective Payment Act (1982)/ Public Law 98-21 of 1983

The PPS for acute hospital care (inpatient) services was implemented in 1983, according to Public Law 98-21.

Under the inpatient PPS, reimbursement for hospital care provided to Medicare patients is based on DRGs. Each case is assigned to a DRG on the basis of the patient's diagnosis at the time of discharge. For example, under inpatient PPS, all the cases of viral pneumonia would be reimbursed at the same predetermined level of reimbursement no matter how long the patients stayed in the hospital or how many services they received.

Prospective payment systems for other healthcare services provided to Medicare beneficiaries have been gradually implemented in the years since 1983. Implementation of the ambulatory payment classification system for hospital outpatient services, for example, began in 2000.

Consolidated Omnibus Budget Reconciliation Act of 1985

The Consolidated Omnibus Budget Reconciliation Act of 1985 made it possible for the Health Care Financing Administration (HCFA) to deny reimbursement for substandard healthcare services provided to Medicare and Medicaid beneficiaries. (HCFA's name was changed to the Centers for Medicare and Medicaid Services [CMS] in 2001.)

Omnibus Budget Reconciliation Act of 1986

The Omnibus Budget Reconciliation Act of 1986 requires PROs to report instances of substandard care to relevant licensing and certification agencies.

Healthcare Quality Improvement Act of 1986

The Healthcare Quality Improvement Act established the **National Practitioner Data Bank (NPDB)**. The purpose of the NPDB is to provide a clearinghouse for information about medical practitioners who have a history of malpractice suits and other quality problems. Hospitals are required to consult the NPDB before granting medical staff privileges to healthcare practitioners. The legislation also established immunity from legal actions for practitioners involved in some peer review activities.

Omnibus Budget Reconciliation Act of 1989

The Omnibus Budget Reconciliation Act of 1989 instituted the Agency for Healthcare Policy and Research (now known as the Agency for Healthcare Research and Quality). The mission of this agency is to develop outcome measures to evaluate the quality of healthcare services.

Omnibus Budget Reconciliation Act of 1990

The Omnibus Budget Reconciliation Act of 1990 requires PROs to report actions taken against physicians to state medical boards and licensing agencies.

Health Insurance Portability and Accountability Act of 1996

The **Health Insurance Portability and Accountability Act (HIPAA)** of 1996 addresses issues related to the portability of health insurance after leaving employment, as well as administrative simplification. One of HIPAA's provisions was the creation of the Healthcare Integrity and Protection Data Bank (HIPDB). Its mission is to inform federal and state agencies about potential quality problems with clinicians and with suppliers and providers of healthcare services.

Mental Health Parity Act of 1996

The Mental Health Parity Act of 1996 (MHPA) is a federal law that may apply to two different types of coverage (CMS 2008a):

- Large group self-funded group health plans (CMS has jurisdiction over self-funded public sector [nonfederal governmental] plans while the Department of Labor has jurisdiction over private sector self-funded group health plans)
- Large group fully insured group health plans.

More than a decade after enactment of the MHPA, Congress is again considering the issue. Today's discussion is occurring in a new environment. Effective new treatment strategies have transformed the practice of behavioral healthcare, and health insurance plans are using a new generation of tools to promote optimal care. Health plans offer customized programs to encourage members to use effective care on an ongoing basis. They provide a variety of flexible benefit options for members, and they use advanced information systems to communicate with behavioral health practitioners about best practices.

American Recovery and Reinvestment Act of 2009

In 2009 Congress passed a diverse set of measures to stimulate economic recovery in the United States. One aspect of the American Recovery and Reinvestment Act (ARRA) focused on accelerating the adoption and use of information technology. ARRA offers economic incentives for healthcare organizations (HCOs) to purchase certified electronic health record systems and demonstrate meaningful use of those systems (AHIMA 2009). A phased rollout beginning in 2011 was developed recognizing that different HCOs were at varying stages of electronic health record (EHR) use. Once the incentive program runs out in 2016, financial penalties take effect for those HCOs treating Medicare beneficiaries. ARRA also extends HIPAA privacy and security provisions beyond healthcare providers and insurers to the business associates with whom they share personally identifiable healthcare information. Title XIII of ARRA is the Health Information Technology for Economic and Clinical Health Act (HITECH), and it contains a number of provisions supporting the adoption and use of EHRs and promoting participation in health information exchanges (HIEs). HITECH created Regional Extension Centers that provide local support for providers through education and training. Workforce development was another component of HITECH with grants offered to develop and provide training for an expanded health information technology workforce. HITECH also officially created the Office of the National Coordinator for Health IT (ONC) and defined the role and scope of the ONC going forward. The ONC has existed by executive order since 2004.

Patient Protection and Affordable Care Act of 2010

ACA was signed into law on March 23, 2010. This comprehensive healthcare reform legislation is intended to improve access through expanded coverage, to control healthcare costs, and to improve the overall healthcare system. ACA requires most US citizens and legal residents to have coverage through increased access to health insurance, tax credits to employers offering health insurance, expansion of the Medicaid programs and tax penalties for those who choose not to purchase coverage (Kovner et al. 2011). ACA calls for the creation of state-based American Health Benefit Exchanges and Small Business Health Options Program (SHOP) Exchanges, administered by a governmental agency or nonprofit organization. These exchanges will offer insurance programs to small businesses (less than 100 employees) and individuals. ACA also provides for the creation of the Consumer Operated and Oriented Plan (CO-OP) program to foster the creation of nonprofit, member-run health insurance companies in all 50 states and the District of Columbia to offer qualified health plans (AHIMA 2010b).

One of the goals of ACA is to improve the quality and performance of the healthcare system in the United States. The act calls for the development of a national quality improvement plan that includes priorities to improve the delivery of healthcare services, patient health outcomes, and population health. It establishes the National Public Health Council to coordinate prevention, wellness, and public health strategies including the development of a national health strategy that addresses the overall health of the population. Along with these initiatives the act also increases benefits for preventative health for Medicare and Medicaid beneficiaries and incents employers to improve wellness benefits for their workers. ACA creates a new patient-centered outcomes research institute with an emphasis on the clinical effectiveness of different healthcare treatments. New Medicare programs include a pilot to launch in 2013 that bundles payment for all services 3 days prior to and 30 days posthospitalization. The new law extends the physician quality reporting system and creates a new value-based purchasing program for hospitals based on performance against quality measures. It also expands quality reporting requirements to long-term care, inpatient rehabilitation, hospice, and cancer care facilities.

Administrative simplification was also addressed in ACA requiring the adoption of standard operating rules for the electronic exchange of information. These requirements expand on previous administrative simplification rules in HIPAA. Where the standards required in HIPAA lack the specificity to insure uniform adoption, those in ACA now require that standard business guidelines be created and adopted. It also charges the secretary of Health and Human Services to reduce the number and complexity of forms required to perform the administrative functions within healthcare. ACA also creates a penalty for noncompliance with the standards and operating rules.

ACA promotes the development of new patient care models through pilots that, based on evaluation, can be expanded through the Medicare and Medicaid programs. These efforts will be led by the newly established Center for Medicare and Medicaid Innovation within CMS, which is charged with testing innovative payment and service delivery models. One new model created in the legislation is the **accountable care organization (ACO)**. An ACO is a group of service providers that work together to manage and coordinate care to Medicare fee-for-service beneficiaries. Guidelines for the establishment of an ACO are under the purview of the secretary of HHS, but they may include quality reporting, e-prescribing, and the use of electronic health records.

Finally, the law addresses the development and training of the healthcare workforce through the newly created National Healthcare Workforce Commission with special emphasis on the underserved areas of the population. The goal of the workforce initiatives is to increase the supply of a qualified healthcare workforce and enhance workforce education and training to improve access and quality of healthcare services. The commission will study issues of workforce, supply, demand, distribution, and financing. Priority areas of study include more integrative training for healthcare workers, increased training in information technology, and the capacity of the educational programs to deliver the required numbers of healthcare workers for the future.

Future Federal Planning

Legislation and federal policy have a significant impact on healthcare. As the largest payer of healthcare services, the US government has a dual role of protecting the health of the population and ensuring that federal money is well spent. Beyond the legislative activities outlined previously, HHS is responsible for almost one-quarter of all federal spending, and its mission is to enhance the health and well-being of Americans by providing for effective health and human services and by fostering sound, sustained advances in the sciences underlying medicine, public health, and social services (HHS 2010). Updated every three years, HHS's strategic plan for the years from 2010 to 2015 contains five goals:

Goal 1: Strengthen healthcare. Improve access particularly to primary care and preventative services.

Improve the quality and safety of healthcare services and protect vulnerable populations. Increase the meaningful use of electronic health records.

Goal 2: Advance scientific knowledge and innovation. Accelerate scientific discovery and foster innovation. Invest in food and medical product safety. Understand what works in public health.

Goal 3: Advance the health, safety, and well-being of the American people. Invest in programs that improve the health and safety of children. Promote economic and social well being. Focus on prevention and wellness.

Goal 4: Increase efficiency, transparency, and accountability of HHS programs. Ensure program integrity, fight fraud and eliminate improp-er payments. Use HHS data to improve the health of Americans. Promote sustainability.

Goal 5: Strengthen the nation's health and human services infrastructure and workforce. Ensure a trained workforce is in place to meet the demands of the future.

Biomedical and Technological Advances in Medicine

Rapid progress in medical science and technology during the late 19th and 20th centuries revolutionized the way healthcare was provided. The most important scientific advancement was the discovery of bacteria as the cause of infectious disease. The most important technological development was the use of anesthesia for surgical procedures. These 19th-century advances formed the basis for the development of antibiotics and other pharmaceuticals and the application of sophisticated surgical procedures in the 20th century.

To further medical advances in the 21st century, the NIH sought the input of more than 300 recognized leaders in academia, industry, government, and the public to create a "Roadmap" program to accelerate biomedical advances, create effective prevention strategies and new treatments, and bridge knowledge gaps. The program, which involves a plethora of NIH institutes and centers, has three main strategic initiatives (NIH 2005):

- New Pathways to Discovery, which includes a comprehensive understanding of building blocks of the body's cells and tissues and how complex biological systems operate; structural biology; molecular libraries and imaging; nanotechnology; bioinformatics and computational biology
- Research Teams of the Future, including interdisciplinary research, high-risk research, and public-private partnerships
- Re-engineer the Clinical Research Enterprise

Figure 2.1.   Key biological and technological advances in medicine

Time	Event
1842	First recorded use of ether as an anesthetic
1860s	Louis Pasteur laid the foundation for modern bacteriology
1865	Joseph Lister was the first to apply Pasteur's research to the treatment of infected wounds
1880s–1890s	Steam first used in physical sterilization
1895	Wilhelm Roentgen made observations that led to the development of x-ray technology
1898	Introduction of rubber surgical gloves, sterilization, and antisepsis
1940	Studies of prothrombin time first made available
1941–1946	Studies of electrolytes; development of major pharmaceuticals
1957	Studies of blood gas
1961	Studies of creatine phosphokinase
1970s	Surgical advances in cardiac bypass surgery, surgery for joint replacements, and organ transplantation
1971	Computed tomography first used in England
1974	Introduction of whole-body scanners
1980s	Introduction of magnetic resonance imaging
1990s	Further technological advances in pharmaceuticals and genetics; Human Genome Project
2000s	NIH creates roadmap to accelerate biomedical advances, create effective prevention strategies and new treatments, and bridge knowledge gaps in the 21st century

Through these efforts, NIH will boost the resources and technologies needed for 21st-century biomedical science.

Figure 2.1 offers a timeline of key biological and technological advances at a glance.

Although surgical procedures were performed before the development of anesthesia, surgeons had to work quickly on conscious patients to minimize risk and pain. The availability of anesthesia made it possible for surgeons to develop more advanced surgical techniques. The use of ether as an anesthetic was first recorded in 1842. At about the same time, nitrous oxide was introduced for use during dental procedures and chloroform was used to reduce the pain of labor. By the 1860s, the physicians who treated the casualties of the American Civil War on both sides had access to anesthetic and pain-killing drugs.

In the 1860s, Louis Pasteur began studying a condition in wine that made it sour and unpalatable. He discovered that the wine was being spoiled by parasitic growths. His research proved that tiny, living organisms (called bacteria) increase through reproduction and cause infectious disease. Pasteur also demonstrated that bacteria could be destroyed by the application of heat and certain chemicals (for example, alcohol). In doing so, he laid the foundation for modern bacteriology. After 20 years of research into the biology of microorganisms, Pasteur began studying human diseases. In 1885, he developed a vaccine that prevented rabies.

Although the importance of cleanliness had been known since early times, the role that microorganisms played in disease was not understood until Pasteur conducted his research. In 1865, Joseph Lister was the first to apply Pasteur's research to the treatment of infected wounds. Lister began by protecting open fractures from infection by treating the wounds with carbolic acid (a disinfectant). His discovery was called the antiseptic principle. Antisepsis reduced the mortality rate in Lister's hospital after 1865 from 45 to 12 percent. He published his results in 1868, and soon carbolic acid was being used to prevent bacterial contamination during surgery.

During the 1880s and 1890s, sterilization of instruments using steam was developed. This technological advance had a major impact on surgery and in other areas throughout the hospital. The sterile operative technique was further advanced through the introduction of rubber surgical gloves in 1898. Other advances included the use of sterile gowns, masks, and antibiotics and other drugs.

In 1895, the well-known physicist Wilhelm Roentgen made observations that led to the development of x-ray technology. He found that he could create images of the bones in his hand by passing x-rays through his hand and onto a photographic plate. Radiographic technology is used extensively today to diagnose illnesses and injuries.

Many advances in laboratory testing occurred during the 20th century. Equipment that allows the rapid laboratory processing of diagnostic and prognostic examinations was developed, and the number of diagnostic laboratory procedures increased dramatically. For example, studies of prothrombin time were first made available in 1940, electrolytes in 1941 through 1946, blood gas in 1957, creatine phosphokinase in 1961, serum hepatitis in 1970, and carcinoembryonic antigen (the first cancer-screening test) in 1974.

Diagnostic radiology and radiation therapy have undergone huge advances in the past 50 years. An enormous advance first used in 1971 in England was an imaging modality called computed tomography (CT). The first CT scanners were used to create images of the skull. Whole-body scanners were introduced in 1974. In the 1980s, another powerful diagnostic tool was added, magnetic resonance imaging (MRI). MRI is a noninvasive technique that uses magnetic and radiofrequency fields to record images of soft tissues.

Surgical advances have been remarkable as well. Cardiac bypass surgery was developed in the 1970s, as were the techniques for joint replacement. Organs are now successfully transplanted and artificial organs are being tested. New surgical techniques have included the use of lasers in ophthalmology, gynecology, and urology. Microsurgery is now a common tool in the reconstruction of damaged nerves and blood vessels. The use of robotics in surgery holds great promise for the future (Sloane et al. 1999, 6–7).

Biotechnology is "the field devoted to applying the techniques of biochemistry, cellular biology, biophysics, and molecular biology to addressing practical issues related to human beings, agriculture, and the environment" (*Stedman's Medical Dictionary* 2000).

A pharmaceutical or drug company is a commercial business and is referred to as *Pharma*. Two examples of the types of companies in the field of biotechnology are Pharma and medical device companies. These companies conduct research on, develop, market, and/or distribute drugs for the healthcare industry.

A medical device company produces **medical devices,** which can be defined as an instrument or apparatus intended for use in the diagnosis of disease or for treatment of a condition. A medical device is used by a physician for a patient who has a condition whereby a body part does not achieve any of its primary intended purposes such as a heart valve. Medical devices can be used for life support, such as anesthesia ventilators, as well as for monitoring of patients, such as fetal monitors, and other uses, such as incubators.

Check Your Understanding 2.2

Instructions: On a separate piece of paper, match the descriptions with the appropriate legislation.

1. ___ Hospital Survey and Construction (Hill-Burton) Act

2. ___ Tax Equity and Fiscal Responsibility Act

3. ___ Public Law 89-79 of 1965

4. ___ Utilization Review Act

5. ___ Omnibus Budget Reconciliation Act of 1989

6. ___ Public Law 92-603 of 1972

7. ___ Healthcare Quality Improvement Act of 1986

8. ___ Omnibus Budget Reconciliation Act of 1990

9. ___ American Recovery and Reinvestment Act of 2009

10. ___ Patient Protection and Affordable Care Act of 2010

   A. Amendments to the Social Security Act that brought Medicare and Medicaid into existence

   B. Authorized grants for states to construct new hospitals

   C. Required concurrent review for Medicare and Medicaid patients

   D. Provides incentives for meaningful use of EHRs.

   E. Required hospitals to conduct continued-stay reviews for Medicare and Medicaid patients

   F. Established the National Practitioner Data Bank

   G. Calls for the development of a national quality improvement plan

   H. Required peer review organizations to report actions taken against physicians to state medical boards and licensing agencies

   I. Required extensive changes in the Medicare program to control the rising cost of providing healthcare services to Medicare beneficiaries (PPS general implementation)

   J. Instituted the Agency for Health Care Policy and Research (now the Agency for Healthcare Research and Quality)

Professional and Trade Associations Related to Healthcare

A number of trade and professional associations currently influence the practice of medicine and the delivery of healthcare services in the United States. Descriptions of a few of the numerous healthcare-related professional and trade associations that currently influence healthcare issues are provided here.

American Medical Association

The **American Medical Association (AMA)** was founded in 1847 as a national voluntary service organization. Today, the AMA has more than 815,000 physician members from every area of medicine. The organization is headquartered in Chicago. For more than 163 years, the AMA has pursued its mission to promote the art and science of medicine and the betterment of public health. Today, that long-standing commitment continues to inspire the AMA's efforts to uphold the highest standards in patient care, practice management, and professionalism. In 2010, as the largest organization of physicians in the country, the AMA marked its 11th consecutive year of financial growth, with net operating results of $34.3 million. Its key focus areas are

- Putting patient care first
- Helping physicians practice medicine
- Bringing people together

In addition, the AMA acts as an accreditation body for medical schools and residency programs. It also maintains and publishes the Current Procedural Terminology (CPT) coding system. CPT codes are used as the basis of reimbursement systems for physician services and other types of healthcare services provided on an ambulatory basis.

American Hospital Association

The **American Hospital Association (AHA)** was founded in 1899. At its first meeting, eight hospital superintendents gathered in Cleveland, Ohio, to exchange ideas, compare methods of hospital management, discuss economics, and explore common interests and new trends. The original group was called the Association of Hospital Superintendents. Its mission was "to facilitate the interchange of ideas, comparing and contrasting methods of management, the discussion of hospital economics, the inspection of hospitals, suggestions of better plans for operating them, and such other matters as may affect the general interest of the membership" (AHA 1999, 110).

The Association of Hospital Superintendents adopted a new constitution in 1906 and a new name, the American Hospital Association. At that time, it had 234 members. Its major concerns were developing hospital standards and building the management skills of its members.

Today, the mission of the AHA is to advance the health of individuals and communities. The association has a current membership of approximately 5,000 hospitals and healthcare institutions, 600 associate member organizations, and 40,000 individual executives active in the healthcare field. Its headquarters are located in Chicago.

The AHA publishes *Coding Clinic,* which provides official ICD-9-CM coding advice.

Joint Commission

Since its beginning in 1952, the **Joint Commission** has continually evolved to meet the changing needs of healthcare organizations. The organization changed its name from the Joint Commission on Accreditation of Hospitals (JCAH) to the Joint Commission on Accreditation of Healthcare Organizations (JCAHO) in the late 1980s to the Joint Commission in 2006 in recognition of changes in the US health delivery system. Today, the Joint Commission is the largest healthcare standards–setting body in the world. It conducts accreditation surveys in more than 19,500 facilities, including ambulatory care facilities, long-term care facilities, behavioral health facilities, healthcare networks, and managed care organizations as well as acute-care hospitals (Joint Commission 2007).

In the late 1990s, the Joint Commission moved away from traditional quality assessment processes and began emphasizing performance and quality improvement. Its ORYX initiative reflected the new approach. The goal of the ORYX initiative was to incorporate the ongoing collection of quality and performance data into the accreditation process.

Today, the Joint Commission's standards give organizations substantial leeway in selecting performance measures and improvement projects. Outcome measures document the results of care for individual patients as well as for specific types of patients grouped by diagnostic category. For example, an acute-care hospital's overall rate of postsurgical infection would be considered an outcome measure. The outcome measures must be reported to the Joint Commission via software from vendors that the Joint Commission has approved for this purpose.

Blue Cross and Blue Shield Association

The forerunner of the **Blue Cross and Blue Shield Association** was a commission instituted by the AHA in 1929. In 1960, the commission was replaced by the Blue Cross Association and ties to the AHA were broken. In 1982, the Blue Cross Association merged with the National Association of Blue Shield Plans to become the Blue Cross and Blue Shield Association. Blue Cross and Blue Shield brands are the nation's oldest and largest family of health benefit companies and among the most recognized brands in the health insurance industry, serving more than 99 million people in the United States and Puerto Rico.

American College of Healthcare Executives

The **American College of Healthcare Executives (ACHE)** is an organization for healthcare administrators. Like most of the organizations previously discussed, it is headquartered in Chicago. Its mission is to "advance our members and healthcare management excellence." ACHE has over 40,000 members internationally. It also publishes books and textbooks on healthcare services management.

American Nurses Association

The ANA was founded in 1897. Headquartered in Washington, D.C., the ANA is a professional association as well as the strongest labor union active in the nursing profession. It represents the interests of the nation's 3.1 million RNs (ANA 2011). The ANA's mission is "Nurses advancing our profession to improve health for all." To achieve that mission the ANA fosters high standards of nursing practice, promoting the rights of nurses in the workplace, projecting a positive and realistic view of nursing, and lobbies Congress and regulatory agencies on healthcare issues affecting nurses and the public (ANA 2011).

American Health Information Management Association

The **American Health Information Management Association (AHIMA)** is the professional membership organization for managers of health record services and healthcare information. It was founded in 1928 under the name of the Association of Record Librarians of North America. In 1929, the association adopted a constitution and bylaws. Its name was changed to the American Medical Record Association in 1970 and then to AHIMA in 1991.

Today, with headquarters in Chicago, the association has more than 63,000 members. Its mission is as follows: "AHIMA leads the health informatics and information management community to advance professional practice and standards" (AHIMA 2011). AHIMA's vision is "leading the advancement and ethical use of quality health information to promote health and wellness worldwide" (AHIMA 2011).

The association is the sponsoring organization for the **Commission on Accreditation of Health Informatics and Information Management Education (CAHIIM)**, which accredits two- and four-year programs in health information management. CAHIIM also accredits master's programs in Health Informatics and HIM. Additionally, it certifies health information professionals as registered health information technicians (RHITs) for graduates of two-year programs and registered health information administrators (RHIAs) for graduates of baccalaureate programs. Finally, AHIMA offers credentialing examinations for coding professionals as certified coding specialists (CCSs), certified coding specialists for physicians' services (CCS-Ps), certified healthcare privacy and security specialists (CHPSs), certified coding associates (CCAs), certified health data analysts (CHDAs), and certified documentation improvement practitioners (CDIPs).

Other Healthcare-Related Associations

Many other healthcare-related associations in the United States serve their professional members by providing educational, certification, and accreditation services. The best known include the following:

- American Osteopathic Association
- American Dental Association
- American College of Surgeons
- American League for Nursing
- American Society of Clinical Pathologists
- American Dietetic Association
- Commission on Accreditation of Rehabilitation Facilities
- American Association of Nurse Anesthetists

Check Your Understanding 2.3

Instructions: On a separate piece of paper, match each organization with the appropriate description.

1. ___ American College of Healthcare Executives

2. ___ American Hospital Association

3. ___ American Medical Association

4. ___ American Nurses Association

5. ___ American Health Information Management Association

6. ___ Blue Cross and Blue Shield Association

   A. Part of this organization's mission is to "advance healthcare management excellence."

   B. This organization was originally called the Association of Hospital Superintendents.

   C. This organization was originally a commission instituted by the AHA in 1929.

   D. This association was founded in 1928 under the name of the Association of Record Librarians of North America.

   E. Part of this organization's mission is to work for the improvement of health standards and the availability of healthcare services.

   F. This organization's mission is to improve health for all.

Healthcare Providers and Settings

According to the US Department of Labor, a healthcare provider or health professional is an organization or person who delivers proper healthcare in a systematic way professionally to any individual in need of healthcare services (29 CFR 825.118).

Healthcare Institutions and Services

Healthcare delivery is more than hospital-related care. It can be viewed as a continuum of services that cuts across services delivered in ambulatory, acute, sub-acute, long-term, residential, and other care environments. This section describes several of the alternatives for healthcare delivery along this continuum.

Organization and Operation of Modern Hospitals

The term *hospital* can be applied to any healthcare facility that has the following four characteristics:

- An organized medical staff
- Permanent inpatient beds
- Around-the-clock nursing services
- Diagnostic and therapeutic services

Most hospitals provide acute-care services to inpatients. **Acute care** is the short-term care provided to diagnose and treat an illness or injury. The individuals who receive acute-care services in hospitals are considered inpatients. Inpatients receive room-and-board services in addition to continuous nursing services. Generally, patients who spend more than 24 hours in a hospital are considered inpatients.

The **average length of stay (ALOS)** in an acute-care hospital is 30 days or less. (Hospitals that have ALOSs longer than 30 days are considered long-term care facilities. Long-term care is discussed in detail later in this chapter.) With recent advances in surgical technology, anesthesia, and pharmacology, the ALOS in an acute care hospital is much shorter today than it was only a few years ago. In addition, many diagnostic and therapeutic procedures that once required inpatient care can now be performed on an outpatient basis.

For example, before the development of laparoscopic surgical techniques, a patient might be hospitalized for 10 days after a routine appendectomy (surgical removal of the appendix). Today, a patient undergoing a laparoscopic appendectomy might spend only a few hours in the hospital's outpatient surgery department and go home the same day. The influence of managed care and the emphasis on cost control in the Medicare and Medicaid programs also have resulted in shorter hospital stays.

In large acute-care hospitals, hundreds of clinicians, administrators, managers, and support staff must work closely together to provide effective and efficient diagnostic and therapeutic services. Most hospitals provide services to both inpatients and outpatients. A hospital outpatient is a patient who receives hospital services without being admitted for inpatient (overnight) clinical care. Outpatient care is considered a kind of ambulatory care. (Ambulatory care is discussed later in this chapter.)

Modern hospitals are extremely complex organizations. Much of the clinical training for physicians, nurses, and allied health professionals is conducted in hospitals. Medical research is another activity carried out in hospitals.

Types of Hospitals

Hospitals can be classified in many different ways according to the

- Number of beds
- Type of services provided
- Type of patients served
- For-profit or not-for-profit status
- Type of ownership

Number of Beds

A hospital's number of beds is based on the number of beds that it has equipped and staffed for patient care. The term *bed capacity* is sometimes used to reflect the maximum number of inpatients for which the hospital can care. Hospitals with fewer than a hundred beds are usually considered small. Most of the hospitals in the United States fall into this category. Some large, urban hospitals have more than 500 beds. The number of beds is usually broken down by adult beds and pediatric beds. The number of maternity beds and other special categories may be listed separately. Hospitals also can be categorized on the basis of the number of outpatient visits per year. Table 2.1 compares the type of ownership and size of hospitals in 1975, 2005, and 2010.

Table 2.1.   Type of ownership and size of hospital, 1975, 2005, and 2010

Type of Ownership and Size of Hospital	1975	2005	2010
Hospitals	Number	Number	Number
All hospitals	7,156	5,756	5,754
Federal	382	226	213
Nonfederal	6,774	5,530	5,523
Community	5,875	4,936	4,985
Nonprofit	3,339	2,958	2,904
For profit	775	868	1,013
State-local government	1,761	1,110	1,068
6–24 beds	299	370	465
25–49 beds	1,155	1,032	1,266
50–99 beds	1,481	1,001	1,191
100–199 beds	1,363	1,129	1,216
200–299 beds	678	619	684
300–399 beds	378	368	399
400–499 beds	230	173	213
500 beds or more	291	244	320

(*continued on next page*)

Table 2.1. Type of ownership and size of hospital, 1975, 2005, and 2010 *(continued)*

Beds	Number	Number	Number
All hospitals	1,465,828	946,997	941,995
Federal	131,946	45,837	44,940
Nonfederal	1,333,882	901,160	897,055
Community			
Nonprofit	941,844	802,311	804,943
For profit	658,195	561,106	555,768
State-local government	73,495	113,510	124,652
6–24 beds	210,154	127,695	124,523
25–49 beds	5,615	6,316	7,932
50–99 beds	41,783	33,726	41,088
100–199 beds	106,776	71,737	85,742
200–299 beds	192,438	161,593	173,915
300–399 beds	164,405	151,290	166,866
400–499 beds	127,728	126,899	137910
500 beds or more	101,278	76,894	94,910
	201,821	173,856	233,632
Occupancy Rate	**Percent**	**Percent**	**Percent**
All hospitals	76.7	69.3	66.6
Federal	80.7	66.0	65.3
Nonfederal	76.3	69.5	66.6
Community			
Nonprofit	75.0	67.3	64.5
For profit	77.5	69.1	66.2
State-local government	65.9	59.6	57.0
6–24 beds	70.4	66.7	64.4
25–49 beds	48.0	33.5	34.3
50–99 beds	56.7	47.1	46.7
100–199 beds	64.7	59.0	58.2
200–299 beds		63.2	63.9
300–399 beds	77.1	67.7	66.3
400–499 beds	79.7	70.1	68.3
500 beds or more	81.1	71.2	70.3
	80.9	75.9	74.7

Sources: AHA Annual Survey of Hospitals. Hospital Statistics, 1976, 1981, 1991–2007, 2011 editions. © 1976, 1981, 1991–2007, 2011: Used with the permission of Health Forum LLC, an affiliate of the AHA; CDS. http://www.cdc.gov/nchs/data/hus/hus07.pdf#092; National Center for Health Statistics Health. United States, With Chartbook on Trends in the Health of Americans, 2007.

Type of Services Provided

Some hospitals specialize in certain types of service and treat specific illnesses. For example:

- *Rehabilitation hospitals* generally provide long-term care services to patients recuperating from debilitating or chronic illnesses and injuries such as strokes, head and spine injuries, and gunshot wounds. Patients often stay in rehabilitation hospitals for several months.
- *Psychiatric hospitals* provide inpatient care for patients with mental and developmental disorders. In the past, the ALOS for psychiatric inpatients was longer than it is today. Rather than months or years, most patients now spend only a few days or weeks per stay.

However, many patients require repeated hospitalization for chronic psychiatric illnesses. (Behavioral healthcare is discussed in detail later in this chapter.)

- *General acute care hospitals* provide a wide range of medical and surgical services to diagnose and treat most illnesses and injuries.
- *Specialty hospitals* provide diagnostic and therapeutic services for a limited range of conditions (for example, burns, cancer, tuberculosis, obstetrics and gynecology).

Type of Patients Served

Some hospitals specialize in serving specific types of patients. For example, children's hospitals provide specialized pediatric services in a number of medical specialties.

For-Profit or Not-for-Profit Status

Hospitals also can be classified on the basis of their ownership and profitability status. Not-for-profit healthcare organizations use excess funds to improve their services and to finance educational programs and community services. For-profit healthcare organizations are privately owned. Excess funds are paid back to the managers, owners, and investors in the form of bonuses and dividends.

Type of Ownership

The most common ownership types for hospitals and other kinds of healthcare organizations in the United States include the following:

- *Government-owned hospitals* are operated by a specific branch of federal, state, or local government as not-for-profit organizations. (Government-owned hospitals are sometimes called public hospitals.) They are supported, at least in part, by tax dollars. Examples of federally owned and operated hospitals include those operated by the Department of Veterans Affairs to serve retired military personnel. The Department of Defense operates facilities for active military personnel and their dependents. Many states own and operate psychiatric hospitals. County and city governments often operate public hospitals to serve the healthcare needs of their communities, especially those residents who are unable to pay for their care.
- *Proprietary hospitals* may be owned by private foundations, partnerships, or investor-owned corporations. Large corporations may own a number of for-profit hospitals, and the stock of several large US hospital chains is publicly traded.
- *Voluntary hospitals* are not-for-profit hospitals owned by universities, churches, charities, religious orders, unions, and other not-for-profit entities. They often provide free care to patients who otherwise would not have access to healthcare services.

Organization of Hospital Services

The organizational structure of every hospital is designed to meet its specific needs. For example, most acute-care hospitals are made up of a board of directors, a professional medical staff, an executive administrative staff, medical and surgical services, patient care (nursing) services, diagnostic and laboratory services, and support services (for example, nutritional services, environmental safety, HIM services).

Board of Directors

The board of directors has primary responsibility for setting the overall direction of the hospital. (In some hospitals, the board of directors is called the governing board or board of trustees.) The board works with the chief executive officer (CEO) and the leaders of the organization's medical staff to develop the hospital's strategic direction as well as its mission, vision, and values:

- *Mission:* A statement of the organization's purpose and the customers it serves
- *Vision:* A description of the organization's ideal future
- *Values:* A descriptive list of the organization's fundamental principles or beliefs

Other specific responsibilities of the board of directors include the following:

- Establishing bylaws in accordance with the organization's legal and licensing requirements
- Selecting qualified administrators
- Approving the organization and makeup of the clinical staff
- Monitoring the quality of care

The board's members are elected for specific terms of service (for example, five years). Most boards also elect officers, commonly a chairman, vice chairman, president, secretary, and treasurer. The size of governing boards varies considerably. Individual board members are called directors, board members, or trustees. Individuals serve on one or more standing committees such as the executive committee, joint conference committee, finance committee, strategic planning committee, and building committee.

The makeup of the board depends on the type of hospital and the form of ownership. For example, the board of a community hospital is likely to include local business leaders, representatives of community organizations, and other people interested in the welfare of the community. The board of a teaching hospital, on the other hand, is likely to include medical school alumni and university administrators, among others.

In the future, boards of directors will continue to face strict accountability in terms of cost containment, performance management, and integration of services to maintain fiscal stability and to ensure the delivery of high-quality patient care.

Medical Staff

The medical staff consists of physicians who have received extensive training in various medical disciplines (for example, internal medicine, pediatrics, cardiology, gynecology and obstetrics, orthopedics, surgery). The medical staff's primary objective is to provide high-quality care to the patients who come to the hospital. The physicians on the hospital's medical staff diagnose illnesses and develop patient-centered treatment regimens. Moreover, physicians on the medical staff may serve on the hospital's governing board, where they provide critical insight relevant to strategic and operational planning and policy making.

The medical staff is the aggregate of physicians who have been granted permission to provide clinical services in the hospital. This permission is called **clinical privileges.** An individual physician's privileges are limited to a specific scope of practice. For example, an internal medicine physician would be permitted to diagnose and treat a patient with pneumonia but not to perform a surgical procedure. Most members of the medical staff are not actually employees of the hospital. However, many hospitals do employ radiologists, anesthesiologists, and critical care specialists.

Medical staff classification refers to the organization of physicians according to clinical assignment. Depending on the size of the hospital and on the credentials and clinical privileges of its physicians, the medical staff may be separated into departments such as medicine, surgery, obstetrics, pediatrics, and other specialty services. Typical medical staff classifications include active, provisional, honorary, consulting, courtesy, and medical resident assignments.

Officers of the medical staff usually include a president or chief of staff, a vice president or chief of staff elect, and a secretary. These offices are authorized by vote of the entire active medical staff. The president presides at all regular meetings of the medical staff and is an ex officio member of all medical staff committees. The secretary ensures that accurate and complete minutes of medical staff meetings are maintained and that correspondence is handled appropriately.

The medical staff operates according to a predetermined set of policies. These policies are called the **medical staff bylaws.** The bylaws spell out the specific qualifications that physicians must demonstrate before they can practice medicine in the hospital. The bylaws are considered legally binding. Any changes to the bylaws must be approved by a vote of the medical staff and the hospital's governing body.

Administrative Staff

The leader of the administrative staff is the **CEO** or **chief executive officer**. The CEO is responsible for implementing the policies and strategic direction set by the hospital's board of directors. He or she also is responsible for building an effective executive management team and coordinating the hospital's services. Today's healthcare organizations commonly designate a **chief financial officer (CFO)**, a **chief operating officer (COO)**, and a **chief information officer (CIO)** as members of the executive management team.

The executive management team is responsible for managing the hospital's finances and ensuring that the hospital complies with the federal, state, and local regulations, standards, and laws that govern the delivery of healthcare services. Depending on the size of the hospital, the CEO's staff may include healthcare administrators with job titles such as vice president, associate administrator, department director or manager, or administrative assistant. Department-level administrators manage and coordinate the activities of the highly specialized and multidisciplinary units that perform clinical, administrative, and support services in the hospital.

Healthcare administrators may hold advanced degrees in healthcare administration, nursing, public health, or business management. A growing number of hospitals are hiring physician executives to lead their executive management teams. Many healthcare administrators are fellows of the American College of Healthcare Executives.

Patient Care Services

Most of the direct patient care delivered in hospitals is provided by professional nurses. Modern nursing requires a diverse skill set, advanced clinical competencies, and postgraduate education. In almost every hospital, patient care services constitute the largest clinical department in terms of staffing, budget, specialized services offered, and clinical expertise required.

Nurses are responsible for providing continuous, around-the-clock treatment and support for hospital inpatients. The quantity and quality of nursing care available to patients are influenced by a number of factors, including the nursing staff's educational preparation and specialization, experience, and skill level. The level of patient care staffing is also a critical component of quality.

Traditionally, physicians alone determined the type of treatment each patient received. However, today's nurses are playing a wider role in treatment planning and **case management.** They identify timely and effective interventions in response to a wide range of problems related to the patients' treatment, comfort, and safety. Their responsibilities include performing patient assessments, creating care plans, evaluating the appropriateness of treatment, and evaluating the effectiveness of care. At the same time that they provide technical care, effective nursing professionals also offer personal caring that recognizes the patients' concerns and the emotional needs of patients and their families.

A registered nurse qualified by advanced education and clinical and management experience usually administers patient care services. Although the title may vary, this role is usually referred to as the **chief nursing officer (CNO)** or vice president of nursing or patient care. The CNO is a member of the hospital's executive management team and usually reports directly to the CEO.

In any nursing organizational structure, several types of relationships can be identified, including the following:

- *Line relationships* identify the positions of superiors and subordinates and indicate the levels of authority and responsibility vested with each position. For example, a supervisor in a postoperative surgical unit would have authority to direct the work of several nurses.
- *Lateral relationships* define the connections among various positions in which a hierarchy of authority is not involved. For example, the supervisors of preoperative and postoperative surgical units would have parallel positions in the structure and would need to coordinate the work they perform.
- *Functional relationships* refer to duties that are divided according to function. In such arrangements, individuals exercise authority in one particular area by virtue of their special knowledge and expertise.

Diagnostic and Therapeutic Services

The services provided to patients in hospitals go beyond the clinical services provided directly by the medical and nursing staff. Many diagnostic and therapeutic services involve the work of allied health professionals. Allied health professionals receive specialized education and training, and their qualifications are registered or certified by a number of specialty organizations.

Diagnostic and therapeutic services are critical to the success of every patient care delivery system. Diagnostic services include clinical laboratory, radiology, and nuclear medicine. Therapeutic services include radiation therapy, occupational therapy, and physical therapy.

Clinical Laboratory Services

The clinical laboratory is divided into two sections: anatomic pathology and clinical pathology. Anatomic pathology deals with human tissues and provides surgical pathology, autopsy, and cytology services. Clinical pathology deals mainly with the analysis of body fluids, principally blood, but also urine, gastric contents, and cerebrospinal fluid.

Physicians who specialize in performing and interpreting the results of pathology tests are called pathologists. Laboratory technicians are allied health professionals trained to operate laboratory equipment and perform laboratory tests under the supervision of a pathologist.

Radiology

Radiology involves the use of radioactive isotopes, fluoroscopic and radiographic equipment, and CT and MRI equipment to diagnose disease. Physicians who specialize in radiology are called radiologists. They are experts in the medical use of radiant energy, radioactive isotopes, radium, cesium, and cobalt as well as x-rays and radioactive materials. They also are expert in interpreting x-ray, MRI, and CT diagnostic images.

Radiology technicians are allied health professionals trained to operate radiological equipment and perform radiological tests under the supervision of a radiologist.

Nuclear Medicine and Radiation Therapy

Radiologists also may specialize in nuclear medicine and radiation therapy. Nuclear medicine involves the use of ionizing radiation and small amounts of short-lived radioactive tracers to treat disease, specifically neoplastic disease (that is, nonmalignant tumors and malignant cancers). Because of the mathematics and physics of tracer methodology, nuclear medicine is widely applied in clinical medicine. However, most authorities agree that medical science has only scratched the surface in terms of nuclear medicine's potential capabilities.

Radiation therapy uses high-energy x-rays, cobalt, electrons, and other sources of radiation to treat human disease. In current practice, radiation therapy is used alone or in combination with surgery or chemotherapy (drugs) to treat many types of cancer. In addition to external beam therapy, radioactive implants and therapy performed with heat (hyperthermia) are available.

Occupational Therapy

Occupational therapy is the medically directed use of work and play activities to improve patients' independent functioning, enhance their development, and prevent or decrease their level of disability. The individuals who perform occupational therapy are credentialed allied health professionals called occupational therapists. They work under the direction of physicians. Occupational therapy is made available in acute-care hospitals, clinics, and rehabilitation centers.

Providing occupational therapy services begins with an evaluation of the patient and the selection of therapeutic goals. Occupational therapy activities may involve the adaptation of tasks or the environment to achieve maximum independence and to enhance the patient's quality of life. An occupational therapist may treat decreased functionality related to developmental deficits, birth defects, learning disabilities, traumatic injuries, burns, neurological conditions, orthopedic conditions, mental deficiencies, and psychiatric disorders. Within the healthcare system, occupational therapy plays various roles. These roles include promoting health, preventing disability, developing or restoring functional capacity, guiding adaptation within physical and mental parameters, and teaching creative problem solving to increase independent function.

Physical Therapy and Rehabilitation

Physical therapy and rehabilitation have expanded into many medical specialties. Physical therapy can be applied in most disciplines of medicine, especially in neurology, neurosurgery, orthopedics, geriatrics, rheumatology, internal medicine, cardiovascular medicine, cardiopulmonary medicine, psychiatry, sports medicine, burn and wound care, and chronic pain management. It also plays a role in community health education. Credentialed allied health professionals administer physical therapy under the direction of physicians.

Medical **rehabilitation services** involve the entire healthcare team: physicians, nurses, social workers, occupational therapists, physical therapists, and other healthcare personnel. The objective is to either eliminate the patients' disability or alleviate it as fully as possible. Physical therapy can be used to improve the cognitive, social, and physical abilities of patients impaired by chronic disease or injury.

The primary purpose of physical therapy in rehabilitation is to promote optimal health and function by applying scientific principles. Treatment modalities include therapeutic exercise, therapeutic massage, biofeedback, and applications of heat, low-energy lasers, cold, water, electricity, and ultrasound.

Respiratory Therapy

Respiratory therapy involves the treatment of patients who have acute or chronic lung disorders. Respiratory therapists work under the direction of qualified physicians and surgeons. The therapists provide such services as emergency care for stroke, heart failure, and shock patients. They also treat patients with chronic respiratory diseases such as emphysema and asthma.

Respiratory treatments include the administration of oxygen and inhalants such as bronchodilators. Respiratory therapists set up and monitor ventilator equipment and provide physiotherapy to improve breathing.

Ancillary Support Services

The ancillary units of the hospital provide vital clinical and administrative support services to patients, medical staff, visitors, and employees.

Clinical Support Services

The clinical support units provide the following services:

- Pharmaceutical services
- Food and nutrition services
- HIM (health record) services
- Social work and social services
- Patient advocacy services
- Environmental (housekeeping) services
- Purchasing, central supply, and materials management services
- Engineering and plant operations

HIM services are managed by credentialed health information management professionals—RHIAs and RHITs. The pharmacy is staffed by registered pharmacists and pharmacy technologists. Food and nutrition services are managed by registered dietitians (RDs), who develop general menus, special-diet menus, and nutritional plans for individual patients. Social work services are provided by licensed social workers and licensed clinical social workers. Patient advocacy services may be provided by several types of healthcare professionals, most commonly, registered nurses and licensed social workers.

Administrative Support Services

In addition to clinical support services, hospitals need administrative support services to operate effectively. Administrative support services provide business management and clerical services in several key areas, including

- Admissions and central registration
- Claims and billing (business office)
- Accounting
- Information services
- Human resources
- Public relations
- Fund development
- Marketing

Organization of Ambulatory Care

Ambulatory care is the provision of preventative or corrective healthcare services on a nonresident basis in a provider's office, clinic setting, or hospital outpatient setting (AHIMA 2010a). Ambulatory care encompasses all the health services provided to individual patients who are not residents in a healthcare facility. Such services include the educational services provided by community health clinics and public health departments. Primary care, emergency care, and ambulatory specialty care (including ambulatory surgery) can all be considered ambulatory care. Ambulatory care services are provided in a variety of settings, including urgent care centers, school-based clinics, public health clinics, and neighborhood and community health centers.

Current medical practice emphasizes performing healthcare services in the least costly setting possible. This change in thinking has led to decreased utilization of emergency services, increased utilization of nonemergency ambulatory facilities, decreased hospital admissions, and shorter hospital stays. The need to reduce the cost of healthcare also has led primary care physicians to treat conditions they once would have referred to specialists.

Physicians who provide ambulatory care services fall into two major categories: physicians working in private practice and physicians working for ambulatory care organizations. Physicians in private practice are self-employed. They work in solo, partnership, and group practices set up as for-profit organizations. Today, the majority of healthcare provided in the United States is by physicians in small physician practices.

Alternatively, physicians who work for ambulatory care organizations are employees of those organizations. Ambulatory care organizations include health maintenance organizations, hospital-based ambulatory clinics, walk-in and emergency clinics, hospital-owned group practices and health promotion centers, freestanding surgery centers, freestanding urgent care centers, freestanding emergency care centers, health department clinics, neighborhood clinics, home care agencies, community mental health centers, school and workplace health service agencies, and prison health services agencies.

Ambulatory care organizations also employ other healthcare providers, including nurses, laboratory technicians, podiatrists, chiropractors, physical therapists, radiology technicians, psychologists, and social workers.

Private Medical Practice

Private medical practices are physician-owned entities that provide primary care or medical and surgical specialty care services in a freestanding office setting. The physicians have medical privileges at local hospitals and surgical centers but are not employees of those healthcare entities.

Hospital-based Ambulatory Care Services

In addition to providing inpatient services, many acute-care hospitals provide various ambulatory care services.

Emergency Services and Trauma Care

Hospital-based emergency departments provide specialized care for victims of traumatic accidents and life-threatening illnesses. In urban areas, many also provide walk-in services for patients with minor illnesses and injuries who do not have access to regular primary care physicians.

Many physicians on the hospital staff also use the emergency care department as a setting to assess patients with problems that may either lead to an inpatient admission or require equipment or diagnostic imaging facilities not available in a private office or nursing home. Emergency services function as a major source of unscheduled admissions to the hospital.

Outpatient Surgical Services

Generally, ambulatory surgery refers to any surgical procedure that does not require an overnight stay in a hospital. It can be performed in the outpatient surgery department of a hospital or in a freestanding ambulatory surgery center. In 2006, there were 34.7 million ambulatory surgery visits with an estimated 53.3 million procedures performed. The rate of visits to freestanding ambulatory surgery centers increased about 300 percent between 1996 and 2006, while the rate of visits to hospital-based surgical centers remained about the same during the period (CDC 2009). The increased number of procedures performed in an ambulatory setting can be attributed to improvements in surgical technology and anesthesia and the utilization management demands of third-party payers.

Outpatient Diagnostic and Therapeutic Services

Outpatient diagnostic and therapeutic services are provided in a hospital or one of its satellite facilities. Diagnostic services are those services performed by a physician to identify the disease or condition from which the patient is suffering. Therapeutic services are those services performed by a physician to treat the disease or condition that has been identified.

Hospital outpatients fall into different classifications according to the type of service they receive and the location of the service. For example, emergency outpatients are treated in the hospital's emergency or trauma care department for conditions that require immediate care. Clinic outpatients are treated in one of the hospital's clinical departments on an ambulatory basis. And referral outpatients receive special diagnostic or therapeutic services in the hospital on an ambulatory basis, but responsibility for their care remains with the referring physician.

Community-Based Ambulatory Care Services

Community-based ambulatory care services refer to those services provided in freestanding facilities that are not owned by or affiliated with a hospital. Such facilities can range in size from a small medical practice with a single physician to a large clinic with an organized medical staff (Masters and Nester 2001).

Among the organizations that provide ambulatory care services are specialized treatment facilities. Examples of these facilities include birthing centers, cancer treatment centers, renal dialysis centers, and rehabilitation centers.

Freestanding Ambulatory Care Centers

Freestanding **ambulatory care centers (ACCs)** provide emergency services and urgent care for walk-in patients. Urgent care centers (sometimes called emergicenters) provide diagnostic and therapeutic care for patients with minor illnesses and injuries. They do not serve seriously ill patients, and most do not accept ambulance cases.

Two groups of patients find these centers attractive. The first group consists of patients seeking the convenience and access of emergency services without the delays and other forms of negative feedback associated with using hospital services for nonurgent problems. The second group consists of patients whose insurance treats urgent care centers preferentially compared with physicians' offices.

As they have increased in number and become familiar to more patients, many of these centers now offer a combination of walk-in and appointment services.

The newest trend in ambulatory care is the growth of clinics in retail outlets. In 2006 there were 175 retail-based convenient care clinics; in 2011 that number grew to about 1,250—two-thirds of which are located in drug stores. These **retail clinics** treat non-life-threatening acute illnesses and offer routine wellness services such as flu shots and sports physicals. Patients who use these clinics frequently do not have a primary care physician, but these visits are covered by most insurers (Marcus 2011).

Freestanding Ambulatory Surgery Centers

Generally, freestanding ambulatory surgery centers provide surgical procedures that take anywhere from 5 to 90 minutes to perform and that require less than a four-hour recovery period. Patients must schedule their surgeries in advance and be prepared to return home on the same day. Patients who experience surgical complications are sent to an inpatient facility for care.

Most ambulatory surgery centers are for-profit entities. They may be owned by individual physicians, managed care organizations, or entrepreneurs. Generally, ambulatory care centers can provide surgical services at lower cost than hospitals can because their overhead expenses are lower.

Public Health Services

Although the states have constitutional authority to implement public health, a wide variety of federal programs and laws assist them. HHS is the principal federal agency for ensuring health and providing essential human services. All its agencies have some responsibility for prevention. Through its 10 regional offices, HHS coordinates closely with state and local government agencies, and many HHS-funded services are provided by these agencies as well as by private-sector and nonprofit organizations.

The Office of the Secretary of HHS has two units important to public health: the Office of the Surgeon General of the United States and the Office of Disease Prevention and Health Promotion (ODPHP). ODPHP has an analysis and leadership role for health promotion and disease prevention.

The surgeon general is appointed by the president of the United States and provides leadership and authoritative, science-based recommendations about the public's health. The surgeon general has responsibility for the **public health service (PHS)** workforce (HHS 2012).

Home Care Services

Home healthcare is the fastest-growing sector to offer services for Medicare recipients. The primary reason for this is increased economic pressure from third-party payers. In other words, third-party payers want patients released from the hospital more quickly than they were in the past. Moreover, patients generally prefer to be cared for in their own homes. In fact, most patients prefer home care, no matter how complex their medical problems. Research indicates that the medical outcomes of home care patients are similar to those of patients treated in **skilled nursing facilities (SNFs)** for similar conditions.

In 1989, Medicare rules for home care services were clarified to make it easier for Medicare beneficiaries to receive such services. Patients are eligible to receive home health services from a qualified Medicare provider when they are homebound; when they are under the care of a specified physician who will establish a home health plan; and when they need physical or occupational therapy, speech therapy, or intermittent skilled nursing care.

Skilled nursing care is defined as both technical procedures, such as tube feedings and catheter care, and skilled nursing observations. Intermittent is defined as up to 28 hours per week for nursing care and 35 hours per week for home health aide care. Many hospitals have formed their own home healthcare agencies to increase revenues and at the same time allow them to discharge patients from the hospital earlier.

Voluntary Agencies

Voluntary agencies provide healthcare and healthcare planning services, usually at the local level and to low-income patients. Their services range from giving free immunizations to offering family planning counseling. Funds to operate such agencies come from a variety of sources, including local or state health departments, private grants, and different federal bureaus.

One common example of a voluntary agency is the community health center. Sometimes called neighborhood health centers, community health centers offer comprehensive, primary healthcare services to patients who otherwise would not have access to them. Often patients pay for these services on a sliding scale based on income or according to a flat rate, discounted fee schedule supplemented by public funding.

Some voluntary agencies offer specialized services such as counseling for battered and abused women. Typically, these are set up within local communities. An example of a voluntary agency that offers services on a much larger scale is the Red Cross.

Long-Term Care

Generally speaking, **long-term care** is the healthcare rendered in a non-acute-care facility to patients who require inpatient nursing and related services for more than 30 consecutive days. Skilled nursing facilities, nursing homes, long-term care facilities, and rehabilitation hospitals are the principal facilities that provide long-term care. Rehabilitation hospitals provide recuperative services for patients who have suffered strokes and traumatic injuries as well as other serious illnesses. Specialized long-term care facilities serve patients with chronic respiratory disease, permanent cognitive impairment, and other incapacitating conditions.

Long-term care encompasses a range of health, personal care, social, and housing services provided to people of all ages with health conditions that limit their ability to carry out normal daily activities without assistance. People who need long-term care often have multiple physical and mental disabilities. Moreover, their need for the mix and intensity of long-term care services can change over time.

Long-term care is mainly rehabilitative and supportive rather than curative. Moreover, healthcare workers other than physicians can provide long-term care in the home or in residential or institutional settings. For the most part, long-term care requires little or no technology.

Long-term Care and the Continuum of Care

The availability of long-term care is one of the most important health issues in the United States today. There are two principal reasons for this. First, thanks to advances in medicine and healthcare practices, people are living longer today than they did in the past. The number of people who survive previously fatal conditions has been growing, and more and more people with chronic medical problems are able to live reasonably normal lives. Second, there was an explosion in birth rate following World War II. Children born during that period, the so-called 'baby-boomer generation,' are in their 50s or 60s today. These factors combined indicate that the need for long-term care can only increase in the years to come.

As discussed earlier, healthcare is now viewed as a **continuum of care.** That is, patients are provided care by different caregivers at several different levels of the healthcare system. In the case of long-term care, the patient's continuum of care may have begun with a primary provider in a hospital and then continued with home care and eventually care in an SNF. That patient's care is coordinated from one care setting to the next.

Moreover, the roles of the different care providers along the patient's continuum of care are continuing to evolve. Health information managers play a key part in providing consultation services to long-term care facilities with regard to developing systems to manage information from a diverse number of healthcare providers.

Post-Acute Care

Post-acute care supports patients who require ongoing medical management or therapeutic, rehabilitative, or skilled nursing care. Patients require frequent physician oversight and advanced nursing care but no longer require the acute interventions and diagnostic services of acute-care settings. It is delivered in a variety of environments, including long-term acute-care hospitals, skilled nursing facilities, rehabilitation centers and at home-by-home health services (AHA 2010b). In 2009 there were 432 long-term acute-care hospitals (LTACHs) in the United States. Covered by Medicare, LTACHs provide intensive long-term services for patients with complex medical problems. To qualify as an LTACH for Medicare payment, a facility must meet Medicare's Conditions of Participation for acute-care hospitals and have an average inpatient length of stay greater than 25 days.

Delivery of Long-Term Care Services

Long-term care services are delivered in a variety of settings. Among these settings are SNFs or nursing homes, residential care facilities, hospice programs, and adult day-care programs.

Skilled Nursing Facilities or Nursing Homes

The most important providers of formal, long-term care services are nursing homes. SNFs, or nursing homes, provide medical, nursing, and, in some cases, rehabilitative care around the clock. The majority of SNF residents are over age 65 and quite often are classified as the frail elderly.

Many nursing homes are owned by for-profit organizations. However, SNFs also may be owned by not-for-profit groups as well as local, state, and federal governments. In recent years, there has been a decline in the total number of nursing homes in the United States but an increase in the number of nursing home beds.

Nursing homes are no longer the only option for patients needing long-term care. Various factors play a role in determining which type of long-term care facility is best for a particular patient, including cost, access to services, and individual needs.

Residential Care Facilities

New living environments that are more homelike and less institutional are the focus of much attention in the current long-term care market. Residential care facilities now play a growing role in the continuum of long-term care services. Having affordable and appropriate housing available for elderly and disabled people can reduce the level of need for institutional long-term care services in the community. Institutionalization can be postponed or prevented when the elderly and disabled live in safe and accessible settings where assistance with daily activities is available.

Hospice Programs

Hospice care is provided mainly in the home to the terminally ill and their families. Hospice is based on a philosophy of care imported from England and Canada that holds that during the course of terminal illness, the patient should be able to live life as fully and as comfortably as possible but without artificial or mechanical efforts to prolong life.

In the hospice approach, the family is the unit of treatment. An interdisciplinary team provides medical, nursing, psychological, therapeutic, pharmacological, and spiritual support during the final stages of illness, at the time of death, and during bereavement. The main goals are to control pain, maintain independence, and minimize the stress and trauma of death.

Hospice services have gained acceptance as an alternative to hospital care for the terminally ill. The number of hospices is likely to continue to grow because this philosophy of care for people at the end of life has become a model for the nation.

Adult Day-Care Programs

Adult day-care programs offer a wide range of health and social services to elderly persons during the daytime hours. Adult day-care services are usually targeted to elderly members of families in which the regular caregivers work during the day. Many elderly people who live alone also benefit from leaving their homes every day to participate in programs designed to keep them active. The goals of adult day-care programs are to delay the need for institutionalization and to provide respite for the caregivers. They are also known as day health centers.

There are currently over 4,600 adult day-care programs serving 150,000 clients each day (NADSA 2011). Most adult day-care programs offer social services, crafts, current events discussions, family counseling, reminiscence therapy, nursing assessment, physical exercise, activities of daily living, rehabilitation, psychiatric assessment, and medical care. The average age of clients is 72, and 52 percent have some kind of cognitive impairment.

Behavioral Health Services

From the mid-19th century to the mid-20th century, psychiatric services in the United States were based primarily in long-stay institutions supported by state governments, and patterns of practice were relatively stable. Over the past 45 years, however, remarkable changes have occurred. These changes include a reversal of the balance between institutional and community care, inpatient and outpatient services, and individual and group practice.

The shift to community-based settings began in the public sector, and community settings remain dominant. The private sector's bed capacity increased in the 1970s and 1980s, including psychiatric units in nonfederal general hospitals, private psychiatric hospitals, and residential treatment centers for children. Substance abuse centers and child and adolescent inpatient psychiatric units grew particularly quickly in the 1980s, as investors recognized their profitability. In the 1990s, the growth of inpatient private mental health facilities leveled off, and the number of outpatient and partial treatment settings increased sharply. The number of mental health organizations providing 24-hour services (hospital inpatient and residential treatment) increased significantly over the 32-year period from 1970 to 2002 (Foley et al. 2004). Today, because of deinstitutionalization and the closure of public psychiatric hospitals, community hospitals are the primary source of inpatient psychiatric care delivered in either designated psychiatric units or in scatter beds throughout the medical units (Mark et al. 2010). In 2010, the AHA reported only 435 dedicated nonfederal psychiatric hospitals (AHA 2012).

Residential treatment centers for emotionally or behaviorally disturbed children provide inpatient services to children under 18 years of age. The programs and physical facilities of residential treatment centers are designed to meet patients' daily living, schooling, recreational, socialization, and routine medical care needs.

Day-hospital or day-treatment programs occupy one niche in the spectrum of **behavioral healthcare** settings. Although some provide services seven days per week, many programs provide services only during business hours, Monday through Friday. Day-treatment patients spend most of the day at the treatment facility in a program of structured therapeutic activities and then return to their homes until the next day. Day-treatment services include psychotherapy, pharmacology, occupational therapy, and other types of rehabilitation services. These programs provide alternatives to inpatient care or serve as transitions from inpatient to outpatient care or discharge. They also may provide respite for family caregivers and a place for rehabilitating or maintaining chronically ill patients. The number of day-treatment programs has increased in response to pressures to decrease the length of hospital stays.

Insurance coverage for behavioral healthcare has always lagged behind coverage for other medical care. Although treatments and treatment settings have changed, rising healthcare costs, the absence of strong consumer demand for behavioral health coverage, and insurers' continuing fear of the potential cost of this coverage have maintained the differences between medical and behavioral healthcare benefits.

Although the majority of individuals who are covered by health insurance have some outpatient psychiatric coverage, the coverage is often quite restricted. Typical restrictions include limits on the number of outpatient visits, higher copayment charges, and higher deductibles.

Behavioral healthcare has changed significantly over the past 40 years, as psychopharmacologic treatment has made possible the shift away from long-term custodial treatment. Psychosocial treatments continue the process of care and rehabilitation in community settings. There are fewer large state hospitals; they have been replaced by psychiatric units in general hospitals, new outpatient clinics, community mental health centers, day-treatment centers, and halfway houses. Treatment has become more effective and specific, based on our growing understanding of the brain and behavior (Kovner et al. 2011).

Check Your Understanding 2.4

Instructions: On a separate piece of paper, match the descriptions provided with the terms to which they apply.

1. ____ Behavioral health service

2. ____ Public health service

3. ____ Home care service

4. ____ Hospice program

5. ____ Skilled nursing facility

6. ____ Voluntary agency

7. ___ Residential care facility

8. ___ Day-treatment program

9. ___ Continuum of care

10. ___ Freestanding ambulatory care center

    A. Fastest-growing sector of Medicare

    B. Provides emergency services and urgent care for walk-in patients

    C. Represents a reversal in the balance between institutional and community care

    D. Designed to meet patients' daily living, schooling, recreational, socialization, and routine medical care needs

    E. Has an analysis and leadership role for health promotion and disease prevention.

    F. Provides healthcare and healthcare planning services usually at the local level and to low-income patients

    G. Provides alternatives to inpatient care or serves as transition from inpatient to outpatient care or discharge

    H. Care provided mainly in the home to the terminally ill and their families

    I. Care provided by different caregivers at several different levels of the healthcare system

    J. Healthcare rendered in a non-acute-care facility to patients who require inpatient nursing and related services for more than 30 consecutive days

Integrated Delivery Systems

Many hospitals have responded to local pressures by rapidly merging, acquiring, and entering into affiliations and other risk-sharing reimbursement agreements with other acute and nonacute providers, hospital-based healthcare systems, physicians and physician group practices, and managed care organizations. Transactions have included mergers of nonprofit organizations into either investor-owned or other nonprofit entities.

The goal of **integrated delivery systems (IDSs)** or **integrated delivery networks (IDNs)** is to organize the entire continuum of care, from health promotion and disease prevention to primary and secondary acute care, tertiary care, long-term care, and hospice care, to maximize its effectiveness across episodes of illness and pathways of wellness. A premium is placed on integration and holistic care.

Managed care and healthcare organization integration have placed enormous pressure on information systems. The need for cost data, as well as the integration of data from the various components of integrated systems, has placed many demands on systems technology and personnel. A healthcare provider that cannot completely analyze the cost of delivery when dealing with an insurer is at a distinct disadvantage. Similarly, an inability to integrate patient data across a system can produce increased costs, inefficiencies, and even medical errors.

An IDS combines the financial and clinical aspects of healthcare and uses a group of healthcare providers, selected on the basis of quality and cost management criteria, to furnish comprehensive health services across the continuum of care (AHIMA 2010b). In an integrated health delivery network, various types of organizations are connected along a continuum of care through horizontal and vertical integration. Depending on where you are in the United States, an IDN may also be called integrated health system, integrated delivery system (network), integrated care system (network), organized delivery system, community care network, integrated healthcare organization, integrated service network, or population-based integrated delivery system. These are all essentially referring to the same thing.

Information Needs of IDNs

The role of computers has changed rapidly in healthcare organizations, just as it has in many service organizations. The more advanced systems, once called data-processing centers, are now called management information systems. As computer operations grew more powerful and complex, it became possible to think about creating new services or greatly improving existing ones. Innovations were considered strategic uses of information systems because they helped an organization to compete or achieve its goals. Hospitals and integrated health systems have begun to use computers to serve in new functions. For example, a hospital can offer physicians the opportunity to connect to its computer system. Thanks to virtual private networks, a physician can connect to an integrated health system's intranet and work within the system in a private and secure environment without worrying about the downtime often experienced on the Internet.

The emergence of IDNs has placed enormous pressure on the need for integrated information systems. The need for financial information, as well as the integration of data from the various components of integrated systems, has placed many demands on systems technology and personnel. An IDN must be able to integrate patient data across a system in an effort to analyze ways to reduce costs and inefficiencies. Healthcare providers must have access to their own data and be able to understand their own cost data to communicate effectively with insurance companies.

The role of IT and information management has changed dramatically for healthcare organizations. Business process improvement and transformation were considered strategic uses of IT because they were converting data to information and analyzing it to their own customized needs. "Interoperable systems provide clinicians with secure and efficient access to the comprehensive patient information they need to make fully informed clinical decisions," said Joyce Sensmeier, vice-president, informatics, at Health Information Management Systems Society (HIMSS). "These systems are the foundation of the comprehensive electronic health record and nationwide and regional health information networks" (e-MDs 2008).

Health information exchange (HIE) is an initiative by healthcare professionals and industry to improve the way computer systems in healthcare share information. HIE promotes the coordinated use of established standards such as Digital Imaging and Communication in Medicine (DICOM) and Health Level seven (HL7) to address specific clinical needs in support of optimal patient care. Systems developed in accordance with HIE communicate with one another better, are easier to implement, and enable care providers to use information more effectively. Physicians, medical specialists, nurses, administrators, and other care providers envision a day when vital information can be passed seamlessly from system to system within and across departments and made readily available at the point of care. HIE is designed to make their vision a reality by improving the state of systems integration and removing barriers to optimal patient care. Health information exchange is discussed in detail in chapter 9.

Attributes of Organized Delivery Systems

The Commonwealth Fund Commission on a High Performance Health System identified six attributes of an ideal healthcare system (Shih et al. 2008):

- Patients' clinically relevant information is available to all providers at the point of care and to patients through electronic health record systems.
- Patient care is coordinated among multiple providers, and transitions across care settings are actively managed.
- Providers (including nurses and other members of care teams) both within and across settings have accountability to each other, review each other's work, and collaborate to reliably deliver high-quality, high-value care.
- Patients have easy access to appropriate care and information including after hours; there are multiple points of entry to the system; and providers are culturally competent and responsive to patients' needs.
- There is clear accountability for the total care of patients.
- The system is continuously innovating and learning in order to improve the quality, value, and patients' experiences of healthcare delivery.

Organized systems like IDNs have the capability to demonstrate these attributes, and the form of organization may continue to be through large local systems. However, new accountable care organizations called for in ACA; independent practice associations that organize independent providers to delivery services under one or more insurers, health maintenance organizations, which combine provider and payer functions; and others may develop to address this challenge.

Check Your Understanding 2.5

Instructions: On a separate piece of paper, indicate whether the statements below are true or false (T or F).

1. ___ Ambulatory care is the short-term care provided to diagnose and treat an illness or injury.
2. ___ The influence of managed care and the emphasis on cost control in the Medicare and Medicaid programs have resulted in shorter hospital stays.
3. ___ Hospitals can be classified on the basis of their type of ownership.
4. ___ Government hospitals are operated by a specific branch of federal, state, or local government as for-profit organizations.
5. ___ The board of directors has primary responsibility for setting the overall direction of the hospital.
6. ___ Medical staff classification refers to the organization of physicians according to clinical assignment.
7. ___ A registered nurse qualified by advanced education and clinical and management experience usually administers patient care services.
8. ___ Physicians who specialize in radiology are called radiology technicians.
9. ___ Occupational therapy is made available in acute-care hospitals, clinics, and rehab centers.
10. ___ The ancillary units of the hospital provide vital clinical and administrative support services to patients, medical staff, visitors, and employees.

Forces Affecting Hospitals

A number of recent developments in healthcare delivery have had far-reaching effects on the operation of hospitals in the United States.

Development of Peer Review and Quality Improvement Programs

The goal of high-quality patient care is to promote, preserve, and restore health. High-quality care is delivered in an appropriate setting in a manner that is satisfying to patients. It is achieved when the patient's health status is improved as much as possible. Quality has several components, including the following:

- Appropriateness (the right care is provided at the right time)
- Technical excellence (the right care is provided in the right manner)

- Accessibility (the right care can be obtained when it is needed)
- Acceptability (the patients are satisfied)

Peer Review

In **peer review,** a member of a profession assesses the work of colleagues within that same profession. Peer review has traditionally been at the center of quality assessment and assurance efforts. The medical profession's peer review efforts have emphasized the scientific aspects of quality. Appropriate use of pharmaceuticals, postoperative infection rates, and accuracy of diagnosis are among the measures of quality that have been used. Peer review is a requirement of both CMS and the Joint Commission.

Quality Improvement

Quality improvement (QI) programs have been in place in hospitals for years and have been required by the Medicare and Medicaid programs and accreditation standards. QI programs have covered medical staff as well as nursing and other departments or processes.

Efforts to encourage the delivery of high-quality care take place at the local and national levels. Such efforts are geared toward assessing the efforts of both individuals and institutions. Currently, professional associations, healthcare organizations, government agencies, private external quality review associations, consumer groups, managed care organizations, and group purchasers of care all play a role in trying to promote high-quality care.

Meaningful Use of Electronic Health Records

The ARRA legislation passed in 2009 provides for economic incentives for hospitals and eligible providers who can demonstrate **meaningful use** of certified electronic health records. The incentive program started in October 2010, and if hospitals have not met the criteria by 2015 they will be subject to payment penalties (AHA 2011). Hospitals must first ensure that they possess a certified EHR. This may be done by acquiring a new system that is certified through an accredited certification body or by having current systems certified by that body. Then hospitals must meet a set of required performance objectives and choose from a list of elective measures that they must attest are being used in their organization. Some of the core objectives include the following:

- Maintain active medical allergy list
- Record standardized patient demographics
- Record vital signs and chart changes
- Maintain an active medication list
- Implement systems to protect patient privacy and security of patient data in the EHR.
- Maintain a current problem list

Finally, the EHR must be able to directly report quality measures to CMS. At least 95 percent of hospitals plan to seek these incentives which will increase the adoption and use of EHRs. This will dramatically change the landscape for health information management practice as an unprecedented investment in technology is under way and must result in systems that are implemented and used to manage care. Because meaningful use impacts many aspects of healthcare delivery, it is discussed in a number of chapters in this book. The primary source for locating information about the Meaningful Use Incentive Payment Program can be found at https://www.cms.gov/ehrincentiveprograms/.

Growth of Managed Care

Managed care is a generic term for a healthcare reimbursement system that manages cost, quality, and access to services. Most managed care plans do not provide healthcare directly. Instead, they enter into service contracts with the physicians, hospitals, and other healthcare providers who provide medical services to enrollees in the plans.

Managed care systems control costs primarily by presetting payment amounts and restricting patient access to healthcare services through precertification and UR processes. (Managed care is discussed in more detail in chapter 16.) Managed care delivery systems also attempt to manage cost and quality by:

- Implementing various forms of financial incentives for providers
- Promoting healthy lifestyles
- Identifying risk factors and illnesses early in the disease process
- Providing patient education

Restructuring initiatives and increased use of technology have streamlined operations and improved operational efficiencies over recent years for the managed care industry. Humana is one of the nation's largest healthcare plan providers in the United States, with approval from CMS to offer the Medicare Part D prescription drug plan (PDP) to the more than 42 million Medicare-eligible beneficiaries. Humana's new product design has, in recent years, focused on meeting the demand for greater self-determination by employers and members for varying levels of copayments, deductibles, coinsurance, benefits levels, and price (Kallos 2008).

Efforts at Healthcare Reengineering

During the 1980s and 1990s, healthcare organizations attempted to adopt **continuous quality improvement (CQI)** processes. Lessons learned from other areas of business were applied to healthcare settings. **Reengineering** came in many varieties, such as focused process improvement, major business process improvement, and business process innovation; total quality management (TQM); and CQI. Regardless of its approach, every healthcare organization attempted to look inside and think "process" as opposed to traditional "department" thinking. Healthcare organizations formed cross-functional teams that collaborated to solve organizational problems. At the same time, the Joint Commission reengineered the accreditation process to increase its focus on process and systems analysis. Gone were the days of thinking in a "silo." All of those silos were turned over, and healthcare teams learned from each other. The drivers of reengineering included cost reduction, staff shortages, and implementation of technology. Healthcare quality improvement is divided into three related activities: quality improvement (including process improvement, CQI, TQM, Six Sigma); quality control (audits, ISO 9001, statistical process control); and quality planning (new products and services) (Carlson 2002).

Value-Based Purchasing

Medicare is officially launching the **Value-Based Purchasing** program in fiscal year 2013 as required by ACA. The intent is to pay for care that rewards better value, patient outcomes, and innovation rather than just the volume of care provided. The Hospital Inpatient Quality Reporting measure infrastructure will be used to identify quality care. Hospitals will be evaluated and assigned points based on their performance compared to peer groups and their own performance improvement over time. Clinical process and patient experience criteria are both included in the evaluation. Because the funding for the incentive increase is taken out of the overall pool of prospective payment funds, hospitals that do not qualify for payment increases may experience reduction in payment. Certainly data collection, management, and reporting will be an important part of successful compliance.

Emphasis on Patient-focused Care

Patient-focused care is a concept developed to contain hospital inpatient costs and improve quality by restructuring services so that more of them take place in the nursing units (patient floors) and not in specialized units in dispersed hospital locations. The emphasis is on cross-training staff in the nursing units to perform a variety of functions for a small group of patients rather than one set of functions for a large number of patients. Some organizations have achieved patient-focused care by assigning multiskilled workers to serve food, clean patients' rooms, and assist in nursing care. However, some organizations have experienced low patient satisfaction with this type of worker because the patients are confused and do not know who to ask to do what.

Hospital staff spend most of their time performing activities in the following nine categories:

- Medical, technical, and clinical procedures
- Hotel and patient services
- Medical documentation
- Institutional documentation
- Scheduling and coordination
- Patient transportation
- Staff transportation
- Management and supervision
- Ready-for-action activities

Hospitals have had difficulty in fully and rapidly implementing patient-focused care for the following reasons: the high cost of conversion; the extensive physical renovations required; resistance from functional departments; and other priorities for management, such as mergers and considering potential mergers.

Check Your Understanding 2.6

Instructions: On a separate piece of paper, write the best terms to complete the following sentences.

1. Today, ___ refers to the level of skilled care needed by patients with complex medical conditions, typically Medicare patients who have multiple medical problems.

   A. acute care
   B. ambulatory care
   C. post acute care
   D. high-quality care

2. Quality has several components, including appropriateness, technical excellence, ___, and acceptability.

   A. accuracy of diagnosis
   B. continuous improvement
   C. connectivity
   D. accessibility

3. ___ programs have been in place in hospitals for years and have been required by the Medicare and Medicaid programs and accreditation standards.

   A. Quality assurance
   B. Peer review
   C. Managed care
   D. Quality improvement

4. ___ is a generic term for a healthcare reimbursement system that manages cost, quality, and access to services.

   A. Quality improvement
   B. Subacute care
   C. Managed care
   D. Patient-focused care

5. Recent evidence indicates that the quality of care provided under managed care systems may differ across ___.

   A. population groups
   B. healthcare settings
   C. medical facilities
   D. integrated delivery systems

6. ___ attempts to contain hospital inpatient costs and improve quality by restructuring services.

   A. Continuous quality improvement
   B. Patient-focused care
   C. Managed care
   D. Acute care

7. Managed care and healthcare organization integration have placed enormous pressure on ___.

    A. integrated delivery systems
    B. acute-care facilities
    C. rehabilitation facilities
    D. information systems

Licensure, Certification, and Accreditation of Healthcare Facilities

Under the 10th Amendment of the US Constitution, states have the primary responsibility for public health, which includes disease and injury prevention, sanitation, water and air pollution, vaccination, isolation and quarantine, inspection of commercial and residential premises, food and drinking water standards, extermination of vermin, fluoridation of municipal water supplies, and licensure of physicians and other healthcare professionals. Each state has a division or an agency that is dedicated to promoting high-quality patient care and safety in healthcare facilities and outpatient services by conducting regular on-site surveys. State and federal licensing and certification programs require that high-performance standards be met in the provision of medical care and in the construction and maintenance of the healthcare facility.

State Licensure

Licensure gives legal approval for a facility to operate or for a person to practice within his or her profession. Virtually every state requires that hospitals, sanatoria, nursing homes, and pharmacies be licensed to operate, although the requirements and standards for licensure may differ from state to state. State licensure is mandatory. Federal facilities such as those of the Department of Veterans Affairs (VA) do not require licensure.

Although licensure requirements vary, healthcare facilities must meet certain basic criteria that are determined by state regulatory agencies. These standards address such concerns as adequacy of staffing, personnel employed to provide services, physical aspects of the facility (equipment, buildings), and services provided, including health records. Licensure typically is performed annually, and facilities must usually meet the minimum acceptable standards for operation.

Certification for Medicare Participation

In 1965, the Social Security Act established both Medicare and Medicaid. Medicare was the responsibility of the Social Security Administration (SSA), but federal assistance to the state Medicaid programs was administered by the Social and Rehabilitation Service (SRS). SSA and SRS were agencies in the Department of Health, Education, and Welfare (HEW). In 1977, HCFA was created under HEW to effectively coordinate Medicare and Medicaid. In 1980, HEW was divided into the Department of Education and the Department of Health and Human Services. In 2001, HCFA was renamed the **Centers for Medicare and Medicaid Services (CMS)**, an agency of HHS.

CMS maintains oversight of the survey and certification of nursing homes and continuing care providers (including hospitals, nursing homes, home health agencies, end-stage renal disease facilities, hospices, and other facilities serving Medicare and Medicaid beneficiaries) and makes available to beneficiaries, providers and suppliers, researchers, and state surveyors information about these activities. In November 2002, CMS began the national Nursing Home Quality Initiative (NHQI). The goals of the initiative are essentially twofold: to give consumers with an additional source of information about the quality of nursing home care by providing a set of MDS-based quality measures on Medicare's Nursing Home Compare website, and to help providers improve the quality of care for their residents by giving them with complementary clinical resources, quality improvement materials, and assistance from the QIOs in every state (CMS 2005). The quality initiative, an important component of CMS's comprehensive strategy to improve the quality of care provided by America's nursing homes, is a four-prong effort that consists of (CMS 2005):

- Regulation and enforcement efforts conducted by state survey agencies and CMS
- Improved consumer information on the quality of care in nursing homes
- Continual, community-based quality improvement programs designed for nursing homes to improve their quality of care
- Collaboration and partnership to leverage knowledge and resources

Many nursing homes have already made significant improvements in the care being provided to residents by taking advantage of these materials and the support of QIO staff (CMS 2005). From the beginning of this Nursing Home Quality Initiative, CMS has insisted that the quality measures be dynamic and continue to be refined as part of CMS's ongoing commitment to quality.

To be eligible for Medicare and Medicaid reimbursement, providers must become Medicare-certified by demonstrating compliance with the **Conditions of Participation**. Certification is the process by which government and nongovernment organizations evaluate educational programs, healthcare facilities, and individuals as having met pre-determined standards. The certification of healthcare facilities is the responsibility of the states. However, Title XVIII of the Medicare amendment specifies that facilities accredited by the Joint Commission and the American Osteopathic Association must be deemed in compliance with the Medicare Conditions of Participation for Hospitals; those accredited are said to have deemed status.

Voluntary Accreditation

Accreditation agencies create standards for medical care, construct measurements of quality, and determine which organizations meet their standards. Provider organizations seek accreditation in order to prove that they meet the standards of legitimate and appropriate medical practice (Kovner et al. 2011, 184).

The Joint Commission operates voluntary accreditation programs for hospitals and other healthcare services. It certifies hospitals as having met the Conditions of Participation required for reimbursement under the federal Medicare program. The definition of federal **deemed status** is as follows:

> In order for healthcare organizations to participate in and receive payment from the Medicare and Medicaid programs, [they] must be certified as complying with the Conditions of Participation, or standards, set forth in federal regulations. (Joint Commission 2007)

A majority of state governments recognize the Joint Commission accreditation as a condition of licensure and receiving Medicaid reimbursement. Inspections are typically triannual with accreditation and survey findings made publicly available. The standards are based on the premise that healthcare organizations exist to maximize the health of the people they serve while using resources efficiently. When an organization is found to be in substantial compliance with the Joint Commission standards, accreditation may be awarded for up to three years. Hospitals must undergo a full survey at least every three years.

The Joint Commission publishes accreditation manuals with standards for hospitals, non-hospital-based psychiatric and substance abuse organizations, long-term care organizations, home care organizations, ambulatory care organizations, and organization-based pathology and clinical laboratory services.

Much like the Joint Commission, the American Osteopathic Association (AOA) Hospital Accreditation Program accreditation is a voluntary program that accredits osteopathic hospitals. Those hospitals that are accredited are recognized by HHS as having deemed status and thus are eligible to receive Medicare funds (AOA 2005).

The AOA has been accrediting healthcare facilities for more than 30 years under Medicare. It is one of only two voluntary accreditation programs in the United States authorized by CMS to survey hospitals under Medicare. In addition, the program is a cost-effective, user-friendly means to validate the quality of care provided by a facility.

The AOA accreditation program was developed in 1943 and 1944 and implemented in 1945. Under this program hospitals were surveyed each year. In this manner, the AOA was able to ensure that osteopathic students received their training through rotating internships and residencies in facilities that provided high-quality patient care. In 1995, the AOA applied for and received deeming authority to accredit laboratories within AOA-accredited hospitals under the Clinical Laboratory Improvement Amendments of 1988. The AOA also has developed accreditation requirements for ambulatory care and surgery, mental health, substance abuse, and physical rehabilitation medicine facilities (AOA 2005).

Reimbursement of Healthcare Expenditures

Together, the Medicare and Medicaid programs and the managed care insurance industry have virtually eliminated fee-for-service reimbursement arrangements.

Evolution of Third-Party Reimbursement

The evolution of third-party reimbursement systems for healthcare services began more than 60 years ago. The evolution created a need for systematic and accurate communications between healthcare providers and third-party payers. Commercial health insurance companies (for example, Aetna) offer medical plans similar to Blue Cross/Blue Shield plans. Traditionally, Blue Cross organizations covered hospital services and Blue Shield covered inpatient physician services and a limited amount of office-based care. Today, Blue Cross plans and commercial insurance providers cover a full range of healthcare services, including ambulatory care services and drug benefits. (Healthcare reimbursement systems are discussed in more detail in chapter 16.)

Most commercial health insurance is provided in the form of group policies offered by employers as part of their fringe benefit packages for employees. Unions also negotiate health insurance coverage during contract negotiations. In most cases, employees pay a share of the cost and employers pay a share.

Individual health insurance plans can be purchased but usually are expensive or have limited coverage and high deductibles. Individuals with preexisting medical conditions often find it almost impossible to get individual coverage.

Commercial insurers also sell major medical and cash payment policies. Major medical plans are directed primarily at catastrophic illness and cover all or part of treatment costs beyond those covered by basic plans. Major medical plans are sold as both group and individual policies. Cash payment plans provide monetary benefits and are not based on actual charges from healthcare providers. For example, a cash payment plan might pay the beneficiary $150 for every day he or she is hospitalized or $500 for every ambulatory surgical procedure. Cash payment plans are often offered as a benefit of membership in large associations such as AARP.

Government-Sponsored Reimbursement Systems

Until 1965, most of the poor and many of the elderly in the United States could not afford private healthcare services. As a result of public pressure calling for attention to this growing problem, Congress passed Public Law 89-97 as an amendment to the Social Security Act. The amendment created Medicare (Title XVIII) and Medicaid (Title XIX). Medicare and Medicaid are not issuers of health insurance. They are public health plans through which individuals obtain health coverage.

Medicare

Medicare was first offered to retired Americans in July 1966. Today, retired and disabled Americans who are eligible for Social Security benefits automatically qualify for Medicare coverage without regard to income. Coverage is offered under two coordinated programs: hospital insurance (Medicare Part A) and medical insurance (Medicare Part B).

Medicare Part A is financed through payroll taxes. Initially, coverage applied only to hospitalization and home healthcare. Subsequently, coverage for extended care in nursing homes was added. Coverage for individuals eligible for Social Security disability payments for over two years and those who need kidney transplantation or dialysis for end-stage renal disease also was added.

Medical insurance under Medicare Part B is optional. It is financed through monthly premiums paid by eligible beneficiaries to supplement federal funding. Part B helps pay for physicians' services, outpatient hospital care, medical services and supplies, and certain other medical costs not covered by Part A. At the present time, Medicare Part B does not provide coverage of prescription drugs. (Medicare Parts A and B are discussed in greater detail in chapter 16.) In January 2006, Medicare Part D was implemented to provide prescription drug coverage for Medicare beneficiaries who select this option.

Medicaid

Medicaid is a medical assistance program for low-income Americans. The program is funded partially by the federal government and partially by state and local governments. The federal government requires that certain services be provided and sets specific eligibility requirements.

Medicaid covers the following benefits:

- Inpatient hospital care
- Outpatient hospital care
- Laboratory and x-ray services
- SNF and home health services for persons over 21 years old
- Physicians' services
- Family planning services
- Rural health clinic services
- Early and periodic screening, diagnosis, and treatment services

Individual states sometimes cover services in addition to those required by the federal government.

Services Provided by Government Agencies

Federal health insurance programs cover health services for several additional specified populations.

TRICARE, which was originally referred to as the Civilian Health and Medical Program for the Uniformed Services (CHAMPUS), pays for care delivered by civilian health providers to retired members of the military and the dependents of active and retired members of the seven uniformed services. The Department of Defense administers the TRICARE program. The program also provides medical services to active members of the military.

The VA provides healthcare services to eligible veterans of military service. The VA hospital system was established in 1930 to provide hospital, nursing home, residential, and outpatient medical and dental care to veterans of the First World War. Today, the VA operates more than 950 medical centers throughout the United States. The medical centers are currently being organized into 22 Veterans Integrated Service Networks (VISNs) to increase the efficiency of their services.

Through the Indian Health Service, HHS also finances the healthcare services provided to Native Americans living on reservations across the country.

State governments often operate healthcare facilities to serve citizens with special needs, such as the developmentally disabled and mentally ill. Some states also offer health insurance programs to those who cannot qualify for private healthcare insurance. Many county and local governments also operate public hospitals to fulfill the medical needs of their communities. Public hospitals provide services without regard to the patient's ability to pay.

Workers' Compensation

Workers' compensation is an insurance system operated by the individual states. Each state has its own law and program to provide covered workers with some protection against the costs of medical care and the loss of income resulting from work-related injuries and, in some cases, illnesses. The first workers' compensation law was enacted in New York in 1910. By 1948, every state had enacted such laws. The theory underlying workers' compensation is that all accidents that occur at work, regardless of fault, must be regarded as risks of industry and that employer and employee should share the burden of loss (Kovner et al. 2011, 55).

Insurance

Healthcare insurance was created to spread risk over a large pool of people and to protect assets in the event of a catastrophic illness or injury. Health insurance guards against financial devastation in the face of serious health problems. In the United States, there are more than 300 million people covered by some form of health insurance (DeNavas-Walt et al. 2011). Of those, 64 percent are covered by private insurance and almost 16 percent are covered by Medicaid. As for employers providing health insurance benefits for their employees, the 2011 data reflected that 60 percent of all employers offered health insurance for their employees, with only 48 percent of small employers (Kaiser 2011).

Managed Care

The growth of managed care in the United States has had a tremendous impact on healthcare organizations and healthcare professionals. Managed care is a broad term used to describe several types of prepaid healthcare plans. Common types of managed care plans include health maintenance organizations (HMOs), preferred provider organizations (PPOs), and point-of-service (POS) plans.

Members of HMOs pay a set premium and are entitled to receive a specific range of healthcare services. In most cases, employers and employees share the cost of the plan. Coverage can be provided for an individual employee or his or her whole family. HMOs control costs by requiring members of the plan to seek services only from a preapproved list of providers, who are reimbursed at discounted rates. The plans also control access to medical specialists, expensive diagnostic and treatment procedures, and high-cost pharmaceuticals. They generally require preapproval for specialty consultations, inpatient care, and surgical procedures.

The development of managed care was an indirect result of the federal government's enactment of the Medicare and Medicaid amendments in 1965. Medicare and Medicaid legislation prompted the development of **investor-owned hospital chains** and stimulated the growth of university medical centers. Both of these furthered the corporate practice of medicine by increasing the number of management personnel and physicians employed by hospitals and medical schools (Kongstevdt 1993, 3–5).

The new healthcare programs for the elderly and poor laid the groundwork for increased corporate control of medical care delivery by third-party payers. This was done through the government-mandated regulation of fee-for-service and indemnity payments for healthcare services. After years of unchecked healthcare inflation, the government authorized corporate cost controls on hospitals, physicians, patients, prospective payment systems, and the resource-based relative value scale.

Further federal support for the corporate practice of medicine resulted from passage of the HMO Act of 1973. Amendments to the act enabled managed care plans to increase in numbers and expand enrollments through healthcare programs financed by grants, contracts, and loans. After passage of the HMO Act, strong support for the HMO concept came from business; the executive,

legislative, and judicial branches of government; and several states where managed care proliferated, such as California, some northeastern states, and particularly Minneapolis and St. Paul, Minnesota.

Bipartisan support for managed care was based on the concept that HMOs can decrease costs and encourage free-market competition in the medical care arena with only limited government intervention. One measure of success of this policy can be found in the virtual disappearance of some 17 national health insurance bills introduced into Congress in the early 1970s (Kongstevdt 1993, 3–5).

Impact of Managed Care Organizations

With more and more Americans receiving their health insurance through **managed care organizations (MCOs)**, the responsibilities of primary care providers have changed. In the fee-for-service model, the primary care provider is responsible only for the patients actually seen in his or her office, and a practice is viewed as being made up of individual patients. In a fully capitated managed care setting, however, particularly when the provider is paid through a capitation system rather than by a modified fee-for-service system, he or she is responsible for providing care to a defined population of patients assigned by the MCO. The MCO may audit the provider's practice to determine whether standards of care are being met. In the capitated MCO setting, providers are often held responsible for each patient on their panels, whether or not the patient ever comes to the office to be seen (Kovner et al. 2011).

The advent of managed care appeared to tame healthcare cost inflation during the early and mid-1990s, but costs are once again rising rapidly. In particular, the total cost of pharmaceuticals is skyrocketing. The managed care industry faces continued financial challenges. At the same time, it remains under intense public scrutiny and is facing continued attempts at increased government legislation and regulation. In addition, for many years costs increased faster than premiums could rise to cover them. Thus, escalating costs have forced employers to ask workers to pay for a larger share of healthcare. Political and market forces and the weakness of any stabilizing influences are eroding the ability of managed care firms to control underlying healthcare costs.

Although managed care deserves much of the credit for taming the rampant, double-digit healthcare inflation of the 1980s and early 1990s, the relief from rising medical bills that Americans enjoyed for several years is over, and increases in premiums have both HMOs and employers, especially smaller ones, scrambling for countermeasures.

Consumer-Driven Healthcare

An emerging issue in the private insurance market is that of consumer-driven healthcare. This strategy seems to be gaining momentum in an effort to both allow employees more choice in their healthcare decisions and to stabilize healthcare costs. The design of consumer-driven plans varies,

Figure 2.2.   Average Annual Firm and Worker Premium Contributions and Total Premiums for Covered Workers for Single and Family Coverage, by Plan Type, 2011

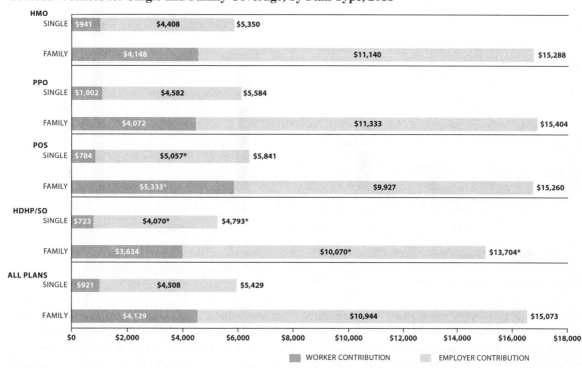

Source: Kaiser/HRET Survey of Employer-Sponsored Health Benefits, 2011.

but, essentially, it focuses on making consumers more price conscious by setting a large deductible before individuals receive insurance benefits. It is very different than managed care in that people have more choice but face sizeable personal financial risk (Kovner et al. 2011, 58). See figure 2.2 for an overview breakdown of the 2011 health insurance premiums for US covered workers.

Health Savings Accounts

Health savings accounts (HSAs), also called medical savings accounts, offer participants the opportunity to control how their healthcare dollars are spent. HSAs were created by the Medicare bill signed by President George W. Bush in December 2003 and are designed to help individuals save for future qualified medical and retiree health expenses on a tax-free basis.

The benefit of an HSA is that the member pays for the deductible with pretax dollars, which allows a member to save the money that ordinarily would have gone to pay taxes. When members pay off the deductible, the insurance company begins to pay. The money in the HSA earns interest and is owned by the member who holds the account (Health Insurance Carriers 2005). Industry estimates indicate that the number of individuals covered by HSA-eligible health plans increased significantly between 2004 and 2007. HSA participation also increased between 2004 and 2005, with estimates of continued growth through 2007. Nevertheless, many

HSA-eligible health plan enrollees have not opened HSAs (GAO 2008). See figure 2.3 for an overview of the estimated lives covered by HSA-eligible plans from September 2004 to January 2007. Between January 2007 and January 2008, the fastest growing market for HSA/high-deductible health plan products was small-group coverage (AHIP 2008).

Continued Rise in Healthcare Costs

The main reason for the continued rise in healthcare costs is that spiraling healthcare costs have, in effect, lessened workers' wages. Even though workers are producing more, inflation-adjusted median family income has dipped 2.6 percent—or nearly $1,000 annually since 2000. Employees and employers are getting squeezed by the price of healthcare. The struggle to control health costs is viewed as crucial to improving wages and living standards for working Americans. Employers are paying more for healthcare and other benefits, leaving less money for pay increases. In 2008, GAO reported that benefits devoured 30.2 percent of employers' compensation costs, with the remaining money going to wages, the Labor Department reported (GAO 2008). That is up from 27.4 percent in 2000. Since 2001, premiums for family health coverage have increased 113 percent, according to a 2011 report by the Kaiser Family Foundation. Premiums for family coverage averaged $15,073, of which workers paid $4,129, according to the report (Kaiser 2011).

Figure 2.3.   Estimated lives covered by HSA-eligible plans, September 2004 to January 2007

4,532,000

3,168,000

1,031,000

438,000

| | | | | | | | | | | | | | | | | | | | | | | | | | | | | | | | | | | | | | |
|Jan.|Feb.|Mar.|Apr.|May|June|July|Aug.|Sept.|Oct.|Nov.|Dec.|Jan.|Feb.|Mar.|Apr.|May|June|July|Aug.|Sept.|Oct.|Nov.|Dec.|Jan.|Feb.|Mar.|Apr.|May|June|July|Aug.|Sept.|Oct.|Nov.|Dec.|Jan.|Feb.|Mar.|

| 2004 | 2005 | 2006 | 2007 |

■ Covered lives

Source: America's Health Insurance Plans.

The catalysts for employers' annual cost for healthcare coverage increases include the cost of prescription drugs, medical innovation, and a growing acceptance of higher-premium health plans that offer greater flexibility in choice of providers. One way that employers attempted to control costs was to implement monitoring and preventive care plans for conditions such as diabetes and heart disease.

As mentioned, the United States continues to spend more on healthcare than any other developed nation. The average per capita healthcare spending among 30 member nations of the Organisation for Economic Co-operation and Development is less than half as much.

Moreover, the United States is seeing greater growth in spending from one year to the next than other developed nations. Despite the higher costs, however, Americans have a much higher incidence of obesity and their average life expectancy is slightly lower than that of people in Japan, Iceland, Sweden, and Canada.

Healthcare prices in the United States are influenced by many factors. Supply and demand are greatly influenced by insurance companies and health plans. Patients' bargaining power is greatly decreased because providers can negotiate different charges depending on the payer. Many cash-strapped Americans abandon their expensive private healthcare plans and choose not to be insured at all.

Payer Changes

Employers are fighting back, partly by establishing new benefit methods that can accomplish much more than simply raising workers' copayments. For example, many major firms are showing their employees how to use the Internet to obtain better information about diseases and prevention. Insurance providers are using the Internet as a resource as well. For example, Humana's web-based Emphesys benefit system puts everything from monthly payments to participating physicians to claims on the Internet at a substantial decrease in cost. Some employers are even hiring in-house physicians and nurses to provide primary care in the workplace.

Cost and Quality Controls

The federal government became involved in the quality-of-care and malpractice issues through the establishment of the NPDB under the Healthcare Quality Improvement Act of 1986. Congress enacted this legislation to

- Moderate the incidence of malpractice
- Allow the medical community to demonstrate new willingness to weed out incompetents
- Improve the base of timely and accurate information on medical malpractice

The act required hospitals to request information from the data bank whenever they hire, grant privileges, or conduct periodic reviews of a practitioner. (See chapter 12 for additional discussion of malpractice and other legal issues affecting HIM.)

Check Your Understanding 2.7

Instructions: Indicate on a separate piece of paper whether the statements below are true or false (T or F).

1. ___ Blue Cross plans and commercial insurance providers cover a full range of healthcare services.

2. ___ Most commercial health insurance is provided in the form of group policies offered by employers as part of their fringe benefit packages for employees.

3. ___ Today, retired and disabled Americans who are eligible for Social Security benefits automatically qualify for Medicare coverage.

4. ___ Medicaid is a medical assistance program for upper-income Americans.

5. ___ The Department of Defense administers the TRICARE program.

6. ___ Employers provide employees with a personal care account in consumer-driven healthcare.

7. ___ The development of managed care was an indirect result of the federal government's enactment of the Medicare and Medicaid amendments in 1965.

8. ___ The federal government became involved in the quality-of-care and malpractice issues through the establishment of the National Practitioner Data Bank under the Healthcare Quality Improvement Act of 1986.

Future of American Healthcare

Six major challenges that face the American healthcare system today include:

- Improving quality and safety
- Improving access and coverage
- Reining in the growth of healthcare costs
- Improving healthy behavior
- Improving public health services
- Improving the coordination and accountability of healthcare services

Although other challenges like health disparity and workforce issues exist, addressing these six would dramatically improve the system (Kovner et al. 2011). The passage of ACA will no doubt have the most profound impact on healthcare since the advent of Medicare and Medicaid in the 1960s. First, it addresses healthcare insurers providing coverage for an additional 32 million Americans through a variety of programs. These changes will impact access, cost, and quality as insured patients use less expensive services and enjoy better health. Second, it enables a variety of new healthcare delivery models such as the **patient-centered medical home (PCMH)**. The PCMH is a physician-directed model where every patient has a personal relationship with a primary care physician who coordinates all of the patient's care from preventative measures to long-term care. In this model the physician works with a group of patients throughout their lives to monitor and improve their overall health.

Another demonstration of a program to change healthcare delivery spelled out in ACA is the accountable care organization. An ACO is an entity comprised of primary care physicians, specialists, hospitalists, and facilities that are accountable for the cost and quality of the care they provide to a population

of patients (Kovner et al. 2011). The ACO would coordinate across a continuum of care for that patient population and receive a predetermined or capitated payment for that care. The physicians and healthcare organizations are expected to work together without being employed by the ACO. It is a partnership between hospitals and physicians to care for a group of patients (AHA 2010a). The ACO must possess the following competencies to coordinate the contributions of each party:

- Leadership
- Organizational culture of teamwork
- Relationships with other providers
- IT infrastructure for population management and care coordination
- Infrastructure for monitoring, managing, and reporting quality
- Ability to manage financial risk
- Ability to receive and distribute payments or savings
- Resources for patient education and support

There are similarities and differences between PCMHs and ACOs. Each deals with improving the care to a population of patients and putting the risk of the cost of care on the provider entity. The PCMH requires a primary care physician who directs the patient care and does not provide the incentives for quality outcomes that are part of ACOs.

Both the ACOs and the PCMH model require enhanced information management. To be successful both need an information technology infrastructure that allows sharing of information across entities. The selection of a population of patients with the functions of a registry that would allow for monitoring the individual's health status, interventions, treatments, and outcomes across time are key to both models. The ability to incorporate clinical and cost information and make meaningful decisions based on both individual and population data is required for successful operation. Both demonstration projects require sharing outcomes data with CMS to demonstrate improved outcomes. To fully monitor the health status of patients, the PCMH requires a patient health record that is interactive with the clinical record. And both systems benefit from enhanced patient education materials and feedback mechanisms.

Biotech Era

Biotechnology is shifting the US healthcare paradigm from a society "struggling to meet the escalating health problems of an aging population to one that focuses on wellness by preventing or delaying the onset of disease" (Burrill 2005). Almost 80 percent of the nation's healthcare spending is for chronic care. With advances in systems biology, this is shifting toward more personalized medicine focused on prevention, and eventually could lead to "a future in which an individual's genetic makeup can be determined to help tailor safer, more effective, cost-efficient treatments" (Burrill 2005).

Figure 2.4.   Americans' healthcare expenditures across the life span

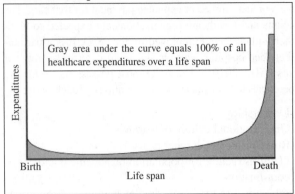

Source: Lynn and Adamson 2003.

New tools and a better understanding of how biological systems work is expected to create new treatments for everything from obesity, memory loss, and aging to cancer and cardiovascular illnesses. However, "safety issues in the pharmaceutical industry will continue to dominate the headlines" (Burrill 2005).

Overall, an outcome of the improvements made to the US healthcare system in the 20th century is a much longer, healthier life. Increased healthcare costs are typically incurred at the end of life. (See figure 2.4.) Much of the focus of biotechnology is directed at improving the care for chronic diseases of the elderly (Lynn and Adamson 2003).

Development of Evidenced-Based Best Practices and Outcomes

Physicians are caught between their desire to achieve high-quality care and the payers' desire for cost control. The cost-versus-care debate has spawned an energetic movement to improve the quality of healthcare in the United States, much of it centered on patients' rights.

Evidence-based medicine is the conscientious, explicit, and judicious use of current best evidence in making decisions about the care of individual patients. The practice of evidence-based medicine means integrating individual clinical expertise with the best available external clinical evidence from systematic research. Evidence-based healthcare extends the application of the principles of evidence-based medicine to all professions associated with healthcare, including purchasing and management (Centre for Evidence-Based Medicine 2005).

Measuring and monitoring healthcare quality is essential, yet quantifying healthcare quality is complex. The entire process of quality assessment requires judgment and choices that should be influenced by physicians' clinical realities of medical care. It is assumed as well as essential that healthcare providers possess the knowledge to participate actively in the assessment of healthcare quality. Assessing quality requires the development and application of performance measures that are explicit standards of care against which actual clinical care is judged. Given the availability of evidenced-based guidelines for the management of patients, there is a natural inclination to use these consensus statements as a basis for developing performance measures for the evaluation of healthcare quality. Guidelines are not performance measures. Rather, they are written to suggest diagnostic or therapeutic interventions for most patients in most circumstances. The use of guideline recommendations in diagnosing and treating individual patients is left to the discretion of the physician. In contrast, performance measures are standards of care that imply that physicians are in error if they do not care for patients according to these standards.

Malpractice Insurance Costs for Physicians

Malpractice is the improper or negligent treatment of a patient, as by a physician, resulting in injury, damage, or loss. Garner (2004) defines malpractice as

The failure of rendering professional services to exercise that degree of skill and learning commonly applied under all the circumstances in the community by the average prudent reputable member of the profession with the result of injury, loss or damage to the recipient of those services or to those entitled to rely upon them.

Medical malpractice liability insurance premiums have increased in recent years, with a trend toward increasingly large plaintiffs' awards and higher losses for insurers. Premiums have risen both because insurance companies face increased costs to pay claims (from growth in malpractice awards) and because of reduced income from the insurance companies' investments and other short-term factors. Rapidly rising malpractice premiums may influence physicians, especially those in high-risk fields, to stop practicing medicine, thus reducing the availability of healthcare in some parts of the country (Beider and Hagen 2004).

Healthcare: No Longer Local

Telehealth is a new platform on which healthcare provision can be reshaped to meet the challenges of an aging population and more demanding and discerning patients and citizens. It involves automating all routine healthcare processes, from monitoring blood sugar levels to administering drugs, and extending the distribution of more complex and expert medical expertise by using videoconferencing to deliver consultations or surgical support. Following both these paths delivers benefits to healthcare provisioning, enabling medical staff to work more effectively, whatever their level of expertise or responsibility. Telehealth provides medical staff with a tool to eradicate mundane and low-value healthcare processes and maximize their core skills and expertise. The same level of automation that is routine among financial and retail verticals, for example, is not as prevalent within the healthcare community. Changes under way have the potential to fundamentally change the delivery of healthcare in the near and long term (HBS Consulting 2003).

Telehealth is now extending beyond the collection of vital signs. The most important factor in any telehealth-based disease management system is its clinical content. Ideally, the clinical content will provide two-way communication of not just physiological information (namely vital signs) but education and compliance information as well. Rich clinical content provides diagnosis-specific information, including programs for comorbidity diagnoses, that takes patient responses into account when determining the next question. For instance, if a congestive heart failure patient does not demonstrate an understanding of the significance of shortness of breath or the importance of taking medications each day, the system uses branching logic to transmit appropriate educational information. This individualizes each encounter the patient has with the telehealth system.

Daily documentation of patient information using telehealth technology allows the care provider to track health patterns over time and detect deviations in patient data that may indicate a decline in health before it becomes acute. A telehealth system can provide alerts that are activated when patient-specific baselines exceed a given parameter–weight, for instance. This is practically impossible in the traditional care delivery model. Having baselines is not enough, though. The home care agency must be able to modify baselines easily to ensure alerts are kept to a minimum and only signify a truly serious situation. Taken together, detailed health tracking and alerts allow agencies to fully understand the overall health of the patient (Utterback 2005).

The evolution of telehealth is expected to reshape not only the delivery of consultations, monitoring, and treatments but also access to healthcare services by healthcare providers, patients, and citizens. Healthcare delivery is no longer controlled—and will be less and less controlled—by secondary and primary healthcare providers.

Medical Tourism

Medical tourism is the practice of traveling from one country, or city, to another to seek healthcare services. Usually this is done to save money and involves high-cost procedures or procedures that are not covered by insurance such as some plastic surgeries. Both developed and underdeveloped countries offer medical tourism, and it has been made possible largely by international accreditation agencies that offer some level of assurance of quality. In 2007 an estimated 750,000 Americans traveled abroad for medical care, and medical tourism is expected to grow to a $21 billion-a-year industry in 2012. Several US insurance companies have implemented medical tourism benefits or pilot programs due to the reduced costs of services. Problems associated with medical tourism are frequently related to aftercare and differing laws regarding malpractice.

Summary

Throughout history, humans have attempted to diagnose and treat illness and disease. As populations settled into towns and cities, early folk medicine traditions eventually led to the establishment of formalized entities specifically designed to care for the sick. In the American colonies, enlightened thinkers such as Benjamin Franklin soon saw the need to establish hospitals and to regulate the practice of medicine. The 19th century saw the growth of organizations dedicated to standardizing medical practice and ensuring consistency in the quality of healthcare delivery. Organizations such as the AMA and the ANA were created to represent the interests of their members and to further ensure the quality of their services.

The 20th century ushered in a completely new concept in the provision of healthcare: prepaid health plans. For the first time, Americans could buy health insurance. However, during the Great Depression of the 1930s and World War II, it became obvious that millions of Americans could not afford to pay for healthcare. After the war, the federal government began to study the problem of healthcare access for all Americans. Finally, during the Johnson administration in the 1960s, Congress passed amendments to the Social Security Act of 1935 that created the Medicare and Medicaid programs. These programs were designed to pay for the cost of healthcare services to the elderly and the poor, respectively.

As the healthcare industry has grown, so have efforts to regulate it. Some regulation has come from professional and trade associations that are associated with the industry. However, much regulation has come from the federal government, particularly with regard to the Medicaid and Medicare programs. Moreover, the types and variety of healthcare services that are available today have increased dramatically. Every new type of service, and every new way to provide it, brings complex issues that must be addressed in order to ensure that Americans receive the highest-quality healthcare possible at the most affordable price.

The passage of healthcare reform legislation in 2010 may well usher in the next phase of American healthcare with broader coverage and new healthcare delivery models. Combined with biotechnology advances and renewed focus on preventive care, there is new hope for renewal in the healthcare system.

References

America's Health Insurance Plans Center for Policy and Research. 2008 (April 1). http://www.ahipresearch.org/pdfs/2008_HSA_Census.pdf.

American Health Information Management Association. 2011. The Vision Mission and Values of the American Health Information Management Association. http://www.ahima.org/about/mission| .aspx.

American Health Information Management Association. 2010a. *Pocket Glossary of Health Information Management and Technology*, 2nd ed. Chicago: AHIMA.

American Health Information Management Association. 2010b. AHIMA Analysis of Healthcare Reform. http://www.ahima.org/downloads/pdfs/advocacy/ARRAReviewDDAFinal4102009.pdf.

American Health Information Management Association. 2009. Review of ARRA. http://www.ahima.org/downloads/pdfs/advocacy/ARRAReviewDDAFinal4102009.pdf.

American Hospital Association. 1999. 100 Faces of Healthcare. Chicago: Health Forum.

American Hospital Association. 2010a (June). Accountable Care Organizations—AHA Research Synthesis Report. http://www.aha.org/research/cor/content/ACO-Synthesis-Report.pdf.

American Hospital Association. 2010b. Maximizing the Value of Post-acute Care. http://www.aha.org/research/reports/tw/10nov-tw-postacute.pdf.

American Hospital Association. 2011 (February). AHA Survey of Hospitals' Ability to Meet Meaningful Use Requirements of the Medicare and Medicaid Electronic Health Records Incentive Programs. http://www.aha.org/content/11/11EHRsurveyresults.pdf.

American Hospital Association. 2012 (Jan. 3). Fast Facts on US Hospitals. http://www.aha.org/research/rc/stat-stat-studies/fast-facts.shtml.

American Nurses Association. 2011. About ANA. http://www.nursingworld.org/FunctionalMenuCategories/AboutANA.

American Osteopathic Association. 2005. http://www.do-online.osteotech.org/index.cfm.

Beider, P., and S. Hagen. 2004 (Jan. 8). Limiting tort liability for medical malpractice. Washington, D.C.: Congressional Budget Office. http://www.cbo.gov.

Burrill, G.S. 2005 (June 20). Healthcare in transition: Biotech drives major changes. Paper presented at BIO 2005, Philadelphia. http://www.sev.prnewswire.com/biotechnology/20050619/NYSU00419062005-1.html.

Carlson, B. 2002 (Oct.). It's Not the Road You Take—It's Getting There That Counts. *Managed Care*. http://www.managedcaremag.com/archives/0210/0210.quality.html.

Cassidy, B.S. 2011. The U.S. Healthcare Delivery System. Chapter 2 in *Health Information Management: Concepts, Principles and Practice*, 3rd ed. Edited by Latour, K.M. and S. Eichenwald Maki. Chicago: AHIMA.

Centers for Disease Control and Prevention (CDC). 2009. Health care in America: Trends in utilization. http://cdc.gov/nchs/datawh/nchsdefs/postacutecare.htm.

Centers for Medicare and Medicaid Services. 2005 (March 4). US Department of Health and Human Services. http://www.cms.hhs.gov/NursingHomeQualityInits.

Centers for Medicare and Medicaid Services. 2012 (March 28). Overview of EHR Incentives Programs. https://www.cms.gov/ehrincentiveprograms/.

Centers for Medicare and Medicaid Services. 2008a. The Mental Health Parity Act. http://www.cms.hhs.gov/HealthInsReformforConsume/04TheMentalHealthParityAct.asp.

Centre for Evidence-Based Medicine. 2005. Glossary of terms in evidence-based medicine. Oxford: Institute of Health Sciences. http://www.cebm.net/glossary.asp.

Cohen, R. and Martinez, M. 2011. (September). Health Insurance Coverage: Early Release of Estimates from the National Health Interview Survey, January–March 2011. National Center for Health Statistics. http://www.cdc.gov/nhis/releases.htm.

Cohen, R. 2007. *PRWORA's Immigrant Provisions*. OLR Research Report. http://www.cga.ct.gov/2007/rpt/2007-R-0705.htm.

Cullen KA, Hall MJ, Golosinskiy A. 2009. Ambulatory Surgery in the United States, 2006. National health statistics reports; no 11. Revised. Hyattsville, MD: National Center for Health Statistics.

Cooke, M., Irby, D., Sullivan, W. Ludmerer, KM. 2006. *American Medical Education 100 Years After the Flexner Report. New England Journal of Medicine* 2006; 355:1339–1344 September 28, 2006.

Davis, K. and A. Shih. 2008 (April). Get Organized: How to Streamline Health Care Delivery. The Commonwealth Fund. http://www.commonwealthfund.org/aboutus/aboutus_show.htm?doc_id=680551.

DeNavas-Walt, C., Proctor, B., and Smith, J. 2011. *US Census Bureau, Current Population Reports, P60-239, Income, Poverty, and Health Insurance Coverage in the United States: 2010*, US Government Printing Office, Washington, D.C.

Department of Health and Human Services (HHS). 2010. Strategic Plan and Priorities. http://www.hhs.gov/secretary/about/priorities/priorities.html.

Department of Health and Human Services (HHS). 2012. Office of the Surgeon General. http://www.surgeongeneral.gov/about/index.html.

e-MDs. 2008 (April 28). e-MDs Participates in 2008 Integrating the Healthcare Enterprise Connectathon. http://www.e-mds.com/news.

Etheredge, L. 2001. *On the Archeology of Health Care Policy: Periods and Paradigms, 1975–2000*. Washington, D.C.: The National Academies Press. http://www.nap.edu/books/NI000569/html/1.html.

Foley, D.J., R.W. Manderscheid, J.E. Atay, J. Maedke, J. Sussman, and S. Cribbs. 2004. Chapter 19: Highlights of Organized Mental Health Services in 2002 and Major National and State Trends. In *Mental Health, United States, 2004*. HHS Publication No. (SMA) 06-4195. http://mentalhealth.samhsa.gov/publications/allpubs/sma06-4195/chapter19.asp.

Garner, B.A., ed. 2004. *Black's Law Dictionary,* 8th ed. St. Paul, MN: West Group.

Hazelwood, A., Cook, E., Hazelwood, S. 2005. *The Joint Commission on Healthcare Organization's Sentinel Events Policy.* Academy of Healthcare Management Journal. Annual.

Health Insurance Carriers. 2005. Health Savings Accounts. http://www.health-insurance-carriers.com/hsa.html.

Joint Commission. 2007. *Comprehensive Accreditation Manual for Hospitals.* Oakbrook Terrace, IL: Joint Commission.

Jonas, S. and A.R. Kovner. 2005. *Healthcare Delivery in the United States.* 8th ed. New York: Springer.

Kaiser Family Foundation. 2011. *Employer Health Benefits 2011 Summary of Findings.* http://ehbs.kff.org/pdf/8226.pdf.

Kaiser Family Foundation. 2009. Statehealthfacts.org. http://www.statehealthfacts.org/comparemaptable.jsp?ind=177&cat=4.

Kallos, C. 2008 (June 10). Zacks Equity Research, Managed Care Industry: Positioned for Growth. http://seekingalpha.com/article/80722-managed-care-industry-positioned-for-growth.

Kongstevdt, P. 1993. *The Managed Care Handbook.* Gaithersburg, MD: Aspen.

Kovner, A., J. Knickman, and V. Weisfeld, 2011 (May 25). Jonas and Kovner's *Health Care Delivery in the United States,* 10th ed. Springer Publishing Company. Kindle Edition. New York.

Lynn, J. and D.M. Adamson. 2003. White paper: Living well at the end of life: Adapting health care to serious chronic illness in old age. Santa Monica, CA: RAND. http://www.rand.org/pubs/white_papers/2005/WP137.pdf.

Marcus, M. 2011. (August 28). Medical clinics in retail settings are booming. *USA Today.*

Mark, T., Stranges, E., and K. Levit. 2010 (September 7). Using Healthcare Cost and Utilization Project State Inpatient Database and Medicare Cost Reports Data to Determine the Number of Psychiatric Discharges from Psychiatric Units of Community Hospitals. Agency for Healthcare Research and Quality (AHRQ). http://www.hcup-us.ahrq.gov/reports.jsp.

Masters, P.A. and C. Nester. 2001 (Jan.). A Study of Primary Care Teaching Comparing Academic and Community-Based Settings. *Journal of General Internal Medicine* 16(1): 9–13.

National Adult Day Services Association 2011. Overview and Facts. http://www.nadsa.org/?page_id=80.

The National Coalition on Health Care. Health Insurance Costs. http://www.nchc.org/facts.

National Institutes of Health. 2005. NIH Roadmap: Accelerating medical discovery to improve health. Frequently asked questions. http://www.nihroadmap.nih.gov/faq.asp.

Shih, A., K. Davis, S. Schoenbaum, A. Gauthier, R. Nuzum, and D. McCarthy. 2008 (August). Organizing the US Health Care Delivery System for High Performance, The Commonwealth Fund. www.commonwealthfund.org.

Siegel, E.L., and D.S. Channin. 2001. Integrating the Healthcare Enterprise: A Primer; Part 1: Introduction. *Radiographics* 21:1339–1341. http://radiographics.rsnajnls.org/cgi/content/full/21/5/1339.

Sloane, R.M., B.L. Sloane, and R. Harder. 1999. *Introduction to Healthcare Delivery Organization: Functions and Management,* 4th ed. Chicago: Health Administration Press.

Starr, P. 1982. *The Social Transformation of American Medicine.* New York: Basic Books.

Stedman's Medical Dictionary. 2000. http://www.stedmans.com.

Sultz, H.A. and K.M. Young. 2004. *Healthcare USA—Understanding its Organization and Delivery,* 4th ed. Sudbury, MA: Jones and Bartlett.

United States Government Accountability Office 2008 (Apr. 1). Health Savings Accounts: Participation Increased and Was More Common among Individuals. GAO Report, GAO-08-744R. http://www.gao.gov/new.items/d08474r.pdf.

Utterback, K. 2005 (Jan./Feb.). Supporting a New Model of Care with Telehealth Technology. *Home Telehealth.* http://tie.telemed.org/articles/article.asp?path=homehealth&article=telehealthTechnology_ku_tpr05.xml.

Wilson, K. 2011 (May). Healthcare Costs 101. California Healthcare Foundation. http://www.chcf.org/publications/2011/05/healthcare-costs-101.

29 CFR 825.118: What is a health care provider? 1995.

chapter 3

The Health Information Management Profession

Susan Parker, MEd, RHIA

Learning Objectives

- Understand the professional definition of health information management (HIM) and technology
- Understand the HIM professional core model and utilize it to further career development for new and experienced health information management professionals
- Identify the functional components of practice roles in HIM as delineated by the Core Model
- Recognize the growing settings of practice available to HIM professionals
- Recognize the components of the American Health Information Management Association Body of Knowledge

- Understand the process and benefits of certification and the requirements for maintaining certification
- Recognize the importance of continuing education and the options available to HIM professionals
- Understand the variety of HIM academic levels and domains within them
- Identify the key HIM and related professional associations
- Understand the importance of a professional code of ethics and what the HIM Code of Ethics means

KEY TERMS

Accountable care organization (ACO)
American Health Information Management Association (AHIMA)
American Medical Informatics Association (AMIA)
American Recovery and Reinvestment Act (ARRA)
Association of Clinical Documentation Improvement Specialists (ACDIS)
Body of knowledge (BoK)
Centers for Medicare and Medicaid Services (CMS)
Certification
Certified coding associate (CCA)
Certified coding specialist (CCS)
Certified coding specialist–physician based (CCS-P)

Certified health data analyst (CHDA)
Certified healthcare privacy and security (CHPS)
Chief knowledge officer
Clinical documentation improvement professional (CDIP)
College of Healthcare Information Management Executives (CHIME)
Commission on Accreditation for Health Informatics and Information Management (CAHIIM)
Compliance officer
Computer-assisted coding
Continuing education
Credentialing
Domain

e-HIM
Electronic health record (EHR)
Health data
Health information exchange (HIE)
Health information management (HIM)
Health Information and Management Systems Society
  (HIMSS)
Health information resource management
Healthcare data organization (HDO)
Healthcare payer organization
Healthcare provider organization

International Federation of Health Information Management
  (IFHIM)
International Medical Informatics Association (IMIA)
National Association for Healthcare Quality (NAHQ)
National Cancer Registrars Association (NCRA)
Personal health record (PHR)
Profession
Registered health information administrator (RHIA)
Registered health information technician (RHIT)
Research
Standard

Introduction

Over the past 80 years, the health information management (HIM) profession has evolved from management of a paper repository to a vibrant, dynamic component of today's healthcare delivery system. **Health information management** is an allied health profession that is responsible for ensuring the availability, accuracy, and protection of the clinical information that is needed to deliver healthcare services and to make appropriate healthcare-related decisions (AHIMA 2012). Or more simply, as the introduction to the AHIMA Core Model states, "Where there is health information, there is HIM."

Professional Core Model

HIM professionals have the opportunity to be involved at all levels of healthcare. Trained HIM managers understand and are able to use technology to serve the provider, the patient, and the payer. Health information management includes the mechanism for collecting health information, ensuring complete documentation, maintaining health data, and appropriately sharing authorized information through electronic as well as paper-based release of information protocol. HIM professionals are involved in policy, design, and implementing workable solutions for making emerging ideas a reality while protecting the individual's privacy and the integrity of collected data. Bonnie Cassidy stated, "During the e-HIM transition, HIM professionals will serve a broad range of roles planning, organizing, and managing clinical content, integrity, accessibility, use, and protection. They will serve as project managers, identifying work process improvements and implementation techniques and redefining information management practices. Privacy coordinators, different from privacy officers, will act as directors, creating policy implementing programs, and directing goals" (Cassidy 2011).

As the electronic health record evolves, the HIM professional also adapts to meet the challenge, expanding the scope of practice well beyond historic borders. Decisions on shaping and training future HIM professionals are based on extensive research and reflect much more than a snapshot view of current trends. A Core Model was developed in 2011 with the intention of specifically identifying the roles, settings, and impact of the profession. This extensive project forecasts the impact, roles, and settings in which the HIM professional would operate for the next decade. The Core Model represents the functions and opportunities open to current and future HIM professionals. (See figure 3.1.) The primary role of the HIM professional is at the heart of the model. This is health information governance and stewardship. Surrounding this primary role are the four drivers of the model: Policy, Standards, Education, and Research. Each one provides a foundational enabler that supports, advances, expands, and contributes to the key functions as identified through HIM governance and stewardship.

Policy

Regulation of health information protects the public and the private individual. Confidentiality laws and regulations related to health information ensure that patient data, paper or electronic, are respected without restricting the access needed for advanced care, treatment, research, and payment. Policy also establishes public health standards by prioritizing health information and health information management best practice. Government regulations and laws related to HIM have their foundation in health information management professional practice.

Standards

To be usable, health information data must be uniform in its interoperability. **Standards** advance this extension of the HIM domain. They streamline the adoption of electronic technology and help ensure consistent data collection. Standards also assist in reduction of costs through mutually recognized methods for the release or transference of information. The Office of the National Coordinator for Health Information Technology has identified unique stakeholders and settings impacted by these standards as provider perspective, consumer prospective, public health perspective; care management and delivery domain; health information domain; confidentiality, privacy, and security domain; infrastructure, interoperability,

Figure 3.1.   The HIM professional core model

Source: AHIMA 2011.

and exchange domain; administrative and financial domain; and quality measurement and assessment domain.

Education

HIM Education is the foundation of the Core Model. The AHIMA Council for Excellence in Education (CEE) designs educational initiatives that address entry-level competencies as well as preparation for senior leadership positions. HIM professionals need a strong foundation and wide span of educational experiences to meet the expectations of the Core Model. HIM Education, in this model, addresses formal academic training provided in colleges and universities as well as continuing professional education for lifelong learning.

Research

Research is a key enabler that extends and advances the HIM profession. Best practices are validated through research. Research in HIM identifies areas of quality and patient safety that are needed in the healthcare industry as a whole, and it identifies practice improvement initiatives and professional advancements. In order to produce meaningful research, HIM professionals need to be competent in statistics and basic research methodology.

Check Your Understanding 3.1

Instructions: Answer the following questions on a separate piece of paper.

1. How is HIM involved in making appropriate healthcare-related decisions?

2. Why was the Professional Core Model developed?

3. Standards streamline the adoption of electronic technology. They also assist in _____ through mutually recognized methods for release or transfer of information.

4. What are the four drivers surrounding the center of the Core Model, equipping and enabling the HIM profession?

Functional Components with Practice Roles

One of the most practical outcomes of the Core Model was a comprehensive study of HIM roles as focused in five main functional areas. Health information begins at birth and ends at death. Health information includes data from individual patient records as well as aggregate data on a patient population that can span the globe. Health information is a diverse collection of information from multiple sources with a wide variety of uses and functional components; therefore the HIM professional has many roles.

Data Capture, Validation, and Maintenance

The role an HIM professional plays in data capture, validation, and maintenance involves uniform standardization of practices, policies, and procedures that will result in reliable, consistent data. This requires a clear understanding of the design and implementation strategies for data quality, data integrity, and management of data structures and terminology as well as a solid understanding and support of the way information flows. The HIM professional, regardless of the setting, is responsible for establishing procedures to capture and maintain **health data.**

Figure 3.2.   Data Capture, Validation, and Maintenance

Roles	Values
Chart correction analyst	• Increased revenue potentially by ensuring accurate coding supported by documentation
Classification editor and exchange expert	
Clinical coding validator	• Improved cash flow caused by first-time claims processing with few denials and appeals required
Clinical content manager	
Clinical documentation improvement specialist/ supervisor	
Coder	• Improved efficiency of data capture through selection and implementation of technology
Coding compliance coordinator/supervisor/ manager	• Decreased operational costs by efficiencies gained in workflow
Computer-assisted coding validation practice leader	
Data architect	• Increased patient safety and satisfaction by reduction of duplicate records
Data capture design specialist	
Data dictionary manager	• Increased patient safety and satisfaction through standardized data collection across systems and sites
Data integrity and transitions specialist/auditor	
Data mapper/translator	• Improved research outcomes through optimized data capture and abstraction
Data quality manager/analyst	
Documentations/EHR trainer	
EHR content manager	• Increased value and accuracy of information through planning for the capture of discrete data
Enterprise patient master index data integrity analyst	
ICD-10 implementation specialist	
Information workflow designer	
Patient identity manager	
Registrar (birth, cancer, device, bone marrow, tissue)	
Research coordinator/ associate	
Research data abstractor	
Terminology asset manager	
Voice capture specialist	

- Develop and maintain data architecture, tools, designs, and exchange models
- Design functional attributes of data structures, data fields, and input templates
- Analyze and design health information–related processes, work, and information flows
- Design and validate appropriate data capture mechanisms
- Design and develop methods for acquisition and integration of externally authored data that maintain the source identity
- Design and implement data quality and integrity validation strategies and methods
- Establish and maintain uniform definitions of data and data dictionaries
- Ensure appropriate protocols to support secondary data uses such as research, quality and safety monitoring, public health, and risk assessment
- Provide nosology, data mapping, and taxonomy support for uniformity, information retrieval, or secondary use
- Code and abstract health record content in both the manual and computer-assisted environments
- Manage, evaluate, and maintain terminology assets including vocabulary and clinical code sets (International Classification of Diseases, Current Procedural Terminology, Systemized Nomenclature of Medicine–Clinical Terminology, RxNORM, Logical Observation Identifiers Names and Codes, Centers for Medicare and Medicaid Services Rules, and such)
- Develop data crosswalks and conversions and test for data quality
- Identify, develop, and operate required registries, repositories, and exchanges
- Manage and influence patient identity mechanisms and frameworks
- Educate and advise on data capture and maintenance functions

An example of a job title related to these elements is clinical documentation improvement (CDI) specialist or supervisor. The CDI specialist would use several of the skills mentioned in the statements related to data capture, validation, and maintenance. CDI programs, and the specialists behind them, play a pivotal role in achieving the goal of recovery audit contractor (RAC) audits, American Recovery and Reinvestment Act (ARRA) and Health Information Technology for Economic and Clinical Health (HITECH) regulations, and developing initiatives related to healthcare quality improvement.

Certainly the jobs of coder, coding compliance coordinator, and **computer-assisted coding** validation practice leader are also part of this element of the AHIMA Core Model, but additional careers using these skills include enterprise patient master index data integrity analyst, electronic health record (EHR) content manager, and information workflow designer.

According to the AHIMA Core Model (AHIMA 2011a), there are 15 statements that further delineate the responsibilities involved in data capture, validation, and maintenance. These statements are aligned with realistic roles and job titles (see figure 3.2). The statements are useful considerations regarding the skills, training, and expectation for current HIM professionals as well as future opportunities.

The value this element brings to the healthcare industry is important to consumers as well as facilities. It includes the very realistic potential to increase revenue through proper documentation and coding, including fewer denials and appeals that result in improved cash flow. Through standardized data collections and reduction of duplicate records, patient safety and satisfaction are improved. Additionally, by optimizing data capture and abstraction, research outcomes are improved, serving multiple users of the data. For a complete capture, validation, and maintenance, refer to figure 3.2.

Data/Information Analysis, Transformation, and Decision Support

The HIM professional is an integral part of data information analysis, transformation, and decision support. Integrated reporting practices, data analysis, and the reporting of accurate health information rely on the knowledge and application of HIM skill sets. As noted in the article "popHealth Primer," "HIM professionals need to ensure building blocks include data validity, relevant standard code sets and accurate, comprehensive documentation are in place to enable electronic reporting of clinical quality measures and continue providing high-quality healthcare for patients, families, and the nation" (Cottington 2011).

The roles applicable to this core element are as diverse as the health information collected itself, but the unifying tie is the function they represent. Listed below are the 10 statements that relate specifically to the functions within the data/information analysis, transformation, and decision support element of the HIM profession.

- Design requirements, criteria, and metrics to meet end users' needs for analysis and interpretation (end users may include clinicians, researchers, executives, purchasers, payers, policymakers or federal and state officials, consumers, and such)
- Develop and support the analysis of data from clinical and other knowledge repositories
- Conduct clinical data and clinical process modeling
- Integrate clinical and business decision support rules into systems
- Evaluate the integrity and comparability of data, and identify gaps in data sources
- Analyze and transform data and information or knowledge to generate findings for clinical financial, operational, research, legal, and regulatory or policy processes and decisions
- Migrate and integrate data from diverse internal and external sources for analysis, for interpretation, and to create new knowledge
- Educate and advise on data analytic techniques and the characteristics of data for analysis, transformation, decision support, and improved health outcomes
- Interpret health data attributes, including data definitions, value sets, and other administrative and clinical coded data content, for analysis, transformation, and decision support
- Apply appropriate statistical methods and data mining techniques

The HIM career options accompanying this core element are many, with anticipated growth as healthcare data become fully integrated with evolving IT systems. Clinical data analyst, data integration manager/analyst, and decision support analyst are certainly in demand as the value of understanding and being able to present strategic data related to payer mix and case mix index increases. Similarly, positions of health data analyst or manager, information warehouse or repository director, or data repository architect or manager are titles that reflect the ability to apply the functions as they relate to securing information and minimizing risk of exposure. Jobs as a regional HIM specialist or administrator, referral specialist, or outcomes and cost analyst are also central to the functions listed as being directly related to providing information to the public and making sure information is available to improve patient care and outcomes. Please refer to figure 3.3 for a full list of roles and value statements regarding data/information analysis, transformation, and decision support.

Figure 3.3. Data/information analysis, transformation, and decision support

Roles	Values
Business analyst	• Increased strategic value of data through informed presentation of payor mix and case mix index
Claims data analyst	
Clinical content manager	
Clinical data analyst	• Compliance with mandated reporting requirements
Data abstractor/coordinator	
Data architect	• Information available to assess and improve patient care delivery and outcomes
Data integration manager/ analyst	
Data integrity and transitions specialist/auditor	• Information provided for marketing to the public
Data quality manager/analyst	
Data repository architect/ manager/analyst	• Minimized risk of exposure to the practice by improving the quality of outcomes
Decision support analyst	
Decision support officer	
Health data analyst/manager/ director	
Health data statistician	
Health outcomes analyst	
Healthcare data quality engineer	

(continued on next page)

Figure 3.3.   Data/information analysis, transformation, and decision support (*continued*)

Roles	Values
Information warehouse/ repository director	
Interface reconciliation specialist	
Patient-centered outcomes researcher	
Physician practice liaison	
Quality outcomes and cost analyst/director	
Record analyst	
Referral specialist	
Regional health information management specialist/ manager/administrator	
Registrar (birth, cancer, device, bone marrow, tissue)	
Report writer	
Research coordinator/ associate	

Information Dissemination and Liaison

Information dissemination and liaison responsibilities involve communication and knowledge of data purpose, use, and allowable users. The HIM professional establishes the reporting procedures and practices for data, information, and knowledge dissemination. This core element also requires skill in formatting as well as providing the data. The following functional statements clarify this topic, and it may be noted that some of the statements overlap with other functional statements, verifying the task as well within the HIM domain and accepted scope of work.

- Design requirements, criteria, and metrics to meet the end users' need for retrieval, reporting, and exchange of data and information (end users may include clinicians, researchers, executives, purchasers, payers, policymakers or federal and state officials, consumers, and such)
- Identify and support the development and operation of required reporting and health data exchange
- Support the integration of clinical and business decision support rules into systems that enable effective and efficient reporting
- Ensure data and information output is usable for the required purpose
- Extract and transfer data from primary sources to meet user needs (including secondary uses such as research, public and population health monitoring, quality and safety monitoring, and continuity of care)

- Migrate, integrate, and measure data from diverse internal and external sources for reporting and health data exchange
- Interpret health data attributes, including data definitions, value sets, and other administrative and clinical coded data content for analysis and output
- Educate and advise on the nature of data including limitations and definitions
- Prepare a health information technology education program to educate all stakeholders

The information and data contemporary HIM professionals are responsible for include far more than any previous HIM director could have imagined. Today's healthcare involves image files (.jpg, .tif, .png). They include audio media that capture heart sounds or voice recordings for speech therapy, video media (.wmv or .mov files) for ultrasounds and electrocardiograms, and there are application media (Octet-Stream or PostScript) images processed by an application before being used, such as a bone scan trending data. Skills in this element do overlap with others, but most definitely are key to management of nontext media data as used and disseminated in healthcare practice.

The roles HIM professionals may pursue related to information dissemination and liaison include clinical documentation analyst and data exchange manager. As **health information exchange (HIE)** becomes more widespread, HIM professionals will find they are well suited for the HIE coordinator role. Careers related to information dissemination and liaison will be able to impact decision making through appropriate decision support tools and opportunities to provide improved data for reporting and quality, such as care measures, outcomes, and research.

For a complete list of dissemination- and liaison-related careers, see figure 3.4.

Check Your Understanding 3.2

Instructions: Answer the following questions on a separate piece of paper.

1. The job title of clinical coding validator would relate to which element of the Core Model?

   A. Data capture, validation, and maintenance
   B. Data/information analysis, transformation, and decision support
   C. Information dissemination and liaison

2. Statements that delineate responsibilities in the practice roles are useful because they

   A. define job titles
   B. identify skill, training, and expectations
   C. provide the research foundation for the future

3. CDI is an acronym for:

   A. Clinical data input
   B. Clinical documentation improvement
   C. Computerized document imaging

Figure 3.4.   Information dissemination and liaison

Roles	Values
Clinical documentation analyst Data exchange manager/ analyst Data report design specialist Data transfer analyst Health information exchange coordinator/ facility representative Information assessment specialist Personal health information exchange manager/ director/administrator Quality information exchange director	• Improved decision making through the appropriate availability of decision support tools • Improved data for reporting and quality in care measures, outcomes, and research

Health Information Resource Management and Innovation

The responsibility for healthcare Information Resource Management and Innovation is a leadership role. The previous three elements contribute to the HI Resource Management and Innovation. HIM professionals manage the health information environment and, as such, are responsible for the education of other health personnel on issues related to health information. The HIM professional's competency in this area impacts both the facility and the patient. **Health information resource management** includes responsibility for the health data life cycle and shapes management of such across the entire enterprise system. Innovation and adoption of advanced management processes related to health information will depend, in part, on the skills of trained HIM professionals.

Research related to the Core Model produced the most functional statements in this core element. There are more job titles related to this area and more values associated with those careers. Obviously Health Information Resource Management and Innovation is a foundational key to the HIM profession now and in the foreseeable future. Appendix A of the Core Model provides functional statements for each of the core elements, and those identified as related to the core element of health information resource management and innovation include the following:

- Contribute to the leadership of, and provide critical input to, the development of strategic information plans to support the organizational mission
- Inform the development of information technology plans to include system integrations, interfaces, implementation plans, and workflow designs to support the strategic initiatives
- Manage the HIM environment including its policies; implementation guidance; and financial, human, technical, and physical resources
- Lead and manage health information management and technology projects and operations (including clinical, financial, and human resources)
- Identify and address change management issues related to the evolution of the health information environment
- Optimize reimbursement through management of the revenue cycle
- Manage process changes required by emerging payment and delivery models on healthcare operations and finance and educate others
- Lead clinical quality improvement and patient safety operations
- Design health information programs that improve healthcare and reduce healthcare costs
- Support information system development, procurement, and implementation that meet public health program needs
- Continuously analyze, evaluate, and communicate the impact of the evolution of the health system and the impact on HIM
- Provide implementation guidance and insight on the deployment of organizational information management policy
- Define functional, technological, and communication requirements for health information
- Lead and perform project and program management initiatives related to health information
- Shape and manage information architecture across EHR, PHR, and HIT enterprise systems
- Advocate for technology solutions and influence the adoption life cycle
- Identify user needs and model user workflow
- Identify and articulate system requirements
- Train users on information technology and information policy
- Evaluate the impact of technology on the quality of data and information
- Ensure the effectiveness of human-technology interfaces to maximize usability of health information
- Evaluate and improve the effectiveness of information systems throughout health information life cycles
- Assess usability and user satisfaction of a health information system or application and its utility including effectiveness and efficiency
- Identify opportunities for and support the use of data, information, or knowledge for business intelligence and decision making throughout the enterprise
- Innovate and optimize the use of information in decision making

- Perform health information resource management research
- Advance information-based process innovation
- Employ performance improvement techniques
- Innovate health information processes and practices using emerging technologies
- Maximize efficiency, effectiveness, accuracy, and quality of information through innovation (AHIMA 2011a)

The leadership element of HIM is clearly a major component of the HIM profession. As stated in *Leading a Business in Anxious Times: A Systems Approach to Becoming More Effective in the Workplace,* "Successful leadership is a relationship process among members of an organization that inspires them to take full advantage of opportunities, recognize and minimize threats to success, and avoid catastrophic failures" (Fox and Gratwick Baker 2009). Leadership is an intentional combination of knowledge, training, and directing. Carolyn Valo, MS, RHIA, FAHIMA, provided an excellent example of this blend of skills utilizing several of the functional statements listed. "Assume that a manager just learned accounts receivables or AR (days or dollars) are outside the target. The manager decides to seek direct input from the staff that performs the day-to-day functions related to AR. When the manager takes, as a first step, engaging the staff to problem-solve the missed AR target, the staff members feel confident that the manager trusts their knowledge, skills, and ability and are more likely to be motivated to reach decisions on how to realign and maintain the AR target" (Valo 2011).

Job titles related to health information resource management and innovation include corporate records manager, **chief knowledge officer,** and clinical information officer. This element also extends to denial appeals coordinator, quality improvement director, reimbursement specialist, and revenue integrity analyst. The **electronic health record (EHR)** opens many doors related to health information resource management with job titles including **e-HIM,** e-health transition manager, and EHR workflow project manager; implementations redesign specialist; and project manager. With experience, health information resource management also includes opportunities to become vice president of data integrity services, vice president of strategic information development, or chief information officer. For a complete list of job titles related to health information resource management and innovation, see figure 3.5.

Figure 3.5.   Health information resource management and innovation

Roles	Values
Accounts receivables manager	• Improved patient care across the continuum through appropriate and timely information access and exchange
Accreditation readiness manager	• Optimized design of EHRs matched to clinical and operational workflow that returns higher value on the investment
Ancillary services systems manager/administrator/officer	• Optimized resource planning through the availability of aggregate clinical information
Application support specialist/coordinator/manager	• Decreased cost created by improved coordination of services and technology
Chief health information officer	• Increased revenue and decreased transaction cost from revenue integrity management programs
Chief information officer	• Enhanced project management through application of broad knowledge of the healthcare delivery system within an organization and with other external organizations
Chief knowledge officer	
Clinical information manager	• Improved patient care outcomes by effective design of information capture and communication systems
Corporate records manager	• Greater empowerment of patients in their own healthcare by advocating for their rights and providing understandable information to them
Data administrator	
Data standards director/administrator	• Increased revenue through assistance with achieving meaningful use requirements
Denial appeals coordinator	• Reduced healthcare costs by ensuring reliable data that eliminate duplicate tests and recordkeeping practices
Director of strategic information management	
eHealth transition specialist/manager/director	
EHR implementation specialist/leader/manager/officer	
EHR model/workflow project manager/director/officer	
Health information implementation specialist	
Health information interoperability and standards specialist/administrator	
Health information project officer	

Figure 3.5. Health Information Resource Management and Innovation (*continued*)

Roles	Values
Health information trainer	• Improved adoption of EHRs through effective training
HIM application support specialist/manager	• Enhanced relationship between hospitals and physicians through coordinated HIM resources
HIM integrity specialist/manager	
HIM manager	
Implementations redesign specialist/tester	
Informatics specialist	
Information operations manager/administrator/officer	
Information resource manager	
Local/regional policy analyst/officer	
National health data coordinator	
Nationwide health information management specialist/manager/director/officer performance improvement specialist	
Physician health information liaison	
Project manager	
Quality improvement coordinator/advisor	
Quality improvement director	
Quality outcomes project manager/analyst/director	
Regional health information management specialist/manager/administrator	
Registrar (birth, cancer, device, bone marrow, tissue)	
Reimbursement specialist	
Revenue integrity analyst	
Systems analyst	
Vice president of data integrity services	
Vice president of strategic information development	
Workflow design analyst	

Information Governance and Stewardship

Governance and responsible stewardship of health information are pivotal to data maintenance, analysis, decisions, dissemination, and leadership. It is a key function of health information management. This element ensures the use and management of health information is compliant with jurisdictional law, regulations, standards, and policies within the organization. HIM professionals lead the development of these organizational policies including compliance, processes, and decisions regarding the rights and responsibilities of good stewardship of health information.

The following functional statements explaining information governance and stewardship elements clarify this practice:

- Ensure compliance with jurisdictional laws and regulations, reimbursement and payer policies, and legal requirements pertaining to health information

- Audit and monitor systems and compliance plans
- Design and administer the content and records management program related to record life cycle management, definition of the legal record, information authentication, alteration management, retention or storage, archiving, destruction, disaster planning, and legacy information management
- Assess, design, and implement business continuity, information integrity, and risk management plans
- Design and administer a data information and record retention program
- Manage access, disclosure, use, and control of protected health information
- Administer organizational infrastructure for privacy, security, confidentiality, access, integrity, availability, and controls
- Verify and control access authorizations and privileges, including emergency access

- Develop, communicate, and ensure compliance with patient identity management policies and procedures
- Support health information exchange through development of data use agreements, and oversee administration of business rules and processes
- Understand and apply ethical principles to the analysis, use, and dissemination of health data and information
- Demonstrate and promote legal and ethical standards of practice
- Build awareness within, educate, and advise the organization on stewardship and governance functions, policies, standards, regulations, and ethics
- Advocate for the rights of consumers around privacy, confidentiality, and security of their health information
- Educate and advise consumers on management of their health information

Clearly the value HIM professional practice brings to healthcare includes a decreased risk of litigation based on appropriate retention of data and the maintenance of an accurate and complete clinical record. This function also offers decreased liability through reduction of privacy breaches through compliance with current laws and regulations. The HIM professional can optimize access to information through proper processes and technology that maintain confidentiality and security.

Some of the job titles associated with the function of information governance and stewardship include **compliance officer,** HIE privacy gatekeeper, and privacy or security officer. This function also applies to more consumer-directed roles with positions such as health record advocate, public relations liaison, patient advocate, and personal health record advisor. With experience, HIM professionals may also hold the title of vice president of health information governance. For a complete list of titles associated with this function, see figure 3.6.

The professional core model also includes a functional component related to quality and patient safety. The job statements and titles in other elements cross into and are related to quality and patient safety. Unique job titles are emerging.

Check Your Understanding 3.3

Instructions: Answer the following questions on a separate piece of paper.

1. Health outcomes analyst is a role that falls into which core element?

2. The function of information dissemination and liaison translates into which of these jobs?

   A. Corporate records manager
   B. eHealth transition manager
   C. Clinical documentation analyst

Figure 3.6.   Information governance and stewardship

Roles	Values
Access manager/auditor	• Decreased risk of litigation based on appropriate retention of data
Accounting disclosures coordinator	• Increased compliance with current laws and regulations
Compliance officer/auditor	• Decreased liability and enhanced reputation through reduction of breaches
Electronic discovery auditor	• Decreased liability through maintenance of an accurate and complete clinical record
Health information exchange privacy gatekeeper	• Optimized access to information through processes and technology that maintain confidentiality and security
Health information security analyst	
Health record advocate	
Healthcare consumer access manager	
Healthcare fraud investigator/analyst	
HIM government relations specialist/consultant	
Information analyst for business continuity	
Patient advocate	
Personal health record advisor	
Privacy and security officer/auditor	
Public relations liaison	
Recovery audit coordinator	
Vice president of health information governance	

3. On what function would a privacy officer focus his or her knowledge?

4. Which of the Core Model elements have the most functional statements and therefore the highest number of career job titles related to HIM?

Settings of Practice

Healthcare Provider Organizations

Traditionally healthcare providers have been the primary employer of HIM professionals. These organizations provide direct patient care including patient diagnosis, treatment, surgical care, and services related to treatment. A healthcare provider is legally responsible for these things and as such is the source for billing and reimbursement claims. HIM professionals hold a wide variety of positions here ranging from coding professional to chief knowledge officer. **Healthcare provider organizations** include, but are not limited to, physician offices, clinics, outpatient facilities, freestanding surgical centers, hospitals, regional health centers, and enterprisewide health systems. Where diagnosis and treatment are given and healthcare provider organizations exist, information is generated and HIM professionals are employed to manage and protect health information.

Healthcare Data Organizations

Healthcare data organizations (HDOs) are groups that maintain healthcare databases in both the public and private sectors. They may be state owned or privately held. These groups use data for reporting systems such as hospital discharge data and all-payer claims databases (APCDs). Healthcare data organizations collect and disseminate health data for users, public and private. HIM professionals employed in healthcare data organizations would assist in development of privacy regulations and control of such. HIM professionals in a healthcare data organization would assist in using the data to provide timely access, trending, and expertise in the healthcare information as well as regulations. Healthcare data organizations include the governmental data organizations, health data banks, HIE organizations, personal health record suppliers, and others.

Healthcare Payer Organizations

Payer organizations are the sources that pay patient healthcare expenses after treatment, diagnosis, or physician visits. *Private pay* is the term used when an individual offers payment without a healthcare payer resource. Healthcare payer organizations are often a strong driving force behind many of the changes in the healthcare system today. HIM professionals have a secure role in helping payers determine necessity,

validity, and billable charges utilizing patient data, codes, clinical documentation improvement, and medical information. HIM professionals have the skills to provide programmatic design, research, procedure development, operational oversight, and data review and appropriate, proper use of data requests. **Healthcare payer organizations** include clearinghouses; the federal and state governments; **accountable care organizations (ACOs)**; and insurance companies including self-insured organizations, medical billing companies, and medical banking. While at this time the **Centers for Medicare and Medicaid Services (CMS)** does not have specific requirements for an HIM professional to be part of the management structure, input and recommendations from the profession are certainly being used.

Healthcare Supplier Organizations

Healthcare supplier organizations are a less cohesive group that supplies a diversity of services to the healthcare industry. These settings provide a wealth of opportunities for HIM professionals to work. Supplier organizations include research within biomedical companies, pharmaceutical firms, and clinical trials. The skills within the HIM profession are critical in development of usable software for information technology and software companies. HIM professionals are the key workforce in consulting firms providing management, transcription, coding, and auditing for healthcare providers.

Planning Organizations, Regulators, and Industry Support

Organizations responsible for planning, regulating, and supporting professionals in the industry are a growing avenue for HIM professionals as the requirement for a more knowledgeable workforce increases. Professional licensing and certifying bodies as well as state and national government regulations depend on reliable HIM professionals for core skills and proven best practices. Settings where one might direct one's career include regional extension centers, state and federal government, standards organizations, private regulators such as the Joint Commission, or professional and trade associations.

Educational Institutions

Health information professionals have an important role in the training of the consumer as well as new HIM professionals and health-related practitioners. A career path in HIM is often found in colleges and universities teaching in HIM and allied health professional programs at every level from certificate programs to doctoral degrees. Distance educational organizations abound, and HIM professionals often direct and teach in these cutting-edge programs. Public health agencies and health foundations as well as organizations providing continuing education rely on HIM professionals and their skills to provide programming.

Research Institutions

One of the secondary functions of health data is research and quality monitoring; therefore, research institutions are an ideal location for the employment of HIM professionals involved in healthcare research. Settings such as colleges and universities, health foundations, government public health agencies, and an increasing number of stand-alone research institutes are common locations for the application of this skill.

Third-Party Compliance Organizations

In HIM, compliance can be defined three ways:

- The process of establishing an organizational culture that promotes the prevention, detection, and resolution of instances of conduct that do not conform to federal, state, or private payer healthcare program requirements or the healthcare organization's ethical and business policies
- The act of adhering to official requirements
- Managing a coding or billing department according to the laws, regulations, and guidelines that govern it (AHIMA 2012)

Third-party compliance organizations are the external firms and companies that provide the framework and implementation of compliance regulations in healthcare. Trained HIM professionals are excellent resources and use their skill in coding, auditing, clinical documentation improvement, process improvement, fraud investigation, quality improvement, and governmental recovery audits. Organizations include auditors, fraud investigation firms, quality improvement organizations, recovery audit companies, and legal offices.

Consumer organizations

As consumers take a stronger role in the healthcare system and responsibility for their own health information, a more informed consumer develops. Organizations to support the consumer abound. The HIM professional can provide insight, data, understanding, and resources for groups such as community awareness programs and faith-based organizations. HIM professionals also play a key role in the design, integrity, use, and control of **personal health records (PHRs).** A complete list of employment settings is included in Appendix D of the Core Model; see figure 3.7.

Figure 3.7.   Practice settings

Healthcare provider settings	Healthcare data organizations
Acute care/critical access hospitals	Governmental data organizations
Ambulatory surgery centers	Health data banks
Behavioral and mental health facilities	Health information exchange organizations
Child care services	Personal health record suppliers
Clinics or physician practices/medical homes	Public health agencies
Community-based healthcare centers	Registries and repositories
Community care retirement centers	Third-party data and analytics services
Continuing education organizations	
Correctional facilities	Healthcare payer organizations
Dental services	Clearinghouses
Employee/student health centers	Government
Home health or hospice	Insurance companies/self-insured organizations
Integrated healthcare delivery systems/accountable care organizations	Large employers
	Medical banking
Long-term care/post-acute care facilities	Medical billing companies
Public health service	
Retail clinics	Healthcare supplier organizations
Retail pharmacies	Biomedical companies
Specialty services—physical therapy/occupational therapy, chiropractic, imaging	Consulting companies
	Information technology and software companies
Tissue/blood banks	Outsourcing transcription/coding companies
Veterinary services/zoos	Pharmaceutical companies
Other provider settings	Recruiters

continued on next page

Figure 3.7. Practice settings (*continued*)

Planning organizations, regulators, and industry support	*Consumer organizaitons*
Government—state and national	Community awareness programs
Private regulators (for example, Joint Commision, AOA)	Faith-based organizations
Professional licensing and certifying bodies	
Professional or trade associations	
Regional extension centers	
Standards organizations	
Educational Institutions	
Colleges and universities	
Distance education organizations	
Government public health agencies	
Health foundations	
Research institutions	
Colleges and universities	
Goverment public health agencies	
Health foundations	
Stand-alone research institutes	
Third-party compliance organizations	
Auditors	
Fraud investigation firms	
Legal offices	
Quality improvement organizations	
Recovery audit companies	

Health Information Management Body of Knowledge

A **body of knowledge (BoK)** (AHIMA 2011b) is the collected resources, knowledge, and expertise within or related to a profession. It is usually made up of specific knowledge areas that represent a taxonomy of concepts pertinent to the profession. Most BoKs also reference a significant amount of supporting literature. The HIM profession has a strong body of knowledge starting at entry-level degree programs and building through AHIMA's online BoK reference library.

The HIM professional BoK is an increasingly diverse requirement. The AHIMA BoK is an online resource available to guests as well as members of the professional association. The information is constantly being updated and new content being added as it is published. Resources in the online BoK encompass practice-related information

that HIM professionals need to perform their jobs as well as theory, research, and links to relevant public materials. The BoK can be found at www.ahima.org.

The AHIMA BoK resource contains

- Journal articles since 1998
- Proceedings from the annual AHIMA Convention & Exhibit
- Practice briefs, toolkits, and position papers
- Reports, guidelines, and white papers
- Leadership models and House of Delegates resolutions
- Job descriptions
- Best Practice statements
- Government publications such as the *Federal Register* and Department of Health and Human Services (HHS) documents.

Because the HIM profession has grown well beyond the borders of the traditional hospital setting, the body of knowledge offered by the profession and required of today's HIM practitioner is much broader than in prior years. ICD-10 requires more clinical foundation (that is, anatomy, physiology, pathophysiology) than ever before, so the body of knowledge has expanded to include vocabulary as well as clinical code sets, data crosswalks, and taxonomy support systems.

Although multiple opportunities exist for relevant HIM knowledge to cross into other healthcare professions, a single example illustrating the explosion of HIM core knowledge today could be the electronic health record. Today, HIM professionals are part of a team with IT professionals and clinicians, steadily expanding the body of professional knowledge to include areas such as informatics and data analytic techniques.

Foundational and graduate curriculum models for educational degrees within the field, such as associate's, baccalaureate, and master's degrees, also have unique bodies of knowledge, which are organized into domains. There are five HIM baccalaureate degree domains:

- Health data management
- Health statistics, biomedical research, and quality management
- Health services organization and delivery
- Information technology and systems
- Organization and management

From these domains, student learning outcomes and the curriculum components or knowledge clusters that support the outcomes are built.

There are two elements making the HIM domains and competencies and knowledge clusters unique: (1) the specialization to healthcare throughout the curriculum and (2) the combination of studies in the biomedical sciences, management, and information fields. Baccalaureate graduates are required to be able to apply, analyze, and in some cases evaluate knowledge from the following biomedical sciences:

- Anatomy
- Physiology
- Medical terminology
- Pathophysiology
- Pharmacotherapy

The master's degree in health information management has three domains that are addressed in the curriculum and build on the knowledge gained in the previous degree:

- Health data management
- Information technology and systems
- Organization and management

Academic Education and Professional Certification

Educational White Paper: "Vision 2016"

"Vision 2016" (AHIMA 2007) is an innovative research-based white paper originally published in 2007. The purpose was to define the state of national HIM education and to outline a plan of action for the future. "Vision 2016" is a guide for new and existing health information management programs to assist in ensuring relevancy and proper direction to support future workforce development. To this end, "Vision 2016" resulted in three key priorities:

- Transform health information management to a graduate-level profession
- Realign the associate's degree with future workforce needs
- Prepare an effective qualified pool of HIM faculty

This white paper resulted in an expansion of traditional educational programs, addition of post-baccalaureate certification programs, development of master's curricula for health information management and health informatics, and realignment of education at the associate's degree level with plans for concentrated study related to workforce needs. It also has provided the foundation for new certifications (for example, certified health data analyst).

Certification and Credentialing

Certification in the HIM profession is different than credentialing. **Certification** is the validation of specific skills and knowledge in a particular aspect of the profession. Certifications are obtained by successfully passing a competency exam and maintaining annual continuing education requirements. The certified coding associate (CCA) certification is entry level and usually requires completion of unique courses of study concentrated in coding. Other certifications such as certified coding specialist–physician based (CCS-P) may be obtained by meeting certain eligibility requirements including knowledge and experience. And other certification examinations such as certified healthcare privacy and security (CHPS) do not specify a specific education but suggest a certain number of years of experience and a certain level of academic training. AHIMA certification is managed and strategic direction for certification is set by AHIMA's Commission on Certification for Health Informatics and Information Management (CCHIIM).

Credentialing in the HIM profession is based on successfully passing a competency exam after completion of a two-year, four-year, or post-baccalaureate course of study.

Undergraduate Degree in HIM

The four-year bachelor's degree in health information management provides entry-level education in preparation for the **registered health information administrator (RHIA)** credential. The 2011 curriculum competencies were developed and approved by the AHIMA Education Strategy Committee. Programs offering an accredited baccalaureate degree in HIM must also meet and maintain the standards as set forth by the **Commission on Accreditation for Health Informatics and Information Management (CAHIIM)**. See Appendix 3A at the end of this chapter for a diagram of the most recent AHIMA baccalaureate degree domains and Curriculum Competency Map (expected student learning outcomes) along with the Knowledge Clusters (components of the curriculum) (AHIMA 2011j).

To become eligible to take the RHIA examination, applicants must meet one of the following educational requirements:

- Hold a baccalaureate degree or post-baccalaureate certification from a CAHIIM-accredited health information management program
- Hold a degree from a foreign HIM baccalaureate program with which AHIMA has a reciprocity agreement
- Be a current student in a CAHIIM-accredited program enrolled in the final term of study

The RHIA exam is offered at computer testing sites located throughout the United States and arrangements can be made for international testing sites. An application must be filed with AHIMA, and details regarding eligibility, test application, and preparation guidance are offered at the AHIMA website.

RHIAs are skilled in the collection, interpretation, and analysis of patient data. Additionally, they receive the training necessary to assume managerial positions related to these functions (AHIMA 2011d). RHIAs are considered experts in managing patient health information, electronic or paper. RHIAs possess comprehensive knowledge of the ethical and legal standards including privacy and related regulations. RHIAs interact with all levels within today's healthcare organizations—administrative, clinical, financial, and information systems. While the majority of HIM professionals still work in acute-care hospitals, integrated delivery systems, clinics, and other provider settings are rapidly offering opportunities for employment. The Core Model also offers an impressive list of job settings and career options for RHIAs. (See figure 3.8.)

Figure 3.8.   RHIA roles

Access manager/auditor	Data integrity and transitions specialist/auditor
Accounting of disclosures coordinator	Data mapper/translator
Accounts receivable manager	Data quality manager/analyst
Accreditation readiness manager	Data report design specialist
Ancillary services systems manager/administrator/officer	Data repository architect/manager/analyst
	Data standards director/administrator
Application support specialist/coordinator/manager	Data transfer analyst
Business analyst	Decision support analyst
Charge capture technician	Decision support officer
Chart correction analyst	Denial appeals coordinator
Chief health information officer	Director of strategic information management
Chief knowledge officer	Documentation/EHR trainer
CIO	eHealth transition specialist/manager/director
Claims data analyst	EHR content manager
Classification editor and exchange expert	EHR implementation specialist/leader/manager/officer
Clinical coding validator	
Clinical content manager	EHR model/workflow project manager/director/officer
Clinical data analyst	
Clinical documentation analyst	Electronic discovery auditor
Clinical documentation improvement specialist/supervisor	Enterprise master patient index data integrity analyst
Clinical information manager	Health data analyst/manager/director
Coder	Health data statistician
Coding compliance coordinator/supervisor/manager	Health information exchange coordinator/facility representative
Compliance officer/auditor	Health information exchange privacy gatekeeper
Computer-assisted coding validation practice leader	Health information implementation specialist

(*continued on next page*)

Figure 3.8.   RHIA roles (*continued*)

Corporate records manager	Health information interoperability and standards specialist/administrator
Data abstractor/coordinator	
Data administrator	Health information project officer
Data architect	Health information security analyst
Data capture design specialist	Health information trainer
Data dictionary manager	Health outcomes analyst
Data exchange manager/analyst	Health record advocate
Data integration manager/analyst	Healthcare consumer access manager
Healthcare data quality engineer	Physician health information liaison
Healthcare fraud investigator/analyst	Physician practice liaison
HIM application support specialist/manager	Privacy and security officer/auditor
HIM government relations specialist/consultant	Project manager
HIM integrity specialist/manager	Public relations liaison
HIM manager	Quality improvement coordinator/advisor
ICD-10 Implementation specialist	Quality improvement director
Implementations redesign specialist/tester	Quality information exchange director
Informatics specialist	Quality outcomes and cost analyst/director
Information analyst for business continuity	Quality outcomes project manager/analyst/director
Information assessment specialist	Record analyst
Information exchange analyst/manager	Recovery audit coordinator
Information operations manager/administrator/officer	Referral specialist
Information resource manager	Regional health information management specialist/manager/administrator
Information warehouse/repository director	Registrar (birth, cancer, device, bone marrow, tissue)
Information workflow designer	
Interface reconciliation specialist	Reimbursement specialist
Local/regional policy analyst/officer	Report writer
National health data coordinator	Research coordinator/associate
Nationwide health information management specialist/manager/director/officer	Research data abstractor
	Researcher
Patient advocate	Revenue integrity analyst
Patient-centered outcomes researcher	Systems analyst
Patient identity manager	Terminology asset manager
Patient portal specialist	Vice president of data integrity services
Performance improvement specialist	Vice president of health information governance
Personal health information exchange manager/director/administrator	Vice president of strategic information development
	Voice capture specialist
Personal health record advisor	Workflow design analyst

There are also a growing number of universities offering post-baccalaureate certification programs leading to eligibility to sit for the RHIA examination. These programs assess the prior degree and adjust future courses appropriately to align the student's education with the competencies and knowledge required to become a credentialed health information management professional at the RHIA level. For a complete list of post-baccalaureate certificate programs, refer to www.HICareers.com or the CAHIIM website at www.cahiim.org.

Graduate Degree in HIM

The HIM professional with a graduate degree in HIM can follow a more flexible curriculum depending on the institution. However, for CAHIIM accreditation, HIM graduate programs may emphasize one or more of the specified domains, but all domains and competencies must be introduced to the student. The **domains** were presented previously and can be found at the AHIMA website.

A master's degree–prepared HIM professional would anticipate a career directed toward enterprise leadership and administration or research. Master's-prepared HIM professionals may also consider a career in government, the pharmaceutical industry, technology, or clinical information resources. According to AHIMA research, a master's degree in HIM is considered valuable by 40 percent of practitioners and employers. As healthcare professionals in general begin to advance toward higher-level degrees, research supports HIM professionals attaining graduate degrees as they compete for positions of leadership, project management, consulting, and academics. According to HICareers.com, one in three healthcare employers finds a graduate degree in health information management or health informatics more valuable than other graduate degrees (AHIMA 2011i).

Master's-prepared HIM professionals usually have a bachelor's degree in HIM or another discipline. They may also have an RHIA credential prior to entering the program. Selected master's degree programs offer the option of additional courses allowing the graduate student to sit for the RHIA credential.

Associate Degree in HIM

A two-year associate's degree in health information technology is generally offered at community colleges or through proprietary programs. The 2012 Standards for Accreditation of Associate Degree Programs help to refine the traditional associate's degree programs and require individual programs to develop their own outcome-focused mission and goals. Every accredited HIM program (at all levels) must demonstrate adherence to CAHIIM standards. This assures students of consistent, reviewed, and approved educational programs.

Accredited associate's degree programs in HIM also follow the five domains that the baccalaureate degree curriculum is built around, but the associate's degree focuses on the technology or application of the knowledge. The domains are

- Health data management—standards, classification systems, and reimbursement
- Health statistics, research, and quality—analysis and evaluation of data, understanding, and using quality assessment tools
- Healthcare delivery systems—laws and roles healthcare practitioners play in the delivery of healthcare
- Information technology—technology, software, and concepts applied within the HIM field including retrieval and security of health data in an electronic environment
- Organizational resources—communication and workflow as well as revenue cycle and resource allocation in an HIM environment

The complete 2011 Curriculum Competencies and Knowledge Clusters can be found on the AHIMA website and include significantly more details.

Graduates of an accredited associate's degree HIM program are eligible to sit for the **registered health information technician (RHIT)** credential. RHITs can look forward to expanding career opportunities in health information. The September 20, 2010 Bureau of Labor Statistics' National Employment Matrix states that the need for health information technicians will grow by 20 percent from 2008 to 2018. RHITs are well trained in technology and coding. As with all careers in HIT, the electronic health record has created unprecedented opportunities. In addition to traditional healthcare facilities, organizations that use patient data or health information, including pharmaceutical companies, law and insurance firms, and health product vendors are growing areas for RHIT employment. Careers in quality, as well as clinical documentation improvement, are expanding. Coding has long been the career of choice for the majority of RHITs and continues to be a very strong specialization area. Technicians are highly recruited for diagnostic and procedural coding for reimbursement as well as research. Cancer registry is also a growing field as the population ages and treatment options become more widespread. With experience, the RHIT credential holds solid potential for advancement to management positions, especially when combined with a bachelor's degree (AHIMA 2011d).

Check Your Understanding 3.4

Instructions: Answer the following questions on a separate piece of paper.

1. An ACO is considered a:

   A. Healthcare data organization
   B. Healthcare payer organization
   C. Healthcare supplier organization

2. Which of the following would NOT be considered a third-party compliance organization?

   A. Recovery audit company
   B. Fraud investigation firm
   C. Blue Cross/Blue Shield insurance company

3. Identify three resources that would be included in the AHIMA Body of Knowledge resources.

4. Distinguish between certification and credentialing in the HIM profession.

Certificate Programs

The HIM field also offers a number of certificate programs, ranging from vocational, entry-level skills training to more advanced post-degree specialty certification. With the growth of opportunities for HIM professionals, there continues to be expanded certifications to validate specific skill sets.

AHIMA-approved coding programs must meet the national curriculum standards and follow an approved academic model. Coding domains and knowledge clusters are as important in the certificate programs as they are in degree programs as they provide the foundation for consistent skills training. Coding domains include

- Biomedical sciences such as anatomy and physiology, medical terminology, pathophysiology, and pharmacology
- Information technology including knowledge applications in the electronic record, meaningful use, and computer-assisted coding, among others
- Healthcare data content, requirements, and standards including knowledge in areas of the health record content, Health Insurance Portability and Accountability Act (HIPAA) standards on privacy and security, data sets, and healthcare delivery organizations and reimbursement systems
- Coding classification systems and reimbursement methodology, which is the key to the credential, focusing on ICD-9 and ICD-10 as well as other diagnostic and procedural coding systems and code sets; this domain also contains the knowledge cluster for current reimbursement methods and compliance requirements

Certified Coding Associate

Certified Coding Associates (CCAs) are entry-level coders certified in the knowledge required to code. They are tested in their understanding of anatomy and physiology, pathophysiology, medical terminology, medical documentation, and the principles of classification systems. This credential creates the first step of a coding career ladder that could lead to a CCS or a CCS-P with more training and experience. Moreover, CCAs may choose to expand their interests in HIM beyond coding and continue their education

by attaining a degree in HIM and applying for the RHIT or RHIA credential.

Certified Coding Specialist

Certified Coding Specialists (CCSs) are professionals skilled in classifying medical data from patient records, generally in the hospital setting (AHIMA 2011d). CCSs review patient records and assign numeric codes for each diagnosis and procedure. They must possess expertise in current coding systems including selected ambulatory and procedural coding systems. In addition, the CCS must be knowledgeable in medical terminology, disease processes, and pharmacology. Hospitals and healthcare providers report coded data to payers such as insurance companies or the government for treatment of Medicare and Medicaid recipients for reimbursement of their expenses. Coding accuracy is highly important to healthcare organizations because of its impact on revenues and in the description of health outcomes. Accordingly, the CCS credential demonstrates tested data quality and integrity skills in a coding practitioner. The CCS certification exam assesses mastery or proficiency in coding rather than entry-level understanding and skills (AHIMA 2011d).

Certified Coding Specialist-Physician Based

Certified coding specialists–physician based (CCS-Ps) specialize in physician-based settings such as physician offices, group practices, multispecialty clinics, or specialty centers. The CCS-P reviews patient records and assigns codes for each diagnosis and procedure. To perform this task, he or she must possess in-depth knowledge of current coding systems related to ambulatory settings (AHIMA 2011d). The CCS-P professional will work with Current Procedural Terminology (CPT) coding systems, Healthcare Common Procedure Coding System (HCPCS), and ICD-9, as well as ICD-10 as new code sets are fully implemented. Because patients' coded data are submitted to payers for expense reimbursement, the CCS-P plays a critical role in the healthcare provider's business operation. Moreover, the employment outlook for this coding specialty looks highly favorable with the growth of nonhospital health services delivery options (AHIMA 2011d).

ARRA Grant Certificates

In 2009 the **American Recovery and Reinvestment Act (ARRA)** was signed into law. This provided federal funding for university-based programs and community college consortia to offer HIT-focused education ranging from six-month certificates to master's degrees in HIT-related areas. While the ARRA grant-funded programs are not required to go through the CAHIIM or AHIMA accreditation and approval process, these programs do offer additional skills training in the health information field and, in some cases, are offered in educational institutions that have accredited HIM programs.

Nine universities are involved and more than 70 community colleges provide training to help meet the predicted workforce demand in health information. These training programs build on prior degrees and offer strategic courses specifically related to areas of health IT and electronic records. After completing a short course of study, usually six months, individuals are eligible to sit for a competency exam of the US HHS (2011) Workforce Development program, called HIT PRO.

Certified Health Data Analyst

The **certified health data analyst (CHDA)** designation denotes advanced competencies in acquiring, managing, analyzing, interpreting, and transforming data into accurate, consistent, and timely information while balancing the "big picture" strategic vision with day-to-day details. CHDA-certified professionals exhibit broad organizational knowledge and the ability to communicate with individuals and groups both internal and external (AHIMA 2011d). Eligibility to write this examination requires the applicant meet one of the following requirements:

- Baccalaureate degree or higher and a minimum of five years of healthcare data experience
- RHIA and a minimum of one year of healthcare data experience

Certified Healthcare Privacy and Security

The **certified healthcare privacy and security (CHPS)** credential denotes advanced competency in designing, implementing, and administering comprehensive privacy and security protection programs in all types of healthcare organizations (AHIMA 2011d). The CHPS certification offers expanded career opportunities as well as credibility and recognition regarding privacy and security of health information. In an AHIMA survey 70 percent of healthcare executives agree that credentialed employees help reduce exposure to fraud and abuse charges (AHIMA 2005a). Those wanting to earn this credential will need to meet one of the following eligibility requirements:

- Baccalaureate degree and minimum of four years' experience in healthcare management
- Master's or related degree (JD, MD, PhD) and two years' experience in healthcare management
- Health information management credential (RHIA or RHIT) with baccalaureate or higher degree and a minimum of two years' experience in healthcare management

Clinical Documentation Improvement Professional

Clinical documentation improvement professional (CDIP) certification is designed for individuals working in the clinical documentation area. The certification offers professionals validation of proficiency in healthcare data integrity, quality, and clinical documentation. Current regulations and initiatives such as ARRA, HITECH, and RAC audits have underscored the growing demand for a well-educated, strategically trained workforce in the area of clinical documentation, and this credential has been designed in response. Eligibility requirements to sit for this exam include a combination of credentials or education and are specified on the AHIMA certification website (AHIMA 2011d, 2011h).

Certification Maintenance

Credentialed HIM professionals are required to maintain a certain level of professional competency through **continuing education.** This requirement helps ensure relevant skills and competency in core professional areas. Continuing education units (CEUs) are based on clock hours. While there is no maximum number of CEUs allowed, there are minimum requirements, which vary with the credential attained.

AHIMA requires all HIM professionals have training related to ICD-10-CM/PCS (AHIMA 2011c):

CHPS: 1 CEU
CHDA: 6 CEUs
RHIT: 6 CEUs
RHIA: 6 CEUs
CCS-P: 12 CEUs
CCS: 18 CEUs
CCA: 18 CEUs

Continuing Education Requirements

AHIMA membership is not dependent upon credentialing. However, all AHIMA credentialed professionals must follow specific requirements for maintenance:

1. Completion of specific number of CEUs in a two year cycle.

   - RHIA: 30 CEUs
   - RHIT: 20 CEUs

   Eighty percent of all CEUs, regardless of RHIA or RHIT, must be within the HIM domain. Please refer to the AHIMA website for explanation on domains. The website also provides an online tracking link for streamlined access and submittal of CEUs. Because RHIAs and RHITs frequently hold multiple credentials, 10 CEUs are required for each additional credential, not to exceed 60 CEUs per two-year cycle. Professionals holding a coding credential will require annual self assessments as part of the CEU maintenance.

2. CE Assessment Fees: AHIMA members are charged an annual continuing education assessment with the annual membership dues. Credentialed HIM professionals not

belonging to AHIMA are assessed a CE fee set by the AHIMA Board of Directors.

3. CE Validation Report: The day after the credential is awarded the two year recertification cycle begins. The cycle for subsequently obtained credentials will begin with the next cycle date, beginning on January 1 and ending on December 31 of the following year. Paper reporting is allowed, but the report may be tracked and submitted online through the AHIMA website. Following submission of the required CE report within the cycle, non-audited participants will receive a CE validation certificate. This is to be retained as evidence of meeting AHIMA CE requirements. If selected for an audit, participants would be asked provide documentation in compliance with the procedure. The CE validation certificate will be provided after the audited documentation has been approved (AHIMA 2011f).

Reporting Time Frames and Costs

CEU forms may be submitted anytime during the two-year cycle. Currently, AHIMA members pay an annual fee at the time of the dues payment. Non-AHIMA members are assessed a CE maintenance fee set by the AHIMA Board of Directors. The fee structure can be found on the AHIMA website, Recertification Guide.

Revocation and Restoration

There are two ways a credentialed professional may lose his or her credentialed status. One is by failure to comply with AHIMA's Code of Ethics. Credentials revoked for this reason may not be restored. The second way is through failure to maintain the credential for two consecutive CE cycles (four years), which will result in notification of revocation of credentials. The candidate will be required to retake the applicable examination. If it is less than four years, or less than two consecutive CE cycles, the candidate has other options. If a credential has been revoked, the individual may not use the credential, even if undergoing the restoration process. CCHIM requires the following to apply for restoration:

- Submit an application, pay a fee, and obtain the required number of CEUs including coding self-assessments if applicable
- Reactivate the credentialed status by portfolio review and required fee payment
- Restore the credential by successfully passing the exam and paying the required fee

Continuing Education Audits

As CE hours are entered into the membership files, a certain percentage of the candidates are randomly selected for audit. An individual selected for audit is required to submit verifiable documentation for each activity listed on the CE form. Auditors will verify attendance or participation and CE credits earned. Therefore, it is important that individuals retain

proof of attendance for at least one year following the cycle end date (AHIMA 2011f).

Prior Approval of Activities

It is not required that programs have prior approval from AHIMA to qualify for CEUs. If the activities do not advertise AHIMA prior approval, candidates can judge for themselves whether it meets AHIMA requirements. The CCHIIM Recertification Guide offers in-depth CE qualifying activities guidance.

Characteristics of a Profession

The term **profession** may be defined in a number of ways. *Merriam-Webster's Collegiate Online Dictionary* (2012) defines it as "a calling requiring specialized knowledge and often long and intensive academic preparation." The world is changing, as are the traditional boundaries associated with professions. Marketplace realities of today did not exist 25 years ago, and they have irreversibly changed the professional climate, especially in the healthcare world. The impact of time, value expectations, market structure, generational differences, competition, and technology has forever changed the way professionals and professional organizations supporting them operate (Coerver and Byers 2011).

Check Your Understanding 3.5

Instructions: Answer the following questions on a separate piece of paper.

1. List and identify the area of focus of the three basic coding credentials.
2. ARRA grant certificates offer additional training in the HIM field. Training is offered specifically to address which skill sets? Certification via competency exam is offered by whom?
3. CDIP is certification offered for specialization in what practice area?
4. With the adoption of ICD-10-CM/PCS on the horizon, what CE requirement was added for those holding an RHIA and RHIT credential?
5. What are the three steps all degree-based AHIMA credentialed professionals must take to maintain their credentials?

Professional Associations

One of the ways to ensure professional success is through membership in a professional association. Professional associations provide a rich environment for learning, contributing, and networking. The following professional associations are particularly important to individuals working in the field of HIM.

American Health Information Management Association

The **American Health Information Management Association (AHIMA)** represents more than 64,000 members. Association membership includes HIM professionals credentialed in the field as well as those with an interest in health information management and a willingness to abide by the AHIMA Code of Ethics (appendix B). AHIMA members play many diverse roles yet share a common purpose: to provide reliable and valid information that drives the healthcare industry. They are specialists in administering information systems, managing healthcare data including the electronic patient record, and coding information for reimbursement and research. As leaders in the field of HIM, AHIMA members work to ensure that healthcare is based on accurate and timely information. AHIMA is the oldest and largest of the membership associations in health information. Since its creation in 1928, AHIMA has undergone numerous changes and significant developments. Building on the profession's strong traditions, AHIMA members also are prepared to be a driving force in a changing healthcare industry. Health information is not a paper document maintained in one location and accessible only through one mechanism. HIM professionals permeate the fabric of healthcare to provide a vital link for practitioners, consumers, and payers. Although much has evolved, the mission of AHIMA provides a distinct summary: "AHIMA leads the health informatics and information management community to advance professional practice and standards" (AHIMA 2011k). AHIMA seeks to attain its vision by fulfilling the following:

- Promote technology advancements that enhance the delivery of quality healthcare
- Promote ethical and appropriate use of health information, in accordance with the AHIMA Code of Ethics
- Working to assure that the health information is valid, accurate, complete, trustworthy, and timely
- Remaining concerned about the effective management of health information from all sources and in all applications
- Recognizing that the application of best health information practices are worldwide and not bound by national borders

AHIMA supports a system of component organizations in every state plus Washington, D.C., and Puerto Rico. Component state associations (CSAs) provide their members with local access to professional education, networking, and representation. They also serve as an important forum for communicating national and emerging issues (AHIMA Foundation, 2012). The House of Delegates within AHIMA is composed of representation from each CSA. The House governs the profession, and the Board of Directors governs the association.

American Medical Informatics Association

The **American Medical Informatics Association (AMIA)** is a professional scientific association that was formed by the merger of three organizations in 1989: the American Association for Medical Systems and Informatics (AAMSI), the American College of Medical Informatics (ACMI), and the Symposium on Computer Applications in Medical Care (SCAMC). Membership is composed of individuals, institutions, and corporations that develop and use biomedical and health informatics to improve healthcare. AMIA represents the United States at the International Medical Informatics Association (IMIA) and sponsors the International Congress on Nursing Informatics. Further AMIA sponsors educational sessions and publishes the *Journal of the American Medical Informatics Association* (AMIA 2011).

Association of Clinical Documentation Improvement Specialists

The **Association of Clinical Documentation Improvement Specialists (ACDIS)** was formed in 2007 as a community in which clinical documentation improvement professionals could communicate resources and strategies to implement successful programs and achieve professional growth. The mission of ACDIS is to bring CDI specialists together for professional improvement. Members receive electronic resources and have access to online discussions and e-learning opportunities. ACDIS also offers annual educational conferences (ACDIS 2011).

College of Healthcare Information Management Executives

The **College of Healthcare Information Management Executives (CHIME)** was formed in 1992 through a collaborative effort by the Health Information and Management Systems Society (HIMSS) and the Center for Health Information Management (CHIM). CHIME serves two purposes: (1) to serve the professional development needs of healthcare chief information officers (CIOs) and (2) to advocate the effective use of information management to improve health and healthcare delivery systems. CHIME offers its members professional development opportunities through its CIO forums, CIO boot camps, online education, and focus groups.

Health Information and Management Systems Society

The **Health Information and Management Systems Society (HIMSS)** provides leadership in healthcare for the management of technology and management systems. Members include healthcare professionals in a variety of settings, including hospitals, corporate healthcare systems, clinical practice groups, vendor organizations, and consulting firms.

HIMSS is a cause-based, not-for-profit organization focusing on providing global leadership for the optimal use of information technology (IT) and management systems for the betterment of healthcare. HIMSS offers a wide variety of education and benefits to members and is arguably best known for its annual conference and exhibition, which is the largest in the industry. HIMSS supports state and local chapters across the United States and Canada. HIMSS also offers certified professional in health information management systems (CPHIMS) certification (HIMSS 2011).

National Cancer Registrars Association

The **National Cancer Registrars Association (NCRA)** was chartered in 1974 and is a nonprofit professional organization with a focus toward education and certification of cancer registry professionals and tumor registrars. NCRA's goal is to ensure that all cancer registry professionals have the required knowledge to contribute better information and accurate data leading to the management of cancer and, ultimately, cures. NCRA sponsors an annual conference designed to improve registrars' professional expertise and offers certified tumor registrar (CTR) certification for individuals working in this field. AHIMA developed the Cancer Registry Management formal educational program in collaborative partnership with NCRA. Additional information on academic training and degrees may be found on the NCRA website (NCRA 2011).

National Association for Healthcare Quality

The **National Association for Healthcare Quality (NAHQ)** provides education, leadership development opportunities, and products to support quality professionals (NAHQ 2011). Healthcare quality professionals are those who are involved in patient safety and ensure facilities meet accreditation standards. NAHQ was founded in 1976, and while it has undergone many transformations, similar to the quality profession itself, NAHQ now is home to more than 10,000 quality and safety professionals in the United States and abroad. The NAHQ offers the professional credential certified professional in healthcare quality (CPHQ).

International Federation of Health Information Management

The **International Federation of Health Information Management (IFHIM)** supports national associations and health record professionals to improve health records and systems. IFHIM was established in 1968 under the name International Federation of Health Record Organizations as a forum to bring national organizations together. IFHIM continues to focus on global issues affecting health information. IFHIM has a partnership with the International Medical Informatics Association and is affiliated with the World Health Organization (WHO).

IFHIM is organized into five regions: Europe, Americas, South East Asia, Western Pacific, Eastern Mediterranean, and Africa. Although national membership is reserved for one association per country, individuals may be associate members. A world congress is sponsored every three years and attracts HIM professionals from all over the globe (IFHIM 2011).

International Medical Informatics Association

The mission of Geneva, Switzerland–based **International Medical Informatics Association (IMIA)** is to promote informatics in healthcare and biomedical research and to advance and nurture international cooperation. IMIA describes itself as an association of associations. Its role is "to bring together, from a global perspective, scientists, researchers, users, vendors, developers, consultants, and suppliers in an environment of cooperation and sharing" (IMIA 2011). IMIA is considered a bridge organization, moving theory into practical application. The membership of IMIA is worldwide and includes organizations, societies, and corporations. IMIA sponsors an international conference—MEDINFO—and engages multiple working groups to advance its mission.

Code of Ethics

An important element of any profession is its commitment to a code of ethics. Today's HIM professionals can face a variety of ethical dilemmas regarding payment and reimbursement systems, confidentiality and privacy, facility accreditation and licensure, and fair practices. A formal code of ethics ensures that professionals understand and agree to uphold an ethical standard that puts the best interests of the profession before their personal interests.

The AHIMA Code of Ethics serves seven purposes:

- Promotes high standards of HIM practice
- Identifies core values on which the HIM mission is based
- Summarizes broad ethical principles that reflect the profession's core values
- Establishes a set of ethical principles to be used to guide decision making and actions
- Establishes a framework for professional behavior and responsibilities when professional obligations conflict or ethical uncertainties arise
- Provides ethical principles by which the general public can hold the HIM professional accountable
- Mentors practitioners new to the field to HIM's mission, values, and ethical principles

Violation of the code of ethics triggers a peer review process. Generally this is separate from legal procedures, allowing the profession to counsel and discipline within AHIMA members. Results can be grounds for disciplinary action including revocation of credentials. In some situations, violation of the code also constitutes an illegal activity, which would result in separate legal actions. AHIMA's Code of Ethics was revised in 2011 and can be found in full in Appendix B (AHIMA 2011e).

Education

An educational requirement is part of the definition of a profession. Indeed, completing a profession's educational requirement is fundamental to gaining entry into the field. Additionally, ongoing education is a responsibility of any professional. This is especially true of HIM professionals challenged by new regulations, innovative technologies, and an industry in transition with the advent of the electronic health record and ICD-10.

For AHIMA members, this commitment to learning was strengthened through a House of Delegates resolution calling for its members to embrace lifelong learning and professional development so that they could continue to be vital players, ensuring quality healthcare through quality information (AHIMA 2005b). This learning may be formal education through the pursuit of a master's or doctoral degree. Ongoing professional development can also be demonstrated through continuing education (CE) gained from conferences, distance learning activities, workshops, or relevant professional journal articles. Seeking challenging work assignments and making lifelong learning a conscious goal contribute to an individual's professional development.

Certification

Certification is a competency validation process for professionals who meet certain qualifications as identified by a nongovernmental agency or an association. Certification is one of the characteristics of the HIM profession. AHIMA certification provides both personal and professional recognition. There are a growing number of certifications available to HIM professionals, some at entry level and others at a mastery level. To achieve AHIMA certification, eligibility requirements and successfully writing a competency exam is required. AHIMA offers seven credential opportunities: HIM, coding (three types), healthcare privacy and security, clinical documentation improvement, and health data analysis (AHIMA 2011d, 2011h).

An AHIMA employer survey conducted in 2005 found that 80 percent of healthcare employers gave a favorable overall rating to industry credentials including credentials for coding professionals, HIM professionals, IT professionals, and privacy and security officers. The employers indicated that credentialed employees help reduce exposure to fraud and abuse and improve the delivery of quality healthcare. In general, the survey found that:

- Hiring and promotion practices are influenced by credentials
- Employers support credential maintenance, both conceptually and financially
- There are financial rewards in the workplace with credentialed employees earning more than non-credentialed employees
- Employers expect a higher level of competence of credentialed employees (AHIMA 2005a)

Professional Cohesion

Another aspect of a profession is professional cohesion, which is characterized by the members of a profession acting in a unified way. The existence of a professional association is one expression of professional cohesion as it embodies the members of the profession who act as a unified body rather than individuals. Professional cohesion can be witnessed in AHIMA's position statements or in advocacy positions that are taken with regulators or legislators. The recognition and adoption of best practices is another example of professional cohesion.

Because health information and data are vital to the healthcare industry, professional cohesion extends to the external community in ways not anticipated by prior generations. AHIMA has a large and growing number of professional affiliates with complementary goals of advancing quality health information to improve healthcare. These affiliates join together, as appropriate, to address specific issues relevant to their mutual goal.

Professional Literature

The final element of a profession is the existence of professional literature. This textbook is one example of professional literature. The *Journal of the American Health Information Management Association* is the best-known source of HIM knowledge. Published since the 1930s, it is distributed to all AHIMA members and is available by subscription to others. With the advent of the electronic record, changing regulations and standards, and a new diagnostic coding system, the opportunity to contribute to the Body of Knowledge through professional research and publication is unprecedented. *Perspectives in Health Information Management* is the scholarly peer-reviewed online research journal published by AHIMA and indexed in PubMed (AHIMA 2011l).

Check Your Understanding 3.6

Instructions: Answer the following questions on a separate piece of paper.

1. Within AHIMA, the Board of Directors governs the association and the House of Delegates governs the _____.

2. Distinguish between ACDIS and AMIA.

3. Which of the associations was specifically designed to serve the needs of healthcare chief information officers?

4. Who has partnered with the International Medical Informatics Association?

5. If you were an HIM practitioner seeking to grow in your understanding of healthcare technology and vendor products, which associations would be beneficial for you?

6. Violation of the AHIMA Code of Ethics triggers

    A. Automatic loss of AHIMA credentials
    B. A review by peers with potential disciplinary actions
    C. Disciplinary actions and a fine

Summary

Workforce research for the professional core model confirmed HIM professionals hold positions in an unprecedented diversity of settings. Over the past 30 years, healthcare delivery settings have become increasingly complex, ranging from ambulatory and specialty settings to diversified healthcare enterprise systems. All of them need and offer multiple opportunities for HIM professionals. Add to these settings factors such as personal health record options, new models for payment, increased auditing, and additional regulations, and the HIM professional workforce in today's healthcare arena has a wealth of options to select. Twenty years ago nearly all HIM professionals worked in hospitals. Today that number is just over 50 percent. For decades, we distinguished "traditional" from "nontraditional" practice; today this distinction is irrelevant. HIM skills and competencies are needed by all organizations that use person-specific or aggregate patient data. The adoption of health IT and the electronic record has further accelerated the demand for a well-qualified HIM workforce.

In 2007, AHIMA published "Vision 2016: A blueprint for Quality Education in Health Information Management" to outline an educational strategy required to bring new professionals into the field with the degree and level of training required to meet the knowledge and competency requirements of the HIM in a healthcare system that is supported by a fully functional and interoperable electronic health information infrastructure (AHIMA 2007). In 2011, AHIMA published the HIM Core Model, further exploring the current and evolving roles and functions of the profession. One of the results of the Core Model research is a comprehensive list of roles. (See figure 3.8.)

In an information-driven healthcare world, roles for HIM professionals shift and expand continuously. The one constant of the HIM profession is its responsibility for advancing the quality of health information and ensuring its availability in response to the needs of the healthcare industry.

References

AHIMA Foundation. 2012. Component State Associations. http://www.ahimafoundation.org/partners/csa.aspx.

American Health Information Management Association. 2005a. Employers Value Credentials in Healthcare: An AHIMA Survey. http://www.ahima.org/downloads/pdfs/certification/EmployeeValuesurvey.pdf.

American Health Information Management Association. 2005b (January). Text of the lifelong learning resolution (2004 Convention Wrap-Up). *Journal of AHIMA* 76(1): 64.

American Health Information Management Association. 2007 (September). Vision 2016: A blueprint for quality education in health information management. http://www.ahima.org.

American Health Information Management Association. 2011a. A new view of HIM: Introducing the Core Model. http://library.ahima.org/xpedio/groups/public/documents/ahima/bok1_049283.pdf.

American Health Information Management Association. 2011b. Body of Knowledge. http://www.ahima.org.

American Health Information Management Association. 2011c. CCHIIM ICD-10 continuing education requirements for AHIMA certified professionals, frequently asked questions for recertification. http://www.ahima.org.

American Health Information Management Association. 2011d. Certification. http://www.ahima.org/certification/default.aspx.

American Health Information Management Association. 2011e. Code of Ethics. http://www.ahima.org/about/ethicscode.aspx.

American Health Information Management Association. 2011f. Commission on Certification of Healthcare Informatics and Information Management recertification guide. http://www.ahima.org/downloads/pdfs/certification/Recertification_Guide.pdf.

American Health Information Management Association. 2011h. New certified documentation improvement practitioner credential. http://www.ahima.org/certification/cdip.aspx.

American Health Information Management Association 2011i. HICareers/masters degree. http://hicareers.com/pathways/mhim.aspx.

American Health Information Management Association. 2011j. School and academics. Faculty resources. Curriculum map. http://www.ahima.org/schools/FacResources/curriculum.aspx.

American Health Information Management Association. 2011k. Vision, mission, and values statement. http://www.ahima.org/about/mission.aspx.

American Health Information Management Association. 2011l. Perspectives in health information management. http://perspectives.ahima.org.

American Health Information Management Association. 2012. *AHIMA Pocket Glossary for HIM and Technology*. Chicago: AHIMA.

American Medical Informatics Association. 2011. http://www.amia.org.

Association of Clinical Documentation Improvement Specialists. 2011. http://www.cdiassociation.com.

Bureau of Labor Statistics. 2010 (December 17). National employment matrix. In *Occupational Outlook Handbook*. http://www.bls.gov/oco/ocos103.htm#outlook.

Cassidy, B. 2011 (September). Stepping into new e-HIM Roles. *Journal of AHIMA* (82)9: 10.

Coerver, H., and M. Byers. 2011. *Race for Relevance, 5 Radical Changes for Associations*. Washington, D.C.: ASAE, The Center for Association Leadership.

Cottington, S. 2011 (September). popHealth Primer, ONC funds open-source software to streamline clinical quality measures reporting for meaningful use program. *Journal of AHIMA* (82)9: 48–50.

Department of Health and Human Services, Office of the National Coordinator for Health Information Technology. (2011). Health information technology competency exams. http://www.hitproexams.org/.

Fox, L.A., and K. Gratwick Baker. 2009. *Leading a Business in Anxious Times: A Systems Approach to Becoming More Effective in the Workplace*. Chicago: Care Communications.

Health Information and Management Systems Society. 2011. http://www.himss.org.

International Federation of Health Information Management. 2011. http://www.ifhima.org.

International Medical Informatics Association. 2011 (October 7). http://www.imia-medinfo.org.

Merriam-Webster's Online Collegiate Dictionary. 2012. http://www.merriam-webster.com.

National Association for Healthcare Quality. 2011. NAHQ home page. http://www.nahq.org.

National Cancer Registrars Association. 2011. http://www.ncra-usa.org.

Valo, C. 2011 (August). Time to lead: Leaders and leadership, building trust. *Journal of AHIMA* (82)8: 26.

Appendix 3A
2011 AHIMA Curriculum Competencies and Knowledge Clusters—Health Information Management Baccalaureate Degree

Approved by AHIMA Education Strategy Committee

HIM Baccalaureate Degree Entry-Level Competencies (Student Learning Outcomes)	CCHIIM Corresponding Domain	Knowledge Clusters (Curriculum Components)	Notes
I. Domain: Health Data Management I.A. Subdomain: Health Data Structure, Content, and Standards 1. Manage health data (such as data elements, data sets, and databases). 2. Ensure that documentation in the health record supports the diagnosis and reflects the patient's progress, clinical findings, and discharge status.	Domain 1: Health Data Mgmt 1.1, III.3 1.3	Health Data Structure, Content, and Acquisition • Capture, structure, and use of health information (Evaluating, 5) • Health information media (paper, electronic) (Evaluating, 5) • Data quality assessment and integrity (Evaluating, 5) • Secondary data sources such as registries and indexes (Applying, 3) • Healthcare data sets (such as HEDIS, UHDDS, OASIS) (Analyzing, 4) • Health information archival and retrieval systems (Evaluating, 5) • Data capture tools and technologies (such as forms; data input screens; templates, other health record documentation tools) (Evaluating, 5)	
I.B. Subdomain: Healthcare Information Requirements and Standards 1. Develop organization-wide health record documentation guidelines. 2. Maintain organizational compliance with regulations and standards. 3. Ensure organizational survey readiness for accreditation, licensing and/or certification processes. 4. Design and implement clinical documentation initiatives.	I.3 IV.1 IV.2; IV. 15	Healthcare Information Requirements and Standards • Standards and regulations for documentation (such as Joint Commission, CARF, COP) (Evaluating, 5) • Health information standards (such as HIPAA, ANSI, HL-7, UMLS, ASTM) (Applying, 3) • Patient Identity Management Policies (MPI) (Applying, 3)	

I.C. Subdomain: Clinical Classification Systems 1. Select electronic applications for clinical classification and coding. 2. Implement and manage applications and processes for clinical classification and coding. 3. Maintain processes, policies, and procedures to ensure the accuracy of coded data.	I.4; VI.1	Clinical Classification Systems • Healthcare taxonomies, clinical vocabularies, nomenclatures (such as ICD-9-CM, ICD-10-CM/PCS, CPT, SNOMED-CT, DSM-IV, LOINC) (Understanding, 2) • Severity of illness systems (Analyzing, 4) • Data integrity, coding audits (Analyzing, 4) • CCI, electronic billing, X12N, 5010 (Applying, 3)	
I.D. Subdomain: Reimbursement Methodologies 1. Manage the use of clinical data required in prospective payment systems (PPS) in healthcare delivery. 2. Manage the use of clinical data required in other reimbursement systems in healthcare delivery. 3. Participate in selection and development of applications and processes for chargemaster and claims management. 4. Implement and manage processes for compliance and reporting. 5. Participate in revenue cycle management.	I.5 I.5 IV.6	Reimbursement Methodologies • Clinical data and reimbursement management (Evaluating, 5) • Compliance strategies and reporting (Analyzing, 4) • Chargemaster management (Analyzing, 4) • Case mix management (Analyzing, 4) • Audit process such as compliance and reimbursement (Evaluating, 5) • Payment systems (such as PPS, DRGs, APCs, RBRVS, RUGs, MSDRGs) (Analyzing, 4) • Commercial, managed care, and federal insurance plans (Analyzing, 4) • Revenue cycle process (Analyzing, 4)	
II. Domain: Health Statistics, Biomedical Research, and Quality Management II.A. Subdomain: Healthcare Statistics and Research 1. Analyze and present data for quality management, utilization management, risk management, and other patient care related studies. 2. Utilize statistical software. 3. Ensure adherence to Institutional Review Board (IRB) processes and policies.	Domain II: Health Statistics and Research Support (No QM) I.7, II.3	Healthcare Statistics and Research • Statistical analysis on healthcare data (Applying, 3) • Descriptive statistics (such as means, standard deviations, frequencies, ranges, percentiles) (Analyzing, 4) • Inferential statistics (such as t-tests, ANOVAs, regression analysis, reliability, validity) (Applying, 3) • Vital statistics (Applying, 3) • Epidemiology (Understanding, 2) • Data reporting and presentation techniques (Evaluating, 5) • Computerized statistical packages (Understanding, 2) • Research design/methods (such as quantitative, qualitative, evaluative, outcomes) (Applying, 3) • Knowledge-based research techniques (such as Medline, CMS, libraries, web sites) (Applying, 3) • National guidelines regarding human subjects' research (Analyzing, 4) • Institutional review board process (Understanding, 2) • Research protocol data management (Understanding, 2)	

II.B. Subdomain: Quality Management and Performance Improvement 1. Provide support for facility-wide quality management and performance improvement programs. 2. Analyze clinical data to identify trends that demonstrate quality, safety, and effectiveness of healthcare. 3. Apply Quality Management tools.	No equivalent Subdomain related to Quality II.3	Quality Management and Performance Improvement • Quality assessment, and management tools (such as benchmarking, Statistical Quality Control, and Risk Management) (Analyzing, 4) • Utilization and resource management (Analyzing, 4) • Disease management process (such as case management, critical paths) (Analyzing, 4) • Outcomes measurement (such as patient, customer satisfaction, disease specific) (Evaluating, 5) • Benchmarking techniques (Creating, 6) • Patient and organization safety initiatives (Applying, 3)	
III. Domain: Health Services Organization and Delivery III.A. Subdomain: Healthcare Delivery Systems 1. Evaluate and implement national health information initiatives in the healthcare delivery system for application to information systems policies and procedures. 2. Interpret, communicate, and apply current laws, accreditation, licensure and certification standards related to health information initiatives at the national, state, local, and facility levels. 3. Analyze and respond to the information needs of internal and external customers throughout the continuum of healthcare services. 4. Revise policies and procedures to comply with the changing health information regulations. 5. Translate and interpret health information for consumers and their caregivers.	Domain IV. Organization and Management 1.2, IV.2 V1.1 II.1 1.2 II.2	Healthcare Delivery Systems • Organization and delivery of healthcare systems (Evaluating, 5) • Components and operation of healthcare organizations including e-health delivery (Evaluating, 5) • Accreditation standards (such as Joint Commission, NCQA, CARF, CHAP, URAC) (Evaluating, 5) • Regulatory and licensure requirements such as COP, state health departments (Evaluating, 5) • Federal initiatives: ONC, CCHIT , Red Flag Rules, Meaningful Use (Evaluating, 5)	

III.B. Subdomain: Healthcare Privacy, Confidentiality, Legal, and Ethical Issues 1. Coordinate the implementation of legal and regulatory requirements related to the health information infrastructure. 2. Manage access and disclosure of personal health information. 3. Develop and implement organization-wide confidentiality policies and procedures. 4. Develop and implement privacy training programs. 5. Assist in the development of security training. 6. Resolve privacy issues and problems. 7. Apply and promote ethical standards of practice. 8. Define and maintain elements of the legal health record. 9. Establish and maintain e-Discovery guidelines.	V.2 V.4 V.3	Healthcare Privacy, Confidentiality, Legal, and Ethical Issues • Legislative and legal system (Analyzing, 4) • Privacy, confidentiality, security principles, policies and procedures (Evaluating, 5) • Identity management (Evaluating, 5) • Health information laws, regulations, and standards (such as HIPAA, HITECH, Joint Commission, State laws) (Evaluating, 5) • Elements of compliance programs (Evaluating, 5) • Professional ethical issues (Evaluating, 5) • Legal Health Record, e-Discovery guidelines (Evaluating, 5) • Information security training (Understanding, 2)
IV. Information Technology and Systems IV.A. Subdomain: Information and Communication Technologies 1. Implement and manage use of technology, including hardware and software to ensure data collection, storage, analysis, and reporting of information. 2. Contribute to the development of networks, including intranet and Internet applications to facilitate the electronic health record (EHR), personal health record (PHR), public health, and other administrative applications. 3. Interpret the use of standards to achieve interoperability of healthcare information systems.	III. Information Technology and Systems III.5; III.1 III.6 III.4	Information and Communication Technologies • Computer concepts (hardware components, network systems architectures, operating systems and languages, and software packages and tools) (Analyzing, 4) • Communications technologies (networks—LANS, WANS, WLANS, VPNs) (Understanding, 2) • Data interchange standards (such as NIST, HL7, 5010, Reference Information Modeling (RIM)) (Analyzing, 4) • Internet technologies (Intranet, web-based systems, standards—SGML, XML) (Analyzing, 4) • Data, information, and file structures (data administration, data definitions, data dictionary, data modeling, data structures, data warehousing, database management systems) (Evaluating, 5) • System interoperability, data sharing, Health Information Exchanges (Evaluating, 5) • Nationwide Health Information Infrastructure NHIN (Applying, 3)

IV.B. Subdomain: Information Systems		Information Systems	
1. Apply knowledge of database architecture and design (such as data dictionary, data modeling, data warehousing) to meet organizational needs.		• Leading development of health information resources and systems (Analyzing, 4) • Database Architecture and Design (Evaluating, 5) • Human factors and user interface design (Applying, 3)	
2. Monitor use of clinical vocabularies and terminologies used in the organization's health information systems.	III.2	• Systems Development Life Cycle (systems analysis, design, implementation, evaluation, and maintenance) (Evaluating, 5)	
3. Manage clinical indices,databases, and registries.	III.3	• Clinical, business, and specialty systems applications (administrative, clinical decision support systems, electronic health record and computer-based health record systems, nursing, ancillary service systems, patient numbering systems at master and enterprise levels) (Evaluating, 5)	
4. Apply appropriate electronic or imaging technology for data and record storage.		• Regional Health Information Exchange (RHIE), Health Information Exchanges (HIE), Regional Health Extension Centers (RHEC) (Evaluating, 5)	
5. Apply knowledge of database querying and data mining techniques to facilitate information retrieval.		• Project management (Evaluating, 5)	
6. Implement and manage knowledge-based applications to meet end-user information requirements.	II.1		
7. Design and generate administrative reports using appropriate software.	II.3		
8. Apply appropriate electronic or imaging technology for data and record storage.			
9. Participate in system selection processes (RFI and RFP).			
10. Evaluate and recommend clinical, administrative, and specialty service applications (RFP vender selection, electronic record, clinical coding).			
11. Apply appropriate systems to life cycle concepts, including systems analysis, design, implementation, evaluation, and maintenance to the selection of healthcare information systems.			

IV.C. Subdomain: Data Security		Data Security	
1. Protect electronic health information through confidentiality and security measures.	III.5	• Data security protection methods (such as authentication encryption, decryption, firewalls) (Analyzing, 4)	
2. Protect data integrity and validity using software or hardware technology.	1.3	• Data security (audits, controls, data recovery, e-security) (Evaluating, 5)	
3. Implement and monitor department and organizational data and information system security policies.	V.1		
4. Recommend elements that must be included in the design of audit trails and data quality monitoring programs.	I.1		
5. Recommend elements that should be included in the design and implementation of risk assessment, contingency planning, and data recovery procedures.			
V. Organization and Management	IV. Organization and Management	Human Resources Management	
V.A. Subdomain: Human Resources Management		• Employment laws (Analyzing, 4)	
1. Manage human resources to facilitate staff recruitment, retention, and supervision.	IV.3	• Principles of human resources management (recruitment, supervision, retention, counseling, disciplinary action) (Evaluating, 5)	
2. Ensure compliance with employment laws.		• Workforce education and training (Creating, 6)	
3. Develop and implement staff orientation and training programs.	IV.3	• Performance standards (Evaluating, 5)	
4. Develop productivity standards for health information functions.	IV.4	• Labor trends, market analysis (Analyzing, 4)	
5. Monitor staffing levels and productivity, and provide feedback to staff regarding performance.	IV.5	• Cost benefit analysis of resource needs (Applying, 3)	
6. Benchmark staff performance data incorporating labor analytics.	IV.3		
7. Develop, motivate, and support work teams.	IV.7		
8. Analyze and report on budget variances.			
9. Evaluate and manage contracts.			
10. Apply principles of ergonomics to work areas.			

V.B. Subdomain: Strategic Planning and Organizational Development		Strategic Planning and Organizational Development	
1. Apply general principles of management in the administration of health information services.	IV.1	• Organizational assessment and benchmarking (Analyzing, 4) • Critical thinking skills, emotional intelligence, employee engagement (Analyzing, 4) • Project management (Evaluating, 5)	
2. Assign projects and tasks to appropriate staff.	IV.14	• Process reengineering and work redesign (Analyzing, 4) • Change management (Analyzing, 4)	
3. Demonstrate leadership skills.		• Facilitation of teams and meetings (Applying, 3)	
4. Apply project management techniques to ensure efficient workflow and appropriate outcomes.	IV.14	• Principles of management (Evaluating, 5) • Negotiation techniques (Analyzing, 4) • Communication and interpersonal skills (Evaluating, 5)	
5. Facilitate project management by integrating work efforts, as well as planning and executing project tasks and activities.		• Team/consensus building (Evaluating, 5) • Professional development for self and staff (Creating, 6) • Problem solving and decision making processes (Evaluating, 5)	
		Biomedical Sciences	
		Anatomy (Applying, 3) Physiology (Applying, 3) Medical Terminology (Evaluating, 5) Pathophysiology (Analyzing, 4) Pharmacotherapy (Analyzing, 4)	

Bloom's Taxonomy: Revised Version
1 = Remembering: Can the student recall or remember the information?
2 = Understanding: Can the student explain ideas or concepts, and grasp the meaning of information?
3 = Applying: Can the student use the information in a new way?
4 = Analyzing: Can the student distinguish between the different parts, break down information, and infer to support conclusions?
5 = Evaluating: Can the student justify a stand or decision, or judge the value of?
6 = Creating: Can the student create new product or point of view?

REV: 08/11 ESC

chapter 4

Health Information Systems: Supporting Technologies and Systems Development

Ryan H. Sandefer, MA, CPHIT, and Patricia B. Seidl, RHIA

Learning Objectives

- Understand the field of informatics as it is being applied in healthcare
- Identify the major issues associated with computerizing health data and information
- Learn the types of computer applications and technologies being used to support the delivery of healthcare and the management of health data and information
- Identify the barriers and limitations associated with computerized health data and information
- Develop a working knowledge of the emerging technologies that support the creation and maintenance of electronic health record (EHR) systems
- Prepare for assuming a leadership role in the development of improved healthcare information systems, integrated patient information systems, and decision support tools

- Understand the importance of strategic information systems planning to healthcare organizations
- Describe the purpose and major activities within each phase of the systems development life cycle: analysis, design, implementation, and maintenance and evaluation
- Identify the resources needed to effectively manage information systems within healthcare organizations
- Know the roles and responsibilities of information system professionals
- Identify the health information manager's role in planning, selecting, and implementing healthcare information systems

Key Terms

Analog
Analysis phase
Application systems analyst
Applied healthcare informatics
Audit trail
Autocoding
Automated forms-processing (e-forms) technology
Bar-coding technology
Bit-mapped data

Chief information officer (CIO)
Chief information security officer (CISO)
Chief information technology officer (CITO)
Chief medical informatics officer (CMIO)
Clinical care plan
Clinical data repository
Clinical information system (CIS)
Clinical messaging system

Clinical systems analyst
Clinical workstation
Clinician/physician web portal
Cloud computing
Computer-assisted coding
Computer output laser disk/enterprise report management
    (COLD/ERM) technology
Continuous speech input
Data repository
Data type
Data warehouse
Data warehousing
Database administrator
Decision support system (DSS)
Design phase
Diagnostic image data
Digital
Digital signature management technology
Discrete data
Document
Document image data
Document imaging technology
Document management technology
e-commerce
e-health
Electronic data interchange (EDI)
Electronic document/content management
    (ED/CM) system
Electronic records management technology
Encryption
Enterprise master patient index (EMPI)
Executive information system (EIS)
Extensible Markup Language (XML)
Extranet
Firewall
Free-text data
Geographic information system (GIS)
Gesture recognition technology
Health 2.0
Healthcare informatics
HyperText Markup Language (HTML)
Identity management
Implementation phase
Informatics
Information management
Information science
Information system (IS)
Intelligent character recognition
    (ICR) technology
Intelligent document recognition
    (IDR) technology
Interoperability
Interoperate
Intranet

Maintenance and evaluation phase
Management information system (MIS)
Mark sense technology
Master patient index (MPI)
Master planning or steering committee
Medical informatics
Metadata
Motion or streaming video/frame data
Multimedia
Natural language processing technology
Network administrator
Neural network
Object-oriented database
Online/real-time analytical processing
    (OLAP)
Online/real-time transaction processing
    (OLTP)
Open source technology
Optical character recognition (OCR)
    technology
Patient/member web portals
Personal digital assistant (PDA)
Personal health record (PHR)
Physiological signal processing system
Pixel
Point-of-care information system
Programmer
Protocol
Public key infrastructure (PKI)
Radio frequency identification
    (RFID)
Raster image
Real audio data
Request for information (RFI)
Request for proposal (RFP)
Secure messaging system
Software engineer
Speech recognition technology
Strategic IS planning
Structured data
Systems analyst
Systems development life cycle
    (SDLC)
Text mining
Unstructured data
Vector graphic (signal tracing) data
Web content management system
Web portal
Web service
Web 2.0
Web 3.0
Webmaster/web developer
Wireless technology
Workflow technology

Healthcare organizations are under increased pressure to control costs and improve efficiency. At the same time, they are experiencing increased demands to ensure patient safety, reduce medical errors, improve the quality of care, promote access, and ensure compliance with privacy and security regulations. Many healthcare organizations are looking to informatics to help them respond to these pressures and provide high-quality services in a more cost-effective manner. The use of computer technology to manage data and information means that well-trained and skilled individuals with knowledge about both healthcare and computerized information technologies are needed to manage (design, develop, select, and maintain) health data and information systems. It also means that healthcare organizations must prioritize the computer technologies and **information systems (IS)** to deploy in their institution.

This chapter introduces the field of informatics as it is currently being applied in the healthcare industry. Also, it describes the current and emerging technologies used to support the delivery of healthcare and the management and communication of patient information. It discusses strategic information systems planning, the **systems development life cycle (SDLC)**, information resource management, and the role of the health information managers in planning, selecting, and implementing healthcare information systems.

The Field of Informatics

Informatics is the science of **information management.** It uses computers to manage data and information and support decision-making activities. In short, informatics can be summarized by the following statement: "A person working in partnership with an information resource is 'better' than a person unassisted" (Friedman 2009, 169). The management of data and information includes the generation, collection, organization, validation, analysis, storage, and integration of data, as well as the dissemination, communication, presentation, utilization, transmission, and safeguarding of information.

The healthcare industry is information intensive. One needs to spend only a day with a healthcare provider or clinician to realize that the largest percentage of healthcare professional activities relates to managing massive amounts of data and information. This includes obtaining and documenting information about patients, consulting with colleagues, staying abreast of the current literature, determining strategies for patient care, interpreting laboratory data and test results, and conducting research. **Healthcare informatics** is the field of **information science** concerned with the management of all aspects of health data and information through the application of computers and computer technologies.

The State of Healthcare Informatics

Historically, the healthcare industry has not valued informatics to the same degree that other industries have.

The healthcare industry has been perceived as slow to both understand computerized information management and to incorporate it effectively into the work environment. Perhaps this is because the data and information requirements of the healthcare industry are more demanding than those of other industries in a number of areas. These areas include implications of violations of privacy, support for personal values, responsibility for public health, complexity of the knowledge base and terminology, perception of high risk and pressure to make critical decisions rapidly, poorly defined outcomes, and support for the diffusion of power (Stead and Lorenzi 1999, 343).

The use of information technologies to improve the healthcare delivery system gained attention in the early 1990s through the early 2000s through the publication of several reports from the Institute of Medicine that highlighted patient safety concerns and discussed how health information technologies can be used to improve care delivery. Momentum was gained with the establishment of the Office of the National Coordinator for Health Information Technology (ONC) in 2004. In 2008, ONC published the Federal Health Information Technology Strategic Plan, which defined a number of goals, objectives, and strategies that bring together all federal efforts in health IT in a coordinated fashion. The purpose of the plan is to guide the advancement of health IT throughout the federal government through 2012.

More recently the Health Information Technology for Economic and Clinical Health (HITECH) provision of the American Recovery and Reinvestment Act of 2009 (ARRA) authorized the Centers for Medicare and Medicaid Services (CMS) to provide reimbursement incentives for eligible professionals and hospitals who are successful in becoming "meaningful users" of certified electronic health record (EHR) technology.

Examples of healthcare informatics successes are steadily growing. Charge collection and billing, automated laboratory testing and reporting, clinical documentation, computerized provider order entry (CPOE), patient and provider scheduling, diagnostic imaging, and secondary data use make up a distinguished list of healthcare informatics successes, proving what is doable and supporting further investment. Today's task for informatics is to design, develop, and implement computer information systems that enable healthcare organizations to accomplish visions for providing the highest-quality care in the most effective way.

Applied healthcare informatics emphasizes the use of the computer-based applications in delivering and documenting healthcare services (AMIA 2005). Therefore, applied healthcare informatics is the application of information technology to functions and activities that are closely aligned with the domains of practice associated with the health information management (HIM) profession.

Instructions: Answer the following questions on a separate piece of paper.

1. How are the disciplines of information management and informatics related? How are they different?

2. Why are data and information so crucial to a healthcare professional's daily work?

3. Why is the healthcare industry perceived as being less proactive than other industries in the area of computerized information systems? How can this perception be changed?

Current and Emerging Information Technologies in Healthcare

To examine the information resources and systems that enable healthcare organizations to accomplish their visions in the most effective way, HIM professionals must possess fundamental knowledge of the components of computer-based information systems. This includes possessing knowledge of system hardware, software, and service components; communication and networking components; the Internet and its derived technologies; and system architectures. For the purposes of this chapter, it is assumed that students have acquired this basic knowledge through other, generic computer system courses and related textbooks.

Next, it is appropriate that HIM professionals review some of the current and emerging information technologies used to specifically support the delivery of healthcare as well as the management and communication of health data and information within the healthcare setting. To do this, five categories of current and emerging technologies in healthcare are discussed in this chapter:

- Supporting capture of various types of data and formats
- Supporting efficient access to, and flow of, data and information
- Supporting managerial and clinical decision making
- Supporting diagnosis, treatment, and care of patients
- Supporting security of data and information

Technologies Supporting the Capture of Different Types of Data and Formats

The information technologies currently in use for healthcare applications, as well as the new technologies being developed, support the capture of many different data types and formats that are all used to support the clinical

services and administrative functions performed in every healthcare setting.

Clinical Data Repository

An EHR system consists of not one or even two or more products. Rather, it is a concept that consists of a host of integrated, component information systems and technologies. The **clinical data repository** is a component of the EHR that captures data. The automated files that make up the EHR system's component information systems and technologies consist of different **data types,** and the data in the files consist of different data formats. Some data formats are structured and some are unstructured. For example, the data elements in a patient's automated laboratory order, result, or demographic or financial information system are coded and alphanumeric. Their fields are predefined and limited. In other words, the type of data is discrete, and the format of these data is structured. Consequently, when a healthcare professional searches a database for one or more coded, **discrete data** elements based on the search parameters, the search engine can easily find, retrieve, and manipulate the element. However, the format of the data contained in a patient's transcribed radiology or pathology result, history and physical (H&P), or clinical note system using word-processing technology is unstructured. **Free-text data,** as opposed to discrete, **structured data,** are generated by word processors, and their fields are not predefined and limited. Consequently, data embedded in unstructured text are not easily retrieved by the search engine. (See the section on speech recognition technology and natural language processing later in this chapter).

Diagnostic image data, such as a digital chest x-ray or a computed tomography (CT) scan stored in a diagnostic image management system, represent a different type of data called **bit-mapped data.** However, the format of bit-mapped data also is unstructured. Saving each bit of the original image creates the image file. In other words, the image is a **raster image,** the smallest unit of which is a picture element or **pixel.** Together, hundreds of pixels simulate the image.

Some diagnostic image data are based on **analog,** photographic films, such as an analog chest x-ray. These analog films must be digitally scanned, using film digitizers, to digitize the data. Other diagnostic image data are based on **digital** modalities, such as computed radiography (CR), CT, magnetic resonance (MR), or nuclear medicine.

Document image data are yet another type of data that are bit mapped and the format of which is unstructured. These data are based on analog paper documents or on analog photographic film documents. Most often, analog paper-based documents contain handwritten notes, marks, or signatures. However, such documents can include pre-printed documents (such as forms), photocopies of original documents, or computer-generated documents available only in hard copy. Analog photographic film-based documents (that is, photographs) are processed using an analog camera and film, similar to analog chest x-rays. Therefore, both the analog paper-based and the photographic film-based documents must be digitally scanned, using scanning devices that are similar to facsimile machines.

In addition, the EHR system's component information systems and technologies consist of other data types, the formats of which are also unstructured. **Real audio data** consist of sound bytes, such as digital heart sounds. **Motion or streaming video/frame data,** such as cardiac catheterizations, consist of digital film attributes, such as fast forwarding. The files that consist of **vector graphic** (or **signal tracing**) **data** are created by saving lines plotted between a series of points, accounting for the familiar electrocardiograms (ECGs), electroencephalograms (EEGs), and fetal heart rate (FHR) tracings.

When more than one **unstructured data** type is present in an information system, the data and system they represent are referred to as **multimedia.** Clearly, the EHR system is multimedia.

Figure 4.1 shows the different types of data and their sources found in EHR system- component information systems. (See chapter 5 for a complete discussion of the types of data captured within the EHR and chapters 6, 7, and 8 for discussion of the practices required to ensure the quality of data collected in EHR systems.)

Speech Recognition Technology

For more than 20 years, the concept of generating an immediately available, legible, final, signed note or report based on computer speech input has been the catalyst for the development and application of different forms of speech recognition technology in healthcare. The technology remains approximately 98 percent accurate (Nuance Communications 2008). Typically, systems offering approximately 98 percent accuracy still may not be acceptable for efficient and often lengthy clinical dictation purposes. Consequently, many still consider speech recognition an emerging technology.

Today, **speech recognition technology** is speaker independent with continuous speech input. Speaker independence does not require extensive training. The software is already trained to recognize generic speech and speech patterns. **Continuous speech input** does not require the user to pause between words to let the computer distinguish between the beginning and ending of words. However, the user is required to be careful in the enunciation of words.

Although speech recognition vocabularies are expanding due to faster and more powerful computer hardware, only limited clinical vocabularies have been developed. Limited vocabulary-based speech recognition systems require the user to say words that are known or taught to the system. In healthcare, limited clinical vocabulary–based specialties such as radiology, emergency medicine, and psychiatry have realized significant benefits for dictation from the technology.

The ultimate goal in speech recognition technology is to be able to talk to a computer's central processor and rapidly create vocabularies for applications without collecting any speech samples (in other words, without training). It includes being able to talk at natural speed and intonation and in no specific manner. It also includes having the computer understand what the user wants to say (the context of the word or words) and then apply the correct commands or words as

Figure 4.1.   EHR data types and their sources

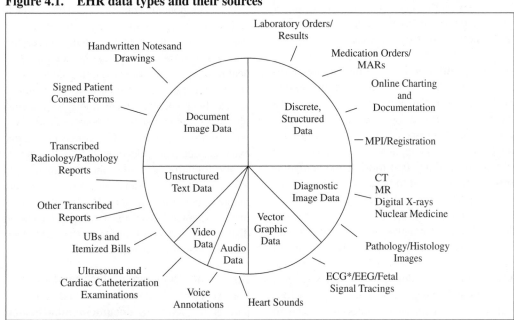

*ECG is the more correct term, but EKG is more widely used.
© Deborah Kohn 2001.

coded data in a structured format. Finally, it includes identifying a user's voice and encrypting the voiceprint. Over the next years and decades, clinical vocabularies and algorithms will continue to improve, true speaker independence will be achieved, and natural language understanding will ultimately make structured dictation a reality.

Natural Language Processing Technology

Natural language processing technology considers sentence structure (syntax), meaning (semantics), and context to accurately process and extract free-text data, including speech data for application purposes. As such, it differs from simple Boolean word search programs (simply combining search terms with AND, OR, NOT, or NEAR) that often complement speech recognition technology–based systems. For example, the narratives "no shortness of breath, chest pain aggravated by exercise" and "no chest pain, shortness of breath aggravated by exercise" look the same to a Boolean word search engine when looking for occurrences of "chest" and "pain" in the same sentence. This Boolean word search approach retrieves approximately 20 percent of the answer 20 percent of the time. It is rife with false positives and false negatives.

On the other hand, **natural language processing technology** knows the difference in the narratives' meanings. For example, for health record coding applications, it teaches computers to understand English well enough to "read" transcribed reports and notes and then find certain key concepts (not merely words) by identifying the many different phrasings of the concept. By "normalizing" these concepts, different phrases of the same content can all be compared with one another for statistical purposes. For example, "the patient thinks he has angina" and "the doctor thinks the patient has angina" have different meanings from a coding perspective (Schnitzer 2000, 96). By employing statistical or rules-based algorithms, natural language processing technology can then compare and code these similar expressions accurately and quickly.

Autocoding and **computer-assisted coding** are the terms commonly used to describe natural language processing technology's method of extracting and subsequently translating dictated and then transcribed free-text data, or dictated and then computer-generated discrete data, into ICD or CPT codes for clinical and financial applications such as patient billing and health record coding. **Text mining** and *data mining* are the terms commonly used to describe the process of extracting and then quantifying and filtering free-text data and discrete data, respectively.

Early results of several formative studies suggest that natural language processing technology improves health record coding productivity and consistency without sacrificing quality (Warner 2000, 78). More recent studies suggest that accuracy of natural language processing varies across applications and it is critical to have processes defined to review, edit, approve, and finalize (AHIMA 2011). Despite the studies' outcomes, vendors continue to integrate natural language processing technology within health record coding reference tools, coding guidelines, drug databases, and legacy information systems to provide complete patient billing, health record coding, and other applications with little or no human intervention.

Electronic Document/Content Management Systems

A **document** is any analog or digital, formatted, and preserved "container" of data or information, collectively referred to as content. The document is a well-worn and very useful human construct, but unless data contained within documents are formatted, accompanied by print-like qualities, such as headings or bolding, data are difficult to interpret. It is for this reason that documents, and not data, are required for evidentiary disclosure and discovery purposes. To settle legal disputes, the transaction *presentation,* not *representation,* is required for all business record documents. In healthcare organizations, this involves the retrieval of the bill document, the consultation report document, the photograph document, the image document, and so on.

An **electronic document/content management (ED/CM) system** is any electronic system that manages an organization's analog and digital documents and content (that is, not just the data) to realize significant improvements in business work processes. Like most information systems, the ED/CM system consists of a number of component technologies that support both digital and analog document and content management. These component technologies are discussed in the following sections.

Document Imaging Technology

Document imaging technology is one of the many ED/CM system component technologies. This technology electronically captures, stores, identifies, retrieves, and distributes documents that are not generated digitally or are generated digitally but are stored on paper for distribution purposes. Currently, in healthcare provider organizations, documents that typically are not generated in a digital format, are stored on paper and are candidates for this technology. They include handwritten physician problem lists and notes; "fill-in-the-blank" typeset nursing forms; preprinted Conditions of Treatment forms; and external documents (documents from the outside).

By digitally scanning the documents, the technology converts the analog data on the document into digital, bit-mapped, document images, discussed in a previous section of this chapter. As more and more documents are created, distributed, and stored digitally, the dependence on, and use of, this technology decreases.

Document Management Technology

For every type of document as well as for every section or part of a document, **document management technology** automatically organizes, assembles, secures, and shares documents. Some of the more common document management technology functions include document version control, check in–check out control, document access control, and text and word searches.

Electronic Records Management Technology

Business records are bound by legal and regulatory requirements. Consequently, formats for long-term preservation, storage media for long-term viability, and strategies for record migration and accessibility are required. **Electronic records management technology** includes components that must ensure the authenticity, security, and reliability of an organization's electronic records. For example, mass storage is required for the massive amounts of structured and unstructured data as well as the large number and kind of documents stored in ED/CM systems. The major, mass storage medium used in ED/CM systems is magnetic, including disk (for example, redundant array of independent disks [RAID], network attached storage [NAS], content addressable storage [CAS]) or tape options. For extraordinarily large amounts of data and lengthy document archive requirements, the optical medium might be used, including compact disk–read only memory (CD-ROM), CD-recordable, digital versatile disk (DVD; read only or recordable), or magneto-optical-based write once read many (WORM) options.

In addition, ED/CM system records must be properly classified under appropriate categories so that appropriate legal and regulatory retention rules can be applied. Users must determine how to identify these records so that the records and record documents can be deleted, purged, or destroyed at a defined point in their life cycle.

Workflow and Business Process Management Technology

Business process management (BPM) technology allows computers to add and extract value from document content as the documents move throughout an organization. The documents can be assigned, routed, activated, and managed through system-controlled rules that mirror business operations and decision processes. For example, in healthcare organizations, **workflow technology** automatically routes electronic documents into electronic in-baskets of its department clerks or supervisors for disposition decisions.

Computer Output Laser Disk/Enterprise Report Management Technology

Computer output laser disk/enterprise report management (COLD/ERM) technology electronically stores, manages, and distributes documents that are generated in a digital format and whose output data are report formatted and print-stream originated. Unfortunately, documents that are candidates for this technology too often are printed to paper or microform for distribution and storage purposes. COLD/ERM technology not only electronically stores the report-formatted documents but also distributes them with fax, e-mail, web, and traditional hard-copy print processes.

One of the more recent trends for ERM is to store the coded, report-formatted output data natively and convert the data to **Extensible Markup Language (XML)** or **HyperText Markup Language (HTML)** when needed. In healthcare provider organizations, such documents generated by COLD/ERM technology typically include "green bar" financial system reports, Uniform Bills (UBs)/CMS 1500s, laboratory cumulative result summary reports, and transcribed, word-processed medical reports.

Automated Forms-Processing Technology

Automated forms-processing (e-forms) technology allows users to electronically enter data into online forms and electronically extract the data from the online forms for various data-manipulation purposes. Powerful contextual verification processes have made such operations highly accurate. In addition, the form document is stored in a form format, as the user sees it on the screen, for ease of interpretation.

Digital Signature Management Technology

Digital signature management technology offers both signer and document authentication for analog or digital documents. Signer authentication is the ability to identify the person who digitally signed the document. Implementation of the technology is such that any unauthorized person will not be able to use the digital signature. Document authentication ensures that the document and the signature cannot be altered (unless both the original document and the change document are shown). As such, document authentication prevents the document signer from repudiating that fact.

Diagnostic Imaging Technologies

Diagnostic imaging technology (medical imaging) consists of using tools to capture images of the human body that can be used for clinical decision making. Picture archiving and communication systems (PACS) provide one example of diagnostic imaging technology where images taken from multiple sources (CT scans or MRIs, for example) are archived electronically for organizational access. Ultrasound technology, such as that used for echocardiography, is also considered imaging technology.

Check Your Understanding 4.2

Instructions: Answer the following questions on a separate piece of paper.

1. Provide an example of structured and unstructured data formats and an example of discrete and free-text data types.

2. What is a key advantage to structured data when searching a database?

3. What are the similarities and differences between a diagnostic image and a document image?

4. Provide a healthcare example for each of the following data types: real audio data, motion or streaming data, and signal or vector graphic data.

5. What is the difference between (a) speech recognition technology and natural language processing technology and (b) natural language processing searching and Boolean searching?

6. What is an ED/CM system?

7. Explain the value of the following technologies: document imaging technology, workflow and BPM technology, COLD/ERM technology, automated forms technology, and digital signature management technology.

Technologies Supporting Efficient Access to, and Flow of, Data and Information

There are many current and emerging information technologies used to support efficient access to, and flow of, healthcare data and information. For purposes of this chapter, the following technologies are highlighted:

- Automatic recognition technologies
- Enterprise master patient indexes and identity management
- Electronic data interchange (EDI) and e-commerce
- Secure messaging systems
- Web-derived technologies and applications

Automatic Recognition Technologies

Several technologies are used in healthcare to recognize analog items automatically, such as tangible materials or documents, or to recognize characters and symbols from analog items. Character and symbol recognition technologies recognize electronically scanned characters or symbols from analog items, enabling the identified data to be quickly, accurately, and automatically entered into digital systems. Other recognition technologies identify the actual items.

Character and Symbol Recognition Technologies

Character and symbol recognition technologies include barcoding, optical character recognition (OCR), and gesture recognition technologies.

Bar-Coding Technology

Almost three decades ago, the bar code symbol was standardized for the healthcare industry, making it easier to adopt **bar-coding technology** and to realize its potential. Since then, bar-coding applications have been adopted for labels, patient wristbands, specimen containers, business/employee/patient records, library reference materials, medication packages, dietary items, paper documents, and more. Benefits have been realized by the uniform consistency in the development of commercially available software systems, fewer procedural variations in healthcare organizations using the technology, and the flexibility to adopt standard specifications for functions while retaining current systems. Because virtually every tangible item in the clinical setting, including the patient, can be assigned a bar code with an associated meaning, it is not surprising to find bar coding as the primary tracking, identification, inventory data-capture, and even patient safety medium in healthcare organizations.

With bar-coding technology, an individual's computer data-entry rate can be increased by 8- to 12-fold in applications such as patient medication tracking, supply requisitioning, or chart/film tracking. For example, a function such as hand-keying paper chart/film locations into a computer that once took a healthcare professional eight hours to perform now can be done in 30 to 45 minutes with bar-coding technology.

In addition to eliminating time spent, bar-coding technology eliminates most of the mounds of paperwork (worksheets, count sheets, identification sheets, and the like) that are still associated with traditional computer keyboard entry. When bar-coding systems are interfaced to these types of healthcare information systems, the bar code can be used to enter the data, especially repetitive data, saving additional processing time and paper generation.

More importantly, the data input error rates with bar coding are as close to zero as most IT professionals think is possible. For all intents and purposes, bar-coded data, with an error rate of approximately three transactions in 1 million, can be considered error free. Thus, it is a most effective remedy for medication errors when used to ensure that the right medication dose is administered to the right patient.

Optical Character Recognition Technology

Like bar coding, **optical character recognition (OCR) technology** was invented to reduce manual data input, or hand-keying. OCR technology recognizes machine-generated characters (for example, preprinted numbers and letters) by interpreting the scanned, bit-mapped shapes of the characters' images and then converting the characters into computer-processable codes. OCR technology was initially used to automatically identify financial accounts consisting of preprinted Arabic numbers and Roman letters using the E13B font on thousands of paper-based documents, such as bank checks.

OCR has since been perfected to recognize the full set of preprinted typeset fonts as well as point sizes. The best OCR systems compensate for imperfectly formed characters and scanned pages by employing characteristics such as de-skewing, broken character repair, and redaction. De-skewing "straightens" oblique characters, broken character repair "fixes" incomplete characters, and redaction "hides" superfluous characters. OCR is used to perform everything from indexing scanned documents to digitizing full text. Its ability to dramatically reduce manual data input, or hand-keying, while increasing input speed represents the best aspect of this technology.

Unfortunately, like other technologies, OCR has been perfected but is not perfect. The approximately 98 percent recognition rate realized by most OCR systems (Prime Recognition 2008) may not be sufficient for the kind of text recognition applications OCR software is designed to perform. In addition, after an analog document is scanned by OCR technology, the data become unstructured, free-text data. As with all unstructured text data, when a healthcare professional needs to search the text, the search engine cannot easily find, retrieve, and manipulate one or more data elements embedded in text.

Gesture Recognition Technology

The recognition of constrained or unconstrained, handwritten, English language free text (print or cursive, upper- or lower-case, characters or symbols) typically stored on paper-based, analog documents is known as **intelligent character recognition (ICR) technology.** The recognition of hand-marked characters in defined areas of, typically, paper-based analog documents is known as **mark sense technology.** Collectively, these technologies are referred to as **gesture recognition technologies.**

Mark sense technology detects the presence or absence of hand-marked characters on analog documents. Consequently, it is used for processing analog questionnaires, surveys, and tests, such as filled-in circles by Number 2 pencils on SAT exam forms.

ICR technology is quite an elaborate information-processing technique. An operation such as the detection of lines or the beginnings of words in sections of handwritten text can be accomplished with relative ease in the normal case. However, subsequent tasks turn out to be extraordinarily complicated. These include segmentation of the words into individual characters and assignment of the individual characters to a definite class of characters, such as words. Consequently, ICR error rates remain high. As such, ICR technology is being adopted slowly, primarily into the data-entry activities of certain types of pen-based computer devices, such as handheld devices.

Neural networks remain the leading ICR technology. These networks are modeled on the way synapses work in the brain: processing information by recognizing patterns of signals. As such, they adapt themselves into shifting configurations based on what they encounter. In other words, they change as they grow and learn.

Consequently, for each handwritten character or symbol recognized by ICR technology, a confidence level is expressed internally as a percentage and a user picks the threshold below which he or she wants to flag uncertain characters or symbols. Like speech recognition technology, a training or setup period is required for this emerging technology.

Other Recognition Technologies

Automatic recognition technologies that identify actual items include radio frequency identification (RFID) and intelligent document recognition (IDR) technologies.

Radio Frequency Identification Technology

Radio frequency identification (RFID) technology works in the following manner: Chips that emit radio signals are embedded in analog items and products. The signals are read and captured by receivers. The receivers act as data collectors and send the signals to PCs on a network, allowing the items and products to be tracked.

RFID's applicability in the healthcare industry is limited only by the imagination. Like bar codes, it is being used to track moveable patients, clinicians, medications, and equipment. As such, in a wireless environment, conceivably, RFID could replace bar codes for these applications. The greatest challenges regarding RFID technology are cost and privacy and security concerns.

Intelligent Document Recognition Technology

Recently, an automatic recognition technology has been developed to recognize types of analog documents or forms, eliminating the need for bar codes or other characters and symbols that identify the documents or forms. **Intelligent document recognition (IDR) technology** trains itself to identify document or form types and to sort the information accordingly for subsequent data entry. This training process requires a period of continuously scanning each type of document or form. As such, the pattern of document and form layouts and information locations educates the system to recognize the document or form for future recognition situations.

Enterprise Master Patient Indexes and Identity Management

Too often, breakdowns in patient identification cause patient record errors that threaten data integrity. The most common error occurs when healthcare provider organization registration personnel fail to locate existing patient information in the organization's **master patient index (MPI)**, including the patient's unique identification number. The patient is then assigned another record (in other words, a duplicate record) and a new file is created in the database. When this error occurs, it is unclear into which database file the patient's data should be entered. This often results in unnecessary duplicate tests, billing problems, and increased legal exposure in the case of adverse treatment outcomes.

Another common error occurs when registration personnel incorrectly register a patient under another person's existing, unique identification number. This error of overlay results in the merging of two different patients' data into one file. The clinical risks are obvious.

As healthcare organizations continue to come together into integrated delivery networks (IDNs), the probability increases that information about a patient is spread across multiple databases and in multiple formats. In addition, the information is updated and accessed by multiple transaction processing systems and personnel. This causes problems when the IDN begins to assemble information about a patient in order to deliver care across diverse systems and encounters. Longitudinal applications, such as the EHR system, cannot be successful.

Consequently, healthcare provider organizations are developing strategic initiatives for **enterprise master patient indexes (EMPIs).** In the broad sense, this involves the increasingly important service referred to as **identity management.**

EMPIs provide access to multiple repositories of information from overlapping patient populations that are maintained in separate systems and databases. This occurs through an indexing scheme to all unique patient identification numbers and information in all the organizations' databases. As such, EMPIs become the cornerstones of healthcare system integration projects.

EMPIs work in two ways. At the back end, EMPIs coordinate recordkeeping. The indexes receive information from multiple systems that need no modification. The receiving is often performed through an integration gateway or engine. The enterprise index tests to see whether the patient is identified in all of the systems; if not, it may assign a unique identification number or other, related identifier as well as correlate records throughout the enterprise.

At the front end, EMPIs receive requests from existing registration systems to send data to these systems. Usually, these existing registration systems need some reprogramming to enable them to request and receive data from the EMPI. Currently, there is no consistent, accepted trigger event and standard data format to do this.

EMPI building is complex. Variations in information systems, data capture, and organizational goals and objectives present multiple challenges to integrating patient data. For example, EMPI building involves a multitude of decision points. These include deciding whether to employ centralized or distributed data storage; whether to maintain limited, additional information such as allergies and encounter histories or robust information such as problem lists; and whether to establish batch processing or real-time communication between the registration system and the EMPI.

In addition, EMPIs include complex capabilities. These capabilities include merging records pertaining to the same person using probabilistic matching and algorithms, maintaining source systems' pointers, removing duplicate records, and providing a common user interface. Finally, after technical and organizational issues are overcome, the purely operational tasks of linking patients across multiple entities and episodes of care and maintaining these linkages are difficult and can be costly.

Secure Messaging Systems

Messaging systems electronically deliver data and information to users. As such, e-mail systems are messaging systems. However, **secure messaging systems** reduce the security concerns that surround e-mail but retain the benefits of proactive, traceable, and personalized messaging.

These systems are not transaction (data) processing systems. Also known as secure notification delivery systems, these systems store and forward content to users in an asynchronous, "anytime" mode.

In healthcare, secure messaging systems are often referred to as **clinical messaging systems** because these systems are important, pervasive tools that are included in a broad set of contextual collaboration tools for clinicians. Other clinical collaboration tools include synchronous, real-time tools, such as instant messaging, chat servers, and web or media conferencing. However, secure clinical messaging is the most heavily used because it crosses time zones, can be done in each clinical user's own time frame, and gives clinical recipients time to think over and then respond to issues, such as notifications of abnormal laboratory test results. In addition, clinical messaging does not require all participants to be available at the same time and eliminates the scheduling problems associated with the real-time tools.

Secure clinical messaging systems work in the following manner: When a **clinical information system (CIS)** generates a patient alert regarding a possible drug interaction or an anomalous test result, the secure clinical messaging system immediately routes the alert, along with patient data, to a caregiver's designated pager number, fax machine number, telephone number, or e-mail address. In turn, clinicians can securely send these alerts to other, related clinicians. Also, messages can be automatically escalated to the next available caregiver if the original caregiver does not respond within a predefined time frame. In addition, messages can be tracked throughout the care delivery network. Most of today's secure clinical messaging systems fall into one of four architectures: peer-to-peer networking, a message staging server installed inside the network's **firewall,** a staging server installed outside the firewall (usually hosted), and a wholly outsourced service (Tabar 2003).

Electronic Data Interchange and E-Commerce

Electronic data interchange (EDI) allows the transfer (incoming and outgoing) of information directly from one computer to another by using flexible, standard formats. These formats function as a common language among many different healthcare "trading" or "business" partners (payers, government agencies, financial institutions, employer groups, healthcare providers, suppliers, and claims processors) who have agreed to exchange the information electronically but use a wide variety of application software with incompatible native formats. In the healthcare industry, with its traditionally strong reliance on paper-intensive processes, the goal of EDI is to eliminate the administrative nightmares of transferring paper documents back and forth between these partners and then hand-keying the information into the partners' disparate computer systems.

With widespread acceptance of the Internet and its derived technologies, such as the web, the term **e-commerce** began to replace the term EDI. Today, e-commerce is used to describe the integration of all aspects of business-to-business (B2B) and business-to-consumer (B2C) activities, processes, and communications, including EDI.

In addition, the term **e-health** is now used to describe the application of e-commerce in the healthcare industry. Several principles and concepts of e-health directly relate to EDI principles and concepts. These include the links among the healthcare trading and business partners; the links to healthcare equipment and supply vendors, providers, and health plans; and the transactions for exchanging data on healthcare eligibility, referrals, claims, and so forth.

Web-Derived Technologies and Applications

Web Portals

No one information system (IS) can provide all the applications, data types, and data formats needed by all of the healthcare industry's diverse healthcare organizations and users. Consequently, most healthcare provider organizations maintain multiple, disparate "feeder" applications for their data repositories. Depending on their size and systems acquisition philosophies, some healthcare provider organizations maintain and often integrate large numbers of disparate feeder applications, and others maintain and integrate at least two or three.

Each disparate feeder application for the repository has a unique user interface, uses different data nomenclature, and takes limited advantage of data standards. Therefore, it is not only difficult to integrate the information from the disparate systems into the repositories, but it is also difficult for the organizations' users to learn and interact with the different systems.

Today, the term **clinical workstation** is still used to describe the presentation of healthcare data and the launching of applications in the most effective way for healthcare providers. However, for all intents and purposes, the concept of web-based, clinician/physician portals has replaced the concept of the clinical workstation.

A **web portal** is a single point of personalized access (an entryway) through which one can find and deliver information (content), applications, and services. Web portals began in the consumer market as an integration strategy rather than a solution. Portals offered users of the large, public, online Internet service provider websites, such as AOL, fast, centralized access (via a web browser) to an array of Internet services and information found on those websites.

Consequently, like clinical workstations, **clinician/physician web portals** first were seen as a way for clinicians to easily access (via a web browser) the healthcare provider organizations' multiple sources of structured and unstructured data from any network-connected device. Like clinical workstations, clinician/physician web portals evolved into

an effective medium for providing access to multiple applications as well as the data. And because clinician/physician portals are based on Internet technologies, they became the access points to sources of data and applications both internal and external to the organization.

In addition, clinician/physician web portals provide simplified, automated methods of creating taxonomy, or classifying data. Consumer portals, such as Yahoo.com, provide good examples of this, whereby files and data corresponding to food, fashion, and travel are organized for easy access. Finally, true clinician/physician web portals have at least one search engine and allow customization at the role and individual level. As such, search engines must be able to search e-mails, file servers, web servers, and databases; and customization must allow users to create individual, relevant views. The clinical benefits of these portal features and functions are obvious.

With the success of clinician/physician web portals and the trend toward improving patient engagement in healthcare through technology, a growing number of healthcare provider and payer organizations have established web portals for their patients/members. Each participant receives an account on the web portal with a unique log-in and password. Typical payer-based portal uses include accessing membership information and choosing a primary care physician. Typical provider-based portal uses include requesting prescription renewals, scheduling appointments, and asking questions of providers via secure messaging. Increasingly, **patient/member web portals** are allowing patients to pay their bills online and to securely view all or portions of their provider-based, electronic health record, such as current medical conditions, medications, allergies, and test results.

Although patients/members access the portals over the Internet, all the information, including the secure messaging applications, resides on the provider's or payer's secured servers. As such, these portals dovetail well with privacy and security regulations, which empower patients/consumers with the authority to determine who can have access to their healthcare information. Also, patients can use the portal to notify providers if their EHR is incorrect. As consumers seek to take a larger role in their healthcare, such patient/member "entryways" to information (content), applications, and services are expected to become more common.

Intranets and Extranets

Web-based information systems and applications cannot continue to proliferate without creating web-based **intranets** designed to enhance communication among an organization's internal employees and facilities and web-based **extranets** designed to enhance communication among an organization's external business partners. This is true because intranets link every employee within an organization via an easy-to-navigate, comprehensive network devoted to internal business operations and extranets link an organization's external business partners with the same comprehensive network but one that is devoted to external business operations. For example, private, secure networks provide every healthcare organization employee with basic information, such as message boards, employee handbooks, manuals, mail, cafeteria menus, newsletters, directories, and contact lists. Also, they are used for the development of the organization's EHR. Restricted access to intranets by authorized users provides assurances that the general Internet public cannot access this private, secure network. However, through its intranet, a healthcare organization can access the Internet's servers for general Internet mail and messaging.

Extranets connect intranets that exist outside an organization's firewall. For example, typically, an IDN's autonomous care facilities (for example, acute care, long-term care, home healthcare), each with its own intranet, need to communicate between and among themselves via secure e-mail or other collaboration tools. As such, the facilities connect the various intranets and form an extranet.

Web Content Management Systems

Web content management systems label and track the exponential increase in and variety of information that is placed on a website so that the information can be easily located, modified, and reused. These systems are a critical component in personalizing an organization's web-based intranet and extranet, web portal, and page content for site users and visitors. They also provide crucial versioning and globalization capabilities. *Versioning* enables each of the website's content components to be tracked individually. Then, as the content changes, each iteration of the content can be identified and the overall website can be recreated as it existed at any specific point in time. *Globalization* enables the look and feel of an organization's website to be managed centrally, while specific content is managed for local requirements, such as regional healthcare language or procedure differences.

Web Services

Web services technology is a platform for software applications (or services) whose basic communication mechanism is XML, the universal language of the web and the accepted format for data exchange over the Internet. In addition, web services technology utilizes web-based infrastructure **protocols,** such as HTTP and transmission control protocol/Internet protocol (TCP/IP). As such, web services technology allows programs written in different languages and on different operating systems to communicate with each other in a standards-based way. In short, web services technology is an open, standardized way of integrating disparate, web browser–based and other applications.

By using XML messages to format and tag data, web services technology allows for data interchange without the need for translation. In addition, the messages use system-independent vocabularies and protocols, such as simple object access protocols (SOAP) to transfer the data; universal description, discovery, and integration (UDDI) to list what services are available; and web services description language (WSDL) to describe the services available. Healthcare organizations have been gradually installing web services to ease integration of disparate web-based and legacy applications, often written in incompatible languages. This ensures that the organizations' applications **interoperate** and that healthcare organizations can more easily choose tools for important interorganizational and regional data sharing. (See figure 4.2.)

Open Source Technology

Open source software products are applications whose source (human-readable) code is freely available to anyone who is interested in downloading the code. Advantages of **open source technology** include its availability, it extensibility to be customized, and the collaborative nature of the product in which a community of developers and users can interact, review, and improve upon each other's ideas. Disadvantages of open source technology include the need for skilled developers within an organization to take advantage of the benefits noted earlier as well as a lack of dependable technical support.

According to the open source definition maintained by Open Source Initiative (2012), ten criteria must be met to qualify a software program as *open source*.

- Free redistribution: Free redistribution is allowed and royalty payments are prohibited
- Source code: The program must include source code
- Derived works: Modifications and derived works are allowed
- Integrity of author's source code: The integrity of the original source code must be preserved
- No discrimination against any person or groups: The license must not discriminate against any person or group
- No discrimination against fields of endeavor: The license must not restrict anyone from making use of the program in a specific field of endeavor
- Distribution of license: The license remains with the program even if it is redistributed
- License must not be specific to a product: The rights attached to the program must not depend on the program's being part of a particular software distribution
- License must not restrict other software: The license must not insist that all other programs distributed on the same medium be open source software
- License must be technology neutral: No provision of the license may be predicated on any individual technology or style of interface

Figure 4.2. Web services

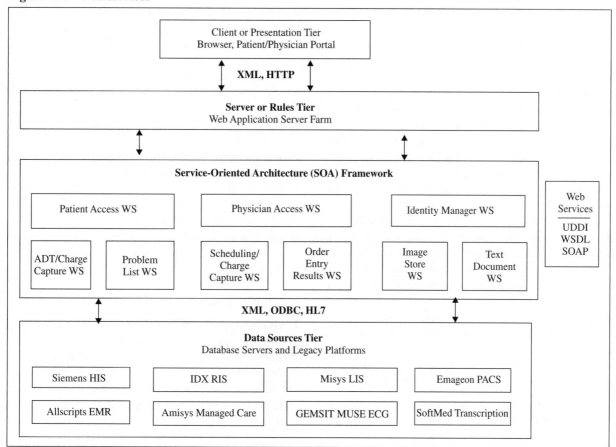

© Deborah Kohn 2005.

 Check Your Understanding 4.3

Instructions: Answer the following questions on a separate piece of paper.

1. Provide a healthcare example for each of the following automatic recognition technologies: bar coding, OCR, ICR, RFID, and IDR.

2. How are the concepts of EDI, e-commerce, and e-health interrelated?

3. What is driving the heightened interest in EMPI technology within the healthcare industry?

4. Explain why secure clinical messaging is often preferred over real-time tools such as instant messaging or chats.

5. What is the primary purpose of the clinical workstation and the clinician/physician portal?

6. How do web portals established by providers or payers assist consumers in taking a larger role in their healthcare?

7. What is the difference between an intranet and an extranet? Provide an example of how each can be used in healthcare.

8. Describe the benefits and drawbacks of open source technology.

Technology Supporting Managerial and Clinical Decision Making

Many current and emerging information technologies are used to support managerial and clinical decision making. For the purposes of this chapter, the following technologies and systems are highlighted:

- Data warehouses and data marts
- Decision support systems

Data Warehouses and Data Marts

Data warehouses are large, centralized, enterprise-wide collections of all the historical, demographic, and transactional data and information about businesses that are used to support managerial or, in the case of healthcare provider organizations, clinical decision-making processes (database data are typically structured and discrete). Generally, only two kinds of operations occur in a data warehouse: data warehousing and data mining. This is referred to as the nonvolatility of warehouse data. **Data warehousing** is the acquisition of all the business data and information from potentially multiple, cross-platform sources, such as legacy databases, departmental databases, and online transaction–based databases, and then the warehouse storage of all the data in one consistent format. Data mining is the probing and extracting of all the business data and information from the warehouse and then the quantifying and filtering of the data for analysis purposes. The model of the data warehouse database is typically subject oriented. In other words, the data within the data warehouse are organized along subject lines (customer, product, patient, clinician) rather than along operational lines (accounting, management, medicine, surgery) in order to be accessible and useful across the enterprise.

Generally, for day-to-day operations, a healthcare organization needs relatively current data and each operational unit needs only its own data. That is why relational and **object-oriented database** models for data repositories are well-suited for **online/real-time transaction processing (OLTP)**. But for large-scale, retrospective data analysis, for which **online/real-time analytical processing (OLAP)** is designed, a healthcare organization generally needs not just its current status but also a historical record over time or time variance, encompassing all the organizational operating units by subject for comparison purposes.

In healthcare, data warehouses have been used primarily for the following applications (Henchey 1998, 68):

- *Clinical management:* For example, every day, patient clinical data are fed into the warehouse from multiple sources to contribute to enterprise-wide best practices and to identify areas of excessive variation from best practices.
- *Operations management*: For example, sophisticated analytical tools, such as cost accounting, case-based budgeting, and variance analysis tools, are included with the warehouse to determine new healthcare market opportunities.
- *Outcomes management:* For example, data mining is conducted to study patient health status or other factors, such as satisfaction, that contribute to clinical outcomes.
- *Population management:* For example, to proactively manage the health of plan members, data mining helps the organization to predict utilization or identify at-risk members requiring case management.
- *Revenue management:* For example, the data warehouse assists healthcare financial analysts in addressing all the different contractual and regulatory reimbursement formulas. With revenue based on a mix of several dimensions, such as fee-for-service, capitation, and risk pooling, only the data warehouse can provide a complete picture of the enterprise's revenue stream and the factors controlling it.

A data warehouse cannot simply be bought and installed. Its implementation requires the integration of many products within its architecture. For example, often data warehouses require advanced data warehousing and mining techniques and tools. The software must be able to locate data that often are stored on multiple servers that may include any type of machine or operating system. The software must be able to maintain **metadata** (indexed data about the data), such as what indexes the acquired data use. Further, the software must be able to recognize data duplication and exceptions as well as issue alerts when data are not present or have been corrupted.

Data marts can be thought of as miniaturized data warehouses. Data marts are usually geared to the needs of a specific department, group, or business operational unit. Because data marts are considerably smaller in both size and complexity than data warehouses, some healthcare organizations build data marts as a way of testing data warehouses on smaller, more focused scales. What many are finding, though, is that data marts can easily proliferate into a collection of incompatible data stores with accessibility or utility limited to the department or operational unit that designed the mart.

Decision Support Systems

Decision support systems (DSSs) are interactive computer systems that intend to help decision makers use data and models to identify and solve problems and make decisions. A great deal of innovation is occurring related to DSSs, and the technologies of which they are comprised are changing rapidly.

Generally, DSSs are based on either a **data repository** model or a data warehouse model. Both transfer data from an operational environment (either in real time or retrospectively, in batches at fixed intervals) to a decision-making environment, and both organize the data in a form suitable to decision support applications.

Power (1997) suggests that DSSs can be classified based on one or more of the following five categories:

- *Communications-driven DSSs* emphasize communications, collaboration, and shared decision-making support. A simple Internet bulletin board or threaded e-mail is the most elementary level of functionality in this type of DSS.
- *Data-driven DSSs* emphasize access to and manipulation of internal, and sometimes external, structured business data. Simple file systems accessed by query and retrieval tools provide the most elementary level of functionality in this type of DSS.
- *Document- or graphics-driven DSSs* focus on the retrieval and management of unstructured business data. Basic document- or graphics-driven DSSs exist in the form of web-based search engines.
- *Knowledge-driven DSSs* can suggest or recommend actions to decision makers. These DSSs are person-to-computer systems with specialized problem-solving expertise. The expertise consists of knowledge about a particular domain, understanding of problems within that domain, and skill at solving some of those problems.

- *Model-driven DSSs* emphasize access to and manipulation of a model, for example, statistical, financial, optimization, and simulation models. Simple statistical and analytical tools provide the most elementary level of functionality in this type of DSS.

A wide variety of DSSs and related tools and technologies exist in healthcare, most of which can be classified as hybrids of the preceding categories. These systems include, but are not limited to, clinical/medical decision support systems, management information systems (MISs), executive information systems (EISs), geographic information systems (GISs), and expert decision support systems. See chapter 5 for an in-depth discussion of clinical/medical decision support systems.

Management Information Systems

Typically, **management information systems (MISs)** refer to the broad range of data-, document-, or knowledge-driven DSSs that provide information concerned with an organization's administrative functions (in other words, those functions that are associated with the provision and utilization of services). In addition, DSS-based MISs enable management to interrogate the computer on an ad hoc basis for various kinds of information within the organization so as to predict the effect of potential decisions. As such, DSS-based MISs provide information to people who must query these systems to make disposition decisions about valuable resources in a timely, accurate, and complete manner. Such systems are crucial for the effective administration of any organization and include, but are not limited to, general accounting and financial systems, customer relationship management (CRM) systems, enterprise resource planning (ERP) systems, and operations and plant management systems.

Executive Information Systems

Executive information systems (EISs) are DSSs that support the decision making of senior managers. As such, they provide direct online access to timely, accurate, and actionable information about aspects of a business that are of particular interest to a senior healthcare manager. Typically, this information is provided in a useful and navigable format so that managers can identify broad strategic issues and then explore the information to find the root causes of those issues. According to Kelly (2001), the following EIS features and functions are essential:

- Specifically tailored to executives' information needs
- Capable of accessing data about specific issues and problems
- Capable of aggregating data into meaningful reports
- Provide extensive online analysis tools, including trend analysis, exception reporting, and drill-down or data-mining capabilities
- Capable of accessing a broad range of internal and external data

- Easy to use (typically mouse or touch screen driven)
- Capable of being used directly by executives without assistance
- Capable of presenting information in a graphical form

Geographic Information Systems

In the strictest sense, **geographic information systems (GISs)** are DSSs capable of assembling, storing, manipulating, and displaying geographically referenced data and information. In other words, GISs identify data according to their locations. The applications of GISs in healthcare extend from practical community-based services to sophisticated studies on a global scale. For example, pediatricians consult community-based GISs to observe neighborhoods with high concentrations of lead and decide whether lead screenings would be appropriate for certain patients.

Technologies Supporting the Diagnosis, Treatment, and Care of Patients

Many current and emerging information technologies are used to support the diagnosis, treatment, and care of patients. For the purposes of this chapter, the following technologies are highlighted:

- Physiological signal processing systems
- Point-of-care information systems
- Mobile and wireless technology and devices
- Automated care plans, clinical practice guidelines, clinical pathways, and protocols
- Telemedicine/telehealth
- EHR systems
- Personal health records
-

Physiological Signal Processing Systems

The human body is a rich source of signals that carry vital information about underlying physiological processes. Traditionally, such signals have been used in clinical diagnosis as well as in the study of the functional behavior of internal organs.

Earlier in this chapter, **physiological signal processing systems**, such as ECG, EEG, and FHR tracing systems, were mentioned because these systems store data based on the body's signals and create output based on the lines plotted between the signals' points. The data type used by these systems is referred to as signal tracing or vector graphic data.

Physiological signal processing systems measure biological signals. Also, they help to integrate the medical science of analyzing the signals with such disciplines as biomedical engineering, computer graphics, mathematics, diagnostic image processing, computer vision, and pattern recognition. The integration of these disciplines allows these systems to electronically compile measurement equations, estimate the signals' parameters, and characterize the feedback elements. For example, the computer-based analysis of the neuromuscular system, the definition of cardiovascular system models, the control of cardiac pacemakers, the regulation of blood sugar levels, and the development of artificial organs not only serve patient diagnostic and care purposes but also support the development and simulation of instrumentation for physiological research and clinical investigation.

Point-of-Care Information Systems

Computer systems that allow healthcare providers to capture and retrieve data and information at the location where the healthcare service is performed have come a long way since hard-wired computer terminals with green screens were first placed at the patient's bedside more than 25 years ago. Functionally, almost every type of patient clinical and administrative application has been introduced to provide care services at the bedside, in the exam room, at the home, or even on the patient, as in medical monitoring. Technologically, massive changes have occurred in these systems' platforms, footprints, and networking capabilities.

For example, many acute care facilities have installed clinical **point-of-care information systems** that, among other services, provide online medication order entry, profiles, administration schedules, and records. The records include information about medications not given (with reasons) as well as related information such as fluid balances, physical assessments, laboratory test results, and vital signs. All medications, including unit doses, are bar coded and scanned at or near the patient's bedside along with the patient's wristband and the caregiver's identification badge. This prompts a safety edit, documents administration of the medication, and generates the charge. Other acute-care facilities have installed administrative point-of-care (or service) systems that have eliminated admitting areas. Inpatients are greeted at the door with their room assignments, and roving admissions representatives visit patients in the assigned rooms to complete all the admission procedures.

Typically, point-of-care information systems use portable, handheld, wireless devices to enable entry of the data by a bar code scanner, keypad, or touch screen. Also, the devices are used to upload and download information to and from hard-wired workstations. Retrieval of the data occurs at the wireless device or on wall-mounted or portable, cart-based computers. The data also can be entered and retrieved on hard-wired workstations located in areas outside the point of care, such as central areas at patient care units, back offices, central or satellite pharmacies, and physician lounges, homes, and offices.

Mobile and Wireless Technology and Devices

Perhaps the biggest influence on, as well as challenge for, point-of-care information systems and their use comes from recent, significant advances in **wireless technology** and smaller, mobile devices. For the healthcare industry, the successful integration of wireless technology and smaller, mobile devices with point-of-care software supports and enhances the clinician's decision-making processes.

True wireless systems use wireless networks and wireless devices to access and transmit data in real time. At the basic level, wireless technology is based on the use of radio waves. For the purposes of this chapter, the technology is divided into two categories: (1) regulated and unregulated, and (2) wide area and in-building.

For years, healthcare organizations have used in-building wireless point-of-care information systems, such as telemetry systems. These systems were based on existing technologies and use a portion of the radio spectrum reserved for industrial, scientific, and medical purposes (ISM band). Individual licenses are not required for these types of systems.

Also, provider organizations have long used wide-area wireless technology to support ISs, such as point-of-care systems. This technology involves microwave systems that are based on fixed, point-to-point wireless technology used to connect buildings in a campus network. Microwave systems are regulated and require licenses and compliance with Federal Trade Commission (FCC) procedures.

Until recently, most in-building wireless systems were proprietary. However, adoption of the Institute of Electrical and Electronic Engineers wireless technology standard (IEEE 802.11) has begun to provide a reasonable level of standardization. The IEEE 802.11 standard allows data transmission speeds of up to 11 megabits per second, is relatively low power, and does not require licenses for installation and use. The IEEE 802.11b is an international standard that provides a method for wireless connectivity to fixed and portable devices within a local area. As such, this standard allows **interoperability** among multiple vendor products.

But it is the widespread adoption of cellular telephone technology that has significantly advanced the development of wireless technology and, consequently, its support for point-of-care systems. A brief look at most healthcare organization today turns up mobile phones, two-way pagers, Internet-enabled telephones (also known as smart phones), tablets, and **personal digital assistants (PDAs).**

Mobile devices improve point-of-care systems by allowing clinicians to use a device personalized to their individual workflows, such as clinical (for example, e-prescribing), dictation, and billing workflows, not functions. In addition, mobile devices provide clinicians the information they need anytime, anywhere, and on any network-addressable device.

Automated Clinical Care Plans, Practice Guidelines, Pathways, and Protocols

The terms used to describe clinical practice mandates, care process guides or pathways, disease management protocols, and decision algorithms are not well standardized. They tend to be used informally and interchangeably, often resulting in miscommunication among healthcare professionals.

Consequently, when **clinical care plans,** practice guidelines, pathways, and protocols are automated and used by multidisciplinary teams, patient care can be adversely affected unless the definitions of these various terms are clearly understood by all. For example:

- Clinical care plans are created for individual patients by healthcare providers for a specific time period. Typically, clinical care plans are based on the healthcare provider's training.
- Clinical practice guidelines are recommendations based on systematic statements or clinical algorithms of proven care options. Often professional organizations and associations, health plans, and government agencies such as the Agency for Healthcare Research and Quality (AHRQ) develop these guidelines.
- Clinical (or critical) pathways (CareMaps) delineate standardized, day-to-day courses of care for a group of patients with the same diagnosis or procedure to achieve consistent outcomes. Typically, pathways (CareMaps) are developed by the local healthcare organization or health plan.
- Clinicians often use the term *protocol* to refer to the written documents that guide or specify a practice, including clinical practice guidelines and clinical pathways. Strictly speaking, however, protocols are more detailed care plans for individual patients based on investigations performed by professional societies, drug companies, or individual researchers (Bufton 1999, 258).

Providers now recognize the enormous variation there is in how they diagnose, treat, and care for patients. Consequently, there is a trend to use guidelines, formalized pathways, and protocols that have emerged from clinical research (evidence-based medicine) in order to reduce variation and improve care outcomes. Automating these guidelines, pathways, and protocols for easier access by healthcare providers is a first step. As automated clinical documentation systems are implemented, there is a trend to incorporate automated clinical pathways and care plans into providers' notes.

In short, clinical care plans, guidelines, pathways, and protocols, as well as drug formularies and other clinical knowledge bases, are becoming automated for easier access and use by healthcare providers, as well as for easier updating and maintenance. Many healthcare organizations purchase subscriptions from agencies, societies, or research companies to gain access to peer-reviewed libraries of clinical practice guidelines and clinical knowledge bases. They do so in order to efficiently download periodic updates of this content into their transaction-based or analytic systems.

The challenge for automated care plans, practice guidelines, pathways, and protocols is that, like clinical workstations and web portals, no one form of clinical documentation or one view of the information suits everyone or all situations. Therefore, automated plans, guidelines, pathways, and protocols require customization capabilities to help individuals and groups better share knowledge to reach similar decisions about patient care. Automated drawing tools and anatomical diagrams are other documentation options.

Telemedicine/Telehealth

Interactive, patient–provider consultations across gulfs of time and space represent what is often referred to as classic telemedicine or telehealth. However, the field has always encompassed a multitude of strategies for moving clinical knowledge and expertise instead of moving people. As such, telemedicine/telehealth systems, like EHR systems, are concepts made up of several cost-effective technologies used to bridge geographic gaps between patients and providers.

In other words, telemedicine/telehealth is not videoconferencing technology. Rather, it is clinically adequate, interactive media conferencing (for example, video conferencing) integrated with other technologies. It can be dynamic and include interactive (or real-time processing) technology, or it can be static and include store-and-forward (or batch processing) technology. It includes telecommunications and remote control–based biomedical technologies. It utilizes in-room systems, roll-abouts, desktop systems, and handheld units. Often it is integrated with component technologies of the EHR system and derived technologies of the Internet. The access and ability to transmit patient records and the integration with reference databases on the Internet all play into the telemedicine/telehealth model.

Telemedicine/telehealth is not a new way to deliver healthcare. It takes existing ways of delivering healthcare and enhances them, such as enhancing patient–provider consultations via "electronic house calls." It extends care to underserved populations, whether they are located in rural or urban areas, and redefines the healthcare organization's community. It transfers clinical information between places of lesser and greater medical capability and expertise.

Like medicine in general, telemedicine/telehealth technology is made up of a number of specialties and subspecialties. Some examples include telecardiology, teledermatology, telesurgery, telepsychiatry, teleradiology, and telepathology, among many others.

The telemedicine/telehealth specialty that has been around for the longest time and, perhaps, is the most notable is teleradiology. Even today, spurred by a rising demand for sophisticated imaging tests as well as a smaller pool of radiologists from which to recruit, teleradiology is taking advantage of the speedy Internet transfer of medical data to outsourced radiologists who provide preliminary interpretations of scans during their normal business hours. In addition, since the early 1990s, the University of Pittsburgh Medical Center, the Mayo Clinic, and other prestigious provider organizations have employed dynamic telepathology interactions. Teleradiology and telepathology specialties are considered first-generation telemedicine/telehealth systems and services because they do not rely on patient interaction.

The second-generation telemedicine/telehealth systems and services involve those specialties relying on patient interaction and consultations. These include teleophthalmology, telepsychiatry, telehome healthcare, and so on.

The latest generation of telemedicine/telehealth systems and services involves patient interaction beyond the consultation. For example, in October 2001, telesurgeons in New York City performed the world's first complete (that is, from start to finish) telesurgery by successfully operating on the gallbladder of a patient in France. This was accomplished by sending high-speed signals through fiber-optic cables across the Atlantic Ocean to robots in a Strasbourg clinic.

As both a clinical and technological endeavor, telemedicine/telehealth plays a key role in the integration of managing patient care and in the more efficient management of the information systems that support it. However, overcoming multiple technical challenges remains a concern. These challenges include the lack of systems interoperability and network integration as well as metropolitan broad bandwidth limitations. Other challenges that require overcoming complex behavioral, economic, and ethical constraints are physician resistance; lack of consistent, proven cost-effectiveness; lack of consistent, proven medical effectiveness; and concerns for safety.

Electronic Health Record Systems

An EHR system is not one or even two or more "products." Rather, it is a concept that consists of a host of integrated, component information systems and technologies. See chapter 5 for a full discussion of electronic health record systems—components, capabilities, selection considerations, and implementation strategies.

Personal Health Records

Personal health records (PHRs) electronically populate elements or subsets of protected health information (PHI) from provider organization databases into the electronic records of authorized patients, their families, other providers, and sometimes health payers and employers. A range of people and groups maintain the records, including the patients, their families, and other providers. The development of PHRs parallels the consumer-centrism described earlier and long evident in other vertical market industries, such as banking, where consumers maintain and examine their activities 24 hours a day in a secure electronic environment.

PHRs come in a variety of forms and formats, with no standard design or model yet to emerge. In recent years, American Health Information Management Association (AHIMA) has vigorously promoted the use of PHRs and has provided definitions and attributes for standardization. For example, AHIMA defines the PHR as "an electronic, lifelong resource of health information needed by individuals to make health decisions. Individuals own and manage the information in the PHR, which comes from healthcare providers and the individual. The PHR is maintained in a secure and private environment, with the individual determining rights of access. The PHR does not replace the legal record of any provider" (AHIMA 2005).

Currently, the most common PHR variations and models include:

- *Shared data record:* The shared data record model consumes the largest number of PHRs and is the most effective. Here, both provider (or employer or health plan) and patient maintain the record. In addition, the provider (or employer or health plan) supports the record. As such, the patient receives and adds information over time. The focus of this model is to keep track of health events, medications, or specific physiological indicators, such as exercise and nutrition.
- *EHR extensions:* The EHR extensions model extends the EHR into cyberspace so that an authorized patient can access the provider's record and check on the record's content. Often this model also allows an authorized patient to extract data from the healthcare provider's record. The record is still maintained by the provider but is available to the patient in an online format.
- *Provider-sponsored information management:* The provider-sponsored information management model represents provider-sponsored information management by creating communication vehicles between patient and provider. Such vehicles can include reminders for immunizations or flu shots, appointment scheduling or prescription refill capabilities, and monitoring tools for disease management in which regular collection of data from the patient is required.

Recently, the preceding models have been enhanced by the introduction of software platforms that propose to store a patient's PHR in a health "vault" or "bank." Under these models, data can be added and viewed electronically by the patient and any other individuals or healthcare providers to whom the patient allows permission.

Several issues are at stake. The first is whether a provider organization will be willing to work with a PHR. For example, increasing consumer demand for useful PHRs will make it mandatory that an EHR system be capable of sending and receiving data from a PHR. Another issue is whether a patient can trust the network that is transmitting his or her information. Currently, large-scale deployment and adoption of Internet-based PHRs remains slow because of ongoing privacy and security challenges, especially with PHR or PHR-related software vendors that are not considered Health Insurance Portability and Accountability Act (HIPAA) "covered entities." Such vendors cannot be held accountable to comply with HIPAA's existing patient privacy and information security regulations.

In 2002, the American Society for Testing and Materials (ASTM) Committee E31 (Healthcare Informatics), Subcommittee 26 established a standard for PHRs on the Internet. Content for the standard was based on the e-health tenets developed by AHIMA in 2000. In 2007, Health Level Seven (HL7) announced the approval of the Personal Health Record System Functional Model (PHR-S FM) as a Draft Standard for Trial Use. The PHR-S FM defines the functions that may be present in PHR systems and provides guidelines that facilitate health information exchange (HIE) among different PHR systems and between PHR and EHR systems.

Web 2.0 and Web 3.0

Web 2.0 is considered the second generation of Internet-based services that emphasizes online collaboration and sharing among users. Some of these applications and technologies include blogs, social networks, content communities, wikis, and podcasts. Web 2.0 tools are characterized by being highly collaborative and participative, using multiple data sources and multimedia, and connecting communities through conversation and an open environment that is virtually available at any time. Although the first generation of Internet services was passive in nature, the Web 2.0 users are actively engaged through the creation of their own content, participating in discussions and communities, and sharing their own videos, photos, and information.

In the healthcare industry, Web 2.0 technologies and tools commonly are referred to as **Health 2.0.** Many consumers and providers are using Health 2.0 tools to better manage their health and that of their patients. Blogs are used to share clinical education information, wikis are used as healthcare reference tools, podcasting is used to provide continuing education for healthcare providers, and social networking is used by patients to develop condition-related communities.

On the other hand, legal and ethical issues must be considered with the use of such technologies and tools. For example, the privacy of the patient and the confidentiality and transparency of the information must be addressed. Additionally, liability issues and the value of intellectual property come into play. Because the nature of Web 2.0/Health 2.0 is inherently open and collaborative, Web 2.0/Health 2.0 restrictions are few, and there is little control over data and information that is available for open distribution. Consequently, while the power of the Web 2.0/Health 2.0 technologies and tools is clear, also is the importance of harnessing its power for the greater good of the healthcare industry.

Technologists are beginning to discuss the concept of Web 2.0/Health 3.0. While the definitions vary widely, **Web 3.0** will likely focus on expanding the participatory and collaborative nature of social networks that defined Web 2.0 to include more real-time video and three-dimensional elements. Other commentators argue that Web 3.0 will adopt semantic web standards, thereby allowing computers to read and generate content similar to humans.

Check Your Understanding 4.4

Instructions: Answer the following questions on a separate piece of paper.

1. What features differentiate a data warehouse from a data repository?

2. Provide at least five distinct examples of diagnostic tests that involve physiological signal processing.

3. What patient data are typically collected and viewed (accessed) by care providers using point-of-care systems?

4. What is driving the increased use of computerized care protocols in healthcare?

5. Describe how second- and third-generation telehealth applications differ in functionality from first-generation applications such as teleradiology.

6. Describe the differences among the following three common models for the PHR: shared data record, EHR extensions, and provider-sponsored information management.

7. Describe the ways consumers use Web 2.0/Health 2.0 tools to manage their health and the subsequent issues that must be managed by healthcare providers.

Technologies Supporting the Security of Data and Information

Many current and emerging information technologies are used to support the security of healthcare data and information. They are the same technologies used to support the security of data and information in most vertical market industries. What sets the healthcare vertical market industry apart is the application of the technologies according to the second portion (Title II) of HIPAA, which mandates the protection of health information.

For the purposes of this chapter, the following technologies are highlighted:

- Encryption and cryptography
- Biometrics technology
- Firewall systems
- Audit trails

Encryption and Cryptography

Computer technology's greatest strengths also are its greatest weaknesses. For example, computer technology, especially the Internet and its derived technologies, easily allows anyone to send and receive information. However, it also easily allows anyone to intercept a transmission.

Cryptography is an applied science in which mathematics transforms intelligible data and information into unintelligible strings of characters and back again. **Encryption** technology uses cryptography to code digital data and information. This is so that the information can be transmitted over communications media and the sender of the information can be sure that only a recipient who has an authorized decoding "key" can make sense of the information.

There are two broad categories of encryption. The first category is symmetric or single-key encryption. Here, each computer uses software that assigns a secret key or code. One computer uses the key to code the message, and the other computer uses the same key to decode the message before the recipient can read it. This form of encryption requires both computers to have the same key.

The second category is asymmetric or **public key infrastructure (PKI)** encryption. PKI does not require that both computers have the same key to decode messages. A private key is known to one computer, which gives a public key to the other computer with which it wants to exchange encrypted data. The public key can be stored anywhere it is convenient, such as on a website or within an e-mail. The second computer decodes the encrypted message by using the public key and its own private key.

To prevent abuse, some type of authority is needed to serve as a trusted third party. A certification authority (CA) is an independent licensing agency that vouches for the individual's identity and relationship to the individual's public key. Acting as a type of electronic notary public, a CA verifies and stores a sender's public and private encryption keys and issues a digital certificate or "seal of authenticity" to the recipient.

These keys come in various strengths or levels of security. The strengths vary not only according to the algorithm that codes the data but also on how well the encoding and decoding keys are maintained. The more bits a key has, the harder it is to break the code without massive computer assistance.

For Internet sites, the use of private and public keys is handled behind the scenes by users' computer browsers and the web servers for the sites. For example, when a healthcare Internet user performs an online, interactive business transaction, a secure socket layer (SSL) PKI is used to exchange sensitive healthcare data and information.

PKI is becoming the de facto encryption technology for secure data transfers and online authentication. As such, its use will enable healthcare organizations to meet HIPAA's regulations concerning the security of data and electronic signatures.

Biometrics Technology

Biometrics technology verifies a person's identity by measuring (comparing different mathematical representations of)

biological and physical features or traits unique to the individual. For example, in signature verification technology, the biometrics of a handwritten signature are measured to confirm the identity of an individual. In data access technology, the biometrics of a hand (hand geometry), fingerprint (fingerprint matching), eye (iris or retinal scanning), voice (voice verification), or facial feature (facial image recognition) are measured to confirm the individual's identity.

Unique, positive identification or verification without the fear of replication or duplication for access to confidential health information is critical. As such, HIPAA requires a mechanism to ensure the authentication of the user and to restrict the user only to those systems that he or she is authorized to access. But because positive identification is so reliable as a personal identifier, individuals might feel that their privacy is threatened or compromised.

Fingerprint matching is the oldest and most popular type of biometrics technology. Everyone has unique, immutable fingerprints made of a series of ridges, furrows, and minute points or contours on the surface of the finger that form a pattern. Retinal scanning is quite accurate because it involves analyzing the layer of blood vessels at the back of the eye. But it is not as popular an identification technology because of the close contact users must make with a scanning device and thus is unfriendly for users wearing eyeglasses or contact lenses. Iris scanning is less intrusive than retinal scanning but is considered clumsy to use.

Facial image recognition requires an unobtrusive, digital camera to develop a dynamic, facial image of the user. Unfortunately, matching dynamic images is not as easy as matching static images, such as two or more fingerprints or iris scans. Therefore, positive identification based on multiple biometrics technologies currently has the most promising potential for authentication purposes.

Firewall Systems

Firewalls are hardware and software security devices situated between the routers of a private and public network. They are designed to protect computer networks from unauthorized outsiders. However, they also can be used to protect entities within a single network, for example, to block laboratory technicians from getting into payroll records. Without firewalls, IT departments would have to deploy multiple-enterprise security programs that would soon become difficult to manage and maintain.

Firewalls originated during the 1980s and were used to screen a network's incoming data from unwanted, outside addresses. At that time, networks were not large and complicated. Consequently, firewalls were not foolproof and were easy to circumvent.

By contrast, today's massive and complex networks demand firewall systems fortified with software applications that, for example, authenticate users, encrypt messages, scan for viruses and spyware, and produce audit trails.

Technically, most firewalls are made up of proxy and filtering services. Proxy services are special-purpose programs allowing network administrators to permit or deny specific applications or features of applications. They screen user names and all information that attempts to enter or leave the private network. Filtering allows the routers to permit or deny decisions for each piece of information that attempts to enter or leave the private network.

Firewalls are based on pre-established rules that allow or deny access to the network or exchange of information between the networks. As such, firewalls enforce security policies so that everything not explicitly permitted is denied. For example, firewall systems determine which inside services may be accessed from the outside, which outsiders are permitted access to the permitted inside services, and which outside services may be accessed by insiders. For a firewall to be effective, all traffic to and from the networks must pass through the firewall, where it can be inspected.

The firewall itself must be immune to penetration. Unfortunately, a firewall cannot offer protection after an attacker has gotten through or around it.

Audit Trails

Audit trails are chronological sets of records that provide evidence of computer system utilization. Data are collected about every system event, such as log-ins, log-outs, file accesses, and data extractions. As such, audit trails are used to facilitate the determination of security violations and to identify areas for improvement. Their usefulness is enhanced when they include trigger flags for automatic, intensified review.

Today, audit trails serve as strong impediments to computer data abuse. For example, the presence of these tools promotes awareness that people who access confidential information can be tracked and held accountable.

Care must be taken to determine which audited data elements are required by law or which ones are exceptions. Following are some suggested data elements to track activity in healthcare information system audit trails:

- Date and time of event
- Patient identification
- User identification
- Access device used
- Type of action (view or read, print, update or add)
- Identification of patient data access by a category of content
- Source of access and software application used
- Reason for access by category (patient care, research, billing)

Practical issues concerning the use of audit trails involve trust. For example, healthcare organizations must be able to distinguish between users who access patient records for patient care and those who access them for unauthorized purposes. Frequent sampling by organizational managers or "tiger teams" is one way to determine system usage within an environment of trust. Delegating to users the responsibility to examine their own audit histories is another way to determine this. It is recommended that the results of audit trails be published and included in employee performance reviews.

Instructions: Answer the following questions on a separate piece of paper.

1. What is public key infrastructure, and why is it receiving so much attention within the healthcare industry?

2. What are the benefits and drawbacks of using each of the following human features for authentication purposes: fingerprints, iris images, and facial images?

3. Firewalls protect network access by employing proxy and filtering services. What are proxy services and filtering services?

4. What are two practical ways to instill user trust in healthcare organizations when deploying IS audit trails?

Today's Environment and Growing Demand for Healthcare Information Systems

Every year the Healthcare Information and Management Systems Society (HIMSS) conducts a leadership survey that provides insight on the priorities, barriers, and future of healthcare IT from a variety of perspectives, including those of chief information officers (CIOs), chief executive officers (CEOs), and physician and nursing executives. When one compares the survey results from year to year, it is apparent that priorities change. The 2011 survey identified the achievement of Stage 1 of meaningful use as the top business objective; this was not even a choice in the 2010 survey. Issues such as healthcare reform (which includes new care models and payment structures) and policy mandates (complying with regulations such as ARRA and ICD-10) caused the top business objective in the 2010 survey of improving patient care to drop to second place (HIMSS 2011).

Healthcare organizations are faced with many potential information systems projects across several categories:

- Clinical systems including a fully functional EHR, CPOE, clinical decision support, and physician documentation
- Financial and administrative systems including new coding systems and new reimbursement models such as value-based purchasing and accountable care organizations

- Leveraging information to support business intelligence and evidence-based medicine
- Patient-centric applications such as patient portals and personal health records
- Interoperability including health information exchange and the Direct Project
- Infrastructure including security and mobile devices

Not surprisingly, healthcare organizations have far more IS priorities than they have resources to allocate to them. How should decisions be made regarding which IS initiatives to support? How can healthcare administrators be reasonably assured that the information systems selected will meet their organization's current and future needs and be accepted by end users? What process will the organization use to select and implement a new system? After the decision is made to implement an IS, what resources are needed to adequately maintain and support it?

These types of questions require that healthcare managers and leaders assume an active role in ensuring that their organizations are well equipped and prepared for change. Healthcare managers need to ask themselves the following questions:

- What are the strategic goals of the organization? What type(s) of information systems are needed to enable the organization to achieve its goals? To what degree are the IS goals aligned with the organization's overall strategic goals?
- How should decisions be made regarding which IS initiatives to support? What criteria or methods will be used? How will the organization make capital budget decisions?
- How can the organization be reasonably assured that the IS selected will meet its current and future needs and be accepted by end users?
- After the decision is made to implement an IS, what resources are needed to adequately maintain and support it?

Strategic Information Systems Planning

No board of directors would ever recommend building a new healthcare facility without an architect's blueprint and a comprehensive assessment of community or market needs and resources. The architect's blueprint helps ensure that the new facility has a strong foundation, a well-planned organizational basis, and the potential for growth and expansion. The assessment helps ensure that there is a need for the new facility and that adequate resources are available to support it.

Similarly, it is critical that the organization's IS plans be well aligned and integrated with its overall organizational strategic plans. To develop a blueprint for IS technology, the healthcare organization should engage in strategic IS planning. **Strategic IS planning** is the process of identifying and prioritizing IS needs based on the healthcare organization's mission and strategic goals.

A recent survey of healthcare information technology (HIT) professionals found that 87 percent reported that a strong level of integration exists between IS strategies and overall organizational strategy. Specifically, 51 percent of respondents indicated that their IS strategic plan is a component of the organization's strategic plan, while 36 percent indicated their IT strategic plan is integrated with the overall strategic plan, although the plans are separate (HIMSS 2011). Different approaches or methods for developing a strategic IS planning process can be used. The following sections present a generic approach. Factors such as the type, size, and complexity of the organization as well as the decision-making philosophy of its leadership team are certainly important components in determining how to establish IS priorities.

Strategic HIT Planning Process

As the senior leadership team engages in strategic planning discussions, they should ensure that IS leadership is also engaged in these discussions. In particular, they should examine the organization's view of the role that IS technology will play in the organization's future. To what extent, if any, will HIT enable the organization to achieve its strategic goals?

Today, it is vital that the leadership team adopt a system-wide perspective on information management and view each major IS acquisition within the context of the larger picture, that is, how the system supports the organization's overall mission and strategic goals. A direct alignment should exist between the strategic goals of the organization and major IS initiatives. The goal is to build systems that support the goals of the organization, not disparate applications that do not "talk to each other."

To help ensure that information systems support the organization's strategic plan and are not acquired in isolation, healthcare leaders examine both the external and internal environment and business plans before establishing IS priorities or making IS investments.

Generic Approach

The following steps represent a generic approach to developing a strategic IS plan (see figure 4.3). This approach can be modified or adapted to meet the healthcare organization's individual needs. The steps include the following:

1. Review the organization's strategic plan and assess the organization's current external and internal environment.
2. Identify the organization's mission, strategic goals, and objectives and assess its IS needs.
3. Establish IS priorities.
4. Gain approval from the organization's leaders (executive management and board of directors) of the prioritized plan for completing IS projects.

Figure 4.3.   Strategic information systems planning process

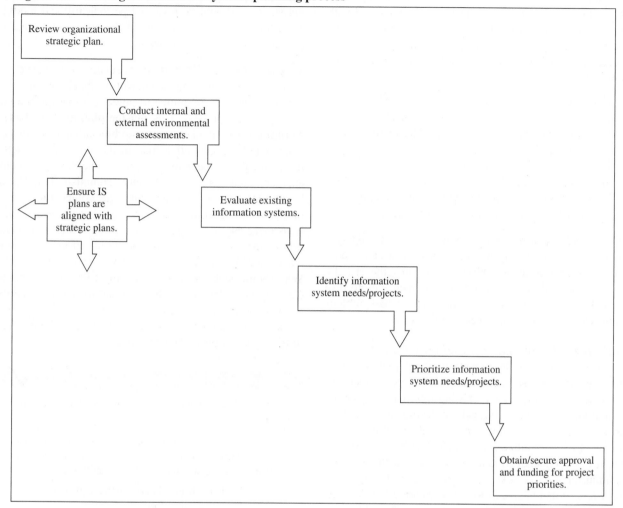

Reviewing the Strategic Plan and Assessing the External and Internal Environment

To begin the planning process, the IS steering committee should review the organization's current strategic plans, goals, and objectives and evaluate its current external environment. The overall strategic plan should include an environmental assessment that analyzes the external forces that may affect the organization. External forces include changes in reimbursement methodologies, new government regulations, and changes in the demographics or healthcare needs of the community.

An environmental assessment should also be performed to explore emerging technologies and their potential impact on the ways the healthcare organization delivers its services. In conducting this assessment, a subgroup of the committee may want to review the literature, visit trade shows, network with colleagues in the field, or meet with leading vendors in the marketplace. A number of consultant groups also can provide vendor or product information to the organization.

In addition to the external environmental assessment, it is equally important that the IS steering committee conduct an internal environmental assessment of the organization's current IS environment. The committee should consider questions such as the following:

- Which information systems are currently used within the organization?
- To what extent do these systems meet the needs of end users?
- Which systems are likely to need replacement or upgrades? Which ones are likely to become obsolete within the next few years?
- To what extent is the organization able to support and maintain its current systems? Does it have the people, equipment, and network infrastructure needed to support its current systems?
- To what degree are the current systems cost-effective and efficient?
- How well do the existing information systems support the organization's strategic goals?

As part of the analysis of the current internal environment, the committee may also compare the organization's IT functionality and performance against external benchmarks.

For example, the committee might compare the organization's ratio of end users to technical support personnel with industry averages. It also might compare the organization's performance in key areas with the performance of other, similar organizations. The committee might want to consider the following questions:

- How secure are patient information systems?
- How much downtime does the facility experience?
- How much IT staff time is spent troubleshooting system problems?
- In what ways, if any, have the major systems adversely affected patient care?
- To what degree are existing systems in compliance with HIPAA privacy and security regulations?

It is essential that the organization evaluate existing systems to accurately identify its needs, problems, and opportunities for improvement. Otherwise, it runs the risk of installing a new IS to fix a perceived problem only to discover that the new system never addressed the actual problem and, instead, created a host of new problems.

Identifying IS Needs and Prioritizing IS Projects

After the committee has developed a thorough understanding of the organization's strategic goals, environment, emerging information technologies, and existing information systems, it should identify IS needs throughout the organization. This internal needs assessment can be formal or informal. For example, if the committee wants to conduct a formal assessment, it might conduct structured interviews with key users or administer surveys in key areas throughout the organization. A less formal approach would be to ask all IS steering committee members to list the information needs within their respective areas. The outcome of this assessment is a fairly comprehensive list of the organization's information management needs. Eventually, the list can be used to identify projects and establish IT priorities.

The next step in the planning process is to establish priorities. Again, the committee might take different approaches to accomplish this important task. One approach is to identify all proposed IS projects and hold an intensive retreat where all interested stakeholders (IS steering committee members and other interested clinicians and staff) score and rank each project. Sufficient information concerning each project should be given to the stakeholders ahead of time to help them make informed choices. (See chapter 5 for a discussion specific to EHR planning considerations and migration strategies.)

Gaining Approval for the Plan

When using either the generic approach or another approach to setting priorities, the strategic IS planning process should result in a list of identified project priorities. These priorities should then be developed further and forwarded to the senior administration and the board of directors for approval

and funding. It is important to note that the priority list is not static. It should be reviewed periodically and modified accordingly based on changes in the environment and the growing needs of the organization.

Role of a Master Planning or Steering Committee

Generally the leadership team will establish an interdisciplinary oversight committee to guide and manage the strategic planning process. This **master planning or steering committee** would likely have representation from the key clinical and administrative areas of the organization such as the medical staff, nursing, pharmacy, radiology, and other ancillary areas as well as finance, administration, IT, and health information management. The composition of the master planning committee may vary, but its primary goal is to make high-level decisions regarding the implementation of the strategic plan and ensure all efforts are coordinated and communicated at all levels within the facility. Who should lead the master planning committee? That too can vary considerably—it is important to select a chairperson who possesses strong leadership skills, is well respected within the organization, and maintains a "big picture" view of the organization's strategic plans.

Check Your Understanding 4.6

Instructions: Answer the following questions on a separate piece of paper.

1. Why is strategic planning for information systems important to organizations in today's healthcare environment? What risks are associated with not having an IS plan?

2. Who should be involved in the strategic planning process? Who should lead the effort?

3. Why is it important for the IS plan to be integrated with the healthcare organization's overall strategic plan?

4. Why is it important for healthcare organizations to examine their existing information systems? What aspects of the existing system(s) should be examined during the planning process?

5. How might a healthcare organization approach prioritizing its IS projects or needs?

Information Systems Development

After establishing IS priorities as part of the strategic plan, the healthcare organization should follow a structured project management process for selecting and implementing new systems. The structured approach enables the organization to identify viable alternatives, gain user buy-in, select a system that meets the needs of the users, and implement the system in a well-organized, systematic way.

Because several new system projects may be going on simultaneously and people may be involved in more than one project, it is important that the projects be organized and managed consistently. Ideally, the IT staff or the project leader should maintain a project repository for every IS initiative. Included in the project repository would be all minutes, notes, survey results, and other relevant information used in managing the project. (See chapter 27 for a full discussion of project management principles, processes, and tools.)

Systems Development Life Cycle

One process for IS development is the SDLC. Although there are many different models of the SDLC, all generally include a variation of the following four phases: analysis, design, implementation, and maintenance and evaluation. As the activities that occur in each phase are discussed, it should become apparent that the process does not end when the new IS is implemented. Rather, the SDLC is an ongoing process that requires continuing assessment and planning. Figure 4.4 illustrates the cyclical nature of the SDLC.

Like the strategic IS planning process, the SDLC involves the participation of numerous people with diverse backgrounds and areas of expertise. Depending on the nature and scope of the project, representatives from the key clinical and administrative areas should be involved. For example, if the organization plans to replace its pharmacy IS, the process might include individuals from the medical staff, nursing, and other ancillary areas that depend on or use pharmacy information, in addition to key people from the pharmacy department. Representatives from IT and HIM services also should be involved.

Analysis Phase

After senior administration or the board gives the go-ahead for the project, the **analysis phase** begins. During the analysis phase, the need for a new IS is explored further, problems with the existing system are solidified, and user needs are identified. The primary focus in this beginning phase of the SDLC is on the business problem, independent of any technology that can or will be used to implement a solution to that problem.

In this phase, it is important to examine the current system and to identify opportunities for improvement or enhancement. Even though an initial assessment was completed as part of the strategic information planning process, the analysis phase of the SDLC involves a more extensive evaluation. Typically, the existing system is evaluated by asking routine users to identify its strengths and limitations. Completion of this task can help ensure that the organization does not make a significant investment in a new system only to later discover that what was needed was better communication, additional training, and more extensive technical support, and not a new information system.

When it is clear that a new IS is needed, the next step is to assess the information needs of users and to define functional requirements. It is best to have a structured method for accomplishing this task. For example, the project team might administer a questionnaire, conduct focus groups, or hold joint-requirements planning sessions. A joint-requirements planning session is a highly structured group meeting that is conducted to analyze problems and define functional requirements. Whatever method or combination of methods is used to solicit user input, the process should result in a detailed list of user specifications.

Design Phase

After the users' needs have been identified, the process generally moves into the **design phase.** During this phase, consideration is given to how the new system will be designed or selected. Questions to ask include the following:

- Will the new system be built in-house?
- Will the organization hire an outside developer to build the system?
- Will the facility purchase an IS from a vendor, lease it from a vendor, or use cloud computing? **Cloud computing** is defined as "a model for enabling convenient, on-demand network access to a shared pool of configurable computing resources (that is, networks, servers, storage, applications, and services) that can be rapidly provisioned and released with minimal management effort or service provider interaction" (NIST 2009).

Due to time, cost, and personnel restraints, most healthcare organizations first look at what IS products are available in the vendor community. For this reason, this discussion focuses on selecting an IS from a vendor rather than building one in-house. In the rare situation that a facility decides to build a system in-house, it is generally because the facility's needs are unique and it has the technical expertise to design and support the system.

A facility that wishes to explore the systems available in the vendor community might begin by obtaining information from exhibits at professional conferences, directories or publications, the Internet, vendor user groups, consulting firms, and contacts with colleagues in the health information

Figure 4.4.   Systems development life cycle

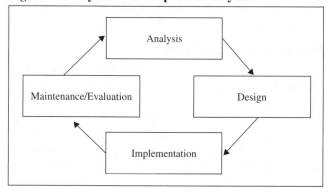

systems (HIS) industry. A **request for information (RFI)** is generally sent to a fairly extensive list of vendors that are known to offer products or systems that meet the organization's needs. The RFI is used to obtain general product information and to prescreen vendors. Responses to the RFI are used to narrow the list to a smaller number of vendors who will be invited to respond to the **request for proposal (RFP).**

The RFP generally includes much more detail on the system's requirements and provides guidelines for vendors to follow in bidding. According to Wager et al. (2009), for a major system acquisition, the RFP generally includes

- Instructions for vendors, including the proposal deadline and contract information, specific instructions for completing the RFP, and any stipulations with which the vendor must comply
- Organizational objectives, including the type of system or application being sought and how it will fit into the organization's strategic plans and goals
- Background of the organization, including a description of the facility (size, type of patient services, patient volume, and so forth) and an inventory of applications and the network infrastructure
- System goals and requirements, including a description of the system characteristics and the features that are desired or required
- Vendor qualifications, including background information, experience, number of installations, annual financial reports, and standard contract
- Proposed solution, including a description of how the vendor believes its product meets the organization's goals and needs
- Criteria to be used in evaluating the RFP
- General contractual requirements, including warranty information, payment, schedule, and penalties for failure to meet schedules specified in the contract
- Pricing and support

Moreover, it is a good idea to ask about the number of planned installations during the same time period and how staffing and other support issues will be managed if multiple implementations are under way at the same time.

Concurrent with development of the RFP, the project team should establish the criteria with which to evaluate the vendors' responses to the RFP. For example, the team may want to evaluate the extent to which each vendor's product meets the functional requirements of the new system, the vendor's track record of performance, and the extent to which the vendor's philosophy of systems development is congruent with the organization's IT strategy. In addition, the team may want to evaluate system reliability, costs, and projected benefits.

Evaluation of the vendor and its products should not depend solely on its response to the RFP. Other formal and informal mechanisms should be used to evaluate each vendor and its products. For example, the project team may hold vendor presentations, check references, attend user group meetings, and make site visits to other facilities that use the product. The purpose of these activities is to gather as much relevant information as possible to make an informed decision. Interested clinicians, administrators, and other end users, as well as members of the project team, should have the opportunity to participate in as many of these activities as possible.

As part of the system selection process, the project team should conduct a cost-benefit analysis for each viable alternative. Costs should include acquisition costs (for example, hardware, software, network, and training) in addition to operating or maintenance costs (for example, system upgrades, technical support, supplies, and equipment). Most costs can be identified and measured reasonably accurately. However, the benefits to implementing an IS can be much more difficult to identify. Some benefits, such as increased productivity or improved access to information, are tangible and can be measured (albeit not easily); others are intangible and very difficult to quantify. For example, a new EHR system might lead to improved employee morale or increased patient satisfaction, but these potential benefits might be more difficult to isolate and quantify. Consequently, when comparing different vendor systems or alternatives, it is important to evaluate and measure costs and benefits to the fullest extent possible. A variety of standard cost-benefit analysis methods may be used to evaluate different IT options that are beyond the scope of this book. The Health IT Body of Knowledge, available through the HIMSS website, provides many references for systems analysis, design, selection, implementation, and evaluation.

When the top two or three vendors have been identified, leadership within the healthcare organization generally initiates the contract negotiation process. It is generally a good idea to begin contract negotiations with more than one vendor. This provides leverage during the negotiation process and affords the organization an alternative should it and the vendor not agree on the terms of the contract. A host of very detailed and technical issues are generally addressed in the contract: everything from when the system is to be delivered and installed to training and support to warranties and guarantees to who is responsible for ensuring that the product interfaces with other institutional systems. Internal legal counsel generally reviews the contract carefully before it is signed and commitments are made.

Implementation Phase

After contract negotiations have been finalized, the **implementation phase** begins. In this phase, a comprehensive plan for implementing the new system is developed. An interdisciplinary implementation team is generally established and led by a project manager. The implementation team will likely include some of the same individuals involved in selecting the new system, but other key people should be involved in the process as well.

Ideally, the project manager should be someone who is well respected and knowledgeable, has experience with implementing new systems, and has the political influence and power to make things happen. He or she also should have strong organizational and communication skills and be able to work effectively with everyone involved in the implementation including the vendor, clinicians, and senior management. The importance of selecting the right person to lead the effort cannot be overemphasized. Even though a good implementation does not guarantee user acceptance of the new system, a poor implementation can lead to frustration, dissatisfaction, and disillusionment. Some organizations never recover fully from a disastrous system implementation.

One of the implementation team's priorities is to identify all the tasks that must be completed before the go-live date. Depending on the type of system, the number of users, and the complexity of the conversion process, the tasks may vary in scope and complexity. However, many system implementation projects require at least the following tasks:

- Preparing the site (for example, workflow patterns, noise, space, telephone lines, and electrical power)
- Installing the necessary hardware and software
- Preparing data tables
- Building interfaces
- Establishing an IT infrastructure (for example, stable network, secure database) to support the system
- Ensuring that adequate security and confidentiality practices are in place
- Training managers, technical staff, and other end users
- Testing the new system
- Identifying and correcting errors
- Preparing documentation to support system use (for example, procedure manuals)
- Implementing conversion plans
- Developing and testing backup and disaster recovery procedures

Although each of these major tasks is very important, a few should be highlighted to stress their relevance to the implementation phase. First, it is critical to thoroughly test any new system before the go-live date. This means testing, testing, and retesting the new system with real patient data, not sample data the vendor may have provided or your institution may have created. Even though it is nearly impossible to identify and correct all the errors before a system goes live, it is essential to identify and correct as many of them as possible. It is often much easier to correct a problem in the test mode than after the system is fully operational.

Second, adequate training is essential. A healthcare organization may be implementing a solid, highly reputable new system, but if the staff who will be using it are not thoroughly trained, the system's implementation can result in dissatisfaction and low morale. For any new system to be successful, it must be accepted and used by the staff. Different organizations and vendors might use different approaches to training, but one common approach is to train the trainer. This approach involves identifying key people in the various functional areas (for example, nursing units, laboratory, and billing), training them on the system, and then having them train others in their area (with guidance from the vendor or a "super user").

The train-the-trainer method can be effective because after the vendor is gone, staff must be available who are comfortable with the system and can assist others. It is equally important to allow adequate time for training. Staff should not have to squeeze in training on their lunch break, with little or no time to practice using the new system. Just as it is important to use real data in testing the system, it is critical to give staff practice using the new system with real patients or real data.

In addition to providing training, the organization must have the IT infrastructure and processes in place to support the system. The infrastructure should include a stable network, a sufficient number of workstations appropriately located throughout the organization, adequate security measures, up-to-date procedural manuals, and a process for reporting problems with the system.

Finally, it is important to develop plans for converting the old system to the new one.

Conversion to a new system often requires major changes in the workflow and organizational structure and places increased demands on staff during this period. Therefore, it is essential to plan appropriately for the conversion and to ensure that adequate technical and support staff members are available to assist managers and end users, as needed.

Throughout the implementation process, many tasks or activities may occur simultaneously; others will need to be completed before other activities can begin. Because of the number of different tasks occurring, it is generally a good idea for the project manager to use a Gantt chart or project management tool that identifies the major tasks, their estimated start and completion dates, the individuals responsible for performing them, and the resources needed to complete them. Again, activities or tasks that depend on the completion of other tasks should be readily identified. Project management software such as Microsoft Project can create Gantt charts that enable managers to track project resources (for example, staff, equipment, and expenditures). Figure 4.5 is an example of a Gantt chart for an IS implementation project.

Maintenance and Evaluation Phase

The final phase of the SDLC is the **maintenance and evaluation phase.** Regardless of how well designed and tested a new system may be, errors or bugs inevitably occur after it goes into operation. IT support staff must be available to find potential problems and take steps to correct them. Whether the technical staff are in-house or employed through a contract service, well-trained staff must be available to maintain or support the new system. For critical systems such as patient care or clinical information systems, technical

Figure 4.5.   Sample Gantt chart of an IS implementation project

Source: Medical University of South Carolina

support should be available 24 hours a day, seven days a week. Sufficient technical staff also should be available to oversee system backups and upgrades, replace outdated equipment, respond to new regulatory requirements, and provide ongoing training and assistance. Nearly 25 percent of the total technical staff time may be devoted to maintenance activities when several information systems are in place.

As the organization hires new people, its technical or support staff must be available to train them on the system. Likewise, all staff will need additional training on a regular basis to ensure that they are current with system upgrades, enhancements, and new features or procedures. Ideally, the organization should have a plan in place outlining how staff will receive initial and ongoing training on any new or existing IS. Many healthcare organizations now appoint an individual within key clinical and administrative departments whose primary role is to ensure that the department staff has adequate training and technical support available to them. For example, the radiology department might have a radiological technician with strong computer skills who serves as the information technician and assists and trains other staff in the department. Such an approach can be effective in increasing response time to user requests and alleviating user frustration.

In addition to providing adequate training and support, the healthcare organization should monitor data quality and integrity and ensure that the system is secure and safe. Specifically, emergency backup procedures should be in place in the event the system fails or goes down for any reason. All staff should know what to do in such circumstances. The backup procedures should be well documented and readily available to staff. If forms are utilized during downtimes, clear instructions on what to do with them should be available when the system is restored.

However, maintaining and supporting the new systems is not enough. Information systems should be evaluated on an ongoing basis to determine if they are contributing to the institution's overall goals and meeting user needs. Healthcare administrators today are demanding to know whether the return on investment (ROI) to the organization has been realized since system implementation. Being able to measure ROI is becoming increasingly important as healthcare institutions struggle to manage limited resources more effectively. Consequently, as a part of the system evaluation process, institutions are looking at the organizational, technological, and economic impact of information systems on the enterprise as a whole. AHRQ recently updated Health Information Technology toolkit can serve as a useful resource in guiding the organization through the evaluation process (Cusack et al. 2009).

Check Your Understanding 4.7

Instructions: Answer the following questions on a separate piece of paper.

1. What is the relationship between strategic information systems planning and the systems development life cycle?

2. Identify the four main phases of the SDLC, and describe the purpose or intent of each.

3. What is the difference between an RFI and an RFP?

Management of Healthcare Information System Resources

Managing information resources is a vital function of any healthcare organization. Within hospitals or health systems, an in-house information services or information systems department often coordinates this function, although a growing number of healthcare organizations outsource IT functions to outside companies. Outsourcing IT might be particularly attractive to small rural hospitals or small physician practices that may not have the in-house technical expertise to implement and support information systems.

Most larger healthcare organizations have an IS department that provides a wide range of technical support functions to users throughout the organization. These functions include systems development and implementation, systems support and maintenance, user support, database administration, communications and network administration, and web support. Figure 4.6 shows a typical organizational structure for an IS department, and the following sections describe some of the key positions within that structure.

IS Management Team Chief Information Officer

Generally, the IS department is managed by the **chief information officer (CIO)** or director of IS, who in turn reports to the CEO or some other senior-level individual. The CIO is responsible for helping to lead the strategic IS planning process, managing the major functional units within the IS department, and overseeing the management of information resources throughout the enterprise.

Chief Medical Informatics Officer

The **chief medical informatics officer (CMIO)** is typically a physician with **medical informatics** training. Generally, the role of the CMIO is to provide physician leadership and direction in the deployment of clinical applications in healthcare organizations.

Chief Information Technology Officer

The role of the **chief information technology officer (CITO)** is to guide the organization's decisions related to technical architecture. For example, the CITO might be involved in determining which operating systems or network technologies the organization will support. This individual also typically keeps current on the latest technology developments and their applicability or potential use in the organization.

Chief Information Security Officer

The need for a **chief information security officer (CISO)** has grown as a direct result of the organization's need to be compliant with HIPAA security regulations. The CISO is responsible for the identification, development, implementation, and maintenance of security programs and processes.

IS Technical Staff

In years past, most of the staff working in the IS department typically had backgrounds in programming and computer science. Today, the department is likely to include individuals with unique sets of skills and specialized areas of interest. These positions include

Figure 4.6.   Typical organizational structure for an IS department

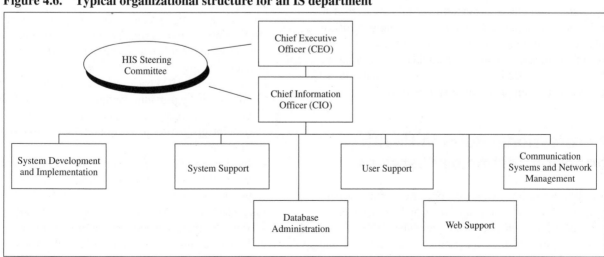

- **Systems analysts:** Systems analysts investigate, analyze, design, develop, install, evaluate, and maintain the healthcare organization's information systems. These individuals typically are involved in all aspects of the SDLC and serve as a liaison among end users and programmers, **database administrators,** and other technical personnel. Systems analysts with a clinical background in nursing, medicine, or other health professions, including HIM, are often called **clinical systems analysts** or **application systems analysts.** They understand the language of clinicians and generally have an in-depth understanding of the patient care process.
- **Programmers:** Programmers are responsible primarily for writing program codes and developing applications. In general, they perform the function of systems development and work closely with system analysts.
- **Software engineers:** Software engineers are in positions that combine aspects of systems analysis and programming. They analyze users' needs and design, test, and develop software to meet those needs.
- **Network administrators:** Network administrators are involved in installing, configuring, managing, monitoring, and maintaining network applications. They are responsible for supporting the network infrastructure and controlling user access.
- Database administrators: Database administrators are involved in database design, management, security, backup, and user access. They are responsible for the technical aspects of managing a database.
- **Webmasters/web developers:** Webmasters and web developers provide support to web applications and to the healthcare organization's intranet and Internet operations. Some of their responsibilities include designing and constructing web pages, managing hardware and software, and linking web-based applications to the organization's existing information systems.

All IS staff must have an opportunity to stay up to date in the IS field by attending conferences, gaining certification in specialized areas, and enrolling in formal academic or continuing education courses. IT applications serving the healthcare industry are emerging at a phenomenal rate, so the professional development of IS staff is critical.

HIM Professional Roles in Health Information Technology Services

Because healthcare informatics is concerned with the management of all aspects of health data and information in computer-based systems, it clearly includes HIM as one of its components. And, as more and more healthcare and healthcare-related data and information are being collected, stored, and transmitted using computer technologies, the HIM discipline is increasingly being integrated into the domain of healthcare informatics.

HIM professionals must be intimate partners with HIT professionals, who, together, form strong alliances with each type of authorized user (physicians, nurses, clinicians, dentists, consumers, and administrators) to develop and implement the required hardware and software and the required data and information infrastructure (content and format) to support their unique needs as well as the overall needs of the healthcare organization. In this context HIM professionals will continue to assume a leadership role in the development, implementation, and use of improved healthcare information systems, integrated patient information systems, accurate decision support tools, or any of the current and emerging information technologies highlighted in this chapter.

Health information managers can make unique contributions to information systems development through their knowledge of

- Existing and emerging requirements related to privacy and confidentiality of health information
- Applicable federal and state EHR-related laws, accreditation standards, and data and vocabulary standards
- Critical activities related to the integrity of the master patient index file
- Clinical data requirements of both internal and external data users
- Interdepartmental and interdisciplinary clinical data and the information workflow

Through HIM leadership there can be successful collaboration and effective promotion of healthcare informatics. HIM professionals can

- Serve as the subject matter expert on managing patient information and clinical documentation, specifically on legal health record and accreditation standards.
- Provide leadership and guidance to process redesign efforts aimed at transforming clinical documentation practices and records management methods from paper to electronic.
  — Translate the HIM basics to electronic practice for colleagues by providing authoritative sources for developing organization standards for forms design, data integrity criteria, and sound documentation practices.
  — Further continuity of care between settings through the facilitation of information transfer between providers.
- Take a leadership role in establishing local health information exchange networks or other committees such as a steering committee regarding electronic health information.

— Promote EHR migration efforts, privacy and security metrics, and other best practices within the organization's leadership structure. Ensure a strong HIM leader is represented on committees such as a computerized order entry steering committee, medication administration committee, and IT steering committee.

— Actively participate on product selection committees and implementation teams for all systems with clinical documentation components. Create HIM acceptance criteria for incorporation into requests for proposals, such as functional requirement for classification of notes when purchasing new information systems.

- Take ownership of the health information management systems within the organization.
- Educate the organization on all the components of the legal health record, including the location, storage media, and locus of responsibility for each legal health record component.
- Educate decision makers about the importance of aligning clinical system projects with organization standards for compliant and effective electronic health records.

— Develop communication strategies to share HIM expertise of EHRs. Publish a monthly newsletter in collaboration with IT (AHIMA 2008).

Summary

In today's environment, healthcare organizations look to IS technology as a way to help them provide high-quality care in a cost-effective manner. However, healthcare managers at all levels often find that they are competing with their colleagues for limited IS resources. Senior administrators are encouraging healthcare managers to work together to build integrated ISs that will support patient care and enable them to control costs across the enterprise. Clearly, in today's environment, information systems should not be developed or selected in isolation. Healthcare organizations should engage in strategic IS planning to ensure that systems are available to support their goals and plans and to prioritize IS needs. The IS plans should be well aligned and integrated with the organization's overall strategic plans. This process should involve key stakeholders throughout the organization, including clinicians and administrators and HIM and information technology leaders.

After the decision has been made to develop or select a new information system, a project manager should be appointed to oversee and manage the SDLC process. Again, key stakeholders throughout the organization should be involved in the analysis, design, implementation, and maintenance and support phases of the SDLC. Adequate technical and organizational resources should be in place to ensure that the new systems are sufficiently maintained and supported. Moreover, systems should be reviewed and evaluated on a continuing basis to determine their technological, organizational, and economic impact on the enterprise.

References

AHIMA e-HIM Personal Health Record Work Group. 2005. Practice brief: Defining the personal health record. *Journal of AHIMA* 76(6): 24–25.

American Health Information Management Association. 2011. CAC 2010-2011 industry outlook and resources report. http://library.ahima.org/xpedio/groups/public/documents/ahima/bok1_048947.pdf.

American Health Information Management Association. 2008. Practice brief: Critical success factors for fostering convergence. *Journal of AHIMA* 79(11).

American Medical Informatics Association. 2005. http://www.amia.com.

Bufton, M. 1999. Electronic health records and implementation of clinical practice guidelines. In *Electronic Health Records: Changing the Vision.* Edited by G.F. Murphy, M.A. Hanken, and K.A. Waters. Philadelphia: W.B. Saunders Company.

Cusack, C.M., C. Byrne, J.M. Hook, J. McGowan, E.G. Poon, and A. Zafar. 2009 (June). Health Information Technology Evaluation Toolkit: 2009 Update (Prepared for the AHRQ National Resource Center for Health Information Technology under Contract No. 290-04-0016.) AHRQ Publication No. 09-0083-EF. Rockville, MD: Agency for Healthcare Research and Quality.

Friedman, C.P. 2009. A "fundamental theorem" of biomedical informatics. *Journal of American Medical Informatics Association* 16: 169–170.

Health Information Management Systems Society. 2011. 22nd Annual HIMSS leadership survey, sponsored by Citrix: Senior executive IT final report. http://www.himss.org/2011Survey/healthcareCIO_final.asp.

Henchey, P. 1998. Maximizing ROI in data warehouses. *Advance for Health Information Executives* 2(1): 60–70.

Kelly, F. 2001. Implementing an executive information system (EIS). http://www.dssresources.com.

National Institute for Standards and Technology. October 2009. The NIST definition of cloud computing. http://www.nist.gov/itl/csd/cloud-102511.cfm.

Nuance Communications. 2008. Dragon Medical: Speech-enable the practice's EMR for faster, more efficient and profitable clinical documentation [Product sheet]. http://www.nuance.com/naturallyspeaking/pdf/ds_DNS10_Medical.pdf.

Open Source Initiative. 2012. The open source definition. http://http://www.opensource.org/docs/osd.

Power, D.J. 1997. What is a DSS? *The Online Executive Journal for Data-Intensive Decision Support* 1(3). http://www.taborcommunications.com/dsstar/971021/100015.html.

Prime Recognition. 2008. OCR software accuracy comparison. http://www.primerecognition.com/augprime/ocr_accuracy_compare.htm.

Schnitzer, G. 2000. Natural language processing: A coding professional's perspective. *Journal of AHIMA* 71(9): 95–98.

Stead, W., and M. Lorenzi. 1999. Health informatics: Linking investment to value. *Journal of the American Medical Informatics Association* 6(5): 341–348.

Tabar, P. 2003. Get the message? *Healthcare Informatics* 20(5): 50.

Wager, K., F. Lee, et al. 2009. *Managing Health Care Information Systems: A Practical Approach for Health Care Executives.* San Francisco: Jossey-Bass.

Warner, H. 2000. Can natural language processing aid outpatient coders? *Journal of AHIMA* 71(8): 78–81.

chapter 5

Electronic Health Records: Conceptual Framework

Margret K. Amatayakul, MBA, RHIA, CHPS, CPEHR, FHIMSS

Learning Objectives

- Describe the evolution of the electronic health record (EHR) and its supporting technologies
- Identify terms and concepts associated with EHRs
- Describe conceptually the overarching functionality, applications, and technologies that support and supplement EHRs
- Discuss EHR system challenges and the supporting roles of health information management (HIM) professionals in addressing these challenges

- Develop an appreciation for the planning and implementation aspects of EHRs
- Provide examples of EHR systems as they may be implemented in various types of care settings

Key Terms

Access control
Accredited Standards Committee X12 (ASC X12)
Administrative application
Adoption
Alert fatigue
Ancillary system
Application service provider (ASP)
Audit log
Automated drug dispensing machine
Availability
Bar code medication administration record (BC-MAR) system
Benefits realization
Best of breed
Best of fit
Break the glass
Bridge technology
Certification Commission for Healthcare Information Technology (CCHIT)

Change control
Charge capture
Chart conversion
Chart tracking
Chief medical informatics officer (CMIO)
Claims data
Clinical analytics
Clinical data analyst
Clinical data repository (CDR)
Clinical data warehouse (CDW)
Clinical decision support (CDS)
Clinical document architecture (CDA)
Clinical knowledge base
Clinical messaging
Clinical transformation
Closed-loop medication management
Cloud computing
Computer output to laser disk (COLD)
Computerized provider order entry (CPOE)

Confidentiality

Consent management

Contingency planning

Continuity of care document (CCD)

Continuity of care record (CCR)

Data administrator

Data conversion

Data exchange standard

Data quality management

Data stewardship

Dependency

Digital Imaging and Communications in Medicine (DICOM)

Discrete reportable transcription (DRT)

Documentation audit

Dual core

Due diligence

e-discovery

e-forms

Electronic document management (EDM) system

Electronic health record (EHR)

Electronic medical record (EMR)

Electronic medication administration record (EMAR) system

Eligibility verification

Encoder

Enterprise (or electronic) content and record management (ECRM)

Enterprise master patient index (EMPI)

e-prescribing (e-Rx)

Evidence-based medicine (EBM)

e-visit

Extensible Markup Language (XML)

Go-live

Health breach notification

Health information exchange (HIE)

Health Information Management and Systems Society (HIMSS)

Health Information Technology for Economic and Clinical Health (HITECH) Act

Health Insurance Portability and Accountability Act (HIPAA)

Health Level Seven (HL7)

Health summary

HIMSS Analytics™ EMR Adoption Model^{SM}

Human–computer interface (HCI)

Hybrid record

Identity management

Identity-matching algorithm

Implementation

Implementation plan

Inference engine

Institute of Medicine (IOM)

Integration

Integrity

Interface

Interface engine

Interoperability

Laboratory information system (LIS)

Legacy system

Legal health record (LHR)

Logical Observation Identifiers Names and Codes (LOINC)

Meaningful use (MU)

Medication list

Medication reconciliation

Message format standard

Migration path

Minimum necessary standard

National Council for Prescription Drug Programs (NCPDP)

National Drug Code (NDC)

Nationwide health information network (NHIN)

Natural language processing (NLP)

Office of the National Coordinator for Health Information Technology (ONC)

Online analytical processing (OLAP)

Online transaction processing (OLTP)

Optimization

Order communication/results reporting (OC/RR)

Patient portal

Personal health record (PHR)

Pharmacy information system

Physician champion

Picture archiving and communication system (PACS)

Point-of-care (POC) patient charting (or documentation)

Policy

Practice management system (PMS)

Predictive modeling

Project manager

Project plan

Protected health information (PHI)

Provider portal

Radio frequency identification (RFID)

Radiology information system (RIS)

Record locator service (RLS)

Redundancy

Registry

Results management system

Revenue cycle management (RCM)

Rip-and-replace

RxNorm

Security risk analysis

Semantics

SMART goals

Smart peripherals

Software as a service (SaaS)

Source system

Specialty clinical application

Storage area network

Storage management

Structured data

Syntax
System build
Technical interoperability
Telehealth
Two-factor authentication
Unstructured data

Usability
Virtualization
Vocabulary
Web portal
Workflow and process management
Workstation on wheels (WOW)

EHR in Practice

Dr. Smith is at home having breakfast with her family. Before heading off to the hospital to check on patients and then to the office, she decides to clear as much from her inbox as possible this morning since she plans to attend a local medical society meeting this evening and wants to leave her office early. She logs onto her computer at home using a secure web portal and first reviews all of the lab results that came in since yesterday. She approves most for posting to her patients' personal health records but asks her office receptionist to arrange a call with one of the patients for today if possible.

In her inbox Dr. Smith sees a message from a colleague, Dr. Jones, who is requesting a consult for a patient with an especially severe condition. Dr. Jones has used his practice management system (PMS) to check and receive prior authorization from the patient's health plan for the consult and used his electronic health record (EHR) to forward the patient's health summary via the Continuity of Care Document (CCD) standard to Dr. Smith for her review. In addition to this message, Dr. Smith's office is also requesting approval for renewal of a medication for a patient who is out of town. In responding to the renewal request, an alert informs Dr. Smith that the patient is also due for a checkup, so this information is sent back to the office scheduling system for contacting the patient to make an appointment within the next 10 days. In using the e-prescribing (e-Rx) component of her EHR, Dr. Smith approves a renewal for only 10 days worth of the medication. Further checking her inbox, Dr. Smith notes that there is an e-mail from another colleague wanting to chat before the meeting this evening about a new treatment regimen that appears promising. Not having seen the literature on this, Dr. Smith checks the National Library of Medicine archives on the Internet for any possible articles. Finding a few, she tags them for printing in the office. Finally, Dr. Smith plans on reviewing and signing the two discharge summaries she dictated yesterday so they may be electronically fed into those patients' records, but before she has a chance to do this she receives an instant message concerning a patient in the hospital whose condition is deteriorating rapidly.

Not wanting to delay treatment for this patient until she arrives at the hospital, Dr. Smith engages the charge nurse in an exchange of information, including a streaming video of the patient's latest vital signs that she is able to combine with lab results and current medications and convert into to a graph using the results management component of the hospital's EHR. Dr. Smith decides to move the patient to critical care and places a series of orders for the patient.

Dr. Smith is able to reconcile all the patient's medication both by using the hospital's bar code medication administration record (BC-MAR) system and by accessing past medication documentation from the patient's health plan's pharmacy benefits manager (PBM) through the community health information exchange organization (HIEO) in which Dr. Smith is a member.

In addition, while placing an order for a specific medication via the hospital's portal to its computerized provider order entry (CPOE) system with its clinical decision support (CDS) system, Dr. Smith is alerted that the medication she entered is contraindicated with another drug the patient is taking, so she makes an adjustment. As it is now time for her to leave, she quickly sets a reminder to review the two transcribed documents at lunch time and logs off the system.

This scenario reflects the growing trends of remote connectivity; clinical messaging; integration of voice, data, and video; use of knowledge sources; workflow tasking, CDS, and integration of the components of the EHR with multiple external sources and uses of health information.

Evolution of the Electronic Health Record

The concept of EHR has been around since the late 1960s; however, it has only been recently that most provider organizations have gotten serious about fully implementing and adopting EHRs. The goal for all Americans to have an EHR by 2014 identified by President George W. Bush in his 2004 State of the Union address has been solidified by the incentives for **meaningful use (MU)** of EHR technology under the **Health Information Technology for Economic and Clinical Health (HITECH)** Act of 2009. The intent of EHR technology is to capture clinical data from multiple sources for use at the point of care in clinical decision making and to exchange such data across the continuum of care for care coordination.

As originally described in its landmark work on patient records, the **Institute of Medicine (IOM)** defined what is today referred to as the EHR as a record "that resides in a system specifically designed to support users by providing accessibility to complete and accurate data, alerts, reminders, clinical decision support systems, links to medical knowledge, and other aids. This definition encompasses a broader view of the patient record than is current today, moving from the notion of a location or device for keeping track of patient care events to a resource with much enhanced utility in patient care (including the ability to provide an accurate, longitudinal account of care—meaning that information is available about all of the patient's health conditions over a lifetime), in management of the healthcare system, and in extension of knowledge" (IOM 1991). In addition, the IOM provided the caveat that "merely automating the form, content, and procedures of current patient records will perpetuate their deficiencies and will be insufficient to meet emerging user needs" (IOM 1991, reaffirmed by the IOM in a 1997 update to its original patient record study).

As with any revolutionary system, the EHR has suffered somewhat from multiple different interpretations and rapid development of products that may not have fully met the vision. In fact, some of them were so disappointing or cumbersome to use that they may have discouraged potential users to such an extent that they may be unwilling to try again. While much has improved, a National Academy of Sciences/IOM study conducted in 2009 examined eight organizations acknowledged as leaders in applying IT to healthcare to assess the current state of affairs. While they identified a number of successes, they also found that EHRs were "rarely well integrated into clinical practice." Care providers felt they were spending a lot of time entering data, but doing so to meet reimbursement requirements or as a defense against potential lawsuits. The report further noted that this state of affairs "does not reflect incompetence on the part of healthcare professionals" but is a "consequence of the intellectual complexity of healthcare and an environment that has not been adequately structured to help clinicians avoid mistakes or to systematically improve their decision making and practice." Consistent with the *Quality Chasm* series of reports on quality of care in the United States conducted by the IOM, the National Academy of Sciences/IOM study concluded that the "nation faces a healthcare IT chasm" (Stead and Lin 2009).

Ultimately, the EHR should be able to

- Improve the quality of healthcare through data availability and links to knowledge sources
- Enhance patient safety with context-sensitive reminders and alerts, clinical decision support, automated surveillance, chronic disease management, and drug and device recall capability
- Support health maintenance, preventive care, and wellness through patient reminders, health summaries, tailored instructions, educational materials, and home monitoring and tracking capability
- Increase productivity through data capture and reporting formats tailored to the user; streamlined workflow support; and patient-specific care plans, guidelines, and protocols
- Reduce hassle factors and improve satisfaction for clinicians, consumers, and caregivers by managing scheduling, registration, referrals, medication refills,

and work queues and by automatically generating administrative data
- Support revenue enhancement through accurate and timely eligibility and benefit information, timely claims adjudication, cost-efficacy analysis, clinical trials recruitment, rules-driven coding assistance, external accountability reporting and outcomes measures, and contract management
- Support predictive modeling and contribute to development of evidence-based healthcare guidance
- Maintain patient confidentiality and exchange data securely among all stakeholders

EHR Terms

As the EHR has evolved, a variety of terms have been used to describe what today the federal government is calling EHR. In fact, there has been considerable confusion between electronic *health* record and electronic *medical* record (EMR). Hospitals sometimes describe that they have both an EMR, which is an electronic document management system, and an EHR, which is composed of applications used by clinicians at the point of care. Physician practices often prefer the term EMR because to many physicians, the term "health" connotes a state of wellness while their practice (and reimbursement) is largely about providing medical care to those who are sick or injured.

In 2008, the federal government asked the National Alliance for Health Information Technology (NAHIT) to develop a set of terms and definitions to help the industry avoid confusion and achieve consensus on terminology. While NAHIT no longer exists, the definitions it published serve as the foundation for the government's adoption of the term *EHR*. NAHIT (2008) distinguished the terms as follows:

- **Electronic health record (EHR)** is defined as "an electronic record of health-related information on an individual that conforms to nationally recognized interoperability standards and that can be created, managed, and consulted by authorized clinicians and staff across more than one healthcare organization."
- **Electronic medical record (EMR)** is defined as "an electronic record of health-related information on an individual that can be created, gathered, managed, and consulted by authorized clinicians and staff within one healthcare organization."

The key difference between the terms *EHR* and *EMR* as suggested by NAHIT is in EHR being interoperable and EMR not. **Interoperability** refers to the ability of two different systems to exchange data with each other. Unfortunately, many care delivery organizations are challenged with systems not being as interoperable as desired within their own organization, let alone with other organizations.

Neither of NAHIT's definitions of EHR or EMR addresses the functionality that contributes to enhanced utility beyond that of paper-based records that the IOM originally envisioned

Figure 5.1.   HL7 EHR-System Functional Model

Direct Care	DC.1	Care Management	
	DC.2	Clinical Decision Support	
	DC.3	Operations Management and Communication	
Supportive	S.1	Clinical Support	
	S.2	Measurement, Analysis, Research and Reports	
	S.3	Administrative and Financial	
Information Infrastructure	IN.1	Security	
	IN.2	Health Record Information and Management	
	IN.3	Registry and Directory Services	
	IN.4	Standard Terminologies & Terminology Services	
	IN.5	Standards-based Interoperability	
	IN.6	Business Rules Management	
	IN.7	Workflow Management	

Source: Health Level Seven 2007. Copyright 2007 by Health Level Seven,® Inc.

in 1991 or which it supplied in its 2003 letter report to the secretary of Health and Human Services (HHS) (IOM 2003). In 2004, the standards development organization **Health Level Seven (HL7)** also helped overcome the lack of a comprehensive description of the EHR in its EHR-System Functional Model, which described a highly functional and interoperable system (see figure 5.1). Still, old habits die hard. For example, the **Health Information Management and Systems Society (HIMSS)** continues to use the term *EMR* in its **HIMSS Analytics™ EMR Adoption Model**[SM] (HIMSS Analytics 2012). This model is widely referenced as it provides a quarterly survey report on the cumulative capabilities of EHRs in hospitals. Figure 5.2 provides the model with data from 2008 and 2011 to illustrate progress being made in EHR adoption. Hospitals in Stage 4 or above would most likely qualify for earning the MU incentives. By the end of 2011, 32.8 percent of hospitals were at Stage 4 or above.

EHR System

As suggested by the HIMSS Analytics report on the current status of EHR adoption, EHR remains a complex system to implement. And it is, indeed, a system—of many elements that must work together to achieve specific goals. For an EHR, these system elements must include not only hardware and software but also attention to people, policy, and process. In fact, David Blumenthal, MD, national coordinator in the **Office of the National Coordinator for Health Information Technology (ONC)** from 2009 to 2011, observed the following in discussing EHR:

Figure 5.2. HIMSS Analytics US EMR Adoption Model

Stage	Cumulative Capabilities	2008 Final	2011 Final
Stage 7	Complete EMR, CCD transactions to share data; Data warehousing; Data continuity with ED, ambulatory, OP	0.3%	1.2%
Stage 6	Physician documentation (structured templates), full CDSS (variance and compliance), full R-PACS	0.5%	5.2%
Stage 5	Closed loop medication administration	2.5%	13.2%
Stage 4	CPOE, Clinical Decision Support (clinical protocols)	2.5%	13.2%
Stage 3	Nursing/clinical documentation (flow sheets), CDSS (error checking), PACS available outside Radiology	35.7%	44.9%
Stage 2	CDR, Controlled Medical Vocabulary, CDS, may have Document Imaging; HIE capable	31.4%	12.4%
Stage 1	Ancillaries-Lab, Rad, Pharmacy-All Installed	11.5%	5.7%
Stage 0	All Three Ancillaries Not Installed	15.6%	9.0%

Data from HIMSS Analytics® Database © 2012 HIMSS Analytics   N=5,166 N=5,337

It's not the technology that's important, but its effect. Meaningful use is not a technology project, but a change management project. Components of meaningful use include sociology, psychology, behavior change, and the mobilization of levers to change complex systems and improve their performance. (Blumenthal 2009)

People are hugely impacted by the EHR. Even for clinicians who use computers frequently (and many to this day still do not), the EHR represents a significantly different way of practicing their professional skills. For instance, most clinicians are taught to quickly assess a patient, take immediate action to stabilize a patient in an emergency, and then gather further information about the patient—through referencing previous records of care, interviewing the patient, and obtaining data diagnostic studies. Only after much of the fact finding is completed is information documented in narrative. As a result, the documentation is largely a summary of findings. Furthermore, where clinicians are generally expected to document an assessment and plan of care, and ideally should engage the patient in making clinical decisions about his or her ongoing care, the result often is simply the recording of a differential or final diagnosis and orders for any additional studies and treatments. Diagnostic studies and treatments are largely based on the provider's training and experience (Ball and Bierstock 2007) rather than evidence from (new) scientific research—although professional judgment must be applied to such evidence (Tonelli 2006).

When EHR is introduced, the clinician is expected to document and even practice in very different ways. Data are to be entered as captured at the point of care, and in standardized and structured form rather than **unstructured data** or narrative form, often taking longer to enter than the typical dictation of a report and without the ability to express nuances important to clinicians (Resnik et al. 2008). The result of this **structured data** often is a bulleted list of findings that clinicians do not find very user friendly. The clinician is expected to receive and be guided by **clinical decision support (CDS)** systems that process the structured data against a drug knowledge database (DKB) and other evidence-based medicine (EBM) into alerts, reminders, and context-sensitive templates for data capture, although often the volume of such "incessant warnings" (Pulley 2010), as some consider these, are frequently ignored. Even giving the patient a **health summary** and certainly supporting a patient in compiling a **personal health record (PHR)** or accepting information from a PHR (Witry et al. 2010) are new concepts for many physicians, who in the past shied away from providing patients with access to their health information. In fact, not providing access to a person's health information is one of the top five Privacy Rule complaints levied against physician practices according to the Office for Civil Rights (OCR 2011).

Workflows and processes clearly are impacted by the EHR. **Workflow and process management** refers to

The application of a focused approach to understanding and optimizing how inputs (in any form—raw data, semi-processed data, and information from knowledge sources such as EBM) are processed (mentally or by computer using algorithms and clinical decision support [CDS] rules) into outputs (information) that contribute to an immediate effect and/or downstream effects (which also contribute to creation of further knowledge). (Amatayakul 2012b)

Even when a change in workflow and process is for the better, such as where medication alerts reduce discrepancies on ordering and medication administration errors (HIMSS 2006) or vocabulary standards support better care coordination (O'Malley et al. 2010), the change is still new and often something of a surprise. Sam Bierstock, MD, has coined the term *thoughtflow* to reflect the "process by which physicians obtain, assess, prioritize, and act on information." He notes that EHR "vendors have long developed systems based on presumptions about the way clinicians work, but without a clear understanding of how clinicians think" (Ball and Bierstock 2007). Because thoughtflow is not observable, it often missed in redesigning workflows and processes. Tools, such as mind mapping (Passuello 2007; Swan 2011) and use case (Constantine and Lockwood 2003), are available to aid care delivery organizations in illustrating new workflows and processes and helping users adapt to them.

Policy considerations are as important as people and process. Policy may be explicit, such as in defining what constitutes a medication error (Lisby et al. 2010), whether rationale must be documented for overriding an alert (Rollins 2005), or how copy and paste may be applied (Amatayakul 2010b). Policy may also be implicit. For example, Phillips and Berner (2004) and Koppel et al. (2008) describe situations where nurses "beat the system" by scanning copies of patients' bar codes at the nursing station instead of at the point of care. While there may not be a written policy requiring that a patient's bar codes be scanned on the patient, the intent is certainly present in the technology. Workarounds, such as scanning bar codes at the nursing station instead of at the bedside, defeat the purpose of the technology and fail to adhere to the five rights of safe medication history as defined by the Institute for Safe Medication Practices: (1) right patient, (2) right route, (3) right dose, (4) right time, and (5) right medication (ISMP 1999). These five rights are now most often described as eight goals by adding these three rights to the first five: (6) right documentation, (7) right reason, and (8) right response (Bonsall 2011).

While potentially not viewed as policy setting, the fact that many organizations implement EHR incompletely, condone workarounds, or do not work to support a culture of patient safety without blame is in effect a form of policy. As more EHR components are implemented and more functionality in the applications creates a dependency on the technology, the risk of unintended consequences significantly increases. For example, ISMP (2004) describes an ICU nurse catching herself retrieving diazepam instead of diltiazem from an automated dispensing cabinet that was not linked to the hospital's pharmacy information system. Without such a link, the contents of the entire cabinet were displayed, not just the medications ordered for the patient. The dispensing cabinet then only served as a locked storage device rather than a patient safety device. In a more recent, and deadly, example (Graham and Dizikes 2011), a pharmacy technician transposed numbers such that 60 times the amount of sodium chloride for a customized IV solution for a newborn was entered into the IV compounding machine, which was not connected to the pharmacy information system. In addition, the automated alerts on the compounding machine that could have identified the error had been turned off, and the label on the IV bag did not contain information on its actual contents. Adding to the problem was a lab technician who saw abnormally high sodium levels on continuous blood testing but assumed there was an error with the auto analyzer and took no action. Such unintended consequences are often blamed on the technology, when they are largely people, policy, and process issues.

EHR Transition

Hospitals and physician practices often start out focusing on technology, then find that just implementing hardware and software is not enough to gain full adoption and achieve the intended benefits. Even when training is included in the implementation process, it is often focused solely on how to turn on and off the computer and enter data into the software. Rarely is attention devoted to fears and concerns of new users, workflow and process redesign, or even establishment of policies with respect to good documentation principles or use of the system as a clinical decision support tool. The result is often that a transition from an implementation phase to an adoption phase and further to an optimization phase is necessary, where

- **Implementation** refers to a system having been installed and configured to meet a specific organization's needs. Users have begun to be trained and are beginning to use the system. However, during implementation an organization may not have rolled out use of the system to all potential users. It may be used on only one or a few nursing units, or on all nursing units but only for certain functions (such as only medication ordering in CPOE). In physician practices, the EHR may be used at one site, or only by primary care physicians, or only by certain physicians who have personally decided to use the system. If workflow and process changes have been introduced, users are still experimenting with them.

- **Adoption** refers to the state of EHR where every intended user is using the basic functionality of the system. Frequently adoption requires a period of acclimation where users need time to work through how they are going to use the system and what further configuration may be desired. Adoption may also require retraining, (further) redesign of workflows and processes, reinforcement (of changes), and even a system of rewards. Unfortunately, some users may never reach full adoption, in which case counseling, workarounds, sanctions, terminating employment, or other strategies may be necessary to achieve the results needed by all.

- **Optimization** includes activities that extend use of EHRs beyond the basic functionality. Optimization includes changes in the clinical practice of medicine. Such a profound change often is referred to as a **clinical transformation** (Pryor 2006). For example, if a physician has always prescribed a certain medication for a given condition, the physician who has optimized use of the EHR will follow evidence-based medicine guidelines in selecting the appropriate medication. Optimization often leads to acquisition of additional technology, such as more sophisticated CDS, different input devices, medical device integration, data analytics, or additional applications as they become available on the market. It could be said that optimization is an ongoing state.

EHR Migration Path

Because an EHR is essentially a set of functional components and the means to get them to work together, each organization should recognize that a migration path is necessary to ultimately reach its goals for clinical transformation through EHR. A **migration path** is a strategic plan but is somewhat different than the traditional IT strategic plan that focuses only on applications and technology. Because the EHR is a tool to use for clinical transformation, the migration path should not only reflect the IT architecture of hardware and software but also reflect the operational elements of people, policy, and process changes to address improvements in clinical quality, patient safety, evidence-based practices, cost of care, productivity, and user satisfaction. The migration path should identify specific, measurable goals along a realistic timeline given the organization's current culture, information technology infrastructure, financial capability, and other strategic imperatives. (See figure 5.3.)

Many hospitals question why they need a migration path when either their vendor pretty much dictates the components to be implemented or MU incentives that are to be implemented in three stages direct required elements. While these circumstances certainly do provide a framework for a strategic plan for EHR, they do not afford a complete picture of all the major elements a healthcare organization must undertake

Figure 5.3.   An example of a migration path for an EHR

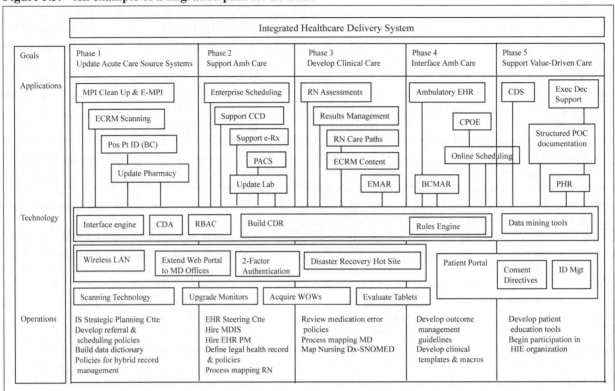

to achieve success with EHR. First, a vendor may not supply all the desired software, and often the hardware, telecommunications, interfaces with medical devices, and other functionality and services are not included. For instance, most EHR vendors do not address data storage, telehealth, health information exchange (HIE), registry utilization, advanced CDS, or clinical analytics and data warehousing. Most EHR vendors will also acknowledge that the people, policy, and process issues associated with gaining adoption and optimizing system use are the responsibility of the healthcare organization. Organizations must determine when certain types of staff are needed, what policies are needed, and how processes need to change to ensure EHR success.

There are also sequencing decisions that the healthcare organization should be making. Again, it is true that the MU incentives are dictating implementation of CPOE and not systems for medication administration records. But this does not mean that a healthcare organization absolutely must follow the incentives. In fact, there are several major hospital systems that have opted out of starting their EHR migration with CPOE. Physician practices are looking very carefully at whether it is prudent from a productivity standpoint to seek the incentives or to opt instead for technology they know will make a difference in their practice and keep their reimbursement at the level desired. Still, the majority of healthcare organizations will want to sequence CPOE sooner rather

than later to take advantage of the incentives. In doing so, however, there are still many other choices, such as when a hospital or physician practice should implement a personal health record; whether a critical access hospital gains more by implementing telehealth than a **bar code medication administration record (BC-MAR) system**, especially when it does not have a full-time pharmacist; or how quickly a hospital can move away from a **hybrid record,** which is part paper and part electronic, adopt an **electronic document management (EDM)** system to go paperless, and then move to full use of EHR for documentation so that the EDM system is only needed to scan occasional paper documents.

In constructing a migration path, the first step should be explicitly documenting what the organization wants to accomplish by automating its clinical systems. For instance, a hospital may have a goal to improve its near-miss medication error rate by 80 percent using a BC-MAR system; to reduce unnecessary diagnostic studies tests by 10 percent by providing results from previous tests to providers at the same time an order is placed; and to have nurses spend 50 percent less time on paperwork by using a single nurse assessment template that distributes data to all other applicable users, which could increase time spent on patient education by half an hour for each patient. Writing **SMART goals** ensures that goals are specific, measurable, attainable, realistic, and timely. These goals set by the hospital or physician practice should identify the needed functionality in the components of the EHR it intends to acquire, identify the specific technology requirements to support those functions, and set expectations for people to adopt new policies and processes to ensure the goals' achievement and, therefore, provide value back to the organization for its investment (Amatayakul 2012a).

The second step in constructing a migration path should be describing the current state of the organization's applications, technology, and operations. It is surprising how many organizations do not have an inventory of their applications and often find their plans result in gaps or duplications as a result. One hospital, for instance, found that it had four separate document imaging systems that did not communicate with one another: one in each of the HIM, radiology, emergency services, and billing departments. Once a full inventory is taken, the organization should determine what applications, technology, and operational elements are needed to achieve each of its goals for clinical transformation. There are often **dependencies** between applications and across applications, technology, and operational elements. These dependencies, such as results management depending on a laboratory information system (LIS) upgrade or successful implementation of CDS depending on physician input, must be addressed for the organization to be successful with EHR. For example, an EHR migration path should address the following:

- What is the organization's current readiness? Is there an EHR steering committee with representation from all stakeholders, including physician champions, the medical director of IS, nurse informaticists, and e-HIM professionals, and are practice guidelines, evidence-based knowledge resource utilization, process mapping, and so on in place?
- What additional applications are needed, and in what sequence? What changes to existing applications must be made? Are there upgrades or replacements needed to source systems?
- Are interfaces required? Is there a repository?
- Will the technical architecture support an EHR, or will a major investment in hardware need to be made first? Is there sufficient bandwidth to support remote hosting of a data center or the use of cloud computing? Is there redundancy in telecommunications?
- Is the network sufficient to support all EHR users and uses, including picture archiving and communication (PAC) and EDM systems, which are composed of very large files, or will this need to be enhanced?
- What operational changes need to be adopted? Will changes need to be made in policies and procedures in support of an EHR? Are enhanced security controls needed? Are staff resources available to support both implementation and ongoing maintenance requirements?

It is important to note that the migration path is a strategic plan, not an implementation plan for each component. **Implementation plans** are used to manage the literally thousands of tasks the implementation of any given application requires. These are tactical, relatively short term, and often repeated with only slight variation for every application implemented.

Once the migration path is developed, it should be reviewed regularly and updated as needed. It becomes the road map for all decisions relative to going forward with clinical transformation. Achieving consensus on the migration path keeps organizations from making reactive decisions. Except for unanticipated changes in current applications, technology, or operations, the migration path should be relatively stable and enable the organization to be proactive in its path to achieving benefits from EHR. Every organization has its own migration path. There is no one right or wrong path, only one that is most or least appropriate for a particular organization given its current situation and future goals. Unfortunately, many organizations are not taking the approach of strategically planning for an EHR but, rather, are responding to external pressures, acquiring whatever their vendor offers, or implementing a system they consider temporary, never retiring any of their information systems. The investment not only in acquiring any technology but also in taking the time and making the effort to implement and gain adoption of a system is immense and often considered too great to ever abandon. Even when a vendor retires a product, a healthcare organization is more likely to find a way to work with the system than to buy a replacement, fearing the effort it will take to get a new system working satisfactorily.

Check Your Understanding 5.1

True/False:

1. ____ An EHR implementation results in all users effectively using basic functions.

2. ____ A migration path is an implementation plan for information systems that connect to the EHR.

3. ____ In an EHR migration path, an example of a dependency might be the need to hire a data administrator when a clinical data repository is acquired.

4. ____ By the end of 2011, HIMSS Analytics determined that over 50 percent of the over 5,000 hospitals responding to its survey had an EHR.

5. ____ The term electronic *health* record is used to denote the fact that hospitals and physicians should use the system to help consumers maintain wellness.

Multiple Choice:

6. What would NOT be included on an EHR migration path?

   A. Acquiring an EHR project manager
   B. Defining what constitutes a reportable medication error
   C. Implementing computerized provider order entry system
   D. Installing a wireless network
   E. Training super users

7. Setting SMART goals for EHR helps healthcare organizations:

   A. Begin to reduce staff not needed after EHR implementation
   B. Define functional requirements
   C. Identify noncompliance with workflows and processes
   D. Implement sanctions for creating workarounds
   E. All of the above

8. The clinical transformation brought about by EHR is expected to:

   A. Create a big change
   B. Eliminate medical errors
   C. Improve the practice of medicine
   D. Standardize information systems across the country

9. Hospitals typically sequence their EHR applications so that:

   A. Clinical data repository is one of the early foundational applications
   B. Computerized provider order entry is implemented before any clinical decision support is used
   C. Personal health records are the first clinical application to be implemented
   D. Physician documentation is the very last application to be implemented
   E. EMR is implemented prior to EHR

10. The ability for two different systems to exchange data with each other is:

    A. Connectivity
    B. Health information exchange
    C. Interoperability
    D. Telecommunications
    E. Telemedicine

EHR Functionality and Technology

It should be clear from the previous discussions that an EHR is not a single application or computer device but a complex set of software and hardware. Figure 5.4 displays a conceptual model that depicts these components.

Source Systems: Financial and Administrative and Ancillary/Clinical Departmental Systems

An important element of EHR includes the ability to communicate data with multiple sources; hence there must be information systems in many, if not all, hospital departments.

Figure 5.4.   EHR system technical components

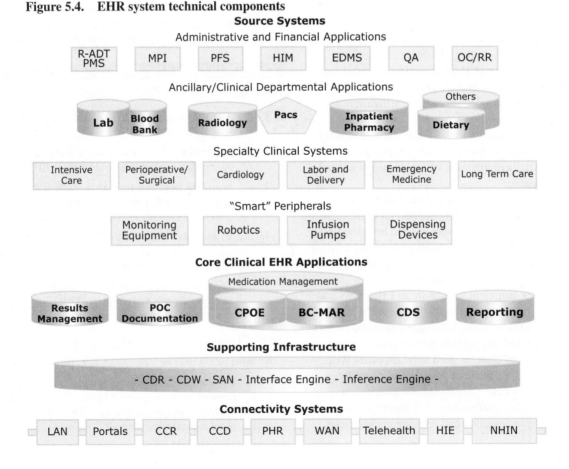

Although physician practices will have fewer systems with which they must communicate, such systems may more commonly be external to the practice. Collectively these are called **source systems,** and there are several types.

Hospitals have numerous financial and administrative applications, and they are no longer solely the domain of the finance department or patient financial services. HIM professionals have long provided input via diagnostic and procedural codes and sometimes chargemaster management to the **revenue cycle management (RCM)** process, which includes creating, submitting, analyzing, and obtaining payment for healthcare services (TripleTree 2006). This link and more direct ties to clinical systems are becoming increasingly important as there is increasing convergence of **claims data** (information required to be reported on a healthcare claim for service reimbursement) with health data. As claims data and clinical data are used together, healthcare quality and cost (value) improvements can be made, and better business intelligence (BI) is available to support better decisions by both the administrative and clinical leadership of healthcare organizations. For example, with more complete clinical information available at the time of admission, a hospital is able to better verify a patient's eligibility for health plan benefits so that it is not faced with a denied claim later. An order placed for a potentially duplicate diagnostic study or therapy can be flagged for physician review, potentially displaying the previous study results simultaneously. While this may appear to be reducing hospital revenue, conducting a duplicate study or treatment is potentially hazardous for the patient and costly to the healthcare delivery system overall. Hospitals will save money and potentially increase their revenues if they are able to demonstrate their quality and cost-effectiveness measures when negotiating discounted fee-for-service contracts with payers. Often it requires staff with clinical backgrounds to aid in understanding where a duplicate test or therapy is efficacious and where it is not. Information that shows the hospital how many and what types of patients are readmitted within 30 days of discharge for the same condition is another example that will enable a hospital to take proactive measures to monitor these patients more closely after discharge and reduce the risk of not being reimbursed by Medicare for the admission.

Financial systems include both general accounting systems (such as general ledger, accounts payable, contract management, procurement, and others) as well as systems specific to patient accounting, often called patient financial services (PFS) systems. RCM starts with **eligibility verification** to determine if a patient's health plan will provide reimbursement for services to be performed, and sometimes prior-authorization management systems where a health plan requires review and approval of a procedure (or referral) prior to performing the service. Once patient care commences, **charge capture** collects information from ancillary systems and the EHR about services performed; claims are generated for reimbursement. Documents may need to be attached to the claim to support the claim. Claims status checking, posting remittance advice reflecting actual fees reimbursed to the organization, receiving electronic funds transfers (EFTs), and sending explanations of benefits (EOBs) to patients, challenging denials, and managing collection are all RCM functions after claims have been sent. Many of these processes utilize standard transaction and code sets (TCSs) mandated under the **Health Insurance Portability and Accountability Act of (HIPAA)** of 1996 Administrative Simplification requirements. Under additional Administrative Simplification provisions of the Affordable Care Act (ACA) of 2010, some of these are just being implemented or are being enhanced with standard operating rules that will significantly reduce the thousands of companion guides, or unique paper rules, that have been used in the past.

Administrative applications that must also connect to EHR systems include admission, discharge, transfer (R-ADT); enterprise master patient index or master patient index (EMPI or MPI); encoders, chart tracking, chart deficiency management, release of information; order communication/results reporting (OC/RR); quality assurance (QA), including core measures abstracting (which pulls specified, quality-related data from health records for reporting to the Joint Commission and Centers for Medicare and Medicaid Services); and many others.

Physician practices may have a **practice management system (PMS)** that provides patient registration, appointment scheduling, and all of the same patient financial services that a hospital performs.

Ancillary systems (clinical department applications) include **laboratory information systems (LISs), radiology information systems (RISs), pharmacy information systems,** and others. As migration toward EHR is considered, it is important to recognize the primary purpose of ancillary systems—to help manage the operations of the departments in which they are used. For example, while LISs obviously produce lab results, they do many other things in order to produce the results: They must receive the order for the test, assign an accession number to the order and specimen if the specimen accompanies the order, generate a specimen collection list and bar code labels for the specimen collection vials, schedule phlebotomists to collect the specimens from the patient, and interface with auto analyzers that run the tests to download the results. Once the results of the tests are available and quality checked, the system prints results or otherwise makes the results available for viewing by the ordering provider. In addition to these basic features, LISs manage workload balancing, supplies inventories, Medicare medical necessity checking, billing, and public health reporting and generate custom reports for clinical or quality management. RISs perform equivalent functions for the radiology department. While the clinical pharmacy in a hospital does not product diagnostic studies results as do the LIS and RIS, it must receive orders for medications, track and maintain inventory, perform quality checks, manage staff, and perform other departmental management functions. In addition, there are other departments that may have their own applications, such as a blood bank, nutrition and food services, housekeeping, and others. These may all ultimately have a connection to EHR through ordering meals, special services, or functions.

Large physician practices may have LIS and/or RIS as well as some other departmental systems. Small practices are likely to use the laboratory and radiology services of the hospital at which the physicians have medical staff privileges, or use commercial labs or imaging centers. Although physician practices may keep some drug samples they give selected patients, they do not maintain a clinical pharmacy. Rather, prescriptions must be written for a retail pharmacy to dispense. (Even if a pharmacy is on the premises of a physician office, by law it must be a separate legal entity to sell drugs directly to patients.)

A special type of system, **picture archiving and communication systems (PACS)**, digitizes medical images. These are becoming increasingly popular in both hospital and physician practice environments. Some vendors offer free PACS viewer software to enable physicians who do not do their own imaging to view images from other sources.

In addition to ancillary systems, there are **specialty clinical applications**. These include many systems for hospitals, but also some for physician practices. Examples include intensive care, perioperative or surgical services, cardiology, oncology, emergency medicine, labor and delivery, infection control, behavioral health, dentistry, and others.

Hospitals and physician practices are also acquiring **smart peripherals,** which are medical instruments that have information processing components including auto analyzers for lab testing, medication dispensing devices, robotics, smart infusion pumps, and vital signs monitoring equipment.

Systems to Support Access to Clinical Information

Many care delivery organizations use **bridge technology** to enhance access to patient information when they do not have a full complement of source systems or have source systems that are not sufficient to support the major clinical components of an EHR. Bridge technology includes interim applications, such as EDM, clinical messaging, electronic knowledge bases, and registries, which are used to provide specific needed functionality until the organization is able to acquire all the necessary source systems that are core to a clinical EHR system. In some cases, clinicians interact fairly well with the bridge technology applications and in other cases the applications primarily enhance financial and administrative processes.

EDM systems greatly improve financial and administrative processes after discharge, where many departments need access to the patient's chart, where there are record completion responsibilities for several providers, and where access to clinical information may be needed in immediate outpatient or emergency department follow-up. It is also possible to add workflow technology to these systems, which can be used to queue work among staff or between departments. Other EDM systems, often then called **enterprise (or electronic) content and record management (ECRM)** systems, also enable digital documents, such as e-mails, e-faxes, transcription files, voice files (from digital and/or speech dictation), and wave forms, to be electronically fed (a process formerly referred to as **computer output to laser disk [COLD]**) into a repository for viewing via the ECRM system (Strong 2008). Coupling electronic, or COLD, feeds from such systems with scanned documents enables the organization to virtually eliminate paper charts. The paperless state, however, does not mean that these organizations have an EHR, as there are no clinical decision support tools embedded in such systems. This is changing somewhat as **discrete reportable transcription (DRT)** is emerging, which combines speech dictation with templates that utilize basic natural language processing tools to capture the speech in structured form (Anderson 2009). **Natural language processing (NLP)** is still in its infancy with respect to being able to parse all unstructured data in an EHR and create structured data from it. However, in the NLP form used in DRT, templates guide the data to be dictated so that structured data fields are populated. If used in real time, clinician decision making can be supported. If not used in real time, the clinical decision support element is missing, but the structured data are still useful for analysis and reporting.

Clinical messaging is another technology that bridges the gap between stand-alone, ancillary systems and a comprehensive EHR. With clinical messaging, secure web-based technology is used to exchange remotely (such as from the hospital to a physician office) scanned or electronically fed documents or results from source systems, as well as e-mail messages among users.

Access to **clinical knowledge bases** is another form of bridge technology, as well as a key part of CDS in an EHR. When used as a stand-alone system, clinicians are provided access to the medical literature, clinical practice guidelines, evidence-based healthcare information, drug knowledge bases, and other clinical information not associated with a given patient. In some cases, this support is simply a predefined set of Internet "favorites" or content that has been specifically gathered and provided through the organization's intranet. In other cases, the knowledge is provided through a subscription service that formats the content in useful ways and keeps it current. For example, access to drug knowledge is popular with both physicians and nurses—and may be updated daily. Once clinical EHR applications are acquired, knowledge bases can be integrated with patient-specific data for CDS. They can also provide instructions for patients that can be produced in a variety of languages, include special instructions where comorbid conditions exists, and even incorporate the patient's picture if so desired by the organization.

Use of a specialized disease registry is a final form of bridge technology. A **registry** is a collection of a limited set of information about a patient and often disease specific—such as for diabetes, heart disease, or other chronic illnesses. These are more popular in physician practices than hospitals as an interim step to a fully functional EHR. Typically, use of a registry requires a staff member to abstract data from the paper patient chart and entering it into an electronic database using a specially designed **e-form** to collect required data for the registry. When the patient is next seen, staff will print out an update of the information from the registry, which usually includes such items as chronic disease reminders. Registries can also be used for quality assessment, patient recall, and research purposes. Because registry data are not collected electronically at the point of care, it cannot provide all the same CDS support that an EHR is capable of doing. Registries also place an added burden on staff to abstract, enter, and retrieve the data.

Core Clinical EHR Applications

Core clinical EHR applications are those used directly by clinicians at the point of care. Although there may be many specific applications, there are five major categories of these applications: results management, point of care documentation, medication management, clinical decision support, and reporting.

Results Management

Results management systems are applications that enable diagnostic studies results to be processed according to the needs of the users. In the past, results review systems enabled clinicians to view lab results. These were generally presented in print file format. While abnormal results were flagged in these reports, the data were not structured, so they could not be graphed or processed in other ways or with other data. Results management assumes that lab results are in structured form, ideally encoded using a standard vocabulary such as **Logical Observation Identifiers Names and Codes (LOINC)**, and placed into a clinical data repository with other clinical data. (The MU incentive program requires that lab results be incorporated into the EHR.) The results management functionality then enables graphing of lab results over time and against medications, vital signs, and/or other data. Given that 70 percent of diagnostic decision making depends on clinical laboratory test results (Wians 2009), results management is an important function to enhance this clinical practice.

Point-of-care Documentation

Also called **Point-of-care (POC) patient charting**, POC documentation applications guide the user in the necessary data to collect in the context of the specific patient (often using **context-sensitive** templates that react to the nature of the data being entered and that tailor the template to the specific data entry needs). Hospitals often initiate POC charting with nursing documentation, such as admission assessments, care planning, nurses notes, vital signs documentation (if not coming directly from a monitoring device), intake/output records, and other documentation. As with lab results, nurse charting is aided by standard vocabularies, such as NANDA International for nursing diagnoses and others (Lundberg et al. 2008), although none are required for the MU incentives at this time.

Physician documentation in a hospital remains largely performed by dictation of history and physical exams, consultations, operative reports, and discharge summaries with handwritten progress notes and problem lists. In order to earn the MU incentives, however, physicians must enter problems on the problem list using either ICD-9-CM or SNOMED-CT to achieve standardization of terminology. In physician practices with an EHR, however, physicians are much more apt to use the EHR for most documentation, utilizing dictation primarily for complicated cases.

POC documentation is intended to capture more complete and accurate data and to avoid duplicative data entry. For example, a nursing admission assessment may include as many as 10 or 11 different forms, each of which must have patient identification recorded and often other clinical data repeated, and taking over an hour to complete. Although nurses sometimes find that automated nursing documentation does not save time, it is acknowledged that the better information is valuable and it can be expected that there is downstream time savings from having such better information. Physicians in their practice also find similar results with POC documentation. Even though initial use of the system takes longer, most physicians are able to return to a normal documentation time or even gain some time after the learning curve.

Medication Management

Applications that support the **closed-loop medication management** process, wherein patient safety is ensured through proper drug ordering, dispensing, administering, and monitoring of reactions, are special forms of POC documentation. These systems include CPOE, e-Rx as a special type of CPOE, electronic (EMAR) or bar code medication administration record, medication reconciliation systems, and automated drug dispensing. Although there is no recommended sequence for implementing these systems, many hospitals have implemented CPOE last because it is difficult to get physicians to use such systems in the hospital. This is changing as MU incentives require use of a CPOE system (although not EMAR or BC-MAR systems at this time). In the ambulatory setting, **e-prescribing (e-Rx)** has sometimes been implemented as a stand-alone system before an EHR (and its CPOE functionality) because some insurers and Medicare were providing incentives for its use.

Computerized provider order entry (CPOE) systems enable ordering of everything from patient admission, laboratory tests, x-rays and other diagnostic studies, dietary/food and nutrition, therapies, nursing services, and consults to discharge of patient, referrals, and even building personal task lists, as well as entering orders for medications. In the past, physicians typically handwrote these orders, which were then faxed to the respective departments or transcribed by nursing personnel into an order communication system. The order communication system, however, only enabled transmission of the order to various departments' information systems. There was no CDS in the order communication system. CPOE systems today have at a minimum drug-allergy checking and drug-drug contraindication checking.

Physicians often dislike CPOE systems, at least initially, because they view order entry as a clerical task. Initial implementations also did not do a very good job of setting the sensitivity of alerts, so **alert fatigue** was often the result of an excessive amount of alerts that were then ignored. Another concern with CPOE systems is that they are based on standard order sets. These order sets reflect the current thinking about patient care from research, referred to as evidence-based medicine. Despite that EBM may reflect the best scientific evidence on how to treat a patient with a specific condition, there is rarely "one size fits all" for human beings (Cerrato 2012). A patient with a specific condition frequently has other conditions, which may not have been taken into account when the research study was performed. As a result, most standard orders need to be modified for each patient. In haste a physician may accept the standard orders or may make an error in modifying them—which may result in unintended consequences.

E-Rx is a special type of CPOE application used to write prescriptions and transmit them to retail pharmacies via the National Council for Prescription Drug Programs (NCPDP) SCRIPT standard that is sent through a pharmacy information exchange, SureScripts being the largest. E-Rx is used in physician practice as well as when a patient is discharged from the hospital or emergency service with a prescription and in hospital outpatient departments or clinics. The e-Rx system includes medication alerts and reminders just as the hospital-based CPOE system, but it also includes formulary information from PBMs that identifies whether the patient's health plan covers the cost of a drug and what copay may be required. Physicians find benefits from e-Rx systems as a result of availability of a medication list, fewer calls from pharmacies not able to read their handwriting or needing to advise the physician that a drug ordered is off formulary for a patient, and being able to receive electronic communications from retail pharmacies for renewal approvals. Recently, the Drug Enforcement Administration (DEA), which had previously banned use of e-Rx for controlled substances (such as narcotics) set special requirements to enable such use.

The medication administration record is used by nurses in a hospital to document the giving of drugs to patients.

The frequency and care that must be taken to ensure that a nurse administers the right drug is critical to avoid medication errors. As a result, computerized systems have been created. Early **electronic medication administration record (EMAR)** systems were simply electronically generated paper lists of medications from the pharmacy information system after it processed physician orders. Later, the lists were retained on the computer and nurses were expected to post the date and time of medication administration to the computer. Any exceptions to or issues with medication administration, however, were still included in handwritten nurses' notes. Most importantly, these systems, while providing a legible list of medications, did not fully address the medication five rights.

Today, many hospitals are moving to BC-MAR systems. These require the hospital to have each patient identified with a bar code (usually on a wrist band) and to package (or buy prepackaged) drugs in unit dose form, each with a bar code or **radio frequency identification (RFID)** tag that identifies the drug, dose, and intended route of administration. At the time the drug is to be administered to a patient, the nurse logs onto the BC-MAR system and scans the patient's wrist band and unit dose package. The system automatically dates and time-stamps the entry made through this process. As a result, the medication five rights have been followed. Most BC-MAR systems also enable notes to describe exceptions, such as the fact that the patient was in surgery at the time the next dose was to be administered. BC-MAR systems provide some CDS, as do CPOE systems, often including links to additional information about drugs.

Although nurses value the more legible medication lists and patient safety assurances that are part of EMAR or BC-MAR, there are issues to be overcome, just as with getting physicians to use CPOE. One issue is that to use a BC-MAR system, nurses must bring a computer, bar code device, and medication to the patient's bedside. Some hospitals use wireless **workstations on wheels (WOWs)** that include these devices as well as a drug dispensing drawer (and a long-life battery). These can be heavy to push once fully loaded. An alternative is to carry, sometimes via a sling, a tablet computer that may be outfitted with a wanding device. Walking around all day with such equipment on one's person, however, is also not comfortable. Another alternative is bedside terminals, although many hospitals express privacy concerns with respect to implementing these. Still another issue with BC-MAR in general is that the bags that contain specially compounded drugs administered intravenously require special labels, which not all hospital pharmacy information systems can accommodate, resulting in a patient safety gap.

Obviously a **medication list** is generated from the closed-loop medication management applications. The MU incentive program requires that the medications be documented using an **RxNorm** terminology. While this is a standard expression of drug names in clinical form, pharmacy information systems typically utilize the **National Drug Code**

(NDC), which is an inventory coding system. (For example, a drug may be described in the NDC with respect to its package size, such as 100 bottles of 100 pills per bottle, information not relevant in clinical administration of the drug.) It is essential that translations are able to be made throughout the closed-loop medication management process so that drug naming conventions are followed appropriately.

The **medication reconciliation** process (often referred to as "medrec" in the clinical setting) also can be automated, although not as easily as the other elements of medication management. Each time a patient is transferred across levels of care, such as when admitted, transferred into an intensive care unit, sent to surgery, and so on, a special review of medications needs to be performed. This is because very often certain medications must be discontinued or a dose changed as a result of the change in level of care. In addition, the clinicians working with the patient are different at different levels of care. Connecting all the systems at the different levels of care has been a challenge that only a few hospitals have been able to fully achieve as yet.

Finally with respect to medication management, **automated drug dispensing machines** are available that are secure and make drugs specific to patient orders readily available to nursing staff. These machines are typically filled by pharmacy department staff based on the physician orders. Although there are several manufacturers of these machines, the most common is Pyxis, sold by CareFusion. As a result, these machines are often better known as "Pyxis machines."

Clinical Decision Support

CDS is perhaps the most important reason for documenting at the point of care and is the functionality that most clearly distinguishes an EHR from paper records. CDS systems are interactive programs designed to assist clinicians in making patient care decisions.

The most common CDS systems are those that are knowledge based. These are composed of four components working in concert:

- A knowledge-based system that provides "facts," or evidence, concerning a domain of practice, such as drug knowledge
- Production rules that are a generic set of "if…then…" structures, or "rules" that draw from the knowledge base
- **An inference engine,** which is the software that controls how the rules are applied to specific facts (about the patient)
- The user interface, which is the presentation of the specific findings relative to application of a rule; this may include a set of questions or template on which to enter data, a process that checks responses for legal answers, a means to supply the user's responses to the inference engine, and alerts or reminders to the user

There are also non-knowledge-based CDS systems. These use a form of artificial intelligence (such as artificial neural networks or genetic algorithms) rather than a knowledge base, enabling the computer to learn from past patterns of clinical data. Non-knowledge-based CDS systems are less frequently found in healthcare for a number of reasons, including that use of systems to capture data (that is, EHRs) is still very new by clinicians. Even if a hospital or physician practice has used an EHR for a long time, the volume of data upon which to create an accurate pattern is often insufficient. Finally, as the name implies, knowledge from clinical trials, experts, and other sources is not included in the CDS provided. Just the same, non-knowledge-based techniques can aid in the system learning practice patterns that may help data entry, such as the system learning "favorite" medications to display first.

CDS is frequently embedded as an integral part of CPOE, e-Rx, EMAR/BC-MAR, point-of-care patient charting, and other applications, such as in a pharmacy information system that provides the pharmacy staff with information on potential drug contraindications. In addition to the CDS that may exist in any one application, more robust CDS applications, often called CDS utilities, are available that can be added to these applications and work with data supplied from multiple applications in an integrated manner. For example, there are companies that are devoted to researching and using clinical evidence to build order sets, nurse care plans, quality forecasters, and practice guidelines (Versel 2011). Researchers reporting in the *Journal of the American Medical Informatics Association* (Wright et al. 2011) identify a taxonomy of six major categories of CDS capabilities, with a total of 53 unique features across the capabilities:

- Medication dosing
- Order facilitators
- POC alerts/reminders
- Relevant information display
- Expert systems
- Workflow support

The same researchers used this taxonomy to compare commercial vendor and homegrown EHR products on what features they integrated into their products. Commercial vendors surveyed ranged widely in the features they accommodated, from 28 percent for one vendor to 94 percent to another vendor. In this survey, researchers also found that medication dosing features were most common (86 percent of vendors had these features) while expert systems were least common (36 percent of vendors had these features). (Homegrown products had slight differences but were not significantly different.) Clearly CDS is an emerging area of health IT.

Tracking the latest scientific information in making patient care decisions is critical. However, while the rewards of CDS use are great, it must be implemented carefully and must be maintained on an ongoing basis. CDS can contribute to EHR user satisfaction because users know there are controls built in to help them apply their professional knowledge in effective and efficient ways. There are also CDS utilities that can be invoked only on demand. Leonhardt (2006) points out that autopsy studies have shown that physicians seriously misdiagnose fatal illnesses about 20 percent of the time, and in fact one such situation led to the creation of a differential diagnosis CDS utility that can scan reams of medical literature much more quickly than a human could, even if willing to take the time, which often is not available. Finally, there are also CDS utilities that are stand-alone. For example, *Infection Control Today* (2010) describes a system that supports infection control nurses reduce incidence of hospital-acquired infections through quick assessments of data to which providers can respond rapidly with targeted treatment. Still, overalerting is common and often results in all alerts being ignored.

The Agency for Healthcare Research and Quality commissioned a report (Berner 2009) on the state of the art of CDS systems. The report cites that CDS is most effective when

- CDS is matched to user intentions, noting that while on-demand reminders are less likely to be overridden, automatic alerts are often ignored
- Tiering alerts so that those that prevent the most harmful results should be displayed for all users, whereas those with less impact may be displayed only for certain categories of clinicians
- Integration of CDS into work processes, as the system is more likely to be used in this configuration, although integration generally requires considerable customization

CDS systems must be kept current. There are many ways such systems can become obsolete or not function properly. Obviously, if a rule directs a clinician to perform certain diagnostic examinations or studies are based on best practices and the best practices change, the rule needs to change as well. The medical literature is replete with examples of where new evidence has suggested that an old treatment modality is not as effective as a newer one or where a correlation once believed to have existed between certain factors no longer appears to be true.

In addition to keeping rules current, it is important to ensure that each rule has the correct information to process. For example, in an emergency situation where a patient presents with chest pain, there are several possible diagnoses, each based in a different bodily system, including cardiac, respiratory, digestive, and so forth. If a CDS system requires a specific set of data to be collected for every patient presenting with chest pain and all data requirements are met, the CDS will operate properly. However, if one data element is not entered, the rule either may not fire when it should or it may fire when unnecessary, causing an annoyance. If clinicians routinely override the rule and identify such

inconsistencies in the rule firing, they will lose trust in all the CDS and the purpose of CDS is lost. Many organizations will not permit a required field to be overridden for this reason. Other organizations allow the override but have the EHR produce an alert that indicates that CDS has been negated due to lack of information, so that the users are advised that they are on their own for making the applicable decision.

However, even in cases where all necessary data are entered and a rule fires appropriately, physicians may need to override a CDS rule. For example, it may be that a patient is allergic to a medication, but having tried other medications and in consultation with the patient it is agreed to give a lower dose of the medication with heightened monitoring. This is a legitimate clinical reason for the override. Some organizations do not require explicit documentation of the rationale for overriding an alert, citing that such rationale was not previously required. However, because EHRs retain metadata indicating that a rule has fired, an attorney may question why attention was not paid to the alert in case of a lawsuit. Even if this never happens, the fired alert is likely to cause a nurse or pharmacist to double-check with the provider, and that ensuing telephone call and potential delay in getting medication to the patient could be eliminated by a simple acknowledgment that the alert was purposely overridden. The EHR should enable a pop-up for the rationale to be recorded by one simple click. Just the same, there are times when rules themselves need to be modified or turned off. In some cases, certain clinicians find certain rules highly repetitive and annoying. In evaluating whether a rule should be changed, a designated clinical committee should review the rule to determine whether its impact on the ultimate result warrants the change. It is also possible, however, to fire rules in accordance with classes of users. For example, when a house staff member logs on, he or she could have more CDS than when an attending physician logs on, or certain specialties may want more rules than others.

There are also concerns about overdependence on alerts where professional judgment may not be applied. For example, always assuming that a drug-allergy alert must be obeyed could lead to delayed or less effective treatment.

Both ignoring alerts and overdependence on alerts have caused vendors to introduce "hold harmless" clauses into their EHR contracts. Unintended consequences from either situation or other ineffective use of EHR has also caused the Food and Drug Administration (FDA) to take notice and observe that it is within its power to regulate EHR as a medical device, although such action has yet to be taken (Raths 2011).

Reporting and Analytics

While reporting and analysis of data have been performed even with paper-based health records, reporting and analytics are considered core clinical EHR applications because heretofore they have required manual abstraction of data—even from electronic systems. A significant level of POC documentation (including CPOE and BC-MAR) of structured data is necessary for the types of analytical reports clinicians need at the POC to make clinical decisions; those that executives need for business decision making; and now, with the ACA health reform legislation, those that allow the organization to promote accountable care organizations (ACOs) and patient-centered medical homes (PCMHs), which are reimbursement and whose care coordination structures are designed to link patient outcomes more closely with risk and reward structures of reimbursement (Kelly 2011).

Reporting and analyzing data have been time-consuming and error-prone tasks. Data are often not required to conform to a standard vocabulary and were therefore virtually incomparable. While the Joint Commission and the Centers for Medicare and Medicaid Services (CMS) have required reporting of core measures and CMS posts the findings on its Hospital Compare website, there was little ability to use the data for real-time or even near-real-time analytics. In fact, it has been observed that healthcare primarily performs quality measurement and reporting, but the improvement aspect is limited and not required to be reported. Physician practices do not fare any better in their quality activities. The Physician Quality Reporting System (PQRS), for example, relies primarily on Current Procedural Terminology (CPT) codes, which are often driven by reimbursement requirements and not necessarily clinically relevance.

As a result of the increasing availability of patient data in the EHR, healthcare is now beginning to use more routinely advanced analytics in clinical decision making—even at the POC and not just in research institutions (Whiting 2001). Analytics may be used in any industry, and the practice has been especially successful in retail, marketing, credit risk, and fraud analysis. Health plans are starting to use **predictive modeling** to evaluate what their future costs will look like in order to develop products accordingly, reduce cost, and ensure adequate resourcing. **Clinical analytics** is the process of gathering and examining data in order to help gain greater insight about patients (Dolan 2011). The examination of the data includes use of statistical techniques, operations research, and probability models on the data as well as data visualization techniques to provide clear and effective graphical presentations of the results.

Clinical analytics is not without its challenges (HIMSS Analytics 2010). The format and comparability of the data, even when in an electronic system, were identified previously. There can be data that are missing, such as lab results from an off-site facility. There are key data that may never be captured, such as whether the patient recovered from an illness. Additionally, there may be insufficient data to ensure the validity and reliability of the results—although this challenge can be overcome, in part, by using an analytics vendor who can pool de-identified data. Lack of staff with skills to perform analytics and train users on their value is another significant challenge. While this can partially be overcome by using a vendor, it does not bring the analytics to the bedside.

Data Quality Management

As more data are now used for clinical decision making and elsewhere for healthcare business decision making, it is becoming increasingly important to ensure the quality of the data, often referred to as **data quality management**. This is true for both direct data entry and data that may reside in database tables and are altered during an upgrade or other system configuration process.

With respect to data entry errors, it is easy to click the wrong item, enter too many or too few digits in a number, copy narrative from one note to create another and not change all the required variables, underuse of structured data in favor of comments fields, or override CDS. HIM professionals should assist their care delivery organizations in updating policies and procedures that describe the required documentation practices for the EHR, which build on and refine documentation practices for paper-based records. The organization should also require checks and balances in the EHR to support data quality (such as valid values for a field, alerts to enter data for a required field, checks for internal consistency for right and left, and so on) and utilize regular data quality audits. For example, if it is found that a comment field is repeatedly used to enter a specific data value that is already on the drop-down menu, this may mean the EHR cannot process that data, defeating the purpose of enhanced utility in EHRs. This is a user training issue that must be addressed. Many clinicians really do not appreciate that the EHR is more than an automated chart. They often are so grateful that they can access data they previously could not that they forget there are many other benefits that rely on structured data. However, if the findings of the audit reveal that the value placed in the comment field is one that is not on the drop-down menu and occurs frequently, there should be consideration for adding the choice or identifying it as a synonym, as applicable. Again, many new users will not think about how the system can be improved. They assume that what they are given is something with which they must work. The result can be some growing unhappiness that the EHR is not doing more than the paper chart is for the level of effort they put forth in learning to use it.

A special case of data quality concern centers on the common practice of data reuse in computer-based systems. Because it is easy to copy and paste, clinicians soon learn to use this capability where it exists. As mentioned earlier, such a practice often results in not fully addressing all the required variables within the documentation. Even if the data element copied from one record to another does not contribute to a medical error, the inconsistency or incomplete documentation can result in the questioning of the entire record if the record is brought to court. Many organizations are disabling this capability where they can, or monitoring for it with applicable sanctions. Yet others have found that the practice

Figure 5.5.   Documentation Audit

- Data Governance
  - Stakeholders
    - Users
    - Developers
    - Consumers
  - Education
    - Awareness
    - Commitment
  - Stewardship
    - Responsibility
    - Accountability
  - Discovery
  - Change Control
    - Document request for change or discovery finding
    - Review information/data models and data dictionary to evaluate risk for making the change
    - Obtain approval from stakeholders to make change
    - Implement and test change
    - Document change
    - Follow up and evaluate impact of change

- Discovery
  - Receiving complaints
    - Why do we have to enter these data?
      - Evaluate us of data against information/data model for need
      - Evaluate alternative sources (e.g., patient/family, other staff)
      - Evaluate for potential repetitive data
    - I can't find the value for this field
      - Evaluate if desired value is valid
      - Look for synonyms
    - This information is out of date or inconsistent with current evidence-based guidelines
  - Observing use
    - Are users entering data at point of care?
    - What data are entered elsewhere?
  - Auditing structured data entries
    - Are data entered in comment fields where structured data choices exist?
    - Are data entered in comment fields because structured values do not exist?
    - Are any values never used, and why not?
    - Are certain values used too frequently, and why (for example, personal preference versus evidence-based guidelines)?
  - Auditing unstructured data entries (for example, comment fields, macros, copy and paste, short dictations)
    - Are entries complete?
    - Are entries unique to patient?
    - Could narrative be generated from structured data for patient story?
  - Auditing corrections, amendments, deletions
    - Visible?
    - Date/time stamped and authenticated?
    - Linked to applicable entry?

is sufficiently useful so they put users on notice that they are individually at risk for errors that may result. Clearly, each organization should do a risk analysis to address such issues for itself.

Documentation audits within the EHR should also look for completeness, timeliness, internal consistency, and other factors that have typically been evaluated in paper documentation (see figure 5.5).

For example, when reviewing patients' data within the EHR, do all patients on a unit appear to have been given their morning meds only seconds apart? This is not feasible in walking from room to room, so it is possible that nurses have found a workaround where they are scanning all the meds at the nursing unit instead of at the point of care—defeating the medication five rights of ensuring right patient, right drug, right dose, right route, and right time.

In addition to reviewing the EHR content itself, it is important to do walkarounds and see how users are using the EHR. This should be done periodically, and not just after go-live but also when upgrades or even slight modifications

are applied. For example, a desired fix may necessitate a slight change in the placement of a data entry field on an assessment form within the EHR, which then may cause an unexpected workflow and process change. While such a change (that is, a change in the placement of a data entry field) to the EHR should be communicated via pop-up at the time of log-in for affected users, choosing that same day to do a walkaround provides the extra emphasis on the commitment and support the organization is making in its EHR and to the clinical transformation initiative and provides an opportunity to observe any unexpected impact on workflow that may be revealed by the EHR users. Walking around also can demonstrate that those responsible for the technology and compliance are approachable. Just as in the paper world, documentation audits and walkarounds should not be punitive but serve to enhance the EHR's usefulness.

Finally, an increasing cause of data error is occurring as a result of heightened use of core clinical applications where source systems are either not connected or an audit of all changes in one application is not traced to potential impact on other applications. ISMP (2007) describes where a hospital's pharmacy information system had recently been upgraded and new medication route codes implemented so they would be more descriptive and use more familiar abbreviations. However, when an order for "Humulin N 40 units" was entered into the computer, the pharmacist did not notice that the route of administration had defaulted to "IJ" on the EMAR. Initially the nurse thought IJ was intrajugular, but the patient did not have a jugular line. After reviewing the original (handwritten) order, which did not include the route of administration, the nurse interpreted the "N" to be IV and administered the drug intravenously. However, Humulin N should never be administered IV and the patient became hypoglycemic. Clearly the changes made to the pharmacy information system were not evaluated to determine their impact on other systems. In addition, of course, this is clearly a case for CPOE that requires all components of the medication order to be entered and for a BC-MAR system that supplies CDS and access to drug knowledge bases.

When technology, software applications, and workflow processes throughout the organization are synchronized to support the work of the system's many end users, the organization has achieved process interoperability, a situation where all its subsystems are able to process data in like manner, with similar access controls and other policy and process constraints.

Supporting Infrastructure for EHR

Many of the basic hardware components that support the EHR were described in chapter 4. Reference has also been made in this chapter for needing standard vocabularies that ensure data comparability, and these are further discussed in chapter 8. There are, however, some important elements of those components that need special attention once the core clinical EHR components are acquired. These include the nature of the databases used in managing EHR data, storage management and e-discovery, special software to support application software, human–computer interfaces, and enhanced security controls.

Databases are obviously the means to hold data for processing. Every application has its own database. But the integration of data from multiple independent systems into a central database is generally considered an essential element for a comprehensive EHR. This not only provides access to data but also integrates them in a manner that makes them more readily processable in real time and for CDS. For example, the CPOE system is able to process drug-allergy and drug-drug contraindication alerts in its own database (although in this case it taps into a separate drug knowledge base to do so). The CPOE database, however, does retain lab results. To support drug-lab checking, such as whether a patient will tolerate a drug known to be contraindicated in patients with poor liver function, there must be the ability to use both drug and lab data. In order to collect

and process data in this integrated manner, a special database is used that incorporates special indexing and management functions to capture, sort, process, and present information back to users—specific to a patient and in a split second of time. Such a database is called a data repository. To distinguish repositories that focus on clinical information (instead of financial or administrative data), the term **clinical data repository (CDR)** is used. CDRs are relational databases that have been optimized to perform **online transaction processing (OLTP)**. Each and every time a user enters data, retrieves data, views data, and is supplied an alert specific to a given patient, that action is considered a transaction.

A CDR is typically used for processing transactions, and even though they may be very complex, each transaction does not require processing an immense amount of data at one time. When complex reporting and analytics are to be performed on data, a **clinical data warehouse (CDW)** may be the more appropriate database structure to use. Data warehouses are often hierarchical or multidimensional and are designed to receive very large volumes of data (often as an extraction of data from a repository) and perform complex, analytical processes on the data. This processing is referred to as **online analytical processing (OLAP)**. Data can be mined and processed in many ways. For example, a data warehouse may be used for clinical quality improvement and best practice guideline development. It is not to suggest that reports cannot be generated from any individual application or from a CDR; however, complex, analytical processing will degrade the processing power of the CDR and frustrate users. Hence, small organizations that do not acquire a CDW tend to generate fewer complex reports, process them at night or on weekends when the CDR is less active, or rely on external CDWs to which they send data for processing. Analytics vendors were described previously.

Storage management is increasingly important in an EHR environment (Hardy 2010). The volume of data captured by information systems in general, and in particular by EHRs, is becoming immense. In addition, there is a growing expectation that data should be accessible in real time for very long periods of time. Finally, as clinicians become dependent on the computer for all their data needs, they will not tolerate downtime or delays for retrieving archived data. As a result, while storage media are becoming less expensive, managing data storage has become increasingly important. Many hospitals are creating specific storage management service units within IT departments. **Storage management** is the process of determining on what type of media to store data, deciding how rapidly data must be accessible, arranging for replication of storage for backup and disaster recovery, and determining where storage systems should be maintained. Storage management requires an understanding of the nature of the data to be maintained and its potential future use.

New technologies should aid storage management. Many healthcare organizations are starting to use **storage area networks**, which are networks whose sole purpose is the transfer of data between computers and storage elements (Tate et al. 2006). Some healthcare organizations are beginning to look at virtualization to reduce both processing and storage hardware costs. **Virtualization** is the emulation of one or more computers within a software platform that enables one physical computer to share resources across other computers (Blokdijk 2010). Even newer to healthcare is **cloud computing**, which is the application of virtualization to a variety of computing resources to enable rapid access to computing services via the Internet (Mell and Grance 2011). Cloud computing is not limited to storage management, as some EHR vendors are providing EHRs as **Software as a service (SaaS)**, a subscription service to EHRs delivered over the cloud. Although more than storage, **redundancy** in servers, networking, and telecommunications capabilities such that there are at least two means of processing, moving, and exchanging data must also be part of **contingency planning** that includes backup, emergency mode operations, and disaster recovery. These are often new strategies for many care delivery organizations as they approach adopting the mission-critical systems that are EHR components.

The introduction of an EHR should trigger a review of the organization's retention schedule, with an eye toward potentially enabling a realistic retention schedule for electronic data. Another element of the retention schedule should be to understand the impact of e-discovery and address what will be retained for what period of time. **E-discovery** refers to the Amendments to Federal Rules of Civil Procedure and Uniform Rules Relating to Discovery of Electronically Stored Information. E-discovery makes audit trails, the source code of software used, metadata ("data about data"), and any other electronic information that is not typically considered the legal health record subject to a motion for compulsory discovery. Three examples serve to illustrate:

- Nurses have long used a card system for annotating their care plans for their patients—written in pencil so they may be updated as needed. On discharge, these have been discarded and were not considered part of the legal health record. This has been the standard of practice, but in an EHR, the care plans are recorded permanently. It may be feasible to delete these from the EHR. But it is yet another new step, which some nurses may always remember to do and others may not, and some nurses may choose to delete or not, based on certain circumstances they perceive to be important. The inconsistency of the practice is very likely subject to question in a court, which may request this information through an e-discovery motion. Because the EHR will record this, it is probably best to retain the information in light of the potential for e-discovery.
- Documentation of system crashes in the IT department is actually a HIPAA requirement (under the Security Rule standard on information system activity review).

There has been more than one incident of a lawsuit lost or large settlement made when an information system activity log could not be produced for the court as proof of the timing of a system crash in comparison to the timing of a specific data entry, dictation, transcription, or signature on a document.

- Documentation associated with CDS systems is increasingly important. This includes what changes are made to the EHR's data dictionary that may impact the firing of a CDS rule, changes made to the rules themselves, as well as documentation of overrides and their rationale. For instance, if a data element is required and users want to make it optional, a data analyst should study the potential impact of this change. If it is very likely to cause a CDS rule to misfire and there is a high risk for a negative result, the change probably should not be made. If a change is made, it should made only with the approval of a clinical committee that has studied the impact and determined that the organization is willing to take whatever risk exists. This should be documented within the data dictionary as the change is made. Likewise, if a CDS rule is turned off or changed, the risk must be understood. Finally, if a clinician is provided with an alert and ignores it, it is possible that an attorney may request a motion to review both the software and an audit trail, asking why the alert was overridden. If not documented, the clinician may not be able to recall or may be found in noncompliance with standards of practice.

Special software to support application software is increasingly needed in an EHR environment. Such software includes interfaces and interface engines and their associated **data exchange standards,** as well as inference engines, registry systems, and knowledge bases previously described.

Because an EHR relies on exchanging data with multiple source (and destination) systems, communication across these systems is essential. But few of these systems are fully integrated. **Integration** in this context means that the systems exchange data seamlessly without the need for an **interface,** or special software to negotiate the exchange. In most cases, however, source systems are from different vendors, or vendors who have acquired different products and "bolted" them together with a strong interface. The result is often that applications do not exchange data easily with one another, or with a CDR into which much of the data should be put for ease of EHR use. In order for an interface to be written, however, the applications' software must be written to conform to a data exchange standard protocol. HL7 is the predominant standards development organization that develops standards for exchange of clinical data. Likewise, the **Accredited Standards Committee X12 (ASC X12)** develops standards for exchange of the HIPAA TCS. **Digital Imaging and Communications in Medicine (DICOM)** develops standards for exchange of clinical images, and the NCPDP develops standards for exchange of retail pharmacy financial and administrative data and for prescriptions. Where a hospital may have as many 200 to 500 different applications and an increasing number of medical devices that now must be connected to information systems (physician practices will have fewer applications, but still the potential exists to have at least 2 if not 20 or more), there are potentially even more interfaces needed, as an application may need to communicate with multiple other applications. Consider only the R-ADT application that must communicate with virtually every other clinical system. The result, then, could be that hospitals may have hundreds of interfaces. While many vendors do write their software to comply with the standard protocols so that interfaces can be written, there are nuances in the standards that do not make them as "standard" as desirable and the interfaces must be kept up-to-date as changes are made to both the underlying applications and the standards themselves. Hence an **interface engine** is a tool to manage the multiplicity of interfaces and track changes.

Recall that data exchange standards only focus on **syntax**, or structure and format, of the data. Data exchange standards are often called **message format standards** for this reason. The interoperability achieved through application of message format standards is often referred to as **technical interoperability.** Technically, the data from one application can be exchanged with another application. Technical interoperability, however, does not address **semantics,** or the meaning of the data. **Semantic interoperability** requires use of a standard **vocabulary** to ensure that when data are exchanged the meaning of the data will be understood.

While data exchange standards are challenging today, there is the expectation that applications will ultimately be moved from a client/server architecture to a web services architecture (WSA) that can take advantage of **Extensible Markup Language** (XML) constructs. XML is a specification for creating custom markup languages that uses a set of annotations to text that gives instructions regarding how text is to be displayed. HL7 Version 3 messages are based on an XML encoding syntax. However, the message standard is not backward compatible with its Version 2.x protocols; hence, until such time that care delivery organizations move from a client/server architecture to WSA, the value of the HL7 Version 3 messaging component is somewhat limited for use in structured data exchange. There are, however, some new uses that are being made of the Version 3 standard, and it is widely deployed in Europe and in countries that did not have the legacy infrastructure as the United States.

Data capture and retrieval technology must also be reassessed in light of EHR and its clinical users. The term **human–computer interface (HCI)** is used to describe these technologies because they are the construct that enables exchange of data between the human and the computer. That interface is improving, but still challenging. HCIs must direct data capture in a clear and concise manner for both the

novice and the power user. Data capture as well as visualization techniques, which were mentioned when describing clinical analytics (how data, alerts, reminders, and other elements of EHR use are displayed), have a significant impact on patient safety. Consideration must be given to screen size and effective use of screen "real estate," the nature of icons and the universality of their meaning, and even sound, animation, and color with respect to the healthcare environment, which has a lot of sounds and different types of lighting. It has been mentioned that clinicians are mobile and often work in teams that require viewing the same information simultaneously. Structured data entry is counterintuitive to most clinicians, so these tools must be easy to use. Especially for documentation of progress notes, clinicians prefer to be able to read narrative, so structured data entry must be able to be converted to a narrative output. Different techniques are available, each with its own benefits and risks. These include the computer wrapping narrative around structured data to produce sentences or paragraphs, DRT, or more sophisticated NLP, or through macros or copy and paste techniques that reuse standard phraseology.

Usability, or the overall ability of a user to capture and retrieve data efficiently and effectively, has been an increasingly recognized issue of importance. The **Certification Commission for Health Information Technology** (CCHIT 2009), which was the original organization that certified EHR products and is now one of several ONC-authorized testing and certifying bodies (ONC-ATCBs), offers a comprehensive certification program—certifying beyond the basic MU criteria. For its comprehensive certification of ambulatory EHRs, CCHIT provides a usability rating it calls PERUSE (from perceived usability).

Enhanced privacy and security controls may be both more available in an EHR and more needed in an EHR environment. This has been recognized by the proposed modifications to the HIPAA privacy and security rules in HITECH. Although most of HIPAA's privacy requirements are accomplished through administrative and operational activities, EHR technology can assist in carrying out a number of the privacy standards. An EHR can provide highly effective **access controls** to meet the HIPAA Privacy Rule **minimum necessary standard** requirements. Role-based access controls (RBACs) are used where only specific classes of persons may access **protected health information (PHI)**. Context-based access controls (CBACs) add the dimensions that control not only class of persons but specific categories of information and under specific conditions for which access is permitted. Because the minimum necessary requirement does not pertain to disclosures for healthcare treatment, some care delivery organizations have interpreted this so broadly as to include that any healthcare professional may have access to any patient, or at least any physician and/or nurse may have such access. (This form of access control is usually referred to as user-based access control [UBAC]). It must be observed, however, that not every clinician has a treatment relationship with every patient. In an emergency, the EHR should have emergency access procedures that can be invoked by a simple additional click on a pop-up window, for instance, indicating the nature of the emergency. This function is often called "**break-the-glass**," a term that is taken from the action one takes to break the glass to reach a fire alarm. This usually also generates a special **audit log** that can be reviewed later to ensure that the situation was truly an emergency. Having such a strong control has been a huge deterrent for the curious. In another example, when a patient requests confidential communication, there needs to be a way to notify providers that an alternate address or phone number must be used to contact the patient concerning certain information. Again, a note on the chart cover may be the only available solution in the paper environment, but a flag that pops up on a computer screen or that automatically routes calls or correspondence would provide much greater assurance that the patient's request is being carried out. Many technical measures are available to help protect patient privacy.

HIPAA's security requirements are generally more technical than the privacy requirements, but they also require establishing policies to direct how the technical tools will be applied. As noted under the privacy discussion, access controls used in healthcare organizations in the past have been quite weak. As a result of heightened concerns on the part of the public and because of an increasing rate of identity theft in general and medical identity theft in particular (Irby 2010), state governments and now the federal government under the HITECH data breach notification requirements (45 CFR Parts 160, 162, and 164, 2009) are cracking down. As a result, many care delivery organizations are adopting more stringent security controls, sanctions, and other formal processes to aid in data protection. Because so many security incidents have occurred surrounding use of laptops, other portable and mobile devices, remote storage services, and remote access capabilities, the federal government issued a HIPAA Security Guidance document in December 2006, providing specific cautions and recommendations for policy development, heightened training, and addressing incidents. It also strongly recommended possible risk management strategies including two-factor authentication, increased backup, password protection for all files, encryption for all portal devices, strong physical security protections for mobile devices, and prohibition against transmission of PHI via open networks, such as the Internet. Yet again in 2009, the federal government issued guidance specifying the technologies and methodologies that render PHI unusable, unreadable, or indecipherable.

More attention is being paid to security, but apparently not considered enough. The MU incentive criteria added a requirement for a **security risk analysis** to be conducted to determine the appropriate level of security controls to put into place to ensure not only **confidentiality** of PHI within EHRs (so it is not wrongfully disclosed), but also data **integrity** (such as encryption and other security controls so data are not altered as they are stored on electronic media or transmitted) and data **availability** (through various forms of contingency planning—backup, emergency operations, and disaster recovery). A risk analysis, as illustrated in figure 5.6, is a systematic process of identifying security measures to afford protections given an organization's specific environment, including where the measures are located, what level of automation they have, how sensitive the information is that needs protection, what remediation will cost, and many other factors. A security risk analysis should lead to ongoing security (and privacy) compliance auditing (Amatayakul 2009).

Other heightened security controls are also being mandated, such as the use of **two-factor authentication** (that is, a password and token) for e-prescribing of controlled substances (21 CFR Parts 1300, 1304, 1306, and 1311, 2010).

Figure 5.6.   A security risk analysis

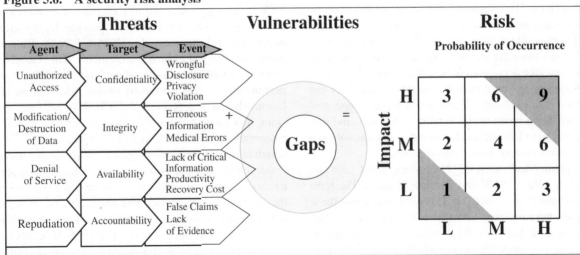

Modifications to the HIPAA privacy and security rules will make business associates directly accountable to the regulations and not just via a contractual obligation with the covered entity. **Health breach notification** from PHRs has also been mandated by the Federal Trade Commission (16 CFR Part 318, 2009).

Systems to Provide Connectivity

The federally sanctioned definition of EHR includes the requirement for use of nationally recognized interoperability standards so data can be shared across more than one healthcare organization. The **MU** incentive criteria require the ability to exchange key clinical information not only with providers but also with patients and includes the provision of electronic copies of discharge instructions, clinical summaries for office visits, and timely electronic access. Coordinating care across the continuum and consumer empowerment are key principles of the federal government's focus on building a better health system.

Clinical messaging was an early form of connectivity, most commonly between providers. If any PHI was exchanged, encryption was sometimes deployed—although the lack of interoperability between encryption software products sometimes made that difficult to do.

Web portals (secure gateways to a local area network [Internet] based on Internet technology) are more commonly used today to provide secure connectivity. This technology is a step up from clinical messaging because not only may messages be exchanged securely but also direct access to certain applications may be provided. For example, if the hospital has a CPOE system, providers may be granted access to the system through a **provider portal**. This enables them to enter orders as if they were in the hospital, based on organizational policy. There may also be a **patient portal** set up by a healthcare organization for use by patients. For example, patients may be able to exchange secure e-mail messages with their providers, such as to request an appointment, for access to lab results, to obtain access to a patient health summary, or for tailored instructions for taking medications, wound care, and so on. **E-visits** are online provider encounters, for which some health plans have started providing reimbursement and which can save patients an office visit and associated costs (Watson et al. 2010). The American Medical Association (Assatourians et al. 2010) and the American Academy of Family Practice (2008), among other specialty groups, have endorsed e-visits, providing guidelines for their use. Although the MU incentive program criteria do not require a portal for exchange of information, physician practices that are seeking recognition as a PCMH will find that a portal is encouraged by the National Committee for Quality Assurance (NCQA 2011).

Continuity of care record (CCR) or **continuity of care document (CCD)** standards are yet another form of connectivity, required in the MU incentive program. The CCR originally was conceived by the Massachusetts Medical Society as a means to standardize referral information and was ratified as a standard under ASTM International (2005) with assistance from HIMSS and other medical societies. The CCR is a specification of data that is most useful as a snapshot of a patient's health condition and the data that should be able to be produced in CCR (or CCD) format directly from the EHR. The CCR may be rendered as a PDF or as an XML file. The CCD is a combination of HL7's Version 3 **clinical document architecture (CDA)** and the CCR.

HL7's CDA is an XML-based markup standard that specifies the encoding, structure, and semantics of a healthcare document (not limited to the content of the CCR). It enables healthcare documents to be transported using HL7 Version 2.x, HL7 Version 3, DICOM, MIME attachments to e-mail, HTTP, or FTP. (When the HIPAA claims attachment standard was first proposed in 2005, the CDA was identified as one format for claims attachments. Today, the ACA requires adoption of a claims attachment standard—although its specification has not yet been finalized.) When the CDA and CCR are combined, the resultant CCD provides an XML-based markup standard to encode, structure, and identify the semantics of the CCR.

PHRs are yet another form of connectivity that is becoming popular with some patients and the federal government, health plans, and employers who are promoting their use for value-driven healthcare. HL7 (2008) has adopted the PHR-System Functional Model, which offers standard content for their use. PHRs come in many forms.

Although fewer than expected, people are adopting PHRs and the majority of individuals who do retain a PHR do so today on paper form, keeping paper copies of discharge summaries or printouts of instructions (Lewis 2011). There are, however, an increasing number of EHRs that support a PHR, as well as commercial PHR vendors selling directly to consumers. In general, PHRs range from being fairly unsophisticated, where patients can direct providers to send an e-fax to a given website or they can upload documents or enter information themselves, to quite comprehensive, where direct feeds from a provider or health plan as well as structured templates for the individual to enter his or her own data are provided. Although many providers remain concerned that the volume of information they may have to review from a PHR is not reimbursable as well as being skeptical about the accuracy of patient-reported data, there is a small but growing interest in having patients more engaged in their healthcare through keeping a PHR.

Health plans are particularly interested in populating PHRs they support with problem lists and medication lists from claims data. While there are some concerns about how clinically relevant diagnosis information may be from claims data, certainly the fact that the health plan can provide this information across all providers is attractive. The health plan can then provide direct disease management support to patients.

Similarly, PHRs that are linked, or tethered, to EHRs enable the provider to direct specific information to the patient's PHR as well as retrieve information from the patient's PHR (Connecting for Health 2006). In more comprehensive forms of PHRs, the source of the data is identifiable and the data entered by any given source is only able to be altered by that source—maintaining the integrity of all data. Although these tethered forms of PHR may only contain the information from the one provider that supports the PHR, the ability for the patient to enter his or her own data can be an aid to the provider. Certainly, the patient can log on in advance of a visit or at a kiosk in the waiting room and enter his or her own medical history, family history, and history of present illness and respond to structured questions that provide a review of systems. Some patient monitoring devices may also be connected to the PHR. These functions save considerable documentation time during the visit, where this information only needs to be reviewed and validated. The time savings can then be spent on more thorough examination, treatment planning, and education (Bachman 2007).

Telehealth may be considered a form of connectivity. Telehealth includes a set of technology and processes that enables delivery of healthcare services (and information) via telecommunications technologies. Telehealth is not new and does not require an EHR. In fact, the Veterans Administration (VA) only requires a dial-up telephone connection. Most organizations performing telehealth have more sophisticated telecommunications, videoconferencing equipment, and other devices than a dial-up telephone line, but the VA obviously must address the lowest common denominator as it reaches out to veterans in remote parts of the country. Telehealth is an excellent means to supplement a healthcare

organization's capabilities such as for remote intensive care unit monitoring (Wright 2005), although there are also questions as to whether critical care outcomes are actually improved (Kahn 2011) or are only supplements to staffing. Telehealth can be used to provide emergency care, offer consultations across great distances (or in limited access areas, even including inner-city areas), monitor local patients with chronic disease, track progress in recovery of certain types of illnesses or injuries (Melville 2012), and bring sign language to the hearing impaired during a local healthcare encounter (Hirsch and Marano 2007).

Health information exchange (HIE), via a local, regional, or state-based HIEO, is yet another means to connect disparate care delivery organizations. The eHealth Initiative 2011 survey identifies that there are 255 HIE initiatives that have been started since 2004, with 24 having sustainable business models. Various models of HIE exist. Figure 5.7 describes the three primary types of HIE models, although most end up with a hybrid structure. The federated model contains no central location of data. Health information is exchanged in a point-to-point manner across organizational participants. The consolidated model is one in which there is a central store of data that are logically separated with access controls requiring specific authorization for sharing the data. The consistent federated model utilizes independent "vaults" or databases so the data are centrally managed but both logically and physically separated.

In general, an HIEO needs to have a governance structure, participation agreements, policies and procedures for exchanging health information, and a funding mechanism—ideally a fee structure for ongoing sustainability. (Many HIEOs were created under and continue

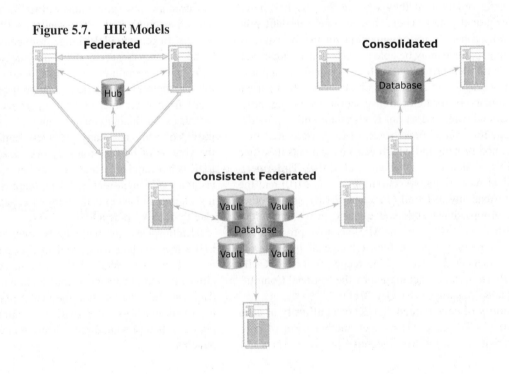

Figure 5.7.   HIE Models

Figure 5.8.   HIEO Services

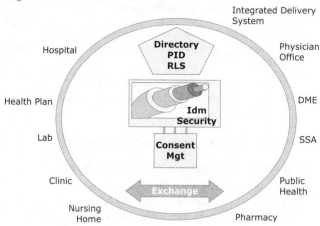

to exist through grants.) The services HIEOs supply are highly varied, but all will supply some basic services, illustrated in figure 5.8. These include patient identification, usually using an **identity-matching algorithm** in which specified patient demographic information is compared to select the patient for whom information is to be exchanged. The algorithmic process is determined by the vendor supplying the service and uses sophisticated probability equations to identify patients. There is increasing interest in using a unique patient identifier, despite the US Congress prohibition on spending any federal money to create such a national identifier. Another basic service is a **record locator service (RLS)**. The RLS is a process that seeks information about where a patient, once identified, may have a health record available to the HIEO. Not to be confused with patient identification, **identity management** provides

security functionality, including determining who (or what information system) is authorized to access information, authentication services, audit logging, encryption, and transmission controls. Consent management is yet another basic HIEO service. In **consent management**, patients may opt in or opt out of having their health information exchanged. As noted before, the patient will often provide a consent directive for this purpose.

Finally, a **nationwide health information network (NHIN)** is under development. The NHIN provides the technology to support exchange across disparate HIEOs. Several projects have been funded by the federal government under the ONC. At this time, the NHIN, as illustrated in figure 5.9, is being used by certain federal agencies and providers using a special participation agreement called a Data Use and Reciprocal Support Agreement (DURSA) in a limited production mode.

See chapter 9 for a full discussion of health information exchange and the nationwide health information network.

EHRs in Other Types of Healthcare Institutions

Hospitals and physician practices have generally been the early adopters of EHRs. They have been discussed together in this chapter because increasingly they are using the EHR systems from the same vendor, they are connecting on a much more regular and intensive basis, and hospitals depend on their physicians to adopt the technology in the hospital as well as in their own practices. Other types of healthcare providers, however, are adopting various forms of EHRs in increasing numbers.

Figure 5.9.   NHIN

Health Bank or
PHR Support Organization

Community Health
Centers

Community #1

CDC

IHS

VA

Common "Dial Tone" and "Chain of Trust" among NHIN Nodes
Enabled by Governance Structure and **DURSA**

SSA

CMS

Integrated
Delivery System

NCI

DoD

Community #2

The Internet

Standards, Specifications and Agreements for Secure Connections

Behavioral health facilities find the integration of data from multiple sources especially helpful in coordination of care. A number of behavioral health EHR products are on the market, and some were certified under the original EHR product certification program. At this time, however, behavioral health professionals who are not physicians do not qualify for MU incentives. Somewhat related to behavioral health are human services agencies. These often have a behavioral health component but also manage assisted living facilities, child care services, adult day care, and many other programs that have at least some need for EHR types of recordkeeping and are, in fact, moving to adopting automated systems to support their needs.

Long-term and post-acute care (LTPAC) has been a relatively early adopter of at least health IT components. Home health agencies have for some time adopted handheld devices to capture data in compliance with regulatory requirements. Nursing home facilities have a difficult time affording systems, but their highly structured data-reporting requirements also make them good candidates for simple EHR systems.

Finally, health plans collect a tremendous amount of data about individuals from claims, direct feeds from commercial labs, and claims attachments. Most health plans are creating databases that can be sorted by patients as their EHRs for disease management or data in aggregate can be used for analytics.

Check Your Understanding 5.2

Match the category of EHR system components to the specific functionality and technology:

    A. Financial and administrative system
    B. Ancillary or clinical departmental system
    C. Core clinical EHR applications
    D. Data quality management
    E. Supporting infrastructure
    F. Systems to provide connectivity

    1. ____ Storage area network

    2. ____ E-prescribing

    3. ____ Eligibility verification

    4. ____ Nutrition and food services system

    5. ____ Clinical analytics

    6. ____ Usability

    7. ____ Data reuse

    8. ____ Continuity of care record

    9. ____ Inference engine

    10. ____ Practice management system

Multiple Choice:

11. The continuity of care document (CCD) enables the continuity of care record (CCR) to be

    A. Compiled from an EHR
    B. Given to the patient
    C. Transported electronically
    D. Used in a personal health record

12. The standards development organization that provides standards for picture archiving and communication systems (PACS) is

    A. Accredited Standards Committee X12 (ASC X12)
    B. Digital Imaging and Communications in Medicine (DICOM)
    C. Health Level Seven (HL7)
    D. Radiological Society of North America (RSNA)

13. A clinical data warehouse (CDW) is optimized to

    A. Archive data for real-time accessibility
    B. Conduct online transaction processing
    C. Perform online analytical processing
    D. Store documents and other digital information

14. Which of the following is NOT a form of clinical decision support (CDS)?

    A. Drug-allergy alert
    B. Interface
    C. Presentation of a context-sensitive template
    D. Workflow support

15. Which of the following provides for the five rights of safe medication administration?

    A. Bar code medication administration record
    B. Computerized provider order entry
    C. Electronic medication administration record
    D. All of the above

EHR System Challenges

The greatest advantage of an EHR is its contribution to the quality of care and patient safety. Greatly enhanced access to data is currently its most important feature. Beyond the ability to retrieve data is the capability to use data. In the past, most clinicians did not truly value information as a tool to help them care for patients, except for limited, short-term results data. For the most part, recording information about patient care was viewed as a necessary evil. However, if such information could guide clinicians' work, help them communicate to others better, and help avoid errors, the EHR should truly become the much-enhanced utility that the IOM originally envisioned.

The greatest disadvantages of an EHR are directly related to its greatest advantages: enhanced use and usability make the EHR a significant investment not only in direct cost but also in gaining executive support, clinician adoption, system configuration, training, and maintenance. In addition, there are still some lingering concerns about legal and regulatory aspects, heightened privacy and security concerns, and new concerns surrounding unintended consequences from poorly implemented or adopted systems.

Cost-Benefit, Return on Investment, and Financing

EHR systems are undoubtedly expensive, even as costs are decreasing. The cost of an EHR system for a hospital is very difficult to generalize because a single system is not purchased. Rather, source systems are integrated into a repository and other applications are acquired that collectively comprise the EHR. Costs also vary over time. However, estimates range from less than $1 million to $3 million for a critical access hospital, $5 to $15 million for a small community hospital with generally a single vendor, $10 to $25 million or more for a small to medium-sized community hospital with a multiplicity of vendors that require either extensive interfacing or complete replacement, to upwards of $100 million for a large IDN to acquire the hardware, software, and human resources to fully implement an EHR. For physician practices, the cost is somewhat easier to estimate because the system being purchased is generally more self-contained. For very small practices (one to three physicians), an EHR may cost around $5,000 to $15,000 per physician. Costs go up as the practice increases in size because of the increase in complexity. There are generally more source systems to interface, and often the practices want greater customizability and more comprehensive functionality. Costs for such systems range from $25,000 to $50,000 or more per physician (also depending on whether a practice management system is acquired or replaced as part of the EHR acquisition) (Hoyt 2011).

As previously noted, the benefits of these systems are often difficult to quantify. Their primary benefits are quality and patient safety. However, there are other benefits that do accrue specific financial rewards. For hospitals, there can be an impact on the clerical workforce, admissions personnel, billers, transcriptionists, couriers, and other support staff, although many staff can be redeployed doing document scanning, data preload prior to go-live, documentation audits, and other activities, especially if staff are interested in acquiring new knowledge and skills. Costs of storing paper charts should be reduced. Although nurses are rarely, if ever, eliminated, overtime and temporary staff costs may be reduced or eliminated. The impact on nursing is much more that their time is freed up to perform more professional nursing functions. This has a downstream benefit to patient safety and quality of care. Hospitals also generally find improvements in charge capture, reduced repetitive tests, use of lower-cost drugs, shorter lengths of stay because actions can be more timely, and other savings from clinical decision support. Bed turnover time may be reduced, discharge planning may be improved, and the ability to handle surges in patient load may be easier. Still, the greatest impact is the reduction in errors of all types, which ultimately impacts the bottom line through better positioning for contracting, improved likelihood of better accreditation and licensure outcomes, and, more recently, incentives offered by Medicare and other payers, especially for physician offices but also for hospitals. For physician offices, many of these same benefits apply. In addition, some offices find that they can see more patients in a day because of productivity improvements. Other offices are able to add physician extenders (for example, nurse practitioners or physician assistants) using freed-up paper chart storage space, thus enhancing revenues to the group. Level of service (evaluation and management) coding support generally improves revenues from 2 to 3 percent to as much as 10 to 20 percent, depending on the quality of coding performed prior to EHR adoption and sometimes the specialty of the practice.

However, the benefits must be weighed against not only the cost of the EHR but also other factors that go into the total cost of ownership (TCO). For example, more staff trained in health informatics may be necessary. Other IT support staff needs may increase or be outsourced. Even the most rudimentary of EHR systems require some effort to implement. Data dictionaries must be created, rules must be reviewed, templates must be reviewed or developed, screen layouts potentially may have to be customized, reports have to be structured, and there is extensive testing. These activities are often referred to as system build, or system configuration. To not just implement the system but to gain full adoption by all intended users, there must be considerable process mapping and workflow analysis and redesign. Training is required for everyone, even for those who may have used another EHR system, because not only is each one different, but also every implementation is different due to the variations in source systems, customizations, and organizational preferences. Today, almost every new physician has done a rotation through a VA facility that has a robust EHR, so as these physicians enter the workforce, there will be an increasing surge of interest in EHRs. In fact, many organizations find that having an EHR is now contributory to successful recruitment of physicians, nurses, and other healthcare professionals. Finally, because an EHR is a clinical system, it must be kept current with the latest evidence-based medicine, new and recalled drugs, new terms for new diseases, and new processes and workflows brought about by external factors, such as reimbursement or patient needs.

The result of a cost-benefit analysis should be the ability to perform return on investment (ROI) analysis. The easiest measure to calculate is the payback period. This is the cash flow (additional cash inflows less cash outflows due to the EHR) compared to the cost of the investment for the period of time it takes to achieve a positive difference. Generally, payback periods of from two to five years are tolerable. Longer payback periods are difficult to justify. Internal rate of return (IRR) also may be calculated. This ROI measure requires a financial calculator or a spreadsheet to factor into the cost-benefit equation the time value of money. If the IRR for an EHR investment is greater than the IRR on other investments, the EHR is considered a good investment. Alternatively, many care delivery organizations are recognizing that an EHR must now be considered a cost of doing business. Reduced costs to abstract data to participate in the increasing quality measurement and reporting requirements plus the emphasis on patient safety and quality are difficult to quantify but are essential to address.

Most vendors will attempt to provide ROI analysis for their clients. However, caution should be applied in interpreting these results because they typically assign a monetary value to every benefit, whether actual savings will result or the benefit will only yield greater value. For example, many vendors will calculate nurse full-time equivalent (FTE) savings, even though no nurses will be eliminated. Although this can provide a good comparison between systems, the expected savings cannot be "taken to the bank." And, in some cases, these savings do need to factor into bank loans or lines of credit for financing the investment.

Another financing option in addition to using cash reserves from operations or loans is to acquire the EHR through an **application service provider (ASP)** model or SaaS (previously described). The ASP and SaaS models are both a financing and an acquisition strategy. With these models the vendor hosts the data center hardware and application software so that upfront and ongoing maintenance costs for the organization are minimized in return for a monthly fee. A good way to compare these financing and acquisition models to the typical license agreement for a client/server EHR is to consider the ASP or SaaS as renting an apartment and the license agreement the purchase of a house. In the ASP or SaaS models, rent accumulates over time to frequently be more than the actual cost of the house. However, costs to maintain the system and acquire all the hardware are reduced.

There are differences, however, between the ASP and SaaS models. The ASP model is built on a client/server architecture, whereas the SaaS model is built on a WSA. Both offer less flexibility than a traditional straight licensure of a client/server EHR, although the SaaS model offers almost no flexibility for customization.

The biggest concern providers have had about either ASPs or SaaS is regarding the security of the data because they reside with the company. Actually, ASP or SaaS may be a more secure environment than a given provider could hope to afford and provide. The bigger concern providers should have is with connectivity. If any part of the connectivity between the provider and the vendor goes down, it is impossible to gain access to the EHR software or data. While both the provider and the vendor can take steps to add redundancy at their respective connection points, absolute 100 percent up time cannot be guaranteed in the event of a major disruption to the Internet. Contingency planning to revert to paper and determining how paper will be fed back to the EHR once up is essential. Another concern providers should have is that many of these vendors are new and often small, and there is a risk of them going out of business, leaving providers without access to their data (worst case) or with their data and no application software to support them (best case). Doing thorough due diligence on not only the product being acquired but the vendor's viability is essential. Contractual agreements need to be carefully worked out so that the provider is assured of getting access to the data and the software needed to at least continue processing until the data can be migrated to another vendor's application. Unfortunately, when an ASP or SaaS company goes out of business, it is often due to bankruptcy, so there is little hope of compensation for disruption of service or conversion.

Executive Commitment

Executives, obviously, are acutely aware of and concerned about ROI and financing issues. They sometimes feel powerless to ensure that the EHR is adopted in a manner that will, in fact, achieve the expected benefits. However, executives can be the crucial factor in adoption and benefits realization if they demonstrate their commitment and support, establish appropriate expectations, and generally foster a culture of quality and productivity improvement. Implementing an EHR system into an adversarial environment is risky. In fact, many believe that implementing only a mediocre EHR product in a good environment can have better results than implementing the best EHR in a poor environment. People, policy, and process are the keys to success and are driven by executive leadership.

Therefore, many ask how executive support can be gained if it is not already present. (If it is present, it is highly likely that the organization is well on its way to achieving a successful EHR already.) Often, without executive leadership recognizing its own issues, little can be done from only a small segment of the organization desiring an EHR. There really needs to be a groundswell of support for the EHR before the executive posture is likely to change. This groundswell must include the medical staff and potentially even the community of patients, health plans, and businesses at large. One of the most successful implementations of an EHR engaged community leaders in helping to fund and motivate adoption.

Clinician Adoption

Although cost and executive commitment are essential ingredients in moving forward with an EHR, clinician adoption is the keystone to achieving results. Clinicians include physicians, nurses, pharmacists, technicians, therapists, and all others who use clinical information to treat patients. Although each may be challenged in special ways, it is probably the physician community that is most challenged, followed by the nursing community that needs the most training.

Physician Concerns with EHR Adoption

For physicians, the EHR represents a monumental change to old habits. Virtually everything physicians do today

Table 5.1.   Differences in hospital and physician's office workflow

	Hospital	**Physician's Office**
Workflow	Tightly coordinated	Loosely coordinated
Communication	Formal	Informal
Primary user	Nurse	Physician
Data content	Comprehensive	Fragmented
Data volume	High density	Low density
Data source	Multiple, disparate	Patient/provider generated
Information flow	Location centric	Geographically dispersed
Data input	Mobile	Stationary
IS decision making	Administration	Physicians

concerning documentation is changed by an EHR. Consider only the need to select the patient for whom to write a medication order. In the paper environment, the correct patient's chart may have been presented to the physician by a member of the nursing staff or a blank sheet of paper could be used to write orders when the chart could not be immediately located. The physician did not have to select Mary Gonzalez from a list of patients that might also include Marie Gomez. The mere fact that care must be taken to distinguish between two relatively similar names is not the norm for the physician and requires a thought process that could be considered distracting from the processing of medication selection and dosage calculation, which is more likely uppermost in the physician's mind. This may seem a minor inconvenience in light of the fact that the system could return contraindication information that normally would have resulted in a phone call from the pharmacist, which simply delays the distraction to another point in time. Yet old habits die hard. The system, then, must be carefully programmed to be intuitive and include as many failsafe measures as possible, but not so many that they are distracting or delay the intended action on the system.

In many cases, physicians must be convinced of the value of the EHR through either using an EHR in their own practice or peer pressure. Typically, **physician champions** are identified and expected to lead the charge. Sometimes, however, physician champions can be looked upon as mavericks by their peers, or they may be brought into the picture too late in the process, which can cause resentment to build in the medical staff. In either case, physician leadership may be required to build trust in the system. Many organizations are beginning to identify the need for a medical director of information systems (MDIS) or chief medical informatics officer (CMIO) who would spend a good portion of time on EHR system selection and implementation and then maintenance, including training peers, ensuring the CDS system is appropriate and kept current, and troubleshooting system issues (Conn 2007). Many MDISs recognize the importance of process improvement, support process mapping, and promote

other strategies to support change. However, hospitals must recognize that engaging the medical staff early is critical to success. Many hospitals still dictate that a CPOE system will be acquired and used without seeking the advice and support of the medical staff. This strategy is rarely successful with clinical information systems. (This strategy is not even successful when the system affects employed physicians and other clinicians, such as an electronic medication administration record system expected to be used by nurses.)

It is interesting to note that physicians tend to be more willing to adopt EHR systems in their own office practice than they are in the hospital or hospitals with which they are affiliated. There are several reasons for this. Perhaps foremost is the fact that the hospital system is just that, a system designed to support an institution, not necessarily an individual. There are significant differences between systems designed for physician offices and hospitals. These differences reflect the many differences in workflow between these two kinds of care. (See table 5.1.)

A physician views the office EHR from an ownership perspective and the hospital EHR from an indentured servant perspective. Couple that with the fact that the hospital system is different from the office system, representing a second system to learn, and one can appreciate the challenge a physician has in using a hospital system. The most successful situation is one in which the office and hospital systems look and function very similarly. This, of course, can be aided by using a standard user interface and providing remote connectivity to accustom the physician to the look and feel of the hospital system.

Physicians also are concerned about security and privacy issues, as well as patient perception issues. Today's information systems have typically been secured by virtue of the fact that they contain minimal patient data, few people know how to use them, and they are closed systems. They do not connect to the outside world. As use and users expand, security must be enhanced to better protect privacy. On the other hand, however, security measures must not be so onerous as to make EHRs even more formidable to learn and use.

Many physicians find loss of productivity, and hence revenue, a major concern as they get ready to use an EHR in their offices. Frequently, it is necessary to schedule fewer patients to be seen in a day for the first few weeks after go-live. If thorough planning, early engagement of all members of the office team, careful attention to processes and workflows, advance preload of key data, and mandatory training are instituted, most offices find that physicians can return to normal workloads within a few weeks or a month or so.

Some physicians, and other clinicians, also have expressed concern about patient acceptance of computers. Will the patient perceive the computer to be a barrier between patient and clinician? Many clinicians are finding that patients actually expect them to use a computer, or at least are not surprised when they do. In fact, some patients are starting to make an EHR a criterion on which they select their doctor. This is as true for elderly patients as young ones, especially as many of the elderly patients have younger members of the family caring for them. They want the convenience of e-mail and even e-visits, being able to schedule appointments themselves, and appreciate the ability to enter blood sugar diaries or medication tracking. Many providers find that computers add value to the patient encounter. Clinicians who make the computer a barrier because they do not use it well will surely create a barrier for their patients. However, the computer can be used to engage and provide the patient with instantaneous information and instructions. Showing the patient a graph of personal data can be a powerful motivator. Instructions tailored specifically to the patient can improve his or her compliance with a treatment regimen.

Nursing Staff Concerns with EHR Adoption

Physicians are not the only users of EHRs. Certainly, their concerns are critical, but attention must be paid to nurse issues, in both hospitals and physician offices.

In hospitals, nursing staff are the primary users of the EHR, yet very few nurses have the opportunity to learn about and evaluate various EHR systems from a nursing perspective. Although many physicians go to conferences and begin to see these systems and hear presentations from peers, nurses have less opportunity for such exposure. Moreover, physicians are starting to acquire EHRs for use in their own offices; hospital-based nurses have no such opportunity. Physician adoption is critical, but it should not be assumed that nurses will necessarily adopt the EHR without issues of their own. A good way to gain nurse support for the EHR is to engage them early in the process. Nurses who represent mainstream nursing need to be prominent members of the EHR selection committee. They need the opportunity to see and hear what issues may arise and how they can be overcome. Amazingly, many systems are not nurse-friendly. Care has not been taken to address special charting issues. For example, nurses depend on trended data to discern changes in their patients' statuses. If corrections made to data cannot be incorporated into the trend lines appropriately, their ability to monitor such trends is at risk. As an example, one system correctly identified where an error had occurred but placed the newly corrected information at the end of the trend line, not at the point of error. This was very difficult for nurses to use because they wanted to see the trend over time, not have to make mental adjustments for the fact that a certain data point should be somewhere else.

It is not uncommon to find nurses left out of the EHR decision-making process in physician offices (much as physicians are left out of the EHR decision-making process in the hospital). Again, this is a mistake because nurses are the ones who will likely use the EHR for a considerable portion of their work and will be expected to support the physician in learning to use the EHR.

Legal and Regulatory, Hybrid Record, and Legal Health Record Issues

Although many states have not adopted specific statutes relating to EHRs, many have updated their statutes to address electronic information in general. Other states are generally silent on whether health information is in paper or electronic form because the statutes are old and generally assumed a paper form. The Federal Rules of Civil Procedure and Uniform Rules Relating to Discovery of Electronically Stored Information that most states have also enacted set the foundation for use of electronic information systems. Every organization needs to review its own state's statutes, but EHRs are generally believed to be legally acceptable for use, so long as special safeguards on their accuracy and integrity are applied. HIM professionals are in the best position to advise their organizations on appropriate ways to carry out these safeguard procedures. As previously mentioned, they may include audits of how templates are completed and how CDS systems are used.

Safeguard procedures also may need to include how hybrid record situations are managed. If part of the official, legal record is deemed electronic and part paper, indications may need to be included in the paper record when content is in electronic form. The location of information also will change over time, as initially only lab results may be available online, and later, nursing notes, and so on. HIM professionals must be vigilant about managing the use of printouts of electronic content as they significantly increase processing time and cost and do pose a patient safety risk if documentation is recorded on the paper. Some organizations have taken to removing printers from nursing stations and physician lounges, or filling printers in such areas with different colored paper to remind users that they should not be used for documentation and must be shredded after use. The opposite concern of using printouts during patient care is that they may be so discouraged that clinicians may avoid reviewing the information at all. This can add a burden to nursing staff, who may be asked to read results to the clinicians, and can pose a risk of misinterpreting information that is read. The worst case is where some results may not be reviewed at all. Decisions also need to be made about whether the electronic part of the record will ultimately be printed and incorporated into the paper chart or will remain online exclusively.

So while many hospitals will live through a hybrid record situation for some period of time, certain portions of EHRs may have to be converted to paper or signed on paper in certain circumstances and in certain states. For example, many courts still require the production of a paper record in response to a subpoena or court order. Taking a laptop into the courtroom to view an EHR is becoming more common but not yet universal. Furthermore, there are issues of connectivity, privacy through incidental disclosures, and the risk that more than the legal health record may be accessible without a motion for further discovery.

AHIMA has been active in helping organizations define their **legal health record (LHR)**, which it defines as the "subset of all patient-specific data created or accumulated by a healthcare provider that may be released to third parties in response to legally permissible requests." (AHIMA 2011). This definition has arisen from the fact that EHRs contain more information than has typically been considered the business record of the organization, representing what was done for the patient and by whom. The EHR contains metadata that are administrative or operational in nature and may also be used to house other forms of communications with patients, health plans, and the like. AHIMA has been instrumental in having HL7 (2007) develop its Legal EHR-System Functional Profile, which is an adjunct to its EHR-System Functional Model (HL7 2009). Released in June 2003 as a draft standard for trial use, it became an ANSI-accredited standard in 2007 and is now in Release 1.1. In addition to specifying what constitutes an LHR, the Functional Profile helps organizations determine how to construct a legal presentation of the EHR that is admissible in court (Servais 2008). See chapter 12 for further discussion of the legal EHR and e-Discovery.

HIM and Roles in EHR

The EHR represents both exciting times and potentially scary times for HIM professionals. Certainly, HIM professionals recognize the burdens of paper records and the important benefits that accrue from EHRs with much enhanced utility. As a result, HIM professionals are concerned that they are sometimes left out of the planning process—at least until it is almost too late to correct an issue discovered after the fact. Finally, HIM professionals may find their departmental base of technical and clerical staff eroding, as many of the traditional functions can be automated, or faced with the challenge of a significant retraining effort. Clerical staff who have traditionally pulled and filed paper charts now need to learn how to use EDM systems. Release of information staff may become patient educators as more patients may be able to access information themselves. Traditional coding activities (especially in physician offices) may give way to automated coding. Transcription services will be decreased with point-of-care charting methods and increased use of speech recognition applications. Some transcriptionists are already doing speech dictation correction rather than transcription, and there will likely be automated ways to monitor for incomplete charts as EHRs begin to provide inboxes to physicians advising them of documentation deficiencies and/or signature requirements.

However, HIM professionals will find many new and interesting roles and functions emerging, as well. The HIM professional is typically the only member of the organization that sees all aspects of the health record systems, its use, and its users, thus the HIM professional is in the best position to urge the organization to adopt a migration path that recognizes when one application depends on another for certain information, rather than reactively acquire applications that have dependencies that are not adequately addressed. HIM professionals are trained in workflow and process improvement and can best anticipate where there may be changes in work patterns that others do not recognize. HIM professionals are intimately familiar with data flows throughout the organization as well. Even where quality management, risk management, and executive decision making may be in separate departments today, the HIM professional is frequently called on to determine the accuracy of reports, interpret findings, and offer suggestions for additional analysis. All of the data quality and documentation auditing described in this chapter are functions for HIM professionals.

HIM professionals have also been the official custodian of the patient record in most organizations, currently maneuvering through all of the hybrid record and LHR issues described earlier. As they continue to fulfill this role, they also need to take on a greater role in **data stewardship**—ensuring the data contained in the EHR are accurate and complete, that the data are privacy- and security-protected, and that users value the data as information assets of the organization. Data stewardship is a function that every person who has access to PHI must take on, but HIM professionals should heavily promote this function. In fact, with HIPAA sometimes being a "dirty word," if not at least a tired mantra, data stewardship that encompasses HIPAA and other accountabilities and responsibilities for data can be one way to refresh the HIPAA principles for the organization. Finally, HIM professionals have traditionally been an interface with patients with respect to information rights, certainly when they are the designated information privacy official, but even when not—and long before HIPAA. As consumer empowerment takes hold and patients have ever greater access to their information and maintain their own PHRs, e-HIM professionals should be there to assist them. AHIMA's myPHR. org website is a good place to start to help patients navigate these new waters.

One important consideration in fulfilling new roles in the EHR environment is the need to be very collegial. Today, some HIM professionals have close working relationships with the IT department and patient financial services in the hospital. However, this is not true in all cases, and the HIM professional may have to work hard to foster better relationships with these departments and others. For some time, the Joint Commission has merged its IT and HIM standards into one IM standard, recognizing that each department has a role to play, but the end result must be a single approach to managing the information assets of the organization. In addition to working closely with the IT department, some HIM professionals find themselves becoming part of the IT department and even in a few cases the chief information officer (CIO).

While the intent of becoming an e-HIM professional should not be to take over the IT department, it is essential to coordinate closely with the IT department. Both IT professionals and HIM professionals have their own unique knowledge and skill sets that are different and essential, while contributing to the overarching goals for IM in general and EHR in particular. In addition to a close working relationship between health information services and IT departments, HIM professionals will find themselves working much more closely with other departments, especially nursing and physicians—in positive rather than adversarial roles of demanding chart completion. Once again, however, HIM professionals may be surprised that these departments also have a stand-alone mentality—believing that only physicians or nurses best know physician and nursing information needs. So HIM professionals will need to prove value to these groups to ensure doctors and nurses see the knowledge and competencies the e-HIM professional brings to the table. Making a sincere effort to regularly join in with different professionals and to understand their concerns and needs is very important. HIM professionals should not only conduct walkarounds to help in an EHR implementation but also make an effort to regularly communicate with the different departments that will be impacted by the EHR. Sometimes this means delegating more routine health information services departmental work to staff within the department, cultivating relationships outside of the health information services department to network with the clinicians and staff, and finding creative ways to earn the gratitude of clinicians and staff in other departments.

In addition to a collegial relationship within the hospital, it is necessary for the HIM professional to cultivate relationships with the clinicians and staff in physician offices. HIM professionals already know the physicians, and there is an opportunity to help them with their EHR vendor selection, implementation, and adoption. Such relationships will strengthen the HIM professional's knowledge of EHRs and their ability to coordinate hospital and physician office communications, garner trust for sharing data, and resolve issues where they occur.

A final consideration for some HIM professionals is deciding how they can participate more fully in the planning, implementation, and benefits realization for EHRs. In this realm, as well, HIM professionals may have to assume a more assertive stance and truly market their services. Similar to marketers, the HIM professional needs to find the right product/service to provide and then target it to the right person in a highly positive manner. HIM professionals who distribute articles of interest, volunteer for a project, or even produce a report on some of the issues currently facing the organization find that they can demonstrate their value in a very positive manner.

Some of the best skills HIM professionals have to offer are in the area of protection—legal, privacy, and data quality—and, though these are important concerns in healthcare organizations, they have not always been highly valued by everyone in the organization. Historically in the evolution of EHR systems, these issues also have not necessarily been well addressed by EHR vendors. As a result, users who are excited about using the EHR sometimes do not want to be bothered with details of what should constitute a legal health record, how corrections should be made in an EHR, and so on. HIM professionals who approach the EHR with such concerns can sometimes be viewed as negative, and this may come across as not supportive of the EHR itself. This is the last thing HIM professionals want, but in order to overcome some of these perceptions it may be necessary to do some soul searching and be flexible. Flexibility, thinking outside the box, and being aware that things can be approached differently and yet produce the same results are important. For example, having a complex process to access the EHR may result in a clinician creating a workaround resulting in not using the record at the point of care and therefore not gaining the benefit of clinical decision support. Accepting that the system login may be sufficient for access to multiple applications rather than requiring a login for each application may be a necessary middle ground (if technically feasible). However, where different processes will not translate into the same desirable and/or required results for the organization, HIM professionals do have a professional obligation to point this out. Doing so in a manner that is constructive may take some fine-tuning of the message and serious consideration of where, when, and how to address the issues. For example, raising the issue that the system being implemented is at risk for loss of data integrity because it does not present the fact that a correction was made with the CIO, an individual with whom HIM professionals need to cultivate a positive relationship, will likely be seen by the CIO as a negative position. A better approach may to be contact the vendor's representative directly and find out how a correction can be made visible when necessary, then update the existing data correction policy and present it as an important contribution to how corrections can be effectively made.

As the adoption rate of EHRs increases in all types of healthcare settings, as organizational experiences with EHR systems mature, and as the standards for and expectations of EHR capabilities evolve, the healthcare industry is beginning to open its eyes to the significant health information management issues that are inherent in EHR systems—critical issues of data quality assurance at the point of capture and throughout the data life cycle, compliance with legal/regulatory mandates, and effective use of these data resources to support clinical and administrative decision making. Progressive and astute HIM professionals are well positioned to fill key roles and assume responsibilities in each of these areas.

EHR System Planning and Acquisition

A key role for HIM professionals to play is as a team member in EHR system planning and acquisition. Many hospitals have already made their vendor choices for their major EHR components. However, it is possible that they have not done so with respect to special components, such as CDS utilities, DRT systems, interfaces, and others, or they may be considering a rip-and-replace strategy for older systems, especially where there are many vendors represented. There are also many adoption and optimization strategies that are needed as technology is rapidly implemented to take advantage of the MU incentives. These strategies will include additional training and reinforcement, workflow and process redesign, change management, potentially different human–computer interfaces, data quality management challenges, and even new or refined goals and benefits realization. Many physician practices, however, are still in the early stages of planning and acquisition and could well benefit from HIM expertise. In fact, it would not be unheard of for the health information services department to become a revenue-generating department through the sale of EHR planning and acquisition services.

EHR Readiness

As an organization approaches the acquisition of an EHR, it is very important to assess its readiness, plot its migration path, and develop a plan of action. Organizations would be well advised to inventory their applications, technical capabilities, staffing resources, and reporting needs. However, there is potentially nothing more important than taking a soul-searching look at the organization's culture of change management and process improvement. It cannot be emphasized enough that the organization's culture of responsiveness is a critical factor in EHR adoption. In fact, there is as key distinction between implementation and adoption. Technology can be installed and applications configured, but getting users to actually use the EHR to its fullest extent is different and takes considerable people skills. Adoption may actually take more time and effort than all of the implementation elements combined.

See chapter 23 for a detailed discussion of change management and chapter 26 for a detailed discussion of workflow design and process improvement.

Organizational Goals for EHR Systems

A large measure of an organization's readiness for the EHR is its understanding and articulation of goals for the EHR. Every member of the organization must understand what an EHR is. There should be a common understanding and clearly stated definition. The EHR is not an administrative or financial system; rather, it is a set of clinical components designed to support direct patient care. Clinicians who bypass the system for printouts or use clerical support for data entry are not achieving the benefit of the EHR and are undermining achievement of its goals. An organization that does not monitor achievement of goals to take corrective action is setting itself up for failure. EHRs can be powerful in helping an organization achieve its strategic initiatives, but they must be managed carefully.

It is not uncommon to find organizations without a migration path floundering in its EHR acquisition. Such organizations typically are reactive rather than proactive. Information systems have typically been requested and used by individual departments, and often this is expected to continue in an EHR environment. This information silo mentality must be changed in an EHR environment, which requires all systems to work together, not be duplicative, and be acquired in the sequence that most appropriately addresses the organization's EHR goals. For example, a hospital with a document-imaging system should not approve a radiology department's request for a separate document-imaging system just because its PACS vendor is attempting to make a sale. Likewise, the health information services department would not need a chart-tracking system if a document-imaging system was going to be implemented within the next year. Yet, an organization without an EHR migration path might not be able to see the overall picture and focus the organization on working together.

EHR Planning and Project Management

An EHR migration path can be developed by an EHR steering committee or can be a precursor to the appointment of an EHR steering committee. If a great deal of infrastructure needs to be put into place prior to EHR acquisition, it may be appropriate to do that prior to forming an EHR steering committee. However, an EHR steering committee can begin to address the operational issues simultaneously with the technical infrastructure issues. Process mapping, gaining acceptance of practice guidelines, and adopting other standards can take considerable time.

An EHR steering committee should be composed of representatives of all direct users as well as those who support such users. The committee is often chaired by a clinician. Other clinical representatives must be present and representatives of IT and HIM are essential for representing IM issues. Responsibility for IM does not shift from health information services to IT or individual departments just because the EHR is a clinical system—it is still the organization's business record, despite the enhanced utility it should provide.

At some point, the organization will need an EHR **project manager.** When direct planning begins, someone needs to provide oversight that all elements are working together. Although an EHR project manager is critical during implementation, an organization is often best served when such an individual starts early in the planning stages and potentially remains in place at least through benefits realization. A project manager can be appointed from within the organization, hired from outside, or contracted with for a period of time. An internal candidate knows the organization but may also carry some "baggage." However, the position can be an excellent opportunity for someone interested in new challenges. An EHR is really a series of ongoing projects, so the project manager rarely needs to be concerned about finishing the project and not having a job. An external candidate has to get up to speed rapidly on the organization's culture but often is viewed as a more neutral party in negotiating among the different departmental silos that reflect current information system use today. The third option, contracting for a project manager, is often used in a small organization where the position of project manager is likely to be short term. The risks in using a contract project manager include that the project manager may not be devoted exclusively to one organization's project and may not impart the learning to existing staff necessary for them to continue to maintain the system. This can be guarded against by requiring staff to be trained, but it is often a secondary part of the project and frequently the outcome is not as successful as desired.

A project manager must have skills that may be different from those required of an operational manager. The project manager must have excellent communication, facilitation, negotiation, and leadership skills, while often not being the project leader (who is more likely the chair of the EHR steering committee). He or she must be skilled at delegating, diligent about following up, comfortable with escalating issues, able to see the big picture, and yet comfortable attending to the highly detailed task of monitoring the **project plan.** A project manager does not have to be highly skilled in information technology but should have a working knowledge of what can and cannot be accomplished. He or she will work with the IT department and the vendor's implementation team, which will provide the IT expertise needed for the specific product. The project manager does not have to be a clinician but should have a thorough understanding of healthcare and the nature of clinical information and associated processes. Finally, the project manager should be well grounded in project management and process-mapping tools. Becoming an EHR project manager is an excellent opportunity for HIM professionals, but it is not a simple promotion. HIM professionals need to demonstrate their ability to adapt to programmatic responsibility and their strong interest in persevering for the duration of the project.

See chapter 27 for a full discussion of project management.

Vendor Selection

Healthcare organizations acquire IT systems in a variety of ways. Figure 5.10 illustrates the different IT acquisition strategies.

Some organizations build their own systems. This is especially true of more academic, research-based environments. Many of these have multiple source systems, some of which are homegrown and others of which are licensed from one or more vendors. If the organization does not believe a product exists on the market that addresses its needs, it may consider acquiring a repository and then creating the applications that will integrate data into the repository, run queries, provide

Figure 5.10.   IT acquisition strategies

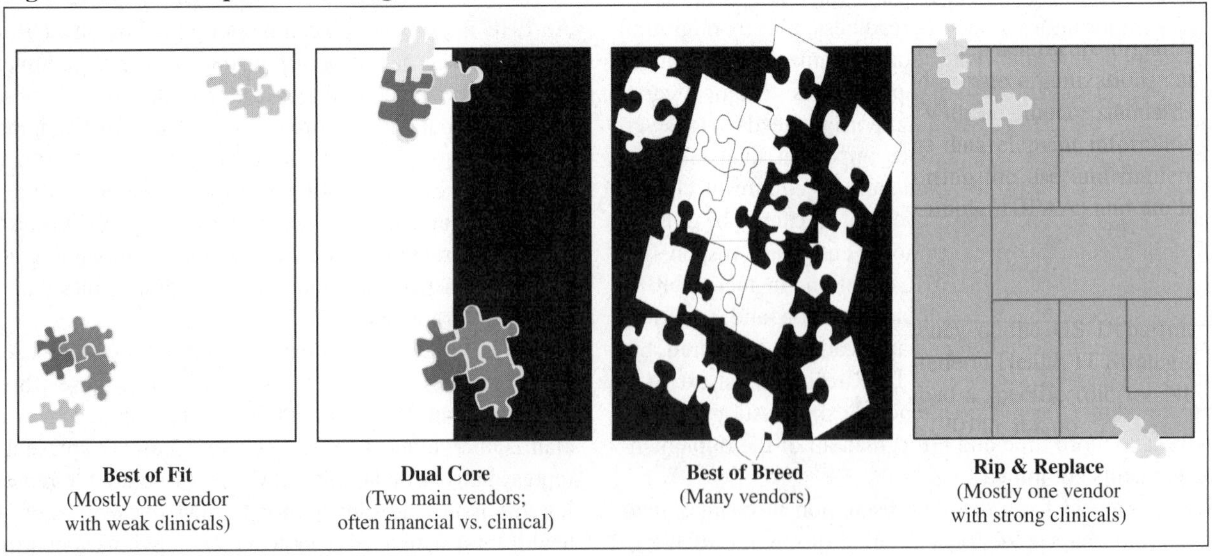

| **Best of Fit** | **Dual Core** | **Best of Breed** | **Rip & Replace** |
| (Mostly one vendor with weak clinicals) | (Two main vendors; often financial vs. clinical) | (Many vendors) | (Mostly one vendor with strong clinicals) |

CDS, and so on. Developing a system from scratch is becoming much less common as more sophisticated commercial products are introduced into the marketplace. Because it is sometimes difficult to hire and retain highly qualified IT staff, building a system from scratch is also costly and time consuming. Vendors can provide commercial-grade products and economies of scale that simply are not available to individual organizations.

Other organizations buy a fully integrated suite of financial and administrative systems and ancillary systems and upgrade as the vendor supplies more functionality toward the ultimate goal of the EHR. This strategy is often called **best of fit** because all components are from the same vendor so should fit well together, enabling smoother exchange of data. Many smaller hospitals and physician practices find this to be a suitable solution. The advantage is that the vendor provides a tried-and-true solution. The disadvantage is that these systems are sometimes fairly basic, meeting minimum requirements of everyone rather than trying to address any special needs, or developing very advanced, customizable applications that are beyond the typical small organizations' capabilities to implement and get adopted. Interestingly, larger hospitals are also adopting a best of fit IT acquisition strategy, but doing so by replacing all **legacy systems,** which are old systems less capable of capturing structured data and often using older programming languages and platforms, with the one vendor that is supplying all of their EHR applications. This is often called a **rip-and-replace** strategy. While it may appear to be a very expensive proposition, the incremental cost may not be as great as expected when the cost of interfacing old systems is considered along with the return on investment from new systems that have much more functionality.

Still other organizations prefer **best of breed** (many different vendors, presumably the best for each type of application) or **dual core** (one vendor for most financial and administrative applications and another vendor for clinical applications) IT acquisition strategies. They go to market to find a vendor or vendors who will supply the clinical applications that comprise an EHR. As previously noted, EHRs for physician offices are much more likely to integrate all components into a bundled package, including the PMS. There may be some individual, often optional, modules, but the vendor selection is more straightforward.

As can be seen from the various IT acquisition strategies discussed and description of EHR implementation that follows, acquiring an EHR is not simply a matter of buying a software package and installing it the next day. While the buying process is generally more complex for hospitals than physician practices, the fact that vendor selection and implementation is a series of many steps over a period of time that could take from months to years is true for both hospitals and physician practices. In addition, many hospitals and some physician practices already have a significant amount of technology and may not go to market for an EHR but acquire the EHR from their incumbent vendor. Others may conduct a vendor selection project primarily to learn about what is new, view competing products to determine how far off the mark their incumbent vendor is, and possibly to decide to rip-and-replace.

An organization approaching EHR vendor selection typically first goes through a process of analyzing EHR functionality. While once it was thought that EHR certification may not require such an extensive requirements analysis, the fact that the MU certification is only considering the minimum criteria for earning the incentives, requirements analysis is as important as, or more important than ever. Furthermore, by the end of January 2012, the ONC Certified Health IT Product List identified 1,132 certified ambulatory EHR products, of which 724 were deemed complete; and 549 certified inpatient EHR products, of which 134 were deemed complete. The number of products on the market makes it especially challenging to distinguish the nuances between the products. In addition, functionality alone is not enough. The organization should look for the vendor's ability to be a good partner in EHR implementation. The vendor must have the core functionality desired and also should be ready to help the organization overcome adoption issues, address process changes, and support ongoing maintenance and upgrades well into the future.

Key vendor selection criteria might include

- Functionality
- Vendor viability
- Vendor support
- Training availability
- Implementation support
- Technology or architecture
- Vision (research and development momentum)
- Integration
- Vendor's clinical culture
- ROI potential

Except for the ROI potential, cost is not identified as a criterion for EHR selection. Cost is undoubtedly very important, but it should not be used in the basic selection. Vendors have many ways to price products, and because the products are not commodities there is considerable room for price negotiation as well as many financing options. The lowest bidder is likely to have the lowest ranking in most of the functionality. When the functionality does not support the user community, ROI will not be achieved, resulting in a significant investment for very little return.

Most organizations use a formal request for proposal (RFP) process to solicit information from vendors on how they can meet the criteria. This then must be accompanied by thorough **due diligence,** usually in the form of product demonstrations, site visits, reference checks, and corporate investigations of the vendor. Throughout the due diligence process, organizations narrow their choices down to a finalist and backup. A final contract is then negotiated to ensure that the organization is getting the product it wants, at the best price, with the best payment schedule, and under the best terms.

EHR System Implementation

After a system has been selected, system implementation includes initial planning, hardware and software installation, system configuration, testing, and user training. Because the EHR directly affects clinical processes, process improvement, workflow redesign, and potentially even space layout are affected.

Initial Planning and Super User Training

After the contract is negotiated for an EHR system, initial planning will take place. This is the time that a comprehensive implementation plan is produced and a communication plan is developed to ensure that all stakeholders are kept up to date with the EHR implementation progress and engaged appropriately in various aspects of the project. A project governance structure may be implemented with various domain teams that support the EHR steering committee. This includes assigning responsibility and accountability for making the myriad decisions that must be made during the course of the implementation. Domain teams must be populated with all applicable representatives of the end users impacted. This is often a process that is not performed well. For example, an EMAR may be viewed as a nursing system; yet without pharmacy working alongside the nurses, differences in how drugs are dispensed, vocabulary differences in drug names, and the like are not fully identified and prepared for. The relationship with the vendor is another planning task. A "war room" may need to be designated where everyone can work on the project. An issues management system needs to be developed so that resolution of the myriad of issues that occur can be made harmoniously with the vendor. Finally, most organizations also set up a formal training room and often start end user training with basic computer skills. During the initial planning super users and other staff are trained by the vendor. Super users are so named because they are actually users who will ultimately be using the system alongside everyone else but will be resourced appropriately so they are available to help new users after their initial training.

Hardware and Software Installation

The next step in implementation is the acquisition and installation of the additional hardware required for the EHR. This often includes upgrades to the network, new servers, additional backup and disaster recovery services, bar code readers, printers, scanning devices, and, of course, human–computer interfaces for various users. Next, the vendor will generally load the software onto the servers. The software is then ready for configuration to the care delivery organization's specific needs. During this time, super users within the organization are identified and trained on system build—usually in an intensive period of time at the vendor's location. Super users typically are clinicians who serve as a bridge between the ultimate end users of the EHR components and the IT staff.

System Configuration

System configuration, sometimes called **system build,** is the structuring of the applications to fit the care delivery organization's environment. System build is the process whereby the organization's unique data and clinical standards are designed into the system. System build can take many months of detailed process mapping, data dictionary build, screen design or screen design refinements, template review and refinement and/or development, review of CDS rules, design of reports, and many other aspects of ultimately being able to use the system. A key element of system build is to ensure that a **change control** process exists—where changes are requested, approved, prioritized, and documented.

System Testing

It should be clear that a system as complex as an EHR must be tested thoroughly. There may be several levels of testing, from evaluating that a screen has been built correctly to the fact that data can be passed from one component to another. Testing should follow the flow of data through all systems and through all decision points. Stress testing also may be performed to ensure that the system works not only in the test environment, where there are minimal data and few users, but also when the system is live and many users are using it simultaneously. Generally, there is an acceptance testing process that addresses all aspects of the system, including adoption rates. This acceptance testing procedure usually triggers a final payment or sign-off on acceptance and should occur from one to three months at a minimum after go-live.

End User Training

End user training is essential. Super users are often used in a train-the-trainer mode. It is important to recognize that users learn in different ways. For example, nurses may do well in a classroom session where the experience can be shared. On the other hand, physicians often require one-on-one, private instruction. In fact, physicians often learn best when a system is intuitive and they can learn on their own. Nevertheless, learning on one's own carries risk—either that he or she will not take the time to learn or that he or she will learn bad habits or only what he or she thinks is necessary to know, which may not be sufficient. To support all end users, there must be some formal training, sufficient online help, and ultimately strong support during go-live. However implementation is managed, training is key to using the system and does not end at go-live. Ongoing training and reinforcement of regular users hones their skills and helps them to learn new things on an ongoing basis. It helps prevent workarounds where users may attempt to revert to old ways of doing things that often can lead to taking more time to use the EHR, and frequently does not afford them all the benefits of the EHR.

Data Conversion, Chart Conversion, Rollout Planning, and Go-Live

The entire implementation process is not totally sequential. Data conversion, chart conversion, rollout planning, and go-live are frequently planned well in advance but then implemented after all system build and end user training take place.

Data conversion is the movement of existing electronic data from an old system to a new system. If the EHR implementation entails new applications for admissions and registration or billing (or practice management in a physician office), there will very likely need to be considerable conversion of data from the old systems to the new ones. An MPI clean-up project is often performed at this time as well, especially if the implementation entails a move to an enterprise-wide MPI. Data housed in various source systems may also need to be converted. Data conversion is not an easy or perfect process. Because the old systems will not have all the functionality of the new system, there may be gaps in data or data fields that do not match from the old to the new. Data conversion is a tedious process that must be thoroughly tested. In some cases, it is so difficult to perform that organizations may start at least some of their new system usage from scratch. For example, while patient demographic data are often converted, the accounts receivable may not be converted—the hospital or office may retain a license to use the old system until the accounts are paid, or it may only do a balance forward.

Chart conversion is a key issue for EHR implementation, especially in physician practices where access to the information from a patient's last visit is critical, particularly for patients with chronic disease. There are several approaches. Some organizations use document imaging as both an interim solution to achieving improved access to information and a means to make old paper charts accessible in an EHR environment. This is the most common way to address the need to bring paper records into the EHR environment. The issue then becomes what parts of the paper record to scan and how far back to scan them. There are no right answers across the board; the organization needs to consider its readmission and revisit rate and use of records (for example, for patient care only or research and education as well). In some cases, the organization may decide to scan the entire records of active patients so that they have a solid archive. In other cases, the organization (typically a physician office) may decide to scan only parts of active patients' paper records and pull the paper records if other information is needed (Amatayakul 2010a).

If an organization is adopting an EHR where there are considerable discrete data and a repository supporting CDS, it may want to abstract some or all of certain records so that the data are not only accessible for viewing but also available for processing. In this case, the organization may hire abstractors or expect clinicians to perform their own abstracting. Again, issues arise concerning what data need to be abstracted and how far back the abstracting must be performed. Abstracting is generally more expensive than scanning, so it should be performed judiciously. Of course, a combination of scanning and abstracting can be used. For example, it may be desirable in an ambulatory environment to abstract the problem list, medication list, allergies, and immunizations and then scan other key documents. Continuing to pull the paper charts is yet another possible way to address how old information is made available to clinicians. Some consider this the least expensive way to make information available, but it may not be if one considers the issues of the hybrid record. Continuing to pull paper charts not only does not reduce this cost but creates patient safety risk if documentation continues to be performed in the paper chart. In addition, there is the potential that continuing to pull the chart continues a dependency on paper for those who are more resistant to using the computer.

There are numerous ways in which installations can be rolled out—by special users, by department, by nursing unit, by site, or by function. Often the vendor has the best recommendation and should be considered an important guide. This issue also should be evaluated during site visits and reference checks. A few organizations have started to consider adopting a "big bang" approach to their rollout. In this case, all of the EHR component applications are implemented at once, although still usually by department, nursing unit, and others. A big bang approach has significant advantages in that it reduces the use of the hybrid record and end users learn and experience the entire process at once. Alternatively, it can be a huge undertaking to train and support even phases of user rollout on all applications. There are concerns that some users cannot learn or at least adapt to this much change at once. Each organization needs to evaluate its organizational culture to help it assess the best approach.

Go-live is the final stage of implementation. This is the time that the applications are turned on and users are expected to start using the system. This needs to be staged very carefully. Testing must have been done thoroughly—although it is likely there will be bugs and process and workflow issues to be ironed out as all the end users start to actually use the system. There is usually a go-live rehearsal. The day of go-live, and for some period of time afterward, usually requires extra support staff to be available near the end users. Go-live is usually performed in an ambulatory environment at a time when it is quieter, although hospitals do not often have such a luxury. Celebrating a successful go-live is also an important element. In fact, celebration of the project's milestones throughout the implementation helps all staff performing the implementation through this tedious and stressful time. Celebrating can take many forms but should be built into the organization's EHR project communication plan.

Benefits Realization, Course Correction and Ongoing Maintenance, Upgrades, and Enhancements

Benefits realization should be the culmination of the implementation. This is the point in time when the organization believes all end users are trained, the system has gone live, and there has been some period of time to get acclimated and adopt as much of the process changes and functionality as possible. The original goals are then reviewed to determine whether they have been met. Some goals may be in the form of financial rewards—where there is a specific return on investment to be achieved. Many goals for EHRs are related to patient safety and quality, yet still need to be specific and measurable, and should be evaluated that they are being met. Goals may be staged over time. For instance, in a physician office, the office may set a goal to reduce transcription by 50 percent within the first year of adoption, then to 85 percent within the second year. In a hospital, it may be that 75 percent of all medication orders and 30 percent of all other orders are entered on the CPOE system within three months of go-live, with full utilization by the end of the first year. If these milestones are not met, the organization then needs to determine why they were not met and take steps to correct course. Is it a system problem, user training issue, resistance to change, or technology issue? Sometimes an organization will not correctly anticipate the bandwidth necessary to support all the new users. Other times, the system configuration needs changing—even after careful system build tasks have been performed. Sometimes also, the goals may have been unrealistic, in which case they should be modified—but still specific and measurable. A solid management theory that "you cannot manage what you cannot measure" is true in an EHR project. If an organization cannot determine whether goals have been met, there is a management issue.

The importance of ongoing system maintenance dovetails directly with benefits realization. As previously mentioned, a clinical system demands constant updating. New drugs, new procedures, new codes, new processes, and many other factors mean continual upgrading of the software itself from the vendor and reconfiguration by the user organization. Even things that may seem minor can be major factors in maintenance. For example, if a particular CDS system alert is set to page a physician and a given physician gets a new pager, the system will need to be reset to send the page to the correct pager. This example may seem minor, but it is a major issue when the alert is a serious situation that is overlooked because the page was not received.

In addition to regular maintenance, the vendor will supply upgrades, and organizations look for enhancements. It seems the EHR project never ends. And, in fact, it must be remembered that the EHR really is not a project, but a clinical transformation program that is much broader and more encompassing of the changes needed to achieve value-driven healthcare.

True False:

1. ____ The analysis that identifies the most comprehensive picture of what an EHR will cost is the cost/benefit analysis.

2. ____ Software as a service (SaaS) utilizes newer architecture than an application service provider (ASP) offering.

3. ____ Pysicians are more likely to adopt POC documentation in their practice than in the hospital.

4. ____ A key ingredient for HIM professionals in fulfilling new roles in the EHR environment is to be especially "tech savvy."

5. ____ Considering the ability for the organization to manage change is an important element of determining readiness for EHR.

List the following in the sequence in which they are most effectively performed:

A. Goal setting
B. Project planning
C. Functional requirements analysis
D. Determining vendor viability
E. System configuration
F. Migration path development
G. Vendor demonstrations
H. Chart conversion
I. Benefits realization
J. Super user training

6. ____
7. ____
8. ____
9. ____
10. ____
11. ____
12. ____
13. ____
14. ____
15. ____

Future Directions of EHR and Health Information Technologies

This chapter describes the conceptual framework for EHR. It is an increasingly complex array of technology, applications, people, policy, and process. EHR is no longer for the academic institution or the "select few." For example, *Forbes* magazine, in an article by Sperling (2009), highlighted Citizens Memorial Healthcare (CMH), a small integrated delivery network with a 74-bed hospital, home care, long term care, and physician practices in Bolivar, Missouri. It had started its strategic planning for EHR in 1999 when it recognized that it was a facility providing longitudinal healthcare services to its community but was unable to integrate information across the continuum of care. By 2003 it had achieved a paperless state in the hospital, and by 2007 its best of fit vendor had helped it achieve a paperless environment across all sites, earning the organization the HIMSS Davies Recognition award for exemplary implementation of an EHR. Subsequently, CMH added emergency services, bar coding for medication administration, in-home telemanagement, e-Rx, additional physician practices, and a patient portal. By 2009, it was at HIMSS Analytics™ Stage 6 and was named by *BusinessWeek* magazine as one of the most wired hospitals. By 2010, the organization achieved the highest Stage 7 on the HIMSS Analytics™ EMR Adoption ModelSM (EMRAM). While only 1 percent of hospitals have achieved Stage 7 as of this writing—so still a unique position for any hospital—this case study highlights what is feasible and becoming increasingly commonplace. It also acknowledges that it is a long journey to EHR, and CMH is the first to observe that the EHR becomes an ongoing program with continual investment, with lines between health information technology and medical devices blurring. CMH notes that while increase in its ongoing IT budget was somewhat anticipated, it has been more than expected.

Factors that are contributing to the push to EHR include, obviously, the MU incentive program but also a critical mass of support systems, more manageable human–computer interfaces, pervasive use of the Internet, the IOM (2000) patient safety report, HIPAA/HITECH/ACA standards enhancements, and, perhaps most important, ever more concern about the value of the healthcare dollar and the push for health reform. The United States spends more money than any other country in the world on its healthcare services yet lags behind even some developing countries on measures such as infant mortality and life expectancy. The government, health plans, and employers are promoting consumer empowerment where the consumer is becoming much more knowledgeable and involved. The government's latest efforts are focused on accountability in healthcare, ensuring quality outcomes so that 30-day readmissions for the same condition do not occur, for example.

An EHR depends on having a critical mass of support systems. All patient care areas, ancillary departments, and support services must be automated and supply data to a CDR (or be fully integrated). More and more hospitals and physician offices are beginning to have the technology in place to support a repository and eventually an EHR. But EHR also requires much more attention to people, policy, and process than anticipated in its early days. CMH points out it made a huge project out of revamping its entire organizational structure to break down both information system silos as well as people and organizational silos. There was huge commitment from executive management. One executive manager indicated that his biggest lessons learned were to (1) talk, talk, talk; (2) listen, listen, listen; and (3) give feedback on results.

Physician leadership is vital, whether formalizing a position for **chief medical informatics officer (CMIO)** or simply cultivating strong physician champions. Additional IT support staff are almost always needed, but very important to the mix are individuals who can marry the information systems aspect with information management/clinical expertise. **Data administrators, clinical data analysts,** clinical analytics specialists, quality auditors, and others who can be the bridge, or translator, between pure IT and pure clinicians are vital.

Other factors that have contributed to expanded adoption of EHR include new technologies to address issues with human-computer interfacing. Because the change is huge and change is always difficult, there is need for a user-friendly human–computer interface and other more manageable (and affordable) technologies. The healthcare industry has always been reactive rather than proactive when it comes to new technology. Even new medical technology undergoes years of testing before it is considered safe enough to use on patients. This reluctance to use new technology, coupled with the lack of effective graphical user interfaces and data capture tools—especially such as NLP and OLAP capabilities for use at the POC—truly has held back EHR adoption, if not implementation. But these deficiencies are starting to be addressed.

The explosion of Internet use, e-commerce, and social media have resulted in not only more widespread use of computers in general and in particular by providers (who are realizing the value of enhanced communications through the Internet) and patients (who are demanding connectivity with their providers), but also greater expectations for EHRs. Clinicians want to be able to browse an EHR like they browse the Internet—and yet that is not a design that has yet been adopted, or adopted well in most EHRs.

The biggest spurt of interest in EHR, and perhaps the most compelling for providers, grew out of the IOM reports on patient safety, now several years old. As a result of these reports describing the extent of medical errors and their cause and potential cure, external pressure has been brought to bear on providers by employers and payer contracting groups. Caution must be applied, however, to recognize that many levels of automation can help reduce medical errors, while new errors may be introduced. CPOE can achieve greater legibility without a full EHR. However, a robust decision support system that is a component of an EHR identifies more contraindications, provides information on more efficacious medications, and offers evidence-based guidance.

Interestingly, HIPAA has had minimal impact on achieving the EHR to date. The goal of HIPAA was to actually "encourage the development of a health information system." The transaction and code sets regulation has required a change in claims but has done little else in the way of promoting information system use. That may well change, however, as the ACA regulations are requiring standard operating rules that will make real-time use of eligibility verification, claims status, remittance advice, and claims attachments much more feasible and meaningful to an organization's bottom line. Privacy and security regulations are written to be more supportive of health information exchange in a secure manner, yet many organizations are either confused or concerned about potential breeches and, in some cases, have used the regulations as an excuse not to proceed with more clinical computing or highly restrictive HIE policies that few are interested in paying for.

Patient medical record information (PMRI) standards, which were a part of HIPAA, have just made it into the MU incentive program requirements. Improvements for achieving interoperability are still very much needed. It is very unlikely that the United States will ever adopt a single EHR vendor across all care settings (in fact, this approach has not been successful in other countries that have tried to do so). Critical to coordinating care is integrating data from disparate systems to support EHRs. Standard vocabularies ensure that content in disparate systems carries the same meaning and have just begun to be adopted under MU and can be expected to be enhanced with the adoption of ICD-10-CM/PCS. Data content standards and data quality standards, however, still are needed to ensure internal consistency, accuracy, completeness, reliability, and timeliness.

There is every indication that the EHR's time has finally come. The future will include complete automation of support systems and use of Internet-based technology to make EHR adoption more affordable and easier to use. The future will also see much more integration of financial and clinical data as the value (quality and cost) of healthcare in the United States remains a critical issue. Individuals who not only can help plan, gain user adoption of, and maintain EHRs but understand the thoughtflow of clinicians, the information contained within the EHR, and how financial and clinical data converge will be highly sought after.

Summary

An EHR is both a reality today and still something of a goal for tomorrow. For some organizations, the reality of an EHR is the minimum necessary to achieve the MU incentives, yet potentially falling short of the goals many have espoused patient safety, quality-of-care improvements, productivity enhancements, rising healthcare costs, and other issues. This is especially true as the future of the incentive program was limited to begin with, and its continued existence let alone expansion potentially uncertain. For others, the EHR reality is a continual migration path, sometimes dictated by internal organizational issues and sometimes limited by vendor offerings. In fact, many of the organizations that are furthest along seem to feel they have a longer migration path ahead them than others that are less fully implemented. Such organizations recognize that there are always new technologies, new challenges, new clinical findings, and new users. Wherever organizations are on their migration path to the EHR, however, the vision of its early pioneers, carried forward

by the IOM and now federal government initiatives, is very much a goal of all healthcare organizations.

References

16 CFR Part 318. Health Breach Notification Rule, Federal Trade Commission.

21 CFR Parts 1300, 1304, 1306, and 1311. Electronic Prescriptions for Controlled Substances, Department of Justice, Drug Enforcement Administration, Office of Diversion Control.

45 CFR Parts 160, 162, and 164 HIPAA Transactions and Code Sets, Security Rule, Privacy Rule, Breach Notification for Unsecured Protected Health Information. Department of Health and Human Services.

American Health Information Management Association. 2011 (February). Fundamentals of the legal health record and designated record set. *Journal of AHIMA* 82(2).

Amatayakul, M.K. 2012a. *Electronic Health Records: A Practical Guide for Professionals and Organizations,* 5th ed. Chicago: AHIMA.

Amatayakul, M.K. 2012b. *Process Improvement with Electronic Health Records: A Stepwise Approach to Workflow and Process Management.* Boca Raton, FL: CRC Press.

Amatayakul, M.K. 2010b. *The No-Hassle Guide to EHR Policies.* Marblehead, MA: HCPro.

Amatayakul, M.K. 2010a. *Electronic Health Records: Transforming Your Medical Practice,* 2nd ed. Englewood, CO: MGMA.

Amatayakul, M.K. 2009. *Guide to HIPAA Privacy and Security Auditing: Practical Tools and Tips to Ensure Compliance*, 2nd ed. Marblehead, MA: HCPro.

American Academy of Family Practice. 2008. E-visits. http://www .aafp.org/online/en/home/policy/policies/e/evists.printerview.html.

Anderson, M.R. 2009 (February 3). DRT-enabled EHRs. http:// www.acgroup.org/images/2009-02_What_is_DRT.pdf.

Assatourians, L. et al. 2010 (February 4). Engaging patients in using technology to manage their personal health care. AMA/ TransforMED webinar. http://www.ama-assn.org/ama1/pub/upload/ mm/472/ama-transformed-engaging-patients-technology.pdf.

ASTM International. 2005. ASTM E2369-05 Standard Specification for Continuity of Care Record (CCR). http://www.astm.org/ Standards/E2369.htm.

Bachman, J. 2007 (July/August). Improving care with an automated patient history. *Family Practice Management* 14(7): 39–43.

Ball, M.J., and S. Bierstock. 2007 (Summer). Clinician use of enabling technology. *Journal of Healthcare Information Management* 21(3): 68–71.

Berner, E.S. 2009. Clinical decision support systems: State of the art. AHRQ Publication No. 09-0069-EF. Rockville, MD: Agency for Healthcare Research and Quality. http://healthit.ahrq.gov/im-ages/jun09cdsreview/09_0069_ef.html.

Blokdijk, G. 2010. *Virtualization—the Complete Cornerstone Guide to Virtualization Best Practices*, 2nd ed. Newstead, Australia: Emereo Pty Ltd.

Blumenthal, D. 2009 (December 27). Presentation to the American Medical Informatics Association. http://www.informationweek.com/blog/healthcare/229204271?printer_friendly=this-page.

Bonsall, L. 2011 (May 27). 8 rights of medication administration. Lippincott's Nursing Center .com. http://www.nursingcwenter.com/Blog/post/2011/05/27/8-rights-of-medication-administration.aspx.

BusinessWeek. 2009. Most wired hospitals: Citizens Memorial Healthcare. http://images .businessweek.com/ss/09/04/0407_ceo_guide_emedical_records/6.htm.

Cerrato, P. 2012 (January 5). Is your clinical database up to speed? *InformationWeek*. http://www.informationweek.com/news/health-care/clinical-systems/232301360.

Certification Commission for Healthcare Information Technology. 2009. *Usability Testing Guide*. http://www.cchit.org/get_certified.

Conn, J. 2007 (July 30). What does a chief medical information officer do? *Modern Healthcare*.

Connecting for Health, Markle Foundation. 2006. Connecting Americans to Their Health Care: A Common Framework for Networked Personal Health Information.

Constantine, L.L., and L.A.D. Lockwood. 2003. Structure and style in use cases for user interface design. forUSE 2003 2nd Int'l Conference on Usage-Centered Design Conference Proceedings. http://www.foruse.com/articles/structurestyle2.pdf.

Dolan, P.L. 2011 (May 2). Electronic medical records: What your data can tell you. amednews.com. http://www.ama-assn.org/amednews/2011/05/02/bisa0502.htm.

Graham, J., and C. Dizikes. 2011 (June 27). Baby's death spotlights safety risks linked to computerized systems. *Chicago Tribune*. http://articles.chicagotribune.com/2011-06-27/news/ct-met-technology-errors-20110627_1_electronic-medical-records-physicians-systems.

Hardy, K. 2010 (May 19). Data storage of top concern to healthcare providers. *Healthcare IT News*.

Health Level Seven. 2009. *EHR System Functional Model, Release 1.1*. Ann Arbor, MI: Health Level Seven.

Health Level Seven. 2008. *PHR-System Functional Model, Release 1 DSTU*. Ann Arbor, MI: Health Level Seven.

Health Level Seven. 2007 (June). *Legal Electronic Health Record-System Functional Profile*. Registration Release 1 (v1.0). Ann Arbor, MI: Health Level Seven.

Health Information and Management Systems Society. 2006. The ROI of EMR-EHR: Productivity soars, hospitals save time and, yes, money. Chicago: Healthcare Information Management and Systems Society. http://www.himss.org/content/files/davies/Davies_WP_ROI.pdf.

Health Information and Management Systems Society. 2005. Full application: Davies Award Program: Citizens Memorial Healthcare. http://www.himss.org/content/files/davies/2005/CMH_FULL_APPLICATION.pdf.

HIMSS Analytics™. 2008, 2012. EMR Adoption Model. Chicago, IL: Healthcare Information Management and Systems Society. http://www.himssanalytics.org/hc_providers/emr_adoption.asp.

HIMSS Analytics™. 2010 (January 7). Clinical analytics: can organizations maximize clinical data? http://www.himssanalytics.org/docs/clinical_analytics.pdf.

Hirsch, J., and F. Marano. 2007. Better patient care through video interpretation. http://www.healthmgttech.com/index.php/solutions/hospitals/better-patient-care-through-video-interpretation/Print.html.

Hoyt, B. 2011. Low cost electronic health records. Health informatics in developing countries. http://www.healthinformaticsforum.com/forum/topics/low-cost-electronic-health.

Infection Control Today. 2010 (July 13). Clinical surveillance system documents interventions to help reduce catheter-related infections. http://www.infectioncontroltoday.com/news/2010/07/clinical-surveillance-system-documents-interventions-to-help-reduce-catheter-related-infections.aspx.

Institute for Safe Medication Practices. 2007 (July). Nurses' rights regarding safe medication administration. *ISMP Medication Safety Alert! Nurse Advise-ERR*. 5(7) Horsham, PA: Institute for Safe Medication Practices.

Institute for Safe Medication Practices. 2004 (November). The *five rights* cannot stand alone. *ISMP Medication Safety Alert! Nurse Advise-ERR*. 2(11). Horsham, PA: Institute for Safe Medication Practices.

Institute for Safe Medication Practices. 1999 (April 7). The "five rights." *ISMP Medication Safety Alert!* Horsham, PA: Institute for Safe Medication Practices. http://www.ismp.org/Newsletters/acutecare/articles/19990407.asp.

Institute of Medicine. 2003. Key capabilities of an electronic health record system. Letter Report. Washington, D.C.: IOM. http://www.nap.edu/books/NI000427/html.

Institute of Medicine. 2000. *To Err Is Human: Building a Safer Health System*. Washington, D.C.: National Academies Press.

Institute of Medicine. 1997. *The Computer-based Patient Record: An Essential Technology for Health Care. Revised Edition*. Washington, D.C.: National Academy Press.

Institute of Medicine. 1991. *The Computer-Based Patient Record: An Essential Technology for Health Care*. Washington, D.C.: National Academies Press.

Irby, L. 2010 (March 23). Medical identity theft on the rise—statistics. http://www.spendonlife.com/blog/medical-identity-theft-statistics.

Kahn, J.M. 2011 (January 1). The use and misuse of ICU telemedicine. *Journal of the American Medical Association* 305(21): 2227–2228.

Kelly, J. 2011 (April 18). Lack of EHR standards hampering healthcare data analytics. http://siliconangle.com/blog/2011/04/18/ehr-standards-healthcare-data-analytics/.

Koppell, R., et al. 2008 (July/August). Workarounds to barcode medication administration systems: Their occurrences, causes, and threats to patient safety. *Journal of the American Medical Informatics Association* (15)4: 408–423.

Leonhardt, D. 2006 (February 22). Why doctors so often get it wrong. *The New York Times*. http://www.nytimes.com/2006/02/22/business/22leonhardt.html.

Lewis, N. 2011 (April 8). Consumers slow to adopt electronic personal health records. *InformationWeek*. http://www.informationweek.com/news/healthcare/EMR/229401249.

Lisby, M., et al. 2010 (December). How are medication errors defined? A systematic literature review of definitions and characteristics. *International Journal of Quality in Health Care* 22(6): 507–18.

Lundberg, C.B. et al. 2008 (June). Selecting a standardized terminology for the electronic health record that reveals the impact of nursing on patient care. *Online Journal of Nursing Informatics* http://ojni.org/12_2/lundberg.pdf.

Mell, P., and T. Grance. 2011 (September). The NIST Definition of Cloud Computing. NIST Special Publication 800-145. Gaithersburg, MD: National Institute of Standards and Technology.

Melville, N.A. 2012 (January 18). Teledermatology sessions improve diagnoses, outcomes. *Medscape Medical News*. http://www.medscape.com/viewarticel/757108.

National Alliance for Health Information Technology. 2008 (April 28). Defining key health information technology terms. http://healthit.hhs.gov/portal/server.pt/...0...0.../10_2_hit_terms.pdf.

National Committee for Quality Assurance. 2011 (February 1). *PCMH 2011 Standards*. Washington, D.C.: National Committee for Quality Assurance.

Office for Civil Rights. 2011 (December 31). Health information privacy rule enforcement highlights. http://www.hhs.gov/ocr/privacy/hipaa/enforcement/highlights/index.html.

O'Malley, A.S., et al. 2010 (March). Are electronic medical records helpful for care coordination? Experiences of physician practices. *Journal of General Internal Medicine* 25(3): 177–185.

Office of the National Coordinator for Health Information Technology. 2012. ONC certified health IT product list. http://onc-chpl.force.com/ehrcert/EHRProductSearch.

Passuello, L. 2007. What is mind mapping? (and how to get started immediately). *The Very Best of Litemind: 2 Years of Mind Explorations*. http://litemind.com/what-is-mind-mapping?.

Phillips, M.T., and E.S. Berner. 2004 (Fall). Beating the system—pitfalls of bar code medication administration. *Journal of Healthcare Information Management* 18(4): 16–18.

Pryor, D.B., et al. 2006. The clinical transformation of Ascension Health: Eliminating all preventable injuries and deaths. *Joint Commission Journal on Quality and Patient Safety* 32(6): 299–308(10).

Pulley, J. 2010 (June 1). EHRs not so user-friendly. *Health IT Update*. http://healthitupdate.nextgov.com/2010/06/the_usability_or_lack_thereof.php.

Raths, D. 2011 (April 8). Report from PharEHR Summit: Will FDA regulate EHRs? *Healthcare Informatics*. http://www.healthcare-informatics.com/article/report-pharmehr-summit-will-fda-regulate-ehrs.

Resnik, P. et al. 2008 (Fall). Communication of clinically relevant information in electronic health records: A comparison between structured data and unrestricted physician language. *Perspectives in HIM, CAC Proceedings*. http://perspectives.ahima.org/index.php?option=com_content&view=article&id=136:communication-of-clinically-relevant-information-in-electronic-health-records-a-comparison-between-structured-data-and-unrestricted-physician-language&catid=58:conference-paper&Itemid=110.

Rollins, G. 2005 (February). The prompt, the alert, and the legal record: Documenting clinical decision support systems. *Journal of AHIMA 76(2): 24–28.*

Servais, C.E. 2008. *The Legal Health Record*. Chicago: AHIMA.

Sperling, E. 2009 (May 25). Prescription for e-health care: How Citizens Memorial Hospital is stepping into the digital age. *Forbes*. http://www.forbes.com/2009/05/22/healthcare-hospital-internet-technology-cio-network-healthcare.html.

Stead, W.W., and H.S. Lin, eds. 2009. *Computational Technology for Effective Health Care: Immediate Steps and Strategic Directions, 2–5*. National Research Council. National Academy of Sciences. Washington, D.C.: National Academies Press.

Strong, K. 2008. Enterprise content and records management. *Journal of AHIMA* 80(2): 38–42.

Swan, H. 2011 (July 15). Mind mapping: A simpler way to capture information. iSixSigma. http://www.isixsigma.com/tools-templates/sampling-data/mind-mapping-simpler-way-capture-information/.

Tate, J. et al. 2006. *Introduction to Storage Area Networks*, 4th ed. IBM Redbooks. http://www.redbooks.ibm.com/redbooks/pdfs/sg245470.pdf.

Tonelli, M. 2006 (February). Evidence-based medicine and clinical expertise: Physicians should incorporate a balance of evidence-based medicine with expertise and experience in their clinical decision-making process. *Virtual Mentor*:71–74. http://virtualmentor.ama-assn.org/2006/02/ccas1–0602.html.

TripleTree. 2006. Healthcare revenue cycle management. Spotlight Report. http://www.connextions.com/files/TripleTreeRevenueCycle.pdf.

Versel, N. 2011 (December 19). 10 innovative clinical decision support programs. *Information Week*. http://www.informationweek.com/news/galleries/healthcare/clinical-systems/232300511.

Watson, A.J. et al. 2010 (April). A randomized trial to evaluate the efficacy of online follow-up visits in the management of acne. *Archives of Dermatology* 146(4): 406–411.

Whiting, R. 2001 (September 24). Data analysis to health care's rescue: IT helps health-care group identify best clinical practices. *Information Week*. http://www.informationweek.com/news/6506582.

Wians, F.H. 2009 (February). Clinical laboratory tests: Which, why, and what do the results mean? *LAB Medicine* 40(2): 105–106.

Witry, M.J., et al. 2010 (Winter). Family physician perceptions of personal health records. Perspectives in HIM. http://perspectives.ahima.org/index.php?option=com_content&view=article&id=169:family-physician-perceptions-of-personal-health-records-&catid=38:education-a-careers&Itemid=84.

Wright, A. et al. 2011 (May). Development and evaluation of a comprehensive clinical decision support taxonomy: Comparison of front-end tools in commercial and internally developed electronic health record systems. *Journal of the American Medical Informatics Association*. 18(3):232–242.

Wright, K. 2005. Home telemonitoring: VNA Western Pennsylvania. 2005 Telehealth Leadership Conference. http://www.homehealthquality.org/hh/medqic/BlobServerc9b3.pdf?blobkey=id&blobwhere=1228861148646&blobheader=application%2Fpdf&blobheadername1=Content-Disposition&blobheadervalue1=attachment%3Bfilename%3D8.+Acute_Care_Hosp_no_tab.pdf&blobcol=urldata&blobtable=MungoBlobs.

part **II**

Healthcare Data Management

chapter 6

Healthcare Data Life Cycle: Governance and Stewardship

Linda Kloss, RHIA, CAE, FAHIMA

Learning Objectives

- Understand foundational data and information management concepts at an organizational level and for a health system
- Describe a model for managing digital information over its life cycle
- Distinguish among data, information technology, and information governance and describe their relationship
- Contrast general approaches and challenges of managing records, data, and information
- Define data stewardship and describe the key challenges of data stewardship at an organizational level and for a health system

- Distinguish between stewardship and governance from a conceptual and a practical level
- Delineate critical information governance functions and criteria for judging their effectiveness
- Describe considerations in organizing for enterprise information management, information governance and stewardship, and life cycle management
- Discuss the role of health information management professionals in enterprise information management, information governance, stewardship, and life cycle management

Key Terms

Content and records management
Data quality
Enterprise information
   management (EIM)
Information
Information asset management (IAM)
Information content

Information governance (IG)
Information integrity
Information life cycle
Information management (IM)
Information science
Information theory
Stewardship

Our Growing Understanding of Information

This chapter briefly steps outside the healthcare industry and considers information as a theory, an entity with properties, and an asset to be preserved and enhanced. James Gleick states that the word *information* began to be used in a scientific context in the late 1940s (Gleick 2011). Contemporary thinking about information theory and information science coincided with the invention of the transistor and the early use of the term *bit* as a unit of measure for information. Information began to be thought of as something that could be modeled, counted, transmitted, and processed, concepts familiar in today's information society.

Gleick captures the foundational value of information when he states, "We can see now that information is what our world runs on: the blood and the fuel, the vital principle ... in the long run, history is the story of information becoming aware of itself" (Gleick 2011). Information is the basis for all sciences. It is now understood that information processing is the key function of DNA and the basis for physics and the structure of the universe. So, it really can be said that information is fundamental to life.

Understanding of information has advanced immensely in the last six decades. **Information theory** today is a branch of applied mathematics and electrical engineering and involves the quantification of information. Information theory impacts fields from mathematics to management, astronomy to physics, and, of course, biology to medicine. Health information management today is the beneficiary of scientific advancement related to information theory in tools such as natural language processing, statistical inference, and other forms of data analysis.

In addition to advancements in understanding and applying the mathematics and engineering of information, **information science** has developed as a multidisciplinary field primarily concerned with the analysis, collection, classification, manipulation, storage, retrieval, and dissemination of information. This is the space in which health information management lives as an applied information science with data and information about health and healthcare at its core.

Contemporary Information Management Concepts

In the 21st century, information is no longer viewed as an incidental by-product of business operations to be catalogued and archived. Today, it is the key to understanding and improving the performance of organizations. The medical record and billing claim can be thought of as by-products of the patient care process, but also the source for data used to improve those processes. Health informatics and information management (HIIM) is concerned with the timely and accurate capture and processing of this transactional information. At the same time, HIIM needs to be concerned with managing information in all its forms and using it to its full potential.

Contemporary information management practices rest on three foundational principles: **information asset management (IAM), information management (IM),** and **information governance (IG).**

Principle One: Information Is an Asset That Must Be Effectively Managed

Information is an asset of the organization that has strategic value. Like other assets such as bricks and mortar properties, people, finances, and intellectual property, information must be deliberately managed. The information assets of the healthcare organization include primary and secondary medical records data, business operations data, images, personal health records, performance review, and other content in both physical and digital form. Information assets are more difficult to envision and quantify, so emphasis continues to be placed on the technology rather than the information content that IT and other technologies capture, store, and process.

The value of the information asset accrues from its use. When information is viewed as an asset and managed accordingly, there is greater trust in it and greater willingness to make information-informed decisions. Without trust, the value of information is diminished. Healthcare organizations are now expanding their use of information to improve care to patient populations and improve organizational performance. They are providing information to patients and the public. These vital uses require greater discipline in managing information assets so they are reliable and available to support use by competent users.

Principle Two: Information Management Is an Organization-wide Function

Ensuring the value of information assets requires an organization-wide perspective of information management functions. It calls for explicit structures, policies, processes, technology, and controls that taken together describe the discipline of enterprise information management (EIM). The scope of EIM may be expanded as information assets come under better control, but the nexus of healthcare EIM is the primary and secondary patient data, structured and unstructured, residing in enterprise and departmental systems regardless of media. Billing and payment information, e-mail, personal health record data, employee and contractor information, quality improvement data, health information exchange, and other information must begin to be viewed as elements of the information asset mosaic and managed accordingly. This includes managing across the life cycle of the information. The **information life cycle** has five stages:

- *Record creation, capture, or receipt.* This phase includes creating, editing, and reviewing work in process as well as capture of content (such as through document imaging technology) or receipt of content (such as through a health information exchange).

- *Record maintenance and use.* Once records are created, they must be maintained in such a way that they are accessible and retrievable. Components of this phase include functions, rules, and protocols for indexing, searching, retrieving, processing, routing, and distributing.
- *Classification and metadata.* Classification is a critical component of records management. Though not a unique point in the lifecycle, it does support the other phases. Record classification creates categories or groups of records necessary for access, search, retrieval, retention, and disposition of records.
- *Metadata* are generated at various points in the records management lifecycle, providing underlying data to describe the document, specify access controls and rights, provide retention and disposition instructions, and maintain the record history and audit trail.
- *Record audit and data controls.* Controls and audits support a variety of phases in the record lifecycle. Functions and processes in this component of records management may include edit checks at the data level, decision support tools, identification of classes of records that require auditing, and checks for record completeness.
- *Record preservation and retention.* Preservation is synonymous with storage. Issues associated with preservation include: technology and media obsolescence, media degradation, media in an archival system, conversion over time, and conversion of standards over time. (AHIMA 2008)

There is still a great deal to be learned about how to manage dynamic healthcare information assets across their life cycle. A career in health information management calls upon professionals to find pragmatic solutions to an array of information management challenges so the right—and right amount—of information is available to support the evolving needs of healthcare.

Principle Three: Information Governance Is a Crucial Building Block of EIM

Governance is about assigning rights and responsibilities and ensuring accountability; governance is an oversight function that makes certain that critical processes and practices are being reasonably carried out. With regard to information governance, experts at the Gartner Group describe **enterprise information management (EIM)** as an essential organizational discipline and information governance as a crucial building block of EIM (Logan 2009). Information governance is like the accountability wrapper for EIM, and it is more fully explained later in this chapter.

Information governance is becoming a key focus for businesses in other information-intensive and regulated sectors, particularly those such as financial services, energy and utilities, and pharmaceuticals. Like all effective governance, information governance begins with the boards of trustees and senior leaders. Hospital boards are now holding senior management accountable for steps being taken to avoid breaches of data. Information exchange and greater transparency and public accountability for outcomes and cost raise the stakes.

Taken together, IAM, EIM, and IG have potential to mitigate risk, improve organizational performance, and reduce costs. In research conducted by *The Economist*, businesses with formalized information governance report improved decision making and business results due to better access to information and improved information sharing (*The Economist* 2008). The researchers cite service and product quality gains because information is more accurate and reliable. They also report improved business risk management and enhanced reputation due to better information security practices. They attribute improved cost control of IT and IT-related services to tighter and more strategic planning and acquisition processes.

The demand for high-quality data and improved governance to support patient care and critical healthcare initiatives is sharply increasing. Health delivery and payment reform will keep information management and information governance in the spotlight. Health informatics and information management professionals are dedicated to ensuring that useful and useable information is available to those who need it to care for patients, manage population and public health, and improve health system performance. In the years to come, some level of information management will be a core competency for all who work in healthcare and for people who manage their health and that of their families and loved ones.

Check Your Understanding 6.1

Instructions: Answer the following questions on a separate piece of paper.

1. Explain the difference between information theory and information science. Where does HIIM fit?

2. Name three key principles for sound contemporary information management and the relationship of the three principles to one another.

3. List the five stages of the information life cycle, and give an example of an information management function that might be performed for each.

4. Describe three implications of the adoption of information technology (IT) by healthcare organizations on the functions of enterprise information management and information governance.

Building Blocks of EIM

Enterprise information management for healthcare organizations can be described as the set of components shown in figure 6.1. Each component is comprised of processes, policies, people, and technology.

Figure 6.1.   Components of EIM

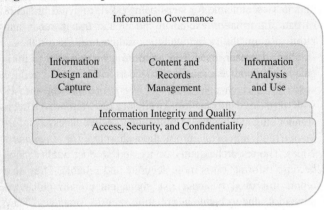

Taken together, the EIM components comprise a managerial system with oversight through information governance. Just as cells are to biology, data, information, and content are to EIM. EIM demands a systems view of managing information over its life cycle. Organizations that take a systems view will have knowledge of the types and definitions of data and its lineage. EIM will have mechanisms to track who uses the data and how it is used. EIM will assess the reliability of information to ensure that it is in line with the criticality of these uses. EIM will ensure that those who view data and information are authorized to do so. EIM will understand how long information should be retained and in what form. And EIM will ensure that there is an internal learning system or feedback loop so information management policies and practices are being adapted and improved continuously.

Figure 6.2 states the overarching goals of each building block of an EIM management system. The pages that follow drill down one level further to explore key policy, process, people, and technology issues associated with each component.

Access, Security, and Confidentiality

For healthcare organizations, privacy, security, and confidentiality are bedrock functions foundational to EIM. Information management in healthcare is grounded in recognition of an individual's right to control the acquisition, use, and disclosure of his or her identifiable health data. All who receive and handle information have obligations to respect the individual's privacy rights. Security refers to the physical, technological, and other tools used to protect identifiable data from unwarranted access or disclosure.

Privacy and security programs are often framed narrowly as the Health Insurance Portability and Accountability Act (HIPAA) compliance rather than more broadly as a critical aspect of information asset management. Failure to implement sound practices can result in damage to the reputation of the organization, its employees, and its affiliates and compromise the trust of patients, stakeholders, and communities. It can result in monetary damages and diminish the value of the information asset.

Examples of how an EIM culture might alter the value and effectiveness of access, security, and confidentiality practices are illustrated in figure 6.3. The value proposition for access, security, and confidentiality practices is increased when framed as a foundational part of EIM with governance oversight. Compliance remains important, but it is not the only rationale.

Figure 6.2.   EIM goals

EIM Building Blocks	
Access, Security, and Confidentiality	To ensure that personal health information and business information are available only to authorized persons and used only for authorized purposes and that security risks and vulnerabilities are proactively managed.
Information Integrity and Quality	To continuously improve the value and trustworthiness of the information asset by ensuring that data and content are valid, accurate, reliable, up to date, and "fit for use."
Information Design and Capture	To continuously improve the standards-based policies and practices for data capture and clinical documentation that supports the full range of uses and enable interoperability, exchange, and linkage.
Content and Records Management	To continuously improve the methods whereby corporate and health records and data content are maintained across their life cycle and regardless of media, to ensure compliance with regulatory, accreditation, and legal best practices.
Information Analysis, Use, and Exchange	To align data and content requirements and availability to the needs of those who rely on information for a range of clinical and business uses and ensure that those who must act on information have the requisite tools and skills to use it effectively.
Information Governance	To ensure leadership and organizational practices, resources, and controls for effective, compliant, and ethical stewardship of information assets to enable best clinical and business practices and serve patients, stakeholders, and the public good.

Figure 6.3.   Comparing access, security, and confidentiality approaches

	Pre-EIM	EIM Culture
Access, Security, and Confidentiality	• Compliance focused • Gaps in policy framework • Focus on threats of punishment for noncompliance • Vulnerabilities in planning for disruptions • Limited connections between related functions, for example, privacy and security have limited crossover	• Stewardship focused • Policy planning integral to process, system changes • Incentives for sound stewardship • Business continuity planning and plan • Safeguards against accidental or deliberate information corruption due to accidental failures or deliberate fraud • Routine audits of compliance leading to improvement

Information Integrity and Quality

This second foundational component, information integrity and quality, is arguably the most underdeveloped and at the same time the most urgently needed of the EIM building blocks. The explosive growth of digital information has led to a state of disorder that makes it difficult to trust, track, and analyze health information. The factors giving rise to these risks are certainly not all attributable to changing the medium from paper to computer, nor are they within the control of the organization as some issues relate to design of the human–machine interface. Information integrity is never easily managed because of the range of factors that must be understood and managed:

1. Change: Depending on how they are designed and executed, organizational structure, regulation, personnel, hardware, and software can compromise or enhance integrity

2. Complexity: The sheer number of systems supporting high-stakes and high-speed work processes and communications carried out across staffs can number in the thousands

3. Conversion: Software and systems upgrades and conversions are a high-risk time for data as well as disruption to work process

4. Corruption: Accidental failures, deliberate fraud, and other situations can profoundly impact the integrity of health information

Information integrity is the dependability or trustworthiness of information—it encompasses the entire framework in which information is recorded, processed, and used (AHIMA 2012). The concept is larger than data quality. Whereas **data quality** focuses on guarding against and correcting bad data, information integrity encompasses three domains and the relationship among them:

- *Information content* includes the data elements including their underlying definitions and relevant data content standards in whatever form they are held, that is, numeric, text, structured, unstructured, digital, paper, e-mail, transaction reports, spreadsheets, analytic reports, databases, and such. Metadata, which are characterized as information about the information, are included in this definition of information content.

- *Process* refers to the functions used to transform an input into a specified output and the policies that guide how they are carried out. Vocabulary mapping, coding, decision support algorithms, and the claims adjudication process are familiar examples of health information processes that have the potential to impact on the quality of information, positively and negatively.

- *System* in this context is the human, IT, organizational, and regulatory environment configured to achieve a specific purpose. Again, how systems and subsystems work together can impact information integrity. Consider the example of a major software upgrade and the attendant risk of new information integrity issues. The transition from ICD-9 to ICD-10 is a classic case study in how all parts of the system must come together to ensure information integrity.

Healthcare organizations must invest in data quality, but they are advised to consider the broader issues of content, process, and system that enhance or impede information integrity as a prerequisite for many other information management initiatives. Examples of how an EIM culture might alter the way in which information integrity and data quality are carried out are highlighted in figure 6.4.

Information Design and Capture

As depicted in figure 6.1, information design and capture is a first cluster of EIM functions. The key requirements of this process depend on who is setting them. For clinicians, data capture and documentation facilitate decision making by individual clinicians and communication with other members of the clinical teams. Patients want their care teams well informed and coordinated. Risk managers require that data capture and documentation produce a

Figure 6.4. Comparing information integrity and quality approaches

	Pre-EIM	EIM Culture
Information Integrity and Quality	• Limited systematic data quality assessment • Reactive response to data quality problems • Lack of trust in data • Lack of standard protocols for error correction • Data scrubbing and cleansing in the creation of data warehouses • Modification of existing systems to accommodate changes such as new regulations	• Standards- and definitions-based data capture • Knowledge of data provenance and lineage • Protocols for monitoring end-to-end impact of conversions and upgrades • Systematic data quality monitoring based on assessed risks • Error correction and amendment processes

complete and logical chronology, quality managers require data that support the measures being tracked, and financial services must ensure that information substantiates the billing claim.

The IM challenge, of course, is to meet the range of needs while also ensuring that information and data standards are being used to the fullest extent and that data are interoperable and understandable by those who receive it. IM must also support efficient data capture of useful data, avoiding redundancy and rework, and provide training and guidance for staff who create the records.

Like other aspects of healthcare IM, the issues relating to efficient capture of information are layered. If designing healthcare information capture from a blank slate, the process would undoubtedly start by assessing data needs, defining data sets based on data content standards and standardized definitions for data elements, and using an information architecture designed for interoperability and information liquidity. But this is not how health IT has evolved, and it is not possible to start over.

Standards development organizations are now working on data content standards, but it will be some time before systems are retrofitted. Meaningful use incentives are imposing greater standardization in how some data are collected. EIM must keep current on these developments to make certain they are well integrated in operations. At

the same time, IM must move forward by making incremental change in areas where there is greatest potential to improve.

As illustrated in figure 6.5, formalized EIM should assess and create policy and learn how best to adapt current practices that compromise data, introduce risk, or impede efficient data capture. Some examples include setting policy for the use of the electronic health record (EHR) copy and paste functionality, improving on formats for standard reports to spotlight important data, and introducing speech recognition and natural language processing solutions to permit clinicians a choice in how they capture data.

There are great opportunities to improve the information design and capture process, improvements that will have quantifiable positive impact on the quality and reliability of information and its value.

Content and Records Management

Health information management professionals understand the goals of the records management component as this has been a core focus for the profession since its inception. The need for more effective management of information content, generally defined as unstructured information, is a newer area of IM focus. This is important because valuable health

Figure 6.5. Comparing information design and capture approaches

	Pre-IAM/EIM	EIM Culture
Information Design and Capture	• Adapted work process to technology constraints • Highly customized solutions with wide personal preference latitude • Documentation improvement as an overlay to the process of data capture • Productivity barriers leading to poor morale • User interface issues impeding safe and effective care	• Process for assessing data needs and improving data capture and documentation over time • Knowledgeable and proactive users behind coordinated efforts to improve the design of technology and the tools used for data capture • Understood and addressed impact on productivity and user acceptability of how structured and unstructured data are captured and available

Figure 6.6.   Content and records management

	Pre-IAM/EIM	EIM Culture
Content and Records Management	• Records management not addressed in specifications for technology acquisition • Permanent retention of all the data • Data silos and data owners unaware of rules for records management • Unmanaged content accumulates in an increasing number of files and applications • The official health record has information holes because valuable unstructured data are inaccessible • Data redundancy expands	• Policies expanded to include the range of record types • Policies linked to business strategy • Retention policies and planning • Audit practices to ensure that policies and practices are being carried out • Records management issues considered as part of technology acquisition

record information lives outside the EHR. There is a spectrum of unstructured data content that needs to be considered, including

- Paper source documents such as record forms received from other providers, consents, and other forms
- Electronic source documents whose data of interest are not structured; e-mail and transcribed reports fall into this category
- Sources that are not documents but rather video, voice, or pictures

While the goals of effective records management remain constant, the transition from paper to computer necessitates revising and restoring some traditionally well-managed practices that are disrupted in the transition. For example, the hospital industry historically agreed on policies for records retention, and these were reflected in law. The definitions of the standard content of the health record have also been set aside and new standards are only now being advanced. Content management is less well developed; taken together, the **content and records management** functions of IM are in need of redesign and greater standardization because digital health information is characterized as follows:

- Rather than a physical record, the health record today is comprised of linked multimedia files and this changes the focus and scope of content and records management.
- The content management functions extend beyond the metaphorical cover of the health record to include secondary data and other sources such as registries, warehouses, e-mail, personal health records, and other content that is not ordinarily part of the legal electronic health record.
- Payment and health delivery reform will further reshape our frame for records management. As ambulatory and inpatient data are merged for population management and bundled payment, traditional inpatient and ambulatory content and record boundaries are breaking down.

The content and records management functions of IM encompass the official health records and range of other ancillary corporate records regardless of media. They focus on the life cycle of these records and content to ensure that such content is being systematically reviewed, classified, retained, and disposed of according to policies and practices that reflect standards, regulations, and laws. Content and records management also addresses the specific protocols and requirements for managing records involved in litigation. Electronic discovery is a critical, complex, and costly process that must be done very well. Figure 6.6 offers some contrast between the current state of content and records management and the desired state possible through an EIM approach.

Information Analysis and Use

Information management plays an important role in supporting the analysis and use of information directly and indirectly. First, major high-stakes applications such as computerized provider order entry (CPOE), patient portals, quality measurement, and information exchange require a systematic approach to IM. This must begin at the definitional stage when data needs are assessed, data content definitions are developed, and decisions are made about the information architecture. It is very difficult to fulfill the user's requirements if the requisite data are not captured or are captured in a way that limits their usefulness.

Information management contributes to the upstream value of information by focusing on the user's data needs and requirements (as distinct from user interface or functionality) and contributing to the design of solutions that enable capture and access to data that meet integrity requirements for that application. It is important to underscore that data quality and integrity requirements may differ depending on the application. CPOE and other applications that are used for real-time clinical decision support require the highest standards, whereas aggregate data applications for general trend analysis can tolerate some data errors.

Information management strives to understand the data issues, including data integrity requirements in each

Figure 6.7. Information analysis and use

	Pre-IAM/EIM	**EIM Culture**
Information Analysis and Use	• Users maintain the information they need • Tools and products are purchased without scrutiny of data properties and information integrity capabilities • Information changes in one system are not replicated in others • New error is introduced because upgrades and interfaces are not consistently tested using standard test databases and test scripts • Users get minimal training in how to capture, analyze, and use information	• Greater trust in the data and willingness to act on information • Greater consistency in information and information policy across the system, lowering the risk and the cost • Information value increases with use because issues are proactively identified and resolved • Competence in the capture, analysis, and use of information is defined by stakeholder; suitable training and support are available • Upgrades and interfaces do not introduce unanticipated information issues

application. Nothing compromises user acceptance as fast as encountering data errors and finding that no one knows or is managing the quality of data. IM also supports the end users with training, guidance, and feedback loops so the experiences of users are brought back through the IM process. See figure 6.7.

Information management helps those who use the data for operations and business management and various secondary uses to understand its availability, meaning, and limitations. "Clinical analytics" and "business intelligence" are contemporary terms describing solutions designed to extract useful properties from data to enable clinical and organizational performance improvement. There is a strong IM component to these functions as the data must be fit for use, available, and understandable to users.

Check Your Understanding 6.2

Instructions: Answer the following questions on a separate piece of paper.

1. Name the five components of EIM.

2. Name three processes that you would expect to see in place for access, security, and confidentiality in an organization with an EIM culture.

3. Name three processes that you would expect to see in place for information integrity and quality in an organization with an EIM culture.

4. What is the purpose of "clinical analytics" or "business intelligence" solutions?

Information Governance

This section addresses information governance and reasons why it is a crucial building block of EIM. In corporate and nonprofit organizations, boards of trustees and senior leaders understand governance principles and practices and

have put in place governance practices for the organization's fiscal, property, compliance, human resource, and other aspects of managing complex organizations. Most do not yet include the organization's information assets within the scope of their governance duties, though this is changing quickly in information-intensive corporations. Healthcare lags, but the explosive growth of digital information with poor information governance impedes trust and willingness to act on data.

A working definition of information governance is

> The leadership and organizational structures, policies, procedures, technology, and controls that ensure that patient and other enterprise data and information sustain and extend the organization's mission and strategies, deliver value, comply with laws and regulations, minimize risk to all stakeholders, and advance the public good (Kloss 2011).

Governance is not about doing; it is about assuring, assessing, and enabling. Boards of directors and senior leaders at organizations that understand the value of information asset management exercise governance by first asking questions and then seeing to it that plans are put in place where they do not exist or are inadequate. Such questions include the following:

- Is there a policy, strategy, and management plan in place for information life cycle management?
- How do we assess the organization's capabilities regarding information security, and what is the plan advancing these capabilities?
- Are our privacy practices sufficient to avoid breaches, and if a breach occurs, what is our plan for managing it?
- How do we inform patients about their information rights, and how we are protecting and using their information?

Information governance also assesses the IM needs in relation to other organizational priorities to make informed decisions about what priorities can be advanced. Constrained and competing resources suggest an incremental approach, and health information management (HIM) leaders should be prepared to outline priorities and sequence and pace change.

Principles for Information Governance and Stewardship

Information governance might best be viewed as a stewardship duty. **Stewardship** is the responsible management of something entrusted to one's care. Healthcare organizations are entrusted with managing patient data, and that responsibility is best performed if the organization's stewardship values are laid out. Starting with guiding principles and the ends to be achieved begins to shape practices in the desired direction. A number of references can serve as a starting point.

The generally accepted recordkeeping principles (GARP) define and describe eight key principles relating to records and information management practices. GARP also include a maturity model to help organizations assess the stage of their development. The Maturity Model describes measures reflecting five levels of development of information governance for each principle. These range from Level 1, Substandard, to Level 5, Transformational. Figure 6.8 overviews

Figure 6.8.   Analysis of the applicability of GARP principles

Cross-Industry GARP Principle	Applicability to Health Information Governance
Accountability	
A senior executive oversees the recordkeeping program and delegates program responsibility to appropriate individuals. The organization adopts policies and procedures to guide personnel and ensure the program can be audited.	Consistent with the recommendation to engage the board and develop an IAM mindset. Healthcare organizations will take different approaches to assigning senior level responsibility depending on program emphasis.
Transparency	
The processes and activities of an organization's recordkeeping program are documented in a manner that is open and verifiable and is available to all personnel and appropriate interested parties.	Highly relevant. Healthcare organizations have very visible privacy policies, but other processes and activities are often not transparent.
Integrity	
A recordkeeping program shall be constructed so the records and information generated or managed by or for the organization have a reasonable and suitable guarantee of authenticity and reliability.	This imperative is far more important in healthcare because the consequence of poor data quality can be life and death. The obligation must include the data content in the record.
Protection	
A recordkeeping program shall be constructed to ensure a reasonable level of protection to records and information that are private, confidential, privileged, secret, or essential to business continuity.	Personally identifiable health information is governed by HIPAA privacy and security laws and regulations and state law. Hence, this imperative too carries great importance for healthcare organizations.
Compliance	
The recordkeeping program shall be constructed to comply with applicable laws and the other binding authorities, as well as the organization's policies.	Highly relevant. Healthcare organizations have complex compliance obligations and the information management and records management is a key element.
Availability	
An organization shall maintain records in a manner that ensures timely, efficient, and accurate retrieval of needed information.	Highly relevant. Electronic health records and related IT can aid retrieval of information, but the design of IT sometimes impedes rapid availability. Access to aggregate data or linking data across systems can be similarly challenging.
Retention	
An organization shall maintain its records and information for an appropriate time, taking into account legal, regulatory, fiscal, operational, and historical requirements.	Highly relevant. Healthcare organizations must redesign retention principles in light of digital media, changing e-discovery and other laws.
Disposition	
An organization shall provide secure and appropriate disposition for records that are no longer required to be maintained by applicable laws and the organization's policies.	Highly relevant and related to lifecycle and retention planning.

Figure 6.9.   NHS acute trust requirements

National Health Service, United Kingdom, Acute Trust Version 8
Information Governance Management
Requires an information governance framework, approved policies with strategies and improvement plans and training for staff; also require in all contracts.
Confidentiality and Data Protection Assurance
The information management agenda is supported by adequate confidentiality and data protection skills, knowledge, and experience including appropriate procedures for informing and securing consents from patients, release of information, monitoring access to personal health information.
Information Security Assurance
The information management agenda is supported by adequate security skills, knowledge, and experience; formal security risk assessment and management programs for key information assets and security incident process and business continuity planning.
Clinical Information Assurance
The information management agenda is supported by adequate information quality and records management skills; procedures for patient and provider identification; and multi-disciplinary audit of clinical records.
Secondary Use Assurance
Applies heavily to the accuracy of coding; national data definitions and standard are incorporated into systems; external data quality reports are used for monitoring and improving data quality; and regular audit cycle for accuracy.
Corporate Information Assurance
Corporate records are handled in a manner consistent with law, including an information lifecycle management strategy.

Source: NHS 2011.

the **GARP principles** and comments on their applicability to healthcare information governance (ARMA 2010). They are certainly all highly relevant, but healthcare organizations carry additional obligations because their essential business is patient care, which has its own laws, regulations, and standards.

Another source of sample principles is the United Kingdom's National Health Service, which require information governance programs in healthcare organizations. Because this was designed for and is applicable to healthcare information management and governance, it is closely related to the components of the EIM model described previously. The principles for acute-care services are summarized in figure 6.9 (NHS 2011). Note the important focus on the adequacy of skills, knowledge, and experience to carry out the various obligations. It is a key focus of information governance to ensure that the functions are appropriately staffed.

Joint Commission (2009) accreditation standards can also serve as a guide for framing principles for information stewardship and governance, as can the principles for stewardship and secondary use of information prepared by the National Committee on Vital and Health Statistics (NCVHS).

Stewardship values should be reflected in health information governance principles and practices to ensure that they reflect the special nature—and special obligations—of safeguarding health data. The benefits accrue not only to the healthcare enterprise but also to patients and to society. The NCVHS stewardship principles are summarized in figure 6.10. These are deliberately written from the patient's perspective.

Change Leadership and Information Management

Taking a systems approach to enterprise information management and governance is not a quick fix for any organization, particularly for healthcare organizations that are not yet fully transitioned to digital records and are often characterized by siloed IT and IM functions. The transition will be incremental and targeted but should be deliberate and guided by an EIM and IG improvement plan.

This work should not be viewed as a project to be commissioned or a technology to be acquired. It is a discipline to be built and improved upon over time. Like all change management, the first step is raising awareness of the benefits and risks of the current state and then initiating a dialogue about points of vulnerability. Given pressure for scarce IM resources, it will be important to follow the tenets of change management, starting with small wins and building from there.

Check Your Understanding 6.3

Instructions: Answer the following questions on a separate piece of paper.

1. Describe the relationship between health data stewardship and information governance.

2. Describe the value of laying out principles to guide information governance.

3. Identify the eight GARP principles.

Figure 6.10. NCVHS health data stewardship key principles

Health Data Stewardship: An NCVHS Primer
Individual Rights
• Access for an individual to his or her own health data
• Opportunity to correct one's own data
• Transparency for the individual about the use(s) of his or her data
• Individual participation and consent for the use of the data
• Education
• Other rights to privacy of personal health information as set forth in state and federal laws and regulations
Responsibilities of the health data steward—Either a formal position or assigned accountability with responsibility
• Adherence to privacy and confidentiality principles and practices
• Appropriate use and interpretation of data
• Limits on the use, disclosure, and retention of information
• Appropriate deidentification of data
• Data quality
Security, safeguards, and controls
• Protect information and minimize the risks of unauthorized or inappropriate access, use or disclosure
Accountability, enforcement, and remedies
• Detection mechanisms for failure to follow policy
• Remediation for the individual whose data are involved

Source: NCVHS 2009.

Summary

Healthcare organizations that understand information as an asset will take steps to introduce principles and practices of effective enterprise information management and information governance. There are substantial benefits to be realized in terms of operational efficiency, cost control, and compliance. There are risks for failing to formally advance the management and governance of healthcare information across the enterprise.

Health information management professionals can advance the vision and benefits of improving the management and governance of information assets and convene the stakeholders needed to shape sound policies and practices. HIM professionals should take part in assessing and developing the IM competencies across the organization. They should advance high-priority improvements and have a firm understanding of areas of vulnerability. Finally, they should be role models for information stewardship.

Healthcare organizations have special obligations as stewards of important patient information. The values of stewardship should be reflected in every aspect of information governance and management. In the end, information asset management, enterprise information management, and information governance will ensure that healthcare organizations are effective stewards of health information to benefit patients and serve the public good.

References

American Health Information Management Association. 2008. Enterprise Content and Record Management for Healthcare. *Journal of AHIMA* (79)10: 91–98.

American Health Information Management Association. 2012. *AHIMA pocket glossary for HIM and technology.* Chicago: AHIMA.

ARMA International. 2010. Information Governance Maturity Model. http://www.arma.org/GARP.

The Economist. 2008 (October). The future of enterprise information governance. Economist Intelligence Unit. http://www.eiu.com.

Gleick, J. 2011. *The Information: A History, A theory, A flood.* New York: Pantheon Books.

Joint Commission. 2009. *Comprehensive Accreditation Manual for Hospitals: The Official Handbook.* Oakbrook Terrace, IL: Joint Commission Resources.

Kloss, L. 2011 (February). Obligation and opportunity. *Trustee* 64(2): 24–25.

Logan, D. 2009 (November). Organizing for information governance. Research ID number G00172224. Gartner, Inc.

National Committee for Vital and Health Statistics. 2009 (December). Health data stewardship: What, why, who, and how. http://www.ncvhs.hhs.gov.

National Health Service. 2011. Acute Trust Version 8 (2010–2011). http://www.igt.connectingforhealth.nhs.uk.

chapter 7

Data Capture, Maintenance, and Quality

Valerie J.M. Watzlaf, PhD, RHIA, FAHIMA

Learning Objectives

- Understand how and what type of data are captured and structured at an organizational level and for a health system
- Examine how data are maintained at the organizational and health system levels
- List and give examples of 10 characteristics of quality data as outlined by AHIMA
- Distinguish among data quality assessment, evaluation, and integrity
- Demonstrate how documentation in the health record supports the overall continuum of care for the patient, including secondary data sources such as registries, databases, data sets, surveys, and core measures
- Differentiate between methods of capturing, maintaining, and evaluating the quality of health information

- Develop standard practices, policies, and procedures that support effective and efficient capture, maintenance, and quality of data
- Design data quality and integrity validation strategies and methods
- Describe appropriate protocols to support secondary data uses in research, patient safety, risk assessment, epidemiology, and public health
- Discuss how healthcare data sets such as the Healthcare Effectiveness Data Set (HEDIS), Uniform Hospital Discharge Data Set (UHDDS), and the Outcome and Assessment Information Set (OASIS) are used to support data capture, maintenance, and quality of healthcare data
- Describe the healthcare information management (HIM) profession Core Model as developed by AHIMA, and explain the functional components

Key Terms

10 characteristics of data quality
Attribute
Authorization management
Clinical documentation improvement (CDI)
Crosswalk
Data
Data dictionary
Data integrity
Data map
Data quality model
Database administrator (DBA) or data administrator (DA)
Database management system (DBMS) data dictionary

Documentation
Enterprise master patient index (EMPI)
Explicit knowledge
Information
Integrity constraint
Knowledge
Knowledge management
Measure applications partnership (MAP)
Patient-centered medical home (PCMH)
Referential integrity
System catalog
Tacit knowledge

Health information managers have numerous roles within the healthcare industry. Most, if not all, of these roles involve managing data and information shared by a diverse and sometimes widely dispersed group of users. These data are the heart of the healthcare environment and vital to decision-making processes surrounding both patient care and the business of healthcare. Meeting the challenge of managing the data and information for these purposes is not a simple task. Users have different information needs and may even have different data definitions. These different needs and definitions must be addressed in developing effective healthcare information systems.

This chapter introduces data capture and maintenance within the healthcare system and how information as an organizational asset must be managed effectively to provide and sustain its value. It examines the relationship between data and information, several models for managing healthcare information, other principles of healthcare information management, issues related to measuring data quality in a healthcare setting, data management roles, ensuring the integrity and validity of data, and some basic principles of data standardization through clinical documentation improvement policies and procedures.

From Data to Information to Knowledge

Where does **information** come from? The simple answer is that information is processed data. **Data** are the raw facts, generally stored as characters, words, symbols, measurements, or statistics. Unprocessed data are not very useful for decision making. Take, for example, the letters and numerals Z, 4, 6, and 1. What do they mean? If seen together as Z461, the data might be processed to resemble the model of a specific car. If one looks further, looking it up in the International Classification of Diseases, Tenth Revision, Clinical Modification (ICD-10-CM) codebook or entering it into an encoder software program, it takes on even more meaning. It is now known that Z46.1 is the code that represents an encounter for a fitting and adjustment for a hearing aid.

Is this information? That depends. When looking for a particular patient's diagnosis to process a claim, Z46.1 may,

in fact, be providing the information an insurance representative needs. However, for the medical researcher looking for patient characteristics that contribute to hearing aid use, Z46.1 on one patient's chart is not yet "processed" enough to provide useful information.

Where does data end and information begin? How are the two concepts related? Do the data collected and stored affect the information available within the organization? To answer these questions, one must first know who needs the data or information to perform what job function or functions. What people and what decisions are involved?

Information as an Organizational Resource

Information is a valuable asset at all levels of the healthcare organization. Personnel, both clinical and support staff, who perform the day-to-day operations related to patient care or administrative functions rely on information to do their jobs. This is truly the information age, and nowhere is this more apparent than in healthcare. Healthcare managers at both the middle management level and the executive level make extensive use of information, both to carry out day-to-day operations and in strategic planning for the organization. An interesting point to think about is that the same data may actually provide different information to different users. In other words, one person's data may be another person's information.

To illustrate this point, consider a small data set that represents some patient demographic data. It might be a subset of data from a hospital's electronic master patient index (MPI) system. (See table 7.1.)

This single set of data could be used at all levels of the hospital, beginning with the admissions process, a day-to-day operation of the facility. Admissions personnel would use the data set to verify previous admissions or the spelling of a patient name. They also would be responsible for data entry and updating the MPI to ensure that it contains accurate, timely data. The MPI data set, as is, would provide useful information to the admissions personnel.

At the middle management level, the director of outpatient services might want information about where recent patients live and how far they travel to use this hospital. He or she might further process or query the data set to classify

Table 7.1.   Subset of a master patient index table

MRN	Last Name	First Name	Middle Name	DOB	Payment Type	Zip Code
096543	Jones	Georgia	Louise	11/21/1957	Self	29425
065432	Lexington	Milton	Robert	08/12/2000	Private	29425
467345	Lovingood	Jill	Karen	10/14/1992	Medicaid	29401
678543	Martin	Chloe	Mary	05/30/1978	Private	29465
234719	Martin	John	Adams	06/22/1961	Private	29401
786543	Nance	Natalie	JoAnn	11/27/1922	Medicare	29464

patients by zip code. After the query is completed, the director of outpatient services has useful information to help identify where patients live.

The chief executive officer (CEO) is interested in patient mix as well, but wants to see trend data over time showing the percentage of Medicare patients vs. the percentage of private-pay and nonpaying patients. Again, the same data set is used, but the query process is more complex and the data set must be linked to another data set that contains payment information. The data in the MPI data set must be processed more extensively before any truly useful information is available to meet the CEO's needs. Moreover, the data from the MPI might be used in strategic planning for the hospital. Any number of complex queries about the patient population could contribute to strategic marketing or development decisions. The organization might even combine the MPI data set with external data sets using sophisticated decision support systems (DSSs) that compare its performance with the performance of other facilities in the region or state. Decision support systems are discussed in chapter 19.

As information systems have evolved and become more complex, organizations are more aware of the importance of managing electronic data among numerous information systems. **Enterprise master patient index (EMPI)** systems include the assignment of an enterprise identifier to link health information systems together across corporations or enterprises. This identifier works behind-the-scenes to identify a patient at the corporate level while the medical record number or other patient identifier links patients together at the local or facility level (AHIMA 2010b).

Knowledge Management

Some texts include a third, higher level in the data-to-information hierarchy: **knowledge** (see figure 7.1). Lau (2004, 2) defines knowledge as "information combined with experience, context, interpretation, and reflection." AHIMA e-HIM Workgroup on Computer-Assisted Coding (2004, 2) defines **knowledge management** as "capturing, organizing, and storing knowledge and experiences of individual workers and groups within an organization and making this

Figure 7.1. From data to knowledge

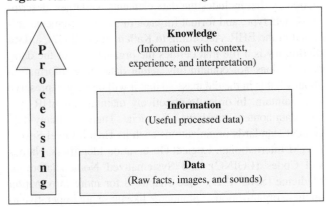

information available to others in the organization." This definition illustrates that there are two types of knowledge: explicit and tacit. **Explicit knowledge** is knowledge that is easily communicated and stored, for example, documents and procedures. **Tacit knowledge** is personal knowledge that is not easily communicated or stored. Employees' experiences, habits, and skills are examples of tacit knowledge. Unless employee tacit knowledge is captured and stored, it is lost when an employee leaves the organization—hence the need for knowledge management.

People use knowledge to make decisions. In the preceding Z46.1 example, the medical researcher might use his or her experience (tacit knowledge), diagnostic rules (written or not), and statistical rules (explicit knowledge) to determine the relationships between patient characteristics and the Z46.1 diagnosis. Computer systems that combine an expert knowledge base and some type of rule-based decision analysis component are sometimes referred to as knowledge management systems to differentiate them from more traditional transaction-based or analytical information systems. Although computerized DSSs in healthcare are not always knowledge management systems, knowledge management systems are almost always used for decision support. (See chapter 19 for more information on decision support systems.)

The value of knowledge management in the healthcare setting is obvious when healthcare explicit and tacit knowledge are identified. To illustrate this, consider the explicit knowledge that may be available in the healthcare setting: policy and procedure manuals, evidence-based research, clinical practice guidelines, computer programs, and training materials. This explicit knowledge is easily recorded, stored, and shared in electronic databases or libraries. Now consider the tacit knowledge, most of which is in the minds of individuals: employee experience, skills, judgment, and guiding principles. The predicted large number of healthcare worker retirements and the shortage of healthcare workers (Bureau of Labor Statistics 2010) illustrate the need to capture, store, and distribute the tacit knowledge of employees.

Dr. Francis Lau (2004) has developed a knowledge management framework for the healthcare environment that addresses both explicit and tacit knowledge. It includes the core concepts of knowledge production, use, and refinement within a social context influenced by individual and organizational values and preferences. Figure 7.2 illustrates how the concepts are interrelated and iterative:

- *Knowledge production* includes the creation, organization, and storage of knowledge.
- *Knowledge use* includes the distribution and sharing of knowledge.
- *Knowledge refinement* includes the evaluation, adaptation, and sustainability of knowledge.

Healthcare faces constant change, and that can be challenging. Consumers are more informed; there is a need to increase efficiency, reduce costs, and improve quality; the

Figure 7.2.   A conceptual knowledge management framework in healthcare

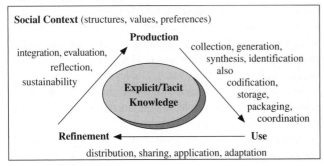

Source: Lau 2004, 3.

industry is changing its focus from curing to preventing illnesses; there is a healthcare worker shortage; and there has been an increase in the generation of medical data, information, and knowledge. Managing this data, information, and knowledge is essential to addressing these changes.

Check Your Understanding 7.1

Instructions: Answer the following questions on a separate piece of paper.

1. Give an example of data that are found in a patient medical record. How could these data become information?

2. Explain the statement that "one person's information can be another person's data."

3. Give specific examples of explicit and tacit knowledge in healthcare. Why would it be important to manage these?

Data Capture

Data capture requires the development and implementation of standard practices, policies, and procedures. There are different types of tools that can be used to capture healthcare data. According to AHIMA (2008), data capture methods identify which methods are permitted for use and who is permitted to use them. For example, structured data capture should be used for positive and negative findings, such as the documentation of positive or negative responses to questions about past history, family history, social history, and the review of systems. Structured text is also appropriate for documentation of diagnostic procedures ordered and the patient's presenting problem. Free-text narrative is appropriate for evaluation and management (E/M) compliance, medical necessity, history of present illness, details about past history, clinical impressions, and treatment options or whenever there needs to be more thorough explanations of findings.

There are many electronic health record (EHR) built-in tools, such as data dictionaries, automated quality measures, patient registries, electronic-referral systems (e-referrals), electronic visit systems (e-visits), and clinical decision support systems. Each of these systems contains methods to capture critical data that can be used for patient scheduling, treatment options, reimbursement, and overall quality of patient care. However, the methods used to capture pertinent data must be standardized.

The Certification Commission for Health Information Technology (CCHIT) provides criteria that an inpatient EHR must contain in order to be certified. Some of the criteria relate to data capture. The criteria are standards that are consistent, organized, reachable, measurable, and valid. For example, one of the criteria states, "The system shall capture and maintain demographic information as discrete data elements as part of the patient record" (CCHIT 2011). Examples of demographic data elements that should be captured as discrete variables include name, address, phone number, and date of birth. Capturing these data elements as discrete variables means being able to reduce the data to whole numbers or some type of categorization so that patient data can be easily queried by more than one form of identification.

Allergy information is another example of CCHIT criteria that must be captured by the EHR. It states "The system shall provide the ability to capture and maintain, as discrete data the reason for inactivating or revising an item from an allergy and adverse reaction list" (CCHIT 2011). This can include revising, marking as erroneous, or marking as inactive rather than deleting this information from the EHR entirely. Again, a specific code or number can be designated so that when the system is mined or queried, the information will be retrieved. For example, 1 = allergy no longer valid, 2 = erroneous allergy information, 3 = allergy is inactive. Once the data are included as discrete or nominal variables they are easy to capture.

Data Maintenance

It is extremely important to be able to employ effective methods to maintain the data once they are captured. Methods to preserve the data include developing appropriate policies and procedures for preservation of data, length of time to maintain the data, who should be responsible for data maintenance and meeting regulations, as well as privacy and security provisions. One method of preserving data is to develop a data dictionary that includes the data elements, variables, descriptions, data type, and format for each of the data elements collected in the EHR. According to Kallem et al. (2007), a **data dictionary** is a file that defines the organization of the database. It does not contain any actual data, only information about what is in the database so that it will be easy to preserve and maintain. In order to effectively maintain an EHR system, data content standards are crucial. There are many data content standards organizations such as Health Level Seven, ASTM International, Logical Observation Identifiers, Names and Codes (LOINC); and Systematized Nomenclature of Medicine (SNOMED). (See chapter 8 for more information on these organizations.) Standards like these are imperative to bridge the gap between qualitative documents and structured, computable data (Kallum et al. 2007).

Data Quality

The concept of data quality is closely tied to the ability of a healthcare information system to support decision making at all levels of the organization. The adage "garbage in, garbage out" is true. This section discusses the importance of establishing data quality standards and introduces two sets of guidelines that can be used for this purpose.

How can one know when data quality has been achieved? The quality of data is tied to the use, or application, of the data. Again, high-quality data are the foundation of high-quality information, and the value of information lies in its application to decision making within the organization.

> Consider for a moment an organization with sophisticated healthcare information systems that affect every type of healthcare information, from patient-specific to knowledge-based. What if the quality of the documentation going into the systems is poor? What if there is no assurance that the reports generated from the systems are accurate or timely? How would the users of the systems react? Are those information systems beneficial or detrimental to the organization in achieving its goals? (Wager et al. 2005, 43)

A healthcare organization cannot have high-quality healthcare information without first establishing that it has high-quality healthcare data. We know that clinical providers and administrative staff gather healthcare information. Much of this clinical information is recorded in patient records and subsequently coded for purposes of reimbursement and research. Poor-quality data collection and reporting can affect patient care, communication among providers and patients, documentation, revenue generation (due to problems with reimbursement), outcomes evaluation, research activities, or public reporting.

The problems with poor-quality patient care data are not strictly limited to the patient health record. In a well-circulated report, the Medical Records Institute (MRI) identified five major functions that are affected by poor-quality documentation (MRI 2002). These functions are found not only at the healthcare organizational level but also throughout the healthcare environment.

> Patient safety is affected by inadequate information, illegible entries, misinterpretations, and insufficient interoperability.
>
> Public safety, a major component of public health, is diminished by the inability to collect information in a coordinated, timely manner at the provider level in response to epidemics and the threat of terrorism.
>
> Continuity of patient care is adversely affected by the lack of shareable information among patient care providers.
>
> Healthcare economics are adversely affected, with information capture and report generation costs currently estimated to be well over $50 billion annually.

> Clinical research and outcomes analysis are adversely affected by a lack of uniform information capture that is needed to facilitate the derivation of data from routine patient care documentation. (MRI 2002, 2)

The MRI report identifies healthcare documentation as having two basic parts: information capture and report generation. Information capture is "the process of recording representations of human thought, perceptions, or actions in documenting patient care, as well as device-generated information that is gathered and/or computed about a patient as part of healthcare" (MRI 2002, 2). Some means of information capture in healthcare organizations are handwriting, speaking, word processing, touching a screen, pointing and clicking on words or phrases, videotaping, audio recording, and generating digital images through x-rays and scans.

Report generation "consists of the formatting and/or structuring of captured information. It is the process of analyzing, organizing, and presenting recorded patient information for authentication and inclusion in the patient's healthcare record" (MRI 2002, 2). In order to have high-quality documentation that results in high-quality data, both information capture and report generation must be considered.

Data Quality Standards

Before an organization can measure the quality of the information it produces and uses, it must establish data standards. That is, data can be identified as high-quality only when they conform to a recognized standard. Ensuring this conformance is not as easy as it might seem because no universally recognized set of healthcare data quality standards exists today. One reason for this is that the quality of the data needed in any situation is driven by how the data or the information that comes from the data will be used. For example, in a patient care setting the margin of error for critical lab tests must be zero or patient safety is in jeopardy. However, a larger margin of error may be acceptable in census counts or discharge statistics. Healthcare organizations must establish data quality standards specific to the intended use of the data or resulting information.

Although no universally adopted healthcare data quality standards exist, two organizations have published guidance that can assist healthcare organizations in establishing their own data quality standards. In *Healthcare Documentation: A Report on Information Capture and Report Generation,* the MRI (2002, 9) has published a set of "essential principles of healthcare documentation," and the American Health Information Management Association (AHIMA) has published the data quality management model (Wager et al. 2005).

MRI Principles of Healthcare Documentation

AHIMA defines **documentation** as "the methods and activities of collecting, coding, ordering, storing, and retrieving information to fulfill future tasks" (AHIMA 2007, 66). The

Figure 7.3.   MRI Consensus Workgroup Essential Principles of Healthcare Documentation

For optimal information capture and report generation, it is important to establish a set of documentation principles to be implemented on a national/international basis. This report recommends that all healthcare documentation must meet the following "Essential Principles of Healthcare Documentation."

Unique identification of patient

Systems, policies, and practices should:

- Provide unique identification of the patient at the time of recording or accessing the information.
- Provide within and across organizations:
  - Simple and easy methods to identify individuals and correct duplicate identities of the same individual.
  - Methods to distinguish among individuals, including those with similar names, birth dates, and other demographic information.
  - Linkages between different identifications of the same individual.

Accuracy

Systems, policies, and practices should:

- Promote accuracy of information throughout the information capture and report generation processes as well as during its transfer among systems.
- Require review to assure accuracy prior to integration in the patient's record.
- Include a means to append a correction to an authenticated document, without altering the original.
- Require the use of standard terminology so as to diminish misinterpretations.

Completeness

Systems, policies, and practices should:

- Identify the minimum set of information required to completely describe an incident, observation, or intent.
- Provide means to ensure that the information recorded meets the legal, regulatory, institutional policy, or other requirements required for specific types of reports (for example, history and physical, operative note).
- Link amendments to the original document (that is, one should not be able to retrieve an original document without related amendments [or vice versa] or notification that such amendments exist and how to access them).
- Discourage duplication of information.
- Discourage nonrelevant and excessive documentation.

Timeliness

Systems, policies, and practices should:

- Require and facilitate that healthcare documentation be done during or immediately following the event so that:
  - Memory is not diminished or distorted.
  - The information is immediately available for subsequent care and decision making.
- Promote rapid system response time for entry as well as retrievability through:
  - Availability and accessibility of workstations.
  - User-friendly systems and policies that allow for rapid user access.

- Provide for automatic, unalterable time, date, and place stamp of each:
  - Documentation entry, such as dictation, uploading, scanning (original, edits, amendments).
  - Access to the documentation.
  - Transmittal of the documentation.

Interoperability

Systems, policies, and practices should:

- Provide the highest level of interoperability that is realistically achievable.
- Enable authorized practitioners to capture, share, and report healthcare information from any system, whether paper- or electronic-based.
- Support ways to document healthcare information so that it can be correctly read, integrated, and supplemented within any other system in the same or another organization.

Retrievability (the capability of allowing information to be found efficiently)

Systems, policies, and practices should:

- Support achievement of a worldwide consensus on the structure of information so that the practitioner can efficiently locate relevant information. This requires the use of standardized titles, formats, templates, and macros, as well as standardized terminology, abbreviations, and coding.
- Enable authorized data searches, indexing, and mining.
- Enable searches with incomplete information (for example, wild card searches, fuzzy logic searches).

Authentication and accountability

Systems, policies, and practices should:

- Uniquely identify persons, devices, or systems that create or generate the information and that take responsibility for its accuracy, timeliness, etc.
- Require that all information be attributable to its source (that is, a person or device).
- Require that unsigned documents be readily recognizable as such.
- Require review of documents prior to authentication. "Signed without review" and similar statements should be discouraged.

• Auditability

Systems, policies, and practices should:

- Allow users to examine basic information elements, such as data fields.
- Audit access and disclosure of protected health information.
- Alert users of errors, inappropriate changes, and potential security breaches.
- Promote use of performance metrics as part of the audit capacity.

<table>
<tr><td>

• **Confidentiality and Security**

Systems, policies, and practices should:

• Demonstrate adherence to related legislation, regulations, guidelines, and policies throughout the healthcare documentation process.

• Alert the user to potential confidentially and security breaches.

</td><td>

RECOMMENDATION #1: Fund, create, and promote a practical implementation guide for the dissemination, teaching, and adoption of the "Essential Principles of Healthcare Documentation" by practitioners, providers, vendors, and healthcare organizations, as well as regulatory bodies and medical schools.

</td></tr>
</table>

Source: MRI 2002.

MRI report states that many steps must be taken to ensure the quality of healthcare documentation (and, thus, the quality of healthcare data). It lists the essential principles to which healthcare organizations should adhere as they establish healthcare documentation and information systems (and their accompanying policies). (See figure 7.3.) The MRI recommends that these principles be uniformly adopted by healthcare organizations.

It is noteworthy that the MRI takes the position that when practitioners interact with electronic resources, their ability to adhere to these principles is increased. All documentation records data and information, which need to be retrieved in order to be used. The MRI argues that all healthcare information should be indexed "to facilitate both clinical and administrative retrieval" (MRI 2002, 16). This is difficult to do with unstructured, free text, such as handwriting, e-mails, and transcription. As electronic medical records are implemented and information capture methods become more interactive, the ability to retrieve information will improve. Table 7.2 shows documentation styles and major information capture methods.

AHIMA Data Quality Model

AHIMA (2012) has published a **data quality model** and an accompanying set of general data characteristics. The model is used as a framework for the design of management processes and data quality measures. There are some similarities between the AHIMA characteristics and the MRI essential principles (refer to figure 7.3). However, one difference is

that AHIMA strives to include all healthcare data and limits characteristics to clinical documentation. (See figures 7.4 and 7.5.)

The AHIMA (2012) model includes the following **10 characteristics of data quality:**

- *Accuracy:* Data that are free of errors are accurate. For example, when the patient's insurance type is recorded as Security Blue, it is accurately recorded as Security Blue and not Medical Assistance.
- *Accessibility:* Data items should be easily obtainable and legal to access with strong protections and controls built into the process.
- *Comprehensiveness*: All required data items are included. Ensure that the entire scope of the data is collected and document intentional limitations.
- *Consistency/Reliability:* Data quality needs to be consistent and reliable. For example, if a patient's blood

Figure 7.4.   AHIMA data quality management model

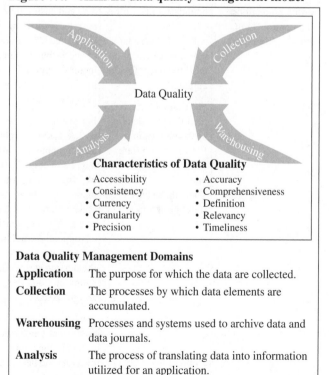

Data Quality Management Domains

Application	The purpose for which the data are collected.
Collection	The processes by which data elements are accumulated.
Warehousing	Processes and systems used to archive data and data journals.
Analysis	The process of translating data into information utilized for an application.

Source: AHIMA 2012.

Table 7.2.   Documentation styles and major information capture methods

	Free Text	Structured Text	Interactive Text
Handwriting	Mostly free text	Paper forms	N/A
Transcription	Mostly free text	Macros and normals	N/A
Speech Recognition	Free text	Templates	Interactive templates
Direct Input	Free text	Mostly structured text	More interactive

Source: MRI 2002.

Figure 7.5. AHIMA characteristics of data quality

Characteristic	Application	Collection	Warehousing	Analysis
Data Quality Management Model Domains and Characteristics				
Data Accuracy The extent to which the data are free of identifiable errors.	To facilitate accuracy, determine the application's purpose, the question to be answered, or the aim for collecting the data element. Standard acceptable values should be used where available. Where possible value flags and constraints should be implemented.	Ensuring accuracy involves appropriate education and training and timely and appropriate communication of data definitions to those who collect data. The applications should constrain entry to allowable values where possible.	To warehouse data, appropriate edits should be in place to ensure accuracy, such as basic field length checks. Also, error reports are generated related to transfers to and from the warehouse. All warehouses should have a correction and change management policy to track any changes.	To accurately analyze data, ensure that the algorithms, formulas, programming, and translation systems are correct. For example, ensure that the encoder assigns correct codes and that the appropriate DRG is assigned for the codes entered.
	For example, data entry of height into EHRs should flag or highlight very small (less than 12 inches) or very tall (over 7 feet) heights.	For example, data accuracy will help ensure that a patient height cannot be entered erroneously as 5 inches when it is in fact 50 inches. In addition to a primary data error, this would impact any calculated fields such as Body Mass Index (BMI).		Continual data validation is important to ensure that each record or entry within the database is correct.
Data Accessibility				
Data items that are easily obtainable and legal to access with strong protections and controls built into the process.	The application and legal, financial, process, and other boundaries determine which data to collect. Ensure that collected data are legal to collect for the application. For example, recording the date of birth and race in the EHR is appropriate and should only occur once with verification. Then, the values should roll forward.	When developing the data collection instrument, explore methods to access needed data and ensure that the best, least costly method is selected. The amount of accessible data may be increased through system interfaces and integration of systems. For example, the best and easiest method to obtain demographic information may be to obtain it from an existing system. Another method may be to assign data collection by the expertise of each team member. For example, the admission staff collects demographic data, the nursing staff collects symptoms, and the HIM staff assigns codes. Data entry should undergo a cost-benefit analysis process to determine which method provides the best data most efficiently.	Technology and hardware impact accessibility. Establish data ownership and guidelines for who may access or modify data and/or systems. Inventory data to facilitate access. In the EHR it may be advisable to establish data ownership or governance at the data element level, especially data which are re-used. For example, allergies are recorded by many different clinicians and come in many forms. Who defines what an allergy is? How does this impact the use of allergies in the EHR, especially for clinical decision support?	Access to complete, current data will better ensure accurate analysis and data mining. Otherwise results and conclusions may be inaccurate or inappropriate. For example, use of the Medicare case mix index (CMI) alone does not accurately reflect total hospital CMI. Consequently, strategic planning based solely on Medicare CMI may not be appropriate.

Data Comprehensiveness				
All required data items are included. Ensures that the entire scope of the data is collected with intentional limitations documented.	Clarify how the data will be used and identify end-users to ensure complete data are collected for the application. Include a problem statement and cost-benefit or impact study when collected data are increased. For example, in addition to outcome it may be important to gather data that impact outcomes.	Cost-effective comprehensive data collection may be achieved via interface to or download from other automated systems. Data definition and data precision impact comprehensive data collection (see these characteristics below).	Warehousing includes managing relationships of data owners, data collectors, and data end-users to ensure that all are aware of the available data in the inventory and accessible systems. This also helps to reduce redundant data collection.	Ensure that all pertinent data impacting the application are analyzed in concert. This is especially important when EHR clinical decision support is utilized. Incomplete data can result in underreporting a numerator or denominator.
Data Consistency				
The extent to which the healthcare data are reliable and the same across applications.	Data are consistent when the value of the data is the same across applications and systems such as, the patient's medical record number. In addition, related data items should agree. For example, data are inconsistent when it is documented that a male patient has had a hysterectomy.	The use of data definitions, extensive training, standardized data collection (procedures, rules, edits, and process) and integrated/interfaced systems facilitate consistency. Static data should be moved between users. For example, once Date of Birth has been definitively established, age at the time of treatment should be calculated, not entered by a user who might make an error.	Warehousing employs edits or conversion tables to ensure consistency. Coordinate edits and tables with data definition changes or data definition differences across systems. Document edits and tables. When new data are loaded it should be checked against existing data for consistency. For example, is someone reporting a different race for a patient?	Analyze data under reproducible circumstances by using standard formulas, scientific equations, programming, variance calculations, and other methods. Compare "apples to apples." Any manipulation of data, aggregating or otherwise, should be documented thoroughly. For example, how is BMI calculated and has the formula been checked?
Data Currency				
The extent to which data are up-to-date; a datum value is up-to-date if it is current for a specific point in time. It is outdated if it was current at some preceding time yet incorrect at a later time.	The appropriateness or value of an application changes over time. In EHRs it is imperative that the guidelines and algorithms be up-to-date. For example, acceptable blood pressure ranges have lowered, as have target HbA1C levels.	Data definitions change or are modified over time. These should be documented so that current and future users know what the data mean. These changes should be made in accordance with data governance policies and practices. Further, they must be communicated in a timely manner to those collecting data and to the end-users.	To ensure current data are available, warehousing involves continually validating systems, tables, and databases. The dates of warehousing events should be documented.	The availability of current data impacts the analysis of data. For example, analyzing the long-term incidence or prevalence of disease requires data in a different timeframe than when trying to track a disease outbreak for bio-surveillance purposes. Validating data from various fiscal and calendar years should also be considered.

(continued on next page)

Figure 7.5. AHIMA characteristics of data quality *(Continued)*

Data Definition	Application	Collection	Warehousing	Analysis
The specific meaning of a healthcare related data element.	The application's purpose, the question to be answered, or the aim for collecting the data element must be clarified to ensure appropriate and complete data definitions. Does the system use the Office of Management and Budget (OMB) standard for race and ethnicity? If not, what are the definitions and acceptable values?	Clear, concise data definitions facilitate accurate data collection. For example, the definition of patient disposition may be "the patient's anticipated location or status following release or discharge." Acceptable values for this data element should also be defined. The instrument of collection should include data definitions and ensure that the application limits data collection to the allowed values.	Warehousing includes archiving documentation and data. Consequently, data ownership documentation and definitions should be maintained over time. Inventory maintenance activities (purging, updates, and others), purpose for collecting data, collection policies, information management policies, and data sources should be maintained over time also.	For appropriate analysis, display data needs to reflect the purpose for which the data were collected. Appropriate comparisons, relationships, and linkages need to be shown.
Data Granularity				
The level of detail at which the attributes and values of healthcare data are defined.	A single application may require varying levels of detail or granularity. For example, census statistics may be utilized daily, weekly, or monthly depending upon the application. Census is needed daily to ensure adequate staffing and food service. However, the monthly trend is needed for long-range planning. Similarly, lab test results may be trended at various levels of detail.	Collect data at the appropriate level of detail or granularity. For example, the temperature of 100° may be recorded. The granularity for recording outdoor temperatures is different from recording patient temperatures. If patient Jane Doe's temperature is 100°, does that mean 99.6° or 100.4°? Appropriate granularity for this application dictates that the data need to be recorded to the first decimal point while appropriate granularity for recording outdoor temperatures may not require it.	Warehouse data at the appropriate level of detail or granularity. For example, exception or error reports reflect granularity based on the application. A spike (exception) in the daily census may show little or no impact on the month-to-date or monthly reports.	Appropriate analysis reflects the level of detail or granularity of the data collected. For example, a spike (exception) in the daily census resulting in immediate action to ensure adequate food service and staffing may have had no impact on analysis of the census for long-range planning. Of particular note for analysis is the impact of any rounding which might be done for numerical data.

Data Precision				
Data values should be strictly stated to support the purpose	The application's purpose, the question to be answered, or the aim for collecting the data element must be clarified to ensure data precision. What level of detail is needed for the data collection purpose? Are age ranges or 4 U.S. regions sufficient?	To collect data precise enough for the application, define acceptable values or value ranges for each data item. For example, limit values for gender to male, female, and unknown; or collect information by age ranges or allow more detailed collection to fully meet the needs.	Are warehouses receiving and storing all data elements being transferred from the source system?	If the precision of the data has been altered in the analysis is the process understood and well-documented?
Data Relevancy				
The extent to which healthcare-related data are useful for the purposes for which they were collected.	The applications purpose, the question to be answered, or the aim for collecting the data element must be clarified to ensure relevant data.	To better ensure relevancy, complete a pilot of the data collection instrument to validate its use. A "parallel" test may also be appropriate, completing the new or revised instrument and the current process simultaneously. Communicate results to those collecting data and to the end-users. Facilitate or negotiate changes as needed across disciplines or users.	Establish appropriate retention schedules to ensure availability of relevant data. Relevancy is defined by the application. It may be appropriate for warehouses to subset data related to its relevancy for certain uses.	For appropriate analysis, display data to reflect the purpose for which the data were collected. This is defined by the application. Show appropriate comparisons, relationships, and linkages.
Data Timeliness				
Concept of data quality that involves whether the data is up-to-date and available within a useful time frame. Timeliness is determined by how the data are being used and their context.	Timeliness is defined by the application. For example, patient census is needed daily to provide sufficient day-to-day operations staffing, such as nursing and food service. However, annual or monthly patient census data are needed for the organization's strategic planning. In the EHR, vitals may be taken once per visit for ambulatory care patients, but every 15 minutes or more often for critically ill patients.	Timely data collection is a function of the process and collection instrument. In the EHR, system performance plays an important role in data timeliness. Data display should be sub-second and data entry should occur instantaneously.	Warehousing ensures that data are available per information management policy and retention schedules. For EHR or clinical data warehouses, is the data updated concurrently or does it occur in a batch process?	Timely data analysis allows for the initiation of action to avoid adverse impacts. For some applications, such as allergy-drug or drug-drug interactions, timely may be seconds. For others, such as the prevalence of a disease over time, it may be years.

Source: AHIMA 2012.

pressure recording within the EHR is listed as 140/90 and three abstractors review the EHR looking for the patient's blood pressure, each of them will record 140/90.

- *Currency:* Many types of healthcare data become obsolete after a period of time. A patient's admitting diagnosis is often changed by the time he or she is discharged. If a clinician needed a current diagnosis, which one would he or she choose?
- *Definition:* Clear definitions should be provided so that current and future data users will know what the data mean. Each data element should have clear meaning and acceptable values.
- *Granularity:* Data granularity is sometimes referred to as data "atomicity," which means that the individual data elements cannot be further subdivided; they are "atomic." For example, a typical patient's name should generally be stored as three data elements—last name, first name, middle name (Smith, John, and Allen)—and not as a single data element (John Allen Smith). Again, granularity can be related to the purpose for which the data are collected. Although it is possible to subdivide a person's birth date into separate fields for the month, date, and year, this is usually not desirable. Birth date is at the lowest level of granularity when used as a patient identifier.
- *Precision:* Precision often relates to numerical data. It denotes how close to an actual size, weight, or other standard a particular measurement is. Some healthcare data must be very precise. For example, in figuring drug dosage, it would be unacceptable to round up to the nearest gram if the drug were to be dosed in milligrams.
- *Relevancy:* Data must be relevant to the purpose for which they are collected. Accurate, timely data may be collected about a patient's color preferences or choice of hairdresser, but are they relevant to the patient's care?
- *Timeliness:* Timeliness is a critical dimension in the quality of many types of healthcare data. Take, for example, a patient's discharge diagnoses recorded as ICD-9-CM codes. These codes must be recorded in a timely manner in order to facilitate reimbursement for the healthcare facility.

Also, data evaluation is important to perform so that all of the listed data characteristics are included and therefore lead to improvements in data quality.

The Agency for Healthcare Research and Quality (AHRQ), AHIMA, and Medical Group Management Association Center for Research (MGMA-CFR) conducted a conference titled Health Care Data Collection and Reporting in 2006 and subsequently published the findings in a report (AHRQ 2007). Data collection issues that cause

duplication of effort, excess cost, and variation in measures across quality reporting are some of the major issues discussed. The need for standardization of national core quality measures that can be collected once and used many times was a major theme in the report, as was the need to utilize the EHR for the effective collection and reporting of key quality data.

Data Quality Requirements for Information Systems

In addition to the 10 characteristics of data quality, AHIMA has published data quality best practices (AHIMA 2007):

- Access permissions: Define and enforce access to the data.
- Data dictionary: A data dictionary exists and each data element is defined. The definitions are communicated to all staff.
- Standardized format: Use a standardized format to ensure consistency.
- State and federal laws: All laws, regulations, accreditation standards, and policies are followed.
- Data integrity: Implement policies and procedures throughout the patient encounter to ensure data integrity.

It already has been noted that users must be involved in defining their information needs and designing information systems. One of the first steps in systems analysis is to identify the users' specific data needs. As a part of this process, it is important to identify the level of quality the user requires for each data element. Another way to view this is to evaluate the use of the data along the AHIMA model's 10 characteristics of data quality. This evaluation eventually will be translated into technical performance requirements for the information system (IS).

Consider a patient encounter documented in an EHR system. Figure 7.6 applies the AHIMA model's 10 characteristics of quality data to the activities of a patient encounter: registration, assessment, treatment, follow-up, information management, and information exchange. Each phase has a data quality checkpoint because ensuring data quality is an ongoing process.

Check Your Understanding 7.2

Instructions: Answer the following questions on a separate piece of paper.

1. Compare and summarize the similarities and differences between the AHIMA Data Quality Model (refer to figure 7.5) and the MRI Essential Principles of Documentation (refer to figure 7.3).

    A. What data quality characteristics do they both list?

    B. What is the major difference between these two sets of guidelines? Are they compatible with one another?

2. List the 10 characteristics of data quality.

Figure 7.6.   Applying AHIMA's 10 data characteristics to a patient encounter

Data Characteristics	Registration Data Quality Checkpoint: Identification (ID) Validation (identity proofing)	Assessment Data Quality Checkpoint: History and physical (H&P)	Treatment Data Quality Checkpoint: Medication reconciliation	Follow-up Data Quality Checkpoint: Discharge/Transfer/ Referral (DTR) record with patient instructions	Information Management Data Quality Checkpoint: Audit log of unauthorized access to the patient record	Information Exchange (external) Data Quality Checkpoint: Information from external sources
Accuracy—Ensures data have the correct value, are valid, and attached to the correct patient record.	Photo ID or two other forms of identification used.	Authentication by author licensed by the state. Patient demographics (five core-data elements (i.e., name [first, middle initial, last], date of birth, gender, Social Security number, medical record number) against that of the record.	List is current and the source of information is noted.	Policies exist defining the components of the DTR record (e.g., correct patient ID, location for follow-up/ ongoing care, patient instructions for self-care, diet, activity, and current medication regimen and allergies).	Periodic system security audits conducted to prevent unauthorized alteration or loss of data.	Incoming records matched against requests for information and validated.
Accessibility—Data items should be easily obtainable and legal to access with strong protections and controls built into the process.	Record of ID validation for each patient encounter exists (i.e., mandatory flag indicating the ID was validated and checked against the master person index).	Available to the right person, in the right place, at right time, for the right purpose as allowed by state and federal law.	Clinical history that pulls the data from previous encounters is available for verification and usage in patient care (e.g., check and verify patient meds with prior record).	Information is made available to patient and patient-authorized organization/ individual responsible for ongoing care at conclusion of visit/ stay.	End user authentication achieved by system signature, date/time stamp.	Data available in PDF format only and linked to appropriate patient record by note in system.
Comprehensiveness—All required data items are included. Ensure that the entire scope of the data is collected and document intentional limitations.	Source and date of ID validation noted. Flag addressed. Multiple discriminations that would further ID the patient such as mother's maiden name included.	Includes all components required by regulatory/ accrediting agencies, medical staff rules, and bylaws.	Data needed for treatment as defined by regulatory/ accrediting agencies, medical staff rules, and bylaws is available at the point of service (e.g., for each medication the name, dosage, route, timing, duration are documented).	Record includes all components required by regulatory agencies/accrediting bodies, medical staff rules, and bylaws. Verification of patient/ SO understanding of instructions is documented by licensed author	Includes user's login ID and date and time of access and the content accessed.	Policies note external data cannot be certified as comprehensive.
Consistency—The value of the data should be reliable and the same across applications.	Standards exist for ID search criteria (e.g., full name search, partial name search).	Required content is the same and available across the encounter and between applications (e.g., the allergy stated in the H&P should the same throughout the patient stay).	Data values are coordinated across the continuum of care (e.g., the translation of a patient's medication list to a required formulary is verified each time a translation occurs).	Process exists ensuring DTR data is consistent with data in other parts of the medical record.	A plan and schedule exists for audits and follow-up.	Policies address the use of external data because it may not meet internal definitions.

(continued on next page)

Figure 7.6.   Applying AHIMA's 10 data characteristics to a patient encounter *(Continued)*

Data Characteristics	Registration Data Quality Checkpoint: Identification (ID) Validation (identity proofing)	Assessment Data Quality Checkpoint: History and physical (H&P)	Treatment Data Quality Checkpoint: Medication reconciliation	Follow-up Data Quality Checkpoint: Discharge/Transfer/ Referral (DTR) record with patient instructions	Information Management Data Quality Checkpoint: Audit log of unauthorized access to the patient record	Information Exchange (external) Data Quality Checkpoint: Information from external sources
Currency—The data should be up-to-date.	Policies exist ensuring the latest ID data is entered and validated.	Information is updated in real-time or within a certain timeframe (i.e., information is synchronized every 30 minutes). When auto-population of data occurs, author validates and updates as necessary and a notation is captured by the system of this occurrence.	Medications taken by the patient are verified against the previous record and updated as necessary.	Policies exist to ensure the most current data are entered and verified for each component.	Verify data classes are clearly and appropriately defined and consistent with current business needs and requirements (e.g., public, sensitive, private, confidential).	Policies note data from external source will not be current. Relying on dates within documentation is suspect in electronic form.
Definition—Clear definitions should be provided so that current and future data users will know what the data mean. Each data element should have clear meaning and acceptable values.	A policy and procedure for updating, communicating, disseminating, and implementing the data dictionary exists (e.g., standards exist to ensure the same patient name and ID flows across all modules of the system including use of hyphens, apostrophes, etc.).	Guidelines defining H&P content (e.g., those by an accrediting agency) are available to authors and noted in the application user guide.	Standardized formulary exists.	Standardized data definitions for each required component of the DTR are clearly defined.	A storage security assessment and audit procedure integrated with other security practices once the major elements of storage security have been defined appropriately for your organizations.	Policies note any agreements with other providers as to definitions of the data.
Granularity—The attributes and values of data should be defined at the correct level of detail.	A policy and procedure for updating, communicating, disseminating, and implementing the data dictionary exists (e.g., truncation does not occur and values are clearly understood).	Components of the H&P as defined by the chosen standard (e.g., CMS E/M guidelines) are documented.	Attributes for each medication (e.g., dosage, form, route, etc) are defined.	Content of the DTR is defined so all required information for each component is captured (e.g., for medications: brand/ generic name, dosage, route, frequency; for activities allowed description of examples).	A storage security assessment and audit procedure is integrated with other security practices once the major elements of storage security have been defined appropriately for your organizations.	Policies note beyond what would be expected from the current standards there is no assurance of the values assigned to data (e.g., laboratory values from another source may not be expressed in the same manner as receiving facility).

Precision—Data values should be just large enough to support the application or process.	Standard policies exist ensuring the same set of rules apply to the ID data values for capture, storage, display, and reporting.	Data obtained by the provider support the degree of patient complexity.	Checks are done to ensure what is ordered is what is given to the patient.	Policies exist to allow prepopulated fields (e.g., discharge medication list, instructions) as well as free text to facilitate data capture (e.g., name/location of organization to provide ongoing care).	Changes are identified and potential security impact assessed.	As directed by HIPAA, the sending organization sends only the minimum necessary information requested.
Relevancy—The data are meaningful to the performance of the process or application for which they are collected.	Standard policies exist requiring the capture of all demographic data that reflects the information needed for ID validation. Standard algorithm for pulling up the patient exists.	Data obtained by the provider support the plan of care (e.g., significant positive/ negative findings).	Express relationships to established standards meet the patient/client needs, achieve the organizations goals and produce benefits exist.	Policies exist requiring the DTR to contain data relevant and necessary for coordination of ongoing care of the patient.	Compliance with specified controls and procedures verified.	Policies note beyond what would be expected from the current standards there is no assurance of the receipt of meaningful data.
Timeliness—Timeliness is determined by how the data are being used and their context.	Real-time updates of ID are performed.	Documented at the time of encounter by the authorized provider and available for patient care.	Patient's medications are available for patient care.	Record is documented at the conclusion of the patient encounter and made available to the patient and patient-authorized organization/ individual responsible for ongoing care.	Conduct audits on a regularly scheduled routine and as needed.	Policies note data from external source will never be timely in the sense of context because the receiver would not be defining the context.

Source: AHIMA e-HIM Workgroup on Assessing and Improving Healthcare Data Quality in the EHR 2007.

Current Initiatives for Data Capture, Maintenance, and Quality in Healthcare

The Patient Protection and Affordable Care Act (PPACA) provides initiatives related to data capture, maintenance, and quality for health information. It requires healthcare organizations to improve health outcomes through the implementation of quality reporting, effective case management, care coordination, chronic disease management, and medication and care compliance initiatives, including the use of the medical homes model. The **patient-centered medical home (PCMH)** is a team-based approach to providing care for patients that includes a primary care physician who coordinates care across the entire continuum by engaging with the patient and family so that patient outcomes are enhanced and the quality of care is improved.

The PPACA also states that organizations must implement programs to improve patient safety and reduce medical errors through best clinical practices, evidence-based medicine, and health information technology. They do this by using three broad mechanisms:

1. A national-level approach to improve healthcare quality, quality measurement, and the use of quality data

2. An incentive for many health service delivery reforms, such as care coordination

3. An effort to target quality improvement reforms across many payers, such as Medicare, Medicaid, and private insurers

Prior to the passage of the PPACA, quality improvement efforts were led by a multitude of public and private agencies, linked somewhat, but not in a systematic way. The PPACA developed five ways in which this could be improved:

- National strategy priorities and a strategic plan to improve healthcare quality
- Coordination of healthcare quality activity at the federal level
- Measurement of development and endorsement

Figure 7.7.   An example of a core measure across the data continuum

Value-Based Measure	Data Capture	Data Maintenance	Data Quality
Vascular Catheter-Associated Infections	Secondary Diagnosis = 2-9 diagnoses on claim ICD-9-CM code: 999.31 (Other and unspecified infection due to central venous catheter) ICD-10-CM code: T80.219A (approximate match—unspecified infection due to central venous catheter, initial encounter) POA = N (not present on admission) or U (unknown)	Number of occurrences of 999.31 as the 2nd-9th diagnosis on the patient claim with a POA code of N or U Number of acute FFS (Fee for Service) Discharges during a specified time period For example: 5 occurrences of 999.31 in 2nd quarter 500 FFS inpatient discharges in 2nd quarter 1% occurrence rate for Vascular Catheter Infections	Patient Safety Measure Sub-conditions: Healthcare Associated Infections (HAI) Common and increase morbidity and cost Effective Practices: *Use of maximum sterile barrier precautions during catheter insertion; *Use of catheters coated with antibacterial or antiseptic agents; *Use of chlorihexidine gluconate at insertion site Additional Effective Practices (efficacy still unclear):*Use of heparin and tunneling at central venous catheter.

Source: AHRQ 2011.

- Public reporting of quality data
- Selection of measures for use in federal quality programs

Data capture, maintenance, and quality are at the forefront of these initiatives. Public reporting of quality data can only be achieved with effective data capture methods, data maintenance and retrieval, and data quality (see figure 7.7).

National Strategy for Quality Improvement in Healthcare

The Department of Health and Human Services (HHS) has developed the National Strategy for Quality Improvement in Healthcare by collecting information from over 300 stakeholders from the healthcare industry and public. Three overarching aims, Better Care, Healthy People/Healthy Communities, and Affordable Care, are identified in the strategy.

There are also six priorities within the National Strategy for Quality Improvement in Healthcare:

- Making care safer by reducing harm caused in the delivery of care
- Ensuring that each person and family is engaged as partners in their care
- Promoting effective communication and coordination of care
- Promoting the most effective prevention and treatment practices for the leading causes of mortality, starting with cardiovascular disease
- Working with communities to promote wide use of best practices to enable healthy living
- Making quality care more affordable for individuals, families, employers, and governments by developing and spreading new healthcare delivery models

Ten guiding principles help to pave the way for meeting the aims and priorities and include

1. Person-centeredness and family engagement
2. Specific health considerations
3. Eliminating disparities in care
4. Aligning the efforts of public and private sectors
5. Quality improvement
6. Consistent national standards
7. Primary care will become a bigger focus
8. Coordination will be enhanced
9. Integration of care delivery
10. Providing clear information

For purposes of this chapter, discussion is limited to the guiding principles that focus on data and information management: Principle 5 Quality Improvement and Principle 10 Providing Clear Information. For example, the strategy states that:

5. Quality improvement will be driven by supporting innovation, evaluating efforts around the country, rapid-cycle learning, and disseminating evidence about what works. The best way to improve healthcare quality is to help health professionals evaluate their own performance and their colleagues' performance, quickly learn how interventions fare in the 'real world,' and see the benefits of innovation firsthand—and then widely share the lessons they learn. For this to happen, health professionals must have rapid access to information about what works in their own care and in care around the country. (AHRQ 2012)

and

10. Providing patients, providers, and payers with the clear information they need to make choices that are right for them will be encouraged.Patients who want to partner with their

healthcare providers in making decisions about their care too often lack the necessary understandable information. The National Quality Strategy will foster transparency so that patients have the information to make choices that are right for them, clinicians have the information they need to improve, and payers have the information to move to value-based payments. (AHRQ 2012)

One major outcome from the strategy is the development of a **measure applications partnership (MAP)** in which performance measures that will be used in public reporting and performance-based payment programs are outlined and described. Some of the performance measures address healthcare-acquired conditions (HCAs) and readmissions, while others focus on clinician and insurance industry performance measurement. The Centers for Medicare and Medicaid Services (CMS) is working with AHRQ and the National Quality Foundation (NQF) to streamline the number of performance measurements so that both public and private concerns are heard and addressed and an open communication plan is provided for those collecting these measures.

An example of one of the measures and how it relates to the data continuum (data capture, maintenance, and quality) is shown in figure 7.7. This figure describes the type of performance measure, what data elements are needed in order for it to be effectively captured, how it can be quantified and continually maintained in a data repository so that outcomes can be easily retrieved, and the effect this type of measure has on the overall quality of patient care.

A major goal of the National Strategy for Quality Improvement in Healthcare is to synthesize the quality measures that exist today so that they are similar across different agencies. Core Clinical Quality Measures/National Quality Measures (CMS), Healthcare Effectiveness Data and Information Set (HEDIS), ORYX Performance Initiative/Core Measures/Accountability Measures (Joint Commission), National Hospice and Palliative Care Organization Standards (NHPCO)—Family Evaluation for Hospice and Bereavement, short-form health surveys, Scales of Independent Behavior-Revised (SIB-R) for Intellectual or Developmental Disabilities, and so forth will be pulled together in one national source so that quality measures are similar across multiple groups.

Data Dictionaries as a Tool in Controlling Data Quality

Important tools for use in controlling the quality of data in healthcare are the database, data dictionary, and data map. A database is an organizational tool that manages data so that it can be easily queried for the data that are included. **Attributes** are characteristics of the data fields that make up the database and may include a name, a medical record number, an address, and such. AHIMA (e-HIM Workgroup on EHR Data Content 2006, 64A) defines a data dictionary as "a descriptive

list of names (also called representations or displays), definitions, and attributes of data elements to be collected in an information system or database." A data dictionary is like a map of the database. Whenever a set of data is created, it should have an accompanying data dictionary. A data dictionary can ensure consistency by standardizing definitions.

Data map and **crosswalk** "are terms used to describe the connections, or paths, between classifications and vocabularies" (Bryant 2006, 9). For example, when a healthcare researcher is studying the effectiveness of an imaging technology, such as magnetic resonance imaging for diagnosing cancer from 1998 to 2013, the researcher uses the magnetic resonance imaging codes from the International Classification of Diseases, 9th Revision, Clinical Modification (ICD-9-CM), and ICD-10-CM to conduct this study. The ICD-9-CM coding classification in 1998 was notably less detailed than ICD-10-CM in 2013. To help the researcher ensure study validity and integrity, the researcher will rely on the data map, or crosswalk, that "connects" the ICD-9-CM codes across the span of the study to ensure that an ICD-9-CM code in 1998 has, in essence, the same meaning as the ICD-10-CM code it is mapped or crosswalked to in 2013. (Chapter 15 provides additional information on classifications and vocabularies.)

Types of Data Dictionaries

There are two general types of data dictionaries: the database management system data dictionary and the organization-wide data dictionary.

Database Management System Data Dictionary

The **database management system (DBMS) data dictionary** is developed in conjunction with development of a specific database. Modern DBMSs have built-in data dictionaries that go beyond data definitions and store information about tables and data relationships. These integrated data dictionaries are sometimes referred to as **system catalogs,** reflecting their technical nature.

Figure 7.8 shows a portion of a designer-defined data dictionary developed in Microsoft Access for a simplified PATIENT table. The database developer would use this portion of the software to define the data to be stored in the database's system catalog.

A typical data dictionary associated with a DBMS allows for at least documentation of the following:

- Table names
- All attribute or field names
- A description of each attribute
- The data type of the attribute (text, number, date, and so on)
- The format of each attribute, such as DD_MM_YYYY for the date

Figure 7.8.   Partial data dictionary for PATIENT table

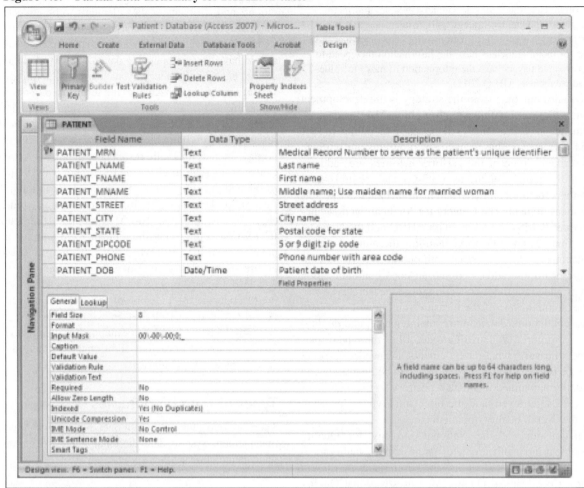

The size of each attribute, such as 12 characters in a phone number with dashes

An appropriate range of values, such as integers 100000–999999 for the health record number

Whether the attribute is required

Relationships among attributes

Other descriptions that might be stored in the data dictionary associated with a database include

Who created the database

When the database was created

Where the database is located

What programs can access the database

Who the end users and administrators of the database are

How access authorization is provided to all users

Organization-wide Data Dictionary

The second type of data dictionary is developed outside the framework of a specific database design process. This data dictionary serves to promote data quality through data consistency across the organization. Individual data element definitions are agreed upon and defined. This leads to better-quality data and facilitates the detailed, technical data dictionaries that are integrated with the databases themselves. Ideally, every healthcare organization will develop a data dictionary to define common data and their formats. This organization-wide document becomes a valuable resource for IS development.

Looking at the MPI example discussed earlier (refer to table 7.1), what would need to be defined for each field? Although everyone may think he or she knows the definition of a last name, can all agree that it will be stored as no more than 25 characters? How should the middle name be handled? Will it be the maiden name for married women? Is the medical record number to be stored with leading zeros? All these issues can be settled with the development of an organization-wide data dictionary.

Another challenge for healthcare managers results from interorganizational projects or the merger of healthcare organizations. Suppose a multifacility organization wanted to merge its MPI systems. Imagine the challenges involved not only in defining data elements but also in uncovering existing definitions. If the organizations in question built other systems based on internal MPI definitions, all of these systems would need to be analyzed and changed.

Development of Data Dictionaries

The health information manager should be a key member of any data dictionary project team. Developing a data dictionary can be an overwhelming task in light of the diversity of data users and the size and scope of some healthcare organizations.

To assist with the development of data dictionaries, AHIMA has published recommended guidelines (AHIMA e-HIM Workgroup on EHR Data Content 2006).

- *Design a plan:* Preplan the development, implementation, and maintenance of the data dictionary.
- *Develop an enterprise data dictionary:* Integrate common data elements across the entire institution to ensure consistency.
- *Ensure collaborative involvement:* Make sure there is support from all key stakeholders.
- *Develop an approvals process:* Ensure a documentation trail for all decisions, updates, and maintenance.
- *Identify and retain details of data versions:* Version control is important.
- *Design for flexibility and growth.*
- *Design room for expansion of field values.*
- *Follow established ISO/International Electrotechnical Commission (IEC) 11179 guidelines for metadata registry:* To promote interoperability, follow standards.
- *Adopt nationally recognized standards.*
- *Beware of differing standards for the same concepts.*
- *Use geographic codes and conform to the National Spatial Data Infrastructure and the Federal Geographic Data Committee.*
- *Test the information system:* Develop a test plan to ensure the system supports the data dictionary.
- *Provide ongoing education and training.*
- *Assess the extent to which the data elements maintain consistency and avoid duplication.*

Safeguards for Ensuring Data Integrity and Security

Nowhere is ensuring the integrity and security of data more important than in healthcare. Healthcare organizations have an obligation to protect patient privacy and to maintain the confidential nature of the physician–patient relationship. Healthcare privacy and confidentiality are regulated by state and federal laws and standards, as well as by standards of care. Other chapters in this text discuss confidentiality and privacy from a legislative and regulatory perspective. This section focuses on the safeguards that should be implemented in a healthcare database system.

Data Integrity

Databases contain rules known as **integrity constraints** that must be satisfied by the stored data. **Data integrity** happens when all of the data in the database conform to all integrity constraint rules. Database integrity constraints include

- *Data type:* The data entered into a field should be consistent with the data type for that field. For example, if a field is a numeric field, it should only accept numbers. If it is a date field, it should only accept a legitimate date.
- *Legal values:* Many fields have a limited number of "legal" values. For example, a health record number may only be entered as 000001 through 999999.
- *Format:* Certain fields, such as dates, must be entered in a certain format, such as MM/DD/YYYY.
- *Key constraints:* Constraints placed on the primary and foreign keys within the database. A foreign key, for example, cannot be entered into the database unless a corresponding primary key already exists. A primary key is an essential attribute within the database that is used to link cases or records together or to query the database for specific information. This concept is called **referential integrity** (Pratt and Adamski 2008).

These constraints help ensure that the originally entered data and changes to these data follow certain rules. DBMSs today include the functionality to enforce integrity constraints (Pratt and Adamski 2008). After the parameters for the types of integrity have been set within the database, users cannot violate them. For example, they cannot enter nonnumeric data into a number field. An error message will result. Likewise, a user cannot add a VISIT entry to the database described earlier unless a corresponding PATIENT has already been entered.

Data Security

Data security ensures the confidentiality, integrity, and availability of the data (Rob and Coronel 2009). Modern DBMSs have built-in mechanisms to enforce security rules. Within healthcare organizations, most of the database systems are shared with multiple users. This makes implementing the security features of the DBMS critical.

Protecting the security and privacy of data in the database is called **authorization management.** Two of the important aspects of authorization management are user access control and usage monitoring (Rob and Coronel 2009).

User access control features within the database are designed to limit access to the database or some portion of it. According to Rob and Coronel (2009), they generally provide the **database administrator (DBA)** or **data administrator (DA)** responsible for security with the tools to

- Define each user of the database. The DBA can create login information for each user.
- Assign passwords to users.
- Define user groups. By defining user groups, the DBA can limit access to certain groups. For example, some users may have read-only privileges. These users can see the data in the database but cannot enter or change them. Other users may be granted read-write privileges, so they can enter and change data.
- Assign access privileges. This can be done according to user groups as described before or on an individual basis. The highest level of privilege is the administrative level, which should be reserved for the DBA. Persons with administrative permissions can change the underlying structure of the database.

This list represents the security features that are part of the DBMS. The database also can be secured at the network operating system level. In many cases, a database user will first log in to the network system with one login and password and then log in to the database with a second login and password. The database also can be secured through physical security protections, such as locked rooms, password-protected workstations, surveillance video, and voice recognition. The level of sensitivity of the data within the database should determine the level of security.

Usage monitoring is another aspect of authorization management. One of the most common ways that database administrators monitor database use is to use audit trails to determine whether there have been any actual or attempted access violations. The audit trails should be able to tell the DBA when and where the attempted breech occurred.

Check Your Understanding 7.4

Instructions: Answer the following questions on a separate piece of paper.

1. What is data integrity?
2. How is data integrity different from data security?
3. What do the authorization management features in a DBMS do?

Other Sources and Uses of Data Capture, Maintenance, and Quality Tools

There are many different healthcare data sets that already provide excellent methods to capture and maintain quality data for effective reporting, epidemiological research, evidence-based medicine, patient-centered outcomes research, patient safety, and overall effectiveness in the quality of patient care.

Healthcare Data Sets

Healthcare data sets that are commonly available in the United States include but are not limited to the following:

- Healthcare Effectiveness Data and Information Set (HEDIS)
- Uniform Hospital Discharge Data Set (UHDDS)
- Uniform Ambulatory Care Data Set (UACDS)
- Minimum Data Set for Long-Term Care and Resident Assessment Protocols (MDS 3.0)
- Outcomes and Assessment Information Set (OASIS)
- Data elements for emergency department systems
- Inpatient Rehabilitation Facility-Patient Assessment Instrument (IRF-PAI)
- Functional Independence Measures (FIM)
- End Stage Renal Disease (ESRD) data sets
- Transplant data through United Network for Organ Sharing (UNOS)
- Mental Health National Outcome Measures (NOMS)
- Drug and Alcohol Services Information System (DASIS)
- Essential Medical Data Set
- Meaningful use requirements

For example, the Functional Independence Measures assess physical and cognitive disability. Items are scored from 1 to 7 based on the patient's ability to perform both functional and cognitive activities of daily living. The items include self-care, such as bathing, grooming, toileting, and such; bowel and bladder management; transfers (bed, chair, wheelchair, toilet, tub, shower); locomotion; communication (comprehension and expression); and social cognition (social interaction, problem solving, memory). The rating levels are broken down into complete dependence (1 to 2), modified dependence (3 to 5), and independence (6 to 7). The ratings are collected upon admission, discharge, and follow-up to see if the patient improves over time. It is important for the health information management (HIM) professional to be knowledgeable in these types of data sets and the data that are necessary for collection, maintenance, and improved quality of health information. It is important for the HIM professional to work with IT staff as well as clinicians to make sure all of the necessary data elements are captured and maintained so that the FIM score can be easily achieved and followed over time. Clinician training is necessary so that the data collected are consistent over time. Standards related to data capture need to be followed specifically so that the data collected is consistent. Specific instructions related to the FIM score are provided by CMS, but it is important that the standards including data elements and data definitions are collected similarly across healthcare facilities. This will enhance data reporting capabilities and requirements for third parties and therefore increase reimbursement amounts and assist with patient-centered outcomes research. These data sets are described in more detail in chapter 8.

Clinical Documentation Improvement

Clinical documentation improvement (CDI), or the ability of physicians and other healthcare providers to document a true picture of what happened to the patient while receiving care so that HIM professionals can take that information and use it to produce accurate classification of diagnoses and procedures into codes, has major implications for improvements in data quality (Gold 2007). CDI can lead to overall improvements in medical record documentation so that coding or classifying diagnoses and procedures into ICD-9-CM or ICD-10-CM and ICD-10-PCS codes becomes easy. If the correct information is collected and maintained, then coding accuracy will increase, reimbursement amounts will be valid, fraud and abuse will decrease, and ultimately overall quality of care will improve. According to AHIMA's CDI toolkit, the CDI review form can include data elements related to clinical indicators and medical evidence, location in the health record and its desired outcome, or impact to patient care. CDI when done right can lead to improvements in the overall methods of data collection, maintenance and data quality (AHIMA 2010a).

Secondary Data Uses

There are many secondary data uses for the healthcare data that is collected and maintained. Clinical practice guidelines or clinical pathways or protocols for specific types of diagnoses and procedures use health related data to measure the outcomes effectiveness of patients who follow the protocols and those patients who do not follow the protocols. Epidemiologists use healthcare data across the continuum of care to examine trends over time for specific diseases. They can conduct prevalence, retrospective, and prospective studies by examining data from the medical record or other data repositories. For example, a study that examined obesity and breast cancer recurrence for postmenopausal Caucasian and African-American women over a period of time used healthcare data, such as height and weight; breast cancer treatment procedures; and follow-up of patients from the medical record, cancer registry, and a hospital database to obtain its results (Watzlaf et al. 1996). Other uses of healthcare data include patient-centered care and outcomes research. The focus is on the patient's needs and concerns so it may lead the clinician to document the feelings of patients in relation to the whole healthcare experience

rather than just diagnostic and procedural outcomes. Different methods to collect data that are patient centered will be needed, and a new focus and training for clinicians on a different way of thinking and documenting may be necessary. Risk assessment and predictive modeling involves using specific types of patient characteristics to determine what types of disease may be forthcoming. Genomic annotation data as well as other types of risk factors can be combined to determine the likelihood of a patient to develop Alzheimer's disease, for example. Predictive modeling will lead to prevention-focused data repositories that can decrease the number of healthcare hospitalizations, length of stay, and overall cost of care. See chapter 14 for discussion of secondary data uses.

Roles in Data Capture, Maintenance, and Quality

This chapter focuses on the importance of maintaining high-quality data that will lead to high-quality information and decisions. High-quality data do not just happen. Healthcare organizations must establish mechanisms and policies for managing their data resources. Such mechanisms and policies must not only encompass the technical aspects of implementing and maintaining the data within the organization, but also ensure that the data conform to established standards of quality. Several roles within the healthcare team can be used to manage the quality of healthcare data. The AHIMA Core Model (AHIMA 2011b) describes the primary role of the HIM professional as focused on five main functional areas of health information:

- Data capture, validation, and maintenance
- Data and information analysis, transformation, and decision support
- Information dissemination and liaison
- Health information resource management and innovation
- Information governance and stewardship

There are also several roles outlined in the AHIMA Core Model that relate to each of these functional areas. For this chapter, roles will focus on the data capture, validation, and maintenance function. See figures 7.9 and 7.10, which demonstrate the roles, functions, and value for the data capture, validation, and maintenance function as well as how these three areas lead to enhancements in the quality of patient care.

Check Your Understanding 7.5

Instructions: Answer the following questions on a separate piece of paper.

1. Discuss the differences and similarities in the roles of the data capture, validation, and maintenance in the AHIMA Core Model.

2. Which of the discussed roles would be most appropriate for a health information manager? Explain your answer.

Figure 7.9 Data capture, validation, and maintenance: AHIMA Core Model

Roles	Functions	Value
Chart Correction Analyst	Develop and maintain data architecture, tools, designs, and exchange models	Increased revenue potential by assuring accurate coding supported by documentation
Classification editor and exchange expert	Design functional attributes of data structures, data fields, and input templates	Improved cash flow caused by first time claims processing with few denials and appeals required
Clinical coding validator	Analyze and design health information related processes, work, and information flows	Improved efficiency of data capture through section and implementation of technology
Clinical content manager	Design and validate appropriate data capture mechanisms	Decreased operational costs by efficiencies gained in workflow
Chart Correction Analyst	Develop and maintain data architecture, tools, designs, and exchange models	Increased revenue potential by assuring accurate coding supported by documentation
Classification editor and exchange expert	Design functional attributes of data structures, data fields, and input templates	Improved cash flow caused by first time claims processing with few denials and appeals required
Clinical coding validator	Analyze and design health information related processes, work, and information flows	Improved efficiency of data capture through section and implementation of technology
Clinical content manager	Design and validate appropriate data capture mechanisms	Decreased operational costs by efficiencies gained in workflow
CDI specialist/supervisor	Design and develop methods for acquisition and integration of externally authored data that maintains the source identity	Increased patient safety and satisfaction by reduction of duplicate records
Coder	Design and implement data integrity validation strategies and methods	Increase in patient safety and satisfaction through standardized data collection across systems and sites
Coding compliance coordinator/supervisor/ manager	Establish and maintain uniform definitions of data, and data dictionaries	Improved research outcomes through optimized data capture and abstraction
Computer-assisted coding validation practice leader	Ensure appropriate protocols to support secondary data uses, such as research, quality/safety monitoring, public health, risk assessment, and such	Increased value and accuracy of information through planning for the capture of discrete data
Data Architect	Provide nosology, data mapping, and taxonomy support for uniformity, information retrieval, or secondary use	
Data capture design specialist	Code and abstract health record content in both the manual and computer-assisted environments	
Data dictionary manager	Manage, evaluate, and maintain terminology assets including vocabulary and clinical code sets	
Data integrity and transition specialist/auditor	Develop data crosswalks and conversions and test for data quality	
Data mapper/translater	Identify, develop and operate required registries, repositories and exchange	
Data quality manager/ analyst	Manage and influence patient identify mechanisms and frameworks	
Documentation /EHR manager	Educate and advise on data capture and maintenance functions	
EHR content manager		
Enterprise patient master index data integrity analyst		

ICD-10 implementation specialist		
Information workflow designer		
Patient identity manager		
Registrar (birth, cancer, device, bone marrow, tissue)		
Research coordinator/ associate		
Research data abstractor		
Terminology asset manager		
Voice capture specialist		

(Note: Functions and value are not specific to each role but encompass all roles related to data capture, validation and maintenance)

Source: AHIMA 2011b.

Figure 7.10. Proper data collection and maintenance methods to achieve data quality

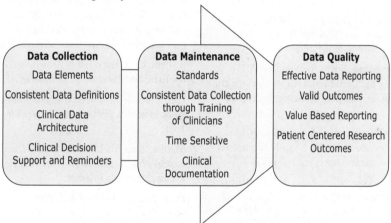

Summary

Health information managers must manage information that is shared by diverse and widely dispersed groups of end users. Information is derived from data, or raw facts. Knowledge is derived from information by combining it with experience and interpretation. Information and knowledge are then used by any number of individuals within a healthcare organization in making decisions about patient care. Thus, data, information, and knowledge are valuable resources that must be managed carefully following certain basic principles. Essential to the management of information is the organization's ability to capture, maintain, and ensure the quality of the data. Data quality is evaluated by comparing its characteristics to recognized standards. Although no single set of nationally recognized standards for healthcare

data quality exists, many organizations have published guidelines. The PPACA is moving toward the coordination of national core measures and standards so that the quality of healthcare can be enhanced.

An important tool in controlling data quality is the data dictionary. There are two general types: the DBMS (database management system) data dictionary, which is developed at the same time the database is developed, and the organization-wide data dictionary, which promotes data consistency throughout the organization.

To manage their data resources, healthcare organizations must set up mechanisms and policies that address not only database implementation and maintenance but also standards of data quality. The roles of HIM professionals continue to evolve. AHIMA has developed the Core Model for Health Information Management, which includes roles, functions, and value for data capture, validation, and maintenance of clinical data. The HIM professional is at the forefront in data management and is a leader in the development and implementation of data capture, maintenance, and quality tools that are effective in promoting healthcare research, patient-centered care, evidence-based practice, and the overall quality of patient care.

References

Agency for Healthcare Research and Quality. 2012. Working for quality: principles for the National Quality Strategy http://www.ahrq.gov/workingforquality/nqs/principles.htm.

Agency for Healthcare Research and Quality. 2011. Prevention of intravascular catheter associated infections. http://www.ahrq.gov/clinic/ptsafety/chap16b.htm.

Agency for Healthcare Research and Quality. 2007. AHRQ conference on healthcare data collection and reporting. Prepared by AHIMA, MGMA-CFR AHRQ Publication No. 07-0033-EF. http://www.ahrq.gov.

American Health Information Management Association. 2011a. A Core Model for the HIM future. http://journal.ahima.org/2011/10/01/a-core-model-for-the-him-future/.

American Health Information Management Association. 2011b. A new view of HIM: Introducing the Core Model (Draft Document). http://library.ahima.org/xpedio/groups/public/documents/ahima/bok1_049283.pdf.

American Health Information Management Association. 2010a. *Clinical Documentation Improvement Toolkit.* http://library.ahima.org/xpedio/groups/public/documents/ahima/bok1_047236.pdf.

American Health Information Management Association. 2010b. Practice brief: Fundamentals for building a master patient index/enterprise master patient index (Updated). *Journal of AHIMA.*

American Health Information Management Association. 2008. Quality data and documentation for EHRs in physician practice. *Journal of AHIMA* 79(8): 43–48.

American Health Information Management Association. 2007. Practice brief: Data standards, data quality, and interoperability. *Journal of AHIMA* 78(2): 65–68.

AHIMA Data Quality Management Task Force. 2012. Practice brief: Data quality management model. *Journal of AHIMA* 83(7).

AHIMA e-HIM Workgroup on Assessing and Improving Healthcare Data Quality in the EHR. 2007. Practice brief: Assessing and improving EHR data quality. *Journal of AHIMA* 78(3): 69–72.

AHIMA e-HIM Workgroup on Computer-Assisted Coding. 2004. Delving into computer-assisted coding. Appendix G: Glossary of Terms. *Journal of AHIMA* 75(10): Web extra.

AHIMA e-HIM Workgroup on EHR Data Content. 2006. Practice brief: Guidelines for developing a data dictionary. *Journal of AHIMA* 77(2): 64A–D.

Bryant, G. 2006. Testimony of Gloryanne Bryant, RHIA, CCS, corporate director for coding and health information management compliance, Catholic Healthcare West, to the Health Subcommittee of the Committee on Ways and Means, US House of Representatives. http://www.ahima.org/icd10/documents/MicrosoftWordTestimonyofGloryanneBryant_4_.pdf.

Bureau of Labor Statistics, US Department of Labor. 2010. *Career Guide to Industries, 2010–11 ed.* http://www.bls.gov/oco/ocos014.htm.

DHHS Annual Progress Report to Congress: National Strategy for Quality Improvement in HealthCare. 2012. http://www.ahrq.gov/workingforquality/nqs/nqs2012annlrpt.pdf.

Certification Commission for Health Information Technology. 2011. Inpatient EHR criteria, 2011, 1–4. http://www.cchit.org/sites/all/files/CCHIT%20Certified%202011%20Inpatient%20EHR%20Criteria%2020100326.pdf.

Gold, R.S. 2007. What clinical documentation improvement is—and what it's not. *For the Record* 19(6). http://www.fortherecord-mag.com/archives/ftr_03192007p8.shtml.

Kallem, C., J. Burrington-Brown, and A. Dinh. 2007. Data content for EHR documentation. *Journal of AHIMA* 78(7): 73–76.

Lau, F. 2004. Toward a conceptual knowledge management framework in health. *Perspectives in Health Information Management* 1(8).

Medical Records Institute. 2002. *Healthcare Documentation: A Report on Information Capture and Report Generation.* Boston: Medical Records Institute.

Pratt, P.J., and J. Adamski. 2008. *Concepts of Database Management,* 6th ed. Cambridge, MA: Course Technology, Thomson Learning.

Rob, P., and C. Coronel. 2009. *Database Systems: Design, Implementation, and Management,* 8th ed. Boston: Course Technology, Thomson Learning.

Wager, K.A., F.W. Lee, and J.P. Glaser. 2005. *Managing Health Care Information Systems: A Practical Approach for Health Care Executives.* San Francisco: Jossey-Bass.

Watzlaf, V., A. Katoh, and F. D'Amico. 1996. Obstacles encountered in the use of the medical record and cancer registry abstract in breast cancer research. *Topics in Health Information Management* 17(1): 25–33.

chapter **8**

Healthcare Informatics Standards

Kathy Giannangelo, MA, RHIA, CCS, CPHIMS, FAHIMA

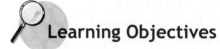

Learning Objectives

- Explain healthcare data sets and describe their purpose
- Recognize the basic data sets used in acute-care, ambulatory care, long-term care, emergency care, and home care settings
- Describe the unique use of the Minimum Data Set for long-term care in defining and addressing the care of residents in long-term care facilities
- Identify the purpose and use of the Healthcare Effectiveness Data and Information Set (HEDIS)
- Explain the intent of the ORYX initiative and give examples of the core measures identified through ORYX
- Recognize the key players in current efforts to develop standards for electronic health records (EHRs)
- Define the term *healthcare informatics standards* and explain vocabulary standards, record structure and content standards, content exchange standards, and privacy and security standards
- Recognize the impact of the Health Insurance Portability and Accountability Act of 1996 (HIPAA) on the development of health informatics standards

- Explain the relationship of core data elements to healthcare informatics standards in electronic environments
- Describe how data standards are developed
- Explain the concepts of interoperability and connectivity as they relate to federal initiatives to provide incentives for the adoption of healthcare informatics standards
- List those involved with standards development, testing, coordination, and harmonization
- Identify prominent healthcare informatics standards development organizations (SDOs)
- Identify key data elements of the continuity of care record core data set
- Define the role of government agencies, such as the Office of the National Coordinator for Health Information Technology (ONC), in healthcare informatics standards development, testing, coordination, and harmonization

Key Terms

Accreditation

Accreditation Standards Committee X12

Aggregate data

American College of Radiology and the National Electrical Manufacturers Association (ACR-NEMA)

American National Standards Institute (ANSI)

ASTM International

ASTM Standard E1384-07

Bills of Mortality

Centers for Medicare and Medicaid Services (CMS)

Clinical Document Architecture (CDA)

Common Formats Version 1.1

Continuity of Care Document (CCD)

Continuity of Care Record (CCR)

Core data element

Core measure

Data

Data dictionary

Data element

Data Elements for Emergency Department Systems (DEEDS) 1.0

Data set

Department of Health and Human Services (HHS)

Digital Imaging and Communications in Medicine (DICOM)

Electronic data interchange (EDI)

Extensible markup language (XML)

Health information exchange (HIE)

Health Information Technology Expert Panel (HITEP)

Health Information Technology Policy Committee (HITPC)

Health Information Technology Standards Committee (HITSC)

Health Insurance Portability and Accountability Act (HIPAA)

Health Level Seven (HL7)

Healthcare Effectiveness Data and Information Set (HEDIS)

Healthcare informatics standards

Hospital discharge abstract system

Identifier standards

Information

Inpatient

Institute of Electrical and Electronics Engineers (IEEE)

International Organization for Standardization (ISO)

Joint Commission

Long-term care

Metadata registry

Minimum Data Set (MDS) Version 3.0

National Center for Health Statistics (NCHS)

National Committee for Quality Assurance (NCQA)

National Committee on Vital and Health Statistics (NCVHS)

National Council for Prescription Drug Programs (NCPDP)

National Institute for Standards and Technology (NIST)

National Provider Identifier (NPI)

Nomenclature

Office of the National Coordinator of Health Information Technology (ONC)

ORYX initiative

Outcomes and Assessment Information Set (OASIS)

Outpatient

Patient-identifiable data

Picture archiving and communication system (PACS)

Privacy standards

Prospective payment system (PPS)

Quality Data Model (QDM)

Security standards

Standard

Standards development organization (SDO)

Standards and Interoperability (S&I) Framework

Structure and content standards

Transaction standards

Unified Medical Language System (MLS)

Uniform Ambulatory Care Data Set (UACDS)

Uniform Hospital Discharge Data Set (UHDDS)

Unique identification number

Vocabulary standards

Data and information pertaining to individuals who use healthcare services are collected in virtually every setting where healthcare is delivered. **Data** represent basic facts and observations about people, processes, measurements, and conditions. In healthcare, these facts usually describe specific characteristics of individual patients. The term *data* is plural. Although the singular form is datum, *data element* is frequently used to describe a single fact or measurement. For example, age, gender, insurance company, and blood pressure are all **data elements** concerning a patient. **Information** refers to data that have been collected, combined, analyzed, interpreted, or converted into a form that can be used for specific purposes. In other words, data represent facts; information represents meaning.

In healthcare settings, data are stored in the individual's health record whether that record is in paper or electronic format or a hybrid combination of paper and electronic documents. The numerous data elements in the health record are then combined, analyzed, and interpreted by the patient's physician and other clinicians. For example, test results are combined with the physician's observations and the patient's description of his or her symptoms to form information about the disease or condition that is affecting the patient. Physicians use both data and information to diagnose diseases, develop treatment plans, assess the effectiveness of care, and determine the patient's prognosis.

Data about patients can be extracted from individual health records and combined as **aggregate data.** Aggregate data are used to develop information about groups of patients. For example, data about all of the patients who suffered an acute myocardial infarction during a specific time period could be collected in a database. From the aggregate data, it would be possible to identify common characteristics that might predict the course of the disease or provide information about the most effective way to treat it. Ultimately, research using the aggregate data might be used for disease prevention. For example, researchers identified the link between smoking and lung cancer by analyzing aggregate data about patients with a diagnosis of lung cancer; smoking cessation programs grew from the identification of the causal effect of smoking on lung cancer and a variety of other conditions. The topic of aggregate data is discussed in chapter 14.

The first known efforts to collect and use healthcare data to produce meaningful statistical profiles date back to the 17th century. In the early 1600s, Captain John Graunt gathered data on the common causes of death in London. He called his study the London **Bills of Mortality** (WHO n.d.). However, few systematic efforts were undertaken to collect statistical data about the incidence and prevalence of disease until the mid-20th century, when technological developments made it possible to collect and analyze large amounts of healthcare data.

Modern efforts at standardizing healthcare data began in the 1960s. At that time, healthcare facilities began to use computers to process larger amounts of data than could be handled manually. The goal was to make comparisons among data from multiple providers. It soon became evident that healthcare organizations needed to use standardized, uniform data definitions in order to arrive at meaningful data comparisons.

The first data standardization efforts focused generally on hospitals and specifically on hospital discharge data. The intent of the efforts was to standardize definitions of key data elements commonly collected in hospitals. Discharge data were collected in **hospital discharge abstract systems.** These systems used databases compiled from aggregate data about all of the patients discharged from a particular facility. The need to compare uniform discharge data from one hospital to the next led to the development of **data sets,** or lists of recommended data elements with uniform definitions.

There is an old saying, "You can't compare apples and oranges." When one attempts to compare terms that do not have the same definition it is like comparing apples and oranges. Standardizing data elements and definitions makes it possible to compare the data collected at different facilities. For example, when data are standardized, the term *admission* means the same thing at City Hospital and at University Hospital. Because both hospitals define admission in the same way, the hospitals can be compared with each other on such things as the number of admissions or the percentage of occupancy each has had.

Today, hospitals and other healthcare organizations collect more data and develop more information than ever before. Moreover, data and information from the health records of individual patients are used for more purposes than ever before. The demand for information is coming from users within the organizations as well as from external users such as third-party payers, government agencies, **accreditation** organizations, and others. The extensive use of information within and across organizational boundaries demands standards that promote interoperable electronic interchange of data and information. Information standards are critical in the migration to electronic health records (EHRs), as described in chapter 5.

The data sets originally developed to support uniform data collection are inadequate for an electronic environment, and many public and private organizations have been actively engaged in the process of developing **healthcare informatics standards** to support EHR development and information interchange. Healthcare information standards development is a dynamic process that evolves on a continuous basis as key players in the standards development community negotiate, refine, and revise standards. The critical importance of healthcare information standards has been recognized in federal initiatives including the legislatively mandated **Office of the National Coordinator of Health Information Technology (ONC)** and the establishment of two official **Department of Health and Human Services (HHS)** advisory committees

as a result of the Health Information Technology for Economic and Clinical Health (HITECH) Act, part of the American Recovery and Reinvestment Act of 2009 (ARRA). The **Health Information Technology Standards Committee (HITSC)** makes recommendations to the National Coordinator on standards, implementation specifications, and certification criteria for the electronic exchange and use of health information for purposes of adoption, consistent with the implementation of the federal Health IT Strategic Plan and in accordance with policies developed by the HIT Policy Committee. In addition, the HITSC provides for the testing of these standards and specifications by the **National Institute for Standards and Technology (NIST)** (ONC 2011a).

According to a report entitled "Toward a National Health Information Infrastructure," by the **National Committee on Vital and Health Statistics (NCVHS),** "if information in multiple locations is to be searched, shared, and synthesized when needed, we will need agreed-upon information guardians that can exchange data with each other . . . we will need equitable rules of data exchange so that competitors (within or between healthcare provider systems, health information management companies, or health web services) will be willing to connect and share data" (NCVHS 2000a).

This chapter describes the initial efforts at developing standardized data sets for use in different types of healthcare settings, including acute care, ambulatory care, long-term care, and home care. It explores the recent national initiatives related to interoperability and connectivity of healthcare information systems that will support widespread implementation of EHR and the ultimate establishment of state health information exchange programs and the Nationwide Health Information Network (NHIN) that will improve patient care, increase safety, and optimize both clinical and administrative decision making. This chapter addresses the evolution of health information standards that are the foundation of this vision. Chapter 9 covers the development of health information exchange (HIE) and the NHIN.

Standards for Data Collection and Reporting

The concept of data standardization became widely accepted during the 1960s, and under the leadership of the **National Center for Health Statistics (NCHS)** and the NCVHS in collaboration with other organizations, data sets were developed for a variety of healthcare settings. Data sets for acute care, long-term care, and ambulatory care were the first to be created. In healthcare, data sets have two purposes: (1) to identify the data elements that should be collected for each patient and (2) to provide uniform definitions for common terms. The use of uniform definitions ensures that data collected from a variety of healthcare settings will share a standard definition.

The standardization of data elements and definitions makes it possible to compare the data collected at different facilities. Comparison data are used for a variety of purposes, including external accreditation, internal performance improvement, and statistical and research studies. However, data sets are not meant to limit the number of data elements that can be collected. Most healthcare organizations collect additional data elements that have meaning for their specific administrative and clinical operations.

Uniform Hospital Discharge Data Set

In 1969, a conference on hospital discharge abstract systems was sponsored jointly by the NCHS, the National Center for Health Services Research and Development, and Johns Hopkins University. Conference participants recommended that all short-term general hospitals in the United States collect a minimum set of patient-specific data elements. They also recommended that these data elements be reflected in all databases formulated from hospital discharge abstract systems. They called the list of patient-specific data items the **Uniform Hospital Discharge Data Set (UHDDS).**

In 1974, the federal government adopted the UHDDS as the standard for collecting data for the Medicare and Medicaid programs. When Section 1886(d) of the Social Security Act was enacted in 1983, UHDDS definitions were incorporated into the rules and regulations for implementing an inpatient prospective payment system based on diagnosis-related groups (DRGs). A key component was the incorporation of the definitions of principal diagnosis, principal procedure, and other significant procedures, into the DRG algorithms. As a result, accurate assignment of a DRG is dependent on accurate selection and coding of the principal diagnosis and principal procedure and the appropriate sequencing of other significant diagnoses and procedures. The NCVHS revised the UHDDS in 1984. The new UHDDS was adopted for all federal health programs in 1986.

The intent of the UHDDS is to list and define a set of common, uniform data elements. The data elements are to be collected in the health records of every hospital inpatient. They are subsequently abstracted from the health record and included in databases that describe aggregate patient characteristics. Because UHDDS data definitions are a component of DRGs and required to accurately calculate DRG payment, short-term, general hospitals in the United States generally collect **patient-identifiable data** in the format recommended by the UHDDS.

The UHDDS has been revised several times since 1986. The current version includes the recommended data elements shown in figure 8.1.

Figure 8.1.   UHDDS data elements

Data Element	Definition/Descriptor
01. Personal identifier	The unique number assigned to each patient within a hospital that distinguishes the patient and his or her hospital record from all others in that institution.
02. Date of birth	Month, day, and year of birth. Capture of the full four-digit year of birth is recommended.
03. Sex	Male or female

04. Race and ethnicity	04a. Race
	        American Indian/Eskimo/Aleut
	        Asian or Pacific Islander
	        Black
	        White
	        Other race
	        Unknown
	04b. Ethnicity
	        Spanish origin/Hispanic
	        Non-Spanish origin/Non-Hispanic
	        Unknown

05. Residence	Full address of usual residence Zip code (nine digits, if available) Code for foreign residence
06. Hospital identification	A unique institutional number used across data collection systems. The Medicare provider number is the preferred hospital identifier.
07. Admission date	Month, day, and year of admission
08. Type of admission	Scheduled: Arranged with admissions office at least 24 hours prior to admission Unscheduled: All other admissions
09. Discharge date	Month, day, and year of discharge
10 & 11. Physician identification • Attending physician • Operating physician	The Medicare unique physician identification number (UPIN) is the preferred method of identifying the attending physician and operating physician(s) because it is uniform across all data systems.
12. Principal diagnosis	The condition established, after study, to be chiefly responsible for occasioning the admission of the patient to the hospital for care.

13. Other diagnoses	All conditions that coexist at the time of admission or that develop subsequently or that affect the treatment received and/or the length of stay. Diagnoses that relate to an earlier episode and have no bearing on the current hospital stay are to be excluded.
14. Qualifier for other diagnoses	A qualifier is given for each diagnosis coded under "other diagnoses" to indicate whether the onset of the diagnosis preceded or followed admission to the hospital. The option "uncertain" is permitted.
15. External cause-of-injury code	The ICD-9-CM code for the external cause of an injury, a poisoning, or an adverse effect (commonly referred to as an E code). Hospitals should complete this item whenever there is a diagnosis of an injury, a poisoning, or an adverse effect.
16. Birth weight of neonate	The specific birth weight of a newborn, preferably recorded in grams.
17. Procedures and dates	All significant procedures are to be reported. A significant procedure is one that is: • Surgical in nature, or • Carries a procedural risk, or • Carries an anesthetic risk, or • Requires specialized training. The date of each significant procedure must be reported. When more than one procedure is reported, the principal procedure must be designated. The principal procedure is one that is performed for definitive treatment rather than one performed for diagnostic or exploratory purposes or is necessary to take care of a complication. If two procedures appear to be principal, the one most closely related to the principal diagnosis should be selected as the principal procedure. The UPIN must be reported for the person performing the principal procedure.
18. Disposition of the patient	• Discharged to home (excludes those patients referred to home health service) • Discharged to acute-care hospital • Discharged to nursing facility • Discharged home to be under the care of a home health service (including a hospice) • Discharged to other healthcare facility • Left against medical advice • Alive, other; or alive, not stated • Died All categories for primary and other sources are: • Blue Cross/Blue Shield • Other health insurance companies • Other liability insurance • Medicare • Medicaid • Workers' Compensation • Self-insured employer plan • Health maintenance organization • CHAMPUS • CHAMPVA • Other government payers • Self-pay • No charge (free, charity, special research, teaching) • Other
19. Patient's expected source of payment	Primary source Other sources
20. Total charges	All charges billed by the hospital for this hospitalization. Professional charges for individual patient care by physicians are excluded.

Source: NCVHS 1992.

Uniform Ambulatory Care Data Set

Ambulatory care includes medical and surgical care provided to patients who return to their homes on the same day they receive the care. The care is provided in physicians' offices, medical clinics, same-day surgery centers, outpatient hospital clinics and diagnostic departments, emergency treatment centers, and hospital emergency departments (EDs). Patients who receive ambulatory care services in hospital-based clinics and departments are referred to as **outpatients.** Patients admitted to hospitals for overnight stays are referred to as **inpatients.**

Since the 1980s, the number and the length of inpatient hospitalizations have declined dramatically. At the same time, the number of healthcare procedures performed in ambulatory settings has increased. There are several reasons for this trend:

• Technological improvements in diagnostic and therapeutic procedures and the development of short-acting anesthetics have made it possible to perform many medical and surgical procedures in ambulatory facilities. Surgical procedures that once required inpatient hospitalization and long recovery periods are now being performed in same-day surgery centers.

• Third-party payers have extended coverage to include most procedures performed on an outpatient basis.

• Medicare's acute inpatient hospital **prospective payment system (PPS)** limits reimbursement for inpatient care and, in effect, encourages the use of ambulatory or outpatient care as an alternative to more costly inpatient services.

Like hospitals, ambulatory care organizations depend on the availability of accurate data and information. A standardized data set to guide the content and structure of ambulatory health records and data collection systems in ambulatory care was needed.

In 1989, the NCVHS approved the **Uniform Ambulatory Care Data Set (UACDS).** The committee recommended its use in every facility where ambulatory care is delivered. Several of the data elements that make up the UACDS are similar to those used in the UHDDS. For example, the UACDS data elements that describe the personal identifier, residence, date of birth, gender, and race and ethnicity of the patient are the same as the definitions in the UHDDS. The purpose of keeping the same demographic data elements is to make it easier to compare data for inpatients and ambulatory patients in the same facility as well as among different facilities.

However, the UACDS also includes data elements specific to ambulatory care, such as the reason for the encounter with the healthcare provider. The UACDS also includes optional data elements to describe the patient's living arrangements and marital status. These data elements (shown in figure 8.2) are unique to the UACDS. Ambulatory care practitioners need information about the living conditions of their patients because patients and their families often need to manage at-home nursing care, for example, activity restrictions after a surgical procedure. Hospital staff provides such nursing services in acute-care settings.

The goal of the UACDS is to improve data comparison in ambulatory and outpatient care settings. It provides uniform definitions that help providers to analyze patterns of care. The data elements in the UACDS are those most likely to be needed by a variety of users. Unlike the UHDDS, the UACDS has not been incorporated into federal regulations. Therefore, it is a recommended, rather than a required, data set and, in practical terms, has been subsumed by other data definition efforts, most notably the **core data elements** recommended as part of the Standards and Interoperability (S&I) Framework, which is described later in this chapter.

Resident Assessment Instrument (RAI) and Minimum Data Set

Uniform data collection is also important in the long-term care setting. **Long-term care** incorporates the healthcare services provided in residential facilities for individuals who are unable to live independently owing to chronic illness or disability. Long-term care facilities also provide dietary and social services as well as housing and nursing care.

Figure 8.2.   UACDS data elements

Data Element	Definition/Descriptor
Provider identification, address, type of practice	Provider identification: Include the full name of the provider as well as the unique physician identification number (UPIN).
	Address: The complete address of the provider's office. In cases where the provider has multiple offices, the location of the usual or principal place of practice should be given. Profession:
	• Physician, including specialty or field of practice • Other (specify)
Place of encounter	Specify the location of the encounter:
	• Private office • Clinic or health center • Hospital outpatient department • Hospital emergency department • Other (specify)
Reason for encounter	Includes, but is not limited to, the patient's complaints and symptoms reflecting his or her own perception of needs, provided verbally or in writing by the patient at the point of entry into the healthcare system or in the patient's own words recorded by an intermediary or a provider at that time.
Diagnostic services	All diagnostic services of any type.
Problem, diagnosis, or assessment	Describes the provider's level of understanding and the interpretation of the patient's reasons for the encounter and all conditions requiring treatment or management at the time of the encounter.
Therapeutic services	List, by name, all services done or ordered:
	• Medical (including drug therapy) • Surgical • Patient education
Preventative services	List, by name, all preventative services and procedures performed at the time of encounter.
Disposition	The provider's statement of the next step(s) in the care of the patient. At a minimum, the following classification is suggested:

	1. No follow-up planned
	2. Follow-up planned
	  • Return when necessary
	  • Return to the current provider at a specified time
	  • Telephone follow-up
	  • Return to referring provider
	  • Refer to other provider
	  • Admit to hospital
	  • Other

Source: NCVHS 1992.

For a long-term care facility to participate in the Medicare and Medicaid programs, the **Centers for Medicare and Medicaid Services (CMS)** requires the development of a comprehensive functional assessment for every resident. From this assessment, a nursing home resident's plan of care is developed.

The Resident Assessment Instrument (RAI) process is a federally mandated standard assessment used to collect demographic and clinical data on residents in a Medicare- or Medicaid-certified long-term care facility. It consists of three components: the **Minimum Data Set (MDS) Version 3.0,** the Care Area Assessment (CAA) process, and the RAI utilization guidelines (CMS 2011).

The MDS is a core set of screening, clinical, and functional status elements based on common definitions. To meet federal requirements, long-term care facilities must complete an assessment for every resident at the time of admission and at designated reassessment points throughout the resident's stay. The MDS is far more extensive and includes more clinical data than either the UHDDS or the UACDS.

The MDS organizes data according to 20 main categories. Each category includes a structured list of choices and responses. The use of structured lists automatically standardizes the data that are collected. The major categories of data collected in the MDS include:

- Identification information
- Hearing, speech, and vision
- Cognitive patterns
- Mood
- Behavior
- Preferences for customary routine and activities
- Functional Status
- Bladder and bowel
- Active disease diagnosis
- Health conditions
- Swallowing/nutritional status
- Oral/dental status
- Skin conditions
- Medications
- Special treatments and procedures
- Restraints
- Participation in assessment and goal setting
- CAA summary
- Correction request
- Assessment administration

The data collected via the MDS are used to develop care plans for residents and to document placement at the appropriate level of care. The MDS is also used as a data collection tool to classify Medicare residents into Resource Utilization Groups (RUGs), a system used in the PPS for skilled nursing facilities, for hospital swing-bed programs, and in many state Medicaid case mix payment systems. Another use of the MDS assessment data is monitoring the quality of care in the nation's nursing homes through MDS-based quality indicators (QIs) and quality measures (QMs).

Outcomes and Assessment Information Set

In 1999, the Health Care Financing Administration (HCFA) (renamed the Centers for Medicare and Medicaid Services) implemented a standardized data set for use in the home health industry. The **Outcomes and Assessment Information Set (OASIS)** is designed to gather and report data about Medicare beneficiaries who are receiving services from a Medicare-certified home health agency. OASIS includes a set of core data items that are collected on all adult home health patients whose care is reimbursed by Medicare and Medicaid with the exception of patients receiving pre- or postnatal services only.

A revised version of the OASIS data set (OASIS-C) became effective January 2010. The data are grouped into the following categories (CMS 2010):

- Patient Tracking Items
- Clinical Record Items
- Patient History and Diagnoses
- Living Arrangements
- Sensory Status
- Integumentary Status
- Respiratory Status
- Cardiac Status
- Elimination Status
- Neuro/Emotional/Behavioral Status
- Activities of Daily Living (ADLs)/Instrumental Activities of Daily Living (IADLs)
- Medications
- Care Management
- Therapy Need and Plan of Care
- Emergent Care
- Discharge

Data collected through OASIS are used to assess the patient's ability to be discharged or transferred from home care services. The data are also used in measuring patient outcomes in order to assess the quality of home healthcare services. Under the prospective payment program for home health, implemented in 2000, data from OASIS also form the basis of reimbursement for provided services. In addition, these data are used to create patient case mix profile reports and patient outcome reports that are used by state survey staff in the certification process. Home health agency quality measures that appear on the CMS Home Health Compare website are also based on OASIS data.

Data Elements for Emergency Department Systems

Emergency and trauma care in the United States have become sophisticated over the past few decades. Emergency services represent a significant part of the healthcare delivery system. As emergency and trauma care services have been developed, it has become increasingly important to collect relevant aggregate data. Many states require the reporting of trauma cases to state agencies.

In 1997, the Centers for Disease Control and Prevention (CDC), through its National Center for Injury Prevention and Control (NCIPC), published a data set called **Data Elements for Emergency Department Systems (DEEDS) 1.0.** This data set was developed with input from the American College of Emergency Physicians, the Emergency Nurses Association, and the American Health Information Management Association (AHIMA). Its stated purpose is to support the uniform collection of data in hospital-based emergency departments and to substantially reduce incompatibilities in emergency department records.

DEEDS recommends the collection of 156 data elements in hospitals that offer emergency care services. As with the UHDDS and UACDS, this data set contains recommendations on both the content and the structure of the data elements to be collected. The data are organized into the following eight sections:

- Patient identification data
- Facility and practitioner identification data
- Emergency department payment data
- Emergency department arrival and first-assessment data
- Emergency department history and physical examination data
- Emergency department procedure and result data
- Emergency department medication data
- Emergency department disposition and diagnosis data

DEEDS incorporates national standards for electronic data interchange so its implementation in an EHR system can facilitate communication and integration with other information systems (NCIPC 2006).

The **Health Level Seven (HL7)** Emergency Care Work Group has begun the process of updating and revising DEEDS 1.0 with the intent to expand the scope of DEEDS to harmonize with the prehospital arena, disaster response systems, and the needs of secondary data users such as the CDC and public health agencies (HL7 2011).

Another group of recommended data elements for health information systems is the emergency department and urgent care data set for syndromic surveillance. In 2011, the International Society for Disease Surveillance (ISDS) working in close collaboration with the CDC published a report defining the core of public health syndromic surveillance (PHSS) practice and the minimum EHR data requirements. Within the report is an emergency department and urgent care core minimum data set for PHSS. The standard list represents data elements commonly used by public health authorities to conduct syndromic surveillance subject to any required revisions in accordance with applicable state and local laws and practices (ISDS 2011).

The 32 core data elements are organized into the following sections:

- Treatment Facility Identifiers
- Patient Demographics
- Patient Health Indicators

The recommendation in the ISDS report is intended to provide the CDC and ONC with business requirements and to support meaningful use stakeholders in meeting the Stage 1 public health surveillance objective (ISDS 2011).

Healthcare Effectiveness Data and Information Set

The **Healthcare Effectiveness Data and Information Set (HEDIS)** is sponsored by the **National Committee for Quality Assurance (NCQA).** HEDIS is a set of standard performance measures designed to provide purchasers and consumers of healthcare with the information they need for comparing the performance of managed healthcare plans.

HEDIS is designed to collect administrative and claims data as well as health record review data. The data are used to analyze and assess the outcomes of treatment. HEDIS collects standardized data about specific health-related conditions or issues so that the success of various treatment plans can be assessed and compared. HEDIS data form the basis of performance improvement efforts for health plans. HEDIS data also are used to develop physician profiles. The goal of physician profiling is to positively influence physician practice patterns.

HEDIS contains more than 70 measures related to conditions such as heart disease, cancer, diabetes, asthma, chlamydia infection, osteoporosis, and rheumatoid arthritis. It includes data related to patient outcomes in addition to data about the treatment process used by the clinician in treating the patient.

Standardized HEDIS data elements are abstracted from health records in clinics and hospitals. The health record data are combined with enrollment and claims data and analyzed according to HEDIS specifications.

An example of a HEDIS measure is comprehensive diabetes care. Other examples of HEDIS effectiveness of care measures include:

- Adolescent immunizations
- Medical assistance with smoking and tobacco use cessation
- Antidepressant medication management
- Breast cancer screening
- Cholesterol management for patients with cardiovascular conditions
- Follow-up care for children prescribed attention deficit hyperactivity disorder medication

Data from HEDIS studies are often released publicly by health plans to document substantial positive effects on the health of their clients. Results are compared over time and with data from other sources. From the data, health plans determine opportunities for performance improvement and develop potential interventions.

HEDIS is an example of a population-based data collection tool. It illustrates the need for developing standardized data definitions and uniform collection methods. It also emphasizes the importance of data quality management.

Core Measures

The **Joint Commission** is one of the largest users of healthcare data and information. Its primary function is the accreditation of hospitals and other healthcare organizations. In 1997, the Joint Commission introduced the **ORYX initiative** to integrate outcomes data and other performance measurement data into its accreditation processes. (The initiative was named ORYX after an African animal that can be thought of as a different kind of zebra.) The goal of the initiative is to foster a comprehensive, continuous, data-driven accreditation process for healthcare facilities.

The ORYX initiative uses nationally standardized performance measures to improve the safety and quality of healthcare.

The goal of the ORYX initiative is to integrate outcomes and other performance measures into the accreditation process through data collection about specific core measures (Joint Commission 2009). In 2001, the Joint Commission announced four initial core measurement areas for hospitals. The **core measures** are based on selected diagnoses and conditions such as diabetes mellitus, the outcomes of which can be improved by standardizing care. They include the minimum number of data elements needed to provide an accurate and reliable measure of performance. Core measures rely on data elements that are readily available or already collected. The Joint Commission is in the process of reclassifying the core measures as accountability measures. Chapter 22 explores current core measures.

Quality Data Model

ARRA and HITECH provided funding to support the adoption of qualified EHRs. Their subsequent regulations define the meaningful use of HIT systems. To meet the meaningful use requirements, the submission of information on clinical quality measures is necessary. Formed by the National Quality Forum (NQF) with support from the Agency for Healthcare Research and Quality (AHRQ), the **Health Information Technology Expert Panel (HITEP)** was tasked with creating a better link between current quality measurement and EHR reporting capabilities. The HITEP Quality Data Set (QDS) Workgroup developed a QDS framework that includes standard elements, quality data elements, and data flow attributes (NQF 2009).

The QDS, now known as the **Quality Data Model (QDM),** has undergone several revisions. However, its underlying purpose remains. According to NQF (2011), the QDM "clearly defines concepts used in quality measures and clinical care and is intended to enable automation of structured data capture in EHRs, PHRs [personal health records], and other clinical applications. It provides a grammar to describe clinical concepts in a standardized format so individuals (i.e., providers, researchers, or measure developers) monitoring clinical performance and outcomes can concisely communicate necessary information."

The QDM element, which is defined as an atomic unit of information that has precise meaning to communicate the data required within a quality measure, provides unambiguous definition and enables consistent capture and use of data for quality measurement (NQF 2011). Figure 8.3 illustrates the QDM element structure.

Figure 8.3. QDM element structure

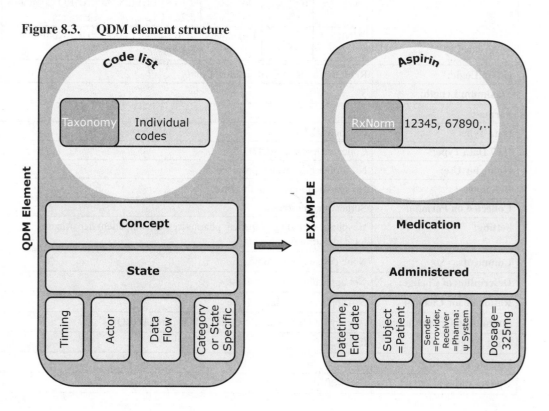

Common Formats for Reporting Patient Safety Events

The Patient Safety and Quality Improvement Act of 2005 and the Patient Safety and Quality Improvement Final Rule authorized the development of common formats for reporting patient safety events. AHRQ is responsible for coordinating this work so the appropriate information can be reported to patient safety organizations. Acute-care hospitals use the AHRQ **Common Formats Version 1.1** when reporting patient safety events. Common formats are "the common definitions and reporting formats, specified by AHRQ, that allow healthcare providers to collect and submit standardized information regarding patient safety events" (AHRQ n.d.). There are two general types: generic and event-specific.

Contained within Version 1.1 are technical specifications that include a **data dictionary.** By defining the Common Formats data elements and their attributes, standardization is possible. This in turn helps to ensure that data collected are clinically and electronically comparable. An example of the data element retained object radiopaque is shown in figure 8.4.

Figure 8.4.   Retained object radiopaque data element

Data Dictionary

Data Element Name:	Retained object radiopaque				
Data Element ISO Name:	Object_Retained-Radiopaque,CD				
Data Element ID:	DE510				
Definition:	Determination of whether the retained object was radiopaque (i.e., detectable by x-ray).				
Version:	1.1				
Synonym:	None defined at this time				
Question:	Was the retained object radiopaque (i.e., detectable by x-ray)?				
Conditionality:	Reserved for future use				
Value Domain:	**Answer Code**	**Answer ID**	**Answer Value**	**Code System**	**Code System Name**
	A15	a	Yes	2.16.840.1.113883.3.263.1.12	AHRQ Common Formats
	A18	b	No	2.16.840.1.113883.3.263.1.12	AHRQ Common Formats
	UNK	c	Unknown	2.16.840.1.113883.5.1008	HL7 NullFlavor
Go-To Logic:	Refer to Common Formats Flow Charts				
Maximum Length:	3				
Format:	N/A				
Data Type:	Character				
HL7 Data Type:	Concept Descriptor (CD)				
Guide for Use:	No further information provided				
References:	No specific reference at this time				
Collected on Form(s):	Surgery or Anesthesia				
Setting:	Hospitals, including outpatient pharmacies and outpatient departments located within the hospital				
Comments:	None defined at this time				
Description of Change:	Not applicable for this release				
Rationale for Change:	Not applicable for this release				
Submitting Organization:	Agency for Healthcare Research and Quality (AHRQ)				
Start Date:	03/31/2010				
End Date:	N/A				
Update Date:	03/31/2010				

Patient Clinical Summary

One of the government's health outcomes policy priorities used to create the framework for meaningful use of EHRs is to improve care coordination. A key to interoperable electronic information exchange is having defined core data sets. **ASTM International** (formerly the American Society for Testing and Materials (ASTM) International) was instrumental in identifying a core data set for a patient's clinical summary with the publication in 2005 of ASTM E2369 - 05e2 Standard Specification for **Continuity of Care Record (CCR)**. The CCR core data set is shown in figure 8.5.

Another organization, HL7, developed the **Clinical Document Architecture (CDA).** The CDA provides an exchange model for clinical documents (such as discharge summaries and progress notes). It also makes documents machine-readable so that they can be processed electronically easily, retrieved easily, and used by the people who need them.

ASTM International and HL7 combined their work to create the **Continuity of Care Document (CCD).** The CCD is an implementation guide for sharing CCR patient summary data using the CDA. The CCD was recognized as part of the first set of interoperability standards.

Continuing the work toward interoperability is the transitions of care (ToC) initiative, one of the projects of the **Standards and Interoperability (S&I) Framework.** According to the initiative's charter (S&I Framework 2011a), "The exchange of clinical summaries is hampered by ambiguous common definitions of what data elements must at a minimum be exchanged, how they must be encoded, and how those common semantic elements map to MU specified formats (C32/CCD and CCR)." An outcome of the initiative is a clinical information model (CIM) "consisting of unambiguous, clinically-relevant definitions of the core data elements that should

Figure 8.5.   Continuity of Care Record core data set

• Patient administrative and clinical data	• Medical devices or equipment need by patient
• Basic information about the patient's payer	• Immunization history
• Advance directives	• Vital signs, as appropriate
• Patient's sources of support	• Results of laboratory, diagnostic, and therapeutic results
• Patient's current functional status	• Diagnostic and therapeutic procedures
• Problems	• Encounters
• Family history	• Plan of care
• Social history	• Healthcare providers
• Alerts	
• Medications	

Source: ASTM 2005.

Figure 8.6.   Active problem list

> *Note: What clinician sending the message has determined to be the patient's active problems and/or diagnoses or determination of no known problems—this list may be reconciled at each ToC.
>
>   Coded Problem(s) or no known problem(s)
>   Start Date (or date of onset) of problem(s)
>   Clinician who added it to the problem list (include date/time stamp)
>   Reconciled (Yes or No)
>   Reconciled by? Date/Time Stamp
>   Resolved and/or changed problems in this encounter

Source: S&I Framework 2011b.

be included in care transitions" (ONC 2011b). The core data element categories are demographics, active medication list, active problem list, and intolerances including allergies. Figure 8.6 lists the core data elements for the active problem list category.

Check Your Understanding 8.1

Instructions: Answer the following questions on a separate piece of paper.

1. What is the difference between patient-identifiable data and aggregate data?

2. Why is it important for data from various sources to be defined in a standardized or uniform way?

3. How do a data set and core data elements make it possible to standardize data in healthcare organizations?

4. What organization initially took the lead in developing a minimum data set for hospitals and continues to play an active role in this area?

5. What role has the growth of technology played in the development of data sets and core content definitions?

6. What are some uses of the MDS data?

Standards to Support Interoperability and Connectivity

The original NCVHS uniform data sets, UHDDS and UACDS, have been the industry standard for data collection, but they were created for use in paper-based (manual) health record systems. These data sets alone can no longer accommodate the data requirements of the current healthcare delivery system. The demands of electronic health records and clinical information systems require a number of minimum data sets and data content standards. Many public and private organizations have been actively engaged in the process of developing healthcare information standards to support EHR development, interoperability, and information exchange. The federal government supports this work in a variety of ways. One example is the S&I Framework. According to Fridsma (2010), the Framework "is the mechanism by which ONC will manage the implementation of specifications and the harmonization of existing health IT standards to promote interoperability nationwide." Many types of standards are being developed and adopted to support the EHR and the NHIN vision. Some involve defining data structure and content, others specify technical approaches for transmitting data, and still others provide rules for protecting the privacy and security of data.

To fulfill current demands for information and to implement a workable nationwide system, information standards are critical, including the following list of standards important to health information management (HIM):

- Content exchange standards (those used to share clinical information)
- Vocabulary standards (including those used to describe clinical problems and procedures, medications, and allergies discussed in chapter 15)

- Transport standards (those used to establish communication protocol between systems)
- Privacy and security standards, including those that were promulgated as part of the Health Insurance Portability and Accountability Act of 1996 (HIPAA). HIPAA privacy and security standards are discussed in Chapter 12.

Data Needs in an Electronic Environment

Healthcare organizations often have evolved into environments where several different computer systems are used at the same time performing different operational requirements. For example, a hospital's laboratory system might be entirely separate from its billing system. In fact, the various departments of large healthcare organizations often use different operating systems and are serviced by different vendors as they purchase the "best of breed systems" for a specific use case, then link them together with interfaces to share data. In addition to operating multiple systems, it is an ongoing challenge to integrate information from legacy systems operating on old platforms with state-of-the-art information systems because of the rapid advancement of information management and communication technologies.

Healthcare organizations must integrate data that originate in various storage locations within facilities as well as in repositories outside the facility affecting operations and decision support. They also must be able to respond to requests to transfer information to other facilities, payers, accrediting and regulating agencies, quality improvement organizations, and other information users. In 2007, the American Medical Informatics Association (AMIA) developed the Secondary

Uses and Reuses of Healthcare Data: Taxonomy for Policy Formulation and Planning document. This document illustrates the broad use of healthcare data for purposes other than direct patient care.

Goals for an interconnected healthcare delivery system can be accomplished only when every system is using common data standards first described in the NCVHS (2000b) report "Uniform Data Standards for Patient Medical Records Information." Thompson and Brailer (2004) expressed the federal commitment to standards in their statement that "a key component of progress in interoperable health information is the development of technically sound and robustly specified interoperability standards and policies." In 2010, states, eligible territories, and qualified State Designated Entities received awards from ONC to assist them in facilitating the secure exchange of health information in order to advance state-level health information exchange while moving toward nationwide interoperability. The ONC expects the funding to be used to increase connectivity, enable patient-centric information flow to improve the quality and efficiency of care, and ensure healthcare providers and hospitals meet national standards (ONC 2011c).

Healthcare Informatics Standards

Healthcare informatics standards describe accepted methods for collecting, maintaining, and transferring healthcare data elements between computer systems. These standards provide a common language that facilitates and supports

- Exchanging information
- Sharing information
- Communicating within and across disciplines and settings
- Integrating disparate data systems
- Comparing information at a regional, national, and international level
- Linking data in a secure environment

Standards are the building blocks of effective health information systems and effective public health and healthcare delivery systems. They lay the foundation for disease surveillance, monitoring the health and healthcare of populations, performing outcomes research, providing data for decision making, and policy development. For almost a decade, the long-term vision for optimal healthcare exchange has been to enhance the comparability, quality, integrity, and utility of health information from a wide variety of public sources through uniform data policies and standards (NCVHS 2000b). Imagine trying to follow a recipe with no standard measurements or instructions that were not organized in any particular order or used any specific structure—standard information models, data structures, and transactions are important to avoid confusion, streamline clinical workflow, and promote better care procedures.

In 2010, the ONC published a final rule establishing standards, implementation specifications, and certification criteria for the certification of EHR technology to support the achievement of meaningful use Stage 1 by eligible professionals and eligible hospitals under the Medicare and Medicaid EHR incentive programs. Stage 1 standards, which took effect in 2011, fall into three categories: content exchange, vocabulary, and privacy and security (ONC 2010a). Transport standards were proposed but removed in the final rule.

Many types of standards are necessary to implement EHRs and a health information technology infrastructure that supports connectivity, interoperability, and seamless data interchange. International, national, state, and regional or local standards ensure communication and efficiency and minimization of duplication of effort along the continuum of healthcare. It is especially important to note that healthcare is provided locally and standards must be adopted at the local level to achieve the full benefit.

The first step for HIM professionals is to be aware of and promote the use of recognized standards when beneficial, even in the absence of a federal mandate. While progress with standards harmonization and consolidation has occurred, there are still hundreds of standards. Thus, it is not possible to discuss them all in this chapter. Those better-known standards HIM professionals may work with are addressed here.

Record Structure and Content Standards

Structure and content standards establish and provide clear and uniform definitions of the data elements to be included in electronic health record systems. Moreover, they specify the type of data to be collected in each data field, the width of each data field, and the content of each data field. Standards are a consistent way to record and share health information.

EHR data standards include various types of standards. Data standards provide the ability to record a certain data item in accordance with the agreed upon standard (Giannangelo 2007). Data content standards are "clear guidelines for the acceptable values for specified data fields" (Fenton et al. 2007). Content exchange standards are protocols that help ensure that data transmitted from one system to another remain comparable. Other EHR standards include identifiers for organizations and individuals, functionality, process, workflow, and information models.

For example, the ASTM International Subcommittee E31.25 on Healthcare Data Management, Security, Confidentiality, and Privacy developed **ASTM Standard E1384-07.** This standard identifies the content and structure for EHRs. The scope of this standard covers all types of healthcare services, including acute care hospitals, ambulatory care, skilled nursing facilities, home healthcare, and specialty environments (ASTM 2007). It applies to short-term contacts such as EDs and emergency medical care services as well as long-term care contacts.

Identifier Standards

Identifier standards recommend methods for assigning **unique identification numbers** to individuals, including patients, healthcare providers (for example, physicians and dentists), corporate providers (healthcare organizations), and healthcare vendors and suppliers. Identifiers usually use a combination of numeric or alphanumeric characters such as a hospital number or a billing number. The **National Provider Identifier (NPI)** is a HIPAA Administrative Simplification Standard. This number is a unique identification number for covered healthcare providers. Covered healthcare providers and all health plans and healthcare clearinghouses will use these identifier numbers in the administrative and financial transactions adopted under HIPAA. The NPI is a 10-position, intelligence-free numeric identifier (10-digit number). Intelligence free means that the numbers do not carry other information about healthcare providers, such as the state where they live or practice, or in which specialty they may be qualified. As of May 2007 (May 2008 for small health plans), the NPI was required in lieu of legacy provider identifiers in the HIPAA standards transactions.

It is generally agreed that unique identification numbers are needed for patients, but there is no consensus on the method of identification. HIPAA regulations require unique identification numbers that can be used across information systems, although a unique patient identifier (UPI) has not been adopted due to a number of factors, specifically privacy and security concerns. With the passage in 1999 of Public Law 105-277 HHS is prohibited from using any of its appropriated funds to develop a UPI without express congressional approval. Nonetheless, a national patient identity solution continues to be studied.

As a result of a **Heath Information Technology Policy Committee (HITPC)** request to the HITSC, several "power teams" were formed to create recommended standards. One team, the Patient Matching Power Team, was responsible for providing best practices guidance for use of demographics in machine-to-machine matching of patient identifiers. This team made four recommendations including assigning patient attributes that could be used for matching, ensuring quality of the data, establishing formats for these data elements, and determining what data are returned from a match request (HITSC 2011).

Content Exchange Standards

Electronic data interchange (EDI) is the electronic transfer of information, such as health claims transmitted electronically, in a standard format between trading partners. EDI originated when a number of industries identified cost savings through the electronic transmission of business information. They were convinced that the standardization of formatted information was the most effective means of communicating with multiple trading partners. EDI allows entities within the healthcare system to exchange medical, billing, and other information and to process transactions in a manner that is fast and cost-effective. With EDI there is a substantial reduction in handling and processing time compared to paper, and the risk of lost paper documents is eliminated. EDI also can eliminate the inefficiencies of handling paper documents, which would significantly reduce administrative burden, lower operating costs, and improve overall data quality. In recent years the term *EDI* has often been replaced by the term *e-commerce.*

Content exchange standards supply the specifications for the format of data exchanges, thereby providing the ability to send and receive medical and administrative data in an understandable and usable manner across information systems. Transmission standards, also referred to as communication, messaging, and **transaction standards,** support the uniform format and sequence of data during transmission from one healthcare entity to another. These standards would indicate where each data element occurs in the electronic file.

One of the purposes of HIPAA's Administrative Simplification rules was to standardize information exchange and in August 2000, HHS published regulations for electronic transactions. These regulations apply to transactions that occur among healthcare providers and healthcare plans and payers (Rode 2001). The long-term goal of the transaction standards is to allow providers and plans or payers to seamlessly transfer data back and forth with little intervention. To do this, HHS adopted the electronic transaction standards of **Accreditation Standards Committee X12** Insurance Subcommittee (Accredited Standards Committee Health Care Task Group X12N). The standards adopted for EDI are called **American National Standards Institute** ANSI ASC X12N.

The HIPAA standards also include code set standards for the electronic exchange of health-related information. To illustrate how the adoption and utilization of standards for data representation and data exchange facilitate billing functions, consider the code sets are data standards used to identify specific data elements such as the diagnosis on a claim. The compendium of data elements on the claim form make up a data set. For example, in order to send the diagnosis and other items that make up the data set electronically, the healthcare provider uses the ASC X12N 837 messaging standard. The 837 specifies the format for each data element. For example, one specification for the format of the diagnosis would be that the diagnosis codes have a maximum size of seven characters.

A new version of the standard for electronic healthcare transactions (Version 5010 of the X12 standard) was approved in 2009 for implementation in 2012. This new version is essential to the use of ICD-10-CM/PCS codes that are expected to be implemented in 2014 pending final publication of implementation date from HHS.

Health Level Seven

HL7 provides a comprehensive framework and related standards for the exchange, integration, sharing, and retrieval of electronic health information that supports clinical practice and the management, delivery, and evaluation of health services. HL7 developed the HL7 Electronic Health Record System (EHR-S) Functional Model and Standards, which address the content and structure of an EHR. The purpose of the functional model is to provide a foundation for common understanding of possible and useful functions of EHR systems.

"Level Seven" refers to the highest level of the **International Organization for Standardization (ISO)** communications model for Open Systems Interconnection (OSI)—the application level. The application level addresses the definition of the data to be exchanged, the timing of the interchange, and the communication of certain errors to the application. The seventh level supports such functions as security checks, participant identification, availability checks, exchange mechanism negotiations, and, most importantly, data exchange structuring.

The HL7 standard consists of rules for transmitting demographic data, orders, patient observations, laboratory results, history, and physical observations and findings. It also includes message rules for appointment scheduling, referrals, problem list maintenance, and care plans.

The HL7 CDA provides an exchange model for clinical documents (such as history and physicals, operative reports, discharge summaries, and progress notes) and brings the healthcare industry closer to the realization of an electronic health record. The CDA utilizes **Extensible Markup Language (XML),** the HL7 Reference Information Model (RIM), and coded vocabularies to make documents machine readable, so they can be easily parsed and processed electronically. It also makes documents human readable so they can be easily retrieved and used by the people who need them. CDA documents can be displayed using XML-aware web browsers or wireless applications such as cell phones. The CDA was adopted in May 2004 as a federal health information interoperability standard used to define the messaging architecture and syntax of clinical text documents (ONC 2006).

With respect to meaningful use Stage 1, one of the two content exchange standard options available for meeting the requirement for EHR technology to be certified as being capable of electronically exchanging a patient summary record is the HL7 CDA Release 2 (R2) (ONC 2010b).

Continuity of Care Record

The ASTM Subcommittee E31.25 on Healthcare Data Management, Security, Confidentiality, and Privacy developed standard E2369 Standard Specification for Continuity of Care Record. The CCR standard is a core data set of relevant current and past information about a patient's health status and healthcare treatment. The CCR was created to help communicate that information from one provider to another for referral, transfer, or discharge of the patient or when the patient wishes to create a personal health record. Data from a CCR may also be incorporated into a personal health record. Because it utilizes XML codes, it enhances interoperability and allows its preparation, transmission, and viewing in multiple ways. The CCR is designed to be organized and transportable. It is sponsored by a consortium of healthcare organizations, practitioners, and other stakeholders. The CCR is the other content exchange option available for meeting the requirement for EHR technology to be certified as being capable of electronically exchanging a patient summary record for stage 1.

Continuity of Care Document

ASTM and HL7 negotiated a memorandum of understanding to bring ASTM's CCR initiative into line with HL7's EHR functionality and CDA standards. The CCD was developed as a collaborative effort between ASTM and HL7 to leverage CDA with the CCR specifications. As the use of the CCD increases, it is likely to become the common **health information exchange (HIE)** methodology between the EHR and PHR systems.

Institute of Electrical and Electronics Engineers 1073

The **Institute of Electrical and Electronics Engineers (IEEE)** 1073 series of standards provides for open systems communications in healthcare applications, primarily between bedside medical devices and patient care information systems, optimized for the acute-care setting. The IEEE 1073 series was adopted as a federal health information interoperability set of standards for electronic data exchange (ONC 2006).

The IEEE 1073 series of standards pertains to connectivity. The standard specifically addresses the requirement for two devices to automatically configure a connection for successful operation, independent of connection type. The standards define a device-to-device internal messaging system that allows hospitals and other healthcare providers to achieve plug-and-play interoperability between medical instrumentation and computerized healthcare information systems, especially in a manner that is compatible with the acute-care environment.

Increasingly there are personal health monitoring devices that interface with other devices including electronic health records for data capture and remote monitoring. As the health record includes more direct interaction with machines and their output, the collaboration and cooperation between device standards and health informatics standards organizations is expected.

Digital Imaging and Communications in Medicine

Through a cooperative effort between the **American College of Radiology** and the **National Electrical Manufacturers Association (ACR-NEMA), Digital Imaging and Communications in Medicine (DICOM)** addresses the exchange of digital information between medical imaging equipment and other systems.

DICOM is used by most medical professions that utilize imaging within the healthcare industry including cardiology, dentistry, endoscopy, mammography, ophthalmology, and orthopedics. DICOM was adopted as the federal health information interoperability messaging standard for imaging

in March 2003 (ONC 2006). Important to the field of medical imaging are **picture archiving and communication systems (PACS).** PACS are computers or networks dedicated to the storage, retrieval, distribution, and presentation of medical images. The most common format today for storage of images is the DICOM standard.

National Council for Prescription Drug Programs SCRIPT

The **National Council for Prescription Drug Programs (NCPDP)** SCRIPT standard is used for transmitting prescription information electronically between prescribers, providers, and other organizations or agents. The standard addresses the electronic transmission of new prescriptions, changes of prescriptions, prescription refills, prescription fill status notifications, cancellation notifications, relaying of medication history, and transactions used in long-term care.

With respect to meaningful use Stage 1, the certification criterion specifies that a complete EHR or EHR module would be compliant if it has the capability of generating and transmitting prescription and prescription-related information according to NCPDP SCRIPT 8.1 while also using the adopted vocabulary standard, or if it is capable of generating and transmitting prescriptions and prescription-related information according to NCPDP SCRIPT 10.6 while also using the adopted vocabulary standard (ONC 2010c).

Structured Product Labeling

Structured Product Labeling (SPL) is an HL7 document markup standard based on CDA and HL7 RIM used by the Food and Drug Administration (FDA) to exchange product information. A number of standard terminologies are used including the Department of Veterans Affairs National Drug File Reference Terminology (NDF-RT), Logical Observation Identifiers Names and Codes (LOINC), and Systematized Nomenclature of Medicine Clinical Terms (SNOMED CT).

Vocabulary Standards

Vocabulary standards include terminologies, classifications, code sets, and **nomenclatures.** These standards go hand in hand with other health informatics standards such as those for information modeling and metadata. Vocabulary standards establish common definitions for medical terms to encourage consistent descriptions of an individual's condition in the health record.

Medical terminology is extremely complex, and establishing universal medical vocabulary standards is a challenging task. Various synonymous medical terms are often used in different areas of the country. In fact, medical terminology often varies between physicians working in the same organization, depending on where and when each physician was trained and in which medical specialty he or she practices. For example, one physician might describe a patient's diagnosis as Parkinson's disease, another might describe it as Parkinsonism, and a third might use the term *paralysis agitans.* All three terms describe the same disease, but using the terms interchangeably would adversely affect data quality and make retrieval more challenging. In addition, data comparison among the physicians' patients would be difficult, if not impossible.

The use of code sets, for example International Classification of Diseases (ICD) or Current Procedural Terminology (CPT), to represent health-related conditions and procedures is common in healthcare for indexing and administrative use. The use of standardized, uniform terminology for data capture and reporting is critical to accurate information storage and retrieval. Vocabulary standards adoption enhanced by technology advancement sets the stage for future automated coding systems that facilitate a higher degree of data integrity than is possible with traditional code assignment and reporting workflow. The development of vocabularies, code sets, and nomenclatures as well as specific systems for drugs, laboratory and clinical observations, information modeling, and metadata are thoroughly explored in chapter 13. Entire code sets are often featured as HL7 standard value sets, allowing an electronic system to restrict data selections to a defined set of valid choices and minimize system changes for code set updates.

Currently there is no "master set" of data elements that would facilitate HIE at the highest level of interoperability. More work toward the adoption of a standard integrated set of data elements and terminologies will advance HIE and enhance clinical representation in electronic environments. For more information about the use of vocabularies, code sets, and nomenclatures see chapter 15.

Privacy and Security Standards

The **Health Insurance Portability and Accountability Act (HIPAA)** mandated the adoption of privacy and security protection for identifiable health information. HIPAA **privacy standards** have been implemented throughout the healthcare industry. They are addressed thoroughly in chapter 12.

Security standards ensure that patient-identifiable health information remains confidential and protected from unauthorized disclosure, alteration, or destruction. Effective security standards are especially important in computer-based environments because patient information is accessible to many users in many locations.

Security standards are addressed in detail in chapter 5 as they relate to the EHR. Many standards organizations—most notably, the ASTM and HL7—have developed security standards, but no single standard currently addresses all of the HIPAA provisions.

Check Your Understanding 8.2

Instructions: Answer the following questions on a separate piece of paper.

1. What is the difference between a structure and content standard and a content exchange standard?

2. What is the relationship between vocabulary standards and the coding of healthcare data?

3. What is the reason for creating a unique identification number for every healthcare consumer?

4. What is the difference between the CCR, CDA, and CCD?

Standards Development, Coordination, Testing, and Harmonization

Developing, coordinating, testing, and harmonizing healthcare standards is a complex process in which many organizations are involved. The following definitions provide further information on standards and harmonization (HITSP 2009):

> The term **standard** … is a well-defined approach that supports a business process
> and:
> has been agreed upon by a group of experts;
> has been publicly vetted;
> provides rules, guidelines, or characteristics;
> helps to ensure that materials, products, processes, and services are fit for their
> intended purpose;
> is available in an accessible format; and
> is subject to an ongoing review and revision process.

Harmonization is the name given to the effort by industry to replace the variety of product standards and other regulatory policies adopted by nations, in favor of uniform global standards. Usually used to in the context of trade agreements, harmonization has recently been adopted by the US government to refer to information technology standards.

Standards Development

Many organizations are directly involved in the development of healthcare informatics standards and invest in resources required to develop, distribute, and maintain the standards for use by others. These organizations are referred to as **standards development organizations (SDOs).** HL7 and ASTM, for example, are both accredited SDOs. Table 8.1 provides a list of several organizations that are actively involved in developing standards for healthcare informatics. Private organizations and government agencies are involved in the process of developing standards, and these groups influence the development of standards by taking positions on proposed standards and setting policies that lend credibility to standards. The government agencies that influence standards development include the ONC, CMS, FDA, AHRQ, the Office of the Assistant Secretary for Planning and Evaluation (ASPE), and CDC.

Most standards are created through a voluntary consensus process that involves identifying the need for a standard, negotiating the content of the standard, and drafting a proposed standard. The final standard is published after undergoing a comment and revision period. This process facilitates wide adoption and improved utility. Figure 8.7 describes the standards value chain.

Table 8.1.   Standards development organizations

Private or government organizations involved in the development of healthcare informatics standards at a national or international level

Resource	Description	Source
AIIM	AIIM is an ANSI (American National Standards Institute)–accredited standards development organization. AIIM also holds the Secretariat for the ISO (International Organization for Standardization) committee focused on information management compliance issues, TC171.	http://www.aiim.org
Accredited Standards Committee (ASC) X12	ASC X12 is a designated committee under the Designated Standard Maintenance Organization (DSMO), which develops uniform standards for cross-industry exchange of business transactions through electronic data interchange (EDI) standards. ASC X12 is an ANSI-accredited standards development organization.	http://www.x12.org
American Dental Association (ADA)	The ADA is an ANSI-accredited standards-developing organization that develops dental standards that promote safe and effective oral healthcare.	http://www.ada.org/prof/ resources/standards/ index.asp
ASTM International	Formerly the American Society for Testing and Materials, ASTM International is an ANSI-accredited standards-development organization that develops standards for healthcare data security, standard record content, and protocols for exchange of laboratory data.	http://www.astm.org
European Committee for Standardization (CEN)	CEN contributes to the objectives of the European Union and European Economic Area with voluntary technical standards that promote free trade, the safety of workers and consumers, interoperability of networks, environmental protection, exploitation of research and development programs, and public procurement.	http://www.cenorm .be/cenorm/index.htm
Clinical and Laboratory Standards Institute (CLSI)	A global, nonprofit standards-development organization that promotes the development and use of voluntary consensus standards and guidelines within the healthcare community. Its core business is the development of globally applicable voluntary consensus documents for healthcare testing.	http://www.clsi.org
Clinical Data Interchange Standards Consortium (CDISC)	CDISC is an open, multidisciplinary, nonprofit organization that has established worldwide industry standards to support the electronic acquisition, exchange, submission, and archiving of clinical trials data and metadata for medical and biopharmaceutical product development.	http://www.cdisc.org/
Designated Standard Maintenance Organization (DSMO)	The DSMO was established in the final HIPAA rule and is charged with maintaining the standards for electronic transactions and developing or modifying an adopted standard.	http://www.hipaa-dsmo.org
Health Industry Business Communications Council (HIBCC)	HIBCC is an industry-sponsored and-supported nonprofit organization. As an ANSI-accredited organization, its primary function is to facilitate electronic communications by developing standards for information exchange among healthcare trading partners.	http://www.hibcc.org/
Health Level Seven (HL7)	An ANSI-accredited standards-development organization that develops messaging, data content, and document standards to support the exchange of clinical information.	http://www.hl7.org
Institute of Electrical and Electronic Engineers (IEEE)	A national organization that develops standards for hospital system interface transactions, including links between critical care bedside instruments and clinical information systems.	http://www .ieee.org
International Organization for Standardization (ISO)	ISO is a nongovernmental organization and network of national standards institutes from 157 countries.	http://www.iso.org/iso/en/ ISOOnline.frontpage

(continued on next page)

Table 8.1.   Standards development organizations *(Continued)*

Resource	Description	Source
National Council for Prescription Drug Programs (NCPDP)	A designated committee under the DSMO that specializes in developing standards for exchanging prescription and payment information.	http://www.ncpdp.org
National Information Standards Organization (NISO)	An ANSI-accredited, nonprofit association that identifies, develops, maintains, and publishes technical standards to manage information. NISO standards address areas of retrieval, repurposing, storage, metadata, and preservation.	http://www.niso.org
National Uniform Billing Committee (NUBC)	A designated committee under the DSMO that is responsible for identifying data elements and designing the CMS-1500 form.	www.nubc.org
National Uniform Claim Committee (NUCC)	The national group that replaced the Uniform Claim Form Task Force in 1995 and developed a standard data set to be used in the transmission of noninstitutional provider claims to and from third-party payers.	www.nucc.org

Standards Coordination

A number of organizations play key roles in coordinating standards development. They do not develop standards but, rather, coordinate the efforts of other SDOs.

For example, the ANSI is a private, nonprofit organization that coordinates voluntary standards in the United States. Many standards developers and participants support ANSI as the central body responsible for the identification of a single consistent set of voluntary standards called American National Standards. ANSI provides an open forum for all concerned interests to identify specific business needs, plan to meet those needs, and agree on standards. Although ANSI itself does not develop standards, its approval of standards does indicate that the principles of openness and due process have been followed in the approval process and that a consensus of those participating in the approval process has been achieved. Most SDOs use the formal balloting process defined by ANSI.

ANSI also is the official US representative to the ISO. The ISO coordinates international standards development. ISO standards are voted on by country rather than individual members. In 1998, ISO created the Technical Committee 215–Health Informatics. AHIMA members are represented in this technical committee charged with advancement of internationally recognized standards. There are currently nine subcommittees/work groups within ISO 215 working on healthcare-related standards.

Some other projects that coordinate healthcare standards are the National Library of Medicines's **Unified Medical Language System** (UMLS) and the United States Health Information Knowledgebase (USHIK).

The UMLS's Metathesaurus® is a centralized vocabulary database that includes more than a hundred vocabularies, classifications, and code sets. The source vocabularies found in the Metathesaurus include those designed for use in patient-record systems such as SNOMED CT, as well as those used for healthcare billing, such as ICD-9-CM. The code sets mandated for use in electronic administrative transactions in the United States under the provisions of HIPAA are found in the Metathesaurus with the exception of the National Drug Codes (NDCs). The NDCs are available from the FDA.

The USHIK contains a listing of health information data element definitions, values, and information models that enable browsing, comparison, synchronization, and harmonization within a uniform query and interface environment. It is a computer-based health metadata registry funded and directed by the AHRQ with CMS and the VA as strategic interagency partners.

A **metadata registry** is used to store characteristics of data that are necessary to clearly describe, inventory, analyze, and classify data. A health metadata registry supports data sharing with cross-system and cross-organization descriptions of common units of health data. This process assists users to form common understanding of a data unit's meaning, representation, and identification.

The USHIK is populated with the data elements and information models of SDOs and other healthcare organizations in such a way that public and private organizations can harmonize information formats with healthcare standards. The knowledge base also contains data element information for government initiatives supporting the use and implementation of data standards (for example, HIPAA) and the federal health architecture program.

Standards Testing

NIST is a nonregulatory agency of the US Department of Commerce. The 2008–2012 federal Health IT Strategic Plan and the HITECH Act described a specific role for NIST in health IT. According to NIST (2011), it is to

- Advance healthcare information enterprise integration through standards and testing.
- Consult on updating the Federal Health IT Strategic Plan.

Figure 8.7. Standards value chain

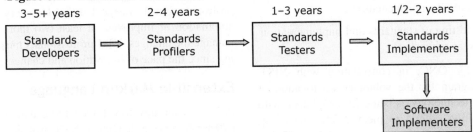

Standards typically go through several stages in a process that can take three or more years. It begins with developers, who draft new standards or update existing ones. Profiling organizations select among applicable standards, combine the work of multiple developers, and create use scenarios for how to apply them. Typically, independent, neutral organizations test the standards, and implementers put them to work.

Advocates

Advocacy organizations influence and facilitate the value chain at every step. National governments are prominent standardization advocates, often sponsoring, funding, and staffing standards activities. Private-sector stakeholders include advocacy organizations such as health IT and finance advocates and software vendors, implementers, and users. Consumers also have a stake in standards, although they are underrepresented in standards advocacy.

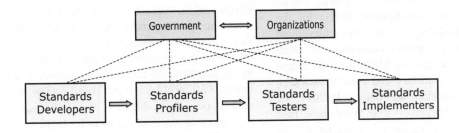

Market Stakeholders

Software vendors, implementers, and users are economic stakeholders. They influence standards development and implementation through participation and funding. Their balance of interest is both strategic and tactical.

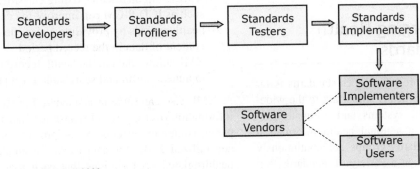

Source: Marshall 2009.

- Consult on voluntary certification programs.
- Consult on health IT implementation.
- Provide pilot testing of standards and implementation specifications, as requested.

ARRA called for ONC, in consultation with NIST, to recognize a program for the voluntary certification of health information technology as being in compliance with applicable certification criteria to meet defined meaningful use requirements. In collaboration with ONC, NIST has developed the necessary functional and conformance testing requirements, test cases, and test tools in support of the health IT certification program.

Standards Harmonization

At present, one of the most challenging aspects of the standards movement is the area of standards harmonization. There are many initiatives occurring in the United States as well as in the international community, resulting in duplication and competition among organizations. Harmonization of these efforts will be critical if the movement toward PHRs for individuals, EHRs at all points of care, and networked health information systems at both the regional and national level are to move forward. The ONC has been charged with the responsibility of leading efforts toward standards harmonization. In 2010, the ONC published standards, implementation specifications, and certification criteria for the certification of EHR technology to support the achievement of meaningful use Stage 1 by eligible professionals and eligible hospitals under the Medicare and Medicaid EHR incentive programs. For some vocabulary and content exchange standards more than one standard was named. In 2011, the HITSC Clinical Quality Workgroup and Vocabulary Task Force were tasked with selecting the minimum number of vocabulary standards with the minimum number of values to meet the requirements of meaningful use stages 2 and 3. Content exchange standards are being reviewed as well with the same goal to harmonize HIT standards. It will take the cooperation and collaboration of many, especially the HIM profession, to harmonize HIT standards and implementation guides for the purpose of interoperability and HIE.

Evolving and Emerging Health Information Standards

The development of healthcare informatics standards is far from complete. The task is critically important to the widespread development of EHR systems and, ultimately, to implementation and use of a national health information infrastructure. Leading standards groups are continuously working to reach consensus on a variety of standards, but many issues are still to be resolved. As breakthroughs occur in communication technology, information management innovation will take advantage of time saving and cost saving

workflow shortcuts. This will affect certain jobs within the profession, but it is expected that for every position lost to automation or improved, at least two more will emerge to manage the changes. HIM professionals must keep on learning since the pace of innovation and change is rapid.

Extensible Markup Language

A key technology tool for enabling data sharing is called extensible markup language. XML was developed as a universal language to facilitate the storage and transmission of data published on the Internet. Markup languages communicate electronic representations of paper documents to computers by inserting additional information into text (Sokolowski 1999). The best-known markup language is hypertext markup language (HTML), which is used to convert text documents into Internet-compatible format.

Pothen and Parmanto (2000) describe XML as "an easy-to-learn, standardized mark-up language with customizable tags that describe data within documents." In other words, XML provides a context for data through the use of a tag. In the context of health data, XML tags each item of data with a descriptor that differentiates, for example, between a number that is a Social Security number from a number that represents the medical record number. XML allows data to be communicated from one computerized system to another without losing the integrity of the data. In addition, XML provides structure and rules that are "important for healthcare informatics because they will provide context for narrative text, a document information model, agreement on high-level structures, and a facility for standardizing formats" (Sokolowski 1999, 22). In other words, XML enables suitably coded documents to be read and understood without difficulty by both humans and machines. It is an open standard for meta languages controlled by the World Wide Web Consortium (W3C) (Schroeter 2008).

As EHRs continue to evolve (as described in chapter 5), XML has the potential to solve some of the difficulties posed by the lack of standardized vocabulary and the need to transmit data among disparate computer systems. Some of the characteristics that make XML relevant to the development of an EHR were described by Pothen and Parmanto (2000):

- XML combined with existing classification systems such as ICD-9-CM can improve the completeness of health records by providing a clear description of the content of data in the record period
- XML allows data in the health record to be organized in a meaningful and searchable form period

XML also can serve as a standard for exchange of health information over the web because it is not impeded by disparate computer systems. A test project conducted in Canada utilized XML for data exchange among three remote health-related organizations that each used a different set of applications, databases, and technology. The organizations mapped each system to standard templates in XML and were able to seamlessly transfer data from one location to the other (Smith 2001). The implementation of XML within the healthcare industry has the potential to address many of the issues of both vocabulary and transmission.

For example, the CCR standard specifies XML coding that allows users to prepare, transmit, and view the CCR in multiple ways such as in a browser, as an element in an HL7 message or a CDA-compliant document, or as a word processing document (ASTM 2009). Another XML-based standard, the Structured Product Labeling (SPL), is a document markup standard approved by HL7 and adopted by the FDA as a mechanism for exchanging product information (FDA 2009).

Metadata Standards

CDA documents are also encoded in XML. CDA is cited throughout an ONC advance notice of proposed rulemaking published on August 9, 2011. This notice solicited comments on metadata standards to support nationwide electronic health information exchange. Initial categories of metadata under consideration as a minimum set include patient identity, provenance, and privacy in association with a patient obtaining his or her summary care record from a healthcare provider (ONC 2011d). Following the notice, the ONC announced the launch of two pilot programs that will test the metadata standards. A decision has not yet been made if, as part of the EHR certification requirements to support meaningful use Stage 2 under the Medicare and Medicaid EHR incentive programs, the EHR technology should be capable of applying the metadata standards.

Check Your Understanding 8.3

Instructions: Answer the following questions on a separate piece of paper.

1. What changes in the healthcare industry have prompted the focus on developing healthcare informatics standards?

2. What SDOs have been most active in developing record structure and content standards for EHRs?

3. What role does ANSI and NIST play in standards work?

4. What characteristics of XML make it a potential solution for many of the problems of storing and transmitting health information?

5. Why is standards harmonization so challenging?

Summary

According to Brandt (2000), "The vision is clear: a longitudinal, or lifetime, health record for each person that is computer-based, secure, readily accessible when needed,

and linked across the continuum of care [is needed]. In reality, we are a long way from that model." At the end of the first decade of the 21st century, a comprehensive electronic health record for every citizen is not yet a reality. It is impossible to develop a longitudinal EHR that meets Brandt's specifications without standards that guide the development. The complexity of technology, the variations in computer platforms from one system to the next, and the differing (and sometimes conflicting) data needs of users demand flexible health data/information systems. The systems must be able to store volumes of data in a standardized format, communicate across vendor-specific systems, and keep data in a secure manner that protects individual privacy and information confidentiality.

The need for standardized data definitions was recognized in the 1960s, and the NCVHS took the lead in developing uniform minimum data sets for various sites of care. As technology has driven the development of the data/information systems, the early data sets have been supplemented with healthcare information standards that focus on electronic health record systems. A number of standards-setting organizations are involved in developing uniform definitions, data fields, and views for health record content and structure. Identifier, clinical representation, technical, medication, privacy, and security standards have been created and implemented. These standards are dynamic and in constant development by various groups. Standards development generally takes place as a consensus-driven process among various interested parties. In the past, implementation has been voluntary. However, one of the major efforts of the ONC is standards harmonization that consolidates a useful and accepted set of national IT standards.

Some data sets and standards have been incorporated into federal law and are thus required for use by affected healthcare organizations. For example, in 1983, when Section 1886(d) of the Social Security Act was enacted, UHDDS definitions were incorporated into the rules and regulations for implementing an inpatient prospective payment system based on DRGs. These definitions are still required for reporting inpatient data for reimbursement under the Medicare program.

HIPAA mandated the incorporation of healthcare information standards into all electronic or computer-based health information systems. Of particular importance under HIPAA are transaction/messaging standards for communication of data across systems, privacy standards that protect individual privacy and confidentiality, security standards that ensure that data are accessed only by those who have a specific right to access, and identifier standards that offer methods of identifying both individual patients and healthcare providers. The rules and regulations for HIPAA are still in development, and, to date, the transaction, privacy, and security standards have been implemented. Other standards are still under development. For example, in 2005 HHS published a proposed rule to adopt a suite of standards for the electronic healthcare claim attachment. A final rule was never published. However, the Affordable Care Act requires the final rule defining standards and operating rules for claim attachments be published no later than January 2014 with compliance no later than January 2016.

The selection of health information standards to support the adoption of electronic health records gained national support through federal initiatives aimed at developing a strategic plan to guide the nation's implementation of interoperable health information technology in both the public and private sectors. The ONC has been given a mandate to advance the development, adoption, and implementation of healthcare information technology nationally through collaboration among public and private interests and to ensure that these standards are consistent with current efforts to set HIT standards for use by the federal government (Thompson and Brailer 2004). In 2010, the ONC published standards, implementation specifications, and certification criteria for the certification of EHR technology to support the achievement of meaningful use Stage 1 by eligible professionals and eligible hospitals under the Medicare and Medicaid EHR incentive programs. The final rule for Stage 2 is expected to be released in June 2012 followed by Stage 3 some years later.

Work will continue on the development of healthcare informatics standards to support continued development of electronic health records and health information exchange. It is a complex task and a dynamic one with constant activity in the development, modification, negotiation, and implementation processes. The rapid growth of technology and the increasing need for healthcare data/information make the task a daunting one. According to Fridsma (2011) "ONC is identifying the vocabularies, the message, and the transport 'building blocks' that will enable interoperability. While vendors should be able to flexibly combine them to support interoperable HIE, these 'building blocks' need to be unambiguous and have very limited (or no) optionality."

References

Agency for Healthcare Research and Quality. n.d. AHRQ releases Common Formats for pateint safety reporting in skilled nursing facilities. http://www.ahrq.gov/research/may11/0511RA30.htm.

American Medical Informatics Association (AMIA). 2007. Secondary Uses and Re-uses of Healthcare Data: Taxonomy for Policy Formulation and Planning Document. http://www.amia.org/inside/initiatives/healthdata/ 2007/amiataxonomyncvhs.pdf.

ASTM International. 2005. http://www.astm.org.

ASTM International. 2007. http://www.astm.org/Standards/E1384.htm.

ASTM International. 2009. http://www.astm.org/Standards/E2369.htm.

Brandt, M.D. 2000. Health informatics standards: A user's guide. *Journal of AHIMA* 71(4):39–43.

Centers for Medicare and Medicaid Services. 2011. Long-Term Care Facility Resident Assessment Instrument User's Manual. http://www.cms.gov/NursingHomeQualityInits/45_NHQIMD-S30TrainingMaterials.asp#TopOfPage.

Centers for Medicare and Medicaid Services. 2010. Outcome and Assessment Information Set: OASIS-C Guidance Manual. http://www.cms.gov/HomeHealthQualityInits/14_HHQIOASISUser-Manual.asp#TopOfPage.

Fenton, S. et al. 2007. Data standards, data quality, and interoperability. *Journal of AHIMA*. 78(2).

Food and Drug Administration. 2009. Structured Product Labeling Resources. http://www.fda.gov/ForIndustry/DataStandards/StructuredProductLabeling/default.htm.

Fridsma, D. 2010. ONC S&I Framework: Coordination and Operations. http://healthit.hhs.gov/portal/server.pt/gateway/PTARGS_0_11673_947553_0_0_18/Fridsma_Harmonization%20Processes%20and%20Governance_v4.pdf.

Fridsma, D. 2011. Standards Are Not Optional. HealthIT Buzz. http://www.healthit.gov/buzz-blog/from-the-onc-desk/standards-optional-2/.

Giannangelo, K. 2007. Unraveling the data set, an e-HIM essential. *Journal of AHIMA*. 78(2):60–61.

Health Information Technology Standards Committee (HITSC). 2011. Patient matching power team recommendations. http://healthit.hhs.gov/portal/server.pt/gateway/PTARGS_0_12811_955311_0_0_18/08_17_11_Patient_Matching_PT_Recomm.pdf.

Health Information Technology Standards Panel. 2009. HITSP Glossary. http://wiki.hitsp.org/docs/REF6/REF6-1.html.

Health Level Seven. 2011. Emergency Care. http://www.hl7.org/Special/committees/emergencycare/projects.cfm?action=edit&ProjectNumber=820.

International Society for Disease Surveillance. 2011. Final Recommendation: Core Processes and EHR Requirements for Public Health Syndromic Surveillance. http://www.syndromic.org/projects/meaningful-use.

Joint Commission. 2009. *Comprehensive Accreditation Manual.* Oakbrook Terrace, IL.

Marshall, G. F. 2009. The standards value chain: Where health IT standards come from. *Journal of AHIMA* 80(10): 54–55, 60–62.

National Center for Injury Prevention and Control. 2006. DEEDS - Data elements for emergency department systems. http://www.cdc.gov/ncipc/pub-res/deedspage.htm.

National Committee on Vital and Health Statistics. 2000a. Toward a national health information infrastructure: Interim report. Washington, D.C.: HHS. http://ncvhs.hhs.gov/nhiilayo.pdf.

National Committee on Vital and Health Statistics. 2000b. Uniform data standards for patient medical records information. http://ncvhs.hhs.gov/hipaa000706.pdf.

National Committee on Vital and Health Statistics. 1992. 1992 Revisions to UHDDS. http://www.cdc.gov/nchs/data/ncvhs/nchvs92.pdf.

National Institute of Standards and Technology (NIST). 2011. Health IT at NIST. http://www.nist.gov/healthcare/hit/upload/Health-IT-Fact-Sheet-09FEB11.pdf.

National Quality Forum. 2009. Health Information Technology Automation of Quality Measurement: Quality Data Set and Data Flow. Washington, D.C.: NQF.

National Quality Forum. 2011. Quality Data Model - Draft October 2011. http://www.qualityforum.org/WorkArea/linkit.aspx?LinkIdentifier=id&ItemID=68545.

Office of the National Coordinator for Health Information Technology. 2006. Consolidated health informatics. http://www.hhs.gov/healthit/chiinitiative.html.

Office of the National Coordinator for Health Information Technology. 2010a. Health Information Technology: Initial Set of Standards, Implementation Specifications, and Certification Criteria for Electronic Health Record Technology. *Federal Register* 75 (144): 44649. http://edocket.access.gpo.gov/2010/pdf/2010-17210.pdf.

Office of the National Coordinator for Health Information Technology. 2010b. Health Information Technology: Initial Set of Standards, Implementation Specifications, and Certification Criteria for Electronic Health Record Technology. *Federal Register* 75 (144): 44649-44650. http://edocket.access.gpo.gov/2010/pdf/2010-17210.pdf.

Office of the National Coordinator for Health Information Technology. 2010c. Health Information Technology: Initial Set of Standards, Implementation Specifications, and Certification Criteria for Electronic Health Record Technology. *Federal Register* 75 (144): 44625. http://edocket.access.gpo.gov/2010/pdf/2010-17210.pdf.

Office of the National Coordinator for Health Information Technology. 2011a. Health IT Standards Committee. http://healthit.hhs.gov/portal/server.pt/community/healthit_hhs_gov__health_it_standards_committee/1271.

Office of the National Coordinator for Health Information Technology. 2011b. HITSC—Standards and Implementation: Update on Standards Effort. http://healthit.hhs.gov/portal/server.pt/gateway/PTARGS_0_16869_955993_0_0_18/HITSC_StandardsUpdate102111.pdf.

Office of the National Coordinator for Health Information Technology. 2011c. Get the Facts about State Health Information Exchange Program. http://healthit.hhs.gov/portal/server.pt?open=512&mode=2&objID=1834.

Office of the National Coordinator for Health Information Technology. 2011d. Metadata Standards to Support Nationwide Electronic Health Information Exchange. *Federal Register* 76 (153): 48769–48776. http://www.gpo.gov/fdsys/pkg/FR-2011-08-09/pdf/2011-20219.pdf.

Pothen, D.J. and B. Parmanto. 2000. XML furthers CPR goals. *Journal of AHIMA* 71(9):24–29.

Rode, D. 2001. Understanding HIPAA transactions and code sets. *Journal of AHIMA* 72(1):26–32.

Schroeter, G. 2008. How XML is Improving Data Exchange in Healthcare. XML—the Site. http://www.softwareag.com/xml/library/schroeter_healthcare.htm.

Smith, D.A. 2001. Data transmission: a world of possibilities. *Journal of AHIMA* 72(5):26–27.

Sokolowski, R. 1999. XML makes its mark. *Journal of AHIMA* 70(10):21–24.

S&I Framework. 2011a. Transitions of care overview. http://wiki.siframework.org/Transitions+of+Care+Overview.

S&I Framework. 2011b. ToC CIM core data elements. http://wiki.siframework.org/ToC+CIM+Core+Data+Elements.

Thompson, T.G. and D.J. Brailer. 2004. The decade of health information technology: Delivering consumer-centric and information-rich healthcare—Framework for strategic action. Washington, D.C.: HHS.

World Health Organization. n.d. History of the Development of ICD. http://www.who.int/classifications/icd/en/HistoryOfICD.pdf.

chapter 9

Health Information Exchange and the Nationwide Health Information Network

Cheryl Stephens, MBA, PhD

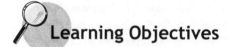

Learning Objectives

- Demonstrate a working knowledge of the concepts of health information exchange (HIE), the Nationwide Health Information Network (NHIN), and the federal policies and legislation that support these concepts
- Explain and cite the benefits and drawbacks of the common clinical data exchange models: centralized, federated, and hybrid
- Demonstrate a working knowledge of the Health Information Technology for Economic and Clinical Health Act
- Discuss meaningful use stages and their impact on health information exchange
- Research the major issues related to integrity, accuracy, and security of health information that is exchanged via the state and federal networks including patient

identity management, data management and data standards, and secure data transport
- Employ use cases to demonstrate effective design of HIE networks and various exchange standards
- Explore variations in HIE network design in states across the country and compare the effectiveness, efficiency, and sustainability of these methods
- Research the efficacy of the opt-in and opt-out models and compare effectiveness of each model
- Analyze relevant issues of security for system configurations including, but not limited to, access controls, encryption, user identification and authentication methodologies, firewalls, and audit trails
- Analyze relevant issues involving the implementation of the Nationwide Health Information Network and state or regional HIE efforts

Key Terms

American Health Information Community (AHIC)
American National Standards Institute (ANSI)
Application programming interface (API)
Beacon Community Program
Centralized model
Common Framework
Continuity of Care Document (CCD)
Continuity of Care Record (CCR)
Data Use and Reciprocal Support Agreement (DURSA)
Direct Project
Federated model
Health information exchange (HIE)

Health Information Exchange Challenge Grant Program
Health Information Security and Privacy Collaboration (HISPC)
Health Information Technology for Economic and Clinical Health Act (HITECH)
Health Information Technology Standards Panel (HITSP)
Hybrid model
Interoperability
Markle Foundation
Master patient index (MPI)
Meaningful use
Medical Internet

217

National Committee on Vital and Health Statistics (NCVHS)
National health information infrastructure (NHII)
Nationwide Health Information Network (NHIN)
Office of the National Coordinator for Health Information Technology (ONC)

Record locator service (RLS)
Regional Health Information Organization (RHIO)
State Health Information Exchange Cooperative Agreement Program
Use case

Overview

Health Information Exchange

Health information exchange (HIE) is the ability to move healthcare information electronically between disparate healthcare information systems while maintaining the accuracy of the information being exchanged (AHIMA 2007a). It is the electronic movement of health information among organizations according to accepted standards and protocols. Health information management (HIM) professionals' skills and knowledge beyond the technical focus are important for achieving success in any HIE initiative. HIM professionals play an important role in asking pertinent HIE questions to ensure data quality, privacy, security, and patient safety. For example, questions should include the following:

- What data or information will be exchanged?
- How will access to the data or information be authorized and authenticated?
- Who will control data authorization and authentication?
- How is data ownership defined?
- What data quality indicators have been established, and how will they be measured?
- What is the plan for data or information communication and interaction with patients and consumers?

State governments and regional public and private partnerships have worked to establish HIE systems that facilitate the transfer of health information among authorized parties to enhance the quality of care and reduce the cost of healthcare services. HIE has the potential to transform nearly every aspect of healthcare delivery in this country.

Nationwide Health Information Network Exchange

The **Nationwide Health Information Network Exchange (NHIN)**, formerly known as the National Health Information Infrastructure (NHII), is a government-sponsored initiative designed to improve the effectiveness, efficiency, and overall quality of health and healthcare in the United States by developing a comprehensive, interconnected, knowledge-based network of interoperable information systems among all sectors of the healthcare industry. It also has been referred to as the **medical Internet**, which allows providers of care

to electronically exchange data among all electronic health records so that a complete electronic health record can be assembled whenever and wherever a patient presents for care.

NHIN was mentioned first by the Institute of Medicine (IOM) in its seminal report, *The Computer-Based Patient Record: An Essential Technology for Health Care* (Dick et al. 1997). A decade later, the National Health Information Infrastructure was defined further by the **National Committee on Vital and Health Statistics (NCVHS)** in its report "Information for Health: A Strategy for Building the National Health Information Infrastructure" (NCVHS 2001). The NHII terminology evolved into the National Health Information Network and then to the Nationwide Health Information Network. Following the September 11, 2001 terror attacks and the much publicized anthrax attacks, NHIN gained national attention in both public and private sectors when the need for enhanced public health surveillance and response became more visible and immediate. Consequently, IOM's fourth quality report, *Patient Safety: Achieving a New Standard for Care*, additionally asserted that an exchange "should be the highest priority for all healthcare stakeholders" (IOM 2003).

Conceptual Framework for HIE

The Department of Health and Human Services (HHS) provided initial guiding principles and requirements for the national network. Based on these and other requirements, in 2004 the Center of Information Technology Leadership determined that over the 10 years required to build a national system of healthcare information exchange a hefty $276 billion would be spent, with another $16.5 billion per year in operating costs. However, a fully implemented and standardized exchange, consisting of machine-interoperable data (that is, structured messages, standardized content or data) would deliver national savings of $77.8 billion per year. This savings takes into account interface and system costs, including acquisition and maintenance, as well as savings primarily due to decreased redundancy and administrative time. Savings from improved patient safety and quality of care are not considered in this number (Center for Information Technology Leadership 2004) (see table 9.1).

Currently, the nationwide health information network is defined as a set of standards, services, and policies referred to as Connect, that enable secure health information exchange over the Internet. The Connect service

Table 9.1. Annual savings with NHIN in place

Provider Type	Net Value Starting at Year 11
Hospitals/Clinician Offices	$33.5 billion
Payers	$21.6 billion
Laboratories	$13.1 billion
Imaging Centers	$ 8.2 billion
Pharmacies	$ 1.3 billion
Public Health	$ 0.1 billion
TOTAL	**$77.8 billion**

Source: Kohn 2006.

allows for health information to be shared through a query process, also called pull technology. It does not require the healthcare provider to know where the patient information is stored as the request queries every participating entity on the NHIN exchange. The approved standard to be used for exchange is the Continuity of Care Document (CCD), and the services and policies are defined in the Data Use and Reciprocal Support Agreement (DURSA). The original version of the DURSA was approved for signature in November 2009, and the most recent version was signed by the founding cooperative participants in May 2011. At the end of 2011, the following entities were securely sharing live health information as part of the NHIN.

- Centers for Medicare & Medicaid Services (CMS) End Stage Renal Disease Center
- Community Health Information Collaborative (CHIC)
- Department of Defense
- Department of Veterans Affairs
- Douglas County Individual Practice Association (DCIPA)
- EHR Doctors
- HealthBridge
- Inland Northwest Health Services
- Kaiser Permanente
- Marshfield Clinic
- MedVirginia
- MultiCare Health System
- North Carolina Healthcare Information and Communication Alliance, Inc. (NCHICA)
- Oregon Community Health Information Network (OCHIN)
- Regenstrief Institute
- Social Security Administration
- South Carolina Health Information Exchange
- South East Michigan Health Information Exchange
- University of California, San Diego
- University of California, San Diego Beacon Community
- Utah Health Information Network
- Western New York Clinical Information Exchange
- Wright State University (ONC 2012)

In the fall of 2011, a governance work group under the Health IT Policy Committee (HITPC) prepared recommendations for governance of the nationwide health information network. Earlier in 2010, the Nationwide Health Information Network Work Group, also a part of the HITPC, presented recommendations for extending the secure exchange of health information using nationwide health information network standards, services, and policies to the broadest audience possible (ONC 2012).

The **Direct Project** was launched in March 2010 to offer a simpler, standards-based way for participants to send authenticated, encrypted health information directly to known recipients over the Internet. Barriers to achieving NHIN by 2014 still exist. Such barriers are insufficient funding, a lack of ongoing economic incentives needed to sustain infrastructure operations, and public concern over privacy.

The interoperability and data-sharing strategies available to support NHIN are fundamentally no different from those available to individual healthcare provider organizations. However, to develop NHIN, healthcare organizations must carefully weigh public concerns over the continued ownership, control, and competitive business advantage their existing data provide them.

In late 2004, HHS stipulated that NHIN must be built incrementally from collaborative, local, and regional efforts in the public and private sectors. As a result, today's exchange focus is to continue to work with networks of connected public and private regional health information organizations (RHIOs) or HIEs, each facilitating exchange of health information in a region. Exchange activities on the national level focus on the development and adoption of standards and economic incentives that will promote the growth of these regional health information exchange infrastructures. A timeline for the development of HIE is provided in figure 9.1 to clarify the key milestones in this initiative since it was introduced in 2001.

Meaningful Use and Health Information Exchange

Meaningful use Stage 1 objectives did not require robust health information exchange; providers are required to test the exchange of health information using a secure encrypted process. The Direct and Connect projects fulfill this requirement, as do other secure e-mail systems that have been in use for years.

The Medicare and Medicaid EHR incentive programs provide payments to hospitals and eligible professionals for the "meaningful use" of certified EHR technology. There are to be three stages of **meaningful use,** each intended to increase the complexity of the measurement or percentage of patient volume that must be involved in the measures—such as e-prescribing or refill automation.

Figure 9.1.   Timeline of key HIE developments 2001–2012

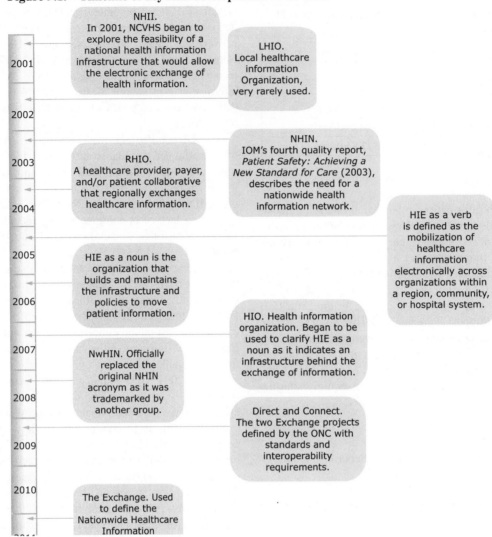

Testing by Eligible Professionals, Eligible Hospitals, and Critical Access Hospitals

The following types of providers fall under the definition of *eligible professional* (EP):

- Doctor of Medicine (MD)
- Doctor of Osteopathy (DO)
- Doctor of Dentistry (DDS)
- Doctor of Oral Surgery or Doctor of Dental Medicine (DDM)
- Doctor of Podiatric Medicine (DPM)
- Doctor of Optometry (OD)
- Doctor of Chiropractic

Some eligible hospitals (EHs) (Medicare and/or Medicaid) may receive EHR incentive payments from both Medicare and Medicaid if they meet all eligibility criteria. What is an eligible hospital under the Medicare EHR Incentive Program?

- Subsection (d) hospitals in the 50 states or Washington, D.C., that are paid under the inpatient prospective payment system (IPPS)
- Critical access hospitals (CAHs)
- Medicare Advantage (MA-affiliated) hospitals

What is an eligible hospital under the Medicaid EHR Incentive Program?

- Acute-care hospitals (including CAHs and cancer hospitals) with at least 10 percent Medicaid patient volume
- Children's hospitals (no Medicaid patient volume requirements)

Some hospitals may be eligible for both; see the Centers for Medicare and Medicaid Services website for more details (CMS 2012).

In Stage 1 of meaningful use both EPs and EHs must attest "yes" to having performed at least one test of certified

EHR technology's capacity to electronically exchange key clinical information prior to the end of the EHR reporting period to meet this measure (CMS 2012).

Stage 2 Meaningful Use and HIE Criteria

As stated in the Notice of Proposed Rule Making (NPRM) released in February 2012, meaningful use Stage 2 does require electronic exchange (CMS 2012). A provider must, when communicating between disparate systems of nonaffiliated organizations, transmit 10 percent of its summary of care documents during transitions of care or for the purposes of referral.

As the proposed rules indicate, the Office of the National Coordinator for Health Information Technology (ONC) is more aggressive in its stage 2 HIE requirements; providers are likely to require additional technical assistance if the true HIE goals are to be realized.

Programs Supporting HIE Development

The **Health Information Technology for Economic and Clinical Health Act (HITECH)** was designed to ensure coordination and alignment between states, establish connectivity to the public health community, and properly train the workforce to be meaningful users of EHRs. The following programs are focused on HIE development and support.

The **Beacon Community Program** is designed to strengthen communities' health information technology (health IT) infrastructure and exchange services (CMS 2012).

The **Health Information Exchange Challenge Grant Program** awarded $16 million to 10 sites in the spring of 2011, providing funding to spur innovative use cases for health information exchange that will be scalable and useful in the sustainability of the nationwide health information exchange and interoperability (CMS 2012).

The **State Health Information Exchange Cooperative Agreement Program** grant program supports states or state-designated entities (SDEs) in establishing HIE services among healthcare providers and hospitals in their regions.

The aim of the grant is to develop exchange capabilities for all healthcare providers that assist them in meeting the requirements of the Medicare and Medicaid EHR incentive programs (CMS 2012).

Early Adopters and Private-Sector Contributions

The Vision of HIE Infrastructure

Regional health information organizations (RHIOs) are collaboratives of healthcare providers, payers, and patients that regionally exchange healthcare information. They serve anywhere from approximately 500,000 to more than 1 million people. Typically, a RHIO is made up of diverse healthcare stakeholders providing and receiving services in a medical referral area (for example, sometimes this area is identified as one served by a regional emergency medical services organization). As such, RHIOs are bigger and fewer than the earlier local health information organizations (LHIOs). However, RHIOs typically are no larger than a state.

Many developing RHIOs and larger HIEs favor a decentralized or federated approach to their technical architectures for exchanging healthcare information. This model is not the fully integrated, monolithic, centralized database model of most healthcare provider organizations. Instead, it consists of distinct, distributed, disparate, and decentralized databases linked together by a centralized **record locator service (RLS)** and, perhaps, with **application programming interfaces (APIs)**. An API is a set of definitions or protocols used by programmers to write applications that allow one piece of computer software to communicate with another (AHIMA 2006).

Models for Health Information Exchange

There are several models that address the architecture of health information exchange:

The Centralized Model

The **centralized model** stores patient records in a single database built to allow queries into the system. This model tends to return results quicker than the other models. Some believe that the management and cost of such a large amount of data would be more expensive. The ownership of the data is a difficult question to settle between all participants, as is how to ensure the accuracy of the data. Changes to the records require multiple transactions and may not occur in a timely fashion (HIMSS 2009).

The Decentralized or Federated Model

The **federated model** maintains the databases at each participant's facility. This allows for easy updates to the record; there is no question about the ownership of the data and who is responsible for the accuracy of the data. Patient matching requires a more sophisticated system and can be a factor in the speed of returning records following a query (HIMSS 2009).

The Hybrid Model

The **hybrid model** is a cross between the centralized and federated models. This usually entails shared patient consent databases, and perhaps the development of shared directories for providers and healthcare facilities for use by all participating organizations (HIMSS 2009).

The ultimate goal of RHIOs and HIEs is to enhance the quality and safety of patient care. Therefore, HIM professionals play a key role by getting involved in RHIOs and HIEs by creating policies, establishing processes, developing communication plans, and ensuring that solid HIM principles are applied.

Efforts of the Markle Foundation: Connecting for Health

The **Markle Foundation's** 2006 Connecting for Health Common Framework, which proposed to facilitate the exchange of healthcare information in RHIOs and HIEs, is a set of standards, policies, and methods intended to ensure secure and reliable connectivity between healthcare systems and to enable RHIOs and HIEs to connect and grow into the Exchange. An RLS is a key infrastructure component of the Common Framework to support this connectivity and interoperability (Connecting for Health 2006).

Distinct, distributed, disparate, and decentralized databases and systems linked by RLSs allow RHIO and HIE participants to search for health records on each of the other systems using patient indexing and identification software. In turn, the records remain intact in source systems where the information is initially created. RLSs only contain information (such as pointers or locators) about where patient-authorized information can be found and not the actual information the records contain.

Authorized users of an established RHIO or HIE can search the RLS, find and select the patient, and then cue the communication application to generate a real-time message to all participating databases that contain data for the patient. The databases receive the request message and send back all appropriate data to the requestor in real time (AHIMA 2007b). Release of information (ROI) from one entity to another is subject to authorization requirements between those parities; in certain sensitive treatment situations patients or providers might choose not to share information. Patients may also choose to opt out of participating in a RLS at all.

Check Your Understanding 9.1

Instructions: Answer the following questions on a separate piece of paper.

1. Describe at least two major reports published by IOM that have each served as a call to action in healthcare informatics.

2. What initiative is referred to as the *medical Internet,* and what is its purpose?

3. What barriers exist to achieving NHIN within the next 10 years?

4. Describe the federated approach that many RHIOs and HIEs are taking to develop their technical architectures for regional healthcare information exchange. What are the advantages and disadvantages of this approach?

Health Information Exchange Initiatives

As the world becomes more connected and its people move around more than at any other time in history, there is an increasing need to exchange information among organizations. Communication and data content standards make it possible to exchange health information using electronic networks that reach across the country and around the world. Technology standards lay the foundation for these networks and data standards enhance the utility and value of the process. Advances in consensus-based standards are making connectivity possible and improving continuity of care and patient safety.

A variety of models and initiatives have been developed and launched with varying degrees of success. As sophistication and utility of the Internet (based on standards) increases, there will be a number of new standards development activities emerging that affect health information management in all settings. The infrastructure requires technology investment for success but also requires fundamental change in business process, information sharing, and adoption of standards. Interoperability is a common thread in all discussion concerning health information technology (HIT). **Interoperability** is the ability of different information systems and software applications to communicate and exchange data. Without the proper standards and infrastructure to facilitate systems that are able to reliably exchange information, an interoperable environment fostering safer and less costly systems cannot occur.

Federal Support Activities for Standards Development

The implementation of standards across the healthcare industry in the United States and creation and continued development of the NHIN establish exchange standards to support electronic health record availability wherever it is needed. All healthcare is delivered at the local level, so a "network of networks" is envisioned to link the location of care with information held on the individual receiving the care wherever it is stored.

The standardized collection of common data elements can provide valuable information about the effectiveness of interventions and treatments for specific diseases. Healthcare providers are able to compare their success rates with those of other providers to determine areas for performance improvement. Measures of quality and effectiveness can be analyzed and compared concerning medications, procedures, or other types of health interventions. This type of analysis can provide critical information that will eventually have a positive impact on clinical outcomes and cost control.

In 1998, the NCVHS produced the concept paper "Assuring a Health Dimension for the National Information Infrastructure," which discussed a conceptual model of a nationwide network of health information. In 2001, NCVHS began to explore the feasibility of a **national health information infrastructure (NHII)** that would allow the electronic exchange of health information. The goal of this initiative was to offer a technology solution that would increase patient safety, reduce medical errors, increase efficiency and effectiveness of healthcare, and contain costs (Mon 2005). The NHII initiative launched an industrywide discussion on how to exchange information electronically in a secure and standard fashion (Mon 2005). This discussion focused attention on the necessity of developing standards to facilitate the definition, collection, exchange, and use of data and information. The NCVHS serves as the statutory public advisory body to the secretary of the HHS in the area of health data and statistics, and work continues to transform the current healthcare delivery system to support enhanced HIE.

According to the NCVHS report "Information for Health: A Strategy for Building the National Health Information Infrastructure" (NCVHS 2001), the NHII included not just the technologies but, more importantly, values, practices, relationships, laws, standards, systems, and applications that support all facets of individual health, healthcare, and public health. It emphasizes the criticality of implementing national health informatics standards as a foundation of a system that supports connectivity and interoperability. The terminology for describing the local or regional networks has evolved over the last decade from subnetworks to the more general use of HIEs to describe the process. Past efforts at standards development have been disparate with varying degrees of industry leadership and limited federal influence or funding. Under NHIN, initial efforts have been focused on creating standards and defining a universal language of health information to flow through networks. As the process spreads and matures, maintaining universality is critical as enhancement and electronic health record (EHR) implementation accelerate. A key tenet for healthcare delivery in the 21st century is to collect information once at the point of care and repurpose it many times for a variety of health-related needs.

There have been diverging opinions on how to accomplish the objective. Consensus building for universal health information interoperability architecture occurs at the federal, state, and local levels. Key public and private organizations are actively working to make the concept of a national health information network a reality while selected regional organizations are successfully sharing data between organizations and care settings. In 2007, through the ONC, six additional contracts were awarded to advance cooperative agreements for additional participants in the trial implementations. These activities advanced the standards and created a suitable infrastructure to support interoperable EHRs.

The American Health Information Community

In 2004, President George W. Bush issued Executive Order 13335. This order called for widespread interoperable EHRs within 10 years (2014), and it established the **Office of the National Coordinator for Health Information Technology (ONC).** The presidential directive to the national coordinator was to develop and implement a strategic plan to guide the nationwide implementation of interoperable HIT in both

the public and private sectors (Thompson and Brailer 2004). The **American Health Information Community (AHIC)**, also referred to as "the Community," was formed in 2005 for leadership toward a connected system and standards development. AHIC initially formed workgroups in the following areas: biosurveillance, consumer empowerment, chronic care, and EHRs. A year later, two additional groups were added: the Biosurveillance Data and Steering Group as a sub-workgroup within the biosurveillance workgroup (since renamed Population Health and Clinical Care Connections workgroup) and the Confidentiality, Privacy, and Security workgroup. The confidentiality workgroup was created as the resource responsible for addressing issues relevant to all the workgroups. Also in 2006, AHIC launched the Quality workgroup to address the need for the development of quality measures, and the Personalized Healthcare workgroup was created to develop and make recommendations on standards for interoperable integration of genomic test information into an individual's EHR. During 2008, this organization was incorporated into a public-private entity to continue its efforts. The new organization was initially called the AHIC Successor, Inc, then was renamed the National eHealth Collaborative (NeHC) in January 2009 to bring the views of consumers, government, and industry into a shared focus on what is needed to enable the development of a secure and reliable exchange of electronic health information nationwide. It is important for HIM professionals to become involved in standards use and, when possible, development; following the activities of this organization is one way to be involved in the process (HHS 2007).

The Community workgroup meetings are open to the public. Notices for each meeting appear in the *Federal Register*. Members of the public can listen to the meetings via the Internet, and the public has the opportunity to submit comments at the end of each meeting. The ONC provides a conference room at HHS in Washington, D.C., so that all who are interested can listen to the meetings. Registration is not required for Internet access to meetings. In order to attend in person a meeting held at an HHS building, a sign-in process at the security desk at the building entrance and proper identification (photograph) are required (HHS 2007).

Soon after the office was established, ONC gathered broad input from key stakeholders about how NHIN should be designed. AHIMA responded as a member of a 13 organization collaborative of major healthcare and information technology organizations. This collaborative recommended general adoption of a set of tools critical to achieving an interoperable environment that supports modern healthcare practice, including precisely defined and uniform technical standards as well as common policies and methods. This set of tools is called the **Common Framework** (Kloss 2005). The nationwide health information network is being constructed incrementally using internet technology with particular emphasis on confidentiality and security of data. A key element is that the network is private, secure, and built on patient control and authorization. Personal information

Table 9.2.   Authorized testing and certification organizations

Organization and Location	Date of Authorization	Scope of Authorization
Surescripts, LLC—Arlington, VA	December 23, 2010	EHR Modules: e-Prescribing, Privacy and Security
ICSA Labs—Mechanicsburg, PA	December 10, 2010	Complete EHR and EHR Modules
SLI Global Solutions—Denver, CO	December 10, 2010	Complete EHR and EHR Modules
InfoGard Laboratories, Inc.—San Luis Obispo, CA	September 24, 2010	Complete EHR and EHR Modules
Certification Commission for Health Information Technology (CCHIT)—Chicago	September 3, 2010	Complete EHR and EHR Modules
Drummond Group, Inc. (DGI)—Austin, TX	September 3, 2010	Complete EHR and EHR Modules

Source: ONC 2012.

would remain with the healthcare provider and accessed and exchange only as needed and with proper authorization and security (Kloss 2005).

The purpose of a RHIO is to give regional healthcare providers access to clinical information for all patients in the defined region across a decentralized technology environment. Such organizations are formed in response to local and regional needs, and each may operate independently, both in the choice of network design and in its access model. The goals of RHIOs are consistent with the goals of NHIN: improved quality of care, increased patient safety, reduction of medical errors, and cost savings. The Electronic Healthcare Network Accreditation Commission (EHNAC) has accredited several HIEs and community health data network partnerships and other groups promoting data sharing across multiple stakeholders.

Advancing a Foundation for Health Information Sharing

Soon after the office was created, the ONC issued a series of three-year government contracts focused on the four key areas identified by the healthcare industry as key to HIE development: EHR certification, data standards, NHIN architecture, and privacy and security (Carol 2005).

Contracts were awarded to public-private groups to address three of the key areas: EHR certification, standards development, and privacy and security.

EHR Certification

Certification by an ONC-authorized testing and certification body (ATCB) signifies that an EHR technology has the capabilities necessary to support efforts to meet the goals and objectives of Meaningful Use. Table 9.2 shows the organizations that have been selected as ATCBs (ONC-ATCB 2012).

Standards Development

The **American National Standards Institute (ANSI)** was awarded a contract to convene the National **Health Information Technology Standards Panel (HITSP)**. This

organization served as a cooperative partnership between the public and private sectors to achieve wide acceptance and usable standards. Table 9.3 shows the body of work accomplished by this committee.

Privacy and Security

The **Health Information Security and Privacy Collaboration (HISPC)** project received federal funding to assess differences in business policies and state laws that would affect health information exchange. The group then focused on identifying solutions while preserving privacy and security requirements in the applicable federal and state laws. Finally, the group was tasked with developing detailed plans and implementing solutions.

HIT Strategic Goals and Objectives

The transition from paper to EHRs has had to include the upgrade from legacy data sets toward a more comprehensive core data set for continuity of care (figure 9.2) that map back to EHR functions. Efforts and workgroups continue in a variety of standards organizations and professional societies toward data content standards that support legal requirements, continuing care, quality-of-care measurement, and patient safety. Table 9.4 describes two goals outlined in the ONC-Coordinated Federal Health Information Technology Strategic Plan: 2008–2012.

Use of the CCR and CCD for Health Summaries

The **Continuity of Care Record (CCR)** standard, created by the American Society for Testing and Materials, is a patient health summary standard. It allows for flexibility in design and ensures that the most relevant and timely core health information about a patient can be sent electronically from one care provider to another. It contains various elements that provide a dated and retrievable record of a patient's health information available at the time of a clinical encounter. The ASTM CCR standard is designed to permit easy creation by any provider using an electronic health record system at the end of an encounter.

Table 9.3.   HITSP interoperability standards

Number	Name	Description
IS 01	**Electronic Health Record (EHR) Laboratory Results Reporting**	The Electronic Health Records Laboratory Results Reporting interoperability specification defines specific standards to support the interoperability between electronic health records and laboratory systems and secure access to laboratory results and interpretations in a patient-centric manner.
IS 02	**Biosurveillance**	The Biosurveillance interoperability specification defines specific standards that promote the exchange of biosurveillance information among healthcare providers and public health authorities.
IS 03	**Consumer Empowerment**	The Consumer Empowerment and Access to Clinical Information via Networks interoperability specification defines specific standards needed to assist patients in making decisions regarding care and healthy lifestyles (that is, registration information, medication history, lab results, current and previous health conditions, allergies, summaries of healthcare encounters, and diagnoses). This interoperability specification defines specific standards needed to enable the exchange of such data between patients and their caregivers via networks.
IS 04	**Emergency Responder Electronic Health Record (ER-EHR)**	The Emergency Responder Electronic Health Record interoperability specification defines specific standards required to track and provide on-site emergency care professionals, medical examiner/fatality managers, and public health practitioners with needed information regarding care, treatment, or investigation of emergency incident victims.
IS 05	**Consumer Empowerment and Access to Clinical Information via Media**	The Consumer Empowerment and Access to Clinical Information via Media interoperability specification defines specific standards needed to assist patients in making decisions regarding care and healthy lifestyles (that is, registration information, medication history, lab results, current and previous health conditions, allergies, summaries of healthcare encounters, and diagnoses). This interoperability specification defines specific standards needed to enable the exchange of such data between patients and their caregivers via physical media or secure email exchange.
IS 06	**Quality**	The Quality interoperability specification defines specific standards needed to benefit providers by providing a collection of data for inpatient and ambulatory care and to benefit clinicians by providing real-time or near-real-time feedback regarding quality indicators for specific patients.
IS 07	**Medication Management**	The Medication Management interoperability specification defines specific standards to facilitate access to necessary medication and allergy information for consumers, clinicians, pharmacists, health insurance agencies, inpatient and ambulatory care, and such.
IS 08	**Personalized Healthcare**	The Personalized Healthcare interoperability specification describes family history and genetic/genomic lab order results that are used to provide personalized treatment specific to genetic makeup.
IS 09	**Consultations and Transfers of Care**	The Consultations and Transfers of Care interoperability specification describes the information flows, issues, and system capabilities that apply to (1) a provider requesting and a patient receiving a consultation from another provider and (2) a provider requesting a transfer of care for a patient and the receiving facility admitting the patient. It is intended to facilitate access to information necessary for consultations and transfers for consulting clinicians, referring clinicians, transferring facilities, receiving facilities, and consumers.
IS 10	**Immunizations and Response Management**	The Immunizations and Response Management interoperability specification focuses on (1) providing information about individuals who need to receive specific vaccines, drugs, or other interventions; (2) the ability to report, track, and manage administration of vaccines, drugs, isolation, and quarantine; (3) the ability to identify and electronically exchange information describing the treatment or prophylaxis status of populations; and (4) the ability to exchange specific resource and supply chain data from public and private sectors.
IS 11	**Public Health Case Reporting**	The Public Health Case Reporting interoperability specification supports the bidirectional information exchanges of the public health case reporting process. It focuses on enabling more efficient data capture at the point of care while allowing for optimizing the information delivery format and content allowing for current SDO efforts to be finalized. In the absence of standards in structured content and associated clinical decision support for alerts and information reporting criteria, this interoperability specification provides options for the secure communication of basic presentation, preserving content to better automate the current paper-based information flows.

(continued on next page)

Table 9.3.   HITSP interoperability standards (*continued*)

Number	Name	Description
IS 12	Patient-Provider Secure Messaging	The Patient-Provider Secure Messaging interoperability specification describes the information flows, processes, and system capabilities that are required for patients to interact with their healthcare clinicians remotely using common computer technologies readily available in homes and other settings.
IS 77	Remote Monitoring	The Remote Monitoring interoperability specification addresses the information exchange requirements for the transfer of remote monitoring information from a device physically attached to or used by a patient in a location that is remote to the clinician to an EHR system or a personal health record system.
IS 91	Maternal and Child Health	The Maternal and Child Health interoperability specification addresses the ability to exchange obstetric and pediatric patient information between EHRs; the ability to incorporate pediatric assessment tools, guidelines, and assessment schedules into EHRs; and the ability to exchange standardized patient assessments for antenatal care, prenatal care, labor and delivery, and postpartum care between EHRs. It also addresses the ability to incorporate assessment tools, guidelines, and assessment schedules into EHRs for antenatal care, prenatal care, labor and delivery, and postpartum care, as well as the ability to exchange this information with appropriate public health programs.
IS 92	Newborn Screening	The Newborn Screening interoperability specification describes the information flows, issues, and system capabilities supporting newborn screening reporting and information exchanges among clinical care settings and public health.
IS 98	Medical Home	The medical home interoperability specification focuses on the information received by the Medical Home (MH) for care coordination and the manner in which this information supports individual patient needs and comorbidity management.
IS 107	EHR-centric	This interoperability specification consolidates all information exchanges and standards that involve an EHR system amongst the 13 HITSP Interoperability specifications in place as of the February 13, 2009 enactment of the American Recovery and Reinvestment Act (ARRA). This interoperability specification is organized as a set of HITSP capabilities, with each capability specifying a business service that an EHR system might address in one or more of the existing HITSP interoperability specifications (for example, the Communicate Hospital Prescriptions capability supports electronic prescribing for inpatient prescription orders). Greater detail on these capabilities is provided as part of this interoperability specification, with their underlying HITSP constructs referenced in the Complete Library on HITSP.org.
IS 158	Clinical Research	The Clinical Research interoperability specification covers clinical research in all its forms as it interoperates with healthcare systems, particularly EHRs. The specification spans two industries, healthcare and clinical research, and incorporates standards from healthcare (HL7 and IHE) and research (CDISC). The design leverages existing HITSP constructs and communication methodologies where applicable, and lays out new constructs as needed. The design also leverages the current players in the clinical research industry such as electronic data capture (EDC) systems and research registries.

Source: HITSP 2012.

Because it is expressed in the standard data interchange language known as XML, a CCR can potentially be created, read, and interpreted by any EHR software application. A CCR can also be exported in other formats, such as PDF and Office Open XML (Microsoft Word 2007 format).

A **Continuity of Care Document (CCD)** is a Health Level Seven (HL7) Clinical Document Architecture (CDA) implementation of the CCR. In general terms, the CCR is the information format and HL7 is the transport mechanism. Conversion of a CCR document into CCD can be accomplished using Extensible Stylesheet Language Transformations (XSLT). It must be noted that it is not always possible to translate a CCD into a CCR as not all CCD features are supported in the CCR.

HIE Trial Implementations

In 2007, HHS awarded contracts to nine regional and state HIEs to begin trial implementations of NHIN. The Nationwide Health Information Network has been built upon a core set of capabilities to enable nationwide information exchange encompassing a diverse set of organizations, technologies, and approaches. These core capabilities include

- Ability to find and retrieve healthcare information within and between health information exchanges and other organizations
- Ability to deliver a summarized patient record to support patient care and to support the patient's health

Figure 9.2.   Core health data elements for standardization

1. Personal/Unique Identifier[2]
2. Date of Birth
3. Gender
4. Race and Ethnicity
5. Residence
6. Marital Status
7. Living/Residential Arrangement[1]
8. Self-Reported Health Status[2]
9. Functional Status[2]
10. Years of Schooling
11. Patient's Relationship to Subscriber/Person Eligible for Entitlement
12. Current or Most Recent Occupation and Industry[2]
13. Type of Encounter[2]
14. Admission Date (inpatient)
15. Discharge Date (inpatient)
16. Date of Encounter (outpatient and physician services)
17. Facility Identification[1]
18. Type of Facility/Place of Encounter[1]
19. Healthcare Practitioner Identification (outpatient)[1]
20. Provider Location or Address of Encounter (outpatient)
21. Attending Physician Identification (inpatient)[1]
22. Operating Clinician Identification[1]

23. Health Care Practitioner Specialty[1]
24. Principal Diagnosis (inpatient)
25. Primary Diagnosis (inpatient)
26. Other Diagnoses (inpatient)
27. Qualifier for Other Diagnoses (inpatient)
28. Patient's Stated Reason for Visit or Chief Complaint (outpatient)[2]
29. Diagnosis Chiefly Responsible for Services Provided (outpatient)
30. Other Diagnoses (outpatient)
31. External Cause of Injury
32. Birth Weight of Newborn
33. Principal Procedure (inpatient)
34. Other Procedures (inpatient)
35. Dates of Procedures (inpatient)
36. Procedures and Services (outpatient)
37. Medications Prescribed
38. Disposition of Patient (inpatient)[1]
39. Disposition (outpatient)
40. Patient's Expected Sources of Payment[1]
41. Injury Related to Employment
42. Total Billed Charges[1]

[1]Element for which substantial agreement has been reached but for which some amount of additional work is needed.
[2]Element that has been recognized as significant but for which considerable work remains to be undertaken.
A lack of footnote indicates that these elements are ready for implementation.
Source: NCVHS 1996.

Table 9.4.   Summary of health IT strategic goals and objectives: 2008–2012

Goal 1: Patient-Focused Healthcare	Objective 1.1: Facilitate electronic exchange, access, and use of electronic health information, while protecting the privacy and security of patients' health information	Objective 1.2: Enable the movement of electronic health information to support patients' health and care needs	Objective 1.3: Promote nationwide deployment of electronic health records and personal health records and other consumer health IT tools	Objective 1.4: Establish mechanisms for multistakeholder priority setting and decision making
Goal 2: Population Health	Objective 2.1: Advance privacy and security policies, principles, procedures, and protections for information access in population health	Objective 2.2: Enable exchange of health information to support population-oriented uses	Objective 2.3: Promote nationwide adoption of technologies to improve population and individual health	Objective 2.4: Establish coordinated organizational processes supporting information use for population health

Source: ONC 2008.

- Ability to support consumer preferences regarding NHIN of his or her information, including the ability to choose not to participate in the NHIN
- Support of secure information exchange
- Support of a common trust agreement that establishes the obligations and assurances to which all NHIN participants agree
- Ability to match patients to their data without a national patient identifier
- Support of harmonized standards, which have been developed by voluntary consensus standards bodies for exchange of health information among all such entities and networks

The current core capabilities of NHIN establish an interoperable infrastructure among distinct networks and systems that allows for different approaches and implementations while ensuring secure information exchange as needed for patient care and population health (CMS 2012).

In 2008, a legal framework was created using existing federal and state law regarding the electronic exchange of health data. This agreement, called the **Data Use and Reciprocal Support Agreement (DURSA),** was first executed by a number of federal agencies and nonfederal organizations in November 2009.

The DURSA is a trust agreement entered into when exchanging information with other organizations using an agreed upon set of national standards, services, and policies developed in coordination with the ONC.

The DURSA describes the responsibilities, obligations, and expectations of all parties under the agreement. Thus it creates a framework for safe and secure health information exchange and is designed to promote trust among participants. It also addresses privacy protection, confidentiality, and security of the health data that are shared (CMS 2012).

Health Information Systems for Other Types of Healthcare Institutions

Although hospitals and clinics have generally been the early adopters of EHRs, other types of healthcare providers, as well as payers, are adopting various forms of EHRs as well. Behavioral health facilities find the integration of data from multiple sources especially helpful in coordination of care. Home health agencies have for some time adopted hand-held devices to capture data in compliance with regulatory requirements. Long-term care facilities have a more difficult time affording systems, but their highly structured data-reporting requirements also make them good candidates for simple EHR systems. Finally, health plans collect a tremendous amount of data about individuals from claims, direct feeds from commercial labs, and claims attachments. These health plans are creating databases that can be sorted by patients as their EHRs for disease management, or data in aggregate can be used for predictive modeling.

Still, it is important to note that the many forms of EHRs that exist in the different health environments are generally stand-alone with respect to the organization in which they reside, with little exchange among different organizations. Even among components of an integrated delivery network (IDN), not all systems communicate with one another. This is changing as HIE organizations form. HIE within the organization is accomplished in a variety of ways, but frequently through portal technology.

Privacy and security measures are especially being scrutinized as care delivery organizations become involved with HIE organizations. HIE organizations are generally not considered covered entities, but rather business associates. Because this is one step removed from covered entity status, many covered entities want to see stronger security controls. For instance, *role-based access control* is the strongest form of access control. It establishes a profile based not only on who the person is and what role he or she is playing, but also on what specific information may or may not be accessed. In some cases, this can be linked to location and time of day as well. For example, Nurse Jones may access patients on floor 3-West during first shift and in the emergency department on second shift if signed in for ED duty.

Consumer Empowerment

In addition, there is increasing emphasis on consumer empowerment and the need to enable consumers to be more directive in who may have access to particular information. Many states have enacted new consent requirements for disclosure, and some states are looking at their existing consent requirements as being too stringent and not permitting HIE. A federal government initiative was HISPC, which is a partnership consisting of a multidisciplinary team of experts and the National Governor's Association (NGA) working with approximately 40 states to assess and develop plans to address variations in organization-level business policies and state laws that affect privacy and security practices that may pose challenges to interoperable health information exchange. The United States has what has been described as a "crazy quilt" of state laws relating to authorizations and consents for uses and disclosure of individually identifiable health information. The disparity in state laws has virtually resulted in every covered entity getting an authorization for every disclosure, including for treatment, payment, and healthcare operations, which is not required under Health Insurance Portability and Accountability Act (HIPAA).

Since HIE organizations serve as the exchange agent for health information, there are increasing concerns about ensuring proper authorization for uses and disclosures. Some HIE organizations are constructing their processes around a personal health record (PHR) service, directly giving consumers total control over who may have access to specific information. The concept is centered around the ability to export patient data from an EHR into a PHR using the CCD standard. Access to records is given by the patient to specific providers of their choice. Other designs utilize patient portals that open up limited data sets for patients to view, offer the ability to schedule appointments or post questions to their providers. Even when a HIE organization is not tightly aligned with a PHR, many are enabling individuals to provide their own consent directions as to whether they want their data to be included in the HIE organization exchange capabilities (called *opt in*); whether they do not want their data to be exchanged via the HIE organization (*opt out*); or, if they do want to be included in the exchange service, to whom data may be disclosed and under what circumstances ("quilted" consent directive). (It should be noted that HIE organizations would not hold health information in one massive database but either would provide direction to where information is located among the participants or would use a bank vault type of structure to manage health information for many different organizations—much like the application service provider or remote connectivity option provided by many information system vendors today.)

Issues in Health Information Exchange

HIE initiatives have been developed in an effort to move toward a longitudinal patient record with complete information about the patient available at any point of care. These patient-specific, rather than aggregate, data are used primarily for patient care. Some researchers have looked at the amount of data available through the health information exchange as a possible source of data to aggregate for research. Since HIE is a fairly new concept, it is important that HIEs take the time to develop policies and procedures covering the use of data collected for patient care for other purposes. Special attention needs to be paid to whether patients included in the HIE need to provide individual consent to be included when the data is aggregated for research or other purposes.

Patient Identity Management

Patient identity management is the accuracy and completeness of data attached to or associated with an individual patient. Data must be reliable, reproducible, and sufficiently extensive for matching purposes. Completeness refers to having not only adequate data elements present but also the correct pairing or linking of all existing records for that individual within and across information systems. Patient identity integrity is of central importance to achieving quality of care, patient safety, and cost control.

While it is relatively easy to see the implications of patient identity integrity on quality, safety, and cost, it is far more difficult to grasp the complexity of maintaining identity integrity in the real operational environment. To solve the problem of ensuring a state of high quality and integrity, one must look at the entire process of patient identity management (PIM). Nine variables have been identified that influence, in varying degrees, our ability to build and sustain a database in a high state of identity integrity. These key influencers are industry standards, interfaces, algorithms, unique identifiers, business processes, data accuracy, data quality, training, and medical devices.

HIE Security and Privacy

HIEs protect patient privacy and security by requiring the use of usernames and passwords or security tokens such as public key infrastructure (PKI) digital certificates to access the system. "PKI security provides the encryption technologies required by electronic data interchange to meet the following security objectives" (Data Interchange Plc. 2005):

- Authentication: The process of proving one's identity
- Confidentiality: Ensuring that no one can read the message except the intended recipient
- Integrity: Assuring the recipient that the received message has not been altered in any way from the original
- Nonrepudiation: A mechanism to prove that the sender or recipient actually sent or received a message (Data Interchange Plc. 2005)

Included in the architecture of HIEs are reporting and auditing tools that provide for tracking of every instance when a patient's data have been accessed and changed, as well as tracking the identity of all users. Role-based access ensures that the HIE takes reasonable steps to limit the use or disclosure of, and requests for, protected health information to the minimum necessary to accomplish the intended purpose

HIPAA regulations require encryption for all protected health information (PHI) transferred over the Internet. To ensure HIPAA compliance, all communication through HIEs is fully encrypted, including client-to-server communications, and the identity of the client and server can be cryptographically verified. Currently, consideration is being given to requiring all data at rest to be encrypted, as well.

As discussed earlier in the chapter, many HIEs support a community opt-in/opt-out system to comply with state statutes requiring patients have control over the sharing of their healthcare data (HIMSS 2009). Security technologies are discussed further in Chapter 4.

HIM Principles in Health Information Exchange: Use Case Scenarios

RHIOs have the challenging task of satisfying the diverse business and personal communication requirements of government and healthcare enterprises and of individual healthcare consumers. Technology development is, at best, driven by use cases or scenarios that articulate, in nontechnical language, how a system should interact with end users to achieve the users' goals. Satisfying the needs of end users is the "acid test" for measuring the utility of valued goals.

Standardization of health information exchange practices and functionality is paramount to NHIN interoperability. Many options are open to an organization seeking to establish a technical infrastructure (network) to exchange health information, but if health information exchange principles are not standardized, the magnitude of the transformation efforts necessary could mean missed opportunities for cost reduction and increased efficiency.

The use case document developed by the American Health Information Management Association (AHIMA) is intended to illustrate a few current and potential use case scenarios that describe how data currently are or may be shared across RHIOs.

Use Case Description and Scope

A **use case** is a set of scenarios that describes an interaction between a user and a system. A use case diagram displays the relationship among actors and use cases. The two main components of a use case diagram are use cases and actors.

- An actor represents a user or another system that will interact with the system being modeled.
- A use case is an external view of the system that represents some action the user might perform in order to complete a task.

HIM and HIE principles have been used to identify, functionality, and standards critical to the success of an NHIN and RHIO. Important considerations include

- Identification of quality improvement needs (that is, back-end reports, audit trails) strategies at the onset of the RHIO project
- Implementation of continuous quality improvement strategies to support quality data and information
- Design of application technology that supports collection of high-quality data at the point of care to optimize data aggregation, exchange, and retrieval with stellar auditing capabilities
- Education of consumers regarding their role in ensuring the quality of healthcare data
- Investigation of all issues surrounding the data's variability to quantify the effect and identify solutions

Issues and Obstacles

As healthcare implementation teams plan for EHRs or exchange of clinical data across competing healthcare provider organizations, key HIM functions are being ignored. Systems that are interfaced within infrastructures and beyond have not facilitated conversations about data validity, integrity, and quality of key data values. The common focus is on the technical exchange of data between systems, not on ensuring the quality of the data exchanged. How are RHIOs developing policies and procedures that ensure data quality attributes? What is the contamination rate of master patient index (MPI) systems? What is the RHIO's rationale for ensuring patient safety and quality patient care that is accessible and traceable? History has shown that EHR implementations demonstrate a direct correlation between data trust, confidence level, and use.

Use Case Scenario

Accurate Patient Identification: This use case illustrates the importance of ensuring accurate patient identification on the front end at the point when the patient's identity data are captured. The challenge of accurately capturing a patient's key demographic data and in preventing duplicate medical records to be created is illustrated. This challenge is severely compounded when those records are electronically transmitted to other clinical databases within that single facility. How then will a RHIO be confident of its ability to accurately link electronic medical records from competing provider organizations? What will it do if participating organizations send it records with data integrity problems or duplicate records? How will these be resolved? What duplicate record standards will participating organizations be held to, and how will this be measured?

Most healthcare information systems do not contain robust algorithms in the patient record search function, or in the electronic record linking function. And if more sophisticated algorithms are used, how does the organization test and validate the accuracy of the record linkage? These, along with many more questions, need to be evaluated and decided upon before electronic record linkage begins in the RHIO.

The diagram in figure 9.3 illustrates how patient identity data are transmitted between systems within a healthcare organization's various registration, billing, and clinical/EHR systems. It also demonstrates how these electronic medical records may be sent to a RHIO. As the MPI of any hospital, clinic, practice management, or ancillary/EHR system is the foundation for each of these systems, the accuracy and completeness of the patient's demographic data is critical to successful clinical data sharing. Table 9.5 provides a detailed explanation of the key steps in the use case scenario for accurate patient identification (AHIMA 2007b).

1. What is the purpose of NHIN and how do the three core content areas support that role?
2. What does PKI mean and what is its purpose?
3. What is a use case?

Figure 9.3.   Use case scenario: Accurate patient identification

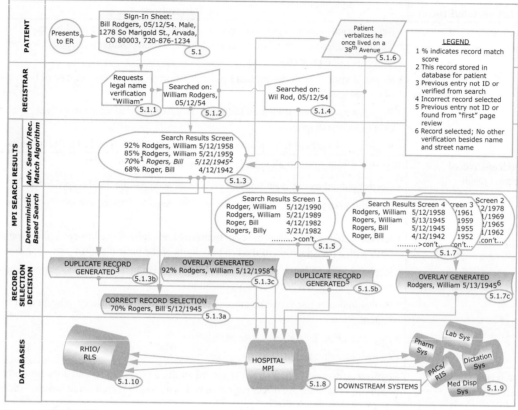

Source: AHIMA 2007b.

Table 9.5.   Explanation of key steps in use case scenario illustration

The table below provides an explanation of the flowchart diagram in figure 9.3 and an explanation of the key steps of this illustration.

Accurate Patient Identification		
Code	**Role/Function/Process**	**Description**
5.1	**Patient**	Patient presents at ER—urgent condition • Patient completes sign-in slip noting name, date of birth, gender, current address, and telephone number • Patient data noted on slip include "Bill Rodgers"; 05/12/19<u>54</u>; Male; 1278 So Marigold St., Arvada, Co 80003; (720) 876-1234 • Data for this patient are stored in database as "Bill Rogers"; 05/12/19<u>45</u>; Male; 873 E. 38th Ave., Westminster., CO 80008; (303) 885-2967. Last previous visit is seven years ago.
5.1.1	**Patient access registrar**	ER registrar picks up slip and calls patient to come up to be registered. Registrar asks patient if his legal name is "William" and patient answers "yes." • Registrar asks patient for his driver's license. • Registrar asks patient if he has ever been treated in any of the health organization's facilities. Patient answers "yes."
5.1.2	**Patient access registrar**	Registrar searches on "William Rodgers"; DOB 05/12/1954; Male; (720) 876-1234. *[Note—correct search performed by registrar.]*
5.1.3	**Advanced algorithm search**	Advanced search/record match algorithm used for searching hospital registration system.

(continued on next page)

Table 9.5.   Explanation of key steps in use case scenario illustration (*continued*)

Code	Role/Function/Process	Description
5.1.3a	Search and record selection result	• Registrar finds patient's previous record. (Patient's correct record is 12th record listed, but only weighted 70%. Algorithm has nickname table and transposition logic and is tolerant of multiple data errors upon search.) • Registrar verifies with patient that his driver's license has his correct date of birth and spelling of his last name. • Registrar asks patient if he used to live on 38th Avenue. Patient answers "yes." (See 5.1.6 on use case flowchart diagram). • Registrar asks patient if his phone number used to be (720) 876-1234. Patient answers "yes."
5.1.5a	Search and record selection result	Registrar scrolls through all records until correct record located. • Correct patient record is on fourth search result screen—the 32nd record listed. • Registrar asks patient if he used to live on 38th Avenue. Patient answers "yes." (See 5.1.6 on use case flowchart diagram.) • Registrar dialogues with patient continuously and realizes she has entered the patient's date of birth with a transposition of the last two digits of the patient's birth year. • Registrar finds patient's correct record, brings up visit history, and asks patient when he had last been a patient in the healthcare organization. • Patient indicates last visit date close to last visit date in visit history in hospital information system. • Registrar reverifies patient's date of birth. • Correct record selected.
5.1.5b	Search and record selection result	Registrar only reviews first screen of record returned (10 patients) and does not find record for which she's searching. (Correct patient record is on fourth search result screen—the 32nd record listed.) • Duplicate created.
5.1.5c	Search and record selection result	14th record in list was for William Rogers, DOB 05/13/1945, and does not verify other data stored on this record with patient. Registrar selects that record. • Overlay created—this is a different patient.
5.1.6	**Patient access registrar**	Registrar asks patient if he ever lived on 38th Avenue.
5.1.7	**Exact match (deterministic) search function**	Registrar searches MPI database for "Wil" in first name. "Rod" in last name. DOB 05/12/19<u>54.</u> (*Typical "3 × 3" search used in deterministic based MPIs.)
5.1.7a	Search and record selection result	Registrar scrolls through all records until correct record located. • Correct patient record is on fourth search screen— the 32nd record listed. • Registrar asks patient if he used to live on 38th Avenue. Patient answers "yes." (See 5.1.6 on use case flowchart diagram.) • Registrar dialogues with patients continuously and realizes she has entered the patient's date of birth with a transposition of the last two digits of the patient's birth year. • Registrar finds patient's correct record, brings up visit history, and asks patient when he had last been a patient in the healthcare organization. • Patient indicates last visit date close to last visit date in visit history in hospital information system. • Registrar reverifies patient's date of birth. • Correct record selected.
5.1.7b	Search and record selection result	Registrar only reviews first screen of records returned (10 patients) and does not find record for which she's searching. (Correct patient record is on fourth search result screen—the 32nd record listed.) • Duplicate created.

Table 9.5.   Explanation of key steps in use case scenario illustration (*continued*)

5.1.7c	Search and record selection result	14th record in list was for William Rogers, DOB 05/13/1945, and registrar does not verify other data stored on this record with patient. Registrar selects that record. • Overlay created—this is a different patient. • Patient armband indicates incorrect patient identify information for this patient. • All autoprinted patient identity labels for various medical record chart forms contain incorrect patient identify information for this patient.
5.1.8	**System record add**	Record for registration is added to or updated in the hospital information system. • New visit added to patient's correct medical record. • Duplicate record added to hospital information system. • Another patient's record is overlaid with this patient's demographic data, and this visit record is added to the other patient's record. • Patient armband indicates either correct or incorrect patient identity information for this patient. • All autoprinted patient identity labels for various medical record chart forms contain either correct or incorrect patient identity information for this patient.
5.1.9	**Record sent to downstream systems**	Depending on whether correct or incorrect patient record is selected at registration: • New visit for correct patient record sent to 20 downstream systems including a radiology information system (and Picture Archiving and Communication System connected to the Radiological Information System), a lab system, a pharmacy system, a medication dispensing system, a dictation system, a transcription system, and a document imaging system for medical records. • Duplicate record sent to 20 downstream systems including a radiology information system (and PACS connected to the RIS), a lab system, a pharmacy system, a medication dispensing system, a dictation system, a transcription system, a document imaging system for medical records. • Overlaid record sent to 20 downstream systems including a radiology information system (and PACS connected to the RIS), a lab system, a pharmacy system, a medication dispensing system, a dictation system, a transcription system, a document imaging system for medical records.
5.1.10	**Record sent to RHIO**	Depending on whether correct or incorrect patient record is selected at registration: • New visit for correct patient record sent to the RHIO. • Duplicate record sent to the RHIO. • Overlaid record sent to the RHIO.

Source: AHIMA 2007b.

Summary

The federal government's strategic health information technology vision includes every American having an interoperable electronic health record (EHR) by the year 2014. The overall goal is to encourage the creation of an environment in which electronic health information moves fluidly through the healthcare system, improving care coordination, reducing healthcare disparities, engaging patients and their families, and improving population health, all while ensuring adequate privacy and security. Fully realized health information exchange will allow providers to have comprehensive, intuitive, high-quality patient information at their fingertips to make the right decision for their patients, from prior patient laboratory tests to medical history, and easy access to research on evidence-based care.

References

American Health Information Management Association. 2006. *Pocket Glossary of Health Information Management and Technology*. Chicago: AHIMA.

American Health Information Management Association. 2007a. Practice brief: HIM principles in health information exchange. *Journal of AHIMA* 78(8).

American Health Information Management Association. 2007b. HIM Principles in Health Information Exchange: Use Case

Scenarios. http://library.ahima.org/xpedio/groups/public/documents/ahima/bok1_035068.pdf.

Carol, R. 2005. Short term forecast: Experts speak up on ONC's RFI. RFPs and the year ahead. *Journal of AHIMA* 76(9): 42–44, 46, 48, 50.

Center of Information Technology Leadership. 2004. *The Value of Healthcare Information Exchange and Interoperability.* Boston: Partners HealthCare.

Centers for Medicare and Medicaid Services. 2012. Electronic health records (EHR) incentive programs.http://www.cms.gov/EHRIncentivePrograms/15_Eligibility.asp#TopOfPage.

Connecting for Health. 2006. Record locator service: Technical background from the Massachusetts Prototype Community. http://www.connectingforhealth.org/commonframework/docs/T6_RecordLocator.pdf.

Data Interchange Plc. 2005. PKI security. http://www.dip.co.uk/downloads/brochures/whitepaper-pki-security.pdf.

Department of Health and Human Services, Centers for Medicare & Medicaid Services. 2012 (March 7). Electronic health record incentive program—stage 2, notice of proposed rulemaking. *Federal Register*, 77 FR 13698.

Dick, R.S., E.B. Steen, and D.E. Detmer. 1997. *The Computer-Based Patient Record: An Essential Technology for Health Care.* Committee on Improving the Patient Record, Division of Health Care Services. Washington D.C.: National Academies Press.

Healthcare Information and Management Systems Society. 2009. *The HIMSS Guide to Participating in a Health Information Exchange.* http://www.himss.org.

Healthcare Information Technology Standards Panel. 2012 (March). Interoperability standards. http://www.hitsp.org/.

Institute of Medicine, Committee on Quality of Health Care in America. 2003. *Patient Safety: Achieving a New Standard of Care.* Washington, D.C.: National Academies Press.

Kloss, L. 2005. The NHIN comes into focus. http:// www.hitsp.org/about_hitsp.aspx.

Mon, D.T. 2005. An update on the NHIN and RHIOs. *Journal of AHIMA* 76(6): 56–57, 59.

National Committee on Vital and Health Statistics. 2001. Information for health: A strategy for building the national health information infrastructure. Washington, D.C.: NCVHS.

National Committee on Vital and Health Statistics. 1996 (August). Core health data elements report. http://ncvhs.hhs.gov/ncvhsr1.htm.

Office of the National Coordinator for Health Information Technology. 2012. Nationwide health information exchange. http://healthit.hhs.gov/portal/server.pt?open=512&objID=1407&parentname=CommunityPage&parentid=8&mode=2&in_hi_userid=11113&cached=true.

Office of the National Coordinator for Health Information Technology. 2008. ONC-coordinated federal health information technology strategic plan: 2008–2012. http://www.hhs.gov/healthit/resources/HITStrategicPlanSummary.pdf.

Office of the National Coordinator for Health information Technology–Authorized Testing and Certification Bodies. 2012 (March). http://healthit.hhs.gov.

Thompson, T.G., and D.J. Brailer. 2004. The decade of health information technology: Delivering consumer-centric and information-rich healthcare. Framework for strategic action. Washington, D.C.: HHS.

part **III**

Development of the Patient Health Record

chapter 10

Content and Structure of Paper and Hybrid Records

Elizabeth D. Bowman, MPA, RHIA, FAHIMA,
and Rebecca B. Reynolds, EdD, RHIA

Learning Objectives

- Describe the traditional (paper-based) health record and the hybrid health record and identify their primary uses and users
- Describe the transition from the paper record to the hybrid record to the electronic health record and the impact of the transition on the flow of health record information
- Identify the factors that determine the content of the health record
- Identify the organizations and standards for the content of the health record
- Describe the major content areas of the health record, including administrative and demographic data, clinical data, and specialized content
- Outline the flow of health record information from initial encounter to final format
- Give examples of general requirements for the primary documentation required in most health records, including the history and physical examination, progress notes, orders, and discharge summary
- Identify forms and documentation requirements specific to facilities other than acute care hospitals, including ambulatory care, home care, hospice care, rehabilitation care, and long-term care facilities
- Compare and contrast the different formats of the paper-based and hybrid health record

- Describe the content of the personal health record
- Define quantitative and qualitative record analysis
- Define the purposes of the following processes: concurrent analysis and discharge analysis, open-record review, record review, point-of-care review, and continuous record review
- Differentiate an incomplete health record and a delinquent health record
- Explain the role of the health information management (HIM) professional in the design and control of forms
- Compare internal and external (contract) medical transcription services
- Summarize how new developments such as telecommuting and voice recognition technology will change the role of the medical transcriptionist
- Define the unit, serial, and serial-unit systems of record numbering and filing and the appropriate use of each, including methods of number assignment
- Explain the basic rules of terminal digit filing and the advantages of using terminal digit filing concepts for productivity
- Describe policies and procedures on health record storage, retention, and destruction
- Define the functions of the master patient index
- Identify issues related to identity management

Key Terms

Accreditation Association for Ambulatory Health Care
  (AAAHC)
Administrative information
Advance directive
American College of Surgeons (ACS)
Association for Healthcare Documentation Integrity (AHDI)
Authentication
Authorization
Autoauthentication
Bar coding technology
Bylaws
Care path
Case manager
Certified medical transcriptionist (CMT)
Chart tracking
Charting by exception
Closed record
Closed-record review
Compliance
Computer output to laser disk (COLD)
Computerized provider order entry (CPOE) system
Concurrent analysis
Conditions of Participation
Consent
Consultation
Continuous record review
Contract service
Deficiency assignment
Delinquent health record
Demographic information
Digital dictation
Discharge analysis
Discharge summary
Disposition
Do not resuscitate (DNR) order
Durable power of attorney
Electronic signature
Emergency Medical Treatment and Active Labor Act
  (EMTALA)
Enterprise master patient index (EMPI)
Family numbering
Format
History
Hybrid record
Incentive pay
Informed consent

Integrated health record
Interval history
Joint Commission
Licensure
Longitudinal health record
Master patient index (MPI)
Meaningful use
Medical transcription
Medicare
Medication administration record (MAR)
Microfilming
National Association for Home Care and Hospice (NAHC)
National Hospice and Palliative Care Organization (NHPCO)
Notice of Privacy Practices
Ongoing records review
Open-record review
Optical imaging technology
Outsourcing
Overlap
Overlay
Patient/member web portal
Personal health record (PHR)
Picture archiving communication system (PACS)
Point-of-care review
Principal diagnosis
Problem-oriented medical record
Progress notes
Qualitative analysis
Quantitative analysis
Queuing
Retention
Retention schedule
Scanning
Serial numbering system
Serial-unit numbering system
Source-oriented health record
Stop order
Straight numeric filing system
Telecommuting
Terminal-digit filing system
Transcription
Unique identifier
Unit numbering system
Universal chart order
Voice recognition technology

The patient health record is in the process of transitioning from a paper-based to an electronic format. Indeed, most healthcare facilities currently maintain their health records using a combination of the two formats (sometimes referred to as a hybrid health record system) in order to accommodate the many different ways in which patient information is provided. Today's health records include computer printouts as well as handwritten notes. A recent survey of the American

Hospital Association's most wired hospitals and health systems in the United States revealed that the majority of these facilities have a hybrid health record. Data now arrive via electronic transfer from computerized laboratory or radiological testing or examination, through direct voice entry into a word-processing system, and from provider wireless devices and handheld personal computers. But as this chapter describes, the paper-based health record is a long way from being obsolete. The momentum to move away from paper is increasing dramatically, but a fully operational electronic health record (EHR) for all types of healthcare providers and facilities remains a future goal for the healthcare system.

This chapter traces the evolution of the health record and describes the different kinds of information it contains and the different formats in which it is kept. The chapter also focuses on the health information management professional's role in managing patient information, from the creation and storage of information to its long-term retention and eventual destruction, and in ensuring its accuracy, completeness, and security. Finally, this chapter describes the functions of the master or enterprise patient index, which is critical for proper patient identification and record linkage.

Evolution of the Health Record

Historical Overview

The patient health record has evolved as medicine and medical technology have evolved. Once simply the notation of the patient's name and a brief description of his or her illness or injury, today's health record evolved into a detailed collection of handwritten entries, transcribed reports, electronic data, and digital images reflecting the contributions of numerous healthcare providers.

Health records have existed as long as there has been a need to communicate information about patient treatment. Archeological evidence indicates that maintaining information on patient care and treatment techniques is an ancient art.

Health records are maintained by all organizations that deliver healthcare services, including physician and provider offices, long-term care facilities, emergency clinics, rehabilitation facilities, home health agencies, behavioral health facilities, correctional institutions, and numerous types of delivery systems and organizations. Records vary depending on the type of facility. Healthcare records in acute-care hospitals, for example, require rapid documentation by many providers. Patients are often in the hospital for life-threatening injuries or conditions, and various healthcare practitioners access and record information in the patients' health records, on average, within a five-day time span. Records in non-acute-care hospital settings have much of the same content found in the acute-care settings. The records also contain specialized content to meet requirements related to those settings. Although format and content of the health record may differ among healthcare settings, all providers of care

must maintain information to meet patient care needs and to comply with relevant laws, standards, and regulations.

Today's health information management (HIM) professional is responsible for records that still contain paper and are maintained in a variety of formats other than paper. There is an increasing demand to share information among providers on a regional basis to improve continuity of care. The multiple formats of today's records are a challenge to the goal of uniform sharing of information. The skills of the HIM professionals are in great demand to ensure the quality of shared information.

Factors Influencing the Content of the Health Record

A variety of factors influence what is included in the health record and how it is formatted. In the physician office, for example, provider preference may influence what and how much data are collected about the patient. The process of providing healthcare is another factor. The healthcare provider must gather enough information to determine a diagnosis and to direct treatment. That data must then be structured in a way that is useful for all users of the record. For many settings, such as acute care, long term care, and home health, data sets have been developed that indicate what data elements should be found in records for that type of facility. Finally, there are accrediting and certifying bodies' external standards and regulations and state licensure standards, in additional to internal standards such as medical staff bylaws that outline requirements for content of the health record.

Documentation and Maintenance Standards for the Health Record

Health records provide proof of what has been done for the patient. As the complexity of care has evolved, so has the need for improved documentation. Standards for record documentation and maintenance have been established and are refined and revised constantly. These standards and regulations have a major impact on what is documented in the health record.

The American College of Surgeons and the Joint Commission

The **American College of Surgeons (ACS)** provided the impetus for standardizing health records when it developed minimum standards for hospitals early in the 20th century. It was evident to the ACS that standards were needed because candidates for membership were unable to produce proof of their experience with various types of surgical cases. Records were either nonexistent or of poor quality. The ACS Minimum Standard of 1917 included specific requirements for maintaining patient health records.

The **Joint Commission** is the successor organization to the ACS in the area of standardization. It assumed responsibility for the accreditation process in 1952 as a joint effort of the ACS, the American College of Physicians, the American Medical Association, and the American Hospital Association. Initially responsible for the accreditation of hospitals, the Joint Commission has since expanded its accreditation process to home health, long-term care, and other types of healthcare facilities.

The major source of information about the hospital or any healthcare facility is the health record. Joint Commission surveyors routinely review the health records of current patients to obtain knowledge about the facility's performance and process of care.

Medicare (CMS) Conditions of Participation

In 1965, the federal government passed legislation creating the **Medicare** program, which provides healthcare insurance coverage to Americans 65 years of age or older. Since then, the legislation has been expanded to cover persons disabled for two years as well as persons with chronic kidney disease. The Centers for Medicare and Medicaid Services (CMS) is the division of the federal Department of Health and Human Services responsible for developing and enforcing regulations regarding the participation of healthcare providers in the Medicare program.

The regulations for health record content and documentation were originally established in the **Conditions of Participation.** As health record documentation became increasingly important, CMS began to focus on reviewing it for medical necessity and compliance with the decision-making rules established by the federal government. In addition, CMS published guidelines for documenting histories and physical examinations and medical decision making that affect physician reimbursement.

State Licensure

Every state has certain **licensure** regulations that healthcare facilities must meet in order to remain in operation. Licensure regulations may include very specific requirements for the content, format, retention, and use of patient records. These regulations are established by state governments, usually under the direction of state departments of health.

Internal Standards

Bylaws, rules, and regulations are developed by the medical staff and approved by the board of trustees or governing body in healthcare facilities. In addition to describing the organization's manner of operation, bylaws outline the content of patient health records, identify the exact personnel who can enter information in health records, and may restate applicable Joint Commission and CMS requirements. In addition, bylaws describe the time limits for completing patient health records. External surveyors review the bylaws to ensure that healthcare facilities abide by their own established rules and regulations and that the bylaws

are in agreement with current standards and regulations. All medical staff personnel are required to abide by the approved bylaws. The HIM professional must be able to work effectively with the medical staff to ensure that they follow the medical staff bylaws and regulations and adhere to the many laws and regulations that specify the need for proper documentation.

Of great importance to the HIM professional is the adherence of individual medical staff members to bylaws related to completion of medical records and compliance with documentation guidelines and requirements. The HIM professional supports the patient care process by ensuring quality and timely documentation in the patient record. This also supports the patient safety and quality efforts of the facility. The typical medical staff bylaws contain provisions for timely and proper completion of medical records, including the requirements to write legibly or utilize the hospital information system to record patient notes; for communicating and coordinating the care of the patient with other members of the staff; and for dictating reports of history and physical examinations, operative notes, and other required documents based on best practices and facility policies. Failure to comply with any of the provisions of medical record documentation may result in progressive discipline up to and including suspension of medical staff membership. One common process is suspending admission privileges until the delinquent health records are completed. Suspension limits the ability of the practitioner or physician to schedule time in the operating room or admit patients. Hospitals typically have procedures to notify the admissions department, surgical care department, and other key hospital departments when a practitioner's privileges are suspended. Sometimes a suspended physician may ask his or her partners to admit patients for him or her. This can create patient care and safety issues for the patients and requires the HIM professional to become an active participant in the patient care team. This is a common situation that involves the HIM professional to provide access to the patient records and generate reports to look at the admission pattern changes to ensure that suspended physicians are following the suspension regulations set forth in the bylaws.

There is generally a medical staff committee responsible for health information management and patient record issues including electronic health records. Information about incomplete and delinquent medical records is typically reported by the director of the health information management department during committee meetings. Because of this, it is important that the HIM professional know the medical staff bylaws, Joint Commission standards, the Medicare and Medicaid Conditions of Participation, any state statutes, and other facility licensure requirements regarding the timely completion of medical records. Physicians and other practitioners may also face disciplinary actions for making inappropriate references to patients and staff in patient records or unacceptable documentation practices.

The Modern Health Record

The modern health record includes the contributions of numerous healthcare providers. In addition, it includes information provided by the patient or a person acting on his or her behalf describing the reasons for the patient's visit to the healthcare provider and other pertinent background facts. The modern health record is patient centered, meaning that the patient is the focus of all documentation of the activities that revolve around him or her while under the provider's care.

Definition of the Health Record

The health record must outline and justify the patient's treatment, support diagnosis of the patient's condition, describe the patient's progress and response to medications and services, and explain the outcomes of the care provided. The health record promotes continuity of care among all the providers who treat the patient by documenting all of the activities that revolve around the patient.

Functions of Health Records and Health Information

To providers, the health record is valuable as the principal source of information in determining care for the patient. To the healthcare facility, it is valuable as a primary source of information in determining the reimbursement for care.

The primary functions of the health record are as follows:

- Facilitate the ongoing care and treatment of individual patients
- Support clinical decision making and communication among clinicians
- Document the services provided to patients in support of reimbursement
- Provide information for the evaluation of the quality and efficacy of the care provided
- Provide information in support of medical research and education
- Help facilitate the operational management of the facility
- Provide information as required by local and national laws and regulations

Ongoing Care and Treatment of Individual Patients

The most important use of the health record is patient care, and the person to whom the record is of most value is the patient. When physicians were the only caregivers, they knew the patient and family and decided how detailed the patient's records needed to be. Often a small card or a ledger listing the patient's problem at a particular time was all the recordkeeping physicians needed. As healthcare has come to depend on technology and the skilled personnel to use it, health records have become more complex. Patients often have multiple caregivers. Providers cannot remember all the information provided by the available technology to a large number of patients, and fast access to past information about the patient's care is vital to the continuity of care.

Clinical Decision Making and Communication

Health information serves the vital function of allowing all the patient's providers to enter and analyze information and to make decisions. Each member of the healthcare team must have equal access to the information and can review what others are doing and communicate with them through the record. Thus, the health record is the healthcare team's primary reference and communication tool.

Reimbursement Including Meaningful Use

Information in the health record is used to document the services provided to the patient so that coding and payment for the care provided can be made by those responsible for creating the bill. Insurance companies, managed care organizations, and CMS require that specific information be submitted to support the bill and to prove that the care provided was medically necessary. The role of the patient record in reimbursement is becoming more complex with the recent **meaningful use** requirements, which can impact reimbursement. See chapter 2 for more information about meaningful use requirements.

Evaluation of the Quality and Efficacy of Care

The health record is used as a legal document to assess the quality of care rendered by the healthcare provider and serves as the legal business record of the organization. The documentation in the record provides information for accrediting and licensing activities. The content of the health record also provides evidence of compliance with evidence-based medicine guidelines.

Medical Research and Education

Data from many health records can be aggregated (combined) and analyzed for research studies and can provide statistical information on medical conditions and treatment modalities. As an example, public health agencies that need health information need data on certain diseases and conditions to develop prevention and control procedures as well as to monitor disease trends. Moreover, the information in health records serves to provide continuing education for students in a variety of health professions.

Operational Management

Information gathered from health records helps facilities plan for the future based on the types of patients and diagnoses treated. Aggregate statistical information provides data on the use of services, provider patterns, and other important issues. Management often uses the information to make comparisons with other facilities. Finally, the quality of information in the health record aids managerial decision making in terms of improving the quality of patient care.

Legal Purposes

The health record serves the legal interests of the patient, the provider, and the facility. It serves as evidence in legal cases addressing the treatment received by the patient or the extent of injuries. It serves to prove the patient's allegations in a malpractice case and also is used by the clinical provider and the facility to defend the care they provided the patient. The record is admissible as evidence in court under the business records provision because the documentation occurs routinely as part of the healthcare facility's daily operation. This is one of the roles of the HIM professional as the custodian of the health record. More information about the role of the record custodian and the admissibility of health records in legal proceedings is found in chapter 12.

The health record itself is the property of the healthcare facility. However, the patient has the right to be informed about the use of his or her protected health information (PHI). Federal Health Insurance Portability and Accountability Act (HIPAA) regulations require that the patient be notified of the uses of PHI through the Notice of Privacy Practices.

The Longitudinal Health Record

The **longitudinal health record** is a record compiled about an individual that contains encounter records from various encounters and from numerous healthcare delivery settings. It is valuable because all the information about a patient is maintained and accessible. It serves as a reference of past history and helps the provider avoid repetition of details and duplication of testing for the same conditions. Moreover, the longitudinal health record helps to prevent medical errors because information on allergies, drug interactions, surgeries, and past medical problems can be made available before treatment decisions are made. The physician can review the details of a patient's care and retrieve information needed at a later date.

A longitudinal health record is difficult to achieve in a paper-based record system because the patient typically has records at a variety of provider locations, such as physician offices, clinics, and hospitals, each of which often has a totally separate record system. The different records are not linked, making it difficult to access all needed patient information. Hybrid records do not improve this access issue as they are generally flat, text files and cannot be integrated into other healthcare provider systems. A longitudinal electronic health record would be especially valuable because it would allow information to be accessed from different locations. Many efforts are presently under way to develop the capability to share patient information electronically in order to improve quality, safety, and continuity of care including the use of personal health records (PHRs).

Responsibility for Quality Documentation

The provider of care is responsible for ensuring that entries made in the record are of high quality. Although the facility's medical staff bylaws establish the rules and regulations for record content, the individual care providers are ultimately responsible for the quality of entries they make and authenticate. Figure 10.1 presents general documentation guidelines that every provider who writes or enters information in the patient health record should follow.

The quality of provider entries includes legibility. If an entry cannot be read, it must be assumed that it cannot be or was not used in the patient care process.

Figure 10.1.   Guidelines for documenting and maintaining the patient health record

These guidelines are considered standard or typical health information practices. Individual facilities develop their own policies based on institutional needs and laws and regulations.

1. All entries in the health record must be authenticated to identify the author (name and professional status) and dated.

2. All entries in the paper health record should be in ink. Photocopying or scanning should be considered when colored ink or colored forms are used because some colors do not reproduce well.

3. No erasures or deletions should be made in the health record.

4. If a correction must be made in a paper health record, one line should be neatly drawn through the error, leaving the incorrect material legible. The error then should be initialed and dated so that it is obvious that it is a corrected mistake.

5. The original report should always be maintained in the health record. Cumulative laboratory reports or computerized nursing notes may be replaced with the latest cumulative report. Faxed copies of admission orders and histories and physicals may be used as originals in the record. The usual signature requirements should be followed.

6. Blank spaces should not be left in progress and nursing notes. If blanks are left, they should be marked out with an X so that additional information cannot be inserted on the paper out of proper date sequence.

7. All blanks on forms should be completed, especially on consent forms.

8. When health records are filed incomplete (as directed by medical staff or health record committee policy), a statement should be attached to indicate that this is the case. The statement should be signed by the chief of staff or chair of the health record committee as specified in the policy.

9. Chart folder labeling, dotting, or other methods of identifying at a glance a particular type of patient, such as one with a drug or alcohol diagnosis or HIV-positive status, should be discouraged to prevent inadvertent breaches of patient confidentiality.

The HIM professional is responsible for ensuring that providers understand the regulations and standards for proper documentation and for educating providers as changes occur. He or she should be involved in training residents and others who enter information so that standards are maintained and the record remains in its proper format.

The facility's administration is responsible for providing the equipment and support personnel to assist physicians in proper documentation. For HIM services, this includes computers, dictation and transcription equipment and services, as well as HIM staff members who assist in creating a high-quality record for accurate coding and billing for the facility's reimbursement.

Except in facilities owned by individuals or the government, a board of trustees or governing board has ultimate legal responsibility for the quality of care rendered in the facility. However, responsibility for patient care decisions and documentation of these decisions is delegated to the physician responsible for the patient. This is discussed more in chapter 12.

Check Your Understanding 10.1

Instructions: Answer the following questions on a separate sheet of paper.

1. What is the primary purpose of patient health information?

2. What are six other purposes or uses of patient health information?

3. What factors influence the content of the health record?

4. What is the role of each of the following in the development of standards for health information: Joint Commission, Centers for Medicare and Medicaid Services, state licensure, and medical staff bylaws?

5. Why is a longitudinal health record valuable, and why is a longitudinal health record in a hybrid system difficult to achieve?

6. Who is responsible for ensuring the quality of health record documentation?

Content of the Health Record

All health records contain information that can be classified into two broad categories: administrative and demographic data and clinical data. All health record entries must be legible, complete, dated, and authenticated according to the healthcare organization's policies. Health records may be paper based, electronic, or hybrid (a combination of formats). As health records evolve from paper to electronic and imaging formats, the term **hybrid record** is used to describe the record information format that includes both paper-based and electronic health information. Because the hospital record is the most complex in content, it will be used in describing the content of the record.

Administrative and Demographic Information

Administrative and demographic information is generally found on the front page of the paper health record and on the login screen in an EHR. The information entered provides facts that identify the patient and data related to payment and reimbursement and other operational needs of the healthcare facility. This information is entered into the system by administrative staff when the patient presents for care or may be entered electronically by the patient or staff from a physician's office.

Demographic Data

Demographic data represent one type of **administrative information.**

Demographic information includes facts such as

- Patient's name
- Patient's address
- Patient's telephone number
- Patient's date of birth
- Patient's next of kin
- Other identifying information specific to the patient

Demographic data are collected prior to, or at the time of, admission or treatment at a healthcare facility. This is the first information the facility collects. Demographic information may be entered directly into the computer by admission or registration personnel. In cases where the patient is coming to the facility for elective, or voluntary, treatment or an operative procedure, he or she can provide this information prior to arrival at the facility. The patient usually provides the information directly, but in cases where the patient is a minor or is incapacitated or in an emergency situation, another individual may provide the information. In such cases, the record must state the name and relationship of the person providing the information in case the information has to be verified or amended. The demographic information in a totally paper-based health record environment is usually on the first page, which is called the face sheet or front sheet. This information is often found on the initial computer screen in facilities that have EHRs.

Payment information also is part of the administrative information. In addition, administrative information includes the various **consents** for treatment and the use of patient information, notification of patient rights, and other nonclinical information.

A **unique identifier** number is assigned to each health record which is often called the medical record number. More information about medical record number assignment is covered later in this chapter. Facilities use the unique identifier to ensure that all information about the patient is entered in the correct record and that the correct record is accessed when a query is entered into the computer system. Demographic information helps to specifically identify the patient and can be aggregated from many patients to provide statistical information that is vital for planning, research, statistics, and other needs.

Consent to Treatment

Through the consent process, the patient agrees to undergo the treatments and procedures to be performed by clinical caregivers. A general consent is often part of the admission or intake process into the healthcare facility and allows the facility to provide routine care. However, this general consent does not replace the individual consent forms the patient must complete and sign for each operation or special procedure to indicate that he or she is fully informed about the care to be provided. Written consents signed by the patient for experimental drugs and treatment and for participation in research also must be included in the health record. Refusal of treatment or procedures likewise must be written to ensure that the consequences of the decision to refuse treatment have been explained and the patient is aware of them.

Consent to Use or Disclose Protected Health Record Information

Under HIPAA, at the time of admission to the facility or prior to treatment by the provider, patients must be informed about the use of individually identifiable health information. This **Notice of Privacy Practices** must explain and give examples of the uses of the patient's health information for treatment, payment, and healthcare operations, as well as other disclosures for purposes established in the regulations. If a particular use of information is not covered in the Notice of Privacy Practices, the patient must sign an **authorization** form specific to the additional disclosure before his or her information can be released. (See figure A.21 in appendix A.) HIPAA and the Privacy Rule are discussed in chapter 12.

Consent to Special Procedures

In cases where the patient is coming to the facility for a specific procedure, an **informed consent** spelling out the exact details of the treatment must be signed by the patient or his or her legally authorized representative. This consent must show that the patient, or the person authorized to act for the patient, understands exactly what the procedure, test, or operation is going to be, including any possible risks, alternative methods, and outcomes.

Advance Directives

An **advance directive** is a written document, such as a living will, that states the patient's preferences for care in the event that the patient's condition prevents him or her from making care decisions. It also can be in the form of a durable power of attorney for healthcare in which the patient names another person to make medical decisions on his or her behalf in the event he or she is incapacitated. When the patient has a written advance directive, its existence must be noted in the health

record. Patients or family members may bring the document to the facility to show the patient's wishes in case of terminal disease, traumatic injury, or cardiac arrest. The advance directive can be included as a part of the health record, although its inclusion may not be required. Rather than a formal written document, there may be documentation by the physician outlining the discussion with the patient or the family about the patient's wishes. Patients must be informed that they have the right to have an advance directive. Further, they must be notified of the provider's policies regarding its refusal to comply with advance directives. Caring Connections (2005) is a program of the National Hospice and Palliative Care Organization and provides links to information about advance directives in each state available at http://www.caringinfo.org/i4a/pages/index.cfm?pageid=3289. This information is helpful for HIM professionals since legal processes and procedures are primarily dictated by state law.

A **durable power of attorney** for healthcare is a document that names someone to make decisions for the patient if the patient is unable to make these decisions. This person is often called a proxy or a healthcare agent and may be a provider, a family member, or a friend of the patient. The advance directive goes into effect when the physician determines the patient is no longer able to communicate about healthcare decisions.

Acknowledgment of Receipt of Patient's Rights Statement

CMS requires that Medicare patients be informed of their rights, including the right to know who is treating them, the right to confidentiality, the right to determine what visitors the patient wants to have, and the right to be informed about treatment. The patient's rights statement also must explain the patient's right to refuse treatment, to participate in care planning, and to be safe from abuse. The patient must sign a statement that these rights have been explained, and the signed statement must be made part of the health record. States often have laws and regulations regarding which rights must be explained to patients, such as the right to privacy in treatment, to refuse treatment, and to refuse experimental treatments and drugs.

Property and Valuables List

Although facilities encourage patients to leave jewelry and other valuables at home, patients often will have clothing, dentures, eyeglasses, hearing aids, and other personal articles. Patients may be asked to list these items and sign a release of responsibility form to absolve the facility of responsibility for loss or damage to their personal property. This form then becomes part of the patient health record.

Clinical Data

Clinical data include information related to the patient's condition, course of treatment, and progress. The patient health record includes mainly clinical data.

Medical History

The **history** is a summary of the patient's illness from his or her point of view. Its purpose is to allow the patient or his or her authorized representative to give the physician as much background information about the patient's illness as possible.

Documentation guidelines for histories and physical examinations and medical decision making published by CMS affect physician reimbursement and are discussed further in chapter 16.

Components of the Medical History

The medical history has several components, including the following:

- *Chief complaint (CC):* Told in the patient's own words (or those of the patient's representative), the chief complaint is the principal reason the patient is seeking care.
- *Present illness or history of present illness (HPI):* This component addresses what the patient feels the problem is and includes a brief description of the duration, location, and circumstances of the complaint.
- *Past medical history:* This section consists of questions designed to gather information about past surgeries and other illnesses that might have a bearing on the patient's current illness. The physician asks about childhood and adult illnesses, operations, injuries, drug sensitivities, allergies, and other health problems.
- *Social and personal history:* The social history uncovers information about habits and living conditions that might have a bearing on the patient's illness, such as marital status, occupation, environment, and so on. Consumption of alcohol or tobacco products also may affect a patient's health, and information about these habits is included in the social history. This section also should address the patient's psychosocial needs.
- *Family medical history:* The questions in this component allow the physician to learn whether the patient's family members have conditions that might be considered genetic. Common questions concern cardiovascular diseases or conditions, renal diseases, history of cancer or diabetes, allergies, health of immediate relatives, and ages of relatives at death and causes of their deaths.
- *Review of systems (ROS):* This component consists of questions designed to cue the patient to reveal symptoms he or she may have forgotten, did not think were important, or neglected to mention when providing the historical information.

It is important that the person recording the history document whether the information was given by the patient or by another person in cases where the patient is unable to communicate.

Physical Examination

The physical examination is the actual comprehensive assessment of the patient's physical condition through examination and inspection of the patient's body by the physician. The physician usually tailors the physical examination to symptoms described in the patient's history and begins an assessment. The end of the physical examination should include the impression, which is a list of the patient's problems based on the information obtained. Thus, the history and physical (H&P) provide a base on which the physician can develop an initial plan of care. Appropriate treatment can then begin.

Components of the Physical Examination

The physical examination is conducted by observing the patient, palpating or touching the patient, tapping the thoracic and abdominal cavities, listening to breath and heart sounds, and taking the blood pressure. In a comprehensive physical examination, each body system of the patient is examined thoroughly. If the patient is admitted for a particular procedure, a more focused physical examination may take place.

Time Frame of the History and Physical Examination

The facility must have a policy that establishes a time frame for completing the history and physical. Most facilities set the time frame as within the first 24 hours following admission and require that the history and physical be completed by the provider who is admitting the patient. CMS requires that the history and physical examination be completed no more than 30 days before or 24 hours after admission and the report must be placed in the record within 24 hours after admission. If the history and physical have been completed within the 30 days prior to admission, there must be an updated entry in the medical record that documents an examination for any changes in the patient's condition since the original history and physical examination, and this entry must be included in the record within the first 24 hours of admission. This is called an **interval history.** CMS rules specify that the history and physical examination be completed by the physician or another qualified individual who has medical staff privileges in accordance with state law and hospital policy. State licensure laws vary on the acceptable time frame for completion of the history and physical.

The Joint Commission requires the history and physical examination to be recorded and made part of the patient health record prior to any operative procedure. When the physician chooses to dictate the history and physical, the dictated report must be transcribed and attached to the chart before the procedure. When the report is dictated but not transcribed, a written preoperative note covering the history and physical is acceptable only in an emergency. The physician must write an explanation of the emergency circumstances (Joint Commission 2011).

The HIM professional is responsible for ensuring that the most stringent time requirements are followed so that the facility is in **compliance** with state and federal laws and regulations, licensure standards, CMS Conditions of Participation, and accreditation requirements for the specific type of facility. Table 10.1 lists the information usually included in a complete medical history, and table 10.2 shows the information usually documented in the report of a physical examination.

Diagnostic and Therapeutic Orders

Physicians' orders direct the healthcare team. Orders may be for treatments, ancillary medical services, laboratory tests, radiological procedures, medications, devices, related materials, restraint, or seclusion. Orders change according to the patient's needs and responses to previous treatment. In the case of medications, the physician orders a specific drug in a particular dosage stating how often the drug is to be given,

Table 10.1.   Information usually included in a complete medical history

Components of the History	Complaints and Symptoms
Chief complaint	Nature and duration of the symptoms that caused the patient to seek medical attention as stated in his or her own words
Present illness	Detailed chronological description of the development of the patient's illness, from the appearance of the first symptom to the present situation
Past medical history	Summary of childhood and adult illnesses and conditions, such as infectious diseases, pregnancies, allergies and drug sensitivities, accidents, operations, hospitalizations, and current medications
Social and personal history	Marital status; dietary, sleep, and exercise patterns; use of coffee, tobacco, alcohol, and other drugs; occupation; home environment; daily routine; and so on
Family medical history	Diseases among relatives in which heredity or contact might play a role, such as allergies, cancer, and infectious, psychiatric, metabolic, endocrine, cardiovascular, and renal diseases; health status or cause of and age at death for immediate relatives
Review of systems	Systemic inventory designed to uncover current or past subjective symptoms that includes the following types of data: • *General:* Usual weight, recent weight changes, fever, weakness, fatigue • *Skin:* Rashes, eruptions, dryness, cyanosis, jaundice; changes in skin, hair, or nails • *Head:* Headache (duration, severity, character, location) • *Eyes:* Glasses or contact lenses, last eye examination, glaucoma, cataracts, eyestrain, pain, diplopia, redness, lacrimation, inflammation, blurring • *Ears:* Hearing, discharge, tinnitus, dizziness, pain • *Nose:* Head colds, epistaxis, discharges, obstruction, postnasal drip, sinus pain • *Mouth and throat:* Condition of teeth and gums, last dental examination, soreness, redness, hoarseness, difficulty in swallowing • *Respiratory system:* Chest pain, wheezing, cough, dyspnea, sputum (color and quantity), hemoptysis, asthma, bronchitis, emphysema, pneumonia, tuberculosis, pleurisy, last chest x-ray • *Neurological system:* Fainting, blackouts, seizures, paralysis, tingling, tremors, memory loss • *Musculoskeletal system:* Joint pain or stiffness, arthritis, gout, backache, muscle pain, cramps, swelling, redness, limitation in motor activity • *Cardiovascular system:* Chest pain, rheumatic fever, tachycardia, palpitation, high blood pressure, edema, vertigo, faintness, varicose veins, thrombophlebitis • *Gastrointestinal system:* Appetite, thirst, nausea, vomiting, hematemesis, rectal bleeding, change in bowel habits, diarrhea, constipation, indigestion, food intolerance, flatus, hemorrhoids, jaundice • *Urinary system:* Frequent or painful urination, nocturia, pyuria, hematuria, incontinence, urinary infections • *Genitoreproductive system:* Male—venereal disease, sores, discharge from penis, hernias, testicular pain, or masses; female—age at menarche, frequency and duration of menstruation, dysmenorrhea, menorrhagia, symptoms of menopause, contraception, pregnancies, deliveries, abortions, last Pap smear • *Endocrine system:* Thyroid disease; heat or cold intolerance; excessive sweating, thirst, hunger, or urination • *Hematologic system:* Anemia, easy bruising or bleeding, past transfusions • *Psychiatric disorders:* Insomnia, headache, nightmares, personality disorders, anxiety disorders, mood disorders

Table 10.2.   Information usually documented in the report of a physical examination

Report Components	Content
General condition	Apparent state of health, signs of distress, posture, weight, height, skin color, dress and personal hygiene, facial expression, manner, mood, state of awareness, speech
Vital signs	Pulse, respiration, blood pressure, temperature
Skin	Color, vascularity, lesions, edema, moisture, temperature, texture, thickness, mobility and turgor, nails
Head	Hair, scalp, skull, face
Eyes	Visual acuity and fields; position and alignment of the eyes, eyebrows, eyelids; lacrimal apparatus; conjunctivae; sclerae; corneas; irises; size, shape, equality, reaction to light, and accommodation of pupils; extraocular movements; ophthalmoscopic exam
Ears	Auricles, canals, tympanic membranes, hearing, discharge
Nose and sinuses	Airways, mucosa, septum, sinus tenderness, discharge, bleeding, smell
Mouth	Breath, lips, teeth, gums, tongue, salivary ducts
Throat	Tonsils, pharynx, palate, uvula, postnasal drip
Neck	Stiffness, thyroid, trachea, vessels, lymph nodes, salivary glands
Thorax, anterior	Shape, symmetry, respiration and posterior
Breasts	Masses, tenderness, discharge from nipples
Lungs	Fremitus, breath sounds, adventitious sounds, friction, spoken voice, whispered voice
Heart	Location and quality of apical impulse, trill, pulsation, rhythm, sounds, murmurs, friction rub, jugular venous pressure and pulse, carotid artery pulse
Abdomen	Contour, peristalsis, scars, rigidity, tenderness, spasm, masses, fluid, hernia, bowel sounds and bruits, palpable organs
Male genitourinary	Scars, lesions, discharge, penis, scrotum, organs epididymis, varicocele, hydrocele
Female reproductive	External genitalia, Skene's glands and organs Bartholin's glands, vagina, cervix, uterus, adnexa
Rectum	Fissure, fistula, hemorrhoids, sphincter tone, masses, prostate, seminal vesicles, feces
Musculoskeletal	Spine and extremities, deformities, swelling, system redness, tenderness, range of motion
Lymphatics	Palpable cervical, axillary, inguinal nodes; location; size; consistency; mobility and tenderness
Blood vessels	Pulses, color, temperature, vessel walls, veins
Neurological system	Cranial nerves, coordination, reflexes, biceps, triceps, patellar, Achilles, abdominal, cremasteric, Babinski, Romberg, gait, sensory, vibratory
Diagnosis(es)	

by what means (orally, intravenously, or by other method), and for how long.

Orders for tests and services must demonstrate the medical necessity and explain the reason for the order. This explanation is required because payers may not reimburse the facility if the reason for the test or treatment is not properly documented.

The legibility of orders is important to ensure that they are clearly understood by the personnel who must carry them out. Some facilities use a **computerized provider order entry (CPOE) system** for providers to directly enter their orders.

Clinicians Authorized to Give and Receive Orders

Orders must be written by the physician or verbally communicated to persons authorized to receive and record verbal orders either in person or by telephone. For verbal orders, the person accepting the order should record the order, sign it and give his or her title, such as RN, PT, LPN, as appropriate. In some states, certified registered nurse practitioners and physician assistants are allowed to write or give verbal orders (AHIMA 2009).

Medical staff policies and procedures must specifically state the categories of personnel authorized to accept orders. Verbal orders for medication are usually required to be given to, and to be accepted only by, nursing or pharmacy personnel. Some categories of personnel that may accept verbal or oral orders for services within the specific area of practice include physical therapists, registered nurse anesthetists, dietitians, and medical technologists.

The time the order was given should be in writing. Some facilities do not allow verbal orders for treatments or procedures that might put the patient at risk. The Joint Commission requires verbal orders to be repeated by the person accepting them to verify that they are clearly understood.

Signatures on Orders

Generally, orders must be dated and authenticated manually or electronically by the treating provider or providers responsible for the patient's care who either wrote or gave the orders. In the case of verbal or telephone orders, the provider should sign them as soon as possible after giving them. Many facilities require the ordering provider to indicate that the telephone orders are accurate, complete, and final by authenticating them in writing or electronically within 24 hours. The timing requirements for signatures on orders are governed by state law, facility policy, accreditation standards, and government regulations and may vary from facility to facility.

For years, HIM department personnel carefully reviewed each order and marked those with missing signatures so that each could be individually signed by the responsible provider after discharge. However, signing orders after discharge does not affect the patient's care process or assist in correcting errors in the orders before they are carried out, so many facilities no longer routinely review orders for signature following patient discharge. A review of orders is part of the concurrent or **open-record review** process; thus, orders can be signed in a timely manner, and providers with patterns of unsigned orders can be detected. A comparison of orders to laboratory and other ancillary reports and to nursing documentation is another way to ensure that all orders are carried out.

Some facilities are developing standing, or standard, orders for certain procedures that all physicians can use when performing the particular procedure. Other facilities require an additional order to implement the standing orders, and still others allow a registered nurse to initiate the standing orders because the medical staff has previously approved them.

CMS regulations allow verbal (telephone or oral) orders to be signed by another provider responsible for the patient's care even if the order did not originate with that provider. The CMS rules retain the current requirements that the use of verbal orders should be infrequent and used only when the orders cannot be written or given electronically. The CMS regulations further state that verbal orders must only be accepted by persons authorized by hospital policies and procedures and state and federal law.

Special Types of Orders

Certain categories of medications, such as narcotics and sedatives, have an automatic time limit or **stop order.** This means that these medications will be discontinued unless the physician gives a specific order to continue the medication. This method prevents patients from receiving drugs for a longer period of time than is necessary.

Do not resuscitate (DNR) orders must contain documentation that the decision to withhold cardiopulmonary resuscitation (CPR) was discussed, when the decision was made, and who participated in the decision. This discussion is often documented in the **progress notes.** Generally,

patients are presumed to have consented to CPR unless a DNR order is present in the record. Do not resuscitate orders may be part of the advance directives in the record.

Orders for seclusion and restraint, including drugs used for restraint, must comply with facility policies and CMS regulations, state laws, and Joint Commission requirements. These should never be standing or as-needed orders; instead, such drugs must be ordered only when necessary to protect the patient or others from injury or harm. Specific time limits for these orders must be followed, and there must be continuous oversight of the patient under restraint or seclusion.

Discharge Orders

Discharge orders for hospital patients must be in writing and can only be issued by a physician. When a patient leaves against medical advice, this fact should be noted in lieu of a discharge order because the patient was not actually discharged. In the case of death, some facilities require that a discharge to the morgue order be written.

Clinical Observations

Clinical observations of the patient are documented in the health record in several areas, including progress notes, consultation reports, and ancillary notes, as described here.

Medical Services

Progress Notes

Progress notes are chronological statements about the patient's response to treatment during his or her stay in the facility. Facility procedures and policies must state exactly what categories of personnel are allowed to write or enter information into progress notes. Generally, these personnel include physicians, nurses, physical therapists, occupational therapists, respiratory therapists, social workers, case managers, registered dietitians (RDs), nurse anesthetists, pharmacists, radiologic technologists, speech therapists, and others providing direct treatment or consultation to the patient. Each person authorized to enter documentation into the progress notes must write or enter his or her own note, authenticate and date it, and indicate authorship by signing his or her full name and title. In some facilities, various practitioners record progress notes on a common form (integrated progress notes) while in other record formats there may be separate sections for physician, nursing, and therapy progress notes.

Each progress note should include changes in the patient's condition, findings based on the facts of the case, test results, and response to treatment, as well as an analysis of the findings. The final part of the note contains the decisions or actions planned for future care. When writing in a paper patient record, providers must avoid leaving blank spaces between progress notes to prevent information from being added out of sequence.

Flowcharts are another effective way to illustrate the patient's progress and can be computerized to demonstrate progress or to keep track of certain data. Many physicians and other providers use mobile devices to maintain ongoing flowchart information about patients, such as blood glucose levels over time.

The patient's condition dictates how often progress notes are recorded, and the frequency is generally established by the healthcare facility or payers of care. In a hospital, the physician primarily responsible for the patient's care is often required to write a progress note daily. Doing so shows the physician's involvement and that he or she is aware of changes in the patient's condition.

Consultation Reports

Consultations are opinions of specialists. If the attending physician requests that a specialist see the patient, the specialist prepares a consultation report, which is included in the health record. Each consultant is responsible for writing, dictating, or entering his or her own report. The report should show evidence of the consultant's review of the record; examination of the patient; and any pertinent findings, opinions, and recommendations. Moreover, the documentation should show that the physician requesting the consultation reviewed the report. Not all patients receive consultations, so a consultation report is not found in every health record.

Nursing Services

Nursing personnel have the most frequent contact with patients, and their notes provide the complete record of the patients' progress and condition and demonstrate the continuity of care. Licensed registered nurses, licensed practical nurses (sometimes called licensed vocational nurses), and nursing assistants record the patient's vital signs and facts of the physician's orders being carried out, observe the patient's response to treatment interventions, nursing interventions, describe the patient's condition and complaints as well as the outcome of care as reflected in the patient's status at discharge or termination of treatment. The method most commonly used by nurses to enter notes is detailed narrative documentation.

Nursing personnel begin recording information in the health record when the patient is admitted to the facility. They coordinate the patient's care to ensure that orders are carried out. The initial nursing assessment must summarize the date, time, and method of admission; the patient's condition, symptoms, and vital signs; and other information. Nurses may use a variation of the SOAP (subjective, objective, assessment, and plan) notes from the **problem-oriented medical record** format (discussed later in this chapter) when recording notes. All nursing notes must be signed by the individuals who provided the service or observed the patient's condition. Full names and titles are required with each entry.

Charting by exception, or focus charting, is a method of documenting only abnormal or unusual findings or deviations from the prescribed plan of care. A complete patient assessment is performed every shift or every eight hours.

When events differ from the assessment or the expected norm for a particular patient, the notes should focus on that particular event and include the data, assessment, intervention, and response. Flow sheets and care plans may be used to illustrate changes in the patient's condition. The purpose of charting by exception is to reduce repetitive recordkeeping and documentation of normal events. Bedside terminals and direct input of monitoring information and other computerization of nursing observations and medication distribution save nurses a great deal of time because information does not have to be rewritten numerous times.

Medication records (also called **medication administration records** or **MARs**) are maintained by nursing staff for all patients and include medications given, time, form of administration, and dosage and strength. The records are updated each time the patient is given his or her medication. The health record must reflect when a medication is given in error, indicating what was done about it and the patient's response. Adverse drug reactions must be fully documented and reported to the provider and to the performance improvement or risk management program according to guidelines established by the facility.

Flow sheets are often used in addition to narrative notes for intake and output records showing how much fluid the patient consumed and how much was eliminated. In addition, blood glucose records are often flowcharted for ease of comparison. Degree of pain is another aspect of the patient's condition that is commonly flowcharted.

Nurses are responsible for maintaining records of patient transfers (to surgery, to another room, or to another level of care) as well as visits to physician or treatment offices and other locations outside the facility.

Case managers are nurses, social workers, or other personnel who are responsible for assisting the patient through the care process. The case management process improves quality of care because care is scheduled in an orderly way and fragmentation is reduced. Hospitals, managed care organizations, and other facilities use case managers to improve coordination of care, scheduling, and discharge planning. Many facilities use predetermined **care paths** that are specific to diagnoses or conditions; case managers ensure that patients receive care according to the care path. Care paths are also called clinical pathways, critical paths, and clinical algorithms.

Ancillary Services

Laboratory and radiology reports and reports from other ancillary services, such as electrocardiographs (EKGs) and electroencephalographs (EEGs), must be signed by the physician responsible for the interpretations. A pathologist is responsible for the work of the pathology laboratory; a radiologist is responsible for the work of the radiology department. The typed interpretations of the radiology or other reports become part of the health record and are kept as long as the health records are kept. Images may be part of a computerized **picture archiving communication system (PACS).**

The laboratory conducts tests on blood, urine, sputum, and other body fluids. Many specialized tests are performed in the laboratory to provide information that the physician can use to make a diagnosis, including analyses of specimens removed during surgery. Laboratory results in a computerized environment are available to the provider as soon as they are entered into the computer. In most facilities, a laboratory summary of computerized results is generated consistently throughout the patient's stay, with a final summary completed after discharge. In paper-based and hybrid records, these multipage summaries are printed and made part of the patient health record. Some facilities use manually completed laboratory forms divided into an original and several copies. The original report is the one that should be included in the record. Most facilities require the original laboratory report to be placed in the health record within 24 hours. In many hybrid systems, this information is **computer output to laser disk (COLD)**-fed into the hospital information system rather than being kept as a printout in the final record. HIM personnel must ensure all COLD-fed reports come from the source of the primary system into the system that maintains the legal health record. This transfer of data may require interfaces and requires oversight to ensure the information becomes part of the permanent record.

Healthcare facility policies and procedures must state that the practitioner approved by the medical staff to interpret diagnostic procedures, such as nuclear medicine procedures, MRIs, EEGs, and EKGs, should sign and date his or her interpretations. The interpretations then become part of the health record. Scans and videotapes, tracings, or other actual recordings are often COLD-fed directly into the hospital information system. Providers may view such recordings, but the recordings do not become part of the permanent record. It is important that all tests or procedures ordered have corresponding reports in the health record.

Orders and records of services rendered to patients from rehabilitation, physical therapy, occupational therapy, audiology, or speech pathology should be included in the record, as appropriate to the patient's condition. These reports must contain evaluations, recommendations, goals, course of treatment, and response to treatment. Nutritional care plans need to be developed in compliance with a physician order, and information on nutrition and diet should be included in the discharge plan and transfer orders.

Surgical Services

The operative section of the health record includes the anesthesia record, the intraoperative record, and the recovery record. The history and physical examination, informed consents signed by the patient or his or her authorized representative, and the postoperative progress note also are part of the documentation about the operative procedure. Every patient's record must include a complete history and physical examination prior to any surgery or invasive procedure unless there is an emergency. When the history and physical report is dictated, it must be included in the record.

Moreover, the anesthesiologist or the certified registered nurse anesthetist must write a preanesthesia evaluation or an updated evaluation prior to surgery. This evaluation must cover information on the anesthesia to be used, risk factors, allergy and drug history, potential problems, and a general assessment of the patient's condition. An intraoperative anesthesia record must be maintained of all events during surgery, including complete information on the anesthesia administration, blood pressure, pulse, respiration, and other monitors of the patient's condition. Finally, after surgery, the appropriate anesthesia personnel must write a postoperative anesthesia follow-up report including any anesthetic complications. Outpatient surgical cases also must include postanesthesia evaluations. CMS regulations state that any individual qualified to administer anesthesia can complete the postanesthesia evaluation rather than limiting the postanesthesia documentation completion to the individual who actually administered the patient's anesthesia.

The operative report itself must be written or dictated by the surgeon immediately after surgery and must include the names of the surgeon and assistants, technical procedures performed, findings, specimens removed, estimated blood loss, and postoperative diagnosis. The surgeon must enter a brief operative progress note in the record immediately after surgery before the patient leaves the operating suite to enable follow-up care. Most facilities have dictation areas near the operative suite or cardiac catheterization laboratories to allow surgeons to dictate the operative reports immediately. However, the written postoperative progress note must be completed to provide information for patient care until the transcribed report is placed in the patient record, usually 12 to 24 hours after surgery. The postoperative progress notes and the dictation and transcription of operative reports must be carefully monitored to ensure that this documentation is placed in the health record in a timely manner.

Pathology reports are required for cases in which a surgical specimen is removed or expelled during a procedure. The medical staff and a pathologist must decide which specimens require both a microscopic and macroscopic (gross or with the naked eye) evaluation of the tissue and which require a gross examination only. These reports are part of the operative section of the health record and must be signed by the pathologist. The preoperative diagnosis and pathological diagnosis can then be compared for quality-of-care purposes.

Information on the patient's discharge from the postoperative or postanesthesia care unit must be documented and signed by the licensed independent practitioner responsible for the discharge or by the provider verifying that the patient is ready for discharge according to specific discharge criteria.

The operative section also will contain data on implants, including product numbers, and additional information for follow-up.

Organ Transplantation

CMS requires hospitals to inform families of the opportunity to donate organs, tissues, or eyes. All patients meeting the United

Network of Organ Sharing (UNOS) criteria must be evaluated and the documentation must be part of the health record. Facilities participating in the transplant program are required to share patient information and provide access to health records to representatives of approved organ procurement organizations (OPOs). Documentation showing that the organ procurement organization has been notified regarding a patient near death must be included in the health record so that anatomical gifts can be preserved and used. Sample forms and other information are available on the UNOS website (UNOS 2012).

Conclusions at Termination of Care

At the time of discharge, the physician must summarize the patient's condition at the beginning of treatment and basic information about tests, examinations, procedures, and results occurring during treatment. This conclusion at termination of care is called the discharge summary.

Discharge Summary

The **discharge summary,** also called the clinical resume, provides details about the patient's stay while in the facility and is the foundation for future treatment. It is prepared when the patient is discharged or transferred to another facility or when the patient expires. The summary states the patient's reason for admission and gives a brief history explaining why he or she needed to be hospitalized. Pertinent laboratory, x-ray, consultation, and other significant findings, as well as the patient's response to treatment or procedures, are included. In addition to a description of the patient's condition at discharge, the discharge summary delineates specific instructions given to the patient or family for future care, including information on medications, referrals to other providers, diet, activities, follow-up visits to the physician, and the patient's final diagnoses. The discharge summary must be authenticated and dated by the physician.

Some facilities require the final diagnoses to be recorded and the discharge summary to be dictated or written at the time of discharge. The information in the discharge summary is extremely important to meet the facility's coding, billing, and reimbursement needs as well as the needs of providers of follow-up care. In some facilities, a paper discharge summary form with an outline of contents is used to ensure that all items are included. A copy of the discharge form, including follow-up instructions, should be provided to the patient or caregivers at discharge.

When a patient expires in the hospital, the facility often requires the physician who pronounced death to write a note that gives the time and date of death. The death note is in addition to the discharge summary, required in all death cases no matter how long the patient was in the facility. In some cases nurses are allowed to declare a patient dead and subsequently complete the necessary documentation.

A discharge summary is not typically required for patients who are in the hospital for 48 hours or less. Such patients usually have a short-stay or short-service record. This one-page form can be used to record the history and physical examination, the operative report, the discharge summary, and discharge instructions. A final discharge progress note may also suffice in these cases to provide a summary of the hospitalization at the patient's discharge. When the patient dies 48 hours or less after admission, the short-stay record is insufficient and a complete discharge summary must be prepared. Also, most facilities do not require a discharge summary for normal newborns and obstetrical cases without complications, as long as there is a final progress note.

Typically, the discharge summary must be completed within 30 days after discharge; however, facility policy may require a quicker completion date. When a patient is transferred, the physician should complete the discharge summary within 24 hours.

At the time of discharge, the **principal diagnosis** and other diagnoses should be recorded completely without symbols or abbreviations on the health record summary sheet (the face sheet) or discharge summary or on another form prescribed by the facility. The principal diagnosis is defined as the condition determined, after study, to be chiefly responsible for occasioning the patient's admission to the hospital.

Healthcare facilities must determine what information goes with the patient when he or she is transferred to another level of care such as a rehabilitation or skilled nursing facility. When the transfer is to an affiliated institution that is part of the same healthcare system, the original patient record is transferred with the patient and new orders are written at the receiving institution to initiate care. A discharge summary is generally required.

Discharge Plan

Discharge planning information regarding further treatment of the patient after discharge should be part of the acute-care health record. The discharge planning process begins at admission and must include information on the patient's ability to perform self-care as well as other services needed by the patient. The case manager, the social worker, utilization review personnel, or nursing personnel may write this plan.

Records Filed with the Health Record

In the past, there was much debate about whether or not patient records received from other facilities should be made part of the receiving facility's health record. HIPAA regulations now require that all information, including information from other facilities, that is used to treat the patient is included as part of the health record when the information was used in treating the patient. It is important for healthcare facilities to develop polices to determine exactly what health information mailed, faxed, or personally brought to the facility by the patient or patient's family becomes part of the receiving facility's designated health record. A good practice is to have the attending physician review copies and note which documents should be made permanent parts of the record. Any extraneous copies, x-rays, or other information should be returned to the patient (AHIMA 2005).

Facilities maintain information on the release of information from the patient record explaining what was released, to whom the information was released, and the date. This required information is often filed with the health record but should not be released when the patient record is released. Federal regulations now require that facilities provide an "accounting of disclosure" under the HIPAA regulations if the patient requests it. Most facilities have traditionally maintained this type of information, excluding information released for treatment, payment, or operations. (See figure A.22 in appendix A.)

The Personal Health Record

Patients frequently maintain information about their own health as well as that of their families. Recently there has been a strong interest in **personal health records (PHRs).** These records may consist of copies of information from providers, insurance companies, pharmacies, and hospitals as well as immunization records and allergy information. Mobile technology allows consumers to readily use technology to create patient information to share with providers. Electronic PHRs may consist of a web-based tool or a PHR offered by the patient's healthcare provider, which is referred to as a **patient/member web portal.** The patient portal allows a patient to access all or part of the health record that is maintained by the patient's provider. Some have limited ability to enter comments that are added to the provider-based record. HIM professionals must work with the medical staff to determine when and how to incorporate patient-created information into the facility's health record. Another issue for the health information professional is the access by patients to the facility's health record in order to download information for their own PHR. This creates new challenges for the HIM professional to interface with patients electronically to share information from the facility's systems (AHIMA 2010).

Social Media and Electronic Communication

Social media include media such as Twitter, Facebook, LinkedIn, blogs, YouTube, and such and provide a method of communication between organizations, patients, and consumers. For HIM professionals, these communications methods can pose a risk of privacy breaches, even if patient names are not used. It is important for facilities to have a policy on managing social media that includes who in the organization can access official social media for the organization. Policies are also needed on disciplinary actions to be taken for inappropriate use of social media. Since social media are used primarily for marketing and communications, their content does not become part of the legal health record.

E-mail may become part of the patient's record when it is used as a method of communicating healthcare information from the physician or facility to a patient. In such cases, e-mail may include information such as laboratory values and other protected health information. The health information professional must ensure that such communications are captured as a permanent part of the patient's health record. Other administrative uses of e-mail, such as verifying an appointment, would not be considered part of the legal record. It is important that the facility have policies indicating which e-mail should become part of the patient's record, how long it must be retained, and how it will be stored. Training staff and other users of e-mail regarding appropriate procedures is also an important role for the HIM professional (Backman et al. 2011).

Specialized Health Record Content

The content of the patient health record varies according to the type of care provided. When specialized services are provided to the patient, additional documentation is required, which may require special templates and custom forms. Joint Commission standards and regulations for the type of facility often specify particular content to include in the record, as do data sets specific to each setting. The following sections describe various specialized services and their records.

Obstetrical Care

The prenatal record, which is kept in the physician's office to document prenatal care as it occurs, serves as the history and physical examination for an obstetrical patient. A copy of the prenatal record is usually forwarded from the physician's office to the hospital for inclusion in the record. When the patient requires a cesarean delivery, however, the record must include a full history and physical report or a detailed admission progress note explaining the need for a cesarean section.

A labor and delivery record indicates the name of the patient, maiden name, date of delivery, sex of infant, name of physician, name of persons assisting, any complications, type of anesthesia used, name of person administering anesthesia, and names of others present at delivery. In the case of a stillborn infant, a separate patient record is not created; rather, information is recorded in the mother's delivery record.

Neonatal Care

Newborns are considered separate patients with separate health records. The newborn patient record must include an admission examination and a discharge examination. Usually, special chart forms for progress notes, orders, and nursing notes are included. When the patient has been in the newborn intensive care unit, a complete discharge summary is required. In situations of stillbirth, often there is no newborn record created; data about the stillborn are maintained in the mother's record.

Emergency Care

Emergency health records may be filed separately or incorporated into the health record when the patient is admitted to the same facility. When the records are filed separately, the emergency record must be available when the patient is readmitted or seeks care in the future. Most of the demographic and clinical information in emergency situations is recorded on one sheet in a paper health record format. Additional sheets may include laboratory, radiology, and other tests; consent forms; and follow-up instructions.

The content of the emergency health record should generally include the following items:

- Identification data
- Time of arrival
- Means of arrival (by ambulance, private automobile, or police vehicle)
- Name of person or organization transporting patient to the emergency department
- Pertinent history, including chief complaint and onset of injury or illness
- Significant physical findings
- Laboratory, x-ray, and EKG findings
- Treatment rendered
- Conclusions at termination of treatment
- Disposition of patient, including whether sent home, transferred, or admitted
- Condition of the patient upon discharge or transfer
- Diagnosis upon discharge
- Instructions given to the patient or the family regarding further care and follow-up
- Signatures and titles of the patient's caregivers

When the patient leaves the emergency department before being seen or against medical advice (AMA), this fact should be noted on the emergency department form. Consent forms for treatment also must be included in the record. A copy of the emergency record should be made available to the provider of follow-up care.

In addition to the emergency department record, most states require facilities to maintain a chronological record or log of all patients visiting the emergency department with name, date, time of arrival, and record number. This register also includes the names of patients who were dead on arrival.

Emergency patients must be made aware of their rights. Transfer and acceptance policies and procedures must be delineated to ensure that facilities comply with the **Emergency Medical Treatment and Labor Act (EMTALA)** and state regulations regarding transfers. Patients cannot be transferred or refused treatment for reasons related to ability to pay or source of payment nor can hospitals determine that space is unavailable based on ability to pay or source of payment. Anyone who requests or requires an examination must be provided an appropriate medical screening examination by hospital staff to determine whether a medical emergency exists. Further, the hospital must stabilize the medical emergency by ensuring an airway and ventilation, by controlling hemorrhage, and by stabilizing or splinting fractures before a patient can be transferred. Appropriate transfer means that the receiving hospital agrees to receive

the patient and provide appropriate medical treatment. Records must be provided to the receiving hospital, and the patient or responsible person must understand the medical necessity of the transfer.

For demonstrating compliance with EMTALA regulations, hospitals must maintain screening examinations for a minimal period of five years. Nonemergency patients presenting to the emergency department are typically examined by the triage nurse or other emergency department staff and referred to a minor medical clinic, a physician office, or another nonemergency patient care facility.

Ambulatory or Outpatient Care

Ambulatory or outpatient care means that patients move from location to location and do not stay overnight. Ambulatory or outpatient care may be given in a freestanding clinic, a clinic that is part of a larger hospital system, or a physician or other provider office. Traditionally, physician office records have been less comprehensive than hospital medical records. Physicians must develop standardized formats and comprehensive documentation practices.

When patients are in a clinic affiliated with a hospital, the entire health record from previous hospital care should be available. The Joint Commission requires ambulatory patients to have a summary list by the third visit that includes known diagnoses, conditions, procedures, drug allergies, and medications. Contents of the ambulatory care record vary depending on the treatment received. The **Accreditation Association for Ambulatory Health Care (AAAHC)** has additional requirements for the content of the ambulatory care record.

Ambulatory facilities that only perform surgery are called ambulatory surgery centers (ASCs). Patients having surgery at any type of ambulatory facility must have a history and physical examination prior to surgery, consents, an operative note, a postoperative progress note, and the same anesthesia information as an operative patient in the hospital. In addition, the record must document instructions for postoperative care and postoperative follow-up. Clinics often call patients after surgery to check on their condition, and these calls should be documented in the record (Accreditation Association for Ambulatory Health Care 2011).

Behavioral Healthcare

Behavioral health records, also known as mental health records or psychiatric records, must include diagnostic and assessment information related to both the patient's mental condition and his or her physical health. The Medicare Conditions of Participation require that the inpatients within a psychiatric hospital receive a psychiatric evaluation (42 CFR 482.61 2011).

Home Health Services

According to the **National Association for Home Care & Hospice (NAHC),** the term *home care* covers many types of services that are delivered at home to patients requiring a variety of medical, nursing, therapy, or other services (NAHC 2011). Physicians order home care services that may include visits from many types of healthcare providers, including physical and occupational therapists and nurses. Patient health records must contain a legible record of each visit describing what was done to or for the patient during the visit. The providers working with patients must develop and document periodic plans of care. Specific documentation required by CMS is included in the home care health record for the attending physician to document and update the plan of care. It is also necessary for the physician to certify the patient's need for the care, and recertification of the need must be documented periodically (NAHC 2011).

Hospice Care Services

The **National Hospice and Palliative Care Organization (NHPCO)** defines hospice care as a "team-oriented approach to expert medical care, pain management, and emotional and spiritual support expressly tailored to the patient's needs and wishes" (NHPCO 2011). Because hospice care is delivered to patients with all types of terminal illnesses, the family is involved in the care, and support is given by the hospice organization. Hospice and palliative care may also consist of pain management, grief counseling, financial planning, and other services provided to the family. Hospice services are provided in numerous types of settings, including homes, hospitals, and long-term care facilities (NHPCO 2011). Special documentation for the election of hospice care is required for CMS to reimburse for services. This includes certification by the patient's attending physician and the hospice that the patient has a terminal illness. Unique documentation issues in hospice care include documentation by volunteers of all patient contacts as well as documentation by bereavement counselors of services provided to the family after the patient's death.

Rehabilitation Services

Rehabilitation covers a wide range of services provided to build or rebuild the patient's abilities to perform the usual activities of daily living. In the rehabilitation setting, the history and physical must include a functional history covering the patient's functional status before and after injury or onset of illness. Additionally, the history should describe the equipment the patient uses at home including orthotics and prosthetics. It is important that the physician outline the goals for the patient's care to coordinate the interdisciplinary team involved in the care.

Services also include physical therapy, occupational therapy, and speech therapy. Physical therapists work in numerous types of facilities, ranging from acute care to long-term care and patient homes, setting goals for patients and helping them reach their goals by building muscle strength and respiratory and circulatory efficiency. Their patients include those who have been disabled for a number of reasons, including birth defects, trauma, and illness. Treatments include exercise, manipulation, heat therapy, light therapy, the use of electricity, and therapeutic massage. In addition to setting treatment goals, physical therapists have to document patient progress.

Occupational therapists are part of the rehabilitation team and work with patients to restore their ability to perform the usual functions of daily life, such as eating, dressing, preparing food, working, and handling other activities specific to the patient.

Speech therapists and other specialized therapists are important members of the rehabilitation team and work together to achieve a variety of patient goals. Rehabilitation professionals must assess patients and provide services based on a plan of care for each patient.

Long-term Care

Long-term care describes the care provided for extended periods of time to patients recovering from illness or injury. Long-term care facilities offer a combination of services, ranging from independent living to assisted living to skilled nursing care. Rehabilitation services are often part of the long-term care plan. The long-term care record must document a comprehensive assessment that includes items in the Minimum Data Set (MDS) to meet CMS requirements stated in 42 CFR 483.20 (2010). (Chapter 8 addresses MDS standards for data collection.)

In addition, long-term facilities must meet state requirements. Individualized patient care plans must be developed and included in the health record. These plans must cover the potential for rehabilitation, the ability to perform activities of daily living, medications prescribed, and other aspects of care.

As with acute-care facilities, the frequency of progress notes depends on the patient's condition. The focus in long-term care is on the achievement of goals. The HIM functions are similar to those in other types of facilities, but a great deal of concurrent review is required to ensure that a complete medical record is maintained throughout the resident's often lengthy stay. Paper records of patients who have been in the facility for an extended period of time may be divided, with the most current information maintained on the nursing unit and the rest filed elsewhere to save space at the nursing station.

Check Your Understanding 10.2

Instructions: On a separate piece of paper, match the contents with the appropriate part of the record by placing the letter for the form in the blank preceding the description of the form's content.

1. ____ Directions given for drugs, devices, and healthcare treatments

2. ____ Comprehensive assessment of patient to determine signs and symptoms

3. ____ Records maintained by physical therapists, speech therapists, respiratory therapists, and other providers of special services

4. ___ Protocol for the process of care

5. ___ Summary of background information about the patient's illness

6. ___ Statement of the patient's wishes or instructions for care

7. ___ Conclusions at the termination of care

8. ___ Observations of the patient's response to treatment

9. ___ Record that must contain the time and means of arrival and the name of the person transporting the patient to the facility

10. ___ Opinions of specialists

    A. Care path

    B. History

    C. Physical examination

    D. Orders

    E. Consultations

    F. Nursing notes

    G. Advance directives

    H. Emergency record

    I. Discharge summary

    J. Ancillary notes

Answer the following questions:

11. What types of information are included in a personal health record?

12. What issues does the personal health record raise for HIM professionals?

13. What is the difference between a personal health record and a patient portal?

Format of the Paper-Based and Hybrid Health Record

The term **format** refers to the organization of information in the health record. There are many possible formats, and most facilities use a combination of formats. During the patient care process, the paper-based health record is often in a different format than after the patient is discharged. This is especially true in facilities with a hybrid health record that in some cases scan the paper portions of the record after the discharge of the patient. Regardless of the media in which the health record is kept, a systematic format for the health record ensures all users of the health record can easily locate the patient information required for their needs.

Source-Oriented Health Records

The **source-oriented health record** is the conventional or traditional method of maintaining paper-based health records. In this method, health records are organized according to the source, or originating, department that rendered the service (for example, all lab reports are filed together, all radiological reports are filed together, and so on).

Figure 10.2 shows the arrangement of forms for records maintained in a large acute-care hospital. Many hybrid health record systems are source oriented and maintain the organization and format of the health record by scanning and indexing the forms based on the "tabs" from the paper-based health record.

Problem-Oriented Health Records

Lawrence Weed developed the problem-oriented medical record (POMR) in the 1970s. The POMR is comprised of the

Figure 10.2. Patient record content

This is not a complete list but does show the types of forms found in most acute-care hospitals.	
Admission record (face sheet)	Prenatal and labor record
Discharge diagnosis information	Labor and delivery summary
Identification data	Admission assessment
General conditions of admission form	Labor progress record
Medicare statements	Infant identification sheet
History	Physician office record
Chief complaint	Copies of records from other facilities
Present illness	Reports of tests and results
Review of systems	Laboratory
Past history	Transfusions
Family history	Bone marrow
Social history	Toxicology
Physical examination	Other special reports
Impression or working diagnosis (part of history and physical or admission notes)	Radiology includes scans, ultrasounds, arteriograms, MRI, and the like
Plan of care (part of history and physical or admission notes)	EEG

(continued on next page)

Figure 10.2.   Patient record content (*continued*)

EKG	Records of donation or receipt of transplants or implants
Echocardiograms	Advance directives (if brought to the facility by the patient)
Treadmills	Living will (if brought to the facility by the patient)
Holter monitor	Power of attorney
Doppler	Special consents
Therapy reports	Anatomical gifts
Physical therapy	AMA release
Occupational therapy	Leave of absence
Cardiac rehabilitation	Consent to photograph
Respiratory therapy	Emergency record
GI lab	Demographic information
Cardiac catheterization	Treatment record
Other specialty areas	Triage assessments
Progress notes, clinical observations, and patient's response to care	Nurses' notes
	EKG
Consultation reports	Newborn records
Informed consent	Admission record
Anesthesia record	Discharge summary
Operative room clinical record	Consultation
Intraoperative report	Consents
Postoperative or recovery record	Physician orders/progress notes
Pathology report	Lab
Discharge summary	Radiology
Final diagnosis	Newborn record
Death	Estimated gestational age
Consent for autopsy	Medication record
Autopsy report, if done	Initial assessment
Release of body	Labor and delivery record
Discharge instructions	Infant identification—footprints and photographs
Discharge medication orders	Newborn ICU delivery room
Nursing notes and observations	Flow sheet
Medication administration records	Observation, neonatal, ICU
Graphic charts	Nursery progress record
Intake-output, temperature, pulse, respirations (vital signs)	Pediatrician selection form
Nursing assessments	
Admission assessments	
Care plans	
Critical pathways	

Source: Methodist Health Systems, Memphis, TN.

problem list, the database (the history and physical examination and initial lab findings), the initial plan (tests, procedures, and other treatments), and progress notes organized so that every member of the healthcare team can easily follow the course of patient treatment (Weed 1970).

A distinctive feature of the POMR is the problem list, which serves as the record's table of contents. All relevant problems—medical, social, or other—that may have an impact on the patient are listed with a number. As problems are resolved, the resolution is noted on the list; new problems are added as they occur. The problem list serves as a permanent index that providers can quickly check to review the status of past and current problems. Entries in the record, such as orders and progress notes, include the number of the problem addressed as provided on the problem list.

The most recognizable component of the POMR is the SOAP format, which is a method for recording progress notes. SOAP is an easy acronym that helps providers remember the specific and systematic decision-making process being documented. *S* stands for subjective findings and includes statements from the patient's viewpoint such as symptoms. The subjective findings are followed by objective findings (the *O* in the acronym) such as laboratory and test results as well as observations and findings from the physical examination. *A* stands for assessment, which consists of appraisals and judgments based on the findings and observations. The *P* stands for plan, which states the methods to be followed in addressing the problems identified. Although the full POMR as championed by Weed has not been adopted universally, many physicians and providers routinely use the SOAP method, or an adaptation of it, to document progress notes and also include a problem list in the record.

Integrated Health Records

The content of the **integrated health record** is arranged in strict chronological order. The order of the record is determined by the date the information was entered, the date of the service, or the date the report was received, rather than by the source department; the record gives the sequence of the patient's care as delivered. Different types of information and sources of information are mixed together according to the dates on the entries. Although this system makes it difficult to find a particular document unless one knows the date, it does provide a better picture of the story of the patient's care. Physician offices often use this format.

Strengths and Weaknesses of Paper-Based Health Records

The main benefit of paper-based health records is that they are the traditional way that records have been maintained and, therefore, are familiar to all users. Providers do not need technological training to begin documenting in the paper record. Another benefit is that written documentation is not affected by system outages.

However, paper-based records have numerous disadvantages. The main disadvantage is that only one person at a time can access information. In addition, there are problems with tracking and monitoring locations of the paper record on the patient floors, within the HIM department, and when it is checked out of the HIM department. The filing of loose and late-arriving reports also presents a problem. Attaching loose reports is not always a priority in a busy patient care area, and this omission can result in numerous loose pieces of paper arriving in the HIM department. HIM personnel must route or deliver the forms to the patient care treatment area if the patient is still present in the facility, or personnel must sort and file stacks of loose paper forms for discharged patients. Organizing loose reports and attaching them to many individual records can be a formidable job. Difficulty in reading and interpreting handwriting of providers can also be a problem.

Another problem with the patient record is that an entire record or a volume of a paper record can be lost or misfiled, making important patient information unavailable to providers when they need it. The creation of shadow or duplicate systems is also a problem with paper-based health record systems. Some providers are concerned about the possibility that records can

be lost or not located in a timely manner; therefore, they create additional records by copying the original records, or keeping a separate set of notes. Providers may want to maintain duplicate information for billing purposes. These notes may never become part of the original record, or the provider may rely on only the duplicate shadow record without referencing the entire original record, which may have additional information.

Strengths and Weaknesses of Hybrid Health Records

The main benefit of hybrid health record systems is that they maintain the format of the paper-based record after the discharge of the patient. Some facilities with hybrid records keep the paper format for the portion of the record that was created on paper while other facilities scan the paper portions of the record after discharge. However, unlike facilities that maintain part of the hybrid record in a paper-based format permanently, those facilities that scan the paper portions of the hybrid record provide many of the advantages of electronic health records. These advantages include more rapid and simultaneous access by providers; less manpower required to file loose paperwork, purge the records, and look for missing paper records; and less space required to archive than paper-based records. Also physicians may remotely access the hybrid record for record completion. Hybrid record systems thus typically reduce the number of incomplete and delinquent health records since physicians do not have to wait until the record is available or come to the HIM department to complete records.

Scanned hybrid records are not as advanced as electronically created records and often cannot be searched for content. They are typically comprised of imaged reports and not separate fields that can be searched. Figure 10.3 lists the steps in the usual flow of the paper-based health and hybrid records in a traditional acute-care facility.

Check Your Understanding 10.3

Instructions: On a separate piece of paper, fill in the blanks with the appropriate terms.

1. ____ This is the conventional or traditional method of maintaining paper-based health records.

2. ____ This record is maintained in the same format while the patient is hospitalized and after discharge.

3. ____ This record is maintained in strict chronological order.

4. ____ This record begins with a problem list that serves as the table of contents for the record.

5. ____ This organization provides care to patients who are terminally ill.

6. ____ These services include physical therapy, occupational therapy, and speech therapy.

7. ____ These services range from independent living to assisted living and skilled nursing care.

8. ____ These duplicate notes or copies often do not become a part of the original record.

Figure 10.3.   Typical steps in the flow of the paper-based and hybrid patient health record following discharge

Paper-Based Record	Hybrid Record
1. Records of discharged patients arrive or are delivered to HIM department.	1. Records of discharged patients arrive or are delivered to HIM department.
2. Receipt of records is verified by comparing discharge lists to actual charts received.	2. Receipt of records is verified by comparing discharge lists to actual charts received.
3. Record is assembled according to prescribed format ensuring that all pages belong to the correct patient and that forms are in correct date order.	3. Record is assembled according to prescribed format ensuring that all pages belong to the correct patient and that forms are in correct date order.
4. Deficiencies such as signatures, reports needing completion, and so on are assigned to the responsible provider.	4. Record is prepped for scanning
5. Record is held for final completion by providers either in incomplete chart area or some other filing area.	5. Record is scanned.
Paper-Based Record	**Hybrid Record**
6. Physician completes the record deficiencies.	6. Record appears in deficiency analyst's queue, and deficiencies such as signatures, reports needing completion, and so on are assigned to the responsible provider.
7. Diagnoses and procedures are coded.	7. Record is made available in the physician's queue for completion.
8. Charts are rechecked after the providers have done their work to ensure that all have been completed.	8. Physician completes the record deficiencies.
9. The complete record is filed in the permanent filing area.	9. Diagnoses and procedures are coded.
	10. Record scanning is verified for accuracy and original paper record is destroyed.
	11. Scanned record is electronically archived.

Management of Health Record Content

The HIM professional manages health record content through oversight responsibilities for **medical transcription** services to produce clinical reports that become part of the health record. The HIM responsibilities for incomplete records include analyzing and monitoring incomplete records to ensure that they are properly completed to meet facility standards and patient healthcare needs, as well as controlling the design and production of forms and electronic templates to ensure that all health records are in a standardized format.

Transcription

Completion of the health record is greatly enhanced by the sophisticated dictation and **transcription** equipment in use today. Physicians and other providers first dictate the necessary reports, including, but not limited to, history and physical examinations, operative reports, discharge summaries, consultation reports, progress notes, clinic notes, pathology reports, and radiology reports. The dictated report then is transcribed to produce final printed output or COLD-fed data into the electronic system to become a part of the legal health record. Personnel who type, that is, transcribe, the dictation are called medical transcriptionists. Facilities should encourage providers to dictate so that reports can be created and later accessed electronically.

Components of a Transcription System

The system encompasses both the dictation and transcription process. The physician or provider dictates into a variety of devices, including a telephone by calling a special number connected to the facility's dictation system or by using a special phone dedicated only to dictation. Whatever the means of input by the dictator, a transcriptionist retrieves the dictated voice input and transcribes the content. The transcription may be performed on-site at the facility or off-site from a remote location. The final product, the transcribed report, is sent for review to the physician or provider, who authenticates it as the final approved original for inclusion in the legal health record. **Authentication** may be done on the printed report or electronically in the computer system. The facility's policies must specify that the signature or authentication indicates that the physician or provider who dictated the report has reviewed and corrected it (if necessary) and approves the content of the report.

Digital dictation is the process by which voice sounds are recorded and converted into a digital format. The physician or provider begins the dictation process using a telephone, a microphone attached to a PC, or a hands-free microphone. The dictator enters digits to indicate certain basic information, such as identification of the dictator, identification of the patient, and the type of report to be dictated (a history and physical examination, a discharge summary, an operative report, and so on).

The dictator then speaks and the dictation is transmitted to a computer that digitizes the voice. After the voice sounds have been digitized, the dictation is accessed by the transcriptionist, who transcribes the report by listening to the voice and converting it to typed output. Special software features allow the transcriptionist to produce reports with as few keystrokes as possible, using techniques such as word expanders. Word expanders are shortened versions of phrases. For example, the keystrokes WDWN are changed to produce typed output as "well-developed, well-nourished." Some facilities use templates for normal reports or macros so that the dictator can direct the transcriptionist to the template or macro to edit and tailor the report to the individual patient.

Digital systems allow the dictated information to be prioritized so that reports that have to be completed quickly are produced first. The dictation can be easily located by utilizing identifying information that is provided by the dictator. Digital systems automatically time-stamp the date and time the work was dictated and the date and time the transcription was started and completed. Random access by the transcriptionist allows the workload to be shared and distributed among several transcriptionists. Providers and other appropriate staff can dial in and listen to the recorded information rather than waiting until the final report is transcribed. Coders can listen to the dictated information and code from the discharge summary and other dictated reports rather than waiting for the actual transcribed reports. The transcribed report can be faxed automatically to the physician's office, printed out in the transcription area, printed out to clinics or patient floors, COLD-fed into the EHR, and integrated with the chart completion system.

Providers can review transcribed documents online and may have editing capabilities. In some systems, both the original and the final edited versions become part of the legal patient health record.

Planning for and Selecting Transcription Equipment

When purchasing or upgrading a dictation and transcription system, the HIM professional must be aware of the long-range consequences of this important decision. Equipment vendors can provide a wealth of information based on their experience working in various facilities. They can help the HIM department determine the number of ports, or entry points, that need to be available based on the number of dictators and transcriptionists requiring simultaneous access. The system needs to have sufficient accessibility to avoid collision, which would prevent a dictator or transcriptionist from gaining access to the system. Immediate access for all

users, whether dictating or transcribing, is critical to the system's success. When dictators call in, a digital channel selector automatically selects an available line without input from the dictator.

The facility must have vendor support to ensure that the system is operational at all times. Transcription systems should be designed so that the transcriptionists can work independently if the general facility information system is not working. Although entering patient information without the connection to the general information system will require greater effort, the work can continue to be generated.

Transcription systems may be designed to archive, or save, dictated information for any length of time. Some facilities archive for 90 days and others for six or more months. Long periods of storage may cause the system to work more slowly, but the advantage is continued access. Even if dictated reports are not attached to the paper or hybrid health records, the people who need the information for coding and billing purposes, quality studies, indexes, registries, and other operational needs can still access and utilize the information.

Transcription services may be centralized or decentralized. In a decentralized system, pathology, radiology, and other departments in addition to health information management may have their own transcriptionists. Some HIM departments have centralized transcription areas that transcribe reports for the entire facility or for all facilities in an integrated system. Moreover, some transcription departments perform work for physician offices in order to generate revenue. The transcription department must consider every possible customer and analyze every possible location for dedicated dictation stations, including nurses' stations, clinics, operative areas, and workrooms in the HIM department. Further, every acceptable format must be determined and policies established for the types of recordings that are allowed. Using a variety of input devices will cause productivity problems and prevent full utilization of the dictation and transcription system's capabilities. In physician offices and clinics, cassette tapes are used more often for dictation than in larger facilities.

The HIM professional must fully understand the dictation and transcription system application. A **certified medical transcriptionist (CMT)** may supervise the transcription area, but the manager of the HIM department is ultimately responsible for the work produced. Before purchasing any large system, the HIM professional should interview references and visit similar facilities to see the system in operation. Often the vendor will arrange these site visits. The HIM professional also might visit facilities that are using the equipment under consideration but have not been specifically recommended by the vendor. Further, he or she might attend trade shows and seminars and narrow the field of products to avoid confusion. In addition, he or she should include the people who will actually use the system in the decision-making process.

Issues in the Management of Transcription Services

Although transcription is just one function of the HIM department, it often requires a great deal of the department's attention and resources. A backlog of dictated minutes waiting to be transcribed is an issue that needs constant monitoring to meet turnaround time. History and physical examination reports and operative reports have accreditation and regulatory time limitations. Quick turnaround time from dictation to transcribed report is important because providers must be able to retrieve information when it is needed for patient care.

Recruitment and retention of qualified medical transcriptionists are major problems for HIM professionals. Transcription equipment is expensive to acquire and maintain, and the equipment and technology are changing rapidly. Skilled medical transcriptionists who can accurately transcribe dictation are in short supply, and the role of the medical transcriptionist is evolving. This evolution is discussed in the following sections.

Internal versus Outsourced Transcription

The facility must decide whether to handle transcription services in-house, to contract with (or outsource to) transcription companies outside the facility, or to use a combination of internal and **contract services.**

Outsourcing to transcription service companies, or contract services, is on the rise. Some healthcare facilities routinely contract all or a portion of their workload; others use the contract service on an as-needed basis for peak times and to accommodate overflow work. The major advantage to a contract service is that it can save the facility money in terms of salaries, fringe benefits, equipment, depreciation, floor space, maintenance, workstations, supplies, and reference materials. Furthermore, use of an outside service can eliminate problems associated with overloading the system with increased dictation prior to a Joint Commission survey or at times when medical residents change clinical service rotations in a teaching facility. Although outsourcing transcription services is an attractive option, it must be analyzed carefully. The major disadvantages to outsourcing are the loss of control over the transcription service, the potential security risks, and the high cost of contract transcription services.

When selecting a contract service, the HIM professional should become as familiar with the company as possible. A growing number of offshore companies or US-based companies send work via the Internet to transcription personnel in other countries. Such companies must provide assurance that their transcriptionists are bonded, trained in confidentiality, and well supervised regardless of their location.

The manner in which the company handles a sudden influx of work is important because this is one of the major reasons why healthcare facilities use outside transcription companies.

The exact method and rationale for billing and counting the final product also is extremely important. The HIM professional should question the exact definitions of a line, a word, a page, a keystroke, minutes, or bytes used for billing. The counting method should be fully explained in the contract. Most companies charge by the line, but the definition of a line may be 65 characters rather than a physical line. For example, if physical lines are counted and the facility is paying $0.13 to $0.18 per line, the costs can add up in situations where one word on a line is considered a line. Using a smaller font to increase the amount of typing per line may be more costly because a smaller type may scan into an imaging system or microfilm poorly. Some companies base their charge on turnaround time, with an increased cost per line when transcription is completed within a shorter time frame. For example, the charge for transcription within 48 hours would be $0.10 a line; within 24 hours, $0.12 a line; and within 8 hours, $0.18 a line. In addition, the company may include electronic storage costs for dictation. The HIM manager should also investigate whether style requirements such as capitalizing, boldface, or underlining are an additional charge.

Billing can be complicated, and the HIM professional must determine the true cost of the outside contract company's service so that he or she can compare alternatives accurately. The distribution and delivery method and the number of copies provided by the company must be evaluated because reprints might cost as much as the original transcribed document. Some companies transmit information back to the facility to be printed by the facility or send information via the Internet, fax, an overnight delivery service, or a courier. The contract needs to state whether the facility or the company will pay for the transmission service. Also, there may be an additional charge for corrections. If the facility allows physicians or providers to dictate on other devices instead of directly into the dictation system, this also may affect the cost.

In addition, the facility must assess how the outside company's equipment will integrate with the facility's current hospital information system, for example, with regard to phone lines, software, and interface with the electronic health record system, if one exists. If the printing is to be done in the facility, responsibility for printer maintenance and supply costs must be determined. The quality of the work performed by the contract company must be evaluated in terms of content, proper abbreviation use, typing and spelling errors, general appearance, correction of grammatical errors, and correct spelling of physician and patient names. Some companies provide several levels of proofreading, including by a physician. However, proofreading also must be performed by the healthcare facility on at least a sample of the reports, and the facility must maintain the voice files so that quality checks can be performed on the outside service's work to ensure that what was dictated was what was actually typed. The HIM professional must make sure the work is closely monitored.

Even with a contract service, the health information manager still has oversight responsibility for the outside contract service and quality control. Facility personnel must file the printed reports in the health record and distribute them to residents, referring physicians, and consultants, as appropriate. Further, contracts must be carefully reviewed to ensure that contract services provide for the security of patient information.

The HIM professional also must ensure fast and easy access to the system. If physicians and coders have the ability to listen to dictation prior to transcribing, this capability should not change when transcription is outsourced.

Staffing of the Transcription Area

When the healthcare facility chooses to do transcription internally, the staff must be carefully selected to ensure that transcription is of high quality. Each applicant for a transcription position should be tested using the kind of work to be performed to confirm that he or she can type from the voice files. In addition, the applicant must have excellent concentration skills, hearing skills, and proofreading and editing skills. CMS has developed guidance for remote workers, and this information is a good resource for developing policies and procedures to provide access for remote workers.

Applicants who are CMTs are in great demand. The Medical Transcription Certification Commission grants certification upon the successful completion of an examination. The requirements for this voluntary examination are experience or formal education or both. The CMT must maintain currency and certification by earning continuing education (CE) hours. Proprietary business schools and community colleges offer formal educational programs and are excellent sources for transcriptionists. A healthcare facility's offer to allow students to obtain clinical experience at the facility is an excellent way to attract applicants. Some healthcare facilities offer on-the-job training to persons with excellent typing skills.

The **Association for Healthcare Documentation Integrity** (AHDI), formerly the American Association for Medical Transcription (AAMT), has a model curriculum for formal educational programs. The curriculum includes the study of medical terminology, anatomy and physiology, medical science, operative procedures, instruments, supplies, laboratory values, reference use and research techniques, and English grammar. All applicants should have knowledge of the areas of the model curriculum.

In addition, the AHDI produces a bimonthly journal and has excellent reference materials. CE opportunities are available for transcription professionals. Transcriptionists must be given the opportunity to participate in CE activities and to be updated in new medical procedures, tests, and terminology.

The AHDI has a model job description with three defined levels for the professional transcriptionist. Some facilities may use these levels as a guide for levels of classification of personnel and promotions (AHDI 2008).

Telecommuting, or telestaffing, is growing. In telecommuting, personnel are allowed to work from home or some other remote location. This has been very successful for healthcare facilities, although remote transcriptionists require special supervisory attention. They need to feel that they are part of the HIM department. The supervisor must ensure ongoing communication with telestaffing employees via e-mail or by bringing them to the facility for CE meetings and interaction with other departmental personnel. Some healthcare facilities offer telecommuting only to employees who have been with them for a period of time, fully understand the system, and are known to be responsible and dependable.

Transcriptionists working outside the healthcare facility use a telephone line or cable connection to access the system. The facility may supply the transcriptionist with the telephone line, the computer workstation, and reference materials. Transcriptionists working from home must be held to the same production and quality standards as in-house transcriptionists and must be fully trained in the security and confidentiality of healthcare information.

Determining the number of transcriptionists needed in relation to the number of providers dictating is challenging and depends on the types and amount of information typed, the specialties of the facility, whether the facility is a teaching hospital or a clinic, and the types of nontranscription duties assigned to the transcriptionists, among other factors. In a clinic or physician office, transcription may be done as part of a larger job. The HIM professional must determine the acceptable turnaround time (TAT) for different types of dictated reports, often referred to as work types. There is a range of definitions of TAT, and often variation occurs at various healthcare facilities and various settings. According to the July 2008 American Health Information Management Association (AHIMA) white paper "Transcription Turnaround Time for Common Document Types," common TAT varies from 8 to 24 hours based on the work type of the dictated report. Most healthcare facilities codify the acceptable TAT for various work types in the medical staff bylaws. The failure of the responsible provider to dictate the report in the required time frame often results in a deficiency in the health record. Once a report is dictated, there are factors that may contribute to noncompliance with approved TATs including staffing, work volume changes, transcription anomalies, implementation of new technology or equipment, and TAT expectation changes.

Productivity Management

Payment methods for transcriptionists vary depending on whether the transcriptionist works for a healthcare facility or a contract service. Entry-level transcriptionists may be paid by the hour. Some contract services pay transcriptionists more per hour for straight production typing, but the transcriptionists may not have the benefits that are available to the employees of a healthcare facility. The AHDI has excellent current information about productivity. This should be referenced to ensure the current standards are utilized.

Quality is a vital part of productivity management in transcription. The supervisor must review the quality of work produced on a regular basis. Among the items to review are punctuation errors, omitted dictation, misspelled words or medical terms, and formatting errors. An analysis of each transcriptionist's errors will target those areas that need improvement. The *Book of Style for Medical Transcription* is often used as the standard for defining and measuring medical transcription errors (AHDI 2008).

Speech and Voice Recognition

Speech or **voice recognition technology** is used increasingly as the accuracy of output improves. In voice recognition technology, the spoken word is transmitted immediately to a database and converted to typed output, which eliminates the need for the transcriptionist to listen to and type the information. The quality of the output is very dependent on the quality of the dictation. The speaker must speak clearly and distinctly. The role of the transcriptionist will change as this new technology increases in accuracy. In time, the transcriptionist will become primarily an editor and a proofreader.

Speech recognition technology may be utilized on the front end, where the person dictates through a microphone or headset apparatus connected to a PC. As the person dictates, the words appear on the screen and are corrected if they are not displayed correctly. The document is correct when completed and the dictator controls the entire process. The facility may still require the document to be sent to a transcriptionist or another person who controls its distribution. This method also requires training of the individual who is dictating, and the dictator may feel that this process is too slow and takes too much physician time. In back-end speech recognition, after the physician dictates in the usual manner, the audio is sent as a draft text along with the voice file to the transcriptionist, who serves as an editor, to listen to the audio in comparison with the displayed text and to make changes to the text document. This document then goes back to the dictating provider for approval. The advantage is that the person dictating does not have to change dictation behavior. Back-end speech recognition (also called *server-based speech recognition*) does not improve productivity because editing is as time consuming as transcribing is. Radiology departments and other departments that have many repetitive reports have utilized speech recognition technology more effectively than the general facility has (AHIMA 2003).

Incentive Programs

Because of the competition for certified medical transcriptionists, many healthcare facilities offer **incentive pay** plans to reward transcriptionists for high productivity. For example, a hospital may require a transcriptionist to type eight hours a day and produce 1,200 lines of typed output for a base monthly salary. Beyond 1,200 lines, the transcriptionist

may earn a bonus of $0.06 per line, with the bonus cents per line increasing to the point where a transcriptionist typing 2,001 lines would receive a bonus of $0.12 per line. However, the quality of the work must remain at 98 percent accuracy based on regular quality review.

For fairness in the incentive system, work must be rotated so that each transcriptionist has the opportunity to perform different kinds of work from different providers. Providers for whom English is a second language may produce dictation that is more difficult to transcribe. Moreover, some providers are not careful in their dictation, which requires more listening and replaying. Operative reports may be more difficult to transcribe than discharge summaries.

The proponents of incentive pay plans believe that monetary incentives increase productivity, reduce turnover, provide fair and equitable pay, and motivate employees. In this payment method, highly productive transcriptionists are paid for what they produce.

Evaluation of the Effectiveness and Efficiency of Transcription Services

The effectiveness and efficiency of transcription services are judged primarily by turnaround time and accuracy in typing the dictation. History and physical examinations and operative reports have time limitations set forth in Joint Commission regulations. Discharge summaries are valuable sources of information for coding, billing, and reimbursement. With EHR systems, the dictated information and transcribed documents are accessible to all providers and healthcare personnel who need to refer to them. The success of the transcription service depends on both the cooperation of the providers who dictate and the skills of the medical transcriptionists.

Check Your Understanding 10.4

Instructions: Answer the following questions on a separate sheet of paper.

1. What are the advantages of using a contract transcription system? What are the advantages of having transcription performed in-house?

2. What are the formal educational requirements for a certified medical transcriptionist?

3. How will speech recognition technology change the job of the medical transcriptionist?

4. What are the four benefits of an incentive pay plan?

5. What factors must be considered when determining the number of transcriptionists a healthcare facility needs?

Abstracting

Abstracting is the compilation, usually in an electronic database, of pertinent information extracted from the patient record. The purpose of abstracting is to make information from the patient record readily available for internal and external reporting needs. Abstracting supports the secondary use of patient data for registries, public reporting, research, and other purposes. It is important for the HIM professional to understand the mission of the facility when determining both the amount of information to abstract from the health record and the appropriate staff required for the abstracting.

Abstracting Process for Paper-Based and Hybrid Health Records

In a facility with paper-based and hybrid health records there are typically administrative systems for registration, coding, and billing and some clinical systems with electronic processes that require data input through an abstracting process. In these cases, the HIM professional may be required to abstract more information than in facilities with more advanced electronic health record systems that provide electronic query functions. The process of abstracting begins with defining the needs and the purposes for the abstracted information. For the creation of indices providing such information as the treating physician and procedures performed, the information included may be a combination of information from other systems that integrate into the abstracting system (Tegan et al. 2005). For example, a paper-based facility may have an ADT (admission, discharge, and transfer) system that captures basic demographic information about the patient and the treating physician. After discharge, this information is available in the abstracting system, and the coder then assigns codes to the encounter. This information is stored with the demographic information; however, the coder may have to enter the names of the physicians who performed the surgeries or procedures during the hospital stay. Also, the coder may verify the discharge status entered in the system with that documented in the health record. If the facility is a teaching facility, the names of the residents and fellows involved in the care of the patient may also be included in the abstracting system.

Incomplete Record Control

Health records must be complete in order to provide all the information that is necessary for patient care, billing, and reimbursement. The HIM department must verify that all records are received from the nursing floor, including records of any previous admissions that were sent to the nursing unit. After the records arrive in the HIM department, their location must be carefully tracked until they reach final storage in the filing area or are scanned.

The business office notifies the HIM department of bills that are waiting for information from the physician so that the record can be coded and the bill prepared. The administration places a great deal of pressure on the HIM department to process bills in a timely manner so that revenue can be generated for the facility. In turn, the HIM professional must motivate physicians to provide the information

the department needs to do its work. Incomplete records are less of a problem in most healthcare facilities with hybrid or electronic health records. However, monitoring incomplete health records is a constant challenge for the HIM professional.

Quantitative Analysis

Quantitative analysis, often called **discharge analysis,** is a review of the health record for completeness and accuracy. It is generally conducted retrospectively, that is, after the patient's discharge from the facility or at the conclusion of treatment. Quantitative analysis also may be done while the patient is in the facility, in which case it is referred to as concurrent review or **concurrent analysis.** Concurrent analysis means that the record is analyzed during the patient's stay in the healthcare facility. It has the advantage of HIM or other personnel being present on the floors where the physicians see patients. HIM personnel can remind providers to complete items in the record and to sign orders and progress notes. Some facilities have HIM personnel physically located on the nursing floors to monitor record completion closely. Other facilities have HIM personnel visit patient care areas to obtain signatures and ensure that loose reports are placed in the health record. Discharge analysis serves as an additional check to ensure that the record is complete and that all information belongs in the patient's record. The concurrent review and discharge analysis review typically analyze the health records for the same documentation.

One component of the discharge analysis process is to assemble the record which is the arrangement of the forms in the paper-based health record in a standard permanent sequence for filing. The order of the forms in the record is unique to each hospital. This order also may differ from the sequencing of forms while patients are under active treatment when convenient reference to certain information is needed. When the patient is in active treatment in the hospital, for example, the record is often maintained in reverse chronological order, with the most recent information in the front of each record section. Tabs for each source allow easy reference to the grouped reports, enabling staff to quickly find the patient's response to treatment.

After the patient is discharged, many facilities rearrange the record in chronological order. However, the arrangement is still source oriented with all labs together, all progress notes together, and all other related reports filed together in date order. Sometimes facilities leave the record in the same format as it was maintained while the patient was in the facility rather than spend the time rearranging the forms. This is called **universal chart order.** The benefits of the universal chart order system are that time is saved in the HIM department and providers can find the parts of the record they need more easily because the arrangement remains the same.

A facility moving to universal chart order must involve nursing and physicians in the decisions about chart arrangement because they use the record as a reference for patient care every day. Labeled dividers and a standard table of contents help ensure that everyone who works with the chart knows the proper arrangement. When the patient is discharged or treatment is terminated, the record arrives in the HIM department, where it is immediately assembled for filing for a paper-based record, or assembled and prepared for scanning in the case of the hybrid health record. The face sheet and demographic information are on top, followed by the history and physical examination, the discharge summary, ancillary reports, consents, operative reports, progress notes in date order with the earliest orders first, orders in date order, nursing notes in date order, and so forth.

Quantitative analysis involves several additional steps. The record forms must be reviewed individually to make sure they belong to that particular patient. Organizing the paper forms is an important step. Forms are often intermingled and usually separated into a source-oriented format. Preliminary laboratory reports may be discarded when there is a final cumulative summary report.

Each facility must develop its own procedures for quantitative analysis. Responsibility for completion of the record must be assigned to each responsible provider. This is called **deficiency assignment.** The deficiencies, or parts of the record needing completion or signature, are entered into the health information system (HIS) or on paper worksheets attached to the incomplete, or deficient, health record.

Moreover, the record must be reviewed to ensure that certain basic reports that are common to all patient records are present, including the history and physical, progress notes, orders, nursing notes, and discharge summary. Other reports (for example, operative reports, diagnostic tests, consultations, and so on) may be included depending on the patient's course of treatment. In the hybrid health record system, the pages of the record are checked for bar codes for indexing according to the labeled dividers and tabs in the paper-based health record.

Quantitative analysis also includes a review for authentication that may be done by written signature, rubber stamp facsimile (unacceptable to CMS), computer password, or initials and must include the professional title of the individual responsible for the entry.

Any corrections to the record must be entered properly. In paper records, the provider should draw a single line through the error, add a note explaining the error, initial and date the error with the date it was discovered, and enter the correct information in chronological order. For electronic entries, a procedure should be followed that explains how to correct errors and enter addenda to the health record. In cases of medical identify theft, when someone presents using another's identity, the record must be identified as such so the appropriate health information is entered into the correct health record. This is a growing area of concern for the HIM professional, and procedures and guidance will continue to evolve until a standard of practice is established.

Criteria for Adequacy of Documentation

Documentation must reflect the care rendered to the patient and the patient's response to care. It must be timely and legible and authenticated by the person who wrote it. The health record is considered a legal document and a business record because it records events at or about the time they happen. Timeliness and legibility are two of the main areas of focus for accreditation and licensure bodies. Personnel in the HIM department analyze the health record for timeliness, accuracy, and completeness of entries in the health record. There are many patient safety concerns as discussed in chapter 22 of this text. However, one patient safety issue that relies on proper documentation is the use of abbreviations in the health record. The health record must be analyzed to ensure that symbols and abbreviations used in documentation have been approved by the medical staff and have only one clear meaning. The HIM department staff often analyze the health record for adequacy of documentation during (concurrent analysis) and after (discharge analysis) the patient's stay in the hospital.

Authentication of Health Record Entries

Authentication means to prove authorship and can be done in several ways. Signatures handwritten in ink are the most common method for signing paper-based health records. The Joint Commission allows rubber-stamp facsimile signatures when there is a statement verifying that the physician is the only one who will use the stamp and will maintain control of it. CMS specifically forbids the use of rubber stamps as an authentication method.

An **electronic signature** or e-signature is defined by AHIMA as "a generic, technology-neutral term for the various ways that an electronic record can be signed (attested)" (AHIMA e-HIM Work Group Best Practices for Electronic Signature and Attestation 2009). Methods of electronically signing documentation include a digital signature, a digitized image of a signature, a biometric identifier such as fingerprint or retinal scan, or a code or password. If a password or code is used, a statement ensuring that the password or code is controlled and used only by the responsible provider should be required to protect patient confidentiality and to ensure that others do not use it. Password security is critical. In the hybrid record, electronic signatures will be used more frequently as more documents in the record are produced by, and remain in, the system rather than becoming part of the paper record. **Autoauthentication** is a policy that allows the physician or provider to state in advance that dictated and transcribed reports should automatically be considered approved and signed when the physician does not make corrections within a certain period of time. Another variation of autoauthentication is that physicians authorize the HIM department to send a weekly list of documents needing signatures. The list is then signed and returned to the HIM department. Some facilities use autoauthentication even though the Joint Commission does not approve it. The objection is that evidence cannot be provided that the physician actually reviewed and approved each report. Facilities that use these methods of autoauthentication state that the physician offices automatically receive copies of transcribed reports and thus providers have the ability to review the reports before the deadline or before signing the list of reports.

Signatures in teaching hospitals are especially important to show that the attending physician responsible for the patient is actively involved in the patient's care. Signatures by attending physicians are generally required on all reports completed by residents and medical students. In electronic signature programs, the attending physician's co-signature should be entered after the resident has reviewed and signed the report to confirm the attending physician's participation.

Record Completion Policies and Procedures

The health record is not complete until all its parts are assembled, organized, and authenticated. The HIM professional, the administration, and the medical staff must develop record completion policies and procedures and include them in the medical staff bylaws. Although the facility's governing body has overall responsibility for patient care, responsibility for the delivery and documentation of patient care is delegated to the medical staff. The medical staff and the individual physician have primary responsibility for completing the health record to document the process of care that was rendered.

Most facilities have a committee in place composed of members of the medical staff, the administration, nursing, and other provider disciplines with responsibility for ensuring that medical staff members follow the established rules and regulations for health records. This committee may be the health record committee, the quality committee, or some other committee responsible for ensuring compliance with rules and regulations. The HIM professional should serve on the committee and generally assist the physician or provider committee chair by preparing the agenda and minutes for meetings.

The HIM professional also assists the committee by preparing reports on the status of record completion and problems with the flow of the record through the facility. Reports regarding the percentage of incomplete and delinquent health records are important to ensure that accreditation standards are met on an ongoing basis. The findings from various types of record review, including concurrent reviews and retrospective reviews, are presented to the committee and discussed. The committee often plays a key role in the approval of forms and electronic templates so that the standard form and format of the health record can be maintained.

The committee chair may communicate directly with physicians or other medical staff members to solve problems related to record completion. The committee can be a valuable resource to the HIM professional because it has representation from every area that enters documents into the patient record. Committee members can often assist the HIM department in acquiring equipment and personnel needed to properly perform its responsibilities. The committee generally reports to the executive committee of the medical staff and makes recommendations for executive staff action to improve patient record services.

Qualitative Analysis

In **qualitative analysis,** HIM personnel carefully review the quality and adequacy of record documentation and ensure that it is in accordance with the policies, rules, and regulations established by the facility; the standards of licensing and accrediting bodies; and government requirements. Like quantitative analysis, qualitative analysis may be done concurrently or retrospectively.

Qualitative analysis is a more in-depth review of health records than quantitative analysis, although the processes may overlap somewhat, depending on the facility. When qualitative analysis is done while the patient is in the facility or under active treatment, it is called open-record review, **ongoing records review, point-of-care review,** or **continuous record review.** Joint Commission requires an open-record review to ensure that its documentation standards are met at the point of care delivery. HIM personnel as well as case management personnel, nurses, physicians, and other providers should participate in the open-record review process. This review process looks at requirements such as presence of the history and physical examination prior to surgery, completion of the postoperative note, and many other aspects of the care process as documented in the health record. Open-record review should be done on an ongoing basis.

Qualitative review also is performed on **closed records,** which are records of discharged patients. **Closed-record review** means that the qualitative review is done retrospectively following discharge or termination of treatment. The benefit of open-record review is that problems in the care process that are revealed through the review can be corrected immediately. Closed-record review is an important way to obtain information about trends and patterns of documentation.

Role of Health Information Management Professionals

CMS and state licensure standards require healthcare facilities to have an HIM department with a designated person having administrative responsibility for health records. This requirement includes having the staff, equipment, and policies and procedures to ensure that records are current and accurate and that information is accessible.

The HIM department works closely with the business department regarding chart completion. The business department and the entire organization depend on the HIM staff to work with physicians and other healthcare professionals to provide the necessary information so that bills can be finalized in a timely manner. Bills are usually sent within two to three days after discharge. The health information manager receives daily notification of accounts that need information, and procedures must be established to expedite the flow of information for payment purposes.

Role of the Medical Staff

Medical staff members are responsible for developing bylaws governing their operation. The requirements for documentation and completion of health records as well as penalties for not adhering to these rules are included in the medical staff bylaws. Each member of the medical staff signs a statement that he or she will abide by the bylaws, and each is responsible for documentation.

Management of Incomplete Records

The HIM professional is responsible for ensuring that health records, whether manual or electronic, are readily accessible and that adequate equipment and personnel are available to facilitate record completion. No matter how well staffed and well organized the HIM department is, it can only facilitate the process. The providers are responsible for the documentation and must dictate, authenticate, and otherwise complete the patient health record.

Storage, Retrieval, and Tracking of Incomplete Records

Facilities provide access to incomplete records in various ways. Paper-based records needing completion must be maintained in an area that is easily accessible to physicians. The records may be arranged alphabetically by the last name of the responsible physician or filed in numerical order. Filing by physician name enables physicians to go directly to their own boxes to access and complete their own records. One disadvantage of alphabetic filing by physician name is that completion is often delayed because the record may remain in one physician's box until it is completed and moved to the next box. In a facility with many specialists or many residents, maintaining incomplete records in numerical order by the patient's record number works well because the records are accessible to all providers who need to complete them. Other facilities file incomplete records alphabetically by the patient's last name. Still other facilities immediately file the records into the general file area, using a combination of filing methods.

In systems with incomplete records filed numerically, clerical staff must be available to assist providers and to ensure that the portions of the record that need to be completed are actually done. With this system, the facility might require physicians to call before arriving at the department so that the needed records can be pulled. Some HIM personnel speed up record completion by taking records to physicians' offices located on the hospital campus.

With the hybrid health record system, the paper-based portion of the record may be scanned at discharge of the patient into the HIS, and providers are allowed to electronically authenticate incomplete records. This method is convenient for the providers as deficient health records may be simultaneously routed to multiple providers via workflow software. It is more efficient than the paper-based routing of health records as it requires fewer HIM personnel to locate, transport, and refile the paper-based health record. It is also more efficient for the providers who may access, authenticate, and complete the hybrid health record remotely. Hybrid health record systems have decreased the health record delinquency rates in many facilities.

Policies and Procedures on Record Completion

CMS, accrediting bodies, and state licensure standards require that the health record be completed in a timely manner. The completion time clock begins running when the patient is discharged, he or she expires, or his or her treatment is terminated. Records are considered deficient or incomplete immediately at discharge. Some facilities choose to begin the time clock after the records are reviewed quantitatively by the HIM staff and made available to the providers; however, regulations and standards do not provide for "extra" time for analysis or transcription delays, computer system downtime, or physician unavailability. Healthcare facility policies and medical staff bylaws must define when incomplete or deficient records become delinquent.

Delinquent health records are those records that are not completed within the specified time frame, for example, within 14 days of discharge. A delinquent record is similar to an overdue library book. The definition of a delinquent chart varies according to the facility, but most facilities require that records be completed within 30 days of discharge as mandated by CMS regulations and Joint Commission standards. Some facilities require a shorter time frame for completing records because of concerns about timely billing. **Chart tracking** of the location of incomplete and delinquent records as they move through the completion process is vital because many people need access to the records of recently treated patients.

Numerous methods may be used to encourage the timely completion of records. The Joint Commission specifies that the number of delinquent records cannot exceed 50 percent of the average number of discharges, so keeping the number of delinquent charts as low as possible is a constant challenge for HIM staff. Concurrent analysis by HIM or other facility personnel can help speed up completion time. Using case managers to work with physicians on chart completion issues while the patient is in the facility, for example, helps reduce the burden on the HIM department. HIM professionals rely on medical staff committees, such as the health record committee, chiefs of medical services, and medical staff leaders, to motivate providers to complete records. As previously discussed, hybrid health records alleviate some of the past issues with completion of the health record.

Many facilities limit the retrospective checking and flagging of incomplete items in the HIM department to the discharge summary, history and physical examination, operative reports, consultations, and clinical reports. Nursing information is not reviewed nor are signatures on progress notes or orders checked. Less detailed analysis is done after discharge due to the increased emphasis on open-record review when patients are in the facility under active treatment. Requiring physicians to sign notes and orders retrospectively does not affect the process of patient care and treatment or ensure that adequate documentation is available at the time patient care is provided. The HIM department should continue to monitor a sample of notes and orders to ensure that signatures are present to comply with established facility policies, accreditation standards, and regulations. Corrective measures should be developed when there is a pattern of missing signatures.

As mentioned earlier, penalties for incomplete health records must be included in medical staff bylaws. Penalties such as suspension of admission privileges or surgical privileges for the individual physician or a physician group and the levying of fines per incomplete chart or per day must be explained in the bylaws. Some hospitals make health record completion a condition of continued membership on the medical staff and suspend physicians from the medical staff who do not comply with the rules regarding completion. Suspended physicians must reapply for staff membership. Some states require that physicians suspended three times in a year be reported to the state medical board. However, in some small facilities or in facilities where a physician is responsible for many admissions, it is difficult to enforce the rules regarding suspension of admitting privileges.

Each facility must have a policy in place for dealing with situations where records remain incomplete for an extended period. The HIM director can be given authority to declare that a record is complete for purposes of filing when a provider relocates, dies, or has an extended illness that would prevent the record from ever being completed. If an incomplete record is filed under such circumstances, the reason for the record remaining incomplete must be documented in the health record. Every effort should be made to have a partner or physician in the same specialty area complete the chart so that coding, billing, and statistical information are available. In teaching hospitals, residents sometimes leave before charts are completed and the residents become difficult to locate. Thus, many facilities require departing residents to obtain clearance from the HIM department before the end of the residency period. The medical staff committee responsible for health record functions also may review long-standing incomplete charts and direct that they be filed even though incomplete.

Physician Notification Processes

With paper records, the physician must be notified when the record is available to be completed. Most healthcare facilities notify physicians of records that need completion on an escalating basis. For example, the first notice reminds the physician that records need completion; the second describes the penalties for noncompliance; the third limits the admission or operative privileges of the physician and might include

suspension of even emergency admission privileges; and the fourth gives a warning regarding suspension or removal from the medical staff. Finally, the physician may be considered to have forfeited staff membership and will have to reapply for membership. Some teaching facilities withhold paychecks for residents or refuse to approve vacations until all of the physician's charts are complete. With the hybrid record, the record is placed in the physician's queue, which serves as notification that it is ready to be completed.

The HIM department is responsible for periodically counting incomplete charts and preparing lists of those providers who have delinquent records and those whose privileges have been suspended. This is now often part of the workflow in the HIM systems, and physicians are often notified electronically of delinquent health records. Extensions are often granted when physicians are out of town, are sick, have a death in the family, and so on. The handling of physician suspensions requires a great deal of tact and cooperation among the HIM professional, the medical staff leadership, and the administration.

Template (Forms) Design and Management

The management and design of forms used in the healthcare environment is a concern of all providers because well-designed forms can facilitate the documentation of care. Forms within the paper record must be developed and approved in a careful, systematic process to ensure that they meet facility standards, are compatible with imaging and microfilming systems, and do not duplicate information on existing forms. (Examples of commonly used health record forms are provided in appendix A of this book.) HIM department personnel must be constantly vigilant to ensure that only approved forms become part of the permanent health record. Unapproved forms do not have the necessary form numbers or bar codes needed for imaging and indexing systems. Small forms and folded flowcharts create problems when records are handled and imaged. Oversized forms also create problems in optical imaging because special preparation is required to ensure that all information is scanned. As health records move toward an electronic format, the forms design process becomes the process of designing computer views and templates for entry of data, but the principles of control still apply. Facilities with hybrid health records have to transition existing forms into templates for the EHR. This transition requires extensive input and expertise from HIM personnel.

Principles of Template Design

A well-designed form improves the reliability of the data entered on it. A form should be designed to collect information in a consistent way and to remind providers of information that needs to be included. Many paper record forms consist of a single sheet. Other specialty forms, such as a unit-set form or a multipart form, have multiple-sheet forms preassembled in either carbon or carbonless sets. With spot carbons in unit-set forms, only part of the information on the original is visible on the copy. For example, when the face sheet is the first page of a unit set and is printed on the computer, the carbon can be positioned so that the copy for a clinical department would have only the patient identification information and not the financial information.

Continuous-feed forms use a series of forms separated with perforations that can be printed by a printer without having to load the paper for each form printed. The forms then can be separated and distributed. Continuous-feed forms can be used for both single sheets and multi-set forms.

Most forms include similar basic components, and all should contain at least a heading to describe the contents and purpose of the form, instructions on how to complete it, and spaces to enter required and optional information. General guidelines to follow when designing forms include the following:

- The form should be easy to complete.
- Instructions on completion and use of the form should be included.
- The form should have a heading with a title that clearly identifies its purpose.
- The facility's name and address should appear on each page of the form.
- The name, patient identification number, and other identifying information should be present on each form. Most facilities now use **bar coding technology** as identifying information.
- Bar coding also should be included in indexing the form for random access in an optical scanner or microfilming system. Bar codes are generally printed directly on the document or on a label affixed to the document.
- The form number and date of revision should be included to ensure that the form being used is the correct and most current version.
- Outdated forms should be recalled and eliminated.
- The physical layout of the form should be logical. When a clerk is entering information as the patient gives it, for example, the form should be organized to match the way the information is requested.
- Personal and address data and other items of information that relate to one another should be placed together (for example, the patient's city, state, and zip code).
- Font selection should be standardized. Some experts recommend all capital letters.
- Additional margin space should be provided for hole punches to allow the documents to be placed in folders or chart holders. The holes may be on the left-hand side of the form, at the top, or both, depending on the types of folders or binders used.
- Ruled lines may be used to outline sections of forms to allow for easy entry of data or to separate areas of the form.
- Check boxes and fields can be used to provide space for the collection of data.

Careful consideration also should be given to not including information on the backs of forms since it may be overlooked.

Facilities that are imaging paper records must have the bar-coded patient identification information on the back of the form to ensure proper indexing into the imaging system. Even though scanners can scan both sides of a document, the ability to index and thus access the information must be ensured.

Electronic Forms Management

Facilities must develop strict guidelines and processes for forms control. Word-processing programs and programs specifically designed for forms design have made the process easier than in the past. Providers often design their own nonapproved forms, which may appear in the paper record when it arrives in the HIM department. These unauthorized forms affect the patient care process as well as procedures in the department. The person who designed the form may be unaware of the interrelated processes that are affected by changing it. A bar code identifying the type of form would not be available for forms that have not gone through the approval process.

Forms control systems must

- Provide for the development of forms according to established guidelines
- Control the printing and use of forms
- Guide providers in designing forms according to established guidelines
- Prevent staff from changing or designing forms that duplicate existing forms or could be combined into other forms

Forms control is critical to the transition toward hybrid and EHR systems. The transition to electronic records usually begins with creating a hybrid health record by using an imaging system to gather information about existing forms and to ensure that all forms can be properly scanned and indexed. Without indexing, the information cannot be easily retrieved. The forms control process also should establish processes for forms inventory, forms identification, forms analysis, and forms purchasing.

Forms Inventory

The first step in the forms control process is the forms inventory. This process involves gathering each form and all of its editions to ensure that the most current version is used. A subject file is a good idea for bringing together all the forms used by each of the areas, such as all admissions or registration forms, all operative forms, and all nursing forms. Organizing in this manner can prevent new forms from being developed when current forms have the needed information, assist in finding ways to combine forms with related information, and serve as a reminder that information changed on one form must be changed on related forms.

Forms Identification

The second part of the forms control process is forms identification. This process involves assigning each form a distinct title that reflects its use. In paper systems, a forms number is also assigned to indicate that the form has been approved.

The date and the source department are usually included with the number. Bar coding and labels with complete bar-coded information about the form are becoming more prevalent as facilities prepare for the computerization of forms. A numerical listing of forms by the forms identification number should be maintained.

Forms Analysis

Forms analysis involves the continuous review and revision of forms. The forms analysis process is often initiated because of procedural problems, such as when providers are not receiving the information they need to do their work. Forms assist in guiding processes and ensuring that complete information is obtained and recorded. Flowcharting the development and distribution of the forms is helpful in determining whether a form is still useful, whether the information it contains is current, and whether it meets the current requirements of the facility.

Forms Purchasing

Purchasing and printing comprise the fourth part of the forms control process. A policy should be in place stating that forms cannot be ordered or reordered without approval of the forms committee or some other group or individual responsible for purchasing and printing approval. Some facilities now use just-in-time production of forms. Just-in-time production is a procedure where copies of forms can be printed at the patient care area rather than having to maintain a large inventory of paper forms. This inventory of forms becomes obsolete when any change is made to the form. This eliminates the possibility that an outdated form is available for use in a health record.

Role for Data Recording During Systems Downtime

Paper forms are critical for data recording in the health record during system downtimes and outages. Forms should be made available for printing in the patient care areas in instances of systems downtime. This allows for easy access to the forms when necessary and also provides a mechanism to manage and update the forms and ensure that only approved forms are available for providers to enter documentation for the health record.

Check Your Understanding 10.5

Instructions: Answer the following questions on a separate sheet of paper.

1. Differentiate between quantitative analysis and qualitative analysis. What purpose do they serve?

2. How does concurrent review facilitate record completion?

3. What is universal chart order, and why is it being adopted by healthcare facilities?

4. What is the difference between open- and closed-record reviews?

5. Why is the finance department concerned about the timely completion of records?

6. In what two ways do HIM departments store incomplete health records? What are the advantages and disadvantages of each method?

7. What is the difference between an incomplete record and a delinquent record?

8. How does the HIM professional help providers to complete health records?

9. Describe the three methods facilities use to authenticate health records.

10. Why have some facilities stopped notifying providers about orders and progress notes needing signatures?

11. Why is forms control a critical responsibility of the HIM professional?

12. What are the four parts of the forms control process?

13. Why is it important for providers wanting a new form to go through the approval process?

14. How are bar codes and labels used in forms? Why are they necessary?

Creation, Storage, and Retention of Paper-Based and Hybrid Health Records

Healthcare organizations need policies covering the distribution and storage of health records to ensure that the records can be located quickly when they are needed for patient care and other uses. Controlling the storage of paper-based and hybrid health records is critical to patient care. The quality of patient care as well as the image and reputation of the HIM department may depend on the speed with which patient health information can be retrieved.

Management of paper-based and hybrid health records includes three processes: creation and identification, storage and retrieval, and retention and disposition.

Health Record Creation and Identification

As discussed earlier, the health record is created when the patient is first admitted to or treated in a healthcare facility. Every patient is assigned a specific identification number, and the health record is initiated with the collection of admission or registration information. As data and information about the patient's care and condition are documented, the record grows. The record remains in active use for the purposes of patient care, clinical coding, billing, statistical analysis, and other operational processes until the episode of care ends.

Health Record Identification Systems

For the correct health record to be quickly retrieved when it is needed, each record must be assigned a unique identifier. The choice of record identification system is tied to the organization's filing system and other core information systems.

Alphabetic versus Numeric Patient Identifiers

Small healthcare facilities, such as physician offices, often use a simple alphabetical identifier: the patient's last and first names. This identifier is also used for filing of medical records in strict alphabetical order by the patient's last name. Alphabetical systems are more appropriate for facilities with a smaller number of records because of the problem of different patients with the same name. Most healthcare organizations use a record identification system that assigns a numerical identifier to each patient. A variety of methods is used in assigning these numbers and using them in filing the record.

Serial Numbering System

In a **serial numbering system,** each patient receives a new number at each visit, and numbers are assigned in straight numerical sequence to consecutive patients in the order in which they arrive for treatment. Each time a patient is treated by the facility, a new number is issued to link the patient to that particular visit or admission. This system is often used by clinics and physician offices.

Unit Numbering System

Most large facilities use a unit numbering system. In a **unit numbering system,** the patient is assigned a number during the first encounter for care and keeps it for all subsequent encounters. The number may be assigned automatically by a computer program. Veterans Affairs (VA) facilities use the patient's Social Security number as the unit number because it is a unique permanent number already assigned to the patient. However, due to patient privacy concerns and increases in identity theft and medical identity theft, the use of the Social Security number is not recommended. If facilities change from a serial to a unit numbering system, it is important to pick a start date and move forward from that point rather than going back in time to assign unit numbers for past encounters. As patients are readmitted, they are assigned a new number that then becomes the permanent unit number and all records are brought forward and linked under the new number.

Serial-Unit Numbering System

In a **serial-unit numbering system,** the patient is issued a different number for each admission or encounter for care and the records of past episodes of care are brought forward to be filed under the last number issued. This creates a unit record that contains information from all the patient's encounters. Because this system requires a great deal of shifting of records and changing of numbers, it is not as commonly used as the unit numbering system.

Family Numbering System

Family numbering is a type of unit numbering system. In this system, the entire family is assigned one number and all information on visits by any family member is filed in one location. This system may be appropriate for use in family practice settings, but care must be taken to preserve patient privacy.

Health Record Filing Systems

Most healthcare facilities use numerical filing systems for permanent storage of paper-based health records. Small facilities, such as physician offices and clinics, often use alphabetic filing; larger facilities generally use numerical filing systems.

Straight Numeric Filing System

In a **straight numeric filing system,** records are filed in numerical order according to the number assigned. The major shortcoming of straight numeric filing is that most of the file activity is where the most recent numbers have been assigned since records of recent hospitalizations or visits are the ones most in use.

Terminal-Digit Filing System

In a **terminal-digit filing system,** records are filed according to a three-part number made up of two-digit pairs. The basic terminal-digit filing system contains 10,000 divisions, made up of 100 sections ranging from 00 to 99 with 100 divisions within each section ranging from 00 to 99. In a terminal-digit filing system, the shelving units (filing space) are equally divided into 100 sections.

In terminal-digit filing, the record number is placed into terminal-digit order when the health record is ready for filing. The number is broken down into two-digit pairs and is read from right to left. For example, the number 670187 would be written as 67-01-87. The first pair of digits on the right (87) is called the primary number or the terminal-digit number, the second pair of digits (01) is called the secondary number, and the third pair of digits (67) is called the tertiary or final number.

The primary number is considered first for filing. The primary numbers range from 00 to 99 and represent the 100 sections of the filing area. Because many records will be filed in each section, each section needs to be further subdivided, first according to the secondary number and then according to the tertiary number. As shown in figure 10.4, a record numbered 67-01-87 would be filed in section 87, in subsection 01, and

Figure 10.4.   Filing of patient record 67-01-87 in a terminal-digit system

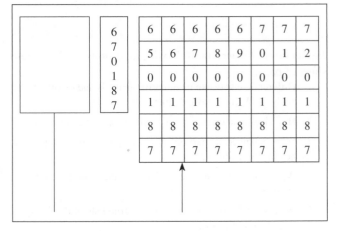

Figure 10.5.   Filing of three consecutive patient records under the terminal-digit system

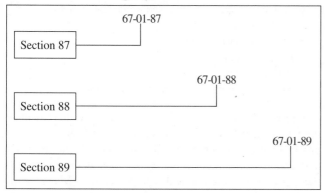

then in numerical sequence for 67 (after 66-01-87 and before 68-01-87). All records with the tertiary and secondary numbers of 01 to 87 would be filed within this part of the file.

Consider three patients who were admitted to a facility and were issued the following numbers in sequence: 67-01-87, 67-01-88, and 67-01-89. In a terminal digit system, these records would be added to three different filing sections of the 100 sections of the file rather than all being filed at the end as in a straight numerical system. (See figure 10.5.) In a standard terminal-digit filing area, there will be 10,000 guides to index the primary number sections and secondary number subdivisions so that behind each guide, all records will have the same final four digits. The guides are set up vertically, with the digits above the line on the guide representing the division (secondary number) and the digits below the line representing the section (primary number). An index guide tab marked with 67 above the line and 80 below would indicate the 67 division of the 80 section.

The advantage of terminal-digit filing is that filing shelves fill equally rather than at the end of the shelving units, as is the case with conventional straight numerical filing. There will be one record with the primary number 00, one with 01, and so on through 99 for every 100 consecutive numbers issued to patients. For every 100 records that are added to the file, each section of the file will be increased by only one record. The task of shifting (moving records) to alleviate overcrowding at the end of the shelving unit is reduced because the sections are filed evenly across the sections. One hundred consecutively numbered folders would be removed from 100 separate locations. Thus, the even distribution of records throughout the filing space can be maintained, and misfiles can be reduced because clerks need to remember only two numbers at a time.

Another advantage of terminal-digit filing is that the department's workload can be evenly distributed among filing personnel. Certain sections can be designated for each employee. For example, if a department has five file clerks, each could be given responsibility for a specific section, with

clerk one responsible for sections 00 to 19, clerk two responsible for sections 20 to 39, and so on. In addition to maintaining the assigned sections, each clerk would file loose reports and keep the records in order, handle requests for information from patient records, and perform other duties.

Terminal-digit filing can be adapted to various types of numbering systems. A six-digit number is most common, but some facilities, such as VA facilities, use a longer number. The VA uses the Social Security number as the basis for terminal-digit filing. For example, number 401-80-1530 could be adapted to serve as a terminal digit by dividing it so that 30 is the primary number, 15 is the secondary number, and 40180 is the tertiary number. The files do not expand as evenly because there is no facility control over the assignment of numbers to patients.

Another advantage of terminal-digit filing is for random distribution of voice files for transcription and health records for coding. The primary digits of the system are randomly assigned to staff so that difficult-to-understand dictators and difficult-to-code records are randomly assigned. Terminal-digit filing concepts may also be utilized to evenly distribute loose paperwork filing and the doctors' incomplete area.

Patient Identity Management

As healthcare delivery becomes more connected, correctly identifying patients and linking patient records is more important and has elevated the role of the HIM professional in patient identity management. HIM professionals have long been charged with the correct assignment of the medical record or health record number, which is used to assimilate, store, and access patient health records.

Master Patient Index

The **master patient index (MPI)** is a permanent database including every patient ever admitted to or treated by the facility. Even though patient health records may be destroyed after legal retention periods have been met, the information contained in the MPI must be kept permanently. The MPI is also referred to as the master person index, master name file, **enterprise master patient index (EMPI),** regional master patient index (RMPI), and master patient database. Whatever it is called, the MPI is an important key to the health record because it contains the patient's identifying information including patient name and health record number.

Each facility has an MPI, which includes information for all patients who have been registered or treated at any location in the facility. The MPI can be a simple manual file containing cards with basic identification information about the patient, or it can be a sophisticated computerized system. Regardless of the format of the MPI, it associates the patient with the particular number under which patient treatment information can be located. The index also helps to control number assignments to ensure that former patients with unit numbers are not inadvertently assigned a new number.

The challenges in maintaining the master patient index are many. For example, patients may not remember previous admissions or may have been admitted under a different name. A person other than the patient may have provided incorrect information, resulting in a new number being assigned when the patient returns for an appointment or is readmitted to the hospital. Sometimes patients use different middle initials or a nickname rather than a given name, or their names may have many possible spellings or may be hyphenated. Babies may have names changed, first and last names can be reversed, and outside laboratories may use different data. Basic demographic information such as addresses can be abbreviated incorrectly. In some cases, patients do not speak the same language as the clerk entering the information, resulting in miscommunication and incorrect data. Facilities that have either merged or separated must keep information on patients treated and often have problems combining information from two computer systems into one master patient index. Facilities may have manual card files that have been microfilmed in the past or may use a variety of formats over time, from index cards to microfilmed cards on rolls or microfiche to a computerized database.

The challenge for facilities is to maintain a correct and current MPI so that each patient has a unique identifier number. Duplication and overlays and overlaps are major problems. An **overlap** occurs when a patient has more than one medical record number assigned across more than one database. An **overlay** occurs when one patient record is overwritten with data from another patient's record. The goal is to have a true longitudinal record from birth to death, and the MPI serves as the link to information and certainty of identification that are critical to the quality and safety of patient care. Healthcare facilities have hired HIM professionals as EMPI coordinators or have hired consultants to clean and maintain EMPI systems to ensure that the correct information on the correct patient is available to the provider and others who need it. With an EMPI, patient information is included from all entities within the enterprise and shared as needed. The sharing of data is a worthy goal, but incorrect information can adversely affect the quality and safety of care; thus, accuracy of the MPI is a critical issue. There has been some interest in a uniform patient identifier that would be used nationwide, but action toward creating such a universal identifier has not progressed because of concerns about compromising patient confidentiality, identity theft, and medical identity theft.

The MPI usually includes the following information:

- Patient's full name and any other names the patient uses
- Patient's date of birth
- Patient's complete address
- Patient's phone numbers including cellular phone number
- Patient's health record number
- Patient's billing or account number

- Name of the attending physician
- Dates of the patient's admission and discharge or the date of the visit or encounter
- Patient's disposition at discharge or the conclusion of treatment
- Patient's marital status
- Patient's gender
- Patient's race
- Name of the patient's emergency contact

Other information may be included to further identify the patient and ensure that his or her name is linked to the proper record number. Some facilities include the mother's maiden name as another way to link the patient health record number and information to the proper patient. Many facilities develop a standard of five common fields to search for each new entry in the MPI and to review the MPI database for potential duplicate entries.

Controls for accuracy of the MPI include limiting access to the index and limiting the ability to make changes to a few key personnel. The first step in maintaining an accurate index is to obtain the correct information at admission or registration, but there are numerous problems, such as situations when the patient is unable to provide the correct information or when items are entered improperly. In the past, when only HIM personnel assigned numbers, there was more control; today, numbers are entered by many different personnel to patients entering the facility through many areas such as the emergency department, the inpatient admissions area, or the outpatient clinic. The more people involved in entering data, the greater the potential for error.

When a patient's record or healthcare information cannot be located, his or her care may be compromised. Without prior information, the physician and other providers might duplicate tests or treatments. A second record for the same patient is then created under a new number, which adds to the problem of bringing the parts of the patient record together. Research to "clean up" duplicate numbers and other errors is among the HIM professional's responsibilities.

As electronic information exchange becomes more prevalent, it is critical that the master patient indexing system correctly identifies the patient. One possible way to exchange healthcare information among facilities would be to utilize an MPI as an additional technical layer infrastructure serving as an umbrella to connect and provide access to electronic patient information at different facilities. Although the MPI consists of demographic information, it is the first step in ensuring that correct clinical information about the correct patient is shared. The MPI becomes the link among multiple computer systems that must be able to share information with each other. This process is complicated within one facility with many computer systems, but when multiple facilities try to share information, the EMPI or RMPI is a prerequisite to linking together the data within their various computer systems (AHIMA 2004).

Instructions: Answer the following questions on a separate piece of paper.

1. Why is the MPI considered the key index in the HIM department?

2. Why is accurate information critical for the MPI?

3. What are some of the reasons why incorrect information is obtained?

4. What is the consequence of a patient having duplicate health record numbers?

Health Record Storage and Retrieval

The HIM department is responsible for ensuring that the health record is available when needed by the provider for patient care. No matter how well organized and well managed the HIM department is, the timeliness of record delivery to providers is the measure of the quality of the department's services. The hybrid state of the health record makes reproduction of the health record more difficult since the health record may be stored in various formats within the same facility.

Health Record Storage

Storage is the application of efficient procedures for the use of filing equipment and storage media to keep records secure and available to those providers and other healthcare personnel authorized to access them. Record storage equipment can range from numerous types of file cabinets to open shelves of various heights and types.

Planning for health record storage is a major responsibility for the HIM professional. He or she must maintain a leadership role in ensuring that sufficient, conveniently accessible space is available for the storage of paper records. Ways must be provided to consistently maintain sufficient filing room by moving inactive records out of the main filing area or imaging records. With hybrid records in which some parts of the record are electronic, the paper sections of the record may be smaller and take less filing space than records that are entirely paper based.

Because space is expensive, administrators and facilities management personnel are always looking for ways to better use it. The HIM professional must make sure that paper health records are not located in poor environmental conditions where they can be either damaged or difficult to locate. For example, health records should not be stored in areas where pipes and flammable substances are located due to the danger of flooding or fire. Subbasements without proper flooring and temperature control, parking garages, and non-temperature-controlled commercial storage units are not appropriate storage locations for health records. Water, pests, and mold are all potential problems. Temperature and humidity control are important to prevent mold. The storage area must be clean and dust free and located away from food and trash in order to prevent bugs such as paper mites. Chemical treatments for mold and pests can cause problems for workers who must sort through and locate records for patient treatment. The HIM professional must be firm in the need to protect the original records for the duration of the legally required period. The potential need for the health records should be considered when deciding to send records to an off-site storage facility. Many companies specialize in the storage of vital records and provide the proper conditions for the protection of records as well as access to records.

HIM professionals have had to deal with the restoration of paper records damaged by water resulting from hurricanes, earthquakes, and tornadoes. There are companies that specialize in the restoration of records and can handle disaster recovery. Moreover, some companies negotiate contracts ensuring that the healthcare provider is first in line for recovery efforts should a disaster occur. Paper is extremely fragile when wet, and indirect circulation of air is critical; dehumidification and perhaps vacuum freezing are considerations in the restoration process. With a hybrid record in which part of the record is in an electronic format, methods must be utilized to ensure the physical security of those parts of the record also (Burrington-Brown et al. 2010).

Health Record Retrieval

Retrieval is concerned with locating requested records and information. It involves signing out or checking out records from the filing area and tracking their location. Those that are not returned within the specified time period must be retrieved. A number of excellent software systems are available for tracking patient records.

HIM professionals are charged with safeguarding patient information by ensuring the person accessing the record has a need to know and an appropriate reason to access the patient record. In both paper and electronic retrievals the HIM professional is responsible for ensuring that access was appropriate.

HIM personnel must be able to quickly determine the exact location of a specific health record at any time. Facilities should have strict policies and procedures in place that specify who is permitted to check out records from the filing area and for what time period. Past records are generally requested when patients are readmitted or appear for appointments. Large clinics create a lot of activity in the filing area because records must be pulled in advance for patient appointments.

The facility or provider is responsible for maintaining the health record. When the facility or provider cannot produce a record, it must be able to prove that the loss was unintentional.

Regardless of the filing system used, the filing area should be audited periodically to ensure that files are in correct order for rapid access and retrieval. Loose reports should be attached, and those awaiting attachment should be sorted and organized to facilitate retrieval. Audits of the record tracking system should be conducted to ensure that the health record is still under the responsibility of the person named in the system.

Statistics on the ratio of number of requests to number of health records in the file should be maintained to demonstrate the activity in the filing area.

Health Record Filing and Storage Equipment

Filing equipment vendors are the HIM professional's best resource in planning a filing area that makes the best use of the available space. Open-shelf filing is the least expensive option for health record storage. Shelves are usually arranged back to back just as shelving is in a library. Shelving uses space more efficiently than file cabinets because only 30 to 36 inches are needed for each aisle. When standard file cabinets with drawers are used, aisles should be at least five feet wide to allow two facing file cabinets to be opened at the same time and to allow personnel who need to work in the same area to pass. Lateral files with drawers and doors also require sufficient aisle space for opening the individual drawers and allowing personnel to pass.

Many facilities use open-shelf files mounted on tracks to conserve valuable space. These are referred to as movable files, and many different styles are available. With movable files mounted on tracks, more sections of files can be installed because the floor space for many fixed aisles is not needed. The files in a mobile unit can be opened one aisle at a time. With permanently installed open shelves, there are fixed aisles between each shelf. Another consideration is whether the files open electronically or manually to create the aisles. Whichever type of shelving is selected, the shelves must handle the heavy weight of paper-based health records, which may require reinforced flooring.

The estimated number of file shelves needed is based on several factors. One consideration is the average size of individual records. The volume of patients and the number of repeat visits or readmissions affect the potential expansion of each individual patient record. The type of facility also affects the size of individual records. Acute-care facilities with extensive ancillary services and more acutely ill patients have larger individual patient records, as do facilities specializing in transplants, cancer, and other chronic diseases. When unit records are organized in a terminal-digit filing system, there must be adequate expansion space in each division of the filing area to allow for expansion of individual records. Hybrid records in which portions of the records are maintained solely in electronic format are smaller than totally paper-based records, so less filing space is needed.

HIM professionals frequently depend on vendors to estimate filing space. It is the responsibility of the HIM professional to ensure that the vendors' estimates for filing space are adequate. The number of linear filing inches is the key factor. When there are existing records, the average size of the individual records can be easily calculated by measuring the number of files on a random sampling of shelves. The usable space must be measured from the inside of the panels so that the true number of linear filing inches is reflected. For example, one standard three-foot-wide shelf would have approximately 33 linear inches available for filing, not 36 linear inches. Allowance also should be made for file guides, which also reduce the number of linear filing inches.

An example might be that of a department expanding into another filing area. The department has selected eight-shelf open shelves that are 36 inches wide with 33 inches of actual filing space on each shelf. The department's present health records have been measured in random areas of the existing files and average two inches in thickness. With 5,000 discharges anticipated each year and a projection of five years, 25,000 records will need to be stored ($5,000 \times 5 = 25,000$). Because records average a two-inch thickness, 50,000 filing inches are needed ($25,000 \times 2 = 50,000$). Because each eight-shelf unit will have 264 linear filing inches available ($33 \times 8 = 264$), the number of inches needed, 50,000, must be divided by 264 to determine the number of filing units that must be purchased, which will be 190.

Storage space is at a premium, and many facilities have several locations for storage of health records. This can create retrieval problems when health records are at distant locations or off-site. Much personnel time can be spent walking or driving to off-site locations. Some facilities contract with commercial storage companies to store inactive records; commercial storage companies can provide transportation of health records to the facility.

Many facilities use color-coded file folders in their filing system—different colors representing numbers or letters depending on the filing system—and the colors appear on the folders and guides. The records in a particular section are in blocks of color. This method allows misfiles to be identified quickly. Vendors of file folders have endless possibilities of color-coding different pairs of numbers and letters. The colors selected to represent particular digits must be permanent and continued when new folders are ordered or else the advantage of color-coding will be lost.

Health Record Retention and Disposition

Health records cannot be stored indefinitely because storage space is expensive. **Retention** involves determining the schedule to be followed to protect and preserve active and inactive records. **Disposition** involves the process of destroying the records once the end of the retention period has been reached. Establishing policies that incorporate state and federal laws and maintaining a disaster plan are part of the disposition process. The transfer and destruction of records, optical scanning, and **microfilming** are all part of this stage.

Facilities must be careful to monitor record maintenance so that health records are moved continuously out of active storage as they become inactive or reach maximum retention periods. Older records also may not be as useful in the patient care treatment process because the patient's health status changes over time. The HIM professional has the challenge of maintaining the location and media types of various health records within the healthcare enterprise. This is often referred to as enterprise content and record management and requires extensive knowledge of standards, regulations, and systems to ensure that the health record is managed through the life cycle of the record. As media is updated and record formats change, the HIM professional must catalog the location of health records that may be stored in a variety of formats.

In looking at retention requirements, it is important to look at the requirements for secondary as well as primary records. Primary records are the original health records in whatever form they are kept; secondary records are by-products of the original information such as indexes, physician profiles, databases, billing information, and other reports or queries.

Accreditation and Legal Health Record Retention Requirements

AHIMA recommends that retention of health information be based on the needs and requirements of the facility, such as legal requirements, continued patient care, research, education, and other legitimate uses (AHIMA 2005). The Joint Commission asserts that the length of health record retention depends on laws, regulations, and the use of health records for care and for other purposes such as research and education (Joint Commission 2011).

State laws, CMS regulations, and other federal regulations, accreditation standards, and facility policies and procedures must also be reviewed when establishing a **retention schedule.** The HIM professional must adhere to the strictest time limit if the recommended retention period varies among different laws and regulations. In addition to the length of time for maintaining health records, the HIM professional must consider the required length of retention for other documentation such as immunization records, mammography records, x-rays, and radiographs. It is important to realize that the retention periods are different for the records of minors and incompetent patients.

CMS requires health records to be maintained for at least five years, according to 42 CFR 482.24(b). This requirement includes committee reports, physician certification and recertification reports, radiologist records (printouts, films, scans, and other images), home health agency records, long-term care records, laboratory records, and any other records that document information about claims. The Occupational Safety and Health Administration (OSHA) requires records of employees with occupational exposure to be maintained for the duration of employment plus 30 years. The statutes

of limitation (deadline for filing a lawsuit) in various types of legal actions are important considerations in developing a retention schedule.

Other departments rely on the expertise of the HIM professional to assist them in developing record retention procedures. A retention plan for the facility must be carefully written and included in the departmental policy and procedure manual to ensure that record destruction is part of the normal course of business and that no one particular health record or group of health records is singled out for destruction.

Retention Requirements for Ancillary Materials

E-mail messages and faxes are used for instructions, information about appointments, and the reporting of information. These must be printed or archived and included in the health record.

Images, such as complete readouts or "strips" from EEGs, EKGs, fetal monitors, Holter monitors, treadmill tests, electromyogram, echocardiograms, videotapes, and other imaging records, do not have to be kept within the physical health record but must be retrievable for as long as legally required. The original interpretations of the results must actually be part of the physical patient health record. Facilities may have computerized systems that COLD-feed the results into the imaging system so that the actual images are available to physicians and other providers. In some scanning systems, these images are not of adequate quality for use in diagnosis, so ancillary departments should maintain the original information for the appropriate retention period. State laws should be reviewed to determine the retention requirement of other images.

Fetal monitoring strips create storage problems for many HIM departments. They are part of the mother's record, but because the strips relate to the newborn, they should be maintained according to the length of time stipulated for a minor's records. Because these strips are not compatible with imaging systems, some facilities have digital systems software to maintain and store fetal monitoring strips within the labor and delivery area.

Magnetic tapes containing the digital versions of MRI and CT studies are not considered permanent health records as long as a hard copy of the final images (radiographic film) is placed in the patient's health record. The signed interpretation of the studies must be maintained in the record for the full retention period required by law. According to 21 CFR 900.12 (c)(4), mammograms must be maintained for 5 to 10 years, depending on whether additional mammograms are performed. State laws may require a retention period for mammograms of 20 to 30 years. This is another example of the HIM professional having to ensure that the longer time period is followed when retention schedules are determined. Microfilming or optical and electronic imaging technology is allowed by most state laws and is an acceptable method of maintaining patient health records (AHIMA 2011a).

Destruction and Transfer of Health Records

After time limits for retention have been reached, the HIM professional must decide on the destruction process for health records, which must ensure that health records are burned, shredded, or destroyed in such a way that protected health information is not revealed. It is important to document the method of destruction, the date, and that fact that record destruction is part of the normal course of business with no one particular health record or group of health records singled out for destruction.

When the facility is closed or sold, its health records are transferred to the successor provider, meaning the entity or individual that purchases the facility. In ambulatory care settings or physician offices, patients are informed of their options to transfer their records to another provider of choice before their health records are transferred to the successor provider. When a physician leaves a group practice, patients should be given the choice to transfer their health records and move with the physician or to have the health records and the responsibility for care transferred to another provider in the group (AHIMA 2011b).

Development of a Record Retention Program

Figure 10.6 lists the objectives of a record retention program. The program must ensure that current health records are retained; that inactive records are maintained; that retention is cost-effective in terms of storage space, equipment, and personnel; that a formal health record destruction process is in place; and that retention periods are established. A task force or committee might be established with representation from administration, medical staff, health information services, risk management, and legal counsel to give consideration to the needs of all groups who use patient health information. Figure 10.7 lists some of the elements to consider in a retention program. These include looking carefully at all of the record's uses and the cost of space.

The HIM director is generally responsible for implementing the retention program. However, other individuals may be charged with the shared responsibility of implementing

Figure 10.6.   Objectives of a record retention program

- To ensure retention and preservation of all valued health records
- To maintain noncurrent records of continuing value for uniform time periods and in designated locations
- To ensure cost-effectiveness in record storage space, equipment, and personnel
- To dispose of unnecessary records by developing an orderly, controlled, and confidential system of record destruction
- To establish record retention periods consistent with patient care, regulatory requirements, and other legal considerations

Figure 10.7.   Elements to consider in the preservation of records

- Patient value for continued care
- Record usage in the facility as guided by the patient population and activity of its medical staff
- Legal value as determined by the statute of limitations
- Research value
- Historical value
- Volume and cost to maintain hard-copy storage versus microfilm, optical disk, or remote storage
- Storage and safety standards
- Contractual arrangements with payers

the program in some facilities. Some facilities establish a task force to oversee the record retention program, sometimes chaired by an HIM professional.

The steps in developing a record retention program include

1. Conducting an inventory of the facility's records
2. Determining the format and location of record storage
3. Assigning each record a retention period
4. Destroying records that are no longer needed

Conducting an Inventory of Records

The first step in establishing a record retention program is to carefully and completely inventory the records or categories of records that are maintained. In this phase, it is important to determine all the locations and formats of patient information, including images, videotapes, e-mails, tracings, computerized records, and other formats. The inventory also must include the records and registries maintained by all departments. Both primary and secondary records must be identified. A comprehensive list of all software and versions used also should be maintained so that health records, documents, and images can be retrieved in the future. Specialized computer systems used by individual departments should be included.

Determining Storage Format and Location

Determining the format and location of storage is the second step in retention program development. Facilities may choose to retain records in paper format or in hard copy and to store them either on-site or in off-site contract storage. Off-site contract storage should be located at a distance far enough away from the facility to ensure that a disaster affecting the facility will not also affect the storage location.

One storage mechanism for inactive records is microfilming. Microfilming is the process of recording miniaturized images of a patient health record on film. The images are usually filmed by a special camera onto rolls of 16-millimeter film. The microfilmed images may be stored permanently on the rolls, which may be stored either in boxes labeling the first and last patient numbers on a roll or inserted into special cartridges. Roll film contains information on many patients and cannot be changed. The images are often indexed according to type of form at the time of filming to allow for quicker retrieval of information.

An alternative to storing microfilm rolls in cartridges is to store images in microfilm jackets. The roll film would be cut into strips and inserted into the channels of the jackets. The microfilm jacket has the advantage of serving as an individual folder for storing the records of one patient. Additional filmed images can be added to the jacket or changed. The jackets are usually four by six inches and have a strip at the top on which to record the patient's name and number. Because the strips can be color-coded, the jackets can be filed in filing cabinets or electric files using the same filing and numbering system the facility uses for paper records.

Microfilm cameras also can film directly onto a microfiche film format. Like the microfilm jacket, the microfiche has the advantage of having only one patient's information available on the sheet of fiche. However, its disadvantage is that patient information cannot be updated because the images are filmed directly onto the microfiche itself. The most common size of fiche is a four- by six-inch sheet, with space for the patient's name and number.

Many facilities use a combination of microfilm formats to accommodate technology and equipment changes. The microfilming of records has many advantages, including the following:

- Microfilming saves space, which is the primary reason why facilities use it.
- Health records can be retrieved and retained for a long period of time.
- It is simple to duplicate microfilm records in order to provide security or backup copies, and paper copies can be printed from reader printer equipment.
- Microfilm is legally admissible as the original document.

The facility also must consider disadvantages when deciding whether to microfilm records. These issues include the following:

- Although microfilming saves a great deal of storage space, it is expensive. For example, preparing the records for filming is a major cost that involves removing staples, checking identification, adjusting oversized or overlapping forms for filming, repairing sheets, and other tasks.
- Special equipment is needed to read and copy microfilm.
- Personnel must be available in patient care areas or in the HIM department to find the microfilm jackets, microfiche, or roll microfilm and to locate the exact information needed.

Microfilming can be done on-site by facility personnel or under contract with a microfilming company. When the facility decides to have the microfilming done in-house, it must take into account the costs of equipment, labor and training, supplies, and maintenance.

On the other hand, when the facility decides to use an outside contract microfilming company, the contract should specify who performs the preparation and packs the boxes of records. After records have been transported to the outside contract company, the facility must be able to retrieve the patient's information at any time in case he or she is readmitted or appears for treatment. When records are to be indexed, the contract should fully explain the indexing procedure to ensure that needed documents are accessible. The contract also should specify the turnaround time for filming. Moreover, film returned to the facility must be carefully analyzed by facility personnel to ensure its quality and legibility before the original record is destroyed. The company microfilming the records usually handles their destruction after the facility has audited the returned film. The cost of microfilming is generally based on the number of images filmed.

A second storage mechanism is optical **scanning.** Records can be scanned into optical scanning equipment or digitally transferred. The imaging process converts paper or microfilm documents into a computer-readable digital format. The facility must determine what information can be fed directly into the imaging system, for example, registration and face sheet, discharge summary, and all other dictated and transcribed reports. Digitized information, including that produced by laboratory and radiology, can be COLD-fed into the imaging system. COLD now refers to a variety of technologies related to digitized input and output. Optical scanning produces an image of the record that can be indexed and quickly retrieved and simultaneously viewed by many providers. This is not a true electronic record because the image cannot be changed after it has been permanently archived. Retrieval from images can be achieved at the report level, for example the history and physical, but more granular queries such as the patient's HbA1c level on a particular date are not possible.

Imaging involves preparing, or prepping, the documents, which must be done before the records are scanned. Staples must be removed, papers repaired, and each page checked to ensure the presence of a bar code on both the front and back of every form in the record. The scanning process involves inserting the paper into the optical scanner so that both the front and back of the forms are scanned at the same time. Two types of scanners are usually used for health records: flatbed scanners and automatic document-feed scanners. The type of scanner used depends on the volume to be scanned. Flatbed scanners are usually slower than automatic document-feed scanners but require less preparation of individual documents.

Indexing involves identifying each individual page according to the type of form such as discharge summary. Indexing is critical. If the image is not indexed to the proper patient and the proper form for that admission, the information cannot be retrieved. The scanner is the device that actually scans a human-readable document and uses software to make a picture of the document. After being scanned, records must be verified and generally are not submitted to the final stored archive until the physician completes them. Verifying that the image is clear and the indexing correct is important to make sure the image can be retrieved and used in the future. Facilities assign personnel to handle the tasks of preparation and scanning. Emergency department reports, outpatient reports, and reports submitted from physicians often do not have the proper patient numbers or encounter numbers, and all of this information must be entered so that each form in the record can be properly indexed and retrieved. A concern for HIM professionals is that scanning equipment from one vendor may not work with equipment from another vendor. The long-term storage capability of optical disk has not been evaluated for long-term quality because the technology is still evolving.

Beginning an imaging system requires detailed planning. Decisions must be made about converting existing records or whether only information from a certain date forward will be imaged. In addition, security backups of images should be available. Health records should be on the type of optical storage using WORM, "write once, read many," technology. This means that the data cannot be erased or altered. Rewritable or erasable **optical imaging technology** is not appropriate for health records. After records are archived in the imaging system, they cannot be changed. While waiting to be archived, images can be added or indexing changed, so it is important that any changes be made before archiving, if possible.

Although imaging has the advantages of rapid retrieval and simultaneous access, it is not an easy process to implement. Loose materials and late-arriving information still must be scanned and indexed. Moreover, problems still exist with recovering charts from the nursing areas after discharge and with unapproved forms being developed and included in the record that cannot be indexed because they do not have bar codes assigned. The HIM department still must perform open-record review and check forms for signatures. In other words, the traditional functions of the HIM department do not change. While the patient is in the facility or in active treatment, the record is paper. The imaging system does not convert the paper into images until after patient discharge or termination of treatment.

Using an imaging system does change the workflow in the facility. The record can be accessed remotely and by more than one provider, which means that physicians spend less time in the HIM department completing records. The record can be queued to HIM employees or others to complete specific tasks such as coding. **Queuing** involves a process of making the record available to a particular user. Because the record is available remotely, HIM employees, such as coders and transcriptionists, are able to work from home or at locations away from the main facility.

Imaging is a key part of the progression to an electronic document management system and ultimately to the electronic health record because it provides providers with quick access to pictures such as x-rays, MRIs, and other documents rather than having to wait for the paper copy. This type of quick access to images improves safety and quality of care.

Assigning a Retention Period

After all departments have been inventoried, the third step is to assign a retention period for each type of record. The retention period should be defined as time in active files, time in inactive storage, and total time before destruction.

As discussed previously, state and federal laws and regulations must be reviewed to ensure that records are maintained for the longest length of time required. Many states recommend that patient health records be retained for 10 years following patient discharge or death. There are usually special requirements for minor patients. For example, the state of Tennessee requires that the records of minors or mentally disabled patients be maintained until the age of majority plus one year, or a total of 10 years, whichever is longer. Therefore, the record of a newborn in Tennessee would be maintained until the patient reaches the age of majority, which is 18 years plus one year or a total of 19 years.

The retention period should reflect the scope and needs of the facility, along with the preliminary costs associated with imaging, microfilming, and other methods of maintaining and storing records. Storage mechanisms should be selected that protect records and provide ease of access and employee safety.

Protection of paper-based, microfilmed, and hybrid health records during the legally required retention period is extremely important and needs to be considered before a disaster occurs or a situation occurs where a health record in storage cannot be found. In addition, as discussed earlier, health records can be destroyed or may be unusable due to water damage, extremes of heat and humidity, and damage caused by airborne chemicals and insects. Natural disasters such as floods, hurricanes, and earthquakes should also be considered when determining how and where to store paper medical records. Records should be stored in areas that have clear aisles and doorways, and boxes or shelves should be well marked and indexed so that needed records can be found. Fire extinguishers should be easily accessible. Transportation and availability of health records back to the facility must also be considered.

Commercial storage vendors should be selected carefully to ensure that records are protected from unauthorized access. Policies for security of all satellite record storage areas must be developed and business associate agreements (discussed in chapter 12) signed regarding timely access to, and retrieval of, health records.

Destroying Unnecessary Records

Destroying records that are not needed is the fourth step in developing a record retention program. In facilities utilizing an imaging system, the general rule is usually that paper records should be boxed up after all paper is scanned, indexed, and released in the electronic document management system (EDMS); stored for no longer than six months; and then destroyed. An organization may influence skeptics of destroying the paper by demonstrating quality processes on the front end—during scanning and indexing. The EDMS totally transitions a facility in terms of the legal medical record, and the legal definition is no longer based upon paper. There must be a rule that no patient health information can be destroyed or thrown away without approval of the HIM director or other authorized committee or person, according to facility policy. The HIM professional must be alert to changes in departmental administration or departmental relocation or remodeling because departments often use these events to clean out files, which could result in the destruction of needed patient information.

The destruction of patient records must be done as part of the facility's usual business. When the required retention schedule has been satisfied, a complete list of records to be destroyed should be compiled and submitted to the individual designated to authorize the destruction. Outsourcing of destruction to shredding companies should be carefully monitored to protect patient confidentiality. The destruction of computerized records should follow security guidelines to ensure that the information is destroyed permanently. Facilities must maintain basic information about the patient in the MPI, which is maintained permanently even though the corresponding health record is destroyed.

AHIMA recommends that records be destroyed in such a way that the information cannot possibly be reconstructed. The destruction should be documented, and the documentation should include the following:

- Date of destruction
- Method of destruction (shredding, burning, or other means)
- Description of the disposed record series of numbers or items
- Inclusive dates covered
- A statement that the records were destroyed in the normal course of business
- The signatures of the individuals supervising and witnessing the destruction

AHIMA further recommends that facilities maintain destruction certification documents permanently. Such certificates may be required as evidence that records were destroyed in the regular course of business. When facilities fail to apply destruction policies uniformly or when destruction is contrary to policy, courts may allow a jury to infer that the facility destroyed its records to hide evidence.

Dealing with Outdated Media

Dealing with various forms and sources of media is not new for HIM professionals and continues to evolve as technological changes impact healthcare delivery. The other side of advances with new media is the dilemma of dealing with outdated media as part of the record retention program. When determining whether or not to maintain records after the retention period has expired, the media type should be considered. As equipment ages and eventually becomes obsolete, the costs for retrieving that information can increase. This should become part of the decision-making process on record retention.

Check Your Understanding 10.7

Instructions: Answer the following questions on a separate piece of paper.

1. What is the difference between a serial numbering system and a unit numbering system?

2. What are two advantages of terminal-digit filing over straight numerical filing?

3. What are the main factors in determining how long to maintain a health record?

4. What is the major advantage of microfilming health records?

5. What is the major advantage of optical imaging in the chart completion process?

6. What are the four primary steps in a record retention program?

Summary

Although healthcare facilities are working toward an electronic health record, many facilities still have paper-based or hybrid records. Regardless of its format, the patient health record is the foundation for most of the decisions made in any healthcare facility. Decisions relative to patient care and financial reimbursement depend on the quality of documentation in the health record. The health record is the communication tool among the members of the patient's healthcare team. It is evidence of what was done for the patient, and the information it contains is used to evaluate the quality of care and to provide important information for research and public health needs. The information in the healthcare record protects the legal interests of both the patient and the facility. The traditional saying, "if it wasn't documented, it wasn't done," is a reminder of how important the record is for the patient, the facility, and the numerous other users of record and the information it contains.

Ensuring that the health record meets current regulatory, legal, accrediting, and licensing standards as well as the facility's bylaws and polices is an ongoing challenge for the HIM professional. He or she must continuously educate and update providers on changes affecting documentation. Records must be reviewed both while the patient is in active treatment and after treatment is concluded to ensure that they meet the current requirements. It is important to analyze and process paper-based or hybrid health records efficiently to ensure that complete information is available for billing and reimbursement purposes. Facilitating the completion of health records by providers is a key factor in ensuring that needed information can be provided to all authorized users.

Facilities use a variety of formats for storing health records to ensure that they are available for future use. Forms must be developed and controlled following good forms design and control principles. As technology has changed, so have the methods of maintaining and storing patient records. Records may be copied onto different types of microfilm stored in cabinets on rolls or on microfiche, scanned and maintained in the HIS. The facility may have a recently installed imaging system. Healthcare information includes videotapes, graphic results, videos, and images from specific computerized test results, which must be included in the paper-based or hybrid record.

The master patient index may be maintained in many formats. The MPI is the key to finding the correct patient's information both within a facility and when patient information is shared outside the facility.

The HIM professional has been incrementally transitioning from managing paper health records to managing information in a variety of media and formats. The transition is ongoing, and HIM professionals must take a leadership role in ensuring that needed health information from the patient's past continues to be available for use in the future.

References

Accreditation Association for Ambulatory Health Care. 2011. *Accreditation Handbook for Ambulatory Health Care*.

AHDI. 2008. *The Book of Style for Medical Transcription* 3rd ed. http://www.ahdionline.org/ProfessionalPractices/BestPracticesandStandardGuidelines/BookofStyleforMedicalTranscription/tabid/282/Default.aspx

AHIMA e-HIM Work Group Best Practices for Electronic Signature and Attestation. 2009 (November–December). Practice brief: Electronic Signature, Attestation and Authorship (Updaed). *Journal of AHIMA*–9-(11).

AHIMA e-HIM Work Group on Maintaining the Legal EHR. 2005(November–December). Update: Maintaining a legally sound health record—paper and electronic. *Journal of AHIMA* 76(10): 64A–L.

AHIMA e-HIM Work Group on Electronic Document Management as a Component of EHR, 2003. Electronic Document Management as a Component of the Electronic Health Record. http://library.ahima.org.

AHIMA e-HIM Work Group on Speech Recognition in the EHR. 2003 (October 20). Practice brief: Speech recognition in the electronic health record. *Journal of AHIMA*–Web exclusive. http://library.ahima.org/xpedio/groups/public/documents/ahima/bok1_022107.hcsp?dDocName=bok1_022107

AHIMA MPI Task Force. 2004. Practice brief: Building an enterprise master person index. *Journal of AHIMA* 75(1):56A–56D.

AHIMA/MTIA Joint Task Force. 2008 (July). Transcription Turnaround Time for Common Document Types. http://library.ahima.org.

American Health Information Management Association. 2011a. Managing Nontext Media in Healthcare Practice. *Journal of AHIMA*, no. 11 (November–December 2011): 54–58.

American Health Information Management Association. 2011b. Retention and Destruction of Health Information. http://library.ahima.org/xpedio/groups/public/documents/ahima/bok1_049252.hcsp?dDocName=bok1_049252

AHIMA. 2010. Role of the Personal Health Record in the EHR (Updated). http://library.ahima.org/xpedio/groups/public/documents/ahima/bok1_048517.hcsp?dDocName=bok1_048517

Association of Healthcare Documentation Integrity (AHDI). http://www.ahdionline.org.

Backman, C., Dolack, S.; Dunyak, D., Lutz, L., Tegen, A., and D. Warner. 2011.Social Media + Healthcare. *Journal of AHIMA* 82(3): 20–25.

Burrington-Brown, J. and G. Hughes. 2010 (December). Practice brief: Disaster planning for health information. *Journal of AHIMA*–Web exclusive. http://library.ahima.org/xpedio/groups/public/documents/ahima/bok1_048638.hcsp?dDocName=bok1_048638

Emergency Medical Treatment & Labor Act (EMTALA). https://www.cms.gov/EMTALA/

Joint Commission. 2011. *Comprehensive Accreditation Manual for Hospitals*. Oak Brook Terrace, IL: Joint Commission.

National Association for Home Care & Hospice. 2011. http://www.nahc.org.

National Hospice and Palliative Care Organization. 2011. http://www.nhpco.org.

Tegan, A., et al. 2005. Practice brief: The EHR's impact on HIM functions. *Journal of AHIMA* 76(5):56C–H.

United Network for Organ Sharing. 2012. http://www.unos.org/data/about/collection.asp.

Weed, L.L. 1970. *Medical Records, Medical Education, and Patient Care*. Cleveland, OH: Case Western Reserve University.

21 CFR 900.12 (c)(4), Mammography. 2012 (April 6).

42 CFR.482.61: Condition of participation: Special medical record requirements for psychiatric hospitals. 2011 (October 1).

42 CFR 483.20: Resident assessment. 2010 (October 1).

chapter 11

Electronic Health Records: Application in Practice

Danika Brinda, MA, RHIA, CHPS, and
Janelle Wapola, MA, RHIA

Learning Objectives

- Identify common functional areas within a health information services department that are impacted significantly by the implementation of an electronic health record (EHR)
- Discuss the specific types of changes in these common functional areas initiated by an EHR implementation
- Demonstrate a matrix tool and sample policy template for defining and maintaining an organization's legal EHR
- Describe how the meaningful use (MU) criteria impact release of information from an EHR system
- Discuss the role(s) health information management (HIM) professionals play in managing patient portal use
- Discuss the types of data integrity issues that must be addressed when patient information is being transferred between and among electronic systems

- Describe the types of data conversion decisions and activities that arise during an EHR implementation
- Differentiate functional training and workflow training in terms of their focus and role in preparing staff for a successful EHR implementation
- Identify best practices in designing electronic forms and templates
- Discuss the implications of an EHR implementation on the knowledge, skills, and roles required within the staff of a health information service
- Identify major activities that must receive the attention post-implementation to ensure proper maintenance of the EHR system from a health information management perspective

Key Terms

Abstracting

Billing software

Chart review

Claims Scrubbing software

Coding workflow

Contingency planning

Data conversion

Disaster recovery plan

Electronic forms and templates

File room activity

Functionality training

Incomplete record process

Legal health record (LHR)

Master patient index (MPI)

Patient/member web portal

Patient registration

Problem list

Release of information (ROI)

Security audit program

Transcription

Workflow analysis

Workflow training

Implementing an electronic health record (EHR) within a healthcare organization is a significant undertaking and also an exciting time for health information management professionals. The health information services department, like all other departments in the organization, must carefully plan and effectively execute many changes in its processes and workflow to achieve a successful implementation effort. This chapter is focused on identifying several of the most common functional areas within a health information services department that require close attention as the organization makes its transition to an electronic health record system: maintenance of the legal EHR, patient registration and master patient index maintenance, file room activities, incomplete record processes, release of information, chart reviews, coding, abstracting and billing, and transcription. In addition, several issues of concern to health information management professionals during EHR planning, implementation, and post-implementation are discussed: data conversion, workflow redesign and training, electronic forms and template design, and electronic forms management; issues related to departmental staffing during implementation and structural changes in the department job descriptions and roles; and key EHR maintenance issues such as disaster recovery, workflow reevaluation, monitoring documentation quality, security auditing, monitoring the enterprise master patient index (EMPI), and the governing of the problem list within the EHR.

Maintenance of a Legal EHR

According to the American Health Information Management Association (AHIMA), the **legal health record (LHR)** is the documentation of healthcare services provided to an individual during any aspect of healthcare delivery in any type of healthcare organization (AHIMA 2011a). An organization's legal health record definition must explicitly identify the sources, medium (paper, images, video, audio, and such), and location of the individually identifiable data that it includes. The documentation that comprises the legal health record may physically exist in separate and multiple paper-based or electronic systems, which complicates the process of pulling the entire legal record together in response to authorized requests to produce the complete patient record. Once the LHR is defined, it is best practice to create a health record matrix that identifies and tracks the physical location of each paper document and the source of each electronic document that constitutes the LHR (AHIMA 2011a). Table 11.1 is an example of an LHR matrix.

In addition to defining the content of the legal health record, it is best practice to establish a policy statement on the maintenance of the legal health record. The policy should include a statement that identifies the title of the individual within the organization who has the primary responsibility for ensuring the maintenance of the legal health record. That individual is commonly the director of the health information management department working in conjunction with the organization's legal counsel and the information technology department. At minimum, they are responsible working together to maintain an accurate matrix, a process for ensuring security of the health record, a process for disclosure of information from the health record, and a health record retention schedule. Figure 11.1 is a sample LHR policy template (McLendon 2012). (See chapters 5 and 12 for further discussion of the legal EHR).

Table 11.1.   Legal health record matrix

Type of Document	Name of Document	Primary Source*	Primary Source System Start Date	Source of Legal Health Record/ Designated Record Set	Legal Health Record, Designated Record Set, or Both	Comments
Nursing	ICU nursing assessment	Electronic nursing documentation system	1/2/2007	Enterprise document management system	Both	Phased implementation
Physician orders	Congestive heart failure order set	Computerized provider order entry system	1/2/2007	EHR	Both	Downtime paper orders scanned
Emergency department	Emergency department treatment record	Paper	3/15/2005	Enterprise document system	Both	
Discharge summary	Discharge summary	Transcription system	12/15/2002	EHR	Both	
Claims	Billing report	Patient financial system	7/1/1998	Patient financial system	Designated record set	

*Includes scanned images.

Figure 11.1.   Sample legal health record policy template

Legal Health Record Policy Template

Policy Name: The Health Record for Legal and Business Purposes

Effective Date:

Departments Affected: HIM, Information Systems, Legal Services, [*any additional departments affected*]

Purpose: This policy identifies the health record of [*organization*] for business and legal purposes and to ensure that the integrity of the health record is maintained so that it can support business and legal needs.

Scope: This policy applies to all uses and disclosures of the health record for administrative, business, or evidentiary purposes. It encompasses records that may be kept in a variety of media including, but not limited to, electronic, paper, digital images, video, and audio. It excludes those health records not normally made and kept in the regular course of the business of [*organization*].

Note: The determining factor in whether a document is considered part of the legal health record is not where the information resides or its format, but rather how the information is used and whether it is reasonable to expect the information to be routinely released when a request for a complete health record is received. The legal health record excludes health records that are not official business records of a healthcare provider. Organizations should seek legal counsel when deciding what constitutes the organization's legal health record.

Policy: It is the policy of [*organization*] to create and maintain health records that, in addition to their primary intended purpose of clinical and patient care use, will also serve the business and legal needs of [*organization*].

It is the policy of [*organization*] to maintain health records that will not be compromised and will support the business and legal needs of [*organization*].

Routine disclosures will only include information needed to fulfill the intent of the request. It excludes information determined to not be included in the legal health record.

Responsibilities

It is the responsibility of the Health Information Management Director, working in conjunction with the Information Services Department (IS) and the Legal Department [*or other appropriate departments*] to:

• Maintain a matrix or other document that tracks the source, location, and media of each component of the health record. [*Reference an addendum or other source where the health record information is found.*]

• Identify any content that may be used in decision making and care of the patient that may be external to the organization (outside records and reports, PHRs, e-mail, and such) that is not included as part of the legal record because it was not made or kept in the regular course of business.

• Develop, coordinate, and administer a plan that manages all information content, regardless of location or form that comprises the legal health record of [*organization*].

• Develop, coordinate, and administer the process of disclosure of health information.

• Develop and administer a health record retention schedule that complies with applicable regulatory and business requirements.

• Ensure appropriate access to information systems containing components of the health record.

• Execute the archiving and retention schedule pursuant to the established retention schedule.

• [*Other responsibilities*]

[*Additional responsibilities for other individuals or departments*]

Source: McLendon 2012.

Patient Registration and Master Patient Index Maintenance

The accurate registration of a patient is critical to an organization whether it functions in a paper-based or an electronic environment. The **patient registration** process provides the organization with the ability to accurately and uniquely identify its patients. It is also the first step in the creation of each patient's record within the EHR and initiates the flow of patient information within the EHR. The data collected at the time of registration contributes to the delivery of quality care and to the operational efficiency of the entire organization; it is also a component of the data set needed to accurately bill for services provided, a component of the data set needed to accurately monitor the organization's performance on its quality measures, and a component of the data set needed to exchange health information among internal clinical and administrative systems as well as between the organization and external healthcare agencies and providers.

The **master patient index** (**MPI**) is a key application within an organization's registration system. It uniquely identifies the individuals who have received services from the organization. As such, maintaining the integrity of the master patient index is critical.

Before implementing an EHR, an organization must make sure that its existing MPI is accurate by first assessing the current level of duplicates and overlays existing within it. With the help of the IT department, determining how many duplicates and overlays currently exist in the system will give the organization the information it needs to determine the time and resources required to do a proper MPI cleanup. With this information in hand, an organization can assess if this task can be completed in-house or through a third-party vendor. The MPI cleanup can be very time consuming and expensive, but it is necessary to ensure the accurate identity of patients and the accurate, complete linkage of patient records created from multiple occasions of service (hospital admissions, outpatient visits, and such) (Martin 2010).

After the MPI cleanup has been accomplished, maintaining the integrity of the master patient index is a critical aspect. Recommendations to sustain an accurate MPI in the EHR environment should include

- Identifying each registration entry point for patients presenting for services
- Standardizing the registration procedures for each of these entry points
- Training all registration staff
- Monitoring the accuracy of registration staff performance
- Having dedicated staff focused on monitoring, investigating, and fixing duplicate medical record numbers (one person with more than one number) and overlays in medical record numbers (two or more persons with the same medical record number)
- Retraining registration staff as necessary

Registration staff must be properly trained in the use of the EHR registration module and on the required workflow to capture accurate and complete patient registration data in the electronic system as well as the underlying policies that apply to the patient registration processes. For example, when searching a patient in the master patient index, registration staff must be knowledgeable about naming conventions required by the system, including efficient methods of searching for and, if necessary, accurately modifying and referencing names due to changes in marital status or associated nicknames. In addition, staff must understand the importance of accurately selecting the appropriate type of service classification for each patient's admission (inpatient, outpatient surgery, observation, emergency, and such) because of the impact it has on triggering workflows in different clinical areas of the organization as well as its impact on administrative activities such as coding, billing, and quality reporting.

Proper training, routine monitoring of registration tasks, feedback on registration errors, and retraining when necessary are all important elements of a registration process quality management program. (See the Data Conversion section later in this chapter for a discussion of the MPI-related issues involved when converting from a legacy EHR system to a new EHR system.)

Check Your Understanding 11.1

Instructions: Answer the following questions on a separate piece of paper.

1. Why could it be difficult for an organization to respond to pulling an entire, legal medical record together for an authorized request for information?
2. Explain why an accurate patient registration is critical to an organization.
3. Identify recommendations for maintaining the integrity of a clean MPI.
4. Identify the elements of an effective registration process quality management program.

File Room Activities

Implementation of an EHR significantly changes the file room activities in a health information management (HIM) department. The main responsibility of the file room staff in a paper environment is to pull patient records for continuity of care, file loose documents into patient records, and file patient records for storage when not in use. With a full implementation of an EHR system the need to pull patient records and maintain a complete paper record will soon be eliminated; however, for some period of time after a full EHR implementation, the file room will continue to pull and file paper records associated with patient visits or admissions that occurred prior to the EHR go-live date. The level of this aspect of file room activity will diminish over time because the creation of additional paper-based patient records has been halted as a result of the EHR implementation. One factor that will continue to impact the level of file room activity even after a full EHR implementation is the approach the organization takes to defining its legal health record (Tegan et al. 2005). For example, if the organization defines the legal health record to include the scanned image documents that are accessible within the EHR, the file room activity will diminish over time. However, if the organization defines the legal health record to include some original paper documents rather than the scanned image of those documents that are accessible within the EHR, the file room will continue being an active area of the department. In the latter case, a process must be defined for maintaining the documents that still exist on paper though they are also available in the EHR. One option is a process that involves creating a duplicate record for a patient that holds all the paper documents also scanned into the system and maintaining the duplicate record in the file room. Another option is to catalog and maintain the paper documents in a date-scanned order. Since these documents may not need to be retrieved very often, cataloging them provides a simple way to maintain the paper documents and to purge them when retention periods have passed (AHIMA 2010b).

Statutes and regulations related to the retention time frame for health record documents vary among states. Therefore, the HIM management team must research them and take that information into consideration when determining the specific methodology for maintaining the paper documents that are also scanned and available within the EHR system in the organization. For example, Minnesota Statute 145.32, 145.30, Minnesota Rule 4642.1000 states that

> Hospitals must maintain the original medical record in its entirety for a minimum of three years. The medical record may be destroyed after three years if it has been microfilmed in its entirety. The hospital governing body must approve destruction of records. After seven years, only the portion of the entire record defined by statute as the "individual permanent medical record" must be retained. For minors, the entire record must be retained for seven years past the age of majority.

Minnesota Rules 4658.0470 Section 1 requires long-term care facility medical records be maintained for a period of at least five years following discharge or death, while Minnesota Rules 4665.4100 Section 4 requires that supervised living facilities maintain records for three years following discharge or death.

Incomplete Record, Deficiency Analysis, and Chart Completion

The **incomplete record processes,** including deficiency analysis and chart completion practices, also change as a result of an EHR implementation. Depending upon the functional capabilities of the EHR system, deficiency analysis may be automated to varying degrees, so evaluating this functionality within the EHR is necessary in order to set up and manage the changes, taking full advantage of the functionalities to improve the efficiencies for the electronic processing of incomplete records (AHIMA 2010b). For example, rules can be built in an EHR to flag a record lacking a history and physical report completed within 24 hours of admission. This type of functionality allows for the system to support a concurrent record analysis rather than strictly rely on a post-discharge record analysis.

In most EHR systems, rules can be built that notify healthcare providers when a transcribed document or verbal orders exist in a patient record that require a signature, essentially eliminating their need to visit the health information services department to complete these types of deficiencies. In spite

of electronic signature capabilities within the EHR, health information services staff will still be required to monitor documentation in the EHR to ensure required reports are present and to identify any remaining unsigned documentation. One of the management benefits of an electronic system is that tasks assigned to staff can be set up in work queues, which allow for easy access by staff to those patient records that have been assigned to them for the day (AHIMA 2010b). For example, rules can be built in the EHR to define how an organization wants to divide out work for deficiency analysis: sending discharges from the emergency department to a particular staff, sending obstetric and newborn discharges to another staff, and sending outpatient surgery discharges to yet another staff. Electronic communication with providers regarding deficiencies that must be addressed can be delivered more quickly to the provider through the EHR system, and in most cases providers are able to complete those deficiencies remotely. As a result an EHR system may significantly shorten the record completion time and reduce the number of deficiencies overall. It is critical for the health information management professional to have a detailed understanding of the deficiency management functionality of the EHR system to ensure providers can effectively and efficiently complete the records and that the official deficiency counts generated from the system are accurate (Tegan et al. 2005).

Release of Information

Health information management departments handle **release of information (ROI)** in different ways. The department may handle this critical HIM function internally, contract it externally with a vendor, or use a blended approach that divides the release of information work volume between internal staff and a contracted company. Regardless of the approach, the health information management department is ultimately responsible for having an advanced understanding of the Health Information Portability and Accountability Act (HIPAA) privacy and security rules, as well as related state regulations. The department is also responsible for having a process in place to track all patient information requested and released from the EHR. Commonly, the request for information paper documents are scanned into a correspondence area of the patient's record within the EHR and kept there electronically as permanent evidence of the request. When the request is completed, a release of information log reflecting when and what was sent in response to the request, to whom it was sent, and how it was sent is maintained within the health information services department. This log is commonly maintained electronically separate from the EHR system (Dunn 2010).

The Centers for Medicare and Medicaid Services (CMS) Meaningful Use Incentive Payment Program provides incentive payments to healthcare providers and hospitals as they adopt, implement, upgrade, or demonstrate meaningful use of certified EHR technology. Within this program

Meaningful Use is defined through a set of functional and quality reporting criteria (see chapter 2 for a full discussion of the CMS Meaningful Use Incentive Payment Program).

One of the biggest changes and challenges associated with the CMS Meaningful Use Incentive Payment Program criteria is the requirement that, if requested, organizations must be able to provide an electronic copy of a patient's health information within three business days of the request. Not only does this require adding electronic media (CD or USB device) to the release of information process, but it also drastically reduces the timeline for responding to the request. With this new standard of performance the health information management department will need to answer some key questions on the electronic release of information:

- How will the department track the number of electronic copies requested, the number of those requests fulfilled, and the number of days to process each request?
- Which electronic media will be used (for example, CD or USB)?
- Will the department encrypt the media prior to providing it to the requestor?
- Does the department have the proper hardware and software to be able to copy patient information from the EHR to the electronic media?
- What are the associated costs or charges permitted by law?

All of these questions must be answered in order to build the best and most efficient workflow to meet the intent of meaningful use and serve patients well.

In the near future, **patient/member web portals** will also be implemented to release health information to patients and facilitate communications between patients and providers through a web connection, utilizing a secure username and password. Portals are becoming mainstream, primarily because Stage 2 criteria tied to the CMS Meaningful Use Incentive Program are likely to require organizations to provide all patients real-time, online access to their health information that is viewable and downloadable. There are many benefits to using a patient portal, such as being able to

- Check and request appointment schedules through the portal
- View lab results
- Examine and pay billing statements
- Request a prescription refill
- Complete new patient intake forms
- Update demographics
- Send a message to the provider

Provider benefits include being able to:

- Send responses to messages from their patients
- Send appointment reminders
- Send healthcare maintenance reminders

- Provide diagnosis-specific education materials
- Communicate preventive care guidelines
- Issue drug recalls (Health Technology Review 2009)

In some organizations, HIM professionals and the health information management department are responsible for managing patient portals. AHIMA describes HIM professionals at Vanderbilt University Medical Center as having a "strong patient advocate role in assisting patients with fast and easy access to their medical information in the portal arena, just as they do in the release of information arena" (Dixon 2012). According to Dixon, responsibilities for managing the release of information through a patient portal may include

- Helping patients who are having problems registering online for an account (patients can come to the department for assistance)
- Helping new employees register for accounts at weekly orientations
- Processing parents' applications for pediatric accounts and creating pediatric accounts (parents must appear in person to gain pediatric account access)
- Answering patient questions that come by phone, e-mail, mail, or direct patient contact
- Responding to assigned help desk tickets (that is, patient questions or problems that come directly through the portal)
- Making service calls to clinics and departments to present a general portal overview at staff meetings or helping train new staff
- Helping to write and update policies, procedures, and application forms
- Resolving patient problems and portal problems with other support areas, such as programmers or IT
- Updating the Frequently Asked Questions section of the portal
- Making suggestions for portal improvements, which are often based on commonly received patient questions or comments

Dixon (2012) notes, "HIM professionals become super-users of the portal, which enables them to answer patient questions. When there is a technical problem with the portal they are often the first to be alerted from patient calls for help."

Chart Reviews

Viewing patient records for various types of **chart reviews** (that is, internal studies and external reviews, including billing audits) are often a daily occurrence in the health information services department. While an EHR system will eliminate the need for health information services staff to pull records from the file room for this purpose, staff will continue to ensure there is proper identification and, where appropriate, signed authorizations on file before giving access to a patient record within the EHR system for case reviews or audits conducted by individuals who are not authorized. Functionality within an EHR system should allow staff to lock down only those patient records the requestor has the right to access in order to protect the personal health information of all other patients in the EHR system. Staff will also be expected to sit with the individual doing the patient record review to help navigate the electronic record and be available to respond to questions from the reviewer (Tegen 2012).

Coding, Abstracting, and Billing

The coding function is greatly impacted by the implementation of an EHR. The EHR system offers many benefits to the coding staff, such as quick access to patient records and remote access to allow for off-site coding, both of which can contribute to reduced turnaround time for completion of the coding activity post-discharge.

To obtain the greatest benefits from the EHR system, **coding workflows** will need to be assessed and revised as an organization implements an EHR. If the organization is going from a completely paper process to a totally electronic process, major redesign of the workflows is required, including education and retraining of staff. One common type of workflow change associated with coding in an EHR environment is described here.

Healthcare organizations with paper-based records that employ coders working in remote settings commonly have all documents required by coders to support their coding effort scanned by HIM department staff to make them available to the coders. When an EHR is implemented, coders working in remote settings can be given secure, direct access into the patient records within the EHR through a specifically designed work queue, which essentially eliminates the need to scan documents for this purpose.

Abstracting data from the patient record is required to support some secondary uses of patient information within the organization. An EHR system presents an opportunity for significantly reducing the amount of manual abstracting that must be done to meet the needs of secondary users of patient data. Patient data can be directly pulled from within the EHR to populate built reports. Patient data can be also be directly pulled from within the EHR to populate a separate electronic database (a data mart) to support a particular secondary use within the organization such as a research study, a quality-of-care study, specialized registries, and such.

Billing software is an application that is used to create a claim for services, to submit charges to third-party payers or patients, to track receipt of payments, and to generate reports of billing- and claims-related activities. Billing software is commonly electronically interfaced with the EHR system and the encoder software to facilitate the accuracy and productivity of the coding staff. The electronic interfacing of these three systems allows data residing in each system to be accessed by the coders and allows data from one system to be downloaded into another in order to eliminate redundant entry of data and reduce the potential for data entry errors.

Many other challenges related to patient billing can result from the implementation of an EHR. For example, if an organization uses a third-party vendor for claims scrubbing, it is important to evaluate how these two systems will work together to ensure the information pulled from the EHR and entering the claims scrubber maintains its integrity. Mapping the data being transferred from one system to the other is essential to ensure that data being transferred are accurately populating the other system. When implementing an EHR, the organization should assign staff to monitor the number of claim denials for up to six months after the EHR implementation and evaluate the claim denial reasons to identify any potential data issues arising from the data transfers occurring between the EHR and the **claims scrubbing software** system.

Transcription

An EHR implementation impacts the current work of transcriptionists and the transcription process at a healthcare organization. **Transcription** remains an integral part of physician documentation; however, the method of documentation and transcription process will change significantly within an EHR environment. For example, within an EHR environment, healthcare providers are encouraged to document directly within the EHR to increase the amount of data that is entered into discrete data fields. The capture of some critical data in discrete format allows the EHR system to support key functionalities such as decision support alerts and graphing of lab values and vital signs, and it enables the organization to pull data directly from the EHR system to support various types of administrative reporting and data analysis activities.

Though there is an increase in the amount of information entered into the EHR through discrete data entry, transcriptionists continue to create text-based documents from dictation. These documents are transferred to the EHR in a variety of different ways. For example, the transcriptionist may type directly into the EHR, which makes the information immediately available and accessible and reduces the need for an interface between the transcription software and the EHR. However, if a healthcare organization outsources transcription, it may be hesitant to provide access to the entire EHR to the transcription vendor. In addition, the EHR vendor may not choose to work directly with EHR software due to the additional training and requirements on the staff. A second process that could be used to transfer documents into the EHR involves developing an electronic interface between the transcription software and the EHR. When the transcription is complete, the document is uploaded into the EHR and available within the EHR for the healthcare provider to review, edit, and electronically sign. The issue to be aware of with this process is that, if the healthcare provider changes information in the document within the EHR, the document in the EHR will be different than the documentation in the transcription software. So, the document in the EHR must always be recognized as the official, authenticated document. And a third process that could be used to enter transcribed documents into the EHR is through scanning. In this case, the transcribed document would be printed in hard copy, signed by the healthcare provider who dictated it, and then scanned into the EHR as an image. This allows for the information to be available electronically for viewing; however, the documentation cannot be edited and the data or information in the scanned image cannot be electronically extracted to populate reports or trigger decision support alerts (Cannon and Lucci 2010).

One of the new technologies being implemented with EHRs is voice/speech recognition software. The technology has made a tremendous impact on the transcription area in recent years. In many organizations, physicians utilize a voice recognition device to create a report that is directly embedded in the EHR. In this scenario, the transcriptionist becomes responsible for text editing the document and conducting quality assurance reviews on reports produced by a voice recognition process. Challenges exist with the implementation of speech recognition technology as well. The biggest challenges include the cost to purchase and implement the software, the diversity of backgrounds and voices of providers that the software must recognize, and the physician's time required to become an efficient user of the application. An ongoing process of reviewing and editing text created through a voice/speech recognition system is a necessity to maintain the quality of documentation in the patient's record. With the proper combination of speech technology and transcription editing, voice/speech recognition can bring added value to an EHR system and the healthcare organization. The benefits that come along with the speech recognition technology include improved turnaround time on dictated reports, reduced transcription costs due to increased productivity, and reduced errors in documents (Cannon and Lucci 2010).

No matter which of these processes is implemented, the processes of planning the workflow changes, identifying the technical requirements, and developing the training to support the new transcription process are fundamental components of a successful implementation.

Document Imaging

Even though an EHR system is being implemented, some types of paper documents are still generated during a patient's stay in or visit to a healthcare facility. In order to incorporate paper documents into the EHR system, document imaging technology is used to convert the paper document to an image, which is then transferred into the EHR through an electronic interface. A properly implemented document imaging process will improve access to paper-generated documents for patient care purposes and administrative activities such as coding, as well as eliminate the need for retrieval of paper files.

The following five steps are recommended when planning for and acquiring document imaging software:

Step 1: Determining the technology strategy
Step 2: Understanding the available technology's options and issues
Step 3: The planning phase
Step 4: The implementation phase
Step 5: The post-implementation phase (AHIMA e-HIM Work Group on Electronic Document Management 2003)

Since document scanning is a new task within the HIM department, proper setup of processes and training of staff is important to ensure a successful implementation and efficient ongoing processes for handling the work volume; to ensure the quality of the scanned images; and to place the images into the correct patient's record and into the correct location within the record in the EHR. The major steps in this process are preparing the documents for scanning, scanning the documents, indexing each document by defined type, and assessing the quality of each imaged document before it is placed into the patient record. Figure 11.2 is a sample workflow for document scanning.

Document imaging software that has an auto-indexing function can facilitate the process of assuring placement of scanned images into the correct patient record, into the correct encounter within the patient record, and into the correct location within that patient based on the document type. To take full advantage of an auto-indexing feature, the paper documents (forms) that will be scanned must be designed with that in mind. For example, one effective design feature is the incorporation of a bar code on each form that will identify the document type and the proper location for the document in the patient record, as well as creating a place on the form where a bar code label, which identifies the specific patient and the specific encounter associated with the form, can be affixed (Rhodes and Dougherty 2003).

HIM departments commonly work with a forms committee that is responsible for the management and maintenance of paper forms in an electronic environment. This committee is also responsible for establishing the organization's policy for retention of the original paper document after it has been scanned. Each state's requirements for retention of patient records must be researched and taken into consideration as the organization's policy is developed.

Figure 11.2.   Sample document scanning workflow

Source: From "Implementing a Document Imaging System" by D'Arcy Myjer, PhD, and Roderick Madamba, RHIA, in the October 2002 (vol. 73, no. 9) *Journal of AHIMA*.

Check Your Understanding 11.2

Instructions: Answer the following questions on a separate piece of paper.

1. Identify at least two types of rules that could be built into the EHR to support the chart deficiency and incomplete record function.

2. List three ways an HIM department might handle the release of information function.

3. What questions should each health information services (HIS) department ask itself when it comes to the e-delivery of ROI?

4. What benefits do patient portals provide to consumers? Providers?

5. How can HIM professionals plan an instrumental part in helping utilize patient portals?

6. Why is it important to monitor the number of claim denials, especially after an EHR implementation?

Data Conversion

Converting the data existing in paper-based health records into an electronic health record system can be a significant expense. When the organization begins to address the **data conversion** questions, it is important that the health information management department be involved in the discussions and decision making because of the department's responsibilities associated with patient data management and role as official custodian of the organization's legal health record.

Some important systemwide decisions will need to be made regarding what information to transfer into the new system from both paper and electronic systems. The reality is that it is not cost-effective to transfer all current information

into the new system, making it important to have a cross-departmental group discussion to establish the best data conversion process for the organization. In order to minimize the expense and meet the needs of the organization, consideration should be given to these questions:

- Which types of information need to be converted?
- How far back in a patient's history does the electronic version need to go?
- If not all information in the paper record is to be placed in the EHR, will the practice need to store the original records and, if so, for how long?
- Will the files be scanned into portable document format (PDF) documents, which may be faster? Or will data be keyed into the EHR itself, which will allow it to be searchable?
- How long will the conversion process take? (HRSA 2012)

Most of the conversion from paper to electronic will happen through direct data entry or scanning. Once an organization decides on the paper-to-electronic conversion process it will implement, it is important for the health information services department to participate in the actual transition of data by conducting regular and complete audits of the historical information being entered into the electronic system for completeness, accuracy, and reliability. Close monitoring of the process will not only facilitate the data transfer but also build confidence in the information being entered into the EHR.

In addition to the paper-to-electronic data conversion, there may also be patient data to transition from a legacy EHR to the new EHR system. One of the main data sources transferred electronically in this situation is the master patient index. During the planning process, the mapping of one or more master patient indices into the EHR system must be given special attention because one minor error can have major negative effects on the integrity of the MPI, which is the primary data source for accurately and uniquely identifying the organization's past and present patient population. Just as with the transition of the data from a paper to an electronic system, it is important that there is significant testing of the transfer protocol and its output to ensure its completeness, accuracy, and availability within the new system. In addition to the MPI data, there are other items to consider for electronic-to-electronic conversion such as dictated reports, immunization information, radiology tests, advance directives, and insurance information (AHIMA Physician Practice Council 2010).

Workflow Analysis, Redesign, and Training

Evaluating EHR functionality, workflow analysis, and workflow redesign efforts is the means for a department to fully understand how the processes and procedures within the department will exist in the electronic world. **Workflow analysis** is a technique used to study the flow of operations. It is the first step in effective workflow redesign: analyzing all functional responsibilities of the department and documenting the current workflow within the department. After the current workflow is documented, department managers and staff who have become system super users should evaluate the functionality of the EHR and determine how the department can capitalize on the functionalities to develop the new workflows. The Health Information and Management Systems Society (HIMSS) offers a workflow redesign toolkit that provides guidance and best practices to organizations that are engaging in an implementation of an EHR (HIMSS 2010).

Once the revised workflows have been defined, the setup work (the "build") required within the EHR to support the new workflows can begin. Clear and constant communication between the EHR build team working in the IT department and the health information services department is critical in this phase of the effort. After the build is done, the workflows must be tested prior to implementation to ensure all of the tasks and activities work as expected to accomplish the desired outcome. Staff buy-in and readiness for the change are enhanced by letting them test the workflows and gain their own sense of the value in the workflow changes. Communication regarding the processes in the EHR department should be done prior to go-live with the understanding that workflow will be evaluated multiple times post-implementation to ensure an effective and efficient process going forward.

The last aspect of workflow development is the creation of the workflow training program for department staff. There are multiple ways to train end users how to use the EHR system. Some key considerations when planning the training program include the timing of the training, type of training, practice in a practice environment, and method of training. The timing and extent of the training is greatly dependent on the number of staff to be trained, the methodology to be used, and the magnitude of change involved. If all training for the department staff is going to happen face to face in a classroom environment, it might take more time and effort than it would take if training could be completed in a virtual environment.

Consideration must be given to both system functionality training and workflow training. **Functionality training** is focused specifically on the capabilities and features of the software: how to navigate through the application, how to enter data into different modules within the application, and such. **Workflow training** is focused on applying the systems capabilities and features within the context of the specific workflow of a person doing a task or series of tasks. There are benefits to both types of training. The training strategy should be clearly defined and documented for all staff to ensure adequate training is received on both functionality and workflow. Commonly, functional training is given greater attention but increasingly, organizations are recognizing that department-specific and interdepartmental workflow training must be completed and practiced prior to the EHR implementation to improve the go-live experience.

Electronic Form and Template Design and Management

The design of **electronic forms and templates** begins with communication between the front-end user and the developer of the form, utilizing a standard data dictionary for the organization. An effective form or template can be created when the front-end user indicates the needs of the form to complete his or her daily work and when the builder shares the functionality of the application within the confines of the software. Specific attention to screen design, data definitions, data collection, flow, print formatting, and reporting capabilities will be necessary.

When designing a new form or template, the designer looks for ways to maximize the space on the screen, taking into consideration the number of clicks and screen space given. In working with the end users of a form, utilize their knowledge and workflow experience for that particular area. This will help create an efficient format that will be utilized to its fullest potential. The form or template should allow the user to choose the discrete data element to capture the information necessary for quality patient care.

In discussion with the user, the designer or builder must determine what the user is trying to capture and in what workflow because there are a variety of ways to gather data within an EHR. For example, if there are multiple answers to one question, a check box of answers may be the best way to design this piece. If there is only one answer to the question, then a radial button could be the most logical choice. Ideally, the designed template should be as user-friendly as possible, requiring minimal clicks and being positioned on one screen so the user can easily move through the document to capture the information necessary without scrolling up and down the screen.

After the form or template has been created and visible in draft format, it is recommended that users of that form or template demonstrate and test its use in a training environment.

Feedback from these users is crucial in moving the document further to its final stage. The users will provide the necessary feedback so that the form or template can be tweaked and finalized. After suggestions have been made, the form can then be finalized and brought into the production environment for all users to utilize. After it is published, training time on the new form should be established with the department that will use the form. Guidelines, instructions, and training (if necessary) should be given to each user of the new form so that the information can be utilized to its fullest potential.

Electronic forms management is a crucial component of creating powerful and efficient record management systems. In the paper environment, a record or forms committee was in place to keep track of forms that reside within the medical record. In the electronic world it is more of a challenge for users to create or change any forms in the electronic record. The electronic record requires special training and access and therefore has restrictions on who can produce, alter, or publish a new form. When a user wishes to initiate the creation of a new form, a policy and procedure should be in place to direct the user so that an organization maximizes the existing data in the system. A strong committee of dedicated and knowledgeable individuals should be formed to review and audit forms that are being placed in the EHR. Individuals such as physicians, nurses, health information managers, and IT staff among others should be involved. An additional task of this committee would be to audit all forms on an annual basis to ensure they are meeting the needs of the organization and its users and are up to date.

Department Staffing during EHR Implementation

Staffing strategies during the implementation of an EHR become important to support staff and make certain enough people are there to get the job completed. Unlike clinical areas, the health information management department cannot reduce its workload for the implementation period because its workload is based on the current census of the healthcare organization. Increasing staff in the department for multiple weeks post-implementation is key to guarantee staffing is adequate to serve the organization as well as adequately supporting staff during the early stages of process and workflow changes. Some organizations will choose to try to increase staffing by 50 to 75 percent for the first few weeks by using current staff as well as temporary staff.

Another aspect of the staffing model during implementation is the use of super users: individuals who have significant levels of training on EHR functionality and associated workflows within the department. Some practices pull the super users out of their normal jobs from a department so they can fully support staff training and user needs for a specified period of time. Other practices keep the super user engaged with his or her normal job during the implementation period but reduce daily productivity expectations for the super user for a certain time period.

Since the health information management department is responsible for managing the completion of the patient record in the electronic environment just as it was in the paper-based environment, department staff may also be involved with provider support during and after the implementation period.

Structural Changes within the Health Information Management Department

The many changes in responsibilities and duties of the health information management department resulting from an EHR implementation will require department staff to have expanded knowledge and skills in use of computers and other technologies, such as scanning equipment, as well as enhanced skills in interacting with other departments and in supporting and assisting providers as they adapt to the EHR system. Due to these changes in required types of knowledge and skills among staff, the management team must include a full review and updating of the following items in their implementation activities:

- Job descriptions
- Job procedures
- Performance expectations
- Reclassifying of pay structures, as appropriate

The changing work activities and processes in the health information services department may also impact the service expectations of those who depend upon the department to support their work and workflow. For example, based on nursing or physician expectations for turnaround time for scanned documents, the department management must evaluate when the documents are available for scanning and how long it takes to do the document preparation and scan it into the EHR. Based on that information it might be determined that the majority of discharges are completed each day between noon and 3:00 p.m., making the documents that must be scanned available to process in the afternoon. Therefore, scanning staff are most needed in the afternoon and early evening in order to complete the work and make it accessible in the EHR by early the following morning.

One of the biggest advantages to the implementation of an EHR is that new jobs will be created within the health information services department. Not only will there be jobs specifically associated with the EHR build and implementation activities, but there will also be many other jobs to support the different tasks associated with the department's routine tasks. Following are some common new health information management jobs primarily created because of the implementation of an EHR within the organization:

- Electro Magnetic Design System scanner/indexer
- EHR builder/analyst

- Clinical documentation improvement specialist
- EHR trainer
- Project manager
- Data quality and integrity analyst
- Electronic forms manager (Dimick 2008)

Throughout the process of planning and implementing an EHR, a departmental communication plan should be drafted and maintained to keep the health information services staff informed of changes, timelines, expectations, and impacts on the department. This communication plan can also be used to keep others in the organization aware of the changes being made in the health information services department.

It is important to have a departmental strategy for documenting and reporting issues that are logged with the organization's help desk. One benefit of having a defined issues logging process within the department is a reduction in the number of duplicate issues reported to the help desk. Having one specific individual identified as the person who will be responsible for communicating issues from the issue log to the help desk benefits the department, as well. It ensures a coordinated effort within the department to obtain resolutions or establish sanctioned workarounds for identified issues.

Check Your Understanding 11.3

Instructions: Answer the following questions on a separate piece of paper.

1. When converting electronic data to electronic data during an EHR implementation, what is the most common type of information that is converted electronically?

2. What are some key considerations when planning for workflow training within the HIM department?

3. What are the differences between functionality training and workflow training?

4. What are two key considerations when creating and designing a new electronic form template?

5. What are two different ways a super user is used during the implementation of an EHR?

6. What are some new jobs created with an EHR implementation?

EHR Maintenance Issues

Disaster Recovery

Contingency planning is an important piece of the overall EHR maintenance and will include a formal **disaster recovery plan** process and downtime planning. An unanticipated loss of patient health records can be detrimental to the patient, organization, and clinical care provider, but having a formal disaster recovery process and action plan in place will help ease the anxiety around any unexpected event such as a natural disaster or power failure. A successful plan will assist organizations in being able to get back to normal business operations more efficiently and effectively with minimal interruptions and loss of information. Every organization must have a comprehensive disaster recovery plan that protects patient safety, secures health information from loss or damage, ensures stability and continuity of care activities, and provides for orderly recovery of information. The AHIMA Practice Brief "Disaster Planning for Health Information" (AHIMA 2010c), can be used to guide an organization in the creation of a plan. Figure 11.3 is a sample contingency plan for maintenance of the MPI in the event of a disaster. This best practice guide encourages the organization to research what other facilities of a similar size are doing and what they have included in their disaster plans. When drafting the initial plan, first create a list of potential disasters that might directly affect the facility such as fire, flood, tornado, or other disasters. Update and maintain a current policy and procedure manual for all core functions in your department. HIM professionals can also refer to the HIPAA rules and regulations for further guidance. After a finalized plan has been approved and adopted, organizations must implement, test, and review the plan with all staff to ensure a successful implementation. The practice brief lists several useful tips when implementing a disaster plan; a few of them are listed here:

- Test the plan
- Retest the plan
- Provide staff with the training and tools necessary to implement the plan
- Reevaluate and revise the plan based on gaps found during test runs
- Include disaster training as part of staff orientation

According to Tegan et al. (2005), having an organizational plan for continuing normal operations when an EHR is unavailable is a critical aspect of contingency planning. The plan includes being prepared to revert to the use of paper-based processes in all clinical and administrative areas of the organization. It must also include established processes for entering data and scanned documents in to the EHR when the system becomes available.

Organizations must develop a plan for worst-case scenarios when the EHR is unavailable and HIM staff should coordinate daily system disaster plans (for example, printing of key documents, maintenance backup, paper systems, coordination of data entry or scanning of key data elements after unplanned down times) as well. Necessary forms revert to paper processes and must be readily available. Staff must be trained in their use. The backup system could be a CD with appropriate documents that can be accessed from a local drive rather than the network. Down time processes could include use of PDAs or tablet PCs with uploading of data when the system has been recovered. (Tegan et al. 2005)

Figure 11.3.   Sample contingency plan

1. Facility name:

2. Department name:

3. Plan originator:

4. Date:

5. Major function: Maintenance of an accurate MPI

6. Disaster: Extended power outage

7. Assumptions: An ice storm has resulted in an extended power outage. Most staff members are able to report to work.

8. Existing process detail: The MPI is generated through entries made by registration and admitting staff and contains detailed patient information, including the patient's name and medical record number. When a patient is registered, the admitting and registration staff access the MPI to determine whether the patient already has a medical record number or whether a new number must be generated. HIM staff also may access the MPI for various functions, such as when they need a medical record number to pull medical records for a current hospitalization, to accompany a bill for payment, for continuing care, for quality monitoring or legal action, and to number documents for placement in the paper record. The accuracy of the numbers assigned is verified by HIM.

9. If/then scenarios: If admitting and registration staff do not have access to the MPI when registering a patient, then the following might result: the registration system or registrars will assign new numbers, creating duplicates that may cost $20 per set to correct, or the registrars will issue no numbers and patient health information will have to be matched to patients by using account numbers, admission or discharge dates, or birth dates. Medical record numbers will have to be assigned and entered into the database at a later date.

   If HIM staff members do not have access to an MPI, then record retrieval for patient care and other healthcare-related purposes cannot occur.

10. Interdependencies: Registration staff, patient care areas, transcription, billing, and external customers, including patients, third-party payers, attorneys, and regulatory agencies, need the medical records, so a functional MPI is required.

Contingency Plan Solutions and Alternatives		
Potential Solutions/Alternatives	Limitations	Benefits
Auxiliary power will be used to access an electronic copy of the MPI on disk	• MPI won't work without auxiliary power • The process is cumbersome • This process will likely generate some duplicate medical record numbers • It is costly for human resources to correct duplicate numbers	• Admitting staff are accustomed to this process • Process produces fewer duplicates than with no back-up system • Process is less cumbersome than totally manual system
Staff members will have to depend on a paper MPI	• Printouts will be cumbersome • Printouts probably will be located in HIM • The process will likely generate duplicate or no numbers • It is costly for human resources to use manual system and correct duplicate numbers	• Process provides a mechanism to look up a patient's number and pull a chart when critical

Contingency Plan Tasks to be Performed for Selected Alternatives (before, during, and after disaster)	
Activity	**Responsibility**
Verify availability of MPI on disk	Associate director, HIM
Implement processes to update disk daily	Associate director, HIM
Develop contingency plan procedures and training materials	Associate director, HIM
Train admitting and registration and HIM staff to use contingency plan	Associate director, HIM
Use post-disaster and implementation contingency plan	Data quality coordinator, HIM
Schedule production and delivery of paper MPI routinely	Associate director, HIM

(Continued on next page)

Figure 11.3.   Sample contingency plan (*continued*)

Create contingency procedures and training materials for manual system	Associate director, HIM
Develop schedule to update contingency plan and training materials	Associate director, HIM
Contact List	**Phone number**
HIM director	
HIM assistant director or managers	
HIM staff members (list each name separately)	

Source: AHIMA 2010c.

Workflow Re-evaluation

Post-implementation, it is important to create a process for the continuous evaluation of the workflow defined prior to implementation. Getting to an optimal workflow does not commonly happen at the moment of implementation. Like most process improvement projects, EHR workflows will need to be reevaluated after the implementation to ensure they are the most efficient and effective way of getting a task completed. Some suggestions are to evaluate a workflow 90 to 180 days after implementation as it will help an organization understand the EHR functionality and staff will become familiar with the EHR. If workflows need to be updated, it is best to go back to the basics when creating the process and test it out prior to implementing. Like any situation, evaluation of processes and workflows should be conducted on a regular basis.

Monitoring Documentation Quality

Monitoring quality documentation is a continuous effort critical to ensuring the integrity of patient data for patient safety, reimbursement, accreditation, and research. The HIM professional's role is evolving away from managing the paper record to driving data standardization within an organization. HIM professionals should continue to be involved in creating EHR auditing and quality improvement programs. Auditing and monitoring databases and data collection processes will help identify gaps in the process that might increase data integrity risks. HIM professionals are trained to ensure that data in the medical record are accurate, timely, consistent, and complete. The ability to use these skills in the electronic environment elevates the importance of HIM knowledge within the organization.

Security Auditing

As data become more electronic, the HIPAA regulations play an important part in the safe keeping of information. After the implementation of an EHR, a process for regular security audits should be implemented. The HIPAA security rule requires an organization to (1) implement a process for regular review of system activity and (2) implement hardware, software, and such to allow the ability to track and review activity on an information system. Security audits can help a healthcare organization proactively ensure that the information it stores and maintains is only being accessed for the normal course of business. As part of becoming a certified EHR for meaningful use, EHR vendors must be able to provide an audit log on an individual user basis over a period of time as well as record different actions that a user is taking within the system (AHIMA 2011b). With the requirements there, a strong **security audit program** consists of a multidisciplinary team. The core steps of an effective program are the following:

- Establish a process and document a procedure
- Define and determine who and what will be audited
- Create and implement effective audit tools
- Define and determine who will conduct the audits and the frequency
- Define the process for confronting employees when audits determine a potential breach
- Define and document the process for documenting audits and how long the data will be kept

With a few steps defined, an organization can make certain it is meeting the requirements of HIPAA and ensuring the protection of patient information.

HIM professionals have always been concerned and involved with privacy and security of health information and have played a vital role in the implementation of HIPAA's privacy and security rules. CMS Meaningful Use Incentive Payment Program criteria require the organization to do an annual risk assessment and take action to mitigate any security issues revealed by the assessment (Dimick 2012). HIM professionals can and should play a lead role in the completion of the privacy and security risk assessments as well as the mitigation process of any identified risks.

Monitoring EMPI (MPI)

Monitoring and managing an MPI also requires constant vigilance from the organization including oversight, evaluation, and correction of errors. The overall responsibility of maintaining the MPI should be centralized and be given to an individual who is detail oriented, is properly trained, has access to adequate tools, and is well versed in the organization's policies and procedures for MPI maintenance.

AHIMA recommends establishing a comprehensive maintenance program to include

- Ongoing processes to identify and address existing errors
- Advanced person search capabilities for minimizing the creation of new errors
- Mechanisms for efficiently detecting, reviewing, and resolving potential errors
- Ability to reliably link different medical record numbers and other identifiers for the same person to create an enterprise view of the person
- Consideration of the types of physical merges (files, film, and such) and the interfaces and correction routines to other electronic systems that are populated or updated by the MPI (AHIMA 2010A)

After the program is in place, MPI management must include continuous maintenance and correction of data integrity problems. Ongoing education of registration and scheduling staff is critical to maintaining low creation rates for duplicates, overlaps, overlays, and other EMPI data integrity problems.

According to AHIMA, the MPI manager should have the following responsibilities:

- Defining data stewardship policies for the organization regarding the EMPI
- Determining policies for access to the EMPI; assisting in the development of privacy and security policies for the organization and other interfacility or enterprise record management program policies
- Working with the organization's integration team to ensure ADT interfaces are properly built and tested
- Representing the organization on health information exchange efforts
- Developing policies and procedures for the exchange of health information data
- Participating in the requirements definition, evaluation, and selection of EHR systems
- Developing and maintaining the organization's naming convention policy; defining the method to follow in entering a patient's name including use of symbols and abbreviations such as hyphens, suffixes, and prefixes
- Advising on patient search routines used by patient access staff
- Defining key demographic data elements captured in the EMPI
- Establishing algorithm-based record auto-matching rules for overlap records within the EMPI and providing recommendations for record-matching rules to be used in each downstream system, based upon the downstream system's record-matching capabilities and types of electronic transactions it receives
- Managing the staff performing the duplicate, overlap, and overlay record validation process; this staff

may also be responsible for merging duplicate or overlap records in the EMPI and various downstream systems
- Communicating completed data integrity corrections to all required downstream system departments
- Reporting data integrity issues identified during routine reviews with adequate breakdown of the issues by cause, location, or system; reporting high-level results to the executive management team
- Providing routine feedback to staff managers creating data integrity issues
- Providing ongoing training to patient access staff regarding EMPI data integrity, duplicate record creation, and the importance of preventing overlaid records
- Monitoring missing, default, or invalid capture of EMPI data
- Reporting on inconsistent capture of key demographic data elements across various departments or facilities
- Defining the quality control processes for auto-linked enterprise records and manual merging of duplicate records or correction of overlaid records
- Determining processes and communication mechanisms for correcting urgent data integrity issues
- Staying abreast of new and better technologies that facilitate accurate patient identity
- Identifying registrations that may involve stolen identities, in accordance with the Red Flags Rule
- Providing education and training for other staff and stakeholder areas whose actions affect the accuracy of the MPI (for example, voluntary physicians who submit inaccurate information for patients)
- Directing the decision-making process related to new, revised, or retired data fields (for example, service type) (AHIMA 2010A)

Governing the Problem List

The **problem list** becomes a challenge in an electronic health record environment. The problem list "is defined as a compilation of clinically relevant physical and diagnostic concerns, procedures, and psychosocial and cultural issues that may affect the health status and care of patients. This information should identify the date of occurrence or discovery and resolution, if known" (AHIMA Best Practices for Problem Lists in an EHR Work Group 2008). The problem list can be extremely beneficial to healthcare providers in the care of a patient as long as it is kept up to date and maintained. Specific challenges to the problem list are the time and effort to maintain from a provider level as well as an administrative level, the functionality constraints within an EHR, and the maintenance of the codes behind the problem list as well as medical terminology and the lack of standards. Clearly, managing and maintaining an effective problem list is quite a challenge for healthcare organizations.

The most effective way to keep an effective and efficient problem list within an EHR is to create a process for governing the problem list. Creating a policy and procedure on the use and data in a problem list can assist an organization with management and governance. Other recommendations to effectively manage a problem list include the following:

- Ensure information added into the problem list is good data
- Ensure that information that is no longer relevant to patient care is removed timely
- Define and specific workflow with information on who is able to add or remove information from the problem list
- Define and create a standardized training program for problem list use
- Define and document the process for maintaining the problem list from an end user and support aspect
- Define an audit process for regular review of the problem lists

With effective management and governance, a problem can be a great tool for interdisciplinary care for healthcare providers (AHIMA Best Practices for Problem Lists in an EHR Work Group 2008).

Check Your Understanding 11.4

Instructions: Answer the following questions on a separate piece of paper.

1. What does a successful contingency plan help an organization do?
2. What is the benefit of reevaluating workflow after the implementation of an EHR?
3. What are the core steps to an effective security audit program?
4. What is the goal of an MPI ongoing maintenance program?
5. What are the biggest challenges when governing the problem list?

Summary

Throughout a healthcare organization's process of planning and implementing an EHR system, actions taken and decisions made significantly impact the activities of, and the workflows within, the HIM department. The HIM department's responsibilities for maintaining the organization's legal patient record is a primary factor that makes it a key stakeholder in the planning process, in the implementation activities, and in the ongoing maintenance of the electronic

health record. In addition, the HIM professionals bring their knowledge of healthcare data and information management principles; of federal, state, and accreditation requirements for the maintenance of patient data and records; and of the organization's healthcare data and information needs to the discussions and decision-making processes. The active engagement of HIM professionals and the HIM department is a major factor in achieving a successful EHR implementation.

References

AHIMA Best Practices for Problem Lists in an EHR Work Group. 2008 (January). Best practices for problem lists in an EHR. *Journal of AHIMA* 79(1): 73–77.

AHIMA e-HIM Work Group on Electronic Document Management as a Component of EHR. 2003 (October). Electronic document management as a component of the electronic health record. http://library.ahima.org/xpedio/groups/public/documents/ahima/bok1_021594.hcsp?dDocName=bok1_021594.

AHIMA Physician Practice Council. 2010 (June). Managing existing patient records in the transition to EHRs in physician practices. *Journal of AHIMA*: web exclusive.

American Health Information Management Association. 2010a (September). Fundamentals for building a master patient index/enterprise master patient index (updated). http://library.ahima.org/xpedio/groups/public/documents/ahima/bok1_048389.hcsp?dDocName=bok1_048389.

American Health Information Management Association. 2010b (November). Managing the transition from paper to EHRs. http://library.ahima.org/xpedio/groups/public/documents/ahima/bok1_048418.hcsp?dDocName=bok1_048418.

American Health Information Management Association. 2010c (December). Disaster planning for health information (updated). http://library.ahima.org/xpedio/groups/public/documents/ahima/bok1_048638.hcsp?dDocName=bok1_048638.

American Health Information Management Association. 2011a (February). Fundamentals of the legal health record and designated record set. *Journal of AHIMA* 82(2). Expanded online version.

American Health Information Management Association. 2011b (March). Security audits of electronic health information (updated). *Journal of AHIMA* 82(3): 46–50.

Cannon, J., and S. Lucci. 2010 (February). Transcription and EHRs: Benefits of a blended approach. *Journal of AHIMA* 81(2): 36–40.

Dimick, C. 2012 (January). Field guide: Seeing the trees through the forest in 2012. *Journal of AHIMA* 83(1): 22–27.

Dimick, C. 2008 (October). HIM jobs of tomorrow: Eleven new and revised jobs illustrate the trends changing HIM and the opportunities that lie ahead. *Journal of AHIMA* 79(10): 26–34.

Dixon, A. 2012 (March). HIM best practices for managing patient portals. *Journal of AHIMA* 83(3): 44–46.

Dunn, R.T. 2010 (November–December). Release of information: Costs remain high in a hybrid, highly regulated environment. *Journal of AHIMA* 81(11): 34–37.

Health Information Technology Review. 2009 (November 17). Benefits of a patient portal. http://www.healthtechnologyreview.com/art10_benefits_of_a_patient_portal.php.

Health Resources and Service Agency. 2012. Rural health IT toolbox. http://www.hrsa.gov/healthit/toolbox/RuralHealthITtoolbox/GettingStarted/paper.html.

Healthcare Information and Management Systems Society. 2010. Workflow redesign in support of the use of information technology within healthcare—a HIMSS toolkit. http://www.himss.org/content/output/D457160B171B43EBA89AFD2AB96DF287.pdf.

Martin, M. 2010 (January). Keys to a clean MPI–advance. http://www.kforce.com/userfiles/files/HC%20Articles/Advance%20for%20Health%20Information%20Professionals%20-%20Keys%20to%20a%20Clean%20MPI%20-%201–18–10.pdf.

McLendon, K. 2012 (January). Creating a legal health record definition. *Journal of AHIMA* 83(1): 46–47.

Minnesota Statutes 145.32, 145.30, Minnesota Rule 4642.1000. Individual permanent medical record. https://www.revisor.mn.gov/rules/?id=4642.1000&keyword_type=all&keyword=4642.1000.

Rhodes, H., and M., Dougherty 2003 (June). Document imaging as a bridge to the EHR (AHIMA Practice Brief). *Journal of AHIMA* 74(6): 56A–56G.

Tegan, A. et al. 2005 (May). The EHR's impact on HIM functions. *Journal of AHIMA* 76(5): 56C–56H.

Tegan, A. 2012 (February 20). Personal communication.

chapter 12

Legal Issues in Health Information Management

Lynda A. Russell, EdD, JD, RHIA, CHP, and
Rita K. Bowen, MA, RHIA, CHPS

Learning Objectives

- Define terms specific to civil litigation
- Diagram the state and federal court systems
- Describe the sources of law
- Explain the difference between civil law and criminal law
- Describe the process for a civil case and the process for a criminal case
- Discuss liability for a tort as it relates to healthcare
- Discuss liability for breach of contract as it relates to healthcare
- Discuss the legal aspects of a health record
- Discuss the purposes of retaining health records
- Outline the basic principles for releasing confidential health information with or without patient authorization

- Identify the required elements of an authorization for the disclosure of confidential health information
- Analyze various requests for confidential health information and determine whether patient authorization is required
- Elaborate on the role of the health record in medical staff appointments and privileges
- Discuss management of the use and disclosure of information process and function
- Explain the health information administrator's relationship with the risk manager in reducing facility liability
- Discuss difficulties and challenges in defining the legal health record (LHR)
- Elaborate on responding to e-Discovery requests

Key Terms

Accreditation
Administrative law
American Recovery and Reinvestment Act (ARRA)
Case law
Circuit
Civil law
Common law
Contract law
Controlled Substances Act
Court of Appeals
Covered entity (CE)
Credentialing process
Criminal law
Default judgment

Defendant
Designated record set
Disclosure
e-Discovery
Electronic health record (EHR)
Evidence
Federal Register
Felony
Freedom of Information Act (FOIA)
Health Insurance Portability and Accountability Act of 1996 (HIPAA)
Incident
Individually identifiable health information
Interrogatories

Judge-made law
Jurisdiction
Legal health record (LHR)
Licensure
Litigation
Metadata
Misdemeanor
Motion for summary judgment
National Practitioner Data Bank
Negligence
Plaintiff
Preemption
Privacy Act of 1974
Privacy Rule

Privilege
Privileging process
Prosecutor
Protected health information (PHI)
Red Flags Rule
Request for production
Restitution
Spoliation
Standard of care
Statutory (legislative) law
Tort
Trier of fact
Use

Introduction to the Legal System

To understand the role of the health information management (HIM) professional in protecting confidential health information, one must first understand the principles for disclosing such information. Because many disclosures are made as part of **litigation,** the HIM professional should be very comfortable with the legal process. The following sections present the basics about the legal system, the sources of American law, the court system, the legal process, and the types of actions encountered in healthcare.

The Legal System

The US legal system consists of three related subsystems: a judicial system, a regulatory system, and an administrative system.

The *judicial system* affords a person or an entity the opportunity to bring a civil action against another person or entity believed to have caused harm to the original party. An individual can bring a wide variety of actions against an alleged wrongdoer. The judicial system also affords a person or an entity charged with criminal wrongdoing the opportunity to defend himself or herself against those charges. In this way, the judicial system provides an avenue for a wronged party to seek retribution or to clear his or her name.

The *regulatory system* controls many activities related to industry, in particular, the healthcare industry. These controls exist as statutes or as regulations derived from, or promulgated pursuant to, statutes. Often the statutes set forth what action is required, and the regulations set forth how that action is to be met.

The *administrative system* controls governmental administrative operations. Federal and state administrative agencies enact regulations that have the same force of law that statutory laws do.

Understanding the American judicial, regulatory, and administrative subsystems within the legal system gives an HIM professional an appreciation for the health record as a legal document and its role in each of these subsystems.

Because it is impossible to summarize the infinite variety of state laws, the text is based on applying the **Privacy Rule** under the **Health Insurance Portability and Accountability Act of 1996 (HIPAA)** (HIPAA-a). HIM professionals must consult their individual state statutes, codes, and regulations for specific applications that may have been declared more stringent than HIPAA and thus not preempted by HIPAA.

Sources of Law

The laws that rule all Americans' lives come from many sources, which results in a rather complex legal system. Overall, there is a federal legal system and 50 individual state legal systems. Regardless of the source, the legal system is a process through which members of society settle disputes. These disputes may be between private individuals and organizations or between either of these entities and the government, whether state, federal, or both.

Constitutional Law

Much of the law governing society is set out in the state and federal constitutions. The Constitution of the United States is the highest law in the land. It takes precedence over constitutions and laws in the individual states and local jurisdictions (Pozgar 2012; Rinehart-Thompson 2009). The US Constitution defines the federal government's general organization and grants powers to it. It also places limits on what federal and state governments may do. State constitutions have the same effect within the borders of each state. Some state constitutions are very elaborate and govern everything from state lotteries to retirement plans for state workers.

Common Law

English common law is the primary source of many legal rules and principles and was based initially on tradition and custom. **Common law,** also known as **judge-made law** or **case law,** is regularly referred to as unwritten law originating from court decisions where no applicable statute exists. Before the Norman Conquest in 1066, English laws primarily addressed violent crimes. After the Norman Conquest, a legal system began to develop that included a jury hearing complaints from the king's subjects (Pozgar 2012). Thus since there were few written laws at this time, the principles that evolved from these court decisions became known as "common law" (Pozgar 2012).

After the American Revolution, Louisiana was the only state that did not adopt all or part of the existing English common-law principles (Pozgar 2012). States created after the Revolution vary in their treatment of English common law, but most have adopted the common law in effect as of a certain date. As a matter of technical legal practice, this date of adoption can make a difference in how a lawsuit is resolved if the only source of law on the subject in the state is the English common law. These cases of "first impression" are rare. Louisiana is the exception because it bases much of its common law on the French (Code of Napoleon) and Spanish civil law systems (Pozgar 2012). States continue to add to the body of common law through court decisions (also referred to as a court's holding) when existing statutes do not apply to the issue before the court. Because each state adds to the common law within its boundaries, there is no body of national common law. Thus, a common-law principle established in one state has no effect in another state unless the second state also adopts the principle. Even then, it may be applied differently. After a court establishes a new common-law principle, that principle becomes a precedent for future cases addressing the same issues in that state. The body of common law in a given state is continually evolving through being modified, overturned, abrogated, or created by court decisions. Although a precedent in State A does not apply to other states, other states may use the State A precedent as a guide in analyzing a specific legal problem (Pozgar 2012). Lower courts must look to higher courts in the same court system for precedent; yet the higher courts are not bound by the decisions held in the lower courts in the same court system. Courts on the same level within the same court system are not obligated to follow each other's decisions (Rinehart-Thompson 2009).

Another legal principle of note is *stare decisis,* which means "let the decision stand" (Rinehart-Thompson 2009). This principle states that in cases in a lower court involving a fact pattern similar to that in a higher court within the court system, the lower court is bound to apply the decision of the higher court (Rinehart-Thompson 2009).

Statutory Law

By contrast, **statutory (legislative) law** is written law established by federal and state legislatures. It may be amended, repealed, or expanded by the legislature. Statutory law also may be upheld or found by a court to violate or conflict with the state or federal constitution. Further, it may be found to conflict with a different state law or a federal law.

Courts also interpret laws in terms of how they apply to a given situation. Thus, statutory law may be "revised" by a court ruling in terms of its constitutionality and applicability. However, if the legislature disagrees with the court's interpretation, it can revise the statute. The legislative revision then becomes the law versus the court's revision based on its interpretation.

Administrative Law

Federal and state legislatures often delegate their legislative authority to regulate in technical or complex areas to appropriate federal and state administrative agencies. These agencies are empowered to enact regulations that have the same force of law that statutory law has and can impose criminal penalties for noncompliance. Accordingly, **administrative law** is the branch of law that controls governmental administrative operations (Pozgar 2012). Such administrative agencies include licensing and accrediting bodies, Medicare, Medicaid, and other federal and state government programs. Additionally, regulatory agencies can function in a legislative, adjudicative, and enforcement role regarding their own regulation in some cases (Pozgar 2012).

Federal administrative agencies function under the Administrative Procedures Act, which sets forth the following (Pozgar 2012):

- The procedures under which administrative agencies must operate
- The procedural responsibilities and authority of administrative agencies
- The legal remedies for individuals or entities harmed by agency actions

The act also requires administrative agencies to make agency rules, opinions, orders, records, and proceedings available to the public (Administrative Procedures Act §552). The publication used to accomplish this is the *Federal Register,* which is issued by the US Government Printing Office every business day. The information that agencies must publish includes the following:

- Their organizational structure and the location where the public can obtain information
- Formal and informal procedures and forms and instructions for using them
- A general statement of applicability
- Amendments, revisions, or repeals of any of this information

Furthermore, agencies must publish proposed administrative rules and revisions to existing rules for which they are delegated the responsibility and authority to enact. These rules or revisions are published in the *Federal Register* for a comment period during which the public is invited to make comments on the applicability and impact of the proposed rules on a given person, group of persons, or entity. After the comment period ends, the applicable administrative agency may or may not finalize the rules. If the rules are finalized, the notice and the final rule are published in the *Federal Register.*

The final rule is also codified and published in the appropriate code section. The Medicare Conditions of Participation regulations and HIPAA's Administrative Simplification rules are examples of healthcare-related information regulations published in the *Federal Register*. Such regulations and administrative decisions can be subject to judicial review when questions arise regarding whether an agency has overstepped its bounds in interpreting the law (Pozgar 2012).

Most states have similar administrative procedure acts, but few have as elaborate a system for the adoption of new regulations as the federal government.

The Court System

The American court system is composed of the state court system and the federal court system. The nature of the issue determines which court has **jurisdiction** over the issue. Jurisdiction means a particular court has the right to hear and decide the controversy in a given case. Matters in the following three categories belong only to federal courts: federal crimes, such as racketeering and bank robbery; constitutional issues; and civil actions where the parties do not live in the same state. Other civil and criminal cases are heard in the state court system.

State Court System

Typically, the state court system has several levels. In most states, the lowest level consists of specialty courts or local courts that hear cases involving traffic, small claims, and justice of the peace issues. State civil and criminal cases are initiated in the lower-level trial courts, which have the authority to first hear a case on a given matter—original jurisdiction. These trial courts are referred to differently in different states, for example, as district trial courts or superior courts. New York's trial courts are called the Supreme Court. Some trial courts at this level have limited jurisdiction and include courts such as probate, family, juvenile, surrogate, and criminal. Other trial courts at this same level have general jurisdiction. Decisions made in a court at this level may be appealed to the intermediate courts, usually known as the state appeals courts. State appellate courts have general jurisdiction; however, some states (such as Texas) divide their appellate courts into civil and criminal appellate jurisdiction, and others divide appellate courts by legal and equitable jurisdiction.

State legal systems also include a court at the highest level. These courts of last resort also are known by different terms in different states. Many are simply the Supreme Court of the state; others are the Supreme Judicial Court, as in Massachusetts, and New York has the **Court of Appeals** as its highest court. These higher courts also have general jurisdiction over all cases heard in the state's trial and appellate courts. Decisions coming from the highest state court hearing a case become the law of that state unless a state legislative process enacts a statute to override the court's decision, or unless it is overturned by another case.

Federal Court System

The 94 trial-level federal courts are referred to as the US District Courts and include the bankruptcy courts (Rinehart-Thompson 2009). Because federal courts have exclusive jurisdiction over bankruptcy matters, such cases cannot be filed in a state court. Special federal courts have jurisdiction over specific matters. These courts include the US Tax Court (hears cases involving federal tax matters only); the US Customs Court (reviews administrative decisions made by customs officials); the US Court of Military Appeals (the jurisdiction of which is limited to hearing appeals from courts-martial under the Uniform Code of Military Justice); the US Court of Appeals for the Federal Circuit (hears appellate cases involving customs and patent issues); and the US Court of Claims (hears certain claims against the government including those for money damages) (Pozgar 2012).

The federal appellate level is composed of the US Courts of Appeals, each court covering a geographic area known as a **circuit** (Pozgar 2012). The appellate courts have several purposes (Pozgar 2012):

- Reviewing cases heard in federal district courts within the court's circuit
- Reviewing orders issued by certain administrative agencies
- Issuing original writs in cases as appropriate

The US Supreme Court is the highest court in the US legal system and hears appeals from the federal appellate courts and the various state courts of last resort.

The Legal Process

The HIM professional can better serve patient privacy interests if he or she has an understanding of the legal process. This understanding should cover both civil and criminal processes, as healthcare facilities sometimes are affected by criminal cases.

Civil Cases

Civil law involves relations between individuals, corporations, government entities, and other organizations. Most actions encountered in the healthcare industry are based on civil law. Typically, the remedy for a civil wrong is monetary in nature but also may include carrying out some action.

The party bringing the action or complaint in a civil case is the **plaintiff.** The plaintiff has the burden of proving the wrong, that the defendant did the wrong act, that the wrong did the plaintiff harm, the harm from the wrong, and the expected **restitution.** The plaintiff presents **evidence** before a judge or a jury that must be more compelling than that of the opposing side, the **defendant.** The plaintiff or an attorney on the plaintiff's behalf begins the process by filing a complaint in the appropriate court. Hereafter in this discussion, the term *plaintiff* refers collectively to the individual or entity bringing the action and that individual or entity's attorney.

The plaintiff has a summons, including a copy of the filed complaint, served on the defendant. The defendant or an attorney on the defendant's behalf prepares an answer and files it in the same court where the original complaint was filed. Hereafter in this discussion, the term *defendant* refers collectively to the person or entity against whom an action has been brought and that person or entity's attorney.

Other actions may be taken before a case is resolved. The defendant may bring a claim against the plaintiff (counterclaim), one party may bring a claim against another party who is on the same side of the litigation (cross-claim), and/or the defendant may bring a claim against an outsider as a codefendant (joinder) (Rinehart-Thompson 2009, citing Garner 2004).

A case may be resolved in five ways:

- A judge can dismiss the plaintiff's case for procedural reasons. The plaintiff's complaint may not set forth a claim recognized by law, the summons and complaint may not have been properly served on the defendant, or the defendant may not be subject to the court's jurisdiction (meaning that the court has no power to compel the defendant to do what it commands). The judge may permit the plaintiff to correct the error and refile the case.
- If the defendant fails to file a timely answer, the court will find in favor of the plaintiff and enter a **default judgment** against the defendant.
- A case may be settled out of court before it goes to trial or at any time during trial before the **trier of fact** (judge or jury) announces the decision.
- Presuming the case does not settle or is not dismissed or no default judgment is entered, the case will proceed with pretrial activities by both plaintiff and defendant. Such activities, known as pretrial discovery, include, but are not limited to, the taking of witnesses' depositions, the serving of **interrogatories** and **requests for production** on the opposing party, and the issuing of subpoenas, as necessary. The court (the judge assigned to the case) will set dates according to the law by which pretrial discovery must be completed. At the conclusion of this stage, in most cases one or both parties present **motions for summary judgment,** in which they argue that there are (or are not) any facts remaining in dispute and that one or the other is (or is not) entitled to a judgment being entered without the intervention of the trier of fact. If the judge grants such a motion, the case is over and has the same effect as if the case had proceeded to trial.
- If a motion for summary judgment is not successful or is not made, the case will proceed to trial before the trier of fact. In most civil cases, the plaintiff must prove his or her case by what is known as a "preponderance of the evidence." In simple terms, this means that there is enough evidence to tip the scales, even slightly, in favor of the plaintiff's case. This is a substantially lower standard of proof than a criminal case, in which the government must prevail "beyond a reasonable doubt." Upon conclusion of the trial, a verdict is given. In civil cases, a verdict is more commonly referred to as being *liable* or *not liable.* If a party is found to be liable, a judgment is rendered against the party determined to be wholly or partially liable for the harm. Either party may appeal the judgment to an appellate court and possibly even to the highest court in that state.

Criminal Cases

Criminal law addresses crimes that are wrongful acts against public health, safety, and welfare. Criminal laws also include punishment for those persons violating the law. Criminal cases involve matters between individuals or groups of people and the government. Crimes are either a felony or a misdemeanor as defined by state or federal law. **Felonies** are the more serious crimes and include, among others, murder, thefts of items or cash in excess of a certain set value (ordinarily $1,000), assault, and rape. **Misdemeanors** are lesser offenses and include disorderly conduct, thefts of small amounts of property, and breaking into an automobile. Information theft crimes (such as hacking, computer destruction, spamming, and the like) can be either misdemeanors or felonies. The criminal provisions of the HIPAA Privacy Rule have only felony crimes.

When law enforcement learns that a crime has or may have been committed, an investigation is begun. The government initiates a criminal action against those individuals or groups of people it believes have committed the crime based on the law enforcement investigation. When the **prosecutor** (prosecuting attorney), also known as the district or state attorney (depending on the state) or the US attorney (in the federal system), determines sufficient evidence is present, he or she files charges against the defendant on behalf of the government. In some states, a grand jury must return an indictment for a felony crime to be prosecuted. The grand jury has the authority to issue subpoenas for its investigative process, and all evidence considered by the grand jury remains confidential unless an indictment is returned. The court arraigns the charged person on the prosecutor's charge, and the prosecutor prosecutes those charges against the defendant. The prosecutor has the burden of proving the charges against the defendant. In virtually all criminal cases, the government must prove the defendant's guilt beyond a reasonable doubt.

The accused defendant may plead guilty and be sentenced to probation or imprisonment and/or pay a fine. He or she also may plead not guilty, which results in a trial. Upon conclusion of the trial, a verdict of either guilty or not guilty is rendered. When a defendant is found not guilty, the charges are dismissed. A defendant found to be guilty is sentenced to probation or imprisonment and/or to pay a fine. In most jurisdictions, only a defendant who is found guilty at trial can proceed through the appellate process.

Actions Encountered in Healthcare

The healthcare industry is involved most often in civil cases and less often in criminal cases. Because government is increasing its investigations into and prosecutions for healthcare fraud and refusal to treat patients based on financial status, the healthcare industry will be faced with more criminal cases. However, this chapter focuses on civil actions. The types of civil legal actions that most typically affect the healthcare industry are torts and contracts. The vast majority of claims founded in tort and **contract law** are resolved without appearing in court, many before a lawsuit is filed.

Torts

A **tort** is an action brought when one party believes that another party caused harm through wrongful conduct and the party bringing the action seeks compensation for that harm. In addition to compensation, a second reason for bringing a tort action is to discourage the wrongdoer from committing further wrongful acts. Three categories of tort liability exist: negligence, intentional torts, and strict and products liability (Pozgar 2012). Most healthcare **incidents** arise in the negligent tort category.

Negligent Torts

Negligence results when a person does not act the way a reasonably prudent person would act under the same circumstances. A negligent tort may result from a person committing an act or failing to act as a reasonably prudent person would or would not in the given circumstances (Pozgar 2012). Typically, negligence is careless conduct that is outside the generally accepted standard of care. **Standard of care** is defined as what an individual is expected to do or not do in a given situation. Standards of care are established in a variety of ways: by professional associations, by statute or regulation, or by practice. Such standards are considered to represent expected behavior unless a court finds differently. Therefore, standards also are established by case law. Standards not established by a governmental body do not by themselves have the force of law.

In healthcare, the standard of care is the exercise of reasonable care by healthcare professionals having similar training and experience in the same or similar communities. However, the trend is a reliance on an industry or national standard versus a community standard because courts are exhibiting a belief that a standard of care should not vary by the area where a person receives care (Pozgar 2012, 36).

Negligence also may occur in cases where an individual has evaluated the alternatives and the consequences of those alternatives and has not exercised his or her best possible judgment. A person can also be found negligent when he or she has failed to guard against a risk that he or she knew could happen. Furthermore, negligence can occur in circumstances where it is known, or should have been known, that a particular behavior would place others in unreasonable danger. Negligence may occur in one of these forms (Pozgar 2012, 33):

- *Malpractice:* Negligence or carelessness of a professional person, such as a nurse, pharmacist, a physician, or an accountant
- *Criminal negligence:* Reckless disregard for the safety of another; the willful indifference to an injury that could follow an act (in this respect, it is possible that conduct could at once create civil and criminal liability)

Negligence can further be categorized in other ways. For example, negligent torts can be categorized as one of the following (Pozgar 2012, 33):

- *Malfeasance:* The execution of an unlawful or improper act
- *Misfeasance:* The improper performance of an act resulting in injury to another
- *Nonfeasance:* The failure to act when there is a duty to act as a reasonably prudent person would act in similar circumstances

Further, negligence can be categorized by the degree of wrongdoing. *Ordinary negligence* is failure to do what a reasonably prudent person would do, or doing something that a reasonably prudent person would not do, in the same circumstances (Pozgar 2012, 33). *Gross negligence* is intentionally omitting care that would be proper or providing care that would be substandard or improper (Pozgar 2012, 33).

To recover damages caused by negligence, the plaintiff must show that all four elements of negligence are present (Pozgar 2012, 33):

- There must be a *duty of care.* For this element to be present in a medical malpractice case, a physician–patient, nurse–patient, therapist–patient, or other caregiver–patient relationship must exist at the time of the alleged wrongful act (there must be an obligation to meet a standard of care).
- There must have been a *breach of the duty of care.* The plaintiff must present evidence that the defendant acted unreasonably under the circumstances (either a failure to follow a standard of care or a deviation from the standard of care).
- The plaintiff must have *suffered an injury* as a result of the defendant's negligent act or failure to act. Injury includes not only physical harm but also mental suffering, pain, loss of income or reputation (Pozgar 2012, 39), and the invasion of a patient's rights and privacy.
- The plaintiff must show that the defendant's conduct *caused* the plaintiff's harm. As an example, varying from a recognized procedure is insufficient to justify

the plaintiff's recovery of damages. The plaintiff must show that the variance was unreasonable and that it caused the harm. Thus the "proximate cause" of the injury must be the breach of duty. (Pozgar 2012, 33)

When no statute exists to define what is reasonable, the trier of fact determines what a reasonably prudent person would have done. According to Pozgar (2012, 36), "the reasonably prudent person concept describes a nonexistent, hypothetical person who is put forward as the community ideal of what would be considered reasonable behavior." The trier of fact considers defendant characteristics such as age, sex, training, education, mental capacity, physical condition, and knowledge in defining the reasonably prudent person. After the behavior of a reasonably prudent person is defined for the given circumstances, the trier of fact compares the defendant's behavior against that definition. If the defendant's behavior meets or exceeds the definition, no negligence has occurred. On the other hand, if the defendant's behavior does not meet the reasonably prudent person standard and injury or damages result, negligence has occurred. In such a case, the trier of fact must determine whether

- The harm that would result from the failure to meet the reasonably prudent person standard could have been foreseen.
- The negligent act caused harm to the plaintiff.

Intentional Torts

Although most torts experienced in healthcare are based on negligence, an occasional intentional tort is committed that includes actions such as assault, battery, libel, slander, invasion of privacy, and false imprisonment. The element of intent is the difference between the intentional tort and the negligent tort. *Intent* means the person committed an act knowing that harm would likely occur.

A quick review of several intentional torts gives the reader an idea of how they may occur in a healthcare setting. These intentional torts include assault and battery, false imprisonment, defamation of character, fraud, invasion of privacy, and reckless infliction of mental distress.

Assault is a deliberate threat that is combined with the apparent present ability to cause physical harm to another person (Pozgar 2012, 43). For example, a large male nurse in the emergency department tells a frail elderly woman that he will break her arm if she does not do what he tells her to do. His comment is a deliberate threat, and his size gives him the apparent ability to harm the woman. In this example, the woman does not need to suffer actual damage or even come in contact with the nurse.

Battery is intentionally touching another person's body in a socially impermissible manner without that person's consent (Pozgar 2012, 43). In healthcare, laws regarding battery are especially important because of the requirement for consent for medical and surgical procedures. The patient does not need to be aware that battery has occurred. For example,

battery occurs to the patient who is sedated and has surgery performed on him or her without either implied or express consent. Thus the hospital and the treating healthcare professionals may be held liable for harm caused by the lack of a proper patient consent. Further, even if the outcome of the procedure benefits the patient, touching the patient without proper consent may make the healthcare professional liable for battery.

False imprisonment is another intentional tort. A healthcare provider's efforts to prevent a patient from leaving a hospital may result in false imprisonment. This is not the case when a patient with a contagious disease or a mentally ill patient who is likely to cause harm to others is compelled to remain in the hospital (Pozgar 2012, 45). There are limits to the actions staff can take to compel a patient not to leave a hospital. For example, staff may confine individuals to protect them from harming themselves or others (Pozgar 2012, 45). The patient's insistence on leaving the facility should be documented in his or her health record, and the patient should be asked to sign a discharge against medical advice form that releases the facility from responsibility. Although physical force is not required to be held liable for false imprisonment, when excessive force is used to restrain a patient, the healthcare provider may be held liable for both false imprisonment and battery (Pozgar 2012, 44).

Defamation of character is a false communication about someone to a person other than the person defamed that tends to injure that person's reputation (Pozgar 2012, 47). The communication may be either oral or written. *Libel* is the written form of defamation, and *slander* is the spoken form. To recover in an action for defamation, the plaintiff must prove that

- The defendant made a false and defamatory statement about the plaintiff
- The statement was not a "privileged" publication and was made to a third person
- At least negligence occurred
- Actual or presumed damages occurred

Proof of special damages, including economic losses, is not required to recover in a defamation case. Special damages include economic losses. Courts also may find that the defamation caused injury to a person's reputation. However, there are four exceptions regarding harm to reputation. In these exceptions, the plaintiff is not required to show proof of actual harm to his or her reputation when the defendant allegedly performs one of the following acts (Pozgar 2012, 47):

- Accuses the plaintiff of a crime
- Accuses the plaintiff of having a loathsome disease
- Uses words that affect the plaintiff's profession or business
- Calls a woman unchaste

When slander is alleged, the plaintiff usually must prove special damages. However, if the slander refers to the plaintiff in a professional capacity, the plaintiff is not required to show actual harm because slanderous references to a person's professional capacity are presumed to be damaging to that person's professional reputation (Pozgar 2012, 47). As to the second exception, healthcare professionals are protected against claims of libel when complying with laws requiring the reporting of communicable diseases that the patient may consider loathsome (Pozgar 2012).

The defendant (the one being accused of defaming another) has two defenses available to a defamation action (Pozgar 2012, 50):

- Truth: The person making an alleged defamatory statement that harms another's reputation will not be liable for that statement if he or she shows the statement was true
- Privilege: The person making the allegedly defamatory communication can claim privilege if he or she is making the communication
  — In good faith
  — On the proper occasion
  — In the proper manner
  — To persons who have a legitimate reason to receive the information

The defense of privilege is based on the person making the communication being charged with a higher duty. For example, in one case, a director of nurses wrote a letter to a nurse's professional registry stating that the hospital wanted to discontinue a particular registry nurse's services because narcotics were disappearing whenever the nurse was on duty (*Judge v. Rockford Memorial Hospital* 1958). The court found the communication to be privileged because the director of nurses had a legal duty to make the communication in the interests of society (Pozgar 2012, 50). Thus, the court denied the nurse's claim for damages.

Fraud is a prevalent concern in today's healthcare environment. It is defined as "a willful and intentional misrepresentation that could cause harm or loss to a person or property" (Pozgar 2012, 51). For example, physicians can be held liable for fraud if they claim that a particular procedure will cure a patient's ailment when they know it will not, or if they charge a third-party payer for a medical procedure they did not actually perform. To prove fraud, the plaintiff must show (Pozgar 2012, 51)

- An untrue statement known to be untrue by the party making the statement and made with an intent to deceive
- The victim's justifiable reliance on the truth of the statement
- Damages resulting from that reliance

Invasion of privacy is another major concern in healthcare. According to Pozgar (2012), a person's right to privacy is "the right to be left alone—the right to be free from unwarranted publicity and exposure to public view, as well as the right to live one's life without having one's name, picture, or private affairs made public against one's will" (Pozgar 2012, 52). The right to privacy is also the right to control personal information (McWay 2010, 101). The United States Constitution does not specifically grant a right to privacy; however, courts have interpreted the Constitution to give privacy rights in various subject matters (Rinehart-Thompson 2009). Although a constitutional right to privacy with respect to health information does not exist, privacy of such information has been established through various court decisions, state laws, and federal laws, specifically the HIPAA Privacy Rule (45 CFR 160, 164) (Rinehart-Thompson 2009). The courts hold healthcare providers liable for negligent disregard for a patient's right of privacy, especially when patients cannot adequately protect themselves (Pozgar 2012, 52). One major actionable offense of concern in healthcare involving invasion of privacy is the release or disclosure of health information without patient authorization in circumstances when it is required.

The *intentional or reckless infliction of mental distress* for which a person can be held liable includes mental suffering resulting from such things as despair, shame, grief, and public humiliation (Pozgar 2012). If the plaintiff shows that the defendant (the one inflicting the distress) intended to cause mental distress and knew or should have known that his or her actions would do so, the plaintiff can recover damages (Pozgar 2012, 52).

The distinction between negligence torts and intentional torts is far from academic. In most state legal systems, punitive damages—those damages awarded to punish or deter wrongful conduct over and above compensation for injury—are limited in negligence cases and may, in fact, be capped in medical malpractice cases. However, most states permit punitive damages as a matter of right in cases of intentional torts, and these damages usually fall outside the scope of state laws capping jury awards or damages. Consequently, it is possible for a battery case involving a failure to obtain surgical consent (an intentional tort) to have more economic value than a medical malpractice case (a negligence tort) due to the presence or absence of punitive damages.

Strict and Products Liability

Strict liability occurs when some person or entity is held "responsible for damages their actions or products cause, regardless of 'fault' on their part" (Pozgar 2012, 53). Products liability is the legal doctrine under which a manufacturer, seller, or supplier of a product may be liable to a buyer or other third party for injuries caused by a defective product (Pozgar 2012, 53). The injured person may bring an action based in negligence; breach of warranty, either implied or express; or strict liability. To prevail in *negligence,* the plaintiff must show all four elements of a negligence case: there was a duty that was breached, causing the injury. The manufacturer will not be held liable for injuries if they resulted from the user's negligent use of the product (Pozgar 2012).

However, manufacturers will be held liable for injuries resulting from a bad product design; thus manufacturers often provide instructions on the proper use of their product (Pozgar 2012, 53). Should a manufacturer not provide these instructions, the manufacturer may be liable for negligence. Defective packaging and a failure to warn of dangers associated with normal, proper use of the product can also result in the manufacturer being held liable in negligence (Pozgar 2012).

To recover under the theory of *breach of warranty,* the plaintiff must show there was an express or implied warranty. Through an *express warranty,* the seller makes specific promises to the buyer, whereas an *implied warranty* exists when the law implies such a warranty exists "as a matter of public policy" to protect the public from harm (Pozgar 2012, 55).

The third basis on which a plaintiff may base a product's liability claim is *strict liability,* which is liability without fault. To prevail, the plaintiff only must show an injury resulted while using the product in the proper manner. The plaintiff does not need to show negligence by the manufacturer. As Pozgar stated, the elements for a strict liability case are (2012, 55) the following:

- The defendant manufactured the product
- The product was defective when it left the hands of the manufacturer or seller; defects typically consist of
  — Manufacturing defects
  — Design defects
  — Absent or inadequate warnings for product use
  — The specific product must have injured the plaintiff
  — The defective product must have been the proximate cause of the injury

Under strict liability, the manufacturer also may be held liable pursuant to *res ipsa loquitur* (the thing speaks for itself). To recover under this concept, the plaintiff must show (Pozgar 2012, 56) that

- The product did not perform in the way intended
- Neither the buyer nor a third person had tampered with the product
- The defect in the product existed when it left the manufacturer

Defenses

A healthcare provider may raise a number of defenses in response to a lawsuit (McWay 2010, 84–87). These include the following:

- *Statute of limitations:* A statutorily set time frame within which a lawsuit must be brought or the court must dismiss the case.
- *Good Samaritan:* Statutes that protect physicians and other rescuers from liability for their acts or omissions in providing emergency care in a nontraditional setting such as at an automobile accident site when no charge for services is made.
- *Charitable immunity:* Charitable institutions such as charity hospitals often were protected from liability for torts occurring on its property or by its employees.
- *Governmental immunity:* Precludes anyone from bringing a lawsuit against a governmental entity unless that entity consents to the lawsuit.
- *Contributory negligence:* The plaintiff's conduct contributed in part to the injury the plaintiff suffered and, if found to be sufficient, can preclude the plaintiff's recovery for the injury.
- *Comparative negligence:* The plaintiff's conduct contributed in part to the injury the plaintiff suffered, but the plaintiff's recovery is reduced by some amount based on his or her percentage of negligence.
- *Assumption of risk:* The plaintiff who voluntarily places himself or herself at risk to a known or appreciated danger may not recover damages for injury resulting from the risk.
- *Apologies:* Several states have passed laws that permit a healthcare provider to apologize to a patient/patient's family for an error without fearing the apology will be considered an admission of liability.

The charitable immunity and governmental immunity defenses have been either significantly limited or abolished as defenses by state and federal laws (McWay 2010, 85).

Pozgar stated that defenses in products liability cases include (Pozgar 2012, 56)

- Assumption of risk
- Intervening cause
- Contributory negligence
- Comparative fault
- Disclaimers

Contract

Lawsuits under contracts are the other type of civil claim arising in the healthcare industry. A contract is an agreement, written or oral, that, in most cases, is legally enforceable through the legal system. Contracts must not violate state or federal policy or state or federal statute, rule, or regulation. Contract law is based on common law. However, some states have replaced common law with statutory law or administrative agency regulations. In those states, the statutes or administrative regulations control. One example of how contractual issues affect healthcare is a contract for services between the hospital and a contracting physician or a physician group, such as pathologists, radiologists, anesthesiologists, and emergency medicine physicians. The parties to a contract must have the capacity to enter into the agreement, such as being a competent adult, being of age of majority, not being incapacitated by medication or alcohol, and not being mentally incapacitated.

The elements of a contract must be stated clearly and specifically. A contract cannot exist unless all the following elements exist. There must be an *agreement* between two or more persons or entities. The agreement must include a valid offer, an exchange of consideration, and acceptance. In an *offer,* one party promises to either do something or not do something if the other party agrees to either do something or not do something (Pozgar 2012). The party making the offer must communicate it to the other party so that it can be accepted or rejected.

A contract must be supported by legal and bargained-for consideration. Each party "must give up something of value in exchange for something of value" (Pozgar 2012, 87).

There also must be *acceptance,* which requires the following to be valid (Pozgar 2012, 87):

- Meeting of the minds (parties must understand and agree on the terms comprising the contract)
- Definite and complete (terms must be sufficiently complete for the parties to understand and agree to the terms)
- Duration (the party making the offer [offeror] may revoke offer prior to a valid acceptance; revocation not effective until the party to whom the offer was made [offeree] receives the revocation; once offeree accepts offer, it cannot be revoked)
- Complete and conforming (acceptance must be mirror image of the offer—not add, change, or delete any of the terms in the offer)

A hospital contract with patients that attempts to limit their right to sue could be a contract to which a court would apply the unconscionable concept and hold the hospital liable.

A contract action arises when one party claims that the other party has failed to meet an obligation set forth in a valid contract. Another way to state this is that the other party has breached the contract. The resolution available is either compensation (money damages) or performance of the obligation. To succeed in a breach of contract action, the plaintiff must show (Pozgar 2012, 87) that

- Parties entered into a valid contract
- Plaintiff performed as specified
- Defendant did not perform as specified
- Plaintiff suffered an economic loss as a result of the defendant's failure to perform

The defendant can raise a variety of defenses to a breach of contract action including waiver and default, conduct of the parties, and waiving rights under the agreement.

Check Your Understanding 12.1

Instructions: Answer the following questions on a separate piece of paper.

1. What are the four sources of laws governing Americans?

2. What types of cases are typically heard in the federal court system?

3. Which court is the court of last resort in the United States legal system?

4. What are the two most common types of civil cases experienced in healthcare?

5. In a court, who is the trier of fact?

6. What is the result of a civil trial called?

7. What types of cases are covered by criminal laws?

8. What are the roles of prosecutor and defendant in a criminal case? Who has the burden of proof?

9. What are the possible outcomes of a criminal case?

10. What are the three categories of tort liability? From which category do most healthcare cases arise?

11. What is the definition of a negligent tort?

12. What are the four elements of negligence?

13. How might false imprisonment occur in a hospital?

14. What defenses are available to a defendant accused of defamation of character?

15. Privacy is difficult to achieve in a healthcare setting. However, courts will hold healthcare providers liable for what type of invasion of privacy?

16. What is a contract?

17. What action must occur for a contract case to arise?

Legal Aspects of Health Information Management

The field of health information management must recognize and treat the patient's health record as a legal document. Thus, the HIM professional must have an understanding of all the regulations and statutes that affect the creation and maintenance of the health record.

Form and Content of the Health Record

The health record is a complete, accurate, and current report of the medical history, condition, and treatment that a particular patient receives during an encounter with a healthcare provider. (See a discussion of a legal health record later in this chapter.) In a hospital, the encounter may be on either an inpatient or outpatient basis. Moreover, it may be defined as one episode of treatment or an accumulation of all episodes of treatment in any setting that is part of the organization.

The health record is composed of two types of information: demographic information and clinical information. Most of the *demographic* information is collected at the time of admission or registration for treatment. It includes, among other items, the patient's name, sex, age, insurance information, and the person to contact in case of emergency. This information may be added to and changed throughout the patient's medical encounters. The *clinical information* comprises the patient's complaint, history of present illness, medical history, family history, social history, continuing documentation of ongoing medical care, report of diagnostic tests, x-ray reports, surgery and other procedure reports, consultant reports, nursing documentation, various graphs, and the final diagnoses. In some states, licensure regulations may specify the contents. In other states, the health record content is defined in broader terms.

Accrediting agency regulations or standards are one source for identifying health record content. The Joint Commission, the American Osteopathic Association (AOA), and other accrediting organizations include some level of requirements for health record content. The Medicare program's Conditions of Participation also include minimum requirements for health record content. However, some sources of regulations for health record content are more prescriptive than others are. For example, some regulations give details on the information to be retained, others specify the broad categories of information required, and still others state simply that the health record must be accurate, adequate, or complete. Most states have statutory or regulatory definitions of what a proper health record must contain, and many third-party payers also dictate how health records for their insured must be maintained and kept. The HIM professional must be aware of the most stringent definition of the health record content to which his or her particular organization is subject.

It also is important to heed agency requirements and various laws that regulate hospitals and have an impact on the process of creating and maintaining health records. The healthcare industry in general and hospitals in particular are extensively regulated by all levels of the government and by numerous agencies within each level of government. Additionally, they are regulated for accreditation purposes by nongovernment agencies. Quite often, hospitals are faced with conflicting requirements because of this multiple-regulation environment.

Regulatory (Licensure) Agencies

Typically, state legislatures have granted authority to a state administrative agency to

- Develop standards hospitals must meet
- Issue licenses to those hospitals that meet the standards
- Monitor continuing compliance with the standards
- Penalize hospitals that violate the standards

Licensure is issued for the organization as a whole. It addresses policies and procedures, staffing, and hospital building integrity among many other facets of the organization. Some states require additional licenses for specific services in the hospital. For example, laboratory, radiology, renal dialysis, and substance abuse services may require separate licenses in addition to the facility license. Additional state and federal laws apply to the use of drugs and medical devices.

Some states require separate licensure for hospital pharmacies whereas other states regulate hospital pharmacies through the general state hospital licensing system.

Typically, the laws address dispensing and administering drugs to patients in the hospital and dispensing take-home drugs through an inpatient or outpatient hospital visit. Additionally, some regulations require sufficient staff members for the hospital pharmacy based on the hospital's size and scope of services.

Finally, some states require certain types of medical equipment to be separately licensed, such as x-ray equipment or medical waste disposal systems.

Hospitals cannot operate without a license. Those that violate the standards may lose their licenses or be penalized in other ways, such as with fines. Thus, licensure is government regulation that is mandatory for hospitals.

Accreditation Agencies

Accreditation is offered through nongovernmental agencies. One of the most important accrediting agencies for hospitals is The Joint Commission. The Joint Commission develops standards that hospitals must meet to be accredited. The healthcare organization applies to The Joint Commission to be accredited, pays an accreditation fee, and submits to an extensive survey to ensure compliance with The Joint Commission's published standards. The Joint Commission addresses privacy, information security, confidentiality, ethical behavior, patient rights training and whether the hospital complies with applicable laws, regulations, and standards. The student should review the most current manual published by The Joint Commission for standards on these topics.

Effective January 2004, The Joint Commission introduced a self-assessment approach to showing compliance with privacy and confidentiality standards and elements of performance. The organization uses 12 months of concrete data to score itself on the elements of performance. The Joint Commission verifies those scores during a regular accreditation visit.

Similarly, the AOA accredits osteopathic hospitals and functions in much the same way that The Joint Commission does.

Accreditation is considered voluntary and is not legally mandated, but it is very important to healthcare organizations. Some states accept The Joint Commission or AOA accreditation as a basis for partial or full licensure with limited or no additional survey by the state agency. This "deeming" authority gives The Joint Commission a significant amount of power it would not otherwise have.

Whereas The Joint Commission and the AOA focus on the entire hospital, other accrediting agencies focus on specific services of the hospital. For example, there is a separate accreditation process for laboratory and radiology services in addition to that of The Joint Commission and the AOA.

The federal Medicare program also sets standards for hospitals in its Conditions of Participation. Although these are government regulations, participation in the Medicare program is considered voluntary. However, few, if any, hospitals elect not to participate in this program. Thus, a hospital must comply with these standards to receive payment from the Medicare program for covered services provided to

Medicare beneficiaries. The Medicare program also recognizes organizations that have The Joint Commission or AOA accreditation as meeting most of the Conditions of Participation, and it grants them deemed status. A hospital would typically undergo an additional survey only if a special Medicare inspection finds noncompliance.

Statutory and Regulatory Law

There are many sources of law mandating the privacy of confidential health information. Some of these sources are discussed here.

Privacy

There is no right to privacy specifically stated in the United States Constitution. However, in 1965, the Supreme Court recognized an implicit constitutional right of privacy in *Griswold v. Connecticut (1965)*. In this case, the court ruled that "the right to privacy limits governmental authority to regulate contraception, abortion, and other decisions affecting reproduction" (Miller 1986, 6–7). Some states also have recognized the right to privacy in their state constitutions (California Constitution, Article 1, Declaration of Rights, Section 1; Arizona Constitution, Section 8, Right to privacy; Florida Constitution, Article I, Section 23, Right of privacy).

On August 21, 1996, Congress enacted HIPAA. This legislation initially focused on making it easier for employees to retain health coverage when they changed jobs or their family status changed. The HIPAA legislation addressed waste, fraud, and abuse in the healthcare system. It also focused on simplifying the administration of health insurance (HIPAA-b).

To address simplification, Congress added the Administrative Simplification provisions, which created a single federal standard electronic claims format for electronic data interchange (HIPAA-c; 45 CFR §162). With these provisions, the legislature intended to improve the efficiency and effectiveness of the healthcare system (HIPAA-d). However, Congress continued to express concerns about privacy and security of patient information in an electronic environment (HIPAA-c). Consequently, HIPAA required the Department of Health and Human Services (HHS) to develop and implement electronic transaction standards and to develop regulations to protect the privacy and security of **individually identifiable health information** (HIPAA-e; 45 CFR §164). As a result, HHS issued three sets of standards: Transactions and Code Sets (45 CFR §§160 and 162), Privacy, and Security (45 CFR §§160 and 164). All rules for these three sets of standards have been promulgated and issued. Covered entities as defined in HIPAA were required to be in compliance with the Privacy Rule by April 14, 2003, with the Transactions and Code Sets Rule by October 16, 2003, and with the Security Rule by April 20, 2005. The compliance dates for small health plans were extended by one year for each set of rules.

In February 2009, President Barack Obama signed the **American Recovery and Reinvestment Act (ARRA)** of 2009, which included the Health Information Technology for Economic and Clinical Health (HITECH) Act provisions. ARRA is discussed in chapter 2 and other chapters throughout this textbook. Only those HITECH provisions that specifically pertain to the use and disclosure of protected health information (PHI) are addressed later in this chapter. This legislation is referred to collectively as ARRA/HITECH in the remainder of this chapter.

Another piece of federal legislation addressing a patient's right to privacy is the **Privacy Act of 1974.** This act gives individuals some control over the information collected about them by the federal government (Hughes 2002). It does not apply to records maintained by institutions in the private sector (McWay 2010). Under the Privacy Act of 1974, people have the right to (Hughes 2002)

- Learn what information has been collected about them
- View and have a copy of that information
- Maintain limited control over the disclosure of that information to other persons or entities

This act also applies to federal government healthcare organizations such as the Veterans Health Administration (VHA) and the Indian Health Service and to record systems operated pursuant to a contract with a federal government agency (Hughes 2002).

Further, the **Freedom of Information Act (FOIA)** is a federal law through which individuals can seek access to information without authorization of the person to whom the information applies. This act applies only to federal agencies and not the private sector. The Veterans Administration and Defense Department hospital systems are subject to this act, but few other hospitals are. The only protection of health information held by federal agencies exists when disclosure would "constitute a clearly unwarranted invasion of personal privacy" (Miller 1986).

Despite the need for patient privacy, healthcare providers disclose health information to subsequent healthcare providers to the extent necessary to ensure continuity of patient care (Hughes 2003). Federal legislation that specifically provides for such disclosures includes, but is not limited to

- Medicare Conditions of Participation for Hospitals
- Conditions of Participation for Clinics, Rehabilitation Agencies, and Public Health Agencies as Providers of Outpatient Physical Therapy and Speech-Language Pathology
- Conditions of Participation for Home Health Agencies
- Confidentiality of Alcohol and Drug Abuse Patient Records

As to privacy rights, the Conditions of Participation for Hospitals rule states that hospitals must have procedures to protect the confidentiality of patient records (Hughes 2002). Under this rule, hospitals must protect records against unauthorized access and alteration. Further, original records may be removed from the facility only in accordance with federal and state laws (Hughes 2002).

The Conditions of Participation for Clinics, Rehabilitation Agencies, and Public Health Agencies as Providers of Outpatient Physical Therapy and Speech-Language Pathology regulations permit the physician to provide medical information to the receiving facility (Hughes 2003).

The Conditions of Participation for Home Health Agencies also requires facilities to have written policies and procedures to safeguard health information against loss or unauthorized use (Hughes 2002). Furthermore, the Requirements for States and Long-Term Care Facilities give the resident or his or her legal representative the right to access information about the resident. Additionally, these regulations give the resident the right to personal privacy and confidentiality of personal and clinical records (Hughes 2002).

The Confidentiality of Alcohol and Drug Abuse Patient Records rule is a federal rule that applies to information created for patients treated in a federally assisted drug or alcohol abuse program (Hughes 2002). This rule specifically protects the identity, diagnosis, prognosis, or treatment of these patients (Hughes 2002). These rules generally prohibit redisclosure of health information related to this treatment except as needed in a medical emergency or when authorized by an appropriate court order or the patient's authorization (Rhodes and Hughes 2009). The rule also specifies the circumstances under which information can be released without patient authorization and requires that language prohibiting redisclosure be attached to all released information concerning drug or alcohol treatment (Hughes 2002).

Other Federal Legislation

The Comprehensive Drug Abuse Prevention and Control Act of 1970, the **Controlled Substances Act,** controls the use of narcotics, depressants, and stimulants (Pozgar 2012). Because this act affects the dispensing and administering of these specific drug categories, pharmacy staff must be well versed in this law and how it interacts with state licensing and regulatory laws and accrediting standards. The controlled substances are classified into schedules according to the extent to which they are controlled. Schedule I drugs are subject to the tightest controls; Schedule I–IV drugs may be dispensed only upon a practitioner's lawful order.

In the outpatient environment, a prescription that meets the requirements of the law is required. In the inpatient setting, an order in the health record satisfies this requirement for a lawful order. The practitioner signing the prescription or the order in the health record must be registered with the Drug Enforcement Administration (DEA) of the Department of Justice (DOJ). State law determines which professionals may be classified as practitioners for this purpose.

The Federal Food, Drug, and Cosmetic Act, which includes the Medical Device Amendments of 1976, covers products that are distributed in federal territory or transported in interstate commerce (Pozgar 2012, 264). Most equipment and supplies used in a hospital for patient care are regulated as devices under these regulations.

Retention of the Health Record

The health record serves several purposes and must be retained to meet those purposes. These purposes include the following:

- Most important, the health record is a tool used in the patient's continuing medical care because it provides complete and accurate information about the patient's previous care and treatment.
- It serves as a means of communication among the patient's healthcare providers—physicians, nurses, therapists, pharmacists, and technologists.
- It is used by the patient's healthcare providers as a basis for developing the plan of care. In addition, the health record may be reviewed after care is rendered to evaluate the quality of the care.
- It is a source of information for statistical, research, and educational purposes.
- It serves as a source of billing and financial reports and information because billing records must be supported by the documentation in the health record.
- It is valuable in legal proceedings because it reflects the care given (the treatments, procedures, and medications the patient received), includes statements made by the patient about the cause of his or her illness or injury, and shows any errors in judgment or treatment made by healthcare facilities or professionals.

These varied purposes influence how long health records must be kept, or their retention period. Federal and state laws and regulations often determine retention periods. In addition to legal sources, nonlegal external organizations such as The Joint Commission, Centers for Medicare and Medicaid Services (CMS), Occupational Safety and Health Administration (OSHA), and others offer guidance (Gaffey and Groves 2011; McWay 2010). Further, the advent of technology, in particular the move toward an electronic health record, will influence retention periods (McWay 2010). The advent of the e-Discovery processes at the federal and some state levels also will impact retention period decisions (McWay 2010). For those periods determined by state law, the state defines what the minimum retention period will be. Some states are more specific than others. For example, some states base the retention period, at least partially, on the statute of limitations for bringing a legal action. Some state and federal statutes and regulations set specific retention requirements for particular parts of the health record (for example, x-rays or mammography studies) or for particular patient types (for example, minors, mentally ill, deceased) (Gaffey and Groves 2011).

The HIM professional must be aware of the retention statutes and retention periods in his or her state of employment.

In some cases, the organization may define a retention period that is longer than the period required by the state. The organization should base its retention policy on hospital and medical needs and any applicable statutes and regulations.

Retention also includes the safeguarding of confidential information maintained in health records. All hospital staff members with the right to access a patient's health record have an obligation to protect the confidentiality of patient information.

Check Your Understanding 12.2

Instructions: Answer the following questions on a separate piece of paper.

1. What are the two types of information collected in the health record? Discuss what information constitutes each type.

2. What is the primary difference between licensure and accreditation of healthcare organizations?

3. What national patient information confidentiality standards were promulgated in December 2000?

4. On what basis can a plaintiff claim unauthorized disclosure of health information against a hospital?

5. What was the holding regarding privacy issued by the court in *Griswold v. Connecticut*?

6. What information can the HIM professional use to determine how long to retain health records?

7. What are the three sets of standards included in the HIPAA Administrative Simplification provisions that are addressed in the text?

8. In addition to HIPAA, what pieces of legislation are discussed that address privacy?

Ownership and Control of the Health Record

Patients often believe they own their health record. The HIM professional must be able to advise the patient regarding the actual ownership and control of the physical health record and the patient's rights to the information contained in it.

Ownership of the Record

The emergence of the electronic health record has clouded the ownership question because the accepted ownership rule has been based on the "original hard copy documents" (Jergesen 2011b). Historically, the physical health record was considered the property of the healthcare provider, the physician, or the hospital that maintains it because it is the healthcare provider's business record. Yet, the patient and others had an interest in the information contained within the health record. Jergesen (2012b, 12) indicated that regardless of whether the medical record format is paper or electronic, the licensed entity originally responsible for creating and maintaining the medical record continues to

have the obligation under licensing and confidentiality laws "to maintain its basic integrity, and particularly to protect it from loss, destruction, or improper alteration." The HIPAA privacy and security rules as well as some state laws and other organizations, such as The Joint Commission, state the hospital or provider has the responsibility for safeguarding the medical record (Jergesen 2011b, 12). Thus the licensed entity originally responsible for the record "owns" the record even if electronically stored.

Redisclosure of health information is of significant concern to the healthcare industry. As such, the HIM professional must be alerted to state and federal statutes addressing this issue (Rhodes and Hughes 2009). A consent obtained by a hospital pursuant to the Privacy Rule in 45 CFR §164.506(a)(5) does not permit another hospital, healthcare provider, or clearinghouse to use or disclose information. However, the authorization content required in the Privacy Rule in 45 CFR §164.508(c)(1) must include a statement that the information disclosed pursuant to the authorization may be disclosed by the recipient and thus is no longer protected (45 CFR §164.508(c)(2)(iii)).

Regardless of the format, the patient and others, as authorized under state and federal laws, rules, and regulations, have the right to access the information and to control the use and disclosure of the information.

Use and Disclosure of Patient Information

Although the original HIPAA Privacy and Security Rules are still in effect, there are significant changes proposed pursuant to ARRA/HITECH that were not finalized as of this publication date. On July 14, 2010, HHS Office for Civil Rights (OCR) published proposed changes to these rules, of which the most significant relate to (HIPAA-j)

- Permitted uses and disclosures and required disclosures by covered entity (CE) and business associate (BA)
- Disclosures to BA and BA contracts
- Minimum necessary
- Deceased individuals
- Marketing and sale of PHI
- Disaster relief
- Public health activities
- Childhood immunizations
- Research and Compound authorizations
- Fundraising and remunerated treatment communications
- Notice of privacy practices
- Restriction request and termination of restriction
- Patient access to PHI

Further, on May 31, 2011, the OCR published proposed changes to the HIPAA Privacy Rule regarding accounting of disclosures pursuant to ARRA/HITECH (HIPAA-i; ARRA/HITECH, Part 1 §13405(c)). The most significant change reflected in these proposed changes is that accounting of disclosures be expanded to include disclosures made for purposes of treatment, payment, and healthcare operations.

ARRA/HITECH also added requirements to the existing HIPAA disclosure rules regarding limiting specific disclosures to the limited data set or the minimum necessary. Guidance from OCR has not been published as of this publication date (ARRA/HITECH, Part 1 §13405(b)).

Final rules for both sets of proposed rules are expected in 2012. The reader can follow the status of these rules and any other OCR-promulgated rules and guidances by accessing the OCR website (http://www.hhs.gov/ocr/privacy/).

Throughout the remainder of the chapter any references to changes made pursuant to ARRA/HITECH that are not noted as "proposed" are considered effective, including the Enforcement Interim Final Rule.

The following discussion reflects the original HIPAA Privacy Rules that are still in effect and the ARRA/HITECH changes where applicable.

The HIPAA Privacy Rule addresses how and for what purposes **protected health information** (**PHI**) can be used. PHI is individually identifiable health information that covered entities or their business associates transmit or maintain in any form or format. The Privacy Rule covers information in oral, electronic, and paper formats (45 CFR §§164.500, 501, and 514). The covered entities include

- Health plans that pay for medical care
- Healthcare clearinghouses that receive health information in a nonstandard format and convert the information into a standard format, or healthcare clearinghouses that receive health information in a standard format and convert the information into a nonstandard format
- Healthcare providers that electronically transmit any health information (45 CFR §§160.102 and 103)

The Privacy Rule is the first attempt at a national set of privacy protections. Although the HIPAA rules provide for preempting state law, it is not a true national standard for patient information privacy. In other words, it is not a ceiling. It is considered a floor because it permits exceptions to the state law **preemption** provisions (45 CFR §§160.201–205).

Prior to HIPAA, many states recognized patients' rights to access their own health records. Many states also recognized that various third parties have a legitimate need to access the confidential health information contained in a health record. These third parties include insurance companies for payment purposes, insurance companies when coverage has been applied for, government agencies to determine eligibility for healthcare programs, and so on. Furthermore, prior to HIPAA, many states also permitted patients to control

access by all third parties except those to which the hospital is required to report information of a medical nature or as otherwise required by law.

The standard HIPAA rule is that it preempts state law if it is contrary to that state law except if one or more of the following conditions is met (45 CFR §§160.201–205):

- The Secretary of HHS determines that the provision of state law is necessary to prevent fraud and abuse related to providing or paying for healthcare; to ensure appropriate state regulation of insurance and health plans; for state reporting on healthcare delivery or costs; or for public health, safety, or welfare if the intrusion into privacy is warranted when balanced against this need.
- The Secretary of HHS determines that the provision of state law is for the purpose of regulating the manufacture, registration, distribution, dispensing, or other control of controlled substances.
- The provision of state law relates to the privacy of individually identifiable health information and is more stringent than a provision in the HIPAA Privacy Rule.
- The provision of state law provides for reporting disease or injury, child abuse, birth, or death or for the conduct of public health surveillance, investigation, or intervention.
- The provision of state law requires a health plan to report, or to provide access to, information for management audits, financial audits, program monitoring and evaluation, or licensure or certification of facilities or individuals.

For purposes of the HIPAA preemption analysis, a state law is more stringent when, in general terms, it affords a patient more access to his or her medical information or more control over the disclosure of his or her medical information to third parties (45 CFR §160.203(b)). As an example, a state statute that requires a patient to consent to any disclosure of his or her medical information to an insurance company for purposes of payment would take precedence over the HIPAA rules, but a statute that prohibited a patient from receiving a copy of his or her health record (other than psychotherapy notes) would not.

Even though HIPAA is the first attempt at national privacy legislation, the HIM professional also must be aware of state laws affecting the use and disclosure of PHI. The Privacy Rule is discussed in the text that follows in terms of patient rights, the types of disclosures that require the patient be given an opportunity to agree or object, uses and disclosures that require patient authorization, and uses and disclosures that do not require patient authorization. HIPAA distinguishes between "use" and "disclosure" in 45 CFR §160.103. **Use** means sharing, employing, applying, utilizing, examining, or analyzing individually identifiable health information *within* an entity that maintains such information (HIPAA-h). **Disclosure** means the release, transfer, provision of, access to, or divulging in any other manner of information *outside* the entity holding such information (HIPAA-h).

Of significant importance is that ARRA/HITECH applied the HIPAA security provisions and penalties to BAs of CEs (ARRA/HITECH, Part 1 §13401(a) – (b)). The penalties apply to BAs that violate any security provision specified in subsection (a), sections 1176 and 1177 of the Social Security Act in the same manner these sections apply to a CE that violates the security provision (SSA). Further, ARRA/HITECH applied the HIPAA privacy provisions and penalties to BAs of CEs. The proposed regulations referred to previously will provide more detail when finalized regarding uses and disclosures of PHI by BAs of CEs (ARRA/HITECH, Part 1 §13404(a) – (c)). The penalties apply to BAs that violate any provisions of sections 1176 and 1177 of the Social Security Act in the same manner the provisions apply to a person who violates a provision of Part C of title XI of such act (SSA). The proposed regulations pursuant to ARRA/HITECH noted earlier in this section address applying the HIPAA rules to BAs in detail (HIPAA-j).

Patient Rights

HIPAA provides patients with certain rights related to protecting their privacy and their PHI. It requires that every patient be provided a Notice of Privacy Practices (Notice) setting forth the following (45 CFR §164.520):

- How covered entities may use and disclose PHI
- The patient's rights regarding the covered entities' uses and disclosures
- The covered entities' obligations for protecting the patient's PHI

The Privacy Rule is very specific about the required contents of the Notice. The Notice must be provided upon request. Covered entities having a direct patient relationship with the patient must provide the patient a copy of the Notice at the time of the first service delivery, including service delivered electronically. In emergency situations, covered entities providing care must provide the Notice as soon as practicable after the emergency treatment situation is resolved. The **covered entity** (**CE**) is to make a good faith effort to obtain the patient's written acknowledgment of receipt of the Notice. This requirement also is delayed until practicable in emergency treatment situations. If receipt is not obtained for any reason, including patient refusal to provide the acknowledgment, the CE is required to document its good faith efforts and the reason why the acknowledgment was not obtained.

With reference to the previous discussion of more stringent state privacy laws, the Notice must be tailored specifically to disclose the effect of these more stringent standards. A generic disclosure that "state laws may affect your rights" is not sufficient.

A second right that the Privacy Rule provides patients is the right to access their own patient information (45 CFR §164.524). Although, as stated earlier, some states had given patients this right, under HIPAA all patients now have it. The information that patients have the right to access is termed the **designated record set.** The types of information that HIPAA does not provide access to are

- Oral information
- Psychotherapy notes
- Information compiled in anticipation of, or for use in, a civil, criminal, or administrative action or proceeding
- PHI the CE maintains that is subject to or exempted from the Clinical Laboratory Improvements Amendment (CLIA) of 1988

The proposed regulations pursuant to ARRA/HITECH noted earlier in this section address the patient's right to access certain information in electronic format (HIPAA-j; ARRA/HITECH, Part 1 §13405(e)). CMS published proposed rule changes on September 14, 2011, to the CLIA Program and HIPAA Privacy Rule regarding patients' access to test reports (CLIA). These proposed revisions would permit laboratory results to be released to authorized persons including the individual or his or her personal representative responsible for using the test results and the laboratory that initially requested the test (76 FR 56712). The proposed changes also permit the laboratory, upon the patient's request, to provide access to completed test reports that using the laboratory's authentication process, can be identified as belonging to that patient (76 FR 56712, 76 FR 56724). The proposed rule would also amend the HIPAA Privacy Rule §164.524 to provide individuals the right to receive their test reports directly from laboratories. This would be accomplished by removing the exceptions for CLIA-certified laboratories and CLIA-exempt laboratories from the provision that provides individuals with the right of access to their protected health information (76 FR 56712, 76 FR 56715, and 76 FR 56724).

This right of access applies to all three categories of CEs that actually create or receive PHI other than as a business associate of another CE.

The patient's request can be denied without giving the patient an opportunity to request review of the denial. In addition to the PHI types noted earlier to which the patient is not given access, access can be denied in the following circumstances:

- When the CE is a correctional institution or a CE acting under the direction of the correctional institution and such access would jeopardize the health, safety, security, custody, or rehabilitation of the individual or others
- When PHI was created or obtained during research that includes treatment (access is suspended while the research is in progress as long as the patient agreed to the access denial when consenting to participate in the research and the patient had been advised that the right would be reinstated upon completion of the research)
- When the PHI is contained in records subject to the Privacy Act of 1974 and is also not available for access under the Privacy Act

The Privacy Rule gives patients a third right, which is to request that the CE amend the designated record set (45 CFR §164.526). It provides that this request also can be granted or denied. Grounds for denying an amendment request include the following:

- The PHI was not created by the CE, unless the patient indicates that the originator is no longer available.
- The PHI is not part of the designated record set.
- The PHI would not be available for the patient to inspect.
- The PHI is accurate and complete.

One of the most striking features of the original legislation is found in 45 CFR §164.528 wherein it gives a patient the right to obtain an *accounting of disclosures* of PHI made by a CE in the six years or less prior to the request date (45 CFR §164.528). Under the original rule, an accounting does not need to include such disclosures as the following:

- To carry out treatment, payment, and healthcare operations (TPO)
- To the patient who is the subject of the PHI
- Those that are incidental to treatment, payment, or healthcare operations
- Those pursuant to patient authorization
- For a facility directory or to family or caregivers
- For national security or intelligence purposes
- To correctional institutions or law enforcement under specific circumstances
- PHI included in a limited data set
- Those made prior to the compliance date for the CE

As noted earlier in this chapter, on May 31, 2011, OCR published proposed changes to the HIPAA Privacy Rule regarding accounting of disclosures to provide more detailed information to patients (individuals) for certain disclosures (HIPAA-i). HITECH required that accounting of disclosures be expanded to include disclosures made for purposes of treatment, payment, and healthcare operations (ARRA/HITECH, Part 1 §13405 (c)).

Another right is that of requesting the CE to restrict the use of PHI to carry out treatment, payment, or healthcare operations; to those involved in the patient care; and for notification purposes (45 CFR §164.522(a)). Again, the CE is not required to agree to the requested restriction. If the CE agrees to the requested restriction, it must document the restriction and must maintain that documentation for six years. A patient also may request health plans and healthcare clearinghouses, which create or receive PHI other than as a business associate, to restrict uses and disclosures. The proposed regulations pursuant to ARRA/HITECH noted earlier in this section address the patient's right to restrict the disclosure of PHI to a health plan for payment or healthcare operations purposes and the PHI pertains solely to a healthcare item or service for which the healthcare provider was paid out of pocket in full (HIPAA-j; ARRA/HITECH, Part 1 §13405(a)).

Moreover, patients are given the right to request that CEs communicate with them in a confidential manner or method (45 CFR §164.522(b)). Confidential communications may be either by an alternative means or at alternative locations. For example, a patient may request that any telephone contact be made only at work or that all written communication be sent to a post office box rather than to his or her home address. A CE that is a healthcare provider

- Must accommodate reasonable requests
- May not require the patient to provide an explanation of the basis for the request
- May require the patient to place the request in writing

A CE that is a health plan also must accommodate reasonable requests. However, the health plan is permitted to require the patient to provide a statement that the disclosure of all or part of the information to which the request pertains could endanger the patient.

Check Your Understanding 12.3

Instructions: Answer the following questions on a separate piece of paper.

1. In light of the electronic health record environment, discuss who "owns" the health record.

2. Who owns the information contained in the health record, whether paper or computer based?

3. What is the primary focus of the HIPAA Privacy Rule?

4. Who are the covered entities covered by the HIPAA Privacy Rule?

5. Does HIPAA preempt all state laws addressing privacy? Discuss your answer.

6. What information must be described in the Notice of Privacy Practices?

7. When are healthcare providers who have a direct relationship with the patient required to provide the patient with a copy of the Notice of Privacy Practices?

8. What formats of information are protected under HIPAA?

9. To what types of information is the patient not provided access?

10. List five types of disclosures under the original rules that do not need to be included in an accounting.

11. Can the patient's request to access his or her own health information be denied? Explain your answer.

12. Under the Privacy Rule, who may sign an authorization for the disclosure of information?

13. Discuss the circumstances listed in the Privacy Rule under which a facility may deny a patient's request for access to his or her own health information without providing the patient the opportunity to have the denial reviewed.

14. Under what circumstances does the Privacy Rule permit disclosure of health information to a patient's employer?

15. What, if any, circumstances might make a healthcare provider liable for breach of confidentiality when reporting public health information?

Types of Disclosures Requiring Opportunity to Agree or Object

The Privacy Rule provides patients an opportunity to agree or object to specific types of disclosures (45 CFR §164.510). These do not require a written authorization; verbal authorization is acceptable. However, communication with the patient regarding these types of disclosures and the patient's decision should be documented in the health record or other appropriate manner of documentation.

Absent the patient's objection, a covered healthcare provider may use specific PHI to maintain a directory of patients in its facility. This information includes the patient's

- Name
- Location in the provider's facility, including the emergency room
- Condition in very general terms that do not include specific medical information about the patient
- Religious affiliation

The general terms that can be used to indicate the condition include *undetermined*, *good*, *fair*, *serious*, *critical*, *stable*, *died*, and *treated and released*. The patient is not required to provide information regarding religious affiliation. The covered provider may disclose the name, location, and condition to anyone asking for the patient by name, including the news media. The covered provider may disclose these elements plus the religious affiliation to members of the clergy even if they do not ask for the patient by name. If the patient does not specifically express an objection to being included in the facility's directory, the PHI may be released as noted without the patient's consent or authorization.

When a patient is incapacitated or in an emergency situation and cannot object to being included in the facility's directory, the covered provider may disclose the information as noted if the disclosure is

- Consistent with any previously expressed preference that is known to the provider
- In the patient's best interest as determined by the provider using professional judgment

If, during the patient's stay in the facility, he or she regains the capacity to make his or her own decisions, the provider must advise the patient about the facility's directory policies and provide the patient the opportunity to object to being included in it.

The covered provider also may obtain the patient's verbal agreement or objection to disclose PHI for the following purposes (45 CFR §164.510):

- Disclosure to family, friends, or other caregivers identified by the patient relevant to their involvement with the patient's care. The requirement for patient authorization typically extends to a request by a patient's family members, including the spouse. However, healthcare providers may discuss general information about the patient's condition with family members without authorization unless the patient has instructed otherwise. If the patient is incapacitated, the physician and other caregivers may discuss health information and treatment plans with the next of kin or the patient's representative (however that is defined by a given state) to the extent necessary to make medical decisions on the incapacitated patient's behalf. The Privacy Rule permits the hospital to disclose to a family member, other relative, close personal friend, or any person identified by the patient health information directly relevant to that person's involvement in the patient's care or payment for healthcare (45 CFR §164.510(b)(1)(i)). (See further discussion under the section on use and disclosure with patient authorization.)
- The hospital may use or disclose health information to notify or assist in notifying (identifying or locating) a family member, a personal representative, or some other person responsible for the patient's care of the patient's location, general condition, or death (45 CFR §164.510(b)(1)(ii)). In such disclosures in situations of incapacity or emergency, the CE may exercise professional judgment to determine whether the disclosure is in the patient's best interest. State law defines who may serve as a personal representative.
- Disclosure to a public or private entity assisting in disaster relief efforts.

Check Your Understanding 12.4

Instructions: Answer the following questions on a separate piece of paper.

1. Explain the access to health information available to the news media.

2. Does releasing information from the directory require the patient's written authorization? Explain your answer.

3. To whom can religious affiliation information be released?

4. Under what circumstances might the hospital disclose information from the directory if the patient is incapacitated or in an emergency situation?

5. Discuss whether the hospital can disclose information to family, friends, or other caregivers.

Use and Disclosure with Patient Authorization

Except as permitted or required under the HIPAA Privacy Rule, a valid patient authorization is required for the use or disclosure of PHI (45 CFR §164.508(a)(1)). This requirement typically extends to a request by a patient's family members, including the spouse. The hospital must have clear policies and procedures for releasing confidential health information with patient authorization. These policies must provide for careful review of each request. They must provide for a careful review of the authorization to ensure that it meets all requirements stated in applicable state and federal statutes and regulations, depending on which requirements are more stringent. As provided in the Privacy Rule, the procedure must permit the opportunity for the patient to revoke an authorization at any time in writing, except to the extent that the hospital has relied on the authorization and taken action as a result of it (45 CFR §164.508(b)(5)(i)). It is good practice to require a patient to sign an authorization for releasing confidential health information to the patient on whom the information is maintained. Finally, all policies and procedures for releasing confidential health information with patient authorization must follow the guidelines established in the Privacy Rule discussed next unless state law supersedes HIPAA.

The Privacy Rule gives very detailed specifications for patient authorization to disclose confidential health information (45 CFR §§164.508(c)(1)–(4)). The authorization must include a specific description of the information to be used or disclosed. In addition, the name or other specific identification of the person(s) authorized to request and receive the requested information must be included. Also, the authorization must include the expiration date or event that relates to the individual or the purpose of the use or disclosure. The patient must be given the right to revoke the authorization in writing, the exceptions to this right, and a description of how he or she may revoke it. The authorization also must advise the patient that information released pursuant to the authorization may be subject to redisclosure by the recipient and no longer protected. Finally, the patient must sign and date the authorization.

If a personal representative signs the authorization, a description of his or her authority to act for the patient must be included in the authorization form. Also, the form must be written in plain language. The patient must be advised that the hospital will not condition treatment, payment, enrollment in a health plan, or eligibility for benefits on his or her providing authorization for the requested information. The authorization must include a description of each purpose for the requested information. Furthermore, the authorization must contain a statement to the effect that the patient may inspect or copy the information and may refuse to sign it. The hospital must disclose to the patient whether disclosure of the information will result in direct or indirect remuneration to the facility from a third party. If there is remuneration, the authorization must state that such remuneration will result. Also, the patient is entitled to a copy of the signed authorization.

Authorizations for uses and disclosures of health information created for research that includes treatment of the patient must contain additional elements. For example, there must be a description of the extent to which the information will be used or disclosed to carry out treatment, payment, or healthcare operations. The authorization must further include a description of any health

information that could be disclosed but will not be disclosed for facility directories or public health purposes. However, the facility may not include a limitation affecting its right to disclose information required by law.

If the facility has or intends to obtain a general consent or has provided or intends to provide the individual with a Notice of Privacy Practices, the authorization must refer to that consent or notice and state that the statements made are binding.

Pursuant to 45 CFR §164.508(b)(2), if any of the following circumstances pertain to the authorization, it is considered "defective":

- The expiration date has passed or the expiration event has occurred.
- The authorization is not completely filled out.
- The authorization has been revoked.
- Any required elements are missing.
- The authorization is combined with any other document to create a "compound authorization" except where permitted.
- The facility knows that material information included in the authorization is false.

For an unemancipated minor, the legal representative is the parent, guardian, or other person acting in *loco parentis*. For the incompetent adult, the conservator of the person (probate or psychiatric) or the attorney-in-fact may serve as the legal representative. The patient's spouse or the person financially responsible for the patient may sign only for the limited purpose of enrolling the patient in a third-party payer plan. For a deceased patient, the executor, the administrator, or another person with authority to act on behalf of the patient or of the patient's estate may sign an authorization for the disclosure of health information. The proposed regulations pursuant to ARRA/HITECH noted earlier in this section address deceased patients (HIPAA-j; ARRA/HITECH, Part 1 §13406(a)). In addition, there are many medical treatments for which a minor (whether or not emancipated) can self-refer under state and federal statutes and regulations. In most states, these treatments include outpatient mental health treatment, drug and alcohol testing and treatment, pregnancy counseling, and treatment for sexually transmitted diseases. In these circumstances, the minor, and not the minor's parent or guardian, controls the disclosure of health information.

To be valid, the written authorization must state the limitations, if any, on the types of health information to be disclosed. Further, it must state the specific uses and limitations, if any, on the use of the health information by the recipients.

The two categories of uses and disclosures that the Privacy Rule specifically refers to as requiring patient authorization are psychotherapy notes and marketing. Psychotherapy notes are those notes recorded in any medium by a mental health professional documenting or analyzing conversations from a private counseling session or a group, joint, or family counseling session (45 CFR

§164.508(a)(2)). These notes are maintained separately from the rest of the patient's health record. Psychotherapy notes exclude medication prescription and monitoring, counseling session start and stop times, the modalities and frequencies of treatment furnished, results of clinical tests, and any summary of the diagnosis, functional status, treatment plan, symptoms, prognosis, and progress to date (45 CFR §164.501). However, HIPAA does provide an exception to the authorization requirements for psychotherapy notes; in these circumstances no patient authorization is required

- In treatment, payment, or healthcare operations, including the following:
  — Use by the originator of the treatment notes
  — Use or disclosure by the CE in its own training programs in which students, trainees, or practitioners in mental health learn under supervision
  — Use or disclosure by the CE to defend itself in a legal action or another proceeding brought by the patient
- As required or permitted as part of oversight of the originator of the psychotherapy notes

As defined in the Privacy Rule, marketing requires an authorization that contains the elements described earlier and an additional statement regarding direct or indirect payment by a third party. HIPAA defines marketing as a communication about a product or service that encourages recipients of the communication to purchase or use the product or service or as an arrangement between a covered entity and any other entity where the covered entity discloses PHI to the other entity, in exchange for direct or indirect remuneration, to permit the other entity to encourage recipients to purchase or use its product or service. The proposed regulations pursuant to ARRA/HITECH noted earlier in this section address marketing in detail (HIPAA-j; ARRA/HITECH, Part 1 §13406(a)). Further, the proposed regulations pursuant to ARRA/HITECH noted earlier in this section address the sale of PHI (HIPAA-j; ARRA/HITECH, Part 1 §13405(d)). Even in these circumstances classified as marketing, HIPAA provides exceptions that are discussed in the next section.

McWay used the *Biddle v. Warren General Hospital* to illustrate breach of confidentiality cases (McWay 2010). In this case for two years, the hospital forwarded all patient registration forms to a law firm without obtaining patient authorization. The hospital's legal counsel contacted certain patients concerning the patient's possible eligibility to receive disability payments. A group of these patients sued the hospital alleging breach of confidentiality. The court held that the hospital was required to obtain patient authorization before releasing this information and thus was liable for breach of confidentiality (McWay 2010, 79–80). McWay indicated similar cases in a variety of jurisdictions ended with the same result (McWay 2010).

Check Your Understanding 12.5

Instructions: Answer the following questions on a separate piece of paper.

1. Does the requirement for a written authorization for use and disclosure apply to obtaining information about family members, including the spouse?

2. List five elements that must be included in a HIPAA-compliant authorization for use and disclosure.

3. Discuss the elements required in an authorization for use and disclosure when health information is created for research that includes treatment.

4. Who can sign an authorization for use and disclosure when the patient is a minor?

5. For what two categories of uses and disclosures does HIPAA specifically require an authorization for uses and disclosures?

Use and Disclosure without Patient Authorization

The basic rule under HIPAA is that the healthcare facility may use or disclose PHI without an authorization for treatment, payment, or healthcare operations purposes (45 CFR §164.506(a)). Although health information can be released without patient authorization in these circumstances, such requests must be scrutinized carefully. Thus, healthcare facilities also must have clear policies and procedures for releasing confidential health information without patient authorization. For example, policies should address

- Reporting required by statutes, whether federal or state
- Specifying information that can be released to the public without patient authorization
- Mandatory disclosures such as those under court order and subpoena, whether served by a party to a suit or administrative proceeding, or by a government agency in the course of an investigation
- Mandatory disclosure pursuant to orders by a board, a commission, or an administrative agency engaged in formal adjudication of a dispute
- Disclosure pursuant to an order by an arbitrator or arbitration panel carrying out arbitration under the law
- Disclosure without patient authorization pursuant to a search warrant
- Disclosure of health information in response to requests in workers' compensation cases (controlled by state law)
- Identifying internal staff categories needing confidential health information to carry out their job duties
- Specifying the types of information needed and the reasons for permitting access
- The opportunity for the patient to restrict how health information is used and disclosed to carry out treatment, payment, or healthcare operations (45 CFR §164.506(c)(4)(i))

All policies and procedures for releasing confidential health information without patient authorization must also follow the guidelines set in the Privacy Rule, again unless state law supersedes HIPAA.

As discussed in the patient's rights section of this chapter, patients and their representatives have access to PHI without signing an authorization form (45 CFR §164.524). In reality, many facilities may have the patient or patient's representative complete the authorization form as a means of documenting the request. Although care should be taken in releasing all health information to a patient, particular care should be taken in releasing specialized information such as information related to mental health, drug and alcohol abuse, and sexually transmitted diseases. Federal and some state statutes address some or all of these types of specialized information. The Privacy Rule in 45 CFR §164.524(a)(1) provides the patient's right of access to inspect and obtain a copy of health information, except for psychotherapy notes and information compiled in reasonable anticipation of, or for use in, a civil, criminal, or administrative action or proceeding.

Further, under the Privacy Rule, the hospital may deny access for other reasons, provided the patient is given a right to have such denials reviewed by a licensed healthcare professional designated by the hospital to act as a reviewing official and who did not participate in the original decision to deny. This reviewer must provide or deny access (45 CFR §164.524(a)(3)).

Numerous other types of disclosures of confidential health information may be made without patient authorization. These include disclosure for direct patient care purposes; for payment purposes; for healthcare operations activities, as required by law; and several others.

Disclosure for *direct patient care (treatment) purposes* is among the most common and most important disclosures without patient authorization. Those involved with patient care must have timely access to health information. In 45 CFR §164.501 and 45 CFR §§164.506(c)(1) and (2), the Privacy Rule permits the facility and healthcare providers to use or disclose confidential information for

- Providing, coordinating, or managing healthcare and related services by one or more healthcare providers, including with a third party
- Consulting among healthcare providers relating to a patient
- Referring a patient for healthcare from one healthcare provider to another

Payment purposes is another important type of disclosure that may be made without patient authorization. The Privacy Rule permits the healthcare provider to use or disclose health information for payment purposes such as health plans obtaining premiums, determining coverage, and providing benefits. It also includes healthcare providers or health plans obtaining or providing reimbursement for services (45 CFR §164.501; 45 CFR §§164.506(c)(1) and (3)).

Healthcare operations consist of a number of activities carried out in a typical provider setting (45 CFR §164.501; 45 CFR §§164.506(c)(1), (4) and (5)). One activity that is important to a hospital is quality improvement (QI). Under HIPAA, QI is a standard healthcare operation and does not require the CE to obtain patient authorization to use confidential health information. Other healthcare operations functions include peer review; underwriting; medical review, legal services, and auditing; business planning, development, management, and administration; educational programs; and licensing and accreditation. Specifically, many organizations participate in educational activities for their medical staff members and their clinical and nonclinical staff members. Some also participate in formalized training programs for physicians, nurses, and allied health professionals. All these trainees require some level of access to confidential health information as part of their training (45 CFR 164.501). However, such access should be on a need-to-know basis. Typically, such use of confidential information does not require patient authorization.

In addition, because health records are considered hospital business records, the information in them has many administrative uses that are considered healthcare operations. Hospital professional, technical, and administrative staff should have access to these records on a need-to-know basis. Administrative uses include, but are not limited to, auditing, billing, filing, replying to inquiries, and defending litigation.

PHI may be disclosed without an authorization as required by law. The use or disclosure is limited to the requirements of the particular law under which is it is used or disclosed (45 CFR §164.512(a)(1)). In some cases, there is a common-law duty to disclose health information, for example, to warn persons of the presence of contagious disease. In many states, there also is a duty to warn an individual against whom a patient has made a credible threat to harm (*Tarasoff v. Board of Regents* 1976). In another case, a physician failed to warn his patient that she had contracted HIV through a blood transfusion. As a result, the hospital and the physician were sued three years later when the patient's sexual partner was exposed to the virus. The court held that the hospital was liable for the physician's failure to warn (Kadzielski 2011; *Reisner v. Regents of the University of California* 1995). These cases should not be confused. *Reisner* involved failure to warn a patient of a serious condition; *Tarasoff* involved failure to warn a third party about potential harm from his patient.

No authorization is needed to use or disclose PHI for public health activities (45 CFR §164.512(b)). Some health records contain information that is important to the public welfare. Such information must be reported to the state's public health service to ensure public safety. The Privacy Rule provides that the hospital or healthcare provider may disclose confidential health information to

- A public health authority authorized to collect or receive information for preventing or controlling disease, injury, or disability

- A public health authority or other government authority authorized to receive reports of child abuse or neglect
- A person subject to the Food and Drug Administration (FDA)
- A person who may have been exposed to a communicable disease or may be at risk of contracting or spreading a disease or condition, if the entity is authorized to notify such person (45 CFR §§164.512(b)(1)(i)–(iii)). Activities that are reported include:
  — Disease and injury reporting
  — Vital statistics reporting (births and deaths)
  — Public health investigation, surveillance, or intervention
  — Child abuse and neglect reporting (HIPAA specifically stated to follow state law) (OCR 2000)
  — Product safety, quality, or effectiveness reporting to the FDA
  — Communicable disease reporting
  — Reporting to an employer in very limited circumstances regarding medical surveillance of the workplace or work-related illness or injury

The Privacy Rule addresses disclosure of health information in the last activity in 45 CFR §164.512(b)(1)(v). The hospital may disclose information to an employer when one of the following conditions is met:

- The care provider is a member of the employer's workforce or provides healthcare to the patient at the employer's request.
- The care relates to a medical surveillance of the workplace or to a work-related illness or injury.
- The information that is disclosed consists of findings concerning a work-related illness or injury or a workplace-related medical surveillance.
- The employer needs the findings to comply with its obligations under federal and state laws.

The Privacy Rule also requires the hospital to provide written notice to the individual that health information relating to the workplace medical surveillance and work-related illnesses and injuries will be disclosed to the employer.

Reporting of other types of abuse, neglect, or domestic violence also is permitted under HIPAA (45 CFR §164.512(c); OCR 2000) when required by law; when the patient agrees to the reporting; and when the CE, in its professional judgment, believes disclosure is necessary to prevent serious harm to the patient or other potential victims. Further, the CE may disclose in situations where the patient is incapacitated and law enforcement or some other public official authorized to receive such information indicates that the disclosure is not to be used against the patient and that immediate enforcement activity depends on the disclosure and would be adversely affected by waiting. Persons complying with reporting statutes are not considered to be making an unauthorized disclosure (HIPAA-f).

Health oversight agencies may receive PHI without authorization for their activities but must be authorized to oversee the healthcare system (public or private) or government programs in which health information is necessary to determine eligibility or compliance or to enforce civil rights laws for which health information is relevant. Health oversight agency activities include audits; civil, criminal, or administrative investigations or proceedings; licensure; disciplinary actions; inspections; or other activities necessary for appropriate oversight of any of the following entities (45 CFR §164.512(d)):

- Healthcare systems
- Government benefit programs for which health information is relevant to beneficiary eligibility
- Entities subject to government regulatory programs for which information is necessary for determining compliance with program standards
- Entities subject to civil rights laws for which health information is necessary for determining compliance

A CE also may disclose PHI in judicial and administrative proceedings. Disclosing confidential health information in compliance with the legal process is typically provided for statutorily. Under the Privacy Rule in 45 CFR §§164.512(e)(i)–(iv), a hospital may disclose health information in the course of any judicial or administrative proceeding in response to any of the following:

- Court or administrative tribunal order if the hospital discloses only the health information expressly authorized by such order
- Subpoena, discovery request, or other lawful process not accompanied by a court or administrative tribunal order if the hospital receives satisfactory assurance that reasonable efforts have been taken to give notice of the request to the person who is the subject of the requested information or to secure a qualified protective order that meets specific requirements

A hospital can disclose health information in response to a lawful process without receiving the satisfactory assurance, discussed earlier, when it makes reasonable efforts to provide notice to the individual or to seek a qualified protective order (45 CFR §164.512(e)(v)).

Pursuant to the Privacy Rule in 45 CFR §164.512(f), the hospital may disclose health information to law enforcement officials without authorization for law enforcement purposes when one of the following conditions is met:

- Disclosure is required by law, including laws that require the reporting of certain types of wounds or other physical injuries
- Disclosure is made in compliance with a court order, court-ordered warrant, subpoena, summons, or grand jury subpoena
- Disclosure is made in response to an administrative request, that is, a subpoena or summons, a civil

demand or an authorized investigative demand, or a similar process authorized under law

- Purpose of the request is to identify or locate a suspect, fugitive, material witness, or missing person (information related to the individual's DNA or DNA analysis, dental records, typing, samples or body fluids, or tissue analysis may not be released)
- Disclosure is made in response to a law enforcement official's request for such information about an individual who is, or is suspected to be, a victim of a crime
- Purpose of the disclosure is to alert law enforcement of the suspicion that a patient's death may have resulted from criminal conduct
- Hospital believes the health information is evidence of criminal conduct that occurred on its premises

When providing healthcare in an emergency situation, other than such emergency on the premises of the healthcare provider, the provider may disclose health information to law enforcement officials when it appears necessary to alert law enforcement to any of the following (45 CFR §164.512(f)(6)):

- Commission and nature of a crime
- Location of the crime or of the victim(s)
- Identity, description, and location of the perpetrator of the crime

Coroners, medical examiners, and funeral directors may receive PHI as necessary to carry out their duties with respect to decedents (45 CFR §164.512(g)). Such duties for a coroner or medical examiner include identifying a deceased person, determining a cause of death, or other duties as authorized by law. If it is necessary for a funeral director to have PHI prior to, and in reasonable anticipation of, the individual's death, the CE may disclose that information necessary to carry out the funeral director's function. The proposed regulations pursuant to ARRA/HITECH noted earlier in this section address deceased patients (HIPAA-j; ARRA/HITECH, Part 1 §13406(a)).

An *organ procurement organization* or a tissue bank processing the tissue of a decedent for transplantation into the body of another person also may be given health information. In 45 CFR §164.512(h) the Privacy Rule provides that a hospital may disclose health information to organ procurement organizations.

Research is another activity for which confidential health information is important. Hospital policy often requires that researchers' access to health information be documented as bona fide research. Such documentation may be provided through a recognized institutional review board's approval of the research. Many states and the federal government have established regulations for the protection of human subjects, including protecting confidential information (45 CFR §46.111(a)(7), protection of human subjects). Any use of confidential health information for research purposes must comply with all such regulations,

including those set forth in the Privacy Rule. Under the Privacy Rule in 45 CFR §164.512(i), researchers may use or disclose health information, as necessary, to prepare a research protocol or for research purposes. This section also provides that researchers may use or disclose health information for the purpose of research on such information for decedents. The facility that creates confidential health information for research that includes treatment of the patient must obtain an authorization for the use or disclosure of that information.

PHI may be disclosed to avert a serious threat to health and safety (45 CFR §164.512(j)). To do so, the CE must, in good faith, believe the use or disclosure is necessary to prevent or lessen a serious and imminent threat to the health and safety of a person or the public and is reasonably able to prevent or lessen the threat. Moreover, the CE may disclose PHI if it believes in good faith that the disclosure is necessary for law enforcement to identify or apprehend an individual because of a statement by a person admitting participation in a violent crime that the CE believes may have caused serious physical harm to the victim. Further, the CE may disclose PHI in cases where the individual has escaped from a correctional institution or from lawful custody.

PHI can be disclosed for specialized governmental functions (45 CFR §164.512(k)). These functions include

- Military and veterans activities
- National security and intelligence activities
- Protective services to the president and heads of state
- Medical suitability determination (for example, security clearance purposes)
- Correctional and law enforcement custodial facilities for the health and safety of the patient, other inmates, or officers or employees at the correctional facility
- Government programs providing public benefits
- Workers' compensation programs to comply with state laws for the provision of benefits for work-related injuries or illness (45 CFR §164.512(l))

With regard to workers' compensation cases, statutes in some states permit the disclosure of health information without patient authorization, but some states require patient authorization or a subpoena from an administrative agency or court for release. It is important to be familiar with a particular state's laws before disclosing any health information in workers' compensation cases.

Without the patient's authorization, an organization may use only demographic data (name, address, and other contact information; date of birth; gender; insurance status; and so on) and dates of service to carry out fundraising activities (45 CFR §164.514(f)(1)). Demographic data do not include information about diagnoses, procedures, or the nature of the patient's illness or services. The organization may disclose this demographic data to a philanthropic foundation that raises funds for the organization (HIPAA-g). The organization also may provide such data to a business associate that conducts fundraising on behalf of the organization. Any fundraising materials sent to a patient must include instructions on how to opt out of receiving future fundraising materials. The proposed regulations pursuant to ARRA/HITECH noted earlier in this section address fundraising (HIPAA-j; ARRA/HITECH, Part 1 §13406(b)).

As stated in the Use and Disclosure with Patient Authorization section, there are marketing exceptions to the requirement for an authorization. When the communication is a face-to-face encounter with a patient or when it involves a promotional gift of nominal value, no authorization is required (45 CFR §164.508(a)(3)). Furthermore, the Privacy Rule describes specific circumstances that are not considered marketing, such as (45 CFR §164.501)

- The covered entity describing its own health-related products and services
- Communications about entities participating in a healthcare provider network or health plan network, replacement of or enhancements to a health plan, and health-related products or services available only to a health plan enrollee that add value to the benefits
- Communications about products and services related to a patient's treatment
- Communications for case management or care coordination
- Recommendations to the patient about alternative treatments, therapies, healthcare providers, or care settings

The Privacy Rule establishes the requirement for verifying the identity of the person receiving the PHI and his or her authority to have access to the requested information.

Penalties

Any person who believes that a CE is violating or has violated the HIPAA Privacy Rule may file a complaint by mail, fax, or e-mail with the HHS OCR, which enforces the Privacy Rules (OCR 2000). Complaints to the OCR must:

- Be filed in writing (either on paper or electronically)
- Name the CE that is the subject of the complaint and describe the acts or omissions believed to be in violation of the applicable requirements of the Privacy Rule
- Be filed within 180 days of when the complainant knew that the act or omission complained of occurred (OCR may extend the 180-day period if "good cause" is shown.)

The OCR will investigate the complaint on behalf of the Secretary of HHS (45 CFR §160.306(a)). The investigation may include the OCR reviewing pertinent policies, procedures, and other documents and the circumstances of the alleged violation (45 CFR §160.306(c)). If the investigation reveals the CE did not violate the HIPAA Privacy Rule, the Secretary will notify the CE. However, should the investigation reveal the CE did not comply with the Privacy Rule, the Secretary will first attempt to enter into

one of the following informal types of resolution (45 CFR §160.312(a)(1)):

- Voluntary compliance
- Corrective action
- Resolution agreement

Most Privacy Rule investigations have been concluded through these types of resolutions. Once the resolution is accepted, the OCR notifies the complainant and the CE in writing of the resolution result (OCR 2006).

If the CE and the Secretary are unable to resolve the issue informally, the Secretary will give the CE an opportunity to provide written evidence of mitigating factors or affirmative defenses (45 CFR §160.312(a)(3)(i)). In the event the CE does not resolve the issue to the OCR's satisfaction, the OCR may impose civil money penalties (CMPs) on the CE. Should CMPs be imposed, the CE may request a hearing before an HHS administrative law judge, who decides if the penalties are supported by the evidence.

The ARRA/HITECH Act strengthened HIPAA enforcement specifically by modifying the HHS Secretary's authority to impose CMPs for HIPAA violations occurring after February 18, 2009. Section 13410(d) of the HITECH Act reflects the significantly increased CMP amounts the HHS Secretary may impose for violations. This provision established a tiered range of increasing minimum penalty amounts and established the maximum penalty of $1,500,000 for all violations of an identical provision (ARRA/HITECH, Part 1 §13410(d)). This ARRA/HITECH Act provision revised §1176(a) of the Social Security Act (SSA).

On October 30, 2009, OCR published the Enforcement Interim Final Rule, which conforms the HIPAA enforcement regulations to the ARRA/HITECH Act revisions (HIPAA-k). In §160.401 of the HIPAA rules, the Enforcement Interim Final Rule provides definitions of *reasonable cause, reasonable diligence, and willful neglect* (HIPAA-k, 56130). Section 160.404 sets forth the violation categories and the tiered CMPs (HIPAA-k, 56131):

- Violations occurring prior to February 18, 2009
  — HHS Secretary may not impose a CMP in excess of $100 for each violation or in excess of $25,000 for identical violations during the calendar year (January 1 through the following December 31)
- Violations occurring on or after February 18, 2009 are categorized with applicable CMP amounts the HHS Secretary may impose:
  — The CE did not know, and by exercising reasonable diligence, would not have known that the CE had violated a provision
    ▪ Not less than $100 or more than $50,000 per violation or
    ▪ Not more than $1,500,000 for identical violations during a calendar year (January 1 through the following December 31)

— The violation was due to reasonable cause and not to willful neglect

- Not less than $1,000 or more than $50,000 per violation or
- Not more than $1,500,000 for identical violations during a calendar year (January 1 through the following December 31)

— The violation was due to willful neglect and was corrected during the 30-day period beginning on the first date the CE liable for the penalty knew, or, by exercising reasonable diligence, would have known the violation occurred

- Not less than $10,000 or more than $50,000 per violation or
- Not more than $1,500,000 for identical violations during a calendar year (January 1 through the following December 31)

— The violation was due to willful neglect and was not corrected during the 30-day period beginning on the first date the CE liable for the penalty knew, or, but exercising reasonable diligence, would have known the violation occurred

- Not less than $50,000 per violation or
- More than $1,500,000 for identical violations during a calendar year (January 1 through the following December 31)

Section 160.404(b)(3) provides that if a requirement or prohibition in one Administrative Simplification provision is repeated in a more general manner in another Administrative Simplification provision in the same subpart, a CMP may be imposed for only one of the Administrative Simplification provisions (HIPAA-k 56131).

Section 160.410 sets forth affirmative defenses the CE may establish. For violations occurring prior to February 18, 2009, HHS Secretary may not impose a CMP if the CE establishes the following:

- The violation is a punishable act under 42 U.S.C. 1320d-6
- CE establishes, to HHS Secretary's satisfaction, that it did not know of the violation, and by exercising reasonable diligence, would not have known the violation occurred or
- The violation is due to reasonable cause and not willful neglect and was corrected either
  — During the 30-day period beginning on the first date the CE liable for the penalty knew, or, by exercising reasonable diligence, would have known the violation occurred or
  — During such other period as the HHS Secretary determines to be appropriate

For violations occurring on or after February 18, 2009, HHS Secretary may not impose a CMP if the CE establishes:

- The violation is a punishable act under 42 U.S.C. 1320d-6 or

- CE establishes, to HHS Secretary's satisfaction, that the violation is not due to willful neglect and was corrected either
  — During the 30-day period beginning on the first date the CE liable for the penalty knew, or, by exercising reasonable diligence, would have known the violation occurred or
  — During such other period as the HHS Secretary determines to be appropriate

The HHS Secretary may waive, in whole or in part, the CMP for violations due to reasonable cause and not willful neglect that are not corrected in either of the periods noted to the extent the CMP payment would be excessive relative to the violation.

The monetary penalties collected are transferred to OCR for purposes of enforcing the ARRA/HITECH provisions and subparts C and E of part 165 of title 45, Code of Federal Regulations (ARRA/HITECH, Part 1 §13410(c)(1)). No later than three years after the enactment of ARRA/HITECH on February 17, 2009, the HHS Secretary is to establish a method by regulation to distribute a percentage of the CMPs collected to an individual harmed by an act that constitutes an offense (ARRA/HITECH, Part 1 §13410(c)(2)–(4)).

The ARRA/HITECH clarified the application of wrongful disclosures criminal penalties by amending §1177(a) of the SSA§1320d-6(a) to state that a person including an employee or other individual shall be considered to have obtained or disclosed individually identifiable health information in violation of this part if the information is maintained by a CE as defined in the HIPAA privacy regulation and the individual obtained or disclosed such information without authorization (ARRA/HITECH, Part 1 §13409).

An exceptionally interesting provision in the ARRA/HITECH Act is the amendment of §1176 of the SSA §1320d-5 adding paragraph (d), which provides enforcement of the HIPAA regulations through state attorneys general (ARRA/HITECH, Part 1 §13410(e)). This provision gives a state attorney general authority to bring a civil action on behalf of a resident(s) whose interest the state attorney general believes has been threatened or adversely affected by any person violating a provision of the ARRA/HITECH Act. The civil action may be to enjoin further violation by the defendant or to obtain damages on behalf of the resident(s) of the state in the amount determined by using the provisions provided in §1320d-5(d)(2) (ARRA/HITECH, Part 1 §13410(e)(2)):

- Multiply number of violations by up to $100 (number of violations determined consistent with the HIPAA privacy regulations)
- Limitation—total damages imposed on the person for all violations of an identical requirement or prohibition during a calendar year may not exceed $25,000
- Reduction of damages—the court may consider the factors the HHS Secretary may consider in determining the amount of CMP

In a successful action, the court may award cost of action and reasonable attorney fees to the state (ARRA/HITECH, Part 1 §13410(e)(3)). The state attorney general must give written notice of any action to the HHS Secretary unless such prior notice is not feasible. Under that circumstance, the state must serve notice immediately upon instituting the action. The HHS Secretary may intervene in the action and be heard on all matters if he or she intervenes and file petitions to appeal (ARRA/HITECH, Part 1 §13410(e)(4)).

There are limitations on bringing a state civil action. If the HHS Secretary has instituted an action against a person regarding a violation of this part, no state attorney general may bring an action under this provision against the person with respect to That violation during the pendency of that action (ARRA/HITECH, Part 1 §13410(e)(7)). A further limitation is that a civil action may not be instituted with respect to a violation of this part unless an action to impose a CMP may be instituted with respect to that violation (ARRA/HITECH, Part 1 §13410(e)(8)).

Originally, CMS was responsible for enforcing the Security Rule (45 CFR Part 160 and Subparts A and C of Part 164) including investigating complaints and performing compliance reviews. As of July 27, 2009, the Secretary of HHS delegated the authority for administration and enforcement of the Security Rule to OCR (OCR 2009). There may be circumstances under which the OCR collaborates in an investigation or refers a matter for investigation to another agency. The OCR may actually refer a complaint to the DOJ for criminal investigation. This might result if the complaint contains information about a CE's action that could be a violation of the criminal provision of HIPAA (42 USC 1320d-6). Such actions involve the knowing disclosure or obtaining of protected health information in violation of the rule (OCR 2006).

Check Your Understanding 12.6

Instructions: Answer the following questions on a separate piece of paper.

1. What three categories of uses and disclosures does HIPAA specifically *not* require an authorization for use and disclosure?

2. Under HIPAA, must a patient sign an authorization for use and disclosure before being permitted access to his or her own record? Explain your answer.

3. May PHI be used and disclosed without patient authorization for a hospital case manager to coordinate care with another healthcare provider such as a long-term care facility? Explain your answer.

4. List at least five uses and disclosures of PHI for which HIPAA does not require an authorization.

5. What common types of information must be reported for public health purposes?

6. What penalties can be enforced against a person or an entity that willfully and knowingly violates the HIPAA Privacy Rule?

Use of Health Records in Litigation

This section discusses how the health record is used in litigation. The health record serves as documentation of care provided when the patient alleges wrongdoing against the hospital and healthcare providers in a lawsuit or seeks damages from another party who caused an injury or illness.

Admissibility of the Health Record

The health record may be valuable evidence in a legal proceeding. To be admissible, the court must be confident that the record

- Is complete, accurate, and timely (recorded at the time the event occurred)
- Was documented in the normal course of business
- Was made by healthcare providers who have knowledge of the "acts, events, conditions, opinions, or diagnoses appearing in it" (AHIMA 2005a, 64A)

The court must accept that the information was recorded as the result of treatment, not in anticipation of a legal proceeding. Furthermore, to be admissible, the health record must be pertinent and proper. The health record is considered hearsay because the healthcare providers made the entries in the record and not in court under oath (McWay 2010, 50). However, the judge or jury uses the exceptions to the hearsay rule of evidence to determine what is pertinent and proper (McWay 2010, 50; AHIMA 2005b).

To have an electronic health record admissible, the court must be confident that the system from which the record was produced is accurate and trustworthy. Characteristics used to support a system's accuracy and trustworthiness are (AHIMA 2005a, 64A)

- The type of computer used and that computer's acceptance as standard and efficient equipment
- The record's method of operation
- The method and circumstances of preparation of the record

Medical witnesses may refer to the health record to refresh their recollection. The custodian of records, typically the health information manager, may be called as a witness to identify the record as the one subpoenaed. He or she also may be called to testify as to policies and procedures relevant to the following:

- Creation of the record including the system or process used
- Maintenance of the record to prevent it from being altered
- Maintenance of the record to prevent it from being accessed without proper authorization

The actual admissibility as evidence depends on the facts and circumstances of the case and the applicable state and federal rules of evidence.

The EHR and Court: e-Discovery

HIM professionals are beginning to experience a completely different approach to responding to requests for health records in litigation whether for depositions or as evidence in court. This new approach applies when the facility has a total electronic record or a hybrid record. What HIM professionals are experiencing is known as **e-Discovery,** which is a pretrial process through which parties obtain and review electronically stored data. The e-Discovery changes to the Federal Rules of Civil Procedure (FRCP) became effective December 1, 2006 (AHIMA 2006). Although the FRCP applies only to cases in federal district courts, states are beginning to implement similar e-Discovery rules that apply to state civil and criminal cases. For example, California enacted its Civil Discovery Act effective in January 2007.

AHIMA has published two articles that are excellent resources for how e-Discovery, whether at the state or federal level, impacts the HIM professional (AHIMA 2006; Horn 2010). Specifically, AHIMA identifies the key issues to be "the impact on disclosure processes, retention and destruction, spoliation, and business continuity planning" (AHIMA 2006, 68E). Horn discussed the Electronic Discovery Reference Model project (EDRM) and states the guidelines and standards for e-Discovery offered in the EDRM have saved those involved in litigation since 2005 cost, time, and manual work in responding to e-Discovery requests (Horn 2010, 44). He further indicated that a subgroup is focusing on "a healthcare-specific viewpoint in the Information Management Reference Model" (Horn 2010, 44).

In the past, HIM professionals could be involved in the pretrial discovery phase through a subpoena for records or for testifying at a deposition. With the advent of e-Discovery, the HIM professional's involvement begins much earlier in the litigation stages with pretrial conferences. During pretrial conferences, attorneys for the parties meet to reach agreement on matters related to discovery, such as document discovery. Thus HIM and information technology (IT) professionals must work with the organization's attorney prior to a pretrial conference to identify relevant information and its availability (AHIMA 2006, 68B). Although the entity producing the electronically stored information (ESI) can object, it must produce the information in "the form in which it is ordinarily maintained or a reasonably usable form" (DeLoss 2008).

The healthcare organization must define what constitutes the legal health record for disclosure purposes (McLendon 2007). This is particularly important in the EHR environment. Through technology, vast volumes of information can be created and stored. Therefore, much more extensive information is subject to discovery than in the paper record environment. Any data stored electronically can serve as evidence, for example, text, information on personal digital assistants (PDAs), calendar files, websites, and the like (AHIMA 2008). The concept of "any and all records" has certainly taken on a whole new connotation with e-Discovery.

HIM professionals must now be familiar with documents stored in what is termed "native file format," including **metadata** (AHIMA 2006, 68D; DeLoss 2008). Metadata are data about the data (AHIMA 2006, 68E; McLendon 2012). They include information not previously available with paper documents such as the time stamp for accessing, creating entries in, or changing electronic records. With the increased prevalence of electronically stored data and the ease of searching these data, the legal discovery process in civil and criminal cases is focusing more on e-Discovery (McLendon 2012, 90). McLendon (2012, 67) further states that organizations should establish policies and procedures that define how to produce "the designated business record, including the native file format and metadata."

The e-Discovery rule will certainly impact retention and destruction of health information. Therefore, HIM professionals must work more closely with IT and other departments to establish and implement information management plans. These plans must address information contained in e-mail, voicemail, instant messages, text messages, document drafts, and shadow records (AHIMA 2006, 68E). Information management plans must also address disaster recovery and business continuity (AHIMA 2006).

The concepts of a legal hold and **spoliation** continue under the e-Discovery rule. A legal hold is typically issued by a court when there is concern that information relevant to a legal proceeding or an audit could be destroyed. This hold would suspend any normal disposition activities, including destruction. The following events can prompt the HIM professional to place a health record under a legal hold (DeLoss 2008):

- Complaints
- Civil investigative demands
- Subpoenas
- Demand letters
- Prelitigation discussions with opposing counsel
- Preservation letters
- Written notices from opposing counsel
- Government investigations or inquiries

Spoliation is the "intentional destruction, mutilation, alteration, or concealment of evidence" (AHIMA 2006, 68E). The organization would have the burden of disputing spoliation allegations by showing that "information lost was a result of a good faith operation of the electronic system" (AHIMA 2006, 68E).

What does the HIM professional do to prepare for the eventuality of having to respond to an e-Discovery request or subpoena? HIM professionals must be familiar not only with what the organization defines as its records (such as legal health record, business record, designated record set) but also with the location and types of information stored within various source systems and databases (AHIMA 2006, 68E; Dimick 2007). Dimick (2007) recommended that HIM professionals start by reviewing the organization's information management plan. The HIM professional knows which departments feed clinical information into the legal health record whether in the paper or electronic format; they must now also become familiar with what systems are used by these different departments. According to DeLoss (2008), the locations in which information can be electronically stored both at home and at work include

- Laptops and desktops
- Servers and shared drives
- Handheld devices such as PDAs and cell phones
- Removable storage devices such as flash drives, thumbnails, CDs (compact discs)
- Websites
- Databases

DeLoss also addressed the location of ESI from the perspective of ancillary services, clinical services, remote access, personal equipment, and e-mail. With regard to ancillary services DeLoss noted the HIM professional must know or determine whether the information is integrated into the EHR or maintained separately. He also states that one should ask if external providers are networked and if data resides on equipment such as an MRI, digital x-ray, IV medication pumps, dictation systems, robotics, equipment for emergency or "crash" situations, or personal health records (PHRs).

Complying with an e-Discovery request or subpoena most likely involves many systems. This is no easy task because as Dimick pointed out, the standards for what will be discoverable and what electronic information needs to be part of the health record are still being developed. Dimick (2007) further stated that HIM professionals should store only what is vital—if it is stored, it is likely subject to e-Discovery. Having good policies, procedures, standards, information management plans, and such that are enforced is the place to start.

AHIMA (2008) stated the organization must also develop a litigation response plan, and it identified five key steps healthcare organizations should take to develop and implement such a plan:

- Evaluate applicable rules—federal-, state-, and local-level e-Discovery rules
- Form a litigation response team—an interdisciplinary group to implement and conduct ongoing review of the e-Discovery process
- Analyze issues, risks, and challenges that may arise from e-Discovery—this analysis is the basis for policy and procedure development
- Develop or revise organizational policies and procedures to incorporate e-Discovery
- Develop and implement an ongoing monitoring and evaluation process to ensure continued compliance with policies and procedures

So just what is the role of the HIM professional in e-Discovery? "While discoverable information will evolve with the creation of complex electronic record systems, the most advanced system means nothing to the e-Discovery process if there aren't people who know how to store, manage, and access the information. That is where HIM professionals come in" (Dimick 2007, 3).

Privileges

Professional relationships between the patient and specific groups of caregivers further affect use of the record and its contents as evidence. These relationships are referred to as **privileges.** The information exchanged between patient and caregiver pursuant to a privilege is a confidential communication that the patient anticipates will be held confidential. One such widely recognized privilege is the physician–patient privilege. This privilege provides that the physician is not permitted to testify as a witness about certain information gained as a result of this relationship without the patient's consent.

The information included in the physician–patient privilege is insulated from the discovery process when there is no patient authorization, waiver, or overriding law or public policy (Gaffey and Groves 2011). The physician–patient relationship usually does not apply to court-ordered examinations or other examinations completed on behalf of other third parties, such as insurance companies (Miller 1986). Depending on the state, similar privileges exist between psychotherapist and patient, sexual assault victim and counselor, and domestic violence victim and counselor.

In states where these professional relationships are recognized, they apply when the caregiver is being compelled to testify as a witness concerning information obtained as a result of the relationship. However, these privileges do not preclude the caregiver from making reports as required by law.

Patient's Waiver of Privilege

The patient may release the caregiver from the privileges discussed through words or actions. This release is known as a waiver of the privilege. For example, a patient who placed his or her treatment at issue in a trial could not continue to claim a privilege to protect the information. The caregiver then could be compelled to testify regarding the information previously considered confidential.

Government's Right of Access to Health Records

The government, whether federal or state, has the right to access health information with or without patient authorization in certain circumstances. Healthcare providers must sign an agreement with HHS to receive payments for care provided to patients covered under the Medicare program (Miller 1986). Medicaid is a joint federal and state program to provide medical care to individuals unable to pay for care. Healthcare providers apply to the responsible state agency for a contract with the state to provide services to Medicaid recipients in return for payment for services provided (Miller 1986). Both

HHS and the state Medicaid agency may request information from the health record to support the healthcare provider's bill submitted for payment. By signing up with Medicare or Medicaid, the patient gives permission for the healthcare provider to disclose confidential health information to the appropriate agency without further authorization.

The government also may require access to health information for other investigative purposes such as pursuant to the federal fraud and abuse statutes that require information-sharing arrangements to be undertaken in an arm's length transaction and pursuant to a written agreement (Kadzielski 2011). An arm's length transaction is a transaction in which "parties are dealing from equal bargaining positions, neither party is subject to the other's control or dominant influence, and the transaction is treated with fairness, integrity, and legality" (Trautmann 2003).

Another important federal statute for which the government may need access to health information as part of an investigation is the Emergency Medical Treatment and Labor Act (EMTALA) (Cohen 2011). This act involves the transfer of uninsured individuals from one hospital emergency department to another for financial reasons (Lickerman and Lickerman 2011, 996).

Individuals are personally liable for their own acts of unauthorized disclosure of confidential health information. The individual's liability is based on fault because he or she did something wrong or failed to do something he or she should have done. Employers also may be held liable for any job-related acts of their employees or agents. It must be distinguished that the hospital is not liable for a breach of confidentiality by the members of its medical staff because they are not employees or agents of the hospital. However, the hospital may be liable for the consequences of any unauthorized disclosure, whether by employees, agents, or medical staff members, because of the breach of its duty to maintain information confidential. The injured person benefits from these concepts of fault because he or she can sue the employer, the employee, or both.

Unauthorized disclosure by various healthcare professionals also may be addressed in professional licensing and certifying laws or regulations. These provisions subject the professional to potential discipline by the licensing or certifying agency for breach of confidentiality because it is considered unprofessional conduct.

Check Your Understanding 12.7

Instructions: Answer the following questions on a separate piece of paper.

1. What are the three methods by which a physician–patient privilege may be created?

2. What actions or requirements can release the care provider from the applicable privilege?

3. Give two examples of government access to health information with or without patient authorization.

4. What are metadata, and why are they important in responding to a subpoena?

5. Discuss why the HIM professional experiences a significant change in responding to legal requests under e-Discovery statutes (state or federal)?

6. If the custodian of records is called to testify pursuant to a subpoena, what can she or he testify to?

Case Law since HIPAA

There are a number of areas of uncertainty in the HIPAA regulations. Interpretation of these areas requires one to make a judgment call, make a good faith effort to follow the regulations, and then take a wait-and-see approach to see if these areas are tested in the courts. The following are some exampes of case law since implementation of the Privacy Rule.

Sample Cases

In *Law v. Zuckerman* (2004), a federal court in Maryland ruled that HIPAA preempted a state law that would have required a plaintiff's current doctor to discuss the patient's condition with the defendants' lawyer without notice to, or consent of, the patient. The court held that Maryland's law was not more stringent than the HIPAA regulations. In *In re PPA Litigation (2003)*, a New Jersey state court ruled that HIPAA did not preempt the state-authorized practice of permitting defendants in personal injury cases to conduct informal interviews with the plaintiff's treating physician where patient authorization requirements are met. In this case, the court required HIPAA-compliant authorization forms.

The first HIPAA privacy criminal prosecution occurred in *US v. Gibson* (2004). In this case, an employee of the Seattle Cancer Care Alliance was charged with illegal disclosure of a patient's PHI in order to fraudulently obtain and make purchases with credit cards in the patient's name. Pursuant to the penalties discussed earlier, this disclosure was for personal gain and potentially subjected the defendant to a fine of up to $250,000 and up to 10 years in prison. The defendant pleaded guilty and entered into a plea bargain with the federal government that recommends 10 to 16 months in prison and requires full restitution to the patient and the credit card companies. In November 2004, under the HIPAA Privacy Rule, US District Judge Ricardo Martinez sentenced the defendant to 16 months in prison, three years of supervised release, and more than $9,000 in restitution.

Of interest in this case is that the defendant is not a covered entity under HIPAA, but rather an employee of a CE that is subject to HIPAA. This case demonstrates that at least one US attorney interprets the HIPAA criminal provisions as applying personally to members of the CE's workforce. There is still considerable debate as to whether the HIPAA criminal provisions apply to persons and organizations that are not CEs.

In the past few years more legal activity has occurred with HIPAA as the basis. While working as a nurse for the Northeast Arkansas Clinic, the defendant, Smith, accessed a patient's health information and gave the information to her husband. Her husband called the patient and threatened to use the information in an impending legal action. In December 2007, both Smith and her husband were indicted for conspiracy to wrongfully disclose individually identifiable information for personal gain and witness tampering (Park 2008). Smith pleaded guilty to the charges of wrongfully disclosing a patient's health information for personal gain.

Latner (2008) described a privacy violation of the kind that HIPAA was designed to avoid. She described a clinic employee (nurse) whose husband had been injured in an automobile accident and was being sued by the driver of the other car. Latner (2008) indicated that while the nurse was straightening medical files, she noted the plaintiff's name. The nurse read the record and made notes, which she shared that evening with her husband. Her husband subsequently called the plaintiff and indicated he had medical information that would weaken the plaintiff's case (Latner 2008). The plaintiff notified the clinic and the district attorney. The complaint was forwarded to a federal prosecutor, who indicted both the nurse and her husband with violating HIPAA (Latner 2008). Latner reported that the nurse pleaded guilty "to one count of wrongful disclosure of individual health information for personal gain" (Latner 2008, 1–2). As a result of the nurse's plea, the charges against her husband were dismissed (Latner 2008). At the time of the writing of the article, Latner indicated the nurse was awaiting sentencing, which included up to 10 years in prison, as much as $250,000 in fines, and up to three years of supervised probation. Latner also indicated the state's board of nursing was seeking to revoke the nurse's license (2008).

A significant recent legal action occurred when Huping Zhou was the first person in the nation to actually receive federal prison time for a misdemeanor HIPAA violation (Dimick 2010a). Dimick indicated that Zhou was a licensed cardiothoracic surgeon from China who the University of California Los Angeles (UCLA) hired as a researcher with the School of Medicine. In 2003 during this employment he was notified that UCLA intended to dismiss him for job performance reasons. That evening and during the next three weeks, Zhou accessed medical records for coworkers, celebrities, and high-profile patients, abusing his access rights to UCLA's EHR system (Dimick 2010a). Dimick noted that according to a press release, Zhou did not improperly use or attempt to sell any of the illegally obtained information. For his actions, Zhou pled guilty to four misdemeanor counts of accessing and reading confidential medical records and was sentenced to four months in prison and fined $2,000 (Dimick 2010a).

Of significance is the fact that on July 16, 2008, HHS entered into its first corrective action plan with a covered entity for potential HIPAA privacy and security regulation violations (Lazzarotti 2008). This action followed the OCR and CMS investigation of more than 30 complaints from persons that the Seattle-based healthcare provider, Providence Health and Services, had notified of data breach occurrences (Lazzarotti 2008). Providence Health and Services agreed to pay $100,000 and entered into a three-year corrective action plan (Lazzarotti 2008). Lazzarotti stated the notifications resulted when backup tapes, optical disks, and laptops that contained unencrypted electronic protected health information of more than 386,000 patients were lost or stolen after being taken from the covered entity's premises and left unattended. Through the Resolution Agreement, Providence Health and Services agreed to ensure it will safeguard patient identifiable electronically stored protected health information (Lazzarotti 2008). Further, because Providence Health and Services entered into the Resolution Agreement, HHS did not impose the potentially significant civil monetary penalties under HIPAA (Lazzarotti 2008).

Of even further significance is the situation addressed in an OCR news release on July 7, 2011 (OCR 2011). In that news release the UCLA Health System (UCLAHS) entered into a resolution agreement to settle potential violations of the HIPAA Privacy and Security Rules (OCR 2011). The resolution resulted from an OCR investigation of two separate complaints regarding repeated accesses to two celebrity patients' confidential information maintained in the EHR without a permissible reason to do so (OCR 2011). The UCLAHS agreed to settle for $865,500 and committed to a corrective action plan to address gaps in its compliance with the rules by improving its policies and procedures to protect patient information (OCR 2011). This resolution agreement was based on the new Enforcement Interim Final Rule.

The Release of Information Process and Function

Managing the release (use and disclosure) of information (ROI) process and function requires an attention to detail and constant vigilance. The ROI manager must constantly stay current with changes in local, state, and federal laws and regulations affecting the use and disclosure of PHI. Further, the ROI manager must be cognizant of The Joint Commission and other regulatory agency requirements regarding protecting a patient's confidentiality and privacy by protecting health information. The manager must constantly ensure that policies and procedures reflect all current local, state, and federal statutes and regulations, as well as regulatory agency requirements.

The ROI manager must provide education that reinforces the organization's policies and the importance of following them. Additionally, ROI staff must be provided with, and express an understanding of, the expectations for them to follow ROI policies and procedures.

The ROI manager must participate in the QI process. This can be used as one means of evaluating staff compliance with policies and procedures. Furthermore, the manager must gather statistics regarding performance (request turnaround time, number of requests processed per employee per month, number of subpoenas processed per employee per month, and so on). These statistics, among others, can be used as the basis for requesting additional staff or as part of the annual evaluation process. Completing requests according to departmental standards, which are based on regulations such as HIPAA or state law, demonstrates the individual employee's competence, or lack thereof, in his or her job.

In some organizations, the ROI functions are decentralized, that is, carried out in other areas in addition to the HIM department. Although having use and disclosure requests processed where the applicable record is maintained may seem the most efficient approach, such an organizational structure presents many management challenges. The ROI manager must ensure that all entities within the organization carrying out the ROI function are following standardized policies and procedures. This requires strong organizational and supervision skills.

The manager is responsible for participating with the organization's privacy officer to investigate any alleged violations of the HIPAA rules by ROI staff. The investigation should be conducted pursuant to the organization's investigation policy and may include involving the human resources (HR) department to impose disciplinary action pursuant to HR policies.

Finally, it is the manager's responsibility to establish an environment in which employees can be successful. Therefore, the ROI manager must develop and implement systems that support the employees' needs.

Check Your Understanding 12.8

Instructions: Answer the following questions on a separate piece of paper.

1. What uses can the ROI manager make of data collected for quality improvement purposes?

2. In addition to the statistics mentioned, list three other categories of statistics that would be useful to the ROI manager in managing this function.

3. What education should the ROI manager provide the ROI staff?

4. Does the ROI manager participate in investigating alleged HIPAA violations by ROI staff? Discuss your answer.

Medical Staff Appointments, Privileges, and Peer Review

Patients expect the physicians who treat them in hospitals to have been evaluated for competency in their selected area of medical practice. Patients expect to receive treatment at or above the acceptable standard of care. Hospitals use the medical staff appointment process to accomplish this evaluation.

Duty to Use Reasonable Care in Granting Staff Appointments

The hospital governing board typically is composed of members from the community and sometimes includes medical staff members. This body has final responsibility for the operation of the hospital. Because of its responsibility for managing the hospital and upholding a satisfactory standard of care, it has the legal duty to select medical staff members. The governing board must use reasonable care in approving a physician's application to be a staff member and grant clinical privileges before the physician can treat patients in the hospital. Typically, after the physician is granted initial medical staff membership, he or she must reapply for membership and privileging every year or every two years. It must be noted that medical staff members are not employees or agents of the hospital. However, even though they are independent of the hospital, they are accountable individually and collectively to the board for the quality of care they provide.

In *Darling v. Charleston Community Memorial Hospital* (1965), the court stated the "corporate negligence doctrine" under which the hospital had a duty to provide an adequately trained medical and nursing staff. The *Darling* case indicated the need for hospitals to have "effective credentialing and continuing medical evaluation and review programs for all members of a professional staff" (Pozgar 2012, 152). This case specifically held that the governing board has the "duty to establish a mechanism for the medical staff to evaluate, counsel, and, when necessary, take action against an unreasonable risk of harm to a patient arising from the patient's treatment by a physician" (Pozgar 2012, 184). Further, the *Darling* court held that based on the hospital's obligation to select high-quality physicians to be medical staff members, the hospital may be held liable for a patient's injury caused by a physician who does not meet those standards but was given medical staff membership and privileges.

Darling involved an 18-year-old college football player studying to be a teacher and coach who suffered a broken leg during a game. He was taken to a small, accredited community hospital where the only physician on duty in the emergency department was a general practitioner who had not treated a severe leg fracture for three years. The physician ordered x-rays that revealed fractures of both bones in the lower leg. The physician reduced the fractures and applied a full-leg plaster cast. The patient complained of pain, and the physician split the cast and visited the patient while in the hospital. However, the physician never called in a specialist because he thought it unnecessary. Two weeks later, the plaintiff was transferred to a larger hospital, where he was treated by an orthopedic surgeon. The specialist found dead tissue in the fractured leg and removed dead tissue several times over the next two months.

Ultimately, he was unable to save the leg and amputated it eight inches below the knee.

The plaintiff's father rejected any settlement and filed suit against the hospital and the physician. The physician was eventually able to settle, but the case against the hospital continued to trial. A judgment was returned against the hospital and upheld in the Illinois Supreme Court.

The hospital's governing board relies on the medical staff structure to conduct the actual evaluation of physicians applying for medical staff membership and to make recommendations regarding their suitability for membership. The mechanisms for selecting medical staff members pursuant to *Darling* and applicable state statutes indicate that peer review is the best system for monitoring physicians. Many states provide that peer review must be conducted in a reasonable and fair manner.

The Credentialing Process

The **credentialing process** is the screening process through which the medical staff evaluates a physician's application for medical staff membership (Hoffman 2011; Glossary 2011). In this process, the medical staff validates the physician's credentials: medical education, including medical school, residencies, postdoctoral studies, and fellowships; license to practice; society memberships; medical practice experience; and references that reflect the individual's qualifications and ability to function as a healthcare provider (Kadzielski 2011). This process also applies to other licensed independent practitioners (for example, nurse practitioners and allied health practitioners).

One major step taken in this process is searching the **National Practitioner Data Bank** (**NPDB**), which is a clearinghouse to collect and release information to qualified healthcare entities regarding professional competence and physician conduct (Kadzielski 2011). The Health Care Quality Improvement Act (HCQIA) established the NPDB in 1990 (Cohen 2011). The following information must be reported to the NPDB for physicians and dentists: "(1) sanctions taken by boards of medical and dental examiners, (2) professional society membership actions, and (3) certain actions taken involving clinical privileges" (Cohen 2011, 1465). A number of other healthcare providers, that is, physician assistants, psychologists, podiatrists, nurse practitioners, and others, are subject to the required reporting to the NPDB regarding (1) paid medical malpractice judgments and settlements of claims regardless of the amount (including no contest pleas); (2) exclusion from the Medicare and Medicaid programs; and (3) registration action taken by the DEA (Cohen 2011, 1465). In 2010, the reporting requirements were expanded in 45 CFR Part 60.2 to include that each state adopt a system of reporting the following to the Secretary of HHS (NPDB 2010, 4676):

- Adverse licensure actions taken against healthcare practitioners and entities

- Negative action or finding which a State licensing authority, peer review organization, or private accreditation entity has concluded against a healthcare practitioner or entity

Hospitals are required to query the NPDB at the time a healthcare provider initially applies for medical staff membership and privileges and every two years thereafter (Cohen 2011, 1466). According to Cohen, if the hospital fails to query the NPDB as required, the hospital puts the medical staff member's confidential information contained therein at risk of discovery by a plaintiff's attorney (Cohen 2011, 1466).

Further, this process includes validating the physician's liability insurance. Having a license to practice medicine in a particular state does not give the physician the right to be a medical staff member in any hospital; rather, it is merely one required criterion (McWay 2010). Credentialing criteria should be related directly to patient care and based on objective factors such as education, experience, and current competence (Kadzielski 2011, 378). To avoid the appearance of discrimination based on profession, credentialing criteria for different types of practitioners (radiologists, psychiatrists, orthopedists, and so on) should be objective and based on community standards of care (Kadzielski 2011, 378). Further Kadzielski (2011) stated that criteria should be facility-specific reflecting the "facility's license capacity and availability of equipment, personnel, and services" (Kadzielski 2011, 378). Having credentialing standards ensures equal treatment of medical staff appointment and reappointment applicants and provides the applicants with "a fair, known, and systematic information collection process" (Kadzielski 2011, 375).

Federal laws in the form of the Medicare Conditions of Participation for hospitals, home health agencies, and long-term care facilities, among others, set forth requirements for medical staff credentialing (Kadzielski 2011). Kadzielski (2011) also pointed out that most states typically address medical staff appointments in licensing statutes or statutes specific for the selection of medical staff members or both and that accreditation standards, such as those published by The Joint Commission, require physician credentialing prior to granting privileges to practice in a healthcare facility.

The Privileging Process

After a physician is determined to meet the criteria to be a medical staff member in a particular hospital, the medical staff must evaluate his or her quality of medical practice and determine the services and procedures he or she is qualified to provide (McWay 2010). This is known as the **privileging process.** A physician's clinical privileges determine the services he or she may provide, such as what operations he or she may perform. The medical staff must have established a written definition of what it means to be granted the privilege to provide a particular service. Some hospitals grant privileges for specific procedures; others grant privileges for categories of procedures. Still other hospitals grant privileges based on levels of care, such as privileges to care for critical care patients. Another approach is to grant privileges by medical specialty based on the services a particular specialty is permitted to perform.

To evaluate a physician for privileging, a hospital may require the physician to obtain a consultation before performing specific procedures. Physicians also may be required to have operative procedures proctored by an observing or assisting physician. For example, California requires all medical staff members to demonstrate their ability to perform the surgical or other procedures they are requesting to be given privileges to perform (Kadzielski 2011, 376). A hospital may require certification beyond a license, such as board certification in a particular medical specialty, before granting privileges for a physician to practice in that specialty.

As stated previously, physicians must periodically reapply for medical staff membership. As part of the reapplication process, their privileges are reevaluated using established criteria. Physicians who have gained additional training since the last appointment may seek privileges not previously held. For any new privileges requested, the physician may be required to have consultation or proctoring performed. Hospitals are required to query the NPDB at least once every two years after the initial medical staff appointment as part of the renewal process of a physician's clinical privileges (Cohen 2011, 1466).

The goal of privileging is to ensure that all physicians have the requisite training and experience to perform the requested services. This process also applies to other licensed independent practitioners (for example, nurse practitioners and allied health practitioners).

Having and following credentialing and privileging processes is important to protecting the hospital or other entities engaged in granting medical staff membership and privileges. Hoffman (2011) indicated that courts have used the doctrine of apparent agency or ostensible agency to hold healthcare institutions vicariously liable for the negligent acts of independent physicians. Healthcare institutions have also been held liable under *respondeat superior* for acts employees committed within the scope of employment (Hoffman 2011; West 2011).

Accessibility and Confidentiality of Credentialing Files

In this discussion, *credentialing* is used as a collective term for the credentialing and privileging processes. In looking at accessibility to credentialing files, third parties, such as The Joint Commission and state and federal regulatory organizations, may review credentialing files as part of their accrediting and licensing functions. Some states statutorily protect credentialing files from discovery in legal proceedings. However, when a plaintiff alleges negligent credentialing against a hospital and as corporate liability theories expand, whether the protection will hold up comes into question (Barton 2011). In such a circumstance, the hospital finds itself in the situation of attempting to protect the information in the credentialing files while at the same time needing those very same documents to defend it. Forwarding such files to the entity's legal counsel may support the protection of such documents (Barton 2011). Although statutory protections, such as in California, may be in place for credentialing information, facilities should be reluctant to share such information "because any subsequent disclosure of peer review committee records could result in a loss of this protection" (Kadzielski 2011, 391).

Further, some states have enacted statutes for peer review protection granting immunity to peer review committee members and protecting the status of documents prepared during the peer review process (Hoffman 2011). Hoffman (2011) stated that typically pursuant to these laws, persons providing information to a peer review committee are protected from criminal and civil liability; however, this may not constitute an absolute immunity. Of course such persons will not be protected if (1) the information provided was false, and the person knew this or had reason to believe it was false; (2) the information provided was unrelated or irrelevant to the peer review committee's purpose; or (3) malice motivated the person to appear before the peer review committee (Hoffman 2011, 68–69). Documents and information recorded and used by a peer review committee are typically not subject to discovery or admissible as evidence in a civil action against the healthcare provider as long as the civil action arises from a matter that the committee has reviewed (Hoffman 2011). Hoffman warns that this protection is also not absolute. If a document used by a peer review committee can be obtained from its original source, the protection will not apply and the document may be disclosed pursuant to applicable law (Hoffman 2011, 69).

Confidentiality of Quality Improvement and Concurrent Review Activities

Quality improvement is the process of improving medical care and potentially decreasing healthcare costs. (This process is discussed more fully in chapter 22.)

QI activities can be carried out on a concurrent review basis or on a retrospective basis. *Concurrent review* consists of evaluating medical care as it is being given. Concurrent review activities can be carried out in a variety of ways. One method is through case management (utilization review) that focuses on the appropriateness of the admission, the level of care, and length of stay (Miller 1986).

Retrospective review occurs after patient discharge. This review may take the form of a focused study based on a pattern of questionable care identified during concurrent review or other retrospective review activities. The questionable care leading to a focused study may be care provided by any caregiver, including physicians. The hospital has a responsibility to address any problems discovered through either review process. If a physician was the caregiver providing the questionable care and it is determined that he or she is not practicing at the expected level of care, an educational session may be conducted with the particular physician. If warranted, more stringent steps, such as suspension of the physician's medical staff privileges or medical staff membership termination, may be taken.

These review activities involve collecting outcomes and performance data on how a physician performed as a physician and may affect continued medical staff membership. Accordingly, the review files are considered confidential. Many states have statutes that specifically provide confidentiality to these types of files (Carroll 2011). California Evidence Code Section 1157 is an example of such a law. This statute protects from discovery the proceedings and records of organized peer review committees responsible for the evaluation and improvement of the quality of care.

Check Your Understanding 12.9

Instructions: Answer the following questions on a separate piece of paper.

1. After he or she completes an application, what is the process for granting a physician membership on the hospital medical staff?

2. What documentation is typically reviewed for the initial membership appointment?

3. What activities may a medical staff require of a physician in order to grant the physician privileges to provide a specific service?

4. As part of the reapplication process, what additional factors may the medical staff review in the privileges component?

5. Discuss circumstances in which confidential information in a credentialing file may be accessed.

6. Distinguish between concurrent and retrospective review activities.

7. What is the basis for maintaining QI and concurrent review files confidential?

Other Liability Issues

Hospitals and other healthcare providers face other liability issues. Hospital staff members have a duty to advise an appropriate member of administration when they become aware of any action or failure to act that is below the standard of care. The standard of care does not just apply to direct patient care. By definition, it applies to the safeguarding of patients' personal belongings whether or not they are placed in the direct care of the facility. For patient and staff personal belongings not placed in the direct care of the facility, the facility must have policies and procedures for addressing questions of theft by staff.

The standard of care also applies to the physical safety of the premises for patients, staff, visitors, vendors, and members of the general public who come onto the premises. Physical safety means being free from physical defects in buildings and grounds and from being harmed by patients, nonstaff members, or staff members. Moreover, the hospital must address staff safety as it relates to treatment of violent or uncontrolled patients (for example, a patient under the influence of drugs or alcohol while being treated in the emergency department).

Electronic Health Records

The move toward a fully **electronic health record** (**EHR**) brings special liability issues with it. In particular, liability issues can be classified in two categories (McWay 2010, 296):

- Those in which the information in the EHR serves as proof in a lawsuit of the quality of patient care provided
- Those that arise from unauthorized access to, or the careless handling of, patient information in a computerized environment

The first issue focuses on whether the EHR can be admitted as evidence. This raises the hearsay rule and how it can be overcome for electronically stored medical records. Although admissibility of such records has been tested on a limited basis, federal courts have allowed a computer printout into evidence where the foundation, trustworthiness, and accuracy requirements were shown to have been met (McWay 2010, 288).

The second issue focuses on the legal requirements to keep EHRs safe and secure. The EHR must be subject to all three components of the HIPAA Security Rule: administrative safeguards (policies, procedures, risk assessment [45 CFR §164.308]); physical safeguards (facility access control [45 CFR §164.310]); and technical safeguards (access control [45 CFR §164.312]). Further, ARRA charges healthcare providers to follow security and privacy regulations issued by HHS (McWay 2010, 289).

The Legal Health Record

The 2006 AHIMA House of Delegates passed a resolution stating, among other supporting statements, that "AHIMA advocates that organizations define one set of health information that meets the legal and business needs of the organization and complies with state and federal laws and regulations" (AHIMA 2007b). However, what constitutes the **legal health record** (**LHR**)? The resolution does not define the specifics of an LHR. Therefore, the HIM professional reading the resolution is probably still uncertain of what constitutes the LHR. Is it the same for all like facilities? Does the format in which it is created and stored (paper, electronic, hybrid) determine what constitutes the LHR? Moving toward an EHR environment adds another dimension to defining the LHR.

Factors the HIM professional should consider in defining or assessing whether the current record is an LHR, regardless of format, include

- Purpose of the health record
- State and federal laws, regulations, and standards defining health record content
- Internal documents
- Risks the organization faces if its health record does not meet business record or legal health record requirements or the rules of evidence, especially if it is an EHR

Pursuant to the Federal Rules of Evidence (FRE) for business records, the health record qualifies as a business record. It is created and kept in the normal course of business, made at or near the time of the matter recorded, and made by a person within the business with knowledge of the events recorded (FRE 803(6)). The business is providing healthcare. As a business record the health record contains documentation of patient care, which can be used for continuity of care and for billing. Further, it serves as a communication tool for caregivers. The organization uses the health record for operational activities such as evaluating quality of care provided. The organization also uses the health record as a resource for medical research and education.

The health record as a business record can also serve as "testimony" in legal proceedings (AHIMA 2007c). The legal standards that control whether a record is admissible in court apply regardless of whether the health record is paper or electronic (AHIMA 2007a). Such standards include the presumption that information recorded in conjunction with business practices is trustworthy and has potential evidentiary value (Rinehart-Thompson et al. 2009). In other words, the rules of evidence requirements and health record content requirements are the standards. Thus the health record is the organization's "legal health record" (Rinehart-Thompson et al. 2009, 125).

State and federal laws, regulations, licensure requirements, and accrediting body standards defining health record content, maintenance, and documentation requirements are covered earlier in this chapter. A review of that section reveals these standards vary widely according to practice setting (Rinehart-Thompson et al. 2009; McLendon 2012). Rinehart-Thompson, Reynolds, and McCain (2009) also point out that internal documents such as the medical staff bylaws, rules, and regulations may contain documentation and retention requirements. These internal documents must also be considered when defining the LHR. Thus there is no boilerplate definition of the LHR—it is as each organization defines it.

The LHR definition was much simpler to arrive at when only paper-based records were used. That definition is much more difficult to arrive at in today's health record environment. Not only is technology in the form of the EHR impacting the definition, but also the changed content of the health record (AHIMA 2011). According to AHIMA (2011), health records now consist of a "facility's record, outpatient diagnostic test results or therapies, pharmacy records, physician records, other care providers' records, and the patient's own personal health record" (AHIMA 2011, 1) AHIMA (2011) also indicated that the health record may also have administrative, financial, and clinical data intermingled. Therefore, those "simple" days are gone for most healthcare organizations. However, the organization can apply the same criteria it used to define the paper legal health record to define its legal heath record in today's environment (AHIMA 2011, 1):

- What information can be stored long term?
- What information is clinically useful for the long term?
- What are the storage costs?
- How can the EHR be effectively and succinctly assembled for long-term use?

McLendon (2007) stated that the healthcare organization may define its LHR in terms of the data set to be released in response to a legal request such as a subpoena by cataloging and using policies and procedures to state what will be divulged pursuant to a legal request. Because most healthcare organizations have moved to some level of electronic health record, the LHR definition may include information in both paper and electronic format, typically referred to as a hybrid health record (McLendon 2012, 21–22). In this situation, the organization must broaden its assessment of what makes up the LHR—consider which "data elements, electronic-structured documents, images, audio files, video files and paper documents" should be included (Rinehart-Thompson et al. 2009, 126). To define the legal EHR, McLendon (2007, 2012) suggests that, in addition to writing new policies as needed, HIM professionals can build on existing policies and procedures and listing of documents defining the paper-based LHR. McLendon (2012) indicated that the organization's legal counsel should participate in policy and procedure development and that organizations should use the policies and procedures as tools to educate the organization's legal counsel so they can provide informed advice (McLendon 2012, 27). AHIMA has developed a legal EHR policy template, located in the AHIMA Body of Knowledge. The HIM professional must remember to also include the details of source EHR systems feeding what the organization has defined as its legal EHR (McLendon 2007). McLendon (2012) further suggested developing and maintaining a source system matrix. Therefore, defining the LHR, regardless of format, is a multidisciplinary responsibility.

According to Amatayakul (2008), HIM professionals are involved in many EHR implementation activities including, but not limited to

- Auditing compliance with clinical guidelines
- Auditing changes in electronic documentation
- Managing the data dictionary
- Designing and modifying templates, screens, and reports

- Managing access controls to EHR systems
- Testing the legal admissibility of records
- Managing amendments to records
- Serving on the EHR development and implementation committees
- Serving as the EHR project manager

Amatayakul (2008) stated that HIM professionals must remember that data quality, which is the HIM professional's responsibility, is the key to ensuring a legal EHR.

Further, in 2003, organizations classified as covered entities under HIPAA were required to determine what constituted their designated record set (DRS). HIPAA defines the DRS as those medical records and billing records about an individual the covered entity maintains or that the covered entity uses to make decisions about individuals (45 CFR §164.501). Because the DRS may include documents from other providers and electronic communications between providers and between provider and patient, the DRS potentially includes more information than what has historically been included in an organization's paper-based LHR. The organization must evaluate this information to determine whether it should be included in the definition of the organization's LHR.

The integrity of the health record is critical to it meeting the standards of evidence in a court of law and thus being classified as the organization's LHR. The integrity of the information stored in the health record means it is correct, accurate, and complete (Rinehart-Thompson et al. 2009, 132). Under the FRE, authenticity of the record means "it is what it purports to be" (Rinehart-Thompson et al. 2009, 133; FRE 901(a)). Rinehart-Thompson Reynolds, and McCain (2009) explain that those using the information stored in the health record rely on it being accurate; that it has not been changed either intentionally or accidentally. Thus the point of record completion (lock down) must be defined (Olenik 2008). Reliability is one of the standards the information must meet to be acceptable as evidence in court.

Rinehart-Thompson, Reynolds, and McCain (2009) further state that authenticity relates both to the information being created and the system being used to create and store that information. As to the system, reliability includes such features as user access controls, system security, access tracking and auditing capabilities, and operational stability (dependability and availability). These features are particularly important because the general concern is that electronically stored information can be easily changed. According to Olenik (2008), the organization must determine what the "original" record is:

- Paper documents
- Electronic information
- Imaged documents

Authenticity also means that in both the paper and EHR environments, there must be methods in place to verify the author of entries made in the health record. This process is typically referred to as authentication. In paper records authentication is most often accomplished by a handwritten signature and initials, both in ink. Authentication in an EHR is another matter. How documents are authenticated in an EHR can significantly impact legal proceedings (McLendon 2012). Electronic or digital signatures and computer keys are examples of authentication methods used in EHRs (Rinehart-Thompson et al. 2009). An organization can also write in its policy that the auto-authentication process can be used. This process states that an entry is considered authenticated if the author fails to review and affirmatively approve or disapprove the entry within a specified time period (Rinehart-Thompson et al. 2009). Whatever approach is decided upon, it must comply with applicable laws and regulations (Olenik 2008). Olenik (2008) provided one such example: "CMS Interpretive Guidelines for Hospitals 482.24(c)(1) *all entries must be legible and complete, and must be authenticated and dated promptly by the person (identified by name and discipline) who is responsible for ordering, providing, or evaluating the service furnished.*"

According to Rinehart-Thompson, Reynolds, and McCain (2009), when defining the LHR, a number of authentication issues must be considered. For example, countersignatures are required when one professional practices under the direct supervision of another. This second provider countersigns documentation authenticating the actions, documentation, and authentication of the first provider. Documents such as assessments require authentication by all staff members involved in the assessment. These multiple authentications may actually occur at different times.

Other issues that need to be considered when defining the LHR include (Rinehart-Thompson et al. 2009; McLendon 2012)

- Accuracy of information—does the information reflect the "true, correct and exact description of the care provided?" (Rinehart-Thompson et al. 2009, 137)
- Abbreviations
- Legibility
- Changes (revisions, additions, deletions, and version management)
- Timeliness and completeness
- Printing

One major concern is the "cut and paste" function included in some systems. According to Olenik (2008), the risks include

- Copying information to the wrong patient
- Copying information to the wrong encounter for the correct patient
- Inadequate identification of the original author and date of the entry
- Could be unethical or illegal in circumstances such as clinical trials

An EHR can be particularly effective in addressing some of these issues, such as abbreviations and legibility. Additionally, there are operational topics to be addressed (McLendon 2007, 2012):

- Alterations to role-based access
- Authorship (attributing information creation to a specific person or entity) and authentication
- Policy and procedure development
- Designating the custodian(s) of records
- Nonrepudiation
- Output formats
- Permanent archiving, retention, and destruction procedures
- System and network security
- Disaster recovery and business continuity

In summary, the definition of an LHR for a specific organization boils down to what documents, data, and the like the organization determines it will disclose pursuant to a legal request and whether that information meets the rules of evidence requirements and health record content, maintenance, and retention requirements. As the LHR transforms from a paper-based record to an EHR, laws and regulations continually change, as does technology. Prudent HIM professionals must monitor these changes to stay current so they can meet their obligations related to maintaining the integrity and security of the organization's LHR and EHR.

The LHR topic is covered in a number of other chapters in this book.

Incident Reports

A happening that is inconsistent with the standard of care is generally defined as an incident. As discussed previously, standards of care are not related only to direct patient care. Therefore, incidents do not relate only to patient care. Anyone witnessing or involved in an incident should complete an incident report as soon as possible after the incident as a way to capture the details of what happened. The incident report is one tool staff can use to report unusual incidents to administration. Data should be collected from the incident reports and analyzed to determine whether trends are developing.

Because incident reports contain facts, hospitals strive to protect their confidentiality. In some states, incident reports are protected under statutes protecting QI studies and activities (Carroll 2011, 204). They also may be protected under attorney–client privilege (Carroll 2011, 204; McWay 2010, 264). Protection under this doctrine may be based on whether the primary purpose of the incident report is to provide information to the hospital's attorney or liability insurer (Carroll 2010, 204; McWay 2010, 264).

Incident reports themselves are not a part of the clinical record and are considered confidential and privileged in many states (Gaffey and Groves 2011; McWay 2010). Even though the facts regarding the incident and the resolution should be documented, there should be no reference to completion of an incident report nor to risk management involvement in the clinical record (Gaffey and Groves 2011; Bunting and Benton 2011). Such a reference to the incident report in the clinical record would likely render the incident report discoverable because it is mentioned in a document that is discoverable in legal proceedings. To further ensure incident report confidentiality, no copies should be made (Carroll 2011, 204).

To encourage staff to complete and submit incident reports, staff must be assured that there will be not be punishment or retribution for reporting according to facility policy (Carroll 2011, 201–202; Woodfin 2011). Carroll (2011) pointed out that incident reports showing a repeated error such as medication errors that lead to patient injury by a single practitioner might involve some form of discipline (Carroll 2011, 201). Carroll (2011) recommended that in such a case, the focus with the practitioner should remain on the practitioner's performance that contributed to the error (Carroll 2011, 201).

Medical Identity Theft (Red Flags Rule)

While the Red Flags Rule is not a requirement in healthcare, the following is an historical discussion of these rules and why they were deemed not to apply to healthcare. The Red Flags Rule originated in the Fair and Accurate Credit Transactions Act of 2003 requiring financial institutions and other institutions considered "creditors" to maintain identity theft preventions programs. These programs were intended to help identify, detect, and respond to patterns or activities, known as red flags, that may indicate identity theft (Dimick 2010c, 22). In November 2007, the Federal Trade Commission (FTC) issued regulations, referred to as the **Red Flags Rule** (Gaffey and Groves 2011, 349). These regulations required certain entities to develop and implement programs to protect consumers from identity theft (Gaffey 2011, 349). The FTC indicated that financial institutions were not the only entities covered; healthcare providers, attorneys and other businesses were also covered because they provide goods or services and bill after the fact or in installments (Dimick 2010c, 22). According to the FTC, such billing practices make these entities a "creditor" under the rule (Dimick 2010c, 22). Gaffey and Groves pointed out that the terms "creditor" and "covered account" determine whether a healthcare organization is subject to the Red Flags Rule (Gaffey and Groves 2011, 349). As noted before "creditor" is defined as any entity that regularly defers payments for goods or services or extends credit (Gaffey and Groves 2011, 349). A "covered account" is "a consumer account that allows multiple payments or transactions or any other account with a reasonably foreseeable risk of identity theft" (Gaffey and Groves 2011, 349). According to Gaffey and Groves (2011) patient accounts opened and maintained by healthcare entities generally fall within this definition.

Although the rule was scheduled for enforcement in November 2008, many delays occurred (Dimick 2010c, provides the historical trail of these regulations). Finally on December 18, 2010, President Obama signed the Red Flags Program Clarification Act of 2010, which redefined "creditor" and excluded most, if not all, healthcare providers from the regulations (Jergesen 2011a; Dimick 2010b). Jergesen (2011a) stated that healthcare providers not covered by the rules at this time should continue to monitor the rules, as the FTC could extend the rule in the future. Jergesen also suggests that as a matter of good business practice, providers should consider implementing programs to identity theft that could lead to "avoiding losses or liability that may result from instances of medical identity theft" (Jergesen 2011a, 1).

Relationship to Risk Manager

The health information manager and the risk manager should work as a team. The risk manager depends on the health information manager to alert him or her to potentially compensable events. These are events that could result in a settlement or judgment against the facility, further resulting in a payout of funds whether through insurance or from facility internal funds. Such events can be identified through coding and abstracting and various health information review activities conducted by HIM department staff. The health information manager also can advise the risk manager when an attorney requests a copy of a health record. The risk manager then can review records identified by any of these methods to determine whether further action is necessary from a risk management standpoint.

Check Your Understanding 12.10

Instructions: Answer the following questions on a separate piece of paper.

1. Define incident as it relates to the healthcare environment.

2. Name one doctrine under which incident reports may be protected.

3. What characteristics of a medical record qualify these records to be "business records"?

4. Differentiate between "authenticity" and "authentication."

5. Discuss the various issues that should be considered when defining the legal health record.

6. Why should incident reports be protected?

7. Discuss the relationship between the health information manager and the risk manager.

Summary

The basic court system is the same from one state to another. However, the health information management professional

should become familiar with the differences that do exist for the state in which he or she works. This knowledge gives the HIM professional the ability to communicate effectively with legal counsel regarding health records and policies and procedures affecting health records when the inevitable lawsuit arises.

Knowledge that is more important and valuable to the HIM professional is of the statutes that control the use and disclosure of confidential health information. These statutes are both federal and state in nature. This area of law is constantly in flux and requires the HIM professional to regularly review the many available resources pertaining to such statutes, including publications and seminars. These resources also should address case law that may affect the ongoing applicability of federal and state statutes and regulations.

E-Discovery statutes at the federal level and at the state level as available are having a significant impact on how HIM professionals respond to subpoenas and other requests for information. E-Discovery goes beyond the data that are visible in systems by including metadata. The concepts of legal hold and spoliation are very important to the HIM professional in responding under e-Discovery statutes to a subpoena or another request. In conjunction with e-Discovery, the HIM professional must have an understanding of what constitutes the organization's electronic health record (EHR), including what systems are contained in the EHR. Included in all of this is knowing what makes up the organization's legal health record (LHR). According to the AHIMA House of Delegates in 2006, the LHR is one set of health information meeting the legal and business needs of the organization (AHIMA 2007b).

Another body of knowledge the HIM professional should develop is a clear understanding of licensure and accreditation standards that affect the creation, completion, maintenance, and protection of health records.

The HIM professional must ensure that health record policies and procedures are in place and enforced and that they reflect all statutes, regulations, and standards pertaining to health records, particularly those pertaining to the use and disclosure of confidential information.

Among the many members of the hospital staff with whom the HIM professional works, he or she must have a close relationship with the facility risk manager. The HIM professional can provide the risk manager tremendous assistance in identifying and addressing incidents that may place the facility at risk.

References

Administrative Procedures Act, 5 U.C.S. §500-576 (Law. Co-op. 1989).

AHIMA e-HIM Work Group on e-Discovery. 2006. New electronic discovery civil rule. *Journal of AHIMA* 77(8): 68A–H.

AHIMA e-Discovery Task Force. 2008. Litigation response planning and policies for e-Discovery. *Journal of AHIMA* 79(2): 69–75. http://www.ahima.org/e-him.

AHIMA e-HIM Work Group on Maintaining the Legal EHR. 2005a. Update: Maintaining a legally sound health record—Paper and electronic. *Journal of AHIMA* 76(10): 64A–L. http://www.ahima.org/e-him.

AHIMA e-HIM Work Group on Defining the Legal Health Record. 2005b. The legal process and electronic health records. *Journal of AHIMA* 76(9): 96A–D.

Amatayakul, M. 2008. EHRs in a changing environment. California Health Information Management Association 2008 State Convention and Exhibit. San Jose, CA: CHIA.

American Health Information Management Association. 2007a. Is your electronic record a legal record? *Journal of AHIMA* 78(1): 54.

American Health Information Management Association. 2007b. Resolution on the legal health record. *Journal of AHIMA* 78(1): 53.

American Health Information Management Association. 2007c. The legal EHR: Trials and errors. *AHIMA Advantage* 11:4. http://www.ahima.org.

American Health Information Management Association. 2011. Fundamentals of the Legal Health Record and Designated Record Set. *Journal of AHIMA* 82(2): expanded online version. http://www.ahima.org.

Arizona Constitution, Article 2, Section 8, Right to privacy. http://azleg.state.az.us/const/2/8.htm.

ARRA/HITECH. American Recovery and Reinvestment Act of 2009. Public Law 111-5.

Barton, E.L. 2011. Claims and Litigation Management. Chapter 12 in *Risk Management Handbook for Healthcare Organizations. Volume 3 Business Risk: Legal, Regulatory, and Technology Issues,* 6th ed. Series edited by Carroll, R. Volume edited by Troyer, G.T. San Francisco: Jossey-Bass.

Biddle v. Warren Gen. Hosp., 715 N.E.2d 518 (Ohio 1999).

Bunting, R.F., Jr. and J.H. Benton. 2011. Managing Risk in the Ambulatory Environment. Chapter 15 in *Risk Management Handbook for Healthcare Organizations. Volume 2 Clinical Risk Management.* 6th ed. Series edited by Carroll, R. Volume edited by Brown, S. M. San Francisco: JosseyBass.

California Civil Discovery Act. http://CaliforniaDiscovery.findlaw.com.

California Constitution, Article 1, Declaration of rights, Section 1. http://leginfo.ca.gov/.const/.article_1.

Carroll, R. 2011. Early Warning Systems for the Identification of Organizational Risks. Chapter 6 in *Risk Management Handbook for Healthcare Organizations. Volume 1 The Essentials.* 6th ed. Series edited by Carroll, R. Volume edited by Nakamura, P.L., and R. Carroll. San Francisco: Jossey-Bass.

Clinical Laboratory Improvement Amendments of 1988 (CLIA). Title 42 Public Health, Part 493 Laboratory Requirements, Subpart K Quality System for Nonwaived Testing §493.1291 Standard: Test report. 76 Fed. Reg. 5672 (September 14, 2011).

Cohen, M. 2011. Statutes, Standards, and Regulations. Chapter 1 in *Risk Management Handbook for Healthcare Organizations.*

Volume 3 Business Risk: Legal, Regulatory, and Technology Issues. 6th ed. Series edited by Carroll, R. Volume edited by Troyer, G.T. San Francisco: Jossey-Bass.

Darling v. Charleston Community Memorial Hospital, 33 Ill.2d 326, 211 N.E. 2d, 253 (1965).

DeLoss, G.E. 2008. Electronic health records: An overview of legal liability, discovery and donation issues. California Health Information Management Association 2008 State Convention and Exhibit. San Jose, CA: CHIA.

Dimick, C. 2007. E-Discovery: Preparing for the coming rise in electronic discovery requests. *Journal of AHIMA* 78(5): 24–29.

Dimick, C. 2010a. Californian sentenced to prison for HIPAA violation. http://journal.ahima.org/2010/04/29/californian-sentenced-to-prison-for-hipaa-violation/.

Dimick, C. 2010b. Red Flags clarification exempts most, not all providers. http://journal.ahima.org/2010/12/16/red-flag-clarification-exempts-most-not-all-providers/.

Dimick, C. 2010c. Red Flags Rule in limbo: Controversy keeps enforcement at bay. *Journal of AHIMA* 81(4): 22–25.

Emergency Medical Treatment and Labor Act (EMTALA). Social Security Act 1867, codified as 42 USC. §1395dd; 42 C.F.R. §489 and others. (Term *active* removed from title in 1989.)

Federal Rules of Evidence (FRE) 803(6): Hearsay Exceptions: Availability of Declarant Immaterial (2000).

Federal Rules of Evidence (FRE) 901: Requirement of Authentication or Identification (1975).

Florida Constitution, Article I, Section 23, Right of privacy. http://www.leg.state.fl.us.

Gaffey, A., and S. Groves. 2011. The Clinical Record. Chapter 13 in *Risk Management Handbook for Healthcare Organizations. Volume 1 The Essentials,* 6th ed. Series edited by Carroll, R. Volume edited by Nakamura, P.L., and R. Carroll. San Francisco: Jossey-Bass.

Garner, B.A. 2004. *Black's Law Dictionary,* 8th ed. (abridged). St. Paul, MN: West.

Glossary. 2011. Glossary in *Risk Management Handbook for Healthcare Organizations. Volume 1 The Essentials.* 6th ed. Series edited by Carroll, R. Volume edited by Nakamura, P.L., and R. Carroll. San Francisco: Jossey-Bass.

Griswold v. Connecticut, 381 U.S. 479 (1965).

Health Care Quality Improvement Act. U.S.C. § 11101; 45 C.F.R. Part 60, Public Law 99-660.

HIPAA. Health Insurance Portability and Accountability Act of 1996. Public Law 104-191.

HIPAA-a. Public Law 104-191, 110 Stat. 1936 (codified in scattered sections of 18, 26, 29, and 42 U.S.C.).

HIPAA-b. Public Law 104-191, preface 110 Stat. at 1936.

HIPAA-c. 65 Fed. Reg. 82463 (Dec. 28, 2000).

HIPAA-d. Public Law 104-191, §261; 65 Fed. Reg. 82463 (Dec. 28, 2000).

HIPAA-e. Public Law 104-191, §§263, 264 (codified at 42 USC 1320d-2 to 1320d-8).

HIPAA-f. 65 Fed. Reg. 82484 (Dec. 28, 2000).

HIPAA-g. 65 Fed. Reg. 82718 (Dec. 28, 2000).

HIPAA-h. 65 Fed. Reg. 82798 (Dec. 28, 2000), as amended at 67 Fed. Reg. 38019, May 31, 2002; 67 Fed. Reg. 53266, Aug. 14, 2002; 68 Fed. Reg. 8374, Feb. 20, 2003; 71 Fed. Reg. 8424, Feb. 16, 2006).

HIPAA-i. 76 Fed. Reg. 31426 (May 31, 2011).

HIPAA-j. 75 Fed. Reg. 40868 (July 14, 2010).

HIPAA-k. 74 Fed. Reg. 56130 (Oct. 30, 2009).

Hoffman, P. 2011. Healthcare Legal Concepts. Chapter 2 in *Risk Management Handbook for Healthcare Organizations. Volume 1 The Essentials.* 6th ed. Series edited by Carroll, R. Volume edited by Nakamura, P.L., and R. Carrol. San Francisco: Jossey-Bass.

Horn, W.S. 2010. Easing e-Discovery: The Electronic Discovery Reference Model and the Information Management Reference Model. *Journal of AHIMA* 81(1): 44.

Hughes, G. 2002. Practice brief: Laws and regulations governing the disclosure of health information (updated).http://library.ahima.org.

Hughes, G. 2003. Transfer of patient health information across the continuum (updated). http://library.ahima.org.

In re PPA Litigation, 2003 WL 22203834 (NJ Super L 2003).

Jergesen, A.D. 2011a. Red Flags law revised to exclude health providers. *CHIA Journal* 62(10): 1, 6, and 9.

Jergesen, A.D. 2011b. Who owns the medical record? *CHIA Journal* 63(5): 1, 12.

Judge v. Rockford Memorial Hospital, 17 Ill. App. 2d 365, 150 N.E. 2d 202 (1958).

Kadzielski, M.A. 2011. Physician and Allied Health Professional Credentialing. Chapter 14 in *Risk Management Handbook for Healthcare Organizations. Volume 1 The Essentials,* 6th ed. Series edited by Carroll, R. Volume edited by Nakamura, P.L., and R. Carroll. San Francisco: Jossey-Bass.

Latner, A.W. 2008. Staff nurse faces jail time for HIPAA violations. *Renal and Urology News.* http://www.renalandurologynews.com/staff-nurse-faces-jail-time-for-hipaa-violations/article/119854/2/.

Law v. Zuckerman, 307 F. Supp. 2d 705 (D. MD 2004).

Lazzarotti, J.J. 2008 (July). Hospital to pay $100,000, comply with 3-year corrective action plan for HIPAA data breach. http://www.jacksonlewis.com/legalupdates/article.cfm?aid=1448.

Lickerman, D., and S. Lickerman. 2011. Emergency Department Risk Management: Promoting Quality and Safety in a Chaotic Environment. Chapter 12 in *Risk Management Handbook for Healthcare Organizations. Volume 2 Clinical Risk Management,* 6th ed. Series edited by Carroll, R. Volume edited by Brown, S.M. San Francisco: Jossey-Bass.

McLendon, K. 2007 (Feb). Record disclosure and the EHR: Defining and managing the subset of data disclosed upon request. *Journal of AHIMA* 78(2): 58–59.

McLendon, W.K. 2012. *The Legal Health Record Regulations, Policies and Guidelines.* Chicago: AHIMA.

McWay, D.C. 2010. *Legal and Ethical Aspects of Health Information Management.* Clifton, NY: Delmar.

Miller, R.D. 1986. *Problems in Hospital Law.* Rockville, MD: Aspen.

National Practitioner Data Bank (NPDB). 75 Fed. Reg. 4656 (January 28, 2010).

National Practitioner Data Bank for Adverse Information on Physicians and Other Health Care Practitioners (NPDB). 45 CFR 60; 42 U.S.C 11101-11152: 42 U.S.C 1396r-2.Office of Civil Rights (OCR). 2000. 65 *Federal Register* 82527.

Office of Civil Rights (OCR). 2006. Compliance and enforcement, how OCR enforces the HIPAA Privacy Rule. http://www.hhs.gov/ocr/privacy/enforcement/hipaarule.html.

Office of Civil Rights (OCR). 2009. HIPAA enforcement. http://www.hhs.gov/ocr/privacy/hipaa/enforcement/index.html.

Office of Civil rights (OCR). 2011. UCLA health system settles potential HIPAA privacy and security violations. http://www.hhs.gov/ocr/privacy/hipaa/news/uclahs.html and http://www.hhs.gov/news/press/2011pres/07/20110707a.html.

Olenik, K. 2008. How to create your legal EHR policy. California Health Information Management Association 2008 State Convention and Exhibit. San Jose, CA: CHIA.

Park, C. 2008 (April 17). Nurse pleads guilty to privacy violation. *Arkansas Democrat Gazette.* http://library.ardemgaz.com/ArchiveSearch.asp?SearchWords=nurse-guilty&eventStartDate=04%2F17%2F2008&eventStopDate=04%2F17%2F2008.

Pozgar, G.D. 2012. *Legal Aspects of Health Care Administration.* Sudbury, MA: Jones and Bartlett.

Reisner v. Regents of the University of California, 31 Cal. App.4th 1995, 37 Cal. Rptr2d 518 (Cal. App. Dist.2 1995).

Rhodes, H., and G. Hughes. 2009. Redisclosure of patient health information (updated). *Journal of AHIMA* 80(2): 51–54. http://www.ahima.org.

Rinehart-Thompson, L.A., 2009. The Legal System in the United States. Chapter 2 in *Fundamentals of Law for Health Informatics and Information Management.* Edited by Brodnick, M.S., L.A. Rinehart-Thompson, M.C. McCain, and R.B. Reynolds. Chicago: AHIMA.

Rinehart-Thompson, L.A., R.B. Reynolds, K. Olenik, and M.C. McCain. 2009. The Legal Health Record: Maintenance, Content, Documentation, and Disposition. Chapter 7 in *Fundamentals of Law for Health Informatics and Information Management.* Edited by Brodnick, M.S., L.A. Rinehart-Thompson, M.C. McCain, and R.B. Reynolds. Chicago: AHIMA.

Social Security Act (SSA). 42 USC. 1320d-5, 1320d-6.

Tarasoff v. Board of Regents, 17 Cal.3d 425, 551 P.2d 334 (Cal. 1976).

Trautmann, C.O. 2003. Dictionary of Small Business. http://www.small-business-dictionary.org/default.asp?.

US v. Gibson, CR 04-0374RFM (W.D. WA 2004).

West, J.C. 2011. Essentials of American Law. Appendix 2.1 in *Risk Management Handbook for Healthcare Organizations. Volume 1 The Essentials.* 6th ed. Series edited by Carroll, R. Volume edited by Nakamura, P.L., and R. Carroll. San Francisco: Jossey-Bass.

Woodfin, K. 2011. Risk Management Considerations in Home Healthcare. Chapter 16 in *Risk Management Handbook for*

Healthcare Organizations. Volume 2 Clinical Risk Management. 6th ed. Series edited by Carroll, R. Volume edited by Brown, S.M. San Francisco: Jossey-Bass.

45 CFR 46.111(a)(7): Research—Protection of Human Subjects, including Protecting Confidential Information. 2006 (Oct. 1).

45 CFR 160: General Administrative Requirements. 2000 (Dec. 28).

45 CFR 160.102: Applicability. 2002 (Aug. 14).

45 CFR 160.103: Definitions. 2006 (Feb. 16).

45 CFR 160.201–205: Preemption Provisions. 2002 (Aug. 14).

45 CFR 160.203(b): General Rules and Exceptions. 2002 (Aug. 14).

45 CFR 160.306(a): OCR Investigations—Right to File a Complaint. 2006 (Feb. 16).

45 CFR 160.306(c): OCR Investigations. 2006 (Feb. 16).

45 CFR 160.312(a)(1): Resolution where Non-Compliance is Indicated. 2006 (Feb. 16).

45 CFR 160.312(a)(3)(i): Mitigating Factors and Affirmative Defenses. 2006 (Feb. 16).

45 CFR 162: Transaction and Code Sets. 2000 (Aug. 17).

45 CFR 164 Subparts A and C: Security Rule. 2003 (Feb. 20).

45 CFR 164 Subpart E: Privacy of Individually Identifiable Health Information. 2003 (Feb. 20).

45 CFR 164.308: Security—Administrative Safeguards. 2005 (Oct. 1).

45 CFR 164.310: Security—Physical Safeguards. 2005 (Oct. 1).

45 CFR 164.312: Security—Technical Safeguards. 2005 (Oct. 1).

45 CFR 164.500: Privacy. 2002 (Aug. 14).

45 CFR 164.501: Definitions. 2003 (Feb. 20).

45 CFR 164.506(a): Permitted Uses and Disclosures. 2002 (Aug. 14).

45 CFR 164.506(a)(5): Consent. 2002 (Aug. 14).

45 CFR 164.506(c)(1): Treatment, Payment, and Health Care Operations. 2002 (Aug. 14).

45 CFR 164.506(c)(2): Treatment Activities of Health Care Provider. 2002 (Aug. 14).

45 CFR 164.506(c)(3): Payment Activities of Health Care Provider. 2002 (Aug. 14).

45 CFR 164.506(c)(4): Health Care Operations of Health Care Provider. 2002 (Aug. 14).

45 CFR 164.506(c)(4)(i): Health Care Operations of Health Care Provider. 2002 (Aug. 14).

45 CFR 164.506(c)(5): Treatment, Payment, and Health Care Operations in Organized Health Care Arrangement. 2002 (Aug. 14).

45 CFR 164.508(a)(1): Authorization—General Rule. 2002 (Aug. 14).

45 CFR 164.508(a)(2): Psychotherapy Notes. 2002 (Aug. 14).

45 CFR 164.508(a)(3): Marketing. 2002 (Aug. 14).

45 CFR 164.508(b)(2): Defective Authorizations. 2002 (Aug. 14).

45 CFR 164.508(b)(5)(i): Authorization Revocation. 2002 (Aug. 14).

45 CFR 164.508(c)(1)–(4): Authorization Content. 2002 (Aug. 14).

45 CFR 164.508(c)(2)(iii): Authorization Content—Core Elements and Requirements. 2002 (Aug. 14).

45 CFR 164.510: Opportunity to Agree or Object to Disclosures. 2002 (Aug. 14).

45 CFR 164.510(b)(1)(i): Uses and Disclosures for Involvement in the Individual's Care. 2002 (Aug. 14).

45 CFR 164.510(b)(1)(ii): Uses and Disclosures for Notification Purposes. 2002 (Aug. 14).

45 CFR 164.512(a)(1): Required by Law. 2002 (Aug. 14).

45 CFR 164.512(b): Public Health Activities. 2002 (Aug. 14).

45 CFR 164.512(b)(1)(i)–(iii): Communicable Disease Notification. 2002 (Aug. 14).

45 CFR 164.512(b)(1)(v): Disclosure to Employer. 2002 (Aug. 14).

45 CFR 164.512(c): Reporting Abuse, Neglect, Domestic Violence. 2002 (Aug. 14).

45 CFR 164.512(d): Health Oversight Activities. 2002 (Aug. 14).

45 CFR 164.512(e)(i)–(iv): Judicial or Administrative Proceeding. 2002 (Aug. 14).

45 CFR 164.512(e)(v): Judicial or Administrative Proceeding–Qualified Protective Order. 2002 (Aug. 14).

45 CFR 164.512(f): Law Enforcement. 2002 (Aug. 14).

45 CFR 164.512(f)(6): Law Enforcement—Perpetrator of Crime. 2002 (Aug. 14).

45 CFR 164.512(g): Decedents. 2002 (Aug. 14).

45 CFR 164.512(h): Procurement Organizations. 2002 (Aug. 14).

45 CFR 164.512(i): Research. 2002 (Aug. 14).

45 CFR 164.512(j): Avert Serious Threat. 2002 (Aug. 14).

45 CFR 164.512(k): Specialized Government Functions. 2002 (Aug. 14).

45 CFR 164.512(l): Workers Compensation. 2002 (Aug. 14).

45 CFR 164.514: De-identified Information. 2002 (Aug. 14).

45 CFR 164.514(f)(1): Fundraising. 2002 (Aug. 14).

45 CFR 164.520: Notice of Privacy Practices. 2002 (Aug. 14).

45 CFR 164.522(a): Restrict Use of Protected Health Information. 2002 (Aug. 14).

45 CFR 164.522(b): Confidential Communications. 2002 (Aug. 14).

45 CFR 164.524: Access to Own Protected Health Information. 2002 (Aug. 14).

45 CFR 164.524(a)(1): Patient Right of Access to Own Protected Health Information. 2002 (Aug. 14).

45 CFR 164.524(a)(3): Reviewable Grounds for Denial of Access to Own Protected Health Information. 2002 (Aug. 14).

45 CFR 164.526: Amend Designated Record Set. 2002 (Aug. 14).

45 CFR 164.528: Accounting of Disclosures. 2002 (Aug. 14).

42 USC 1320d-5: General Civil Money Penalties. 1996.

42 USC 1320d-6(a): Criminal Provisions. 2000.

42 USC 1320d-6(b): Maximum Penalties. 2000.

chapter 13

Ethical Issues in Health Information Management

Laurinda B. Harman, PhD, RHIA, FAHIMA

Learning Objectives

- Recognize and respond to health information ethical problems, including those related to privacy and confidentiality; compliance, fraud, and abuse; clinical code selection and use; quality review; research and decision support; public health; managed care; clinical care; electronic health information systems; the management of sensitive information; the roles of manager, entrepreneur, and advocate; and business relationships with vendors
- Recognize the historical problems of research and ethics and the importance of diligence for future research endeavors

- Recognize the problems associated with the emerging ethical problem of medical identity theft
- Identify ethical principles and professional values that can guide health information management (HIM) professionals who must confront and respond to ethical problems
- Apply the American Health Information Management Association (AHIMA) Code of Ethics to guide behaviors such as protecting privacy, advancing HIM knowledge and practice, advocating for others, and refusing to participate in or conceal unethical behaviors
- Follow the steps in an ethical decision-making process that can be used to resolve complex ethical problems

Key Terms

Autonomy
Beneficence
Blanket authorization
Confidentiality
Ethical agent
Ethical decision making
Ethicist
Ethics

Justice
Medical identity theft
Moral values
Need-to-know principle
Nonmaleficence
Privacy
Secondary release of information
Security

Introduction

The responsibilities of the health information management (HIM) professional include a wide range of functions and activities. Regardless of the employer—such as healthcare facility, vendor, pharmaceutical company, or research firm—the HIM professional's core ethical obligations are to protect patient privacy and confidential information and to ensure security of that information. The documentation in the paper and electronic health record (EHR) systems include many sacred stories that must be protected on behalf of the individual patient and the aggregate community of patients and consumers served by the healthcare system. The obligation to protect this information is at the center of the decisions made on behalf of patients, the healthcare team, peers, colleagues, the public, or the many other stakeholders who seek access to patient and consumer information (AHIMA 2011).

Moral intelligence is important for our understanding of the complexity of the issues that we face and how we can apply our values, goals, and actions in ethical decision making (Lennick and Kiel 2008). There is also an increased understanding that technological systems require moral guidance in design and application. The focus on technology and human relationships increases ethical imperatives because what is done, how it is done, and what the intended (and sometimes unintended) outcomes are must be carefully examined (Van den Hoven and Weckert 2008).

The terms in this chapter describe ethical principles that most people already know, although the terms themselves may not be familiar. For example, recognizing the importance of individuals being able to decide what happens to them is autonomy, doing good is included in the ethical principle of beneficence, not harming others is nonmaleficence, and treating people fairly is justice (Beauchamp and Childress 2001). With regard to one of the HIM professional's primary functions, how might ethical principles apply in the case of deciding whether to release patient information?

- **Autonomy** would require the HIM professional to ensure that the patient, and not a spouse or third party, makes the decisions regarding access to his or her health information.
- **Beneficence** would require the HIM professional to ensure that the information is released only to individuals who need it to do something that will benefit the patient (for example, to an insurance company for payment of a claim).
- **Nonmaleficence** would require the HIM professional to ensure that the information is not released to someone who does not have authorization to access it and who might harm the patient if access were permitted (for example, a newspaper seeking information about a famous person).
- **Justice** would require the HIM professional to apply the rules fairly and consistently for all and not to make special exceptions based on personal or organizational perspectives (for example, releasing information more quickly to a favorite physician's office).

This chapter provides the language and framework for understanding more about ethics within the context of dealing with complex health information issues. It also offers a step-by-step process that HIM professionals can use to make appropriate ethical choices and to analyze what is and is not justified from an ethical perspective.

Theory into Practice

The following discussion is extracted from "What the Seven Signs of Ethical Collapse Can Teach Us about Quality in Healthcare" (Tomzik 2008):

Healthcare has much in common with the traditional business marketplace. What began as a means to meet the healthcare needs of the individual and promote health within the community has mushroomed into a steadily increasing $2.3 trillion dollar business enterprise. The temptations and ethical afflictions of traditional business activities are occurring within healthcare, setting a course for equally disastrous results. One strong indicator of impending demise is eroding quality. Healthcare can learn from its traditional counterparts who slowly drifted away from ethical values and failed to recognize or heed the ethical warning signs that eventually set the stage for their own demise. Restoring patient confidence and trust in quality of healthcare delivery requires more than adequate benefit coverage. Restoring patient confidence and trust in the quality of the healthcare delivery system requires a return to core values and a willingness to heed the ethical warning signs present in our midst to change course and position itself for return to solvency and success.

Moral Values and Ethical Competencies

Although most people probably have never undertaken a formal study of ethics, everyone is exposed to ethical principles, moral perspectives, and values throughout a lifetime. Individuals learn about basic **moral values** from families, religious leaders, teachers, the government, community organizations, and other groups that influence experiences and perspectives. Moral values are taught as "this is right and that is wrong." For example, some might consider it right to be nice to a neighbor and wrong to destroy the neighbor's property. However, these are not universal values. Others might consider it acceptable to be rude or mean to a neighbor they do not like and to destroy the neighbor's property. Applying this language to health information management, it is right—and a moral obligation—to protect the neighbor's privacy when you learn about diseases and conditions while working, and it is wrong to share the neighbor's medical information with other neighbors, family, and friends.

HIM professionals should not make ethical decisions on behalf of others based solely on personal moral values or perspectives because not everyone shares the same moral perspectives or values. Professional responsibilities often require an individual to move beyond personal values. For example, an individual might demonstrate behaviors that are based on the values of honesty, providing service to others, or demonstrating loyalty. In addition to these, professional values might require promoting confidentiality, facilitating interdisciplinary collaboration, and refusing to participate or conceal unethical practices. Professional values could require a more comprehensive set of values than what an individual needs as an **ethical agent** in his or her personal life. For example, an HIM professional who hears information about a friend at a party has a range of options. He or she can share the information, share only part of it, change it, or not confirm or share it with anyone. However, that same individual in his or her role as an HIM professional cannot share overheard information under any circumstances. Optimally, the HIM professional will apply the same high standards in both personal and professional situations.

Ethics provides a language and a framework for formally discussing ethical issues, taking into account the values and obligations of others. Ethical discussion offers an opportunity to resolve conflicts when competing values are at stake. **Ethical decision making** requires people to explore choices beyond the perspective of simple right or wrong (moral) options. According to Glover, "ethics refers to the formal process of intentionally and critically analyzing the basis for our moral judgments for clarity and consistency" (Glover 2006, 34). When making health information decisions, HIM professionals must go beyond the personal right or wrong moral perspective and evaluate the many values and perspectives of others who are engaged in the decision to be made.

Ethical discussions outside the healthcare environment can be theoretical in nature, and the analysis of a problem does not necessarily result in an action. For example, **ethicists** could discuss whether to require all citizens living in a certain community to donate 10 hours a week to people in need as part of their civic duty. One ethicist might argue for a decision based on the ethical principle of beneficence, which would guide action to do good things for others. Another ethicist might argue for the same decision based on the principle of justice in which every citizen should contribute his or her fair share for the good of the community. These discussions and decisions would not necessarily require an action but would help frame the ethical justification for a certain action.

In contrast, bioethics involves problems or issues regarding clinical care or the health information system that are never strictly theoretical in nature and must always result in a decision and an action. HIM professionals cannot merely deliberate whether to release patient information, assign the correct code, or purchase a new software system. Rather, they must apply ethical principles and then do something. In short, ethics applied in the work environment cannot remain theoretical and must result in an action.

Ethical Foundations in Health Information Management

Ethical principles and values have been important to the HIM profession since its beginning in 1928. The first ethical pledge was presented in 1934, by Grace Whiting Myers, a visionary leader who recognized the importance of protecting information in medical records. The HIM profession was launched with recognition of the importance of privacy and the requirement of an authorization for the release of health information:

> I pledge myself to give out no information from any clinical record placed in my charge, or from any other source to any person whatsoever, except upon order from the chief

executive officer of the institution which I may be serving. (Huffman 1972, 135)

Today, it is the patient who authorizes the release of information and not the chief executive officer (CEO) of the healthcare organization, as was stated in the original pledge. The most important values embedded in this pledge are to protect patient privacy and confidential information and to recognize the importance of the HIM professional as a moral agent in protecting patient information (Rinehart-Thompson and Harman 2006). The HIM professional has a clear ethical and professional obligation not to give any information to anyone unless the release has been authorized.

Protection of Privacy, Maintenance of Confidentiality, and Assurance of Data Security

The terms *privacy*, *confidentiality*, and *security* are often used interchangeably. However, there are some important distinctions, including the following:

- **Privacy** is "the right of an individual to be let alone. It includes freedom from observation or intrusion into one's private affairs and the right to maintain control over certain personal and health information" (Harman 2006, 634).
- **Confidentiality** carries "the responsibility for limiting disclosure of private matters. It includes the responsibility to use, disclose, or release such information only with the knowledge and consent of the individual" (Harman 2006, 627–628). Confidential information may be written or verbal.
- **Security** includes "physical and electronic protection of the integrity, availability, and confidentiality of computer-based information and the resources used to enter, store, process, and communicate it; and the means to control access and protect information from accidental or intentional disclosure" (Harman 2006, 635).

The HIM professional's responsibilities include ensuring that patient privacy and confidential information are protected and that data security measures are used to prevent unauthorized access to information. This responsibility includes ensuring that the release policies and procedures are accurate and up to date, that they are followed, and that all violations are reported to the proper authorities.

The Health Insurance Portability and Accountability Act (HIPAA) of 1996 established national standards for the protection of privacy and the assurance of the security of health information. This law deals with privacy, information standards, data integrity, confidentiality, and data security (Rinehart-Thompson and Harman 2006). Although HIPAA was passed in 1996, it took five years before the Privacy Rule became effective in April 2001, with an April 2003 compliance date. Congress passed the statute, and the US Department of Health and Human Services (HHS) developed the regulations contained within the Privacy Rule (HHS 2003). The final HIPAA Security Rule regulations were published in the *Federal Register* in February 2003 and became effective in April 2005.

This legislation, which includes Administrative Simplification standards and security and privacy standards, has had a major impact on the collection and dissemination of information, and will continue to have this impact for years to come. This legislation has an enforcement program, and HIM professionals serve an important role that ensures compliance. Preemptive federal legislation was needed so that all patient information would be protected regardless of where a patient lived or received healthcare. Moreover, this legislation protects individuals from losing their health insurance when leaving or changing jobs by providing insurance continuity (portability) and increases the federal government's authority over fraud and abuse in the healthcare arena (accountability) (Harman 2005). In addition to federal legislation, each state can pass its own legislation regarding access to patient information.

The American Recovery and Reinvestment Act of 2009 (ARRA) contains multiple provisions that affect the rights and obligations of certain parties under the privacy and security provisions of HIPAA. These changes relate to the application of the security and privacy provisions to business associates; the notification requirements in the event of a breach; the educational requirements regarding health information privacy; the restrictions on the disclosure and sale of health information; the accounting requirements of certain protected health information disclosures; auditing standards; and other related issues. HHS promulgated regulations to implement the provisions of this legislation over a multi-year period. It will be important to monitor these developments as they relate to the obligations of all parties affected by HIPAA. (HIPAA privacy and security standards are discussed more fully in chapters 12 and 28.)

Part of the impetus for HIPAA was the development of the EHR (Amatayakul 2009; Dick et al.1997; Hanken and Murphy 2006; Jones 2006; Murphy et al. 1999). As patient information was moved to the electronic medium, integrated systems across the continuum of care were developed and information was released and redisclosed to many people and agencies needing access to it. Thus, standardized federal legislation became an imperative. HIPAA was designed to guarantee that information transferred from one facility to the next would be protected. The National Committee on Vital and Health Statistics (NCVHS) supports a national health information infrastructure (NHII) so that patient care information can be transferred and protected in our integrated healthcare systems. As a result, patients benefit from the continuity of care and can control their personal health information (NCVHS 2001; Gellman 2004). In an electronic environment, protecting privacy has become extremely difficult and patients are becoming increasingly concerned about the loss of privacy and their inability to control the dissemination of information about them. As patients become more aware of the misuses of information, they may become reluctant to share information with their healthcare team. This may, in turn, result in problems with the healthcare provided and the information given to researchers, insurers, the government, and the many other stakeholders who legitimately need to access to the information. Increasingly, patients are seeking anonymity and are responding to issues related to the use and disclosure of health information for directory purposes; to family and close personal friends; for notification purposes such as disasters; and for other disclosures required by law such as public health, employer medical surveillance, and funeral directors (Hughes 2002a, 2002b; Rhodes 2001; AHIMA 2002). Perhaps more importantly, ARRA, which was signed February 14, 2009, by President Barack Obama, includes legislative language that makes it clear that one of the key purposes of the act is that it "advances the delivery of patient-centered care." Part of laying that foundation includes some in-depth analysis about what it means to get consumers engaged in managing their health. It is imperative that principles such as patient-centered care get translated into policies that actually help to deliver it (Seidman 2009, 34). Accountable care organization (ACOs) are intended to pay providers in a way that will encourage collaboration, discourage supplier-induced demand, and reward high-quality care (http://www.ahima.org/advocacy/arrahitech.aspx).

Professional Code of Ethics

HIM professionals used the pledge as the basis for guiding ethical decision making until 1957, at which time the American Association of Medical Record Librarians' (AAMRL) House of Delegates passed the first Code of Ethics for the Practice of Medical Record Science (see figure 13.1). The first code of ethics combined ethical principles with a set of professional values to help support the decisions that HIM professionals had to make at work. The original code of ethics has been revised several times since 1957. Codes passed in 1977, 1988, and 1998 are included as good representations of how the codes changed to reflect the changes in the work responsibilities for the HIM professional. (see figures 13.2, 13.3, 13.4). Other codes were passed during the time frame but are not included in this chapter. The 2011 American Health Information Management Association (AHIMA) Code of Ethics—Preamble and Ethical Principles are presented in figure 13.5. The entire 2011 AHIMA Code of Ethics, including its Guidelines, is presented in Appendix B.

Upon being awarded the credential of Registered Health Information Technician (RHIT) or Registered Health Information Administrator (RHIA); the coding credentials of Certified Coding Assistant (CCA), Certified Coding Specialist (CCS); Certified Coding Specialist-Physician (CCS-P); the health data analytics credential Certified Health Data Analyst (CHDA); the privacy and security

Figure 13.1.   1957 Code of Ethics for the Practice of Medical Record Science

As a member of one of the paramedical professions he shall:

1. Place service before material gain, the honor of the profession before personal advantage, the health and welfare of patients above all personal and financial interests, and conduct himself in the practice of this profession so as to bring honor to himself, his associates, and to the medical record profession.

2. Preserve and protect the medical records in his custody and hold inviolate the privileged contents of the records and any other information of a confidential nature obtained in his official capacity, taking due account of the applicable statutes and of regulations and policies of his employer.

3. Serve his employer loyally, honorably discharging the duties and responsibilities entrusted to him, and give due consideration to the nature of these responsibilities in giving his employer notice of intent to resign his position.

4. Refuse to participate in or conceal unethical practices or procedures.

5. Report to the proper authorities, but disclose to no one else, any evidence of conduct or practice revealed in the medical records in his custody that indicates possible violation of established rules and regulations of the employer or of professional practice.

6. Preserve the confidential nature of professional determinations made by the staff committee which he serves.

7. Accept only those fees that are customary and lawful in the area for services rendered in his official capacity.

8. Avoid encroachment on the professional responsibilities of the medical and other paramedical professions, and under no circumstances assume or give the appearance of assuming the right to make determinations in professional areas outside the scope of his assigned responsibilities.

9. Strive to advance the knowledge and practice of medical record science, including continued self-improvement, in order to contribute to the best possible medical care.

10. Participate appropriately in developing and strengthening professional manpower and in representing the profession to the public.

11. Discharge honorably the responsibilities of any Association post to which appointed or elected, and preserve the confidentiality of any privileged information made known to him in his official capacity.

12. State truthfully and accurately his credentials, professional education, and experiences in any official transaction with the American Association of Medical Record Librarians and with any employer or prospective employer.

Copyright © 1957 by the American Association of Medical Record Librarians.

Figure 13.2.   1977 AMRA Bylaws and Code of Ethics

The medical record practitioner is concerned with the development, use, and maintenance of medical and health records for medical care, preventive medicine, quality assurance, professional education, administrative practices and study purposes with due consideration of patients' right to privacy. The American Medical Record Association believes that it is in the best interests of the medical record profession and the public which it serves that the principles of personal and professional accountability be reexamined and redefined to provide members of the Association, as well as medical record practitioners who are credentialed by the Association, with definitive and binding guidelines of conduct. To achieve this goal, the American Medical Record Association has adopted the following restated Code of Ethics:

1. Conduct yourself in the practice of this profession so as to bring honor and dignity to yourself, the medical record profession and the Association.

2. Place service before material gain and strive at all times to provide services consistent with the need for quality health care and treatment of all who are ill and injured.

3. Preserve and secure the medical and health records, the information contained therein, and the appropriate secondary records in your custody in accordance with professional management practices, employer's policies, and existing legal provisions.

4. Uphold the doctrine of confidentiality and the individual's right to privacy in the disclosure of personally identifiable medical and social information.

5. Recognize the source of the authority and powers delegated to you and conscientiously discharge the duties and responsibilities thus entrusted.

6. Refuse to participate in or conceal unethical practices or procedures in your relationship with other individuals or organizations.

7. Disclose to no one but proper authorities any evidence of conduct or practice revealed in medical reports or observed that indicates possible violation of established rules and regulations of the employer or professional practice.

(continued on next page)

Figure 13.2.   1977 AMRA Bylaws and Code of Ethics *(continued)*

8. Safeguard the public and the profession by reporting to the Ethics Committee any breach of this Code of Ethics by fellow members of the profession.

9. Preserve the confidential nature of professional determinations made by official committees of health and health-service organizations.

10. Accept compensation only in accordance with services actually performed or negotiated with the health institution.

11. Cooperate with other health professions and organizations to promote the quality of health programs and advancement of medical care, ensuring respect and consideration for the responsibility and the dignity of medical and other health professions.

12. Strive to increase the profession's body of systematic knowledge and individual competency through continued self-improvement and application of current advancements in the conduct of medical record practices.

13. Participate in developing and strengthening professional manpower and appropriately represent the profession in public.

14. Discharge honorably the responsibilities of any Association position to which appointed or elected.

15. Represent truthfully and accurately professional credentials, education, and experience in any official transaction or notice, including other positions and duality of interests.

credentials Certificate in Healthcare Privacy and Security (CHPS) or, for clinical documentation improvement, Certified in Healthcare Documentation Improvement (CDIP) by AHIMA, the HIM professional agrees to follow the principles and values discussed in this chapter and to base all professional actions and decisions on those principles and values. Even if federal or state laws did not require the protection of patient privacy, the HIM professional would be responsible for protecting it according to AHIMA's Code of Ethics (see Appendix B).

Professional Values and Obligations

The ethical obligations of the HIM professional include the protection of patient privacy and confidential information. Important health information issues include what information should be collected, how the information should be handled, who should have access to the information, and under what conditions the information should be disclosed.

Ethical obligations are central to the professional's responsibility, regardless of the employment site or the method of collection, storage, and security of health information.

Figure 13.3.   1988 AMRA Code of Ethics and Bylaws

The medical record professional abides by a set of ethical principles developed to safeguard the public and to contribute within the scope of the profession to quality and efficiency in health care. This code of ethics, adopted by the members of the American Medical Record Association, defines the standards of behavior which promote ethical conduct.

1. The Medical Record Professional demonstrates behavior that reflects integrity, supports objectivity, and fosters trust in professional activities.

2. The Medical Record Professional respects the dignity of each human being.

3. The Medical Record Professional strives to improve personal competence and quality of services.

4. The Medical Record Professional represents truthfully and accurately professional credentials, education, and experience.

5. The Medical Record Professional refuses to participate in illegal or unethical acts and also refuses to conceal the illegal, incompetent, or unethical acts of others.

6. The Medical Record Professional protects the confidentiality of primary and secondary health records as mandated by law, professional standards, and the employer's policies.

7. The Medical Record Professional promotes to others the tenets of confidentiality.

8. The Medical Record Professional adheres to pertinent laws and regulations while advocating changes which serve the best interest of the public.

9. The Medical Record Professional encourages appropriate use of health record information and advocates policies and systems that advance the management of health records and health information.

10. The Medical Record Professional recognizes and supports the association's mission.

Figure 13.4.   1998 AHIMA Code of Ethics and Bylaws

AHIMA's Mission

The American Health Information Management Association is committed to the quality of health information for the benefit of patients, providers, and other users of clinical data. Our professional organization:

- Provides leadership in HIM education and professional development
- Sets and promotes professional practice standards
- Advocates patient privacy rights and confidentiality of health information
- Influences public and private policies including educating the public regarding health information
- Advances health information technologies

Guiding Principles

We are committed to the:

- Creation and utilization of systems and standards to ensure quality health information
- Achievement of member excellence
- Development of a supportive environment and provision of the resources to advance the profession
- Provision of the highest-quality service to members and healthcare information users
- Investigation and application of new technology to advance the management of health information

We value:

- The balance of patients' privacy rights and confidentiality of health information with legitimate uses of data
- The quality of health information as evidenced by its integrity, accuracy, consistency, reliability, and validity
- The quality of health information as evidenced by its impact on the quality of healthcare delivery

This Code of Ethics sets forth ethical principles for the HIM profession. Members of this profession are responsible for maintaining and promoting ethical practices. This Code of Ethics, adopted by the American Health Information Management Association, shall be binding on health information management professionals who are members of the Association and all individuals who hold an AHIMA credential.

    I. Health information management professionals respect the rights and dignity of all individuals.

    II. Health information management professionals comply with all laws, regulations, and standards governing the practice of health information management.

    III. Health information management professionals strive for professional excellence through self-assessment and continuing education.

    IV. Health information management professionals truthfully and accurately represent their professional credentials, education, and experience.

    V. Health information management professionals adhere to the vision, mission, and values of the Association.

    VI. Health information management professionals promote and protect the confidentiality and security of health records and health information.

    VII. Health information management professionals strive to provide accurate and timely information.

    VIII. Health information management professionals promote high standards for health information management practice, education, and research.

    IX. Health information management professionals act with integrity and avoid conflicts of interest in the performance of their professional and AHIMA responsibilities.

Health information ethical and professional values are based on obligations to the patient, the healthcare team, and the employer and the interests of the public, oneself, one's peers, and one's professional associations (Harman 1999).

Based on an analysis of the AHIMA Code of Ethics for 1957, 1977, 1988, 1998, and 2004, the themes and values discussed in the following sections were identified (Harman and Mullen 2006).

Obligations to the Patient and the Healthcare Team

With regard to the patient and the healthcare team, the HIM professional is obligated to

- *Protect health, medical, genetic, social, personal, and adoption information:* Clinical information (for example, diagnoses, procedures, pharmaceutical

Figure 13.5.   2011 American Health Information Management Association Code of Ethics—Preamble and Ethical Principles

---

Preamble

The ethical obligations of the health information management (HIM) professional include the safeguarding of privacy and security of health information; disclosure of health information; development, use, and maintenance of health information systems and health information; and ensuring the accessibility and integrity of health information.

Healthcare consumers are increasingly concerned about security and the potential loss of privacy and the inability to control how their personal health information is used and disclosed. Core health information issues include what information should be collected; how the information should be handled, who should have access to the information, under what conditions the information should be disclosed, how the information is retained and when it is no longer needed, and how is it disposed of in a confidential manner. All of the core health information issues are performed in compliance with state and federal regulations, and employer policies and procedures.

Ethical obligations are central to the professional's responsibility, regardless of the employment site or the method of collection, storage, and security of health information. In addition, sensitive information (e.g., genetic, adoption, drug, alcohol, sexual, health, and behavioral information) requires special attention to prevent misuse. In the world of business and interactions with consumers, expertise in the protection of the information is required.

Code of Ethics 2011 Ethical Principles

Ethical Principles: The following ethical principles are based on the core values of the American Health Information Management Association and apply to all AHIMA members and certificants.

A health information management professional shall:

1. *Advocate, uphold, and defend the individual's right to privacy and the doctrine of confidentiality in the use and disclosure of information.*

2. *Put service and the health and welfare of persons before self-interest and conduct oneself in the practice of the profession so as to bring honor to oneself, their peers, and to the health information management profession.*

3. *Preserve, protect, and secure personal health information in any form or medium and hold in the highest regards health information and other information of a confidential nature obtained in an official capacity, taking into account the applicable statutes and regulations.*

4. *Refuse to participate in or conceal unethical practices or procedures and report such practices.*

5. *Advance health information management knowledge and practice through continuing education, research, publications, and presentations.*

6. *Recruit and mentor students, peers, and colleagues to develop and strengthen professional workforce.*

7. *Represent the profession to the public in a positive manner.*

8. *Perform honorably health information management association responsibilities, either appointed or elected, and preserve the confidentiality of any privileged information made known in any official capacity.*

9. *State truthfully and accurately one's credentials, professional education, and experiences.*

10. *Facilitate interdisciplinary collaboration in situations supporting health information practice.*

11. *Respect the inherent dignity and worth of every person.*

Copyright © 2011 by the American Health Information Management Association

dosages, or genetic risk factors) must be protected as well as behavioral information (for example, use of drugs or alcohol, high-risk hobbies, sexual habits). It is increasingly important to protect genetic and social information so that patients will not be vulnerable to the risks of discrimination.

- *Protect confidential information:* This involves ensuring that the information collected and documented in the patient information system is protected by all members of the healthcare team and by anyone with access to the information. This responsibility also includes

protection of verbal communications on behalf of a patient and can involve communication with those in the legal profession, the media, or others who seek patient information.

- *Provide service to those who seek access to patient information:* Individuals who may request access to patient information include healthcare providers; insurance, research, or pharmaceutical companies; government agencies; and employers. Disclosure and redisclosure policies and procedures must be developed and followed. The HIM professional must ensure the honor of the profession before personal advantage and to safeguard the health and welfare of patients before all other interests. He or she also must balance the many competing interests of all the stakeholders who want patient information, avoiding conflicts of interest.

- *Preserve and secure health information:* This includes obligations to maintain and protect the medium that stores the information, such as paper documentation and information stored in EHRs, including the protection of all databases and detailed secondary records and registries.
- *Promote the quality and advancement of healthcare:* As an important member of the healthcare team, the HIM professional provides valuable expertise in the collection of health information that will help providers improve the quality of care they deliver. The HIM professional might need to develop expertise in clinical medicine, pharmacology, biostatistics, and quality improvement methodologies so as to interpret clinical information and support research based on work responsibilities.
- *Function within the scope of responsibility and restrain from passing clinical judgment:* Sometimes healthcare data may indicate a problem with a provider of care, the treatment of a diagnosis, or some other problem. The HIM professional's obligation is to provide the data; the obligation of evaluating the significance of the data rests with those held accountable for the review of the data. The HIM professional should repeatedly, consistently, and accurately report the results of studies, regardless of the volatility of the research outcomes.

Obligations to the Employer

With regard to the employer, the HIM professional is obligated to

- *Demonstrate loyalty to the employer.* The HIM professional can do this by respecting and following the policies, rules, and regulations of employment unless they are illegal or unethical.
- *Protect committee and task force deliberations.* The HIM professional should be as committed to protecting committee conversations and decisions as he or she is to protecting patient information. These can include medical staff and employer committees.
- *Comply with all laws, regulations, and policies that govern the health information system.* The HIM professional should keep up to date with state and federal laws, accrediting and licensing standards, employer policies and procedures, and any other standards that affect the health information system.
- *Recognize both the authority and the power associated with the job responsibility.* The HIM professional is the expert on privacy and confidentiality and must

be present at strategic meetings with clinical providers, administrative staff, and financial and operations management personnel to be sure that HIM expertise is presented and understood. Unethical behaviors would include avoidance of strategic meetings, waiting for the outcomes and decisions made by others, and then complaining about the decisions that were made. The HIM professional cannot remain quiet and let others have the power to decide what information is released, what software is installed, or other important HIM decisions. HIM professionals do have both the power and the authority to say, "This is inappropriate action and it is unethical."

- *Accept compensation only in relationship to work responsibilities.* Increasingly, there are groups or individuals who could benefit by gaining access to patient information and are willing to pay for such information. Access to databases with patient information on certain diagnoses such as AIDS or cancer could be sought by employers, commercial vendors, or others. The HIM professional must avoid the temptation to accept money for disclosing patient information or proprietary vendor secrets. This is especially important in the context of medical identity theft, which is discussed later in this chapter.

Obligations to the Public

With regard to the public interest, the HIM professional is obligated to

- *Advocate change when patterns or system problems are not in the best interests of the patients.* The HIM professional should be a change agent and lead initiatives to change laws, rules, and regulations that do not ensure the integrity of patient information, including the protection of privacy and confidentiality. Moreover, the HIM professional should be proactive about protecting patients, the healthcare team, the organization, the professional association, peers, and himself or herself. State and national policy and legislative advocacy activities support this ethical obligation.
- *Report violations of practice standards to the proper authorities.* The HIM professional should not share information learned at work with family or friends or discuss such information in public places. The HIM professional should report the results of audits to the proper authorities only and bring potential or actual problems to the attention of those individuals responsible for the delivery and assessment of care and services.
- *Promote interdisciplinary cooperation and collaboration.* As an important member of the healthcare team, the HIM professional should work with others to analyze and address health information issues, facilitate conflict resolution, and recognize the expertise and dignity of his or her fellow team members.

Obligations to Self, Peers, and Professional Associations

With regard to self, peers, and professional associations, the HIM professional is obligated to

- *Be honest about degrees, credentials, and work experiences.* The HIM professional should only report an acquired degree (such as a BS or MS) or successfully earned credentials (such as RHIT, RHIA, or CCS). Work experiences must be reported accurately and honestly.
- *Bring honor to oneself, one's peers, and one's profession.* This obligation refers to personal competency and professional behavior. The HIM professional should ensure that peers and colleagues are proud to have him or her on the health information team.
- *Commit to continuing education and lifelong learning.* The HIM professional's education should not stop when he or she has earned a degree or a credential. Rather, the HIM professional should continue to attend educational sessions to keep abreast of changing laws, rules, and regulations that affect the health information system. The HIM professional should be a lifelong learner and contribute to improving the quality of healthcare service delivery. HIM professionals can keep their credentials by meeting the ongoing certification requirements of AHIMA. Maintaining competency through self-improvement is an important directive that ensures the continuance of the profession.
- *Strengthen health information professional membership.* This obligation includes belonging to professional associations, actively participating on committees, making presentations, writing for publications, and encouraging others to seek health information management as a career.
- *Represent the health information profession to the public.* The HIM professional has a responsibility to advocate for the public interest in areas related to the principles and values of HIM practice. For example, HIM professionals serve an important role when advocating for needed legislation to protect privacy and confidentiality, educational manpower funding, or appropriate EHR applications.
- *Promote and participate in health information research.* For example, when problems are discovered with the health information system, the HIM professional should conduct research to clarify the sources and potential solutions.

Ethical Responsibilities of the HIM Professional

In general, the HIM professional's primary responsibilities include those related to designing and implementing a system to ensure the completeness, accuracy, integrity, and timeliness of health information. In support of these responsibilities, the HIM professional is accountable for complying with laws, rules, regulations, standards, and policies from many sources, including the government, accreditation and licensure organizations, and the healthcare facility. Some of the HIM professional's core ethical responsibilities include the following:

- Protecting patient privacy and confidential information (Rinehart-Thompson and Harman 2006)
- Making appropriate decisions regarding the selection and use of clinical diagnostic and procedural codes (Schraffenberger and Scichilone 2006)
- Developing policies and procedures that ensure coding accuracy that supports clinical care and research and meets the requirements for reimbursement while avoiding fraud and abuse violations (Rinehart-Thompson 2006)
- Reporting quality review outcomes honestly and accurately, even when the results might create conflict for an individual or an institution (Spath 2006)
- Ensuring that research and decision support systems are reliable (Johns and Hardin 2006)
- Releasing accurate information for public health purposes for patients with communicable diseases, such as AIDS or venereal disease, and assisting with the complexities of information management in the context of bioterrorism and the threat or reality of global diseases, such as smallpox or avian flu (Neuberger 2006)
- Supporting managed care systems by providing accurate, reliable information about patients and consumers, clinicians, healthcare organizations, and patterns of care, with special care devoted to issues related to access to information (Schick 2006)
- Facilitating the exchange of information for patients, families, and providers of care, especially for those affected by chronic and terminal illness, that ensures patient autonomy and beneficence (Tischler 2006)
- Ensuring that the EHR meets the standards of privacy and security according to HIPAA and other federal and state laws (Hanken and Murphy 2006), the standards of information security (Czirr et al. 2006), and software development (Fenton 2006)
- Ensuring that clinical data repositories, data marts, data warehouses, and EHRs meet the standards of the best practices of health information and database management (Lee et al. 2006)
- Participating in the development of integrated delivery systems so that patients can move across the continuum of care and the right information can be provided to the right people at the right time (Olson and Grant 2006)
- Working in the context of e-health technologies that allow consumers, patients, and caregivers to search for health information and advice, create and maintain

personal health records, and conduct virtual consultations with their care providers (Baur and Deering 2006)

- Ensuring that health information technology systems, including EHRs, electronic prescribing, bedside bar coding, computerized provider order entry (CPOE), and clinical decision support systems reduce errors and improve quality (Bloomrosen 2006)
- Managing the protection of sensitive information, including genetic information (Fuller and Hudson 2006); drug, alcohol, sexual, and behavioral information (Randolph and Rinehart-Thompson 2006); and adoption information (Jones 2006)
- Developing moral awareness and nurturing an ethical environment in the context of managing a health information system (Flite and Laquer 2006)
- Serving as entrepreneur and advocate for patients, the healthcare team, and others who have interests in the health information system (Gardenier 2006; Helbig 2006)
- Working with vendors in the development of business relationships that ensure ethical processes when selecting and communicating with vendors, managing vendor relationships, and dealing with the contract negotiation process (Olenik 2006)

Ethical Issues Related to Medical Identity Theft

According to the Federal Trade Commission (FTC), medical identity theft is one of the fastest growing ethical issues and is an information crime. Identity theft affected almost 10 million victims in 2008 (a 22 percent increase from 2007). It is relatively easy to do, the stakes are high, the financial temptations are huge, it is difficult to detect, and there are virtually no protections for the patient or providers who are victimized. The HIM professional must be familiar with what medical identity theft is, who commits the crime, what protections can be put into place, and what HIM advocacy roles are needed (AHIMA e-HIM Workgroup on Medical Identity Theft 2008; Nichols et al. 2008).

Medical identity theft occurs when someone uses a person's name and sometimes other parts of that person's identity—such as insurance information or Social Security number—without the victim's knowledge or consent to obtain medical services or goods, or when someone uses the person's identity to obtain money by falsifying claims for medical services and falsifying Medicare records to support those claims (World Privacy Forum 2006b, 16).

Medical identity theft can be committed by family, friends, or acquaintances. It can also be committed by strangers who steal someone's identity in order to obtain medical care, services, or equipment, either because they do not have access to medical care or their insurance does not cover the needed services. Medical identity theft creates an ethical dilemma for the healthcare system because

those involved can be working within the healthcare delivery system, including doctors, nurses, administrative staff, and health information and billing employees. The World Privacy Forum (2006b, 14) notes that

All levels of the medical system may be involved in medical identity theft. Doctors, clinics, billing specialists, nurses and other members of the medical profession have taken part in this crime, as have criminals who work in administrative positions inside the healthcare system to collect information and to carry out their crimes.

There was one case in California in which it was determined that medical record and billing employees had copied the identity information for as little as $100 (FTC 2000). Those who commit the crime can earn money by using the patient information fraudulently. Medical information systems have multiple access points across the continuum of the healthcare system, making it almost impossible to detect and correct fraud. Medical identify theft deserves the attention of the HIM professional because the central problem is falsification of medical documentation that could adversely affect patient safety. Inaccurate information, such as an incorrect blood type or inaccurate documentation of prescriptions can kill patients (World Privacy Forum 2006b; Weaver 2000; Office of Inspector General 2005; *United States v. Sample* 2000). Also, the "real" patients can be denied needed equipment (wheelchairs or walkers and the like) because their records show that they have already received the equipment, when, in fact, the fraudulent user of their health information received the equipment. Increasingly, physicians are becoming victims of this crime. Their name and license numbers stolen, and their signatures are forged for writing prescriptions and documentation that will help criminals bill for services never rendered to patients.

The national health information network (NHIN) and EHRs could exacerbate the ease of committing this crime. Electronic systems with multiple centralized and decentralized databases could facilitate both the commission and hiding of this crime. The government has passed "red flag rules" that require healthcare organizations to shelter patients from identity theft, which went into effect August 1, 2010. Healthcare facilities will need to identify patterns, practices, and activities that could indicate identity theft, such as suspicious documents (altered or potentially forged), photographs or identification data that do not match, returned mail complaints, or other similar occurrence (http://www.ftc.gov).

HIPAA provides some modicum of protection, but it cannot begin to truly protect patient information or patients from being harmed. The problem becomes almost unsolvable in the context of secondary releases of false information for insurance, the increasing number of integrated systems, and the development of medical clearinghouses. HIM professionals are in a strong position to be advocates on behalf of patients who are victimized by this crime. In addition, it places an obligation on the profession to be diligent in hiring practices, especially with the employees who report directly to HIM professionals. Once hired, the employees must have ongoing educational sessions on the importance of ethical behavior.

The Patient's Perspective

Many patients have been victimized by medical identity theft, and the overwhelming reality is that there are few who can assist them in resolving the problem, as opposed to those who are victimized by financial identity theft. There are inadequate resources and knowledge in the private sector (police departments, insurance companies, bankers, and the like) as well as the lack of laws specific to medical identity theft. There have been preliminary protective and corrective recommendations for patients that have been initiated by the Federal Trade Commission (2005) and the Government Accountability Office (2005).

The HIM Professional's Perspective

Because of the unique aspects of this crime, HIM professionals must be vigilant in the case of medical identity theft and work with the "real" patient to confirm and correct inaccurate information. If there is no previous medical record, there must be a way to identify the record as being fraudulent and refuse further release of the false information. The HIM professional must be an advocate for the patient and find the time, resources, and expertise to substantiate valid identification. The HIM professional must seek assistance in this process, if necessary, rather than just sending the patient away. HIM professionals can exacerbate the problem by refusing to work with the "real" patient. Legal counsel should be sought.

Once information is in a patient's medical record, it is difficult to amend or remove that information. HIM professionals cannot ignore the false documentation in the paper medical records and electronic information systems. Duplicating these false entries in multiple databases as a result of secondary data uses will increase the problem. The Code of Ethics requires attestation as to the accuracy and validity of the data.

Patients need to be able to access and amend their medical records if fraud has occurred. As patients maintain their own personal health record (PHR), they will become more aware of the fraud. They are in the best position to know that the documentation belongs to someone else, based on a review of medical or financial reports (AHIMA n.d.; World Privacy Forum 2006a).

Given this, HIM professionals should work toward the solution that all HIM systems should track all disclosures, even if not required by HIPAA, and there should be guaranteed protection of all information. In addition, audit trails should be developed that identify both internal and external disclosures to prevent fraud, rather than allowing the EHR system to exacerbate the problem (Sparrow 2000).

The health information system is extremely complex. Data can be entered manually, electronically, through PDAs (personal digital assistants), through wireless systems, or from laptops. Information systems cross geographical boundaries and utilize many different software and hardware applications for patient care and research. The AHIMA Code of Ethics requires the protection of information across this continuum. The adage a few years ago was "follow the money." Today, the mantra must be "follow the information" (AHIMA e-Learning 2012).

What can HIM professionals do as part of advocacy roles? They can:

- Facilitate the patient's ability to review and correct errors in their medical records (not just the entries with which they disagree but those that are due to fraud and do not belong to their medical or treatment history). This information might also be in the pharmaceutical information system or within the insurance agency database.
- Prevent discrimination. Not only can medical errors affecting patient safety occur with medical identity theft, but there can also be discrimination in the life and health insurance systems. Do not obstruct patients' ability to review their records. Pay attention to their pleas if they think that they are victims of medical identity theft, make sure that patients have the right to amend their documentation, and ensure systems are in place that will facilitate this process.
- Reconsider the importance of analysis. The entire medical record used to be analyzed for accuracy, and the medical record analyst could learn to identify falsification of information. Now, analysis often is limited to discharge summaries, operative reports, and other critical documents. Does the organization have systems in place, within the context of the EHR system, that will prevent medical identity theft?
- Consider advocacy to amend the HIPAA rules and regulations related to the accounting of disclosures to include problems related to internal participants.
- Participate in HIM research studies that will help identify occurrences and sources of medical identity theft. Build interdisciplinary collaborative teams to conduct this research, including healthcare providers; HIM professionals; privacy and security experts; legal representatives (both prosecution and defense); ethicists; HIPAA, identify theft, and fraud experts; and patients who have been victimized.
- Conduct needed risk assessments as the NHIN becomes more of a reality—the EHR, can make this crime easier. Document and quantify this problem. Improper access to information and disclosures of false information could increase in the future as a result of the EHR.
- Design systems that can assess employees' integrity and accountability. Make sure the healthcare team and employees who work on behalf of patients respect the importance and sacredness of the information in a

patient's medical record. Give them an understanding of the importance of ethics so that they will avoid the temptation of taking money for the information in the system. Ensure that there are no pressures on employees that will tempt them to participate in the fraud.

- Design educational programs to ensure that colleagues understand and value the HIM Code of Ethics, which sets forth values and ethical principles and offers ethical guidelines to which professionals aspire and by which their actions can be judged. A code is important in helping guide the decision-making process and can be referenced by individuals, agencies, organizations, and bodies (such as licensing and regulatory boards, insurance providers, courts of law, agency boards of directors, government agencies, and other professional groups), among others (AHIMA 2011).

- Consider establishing policies so that patients who are victims of medical identity fraud do not have to pay for the costs of duplicating their files. In 2006, an AHIMA survey found that 63 percent of providers charge patients for copies, and these costs can be up to $5 per page (although $1 is more common) (AHIMA 2006). Increasingly, healthcare facilities have abandoned the practice of charging patients for copies of their medical information, based on a rationale that the information belongs to them and providing copies is an important customer service.

When HIM professionals think about identity, they typically think about the person and the story in an individual medical record. Emerging technologies are changing perceptions of a person's identity—the sum of our genetic and health information. HIM professionals are being challenged to understand and deal with issues that they have never faced before, and they must stay abreast of new and evolving issues that deal with identity. HIM professionals have ethical obligations to prevent problems with medical identity theft and to report those who participate in this crime. See chapter 12 for more detail on medical identity theft and red flags.

Ethical Issues Related to Documentation and Privacy

Just a few decades ago, only a few people created documentation in patient health records, and still fewer wanted access to patient information after the episode of care was completed. In today's healthcare system, many providers document their decision-making process and patient outcomes in the health information system, and many more people want access to that information. The HIM professional plays a critical role in developing policies and procedures to ensure the integrity of patient information, including appropriate and authorized access.

In addition to writing policies and procedures to ensure compliance with federal and state laws, accrediting and licensing agencies, and the bylaws of the healthcare facility, the HIM professional can serve many functions that support the integrity of data and the protection of privacy. The HIM professional can design and deliver educational sessions to the healthcare team to make them aware of the documentation and access rules and regulations. Sometimes educational sessions address the issue of avoiding participation in fraudulent or retrospective documentation practices. Retrospective documentation practices are those where healthcare providers add documentation after care has been given for the purpose of increasing reimbursement or avoiding a medical legal action.

Unacceptable documentation practices include backdating progress notes or other documentation in the patient's record and changing the documentation to reflect the known outcomes of care (versus what was done at the time of the actual care). It is the HIM professional's responsibility to work with others to ensure that patient documentation is accurate, timely, and created by authorized parties. The professional Code of Ethics requires the HIM professional to ensure accurate and timely documentation. Clinical documentation is essential to the expertise of HIM professionals. Increasingly, there are ethical issues that surface as a result of documentation, such as issues related to coding, reporting of data, and inappropriate documentation and billing practices. AHIMA passed the Ethical Standards for Clinical Documentation Improvement (CDI) Professionals (2010). This ethical code is based on the principles and framework of the AHIMA Code of Ethics (2011). The complete set of CDI ethical standards is presented in Appendix B.

Ethical Issues Related to Release of Information

Three primary ethical problems are pertinent to the release of information (ROI):

- Violations of the need-to-know principle
- Misuse of blanket authorizations
- Violations of privacy that occur as a result of secondary release of information procedures

In the past, the standard for ROI was the need to know. If an insurance company had a patient request to pay for surgery, the request was sent to the healthcare facility and the HIM professional carefully examined it for legitimacy. He or she would

- Compare the patient's signature to the one collected upon admission to the facility
- Check the date to ensure that the request was dated after the occurrence so that the patient was aware of what was being authorized and released
- Verify the insurance company as the one belonging to the patient
- Review the request for what was wanted and whether the requestor was entitled to the information

The HIM professional then reviewed the documentation and provided the information requested. For example, the admission and discharge dates, the diagnoses of cholecystitis and cholelithiasis, and the surgical procedure of cholecystectomy were provided to the insurance company so that the bill could be paid.

Today, the process of abstracting needed information is virtually nonexistent, except for disability cases, and documentation is copied above and beyond the criterion of the **need-to-know principle.** For example, in response to the request to verify an admission for a cholecystectomy, the history and physical, the operative report, the discharge summary, and the laboratory report could be copied. That documentation could reveal social habits, genetic risks, and family history of disease that have nothing to do with the surgery. Patient privacy could be violated as a result of the release of the information through subsequent discrimination.

Another common ethical problem is misuse of **blanket authorizations.** Patients often sign a blanket authorization, which authorizes the release of information from that point forward, without understanding the implications. The requestor of the information then could use the authorization to receive health information for many years. The problem with the use of blanket authorizations is that there is no way for the patient to know that the information is being accessed. Patients cannot authorize the release of information in 2003 for diagnoses or care that has not yet been provided. For example, by 2011, the patient might have AIDS or cancer and might not want this information released.

A third problem is **secondary release of information** to others by the authorized recipient to an unauthorized party. This problem has increased in frequency in the context of EHR systems. A legitimate request might be processed to pay for an insurance claim, but adequate safety measures and protections may not be in place for the information after it has been released. The initial requestor could then forward the information to others without patient authorization. The HIM professional cannot merely think about ROI within the context of the single request. The responsibility to "follow the information beyond the walls of the healthcare facility" is much more serious today than it was a few years ago. Does the HIM professional know who gains access to the information after it is released to an authorized requestor? If not, he or she may be contributing to the violations of patient privacy and of discrimination by employers or insurance companies based on the information that was released.

Patients have increasingly expressed concerns about the use of blanket authorizations and secondary ROI by the initial requestor or receiving party. They fear that more information is being given out than is necessary and that they do not know about the many people and agencies that are gaining access to this information.

HIPAA has been designed to address several issues related to patient privacy, including a return to the need-to-know principle. The HIM professional needs to participate in the development of electronic systems that can replicate the original human decisions regarding ROI to release what is needed but not more. Although it is easier to just photocopy the information, the HIM professional needs to carefully consider the implications of doing this within the context of patient privacy. This situation has created an opportunity for HIM professionals to participate with other HIM professionals in efforts to correct these problems.

Because the HIM professional works in many employment sites throughout the healthcare delivery system, the ethical obligations extend into a variety of areas, as noted previously. In fulfilling the responsibilities of the position, the HIM professional must apply ethical values when making decisions wherever he or she is positioned within the organization.

Check Your Understanding 13.1

1. The term that means the HIM professional applies rules fairly and consistently is:

   A. Nonmaleficence
   B. Beneficence
   C. Justice
   D. Moral values

2. An HIM professional's ethical obligations:

   A. Apply regardless of employment site
   B. Are limited to the employer
   C. Apply to only the patient
   D. Are limited to the employer and patient

3. Which of the following is the concept of the right of an individual to be left alone?

   A. Privacy
   B. Bioethics
   C. Security
   D. Confidentiality

4. An individual stole and used another person's insurance information to obtain medical care. This action would be considered:

   A. Nonmaleficence
   B. Fraud and abuse
   C. Medical identify theft
   D. Beneficence

5. Which of the following threatens the need-to-know principle?

   A. Backdating progress notes
   B. Blanket authorizations
   C. HIPAA regulations
   D. Informed consent

Instructions: Match the HIM professional's obligations to the following groups with the professional values expressed in AHIMA's Code of Ethics.

   A. Patient and healthcare team
   B. Employer

C. Public interest

D. Oneself, one's peers, and professional associations

_____6. Accept compensation only in relationship to responsibilities

_____7. Advocate change

_____8. Preserve and secure health information

_____9. Be honest

____10. Commit to continuing education and lifelong learning

Ethical Decision-Making Matrix

HIM professionals must factor several criteria into their decision making, as illustrated in figure 13.6. These include, but are not limited to

- *Cost:* Can the facility and the health information system afford the improvement in the system?
- *Technological feasibility:* Will the technological application provide accurate and reliable information for the decision-making process?
- *Federal and state laws:* Are there federal or state laws that must be considered before a change is made in the system?
- *Medical staff bylaws:* Are there rules or regulations unique to the facility that require or prohibit an action?
- *Accreditation and licensing standards:* Which agencies have standards that are important to the decision being made? Do the standards allow or prohibit a certain action?
- *Employer policies, rules, or regulations:* Does the facility have policies, rules, or regulations that require or prohibit a decision?

Although these criteria must be assessed in the decision-making process, they cannot be used alone. Virtually every decision the HIM professional makes also must be based on ethical principles and professional values.

Ethicists provide assistance in this process. Glover (2006, 35, 38, 50) has proposed a seven-step process to guide ethical decision making. When faced with an ethical issue, the HIM professional should ask and answer all of the following questions. The questions represent the steps in the ethical decision-making process.

1. What is the ethical question?
2. What facts do you know, and what do you need to find out?
3. Who are the different stakeholders, what values are at stake, and what are the shared and different obligations and interests of each of the stakeholders?
4. What options for action do you have?
5. What decision should you make, and what core HIM values are at stake?
6. What justifies the choice, and what are the values-based reasons to support the decision? What choice or choices cannot be justified?
7. What prevention options can be put into place so that this issue will not come up again?

When a decision must be made about an issue and only one choice is identified, the decision most likely will be based on an individual's narrow moral perspective of right or wrong. If it is an ethical problem, the decision makers must take into account the perspectives of competing stakeholders and their values. Decisions made without this model will not benefit from an ethical decision-making process that considers multiple options.

Figure 13.6.   Ethical decision-making matrix

ETHICAL PROBLEM		
Steps	**Information**	
1. What is the question?		
2. What are the facts?	**KNOWN**	**TO BE GATHERED**
3. What are the values? Examine the shared and competing values, obligations, and interests in order to fully understand the complexity of the ethical problem(s).	**Patient:** **HIM Professional:** **Healthcare professionals:** **Administrators:** **Society:** **Other, as appropriate:**	
4. What are my options?		
5. What should I do?		
6. What justifies my choice?	*JUSTIFIED*	*NOT JUSTIFIED*
7. What can I do to prevent this ethical problem?		

Source: Harman 2006.

1. Using A, B, C, and so on, rearrange the steps of the ethical decision-making process in the correct order.

   ___ What decisions should you make, and what core HIM values are at stake?

   ___ What facts do you know, and what do you need to find out?

   ___ What options for action do you have?

   ___ What is the ethical question?

   ___ What justifies the choice, and what are the values-based reasons to support the decision, based on values? What choice(s) cannot be justified?

   ___ What prevention options can be put into place so that this issue will not happen again?

   ___ Who are the different stakeholders, what values are at stake, and what are the different obligations and interests of each of the stakeholders?

Important Health Information Ethical Problems

Several problems face HIM professionals in today's complex world or work, including issues related to the use of information; electronic health information systems; the management of sensitive health information; process and strategies for decision making; and the HIM roles as manager, entrepreneur, and advocate. The business relationships with vendors can also create ethical tensions. There are issues raised because of the uses of information, including clinical code selection and use, quality review, research and decision support, public health, managed care, and clinical care (Harman 2006).

Ethical Issues Related to Coding

In the past, coding was done almost exclusively for clinical studies and quality assurance review processes. Although codes were provided for reimbursement purposes, the healthcare facility was reimbursed on the basis of usual, customary, and reasonable costs. The codes that were assigned became the basis of retrieval for clinical studies, quality reviews, and the reimbursement system. After the codes became the basis for reimbursement, there were inherent incentives to code so that the greatest amount of reimbursement could be acquired. This placed the importance of accurate coding at the forefront of the ethical issues facing HIM professionals.

Ethical problems have risen in the past few years as a result of the direct linkage between coding and payments for care. Increased pressure has been put on HIM professionals who are coding to transmit inaccurate information, creating problems that are legal and ethical in nature. Problems

include pressure to code inappropriate levels of service, discovering misrepresentation in physician documentation, miscoding to avoid conflicts, discovering miscoding by other staff, lacking the tools and educational background to code accurately, and being required by employers to engage in negligent coding practices (Schraffenberger and Scichilone 2006). In response to these issues, AHIMA passed standards that specifically address coding issues. The AHIMA Standards of Ethical Coding are presented in Appendix B.

Failure to heed the complex rules of coding for reimbursement can lead to problems with compliance and with fraud and abuse for the HIM professional. If the HIM professional fails to establish adequate monitoring systems for accurate code assignment or submits a false claim, the consequences could include penalties such as fees and prison. The HIM professional must know the laws and the penalties for failure to follow the laws and have the expertise to develop preventative programs to ensure that submission of the false claim does not happen. Fraud and abuse problems include documentation that does not justify the billed procedure, acceptance of money for information, fraudulent retrospective documentation on the part of the provider to avoid suspension, and code assignment without physician documentation. An important role for the HIM professional is that of compliance officer (Rinehart-Thompson 2006).

Ethical Issues Related to Quality Management, Decision Support, Public Health, Managed Care, and Clinical Care

The pressures to conceal information that was discovered as an outcome of quality reporting systems and that could be potentially harmful to an employer, and problems with patient safety require constant diligence and the courage to repeatedly report the truth. Many factors contribute to the ethical problems faced by quality management professionals, including the rising cost of healthcare, limited resources, and concerns with patient safety. Some of the common quality outcome problems include (Spath 2006):

- Inaccurate performance data that are inappropriately shared with the public
- Negative care outcomes, such as infections, that occurs in the course of providing home healthcare
- Failure to check a physician's licensure status
- Incomplete health records hidden in preparation for accreditation or licensure surveys
- Patterns of inappropriate healthcare

Research and decision support responsibilities include ensuring data integrity and confidentiality, ensuring compliance with human subject research protocols, and maintaining and enhancing professional competence (Johns and Hardin 2006).

Career opportunities for the HIM professional are growing in public health systems. Careers in this area require an understanding of the government's role in the collection and use of health information. The government's responsibility to protect the health of the public sometimes competes with the need to protect patient privacy, such as in the case of reporting HIV status. State and local mandatory reporting requirements exist for certain conditions, including infectious and communicable diseases. The government needs this information to monitor, investigate, and implement interventions when necessary. Sometimes problems arise when the public's right to know or duty to one's employer conflicts with patient privacy (Neuberger 2006). The HIM professional can provide invaluable assistance with public health initiatives that will contribute to environmental and personal health. This role requires constant advocacy so that the interests of both the public and the individual patient can be served. New threats of bioterrorism and global infections (such as anthrax, SARS, H1N1, or avian flu) pose new ethical dilemmas in the management of health information. There will need to be a balance between protecting privacy of those injured and providing information to the government and healthcare professionals so that the medical crisis can be resolved.

There are many important ethical issues faced by the HIM professional working on behalf of managed care organizations. Problems arise if high-quality information is not provided so that commitments to patients, clinicians, and communities cannot be met. Access to information is key to the problems faced by the HIM professional as he or she helps with the organization's strategies regarding pricing, access to providers, and quality of care. Job responsibilities in this work context include providing information about provider practices, providing patient clinical and demographic information, and establishing policies and procedures that provide for patient privacy (Schick 2006).

There are an increasing number of patients who will require information in order to make difficult end-of-life decisions. Problems dealing with aging, frailty, autonomy of those near death, physician bias and equity, treatment choices, treatment goals and beneficence, advance care planning, palliative care, and managing pain are a few of the difficult decisions that must be made, and the availability of accurate information requires ethical decision making (Tischler 2006).

Ethical Issues Related to Sensitive Health Information

All health information must be protected, but additional ethical issues have emerged around the release of sensitive information such as genetic, drug and alcohol, and psychiatric; communicable disease; and adoption information. At least two levels of genetic information can be reported in an information system: presence of a disease, such as cystic fibrosis, and presence of a risk of disease, such as a genetic risk for breast cancer. Various state laws govern the use and release of genetic information, and the HIM professional must be aware

of them. In recent years, there have been growing concerns about discrimination in employment and insurance based on the misuse of genetic information (Fuller and Hudson 2006).

According to Fuller and Hudson (2006, 434), the HIM professional must be aware of the following issues related to genetic information:

1. Genetic research and testing can give researchers, clinicians, and patients a means to prevent, treat, or screen for a disease. Often, however, individuals are reluctant to participate in genetic research and testing because they believe they cannot be sure of the privacy of the genetic information that will be obtained from them and placed in their medical records or in research records.

2. Insurers and employers may seek genetic information to identify at-risk individuals and deny them employment or insurance coverage, fire them, or raise their insurance premiums. Genetic information may also be sought in custody battles or in cases of third-party liability. Even when this information is not used to discriminate, individuals may be concerned about its disclosure because of its possibility of causing psychosocial harm, such as harm to family relationships.

3. It is difficult to provide special protections for genetic information as a category because it cannot be clearly separated from other medical information. Therefore, the best way to protect genetic information is to strengthen privacy and confidentiality protections for medical information in general and to enact antidiscrimination legislation.

4. The HIPAA Privacy Rule provides a basic level of privacy and confidentiality protection for protected health information. The Privacy Rule does not preempt state laws (including genetic antidiscrimination laws) that offer a higher level of privacy protection.

5. The generation of experimental data by a research protocol is not specifically addressed by most state laws.

6. HIM professionals have the responsibility to ensure that their practices are guided by state and federal laws and regulations to protect genetic information and by the ethical imperative to protect the privacy and confidentiality of patients.

The Genetic Information Nondiscrimination Act was passed in 2008 (HHS 2008). This took many years to approve, and AHIMA worked extensively to facilitate passage of this important legislation. Other federal and state laws will need to be passed in order for patients to be fully protected in the context of genetic information, and this is an important first step.

Federal and state laws also govern the use of behavioral health information and special concerns with its use. The HIM professional must respond to the government, the police, and other agencies that seek drug, alcohol, sexual, or other behavioral information (Randolph and Rinehart-Thompson 2006). The inappropriate release of information can have serious discriminatory consequences, such as in the following scenarios:

- The police officer presents an arrest warrant to a behavioral health facility. Do you confirm that the patient has been treated? What are the implications for patient privacy if you do?
- A patient with schizophrenia and assaultive behavior is about to be released from a healthcare facility. Do you have a responsibility to inform the patient's girl-friend, who has been assaulted in the past? What are your obligations to protect the privacy of the patient being released?

The ROI dealing with substance abuse, sexually trans-mitted diseases, and mental health require extra caution on the part of the HIM professional when developing release policies and procedures. There are often competing inter-ests between public safety and patient privacy. How does one deal with law enforcement officials within this context? Federal and state legislation can provide some guidance, but often additional legal counsel must be sought.

The release of adoption information is another example of an issue in which laws are necessary, but insufficient, for solving the problems. Decisions cannot be made merely by following the legal rules. More and more often, access to adoption information is being requested by adopted children seeking their biological parents, and vice versa. Biological parents often look for children who could be organ donors or for other assistance. This issue reflects the complexities of releasing genetic and behavioral information because,

increasingly, "self" is defined within genetic parameters and biological heritage. Access to adoption information raises the larger issue of familial access to information, regardless of adoptive status. If biological children can gain access to health information for their biological parent(s), why can't all children gain access to familial information (Jones 2006)? HIM professionals must be alert to these special needs and refrain from processing requests for adoption information without carefully considering the risks for violations of patient privacy, discrimination, or inappropriate access.

Ethical Issues Related to Research

There are many past and present problems with research and ethics. Human subjects have been mistreated, misin-formed, and harmed in recent years, even though there are ethical codes, national and international agreements, and agencies that review research proposals with a focus of pro-tecting research participants. These include the Nuremberg Code, the Helsinki Agreement (also known as the Declara-tion of Helsinki), the National Research Act of 1974 (Public Law 93-348), the Belmont Report, bioethics commissions, HIPAA, and IRB processes (Harman and Nielsen 2008, 341).

The primary ethical principles that are engaged in research include respect for autonomy (self-determination); benefi-cence (promoting good); nonmaleficence (doing no harm); and justice (fairness) (Beauchamp and Childress 2001). The respect for autonomy requires an ability of the participant to understand and authorize the research through informed con-sent; beneficence means that benefit is possible; nonmalefi-cence means that patients will not be intentionally harmed; and justice requires fairness in the enrollment of participants (Harman and Nielsen 2008, 337). Table 13.1 highlights ethi-cal issues with vulnerable populations and research projects.

As noted in table 13.1, mistreatment of vulnerable popu-lations has happened too often. These populations include

Table 13.1.   Ethical issues with vulnerable populations and research projects

Vulnerable populations	
Vulnerable Populations	Issues to Consider Regarding Consent and How Attributes of the Vulnerable Population Manifest Themselves in the Consent Process
Children	Protected class of persons who cannot voluntarily consent without parental consent. Children may sign assent form depending on age; See Subpart D of Title 45, Part 46 of the Code of Federal Regulations contain the federal policy on research that involves children: http://www.hhs.gov/ohrp/humansubjects/guidance/45cfr46.htm#subpartd
Cognitively Impaired Persons	Cognitive skills may vary on a day-to-day basis and therefore the ability to understand consent form and ongoing participation may change from week to week; ability to understand consent form may be permanently impaired; judgment and reasoning affected. Assessment must occur so that the investigator knows the condition of each participant. Sometimes assessment must occur each time subject is seen as part of the study. Sometimes a legally authorized surrogate is utilized when research studies include persons with cognitive impairment.
Comatose Persons	Cannot give consent; need appropriate and legally authorized surrogate. Some research with comatose persons could be considered emergency research. See the OHRP guidance from 1996 on this topic: http://www.hhs.gov/ohrp/humansubjects/guidance/hsdc97-01.htm

Vulnerable populations	
Vulnerable Populations	**Issues to Consider Regarding Consent and How Attributes of the Vulnerable Population Manifest Themselves in the Consent Process**
Drug Addicts	Involved in illegal activities; Certificate of Confidentiality should be considered. Information on Certificates of Confidentiality can be found at: http://grants.nih.gov/grants/policy/coc/

"Certificates of Confidentiality are issued by the National Institutes of Health (NIH) to protect identifiable research information from forced disclosure. They allow the investigator and others who have access to research records to refuse to disclose identifying information on research participants in any civil, criminal, administrative, legislative, or other proceeding, whether at the federal, state, or local level." |
Economically Disadvantaged Persons	May agree to be involved in a study only for free medical care or for payment made for participation when it may not be in the best interests of the individual.
Elderly Persons	Cognition levels may vary during the course of the study. Is informed consent still valid throughout the research study?
Employees	May feel coerced by employer to participate. Sometimes lab staff are asked to be "normal subjects." There must not be any requirements of employment that coerce employees to participate if they don't want to.
Hearing-Impaired Persons	If a deaf person wishes to enroll in a study, how will the investigator make sure the consent process has been complete? It is not enough to have the consent form for the subject to read. How will questions be handled? How will future visits be handled? Does someone on the study staff know sign language? Note: The Deaf Pride movement may clash with the IRBs definitions of the hearing impaired and their ability to participate in research studies.
Institutionalized Persons	May not understand consent form, may be cognitively impaired, may not have autonomy, and may not be able to exercise free will (voluntariness).
Low Literacy Persons	May not understand the consent form.
Minorities	Not all minorities are considered vulnerable populations. The context of the study, why minorities are included, whether they are the targeted focus of the study are factors that must be considered and may impact informed consent.
Non-English speaking Persons	Even though consent forms must be translated into the native language, without research staff that are fluent in the language, there is difficulty ascertaining whether non-English speaking participants truly understand their study involvement. How are participants informed, if they are illiterate in their native language?
Persons Involved in Illegal Activities	Could include: computer hackers, drug addicts, prostitutes, illegal immigrants, and other types of illegal activities. Collecting data from persons who are involved in illegal activities can be challenging. A foremost consideration must be that by signing a consent form, the subject is, in effect, agreeing to participate in a study about their illegal activities. Therefore the act of protecting subjects, making sure they understand their rights and explaining the study, and executing legally authorized consent may lead to disclosure and place the subject in more harm than non-participation would. Investigators need to carefully weigh what problems may be encountered if subjects are required to sign consent forms. It may be appropriate to ask for a waiver of written consent and employ the use of an information sheet for this type of research. A Certificate of Confidentiality may also be appropriate. See "Drug Addicts" for additional information on COC.
Pregnant Women, Fetuses, Neonates, In-Vitro	In some instances, pregnant women must be included as would any other population; in other instances special protections for pregnant woman must be in place. Investigators who plan to use pregnant women, human fetuses, and neonates in research should be familiar with the government regulations described in 45 CFR 46, Subpart B. http://www.hhs.gov/ohrp/humansubjects/guidance/45cfr46.htm#subpartb

There are specific requirements for the wording in the consent form when using pregnant women in research. Problems with ethical research involving this population occur in "third world research"—promises of pregnancy care, if participant in research. |
| Prisoners | Do not have free will as they are incarcerated. Prisoners may feel coerced into participating because they think the authorities may grant them special privileges. May agree to participate because they think it will reduce their sentence, earn favors with guards; See Subpart C of Title 45, Part 46 of the Code of Federal Regulations containing the federal policy on research that involves prisoners: http://www.hhs.gov/ohrp/humansubjects/guidance/45cfr46.htm#subpartc |
| Students (over the age of 18) | May feel coerced because they think their grade may be affected if they don't agree to participate. The professor is always in power position over the student. Usually have another option for participation. Grade cannot be affected by non-participation. |

Note: Vulnerable populations cannot be studied under an exemption certification. Additional current ethical violations are online from the Alliance for Human Research Protection (AHRP) (2007).

Source: Harman, L.B. and Nielsen, C.S. 2008. Research and ethics. In Layman, E. and V. Watzlaf, eds. *Health informatics research methods: Principles and practice*. Chicago: AHIMA, 342.

children and persons who are cognitively impaired, comatose, drug addicts, economically disadvantaged, elderly, institutionalized, non-English-speaking employees, low-literacy persons, minorities, or involved in illegal activities. Other groups include pregnant women, fetuses, neonates, and in-vitro; prisoners; and students (over the age of 18) (Harman and Nielsen 2008). In 2010, the US government formally apologized for medical research on syphilis that was conducted from 1946 to 1948 because doctors had infected soldiers, prostitutes, prisoners, and mental patients with syphilis without informed consent (McGreal 2010).

HIM professionals must be cautious when reviewing research protocols and take patient safety and protection seriously, so that unethical problems do not occur.

Ethical Issues Related to Electronic Health Record Systems

With a paper-based health record, access issues were relatively simple. Only one person at a time could access the information, and it was extremely difficult to collect and use data of an aggregate nature. With electronic systems, many requestors are allowed multiple, simultaneous access, and it is relatively easy to share information across a continuum of care and with computerized systems well outside the boundaries of any individual care site. The advent of the electronic information system has presented complex challenges with regard to record integrity and information security, integrated linkage of information systems across a continuum of care, software development and implementation, and the protection of information in e-health systems. It is imperative for HIM professionals be a part of the implementation team in order to advise their facilities on state and federal regulations regarding privacy/security so that these core principles are built into the system itself. At a very minimum, the HIM professional should ensure that the issues have been addressed by the team implementing the EHR system.

In both the public and private sectoris, e-HIM affords information exchange that necessitates active participation on the part of HIM professionals. There are many ethical challenges, including developing and maintaining information and systems security, exchanging information within and across jurisdictions, executing technical and clinical services contracts, handling release of information, implementing and managing telehealth applications, maintaining and documenting compliance with HIPAA and state privacy rules, and maintaining the legal electronic health record (Bloomrosen 2006).

As EHR systems were developed and healthcare facilities began to link various health information systems, the temptation increased to sacrifice privacy and data integrity for the sake of business efficiency and timely access to information. There is an exponential increase in the risk to privacy and the protection of confidential information

(Hanken and Murphy 2006). The HIM professional must do a thorough systems analysis of the independent systems and ensure that the merged systems meet the criteria of data integrity, information security, and the ethical use of the information.

Information security carries additional burdens of ethical decision making. Many requestors such as insurance companies, government agencies, managed care organizations, and employers need health information to do their jobs. Unauthorized access to patient information becomes a constant challenge, given the need to balance the responsibility to protect information with giving others access to information within the context of job responsibilities. Internal requestors include, but are not limited to, patients, providers of care, financial agencies, and administrative and clinical personnel such as quality or risk management professionals. External stakeholders include other healthcare facilities, research institutes, accrediting and licensing agencies, and fiscal intermediaries (Czirr et al. 2006). The HIM professional must develop a comprehensive information security policy, including detailed audit trails of access and actions. Moreover, the policy must be monitored with consequences for violations. Increasingly, HIM professionals are being designated as the information security officers within a healthcare facility or healthcare system.

Development and implementation of software systems are inherently interdisciplinary in nature, and the process requires collaboration and conflict resolution. The physicians, the HIM professional, the information technology experts, and administrative personnel often have competing interests. The HIM professional is often in the position of carefully delineating the details of competing interests so that appropriate decisions can be made. This role of being able to see the systems' implications within the context of protecting privacy is invaluable (Fenton 2006). The HIM professional's role as interdisciplinary facilitator is crucial, which is why educational sessions on organizational development, team building, and conflict resolution are often key components of the HIM professional's continuing education program.

The expertise of the HIM professional includes data resource management because EHR systems generate data repositories and huge amounts of health information of interest to many people. A primary focus of the HIPAA legislation is to ensure that systems are developed that protect privacy, threats of violations of information integrity, and unauthorized access. Data resource managers must have both HIM technical expertise and information technology expertise so that they can design and monitor systems that ensure data security and patient privacy. These functions are accomplished through the use of many decision-making tools, including databases, clinical data repositories, and data-mining tools, among others. The primary ethical dilemma involves balancing the competing interests of access and appropriate use of information (Lee et al. 2006).

EHR systems facilitated the capacity for developing integrated delivery systems across a continuum of care. HIM systems that relied on paper-based systems could only transmit information from one site of care to another through copying procedures or faxing. Now, information can follow the patient and be instantly and simultaneously shared and made available as needed. The integrated electronic systems require HIM professional diligence to ensure protection of information and access to only those who have a need to know. Information management policies, rules, and procedures for individual healthcare entities must be compatible with those of other facilities, and often the issues of competing interests can create major ethical conflicts as to the appropriate action.

The master patient index presents a major problem because there is often no consistency among facilities in terms of how and what information is collected. If the information is to follow the patient, the individual systems must be accurate and compatible. Data quality issues include accuracy, comprehensiveness, consistency, currency, granularity, precision, relevancy, and timeliness (AHIMA 1998). Negotiation and problem-solving skills are an inherent requirement for the HIM professional working in an integrated delivery system (Olson and Grant 2006). The HIM professional must lead the organization in addressing data quality issues associated with implementing integrated information systems.

Last, but not least, the HIM professional's ethical expertise is needed in the burgeoning e-health systems. Some of the ethical issues the HIM professional faces in the work environment include the quality of online health data, privacy protections, and equity. The issue of equity is important to e-health systems because not everyone has access to the information on the electronic systems. There cannot be equity when some patients can easily gain access to invaluable and voluminous information about symptoms, diseases, pharmaceutical interventions, and treatment options and others cannot. Privacy can be an issue when patients reveal sensitive information to a website and have no idea what will happen to the information or who will have access to it. The opportunities for the HIM professional are unlimited given the problems of consumer access to information, the potential for loss of privacy of information, and the variability in the quality of health data/information provided in e-health systems. This type of advocacy role for HIM professionals is important in this era of emerging technological advancement (Baur and Deering 2006).

Roles of Manager, Entrepreneur, and Advocate

The HIM professional deals with daily complexities that require the need for understanding ethics. Problems such as late and absent employees, temptations at conventions and meetings, employees who should be terminated, and poor work performance are a few of the many dilemmas facing the busy HIM manager (Flite and Laquer 2006). As an entrepreneur, the HIM professional must understand the complexities of business practices intersecting with professional values and ethical principles. Common ethical dilemmas occur when establishing contracts, clarifying the roles of intrapreneur and entrepreneur, or acting as an independent contractor. Difficulties may arise when consulting for competitors (having access to sensitive information that might be of value to the competition), dealing with advertising, confronting unrealistic client expectations, or confusing profit with not-for-profit motivations for decisions (Gardenier 2006).

HIM professionals have always been advocates for patients and providers, and the advocacy role is important in today's healthcare delivery system. For the HIM professional, advocacy "is ethics in action: choosing to take a stand for and speak out for the rights or needs of a person, group, organization, or community" (Helbig 2006). For example, HIM problems that require advocacy include

- Protecting the privacy of prominent citizens because it is more tempting to want access to the information of prominent citizens, such as elected officials, famous actors, or sports heroes
- Demonstrating compassion for drug-dependent peers
- Protecting the work environment for HIM employees
- Ensuring that consent forms are properly designed so that patients understand what they are signing and so that patient information is protected from unauthorized secondary disclosure

The advocacy role requires HIM expertise, ethical expertise, and an understanding of the patient's bill of rights (Helbig 2006).

Business relationships with vendors also pose ethical dilemmas (Olenik 2006). What issues are raised when vendors are also friends? What is the appropriate use of gifts? Should some vendors be "preferred" when dealing with requests for proposals? How can you ensure ethical dealings when negotiating contracts?

Check Your Understanding 13.3

1. Which of the following is an example of ethical issues related to coding?

   A. Inaccurate performance data
   B. Fraud and abuse
   C. Release of sensitive data
   D. Mistreatment of a vulnerable population

2. What has created ethical issues based on access, security, and linking data?

   A. The electronic health record
   B. Entrepreneurship
   C. HIPAA
   D. Adoption information systems

Instructions: Indicate whether the statements below are true or false (T or F).

3. _____ Protecting the work environment for HIM staff is part of advocacy.

4. _____ The advocacy role requires an HIM professional to understand HIM practices, ethics, and patient bill of rights.

Instructions: Match the ethical principle with its definition.

Autonomy

Beneficence

Justice

Nonmaleficence

Privacy

5. _____ Do good for others, promote good

6. _____ Do no harm

7. _____ Fairness

8. _____ Right to be left alone, to maintain control over personal information

9. _____ Self-determination

Summary

Ethical decision making is one of the health information professional's most challenging and rewarding job responsibilities. It requires courage because there will always be people who choose not tell the truth or do the right thing. HIM professionals must discuss these issues with their peer professionals and seek the advice of the professional association when necessary.

The HIM professional's job responsibilities inherently require an understanding of ethical principles, professional values and obligations, and the importance of using an ethical decision-making matrix when confronting difficult challenges at work. With this knowledge, the informed HIM professional can move from understanding problems based on a moral perspective to understanding the importance of applying an ethical decision-making process. Ethical decision making takes practice, and discussions with peers will help the HIM professional to build competency in this important area.

When making ethical decisions, the HIM professional should use the complete ethical decision-making matrix to consider all the stakeholders and their obligations and the important HIM professional values. More than one response can be given for any ethical issue as long as the complete matrix is applied. Just as there can be more than one "right" answer to a problem, there can be "wrong" answers, especially when an answer is based only on a moral value or the perspective of one individual or when the action violates ethical principles.

There will always be ongoing ethical problems, such as the protection of human subjects in research, and emerging or new ethical problems, such as medical identity theft, that require the constant diligence of the HIM professional. HIM professionalism and the Code of Ethics will help with emerging issues, now and in the future.

Bioethical decisions involving the use of health information require action, and such actions always require courage. The healthcare team, the patients, and the others who are served need to know that the HIM professional has the expertise and the courage to make appropriate ethical decisions.

References

AHIMA e-HIM Workgroup on Medical Identity Theft. 2008. Practice brief: Mitigating medical identity theft. *Journal of AHIMA* 79(7):63–69.

AHIMA e-Learning. 2012. Medical identity theft: Prevention in the EHR environment http://www.ahima.org/advocacy.

AHIMA House of Delegates. 2008. Standards of ethical coding. Chicago: AHIMA.

Amatayakul, M.K. 2009. Electronic Health Records: A Practical Guide for Professionals and Organizations, 4th ed. Chicago: AHIMA.

American Health Information Management Association. n.d. Personal health record (PHR). http://www.myphr.com.

American Health Information Management Association. 1998. Practice brief: Data quality management model. Chicago: AHIMA.

American Health Information Management Association. 2002. Practice brief: Consent for uses and disclosures of information. Chicago: AHIMA.

American Health Information Management Association. 2006. HIPAA privacy and security compliance: A report by the American Health Information Management Association. Chicago: AHIMA.

American Health Information Management Association. 2010. AHIMA Ethical Standards for Clinical Documentation Improvement (CDI) Professionals. http://library.ahima.org/xpedio/groups/public/documents/ahima/bok1_047842.hcsp?dDocName=bok1_047842.

American Health Information Management Association. 2011. AHIMA Code of Ethics. http://library.ahima.org/xpedio/groups/public/documents/ahima/bok1_024277.hcsp?dDocName=bok1_024277.

Baur, C., and M.J. Deering. 2006. E-Health for Consumers, Patients and Caregivers. Chapter 16 in *Ethical Challenges in the Management of Health Information,* 2nd ed. Harman, L.B. Sudbury, MA: Jones and Bartlett.

Beauchamp, T., and J. Childress. 2001. *Principles of Biomedical Ethics.* New York: Oxford University Press.

Bloomrosen, M. 2006. E-HIM: Information Technology and Information Exchange. Chapter 17 in *Ethical Challenges in the*

Management of Health Information, 2nd ed. Edited by Harman, L.B. Sudbury, MA: Jones and Bartlett.

Czirr, K., K. Rosendale, and E. West. 2006. Information Security. Chapter 12 in *Ethical Challenges in the Management of Health Information,* 2nd ed. Edited by Harman, L.B. Sudbury, MA: Jones and Bartlett.

Department of Health and Human Services. 2003. Summary of the HIPAA Privacy Rule. *OCR Privacy Brief.* http://www.hhs.gov/ocr/privacy/hipaa/understanding/summary/privacysummary.pdf.

Department of Health and Human Services. 2008. Genetic Information Nondiscrimination Act of 2008. http://www.eeoc.gov/laws/statutes/gina.cfm.

Dick, R.S., E.B. Steen, and D.E. Detmer, eds. 1997. *The Computer-Based Patient Record: An Essential Technology for Health Care,* Rev. ed. Washington, D.C.: The National Academies Press.

Federal Trade Commission. 2005. Take charge: Fighting back against identity theft. http://www.ftc.gov/bcp/conloine/pubs/credit/idtheft.htm.

Fenton, S.H. 2006. Software Development and Implementation. Chapter 13 in *Ethical Challenges in the Management of Health Information,* 2nd ed. Edited by Harman, L.B. Sudbury, MA: Jones and Bartlett.

Flite, C., and S. Laquer. 2006. Management. Chapter 21 in *Ethical Challenges in the Management of Health Information,* 2nd ed. Edited by Harman, L.B. Sudbury, MA: Jones and Bartlett.

Fuller, B.P., and K.L. Hudson. 2006. Genetic Information. Chapter 18 in *Ethical Challenges in the Management of Health Information,* 2nd ed. Edited by Harman, L.B. Sudbury, MA: Jones and Bartlett.

Gardenier, M. 2006. Entrepreneurship. Chapter 22 in *Ethical Challenges in the Management of Health Information,* 2nd ed. Edited by Harman, L.B. Sudbury, MA: Jones and Bartlett.

Gellman, R. 2004. When HIPAA meets NHII: A new dimension for privacy. Presentation to U.S. Department of Health and Human Services Data Council Privacy Committee, Washington, D.C.

Glover, J.J. 2006. Ethical Decision-Making Guidelines and Tools. Chapter 2 in *Ethical Challenges in the Management of Health Information,* 2nd ed. Edited by Harman, L.B. Sudbury, MA: Jones and Bartlett.

Government Accountability Office. 2005. Identity theft rights: Some outreach efforts to promote awareness of new consumer rights are underway. GAO-05-710. http://www.gao.gov/new.items/d05710.pdf.

Hanken, M.A., and G. Murphy. 2006. Electronic Patient Record. Chapter 11 in *Ethical Challenges in the Management of Health Information,* 2nd ed. Edited by Harman, L.B. Sudbury, MA: Jones and Bartlett.

Harman, L.B. 1999. HIM and ethics: Confronting ethical dilemmas on the job, an HIM professional's guide. *Journal of AHIMA* 71(5):45–49.

Harman, L.B. 2005. HIPAA: A few years later. *Online Journal of Issues in Nursing* 10(2). http://www.nursingworld.org/MainMenu-Categories/ANAMarketplace/ANAPeriodicals/OJIN/TableofContents/Volume102005/No2May05/tpc27_216018.html.

Harman, L.B., ed. 2006. *Ethical Challenges in the Management of Health Information,* 2nd ed. Sudbury, MA: Jones and Bartlett.

Harman, L.B., and V.L. Mullen. 2006. Professional Values and the Code of Ethics. Chapter 1 in *Ethical Challenges in the Management of Health Information,* 2nd ed. Edited by Harman, L.B. Sudbury, MA: Jones and Bartlett.

Harman, L.B., and C.S. Nielsen. 2008. Research and Ethics. In *Health Informatics Research Methods: Principles and Practice.* Edited by Layman, E.J., and V.J. Watzlaf. Chicago: AHIMA.

Helbig, S. 2006. Advocate. Chapter 24 in *Ethical Challenges in the Management of Health Information,* 2nd ed. Edited by Harman, L.B. Sudbury, MA: Jones and Bartlett.

Huffman, E.K. 1972. *Manual for Medical Record Librarians,* 6th ed. Chicago: Physician's Record Company.

Hughes, G. 2002a. Practice brief: Laws and regulations governing the disclosure of health information. Chicago: AHIMA.

Hughes, G. 2002b. Practice brief: Required content for authorizations to disclose. Chicago: AHIMA.

Johns, M.L., and J.M. Hardin. 2006. Research and Decision Support. Chapter 7 in *Ethical Challenges in the Management of Health Information,* 2nd ed. Edited by Harman, L.B. Sudbury, MA: Jones and Bartlett.

Jones, M.L. 2006. Adoption Information. Chapter 19 in *Ethical Challenges in the Management of Health Information,* 2nd ed. Edited by Harman, L.B. Sudbury, MA: Jones and Bartlett.

Lee, F.W., A.W. White, and K.A. Wager. 2006. Data Resource Management. Chapter 14 in *Ethical Challenges in the Management of Health Information,* 2nd ed. Edited by Harman, L.B. Sudbury, MA: Jones and Bartlett.

Lennick, D., and F. Kiel. 2008. *Moral Intelligence: Enhancing Busines Performance and Leaderwship Success.* New York: Wharton School Publishing.

McGreal, C. 2010 (October 1). U.S. says sorry for "outrageous and abhorrent" Guatemalan syphilis tests. *The Guardian.* http://www.guardian.co.uk/world/2010/oct/01/us-apology-guatemala-syphilis-tests.

Murphy, G., M.A. Hanken, and K.A. Waters. 1999. *Electronic Health Records: Changing the Vision.* Philadelphia: W.B. Saunders.

National Committee on Vital and Health Statistics. 2001. Information for health: A strategy for building the national health information infrastructure. http://www.aspe.hhs.gov/sp/nhii/Documents/NHIIReport2001/report11.htm.

Neuberger, B.J. 2006. Public Health. Chapter 8 in *Ethical Challenges in the Management of Health Information,* 2nd ed. Edited by Harman, L.B. Sudbury, MA: Jones and Bartlett.

Nichols, C., N. Davis, C. Lemery, and C. Smith. 2008. *Medical Identity Theft.* Chicago: AHIMA.

Office of Inspector General, Department of Health and Human Services 2005. Criminal and Civil Enforcement. http://oig.hhs.gov/fraud/enforcement/criminal/.

Olenik, K. 2006. Vendor Relationships. Chapter 23 in *Ethical Challenges in the Management of Health Information,* 2nd ed. Edited by Harman, L.B. Sudbury, MA: Jones and Bartlett.

Olson, B., and K.G. Grant. 2006. Integrated Delivery Systems. Chapter 15 in *Ethical Challenges in the Management of Health Information,* 2nd ed. Edited by Harman, L.B. Sudbury, MA: Jones and Bartlett.

Randolph, S.J., and L.A. Rinehart-Thompson. 2006. Drug, Alcohol, Sexual, and Behavioral Health Information. Chapter 20 in *Ethical Challenges in the Management of Health Information,* 2nd ed. Edited by Harman, L.B. Sudbury, MA: Jones and Bartlett.

Rhodes, H. 2001. Practice brief: Patient anonymity. Chicago: AHIMA.

Rinehart-Thompson, L.A. 2006. Compliance, Fraud, and Abuse. Chapter 4 in *Ethical Challenges in the Management of Health Information,* 2nd ed. Edited by Harman, L.B. Sudbury, MA: Jones and Bartlett.

Rinehart-Thompson, L.A., and L.B. Harman. 2006. Privacy and Confidentiality. Chapter 3 in *Ethical Challenges in the Management of Health Information,* 2nd ed. Edited by Harman, L.B. Sudbury, MA: Jones and Bartlett.

Schick, I.C. 2006. Managed care: Lessons in Integration. Chapter 9 in *Ethical Challenges in the Management of Health Information,* 2nd ed. Harman, L.B. Sudbury, MA: Jones and Bartlett.

Schraffenberger, L.A., and R.A. Scichilone. 2006. Clinical Code Selection and Use. Chapter 5 in *Ethical Challenges in the Management of Health Information,* 2nd ed. Edited by Harman, L.B. Sudbury, MA: Jones and Bartlett.

Seidman, J.J. 2009. Big gamble: Will stimulus dollars pay off in health information consumers can use? *Journal of AHIMA* 80(6):34–36.

Sparrow, M.K. 2000. *License to Steal: How Fraud Bleeds America's Health Care System.* Boulder, CO: Westview Press.

Spath, P.L. 2006. Quality Review. Chapter 6 in *Ethical Challenges in the Management of Health Information,* 2nd ed. Edited by Harman, L.B. Sudbury, MA: Jones and Bartlett.

Tischler, J.F. 2006. Clinical Care: End of Life. Chapter 10 in *Ethical Challenges in the Management of Health Information,* 2nd ed. Edited by Harman, L.B. Sudbury, MA: Jones and Bartlett.

Tomzik, Kristine M. 2008. "What the Seven Signs of Ethical Collapse Can Teach Us about Quality in Healthcare." 2008 AHIMA Convention Proceedings.

United States v. Sample, 213 F. 3d 1029 (2000).

Van den Hoven, J., and J. Weckert. 2008. *Information Technology and Moral Philosophy.* New York: Cambridge University Press.

Weaver, L. 2000. Identity theft victim assistance workshop. Federal Trade Commission. http://www.ftc.gov/bcp/workshops/idtheft/transcripts/001023.htm.

World Privacy Forum. 2006a. Access, amendment, and accounting of disclosures: FAQs for medical ID theft victims. http://www.worldprivacyforum.org/FAQ_medicalrecordprivacy.html.

World Privacy Forum. 2006b. Medical identity theft: What to do if you are a victim (or are concerned about it). http://www.worldprivacyforum.org/medidtheft_consumertips.html.

Additional Resources

American Health Information Management Association. 2006. The state of HIPAA privacy and security compliance. http://library.ahima.org/xpedio/groups/public/documents/ahima/bok1_047499.pdf.

Dixon, P. 2006 (May 3). Medical identity theft: The information crime that can kill you. The World Privacy Forum.

Federal Trade Commission. 2003 (Sept.). Identity theft survey report. http://www.ftc.gov/os/2003/09/synovatereport.pdf.

Harman, L.B., and V.L. Mullen. 2007. Emerging HIM identity ethical issues. AHIMA's 79th National Convention and Exhibit Proceedings, October.

Hornblum, A.M. 1999. *Acres of Skin: Human Experiments at Holmesburg Prison.* New York: Routledge.

Hornblum, A.M. 2007. *Sentenced to Science: One Black Man's Story of Imprisonment in America.* University Park, PA: Pennsylvania State University.

part **IV**

Aggregate Healthcare Data

Secondary Records and Healthcare Databases

Marcia Y. Sharp, EdD, RHIA

 ## Learning Objectives

- Distinguish between primary and secondary data and between patient-identifiable and aggregate data

- Identify the internal and external users of secondary data

- Compare the facility-specific indexes commonly found in hospitals

- Describe the registries used in hospitals according to purpose, methods of case definition and case finding, data collection methods, reporting and follow up, and pertinent laws and regulations affecting registry operations

- Define the terms pertinent to each type of secondary record or database

- Discuss agencies for approval and education and certification for cancer, immunization, trauma, birth defects, diabetes, implant, transplant, and immunization registries

- Distinguish among healthcare databases in terms of purpose and content

- Compare manual and automated methods of data collection and vendor systems with facility-specific systems

- Assess data quality issues in secondary records

- Recognize appropriate methods for ensuring data security and the confidentiality of secondary records

- Discuss some of the other issues related to the collection and maintenance of secondary data such as transparency, ownership, and deidentification

- Identify the role of the health information management professional in creating and maintaining secondary records

Key Terms

Abbreviated Injury Scale (AIS)
Abstracting
Accession number
Accession registry
Activities of daily living (ADLs)
Agency for Healthcare Research and Quality (AHRQ)
Aggregate data
Autodialing system
Case definition
Case finding
Claim
Clinical trial
Collaborative Stage Data Set

Computer virus
Credentialing
Data confidentiality
Data dictionary
Data security
Database
Deidentification
Demographic information
Disease index
Disease registry
Edit
Encryption
Facility-based registry

Food and Drug Administration (FDA)
Health services research
Healthcare Cost and Utilization Project (HCUP)
Healthcare Integrity and Protection Data Bank
    (HIPDB)
Histocompatibility
Incidence
Index
Injury Severity Score (ISS)
Interrater reliability
Master population/patient index (MPI)
Medical Literature, Analysis, and Retrieval System Online
    (MEDLINE)
Medicare Provider Analysis and Review (MEDPAR)
National Center for Health Statistics (NCHS)
National Health Care Survey

National Practitioner Data Bank (NPDB)
National Vaccine Advisory Committee (NVAC)
Operation index
Patient-identifiable data
Physician index
Population-based registry
Primary data source
Protocol
Public health
Registry
Secondary data source
Staging system
Transparency
Traumatic injury
Unified Medical Language System (UMLS)
Vital statistics

As a rich source of data about an individual patient, the health record fulfills the uses of patient care and reimbursement for individual encounters. However, it is not easy to see trends in a population of patients by looking at individual records. For this purpose, data must be extracted from individual records and entered into specialized **databases** that support analysis across individual records. These data may be used in a facility-specific or population-based registry for research and improvement in patient care. In addition, they may be reported to the state and become part of state- and federal-level databases that are used to set health policy and improve healthcare.

The health information management (HIM) professional can play a variety of roles in managing secondary records and databases. He or she plays a key role in helping to set up databases. This task includes determining the content of the database or registry and ensuring compliance with the laws, regulations, and accrediting standards that affect the content and use of the registry or database. All data elements included in the database or registry must be defined in a data dictionary. In this role, the HIM professional may oversee the completeness and accuracy of the data abstracted for inclusion in the database or registry.

This chapter explains the difference between primary and secondary data sources and their uses. It also offers an in-depth look at various types of secondary databases, including indexes and registries, and their functions. Finally, the chapter discusses how secondary databases are processed and maintained.

Primary versus Secondary Data Sources and Databases

The health record is considered a **primary data source** because it contains information about a patient that has been documented by the professionals who provided care or services to that patient. Data taken from the primary health

record and entered into registries and databases are considered a **secondary data source.**

Data also are categorized as either **patient-identifiable data** or **aggregate data.** The health record consists entirely of patient-identifiable data. In other words, every fact recorded in the record relates to a particular patient identified by name. Secondary data also may be patient identifiable. In some instances, data are entered into a database, along with information such as the patient's name, and maintained in an identifiable form. Registries are an example of patient-identifiable data on groups of patients.

More often, however, secondary data are considered aggregate data. Aggregate data include data on groups of people or patients without identifying any particular patient individually. Examples of aggregate data are statistics on the average length of stay (ALOS) for patients discharged within a particular diagnosis-related group (DRG).

Purposes and Users of Secondary Data Sources

Secondary data sources consist of facility-specific indexes; registries, either facility or population based; and other healthcare databases. Healthcare organizations maintain those indexes, registries, and databases that are relevant to their specific operations. States as well as the federal government also maintain databases to assess the health and wellness of their populations.

Secondary data sources provide information that is not easily available by looking at individual health records. For example, if the HIM director doing a research study wanted to find the health records of 25 patients who had the principal diagnosis of myocardial infarction, he or she would have to look at numerous individual records to locate the number needed. This would be a time-consuming and laborious project. With a diagnosis index, the task would involve simply looking at the list of diagnoses in numerical order and selecting those with the appropriate diagnosis code for myocardial infarction for inclusion in the study.

Data extracted from health records and entered into disease-oriented databases can, for example, help researchers determine the effectiveness of alternate treatment methods. They also can quickly demonstrate survival rates at different stages of disease.

Internal users of secondary data are individuals located within the healthcare facility. For example, internal users include medical staff and administrative and management staff. Secondary data enable these users to identify patterns and trends that are helpful in patient care, long-range planning, budgeting, and benchmarking with other facilities.

External users of patient data are individuals and institutions outside the facility. Examples of external users are state data banks and federal agencies. States have laws that mandate cases of patients with diseases such as tuberculosis and AIDS be reported to the state department of health. Moreover, the federal government collects data from the states on vital events such as births and deaths.

The secondary data provided to external users is generally aggregate data and not patient-identifiable data. Thus, these data can be used as needed without risking breaches of confidentiality.

Check Your Understanding 14.1

Instructions: Answer the following questions on a separate piece of paper.

1. What is the difference between a primary data source and a secondary data source?
2. What is the difference between patient-identifiable data and aggregate data?
3. Why are secondary data sources developed?
4. What are the differences between internal users and external users of secondary data sources?

Facility-Specific Indexes

The secondary data sources that have been in existence the longest are the indexes that have been developed within facilities to meet their individual needs. An **index** is simply a report from a database that enables health records to be located by diagnosis, procedure, or physician. Prior to extensive computerization in healthcare, these indexes were kept on cards with handwritten data. They now are usually computerized reports available from data included in databases routinely maintained in the healthcare facility. Most acute-care facilities maintain indexes described in the following subsections.

Master Population/Patient Index

The **master population/patient index (MPI)**, which is sometimes called the master person index, contains patient-identifiable data such as name, address, date of birth, dates of hospitalizations or encounters, name of attending physician, and health record number. Because health records are filed numerically in most facilities, the MPI is an important source of patient health record numbers. These numbers enable the facility to quickly retrieve health information for specific patients.

Hospitals with a unit numbering system also depend on the MPI to determine whether a patient has been seen in the facility before and, therefore, has an existing medical record number. Having this information in the MPI avoids issuance of duplicate record numbers. Most of the information in the MPI is entered into the facility database at the time of the admission, preadmission, or registration process.

Disease and Operation Indexes

In an acute care setting, the **disease index** is a listing in diagnosis code number order for patients discharged from the facility during a particular time period. Each patient's diagnoses are converted from a verbal description to a numerical code, usually using a coding system such as the International Classification of Diseases (ICD). In most cases, patient diagnosis codes are entered into the facility health information system as part of the discharge processing of the patient health record. The index always includes the patient's health record number as well as the diagnosis codes so that records can be retrieved by diagnosis. Because each patient is listed with the health record number, the disease index is considered patient-identifiable data. The disease index also may include other information such as the attending physician's name or the date of discharge. In nonacute settings, the disease index might be generated to reflect patients currently receiving services in the facility.

The **operation index** is similar to the disease index except that it is arranged in numerical order by the patient's procedure code(s) using ICD or Current Procedural Terminology (CPT) codes. The other information listed in the operation index is generally the same as that listed in the disease index except that the surgeon may be listed in addition to, or instead of, the attending physician.

In many cases, facilities no longer have an actual listing for the diagnosis and operation indexes. Instead, they query the health information system utilizing the ICD code for the condition or operation needed.

Physician Index

The **physician index** is a listing of cases in order by physician name or physician identification number. It also includes the patient's health record number and may include other information, such as date of discharge. The physician index enables users to retrieve information about a particular physician, including the number of cases seen during a particular time period. As with the disease and operation indexes, facilities generally query the health information system (HIS) to obtain physician data.

Instructions: Answer the following questions on a separate piece of paper.

1. How do HIM departments use facility-specific indexes?

2. What is the purpose of the master population/patient index? What types of information does it include?

3. What is the purpose of disease and operation indexes? What types of information do they include?

4. What is the purpose of the physician index? What types of information does it include?

Registries

Disease registries are collections of secondary data related to patients with a specific diagnosis, condition, or procedure. **Registries** are different from indexes in that they contain more extensive data. Index reports can usually be produced using data from the facility's existing databases. Registries often require more extensive data from the patient record. Each registry must define the cases that are to be included in it. This process is called **case definition.** In a trauma registry, for example, the case definition might be all patients admitted with a diagnosis falling into ICD code numbers 800 through 959, the trauma diagnosis codes.

After the cases to be included have been determined through the case definition process described earlier, the next step in data acquisition is usually **case finding.** Case finding includes the methods used to identify the patients who have been seen and treated in the facility for the particular disease or condition of interest to the registry. After cases have been identified, extensive information is abstracted from the paper-based patient record into the registry database or fed from other databases and entered into the registry database.

The sole purpose of some registries is to collect data from the patient health record and to make them available to users. Other registries take further steps to enter additional information in the registry database, such as routine follow-up of patients at specified intervals. Follow-up might include rate and duration of survival and quality-of-life issues over time.

Cancer Registries

Cancer registries have a long history in healthcare. According to the National Cancer Registrars Association (NCRA),

the first hospital registry was founded in 1926, at Yale-New Haven Hospital. It has long been recognized that aggregate clinical information is needed to improve the diagnosis and treatment of cancer. Cancer registries were developed as an organized method to collect these data. The registry may be a **facility-based registry** (located within a facility such as a hospital or clinic) or a **population-based registry** (gathering information from more than one facility within a geographic area such as a state or region).

The data from facility-based registries are used to provide information for the improved understanding of cancer, including its causes and methods of diagnosis and treatment. The data collected also may provide comparisons in survival rates and quality of life for patients with different treatments and at different stages of cancer at the time of diagnosis. In population-based registries, emphasis is on identifying trends and changes in the **incidence** (new cases) of cancer within the area covered by the registry.

The Cancer Registries Amendment Act of 1992 provided funding for a national program of cancer registries with population-based registries in each state. According to the law, these registries were mandated to collect data such as

- Demographic information about each case of cancer
- Information on the industrial or occupational history of the individuals with the cancers (to the extent such information is available from the same record)
- Administrative information, including date of diagnosis and source of information
- Pathological data characterizing the cancer, including site, stage of neoplasm, incidence, and type of treatment

Case Definition and Case Finding in the Cancer Registry

As defined previously, case definition is the process of deciding what cases should be entered in the registry. In a cancer registry, for example, all cancer cases except certain skin cancers might meet the definition for the cases to be included. Skin cancers such as basal cell carcinomas might be excluded because they do not metastasize and do not require the follow-up necessary for other cancers included in the registry. Data on benign and borderline brain or central nervous system tumors also must be collected by the National Program of Cancer Registries (CDC 2008a).

In the facility-based cancer registry, the first step is case finding. One way to find cases is through the discharge process in the HIM department. During the discharge procedure, coders or discharge analysts can easily identify cases of patients with cancer for inclusion in the registry. Another case-finding method is to use the facility-specific disease indexes or the health information system to identify patients with diagnoses of cancer. Additional methods may include reviews of pathology reports and lists of patients receiving radiation therapy or other cancer treatments to determine cases that have not been found by other methods.

Population-based registries usually depend on hospitals, physician offices, radiation facilities, ambulatory surgery centers (ASCs), and pathology laboratories to identify and report cases to the central registry. The population-based registry has a responsibility to ensure that all cases of cancer in the target area have been identified and reported to the central registry.

Data Collection for the Cancer Registry

Data collection methods vary between facility-based registries and population-based registries. When a case is first entered in the registry, an **accession number** is assigned. This number consists of the first digits of the year the patient was first seen at the facility, with the remaining digits assigned sequentially throughout the year. The first case in 2012, for example, might be 12-0001. The accession number may be assigned manually or by the automated cancer database used by the organization. An **accession registry** of all cases can be kept manually or provided as a report by the database software. This listing of patients in accession number order provides a way to monitor that all cases have been entered into the registry.

In a facility-based registry, data are initially obtained by reviewing and collecting them from the patient's health record. In addition to **demographic information** (such as name, health record number, address), patient data in a cancer registry include

- Type and site of the cancer
- Diagnostic methodologies
- Treatment methodologies
- Stage at the time of diagnosis

The stage provides information on the size and extent of spread of the tumor throughout the body. Historically, several different **staging systems** have been used. The American Joint Committee on Cancer (AJCC) has worked, through its Collaborative Stage Task Force, with other organizations with staging systems to develop a standardized data set, the **Collaborative Stage Data Set,** which uses computer algorithms to describe how far a cancer has spread (AJCC 2008).

After the initial information is collected at the patient's first encounter, information in the registry is updated periodically through the follow-up process discussed in the following section.

Frequently, the population-based registry only collects information when the patient is diagnosed. Sometimes, however, it receives follow-up information from its reporting entities. These entities usually submit the information to the central registry electronically.

Reporting and Follow-up for Cancer Registry Data

Formal reporting of cancer registry data is done through an annual report. The annual report includes aggregate data on the number of cases in the past year by site and type of cancer. It also may include information on patients by gender, age, and ethnic group. Often a particular site or type of cancer is featured with more in-depth data provided.

Other reports are provided as needed. Data from the cancer registry are frequently used in the quality assessment process for a facility as well as in research. Data on survival rates by site of cancer and methods of treatment, for example, would be helpful in researching the most effective treatment for a type of cancer.

Another activity of the cancer registry is patient follow-up. On an annual basis, the registry attempts to obtain information about each patient in the registry, including whether he or she is still alive, status of the cancer, and treatment received during the period. Various methods are used to obtain this information. For a facility-based registry, the facility's patient health records may be checked for return hospitalizations or visits for treatment. The patient's physician also may be contacted to determine whether the patient is still living and to obtain information about the cancer.

When patient status cannot be determined through these methods, an attempt may be made to contact the patient directly, using information in the registry such as address and telephone number of the patient and other contacts. In addition, contact information from the patient's health record may be used to request information from the patient's relatives. Other methods used include reading newspaper obituaries for deaths and using the Internet to locate patients through sites such as the Social Security Death Index and online telephone books. The information obtained through follow-up is important to allow the registry to develop statistics on survival rates for particular cancers and different treatment methodologies.

Population-based registries do not always include follow-up information on the patients in their databases. They may, however, receive the information from the reporting entities such as hospitals, physician offices, and other organizations providing follow-up care.

Standards and Approval Agencies for Cancer Registries

Several organizations have developed standards or approval processes for cancer programs. (See table 14.1.) The American College of Surgeons (ACS) Commission on Cancer has an approval process for cancer programs. One of the

Table 14.1. Standard-setting or approval agencies for cancer registries

Agency	Type of Registry
American College of Surgeons (ACS)	Facility based
North American Association of Central Cancer Registries (NAACCR)	Population based
Centers for Disease Control and Prevention	Population based

requirements of this process is the existence of a cancer registry as part of the program. The ACS standards are published in the Cancer Program Standards (ACS 2008a). When the ACS surveys the cancer program, part of the survey process is a review of cancer registry activities.

The North American Association of Central Cancer Registries (NAACCR) has a certification program for state population-based registries. Certification is based on the quality of data collected and reported by the state registry. The NAACCR has developed standards for data quality and format and works with other cancer organizations to align their various standards sets.

The Centers for Disease Control and Prevention (CDC) also has national standards regarding completeness, timeliness, and quality of cancer registry data from state registries through the National Program of Cancer Registries (NPCR). The NPCR was developed as a result of the Cancer Registries Amendment Act of 1992. The CDC collects data from the NPCR state registries.

Education and Certification for Cancer Registrars

Traditionally, cancer registrars have been trained through on-the-job training and professional workshops and seminars. The NCRA has worked with colleges to develop formal educational programs for cancer registrars either through a certificate or an associate's degree program. A cancer registrar may become certified as a certified cancer registrar (CTR) by passing an examination provided by the National Board for Certification of Registrars (NBCR). Eligibility requirements for the certification examination include a combination of experience and education (NCRA 2008).

Trauma Registries

Trauma registries maintain databases on patients with severe traumatic injuries. A **traumatic injury** is a wound or another injury caused by an external physical force such as an automobile accident, a shooting, a stabbing, or a fall. Examples of such injuries would include fractures, burns, and lacerations. Information collected by the trauma registry may be used for performance improvement and research in the area of trauma care. Trauma registries are usually facility based but may, in some cases, include data for a region or state.

Case Definition and Case Finding for Trauma Registries

The case definition for the trauma registry varies from registry to registry. To find cases with trauma diagnoses, the trauma registrar may query the HIS system looking for cases with codes in the trauma section of ICD. In addition, the registrar may look at deaths in services with frequent trauma diagnoses such as trauma, neurosurgery, orthopedics, and plastic surgery to find additional cases.

Data Collection for Trauma Registries

After the cases have been identified, information is abstracted from the health records of the injured patients and entered into the trauma registry database. The data elements collected in the abstracting process vary from registry to registry but usually include

- Demographic information on the patient
- Information on the injury
- Care the patient received before hospitalization (such as care at another transferring hospital or care from an emergency medical technician who provided care at the scene of the accident or in transport from the accident site to the hospital)
- Status of the patient at the time of admission
- Patient's course in the hospital
- ICD diagnosis and procedure codes
- Abbreviated Injury Scale (AIS)
- Injury Severity Score (ISS)

The **Abbreviated Injury Scale** (AIS) reflects the nature of the injury and the severity (threat to life) by body system. It may be assigned manually by the registrar or generated as part of the database from data entered by the registrar. The **Injury Severity Score** (ISS) is an overall severity measurement calculated from the AIS scores for the three most severe injuries of the patient (Trauma.org 2008).

Reporting and Follow-up for Trauma Registries

Reporting varies among trauma registries. An annual report is often developed to show the activity of the trauma registry. Other reports may be generated as part of the performance improvement process, such as self-extubation (patients removing their own tubes) and delays in abdominal surgery or patient complications. Some hospitals report data to the National Trauma Data Bank, a large database of aggregate data on trauma cases (ACS 2008b). An example of the use of such population data is the number of head injuries from motorcycle accidents in a state to encourage passage of a helmet law.

Trauma registries may or may not do follow-up of the patients entered in the registry. When follow-up is done, emphasis is frequently on the patient's quality of life after a period of time. Unlike cancer, where physician follow-up is crucial to detect recurrence, many traumatic injuries do not require continued patient care over time. Thus, follow-up is often not given the emphasis it receives in cancer registries.

Standards and Agencies for Approval of Trauma Registries

The American College of Surgeons certifies levels I, II, III, and IV trauma centers. As part of its certification requirements, the ACS states that the level I trauma center, the type of center receiving the most serious cases and providing the highest level of trauma service, must have a trauma registry (ACS 2008b).

Education and Certification of Trauma Registrars

Trauma registrars may be registered health information technicians (RHITs), registered health information administrators (RHIAs), registered nurses (RNs), licensed practical nurses (LPNs), emergency medical technicians (EMTs), or other health professionals. Training for trauma registrars is accomplished through workshops and on-the-job training. The American Trauma Society (ATS), for example, provides core and advanced workshops for trauma registrars. It also provides a certification examination for trauma registrars through its Registrar Certification Board. Certified trauma registrars have earned the certified specialist in trauma registry (CSTR) credential.

Birth Defects Registries

Birth defects registries collect information on newborns with birth defects. Often population based, these registries serve a variety of purposes. For example, they provide information on the incidence of birth defects to study causes and prevention of birth defects, to monitor trends in birth defects to improve medical care for children with birth defects, and to target interventions for preventable birth defects such as folic acid to prevent neural tube defects.

In some cases, registries have been developed after specific events have put a spotlight on birth defects. After the initial Persian Gulf War, for example, some feared an increased incidence of birth defects among the children of Gulf War veterans. The Department of Defense subsequently started a birth defects registry to collect data on the children of these veterans to determine whether any pattern could be detected.

Case Definition and Case Finding for Birth Defects Registries

Birth defects registries use a variety of criteria to determine which cases to include in the registry. Some registries limit cases to those birth defects found within the first year of life. Others include those children with a major defect that occurred in the first year of life and was discovered within the first five years of life. Still other registries include only children who were liveborn or stillborn babies with discernible birth defects.

Cases may be detected in a variety of ways, including review of disease indexes, labor and delivery logs, pathology and autopsy reports, ultrasound reports, and cytogenetic reports. In addition to information from hospitals and physicians, cases may be identified from rehabilitation centers and children's hospitals and from vital records such as birth, death, and fetal death certificates.

Data Collection for Birth Defects Registries

A variety of information is abstracted for the birth defects registry, including

- Demographics
- Codes for diagnoses
- Birth weight
- Status at birth, including liveborn, stillborn, aborted
- Autopsy
- Cytogenetics results
- Whether the infant was a single or multiple birth
- Mother's use of alcohol, tobacco, or illicit drugs
- Father's use of drugs and alcohol
- Family history of birth defects

Diabetes Registries

Diabetes registries collect data about patients with diabetes for the purpose of assistance in managing care as well as for research. Patients whose diabetes is not kept under good control frequently have numerous complications. The diabetes registry can keep up with whether the patient has been seen by a physician in an effort to prevent complications.

Case Definition and Case Finding for Diabetes Registries

There are two types of diabetes mellitus: insulin-dependent diabetes (type I) and non-insulin-dependent diabetes (type II). Registries sometimes limit their cases by type of diabetes. In some instances, there may be further definition by age. Some diabetes registries, for example, only include children with diabetes.

Case finding includes the review of health records of patients with diabetes. Other case-finding methods include the reviews of the following types of information:

- ICD diagnostic codes
- Billing data
- Medication lists
- Physician identification
- Health plans

Although facility-based registries for cancer and trauma are usually hospital based, facility-based diabetes registries are often maintained by physician offices and clinics because they are the main location for diabetes care. Thus, the data about the patient to be entered into the registry are available at these sites rather than at the hospital. Patient health records of diabetes patients in the physician practice may be identified through ICD code numbers for diabetes, billing data for diabetes-related services, medication lists for patients on diabetic medications, or identification of patients as the physician sees them.

Health plans also are interested in optimal care for their enrollees because diabetes can have serious complications when not managed correctly. They may provide information to the office or clinic on diabetic enrollees in the health plan.

Data Collection for Diabetes Registries

In addition to demographic information about the cases, other data collected may include laboratory values such as HbA1c. This test is used to determine the patient's blood glucose level for a period of approximately 60 days prior to the time of the test. Moreover, facility registries may track patient visits to follow up with patients who have not been seen in the past year.

Reporting and Follow-up for Diabetes Registries

A variety of reports may be developed from the diabetes registry. For facility-based registries, one report may keep up with laboratory monitoring of the patient's diabetes to allow intensive intervention with patients whose diabetes is not well controlled. Another report might be of patients who have not been tested within a year or who have not had a primary care provider visit within a year.

Population-based diabetes registries might provide reporting on the incidence of diabetes for the geographic area covered by the registry. Registry data also may be used to investigate risk factors for diabetes.

Follow-up is aimed primarily at ensuring that the diabetic is seen by the physician at appropriate intervals to prevent complications.

Implant Registries

An implant is a material or substance inserted in the body, such as breast implants, heart valves, and pacemakers. Implant registries have been developed for the purpose of tracking the performance of implants, including complications, deaths, and defects resulting from implants, as well as longevity.

In the recent past, the safety of implants has been questioned in a number of highly publicized cases. In some cases, implant registries have been developed in response to such events. For example, there have been questions about the safety of silicone breast implants and temporomandibular joint implants. When such cases arise, it has often been difficult to ensure that all patients with the implant have been notified of safety concerns.

A number of federal laws have been enacted to regulate medical devices, including implants. These devices were first covered under Section 15 of the Food, Drug, and Cosmetic Act. The Safe Medical Devices Act of 1990 was passed and then amended through the Medical Device Amendments of 1992. These acts required facilities to report deaths and severe complications thought to be due to a device to the manufacturer and the **Food and Drug Administration (FDA)** through its MedWatch reporting system. Implant registries can help in complying with the legal requirement for reporting for the sample of facilities required to report.

Case Definition and Case Finding for Implant Registries

Implant registries sometimes include all types of implants but often are restricted to a specific type of implant such as cochlear, saline breast, or temporomandibular joint.

Data Collection for Implant Registries

Demographic data on patients receiving implants are included in the registry. The FDA requires that all reportable events involving medical devices include information on the following (FDA 2008):

- User facility report number
- Name and address of the device manufacturer
- Device brand name and common name
- Product model, catalog, and serial and lot number
- Brief description of the event reported to the manufacturer or the FDA

Thus, these data items also should be included in the implant registry to facilitate reporting.

Reporting and Follow-up for Implant Registries

Data from the implant registry may be used to report to the FDA and the manufacturer when devices cause death or serious illness or injury. Follow-up is important to track the performance of the implant. When patients are tracked through the registry, they can be easily notified of product failures, recalls, or upgrades.

Transplant Registries

Transplant registries may have varied purposes. Some organ transplant registries maintain databases of patients who need organs. When an organ becomes available, an equitable way then may be used to allocate the organ to the patient with the highest priority. In other cases, the purpose of the registry is to provide a database of potential donors for transplants using live donors, such as bone marrow transplants. Posttransplant information also is kept on organ recipients and donors.

Because transplant registries are used to match donor organs with recipients, they are often national or even international in scope. Examples of national registries include the UNet of the United Network for Organ Sharing (UNOS) and the registry of the National Marrow Donor Program (NMDP).

Data collected in the transplant registry also may be used for research, policy analysis, and quality control projects.

Case Definition and Case Finding for Transplant Registries

Physicians identify patients needing transplants. Information about the patient is provided to the registry. When an organ becomes available, information about it is matched with potential donors. For donor registries, donors are solicited through community information efforts similar to those carried out by blood banks to encourage blood donations.

Data Collection for Transplant Registries

The type of information collected varies according to the type of registry. Pretransplant data about the recipient include

- Demographics
- Patient's diagnosis
- Patient's status codes regarding medical urgency
- Patient's functional status
- Whether the patient is on life support
- Previous transplantations
- **Histocompatibility**—"a state of immunologic similarity (or identity) that permits successful homograft transplantation" (*Stedman's Online Dictionary*)

Information on donors varies according to whether the donor is living. For organs harvested from patients who have died, information is collected on

- Cause and circumstances of the death
- Organ procurement and consent process
- Medications the donor was taking
- Other donor history

For a living donor, information includes

- Relationship of the donor to the recipient (if any)
- Clinical information
- Information on organ recovery
- Histocompatibility

Reporting and Follow-up for Transplant Registries

Reporting includes information on donors and recipients as well as survival rates, length of time on the waiting list for an organ, and death rates. Follow-up information is collected for recipients as well as living donors. For living donors, the information collected might include complications of the procedure and length of stay (LOS) in the hospital. Follow-up information about recipients includes information on status at the time of follow-up (for example, living, dead, lost to follow-up), functional status, graft status, and treatment, such as immunosuppressive drugs. Follow-up is carried out at intervals throughout the first year after the transplant and then annually after that.

Immunization Registries

Children are supposed to receive a large number of immunizations during the first six years of life. These immunizations are so important that the federal government has set several objectives related to immunizations in Healthy People 2010, a set of health goals for the nation (HHS 2000). These include increasing the proportion of children and adolescents who are fully immunized (Objective 14-24) and increasing the proportion of children in population-based immunization registries (Objective 14-26).

Immunization registries usually have the purpose of increasing the number of infants and children who receive proper immunizations at the proper intervals. To accomplish this goal, they collect information within a particular geographic area about children and their immunization status. They also help by maintaining a central source of information for a particular child's immunization history, even when the child has received immunizations from a variety of providers. This central location for immunization data also relieves parents of the responsibility of maintaining immunization records for their own children.

Case Definition and Case Finding for Immunization Registries

All children in the population area served by the registry should be included in the registry. Some registries limit their inclusion of patients to those seen at public clinics, excluding those seen exclusively by private practitioners. Although children are usually targeted in immunization registries, some registries do include information on adults for influenza and pneumonia vaccines.

Children are often entered in the registry at birth. Registry personnel may review birth and death certificates and adoption records to determine what children to include and what children to exclude because they died after birth. In some cases, children are entered electronically through a connection with an electronic birth record system. Accuracy and completeness of the data in the registry are dependent on the thoroughness of the submitters in reporting immunizations.

Data Collection for Immunization Registries

The National Immunization Program at the CDC has worked with the **National Vaccine Advisory Committee (NVAC)** to develop a set of core immunization data elements to be included in all immunization registries. The data elements are divided into required and optional. The required data elements include (CDC 2008b)

- Patient's name (first, middle, and last)
- Patient's birth date
- Patient's sex
- Patient's birth state and country
- Mother's name (first, middle, last, and maiden)
- Vaccine type
- Vaccine manufacturer
- Vaccination date
- Vaccine lot number

Other optional items may be included, as needed, by the individual registry.

Reporting and Follow-up for Immunization Registries

Because the purpose of the immunization registry is to increase the number of children who receive immunizations in a timely manner, reporting should emphasize immunization rates, especially changes in rates in target areas. Immunization registries also can provide automatic reporting of children's immunization to schools to check the immunization status of their students.

Follow-up is directed toward reminding parents that it is time for immunizations as well as seeing whether the parents do not bring the child in for the immunization after a reminder. Reminders may include a letter or postcard or telephone calls. **Autodialing systems** may be used to call parents and deliver a prerecorded reminder. Moreover, registries must decide how frequently to follow up with parents who do not bring their children for immunization. Maintaining up-to-date addresses and telephone numbers is an important factor in providing follow-up. Registries may allow parents to opt out of the registry if they prefer not to be reminded.

Standards and Agencies for Approval of Immunization Registries

The CDC, through its National Immunization Program, provides funding for some population-based immunization registries. The CDC has identified 12 minimum functional standards for population-based immunization registries (CDC 2008b), including the following:

- Electronically store data on all NVAC-approved core data elements
- Establish a registry record within six weeks of birth for each newborn child born in the catchment area
- Enable access to and retrieval of immunization information in the registry at the time of the encounter
- Receive and process immunization information within one month of vaccine administration
- Protect the confidentiality of healthcare information
- Ensure the security of healthcare information
- Exchange immunization records using Health Level Seven (HL7) standards
- Automatically determine the routine childhood immunization(s) needed, in compliance with current Advisory Committee on Immunization Practices (ACIP) recommendations, when an individual presents for a scheduled immunization
- Automatically identify individuals due or late for an immunization(s) to enable the production of reminder or recall notifications
- Automatically produce immunization coverage reports by providers, age groups, and geographic areas
- Produce official immunization records
- Promote the accuracy and completeness of registry data

The CDC provides funding for population-based immunization registries.

Other Registries

Registries may be developed for any type of disease or condition. Examples of other types of registries that are commonly kept include HIV/AIDS and cardiac registries.

In 2007 the state of Nebraska initiated a partnership within the state called the Nebraska Registry Partnership (NRP) to introduce, sustain, and gradually expand a registry for chronic disease management for cardiovascular diseases and diabetes care improvement for patients seen in rural health clinics.

In addition, the American Gastroenterological Association (AGA) sponsors the AGA Registry. The AGA Registry is the only gastroenterology registry sponsored by the Centers for Medicare and Medicaid Services (CMS), enabling practices to directly submit data for the CMS Physician Quality Reporting System (AGA 2011). It is a national outcomes-driven registry that allows clinicians to monitor and improve patient care while generating data to compare the efficacy of treatments.

A new registry used to track cases of sudden unexpected infant deaths (SUIDs) is being piloted in five states (Georgia, Colorado, Michigan, New Jersey, and New Mexico) over a three-year period, and it represents a collaboration between the Centers for Disease Control and Prevention and the National Center for Child Death Review. The SUID Registry, now in the third year (2012), aims to improve knowledge of factors surrounding SUID events, create prevention strategies and interventions, and ultimately reduce SUIDs and injury-related infant deaths (Shapiro-Mendoza et al. 2012).

Registries may be developed for administrative purposes also. The National Provider Identifier (NPI) Registry is an example of an administrative registry. The NPI Registry enables users to search for a provider's national plan and provider enumeration system information, including the national provider identification number. The NPI number is a 10-digit unique identification number assigned to healthcare providers in the United States. There is no charge to use the registry, and it is updated daily. Data collected for healthcare administrative purposes are discussed in the next subsection.

Check Your Understanding 14.3

Instructions: Answer the following questions on a separate piece of paper.

1. What is a registry? What is the purpose of a registry?

2. How is case definition different from case finding?

3. What is the difference between a facility-based registry and a population-based registry?

Answer questions 4 through 10 for each of the following registries: cancer, trauma, birth defects, diabetes, implant, transplant, and immunization.

4. What methods are used for case definition and case finding?

5. What methods of data collection are used?

6. What methods of reporting are used?

7. What methods of follow-up are used?

8. What standards are applicable, and what agencies approve or accredit the registry?

9. What education is required for registrars?

10. What certification is available for registrars? What agency/organization provides certification? What are the certification requirements?

Healthcare Databases

Databases may be developed for a variety of purposes. The federal government, for example, has developed a wide variety of databases to enable it to carry out surveillance, improvement, and prevention duties. Health information managers may provide information for these databases through data abstraction or from data reported by a facility to state and local entities. They also may use these data to do research or work with other researchers on issues related to reimbursement and health status.

There are concerns about collecting healthcare data in an environment without clear guidance about ownership of secondary data, unauthorized reuse of data, and spotty confidentiality and security regulations. Patients have concerns that secondary data collected about them may adversely affect their employment or ability to obtain health insurance. It is much more difficult for patients to determine what information about them is maintained in secondary databases than it is to view their primary health records. Although facilities utilize secondary data under the "healthcare operations" section of the Health Insurance Portability and Accountability Act (HIPAA), patients must be made aware of this practice through the Notification of Privacy Practices. Also, not all secondary data are protected under HIPAA.

National and State Administrative Databases

Some databases are established for administrative rather than disease-oriented reasons. Data banks are developed, for example, for **claims** data submitted on Medicare claims. Other administrative databases assist in the **credentialing** and privileging of health practitioners.

Medicare Provider Analysis and Review File

The **Medicare Provider Analysis and Review (MEDPAR)** file is made up of acute-care hospital and skilled nursing facility (SNF) claims data for all Medicare claims. It consists of the following types of data:

- Demographic data on the patient
- Data on the provider
- Information on Medicare coverage for the claim
- Total charges
- Charges broken down by specific types of services, such as operating room, physical therapy, and pharmacy charges
- ICD-9-CM diagnosis and procedure codes
- DRGs

The MEDPAR file is frequently used for research on topics such as charges for particular types of care and analysis by DRG. The limitation of the MEDPAR data for research purposes is that it only contains data about Medicare patients.

National Practitioner Data Bank

The **National Practitioner Data Bank (NPDB)** was mandated under the Health Care Quality Improvement Act of 1986 to provide a database of medical malpractice payments; adverse licensure actions including revocations, suspensions, reprimands, censures, probations, and surrenders of licenses for quality-of-care purposes only; and certain professional review actions (such as denial of medical staff privileges) taken by healthcare entities such as hospitals against physicians, dentists, and other healthcare providers (NPDB 2006). The NPDB was developed to address the lack of information on malpractice decisions, denial of medical staff privileges, or loss of medical license. Because these data were not widely available, physicians could move to another state or another facility and begin practicing again with the current state or facility unaware of the previous actions against the physician.

Information in the NPDB is provided through a required reporting mechanism. Entities making malpractice payments, including insurance companies, boards of medical examiners, and entities such as hospitals and professional societies, must report to the NPDB. The information to be reported includes information on the practitioner, the reporting entity, and the judgment or settlement. Information on physicians must be reported. A recent change to the law now requires entities such as private accrediting organizations and peer review organizations to report adverse actions to the data bank. In addition, adverse licensure and other actions against any healthcare entity must be reported, not just physicians and dentists. Monetary penalties may be assessed for failure to report.

The law requires healthcare facilities to query the NPDB as part of the credentialing process when a physician initially applies for medical staff privileges and every two years thereafter.

Healthcare Integrity and Protection Data Bank

Part of HIPAA of 1996 mandated the collection of information on healthcare fraud and abuse because there was no central place to obtain this information. As a result, the national **Healthcare Integrity and Protection Data Bank (HIPDB)** was developed. The types of items that must be reported to the data bank include reportable final adverse actions such as (HHS 2008)

- Federal or state licensing and certification actions, including revocations, reprimands, censures, probations, suspensions, and any other loss of license, or the right to apply for or renew a license, whether by voluntary surrender, nonrenewability, or otherwise
- Exclusions from participation in federal or state healthcare programs
- Any other adjudicated actions or decisions defined in the HIPDB regulations

There may be some overlap with the National Practitioner Data Bank, so a single report is made and then sorted to the appropriate data bank. Information to be reported includes information on the healthcare provider, supplier, or practitioner that is the subject of the final adverse action, the nature of the act, and a description of the actions on which the decision was based. Only federal and state government agencies and health plans are required to report, and access to the data bank is limited to these organizations and to practitioners, providers, and suppliers, who may only query about themselves.

State Administrative Data Banks

States also frequently have health-related administrative databases. Many states, for example, collect either Uniform Hospital Discharge Data Set (UHDDS) or UB-04 data on patients discharged from hospitals located within their area. The Statewide Planning and Research Cooperative System (SPARCS) in New York is an example of this type of administrative database. It combines UB-04 data with data required by the state of New York.

National, State, and County Public Health Databases

Public health is the area of healthcare dealing with the health of populations in geographic areas such as states or counties. Publicly reported healthcare data vary from quality and patient safety measurement data to patient satisfaction results. The aggregated data range from a local to national perspective, such as state-specific public health conditions to national morbidity and mortality statistics. In addition, consumers are becoming more actively involved in their healthcare. Publicly reported data may be presented for consumer use through various star ratings on different quality measures via organizations such as the Leapfrog Group, HealthGrades, or Hospital Compare. One of the duties of public health agencies is the surveillance of health status within their jurisdiction.

Databases developed by public health departments provide information on the incidence and prevalence of diseases,

possible high-risk populations, survival statistics, and trends over time. Data for these databases may be collected using a variety of methods including interviews, physical examination of individuals, and review of health records. At the national level, the **National Center for Health Statistics (NCHS)** has responsibility for these databases.

National Health Care Survey

One of the major national public health surveys is the **National Health Care Survey.** To a large extent, it relies on data from patient health records. It consists of a number of databases, including

- National Hospital Discharge Survey
- National Ambulatory Medical Care Survey
- National Survey of Ambulatory Surgery
- National Nursing Home Survey
- National Home and Hospice Care Survey

Table 14.2 lists the component databases of the National Health Care Survey, along with their corresponding data sources.

Data in the National Hospital Discharge Survey are abstracted manually from a sample of acute-care hospitals or from discharged inpatient records or are obtained from state or other discharge databases. Items collected follow UHDDS, including demographic data, admission and discharge dates, and final diagnoses and procedures.

The National Ambulatory Medical Care Survey includes data collected by a sample of office-based physicians and their staffs from the records of patients seen in a one-week reporting period. Data included are demographic data, the patient's reason for visit, the diagnoses, diagnostic and screening services, therapeutic and preventive services, ambulatory surgical procedures, and medications and injections, in addition to information on the visit disposition and time spent with the physician.

Data for the National Survey of Ambulatory Surgery are collected on a representative sample of hospital-based and freestanding ambulatory surgery centers. Data include patient demographic characteristics; source of payment; information on anesthesia given; the diagnoses; and the surgical and nonsurgical procedures on patient visits to hospital-based and freestanding ambulatory surgery centers. The survey consists of a mailed survey about the facility and abstracts of patient data.

The National Nursing Home Survey provides data on the facility, current residents, and discharged residents. Information is gathered through an interview process. The administrator or designee provides information about the facility. For information on the residents, the nursing staff member most familiar with the resident's care is interviewed. The staff member uses the resident's health record for reference in the interview. Data collected on the facility include information on ownership, size, certification status, admissions, services, full-time equivalent employees, and basic charges.

Table 14.2.   Components of the National Health Care Survey

Database	Type of Setting	Content	Data Source	Method of Data Collection
National Hospital Discharge Survey Note: this survey ended in 2010. See note 1 below	Hospital inpatient	Uniform Hospital Discharge Data Set	Discharged patient records	Abstract
National Ambulatory Medical Care Survey	Office-based physician practice	Data on the patient and the visit	State discharge databases Office-based physician records	Abstract
National Survey of Ambulatory Surgery	Hospital-based and freestanding ambulatory surgery centers	Data on the facility and patients	Facility response to survey and patient records	Survey and abstract
National Nursing Home Survey	Nursing home	Data on the facility and current and discharged residents	Administrator Nurse caregiver	Interview
National Home and Hospice Care Survey	Home health and hospice	Facility data and patient data	Administrator Caregiver	Interview
National Electronic Disease Surveillance System (NEDSS)	Public health departments	Possible bioterrorism incidents	Local and state public health departments	Electronic surveillance
National Hospital Care Survey (NHCS) Note: Will replace NHDS beginning 2013. See note 2 below	Emergency, outpatient, ambulatory surgery centers	Uniform Hospital Discharge Data Set and data on the patient and the visit	Discharged patient records	Abstract

[1] The National Hospital Discharge Survey (NHDS) was conducted annually from 1965 to 2010. The NHDS is being transitioned to the National Hospital Care Survey, and data collection began in 2011 with inpatient data from 500 hospitals. Other care areas will be added in 2013. http://www.cdc.gov/nchs/nhds/about_nhds.htm.
[2] Data collection began in 2011 with inpatient data from 500 hospitals. Expansion will occur in 2013. http://www.cdc.gov/nchs/nhcs.htm.

Both the current and discharged resident interviews provide demographic information on the resident as well as LOS, diagnoses, level of care received, **activities of daily living (ADLs)**, and charges.

For the National Home and Hospice Care Survey, data are collected on the home health or hospice agency as well as on its current and discharged patients. Data include referral and length of service, diagnoses, number of visits, patient charges, health status, reason for discharge, and types of services provided. Facility data are obtained through an interview with the administrator or designee. Patient information is obtained from the caregiver most familiar with the patient's care. The caregiver may use the patient's health record in answering the interview questions.

Because of the bioterrorism scares in recent years, the CDC is developing the National Electronic Disease Surveillance System (NEDSS), which serves as a major part of the Public Health Information Network (PHIN). It will provide a national surveillance system by connecting the CDC with local and state public health partners. This integrated system will allow the CDC to monitor trends from disease reporting at the local and state level to look for possible bioterrorism incidents.

The National Center for Health Statistics, Centers for Disease Control announced plans to conduct a new survey beginning in 2013, the National Hospital Care Survey (NHCS). This survey combines the National Hospital Discharge Survey (NHDS) and the National Hospital Ambulatory Medical Care Survey (NHAMCS). The newly formed initiative aims to request data on the utilization of healthcare provided in emergency departments, outpatient departments, and ambulatory surgery centers, thus integrating the NHDS and NHAMCS into NHCS. NHCS will replace NHDS and NHAMCS but continue to provide nationally representative data on utilization of hospital care and general purpose healthcare statistics on inpatient care as well as care delivered in emergency departments, outpatient departments, and ambulatory surgery centers.

Other national public health databases include the National Health Interview Survey, which is used to monitor the health status of the population of the United States, and the National Immunization Survey, which collects data on the immunization status of children between the ages of 19 months and 35 months living in the United States.

State and local public health departments also develop databases as needed to perform their duties of health surveillance, disease prevention, and research. An example of a state database is the infectious and notifiable disease database. Each state has a list of diseases that must be reported to the state, such as AIDS, measles, and syphilis, so that containment and prevention measures may be taken to avoid large outbreaks. As mentioned before, these state and local reporting systems will be connected with the CDC through NEDSS to evaluate trends in disease outbreaks. Statewide databases and registries also may collect extensive information on particular diseases and conditions such as birth defects, immunization, and cancer.

Vital Statistics

Vital statistics include data on births, deaths, fetal deaths, marriages, and divorces. Responsibility for the collection of vital statistics rests with the states. The states share information with NCHS. The actual collection of the information is carried out at the local level. For example, birth certificates are completed at the facility where the birth occurred. They are then sent to the state. The state serves as the official repository for the certificates and provides vital statistics information to NCHS. From the vital statistics collected, states and the national government develop a variety of databases and statistics about vital events in the state or country.

One vital statistics database at the national level is the Linked Birth and Infant Death Data Set. In this database, the information from birth certificates is compared to death certificates for infants who die under one year of age. This database provides data to conduct analyses for patterns of infant death. Other national programs that use vital statistics data include the National Mortality Followback Survey, the National Survey of Family Growth, and the National Death Index (CDC 2008c). In some of these databases, such as the National Mortality Followback Survey, additional information is collected on deaths originally identified through the vital statistics system.

Similar databases using vital statistics data as a basis are found at the state level. Birth defects registries, for example, frequently use vital records data with information on the birth defect as part of their data collection process.

Clinical Trials Databases

A **clinical trial** is a research project in which new treatments and tests are investigated to determine whether they are safe and effective. The trial proceeds according to a **protocol,** which is the list of rules and procedures to be followed. Clinical trials databases have been developed to allow physicians and patients to find clinical trials. A patient with cancer or AIDS, for example, might be interested in participating in a clinical trial but not know how to locate one applicable to his or her type of disease. Clinical trials databases provide the data to enable patients and practitioners to determine what clinical trials are available and applicable to the patient.

The Food and Drug Administration Modernization Act of 1997 mandated that a clinical trials database be developed. The National Library of Medicine has developed the database, called ClinicalTrials.gov, which is available on the Internet for use by both patients and practitioners (NLM 2008). Information in the database includes the following:

- Abstracts of clinical study protocols
- Summary of the purpose of the study
- Recruiting status
- Criteria for patient participation
- Location of the trial and specific contact information
- Additional information (may help a patient decide whether to consider a particular trial)
- Research study design
- Phase of the trial
- Disease or condition and drug or therapy under study

Each data element has been defined. For example, the brief summary gives an overview of the treatments being studied and types of patients to be included. The location of the trial tells where the trial is being carried out so that patients can select trials in convenient locations. Recruitment status indicates whether subjects are currently being entered in the trial or will be in the future or whether the trial is closed to new subjects. Eligibility criteria include information on the type of condition to be studied, in some cases the stage of the disease, and what other treatments are allowed during the trial or must have been completed before entering the trial. Age is also a frequent eligibility criterion. Study types include diagnostic, genetic, monitoring, natural history, prevention, screening, supportive care, training, and treatment (McCray and Ide 2000, 316). Study design includes the research design being followed.

A clinical trial consists of four study phases. Phase I studies research the safety of the treatment in a small group of people. In phase II studies, emphasis is on determining the treatment's effectiveness and further investigating safety. Phase III studies look at effectiveness and side effects and make comparisons to other available treatments in larger populations. Phase IV studies look at the treatment after it has entered the market.

Some clinical trials databases concentrate on a particular disease. The Department of Health and Human Services, for example, has developed the AIDS Clinical Trials Information Service (ACTIS). The National Cancer Institute sponsors the Physician Data Query (PDQ), a database for cancer clinical trials. These databases contain information similar to ClinicalTrials.gov. Although ClinicalTrials.gov has been set up for use by both patients and health practitioners, some databases are more oriented to practitioners. Clinical trials are discussed in chapter 21.

Health Services Research Databases

Health services research is research concerning healthcare delivery systems, including organization and delivery and care effectiveness and efficiency. Within the federal government, the organization most involved in health services research is the **Agency for Healthcare Research and Quality (AHRQ).** AHRQ looks at issues related to the efficiency and effectiveness of the healthcare delivery system, disease protocols, and guidelines for improved disease outcomes. AHRQ also provides access to different types of data that are primarily used for quality and utilization management purposes.

A major initiative for AHRQ has been the **Healthcare Cost and Utilization Project** (HCUP). HCUP uses data collected at the state level from either claims data from the UB-04 or discharge-abstracted data, including UHDDS items reported by individual hospitals and, in some cases, by freestanding ambulatory care centers. Which data are reported depends on the individual state. Data may be reported by the facilities to a state agency or to the state hospital association, depending on state regulations. The data are then reported from the state to AHRQ, where they become part of the HCUP databases.

HCUP consists of the following set of databases:

- Nationwide Inpatient Sample (NIS) consists of inpatient discharge data from a sample of hospitals in 35 states throughout the United States
- State Inpatient Database (SID) includes data collected by states on hospital discharges
- State Ambulatory Surgery Databases (SASD) include information from a sample of states on hospital-affiliated ASCs and, from some states, data from freestanding surgery centers
- State Emergency Department Databases include data from hospital-affiliated emergency departments (EDs)
- Abstracts for visits that do not result in a hospitalization
- Kids Inpatient Database (KID) is made up of inpatient discharge data on children younger than 19 years old

These databases are unique because they include data on inpatients whose care is paid for by all types of payers including Medicare, Medicaid, and private insurance as well as by self-paying and uninsured patients. Data elements include demographic information, information on diagnoses and procedures, admission and discharge status, payment sources, total charges, LOS, and information on the hospital or freestanding ambulatory surgery center. Researchers may use these databases to look at issues such as those related to the costs of treating particular diseases, the extent to which treatments are used, and differences in outcomes and cost for alternative treatments.

National Library of Medicine

The National Library of Medicine produces two databases of special interest to the HIM professional: MEDLINE and UMLS.

Medical Literature, Analysis, and Retrieval System Online

Medical Literature, Analysis, and Retrieval System Online (MEDLINE) is the best-known database from the National Library of Medicine. It includes bibliographic listings for publications in the areas of medicine, dentistry, nursing, pharmacy, allied health, and veterinary medicine. HIM professionals use MEDLINE to locate articles on HIM issues as well as articles on medical topics necessary to carry out quality improvement and medical research activities.

Unified Medical Language System

The **Unified Medical Language System (UMLS)** provides a way to integrate biomedical concepts from a variety of sources to show their relationships. This process allows links to be made between different information systems for purposes such as the electronic health record. UMLS is of particular interest to the HIM professional because medical classifications such as ICD-9-CM, CPT, and the Healthcare Common Procedure Coding System (HCPCS) are among the items included. UMLS is covered extensively in chapter 15.

Health Information Exchange

Health information exchange (HIE) initiatives have been developed in an effort to move toward a longitudinal patient record with complete information about the patient available at any point of care. The data from an HIE are patient specific rather than aggregate and are used primarily for patient care. Some researchers have looked at the amount of data available through the health information exchanges as a possible source of data to aggregate for research. Since HIE is a fairly new concept, it is important that HIEs take the time to develop policies and procedures covering the use of data collected for patient care for other purposes. Special attention needs to be paid to whether patients included in the HIE need to provide individual consent to be included when the data are aggregated for research or other purposes. Aggregated data can be deidentified to add another layer of protection for the patient's identity. A full discussion of HIE is included in chapter 9.

Data for Performance Measurement

The Joint Commission, CMS, and some health plans are requiring healthcare facilities to collect data on core performance measures. These measures are "quantitative tools used to assess the clinical, financial, and utilization aspects of a healthcare provider's outcomes of processes" (AHIMA 2010). As such, they are secondary data. Facilities must determine how to collect these measures and how to aggregate the data for reporting purposes. Such measures may be used in the future as a basis for pay for performance. It is, therefore, extremely important that the data accurately reflect the quality of care provided in the facility.

Check Your Understanding 14.4

Instructions: Answer the following questions on a separate piece of paper.

1. What information is included in the Medicare Provider Analysis and Review file?

2. What limitations are encountered when using MEDPAR data in research?

3. Why was the National Practitioner Data Bank developed? What law requires its use? Why was the Healthcare Integrity and Protection Data Bank developed? What law requires its use?

4. What types of information must be reported to the National Practitioner Data Bank and the Healthcare Integrity and Protection Data Bank? Do the two data banks overlap in any way?

5. How do healthcare organizations use the National Practitioner Data Bank? Who may use the HIPDB?

6. How can the health information manager contribute to public health databases?

7. Which of the five National Health Care Survey databases use data from health records?

8. What is a clinical trial? Why are clinical trials databases developed? Which law mandated development of a national clinical trials database?

9. What is the source of data for the Healthcare Cost and Utilization Project?

10. Why is UMLS of interest to HIM professionals?

11. Why have health information exchange efforts been developed?

12. What type of data is included in HIEs?

Processing and Maintenance of Secondary Databases

Several issues surround the processing and maintenance of secondary databases. HIM professionals are often involved in decisions concerning these issues.

Manual versus Automated Methods of Data Collection

Although registries and databases are almost universally computerized, data collection is commonly done manually. The most frequent method is **abstracting.** Abstracting is the process of reviewing the patient health record and entering the required data elements into the database. In some cases, the abstracting may initially be done on an abstract form. The data then would be entered into the database from the form. In many cases, it is done directly from the primary patient health record into a data collection screen in the computerized database system.

Not all data collection is done manually. In some cases, data can be downloaded directly from other electronic systems. Birth defects registries, for example, often download information on births and birth defects from the vital records system. In some cases, providers such as hospitals and physicians send information in electronic format to the registry or database. The National Discharge Survey from the National Center for Health Statistics uses information in electronic format from state databases. As the electronic health record (EHR) develops further, less and less data will need to be manually abstracted since it will be available electronically through the EHR.

Vendor Systems versus Facility-Specific Systems

Each registry must determine what information technology solution best meets its needs. In some cases that will be a vendor-created product specifically for registries. In other cases, the registry system may be part of an overall facility health information system. It is important that either type of product is able to incorporate demographic and other pertinent information from the facility health information system. In this way, time is saved and data integrity between the registry information and the health information system is maintained. If registries utilize registry applications as part of a facility-wide health information system, it is important that the registry manager be included in the decision of which health information system to purchase for the facility as well as in pertinent training and implementation decisions.

Data Quality Issues

Indexes, registries, and databases are only helpful when the data they contain are accurate. Decisions concerning new treatment methods, healthcare policy, and physician credentialing and privileging are made based on these databases. Incorrect data will likely result in serious errors in decision making. Several factors must be addressed when assessing data quality, including data validity, reliability, completeness, and timeliness.

Validity of the Data

Validity refers to the accuracy of the data. For example, in a cancer registry, the stage of the neoplasm must be recorded accurately because statistical information on survival rates by stage is commonly reported.

Several methods may be used to ensure validity. One method is to incorporate **edits** in the database. An edit is a check on the accuracy of the data, such as setting data types. When a particular data element, such as admission date, is set up with a data type of date, the computer will not allow other types of data, such as name, to be entered in that field. Other edits may use comparisons between fields to ensure accuracy. For example, an edit might check to see that all patients with the diagnosis of prostate cancer are listed as males in the database.

Reliability of the Data

Another factor to be considered in looking at data quality is reliability. Reliability refers to the consistency of the data. For example, all patients in a trauma registry with the same level, severity, and site of injury should have the same Abbreviated Injury Scale. Reliability is frequently checked by having more than one person abstract data for the same case. The results are then compared to identify any discrepancies. This is called an **interrater reliability** method of checking. Several different people may be used to do the checking. In the cancer registry, physician members of the cancer committee are called on to check the reliability of the data.

The use of uniform terminology is an important way to improve data reliability. This has been evident in case definition for registries. The criteria for including a patient in a registry must have a clear definition. Definitions for terms such as *race*, for example, must include the categories to be used in determining race. When uniform terms are not used, the data will not be consistent. Also, it will be impossible to make comparisons between systems when uniform terms have not been used for all data. A **data dictionary** in which all data elements are defined helps ensure that uniform data definitions are being followed. An example would be the term *discharge time*. Discharge time could be the time the physician writes the discharge order, the time the information about the discharge is entered into the admission, discharge, transfer (ADT) system, or the time the patient leaves the floor. The data dictionary could define it as the time the information is entered in the ADT system, and then everyone recording discharge time would be using the same time reference for that data element.

Completeness of the Data

Completeness is another factor to be considered in data quality. Missing data may prevent the database from being useful for research or clinical decision making. To avoid missing data, some databases will not allow the user to move to the next field without making an entry in the current one, especially for fields considered crucial. Looking at a variety of sources in case finding is a way to avoid omitting patients who should be included in a registry.

Timeliness of the Data

Another concept important in data quality is timeliness. Data must be available within a time frame helpful to the user. Factors that influence decisions may change over time, so it is important that the data reflect up-to-date information.

Data Security and Confidentiality Issues

Data security usually refers to the tools, including technological safeguards, used to ensure confidentiality of personal health information. **Data confidentiality** usually refers to an individual's right to information privacy and is accomplished through well-managed administrative privacy policies and practices and technology tools.

HIPAA-Covered Entities

When looking at data security and confidentiality issues, it is important to consider the HIPAA regulations for privacy and security. For HIPAA-covered entities, the data collection done by registries is considered part of "healthcare operations." The patient does not, therefore, have to sign an authorization for release of protected health information (PHI) to be included in the registry. Reporting of notifiable diseases to the state comes under "required reporting" and does not require patient authorization for release (Handling Cancer Registry Requests 2003, 7). Release of information to requestors other than the state will depend on the requestor. Data may be released to internal users, such as physicians for research, without the patient's consent as well because research also comes under healthcare operations. External users, such as the American College of Surgeons, collect aggregate data from facilities, so individual patient authorization is not required. Information about patients that may be included in registries or other secondary data sources and reported to outside entities must be included in the facility's Notice of Privacy Practices given to each patient on his or her initial encounter. Through this mechanism, patients are made aware that data about them may be reported to outside entities.

HIPAA security regulations also apply to data in registries and indexes. These regulations require policies in the areas of administrative, technical, and physical security, which are discussed here. (See chapter 12 for further discussion of privacy, security, and confidentiality.)

Entities Not Covered by HIPAA

Not all registries and databases are covered under HIPAA if they do not bill for patient care services. Central registries would be an example of a registry that is not covered under HIPAA. In such cases, the general norms for data security and confidentiality should be followed.

Data Security

Registries and secondary databases must ensure the security of the information that they maintain. A number of methods such as passwords and role-based access may be used to ensure that only authorized people have access to patient data in the facility's computer system. Loss of data is another important consideration in data security that could severely affect registries and secondary data sources. Although data sometimes are lost as a result of unauthorized access, more often they are lost in more routine ways such as computer malfunction or **computer viruses** that can cause data to be erased or lost.

Physical security of the system is a consideration that is required under the HIPAA security regulations. Computer terminals must be kept in areas that are not physically accessible to unauthorized people. Reports and printouts from the system should not be left where they can be seen. When they are no longer needed, they should be destroyed.

Technical security under HIPAA involves issues such as whether sensitive data need to be encrypted. **Encryption** is a method of scrambling data so that they cannot be read without first being decoded. An AIDS registry, for example, might want to use an encryption method to protect patient-identifiable information since AIDS data are considered sensitive.

Data Privacy and Confidentiality

Maintaining the privacy and confidentiality of health data is a traditional role of HIM professionals. When looking at methods to protect secondary records, patient-specific information requires more control than secondary databases that include only aggregate data because individual patients cannot be identified in aggregate data. Policies on who may access the data provide the basic protection for confidentiality.

The type of data maintained also may affect policies on confidentiality. For many of the government databases discussed previously, the information is aggregate and the data are readily available to any interested users. For example, public health data are frequently published in many formats, including printed reports, Internet access, and direct computer access.

As is true of all employees working with patient data, employees working with data in indexes, registries, and databases should receive training on confidentiality. Further, they should be required to sign a yearly statement indicating that they have received the training and understand the implications of failure to maintain confidentiality of the data.

Deidentification

In some cases, users of secondary data will need to remove identifying data so that data can be used without violating the patient's privacy. This process is called **deidentification**. The HIPAA privacy regulations indicate two ways to accomplish the deidentification:

- The covered entity can strip off certain elements to ensure that the patient's information is truly deidentified (45 CFR 164)

- The covered entity can have an expert apply generally accepted statistical and scientific principles and methods to minimize the risk that the information might be used to identify an individual (Brodnik et al. 2009)

Whichever method is utilized, it is important that a data set released as deidentified contain no information that would enable patients to be individually identified.

Transparency

Transparency refers to the degree to which patients included in secondary data sets are aware of their inclusion. In its report *Toward a National Framework for the Secondary Use of Health Data*, the American Medical Informatics Association (2006) has recommended that full disclosure be the policy for all secondary uses of data.

Trends in the Collection of Secondary Data

The most significant trend in collecting secondary data is the increased use of automated data entry. Registries and databases are more commonly using data already available in electronic form rather than manually abstracting all data. As the EHR becomes more common, separate databases for various diseases and conditions such as cancer, diabetes, and trauma will become unnecessary. The patient health record itself will be a database that can be queried for information currently obtained from specialized registries.

Since not all data can currently be entered through automated means, other facilities are using existing technologies such as point-of-care data collection at the patient's bedside using wireless technology (Eisenhower et al. 2005). Finally, secondary data collection is becoming more common and more secondary data are being collected about patients. Because of this fact, national stakeholders such as the American Medical Informatics Association and the National Center for Vital and Health Statistics are becoming more involved in setting national policy related to secondary data. One of the issues of concern is the ownership of secondary data. As stated in an AHIMA practice brief, "'Who can do what to which data and under which circumstances' is really the central question that must be asked in determining the rights and responsibilities of each stakeholder" (Burrington-Brown and Hjort 2007). Stakeholders include patients, health facilities, HIE organizations, vendors, governmental agencies, employers, and researchers. There is currently no clear-cut guidance on the sometimes conflicting rights and responsibilities of each stakeholder of the data. Additional issues include transparency, deidentification, and data privacy and confidentiality, which were previously discussed.

As more secondary data are collected, the role of the HIM professional remains that of data steward. According to the American Medical Informatics Association, data stewardship "encompasses the responsibilities and accountabilities associated with managing, collecting, viewing, storing, sharing, disclosing, or otherwise making use of personal health information" (NCVHS 2007). These are traditional roles for the HIM professional in relationship to primary data. It will be necessary for these roles to be expanded to encompass secondary data.

Check Your Understanding 14.5

Instructions: Answer the following questions on a separate piece of paper.

1. What factors must be considered when determining the quality of data?

2. Which errors in registries and other secondary databases can cause serious problems?

3. What methods and systems can be used to ensure the quality of secondary healthcare data?

4. What is the difference between security and confidentiality?

5. What methods might be used to control access to a health information system?

6. What types of data should be encrypted?

7. What methods can be used to ensure data confidentiality?

8. What trends are evident in the collection of secondary data?

9. Which types of registries and secondary data sources would be covered by HIPAA privacy and security regulations?

10. How are patients notified that data about them may be included in registries and databases and released to outside entities?

11. What is deidentification, and what are two ways under HIPAA that deidentification may be accomplished?

Summary

Health records contain extensive information about individual patients but are difficult to use when attempting to perceive trends in care or quality. For that reason, secondary records were developed. One type of secondary record is the index. An index is a report from a database that provides information on patients and supports retrieval by diagnosis, procedure, or physician. Health information management departments routinely produce indexes.

Disease registries are developed when extensive information is needed about specific diagnoses, procedures, or conditions. They are commonly used for research and to improve patient care and health status. From the database created through the data collection process, reports can be developed to answer questions regarding patient care or issues such as rates of immunization and birth defects. In some cases, patient follow-up is done to assess survival rates and quality of life after a disease or an accident.

HIM professionals perform a variety of roles in relation to registries. In some cases, they work on setting up the registry.

Moreover, they may work in data collection and management of registry functions. HIM professionals are well suited to such positions because of their background and education in management, health record content, regulatory and legal compliance, and medical science and terminology.

Today, organizations and institutions of all types commonly maintain databases pertaining to healthcare. At the federal level, some administrative databases provide data and information for decisions regarding claims and practitioner credentialing. Other databases focus on the public health area, using data collected at the local level and shared with states and the federal government. These databases assist in government surveillance of health status in the United States. Some databases, such as the clinical trials database, are mandated by law and help patients and providers locate clinical trials regardless of source or location.

Registries and databases raise a number of managerial issues. Data collection is often time-consuming, so some databases now use automated entry methods. In addition, decisions must be made between vendor and facility-specific products. Finally, the quality of the data is an important issue because the decisions made based on data in registries and databases depend on the data's validity, reliability, accuracy, and timeliness.

Another important issue related to registries and databases is data security. Facilities must adopt methods that will ensure controlled access to data as well as prevent the loss of data. Confidentiality is always of concern to the HIM professional, and steps must be taken to protect it.

In the future, separate registries and databases may become less common with the advent of the computer-based patient record. Essentially a large database, the electronic health record can be queried directly rather than having to first abstract data from the primary record into a secondary record.

References

American College of Surgeons. 2008a. Commission on Cancer. http://www.facs.org/cancer.

American College of Surgeons. 2008b. Trauma programs. http://www.facs.org/trauma/index.html.

American Gastroenterological Association. 2011. AGA digestive health outcomes registry. http://www.gastro.org/practice/digestive-health-outcomes-registry.

American Health Information Management Association. 2010. *Pocket Glossary of Health Information Management and Technology,* 2nd ed. Chicago: AHIMA.

American Joint Committee on Cancer. 2008. http://www.cancerstaging.org.

American Medical Informatics Association. 2006. *Toward a National Framework for the Secondary Use of Health Data.* Bethesda, MD: American Medical Informatics Association.

Brodnik, M., et al. 2009. *Fundamentals of Law for Health Informatics and Information Management.* Chicago: AHIMA.

Burrington-Brown, J., and B. Hjort. 2007. Health data access, use and control. *Journal of AHIMA* 78(5): 63–66.

Centers for Disease Control and Prevention. 2008a. National Program of Cancer Registries. http://www.cdc.gov/cancer/NPCR/publications.

Centers for Disease Control and Prevention. 2008b. National immunization program. http://www.cdc.gov/vaccines/programs/iis/stds/coredata.html.

Centers for Disease Control and Prevention. 2008c. National Center for Health Statistics. http://www.cdc.gov/nchs/nvss.htm.

Department of Health and Human Services. 2000. Healthy people 2010: Tracking healthy people 2010.

Department of Health and Human Services. 2008. Fact sheet on the Healthcare Protection and Integrity Data Bank.

Eisenhower, C., et al. 2005. Data abstraction unplugged: Taking trauma registry to the point of care with wireless technology. *Journal of AHIMA* 76(7): 42–45.

Food and Drug Administration. 2008. http://www.fda.gov/downloads/MedicalDevices/DeviceRegulationandGuidance/GuidanceDocuments/UCM095266.pdf.

Handling cancer registry requests for information. 2003. *In Confidence* 11(8):7.

McCray, A., and N.C. Ide. 2000. Design and implementation of a national clinical trials registry. *Journal of the American Medical Informatics Association* 7(3):313–323.

National Committee on Vital and Health Statistics. 2007. Report to the Secretary of the U.S. Department of Health and Human Services on Enhanced Protection for Uses of Health Data: A stewardship framework for "Secondary Uses" of Electronically Collected and Transmitted Health Data.

National Library of Medicine. 2008. http://www.clinicaltrials.gov.

National Practitioner Data Bank. 2006 (Mar. 21). National Practitioner Data Bank for Adverse Information on Physicians and Other Health Care Practitioners: Reporting on adverse and negative actions. *Federal Register* 71 FR 14135.

Shapiro-Mendoza, C.K., et al. 2012. http://pediatrics.aappublications.org/content/early/2012/01/04/peds.2011-0854.abstract.

Stedman's Medical Dictionary Online. 2008. http://www.stedmans.com/section.cfm/45.

Trauma.org. 2008. http://www.trauma.org.

45 CFR 164: Health Insurance Portability and Accountability security regulations. 2007.

chapter 15

Clinical Classifications and Terminologies

Brooke Palkie, MA, RHIA

Learning Objectives

- Differentiate among and identify the correct uses of classifications, nomenclatures, and terminologies
- Discuss the strengths and weaknesses of the classification systems currently required in the United States
- Identify key elements in the transition from ICD-9-CM to ICD-10-CM/PCS
- Describe the characteristics of ICD-10-CM and ICD-10-PCS

- Identify clinical data representation and data retrieval needs, and select a terminology most likely to meet these needs
- Understand the need for a terminology in an electronic health record (EHR) system
- Discuss the role of mapping among clinical terminologies
- Describe the characteristics of a sound clinical terminology

Key Terms

American Medical Association (AMA)
American Society for Testing and Materials (ASTM)
Centers for Medicare and Medicaid Services (CMS)
Clinical Care Classification (CCC)
Clinical terminology
Community of Practice (CoP)
Concept
Consolidated Health Informatics (CHI)
Context
Current Dental Terminology (CDT)
Current Procedural Terminology (CPT)
Digital Imaging and Communications in Medicine (DICOM)
Food and Drug Administration (FDA)
Functional interoperability
General Equivalence Mapping (GEM)
Granularity
Health Insurance Portability and Accountability Act (HIPAA)
Health Level Seven (HL7)
Healthcare Common Procedure Coding System (HCPCS)
Interface terminology
International Classification of Diseases (ICD)

International Classification of Diseases, 9th Revision, Clinical Modification (ICD-9-CM)
International Classification of Diseases, 10th Revision, Clinical Modification (ICD-10-CM)
International Classification of Diseases, 10th Revision, Procedure Coding System (ICD-10-PCS)
International Classification of Diseases, 11th Revision (ICD-11)
International Classification of Diseases for Oncology, 3rd Revision (ICD-O-3)
International Classification on Functioning, Disability, and Health (ICF)
International Classification of Primary Care (ICPC-2)
International Health Terminology Standards Development Organisation (IHTSDO)
Interoperability
Lexicon
Logical Observation Identifiers Names and Codes (LOINC)
Medical Subject Headings database (MeSH)
Morbidity
Morphological

Morphology
Mortality
Multiaxial
National Center for Health Statistics (NCHS)
National Drug Codes (NDC)
National Library of Medicine (NLM)
Nomenclature
Not Elsewhere Classified (NEC)
Not Otherwise Specified (NOS)
Orthographic
Patient medical record information (PMRI)
Permanence
Polyhierarchy
Reference terminology
Relationship
RxNorm
Semantic interoperability
Structured Product Labeling (SPL)
Syntactic

Systemized Nomenclature of Medicine– Clinical
    Terminology (SNOMED CT)
Systematized Nomenclature of Medicine– Reference
    Terminology (SNOMED RT)
Terminology
Topography
Unified Medical Language System (UMLS)
Unified Medical Language System (UMLS) Metathesaurus
Unified Medical Language System (UMLS) Semantic
    Network
Unified Medical Language System (UMLS) SPECIALIST
    Lexicon
Vendor neutral
Vocabulary
World Health Organization (WHO)
World Organization of National Colleges, Academies, and
    Academic Associations of General Practitioners/Family
    Physicians (WONCA)

Healthcare is faced with many challenges, including an aging population, the need to conserve resources, medical knowledge that is increasing exponentially, and a consumer population with Internet access. To meet these challenges, healthcare organizations must have the ability to operate effectively and efficiently using the latest medical data and knowledge. Unfortunately, the healthcare industry in the United States has yet to fully agree on common terminologies that would allow healthcare facilities and practitioners throughout the country to exchange and use information reliably.

It is difficult to believe that the quest to classify **morbidity** and **mortality** is quite old. London parishes first began to keep death records in 1532. In 1662, John Graunt, a merchant, wrote *Natural and Political Observations ... Made upon the Bills of Mortality.* His friend, Sir William Petty, was able to extrapolate from mortality rates an estimate of community economic loss caused by deaths (Encyclopedia Britannica Online 2012). Two hundred years later, in *Notes on a Hospital,* Florence Nightingale wrote, "In attempting to arrive at the truth, I have applied everywhere for information, but in scarcely an instance have I been able to obtain hospital records fit for any purposes of comparison. If they could be obtained ... they would show subscribers how their money was being spent, what amount of good was really being done with it, or whether the money was not doing mischief rather than good" (Barnett et al. 1993, 1046).

Many of the same issues remain in healthcare today. It is vitally important to be able to compare data for outcomes measurement, quality improvement, resource utilization, best practices, and medical research. These tasks can be accomplished only when healthcare has a common terminology that is easily integrated into the electronic health record (EHR).

This chapter examines the history and current practices of classification in the healthcare industry. It also addresses various clinical terminologies and the desired characteristics of a terminology.

Development of Classification Systems and Terminologies for Healthcare Data

As the discussion of classification systems and terminologies for healthcare data begins, it is important to have an understanding of several terms related to clinical content representation. Unfortunately, it is difficult to get complete agreement on definitions for even these basic concepts. However, there are some commonly accepted definitions. A classification is a clinical vocabulary, terminology, or nomenclature that lists words or phrases with their meanings; provides for the proper use of clinical words as names or symbols; and facilitates mapping of standardized terms to broader classifications for administrative, regulatory, oversight, and fiscal requirements (AHIMA 2010). A classification system provides easy storage, retrieval, and analysis of data for the purposes of transmitting and comparing data. A **nomenclature** is a recognized system of terms used in a science or an art that follows preestablished naming conventions (AHIMA 2010). The terms *classification* and *nomenclature* are often used interchangeably. However, Chute (2000, 298) distinguishes the two: "classifications and nomenclatures can be more helpfully regarded as lying along a continuum, where the first categorizes and aggregates while the second supports detailed descriptions." The Diagnostic Statistical Manual (DSM) is an example of a nomenclature

Figure 15.1.   Comparative level of detail in nomenclatures, terminologies, and languages

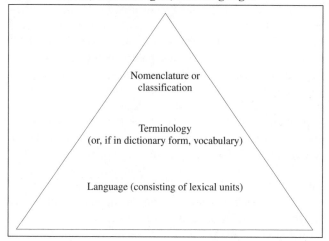

that provides a listing of the terms and definitions (criteria) used to describe mental health disorders. The International Classification of Diseases, 10th Revision is a classification system that organizes (categorizes) many of its disease entries by body system or etiology. For example, disorders related to the circulatory system are organized and classified within a single chapter.

In the generic sense a **terminology** is a "set of terms representing the system of concepts of a particular subject or field" (AHIMA 2010, 291). Obviously when working in healthcare, medical or clinical terminologies are of interest. Another generic term often used when discussing terminologies is **lexicon,** which refers to the listings of words or expressions in a language (terminology) and information about the language such as definitions, related principles, and description of (grammatical) structure (NLM 2012a). The pyramid in figure 15.1 illustrates how these terms are all related. A nomenclature can be less specific than a terminology, which is less specific than a language. So, while a classification or nomenclature categorizes and aggregates, a terminology represents the whole of a subject field.

It is important to recognize that the problem of multiple definitions and names is endemic in the field of healthcare terminology. A **clinical terminology** is defined as a set of standardized terms and their synonyms that record patient findings, circumstances, events, and interventions with sufficient detail to support clinical care, decision support, outcomes research, and quality improvement (AMIA and AHIMA Terminology and Classification Policy Task Force 2007, 41). A *clinical vocabulary* is "a formally recognized list of preferred medical terms" (AHIMA 2010, 55). The definition for the **vocabulary** is similar to that of terminology except that it includes the meanings or definitions of words. Because of their very similar meanings, the terms *clinical terminology* and *clinical vocabulary* are often used interchangeably in practice. To further complicate the issue,

many working within the field also often use *terminology* to refer to the entire spectrum of issues related to clinical data representation from classifications and nomenclatures to clinical terminologies (Chute 2000, 299).

Clinical classifications and terminologies serve different functions. For example, the classification systems ICD-10-CM/PCS (Clinical Modification/Procedure Coding System) and Current Procedural Terminology (CPT) represent similar procedures and diagnoses with single codes. This broad categorization of information is useful for functions such as billing and monitoring resource utilization. In contrast, terminologies support the capture and representation of information collected within an EHR at the time of documentation (Bowman 2005). Terminologies exist to represent topics ranging from nursing documentation and laboratory data to medical devices. This detailed level of data capture is useful to support functions such as clinical decision support and clinical alerts.

Depending on the purpose of a given classification or terminology, differences are also seen at the level of **granularity** (detail) used to represent content. For example, the CPT classification system has a single code (86003 Allergen specific IgE: quantitative or semiquantitative, each allergen) to report a laboratory test to detect a specific allergen. The same code is used regardless of the allergen (for example, food, weeds, dust). On the other hand, Logical Observation Identifier Names and Codes (LOINC), a clinical terminology, provides many different codes (for example, 11195-5, 11196-3, 11197-1) to represent the test for each unique allergen (NLM 2012b). In this case, the LOINC representation of the allergen tests is more granular, that is, more specific.

Check Your Understanding 15.1

Instructions: Answer the following questions on a separate piece of paper.

1. What are the general functions of classifications and nomenclatures? Give examples of each.

2. How does a clinical terminology differ from a classification or nomenclature?

3. Describe the general differences of clinical classifications and terminologies, providing examples of these differences.

Current Systems of Classification and Nomenclature

Systems for classifying diseases have progressed through various stages since the first classification system was developed in the late 19th century. The following sections describe past, current, and near-future developments for a variety of classification systems.

International Classification of Diseases

The **International Classification of Diseases (ICD)** began as the Bertillon Classification of Diseases in 1893. In 1900, the French government convened an international meeting to update the Bertillon classification to the International List of Causes of Death. The goal was to develop a common system for describing the causes of mortality. The **World Health Organization (WHO)** became responsible for maintaining ICD in 1948. Currently, ICD is used by more than 100 countries worldwide to classify diseases and other health issues. The classification system facilitates the storage and retrieval of diagnostic information and serves as the basis for compiling mortality and morbidity statistics reported by WHO members. The latest version of the International Classification of Diseases, the 10th edition (ICD-10), has been in use since 1994. In 1999, the United States began using ICD-10 to report mortality statistics under its agreement with WHO. The United States is the only developed country that has not yet implemented ICD-10 for capturing morbidity. However, the United States is slated to transition to a clinical modification of ICD-10 (meaning capturing diseases or causes of illness) by the mandated date of October 1, 2013. ICD-10 is routinely updated by WHO and allows for data comparability internationally. The development of an 11th edition of ICD is currently underway. A significant difference in **International Classification of Diseases, 11th Revision (ICD-11)** is that it will be designed to include linkages to standardized healthcare terminologies to facilitate processing and use of the data for a variety of purposes such as research (WHO 2007). It is anticipated that the process of transition from ICD-10 to ICD-11 will be much more efficient than the transition from the current version of ICD-9 to ICD-10.

International Classification of Diseases, 9th Revision, Clinical Modification

Developed by the **National Center for Health Statistics (NCHS)**, the **International Classification of Diseases, 9th Revision, Clinical Modification (ICD-9-CM)** is a derivative work of the International Classification of Diseases, 9th Revision, as developed by WHO. ICD-9-CM is used in the United States only to code and classify diagnoses from inpatient and outpatient records, as well as inpatient procedures. Although diagnostic and procedural coding were the original functions of the system, ICD-9-CM also has been used to communicate provider reimbursement information on healthcare services since 1983. Today, coding for reimbursement is a vital part of healthcare operations. The official ICD-9-CM coding guidelines are published quarterly in *Coding Clinic for ICD-9-CM* by the Central Office on ICD-9-CM Coding of the American Hospital Association (AHA).

Changes and updates to ICD-9-CM are managed by the ICD-9-CM Coordination and Maintenance Committee, a federal committee co-chaired by representatives from the NCHS and the **Centers for Medicare and Medicaid Services (CMS)**. The NCHS is responsible for Volumes 1 and 2 (diagnoses), and CMS is responsible for Volume 3 (procedures). Both the public and private sectors are invited to make suggestions for modifications to ICD-9-CM, and meetings are open to the public. Modifications may be implemented on April 1 and October 1 of each year. However, based on the impending transition to ICD-10, the ICD-9-CM Coordination and Maintenance Committee implemented a partial freeze of the ICD-9-CM and ICD-10 codes prior to the pending implementation of ICD-10. According to CMS (2012a) "the development of WHO's ICD-10 was based on the realization that the great expansion in the use of the ICD necessitated a thorough rethinking of its structure and an effort to devise a stable and flexible classification that would not require fundamental revision for many years." The National Committee on Vital and Health Statistics (NCVHS) reported that ICD-9-CM was outdated and made the recommendation that the US transition to ICD-10-CM for morbidity and mortality coding. Similarly, CMS recommended that ICD-9-CM be replaced with a more flexible option.

International Classification of Diseases, 10th Revision, Clinical Modification

As with ICD-9-CM, the US government modified the **International Classification of Diseases, 10th Revision, Clinical Modification (ICD-10-CM)** for the reporting of morbidity data. In 2008, the Department of Health and Human Services (HHS) published a notice of proposed rulemaking that identified the replacement of ICD-9-CM with ICD-10-CM for diagnosis coding and ICD-10-PCS (International Classification of Diseases, 10th Revision, Procedure Coding System) for procedure coding. In 2008, the Department of Health and Human Service(HHS) published a notice of . . . effective October 1, 2013. However, implementation has been delayed and it is anticipated that the new effective date for ICD-10 code sets will be October 1, 2014.

When the United States modified ICD-9 to create ICD-9-CM more than 30 years ago, a third volume was added to capture procedure codes. However, instead of appending a short volume to ICD-10-CM, a complete classification, ICD-10-PCS, was developed. This procedure coding system is much more detailed and specific than the short volume of procedure codes included in ICD-9-CM (CMS 2012a).

CMS (2012a) identifies ICD-10-CM as a system that consists of more than 86,000 diagnosis codes, compared to approximately 13,000 ICD-9-CM diagnosis codes. ICD-10-PCS consists of 87,000 procedure codes. Together, the ICD-10 codes have the potential to reveal more about quality of care, so that data can be used in a more meaningful way to better understand complications, better design clinically robust algorithms, and better track the outcomes of care (CMS 2012a). ICD-10-CM and ICD-10-PCS incorporate greater specificity and clinical detail to provide information for clinical decision making and outcomes research. CMS (2012a) defines ICD-10 as follows:

- ICD-10-CM is a US clinical modification of WHO's ICD-10 and is maintained by the National Center for Health Statistics (NCHS). It is a morbidity classification system that classifies diagnoses and other reasons for healthcare encounters. The code structure is alphanumeric, with codes comprised of 3 to 7 characters.
- ICD-10-PCS is a procedure coding system developed under contract by the Centers for Medicare and Medicaid Services (CMS) as a replacement of the ICD-9-CM procedure coding system for hospital reporting of inpatient procedures. It has a 7-character alphanumeric code structure.

The value of transitioning to ICD-10-CM is broad and contains a substantial increase in content over ICD-9-CM. Improvements in the content and format of ICD-10-CM will result in

- Additional information relevant to ambulatory care
- Expanded cause of injury codes
- New combination diagnosis/symptom codes to reduce the number of codes needed to fully describe a condition and reduce coding errors
- Greater specificity in code assignment
- Laterality information (right and left)
- Greater achievement of the benefits of an electronic health record

- Enhanced ability to meet the Health Insurance Portability and Accountability Act (HIPAA) electronic transaction/code set requirements
- Increased value in the US investment in Systematized Nomenclature of Medicine–Clinical Terminology (SNOMED CT)
- Use of seven-digit alphanumeric format, which facilitates expansion and revision of classification (space to accommodate future expansion)

Figure 15.2 provides an example of an entry in the Tabular List of Diseases, ICD-10-CM.

ICD-10-CM Field Test Study

The American Health Management Association (AHIMA) and the AHA collaborated on an ICD-10-CM Field Testing Project in 2003. The goal of this project was to assess the functionality of ICD-10-CM and its ability to describe conditions better than ICD-9-CM. Volunteers with adequate coding knowledge and experience with ICD-9-CM were recruited to code 50 records using both ICD-9-CM and ICD-10-CM. Procedural coding was not included in this study. Volunteers selected for the study were required to undergo several hours of training in regards to ICD-10-CM coding guidelines and how to use the reporting tool. After training, the volunteers were advised to select 50 medical records from various care settings to code. They were then required to submit the codes from both systems, the amount of time required to code each case in both systems, and any difficulties that they experienced with the ICD-10-CM system.

Figure 15.2.   Example of an ICD-10-CM entry

T40   Poisoning by, adverse effect of and underdosing of narcotics and psychodysleptics [hallucinogens]
Excludes2: drug dependence and related mental and behavioral disorders due to psychoactive substance use (F10.-F19.-)
The appropriate 7th character is to be added to each code from category T40
A   initial encounter
D   subsequent encounter
S   sequela
T40.0   Poisoning by, adverse effect of and underdosing of opium
T40.0x   Poisoning by, adverse effect of and underdosing of opium
T40.0x1   Poisoning by opium, accidental (unintentional)   Poisoning by opium NOS
T40.0x2   Poisoning by opium, intentional self-harm
T40.0x3   Poisoning by opium, assault
T40.0x4   Poisoning by opium, undetermined
T40.0x5   Adverse effect of opium
T40.0x6   Underdosing of opium

Source: CMS 2012b.

The findings included the following key observations (AHIMA and AHA 2003):

- Clinical descriptors were found to be 71.7 percent better in ICD-10-CM than ICD-9-CM
- 76.3 percent of the respondents reported that ICD-10-CM was an improvement over ICD-9-CM
- 78.6 percent of the respondents suggested that ICD-10-CM should be implemented for coding conditions in three years or less
- 60 percent of the respondents recommended that coders would require 16 hours or less of training before using ICD-10-CM
- Over 50 percent of the respondents reported that there was no time difference required to code in both systems
- The respondents also reported that coding in ICD-10-CM may require less time if adequate coding tools and training are provided and when the coders become familiar with ICD-10-CM

International Classification of Diseases, 10th Revision, Procedure Coding System

In the mid-1990s, CMS awarded a contract to the 3M Health Information Systems group to develop a new procedure coding system to replace the Tabular List of Procedures, Volume 3 of ICD-9-CM. The classification developed, the **International Classification of Diseases, 10th Revision, Procedure Coding System (ICD-10-PCS)**, is considered an improvement over ICD-9-CM, Volume 3 for many reasons including the use of standardized definitions, ease of expandability, ease of use, and comprehensiveness. ICD-10-PCS uses very precise definitions. For example, a percutaneous approach is defined as "entry, by puncture or minor incision, of instrumentation through the skin or mucous membrane and any other body layers necessary to reach the site of the procedure" (CMS 2008a). This is a substantial improvement over ICD-9-CM in which a term could have a different meaning in different sections of the classification. For example, when referring to a percutaneous liver biopsy in ICD-9-CM, *percutaneous* means through the skin. However, percutaneous in the term *percutaneous coronary angioplasty* refers to an endoscopic percutaneous approach. The greater coverage of ICD-10-PCS is illustrated by the significantly larger number of codes. ICD-9-CM contains approximately 4,000 procedure codes and ICD-10-PCS contains over 86,000 (Averill et al. 2005; CMS 2008a).

ICD-10-PCS is composed of seven-character alphanumeric codes. Each character can be one of 34 values (numbers 0 through 9 and the letters of the alphabet excluding I and O). The classification is divided into 16 sections, each of which covers a specific diagnostic area (for example, medical and surgical, radiation oncology, and mental health). Depending on the requirements of each section, the seven characters are assigned different meanings. For example,

Figure 15.3.   ICD-10-PCS Code Structure

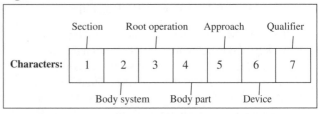

Source: Reprinted from CMS. 2012. https://www.cms.gov/Medicare/Coding/ICD10/downloads//pcs_refman.pdf.

in the medical and surgical section, the fourth character represents the body part or region involved in the procedure; in the placement section, it represents the body region or orifice; and in the chiropractic section, it represents the body region (CMS 2012a).

Figure 15.3 illustrates the meanings of each character of ICD-10-PCS codes in the medical surgical section of the classification.

Table 15.1 is an excerpt from a table used for code assignment in the medical and surgical and section of ICD-10-PCS. All codes represented in the table begin with the three characters identified in the header and are completed with characters selected from each of the four columns depending upon the nature of the procedure being coded.

To facilitate the transition from ICD-9-CM, maps have been developed, which link valid relationships between ICD-9-CM codes with those in the ICD-10-CM or ICD-10-PCS classification. The maps, called **General Equivalence Mappings (GEMs)**, were developed by a coordinated effort of NCHS, CMS, AHIMA, AHA, and 3M Health Information Systems and can be found on the CMS website. Additionally, disease-specific GEM files can be found on the NCHS website. Four GEMs were created to handle translation of data between the 9th and 10th versions of the code sets. Two of the crosswalks include mappings from ICD-9-CM to the ICD-10 code sets for diagnoses and procedures. The GEMs are data files that list the ICD-9 and ICD-10 codes and the attributes of the mapping between the two code sets. Mapping from ICD-9 to ICD-10 is called "forward mapping," and mapping from ICD-10 to ICD-9 is "backward mapping" (AMA 2010). In the remaining two GEMs, ICD-10-CM and ICD-10-PCS serve as the source classifications. A clear one-to-one map between an ICD-9-CM and ICD-10-CM code does not occur very often. Therefore, the GEMs provide information regarding the type of match such as a direct match, no match, an approximate match, or a one-to-many code linkage (Butler 2007).

International Classification of Diseases for Oncology, 3rd Revision

The **International Classification of Diseases for Oncology (ICD-O-3)** is currently in its third revision. This classification is used for coding diagnoses of neoplasms in tumor and cancer registries and in pathology laboratories.

Table 15.1.   PCS Table

Within a PCS table, valid codes include all combinations of choices in characters 4 through 7 contained in the same row of the table. In the example below, **0JHT3VZ** is a valid code, and 0JHW3VZ is *not* a valid code.

Section: 0 Medical and Surgical

Body System: J Subcutaneous Tissue and Fascia

Operation: H Insertion: Putting in a nonbiological appliance that monitors, assists, performs, or prevents a physiological function but does not physically take the place of a body part

Body Part	Approach	Device	Qualifier
S Subcutaneous Tissue and Fascia, Head and Neck **V** Subcutaneous Tissue and Fascia, Upper Extremity **W** Subcutaneous Tissue and Fascia, Lower Extremity	**0** Open **3** Percutaneous	**1** Radioactive Element **3** Infusion Device	**Z** No Qualifier
T Subcutaneous Tissue and Fascia, Trunk	**0** Open **3** Percutaneous	**1** Radioactive Element **3** Infusion Device **V** Infusion Pump	**Z** No Qualifier

Source: CMS 2012c.

The **topography** code describes the site of origin of the neoplasm and uses the same three- and four-character categories as in the neoplasm section of the second chapter of ICD-10. The **morphology** code describes the characteristics of the tumor itself, including cell type and biologic activity (Percy et al. 2000). The topography codes remain the same as in the previous edition, but the morphology codes have been thoroughly revised where necessary in the third edition.

To the greatest extent possible, ICD-O uses the nomenclature published in the WHO series, International Histological Classification of Tumors. ICD-O is under the purview of the heads of WHO Collaborating Centres for Classification of Disease (WHO 2010).

International Classification on Functioning, Disability, and Health

The **International Classification on Functioning, Disability, and Health (ICF)** is a classification of health and health-related domains that describe body functions and structures, activities, and participation. Three lists exist within ICF:

- Body functions and structure
- Domains of activity and participation
- Environmental factors that interact with all these components

ICD-10 and ICF are complementary, and users are encouraged to use them together to create a broader and more meaningful picture of the experience of health of individuals and populations (WHO 2012c). Table 15.2 provides examples of ICF self-care codes.

Current Procedural Terminology

The **American Medical Association (AMA)** publishes the **Current Procedural Terminology (CPT)**. According to the AMA (2012), the purpose of CPT is "to provide a uniform language that accurately describes medical, surgical, and diagnostic services, and thereby serves as an effective means for reliable nationwide communication among physicians, patients, and third parties." CPT was first developed and published by the AMA in 1966. In 1983, the system was adopted by CMS as Level I of the Healthcare Common Procedure Coding System (HCPCS). Since that time, CPT has become widely used as a standard for outpatient and ambulatory care procedural coding in contexts related to reimbursement.

CPT is updated every year on January 1. The codebook is organized into chapters by specialty, body system, and service provided. The codes themselves consist of five digits, and the descriptions of the codes are often accompanied by inclusion and exclusion notes. Modifiers to the five-digit codes also are used extensively. CPT also contains two supplemental sections. The first, Category II codes, contains optional codes used for performance measurement reporting purposes. The CPT Category III codes are temporary codes assigned to facilitate data collection for emerging technologies.

CPT is maintained by the CPT Editorial Panel, which is authorized to revise, update, and modify CPT. The majority of the panel are physicians, with the rest coming from industry and government. Supporting the work of the CPT Editorial Panel is the CPT Health Care Professionals Advisory Committee (HCPAC). The HCPAC includes participation in

Table 15.2   Examples of ICF self-care codes 2010 Version

Chapter	Description	Categories	Category Description	Subcategories
Self-Care	This chapter is about caring for oneself; washing and drying oneself; caring for one's body and body parts; dressing, eating, and drinking; and looking after one's health	d530 Toileting	Planning and carrying out the elimination of human waste (menstruation, urination, and defecation) and cleaning oneself afterwards.	**d5300** Regulating urination **d5301** Regulating defecation **d5302** Menstrual care **d5308** Toileting, other specified **d5309** Toileting, unspecified
		d540 Dressing	Carrying out the coordinated actions of putting on and taking off clothes and footwear in sequence and in keeping with climatic and social conditions, such as by putting on, adjusting, and removing shirts, skirts, blouses, pants, undergarments, saris, kimono, tights, hats, gloves, coats, shoes, boots, sandals, and slippers.	**d5400** Putting on clothes **d5401** Taking off clothes **d5402** Putting on footwear **d5403** Taking off footwear **d5404** Choosing appropriate clothing **d5408** Dressing, other specified **d5409** Dressing, unspecified

Source: WHO 2012c.

the CPT process from organizations representing limited-license medical practitioners and allied health professionals.

The AMA is responsible for developing and publishing the official guidelines for CPT. The association provides support in several ways. It publishes *CPT Assistant*, a monthly newsletter, and offers CPT Information Services, a telephone service that provides users with expert advice on code use. The association also conducts an annual CPT coding symposium (AMA 2012).

Healthcare Common Procedure Coding System

The **Healthcare Common Procedure Coding System (HCPCS)** is used to report services and supplies primarily for reimbursement purposes. The system is divided into two sections referred to as levels. Level I of HCPCS is composed of the CPT codes as published by the AMA and represents medical services and procedures performed by physicians and other healthcare providers. Level II of HCPCS contains codes that represent products, supplies, and services not included in the CPT codes. The Level I (CPT) codes (other than the Category II and III codes) are five-digit numeric codes, whereas Level II codes are five-character alphanumeric codes. HCPCS codes may be reported with two-character modifiers.

Except for temporary codes (those beginning with G, K, or Q), HCPCS codes are updated every year on January 1. The HCPCS Level II codes can be downloaded from the HCPCS website. Table 15.3 contains examples of various types of HCPCS Level II codes (CMS 2008b).

Diagnostic and Statistical Manual of Mental Diseases

The Diagnostic and Statistical Manual of Mental Diseases (DSM) was first published by the American Psychiatric Association (APA) in 1952. The fourth and most recent complete revision was introduced in 1994. In 2000, the APA introduced DSM-IV-TR (Fourth Edition, Text Revision), which is the most current version available. The next edition of the DSM, DSM-V, is scheduled for publication in 2013

Table 15.3.   Examples of HCPCS Level II codes

HCPCS Level II Code	Code Title
A0130	Non-Emergency Transportation: Wheel-Chair Van
A4918	Venous Pressure Clamp, For Hemodialysis, Each
B4036	Enteral Feeding Supply Kit; Gravity Fed, per Day, Includes but not limited to Feeding/Flushing Syringe, Aministration Set Tubing, Dressings, Tape
E0619	Apnea Monitor, with Recording Feature
J3370	Injection, Vancomycin Hcl, 500 mg
Q0480	Driver For Use with Pneumatic Ventricular Assist Device, Replacement Only
S0274	Nurse Practitioner Visit, Outside of a Capitation Arrangement

Source: CMS 2008b.

(APA 2012a). A strategy is in place to align the mental and behavioral disorders in ICD-11 and DSM-V. There is strong support from the International Advisory Group (AG) and the ICD-DSM Harmonization Coordination Group for the harmonization effort of these two systems.

DSM is a **multiaxial** coding system with five axes. Axis I includes the mental disorders or illnesses comparable to general medical illnesses. Axis II includes personality disorders. Axis III includes general medical illnesses. Axis IV covers life events or social problems that affect the patient. Axis V is the overall level of the patient's functioning, usually as determined by the Global Assessment of Functioning (GAF). Figure 15.4 provides an example of DSM-IV-TR codes and instructions.

Figure 15.4.   Example of DSM-IV-TR codes

Diagnostic Criteria for Mental Retardation

A.   Significantly subaverage intellectual functioning: an IQ of approximately 70 or below on an individually administered IQ test (for infants, a clinical judgment of significantly subaverage intellectual functioning).

B.   Concurrent deficits or impairments in present adaptive functioning (i.e., the person's effectiveness in meeting the standards expected for his or her age by his or her cultural group) in at least two of the following areas: communication, self-care, home living, social/interpersonal skills, use of community resources, self-direction, functional academic skills, work, leisure, health, and safety.

C.   The onset is before age 18 years.

Code based on degree of severity reflecting level of intellectual impairment:

317 Mild Mental Retardation: IQ level 50–55 to approximately 70

318.0 Moderate Mental Retardation: IQ level 35–40 to 50–55

318.1 Severe Mental Retardation: IQ level 20–25 to 35–40

318.2 Profound Mental Retardation: IQ level below 20 or 25

319 Mental Retardation, Severity Unspecified: when there is strong presumption of Mental Retardation but the person's intelligence is untestable by standard tests

Reprinted with permission from the *Diagnostic and Statistical Manual of Mental Disorders, Text Revision, Fourth Edition* (copyright 2000). American Psychiatric Association.

The APA states two general uses for DSM: as a source of diagnostic information that enhances clinical practice, research, and education and as a tool for collecting and communicating accurate public health statistics. The APA updates DSM information to correspond to ICD-9-CM. According to the APA, the DSM will be updated to ICD-10-CM when it is implemented in the United States (APA 2012b).

International Classification of Primary Care

The **International Classification of Primary Care (ICPC-2)** is a coding terminology for the classification of primary care developed by the **World Organization of National Colleges, Academies, and Academic Associations of General Practitioners/Family Physicians (WONCA)** International Classification Committee (WHO 2012a). According to WONCA, ICPC-2 has been developed as a tool for general practitioners and family doctors throughout the world. It has been mapped to ICD-10 so that conversion systems can be used. Extensive use has confirmed that it and ICD-10 are complementary rather than in competition. ICPC-2 includes a severity of illness checklist and functional status assessment charts (Jamoulle 1998). Table 15.4 depicts the four categories of diagnosis in primary care in ICPC.

Table 15.4.   ICPC-2-E: four categories of diagnosis in primary care

Category	Description	Examples
1. Aetiological and pathological	The diagnosis has proven pathology or aetiology	Appendicitis, acute myocardial infarction
2. Pathophysiological	The diagnosis has a proven pathophysiological substrate	Presbycusis, hypertension
3. Nosological	The diagnosis depends on a symptom complex based on consensus between physicians	Depression, irritable bowel syndrome
4. Symptom	A symptom or complaint is the best medical label for the episode	Fatigue, eye pain

Current Dental Terminology

The **Current Dental Terminology (CDT)** is a reference manual maintained and updated annually by the American Dental Association. Included in the manual is the Code on Dental Procedures and Nomenclature (the Code), which is a classification system for dental treatment procedures and services. The Code, has been designated as the national standard for reporting dental services by the federal government under the **Health Insurance Portability and Accountability Act (HIPAA)**, and is recognized by third-party payers nationwide. The code set is organized into 12 categories of service, each with its own series of five-digit alphanumeric codes (see table 15.5). Each category of service is divided into subcategories of generally recognized related procedures (ADA 2012).

National Drug Codes

The **Food and Drug Administration (FDA)** developed the **National Drug Codes (NDCs)** to serve as a universal product identifier for human drugs. It identifies the labeler/vendor, product, and trade package size. It is an approved HIPAA billing/financial transaction code set for reporting

Table 15.5. Examples of CDT-4 2011/2012 codes

Category of Service	Code Series	Example Code	Nomenclature	Descriptor (if applicable)
I. Diagnostic	D0100–D0999	D0277	Vertical bitewings–7 to 8 films	This does not constitute a full mouth intraoral radiographic series.
II. Preventive	D1000–D1999	D1320	Tobacco counseling for the control and prevention of oral disease	Tobacco prevention and cessation services reduce patient risks of developing tobacco-related oral diseases and conditions and improves prognosis for certain dental therapies.
III. Restorative	D2000–D2999	D2390	Resin-based composite crown, anterior	Full resin-based composite coverage of tooth.
IV. Endodontics	D3000–D3999	D3410	Apicoectomy/periradicular surgery–anterior	For surgery on root of anterior tooth. Does not include placement of retrograde filling material.
V. Periodontics	D4000–D4999	D4355	Full mouth debridement to enable comprehensive evaluation and diagnosis	The gross removal of plaque and calculus that interfere with the ability of the dentist to perform a comprehensive oral evaluation. This preliminary procedure does not preclude the need for additional procedures.
VI. Prosthodontics, removable	D5000–D5899	D5110	Complete denture–maxillary	
VII. Maxillofacial Prosthetics	D5900–D5999	D5984	Radiation shield	Synonymous terminology: radiation stent, tongue protector, lead shield. An intraoral prosthesis designed to shield adjacent tissues from radiation during orthovoltage treatment of malignant lesions of the head and neck region.
VIII. Implant Services	D6000–D6199	D6010	Surgical placement of implant body: endosteal implant	Includes second-stage surgery and placement of healing cap.
IX. Prosthodontics, fixed	D6200–D6999	D6794	Crown–titanium	
X. Oral Surgery	D7000–D7999	D7220	Removal of impacted tooth–soft tissue	Occlusal surface of tooth covered by soft tissue; requires mucoperiosteal flap elevation.
XI. Orthodontics	D8000–D8999	D8691	Repair of orthodontic appliance	Does not include bracket and standard fixed ortho appliances. It does include functional appliances and palatal expanders.
XII. Adjunctive General Services	D9000–D9999	D9230	Inhalation of nitrous oxide/anxiolysis, analgesia	

Source: ADA 2012.

Table 15.6. Examples of NDC codes

Drug	NDC Code
Fluoxetine 100 mg Caps	00172-4363-70
Prenatal Plus Tab	0093-9111-01
Hydrocodone/APAP 7.5/500 mg Tab	00591-0385-05
Glycolax 3350 NF POW	62175-442-31
Flonase 0.05% Nasal Spray	00173-0453-01
Progesterone 600 mg Supp	51927-1046-00
Seraquel 100 mg Tab	00310-0271-10
Axert 12.5 mg Tab	00062-2085-06
Amitriptyline 25 mg Tab	00603-2213-32
Amoxicillin 400 mg/5 Susp	63304-0970-04

Source: CMS 2012b.

drugs and biologicals. In 2004, the NDCs were adopted as a federal healthcare information interoperability standard to enable the federal healthcare sector to share information regarding drug products (USHIK 2008).

Each drug product is assigned a unique 10-digit, 3-segment number. The three segments of an NDC represent the following:

- First segment—labeler code, assigned by the FDA. A labeler is a firm that manufactures, repacks, or distributes a drug product
- Second segment—product code, identifies a specific strength, dose form, and formulation for a particular firm
- Third segment—package code, identifies package sizes; both the product and package codes are assigned by the firm

The NDC will be in one of the following configurations: 4-4-2, 5-3-2, or 5-4-1 (see table 15.6). Each manufacturer defines the specific codes for its own products. Therefore, there is no uniform class hierarchy for the codes, and codes may be reused at the manufacturer's discretion (Hammond and Cimino 2001).

Check Your Understanding 15.2

Instructions: Answer the following questions on a separate piece of paper.

1. Identify at least five essential improvements in content and format of ICD-10-CM over ICD-9-CM.

2. Name and describe the four characteristics of ICD-10-PCS that makes it an improvement over ICD-9-CM for a procedural coding system.

3. What is the primary function of CPT?

4. What does the topography code in ICD-O describe?

Healthcare Terminologies

Along with the many data standards discussed in chapter 8, healthcare terminologies facilitate health information exchange by standardizing the data collected. Through this

standard representation of data, terminologies provide shared meaning and a sense of context for the information being used. In simple terms, this ability to exchange information between computer systems is referred to as **interoperability.**

A 2006 Presidential Executive Order calling for the promotion of quality and efficient healthcare provides a more detailed definition for interoperability as "the ability to communicate and exchange data accurately, effectively, securely, and consistently with different information technology systems, software applications, and networks in various settings, and exchange data such that clinical or operational purpose and meaning of the data are preserved and unaltered" (Bush 2006). Many experts have identified a lack of interoperability as a major obstacle to realizing the full potential of EHR systems and the exchange of health information (Ash and Bates 2005; NCVHS 2005; AMIA and AHIMA Terminology and Classification Policy Task Force 2007).

Interoperability is often described in levels. The NCVHS has identified three levels: basic, functional, and semantic. Basic interoperability relates to the ability to successfully transmit and receive data from one computer to another. The ability to understand or interpret the information being transmitted is not essential to basic interoperability. **Functional interoperability** refers to sending messages between computers with a shared understanding of the structure and format of the message. With functional interoperability, the receiving computer can store information in a similar data field because the nature (context) of the data being sent is understood. For example, the receiving computer could recognize that the information being sent is a lab result and store it accordingly. The NCVHS definition of **semantic interoperability** is similar to that of the Health Level Seven (HL7) EHR Interoperability Work Group, in which the information being transmitted is understood (EHR Interoperability Work Group 2007). So, building on the previous example, the receiving system would not only recognize that what was being sent is a lab value but would also understand the method used to calculate the value and the reference ranges for a normal result. The use of clinical terminologies in EHRs to provide standardized data is essential to achieving semantic interoperability. Progress is being made in the incorporation of clinical terminologies into EHR systems.

There are different types of clinical terminologies, each of which serves unique purposes. Spackman and colleagues (1997) defined a **reference terminology** for clinical data as "a set of concepts and relationships that provides a common reference point for comparison and aggregation of data about the entire healthcare process, recorded by multiple different individuals, systems, or institutions." A reference terminology provides a common source to which data captured through other terminologies and classifications can be mapped. This linkage back to a common source facilitates aggregation and comparison of data. SNOMED CT, a widely used reference terminology, is discussed later in this chapter. An **interface terminology** is concerned with facilitating clinician documentation within the standardized structure (for example, menus, drop-down boxes) needed for an EHR. An interface terminology provides a limited set of words and phrases in a manner that is consistent with a clinician's thought process used while documenting. Information represented by an interface terminology is often mapped to similar concepts in a comprehensive reference terminology. In this sense the interface terminology serves as a conduit between the natural language expression of the healthcare provider and the data as they are represented by the reference terminology (Rosenbloom et al. 2006).

The following section describes some of the terminologies being used more commonly in EHRs and their uses.

Systematized Nomenclature of Medicine-Clinical Terms

The **Systematized Nomenclature of Medicine–Clinical Terminology (SNOMED CT)** is a comprehensive, multi-hierarchical, concept-oriented clinical terminology owned, maintained, and distributed by the **International Health Terminology Standards Development Organisation (IHTSDO)**, an international nonprofit organization based in Denmark. Figure 15.5 lists the top-level hierarchies into which SNOMED CT is organized.

The size of the terminology conveys how extensive it is. The 2010 release of SNOMED CT includes more than 315,000 active concepts, 806,000 active descriptions, and 945,000 defining relationships (IHTSDO 2010). A **concept** is the most granular unit within a terminology. In SNOMED CT, it is specifically defined as "a single clinical meaning identified by a unique numeric identifier" (College of American Pathologists 2008). Multiple descriptions are oftentimes assigned to a single concept. For example, the descriptions heart attack, myocardial infarction, and cardiac infarction would all be linked to a single concept. **Relationships** describe how the concepts within SNOMED CT are linked to one another. An example of a relationship is that the concept *diabetes mellitus* is an *endocrine disorder*, another concept with a broader meaning (IHTSDO 2008b).

The current terminology—SNOMED CT—is the result of the evolution and combination of various classifications and terminologies over the past several decades. SNOMED was originally built on the Systematized Nomenclature of Pathology (SNOP), which was introduced in 1965. Like SNOP, SNOMED uses an alphanumeric, multiaxial coding scheme (Kudla and Blakemore 2001). In 1997, the College of American Pathologists (CAP) worked with a team of physicians and nurses from Kaiser Permanente to begin development of the **Systematized Nomenclature of Medicine–Reference Terminology (SNOMED RT)**. One

Figure 15.5.   Example of SNOMED CT hierarchies

Clinical finding
- Finding *(Swelling of arm)*
- Disease *(Pneumonia)*

Procedure *(Biopsy of lung)*

Observable entity *(Tumor stage)*

Body structure *(Structure of thyroid)*
- Morphologically abnormal structure *(Granuloma)*

Substance *(Gastric acid)*

Pharmaceutical/biologic product *(Tamoxifen)*

Specimen *(Urine specimen)*

Qualifier value *(Right)*

Record artifact *(Death certificate)*

Physical object *(Suture needle)*

Physical force *(Friction)*

Environments/geographical locations *(Intensive care unit)*

Social context *(Organ donor)*

Situation with explicit content *(No nausea)*

Staging and scales *(Barthel index)*

Linkage concept
- Link assertion *(Has etiology)*
- Attributes *(Finding site)*

Special concept *(Inactive concept)*

Source: IHTSDO 2012.

of the ways that SNOMED RT came to be recognized as a reference terminology was by the inclusion of an elementary mapping to ICD-9-CM (Kudla and Blakemore 2001). SNOMED also worked with the **Digital Imaging and Communications in Medicine (DICOM)** community, the LOINC system, and the various nursing vocabularies to further expand its content. In 2002, SNOMED RT and Clinical Terms, Version 3 (CTV3), also known as the Read Codes, merged to create the SNOMED–Clinical Terminology (CT) system. In 2007, the SNOMED CT intellectual property rights were transferred from the College of American Pathologists to IHTSDO.

HHS recommended SNOMED CT as part of a core set of **patient medical record information (PMRI)** terminology in 2003. Then in 2004, SNOMED CT was adopted as a federal information technology interoperability standard (IHTSDO 2008a):

- Describe specific nonlaboratory interventions and procedures performed or delivered
- Exchange results of laboratory tests between facilities

Table 15.7. SNOMED CT ICD clinical detail comparison

SNOMED CT	Description	ICD 10
49455004	Diabetic polyneuropathy (disorder)	E08.42
		E09.42
		E10.42
		E11.42
	Model (one to many)	E13.42
190502001	Pituitary-dependent Cushing's Disease (disorder)	E24.0
	Exact Match	
102572006	Ankle edema (finding)	R60.0
	Inexact Match	

Source: *Online Research Journal* 2012.

- Describe anatomical locations for clinical, surgical, pathological, and research purposes
- Diagnosis and problem lists
- Define terminology of the delivery of nursing care

Tables 15.7 and 15.8 illustrate level of detail comparisons between SNOMED CT concepts and codes to ICD-10-CM and CPT, respectively.

Examples of Implementations of SNOMED CT

SNOMED CT is currently being used in EHR systems as a clinical reference terminology to capture data for problem lists and patient assessments at the point of care. It also supports alerts, warnings, or reminders used for decision support. The Department of Veteran Affairs (VA) is using SMOMED CT for standardization of problem list entries, allergic reactions, and anatomy coding in autopsy reports. A subset of SNOMED CT terms that can be used to represent problem list entries documented within an EHR is available for download at the Unified Medical Language System's website. The list is being provided without any licensing or intellectual property restrictions in an effort to facilitate use of the SNOMED CT terms for problem list data representation (NLM 2008a). The incorporation of SNOMED CT into EHR applications is increasing (IHTSDO 2008c).

Logical Observation Identifiers Names and Codes

Development of the **Logical Observation Identifiers Names and Codes (LOINC)** began in February 1994. LOINC is generally accepted as the exchange standard for laboratory results. The Regenstrief Institute maintains the LOINC database and its supporting documentation. Most healthcare facilities and reference laboratories use their own protocols for storing lab test and result information. The goal for LOINC is not to replace the laboratory fields in facility databases but, rather, to provide a mapping mechanism. The LOINC committee hoped that laboratories would create fields in their master files for storing LOINC codes and names as attributes of their own data elements (Regenstrief Institute 2012). Each LOINC name identifies a distinct laboratory observation and is structured to contain up to six parts, including

- Analyte/component (for example, potassium, hemoglobin)
- Kind of property measured or observed (for example, mass, mass concentration, enzyme concentration)
- Time aspect of the measurement or observation (a point in time vs. an observation integrated over time)
- System and sample type (for example, urine, blood, serum)

Table 15.8. SNOMED CPT clinical detail comparison: Procedures

SNOMED-CT	Description	CPT
	Total abdominal hysterectomy with or without removal of tubes, with or without removal of ovaries	58150
86477000	–with removal of tube and ovary	
27950001	–with unilateral removal of ovary	
31545000	–with unilateral removal of tube	

Source: CAP (n.d.).

Table 15.9.   Example of a LOINC code and its attributes

LOINC number	10968-6
Component/Analyte	Smudge cells/100 leukocytes
Property	NFr (number fraction)
Time aspect	Pt (point in time)
System (sample type)	Bld (whole blood)
Scale type	Qn (quantitative—continuous numeric scale)
Method type	Manual count

Source: LOINC 2012.

- Type of measurement or observation scale (quantitative [a number] vs. qualitative [a trait such as cloudy])
- Type of measurement or observation method used (for example, clean catch or catheter)

Table 15.9 provides an example of a LOINC code and the characteristics with its corresponding attributes.

The primary disadvantage to LOINC is that it may require significant modifications to work with a current laboratory information system that has been previously using its own protocols for lab data representation. A distinct advantage to using LOINC is that it enables the standardized communication of laboratory results. Large integrated delivery systems that have very diverse laboratory processing systems (the machines that perform the tests) will find it easier to maintain and use an EHR with LOINC-identified laboratory results.

LOINC is divided into two major sections: Lab LOINC and Clinical LOINC. Clinical LOINC includes entries for vital signs, hemodynamics, intake/output, EKG, obstetric ultrasound, cardiac echo, urologic imaging, gastroendoscopic procedures, pulmonary ventilator management, selected survey instruments, and other clinical observations.

In 2003, LOINC was adopted as a federal health information interoperability standard for the electronic exchange of laboratory test orders and drug label section headers using **Structured Product Labeling (SPL)** (Regenstrief Institute 2012).

Examples of LOINC Implementations

LOINC has been implemented in a number of different healthcare settings. Many large commercial laboratories have adopted LOINC as an alternate format for reporting lab data. The VA has implemented Lab LOINC as their primary coding system for laboratory tests and HL7 messages. The **Consolidated Health Informatics (CHI)** initiative recommended in May 2004 the use of Clinical LOINC to fully specify document titles in text-based documentation (HHS 2012). Several

healthcare facilities have reported successful use of LOINC to standardize the reporting of laboratory data (Baorto et al. 1998; Khan et al. 2006).

Clinical Care Classification

The **Clinical Care Classification (CCC)** system is two interrelated taxonomies, the CCC of Nursing Diagnoses and Outcomes and the CCC of Nursing Interventions and Actions, that provide a standardized framework for documenting patient care in hospitals, home health agencies, ambulatory care clinics, and other healthcare settings (AHIMA 2012). This system increases the opportunities for health information and interoperability in the important area of nursing.

The CCC system can be used for a number of purposes. Primarily, it facilitates capturing standardized data with the electronic documentation of patient care at the point of care. It can be used to track nursing activities in patient care, clinical pathways, decision support, and the effect of nursing care on patient outcomes. Furthermore, it can be used to predict workload, assess resource needs, and determine costs of nursing care. This is difficult to capture without a standardized method for codifying nursing data.

The CCC also has applications in nursing education. It can be used to teach students how to document patient care electronically and the characteristics of a nursing terminology for documentation purposes. For the most part, nursing documentation is still primarily done on paper. Future nurses need to transition to the electronic health record, and education is key.

Another important functionality the CCC provides is in the area of nursing research (table 15.10). It supports analysis and evaluation of patient outcomes, facilitates the design of expert systems, and advances nursing practice knowledge. The CCC's standardized terminology allows much higher quality data for the research. It also allows the data to be captured and reviewed more quickly than paper documentation. Thus, the knowledge gained can be utilized to improve the nursing care provided to patients at the point of care (Saba 2012).

RxNorm

RxNorm is a standardized nomenclature for clinical drugs that provides information on a drug's ingredients, strengths, and form in which it is to be administered or used. It is produced by the National Library of Medicine and allows various systems using different drug nomenclatures to share data efficiently at the appropriate level of detail. RxNorm's standard names for clinical drugs are connected to the names of drugs present in many other controlled vocabularies, including those available in drug information sources today. These connections facilitate interoperability among the electronic health record systems that record or process data dealing with clinical drugs (NLM 2008b). Examples of the linkages provided through RxNorm include from brand-named and generic-named

Table 15.10.   Examples of CCC system nursing diagnoses

Code	Category	Diagnosis
A01.0	Activity Alteration	Change in or modification of energy used by the body
A01.1	Activity Intolerance	Incapacity to carry out physiological or psychological daily activities
A01.2	Activity Intolerance Risk	Increased chance of an incapacity to carry out physiological or psychological daily activities
O38.1	Activities of Daily Living (ADLs) Alteration	Change in modification of ability to maintain oneself
Q45.1	Acute Pain	Physical suffering or distress; to hurt
E12.1	Adjustment Impairment	Inadequate adaptation to condition or change in health status
U61.4	Adolescent Behavior Alteration	Change in or modification or normal standards of performing developmental skills and behavior of a typical adolescent from 12 years through 20 years of age
U61.5	Adult Behavior Alteration	Change in or modification or normal standards of performing developmental skills and behavior of a typical adult from 21 years through 64 years of age
L26.1	Airway Clearance Impairment	Inability to clear secretions/obstructions in airway
N58.2	Alcohol Abuse	Excessive use of distilled liquors

Source: Clinical Care Classification System 2012.

clinical drugs to their active ingredients, drug components, and related brand names. They can also be connected to the FDA's NDCs (refer to table 15.6) for specific drug products and many of the drug vocabularies commonly used in pharmacy management and drug interaction (NIST 2012b). This nomenclature provides a detailed level of codified data that facilitates interoperability between pharmacy systems. It allows these systems to check for drug–drug or drug–allergy interactions so that providers can avoid prescribing certain drugs and to give them other prescription choices with no adverse effects. This functionality is available today on a limited basis for patients who are treated in both the VA and Department of Defense (DoD) medical treatment facilities. It has already been shown to significantly decrease medication errors, reduce duplicate prescriptions, and most importantly, improve patient safety.

MEDCIN

MEDCIN is a proprietary clinical terminology owned and maintained by Medicomp Systems. The system was initially developed by Peter Goltra in 1978 and has been

updated regularly (NLM 2012d). Table 15.11 contains examples of a few of MEDCIN'S approximately 270,000 clinical elements created with a strong focus on facilitating documentation by providing clinically relevant choices in a format that is consistent with the provider's clinical thought processes. Because of this feature, the system is considered to be an interface terminology (Bowman 2005; Fraser 2005). MEDCIN is licensed by EHR developers that incorporate the terminology into their EHR systems. For example, MEDCIN is the clinical terminology used by the DoD in its Armed Forces Health Longitudinal Technology Application (AHLTA) system. MEDCIN also identifies relationships through multiple hierarchies for each of its clinical elements. These linkages support other functionalities of the system such as clinical alerts, automated note generation, and computer-assisted coding for CPT evaluation and management codes (Goltra 1997; Medicomp Systems 2012).

Table 15.11.   Examples of MEDCIN clinical elements

Code Number	Clinical Element
1931	Joint swelling, fingers, right hand
34183	Chronic interstitial cystitis
49339	Mechanical vitrectomy by pars plana approach
48618	Acetaminophen + Diphenhydramine
35034	Accident involving a motor vehicle, collision with another motor vehicle on the road

Source: Goltra 1997.

Check Your Understanding 15.3

1. What is semantic interoperability?

2. Identify a clinical terminology that would be a good candidate to represent:
   (a) laboratory data, (b) nursing documentation, and
   (c) problem list documentation.

3. What do the terms *concept* and *relationship* mean in the context of SNOMED CT?

4. Provide a description of the intent and identify the attributes of the LOINC codes.

5. Identify the major difference between RxNorm and MEDCIN, providing examples of each.

Other Emerging Healthcare Terminologies, Classifications, and Nomenclatures

No single terminology, classification, or nomenclature has the depth and breadth to represent the broad spectrum of medical knowledge; thus, a core group of well-integrated,

nonredundant methods will be needed to serve as the backbone of clinical information (Open Clinical 2012).

Table 15.12 provides a reference to many of the specialized terminologies, classifications, and nomenclatures available for use in healthcare. Tables 15.13 through 15.17 provide examples of the coding methodologies for several of these systems.

Table 15.12   Emerging healthcare terminologies, classifications, and nomenclatures

Name	Description
The **National Cancer Institute** (NCI) **Thesaurus** (Table 15.13)	Contains the working vocabulary used in NCI data systems. It covers clinical, translational, and basic research as well as administrative terminology. In May 2004, the NCI Thesaurus was adopted as a federal healthcare information interoperability standard to describe anatomical locations for clinical, surgical, pathological, and research purposes (NAHIT 2005).
The **Human Genome Nomenclature** (HUGN) (Table 15.14)	Provides data for all human genes that have approved symbols. It is managed by the Human Genome Organisation (HUGO) Gene Nomenclature Committee (HGNC) as a confidential database containing over 16,000 records. Web data are integrated with other human gene databases, and approved gene symbols are carefully coordinated with the Mouse Genome Database (MGD). HUGN was adopted as a federal health information interoperability standard for exchanging information regarding the role of genes in biomedical research and healthcare (NAHIT 2005).
The **Global Medical Device Nomenclature** (GMDN) (Table 15.15)	Medical devices consist of such things as home blood pressure monitors, blood glucose devices, and ventilators. A standard is needed to inventory devices, document their use by healthcare providers, and regulate their availability and use in the community by public health agencies. Regulation involves approval and classifications of devices as well as ensuring the safety and effectiveness of these products.

GMDN is a collection of internationally recognized terms used to describe and catalogue medical devices and supplies. GMDN is currently divided into 12 categories that encompass all of these products (Table 15.15). It is strongly supported by the FDA for communicating these data. The agency also recommends that the GMDN eventually replace the FDA terminology for devices. The nomenclature is used extensively outside the US and is recognized by the European Committee for Standardization (CEN) and other international bodies.

The FDA and **Emergency Care Research Institute** (ECRI) are currently producing a map of UMDNS to GMDN to coordinate their practices, which may lead to a merger in the near future. This should result in a terminology that enables the US federal system to utilize one set of medical device names, definitions, and codes. These identifiers may also be used to communicate with foreign entities. |
| The **Universal Medical Device Nomenclature System** (UMDNS) | Is a standard international nomenclature and computer coding system for medical devices. It facilitates identifying, processing, filing, storing, retrieving, transferring, and communicating data about medical devices. It is primarily used by healthcare institutions. It has been adopted by many nations, including the entire European Union (EU). It is used in applications ranging from hospital inventory and work-order controls to national agency medical device regulatory systems. It is incorporated into the UMLS. UMDNS has been merged with the GMDN. |
| The **Environmental Protection Agency** (EPA) **Substance Registry System** (SRS) (Table 15.16) | Provides information on substances and how they are represented in the EPA's regulations and information systems. It provides a common basis for identification of chemicals, biological organisms, and other substances listed in EPA regulations and data systems, as well as substances of interest from other sources, such as publications. The EPA SRS was adopted as the federal health information interoperability standard for chemicals in May 2004 (NAHIT 2005). |
| The **Breast Imaging Reporting and Data System Atlas** (BI-RADS) (Table 15.17) | Designed to serve as a comprehensive guide providing standardized breast imaging terminology, a report organization, an assessment structure, and a classification system for mammography, ultrasound, and MRI of the breast (NAHIT 2005). BI-RADS assessment categories are listed in table 15.17.

BI-RADS is the product of a collaboration effort among members of various committees of the American College of Radiology with cooperation from the National Cancer Institute, the Centers for Disease Control and Prevention, the FDA, and the College of American Pathologists. Results are compiled in a standardized manner that permits the maintenance and collection analysis of demographic, mammographic, and outcome data (ACR 2003). |

Table 15.12   Emerging healthcare terminologies, classifications, and nomenclatures (*continued*)

Name	Description
The **Medical Dictionary for Regulatory Activities** (MedDRA)	Is a pragmatic, medically valid terminology with an emphasis on ease of use for data entry, retrieval, analysis, and display, as well as a suitable balance between sensitivity and specificity within the regulatory environment. It was developed by the International Conference on Harmonisation (ICH) and is owned by the International Federation of Pharmaceutical Manufacturers and Associations (IFPMA) acting as trustee for the ICH steering committee. MedDRA terminology applies to all phases of drug development, excluding animal toxicology. It also applies to the health effects and malfunction of devices. Who should subscribe to MedDRA? • Pharmaceutical companies • Biotechnology companies • Device manufacturers • Regulatory authorities • Contract research organizations • Systems developers • Other support service organizations The Maintenance and Support Services Organization (MSSO) serves as the repository, maintainer, and distributor of MedDRA as well as the source for the most up-to-date information regarding MedDRA and its application within the biopharmaceutical industry and regulators.
The **Systematized Nomenclature of Dentistry** (SNODENT)	Is a clinical vocabulary developed by the American Dental Association (ADA) for data representation of clinical dentistry content. The need for interoperable dental information is increasing as the field of dentistry is moving more into the medical management of oral diseases. For example, dentists now sometimes perform saliva testing for the purpose of substance abuse and disease monitoring. This type of information may need to be shared with other healthcare providers.

Evaluation of Clinical Terminologies and Classification Systems

As health information management (HIM) professionals search for ways to formalize the myriad types of data contained in EHRs, it helps to be able to evaluate the different classifications and terminologies. Certain characteristics are desirable. The first 12 characteristics listed below are taken from Cimino (1998). The final six are taken from Campbell, who presented additional requirements after his experience with implementing a terminology for Kaiser Permanente (Campbell et al. 1999). The characteristics are as follows:

- Content: The content of clinical classifications and terminologies should be determined by their intended use. It is wise to assume that the first identified need will never be the last or only need. It is far better to have too much content initially than to have too little to meet subsequent needs.
- Concept orientation: The content of terminologies and classifications should be oriented toward concepts rather than terms or code numbers. For example, "cold" can either be a disease (chronic obstructive lung disease or the common cold) or a feeling of temperature—these are three separate concepts.

- Concept **permanence:** Terminologies and classifications must be permanent if they are to be useful for longitudinal reporting. Concepts may be inactivated but must never be deleted.

Table 15.13.   NCI Thesaurus taxonomy concept details

Identifiers:	
Name	Pancreas
Code	C12393
Relationships to other concepts:	
Anatomic_Structure_Has_Location	Epigastric Region
Anatomic_Structure_is_Physical_Part_of	Gastrointestinal System
Information about this concept:	
Display_Name	Pancreas
Mitelman_Code	218
Preferred_Name	Pancreas
Semantic_Type	Body Part, Organ, or Organ Component
Subsource	ICD
Subsource	LASH
Subsource	Mitelman
Unified Medical Language System	C0030274

Source: NCI 2012.

Table 15.14.   Human genes with approved symbols: Single-letter amino acid codes

Amino Acid	Three-Letter Symbol	One-Letter Symbol
Alanine	Ala	A
Arginine	Arg	R
Asparagine	Asn	N
Aspartic Acid	Asp	D
Cysteine	Cys	C
Glutamine	Gln	Q
Glutamic Acid	Glu	E
Valine	Val	V
Glycine	Gly	G

Source: NLM 2011.

- Nonsemantic concept identifier: No implicit or explicit meaning can be associated with the code numbers used in a classification system. Because primary healthcare systems are now computerized, the human ability to use a classification system without a computer is no longer necessary. For example, in ICD-9-CM, code 250 xx is related to diabetes regardless of when the condition was put into ICD-9-CM. Thus, 250 has meaning.

Table 15.15.   GMDN device categories

The Standard allocates codes for a possible 20 categories. For this version of the GMDN 13 device categories are now established. These are:

01	Active implantable devices
02	Anaesthetic and respiratory devices
03	Dental devices
04	Electro mechanical medical devices
05	Hospital hardware
06	In vitro diagnostic devices (IVD)
07	Nonactive implantable devices
08	Ophthalmic and optical devices
09	Reusable instruments
10	Single use devices
11	Technical aids for disabled persons
12	Diagnostic and therapeutic radiation devices
13	Obsolete terms
14	Vacant
15	Vacant
16	Vacant
17	Vacant
18	Vacant
19	Vacant
20	Vacant

Source: NCHVS 2012.

Table 15.16.   Example of an EPA SRS substance list

Name	Liquid Nitrogen (Containing)
Molecular Formula	[No Criteria Specified]
Type	All
Classification	All
Display Option	Substance Name
Sort Option	Name
Systematic Name	Nitrogen
EPA Registry Name	Nitrogen
Classification	Chemical
CAS number	7727-37-9
TSN	
ICTV	
EPA ID	

Source: EPA 2012.

- **Polyhierarchy:** Multiple relationships should exist for every concept. For example, bacterial pneumonia is both a pulmonary disease and an infectious disease.
- Formal definitions: Standardized definitions are necessary to ensure comparability among terminologies and classifications. They also reduce confusion.

Table 15.17.   BI-RADS mammography assessment categories

Assessment	Category
a. Mammographic Assessment is Incomplete	0: Need to review prior studies and/or complete additional imaging
b. Mammographic Assessment is Complete–Final Categories	1: Negative Continue routine screening
	2: Benign finding Continue routine screening
	3: Probably Benign Finding Short-term follow-up mammogram at 6 months, then every 6 to 12 months for 1 to 2 years
	4: Suspicious Abnormality Perform biopsy, preferably needle biopsy
	5: Highly Suggestive of Malignancy–Appropriate Action Should Be Taken (Biopsy and treatment, as necessary)
	6: Known Biopsy–Proven Malignancy–treatment pending (ensure that treatment is completed)

Source: ACR 2012.

- Reject Not Elsewhere Classified: **Not Elsewhere Classified (NEC)** is not the same as **Not Otherwise Specified (NOS)**. NOS means that there is no additional information. NEC means you have more information but no place to put it. It also means that any additional information will be lost forever if it is assigned the NEC label (for example, assigning "Pneumonia, NEC" when you know the bacterial agent causing the pneumonia but ICD-9-CM doesn't accommodate it).

- Multiple granularities: Because classifications and terminologies must fulfill multiple purposes, the information in them may be specific or general so that all needs can be met.

- Multiple consistent views: Classifications and terminologies must accommodate more than one viewpoint to allow them to be multipurpose as well as to ensure continuity of care. When caring for the same patient, nurses want to use nurse speak and physicians want to use physician speak.

- Context representation: Words have different meanings when used in different contexts or as different grammatical parts of language. **Context** is determined by how the concepts relate to each other. For example, consider the term *cold*. In the phrase "the patient is cold," cold is how the patient feels. In the phrase "the patient has a cold," cold is a disease. The difference between the two phrases reflects the two different contexts of the word *cold*.

- Graceful evolution: The days of yearly updates need to end soon. Future updates will have to be made monthly or, more likely, weekly. The growth of medical knowledge is exponential; classification systems and terminologies must to be able to keep up.

- Recognized redundancy: Classifications and terminologies need to accommodate redundancy.

- Licensed and copyrighted: Terminologies and classifications need to be copyrighted and licensed to control local modifications, which result in semantic drift and produce incomparable data.

- **Vendor neutral:** Classifications and terminologies must be vendor neutral so that they can be readily used as national standards by all vendors without conferring a competitive advantage to any one of them.

- Scientifically valid: Terminologies and classifications should be understandable, reproducible, and useful and should reflect the current understanding of the science.

- Adequate maintenance: A central authority that provides a rapid response to requests for new terms is essential to minimize the need for local enhancements and to keep terminologies and classifications current.

- Self-sustaining: Classifications and terminologies should be supported by public or endowment funding. Alternatively, licensing fees should be proportional to the value the system provides to users.

- Scalable infrastructure and process control: The tools and processes for maintaining a terminology or classification should be scalable, especially for a nationally standardized terminology.

ASTM Standard E2087-00

HIM professionals should use all of their system analysis and data management skills when evaluating the appropriateness of a clinical terminology for a particular function or need. A helpful reference for evaluating the quality of a clinical terminology is the **American Society for Testing and Materials (ASTM)** Standard E2457-07, Standard Terminology for Healthcare Informatics.

> This international standard is intended to document principal ideas that are necessary and sufficient to assign value to a classification. The standard will serve as a guide for governments, funding agencies, terminology developers, terminology integration organizations, and the purchasers and users of classification systems toward improved terminological development and recognition of value in a classification. It is applicable to all areas of health about which information is kept or utilized. Appropriately, classifications should be evaluated within the context of their stated scope and purpose. It is intended to complement and utilize those notions already identified by other national and international standards bodies. This standard explicitly refers only to classifications. This international standard will also provide classification developers and authors with the quality guidelines needed to construct useful, maintainable classifications. These tenets do not attempt to specify all of the richness that can be incorporated into a classification. However, this standard does specify the minimal requirements, which if not adhered to will ensure that the classification will have limited generalizability and will be very difficult if not impossible to maintain (ASTM International 2012).

National Library of Medicine's Role in Healthcare Terminologies

The **National Library of Medicine (NLM)** is the world's largest medical library. It collects materials in all aspects of biomedicine and healthcare, as well as works on biomedical aspects of technology, the humanities, and the physical, life, and social sciences. It is a standards-supporting/promoting organization that explores the uses of computer and communication technologies to improve organizations and the use of biomedical information. It is responsible for publishing Medical Subject Headings (MeSH), RxNorm, Semantic Clinical Drug (SDC) of RxNorm, and the Unified Medical Language Systems (NAHIT 2005).

Unified Medical Language System

The **Unified Medical Language System (UMLS)** is a government-funded project from the NLM. The UMLS has been in development since 1986. The purpose of the UMLS is "to facilitate the development of computer systems that behave as if they 'understand' the meaning of the language of biomedicine and health. The UMLS provides data for system developers as well as search and report functions for less technical users" (NLM 2008c). This goal is achieved through the three knowledge sources found in the UMLS: (1) the UMLS Metathesaurus, (2) the SPECIALIST Lexicon, and (3) the UMLS Semantic Network. More information on the UMLS can be obtained from the NLM website. When looking in-depth at the UMLS, it is important to keep in mind that it has been designed for computer use; its layouts and other structures are meant to be read by machines. It is not structured to be readable by humans.

Unified Medical Language System Metathesaurus

The **Unified Medical Language System (UMLS) Metathesaurus** is a list containing information on biomedical concepts and terms from more than 100 healthcare vocabularies and classifications, administrative health data, bibliographic and full-text databases, and expert systems (AHIMA 2012).

The National Library of Medicine (NLM) explains further:

> Computer programs can use information in the Metathesaurus to interpret user inquiries, interact with users to refine their questions, identify the databases that contain information relevant to particular inquiries, and convert the users' terms into the vocabulary used by relevant information sources. The scope of the Metathesaurus is determined by the combined scope of its source vocabularies.
>
> The Metathesaurus is produced by the automated processing of machine-readable versions of its source vocabularies, followed by human review and editing by subject experts. It is intended primarily for use by system developers but also can be a useful reference tool for database builders, librarians, and other information professionals (NLM 2003).

Unified Medical Language System SPECIALIST Lexicon

The **Unified Medical Language System (UMLS) SPECIALIST Lexicon** is an English-language lexicon containing many biomedical terms. It has been developed in the context of the SPECIALIST natural language processing project at the NLM. The current version includes over 200,000 terms.

The lexicon entry for each word or term records syntactic, morphological, and orthographic information. (**Syntactic** refers to the formal properties of language; **morphological** refers to the study and description of word formation in a language, including inflection, derivation, and compounding; and **orthographic** refers to the correctness of spelling or the representation of the sounds of a language by written or printed symbols.) Lexical entries may be single-word or multiword terms. Entries

that share their base form and spelling variants, if any, are collected into a single lexical record. The base form is the uninflected form of the lexical item—the singular form in the case of a noun, the infinitive form in the case of a verb, and the positive form in the case of an adjective or adverb (NIST 2012a).

Unified Medical Language System Semantic Network

The **Unified Medical Language System (UMLS) Semantic Network,** "through its 135 semantic types, provides a consistent categorization of all concepts represented in the UMLS Metathesaurus. The 54 links between semantic types provide the structure for the network and represent important relationships in the biomedical domain." (McCray 2002) All information on specific concepts is found in the Metathesaurus; the network provides information on the basic semantic types assigned to these concepts and defines their possible relationships.

Examples of Unified Medical Language System Implementation

The VA has used the UMLS Metathesaurus as a lookup tool for finding concepts, synonyms, and linkages to other terminologies in the data standardization of allergies data. It is also using the UMLS RxNorm for standardizing pharmacy data and are sharing those data with the Department of Defense as part of the Consolidated Health Data Repository (CHDR) interagency project. It has also been proposed to use UMLS as the mediation terminology for VA drug classes in the CHDR project. Vanderbilt University has used the UMLS in its WizOrder order entry and decision support system.

Medical Subject Headings

The **Medical Subject Headings database (MeSH)** is the NLM's controlled vocabulary thesaurus. It consists of terms naming descriptors in a hierarchical structure that permits searching at various levels of specificity (NAHIT 2005). The descriptors exist in both alphabetic and hierarchical structures. It contains very broad headings, such as "Mental Disorders," and more specific levels, such as "Conduct Disorder." There are 22,568 descriptors in MeSH and more than 139,000 headings, called Supplementary Concept Records, within a separate thesaurus. Thousands of cross-references also exist. MeSH is used by the NLM for indexing articles from 4,600 of the world's leading biomedical journals for the MEDLINE/PubMed database. Each bibliographic reference is associated with a set of MeSH terms that describe the content of the item. Staff subject specialists are responsible for revising and updating the vocabulary on a continuous basis. MeSH is available in electronic format at no charge at http://www.nlm.nih.gov/mesh and a hard copy version is published each January (UMLS 2012).

Mapping Initiatives

As illustrated by this chapter's descriptions of widely varying clinical classifications and terminologies, no single system meets all needs. "Mappings are sets of relationships of varying complexity established between two vocabularies in order to allow automated translation or connection between them. More specific concepts can generally be mapped accurately to more general concepts." (NLM 2012c) Maps that link related content in classifications and terminologies allow data collected for one purpose to be used for another. For example, a laboratory system that manages data using the LOINC terminology can map the LOINC terms to CPT codes to be used for billing purposes. The NLM, within the framework of the UMLS, contains many sets of mapping among terminologies including LOINC to CPT mapping and SNOMED CT to ICD-10-CM mapping (WHO 2012b). Many maps are created to support a specific use case. For example, the map created for a reimbursement use case might be very different from that for a public health use case. This is even true if the two use cases were mapping between the same two systems. Therefore, successful mapping requires a thorough understanding of the intended use of the map (use case), the structure and purpose of the source, and target terminologies (Foley et al. 2007).

Most often, the links created in a map are categorized according the how closely the terms in each system are related (Imel 2002). Examples of these categories are:

- *One-to-one:* An exact match is made between the systems
- *Narrow-to-broad:* A more granular term in the starting system maps to a more general term in the receiving system
- *Broad-to-narrow:* A more general term in the starting system maps to a more granular term in the receiving system
- *Unmappable:* There is no match in the receiving system

Developing and maintaining maps that have been created between classifications and terminologies is a relatively new field, and best practices for validation and routine maintenance are still being developed. Maintenance of maps is resource intensive, requiring review and updating, as necessary, of established links whenever a source or target terminology is updated. As electronic health records continue to evolve, the need for cross-system maps and for persons who understand map creation, validation, and maintenance will increase. See figure 15.6.

Health Level Seven Vocabulary Workgroup

The objective of the **Health Level Seven (HL7)** Vocabulary Workgroup was to identify, organize, and maintain coded

Figure 15.6.   The Canadian Institute for Health Inforamation: CCICD-10 implementation tool kit

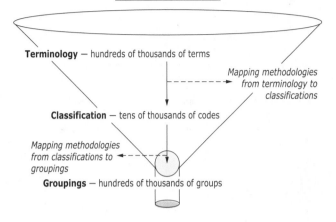

Source: Canadian Institute for Health Information 1996.

vocabulary terms used in HL7 messages. This workgroup disbanded in 2010; however, its goal is to

> provide an organization and a repository for maintaining a coded vocabulary that, when used in conjunction with HL7 and related standards, will enable the exchange of clinical data and information so that sending and receiving systems have a shared, well-defined, and unambiguous knowledge of the meaning of the data transferred. The purposes of the exchange of clinical data include, but are not limited to, provision of clinical care, support of clinical and administrative research, execution of automated transaction–oriented decision logic (medical logic modules), support of outcomes research, support of clinical trials, and support of data reporting to government and other authorized third parties. To achieve this goal, the workgroup worked cooperatively with all other groups that have an interest in coded vocabularies used in clinical computing (HL7 2012).

These groups include standards development organizations, creators and maintainers of vocabularies, government agencies and regulatory bodies, clinical professional specialty groups, vocabulary content providers, and vocabulary tool vendors (HL7 2012).

AHIMA Clinical Terminology and Vocabulary Community of Practice

The AHIMA Clinical Terminology and Vocabulary **Community of Practice (CoP)** is the community for those interested in clinical terminologies and vocabularies. It contains information of interest to health information management professionals as well as others interested in this topic. Like other CoPs, it includes sections for announcements, FAQs, links, resources, document collaboration, the HIM Body of Knowledge, and discussion. Contributions to content and questions are always welcome and improve the usefulness of the community.

Check Your Understanding 15.4

Instructions: Answer the following questions on a separate piece of paper.

1. Why is the concept of permanence important in clinical terminologies and classifications?

2. What is another name for context representation? What does the term mean?

3. What is the role of mapping in relation to clinical terminologies?

Summary

Medical coding and classification systems form part of the current movement toward implementing a standardized "language of health": a common (computerized) medical language for global use (Open Clinical 2012). The Institute of Medicine (Aspen et al. 2003) report, *Patient Safety: Achieving a New Standard for Care*, highlights the importance of terminologies to healthcare and provides the following summary of their purpose and a likely outcome of current efforts in the field:

> If health professionals are to be able to send and receive data in an understandable and usable manner, both the sender and the receiver must have common clinical terminologies for describing, classifying, and coding medical terms and concepts. Use of standardized clinical terminologies facilitates electronic data collection at the point of care; retrieval of relevant data, information, and knowledge; and reuse of data for multiple purposes. (Aspen et al. 2003)

A variety of classifications and terminologies exist to support different healthcare functions. Classifications are used to aggregate data for functions such as data analysis and reimbursement. Clinical terminologies play an essential role in capturing and sharing data in a manner that meets the requirements of semantic interoperability, which is essential for reliable health information exchange. Mapping is a function that allows for the reuse of data captured for one purpose to be used for other purposes. In order to reach the full potential of health information exchange, HIM professionals must participate in the development, implementation, and maintenance of information systems that use standard terminologies, nomenclatures, and classification systems.

References

American College of Radiology. 2003. *BI-RADS Atlas.* http://www.acr.org.

American Dental Association. 2012. Current Dental Terminology, CDT 2011-2012. Chicago: ADA.

American Health Information Management Association. 2012. *Pocket Glossary of Health Information Management and Technology*, 3rd ed. Chicago, IL: AHIMA.

American Health Information Management Association and American Hospital Association. 2003 (Sept. 23). *ICD-10-CM Field Testing Project: Report on Findings.* Chicago: AHIMA and AHA.

American Medical Association. 2012. CPT (Current Procedural Terminology). http://www.ama-assn.org/ama/pub/category/3113.html.

American Medical Association, 2010. Preparing for the ICD-10 Code Set: Crosswalking Between ICD-9 and ICD-10. http://www.ama-assn.org/ama1/pub/upload/mm/399/crosswalking-between-icd-9-and-icd-10.pdf.

American Medical Informatics Association and American Health Information Management Association Terminology and Classification Policy Task Force. 2007 (June 27). Healthcare terminologies and classifications: An action agenda for the United States. *Perspectives in Health Information Management.* http://library.ahima.org/xpedio/groups/public/documents/ahima/bok1_032401.html.

American Psychiatric Association. 2012a. DSM-V Development.

American Psychiatric Association. 2012b. Diagnostic and Statistical Manual. http://www.psych.org/MainMenu/Research/DSMIV.aspx.

Ash, J. S. and D.W. Bates. 2005. Factors and forces affecting EHR system adoption: Report of a 2004 ACMI discussion. *Journal of the American Medical Informatics Association* 12(1):8–12.

Aspen, P., J.M. Corrigan, J. Wolcott, and S.M. Erickson. 2002. *Patient Safety: Achieving a New Standard of Care.* Institute of Medicine of the National Academies Committee on Data Standards for Patient Safety. Institute of Medicine of the National Academies: Washington, D.C.

ASTM International. 2012. ASTM E2522-07: Standard guide for quality indicators for health classification. http://www.astm.org/Standards/E2522.htm.

Averill, R.F., R.L., Mullin, B.A., Steinbeck, N.I., Goldfield, T.M., Grant,and R.R. Butler. 2005. *Development of the ICD-10 Procedure Coding System (ICD-10-PCS).* 3M HIS Research Report 1-05. St. Paul, MN: 3M.

Baorto, D.M., J J., Cimino, C A., Parvin, and M.G. Kahn. 1998. Combining laboratory data sets from multiple institutions using the Logical Observation Identifier Names and Codes (LOINC). *International Journal of Medical Informatics* 51(1): 29–37.

Barnett, O.G., et al. 1993. The computer-based clinical record: Where do we stand? *Annals of Internal Medicine* 119(10): 1046–1048.

Bowman, S. 2005 (Spring). Coordination of SNOMED-CT and ICD-10: Getting the most out of electronic health record systems. *Perspectives in Health Information Management.* Chicago: AHIMA.

BSI Group. 2004. Global Medical Device Nomenclature (GMDN). http://www.gmdn.org.

Bush, G.W. 2006. Executive Order: Promoting quality and efficient health care in federal government administered or sponsored health care programs. Washington, D.C.: White House.

Butler, R. 2007. The ICD-10 general equivalence mappings: Bridging the translation gap from ICD-9. *Journal of AHIMA* 78(9): 84–86.

Campbell, K.E., B., Hochhalter, J., Slaughter, and J. Mattison. 1999. Enterprise issues pertaining to implementing controlled terminologies. IMIA Conference Proceedings. Edmonton, AB: IMIA.

Canadian Institute for Health Information. 1996. Working Group 2: Health terminology, classification and nomenclatures. Background Document. http://www.cihi.com.

Centers for Medicare and Medicaid Services. 2012a. Development of the ICD-10 Procedure Coding System (ICD-10-PCS). http://www.cms.gov/Medicare/Coding/ICD10/downloads// pcs_final_report2012.pdf.

Centers for Medicare and Medicaid Services. 2012b. CMS ICD-10-CM 2012 Official Code Set. http://www.cdc.gov/nchs/icd/ icd10cm.htm#10update.

Centers for Medicare and Medicaid Services. 2012c. CMS ICD-10-PCS 2012 Official Coding Guidelines. https://www.cms.gov/ ICD10/Downloads/PCS_2012_guidelines.pdf.

Centers for Medicare and Medicaid Services. 2008a. ICD-10-PCS 2008 Version: What's new in this release. http://www.cms.hhs.gov/ ICD10/Downloads/pcs_whats_new_2008.pdf.

Centers for Medicare and Medicaid Services. 2008b. HCPCS general information. http://www.cms.hhs.gov/MedHCPCSGenInfo/.

Chute, C.G. 2000. Clinical classification and terminology: Some history and current observations. *Journal of the American Medical Informatics Association* 70(3): 298–303.

Cimino, J.J. 1998. Desiderata for controlled medical vocabularies in the twenty-first century. *Methods of Information in Medicine* 37: 394–403.

Clinical Care Classification System. 2012. Terminology tables. http://www.sabacare.com/Tables/Diagnoses.html?SF=DiagCode &SO=Asc.

College of American Pathologists. 2008. SNOMED Terminology Solutions. http://www.cap.org/apps/cap.portal?_nfpb=true&_ pageLabel=snomed_page.

Department of Health and Human Services. 2008. HIPAA Administrative Simplification: Modifications to medical data code set standards to adopt ICD-10CM and ICD-10-PCS. *Federal Register* 73(164): 49796–49832.

Department of Health and Human Services. 2012. Office of the National Coordinator for health information Technology: Consolidated health informatics. http://www.hhs.gov/healthit/chiinitiative.html.

EHR Interoperability Work Group. 2007. Coming to terms: Scoping interoperability for health care. Ann Arbor, MI: HL7. Health Level Seven.

Encyclopedia Britannica Online. 2012. http://www.eb.com.

Environmental Protection Agency Substance Registry Services. 2012. Substance details. http://iaspub.epa.gov/sor_internet/ registry/substreg/searchandretrieve/substancesearch/search. do?details=displayDetails.

Fenton, Susan. 2004. "Clinical Vocabularies: Essential to the Future of Health Information Management." *2004 IFHRO Congress & AHIMA Convention Proceedings.* http://library. ahima.org/xpedio/groups/public/documents/ahima/bok3_005532. hcsp?dDocName=bok3_005532.

Foley, M.M., C., Hall, K., Perron, and R. D'Andrea. 2007. Translation please: Mapping translates clinical data between the many languages that document it. *Journal of AHIMA* 78(2): 34–38.

Fraser, G. 2005. Problem list coding in e-HIM. *Journal of AHIMA* 76(7): 68–70.

Goltra, P.S. 1997. *MEDCIN: A New Nomenclature for Clinical Medicine.* New York: Springer-Verlag.

Hammond, W.E., and J.J. Cimino. 2001. Standards in medical informatics. In *Health Informatics.* Edited by Hannah, K.J., and M.J. Ball. New York: Springer-Verlag.

Health Level Seven International. 2012. HL7 Unlocking the power of health information. http://www.hl7.org/search/index. cfm?x=0&y=0&criteria=NLM.

Imel, M. 2002. A closer look: The SNOMED clinical terms to ICD-9-CM mapping. *Journal of AHIMA* 73(6): 66–69.

International Health Terminology Standards Development Organisation. 2010. About SNOMED CT: http://www.ihtsdo.org/ snomed-ct/snomed-ct0/.

International Health Terminology Standards Development Organisation. 2008a. *SNOMED CT User Guide—July 2008 International Release.*

International Health Terminology Standards Development Organisation. 2008b. Who is using SNOMED-CT? http://www. ihtsdo.org/snomed-ct/who-is-using-snomed-ct.

Jamoulle, M. 1998. ICPC-2: The international classification of primary care: An introduction. http://www.ulb.ac.be/esp/wicc/ icpc2.html.

Khan, A.N., S.P., Griffith, C., Moore, D., Russell, A.C., Rosario, Jr., and J. Bertolli. 2006. Standardizing laboratory data by mapping to LOINC. *Journal of the American Medical Informatics Association* 13(3): 353–355.

Kudla, K.M., and M., Blakemore. 2001. SNOMED takes the next step. *Journal of AHIMA* 72(7): 62–68.

Logical Observation Identifiers Names and Codes. 2012. LOINC home page. http://www.loinc.org.

McCray, A.T. 2002. An upper-level ontology for the biomedical domain. http://ukpmc.ac.uk/articles/PMC2447396/pdf/CFG-04 -080.pdf

Medicomp Systems, Inc. 2012. *MEDCIN.* http://www.medicomp .com/products/medcinengine/.

National Alliance for Health Information Technology. 2005. *Alliance Standards Directory.* http://www.hitsdir.org.

National Cancer Institute. 2012. NCI Thesaurus: Pancreas. http:// ncit.nci.nih.gov/ncitbrowser/ConceptReport.jsp?dictionary=NCI% 20Thesaurus&code=C12393.

National Committee on Vital and Health Statistics. 2012. The Global Medical Device Nomenclature. http://www.ncvhs.hhs.gov/030819p2.pdf.

National Committee on Vital and Health Statistics. 2005. NCVHS Subcommittee on Standards and Security. http://www.ncvhs.hhs.gov/stdschrg.htm.

National Institute of Standards and Technology. 2012a. An Analysis of Existing Ontological Systems for Applications in Manufacturing and Healthcare. http://www.mel.nist.gov/msidlibrary/doc/nistir6301.pdf.

National Institute of Standards and Technology. 2012b. HIT implementation support and testing. http://xreg2.nist.gov/hit-testing/.

National Library of Medicine. 2012a. Unified Medical Language System Glossary. http://www.nlm.nih.gov/research/umls/new_users/glossary.html#l.

National Library of Medicine. 2012b. UMLS Knowledge Source Server Mappings: Draft LNC215 to CPT2005 Mapping. http://umlsks.nlm.nih.gov/uPortal/tag.b19c0fb661fa2381.render.userLayoutRootNode.uP?uP_fname=mappings-download.

National Library of Medicine 2012c. Basic mapping project assumptions. http://www.nlm.nih.gov/research/umls/knowledge_sources/metathesaurus/mapping_projects/index.html.

National Library of Medicine. 2012d. 2011 AB MEDCIN Source Information. http://www.nlm.nih.gov/research/umls/sourcereleasedocs/current/MEDCIN/termtypes.html.

National Library of Medicine. 2011 (May). Guidelines for human gene nomenclature. http://www.ncbi.nlm.nih.gov/pubmed/11944974.

National Library of Medicine. 2008a. UMLS enhanced VA/KP problem list subset of SNOMED CT. http://www.nlm.nih.gov/research/umls/Snomed/snomed_problem_list.html.

National Library of Medicine. 2008b. RxNorm overview. http://www.nlm.nih.gov/research/umls/rxnorm/overview.html.

National Library of Medicine. 2008c. UMLS 2008AA Documentation, Section 2 Metathesuarus. http://www.nlm.nih.gov/research/umls/meta2.html.

National Library of Medicine. 2003. UMLS Metathesaurus Fact Sheet. http://www.docstoc.com/docs/22579330/UMLS-Metathesaurus-Fact-Sheet.

Online Research Journal Perspectives in Health Informaiton Management. 2012. A comparison between a SNOMED CT problem list and the ICD-10-CM/PCS HIPAA code sets. http://perspectives.ahima.org/index.php?option=com_content&view=article&id=231:a-comparison-between-a-snomed-ct-problem-list-and-the-icd-10-cmpcs-hipaa-code-sets&catid=45:icd-9icd-10&Itemid=93.

Open Clinical. 2012. Medical terminologies, nomenclatures, coding and classification systems: An introduction. http://www.openclinical.org/medicalterminologies.html.

Percy, C., A. Fritz, A. Jack, S. Shanmugarathan, L. Sobin, D.M. Parkin, and S. Whelan. 2000. International Classification of Diseases for Oncology (ICD-O). World Health Organization.

Regenstrief Institute, Inc. 2012. Logical Observation Identifiers Names and Codes. http://loinc.org.

Rosenbloom, S.T., R.A., Miller, K.B., Johnson, P.L., Elkin, and S.H. Brown. 2006. Interface terminologies: Facilitating direct entry of clinical data into electronic health record systems. *Journal of the American Informatics Association* 13(3): 277–288.

Spackman, K.A., K.E., Campbell, and R.A. Cote. 1997. SNOMED RT: A reference terminology for health care. *Proceedings/AMIA Annual Fall Symposium* 640: 4.

Unified Medical Language System. 2012. RxNorm. http://www.nlm.nih.gov/research/umls/rxnorm/.

United States Health Information Knowledgebase. 2008. Consolidated health informatics. http://www.dcg.dnsalias.net/chi.

World Health Organization. 2012a. *International Classification of Primary Care, Second Edition (ICPC-2).* http://www.who.int/classifications/icd/adaptations/icpc2/en/index.html.

World Health Organization. 2012b. SNOMED CT to ICD-10 cross map release. http:www.who.int/classifications/icd/snomedCT-TOICD10Maps/en/.

World Health Organization. 2012c. ICF Browser Self-Care Codes. http://apps.who.int/classifications/icfbrowser/.

World Health Organization. 2010. History of the development of ICD. http://www.who.int/classifications/icd/en/HistoryOfICD.pdf.

World Health Organization. 2007. Production of ICD-11: The overall revision process.

chapter 16

Reimbursement Methodologies

Anita C. Hazelwood, MLS, RHIA, FAHIMA,
and Carol A. Venable, MPH, RHIA, FAHIMA

Learning Objectives

- Understand the historical development of healthcare reimbursement in the United States
- Describe current reimbursement processes, forms, and support practices for healthcare reimbursement
- Describe the difference between commercial health insurance and employer self-insurance
- Describe the purpose and basic benefits of the following government-sponsored health programs: Medicare Part A, Medicare Part B, Medicare Advantage, Medicaid, CHAMPVA, TRICARE, IHS, TANF, PACE, CHIP, workers' compensation, and FECA
- Understand the concept of managed care and provide examples of different types of managed care organizations

- Identify the different types of fee-for-service reimbursement methods
- Understand ambulatory surgery center rates
- Describe prospective payment systems for various types of healthcare facilities and services
- Explain the elements of coding quality
- Differentiate between encoders, automated code assignment, and computer-assisted coding
- Describe the purpose of the fee schedules, chargemasters, and auditing procedures that support the reimbursement process

Key Terms

Accept assignment

Accounts receivable

Acute-care prospective payment system

Administrative services only (ASO) contract

Advance Beneficiary Notice of Noncoverage (ABN)

All-patient diagnosis-related group (AP-DRG)

All-patient refined diagnosis-related group (APR-DRG)

Ambulatory payment classification (APC) system

Ambulatory surgery center (ASC)

Ambulatory surgery center prospective payment system (ASC PPS)

Auditing

Automated code assignment

Balance billing

Balanced Budget Refinement Act (BBRA) of 1999

Blue Cross and Blue Shield (BC/BS)

Blue Cross and Blue Shield Federal Employee Program (FEP)

Bundled payment

Capitation

Case-mix group (CMG)

Case-mix group (CMG) relative weight

Case-mix index

Categorically needy eligibility group

Chargemaster

Children's Health Insurance Program (CHIP)

Civilian Health and Medical Program of the Uniformed Services (CHAMPUS)

Civilian Health and Medical Program–Veterans Administration (CHAMPVA)

Claim

Clinical documentation improvement (CDI) program

CMS-1500

Coding

Coinsurance

Comorbidity

Compliance

Compliance program guidance

Complication

Computer-assisted coding (CAC)

Coordination of benefits (COB) transaction

Cost outlier

Cost outlier adjustment

Current Procedural Terminology (CPT)

Department of Health and Human Services (HHS)

Diagnosis-related group (DRG)

Discharge planning

Discounting

DRG grouper

Emergency Maternal and Infant Care (EMIC) Program

Employer-based self-insurance

Encoder

Episode-of-care (EOC) reimbursement

Exclusive provider organization (EPO)

Explanation of Benefits (EOB)

External review (audits)

Federal Employees' Compensation Act (FECA)

Fee schedule

Fee-for-service basis

Fraud and abuse

Geographic practice cost index (GPCI)

Global payment

Global surgery payment

Group health insurance

Group model HMO

Group practice without walls (GPWW)

Hard-coding

Health maintenance organization
  (HMO)

Healthcare Effectiveness Data and Information Set (HEDIS)

Healthcare Common Procedure Coding System (HCPCS)

Healthcare provider

Home Assessment Validation and Entry (HAVEN)

Home health agency (HHA)

Home health prospective payment system (HH PPS)

Home health resource group (HHRG)

Hospice

Hospital-acquired conditions (HAC)

Hospitalization insurance (HI) (Medicare Part A)

ICD-9-CM

Indemnity plan

Independent practice association (IPA)

Indian Health Service (IHS)

Inpatient psychiatric facility (IPF)

Inpatient rehabilitation facility (IRF)

Inpatient Rehabilitation Validation and Entry (IRVEN) system

Insured

Insurer

Integrated delivery system (IDS)

Integrated provider organization (IPO)

Long-term care hospital (LTCH)

Low-utilization payment adjustment (LUPA)

Major diagnostic category (MDC)

Major medical insurance

Managed care

Management service organization (MSO)

Medicaid

Medical foundation

Medically needy option

Medicare

Medicare Administrative Contractor (MAC)

Medicare Advantage

Medicare fee schedule (MFS)

Medicare severity diagnosis-related groups (MS-DRGs)

Medicare Summary Notice (MSN)

Medigap

Minimum Data Set 3.0 (MDS)

National Committee for Quality Assurance (NCQA)

National conversion factor (CF)

National Correct Coding Initiative (NCCI)

Network model HMO

Network provider

Nonparticipating provider

Omnibus Budget Reconciliation Act (OBRA)

Outcome and Assessment Information Set (OASIS)

Out-of-pocket expense

Outpatient code editor (OCE)

Outpatient prospective payment system (OPPS)

Packaging

Partial hospitalization

Patient Protection and Affordable Care Act

Payer of last resort

Payment status indicator (PSI)

Per member per month (PMPM)

Per patient per month (PPPM)

Physician–hospital organization (PHO)

Point-of-service (POS) plan

Policyholder

Preferred provider organization (PPO)

Premium

Present on admission (POA)

Primary care manager (PCM)

Primary care physician (PCP)

Principal diagnosis

Principal procedure

Professional component (PC)

Programs of All-Inclusive Care for the Elderly (PACE)

Prospective payment system (PPS)

Public assistance

Relative value unit (RVU)

Religious non-medical health care institution (RNHCI)
Remittance advice (RA)
Resident Assessment Validation and Entry (RAVEN)
Resource Utilization Groups, Version IV (RUG-IV)
Resource-based relative value scale (RBRVS)
Respite care
Retrospective payment system
Revenue code
Skilled nursing facility prospective payment system (SNF PPS)
Social Security Act
Staff model HMO
State workers' compensation insurance fund
Supplemental Medical Insurance (SMI) (Medicare Part B)
Tax Equity and Fiscal Responsibility Act of 1982 (TEFRA)
Technical component

Temporary Assistance for Needy Families (TANF)
Traditional fee-for-service reimbursement
TRICARE
TRICARE Extra
TRICARE Prime
TRICARE Prime Remote
TRICARE Senior Prime
TRICARE Standard
UB-04
Unbundling
Upcoding
Usual, customary, and reasonable (UCR) charges
Voluntary Disclosure Program
Workers' compensation

In the United States, very complex systems are used to pay healthcare organizations and individual healthcare professionals for the services they provide. This complexity is due in part to the variety of reimbursement methods in use today as well as the strict requirements for detailed documentation to support medical claims. The government and other third-party payers also are concerned about potential fraud and abuse in claims processing. Therefore, ensuring that bills and claims are accurate and correctly presented is an important focus of healthcare **compliance.**

A reimbursement **claim** is a statement of services submitted by a **healthcare provider** (for example, a physician or a hospital) to a third-party payer (for example, an insurance company or Medicare). The claim documents the medical and surgical services provided to a specific patient during a specific period of care. Accurate reimbursement is critical to the operational and financial health of healthcare organizations. In most healthcare organizations, health insurance specialists process reimbursement claims. Health information management (HIM) professionals also play an important role in healthcare reimbursement by

- Ensuring that health record documentation supports services billed
- Assigning diagnostic and procedural codes according to patient record documentation
- Applying coding guidelines and edits when assigning codes or auditing for coding quality and accuracy
- Appealing insurance claims denials

This chapter reviews the history of healthcare reimbursement in the United States and explains the different reimbursement systems commonly used since the adoption of various types of prospective payment systems. It then discusses a variety of healthcare reimbursement methodologies with a focus on Medicare prospective payment

systems. Finally, it explains how reimbursement claims are processed and the support processes involved.

History of Healthcare Reimbursement in the United States

Healthcare reimbursement in the United States has a long and complex history. Until the late 1800s, Americans paid their own healthcare expenses. Many people without the means to pay for care received charity care or no care at all. Over the past 100 years, a number of groups attempted to develop systems that would ensure adequate healthcare for every American. But the development of prepaid insurance plans and third-party reimbursement systems did not follow a straight path. The result is the complicated reimbursement system in place today.

Campaigns for National Health Insurance

The American Association of Labor Legislation (AALL) began the campaign for health insurance in the United States with the creation of a committee on social welfare. The committee held its first national conference in 1913 and drafted model health insurance legislation in 1915. The proposed legislation limited coverage to the working class and others who earned less than $1,200 a year, including their dependents. Coverage included the services of physicians, nurses, and hospitals; sick pay; maternity benefits; and a death benefit of $50 to pay for funeral expenses. Although the plan was supported by the American Medical Association (AMA), it was never passed into law.

During the 1930s, expanding access to medical care services became the focus of healthcare reforms. Hospital costs increased as the middle class used more hospital services. Medical care, especially hospital care, became a larger item in family budgets. The Committee on the Cost of Medical Care (CCMC) was formed to address concerns about the cost and distribution of medical care. It was funded by eight philanthropic organizations, including the Rockefeller, Millbank, and Rosenwald foundations. It first met in 1926 and stopped meeting in 1932. The CCMC's published research findings demonstrated the need for additional healthcare services. The committee recommended that national resources be allocated for healthcare and that voluntary health insurance be provided as a means of covering medical costs. However, like the AALL's earlier efforts, nothing came of the CCMC initiative.

In 1937, the Tactical Committee on Medical Care was formed. It drafted the Wagner National Health Act of 1939. The act supported a federally funded national health program to be administered by states and localities. The Wagner Act evolved from a proposal for federal grants-in-aid to a plan for national health insurance. The proposal called for compulsory national health insurance and a payroll tax. Although the proposed legislation generated extensive national debate, Congress did not pass it into law.

In 1945, the healthcare issue received the support of an American president for the first time when Harry Truman introduced a plan for universal comprehensive national health insurance. Proposed compromises included a system of private insurance for those who could afford it and public welfare services for the poor. Truman's plan died in a congressional committee in 1946.

After the Second World War, private insurance systems expanded and union-negotiated healthcare benefits served to protect workers from the impact of unforeseen healthcare expenses. The Hill-Burton Act (formally called the Hospital Survey and Construction Act) was passed in 1946. This health facility construction program was instituted under Title VI of the Public Health Service Act. The program was designed to provide federal grants for modernizing hospitals that had become obsolete due to a lack of capital investment from the onset of the Great Depression (1929) to the end of World War II (1945). The program later evolved to address other types of infrastructure needs. In return for federal funds, facilities agreed to provide medical services free or at reduced rates to patients who were unable to pay for their own care.

Congress first introduced a bill to fund coverage of hospital costs for Social Security beneficiaries in 1948. In response to criticism from the AMA, the proposed legislation was expanded to cover physician services. The concept of federal health insurance programs for the aged and the poor was highly controversial. It was not until 1965 that President Lyndon Johnson signed the law that created federal healthcare programs for the elderly and poor as part of his Great Society legislation (also called the War on Poverty).

Title XVIII of the **Social Security Act,** or Health Insurance for the Aged and Disabled, is commonly known as Medicare. Medicare legislation was enacted as one element of the 1965 amendments to the Social Security Act. Medicare is a health insurance program designed to complement the retirement, survivors, and disability insurance benefits enacted under Title II of the Social Security Act. When it was first implemented in 1966 it covered most Americans age 65 or older. In 1973, several additional groups became eligible for Medicare benefits, including those entitled to Social Security or Railroad Retirement disability cash benefits for at least 24 months, most persons with end-stage renal disease (ESRD), and certain individuals over 65 who were not eligible for paid coverage but elected to pay for Medicare benefits.

Medicaid was designed as a cost-sharing program between the federal and state governments. It pays for the healthcare services provided to many low-income Americans. The program became effective in 1966 under Title XIX of the Social Security Act. It allowed states to add health coverage to their **public assistance** programs for low-income groups, families with dependent children, the aged, and the disabled. Because Medicaid eligibility is based on meeting criteria other than income, today the program covers only about 40 percent of the population living in poverty.

The Medicare and Medicaid programs were originally the responsibility of the Department of Health, Education, and Welfare, the predecessor to the **Department of Health and Human Services (HHS)**. The Social Security Administration (SSA) administered the Medicare program, and the Social and Rehabilitation Service (SRS) administered the Medicaid Program. In 1977, administration of Medicare and Medicaid was transferred to a newly created administrative agency within HHS, the Health Care Financing Administration (HCFA). HCFA's name changed in 2001, and the agency is now the Centers for Medicare and Medicaid Services (CMS).

The demand for medical services grew tremendously during the 1970s and early 1980s. As a result, health insurance premiums and the cost of funding Medicare and Medicaid programs skyrocketed. By the mid-1980s, both private and government-sponsored healthcare programs had instituted cost-cutting programs.

Since 1983, CMS has developed the **prospective payment system (PPS)** to manage the costs of the Medicare and Medicaid programs. The PPS for inpatient acute care was the first to be implemented, followed by several others ranging from home health services to outpatient facility services. The most recently implemented system is the inpatient psychiatric facilities. Medicare and Medicaid reimbursement is discussed in more detail later in the chapter.

Private and self-insured health insurance plans have also implemented a number of cost-containing measures, most notably, **managed care** delivery and reimbursement systems. Managed care has virtually eliminated **traditional**

fee-for-service reimbursement systems in just two decades. The implementation of managed care systems has had far-reaching effects on healthcare organizations and providers in every setting. However, hospitals have experienced the greatest financial pressure. Managed care is discussed in detail later in this chapter.

Development of Prepaid Health Plans

In 1860, Franklin Health Assurance Company of Massachusetts became the first commercial insurance company in the United States to provide private healthcare coverage for injuries that did not result in death. Within 20 years, 60 other insurance companies offered health insurance policies, and by 1900, both accident insurance companies and life insurance companies were offering policies. These early policies covered loss of income and provided benefits for a limited number of illnesses (such as typhus, typhoid, scarlet fever, and smallpox).

Modern health insurance was born in 1929, when Baylor University Hospital in Dallas, Texas, agreed to provide healthcare services to Dallas schoolteachers. The hospital agreed to provide room, board, and certain ancillary services to the teachers for a set monthly fee of 50 cents. This plan is generally considered to be the first Blue Cross plan. Such plans were attractive to consumers and hospitals alike because they provided a way to ensure that patients would be able to pay for hospital services when they needed them. Payment was made directly to the hospital, not to the patient. In addition, coverage usually included a hospital stay for a specified number of days or for specific hospital services.

The Blue Cross plans contrasted with standard **indemnity plans** (insurance benefits provided in the form of cash payments) offered by private insurance companies that reimbursed, or indemnified, the patient for covered services up to a specified dollar limit. It was then the responsibility of the hospital to collect the money from the patient. Blue Shield plans were eventually developed by physicians. The plans were similar to Blue Cross plans except that they offered coverage for physicians' services.

Starting in the 1930s, and continuing through World War II, traditional insurance companies added health insurance coverage for hospital, surgical, and medical expenses to their accident and life insurance plans. During World War II, **group health insurance** was offered as a way to attract scarce wartime labor. Group health insurance plans provide healthcare benefits to full-time employees of a company. This trend was strengthened by the favorable tax treatment for fringe benefits. Unlike monetary wages, fringe benefits were not subject to income or Social Security taxes. Therefore, a pretax dollar spent on health insurance coverage was worth more than an after-tax dollar spent directly on medical services. After the war, the Supreme Court ruled that employee benefits, including health insurance, were a legitimate part of the labor–management bargaining process. Health insurance quickly became a popular employee benefit.

Although early health insurance policies covered expenses associated with common accidents and illnesses, they were inadequate for coverage of extended illnesses and lengthy hospital stays. To correct this deficiency, insurance companies in the early 1950s began offering **major medical insurance** coverage for catastrophic illnesses and injuries. Major medical insurance provides benefits up to a high-dollar limit for most types of medical expenses. However, it usually requires patients to pay large deductibles. It also may place limits on charges (for example, room and board) and may require patients to pay a portion of the expenses. Blue Cross and Blue Shield soon followed suit by offering similar plans.

Typically, the major medical insurance **policyholder** (or **insured**) paid a specified deductible—the amount the insured pays before the **insurer** assumes liability for any remaining costs of covered services. After the deductible had been paid, insured and insurer (third-party payer) shared covered losses according to a specified ratio, and the insured paid a **coinsurance** amount. Coinsurance refers to the amount the insured pays as a requirement of the insurance policy. For example, an insurance company may require the insured to pay a percentage of the daily costs for inpatient care.

Health insurance coverage continued to expand throughout the mid-20th century and eventually 77 million Americans were covered by either an indemnity plan or a major medical plan. In subsequent years, insurance companies introduced high-benefit-level major medical plans, which limited out-of-pocket expenses. **Out-of-pocket expenses** are the healthcare expenses the insured is responsible for paying. After the insured pays an amount specified in the insurance plan (that is, the deductible plus any copayments), the plan pays 100 percent of covered expenses. Such health insurance plans are common today and have been expanded to include coverage for advanced medical technology.

According to the US Census Bureau, the percentage of people covered by health insurance in 2010 was 83.7 percent, lower than in previous years. (See table 16.1.)

The lack of health insurance for so many Americans continues to be a serious concern. Because of the financial constraints brought about by changes in Medicare and Medicaid as well as managed care reimbursement, many hospitals are no longer able to provide charitable services. As a result, underfunded and overcrowded public hospitals are struggling to provide services to uninsured patients who cannot pay for their own care. In addition, many uninsured patients delay seeking medical treatment until they are extremely ill, with long-term consequences for their own health and for the healthcare system. Thousands of patients with chronic diseases such as diabetes and asthma are brought to hospital emergency departments

Table 16.1. Health insurance coverage status: 1990–2010

Year	Total U.S. Population (000)	Number Covered (000)	Percentage Covered
2010	306,110	256,206	83.7
2009	304,280	255,295	83.9
2008	301,483	256,702	85.1
2007	299,106	255,018	85.3
2006	296,824	251,610	84.8
2005	293,834	250,799	85.4
2004	291,166	247,669	85.1
2003	288,280	246,332	85.4
2002	285,933	246,157	86.1
2001	282,082	244,059	86.5
2000	279,517	242,932	86.9
1999	274,087	231,533	84.5
1998	271,743	227,462	83.7
1997	269,094	225,646	83.9
1996	266,792	225,077	84.4
1995	264,314	223,733	84.6
1994	262,105	222,387	84.8
1993	259,753	220,040	84.7
1992	256,830	218,189	85.0
1991	251,447	216,003	85.9
1990	248,886	214,167	86.1

Source: Based on US Census Bureau information: www.census.gov/.

every day because they do not have access to basic healthcare services.

One solution to the problem may be to expand government-sponsored healthcare programs. Another may be to create tax incentives to help individuals and small employers purchase private health insurance. For example, tax deductions could be offered to low-income people who buy their own insurance, or tax credits could be offered to small employers that offer health insurance coverage to employees. On March 23, 2010, President Barack Obama signed comprehensive health reform, the **Patient Protection and Affordable Care Act,** into law. This law includes mandate requirements, expansion of public programs, health insurance exchanges, changes to private insurance, employer requirements, and cost and coverage estimates. Several states and specialty groups nationwide have challenged this law with lawsuits still pending at this time.

Check Your Understanding 16.1

Instructions: Answer the following questions on a separate piece of paper.

1. How did the uninsured pay for healthcare services prior to implementation of government programs (for example, Medicare)?

2. Why did the Centers for Medicare and Medicaid Services develop prospective payment systems?

3. Using table 16.1, calculate the percentage change in health insurance coverage status from 2009 to 2010.

4. Which government agency administers the Medicaid and Medicare programs?

5. During World War II, how did employers try to increase wartime labor?

Healthcare Reimbursement Systems

Before the widespread availability of health insurance coverage, individuals were assured access to healthcare only when they were able to pay for the services themselves. They paid cash for services on a retrospective **fee-for-service basis,** in which the patient was expected to pay the healthcare provider after a service was rendered. Until the advent of managed care, capitation, and other PPSs, private insurance plans and government-sponsored programs also reimbursed providers on a retrospective fee-for-service basis.

Fee-for-service reimbursement is now rare for most types of medical services. Today, most Americans are covered by some form of health insurance, and most health insurance plans compensate providers according to predetermined discounted rates rather than fee-for-service charges. However, some types of care are not covered by most health insurance plans and are still paid for directly by patients on a fee-for-service basis. Cosmetic surgery is one example of a medical service that is not considered medically necessary and so is not covered by most insurance plans. Many insurance plans also limit coverage for psychiatric services, substance abuse treatment, and the testing and correction of vision and hearing.

Commercial Insurance

Most Americans are covered by private group insurance plans tied to their employment. Typically, employers and employees share the cost of such plans. Two types of commercial insurance are commonly available: private insurance and employer-based self-insurance.

Private Health Insurance Plans

Private commercial insurance plans are financed through the payment of **premiums**. Each covered individual or family pays a pre-established amount (usually monthly), and the insurance company sets aside the premiums from all the people covered by the plan in a special fund. When a claim for medical care is submitted to the insurance company, the claim is paid out of the fund's reserves.

Before payment is made, the insurance company reviews every claim to determine whether the services described on the claim are covered by the patient's policy. The company also reviews the diagnosis codes provided on the claim to ensure that the services provided were medically necessary. Payment then is made to either the provider or the policyholder.

When purchasing an insurance policy, the policyholder receives written confirmation from the insurance company when the insurance goes into effect. This confirmation document usually includes a policy number and a telephone number to be called in case of medical emergency. An insurance policy represents a legal contract for services between the insured and the insurance company.

Most insurance policies include the following information:

- What medical services the company will cover
- When the company will pay for medical services
- How much and for how long the company will pay for covered services
- What process is to be followed to ensure that covered medical expenses are paid

Employer-Based Self-Insurance Plans

During the 1970s, a number of large companies discovered that they could save money by self-insuring their employee health plans rather than purchasing coverage from private insurers. Large companies have large workforces, and so aggregate (total) employee medical experiences and associated expenses vary only slightly from one year to the next. Periods of rapid inflation in healthcare charges are the exception to this. The companies understood that it was in their best interest to self-insure their health plans because yearly expenses could be predicted with relative accuracy.

The cost of self-insurance funding is lower than the cost of paying premiums to private insurers because the premiums reflect more than the actual cost of the services provided to beneficiaries. Private insurers build additional fees into premiums to compensate them for assuming the risk of providing insurance coverage. In self-insured plans, the employer assumes the risk. By budgeting a certain amount to pay its employees' medical claims, the employer retains control over the funds until the time when group medical claims need to be paid.

Employer-based self-insurance has become a common form of group health insurance coverage. Many employers enter into **administrative services only (ASO) contracts** with private insurers and fund the plans themselves. The private insurers administer self-insurance plans on behalf of the employers.

Blue Cross and Blue Shield Plans

Blue Cross and Blue Shield (BC/BS) plans, also known as the Blues, were the first prepaid health plans in the United States. Originally, Blue Cross plans covered hospital care and Blue Shield plans covered physicians' services.

The first Blue Cross plan was created in 1929. In 1939, a commission of the American Hospital Association (AHA) adopted the Blue Cross national emblem for plans that met specific guidelines. The Blue Cross Association was created in 1960, and the relationship with the AHA ended in 1972.

The first Blue Shield plan was created in 1939, and the Associated Medical Care Plans (later known as the National Association of Blue Shield Plans) adopted the Blue Shield symbol in 1948. In 1982, the Blue Cross Association and the National Association of Blue Shield Plans merged to create the Blue Cross and Blue Shield Association.

Today, the Blue Cross and Blue Shield Association includes over 60 independent, locally operated companies with plans in 50 states, the District of Columbia, and Puerto Rico. The Blues offer health insurance to individuals, small businesses, seniors, and large employer groups. In addition, federal employees are eligible to enroll in the **Blue Cross/ Blue Shield Federal Employee Program (FEP)** (also called the BC/BS Service Benefit Plan). The plan offers these two products to federal employees:

- **Preferred provider organization (PPO) plan:** Healthcare providers provide healthcare services to members of the plan at a discounted rate
- **Point-of-service (POS) plan:** Subscribers are encouraged to select providers from a prescribed network but are allowed to seek healthcare services from providers outside the network at a higher level of copayment

Government-Sponsored Healthcare Programs

The federal government administers several healthcare programs. The best known are Medicare and Medicaid. The Medicare program pays for the healthcare services provided to Social Security beneficiaries 65 years old and older as well as permanently disabled people, people with end-stage renal disease, and certain other groups of individuals. State governments work with the federal Medicaid program to provide healthcare coverage to low-income individuals and families.

In addition, the federal government offers three health programs to address the needs of military personnel and their dependents as well as Native Americans. The Civilian Health and Medical Program–Veterans Administration (CHAMPVA) provides healthcare services for dependents and survivors of disabled veterans, survivors of veterans who died from service-related conditions, and survivors of military personnel who died in the line of duty. TRICARE (formerly CHAMPUS, the Civilian Health and Medical Program of the Uniformed Services) provides coverage for the dependents of armed forces personnel and retirees receiving care outside a military treatment facility. The Indian Health Service (IHS) provides federal health services to American Indians and Alaska Natives.

Medicare

The original **Medicare** program was implemented on July 1, 1966. In 1973, Medicare benefits were expanded to include individuals of any age who suffered from a permanent disability or end-stage renal disease.

For Americans receiving Social Security benefits, Medicare automatically provides **Hospitalization Insurance (HI) (Medicare Part A)**. It also offers voluntary **Supplemental Medical Insurance (SMI) (Medicare Part B)** to help pay for physicians' services, medical services, and medical–surgical supplies not covered by the hospitalization plan. Enrollees pay extra for Part B benefits. To fill gaps in Medicare coverage, most Medicare enrollees also supplement their benefits with private insurance policies. These private policies are referred to as Medigap or supplemental insurance. **Medicare Advantage** (formerly Medicare + Choice) was established by the Balanced Budget Act (BBA) of 1997 to expand the options for participation in private healthcare plans. Established in 2003, Medicare Part D covers prescription drugs.

According to CMS, approximately 19 million Americans were enrolled in the Medicare program in 1966. In 2008, approximately 45 million people were enrolled in Parts A or B (or both) of the Medicare program. By February 2012, 12.8 million of the enrollees participated in a Medicare Advantage plan.

Medicare Part A

Medicare Part A is generally provided free of charge to individuals age 65 and over who are eligible for Social Security or Railroad Retirement benefits. Individuals who do not claim their monthly cash benefits are still eligible for Medicare. In addition, workers (and their spouses) who have been employed in federal, state, or local government for a sufficient period of time qualify for Medicare coverage beginning at age 65.

Similarly, individuals who have been entitled to Social Security or Railroad Retirement disability benefits for at least 24 months and government employees with Medicare coverage who have been disabled for more than 29 months are entitled to Part A benefits. This coverage also is provided to insured workers (and their spouses) with end-stage renal disease as well as to children with end-stage renal disease. In addition, some otherwise-ineligible aged and disabled beneficiaries who voluntarily pay a monthly premium for their coverage are eligible for Medicare Part A.

The following healthcare services are covered under Medicare Part A: inpatient hospital care, skilled nursing facility (SNF) care, home healthcare, hospice care, and inpatient care in a religious non-medical health care institution. (See table 16.2.) Medicare Part A pays for inpatient hospital care and skilled nursing care when such care is medically necessary. An initial deductible payment is required for each hospital admission, plus copayments for all hospital days following day 60 within a benefit period.

Each benefit period begins the day the Medicare beneficiary is admitted to the hospital and ends when he or she has not been hospitalized for a period of 60 consecutive days. Inpatient hospital care is usually limited to 90 days during each benefit period. There is no limit to the number of benefit periods covered by Medicare Hospital Insurance during a beneficiary's lifetime. However, copayment requirements apply to days 61 through 90. When a beneficiary exhausts the 90 days of inpatient hospital care available during a benefit period, a nonrenewable lifetime reserve of up to a total of 60 additional days of inpatient hospital care can be used. Copayments are required for such additional days.

SNF care is covered when it occurs within 30 days of a three-day-long or longer hospitalization and is certified as medically necessary. The number of SNF days provided

Table 16.2. Medicare Part A benefit period, beneficiary deductibles and copayments, and Medicare payment responsibilities according to healthcare setting

Healthcare Setting	Benefit Period	Patient's Responsibility	Medicare Payments
Hospital (Inpatient)	First 60 days Days 61–90 Days 91–150 (these reserve days can be used only once in the patient's lifetime) Beyond 150 days	$1,156 annual deductible $289 per day $578 per day All costs	All but $1,156 All but $289/day All but $578/day Nothing
Skilled Nursing Facility	First 20 days Days 21–100 Beyond 100 days	Nothing $144.50 per day All costs	100% approved amount All but $144.50 per day Nothing
Home Healthcare	For as long as patient meets Medicare medical necessity criteria	Nothing for services, but 20% of approved amount for durable medical equipment (DME)	100% of the approved amount, and 80% of the approved amount for DME
Hospice Care	For as long as physician certifies need for care	Limited costs for outpatient drugs and inpatient respite care ($5 per outpatient prescription and 5% for respite care)	All but limited costs for outpatient drugs and inpatient respite care
Blood Banks	Unlimited if medical necessity criteria are met	First 3 pints unless patient or someone else donates blood to replace what patient uses	All but first 3 pints per calendar year

Source: www.medicare.gov/costs.

under Medicare is limited to 100 days per benefit period, with a copayment required for days 21 through 100. Medicare Part A does not cover SNF care when the patient does not require skilled nursing care or skilled rehabilitation services.

Care provided by a **home health agency (HHA)** may be furnished part-time in the residence of a homebound beneficiary when intermittent or part-time skilled nursing or certain other therapy or rehabilitation care is needed. Certain medical supplies and durable medical equipment (DME) also may be paid for under the Medicare home health benefit.

The Medicare program requires the HHA to develop a treatment plan that is periodically reviewed by a physician. Home healthcare under Medicare Part A has no limitations on duration, no copayments, and no deductibles. For DME, beneficiaries must pay 20 percent coinsurance, as required under Medicare Part B.

Terminally ill persons whose life expectancies are six months or less may elect to receive **hospice** services. To qualify for Medicare reimbursement for hospice care, patients must elect to forgo standard Medicare benefits for treatment of their illnesses and agree to receive only hospice care. When a hospice patient requires treatment for a condition that is not related to his or her terminal illness, however, Medicare does pay for all covered services necessary for that condition. The Medicare beneficiary pays no deductible for hospice coverage but does pay coinsurance amounts for

drugs and inpatient **respite care.** (Respite care is any inpatient care provided to the hospice patient for the purpose of providing primary caregivers a break from their caregiving responsibilities.)

Medicare Part B

Medicare Part B (Supplemental Medical Insurance) covers the following services and supplies:

- Physicians' and surgeons' services, including some covered services furnished by chiropractors, podiatrists, dentists, and optometrists and services provided by the following Medicare-approved practitioners who are not physicians: certified registered nurse anesthetists, clinical psychologists, clinical social workers (other than those employed by a hospital or an SNF), physician assistants, nurse practitioners, and clinical nurse specialists working in collaboration with a physician
- Services in an emergency department or outpatient clinic, including same-day surgery and ambulance services
- Home healthcare not covered under Medicare Part A
- Laboratory tests, x-rays, and other diagnostic radiology services, as well as certain preventive care screening tests
- Ambulatory surgery center (ASC) services in Medicare-approved facilities

- Most physical and occupational therapy and speech pathology services
- Comprehensive outpatient rehabilitation facility services and mental healthcare provided as part of a partial hospitalization psychiatric program when a physician certifies that inpatient treatment would be required without the partial hospitalization services. (A **partial hospitalization** program offers intensive psychiatric treatment on an outpatient basis to psychiatric patients, with an expectation that the patient's psychiatric condition and level of functioning will improve and that relapse will be prevented so that rehospitalization can be avoided.)
- Radiation therapy, renal dialysis and kidney transplants, and heart and liver transplants under certain limited conditions
- DME approved for home use, such as oxygen equipment; wheelchairs; prosthetic devices; surgical dressings, splints, and casts; walkers; and hospital beds needed for use in the home
- Drugs and biologicals that cannot be self-administered, such as hepatitis B vaccines and transplant and immunosuppressive drugs (plus certain self-administered anticancer drugs)
- Preventive services such as bone mass measurements, cardiovascular screening blood tests, colorectal cancer screening, diabetes services, glaucoma testing, Pap test and pelvic exam, prostate cancer screening, screening mammograms, and vaccinations (flu, pneumococcal, hepatitis B)

To be covered, all Medicare Part B services must be either documented as medically necessary or covered as one of several prescribed preventive benefits. Also, Part B services are generally subject to deductibles and coinsurance payments. (See table 16.3.) Certain medical services and related care are subject to special payment rules, for example:

- Deductibles for administration of blood and blood products
- Maximum approved amounts for Medicare-approved physical or occupational therapy services performed in settings other than hospitals
- Higher cost-sharing requirements, such as those for outpatient psychiatric care

Table 16.3.   Medicare Part B benefit deductibles and copayments and Medicare payment responsibilities according to type of service

Type of Service	Benefit	Deductible and Copayment	Medicare Payment
Medical expense	Physicians' services, inpatient and outpatient medical and surgical services and supplies, and durable medical equipment (DME)	$140 annual deductible, plus 20% of approved amount after deductible has been met, except in outpatient setting	80% of approved amount (after patient has paid $110 deductible)
	Mental healthcare	40% of most outpatient care	60% of most outpatient care
Clinical laboratory services	Blood tests, urinalysis, and more	Nothing	100% of approved amount
Home healthcare	Intermittent skilled care, home health aid services, DME and supplies, and other services	Nothing for home care service, 20% of approved amount for DME	100% of approved amount 80% of approved amount for DME
Outpatient hospital services	Services for diagnosis and treatment of an illness or injury	A coinsurance (for doctors' services) or a copayment amount for most outpatient hospital services. The copayment for a single service cannot be more than the amount of the inpatient hospital deductible. Charges for items or services that Medicare does not cover	Payment based on ambulatory patient classifications/outpatient prospective payment system
Blood	Unlimited if medical necessity criteria are met	First 3 pints or have blood donated by someone else (if met under Part B, does not have to be met again under Part A)	All but first 3 pints

Source: www.medicare.gov/costs.

It should be noted that the following healthcare services are usually not covered by Medicare Part A or B and are only covered by private health plans under the Medicare Advantage program:

- Long-term nursing care
- Cosmetic surgery
- Dentures and dental care
- Accupuncture
- Hearing aids and exams for fitting hearing aids

Medicare Advantage

Medicare Advantage provides expanded coverage of many healthcare services. Although any Medicare beneficiary may receive benefits through the original fee-for-service program, most beneficiaries enrolled in both Parts A and B can choose to participate in a Medicare Advantage plan instead. Organizations that offer Medicare Advantage plans must meet specific requirements as determined by CMS.

Primary Medicare Advantage products include the following types of plans:

- *Health maintenance organization (HMO) plans:* In most HMOs, you can only go to doctors, other healthcare providers, or hospitals on the plan's list, except in an emergency. You may also need to get a referral from your primary care doctor.
- *PPO plans:* In a PPO plan, patients use doctors, specialists, and hospitals in the plan's network and can go to doctors and hospitals not on the list, usually at an additional cost. Patients do not need referrals to see doctors or go to hospitals that are not part of the plan's network and may pay lower copayments and receive extra benefits.
- *Private fee-for-service plans:* These plans are similar to original Medicare in that you can generally go to any doctor, other healthcare provider, or hospital as long as they agree to treat you. The plan determines how much it will pay doctors, other healthcare providers, and hospitals and how much you must pay when you get care.
- *Special needs plans:* These plans provide focused and specialized healthcare for specific groups of people, such as those who have both Medicare and Medicaid, who live in a nursing home, or who have certain chronic medical conditions.

Medicare Prescription Drug Improvement and Modernization Act

The Medicare Prescription Drug Improvement and Modernization Act, also known as the Medicare Reform Bill, was signed into law by President George W. Bush in December 2003. This legislation provides seniors and individuals with disabilities with a prescription drug benefit, more choices, and better benefits under Medicare. Medicare drug plans are run by insurance companies and other private companies approved by Medicare. Each plan can vary in cost and drugs covered, and beneficiaries select their preferred plan.

Out-of-Pocket Expenses and Medigap Insurance

Medicare beneficiaries who elect the fee-for-service option are responsible for charges not covered by the Medicare program and for various cost-sharing aspects of Parts A and B. These liabilities may be paid by the Medicare beneficiary; by a third party, such as an employer-sponsored health plan or private Medigap insurance; or by Medicaid, when the person is eligible.

Medigap or supplemental insurance is private health insurance that pays, within limits, most of the healthcare service charges not covered by Medicare Parts A or B. These policies must meet federal and state laws.

The payment share for beneficiaries enrolled in Medicare Advantage plans is based on the cost-sharing structure of the specific plan they select. Most plans have lower deductibles and coinsurance than are required of Medicare fee-for-service beneficiaries. Such beneficiaries pay the monthly Part B premium and may pay an additional plan premium, depending on the plan.

For hospital care covered under Medicare Part A, a fee-for-service beneficiary's payment share includes a one-time deductible amount payable at the beginning of each benefit period. For 2012, the deductible is $1,156. This deductible covers the beneficiary's part of the first 60 days of each inpatient hospital stay. When continued inpatient care is needed beyond the 60 days, additional coinsurance payments ($289 per day in 2012) are required through the 90th day of a benefit period. Each Part A beneficiary also has a lifetime reserve of 60 additional hospital days, which may be used when the covered days within a benefit period have been exhausted. Lifetime reserve days may be used only once, and coinsurance payments ($578 per day in 2012) are required.

For SNF care covered under Part A, Medicare fully covers the first 20 days in a benefit period. For days 21 through 100, a copayment ($144.50 per day in 2012) is required. Medicare benefits expire after the first 100 days of SNF care during a benefit period.

Home healthcare services require no deductible or coinsurance payment by the beneficiary. For any Part A service, the beneficiary is responsible for paying fees to cover the first three pints or units of nonreplaced blood per calendar year. The beneficiary has the option of paying the fee or arranging for the blood to be replaced by family and friends.

Most beneficiaries covered by Medicare Part A pay no premiums. Eligibility is generally earned through the work experience of the beneficiary or of his or her spouse. In addition, most individuals over 65 who are otherwise ineligible for Medicare Part A coverage can enroll voluntarily by paying a monthly premium when they also enroll in Part B.

For Part B (refer to table 16.3), the beneficiary's payment share includes

- One annual deductible ($140 in 2012)
- Monthly premiums ($99.90 to $319.70 per month depending on income in 2012)
- Coinsurance payments for Part B services (usually 20 percent of medically allowable charges)
- Any deductibles for blood products
- Certain charges above approved charges (for claims not on assignment)
- Payment for any services that are not covered by Medicare

Medicaid

Title XIX of the Social Security Act enacted **Medicaid** in 1965. The Medicaid program pays for medical assistance provided to individuals and families with low incomes and limited financial resources. Individual states must meet broad national guidelines established by federal statutes, regulations, and policies to qualify for federal matching grants under the Medicaid program. Individual state medical assistance agencies, however, establish the Medicaid eligibility standards for residents of their states. The states also determine the type, amount, duration, and scope of covered services; calculate the rate of payment for covered services; and administer local programs.

Medicaid policies on eligibility, services, and payment are complex and vary considerably among states, even among states of similar size or geographic proximity. Therefore, an individual who is eligible for Medicaid in one state may not be eligible in another. In addition, the amount, duration, and scope of care provided vary considerably from state to state. Moreover, Medicaid eligibility and services within a state can change from year to year.

Medicaid Eligibility Criteria

Low income is only one measure for Medicaid eligibility. Other financial resources also are compared against eligibility standards. Each state determines these standards according to federal guidelines.

Generally, each state can determine which groups Medicaid will cover. Each state also establishes its own financial criteria for Medicaid eligibility. However, to be eligible for federal funds, states are required to provide Medicaid coverage to certain individuals. These individuals include recipients of federally assisted income maintenance payments as well as related groups of individuals who do not receive cash payments. The federal **categorically needy eligibility groups** include the following:

- Individuals eligible for Medicaid when they meet requirements for **Temporary Assistance for Needy Families (TANF)**
- Children below age six whose family income is at or below 133 percent of the federal poverty level (FPL)

(the income threshold established by the federal government)
- Pregnant women whose family income is below 133 percent of the FPL (services are limited to those related to pregnancy-related medical care)
- Supplemental Security Income (SSI) recipients in most states
- Recipients of adoption or foster care assistance under Title IV-E of the Social Security Act
- Specifically protected groups (typically individuals who lose their cash assistance due to earnings from work or from increased Social Security benefits but who may keep Medicaid for a period of time)
- Infants born to Medicaid-eligible pregnant women
- Certain low-income Medicare beneficiaries

States also have the option of providing Medicaid coverage to other categorically related groups. Categorically related groups share the characteristics of the eligible groups (that is, they fall within defined categories), but the eligibility criteria are somewhat more liberally defined. A **medically needy option** also allows states to extend Medicaid eligibility to persons who would be eligible for Medicaid under one of the mandatory or optional groups except that their income and resources are above the eligibility level set by their state. Individuals may qualify immediately or may "spend down" by incurring medical expenses that reduce their income to or below their state's income level for the medically needy.

In 1996, Congress passed the Personal Responsibility and Work Opportunity Reconciliation Act (also known as welfare reform). The act made restrictive changes in the eligibility requirements for SSI coverage. These changes also affected eligibility for participation in the Medicaid program.

The welfare reform act also affected a number of disabled children. Many lost their SSI benefits as a result of the restrictive changes. However, their eligibility for Medicaid was reinstituted by the BBA.

In addition, the welfare reform act repealed the open-ended federal entitlement program known as Aid to Families with Dependent Children (AFDC). TANF, which replaced AFDC, provides states with grant money to be used for time-limited cash assistance. A family's lifetime cash welfare benefits are generally limited to a maximum of five years. Individual states also are allowed to impose other eligibility restrictions.

Medicaid Services

To be eligible for federal matching funds, each state's Medicaid program must offer medical assistance for the following basic services:

- Inpatient hospital services
- Outpatient hospital services
- Emergency services
- Prenatal care and delivery services
- Vaccines for children

- Physicians' services
- SNF services for persons age 21 or older
- Family planning services and supplies
- Rural health clinic services
- Home healthcare for persons eligible for skilled nursing services
- Laboratory and x-ray services
- Medical and surgical services of a dentist
- Pediatric and family nurse practitioner services
- Nurse-midwife services
- Federally qualified health center (FQHC) services and ambulatory services performed at the FQHC that would be available in other settings
- Early and periodic screening and diagnostic and therapeutic services for children under age 21

States also may receive federal matching funds to provide some of the optional services, the most common being:

- Diagnostic services
- Clinic services
- Prescription drugs and prosthetic devices
- Transportation services
- Rehabilitation and physical therapy services
- Prosthetic devices
- Home care and community-based care services for persons with chronic impairments

The BBA also called for implementation of a state option called **Programs of All-Inclusive Care for the Elderly**

(PACE). PACE provides an alternative to institutional care for individuals 55 years old or older who require a level of care usually provided at nursing facilities. It offers and manages all of the health, medical, and social services needed by a beneficiary and mobilizes other services, as needed, to provide preventive, rehabilitative, curative, and supportive care.

PACE services can be provided in day healthcare centers, homes, hospitals, and nursing homes. The program helps its beneficiaries to maintain their independence, dignity, and quality of life. PACE also functions within the Medicare program. Individuals enrolled in PACE receive benefits solely through the PACE program.

Medicaid-Medicare Relationship

Medicare beneficiaries who have low incomes and limited financial resources also may receive help from the Medicaid program. For persons eligible for full Medicaid coverage, Medicare coverage is supplemented by services that are available under their state's Medicaid program according to their eligibility category. Additional services may include, for example, nursing facility care beyond the 100-day limit covered by Medicare, prescription drugs, eyeglasses, and hearing aids. For those enrolled in both programs, any services covered by Medicare are paid for by the Medicare program before any payments are made by the Medicaid program because Medicaid is always the **payer of last resort**. Table 16.4 provides a comparison of the Medicare and Medicaid programs.

Table 16.4. Comparison of Medicare and Medicaid programs

Medicare	Medicaid
Health insurance for people age 65 and older, or people under 65 who are entitled to Medicare because of disability or are receiving dialysis for permanent kidney failure	Health assistance for people of any age
Administered through fiscal intermediaries, insurance companies under contract to the government to process Medicare claims	Administered by the federal government through state and local governments following federal and state guidelines
Medicare regulations are the same in all states	Medicaid regulations vary from state to state
Financed by monthly premiums paid by the beneficiary and by payroll tax deductions	Financed by federal, state, and county tax dollars
For people age 65 and over, eligibility is based on Social Security or Railroad Retirement participation. For people under age 65, eligibility is based on disability. For people who undergo kidney dialysis, eligibility is not dependent on age	Eligibility based on financial need
Beneficiary responsible for paying deductibles, coinsurance or copayments, and Part B premiums	Medicaid can help pay Medicare deductible, coinsurance or copayment, and premiums
Hospital and medical benefits; preventive care and long-term care benefits are limited	Comprehensive benefits include hospital, preventive care, long-term care, and other services not covered under Medicare such as dental work, prescriptions, transportation, eyeglasses, and hearing aids

Children's Health Insurance Program

The **Children's Health Insurance Program** (CHIP) (Title XXI of the Social Security Act) is a program initiated by the BBA. CHIP allows states to expand existing insurance programs to cover children up to age 19. It provides additional federal funds to states so that Medicaid eligibility can be expanded to include a greater number of children.

CHIP became available in October 1997 and is jointly funded by the federal government and the states. Following broad federal guidelines, states establish eligibility and coverage guidelines and have flexibility in the way they provide services. Recipients in all states must meet three eligibility criteria:

- They must come from low-income families.
- They must be otherwise ineligible for Medicaid.
- They must be uninsured.

States are required to offer the following services:

- Inpatient hospital services
- Outpatient hospital services
- Physicians' surgical and medical services
- Laboratory and x-ray services
- Well-baby and child care services, including age-appropriate immunizations

TRICARE

TRICARE is a healthcare program for active-duty members of the military and other qualified family members. Eligible retirees and their family members, as well as eligible survivors of members of the uniformed services, also are eligible for TRICARE.

The idea of medical care for the families of active-duty members of the uniformed military services dates back to the late 1700s. It was not until 1884, however, that Congress directed Army medical officers and contract surgeons to care for the families of military personnel free of charge.

There was very little change in the provision of medical care to members of the military and their families until the Second World War, when the military was made up mostly of young men who had wives of childbearing age. The military medical care system could not handle the large number of births or the care of young children. So, in 1943, Congress authorized the **Emergency Maternal and Infant Care (EMIC) Program.** The program provided maternity and infant care to dependents of service members in the lowest four pay grades.

During the early 1950s, the Korean conflict also strained the capabilities of the military healthcare system. As a result, the Dependents Medical Care Act was signed into law in 1956. Amendments to the act created the **Civilian Health and Medical Program of the Uniformed Services (CHAMPUS)** in 1966.

During the 1980s, the search for ways to improve access to top-quality medical care and at the same time control costs led to implementation of CHAMPUS demonstration projects in various parts of the country. The most successful of these projects was the CHAMPUS Reform Initiative (CRI) in California and Hawaii. Initiated in 1988, the CRI offered military service families a choice in the way their military healthcare benefits could be used. Five years of successful operation and high levels of patient satisfaction persuaded Department of Defense officials that they should extend and improve the CRI concepts as a uniform program nationwide.

The new program, known as TRICARE, was phased in nationally by 1998. TRICARE offers three options: TRICARE Prime, TRICARE Extra, and TRICARE Standard.

TRICARE Prime

Of the three options, **TRICARE Prime** provides the most comprehensive healthcare benefits at the lowest cost. Military treatment facilities, such as military base hospitals, serve as the principal source of healthcare, and a **primary care manager (PCM)** is assigned to each enrollee.

Two specialized programs supplement TRICARE Prime. **TRICARE Prime Remote** provides healthcare services to active-duty military personnel stationed in the United States in areas not served by the traditional military healthcare system. (Active-duty personnel include members of the Army, Navy, Marine Corps, Air Force, Coast Guard, and active National Guard.) **TRICARE Senior Prime** is a managed care demonstration program designed to serve the medical needs of military retirees who are 65 years old or over, as well as their dependents and survivors.

TRICARE Extra

TRICARE Extra is a cost-effective preferred provider network (PPN) option. Healthcare costs in TRICARE Extra are lower than for TRICARE Standard because beneficiaries must select physicians and medical specialists from a network of civilian healthcare professionals working under contract with TRICARE. The healthcare professionals who participate in TRICARE Extra agree to charge a preestablished discounted rate for the medical treatments and procedures provided to participants in the plan.

TRICARE Standard

TRICARE Standard incorporates the services previously provided by CHAMPUS. TRICARE Standard allows eligible beneficiaries to choose any physician or healthcare provider. It pays a set percentage of the providers' fees, and the enrollee pays the rest. This option permits the most flexibility but may be the most expensive for the enrollee, particularly when the provider's charges are higher than the amounts allowed by the program.

CHAMPVA

The **Civilian Health and Medical Program–Veterans Administration (CHAMPVA)** is a healthcare program for dependents and survivors of permanently and totally disabled veterans, survivors of veterans who died from service-related conditions, and survivors of military personnel who died in the line of duty. CHAMPVA is a voluntary program that allows beneficiaries to be treated for free at participating VA healthcare facilities, with the VA sharing the cost of covered healthcare services and supplies. Because of the similarity between CHAMPVA and TRICARE, people sometimes confuse the two programs. However, CHAMPVA is separate from TRICARE, and there are distinct differences between them. TRICARE is for individuals currently serving in the armed forces, and CHAMPVA is for retired military personnel.

Indian Health Service

The provision of health services to Native Americans originally developed from the relationship between the federal government and federally recognized Indian tribes established in 1787. It is based on Article I, Section 8, of the US Constitution and has been given form and substance by numerous treaties, laws, Supreme Court decisions, and executive orders.

The **Indian Health Service (IHS)** is an agency within the HHS. It is responsible for providing healthcare services to American Indians and Alaska Natives. The American Indians and Alaska Natives served by the IHS receive preventive healthcare services, primary medical services (hospital and ambulatory care), community health services, substance abuse treatment services, and rehabilitative services. Secondary medical care, highly specialized medical services, and other rehabilitative care are provided by IHS staff or by private healthcare professionals working under contract with the IHS.

A system of acute- and ambulatory care facilities operates on Indian reservations and in Indian and Alaska Native communities. In locations where the IHS does not have its own facilities or is not equipped to provide a needed service, it contracts with local hospitals, state and local healthcare agencies, tribal health institutions, and individual healthcare providers.

Workers' Compensation

Most employees are eligible for some type of **workers' compensation** insurance. Workers' compensation programs cover healthcare costs and lost income associated with work-related injuries and illnesses. Federal government employees are covered by the **Federal Employees' Compensation Act (FECA)**. Individual states pass legislation that addresses workers' compensation coverage for nonfederal government employees. Some states exclude certain workers, for example, business owners, independent contractors, farm workers, and so on. Texas employers are not required to provide workers' compensation coverage.

Federal Workers' Compensation Funds

In 1908, President Theodore Roosevelt signed legislation to provide workers' compensation for certain federal employees in unusually hazardous jobs. The scope of the law was narrow and its benefits were limited. This law represented the first workers' compensation program to pass the test of constitutionality applied by the US Supreme Court.

FECA replaced the 1908 statute in 1916. Under FECA, civilian employees of the federal government are provided medical care, survivors' benefits, and compensation for lost wages. The Office of Workers' Compensation Programs (OWCP) administers FECA as well as the Longshore and Harbor Workers' Compensation Act of 1927 and the Black Lung Benefits Reform Act of 1977.

FECA also provides vocational rehabilitation services to partially disabled employees. Employees who fully or partially recover from their injuries are expected to return to work. FECA does not provide retirement benefits.

State Workers' Compensation Funds

According to the American Association of State Compensation Insurance Funds (AASCIF), state workers' compensation insurance was developed in response to the concerns of employers. Before state workers' compensation programs became widely available, employers faced the possibility of going out of business when insurance companies refused to provide coverage or charged excessive premiums. Legislators in most states have addressed these concerns by establishing **state workers' compensation insurance funds** that provide a stable source of insurance coverage and serve to protect employers from uncertainties about the continuing availability of coverage. Because state funds are provided on a nonprofit basis, the premiums can be kept low. In addition, the funds provide only one type of insurance: workers' compensation. This specialization allows the funds to concentrate resources, knowledge, and expertise in a single field of insurance.

State workers' compensation insurance funds do not operate at taxpayer expense because, by law, the funds support themselves through income derived from premiums and investments. As nonprofit departments of the state or as independent nonprofit companies, they return surplus assets to policyholders as dividends or safety refunds. This system reduces the overall cost of state-level workers' compensation insurance. Numerous court decisions have determined that the assets, reserves, and surplus of the funds are not public funds but, instead, the property of the employers insured by the funds.

In states where state funds have not been mandated, employers purchase workers' compensation coverage from private carriers or provide self-insurance coverage.

Managed Care

Healthcare costs in the United States rose dramatically during the 1970s and 1980s. As a result, the federal government, employers, and other third-party payers began investigating more cost-effective healthcare delivery systems. The federal government decided to move toward PPSs for the Medicare program in the mid-1980s. Prospective payment as a reimbursement methodology is discussed later in this chapter. Commercial insurance providers looked to managed care.

Managed care is the generic term for prepaid health plans that integrate the financial and delivery aspects of healthcare services. In other words, managed care organizations work to control the cost of, and access to, healthcare services at the same time that they strive to meet high-quality standards. They manage healthcare costs by negotiating discounted providers' fees

and controlling patients' access to expensive healthcare services. In managed care plans, services are carefully coordinated to ensure that they are medically appropriate and needed.

The cost of providing appropriate services is also monitored continuously to determine whether the services are being delivered in the most efficient and cost-effective way possible.

Since 1973, several pieces of federal legislation have been passed with the goal of encouraging the development of managed healthcare systems. (See table 16.5.) The

Table 16.5.   Federal legislation relevant to managed care

Year	Legislative Title	Legislative Summary
1973	Federal Health Maintenance Organization Assistance Act of 1973 (HMO Act of 1973)	• Authorized grants and loans to develop HMOs under private sponsorship • Defined a federally qualified HMO (certified to provide healthcare services to Medicare and Medicaid enrollees) as one that has applied for and met federal standards established in the HMO Act of 1973 • Required most employers with more than 25 employees to offer HMO coverage when local plans were available
1974	Employee Retirement Income Security Act of 1974 (ERISA)	• Mandated reporting and disclosure requirements for group life and health plans (including managed care plans) • Permitted large employers to self-insure employee healthcare benefits • Exempted large employers from taxes on health insurance premiums
1981	Omnibus Budget Reconciliation Act of 1981 (OBRA)	• Provided states with flexibility to establish HMOs for Medicare and Medicaid programs • Resulted in increased enrollment
1982	Tax Equity and Fiscal Responsibility Act of 1982 (TEFRA)	• Modified the HMO Act of 1973 • Created Medicare risk programs, which allowed federally qualified HMOs and competitive medical plans that met specified Medicare requirements to provide Medicare-covered services under a risk contract • Defined risk contract as an arrangement among providers to provide capitated (fixed, prepaid basis) healthcare services to Medicare beneficiaries • Defined competitive medical plan (CMP) as an HMO that meets federal eligibility requirements for a Medicare risk contract but is not licensed as a federally qualified plan
1985	Preferred Provider Health Care Act of 1985	• Eased restrictions on preferred provider organizations • Allowed subscribers to seek healthcare from providers outside the PPO
1985	Consolidated Omnibus Budget Reconciliation Act of 1985 (COBRA)	• Established an employee's right to continue healthcare coverage beyond scheduled benefit termination date (including HMO coverage)
1988	Amendment to the HMO Act of 1973	• Allowed federally qualified HMOs to permit members to occasionally use non-HMO physicians and be partially reimbursed
1989	Healthcare Effectiveness Data and Information Set (HEDIS)—developed by National Committee for Quality Assurance (NCQA)	• Created standards to assess managed care systems in terms of membership, utilization of services, quality, access, health plan management and activities, and financial indicators
1994	HCFA's Office of Managed Care established	• Facilitated innovation and competition among Medicare H MOs
2010	Patient Protection and Affordable Care Act	• Individual mandate requirements; expansion of public programs; health insurance exchanges; changes to private insurance; employer requirements; and cost and coverage estimates

Health Maintenance Organization Assistance Act of 1973 authorized federal grants and loans to private organizations that wished to develop **health maintenance organizations (HMOs)**. Another important advancement in managed care was development of the **Healthcare Effectiveness Data and Information Set (HEDIS)** by the **National Committee for Quality Assurance (NCQA)**.

The NCQA is a private, not-for-profit organization that accredits, assesses, and reports on the quality of managed care plans in the United States. It worked with public and private healthcare purchasers, health plans, researchers, and consumer advocates to develop HEDIS in 1989. HEDIS (formerly known as the Health Plan Employer Data and Information Set) is a set of standardized measures used to compare managed care plans in terms of the quality of services they provide. The standards cover areas such as plan membership, utilization of and access to services, and financial indicators. The goals of the program include

- Helping beneficiaries make informed choices among the numerous managed care plans available
- Improving the quality of care provided by managed care plans
- Helping the government and other third-party payers make informed purchasing decisions

CMS offers several managed care options to Medicare and Medicaid enrollees. It began collecting HEDIS data from Medicare managed care plans in 1996.

Several kinds of managed care plans are available in the United States, including

- HMOs
- PPOs
- POS plans
- Exclusive provider organizations (EPOs)
- Integrated delivery systems (IDSs)

Health Maintenance Organizations

An HMO is a prepaid voluntary health plan that provides healthcare services in return for the payment of a monthly membership premium. HMO premiums are based on a projection of the costs that are likely to be involved in treating the plan's average enrollee over a specified period of time. If the actual cost per enrollee were to exceed the projected cost, the HMO would experience a financial loss. If the actual cost per enrollee turned out to be lower than the projection, the HMO would show a profit. Because most HMOs are for-profit organizations, they emphasize cost control and preventive medicine.

Today, most employers and insurance companies offer enrollees some type of HMO option. The benefit to third-party payers and enrollees alike is cost savings. Most HMO enrollees have significantly lower out-of-pocket expenses than enrollees of traditional fee-for-service and other types of managed care plans. The HMO premiums shared by employers and enrollees also are lower than the premiums for other types of healthcare plans.

HMOs can be organized in several different ways, including the group model HMO, the independent practice association (IPA), the network model HMO, and the staff model HMO, or there can also be a combination of the staff, group, and network models.

Group Model HMOs

In the **group model HMO,** the HMO enters into a contract with an independent multispecialty physician group to provide medical services to members of the plan. The providers usually agree to devote a fixed percentage of their practice time to the HMO. Alternatively, the HMO may own or directly manage the physician group, in which case the physicians and their support staff would be considered its employees.

Group model HMOs are closed-panel arrangements. In other words, the physicians are not allowed to treat patients from other managed care plans. Enrollees of group model HMOs are required to seek services from the designated physician group.

Independent Practice Associations

In an **independent practice association** (IPA) model, the HMO enters into a contract with an organized group of physicians who join together for purposes of fulfilling the HMO contract but retain their individual practices. The IPA serves as an intermediary during contract negotiations. It also manages the premiums from the HMO and pays individual physicians as appropriate. The physicians are not considered employees of the HMO. They work from their own private offices and continue to see other patients. The HMO usually pays the IPA according to a prenegotiated list of discounted fees. Alternatively, physicians may agree to provide services to HMO members for a set prepaid capitated payment for a specified period of time. Capitation is discussed later in this chapter.

The IPA is an open-panel HMO, which means that the physicians are free to treat patients from other plans. Enrollees of such HMOs are required to seek services from the designated physician group.

Network Model HMOs

Network model HMOs are similar to group model HMOs except that the HMO contracts for services with two or more multispecialty group practices instead of just one practice. Members of network model HMOs receive a list of all the physicians on the approved panel and are required to select providers from the list.

Staff Model HMOs

Staff model HMOs directly employ physicians and other healthcare professionals to provide medical services to members. Members of the salaried medical staff are considered employees of the HMO rather than independent practitioners.

Premiums are paid directly to the HMO, and ambulatory care services are usually provided within the HMO's corporate facilities. The staff model HMO is a closed-panel arrangement.

Preferred Provider Organizations

PPOs represent contractual agreements between healthcare providers and a self-insured employer or a health insurance carrier. Beneficiaries of PPOs select providers such as physicians or hospitals from a list of participating providers who have agreed to furnish healthcare services to the covered population. Beneficiaries may elect to receive services from nonparticipating providers but must pay a greater portion of the cost (in other words, higher deductibles and copayments). Providers are usually reimbursed on a discounted fee-for-service basis.

Point-of-Service Plans

POS plans are similar to HMOs in that subscribers must select a **primary care physician (PCP)** from a network of participating physicians. The PCP is usually a family or general practice physician or an internal medicine specialist. The PCP acts as a service gatekeeper to control the patient's access to specialty, surgical, and hospital care as well as expensive diagnostic services.

POS plans are different from HMOs in that subscribers are allowed to seek care from providers outside the network. However, the subscribers must pay a greater share of the charges for out-of-network services. POS plans were created to increase the flexibility of managed care plans and to allow patients more choice in providers.

Exclusive Provider Organizations

Exclusive provider organizations (EPOs) are similar to PPOs except that EPOs provide benefits to enrollees only when the enrollees receive healthcare services from **network providers.** In other words, EPO beneficiaries do not receive reimbursement for services furnished by nonparticipating providers. In addition, healthcare services must be coordinated by a PCP. EPOs are regulated by state insurance departments. In contrast, HMOs are regulated by state departments of commerce or departments of incorporation.

Integrated Delivery Systems

An **integrated delivery system (IDS)** is a healthcare provider consisting of a number of associated medical facilities that furnish coordinated healthcare services. Most IDSs include a number of facilities that provide services along the continuum of care, for example, ambulatory surgery centers, physicians' office practices, outpatient clinics, acute care hospitals, SNFs, and so on.

Integrated delivery systems can be structured according to several different models, including

- Group practices without walls (GPWWs)
- Integrated provider organizations (IPOs)
- Management service organizations (MSOs)
- Medical foundations
- Physician–hospital organizations (PHOs)

Group Practices without Walls

Group practices without walls (GPWWs) is an arrangements that allows physicians to maintain their own offices but to share administrative, management, and marketing services (for example, medical transcription and billing) for the purpose of fulfilling contracts with managed care organizations.

Integrated Provider Organizations

Integrated provider organizations (IPOs) manage and coordinate the delivery of healthcare services performed by a number of healthcare professionals and facilities. IPOs typically provide acute care (hospital) services, physicians' services, ambulatory care services, and skilled nursing services. The physicians working in an IPO are salaried employees. IPOs are sometimes referred to as delivery systems, horizontally integrated systems, health delivery networks, accountable health plans, integrated service networks (ISNs), vertically integrated plans (VIPs), and vertically integrated systems.

Management Service Organizations

Management service organizations (MSOs) provide practice management (administrative and support) services to individual physicians' practices. They are usually owned by a group of physicians or a hospital.

Medical Foundations

Medical foundations are nonprofit organizations that enter into contracts with physicians to manage the physicians' practices. The typical medical foundation owns clinical and business resources and makes them available to the participating physicians. Clinical assets include medical equipment and supplies as well as treatment facilities. Business assets include billing and administrative support systems.

Physician-Hospital Organizations

Physician–Hospital Organizations (PHOs), previously known as medical staff–hospital organizations, provide healthcare services through a contractual arrangement between physicians and hospital(s). PHO arrangements make it possible for the managed care market to view the hospital(s) and physicians as a single entity for the purpose of establishing a contract for services.

Check Your Understanding 16.2

Instructions: Answer the following questions on a separate piece of paper.

1. What is fee-for-service reimbursement? Why is it rarely used today as a reimbursement method?

2. How are private commercial insurance plans financed?

3. What process do most insurance companies use to reimburse healthcare services?

4. What are administrative services only contracts?

5. What federal program pays for healthcare services provided to financially needy individuals?

6. For which populations of individuals do TRICARE and CHAMPVA reimburse healthcare services?

7. Why is Medicare Part B referred to as Supplemental Medical Insurance?

8. What federal legislation expanded Medicare options by creating Medicare Advantage?

9. What private health insurance pays (within limits) for most healthcare services not covered by Medicare Part A?

10. How did the Medicare and Medicaid programs come into effect? How are the two programs different?

11. How are Medicaid eligibility standards established?

12. What is the difference between a preferred provider organization and a point-of-service plan?

13. What is the purpose of the Children's Health Insurance Program?

14. What type of Medicare coverage applies to inpatient hospitalization? To prescription eyeglasses? To emergency department visits? To dental care? To ambulatory surgery center service? To hospice care?

15. What is the difference between TRICARE Extra and TRICARE Prime?

16. How does state workers' compensation coverage differ from federal workers' compensation coverage?

17. What type of HMO model employs physicians and other healthcare professionals to provide healthcare services to members?

18. What is the difference between an independent practice association and a staff model HMO?

19. Define managed care and describe the various types of managed care programs available in the United States.

20. What do management service organizations do?

Healthcare Reimbursement Methodologies

As mentioned earlier in this chapter, about 85 percent of Americans are covered by some type of private prepaid health plan or federal healthcare program. Therefore, most healthcare expenses in the United States are reimbursed through third-party payers rather than by the actual recipients of the services. The recipients can be considered the "first parties" and the providers the "second parties." Third-party payers include commercial for-profit insurance companies, nonprofit Blue Cross and Blue Shield organizations, self-insured employers, federal programs (Medicare, Medicaid, CHIP, TRICARE, CHAMPVA, and IHS), and workers' compensation programs.

Providers charge their own determined amounts for services rendered. However, providers are rarely reimbursed this full amount because third-party payers may have a unique reimbursement methodology. For example, commercial insurance plans usually reimburse healthcare providers under some type of **retrospective payment system.** In retrospective payment systems, the exact amount of the payment is determined after the service has been delivered. In a PPS, the exact amount of the payment is determined before the service is delivered. The federal Medicare program uses PPSs.

Fee-for-Service Reimbursement Methodologies

Fee-for-service reimbursement methodologies issue payments to healthcare providers on the basis of the charges assigned to each of the separate services that were performed for the patient. The total bill for an episode of care represents the sum of all the itemized charges for every element of care provided. Independent clinical professionals such as physicians and psychologists who are not employees of the facility issue separate itemized bills to cover their services after the services are completed or on a monthly basis when the services are ongoing.

Before prepaid insurance plans became common in the 1950s and the Medicare and Medicaid programs were developed in the 1960s, healthcare providers sent itemized bills directly to their patients. Patients were held responsible for paying their own medical bills. When prepaid health plans and the Medicare and Medicaid programs were originally developed, they also based reimbursement on itemized fees.

Traditional Fee-for-Service Reimbursement

In traditional fee-for-service (FFS) reimbursement systems, third-party payers or patients issue payments to healthcare providers after healthcare services have been provided (for example, after the patient has been discharged from the hospital). Payments are based on the specific services delivered. The fees charged for services vary considerably by the type of services provided, the resources required, and the type and number of healthcare professionals involved.

Payments can be calculated on the basis of actual billed charges, discounted charges, prenegotiated rate schedules, or the usual or customary charges in a specific community.

For example, some third-party payers pay only the maximum allowable charges as determined by the plan. Maximum allowable charges may be significantly lower than the provider's billed charges. Some payers issue payments on the basis of **usual, customary, and reasonable (UCR) charges.** Commercial insurance and Blue Cross/Blue Shield plans often issue payments based on prenegotiated discount rates and contractual cost-sharing arrangements with the patient.

For many plans, the health plan and the patient share costs on an 80/20 percent arrangement. The portion of the claim covered by the patient's insurance plan would be 80 percent of allowable charges. After the third-party payer transmits its payment to the provider, the provider's billing department issues a final statement to the patient. The statement shows the amount for which the patient is responsible (in this example, 20 percent of allowable charges).

The traditional FFS reimbursement methodology is still used by many commercial insurance companies for visits to physicians' offices.

Managed Fee-for-Service Reimbursement

Managed FFS reimbursement is similar to traditional FFS reimbursement except that managed care plans control costs primarily by managing their members' use of healthcare services. Most managed care plans also negotiate with providers to develop discounted **fee schedules.** Managed FFS reimbursement is common for inpatient hospital care. In some areas of the country, however, it also is applied to outpatient and ambulatory services, surgical procedures, high-cost diagnostic procedures, and physicians' services.

Utilization controls include the prospective and retrospective review of the healthcare services planned for, or provided to, patients. For example, a prospective utilization review of a plan to hospitalize a patient for minor surgery might determine that the surgery could be safely performed less expensively in an outpatient setting. Prospective utilization review is sometimes called precertification.

In a retrospective utilization review, the plan might determine that part or all of the services provided to a patient were not medically necessary or were not covered by the plan. In such cases, the plan would disallow part or all of the provider's charges and the patient would be responsible for paying the provider's outstanding charges.

Discharge planning also can be considered a type of utilization control. The managed care plan may be able to move the patient to a less intensive, and therefore less expensive, care setting as soon as possible by coordinating his or her discharge from inpatient care.

Episode-of-Care Reimbursement Methodologies

Plans that use **episode-of-care (EOC) reimbursement** methods issue lump-sum payments to providers to compensate them for all the healthcare services delivered to a patient for a specific illness or over a specific period of time. EOC payments also are called **bundled payments.** Bundled payments cover multiple services and also may involve multiple providers of care. EOC reimbursement methods include capitated payments, global payments, global surgery payments, Medicare ambulatory surgery center rates, and Medicare PPSs.

Capitation

Capitation is based on per person premiums or membership fees rather than on itemized per-procedure or per-service charges. The capitated managed care plan negotiates a contract with an employer or a government agency representing a specific group of individuals. According to the contract, the managed care organization agrees to provide all the contracted healthcare services that the covered individuals need over a specified period of time (usually one year). In exchange, the individual enrollee or third-party payer agrees to pay a fixed premium for the covered group. Like other insurance plans, a capitated insurance contract stipulates as part of the contract exactly which healthcare services are covered and which ones are not.

Capitated premiums are calculated on the projected cost of providing covered services **per patient per month (PPPM)** or **per member per month (PMPM).** The capitated premium for an individual member of a plan includes all the services covered by the plan, regardless of the number of services actually provided during the period or their cost. If the average member of the plan actually used more services than originally assumed in the PPPM calculation, the plan would show a loss for the period. If the average member actually used fewer services, the plan would show a profit.

The purchasers of capitated coverage (usually the member's employer) pay monthly premiums to the managed care plan. The individual enrollees usually pay part of the premium as well. The plan then compensates the providers who actually furnished the services. In some arrangements, the managed care plan accepts all the risk involved in the contract. In others, some of the risk is passed on to the PCPs who agreed to act as gatekeepers for the plan.

The capitated managed care organization may own or operate some or all of the healthcare facilities that provide care to members and directly employ clinical professionals. Staff model HMOs operate in this way. Alternatively, the capitated managed care organization may purchase services from independent physicians and facilities, as do group model HMOs.

Global Payment

Global payment methodology is sometimes applied to radiological and similar types of procedures that involve professional and technical components. Global payments are lump-sum payments distributed among the physicians who performed the procedure or interpreted its results and the healthcare facility that provided the equipment, supplies, and technical support required. The procedure's **professional component** is supplied by physicians (for example, radiologists), and its **technical component** (for example, radiological supplies, equipment, and support services) is supplied by a hospital or freestanding diagnostic or surgical center. For example:

Larry Timber underwent a scheduled carotid angiogram as a hospital outpatient. He had complained of ringing in his ears and dizziness, and his physician scheduled the procedure to determine whether there was a blockage in one of Larry's carotid arteries. The procedure required a surgeon to inject radiopaque contrast material through a catheter into Larry's left carotid artery. A radiological technician then took an x-ray of Larry's neck. The technician was supervised by a radiologist and both were employees of the hospital.

Professional component: Injection of radiopaque contrast material by the surgeon

Technical component: X-ray of the neck region

Global payment: The facility received a lump-sum payment for the procedure and paid for the services of the surgeon from that payment.

Global Surgery Payments

A single **global surgery payment** covers all the healthcare services entailed in planning and completing a specific surgical procedure. In other words, every element of the procedure from the treatment decision through normal postoperative patient care is covered by a single bundled payment. For example:

Tammy Murdock received from Dr. Thomas Michaels all the prenatal, perinatal, and postnatal care involved in the birth of her daughter. She received one bill from the physician for a total of $2,200. The bill represented the total charges for the obstetrical services associated with her pregnancy. However, the two-day inpatient hospital stay for the normal delivery was not included in the global payment, nor were the laboratory services she received during her hospital stay. Tammy received a separate bill for these services. In addition, if she had suffered a postdelivery complication (for example, a wound infection) or an unrelated medical problem, the physician and hospital services required to treat the complication would not have been covered by the global surgical payment.

Check Your Understanding 16.3

Instructions: Answer the following questions on a separate piece of paper.

1. What type of payment system is in place when the amount of payment is determined before the service is delivered?

2. What are usual, customary, and reasonable (UCR) charges based on?

3. Many insurance plans require patients to share costs for healthcare services. What is the most typical cost-sharing ratio?

4. Which utilization control is most closely associated with managed fee-for-service reimbursement?

5. What would a managed care plan likely show when a group of patients uses more services than the plan originally calculated in its contract with the group?

6. What are bundled payments? What is another name for bundled payments?

7. Describe the concept of capitation.

Medicare's Prospective Payment Systems

Congress enacted the first Medicare prospective payment system in 1983 as a cost-cutting measure. Implementation of the **acute care prospective payment system** resulted in a shift of clinical services and expenditures away from the inpatient hospital setting to outpatient settings. As a result, spending on nonacute care exploded.

Congress responded by passing the **Omnibus Budget Reconciliation Act (OBRA)** of 1986, which mandated that CMS develop a prospective system for hospital-based outpatient services provided to Medicare beneficiaries. In subsequent years, Congress mandated the development of PPSs for other healthcare providers.

Medicare's Acute-Care Prospective Payment System

As mentioned, prior to 1983, Medicare Part A payments to hospitals were determined on a traditional FFS reimbursement methodology. Payment was based on the cost of services provided, and reasonable cost or per diem costs were used to determine payment.

During the late 1960s, just a few years after the Medicare and Medicaid health programs were implemented, Congress authorized a group at Yale University to develop a system for monitoring quality of care and utilization of services. This system was known as **diagnosis-related groups (DRGs).** DRGs were implemented on an experimental basis by the New Jersey Department of Health in the late 1970s as a way to predetermine reimbursement for hospital inpatient stays.

At the conclusion of the New Jersey DRG experiment, Congress passed the **Tax Equity and Fiscal Responsibility Act of 1982 (TEFRA).** TEFRA modified Medicare's retrospective reimbursement system for inpatient hospital stays by requiring implementation of the DRG PPS in 1983. Under DRGs, Medicare paid most hospitals for inpatient hospital services according to a predetermined rate for each discharge. Very simply, the DRG system was a way of classifying patients on the basis of diagnosis. Patients within each DRG were said to be "medically meaningful"—that is, patients within a group were expected to evoke a set of clinical responses that statistically would result in an approximately equal use of hospital resources. Originally there were 470 DRGs with changes made to the system each year. On October 1, 2007, the DRG system became the **Medicare severity diagnosis-related groups (MS-DRGs).**

At this time, several types of hospitals are excluded from Medicare's acute-care PPS. The following facilities are still paid on the basis of reasonable cost, subject to payment limits per discharge or under a separate PPS:

- Psychiatric and rehabilitation hospitals and psychiatric and rehabilitation units within larger medical facilities

- **Long-term care hospitals (LTCHs)**, which are defined as hospitals with an average length of stay of 25 days or more
- Children's hospitals
- Cancer hospitals
- Critical access hospitals
- **Religious non-medical health care institutions** (RNHCI)

To determine the appropriate MS-DRG, a claim for a healthcare encounter is first classified into one of 25 **major diagnostic categories (MDCs)**. Most MDCs are based on body systems and include diseases and disorders relating to a particular system. However, some MDCs include disorders and diseases involving multiple organ systems (for example, burns). The number of MS-DRGs within a particular MDC varies.

The **principal diagnosis** is defined as the condition that, after study, is determined to have caused the admission of the patient to the hospital for care, and it determines the MDC assignment. Within each MDC, decision trees are used to determine the correct MS-DRG. Within most MDCs, cases are divided into surgical MS-DRGs (based on a surgical hierarchy that orders individual procedures or groups of procedures by resource intensity) and medical MS-DRGs. Medical MS-DRGs generally are differentiated on the basis of diagnosis and age. Some surgical and medical MS-DRGs are further differentiated on the basis of the presence or absence of complications or comorbidities (CCs).

A **complication** is a secondary condition that arises during hospitalization and is thought to increase the length of stay by at least one day for approximately 75 percent of patients. A **comorbidity** is a condition that existed at admission and is thought to increase the length of stay at least one day for approximately 75 percent of patients. During the initial years of DRGs there was a standard list of diagnoses that were considered CCs. Each year new CCs are added and others deleted from the CC list.

Prior to the implementation of MS-DRGs, a comprehensive review of the CC list was performed and an important change to the CC concept was made. Each base MS-DRG can be subdivided in one of three possible alternatives:

- MS-DRGs with three subgroups [Major Complication/Comorbidity (MCC, CC, and non-CC; referred to as "with MCC, "with CC," and "w/o CC/MCC")]
  — MS-DRG 682 Renal Failure w MCC
  — MS-DRG 683 Renal Failure w CC
  — MS-DRG 684 Renal Failure w/o CC/MCC

- MS-DRGs with two subgroups (MCC and CC/non-CC; referred to as "with MCC" and "w/o MCC")
  — MS-DRG 725 Benign Prostatic Hypertrophy w MCC
  — MS-DRG 726 Benign Prostatic Hypertrophy w/o MCC

- MS-DRGs with two subgroups (non-CC and CC/MCC; referred to as "with CC/MCC" and "w/o CC/MCC")
  — MS-DRG 294 Deep Vein Thrombophlebitis w CC/MCC
  — MS-DRG 295 Deep Vein Thrombophlebitis w/o CC/MCC

The increased number of classifications is intended to differentiate between the levels of resource consumption within a base MS-DRG group.

Under the acute-care prospective payment system, a predetermined rate based on the MS-DRG (only one is assigned per case) assigned to each case is used to reimburse hospitals for inpatient care provided to Medicare and TRICARE beneficiaries. Hospitals determine MS-DRGs by assigning **ICD-9-CM** codes to each patient's principal diagnosis, comorbidities, complications, major complications, **principal procedure,** and secondary procedures. These code numbers and other information on the patient (age, gender, and discharge status) are entered into a grouper. A MS-**DRG grouper** is a computer software program that assigns appropriate MS-DRGs according to the information provided for each episode of care.

Reimbursement for each episode of care is based on the MS-DRG assigned. Different diagnoses require different levels of care and expenditures of resources. Therefore, each MS-DRG is assigned a different level of payment that reflects the average amount of resources required to treat a patient assigned to that MS-DRG. Each MS-DRG is associated with a description, a relative weight, a geometric mean length of stay (LOS), and an arithmetic mean LOS. The relative weight represents the average resources required to care for cases in that particular MS-DRG relative to the national average of resources used to treat all Medicare patients. A MS-DRG with a relative weight of 2.000, on average, requires twice as many resources as a MS-DRG with a relative weight of 1.000. The geometric mean LOS is defined as the total days of service, excluding any outliers or transfers, divided by the total number of patients; the arithmetic mean LOS is defined as the total days of service divided by the total number of patients.

For example, MS-DRG 1, organized within MDC 01, is described as heart transplant or implant of heart assist system w MCC and has a relative weight of 24.2794, a geometric mean LOS of 28.6, and an arithmetic mean LOS of 37.4.

CMS adjusts the Medicare MS-DRG list and reimbursement rates every fiscal year (October 1 through September 30). There are currently 751 MS-DRGs.

In some cases, the MS-DRG payment received by the hospital may be lower than the actual cost of providing Medicare Part A inpatient services. In such cases, the hospital must absorb the loss. In other cases, the cost of providing care is lower than the MS-DRG payment, and the hospital may receive a payment for more than its actual cost and, therefore, make a profit. It is expected that, on average, hospitals will be reimbursed for their total costs in providing services to Medicare patients.

Special circumstances can also apply to inpatient cases and result in an outlier payment to the hospital. An outlier case results in exceptionally high costs when compared with other cases in the same DRG. To qualify for a **cost outlier,** a hospital's charges for a case (adjusted to cost) must exceed the payment rate for the MS-DRG by a fixed dollar amount, which changes each year. The additional payment amount is equal to 80 percent of the difference between the hospital's entire cost for the stay and the threshold amount.

There can be further hospital-specific adjustments resulting in add-on payments:

- Disproportionate share hospital (DSH): If the hospital treats a high percentage of low-income patients, it receives a percentage add-on payment applied to the MS-DRG-adjusted base payment rate.
- Indirect medical education (IME): If the hospital is an approved teaching hospital, it receives a percentage add-on payment for each case paid under MS-DRGs. This percentage varies depending on the ratio of residents to beds.
- New technologies: If the hospital can demonstrate the use of a new technology that is a substantial clinical improvement over available existing technologies and the new technology is approved, additional payments are made. Hospitals must submit a formal request to CMS with a significant sample of data to demonstrate that the technology meets the high-cost threshold.

The MS-DRG system creates a hospital's **case-mix index** (types or categories of patients treated by the hospital) based on the relative weights of the MS-DRG. The case-mix index can be figured by multiplying the relative weight of each MS-DRG by the number of discharges within that MS-DRG. This provides the total weight for each MS-DRG. The sum of all total weights divided by the sum of total patient discharges equals the case-mix index. A hospital may relate its case-mix index to the costs incurred for inpatient care. This information allows the hospital to make administrative decisions about services to be offered to its patient population. For example:

> The hospital's case-mix report indicated that a small population of patients was receiving obstetrical services, but that the costs associated with providing such services was disproportionately high. This report along with other data might result in the hospital's administrative decision to discontinue its obstetrical services department.

An **all-patient diagnosis-related group (AP-DRG)** system was developed in 1988 by 3M Health Information Systems as the basis for New York's hospital reimbursement program for non-Medicare discharges. AP-DRGs are still used in a number of states as a basis for payment of non-Medicare claims. AP-DRGs use the patient's age, sex, discharge status,

and ICD-9-CM diagnosis and procedure codes to determine a DRG that, in turn, determines reimbursement. 3M also has developed **all-patient refined DRGs (APR-DRGs)** as an extension of the DRG concept. APR-DRGs adjust patient data for severity of illness and risk of mortality, help to develop clinical pathways, are used as a basis for quality assurance programs, and are used in comparative profiling and setting capitation rates (3M HIS 2002).

Hospital-Acquired Conditions and Present on Admission Indicator Reporting

The Deficit Reduction Act of 2005 (DRA) mandated a quality adjustment in the MS-DRG payments for certain hospital-acquired conditions. CMS titled the program "Hospital-Acquired Conditions and Present on Admission Indicator Reporting" (HAC and POA). Inpatient hospitals were required to submit POA information on diagnoses for inpatient discharges on or after October 1, 2007. The following hospitals are exempt from the POA indicator requirement: critical access hospitals, long-term care hospitals, Maryland waiver hospitals, cancer hospitals, children's inpatient facilities, inpatient rehabilitation facilities, and psychiatric hospitals.

Present on admission (POA) is defined as a condition present at the time the order for inpatient admission occurs— conditions that develop during an outpatient encounter, including in the emergency department, observation, or outpatient surgery, are considered as present on admission. A POA indicator is assigned to principal and secondary diagnoses and the external cause of injury codes. The reporting options that are available are

- Y = Yes, diagnosis was present at the time of inpatient admission.
- N = No, diagnosis was not present at the time of inpatient admission.
- U = Unknown, documentation is insufficient to determine if condition was present at the time of inpatient admission.
- W = Clinically undetermined. The provider is unable to clinically determine whether the condition was present at the time of admission.
- 1 = Unreported/not used = Exempt from POA reporting.

Complete guidelines with examples are part of the *ICD-9-CM Official Guidelines for Coding and Reporting* and should be reviewed. The POA indicator guidelines do not provide guidance on when a condition should be coded but, rather, how to apply the POA indicator to the final set of diagnosis codes that have been assigned.

CMS identified eight **hospital-acquired conditions (HACs)** (not present on admission) as "reasonably preventable," and

Table 16.6.   Sample 2011 RVUs for selected HCPCS codes

HCPCS Code	Description	Work RVU	Facility Practice Expense RVU	Malpractice Expense RVU
99203	Office visit	1.42	0.72	0.14
99204	Office visit	2.43	1.21	0.23
11010	Debridement skin at fracture site	4.19	3.49	0.76
45380	Colonoscopy with biopsy	4.43	2.73	0.67
52601	TURP, complete	15.26	8.09	1.49

hospitals will not receive additional payment for cases in which one of the eight selected conditions was not present on admission. This is termed the HAC payment provision. The eight originally selected conditions include

- Foreign object retained after surgery
- Air embolism
- Blood incompatibility
- Stage III and IV pressure ulcers
- Falls and trauma
- Catheter-associated urinary tract infection
- Vascular catheter-associated infection
- Surgical site infection—mediastinitis after coronary artery bypass graft

Additional conditions were added in 2010 and remain in effect:

- Surgical site infections following certain orthopedic procedures and bariatric surgery
- Manifestations of poor glycemic control
- Deep vein thrombosis (DVT)/pulmonary embolism (PE) following certain orthopedic procedures

The HAC and POA webpage at http://www.cms.gov/HospitalAcqCond/ provides up-to-date information on these topics.

Resource-Based Relative Value Scale System

In 1992, CMS implemented the **resource-based relative value scale (RBRVS)** system for physician's services such as office visits covered under Medicare Part B. The system reimburses physicians according to a fee schedule based on predetermined values assigned to specific services.

The **Medicare fee schedule (MFS)** is the listing of allowed charges that are reimbursable to physicians under Medicare. Each year's MFS is published by CMS in the *Federal Register.*

To calculate fee schedule amounts, Medicare uses a formula that incorporates the following **relative value units (RBUs)** for

- Physician work (RVUw)
- Practice expenses (RVUpe)
- Malpractice costs (RVUm)

Sample 2011 RVUs for selected Healthcare Common Procedure Coding System (HCPCS) codes are shown in table 16.6.

Payment localities are adjusted according to three **geographic practice cost indices** (GPCIs):

- Physician work (GPCIw)
- Practice expenses (GPCIpe)
- Malpractice costs (GPCIm)

Sample GPCIs for selected US cities are shown in table 16.7.

A geographic cost index is a number used to multiply each RVU so that it better reflects a geographical area's relative costs. For example, costs of office rental prices, local taxes, average salaries, and malpractice costs are all affected by geography.

A **national conversion factor (CF)** converts the RVUs into payments. In 2011, the CF was $33.9764.

The RBRVS fee schedule uses the following formula:

$$[(RVUw \times GPCIw) + (RVUpe \times GPCIpe) + (RVUm \times GPCIm)] \times CF = Payment$$

As an example, payment for performing a repair of a nail bed (code 11760) in Birmingham, Alabama, can be calculated. RVU values include

- RVUw = 1.60
- RVUpe = 1.43
- RVUm = 0.21

Table 16.7.   Sample GPCIs for selected US cities

City	Work GPCI	Practice Expense GPCI	Malpractice Expense GPCI
St. Louis	0.991638	0.939923	1.059442
Dallas	1.011353	0.99943	0.825433
Spokane	0.989894	0.932469	0.861289
Philadelphia	1.017097	1.070284	1.670886

GPCI values include:

- GPCIw = 1.00
- GPCIpe = 0.850
- GPCIm = 0. 617
- National CF = $33.9764

The calculation is as follows:

$$(1.60 \times 1.00) + (1.43 \times 0.850) + (0.21 \times 0.617) \times \$33.9764$$

$$1.60 + 1.2155 + 0.1295$$

$$2.945 \times \$33.9764$$

Fee schedule payment of $100.06

Medicare Skilled Nursing Facility Prospective Payment System

The BBA mandated implementation of a **skilled nursing facility prospective payment system (SNF PPS)**. The system was to cover all costs (routine, ancillary, and capital) associated with covered SNF services furnished to Medicare Part A beneficiaries. Certain educational activities were exempt from the new system.

The SNF PPS was implemented on July 1, 1998. Under the PPS, SNFs are no longer paid under a system based on reasonable costs. Instead, they are paid according to a per-diem PPS based on case mix–adjusted payment rates. Per diem rates range from a high of about $737 to a low of about $183.

Medicare Part A covers posthospital SNF services and all items and services paid under Medicare Part B before July 1, 1998 (other than physician and certain other services specifically excluded under the BBA). Major elements of the SNF PPS include rates, coverage, transition, and consolidated billing. OBRA required CMS to develop an assessment instrument to standardize the collection of SNF patient data. That document is called the **Minimum Data Set 3.0 (MDS)**. The MDS is the minimum core of defined and categorized patient assessment data that serves as the basis for documentation and reimbursement in an SNF. The MDS form contains a face sheet for documentation of resident identification information, demographic information, and the patient's customary routine.

Resource Utilization Groups

SNF reimbursement rates are paid according to **Resource Utilization Groups, Version IV (RUG-IV)**, a case mix–adjusted resident classification system based on MDS used in skilled nursing facilities for resident assessments.

The RUG-IV classification system uses resident assessment data from the MDS collected by SNFs to assign residents to one of 66 groups.

Resident Assessment Validation and Entry

CMS developed a computerized data-entry system for skilled nursing facilities that offers users the ability to collect MDS assessments in a database and transmit them in CMS-standard format to their state database. The data-entry software is entitled **Resident Assessment Validation and Entry (RAVEN)**. RAVEN imports and exports data in standard MDS record format; maintains facility, resident, and employee information; enforces data integrity via rigorous edit checks; and provides comprehensive online help. It includes a data dictionary and a RUG calculator.

Consolidated Billing Provision

The BBA includes a billing provision that requires an SNF to submit consolidated Medicare bills for its residents for services covered under either Part A or Part B except for a limited number of specifically excluded services. For example, when a physician provides a diagnostic radiology service to an SNF patient, the SNF must bill for the technical component of the radiology service because this is included in the SNF consolidated billing payment. The rendering physician must develop a business relationship with the SNF in order to receive payment from the SNF for the services he or she rendered. The professional component of the physicians' services is excluded from SNF consolidated billing and must be billed separately to the Medicare Administrative Contractor. There are, of course, other exclusions to this provision, including physician assistant services, nurse practitioner services, and clinical nurse specialist services when these individuals are working under the supervision of, or in collaboration with, a physician, certified midwife services, qualified psychologist services, and certified registered nurse anesthetist services. Other exclusions include hospice care, maintenance dialysis, selected services furnished on an outpatient basis such as cardiac catheterization services, CT elsewhere scans and MRIs, radiation therapy, and ambulance services. In addition, SNFs report **Healthcare Common Procedure Coding System (HCPCS)** codes on all Part B bills.

Medicare and Medicaid Outpatient Prospective Payment System

The **outpatient prospective payment system** (OPPS) was first implemented for services furnished on or after August 1, 2000. Under the OPPS, the federal government pays for hospital outpatient services on a rate-per-service basis that varies according to the **ambulatory payment classification (APC)** group to which the service is assigned. The HCPCS identifies and groups the services within each APC group. Services included under APCs follow:

- Surgical procedures
- Radiology including radiation therapy
- Clinic visits (evaluation and management, or E/M)
- Emergency room visits
- Partial hospitalization services for the mentally ill
- Chemotherapy
- Preventive services and screening exams
- Dialysis for other than ESRD
- Vaccines, splints, casts, and antigens
- Certain implantable items

The OPPS does not apply to critical access hospitals (CAHs), hospitals in Maryland that are excluded, IHS hospitals, or hospitals outside the 50 states, the District of Columbia, and Puerto Rico.

The calculation of payment for services under the OPPS is based on the categorization of outpatient services into APC groups according to **Current Procedural Terminology (CPT)/HCPCS** codes. ICD-9-CM coding is not utilized in the selection of APCs. The more than 850 APCs are categorized into significant procedure APCs, radiology and other diagnostic APCs, medical visit APCs, and a partial hospitalization APC. Services within an APC are similar, both clinically and with regard to resource consumption, and each APC is assigned a fixed payment rate for the facility fee or technical component of the outpatient visit. Payment rates are also adjusted according to the hospital's wage index. Multiple APCs may be appropriate for a single episode of care as the patient may receive various types of services such as radiology or surgical procedures.

The OPPS **payment status indicators (PSIs)** (see table 16.8) that are assigned to each HCPCS code and APCs play an important role in determining payment for services under the OPPS. They indicate whether a service represented by a HCPCS code is payable under the OPPS or another

Table 16.8.   OPPS payment status indicators and description of payment under OPPS

Status Indicator	Description of Payment under OPPS
SI A	Services paid under some other method (such as a fee schedule): • Ambulance services • Clinical diagnostic laboratory services • Nonimplantable prosthetic and orthotic devices • EPO for ESRD patients • Physical, occupational, and speech therapy • Routine dialysis services for ESRD patients provided in a certified dialysis unit of a hospital • Diagnostic mammography • Screening mammography
SI B	Codes that are not recognized by OPPS when submitted on an outpatient hospital Part B bill type
SI C	Inpatient procedures
SI D	Discontinued codes
SI E	Items, codes, and services not covered by Medicare
SI F	Corneal tissue acquisition; certain Certified Registered Nurse Anesthetist services and hepatitis B vaccines
SI G	Pass-through drugs and biologicals
SI H	Pass-through device categories
SI K	Non-pass-through drugs and nonimplantable biologicals, including therapeutic radiopharmaceuticals
SI L	Influenza vaccine; pneumococcal pneumonia vaccine
SI M	Items and services not billable to the fiscal intermediary
SI N	Items and services packaged into APC rates
SI P	Partial hospitalization
SI Q1	STVX packaged codes
SI Q2	T packaged codes
SI Q3	Codes that may be paid through a composite APC
SIR	Blood and blood products
SI S	Significant procedure, not discounted when multiple
SI T	Significant procedure, multiple reduction applies
SIU	Brachytherapy
SI V	Clinic or emergency department visit
SI Y	Nonimplantable durable medical equipment
SI X	Ancillary services

payment system and also whether particular OPPS policies apply to the code. Status indicator "N" refers to items and services that are "packaged" into APC rates. **Packaging** means that payment for that service is packaged into payment for other services and, therefore, there is no separate APC payment. Packaged services might include minor ancillary services, inexpensive drugs, medical supplies, and implantable devices.

Discounting applies to multiple surgical procedures furnished during the same operative session. For discounted procedures, the full APC rate is paid for the surgical procedure with the highest rate, and other surgical procedures performed at the same time are reimbursed at 50 percent of the APC rate. When a surgical procedure is terminated after a patient is prepared for surgery but before induction of anesthesia, the facility is reimbursed at 50 percent of the APC rate. Modifier 73 should be appended to the procedure code indicating that the procedure was discontinued. Modifier 74 is appended to the procedure code when a procedure is interrupted after its initiation or the administration of anesthesia. The facility receives the full APC payment.

The OPPS does pay outlier payments on a service-by-service basis when the cost of furnishing a service or procedure by a hospital exceeds 1.75 times the APC payment amount and exceeds the APC payment rate plus a fixed-dollar threshold. If a provider meets both of these conditions, the outlier payment is calculated as 50 percent of the amount by which the cost of furnishing the service exceeds 1.75 times the APC payment rate. The fixed-dollar threshold changes each year.

Services that are identified with a status indicator "C" have been identified as inpatient only services and will not be reimbursed by Medicare when they are provided on an outpatient basis. This "inpatient only" list is updated each year.

Special payments are also made for new technology in one of two ways. Transitional pass-through payments are temporary additional payments that are made when certain drugs, biological agents, brachytherapy devices, and other expensive medical devices new to medicine are used. These new technology APCs were created to allow new procedures and services to enter the OPPS quickly even though their complete costs and payment information are not known. New technology APCs house modern procedures and services until enough data are collected to properly place the new procedure in an existing APC or to create a new APC for the service/procedure. Coding for E/M medical visits is difficult under the APC system. CMS states that each facility should develop a system for mapping the provided services furnished to the different levels of effort represented by E/M codes. As long as services furnished are documented and medically necessary and the facility is following its own system, which reasonably relates the intensity of hospital resources to the different levels of codes, CMS assumes that the hospital is in compliance with its reporting requirements.

Ambulatory Surgery Centers

For Medicare purposes, an **ambulatory surgery center (ASC)** is a distinct entity that operates exclusively for the purpose of furnishing outpatient surgical services to patients. An ASC is either independent or operated by a hospital. If it is operated by a hospital, it has the option of being covered under Medicare as an ASC or can continue to be covered as an outpatient surgery department. To be considered an ASC of a hospital it has to be a separately identifiable entity physically, administratively, and financially.

The Medicare Modernization Act (MMA) of 2003 extensively revised the ASC payment system with changes going into effect on January 1, 2008. The system is called the **ambulatory surgery center prospective payment system (ASC PPS)**.

ASCs must accept assignment as payment in full. Eighty percent of the payment comes from the government and 20 percent from the beneficiary.

Under the ASC payment system, Medicare will make payments to ASCs only for services on the ASC list of covered procedures. The surgical procedures included in the list are those that have been determined to pose no significant risk to beneficiaries when furnished in an ASC. The ASC payment includes services such as medical and surgical supplies, nursing services, surgical dressings, implanted prosthetic devices not on a pass-through list, and splints and casts. Examples of services not included in the ASC payment are brachytherapy, procurement of corneal tissue, and certain drugs and biologicals.

The payment rates for most covered ASC procedures and covered ancillary services are established prospectively based on a percentage of the OPPS payment rates while a small number of services are contractor based, such as the pass-through items.

The HCPCS code is used as the basis for payment. Each HCPCS code falls into one of more than 1,500 ASC groups, with each group having a unique payment. Medicare pays 80 percent of the wage-adjusted rate, and the beneficiary is responsible for the other 20 percent. Similar to the OPPS, each HCPCS has a payment indicator that determines whether the surgical procedure is on the ASC list (A2); device-intensive procedure paid at adjusted rate (J8); or packaged service or item for which no separate payment is made (N1). These are just a few examples of some of the payment indicators; there are others.

Again, like the OPPS, there are guidelines for payment of terminated procedures. The following rules apply:

- 0 percent payment for procedures terminated for unforeseen circumstances before the ASC has expended substantial resources
- 50 percent payment for procedures that are terminated due to medical complications prior to anesthesia
- 100 percent payment for procedures that have started but are terminated after anesthesia is induced

Home Health Prospective Payment System

The BBA called for the development and implementation of a **home health prospective payment system** (HH PPS) for reimbursement of services provided to Medicare beneficiaries. The PPS for HHAs was implemented on October 1, 2000. Extensive changes were made in 2008.

OASIS and HAVEN

HHAs use the OASIS data set and HAVEN data-entry software to conduct all patient assessments, not just the assessments for Medicare beneficiaries. **OASIS** stands for **Outcome and Assessment Information Set.** It consists of data elements that (1) represent core items for the comprehensive assessment of an adult home care patient and (2) form the basis for measuring patient outcomes for the purpose of outcome-based quality improvement (OBQI). OASIS is a key component of Medicare's partnership with the home care industry to foster and monitor improved home healthcare outcomes. The Conditions of Participation for HHAs require that HHAs electronically report all OASIS data.

CMS also developed the OASIS data-entry system called **HAVEN (Home Assessment Validation and Entry).** HAVEN is available to HHAs at no charge through CMS's website or on CD-ROM. HAVEN offers users the ability to collect OASIS data in a database and transmit them in a standard format to state databases. The data-entry software imports and exports data in standard OASIS record format; maintains agency, patient, and employee information; maintains data integrity through rigorous edit checks; and provides comprehensive online help.

Home Health Resource Groups

Home health resource groups (HHRGs) represent the classification system established for the prospective reimbursement of covered home care services to Medicare beneficiaries during a 60-day episode of care. Covered services include skilled nursing visits, home health aide visits, therapy services (for example, physical, occupational, and speech therapy), medical social services, and nonroutine medical supplies. DME is excluded from the episode-of-care payment and is reimbursed under the DME fee schedule.

The classification of a patient into 1 of 153 HHRGs is based on OASIS data, which establish the severity of clinical and functional needs and services utilized. Grouper software is used to determine the appropriate HHRG (see table 16.9). For example:

> OASIS data collected on a 76-year-old male home care patient resulted in an HHRG of C2, F3, and S2. This HHRG is interpreted as a clinical domain of low severity, a functional domain of moderate severity, and a service utilization domain of low utilization.

The HHRG assigned as well as the type of supplies provided and the number of home health visits comprise the

Table 16.9.   HHRG severity levels in three domains: clinical, functional, and service utilization

Domain	Score	Severity Level
Clinical	C1	Minimum severity
	C2	Low severity
	C3	Moderate severity
Functional	F1	Minimum severity
	F2	Low severity
	F3	Moderate severity
Service utilization	S1	Minimum utilization
	S2	Low utilization
	S3	Moderate utilization
	S4	High utilization
	S5	Maximum utilization

Health Insurance Prospective Payment System (HIPPS) code, which is the unit of payment for the episode of care.

Episode-of-care reimbursements vary from $1,700 to almost $7,000 and are affected by treatment level and regional wage differentials. There is no limit to the number of 60-day episodes of care that a patient may receive as long as Medicare coverage criteria are met.

Low Utilization and Outlier Payments

When a patient receives fewer than four home care visits during a 60-day episode, an alternate (reduced) payment, or **low-utilization payment adjustment (LUPA),** is made instead of the full HHRG reimbursement rate. HHAs are eligible for a **cost outlier adjustment,** which is a payment for certain high-cost home care patients whose costs are in excess of a threshold amount for each HHRG. The threshold is the 60-day episode payment plus a fixed-dollar loss that is constant across the HHRGs.

Ambulance Fee Schedule

A new Medicare payment system for medically necessary transports effective for services provided on or after April 1, 2002, was included as part of the BBA. The payment system applies to all ambulance services including volunteer, municipal, private, independent, and institutional providers (hospitals, critical access hospitals, SNFs, and HHAs).

Ambulance services are reported on claims using HCPCS codes that reflect the seven categories of ground service and two categories of air service. Mandatory assignment is required for all ambulance service providers.

The seven categories of ground (land and water) ambulance services include

- Basic life support
- Advanced life support, level 1
- Advanced life support, level 2
- Specialty care transport
- Paramedic intercept
- Fixed wing air ambulance
- Rotary wing air ambulance

Inpatient Rehabilitation Facility Prospective Payment System

The BBA (as amended by the Balanced Budget Refinement Act of 1999) authorized implementation of a per discharge PPS for care provided to Medicare beneficiaries by inpatient rehabilitation hospitals and rehabilitation units, referred to as **inpatient rehabilitation facilities (IRFs)**. The PPS for IRFs became effective on January 1, 2002.

IRFs must meet the regulatory requirements to be classified as a rehabilitation hospital or rehabilitation unit that is excluded from the PPS for inpatient acute care services. To meet the criteria, an IRF must operate as a hospital. Requirements state that during the most recent, consecutive, and appropriate 12-month time period, the hospital will have treated an inpatient population of whom at least 75 percent required intensive rehabilitative services for treatment of one or more of the medical conditions specified in figure 16.1.

Patient Assessment Instrument

IRFs are required to complete a patient assessment instrument (PAI) upon each patient's admission and also discharge from the facility. CMS provides facilities with the **Inpatient Rehabilitation Validation and Entry (IRVEN)** system to collect the IRF-PAI in a database that can be transmitted electronically to the IRF-PAI national database. These data are used in assessing clinical characteristics of patients in rehabilitation settings. Ultimately, they can be used to provide survey agencies with a means to objectively measure and compare facility performance and quality and to allow researchers to develop improved standards of care.

Figure 16.1. Medical conditions that are criteria for classification as inpatient rehabilitation facility

- Stroke
- Spinal cord injury
- Congenital deformity
- Amputation
- Major multiple trauma
- Fracture of femur (hip fracture)
- Brain injury
- Neurological disorders including multiple sclerosis, motor neuron
  diseases, polyneuropathy, muscular dystrophy, and Parkinson's disease
- Burns
- Rheumatoid arthritis, osteoarthritis, polyarthritis
- Systemic vasculidities with joint inflammation
- Knee or hip replacement

Source: CMS 2011.

The IRF PPS uses information from the IRF-PAI to classify patients into distinct groups on the basis of clinical characteristics and expected resource needs. Data used to construct these groups, called **case-mix groups (CMGs)**, include rehabilitation impairment categories (RICs), functional status (both motor and cognitive), age, comorbidities, and other factors deemed appropriate to improve the explanatory power of the groups. There are currently 92 CMGs into which patients are classified.

Case-mix group Relative Weight

An appropriate weight, called the **case-mix group (CMG) relative weight,** is assigned to each case-mix group and measures the relative difference in facility resource intensity among the various groups. Separate payments are calculated for each group, including the application of case- and facility-level adjustments. Facility-level adjustments include wage-index adjustments, low-income patient adjustments, and rural facility adjustments. Case-level adjustments include transfer adjustments, interrupted-stay adjustments, and cost outlier adjustments.

Long-Term Care Hospital Prospective Payment System

The **Balanced Budget Refinement Act (BBRA) of 1999** amended by the Benefits Improvement Act of 2000 mandated the establishment of a per discharge, DRG-based PPS for longer-term care hospitals beginning on October 1, 2002.

LTCHs are defined as having an average inpatient LOS greater than 25 days. Typically, patients with the following conditions are treated in LTCHs:

- Chronic cardiac disorders
- Neuromuscular and neurovascular diseases such as after-effects of strokes or Parkinson's disease
- Infectious conditions requiring long-term care such as methicillin-resistant *Staphylococcus aureus*
- Complex orthopedic conditions such as pelvic fractures or complicated hip fractures
- Wound care complications (traumatic, pressure, diabetic, and venous)
- Multisystem organ failure
- Immunosuppressed conditions
- Respiratory failure and ventilation management and weaning
- Dysphagia management
- Postoperative complications
- Multiple intravenous therapies
- Chemotherapy
- Pre and postoperative organ transplant care
- Chronic nutritional problems and total parenteral nutrition issues
- Spinal cord injuries
- Burns
- Head injuries

MS-LTC-DRGs

Patients are classified into distinct diagnosis groups based on clinical characteristics and expected resource use. These groups are based on the current inpatient MS-DRGs. There are approximately 750 LTC-DRGs. The payment system includes the following three primary elements:

- Patient classification into a MS-LTC-DRG weight.
- Relative weight of the MS-LTC-DRG. The weights reflect the variation in cost per discharge as they take into account the utilization for each diagnosis.
- Federal payment rate. Payment is made at a predetermined per discharge amount for each MS-LTC-DRG.

Adjustments

The PPS does provide for case (patient)–level adjustments such as short-stay outliers, interrupted stays, and high-cost outliers. Facility-wide adjustments include area wage index and cost of living adjustments.

A short-stay outlier is an adjustment to the payment rate for stays that are considerably shorter than the average length of stay (ALOS) for a particular MS-LTC-DRG. A case would qualify for short-stay outlier status when the LOS is between one day and up to and including five-sixths of the ALOS for the MS-LTC-DRG. Both the ALOS and the five-sixths of the ALOS periods are published in the *Federal Register.* Payment under the short-stay outlier is made using different payment methodologies. (See table 16.10 for examples of MS-LTC-DRGs and the ALOS for each.)

An interrupted stay occurs when a patient is discharged from the long-term care hospital and then is readmitted to the same facility for further treatment after a specific number of days away from the facility. There are different policies if the patient is readmitted to the facility within three days (called three-day or less interrupted-stay policy) or if the patient is away from the facility more than three days (called the greater than three-day interrupted-stay policy).

A high-cost outlier is an adjustment to the payment rate for a patient when the costs are unusually high and exceed the typical costs associated with a MS-LTC-DRG. High-cost outlier payments reduce the facility's potential financial losses that can result from treating patients who require more costly care than is normal. A case qualifies for a high-cost

outlier payment when the estimated cost of care exceeds the high-cost outlier threshold, which is updated each year.

Inpatient Psychiatric Facilities Prospective Payment System

The Balanced Budget Refinement Act of 1999 mandated the development of a per diem PPS for inpatient psychiatric services furnished in hospitals and exempt units. The PPS became effective on January 1, 2005, establishing a standardized per diem rate to **inpatient psychiatric facilities (IPFs)** based on the national average of operating, ancillary, and capital costs for each patient day of care in the IPF. The system uses the same MS-DRGs as the acute-care hospital inpatient system.

CMS is phasing in the PPS for existing facilities over a three-year period with full payments under the PPS beginning in the fourth year. The per diem payment is adjusted to reflect both patient and facility characteristics that cause significant cost increases.

Adjustments

Patient-level or case-level adjustments are provided for age, specified MS-DRGs, and certain comorbidity categories. Payment adjustments are made for eight age categories beginning with age 45 at which point, statistically, costs are increased as the patient ages.

The IPF receives an MS-DRG payment adjustment for a principal diagnosis that groups to one of 15 psychiatric MS-DRGs. (See table 16.11.) Seventeen comorbidity categories that require comparatively more costly treatment during an inpatient stay also generate a payment adjustment. The list of comorbidity categories and their associated ICD-9-CM diagnosis codes can be found in table 16.12.

In addition, there is a variable per diem adjustment to recognize higher costs in the early days of a psychiatric stay.

The IPF PPS also includes an outlier policy for those patients who require more expensive care than expected in an effort to minimize the financial risk to the IPF. Although the basis of the system is a per diem rate, outlier payments are made on a per case basis rather than on the per diem basis. Payment is also adjusted for patients who are given electroconvulsive therapy (ECT).

Table 16.10.   Examples of MS-LTC-DRGs, relative weights, geometric ALOS, and arithmetic ALOS

MS-LTC-DRG	Description	Relative Weight	Geometric ALOS	Arithmetic ALOS
28	Spinal procedures w MCC	1.7420	36.0	30.0
114	Orbital procedures w/o CC/MCC	0.7789	23.4	19.5
132	Cranial/facial procedure w/o CC/MCC	0.4607	17.9	14.9
150	Epistaxis w MCC	0.6931	21.9	18.30
163	Major chest procedure w MCC	2.2110	38.5	32.1
181	Respiratory neoplasm w CC	0.5810	17.4	14.5
194	Simple pneumonia and pleurisy w MCC	0.6173	18.9	15.8

Table 16.11.   Psychiatric DRGs

MS-DRG	MS-DRG Description
056	Degenerative nervous system disorders w MCC
057	Degenerative nervous system disorders w/o MCC
080	Nontraumatic stupor and coma w MCC
081	Nontraumatic stupor and coma w/o MCC
876	OR procedure w principal diagnoses of mental illness
880	Acute adjustment reaction and psychosocial dysfunction
881	Depressive neuroses
882	Neuroses except depressive
883	Disorders of personality and impulse control
884	Organic disturbances and mental retardation
885	Psychoses
886	Behavioral and developmental disorders
887	Other mental disorder diagnoses
894	Alcohol/drug abuse or dependence, left AMA
895	Alcohol/drug abuse or dependence with rehabilitation therapy
896	Alcohol/drug abuse or dependence w/o rehabilitation therapy w MCC Alcohol/drug abuse or dependence w/o rehabilitation therapy w/o MCC
897	

The PPS also includes regulations on payments when there is an interrupted stay, meaning the patient is discharged from an IPF and returns to the same or another facility before midnight on the third consecutive day. The intent of the policy is to prevent a facility from prematurely discharging a patient after the maximum payment is received and subsequently readmitting the patient.

Facility adjustments include a wage-index adjustment, a rural location adjustment, a teaching status adjustment, a cost-of-living adjustment for Alaska and Hawaii, and a qualifying emergency department adjustment.

Check Your Understanding 16.4

Instructions: Answer the following questions on a separate piece of paper.

1. When did Congress enact the first Medicare prospective payment system?

2. What were Medicare Part A payments to hospitals based on prior to implementation of the diagnosis-related group PPS?

3. What type of diagnosis is the MS-DRG prospective payment rate based on?

4. What is the name of the computer software program that assigns appropriate MS-DRGs according to information provided for each episode of care?

Table 16.12.   Comorbidity categories affecting IPF-PPS payments

Category	ICD-9-CM Diagnosis Codes
Developmental disabilities	317, 318.0, 318.1, 318.2, 319
Coagulation factor deficit	286.0 through 286.4
Tracheostomy	519.00 through 519.09; V44.0
Renal failure, acute	584.5 through 584.9, 636.30, 636.31, 636.32, 637.30, 637.31, 637.32, 638.3, 639.3, 669.32, 669.34, 958.5
Renal failure, chronic	403.01, 403.11, 403.91, 404.02, 404.03, 404.12, 404.13, 404.92, 404.93, 585.3, 585.4, 585.5, 585.6, 585.9, 586, V45.1, V56.0, V56.1, V56.2
Oncology treatment	140.0 through 239.9 with either 99.25 or a code from 92.21 through 92.29
Uncontrolled diabetes mellitus w or w/o complications	250.02, 250.03, 250.12, 250.13, 250.22, 250.23, 250.32, 250.33, 250.42, 250.43, 250.52, 250.53, 250.62, 250.63, 250.72, 250.73, 250.82, 250.83, 250.92, 250.93
Severe protein calorie malnutrition	260 through 262
Eating and conduct disorders	307.1, 307.50, 312.03, 312.33, 312.34
Infectious diseases	010.00 through 041.10, 042, 045.00 through 053.19, 054.40 through 054.49, 055.0 through 077.0, 078.2 through 078.89, 079.50 through 079.59
Drug- or alcohol-induced mental disorders	291.0, 292.0, 292.12, 292.2, 303.00, 304.00
Cardiac conditions	391.0, 391.1, 391.2, 402.01, 404.03, 416.0, 421.0, 421.1, 421.9
Gangrene	440.24, 785.4
Chronic obstructive pulmonary disease	491.21, 494.1, 510.0, 518.83, 518.84, V46.11, V46.12, V46.13, V46.14
Artificial openings—digestive and urinary	569.60 through 569.69, 997.5, V44.1 through V44.6
Severe musculoskeletal and connective tissue disorders	696.0, 710.0, 730.00 through 730.09, 730.10 through 730.19, 730.20 through 730.29
Poisoning	965.00 through 965.09, 965.4, 967.0 through 969.9, 977.0, 980.0 through 980.9, 983.0 through 983.9, 986, 989.0 through 989.7
Schwannomatosis	237.73
Other neurofibromatosis	237.79

5. What kinds of hospitals are excluded from the Medicare acute-care PPS?

6. What are major diagnostic categories, and how many are there?

7. What does case mix refer to? What is the relationship between MS-DRGs and case-mix groups?

8. What act mandated implementation of the skilled nursing facility PPS?

9. What are resident assessment data? From what are they collected?

10. What is the purpose of the resource-based relative value scale?

11. What types of hospitals are not reimbursed according to the outpatient prospective payment system?

12. What concept is applied when multiple surgical procedures are furnished during the same operative session?

13. Which data set for patient assessments is used by the home health PPS?

14. What types of services are covered by the home health resource group classification system?

15. What PPS uses a patient assessment instrument to gather data on patients?

16. What is the purpose of the IRVEN software?

17. To meet the definition of a long-term care hospital, what must the average length of stay be?

18. What is a short-stay outlier in relation to the LTCH PPS, and how is it calculated?

19. What other PPSs use the MS-DRGs currently used for inpatient hospitals?

20. The IPF prospective payment system identifies comorbidities that generate a payment adjustment. What are some of the other factors that generate adjustments with the IPF PPS?

Coding

Coding is the process of assigning numerical representations to clinical documentation (AHIMA 2010). As mentioned, many of the prospective payment systems are based on the ICD-9-CM (it is expected that CMS will mandate ICD-10-CM/PCS in October 2014), CPT, or HCPCS codes. Therefore, complete and accurate coding has become central to the financial survival of healthcare provider organizations. These classifications and others are discussed in chapter 15.

The coding professional's first responsibility is to ensure the accuracy of coded data. To this end, AHIMA has established a code of professional ethics by which coders must abide.

Elements of Coding Quality

The quality of coded clinical data depends on a number of factors, including

- Adequate training for everyone involved in the coding process, including coders, coding supervisors, clinicians, and financial personnel
- Adequate references and support resources, including up-to-date coding books, as well as subscription publications that communicate official guidelines (namely, *Coding Clinic for ICD-9-CM* and *CPT Assistant*) and, in some cases, encoders or other support software
- Accurate and complete clinical documentation that includes every pertinent condition and service provided to the patient
- The support of senior managers, who must understand how important the coding function is to the organization's continued existence
- A performance improvement plan for the coding function that ensures continuous quality improvement processes

There are seven criteria that define high-quality clinical documentation as listed in table 16.13.

The Role of a CDI Program

A **Clinical Documentation Improvement (CDI) program** is designed to provide a link between coders and physicians and to ensure completeness and accuracy of patient care documentation. A documentation specialist reviews the record and consults with physicians regarding nonspecific or incomplete documentation (Schraffenberger and Kuehn 2011). Query forms have proven to be an effective means of communication with physicians. AHIMA cautions coders that these forms are used to improve documentation and understanding of the clinical situation, but not to increase reimbursement (Bowman 2008).

The facility should develop a standard form to be used in communicating with physicians. Characteristics of a good query form are noted in figure 16.2.

Quality Assessment for the Coding Process

Quality assessment for the coding process is also referred to as performance improvement for the coding process. It involves looking at more than just the assigned codes. As stated previously, accurate coding is essential to the economic survival of the healthcare organization; hence, ongoing efforts to improve the coding process should yield better economic benefits.

Baseline measurements of the current coding process need to be taken, and benchmarks for improvement should be set up. For example, if the current process results in records being coded an average of 10 work-hours after arriving in the HIM department, a benchmark for improvement might be to code records in less than 8 hours. To establish valid internal coding data monitors,

Table 16.13. Criteria for high-quality clinical documentation

The seven criteria for high-quality clinical documentation require that all entries in the patient record be

1. Legible

2. Reliable

3. Precise

4. Complete

5. Consistent

6. Clear

7. Timely

The first six criteria are focused on in a review process because, if necessary, they can be corrected after the fact; however, the last, timeliness, is one criteria that cannot be corrected after the fact because once an entry is late, it remains late. Each of the seven criteria is discussed next, with a definition from the *Oxford English Dictionary* (6th edition, 2005) and a brief description of how the criterion applies to health record documentation.

1. **Legible:** *Clear enough to be read and easily deciphered*

   A record entry must be understandable to all future readers to have value. Indecipherable handwriting, frequently from the physician, is the coding challenge.

2. **Reliable:** *Trustworthy, safe, yielding the same result when repeated*

   Reliability of documentation is demonstrated when all of the treatments given are supported by a valid diagnostic statement, such as a bleeding gastric ulcer with acute blood loss as the diagnosis supporting the provision of a transfusion.

3. **Precise:** *Accurate, exact, strictly defined*

   Precise documentation is evidenced by the detail found in the clinical documentation. The more detailed the physician's documentation, the more representative and accurate the clinical documentation in the patient's record is likely to be, as exemplified in the differentiation between "pneumonia" and "aspiration pneumonia."

4. **Complete:** *Having the maximum content, thorough*

   Complete documentation means that the physician has fully addressed all concerns in the patient record. Completeness also includes the appropriate authentication by the physician or clinician, which generally includes a signature and a date.

5. **Consistent:** *Not contradictory*

   All documentation, from history and physical, to progress notes, to discharge summary, contains entries that are consistent and have no unexplained differences of opinion in the diagnostic statements.

6. **Clear:** *Unambiguous, intelligible, not vague*

   Documentation is clear when it states the cause of the patient's symptoms. For example, if a patient presents with a symptom such as chest pain and the physician provides no other insight in his documentation, it would be considered vague. If there is no clinical evidence for any diagnosis, then the appropriate documentation would be "chest pain, etiology undetermined."

7. **Timely:** *At the right time*

   The lack of a timely entry cannot be rectified later—late will always be late. The record is the primary communication tool of healthcare, and timeliness of documentation is essential to the best treatment of the patient.

Source: Adapted from Russo 2010.

comparative data will be necessary. Comparative data can be obtained from a variety of sources, including state data organizations, hospital associations, peer review organizations, and the Medicare MEDPAR data, which can be obtained from CMS. The National Health Information Resource Center and the National Association of Health Data Organizations are additional sources of information on health data.

Quality assessment of a process is generally ongoing. Even when the most ambitious goals for the most important measures have been accomplished, the measures should continue to be monitored. In addition, management should continually search for ways to improve the coding process through computerization or other methods.

Check Your Understanding 16.5

Instructions: Answer the following questions on a separate piece of paper.

1. What is the coder's primary responsibility?

2. What is the main factor in ensuring the quality of clinical coding?

3. Describe the quality assessment process for coding.

Figure 16.2.   Characteristics of a good query format

> The query form should
>
> - Be clearly and concisely written
> - Contain precise language
> - Present the facts from the medical record and identify why clarification is needed
> - Present the scenario and state a question that asks the physician to make a clinical interpretation of a given diagnosis or condition based on treatment, evaluation, monitoring, and/or services provided. "Open-ended" questions that allow the physician to document the specific diagnosis are preferable to multiple-choice questions or questions requiring only a "yes" or "no" response. Queries that appear to lead the physician to provide a particular response could lead to allegations of inappropriate upcoding.
> - Be phrased such that the physician is allowed to specify the correct diagnosis. It should not indicate the financial impact of the response to the query.
> - The form should be designed to include the health record number, name and contact information (phone number and e-mail address) of the individual initiating the query, specific questions and rationale, place for the physician to document his or her response, place for the physician to sign and date his or her response.

Source: AHIMA 2008.

Application of Technology to the Coding Process

Recent technologies are having a considerable impact on the coding process, and new technologies hold promise for the future. Some of the most significant advances are discussed here.

Encoders

An **encoder** is a software program that enables coders to assign codes based on using text typed into a look-up screen analogous to the coder looking up a term in the index of the printed codebook (Schraffenberger and Kuehn 2011).

Encoders come in two distinct categories: logic-based and automated codebook formats. A logic-based encoder prompts the user through a variety of questions and choices based on the clinical terminology entered. The coder selects the most accurate code for a service or condition (and any possible complications or comorbidities).

An automated codebook provides screen views that resemble the actual format of the coding system. This allows the coder to review code selections, notes, look-up tables, edits, and various other automated notations that help him or her choose the most accurate code for a condition or service. Although encoders can cite official coding guidelines and provide code optimization guidance, they require user interaction. Encoders promote accuracy as well as consistency in the coding of diagnoses and procedures.

Computer-Assisted Coding

AHIMA defines **computer-assisted coding (CAC)** as the use of computer software that automatically generates a set of medical codes for review, validation, and use based upon the documentation provided by the various providers of healthcare (AHIMA 2010, 62). With CAC, an electronic document is processed through a computer application to generate a list of procedure and diagnosis codes. There are two CAC applications designs: natural language processing (NLP) and structured data input. NLP uses a technology based on artificial intelligence that extracts pertinent data and terms from a text-based document and converts them into medical codes. The natural language processing technology used might be algorithmic (rules based) or statistical. Schnitzer (2000) has stated that statistical approaches that can predict how an experienced coder might code a record and use machine learning techniques are superior to rigid rule sets. This opinion is congruent with the oft-heard argument that "coding is subjective." NLP is most commonly used in the medical specialties of radiology, pathology, and emergency medicine. According to the 2004 report of the AHIMA e-HIM Workgroup on Computer-Assisted Coding, "CAC works best within medical domains that have a limited vocabulary. NLP-based tools in particular work best when there is a limited number of source documents that must be analyzed for code selection and less extensive coding guidelines."

Structured data input is used when menu selections and drop-down pick lists are used for documentation rather than handwritten or dictated notes. When a practitioner selects a certain term from a drop-down list, a code is automatically generated, which is then reviewed by a coding professional.

According to Schnitzer, the advantages to using **automated code assignment** include

- *Consistency:* Automated code assignment is consistently correct and consistently incorrect; thus, errors are easier to locate and fix once they are detected.
- *Accuracy:* As with medical knowledge, the amount of information that must be synthesized to correctly code patient records has increased substantially. Expert computer software programs can apply these rules and guidelines accurately.
- *Speed:* The computational power of computers can apply the many coding rules and guidelines efficiently.

Another benefit is the potential decrease in coding costs as overtime, vacation, and other benefits might be decreased. In addition, when codes are available for billing more quickly, accounts receivables are improved and revenue increases.

It is important to note, however, that computer-assisted coding is not a magic bullet. For example, it cannot address the major obstacle facing today's human coder: the lack of accurate, complete clinical documentation. As Schnitzer (2000) put it, "If a service isn't appropriately documented, there no way for NLP to find it, assume it, or infer it." In addition, automated code assignment has not developed to the point where it can operate without substantial human interaction (Warner 2000).

There are advantages and disadvantages to implementing CAC. Each individual facility should determine if CAC would be beneficial to its operation. As CAC evolves, so will the role of the HIM professional. However, the fear that coding professionals will become obsolete is unfounded. The expertise of coders will always be needed both for the review and the teaching of the software. Coders' positions will be elevated rather than eliminated.

Emerging Technologies

As is apparent from the preceding subsection, the status quo will not continue for coding. A number of emerging technologies will likely be used to support the coding function.

Speech recognition is one candidate for improving the coding process as well as coding accuracy. As speech recognition improves and has the ability to accurately document what the clinician is saying, the ease of completely documenting healthcare services also improves. Schwager (2000) maintains that "speech recognition, combined with technology designed to extract and structure medical information (natural language processing) contained in narrative text, can automate the coding process used in reimbursement." He also discusses the possibility that the computerized patient record software could analyze the record in an interactive fashion, prompting the clinician for higher-quality documentation.

Check Your Understanding 16.6

Instructions: Answer the following questions on a separate piece of paper.

1. What is the difference between encoders and automated code assignment?

2. Name two emerging technologies, and describe their impact on coding.

Processing of Reimbursement Claims

Understanding payment mechanisms is an important foundation for accurately processing claims forms. However, it is not enough just to understand payment mechanisms.

A facility's patient accounts department is responsible for billing third-party payers, processing **accounts receivable,** monitoring payments from third-party payers, and verifying insurance coverage. Medicare Administrative Contractors (MACs) contract with CMS to serve as the financial agent between providers and the federal government to locally administer Medicare's Part A and Part B.

Coordination of Benefits

In many instances, patients have more than one insurance policy, and the determination of which policy is primary and which is secondary is necessary so that there is no duplication of benefits paid. This process is called the coordination of benefits (COB) or the **coordination of benefits transaction.** The monies collected from third-party payers cannot be greater than the amount of the provider's charges.

Submission of Claims

According to the National Uniform Billing Committee (NUBC), more than 98 percent of hospital claims are submitted electronically to Medicare. The Administrative Simplification Compliance Act (ASCA), which was part of the Health Insurance Portability and Accountability Act (HIPAA), mandated the electronic submission of all healthcare claims with a few exceptions.

Healthcare facilities submit claims via the 837I electronic format, which replaces the **UB-04** (CMS-1450) paper billing form. Physicians submit claims via the 837P electronic format, which takes the place of the **CMS-1500** billing form. For those healthcare facilities with a waiver of the ASCA requirements, UB-04 and CMS-1500 are used.

Explanation of Benefits, Medicare Summary Notice, and Remittance Advice

An **Explanation of Benefits** (EOB) is a statement sent by a third-party payer to the patient to explain services provided, amounts billed, and payments made by the health plan. Medicare sends a **Medicare Summary Notice (MSN)** to a beneficiary to show how much the provider billed, how much Medicare reimbursed the provider, and what the patient must pay the provider by way of deductible and copayments. (See figure 16.3 for a sample Part B MSN.)

A **remittance advice (RA)** is sent to the provider to explain payments made by third-party payers (see figure 16.4). Payments are typically sent in batches with the RA sent to the facility and payments electronically transferred to the provider's bank.

Medicare Administrative Contractors

Medicare Administrative Contractors (MACs) process Part A and Part B claims from hospitals, physicians, and other providers. Currently there are 15 MAC jurisdictions with an additional four jurisdictions for home health and four for DME.

There are plans to decrease this to ten MAC jurisdictions over the next few years. Examples of carriers might include a state Blue Shield plan or commercial insurance companies or other organizations under contract with Medicare. The intent of decreasing the number of entities responsible for processing claims is to allow greater consistency in the interpretation of CMS policies for payment and coverage.

Figure 16.3.   Sample Medicare Summary Notice

	Page 1 of 2
Medicare Summary Notice	
	July 1, 2006

CUSTOMER SERVICE INFORMATION

BENEFICIARY NAME
STREET ADDRESS
CITY, STATE   ZIP CODE

Your Medicare Number: 111-11-1111A

If you have questions, write or call:
   Medicare (#12345)
   555 Medicare Blvd., Suite 200
   Medicare Building
   Medicare, US XXXXX-XXXX

BE INFORMED: Beware of "free" medical services or products. If it sounds too good to be true, it probably is.

Call: 1-800-MEDICARE (1-800-633-4227)
Ask for Hospital Services
TTY for Hearing Impaired: 1-877-486-2048

This is a summary of claims processed from 05/15/2006 through 08/10/2006.

PART A HOSPITAL INSURANCE – INPATIENT CLAIMS

Dates of Service	Benefit Days Used	Non-Covered Charges	Deductible and Coinsurance	You May Be Billed	See Notes Section
Claim Number: 12435-84956-84556-45621					a
Cure Hospital, 213 Sick Lane, Dallas, TX 75555					
Referred by: Paul Jones, M.D.					
04/25/06 – 05/09/06	14 days	$0.00	$876.00	$876.00	b, c
Claim Number: 12435-84956-845556-45622					
Continued Care Hospital, 124 Sick Lane, Dallas, TX 75555					
Referred by: Paul Jones, M.D.					
05/09/06 – 06/20/06	11 days	$0.00	$0.00	$0.00	

PART B MEDICAL INSURANCE – OUTPATIENT FACILITY CLAIMS

Dates of Service	Services Provided	Amount Charged	Non-Covered Charges	Deductible and Coinsurance	You May Be Billed	See Notes Section
Claim Number: 12435-8956-8458						d
Medicare Hospital, 123 Medicare Lane, Dallas, TX 75209						
Referred by: Paul Jones, M.D.						
04/02/06	L.V. Therapy (Q0081)	$33.00	$0.00	$6.60	$6.60	
	Lab (3810)	1,140.50	0.00	228.10	228.10	
	Operating Room (31628)	786.50	0.00	157.30	157.30	
	Observation Room (99201)	293.00	0.00	58.60	58.60	
	Claim Total	**$2,253.00**	**$0.00**	**$450.60**	**$450.60**	

(continued)

THIS IS NOT A BILL – Keep this notice for your records.

Your Medicare Number: 111-11-1111A

Notes Section:

a The amount Medicare paid the provider for this claim is $XXXX.XX.

b $776.00 was applied to your inpatient deductible.

c $30.00 was applied to your blood deductible.

d The amount Medicare paid the provider for this claim is $XXXX.XX.

Deductible Information:

You have met the Part A deductible for this benefit period.

You have met the Part B deductible for 2006.

You have met the blood deductible for 2006.

General Information:

You have the right to make a request in writing for an itemized statement which details each Medicare item or service which you have received from your physician, hospital, or any other health supplier or health professional. Please contact them directly, in writing, if you would like an itemized statement.

Compare the services you receive with those that appear on your Medicare Summary Notice. If you have questions, call your doctor or provider. If you feel further investigation is needed due to possible fraud and abuse, call the phone number in the Customer Service Information Box.

Appeals Information – Part A (Inpatient) and Part B (Outpatient)

If you disagree with any claims decisions on either Part A or Part B of this notice, your appeal must be received by **November 1, 2006**. Follow the instructions below:

1) Circle the item(s) you disagree with and explain why you disagree.

2) Send this notice, or a copy, to the address in the "Customer Service Information" box on Page 1. (You may also send any additional information you may have about your appeal.)

3) Sign here _____ Phone number _____

Revised 08/06

National Correct Coding Initiative

CMS implemented the **National Correct Coding Initiative (NCCI)** in 1996 to develop correct coding methodologies to improve the appropriate payment of Medicare Part B claims.

NCCI policies are based on:

- Coding conventions defined in the CPT codebooks
- National and local policies and coding edits
- Analysis of standard medical and surgical practice
- Review of current coding practices

Figure 16.4.   Sample single-chain remittance advice

```
Medicare National Standard Intermediary Remittance Advice
FPE:                                      07/30/07
PAID:                                     01/25/08
CLM#                                      2
TOB:                                      111
--------------------------------------------------------------------------------

PATIENT:      JOHN DOE                                        PCN:   235617
HIC:          123456                  SVC FROM:   01/05/08    MRN:   124767
PAT STAT:     01     CLAIM STAT:   1   THRU:      01/06/08    ICN:   987654
--------------------------------------------------------------------------------

CHARGES:                      PAYMENT DATA: 140=DRG      0.000    =REIM RATE
1939.90       =REPORTED       2741.69  =DRG AMOUNT       0.00     =MSP PRIM PAYER
0.00          =NONCOVERED     2497.26  =DRG/OPER         0.00     =PROF COMPONENT
0.00          =DENIED         244.43   =DRG/CAPITAL      0.00     =ESRD AMOUNT
1939.90       =COVERED        0.00     =OUTLIER          0.00     =HCPCS AMOUNT
DAYS/VISITS:                  0.00     =CAP OUTLIER      0.00     =ALLOWED AMOUNT
1             =COST REPT      768.00   =CASH DEDUCT      0.00     =G/R AMOUNT
1             =COVD/UTIL      0.00     =BLOOD DEDUCT     0.00     =INTEREST
0             =NONCOVERED     0.00     =COINSURANCE      -801.79  =CONTRACT ADJ
0             =COVD VISITS    0.00     =PAT REFUND       675.00   =PER DIEM AMT
0             =NCOV VISITS    0.00     =MSP LIAB MET     1973.69  =NET REIM AMT
ADJ REASON CODES:     CO  A2 -801.79
                      PR       1
                      768
REMARK CODES:         MA02
--------------------------------------------------------------------------------
```

The NCCI edits explain what procedures and services cannot be billed together on the same day of service for a patient. The mutually exclusive edit applies to improbable or impossible combinations of codes. For example, code 58940, Oophorectomy, partial or total, unilateral or bilateral, would never be used with code 58150, Total abdominal hysterectomy (corpus and cervix), with or without removal of tube(s), with or without removal of ovary(s). Modifiers may be used to indicate circumstances in which the NCCI edits should not be applied and payment should be made as requested. Modifier-59, for example, is used when circumstances require that certain procedures or services be reported together even though they usually are not.

Portions of the NCCI are incorporated into the **outpatient code editor (OCE),** against which all ambulatory claims are reviewed. The OCE also applies a set of logical rules to determine whether various combinations of codes are correct and appropriately represent services provided. Billing issues generated from these NCCI and OCE edits often result in claim denials.

Check Your Understanding 16.7

Instructions: Answer the following questions on a separate piece of paper.

1. What is a COB transaction, and what is its purpose?

2. What purpose does the remittance advice serve?

3. What is CMS-1500 used for? What is another name for this form?

4. What is a Medicare Administrative Contractor?

5. What is the purpose of the NCCI edits?

6. On what are the NCCI policies implemented in 1996 to develop correct coding methodologies to improve appropriate payment of Medicare Part B claims based?

Reimbursement Support Processes

Reimbursement support processes are routinely reviewed and revised by third-party payers to control payments to providers. Healthcare facilities also implement reimbursement support processes to make sure that they are receiving the level of reimbursement to which they are entitled. Third-party payers revise fee schedules, and healthcare facilities revise chargemasters, evaluate the quality of documentation and coding, conduct internal audits, and implement compliance programs.

Management of the Fee Schedules

Third-party payers that reimburse providers on a fee-for-service basis generally update fee schedules on an annual

Table 16.13. Partial 2011 Medicare physician fee schedule payment amounts for Chicago, Illinois

MAC	CPT Code	Nonfacility Fee Schedule Amount	Facility FeeSchedule Amount
95215	10040	109.21	95.93
95215	10060	115.85	98.26
95215	10061	194.89	171.21
95215	10080	178.50	106.02
95215	10081	277.58	182.86
95215	10120	143.55	97.26
95215	10121	280.42	197.54

Source: CMS 2011.

basis. A fee schedule is a list of healthcare services and procedures (usually CPT/HCPCS codes) and charges associated with each. (See table 16.13.) The fee schedule (sometimes referred to as a table of allowances) represents the approved payment levels for a given insurance plan (for example, Medicare, Medicaid, and BC/BS).

Physicians, practitioners, and suppliers must notify Medicare by December 31 of each year whether they intend to participate in the Medicare program during the coming year. Medicare participation means that the provider or supplier agrees to accept assignment for all covered services provided to Medicare patients. To **accept assignment** means the provider or supplier accepts, as payment in full, the allowed charge (from the fee schedule). The provider or supplier is prohibited from **balance billing,** which means the patient cannot be held responsible for charges in excess of the Medicare fee schedule.

However, participating providers may bill patients for services that are not covered by Medicare. Physicians must notify a patient that the service will not be paid for by giving the patient a Notice of Exclusions from Medicare Benefits.

If a provider believes that a service may be denied by Medicare because it could be considered unnecessary, he must notify the patient before the treatment begins using an **Advance Beneficiary Notice of Noncoverage (ABN)**. (See figure 16.5.) CMS has created ABNs for various care settings such as home health and SNF facilities.

Nonparticipating providers (nonPARs) do not sign a participation agreement with Medicare but may or may not accept assignment. If the nonPAR physician elects to accept assignment, he or she is paid 95 percent (5 percent less than participating physicians) of the MFS. For example, if the MFS amount is $200, the PAR provider receives $160 (80 percent of $200), but the nonPAR provider receives only $152 (95 percent of $160).

NonPAR providers who choose not to accept assignment are subject to Medicare's limiting charge rule, which states that a physician may not charge a patient more than 115 percent of the nonparticipating fee schedule. The provider collects the full amount from the patient, and Medicare reimburses the patient. Figure 16.6 illustrates the various fee schedules by type of provider.

Management of the Chargemaster

The **chargemaster** (table 16.14), also called the charge description master (CDM), contains information about healthcare services (and transactions) provided to a patient. Its primary purpose is to allow the provider to accurately charge routine services and supplies to the patient. Services, supplies, and procedures included on the chargemaster generate reimbursement for almost 75 percent of claims submitted for outpatient services alone.

The information that makes up a chargemaster line item may vary from one facility to another. There are, however, some common elements found in a typical chargemaster (Shraffenberger and Kuehn 2011). These include

- *Item description:* The actual name of the service or supply. Examples might be the evaluation and management visit, observation, or emergency room visit.
- *CPT/HCPCS code:* This code must correspond to the description of the service.
- *Revenue code*: The **revenue code** is a three-digit code that describes a classification of a product or service provided to the patient. These revenue codes are required by CMS for reporting services. (See table 16.15 for examples of revenue codes.)
- *Charge amount*: This is the amount the facility charges for the procedure or service. It is not necessarily what the facility will be reimbursed by the third-party payer.
- *Charge code*: The charge or service code is an internally assigned number that is unique to the facility. It identifies each procedure listed on the chargemaster and identifies the department or revenue center that initiated the charge. The charge code can be very useful for revenue tracking and budget analysis.
- *General ledger key*: The general ledger key is a two- or three-digit number that assigns a line item to a section of the general ledger in the hospital's accounting system.
- *Activity/status date:* The activity/status date indicates the most recent activity of an item.

Figure 16.5 Advance Beneficiary Notice Of Noncoverage

A. Notifier:

B. Patient Name: **C. Identification Number:**

Advance Beneficiary Notice of Noncoverage (ABN)

NOTE: If Medicare doesn't pay for **D.** _____ below, you may have to pay. Medicare does not pay for everything, even some care that you or your health care provider have good reason to think you need. We expect Medicare may not pay for the **D.** _____ below.

D.	E. Reason Medicare May Not Pay:	F. Estimated Cost

WHAT YOU NEED TO DO NOW:

• Read this notice, so you can make an informed decision about your care.

• Ask us any questions that you may have after you finish reading.

• Choose an option below about whether to receive the **D.** _____ listed above.

Note: If you choose Option 1 or 2, we may help you to use any other insurance that you might have, but Medicare cannot require us to do this.

G. OPTIONS: Check only one box. We cannot choose a box for you.

❏ **OPTION 1.** I want the **D.** _____ listed above. You may ask to be paid now, but I also want Medicare billed for an official decision on payment, which is sent to me on a Medicare Summary Notice (MSN). I understand that if Medicare doesn't pay, I am responsible for payment, but **I can appeal to Medicare** by following the directions on the MSN. If Medicare does pay, you will refund any payments I made to you, less co-pays or deductibles.

❏ **OPTION 2.** I want the **D.** _____ listed above, but do not bill Medicare. You may ask to be paid now as I am responsible for payment. **I cannot appeal if Medicare is not billed.**

❏ **OPTION 3.** I don't want the **D.** _____ listed above. I understand with this choice I am **not** responsible for payment, and **I cannot appeal to see if Medicare would pay.**

H. Additional Information:

This notice gives our opinion, not an official Medicare decision. If you have other questions on this notice or Medicare billing, call **1-800-MEDICARE** (1-800-633-4227/**TTY:** 1–877-486-2048). Signing below means that you have received and understand this notice. You also receive a copy.

I. Signature:	I. Signature:

According to the Paperwork Reduction Act of 1995, no persons are required to respond to a collection of information unless it displays a valid OMB control number. The valid OMB control number for this information collection is 0938-0566. The time required to complete this information collection is estimated to average 7 minutes per response, including the time to review instructions, search existing data resources, gather the data needed, and complete and review the information collection. If you have comments concerning the accuracy of the time estimate or suggestions for improving this form, please write to: CMS, 7500 Security Boulevard, Attn: PRA Reports Clearance Officer, Baltimore, Maryland 21244-1850.

Form CMS-R-131 (03/11)   Form Approved OMB No. 0938-0566

Figure 16.6.   Examples of physician reimbursement methodologies

Participating Provider	
Physician's fee	$180.00
MFS	$105.00
Medicare pays 80% of MFS or	$ 84.00
Patient pays 20% of MFS or	$ 21.00
Physician write-off ($180 – $105)	$ 75.00
Nonparticipating provider who accepts assignment	
Physician's fee	$180.00
MFS	$105.00
Medicare nonPAR fee (95% of $105)	$ 99.75
Medicare pays 80% of nonPAR fee	$ 79.80
Patient pays 20% of nonPAR fee	$ 19.95
Physician write-off ($180 – $99.75)	$ 80.25
Nonparticipating provider who does not accept assignment	
Physician's normal fee	$180.00
MFS	$105.00
Medicare nonPAR fee (95% of $105)	$ 99.75
Limiting charge (115% of $99.75)	$114.71
Patient billed	$114.71
Medicare pays patient (80% of nonPAR fee)	$ 79.80
Patient out of pocket ($114.71 – $79.80)	$ 34.91

Chargemasters may allow more than one CPT/HCPCS code per item to differentiate between payment schedules for different payers.

The CDM can also be a tool for collecting workload statistics that can be used to monitor production and compile budgets. It is often used as a decision support tool to evaluate costs related to resources and to prepare for contract negotiations with managed care organizations.

The CDM relieves coders from coding repetitive services and supplies that require little, if any, formal documentation analysis. In these circumstances, the patient is billed automatically by linking the service to the appropriate CPT/HCPCS code (referred to as **hard-coding**). The advantage of hard-coding is that the code for the procedure will be reproduced accurately each time that a test, service, or procedure is ordered. (Schraffenberger and Kuehn 2011).

Maintenance of the Chargemaster

The chargemaster must be updated routinely. Maintenance of the chargemaster is best accomplished by representatives from health information management, clinical services, finance, the business office or patient financial services, compliance, and information systems. The HIM professionals are generally consulted regarding the update of CPT codes. The CDM is updated when new CPT codes become available, when departments request a new item, and when the medical fee schedules or PPS rates are updated.

Table 16.14.   Sample section from a chargemaster

Charge Code	Item Description	CPT/HCPCS Code			Revenue Code	G/L Key	Activity Date
		Insurance Code A	Insurance Code B	Insurance Code C			
2110410000	ECHO ENCEPHALOGRAM	76506	76506	Y7030	320	15	12/2/2011
2110410090	F/U ECHO ENCEPHALOGRAM	76506	76506	Y7040	320	15	12/2/2011
2110413000	PORT US ECHO ENCEPHALOGRAM	76506	76506	Y7050	320	15	12/2/2011
2120411000	ULTRASOUND SPINAL CONTENTS	76800	76800	Y7060	320	15	12/2/2011
2130401000	THYROID SONOGRAM	76536	76536	Y7070	320	15	1/1/2010
2151111000	TM JOINTS BILATERAL	70330	70330	Y7080	320	15	8/12/2010
2161111000	NECK LAT ONLY	70360	70360	Y7090	320	15	10/1/2011
2162111000	LARYNX AP & LATERAL	70360	70360	Y7100	320	15	10/1/2011
2201111000	LONG BONE CHLD AP	76061	76061	Y7110	320	15	8/12/2010
2201401000	NON-VASCULAR EXTREM SONO	76880	76880	Y7120	320	15	10/1/2011
2210111000	SKULL 1 VIEW	70250	70250	Y7130	320	15	1/1/2009
2210112000	SKULL 2 VIEWS	70250	70250	Y7140	320	15	8/12/2010
2210114000	SKULL 4 VIEWS	70260	70260	Y7150	320	15	8/12/2011
2211111000	MASTOIDS	70130	70130	Y7160	320	15	1/1/2011
2212111000	MANDIBLE	70110	70110	Y7170	320	15	12/2/2010
2213111000	FACIAL BONES	70140	70140	Y7180	320	15	12/2/2010
2213114000	FACIAL BONES MIN 4	70150	70150	Y7190	320	15	12/2/2011
2214111000	NASAL BONES	70160	70160	Y7200	320	15	1/1/2011
2215111000	ORBITS	70200	70200	Y7210	320	15	1/1/2011
2217111000	PARANASAL SINUSES	70220	70220	Y7220	320	15	1/1/2011

Table 16.15.　Examples of UB–04 revenue codes

Revenue Code	Description
250	Pharmacy—General
251	Pharmacy—Generic Drugs
252	Pharmacy—Nongeneric Drugs
253	Pharmacy—Take-Home Drugs
260	IV Therapy—General
261	IV Therapy—Infusion Pump
262	IV Therapy—IV Therapy/Pharmacy Services
263	IV Therapy—IV Therapy/Drug/Supply Delivery
270	Medical/Surgical Supplies and Devices—General
271	Medical/Surgical Supplies and Devices—Nonsterile Supply
272	Medical/Surgical Supplies and Devices—Sterile Supply
273	Medical/Surgical Supplies and Devices—Take-Home Supplies
280	Oncology—General
289	Oncology—Other
290	DME—General
291	DME—Rental
292	DME—Purchase of New DME
293	DME—Purchase of Used DME
300	Laboratory—General
301	Laboratory—Chemistry
302	Laboratory—Immunology
303	Laboratory—Renal Patient (Home)
310	Laboratory Pathological—General
311	Laboratory Pathological—Cytology
312	Laboratory Pathological—Histology
320	Radiology—Diagnostic—General
321	Radiology—Diagnostic—Angiocardiography
322	Radiology—Diagnostic—Arthrography
360	Operating Room Services—General
361	Operating Room Services—Minor Surgery
362	Operating Room Services—Organ Transplant—Other Than Kidney
370	Anesthesia—General
371	Anesthesia—Incident to Radiology
372	Anesthesia—Incident to Other Diagnostic Services
410	Respiratory Services—General
411	Respiratory Services—Inhalation Services
412	Respiratory Services—Hyperbaric Oxygen Therapy

An inaccurate chargemaster adversely affects facility reimbursement, compliance, and data quality. According to an AHIMA practice brief (Rhodes 1999), negative effects that may result from an inaccurate chargemaster include overpayment, underpayment, undercharging for delivery of healthcare services, claims rejections, and fines or penalties. Chargemaster programs are automated and involve the billing of numerous services for high volumes of patients, often without human intervention. Therefore, it is highly likely that a single error on the chargemaster could result in multiple errors before it is identified and corrected, resulting in a serious financial impact.

Coding and Corporate Compliance

The federal government has initiated efforts to investigate healthcare fraud and to establish guidelines to ensure corporate compliance with the government guidelines. Part of the initiative involved providing healthcare organizations with guidelines for developing comprehensive compliance programs with specific policies and procedures.

History of Fraud and Abuse and Corporate Compliance in Healthcare

Probably the most pertinent fact in the history of corporate compliance related to healthcare organizations is that the federal government, specifically HHS, is the largest purchaser of healthcare in the United States. Because one of the federal government's duties is to use the taxpayers' monies wisely, federal agencies must ensure that the healthcare provided to enrollees in federal healthcare programs is appropriate and is actually provided.

Several federal initiatives and pieces of legislation related to investigating, identifying, and preventing healthcare **fraud and abuse** have been passed. Interestingly, the basis of these initiatives and laws lies within the Civil False Claims Act, which was passed during the Civil War to prevent government contractors from overbilling for services provided. The original law was updated and reinforced in subsequent legislation and is still used to prosecute offenders.

Several government agencies are involved in detecting, prosecuting, and preventing fraud and abuse. Among them are HHS, the Office of Inspector General (OIG), the Department of Justice (the US attorney general), the Federal Bureau of Investigation (FBI), CMS, the Drug Enforcement Agency (DEA), the Internal Revenue Service (IRS), and state attorneys general.

Many initiatives are joint efforts among the agencies. For example, Operation Restore Trust, which began in 1995, is a joint effort of HHS, OIG, CMS, and the Administration on Aging. Operation Restore Trust spent only $7.9 million in the first two years to identify $188 million in overpayments to providers. It also led to implementation of special fraud alerts notifying providers of current investigative findings and to the **Voluntary Disclosure Program.**

The federal government began to actively investigate fraud in the Medicare program in 1977 with passage of the Anti-Fraud and Abuse Amendments of 1977 to Title XIX of the SSA. However, detecting, preventing, and prosecuting fraud and abuse did not reach true prominence until HIPAA established Sections 1128C and 1128D of the SSA. Sections 1128C and 1128D authorized the OIG to conduct investigations, audits, and evaluations related to healthcare fraud. The BBA focused on fraud and abuse issues specifically relating to penalties.

The BBA also required that physicians and practitioners provide diagnostic information (to show medical necessity) prior to a facility performing lab or radiology services for a patient.

As previously mentioned, HIPAA expanded the OIG's duties to include

- Coordination of federal, state, and local enforcement efforts targeting healthcare fraud
- Provision of industry guidance concerning fraudulent healthcare practices
- Establishment of a national data bank for reporting final adverse actions against healthcare providers

Significantly, HIPAA authorizes the OIG to investigate cases of healthcare fraud that involve private healthcare plans as well as federally funded programs. However, according to information on the OIG website, present policies restrict the OIG's investigative focus to cases of fraud that affect federally funded programs.

A major portion of HIPAA focused on identifying medically unnecessary services, upcoding, unbundling, and billing for services not provided. **Upcoding** is the practice of assigning a diagnosis or procedure code specifically for the purpose of obtaining a higher level of payment. It is most often found when reimbursement-grouping systems are used.

Unbundling is the practice of using multiple codes that describe individual components of a procedure rather than an appropriate single code that describes all steps of the procedure performed. Unbundling is a target of the NCCI.

HIPAA also expanded sanctions related to mandatory exclusion from Medicare, length of exclusion, failure to comply with statutory obligations, and anti-kickback penalties (Schraffenberger and Kuehn 2011).

Since February 1998 the OIG has continued to issue **compliance program guidance** for various types of healthcare organizations. The OIG website posts the documents that most healthcare organizations need to develop fraud and abuse compliance plans. The goal of compliance programs is to prevent accusations of fraud and abuse, make operations run more smoothly, improve services, and contain costs (Anderson 2000).

Elements of Corporate Compliance

In the February 23, 1998 *Federal Register*, the OIG outlined the following seven elements as the minimum necessary for a comprehensive compliance program:

- The development and distribution of written standards of conduct, as well as written policies and procedures that promote the hospital's commitment to compliance and address specific areas of potential fraud, such as claims development and submission processes, code gaming, and financial relationships with physicians and other healthcare professionals
- The designation of a chief compliance officer and other appropriate bodies, for example, a corporate compliance committee, charged with the responsibility for operating and monitoring the compliance program, and who report directly to the CEO and the governing body
- The development and implementation of regular, effective education and training programs for all affected employees
- The maintenance of a process, such as a hotline, to receive complaints and the adoption of procedures to protect the anonymity of complainants and to protect whistleblowers from retaliation
- The development of a system to respond to allegations of improper or illegal activities and the enforcement of appropriate disciplinary action against employees who have violated internal compliance policies, applicable statutes, regulations, or federal healthcare program requirements
- The use of audits or other evaluation techniques to monitor compliance and assist in the reduction of identified problem areas
- The investigation and remediation of identified systemic problems and the development of policies addressing the nonemployment or retention of sanctioned individuals

The OIG believes that a compliance program conforming to these elements above will not only "fulfill the organization's legal duty to ensure that it is not submitting false or inaccurate claims to government and private payers" but will also result in additional potential benefits, including, among others

- Demonstration of the organization's commitment to responsible conduct toward employees and the community
- Provision of a more accurate view of behavior relating to fraud and abuse
- Identification and prevention of criminal and unethical conduct
- Improvements in the quality of patient care

The *Federal Register* published the supplemental compliance program guidance for hospitals in the January 31, 2005

Figure 16.7. Online compliance resources

Department of Health and Human Services, Office of Inspector General	www.oig.hhs.gov
American Health Information Management Association	www.ahima.org
Health Care Compliance Association	www.hcca-info.org
National Health Care Anti-Fraud Association	www.nhcaa.org
Centers for Medicare and Medicaid Services	www.cms.govCMS Fraud Page
CMS Fraud Page	www.medicare.gov

issue. This document supplements rather than replaces the 1998 compliance program guidance (CPG) document. The supplemental CPG contains new compliance recommendations and an expanded discussion of risk areas, current enforcement priorities, and lessons learned in the area of corporate compliance.

For additional resources on compliance and fraud and abuse, see figure 16.7.

Relationship between Coding Practice and Corporate Compliance

Any corporate compliance program must contain references to complete and accurate coding. Many of the documented fraud and abuse convictions have centered on the coding function.

OIG Work Plan

At the beginning of each fiscal year, the OIG publishes guidance on its "special areas of concern" for the upcoming year. The OIG refers to this as its workplan. The current year's workplan can be found at http://oig.hhs.gov under Reports and Publications.

HIM Compliance Program

As mentioned previously, one element of the corporate compliance program addresses the coding function. Because the accuracy and completeness of ICD-9-CM and CPT code assignment determine the provider payment, the reference to coding is not surprising. Thus, it is important that healthcare organizations have a strong coding compliance program. This coding compliance plan should be based on the same principles as that of the corporate-wide program. The basic elements of a coding plan should include

- Code of conduct
- Policies and procedures
- Education and training
- Communication
- Auditing
- Corrective action
- Reporting

Code of Conduct

The HIM department should develop a code of conduct that reflects the principles in AHIMA's Standards of Ethical Coding, which can be found in Appendix B.

Policies and Procedures

Policies and procedures that describe the facility's coding standards and functions should be documented in a coding compliance manual. Some of the items that should be included in this manual include policies on the following: ambiguous or incomplete documentation, rebilling of problem claims, use of official coding guidelines, issues where no official guidelines exist, and clarification of new or confusing coding issues.

Education and Training

Periodic and staff-appropriate education of staff is a key factor in a successful coding compliance program. Education for coders should be provided monthly (Schraffenberger and Kuehn 2011).

Areas that could be covered at training sessions include

- The OIG work plan
- Clinical information related to problematic body systems, diagnoses, and procedures
- Changes to the PPSs
- Changes to ICD-9-CM, HCPCS Level II, and CPT codes
- Application of the official coding guidelines
- Issues in *Coding Clinic for ICD-9-CM*
- Issues in *CPT Assistant*

All newly hired coding personnel should receive extensive training on the facility's and HIM department's compliance programs.

Education of the medical staff on documentation is likewise important to the success of any coding compliance program. Documentation education may be provided monthly, bimonthly, or quarterly depending on the importance of the issues covered (Schraffenberger and Kuehn 2011).

Examples of documentation problems that may need to be addressed with physicians include

- Inconsistent documentation
- Incomplete progress notes
- Undocumented care
- Test results not addressed in physician documentation
- Historical diagnoses being documented as current diagnoses
- Long-standing, chronic conditions that are not documented
- Lack of documentation of postoperative complications
- Illegibility
- Documentation not completed on time (Bowman 2008)

Communication

Communication between the coding supervisor and the coding professionals is vital to ensure consistency in following coding policies and issues.

Internal Audits

Ongoing evaluation is critical to successful coding and billing for third-party payer reimbursement. In the past, the goal of internal audit programs was to increase revenues for the provider. Today, the goal is to protect providers from sanctions or fines. Healthcare organizations can implement monitoring programs by conducting regular, periodic audits of (1) ICD-9-CM and CPT/HCPCS coding and (2) claims development and submission. In addition, audits should be conducted to follow up on previous reviews that resulted in the identification of problems (for example, poor coding quality or errors in claims submission).

Auditing involves the performance of internal and **external reviews** to identify variations from established baselines (for example, review outpatient coding as compared with CMS outpatient coding guidelines). Internal reviews are conducted by facility-based staff (for example, HIM professionals), and external reviews are conducted by either consultants hired for this purpose (for example, corporations that specialize in such reviews and independent health information consultants) or third-party payers.

The scope and frequency of audits and the size of the sample depend on the size of the organization, available resources, the number of coding professionals, the history of noncompliance, risk factors, case complexity, and the results of initial assessments (Bowman 2008).

One of the elements of the auditing process is identification of risk areas. Some major risk areas include

- MS-DRG coding accuracy
- Variations in case mix
- Discharge status (transfers versus discharges)
- Services provided under arrangement
- Three-day payment window, formerly called the 72-hour rule (Under this rule, diagnostic services provided within three days of admission should be included, or bundled, in the DRG, whether or not they are related to the admission. Non-diagnostic services provided within three days of admission should be included in the DRG only if they are related to the admission.)
- All nondiagnostic services that are unrelated to the admission can be billed separately
- Medical necessity
- Evaluation and management services
- Chargemaster description

Selecting types of cases to review also is important. Some examples of various case selection possibilities are found in figure 16.8.

Figure 16.8. Examples of various case selections for auditing

- Simple random sample
- Medical MS-DRGs by high dollar and high volume
- Surgical MS-DRGs by high dollar and high volume
- Medical MS-DRGs without comorbid conditions or complications
- Surgical MS-DRGs without comorbid conditions or complications
- Major diagnostic category by high dollar and high volume
- Most common diagnosis codes
- Most common procedure codes
- Significant procedure APCs by high dollar and high volume
- Unlisted CPT codes
- "Separate procedure" CPT codes reported in conjunction with related CPT codes
- Unusual modifier usage patterns
- Not elsewhere classified (NEC) and not otherwise specified (NOS) codes
- Highest-level evaluation and management (E/M) codes
- Consultation E/M codes
- Critical care E/M codes
- Chargemaster review by service

The frequency of audits depends on the individual facility; daily, weekly, monthly, or quarterly audits may be considered.

The results of the audits must be analyzed to determine the reason(s) for the coding errors. Focused reviews in one particular area may be necessary to review a higher volume of cases in which there were frequent errors. Certainly, focused reviews aimed at OIG target areas would be appropriate. Significant variations from baselines should prompt an investigation to determine cause(s).

Feedback on the results of audits should be presented to interested parties such as coding staff, supervisors, and physicians.

Corrective Action

Certainly, the goal of corrective action activities is the prevention of the same or a similar problem in the future. Typical corrective actions for resolving problems identified during coding audits include

- Revisions to policies and procedures
- Development of additional policies and procedures
- Process improvements
- Education of coders, physicians, or other organizational staff depending on the nature of the identified problem
- Revision or addition of routine monitoring activities
- Additions, deletions, or revisions to systems edits

- Documentation improvement strategies
- Disciplinary action (Bowman 2008)

Reporting

Documentation on coding compliance activities should be maintained and reported as stated in the policies and procedures. Certainly, adverse findings should be reviewed with the corporate compliance officer and steps taken as necessary to report these findings.

Check Your Understanding 16.8

Instructions: Answer the following questions on a separate piece of paper.

1. How often do third-party payers update fee schedules?

2. What does the term *accept assignment* mean?

3. Explain the difference between a participating provider, a nonparticipating provider who accepts assignment, and a nonparticipating provider who does not accept assignment.

4. What is the limiting charge rule?

5. What is a chargemaster, and why do healthcare facilities develop chargemasters?

6. How might an inaccurate chargemaster affect facility reimbursement?

7. What are the typical items on the charge description master?

8. Who is responsible for maintaining the charge description master?

9. What are some characteristics of a good physician query form? What is the purpose of a physician query form?

10. What do coding compliance programs concentrate on preventing? Which federal agency has established the precise steps that each healthcare facility must follow in establishing its compliance program?

11. What do the terms *upcoding* and *unbundling* mean in relation to coding?

12. What items might be covered during educational programs for the medical staff?

13. What major risk areas are related to coding and billing?

14. Describe some of the benefits of effective corporate compliance programs for healthcare organizations.

Summary

From its very beginnings, financial reimbursement for healthcare services has followed several paths. Among these are private pay, commercial insurance, employer self-insurance, and various government programs. The mixture of payment mechanisms has made healthcare reimbursement in the United States very complex.

As a consequence, the processing of medical claims can be complicated. How a claim is processed, what documentation is required, and how much reimbursement will be paid depend on the payer and the type of claim. Many attempts have been made to create a uniform healthcare claim that would accommodate all payment mechanisms. Claims processed for payment under Medicare have been consolidated into a uniform bill.

Healthcare organizations have developed several tools to help manage the billing and reimbursement process, including development of fee schedules and chargemasters. The HIM professional is frequently called on to provide expertise in the development, management, and auditing of these tools. In addition, organizations have recognized that ongoing evaluation of the entire billing process is essential to ensure accurate payment as well as to avoid fraud and abuse sanctions or fines. The HIM professional's work is likely to involve helping to develop such audit programs in addition to conducting the audits themselves.

Over the past two decades, the billing and reimbursement process has become an integral part of the job functions of many HIM professionals. The expertise given to the process to ensure accurate and timely claims submission is critical to the operations of any healthcare organization.

Payments for the delivery of healthcare services increased from $27 billion in 1960 to more than $2.5 trillion in 2009. In response, private insurers introduced managed care programs and the federal government implemented prospective payment systems to replace the costly per diem (or traditional fee-for-service) reimbursement methods. The federal government also incorporated managed care into its healthcare programs.

Health claims reimbursement processing has evolved from the submission of a handwritten CMS-1500 form to specially designed forms used for optical scanning purposes to electronic data interchange. Of recently enacted federal legislation affecting claims reimbursement processing, the NCCI and the OIG coding compliance programs have had the most effect on HIM professionals.

References

AHIMA e-HIM Workgroup on Computer-Assisted Coding. 2004. Delving into computer-assisted coding. *Journal of AHIMA* 75(10): 48A–H.

American Association of State Compensation Insurance Funds (2012). About Us – History. http://www.aascif.org/index.php?page=history

American Health Information Management Association. 2010. *Pocket Glossary of Health Information Management and Technology*, 2nd ed. Chicago: AHIMA.

American Health Information Management Association. 2008. Managing an Effective Query Process. *Journal of AHIMA* 79(10):

83-88.

American Medical Association. 2012. *Current Procedural Terminology,* 2012 ed. Chicago: AMA.

Anderson, S. 2000. Audit outpatient bills to get all the money you deserve. *Medical Records Briefing* 15(12): 6.

Bowman, S. 2008. *Health Information Management Compliance: Guidelines for Preventing Fraud and Abuse,* 4th ed. Chicago: AHIMA.

Centers for Medicare and Medicaid Services. 2011. http://www.cms.gov.

Federal Register. 1998. https://www.federalregister.gov/articles/1998/02/23/98-4399/publication-of-the-oig-compliance-program-guidance-for-hospitals.

National Uniform Billing Committee (2012). The History of the NUBC. http://www.nubc.org/history.html.

Rhodes, H. 1999. Practice brief: The care and maintenance of charge masters. *Journal of AHIMA*, 70(7):supplement 2.

Russo, R. 2010. *Clinical Documentation Improvement*. Chicago: AHIMA.

Schnitzer, G.L. 2000. Natural language processing: A coding professional's perspective. *Journal of AHIMA* 71(9):95–98.

Schraffenberger, L. and L. Kuehn. 2011. *Effective Management of Coding Services.* Chicago: AHIMA.

Schwager, R. 2000. Speech recognition propels transcription revolution. *Journal of AHIMA* 71(9): 64–68.

3M Health Information Systems. 2002. http://www.3Mhis.com.

Warner, H.R. 2000. Can natural language processing aid outpatient coders? *Journal of AHIMA* 71(8):78–81.

chapter 17

Revenue Cycle Management

Colleen Malmgren, MS, RHIA, and C. Jeanne Solberg, MA, RHIA

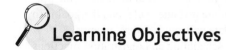

Learning Objectives

- Describe revenue cycle management's key phases
- Define and calculate key performance indicators to compare performance among peers and with the industry
- Identify critical points in the revenue cycle processes
- Understand the revenue life cycle from point-of-service collections to claims adjudication
- Define the impact of a clinical documentation improvement program on the revenue cycle
- Articulate case management's and utilization review's impact on the revenue cycle
- Identify and correct issues at the source of denial
- Identify proper claims denial management tactics
- Create a successful denials management team

Key Terms

Accounts receivable (A/R) Days
Bill hold
Case management
Case mix index (CMI)
Charge capture
Charge Description Master (CDM)
Charity care
Claims scrubber software
Clean claim
Clinical documentation improvement (CDI)
Denial
Discharge, no final bill (DNFB)
Facility charge
Financial counselor

Insurance verification
Key performance indicator (KPI)
Local coverage determination (LCD)
MAP key
Medical necessity
National coverage determination (NCD)
Point-of-service (POS) collection
Preauthorization (or prior approval, authorization, or predetermination)
Revenue cycle
Steerage
Utilization management
Utilization review

Introduction

There is significant financial pressure on healthcare organizations to manage their costs as consumers of services take on an increased financial responsibility for their healthcare costs. The **revenue cycle** is the process that begins when a patient comes into the healthcare system and includes those activities that have to occur in order for a provider of the care to bill at the end of the patient's service encounter. The healthcare revenue cycle encompasses people, tools, methodologies, and techniques that medical institutions use to manage their patients' financial status. Revenue cycle management is a complex process that involves balancing people, processes, technology, and the environment in which the processes take place.

The revenue management life cycle can be broken down into three phases—the front-end, middle, and back-end (see figure 17.1). The front-end of the revenue cycle includes patient access functions such as scheduling of the patient for services, registration of the patient, prior or preauthorization for services, insurance verification, service estimates, and financial counseling. During this phase, healthcare organizations need to ascertain the source of payment for the service, follow requirements specified by the payer, accurately collect the patient's demographic information, and ensure a positive patient experience. Contract negotiations and re-negotiations with third-party payers are also included in the front-end process. Specific terms negotiated with payers drive patient services covered for reimbursement. These terms need to be defined and understood by staff to properly support the front-end of the revenue cycle.

The middle process of the revenue cycle includes case management, capture of charges for the services rendered, and coding for those services based on clinical documentation. The key objectives in this phase are to manage clinical practice according to accepted medical guidelines, identify reimbursable services and ensure that documentation supports those services, and ensure coding of the documented services is accurate and complete.

Figure 17.1.   Revenue management life cycle

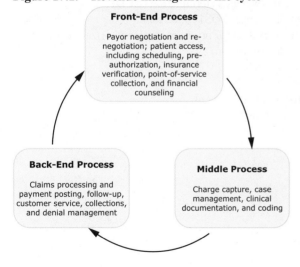

The back end of the revenue cycle is typically viewed as the business office or patient financial service process and includes claims processing and payment posting, follow-up, customer service, collections of unpaid bills, and denial management (HIMSS 2009). In this phase, organizations focus on releasing claims to the payers as quickly as possible after service is rendered and generating accurate and complete claims resulting in reimbursement of the amount expected by the payer.

Revenue Cycle Front-End Process

Scheduling and Registration

The scheduling of patient visits requires optimal assignment of patients to the available healthcare resources. Accuracy of information captured in this stage is vital to many of the processes occurring later in the revenue cycle, and the goal is to continuously improve data collection and accuracy.

Staff responsible for scheduling and registration functions requires a significant amount of knowledge regarding the medical services provided, insurance carrier requirements, provider preferences, and operational hours of services to be rendered. The registration staff is tasked with gathering and entering the required patient visit information. This staff also takes an active role in promoting positive public relations with patients to increase community trust in the facility. Examples of demographic data collected include name, date of birth, residence, sex, marital status, race and ethnicity, employer, insurance carrier, and guarantor. Incomplete or inaccurate information can delay care and negatively impact the revenue cycle (Corrigan 2009). When a patient arrives for services, the registration staff is responsible for validating the patient's identify, for example by photo identification; obtaining copies of insurance card(s); and obtaining patient (responsible party) signatures for insurance payment and release of medical information.

Initiating patient registration at the time of scheduling saves time and is more user-friendly for patients when they arrive for services. Each time a patient presents for clinical services, the prior collected data need to be verified for accuracy and updated with any changes.

The most common registration errors that affect the revenue cycle are noted in table 17.1.

Insurance Verification

Insurance verification is a vital component of the pre-arrival process for scheduled patients. Verification of the patient's insurance for unscheduled patients occurs at the time of their registration for clinical services or shortly thereafter. The verification process entails validating that the patient is a member of the insurance plan given and is covered for the scheduled service date. It is also important to determine whether the patient's insurance plan is

Table 17.1.   Most common registration errors

- Incorrect insurance plan listed
- Policy number or group number missing or invalid
- Patient not eligible on date of service
- Patient with insurance listed as private pay
- Medicare listed when plan is Medicare health maintenance organization (HMO)
- Medicare listed as primary when should be secondary
- Minors listed as guarantors
- More than one medical record number per patient
- Accident claims without occurrence codes
- Patient relationship to insurance subscriber code errors
- Failure to list medical necessity
- Missing guarantor or employer information
- Physician orders incomplete or missing
- Internal coding mismatches (for example, financial class to patient type to stay type to service code to admit code)
- Missing prior authorization or precertification required for service provided
- Transposed digits: Social Security number, date of birth, policy number, group number
- Invalid punctuation in specified text fields
- Misspelled name
- Insurance eligibility verification failure
- Address verification failure (returned mail cost)
- Observation patient with inpatient stay type
- Point-of-service collection failure
- Incomplete or inaccurate Medicare secondary payer questionnaire

Source: Shorrosh 2011.

in-network vs. out-of-network, whether the scheduled service expenses will be covered, whether a referral or an authorization is required prior to the service being rendered, and whether the patient will incur an out-of-pocket expense (Langford et al. 2010).

Patient demographic and insurance information needs to be complete and correct. In the absence of proper eligibility determination, payment for services may be delayed or denied; claims may need to be reprocessed or reworked, adding delays in receiving payment for services; and patients may become dissatisfied due to late statements and increased financial responsibility for services (Anderson 2009).

Preauthorization

Preauthorization is also referred to as **prior approval, authorization, precertification,** or **predetermination** and is the requirement that a healthcare provider obtain permission from the health insurer prior to predefined services being provided to the patients. Insurers have established more

stringent guidelines with the increase in high-technology and high-cost procedures and tests.

Scheduling or preauthorization teams need to understand medical procedures and tests, initial diagnoses, and scheduled treatments in order to obtain the necessary preauthorization by the insurance company. There is a wide variation in prior authorization requirements and criteria among payers (HASC Summit 2009). It is important for healthcare providers to have current lists of procedures and tests requiring prior authorization from all health insurers and have processes in place to obtain the authorization prior to services being rendered. Reimbursement for services without preauthorization is often denied by insurers and results in significant negative financial impact to the healthcare organization.

Financial Counseling

A healthcare organization needs to ensure the patient understands the financial aspects of his or her encounter of care and the process for resolving any fiscal responsibility. **Financial counselors** are staff dedicated to helping patients and physicians determine sources of reimbursement for healthcare services. The counselors are responsible for identifying and verifying the method of payment and debt resolution for services rendered to patients. Counselors need to understand a patient's financial assets and discuss payment alternatives with patients. Some patients are eligible for **charity care,** which is defined as healthcare services that have been or will be provided but are never expected to result in cash inflows. Charity care results from a provider's policy to provide healthcare services free or at a discount to individuals who meet the established criteria (HFMA 2010). The counselors can establish payment arrangements such as credit card payments, bank loans, and interest-bearing, hospital-funded payment arrangements as necessary.

Strategies for financial counselors can include the ability to provide discounts on hospital bills for patients who do not have health insurance and who meet certain eligibility criteria. The amount of the discount is determined after an assessment of the patient's or a family's financial need and is typically based on current federal poverty guidelines. Incentives for prompt-payment discounts can also be offered to patients. Healthcare facilities need to follow consistent procedures and steps to obtain appropriate payment and to enhance revenue cycle processes (Guyton et al. 2005).

Point of Service Collection

Patients have taken on an increasing amount of financial responsibility for their healthcare costs. Insurance companies determine that the annual copayments and deductibles for which the patient is responsible account for 5 to 6 percent of total net revenue and 16 to 17 percent of outstanding receivables (Page 2010). **Point-of-service (POS) collection** is defined as the collection of the portion of the bill that is likely the responsibility of the patient prior to the provision of service (Goudzwaard 2007). POS collection works well with scheduled and nonemergent patient visits. Access to billing data from both payers and the healthcare's own system is needed to be able to estimate what a patient owes at the point of service. Healthcare staff needs to communicate with the patient to set expectations regarding the cost of the services, insurance coverage, and the expected payment at the time of service (Yarbrough 2007). It is also important that the healthcare providers be educated about the POS policy and procedures within the hospital so they may support the process.

Medical Necessity Coverage Issues

Health insurance companies provide coverage only for health-related services that they define or determine to be medically necessary. Medicare defines **medical necessity** as a determination that a service is reasonable and necessary for the related diagnosis or treatment of illness or injury.

The American College of Medical Quality (ACMQ) further defines the application of appropriate services and supplies as those that are neither more nor less than what the patient requires at a specific point in time. The ACMQ (2010) has also adopted the following nine principles as part of their policy related to the application of medical necessity:

1. Determinations of medical necessity must adhere to the standard of care that applies to the actual direct care and treatment of the patient.

2. Medical necessity is the standard terminology that all healthcare professionals and entities will use in the review process when determining if medical care is appropriate and essential.

3. Determinations of medical necessity must reflect the efficient and cost-effective application of patient care including, but not limited to, diagnostic testing, therapies (including activity restriction, after-care instructions, and prescriptions), disability ratings, rehabilitating an illness, injury, disease or its associated symptoms, impairments or functional limitations, procedures, psychiatric care, levels of hospital care, extended care, long-term care, hospice care, and home healthcare.

4. Determinations of medical necessity made in a concurrent review should include discussions with the attending provider as to the current medical condition of the patient whenever possible. A physician advisor or reviewer can make a positive determination regarding medical necessity without necessarily speaking with the treating provider if the advisor has enough available information to make an appropriate medical decision. A physician advisor cannot decide to deny care

as not medically necessary without speaking to the treating provider and these discussions must be clearly documented.

5. Determinations of medical necessity must be unrelated to payors' monetary benefit.

6. Determinations of medical necessity must always be made on a case-by-case basis consistent with the applicable standard of care and must be available for peer review.

7. Recommendations approving medical necessity may be made by a non-physician reviewer. Negative determinations for the initial review regarding medical necessity must be made by a physician advisor who has the clinical training to review the particular clinical problem (clinically matched) under review. A physician reviewer or advisor must not delegate his or her review decisions to a non-physician reviewer.

8. The process to be used in evaluating medical necessity should be made known to the patient.

9. All medical review organizations involved in determining medical necessity shall have uniform, written procedures for appeals of negative determinations that services or supplies are not medically necessary.

Medicare's national coverage policies are known as **national coverage determinations (NCDs)**, and local fiscal intermediary policies are known as **local coverage determinations (LCDs)**. These policies define the specific International Classification of Diseases (ICD) diagnosis codes that support medical necessity for many services provided. There are not NCD or LCD policies for every type of procedure or service that could be provided for a patient, so healthcare organizations must stay current with the regulatory requirements and revisions that are contained in the following documents in order to reduce billing denials and ensure that payment is received for the services rendered.

- Payer billing manuals
- Medicare billing manuals
- Local fiscal intermediary policies
- Local Part B carrier policies

Pre-encounter Services

Many healthcare facilities have combined staff resources related to the revenue cycle front-end process and developed pre-encounter service centers for patients. The centers handle preregistration, insurance eligibility and benefit verification, payer authorizations, and preservice collections for all scheduled diagnostic testing and surgery patients. Organizations have developed the following operating characteristics to support the front-end processes.

- Ninety-five percent of all scheduled services will be preregistered.
- All areas performing registration functions will be guided by the same operating characteristics.
- Procedures will be standardized and all staff trained accordingly.
- Lack of preregistration will not contribute to treatment delays.
- Insurance clearance processes will drive a decrease in payer denials.
- Patient payment expectations will be communicated to the patients and (except for emergency department services) will be collected prior to or at the time of service.
- All uninsured patients will be offered a self-pay discount package or will be screened for either medical assistance or charity care, or both.
- Quality monitoring will be performed on a monthly basis with feedback to the employees.
- Physician offices will be notified of any noncovered services to make decisions regarding continuing with services.
- Denials will be work-listed for identification and resolution.
- Preregistration and financial clearance of scheduled services will be completed five days before the patient's appointment.
- Staff will use automated credit-scoring and address-checking software to identify a patient's potential to pay and potential eligibility for charity care (Butcher 2012).

Results from combining the front-end processes have eliminated last-minute cancellations of scheduled services, improved patient flow, and increased patient satisfaction.

Contract Management

The management of contracts is an integral part of the revenue life cycle. Healthcare facilities negotiate contract terms with third-party insurers for payment of services rendered to patients. This is where allowable costs or chargeable services or supplies provided by a hospital or physician that qualify as covered expenses are defined. The contract terms need to benefit and be cost-effective for the facility, its patients, and the insurer.

Contract management has its own life cycle. Persons responsible for contract management must first understand service lines provided within their facility and then analyze the financial needs to provide the services. Contract managers need to be able to analyze steerage vs. discounts. **Steerage** is when an insurer provides financial incentive or discounted rates to a facility to obtain a flow of patients it would not otherwise receive. Contract management also includes a comprehensive understanding of competitors and the local market rates, for instance, what other providers of services are charging. Managers need to negotiate contract

language and rates and be able to define payers' and providers' duties. Additional steps in the contract life cycle include claims submission and follow-up; denial management; analysis of payment variances; the collection of accounts and posting of payments; and, finally, analysis of the contract performance (Hammer 2009).

Technology Tools

Hospitals and healthcare systems need to accurately forecast, calculate, and capture all net revenue contractually owed to them. Contract management technology can assist with understanding the expected net revenue of every patient at discharge regardless of payer. Contract management software systems enable organizations to coordinate all phases of contracted payer business (negotiations, payment compliance, performance review); recover prior contract management underpayments by identifying payment variances; ensure proper payments on all subsequent claims as the system accurately calculates expected reimbursement; model complex contracts with multiple reimbursement formulas in a simple and timely manner; and take appropriate action when expected results are not achieved.

Technology tools to support the patient access workflows are important to support quality of work and productivity of staff. Tools identified by the 2008–2009 HIMSS Revenue Cycle Improvement Task Force (2009) to support the front-end process include

- Enterprise-wide scheduling system
- Order tracking and management system
- Telephony system in order to measure call activity
- Registration quality assurance tools
- Online third-party eligibility and coverage limitations
- Workflow drivers to ensure all financial clearance functions are completed
- Estimation tools for patient out-of-pocket financial responsibility
- Electronic financial assistance applications

Check Your Understanding 17.1

Instructions: Answer the following questions on a separate piece of paper

1. List five common registration errors that affect the revenue cycle.

2. Name the Medicare coverage policies that list diagnoses supporting medical necessity?

3. What information does the scheduling staff need in order to obtain authorization prior to services being rendered?

4. What strategies are employed by the financial counseling staff to obtain appropriate payment for services provided to the patient?

5. Identify five steps of the contract life cycle.

Revenue Cycle Middle Process

Case and Utilization Management

The Case Management Society of America (CMSA) defines **case management** as "…a collaborative process of assessment, planning, facilitation, care coordination, evaluation, and advocacy for options and services to meet an individual's and family's comprehensive health needs through communication and available resources to promote quality cost effective outcomes" (CMSA 2012). The American Case Management Association (ACMA) defines case management as "…a collaborative practice model including patients, nurses, social workers, physicians, other practitioners, caregivers and the community. The case management process encompasses communication and facilitates care along a continuum through effective resource coordination. The goals of case management include the achievement of optimal health, access to care, and appropriate utilization of resources, balanced with the patient's right to self-determination" (ACMA 2012). Both organizations support professionals who evaluate the appropriateness of hospital admissions according to pre-established criteria.

Case managers' responsibilities were initially to manage and ensure the appropriate utilization of acute care resources with a focus on improving quality and reducing costs. Today's case manager role has evolved further and involves:

- Partnering with physicians during rounds to participate in treatment plan progress reporting
- Questioning duplicative interventions or interventions that may be contrary to evidence-based protocols
- Collaborating with the nurses to identify any obstacles to move the treatment plan forward and bring that information to the bedside to resolve with the physician
- Facilitating communication among attending physicians and consultants
- Advocating for the patient and family to ensure that prescribed interventions are suitable to the patient's preferences and economic circumstances
- Prompting a planning discussion for transitioning patients from one level of care to another—whether from a critical care area to a medical unit or from a medical unit to the patient's home (Daniels and Frater 2011).

These responsibilities allow the case managers to quickly identify barriers that may impede the efficient progression of the patient through the healthcare service process. Unexpected delays in care or discharge can be prevented, and unnecessary consumption of resources such as additional patient days can be avoided (Daniels 2007). The case manager can have a positive impact on the revenue cycle by avoiding the delays, navigating the patient through the healthcare process, and acting as an advocate for the patient resulting in higher patient satisfaction with the healthcare facility (Miodonski 2011).

Utilization management works in conjunction with case management, and, at times, the terms and responsibilities are used interchangeably. **Utilization management** is the evaluation of the medical necessity, appropriateness, and efficiency of the use of healthcare services, procedures, and facilities under the provisions of the applicable health benefits plan; it is sometimes called **utilization review** (URAC 2012). The utilization review (UR) staff is responsible for the day-to-day provisions of the hospital's utilization plan as required by the Medicare Conditions of Participation. Utilization personnel are required to perform the following functions:

- Review the medical record thoroughly to obtain information necessary to make UR decisions
- Apply criteria objectively for admissions, continued stay, level of care, and discharge readiness
- Provide services 24 hours a day, 7 days a week, to all relevant hospital departments, acting as a resource
- Review, within 24 hours, all patients placed in a bed
- Screen and coordinate elective and emergency admissions and transfers, outpatient observations, and conversions of status as appropriate and compliant
- Provide UR to all admissions, regardless of payer status
- Review all continued stays at a scheduled frequency, but not less than every three days or sooner
- Screen for timeliness, safety, and appropriateness of the rendering or use of hospital services or resources
- Meet weekly for complex case (high-dollar or long length of stay) problem solving
- Complete retrospective or focused reviews as directed by the UR committee. (McLean 2011a)

The staff works with external review organizations and should establish working relations with third-party reviewers, provide requested clinical information as required, facilitate medical record access and supervision of insurance reviewers, and ensure communication to patients and their families resulting from the external review organization communications.

According to the Centers for Medicare and Medicaid Services (CMS 2012), hospitals have the responsibility to issue Hospital-Issued Notices of Noncoverage (HINNs) to Medicare beneficiaries prior to admission, at admission, or at any point during an inpatient stay if the hospital determines that the care the beneficiary is receiving, or is about to receive, is not covered because it:

- is not medically necessary,
- is not delivered in the most appropriate setting, or
- is custodial in nature.

Medicaid requirements vary from state to state for notification of denial of care or termination of benefits. The healthcare facility's utilization plan should include the state's specific requirements associated with denial or termination of benefits coverage (McLean 2011b).

Commercial payers are responsible for informing the patient or the patient's family, attending physician, and facility department responsible for utilization review of adverse determinations. Utilization personnel take an active role in monitoring, reporting, and communicating adverse determination to patients and their families and ensuring all procedures are followed in rendering the communication. These procedures are important to ensure financial responsibility of services provided and are important in a well-managed revenue cycle process.

Charge Capture

Charge capture is a method of recording services and supplies or items delivered to the patient and directing them to be billed on a claim form. It is the process of documenting, posting, and reconciling the charges for services rendered to patients. Organizational success is directly dependent upon accurately documenting and reporting charges in a timely manner, and the aim is to have policies, procedures, and resources in place to ensure quality charge capture that enhances revenue and adheres to compliance and other standards.

Quality charge capture is critical for the following reasons:

- Payments are often related to charges; reimbursement for outpatient services is often driven by the specific charges along with Current Procedural Terminology (CPT) and Healthcare Common Procedure Coding System (HCPCS) codes listed on the claim.
- Charges drive prices and rates for reimbursement; payment rates established for diagnosis-related groups (DRGs) and ambulatory patient classifications (APCs) is determined by analyzing historical cost data, and if true costs are not being reflected, reimbursement rates are set too low.
- Charges reflect resource utilization; this allows analysis and comparison of the resources used for patients with similar diagnoses treated in similar service lines or receiving similar treatments.
- Charges help in the measurement of labor cost and productivity; this assists the organization in monitoring the cost of doing business and determining staffing needs.
- Errors in charge capture create significant rework and billing delays; errors may also go undetected and result in loss of revenue or put the organization at risk by not meeting regulatory requirements.

A variety of charge capture mechanisms may be in place to get charges entered into the billing system. Charges may be entered from paper or electronic charge tickets or encounter forms, or they may be interfaced from source systems used in areas, such as a lab or pharmacy, that submit large volumes of charges. Electronic health record systems may also be configured to apply charges to patient accounts, and health information management coding staff often has responsibility for some charge entry based on clinical documentation. Regardless of the mechanism for charge entry, it is important to verify the accuracy of the charge codes being entered and to ensure they are posted to the correct patient accounts for the correct dates of service.

The primary responsibility for charge capture is assigned to staff in the departments providing the services, but there are complex regulatory requirements surrounding compliant charge capture, so ongoing charge capture education with well-documented policies and procedures is vital.

Organizations may utilize internal billing system edits designed to detect and correct charge capture errors before claims are submitted to the third-party payers. They may also utilize APC grouper software or Medicare **claims scrubber software** designed to detect errors that would result in payer denials. As errors are detected, they should appear on reports and be reviewed by the appropriate departments so corrections can be made and issues or problems can be detected and resolved.

Timely submission of charges is also critical for revenue cycle success. Each facility has a defined number of **bill hold** days. These are the number of days in which accounts will be held from billing so charges can be entered after the patient is discharged. Bill hold assumes that there will be a delay in accumulating the charges incurred by a patient. By incorporating this predicted delay into normal operations, the facility creates a preventive control to avoid underbilling or having to submit late charges to the payer. Charges added after this suspense period (typically two to five days) are considered late charges.

Third-party payers generally will not reimburse a claim that does not include the clinical diagnostic and procedural codes. This is true whether the reimbursement is based on a prospective payment system (PPS), actual charges, or some other method. For this reason, the patient accounts department cannot drop a bill until the patient record has been coded. Therefore, timely, accurate coding is critical to the reimbursement process and directly affects the facility's cash flow.

An additional responsibility in revenue cycle management is determining items or services that are not separately billable. Routine supplies are commonly defined as a supply used as part of the normal course of service where the care is delivered, given to most patients treated in a particular setting or incidental to the procedure, or inherent to a procedure. These supplies are not billable and are considered part of the room and board charge for a hospital or an overhead cost for the healthcare facility. Examples of routine supplies include specimen collection containers, syringes, needles, gloves, pillows, sponges, heating pads, and irrigation solutions. Equipment available to all patients in an area or commonly used during a procedure is also considered not separately billable. Examples of equipment not separately billable include cardiac monitors, blood pressure monitors, wall suction units, and intravenous pumps.

Another important aspect of charge capture includes facility charge capture. Since April 7, 2000, CMS has instructed hospitals to report facility resources for clinic hospital outpatient visits using the CPT evaluation and management (E/M) codes (CMS 2008). The **facility charge** allows capture of an E/M charge that represents those resources not included with the CPT code for the clinic environment. Hospitals were also instructed to develop internal hospital guidelines for reporting the appropriate visit level. Three options are allowed for capture of the facility evaluation and management charge:

- Guidelines based on the number or type of staff interventions
  — Number and type of interventions
  — Based upon diagnosis—evaluating most common vs. extreme trauma
  — Interventions not identified by CPT
- Guidelines based on the time staff spent with the patient
  — Nursing time spent with patient
- Guidelines based on a point system
  — Resource intensity points
  — Severity acuity based upon patient complexity

CMS does not provide national guidelines but expects a hospital's internal guidelines to follow the principles listed here.

1. The coding guidelines should follow the intent of the CPT code descriptor in that the guidelines should be designed to reasonably relate the intensity of hospital resources to the different levels of effort represented by the code (65 FR 18451).

2. The coding guidelines should be based on hospital facility resources. The guidelines should not be based on physician resources (67 FR 66792).

3. The coding guidelines should be clear to facilitate accurate payments and be usable for compliance purposes and audits (67 FR 66792).

4. The coding guidelines should meet the Health Insurance Portability and Accountability Act (HIPAA) requirements (67 FR 66792).

5. The coding guidelines should only require documentation that is clinically necessary for patient care.

6. The coding guidelines should not facilitate upcoding or gaming (67 FR 66792).

7. The coding guidelines should be written or recorded, be well documented, and provide the basis for selection of a specific code.

8. The coding guidelines should be applied consistently across patients in the clinic or emergency department to which they apply.

9. The coding guidelines should not change with great frequency.

10. The coding guidelines should be readily available for fiscal intermediary (or, if applicable, medicare administrative contractor) review.

11. The coding guidelines should result in coding decisions that could be verified by other hospital staff as well as outside sources.

CMS provided additional clarification surrounding some of the principles.

- The first principle states coding guidelines should follow the intent of the CPT code descriptor to relate to the intensity of resources to different levels of effort represented by the code, not that the hospital's guidelines need to specifically consider the three factors included in the CPT E/M codes for consideration regarding physician visit reporting.

- Regarding principle two, hospitals are responsible for reporting the CPT E/M visit code that appropriately represents the resources utilized by the hospital rather than the resources utilized by the physician. This does not preclude the hospital from using or adapting the physician guidelines if the hospital believes that such guidelines adequately describe hospital resources.

- In principle eight, a hospital with multiple clinics (for example, primary care, oncology, wound care, and such) may have different coding guidelines for each clinic, but the guidelines must be applied uniformly within each separate clinic. The hospital's various sets of internal guidelines must measure resource use in a relative manner in relation to each other. For example, resources required for a Level 3 established patient visit under one set of guidelines should be comparable to the resources required for a Level 3 established patient visit under all other sets of clinic visit guidelines used by the hospital.

- Regarding principle nine, CMS would generally expect hospitals to adjust their guidelines less frequently than every few months, and CMS believes it would be reasonable for hospitals to adjust their guidelines annually, if necessary.

- Regarding the tenth principle, hospitals should use their judgment to ensure that coding guidelines are readily available in an appropriate and reasonable format. CMS would encourage fiscal intermediaries and medicare administrative contractors to review a hospital's internal guidelines when an audit occurs.

- Regarding the 11th principle, hospitals should use their judgment to ensure that their coding guidelines can produce results that are reproducible by others. In the absence of national visit guidelines, hospitals have the flexibility to determine whether or not to include separately payable services as a proxy to measure hospital resource use that is not associated with those separately payable services. The costs of hospital resource use associated with those separately payable services would be paid through separate outpatient PPS payment for the other services (Bowman 2008).

CMS also noted that facilities must also make the determination as to whether the patient is "new" or "established." CMS stated, "effective January 1, 2009, as stated in the November 24, 2008 OPPS Final Rule (73 FR 68679), under the OPPS, the meanings of 'new' and 'established' pertain to whether or not the patient has been registered as an inpatient or outpatient of the hospital within the past 3 years. If a patient has been registered as an outpatient in a hospital's off-campus provider-based clinic or emergency department within the past 3 years that patient would still be considered an 'established' patient to the hospital for an on-campus or off-campus clinic visit even if the medical record was initially created by the hospital prior to the past 3 years" (CMS 2008).

Charge Description Master

The **Charge Description Master (CDM)** is an electronic file that represents a master list of all services, supplies, devices, and medications charged for inpatient or outpatient services (see table 17.2). The CDM contains the basic elements for identifying, coding, and billing items and services provided to patients, and it is the mechanism for representing captured charges on the billing claim.

Each billable service or supply is set up in the CDM and assigned an internal charge code number, which links it to the various data elements necessary for billing and for tracking charge activity within the organization. All charges that are set up in charging source systems or charges that are listed on paper or electronic charge tickets must be identical to those set up in the Charge Description Master file in the billing system.

The CDM contains the following general data elements:

- Charge code—a unique identifier to identify and represent each billable service or supply. The number is meaningful only to the organization and does not appear on the billing claim.
- Charge code description—a narrative description of the service or supply. It does not appear on the billing claim but would be available on an itemized patient statement.
- CPT or HCPCS code—a nationally recognized five-digit code. Not all CDM line items have a CPT or HCPCS code because there are services and supplies for which no code has been developed. These charges are represented on the claim using only the revenue code. When a CPT or HCPCS code does exist to represent a chargemaster line item, it is reported on the outpatient billing claim.
- Modifiers—two-digit numeric or alphanumeric extensions that are added to the CPT or HCPCS codes to provide further information about the code. The claim form allows room for one or two modifiers to be attached to a CPT or HCPCS code.
- Revenue code—a nationally recognized four-digit code that provides a general identification of what the line item charge represents (that is, room and board, lab services, radiology services, pharmacy items, supply items, surgical procedures). The revenue code and its description are required on each line item of a billing claim for both inpatients and outpatients.

Table 17.2. Sample chargemaster description

Charge Code	Charge Code Description	CPT/HCPCS Code	Modifier	Revenue Code	Price
2721159	CATHETER, DRAINAGE			272	79.00
2786337	CATHETER, HEMODIALYSIS LONG TERM	C1750		278	438.00
3008423	DRUG SCREEN QUALITATIVE, SINGLE DRUG CLASS	80101		300	41.00
3007215	CBC COMPLETE, WITH DIFFERENTIAL	85025		300	123.00
3207721	VENOGRAM EXTREMITY BILATERAL	75822		320	1,320.00
3406973	PARATHYROID SCAN	78070		340	798.00
3618306	DRAINAGE OF HEMATOMA/SEROMA	10140		361	1,517.00
3612905	INJECTION SACROILIAC JOINT	27096		361	786.00
4245986	PHYSICAL THERAPY EVALUATION	97001	GP	424	196.00
4302398	OCCUPATIONAL THERAPY RE-EVALUATION	97004	GO	430	134.00
4802563	ECHO TRANSTHORACIC, CONGENITAL W/CONTRAST	93303		480	1,232.00

• Price—the charge that is established for the line item service, item, or supply. Factors that may determine the price that is established include

— The Medicare and Medicaid reimbursement rates (set by federal and state government agencies)

— Reimbursement provided by other third-party payers (set by contract negotiations with the payers)

— Cost information that is calculated by the accounting or finance area (the cost to the organization to provide that service, such as supplies, equipment, and labor).

— Standard markup rates for services or supplies (to factor in indirect costs to the organization or discount rates that are negotiated with the third-party payers)

— Benchmark data on pricing in comparable organizations

— Market competitive services.

Additional data elements may include the date the charge code was created or made active; the date the charge code was deactivated; a code that uniquely identifies the department cost center that uses the code; and payer-specific requirements for reporting the charge, for example, a different CPT, HCPCS, or modifier that needs to be reported to the payer for the charge submitted.

The chargemaster must continually be updated to ensure that it represents all billable services and supplies and to keep up with changes in CPT or HCPCS codes, revenue code assignment, and payer-specific requirements. Any number of events may trigger a need for CDM modifications. Examples include

1. Regulatory changes such as CPT or HCPCS code changes
2. Changes in CMS reimbursement guidelines
3. New department services
4. New product lines
5. Identification that the existing code does not match the service being provided
6. Recurring claim scrubber or APC edits identifying inappropriate setup in the CDM
7. Payer denials identifying inappropriate revenue code or CPT or HCPCS code assignment in the CDM (HFMA 2007).

A variety of resources are used to support the maintenance of the CDM. Internet resources are listed in table 17.3.

Many larger organizations use a software system to assist with maintenance of the CDM and to view items that are set up in a department or cost center's chargemaster. The software is primarily designed to continuously apply edits that point out compliance issues, validity of elements such as CPT codes and revenue codes, and identification of items priced below national reimbursement levels.

Maintenance of the CDM is a multidisciplinary activity. Proper chargemaster maintenance requires expertise in coding, clinical procedures, health record or clinical documentation, and billing regulations. For example, the health information management (HIM) department is knowledgeable of the codes, the patient accounts department knows the general ledger codes, the pharmacy department is familiar with the drugs and their costs, and the finance or revenue integrity department knows the associated charge formulas. Pharmacy cannot realistically update radiology's data nor can finance update charges without knowledge of underlying costs and input from the specific department (OptumInsight 2011).

Representatives from various areas that impact the revenue life cycle are critical to the success of the team. It is equally beneficial to include representatives from those departments that capture and generate charges; additional representatives may be included depending upon the facility structure. Department representation typically includes the chargemaster coordinator; patient access including admitting, registration, and scheduling; compliance; revenue integrity; patient financial service (billing department); contracting; finance; information services; HIM; ancillary departments such as radiology, laboratory, surgery, or pharmacy; and physicians as needed.

Table 17.3. CDM resources

• Medicare contractor bulletins and advisories
• Medicare manuals
— Claims Processing Manual (combination of the old hospital, intermediary, and carrier manuals)
— Benefit Policy Manual
— Provider Reimbursement Manual
— National Coverage Determinations Manual
• Transmittals related to
— Hospital OPPS
— Fraud and abuse
— Coverage determinations
— Durable medical equipment regional carriers (DMERCs)
— Orthotics, prosthetics, and supplies
— Ambulance billing
— HIPAA
— Clarifications of previous transmittals
• Office of Inspector General
• National Correct Coding Initiative (NCCI) edits
• Medicare Addendum B

Source: Shuler 2011.

Responsibilities of the chargemaster committee include:

- Developing policies and procedures for the chargemaster review process
- Performing chargemaster review at least annually when new CPT and HCPCS codes are available or changes are made throughout the year
- Attending to key elements of the annual chargemaster review, including
  - Reviewing all CPT and HCPCS codes for accuracy, validity, and relationship to charge description number
  - Reviewing all charge descriptions for accuracy and clinical appropriateness
  - Reviewing all revenue codes for accuracy and linkage to charge description numbers
- Ensuring that the usage of all CPT, HCPCS, and revenue codes are in compliance with Medicare guidelines or other existing payer contracts
- Reviewing all charge dollar amounts for appropriateness by payer
- Reviewing all charge codes for uniqueness and validity
- Reviewing all department code numbers for uniqueness and validity
- Performing ongoing chargemaster maintenance as the facility adds or deletes new procedures, updates technology, or changes services provided
- Ensuring that all necessary maintenance to systems affected by changes to the chargemaster (such as order entry feeder systems, charge tickets, and interfaces) is performed when chargemaster maintenance is performed
- Performing tests to make sure that changes to the chargemaster result in the desired outcome
- Educating all clinical department directors on the chargemaster and the effect of the chargemaster on corporate compliance
- Establishing a procedure to allow clinical department directors to submit chargemaster change requests for new, deleted, or revised procedures or services
- Ensuring there is no duplication of code assignment by coders and chargemaster-assigned codes in any department (for example, interventional radiology or cardiology catheterization laboratory)
- Reviewing all charge ticket and order entry screens for accuracy against the chargemaster and appropriate mapping to CPT or HCPCS codes when required
- Reviewing and complying with directives in Medicare transmittals, Medicare manual updates, and official coding guidelines
- Complying with guidelines in the National Correct Coding Initiative, Outpatient Code Editor edits, and any other coding or bundling edits
- Considering carefully any application that involves one charge description number that expands into more than one CPT or HCPCS code to prevent inadvertent unbundling and unearned reimbursement for services
- Reviewing and taking action on all remittance advice denials involving HCPCS or CPT coding rules and guidelines or CMS payer rules
- Educating all staff affected by changes to the chargemaster in a timely fashion (AHIMA 2010b)

The CDM staff must also communicate with staff who negotiates commercial and managed care contracts for the hospital to ensure that data elements meet specific payer requirements. Chargemaster maintenance also involves good communication with the billing staff with regard to payment denials related to an incorrect revenue code or CPT or HCPCS code, so that necessary changes get made to the chargemaster.

Consequences of improperly maintained or inaccurate chargemaster are the following:

- Services are provided, but associated charges are not set up in the CDM, so the organization is unable to bill and is providing free service.
- If a charge is not set up in the CDM until after the service is provided, the charge might not get posted to the patient's account during the bill hold time.
- When all services are not set up in the CDM, the department is only capturing part of its charges, and the result is reduced revenue.
- If charges are not set up in the CDM or if there are errors in the way they are set up, billing edits and APC edits may be generated, holding up processing of the claim. All billing delays result in increased accounts receivable (A/R) days.
- APC and billing edits result in multiple individuals investigating the issues and making necessary changes, which results in increased cost to the organization.

An up-to-date, complete, and well-maintained chargemaster is a significant financial, operational, and compliance asset to a healthcare organization.

Clinical Documentation

Complete, accurate, and timely documentation of patient history, assessment, surgical and procedure notes, and clinical plan are important aspects of the revenue cycle. Clinicians need to document the services that are performed and the medical necessity of the services, and staff needs to verify the charges are matching the services that are being performed prior to bill submission. CMS regulations require documentation to support the care provided to the patient. In order to comply with these regulations, hospitals have placed an increased focus on clinical documentation management and coding practices due to their direct impact on the healthcare facility's revenue.

Hospitals have invested in **clinical documentation improvement (CDI)** programs to assure the health record accurately reflects the actual condition of the patient. The American Health Information Management Association (AHIMA) developed a toolkit for clinical documentation improvement, stating its purpose is to "…initiate concurrent and, as appropriate, retrospective reviews of inpatient health records for conflicting, incomplete, or nonspecific provider documentation" and identified the following key goals for a CDI program:

- Identify and clarify missing, conflicting, or nonspecific physician documentation related to diagnoses and procedures
- Support accurate diagnostic and procedural coding, DRG assignment, severity of illness, and expected risk of mortality, leading to appropriate reimbursement
- Promote health record completion during the patient's course of care
- Improve communication between physicians and other members of the healthcare team
- Provide education
- Improve documentation to reflect quality and outcome scores
- Improve coders' clinical knowledge (AHIMA 2010a)

A focus on appropriate clinical documentation can reduce the risks from incomplete and unclear documentation resulting in lost revenue for the healthcare facility. Accurate and thorough clinical documentation that is properly coded and billed to payers results in benefits such as increased third-party payer billing compliance, improved quality reporting to external parties, and increased revenues by coding the most appropriate DRG and minimizing denials.

Coding

The HIM department performs a variety of functions, but the primary one related to the revenue cycle is code assignment. Upon a patient's discharge, the clinical documentation is reviewed and ICD diagnosis codes are assigned for inpatient and outpatient claims, and CPT or HCPCS codes are assigned only for outpatient claims. It is very important to have experienced, well-trained coders in order to ensure accurate and complete code assignment and optimum reimbursement. Coders must be skilled at reading through documentation on a variety of different forms and formats and interpreting that documentation to arrive at the correct code assignment. When documentation is vague or ambiguous, they may need to query the physician for clarification. The physician query process can create significant delays in the revenue cycle when the coder is waiting for the physician response and cannot complete the coding until it is received.

A bill cannot be generated until the coding is complete, so organizations routinely monitor the **discharged, no final bill (DNFB)** days. The goal for an efficient revenue cycle is to eliminate any backlog of uncoded charts and to complete the coding process within the time frame of the bill hold days that have been established for the organization.

The hospital's **case mix index (CMI)** is also measured and analyzed. The case mix index allows an organization to compare its cost of providing care to its DRG mix of patients compared to other hospitals. Medicare determines DRG weights by comparing the average cost of treating patients in one DRG to the average cost of all patients receiving hospital inpatient care. The DRG weights do not reflect an individual hospital's costs relative to another hospital or peer group. The CMI is calculated by summing the Medicare DRG weight for every inpatient discharge and dividing by the number of discharges. Medicare DRG weights are used and applied to patients within all payers. The accuracy of clinical documentation and of code assignment can influence a facility's case mix index. By missing diagnoses or procedures that should be coded, or failing to assign the most specific coding possible, the coding staff can cause the case mix index to be lower than it should be.

Technology Tools

Similar to the front-end process of the revenue cycle, technology tools play a vital role in the efficiency and quality of work produced by healthcare staff. The following tools and techniques were identified by the HIMSS Revenue Cycle Improvement Task Force (2009) to support the middle process:

- Clinical documentation may first originate as written text, dictation, or text keyed directly to the system. Ultimately, clinical documentation must result in codified procedures and diagnoses to support billing.
- Charge capture may be completed with a mix of forms, online entry (keyed or scanned), and automatic triggering.
- Electronic or e-tools help with maintenance of chargemasters. Optimal software packages include online reference tools that compile the latest coding and regulatory information, have a complete and active code book feature, and include a browser-based, cross-reference toolkit enabling users to research coding, regulations, and pricing information.
- HIM processes are dependent on access to all clinical documentation and any precoded data. Reference materials may be required to support the coding process; once determined, coded values must be input into systems for inclusion in claims processing. Automated edits may be imbedded in transactions systems to identify discrepancies at the time of entry (prior to submission into the claim cycle). Final coded records must be submitted through DRG tools to calculate and assign DRGs. Systems tools may include a mix of health information system (HIS) applications or an HIM-specific application that is integrated with other HIS applications.

Check Your Understanding 17.2

Instructions: Answer the following questions on a separate piece of paper.

1. To ensure appropriate and effective resource coordination, what roles should be performed by the case management or utilization review staff?

2. What effect does the charge capture process have on the reimbursement received for services?

3. What is the relationship between charging source systems and the CDM?

4. To ensure multidisciplinary representation, what areas should be involved in the chargemaster committee?

5. What are the key goals of a clinical documentation improvement program?

6. How is the hospital case mix index calculated?

Revenue Cycle Back-End Process

Claims Processing

Claims processing involves accumulating charges for services, submitting claims for reimbursement, and ensuring that claims are satisfied. The patient financial services or billing area has the responsibility for the collection of revenue for the patient encounter. Once a patient has been discharged, the goal is to get a complete and accurate claim generated and submitted for payment as quickly as possible. Organizations routinely measure **accounts receivable (A/R) days**—the average number of days between the provision of services and the receipt of payment for those services as a measure of how successful their revenue cycle is. An efficient revenue cycle helps the organization lower the A/R days, which in turn improves cash flow.

Claims processing is sometimes outsourced in nonhospital ambulatory care because physician offices and other small facilities often do not have the resources to perform this complex activity effectively. The activity of submitting a claim is often called dropping a bill. Because reimbursement for clinical services provided is the healthcare facility's largest source of revenue, timely, accurate claims processing is necessary.

Most billing systems are programmed to automatically submit claims to the payers (after the bill hold time frame) if the account is not being held for any type of edit resolution, and these are often referred to as **clean claims**. Because there are so many complex rules and edits, manual intervention is required for many claims, but the goal is to continually increase the percentage of clean claims that can be billed with no intervention. The sophistication level of the organization's billing system determines how much is able to be programmed into the system vs. how much has to be handled manually by the billing staff.

America's Health Insurance Plans, Washington, D.C., released a study to show the percentage of claims received electronically was 82 percent in 2009, up from 75 percent in 2006 and 44 percent in 2002 (AHIP 2009). The study also showed a notable lag before health insurance plans receive claims from healthcare providers. Twenty-two percent of claims received from healthcare providers were greater than 30 days after the date of patient service, and 12 percent of claims were received more than 60 days after the date of the patient's service. The 2009 survey also showed health insurance plans processed nearly 99 percent of clean claims within 60 days, and 97 percent within 30 days.

Payment Posting

Payment is received from third-party payers and patients in various ways, and the payments must be posted to the correct individual patient accounts. Internally, some allocation of the revenue must be made to the various areas that provided services. This process is established by the organization's financial accounting area, and the methods of allocation may vary. Since payment received does not equal the amount that was billed, it is a complex process to determine the correct allocations and to post the necessary payments, adjustments, and discounts to the correct accounts. Ultimately, the account balance on each patient's account must equal zero (Nelson 2011). There are instances when too many payments are posted to the accounts because there can be multiple payments from one or more insurance companies and copayment or coinsurance payments received from the patient. In these cases, the account has a negative balance, and it must be determined where the overpayments occurred, so funds can be refunded to the correct payer or to the patient.

Follow-up

Once payment is received from third-party payers and the discounts and adjustments are applied to the balance on the account, there may still be a portion that is due from the patient (related to deductibles, coinsurance, and copayments). The patient financial services staff works to collect this portion from the patient and to appropriately refer patients to medical assistance or other programs or apply charge discounts as applicable.

Organizations may also utilize third-party collection agencies to assist with collection of payment on problem accounts. These engagements may also necessitate a relationship with a third-party collection attorney and an internal legal review team that reviews all accounts prior to legal collection.

Denial Management

Denials may simply be defined as a payer's refusal to provide payment. According to the Advisory Board Company, the nation's largest hospital research organization, the cost of denials to healthcare organizations ranges from 1 to 3 percent of total revenue. Approximately 90 percent of denials are preventable and 67 percent are recoverable (Fontaine n.d.). The most common reasons for the denials include

- Beneficiary not covered
- Lack of medical necessity—not reasonable or necessary
- Lack of precertification
- Inappropriate utilization
- Noncovered services
- Incorrect charging—unbundled code
- Incorrect coding
  - Procedure code does not match patient sex
  - Diagnosis procedure code does not match service provided
  - Procedure code inconsistent with modifier used
  - Procedure code inconsistent with place of service
  - Diagnosis inconsistent with age, sex, and procedure
  - Modifier not provided
- Late charges or untimely filing

A denial management program requires facilities to seek both prevention and recovery. Denials management requires a cross-functional team to evaluate reasons for the denials and to facilitate changes in work processes to prevent further denials from occurring. Denial team stakeholders often include staff or managers from departments such as patient financial services or billing; HIM; compliance; revenue integrity or chargemaster; patient access, including registration, admissions, and surgery scheduling; utilization or case management; contracting; finance; and various ancillary services and clinics where the denials may be occurring. A successful denial management program includes the following:

- Focus on recovery of lost reimbursement and prevention of further denial
- Teamwork to manage the denials
- Need to appropriately value the staff and provide appropriate and clear work guidelines, standards, and expectations
- Investment in staff training and education
- Utilization of technology to assist with processes
- Creation of a departmental dashboard to monitor progress of team efforts used to
  - Measure individual department against a benchmark
  - Compare individual departments against the organization as a whole
  - Trend success within a department
- Denial tracking by payer
- Identification, quantification, and sorting by carrier
- Identification of trends that are not "true" denials but potential stall tactics
- Sharing of specific examples with managed care or contracting departments (Dunn 2009)

Revenue Audit and Recovery

After payment has been received, it is audited against the terms of the contract to determine whether the organization has received the correct reimbursement. Since the terms of payer contracts are usually very complex, the revenue audit and recovery function is greatly enhanced by the use of software systems that model the contracts and produce reports of accounts with variation to the expected reimbursement.

To achieve optimum benefit, audits should occur for all payment relationships that can be modeled. The government payers and most commercial payers have fairly straightforward terms of reimbursement without a lot of specific language. Those payers that negotiate specific terms of a contract with the organization's contracting team usually have more complex terms of payment and variations for various plans or products offered by their company. It is particularly helpful to model the specific terms of these contracts in a software system in order to detect variation in payment.

In organizations utilizing modeling software, the information about expected reimbursement is calculated after all charges have been posted to the account and the bill has been submitted to the payer. The level of detail specified in negotiated contracts requires the software modeling programs to create a hierarchy when there are multiple types of services provided to the patient. Once payment is received and the reimbursement amounts are posted to the account, the software system generates a weekly or monthly report of all accounts with payment variation. A threshold is usually established for the percentage of variation that must exist in order for an account to be included on the variation report. The number of accounts may be too high to enable a 100 percent review, so guidelines should be established to determine which accounts will be reviewed. Reports can be generated to allow review of accounts by a specific payer, a payer plan, inpatients vs. outpatients, accounts with high dollar amount, and such.

Payments are examined against the Explanation of Benefits (EOB) to see if specific items were paid or if they were considered to be bundled services or were denied or returned to the provider for correction. The audit may detect errors in the modeling that was applied or errors in insurance assignment at the time of registration. This provides an opportunity to provide feedback and further staff education. The audit may also detect patterns of underpayments or overpayments, which can initiate a focus on accounts with similar charges.

Technology Tools

Tools identified by the HIMSS Revenue Cycle Improvement Task Force (2009) to support the back-end process include

- Workflow claims management system for follow-up
- Denial management system
- Contract management system
- Claims editing system
- Integration to payers for automated claims status and cash posting
- Telephony system in order to measure call activity
- Electronic financial assistance application

Instructions: Answer the following questions on a separate piece of paper

1. How are an organization's accounts receivable days impacted by its bill hold days and its percentage of clean claim submissions?

2. What factors can cause a patient account balance to display a negative amount?

3. What are four of the most common reasons for billing denials?

4. What criteria are used to select claims that should be audited to determine whether proper reimbursement has been received?

Strategies for Revenue Cycle Success

Quality Measures for Improvement

Increasing revenue cycle performance can have a positive impact on a healthcare organization's financial bottom line (see table 17.4). Measuring the various processes of the revenue cycle against established benchmarks provides an opportunity for organizations to focus on areas to improve. Influences such as geographical location, bed size, payer mix, net patient revenue, and the mix of inpatient, outpatient, and emergency room visits can impact the revenue cycle (HFMA 2011). The Healthcare Financial Management Association (HFMA) defined key measures to evaluate revenue cycle performance. The tool allows hospitals to track its revenue cycle performance using industry-standard metrics and compare the results with peer groups based upon the aforementioned influences (table 17.5).

Key performance indicators (KPIs) allow healthcare facilities to measure and benchmark their data against best practice. The KPIs were developed by the HFMA based upon research from HFMA publications, forums, and website; the American Health Information Management Association publications and website; accounting firms; vendor internal standards and client data; and hospital accounts receivable analysis report standards (Hammer 2007).

Table 17.4.   Benchmarking

Use of Benchmarking Can Drive Significant Improvements			
Key Performance Indicator	Top Quartile	Median	Difference
Days in A/R	37.7	43.1	5.4
Point-of-Service Cash Collection	46%	30%	16%

Source: Analysis of HFMA's MAP App^SM, September 2010.

In addition to measuring key revenue cycle tasks, seven additional strategies for success include the following:

- There needs to be an organization focus on revenue cycle improvement, and a dedicated team should be put into place to maintain the focus.
- Metrics need to be used to conduct root cause analysis to facilitate changes throughout the healthcare system.
- There needs to be a shared sense of accountability for revenue cycle performance.
- Collaboration with other departments to enhance the revenue cycle performance needs to become an organizational focus.
- A comprehensive approach needs to be developed to address uncompensated care.
- The organization needs to find innovative ways to enhance customer service.
- The organization must focus on improving the total patient experience (Williams 2011).

Technology plays a key role in successful revenue cycle management by supporting effective and efficient operational practices. Healthcare financial improvement can be enhanced by employing the following tools and techniques:

- Enforce accountability.
- Monitor goals in a timely manner.
- Report results using a balanced scorecard technique.
- Establish a goal of overhead costs as a percentage of total costs.
- Adopt flexible budgeting.
- Adopt benchmarking.
- Develop percentile goals.
- Determine labor ratio goals.
- Reduce resource consumption.
- Purchase and use effective cost-management tools. (Berger 2007)

HFMA developed additional indicators to consistently measure the key performance indicators known as **MAP keys**. The purpose was to develop the standard for revenue cycle excellence. Each MAP key measures a specific revenue cycle function and provides the purpose for the measurement, the value of the measure, and the specific equation (numerator and denominator) to consistently calculate the measure. Examples of MAP keys are found in table 17.6.

Instructions: Answer the following questions on a separate piece of paper

1. What is the purpose of MAP keys?

2. Name four key strategies of success for the revenue cycle.

3. How do you measure late charges as a percentage of total charges?

Table 17.5. HFMA denial key performance indicators

Denial Type	Percent
Overall initial denials rate (% of gross revenue)	≤ 4%
Clinical initial denials rate (% of gross revenue)	≤ 5%
Technical initial denials rate (% of gross revenue)	≤ 3%
Underpayments additional collection rate	≥ 75%
Appealed denials overturned rate	40–60%
Electronic eligibility rate	≥ 75%
Physician precertification double-check rate	100%
Case managers' time spent securing authorization	≤ 20%
Total denial reason codes	≤ 25%
Scheduling	**Percent**
Overall scheduling rate of potentially eligible patients	100%
• Scheduling rate for elective and urgent inpatients	100%
• Scheduling rate for ambulatory surgery patients	100%
• Scheduling rate for high-dollar outpatient diagnostic patients	100%
Scheduled patients' preregistration rate	98%
Registration/Preregistration	**Percent**
Overall preregistration rate of scheduled patients	≥ 98%
Overall insurance verification rate of preregistered patients	≥ 98%
Data quality compared with pre-established department standards	≥ 99%
Health Information	**Percent**
Copies of medical records pursuant to payers' requests	≥ 2 days
Potential "over codes" beyond 75th percentile	≥ 2%
Potential "under codes" below 10th percentile	≥ 2%
Data quality compared with pre-established department standards	≥ 99%
Chargemaster	**Percent**
Chargemaster duplicate items	0%
Chargemaster incorrect or missing HCPCS/CPT-4 codes	0%
Chargemaster incorrect or invalid revenue codes	0%
Chargemaster revenue code lacks necessary HCPCS/CPT-4 code	0%
Chargemaster item has invalid or incorrect modifier	0%
Chargemaster item has missing modifier	0%
Chargemaster item description is "miscellaneous"	0%

Table 17.6. Examples of MAP keys

Measure	Purpose	Value	Equation
Point-of-Service Cash Collections	Trending indicator of point-of-service collection efforts	Indicates revenue cycle efficiency and effectiveness	N: Number of patient encounters preregistered
			D: Number of scheduled patient encounters
Preregistration Rate	Trending indicator that patient access processes are timely, accurate, and efficient	Indicates revenue cycle efficiency and effectiveness	N: Number of patient encounters preregistered
			D: Number of scheduled patient encounters
Insurance Verification Rate	Trending indicator that patient access functions are timely, accurate, and efficient	Indicates revenue cycle process efficiency and effectiveness	N: Total number of verified encounters
			D: Total number of registered encounters
Service Authorization Rate	Trending indicator that patient access functions are timely, accurate, and efficient	Indicates revenue cycle process efficiency and effectiveness	N: Number of encounters authorized
			D: Number of encounters requiring authorization
Days in Total Discharged, No Final Bill (DNFB)	Trending indicator of claims generation process	Indicates revenue cycle performance and can identify performance issues impacting cash flow	N: Gross dollars in A/R (no final billed)
			D: Average daily gross revenue
Days in Total Discharged, Not Submitted to Payer (DNSP)	Trending indicator of total claims generation and submission process	Indicates revenue cycle performance and can identify performance issues impacting cash flow	N: gross dollars in DNFB + gross dollars in FBNS
			D: Average daily gross revenue
Late Charges as % of Total Charges	Measure of revenue capture efficiency	Indicates revenue cycle performance and can identify performance issues impacting cash flow	N: Charges with post date greater than 3 days from last service date
			D: Total gross charges
Net Days Revenue in Credit Balance	Trending indicator to accurately report account values, ensure compliance with regulatory requirements, and monitor overall payment system effectiveness	Indicates whether credit balances are being managed to appropriate levels and are compliant with regulatory requirements	N: Dollars in credit balance
			D: Average daily net patient services revenue

Source: HFMA 2012.

Summary

Effective management of the revenue cycle is an important piece of improving the net revenue for a facility. Successful revenue cycle management requires streamlined workflow processes throughout the life cycle. The goal is to get revenue to flow quickly and efficiently through all steps in the cycle. To achieve that goal, it is necessary to understand each of the steps and the detailed processes that take place within them. It is also important to monitor and audit all the steps to uncover processes that are inefficient or are in need of improvement. Organizations should conduct research to identify best practices in each area and attempt to model those practices where possible. When conducting evaluation of processes, it is necessary to examine the flow of events and the interrelationships among them, as opportunities for improvement may exist there. Once improvement efforts are initiated and efficiency of processes and workflow has been achieved, there must be controls in place to sustain those improvements.

References

2008–2009 Healthcare Information and Management Systems Society Financial Systems Revenue Cycle Task Force. 2009. Revenue cycle management: A life cycle approach. http://www.himss.org/content/files/20090909RCMTFwhitepaper.pdf.

America's Health Insurance Plans Center for Policy and Research. 2009. An updated survey of health care claims receipt and processing times. http://www.ahipresearch.org/pdfs/SurveyHealthCare-Jan252010.pdf.

American Case Management Association. 2012. Definition of case management. American Case Management Association. http://acmaweb.org/section.asp?sID=4&mn=mn1&sn=sn1&wpg=mh.

American Health Information Management Association. 2010a. Clinical documentation tool kit. Chicago: AHIMA. http://library.ahima.org/xpedio/groups/public/ documents/ahima/bok1_047236.pdf.

American Health Information Management Association. 2010b. Care and maintenance of chargemasters (Updated). Chicago: AHIMA. http://library.ahima.org/xpedio/ groups/public/ documents/ahima/bok1_047258.hcsp?dDocName=bok1_047258.

Anderson, H.J. 2009 (March). Unraveling the claims snarl. Health-Data Management.com. http://www.healthdatamanagement.com/issues/2009_62/27764-1.html.

Berger, S. 2007. Treating technology as a luxury? 10 necessary tools. Healthcare Financial Management Association. http://www.hfma.org/Templates/InteriorMaster.aspx?id=341.

Bowman, S. 2008. Analysis of final rule for 2008 revisions to the Medicare hospital outpatient prospective payment system. Chicago: AHIMA. http://library.ahima.org/xpedio/groups/public/documents/ahima/bok1_044014.pdf.

Butcher, L. 2012. Centralizing registration boosts collections, patient experience at Crozer-Keystone. Healthcare Financial Management Association. http://www.hfma.org/Templates/InteriorMaster.aspx?id=30451.

Case Management Society of America. 2012. What is case management? http://cmsa.org/Home/CMSA/WhatisaCaseManager/tabid/224/Default.aspx.

Centers for Medicare and Medicaid Services. 2012. FFS HINNs. https://www.cms.gov/BNI/05_HINNs.asp.

Centers for Medicare and Medicaid Services. 2008. OPPS Final Rule. http://www.cms.gov/Medicare/Medicare-Fee-for-Service-Payment/HospitalOutpatientPPS/downloads//CMS-1404-FC.pdf.

Corrigan, J. 2009. Improving patient access. Healthcare Financial Management Association. http://findarticles.com/p/articles/mi_m3257/is_6_63/ai_n35529547/.

Daniels, S. 2007. The business case for hospital case management. http://phoenixmed.net/articles/the-business-case-for-hospital-case-management.html.

Daniels, S., and J. Frater. 2011. Hospital case management and progression of care. Healthcare Financial Management Association. http://www.hfma.org/Templates/ InteriorMaster.aspx?id=28178.

Dunn, R. 2009. Improving cash flow in a down economy: How HIM can help reduce denial. Journal of AHIMA 80(3).

Fontaine, C. n.d. Implementing a culture of denial prevention. Optum Health Webinar. http://go.ingenix.com/provider/webinar/denialprevention_3_15.pdf.

Goudzwaard, L. 2007. Point-of-service collections in healthcare. http://www.fhscorp.net/FHSCorp_POSCollectionsInHealthcare.pdf.

Guyton, E., R. Madison, and T. DeMarco. 2005. Time for patient payment strategies. Healthcare Financial Management Association. http://www.hfma.org/Templates/InteriorMaster.aspx?id=301.

Hammer, D. 2009. Using key performance indicators to prepare for contract renegotiation. Northeast New York HFMA Education Session. http://www.hfmaneny.org/Key%20Performance%20Indicators%20by%20David%20Hammer.ppt.

Hammer, D. 2007. The next generation of revenue cycle management: The revenue cycle universe is changing. Are your revenue cycle operations keeping up? Healthcare Financial Management July 01: 51–57.

HASC Summit on Administrative Simplification Final Report. 2009. Bringing better value: Recommendations to address the costs and causes of administrative complexity in the nation's healthcare system. http://www.ahima.org/downloads/pdfs/advocacy/ HASCReport20090717.pdf.

Healthcare Financial Management Association. 2011. Research shows path to revenue cycle gains through effective benchmarking. Special Research Report. http://www.hfma.org/Templates/InteriorMaster.aspx?id=29124.

Healthcare Financial Management Association. 2012. hfmap: Revenue cycle excellence. HFMA recently released 8 new MAP keys for physician practice management. http://www.hfmamap.org/mapkeys/.

Healthcare Financial Management Association. 2007 (June). Missed opportunities—your strategy for correct—and complete—charge capture. Educational Report. http://www.hfma.org/Templates/ InteriorMaster.aspx?id=2690.

HFMA 2008–2009 Principles and Practices Board. 2010. P&P Board Sample 501(c)(3) Hospital Charity Care Policy and Procedures. Healthcare Financial Management Association. http://www.hfma.org/Templates/InteriorMaster.aspx?id=240.

Langford, A., L. Dye, J. Moresco, and D. Riefner. 2010. Improving the revenue cycle by taking the patient's perspective. Healthcare Financial Management Association. http://www.hfma.org/Templates/InteriorMaster.aspx?id=22654.

McLean, D. 2011a. Authority and responsibility for the utilization management (UM) plan. RACmonitor. http://racmonitor.com/news/33-top-stories/696-authority-and-responsibility-for-the-utilization-management-um-plan.html.

McLean, D. 2011b. The essential requirements for effective utilization review. RACmonitor. http://racmonitor.com/news/27-racenews/724-the-essential-requirements-for-effective-utilization-review.html.

Miodonski, K. 2011. The role of case managers in controlling hospital costs. Fierce Health Finance. http://www.fiercehealthfinance.com/story/role-case-managers-controlling-hospital-costs/2011-05-31.

Nelson, R. 2011. What's this about revenue cycle management? http://www.medpagetoday.com/Columns/PracticePointers/24796.

OptumInsight. 2011 (November). Hospital chargemaster guide. Real life applications. November 11, 43–45.

Page, L. 2010. Five tips on point-of-service collections. Hospital Management Administration. Association. http://www.beckershospitalreview.com/hospital-management-administration/five-tips-on-point-of-service-collections.html.

Shorrosh, P. 2011. The hidden KPI: Registration accuracy. Healthcare Financial Management Association. http://www.hfma.org/Templates/ InteriorMaster.aspx?id=28451.

Schraffenberger, L.A., ed. 2011. *Effective Management of Coding Services*, 4th ed. Chicago: AHIMA.

Shuler, G. 2011 (August 12). Chargemaster 101—let's start at the beginning. Minnesota Hospital Association Education Program.

Utilization Review Accreditation Commission. 2012. What is utilization management? https://www.urac.org/resources/caremanagement.aspx#um.

Williams, J. 2011. Mapping out strategies for improving value in the revenue cycle. Health care Financial Management Association. http://www.hfmamap.org/wp-content/uploads/2011/09/0911_HFM_Map.pdf.

Yarbrough, L. 2007. Improving Point-of-service collections. For the Record. http://www.fortherecordmag.com/archives/ftr_07232007p10.shtml.

part **V**

Comparative Healthcare Data

chapter 18

Healthcare Statistics

Loretta A. Horton, MEd, RHIA

Learning Objectives

- Define measurement
- Differentiate among nominal-level, ordinal-level, interval-level, and ratio-level data
- Identify various ways in which statistics are used in healthcare
- Differentiate between descriptive and inferential statistics
- Define hospital-related statistical terms
- Calculate hospital-related inpatient and outpatient statistics
- Define community-based morbidity and mortality rates
- Calculate community-based morbidity and mortality rates

- Define and calculate measures of central tendency and variability
- Describe the characteristics of the normal distribution
- Identify the relationships of measures of central tendency and variation to the normal distribution
- Display healthcare data using tables, charts, and graphs, as appropriate
- Calculate the case-mix index
- Locate healthcare-related state and federal databases on the Internet
- Use healthcare data collected from online databases in comparative statistical reports

Key Terms

Acute care
Ambulatory surgery center (ASC)
Average daily census
Average length of stay (ALOS)
Bar chart
Bed count
Bed count day
Bed turnover rate
Boxplot
Bubble chart
Case fatality rate
Case mix
Case-mix index (CMI)
Cause-specific death rate
Census
Clinic outpatient
Consultation rate
Continuous variable

Crude birth rate
Crude death rate
Daily inpatient census
Descriptive statistics
Discrete variable
Emergency outpatient
Encounter
Fetal autopsy rate
Fetal death
Fetal death rate
Frequency distribution
Frequency polygon
Gross autopsy rate
Gross death rate
Histogram
Hospital ambulatory care
Hospital autopsy
Hospital autopsy rate

Hospital death rate
Hospital inpatient
Hospital inpatient autopsy
Hospital newborn inpatient
Hospital outpatient
Hospital-acquired (nosocomial) infection rate
Incidence rate
Infant mortality rate
Inferential statistics
Inpatient admission
Inpatient bed occupancy rate (percentage of occupancy)
Inpatient discharge
Inpatient hospitalization
Inpatient service day (IPSD)
Interval-level data
Length of stay (LOS)
Line graph
Maternal death rate
Maternal mortality rate
Mean
Measure of central tendency
Median
Mode
National Vital Statistics System (NVSS)
Neonatal mortality rate
Net autopsy rate
Net death rate
Newborn (NB)
Newborn autopsy rate
Newborn death rate

Nominal-level data
Normal distribution
Nosocomial infection
Notifiable disease
Occasion of service
Ordinal-level data
Outpatient
Outpatient visit
Pie chart
Population-based statistics
Postneonatal mortality rate
Postoperative infection rate
Prevalence rate
Proportion
Proportionate mortality ratio (PMR)
Range
Rate
Ratio
Ratio-level data
Referred outpatient
Scale of measurement
Scatter chart
Standard deviation
Stem and leaf plot
Surgical operation
Surgical procedure
Total length of stay
Variability
Variance
Vital statistics

Complete and accurate information is at the heart of good decision making. The health information management (HIM) professional has responsibility for ensuring that the data collected are accurate and organized into information that is useful to healthcare decision makers.

The primary source of clinical data in a healthcare facility is the health record. To be useful in decision making, data taken from the health record must be as complete and accurate as possible. Data are compiled in various ways to help in making decisions about patient care, the facility's financial status, and facility planning, to name a few issues.

This chapter discusses common statistical measures and types of data used by organizations in different healthcare settings and data collection and reporting on a community, regional, and national basis. Methods and tools for graphically displaying data are then presented along with a discussion of normal distribution and descriptive statistics.

Introduction to Measurement

Before discussing statistical measures used in healthcare, it is important to understand what measurement is and how the data collected are classified. Measurement simply refers to measuring an "attribute or property of a person, object, or event according to a particular set of rules" (Osborn 2005, 66). The result of the measurement will be numbers. And the "particular set of rules" refers to what will be collected and how it will be collected so that the resulting numbers "will be meaningful, accurate, and informative" (Osborn 2005, 66). In other words, the process of collecting the data must be consistent in order to ensure the results are the same no matter who is collecting the data. If there is consistency in the data collection we will be able to make comparisons in our own facilities and across facilities.

Data collected falls on one of four **scales of measurement:** nominal, ordinal, interval, or ratio. Furthermore, the data collected are described as either continuous or discrete. These characteristics influence the type of graphic technique that can be used to display the data and the types of statistical analyses that can be performed.

Nominal-level data fall into groups or categories. This is a scale that measures data by name only. The groups or categories are mutually exclusive, that is, a data element cannot be classified to more than one group. Some examples of nominal data collected in healthcare are related to patient demographics such as third-party payer, race, and sex. There is no order to the data collected within these categories.

Data that fall on the ordinal scale have some inherent order, and higher numbers are usually associated with higher values. In **ordinal-level data,** the order of the numbers is meaningful, not the number itself. Staging of a pressure ulcer is an example of a variable that has order. A pressure ulcer has four stages, with stage I being the least severe ulcer and stage IV being the most severe. In this example, the higher number is associated with the most severe type of pressure ulcer; however, we cannot measure the difference between the levels in exact numerical terms.

The most important characteristic of **interval-level data** is that the intervals between successive values are equal. On the Fahrenheit scale, for example, the interval between 20°F and 21°F is the same as between 21°F and 22°F. But because there is no true zero on this scale, we cannot say that 40°F is twice as warm as 20°F.

The **ratio-level data scale** is the highest level of measurement. On the ratio scale there is a defined unit of measure, a real zero point, and the intervals between successive values are equal. A real zero point means that there is an absolute zero. Only when a zero on a scale truly means the total absence of a property being assessed can that scale be described as ratio level. For example, consider the variable "length of stay." **Length of stay (LOS)** has defined unit of measurement, day, and a real zero point—0 days. Because there is a real zero point, we can state that an LOS of six days is twice as long as an LOS of three days. Multiplication on the ratio scale by a constant does not change its ratio character, but addition of a constant to a ratio measure does. For example, if we add two days to each LOS so that the stays are 8 and 5 days, respectively, the ratio of their stays is no longer 2:1. However, if we multiply the respective lengths of stay by 2 (for example, 6 × 2 and 3 × 2), the ratio between the two lengths of stay remains 2:1.

The difference between the ratio and interval scales of measurement is that there is no true zero point on the interval scale.

This fourfold structure is a useful classification for data, and the four levels are hierarchically arranged so that higher levels include the key properties of the levels so that ratio-level data include the three key properties found in nominal-, ordinal-, and interval-level data.

Discrete versus Continuous Data

Another way to classify data involves categorizing them as either being *discrete* or *continuous*. Data that are nominal or ordinal are also considered discrete. **Discrete variables** are those that fall into categories. For example, the variable "gender" has two categories: male and female. The variable "third-party payer" has a number of categories, depending on the healthcare facility. Examples include Medicare, Medicaid, commercial insurance, and private insurance or self-pay.

Discrete variables can only take on a limited number of values and have gaps between successive values. In the pressure ulcer example, the ulcer can be a stage I, II, III, or IV (limited number of values). It cannot be staged as 2.5 or 3.2, as there are "gaps" between each stage. This is an example of a discrete variable that has order to its categories.

Continuous variables are either interval or ratio level, but some ratio-level variables are discrete. For example, if you wanted to compare the number of patients on two different nursing units you could count 5 on one unit and 10 on another. These data are discrete. But you could also say that there are twice as many patients on one unit as there are on the other. And there could be zero patients on one unit; this would be a true zero because it absolutely corresponds to the total absence of the variable you are assessing—the number of patients on each unit. With **continuous variables** there are no gaps in the measurement data. For example, an individual's weight may be 120 or 121 or any weight between 120 and 121. Continuous variables include fractions. Arithmetic operations—addition, subtraction, multiplication, and division—may be performed on continuous variables.

Check Your Understanding 18.1

Instructions: On a separate piece of paper, identify the scale of measurement for each of the following variables and indicate which scale of measurement each variable listed below represents.
Scales of Measurement:

Interval

Nominal

Ordinal

Ratio

1. ___ Zip code
2. ___ Blood pressure
3. ___ Heart failure classification I, II, III, IV
4. ___ Age
5. ___ Ethnicity
6. ___ Marital status
7. ___ Length of stay
8. ___ Discharge disposition (home, skilled nursing facility, and so on)
9. ___ Weight
10. ___ Level of education
11. ___ Race
12. ___ Temperature in degrees Fahrenheit
13. ___ Types of third-party payers
14. ___ Gender
15. ___ Height

Common Statistical Measures Used in Healthcare

Healthcare data are collected to describe the health status of groups or populations. The data reported about healthcare facilities and communities describe the occurrence of illnesses, births, and deaths for specific periods of time. Data that are collected may be either facility based or population based. The sources of facility-based statistics are **acute-care** facilities, long-term care facilities, and other types of healthcare organizations. The population-based statistics are gathered from cities, counties, states, or specific groups within the population, such as individuals affected by diabetes.

Reporting statistics for a healthcare facility is similar to reporting statistics for a community. Rates for healthcare facilities are reported as per 100 cases or percent; a community rate is reported as per 1,000, 10,000, or 100,000 people. For example, if a hospital experienced 2 deaths in a given month and 100 patients were discharged in the same month, the death rate would be 2 percent ([2/100]/100). If there were 200 deaths in a community of 80,000 for a given period of time, the death rate would be reported as 25 deaths per 10,000 population ([200/10,000]/80,000) for the same period of time.

Ratios, Proportions, and Rates: Three Common Examples of Ratio-Level Data Worth Knowing

Many healthcare statistics are reported in the form of a ratio, proportion, or rate. These measures are used to report morbidity (illness), mortality (death), and natality (birthrate) at the local, state, and national levels. Basically, these measures indicate the number of times something happened relative to the number of times it could have happened. All three measures are based on formula 18.1. In this formula, x and y are the quantities being compared, and x is divided by y. Further, 10^n is 10 to the nth power. The size of 10^n may equal 10, 100, 1,000, 10,000, and so on, depending on the value of n:

$$10^0 = 1$$
$$10^1 = 10$$
$$10^2 = 10 \times 10 = 100$$
$$10^3 = 10 \times 10 \times 10 = 1,000$$

Formula 18.1.   General formula for calculating rates, proportions, and ratios

Ratio, proportion, rate = $x/y \times 10^n$

Ratios

In a **ratio**, the quantities being compared, such as patient discharge status (x = alive, y = dead), may be expressed so that x and y are completely independent of each other, or x may be included in y. For example, the outcome of patients

Figure 18.1.   Calculation of a ratio; discharge status of patients discharged in a month

1. Define x and y:
    x = number of patients discharged alive
    y = number of patients who died

2. Identify x and y:
    x = 235
    y = 22

3. Set up the ratio x/y:
    235/22

4. Reduce the fraction so that either x or y equals 1:
    10.68/1

There were 10.68 live discharges for every patient who died.

discharged from Community Hospital could be compared in one of two ways:

Alive/dead, or x/y

Alive/(alive + dead), or $x/(x + y)$

In the first example, x is completely independent of y. The ratio represents the number of patients discharged alive compared to the number of patients who died. In the second example, x is part of the whole ($x + y$). The ratio represents the number of patients discharged alive compared to all patients discharged. Both expressions are considered ratios.

Proportions

A **proportion** is a particular type of ratio in which x is a portion of the whole ($x + y$). In a proportion, the numerator is always included in the denominator. Figures 18.1 and 18.2 describe the procedures for calculating ratios and proportions, respectively.

Rates

Rates are often used to measure events over a period of time. Sometimes they also are used in performance improvement studies. Like ratios and proportions, rates may be reported daily, weekly, monthly, or yearly. This allows for trend analysis and comparisons over time. The basic formula for calculating a rate is shown in formula 18.2.

Figure 18.2.   Calculation of a proportion; discharge status of patients discharged in a month

1. Define x and y:
    x = number of patients discharged alive
    y = number of patients who died

2. Identify x and y:
    x = 235
    y = 22

3. Set up the proportion $x/(x + y)$:
    235/(235 + 22) = 235/257

4. Reduce the fraction so that either x or y equals 1:
    0.91/1

The proportion of patients discharged alive was 0.91.

Formula 18.2. Calculating risk for contracting a disease

$$\text{Risk rate} = \frac{\text{Number of cases occurring during a given time period}}{\text{Total number of cases or population at risk during the same time period}}$$

Healthcare facilities calculate many types of morbidity and mortality rates. For example, the C-section rate is a measure of the proportion, or percentage, of C-sections performed during a given period of time. C-section rates are closely monitored because they present more risk to the mother and baby and because they are more expensive than vaginal deliveries. In calculating the C-section rate, the number of C-sections performed during the specified period of time is counted, and this value is placed in the numerator. The number of cases, or the population at risk, is the number of women who delivered during the same time period. This number is placed in the denominator. By convention, inpatient hospital rates are reported as the rate per 100 cases ($10^n = 10^2 = 10 \times 10 = 100$) and are expressed as percentages.

Figure 18.3 shows the procedure for calculating a rate. In the example, 30 of the 263 deliveries at Community Hospital during the month of May were C-sections. In the formula, the numerator is the number of C-sections performed in May (given period of time) and the denominator is the total number of deliveries including C-sections (the population at risk) performed within the same time frame. In calculating the rate, the numerator is always included in the denominator. Also, when calculating a facility-based rate, the numerator is first multiplied by 100 and then divided by the denominator.

Because hospital rates rarely result in a whole number, they usually must be rounded. The hospital should set a policy on whether rates are to be reported to one or two decimal places. The division should be carried out to at least one more decimal place than desired.

When rounding, if the last number is five or greater, the preceding number should be increased one digit. In contrast, if the last number is less than five, the preceding number remains the same. For example, when rounding 25.56 percent to one decimal place, the rate becomes 25.6 percent because the last number is greater than five. When rounding 1.563 percent to two places, the rate becomes 1.56 percent because the last digit is less than five. Rates of less than 1 percent are usually carried out to three decimal places and rounded to two. For rates less than 1 percent, a zero should precede the decimal to emphasize that the rate is less than 1 percent, for example, 0.56 percent.

Check Your Understanding 18.2

Instructions: On a separate piece of paper, identify the following statements as a rate, a ratio, or a proportion.

1. Medicare admissions outnumber commercial insurance admissions 3 to 2.

2. At the annual state HIM meeting, 85 of the registrants were female and 35 were male. Therefore 0.71 percent of the registrants were female.

3. Of the 250 patients admitted in the last six months, 36 percent had Type II diabetes mellitus.

Figure 18.3. Calculation of a rate; C-section rate for May 20XX

During May, 263 women delivered; of these, 33 deliveries were by C-section. What is the C-section rate for May?

1. Define the numerator (number of times an event occurred) and the denominator (number of times an event could have occurred):
   Numerator = total number of C-sections performed during the time period
   Denominator = total number of deliveries, including C-sections, in the same time period

2. Identify the numerator and the denominator:
   Numerator = 33
   Denominator = 263

3. Set up the rate:
   33/263

4. Multiply the numerator by 100 and then divide by the denominator:
   $[(33 \times 100)/263] = 12.5\%$

The C-section rate for May is 12.5 percent.

Statistical Data Used in Healthcare Facilities

Acute-Care Statistical Data

In the daily operations of any organization, whether in business, manufacturing, or healthcare, data are collected for decision making. To be effective, the decision makers must have confidence in the data collected. Confidence requires that the data collected be accurate, reliable, and timely. The types of data collected in the acute-care setting are discussed in the following section.

Administrative Statistical Data

Hospitals collect data on both inpatients and outpatients on a daily basis. They use these statistics to monitor the volume of patients treated daily, weekly, monthly, or within some other specified time frame. The statistics give healthcare decision makers the information they need to plan facilities and services and to monitor inpatient and outpatient revenue streams. For these reasons, the HIM professional must be well versed in data collection and reporting methods.

Standard definitions have been developed to ensure that all healthcare providers collect and report data in a consistent manner. The *Pocket Glossary of Health Information Management and Technology,* developed by the American Health Information Management Association (AHIMA 2012), is a resource commonly used to describe the types of healthcare events for which data are collected. It includes definitions of terms related to healthcare organizations, health maintenance organizations (HMOs), and other health-related programs and facilities. Some basic terms that HIM professionals should be familiar with include the following:

- **Hospital inpatient:** A patient who is provided with room, board, and continuous general nursing service in an area of an acute-care facility where patients generally stay at least overnight
- **Hospital newborn inpatient:** A patient born in the hospital at the beginning of the current inpatient hospitalization.
  — Newborns are usually counted separately because their care is so different from that of other inpatients
  — Infants born on the way to the hospital or at home are considered hospital inpatients, not hospital newborn inpatients
- **Inpatient hospitalization:** The period during an individual's life when he or she is a patient in a single hospital without interruption except by possible intervening leaves of absence
- **Inpatient admission:** An acute-care facility's formal acceptance of a patient who is to be provided with room, board, and continuous nursing service in an area of the facility where patients generally stay overnight
- **Inpatient discharge:** The termination of hospitalization through the formal release of an inpatient by the hospital
  — The term includes patients who are discharged alive (by physician's order), who are discharged against medical advice (AMA), or who died while hospitalized
  — Unless otherwise indicated, inpatient discharges include deaths
- **Hospital outpatient:** A hospital patient who receives services in one or more of the hospital's facilities when he or she is not currently an inpatient or home care patient.
  — An outpatient may be classified as either an emergency outpatient or a clinic outpatient

- An emergency outpatient is admitted to the emergency department of a hospital for diagnosis and treatment of a condition that requires immediate medical, dental, or other emergency services
- A clinic outpatient is admitted to a clinical service of the clinic or hospital for diagnosis and treatment on an ambulatory basis

Inpatient Census Data

Even though much of the data collection process has been automated, an ongoing responsibility of the HIM professional is to verify the **census** data that are collected daily. The census reports patient activity for a 24-hour reporting period. Included in the census report are the number of inpatients admitted and discharged for the previous 24-hour period and the number of intrahospital transfers. An intrahospital transfer is a patient who is moved from one patient care unit to another (for example, a patient may be transferred from the intensive care unit [ICU] to the medicine unit). The usual 24-hour reporting period begins at 12:01 a.m. and ends at 12:00 midnight. In the census count, adults and children (A&C) are reported separately from newborns.

Before compiling census data, however, it is important to understand their related terminology. The census is the number of hospital inpatients present at any one time. For example, the census in a 300-bed hospital may be 250 patients at 2:00 p.m. on May 1 but 245 an hour later. Because the census may change throughout the day as admissions and discharges occur, hospitals designate an official census-taking time. In most facilities, the official count takes place at midnight. The census-reporting time can be any other time, but it must be consistent throughout the healthcare facility.

The result of the official count taken at midnight is called the **daily inpatient census**. This is the number of inpatients present at the official census-taking time each day. Also included in the daily inpatient census are any patients who were admitted and discharged that same day. For example, if a patient was admitted to the cardiac care unit (CCU) at 1:00 p.m. on May 1 and died at 4.00 p.m. on May 1, he would be counted as a patient who was both admitted and discharged the same day.

Because patients admitted and discharged the same day are not present at the census-taking time, the hospital must account for them separately. If it did not, credit for the services provided these patients would be lost. The daily inpatient census reflects the total number of patients treated during the 24-hour period. Figure 18.4 displays a sample daily inpatient census report.

A unit of measure that reflects the services received by one inpatient during a 24-hour period is called an **inpatient service day (IPSD).** The number of IPSDs for a 24-hour

Figure 18.4. Daily inpatient census report—adults and children

May 2	
Number of patients in hospital at midnight, May 1	230
+ Number of patients admitted May 2	+35
– Number of patients discharged, including deaths, May 2	–40
Number of patients in hospital at midnight, May 2	225
+ Number of patients both admitted and discharged, including deaths	+5
Daily inpatient census at midnight, May 2	230
Total inpatient service days, May 2	230

period is equal to the daily inpatient census, that is, one service day for each patient treated. In figure 18.4, the total number of inpatient service days for May 2 is 230.

IPSDs are compiled daily, weekly, monthly, and annually. They reflect the volume of services provided by the healthcare facility: the greater the volume of services, the greater the revenues to the facility. Daily reporting of the number of IPSDs is an indicator of the hospital's financial condition.

As mentioned, the daily inpatient census is equal to the number of IPSDs provided for that day as shown in table 18.1. Thus, the total number of IPSDs for a week, a month, and so on can be divided by the total number of days in the period of interest to obtain the **average daily census.** In the preceding example, 730 IPSDs is divided by three days to obtain an average daily census of 243.3.

Table 18.1. Inpatient service days

Day	Census	Same-Day Admissions and Discharges	Inpatient Service Days
Day 1	240	0	240
Day 2	253	0	253
Day 3	235	2	237
Total			730

Formula 18.3. Calculating the average daily census

$$\text{Average daily census} = \frac{\text{Total number of inpatient service days for a given period}}{\text{Total number of days in the same period}}$$

The average daily census is the average number of inpatients treated during a given period of time. The general formula for calculating the average daily census is shown in formula 18.3.

In calculating the average daily census, A&C and **newborns (NBs)** are reported separately. This is because the intensity of services provided to adults and children is greater than it is for newborns. To calculate the A&C average daily census, the general formula is modified as shown in formula 18.4. Many facilities use a whole number when calculating the census.

Formula 18.4. Calculating the average daily census for adults and children

$$\text{Average daily census for A\&C} = \frac{\text{Total number of inpatient service days for A\&C for a given period}}{\text{Total number of days for the same period}}$$

The formula for the average daily census for newborns is shown in formula 18.5. For example, the total number of IPSDs provided to adults and children for the week of May 1 is 1,729, and the total for newborns is 119. Using the formulas, the average daily census for adults and children is 247 (1,729/7) and for newborns it is 17 (119/7). The average daily census for all hospital inpatients for the week of May 1 is 264 ([1,729 + 119]/7). Table 18.2 compares the various formulas for calculating the average daily census.

Formula 18.5. Calculating the average daily census for newborns

$$\text{Average daily census for NBs} = \frac{\text{Total number of inpatient service days for NBs for a given period}}{\text{Total number of days for the same period}}$$

Table 18.2. Calculation of census statistics

Indicator	Numerator	Denominator
Average daily inpatient census	Total number of inpatient service days for a given period	Total number of days for the same period
Average daily inpatient census for A&C	Total number of inpatient service days for A&C for a given period	Total number of days for the same period
Average daily inpatient census for NBs	Total number of inpatient service days for NBs for a given period	Total number of days for the same period

Instructions: Answer the following questions on a separate piece of paper.

1. Community Hospital reported the following statistics for adults and children at 12:01 a.m. April 1: census 150; admissions 20; discharges 15; 1 patient admitted and died the same day; 1 patient admitted and discharged alive the same day. Calculate the following for April 2:

      A. Inpatient census
      B. Daily inpatient census
      C. Inpatient service days

2. Community Hospital reported the following statistics for their newborn unit at 12:01 a.m. April 1: census 14: births 5; discharges 3; 1 newborn born and transferred to University Hospital. Calculate the following for April 2:

      A. Inpatient census
      B. Daily inpatient census

3. Community Hospital reported the following statistics for its intensive care unit at 12:01 a.m. April 1: census 10; 1 patient admitted directly from the ESD; 1 patient transferred from surgery unit; 1 patient transferred from the medicine unit; 1 patient transferred to the Medicine unit; 1 patient admitted and died the same day. Calculate the following for April 2:

      A. Inpatient census
      B. Daily inpatient census

Inpatient Bed Occupancy Rate

Another indicator of the hospital's financial position is the **inpatient bed occupancy rate,** also called the **percentage of occupancy.** The inpatient bed occupancy rate is the percentage of official beds occupied by hospital inpatients for a given period of time. In general, the greater the occupancy rate, the greater the revenues for the hospital. For a bed to be included in the official count, it must be set up, staffed, equipped, and available for patient care. The total number of inpatient service days is used in the numerator because it is equal to the daily inpatient census or the number of patients treated daily. The occupancy rate compares the number of patients treated over a given period of time to the total number of beds available for the same period of time.

For example, if 200 patients occupied 280 beds on May 2, the inpatient bed occupancy rate would be 71.4 percent ([200/{280 × 1}] × 100). If the rate were for more than one day, the number of beds would be multiplied by the number of days within that particular time frame. For example, if 1,729 IPSDs were provided during the week of May 1, the inpatient bed occupancy rate for that week would be 88.2 percent ([1,729/{280 × 7}] × 100).

The denominator in this formula is actually the total possible number of IPSDs. That is, if every available bed in the hospital were occupied every single day, this would be the maximum number of IPSDs that could be provided. This is an important concept, especially when the official **bed count** changes for a given reporting period. For example, if the bed count changed from 280 beds to 300, the bed occupancy rate would reflect the change. The total number of inpatient beds times the total number of days in the period is called the total number of **bed count days.** The general formula for the inpatient bed occupancy rate is shown in formula 18.6.

Formula 18.6. Calculating the inpatient bed occupancy rate

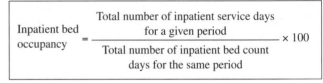

$$\text{Inpatient bed occupancy} = \frac{\text{Total number of inpatient service days for a given period}}{\text{Total number of inpatient bed count days for the same period}} \times 100$$

For example, in May the total number of inpatient service days provided was 7,582. The bed count for the month of May changed from 280 beds to 300 on May 20. To calculate the inpatient bed occupancy rate for May, the total number of bed count days must be determined. There are 31 days in May; therefore, the total number of bed count days is calculated as

Number of beds, May 1–May 19 = 280 × 19 days = 5,320 bed count days
Number of beds, May 20–May 31 = 300 × 12 days = 3,600 bed count days
5,320 + 3,600 = 8,920 bed count days

The inpatient bed occupancy rate for the month of May is 85.0 percent ([7,582/8,920] × 100).

As with the average daily census, the inpatient bed occupancy rate for adults and children is reported separately from that of newborns. To calculate the total number of bed count days for newborns, the official count for newborn bassinets is used. Table 18.3 reviews the formulas for calculating inpatient bed occupancy rates.

It is possible for the inpatient bed occupancy rate to be greater than 100 percent. This occurs when the hospital faces an epidemic or a disaster. In this type of situation, hospitals set up temporary beds that usually are not included in the official bed count. As an example, Community Hospital experienced an excessive number of admissions in January because of an outbreak of influenza. In January, the official bed count was 150 beds. On January 5, the daily inpatient census was 156. Therefore, the inpatient bed occupancy rate for January 5 was 104 percent ([156/150] × 100).

Bed Turnover Rate

The **bed turnover rate** is a measure of hospital utilization. It includes the number of times each hospital bed changed occupants. The formula for the bed turnover rate is shown in formula 18.7. For example, Community Hospital had 2,060 discharges and deaths for the month of May. Its bed count for May averaged 677. The bed turnover rate is 3.0 (2,060/677).

Table 18.3.   Calculation of inpatient bed occupancy rates

Rate	Numerator	Denominator
Inpatient bed occupancy rate	Total number of inpatient service days for a given period × 100	Total number of inpatient bed count days for the same period
Inpatient bed occupancy rate for A&C	Total number of inpatient service days for A&C for a given period × 100	Total number of inpatient bed count days for A&C for the same period
NB bed occupancy rate	Total number of NB inpatient service days for a given period × 100	Total number of bassinet bed count days for the same period

This simply means that on average, each hospital bed had three occupants during May.

Formula 18.7.   Calculating the bed turnover rate

$$\text{Bed turnover rate} = \frac{\text{Total number of discharges, including deaths, for a given time period}}{\text{Average bed count for the same time period}}$$

Check Your Understanding 18.4

Instructions: Answer the following questions on a separate piece of paper.

1. What is the inpatient bed occupancy rate for each of the following patient care units at Community Hospital for the month of June? Calculate to one decimal point.

Inpatient Unit	Service Days	Bed Count	Occupancy Rate
Medicine	580	36	_____
Surgery	689	42	_____
Pediatric	232	18	_____
Psychiatry	889	35	_____
Obstetrics	222	10	_____
Newborn	212	15	_____

2. Use the preceding information to determine the occupancy rate for Community Hospital—all adults and children (exclude newborns). Calculate to one decimal point.

3. On June 1, Community Hospital expanded the number of patient beds from 156 to 200. Use the following information to determine the occupancy rate for January to June; July to December; and the total for the year (non-leap year).

Months	Service Days	Bed Count
January–June	15672	156
July–December	25876	200

Length of Stay Data

LOS data are calculated for each patient after he or she is discharged from the hospital. It is the number of calendar days from the day of patient admission to the day of patient discharge. When the patient is admitted and discharged in the same month, the LOS is determined by simply subtracting the date of admission from the date of discharge. For example, the LOS for a patient admitted on May 12 and discharged on May 17 is five days (17 − 12 = 5)

When the patient is admitted in one month and discharged in another, the calculations must be adjusted. One way to calculate the LOS in this case is to subtract the date of admission from the total number of days in the month the patient was admitted and then add the total number of hospitalized days for the month in which the patient was discharged. For example, the LOS for a patient admitted on May 28 and discharged on June 6 is nine days ([May 31–May 28 = 3 days] + [June 1–June 6 = 6 days]; LOS = 9 days).

When a patient is admitted and discharged on the same day, the LOS is one day. A partial day's stay is never reported as a fraction of a day. The LOS for a patient discharged the day after admission also is one day. Thus, the LOS for a patient who was admitted to the ICU on May 10 at 9:00 a.m. and died at 3:00 p.m. on the same day is one day. Likewise, the LOS for a patient admitted on May 12 and discharged on May 13 is one day.

When the LOS for all patients discharged for a given period of time is summed, the result is the **total length of stay.** As an example, five patients were discharged from the pediatric unit on May 9. The LOS for each patient was as follows:

Patient	LOS
1	5
2	3
3	1
4	8
5	10
Total LOS	**27**

In the preceding example, the total LOS is 27 days (5 + 3 + 1 + 8 + 10). The total LOS is also referred to as the number

Table 18.4.   Calculation of LOS statistics

Indicator	Numerator	Denominator
Average LOS	Total LOS (discharge days) for a given period	Total number of discharges, including deaths, for the same period
Average LOS for A&C	Total LOS for A&C (discharge days) for a given period	Total number of discharges, including deaths, for A&C for the same period
Average LOS for NBs	Total LOS for all NB discharges and deaths (discharge days) for a given period	Total number of NB discharges, including deaths, for the same period

of days of care provided to patients who were discharged or died (discharge days) during a given period of time.

The **average length of stay (ALOS)** is calculated from the total LOS. The total LOS divided by the number of patients discharged is the ALOS. Using the data in the preceding example, the ALOS for the five patients discharged from the pediatric unit on May 9 is 5.4 days (27/5)

The general formula for calculating ALOS is shown in formula 18.8. As with the measures already discussed, the ALOS for adults and children is reported separately from the ALOS for newborns. Table 18.4 reviews the formulas for ALOS. Table 18.5 displays an example of a hospital statistical summary prepared by the HIM department using census and discharge data.

Formula 18.8.   Calculating the average length of stay

$$\text{Average length of stay} = \frac{\text{Total length of stay for a given period}}{\text{Total number of discharges, including deaths, for the same period}}$$

Check Your Understanding 18.5

Instructions: Complete the following exercise on a separate piece of paper.

	Number of Patients	
Day	**Discharged**	**Discharge Days**
August 1	12	72
August 2	10	70
August 3	12	72
August 4	17	136
August 5	8	32
August 6	9	81
August 7	11	68
August 8	10	80
August 9	14	63
August 10	12	84

1. Calculate the total length of stay for the patient discharges and the average length of stay. Calculate to one decimal point.

   A. Total length of stay _____
   B. Number of patients discharged _____
   C. Average length of stay _____

Patient Care and Clinical Statistical Data

Thus far, this chapter has discussed statistical measures that are indicators of volume of services and utilization of services. The collection of data related to morbidity and mortality is also an important aspect of evaluating the quality of hospital services. Morbidity and mortality rates are reported for all patient discharges within a certain time frame. They also may be reported by service or by physician or other variable of interest in order to identify trends, issues, or opportunities for improvement that may require corrective action. The most frequently collected morbidity and mortality rates are presented in this section.

Hospital Death (Mortality) Rates

The **hospital death rate** is based on the number of patients discharged, alive and dead, from the hospital. Deaths are considered discharges because they are the end point of a period of hospitalization. In contrast to the rates discussed in the preceding section, newborns are not counted separately from adults and children.

Gross Death Rate

The **gross death rate** is the proportion of all hospital discharges that ended in death. It is the basic indicator of mortality in a healthcare facility. The gross death rate is calculated by dividing the total number of deaths occurring in a given time period by the total number of discharges, including deaths, for the same time period. The formula for calculating the gross death rate is shown in formula 18.9.

Formula 18.9.   Calculating the gross death rate

$$\text{Gross death rate} = \frac{\text{Total number of inpatient deaths (including NBs) for a given period}}{\text{Total number of discharges, including A\&C and NB deaths, for the same period}} \times 100$$

As an example, Community Hospital experienced 21 deaths (A&C and NBs) during the month of May. There were 633 total discharges, including deaths. The gross death rate is 3.3 percent ([21/633] × 100).

Table 18.5. Statistical summary, Community Hospital, period ending July 20XX

Admissions	July 20XX		Year-to-Date 20XX	
	Actual	Budget	Actual	Budget
Medical	728	769	5,075	5,082
Surgical	578	583	3,964	3,964
OB/GYN	402	440	2,839	3,027
Psychiatry	113	99	818	711
Physical Medicine & Rehab	48	57	380	384
Other Adult	191	178	1,209	1,212
Total Adult	2,060	2,126	14,285	14,380
Newborn	294	312	2,143	2,195
Total Admissions	2,354	2,438	16,428	16,575

Average Length of Stay	July 20XX		Year-to-Date 20XX	
	Actual	Budget	Actual	Budget
Medical	6.1	6.4	6.0	6.1
Surgical	7.0	7.2	7.7	7.7
OB/GYN	2.9	3.2	3.5	3.1
Psychiatry	10.8	11.6	10.4	11.6
Physical Medicine & Rehab	27.5	23.0	28.1	24.3
Other Adult	3.6	3.9	4.0	4.1
Total Adult	6.3	6.4	6.7	6.5
Newborn	5.6	5.0	5.6	5.0
Total ALOS	6.2	6.3	6.5	6.3

Patient Days	July 20XX		Year-to-Date 20XX	
	Actual	Budget	Actual	Budget
Medical	4,436	4,915	30,654	30,762
Surgical	4,036	4,215	30,381	30,331
OB/GYN	1,170	1,417	10,051	9,442
Psychiatry	1,223	1,144	8,524	8,242
Physical Medicine & Rehab	1,318	1,310	10,672	9,338
Other Adult	688	699	4,858	4,921
Total Adult	12,871	13,700	95,140	93,036
Newborn	1,633	1,552	12,015	10,963
Total Patient Days	14,504	15,252	107,155	103,999

Other Key Statistics	July 20XX		Year-to-Date 20XX	
	Actual	Budget	Actual	Budget
Average Daily Census	485	492	498	486
Average Beds Available	677	660	677	660
Clinic Visits	21,621	18,975	144,271	136,513
Emergency Visits	3,822	3,688	26,262	25,604
Inpatient Surgery Patients	657	583	4,546	4,093
Outpatient Surgery Patients	603	554	4,457	3,987

Net Death Rate

The **net death rate** is an adjusted death rate. It is calculated with the assumption that certain deaths should not "count against the hospital." The net death rate is an adjusted rate because it does not include patients who die within 48 hours of admission. The reason for excluding these deaths is that 48 hours is not enough time to positively affect patient outcome. In other words, the patient was not admitted to the hospital in a manner timely enough for treatment to have an effect on his or her outcome. The formula for calculating the net death rate is shown in formula 18.10.

Formula 18.10. Calculating the net death rate

$$\text{Net death rate} = \frac{\text{Total number of inpatient deaths (including NBs) minus deaths} < 48 \text{ hours for a given period}}{\text{Total number of discharges (including A\&C and NB deaths) minus deaths} < 48 \text{ hours for the same period}} \times 100$$

Continuing with the preceding example of the 21 patients who died at Community Hospital, three died within 48 hours of admission. Therefore, the net death rate is 2.9 percent ([{21 − 3}/{633 − 3}] × 100 = 2.9%). The fact that the net death rate is less than the gross death rate is favorable to Community Hospital because lower death rates may be an indicator of better care.

Newborn Death Rate

Even though newborn deaths are included in the hospital's gross and net death rates, the **newborn death rate** can be calculated separately. Newborns include only infants born alive in the hospital. The newborn death rate is the number of newborns who died in comparison to the total number of newborns discharged, alive and dead. To qualify as a newborn death, the newborn must have been delivered alive. A stillborn infant is not included in either the newborn death rate or the gross or net death rate. The formula for calculating the newborn death rate is shown in formula 18.11.

Formula 18.11. Calculating the newborn death rate

$$\text{Newborn death rate} = \frac{\text{Total number of NB deaths for a given period}}{\text{Total number of NB discharges (including deaths) for the same period}} \times 100$$

For example, Community Hospital experienced two newborn deaths during the month of May. There were 53 newborn discharges (including these two deaths). The newborn death rate is 3.8 percent ([2/53] × 100).

Fetal Death Rate

In healthcare terminology, the death of a stillborn baby is called a **fetal death.** A fetal death is a death prior to the

Table 18.6.   Classifications of fetal death

Classification	Length of Gestation	Weight
Early fetal death	Less than 20 weeks' gestation	500 g or less
Intermediate fetal death	20 weeks' completed gestation, but less than 28 weeks	501 to 1,000 g
Late fetal death	28 weeks' completed gestation	Over 1,000 g

fetus's complete expulsion or extraction from the mother in a hospital facility, regardless of the length of the pregnancy. Thus, stillborns are neither admitted nor discharged from the hospital. A fetal death occurs when the fetus fails to breathe or show any other evidence of life, such as a heartbeat, a pulsation of the umbilical cord, or a movement of the voluntary muscles.

Fetal deaths also are classified into categories based on length of gestation or weight. (See table 18.6.) To calculate the **fetal death rate,** divide the total number of intermediate and late fetal deaths for the period by the total number of live births and intermediate and late fetal deaths for the same period. The formula for calculating the fetal death rate is shown in formula 18.12. For example, during the month of May, Community Hospital experienced 269 live births and 7 intermediate and 6 late fetal deaths. The fetal death rate is 4.6 percent ([7 + 6/{269 + 7 + 6}] ×100).

Formula 18.12.   Calculating the fetal death rate

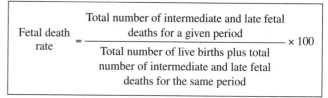

$$\text{Fetal death rate} = \frac{\text{Total number of intermediate and late fetal deaths for a given period}}{\text{Total number of live births plus total number of intermediate and late fetal deaths for the same period}} \times 100$$

Maternal Death Rate

Hospitals are also interested in calculating their **maternal death rate.** A maternal death is the death of any woman from any cause related to, or aggravated by, pregnancy or its management, regardless of the duration of the pregnancy or the site of death. Maternal deaths that result from accidental or incidental causes are not included in the maternal death rate.

Maternal deaths are classified as either direct or indirect. A direct maternal death is the death of a woman resulting from obstetrical (OB) complications of the pregnancy state, labor, or puerperium (the period including the six weeks after delivery). Direct maternal deaths are included in the maternal death rate. An indirect maternal death is the death of a woman from a previously existing disease or a disease that developed during pregnancy, labor, or the puerperium that was not due to obstetric causes, although the physiologic effects of pregnancy were partially responsible.

Table 18.7.   Calculation of hospital-based mortality rates

Rate	Numerator (x)	Denominator (y)
Gross death rate	Total number of inpatient deaths, including NBs, for a given period × 100	Total number of discharges, including A&C and NB deaths, for the same period
Net death rate (institutional death rate)	Total number of inpatient deaths, including NBs, minus deaths < 48 hours for a given period × 100	Total number of discharges, including A&C and NB deaths, minus deaths < 48 hours for the same period
Newborn death rate	Total number of NB deaths for a given period × 100	Total number of NB discharges, including deaths, for the same period
Fetal death rate	Total number of intermediate and late fetal deaths for a given period × 100	Total number of live births plus total number of intermediate and fetal deaths for the same period
Maternal death rate	Total number of direct maternal deaths for a given period × 100	Total number of maternal (obstetric) discharges, including deaths, for the same period
Infant death rate	Number of deaths under one year of age during a given time period	Number of live births during the same time period

The maternal death rate may be an indicator of the availability of prenatal care in a community. The hospital also may use it to help identify conditions that could lead to a maternal death. The formula for calculating the maternal death rate is shown in formula 18.13. For example, during the month of May, Community Hospital experienced 275 maternal discharges. Two of these patients died. The maternal death rate for May is 0.73 percent ([2/275] × 100). Table 18.7 summarizes hospital-based mortality rates.

Formula 18.13.   Calculating the maternal death rate

$$\text{Maternal death rate} = \frac{\text{Total number of direct maternal deaths for a given period}}{\text{Total number of maternal (OB) discharges, including deaths, for the same period}} \times 100$$

Check Your Understanding 18.6

Instructions: Using the data provided on deaths and discharges at Community Hospital for the past calendar year, answer the following questions on a separate sheet of paper. Calculate to two decimal points.

Total discharges, including deaths (A&C)	1,250
Total deaths (A&C)	20
Deaths less than 48 hours after admission (A&C)	3
Fetal deaths (intermediate and late)	4
Live births	155
Newborn deaths	2
Newborn discharges, including deaths	155
Maternal deaths (direct)	1
OB discharges, including deaths	155

1. ___ What is the gross death rate for adults and children?

2. ___ What is the net death rate for adults and children?

3. ___ What is the fetal death rate?

4. ___ What is the newborn death rate?

5. ___ What is the gross death rate for adults and children and newborns combined?

6. ___ What is the maternal death rate (direct)?

Autopsy Rates

An autopsy is an examination of a dead body to determine the cause of death. Another name that may be used is a postmortem examination. Autopsies are very useful in the education of medical students and residents. In addition, they can alert family members to conditions or diseases for which they may be at risk.

Two categories of hospital autopsies are conducted in acute-care facilities: hospital inpatient autopsies and hospital autopsies. A **hospital inpatient autopsy** is an examination of the body of a patient who died while being treated in the hospital. The patient's death marked the end of his or her stay in the hospital. A pathologist or some other physician on the medical staff performs this type of autopsy in the facility.

A **hospital autopsy** is an examination of the body of an individual who at some time in the past had been a hospital patient and was not a hospital inpatient at the time of death. A pathologist or some other physician on the medical staff performs this type of autopsy as well. The following sections describe the different types of autopsy rates calculated by acute-care hospitals.

Gross Autopsy Rates

A **gross autopsy rate** is the proportion or percentage of deaths that are followed by the performance of autopsy. The formula for calculating the gross autopsy rate is shown in formula 18.14. For example, during the month of May, Community Hospital experienced 21 deaths. Autopsies were performed on four of these patients. The gross autopsy rate is 19.0 percent ([4/21] × 100).

Formula 18.14.   Calculating the gross autopsy rate

$$
\text{Gross autopsy rate} = \frac{\text{Total inpatient autopsies for a given period}}{\text{Total number of inpatient deaths for the same period}} \times 100
$$

Net Autopsy Rates

The bodies of patients who have died are not always available for autopsy. For example, a coroner or medical examiner may claim a body for an autopsy for legal reasons. In these situations, the hospital calculates a **net autopsy rate.** In calculating the net autopsy rate, bodies that have been removed by the coroner or medical examiner are excluded from the denominator. The formula for calculating the net autopsy rate is shown in formula 18.15. Continuing with the example in the preceding section, the medical examiner claimed three of the patients for autopsy. The numerator remains the same because four autopsies were performed by the hospital pathologist. However, because three of the deaths were identified as medical examiner's cases and removed from the hospital, 3 is subtracted from 21. The net autopsy rate is 22.2 percent ([4/{21 − 3}] × 100).

Formula 18.15.   Calculating the net autopsy rate

$$
\text{Net autopsy rate} = \frac{\text{Total number of autopsies on inpatient deaths for a period}}{\text{Total number of inpatient deaths minus unautopsied coroners' or medical examiners' cases for the same period}} \times 100
$$

Hospital Autopsy Rates

A third type of autopsy rate is called the **hospital autopsy rate.** This is an adjusted rate that includes autopsies on anyone who may have at one time been a hospital patient. The formula for calculating the hospital autopsy rate is shown in formula 18.16. The hospital autopsy rate includes autopsies performed on any of the following:

Formula 18.16.   Calculating the hospital autopsy rate

$$
\text{Hospital autopsy rate} = \frac{\text{Total number of hospital autopsies for a given period}}{\text{Total number of deaths of hospital patients whose bodies were available for autopsy for the same period}} \times 100
$$

- Bodies of inpatients, except those removed by the coroner or medical examiner. When the hospital pathologist or other designated physician acts as an agent in the performance of an autopsy on an inpatient, the death and the autopsy are included in the percentage.
- Bodies of other hospital patients, including ambulatory care patients, hospital home care patients, and former hospital patients who died elsewhere but whose bodies have been made available for autopsy to be performed by the hospital pathologist or other designated physician. These autopsies and deaths are included in computations of the percentage.

Generally, it is difficult to determine the number of bodies of former hospital patients who may have died in a given time period. In the formula, the phrase "available for autopsy" involves several conditions, including the following:

- The autopsy must be performed by the hospital pathologist or a designated physician on the body of a patient treated at some time at the hospital.
- The report of the autopsy must be filed in the patient's health record and in the hospital laboratory or pathology department.
- The tissue specimens must be maintained in the hospital laboratory.

Figure 18.5 explains how to calculate the hospital autopsy rate.

Newborn Autopsy Rates

Autopsy rates usually include autopsies performed on newborn infants unless a separate rate is requested. The formula for calculating the **newborn autopsy rate** is shown in formula 18.17. For example, there were two newborn deaths at Community Hospital in May, and one of the deaths was autopsied. This represents 50 percent ([1/2] × 100).

Formula 18.17.   Calculating the newborn autopsy rate

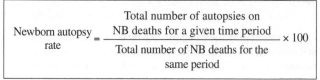

$$
\text{Newborn autopsy rate} = \frac{\text{Total number of autopsies on NB deaths for a given time period}}{\text{Total number of NB deaths for the same period}} \times 100
$$

Fetal Autopsy Rates

Hospitals sometimes also calculate the **fetal autopsy rate.** Fetal autopsies are important for the clinician to determine the cause of the fetal loss and to the parents to determine if they need genetic counseling. Fetal autopsies are performed on stillborn infants who have been classified as either intermediate or late fetal deaths. This is the proportion or percentage of autopsies done on intermediate or late fetal deaths out of the total number of intermediate or late fetal deaths. The formula for calculating the fetal autopsy rate is shown in formula 18.18.

Figure 18.5.   Calculation of the hospital autopsy rate

In June, 33 inpatient deaths occurred. Three of these were medical examiner's cases. Two of the bodies were removed from the hospital and so were not available for hospital autopsy. One of the medical examiner's cases was autopsied by the hospital pathologist. Fourteen other autopsies were performed on hospital inpatients who died during the month of June. In addition, autopsies were performed in the hospital on

- A child with congenital heart disease who died in the emergency department

- A former hospital inpatient who died in an extended care facility and whose body was brought to the hospital for autopsy

- A former hospital inpatient who died at home and whose body was brought to the hospital for autopsy

- A hospital outpatient who died while receiving chemotherapy for cancer

- A hospital home care patient whose body was brought to the hospital for autopsy

- A former hospital inpatient who died in an emergency vehicle on the way to the hospital

Calculation of total hospital autopsies:

```
    1  autopsy on medical examiner's case
 +14  autopsies on hospital inpatients
  +6  autopsies on hospital patients whose bodies were
available for autopsy
_____
   21  autopsies performed by the hospital pathologist
```

Calculation of number of deaths of hospital patients whose bodies were available for autopsy:

```
  33  inpatient deaths
  -2  medical examiner's cases
  +6  deaths of hospital patients
_____
  37  total bodies available for autopsy
```

Calculation of the hospital autopsy rate:

$$\frac{\text{Total number of hospital autopsies for the period}}{\text{Total number of deaths of hospital patients with bodies available for hospital autopsy for the period}} \times 100 \quad (21 \times 100)/37 = 56.8\%$$

For example, there were 13 intermediate and late fetal deaths at Community Hospital in May. Three of those deaths were autopsied. The fetal autopsy rate is 23.1 percent ([3/13] × 100).

Formula 18.18.   Calculating the fetal autopsy rate

$$\text{Fetal autopsy rate} = \frac{\begin{array}{c}\text{Total number of autopsies on intermediate}\\\text{and late fetal deaths for a given period}\end{array}}{\begin{array}{c}\text{Total number of intermediate and late}\\\text{fetal deaths for the same period}\end{array}} \times 100$$

Table 18.8 summarizes the different hospital autopsy rates.

Instructions: Read the following scenario and answer the questions on a separate sheet of paper.

In April, Community Hospital experienced 25 inpatient deaths. Two of these were coroner's cases. One additional death was a former hospital patient who died in hospice and was autopsied by the hospital pathologist. Twelve autopsies were performed on the remaining deaths. Calculate to one decimal point.

1. ___ What is the gross autopsy rate for this month?

2. ___ What is the net autopsy rate for this month?

3. ___ What is the hospital autopsy rate?

Hospital Infection Rates

The most common morbidity rates calculated for hospitals are related to hospital-acquired infections, called **nosocomial infections.** The hospital must continuously monitor the number of infections that occur in its various patient care units because infection can adversely affect the course of a patient's treatment and possibly result in death. The Joint Commission requires hospitals to follow written guidelines for reporting all types of infections. Examples of the different types of infections are respiratory, gastrointestinal, surgical wound, skin, urinary tract, septicemias, and infections related to intravascular catheters.

Hospital-Acquired Infection Rates

Hospital-acquired (nosocomial) infection rates may be calculated for the entire hospital or for a specific unit in the hospital. They also may be calculated for the specific types of infections. Ideally, the hospital should strive for an infection rate of 0.0 percent. The formula for calculating the hospital-acquired or nosocomial infection rate is shown in formula 18.19. For example, Community Hospital discharged 725 patients during the month of May. Thirty-two of these patients experienced hospital-acquired infections. The hospital-acquired infection rate is 4.4 percent ([32/725] × 100).

Formula 18.19.   Calculating the nosocomial infection rate

$$\begin{array}{c}\text{Hospital-acquired}\\\text{infection rate}\end{array} = \frac{\begin{array}{c}\text{Total number of hospital-acquired}\\\text{infections for a given period}\end{array}}{\begin{array}{c}\text{Total number of discharges, including}\\\text{deaths, for the same period}\end{array}} \times 100$$

Postoperative Infection Rates

Hospitals often track their **postoperative infection rate.** The postoperative infection rate is the proportion or percentage of infections in clean surgical cases out of the total number of

Table 18.8. Calculation of hospital autopsy rates

Rate	Numerator	Denominator
Gross autopsy rate	Total number of autopsies on inpatient deaths for a given period × 100	Total number of inpatient deaths for the same period
Net autopsy rate	Total number of autopsies on inpatient deaths for a given period × 100	Total number of inpatient deaths minus unautopsied coroner or medical examiner cases for the same period
Hospital autopsy rate	Total number of hospital autopsies for a given period × 100	Total number of deaths of hospital patients whose bodies are available for hospital autopsy for the same period
Newborn (NB) autopsy rate	Total number of autopsies on NB deaths for a given period × 100	Total number of NB deaths for the same period
Fetal autopsy rate	Total number of autopsies on intermediate and late fetal deaths for a given period × 100	Total number of intermediate and late fetal deaths for the same period

surgical operations performed. A clean surgical case is one in which no infection existed prior to surgery. The postoperative infection rate may be an indicator of a problem in the hospital environment or of some type of surgical contamination.

The individual calculating the postoperative infection rate must know the difference between a surgical procedure and a surgical operation. A **surgical procedure** is any separate, systematic process on or within the body that can be complete in itself. A physician, dentist, or some other licensed practitioner performs a surgical procedure, with or without instruments, to

- Restore disunited or deficient parts
- Remove diseased or injured tissues
- Extract foreign matter
- Assist in obstetrical delivery
- Aid in diagnosis

A **surgical operation** involves one or more surgical procedures that are performed on one patient at one time using one approach to achieve a common purpose. An example of a surgical operation is the resection of a portion of both the intestine and the liver in a cancer patient. This involves two procedures, removal of a portion of the liver and removal of a portion of the colon, but it is considered only one operation because there is only one operative approach or incision. In contrast, an esophagoduodenoscopy (EGD) and a colonoscopy performed at the same time are two procedures with two different approaches. In the former, the approach is the upper gastrointestinal tract; in the latter, the approach is the lower gastrointestinal tract. In this case, the two procedures do not have a common approach or purpose. The formula for calculating the postoperative infection rate is shown in formula 18.20.

Formula 18.20. Calculating the postoperative infection rate

$$\text{Postoperative infection rate} = \frac{\text{Number of infections in clean surgical cases for a given period}}{\text{Total number of surgical operations for the same period}} \times 100$$

Consultation Rates

A consultation occurs when two or more physicians collaborate on a particular patient's diagnosis or treatment. The attending physician requests the consultation and explains his or her reason for doing so. The consultant then examines the patient and the patient's health record and makes recommendations in a written report. The formula for calculating the **consultation rate** is shown in formula 18.21.

Formula 18.21. Calculating the consultation rate

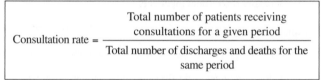

$$\text{Consultation rate} = \frac{\text{Total number of patients receiving consultations for a given period}}{\text{Total number of discharges and deaths for the same period}}$$

During May, Community Hospital had 725 discharges and deaths. Fifty-seven patients received consultations. The consultation rate for May is 7.9 percent ([57/725] × 100).

Case-Mix Statistical Data

Case mix is a method of grouping patients according to a predefined set of characteristics. Medicare severity diagnosis-related groups (MS-DRGs) are often used to determine case mix in hospitals.

When calculating case mix using MS-DRGs, the **case-mix index (CMI)** is the average MS-DRG weight for patients discharged from the hospital. The CMI is a measure of the resources used in treating the patients in each hospital or group of hospitals. It may be calculated for all patients discharged, discharges by payer (see table 18.9), or discharges by particular physicians (see table 18.10).

Table 18.11 provides an example of a case-mix calculation for the top 10 MS-DRGs at Community Hospital. The CMI is calculated by multiplying the number of cases for each MS-DRG by the relative weight of the MS-DRG, summing the result (687.8310), and dividing by the total number of cases (484). By convention, the CMI is calculated to five decimal points and rounded to four.

Table 18.9. Case-mix index by payer, Community Hospital, 20XX

Payer	CMI	N
Commercial	1.8830	283
Government managed care	0.9880	470
Managed care	1.4703	2,326
Medicaid	1.3400	962
Medicare	2.0059	1,776
Other	1.3251	148
Self-pay	1.3462	528
Total	**1.5670**	**6,503**

Table 18.10. Case-mix of one physician, 20XX

Physician	CMI	N
A	1.0235	71
B	1.6397	71
C	1.1114	86
Total	**1.2501**	**228**

Table 18.11. Calculation of case-mix index for 10 MS-DRGs, Community Hospital, 20XX

MS-DRG	Number (N)	MS-DRG Weight	N × MS-DRG Weight
286	84	1.6667	140.0028
287	41	1.1412	46.7892
293	61	0.8765	53.4665
378	41	1.0195	41.7995
391	43	0.9565	41.1295
434	45	1.0125	45.5625
689	26	1.0587	27.5262
871	31	1.7484	54.2004
982	61	3.5417	216.0437
986	51	1.6706	85.2003
Total	**484**		**751.7206**
CMI			**1.5531**

The CMI can be used to indicate the average reimbursement for the hospital. From table 18.9, the reimbursement is approximately 1.5670 multiplied by the hospital's base rate. It also is a measure of the severity of illness of Medicare patients. In table 18.9, you can see that Medicare patients, as expected, have the highest CMI at 2.0059.

Other data analyzed by MS-DRG include LOS and mortality rates. LOS and mortality data are benchmarked against the hospital's peer group and national data. The process of benchmarking involves comparing the hospital's performance against an external standard or benchmark. An excellent source of information for benchmarking purposes is the Healthcare Cost Utilization Project database (HCUPnet), which is available online. A comparison of hospital and national data for MS-DRG 293 appears in table 18.12.

Gross analysis of the data indicates that Community Hospital's mortality rate and ALOS are slightly better than the national average. But, at the same time, the hospital's average charges are higher than the national average.

Table 18.12. Benchmark data, Community Hospital vs. national average for MS-DRG 293, Heart failure and shock w/o CC/MCC

	ALOS	Mortality Rate	Average Charges
Community Hospital	4.8	0.3%	$20,042
National average	4.6	2.1%	$27,731

Check Your Understanding 18.8

Instructions: Using the following table, answer the following questions on a separate piece of paper. Round to four decimal points.

MS-DRG	MS-DRG Title	Rel. Wt.	No. of Pts.	Total Wt.
179	Respiratory infections and inflammations w/o CC/MCC	1.0088	5	
187	Pleural effusion w/ CC	1.0620	2	
189	Pulmonary edema and respiratory failure	1.3455	3	
194	Simple pneumonia and pleurisy w/ CC	0.9976	1	
208	Respiratory system diagnosis w/ ventilator support <96 hours	2.2358	1	
280	Acute myocardial infarction, discharged alive w/ MCC	1.8313	3	
299	Peripheral vascular disorders w/ MCC	1.4045	2	
313	Chest pain	0.5404	4	
377	G.I. hemorrhage w/ MCC	1.6149	1	
391	Esophagitis, gastroent and misc. digest disorders w/ MCC	1.0958	1	
547	Connective tissue disorders w/o CC/MCC	0.7475	1	
552	Medical back problems w/o MCC	0.7937	1	
684	Renal failure w/o CC/MCC	0.6746	1	
812	Red blood cell disorders w/o MCC	0.7751	2	

872	Septicemia w/o MV 96 + hours w/o MCC	1.1155	1	
918	Poisoning and toxic effects of drugs w/o MCC	0.5839	1	
Total			**30**	

Case-mix index = 33/0785/30 = 1.1026

1.___ Last month, Community Hospital had 57 discharges from its medicine unit. Six patients developed a urinary tract infection while in the hospital. Calculate the nosocomial infection rate for the last month.

2.___ During June, Community Hospital had 149 discharges. Fifty-seven patients had consultations from specialty physicians. What was the consultation rate for June?

3.___ Dr. Green discharged 30 patients from Medicine Service during the month of August. The table presents the number of patients discharged by MS-DRG. Calculate the total weight for each MS-DRG and the CMI for Dr. Green.

4.___ A name given to describe an infection acquired in a healthcare facility is _____.

Ambulatory Care Statistical Data

Ambulatory care includes healthcare services provided to patients who are not hospitalized (that is, who are not considered inpatients or residents and do not stay in the healthcare facility overnight). Such patients are referred to as outpatients. Most ambulatory care services today are provided in freestanding physicians' offices, emergency care centers, and ambulatory surgery centers that are not owned or operated by acute-care organizations. Hospitals do, however, provide many hospital-based healthcare services to outpatients. Hospital outpatients may receive services in one or more areas within the hospital, including clinics, same-day surgery departments, diagnostic departments, and emergency departments.

Outpatient statistics include records of the number of patient visits and the types of services provided. Many different terms are used to describe outpatients and ambulatory care services, including

- **Hospital ambulatory care:** All hospital-directed preventive, therapeutic, and rehabilitative services provided by physicians and their surrogates to patients who are not hospital inpatients
- **Outpatient:** A patient who receives ambulatory care services in a hospital-based clinic or department
- **Hospital outpatient:** A hospital patient who receives services in one or more of a hospital's facilities when he or she is not currently an inpatient or a home care patient

- **Emergency outpatient:** A patient who is admitted to the emergency department of a hospital for diagnosis and treatment of a condition that requires immediate medical, dental, or allied health services in order to sustain life or to prevent critical consequences
- **Clinic outpatient:** A patient who is admitted to a clinical service of a clinic or hospital for diagnosis or treatment on an ambulatory basis
- **Referred outpatient:** An outpatient who is provided special diagnostic or therapeutic services by a hospital on an ambulatory basis but whose medical care remains the responsibility of the referring physician
- **Outpatient visit:** A patient's visit to one or more units or facilities located in the ambulatory services area (clinic or physician's office) of an acute care hospital in which an overnight stay does not occur
- **Encounter:** The professional, direct personal contact between a patient and a physician or other person who is authorized by state licensure law, and if application, by medical staff bylaws to order or furnish healthcare services for the diagnosis or treatment of the patient; face-to-face contact between a patient and a provider who has primary responsibility for assessing and treating the condition of the patient at a given contact and exercise
- **Occasion of service:** A specified, identifiable service involved in the care of a patient that is not an encounter (for example, a lab test ordered during an encounter)
- **Ambulatory surgery center or ambulatory surgical center (ASC):** Under Medicare, an outpatient surgical facility that has its own national identifier; is a separate entity with respect to its licensure, accreditation, governance, professional supervision, administrative functions, clinical services, recordkeeping, and financial and accounting systems; has as its sole purpose the provision of services in connection with surgical procedures that do not require inpatient hospitalization; and meets the conditions and requirements set forth in the Medicare Conditions of Participation
  — May be referred to as short-stay surgery, one-day surgery, same-day surgery, or come-and-go surgery services

Check Your Understanding 18.9

A. Ambulatory surgery center

B. Outpatient visit

C. Encounter

D. Occasion of service

E. Referred outpatient

F. Clinic outpatient

G. Emergency outpatient

H. Hospital outpatient

I. Hospital ambulatory care

J. Outpatient

Match the definitions with the choices (A through K):

1. _____ A patient's visit to one or more units or facilities located in the ambulatory services area (clinic or physician's office) of an acute-care hospital in which an overnight stay does not occur

2. _____ A specified, identifiable service involved in the care of a patient that is not an encounter (for example, a lab test ordered during an encounter)

3. _____ All hospital-directed preventive, therapeutic, and rehabilitative services provided by physicians and their surrogates to patients who are not hospital inpatients

4. _____ A patient who receives ambulatory care services in a hospital-based clinic or department

5. _____ An outpatient who is provided special diagnostic or therapeutic services by a hospital on an ambulatory basis but whose medical care remains the responsibility of the referring physician

6. _____ The professional, direct personal contact between a patient and a physician or other person who is authorized by state licensure law, and if applicable, by medical staff bylaws to order or furnish healthcare services for the diagnosis or treatment of the patient; face-to-face contact between a patient and a provider who has primary responsibility for assessing and treating the condition of the patient at a given contact and exercise

7. _____ A patient who is admitted to a clinical service of a clinic or hospital for diagnosis or treatment on an ambulatory basis

8. _____ A hospital patient who receives services in one or more of a hospital's facilities when he or she is not currently an inpatient or a home care patient

9. _____ A patient who is admitted to the emergency department of a hospital for diagnosis and treatment of a condition that requires immediate medical, dental, or allied health services in order to sustain life or to prevent critical consequences

10. _____ An outpatient surgical facility that has its own national identifier; is a separate entity with respect to its licensure, accreditation, governance, professional supervision, administrative functions, clinical services, recordkeeping, and financial and accounting systems.

Public Health Statistics and Epidemiological Information

Just as statistics are collected in the healthcare organizational setting, they also are collected on a community, regional, and national basis. **Vital statistics** are an example of data collected and reported at these levels. The term *vital statistics* refers to the collection and analysis of data related to the crucial events in life: birth, death, marriage, divorce, fetal death, and induced terminations of pregnancy. These statistics are used to identify trends. For example, a higher-than-expected death rate among newborns may be an indication of the lack of prenatal services in a community. A number of deaths in a region due to the same cause may indicate an environmental problem.

These types of data are used as part of the effort to preserve and improve the health of a defined population—the public health. The study of factors that influence the health status of a population is called epidemiology.

National Vital Statistics System

The **National Vital Statistics System (NVSS)** is responsible for maintaining the official vital statistics of the United States. These statistics are provided to the federal government by state-operated registration systems. The NVSS is housed in the National Center for Health Statistics (NCHS) of the Centers for Disease Control and Prevention (CDC).

To facilitate data collection, standard forms and model procedures for the uniform registration of events are developed and recommended for state use through cooperative activities of the individual states and the NCHS. The standard certificates represent the minimum basic data set necessary for the collection and publication of comparable national, state, and local vital statistics data. The standard forms are revised about every 10 years, with the last revision completed in 2003. To effectively implement these new certificates, the NCHS collaborates with its state partners to improve the timeliness, quality, and sustainability of the vital statistics system, along with collection of the revised and new content of the 2003 certificates.

The certificate of live birth is used for registration purposes and is composed of two parts. The first part contains the information related to the child and the parents. The second part is used to collect data about the mother's pregnancy. This information is used for the collection of aggregate data only. No identification information appears on this portion of the certificate nor does it ever appear on the official certificate of birth. Pregnancy-related information includes complications of pregnancy, concurrent illnesses or conditions affecting pregnancy, and abnormal conditions and/or congenital anomalies of the newborn. Lifestyle factors such as use of alcohol and tobacco also are collected. Thus, the birth certificate is the major source of maternal and natality statistics. A listing of pregnancy-related information appears in figure 18.6.

Data collected from death certificates are used to compile causes of death in the United States. The certificate of death contains decedent information, place of death information, medical certification, and disposition information. Data on causes of death are classified and coded using the International Classification of Diseases (ICD). Beginning in 1999, the United States implemented ICD-10 for the coding of causes of death. Examples of the content of death certificates appear in figure 18.7.

Figure 18.6.   Content of US certificate of live birth, 2003

Child's Information	**Pregnancy History**
Child's name	Date of first prenatal care visit
Time of birth	Date of last prenatal care visit
Sex	Total number of prenatal visits for this pregnancy
Date of birth	Number of previous live births
Facility (hospital) Name (if not an institution, give street address)	Mother's height
City	Mother's pregnancy weight
County	Mother's weight at delivery
	Did mother get WIC food for herself during this pregnancy?
Mother's Information	Number of previous live births
Current legal name	Number of other pregnancy outcomes
Date of birth	Cigarette smoking before and during pregnancy
Mother's name prior to first marriage	Principal source of payment for this delivery
Birthplace	Date of last live birth
Residence (state)	Date of last other pregnancy outcome
County	Date last normal menses began
City	Risk factors in this pregnancy
Street number	Infections present and/or treated during this pregnancy
Zip code	Obstetric procedures
Inside city limits?	Onset of labor
Mother married?	Characteristics of labor and delivery
If no, has paternity acknowledgment been signed in the hospital?	Method of delivery
Social Security number (SSN) requested for child?	Maternal mortality
Mother's SSN	
Father's SSN	**Newborn's Information**
Education	Birth weight
Hispanic origin?	Obstetric estimate of gestation
Race	Apgar score (1 and 5 minutes)
	Plurality
Father's Information	If not born first (born first, second, third, etc.)
Current legal name	Abnormal conditions of newborn
Date of birth	Congenital anomalies of newborn
Birthplace	Was infant transferred within 24 hours of delivery?
Education	Is infant living at time of report?
Hispanic origin?	Is infant being breast fed at discharge?
Race	

Source: CDC 2011a.

A report of fetal death is completed when a pregnancy results in a stillbirth. This report contains information on the parents, the history of the pregnancy, and the cause of the fetal death. Information collected on the pregnancy is the same as that recorded on the birth certificate. To assess the effects of environmental exposures on the fetus, the parents' occupational data are collected. A listing of the content of the fetal death certificate appears in figure 18.8

The report of induced termination of pregnancy records information on the place of the induced termination of pregnancy, the type of termination procedure, and the patient. (See figure 18.9.)

Figure 18.7.   Content of US certificate of death, 2003

Decedent Information

Name

Sex

Social Security number

Age

Date of birth

Birthplace

Residence (state)

County

City or town

Street and number

Zip code

Inside city limit?

Ever in US armed forces?

Marital status at time of death

Surviving spouse's name (If wife, give name prior to first marriage)

Father's name

Mother's name (prior to first marriage)

Decedent's education

Hispanic origin?

Race

Informant's name

Relationship to decedent

Mailing address

Disposition Information

Method of disposition

Place of disposition (cemetery, crematory, other)

Location

Name and address of funeral facility

Place of Death Information

Place of death

If hospital, indicate inpatient, emergency room/outpatient, dead on arrival

If somewhere other than hospital, indicate hospice, nursing home/long-term care facility, decedent's home, other

Facility name

City, state, zip code

County

Medical Certification

Date pronounced dead

Time pronounced dead

Signature of person pronouncing death

Date signed

Actual or presumed date of death

Actual or presumed time of death

Was medical examiner contacted?

Immediate cause of death

Due to _____

Due to _____

Due to _____

Other significant conditions contributing to death

Was an autopsy performed?

Were autopsy findings available to complete the cause of death?

Did tobacco use contribute to death?

If female, indicate pregnancy status

Manner of death

For deaths due to injury:

Date of injury

Time of injury

Place of injury

Injury at work?

Location of injury

Describe how injury occurred

If transportation injury, specify if driver/operator, passenger, pedestrian, other

Source: CDC 2011a.

A tool for monitoring and exploring the interrelationships between infant death and risk factors at birth is the linked birth and infant death data set. This is a service provided by the NCHS. In this data set, the information from the death certificate (such as age and underlying or multiple causes of death) is linked to the information in the birth certificate (such as age, race, birth weight, prenatal care usage, maternal education, and so on) for each infant who dies in the United States, Puerto Rico, the Virgin Islands, and Guam. The purpose of the data set is to use the many additional variables available from the birth certificate to conduct a detailed analysis of infant mortality patterns.

Birth, death, fetal death, and termination of pregnancy certificates provide vital information for use in medical research, epidemiological studies, and other public health programs. In addition, they are the source of data for compiling morbidity, birth, and mortality rates that describe the health of a given population at the local, state, or national level. Because of their many uses, the data on these certificates must be complete and accurate.

Figure 18.8.   Content of US standard report of fetal death, 2003

Mother's information	Other outcomes
Name of fetus (optional—at the discretion of the parents)	Date of last other pregnancy outcomes
Time of delivery	Cigarette smoking before and during pregnancy
Sex	Date last normal menses began
Date of delivery	Plurality
City, town or location of delivery	If not born first (born first, second, third, etc.)
Zip code of delivery	Mother transferred for maternal medical or fetal indications for delivery?
County of delivery	**Medical and Health Information**
Place where delivery occurred	Risk factors in this pregnancy
Facility name	Infections present and/or treated during this pregnancy
Facility ID	Method of delivery
Mother's current legal name	Maternal mortality
Date of birth	Congenital anomalies of the fetus
Mother's name prior to first marriage	**Father's Information**
Birthplace	Father's current legal name
Residence of mother—state	Date of birth
County	Birthplace
City, town, or location	**Disposition**
Street number	Method of disposition
Apartment number	**Attendant and Registrant Information**
Zip code	Attendant's name, title, and NPI
Inside city limits?	Name of person completing report
Education	Date report completed
Hispanic origin?	Date received by registrar
Race	**Cause of Fetal Death**
Mother married at delivery, conception, or any time between?	Initiating cause/condition
Date of first prenatal care visit	Other significant causes or conditions
Date of last prenatal care visit	Weight of fetus
Total number of prenatal visits for this pregnancy	Obstetric estimate of gestation at delivery
Mother's height	Estimated time of fetal death
Mother's prepregnancy weight	Was an autopsy performed?
Mother's weight at delivery	Was a histological placental examination performed?
Did mother get WIC food for herself during this pregnancy?	Were autopsy or histological placental examination results used in determining the cause of fetal death?
Number of previous live births	
Number now living	
Number now dead	
Date of last live birth	
Number of other pregnancy outcomes	

Source: CDC 2011a.

Population-Based Statistics

Population-based statistics are based on the mortality and morbidity rates from which the health of a population can be inferred. The entire defined population is used in the collection and reporting of these statistics. The size of the defined population serves as the denominator in the calculation of these rates.

Birth Rates and Measures of Infant Mortality

Two community-based rates that are commonly used to describe a community's health are the crude birth rate and measures of infant mortality. The World Health Organization's definition of a live birth is the complete expulsion or extraction from its mother of a product of conception, irrespective of the duration of the pregnancy, which after

Figure 18.9.   Content of US standard report of induced termination of pregnancy, 1997

Place of Induced Termination

  Facility name

  Address (city, town, state, county)

Patient Information

  Patient identification

  Age at last birthday

  Marital status

  Date or pregnancy termination

  Residence (city, town, state, county)

  Inside city limits?

  Zip code

  Hispanic origin?

  Race

  Education

  Date last normal menses began

  Clinical estimate of gestation

  Previous pregnancies

  Live births

  Other terminations

  Type of termination procedure

Source: CDC 2011b.

such separation, breathes or shows other evidence of life, such as beating of the heart, pulsation of the umbilical cord, or definite movement of voluntary muscles, whether or not the umbilical cord has been cut or the placenta is attached.

Rates that describe infant mortality are based on age. Therefore, the definitions for the various age groups must be strictly followed. Table 18.13 summarizes the calculations for community-based birth and infant mortality

rates. These mortality or death rates are broken down as follows:

- **Crude birth rate:** As shown in Table 18.13, the crude birth rate is the number of live births divided by the population at risk. Community rates are calculated using the multiplier 1,000, 10,000, or 100,000. The purpose is to bring the rate to a whole number, as discussed earlier in the chapter. The result of the formula would be stated as the number of live births per 1,000 population. For example, if there were 7,532 live births in a community of 600,000 in 2011, the crude birth rate for that year would be 13 per 1,000 population ($[7,532/600,000] \times 1,000$).

- **Neonatal mortality rate:** The neonatal mortality rate can be used as an indirect measure of the quality of prenatal care or the mother's prenatal behavior (for example, alcohol, drug, or tobacco use). The neonatal period is the period from birth up to, but not including, 28 days of age. In the formula for calculating the neonatal mortality rate, the numerator is the number of deaths of infants from birth up to but not including 28 days of age during a given time period and the denominator is the total number of live births during the same time period. For example, in your community there were 7,532 live births in 20XX and 21 infants under age 28 days who died in that year. The neonatal mortality rate is 3 per 1,000 live births for the period ($[21/7,532] \times 1,000$).

- **Postneonatal mortality rate:** The postneonatal mortality rate is often used as an indicator of the quality of the home or community environment of infants. The postneonatal period is from 28 days of age up to, but not including, one year of age. In the formula for calculating the postneonatal mortality rate, the numerator is the number of deaths among infants from 28 days of age up to, but not including, one year of age during a given time period and the denominator is the total number of live births minus the number of neonatal deaths during the same time period. For

Table 18.13.   Calculation of community-based birth and infant death (mortality) rates

Measure	Numerator (x)	Denominator (y)	10^n
Crude birth rate	Number of live births for a given community for a specified time period	Estimated population for the same community and the same time period	1,000
Neonatal death rate	Number of deaths under 28 days up to, but not including, one year of age during a given time period	Number of live births during the same time period	1,000
Postneonatal death rate	Number of deaths from 28 days up to, but not including, one year of age during a given time period	Number of live births during the same time period less neonatal deaths	1,000
Infant death rate	Number of deaths under one year of age during a given time period	Number of live births during the same time period	1,000

Table 18.14.   Cause-specific mortality rates by sex, due to influenza and pneumonia (ICD-10 codes J10–J18.9), age 45+ in the United States, 2005

Age Group	Women			Men		
	Population	Deaths	Rate/100,000	Population	Deaths	Rate/100,000
45–54	21,586,910	881	4.08	20,895,355	1,302	6.23
55–64	15,728,823	1,434	9.12	14,626,718	1,988	13.59
65–74	10,110,417	2,975	29.43	8,529,396	3,640	42.68
75–84	7,774,917	9,360	120.39	5,279,445	9,198	174.22
85+	3,492,142	19,465	557.39	1,603,796	10,797	673.22
Total	58,693,209	34,115	58.12	50,934,710	26,925	52.86

Source: CDC 2008.

example, in your community there were 7,532 live births, 21 neonatal deaths, and 17 postneonatal deaths during 20XX. The postneonatal mortality rate is 2 per 1,000 live births minus neonatal deaths for the period (17/[7,532 − 21] × 1000).

- **Infant mortality rate:** The infant mortality rate is the summary of the neonatal and postneonatal mortality rates. In the formula for calculating the infant mortality rate, the numerator is the number of deaths among infants under one year of age and the denominator is the number of live births during the same period. The infant mortality rate is the most commonly used measure for comparing health status among nations. All the rates are expressed in terms of the number of deaths per 1,000 live births. For example, in your community there were 21 neonatal deaths, 17 postneonatal deaths, and 7,532 live births in 20XX. The infant mortality rate is 5 per 1,000 live births in that year ([17 + 21]/7,532 × 1,000).

Death (Mortality) Rates

Other measures of mortality with which the HIM professional should be familiar include the following:

- **Crude death rate:** The crude death rate is a measure of the actual or observed mortality in a given population. Crude death rates apply to a population without regard to characteristics such as age, race, and sex. They measure the proportion of the population that has died during a given period of time (usually one year) or the number of deaths in a community per 1,000 for a given period of time. In the formula, the numerator is the total number of deaths in a population for a specified time period and the denominator is the estimated population for the same time period. For example, a community has a population of 600,000. There were 1,498 deaths in 20XX. Dividing 1,498 by 600,000 equals 0.024966. Using a multiplier of 1,000 gives a crude death rate of 3 deaths per 1,000 population for 20XX ([1,498/600,000] × 1,000).

- **Cause-specific death rate:** As its name indicates, the cause-specific death rate is the rate of death due to a specified cause. It may be calculated for an entire population or for any age, sex, or race. In the formula, the numerator is the number of deaths due to a specified cause for a given time period and the denominator is the estimated population for the same time period. Table 18.14 displays cause-specific death rates for men and women due to influenza and pneumonia for the year 2005. The cause-specific death rates for each age group are consistently higher for men than for women. This information could lead to an investigation of why men are more susceptible to death from influenza and pneumonia than are women.

- **Case fatality rate:** The case fatality rate measures the total number of deaths among the diagnosed cases of a specific disease, most often acute illness. In the formula for calculating the case fatality rate, the numerator is the number of deaths due to a specific disease that occurred during a specific time period and the denominator is the number of diagnosed cases during the same time period. The higher the case fatality rate, the more virulent the infection. For example, in a community there were 15 cases of meningitis and 2 deaths. The case fatality rate of meningitis is 13.3 percent ([2/15] × 100).

- **Proportionate mortality ratio (PMR):** The proportionate mortality ratio is a measure of mortality due to a specific cause for a specific time period. In the formula for calculating the PMR, the numerator is the number of deaths due to a specific disease for a specific time period and the denominator is the number of deaths from all causes for the same time period. Table 18.15 displays the PMRs for influenza and pneumonia in the United States in 2005 by age group.

- **Maternal mortality rate:** The maternal mortality rate measures the deaths associated with pregnancy for a specific community for a specific period

Table 18.15.   Proportionate mortality ratios for influenza and pneumonia (ICD-10 codes J10–J18.9), all ages, in the United States, 2005

Age Group	Influenza and Pneumonia Deaths	Total Deaths	PMR/100
0–4	375	33,196	1.13
5–14	106	6,602	1.61
15–24	172	34,234	0.50
25–34	354	41,925	0.84
35–44	934	84,785	1.10
45–54	2,183	183,530	1.19
55–64	3,422	275,301	1.24
65–74	6,623	398,355	1.66
75–84	18,563	686,665	2.70
85+	30,267	703,169	4.30

Source: CDC 2008.

of time. It is calculated only for deaths that are directly related to pregnancy. In the formula for calculating the maternal mortality rate, the numerator is the number of deaths attributed to causes related to pregnancy during a specific time period for a given community and the denominator is the number of live births reported during the same time period for the same community. The maternal mortality rate is expressed as the number of deaths per 100,000 live births. For example, in the United States in 2007 there were 4,317,119 live births and 548 maternal deaths. This is a maternal mortality rate of 13 maternal deaths per 100,000 live births ([548/4,317,119] × 100,000).

Table 18.16 summarizes the calculations for these rates.

Instructions: Review the mortality data in the following table and then answer the following questions on a separate piece of paper.

Mortality Rates, United States, 2007

Age Group (years)	Female Population	Female Deaths	Male Population	Male Deaths
Less than 1	2,078,212	12,845	2,178,808	16,293
1–4	8,043,056	2,069	8,424,049	2,634
5–9	9,701,050	1,192	10,148,578	1,519
10–14	9,914,382	1,370	10,399,927	2,066
15–19	10,466,821	3,741	11,006,869	9,558
20–24	10,179,459	4,925	10,852,937	15,758
25–34	19,908,376	12,780	20,682,550	29,792
35–44	21,542,555	29,501	21,618,734	50,105
45–54	22,279,847	70,230	21,594,913	114,456
55–64	16,936,988	113,492	15,775,088	173,618
65–74	10,465,176	170,894	8,888,973	218,344
75–84	7,710,838	331,879	5,312,673	320,803
85+	3,735,499	464,781	1,776,799	248,866
Total	152,962,259	1,219,699	148,660,898	1,203,812

Source: CDC Wonder. 2010.

1. ___ What is the crude death rate per 10,000 for men?
2. ___ What is the crude death rate per 10,000 for women?
3. ___ What is the crude death rate per 10,000 for the entire group?
4. ___ What is the crude death rate per 10,000 for men ages 35–44?
5. ___ What is the crude death rate per 10,000 for women ages 35–54?

Table 18.16.   Calculation of community-based death (mortality) rates

Rate	Numerator (x)	Denominator (y)	10^n
Crude death rate	Total number of deaths for a population during a specified time period	Estimated population for the same time period	1,000 or 10,000 or 100,000
Cause-specific death rate	Total number of deaths due to a specific cause during a specified time period	Estimated population for the same time period	100,000
Case fatality rate	Total number of deaths due to a specific disease during a specified time period	Total number of cases due to a specific disease during the same time period	100
Proportionate mortality (ratio)	Total number of deaths due to a specific cause during a specified time period	Total number of deaths from all causes during the same time period	NA
Maternal mortality rate	Total number of deaths due to pregnancy-related conditions during a specified time period	Total number of live births during the same time period	100,000

Measures of Morbidity

Two measures are commonly used to describe the presence of disease in a community or specific location (for example, a nursing home): incidence rates and prevalence rates. Disease is defined as any illness, injury, or disability. Incidence and prevalence measures can be broken down by race, sex, age, or other characteristics of a population.

An **incidence rate** is used to compare the frequency of disease in populations. Populations are compared using rates instead of raw numbers because rates adjust for differences in population size. The incidence rate is the probability or risk of illness in a population over a period of time. The formula for calculating the incidence rate is shown in formula 18.22. The denominator represents the population from which the case in the numerator arose, such as a nursing home, a school, or an organization. For $10n$, a value is selected so that the smallest rate calculated results in a whole number. For example, in a small population such as a nursing home you might select 100, in studying a larger population you might select 1,000. For example, in a nursing home of 110 patients, two were confirmed as having H1N1, a strain of influenza A virus. Using this formula, the incidence rate is 2 percent ($[2/110] \times 100$).

Formula 18.22.   Calculating the incidence rate

$$\text{Incidence rate} = \frac{\begin{array}{c}\text{Total number of new cases of a specific}\\\text{disease during a given time period}\end{array}}{\begin{array}{c}\text{Total population at risk during the same}\\\text{time period}\end{array}} \times 100^{n}$$

The **prevalence rate** is the proportion of persons in a population who have a particular disease at a specific point in time or over a specified period of time. The formula for calculating the prevalence rate is shown in formula 18.23. The prevalence rate describes the magnitude of an epidemic and can be an indicator of the medical resources needed in a community for the duration of the epidemic. For example, in a community of 600,000 individuals, there were 2,486 individuals identified as having AIDS and an additional 309 cases identified. The prevalence rate is 4.66 cases per 1,000 population ($[2,486 + 309]/600,000 \times 1,000$).

Formula 18.23.   Calculating the prevalence rate

$$\text{Prevalence rate} = \frac{\begin{array}{c}\text{All new and preexisting cases of a specific}\\\text{disease during a given time period}\end{array}}{\text{Total population during the same time period}} \times 10^{n}$$

It is easy to confuse incidence and prevalence rates. The distinction is in the numerators of their formulas. The numerator in the formula for the incidence rate is the number of new cases occurring in a given time period. The numerator in the formula for the prevalence rate is all cases present during a given time period. In addition, the incidence rate includes only patients whose illness began during a specified time period whereas the prevalence rate includes all patients from a specified cause regardless of when the illness began. Moreover, the prevalence rate includes a patient until he or she recovers.

National Notifiable Diseases Surveillance System

In 1878, Congress authorized the US Marine Hospital Service, the precursor to the Public Health Service, to collect morbidity reports on cholera, smallpox, plague, and yellow fever from US consuls overseas. This information was used to implement quarantine measures to prevent the spread of these diseases to the United States. In 1879, Congress provided for the weekly collection and publication of reports of these diseases. In 1893, Congress expanded the scope to include weekly reporting from states and municipalities. To provide for more uniformity in data collection, Congress enacted a law in 1902 that directed the surgeon general to provide standard forms for the collection, compilation, and publication of reports at the national level. In 1912, the states and US territories recommended that infectious disease be immediately reported by telegraph. By 1928, all states, the District of Columbia, Hawaii, and Puerto Rico were participating in the national reporting of 29 specified diseases. In 1961, the CDC assumed responsibility for the collection and publication of data concerning nationally notifiable diseases.

A **notifiable disease** is one for which regular, frequent, and timely information on individual cases is considered necessary to prevent and control disease. The list of notifiable diseases varies over time and by state. The Council of State and Territorial Epidemiologists (CSTE) collaborates with the CDC to determine which diseases should be reported. State reporting to the CDC is voluntary. However, all states generally report the internationally quarantinable diseases in accordance with the World Health Organization's International Health Regulations. Completeness of reporting varies by state and type of disease and may be influenced by any of the following factors:

- Type and severity of the illness
- Whether treatment in a healthcare facility was sought
- Diagnosis of an illness
- Availability of diagnostic services
- Disease-control measures in effect
- Public awareness of the disease
- Resources, priorities, and interests of state and local public health officials

Information that is reported includes date, county, age, sex, race and ethnicity, and disease-specific epidemiologic information; personal identifiers are not included. A strict CSTE Data Release Policy regulates dissemination of the data. A list of nationally notifiable infectious diseases appears in figure 18.10. The list is updated annually.

National morbidity data are reported weekly. Public health managers and providers use the reports to rapidly

Figure 18.10.   Nationally notifiable infectious diseases in the United States, 2012

Acquired immunodeficiency syndrome (AIDS)
Anthrax
Arboviral neuroinvasive and non-neuroinvasive diseases California serogroup virus disease Eastern equine encephalitis virus disease Powassan virus disease St. Louis encephalitis virus disease West Nile virus disease Western equine encephalitis virus disease
Botulism Botulism, foodborne Botulism, infant Botulism, other (wound and unspecified)
Brucellosis
Chancroid
Chlamydia trachomatis, genital infections
Cholera
Coccidioidomycosis
Cryptosporidiosis
Cyclosporiasis
Diphtheria
Ehrlichiosis/anaplasmosis *Ehrlichia chaffeensis* *Ehrlichia ewingii* *Anaplasma phagocytophilum* Undetermined
Giardiasis
Gonorrhea
Haemophilus influenzae, invasive disease
Hansen disease (leprosy)
Hantavirus pulmonary syndrome
Hemolytic uremic syndrome, postdiarrheal
Hepatitis, viral, acute Hepatitis A, acute Hepatitis B, acute Hepatitis B, virus, perinatal infection Hepatitis C, acute
Hepatitis, viral, chronic Chronic hepatitis B Hepatitis C virus infection (past or present)
Human immunodeficiency virus (HIV) infection HIV infection, adult (≥13 years) HIV infection, pediatric (<13 years)

Influenza-associated pediatric mortality
Legionellosis
Listeriosis
Lyme disease
Malaria
Measles
Meningococcal disease
Mumps
Novel influenza A virus infections
Pertussis
Plague
Poliomyelitis, paralytic
Poliovirus infection, nonparalytic
Psittacosis
Q fever
Rabies Rabies, animal Rabies, human
Rocky Mountain spotted fever
Rubella
Rubella, congenital syndrome
Salmonellosis
Severe acute respiratory syndrome–associated Coronavirus (SARS–CoV) disease
Shiga toxin-producing *Escherichia coli* (STEC)
Shigellosis
Smallpox
Streptococcal disease, invasive, group A
Streptococcal toxic-shock syndrome
Streptococcus pneumoniae, drug resistant, invasive disease
Streptococcus pneumoniae, invasive disease non-drug resistant, in children less than 5 years of age
Syphilis Syphilis, primary Syphilis, secondary Syphilis, latent Syphilis, early latent Syphilis, late latent Syphilis, latent, unknown duration Neurosyphilis Syphilis, late, non-neurological Syphilitic stillbirth

Figure 18.10.   Nationally notifiable infectious diseases in the United States, 2012 *(continued)*

Syphilis, congenital
Tetanus
Toxic-shock syndrome (other than streptococcal)
Trichinellosis (trichinosis)
Tuberculosis
Tularemia
Typhoid fever

Vancomycin, intermediate *Staphylococcus aureus* (VISA)
Vancomycin, resistant *Staphylococcus aureus* (VRSA)
Varicella (morbidity)
Varicella (deaths only)
Vibriosis
Yellow fever

Source: CDC 2012.

identify disease epidemics and to understand patterns of disease occurrence. Case-specific information is included in the reports. Changes in age, sex, race and ethnicity, and geographic distributions can be monitored and investigated as necessary.

Check Your Understanding 18.11

Instructions: Answer the following questions on a separate piece of paper.

1. Define incidence rate and prevalence rate.

2. What is a notifiable disease?

3. Calculate the incidence rate, per 100,000, for the following hypothetical data: In 20XX, 189,000 new cases of coronary artery disease were reported in the United States. The estimated population for 20XX was 301,623,157.

Presentation of Statistical Data

Collected data are often more meaningful when presented in graphic form (consider any of the acute- or ambulatory care data previously described). How one presents such data will be governed by whether they are nominal, ordinal, interval, or ratio.

Tables, charts, and graphs offer the opportunity to analyze data sets and to explore, understand, and present frequency distributions, trends, and relationships in the data. The purpose of tables, charts, and graphs is to communicate information about the data to the user of the data.

Whatever type of graphic form is used, it should do the following:

- Display the data
- Allow the user to think about the meaning of the data
- Avoid distortion of the data
- Encourage the user to make comparisons
- Reveal data at several levels, from a broad overview to the fine detail

Methods of displaying the data in graphic form are discussed in the following subsections.

Tables

A table is an orderly arrangement of values that groups data into rows and columns. Almost any type of quantitative information can be organized into a table. Tables are useful for demonstrating patterns and other kinds of relationships. In addition, they may serve as the basis for more visual displays of data, such as charts and graphs, where some of the detail may be lost. However, because tables are not very interesting, they should be used sparingly.

A useful first step is to prepare a table shell that shows how the data will be organized and displayed. A *table shell* is the outline of a table with everything in place except for the data. (See table 18.17.) A table should contain all the information the reader needs to understand the data in it. It should have the following characteristics:

- It is a logical unit.
- It is self-explanatory and can stand on its own when photocopied or removed from its context.
- All sources are specified.
- Specific, understandable headings are provided for every column and row.
- Row and column totals are checked for accuracy.
- Blank cells are not left empty. When no information is available for a particular cell, the cell should contain a zero or a dash.
- Categories are mutually exclusive and exhaustive.

The data contained in tables should be aligned. Guidelines for aligning text and numbers include the following:

- Text in the table should be aligned at left.
- Text that serves as a column label may be centered.
- Numeric values should be aligned at right.
- When numeric values contain decimals, the decimals should be aligned.

The essential components of a table are summarized in figure 18.11.

Tables may contain information on one, two, or three variables. Tables 18.18 and 18.19 are examples of one- and two-variable tables, respectively.

Table 18.17. Table shell

TITLE								
		Sex				**Total**		
		Male		**Female**				
Box Head	**Age**	**Number**	**%**	**Number**	**%**	**Number**	**%**
Stub	*Row Variable*	→→→→→	→→→→→	→→→→→	→→→→→	→→→→→	→→→→→
	<45			*Column Variable*			
↓	45–54			↓			
↓	55–64			↓			
↓	65–74			↓			
↓	75+			↓			

Source: HHS 1994.

Figure 18.11.   Essential components of a table

Title	The title should be as complete as possible and should clearly relate to the content of the table. It should answer the following questions: • What are the data (e.g., counts, percentages)? • Who (e.g., white females with breast cancer; black males with lung cancer)? • Where are the data from (e.g., hospital, state, community)? • When (e.g., year, month)? A sample title might be: Site Distribution by Age and Sex of Cancer Patients upon First Admission to Community Hospital, 2000–2004
Box Head	The box head contains the captions or column headings. The heading of each column should contain as few words as possible but should explain exactly what the data in the column represent.
Stub	The row captions are knows as the stub. Items in the stub should be grouped to make it easy to interpret the data, for example, ages grouped into five-year intervals.
Cell	The cell is the box formed by the intersection of a column and a row.
Optional Items:	
Note	Notes are used to explain anything in the table that the reader cannot understand from the title, box head, or stub. They contain numbers, preliminary or revised numbers, or explanations of any unusual numbers. Definitions, abbreviations, and/or qualifications for captions or cell names should be footnoted. A note usually applies to a specific cell(s) within the table, and a symbol (e.g., ** or #) may be used to key the cell to the note. If several notes are used, it is better to use small letters than symbols or numbers. Note any numbers that may be confused with the numbers within the table.
Source	If data are used from a source outside the research, the exact reference to the source should be given. The source lends authenticity to the data and allows the reader to locate the original information if he or she needs it.

Source: HHS (1994).

Table 18.18.   One-variable table, Community Hospital admissions by gender, 20XX

Gender	Number	Percentage
Male	3,141	46.0
Female	3,683	54.0
Total	6,824	100.0

Table 18.19.   Two-variable table, Community Hospital admissions by race and gender, 20XX

Race	Gender		Total
	Male	**Female**	
White	2,607	2,946	5,553
Nonwhite	534	737	1,271
Total	3,141	3,683	6,824

Charts and Graphs

Charts and graphs of various types are the best means for presenting data for quick visualization of relationships. They emphasize the main points and analyze and clarify relationships among variables.

Several principles are involved in the construction of charts and graphs. When constructing charts and graphs, the following points should be considered:

- *Distortion:* To avoid distorting the data, the representation of the numbers should be proportional to the numerical quantities represented.
- *Proportion and scale:* Graphs should emphasize the horizontal. It is easier for the eye to read along the horizontal axis from left to right. Also, graphs should be greater in length than height. A useful guideline is to follow the three-quarter-high rule. This rule states that the height (*y*-axis) of the graph should be three-fourths the length (*x*-axis) of the graph.
- *Abbreviations:* Any abbreviations should be spelled out in notes.
- *Color:* Color may be used to highlight groupings that appear in the graph.
- *Print:* Both upper- and lowercase letters should be used in titles; the use of all capital letters can be difficult to read.

Bar Charts

Bar charts are used to display data from one or more variables. The bars may be drawn vertically or horizontally. The simplest bar chart is the one-variable bar chart. In this type of chart, a bar represents each category of the variable. For example, if the data in table 18.18 were displayed in a bar chart, "gender" would be the variable and "male and female" would be the variable categories. Bar charts are used for nominal or ordinal variables. Sometimes ratio data that are discrete tend to be represented with bar charts rather than histograms because they are not continuous. Figure 18.12 displays the data from table 18.18 as a bar chart. The length or height of each bar is proportional to the number of males and females admitted. Presentation of the data in a bar chart makes it easy to see that more females than males were admitted to Community Hospital.

Figure 18.13 displays the two-variable data from table 18.19 as a two-variable chart. Computer software makes it easy to create bar graphs. Be careful, though, if you choose to present data in a three-dimensional format. The reader may not always be able to estimate the true height of the bar. In a three-dimensional bar chart, the back edges of the bar appear higher than the front edge. To make sure the reader correctly interprets the chart, the bars should include the actual values for each category.

Figure 18.14 presents guidelines for constructing bar charts.

Pie Charts

A **pie chart** is an easily understood chart in which the sizes of the slices of the pie show the proportional contribution of each part. Pie charts can be used to show the component parts of a single group or variable. Pie charts are intended for interval or ratio data.

To calculate the size of each slice of the pie, first determine the proportion that each slice is to represent. Multiplying the proportion by 360 (the total number of degrees in a circle) will give the size of each slice of the pie in degrees.

Figure 18.12.   One-variable bar chart, Community Hospital admissions by gender, 20XX

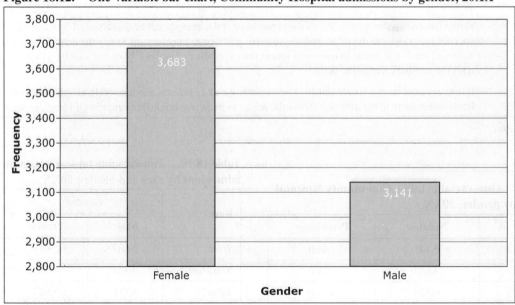

Figure 18.13.   Two-variable bar chart, Community Hospital admissions by race and gender, 20XX

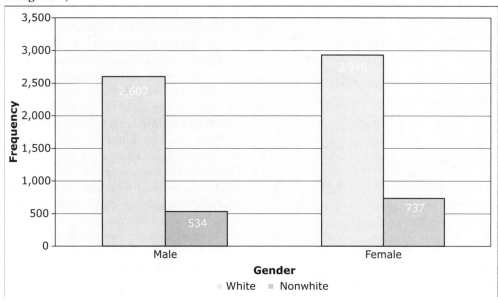

Figure 18.14.   Guidelines for constructing a bar chart

When constructing a bar chart, keep the following points in mind:

- Arrange the bar categories in a natural order, such as alphabetical order, order by increasing age, or an order that will produce increasing or decreasing bar lengths.

- The bars may be positioned vertically or horizontally.

- The length of the bars should be proportional to the frequency of the event.

- Avoid using more than three bars (categories) within a group of bars.

- Leave a space between adjacent groups of bars, but not between bars within a group.

- Code different categories of variables by differences in bar color, shading, and cross-hatching. Include a legend that explains the coding system.

Figure 18.15 shows payer data collected on admissions to Community Hospital. The summary data for one year show that managed care was the payer for 39 percent of the patients, Medicare was the payer for 30 percent, Medicaid was the payer for 18 percent, government-managed care was the payer for 8 percent of the patients, and 5 percent of the patients had commercial insurance.

With 39 percent of the pie chart, the managed care category equals approximately 140° (360° × 0.39 = 140°). The Medicare category equals 108° (360° × 0.30 = 108°). The Medicaid category equals 65° (360° × 0.18 = 65°). The government-managed care category equals approximately 29° (360° × 0.08 = 29°). And commercial insurance equals 18° (360° × 0.05 = 18°). Taken together, the slices equal 360° (140° + 108° + 65° + 29° + 18° = 360°).

The slices of the pie should be arranged in some logical order. By convention, the largest slices begin at twelve o'clock. Computer software is available to make the construction of pie charts easy. The pie chart in Figure 18.15 was prepared using Microsoft Excel software.

Line Graphs

A **line graph** may be used to display time trends. A line graph can show trends or patterns of quantitative data over time. The x-axis shows the unit of time from left to right, and the y-axis measures the values of the variable

Figure 18.15.   Pie chart, Community Hospital admissions by payer, 20XX

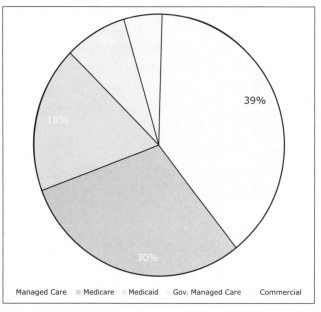

Figure 18.16.   Line graph with point data, Community Hospital admissions, 2008–2012

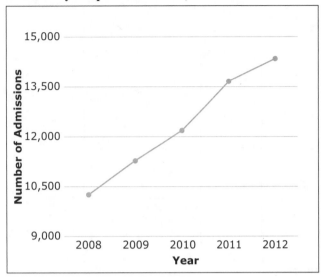

Either actual numbers or percentages may be used on the *y*-axis of the graph. Percentages should be used on the *y*-axis when more than one distribution is to be shown. A percentage distribution allows comparisons among groups where the actual totals are different.

When two or more sets of data are plotted on the same graph, the lines should be made different—solid or broken—for each set. However, the number of lines should be kept to a minimum to avoid confusion. Each line then should be identified in a legend located on the graph.

There are two kinds of time-trend data: point data and period data. Point data reflect an instant in time. Figure 18.16 displays point data—the total number of admissions for each year represented in the graph. Period data are averages or totals over a specified period of time, such as a five-year time frame. Table 18.20 summarizes period data for survival rates of patients diagnosed with kidney cancer at Community Hospital. Figure 18.17 displays these period data in a line graph.

being plotted. A line graph does not represent a **frequency distribution.**

A line graph consists of a line connecting a series of points. Like all graphs, a line graph should be constructed so that it is easy to read. Selection of the proper scale, a complete and accurate title, and an informative legend is important. When a graph is too long and narrow, either vertically or horizontally, it has an awkward appearance and may exaggerate one aspect of the data.

A line graph is especially useful for plotting a large number of observations. It also allows several sets of data to be presented on one graph.

Table 18.20.   Sample five-year survival rates for kidney cancer by stage, for patients diagnosed between 2000 and 2008

Year of Diagnosis	Midpoint of Interval	Survival Rate (%)		
		Localized	Regional	Distant
2000–2002	2001	80	71	28
2003–2005	2004	84	74	29
2006–2008	2007	85	74	31

Figure 18.17.   Period data trend line: Survival rates for kidney cancer by stage for patients diagnosed from 2000 to 2009

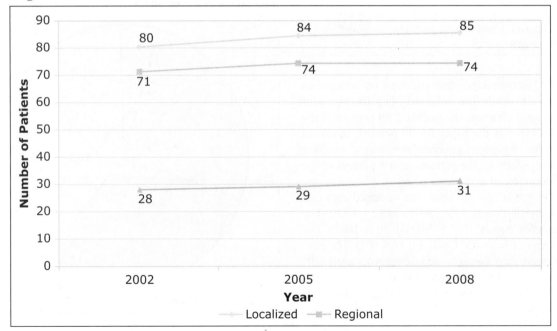

Figure 18.18.   Histogram, Community Hospital LOS of patients discharged from DRG 127, 20XX

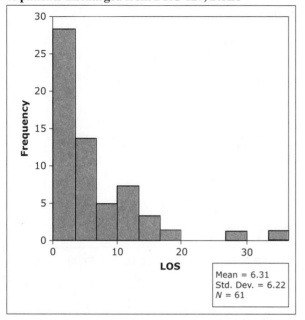

Mean = 6.31
Std. Dev. = 6.22
N = 61

Histograms

A **histogram** is used to display a frequency distribution. It is different from a bar graph in that a bar graph is used to display data that fall into groups or categories (nominal or ordinal data). The categories are noncontinuous, or discrete. In a bar chart, the bars representing the different categories are separated. (Refer to figures 18.12 and 18.13.) On the other hand, histograms are used to illustrate frequency distributions of continuous variables, such as age or LOS. A continuous variable can take on a fractional value (for example, 75.345°F). With continuous variables, there are no gaps between values because the values progress fractionally. Histograms are used for interval or ratio variables.

In a histogram, the frequency distribution may be displayed as a number or a percentage. The histogram consists of a series of bars. Each bar has one class interval as its base and the number (frequency) or percentage of cases in that class interval as its height. A class interval is a type of category. It can represent one value in a frequency distribution (for example, three years of age) or a group of values (for example, ages three to five).

In histograms, there are no spaces between the bars. (See figure 18.18.) The lack of spaces between bars depicts the continuous nature of the distribution. The sum of the heights of the bars represents the total number, or 100 percent, of the cases. Histograms should be used when the distribution of the data needs to be emphasized more than the values of the distribution.

Frequency Polygons

A **frequency polygon** is an alternative to a histogram. Like a histogram, it is a graph of a frequency distribution, but in line form rather than bar form, and is intended for interval or ratio data. The advantage of frequency polygons is that several of them can be placed on the same graph to make comparisons. Another advantage is that frequency polygons are easy to interpret.

When constructing a frequency polygon, the x-axis should be made longer than the y-axis to avoid distorting the data. The frequency of observations is always placed on the y-axis and the scale of the variable on the x-axis. The frequency polygon in figure 18.19 plots the same data that appear in the histogram in figure 18.18. Because the x-axis represents the entire frequency distribution, the line starts at zero cases and ends with zero cases. Frequency polygons are used for interval or ratio variables

Scatter Charts

Scatter charts, also called scatter plots or scatter diagrams, are used when one wants to determine if there is a relationship between two variables, such as charges and LOS.

Figure 18.19.   Frequency polygon, Community Hospital LOS of patients discharged from DRG 127, 20XX

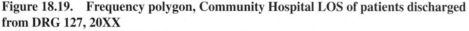
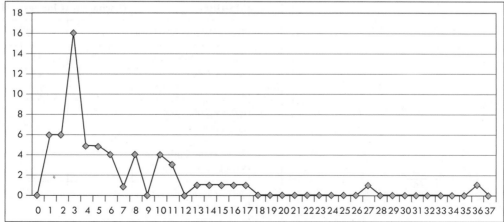

Figure 18.20.   Scatter chart, perfect positive relationship

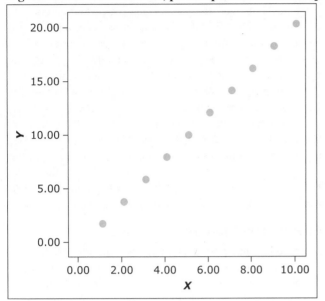

Figure 18.22.   Scatter chart, no relationship

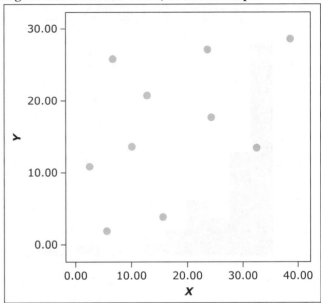

Data collected for scatter charts must be at the interval or ratio level of measurement. The data for the two variables are arranged in pairs; one of the two variables is plotted on the *x*-axis and the other variable is plotted on the *y*-axis. The closer the data points come to making a straight line, the stronger the relationship between the two variables. If the data points form a straight line from the lower left of the *x*-axis to the upper right on the *y*-axis, the relationship is positive. (See figure 18.20.) If the line begins at a high value on the *y*-axis and descends to a low value on the *x*-axis, the relationship is negative. (See figure 18.21.) If the data points are widely scattered, there is no relationship between the two variables. (See figure 18.22.)

Figure 18.21.   Scatter chart, perfect negative relationship

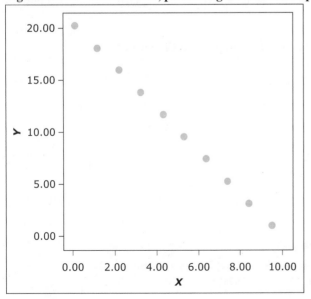

Bubble Charts

A **bubble chart** is a type of scatter plot with circular symbols used to compare three variables; the size of the symbol indicates the value of a third variable. In developing the chart, one variable is displayed on the vertical or *y*-axis, and two variables are displayed on the horizontal or *x*-axis. Data must be at the interval or ratio level of measurement.

As an example, an administrator at Community Hospital is interested in displaying the average charges for the five highest-volume MS-DRGs in the organization. The number of discharges will be displayed on the *x*-axis, and average charges will be displayed on the *y*-axis. The size of the bubble indicates the percentage of total discharges for each MS-DRG. The data are displayed in table 18.21,

Table 18.21.   Top five high-volume discharges, average charges, and percent of total discharges, Community Hospital, 20XX

MS-DRG	Number of Discharges	Average Charges	Percent of Total Discharges
795—Normal Newborn	637	$1,239	9.8
946—Rehabilitation w/o CC/MCC	542	$21,517	8.4
775—Vaginal Delivery w/o Complicating Diagnoses	505	$5,576	7.8
293—Heart Failure and Shock w/o CC/MCC	287	$12,043	4.4
766—Cesarean Section w/o CC/MCC	189	$7,626	2.9

Figure 18.23. Bubble chart, top five high-volume discharges, average charges, and percent of total discharges, Community Hospital, 20XX

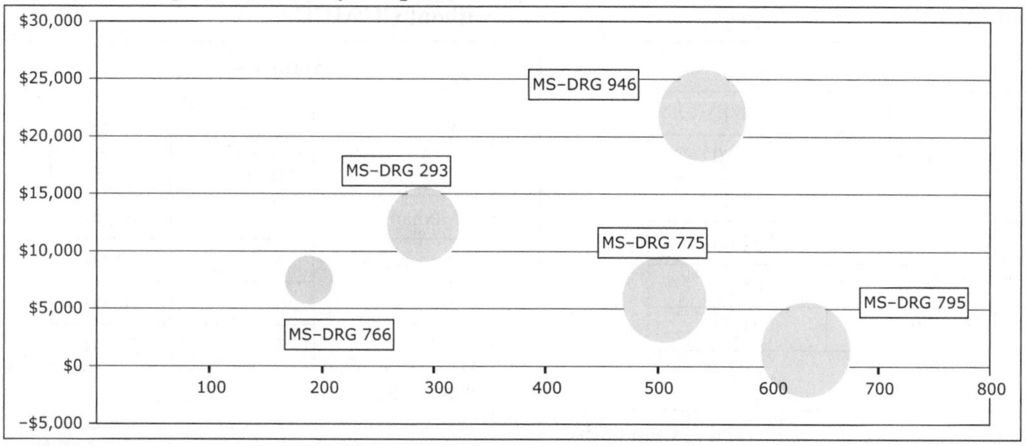

and the corresponding bubble chart is displayed in figure 18.23. It can easily be seen that MS-DRG 795, Normal Newborn, has the highest proportion of overall discharges and the lowest average charges among the top-volume MS-DRGs.

Stem and Leaf Plots

In **stem and leaf plots,** data can be organized so that the shape of a frequency distribution is revealed. As an example, a stem and leaf plot will be constructed on the age of 12 patients discharged from MS-DRG 68, Nonspecific CVA and Precerebral Occlusion w/o Infarct w/o MCC. The ages are ranked in order from lowest to highest:

44   51   52   52   62   65   65   66   68   72   76   82

To develop the plot, break each number into two parts. The last number is called the leaf and the rest of the number is called the stem. Thus, for the number 51, 1 is the leaf and 5 is the stem, and for the number 125, 5 is the leaf and 12 is the stem. The data are then arranged in a table that looks somewhat like a T, with the stem portion in the first column and the leaf portion in the second column. For our data set, the stems are 4, 5, 6, 7, and 8. The leaf portion is then filled in with the last digits that correspond to each stem as shown in table 18.22.

The completed plot reveals the distribution of the data set. It can immediately be seen that the lowest value in the distribution is 44 and the highest is 82 and that there are

five observations in the 60s age group. With this type of display you can quickly see that most patients are in their 60s. Turning the table on its side shows a fairly normal bell-shaped distribution (see table 18.23). These can be used for interval data.

Boxplots

Boxplots are useful in summarizing a data set. In a box-plot, a single variable in two categories can be compared. The boxplot reveals the range, the median, and the 25th and 75th percentiles for the distribution. They can be used to show interval data. To illustrate, patients discharged from MS-DRGs 66, Intracranial Hemorrhage or Cerebral Infarction w/o CC/MCC, and 68, Nonspecific CVA & Precerebral Occlusion w/o Infarct w/o MCC, are compared with age as the variable.

The frequency distributions appear in figures 18.24 and 18.25. Twelve patients were discharged from MS-DRG 68 ranging in age from 44 to 82; 38 patients were discharged from MS-DRG 66 ranging in age from 22 to 86. The boxplot, shown in figure 18.26, displays these data side by side. Even though there are more discharges from MS-DRG 66 with a wider range in age, the median age for both MS-DRGs is similar, 62 and 65, respectively. The interquartile range (25th to 75th quartile) for both groups is age 52 to 72 for MS-DRG 66 and age 51 to 73 for MS-DRG 68.

Table 18.22   Stem and leaf plotting—step 1

Stem	Leaf
4	4
5	122
6	25568
7	26
8	2

Table 18.23   Stem and leaf plotting—step 2

			8		
L			8		
e			6		
a		2	5		
f		2	5	6	
	4	1	2	2	2
Stem	4	5	6	7	8

Figure 18.24.   Frequency distribution for age, MS-DRG 68 Nonspecific CVA and Precerebral Occlusion without Infarct without MCC

Age

N	Valid	12
	Missing	0
Median		65.00
Percentiles	25	52.00
	50	65.00
	75	71.00

Age

		Frequency	Percent	Valid Percent	Cumulative Percent
Valid	44	1	8.3	8.3	8.3
	51	1	8.3	8.3	16.7
	52	2	16.7	16.7	33.3
	62	1	8.3	8.3	41.7
	65	2	16.7	16.7	58.3
	66	1	8.3	8.3	66.7
	68	1	8.3	8.3	75.0
	72	1	8.3	8.3	83.3
	76	1	8.3	8.3	91.7
	82	1	8.3	8.3	100.0*
	Total	12	100.0*	100.0*	

*rounded

Spreadsheets and Statistical Packages

Electronic spreadsheets, such as Microsoft Excel, and statistical packages, such as SPSS or SAS, can be used to facilitate the data collection and analysis processes. The advantage of using one of these tools is that charts and graphs can be formulated at the time the data are being analyzed. Instruction on the use of these tools is beyond the scope of this chapter; however, they are available on the market, and readers are encouraged to learn how to use them.

Check Your Understanding 18.12

Instructions: Complete the following sentences on a separate sheet of paper.

1. A presentation of data in rows and columns is a ___.

2. A graphic display technique used to display parts of a whole is a ___.

3. A graphic display technique used to show trends over time is a ___.

Figure 18.25.   Frequency distribution for age, MS-DRG 66 Intracranial hemorrhage or cerebral infarction without CC/MCC

Age

Statistics

N	Valid	38
	Missing	0
Median		62.00
Percentiles	25	51.50
	50	62.00
	75	73.50

Age

		Frequency	Percent	Valid Percent	Cumulative Percent
Valid	22	1	2.6	2.6	2.6
	23	1	2.6	2.6	5.3
	26	1	2.6	2.6	7.9
	39	1	2.6	2.6	10.5
	44	1	2.6	2.6	13.2
	46	1	2.6	2.6	15.8
	47	1	2.6	2.6	18.4
	49	1	2.6	2.6	21.1
	50	1	2.6	2.6	23.7
	52	1	2.6	2.6	26.3
	55	1	2.6	2.6	28.9
	56	1	2.6	2.6	31.6
	57	3	7.9	7.9	39.5
	58	2	5.3	5.3	44.7
	60	2	5.3	5.3	50.0
	64	1	2.6	2.6	52.6
	68	2	5.3	5.3	57.9
	70	2	5.3	5.3	63.2
	71	2	5.3	5.3	68.4
	72	2	5.3	5.3	73.7
	73	1	2.6	2.6	76.3
	75	1	2.6	2.6	78.9
	76	1	2.6	2.6	81.6
	77	2	5.3	5.3	86.8
	78	1	2.6	2.6	89.5
	83	1	2.6	2.6	92.1
	84	1	2.6	2.6	94.7
	86	2	5.3	5.3	100.0*
	Total	38	100.0*	100.0*	

*rounded

Figure 18.26.   Boxplot of age, DRGs 14 and 15

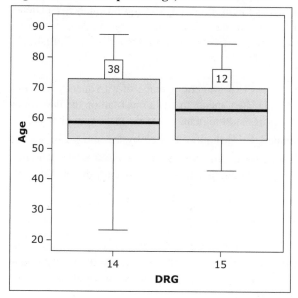

4. A graphic display technique used to display categories of a variable is a ___.

5. A graphic display technique that may be used to show the age distribution of a population is a ___.

6. A graphic technique that can visually compare the range of a variable between two categories is a ___.

7. A graphic display that can help one determine if there is a relationship between two variables is a _____.

Descriptive Statistics

Measures of central tendency and measures of **variability** are used to describe frequency distributions. Measures of central tendency are measures of location; they indicate the typical value of a frequency distribution. Variation emphasizes differences and scattering around the typical value of a data set. Inferences about populations from samples are based on the variation of the observations in the data set.

Descriptive measures are computed from both populations and samples. A population is a group of persons or objects about which an investigator wants to draw a conclusion. A sample is a subset of a population. Measures that result from a compilation of data from populations are called parameters. Measures that result from samples are called statistics. For example, if an organization is interested in the average age of undergraduates enrolled at City University, all registered undergraduates would be the defined population. If the average age of the entire population of undergraduate students is calculated, the resultant average is a population parameter. However, if a sample is drawn from the registered undergraduate students and the average age is calculated, the resultant average is a sample statistic.

A variety of **descriptive statistics** are available to help a researcher summarize data for a variable in a frequency distribution. The choice of which descriptive statistics to use is determined, for the most part, by a variable's scale of measurement. Later, the shape of a variable's frequency distribution will be identified as another relevant factor.

Measures of Central Tendency—The Center of a Variable's Values

Measures of central tendency and variability also can be used to describe populations. Measures of central tendency discussed in this subsection are the mean, median, and mode. There are three measures of the center of a distribution of values. The most appropriate center to use can often be determined on the basis of the scale of measurement of the variable considered. Modes are used for nominal-level variables; medians are used for ordinal-level variables; and means are used for interval- and ratio-level variables.

A frequency distribution shows the values that a variable can take and the number of observations associated with each value. For example, using LOS as the variable, five patients were discharged with the following lengths of stay:

Patient	LOS
1	2 days
2	3 days
3	4 days
4	2 days
5	3 days

The data displayed here are referred to as a frequency distribution. A frequency distribution displays the number of times a particular observation occurs for the variable being measured. In this example, the number of times a certain LOS occurs is the variable of interest. The frequency distribution for LOS, in ascending order, is 2, 2, 3, 3, and 4 days.

Frequency distributions may be constructed for both discrete and continuous data. As an example, Community Hospital wants to construct a frequency distribution showing the LOS of patients who were discharged on May 10. LOS is a continuous variable falling on the ratio scale of measurement. The hospital wants to see how many of these patients were in the hospital for a particular LOS (for example, four days). The variable is the LOS, and the frequency is the number of times a particular LOS occurred among the patients discharged on May 10.

To construct the frequency distribution, list all the values that the particular LOS can take, from the lowest observed value to the highest. Then enter the number of times a discharged patient had that particular LOS. Table 18.24 shows a frequency distribution for LOS on May 10. Notice that the frequency distribution lists all the values for LOS between the lowest and the highest, even when there are no observations

Table 18.24.   Calculation of the variance, LOS data

LOS	LOS – Mean (5.8) $(X - \overline{X})$	(LOS – Mean)² $(X - \overline{X})^2$
1	–4.8	23.04
1	–4.8	23.04
2	–3.8	14.44
2	–3.8	14.44
4	–1.8	3.24
4	–1.8	3.24
4	–1.8	3.24
4	–1.8	3.24
4	–1.8	3.24
4	–1.8	3.24
5	–0.8	0.64
5	–0.8	0.64
5	–0.8	0.64
5	–0.8	0.64
5	–0.8	0.64
5	–0.8	0.64
6	0.2	0.04
6	0.2	0.04
6	0.2	0.04
6	0.2	0.04
6	0.2	0.04
6	0.2	0.04
6	0.2	0.04
6	0.2	0.04
6	0.2	0.04
6	0.2	0.04
7	1.2	1.44
7	1.2	1.44
7	1.2	1.44
7	1.2	1.44
7	1.2	1.44
7	1.2	1.44
8	2.2	4.84
8	2.2	4.84
8	2.2	4.84
8	2.2	4.84
8	2.2	4.84
9	3.2	10.24
9	3.2	10.24
9	3.2	10.24
10	4.2	17.64
Total	0*	179.88

*rounded

$$s^2 = \sum_{i}^{n}(X_1 - X)^2/N - 1$$
$$= 179.88/41$$
$$= 4.39$$

for some of the values. For example, there are no observations of patients spending three days in the hospital. Six patients have LOS of four days. The data in table 18.24 can be used to calculate measures of both central tendency and variability.

Mean

The **mean** is the arithmetic average of a frequency distribution. To calculate a mean, the data must fall on the interval or ratio scales of measurement. The mean is the sum of all scores in a frequency distribution divided by the number of scores. The symbol for the mean is $\overline{X}i$ (pronounced x-bar). The formula for calculating the mean in a frequency distribution is

$$\overline{X} \bullet \sum_{i}^{n} X_1/N$$

where $\sum$ is summation; Xi is each successive observation from the first one in the frequency distribution, $i = 1$, to the last observation; and N is the total number of observations.

To calculate the ALOS for the data in table 18.24, substitute the appropriate figures into the formula shown in formula 18.24. The ALOS for patients discharged from Community Hospital on May 10 is 5.8 days (rounded).

Formula 18.24   Calculating the mean of a frequency distribution

$$\overline{X} = \sum_{i}^{n} X_1/N$$

$$\overline{X} = \frac{\begin{matrix}1+1+2+2+4+4+4+4+4+4\\+5+5+5+5+5+5\\+6+6+6+6+6+6+6+6+6+6\\+7+7+7+7+7+7\\+8+8+8+8+8+9+9+9+10\end{matrix}}{42}$$

$$\overline{X} = 245/42$$
$$\overline{X} = 5.8$$

Two disadvantages are associated with using the mean as the most typical value in a frequency distribution. First, in this example, the LOS for the 42 patients are integers (whole numbers). However, the ALOS is fractional (5.8), even though there is no fractional LOS. Fractional values are considered more a problem of interpretation than a result that is not meaningful. In this case, the ALOS is interpreted as, "On average, the length of stay for the patients discharged from the Community Hospital on May 10 is between 5 and 6 days."

Second, the mean is sensitive to extreme measures. That is, it is strongly influenced by outliers. For example, if the 10-day LOS were actually a 25-day LOS, the ALOS would increase to 6.2 days.

Thus, the average or arithmetic mean may not always be the most appropriate way to summarize the most typical value of a frequency distribution. The measure of central tendency selected to describe the typical value of a frequency distribution should be based on the characteristics of that particular frequency distribution.

Median

The **median** is the midpoint of a frequency distribution and falls in the ordinal scale of measurement. It is the point at which 50 percent of the observations fall above and 50 percent fall below. If an odd number of observations is in the frequency distribution, the median is the middle number. In the following frequency distribution, the median is 13. Three observations fall above the value of 13, and three fall below it:

$$10 \quad 11 \quad 12 \quad \mathbf{13} \quad 14 \quad 15 \quad 16$$

If an even number of observations is in the frequency distribution, the median is the midpoint between the two middle observations. It is found by averaging the two middle scores ($[x + y]/2$). In the following example, the median is 13.5 ($[13 + 14]/2$):

$$10 \quad 11 \quad 12 \quad \mathbf{13} \quad \mathbf{14} \quad 15 \quad 16 \quad 17$$

If the two middle observations take on the same value, the median is that value. When determining the median, it does not matter whether there are duplicate observations in the frequency distribution. Consider the following frequency distribution:

$$10 \quad 11 \quad 11 \quad 12 \quad \mathbf{13} \quad \mathbf{13} \quad 14 \quad 15 \quad 16 \quad 17$$

In this frequency distribution, the median falls between the fifth and sixth observations. Therefore, the median is 13 ($[13 + 13]/2$).

Table 18.23 records LOS data for 42 patients. In this example, the median falls between the 21st and 22nd observations. Placed in order from lowest to highest, the distribution is as follows:

1 1 2 2 4 4 4 4 4 5 5 5 5 5 6 6 6 6 6 6 **6**
6 6 6 6 6 7 7 7 7 7 7 8 8 8 8 9 9 9 10

The median is 6 ($[6 + 6]/2$).

The median offers the following three advantages:

- It is relatively easy to calculate
- It is based on the whole distribution and not just a portion of it, as is the case with the mode
- Unlike the mean, it is not influenced by extreme values or unusual outliers in the frequency distribution

Mode

The **mode** is the simplest measure of central tendency. It is used to indicate the most frequent observation in a frequency distribution. The mode offers several advantages, including the following:

- It is easy to obtain and interpret
- It is not sensitive to extreme observations in the frequency distribution
- It is easy to communicate and explain to others
- It can be used with nominal-level data

However, there are also disadvantages:

- It may not be descriptive of the distribution when the most frequent observation does not occur very often, especially when the number of observations is large.
- It may not be unique. That is, more than one mode may be in a distribution. A frequency distribution may be unimodal, bimodal, or multimodal. When each observation occurs an equal number of times, the distribution does not have a mode.
- It does not provide information about the entire distribution, only the observation that occurs most frequently.

In table 18.24, the mode is 6 because 11 patients had a length of stay of 6 days. To summarize, for the LOS data in table 18.24, the measures of central tendency are similar. The mean is 5.8 days, the median is 6 days, and the mode is 6 days. These statistics are summarized in table 18.25.

Measures of Variability—Spread of a Variable's Values

In addition to measures of central tendency, the hospital can use measures of variability to describe frequency distributions. These measures indicate how widely the observations are spread out around the measures of central tendency. The measures of spread increase with greater variation in the frequency distribution. The spread is equal to zero when there is no variation. The spread of a nominal-level's variable can only be depicted by frequency data. Ordinal-level data may also be displayed as frequencies, but sometimes it may help to calculate a range. Standard deviations

Table 18.25. Descriptive statistics for LOS data

N	Valid	42
	Missing	0
Mean		5.8333
Median		6.0000
Mode		6.00
Standard deviation		2.09432
Variance		4.386
Range		9.00
Minimum		1.00
Maximum		10.00

and their squared values are used to represent interval- and ratio-level data so long as such data are normally distributed; otherwise ranges are used for these kinds of data as well. This subsection discusses the following measures of spread: the range, the variance, and the standard deviation.

Range

The **range** is the simplest measure of spread. It is the difference between the smallest and largest values in a frequency distribution:

$$\text{Range} = X_{max} - X_{min}$$

The range for the LOS data in table 18.24 is 9 (10 – 1 = 9).

One disadvantage of the range is that it can be affected by extreme values, or outliers, in the distribution. Also, the range varies widely from sample to sample. Only the two most extreme observations affect its value, so it is not sensitive to other observations in the distribution.

Two frequency distributions may have the same range but differ greatly in variation. For example, the range for the following frequency distributions is 9 (10 – 1 = 9):

Distribution 1: 1 2 3 4 5 6 7 8 9 10
Distribution 2: 1 1.5 3 3.5 3.7 7 8 8.26 10 10

However, when the two distributions are compared, the second distribution has more variation than the first distribution. This is demonstrated when the variance is calculated. The variance for the first distribution is 9.1, and the variance for the second distribution is 11.8.

Variance

The **variance** of a frequency distribution is the average of the squared deviations from the mean. The variance of a sample is symbolized by s^2. The variance of a distribution is larger when the observations are widely spread. The formula for calculating the variance:

$$\overline{X} = \sum_{i}^{n} X_i / N$$

The squared deviations of the mean are calculated by subtracting the mean of the frequency distribution from each value in the distribution. The difference between the two values is squared, $(X - \overline{X})^2$. The squared differences are summed and divided by $N - 1$. The calculations for the variance for the LOS data in table 18.24 are shown in formula 18.25

Formula 18.25   Calculation of the Variance of a Frequency Distribution

$$s^2 = \sqrt{\frac{\Sigma(X - \overline{X})^2}{N - 1}}$$
$$= 179.88/41$$
$$= 4.39$$

In the calculations for the variance, the sum of $(X - \overline{X})$ is equal to zero. This is because the mean is the balance point in the distribution. When a value is less than the mean, the difference is negative (1 – 5.8 = – 4.8); when the value is greater than the mean, the difference is positive (6 – 5.8 = 0.2). Therefore, the sum of the differences from the mean is equal to zero. In this example, the sum approximates zero because the actual mean of 5.8333 was rounded to 5.8 for ease in calculation.

The concept of variance is meaningful in more advanced procedures, but in the case of describing the distribution of a single variable, the standard deviation is preferred.

Standard Deviation

The variance for the LOS data in table 18.24 is 4.39, but what does this mean? The interpretation of the variance is not meaningful at the descriptive level because the original units of measure—the lengths of stay—are squared to arrive at the variance. By calculating the square root of the variance, the data are returned to the original units of measurement. This is called the **standard deviation**, which is symbolized by s. The formula for the standard deviation is

$$s = \sqrt{\frac{\Sigma(X - \overline{X})}{N - 1}}$$

The standard deviation for the LOS data is 2.1.

The standard deviation is the most widely used measure of variability in descriptive statistics. Because it is easy to interpret, it is the preferred measure of dispersion for frequency distributions. Most handheld calculators include features for calculating the variance and the standard deviation.

The measures of central tendency and variation may be calculated using a handheld calculator. Also, statistical packages such as SPSS are available for performing these and other descriptive and **inferential statistics.** The histograms were prepared using SPSS. The SPSS output for the LOS data appears in table 18.25. The slight differences between the handheld calculator results and the SPSS results in the mean, variance, and standard deviation are because of rounding.

Check Your Understanding 18.13

Instructions: Fifteen infants were born at Community Hospital during the week of December 1. Using a handheld calculator, determine the measures of central tendency and variability for the following infant birth weights (in grams):

2,450	2,750	2,600
2,540	2,815	2,540
2,300	1,735	1,720

2,715   1,800   2,780

2,400   2,485   2,640

1. ___ Mean

2. ___ Median

3. ___ Mode

4. ___ Range

5. ___ Variance

6. ___ Standard deviation

Normal Distribution

The **normal distribution** is actually a theoretical family of distributions that may have any mean or any standard deviation. It is bell-shaped and symmetrical about the mean. Because it is symmetrical, 50 percent of the observations fall above the mean and 50 percent fall below it. In a normal distribution, the mean, median, and mode are equal. The values of the normal distribution range from minus infinity ($-\infty$) to plus infinity ($+\infty$).

In the normal distribution, the **standard deviation** indicates how many observations fall within a certain range of the mean. The areas under the curve corresponding to one, two, and three standard deviations are 68.3 percent, 95.4 percent, and 99.7 percent.

Figure 18.27 shows an example of a normal distribution superimposed on a histogram. The center of the distribution, or mean, is 6. (The median and the mode also

Figure 18.28.   Histogram of LOS with superimposed normal curve

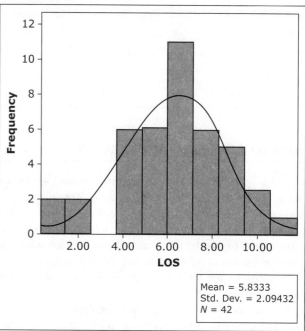

Mean = 5.8333
Std. Dev. = 2.09432
N = 42

are 6.) The standard deviation is 2.45. This means that 68 percent of the observations in the frequency distribution fall within 2.45 standard deviations of 6 (6 ± 2.45). Thus, 68 percent fall between 3.55 and 8.45; 95 percent fall between 1.1 and 10.9; and 99.7 percent fall between 21.35 and 13.35.

As shown in figure 18.27, a characteristic of the normal distribution is that each tail of the curve approaches the *x*-axis but never touches it, no matter how far from center the line is.

A histogram of the frequency distribution for the LOS data in table 18.24 is shown in figure 18.28. The distribution is more peaked than the normal distribution and so is considered kurtotic. *Kurtosis* is the vertical stretching of a distribution.

A skewed distribution is asymmetrical. Skewness is the horizontal stretching of a frequency distribution to one side or the other so that one tail is longer than the other. The longer tail has more observations. Because the mean is sensitive to extreme observations, it moves in the direction of the long tail when a distribution is skewed. When the direction of the tail is off to the right, the distribution is positively skewed, or skewed to the right. When the direction of the tail is off to the left, the distribution is negatively skewed, or skewed to the left. When the mean and the median approximate one another (as with the LOS data), the distribution is not significantly skewed. A perfect normal distribution has a zero skew. If an interval or ratio-level distribution is skewed, the median may be more appropriate than the mean in representing the center of such a distribution.

Figure 18.27.   Histogram of normal distribution

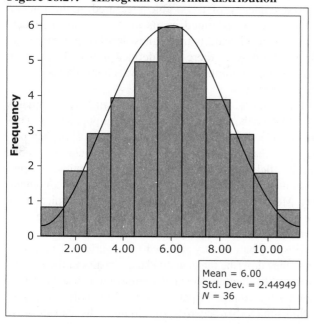

Mean = 6.00
Std. Dev. = 2.44949
N = 36

Instructions: Answer the following questions on a separate piece of paper.

1. What are the characteristics of a normal distribution?

2. What is the definition of the term *skewness?*

3. What is kurtosis?

How to Analyze Information

As health information management professionals we are be able to access so much patient information. The information in a healthcare facility is vital to the health and future of that facility. Because of the quantity of the information, we need to know how to use the information to its best advantage. It is not the amount of information that will help administrators make decisions but the knowledge within that information that is important.

We make decisions everyday based on the information we have. For example, if you receive a failing grade on a test, you know you must study harder to receive a passing grade in a class. Personal decisions we make have a powerful effect on our lives. If you receive that failing grade and do not study harder, you may not pass your classes and be forced to leave school, thereby not fulfilling your dreams. Just as personal decisions have an impact on us, professional decisions can affect a healthcare facility. If a hospital board of directors decides not to take into consideration changes in payment methodologies for its patients, there could be widespread ramifications. So, just how can we analyze information?

In his book, *How to Analyze Information* (2010), Herbert Meyers suggests that there is a seven-step process to follow that will help someone make the best decision he or she can with the information available.

- First, figure out where you are. You will need to know where your business is currently in order to make decisions about it. You do not need all the detail in this step, but having a good idea how your business is doing will allow you to move forward.
- Second, be sure you are seeing clearly. You need to have a generally accurate idea of the issues at hand.
- Third, decide what you need to decide. In this step you need to be certain that you are asking the right questions. What is it you are really trying to accomplish?
- Next, determine what you need to know. Make a list of the information you need in order to make a decision. Take your time; list everything and if you miss something you discover later on, just go back to this step and add it to the list.
- Fifth, collect the information. But, first ask yourself, what is the most reliable source for the information? Go to the best source you know. This may include checking all your indices or interviewing individuals. Get all the information you can.
- Next, turn the information into knowledge. After you have collected the information, turn these into facts and keep an eye out for any patterns that may occur. When determining facts and patterns this becomes knowledge.
- Finally, add your own judgment. Your judgment is made up of the knowledge you gleaned from the information you gathered and you—your character, your personality and your instincts. You can see from this last step that faced with the same knowledge, two people may make entirely different decisions.

The effect of the decisions made by healthcare administrators through the analysis of data is enormous and can affect the viability of the facility.

Summary

The nominal, ordinal, interval, and ratio scales of measurement are discussed in this chapter. In nominal measure, names are given to objects or categories. Nominal data's measure of central tendency is the mode. Examples of nominal data include gender, marital status, health insurance type, race, and place of residence. In ordinal data the numbers given to categories represent rank order. The central tendency of ordinal data can be represented by its mode or its median. Examples of ordinal data include patient health status (for example, critical, stable, good) or opinion scales (strongly agree to strongly disagree). The most important characteristic of interval-level data is that the intervals between successive values are equal. Examples include temperature and years. The central tendency of a variable measured at the interval level can be represented by its mode, median, or mean. The ratio-level scale is the highest level of measurement. On the ratio scale there is a defined unit of measure, it has a real zero point, and the intervals between successive values are equal.

Rates, ratios, proportions, and statistics are commonly used to describe community and hospital populations. They are considered to be descriptive statistics because they portray the characteristics of a group or population. Public health officials use community-based rates, ratios, and proportions to evaluate the general health status of a community. Morbidity and mortality rates are used as indicators of the accessibility and availability of healthcare services in a community.

Hospital-based rates are used for a variety of purposes. First, they describe the general characteristics of the patients treated at the facility. Hospital administrators use the data to monitor the volume of patients treated monthly, weekly, or within some other specified time frame. The statistics give healthcare decision makers the information they need to plan facilities and to monitor inpatient and outpatient revenue streams.

Graphic techniques are often used to summarize and clarify data. Data may be displayed in a variety of ways, for example, as charts, graphs, and tables. Graphic forms are effective ways to present large quantities of information.

Analysis of data is a seven-step process that can assist health information professionals in learning how to think about the data presented and allow them to help the facility's administration in their decision-making processes.

The health information management professional is in a position to serve as a data broker for the healthcare organization. To do this, he or she must fully understand the clinical data that are collected and their application to the decision-making process. In addition, he or she must know what information is needed and how to provide it in a timely manner. The seven-step process suggested by Herbert Meyers can help health information professionals think about what data are needed and how they should be presented to be most valuable to the person who needs them for making specific decisions. With this knowledge, the HIM professional is an invaluable member of the healthcare team.

References

American Health Information Management Association. 2012. *Pocket Glossary of Health Information Management and Technology*, 3rd ed. Chicago: AHIMA.

Centers for Disease Control and Prevention. 2012. Division of Public Health Surveillance and Informatics. Nationally notifiable infectious diseases. United States, 2012. http://www.cdc.gov/osels/ph_surveillance/nndss/phs/infdis.htm.

Centers for Disease Control and Prevention. 2011a. National Center for Health Statistics. 2003 Revisions of the U.S. Standard Certificates of Live Birth and Death and the Fetal Death Report. http://www.cdc.gov/nchs/nvss/vital_certificate_revisions.htm.

Centers for Disease Control and Prevention. 2011b. National Center for Health Statistics. Handbook on the reporting of induced termination of pregnancy. http://www.cdc.gov/nchs/data/misc/hb_itop.pdf.

Centers for Disease Control and Prevention. 2010. CDC Wonder Data Base. http://wonder.cdc.gov.

Centers for Disease Control and Prevention. 2008. "Deaths: Final Data for 2005." National Vital Statistics Report. 56 (10).

Department of Health and Human Services, Public Health Service. 1994. *Self-Instructional Manual for Tumor Registrars, Book 7: Statistics and Epidemiology for Cancer Registries.* NIH Publication No. 94-3766. Washington, D.C.: HHS. http://seer.cancer.gov/training/manuals/Book7.pdf.

Meyers, H.E. 2010. *How to Analyze Information.* Friday Harbor, WA: Storm King Press.

National Vital Statistics System. 2011. Centers for Disease Control and Prevention. http://cdc.gov.nchs.nvss.htm.

Osborn, C.E. 2005. *Statistical Applications for Health Information Management.* Sudbury, MA: Jones and Bartlett.

chapter 19

Healthcare Data Analytics

Susan White, PhD, CHDA

Learning Objectives

- Describe the role of data analytics in healthcare operations
- Apply statistical techniques to healthcare data
- Define statistical inference
- Calculate hypothesis tests and confidence intervals
- Understand the role of HIM professionals in healthcare data analytics

Key Terms

Accountable care organization (ACO)
Benchmarking
Coefficient of determination
Confidence interval
Continuous variable
Correlation
Dashboard
Data analytics
Data mining
Descriptive statistics
Healthcare data analytics
Hypothesis test
Indirect standardization
Inferential statistics
Key performance indicator

Mean
Median
Mode
One-sample *t*-test
Pay for performance (P4P)
Predictive modeling
P-value
RAT-STATS
Revenue cycle
Simple linear regression (SLR)
Standard deviation
Standardized mortality ratio (SMR)
Type I error
Variance

Data Analytics in Healthcare

The term **data analytics** is used to describe a variety of approaches to using data to make business decisions. **Healthcare data analytics** is therefore the practice of using data to make business decisions in healthcare. More specifically, healthcare data analytics is the application of statistical techniques to allow informed decisions to be made based on the data. A variety of descriptive statistics were discussed in chapter 18. They included rates and proportions as well as measures of central tendency such as the mean, median, and mode. In Chapter 20, the concept of inferential statistics is introduced in the context of research methods. In this chapter, both sets of statistical techniques will be applied in the healthcare operations and business context.

The business of healthcare requires the management of both clinical and financial decisions. Healthcare is rich with a wide variety of data sources that may be analyzed to drive those decisions. Professionals working in the field of analytics do not typically perform primary research and design experiments to prove or disprove theories. The field of analytics often leverages the use of secondary data to help improve business decisions going forward. Sampling and experimental design may be used to collect primary data to answer specific business analysis needs.

Electronic health records (EHRs) bring a flood of data into the already data-rich healthcare environment. The true value of that data may only be realized through applying analytic techniques to distill the raw data into information that can support decision making. The results of data analytics can have a significant impact on both the clinical and financial outcomes of the healthcare system.

The SAS Institute is an industry leader in the area of business analytics and distributes a statistical software program, called SAS, that is used by many business and government entities. In a 2006 white paper, the SAS Institute listed the following framework for the effective use of EHR data (SAS 2006):

- A centralized data repository that synthesizes data from currently incompatible data silos on any platform and format
- Sophisticated extract, transform, and load (ETL) processes that maintain data quality, so that you can have faith in the accuracy of research based on that data
- Healthcare-specific analytics that enable nonstatisticians to surface meaningful intelligence from vast amounts of information about patients, populations, providers, procedures, and risks
- Predictive analytics to deliver more accurate research forecasts, evidence-based treatment protocols, and improved patient outcomes
- Query, reporting, and visualization tools that give various types of users the highest quality of information, where and when needed, via multiple platforms and channels

Many recent federal initiatives have put the spotlight on the importance of data analytics in healthcare. A few samples are discussed in the following paragraphs.

Pay for performance (P4P) programs are based on data-driven metrics to measure both the quality and efficiency of a healthcare provider. Bonus payments may be awarded or penalties imposed on providers that do not perform at a high level. The Centers for Medicare and Medicaid Services (CMS) implemented the first stages of its P4P program in July 2003 with the National Voluntary Hospital Reporting Initiative (CMS 2009). In its 2009 report titled "Roadmap for Implementing Value Driven Healthcare in the Traditional Medicare Fee-for-Service Program," CMS listed six key steps in the implementation of P4P:

1. Identification and promotion of the use of quality measures through pay for reporting
2. Payment for quality performance
3. Measures of physician and provider resource use
4. Payment for value—promote efficiency in resource use while providing high quality care
5. Alignment of financial incentives among providers
6. Transparency and public reporting

Each of these steps is related to the use of healthcare data and analytic techniques. CMS is in various stages of the implementation of these steps throughout the Medicare system. In the hospital setting, the inpatient prospective payment system (IPPS) and outpatient prospective payment system (OPPS) both include a penalty for providers that do not report the required quality indicators. The targets for incentive payments have not been implemented, but a proposed rule for the implementation of such payments is open for comment.

In the area of financial analytics, the Healthcare Financial Management Association (HFMA) developed a set of indicators to measure **revenue cycle** performance. These so-called MAP (measure, apply, perform) indicators include financial metrics that may be derived from healthcare data. They provide a framework for **benchmarking** the ability of a healthcare provider to collect the money owed for the treatment of patients. The MAP indicators measure performance in four key areas (HFMA 2011):

- Patient access
- Revenue integrity
- Claims adjudication
- Management

The arrival of the **accountable care organization (ACO)** begins to tie together the use of clinical and financial analytics throughout the healthcare delivery system (White et al. 2011). The ACO is essentially an integrated delivery system that includes physicians, hospitals, and other providers all focused on the delivery of care to a particular geographic segment of the Medicare population. The ACO receives incentive payments for delivering care in an efficient manner and providing a level of preventive care and education that may avoid subsequent treatment for chronic diseases. The intent of the ACO program is to improve the efficiency of care delivered to Medicare beneficiaries. In order to do so effectively, the ACO must have a robust database regarding the care delivered to the beneficiaries they are to serve as well as a broad spectrum of analytics to understand the patterns of care and chronic diseases present in the population.

All of the examples presented in this section highlight the growth of analytics in the healthcare setting. The demand for professionals with solid analytic skills and the ability to interpret the results of analysis to nonanalytics staff is outpacing availability at this time. HIM professionals who can demonstrate these skills will become an invaluable resource in their organization.

Descriptive versus Inferential Statistics

The science of statistics is segmented into two broad categories: descriptive and inferential. **Descriptive statistics** are used to describe the distribution of the variable of interest. **Inferential statistics** are used to test hypotheses or make decisions. These hypotheses have a probability or risk of making an error based on the data collected. In Chapter 20, this probability is referred to as the **Type I error** or *p*-value. Inferential statistics help analysts trend and summarize the data to determine whether or not they are seeing significant results in the sample or simply observing an event that occurred due to chance.

The appropriate descriptive statistic is determined by the type of data analyzed. If the intent is to describe how often an event of interest occurs, then rates and proportions are often used. For instance, a mortality rate is used to measure how many subjects died compared to the total number of subjects. A proportion is the appropriate statistical measure to use when describing the breakout of Medicare severity diagnosis-related group (MS-DRG) cases with no complication or comorbidities, with complications or comorbidities, and with major complications or comorbidities. If the intent is to analyze a variable that is interval or ratio in nature, then the appropriate descriptive statistic is likely the mean, median, or mode. For instance, length of stay for inpatient services is described using mean (average) or median. Table 19.1 lists types of data and the appropriate descriptive statistics.

The appropriate inferential statistical method is determined by the hypothesis to be tested or the question to be answered. An analyst may be asked to compare his or her facility's length of stay or mortality rate to a state standard or determine if the MS-DRG change rate is different from the value typically observed at the facility. These questions may be answered using inferential techniques. The appropriate statistical method is dependent on the question and the type of data available for the analysis.

Basic healthcare operations questions may often be analyzed using confidence intervals or hypothesis tests. A **confidence interval** is a range of values, such that the probability of that range covering the true value of a parameter is a set probability or confidence. A **hypothesis test** allows the analyst to determine the likelihood that a hypothesis is true given the data present in the sample with a predetermined acceptable level of making an error.

For instance, suppose the goal of a study is to determine the typical wait time in a hospital's emergency department (ED). A random sample of patients is selected from the population of patients visiting the ED during the previous month. The average wait time, 53.5 minutes, is a statistic that describes the typical wait time, but that statistic alone does not give any information about the precision of the estimate or how sure we are that the true population ED wait time in some EDs is about 53.5 minutes.

A confidence interval may be used to provide that additional information. A 95 percent confidence interval for the ED wait time was calculated and found to be (50.1, 56.9). The value 95 percent is the confidence level or the probability that the confidence interval contains the true population average. In this case, there is a probability of 95 percent that the interval (50.1, 56.9) includes the true population average ED wait time. Recall that these figures are based on a sample and we do not know the entire population value. The sample is used to make an inference or conclusions about the population. The width of the confidence interval is a measure of the precision of the estimate. A narrower interval is more precise.

Continuing with this same ED wait time example, suppose the goal was to test to determine if the average wait time was meeting a facility standard of 60 minutes. In this case, a hypothesis test is the correct statistical method. The

Table 19.1. Data types and appropriate descriptive statistics

Data Type	Definition	Examples	Appropriate Descriptive Statistics
Nominal	Categorical data where the categories are mutually exclusive but do not have a natural order	Gender, HCPCS codes, department or unit	Frequency counts, proportions, mode
Ordinal	Categorical data where the categories are mutually exclusive and they do have a natural order	Patient satisfaction scores, severity scores, trauma center level, surveys measured on a Likert scale	Frequency counts, proportions, mode, range
Interval	Naturally numeric data where the distance between two values has meaning, but multiplying values and zero value has no interpretation	Temperature, pH level, dates	Mean, median, standard deviation, range
Ratio	Naturally numeric data where zero has an interpretation and the values may be doubled or multiplied by a constant and still have meaning	Charges, length of stay, age	Mean, median, standard deviation, range, geometric mean, coefficient of variation

null hypothesis is that the ED wait time is less than or equal to 60 minutes; the alternative hypothesis is that the ED wait time is greater than 60 minutes. In hypothesis testing, an acceptable Type I error level should be selected prior to calculating the result. Type I error is the probability of incorrectly rejecting the null hypothesis given the values present in the sample. In this example, Type I error is making the conclusion that the wait time is longer than 60 minutes when it is truly less than or equal to 60 minutes. (See chapter 20 for additional discussion about Type I error.)

The practical implication of making a Type I error in this situation is the expense that may be incurred to study the root cause of the long wait times and make operational corrections. For this example the Type I error is set to be 5 percent or 0.05. The probability of making a Type I error may be calculated using the sample data and the appropriate test statistic. The probability of making a Type I error based on a particular set of data is called the *p*-**value**. If the *p*-value or probability of making a Type I error is less than the Type I error level set prior to testing, then the null hypothesis may be rejected. After calculating the test statistic and determining the *p*-value is 0.03, the null hypothesis is rejected and the conclusion is made that the ED wait time is longer than the standard.

As discussed in the research methods chapter, the first step in any study is to identify the research question. This may seem obvious, but many data analysis projects start without a clear idea of the exact question to be answered. The analyst becomes so concerned with summarizing the data and producing reports that they forget their efforts may be wasted if the question is not well defined at the outset. Examples of some of the research question that may be of interest include the following:

- What is the typical ED wait time?
- Does our ED wait time meet our facility standard?
- What is the percentage of lab orders that are not signed by a physician?
- What is the coding accuracy rate for secondary diagnosis codes?

Once the research question is defined, the unit of analysis must also be determined. For example, to determine the percentage of lab orders that are not signed by a physician, the unit of analysis is the set of lab orders for the time period of interest. This set of lab orders serves as the population of interest. It is practically impossible to collect the entire population of lab orders to definitively answer the questions posed. The data required are often selected via a sampling plan and then analyzed to make inferences or conclusions about the percentage of lab orders unsigned in the population.

In practice, it is sometimes difficult to determine the unit of analysis. For instance, in determining the coding accuracy rate for secondary diagnosis codes, should the unit of analysis be each code or the claim on which the code appears?

There is a critical difference between the two units of analysis. If the unit of analysis is the code, then the resulting rate would be the proportion of correct codes and not the proportion of correct claims. If the research question is to estimate the number of claims correctly coded, then the claim should be the unit of analysis.

Impact of Sampling

If the entire population of units of analysis were available for a study, then there would be no reason to use inferential statistics. Consider the previous lab order example. If the entire population of lab orders submitted at the facility during the time period of interest could be profiled, then the signature rate could be calculated exactly and compared to a standard. Unfortunately, the availability of the population or the time required to review the population is often not practical to achieve.

The most common types of random sampling are simple, stratified, systematic, and cluster sampling. These are discussed further in chapter 20. The particular statistical method used is dependent on the sampling method used to collect the data. Stratified and cluster sampling require a more complex set of statistical methods than simple random sampling.

Sampling techniques are used frequently in the healthcare setting. For instance, CMS allows hospitals to report many of the 28 required quality indicators based on a sample of claims and not the full population. Figure 19.1 shows the sample size requirements outlined in the QualityNet Hospital Inpatient Measures Specification Manual (QualityNet 2011).

Figure 19.1.   AMI measure set sample size requirements

Quarterly Sample Size Based on Initial Patient Population Size for the AMI Measure Set	
Hospital's Measure	
Average Quarterly Initial Patient Population Size "N"	*Minimum Required Sample Size* "n"
≥ 1551	311
391–1550	20% of Initial Patient Population Size
78–390	78
6–77	No sampling; 100% Initial Patient Population required
0–5	Submission of patient level data is encouraged but not required: • CMS: if submission occurs, 1–5 cases of the Initial Patient Population may be submitted • The Joint Commission: if submission occurs, 100% Initial Patient Population required

Source: CMS 2011. Statistical methods used to calculate rates.

Table 19.2.   Example of a hospital comparison based on sample

Hospital Process of Care Measures Tables	Average for All Reporting Hospitals in the US	Average for All Reporting Hospitals in the State	General Hospital	University Hospital	Data Collected	
					From	To
Heart Attack Patients Given Aspirin at Arrival	99%	99%	99% of 747 patients	100% of 173 patients2	1/1/2010	12/31/2010
Heart Attack Patients Given ACE Inhibitor or ARB for Left Ventricular Systolic Dysfunction (LVSD)	96%	97%	100% of 116 patients	97% of 71 patients[2]	1/1/2010	12/31/2010
Heart Attack Patients Given PCI Within 90 Minutes Of Arrival	91%	93%	96% of 154 patients	88% of 16 patients[1,2]	1/1/2010	12/31/2010

[1] The number of cases is too small to be sure how well a hospital is performing.

[2] The hospital indicated that the data submitted for this measure were based on a sample of cases.

Source: http://www.hospitalcompare.hhs.gov.

CMS reports the sample size and rate for measures that are based on samples rather than full population statistics. In table 19.2 the values for University Hospital are based on a sample. Notice that one of the footnotes on the heart attack patients given PCI within 90 minutes of arrival category states that "The number of cases is too small to be sure how well a hospital is performing."

CMS also includes guidance on how to calculate a confidence interval for rates based on samples. These instructions may be found in figure 19.2.

Using the guidance in figure 19.2 and the data presented in table 19.2, confidence intervals may be formed for the sample quality indicators. For example, a 95 percent confidence interval for the proportion of heart attack patients given ACE inhibitor or ARB for left ventricular systolic dysfunction (LVSD) for University Hospital is 97 percent +/– 8.3 percent.

The 8.3 percent comes from figure 19.2 looking up the value for the row with a sample size of 71 or 25–75 and the column for the observed rate of 90 percent (highest available in the table). Based on the sample selected, we are 95 percent sure that the population compliance with this quality indicator is between 88.7 percent and 100 percent at University Hospital. Notice that the upper bound on the confidence interval should be 97 percent + 8.3 percent, but in practical terms the percentage cannot be more than 100 percent, and therefore that is the reported upper limit.

Notice the pattern of the values presented in figure 19.2. The values in the table represent the half-widths of the confidence interval or the amount to be added and subtracted from the observed rate to formulate the 95 percent confidence interval. For a fixed value of the observed rate (column in the figure), the half-width values decrease as the

Figure 19.2. Estimating confidence intervals for the process of care measures: Estimated values for proportion data

Sample Size	Observed Rate								
	10%	20%	30%	40%	50%	60%	70%	80%	90%
<25	—	—	24.9%	26.6%	27.2%	26.6%	24.9%	—	—
25–75	8.3%	11.1%	12.7%	13.6%	13.9%	13.6%	12.7%	11.1%	8.3%
76–125	5.9%	7.8%	9.0%	9.6%	9.8%	9.6%	9.0%	7.8%	5.9%
126–175	4.8%	6.4%	7.3%	7.8%	8.2%	7.8%	7.3%	6.4%	4.8%
176–225	4.2%	5.5%	6.4%	6.8%	6.9%	6.8%	6.4%	5.5%	4.2%
226–275	3.7%	5.0%	5.7%	6.1%	6.2%	6.1%	5.7%	5.0%	3.7%
276+	2.9%	3.9%	4.5%	4.8%	4.9%	4.8%	4.5%	3.9%	2.9%

Source: CMS/OCSQ/QIG: The values in the table are the approximate amount to add and subtract from the observed rate to estimate a 95 percent confidence interval for the given sample size. (Interpolation between the values in the table is appropriate.) Estimates of an interval in these cells exceed the natural limits for proportions.

sample size increases. This makes intuitive sense. As the sample size increases, the analyst knows more about the population and therefore may formulate narrower or more precise intervals for the rate. For a fixed sample size (row in the figure), the half-width values increase until the observed rate is 50 percent and then decreases across the row as the observed rate decreases. This pattern is due to the fact that the standard deviation of the rate statistic is equal to the rate times one minus the rate, which is maximized at 50 percent. This also makes intuitive sense. If an event has an equal chance of occurring or not, like flipping a coin, then it is difficult to make precise estimates, and therefore the confidence interval must be wider or less precise for a fixed sample size.

Tools for Sampling and Design

The sample size for a study is determined by the amount of precision desired for the study. There are a number of tools available to assist analysts in calculating the required sample size. Traditional statistical software packages such as SPSS and SAS both offer modules for sample size calculation. G-Power (2012) is a public domain software application that may be used to calculate sample size for a number of statistical methods. The Office of Inspector General (OIG) offers a statistical package called **RAT-STATS** (OIG 2007) that is free to download and use for both sample size determination and the generation of the random numbers required for sampling.

The OIG developed RAT-STATS to help providers select samples for audits required for those under corporate integrity agreements. The OIG also requires random sample audits to support the estimation of amounts subject to repayment under self-disclosure agreements. The claim error rate and overpayment per claim are estimated from the sample and then extrapolated to determine the repayment amount. CMS Medicare integrity contractors use a similar methodology to determine amounts of over- or underpayments during their audits.

Using RAT-STATS to Determine Appropriate Sample Size

Suppose a health data analyst at a recovery audit contractor is asked to select a sample of medical records to determine if a provider is accurately coding the CC and MCCs for their congestive heart failure (CHF) cases for discharges

Figure 19.3.   Variable sample size determination

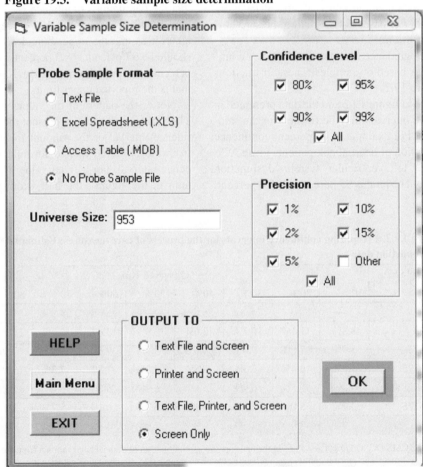

Source: OIG 2007.

Figure 19.4.   Example variable sample size output

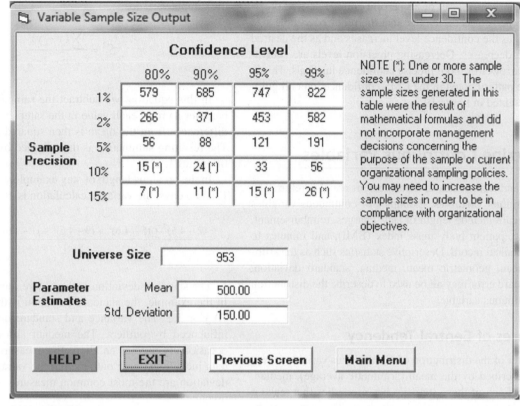

Source: OIG 2007.

from October 1, 2009, to September 30, 2010. The analyst knows that CHF groups to MS-DRGs 291, 292, and 293. She also knows that the provider of interest submitted 953 claims for these MS-DRGs during the time period. The RAC's medical record reviewers will make a correct or incorrect coding determination for each claim and then estimate the total amount of payment error for this MS-DRG set. The Medicare Integrity Manual (CMS 2010) suggests that contractors use a one-sided lower 90 percent confidence interval to determine the amount of the payment error. They claim this is a conservative estimate of overpayment since there is a 90 percent probability that the true overpayment amount is more than the one-sided lower 90 percent confidence bound.

The unit of analysis in this study is the claim. The population to be sampled is the 953 claims that the provider submitted during the study period for the MS-DRGs of interest. The research question is to determine the average amount of payment error for claims assigned to an incorrect MS-DRG. In RAT-STATS this is referred to as a variable study since the goal is to measure a continuous variable for each sampling unit.

To determine the sample size required for this audit, the analyst must set a precision range and confidence level. Suppose she wishes to draw a simple random sample, with a precision range of ±5 percent and a confidence level of

80 percent. This level is selected since an 80 percent confidence level in RAT-STATS is equivalent to the one-sided 90 percent confidence interval suggested for RAC use in the CMS Program Integrity Manual (CMS 2010). The sample size calculation also requires a prior estimate of the overpayment amount average and standard deviation. These statistics are typically determined via a probe sample or pilot study. From previous studies the analyst knows that the typical provider audit yields an average overpayment of $500 with a standard deviation of $150.

To determine the required sample size,

1. Open RAT-STATS
2. Click on "Sample Size Determination"
3. Click on "Variable Sample Size Determination"
4. Click on "Unrestricted"
5. Click on "Using a Probe Sample"
6. Select the "No Probe Sample" radio button since the mean and standard deviation from the probe sample are known and do not need to be calculated
7. Enter the universe size and select all confidence and precision levels (figure 19.3)
8. Click "OK"
9. The mean ($500) and standard deviation ($150) from the probe sample should be entered when requested
10. The required sample sizes are then presented (see figure 19.4)

The sample size required for the audit to result in the desired confidence level of 80 percent and the desired precision of 5 percent is 56. Notice that the required sample size increases as the confidence level increases and as the desired precision decreases. Decreasing precision levels are equivalent to narrower or more precise confidence intervals. This is the same pattern noted in the CMS confidence interval guidance presented in figure 19.2.

Analyzing Continuous Variables

Interval and ratio scales of measurement are also referred to as **continuous variables.** Examples of continuous variables in healthcare include length of stay, charges, reimbursement, wait time, patient body mass index (BMI), and minutes to code a medical record. Descriptive statistics such as the arithmetic mean, geometric mean, median, standard deviation, and standard error may all be used to describe the distribution of a continuous variable.

Measures of Central Tendency

The center of the distribution of a continuous variable is typically described by the mean (arithmetic average), median, or mode. Each of these statistics has properties that make it the correct choice in a particular situation. The mean is probably the most common statistic used in practice. To find the **mean** you add up all of the values and divide by the number of observations in the sample. The median is the middle value in the sample. To find the **median**, sort the sample from smallest to largest value and choose the middle value as the median. If the sample has an even number of observations, then the two middle values are averaged to determine the median. The **mode** is the value with the highest frequency of occurrence.

The mean can be heavily influenced by extreme values. If the sample has extreme values on either the high or low end of the scale, then the median may be the better choice for describing the center of the distribution. The median is less influenced by outliers. For example consider the mean length of stay for a set of patients with the following values: 2, 5, 9, 1, 6 days. The mean length of stay is 4.6 days and the medial length of stay is 5 days. If the patient who stayed 9 days is replaced by a patient with a 20-day stay, the mean length of stay becomes 6.8 days while the median is still 5 days. The outlier value of 20 pulls the mean higher, but the median is unchanged by the extreme value. The mode is most often used when summarizing categorical data.

Measures of Spread

The most common measures of spread of a continuous variable are the **variance, standard deviation,** and range. The sample variance is calculated as the average squared deviation from the mean. The following formula is used for the sample variance:

$$S^2 = \frac{\sum (y - \bar{y})^2}{n - 1}$$

In this equation, we subtract the sample mean (y with a bar over it) from each value in the sample (y). Each of these differences from the mean is then squared and summed up. The resulting summation is then divided by the sample size (n) minus 1.

In the previous length of stay example with values 2, 5, 9, 1, and 6 days, the variance calculation is as follows:

$$S^2 = \frac{(2 - 4.6)^2 + (5 - 4.6)^2 + (9 - 4.6)^2 + (1 - 4.6)^2 + (6 - 4.6)^2}{5 - 1} = 10.3$$

The standard deviation is the square root of the variance. In the example, the standard deviation is the square root of 10.3 or 3.2. The variance and standard deviation are both influenced by outliers. The median absolute deviation is occasionally used as an alternative measure of spread if the data include extreme outliers, but the variance and standard deviation are the most common measures of spread used in practice.

The range is the difference between the minimum and maximum values. The range is by definition very sensitive to outliers, since it is calculated as the difference between the two most extreme values.

Inferential Statistics for Continuous Data

The presentation of the full spectrum of inferential techniques used with continuous variables is beyond the scope of this text. The following sections present two common methods that demonstrate the utility of statistical inference in the healthcare setting.

Inference Example: One Sample T-test

Hypothesis tests are a common technique used to determine if the results for the sample are truly significant or if they are simply due to random chance. The **one-sample *t*-test** is used to compare a population to a standard value. An example regarding the wait times in an ED was presented earlier in this chapter. That example is an application of the one-sample *t*-test.

The first step in performing any hypothesis test is to determine the null and alternative hypotheses. Suppose in the ED wait time example, the ED director is concerned that the wait times exceed the standard of 60 minutes. The marketing director would like to run a new campaign that touts ED wait times that are significantly shorter than the standard of 60 minutes. In this case, the research question is to determine if the ED wait times are significantly shorter or longer than 60 minutes, and we will use a two-sided alternative hypothesis. The null and alternative hypotheses are:

$$H_0: \ = 60$$

$$H_1: \ \neq 60$$

The lower case Greek letter μ (*mu*) represents the true population mean. The next step is to determine the acceptable level of Type I error. Recall that Type I error is the probability of rejecting the null hypothesis when it is actually true. In this example, the Type I error level is set to be 5 percent. This is a two-sided hypothesis test since the alternative is not equal.

A sample of 20 patients is selected and the sample mean ED wait time is 53.5 minutes with a standard deviation of 7.23 minutes. The null hypothesis may be tested using the following formula:

$$t = \frac{(\bar{x} - \ _0)}{s/\sqrt{n}}$$

Studying the anatomy of the *t*-test can help formulate the intuition regarding hypothesis tests in general. In general the null hypothesis is rejected when the test statistic, *t* in this case, is an extremely large positive value or extremely small negative value. The numerator of the *t* statistic is the difference between the sample mean and the null hypothesis value. If that difference is large (positive or negative), then the *t* statistic is large. The denominator of the *t* statistic is the standard error, or the standard deviation divided by the square root of the sample size. This value is directly proportional to the standard deviation and indirectly proportional to the sample size. In other words, the standard error gets larger if the standard deviation is larger and smaller as the sample size grows. The *t* statistic increases as the standard error decreases. The *t* statistic is comparing the difference between the sample mean and the null hypothesis value relative to the spread in distribution and the sample size.

Determining what extreme is large enough of a *t* statistic to reject the null hypothesis is dependent on the distribution of the *t* statistic? The *t* statistic is compared to the *t* distribution which is similar in shape to the standard normal distribution. Using the *t* distribution, a cut off or critical value can be determined so that the probability of observing a value that large by chance is the Type I error level. The critical value is determined by the Type I error level and the degrees of freedom or the sample size minus one ($n - 1$). In this example, the degrees of freedom are $20 - 1 = 19$ and the level is 0.05. The test statistic must be greater than 2.09 or less than −2.09 to reject the null hypothesis. This value may be derived from a table of the *t* distribution found in most statistical tests or from Excel by using this function: = TINV(0.05,19). Figure 19.5 shows the shape of the *t* distribution and the probability represented by the 2.09 and −2.09 critical values. The probability of observing a value outside of −2.09 and 2.09 on the *t* distribution with 19 degrees of freedom is 2.5 percent + 2.5 percent = 5 percent. Based on the sample the *t* statistic is

$$t = \frac{(53.5 - 60)}{7.23/\sqrt{20}} = \frac{-6.5}{1.62} = -4.02$$

Since −4.02 is less than −2.09, the null hypothesis is rejected and the conclusion is that the ED wait time is less than the 60 minute standard. (Note: In hypothesis testing, the null hypothesis is either rejected or not rejected. The null hypothesis is never accepted.)

Inference Example: Confidence Interval for Mean

Since the null hypothesis was rejected in favor of the alternative that the ED wait times are significantly lower than the standard, the marketing director is interested in finding out how far below the standard the ED wait times might be. She is interested in publishing a figure in the new campaign but needs to be sure the value is defensible. A confidence interval will result in a range of values with an associated level of confidence that

Figure 19.5. T distribution with 19 degrees of freedom

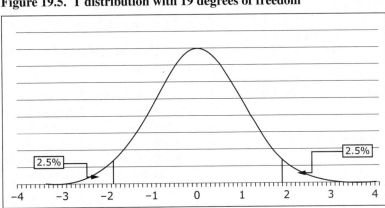

the interval contains the population average ED wait time. The confidence level is designated to be 95 percent. The formula for the 95 percent confidence interval for the mean is

$$\bar{x} - t_{\alpha/2,\,n-1} \times \frac{s}{\sqrt{n}},\ \bar{x} + t_{\alpha/2,\,n-1} \times \frac{s}{\sqrt{n}}$$

The confidence interval is centered at the sample mean. The width of the confidence interval is a function of the t distribution (confidence level), the sample standard deviation, and the sample size. Notice that a larger standard deviation results in a wider interval. A larger sample size results in a narrower or more precise interval. Recall from the earlier discussion that sample size selection was dependent on the sample standard deviation, the desired precision, and the confidence level. The concept of sample size selection is directly related to the width or precision of the desired confidence interval. $t_{\alpha/2,n-1}$ is the value from the t distribution with $n-1$ degrees of freedom where there is an $\alpha/2$ chance of observing a value that extreme by chance. A 95 percent confidence interval may also be expressed as a $(1-\alpha)$ percent confidence interval. In this case, α is 0.05 and the degrees of freedom are $20-1 = 19$ so $t_{\alpha/2,n-1} = 2.09$.

$$53.5 - 2.09 \times \frac{7.23}{\sqrt{20}},\ 53.5 + 2.09 \frac{7.23}{\sqrt{20}}$$
$$(53.5 - 3.4,\ 53.5 + 3.4)$$
$$(50.1,\ 56.9)$$

The result of this analysis is that the marketing director can be 95 percent sure that the true population average ED wait time is between 50.1 and 56.9 minutes.

The two-sided hypothesis test and confidence interval for the population mean are related. The formulas contain the same sample statistics, and if the confidence level is one minus the Type I error rate, then the null hypothesis will be rejected for any value outside of the confidence intervals. For the ED wait time example, notice that the 95 percent confidence interval does not contain 60 minutes. The null hypothesis that the ED wait time was equal to 60 minutes was rejected at the 5 percent level. The confidence interval end points tell us that any null hypothesis greater than 56.9 minutes or less than 50.1 minutes would be rejected at the 5 percent level since those values are outside of the upper and lower bounds of the 95 percent confidence interval.

Check Your Understanding 19.1

Answer the following questions on a separate piece of paper.

1. Which of the following is a measure of central tendency?

   A. Standard deviation
   B. Variance
   C. Median
   D. Range

2. When describing the typical length of stay for patients admitted for congestive heart failure, which is the most appropriate measure of central tendency when there are a number of long-stay outliers?

   A. Mean
   B. Median
   C. Mode
   D. Minimum

3. The one-sample *t*-test may be used to:

   A. Determine if a population mean is likely to be different from a standard value
   B. Determine if a distribution is highly variable
   C. Determine the most likely value of the population mean
   D. Define a range of likely values for the population mean

4. Type I error in an hypothesis test is:

   A. The probability of rejecting the null hypothesis when it is false
   B. The probability of not rejecting the null hypothesis when it is true
   C. The probability of not rejecting the null hypothesis with it is false
   D. The probability of rejecting the null hypothesis when it is true.

5. If the average length of stay for a sample of 15 patients is 2.3 days and the standard deviation is 1.5 days, which of the following statements is true?

   A. A 95 percent confidence interval will be narrower than a 90 percent confidence interval
   B. A 95 percent confidence interval will be wider than a 90 percent confidence interval
   C. A 95 percent confidence interval and 90 percent confidence interval will be the same width
   D. Not enough information is provided to answer

Analyzing Rates and Proportions

Rates and proportions are actually summary statistics based on either a sample or population. A rate is the number of times an event of interest occurs divided by the number of times that event could have occurred. The event and the number eligible must be carefully defined so that the calculations of rates are valid and reproducible.

Descriptive Statistics for Rates and Proportions

Rates may be reported as percentages or counts per 1,000 or as a fraction, as in *x* out of *y*. When calculating a rate, the numerator (top number in a fraction) is the number of subjects with the trait of interest. The denominator (bottom number in a fraction) is the number of subjects that could have had the trait of interest.

Consider the example of measuring the mortality rate at a facility. The mortality rate may be interpreted as the probability of any one of 100 patients dying. In other words, in the context of this analysis each patient has two outcomes: living or dying. The mortality rate calculated from a sample is an estimate of the population probability of dying or p.

It is always good practice to not only estimate the probability or p of an event but also estimate the variance or spread around the sample proportion estimate. If our sample of size n produces a proportion estimate of p, denoted as $\hat{p}$, then standard error of a proportion estimate is

$$SE_p = \sqrt{\frac{\hat{p} \times (1 - \hat{p})}{n}}$$

The standard error of the sample proportion is the standard deviation divided by the square root of the sample size. In this formula, $\hat{p}$ is the estimated proportion based on the random sample. Therefore, both the mean and the standard error of the sample proportion depend on the estimated value. Notice that the standard error decreases and the sample size increases. The value of SE_p is maximized when the sample proportion is 0.5 or 50 percent. Recall from the discussion of the CMS quality indicators that the confidence intervals using their guidance were the widest when the observed rate was 50 percent.

Inferential Statistics for Rates and Proportions

The most common types of inferential statistical techniques used with rates and proportions are hypothesis tests to compare rates to a standard or confidence intervals. If an analyst is trying to determine if a rate is higher or lower than a standard, then a hypothesis is the correct statistical technique. In hypothesis testing, the first step is to define the null hypothesis (status quo) and the alternative or research hypothesis.

$$H_0: p = p_0$$

$$H_1: p \uparrow p_0$$

The test is performed to determine if the analyst should reject the null hypothesis at a given error level. This is called the Type I

error level. The error level should be set low (0.01 or 0.05) if the action to be taken is costly in terms of money, time, or patient lives. If the question is less critical, then the error level may be set higher. The test statistic used in this situation is a z-test:

$$z = \frac{(\hat{p} - p_0)}{\sqrt{p_0 \times (1 - p_0)/n}}$$

In this formula, n is the sample size, p_0 is the null hypothesis value, and $\hat{p}$ is the estimated proportion based on the random sample. If the test statistic z is greater than $z_{\alpha/2}$ or less than $-z_{\alpha/2}$ where α is the predefined Type I error level, then the null hypothesis is rejected. For this test, the standard normal distribution is used to determine a critical value beyond which the null hypothesis should be rejected. If the error level of the test is 0.05 or 5 percent, then the critical value or $z_{\alpha/2}$ is 1.96. This may be derived from the standard normal table found in most statistics textbooks or from using the following formula in Excel: =NORMSINV(0.025). Figure 19.6 shows the critical values on the probability curve of the standard normal distribution. As with the t-test, one half of the Type I error is allocated to each side of the curve. Notice that the critical value for the standard normal distribution is slightly smaller than that from the t distribution with 19 degrees of freedom. As the degrees of freedom for the t distribution increases, it becomes closer to the standard normal distribution.

One of the CMS quality indicators measures the proportion of pneumonia patients assessed and given influenza vaccination. A facility may wish to compare its rate to the national vaccination rate. If 80 percent of the patients out of a sample of 74 eligible patients received a flu vaccine at University Hospital, can we conclude that its vaccination rate is significantly different from the national rate of 91 percent?

The hypothesis to be tested here is

$$H_0: p = 0.91$$

$$H_1: p \uparrow 0.91$$

Figure 19.6. Standard normal distribution

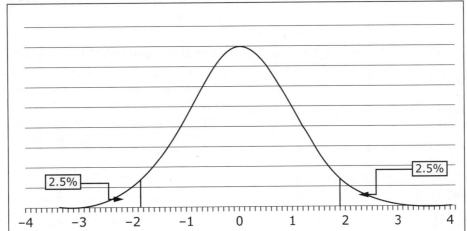

The test statistic is

$$z = \frac{(0.80 - 0.91)}{\sqrt{0.91 \times (1 - 0.91)/74}} = \frac{-0.110}{0.033} = -3.33$$

Since the test statistic, $z = -3.33$, is less than the critical value, -1.96, the null hypothesis is rejected. The conclusion is that University Hospital's flu vaccine rate for pneumonia patients is significantly lower than the national rate.

The $z_{\alpha/2}$ is the same critical value identified for the two-sided hypothesis test presented before. A 95 percent confidence interval for the flu vaccine rate at University Hospital is

$$\hat{p} - z_{\alpha/2} \times \sqrt{\frac{\hat{p} \times (1 - \hat{p})}{n}}, \hat{p} + z_{\alpha/2} \times \sqrt{\frac{\hat{p} \times (1 - \hat{p})}{n}}$$

$$0.80 - 1.96 \times \sqrt{\frac{0.80 \times (1 - 0.80)}{74}},$$

$$0.80 + 1.96 \times \sqrt{\frac{0.80 \times (1 - 0.80)}{74}}$$

$$(0.80 - 0.09, 0.80 + 0.09) \; or \; (0.71, 0.89)$$

The 95 percent confidence interval for the population pneumonia patient flu vaccine rate is from 71 percent to 89 percent. This precision for this interval is +/–9 percent. If a more precise interval is desired, then a large sample size should be collected for the next measurement period.

Check Your Understanding 19.2

Answer the following questions on a separate piece of paper.

1. The sample mean and standard error of a proportion is dependent on

    A. The sample size
    B. The estimated proportion
    C. Both of these values
    D. Neither of these values

2. Which distribution is used to test a hypothesis regarding proportions?

    A. T distribution
    B. Normal distribution
    C. F distribution
    D. Uniform distribution

3. If we wish to test the hypothesis that a facility's mortality rate is significantly different than the state average of 5 percent, which of the following null and alternative hypotheses are appropriate?

    A. $H_0: p > 5\%; H_1: p \le 5\%$
    B. $H_0: p = 5\%; H_1: p \ne 5\%$

    C. $H_0: p \ne 5\%; H_1: p = 5\%$
    D. $H_0: p \le 5\%; H_1: p \ge 5\%$

4. If a 95 percent confidence interval for the proportion of postoperative infections is (0.9 percent, 1.5 percent), what is the precision of that interval?

    A. ±0.9%
    B. ±0.6%
    C. ±0.3%
    D. ±1.5%

5. If the test statistic for testing the hypothesis that the readmission rate at General Hospital is different from zero is $z = 3.45$, what would the conclusion of the test be at the 0.05 level?

    A. Reject H_0
    B. Reject H_1
    C. Do not reject H_0
    D. Accept H_0

Analyzing Relationships between Two Variables

A data analyst may need to explore the relationship between two variables. Examples include the relationship between length of stay and charges, patient age, and mortality or number of coding staff members and number of records coded per shift.

Correlation

Correlation is the statistic that is used to describe the association or relationship between two variables. In the healthcare setting, we may note that length of stay and charges are highly related, or correlated. Since charges increase as length of stay increases, we say that the two variables are positively correlated. An example of two variables that are negatively correlated may be years of coder experience and time to code a medical record. If the more experienced coders have shorter review times, then the two variables are negatively correlated.

Pearson's Correlation Coefficient

Pearson's correlation coefficient or r measures the strength of the linear relationship between two variables. The statistic can range from -1 to $+1$. Negative one is perfect negative correlation while positive one is perfect position correlation. The formula for calculating Pearson's correlation coefficient is

$$r = \frac{\sum_{i=1}^{n} (X_i - \overline{X}) \times (Y_i - \overline{Y})}{\sqrt{\sum_{i=1}^{n} (X_i - \overline{X})^2} \times \sqrt{\sum_{i=1}^{n} (Y_i - \overline{Y})^2}}$$

Table 19.3. Calculation of Pearson's *r* of coder experience and time

Subject	*X*: Experience (yr)	*Y*: Time (min)			
1	5.00	30.00	(20.94)	3.72	117.88
2	1.00	55.00	(29.30)	4.29	200.02
3	2.50	45.00	(2.37)	0.33	17.16
4	4.50	35.00	(8.37)	2.04	34.31
5	3.50	45.00	1.78	0.18	17.16
6	2.00	39.00	1.99	1.15	3.45
7	3.00	37.00	0.28	0.01	14.88
Total	**21.50**	**286.00**	**(56.93)**	**11.71**	**404.86**

Notice that the numerator of the statistic will determine the sign of the correlation. Confidence intervals and hypothesis tests may be performed to make inferences about the strength of association between two variables. Pearson's *r* is a measure of correlation and not causation. Causation is far more difficult to prove via data and really requires a carefully designed and controlled experiment to prove.

Suppose an analyst wishes to study the relationship between number of years of coding experience and time required to code an outpatient medical record. The analyst selects a random sample of seven coders and collects the data presented in table 19.3 (values are rounded to two decimal places).

The Pearson's *r* for experience and time is

$$r = \frac{-56.93}{\sqrt{21.50} \times \sqrt{286.00}} = -0.83$$

The interpretation of the negative value of the correlation coefficient is that time to code records decreases as experience increases. A scatter plot of two variables is a useful tool for exploring the relationship. Figure 19.7 shows the

decreasing trend in coding time as the years of experience increase for each subject in the sample.

Pearson's *r* may be converted to the **coefficient of determination** or r^2. The r^2 measures how much of the variation in one variable is explained by the second variable. In this example, $r^2 = (-0.83)^2 = 0.68$. Therefore, 68 percent of the variance in coding time may be explained by the years of experience.

Simple Linear Regression

Simple linear regression (SLR) is another type of statistical inference that not only measures the strength of the relationship between two variables but also estimates a functional relationship between them. SLR may be used when one of the two variables of interest is dependent on the other. For instance, the total charge incurred during an inpatient stay is often dependent on the length of time spent in the hospital. Regression may also be used to describe the relationship between coder experience and time per record beyond simply stating that these two factors have a negative correlation or an inverse relationship.

SLR is typically performed by fitting a line via a least squares algorithm. Basically, the least squares method selects the line that minimizes the vertical (*Y*) distance between all points and the selected line. The result is a line that may not actually go through any points but comes as close as possible to all points. The least squares line for this example is displayed in figure 19.8.

The slope of the least squares line is always the same sign as the correlation between the two variables. The formula for the least squares line for these data is

coding time = −4.86 × experience + 55.78

The SLR line represents the predicted or expected values of the dependent variable given various values of the independent variable. The interpretation of this relationship is that the predicted coding time for a coder with no experience is 55.78 minutes. This value, 55.78, is referred to as the

Figure 19.7. Relationship between coder experience and time per record

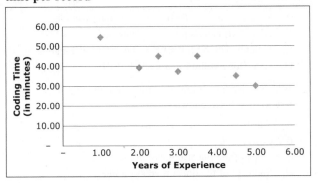

Figure 19.8. Relationship between coder experience and time per record

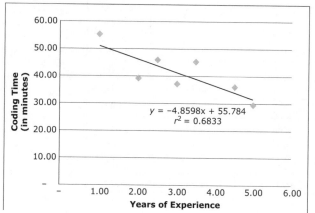

$y = -4.8598x + 55.784$
$r^2 = 0.6833$

y-intercept of the line. Each year of experience reduces the predicted time to code records by 4.86 minutes. This value, −4.86, is referred to as the slope of the line. The slope is an estimate of the change in the dependent variable, *y*, which is expected for each one unit change in the independent variable, *x*. The line displayed in figure 19.8 states that the expected coding time for a coder with four years of experience is y = −4.86 × 4 + 55.78 = 36.34 minutes. The coefficient of determination is used to measure the explanatory power of the linear regression line. As previously calculated, $r^2 = 0.68$. The years of experience of a coder explains 68 percent of the variance in coding time. One application of this regression line is to create personalized workload expectations for each coder based on experience. A performance ratio could then be calculated as the observed coding time divided by the expected coding time for each coder to monitor performance and provide feedback for improvement. A performance ratio greater than one would indicate better-than-expected performance, and a performance ratio less than one would indicate a performance that requires improvement.

Another interesting application of SLR is studying the relationship between charge per inpatient visit and length of stay for inpatient stays. The least squares line may be used to break out the fixed and variable portions of the charges.

Figure 19.9 displays the relationship between patient length of stay and total charges for congestive heart failure. The relationship between length of stay and total charge is very strong with an r^2 of 0.93. In other words, length of stay explains 93 percent of the variance in total charge. This strong relationship between total charge and length of stay is true for many medical inpatient stays. The relationship between these two variables may be less strong for surgical inpatient stays if the charge for the surgery is a large proportion of the total charge.

The model in figure 19.9 states y = 3829.7x − 1520.6, which means that the predicted total charge (*y*) equals $1,521 + $3,830x. (Note: $1,521 is rounded from 1,520.6, 3,830 is rounded from 3,829.7, and x = LOS). The intercept of the line, $1,521, represents the fixed charge of a CHF inpatient stay. Fixed charge items are registration, administration, initial laboratory, or radiology workups that are not dependent on how long the patient stays. The slope of the line represents the variable component of the charge. Variable charge items are nursing care, dietary, maintenance medications, and other resources that are used each day of the stay. Breaking the charges into the fixed and variable components facilitates root-cause analysis studies into the variation in resources used to treat various types of patients. For instance, the charges for CHF patients are clearly driven more by the variable component than the fixed component. CHF treatment protocols that concentrate on length of stay reduction may be an effective way to ensure proper resources are used to treat these patients. For a joint replacement or an other surgical case with significant medical supply costs, it is unlikely that a length of stay study would be very effective.

Figure 19.9. Relationship between length of stay and total charge for CHF inpatient stays

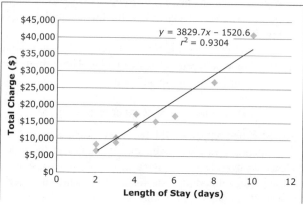

$y = 3829.7x − 1520.6$
$r^2 = 0.9304$

Check Your Understanding 19.3

Answer the following questions on a separate piece of paper.

1. If the correlation between patient lung volume level and body mass index (BMI) is 0.6, which of the following conclusions is correct?

    A. Patients with low BMI have large lung volume
    B. High BMI causes large lung volume
    C. Patients with high BMI have large lung volume
    D. Large lung volume causes high BMI

2. Which statistic measures the strength of the linear relationship between two variables?

    A. T-test
    B. Correlation
    C. Slope of the linear regression line
    D. Intercept of the linear regression line

3. If the coefficient of determination for this SLR model is Cost = 1,500 + 300 × LOS = 0.8, then which of the following statements is correct?

   A. 20 percent of the variance in cost is explained by length of stay

   B. 80 percent of the variance in length of stay is explained by cost

   C. 80 percent of the variance in cost is explained by length of stay

   D. 20 percent of the variance in length of stay is explained by cost

4. Using the model in question 3, what is the interpretation of the slope of the line?

   A. For every one-day increase in length of stay, the cost will decrease by $300

   B. For every one-day increase in length of stay, the cost will increase by $300

   C. The typical cost of care is $1,500

   D. The cost of care and length of stay are not related

5. Using the model in question 3, what is the interpretation of the intercept of the line?

   A. For every one-day increase in length of stay, the cost will decrease by $1,500

   B. For every one-day increase in length of stay, the cost will increase by $1,500

   C. The fixed cost of admitting a patient is $1,500

   D. The fixed cost of admitting a patient is $300

Analytics in Practice

Data Mining

The techniques of data analytics may be used to perform **data mining.** In data mining, the analyst performs exploratory data analysis to determine trends and identify patterns in the data set. Data mining is sometimes referred to as knowledge discovery. In any business, including healthcare, data mining may be used to support (Fayyad 1996)

- Marketing: Identification of groups of customers or prospective patients who may use a particular product.
- Investment: Determine optimal investment strategy given the history of various alternatives
- Fraud detection: Find unusual purchase patterns of customers or unusual billing patterns of providers
- Manufacturing: Finding patterns in system failures

In healthcare, data mining may be used to determine if it is cost-effective to expand facilities. An analysis of appointment wait times for patients to see a certain type of specialist or to receive a particular diagnostic test might indicate a need to expand that service. Data mining may also be used to analyze referral patterns of physicians within a particular network.

In traditional data analytics, data are collected for a specific purpose to answer a business or research question. In data mining, data are often used for secondary analysis. That is, the data are used for a purpose that was not the primary reason for collection. Claims data are an excellent data source for mining and finding patterns, but the primary purpose of claims data is for submission to ask for payment and not data mining.

Predictive Modeling

Predictive modeling is another application of data analytics in healthcare. Predictive modeling is actually a special application of data mining. CMS is using predictive modeling to identify potential fraudulent Medicare claims (White 2011). The pattern of claims submitted by a provider is analyzed to identify trends that are unlikely given the claims history of the provider or the patient. For instance, predictive modeling may be used to identify a provider that submits a claim for a service that is unrelated to its specialty or a high-cost service for which it has not submitted a previous claim. The goal of this technique is to target claims that are unlikely to be valid and select them for further review.

Predictive modeling applies statistical techniques to determine the likelihood of certain events occurring together (White 2011). Statistical methods are applied to historical data to "learn" the patterns in the data. These patterns are used to create models of what is most likely to occur. Predictive modeling is used by credit card issuers to determine if transactions are likely fraudulent. Customers who receive a phone call from their credit card company verifying that they authorized a transaction were the subjects of a predictive model.

For example, a customer's typical credit card transaction is $100. The credit card issuer notices that the customer submitted three $5,000 transactions in one day. Given the customer's history and the credit card issuer's historical data regarding fraudulent transactions, those transactions look suspicious. The credit card company may then put a hold on the card and call to verify that the customer really did authorize the suspect transactions. The triggers that tell the credit card company when to suspect a fraud issue are created via predictive modeling techniques.

Predictive modeling techniques use multiple data sources. Data such as the provider's claim history, the patient's demographics and health status, the services included on the claim, and the attributes associated with previously identified fraudulent claims may all be used to develop a statistical model. Statistical techniques used to create the model may include logistical regression, cluster analysis, or decision trees. All of these statistical techniques allow the user to combine multivariate historical data into a model that may be used to assess the probability or likelihood that current claims are fraudulent.

In logistical regression, the likelihood that a claim is fraudulent is estimated based on a series of historical data. In cluster analysis, historical data are used to build a model that will measure the distance of a claim from the typical claims submitted by that provider or for that type of service. Decision trees use a series of screens or yes and no questions to determine the probability that a claim is valid. The output of each of these methods is the probability of a claim's validity, which is expressed as a score.

The claim score is typically structured so that it is directly related to the probability that a claim is in error. A high score may indicate a high probability that a claim is not legitimate. If the score meets a criteria (either above or below a cutoff value), then it is identified as a potential error. The criteria or cutoff value may be used to tune the model to control the sensitivity and specificity of the model. If the cutoff is too extreme, then the model may not be sensitive enough and will allow fraudulent claims to be paid. If the cutoff is not extreme enough, then the model may not be specific enough and identify a large number of false positives.

In the healthcare setting the cost of paying fraudulent claims must be weighed against the cost of withholding payment and reviewing the claim prior to payment. For high-cost and low-volume claims, the cutoff may be set lower to ensure that no questionable claims are paid. The cost of paying an invalid claim outweighs the cost of reviewing a few false positive claims. The model may be adapted and adjusted as more claims history is aggregated.

Many commercial payers currently use predictive modeling as one of their fraud prevention techniques. The UnitedHealth Group (UnitedHealth Center for Health Reform and Modernization 2009) estimated that the use of predictive modeling in the Medicare and Medicaid programs could save the programs $113 billion over the first 10 years of use. A study from the Lewin Group (2009) validated the UnitedHealth Group's estimates and further estimated savings of $128.6 billion over the same first 10 years of use. Predictive modeling will be combined with prepayment edits and the current activities of the payment integrity contractors to provide CMS with a state-of-the-art fraud prevention program.

Risk-Adjusted Quality Indicators

The values for some quality and outcomes indicators in healthcare are dependent on the mix of patients treated at that facility. For example, the 30-day mortality rate at a major academic medical center cannot be directly compared to the 30-day mortality rate at a rural community hospital without some sort of adjustment for the difference in acuity of the patients. CMS uses a hierarchical regression model to adjust for both individual patient characteristics and hospital characteristics. The model calculates an expected 30-day mortality rate for each hospital and then compares the expected rate

to the observed rate when reporting statistics on CMS's Hospital Compare website. The method is similar to the observed versus expected productivity ratio presented in the simple linear regression portion of this chapter. The model used to calculate the expected mortality is far more complex, but the interpretation is the same. CMS (2011) calculates a risk standardized mortality rate (RSMR) based on the expected mortality rate and the observed mortality rate for each condition and hospital profiled. Lower RSMR implies a hospital has better quality as measured by these rates.

Although the details involved in hierarchical regression are beyond the scope of this text, the concept that an observed rate is compared to an expected rate to determine relative performance makes intuitive sense. The exact methodology to derive the expected rate may vary depending on the research question and the data available for modeling.

A more straightforward method for calculating RSMR is to use **indirect standardization** (Osborn 2005) to derive the expected rate for an outcome variable. Indirect standardization is appropriate to use for risk adjustment when the risk variables are categorical and the rate or proportion for the variable of interest is available for the standard or reference group at the level of the risk categories. The expected outcome rate for each risk category is calculated based on the reference group and then weighted by the volume in each risk group at the population to be compared to the standard. Indirect standardization is not useful when trying to compare the outcomes at two facilities but is useful when comparing a facility to a standard.

The sample data presented in table 19.4 present the in-hospital mortality rate for the family of cardiac arrhythmia and conduction disorder MS-DRGs for the United States as well as The Hospital. The observed overall in-hospital mortality rate for The Hospital, 1.6 percent, is higher than the national rate, 1.3 percent. The Hospital actually recorded lower mortality rates for patients assigned to two of the three individual MS-DRGs. The Hospital had lower mortality in MS-DRG 308, which includes patients with major complications and comorbidities. The proportion of the patients in each MS-DRG is not available for the national statistics, so we do not know if The Hospital's mix is more concentrated in the MS-DRGs with major complications or comorbidities. The national rates for each MS-DRG may be used to estimate the expected mortality rate for The Hospital using indirect standardization.

The first step in indirect standardization is to use the hospital's volume and the national in-hospital mortality rate for each risk category to calculate the expected number of deaths. In this example, the MS-DRGs represent the risk categories. Based on the data in table 19.4 the expected number of deaths for each of the MS-DRGs is

- MS-DRG 308: $0.049 \times 152 = 7.39$
- MS-DRG 309: $0.008 \times 158 = 1.31$
- MS-DRG 310: $0.002 \times 191 = 0.46$

Table 19.4. In-hospital mortality rate for the family of cardiac arrhythmia and conduction disorder MS-DRGs for the United States as well as The Hospital

MS-DRG and Name		The Hospital's Statistics				
		Estimated US In-Hospital Mortality Rate	The Hospital Discharges	Observed In-Hospital deaths	Observed Mortality Rate	Expected Deaths
308	Cardiac arrhythmia and conduction disorders w/mcc	4.9 percent	152	6	3.9 percent	7.39
309	Cardiac arrhythmia and conduction disorders w/cc	0.8 percent	158	2	1.3 percent	1.31
310	Cardiac arrhythmia and conduction disorders w/o cc/mcc	0.2 percent	191	0	0.0 percent	0.46
Totals		1.3 percent	501	8	1.6 percent	9.16

Source: US figures from HHS (2009) data: http://hcupnet.ahrq.gov/HCUPnet.jsp.

The three MS-DRG expected death rates are then added together to yield the expected number of deaths at the hospital: 7.39 + 1.31 + 0.46 = 9.16. The expected in-house mortality rate for the hospital is then 9.16/501 = 1.8 percent. The observed and expected mortalities may then be used to calculate a **standardized mortality ratio (SMR).**

$$SMR = \frac{\text{observed mortality rate}}{\text{expected mortality rate}}$$

The SMR for the hospital is 1.6 percent/1.8 percent or 0.89. An SMR value less than one means the observed mortality rate is lower than expected, and an SMR greater than one means the observed mortality rate is higher than expected. The SMR for the hospital is 0.89, indicating that the observed in-hospital mortality rate is lower than expected. Note that the unadjusted observed mortality rate for the hospital was actually higher than the national rate. Indirect standardization gave the hospital credit for the lower mortality rate in the most resource-intensive cases and therefore allowed an apples-to-apples comparison to the national rate.

Real-Time Analytics

As data analysis tools mature and the granularity of the data available in a healthcare entity increases, real-time analytics and performance **dashboards** based on **key performance indicators (KPIs)** are becoming the norm. Once a set of KPIs is identified, data elements to drive those indicators are created in real time and not based on static historical databases. For example, a KPI for a health information management (HIM) manager at a hospital may be the level of charges in the set of discharged and not final billed (DNFB) charts. If the level of charges goes above a predefined threshold, then an e-mail is sent to the manager to notify him of that fact so that action may be taken quickly. Without real-time analytics producing the KPI and alert, the manager may not have been alerted of the high level of DNFB until a weekly or monthly report was produced.

Some of the KPIs that may be included in real-time dashboards include both financial and clinical indicators, such as

- Days in accounts receivable
- Charges in DNFB
- Patient census by unit
- Number of patients in ED waiting for inpatient bed
- ED wait time
- Number of patients waiting for discharge
- Time for housekeeping to return a bed to service

KPI dashboards are now used throughout healthcare organizations. Many healthcare IT vendors now include at least some level of KPI dashboard functionality in their systems. The difficulty in implementing such systems effectively is setting thresholds for the various KPIs that are meaningful and do not identify false positives. Many hospital performance indicators such as volume, length of stay, and emergency department wait times have a certain amount of typical variability. Setting thresholds that are too sensitive could result in management investigating issues that are not unusual. Combining KPIs with the concepts of analytics such as confidence intervals and other statistical inference tools can produce a system of real-time alerts that are both sensitive enough to identify performance issue and yet specific enough to avoid false positives.

Opportunities for Health Information Management Professionals in Healthcare Data Analytics

HIM professionals are uniquely positioned to take on a variety of roles related to healthcare data analytics. Combining the following skills transforms the traditional HIM role into one of a business analyst:

- Understand data structures and coding systems
- Understand available data and methods for integration
- Can communicate with both finance and IT staff
- Act as a business analyst—far more valuable than a pure data analyst

For instance, in revenue cycle management the identification of missed charges is challenging. The traditional approach to identifying missed charges is to perform a charge description master (CDM) review and interview unit staff to ensure charge codes are utilized as designed. The staff may also review departmental order sheets to ensure they include complete and accurate listings of the services available in the department. An HIM professional with strong analytic skills may take a data-driven approach to study this issue.

The charge codes that occur together often may be identified through profiling of the historical claims data. Claims with only one of those codes may be selected for focused review. A chart review on that set of records that is most likely to include missed charges may then be completed to understand the root cause of the missing charges. The use of analytics on the historical claims may save a significant amount of time in the identification of particular codes that are problematic. Corrective action may be designed and implemented in a much more efficient manner.

Opportunities to apply analytics to common operational issue are present throughout the healthcare business setting. The American Health Information Management Association's *Health Data Analysis Toolkit* (Bronnert et al. 2011) lists a number of responsibilities that may be required of HIM professionals to perform analysis-based jobs in healthcare.

An entry-level health data analyst position may include the following analytic responsibilities:

- Identify, analyze, and interpret trends or patterns in complex data sets
- In collaboration with others, interpret data and develop recommendations on the basis of findings
- Develop graphs, reports, and presentations of project results, trends, and data mining
- Perform basic statistical analyses for projects and reports
- Create and present quality dashboards
- Generate routine and ad hoc reports

A mid-level health data analyst position may include the following additional analytic responsibilities:

- Work collaboratively with data and reporting and the database administrator to help produce effective production management and utilization management reports in support of performance management related to utilization, cost, and risk with the various health plan data; monitor data integrity and quality of reports on a monthly basis
- Work collaboratively with data and reporting in monitoring financial performance in each health plan

- Develop and maintain claims audit reporting and processes
- Develop and maintain contract models in support of contract negotiations with health plans
- Develop, implement, and enhance evaluation and measurement models for the quality, data and reporting, and data warehouse department programs, projects, and initiatives for maximum effectiveness
- Recommend improvements to processes, programs, and initiatives by using analytical skills and a variety of reporting tools
- Determine the most appropriate approach for internal and external report design, production, and distribution, specific to the relevant audience

A senior-level health data analyst position may include the following additional analytic responsibilities:

- Understand and address the information needs of governance, leadership, and staff to support continuous improvement of patient care processes and outcomes
- Lead and manage efforts to enhance the strategic use of data and analytic tools to improve clinical care processes and outcomes continuously
- Work to ensure the dissemination of accurate, reliable, timely, accessible, actionable information (data analysis) to help leaders and staff actively identify and address opportunities to improve patient care and related processes
- Work actively with information technology to select and develop tools to enable facility governance and leadership to monitor the progress of quality, patient safety, service, and related metrics continuously throughout the system
- Engage and collaborate with information technology and senior leadership to create and maintain a succinct report (for example, dashboard), as well as a balanced set of system assessment measures, that conveys status and direction of key system-wide quality and patient safety initiatives for the trustee quality and safety committee and senior management; present this information regularly to the quality and safety committee of the board to ensure understanding of information contained therein
- Actively support the efforts of divisions, departments, programs, and clinical units to identify, obtain, and actively use quantitative information needed to support clinical quality monitoring and improvement activities
- Function as an adviser and technical resource regarding the use of data in clinical quality improvement activities
- Lead analysis of outcomes and resource utilization for specific patient populations as necessary
- Lead efforts to implement state-of-the-art quality improvement analytical tools (that is, statistical process control)

- Play an active role, including leadership, where appropriate, on teams addressing system-wide clinical quality improvement opportunities

The level of understanding of the relationship between the variables analyzed and the complexity of the analytic techniques increases as an HIM professional advances from the entry to senior level. The common thread through all of these job responsibilities is strong basic analytic skills and understanding of the healthcare application of those techniques. HIM professionals who have a solid grasp of statistical techniques can combine those skills with their knowledge of the clinical application of data to assist with the interpretation and application of the results of analysis projects.

References

Bronnert, J., J. Clark, L. Hyde, J. Solberg, S. White, and M. Wolin. 2011. *Health Data Analysis Toolkit*. Chicago, IL: AHIMA.

Centers for Medicare and Medicaid Services. 2011. Statistical methods used to calculate rates. http://www.hospitalcompare.hhs.gov/staticpages/for-professionals/ooc/statistcal-methods.aspx.

Centers for Medicare and Medicaid Services. 2010. *Program Integrity Manual*. https://www.cms.gov/Regulations-and-Guidance/Guidance/Transmittals/downloads/R114PI.pdf.

Centers for Medicare and Medicaid Services. 2009. *Roadmap for Implementing Value Driven Healthcare in the Traditional Medicare Fee-for-Service Program*. Technical Report. Baltimore, MD: CMS.

Department of Health and Human Services. 2009. HCUP nationwide inpatient sample. http://hcupnet.ahrq.gov/HCUPnet.jsp.

Fayyad, U.M. 1996 (October). Data mining and knowledge discovery: Making sense out of data. *IEEE Expert*. 11.5. Piscataway, NY: IEEE Educational Activities Department.

Healthcare Financial Management Association. 2011. HFMA MAP revenue cycle excellence. http://www.hfmamap.org/.

Lewin Group. 2009. Comprehensive application of predictive modeling to reduce overpayments in Medicare and Medicaid. The Lewin Group. http://www.lewin.com/~/media/lewin/site_sections/publications/predictivemodelingmedicaidoverpymnt.pdf.

Office of Inspector General. 2007. RAT-STATS statistical software. http://oig.hhs.gov/compliance/rat-stats/index.asp.

Osborn, C. 2005. *Statistical Applications for Health Information Management*, 2nd ed. Sudbury, MA: Jones and Bartlett.

QualityNet. 2011. Specifications Manual, Version 4.0b. Users Manual, QualityNet.

SAS Institute. 2006. SAS white paper: Analytics in healthcare. Cary, NC: SAS.

UnitedHealth Center for Health Reform and Modernization. 2009 (June). Health care cost containment—how technology can cut red tape and simplify health care administration. http://www.unitedhealthgroup.com/hrm/UNH_WorkingPaper2.pdf.

White, S. 2011 (September). Predictive modeling 101. *Journal of AHIMA* 82(9): 46–47.

White, S., C. Kallem, C. Viola, and J. Bronnert. 2011 (June). An ACO primer. *Journal of AHIMA* 6(82): 48–49.

chapter 20

Research Methods

Elizabeth Forrestal, PhD, RHIA, CCS, FAHIMA

Learning Objectives

- Describe basic research designs and methods used in the practice of health information management
- Formulate research problems in terms of research questions
- Search knowledge bases such as bibliographic databases
- Plan research projects appropriate to the research questions
- Conduct research projects using standard and suitable tools and techniques
- Present research findings in formats consistent with the purpose of the research
- Critically evaluate research studies in health-related fields

Key Terms

Abstract
Alternative hypothesis
Applied research
Basic research
Bivariate
Case study
Case-control (retrospective) study
Categorical data
Causal relationship
Causal-comparative research
Census survey
Cluster sampling
Common Rule
Comparative effectiveness research (CER)
Confidence interval (CI)
Confidence limit
Confounding (extraneous, secondary) variable
Construct validity
Content analysis
Content validity
Continuous data
Control group
Convenience sampling

Correlational research
Coverage error
Covert observation
Cross-sectional study
Data cleansing
Data mining
Deductive reasoning
Dependent variable
Descriptive research
Descriptive (summary) statistics
Discrete data
Double-blind study
Effect size
Empiricism
Ethnography
Evaluation research
Experimental (study) group
Experimental research
External validity
Focus group
Focused study
Generalizability
Grounded theory

Health services research
Health technology assessment
Heterogeneity
Historical research
Hypothesis
Imputation
Independent variable
Inductive reasoning
Inferential statistics
Institutional review board (IRB)
Instrument
Internal validity
Interrater reliability
Interval data
Intervention
Interview guide
Interview survey
Intrarater reliability
Level of significance
Likert scale
Literature review
Longitudinal
Meta-analysis
Metric
Missing values
Mixed methods research
Model
Mortality (attrition)
Multivariate
Naturalism
Naturalistic study
Negative (inverse) relationship
Nominal data
Nonparametric (distribution-free) technique
Nonparticipant observation
Nonrandom sampling
Null hypothesis
Observational research
One-tailed hypothesis
Operational definition
Operationalize
Ordinal data
Outcomes research
Paradigm
Parametric technique
Parsimony
Participant observation
Peer review
Peer-reviewed (refereed) journal
Pilot study
Placebo
Population
Positive (direct) relationship
Positivism
Power

Primary analysis
Primary source
Prospective
Protocol
Purposive sampling
Qualitative approach
Quantitative approach
Questionnaire survey
Random sampling
Randomization
Randomized clinical trial (RCT)
Ratio data
Receiver operating characteristic (ROC) analysis
Reliability
Research
Research design
Research frame
Research method
Research methodology
Retrospective
Sample
Sample frame
Sample size
Sample size calculation
Sample survey
Sampling
Scale
Scientific inquiry
Secondary analysis
Secondary source
Semantic differential scale
Semistructured question
Sensitivity
Simple random sampling
Simulation observation
Specificity
Stratified random sampling
Structured (closed-ended) question
Survey
Systematic literature review
Systematic sampling
Target population
Test statistics
Theory
Translational research
Treatment
Triangulation
Two-tailed hypothesis
Type I error
Type II error
Univariate
Unstructured (open-ended) question
Validity
Variable

Health information management (HIM) is an intersection of many different fields of study. Health information managers are business people in a health-related profession. Thus, health information managers draw on theories from the many fields associated with both business and healthcare, including management, organizational behavior, sociology, psychology, medical sciences, computer science, and decision support. In this chapter, research concepts are applied to healthcare settings and the role of the HIM professional as a researcher is explored.

Research is thoughtful, planned activity that expands or refines knowledge. The purpose of research is to create generalizable knowledge. Research answers questions and provides solutions to everyday problems. Research is not some vague, mysterious activity for geniuses, as some people believe; rather, it is a step-by-step method that ordinary people can use to collect reliable and accurate facts in order to generate valuable information.

HIM professionals are contributors to research studies. (See table 20.1.) They are experts on health data; the data's location, accuracy, and format; and other aspects of HIM practice. Their training and education provide specific research skills, and their professional values are supportive of research.

Knowledge of research also supports HIM practice. Understanding research methods aids HIM professionals whenever they use data or information to answer a question or to make a decision.

This chapter provides an overview of the role of research in HIM and healthcare and the development of theories and models. It also presents a step-by-step process for conducting research. Finally, the chapter addresses how HIM

Table 20.1.   HIM contributions to research teams

HIM-Specific Skills	Research-Specific Skills	HIM Values
Knowledge of health record content Form and view design Expertise in classifications and nomenclatures Database query skills Professional collegiality	Ability to conduct literature reviews Knowledge of research protocols Capability to devise case-based algorithms Understanding of procedures of institutional review boards Knowledge of data collection protocols Written and oral communication of data, information, and knowledge	Accuracy Attention to detail Respect for patient rights and confidentiality Commitment to protecting health data privacy and security

professionals can use the techniques of research to improve HIM practice and data quality.

Research Frame

A **research frame** is the overarching structure of the research project. Another term for the research frame is **paradigm**. A research frame comprises the theory or theories underpinning the study, the models illustrating the factors and relationships of the study, the assumptions of the field and the researcher, the methods, and the analytical tools. Research is conducted within frames.

Theories and Models

A **theory** is the systematic organization of knowledge that predicts or explains behavior or events. Theories and research have a chicken-and-egg relationship. Theories are both the result and the foundation of research. Researchers begin with informed predictions or raw theories of what they believe will happen. As they collect observations and data, they refine their theories. Over time, the refined theories become more predictive of subsequent events than their previous embryonic versions.

Theories help people understand their world. Without theories, people are merely speculating. Although speculation may be informed by experiences and some facts, it is nevertheless speculation.

Apparent in all fields of study, theories explain what people have observed. In addition, they provide definitions, relationships, and boundaries. In other words, theories systematically organize everything people know about a concept. Formally defined, theories are

- Concepts that are abstract ideas generalized from particular instances
- Interrelationships that are assumed to exist among these concepts
- Consequences that are assumed to follow logically from the relationships proposed in the theory (Amatayakul and Shah 1992, 8)

The best theories simplify the situation, explain the most facts in the broadest range of circumstances, and most accurately predict behavior (Singleton and Straits 2005, 20). Researchers in health information management use several different theories (see figure 20.1).

Overall, research theories are practical and efficient because they help researchers explain and predict many events in simple and precise terms. In other words, theories organize knowledge. When knowledge is organized, ordinary people can access and use it. Thus, everyone benefits.

A **model** is a representation of a theory in visual format. Models can portray theories with objects, can be smaller-scaled versions, or can be graphic representations. A model includes all of a theory's known properties. Models aid in comprehension of a theory.

Figure 20.1.   Theories used in health informatics and HIM research

- Adult learning theories
- Behavioral theories
- Change theories
- Diffusion of innovation
- Information processing or cognitive learning theories
- Information theories (Shannon and Weaver's Information–Communication Model and Blum's model)
- Learning styles
- Learning theories
- Systems theory

Source: Constructed by author based on content in Englebardt and Nelson 2002.

Research Methodology

Research methodology is the study and analysis of **research methods** and theories. Generally, there are two types of research: basic research and applied research. These two types are ends of a continuum, not separate entities. Therefore, the distinction between them is sometimes unclear. In essence, basic research focuses on the development of theories and their refinement (Gay et al. 2012, 16). Because **basic research** often occurs in laboratories, it is sometimes called "bench science." Basic research answers the question: Why? On the other hand, **applied research** focuses on the implementation of theories into practice (Gay et al. 2012, 16). Applied research answers the questions: What? and How? Applied research, particularly clinical applied science, may occur in healthcare settings, such as at the bedside in hospitals.

For the past several years, **translational research,** which specifically spans the continuum, has received attention. Translational research effectively translates "new knowledge, mechanisms, and techniques generated by advances in basic science research into new approaches for prevention, diagnosis, and treatment of disease" (Fontanarosa and DeAngelis 2002, 1728). For example, translational research may take knowledge from basic science, such as a newly discovered property of a chemical, and may convert that knowledge into a practical application, such as a new drug. Therefore, sometimes people describe translational research as "bench-to-bedside" (Woolf 2008, 211). Of interest to health information professionals is the subspecialty translational bioinformatics. Translational bioinformatics is "the development of storage, analytic, and interpretive methods to optimize the transformation of increasingly voluminous biomedical data...into proactive, predictive, preventive, and participatory health" (AMIA 2012).

In practice as applied researchers, some HIM professionals study questions they believe will improve health information practices in the continuum of care. For example, HIM professionals explored whether the data in health records

are adequate to support coding using the ICD-10-CM classification (Moczygemba and Fenton 2012, 1). This initial exploratory study involving three diagnoses—heart disease, pneumonia, and diabetes—revealed that over 25 percent of the time the documentation's level of detail was insufficient for ICD-10-CM coding (Moczygemba and Fenton 2012, 3). This type of study is representative of applied research in health informatics and information management.

Also, at a general level, researchers in research methodology have described two overarching approaches to research: the quantitative approach and the qualitative approach.

The **quantitative approach** is the explanation of phenomena through scientific inquiry and empiricism. **Scientific inquiry** involves making predictions, collecting and analyzing evidence, testing alternative theories, and choosing the best theory. **Empiricism** means "based on observed and validated evidence." For example, research based on experiments is empirical. Objective knowledge is the desired end result. As the word *quantitative* implies, the data often can be quantified and result in statistical or numerical results. Another name for the quantitative approach is **positivism.** A classic example of quantitative research is the human genome project.

Researchers in the **qualitative approach** interpret non-numerical observations. These non-numerical observations include words, gestures, activities, time, space, images, and perceptions. These observations are placed in context. Another term for the qualitative approach is **naturalism.** A classic example of qualitative research is Margaret Mead's anthropological study of the Polynesian culture of American Samoa in the early 1920s. Examples in medicine involve studies of near-death experiences, dying, and being a patient. Without qualitative research, healthcare personnel would not have learned that elderly, married patients cut their pills in half in order to share their prescriptions when they run out of money.

These two approaches to research are frames on a grand scale. Within both approaches, researchers make certain basic assumptions. (See table 20.2.) Some large topics require both approaches with many researchers conducting complementary studies.

Table 20.2.   Comparison of assumptions in quantitative and qualitative research approaches

Quantitative	Qualitative
Single truth exists	Multiple truths exist simultaneously
Single truth applies across time and place	Truths are bound to place and time (contextual)
Researchers can adopt neutral, unbiased stances	Neutrality is impossible because researchers choose their topics of investigation
Chronological sequence of causes can be identified	Influences interact with one another to color researchers' views of the past, present, and future

An emerging third approach is called **mixed methods research** (Johnson and Onwuegbuzie 2004, 15). Mixed methods research combines quantitative and qualitative techniques within a single study and across related studies. Mixed methods research may be suited to investigations into complex phenomena in healthcare (McKibbon and Gadd 2004). An example is a study of current practices, in admitting and registration departments, to reduce the occurrence of medical identify theft (Mancilla and Moczygemba 2009, 2). The researchers used both quantitative and qualitative methods to collect data on the procedures that healthcare staff members follow to establish and confirm patients' identities. The researchers found that procedures and technology in admitting and registration departments did not support organizational policies and federal regulations designed to protect patients' identities (Mancilla and Moczygemba 2009, 7).

The purpose of the research determines the approach. Research that investigates numerically measurable observations or tests a **hypothesis** is often quantitative, while research that is exploratory and preliminary often begins with a qualitative investigation.

Most advances in medicine have been the result of quantitative research. Quantitative research, with its scientific and evidence-based approach, is also the approach that HIM researchers often select.

Within both the quantitative and the qualitative approaches, researchers use inductive reasoning and deductive reasoning. **Inductive reasoning,** or induction, involves drawing conclusions based on a limited number of observations. For example, during his professional practice experience, a student might observe that all coders in the coding department at XYZ hospital had the RHIT credential. Thus, he might conclude that all coders have the RHIT credential. **Deductive reasoning,** or deduction, involves drawing conclusions based on generalizations. For example, all coders have the RHIT credential. Jane Doe is a coder. Therefore, Jane Doe must have the RHIT credential.

As the examples demonstrate, neither induction nor deduction alone is completely satisfactory. Used together, however, they are very effective and are the basis of the research.

Check Your Understanding 20.1

Instructions: Answer the following questions on a separate piece of paper.

1. What is research?

2. What are the three characteristics of a theory?

3. How does the phrase "keep it simple" apply to theories?

4. What are the advantages of models?

5. Why is the research conducted by HIM professionals considered applied research?

6. Why is it so important for researchers to know their purpose?

7. How do inductive reasoning and deductive reasoning differ?

Research Process

Conceptually, researchers participate in the following major activities:

- Defining the research question (problem)
- Summarizing prior pertinent knowledge
- Gathering data
- Analyzing the data
- Interpreting and presenting findings

However, because these major activities are so broad, most researchers divide them into more manageable components. Thus, the research process becomes orderly problem solving. In the verbal shorthand of researchers, these basic components are

- Defining the research question (problem)
- Performing a literature review
- Determining a research design and method
- Selecting an instrument
- Gathering data
- Analyzing the data
- Presenting results

Defining the Research Question (Problem)

Research begins with defining the problem. Defining the problem is also known as specifying the research question. Whichever phrase is used, both mean that researchers must be crystal clear about what they are investigating. Vague notions lead to substandard research, which is a waste of time, effort, and energy for both researchers and participants.

The importance of investing time and effort in developing the research question cannot be overstated. Experts agree that "the key element, the starting point and the most important issue in developing research, is the research question" (Metz 2001, 13).

According to Metz, the criteria for a well-developed research question are

- The question is clearly and exactly stated.
- The question has theoretical significance, practical worth, or both.
- The question has obvious and explicit links to a larger body of knowledge, such as a theory or a research model.
- The research's results advance knowledge in a definable way.
- The answer to the question or the solution to the problem is worthwhile.

The first step in developing the research question is to identify a general problem in an area of interest and expertise. Three excellent sources of meaningful problems exist:

Research models: Research models show all the factors and relationships in a theory. Researchers can

Figure 20.2.   AHIMA's model of data quality

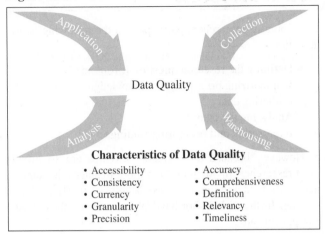

Characteristics of Data Quality

• Accessibility	• Accuracy
• Consistency	• Comprehensiveness
• Currency	• Definition
• Granularity	• Relevancy
• Precision	• Timeliness

Source: AHIMA 2012.

Figure 20.3.   Examples of topics of literature reviews in health informatics and HIM

- Findings of evaluation studies of health information systems and technology (Lau et al. 2010)
- Information technology and improvement of clinicians' performance, clinical care, and health outcomes
  (Buntin et al. 2011; Eslami et al. 2008; Georgiou et al. 2011; Jaspers et al. 2011)
- Factors in the adoption and use of health information technologies and systems (Lluch 2011; Police et al. 2010)
- Standards for reporting on studies in health informatics (Augestad et al. 2012)
- Access, use, quality, and types of consumer e-health initiatives (Archer et al. 2011; Brouwer et al. 2011; Cugelman et al. 2011)
- Classifications, terminologies, coded data, and structured reports (Byrne et al. 2010; Stanfill et al. 2010)

select one or two factors that other researchers have raised questions about or have found problematic. An added benefit is that the model suggests the relationships among all the factors. For example, researchers in health information management could use AHIMA's Model of Data Quality to develop a research problem. (Refer to figure 20.2.) These hypothetical researchers could investigate the relationship between collection and data quality. Finally, research models explicitly link to a larger body of knowledge, one of the criteria for a well-developed research question.

- *Recommendations of earlier researchers:* In journal articles, researchers specifically make recommendations for later research. Their research raises yet more questions that future researchers can answer.
- *Gaps in the body of knowledge:* A comprehensive review of the literature related to the problem or question will identify gaps or problematic areas. (See next section on performing a literature review.) For example, in journal articles, researchers often identify unintentional flaws in their own study that future researchers could correct in a replication study. Correcting the flaw in the subsequent study could produce more accurate and predictive results than were found in the original study. In health information management and other fields, entire articles have been dedicated to reviewing the literature. These literature review articles can be examined for research questions. Literature review articles related to health informatics and health information management have covered a wide range of topics. (See figure 20.3.)

In addition, researchers make recommendations for future research in master's theses and doctoral dissertations. Therefore, a careful and thoughtful reading of journal articles, literature review articles, master's theses, and doctoral dissertations can identify meaningful research problems.

The next step is to narrow the focus of the question to a manageable and researchable issue. Researchers clearly state the research problem or question in their article or paper in order to draw the reader into the topic. A helpful metaphor is the funnel. Researchers begin with a broad, general question and then gradually pinpoint the topic to their precise problem or question.

Moreover, an effective problem statement delimits or sets the boundaries of the problem. By clearly stating the study's area of investigation, researchers also specify the aspects of the problem that are beyond or outside the scope of their research. For example, the researcher might begin the problem statement with a general societal concern. Supporting citations would then come from the popular literature, opinion articles, and journal articles. Next, he or she would concentrate the discussion by explaining how this problem or question affects the field of health information management. Finally, he or she would state the research problem or question succinctly and accurately.

Clearly delineating the problem helps the researcher later in the research process when he or she is writing the hypothesis. The hypothesis is written after the researcher completes the literature review. In the hypothesis, the researcher operationalizes his or her research question. (See later section on statement of hypothesis.). **Operationalize** means formulating the question in terms that are capable of generating data and that satisfactorily capture the issues of the question or problem.

The last step in developing the research question or problem is to ensure that the issue has merit. Similar to substandard research, research on a trite issue about which no one cares is a waste of time, effort, and energy. Therefore, the key to defining the problem statement is to find a meaningful problem that needs a solution or a significant question that needs an answer.

Table 20.3. Three meanings of *literature review*

Meaning	General Description	Example
One	Process	Identifying, reading, analyzing, summarizing, and synthesizing the works of researchers and experts
Two	Product—Portion of study's presentation	Excerpt from research article, Kesh, Someswar, and Wullianallur Raghupathi. 2004. Critical issues in bioinformatics and computing. *Perspectives in Health Information Management* 1(9): 1–8. Bioinformatics is defined by the National Institutes of Health as the "research, development, or application of computational tools and approaches for expanding the use of biological, medical, behavioral or health data, including those to acquire, store, organize, archive, analyze, or visualize such data." The exponential growth in the amount of such data has necessitated the use of computers for information cataloging and retrieval; a more global perspective in the quest for new insights into health and disease and the resulting data mining also underscore the need for bioinformatics. Both sophisticated hardware and complex software play an increasingly critical role in the analysis of genomic data, and the accelerated maturation of the field of bioinformatics has implications for computing and life sciences professionals as well as the general public. Like computational biology, bioinformatics is anchored in the life sciences as well as computer and information sciences and technologies. Its interdisciplinary and integrative approach draws from fields such as mathematics, physics, computer science and engineering, biology, and behavioral science. The generally accepted subdisciplines include (1) development of new algorithms and statistics with which to assess relationships among members of large data sets; (2) analyses and interpretation of various types of sequences, domains, and structures; and (3) development and implementation of tools that enable efficient access and management of different types of information.
Three	Product—Entire research article or book	Citation in bibliographic databases includes publication type of "review" and number of references Edmonson, S.R., K.A. Smith-Akin, and E.V. Bernstam. 2007. Context, automated decision support, and clinical practice guidelines: Does the literature apply to the United States practice environment? [Review] [36 refs] *International Journal of Medical Informatics* 76(1): 34–41. Dorr, D., L.M. Bonner, A.N. Cohen, R.S. Shoai, R. Perrin, E. Chaney, and A.S. Young. 2007. Informatics systems to promote improved care for chronic illness: A literature review. [Review] [40 refs] *Journal of the American Medical Informatics Association* 14(2): 156–163. Systematic (integrative) review Meta-analysis

Performing a Literature Review

A **literature review** is a systematic and critical investigation of the important information about a topic. After completing this orderly and organized approach to the literature, researchers know the following about a topic:

- Mainstream and lesser-known theories, theorists, and factors
- Key turning points in the development of ideas about the topic
- Typical research methods
- Major research instruments
- Appropriate analytical approaches

From the literature review, researchers are able to assess the competency of research studies and to identify gaps or holes in the field's body of knowledge. Because overviews identify gaps or discrepancies in a field's knowledge, they are both sources of problems or research questions that researchers can investigate and an excellent means to refine and focus a research question into a previously unexplored issue.

Literature review has three meanings (see table 20.3). In the first meaning, it is the process of identifying, reading, analyzing, summarizing, and synthesizing the writings of other researchers and thinkers. In the second and third meanings, the literature review is a product. It is the portion of a manuscript or an article in which researchers record their analysis and summary of the literature they have read. A literature review article is a separate and independent peer-reviewed article. In a literature review article, the previously mentioned "portion" is expanded and refined into an entire article.

Both as a process and as a product, these overviews identify gaps or discrepancies in the body of knowledge for researchers.

Purpose of the Literature Review

The purpose of a literature review is to develop and present a strong knowledge base. The strong knowledge base can be used to

- Conduct research
- Generate and analyze theories
- Develop evidence-based practice guidelines
- Develop curriculum
- Perform strategic planning
- Develop white (position) papers

The researcher comes to a complete understanding of the topic. This means that he or she can:

- Determine applicable theories, pertinent factors, and appropriate research designs and methods
- Outline a historical overview of a topic
- Explain the development and evolution of relevant theories
- Assess the thoroughness of literature reviews in published studies
- Relate theorists and researchers with their ideas and findings
- Differentiate between accepted theories and those outside the mainstream
- Discriminate between relevant and irrelevant factors
- Clarify concepts, recognize trends, explain debates, and identify confounding factors
- State advantages and disadvantages of various research methods
- Cite the strengths and weaknesses of various instruments
- Select appropriate techniques for analysis
- Identify competently conducted research and inadequately conducted research
- Detect the holes in the body of knowledge that his or her research can fill

Thus, the literature review results in the researcher "owning" this particular slice of the body of knowledge. He or she knows the theories; the names of the researchers, theorists, and collaborators; the sources of the data; common research designs; and gaps in the body of knowledge.

Process of the Literature Review

Researchers conducting a literature review identify, read, analyze, summarize, and synthesize knowledge and research of a topic and closely related topics. The process of a literature review is a systematic plan consisting of four steps:

1. Determine the literature to review.
2. Identify, categorize, organize, and obtain the literature.
3. Analyze the research questions, methods, and results presented in the literature.
4. Synthesize the information in the literature.

Sources of Information

In the first step, the researcher determines the literature to review. Sources of information include journals; periodicals; books, brochures, and book chapters; technical and research reports; proceedings of conferences; doctoral dissertations and master's theses; unpublished works; reviews; audiovisual media; and electronic media. (See figure 20.4.) These sources can be found in many bibliographic databases that

Figure 20.4. Sources of information

Periodicals	Product insert	**Doctoral Dissertations and Master's Theses**	Performance
Abstract	Published or archived letter		Published interview
Annual review		Abstract of dissertation	Recorded interview
Cartoon	**Technical and Research Reports**	Abstract of thesis	Slide
Journal		Dissertation	Speech
Magazine	Government bulletin	Thesis	Television broadcast and transcript
Monograph	Government report		Television series and transcript
Newsletter	Industry report	**Unpublished Works**	Unpublished interview
Newspaper	Issue brief	Submitted manuscript	Work of art
Press release	Monograph	Unpublished letter	
	Nongovernment agency report	Unpublished manuscript	**Electronic Media**
Books, Brochures, and Book Chapters	Position paper	Unpublished raw data	Abstract on CD-ROM
Book	Reference report	**Reviews**	CD-ROM
Book chapter	University report	Book	Computer program
Brochure	White paper	Film	Computer software
Dictionary	Working paper	Video	Electronic database
Encyclopedia			Internet website
Legal citation	**Proceedings of Meetings**	**Audiovisual Media**	Online abstract
Manual	Conference	Address	Online book
Map or chart	Meeting	Audiotape	Online journal
Pamphlet	Poster session	Chart	Software manual
	Symposium	Film	
	Unpublished proceeding paper	Lecture	
		Music recording	

index them. Because health information management combines theories from many academic fields, HIM researchers need to search a wide variety of databases that include sources related to management, organizational behavior, sociology, psychology, medical sciences, computer science, and decision support. Particularly helpful are databases that access the articles in journals related to medicine, health, health information management, health services administration, and bioinformatics. (See table 20.4.)

The literature comprises primary and secondary sources. **Primary sources** are the original works of the researchers who conducted the investigation. Research-based articles in the *New England Journal of Medicine* or *Science* are examples of primary sources. **Secondary sources** are summaries of the original works. Encyclopedias and textbooks are familiar secondary sources. Other examples of secondary sources are annual reviews (also sometimes called tertiary sources). Annual reviews summarize and synthesize current and recent knowledge on a topic. Examples from over 30 disciplines in the biomedical, life, physical, and social sciences are available online (Annual Reviews 2008). They may be special issues of print or electronic journals or entire

Table 20.4.   Selected bibliographic databases with emphases in medicine, health, HIM, health services administration, and health informatics

Bibliographic Database	Description
ACM Digital Library (Association for Computing Machinery)	Journals, magazine, and conference proceedings from 1985, many full text
Allied and Complementary Medicine (AMED)	Biomedical journals focused on alternative and complementary with relevant articles taken from other journals plus newspapers and books; includes English-language and European sources
AltHealth Watch	International peer-reviewed and professional journals, many full text from 1990; also includes magazines, reports, proceedings, association and consumer newsletters, pamphlets, booklets, special reports, original research, and book excerpts
Annual Reviews	Definitive academic resource for reviews in topics from biomedical, physical, and social sciences
BioMed Central	Peer-reviewed research of biology and medicine with immediate, barrier-free access from 1997
BioMedical Reference Collection, Comprehensive	Full-text journals including clinical medicine, psychiatry, psychology, nursing, allied health, public health, nutrition, and HIM
CINAHL (Cumulative Index of Nursing and Allied Health Literature)	Journals and publications in nursing, biomedicine, health sciences librarianship, consumer health, and allied health disciplines
Health Business FullTEXT Elite	Full-text journals on healthcare administration and other non-clinical aspects of healthcare management
Health Services Technology/Assessment Texts (HSTAT)	Free, web-based full-text documents on health information for healthcare decision making
Health Source: Nursing/Academic	Scholarly full-text journals, many focused on nursing and allied health; indexing, 1984–present; full text, 1990–present
IEEE Xplore (Institute of Electrical and Electronics Engineers)	Full-text access to transactions, journals, magazines, and conference proceedings since 1952
LISTA (Library Information Science and Technical Abstracting)	Open access to periodicals, books, research reports, and conference proceedings from mid-1960s
MEDLINE	Authoritative source of information on medicine, nursing, allied health, dentistry, veterinary medicine, healthcare system, and preclinical sciences
Ovid HealthSTAR	More than 3 million citations addressing health services, technology, administration, and research, published from 1975 to present, from the National Library of Medicine. Includes both clinical and nonclinical topics in journal articles, government documents, newspaper articles, monographs, book chapters, technical reports, and meeting abstracts and papers
PubMed	Preeminent bibliographic biomedical database of the National Library of Medicine
SIAM Journals Online (Society for Industrial and Applied Mathematics)	Access to full-text journals from 1994

books. For literature reviews, primary sources are preferable to secondary sources.

The gold standard for a literature review is primary research in **peer-reviewed (refereed) journals. Peer review** is the process that ensures that the information reported in the journal is of the highest quality (Colaianni 1994, 156). Journals may be peer-reviewed (also called research, refereed, academic, and professional) or non-peer-reviewed (also called popular). In peer-reviewed journals, the articles are evaluated in manuscript form by experts in the field (peers) for quality prior to publication.

Both print and electronic journals are peer-reviewed. Examples of peer-reviewed journals are the *Journal of the American Medical Association,* the *New England Journal of Medicine, Science,* and the *Journal of the American Medical Informatics Association.* In the field of health information management, the major peer-reviewed journals are the *Journal of the American Health Information Management Association* and *Perspectives in Health Information Management.* Thus, researchers must make a distinction between research (professional) literature and popular literature. Properly conducted and written literature reviews focus on primary sources in peer-reviewed journals.

Search Techniques

In the second step, researchers identify, categorize, organize, and obtain the literature. A systematic plan identifies the databases to search as well as all the terms used to query the databases. Categorizing includes listing all types of sources of information on the topic. Although traditional literature may constitute the major portion of the plan, other sources (such as videos, newscasts, and the Internet) can contribute and should be considered. Tables and lists are essential tools. The plan also includes organizing the documentation of the queries, the search terms, the results of the queries for each database, and the literature itself as it is received. This section focuses on the search techniques.

Procedure

The following steps describe the search procedure for referreed journal articles. Researchers can use similar tactics in other media and for popular literature.

1. Generate a list of key terms and synonyms (in the databases of medical literature these are medical subject headings or MeSH headings). Include synonyms and alternative formats and spellings (quality management, continuous quality improvement, performance improvement; manage, management; **meta-analysis**).

2. Generate a list of target databases (such as Ovid Health-STAR , MEDLINE, CINAHL). An excellent database for health-related research is PubMed from the National Library of Medicine. HIM researchers provide detailed instructions on how to query this database (Fenton and Williams 2005, 60A).

3. Search each database with each term. Use an advanced "All Fields" search and document each search.

4. Use the "Limit" function to narrow the searches to referreed journals (also sometimes called academic journals). You can also "limit" to human subjects, English language, and time periods.

5. Scan the **abstracts** of the articles to determine whether the articles are applicable. Abstracts summarize research studies' major parts: context; objective; design, setting, and participants; **interventions;** main outcome measures; results; and conclusions.

6. Save applicable articles (online and print) to a computer or an external storage device. Use a naming convention, such as the author's last name, a word or two on the topic, year of publication, and month (or season). For ease of reading, consider printing the articles as well. Be sure to consult a librarian about limits on and fees for printing.

7. Photocopy articles that are unavailable electronically. Note that although it may be convenient or expedient to only use online articles, the resulting literature review will be incomplete and biased. In some cases, academic libraries offer document delivery in which the library staff scan the articles and send the articles electronically to the requester. Be sure to investigate the costs of this procedure as it may be expensive.

8. Read and analyze the literature obtained to date.

9. Identify key journal articles.

10. Obtain the references cited at the end of the key articles. Track their order and receipt.

11. Note the MeSHs of the key articles. If the original list missed these terms, rerun the searches of the databases on the new terms.

12. Identify key researchers in the topic. Run advanced searches on "author." Obtain every researcher's articles and books on the topic.

13. Alphabetize all the copies of the articles by author. This strategy avoids duplication and allows prompt access.

To avoid rework during the manuscript's composition, researchers should capture all data about the source when they first obtain it. The various style manuals have different requirements. To meet all the requirements, researchers should be sure to note the following information about their sources:

- Full name of the author, including first name and middle initial or name (be aware that some entries in websites have authors)
- Full title of the journal, book, video, or website
- Complete information about dates of publication, including the year, month, and season (be aware that some entries in websites are dated)
- Complete name and address of the publisher (for books and videos)
- Inclusive page numbers

- Volume number and issue number (sometimes these data are only on the front of the publication)
- Accurate URL and access date (for Internet sources)
- Accurate DOI (Digital Object Identifier) for all articles that have them. The DOI is a unique, stable (persistent) identifier for articles in an online environment. The DOI is alphanumeric, beginning with the number 10, then a prefix (four or more digits representing the publisher), a forward slash, and a suffix (numbers assigned to the article by the publisher)

As a means to organize the literature review, researchers are strongly encouraged to invest in a bibliographic software package at the beginning of their research. Bibliographic software packages greatly assist researchers. Helpful features of these packages allow researchers to

- Create their own personal bibliographic databases
- Utilize the packages' search engines that directly download citations into the researchers' personal bibliographic databases
- Import the contents of databases into word-processing software
- Transform bibliographic entries into the required style of the journal (styles editor)

Commonly used bibliographic packages include Reference Manager, EndNote, RefWorks, and ProCite. Reference manager "freeware" includes BiblioExpress and Scholar's Aid 4 Lite. Zotero runs on Mozilla Foxfire and is easy to use.

Retrieval of Information

Students and instructors may retrieve information from many sources. The libraries at their educational institutions have extensive holdings. These holdings include bibliographic databases, other databases, books, electronic books, reference manuals, maps, videotapes, and audiotapes. Libraries typically list their holdings on webpages. Many of the library's holdings can be accessed through the library's catalogs. The databases, electronic books, and online journals usually can be found under electronic resources. Libraries purchase licenses that allow their users access to the various databases. Just as different libraries have purchased different books, different libraries have purchased different licenses.

In addition, AHIMA members have access to the holdings of the Body of Knowledge (BoK). These holdings include over 6,500 documents covering

- Full-text articles from the *Journal of the American Health Information Management Association* since 1998
- Proceedings from AHIMA's Annual Convention and Exhibit
- *AHIMA Advantage* articles published since January 2002
- AHIMA practice briefs, toolkits, position statements, reports, guidelines and white papers, leadership

models, job descriptions, and other association information
- Government publications such as parts of the *Federal Register* and Department of Health and Human Services (HHS) documents

There is also document delivery for a fee that varies by availability. Practice guidelines about e-HIM, the transition from paper health records to electronic health records (EHRs), also are available at the AHIMA website (AHIMA 2012).

Practitioners also may access sources of information and databases through their workplaces. Healthcare organizations have libraries or some arrangement for access to libraries. As employees, practitioners may access these resources.

Although websites may have information that has not been peer reviewed, they may have valuable government reports and other documents. Many libraries of colleges and universities, such as the University of South Carolina Beaufort Library (2010), have developed online tutorials on their websites that explain the features of various Internet search engines.

In the steps of the search procedure, this brief statement is made: "Read and analyze the literature obtained to date." The brevity of this statement in no way represents the task of reading and analyzing the literature. In this analytical task, researchers should be noting

- Major theories and theorists
- Trends
- Concepts, factors, and variables
- Research designs and methods
- Populations and sampling techniques
- Accepted and commonly used instruments
- Appropriate statistical techniques
- Controversial issues within the topic

Researchers can record the key features of each article in a table. (See table 20.5.) From this tool, they can identify trends, common characteristics, and gaps.

Development of Literature Review

The development of the literature review is the synthesis of the data and information captured in the process of the literature review. The word *synthesize* cannot be emphasized enough. In today's world of data and information overload, mere narrative reviews, which are long summaries of previous studies, are not adequate. Readers require the knowledge that comes from the analysis and synthesis of the literature.

After completing the literature review, researchers develop its products. These products are written and may be either a portion of a journal article, paper, or presentation or an entire article or paper. However, in both forms, the well-developed literature review concisely and logically states what is known and unknown about a topic.

Table 20.5. Summary of the literature

Author	Year	Design & Method	Time Frame	Sample & Response Rate	Statistical Techniques	Key Findings, Limitations, & Recommendations
X and Y	1980	Descriptive	One-shot	20 patients, convenience 100%	Means and percentages	• More smokers in dermatology clinic • Small convenience sample limits generalizability • Recommends larger random sample
A and B	1995	Correlational	One-shot	70 random subjects, 30%	Bivariate correlation	• Relationship between smoking and skin tone • Limitations of self-report and one-shot approach • Recommends longitudinal, experimental research
L, M, and N	2001	Quasi-experimental	1 year	40 subjects, 100%	ANOVA	• Skin tone of nonsmokers significantly more toned than skin tone of smokers • Generalizability limited because subjects come from one socioeconomic class and one clinic • Recommends larger and more heterogeneous sample

For both forms, the characteristics of a good literature review are

- Comprehensiveness that is also relevant and focused
- Critique that includes strengths, weaknesses, limitations, and gaps
- Analysis
- Summary that is succinct and logical and comprises mainly primary sources
- Synthesis

Several common conventions guide the development of both forms of literature reviews. These conventions are detailed in the following paragraphs, with unique aspects of each form concluding this section.

In a complex or broad topic, researchers should briefly describe the strategy they used to identify literature. In addition, they should explain the scope of the literature review by explicitly stating both their inclusion and exclusion criteria. For example, a researcher could state, "The topic of health information systems is broad. This literature review focused on research articles related to mental health."

Researchers should make a conscious effort to identify, consider, and use an organizing function or factor for the literature review. Using the research model is one organizing function; chronology is another. Explicitly stating the order helps to guide and direct the reader. A coherent and logical order clarifies the topic.

In the literature review, the researcher identifies the key points or turning points in the development of knowledge about a topic. The literature included should be the research studies that either moved the topic forward or added new factors to the topic. However, important studies with contradictory findings also should be included. Otherwise, readers could interpret the absence of contradictory studies as bias. Evidence of bias detracts from the credibility of the literature review. Explanations of the contradictory findings, based on evaluation and analysis, might be suggested.

Moreover, the studies included in the research study should be pertinent. When tangential studies are included, their relevance should be explicitly stated. Generally, the least-related studies should be discussed first and the most-related studies discussed last.

Research studies that either were conducted inadequately or resulted in gaps or conflicting results should be included, especially if the researcher is rectifying the errors. Again, the researcher should specifically point out the inadequacies, gaps, or conflicting results.

Key research studies or turning-point studies should be described in greater detail than replication or duplicative studies. Enough information about the key studies (design, time frame, method, sample, response rate, statistical techniques, and findings) should be included so that the reader can evaluate their quality. Research that has the same findings with the same factors should be bundled. For example, the author could state, "Research (citation one, citation two, citation three, and so on) has shown that smoking is bad for skin tone."

Tradition and logic demand that researchers pay close attention to verb tense when they write the literature review. The tense of the verb situates the event or idea in time. Present tense expresses truths, accepted theories, and facts. Recent, valid studies also are explained in the present tense. For example:

- *Accepted theory:* Specific goals motivate employees more than vague goals.
- *Recent study:* Johnson's results illustrate the importance of specific goals.

Past studies with continued historical value can be described in the past tense. Including the date to situate the study is a common practice. For example:

- *Study of historical importance:* In 1972, the study of Smith et al. showed the importance of expectancy in motivation.

However, the easiest and safest rule is to use present tense for published studies and theories.

A table that briefly summarizes and highlights the important elements of each of the studies included in the literature review is an effective tool. Readers can quickly see trends and gaps in the literature. The table lists each study in a row, with columns displaying its summary, advantages, and disadvantages. Another possible structure for the table is to use rows for the studies but substitute features of the studies in the columns (refer to table 20.5).

As a portion of a journal article, paper, or presentation, the purpose of the literature review is to persuade the reader or audience of the necessity of the research study. The literature review should guide the reader and audience to reach the same conclusions that the researchers reached and the same question or problem. Moreover, the reader and audience should conclude that the logical and necessary next step is the research proposed by the researchers. A secondary purpose is to assure the reader or audience that the researcher has conducted a thorough and diligent review of all aspects of the topic. The thoroughness of the literature review lends credibility to both the researcher and the entire investigation. Finally, the literature review should conclude with a clear and exact statement of the hypothesis.

As an entire article, the literature review is a specialized type of research. Terms for this type of research are *systematic literature review*, *integrative review*, or *meta-analysis*. The **systematic literature review** is a methodical approach to literature review that reduces the possibility of bias. It is characterized by

- Explicit search criteria to identify literature
- Inclusion and exclusion criteria to select articles and information sources
- Evaluation against consistent methodological standards

This analytical summary of the literature is an amplified and enhanced version of the paragraphs that form the literature review in other research articles.

The meta-analysis is a specialized kind of systematic review that introduces statistical techniques to combine the results of several studies. This type of review is discussed in greater detail in the subsection on research methods.

The literature review article is a distillation and synthesis of the current status of knowledge on a topic. "Systematic reviews establish whether scientific findings are consistent and can be generalized across populations, settings, and treatment variations" (Mulrow 1994, 597). Annual reviews are examples of analytical summaries of the literature. Examples of annual reviews can be found in journal articles or entire books.

More information on performing literature reviews is available in *Health Sciences Literature Review Made Easy* (Garrard 2011), which focuses on literature reviews in the health sciences.

Check Your Understanding 20.2

Instructions: Answer the following questions on a separate piece of paper.

1. What are the seven basic steps of research?
2. What are five characteristics of a well-developed research question?
3. What are three rich sources of meaningful research questions?
4. Why is conducting a literature review important for a researcher?
5. List five data sources, other than journal articles, that a researcher should consider when doing a comprehensive search.
6. Why would a researcher limit the search of journal articles to peer-reviewed (refereed) journals?
7. Why would the director of health information services select the productivity standard recommended in a peer-reviewed journal rather than the productivity standard recommended in a popular magazine?
8. How do researchers use key terms (MeSH headings)?
9. Why would a researcher use bibliographic software?
10. Why should studies with contradictory results be included in the review of the literature?
11. In the review of the literature, what information about key studies should readers expect?

Determining a Research Design and Method

The research design is the infrastructure of a study. The purpose of the research design is to increase the likelihood that the data (evidence) collected are relevant, high quality, and directly related to the research question or problem. A research design is a plan for conducting research that appropriately manages variations and provides answers to the research question or problem. Researchers can investigate the same broad question or problem using several different research designs. The design chosen depends on the purpose of the research. An important point to remember is that how the problem or question is defined in the problem statement indicates the appropriate research design.

Researchers can choose from among many research designs. Moreover, different disciplines, such as history, medicine, and anthropology, tend to emphasize and use different designs. Certain designs are better suited to answer certain types of questions or to solve certain types of problems than other designs are. (See table 20.6.)

Similarly, certain research methods are more closely associated with one design than another. However, there is considerable overlap among the methods and their designs. Again, the purpose of the research determines the appropriate research method. Thus, the choice of both the research design and the research method depends on the research question or problem.

Research Designs

There are six common **research designs:** *historical, descriptive, correlational, evaluation, experimental,* and *causal-comparative.* These designs are particularly well suited to research in topics related to healthcare and, specifically, health information management. Which design is appropriate depends on the problem and the researcher's definition of the problem.

Historical Research

Historical research investigates the past. Researchers examine primary and secondary sources. Primary sources include wills, charters, reports, minutes, eyewitness accounts, letters, and e-mail records. Secondary sources are derived from primary sources; secondary sources summarize, critique, or analyze the primary sources. This chapter is a secondary source because it describes and summarizes the original reports of others. Primary sources are superior to secondary sources. An example of historical research in healthcare would be an investigation of the development of health insurance in the United States. Examining both primary and secondary sources, researchers in health information management could explore the founding of the professional association, the development of the code of ethics, or the establishment of the technical-level and the various specialty credentials.

Table 20.6.   Designs of research, their applications, and their methods

Design	Application	Method	Example in Healthcare
Historical	Understand past events	• Case study • Bibliography	• What factors led to the enactment of Medicare legislation? • How did events in the history of the American College of Surgeons affect the development of the field of health information management?
Descriptive	Describe current status	• Survey • Observation	• What barriers prevent healthcare personnel from using computers during the delivery of patient care? • How do coders use references and help screens when they code?
Correlational	Determine existence and degree of relationship	• Survey • Secondary analysis	• How are credential and performance related? • What is the relationship between provider satisfaction and EHR systems?
Evaluation	Evaluate effectiveness	• Case study	• How has implementation of an EHR system affected the enterprise's ability to deliver healthcare to underserved populations? • How has EDI reduced the costs of delivery of healthcare to Medicare patients?
Experimental	Establish cause and effect	• Randomized, double-blind, clinical trial • Pretest–posttest control group method • Solomon four-group method • Posttest-only control group	• Which group of molecules with innate immunity affects the risk and severity of invasive *Blastomyces dermatitidis* infection? • Which dosage level of the medication is more efficacious and safer for immunocompromised patients with uncomplicated herpes zoster?
Causal-Comparative (Quasi-Experimental)	Detect causal relationship	• One-shot case study • One-group pretest–posttest • Static group comparison • Nonparticipant observation	• What is the effect of a coder training program on the case mix index? • What is the effect of having a working mother on childhood obesity?

Descriptive Research

Descriptive research determines and reports the current status of topics and subjects. Common tools used to collect descriptive data are surveys, interviews, and observations. The shortcomings of descriptive research include the lack of standardized questions, trained observers, and high response rates. Examples of descriptive studies include polls of Americans' opinions concerning abortion, the patient's bill of rights, stem-cell research, and bioengineering.

In health information management, researchers also conduct descriptive studies. A very limited list of examples includes studies on the status of the composition of the HIM workforce, employee morale in health information systems (HIS) departments, coding accuracy, the extent of EHR implementation, and the types of tasks that HIM technicians and administrators perform.

Correlational Research

Correlational research determines the existence, the direction, and the degree of relationships among factors. For example, HIM professionals have conducted correlational studies on factors related to the adoption of health information technologies (Rosenthal and Layman 2008, 6) and to e-learning (Bell 2006, 4). Other correlational studies in health information management might investigate relationships between credential and coding accuracy, job satisfaction and educational level, and increased patient volumes and the level of organizational computerization.

The factors in correlational research and other research designs are called **variables.** The degree or strength of the relationship can range from 0.00 to 1.00 (or –1.00). A strength of 0.00 means absolutely no relationship. On the other hand, a strength of 1.00 (or –1.00) means a perfect relationship. For example a **positive (direct) relationship** 0.313 exists between the size of a physician practice and its utilization of the EHR (Rosenthal and Layman 2008, 19). A positive relationship means that the larger the physician practice, the more likely the practice is to utilize an EHR. This direct relationship could also be expressed as the smaller the physician practice, the less likely its utilization of the EHR. Conversely, in a **negative (inverse) relationship,** the directions of the relationship are opposite (inverse). For example, researchers found increased adoption of health information technologies, particularly clinical information technologies, was associated with improved health outcomes (Menachemi et al. 2008, 56). The relationship between overall health information technology adoption and the post–pancreatic resection mortality rate was –0.403. Thus, the higher the adoption of health information technologies, the lower the mortality rate after pancreatic resections.

Correlational research cannot establish causation. Correlational research can only detect the existence, the direction, and the degree of relationship. For example, in the research on utilization of EHRs in physician practices, the researchers could *not* state whether the practice size causes the use of EHRs or whether the use of EHRs causes the practice size (Rosenthal and Layman 2008). Adding to the correlational researchers' difficulties, a third unlisted factor, such as geographic location, could affect both the practice size and the utilization of the EHR. This third unlisted factor is called a **confounding (extraneous, secondary) variable** because it confounds (confuses) interpretation of the data.

Researchers conducting correlational studies use surveys, standardized tests, observations, and secondary data. The important point to remember is that correlational research never establishes causal relationships.

Evaluation Research

Evaluation research examines the effectiveness and efficiency of programs, organizations, interventions, policies, technologies, or products. Other terms for the large umbrella of evaluation research are *outcomes research*, *health services research*, *health technology assessment*, and *comparative effectiveness research (CER)*. The term used depends upon focus of the research, program versus technology. Other influences on the choice of term are the discipline of the researcher, such as education or bioinformatics, and the funding source.

Evaluation research is the systematic application of criteria to assess value (Ovretveit 1998, 5). In evaluation research, investigators examine several aspects of the objects (topics) of research, such as conceptualization, design, implementation, impact, and **generalizability** (Shi 2008, 212). New programs often are evaluated in terms of the achievement of their goals and objectives. For example, new educational degree programs may be evaluated by the pass rates of their graduates on licensure or certification examinations. Public service programs and health outreach initiatives may be evaluated by their success in reaching their target populations. Evaluation research studies may be quantitative, qualitative, or mixed methods. For example, in a quantitative study, researchers might investigate the effectiveness of a community health program to educate families with low incomes on the availability of pediatric dental services. In a qualitative study, researchers may explore mothers' acceptance of the educational program. In a mixed methods study, researchers could investigate factors associated with the health directors' selection of the educational materials and the directors' views on barriers and facilitators of the program's implementation. Case studies are often associated with evaluation research.

Outcomes research is related to evaluation research. Some extremists believe that all research is outcomes research because all results are outcomes (Lee et al. 2000, 195). As early as 1910, Codman promoted measuring outcomes or, in his words, "ends results" (Donabedian 1989, 234; Lee et al. 2000, 195). Today, **outcomes research** is defined as studies "aimed at assessing the quality and effectiveness of health-care as measured by the attainment of a specified end result or outcome, improved health, lowered morbidity or mortality, and improvement of abnormal states (such as elevated blood pressure)" (National Library of Medicine 2012; Lee et al. 2000, 198). An example of outcomes research would be a study that investigated whether a vertebroplasty (back surgery) reduced patients' pain and improved their quality of life.

Health services research is closely related to outcomes research (Lee et al. 2000, 195). Health services research is defined as research that integrates "epidemiologic, sociological, economic, and other analytic sciences in the study of health services. Health services research is usually concerned with relationships between need, demand, supply, use, and outcome of health services" (National Library of Medicine 2012; Lee et al. 2000, 195). An example of health services research is a study that investigates the differential impact of copayments on various subgroups of Medicare beneficiaries, such as females and the poor.

Health technology assessment is the evaluation of the usefulness (utility) of health technologies. Technology is broadly defined as pharmaceuticals, medical devices, medical equipment, medical processes and procedures, and health information technologies (Williams and Torrens 2008, 21). Technology assessments are based on systematic reviews of the literature, meta-analyses, and appropriate qualitative methods of synthesizing data from multiple studies (AHRQ n.d.). The purpose of health technology assessment is to provide individual patients, clinicians, funding bodies, and policymakers with high-quality information on the benefits and cost effectiveness of health interventions (Ware and Hicks 2011, 64S). The website of the Agency for Healthcare Research and Quality provides links to technology assessment currently in progress and to many assessments completed since the 1990s. A recent example of a technology assessment is one that reviewed the effectiveness of cochlear implants in adults with sensorineural hearing loss.

Currently, there is much interest in **comparative effectiveness research (CER).** In the American Recovery and Reinvestment Act of 2009, Congress charged the Institute of Medicine with developing a list of research priorities for comparative effectiveness research (Sox and Greenfield 2009, 203). Subsequently, the Affordable Care Act of 2010 contained provisions related to comparative effectiveness research. The Institute of Medicine defines CER as the "generation and synthesis of evidence that compares the benefits and harms of alternative methods to prevent, diagnose, treat, and monitor a clinical condition, or to improve the delivery of care. The purpose of CER is to assist consumers, clinicians, purchasers, and policy makers to make informed decisions that will improve healthcare at both the individual and population levels" (Sox and Greenfield 2009, 203). For example, a potential CER project could compare therapies for children with autism.

In an example of an evaluation study, researchers appraised the functioning of health information technologies and systems in a field hospital during an emergency (Levy et al. 2010, 626). Specifically, the researchers were evaluating the feasibility of deploying computerized administrative and clinical systems to disaster areas with mass casualties. In January 2010, Haiti experienced an earthquake with a magnitude of 7.0. The Israel Defense Force sent its field hospital and set it up near the airport in Port-au-Prince. The field hospital is capable of providing the following medical services: medicine, surgery (including an operating room and intensive care), orthopedics, pediatrics (including neonatal intensive care), obstetrics and gynecology, ambulatory care, and auxiliary services (x-ray, ultrasound, laboratory, medical engineering and equipment, mental health, medical informatics, and logistics). The information systems for the field hospital included both an administrative application and an EHR. For 10 days the field hospital operated, serving 1,111 patients (737 inpatients). Types of services included 242 operations in the operating room and the delivery of 16 babies (Levy et al. 2010, 627). Within six hours of arrival in Port-au-Prince and within 89 hours of the earthquake, the field hospital's computer systems were fully operational. The system was up 99.9 percent of the time. Upon arrival, patients were assigned an identification number and their photograph taken. Patients were tracked throughout the field hospital. The researchers concluded that an EHR in a disaster with mass casualties helps ensure the adequacy of healthcare provided by multiple clinicians (Levy et al. 2010, 628). Furthermore, the researchers recommended that emergency response teams consider adding health information technologies to their plans.

Experimental Research

Experimental research establishes causal relationships. A **causal relationship** shows cause and effect. For example, smoking (the cause) results in lung cancer (the effect). Characteristics of experimental research are

- Control
- Manipulation of treatment
- Random assignment of subjects to groups

The key and defining characteristic of experimental research is control. Experimental researchers follow strict protocols to maintain control. Experimental research is the gold standard.

Researchers conducting experimental research select both independent variables and dependent variables. **Independent variables** are the factors that researchers manipulate directly; independent variables are antecedent or prior factors. **Dependent variables** are the measured variables; they depend on the independent variables. The dependent variables reflect the results that the researcher theorizes. They occur subsequently or after the independent variables. Therefore, the independent variable causes an effect in the dependent variable.

The independent variables that researchers manipulate are also called interventions or **treatments.** Researchers use the term *treatment* generically or broadly, beyond its usual meaning of therapy. Therefore, treatment could mean a physical conditioning program, a computer training program, a particular laboratory medium, or the timing of prophylactic medications.

In experimental research, researchers select subjects for comparison groups. The **experimental (study) group** comprises the research subjects. Another group, the **control group,** comprises the control subjects. The experimental subjects undergo the intervention of the research study. For comparison, the control subjects do not.

Important elements of experimental research are random sampling and randomization. Although the terms are similar, they represent two different procedures. **Random sampling** is the unbiased selection of subjects from the **population** of interest. (Random sampling is discussed in greater detail in the section on gathering data.) **Randomization** is the random allocation of subjects between experimental groups and control groups. Thus, step one is to select subjects from the population using random sampling, and step two is to randomly assign these randomly selected subjects to experimental or control groups.

Random sampling and randomization characterize double-blind studies. A **double-blind study** is an extremely rigorous form of experimental research in which neither the researcher nor the subject knows to which group the subject belongs. Random selection and random allocation eliminate the effects of expectations and perceptions. For instance, a participant receiving a new heart medication may expect to have more energy and actually believe that he or she does have more energy. In addition, the researcher who knows the participant is receiving the new heart medication may perceive that the participant's color has improved. Thus, double-blind studies control bias because of false expectations and perceptions.

Double-blind studies are often used in the investigation of new drugs. When experimental and control groups are created, neither the participants nor the researchers know to which group the individual participants belong. In order to receive what appears to be the new drug, the participants in the control group are given a **placebo.** A placebo looks exactly like the new drug but, instead, contains harmless ingredients (sometimes called a sugar pill). Therefore, the expectations of the researchers and the participants do not bias the results.

Causal-Comparative Research

Causal-comparative research is a type of quasi-experimental design. *Quasi* means resembling or having some of the characteristics. Therefore, causal-comparative research resembles experimental research by having many, but not all, of its characteristics. However, causal-comparative research lacks two key characteristics of experimental research: manipulation of treatment and random assignment to a group.

Choosing causal-comparative research is correct when one of the three following situations exist

- The variables cannot be manipulated (gender, age, race, birthplace)
- The variables should not be manipulated (accidental death or injury, child abuse)
- The variables represent different conditions that have already occurred (medication error, heart catheterization performed, smoking)

This research design is also called *ex post facto*, meaning **retrospective.** Examples of quasi-experimental research are *case-control (retrospective) studies, field experiments, and natural experiments.*

Epidemiologists investigating the development of disease often use **case-control (retrospective) studies.** In case-control studies, the epidemiologists look for characteristics and occurrences that are related to the subsequent development of a disease. In these studies, epidemiologists collect masses of data from health records and through interviews with both persons with the disease (cases) and persons without it (controls). HIM professionals are often involved with case-control studies because they are experts on the content of health records and at finding cases and controls using various clinical and administrative classification systems, such as ICD-9-CM, ICD-10 CM/PCS, DSM, and SNOMED CT.

Researchers investigating the sociology of medicine often conduct field experiments by going into the site (field) and observing activities. The strength of this type of research is that participants tend to act more naturally in their real setting. An outstanding example of field research is the research on health practitioners' conversations overheard in elevators. Researchers rode hospital elevators all day, listening to and recording conversations. They found that patient confidentiality was severely breached.

Researchers conducting natural experiments wait for the event to occur naturally. For example, researchers interested in the effectiveness of triage in emergencies would wait for a disaster. Prior to the disaster, they would establish baseline data and tools for data collection. When the disaster occurs, they would record their observations of the actions and results.

In case-control studies, field experiments, and natural experiments, researchers relinquish control of the situations. For purists, however, the lack of randomization and control of treatment lessens the value of causal-comparative (quasi-experimental) research. The research only weakly determines causation. However, as the examples illustrate, in some situations, causal-comparative research is the only design that is logistically and ethically feasible. Causal-comparative research, then, determines the possibility of causal relationships.

Time Frame as an Element of Research Design

Another element of design cuts across all six types of design. This element is the time frame of the study. There are two pairs of time frames: *retrospective versus prospective* and *cross-sectional versus longitudinal.*

Studies within a retrospective time frame look back in time. For example, many early research studies of stress were retrospective. In these retrospective studies, the researchers measured the participant's level of stress and then asked the participant to reconstruct events that had occurred in a past period of time. Leadership studies in which the researcher asked the leader to list factors that led to his or her success are another example of a retrospective time frame. For some types of questions, such as those related to historic events, a retrospective design is the only possible design.

In **prospective** research studies, subjects are followed into the future to examine relationships between variables and later occurrences. For example, researchers identify individuals or subjects with certain variables and then follow these individuals or subjects into the future to see what occurs. Researchers conducted a study in which they prospectively assigned consecutively admitted patients to one of two groups (Oniki et al. 2003, 179). The nurses caring for one group of patients received periodic electronic reminders about the status of documentation on routine nursing tasks; the nurses caring for the other group did not receive the reminders (Oniki et al. 2003, 180). The researchers found fewer deficiencies in documentation for the electronic reminder group (Oniki et al. 2003, 181). Research studies with a cross-sectional design collect data at one point in time. For example, the previously mentioned exploratory study on whether data in current health records are adequate to support ICD-10-CM/PCS coding was a cross-sectional study (Moczygemba and Fenton 2012, 2). **Cross-sectional studies** are snapshots and, as such, may collect data at an entirely unrepresentative point in time. The great advantage of cross-sectional studies is that they are efficient.

Longitudinal studies collect data from the same participants at multiple points in time. Cancer registries that collect data on cancer patients throughout their lifetimes are prime examples of longitudinal studies. Other longitudinal studies include studies of breast cancer and cardiovascular disease. For example, since 1976, the Nurses' Health Study has followed the health of more than 120,000 nurses (Field et al. 2007, 968).

The six types of research designs are not rigid boxes. Researchers often combine designs to address their particular research questions or problems. For instance, many studies include both descriptive and correlational findings. In describing their study, researchers also often state its time frame. Thus, a researcher would state that the study was descriptive, correlational, and cross-sectional. However, the key to classifying the design is to understand the purpose of the research.

Check Your Understanding 20.3

Instructions: Answer the following questions on a separate piece of paper.

1. What determines a researcher's choice of a research design?

2. Which research design would a researcher use to investigate the relationship between a supervisor's level of stress and the number of his or her subordinates?

3. What would be a direct relationship between the supervisor's level of stress and the number of his or her subordinates?

4. What is the key characteristic of experimental research?

5. How does quasi-experimental research differ from experimental research?

6. How do independent variables and dependent variables differ?

7. In a double-blind study, who knows which subjects are in the study group and which subjects are in the control group?

8. Why would a researcher choose a longitudinal study rather than a cross-sectional study?

Research Methods

A research method is the particular strategy that a researcher uses to collect, analyze, and present data. Particular methods are associated with certain research designs, although considerable overlap exists. (Refer to table 20.6.) For example, researchers can use surveys in both descriptive and correlational research designs.

Surveys

A survey is a common research method. **Surveys** are a form of self-report research in which the individuals themselves are the source of data. Surveys collect data about a population to determine its current status with regard to certain factors (Gay et al. 2012, 9). Surveys that collect data from all the members of the population are **census surveys;** surveys that collect data from representative members of the population are **sample surveys.**

HIM professionals conduct both types of surveys. For example, when surveying HIM program directors, researchers surveyed all the directors (Sasnett and Ross 2007, 4). On the other hand, when information about the members of the national association (a population of more than 40,000) is needed, researchers conduct only a sample survey. A census survey of a large population is generally beyond the resources of a solitary researcher or a small research team. For example, in an exploratory descriptive study, an HIM researcher surveyed a representative sample of 250 "most-wired" hospitals to investigate their record retention practices (Rinehart-Thompson 2008, 2).

Survey research is further categorized as interview or questionnaire. Researchers conduct **interview surveys** by personally questioning the members of the **target population.** In **questionnaire surveys,** researchers create electronic or paper forms that include the questions.

Interview Surveys

In interview surveys, researchers orally question the members of the population. Examples of interview surveys are telephone surveys, exit polls, and **focused studies.** Researchers can question members of the population as individuals or as a **focus group.** In focused studies, the researcher and the group members have a group discussion.

In this research method, researchers may choose a structured interview because it is easier to quantify, tabulate, and analyze than an unstructured interview. In a structured interview, the researcher uses a written list of questions called an **interview guide.** Using an interview guide ensures that all individuals or focus groups are asked the same questions. Researchers can strictly control the questions and responses or can allow a free-flowing conversation. They often record sessions and then transcribe the comments.

For example, using telephone interviews, researchers explored the public's attitudes concerning the potential of health information technologies, particularly EHRs, to improve healthcare (Gaylin et al. 2011, 920, 923). The researchers interviewed a random sample of 1,015 US households with telephones or cell phones. The interviewers had in-depth training and followed a strict protocol with rigorous callback rules. The design of the study allowed the researchers to differentiate the attitudes by sociodemographic characteristics and by affinity for technology. They achieved a final response rate of 43 percent (Gaylin et al. 2011, 923). The researchers found that the respondents believed that EHRs could improve healthcare and reduce its costs (78 percent and 59 percent, respectively) (Gaylin et al. 2011, 927). Specifically, respondents 65 years or older and African American respondents believed that e-prescribing could improve healthcare (Gaylin et al. 2011, 932). Additionally, most of the respondents believed that the benefits of EHRs outweigh potential risks to privacy (Gaylin et al. 2011, 928). Finally, the researchers found that positive attitudes toward health information technologies and EHRs were related to higher incomes and affinity for technology (Gaylin et al. 2011, 928).

In another example, researchers used focus groups. These researchers explored family physicians' perceptions of personal health records (Witry et al. 2010, 2). The researchers conducted a focus group at four different sites. The sites were both urban and rural, and all four sites used a combination of paper and electronic records. At each site, the researchers used the same script with introductory comments, questions, prompts, and probes (comments or questions to elicit additional explanatory statements or details). Overall, the focus groups included 12 physicians, 8 residents, 8 nurses, and 1 pharmacist. Transcripts and detailed notes from the focus groups were analyzed in a multistep process. Each of the four members of the research team independently organized and analyzed the transcripts and notes for concepts (themes) that they coded. Aggregating their independent analyses, the members reached consensus on the main themes. Summarizing and interpreting the analyses, the researchers concluded that providers view patients' health records as a backup source of medical information secondary to patients' medical records. Thus, providers primarily view personal health records as a tool for providers and not as a tool for patients (Witry et al. 2010, 8).

Finally, in a third example, researchers conducted a cognitive work analysis (Effken et al. 2011, 699). The purpose of the study was to describe nurse managers' work environment, to determine data available in existing sources for a decision support tool, and to assess how the decision support tool could best be incorporated into existing workflows. One level of a cognitive work analysis is a work domain analysis. The researchers conducted the work domain analysis at three sites by interviewing 10 nurse managers, 2 nursing directors, 2 nurse executives, 3 information technology managers, and 3 quality managers. Each interview was one hour, in the informant's (participant's) office, and audio-recorded. The researchers used a semi-structured interview. The informants were asked about their typical day (they could consult their calendars); current quality and safety initiatives at the organizational and unit levels; and a specific, recent safety or quality issue, how they learned of it, their information resources, and interventions they used to resolve it (Effken et al. 2011, 700). The information technology managers were also asked about current information and communication technologies, and the quality managers about quality and safety report formats. The interviewers (researchers) asked additional questions as needed (the "semi-structure"). The interviews were transcribed verbatim (word-for-word). Reading the transcripts, researchers identified themes. Similar themes were aggregated into concepts ("main themes" in the previous example). Improvements quality and safety were organization-level priorities. However, nurse managers were called upon to implement various initiatives, even when nursing was not the initiative's focus. One six-month initiative, patient satisfaction, required that nurse managers round (check on patients at their bedsides) daily and every patient. At one hospital, this rounding almost entirely consumed the nurse manager's time. Nurse managers were involved with multiple meetings at the unit, division, and organizational levels. When patient censuses were high, three meetings per day were dedicated to managing lengths of stay and availability of beds (Effken 2011, 701). Nurse managers spent much time accessing, reviewing, and integrating electronic data that resided in multiple systems. The nurse informants viewed accessing data in multiple systems as cumbersome. Generally, the quality and safety data needed for the decision support system were available in spreadsheets. Resolving problems often involved quick investigations into their causes, quick decisions, and quick solutions, typically staff remedial education (Effken 2011, 703, 706). The researchers concluded that the nurse managers' current decision tool—spreadsheets—was inadequate for the complex environment and multifactorial problems that they face. Therefore, a sophisticated decision support tool that can synthesize data and test hypotheses could assist nurse managers (Effken 2011, 706).

Questionnaire Surveys

Questionnaire surveys also query members of the population. Rather than asking questions orally, researchers mail participants an electronic or print form to complete and return.

Questionnaire studies are efficient because they require less time and money than interview studies do and because they allow the researchers to collect data from many more members of the target population. For additional discussion, see the paragraph on response rates in the Gathering the Data section.

For example, HIM researchers conducted a web-based survey (questionnaire) to explore the factors affecting physicians' attitudes toward EHR adoption (Morton and Wiedenbeck 2010, 1). Specifically, the researchers investigated the association between the physicians' individual characteristics and specific factors. The specific factors included management support, physician involvement, adequate training, physician autonomy, doctor–patient relationship, perceived ease of use, perceived usefulness, and attitude about EHR usage. The survey was distributed to 802 physicians and obtained an overall response rate of 29.8 percent. The researchers found no significant relationships between physicians' individual characteristics, such as age, years in practice, clinical specialty, or prior computer experience, and EHR acceptance (Morton and Wiedenbeck 2010, 3–4).

In another example, researchers sent directors of regional health information organizations (RHIOs) an Internet link to a web-based survey (Adler-Milstein et al. 2011, 667). The purpose of the research was to ascertain the status of the RHIOs and to assess their ability to assist physicians and hospitals to meet meaningful use requirements. Subjects were offered a $25 gift card to complete the survey. Nonresponders received a minimum of three follow-up e-mails and three telephone calls. Of the 247 organizations initially identified as RHIOs, 50 did not meet the criteria for inclusion in the study because they did not plan to facilitate the exchange of clinical data between independent entities. Of the remaining 197, 15 respondents partially completed the survey, reporting only their status, and 165 respondents fully completed the survey (84 percent response rate). Of these 165 respondents, 75 were operational, covering 14 percent of US hospitals and 3 percent of ambulatory physician practices (Adler-Milstein et al. 2011, 668–669). Furthermore, only 14 respondents met the definition of a basic RHIO; no respondent met the definition of comprehensive RHIO (Adler-Milstein 2011, 669). Finally, of the 75 operational RHIOs only 25 (33 percent) reported "being financially viable (able to covering [sic] operating expenses with revenues from participating entities)" (Adler-Milstein et al. 2011, 669). The researchers concluded that few RHIOs could support meaningful use, which limited their ability to assist physicians and hospitals in meeting the requirements (Adler-Milstein et al. 2011, 671).

Observational Research

In **observational research,** researchers observe, record, and analyze behaviors and events. Highly detailed, observational research provides insights into what subjects do, how they do it, and why they do it. Usually classified as qualitative research, observational studies include a wide range of research techniques. Observational researchers may use triangulation to support their findings. **Triangulation** is the use of multiple sources or perspectives to investigate the same phenomenon. The multiple sources or perspectives include data (multiple times, sites, or respondents), investigators (researchers), theories, and methods (Bednarz 1985, 304). The results or conclusions are validated if the multiple sources or perspectives arrive at the same results or conclusions. This process lends credence to the research.

Observational research is used in many designs. For example, sociologists used a descriptive design to describe the culture of medical students (Becker et al. 1961). There are three common types of observational research: *nonparticipant observation, participant observation,* and *ethnography.*

Nonparticipant Observation

In **nonparticipant observation,** researchers act as neutral observers who neither intentionally interact with nor affect the actions of the population being observed. Of the three types of observational research, HIM professionals are more likely to encounter nonparticipant observation. Nonparticipant observation takes three common forms: *naturalistic observation, simulation observation, and case study.*

In nonparticipant observation, researchers also analyze the content of modes of communication, such as documentation, speech, body language, music, television shows, commercials, and movies. Research on the content of websites has become common. For example, researchers evaluated the web accessibility of state vocational rehabilitation agencies (Sligar and Zeng 2008, 13). The purpose of the research was to assess whether the 80 websites (50 state sites, District of Columbia, and 29 sites for the blind) were accessible to people with disabilities. The researchers used software that incorporated web Content Accessibility Guidelines (WCAG). Of the websites, seven (9 percent) did not comply with WCAG checkpoints (Sligar and Zeng 2008, 15). The researchers noted that because of the dynamic nature of the Internet, ongoing monitoring of the accessibility of websites is needed (Sligar and Zeng 2008, 17).

Also, using nonparticipant observation, researchers investigated the feasibility of implementing an EHR at an international athletic event (Wells et al. 2010, 377). The international athletic event was an annual 10K run held in a northeastern state in the United States. Prior to the event, in the packet that went to the runners, the researchers included information about a free online subscription to a secure web-based EHR. This information was also on the event's website. The event's medical director also sent a follow-up letter to the runners encouraging them to subscribe to the online EHR. Of the 6,000 runners, only 320 (5 percent) subscribed to the EHR. Of these 320 participants, only 2 required medical attention during the event. Unfortunately, in a test prior to the event, Internet connectivity was not reliable. Because of this unreliability, a redundant paper record was implemented. Fortunately, during the 10K, connectivity was stable, but the problem of the redundant paper record remained. Moreover, during the run, the nonparticipant observers saw another potential problem. The "medical records" of the runners were matched to their "bib numbers" (numbers for the run). The observers saw that the runners swapped bib numbers; the bib numbers and the medical records were now mismatched. This mismatch could have resulted in serious medical errors (Wells et al. 2010, 378). The researchers concluded that their study identified barriers to successfully implementing an EHR at a large public event (Wells et al. 2010, 378).

In a **naturalistic study,** researchers reviewed the performance of collision avoidance systems from 73 real rear-end striking crashes (13) or rear-end striking near-crashes (60) (McLaughlin et al. 2008, 10). Collision avoidance systems rely on driving data from various sensors and indicators including radar, infrared laser, ultrasonic, machine vision, accelerator, speedometer, and brake and turn signals. Types of systems include parking assistance, forward collision warning (rear-end), and lane change and warning. Systems provide varying degrees of control from issuing warnings to taking control of the vehicle. The systems' driving data were entered into software that allowed the frame-by-frame review and analysis of the events. The researchers concluded that, based on the timing of the systems' alerts and human reaction times in the driving literature, just over 60 percent of the population would be able to avoid a collision (McLaughlin et al. 2008, 14).

Simulation observation is very similar to naturalistic observation except that the researchers stage the events rather than allowing them to occur naturally. Researchers can invent their own simulations or use standardized vignettes to stage the events. For example, researchers investigated how institutional policies and federal regulations for clinical research affect the configuration of an EHR (Kahn et al. 2007, 661–662). To identify potential problems in workflows, the researchers created a detailed clinical vignette (Kahn et al. 2007, 662). Included in the vignette were all the key steps of a prospective clinical trial. (See chapter 21.) Discussing policies, procedures, and workflows in terms of EHR configurations resulted in definitions of the users' roles and access and the system's workflows and functional capabilities (Kahn et al. 2007, 663). Reviewing the vignette also revealed a lack of functionality in the commercial EHR. In the EHR, orders, results, and progress notes related to the research study could *not* be separated and restricted from the patients' ongoing care as could occur in the paper based health record. This research finding resulted in modifications of some of the healthcare organization's processes. For example, order entry for research-related care remained paper based (Kahn et al. 2007, 665). Additionally, as a result of this finding, the EHR vendor created a clinical research advisory council to provide input into future product development (Kahn et al. 2007, 666). Finally, the researchers noted that the vignette assisted discussion by making generalized concepts concrete, tangible, and accessible to the responsible clinicians and executives (Kahn et al. 2007, 665).

The **case study** is another type of nonparticipant observation. Case studies are in-depth investigations of one person, one group, or one institution. Researchers conduct case studies to determine characteristics associated with a person, group, or institution. The characteristics then can shed light on similar persons, groups, or institutions. Often case studies suggest hypotheses that researchers subsequently investigate using other methods. Case studies are intensive, and researchers amass extensive details. Sources of data include administrative records, financial records, policy and procedure manuals, legal documents, government documents, surveys, and interviews. These many sources result in layer upon layer of detailed data, often called rich data.

Sigmund Freud conducted case studies at the individual person level (Flyvbjerg 2006, 229). This type of case study is called a clinical case study. From a physician's presentation of detailed information about an individual patient, other physicians learned about similar patients.

Other case studies are at the group level and the institutional level. For example, at the group level researchers could investigate the influence that AIDS action groups have had on funding practices of the National Institutes of Health. At the institutional level, researchers studied the characteristics of ambulatory medical practices that were associated with the implementation and use of e-prescribing systems (Crosson et al. 2008, 365). Twelve medical practices representing a range of sizes and physician specialties were in the study. In the field, the researchers collected data through observation and interview before and after the implementation of an e-prescribing system. The data were entered into specialized software for the analysis of textual, graphical, audio, and visual data. The analyses revealed that successful implementations were associated with modest expectations, such as improved workflow, while unsuccessful implementations were associated with high expectations, such as flawless functioning and minimal disruption of routines. Finally, the researchers concluded that successful implementation of e-prescribing systems were associated with effective communication of the actual capabilities and limitations of the technology, with knowledge of the anticipated effects on the clinical workflow, and with timely access to high-quality technical support (Crosson et al. 2008, 368).

Participant Observation

In **participant observation,** researchers are also participants in the observed actions. They can participate overtly (openly) or covertly (secretly). For example, researchers in Australia wanted to determine the optimum time to repeat feedback on rates of hand washing to maximize the effects of the feedback and to most improve the rates (van de Mortel et al. 2000, 91). The researchers covertly observed the incidence of hand washing to establish a baseline. The researchers then posted feedback—bar charts displaying the rates of hand washing. Immediately after posting the feedback, the researchers overtly observed hand washing to assess the effect of their posting (intervention of providing feedback). Then, 6 months and 12 months later, the researchers again covertly observed the rates of hand washing. The baseline rate of hand washing was 61 percent; the rate was 83 percent immediately after intervention; and the 6-month and 12-month rates were 76 percent and 65 percent, respectively (van de Mortel et al. 2000, 93–94). Based on this pattern, the researchers concluded that feedback on the rates of hand washing should be provided every 12 months (van de Mortel et al. 2000, 95). Researchers using participant observation reflect the insiders' perspectives. This reflection can be both an advantage and a disadvantage. As insiders, the researchers have unique insights into the environment and context of the action. At the same time, however, as insiders, the researchers may share the biases and blind spots of insiders. Therefore, in participant observation, researchers attempt to maintain neutrality while in the "thick of the action."

Another aspect of participant observation is the ethical ambiguity of covert observation (Johnson 1992, 218). **Covert observation** is the deception of participants, and specifically in the previous research, deception of coworkers. It breaches the right to privacy and the principle of informed consent (Johnson 1992, 217–219; Herrera 1999, 332). Additionally, covert observation undermines human relationships by eroding trust and disregarding honesty. On the other hand, the ethical principal of utility—the greatest good for the greatest number—and the advancement of science may override the ethical breaches of covert observation (Johnson 1992, 220; Herrera 1999, 332). In general, researchers who are considering covert observation as their research method should assess whether the data could be collected using another method and should seek counsel from appropriate research oversight entities.

Ethnography

Ethnography is observational research that came to the life sciences from anthropology. It includes both qualitative and quantitative approaches and both participant and non-participant observation. Ethnographers typically investigate aspects of culture in naturalistic settings. For example, an HIM professional could choose ethnography to investigate how the culture of a nursing unit or clinic affects the timeliness and comprehensiveness of provider documentation. Are areas of the unit or clinic set aside for documentation, indicating that the culture of the unit or clinic values accurate and comprehensive documentation? Or do providers attempt documenting in health records in corners or on ledges of the unit or clinic, indicating less attention to documentation?

Two key differences exist between ethnography and other types of research. First, in ethnography, the literature review results in initial research questions rather than clearly defined problems or focused research questions (Gay et al. 2012, 424). Second, ethnography is iterative, or cyclical (Byrne 2001, 82). As ethnographers collect data, they analyze them,

revising their initial questions and creating new interpretations. They may seek other sources of data and participants and add alternate techniques for data collection. Therefore, ethnographers work in a cycle beginning with initial questions. They collect data about those questions. Based on their analysis of the initial data, they then revise their questions, interpretations, and techniques and collect more data about those revisions. This cyclical process contrasts with the linear processes of other research methods discussed in this chapter.

In order to understand cultures, ethnographers amass great volumes of detailed data while studying in the field. Therefore, another characteristic of ethnography is that the researchers live or work with the population they are studying. For example, researchers investigated the culture of clinical teaching conferences (Hill and Tyson 1997, 594). They attended 52 sessions of morning report with the faculty physicians, house officers, and medical students and timed the length of people's comments, the commentator's status, and the content of the comments (Hill and Tyson 1997, 594). In addition to the sessions of morning report, the researchers conducted 34 interviews lasting between 30 and 60 minutes with people from the three groups (Hill and Tyson 1997, 595). The quantitative aspect of this study is that the researchers tabulated the minutes and averaged the time that members of each group spoke. The qualitative aspect of this study is that the researchers analyzed the comments for themes.

Ethnography has other unique characteristics, such as the attention that ethnographers pay to the environment (furniture, instruments, space, lighting, schedules, brochures, and clothing). For example, the ethnographers in the previously described study recorded data on x-ray equipment and the placement of a table and a sign-in sheet (Hill and Tyson 1997, 596). In general, ethnographers also record details about members of the population, including jargon, feelings, points of view, beliefs, practices, and goals. In conclusion, the strength of ethnography is that researchers obtain insights not discoverable in other methods. Its weaknesses include volumes of data that are difficult to analyze, large investments of money and time, and the lack of generalizability and replicability.

Experimental Research

Experiments are another major category of research methods. These methods classify into two subcategories: *experimental studies* and *quasi-experimental studies*. Both subcategories involve treatments using the broad meaning of the term as some sort of intervention. The level of control that researchers establish differentiates experiments between experimental studies and quasi-experimental studies.

Campbell and Stanley (1963) wrote the classic text on experiments, defining and describing six major types of experiments, with three in the subcategory of experimental and three in the subcategory of quasi-experimental.

Experimental studies include

- Pretest–posttest control group method
- Solomon four-group method
- Posttest-only control group method

Quasi-experimental studies include

- One-shot case study
- One-group pretest–posttest method
- Static group comparison

The key elements in the descriptions of these experiments are

- Randomization
- Observation (pretest or posttest)
- Control group
- Treatment

Readers should be aware that, similar to the term *treatment,* researchers use the terms *pretest, posttest,* and *observation* broadly. They simply mean that they have measured the variable in some way.

To demonstrate the differences among these six subcategories, descriptions of research studies conducted in each of the six subcategories will be described. (See table 20.7.) The description will include how the studies representing the subcategories conform with or deviate from the four key elements. To highlight the differences, the research studies all involve the same research topic. This topic is the medical students' utilization of voice recognition software.

Experimental Studies

Researchers conducted a pretest–posttest control group method to investigate medical students' utilization of voice recognition software. The researchers randomly assigned the first-year medical students to experimental and control groups. The researchers performed a pretest in which they established both groups' levels of utilization of voice recognition software. The researchers then conducted a two-hour training session (treatment). At the end of the academic year, the researchers measured both groups' utilization of voice recognition software. They could reasonably attribute differences in utilization to their treatment. However, the researchers should be cautious because the possibility exists that the students' higher level of utilization of the software is a function of their exposure during the pretest observation. Familiarity with the software from exposure could predispose the students to use it.

The key elements of this study include

- Randomization (randomly assigned medical students to groups)
- Pretest and posttest observation (levels of utilization of voice recognition software before and after the training session)
- Control group
- Treatment (two-hour training session)

The Solomon four-group method is a complex variation of the pretest–posttest control group method. The purpose of the Solomon four-group method is to provide a way to control for the potential effect of exposure. For example, as noted in the previous study, taking a pretest may affect performance on a posttest. In the previous study of utilization of voice recognition software, how much of the utilization is due to mere familiarity with the software related to the original exposure? Using the Solomon four-group method, researchers create two experimental groups and two control groups rather than only one of each. They then administer the pretest to only one of the experimental groups and to only one of the control groups. However, they administer the posttest to *all* four groups. The difference in level of utilization between the two experimental groups would be the effect of the familiarity from pretesting. Therefore, the Solomon four-group method provides a valuable additional control. However, this additional control comes at a high price: everything is doubled.

The key elements of the Solomon four-group method are the same as those for the pretest–posttest control group method.

The posttest-only control group method is another method to offset the potential effect of familiarity related to exposure through pretesting. The posttest-only control group method is similar to the pretest–posttest control group method except that there is no pretest. In the research on utilization of voice recognition software, the researchers randomly assign half the first-year medical students to the experimental group and half to the control group. The researchers do not observe an initial level of utilization through a pretest. The experimental group receives the treatment of the training session, and the control group does not. Then, at the end of the academic year, the researchers measure the students' level of utilization of the software. This fairly simple method eliminates the potential bias introduced by pretesting.

The key elements of the posttest-only control group are randomization, posttest observation, control group, and treatment. For example, health educators used this method to observe the effects of endorsements by local opinion leaders and testimonials by teachers on schools' use of a web-based smoking prevention program (Buller et al. 2007, 610–612). Randomization of the 394 public secondary schools occurred by region. There were three experimental groups that received the treatment—(1) received the endorsement and the testimonial, (2) received the endorsement only, and (3) received the testimonial only—as well as one control group that received neither the endorsement nor the testimonial. All four groups received the information on the web-based smoking prevention program. The researchers found that the second experimental condition, the endorsements of opinion leaders such as directors of tobacco control coalitions, resulted in more teachers visiting the program's website and assigning their students to use it (Buller et al. 2007, 614).

Table 20.7.   Key elements of experimental and quasi-experimental studies*

Category/ Subcategory	Study Features	Randomization	Observation	Control Group	Treatment
		Elements			
Experimental					
Pretest–Posttest Control Group Method	• Random assignment to experimental and control groups • Observation to establish initial level of utilization (pretest) • Two-hour training session (treatment) • Observation to determine posttreatment utilization (posttest) • Potential that pretest exposure affected posttreatment performance	X	X	X	X
Solomon Four-Group Method	• Random assignment to two experimental and two control groups • Observation to establish initial level of utilization (pretest) • Two-hour training session (treatment) • Observation to determine posttreatment utilization (posttest) • Controls for pretest exposure, but at the cost of double work because of double groups	X	X	X	X
Posttest-Only Control Group Method	• Random assignment to experimental and control groups • Two-hour training session (treatment) • Observation to determine posttreatment utilization (posttest) • Controls the for pretest exposure by eliminating pretest, but at the cost of establishment of initial utilization level	X	P	X	X
Quasi-experimental					
One-Shot Case Study	• Two-hour training session (treatment) • Observation to determine posttreatment utilization (posttest) • Flaws of no pretest, no randomization, and no control group	0	P	0	X
One-Group Pretest–Posttest Method	• Investigation of medical students' utilization of voice recognition software • Observation to establish initial level of utilization (pretest) • Two-hour training session (treatment) • Observation to determine posttreatment utilization (posttest) • Flaws of no control group and no randomization	0	X	0	X
Static Group Comparison	• Investigation of medical students' utilization of voice recognition software • Assignment to experimental and control groups • Two-hour training session (treatment) • Observation to determine posttreatment utilization (posttest) • Flaws of no pretest and no randomization	0	P	X	X

*X = Fully met; P = Partially met; 0 = Absent.

Quasi-experimental Studies

In the one-shot case study, researchers study one group only once following the treatment. For example, in the study of utilization of voice recognition software, researchers provide a two-hour training session on utilization of voice recognition software to all the first-year medical students at some point in the academic year. Then, at the end of the academic year, the researchers measure the students' level of utilization of the software. The researchers can make no credible statement about the effect of the training session on the utilization of voice recognition software because they (1) have not established with an observation (pretest) the level of utilization prior to the training (treatment) to use as a comparison and (2) have no other group of medical students (control group) to use as a comparison.

The key elements in this case are posttest observation and treatment.

The one-group pretest–posttest method corrects one flaw of the one-shot case study with the addition of the pretest. Therefore, the researchers investigating utilization of voice recognition software improve their experiment by adding some measurement, or pretest, that establishes the medical students' level of utilization prior to the training session. However, adding the pretest only minimally improves their investigation. Statements made by the researchers about the utilization of voice recognition software are still highly suspect because the researchers included no control group. Therefore, readers of this research could reasonably wonder whether other factors in the hospital or in society caused the level of utilization.

The key elements of this method are pretest and posttest observation and treatment.

The static group comparison corrects for the lack of a control group. Therefore, the static group comparison is similar to the one-shot case study except that researchers using the static group comparison add a second group, the control group. In the research on utilization of voice recognition software, the researchers allow half the students to choose to attend the training session. This group is the experimental group, and the half who choose not to receive the training are the control group. Then, at the end of the academic year, the researchers measure the students' level of utilization of the software. Unfortunately, a flaw of this study is that there is no random assignment to the groups. Perhaps all the technophiles joined the experimental group and all the technophobes joined the control group. In that case, the increased level of utilization of the experimental group could just be an effect of the group's inherent love of computers and not of the training session.

The key elements of the static group comparison are posttest observation, control group, and treatment.

Experimental research is important because this major category of research allows researchers to investigate cause and effect. It should be clear from these examples of research studies that true experimental studies are difficult to conduct. Nevertheless, experimental research studies are extremely powerful research methods because only they can establish cause and effect (causal relationship). The types classified as quasi-experimental studies begin to determine that a causal relationship could exist. Some experts state that very large quasi-experimental studies weakly determine a causal relationship. However, to truly establish causal relationships, researchers must use one of the types classified as an experimental study.

Secondary Analysis

Secondary analysis is the analysis of the original work of another person or organization. In secondary analysis, researchers reanalyze original data by combining data sets to answer new questions or by using more sophisticated statistical techniques (Cohen 1992, 172). Researchers make the distinction between primary analysis and secondary analysis. **Primary analysis** refers to analysis of original research data by the researchers who collected them. There are two types of secondary analysis: *data mining* and *meta-analysis*.

Reanalysis of secondary data is a powerful tool for health information managers because it allows them to compare their performance data with local, regional, state, and national benchmarks. For healthcare organizations in general, secondary analysis is an important tool because it allows organizations to compare their outcomes with the outcomes of industry leaders.

Data mining is the extraction and enumeration of patterns from data using algorithms (Fayyad 1997, 9). These patterns are nontrivial, previously undiscerned, and potentially useful (Fayyad 1997, 7). Data mining is considered secondary data analysis because data miners use databases created by others, often for purposes unrelated to research and data mining.

For example, researchers explored data from the clinical information system of the Ulster Community and Health Trust (Huang et al. 2007, 254). The clinical information system was used routinely for patient management (Huang et al. 2007, 254). The researchers' purpose was to improve the quality of diabetic treatment. They analyzed the clinical data of 2,064 type 2 diabetic patients. Data mining allowed the researchers to determine the top 15 features (factors) that predicted patients' blood glucose control (Huang et al. 2007, 256). The researchers concluded that their model could become a part of routine medical practice, especially as the model provided support for evidence-based practice (Huang et al. 2007, 261).

Meta-analysis is the integrative analysis of findings from many studies that examined the same question. Studies that are included in a meta-analysis have common underlying characteristics (Cohen 1992, 172). Gene Glass coined the term *meta-analysis* (Cohen 1992, 172) and defined it as "the statistical analysis of a large collection of results from individual studies for the purpose of integrating findings"

(Glass 1976, 3). Meta-analysis began as a sophisticated way to present a literature review but has become a research method in its own right.

The advantage of meta-analysis is that it weighs findings from many studies, some of which are contradictory. Researchers who use meta-analysis must specify their inclusion criteria; explain how they searched and found articles; code the studies' designs, methods, and outcomes; and analyze the coded data (Cohen 1992, 173–174).

For example, researchers conducted a meta-analysis that synthesized studies on the effects of decision aids on breast cancer patients' choices of surgical procedure and their knowledge of treatments for breast cancer (Waljee et al. 2007, 1068). Decision aids include brochures, pamphlets, audio and video tapes, and computer programs (Waljee et al. 2007, 1069). First, the researchers specified their inclusion criteria: to be included, the study must be an evaluation of a decision aid for stage I or II breast cancer treatment of breast-conserving surgery versus mastectomy. Second, the researchers explained their strategies to find all the studies. They listed their 16 search terms noting that their search terms were medical subject heading terms that the researchers "exploded" (librarians' term meaning expanding the search to the general topic). The researchers specified which reference databases they searched (MEDLINE, EMBASE, CINAHL, the Cochrane Network, and Health and Psychosocial Instructions [HAPI]). They also noted that they manually reviewed the reference lists of all the articles to identify additional studies. They also searched for unpublished works and abstracts from associations related to cancer and decision support. They included articles in all languages. Their search resulted in 116 articles and 7 unpublished abstracts, of which 11 articles (9 studies) met the search criteria: (a) three studies were **randomized clinical trials (RCTs)**, (b) two studies

were nonrandomized trials with control groups of which one study yielded three articles, and (c) four studies were nonrandomized trials without control groups. Third, all three researchers then extracted data independently. In cases of disagreement, consensus was obtained through discussion (Waljee et al. 2007, 1068). Finally, they conducted the meta-analysis statistical procedure called effect size analysis. **Effect size** is the strength of the impact of one factor on another (Shi 2008, 120). Integrating the results of these studies revealed that women who used a decision aid were 25 percent more likely to choose breast-conserving surgery over mastectomy than women who did not use a decision aid (Waljee et al. 2007, 1068). The analysis also indicated that average knowledge of treatment options was significantly increased, by 24 percent, for patients who received the decision aid as compared to the controls. Thus, using meta-analysis, the researchers synthesized the results from multiple studies in order to reach overall conclusions.

Several key points are important to remember about research design and methods. **Research** is the systematic, orderly set of procedures that individuals choose to expand their knowledge or to answer their question. They can investigate the same broad question or problem using several of the research designs. (See table 20.8.) Preliminary, exploratory investigations are often descriptive or correlational. As researchers refine these investigations, they conduct causal-comparative and experimental studies. The research design chosen depends on the purpose of the research. Certain methods, such as surveys and laboratory experiments, are associated with particular designs. However, methods can be associated with more than one design and overlap occurs. The key point is that how the problem or question is defined indicates the appropriate research design and method.

Table 20.8.   Research designs in a progression of studies within one topic

Design	Example of Progression of Studies
Historical	The factors leading to the creation and expansion of The Medical Record (TMR) and the Regenstrief Medical Record System (RMRS) between 1970 and 1990
Descriptive	A survey of physicians to determine how and to what degree they use the computer-based patient record
Correlational	A study to determine the relationship among physicians' attributes, the setting, and use of the computer-based patient record
Evaluation	A study to evaluate the efficacy of the implementation of the computer-based patient record in an academic health center
Causal-Comparative (Quasi-experimental)	A study to compare the use of the computer-based patient record of a group of physicians in a setting classified as low barrier and a group of physicians in a setting classified as high barrier
Experimental	A study to compare use of the computer-based patient record of two matched physician groups: one group trained in a low-barrier experimental computer laboratory and one group trained in a high-barrier experimental computer laboratory

Instructions: Answer the following questions on a separate piece of paper.

1. Which research method uses self-report data?

2. What type of question is question 1?

3. Why would researchers choose to conduct a structured interview using an interview guide?

4. If researchers wanted to investigate the impact of changes in Medicare reimbursement on a region's healthcare, which method would they choose?

5. Why would researchers choose to conduct a questionnaire survey?

6. If researchers wanted to establish that a new drug caused a reduction in blood pressure, which research method would they choose?

7. When would researchers choose to conduct a meta-analysis?

8. In questions 3 through 7, what common characteristic determined the researchers' choice of method?

Statement of Hypothesis

Hypotheses are working possibilities that guide the initial data collection and are revised during the study based on the data obtained. Hypotheses differ between quantitative and qualitative research. In quantitative research, hypotheses are concrete and written in specific terms that are testable. In qualitative research, hypotheses are tentative suppositions. This section discusses hypotheses in quantitative research.

Formulation of Hypotheses

Formulation of precise and accurate hypotheses is a difficult task. The statement of the hypothesis is more specific than the research question. In the statement of hypothesis, the researcher states the research question using operational definitions. **Operational definitions** are measurable terms that come from the literature and are capable of generating data. (See figure 20.5.) The hypothesis states the research question in a way that is quantifiable, is computable, and uses defined variables. Therefore, some experts say that the statement of the hypothesis operationalizes the research question. Moreover, the statement of the hypothesis becomes the basis of the statistical tests. Therefore, there are two errors to

Figure 20.5. Components of hypotheses

- Variables of the study as defined in the literature
- Predicted relationship(s) or difference(s) between and among variables
- Measurement (quantifiable, computable)
- Intent of research

avoid in the statement of the hypothesis: writing an ambiguous hypothesis and writing an untestable hypothesis. Finally, researchers should take care that the hypothesis actually reflects the intent of the research.

Researchers write null hypotheses and alternative hypotheses. The **null hypothesis** states that there is no association between the independent and dependent variables. (The word *null* means none.) The **alternative hypothesis** states that there is an association between the independent and dependent variables. Alternative hypotheses are one-tailed or two-tailed. If the researcher states that the association is more or less, the alternative hypothesis is a **one-tailed hypothesis.** If the researcher makes no prediction about the direction of the results (more or less), the alternative hypothesis is a **two-tailed hypothesis.** These hypotheses are matched pairs. For example:

- *Null hypothesis:* There is no difference in the levels of utilization of voice recognition software between the group of physicians receiving the training and the group not receiving it.
- *Alternative hypothesis (one-tailed):* The level of utilization of the group receiving the training is 10 percent higher than the level of the group not receiving it.
- *Alternative hypothesis (two-tailed):* There is a 10 percent difference in the levels of utilization of voice recognition software between the group of physicians receiving the training and the group not receiving it.

Researchers state what they believe in alternative hypotheses. Unfortunately, the properties of statistical techniques do not allow them to directly test the accuracy of the alternative hypotheses. Instead, statistical techniques test null hypotheses. Therefore, researchers also must write null hypotheses in order to conduct statistical analysis. If the null hypothesis is rejected, the alternative hypothesis is accepted.

Significance

Researchers properly use the term *significance* in two ways (see table 20.9). There is *statistical significance,* which is related to significance testing determined from statistical techniques. This meaning signifies that the association or difference is actual and not a random chance. This meaning is related to the reliability of the research findings. Statistical significance is based on calculations. The size of the sample is an element in the calculation. Because of its sheer size, a very large sample can create statistical significance. However, statistical significance *does not* guarantee clinical or practical significance. Statistically significant findings can be trivial. For example, researchers studying a managerial decision support system could find that an improved algorithm increased the speed of calculating staffing needs by a statistically significant 0.5 seconds. While statistically significant, managers are not likely to purchase a new decision support system for staffing based on half a second. However, in the previous study of collision avoidance systems where

Table 20.9.   Meanings of significance in research

Use	Meaning
Statistical significance	Probability that a given finding actually exists and is not the result of a biased sample or random chance
	Reliable finding
	Not necessarily meaningful—because of the statistical formula for computation, the outcome may be the result of a large sample size
Significance	Dictionary meaning of important, meaningful, or consequential
	Sometimes stated as clinical significance or practical significance
	Having implications for decision making, practice, or policy

one second made the difference between a near-crash and a crash, 0.5 seconds would be both statistically significant and *significant* (McLaughlin et al. 2008, 14).

Researchers also use the term *significance* alone to mean clinical or practical significance. The word *significance* alone is the common, dictionary definition of the word as importance or meaningfulness (or important and meaningful, in its adjective form). This use relates to the importance of the finding and whether the association or difference can or should affect practice or policy. Therefore, researchers should take care to write out the full phrase *statistical significance* when referring to the likelihood that their findings were not the result of random chance or a biased sample and use the word *significance* alone when they mean importance or meaningfulness.

Researchers establish an appropriate **level of significance** before performing statistical analyses. This level of significance is known as the alpha (α) level. The level of significance is the criterion used for rejecting the null hypothesis. Common alpha levels are 0.05 and 0.01. Researchers set the lower alpha level when they want to minimize the chance that they might erroneously reject the null hypothesis when it is actually true.

Power is the probability of identifying real relationships or differences between groups (Goodman and Berlin 1994, 200). Specifically, power is the likelihood of failing to reject a false null hypothesis. When researchers fail to reject a false null hypothesis, the researchers have wrongly determined that there is no relationship or difference when, in fact, there is. However, for researchers (and the public), the ramifications of failing to assert a difference (power) are less than falsely asserting a difference (level of significance). Therefore, typically, power is less stringent than the level of significance and is often set at 0.80.

Researchers can make two types of errors associated with rejecting or failing to reject null hypotheses (see table 20.10).

A **type I error** occurs when the researcher erroneously rejects the null hypothesis when it is true; in actuality, there is no difference. A **type II error** occurs when the researcher erroneously fails to reject the null hypothesis when it is false; in actuality, there is a difference. For example:

- *Null hypothesis:* There is no difference in blood pressure levels between the group of patients receiving the new drug and the group receiving the placebo.
- *Alternative hypothesis (one-tailed):* The blood pressure of the group of patients receiving the new drug is 15 percent lower than the blood pressure of the group receiving the placebo.

A researcher committing a type I error would reject the null hypothesis. Continuing in the error, he or she would report the efficacy of the new drug. Unfortunately, the fact is that there is no difference between the blood pressures of the two groups of patients; the new drug does not work as predicted. Researchers who set the alpha level at 0.05 have a 5 percent chance of making this error whereas those who set the alpha level at 0.01 have a 1 percent chance of making the error. Thus, an alpha level of 0.01 is stricter than an alpha level of 0.05.

Beta (β) designates the probability of making a type II error. In the previous example, the researcher would make a type II error if he or she failed to reject the null hypothesis and it was indeed false. The researcher would erroneously state that there was no difference between the blood pressure of the group taking the new drug and the blood pressure of the group taking the placebo. In fact, there was a difference and the new drug was working as predicted. Beta is related to power because power is 1 − β. Reflecting its relationship to power, β is often set at 0.20, meaning that the researcher has a 20 percent chance of failing to reject the null hypothesis when an association or difference actually exists.

Table 20.10.   Type I and type II errors in significance testing

Error	Truth or Actuality
Fail to reject null hypothesis	Incorrect: Type II error (b) (false negative) Difference or association between groups' performance
	Correct: No difference or association between groups' performance
Reject null hypothesis	Incorrect: Type I error (a) (false positive) No difference or association between groups' performance
	Correct (power): Actual difference

Statistical tests for significance result in a *p*-value. A *p-value* indicates the probability of obtaining the result by chance if the null hypothesis is true. Therefore, if the *p*-value is 0.05, the probability that the difference occurred by pure chance is 5 percent. If the *p*-value obtained from the statistical test is less than or equal to the level of predetermined alpha value, the study's results are considered unlikely to be mere chance and the null hypothesis is rejected.

The increasing sophistication of analytical techniques has led methodological experts to discount the use of *p*-values by themselves in significance testing. As previously explained, statistical significance (rejection of the null hypothesis) can occur just because the number of responders is very large (sheer size rules). Also, as previously explained, statistical significance does not always equate to practical (clinical) significance. Therefore, experts recommend other statistical techniques, such as **confidence intervals (CIs), receiver operating characteristic (ROC) analysis,** and other techniques.

A CI is a range of values for a sample's characteristic within which it is estimated that the population's characteristic lies. CIs indicate the reliability of the estimate. On each end of the range is the **confidence limit** (upper limit and lower limit). Researchers set their confidence levels to represent their desired level of certainty. Desired certainty can be set at any percentage, but common percentages are 90 percent confidence level (10 percent significance level), 95 percent confidence level (5 percent significance level), and 99 percent confidence level (1 percent significance level) (see previous discussion of alpha levels).

CIs convey three key pieces of information:

- Statistical significance—intervals do not overlap
- Practical (clinical) significance or importance— magnitude of the values
- Precision—range of the confidence interval

For example, the results of a national computer proficiency examination for a random sample of 25 entering students were obtained. The mean score was 85.0. For this situation, the CI, at a 95 percent confidence level, is plus or minus 6.2 (±6.2) and combined with the mean, 85.0 (±6.2). The upper confidence limit is 91.2 (85.0 plus 6.2) and the lower confidence limit is 78.8 (85. 0 minus 6.2). In research papers, this information would be provided as follows: (95 percent CI, 78.8 to 91.2). In addition, CIs are reported in the unit of measure of the dependent variable (days, minutes, and such). Reporting results in the unit of measure of the dependent variables promotes ease of use and interpretation by practitioners. Using the unit of measure of the dependent variable allows the results to be put in context.

ROC analysis measures performance. Commonly, ROC analysis is used to measure the performance of predictive algorithms (such as in decision support systems), diagnostic tests (such as sputum tests), screening exams (such as mammograms), and other detection technologies. **Sensitivity** and **specificity** are the most common measures to detect accuracy (Joy et al. 2005, 314).

A sensitive measure has the ability to detect a characteristic (such as disease) when the characteristic exists. In a population with a characteristic, sensitivity is the proportion of people with the characteristic that will have a *positive* result (Akobeng 2007, 339). A specific measure has the ability to detect the absence of a characteristic (again such as disease) when the characteristic is absent. In a population *without* a characteristic, specificity is the proportion of people without a characteristic that will have a *negative* result. Sensitivity and specificity are related to type 1 and type II errors. Therefore, a 100 percent sensitive measure would identify everyone who has a disease. Similarly, a 100 percent specific measure would identify everyone *without* the disease. Sensitivity and specificity are reported as percentages.

In the real world, an inherent trade-off exists between sensitivity and specificity. Performance measures attempt to strike a reasonable balance. This reasonable balance is often based on the consequences of being wrong, a false positive or a false negative (Kocher and Zurakowski 2004, 611). Often, people would prefer to err on the side generating excess false positives. With many false positives, it is more likely that *all* possible cases are identified, but few cases are missed.

The relationship between sensitivity and specificity is graphically shown in ROC curves (graphs). ROC curves visualize the trade-off between sensitivity and specificity. ROC curves graph all different possible cut points between sensitivity (true positive rate) and the false positive rate (1 − specificity). In terms of the graph, the *y*-axis is the sensitivity (true positive rate) and the *x*-axis is the false positive rate (1 − specificity). In interpreting ROC curves, the area under the curve is the performance of the predictive algorithm or other detection technology (Kocher and Zurakowski 2005, 611). Perfect performance yields 100 percent (1.0) of the area under the curve and is shown by a point at the upper left corner (perfect classification). On the other hand, totally random guessing yields 50 percent (0.5) and a diagonal line from the bottom left corner to the top right corner (line of no discrimination).

Other techniques include measures of effect size. Effect size is the extent to which the null hypothesis is false. It represents the degree to which the sample results differ from the null hypothesis. It shows the practical (clinical) significance of a study's findings. Measures of effect size can be used to determine statistical significance. They also put the results of a study in context for practitioners. Measures of effect provide information about the magnitude of the association or difference. A common measure of effect is the odds ratio. The odds ratio is discussed in chapter 21. Other measures of effect size include Cohen's *d*, Glass' delta, and adjusted *R*2 (Thompson 2002, 25).

The statement of the hypothesis is a crucial step in the development of the research plan. It leads to the establishment of the appropriate statistical techniques and the determination of the level of significance. These two actions, in turn, affect the interpretation of the consequences of the treatment.

Selection of a Research Method

In selecting a research method, researchers first and foremost should consider their purpose as reflected in their research question. If they want to establish a causal relationship, they should conduct one of the experimental studies. If they are breaking new ground in a poorly understood area of practice, they may want to consider an exploratory study in a qualitative design.

Other factors are associated with the researchers' expertise and resources. Researchers should establish a match between the method and the following factors:

- *Expertise:* Can the researcher conduct, interpret, and explain sophisticated statistical techniques, or are more basic statistical techniques within the researcher's comfort zone?
- *Skills:* Can the researcher conduct the laboratory experiments necessary for research? For example, to investigate physicians' utilization of clinical guidelines, is the researcher able to insert codes into an EHR? Is the researcher able to insert a time clock into the software and design a query mechanism?
- *Personal attributes:* If the researcher is considering interviewing people, is he or she able to easily establish rapport with people? Or do conversations with strangers make the researcher feel awkward?
- *Time:* Does the researcher have the time to devote to conducting the research plan well? For example, investigating the change in attitude of students in HIM programs from freshman year through graduation is a meritorious idea. However, graduate programs have time frames within which students must complete their studies. A four-year research study may not fit the time frame.
- *Money:* Can the researcher afford the postage for a census survey of 64,000 AHIMA members?
- *Potential subjects:* The Solomon four-group method is excellent and beautifully controlled; however, it requires double the number of subjects. If subjects are in short supply, would this method be feasible?

Finally, researchers should strive for parsimony or elegance. **Parsimony** means that explanations of phenomena should include the fewest assumptions and conditions. Researchers who have achieved parsimony have eliminated extraneous, unnecessary complications. Just as the best theory is the simplest, so too is the best method.

Validity and Reliability

There are three types of **validity.** Internal validity and external validity involve the integrity of the research plan. Validity without a modifier refers to an attribute of measurement instruments. Reliability involves the consistency of measurements.

Figure 20.6.   Threats to internal validity

History:	Unplanned events occur during the research and affect the results
Maturation:	Subjects grow or mature during the period of the study
Testing:	Taking the first test affects subsequent tests; "practice effect"
Instrumentation:	Lack of consistency in data collection
Statistical Regression:	Subjects selected because of their extreme scores
Differential Selection:	Control group and experimental group differ, and the difference could affect the study's findings
Experimental Mortality:	Loss of subjects during the study
Diffusion of Treatment:	Members of the control group learn about the treatment of the experimental group

Validity

Internal validity and external validity are key issues when implementing a research plan. **Internal validity** is an attribute of a study's design that contributes to the accuracy of its findings. Campbell and Stanley (1963, 5) identified eight threats to internal validity. (See figure 20.6.) Threats to internal validity are potential sources of error that contaminate the study's results. These sources of error come from factors outside the study (confounding variables). Therefore, if internal validity is breached, researchers cannot state for certain that the independent variable caused the effect. **External validity** refers to the extent to which the findings can be generalized to other people or groups. *Generalizability* is the term that researchers use to mean the ability to apply the results to other groups, such as hospitals, patients, and states. Are the findings representative of many people or groups? Internal validity represents the bare minimum; internal validity combined with external validity is the ideal.

For example, researchers within the Department of Veterans Affairs (VA) evaluated the use of automated encoders in the VA system (Lloyd and Layman 1997, 73–74). Eight VA medical centers tested encoding software programs from three vendors. During the course of the study, an earthquake badly damaged one of the VA medical centers, which never reopened. Therefore, no final data on the software program were available from that center. This event represents the threat to internal validity of **mortality (attrition),** meaning the loss of subjects. In addition, the VA centers were not covered by Medicare's inpatient prospective payment system (PPS) at the time. This uniqueness represents a threat to external validity because most hospitals are covered by the PPS. Thus, the findings lacked generalizability. Therefore, both internal validity and external validity are important considerations for researchers.

In terms of an instrument, validity means the extent to which the instrument measures what it is intended to measure. Multiple aspects of an instrument's validity are assessed. Two important aspects are content validity and construct validity. **Content validity** concerns whether the instrument's items relate to the topic (content). For example, an ICD-9-CM coding test with content validity would have items related to key aspects of coding, such as the definition of principle diagnosis, fifth digits, complications and comorbidities, V codes, E codes, and the neoplasm table. Construct validity is the instrument's ability to measure hypothetical, nonobservable traits called constructs. Classic examples of constructs are psychological concepts, such as intelligence, motivation, and anxiety. Although intelligence itself is not visible, its effects are. Therefore, if an instrument is intended to measure patient satisfaction, it should include issues associated with patient satisfaction. Researchers state in their journal articles the validity of the instruments they use. References about instruments also provide the validity of instruments.

Reliability

Reliability represents consistency. Instruments that have reliability are stable. Repeated administrations will result in reasonably similar findings. **Intrarater reliability** means that the same person repeating the test will have reasonably similar findings. **Interrater reliability** means that different persons taking the test will have reasonably similar findings. Thus, reliability means that, over time, a test or an observation dependably measures whatever it was intended to measure.

Check Your Understanding 20.5

Instructions: Answer the following questions on a separate piece of paper.

1. In which hypothesis does the researcher state what he or she believes?

2. If the researcher believes that the treatment increases output, would he or she write a one-tailed or a two-tailed hypothesis?

3. What is the difference between a type I error and a type II error?

4. What does the *p*-value represent?

5. What issues are involved in internal validity?

6. Why is reliability important in tests?

Selecting an Instrument

An **instrument** is a standardized, uniform way to collect data. Common examples of instruments are interview guides and questionnaires, although many other types exist. (See figure 20.7.) Researchers can find standardized instruments

Figure 20.7.   Types of measurement instruments

Checklists	Personality tests
Clinical screenings and assessments	Projective techniques
Coding schemes and manuals	Psychological tests
Educational tests	Questionnaires
Index measures	Rating scales
Interview guides (schedules)	Scenarios
	Vignettes

in several reference books (see figure 20.8) and in electronic databases. Of particular interest to HIM professionals are two electronic databases: HAPI and Buros Institute of Mental Measurements. These databases provide descriptions and critiques of instruments.

Factors in Selection

Factors that determine the selection of an instrument include

- Purpose
- Satisfactory ratings for reliability and validity

Figure 20.8.   Print sources of measurement instruments

Bowling, A. 2005. *Measuring Health: A Review of Quality of Life Measurement Scales*, 3rd ed. New York: Open University Press.

Chun, K, S. Cobb, and J.R.P. French, Jr. 1975. *Measures for Psychological Assessment: A Guide to 3,000 Original Sources and Their Applications*. Ann Arbor, MI: Survey Research Center, Institute for Social Research.

Herndon, R.M., ed. 1997. *Handbook of Neurologic Rating Scales*. New York: Demos Vermande.

Keyser, D.J., and R.C. Sweetland, eds. 1991. *Test Critiques*. Kansas City, MO: Test Corporation of America.

Maddox, T., ed. 2003. *Tests: A Comprehensive Reference for Assessments in Psychology, Education, and Business*, 5th ed. Austin, TX: Pro-Ed.

McDowell, I., and C. Newell. 1996. *Measuring Health: A Guide to Rating Scales and Questionnaires*, 2nd ed. New York: Oxford University Press.

Murphy, L.L., R.A. Spies, and B.S. Plake, eds. 2006. *Tests in Print VII: An Index to Tests, Test Reviews, and the Literature on Specific Tests*. Lincoln, NE: University of Nebraska Press.

Redman, B.K., ed. 2003. *Measurement Tools in Patient Education*, 2nd ed. New York: Springer.

Redman, B.K., ed. 2002. *Measurement Tools in Clinical Ethics*. New York: Springer.

Spies, R.A., and B.S. Plake, eds. 2005. *The Sixteenth Mental Measurements Yearbook* (Buros Mental Measurements Yearbooks). Lincoln, NE: University of Nebraska Press.

Strauss, E., Sherman, E.M.S., and O. Spreen. 2006. *A Compendium of Neuropsychological Tests: Administration, Norms, and Commentary*, 3rd ed. New York: Oxford University Press.

- Clarity of language
- Brevity and attractiveness
- Match between the theories underpinning the instrument and the researcher's investigation
- Match between the level of measurement (nominal, ordinal, interval, or ratio scales of data) and the proposed statistical analyses
- Public domain or proprietary
- Cost

Of these factors, purpose is the most important. Researchers should match their purpose and the instrument's purpose. They should obtain the instrument and then read it in its entirety to be sure that it is collecting what they want to collect and that the terms in it match their meaning for the terms. For example, if the instrument is measuring social support, does it mean social support in the workplace or social support in the family and home? A researcher studying the effect of social support from colleagues and coworkers in the workplace should select an instrument about social support in the workplace. Selecting an instrument about social support in the family would be a grave error with negative consequences for the validity of the research. Thus, merely reading the description and critique in the reference database is insufficient.

Researchers should select instruments that other researchers have already developed and refined. The reliability and validity of these instruments are established. Development of a reliable and valid measure is a research project in and of itself. For example, construction of a questionnaire includes developing potential items (questions), conducting focus groups to explore the comprehensiveness of the instrument and its readability, analyzing the validity and reliability of the instrument, and pilot testing (Garvin 2005, 3–4). This list of tasks appears deceptively simple. However, regarding another instrument, establishing its content validity *alone* required a multiphase research study (Sharp 2010, 3). First, the HIM researcher created a preliminary draft instrument drawing items from several sources. Second, the HIM researcher sent the draft instrument to a panel of seven expert judges. She also made a follow-up telephone call to the expert judges to review their role. The expert judges rated the draft survey's items in terms of their clarity, relevance, and content. Third, the judges' scores on each of the items were statistically analyzed. Fourth, revisions to the instrument were made based on the analysis and the judges' comments. Fifth, a focus group (six of the seven expert judges) evaluated the overall comprehensiveness of the instrument. Finally, after five phases, the content validity alone of the instrument was validated (Sharp 2010, 4). Therefore, researchers should undertake the difficult task of developing an instrument only after they have investigated and verified that one does not already exist.

Instruments may be in the public domain or proprietary. Instruments in the public domain can be copied and used freely. Instruments that are proprietary must be purchased and cannot be copied. However, researchers can often obtain samples of instruments for review at little or no cost. In addition, researchers must consider the quality of the research. Of what use is an instrument that collects inaccurate data only tangentially related to the researcher's topic? The instrument must match the purpose and contribute to the collection of accurate data that build knowledge.

Features of Instruments

Questions on instruments may be structured, semistructured, or unstructured. **Structured (closed-ended) questions** list all the possible responses. **Unstructured (open-ended) questions** allow free-form responses. In **semistructured questions,** researchers first ask structured questions and then follow with open-ended questions to clarify. The advantages of structured questions are that they are easier for the participant to complete and for the researcher to tabulate and analyze than unstructured questions. The disadvantages of structured questions are that they are restrictive and may not be the right questions (questionable validity). The advantages of unstructured questions are that they allow in-depth questions and may uncover aspects of a problem unknown to the researcher. The disadvantages of unstructured questions are that they are less reliable and are more difficult to quantify, tabulate, and analyze than structured questions.

Structured questions may be numeric items or categorical items. Numeric items request the respondent to enter a number. When feasible, numeric items are preferable to categorical items (Alreck and Settle 2004, 113). In writing a numeric item, researchers must be careful to be clear and to specify the unit of measure. For example, the question "How long ago was your last visit to the dentist?" does not give the respondent an explicit unit of measure. The respondent may write 365 days, 52 weeks, or one year.

Categorical items classify respondents into groupings. It is important to construct categories that

- *Are all-inclusive:* All respondents must fit into a category, even if it is "other."
- *Are mutually exclusive:* Categories should not overlap and, thereby, confuse the respondents.
- *Form meaningful clusters:* Categories should make sense and be meaningfully distinct. The following set of categories does not form a reasonable, balanced progression: kindergarten to 12th grade, freshman, sophomore, junior, senior, and graduate school. A more meaningful set of categories is: high school education, associate's degree, baccalaureate degree, and graduate degree.
- *Are sufficiently narrow or broad:* The number of categories for a question may range from two (yes or no, true or false) to six or eight. Respondents have difficulty seeing meaningful shades of meaning beyond eight categories. Alreck and Settle (2004, 112–113) recommend that, when in doubt, use the narrower

Table 20.11. Common scales

Scale	Purpose	Example
Two-Point	Dichotomous question	Yes, no Favor, oppose True, false
Three-Point	Importance, interest, or satisfaction Satisfaction with amounts	Very, fairly, not at all Too much (many), just (about) right, not enough (too few)
Four-Point	Generic Measurement of amounts	Excellent, good, fair, poor Very much, quite a bit, some, very little
Likert (Five-Point)	Indication of agreement or disagreement	Strongly agree, agree, neutral, disagree, strongly disagree
Verbal Frequency (Five-Point)	Frequency	Always, often, sometimes, rarely (seldom), never
Expanded Likert (Seven-Point)	Extra discrimination desirable	Very strongly agree, strongly agree, agree, neutral, disagree, strongly disagree, very strongly disagree

(greater number) categories. Researchers can always combine categories, but they cannot disaggregate broad categories into fine-grained categories if the detailed data were not collected. On the other hand, requesting participants to respond to too many, and unnecessarily narrow, categories may depress the response rate and introduce inaccuracy.

A type of categorical item is a scaled item. **Scales** are progressive categories such as size, amount, importance, rank, or agreement. (See table 20.11.) For example, an HIM researcher used a scale on her questionnaire that allowed respondents to categorize their feelings of capability regarding various skills related to coding (Garvin 2001, 30–31). (See figure 20.9.)

A commonly used scale is the **Likert scale,** named for its developer, Rensis Likert. A Likert scale records the respondents' level of agreement or disagreement. On a Likert scale, the categories are along a range: strongly agree, agree, neutral, disagree, and strongly disagree. Each category is also called a point. Therefore, a scale with five categories is a five-point scale.

Researchers, marketers, and others use a **semantic differential scale** to ascertain a group's perspective or image of a product, healthcare organization, or program. (See figure 20.10.) A semantic differential scale uses adjectives to rate the product, organization, or program. Adjectives that are

Figure 20.9. Excerpt from survey questionnaire

Questionnaire on Coding Skills Contained in AHIMA's Vision 2006

On a scale of 1 to 5, 5 being the most capable, please designate how capable you feel in the following areas:

1. Understanding the current clinical coding systems relevant to the organization:

  A. ICD-9-CM   5   4   3   2   1

  B. CPT   5   4   3   2   1

  C. DSM-IV   5   4   3   2   1

  D. SNOMED   5   4   3   2   1

  E. ICD-O   5   4   3   2   1

  F. ICD-10   5   4   3   2   1

2. Ability to gather clinical data from primary data sources
     5   4   3   2   1

3. Understanding of the elements required for research and outcomes   5   4   3   2   1

4. Ability to participate in the design of studies
     5   4   3   2   1

Source: Garvin 2001.

polar opposites are placed on the ends of the continua. Up to 20 adjective pairs may be used. Half the items should begin with the positive adjective of the pair and the other half with the negative adjective. Identifying polar opposite adjectives and capturing the major attributes make this scale difficult to construct. However, a well-constructed semantic differential scale can provide a valuable profile of a product, an organization, or a program's image (Alreck and Settle 2004, 132–134).

Availability of an Internet format is another important feature. Internet-based instruments have been developed for many paper-based instruments. Researchers are evaluating whether Internet-based instruments have similar reliability to their paper-based versions. Researchers found that for 16 existing self-report instruments, their Internet and paper-based versions had similar reliabilities (Ritter et al. 2004). Prior to using an instrument, researchers should validate that

Figure 20.10. Example of a semantic differential scale

Please mark with an "X" the space on each line below to show your opinion of the education received in your academic program.

Up-to-Date	___:___:___:___:___:___	Outdated
	1 2 3 4 5 6 7	
Low-Tech	___:___:___:___:___:___	High-Tech
	1 2 3 4 5 6 7	
Expensive	___:___:___:___:___:___	Economical
	1 2 3 4 5 6 7	
Easy	___:___:___:___:___:___	Hard
	1 2 3 4 5 6 7	

its reliability has been established for the format they intend to use. For additional discussion, see paragraphs on response rate in the next section, Gathering the Data.

In summary, obtaining or developing the proper instrument is a key step. Researchers should carefully consider the various factors as they review and select instruments. Carelessness or haste during this step can lead to unusable, unanalyzable data. Purpose should drive the decision.

Gathering the Data

All too often, researchers fail to plan how to gather data. Researchers who make mistakes during this phase of the research violate one of the factors of internal validity: instrumentation. They have contaminated data and may have compromised their ability to analyze their data. Researchers must write a step-by-step, day-by-day plan for gathering data prior to implementation.

Target Population and Sample

A target population is the large group that is the focus of the research study. Target populations can be health information professionals, physicians, US patients, households, hospitals, schools, university students, US citizens, voters, people with diabetes, and websites. A **sample** is a portion of a target population; it is a set of units. Researchers often use samples because studies involving entire populations can be impractical or unfeasible. For example, very few researchers would have enough funding to poll all US citizens for their opinions on storing their health data on the Internet. Researchers, however, can identify a sample, meaning a group of citizens representative of the entire population. Individuals are one set of units. In other studies, the sets of units could be bacteria, mice, families, schools, television shows, historical documents, websites, and so on.

Data Sampling Methods

Sampling is the process of selecting the units to represent the target population. In sampling, the **sample frame** is an important issue. The sample frame is the list of subjects from which the sample is drawn (Dillman 2007, 196). The list must be representative of all the elements of the target population. If elements of the population are missing from the sample frame, a **coverage error** may occur. A coverage error is a systematic (nonrandom) discrepancy between the target population and the sample frame (Dillman 2007, 196). For example, a coverage error could occur if researchers used web access to determine the sample frame for a study of Medicare beneficiaries' opinion of using an electronic personal health record. Not all people have access to the Internet. Researchers must be careful to avoid this systematic error.

Researchers use various methods to obtain their samples. The data sampling method matches the purpose of the research study. There are two major types of samples: random and nonrandom.

Random Samples

Random sampling underpins many statistical techniques that HIM professionals encounter. To generate random samples, researchers can use either a feature of spreadsheet applications called the random number generator, an option of statistical packages called select cases, or a table of random numbers from a basic statistics textbook. The four types of random sampling are **simple random sampling, stratified random sampling, systematic sampling,** and **cluster sampling.** (See table 20.12.) Researchers using these methods attempt to make the sample as representative of the population as possible.

Nonrandom Samples

Two common types of **nonrandom sampling** are **convenience sampling** and purposive sampling. Convenience samples cast doubt on the generalizability and usefulness of the research. **Purposive sampling,** on the other hand, serves a valuable function in qualitative research.

Researchers use convenience samples when they "conveniently" use any unit that is at hand. For example, HIM professionals investigating physician satisfaction with departmental services could interview physicians who came to the department. Unfortunately, this convenience sample ignores the opinions of all the physicians who did not come to the department, and these physicians may find services substandard.

Table 20.12.   Types of random sampling

Type of Sampling	Description
Simple	The selection of units from a population so that every unit has exactly the same chance of being included in the sample. When a unit has been selected, it is returned to the population so that the other units' chances remain identical.
Stratified	Some populations have characteristics that divide them. For example, the human population is male and female. The male and female subgroups are called strata (singular, stratum). The percentage of the stratum in the population should equal the percentage of the stratum in the sample. Therefore, the sample should be 50% male and 50% female. Other percentages would cast doubt on the results.
Systematic	Units of the sample are selected from a list by drawing every nth unit. For example, health information professionals could choose every fourth surgery on the surgical schedule for surgical case review.
Cluster	The sample is clusters of units. The population is first divided into clusters of units, such as family, school, or community.

Therefore, use of a convenience sample diminishes the credibility of the research.

Purposive sampling is a strategy of qualitative research. In purposive sampling, researchers use their expertise to select both representative units and unrepresentative units. This strategy reflects the qualitative view that there are many truths. For example, Freud's work is purposive sampling because it focuses on unusual cases. Psychiatrists investigating the psychopathology of mass murderers would use purposive sampling because mass murder is not generalizable (Chadwick et al. 1984, 66). In an HIM example, the previously discussed study on the implementation and use of e-prescribing systems, the researchers used purposive sampling of the ambulatory medical practices (Crosson et al. 2008, 365). The researchers wanted to ensure that their study included practices in a range of sizes and physician specialties (Crosson et al. 2008, 365). Thus, purposive sampling has very specific applications.

Adequacy of the Sample Size

Sample size is the number of subjects the researcher determines should be included in the study in order to represent the population. The adequacy of the sample's size is a common concern. The size of the sample depends on the purpose of the study, the nature of the population, and the researchers' resources (Chadwick et al. 1984, 67). Some experts state that the general rule is to use the largest sample possible (Gall et. al 2007, 176; Gay et al. 2012, 139). However, Kish (1995/1965) factored in utility to arrive at economic samples. An economic sample provides the level of detail needed to answer the question. Overall, although no absolute rule dictates the size of the sample, researchers should strive for a level of accuracy that makes the study worth conducting.

If a researcher's purpose is to explore areas of inconsistency between paper and electronic records, 90 randomly selected records at one academic health center may be sufficient (Mikkelsen and Aasly 2001). However, a study comparing the efficacy of various treatment **protocols** for breast cancer warrants a sample size in the thousands. If the researcher's purpose includes many variables, the sample size needs to be larger. Thus, purpose is a critical concern.

The nature of the population includes **heterogeneity** and typical response and attrition rates. Heterogeneity means variation or diversity. The more heterogeneous a population, the larger the sample. The sample needs to be larger to ensure that it includes all the diverse units in the population. Typical response rate is a factor for surveys. In the literature, other researchers report their response rates. The response rate is the number of people who returned the questionnaire or were reached for interview. If the typical response rate is 50 percent, the researcher will need to distribute twice as many surveys to achieve an adequate response. Attrition (mortality) rates are the numbers of subjects lost during the course of the study. Attrition is a threat to internal validity.

High attrition rates also require a larger sample. Understanding the nature of the population contributes to the accuracy of the research.

Resources, namely time and money, also can affect sample size. Sometimes researchers must provide answers within a short time frame. For example, to respond in a timely fashion to a legislative initiative regarding photocopy charges, HIM professionals may conduct a quick survey of a small sample. Individual researchers often face financial constraints. These constraints sometimes result in smaller samples than purists would prefer.

Sample size calculation refers to the qualitative and quantitative procedures used to determine the appropriate sample size. Some experts have offered rules of thumb to calculate sample size. (See table 20.13.) These rules of thumb try to account for frequency of the behavior, number of variables, and statistical technique. Statistical formulae are also used to calculate adequate sample sizes (Osborn 2006, 145–149). Formulae depend on the sampling method used, such as simple random sampling or stratified random sampling, and on the amount of information the researcher has about the population. For health information managers, Osborn's (2006) text offers excellent examples and step-by-step procedures. Finally, however, specific considerations should override reliance on these rules of thumb and formulae.

One commonly used formula for determining optimal sample size requires the researcher to know or to decide on the size of the population, the proportion of subjects needed, and an acceptable amount of error. The formula results in the number of responses needed from the sample. This number must be adjusted by the target audience's typical response rate to arrive at the number of instruments to be distributed.

Table 20.13.   Rules of thumb for sample size

Rule of Thumb	Source
General: minimum of 30 cases or responses	Bailey (1994, 97)
Pilot study: 20–50 cases	Sudman (1976, 87)
Descriptive study: minimum 10% of population	Gay et al. (2006, 110)
Descriptive study: population 100 of fewer, survey entire population	Gay et al. (2006, 110)
Descriptive study: minimum 20 percent of small population (~1,500)	Gay et al. (2006, 110)
Correlational study: minimum of 30 cases or responses	Gall et al. (2007, 176)
Causal-comparative and experimental research: 15–30 cases/comparison group	Gall et al. (2007, 176) Gay et al. (2006, 110)
Major subgroup: minimum of 100 each Minor subgroups: minimum of 20–50 each/subgroup	Sudman (1976, 30)
General: 200 cases or responses	Chadwick et al. (1984, 68)

Figure 20.11. Basic example of sample size calculation

Sample size = n

Size of the population = N

Proportion of subjects needed = p

Acceptable amount of error = β

Formula

$$n = \frac{Np(1-p)}{(N-1)\dfrac{(B^2)}{4} + (p)(1-p)}$$

Calculations

Data from the case

$$n = \frac{(800)(.5)(1-5)}{(800-1)\dfrac{(.05^2)}{4} + (.5)(1-5)}$$

$N = 800$

$p = .5$

$$n = \frac{200}{(799)(.000625) + 25}$$

$\beta = .05$

$$n = \frac{200}{.75}$$

$$n = 267$$

The following example walks through the formula for arriving at the sample size. (See figure 20.11.) Suppose the HIS director at a large academic health center wanted to determine the sample size for a study on the medical staff's opinion of electronic health records. In this instance, the director knows that the number of attending physicians on the medical staff is 800 but has little other information. Therefore, p = 0.5 and β = 0.05. Using the basic formula, the director calculates that, in this situation, a sample of 267 is needed if he or she is willing to accept 5 percent error due to variability in the sampling. Finally, the director determines the number of surveys to distribute by multiplying the sample size by the typical response rate. Thus, if half of the attending physicians typically respond to surveys, the director must double the sample and distribute 534 surveys for the opinion study.

Data Collection Procedures

The research plan should consider every logistical detail of the collection of the data from start to finish. Lack of attention to detail at this point will breach factors of internal validity. Some issues related to data collection affect many of the methods; other issues are unique to the method. Data collection issues include

- Obtaining approvals of oversight committees
- Listing each data element required to perform the appropriate statistical techniques
- Training for data collection procedures
- Performing a pilot study
- Considering the response rate
- Conducting the treatment
- Collecting the data
- Assembling the data for analysis

Federal regulations govern research on human subjects (Penslar and Porter 2001). The purpose of the regulations is to protect humans from researchers' abuses, such as those that occurred in the US Public Health Services Syphilis Study (also known as the Tuskegee Syphilis Study; see chapter 21). To comply with federal regulations, organizations have **institutional review boards (IRBs)**. IRBs (sometimes called human subjects committees) are administrative bodies established to protect the rights and welfare of human subjects recruited to participate in research activities associated with institutions. IRBs provide oversight for the research studies conducted within their institutions. As specified by both federal regulations and institutional policies, IRBs have the authority to review and to approve or reject research studies within their jurisdictions. They also may require modifications in research protocols. As human health and life are at stake, the federal government imposes severe penalties on institutions and individuals who fail to comply.

Prior to conducting studies, researchers must obtain written approvals from the IRB and other oversight entities of their organizations. To obtain approvals, researchers complete the organization's documentation, providing descriptions of their research plan and copies of their informed consent forms. (See chapter 21 for a complete discussion of IRBs.) Sufficient time must be allowed in their plan for the board to review the research, meet, and respond.

Researchers should compile a list of each data element required for each statistical analysis they plan to conduct. Prior to beginning data collection, researchers should ensure that their data collection strategies will obtain all the data. Therefore, it is advisable to conduct mock statistical analyses on fabricated data and to create tables and figures for the manuscript early in the planning of the research. For example, suppose researchers were investigating whether the time from heart transplant to the first rejection episode differed by ABO blood type and Rh factor. The blood types and Rh factors are not evenly distributed in the general population nor are they evenly distributed by national origin. Running mock statistical analyses would reveal that the researchers need a large sample size. Too often, graduate students have had to write in their theses or dissertations, "I did not have sufficient cases to run the statistical analysis." Planning can avoid this embarrassment.

Researchers and those they employ to assist them may require special training. For example, publishers of some psychological tests require verification of training to administer the tests. The researchers must obtain this verification (or select another instrument). To effectively conduct interviews or to observe vignettes, researchers and their assistants also need training.

Performing a **pilot study** (trial run) enhances the likelihood of its successful completion. When researchers conduct pilot studies, they work out the details of their research plan. The maxim, "The devil is in the details," is only too true. Pilot studies can reveal the following information:

- Biases in sample selection
- Volumes required

- Associated costs
- Performance features of equipment, hardware, and software
- Defects, such as poorly worded cover letters, unclear questionnaire items, and leading questions in interviews
- Possible log jams (gridlock) in the mailing method or problems with the Internet site
- Errors in the scoring key
- Discrepancies between the order of items on the data collection instrument and the order on the data entry screen

Pilot studies demonstrate whether the research study is logistically feasible. Even researchers conducting naturalistic studies perform simulations that test their instruments prior to the event. Pilot studies are as necessary as disaster drills.

Figure 20.12.   Summary of Berdie and Anderson's strategies to increase the response rate in questionnaire surveys

General

1. Physical attractiveness of cover letter, postcard, and questionnaire

2. Quality of printing and paper

3. Pleasingly colored paper

4. Error-free documents

5. Incentives, such as an offer of the study's results or money ($0.25 maximum)

Cover Letter

1. Salutation's formality is tailored to the target population.

2. Prestigious sponsor

3. Time frame for response is exact (10 days) or "as soon as possible," depending on the population.

4. Tone of sincerity and honesty

5. Assurance of confidentiality

Questionnaire

1. Title

2. Easy to complete

3. Clear instructions included in the body of the questionnaire

4. Reasonable length

5. Contact information and return mailing address at the bottom

Mailing

1. Initial contact (postcard) that is an appeal for participation

2. Self-addressed, stamped return envelope

3. Properly timed follow-up

Ensuring an adequate response rate is of particular concern for surveys. Low response rates jeopardize study accuracy and generalizability. Therefore, researchers strive to increase their response rates. To increase response rates, researchers can use the findings of Berdie and Anderson (1974). These researchers conducted the classic research study on the process of questionnaire surveys. Their research revealed many strategies to increase the response rate. (See figure 20.12.) Their primary recommendation was that researchers know their topic and their target population. This knowledge underpins decisions about the strategies and techniques to increase response rates.

Strategies to increase the response rate for questionnaire research include using a brief cover letter and multiple mailings. The cover letter should explain the purpose of the study and its benefits for the participants. Obtaining the sponsorship of a professional association or officials is desirable. Moreover, the letter should thank the responder, provide a deadline, and offer the study results. In the field of health information management, ensuring the confidentiality of the response also is particularly important. Key characteristics of effective cover letters are shown in figure 20.13. Multiple mailings in a timed sequence can significantly improve the response rate. For example, the tailored (total) design method on average achieves response rates of 74 percent (Dillman 2007, 27–28).

Internet surveys are becoming more prevalent because they are able to gather data from large samples directly and relatively inexpensively (Bethell et al. 2004). They are now being used to gather data on health outcomes; adoption of information technologies; and a wide variety of characteristics of healthcare organizations, health professionals, and health consumers. Researchers should *not* assume that conducting a survey on the Internet ensures a higher response rate than ground mail surveys or telephone surveys.

Instead, researchers specifically studying response rates have reported that various survey strategies, including Internet surveys, provided mixed results in their response rates. In terms of an Internet survey versus a telephone survey, Bethell and colleagues reported that their one-time contact via e-mail resulted in a higher response rate than a telephone survey with six follow-up telephone calls. Survey administration, statistical sampling, and weighted approaches to ensure representativeness were similar for the two survey strategies. The researchers concluded that, with the increasing resistance to telephone solicitations, Internet surveys represent an efficient, real-time strategy for data collection (Bethell et al. 2004). On the other hand, Leece and colleagues obtained a lower response rate to an Internet questionnaire than to a ground-mailed questionnaire (Leece et al. 2004, e39). Leece and colleagues used ground mail to deliver the questionnaire to half of the subjects and an e-mail to invite the other half of the subjects to complete the questionnaire on the Internet. The response rate to the ground-mail-delivered questionnaire was 58 percent while

Figure 20.13. Sample cover letter

Letterhead	ZHIMA	
	1800 Carriage	
	Oxford, ZB 31002	
	October 1, 20xx	
	Dear Colleague:	
Purpose	The healthcare system and our field are rapidly changing. These changes place increasing demands on health information practitioners. Little research exists that explores stress and the buffers in directors of hospital health information management departments.	
Study's Importance Participant's Importance	Therefore, you have been randomly selected to participate in a national survey on stress in the workplace. Please take the time to complete and return the survey. The accuracy of the results and the possible benefits for the profession depend on your participation.	
Sponsor Time to Complete	This research is being sponsored by AHIMA. The entire survey should take 15 to 20 minutes of your time. A detailed, personalized report on your coping resources is available. Should you wish to receive it, please write your name and address at the bottom of the pink Demographic Form.	Offer of Results
Time Frame	Please return the survey within 10 days in the postage-paid envelope.	SASE
	A vital concern of the health information management profession is confidentiality in research. The code number on your questionnaire is for mailing and follow-up purposes only. Only aggregate data will be reported, and at no time will the questionnaires be identified by respondent.	Confidentiality
Appreciation Contact Instruction	I truly appreciate your participation, and I think the findings of the survey will benefit many members of our profession in these stressful times. If you have any questions about the survey, please write or call me.	
	Sincerely	
	Jane Edwards, PhD	
	123 Anyplace Street	
	Anytown, IL 12345	
	(123) 456-7890	
	Enclosures	

the response rate to the Internet-based questionnaire was 45 percent (Leece et al. 2004, e39). The subjects of Leece and colleagues were physicians. Another study investigated patients' response rates between paper questionnaires and Internet questionnaires (Kongsved et al. 2007, e25). Half of the subjects received the paper questionnaire and the other half the Internet questionnaire. The difference between the two response rates was larger than the study involving physicians. The initial response rate for the paper questionnaire was 73.2 percent and for the Internet questionnaire, 17.9 percent. After a reminder to each group, the paper response rate was 76.5 percent and the Internet response rate was 64.2 percent (Kongsved et al. 2007, e25). The researchers noted that the questionnaires completed on the Internet were more complete than the paper questionnaires.

Therefore, as Internet-based surveys have become more common, their novelty has worn off and their response rates for some groups have declined. On the other hand, Internet-based instruments offer three key advantages related to efficiency:

- Ease of follow-up
- Automated data entry into the researcher's database
- Direct data entry or capability of being uploaded into the analytical software

Researchers should carefully review the literature for the response rates of their intended audience and factors affecting response rates. The pilot study may also provide key information on the likelihood of a high response rate. Thus, determining whether to use an Internet-based or paper-based instrument requires careful weighing of the disadvantages versus the advantages and knowledge of the target audience.

Researchers also must be on guard for bias in response. For example, do persons who volunteer to participate in the research differ from those who do not volunteer? Do the persons who responded to the survey (responders) differ from those who did not (nonresponders)? Finally, how similar are the participants, nonparticipants, responders, and nonresponders to the population?

In conducting the study, researchers must be careful to follow the plan they have written. Deviations from the protocol result in potential bias and inaccurate data. For example, in questionnaire research, the Dillman (2007, 151) method depends on a timed series of five contacts. Does the researcher have staff to track the responses and to make the multiple contacts?

Researchers must include a mechanism in the plan for compiling their data. If videotapes are involved, where will they be stored? Because sensitive data may be on personality tests, how will confidentiality be maintained? If the research includes measurement instruments, who will score them?

After researchers have collected the data, they must organize them in a way that allows analysis. In this step, the researchers must decide how they will enter the data into a software package. Who will enter the data? How will they ensure accuracy of data entry? Who will transcribe the contents of videotapes or audiotapes?

Data collection is a systematic, planned procedure that results in internal validity. Conducting a pilot study is a key step in ensuring a thorough and carefully conceived plan. The methods section of the study report documents the plan's execution. The methods section is also a recipe that other researchers can use to replicate the study. Therefore, careful attention to documentation and vigilant adherence to procedures are demanded.

Sources of Secondary Data

Researchers may choose to analyze or mine data that other researchers or agencies have gathered. As noted, analysis of secondary data is a powerful tool because it allows researchers to mine large databases at the regional, state, and national level. For example, researchers at an academic health center mined 667,000 deidentified EHRs, representing over 1 million inpatient and outpatient visits (Mullins et al. 2006, 1353–1356). These data were compiled in clinical data repositories that received data from a variety of clinical and administrative sources (Mullins et al. 2006, 1352). The data mining software included three components: association analysis, predictive analysis, and pattern discovery. After discovering associations, the researchers verified them in the medical literature. Many of the associations were expected. However, the researchers listed novel (new) associations that they believed warranted further investigation (Mullins et al. 2006, 1362–1370). One such novel association was among psychoses, peptic ulcer disease, and paralysis (Mullins et al.

2006, 1370). The researchers concluded that non-hypothesis-driven (unsupervised) data mining of large clinical repositories is feasible (Mullins et al. 2006, 1370).

Health services researchers used Florida's Medicaid claims data (Harman et al. 2011, 787). The researchers examined the effects of Florida's Medicaid Reform Demonstration on Medicaid expenditures. Implemented in specific counties, the reform was a program that provided Medicaid enrollees with education and outreach to assist them in (1) choosing the best health plan (health maintenance organization or preferred provider organization) and (2) adopting healthy lifestyles (Harman et al. 2011, 789). Medicaid enrollees in counties where the reform was not implemented (nonreform counties) could choose a health maintenance plan or a fee-for-service case management plan. The researchers compared data from the reform counties to data from the nonreform counties. The data were from two fiscal years before the reform's implementation and from two fiscal years after its implementation (Harman et al. 2011, 787). The researchers found that the reform demonstration did not result in significant savings in Medicaid expenditures (Harman et al. 2011, 802). Finally, though, the researchers noted that for specific populations expenditures were reduced and that two years postimplementation may have been insufficient to see the long-term effects of the reform project (Harman et al. 2011, 802).

Biomedical informatics researchers mined usage patterns from EHR systems (Malin et al. 2011, 333). The EHR systems of healthcare organizations generate access logs so that audit trails may be constructed. The researchers mined 7,575,434 accesses of patient information during a five-month period at one academic health center. From the mined access logs, the informatics researchers created rules related to EHR users' patterns of access. From these patterns of access, healthcare administrators could develop meaningful access control policies. The researchers concluded that their data-driven method of automatically extracting policies from EHR access logs could be expanded to other healthcare organizations (Malin et al. 2011, 341).

Several other sources of data are available to researchers. For example, several states post Medicaid data on the Internet. Specific examples of available data include

- Labor force, earnings, and prices (Bureau of Labor Statistics)
- Crime, demographics, education, and health (Social Statistics Briefing Room)
- Statistics and information from more than 100 federal agencies (FedStats)
- Behavioral health (Behavioral Risk Factor Surveillance System [BRFSS] of the Centers for Disease Control and Prevention)
- Health statistics (National Center for Health Statistics, FASTATS A–Z)
- Health statistics, social indicators, and population health research (Area Resource File [ARF] of the

Health Resources and Services Administration of the US Department of Health and Human Services)
- Health information national trends survey (HINTS) (US National Institutes of Health, National Cancer Institute)
- Medicare data (Medicare Provider Analysis and Review [MEDPAR] of Short-Stay Hospitals)
- Demographic data on domestic and international populations (Population Reference Bureau)
- Hundreds of files from various state and federal governmental agencies (Statistical Resources on the web)
- US census data (US Census Bureau)
- Medicaid data by state (see Medicaid programs of each state)

The problem is that in order to transform the data into information, researchers must understand the underlying structure of the data and how they were collected. Each data source has unique characteristics.

For example, one hospital database contained a field related to death, which is typically a discharge status. However, with its death field (Field 342), the hospital could track the number of intraoperative deaths, postoperative deaths, autopsied deaths, and medical examiner's cases. The death field was a multiple-entry field, with each category having a number (intraoperative death = 1; postoperative death = 2; autopsied death = 3; and medical examiner's case = 4). A surgeon requested a report on the number of intraoperative deaths. The worker who usually ran reports was on vacation and another worker attempted to run the query. This worker wrote the query as Field 342 = "1." As a multiple-entry field, the query should have been written as Field 342 contains "1." The erroneously written query excluded all intraoperative deaths that were also postoperative deaths (2), autopsied deaths (3), and medical examiner's cases (4). Some cases are all four. The case of a multiple stabbing victim illustrates the point. From the emergency room, the patient is initially brought to the operating room (OR). His wounds are explored and sutured. Postoperatively, the patient is sent to the intensive care unit. While in the ICU, he begins to bleed internally again and is brought back to the OR. While in the OR the second time, the patient dies. This patient is both a postoperative death and an intraoperative death (2 and 1). In addition, the body was sent for autopsy, and as a crime victim, the patient is a medical examiner's case (3 and 4). Therefore, researchers must either learn the underlying structure of the database and query it directly or download the data into a database or spreadsheet with which they are familiar.

Similar to the approach to literary databases, researchers must take a systematic and orderly approach. Researchers from multiple disciplines have queried large databases to analyze health data. As HIM researchers develop their areas of interest, secondary analysis may be a productive and rewarding research method.

Check Your Understanding 20.6

Instructions: Answer the following questions on a separate piece of paper.

1. Why would a researcher choose to use an instrument that someone else has created?
2. What is an adequate sample?
3. Would directors of departments of health information services be considered a heterogeneous population or a homogeneous population?
4. Why are IRBs important?
5. What is a pilot study?
6. Why are survey researchers concerned about their response rates?
7. What common mistake do researchers make in data collection?

Preparing Data for Analysis

In the design of studies, researchers use procedures to maximize the integrity of their data. They attempt to prevent errors by constructing instruments that facilitate accurate and complete responses. They may insert field edits into their spreadsheet or database to support accurate data entry. However, despite researchers' best efforts, many different types of errors may occur. For example, researchers can transpose numbers in their data entry or participants can skip items. Thus, data must be prepared prior to analysis. In this preparation, researchers assess the quality of their data. They verify the accuracy and completeness of the data. This preparation minimizes the effects of these errors on their studies' results. All data require preparation; however, the data from data sources for secondary analysis and data mining require extensive preparation. Important aspects of data preparation are handling missing values and data cleansing.

Missing Values

Missing values are variables that do not contain values for some cases. For example, in the previously discussed study on breast cancer, occupation, menopausal status, and estrogen and progesterone receptor values were missing values (Watzlaf et al. 1996, 30–31). Missing values is a type of incomplete or coarse data (Heitjan and Rubin 1991, 2244).

Missing values must be resolved before statistical techniques can be applied. Methods to resolve missing values are case deletion, single imputation, and multiple imputation. Each of these methods has multiple techniques. A few representative and explanatory techniques are discussed.

In case deletion, a case with missing values is deleted entirely from the study. In a modified form of case deletion, a case is only excluded from calculations for which it has missing data. **Imputation** is the substitution of values for the missing values. A common single imputation is the substitution of the mean of the available values for the missing data. Both case deletion and single imputation have the advantage of simplicity. The disadvantages of both techniques are the loss of cases and the potential for bias because the missing data may not be random.

Techniques of multiple imputation involve several complex calculations, creation of subgroups, and multiple simulations. Statistical packages include multiple imputation. The advantages of multiple imputation are greater accuracy and less bias. One disadvantage is that large samples may be required.

Missing values are a common problem for researchers. However, this problem is important to address because, until shown otherwise, missing values are considered systematically biased. This systematic bias would corrupt the analysis of the data and undermine the integrity of the study. Finally, researchers should document the technique they use to resolve missing values.

Data Cleansing

Data cleansing (data cleaning, data scrubbing) is the "process of detecting, diagnosing, and editing faulty data" (Van den Broeck et al. 2005, 0966). Researchers note that data cleansing can consume 80 percent of the time of data mining (Sokol et al. 2001, 2). For other types of research, data cleansing may not be quite as arduous and time consuming. However, the process still requires many hours of detailed work for which researchers should allow time.

Methods of data cleansing include finding duplications, checking internal consistency, and identifying outliers:

- Finding duplication often occurs during data entry when two completed questionnaires from the same subject are encountered (researchers need to have a method of determining which questionnaire to use— first received or most complete)
- Checking for internal consistency involves assessing gender and age against diagnosis or procedure, city against zip code, or other comparable attributes
- Detecting statistical outliers identifies values outside the expected range and may occur during the participants' completion of the instrument or the researchers' data entry (see box and whisker plot in the next section)

Once errors are detected they are corrected during data editing. According to Van den Broeck et al. (2005, 0966), data editing is "changing the value of data shown to be incorrect." Only errors shown to be wrong should be corrected in data editing. Care should be taken not to manipulate the data.

As researchers clean their data, they should record their methods, the error types and rates, the error deletion and correction rates, and the outcomes with and without outliers (Van den Broeck et al. 2005, 0966). This information should then be documented in the scientific paper. This documentation thus avoids the appearance of data manipulation.

For example, in the previously described study on 667,000 individuals' health records, the researchers stated several procedures that they had performed to clean the data (Mullins et al. 2006, 1356–1357). To meet Health Insurance Portability and Accountability Act (HIPAA) requirements for deidentification, 18 identifiers were removed. The researchers omitted "time" as a variable because of formatting and extracted "first values" for several laboratory values. Narrative variables were converted to numeric (for example, yes, don't know, no were converted to –1, 0, +1, respectively).

Data preparation is integral to the quality of the study's results. It is important to allow sufficient time to resolve missing values and to conduct data cleansing.

Analyzing the Data

In this phase of the research process, researchers try to determine what they have found or what the data reveal. Many researchers fall into the common error of allowing too little time for analysis. Researchers should be sure to allocate sufficient time in their research plan to analyze and interpret the data.

Before conducting their study, researchers should determine which analytical techniques they will use. These techniques are specified in the methods section of the manuscript. The description of the analytical techniques should be clear so that other researchers can duplicate them.

Techniques for Quantitative Data Analysis

This section briefly describes a few common statistical techniques. For a detailed discussion, see a standard statistical text, such as *Statistical Applications for Health Information Management* (Osborn 2006). The purpose here is to suggest appropriate statistical techniques for general situations. The following three broad categories of statistical analysis are addressed:

- **Descriptive (summary) statistics** describe the data. Generally, researchers should begin with descriptive techniques to verify the accuracy of their data entry and to provide an overview of their respondents. Exploratory data analysis looks at the raw data. The raw data are presented in graphic displays. Two techniques of exploratory data analysis are box and whisker plots and stem and leaf diagrams. The stem and leaf diagram shows all the individual scores on a particular measure (Gall et al. 2007, 152). Box and whisker plots are especially useful when the sets of data have hundreds or thousands of scores or the sets of data have unequal numbers of values. The shapes of these graphic displays allow researchers to see the range and distribution of scores (see figure 20.14 and chapter 18). Outliers become visible. Descriptive techniques include means, frequency distributions, and standard deviations. These statistical techniques are also called **univariate** because they involve one variable.

Figure 20.14.   Box and whisker plot

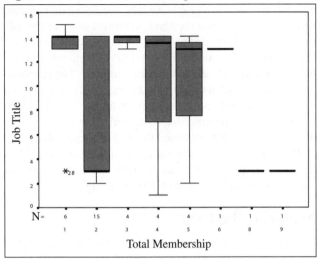

Table 20.14.   Statistical test by characteristics of data

No. of Variables	Characteristics	Test
1+	One group, normal*	Mean and standard deviation
	One group, nonnormal	Binomial test
	Two groups, normal	*t*-test
	Two groups, nonnormal	Chi-square
	Three+ groups, normal	ANOVA
	Three+ groups, nonnormal	Nonparametric
2+	Both continuous	Correlation
	1 continuous, 1 discrete	ANOVA
	Both categorical	Chi-square
3+	One group	Multiple regression, factor analysis, repeated measures ANOVA, analysis of covariance
	Two+ groups	Multivariate ANOVA, discriminant function

*Normal distribution.

- **Inferential statistics** allow the researchers to make inferences about the population characteristics (parameters) from the sample's characteristics. Examples of inferential statistics include the paired *t*-test and the analysis of variance (ANOVA). Researchers investigating the differences between groups would use these statistical techniques.
- **Test statistics** examine the psychometric properties of measurement instruments. They describe and explore the validity and reliability of tests. Researchers conducting test statistics calculate the validity coefficient (correlation coefficient) and each item's validity. They also could perform factor analysis. Examples of approaches to verify reliability include test–retest and Kuder-Richardson formulae. Finally, test statistics include an index of difficulty, which is the percentage of persons correctly answering each item.

Most research data can be subjected to more than one statistical technique. Table 20.14 shows potential statistical tests for various combinations of data characteristics. The suggested statistical tests in the table are merely a starting point. Researchers should maximize the use of their data by using a variety of techniques to look at their data from multiple views. Multiple views of the data shed light on different aspects of the issue and expand the body of knowledge.

Appropriate statistical techniques vary by

- Purpose of the research (research design)
- Number of variables
- Type of data
- Nature of the target population
- Number, size, and independence of the groups

Purpose of the Research
Researchers should match their purpose and their statistical technique. Researchers whose purpose is to investigate the differences between groups would use statistical techniques of the paired *t*-test and ANOVA. On the other hand, researchers might be looking for relationships, such as in a correlational design. These researchers would want to know how the variables relate to one another. Therefore, these researchers would use correlational statistics. One correlational technique is the **bivariate** correlational coefficient. The bivariate correlational coefficient allows the researcher to describe the strength of the relationship between two variables in mathematical terms.

Number of Variables
The number of variables also affects the choice of statistical technique. **Multivariate** correlational methods involve many variables. For example, multiple linear regression examines the strength of relationship between several independent variables and one dependent variable. Other, more complex forms of regression exist.

Type of Data
Another factor in the choice of statistical technique is the type of data. There are five types of data:

- **Discrete data** are separate and distinct values or observations. Patients in the hospital represent discrete data because each patient can be counted.

- **Categorical data** are values or observations that can be sorted into a category (for example, gender).
- **Nominal data** are values or observations that can be labeled or named (*nom* = name). Therefore, the data can be coded (for example, Married = Y and Single = N or Male = 0 and Female = 1). Nominal data cannot be ranked or measured.
- **Ordinal data** represent values or observations that can be ranked (ordered). Ranking scales are common examples of ordinal data. For example, physicians often ask patients to evaluate the severity of their pain on a scale from 1 to 10. HIM professionals could use ordinal data when investigating customer satisfaction. For example, a health information manager could ask physicians how satisfied they are with the department's service on a scale from 1 to 5. However, because these rankings are subjective, the difference in satisfaction between 2 and 3 may be much less than the difference between 4 and 5.
- **Metric** data can be measured on some scale. Two subtypes are interval and ratio. The scale for **interval data** does not begin with a true zero. Time, as humans measure it, does not begin with a true zero. Interval data represent values or observations that occur on an evenly distributed scale. Time in years is an evenly distributed scale. The interval between 1985 and 1990 is the same as the interval between 1991 and 1996. On the other hand, the scale for **ratio data** does begin at a true zero. Height, weight, and temperature are examples of ratio data.

Metric data are **continuous data.** They represent values or observations that have an indefinite number of points along a continuum. For example, measurements made with a ruler can be a foot, an inch, a half-inch, a quarter, an eighth, to infinity. Continuous data also exhibit characteristics of the other types of data; they can be counted (discrete) and ordered (ordinal) and can be grouped.

The type of data depends on the way the variable is measured, not some inherent attribute of the variable. For example, height can be measured in inches or categorized as short or tall. Therefore, researchers should be careful to collect data in the form that matches their intended statistical technique.

Nature of the Target Population

The nature of the target population also affects the choice of statistical technique. For example, some statistical techniques are based on the assumption that the variable is normally distributed in the population. **Parametric techniques,** such as the *t*-test, ANOVA, and Pearson *r* correlation efficient, are used in these cases. However, this assumption is not always true. In some cases, researchers use **nonparametric (distribution-free) techniques** (for example, chi-square and Spearman's rho). Nonparametric techniques also are used for nominal and ordinal data. Osborn (2006, 251–253) provides a powerful discussion on the use of parametric and nonparametric statistical tests by type of data (level of measurement, nominal to metric).

Number, Size, and Independence of Groups

The selection of statistical test also depends on the number of samples or groups. In many instances, researchers want to compare two groups, the control group and the study group. However, in other types of studies, researchers may want to compare results from 10 different communities or all 50 states. The number of groups affects the choice of statistical test. Disparate sizes of groups also sometimes affect the choice of statistical test. Some statistical tests, however, are quite robust and can handle differences in sizes. For example, in many instances analysis of variance (ANOVA) can handle unequal group sizes. Researchers must take into account the inequality of sizes. For example, the smallest group size determines the precisions of estimates. The independence of the samples is also an issue. For instance, matched pairs of graduates and supervisors are used when an academic program wants to know the graduates' perspectives on the quality of the education and the supervisors' perspectives on the capabilities of graduates.

Techniques for Qualitative Data Analysis

Grounded Theory

Grounded theory is commonly used to analyze qualitative data. Researchers using grounded theory code, categorize, and compare their data. Grounded theory refers both to the theories generated using this technique and the technique itself. The term evolved because its early users spoke of their work being "grounded in data." Thus, the term emphasizes that the data generate the theories.

Grounded theory is an iterative or cyclical process. During data collection, researchers using grounded theory record and code their observations (called incidents). However, analysis begins during data collection. From the analysis, the researchers begin creating conceptual categories to fit their data. Both data collection and analysis may uncover gaps or discrepancies that require additional data collection or participants. The grounded theory technique has four stages:

1. Comparing incidents applicable to each category (includes comparing categories' relationships)
2. Integrating categories and their properties (cyclical process)
3. Delimiting theory (reducing and integrating core categories, tying theory to core categories, and achieving higher-level conceptualizations)
4. Writing theory (validating theory by pinpointing data behind it) (Glaser 1965, 439–443)

Development of grounded theory consists of intertwined and concurrent data collection, data coding, categorization, and analysis. Because of the constant analysis and comparisons of categories, the theory and technique are sometimes called *constant comparative method*.

This process results in complex theories that fit the data closely. In grounded theory, researchers seek to develop theories that are unique to groups or settings, unlike quantitative researchers, who seek to develop theories that are generalizable.

Content Analysis

Content analysis is the systematic and objective analysis of communication. Most often, researchers analyze written documentation. However, they may analyze other modes of communication, such as speech, body language, music, television shows, commercials, and movies. The purpose of content analysis is to describe and to make inferences and predictions about communication and its characteristics. Consumer groups who notify the public about the "most violent" or the "most sexually graphic" shows on television have used content analysis to compile their reports.

Researchers code the text or other means of communication. Coding is the labeling of words or word groups (segments) with annotations or scales. These labels are characteristics of the segments. To assess reliability, the agreement between and among coders may be checked. From the coding, researchers identify key terms, characteristics, or other attributes. The coded text (or communication) becomes the data. The data are then categorized into overarching themes. Some researchers also tabulate the frequency of coded data. Content analysis is "essentially a coding operation" (Babbie 2004, 318).

Healthcare personnel use content analysis. For example, researchers at a library of an academic health center conducted a study on the process of information retrieval (Crystal and Greenberg 2006, 1368). Specifically, the researchers explored how users judged the relevance of health information on the web (Crystal and Greenberg 2006, 1368). The researchers explained that developers of search engines need to understand the criteria that users employ to judge the relevance of their "hits" (Crystal and Greenberg 2006, 1368). Given that searchers generate thousands to millions of "hits," developing search engines that make the process more efficient than the current process would serve users. The 12 participants in the study were students and various types of professionals. The participants searched the web on 12 different health-related topics (Crystal and Greenberg 2006, 1372). The researchers helped the participants develop suitable queries, such as "health effects power lines," "cell phone cancer," "asthma car exhaust," "lead poisoning," and "pesticide risk developing countries" (Crystal and Greenberg 2006, 1372, 1382). The participants searched both surrogates (researcher developed mock document summaries) and the web. The participants highlighted with their mouse any terms of interest. Additionally, the participants' interactions with the search engines were video captured (Crystal and Greenberg 2006, 1372). After the

search, the researchers conducted and audiotaped "think-aloud" sessions with the participants. In these sessions, as the researchers and the participants jointly viewed the video record, the participants described their reactions to the document or summary. Finally, the researchers performed content analysis on the video logs and the audio tapes (Crystal and Greenberg 2006, 1373). The researchers found that the participants used many diverse stratagems. The researchers classified the stratagems into categories. These categories were the participants' criteria for assessing the relevance of the web document. The most common criterion was topic (Crystal and Greenberg 2006, 1378). Other criteria included affiliation (such as institution), authority (such as author or reference), and scope category (such as level or audience) (Crystal and Greenberg 2006, 1375). The researchers concluded that web search engines could be improved by incorporating the criteria upon which users tend to rely (Crystal and Greenberg 2006, 1380–1381).

Statistical Software Packages

Many software packages are available to assist researchers in the analysis of quantitative and qualitative data. For basic descriptive statistics, researchers can use spreadsheet software, such as Excel. However, most researchers will choose to use dedicated analytical packages because these packages require less manipulation of the data than spreadsheet packages and because they perform many more analytical procedures. Other factors that influence the choice of software are type of data, planned analytical techniques, and cost.

Quantitative

Several software packages are commonly used to analyze data in quantitative studies. Freeware is also available on the web, such as Amelia II. Amelia II includes the statistical technique of multiple imputation.

- Epi-Info is freeware from the Centers for Disease Control and Prevention. This integrated package, which includes word processing, database, and statistics, is designed for public health. The software allows the handling of epidemiological data in questionnaire format, calculating the required sample size, analyzing data, and presenting results.
- LISREL is a software package that conducts factor analysis. Factor analysis is used to evaluate the psychometric properties of measurement instruments. LISREL generates test statistics. For example, researchers used LISREL to evaluate the properties of a psychological test that predicts suicidal behavior (Aish and Wasserman 2001, 368).
- STATISTICA is a suite of analytical software. The suite provides a comprehensive array of software for data analysis, data management, data visualization, and data mining procedures. The suite includes techniques for predictive modeling, clustering, classification, and exploration.

- Statistical Analysis System (SAS) is a powerful software package that integrates data access, data management, data analysis, and data presentation. Researchers use SAS to enter data, retrieve and manage data, analyze data with statistical and mathematical techniques, write reports, and generate graphics.
- Statistical Package for Social Sciences (SPSS) offers a broad array of analytical and graphic software. Its many components range from basic statistical techniques to advanced, specialized techniques. The basic statistics package performs counts and cross-tabs. Advanced techniques include factor analysis, regression, cluster analysis, binomial and multinomial logistic regression, and correspondence analysis.

Qualitative

Analytical software exists for qualitative studies. These software support the analysis of the multitudes of data in multiple media obtained during qualitative studies.

- ATLAS.ti is used to code and analyze text-based data from open-ended surveys, transcriptions of focus groups, or other sources. ATLAS.ti can be used to code other types of qualitative data, such as photographs. ATLAS.ti allows the retrieval of specific information based on search criteria. ATLAS.ti also has the ability to export data as an SPSS data set.
- CDC EZ-Text is a free software program from the US Centers for Disease Control and Prevention (CDC). EZ-Text assists researchers to create, manage, and analyze semistructured qualitative databases. Investigators can use the software to enter data, create online code books, apply codes to specific response packages, develop case studies, conduct database searches to identify text passages, and export data in a wide array of formats for future analysis with other analytical software programs.
- Code-A-Text Integrated System for the Analysis of Interviews and Dialogues (C-I-SAID) is used to code, to label, and to analyze documents, transcripts, and sound files. This software allows researchers to specify codes and labels and to insert them into the document or sound file. Coded content of documents, transcripts, and sound files then can be analyzed. C-I-SAID produces descriptive statistics and tables and charts that support analysis. The software also assists researchers in categorizing the segments into themes, known as content analysis. C-I-SAID can be applied to field notes, open-ended questionnaires, and interviews. A multimedia version codes video and pictures.
- NVivo is a software that is used to analyze unstructured, qualitative data. It is used to code and analyze text-based data from open-ended surveys, transcriptions of focus groups, or other sources. NVivo allows researchers to retrieve specific quotes based on search criteria. The software can also create tabular data

representing the counts of specific codes. The data can be exported to quantitative statistical packages.

In summary, analytical software packages exist for both quantitative and qualitative researchers. Researchers are encouraged to explore the capabilities of several packages. The choice of software depends on the type of data, the planned analytical techniques, and skills of the researcher.

Check Your Understanding 20.7

Instructions: Answer the following questions on a separate piece of paper.

1. How do descriptive and inferential statistics differ?
2. How many variables do bivariate statistical techniques involve?
3. What inferential statistical techniques emphasize differences in groups?
4. What are two types of continuous data?
5. Why must researchers know the type of data they are collecting?
6. Why might a researcher use Epi-Info as his or her statistical package?

Presenting Results

Researchers follow a two-step process when presenting their results. In the first step, they report their research findings with no commentary, explanation, or interpretation. This section of a manuscript is called research findings. In the second step, the researchers comment on, explain, and interpret their findings. This section of the manuscript is called discussion. Also included in the discussion are conclusions and recommendations for future research.

Researchers describe their results in the past tense; general truths are stated in the present tense. The style of writing for scientific manuscripts is objective, precise, and factual. Researchers avoid subjective interjections and emotional hyperbole. In the research findings, researchers must be careful to maintain a neutral tone. They are merely recording their findings in narrative form.

In research findings, researchers describe the results for each hypothesis. Restating the hypothesis aids the readers. Researchers state whether or not the results support the hypotheses. They also record characteristics about the sample and describe the results of the statistical analyses that investigate whether the sample is similar to or different from the population. Supplemental statistical analyses also are described. Researchers are careful to use the term *statistical significance*, as appropriate (refer to table 20.9).

For research findings, researchers generate tables and graphs to support the readers' understanding of their findings. (See chapter 18 for more detailed descriptions of

Figure 20.15.   Considerations for effective graphics

- Tables, graphs, and figures have titles.
- Tables have stubheads, spanner heads, and column heads for clarification.
- Sources are cited.
- Time frames and dates are noted.
- Multiple tables, charts, graphs, and figures are numbered.
- Both axes of graphs are labeled (bar titles, legends, scale captions).
- Keys show the meaning of shadings and colors.
- Scales start at zero.
- Wedges (slices) of a pie chart represent percentages, and the percentages convert to 360 degrees.
- Graphics are for emphasis; do not dilute the effect with clutter.

some common tables and graphs.) One rule of thumb is that data should be presented in only one way or mode (Day and Gastel 2011, 92). Researchers should present the particular data element in narrative text, in a table, or in a figure, but not in multiple modes. Graphics should clarify the data, not confuse the readers. Figure 20.15 lists 10 important points to remember when constructing graphics. Researchers must carefully consider which mode of communication is most effective for the particular data element. For example,

- *Tables* summarize data in a grid or matrix. The elements and numbers should be in the columns, not in the rows.
- *Pie charts* with their segments visually show the relationships among variables and the whole. They also can represent categorical data.
- *Bar charts* show comparisons between and among items. They often illustrate major characteristics in the distribution of data (male or female, age ranges). They can be used to represent categorical, nominal, or ordinal data.
- *Line charts* show comparisons over time.
- *Histograms* are similar to bar charts. They show major characteristics in the distribution of data and summarize data about variables whose values are numerical and measured on an interval scale. Histograms are used for large data sets.

Writing the discussion section requires energy and creativity. Too often, researchers shortchange this section. The discussion section is not a superficial repetition of the findings section. Rather, it is where researchers create new knowledge.

In the discussion section, researchers should compare their findings to the findings in the literature, explaining similarities and discrepancies. More important, they should provide some rationale to explain why their findings were the same or different. In writing this section, researchers should return to why they conducted the study in the first place. They should answer the following questions:

- What theoretical significance do their findings have?
- What practical significance do their findings have? (Refer to table 20.9.)
- How do their findings explicitly link to the larger body of knowledge?
- How have their findings improved the field's research model?
- How have their findings expanded the body of knowledge?
- What new definitions have they added to the field's area of practice?
- How do their findings support practitioners in the workplace?
- What problems do their findings solve?
- What valid conclusions can the researchers and the readers draw?

Researchers also state their assumptions and the limitations of their research. A researcher describing a questionnaire study might state that one assumption is that people are honest and that one limitation is that the study only reflects one point in time. Also, research always raises new questions. These new questions become the recommendations for further research.

The discussion section closes the presentation of the findings. To accurately represent the time and effort that went into the research study, the discussion section should be rich and insightful. Sufficient time for reflection and contemplation should be scheduled into the research plan. The researchers' goal should be to put usable information into the hands of practitioners in the workplace.

Disseminating Research

Knowledge is disseminated and examined through poster sessions, presentations at professional meetings, and journal articles. Researchers have an ethical obligation to disseminate their research because this new knowledge advances the health information profession and helps practitioners in the workplace. It is only common sense that in order for the researchers' information to be useful, it must be available and accessible to practitioners.

Poster sessions and presentations occur at professional meetings, conferences, and symposia. Often these events have been planned far in advance. Up to 12 months before a professional meeting, professional associations will issue a call for session proposals. (See figure 20.16.) In response to the call, researchers send brief descriptions of their proposed session. The meeting planners determine which proposals to accept based on the quality, number, and relevance of the topic to the theme of the conference.

Figure 20.16.   Sample call for proposals

Call for Research Abstracts
Deadline for Abstracts: January 1, 20XX.

   Abstracts for the Summer Symposium are being solicited.
Topics:

• Workforce initiatives

• Innovations in service delivery

• Organizational or administrative issues in healthcare
  enterprises

• HIM best practices or performance improvement

• E-health implementations

Content of the research abstract should include

• Title of presentation

• Name(s) of author(s) with title, credentials, and organization

• Method

• Brief results

Abstracts should be limited to 250 words. To be considered,
abstracts must be submitted by January 1, 20XX via the online
submission form on the symposium website, www.fictitious-
URL.org/symposium 20XX. (Questions should be sent to
Liz Qualef at the e-mail address listed at the bottom of this
message.)

Selection of abstracts will be made through a peer-reviewed
process.

Authors of accepted abstracts will then be asked to submit the
complete scholarly paper by February 15, 20XX. Scholarly
papers will be published in *Symposium Proceedings*. Content
for the scholarly paper includes (a) abstract; (b) title; (c)
name(s) of author(s) with title, credentials, and organization;
(d) literature review; (e) purpose or problem statement;
(f) methods including analytical technique; (g) results; (h)
discussion; and (i) conclusions and recommendations for future
research.

Authors of accepted papers will also be asked to submit
handouts for their presentation. The deadline for handouts is
April 15. Presentations will be limited to 12 minutes, inclusive
of questions. Due to the time constraints, authors are asked
to focus their presentation and corresponding handouts on
the sections of Results, Discussion, and Conclusions. For
reference, interested parties will have the entire scholarly paper
in the *Symposium Proceedings*.

For authors of accepted abstracts, half the symposium
registration fee will be waived.

Address to submit Research Abstracts:

Liz Qualef, PhD, RHIA
Professor and Chair
Blank University
Department of Health Information Management
School of Allied Health Sciences
City, ST 12345
School Fax: 252.428.XXXX
E-mail: qualefl@xxxx.edu

Poster Sessions

Researchers must conform to poster guidelines when participating in a poster session. Prior to the event, meeting
planners send out the requirements for the poster. These
requirements state the size of the poster. Common size
requirements are often three feet by five feet or four feet
by six feet. Meeting planners will also state the session's
time slot on the meeting agenda. Typically, poster sessions
are three to five hours on one day. During that time, the
researcher stands near the poster and answers questions
about the research study.

Institutional printing departments offer services that
enhance posters. Commercial printing companies with
staffs of commercial artists and graphic designers also will
print the posters. Researchers need to submit word documents or PowerPoint slides. Websites that offer printing of
posters may be a cost-effective alternative. These websites
may have templates that researchers can use. Posters typically include

- Banner (header) with title of study, names of
  researchers, and institutional affiliation
- Abstract
- Purpose
- Method
- Results
- Discussion and conclusions

Posters should be colorful and readable at 10 feet. Charts
and graphics are particularly striking. The posters can
be laminated or mounted on poster board. Moreover, the
researcher should take the time necessary to create a poster
that looks professional.

Presentation

Professional presentations occur during sessions of regional,
state, national, and international meetings. As described previously, researchers submit proposals in response to a call.
Linking the response to the theme of the meeting increases
the likelihood that the proposal will be accepted.

Presenters should remember their audience as they
create and present their papers and PowerPoint slides. One
researcher conducted research on the delivery of research
papers (Edirisooriya 1996, 25). Over seven years, she attended
126 sessions and viewed 748 presenters. Most presenters
were allowed 12 minutes and found this limit inadequate.
She found that 42 percent of presenters had not synthesized
their data into information and, thus, wasted their time on
unnecessary and trivial details (Edirisooriya 1996, 27).
These presenters never reached the important points of their
research. Edirisooriya recommended that presenters prepare
for oral presentations by

- Practicing their presentation
- Bringing all their materials
- Distilling their paper to four or five pages

Figure 20.17.   Guidelines for effective PowerPoint presentations

- High contrast for visibility (black text on white background or dark blue background with white text and yellow highlights)
- Lots of white space
- Six-by-six rule (six words per line, six lines per slide)
- Upper- and lowercase (all caps hard to read)
- 18 minimum point size (24 recommended and 28 to 36 preferable)
- Two inches character height for every 20 feet between visual and audience
- Clear, simple fonts (Helvetica or Ariel)
- Colors limited to 2 or 3
- Colors' subliminal messages ("in the red")
- Red-green color blindness
- Color opposites on color wheel create "shimmer"
- Transitions limited to 1 or 2 and nondistracting
- Overuse of sounds annoying
- Bullets are points of the outline
- No paragraphs
- Consistent verb tenses
- Consistent tense of first words of parallel lines
- Simple graphs
- Proofread for spelling, math, grammar, numbering
- Handouts should have three slides and room for notes

- Showing eye-catching graphics (not tables with miniscule numbers)
- Focusing on results, discussion, and implications rather than background, theoretical framework, and rationales for analytical techniques

A more recent article reiterated these ideas for effective presentations (Wineburg 2004, 13–14). Generally, presenters should be prepared to talk about their research. Merely reading the notes is inadequate. Rather, presenters should try to be animated and talk to the people in the room. Other details regarding the mechanics of creating an effective PowerPoint presentation are listed in figure 20.17.

Publication

Publication is important because it makes knowledge public. Practitioners, other researchers, and professionals in related fields can examine and critically analyze the research. Through publication, the HIM body of knowledge and the expertise of its professionals become available to the world.

Scientific manuscripts commonly are organized in a prescribed structure. An unpublished paper is known as a *manuscript*. A manuscript or paper that has been published in a journal is known as an *article*. The prescribed structure of scientific papers is called *IMRAD* (introduction, methods, results, and discussion) (Sollaci and Pereira 2004, 364).

This chapter has moved through the steps of research. In each step, the associated documentation is described. This documentation correlates with many sections of a research paper or journal article, including

- Problem statement (introduction)
- Literature review
- Statement of hypothesis
- Method
- Results (including discussion)

At this time, the researcher must complete the documentation by writing the abstract and expanding and detailing the sections already written.

It seems strange that the abstract, the first section of a journal article, is written last. However, the abstract is written last because it encompasses the entire study, including the study's findings.

An abstract is a brief summary of the major parts of a research study. It only reports the contents of the research; no additional information is included. An abstract is important because it is used in bibliographic databases to index and retrieve an article. Readers use it to decide whether the article contains valuable information and whether they should read the entire article. In writing an abstract, an author should focus on the research's important information, objectives, results, and conclusions. Brevity and directness are keys to a good abstract.

Table 20.15 serves as a final checklist for the composition and revision of the manuscript. Authors submitting manuscripts to journals in the field of health information management should take note that the peer reviewers highly value the following characteristics of manuscripts: (1) accuracy, (2) potential for contribution, (3) reasonableness of conclusions, (4) readability and style, and (5) organization (Layman and Watzlaf 2003, 61). Common pitfalls are listed in figure 20.18. Careful attention to detail at this point has a high return on investment in terms of having journals accept the manuscripts. In preparing their manuscript for publication, researchers face two major remaining tasks: selecting the appropriate journal and following its submission guidelines.

Selecting the Appropriate Journal

Selecting the appropriate journal requires thought and investigation. Depending on the topic, researchers should consider journals in other disciplines, such as informatics, computer science, public health, epidemiology, healthcare management, allied health, nursing, bioethics, health services, health policy, and health education. As mentioned earlier, in health information management, research is published in two journals: the *Journal of the American Health Information Management Association* (*Journal of AHIMA*) and *Perspectives in Health Information Management* (*PHIM*).

Table 20.15. Organization of research publications

Section	Contents
Title Page	Concise and descriptive title, author, author's affiliation, grant information, disclaimer, corresponding author's address, telephone, fax, and e-mail
Abstract	Background, purpose, methods, results, conclusions or Context; objective; design, setting, and participants; interventions; main outcome measures; results, conclusions 45 to 250 words dependent upon call for papers or journal instructions 3 to 10 key words using medical subject headings (MeSH)
Introduction	Background; pertinent literature review that provides rationale for research; brief statement of research plan; purpose, objectives, or research question
Methods	Protocol with detail for replication Design, setting, and participants Definition of variables Reference to established methods Sampling strategy Collection of data Statement about approval of IRB or other oversight entity Analytical strategy
Results	Core Important results followed by less important results Neutral reporting
Discussion	Relationship between results and purpose, objectives, or research question Evidence of relationship Similarities to and differences from previous research New knowledge in terms of theoretical framework Limitations Conclusions as related to purpose, objectives, or research question Implications for future research Recommendations as warranted Summary
Acknowledgment	Contributors whose level of involvement does not justify authorship
References	Citations per format in instructions
Tables	Consistent with narrative Expand abbreviations Format per instructions
Figures	Consistent with narrative Expand abbreviations Legend Format per instructions

Figure 20.18. Pitfalls in presenting research

- Allowing insufficient time to write the results or to develop the presentation
- Interjecting subjective commentary and emotional hyperbole
- Duplicating information in narrative and graphic forms
- Creating confusing or inconsistent graphics
- Believing that verbosity and inflated statements substitute for clarity and accuracy

Researchers can obtain lists of journals from a college or university library. They may also want to spend time at the library skimming through a number of journals. Reviewing the journals allows them to determine the journals' mission, foci, and audiences. This determination allows them to match their purpose, topic, research design, and style to the journal's scope, content, and audience.

First, researchers should determine their purpose. Is it altruism, service, or scholarship? Certain journals are better suited to one purpose than another. For example, some journals have a practice orientation and others have a research orientation.

For altruism and service, researchers may send their manuscripts to journals oriented to practice, such as the *Journal of AHIMA*. The researchers want to help their profession by putting effective techniques into the hands of practitioners. For example, if the researcher found that a particular graphical interface increased coder accuracy by 10 percent, he or she may decide to send that manuscript to the *Journal of AHIMA*.

In addition to altruism and service, some researchers want to advance scholarship in health information management. These researchers are building the field's body of knowledge. To build a body of knowledge, publication in high-quality journals is essential. Quality, however, is not easily quantified and is more difficult to determine. For journals, direct measures of quality include

- Being referenced in bibliographic databases, such as MEDLINE
- Having high rejection rates
- Scoring high impact factors (rate of citation of the journal's articles in a year)
- Being refereed

An indirect measure is the prestige of the journal. Prestige is the field's members' general opinion of the journal in comparison to other journals in the discipline. Thus, researchers publishing for scholarship should consider indexed and refereed journals with high rejection rates and high impact factors.

Second, researchers should match the content of their manuscript with the focus of the journal. For example, they should send manuscripts about research on the management of health information services to journals in the field of health information management. If their results have an impact on reimbursement or health policy, the researchers should consider journals with a broader base.

Third, researchers must match the design and method of their research to the types of designs and methods in the journal. Some journals include mostly experimental and quasi-experimental research; others include ethnographies, case studies, and personal histories. Researchers who match the design and method of their study with the typical designs and methods in the journal increase the likelihood of their manuscripts being accepted.

Fourth, researchers should strive for a match between their writing style and the preferences of the journal's audience. Journals that are oriented toward practice prefer brief articles written in simple, direct sentences. On the other hand, journals oriented toward scholarly work prefer a more formal and pedantic tone.

Finally, understanding the journal's audience combines the issues of topic and design. Researchers should submit their manuscripts to journals with audiences that would be

Figure 20.19.   Common style manuals

American Psychological Association. 2010. *Publication Manual of the American Psychological Association,* 5th ed. Washington, DC: APA. [Referred to as **APA style.**]

Gibaldi, J. 2009. *MLA Handbook for Writers of Research Papers,* 6th ed. New York: Modern Language Association of America. [Referred to as **MLA style.**]

Iverson, C. ed., 2007. *American Medical Association Manual of Style: A Guide for Authors and Editors,* 10th ed. New York: Oxford University Press. [Referred to as **AMA style.**]

University of Chicago Press. 2010. *Chicago Manual of Style,* 16th ed. Chicago: University of Chicago Press. [Referred to as **Chicago style.**]

interested in the topic. If the intended audience includes a broad range of fields, researchers should write manuscripts that are of interest to all potential readers. Moreover, researchers should clearly state how their manuscript affects and benefits the journal's intended audience.

Following the Journal's Submission Guidelines

Journals have rules for the format of manuscripts. The rules are both explicit and implicit. Explicit rules are openly stated; implicit rules are unwritten, but important. Editors and peer reviewers assume that researchers will naturally know and follow them. Different fields tend to have their own unique sets of implicit rules.

Journal editors state their explicit requirements for manuscripts in their style manual and submission guidelines. There are four common style manuals. (See figure 20.19.) Selection of style manual relates to the field. For example, journals in education generally require APA style whereas biomedical journals require AMA style. Journals in health information management use an adapted Chicago style. The variance in style manuals is illustrated in table 20.16.

The journal's submission guidelines include details such as the word-processing package, width of margins, length, and organizational structure. (See figure 20.20.) For instance, the editors of *PHIM* prefer an organizational structure that generally includes the following elements:

- Abstract (150 words or less and up to 10 key words)
- Introduction
- Background (literature review)
- Research question or hypothesis
- Methods
- Results
- Discussion
- Conclusion
- References

However, most editors state that the organizational structure is flexible and that researchers should adapt the structure to suit their research. Researchers can find guidelines in journals or on the publishers' websites.

Table 20.16. Variation in style manuals

Organization	Book	Journal
AMA	Jencks C, Riesman D. *The Academic Revolution.* Chicago: University of Chicago Press; 1977.	Lloyd SC, Layman E. The effects of automated encoders on coding accuracy and coding speed. *Top Health Inf Manage* February 1997; 17(3): 72–79.
APA	Jencks, C., & Riesman, D. (1977). *The academic revolution.* Chicago: University of Chicago Press.	Lloyd, S. C., & Layman, E. (1997, February). The effects of automated encoders on coding accuracy and coding speed. Topics in *Health Information Management,* 17(3), 72–79.
Chicago	Jencks, Christopher, and David Riesman. 1977. *The Academic Revolution.* Chicago: University of Chicago Press.	Lloyd, Susan C., and Elizabeth Layman. 1997. "The Effects of Automated Encoders on Coding Accuracy and Coding Speed." *Topics in Health Information Management* 17 (3): 72–79.
MLA	Jencks, Christopher, and David Riesman. *The Academic Revolution.* Chicago: University of Chicago Press, 1977.	Lloyd, Susan C., and Elizabeth Layman. "The Effects of Automated Encoders on Coding Accuracy and Coding Speed." *Topics in Health Information Management* 17.3 (1997): 72–79.

Figure 20.20. Content of submission guidelines

- Information needed about the author and contact
- Style manual
- Length and representativeness of title
- Length of abstract in words
- Length of manuscript in maximum number of pages or number of words
- Font and font size
- Line spacing
- Justification
- Margins
- Pagination
- Inclusive (nonsexist) language
- Blinding (names of authors on separate page)
- Format of charts and tables
- Format of citations in text
- Format of references (sometimes vary slightly from style manual)
- General organizational structure of manuscript
- Word-processing software
- Number of paper copies
- Diskette or electronic submission

A journal's implicit rules reflect the culture of its audience. Culture is reflected in the use of the first person, anthropomorphism, passive voice, and tone. For example, an audience of qualitative researchers would accept use of the first person whereas its use probably would cause an audience of experimental researchers to doubt the article's credibility. Purists reject anthropomorphism as giving human traits to inanimate objects. Audiences that reject first person and anthropomorphism also tend to prefer passive voice and a detached, neutral tone. Time spent skimming journals would provide insight into their implicit rules.

Some editors and peer reviewers assume that sloppy writing indicates sloppy research. Moreover, some editors and peer reviewers believe that the inability to follow submission guidelines indicates the inability to follow research protocols. Therefore, attention to detail is important. Researchers seeking more information about writing and publishing manuscripts should read the style manuals and review samples of submission guidelines. For grammar and clarity, Strunk and White's (2000) book on writing is a classic. First published in 1959 and periodically revised, its succinct discussions and precise examples provide clear guidance. Finally, researchers should carefully read *How to Write and Publish a Scientific Paper* by Day and Gastel (2011), which is dedicated to research writing and publishing.

Check Your Understanding 20.8

Instructions: Answer the following questions on a separate piece of paper.

1. How do the research findings and discussion sections differ?
2. What two factors should researchers consider when determining how to present a particular data element?
3. What three questions should a researcher answer when writing the discussion section?
4. What three factors should researchers consider when selecting a journal for manuscript submission?

Data Access and Confidentiality

When they access data, researchers pledge that they will keep them confidential. In their code of ethics, HIM professionals affirm that they will "uphold and defend the individual's right to privacy and the doctrine of confidentiality in the use and disclosure of information." This section describes the intersection of data access and protection of confidentiality.

Practical Considerations

Access to data depends on the type of data and their location. Data can range from totally uncontrolled to highly protected. For example, data on the Internet are easily accessed whereas data in health records require approvals from IRBs.

Data can be public or proprietary. Public data are often accessible under the Freedom of Information Act; some have been posted on the Internet. State registry data also are often accessible. Proprietary data require permission of the owner of the database.

Data can be individual or aggregate. Data that identify one individual are less accessible than aggregate data. Protections exist for identifiable data. To use identifiable data, researchers must obtain approvals from all involved IRBs. For example, researchers may need to obtain the approval of the IRB of the university where they work and from the IRB of the healthcare organization from which they received the identifiable data. Some organizations may require informed consents to review data. In addition, access to personally identifiable data has become more complex with the implementation of HIPAA. (See chapter 21 for additional information.)

After approvals or permissions are obtained, the location of data also affects ease of access. For data in databases, researchers can transfer the files over the Internet. For paper records, researchers must physically go to the site of storage where they must abide by the hours of operation and rules for security. In addition, they must arrange in some way to collect their data, for example, by entering them into a laptop.

Access to data becomes critical for researchers who conduct secondary analyses or combine their primary research with public databases. When using large databases for secondary analysis, researchers should know whether the database is public or proprietary, whether the data are individual or aggregate, and the means of access. In all cases, they will need to obtain approvals or permissions from relevant oversight entities and, in the case of individually identifiable data, additional approvals or permissions may be required. The key points for researchers who want to mine these rich data resources are obtaining the approvals and allowing sufficient time.

Confidentiality

Confidentiality and anonymity are closely related concepts. *Confidentiality* pertains to the handling and maintenance of data so that the data are not divulged to others without the research participant's permission or divulged in ways contrary to the participant's understanding of the original disclosure. *Anonymity* pertains to data that have no identifiers linked to them and that cannot be traced back to the research participant.

Thus, confidentiality and anonymity are not synonymous and cannot be used interchangeably. Researchers must be careful in their use of the terms and not promise the more stringent concept of anonymity when they mean confidentiality.

The HIPAA regulations and its clauses related to deidentified data revolve around the concepts of confidentiality and anonymity.

Medical research, and by extension many other types of research in the United States, is covered under the Federal Policy for the Protection of Human Subjects (45 *CFR* Part 46, subparts A through D) (Office for Human Research Protections n.d.). This federal policy is a set of regulations regarding research that 18 federal agencies share (NSF 2008). Because this federal policy is shared among many agencies, it is also known as the **Common Rule**. These agencies fund research at institutions that provide written assurance to the funding agency that the institutions will comply with the requirements of the Common Rule.

At a minimum, the Common Rule requires the following (Burrington-Brown and Wagg 2003, 56A):

- Institutional statement of principles regarding the institution's responsibilities in the protection of human subjects involved in its research studies
- IRB with sufficient staff
- List of IRB members that demonstrates representative capacity to contribute to IRB deliberations
- Written procedures that the IRB follows for reviewing proposed research and ongoing oversight
- Written procedures that ensure prompt reporting of unanticipated problems, serious or continuing noncompliance, and suspension or termination of IRB approval

Institutions that are covered entities under HIPAA and that conduct federally funded research must comply with the regulations of both HIPAA and the Common Rule. The regulations of HIPAA articulate with the Common Rule. For example, under the Common Rule, researchers must obtain informed consent. HIPAA adds that the researcher also must obtain a signed authorization before protected health information may be used or disclosed for research. Further, HIPAA expands the role of the IRB by giving it authority, under specific stipulations, to approve waivers or alterations to the requirement to obtain authorization.

Health data that have been deidentified may be used without restriction for research purposes. However, the IRB must ensure that the data have been deidentified in the correct manner, that is, deidentified using statistical verification or all of the following identifiers removed: names, addresses (except state), date (except year), telephone and fax numbers, e-mail addresses, Social Security numbers, health record numbers, health plan numbers, account numbers, certificate and license numbers, vehicle identifiers and serial numbers, device identifiers and serial numbers, URLs, IP addresses, biometric identifiers, full-face photographic images, and any other unique identifying number, characteristic, or code unless permitted by the privacy rule for reidentification (Gilles 2004, 52).

A disadvantage to using deidentified data is that contacting the patient or client to improve the response rate or to notify the patient about some malfunction of a device or side effect of a drug is impossible.

Researchers who are preparing to conduct research with health information are encouraged to read the in-depth discussions provided by Burrington-Brown and Wagg (2003), Gilles (2004), and Roth (2004a, 2004b, 2004c). Finally, researchers should familiarize themselves with state laws protecting privacy. Some state laws are more restrictive than HIPAA. Researchers must comply with the more restrictive regulations.

Research and the Practitioner

Research is a potential career for HIM professionals, according to Biedermann and Burrington-Brown (2004, 44), who state that "HIM professionals are naturals for careers in research." Moreover, an HIM researcher describes how HIM professionals can incorporate research into their roles as leaders of HIM services departments (Watzlaf 1995, 47–48). In practice, the roles of HIM professionals in research sort into four types:

- Researcher
- Support staff to researchers in healthcare organizations or health-related settings
- Employee of a research company or agency
- User of research in implementations of best practices in the workplace or in continuing education

First, many HIM professionals are researchers. They conduct research for several reasons, including service to the profession, personal interest, and condition of employment. HIM researchers have been involved in a wide array of research projects, such as

- Developing a web-based reporting system for medication errors
- Coordinating a statewide patient safety education program
- Developing an information infrastructure to link rural hospitals to a tertiary care center (Bailey and Rudman 2004, 2)

Additionally, many of the citations in this chapter represent HIM professionals in the role of researcher.

Second, HIM professionals in the health information services departments of healthcare enterprises assist researchers in many ways, including

- Assisting members of IRBs in the review of proposed studies that relate to data in health databases or paper records
- Evaluating and summarizing for administration the content of proposed studies that relate to data in health databases or paper records
- Identifying the location of the desired health data in databases, records, logs, reports, registers, or indexes
- Directing researchers and other authorized users to the location of health data

- Discussing with researchers the format of the data, such as paper records, microfilm, microfiche, and database
- Noting caveats, such as time frames and residual codes, related to the data
- Running computer queries to find cases
- Arranging access to computer databases and paper records
- Managing the work area reserved for researchers
- Obtaining signed confidentiality statements

Third, HIM professionals are employees of research companies or agencies. Research companies conduct various research-related activities, such as clinical trials or development of new pharmaceuticals. Research agencies often provide outcomes research that supports policymaking in healthcare. In these settings, HIM professionals may be responsible for collecting and coding data, managing clinical databases and protocols, providing decision support, and writing reports. HIM researchers note that these positions "blend [HIM] professional, clinical, and research skills with knowledge of business operations and insight into management of information systems" (Bailey and Rudman 2004, 2).

All HIM professionals can use the steps of research. Research provides a thorough, systematic approach. The problem-solving models of management and the decision-making models of decision sciences are based on the steps of research. Therefore, the logic of the approach allows HIM professionals to use research in their day-to-day activities. To find answers to common questions or solutions to everyday problems, research is a practical and effective tool. In the long term, the orderliness of the step-by-step approach saves time and results in the best decision.

Research results are made public in professional presentations, proceedings of meetings, and journals. The availability and accessibility of these results allow all HIM professionals to benefit. HIM professionals can put the results of the research into practice. For example, as a consequence of the medical sociologist's research on the chatter about patients in hospital elevators, orientation sessions specifically address the need to maintain confidentiality in all conversations and in all settings.

Relationship with the Professional Body of Knowledge

One of the defining characteristics of a profession is that it has a body of knowledge. By definition, a field of work without a body of knowledge becomes an occupation or a job. Therefore, as a means to build and expand knowledge, research is the foundation of a profession.

As an emerging profession, health information management is developing and articulating its body of knowledge. Leaders of AHIMA recognize the importance of knowledge in advancing practice and professional learning (Kloss 2000, 27). HIM professionals are conducting research in issues and topics

Figure 20.21.   Research topics in HIM

Compliance	Best practices in health
Use of computer applications	information services
in HIM education	Unique HIM instructional
Information security	techniques
Distance learning	Information technology
Vocabularies and	Adoption and implementation
terminologies	of electronic health record
Clinical education	Role of technology in
Management issues	healthcare
Graduate education	Quality and use of coded data
Workforce retention and	Impact of data quality in
satisfaction	health outcomes
Impact of HIPAA	Data mining
Managed care	
HIM curricular changes and	
their effectiveness	

related to health information. These topics and issues involve health information technology and systems, health data security and quality, management, benchmarks in practice and education, and informatics. (See figure 20.21.) This research is defining, expanding, and refining the body of knowledge for the HIM profession.

Use in HIM Practice: Evaluating Published Research Findings

HIM practitioners can use research to improve their department's efficiency and effectiveness. They also can use research to improve their own performance as managers and administrators. But which research results should they rely on? This section gives HIM practitioners pointers and information on how to identify high-quality data in research reports.

Evaluating research begins with carefully, critically, and analytically reading the journal article. Cohen (1991) provides questions that analytical readers of research should ask themselves. (See figure 20.22.)

As a demonstration, these questions are applied here to a journal article in *Perspectives in Health Information Management*. In this published study HIM researchers conducted a study to measure the awareness, use, and validity of the minimum content for EHRs as recommended by the American Society for Testing and Materials (ASTM) (Watzlaf et al. 2004, 3).

1. Is the problem clearly stated? Are terms defined as needed? Has the problem been appropriately delimited?

   • Statements: *"Therefore, it is important to assess if those who purchase and use these systems are aware that these standards exist, and to measure the extent of usage of these standards. It will also be helpful to see if the content of the standards is meeting users'*

Figure 20.22.   Key questions to evaluate research

1. Is the problem clearly stated? Are terms defined as needed? Has the problem been appropriately delimited?

2. Is the hypothesis stated? Does the hypothesis relate to the problem? Is the way the researcher intends to test the hypothesis clear?

3. To the best of the student's knowledge, is the literature review thorough, complete, and pertinent? Is the literature review clear and organized? Is the student convinced this problem is important? Does the literature review synthesize rather than merely summarize?

4. Does the study's design relate to the problem? Is the population clearly defined? Is the method of creating the sample clearly explained? Is bias reduced in sampling? Is the sample representative of the population?

5. Is the instrument specified? Is the instrument related to the problem? Does the researcher state the instrument's reliability and validity?

6. Does the researcher explain the method clearly enough and with sufficient detail that another person could replicate the study? Are confidential data protected?

7. Does the researcher use the best mode to present the results? Do tables, figures, and graphs have clear titles? Do the numbers "add up"?

8. Do the conclusions relate to the findings? Does the researcher provide alternative explanations? Does the researcher relate the findings back to the larger body of knowledge or theory?

9. Are all citations in the body of the article in the reference list? Is jargon kept to a minimum?

Source: Cohen 1991.

needs, so future revisions can address any deficiencies or problem areas." "To our knowledge, no other survey-based study has been performed that examines the awareness, use, and fulfillment of users' needs of the most recent ASTM E1384 standards and E1633 coded values for the EHR."

   • Based on these statements, it appears the conditions of the first set of questions are met.

2. Is the hypothesis stated? Does the hypothesis relate to the problem? Is the way the researcher intends to test the hypothesis clear?

   • *"The study is descriptive. Because there is no intent to make inferences, no hypothesis is needed."*

   • The conditions of the second set of questions are not applicable.

3. To the best of the student's knowledge, is the literature review thorough, complete, and pertinent? Is the literature review clear and organized? Is the student

convinced this problem is important? Does the literature review synthesize rather than merely summarize?

- The authors explain the advantages of the EHR based on the *Standard Guide*. They cite Mary Brandt and Gretchen Murphy, AHIMA leaders. The authors also state, "*To our knowledge, no other survey-based study has been performed that examines the awareness, use, and fulfillment of users' needs of the most recent ASTM E1384 standards and E1633 coded values for the EHR.*" "*It is therefore important and timely to determine the awareness, use, and validity of the ASTM standards for the content and structure of EHRs and their corresponding coded values.*"

- The final statement is most convincing. Based on these statements and the citation of professional leaders, it appears the conditions of the third set of questions are met.

4. Does the study's design relate to the problem? Is the population clearly defined? Is the method of creating the sample clearly explained? Is bias reduced in sampling? Is the sample representative of the population?

- Yes, the design relates to the problem because there is little known on the topic. When little is known, the descriptive, cross-sectional design is appropriate. The population is stated in the article: US healthcare facilities identified by the American Hospital Association; vendors of EHR/Cardiopulmonary Resuscitation systems as identified in *Healthcare Informatics;* vendors reviewed by the American Academy of Family Physicians, volunteers, and organizations recognized by CPRI-HOST. Yes, sample creation is clearly explained.

- Stratified random sample (stratification by state and type) is representative of the population and it reduces bias.

5. Is the instrument specified? Is the instrument related to the problem? Does the researcher state the instrument's reliability and validity?

- The authors explain that they designed their own survey. The survey was piloted on a random sample of 5 to 10 facilities and organizations. To detect potential problems, two individuals were shadowed when completing the online survey. A draft of the survey was presented to the ASTM E1384 committee. Changes were made based on the comments. From the piloting it appears that the instrument relates to the problem. The instrument's reliability and validity were not stated. As a new instrument, reliability and validity would need to be established, particularly if the researchers wanted to use this instrument again. Based on this information, it appears the conditions of the fifth set of questions are partially met.

6. Does the researcher explain the method clearly enough and with sufficient detail that another person could replicate the study? Are confidential data protected?

- Yes, because the method is very detailed, another researcher could replicate this study. It does not appear that confidential data were obtained; however, the researchers did go through their IRB.

- Based on the clarity, I believe that the article meets the conditions of the sixth set of questions.

7. Does the researcher use the best mode to present the results? Do tables, figures, and graphs have clear titles? Do the numbers "add up"?

- Tables appear to be the best mode to present the results. Tables have clear titles. Authors explain when the numbers do not "add up."

- Tables contain lots of data and seem long. Perhaps selected findings relevant to the audience could have been extracted. Overall, the article appears to meet conditions of the seventh set of conditions.

8. Do the conclusions relate to the findings? Does the researcher provide alternative explanations? Does the researcher relate the findings back to the larger body of knowledge or theory?

- The authors concluded, "*This study was able to provide some beginning information on the type of EHR system healthcare facilities have in place, as well as their awareness of ASTM standards and the specific minimum data elements they believe should be included in an EHR.*"

- Comparing these conclusions, the problem statement, and the findings, it appears that they all relate.

- The authors did not provide alternative explanations as they were conducting a descriptive study. They linked to the larger body of knowledge by extrapolating how their study supported the development of the longitudinal record. Overall, the article appears to have met the conditions of the eighth set of questions.

9. Are all citations in the body of the article in the reference list? Is jargon kept to a minimum?

- All citations in the body of the article are in the reference list. ASTM and healthcare jargon is employed; however, it may have been difficult to communicate with the study participants without employing jargon. Also, the fields of healthcare and informatics seem particularly prone to jargon.

- Overall, the article appears to have partially met the conditions of the eighth set of questions.

Reviewing a journal article requires that readers synthesize all they know about research with much of what they know about a topic. Practicing these skills keeps readers sharp and attuned to results that do not meet the characteristics of data quality.

Another skill to evaluate research is to sort out the meaning of statistics on the tables that report them. A sample statistical table from a research article is dissected in table 20.17.

Table 20.17.   Pearson product–moment correlation of burnout subscales and selected coping mechanisms

	Self-Disclosure	Self-Directed	Confidence	Acceptance	Solving Structuring	Problem Resources	Coping
EE	2.2489 (287) p = .000***	2.3245 (287) p = .000***	2.3993 (287) p = .000***	2.2821 (287) p = .000***	2.2948 (287) p = .000***	2.3048 (287) p = .000***	2.4536 (287) p = .000***
DP	2.2952 (287) p = .000***	2.2172 (287) p = .000***	2.3004 (287) p = .000***	2.2895 (287) p = .000***	2.1808 (287) p = .002**	2.2712 (287) p = .000***	2.3653 (287) p = .000***
PA	.2984 (287) p = .000***	.3731 (287) p = .000***	.5332 (287) p = .000***	.3398 (287) p = .000***	.3904 (287) p = .000***	.4970 (287) p = .000***	.5576 (287) p = .000***

Note. (coefficient / (cases) / two-tailed test).
*p < .05. **p < .01. ***p < .001.

Source: Layman and Guyden 1999.

In this published research study, the researchers investigated the relationships between independent variables and dependent variables (Layman and Guyden 1999, 34). The independent variables were the coping mechanisms of self-disclosure, self-directed, confidence, acceptance, structuring, problem solving, and coping resources. The dependent variable was burnout with its three subscales of emotional exhaustion (EE), depersonalization (DP), and personal accomplishment (PA). The word *relationship* clues the reader that correlational statistical techniques are likely. The table's title lists the statistical technique as Pearson product–moment correlation. This title confirms the initial impression that correlational statistical techniques were used in this study.

In the footnote to the table, the researchers provide a key to the symbols (*, **, and ***). The asterisks mean the p-values were less than would be encountered through chance. The p < 0.05 means that the probability of obtaining this extreme of a test statistic is 5 percent. The p < 0.01 means that the probability of obtaining this extreme of a test statistic is 1 percent. The p < 0.001 means that the probability of obtaining this extreme of a test statistic is 0.1 percent. Therefore, the researchers' findings were unlikely to be due to chance. A relationship existed between the emotional exhaustion and the coping resources (–0.4536).

Some of the findings have minus (–) signs in front of them. The minus signs show that an inverse relationship exists between the emotional exhaustion and coping resources (–0.4536). An inverse relationship means that the *more* emotionally exhausted the respondent was, the *fewer* coping resources the respondent had. Inverse relationships move in opposite directions. An alternative explanation of the relationship between emotional exhaustion and coping resources could be that the more

coping resources the respondent had, the less emotionally exhausted the respondent was. Correlations cannot indicate which came first, the emotional exhaustion or the coping resources. We only know that the two variables are related.

The researchers state that the study was a cross-sectional, correlational design. As a quasi-experimental design, the study cannot show causation. Thus, the researchers cannot state what caused the lower levels of emotional exhaustion for some respondents. The researchers do not know whether the high levels of coping resources caused the lower levels of emotional exhaustion. The most the researchers can say is that the more coping resources the respondent recorded, the less emotionally exhausted the respondent was.

Astute readers may note that the row of data labeled PA (personal accomplishment) does not have minus signs. The absence of the minus signs indicates that a positive relationship exists between the two variables. In positive relationships, the variables both move in the same direction. The *more* coping resources a respondent has, the *more* personally accomplished the respondent feels. To reiterate, the correlational design of the study precludes statements about causation.

Being able to determine the meaning of tables with statistical data is a powerful skill. Articles report data in tables and other graphics because these formats efficiently deliver information. However, if one cannot decode the table, the benefit is lost.

Researchers disseminate the findings from their studies in journal articles. Skills in evaluating the quality of information reported in journal articles and skills in analyzing the statistical data presented are valuable competencies for HIM professionals to bring into their professsional practice.

Check Your Understanding 20.8

Instructions: Answer the following questions on a separate piece of paper.

1. What should researchers who use large databases for secondary analysis know about them?

2. How do public databases and proprietary databases differ?

3. The researcher's informed consent form stated that the patients' information would be anonymous. Later, in the application form for IRB approval, the researcher described a coding system to track respondents and nonrespondents. The IRB returned the application to the researcher with the stipulation that the informed consent be changed. What raised the red flag?

4. What is the Common Rule?

5. A researcher is at an institution that is a covered entity and received federal funding for research. Which set of regulations applies to the researcher?

6. Why is research particularly important to an emerging profession, such as health information management?

Summary

High-quality research depends on a carefully conceived plan and impeccable execution. Researchers' plans are similar to the blueprints that architects use to construct buildings. Researchers use their plans to conduct their studies and to build new knowledge. Research is systematic, and health information professionals can adapt its step-by-step approach to practical problems in the workplace.

Knowing the purpose of the research is a consistent theme in this chapter. Purpose drives decisions in each of the steps of research. These steps are defining the problem, reviewing the literature, determining the design and method, selecting the instrument, collecting and analyzing the data, presenting the results, and interpreting the findings.

The purpose of research determines the approach, whether qualitative or quantitative. Qualitative research is often exploratory and preliminary; quantitative research investigates numerically measurable observations or tests hypotheses.

Purpose also assists researchers in clarifying their research question. Considering their purposes helps researchers to concentrate or narrow the focus of the question to a researchable issue. Purpose also can ensure that researchers investigate meaningful problems that need solutions or significant questions that need answers.

The literature review is guided by purpose. In research, preference is given to articles in refereed journals. Purpose aids researchers in discriminating between relevant and irrelevant articles and between related and tangential articles.

Finally, one purpose of the literature review is to identify gaps in the body of knowledge that researchers can fill with their studies.

There are six common designs of research: historical, descriptive, correlational, evaluation, experimental, and causal-comparative. The design a researcher chooses depends on the purpose of the research. Associated with each design are many methods of research, including survey, observation, case study, ethnography, experiments, secondary analysis, and meta-analysis. As with the choice of design, purpose is crucial in the choice of method.

Purpose is also crucial in selecting the research instrument. Instruments are standardized means to collect data. Although many factors should be considered in the selection of an instrument, the most important is the researchers' purpose.

The importance of purpose may be less obvious in the collection and analysis of data. However, the higher the stakes, the larger the sample. Moreover, research that involves many variables also needs larger sample sizes. Therefore, purpose is a critical concern in the collection of data. Purpose also is involved in the analysis of data because statistical approaches vary by research design.

Moreover, purpose underlies the presentation of results and interpretation of findings. Researchers provide other HIM professionals with knowledge and techniques to answer questions and to solve problems in the workplace. Without presentation and interpretation, the knowledge and techniques would be unavailable to practitioners. Thereby, research in the field of health information management improves health information practices in the continuum of care.

HIM professionals are well suited to the role of researcher. Typically, persons in the field recognize their abilities to plan and organize. Their abilities with analytical expertise create a powerful toolbox of skills that HIM professionals can use to increase the field's body of knowledge.

References

Adler-Milstein, J., D.W. Bates, and A.K. Jha. 2011 (May 17). A survey of health information exchange organizations in the United States: Implications for meaningful use. *Annals of Internal Medicine* 154(10): 666–671.

Agency for Healthcare Quality and Research. n.d. Technology assessments. http://www.ahrq.gov/clinic/techix.htm.

AHIMA Data Quality Management Task Force. 2012. Practice brief: Data quality management model. *Journal of AHIMA* 83(7).

Aish, A.M., and D. Wasserman. 2001. Does Beck's Hopelessness Scale really measure several components? *Psychological Medicine* 31(2): 367–372.

Akobeng, A.K. 2007 (March). Understanding diagnostic tests 1: Sensitivity, specificity and predictive values. *Acta Paediatrica* 96(3): 338–341.

Alreck, P.L., and R.B. Settle. 2004. *The Survey Research Handbook,* 3rd ed. New York: McGraw-Hill/Irwin.

Amatayakul, M.K., and M.A. Shah. 1992. *Research Manual for the Health Information Profession.* Chicago: AHIMA.

American Health Information Management Association. 2012. e-HIM. http://www.ahima.org/ehim.

American Medical Informatics Association. 2012. Informatics areas, translational bioinformatics. http://www.amia.org/applications-informatics/translational-bioinformatics.

American Psychological Association. 2010. *Publication Manual of the American Psychological Association,* 6th ed. Washington, D.C.: American Psychological Association.

Annual Reviews. 2008. Welcome to Annual Reviews. http://www.annual reviews.org.

Archer N., U. Fevrier-Thomas, C. Lokker, K.A. McKibbon, and S.E. Straus. 2011 (July–August). Personal health records: a scoping review. *Journal of the American Medical Informatics Association* 18(4): 515–522.

Augestad, K.M., G. Berntsen, K. Lassen, J.G. Bellika, R. Wootton, and R.O. Lindsetmo. 2012 (January). Standards for reporting randomized controlled trials in medical informatics: A systematic review of CONSORT adherence in RCTs on clinical decision support. *Journal of the American Medical Informatics Association* 19(1): 13–21.

Babbie, E. 2004. *The Practice of Social Research,* 10th ed. Belmont, CA: Wadsworth/Thomson Learning.

Bailey, J., and W. Rudman. 2004 (September 20). The expanding role of the HIM professional: Where research and HIM roles intersect. *Perspectives in Health Information Management* 1(7): 1–6.

Bailey, K.D. 1994. *Methods of Social Research,* 4th ed. New York: Free Press.

Becker, H.S., B. Geer, E.C. Hughes, and A.S. Strauss. 1961. *Boys in White: Student Culture in Medical School.* Chicago: University of Chicago Press.

Bednarz, D. 1985. Quantity and quality in evaluation research: A divergent view. *Evaluation and Program Planning* 8(4): 289–306.

Bell, P.D. 2006 (Summer). Can factors related to self-regulated learning and epistemological beliefs predict learning achievement in undergraduate asynchronous web-based courses? *Perspectives in Health Information Management* 3(7): 1–17.

Berdie, D.R., and J.F. Anderson. 1974. *Questionnaires: Design and Use.* Metuchen, NJ: Scarecrow Press.

Bethell, C., J. Fiorillo, D. Lansky, M. Hendryx, and J. Knickman. 2004. Online consumer surveys as a methodology for assessing the quality of the United States health care system. *Journal of Medical Internet Research* 6(1): e2. http://www.jmir.org/2004/1/e2.

Biedermann, S.E., and J. Burrington-Brown. 2004. The research track: Career progressions in research for HIM professionals. *Journal of AHIMA* 75(10): 44–46.

Bowling, A. 2005. *Measuring Health: A Review of Quality of Life Measurement Scales,* 3rd ed. New York: Open University Press.

Brouwer, W., W. Kroeze, R. Crutzen, J. de Nooijer, N.K. de Vries, J. Brug, and A. Oenema. 2011 (January-March). Which intervention characteristics are related to more exposure to Internet-delivered health lifestyle promotion interventions? A systematic review. *Journal of Medical Internet Research* 13(1): e2.

Buller, D.B., W.F. Young, K.H. Fisher, and J.A. Maloy. 2007. The effect of endorsement by local opinion leaders and testimonials from teachers on the dissemination of a web-based smoking prevention program. *Health Education Research* 22(5): 609–618.

Buntin, M.B., M.F. Burke, M.C. Hoaglin, and D. Blumenthal. 2011 (March). The benefits of health information technology: A review of the recent literature shows predominantly positive results. *Health Affairs* 30(3): 464–471.

Burrington-Brown, J., and D.G. Wagg. 2003. Practice brief: Regulations governing research. *Journal of AHIMA* 74(3): 56A–56D.

Byrne, M. 2001. Ethnography as a qualitative research method. *Association of Operating Room Nurses Journal* 74(1): 82–84.

Campbell, D.T., and J.C. Stanley. 1963. *Experimental and Quasi-experimental Designs for Research.* Chicago: Rand McNally.

Chadwick, B.A., H.M. Bahr, and S.L. Albrecht. 1984. *Social Science Research Methods.* Englewood Cliffs, NJ: Prentice-Hall.

Chun, K., S. Cobb, and J.R.P. French Jr., eds. 1975. *Measures for Psychological Assessment: A Guide to 3,000 Original Sources and Their Applications.* Ann Arbor, MI: Survey Research Center, Institute for Social Research.

Cohen, P.A. 1992. Meta-analysis: Application to clinical dentistry and dental education. *Journal of Dental Education* 56(3): 172–175.

Cohen, P.A. 1991. Criteria for evaluating research reports. Handout, educational research course. Augusta, GA: Medical College of Georgia.

Colaianni, L.A. 1994. Peer review in journals indexed in Index Medicus. *Journal of the American Medical Association* 272(2): 156–158.

Crosson, J.C., N. Isaacson, D. Lancaster, E.A. McDonald, A.J. Schueth, B. DiCicco-Bloom, J.L. Newman, C.J. Wang, and D.S. Bell. 2008 (April). Variation in electronic prescribing implementation among twelve ambulatory practices. *Journal of General Internal Medicine* 23(4): 364–371.

Crystal, A., and J. Greenberg. 2006. Relevance criteria identified by health information users during web searches. *Journal of the American Society for Information Science and Technology* 57(10): 1368–1382.

Cugelman, B., M. Thelwall, and P. Dawes. 2011 (January–March). Online interventions for social marketing health behavior change campaigns: A meta-analysis of psychological architectures and adherence factors. *Journal of Medical Internet Research* 13(1): e17.

Day, R.A., and B. Gastel. 2011. *How to Write and Publish a Scientific Paper,* 7th ed. Santa Barbara, CA: Greenwood Press.

Dillman, D.A. 2007. *Mail and Internet Surveys: The Tailored Design Method,* 2nd ed. Hoboken, NJ: John Wiley & Sons.

Donabedian, A. 1989. The end results of health care: Ernest Codman's contribution to quality assessment and beyond. *Milbank Quarterly* 67(2): 233–256.

Dorr, D., L.M. Bonner, A.N. Cohen, R.S. Shoai, R. Perrin, E. Chaney, and A.S. Young. 2007 (March–April). Informatics systems to promote improved care for chronic illness: A literature review. *Journal of the American Medical Informatics Association* 14(2): 156–163.

Edirisooriya, G. 1996. Research presentations in a democratic society: A voice from the audience. *Educational Researcher* 25(6): 25–30.

Edmonson, S.R., K.A. Smith-Akin, and E.V. Bernstam. 2007 (January). Context, automated decision support, and clinical practice guidelines: Does the literature apply to the United States practice environment? *International Journal of Medical Informatics* 76(1): 34–41.

Effken, J.A., B.B. Brewer, M.D. Logue, S.M. Gephart, and J.A. Verran. 2011 (October). Using cognitive work flow analysis to fit decision support tools to nurse managers' work flow. *International Journal of Medical Informatics* 80(10): 698–707.

Englebardt, S.P., and R. Nelson. 2002. *Health Care Informatics: An Interdisciplinary Approach.* St. Louis, MO: Mosby, Inc.

Eslami, S., N.F. de Keizer, and A. Abu-Hanna. 2008 (June). The impact of computerized physician medication order entry in hospitalized patients—a systematic review. *International Journal of Medical Informatics* 77(6): 365–376.

Fayyad, U. 1997. Knowledge discovery in databases: An overview. *Inductive Logic Programming: Proceedings of the 7th International Workshop.* Book series: Lecture notes in computer science, vol. 1297. New York: Springer. http://www.springerlink.com/content/a07u771435m35318/fulltext.pdf.

Fenton, S., and M. Williams. 2005. Getting to know PubMed: An overview. *Journal of AHIMA* 76(3): 60A–60D.

Field, A.E., W.C. Willett, L. Lissner, and G.A. Colditz. 2007. Dietary fat and weight gain among women in the Nurses' Health Study. *Obesity* 15(4): 967–976.

Flyvbjerg, B. 2006. Five misunderstandings about case-study research. *Qualitative Inquiry* 12(2): 219–245.

Fontanarosa, P.B., and C.D. DeAngelis. 2002 (April 3). Basic science and translational research. *Journal of the American Medical Association* 287(13): 1728.

Gall, M.D., J.P. Gall, and W.R. Borg. 2007. *Educational Research: An Introduction,* 8th ed. Boston: Allyn & Bacon.

Garrard, J. 2011. *Health Sciences Literature Review Made Easy: The Matrix Method,* 3rd ed. Sudbury, MA: Jones and Bartlett.

Garvin, J.H. 2005 (Fall). Development of a public health assessment tool to prevent lyme disease: Tool construction and validation. *Perspectives in Health Information Management* 2(10): 1–25.

Garvin, J.H. 2001. Building on the vision: Exploratory research in future skill areas of the clinical data specialist as described in evolving HIM careers. *Educational Perspectives in Health Information Management* 4(1): 19–32.

Gay, L.R., and P.W. Airasian. 2006. *Educational research: Competencies for analysis and application,* 6th ed. Upper Saddle River, NJ: Pearson Education.

Gay, L.R., G.E. Mills, and P. Airasian. 2012. *Educational Research: Competencies for Analysis and Application,* 10th ed. Upper Saddle River, NJ: Pearson Education.

Gaylin, D.S., A. Moiduddin, S. Mohamoud, K. Lundeen, and J.A. Kelly. 2011 (June). Public attitudes about health information technology and its relationship to health care quality, costs, and privacy. *Health Services Research* 46(3): 920–938.

Georgiou, A., M. Prgomet, A. Markewycz, E. Adams, and J.I. Westbrook. 2011 (May). The impact of computerized provider order entry systems on medical-imaging services: A systematic review. *Journal of the American Medical Informatics Association* 18(3): 335–340.

Gibaldi, J. 2009. *MLA Handbook for Writers of Research Papers,* 7th ed. New York: Modern Language Association of America.

Gilles, K. 2004. Uncovering the relationship between IRBs and the HIPAA privacy rule. *Journal of AHIMA* 75(10): 48–49, 52.

Glaser, B.G. 1965 (Spring). The constant comparative method of qualitative analysis. *Social Problems* 12(4): 436–445.

Glass, G.V. 1976. Primary, secondary, and meta-analysis of research. *Educational Researcher* 5(10): 3–8.

Goodman, S.N., and J.A. Berlin. 1994 (Auguest. 1). The use of predicted confidence intervals when planning experiments and the misuse of power when interpreting results. *Annals of Internal Medicine* 121(3): 200–206.

Harman, J.S., C.H. Lemak, M. Al-Amin, A.G. Hall, and R.P. Duncan. 2011 (June). Changes in per member per month expenditures after implementation of Florida's Medicaid Reform Demonstration. *Health Services Research* 46(3): 787–804.

Heitjan, D.F., and D.B. Rubin. 1991 (December). Ignorability and coarse data. *Annals of Statistics* 19(4): 2244–2253.

Herndon, R.M., ed. 2006. *Handbook of Neurologic Rating Scales,* 2nd ed. New York: Demos Vermande.

Herrera, C.D. 1999 (June). Two arguments for 'covert methods' in social research. *British Journal of Sociology* 50(2): 331–343.

Hill, R.F., and E.P. Tyson. 1997. The culture of morning report: Ethnography of a clinical teaching conference. *Southern Medical Journal* 90(6): 594–600.

Huang, Y., P. McCullagh, N. Black, and R. Harper. 2007 (November). Feature selection and classification model construction on type 2 diabetic patients' data. *Artificial Intelligence in Medicine* 41(3): 251–262.

Iverson, C., ed. 2007. *American Medical Association Manual of Style: A Guide for Authors and Editors,* 10th ed. New York: Oxford University Press.

Jaspers, M.W.M., M. Smeulers, H. Vermeulen, and L.W. Peute. 2011 (May). Effects of clinical decision-support systems on practitioner performance and patient outcomes: A synthesis of high-quality systematic review findings. *Journal of the American Medical Informatics Association* 18(3): 327–334.

Jencks, C., and D. Riesman. 1977. *The Academic Revolution.* Chicago: University of Chicago Press.

Johnson, M. 1992. A silent conspiracy? Some ethical issues of participant observation in nursing research. *International Journal of Nursing Studies* 29(2): 213–223.

Johnson, R.B., and A.J. Onwuegbuzie. 2004. Mixed methods research: A research paradigm whose time has come. *Educational Researcher* 33(7): 14–26.

Joy, J.E., E.E. Penhoet, and D.B. Petitti, eds. 2005. *Saving Women's Lives: Strategies for Improving Breast Cancer Detection and Diagnosis.* Washington, D.C.: National Academies Press.

Kahn, M.G., D. Kaplan, R.J. Sokol, and R.P. DiLaura. 2007. Configuration challenges: Implementing translational research policies in electronic medical records. *Academic Medicine* 82(7): 661–669.

Kesh, S., and W. Raghupathi. 2004. Critical issues in bioinformatics and computing. *Perspectives in Health Information Management* 1(9): 1–8.

Keyser, D.J., and R.C. Sweetland, eds. 1991. *Test Critiques.* Kansas City, MO: Test Corporation of America.

Kish, L. 1995/1965. *Survey Sampling.* New York: John Wiley & Sons.

Kloss, L. 2000. Growing the HIM body of knowledge. *Journal of AHIMA* 71(10): 27.

Kocher, M.S., and D. Zurakowski. 2004 (March). Clinical epidemiology and biostatistics: A primer for orthopedic surgeons. *Journal of Bone and Joint Surgery* 86(3): 607–620.

Kongsved, S.M., M. Basnov, K. Holm-Christensen, and N.H. Hjollund. 2007 (September). Internet versus mailed questionnaires: A controlled comparison. *Journal of Medical Internet Research* 9(3): e25.

Lau, F., C. Kuziemsky, M. Price, and J. Gardner. 2010 (November–December). A review of systematic reviews of health information system studies. *Journal of the American Medical Informatics Association* 17(6): 637–645.

Layman, E.J., and J.A. Guyden. 1999 (Spring). The relationships among psychological type, coping mechanisms, and burnout in directors of hospital health information management departments. *Educational Perspectives in Health Information Management* 1(2): 29–41.

Layman, E., and V. Watzlaf. 2003. Manuscript characteristics affecting reviewers' decisions for journals in health information management. *Educational Perspectives in Health Information Management* 5(1): 48–85.

Lee, S.J., C.C. Earle, and J.C. Weeks. 2000 (February 2). Outcomes research in oncology: History, conceptual framework, and trends in the literature. *Journal of the National Cancer Institute* 92(3): 195–204.

Leece P., M. Bhandari, S. Sprague, M.F. Swiontkowsi, E.H. Schemitsch, P. Tornetta, P.J. Devereaux, and G.H. Guyatt. 2004 (October). Internet versus mailed questionnaires: A controlled comparison. *Journal of Medical Internet Research* 6(4): e39.

Levy, G., N. Blumberg, Y. Kreiss, N. Ash, and O. Merin. 2010 (November–December). Application of information technology within a field hospital deployment following the January 2010 Haiti earthquake disaster. *Journal of the American Medical Informatics Association* 17(6): 626–630.

Lloyd, S.C., and E. Layman. 1997. The effects of automated encoders on coding accuracy and coding speed. *Topics in Health Information Management* 17(3): 72–79.

Lluch, M. 2011 (December). Healthcare professionals' organizational barriers to health information technologies: A literature review. *International Journal of Medical Informatics* 80(12): 849–862.

Maddox, T., ed. 2008. *Tests: A Comprehensive Reference for Assessments in Psychology, Education, and Business,* 6th ed. Austin, TX: Pro-Ed.

Malin, B., S. Nyemba, and J. Paulett. 2011 (April). Learning relational policies from electronic health record access logs. *Journal of Biomedical Informatics* 44(2): 333–342.

Mancilla, D., and J. Moczygemba. 2009 (Fall). Exploring medical identity theft. *Perspectives in Health Information Management* 6: 1–11.

McDowell, I., and C. Newell. 1996. *Measuring Health: A Guide to Rating Scales and Questionnaires,* 2nd ed. New York: Oxford University Press.

McKibbon, K.A., and C.S. Gadd. 2004 (July 22). A quantitative analysis of qualitative studies in clinical journals for 2000 publishing year. *BMC Medical Informatics and Decision Making* 4: 11. http://www.biomedcentral.com/content/pdj/1472-6947-4-11.pdf.

McLaughlin, S.B., J.M. Hankey, and T.A. Dingus. 2008. A method for evaluating collision avoidance systems using naturalistic driving data. *Accident Analysis and Prevention* 40(1): 8–16.

Menachemi, N., A. Chukmaitov, C. Saunders, and R.G. Brooks. 2008. Hospital quality of care: Does information technology matter? The relationship between information technology adoption and quality of care. *Health Care Management Review* 33(1): 51–59.

Metz, M.H. 2001. Intellectual border crossing in graduate education: A report from the field. *Educational Researcher* 30(5): 12–18.

Mikkelsen, G., and J. Aasly. 2001 (October). Concordance of information in parallel electronic and paper-based patient records. *International Journal of Medical Informatics* 63(3): 123–131.

Moczygemba, J., and S.H. Fenton. 2012 (Winter). Lessons learned from an ICD-10-CM clinical documentation pilot study. *Perspectives in Health Information Management* 9: 1–11.

Morton, M.E., and S. Wiedenbeck. 2010 (Winter). EHR acceptance factors in ambulatory care: A survey of physician perceptions. *Perspectives in Health Information Management* 7: 1–17.

Mullins, I.M., M.S. Siadaty, J. Lyman, K. Scully, C.T. Garrett, W.G. Miller, R. Muller, B. Robson, C. Apte, S. Weiss, I. Rigoutsos, D. Platt, S. Cohen, and W.A. Knaus. 2006. Data mining and clinical data repositories: Insights from a 667,000 patient data set. *Computers in Biology and Medicine* 36(12): 1351–1377.

Mulrow, C.D. 1994. Systematic reviews: rationale for systematic reviews. *British Medical Journal* 309(6954): 597–599.

Murphy, L.L., K.F. Geisinger, J.F. Carlson, and R.A. Spies, eds. 2011. *Tests in Print VIII: An Index to Tests, Test Reviews, and the Literature on Specific Tests.* Lincoln, NE: University of Nebraska Press.

National Library of Medicine. 2012. MeSH browser, online searching. http://www.nlm.nih.gov/mesh/.

National Science Foundation. 2008 (November 13). Interpreting the Common Rule for the Protection of Human Subjects for Behavioral and Social Science Research. http://www.nsf.gov/bfa/dias/policy/hsfaqs.jsp.

Office for Human Research Protections, US Department of Health and Human Services. n.d. Human Subject Research. http://www.hhs.gov/ohrp/humansubjects/guidance/.

Oniki, T.A., T.P. Clemmer, and T.A. Pryor. 2003 (March–April). The effect of computer-generated reminders on charting deficiencies in the ICU. *Journal of the American Medical Informatics Association* 10(2): 177–187.

Osborn, C.E. 2006. *Statistical Applications for Health Information Management,* 2nd ed. Sudbury, MA: Jones and Bartlett.

Ovretveit, J. 1998. *Evaluating Health Interventions.* Maidenhead, England: Open University Press.

Penslar, R.L., and J.P. Porter. 2001. *IRB Guidebook.* Office for Human Research Protections. http://www.hhs.gov/ohrp/irb/irb_guidebook.htm.

Police, R.L., Foster, T., and K.S. Wong. 2010. Adoption and use of health information technology in physician practice organizations: Systematic review. *Informatics in Primary Care* 18(4): 248–258.

Redman, B.K., ed. 2003. *Measurement Tools in Patient Education,* 2nd ed. New York: Springer.

Redman, B.K., ed. 2002. *Measurement Tools in Clinical Ethics.* New York: Springer.

Rinehart-Thompson, L.A. 2008. Storage media profiles and health record retention practice patterns in acute care hospitals. *Perspectives in Health Information Management* 5(9): 1–13.

Ritter, P., K. Lorig, D. Laurent, and K. Matthews. 2004. Internet versus mailed questionnaires: A randomized comparison. *Journal of Medical Internet Research* 6(3): e29. http://www.jmir.org/2004/3/e29/html.

Rosenthal, D.A., and E.J. Layman. 2008. Utilization of information technology in eastern North Carolina physician practices: Determining the existence of a digital divide. *Perspectives in Health Information Management* 5(3): 1–20.

Roth, J.A. 2004a. Getting "hip" to other privacy laws, Part 1. *Journal of AHIMA* 75(2): 50–52.

Roth, J.A. 2004b. Getting "hip" to other privacy laws, Part 2. *Journal of AHIMA* 75(3): 48–50.

Roth, J.A. 2004c. Overdose of privacy law creates headaches for student health clinics. *Journal of AHIMA* 75(8): 64–65, 67.

Sasnett, B., and T. Ross. 2007 (Fall). Leadership frames and perceptions of effectiveness among health information management program directors. *Perspectives in Health Information Management* 4(8): 1–15.

Sharp, M. 2010 (Summer). Development of an instrument to measure students' perceptions of information technology fluency skills: Establishing content validity. *Perspectives in Health Information Management* 7: 1–10.

Shi, L. 2008. *Health Services Research Methods*, 2nd ed. Albany, NY: Delmar.

Singleton, R.A., Jr., and B.C. Straits. 2005. *Approaches to Social Research,* 4th ed. New York: Oxford University Press.

Sligar, S.R., and X. Zeng. 2008. Evaluation of website accessibility of state vocational rehabilitation agencies. *Journal of Rehabilitation* 74(1): 12–18.

Sokol, L., B. Garcia, J. Rodriguez, M. West, and K. Johnson. 2001 (August). Using data mining to find fraud in HCFA health care claims. *Topics in Health Information Management* 22(1): 1–13.

Sollaci, L.B., and M.G. Pereira. 2004. The introduction, methods, results, and discussion (IMRAD) structure: A fifty-year survey. *Journal of the Medical Library Association* 92(3): 364–371.

Sox, H.C., and S. Greenfield. 2009 (August 4). Comparative effectiveness research: A report from the Institute of Medicine. *Annals of Internal Medicine* 151(3): 203–205.

Spies, R.A., J.F. Carlson, and K.F. Geisinger, eds. 2010. *The Eighteenth Mental Measurements Yearbook* (Buros Mental Measurements Yearbooks). Lincoln, NE: University of Nebraska Press.

Stanfill, M.H., M. Williams, S.H. Fenton, R.A. Jenders, and W.R. Hersh. 2010 (November–December). A systematic literature review of automated clinical coding and classification systems. *Journal of the American Medical Informatics Association* 17(6): 646–651.

Strauss, E., Sherman, E.M.S., and O. Spreen. 2006. *A Compendium of Neuropsychological Tests: Administration, Norms, and Commentary,* 3rd ed. New York: Oxford University Press.

Strunk, W., Jr., and E.B. White. 2000. *The Elements of Style,* 4th ed. New York: Longman.

Sudman, S. 1976. *Applied Sampling.* New York: Academic Press.

Thompson, B. 2002 (April). What future quantitative social science research could look like: Confidence intervals for effect sizes. *Educational Researcher* 31(3): 25–32.

University of Chicago Press. 2010. *The Chicago Manual of Style,* 16th ed. Chicago: University of Chicago Press.

University of South Carolina Beaufort Library. 2010. Bare bones 101: A basic tutorial on searching the web. http://sc.edu/beaufort/library/pages/bones/bones.shtml.

Van de Mortel, T., Bourke, R. Fillipi, L., McLoughlin, J., Molihan, C., Nonu, M., and M. Reis. 2000 (August). Maximizing handwashing rates in the critical care unit through yearly performance feedback. *Australian Critical Care* 13(3): 91–95.

Van den Broeck, J., Cunningham, S.A., Eeckels, R., and K. Herbst. 2005 (October). Data cleaning: Detecting, diagnosing, and editing data abnormalities. *PLoS [Public Library of Science] Medicine* 2(10)(e267): 0966–0970.

Waljee, J.F., Rogers, M.A.M., and A.K. Alderman. 2007 (March 20). Decision aids and breast cancer: Do they influence choice of surgery and knowledge of treatment options? *Journal of Clinical Oncology* 25(9): 1067–1073.

Ware, R.E., and R.J. Hicks. 2011 (December). Doing more harm than good? Do systematic reviews of PET by health technology assessment agencies provide an appraisal of the evidence that is closer to the truth than the primary data supporting its use? *Journal of Nuclear Medicine* 52 (12, Suppl 2): 64S–73S.

Watzlaf, V.J.M. 1995. The leadership role of the health information management professional in research. *Topics in Health Information Management* 15(3): 47–58.

Watzlaf, V., Katoh, A., and F. D'Amico. 1996. Obstacles encountered in the use of medical record and cancer registry abstract in breast cancer research. *Topics in Health Information Management* 17(1): 25–33.

Watzlaf, V., Zeng, X., Jarymowycz, C., and P.A. Firouzan. 2004. Standards for the content of the electronic health record. *Perspectives in Health Information Management* 1(1): 1–21.

Wells, H.J., Higgins, G.L., and M.R. Baumann. 2010 (September). Implementing an electronic point-of-care medical record at an organized athletic event: Challenges, pitfalls, and lessons learned. *Clinical Journal of Sport Medicine* 20(5): 377–378.

Williams, S.J., and P.R. Torrens. 2008. *Introduction to Health Services*, 7th ed. Clifton Park, NY: Thomson Delmar Learning.

Wineberg, S. 2004. Must it be this way? Ten rules for keeping your audience awake during conferences. *Educational Researcher* 23(4): 13–14.

Witry, M.J., Doucette, W.R., Daly, J.M., Levy, B.T., and E.A. Crischilles. 2010 (Winter). Family physician perceptions of personal health records. *Perspectives in Health Information Management* 7: 1–12.

Woolf, S.H. 2008 (January). The meaning of translational research and why it matters. *Journal of the American Medical Association* 299(2): 211–213.

chapter 21

Biomedical and Research Support

Valerie J.M. Watzlaf, PhD, RHIA, FAHIMA

Learning Objectives

- Explain the role of biomedical research in evaluating the safety and efficacy of diagnostic and therapeutic procedures in order to solve human problems
- Relate the measures outlined by the Nuremberg Code, the Declaration of Helsinki, and the Belmont Report for the protection of human subjects
- Describe the purpose and responsibilities as well as the overall management of the Institutional Review Board (IRB) for biomedical research
- Illustrate the different types of IRB submissions and the procedures that must be followed when conducting biomedical research
- Outline the contents of informed consent for the protection of human subjects as required by federal regulation
- Explain the procedures that should be followed when handling problems that include risks to human subjects engaged in biomedical research

- Outline the recordkeeping and retention requirements that are required by the IRB
- Discuss the role of the health information management (HIM) professional both as a researcher and in a supportive role to research conducted in healthcare facilities
- Discuss the Health Insurance Portability and Accountability Act (HIPAA) and its privacy provisions for the protection of human subjects
- Outline the various research designs for conducting biomedical research
- Describe the purpose of outcomes and effectiveness research as it relates to the Patient Protection and Affordable Care Act
- Describe the various types of outcomes and effectiveness measures

Key Terms

Agency for Healthcare Research and Quality (AHRQ)
Attributable risk (AR)
Beneficence
Case-control study
Clinical trial
Cohort study
Control
Cross-sectional study
Double-blind study
Epidemiological study
Experimental study
Food and Drug Administration (FDA)

Health Research Extension Act
Health services research
Healthcare Cost and Utilization Project (HCUP)
Human subjects
Informed consent
Institutional Review Board (IRB)
Justice
Morality
National Committee for Quality Assurance (NCQA)
Observational study
Odds ratio
Office for Human Research Protections (OHRP)

607

Office of Management and Budget (OMB)
Office of Research Integrity (ORI)
Outcomes and effectiveness research (OER)
Patient-Centered Outcomes Research Institute (PCORI)
Patient Protection and Affordable Care Act (PPACA)
Principal investigator
Privacy Rule
Prospective study
Protected health information (PHI)
Protocol

Quality indicator (QI)
Randomized clinical trial (RCT)
Relative risk (RR)
Research
Respect for persons
Retrospective study
Single-blind study
Sponsor
Vulnerable subjects

Biomedical research is a search for knowledge that often leads to advances in medicine. It determines what new drugs and other types of treatments, as well as new technology, are safe and effective for patients. When new treatments and technologies ultimately reach the consumers of healthcare, long-term studies of outcomes and effectiveness begin.

This chapter explores the various methods by which biomedical research is conducted. It also examines methods of assessing outcomes and effectiveness, including programs initiated by the Agency for Healthcare Research and Quality (AHRQ), the Joint Commission, the National Committee for Quality Assurance (NCQA), and the Patient-Centered Outcomes Research Institute (PCORI).

Clinical and Biomedical Research

Clinical and biomedical research studies are conducted to evaluate disease processes and interventions and the safety, effectiveness, and usefulness of drugs, diagnostic procedures, and preventive measures such as vaccines, mammography, and diets. The broad objective of these studies is to establish reproducible facts and theory that help solve human problems. The most common examples of these research studies are called **clinical trials,** in which a specific type of clinical or biomedical intervention is tested to determine its effectiveness. **Health services research** examines the quality, access, cost, staffing, utilization, and safety of healthcare services in order to improve the overall quality of care provided to patients. For example, health services research studies may focus on examining the number and type of infections in an elderly cohort in order to determine the effect the infection has on extended length of stay, cost, coding, and reimbursement. Further research in this area may include siphoning out which infections are hospital acquired and which are community acquired and then determining which lead to additional cost, treatment, staffing, and length of stay while not providing additional reimbursement for the hospital and certainly not providing additional safety and quality for the patient (Watzlaf et al. 1998).

Ethical Treatment of Human Subjects

Human subjects are used in biomedical research studies. Because human subjects are involved, researchers are

required to follow certain ethical principles that guide their behavior, **morality,** and character traits. Morality includes two separate requirements related to research: the requirement to acknowledge autonomy (being capable of making decisions) and the requirement to protect those with decreased autonomy (due to changes in their health capacity) (NIH 1979).

Research ethics

- Provide a structure for analysis and decision making
- Support and remind researchers to protect human subjects
- Provide workable definitions of benefits and risks

Risk versus benefit is critical in weighing the advantages of biomedical research. A benefit is a positive value of being part of the clinical research study. A benefit may be specific to the individual subject in that it provides a good therapeutic outcome, or it may be a direct advantage to society as a whole rather than to the individual subject.

Risks are concerned with the probability or magnitude of harm to the research subject. Stating that 1 in 100 patients may experience a certain risk suggests probability of harm. A rash as a minor effect of the treatment or liver failure as a major effect of the treatment suggests magnitude of harm.

The challenge for the researcher is to weigh risks to the subject against potential benefits. This is difficult because not all potential benefits and risks are known in advance and, as stated earlier, the benefit may be for society at large rather than for the individual subjects who assumed the risks. However, there are many clinical and biomedical research studies in which the benefits far outweigh the risks to the individual. For example, an individual with stage IV pancreatic cancer may only see how the benefits outweigh the risks to enroll in a clinical trial that examines the effectiveness of a medication to stop the advancement of this devastating illness.

The Nuremberg Code and the Declaration of Helsinki

International guidelines also govern the ethical conduct of human research. The Nuremberg Code outlines research ethics that were developed during the trials of Nazi war criminals following World War II. The code was widely adopted as a standard for protecting human subjects in the 1950s and

1960s. The basic tenet of the Nuremberg Code is that "voluntary consent of the human subject is absolutely essential" (Nuremburg Code 1949, 181). It is the duty and responsibility of the individual initiating, directing, or conducting the experiment to ensure the quality of the informed consent. Additionally, the Nuremburg Code requires that research be based on animal work, the risks be justified by the anticipated benefits, only qualified scientists conduct the research, and physical and mental suffering be avoided. Research in which death is expected should not be conducted.

The Declaration of Helsinki is a code of ethics for clinical research approved by the World Medical Association in 1964. It was a reinterpretation of the Nuremberg Code directed toward medical research with a therapeutic intent. It is a statement of ethical principles that provides guidance to physicians and other participants in medical research involving human subjects, including research on identifiable human material or identifiable data. The document has been revised a number of times, most recently in October 2000 at the 52nd World Medical Association Assembly held in Edinburgh, Scotland.

Despite the Nuremberg Code and the Declaration of Helsinki, controversial ethical practices in biomedical research continued to be a problem. In 1966, Dr. Henry K. Beecher, an anesthesiologist, described 22 examples of research studies with controversial ethics that had been published by prominent researchers in major journals. Beecher's article increased public awareness of the ethical problems related to biomedical research, including

- Lack of informed consent
- Coercion of, or undue pressure on, volunteers
- Use of a vulnerable population
- Information being withheld
- Available treatment being withheld
- Information about risks being withheld
- Subjects put at risk
- Risks to subjects that outweigh the benefits
- Deception
- Violation of rights

The US Public Health Services Syphilis Study

A study conducted in the United States that brought ethical issues in research to the forefront was the US Public Health Services Syphilis Study. This study was designed to study the natural history of syphilis in African-American men (see figure 21.1). At the time the study began, there was no treatment for syphilis. However, by the 1940s penicillin had proved to be safe and effective. The men enrolled in the study were denied treatment. They continued to be followed until 1972, when the first public accounts began to appear in the national press. The study resulted in 28 deaths, 100 cases of disability, and 19 cases of congenital syphilis.

After the press blew the whistle, Congress formed an ad hoc panel that determined the study should be stopped

Figure 21.1.   Tuskegee syphilis study

The Tuskegee Syphilis Study is a notorious chapter in medical research in the United States. From 1932 to 1972, the US Public Health Service conducted research that had the stated purpose of obtaining more information about the clinical course of syphilis. The medical researchers from the US Public Health Service experimented on 399 African American males in Macon County, Alabama. The medical researchers told the men that they were being treated for "bad blood." In fact, the researchers were deceiving the men and were denying them treatment for syphilis. Many of the men's wives were infected, and their children were subsequently born with congenital syphilis. The US Public Health Service continued the study despite the advent of penicillin in 1947. The Tuskegee Syphilis Study is a symbol of unethical research.

immediately and that oversight of human research was inadequate. It was recommended that federal regulations be implemented to protect human research in the future. In 1974, Congress authorized formation of the National Commission for the Protection of Human Subjects in Biomedical and Behavioral Research. The commission was charged with identifying the basic ethical principles that underlie the conduct of human research.

In 1979, the commission published the *Belmont Report: Ethical Principles and Guidelines for the Protection of Human Subjects of Research. (Dept. of HHS, 1979)* This report identifies the following three basic ethical principles that underlie all human subject research:

Respect for persons requires that individuals be treated as autonomous human beings and not used as a means to an end. Elements of autonomy include the ability to understand and process information and the freedom to volunteer for research without coercion or undue influence from others. Respect for persons requires informed consent and respecting the privacy of research subjects.

Beneficence is minimizing harms and maximizing benefits. Beneficence requires the best possible research design to achieve its goals. It also requires that researchers be able to perform the research and handle the risks.

Justice requires that people be treated fairly and that benefits and risks be shared equitably among the population. Justice requires that subjects be selected equitably and that vulnerable populations or populations of convenience not be exploited.

In 1981, the Department of Health and Human Services (HHS) revised its regulations on the protection of human subjects and made them available within the Code of Federal Regulations (45 CFR part 46). In 1991, subpart A of those regulations, was broadened to include 14 other federal departments, creating the Common Rule. However, even though research has increased and changed dramatically since the early 1980s, with increases in multisite and health services research as well as new technologies such as genomics and informatics, there has been no change to the Common Rule. Therefore, the **Office of Management and Budget (OMB)** developed a working group to examine possible revisions to the Common Rule. Its draft, Advance Notice of Proposed Rulemaking (ANPRM), was circulated for comment, and the ANPRM entitled "Human Subjects Research Protections: Enhancing Protections for Research Subjects and Reducing Burden, Delay and Ambiguity for Investigators" was developed. The goal is to provide options for broadening protections for research subjects and to focus more oversight on those studies that hold more risk for the research subject and less oversight on those that pose less risk. At this writing, no changes to the Common Rule have been made. The ANPRM received public comment. Public comments will be used in the process of developing proposed revisions to the Common Rule. The draft revisions will be publicized in a Notice of Proposed Rule Making (NPRM), and the public will have additional time to comment before changes to the Common Rule are finalized (Emanuel and Menikoff 2011; HHS 2011).

The **Office for Human Research Protections (OHRP)** of the HHS monitors compliance with the federal regulations that govern the conduct of research conducted or supported by HHS (HHS 2009). OHRP is a federal agency that provides leadership and oversight on all matters related to the protection of human subjects participating in research conducted or supported by HHS, as outlined in the regulations. OHRP provides clarification and guidance, develops educational programs, maintains regulatory oversight, and provides advice on ethical and regulatory issues in biomedical and behavioral research. The federal regulations for the protection of human subjects include Title 45 of CFR 46. The **Food and Drug Administration (FDA)** has a separate set of regulations governing human subjects research (21 CFR Part 56 IRBs and 21 CFR Part 50 Informed Consent). The basic requirements for IRBs and informed consent are similar between the HHS and FDA regulations (21 CFR Parts 101–124).

Check Your Understanding 21.1

Instructions: Answer the following questions on a separate piece of paper.

1. What is the origin of the Nuremberg Code? What are its basic tenets?

2. List the three principles outlined in the *Belmont Report.*

3. A researcher fails to inform a study participant of the reasonable risks in a study on the effectiveness of a new chemotherapy agent. What ethical principle was violated?

4. List five ethical issues in the conduct of biomedical research in the United States cited by Beecher.

5. What study led to creation of the *Belmont Report* and ultimate federal regulations for human subject protection?

Protection of Human Subjects

The HHS regulations contain three basic provisions for the protection of human subjects:

- Institutional assurances of compliance
- Institutional review board review and approval
- Informed consent

Institutional Assurances of Compliance

An institutional assurance of compliance is a commitment of an institution to comply with HHS regulations for the protection of human subjects by documenting this commitment. HHS will support nonexempt research covered by the regulations only if the organization has an OHRP-approved assurance on file; the research has been reviewed and approved by the organization's IRB; and the IRB will continue to review the research, as necessary (HHS 2009).

Office for Human Research Protections

Protection of human subjects is required under the HHS Code of Federal Regulations (45 CFR 46). OHRP has formal agreements with more than 10,000 federally funded universities, hospitals, and other medical and behavioral research institutions in the United States and abroad. These organizations must agree to abide by the human subject protection regulations found in the Code of Federal Regulations. The OHRP's duties include

- Establishing criteria for, and approving assurance of, compliance for the protection of human subjects with institutions engaged in HHS-conducted or HHS-supported human subject research
- Providing clarification and guidance on involving humans in research
- Developing and implementing educational programs and resource materials
- Promoting the development of approaches to enhance human subject protections

The OHRP also evaluates substantive allegations or indications of noncompliance with HHS regulations regarding the conduct of research involving human subjects (45 CFR 46.103). It also provides education and development on the complex ethical and regulatory issues relating to human subjects protection in medical and behavioral research. The OHRP helps institutions assess and improve their own procedures for protecting human subjects through a quality improvement program.

Institutional Review Board

The **Institutional Review Board (IRB)** is a committee established to protect the rights and welfare of human research subjects involved in research activities. The IRB members are appointed by the specific organization conducting the research.

The IRB determines whether research that is conducted is appropriate and that it protects human subjects as they participate in this research. The primary focus of the IRB is not on whether the type of research is appropriate for the organization to conduct but upon whether or not human subjects are adequately protected. (45 CFR 46.111).

The purpose and responsibility of the IRB is to protect the rights and welfare of human subjects as they engage in research activities. The IRB must abide by the regulations as listed in 45 CFR 46.111 and 21 CFR 56.111. The IRB must first determine if research is being conducted and then determine if human subjects are being protected. **Research** is defined by the regulations as "a systematic investigation, including research development, testing and evaluation, designed to develop or contribute to generalizable knowledge" (Federal Policy §46.102 (d)). **Human subjects** are defined by the regulations as "living individual(s) about whom an investigator (whether professional or student) conducting research obtains (1) data through intervention or interaction with the individual, or (2) identifiable private information" [Federal Policy §46.102 (f)] (45 CFR 46.102). Research as defined here is different than quality improvement studies because quality improvement studies are not designed to contribute to "generalizable knowledge" but to add to the internal evaluation of healthcare organizations. Quality improvement is presented in chapter 22.

An IRB must review all research activities covered by the HHS regulations and either (1) approve, (2) require changes to obtain approval, or (3) disapprove any research activity. An IRB must perform continuing reviews of ongoing research as often as necessary per degree of risk, but not less than one year. The IRB has the authority to suspend or terminate approved research that is not being conducted in accordance with IRB requirements or that has caused unexpected or serious harm to the subject. If a suspension or termination occurs, the IRB must include a documented statement for the reason and must report this immediately to the investigator, appropriate institutional officials, and HHS.

The protection of human subjects is a shared responsibility between the institutional officials, the IRB, and the investigator. It should not rest solely with the IRB. The institutional official is responsible for choosing one or more IRBs to review research; providing enough space, staff, and other resources to support the IRB's review and recordkeeping responsibilities; providing education and training for the IRB staff and investigators; providing effective communication and guidance on human subject research; ensuring that investigators carry out their research responsibilities with the utmost respect for human subjects; and serving as the point of contact for OHRP or designating another individual to undertake this responsibility.

The IRB is made up of at least five members with diversified backgrounds per federal regulation, such as including at least one member with a scientific background and at least one member in a nonscientific area. However, most organizations have more than that number. For example, many large universities are composed of 10 IRB committees, each functioning as a separate IRB under a central administration and support from the main IRB office. An IRB vice chairperson and several members with expertise in many diversified areas comprise the IRB committee. Also, the IRB office includes additional staff that reviews exempt or expedited research proposals.

A typical IRB in a large university may consist of the following individuals:

- *Chairperson:* Has ultimate responsibility for the review and approval of the research study protocol as it relates to human subject research.
- *Director, IRB office:* Manages the entire IRB office. Develops policies and procedures as they pertain to appropriate federal and state regulations pertaining to human subject research and protection. Provides continuing education to the organization at large.
- *Legal counsel:* Advises the entire IRB office staff on legal issues pertaining to human subject research and protection.
- *Committee vice chairpersons:* Conduct the IRB committee to review and approve research study protocol as it pertains to human subject protections.
- *Exempt/expedited vice chairpersons:* Conduct the organization and management of the review and approval of exempt or expedited research study protocols.
- *Education coordinator:* Provides orientation and continuing education to IRB committee members, researchers, IRB staff, and the research community.
- *Research review coordinators:* Review all IRB applications, attends all IRB committee meetings, ensures compliance with IRB policies and procedures, and records all minutes.
- *Adverse event coordinators:* Review and develop the response to all adverse-related events that may occur as part of the research study protocol. Provides c\ontinuing education (University of Pittsburgh 2012a).

Conflict of Interest

No IRB member may participate in the review of a research project in which he or she has a conflict of interest. A conflict of interest may include serving as an IRB committee member to review a research study protocol in which one has a definite interest in the outcome of the specific medical device or medication. If this situation arises, the IRB committee member should remove himself or herself from the composition of the committee.

Before IRB submissions are reviewed, investigators may be required or recommended to complete different educational modules. These modules may include research integrity, conflict of interest, use of lab animals in research and education, human embryonic and stem cell research, Health Insurance Portability and Accountability Act (HIPAA) researchers' privacy requirements, blood-borne pathogens, chemical hygiene, responsible literature searching, IRB member education, research with children, and Good Clinical Practices module (recommended for those investigators involved in FDA-regulated research) (University of Pittsburgh 2012b).

Procedures for IRB submission

Exempt, expedited, and full board approval are the three major categories of IRB review for research study proposals. OHRP recommends that clear procedures be developed by organizations so that IRBs can determine whether research is exempt.

Exempt research activities include the involvement of human subjects in one or more of the listed categories according to the HHS Federal Policy regulations (45 CFR 46.101(b) (1–6)). Research that is exempt does not mean that the researchers have no ethical obligations to the participants but that the regulatory requirements such as informed consent and yearly renewal from IRB do not apply to this type of research. The IRB still reviews research protocols to determine their exempt status.

Exempt research activities may include the involvement of human subjects in one or more of the following categories:

- Educational settings (45 CFR 46.101(b)(1)): Research conducted in educational settings involving normal educational practices such as testing different instructional methods (for example, differences in learning outcomes between distance education and traditional classroom)
- Use of educational tests, surveys, interviews, or observation (45 CFR 46.101 (b)(2)): Research conducted in any setting in which educational tests such as aptitude or achievement tests are conducted unless participants are identified in any way when data are collected
- Use of educational tests, surveys, interviews, or observation (45 CFR 46.101 (b)(3)): Research conducted that is not exempt under paragraph (b)(2) if (i) the human subjects are elected or appointed public officials or candidates for public office; or (ii) federal statute(s) require(s) without exception that the confidentiality of the personally identifiable information be maintained throughout the research and thereafter
- Research involving the collection or study of existing data, documents, records, pathological specimens, or diagnostic specimens (45 CFR 46.101 (b)(4)): if these sources are publicly available or if the information is recorded by the investigator in such a manner that subjects cannot be identified, directly or through identifiers linked to the subjects
- Research and demonstration projects that are conducted by or subject to the approval of department or agency heads, and are designed to study, evaluate, or otherwise examine (45 CFR 46.101 (b)(5)): (i) Public benefit or service programs; (ii) procedures for obtaining benefits or services under those programs; (iii)

possible changes in or alternatives to those programs or procedures; or (iv) possible changes in methods or levels of payment for benefits or services under those programs

- Taste and food quality evaluation and consumer acceptance studies (45 CFR 46.101 (b)(6)): (i) if wholesome foods without additives are consumed; or (ii) if a food is consumed that contains a food ingredient at or below the level and for a use found to be safe, or agricultural chemical or environmental contaminant at or below the level found to be safe, by the Food and Drug Administration or approved by the Environmental Protection Agency or the Food Safety and Inspection Service of the U.S. Department of Agriculture

Expedited research include those activities that (1) present no more than minimal risk to human subjects and (2) involve only procedures listed in one or more of the following categories as authorized by 45 CFR 46.110 and 21 CFR 56.110. The categories for expedited IRB review include:

1. Clinical studies of drugs and medical devices only when an investigational new drug application or medical device application is not required or when the medical device is cleared or approved for marketing and the medical device is being used in accordance with its cleared or approved labeling.
2. Collection of blood samples by finger stick, heel stick, ear stick, or venipuncture.
3. Prospective collection of biological specimens for research purposes by noninvasive means. Examples include hair and nail clipping or placenta removed at delivery.
4. Collection of data through noninvasive procedures (not involving general anesthesia or sedation) routinely employed in clinical practice, excluding procedures involving x-rays or microwaves. Examples include magnetic resonance imaging, electrocardiography, exercise testing, muscle strength testing, and so forth.
5. Research involving materials (data, documents, records, or specimens) that have been collected, or will be collected solely for nonresearch purposes (such as medical treatment or diagnosis). (*Note*: Some research in this category may be exempt from the HHS regulations for the protection of human subjects (45 CFR 46.101(b)(4)). This listing refers only to research that is not exempt.)
6. Collection of data from voice, video, digital, or image recordings made for research purposes.
7. Research on individual or group characteristics or behavior (including, but not limited to, research on perception, cognition, motivation, identity, language, communication, cultural beliefs or practices, and social behavior) or research employing survey, interview, oral history, focus group, program evaluation, human factors evaluation, or quality assurance methodologies. (*Note*: Some research in this category may be exempt from the HHS

regulations for the protection of human subjects [45 CFR 46.101(b)(2) and (b)(3)]. This listing refers only to research that is not exempt.)

8. Continuing review of research previously approved by the convened IRB as follows:
   — where (i) the research is permanently closed to the enrollment of new subjects; (ii) all subjects have completed all research-related interventions; and (iii) the research remains active only for long-term follow-up of subjects; or
   — where no subjects have been enrolled and no additional risks have been identified; or
   — where the remaining research activities are limited to data analysis.

9. Continuing review of research, not conducted under an investigational new drug application or investigational device exemption where categories two (2) through eight (8) do not apply but the IRB has determined and documented at a convened meeting that the research involves no greater than minimal risk and no additional risks have been identified.

10. An *expedited review procedure* consists of a review of research involving human subjects by the IRB chairperson or by one or more experienced reviewers designated by the chairperson from among members of the IRB in accordance with the requirements set forth in 45 CFR 46.110.

All other research projects that do not qualify under exempt or expedited review must be reviewed and approved at the full board level.

Once the category of submission is determined, the investigator must complete the proper forms for submission to the IRB. The types of forms that must be completed depend upon the level of review. Most IRBs are requiring research protocols be submitted electronically. An IRB protocol checklist is usually provided so that the investigator can determine what types of documents need to be completed and submitted. See figure 21.2 for a copy of the IRB checklist used at the University of Pittsburgh IRB office.

Once the appropriate forms are submitted to the IRB, the investigator awaits a decision from the IRB committee. The decisions from the IRB can include one of the following four categories:

- Full approval
- Approval subject to modifications—protocol is recommended for approval pending inclusion of changes
- Reconsideration—when there are a number of questions and concerns regarding the protocol and full board review and approval may be necessary once all questions and concerns are addressed
- Disapproval—when major scientific or ethical problems cannot be resolved (University of Pittsburgh 2012c)

Management of Handling Problems Related to Risk to Human Subjects

Sometimes during the course of the research study protocol adverse events occur. When this happens the investigator must notify the IRB and complete an adverse or reportable event report. The adverse event report should include the following (University of Pittsburgh 2008):

- Principal investigator's (PI) name
- Title of the study
- IRB study number
- Date of the adverse event
- Date the adverse event was reported to the PI
- Subject ID
- Probability of the adverse event occurring
- Severity of the event
- Causality of the event (Was it due to the study protocol or procedure?)
- Seriousness or outcome of the event, such as death, life-threatening episode, hospitalization, and so forth
- Whether the adverse event was seen before
- Number of subjects exposed to the intervention related to this adverse event
- Whether protocol modification is necessary and if so, a revised protocol and informed consent must be submitted
- Signature of the PI and date

Recordkeeping and Retention

The IRB should prepare and maintain adequate documentation of all IRB activities. This documentation may include (45 CFR 46.115)

- Copies of all research study protocols reviewed, sample consent forms, progress reports, and reports of injuries to subjects or adverse event reports
- Minutes of IRB committee meetings
- Records of continuing review activities
- Listing of IRB members and their responsibilities
- All written procedures for the IRB
- Statements of significant new findings provided to subjects

The records related to this policy should be retained for at least three years, and records relating to research conducted should be retained for at least three years after completion of the research. All records shall be accessible for inspection and copying by authorized representatives of the department or agency at reasonable times and in a reasonable manner.

Informed Consent

Informed consent is more than just completing a form. It is a thoughtful and respectful explanation of information so that a person can decide whether to participate in a research study. The process that encompasses informed consent should not just regurgitate research study information

Figure 21.2.   IRB Scientific Reviewer Checklist

University of Pittsburgh IRB Checklist for Scientific Reviewers Revised May 2008				
OSIRIS Section				
	TRIAGE	**Yes**	**No**	**NA**
T 3.0	Is risk level noted by investigators consistent with risks the study poses to subjects?	❏	❏	
	COVER SHEET	**Yes**	**No**	**NA**
CS 9.0	If not already listed, does this study require an IND or IDE?	❏	❏	❏
	OBJECTIVE, AIMS, BACKGROUND AND SIGNIFICANCE	**Yes**	**No**	**NA**
1.4	Is the research design adequate to yield scientifically sound data?	❏	❏	
	RESEARCH DESIGN AND METHODS	**Yes**	**No**	**NA**
2.1	Is the duration of the study drug intervention limited appropriately to that which is minimally necessary to evaluate efficacy?	❏	❏	❏
2.18	Is there a statistical justification for the sample size?	❏	❏	❏
2.18	Is the proposed statistical treatment of the data appropriate for the design of the study?	❏	❏	❏
2.3.1	Is a placebo being used where an effective treatment exists?	❏	❏	❏
2.6	Are the study procedures and study visits clearly outlined and described?	❏	❏	❏
2.6	Are all procedures described clearly defined as either research related or completed as part of the subject's clinical care? (regardless of study participation)	❏	❏	❏
	HUMAN SUBJECTS	**Yes**	**No**	**NA**
3.0	Is the study population appropriate for the goals of the study? (consider both the nature and size of the sample)	❏	❏	❏
3.5–3.11	Are adequate safeguards in place to protect any subject that would be categorized as vulnerable as defined by Subparts B, C and D? 46.111 (b)	❏	❏	❏
3.13	Are the criteria for inclusion of subjects appropriate?	❏	❏	
3.14	Are the criteria for exclusion of subjects appropriate?	❏	❏	
	RECRUITMENT	**Yes**	**No**	**NA**
4.4	Are methods of subject recruitment equitable, taking into consideration the nature and setting in which the research is being conducted? (46.111 (a) (3))	❏	❏	
4.4	Are the methods of recruitment legal, ethical and free from coercion or undue influence?	❏	❏	❏
	INFORMED CONSENT DOCUMENT--REQUIRED ELEMENTS	**Yes**	**No**	**NA**
4.9	Is there a clear statement that the study involves research?	❏	❏	
4.9	Is there a clear statement of the purpose of the study?	❏	❏	
4.9	Is the expected duration of the subject's participation included?	❏	❏	
4.9	Is there a description of procedures to be following during subject's participation?	❏	❏	
4.9	Are procedures which are experimental identified?	❏	❏	
4.9	Is there a complete and clear description of the potential risks (i.e., is quantitative information on the expected frequency of the listed side effects provided)?	❏	❏	
4.9	Are the potential benefits to the subjects (if any) clearly described? If there are no benefits is this clearly stated?	❏	❏	
4.9	If applicable, have all alternative treatments or courses of treatment that might be advantageous to the subject been satisfactorily described?	❏	❏	
4.9	Is there a statement describing the extent to which the confidentiality of subjects' records will be maintained?	❏	❏	
4.9	For research that is more than minimal risk, is there an explanation of whether compensation for injury will be provided?	❏	❏	
4.9	Is there an explanation of whom to contact for questions about the research, research subject's rights, and in the event of a research-related injury?	❏	❏	
4.9	For research that is more than minimal risk, is there a statement regarding treatment that is available if an injury were to occur as a result of the research?	❏	❏	

		Yes	No	NA
4.9	Is there a statement that participation in the research study is voluntary?	❑	❑	
4.9	Is there a statement that refusal to participate will involve no penalty or loss of benefits to which the subject is otherwise entitled?	❑	❑	
4.9	Is there a statement that the subject may discontinue participation at any time without penalty of loss of benefits to which the subject is otherwise entitled?	❑	❑	
4.9	Does the consent form contain exculpatory language?	❑	❑	
INFORMED CONSENT DOCUMENT—ADDITIONAL ELEMENTS		**Yes**	**No**	**NA**
4.9	Is there a statement that the treatment or procedure may involve risks to the subject (or embryo or fetus, if the subject is or may become pregnant) which is currently unforeseeable?	❑	❑	❑
4.9	Is there a statement that indicates the anticipated circumstances under which the subject's participation may be terminated by the investigator without regard to the subject's consent?	❑	❑	❑
4.9	If subjects are expected to bear any additional costs for participation, are the costs identified?	❑	❑	❑
4.9	Are the consequences of a subject's decision to withdraw from the research and procedures for orderly termination of participation included?	❑	❑	❑
4.9	Is there a statement that significant new findings developed during the course of the research which may relate to the subject's willingness to continue participation will be provided to subjects?	❑	❑	❑
4.9	Is the approximate number of subjects involved in the study included?	❑	❑	❑
INFORMED CONSENT PROCESS		**Yes**	**No**	**NA**
4.12	Is sufficient information provided about the informed consent process that will take place (including who will conduct the consent interview, whether there will be a waiting period between informing the prospective participant and obtaining consent and steps that will be taken to minimize the possibility of coercion or undue influence)?	❑	❑	❑
4.12	Will informed consent be sought from each prospective subject or the subject's legally authorized representative to the extent required by §46.116? (46.111 (a) (4))	❑	❑	❑
4.12	Will informed consent be appropriately documented in accordance with and to the extent required by §46.117? (46.111 (a) (5))	❑	❑	❑
POTENTIAL RISKS AND BENEFITS		**Yes**	**No**	**NA**
5.1–5.5	Are the risks to subjects reasonable in relation to the anticipated benefits, if any? (46.111 (a) (2))	❑	❑	❑
5.1–5.5	Are risks and benefits in the protocol consistent with risks/benefits in the consent?	❑	❑	❑
5.12	Are the potential benefits to the subject and/or society clearly described and outweigh the risks being incurred? (46.111 (a) (2))	❑	❑	
5.13	Does the research plan have adequate provision for monitoring the data collected to ensure the safety of the subjects? (46.111 (a) (6))	❑	❑	
5.2.2	Are the risks to the subject minimized by using procedures that are consistent with sound research design and, whenever appropriate, by using procedures already being performed on the subjects for diagnostic or treatment purposes? (46.111 (a) (1))	❑	❑	
5.4	Have appropriate statements regarding reproductive risks and birth control been included?	❑	❑	❑
5.8	Are there adequate provisions to protect the privacy of subjects and to maintain the confidentiality of data? (46.111 (a) (7))	❑	❑	❑
COSTS AND PAYMENTS		**Yes**	**No**	**NA**
6.0	Are the financial obligations of the subject, the sponsor and the institution clearly described?	❑	❑	❑
6.1	Are costs/availability of the experimental drug/device following study completion addressed?	❑	❑	❑
6.1	Is there a clear description distinguishing between the costs related to research procedures versus clinical care procedures (done regardless of study participation)?	❑	❑	❑
6.2	Do all payments seem sufficient yet not large enough to be coercive?	❑	❑	❑
QUALIFICATIONS AND SOURCE(S) OF SUPPORT/REFERENCES		**Yes**	**No**	**NA**
7.1	Do the principal investigator and co-investigators have the appropriate academic/clinical credentials and experience for this study?	❑	❑	
7.2	Were appropriate references cited in the research protocol to support the research design and the risks and benefits of the study?	❑	❑	❑

but educate possible participants in terms they can understand. Informed consent should contain three fundamentals: information, comprehension, and voluntariness. The written presentation of information should document the basis for consent and for the participant's future reference. The consent document should also be revised when necessary to include changes to improve the consent procedure (45 CFR 46.116).

In most cases, biomedical research requires that subjects be given informed consent. Informed consent is a person's voluntary agreement to participate in research or to undergo a diagnostic, therapeutic, or preventive procedure. It is based on adequate knowledge and an understanding of relevant information provided by the investigators. In giving informed consent, subjects do not waive any of their legal rights nor do they release the investigator, sponsor, or institution from liability for negligence. Federal regulations require that certain information be provided each human subject. This information includes the following:

- A statement that the study involves research, the purpose of the research, the expected duration of subject participation, a description of the procedures to be followed, and the identification of procedures that are experimental.
- A description of reasonably foreseeable risks or discomforts. The description must be accurate and reasonable, and subjects must be informed of previously reported adverse events.
- A description of the benefits to the subject or others who may reasonably benefit from the research.
- A disclosure of the appropriate alternative procedures or courses of treatment, if any, that might be advantageous to the subject. When appropriate, a statement that supportive care with no additional disease-specific treatment is an alternative.
- A statement describing the extent to which confidentiality of records identifying the subject will be maintained. The statement should include full disclosure and description of approved agencies such as the FDA that may have access to the records.
- For research involving more than minimal risk, an explanation as to whether any compensation or medical treatments are available if injury occurs and, if so, what they consist of or where further information may be obtained. Injury is not limited to physical injury. Research-related injury may include physical, psychological, social, financial, or otherwise.
- An explanation of whom to contact for answers to pertinent questions about the research and research subjects' rights and who to contact in the event of a research-related injury to the subject.
- A statement that participation is voluntary and that the subject may discontinue participation at any time without penalty or loss of benefits to which he or she is otherwise entitled.

The regulations further require that additional consent information be provided when appropriate (45 CFR 46.116), including

- A statement that the treatment or procedure may involve risks to the subject (or embryo or fetus if the subject is pregnant) that are unforeseeable
- Anticipated circumstances under which the subject's participation may be terminated by the investigator without regard to the subject's consent
- Any additional costs that a subject may incur as a result of participating in the research
- The consequences of a subject's decision to withdraw from the research and procedures for orderly termination of participation by the subject
- A statement that significant new findings developed during the course of the research that may relate to the subject's willingness to continue participation will be provided to the subject
- The approximate number of subjects involved in the study

Federal regulations also require that informed consent be presented in a language that is understandable to the subject. If it is not, the consent form must be translated into the appropriate language. Subjects who are illiterate must have an interpreter present to explain the study and translate questions and answers between subject and investigator. A model consent form appears in appendix 21A, at the end of this chapter. In institutions where biomedical research is conducted, consent forms are usually maintained in storage facilities monitored by the **principal investigator.** Copies of the consent may or may not be kept in the medical record depending upon organizational policy. Consent forms often contain sensitive information such as that related to genetic testing. Results of tests related to genetic testing are not to be provided to insurers or other parties, and sometimes not to the subject. To help ensure that this information is not released inadvertently in the regular course of business related to the release of information process, some organizations choose to maintain these important documents separately. Examples of documents that are kept in the study center files are listed in figure 21.3.

The Joint Commission also has specific requirements regarding the protection of human research subjects. These are identified in the patients' rights chapter of the Joint Commission accreditation manual (Joint Commission 2012). The specific requirements related to human subject research appear in figure 21.4.

Vulnerable Subjects

HHS regulations include additional protections for vulnerable or special subject populations as subparts of 45 CFR Part 46. Federal regulations (45 CFR 46.111(b) and 21 CFR

56.111(b)) require that "when some or all of the subjects are likely to be vulnerable to coercion or undue influence, additional safeguards have been included in the study to protect the rights and welfare of these subjects." When a subject has limited mental capacity or is unable to freely volunteer, the subject is considered vulnerable. Examples of **vulnerable subjects** include the following:

- *Children* may be vulnerable depending on age, maturity, and psychological state. There is potential for control, coercion, undue influence, or manipulation by parents, guardians, or investigators. The risk is greater for particularly young children.
- *Pregnant women, human fetuses, and neonates* may be vulnerable because of the increased potential risk to them. There is potential for interventions or procedures to cause greater risk for both the pregnant woman and the fetus or neonate.
- *Mentally disabled individuals* have problems with capacity. They may not have freedom to volunteer because they may be institutionalized or hospitalized, are economically and educationally disadvantaged, and suffer from chronic diseases.

Figure 21.3. Study center file contents

- Investigator's brochure
- Signed protocol
- Revised protocols (if applicable)
- Protocol amendments (if applicable)
- Continuing review documents
- Informed consent form (blank)
- HIPAA consent form (blank)
- Copies of signed consent forms
- Curriculum vitae (resumes) of principal investigator and coinvestigators
- Documentation of IRB or ethical review board (ERB) compliance
- All correspondence between the investigator, IRB or ERB, and study sponsor or contract research organization relating to study conduct
- Copies of safety reports sent to the FDA
- Lab certifications
- Normal laboratory value ranges for tests required by the protocol
- The FDA's Clinical Investigator Information Sheet
- Clinical research associate monitoring log
- Drug invoices
- Study site signature log
- Financial disclosure statement

- *Educationally disadvantaged subjects* may have limitations on understanding the study they will be participating in; some may be illiterate. There is potential for undue influence and manipulation.
- *Economically disadvantaged subjects* may volunteer only because they will benefit economically. That is,

Figure 21.4. The Joint Commission standards for human subjects' research

Standard RI.01.03.05: The organization protects the patient and respects his or her rights during research, investigation, and clinical trials.

Elements of Performance:

1. The hospital reviews all research protocols and weighs the risks and benefits to the patient participating in the research.

2. To help the patient determine whether or not to participate in research, investigation, or clinical trials, the hospital provides the patient with all of the following information:
   - An explanation of the purpose of the research
   - The expected duration of the patient's participation
   - A clear description of the procedures to be followed
   - A statement of the potential benefits, risks, discomforts, and side effects
   - Alternative care, treatment, and services available to the patient that might prove advantageous to the patient

3. The hospital informs the patient that refusing to participate in research, investigation, or clinical trials, or discontinuing participation at any time, will not jeopardize his or her access to care, treatment, and services unrelated to the research.

4. The hospital documents the following in the research consent form: That the patient received information to help determine whether or not to participate in the research, investigation, or clinical trial.

5. The hospital documents the following in the research consent form: That the patient was informed that refusing to participate in research, investigation, or clinical trials, or discontinuing participation at any time will not jeopardize his or her access to care, treatment, and services unrelated to research.

6. The hospital documents the following in the research consent form: The name of the person who provided the information and the date the form was signed.

7. The research consent form describes the patient's right to privacy, confidentiality, and safety.

8. The hospital keeps all information given to subjects in the medical record or research file along with the consent forms.

Source: The Joint Commission. 2008. Rights and Responsibilities of Individuals: Pre-publication version. In *The Joint Commission Hospital Accreditation Program 2009* http://www.jointcommission.org.

because they will receive payment for participating in the research, they may "volunteer." They may enroll in research only to receive monetary compensation or medical care they cannot otherwise afford.

- *Individuals with incurable or fatal diseases* may volunteer to participate out of desperation. In many cases, these individuals have failed many treatments and view volunteering in biomedical research as their last chance at surviving their illness. Also, because of disease progression or effects of medications, they may not have the mental capacity necessary to make an informed decision. These individuals may accept high risk because they are desperate for a cure, even when there is little or no prospect of direct benefit.

- *Prisoners* have limited autonomy and may not be able to exercise free choice. They may believe that they will receive adverse treatment or be denied certain privileges if they refuse to participate in the research study. In addition, cash payments may be an inducement to participate in research; thus, it could be said that they are not truly volunteering but only participating for the cash benefit. Prisoners represent a population of convenience; that is, they are readily accessible and available. Studies on a contained population can be done more quickly and more cheaply. Lastly, prisoners may not realize benefits from their participation in research because of their incarceration and social and economic status.

Role of HIM Professionals

Research

The role of the health information management (HIM) professional and the IRB can take on two different functions. First, the HIM professional may serve as the PI for a particular research project. In this capacity, it is the responsibility of HIM professionals to submit their research study to the appropriate level of IRB review and approval. HIM professionals should follow the IRB checklist (refer to figure 21.2). They should also complete any appropriate consent forms (Appendix 21A) so that the forms meet all of the essential rules and regulations that govern the IRB. As the PI of a research project, HIM professionals must follow all of the procedures just as they are written in their research study protocol. Since this is the original protocol that was approved by the IRB, any changes to this protocol should be submitted to the IRB again for review and approval. Second, HIM professionals can serve in a supportive role to investigators conducting research in healthcare facilities. In this capacity, they can provide education and information regarding the necessary policies and procedures that an investigator must follow when conducting research. They can also inform the PI about the proper procedures to follow when undergoing IRB review and approval and provide consultation on

the development of the research study protocol and consent forms. They can also serve as a patient advocate by educating patients about their rights when involved in research. Finally, HIM professionals may be asked to serve as members of or consultants to the IRB as subject matter experts in data and information handling as well as the protection of patient privacy and confidentiality.

Privacy Considerations in Clinical and Biomedical Research

In response to a congressional mandate in HIPAA, HHS issued regulations entitled Standards for Privacy of Individually Identifiable Health Information. Known as the **Privacy Rule,** the regulations protect medical records and other individually identifiable health information from being used or disclosed in any form. The rule became effective in April 2001, and organizations covered by the rule (covered entities) were expected to be in compliance by April 2003.

The Privacy Rule establishes a category of **protected health information (PHI)**, which may be used or disclosed only in certain circumstances or under certain conditions. PHI is a subset of what is called individually identifiable health information. It includes information in the patient's medical records as well as billing information for services rendered. PHI also includes identifiable health information about subjects of clinical research. Patient information considered "protected" is listed in figure 21.5. Deidentification (as referenced in figure 21.5) includes removing identifying information from patient records so that patients' privacy is protected and can include patient name, zip code, and so forth.

The Privacy Rule defines the means by which human research subjects are informed of how their protected medical information will be used or disclosed. It also outlines their rights to access the information. The Privacy Rule protects the privacy of individually identifiable information while ensuring that researchers continue to have access to the medical information they need to conduct their research. Investigators are permitted to use and disclose PHI for research with individual authorization or without individual authorization under limited circumstances.

A valid Privacy Rule authorization is an individual's signed permission that allows a covered entity to use or disclose the patient's PHI for the purpose(s) and to the recipient(s) stated in the authorization (HHS 2004b). When an authorization is obtained for biomedical research purposes, the Privacy Rule requires that it pertain only to a specific research study, not to future unspecified projects. Following are the core elements of the Privacy Rule authorization:

- A description of the PHI to be used or disclosed, identifying the information in a specific and meaningful manner
- The names or other specific identification of the person or persons authorized to make the requested use or disclosure

Figure 21.5.   Deidentifying protected health information

The Privacy Rule allows covered entities to deidentify data by removing the following 18 elements that may be used to identify the individual or the individual's relatives, employers, or household members.

1. Names

2. All geographic subdivisions smaller than a state, including street address, city, county, precinct, ZIP code, except for the initial three digits of a ZIP code if, according to the current publicly available data from the Bureau of the Census:

   a. The geographic unit formed by combining all ZIP codes with the same three initial digits contains more than 20,000 people.

   b. The initial three digits of a ZIP code for all such geographic units containing 20,000 or fewer people are changed to 000.

3. All elements of dates (except year) for dates directly related to an individual, including birth date, admission date, discharge date, date of death; and all ages over 89 and all elements of dates (including year) indicative of such age, except that such ages and elements may be aggregated into a single category of age 90 or older.

4. Telephone numbers

5. Facsimile numbers

6. Electronic mail addresses

7. Social Security numbers

8. Medical record numbers

9. Health plan beneficiary numbers

10. Account numbers

11. Certificate/license numbers

12. Vehicle identifiers and serial numbers, including license plate numbers

13. Device identifiers and serial numbers

14. Web universal resource locators (URLs)

15. Internet protocol (IP) address numbers

16. Biometric identifiers, including fingerprints and voiceprints

17. Full face photographic images and any comparable images

18. Any other unique identifying number, characteristic, or code, unless permitted by the Privacy Rule for reidentification

Source: HHS 2004a.

- The names or other specific identification of the person or persons to whom the covered entity may make the requested use or disclosure
- A description of each purpose of the requested use or disclosure
- Authorization expiration date or expiration event that relates to the individual or to the purpose of the use or disclosure
- Signature of the individual and date (if the individual's legally authorized representative signs the authorization, a description of his or her authority to act for the individual also must be provided)

In addition, the authorization must include statements indicating the following:

- The individual has the right to revoke the authorization at any time and must be provided with the procedure for doing so

- Whether treatment, payment, enrollment, or eligibility of benefits can be contingent upon authorization, including research-related treatment and consequences of refusing to sign the authorization, if applicable
- Any potential risk that PHI will be redisclosed by the recipient and no longer protected by the Privacy Rule

In addition, the authorization must be written in plain language and a copy provided to the individual. Elements that are required in the HIPAA consent are shown in figure 21.6; optional elements are listed in figure 21.7.

For some types of research, it is impracticable for researchers to obtain written authorization from research participants. Therefore, the Privacy Rule contains criteria for waiver or alteration of the authorization requirement by an IRB or a privacy board. Under the Privacy Rule, either board may waive or alter, in whole or in part, the Privacy Rule's authorization requirements for the use and disclosure of PHI in connection with a particular research project. For example, an IRB may partially waive the authorization requirement so that the covered entity can provide contact information to investigators so that they can contact and recruit subjects into their research study (HHS 2004c).

It is believed that the Privacy Rule will promote participation in clinical trials. Reasons cited most often are concern about health insurance discrimination and loss of privacy should the information be released.

Oversight of Biomedical Research

Because of past abuses of human subjects in the conduct of biomedical research in the United States, Congress began hearings in 1981 to investigate scientific misconduct. Twelve cases of scientific misconduct were reported in the country between 1974 and 1981. Representative Albert Gore Jr., chairman of the Investigations and Oversight Subcommittee of the House Science and Technology Committee, held the first hearing. Continued abuses were reported throughout the 1980s, which resulted in the creation of the Office of Research Integrity to provide oversight of biomedical research.

Office of Research Integrity

In response to the public outcry over scientific misconduct in biomedical research, Congress passed the **Health Research Extension Act** in 1985 (Public Health Service regulation 42 CFR 493). The act requires the secretary of HHS to issue a regulation requiring applicant or awardee institutions to establish "an administrative process to review reports of scientific fraud" and "report to the Secretary any investigation of scientific fraud which appears substantial" (42 CFR 493).

Before 1986, reports of scientific misconduct were received by funding institutes within the Public Health Service (PHS). In 1986, the National Institutes of Health (NIH) assigned responsibility for receiving and responding to complaints of scientific misconduct to its Institutional Liaison Office. This was the first step in creating a central locus of responsibility for scientific misconduct within HHS. In March 1989, the PHS created the Office of Scientific Integrity (OSI) and the Office of Scientific Review (OSIR) in the Office of the Assistant Secretary for Health (OASH). In 1992, the OSI and the OSIR were consolidated to form the **Office of Research Integrity (ORI)** in the OASH. The creation of these groups removed responsibility

Figure 21.6. Model HIPAA consent—required elements

**Authorization to Use or Disclose (Release) Health Information
That Identifies You for a Research Study**

If you sign this document, you give permission to (name of healthcare providers) at (name of covered entity) to use or disclose (release) your health information that identifies you for the research study described here:

(Provide a description of the research study, such as title and purpose.)

The health information that we may use or disclose (release) for this research includes:

The health information listed above may be used by and/or disclosed (released) to:

(Name of covered entity) is required by law to protect your health information. By signing this document, you authorize (name of covered entity) to use and/or disclose (release) your information for this research. Those persons who receive your health information may not be required by federal privacy laws (such as the Privacy Rule) to protect it and may share your information with others without your permission, if permitted by laws governing them.

Please note that (include the appropriate statement)

- You do not have to sign this Authorization, but if you do not, you may not receive research-related treatment (when the research involves treatment and is conducted by the covered entity or when the covered entity provides healthcare solely for the purpose of creating protected health information to disclose to a researcher).

- (Name of covered entity) may not condition (withhold or refuse) treating you on whether you sign this Authorization (when the research does not involve research-related treatment by the covered entity or when the covered entity is not providing healthcare solely for the purpose of creating protected health information to disclose to a researcher).

- Please note that (include the appropriate statement)

- You may change your mind and revoke (take back) this Authorization at any time, except to the extent that (name of covered entity) has already acted based on this Authorization. To revoke this Authorization, you must write to: (name of covered entity and contact information) (where the research study is conducted by an entity other than the covered entity).

- You may change your mind and revoke (take back) this Authorization at any time. Even if you revoke this Authorization, (name of persons at the covered entity involved in the research) may still use or disclose health information they already have obtained about you as necessary to maintain the integrity or reliability of the current research. To revoke this Authorization, you must write to: (name of covered entity and contact information)

- This Authorization does not have an expiration date.

Figure 21.7. Model HIPAA consent—optional elements

**Authorization to Use or Disclose (Release) Health Information
That Identifies You for a Research Study**

- Your health information will be used or disclosed when required by law.

- Your health information may be shared with a public health authority that is authorized by law to collect or receive such information for the purpose of preventing or controlling disease, injury, or disability and conducting public health surveillance, investigations, or interventions.

- No publication or public presentation about the research described above will reveal your identity without another authorization from you.

- All information that does or can identify you is removed from your health information; the remaining information will no longer be subject to this authorization and may be used or disclosed for other purposes.

- **When the research for which the use or disclosure is made involves treatment and is conducted by a covered entity:** To maintain the integrity of this research study, you generally will not have access to your personal health information related to this research until the study is complete. At the conclusion of the research and at your request, you generally will have access to your health information that (name of covered entity) maintains in a designated record set that includes medical information or billing records used in whole or in part by your doctors or other healthcare providers at (name of covered entity) to make decisions about individuals. Access to your health information in a designated record set is described in the Notice of Privacy Practices provided to you by (name of covered entity). If it is necessary for your care, your health information will be provided to you or your physician.

for reviewing complaints of scientific misconduct from the funding agencies.

In 1993, the NIH Revitalization Act established the ORI as an independent agency within HHS. The role, mission, and structure of the ORI are focused on preventing misconduct and promoting research integrity principally through oversight, education, and review of institutional findings and recommendations. Responsibilities of the ORI include

- Developing policies, procedures, and regulations related to the detection, investigation, and prevention or research misconduct and the responsible conduct of research
- Reviewing and monitoring research misconduct investigations conducted by applicant and awardee institutions
- Implementing activities and programs to teach the responsible conduct of research, promote research integrity, prevent research misconduct, and improve the handling of allegations of research misconduct
- Providing technical assistance to institutions that respond to allegations of research misconduct
- Conducting policy analyses, evaluations, and research to build the knowledge base in research misconduct and research integrity

The ORI within HHS conducted a study that examined scientists' reports on suspected research misconduct. From this study, it found that investigators believe that the best way to detect and prevent research misconduct is to have the PI supervise research work closely by reviewing data and applying quality control procedures or audits on the data. The ORI also found that more open communication is necessary to detect research misconduct and that

anonymity is necessary for the person reporting the possible misconduct. Polices and an effective training guide with a system for reporting were also found to be important (HHS 2008).

Check Your Understanding 21.2

Instructions: Answer the following questions on a separate piece of paper.

1. In signing an informed consent, a subject releases the research sponsor from any liability or negligence. True or false?

2. A patient agrees to be a subject in a clinical trial assessing the effectiveness of the combination of two cancer agents. Because the patient is part of this research, all medical expenses are covered by the sponsoring organization. True or false?

3. Medical records of subjects in a research study may be released without patient authorization. True or false?

4. A subject may withdraw from a research study at any time. True or false?

5. Individuals who may be subject to undue influence to enroll in biomedical research are considered vulnerable. True or false?

6. Individuals who participate in clinical trials and biomedical research must sign the HIPAA consent form. True or false?

7. A patient's medical record number is considered protected health information (PHI). True or false?

8. Describe the relationship of the HIPAA Privacy Rule to clinical research.

9. What federal agency provides oversight to biomedical research and when was it formed?

Types of Biomedical Research Designs

The more common types of designs for research involving human subjects include

- Epidemiological studies
- Cross-sectional study
- Case-control studies
- Cohort studies
- Clinical trials

Epidemiological Studies

Epidemiology is the study of health and disease in populations rather than individuals. It examines epidemics as well as chronic diseases. The purpose of an **epidemiological study** is to compare two groups or populations of individuals, one group with the risk factor of interest and one without it. In such studies, the investigator attempts to identify risk factors for diseases, conditions, behaviors, or risks that result from particular causes, such as environmental factors and industrial agents.

The goals are to quantify the association between exposures and outcomes and to test hypotheses about causal relationships. Epidemiological research has several objectives:

- Identify the cause of disease and its associated risk factors
- Determine the extent of disease in a given community
- Study the natural history and prognosis of disease
- Evaluate new preventive and therapeutic measures and new modes of healthcare delivery
- Provide the foundation for public policy and regulatory decisions relating to environmental problems

Epidemiological studies may be observational or experimental. In an **observational study**, the exposure and outcome for each individual in the study is studied (observed). In an **experimental study**, the exposure status for each individual in the study is determined and the individuals are then followed to determine the effects of the exposure.

Observational studies are used to generate hypotheses for later experimental studies. They may consist of clinical observations at a patient's bedside. For example, Alton Ochsner observed that every patient he operated on for lung cancer had a history of cigarette smoking (Gordis 1996). If he had wanted to explore the relationship further, he would have compared the smoking histories of a group of his lung cancer patients with a group of his patients without lung cancer. This would be a case-control study. Research designs that are considered observational are cross-sectional studies, prospective cohort studies, retrospective cohort studies, and case-control studies.

In biomedical research, experimental studies consist primarily of randomized clinical trials. In randomized clinical trials, individuals are randomly assigned to experimental and control groups in order to study the effect of an intervention, such as an experimental drug.

A major purpose of epidemiological studies is to determine risk. In prospective studies, a 2 × 2 table is a tool that is used to evaluate the association between exposure and disease. (See table 21.1.) The table is a cross-classification of exposure status and disease status. The total number of individuals with the disease is $a + c$, and the total number without disease is $b + d$. The total number exposed is $a + b$, and the total number not exposed is $c + d$.

The number of individuals who had both exposure and the disease is recorded in cell a; the number who had exposure, but no disease, is recorded in cell b; the number who had the disease, but no exposure, is recorded in cell c; and the number who had neither the disease nor exposure is recorded in cell d.

Cross-Sectional Studies

In a **cross-sectional study,** both the exposure and the disease outcome are determined at the same time in each subject. A cross-sectional study may also be referred to as a prevalence study because it describes characteristics and health outcomes at a particular point in time. It provides quantitative estimates of the magnitude of a problem. After the population has been defined, the presence or absence of exposure and of disease can be established for each individual in the study. Each subject is then categorized into one of four subgroups that correspond to the 2 × 2 table that appears in table 21.2. An example of a cross-sectional study is determining the prevalence rate of individuals who receive yearly eye exams with type 2 diabetes mellitus.

The prevalence of disease in persons with exposure (a/a + b) is compared with persons without exposure (c/c + d). Alternatively, the prevalence of exposure in persons with the disease (a/a + c) is compared to the prevalence of exposure to persons without the disease (b/b + d).

A major advantage of the cross-sectional study is that it is relatively easy to conduct and may produce results in a short period of time. The disadvantage is that because exposure

Table 21.1.   2 × 2 table for classifying disease status and exposure status

		Disease Status		
		Yes	No	Total
Exposure Status	Yes	a	b	$a + b$
	No	c	d	$c + d$
		$a + c$	$b + d$	$a + b + c + d$

and disease are determined at the same time in each subject, the time relationship between exposure and onset of the disease cannot be established. It describes only what exists at the time of the study.

Case-Control Studies

Case-control studies are a major component of epidemiological research. In them, persons with a certain condition (cases) and persons without the condition (**controls**) are studied by looking back in time. The objective is to determine the frequency of the risk factor among the cases and the frequency of the risk factor among the controls in order to determine possible causes of the disease. In a case-control study, if there is an association between exposure and disease, the prevalence of history of exposure will be higher in persons with the disease (cases) than in those without it (controls). For a case-control study, the 2×2 table in table 21.1 is modified in table 21.3. The proportion of cases exposed is $a/a + c$, and the proportion of controls exposed is $b/b + d$. For example, a researcher may be interested in examining the relationship between cell phone use and brain cancer. The researcher selects the cases as those individuals with brain cancer and the controls as those individuals without brain cancer but very much like the cases in all other characteristics. So, when selecting the controls, the researcher may choose a sibling or friend of the cases, as long as he or she does not have brain cancer. Then, the researcher may review cell phone records or conduct a person-to-person interview asking them questions about their past cell phone use. Odds ratios will be determined. If the odds ratio is 5, the researcher can conclude that those individuals who use cell phones are five times more likely to develop brain cancer than those individuals who do not use cell phones (see "Risk Assessment" later in the chapter).

The advantages of case-control studies are that they are easy to conduct and cost-effective, with minimal risk to the subjects. Also, existing records may be used to conduct the studies. Case-control studies also allow the researcher to study multiple causes of disease. Although the use of existing medical records is advantageous, there are problems

Table 21.3. 2×2 table for case-control studies

	Cases (with disease)	Controls (without disease)
Exposed	a	b
Not exposed	c	d
Total	$a + c$	$b + d$
Proportions exposed	$a/a + c$	$b/b + d$

associated with using them for retrospective research. One major problem is that the cases are based on hospital admissions. Admissions are based on patient characteristics, severity of illness and associated conditions, and admission policies. All of these vary from hospital to hospital, making standardization of the study difficult. In addition, there are problems related to poor documentation, illegibility, and missing records. Lack of consistency in diagnostic and clinical services between hospitals also makes comparability difficult. Further, validation of the information can be difficult. An important aspect of epidemiological studies is the identification of risk. In studies using medical records, the population at risk is generally not defined.

Cohort Studies

A **cohort study** is a prospective study in which the investigator selects a group of exposed individuals and unexposed individuals who are followed for a period of time to compare the incidence of disease in the two groups. The length of time for follow-up varies from a few days for acute diseases to several decades for cancer and cardiac diseases. If there is an association between exposure and disease, the incidence of disease is greater in the exposed group ($a/a + b$) than in the unexposed group ($c/c + d$). New cases of the disease are identified as they occur so that it can be determined whether a time relationship exists between exposure to disease and development of disease. The time relationship must be established if the exposure is to be considered the cause of the disease. For a cohort study, the 2×2 table in table 21.1 is modified in table 21.4.

Table 21.2. 2×2 table for cross-sectional studies

	Disease	No Disease	Totals	Prevalence of Disease for Exposed/Not Exposed
Exposed	a	b	$a + b$	$a/a + b$
Not Exposed	c	d	$c + d$	$c/c + d$
Totals	$a + c$	$b + d$	$a + b + c + d$	$a + b + c + d$
Prevalence of Exposure for Disease/No Disease	$a/a + c$	$b/b + d$		

Group a: Persons exposed with the disease
Group b: Persons exposed without the disease
Group c: Persons with the disease, but not exposed
Group d: Persons without disease and without exposure

One of the most famous cohort studies is the Framingham Study, which began in the 1950s. The research project was designed to monitor the incidence of coronary artery disease in more than 5,000 residents who were examined every two years for a period of 20 years. This study has provided important data demonstrating the relationship between the development of heart disease and risk factors such as smoking, obesity, diet, and high blood pressure.

Cohort studies offer several advantages. First, the researcher can control the data collection process throughout the study. Also, outcome events can be checked as they occur; many outcomes can be studied, including those that were not anticipated at the start of the study. The disadvantages of cohort studies are that they are costly and there is a long wait for the study results. Also, subjects may be lost to death, withdrawal, or follow-up.

One difference between case-control and cohort studies is that the former is a retrospective study and the latter is a prospective study. A **retrospective study** is conducted by reviewing records from the past; a **prospective study** is designed to observe events that occur after the subjects have been identified. The advantages and disadvantages of retrospective and prospective studies are outlined in tables 21.5 and 21.6.

Another difference is that in a cohort study the subjects are individuals with or without the disease and the focus is disease status; in the case-control study, the subjects are individuals who have been exposed or not exposed to the disease and the focus is exposure status.

Clinical Trials

Clinical (medical) research is a specialized area of research that primarily investigates the efficacy of preventive, diagnostic, and therapeutic procedures. Efficacy involves both safety and effectiveness.

Clinical trials are the specific, individual studies within the field of clinical research. They offer a systematic way to introduce, evaluate, and monitor new drugs, treatments, and devices prior to their dissemination throughout the healthcare system. As a result, they have proved to be effective means of advancing knowledge about medicine and health and, thus, improving the quality of healthcare in the United States. Because clinical trials involve patients, they can begin only after the researcher has shown promising results in the laboratory or the results have been well documented in the literature.

Table 21.4.   2 × 2 table for cohort studies

	Disease Develops	Disease Does Not Develop	Totals	Incidence Rates of Disease
Exposed	*a*	*b*	*a + b*	*a/a + b*
Not Exposed	*c*	*d*	*c + d*	*c/c + d*

Table 21.5.   Advantages and disadvantages of retrospective studies

Advantages	Disadvantages
Short study time	Control group subject to bias in selection
Relatively inexpensive	Biased recall possible
Suitable for rare diseases	Cannot determine incidence rate
Ethical problems minimal	Relative risk is approximate
Hospital medical record may be used	
Small number of subjects	
No attrition problems	

The NIH supports thousands of clinical trials (NIH 2012). Private organizations such as drug companies and health maintenance organizations (HMOs) also support them. Trial sites are teaching and community hospitals, physician group practices, or health departments. Many clinical trials are multicentered; that is, a number of research institutions cooperate in conducting the study. In **randomized clinical trials (RCTs)**, participants are assigned to a treatment or a control group. They may be **single-** or **double-blind studies,** in which case the investigator, the participants, or both do not know who is in the treatment or control group until the end of the study.

Researchers conduct clinical trials using **protocols.** Protocols are sets of strict procedures that specify the language of informed consent, the types of subjects, the timing of treatments, the period of participation, and the evaluation of efficacy. For example, in RCTs, researchers must follow strict rules in assigning patients to groups. The rules ensure that both known and unknown risk factors will occur in

Table 21.6.   Advantages and disadvantages of prospective studies

Advantages	Disadvantages
Control group less susceptible to bias	Requires more time
No recall necessary	Costly
Incidence rate can be determined	Relatively common diseases only
Relative risk is accurate	Ethical problems may be considerable and influence study design
	Volunteers needed
	Results may not be generalizable to a larger population
	Requires a large number of subjects
	Problems with attrition

approximately equal numbers between the group of patients receiving the treatment and the group of patients not receiving it.

Most clinical trials consist of three phases. In a phase 1 drug trial, studies are performed on 20 to 80 healthy volunteers who are closely monitored. The objectives of phase 1 drug trials are to determine the metabolic and pharmacological actions of the drug in humans, to determine the side effects associated with increasing dosages, and to gain early evidence of effectiveness. Historically, phase 1 trials are considered the safest and usually involve administering a single dose to healthy volunteers. But they also can pose a high level of unknown risk because this is the first administration of a drug to a human. When the drug is highly toxic, such as cancer chemotherapies, cancer patients are usually the subjects for phase 1 trials.

In the phase 2 drug trial, the number of participants is usually increased to between 100 and 200. The purposes of this trial are to evaluate the drug's effectiveness for a certain indication in patients with the condition under study and to determine the short-term side effects and risks associated with the drug. Subjects included in phase 2 studies are usually those with the condition the drug is intended to treat. Phase 2 studies are randomized, well controlled, and closely monitored. They may include randomization to treatment and control groups and be double-blinded. Treatment and control groups allow for comparison between subjects who received the drug and those who did not.

Phase 3 drug trials involve the administration of a new drug to a larger number of patients in different clinical settings to determine its safety, effectiveness, and appropriate dosage. The number of subjects involved may range from several hundred to several thousand. Phase 3 trials are conducted only after evidence of effectiveness has been obtained. Phase 3 studies are designed to collect more information on drug effectiveness and safety for evaluating the drug's overall risk benefit.

The FDA, in collaboration with the **sponsor,** may decide to conduct a phase 4 postmarketing study to obtain more information about the drug's risks, benefits, and optimal use. Phase 4 studies may include studying different doses or schedules of administration than what was used in phase 2 studies, the use of the drug in other patient populations or other stages of the disease, or the use of the drug over a longer period of time. See table 21.7.

Risk Assessment

As stated earlier, one objective of epidemiological studies is to assess risk. Risk is the probability that an individual will develop a disease over a specified period of time, provided that he or she did not die as a result of some other disease process during the same time period. It is usually expressed as **relative risk (RR)**. Before risk can be assessed properly, prevalence and incidence should be defined. Prevalence refers to the number of existing cases of a particular disease. Incidence refers to the number of new cases of a disease. The *prevalence rate* is therefore the number of existing cases of disease in a particular region during a specific time period divided by the number of individuals in the specific region for a specific time period. The *incidence rate* is the number of new cases of disease in a particular region during a specific time period divided by the number of individuals in the specific region for a specific time period. RR is calculated from cohort studies and compares the risk of some disease in two groups differentiated by some demographic variable such as sex or race. The group of interest is referred to as the exposed group and the comparison group is the unexposed group. The risk ratio is calculated as

$$\frac{\text{Risk for exposed group or the incidence rate}}{\text{of the exposed group}}{\text{Risk for unexposed group or the incidence rate}}{\text{of the unexposed group}}$$

A relative risk of 1.0 indicates that there is identical risk in both groups. A RR that is greater than 1.0 indicates an increased risk for the exposed group; a RR of less than 1.0 indicates a decreased risk for the exposed group.

Odds Ratio

In a case-control study, the objective is to identify differences in exposure frequency associated with one group

Table 21.7.   Phases of clinical trials

Phase	1	2	3	4
Number of Subjects	20–80	100–300	1,000–3,000	Multitudes postmarketing
Purpose	Evaluate safety Determine dosage Identify side effects	Evaluate safety Determine effectiveness	Collect more information about safe usage Confirm effectiveness Monitor side effects Compare to alternatives	Collect data on effect on specific groups (population) Monitor long-term side effects

having the disease under study and the other group not having it. The incidence of disease in the exposed and unexposed populations is not known because persons with the disease (cases) and without the disease (controls) are identified at the onset of the study. Thus, RR cannot be calculated directly. So the question becomes: what are the odds that an exposed person will develop the disease? Or, put another way, what are the odds that a nonexposed person will develop the disease?

In a case-control study, the **odds ratio** compares the odds that the cases were exposed to the disease with the odds that the controls were exposed. Using the 2 × 2 table in table 21.1 as a reference, the odds ratio is calculated as

$$\frac{(a/a + c)}{(b/b + d)}$$

or

$$\frac{(ad)}{(bc)}$$

The odds ratio measures the odds of exposure of a given disease. For example, an odds ratio of 1.0 indicates that the incidence of disease is equal in each group; thus, the exposure may not be a risk factor for the disease of interest. An odds ratio of 2.0 indicates that the cases were twice as likely to be exposed as the controls. This implies that the exposure is associated with twice the risk of disease.

Attributable Risk

The **attributable risk (AR)** is a measure of the public health impact of a causative factor on a population. In this measure, the assumption is that the occurrence of a disease in an unexposed group is the baseline or expected risk for that disease. Any risk above that level in the exposed group is attributed to exposure to the risk factor. It is assumed that some individuals will acquire a disease, such as lung cancer, whether or not they were exposed to a risk factor such as smoking. The AR measures the additional risk of illness as a result of an individual's exposure to a risk factor. The AR is calculated as risk for the exposed group minus the risk for the unexposed group. AR percent is calculated as follows:

$$AR = \frac{(\text{Risk for exposed group}) - (\text{Risk for unexposed group})}{\text{Risk for exposed group}} \times 100$$

Instructions: Answer the following questions on a separate piece of paper.

1. Describe the relationship of the Privacy Rule to clinical research.

2. What are some of the common types of research designs used in studies of human subjects?

3. What are the objectives of epidemiological studies?

4. In what type(s) of studies are medical records used?

5. What are the characteristics of a case-control study?

6. What are the characteristics of randomized clinical trials?

7. What is relative risk?

8. What is attributable risk?

Outcomes and Effectiveness Research in Healthcare

The major objective of **outcomes and effectiveness research (OER)** is to understand the end results (outcomes) of particular healthcare practices and interventions. Examples of patient outcomes include ability to function, quality of life, satisfaction, and mortality. By linking the care that patients receive to the outcomes they experience, OER has become the key to developing better ways to monitor and improve the quality of care. Comparative effectiveness research is the ability to demonstrate the effectiveness or end results of specific types of treatments, medications, procedures, therapies, assistive technologies, and the like on certain types of patient care or illness.

The history of outcomes research can be traced back to the 1860s when Florence Nightingale laid the foundation for collecting and evaluating hospital statistics (Burns and Grove 2005). Hospital mortality rates were the basic measures used for evaluating patient outcomes. The major finding was that mortality rates varied significantly from hospital to hospital.

The Flexner Report (1910), the Codman studies (1914), the establishment of hospital standards by the American College of Surgeons (1913), and the founding of the Joint Commission (1952) are landmarks in the development of outcomes research. More recently, the passage of Medicare (1965), the American Recovery and Reinvestment Act (ARRA) and the Health Information Technology for Economic Clinical Health Act (HITECH) (2009), and the Patient Protection and Affordable Care Act (2010) has accelerated interest in outcomes and comparative effectiveness research with a focus on health information technology and patient-centered care.

Outcomes and Effectiveness Research Strategies

OER may be conducted at the community, system, institutional, or patient level. At the community level, outcomes research focuses on the population as a whole or on specific communities. For example, the "Dartmouth Atlas Report: Improving Patient Decision Making in Health Care" (2011) has found that the rate for mastectomy for early stage breast cancer in women over 65 in Victoria, Texas, was more than seven times higher than for women living in Muncie, Indiana. The average rate of mastectomy was 1.1 per 1,000 females Medicare beneficiaries in the entire United States compared to 2.5 per 1,000 females in Victoria and 0.3 per 1,000 females in Muncie.

OER at the system level refers to the healthcare system as a whole. It may include the entire country or a specific region. Examples of geographic variations in medical care at the national level cited by the *Dartmouth Atlas of Health Care* include the following:

- In Casper, Wyoming, the rate for back surgeries is 10.0 for every 1,000 Medicare recipients, more than six times higher than in Honolulu, Hawaii, where there are 1.7 surgeries for every 1,000 Medicare recipients.
- Heart patients in Albuquerque, New Mexico, receive carotid endarterectomies at a rate four times higher than in Roswell, New Mexico, a difference of about 200 miles away.
- Men in Wilmington, North Carolina, receive prostate-specific antigen (PSA) at a rate more than ten times higher than do men in Minot, North Dakota.

OER at the institutional level refers to the sites in which healthcare is delivered: hospitals, clinics, or HMOs. At the patient level, interest is on the interaction between one provider and one patient. An example outcome study performed at the institutional level is a review of medical records and clinical data of patients with a principal diagnosis of acute myocardial infarction who expire during hospitalization. A second example is the ongoing assessment of patient satisfaction.

There is no standard method for conducting outcomes research at the institutional level or any level. Donabedian (1966) proposed the first model for evaluating patient outcomes. His model focused on measuring the structure, process, and outcomes of medical care. Structure is the setting in which the healthcare is provided and the resources available to provide it. Process is the extent to which professionals perform according to accepted standards. Process also is a set of activities that take place between providers. Outcomes include changes in the patient's condition, quality of life, and level of satisfaction. Characteristics of structure, process, and outcome appear in table 21.8. Other models used for the study of outcomes include the disease model and the health and wellness model. Epidemiological approaches are often used to study outcomes. In the hospital setting, the medical record often serves as the data source for outcomes studies.

Outcomes and Effectiveness Measures

Several types of measures are used in OER:

- *Clinical performance* measures are designed to evaluate the processes or outcomes of care associated with

Table 21.8.   Characteristics of structure, process, and outcome

Structure	Process	Outcome
System characteristics: Organization Specialty mix Workload Access/convenience	Technical: Visits Medications Referrals Test ordering Hospitalizations	Clinical endpoints: Symptoms and signs Laboratory values Death
Provider characteristics: Specialty training Preferences Job satisfaction	Interpersonal: Interpersonal manner Counseling Communication level	Health-related quality of life: Physical Mental Social Role
Patient characteristics: Diagnosis/condition Severity Comorbidity Health habits		Satisfaction with care: Access Convenience Quality General

Figure 21.8.   Sample objectives and outcome variables for clinical research

Objective: to determine whether the treatment drug is safe and effective in patients with advanced chronic heart failure and is effective in reducing the incidence of cardiovascular hospitalization and/or mortality due to all causes.

Primary Outcome Variable: The primary outcome variable is the time from entry into the study to mortality from all causes of cardiovascular hospitalization. A hospitalization is a nonelective admission for medical therapy that results in at least one overnight stay. A cardiovascular hospitalization is one that is due to heart failure, myocardial infarction, coronary insufficiency, stroke, atrial or ventricular dysrhythmias, or symptomatic heart block.

Secondary Outcome Variable:

Time from study entry to all-cause mortality or all-cause hospitalization

Time from study entry to all-cause mortality or worsening heart failure hospitalization

Patient global assessment at the six-month visit

Six-minute walk test at the six-month visit

Other Outcomes of Interest:

All hospitalizations, classified by cause (heart failure, cardiovascular, vascular, nonvascular) in regard to frequency, length of stay, and cost

Number of emergency department visits classified by cause (heart failure or non–heart failure)

Mortality classified by cause (heart failure, cardiovascular, vascular, nonvascular)

All-cause mortality, all-cause hospitalization, cardiac transplant, and left ventricular assist device insertion

Myocardial infarction and cardiac revascularization

The safety and tolerability of the drug as determined by the occurrence of adverse events, permanent treatment withdrawals, changes in laboratory tests, physical exam, and ECG (electrocardiogram)

the delivery of clinical services. They allow for intra-organizational and interorganizational comparisons to be used to improve patient health outcomes. Clinical measures should be condition specific or procedure specific or should address important functions of patient care, such as medication use and infection control.

- *Patient perceptions of care* and services focus on the delivery of clinical services from a patient's perspective. Aspects of care that may be addressed are patient education, wait times, medication use, pain management, practitioner bedside manner, communication regarding current care and future plans for care, and improvement in health status.

- *Health status* measures address the functional well-being of specific populations, both in general and in relation to specific conditions. They indicate changes that have occurred in physical functioning, bodily pain, social functioning, and mental health over time.

- *Administrative and financial performance* measures address the organizational structure for coordinating and integrating service, functions, or activities across organizational components. Examples of administrative and financial measures are those related to financial stability, utilization, length of stay (LOS), and credentialing.

Defining expected clinical outcomes is a major section of the protocols for clinical trials. The principal investigator or organization sponsoring the study must specifically state the expected outcomes of the clinical trial before the investigation can begin. Investigators also must state at what point the research study will stop if adverse events occur. Examples of study objectives and outcome variables are listed in figure 21.8.

Current Outcomes Movement

The current outcomes movement gained momentum in the 1980s when the prospective payment system (PPS) for Medicare inpatient care was implemented. The public and policymakers were concerned that Medicare patients were being forced out of hospitals because "their DRG had run out." The fear was that patients were being discharged based on their LOS rather than when they were clinically ready for discharge. William Roper, who became HCFA (Health Care Financing Administration, now the Centers for Medicare and Medicaid Services [CMS]) administrator in 1986, promoted the use of Medicare databases to monitor the quality of care through measurement of mortality rates, readmission rates, and other adverse outcomes.

Simultaneously, others were advancing the outcomes movement, which contained elements of research, measurement, and management. John Wennberg, director of the

Center for the Evaluative Clinical Sciences at the Dartmouth Medical School, and others developed methods for exploring the impact of healthcare services on patient outcomes. Other research efforts on geographic variations in medical practice, appropriateness of care, and the poor quality of medical evidence to support various interventions and treatments resulted in establishment of the Agency for Health Care Policy and Research (AHCPR) in 1989. The Healthcare Research and Quality Act of 1999 changed the agency's name to the **Agency for Healthcare Research and Quality (AHRQ).** The mission of AHRQ is to support health services research designed to improve the outcomes and quality of healthcare, reduce its costs, address patient safety and medical errors, and broaden access to effective services. The research sponsored by AHRQ provides information that helps people make better decisions about healthcare. The goals and research priorities of AHRQ include

- Supporting improvement in health outcomes
- Strengthening quality measurement and improvement
- Identifying strategies to improve access, foster appropriate use, and reduce unnecessary expenditures

A component of AHRQ is the AHRQ **quality indicators (QIs).** QIs are measures that address various aspects of quality. The various types of QIs include the following:

- *Prevention QIs* identify hospital admissions that could have been avoided, at least in part, through high-quality outpatient care (AHRQ 2011b).
- *Inpatient QIs* reflect quality of care inside hospitals, including inpatient mortality for medical conditions and surgical procedures. Four dimensions are used to assess inpatient quality: volume, mortality for inpatient procedures, mortality for inpatient conditions, and utilization indicators (AHRQ 2011a).

- *Patient safety indicators* also reflect quality of care inside hospitals but focus on potentially avoidable complications and iatrogenic (caused by treatment) events. Patient safety indicators screen for problems that patients experience as a result of exposure to the healthcare system and that can be prevented by changes at the provider level or the area level. Provider-level indicators include only those cases where a secondary ICD-9-CM diagnosis code flags a potentially preventable complication. Area-level indicators capture all cases of potentially preventable complications in a given area either during a hospitalization or resulting in subsequent hospitalization. Area-level indicators are identified by both principal and secondary ICD-9-CM diagnosis codes (AHRQ 2011c).
- *Pediatric quality indicators* use one or more of the other indicators listed previously and adapt them for use with children and neonates to reflect quality of care inside hospitals in different geographic areas across the United States to identify potentially avoidable hospitalizations (AHRQ 2011d).

Examples of AHRQ quality indicators appear in tables 21.9 through 21.11.

One must use caution when evaluating the results of assessments using the inpatient quality indicators. The data collected for these indicators were collected using the ICD-9-CM codes that appear on the UB-04. This represents administrative data and not research data. Limitations associated with using administrative data include

- *Coding differences across hospitals:* Some hospitals code more thoroughly than others, making "fair" comparisons across hospitals difficult.

Table 21.9. AHRQ inpatient quality indicators

Type of Indicator	Definition	Indicators
Volume	Indirect measure of quality based on evidence suggesting that hospitals performing more of certain intensive, high-technology, or highly complex procedures may have better outcomes for these procedures.	Esophageal resection volume Pancreatic resection volume Pediatric heart surgery volume Abdominal aortic aneurysm (AAA) repair volume Coronary artery bypass graft (CABG) volume Percutaneous transluminal coronary angioplasty (PTCA) volume Carotid endarterectomy (CEA) volume
Mortality Indicators for Inpatient Conditions	Conditions where mortality has been shown to vary substantially across institutions and where evidence suggests that high mortality may be associated with deficiencies in the quality of care.	Acute myocardial infarction (AMI) mortality rate Congestive heart failure mortality rate Acute stroke mortality rate Gastrointestinal hemorrhage mortality rate Hip fracture mortality rate Pneumonia mortality rate

(Continued on next page)

Table 21.9.   AHRQ inpatient quality indicators (*Continued*)

Mortality Indicators for Inpatient Procedures	Procedures where mortality has been shown to vary substantially across institutions and where evidence suggests that high mortality may be associated with deficiencies in the quality of care.	Esophageal resection mortality rate Pancreatic resection mortality rate Pediatric heart surgery mortality rate AAA repair mortality rate CABG mortality rate PTCA mortality rate CEA mortality rate Craniotomy mortality rate Hip replacement mortality rate
Utilization	Procedures whose use varies significantly across hospitals and for which questions have been raised about overuse, underuse, or misuse. High or low rates are likely to represent inappropriate or inefficient delivery of care.	Cesarean delivery rate Primary cesarean delivery rate Vaginal birth after cesarean (VBAC) rate VBAC rate, uncomplicated Laparoscopic cholecystectomy rate Incidental appendectomy in the elderly rate Bilateral cardiac catheterization rate

Source: AHRQ 2011b.

Table 21.10.   AHRQ patient safety indicators

Complications of anesthesia
Death in low-mortality diagnosis-related groups (DRGs)
Decubitus ulcer
Failure to rescue
Foreign body left during procedure
Iatrogenic pneumothorax
Selected infections due to medical care
Postoperative hip fracture
Postoperative infection or hematoma
Postoperative physiologic and metabolic derangements
Postoperative respiratory failure
Postoperative pulmonary embolism or deep vein thrombosis
Postoperative sepsis
Postoperative wound dehiscence
Accidental puncture or laceration
Transfusion reaction
Birth trauma—injury to neonate
Obstetric trauma—vaginal with instrument
Obstetric trauma—vaginal without instrument
Obstetric trauma—cesarean delivery
Obstetric trauma with 3rd-degree lacerations—vaginal with instrument
Obstetric trauma with 3rd-degree lacerations—vaginal without instrument
Obstetric trauma with 3rd-degree lacerations—cesarean delivery

Source: AHRQ 2011c.

Table 21.11.   AHRQ prevention quality indicators

Indicator Name
Diabetes short-term complication admission rate
Perforated appendix admission rate
Diabetes long-term complications admission rate
Pediatric asthma admission rate
Chronic obstructive pulmonary disease (COPD) admission rate
Pediatric gastroenteritis admission rate
Hypertension admission rate
Congestive heart failure (CHF) admission rate
Low birth weight rate
Dehydration admission rate
Bacterial pneumonia admission rate
Urinary tract infection admission rate
Angina without procedure admission rate
Uncontrolled diabetes admission rate
Adult asthma admission rate
Rate of lower-extremity amputation among patients with diabetes

Source: AHRQ 2011b.

- *Limitations in ICD-9-CM coding:* The codes are often not specific enough to adequately describe a patient's condition, which makes it impossible to perfectly risk-adjust any administrative data set. This makes fair comparisons across hospitals difficult.

However, despite these limitations, QIs can assist individual hospitals in comparing their organizations with averages at the national, regional, or state level. The information can be used to investigate potential quality problems. Investigation may reveal quality problems for which quality improvement programs may be initiated, uncover problems in data

- *Ambiguity about when a condition occurs:* Most administrative data cannot distinguish whether a specific condition was present at admission or whether it occurred during the inpatient stay.

Figure 21.9. Text from HCUPnet web page (partial)

National Statistics	Create your own statistics for national and regional estimates on hospital use for all patients from the HCUPNationwide Inpatient Sample (NIS).
For Children Only	Create your own statistics for national estimates on use of hospitals by children (age 0–17 years) from the HCUPKids' Inpatient Database (KID).
State Statistics	Create your own statistics on stays in hospitals for participating States from the HCUPState Inpatient Databases (SID).
Quick Statistics	Ready-to-use tables on commonly requested information from the HCUPNationwide Inpatient Sample (NIS), the HCUPKids' Inpatient Database (KID), or the HCUPState Inpatient Databases (SID).
AHRQ Quality Indicators	Ready-to-use national information on measures of healthcare quality based on the NIS, using theAHRQ Quality Indicators (QIs).

Source: AHRQ 2012.

collection that can be remedied through coding education, or determine what additional clinical information is required to understand the quality issues, beyond that obtained through administrative data alone.

An analytical tool that AHRQ supports is the **Healthcare Cost and Utilization Project (HCUP)**. The HCUP database, called HCUPnet, is an online query system that gives instant access to the largest set of all payer healthcare databases that are publicly available (AHRQ 2012). It contains web-based tools that can be used to identify, track, analyze, and compare trends in hospital care at the national, regional, and state levels. HCUP data are used for research on hospital utilization, access, charges, quality, and outcomes. This database can be queried for information when doing internal assessments related to the AHRQ QIs. Figure 21.9 provides a snapshot of the interactive databases available at HCUPnet.

As an example, an organization wants to evaluate its congestive heart failure (CHF) mortality rate. CHF is a progressive, chronic disease with substantial short-term mortality, which varies across organizations. To begin the process, the researcher must review the definition of CHF mortality rate, which appears in table 21.12, and the ICD-9-CM codes used to retrieve the CHF information (table 21.13). The organization's data then can be compared with AHRQ QIs available at the HCUPnet website. (National data for the CHF mortality rate are displayed in figure 21.10.)

Use of Comparative Data in Outcomes Research

Healthcare organizations such as the **National Commission for Quality Assurance (NCQA)** and the Joint Commission have developed measures for evaluating the effectiveness of healthcare providers. The purpose of the measures developed by the NCQA is to provide purchasers of healthcare, primarily employers, with information about the cost and

Table 21.12. Congestive heart failure mortality rate

Relationship to quality	Better processes of care may reduce short-term mortality, which represents better quality
Benchmark	State, regional, or peer group average
Definition	Number of deaths per 100 discharges with principal diagnosis code of CHF
Numerator	Number of deaths with a principal diagnosis code of CHF
Denominator	All discharges with a principal diagnosis of CHF Age 18 years and older Exclude patients with missing discharge disposition, transferring to another short-term hospital, MDC 14 and MDC 15
Type of indicator	Mortality indicator for inpatient conditions
Empirical performance	Population rate (2002): 4.61 per 100 discharges at risk

Source: AHRQ 2011a.

effectiveness of organizations with which they contract for services. The Joint Commission measures also are designed primarily to encourage organizations to improve their own performance and to provide a comprehensive picture of the care provided within the organization. A full discussion of NCQA's HEDIS measures and the Joint Commission's ORYX measures, as well as other performance measures used in healthcare and by healthcare providers, is presented in chapter 22.

Patient-Centered Outcomes Research

The **Patient Protection and Affordable Care Act (PPACA)** established the **Patient-Centered Outcomes Research Institute (PCORI)**. PCORI was established to provide evidence that will assist patients and healthcare providers about

Table 21.13.   ICD-9-CM codes for congestive heart failure

Code	Description	Code	Description
398.31	Rheumatic heart failure	428.21	Acute systolic heart failure
402.01	Malignant hypertensive heart disease w/ CHF	428.22	Chronic systolic heart failure
402.11	Benign hypertensive heart disease w/ CHF	428.23	Acute or chronic systolic heart failure
402.91	Hypertensive heart disease w/ CHF	428.9	Heart failure NOS
404.01	Malignant hypertensive heart/renal disease w/ CHF	428.30	Diastolic heart failure NOS
404.03	Malignant hypertensive heart/real disease w/ CHF and renal failure	428.31	Acute diastolic heart failure
404.11	Benign hypertensive heart/renal disease w/ CHF	428.32	Chronic diastolic heart failure
404.13	Benign hypertensive heart/renal disease w/ CHF and renal failure	428.33	Acute or chronic diastolic heart failure
404.91	Hypertensive heart/renal disease NOS w/ CHF	428.40	Systolic/diastolic heart failure NOS
404.93	Hypertensive heart/renal disase w/ CHF and renal failure	428.41	Acute systolic/diastolic heart failure
428.0	Congestive heart failure	428.42	Chronic systolic/diastolic heart failure
428.1	Left heart failure	428.43	Acute/chronic systolic/diastolic heart failure
428.20	Systolic heart failure NOS		

Figure 21.10.   Agency for Healthcare Research and Quality (AHRQ), Center for Delivery, Organization, and Markets, Healthcare Cost and Utilization Project, State Inpatient Databases, disparities analysis file, 2007, and AHRQ Quality Indicators, version 3.1: Deaths per 1,000 hospital admissions with congestive heart failure as principal diagnosis, [a] age 18 and over, by race/ethnicity, United States, 2007

Population group		Total Rate	Total SE	Non-Hispanic White Rate	Non-Hispanic White SE	Non-Hispanic Black Rate	Non-Hispanic Black SE	Non-Hispanic API Rate	Non-Hispanic API SE	Hispanic, all races Rate	Hispanic, all races SE
Total		28.6	0.2	30.5	0.2	22.1	0.4	27.2	1.2	23.6	0.7
Age	18–44	13.0	0.5	14.8	1.0	11.9	0.7	DSU	DSU	13.2	1.7
	45–64	14.5	0.3	17.3	0.4	11.6	0.4	14.4	2.0	11.7	0.9
	65 and over	34.4	0.2	37.5	0.3	22.0	0.5	32.3	1.5	26.0	0.8
	65–69	18.9	0.5	21.0	0.6	13.3	1.0	15.5	3.4	18.9	1.6
	70–74	23.5	0.5	26.2	0.6	17.1	1.1	24.6	3.3	17.0	1.6
	75–79	28.4	0.5	30.6	0.5	20.6	1.2	24.1	3.3	24.3	1.7
	80–84	35.1	0.5	37.3	0.5	25.0	1.4	35.2	3.2	24.7	1.9
	85 and over	48.6	0.4	50.2	0.5	36.4	1.4	47.9	3.2	42.6	2.0
Gender	Male	28.8	0.2	34.0	0.3	16.0	0.5	28.1	1.8	20.3	0.8
	Female	29.1	0.2	33.9	0.3	16.8	0.4	25.5	1.6	21.7	0.8
Median income of patient's ZIP Code	First quartile (lowest income)	30.0	0.3	34.4	0.4	23.1	0.6	23.4	2.6	22.9	1.0
	Second quartile	29.5	0.4	31.5	0.4	20.0	1.0	31.6	2.7	25.6	1.5
	Third quartile	27.3	0.3	28.4	0.4	21.0	1.1	28.7	2.4	22.1	1.4
	Fourth quartile (highest income)	27.3	0.4	27.7	0.4	22.7	1.4	26.2	2.0	25.6	1.8

(continued on next page)

Location of patient residence	Large central metropolitan	25.3	0.3	27.8	0.4	20.8	0.6	25.8	1.5	22.8	0.9
	Large fringe metropolitan	25.8	0.3	26.8	0.4	19.9	0.9	31.3	3.0	21.1	1.8
	Medium metropolitan	28.2	0.4	29.6	0.5	21.0	1.3	28.9	3.1	23.0	1.5
	Small metropolitan	31.6	0.6	32.1	0.6	27.9	1.6	DSU	DSU	35.1	3.3
	Micropolitan (nonmetropolitan)	35.8	0.5	37.0	0.6	28.2	1.9	31.3	4.9	29.7	2.9
	Noncore (nonmetropolitan)	40.6	0.6	41.5	0.7	35.9	2.1	DSU	DSU	28.3	4.0
Expected payment source	Private	33.5	0.6	38.7	0.7	23.3	1.3	23.3	4.2	21.5	2.1
	Medicare	27.7	0.2	29.1	0.2	21.5	0.5	28.5	1.4	23.8	0.8
	Medicaid	27.8	0.9	37.6	1.6	23.4	1.4	21.9	3.5	22.6	2.0
	Other	58.5	1.6	71.1	2.0	30.4	3.7	DSU	DSU	33.5	5.9
	Uninsured/self-pay/no charge	33.8	1.4	44.2	2.1	25.5	2.5	DSU	DSU	25.2	3.5
Region where inpatient treatment was obtained	Northeast	31.8	0.4	33.3	0.4	25.9	1.2	30.4	3.0	22.0	1.5
	Midwest	26.8	0.3	29.0	0.4	17.2	0.8	20.4	5.6	21.6	3.8
	South	28.2	0.3	30.2	0.3	23.7	0.6	19.6	3.2	23.0	1.0
	West	28.3	0.4	29.6	0.5	22.2	1.6	28.5	1.5	25.7	1.2
Ownership/ control of hospital	Private, not for profit	27.8	0.2	29.7	0.2	20.3	0.5	26.6	1.4	22.8	0.8
	Private, for profit	29.3	0.4	30.6	0.5	28.0	1.2	23.5	3.1	24.0	1.3
	Public	33.3	0.5	35.7	0.6	26.0	1.2	35.2	3.4	26.9	1.8
Teaching status of hospital	Teaching	27.1	0.3	29.3	0.4	22.0	0.7	27.5	2.1	23.2	1.2
	Nonteaching	29.2	0.2	30.9	0.2	22.3	0.6	27.1	1.5	23.8	0.8
Location of hospital	Large central metropolitan	25.5	0.3	27.6	0.4	21.2	0.6	25.5	1.5	22.9	0.9
	Large fringe metropolitan	25.6	0.3	26.8	0.4	19.5	0.9	32.0	3.1	20.5	1.8
	Medium metropolitan	28.2	0.4	29.5	0.5	21.9	1.3	26.5	3.1	23.8	1.4
	Small metropolitan	31.5	0.5	32.3	0.6	26.8	1.5	DSU	DSU	33.1	3.2
	Micropolitan (nonmetropolitan)	37.5	0.6	38.7	0.6	28.1	2.0	38.8	5.2	31.6	3.4
	Noncore (nonmetropolitan)	48.5	0.9	49.5	0.9	42.2	3.1	DSU	DSU	31.0	6.2
Bed size of hospital	Less than 100	39.0	0.5	40.2	0.5	29.4	1.9	32.0	5.1	28.8	2.5
	100–299	29.1	0.3	30.5	0.3	23.1	0.8	27.6	1.7	25.5	1.0
	300–499	24.9	0.3	26.5	0.4	20.0	0.7	23.3	2.3	22.8	1.2
	500 or more	26.8	0.4	28.9	0.5	22.5	0.8	30.9	3.0	20.5	1.3

[a]Excludes obstetric admissions and transfers to another hospital. Rates are adjusted by age, gender, age-gender interactions, and All Patient Refined-Diagnosis Related Group (APR-DRG) risk of mortality score. When reporting is by age, the adjustment is by gender and APR-DRG risk of mortality score; when reporting is by gender, the adjustment is by age and APR-DRG risk of mortality score.

DSU—Data do not meet the criteria for statistical reliability, data quality, or confidentiality.

Key: API: Asian or Pacific Islander; SE: standard error.

Source: Agency for Healthcare Research and Quality (AHRQ), Center for Delivery, Organization, and Markets, Healthcare Cost and Utilization Project, State Inpatient Databases, disparities analysis file, 2007, and AHRQ Quality Indicators, version 3.1. The analysis file is designed to provide national estimates on disparities using weighted records from a sample of hospitals from the following 26 States: Arkansas, Arizona, California, Colorado, Connecticut, Florida, Georgia, Hawaii, Kansas, Massachusetts, Maryland, Michigan, Missouri, New Hampshire, New Jersey, New York, Oklahoma, Rhode Island, South Carolina, Tennessee, Texas, Utah, Virginia, Vermont, Wisconsin, and Wyoming.

prevention and treatment care options and the research or comparative evidence that supports these decisions. The major difference in this type of research is that patients will play a major role in the types of research that are conducted as well as receiving information and research results that are clear and easy to understand. These studies will compare medications, medical devices, assistive technologies, surgeries, and such to determine the best ways to provide healthcare to patients. The National Strategy for Quality Improvement of Healthcare (2011) was developed by HHS as part of the PPACA. It sets priorities and a strategic plan for quality improvement of healthcare in the United States. The Hospital Consumer Assessment of Healthcare Providers and Systems (HCAHPS), under Medicare, now requires all hospitals to publicly report standardized information on the perspectives of all patients to include the patient experience and patient satisfaction in the quality reporting. AHRQ has established a patient-centered care improvement guide. It provides best practices to assist hospitals in moving toward patient-centered care. It also provides evidence behind these best practices and examines barriers to establishing patient-centered care.

Patient-Centered Research Questions

A major part of patient-centered research is developing questions that are important to patients and providers of care. Such questions include the following:

- Given my personal characteristics, conditions, and preferences, what should I expect will happen to me?
- What are my options, and what are the benefits and harms of those options?
- What can I do to improve the outcomes that are most important to me?
- How can the healthcare system improve my chances of achieving the outcomes I prefer?

To answer these questions, PCORI will

1. Assesses benefits and harms to inform decision making, highlighting comparisons that matter to people
2. Focus on outcomes that people notice and care about
3. Incorporate a wide variety of settings and diversity of participants

A patient-centered research question should include the following elements:

1. Population of patients and research participants
2. Intervention(s) relevant to patients in target population
3. Comparator(s) relevant to patients in target population
4. Outcomes meaningful to patients in target population
5. Timing: outcomes and length of follow-up
6. Setting and providers

PCORI explains that people sometimes care about outcomes that are different than the outcomes of interest to investigators. They care about things they notice such as pain and fatigue levels even though these elements may be more difficult to measure. For example, when measuring the outcomes related to a new drug for cancer, investigators may measure the difference in blood markers, while patients will focus on an end result of nausea.

The role and goal of PCORI is to redirect research investigations so that they include patient-centered outcomes such as nausea, pain, and functional status as well as the other scientific elements that may be important. PCORI strives to engage the end users to help shape the research so that the outcomes are going to matter to them: survival, function, symptoms, health-related quality of life versus biomarkers, chemistry panels, and cost of end-of-life care.

A priority of the National Quality Strategy in Person and Family-Centered Care is to increase the use of electronic health records (EHRs) that capture the voice of the patient by integrating patient-generated data in EHRs and routinely measuring patient engagement, self-management, shared decision making, and patient-reported outcomes. One of its indicators for doing this is to collect the percentage of patients asked for feedback. This is an example of how the EHR will be used to demonstrate at what rate the patient is involved in his or her care, and patient-centered outcomes research will be a major component in this data analysis.

Therefore, the HIM professional will play a vital role in making effective decisions about how to incorporate patient- and family-centered data within the EHR so that research in this area can be continued and needed outcomes generated.

Check Your Understanding 21.4

Instructions: Answer the following questions on a separate piece of paper.

1. What is the purpose of outcomes and effectiveness research?
2. What types of outcomes are studied?
3. What is the mission of the Agency for Healthcare Research and Quality (AHRQ)?
4. Who sponsors the Health Care Utilization Project (HCUP)? What is the purpose of its database?
5. What is the focus of the AHRQ quality indicators?
6. What types of performance measures are used in outcomes and effectiveness research?
7. How is patient-centered outcomes research different than research historically performed by investigators?

Summary

Biomedical and health services research conducted on human subjects should follow guidelines set forth in the *Belmont Report,* the Nuremberg Code, and the Declaration of Helsinki. Furthermore, biomedical research on human subjects requires a thorough evaluation and approval from the IRB. The IRB is a review board that examines research studies to determine if the rights of human subjects involved in the research are protected. The different levels of IRB approval depend upon the type of research conducted. Exempt, expedited, and full-study protocols are the different levels of review. Informed consent is necessary when individuals are involved in research. Consent forms are necessary for research that is invasive or includes some type of intervention. The Office of Research Integrity and the Office for Human Research Protections are federal agencies that provide oversight of biomedical research.

Many study designs are used to conduct biomedical research, including cross-sectional studies, case-control studies, cohort studies, and clinical trials. In a cross-sectional study, the frequency of a risk factor and an outcome of interest in a geographically defined population are studied at one point in time. In a case-control study, the frequency of the exposure in the diseased cases is compared with the frequency of exposure in the controls. In a cohort study, individuals with the risk factor and individuals without the risk factor are followed over time for specific outcomes. Clinical trials are controlled studies that involve human subjects. They are designed to evaluate prospectively the safety and effectiveness of new drugs, devices, or behavioral interventions.

A major objective of biomedical and health services research is to quantify the risk of obtaining a particular disease resulting from exposure to a risk factor. Relative risk, odds ratio, and attributable risk are measures used to quantify or assess risk. Relative risk compares the incidence of disease in the exposed group to the incidence of disease in the control group. The odds ratio, the odds of exposure in a diseased group, is divided by the odds of exposure in the nondiseased group. Odds ratios are assessed in case-control studies while relative risk is assessed in cohort studies. Attributable risk is the proportion of total risk for a disease or an outcome attributable to a particular exposure.

Various models for outcomes and effectiveness research are available and are commonly used in performance improvement (quality improvement) programs within healthcare organizations. AHRQ sets a national agenda for the types of outcomes research that should be conducted and serves as a resource for individuals engaged in outcomes and health services research. The PPACA has also set a comparative effectiveness research agenda with a focus on patient-centered outcomes research with the development of the PCORI and the National Quality Strategy.

References

21CFR 56.101 Scope.2011 (April 1).

21 CFR 56.110 Expedited review procedures for certain kinds of research involving no more than minimal risk, and for minor changes in approved research.2011 (April 1).

45 CFR 46.102.Definitions.2009 (July 14)

45 CFR 46.103. Assuring compliance with this policy--research conducted or supported by any Federal Department or Agency. 2009 (July 14)

45 CFR 46.111. Criteria for IRB approval of research.2009 (July 14)

45 CFR 46.115. IRB records 2009 (July 14)

45 CFR 46.116 General requirements for informed consent. 2009 (July 14).

42 CFR 493. Public Health Service Act § 493, 42 U.S.C. § 289b ("the PHS Act"). PHS Act § 493(a) (1985) § 493(b).

Agency for Healthcare Research and Quality. 2011a. *AHRQ Quality Indicators—Guide to Inpatient Quality Indicators:* Revision 4.3 AHRQ Pub. No. 290-04-0020 (AHRQ SQI-II). Rockville, MD: AHRQ. http://www.qualityindicators.ahrq.gov/Downloads/Software/SAS/V43/Composite_User_Technical_Specification_IQI_4.3.pdf.

Agency for Healthcare Research and Quality. 2011b. *AHRQ Quality Indicators—Guide to Prevention Quality Indicators: Hospital Admission for Ambulatory Care Sensitive Conditions.* Revision 4.3. AHRQ No. 290-04-0020 (AHRQ SQI-II). Rockville, MD: AHRQ. http://www.qualityindicators.ahrq.gov/Downloads/Software/SAS/V43/Composite_User_Technical_Specification_PQI_4.3.pdf.

Agency for Healthcare Research and Quality. 2011c. *AHRQ Quality Indicators—Guide to Patient Safety Indicators.* Version 4.3. AHRQ Pub. No. 290-04-0020 (AHRQ SQI-II). Rockville, MD: AHRQ. http://www.qualityindicators.ahrq.gov/Downloads/Software/SAS/V43/Composite_User_Technical_Specification_PSI_4.3.pdf.

Agency for Healthcare Research and Quality. 2011d. *AHRQ Quality Indicators—Guide to Pediatric Quality Indicators.* Version 4.3. AHRQ Pub. No. 290-04-0020 (AHRQ SQI-II). Rockville, MD: AHRQ. http://www.qualityindicators.ahrq.gov/Downloads/Software/SAS/V43/Composite_User_Technical_Specification_PDI_4.3.pdf.

Agency for Healthcare Research and Quality. 2012. *HCUPnet, Healthcare Cost and Utilization Project.* Rockville, MD: AHRQ.

Beecher, HK. 1966 (January). Consent in clinical experimentation: myth and reality. *JAMA: The Journal of the American Medical Association.*" 195(1):34–5. http://www.ncbi.nlm.nih.gov/pubmed/5951827.

Burns, N., and S. Grove. 2005. *The Practice of Nursing Research: Conduct, Critique, and Utilization* 17. Elsevier Saunders.

Dartmouth Medical School Center for the Evaluative Clinical Sciences. 2000. *Dartmouth Atlas* of *Health Care.* Hanover, NH: CECS. http://www.dartmouthatlas.org.

Department of Health and Human Services. 1979. *The Belmont Report: Ethical Principles and Guidelines for the Protection of Human Subjects of Research.* http://www.hhs.gov/ohrp/policy/belmont.html.

Department of Health and Human Services. 2011. Office of Human Research Protections, ANPRM frequently asked questions. http://www.hhs.gov/ohrp/humansubjects/anprmqanda.html.

Department of Health and Human Services. 2009. Office of Human Research Protections OHRP fact sheet. http://www.hhs.gov/ohrp/about/facts/ohrpfactsheetdec09.pdf.

Department of Health and Human Services. 2008. The Office of Research Integrity observing and reporting suspected misconduct in biomedical research. The Gallup Organization, James A. Wells, Project Director.

Department of Health and Human Services. 2004a. Clinical research and the HIPAA Privacy Rule. NIH Pub. No. 04-5495. http://www.privacyruleandresearch.nih.gov/clin_research.asp.

Department of Health and Human Services. 2004b. HIPAA authorization for research. NIH Pub. No. 04-5529. http://www.privacyruleandresearch.nih.gov/authorization.asp.

Department of Health and Human Services 2004c. Institutional review boards and the HIPAA Privacy Rule. NIH Pub.No. 03-5428. http://www.privacyruleandresearch.nih.gov/irbandprivacyrule.asp.

Donabedian, A. 1966. Evaluating the quality of medical care. *Milbank Memorial Fund Quarterly: Health and Society* 44(3): 166–203.

Emanuel, E. and J. Menikoff, 2011. Reforming the regulations governing research and human subjects. *New England Journal of Medicine* 365:1145–1150.

Gordis, L. 1996. *Epidemiology.* Philadelphia: W.B. Saunders.

Joint Commission. 2012. *Comprehensive Accreditation Manual for Hospitals.* Oakbrook Terrace, IL: Joint Commission.

National Institutes of Health. 2012. Clinicaltrials.gov. http://clinicaltrials.gov.

National Institutes of Health, Office of Human Subjects Research. 1979. *The Belmont Report: Ethical Principles and Guidelines for the Protection of Human Subjects of Research.* The National Commission for the Protection of Human Subjects of Biomedical and Behavioral Research. http://ohsr.od.nih.gov/guidelines/belmont.html.

National Strategy for Quality Improvement in Healthcare. 2011. Healthcare.gov. http://www.healthcare.gov/law/resources/reports/quality03212011a.html.

Patient Centered Outcomes Research Institute (PCORI). 2012. http://www.pcori.org/about/.

Patient Protection and Affordable Care Act (PPACA). 2010. http://housedocs.house.gov/energycommerce/ppacacon.pdf.

The Nuremberg Code. 1949. Washington, D.C.: US Government Printing Office. Reprinted in *Trials of War Criminals before the Nuremberg Military Tribunals under Control Council Law* 2(10): 188–182. http://www.nihtraining.com/ohsrsite/guidelines/nuremberg.

University of Pittsburgh. 2012a. *Institutional Review Board Reference Manual.* human subject research and the authority and jurisdiction of the University of Pittsburgh IRB. http://www.irb.pitt.edu/PandP/default.asp#3.

University of Pittsburgh. 2012b. Conflict of interest policies: http://www.coi.pitt.edu/index.htm.

University of Pittsburgh. 2012c. *Institutional Review Board Reference Manual.* General procedures for all IRB submissions. http://www.irb.pitt.edu/PandP/default.asp#8.

University of Pittsburgh. 2008. Adverse event reporting form. www.irb.pitt.edu/irbforms/Int%20AE%20form6.08.doc.

Watzlaf, V., L. Kuller, and F. Ruben. 1998 (July). The use of medical record and financial data to examine the cost of infections in the elderly. *Pharmacy Practice Management Quarterly* 18(2).

Appendix 21A
Sample Informed Consent Document

Revised 6/2/08

SAMPLE INFORMED CONSENT DOCUMENT

Please note that some of the language contained in this sample consent document may not be appropriate for the type of study that you are conducting. If you would like assistance on how to modify the document for your study, please contact the IRB Office.

ONLY INCLUDE THIS HEADER ON ALL CONSENT PAGES IF YOU ARE SUBMITTING A PAPER APPLICATION. IF YOU ARE SUBMITTING AN ELECTRONIC SUBMISSION THROUGH OSIRIS (CURRENTLY REQUIRED FOR ALL NEW PROTOCOLS), PLEASE USE THE WATERMARK THAT IS AVAILABLE THROUGH THE SYSTEM.

(Division, Department, School, or Center Letterhead)

University of Pittsburgh
Institutional Review Board
Approval Date:
Renewal Date:
IRB Number:

CONSENT TO ACT AS A PARTICIPANT IN A RESEARCH STUDY

TITLE: Phase III Evaluation of Iometinol-300 as a Contrast Medium for CT Scans

PRINCIPAL INVESTIGATOR:

Cynthia Curie, M.D.
Professor of Radiology
University of Pittsburgh
Room B-319, UPMC Presbyterian
Telephone: 412-647-xxxx

CO-INVESTIGATORS:

Ray Rembrant, M.D.
Associate Professor of Radiology
University of Pittsburgh
Room B-325, UPMC Presbyterian
Telephone: 412-647-xxxx

SOURCE OF SUPPORT:

January Laboratories, Inc.
Department of Radiology, UPMC

Page 1 of 11

Participant's Initials_____

Revised 6/2/08

Why is this research being done?

You are being asked to participate in a research study in which we will test whether an "investigational" drug, called Iometinol-300, can further improve the pictures taken during CT scans, compared to drugs used currently. We will also test the safety of this "investigational drug". Computerized tomography (CT scan) is a method to take pictures of internal organs using X-rays. To increase the quality of these pictures, a drug ("X-ray dye") is often given by injection into a vein prior to the CT scan. Iometinol-300 is an "investigational" X-ray dye. This drug is considered "investigational" because it has not received approval from the Food and Drug Administration for general use.

In this research study, we will compare the CT scan pictures taken with the study drug, Iometinol-300, to those taken with the standard drug currently used in the radiology department. We will also evaluate if the study drug causes any changes to your body or blood.

Who is being asked to take part in this research study?

You are being invited to take part in this research study because you have already been scheduled for a CT scan of your head using the standard drug. The results of the CT scan using the standard drug will be compared to the results of an extra, research CT scan using the study drug to show us which of the two drugs was better for your particular case.

People invited to participate in this study must be between 18-60 years of age and, if female, cannot be pregnant. The study is being performed on a total of 60 individuals in three different medical centers in the United States. At this medical center, 20 individuals will participate.

What procedures will be performed for research purposes?

If you decide to take part in this research study, you will undergo the following procedures that are not part of your standard medical care:

Screening Procedures:

Procedures to determine if you are eligible to take part in a research study are called "screening procedures". For this research study, the screening procedures include:

1. For women who could possibly be pregnant, a small sample (about 1 teaspoonful) of blood will be taken from a vein in your arm for a pregnancy test. Pregnant women, or women who are currently breast-feeding an infant, will not be allowed to take part in this study.

Page 2 of 11   Participant's Initials_____

Revised 6/2/08

<u>Experimental Procedures:</u>
If you qualify to take part in this research study, you will undergo the experimental procedures listed below. These procedures will take place in the radiology department.

1. Prior to the injection of the study drug and the extra, research CT scan, we will measure your blood pressure, temperature, and heart rate. In addition, we will obtain a blood sample (about 1 teaspoonful) from a vein in your arm for safety tests. This will require about 30 minutes of your time.

2. The study drug will be injected by vein followed by the extra, research CT scan.

<u>Monitoring/Follow-up Procedures:</u>
Procedures performed to evaluate the effectiveness and safety of the experimental procedures are called "monitoring " or "follow-up" procedures. For this research study, the monitoring/follow-up procedures include:

1. One hour after the injection of the study drug, we will again measure your blood pressure, temperature, and heart rate. Thus, the study drug injection, research CT scan, and repeat safety measures will require about 1 hour of your time.

   You are free to leave the radiology department after these measures, but you will need to return 3 hours later for additional safety tests.

2. Four hours after the injection of the study drug, we will once again measure your blood pressure, temperature, and heart rate. These repeat safety measures will require about 15 minutes of your time.

   You are free to go home after these measures, but you will need to return the next day for final safety tests.

3. At about 24 hours (1 day) following injection of the study drug, we will measure your blood pressure, temperature, and heart rate. We will also obtain another sample (about 1 teaspoonful) of blood from your vein for follow-up safety tests. These procedures will require about 30 minutes of your time and will be performed in the radiology department.

4. The investigators will compare your scheduled CT scan using the standard drug to the research CT scan using the study drug.

Page 3 of 11   Participant's Initials_____

Revised 6/2/08

What are the possible risks, side effects, and discomforts of this research study?
The possible risks of this research study may be due to the study drug, the blood tests, and/or the radiation exposure from the extra CT scan.

Risks of the Study Drug:
Previous human research studies using the study drug have shown that the nature and number of adverse events associated with its use are similar to those which occur with the standard drugs used for CT scans.

> Infrequent adverse events (occur in 1–10%, or 1–10 out of 100 people): Itching, hives, nausea, and vomiting may be expected in 1-2% of the individuals who receive the study drug. These adverse events are usually mild in severity.
>
> Rare adverse events (occur in less than 1%, or less than 1 out of 100 people): In about 1 out of every 10,000 injections (0.01%), more severe reactions (e.g., shortness of breath, chest pain, seizure) may occur. In some cases these reactions can be life-threatening.
>
> As with any experimental procedure, there may be adverse events or side effects that are currently unknown and certain of these unknown risks could be permanent, severe, or life threatening.
>
> A physician and emergency drugs and equipment will be readily available should you experience any adverse reactions from administration of the study drug.
>
> Because participation in this study may harm a pregnancy, you and any person with whom you have sex must use an approved form of birth control. If you become pregnant or father a child while you are in this study, you must tell your doctor at once. Also, women must not breast feed while in this study. If you are a woman and you are able to become pregnant, you will have a *(insert the appropriate measurement: blood or urine)* test to make sure that you are not pregnant before you are permitted to undergo the experimental procedures. If you have questions, you are encouraged to speak with either the study doctor or your personal physician. **(Note: Additional examples of acceptable reproductive risk language appear on the IRB web site in a document entitled "Guidance for Reproductive Risk Language for Consents Revised February 22, 2008.")**

Risks of the Blood Tests:
Bruising, soreness, or rarely, infection may occur as a result of the needle sticks to obtain blood from your vein.

Page 4 of 11   Participant's Initials_____

Revised 6/2/08

Risks of Radiation Exposure:
Participation in this research study will involve exposure to radiation from the extra, research CT scan. The amount of radiation exposure that you will receive from this extra CT scan is about 1 rem (a unit of radiation exposure) to your head, with minimum exposure of other areas of your body. For comparison, radiation
\workers are permitted, by federal regulation, a maximum radiation exposure of 50 rems per year to any single body organ. There is no minimum amount of radiation exposure that is recognized as being totally free of the risk of causing genetic mutations (abnormal cells) or cancer. However, the risk associated with the amount of radiation exposure that you will receive from taking part in this study is felt to be low and comparable to everyday risks.

What are possible benefits from taking part in this study?
You will likely receive no direct benefit from taking part in this research study. Should the study drug be better than the standard drug, it is possible that you may receive some benefit from the higher quality CT scan. However, such a benefit cannot be guaranteed.

What treatments or procedures are available if I decide not to take part in this research study?
If you decide not to take part in this research study, you will have only the routine CT scan for which you were scheduled, using the standard drug.

If I agree to take part in this research study, will I be told of any new risks that may be found during the course of the study?
You will be promptly notified if, during the conduct of this research study, any new information develops which may cause you to change your mind about continuing to participate.

Will my insurance provider or I be charged for the costs of any procedures performed as part of this research study?
Neither you, nor your insurance provider, will be charged for the costs of any of the procedures performed for the purpose of this research study (i.e., the Screening Procedures, Experimental Procedures, or Monitoring/Follow-up Procedures described above). You will be charged, in the standard manner, for any procedures performed for your routine medical care (e.g., the CT scan for which you were already scheduled).
(NOTE—IF THE RESEARCH SUBJECTS OR THEIR HEALTH INSURANCE PROVIDER WILL BE RESPONSIBLE FOR ANY COSTS ASSOCIATED WITH THE RESEARCH, PLEASE INCLUDE THE FOLLOWING STATEMENTS):

Page 5 of 11   Participant's Initials_____

Revised 6/2/08

If you participate in this research study, the cost of the experimental (device or drug, as applicable) and/or the costs of certain procedures performed for the purpose of the research study may be billed to your health insurance provider. You will be notified, in advance of undergoing the research procedures should your health insurance provider refuse to cover certain or all of these research costs and if any of these uncovered research costs will be billed directly to you. In this situation, you will be provided with a price estimate for the uncovered research costs that will be billed to you. If you decide to continue your participation in this research study, you will be required to meet with a hospital financial counselor to arrange for your advance payment of these uncovered research costs. If you do not have health care insurance, you will be provided with a price estimate for the research costs that will be billed to you. If, you decide to continue your participation in this research study, you will be required to meet with a hospital financial counselor to arrange for your advance payment of these research costs.

Will I be paid if I take part in this research study?
You will be paid a total of $150 if you complete all parts of this study. If, for whatever reason, you complete part but not all of the study, the terms of this payment will be as follows: 1) $20 for completing the initial temperature, blood pressure, and heart rate measurements and blood sample (if applicable); 2) an additional $50 for completing the extra, research CT scan using the new drug; 3) an additional $20 for completing the repeat measurements at 1 hour after injection of the study drug; 4) an additional $20 for completing the repeat measurements at 4 hours after injection of the study drug; and 5) an additional $40 for completing the repeat measurements and blood sample at 24 hours after injection of the study drug.
In addition, any parking fees related to your participation in this study will be paid for by the study.

Who will pay if I am injured as a result of taking part in this study?
For research that is NOT commercially sponsored but is conducted at Pitt or UPMC facilities utilize the following language:
If you believe that the research procedures have resulted in an injury to you, immediately contact the Principal Investigator who is listed on the first page of this form. Emergency medical treatment for injuries solely and directly related to your participation in this research study will be provided to you by the hospitals of UPMC. Your insurance provider may be billed for the costs of this emergency treatment, but none of those costs will be charged directly to you. If your research-related injury requires medical care beyond this emergency treatment, you will be responsible for the costs of this follow-up care. At this time, there is no plan for any additional financial compensation.

                    Page 6 of 11   Participant's Initials_____

Revised 6/2/08

For research that IS commercially sponsored and the protocol is provided by the sponsor, please see Chapter 8 of the IRB Reference Manual for instructions.

Who will know about my participation in this research study?

Any information about you obtained from this research will be kept as confidential (private) as possible. All records related to your involvement in this research study will be stored in a locked file cabinet. Your identity on these records will be indicated by a case number rather than by your name, and the information linking these case numbers with your identity will be kept separate from the research records. You will not be identified by name in any publication of the research results unless you sign a separate consent form giving your permission (release).

Will this research study involve the use or disclosure of my identifiable medical information?

This research study will involve the recording of current and/or future identifiable medical information from your hospital and/or other (e.g., physician office) records. The information that will be recorded will be limited to information concerning the purpose of the CT scan that you were scheduled to undergo for your medical care, the results of this CT scan, and any adverse events that may have been associated with the approved X-ray dye used in this CT scan. This information will be compared to the research CT scan performed using the study drug for the purpose of evaluating the safety and effectiveness of the study drug.

This research study will result in identifiable information that will be placed into your medical records held at UPMC Presbyterian. The nature of the identifiable information resulting from your participation in this research study that will be recorded in your medical record includes the results of the additional CT scan performed for research purposes and information related to any adverse events you may suffer following the injection of the study drug.

Who will have access to identifiable information related to my participation in this research study?

In addition to the investigators listed on the first page of this authorization (consent) form and their research staff, the following individuals will or may have access to identifiable information (which may include your identifiable medical information) related to your participation in this research study:

Authorized representatives of the University of Pittsburgh Research Conduct and Compliance Office may review your identifiable research information (which may include your identifiable medical information) for the purpose of monitoring the appropriate conduct of this research study.

Page 7 of 11   Participant's Initials_____

Revised 6/2/08

In unusual cases, the investigators may be required to release identifiable information (which may include your identifiable medical information) related to your participation in this research study in response to an order from a court of law. If the investigators learn that you or someone with whom you are involved is in serious danger or potential harm, they will need to inform, as required by Pennsylvania law, the appropriate agencies.

Authorized representatives of the sponsor of this research study, January Laboratories, Inc., will review and/or obtain identifiable information (which may include your identifiable medical information) related to your participation in this research study for the purpose of monitoring the accuracy and completeness of the research data and for performing required scientific analyses of the research data. Authorized representatives of the study sponsor may also be present during your participation in CT procedures performed as part of this research study. While the study sponsor understands the importance of maintaining the confidentiality of your identifiable research and medical information, the UPMC and University of Pittsburgh cannot guarantee the confidentiality of this information after it has been obtained by the study sponsor. The investigators involved in the conduct of this research study may receive funding from the sponsor to perform the research procedures and to provide the sponsor with identifiable research and medical information related to your participation in the study.

Authorized representatives of the U.S. Food and Drug Administration may review and/or obtain identifiable information (which may include your identifiable medical information) related to your participation in this research study for the purpose of monitoring the accuracy of the research data. While the U.S. Food and Drug Administration understands the importance of maintaining the confidentiality of your identifiable research and medical information, the University of Pittsburgh and UPMC cannot guarantee the confidentiality of this information after it has been obtained by the U.S. Food and Drug Administration.

Authorized representatives of the UPMC hospitals or other affiliated health care providers may have access to identifiable information (which may include your identifiable medical information) related to your participation in this research study for the purpose of (1) fulfilling orders, made by the investigators, for hospital and health care services (e.g., laboratory tests, diagnostic procedures) associated with research study participation; (2) addressing correct payment for tests and procedures ordered by the investigators; and/or (3) for internal hospital operations (i.e. quality assurance).

Page 8 of 11   Participant's Initials_____

Revised 6/2/08

For how long will the investigators be permitted to use and disclose identifiable information related to my participation in this research study?

The investigators may continue to use and disclose, for the purposes described above, identifiable information (which may include your identifiable medical information) related to your participation in this research study for a minimum of seven years after final reporting or publication of a project.

May I have access to my medical information that results from my participation in this research study?

In accordance with the UPMC Notices of Privacy Practices document that you have been provided, you are permitted access to information (including information resulting from your participation in this research study) contained within your medical records filed with your health care provider.

Is my participation in this research study voluntary?

Your participation in this research study, to include the use and disclosure of your identifiable information for the purposes described above, is completely voluntary. (Note, however, that if you do not provide your consent for the use and disclosure of your identifiable information for the purposes described above, you will not be allowed to participate in the research study.) Whether or not you provide your consent for participation in this research study will have no effect on your current or future relationship with the University of Pittsburgh. Whether or not you provide your consent for participation in this research study will have no effect on your current or future medical care at a UPMC hospital or affiliated health care provider or your current or future relationship with a health care insurance provider.

Your doctor is involved as an investigator in this research study. As both your doctor and a research investigator, s/he is interested both in your medical care and the conduct of this research study. Before agreeing to participate in this research study, or at any time during your study participation, you may discuss your care with another doctor who is not associated with this research study. You are not under any obligation to participate in any research study offered by your doctor.

Page 9 of 11   Participant's Initials_____

Revised 6/2/08

May I withdraw, at a future date, my consent for participation in this research study?
You may withdraw, at any time, your consent for participation in this research study, to include the use and disclosure of your identifiable information for the purposes described above. (Note, however, that if you withdraw your consent for the use and disclosure of your identifiable medical record information for the purposes described above, you will also be withdrawn, in general, from further participation in this research study.) Any identifiable research or medical information recorded for, or resulting from, your participation in this research study prior to the date that you formally withdrew your consent may continue to be used and disclosed by the investigators for the purposes described above.

To formally withdraw your consent for participation in this research study you should provide a written and dated notice of this decision to the principal investigator of this research study at the address listed on the first page of this form.

Your decision to withdraw your consent for participation in this research study will have no effect on your current or future relationship with the University of Pittsburgh. Your decision to withdraw your consent for participation in this research study will have no effect on your current or future medical care at a UPMC hospital or affiliated health care provider or your current or future relationship with a health care insurance provider.

If you decide to withdraw from study participation after you have received the study drug, you should participate in described monitoring follow-up procedures directed at evaluating the safety of the study drug.

If I agree to take part in this research study, can I be removed from the study without my consent?
It is possible that you may be removed from the research study by the researchers if, for example, your pregnancy test proves to be positive. If you are withdrawn from participation in this research study, you will continue to undergo the CT scan for which you were scheduled using the currently approved X-ray dye.

****

VOLUNTARY CONSENT
The above information has been explained to me and all of my current questions have been answered. I understand that I am encouraged to ask questions about any aspect of this research study during the course of this study, and that such future questions will be answered by a qualified individual or by the investigator(s) listed on the first page of this consent document at the telephone number(s) given. I understand that I may always request that my questions, concerns or complaints be addressed by a listed investigator.

Page 10 of 11   Participant's Initials_____

Revised 6/2/08

I understand that I may contact the Human Subjects Protection Advocate of the IRB Office, University of Pittsburgh (1-866-212-xxxx) to discuss problems, concerns, and questions; obtain information; offer input; or discuss situations that have occurred during my participation.

By signing this form, I agree to participate in this research study. A copy of this consent form will be given to me.

_____

Participant's Signature   Printed Name of Participant   Date

CERTIFICATION of INFORMED CONSENT

I certify that I have explained the nature and purpose of this research study to the above-named individual(s), and I have discussed the potential benefits and possible risks of study participation. Any questions the individual(s) have about this study have been answered, and we will always be available to address future questions as they arise."

_____

Printed Name of Person Obtaining Consent   Role in Research Study

_____

Signature of Person Obtaining Consent   Date

IF THE RESEARCH STUDY INVOLVES CHILDREN OR DECISIONALLY IMPAIRED SUBJECTS, PLEASE SEE CHAPTER 6.0 FOR THE APPROPRIATE LANGUAGE/SIGNATURE SPACES.

Page 11 of 11   Participant's Initials_____

chapter 22

Clinical Quality Management

Chris R. Elliott, MS, RHIA

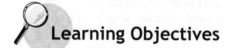

Learning Objectives

- Explain performance improvement (PI) principles
- Describe team-based performance improvement processes
- Summarize the concept of quality and its importance in healthcare
- Summarize the importance of patient safety and the Joint Commission's National Patient Safety Goals
- Identify major organizations that publish clinical quality standards and guidelines
- Explain common ways that healthcare organizations manage the prevention and occurrence of infections

Key Terms

Accountable care organization (ACO)
Agency for Healthcare Research and Quality (AHRQ)
Allied health professional performance review
Benchmark
Board of directors (BOD)
Case management
Clinical guideline
Commission on the Accreditation of Rehabilitation Facilities (CARF)
Common cause variation
Consumer Assessment of Healthcare Providers and Systems (CAHPS)
Continuous quality improvement
Core performance measure
Credentialing process
Dashboard
Evidence-based medicine
External customer
Ground rule
Health Care Quality Improvement Program (HCQIP)
Infection review
Internal customer
ISO 9000
Medication usage review
Mortality review
National CAHPS Benchmarking Database (NCBD)

National Committee for Quality Assurance (NCQA)
National Patient Safety Goals (NPSGs)
Nursing staff performance review
Outcome indicator
Outcome measure
Pay for performance
Performance
Performance improvement (PI)
Performance measure
Privileges
Process indicator
Quality improvement organization (QIO)
Quality indicator
Quality management
Quality management board (QMB)
Quality management liaison group (QMLG)
Scorecard
Sentinel event
Six Sigma
Special cause variation
Stakeholder
Standard
Standard of care
Structure indicator
Tracer methodology

Introduction

The concept of achieving something better is a mainstay of American life. American people expect that the quality of their lives and the lives of their offspring will become better, that is, improve, over the course of their lifetimes. It is the pursuit of the better life that has driven the development of American society: development of educational systems, conformation of political processes, personal and family habits of product consumption, innovation of new products and services, and, most importantly for this text, expectations of interactions with the US healthcare delivery system.

When people go to a doctor they expect to be made better or at least to be assured of maintaining a state of good health. If they receive services from one of the myriad healthcare organizations, they expect the experience to be as comfortable as possible and the end results of the services to be beneficial. Recent and continuing public debate about healthcare access, eligibility, and economics demonstrates that this is not the case.

Those who provide healthcare services in the United States also have expectations of themselves. Caregivers were concerned about the quality of care they provided to people even in ancient times. Around the 5th century B.C., for example, the Greek physician Hippocrates advised young physicians to "First, do no harm." That directive is still part of the physician's oath today. Throughout the history of medicine, providers have had benefit to their patients and clients at the heart of their desire to practice and by and large still do so today. As scientific inquiry advanced in its process, healthcare providers were interested in improving the outcomes of patient care. Florence Nightingale, for instance, is considered to have been the founder of modern nursing in the mid-19th century. She advocated the use of a uniform scientific method of collecting and evaluating statistics that compared mortality rates among hospitals. The results of her measurement efforts showed wide variation among hospitals. She implemented sanitary procedures such as simple handwashing that greatly improved the results or outcomes of hospital care. Throughout history we can find individuals involved in the provision of healthcare services making minor as well as major improvements in the way the services are provided, up to and including those involved in the healthcare delivery system today.

The recent debate regarding the issues in our healthcare delivery system from the access, eligibility, and economic perspectives has made Americans recognize the complexity of the system. Even before the recent debate, the healthcare system had recognized in the late 20th century that it had significant issues around the quality of its processes and results. It also recognized that everyone who worked in the system potentially affected that quality. Obviously, individuals who actually interact and assist patients can affect healthcare quality. But because of the complexity of the system, individuals who basically have little to no contact with the

patient or client can also impact the perceptions of patients regarding their healthcare, whether the experience was better or worse. This recognition now becomes the reason why this chapter must be undertaken in this textbook. You, the developing health information technician, along with all of your colleagues in health professions programs, and with all of the practicing nurses, doctors, and therapists in all the healthcare organizations in the country, make contributions to the perceptions of the quality of healthcare services with which patients and clients come away from the healthcare system every day.

Performance Measurement and Quality Improvement

The most important concept in an introductory discussion of quality is that of measurement. Over the decades of attempting to deal with the issues involved in healthcare quality, healthcare professionals have struggled with where to put the emphasis of their resources. Ultimately, they recognized—with the assistance of the theoretical writings of general industry quality masters—that the key to improvement lay in the measurement of the important characteristics of their practice (figure 22.1). The characteristics could be related to the practice of a physician, nurse, or therapist, or it could be the practice of an organization. The important thing to notice is that the model fits for most individuals, groups, and levels of a healthcare organization.

Definition of Performance Improvement

The word **performance** has been defined as "the execution of an activity or pattern of behavior; the application of inherent or learned capabilities to complete a process according to prescribed specifications or standards" (Meisenheimer 1997). Performance is measured using one or more performance indicators. For example, performance can be measured against financial indicators, such as the average cost per laboratory test, or productivity indicators, such as the number of patients seen per physician per day. It is important to measure the aspects of performance that exemplify its quality and that point conclusively to the aspects of performance that require improvement.

The term **performance improvement (PI)** is a "process for involving personnel in planning and executing a continuous flow of improvements to provide quality healthcare that meets or exceeds expectations" (McLaughlin and Kaluzny 2006). Although a number of terms and acronyms are frequently used to represent this PI concept (for example, continuous quality improvement [CQI] and total quality management [TQM]), this chapter uses *performance improvement*. Numerous improvement models and quality philosophies have been developed over the years. The key feature of performance improvement as implemented

Figure 22.1.   Quality masters

A number of individuals have contributed to the theoretical underpinnings of continuous performance improvement. Over the decades, various aspects of their writings have been integrated into the current philosophy of improving quality in the healthcare arena. Go online and see what you can find about two or three of these theoreticians.

Walter A. Shewhart

Walter Shewhart was a statistician and research engineer for Bell Telephone Laboratories from 1925 until 1956. During that time, he pioneered the use of a quality control mechanism called statistical process control. Its purpose was to reduce variation in processes. Shewhart was the first person to suggest that two types of variation could be at work in a process: variation that was the result of chance, and variation that was the result of a definable cause. He used this method to improve the stability of processes.

He also was the first to develop what he called the "act of control." This concept evolved into the plan–do–check–act cycle. W. Edwards Deming built on Shewhart's work.

W. Edwards Deming

W. Edwards Deming was an American statistician. He is often credited with revitalizing the Japanese economy after the Second World War. He wrote the book *Out of the Crisis* in 1983. In his book, he described his methods for improving quality. Like Shewhart, Deming discussed variation and identified two types: common cause variation (variation caused by chance) and special cause variation (variation assigned a cause).

Deming believed that quality must be built into the product. He made a number of controversial statements about standard management techniques. For example, he declared that he did not believe in performance appraisals, management by objectives, or work standards.

Deming also developed a 14-point plan to help executives lead their organizations. Several of his points can be recognized in the principles of performance improvement. He believed that senior administrators need to communicate a constancy of purpose in which the vision and mission statements are made known. He proposed focusing on the process and not the results. Another of the 14 points was that organizations must not rely on inspection for defects but, rather, continually work to improve production and service.

According to Deming, the organization's leadership also must provide training, education, and self-improvement opportunities for employees and work to help employees achieve excellence in their jobs. Fear must be driven out of the organization because it impedes self-actualization. Barriers among departments and staff must be broken because barriers prevent people from communicating effectively and processes from being improved.

Joseph M. Juran

Joseph Juran also consulted with the Japanese in the 1950s and wrote several books on quality control. In the 1980s, he claimed that management could control over 80 percent of quality defects by using the three central principles of quality: planning, control, and improvement. He believed that training and hands-on management are basic requirements for meeting the needs of customers.

Armand F. Feigenbaum

Armand Feigenbaum built on Deming's statistical approach. In the early 1980s, he emphasized the necessity of integrating the functions of total quality control. Feigenbaum stated that the planning, design, and setup of the product or service must be integrated with its production and distribution. In turn, the product's production and distribution must be integrated with training, data analysis, and user feedback. Thus, customers and suppliers are all incorporated into the total quality concept. The goal is to meet the expectations and requirements of the organizations' customers.

Philip B. Crosby

Philip Crosby was a quality consultant working in the 1980s. He did not agree with his predecessors' focus on statistics. Instead, he proposed the concepts of zero defects and conformance to requirements. Crosby also proposed four absolutes of quality:

• Do it right the first time.

• Defect prevention is the only acceptable approach.

• Zero defects is the only performance standard.

• The cost of quality is the only measure of quality. This means that it is less costly to produce a high-quality product the first time than to manage the losses that result from producing a low-quality product.

Brian Joiner

Brian Joiner, also consulting in the 1980s, maintained that quality begins at the top and funnels down through the organization. He developed the Joiner triangle. This concept has three basic elements:

• Quality to ensure customer satisfaction and loyalty

• A scientific approach to root out underlying causes of problems

• The all-one-team method that encourages and empowers employees to work together to break down departmental barriers and creates buy-in to improvement, ownership in the process, and commitment to quality

in today's healthcare organizations is that it is a continuous cycle of measurement, analysis, monitoring, planning, designing, and evaluating.

Performance monitoring is data driven. Monitoring performance based on internal and external data is the foundation of all PI activities. Each healthcare organization must identify and prioritize the processes and outcomes (in other words, types of data) that are important to monitor based on its mission and the scope of care and services it provides. A logical starting point for performance improvement activities is identifying areas to monitor. Monitoring should include important organization functions, particularly those that are high risk, high volume, or problem prone. Outcomes of care, customer feedback, and the requirements of regulatory agencies are additional areas that organizations consider when prioritizing performance measures. Once the scope and focus of performance monitoring are determined, the leaders define the data collection requirements for each performance measure (Shaw and Elliott 2013).

As shown in figure 22.2, measuring performance depends on the identification of performance measures for each service, process, or outcome determined important to track. A **performance measure** is a quantitative tool (for example, a rate, ratio, index, percentage) that provides an indication of an organization's performance in relation to a specified process or outcome. Monitoring selected performance measures can help an organization determine process stability or can identify improvement opportunities. Specific criteria are used to define the organization's performance measures. Components of a good performance measure include a documented numerator statement, a denominator statement, and a description of the population to which the measure is applicable. In addition, the measurement period, baseline goal, data collection method, and frequency of data collection, analysis, and reporting must be identified (Shaw and Elliott 2013). The sum total of the performance measures selected as applicable to a healthcare organization make up the "Performance Measurement System" required by the Joint Commission for use in accreditation processes (Joint Commission 2009a).

For example, one indicator of quality might be that a physician sees patients within 30 minutes after their arrival at the facility. The organization could measure the minutes that it took from the time the patient stated his or her name to the time the physician first saw the patient. As long as patients were seen within that 30-minute time frame, the organization could assume that it was providing high-quality care. No attempts would be made to analyze the process or take corrective action unless the number of minutes increased beyond the 30-minute threshold. In this traditional approach, organizations actively address quality and performance issues only when they fail to meet the level of quality defined in performance measures (Shaw and Elliott, 2013).

An example of an outcome that hospitals are required to continuously monitor is the monthly delinquent health record rate. The elements included in this performance measure are the medical staff and inpatient health records. Tracking this outcome allows the hospital to continuously monitor its

Figure 22.2.   Organization-wide performance improvement process

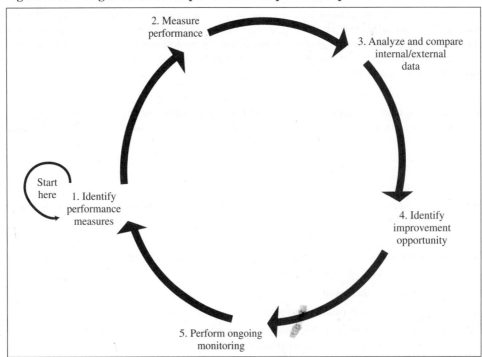

rate or percentage of delinquent health records. If the health record delinquency rate exceeds the hospital's established performance standards (an internal comparison) or nationally established performance standards (external comparison), an opportunity for improvement has been identified. Once an issue has been identified, a team-based performance improvement process may be initiated.

When an organization compares its current performance to its own internal historical data, or uses data from similar external organizations across the country, it helps establish a **benchmark,** also known as a standard of performance or best practice, for a particular process or outcome. Establishing a benchmark for each monitored performance measure assists the healthcare organization in setting performance baselines, describing process performance or stability, or identifying areas for more focused data collection. The Joint Commission is one available external resource that can be used to establish the performance measure of the average monthly health record delinquency rate for a hospital. The Joint Commission will cite a healthcare organization with a requirement for improvement if the total average health record delinquency exceeds 50 percent of the average monthly discharges in any one quarter. Hospitals commonly set the benchmark for their health record delinquency rate at less than 50 percent.

Every department in a healthcare organization should continuously monitor its key performance indicators on a regular basis. Some of the guidelines for data collection for key performance indicators used to monitor health information management (HIM) functions are

- Collecting information that is neither too specific nor too general
- Monitoring the overall performance of the department, using an optimal number of work processes
- Evaluating department units where specialized work is performed, such as a filing unit, report sorting unit, or record pulling unit
- Identifying measures that describe the unit's performance over time, recording on a daily basis but reporting on a weekly basis
- Designing a report that can track data over time, including percentage measures to identify problem areas

Quality Dimensions

Donabedian (1988) contributed significantly to the understanding of measuring quality. He recognized that quality had multiple dimensions that needed to be measured using various types of indicators and proposed three types of quality indicators:

Structure indicators measure the attributes of the setting, such as number and qualifications of the staff, adequacy of equipment and facilities, and adequacy of organizational policies and procedures.

Process indicators measure the actions by which services are provided, that is, the things people or devices do, from conducting appropriate tests to making a diagnosis to actually carrying out a treatment.

Outcome indicators measure the actual results of care for patients and populations, including patient and family satisfaction.

In addition to identifying types of quality indicators, Donabedian introduced the idea that quality has both a technical and an interpersonal dimension. The technical dimension recognizes that caregivers must have the knowledge and judgment to arrive at an appropriate strategy for providing service and the technical skills to carry it out. The interpersonal aspect recognizes that caregivers must have the communication skills and social attributes necessary to serve patients appropriately. The interpersonal aspect of quality recognizes the importance of empathy, honesty, respectfulness, tact, and sensitivity to others. Donabedian acknowledged that it was far easier to measure quality's technical dimension than its interpersonal dimension.

Contemporary Approach to PI

The contemporary approach to PI is much more proactive than the traditional quality management approach. Although PI uses several traditional quality management techniques such as quality indicators, its primary focus is on continually making small, targeted changes for improvement, which over time lead to significant overall improvement. Performance improvement is not a philosophy that is satisfied with the status quo; it is not based on the "if it is not broke, don't fix it" assumption. Nor does PI operate on the theory of identifying poor performers where one conducts inspections to identify defects. PI does not attempt to assign individual blame and punish lapses in quality. Instead, PI is based on the assumption that organizations should continuously and systematically identify and test small, planned changes in processes and systems. Over time, the theory proposes, these changes will improve the quality of care provided to patients (Berwick 1989). Opportunities for improvement are identified by gathering and analyzing data on an ongoing basis.

Creating a Culture of Service Excellence

Providing healthcare services requires safe, accurate, and caring behaviors and attitudes to provide healthcare that meets the expectations of patients, clients, or customers. Healthcare organizations strive to emphasize serviced-based patient-focused care. The mission of most healthcare facilities is to provide superior healthcare in a compassionate manner mindful of the dignity of each individual person. In order to foster an environment of customer service, all levels of the organization must be involved and committed.

Generating pride in work performed by all employees and healthcare providers is key to providing excellent service. A culture that pays attention to details and treats all individuals with respect sounds simple, but in reality it can be challenging. In addition, continual affirmation of a service of excellence culture is required of the organization. This is achieved by managing in a way that gives employees a chance to succeed by recognizing and rewarding employees.

Managers can use various strategies to help determine whether or not service excellence is present. Red flags indicating low service standards include such things as high employee turnover, training that is "one time" in nature, and training to regulations rather than to the needs of the patient population. Ideas that help create an organization or a department that strives for service excellence include: hiring the right person for the right role, orienting employees thoroughly, developing leaders within the organization, sharing information so staff understand the impact of their behaviors on the business of healthcare, managing people with success strategies in mind, recognizing employees for work well done, providing rapid feedback and responses to employees, and supporting improvement teams. Services and products are enhanced and a culture of service excellence established when managers understand the quality goals of the organization.

The goal of creating a culture of service excellence is to provide an environment that recognizes and accepts the limitations of human performance. Technology and systems are developed with the spirit of service excellence and used to support and enhance care providers. The end result is that healthcare delivery is of high quality and consistently predictable with efficient use of all quality improvement methods.

Focus on the Customer

It becomes apparent as one works through the definition of an organization's quality monitors that many cannot be measured without the input of the individuals who are the consumers of the product or service or the receiver of a process's output. As performance improvement practices have evolved, gathering feedback and opinions of customers has become a focus. Many organizations and quality experts define quality as meeting or exceeding customer expectations.

The term *customer* is used frequently in performance management activities. **External customers** are those people outside the organization for whom it provides services. For example, the external customers of a hospital would include patients, physicians, and third-party payers. Organizations also have **internal customers.** Employees are internal customers. They receive services from other areas in the organization that make it possible for them to do their jobs. For example, a nurse on an intensive care unit would be an internal customer of the hospital pharmacy. The nurse depends on the pharmacy to provide the medications needed to fill the physicians' orders for his or her patients.

Employees in one system or subsystem use the outputs from other systems or subsystems of the organization as inputs to their own system or subsystem. The employees then produce new outputs, which in turn may become inputs for still another system or subsystem. In this way, the performance of one system can affect the performance of many others.

To measure the requirements and perceptions of external customers, many healthcare organizations utilize polling methods to obtain opinions of their patients and clients following an episode of care. This is often done through an external survey vendor. The Centers for Medicare and Medicaid Services also publish quality information that it gleans from data reported during the reimbursement cycle regarding hospitals that provide services to its beneficiaries (see table 22.1 for a sampling of vendors of patient satisfaction surveys.).

Another means by which customers can see how a healthcare organization performs is through the publication of dashboards and scorecards. As discussed earlier, quality has many dimensions. Healthcare leaders cannot just focus on one aspect of quality (such as financial) without also considering other aspects (such as patient satisfaction or clinical quality) or they miss the whole picture. Dashboards and scorecards are tools that present metrics from a variety of quality aspects in one concise report. They may present measures of clinical quality (such as infection rates), financial quality, volume, and patient satisfaction. The indicators provide snapshots of all areas of quality to give leaders and communities of interest an overall perspective of the service the organization is providing.

The terms *dashboard* and *scorecard* are often used interchangeably, but technically, **dashboards** (like dashboards on a car) are reports of process measures that help leaders know what is currently going on so that they can plan strategically where they want to go next, and **scorecards** (like baseball scorecards) are reports of outcomes measures to help leaders know what they have accomplished. These concise reports help leaders "align organizational effort to achieve higher levels of organizational performance" (Pugh 2005).

The primary focus of PI efforts must be on the customer. The expectations and needs of both external and internal customers must be kept in mind throughout the PI process. Those involved in PI projects must know and understand their customers and involve them in the process so they can express their needs.

Consumer Assessment of Healthcare Providers and Systems

The **Consumer Assessment of Healthcare Providers and Systems (CAHPS)** is a program sponsored and administered by the Agency for Healthcare Research and Quality

Table 22.1. Sampling of vendors of patient satisfaction surveys

Vendor Name/ Contact Information	Vendor Name/ Contact Information
NRC+Picker 1245 Q Street Lincoln, NE 68508 http://www.nationalresearch.com	LSUS Institute for Human Services and Public Policy One University Place Bronson Hall 123 Shreveport, LA 71115 http://www.lsus.edu
Avatar International, LLC 1000 Primera Blvd., Ste 3144 Lake Mary, FL 32746 http://www.avatar-intl.com	Beacon Technologies, Ltd. 3958 Dundee Rd. Northbrook, IL 60062 http://www.beacontouch.com
Press Ganey Associates 404 Columbia Place South Bend, IN 46601 http://www.pressganey.com	Conifer Patient Communications, LLC 140 Fountain Parkway Suite 500 St. Petersburg, FL 33716 http://www.coniferhealth.com
CTQ Solutions, LLC 500 East Main Street Suite 340 Branford, CT 06405 http://www.ctqsolutions.com	J. D. Power and Associates 5435 Corporate Drive Ste. 300 Troy, MI 48098 http://www.jdpa.com
Data Recognition Corporation 13490 Bass Lake Road Maple Grove, MN 55311 http://www.datarecognitioncorp.com	Regenstrief Institute Inc. 1050 Wishard Blvd RG6 Indianapolis, IN 46202-2872 http://www.regenstrief.org
Professional Research Consultants, Inc. 11326 P Street Omaha, NE 68137 http://www.prconline.com	CAMC Institute 3200 MacCorkle Avenue, SE Charleston, WV 25304 http://www.camcinstitute.org/
Fields Research, Inc. 3814 West St., Suite 110 Cincinnati, OH 45227-3743	HealthStream Research 209 10th Avenue South Suite 536 Nashville, TN 37203 http://www.healthstream.com
Alexandria Marketing Research Group, Inc. 212 1/2 West 5th Street, Suite 209 Joplin, MO 64801 http://www.alexandriamarketing.com	Minnesota Rural Health Cooperative 190 East 4th Street North P.O. Box 155 Cottonwood, MN 56229 http://www.mrhc.net
Center for the Study of Services 1625 K Street, NW, 8th Floor Washington, D.C. 20006 http://www.cssresearch.org	Quality Data Management, Inc. 4015 East Royalton Broadview Heights, OH 44147 http://www.qdmnet.com
Gallup 1001 Gallup Drive Omaha, NE 68102 http://www.gallup.com	WestGroup Research 2702 North 44th Street, Suite 100a Phoenix, AZ 85008 http://www.westgroupresearch.com
Gilmore Research Group 2324 Eastlake Ave E #300 Seattle, WA 98102 http://www.gilmore-research.com	RAND Health Communications 1776 Main St. Santa Monica, CA 90407 http://www.rand.org/health

Source: HCAHPS Approved Vendor List. http://www.hcahpsonline.org/app_vendor.aspx.

(AHRQ). CAHPS has evolved into a source of coordinated survey instruments and reports intended to measure and communicate information on healthcare quality from the consumers' perspective. The original program (CAHPS I, mid-1990s to 2001) succeeded in developing questionnaires and reports for consumers enrolled in health plans. In 2002, the focus expanded and CAHPS II conducted research and developed survey products targeting ambulatory, hospital, nursing home, and dialysis center patients. During this second phase, surveys to assess consumer reaction were developed in various settings including physician offices, managed behavioral healthcare organizations, dental plans, and tribal clinics. In 2007, CAHPS III shifted focus to the development of tools and resources supporting the use of CAHPS surveys. These tools are used by public and private purchasers (employers, state and federal agencies), quality measurement organizations (accrediting organizations, state healthcare organizations), provider organizations, health plans, and consumers and patients.

The **National CAHPS Benchmarking Database (NCBD)** contains 10 years' worth of data from the Health Plan Survey as well as two years of data from the new Hospital Survey. CAHPS is best known for its Health Plan Survey, which is well respected in the healthcare industry for obtaining consumers' perspective of their health plans (AHRQ 2008). The CAPHS survey is currently administered to commercial, Medicaid, Children's Health Insurance Program (CHIP), and Medicare plans. More than 120 million enrollees have taken the CAHPS survey. The intent is to promote the comparison of results among users as a quality improvement tool, using the standardized data to identify relative strengths and weaknesses in performance, to determine where to improve and track progress over time. The data can also be used to make comparisons between Medicaid agencies using the benchmarks from the database. The NCBD is the source of CAHPS information for all types of care. Another role of the NCBD is as a supplier of primary data for conducting research on survey design and health plan and enrollee characteristics. CAHPS is another tool that can be used to improve the quality of healthcare in the United States. AHRQ's Report Card Compendium provides profiles of projects, organizations, and initiatives.

Patients bring a unique perspective to the evaluation of healthcare services. Patients have an opinion and, as consumers of services, are increasingly aware of and informed about their healthcare services and providers. The move to obtain opinions from consumers is growing. The Centers for Medicare and Medicaid Services (CMS) is requiring that facilities that are part of the inpatient prospective payment system must submit the CAHPS. The data from the CAHPS survey will be posted for public review on the Hospital Compare website. This survey has been endorsed by the National Quality Forum. The CAHPS survey is a tool used by many hospitals to meet the CMS requirement. Hospitals are taking this patient evaluation tool seriously. Some hospitals have used the survey then

included additional questions to personalize the survey. This tool can be useful as a quality measure of patient experience. Patients will have access to patient-centered information to help them decide where to get their care. The CAHPS and HCAHPS tools have become the standard for patient satisfaction surveying.

Instructions: Answer the following questions on a separate piece of paper.

1. Which of the following provide process measure metrics in a precise format?

    A. Dashboard
    B. Scoreboard
    C. Structured indicator
    D. Outcome indicator

2. The focus of performance improvement should be on:

    A. Employees
    B. Financial stability of the organization
    C. Customers
    D. Interpersonal skills

3. Fifty percent of an HIM department's staff have a nationally recognized credential. This is an example of what type of indicator:

    A. Structure
    B. Process
    C. Outcome
    D. Internal

Instructions: Indicate whether the following statements are true or false.

4. ____ Performance monitoring is outcomes driven.

5. ____ Performance improvement is something that is done periodically.

6. ____ An outcome indicator measures results of care provided to the patient.

Fundamental Principles of Continuous Performance Improvement

Performance improvement is based on several fundamental principles, including the following:

- The structure of a system determines its performance. Therefore, problems are more often within systems than within individual people.
- All systems demonstrate variation. Some variation occurs because of common causes and some because of special causes.

- Improvements rely on the collection and analysis of data that increase knowledge.
- PI requires the commitment and support of top administration.
- PI works best when leaders and employees know and share the organization's mission, vision, and values.
- PI efforts take time and require a big investment in people.
- Excellent teamwork is essential.
- Communication must be open, honest, and multidirectional.
- Success must be celebrated to encourage more success.

The Problem Is Usually the System

Problems in patient care and other areas of the healthcare organization are usually symptoms of shortcomings inherent in a system or a process. Kelly defines a system as "a collection of parts that interact with each other to form an interdependent whole" (Kelly 2003). Practically everything one can think of (both entities and processes) can be viewed as a system. Human beings are systems (very complicated systems made up of a lot of subsystems). Families are systems. Healthcare organizations are very large systems. Each department in a healthcare facility is a system with numerous subsystems.

Every system has inputs. The system processes the inputs and eventually produces outputs. One system's outputs may then become inputs for another system.

The hospital's admitting department is an example of a system. When a patient enters the hospital, he or she presents to the admitting clerk. The clerk uses a computer to collect data for the admitting system. The patient with knowledge of his or her condition, the admitting clerk with knowledge of the admitting process, and the computer with its admitting template can all be considered inputs for the admitting system. When the clerk begins asking for the patient's address, insurance coverage, and reason for admission and the patient begins responding, the admitting process is under way. The output of the process is the patient's admission to the hospital and a completed face sheet for his or her medical record. These outputs can then be viewed as inputs into the next system in the hospital, the patient care system.

Systems thinking is a vital part of performance improvement. Systems thinking requires individuals to think about patterns and interrelationships rather than simple units. Performance problems often occur because sources of problems were actually built into the system (Batalden and Stoltz 1993). More recently, the National Academy of Engineering and the Institute of Medicine jointly published *Building a Better Delivery System* (2005) in which means of utilizing systems engineering concepts to improve the healthcare system are demonstrated. Improvements must address the system's shortcomings. For example, if the admitting clerk had to follow a series of cumbersome procedures to obtain data about referring physicians in order to enter them into the admitting template, this could seriously affect the clerk's performance and produce a less-than-desirable output. Examples of poor-quality output might be inaccurate information or long delays in admissions. The problems in the admitting department may then create problems for other systems in the hospital.

Variation Is Constant

Every system has some degree of variation built into it. No system produces the exact same output every time. It would be desirable to reduce variation within systems as much as possible so that system output could be more predictable or better controlled. However, there will always be some variation, albeit sometimes minor (Omachonu 1999). Variation that is inherent within the system is known as **common cause variation**. For example, when a nurse takes a patient's blood pressure, she may believe that she is performing the procedure in exactly the same way every time, but she will get slightly different readings each time. Although the blood pressure cuff, the patient, and the nurse are all the same inputs into the system, variations can occur. For example, the cuff may be applied to a different place on the patient's arm. The patient may have a slightly different emotional or physiological status at the time of the measurement. The nurse may have a different level of focus or concentration. Any one of these factors, plus countless others, can affect the values obtained. However, they are potentially present in every single episode of blood pressure measurement in every single patient. It is important to recognize that not every variation is a defect. The variation may just be an example of common cause variation found inherently in the process.

Some variations are caused by factors outside the system. This type of variation is known as **special cause variation**. If the special cause produces a negative effect, we will want to identify the special cause and eliminate it. If the special cause produces a positive effect, we will want to reinforce it so the good effect will continue and perhaps be expanded into the processes of others in the organization. An example of this type of variation occurs when a patient is taking blood pressure medication and there is a substantial drop in the measurement. The medication has caused the decrease in blood pressure values and can clearly be considered a special cause. In this situation, the variation is intentional and desired. In other situations, the variation may produce an undesirable and unintentional effect. For example, if a patient is upset about a phone call he received just before the nurse came in to take his vitals, his blood pressure could be exceptionally high. The change in values occurred due to a special cause (the phone call) and resulted in a blood pressure reading much higher than normally expected.

Similar examples of special cause variation can be identified in our hospital systems. In the HIM department, for example, there is always some common cause variation in the number of records that can be coded each day. On a day when one of the regular coders is out sick, however, the number of records coded might drop significantly. This would be an example of special cause variation. As much as is possible, the goal should be to remove special causes if they are creating an undesirable effect.

Data Must Support PI Activities and Decisions

Data drives performance improvement. Omachonu states that "the ability to collect, analyze, and use data is a vital component of a successful performance improvement process. Healthcare organizations that do not devote sufficient attention to data collection may be able to speak of only marginal success in their process improvement journey" (Omachonu 1999).

In the past, healthcare organizations relied on unsupported assumptions about which processes were functioning well and which ones were not. Without real data, however, no objective and accurate assessment can take place. Collecting data provides information about the current level of customer satisfaction, potential areas for improvement efforts, and the effectiveness of changes already implemented.

A number of methods can be used in data collection. PI activities must include the best method for obtaining timely, accurate, and relevant data.

Examples of data collection methods and instruments include retrospective record review with specific quality criteria, written surveys, direct observation, and individual or focus group interviews.

After adequate data have been collected, they must be carefully analyzed. Improvement efforts must be built on knowledge, and knowledge is gained through data analysis.

Support Must Come from the Top Down

PI as a vital, continuous process must be built into the organization's culture. The executive leaders of the organization must believe in its value in order for it to permeate the entire organization. Moreover, they must ensure that their management teams are well versed in the principles and techniques of continuous performance improvement.

Training for managers and supervisors can be provided by outside consultants or through in-service training. Managers and supervisors are then able to train their own employees and model the continuous improvement philosophy. Every employee must understand the importance of continually improving processes so as to provide better service to the organization's customers.

The Organization Must Have a Shared Vision

The organization's executive leaders and board of directors are responsible for developing and communicating a clear vision of the organization's future. The organization's vision, mission, and values set its direction and support the norms it considers important. They communicate a constancy of purpose. Vision,

mission, and values statements help employees to understand the vision and embrace it as their own. The statements also guide employees as they make their own contributions to the organization by fulfilling their professional responsibilities.

Staff and Management Must Be Involved in the Process

As mentioned earlier, executive leaders must be committed to the philosophy of **continuous quality improvement** and work to ensure that every manager and every employee is committed to its value. This commitment demands an investment in people and requires substantial time and training. PI depends on everyone in the organization actively seeking to meet internal and external customers' spoken or anticipated needs.

This is particularly important for employees who have direct contact with external customers. These employees are perhaps in the best position to recognize which needs of the customer are not being met. They often offer helpful ideas for improvement. It works to the organization's benefit when staff are empowered to make a difference for their fellow workers and the patients they serve.

Setting Goals Is Crucial

All PI programs must have established goals. Goals are essentially targets that the organization strives to achieve in a given PI program year. They should be specific and define measurable end results. An example of an organizational goal might be "To provide high-quality patient care that is cost-effective."

After goals are established, it is important to identify specific, measurable objectives that can be completed within a certain time frame. An objective associated with the example goal might be "By the end of the year, a high-quality, cost-effective care program will be designed for the management of diabetes patients."

Effective Communication Is Important

Effective communication is absolutely essential for the PI process to work. It must exist at all levels of the organization and in all directions. Managers must hear from staff how the organization is functioning. Staff must feel comfortable in telling management when things are going well and when there are problems. This level of communication requires trust and respect for all individuals and the recognition that everyone wants to do the best job possible.

Obviously, openly identifying and discussing problems is not always comfortable or easy. However, an organization that is committed to serving its customers must view problems as opportunities for improvement. The Japanese call this *kaizen:* the continuous search for opportunities for all processes to get better (Imai 1986). Defects are looked on as treasures because a chance for improvement lies in the discovery of imperfection (Berwick 1989). None of this can happen without effective communication.

Effective communication is two-way communication. It requires clear, articulate, and tactful speaking. Even more important, it requires careful, attentive listening and understanding. Organizations must take the time to listen to their customers, both internal and external, so they can hear information about where services need improvement.

Success Should Be Celebrated

Although PI demands that organizations focus on identifying and addressing problems, it also must celebrate the organization's successes. A celebration of success communicates to everyone that the participants' efforts are applauded, that success can occur from such efforts, and that others should be encouraged to participate in PI initiatives. Those people involved in improving the process need to be recognized and appreciated. One of the reasons organizations collect and analyze data is to let them know when they have reasons to celebrate. Achieving service excellence is certainly a great reason to celebrate.

Formal Performance Improvement Activities

Performance improvement is always some combination of everyday managerial improvements and more formal performance improvement activities. The mix may at times conform with the types of activities discussed thus far in this chapter, which can be undertaken by managers and staff in a more informal manner, and at other times the issues at hand may require a more formal approach due to the significance of the issues identified, the multidepartment effects of the issues identified, or the complexity of the processes involved in the issues identified. At that point, a formal performance improvement team can be convened to examine the issues and make recommendations utilizing the classic techniques of continuous quality and performance improvement.

Formal performance improvement activities tend to be cyclical in nature. They are based on the kinds of monitoring of internal and external data, or performance measures, discussed previously in this chapter.

When an organization compares its current performance to its own internal historical data, or uses data from similar external organizations, it helps establish an organizational benchmark. A benchmark is a systematic comparison of one organization's measured characteristics with those of another similar organization or with regional or national standards. Once a benchmark for a performance measure is determined, analyzing data collection results becomes more meaningful. Often, further study or more focused data collection on a performance measure is triggered when data collection results fall outside the established benchmark. This is cycle #1 of the common performance improvement model discussed by Shaw and Elliott, as graphically depicted in figure 22.3. When variation is discovered through continuous monitoring

Figure 22.3. Performance improvement model, cycle #1 example: Monitoring and improving customer satisfaction

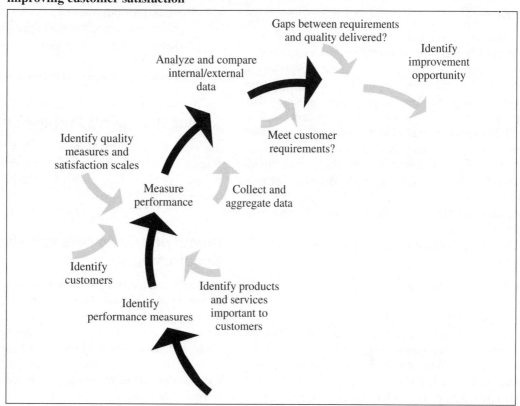

Figure 22.4. Team-based performance improvement process

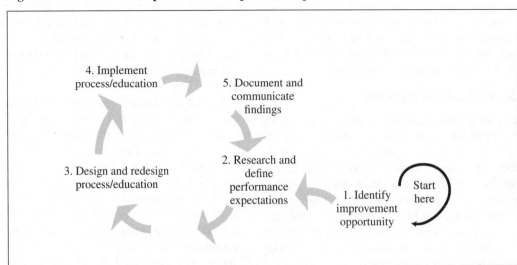

or when unexpected events suggest performance problems, the organization may decide that there is an opportunity for improvement and institute a team performance improvement process. This is cycle #2 of the common performance improvement model discussed by Shaw and Elliott, as graphically depicted in figure 22.4 and discussed in detail below (Shaw and Elliott 2013).

Team-Based Performance Improvement Processes

The first step in a formal process improvement effort is to assemble the team. If a performance improvement team is to be undertaken, staff with knowledge and a background in the process under examination should be involved. Because staff have fundamental knowledge of the process, they are vital to the success of process redesign activities. It is important to empower staff members to change processes and then to recognize them for their part in the improvements. In addition, staff members accept change much more easily when they have been part of the decision-making process. By being part of the process redesign team, staff also will have an easier time going through the early phases of the transition period.

The team's success depends on the following seven elements:

- Establishing ground rules
- Stating the team's purpose or mission
- Identifying customers and their requirements
- Documenting current processes and identifying barriers
- Collecting and analyzing data
- Identifying possible solutions by brainstorming or using other PI techniques
- Making recommendations for changes in the process

Establishing Ground Rules

Ground rules must be agreed upon at the very beginning. All members of the team should have input into the ground rules. They should agree to abide by them for the sake of the team's success. Some ground rules that team members should consider are

- To arrive on time for meetings
- To complete and present the results of assignments from the previous meeting
- To respect the opinions of all team members
- To listen to other team members' points of view without criticism
- To abide by decisions made by the team

Stating the Team's Purpose or Mission

The team must answer this question: Why has this team been formed? The team must define its mission in order to create a "map" or plan of the means by which it will examine the issues and plan its activities.

Identifying Customers and Their Requirements

The performance improvement team must identify the customers associated with the processes under discussion. Customers are both internal (for example, the facility's business office) and external (for example, third-party payers). The process improvement team identifies these customers as well as their requirements. Having identified its customers, the team works toward modifying the process to meet the customers' requirements.

Documenting Current Processes and Identifying Barriers

The process improvement team members work together to discuss and document current processes. For this step, the team's knowledge is vital because members must answer the following questions:

- What is the current process?
- Where are the start and end points of the process?
- What are the barriers to the process?

Collecting Current Process Data

Once an improvement opportunity has been identified through performance monitoring and a team that consists of staff involved in the process under study has been assembled, the first task is to research and define performance expectations for the process targeted. Performance improvement teams have a variety of tools that they can use to accomplish their goals. The tools make it easier to gather and analyze information, and they help team members stay focused on PI activities and move the process along efficiently. If the organization has already been routinely monitoring the process under examination as discussed earlier, it is important to remember that that information is available for use by the assembled PI team as well. Tools for process improvement are addressed fully in Chapter 26.

Analyzing Process Data

Following the collection of data, it is important for the team to be able to consider it in a meaningful way. Obviously if the team is handed reams and reams of check sheets, time ladders, or abstracts and asked to prioritize problem areas for focused improvement, there will be no meaningful decisions made. Again, the PI tools and techniques can be of some assistance in providing the team with meaningful documents from which it can draw some conclusions.

Identifying Process Redesign Solutions

Following in-depth examination of all the data, policies and procedures, interviews, and so forth that have been collected regarding the issue under examination, the team must make decisions about either leaving the situation as it is with minor adjustments or developing major restructuring of the process to make it meet its customer's expectations.

If the solution is the latter, the following steps are undertaken next:

1. Incorporate findings or changes identified in the research phase of the improvement process.
2. If necessary, collect focused data from the prioritized problem areas to further clarify process failure or variation.
3. Create a flow chart of the redesigned process.

4. Develop policies and procedures that support the redesigned process.
5. Educate involved staff about the new process.

Making Recommendations for Process Change

The process improvement team is responsible for putting the outcome of its work in a report format, along with recommendations for improving the process. The recommendations are finalized after all data have been received and analyzed. These data include findings from the benchmarking studies as well as from productivity and other measurements. The recommendations should take into account anything that might have an impact on the organization, such as:

- Utilization of staff
- Effect on the budget
- Change in productivity
- Effects on customer requirements

Recommendations are considered by the leadership group and top management for an organization-wide problem or by the management group heading up the HIM department if the problem is confined to just that unit of the organization. The relationship between organization-wide performance monitoring and team-based PI processes is illustrated in figure 22.5. Leadership and top management must be kept aware of all developments however, no matter at what level they are occurring. Implementation resources and timing must be supported and committed by them.

After implementing a new process, the team continues to measure performance against customers' expectations and established performance standards. The team may then need to redesign the process or product if measurements indicate that there is room for further improvement. When measurement data indicate that the improvement is effective, ongoing monitoring of the process is resumed (as in figure 22.3). The team documents and communicates its findings to the leadership group and other interested parties in the organization. Results also may be communicated to interested groups in the community.

The team is usually disbanded at this point in the cycle, and routine organizational monitoring of the performance measures is resumed. If another opportunity for improvement arises, the team-based improvement process may be reinstituted.

Check Your Understanding 22.2

Instructions: Answer the following questions on a separate piece of paper.

1. Staff members adapt to change more readily when:

    A. Change is mandated by the administration.
    B. They have been part of the decision.

Figure 22.5.   Organizationwide and team-based performance improvement model

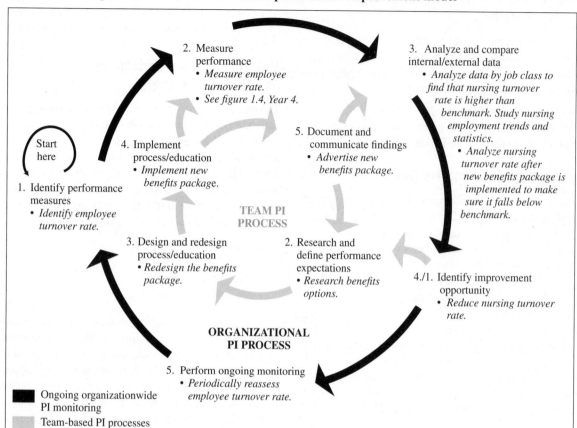

C. Change is the result of change in accreditation or legislation.
D. They have seen the value of the desired outcome.

2. In order to expedite basic performance improvement team functioning, the team should:

A. Establish ground rules.
B. Perform force field analysis
C. Use unstructured brainstorming
D. Use structured brainstorming

3. Which of the following is the most important to guide the performance improvement team's process?

A. Organizational vision statement.
B. Organizational mission statement.
C. Customer process requirements.
D. Top management's requirements.

Managing Quality and Performance Improvement

Quality and superior performance within an organization do not just happen. Quality and the process of performance improvement must be managed to ensure that these activities accomplish important and vital changes needed by the

organization's internal and external customers. This means that traditional management functions such as planning, organizing, directing, and controlling must be applied to PI initiatives. In addition, those responsible for quality and performance improvement in healthcare organizations must bring the perspectives of entities external to the organization into play within the organization's quality deliberations, discussions, and decision making. External entities that must be considered include agencies offering voluntary accreditation services, agencies involved in the reimbursement cycle, agencies administering licensure services, and agencies offering national quality policy and direction. All must be considered and reflected in an organization's approach to improving its quality and professional performance in order for the quality program to be considered an effective asset to the attainment of the organization's mission and goals as a healthcare organization of superior quality.

Organizational Components of Performance Improvement

To be successful in implementing PI programs, healthcare organizations may have to restructure and create a new culture to accommodate the enormous changes and competition that exist in today's healthcare environment. Changes in customer expectations and the way that healthcare is financed may demand organizational restructuring. Traditional, hierarchical management methods do not necessarily meet the needs of today's customers, the organization's employees, or the organization's operations.

PI thrives in an environment of cooperation. It is most successful in organizations that have an interdisciplinary and participative management approach. As discussed previously, shared vision is one of the cornerstones of a successful PI program. A shared vision puts everyone, including the governing board, upper management, and employees, on the same path to organizational success. Changing to a shared leadership environment can create a new organizational culture of shared vision, responsibility, and accountability. Because every employee is a vital part of this shared leadership, this type of environment helps to increase employee motivation and empowerment.

In addition to an enterprisewide vision, a shared leadership framework is essential for implementing PI. Shared leadership essentially means that organizations ensure that all employees participate in an integrated, continuous PI program. Various organizational frameworks or structures can be developed that encourage shared leadership. One suggested framework includes the following components:

- Governing **board of directors (BOD)** or board of trustees (BOT): A BOD has overall responsibility and accountability for the successful operation of the organization's quality and PI activities and should include membership from the communities of interest, the medical staff, and top organizational administration. The governing board should regularly review current status of quality and PI initiatives and approve all strategic decisions and organizational expenditures of resources concerning them.
- **Quality management board (QMB)**: A QMB has responsibility for the PI program across all subunits of the organization and should include membership from top administration, medical staff officers, top clinical operations staff, and top quality management staff. It should be facilitating all proposals for quality and PI initiatives, making recommendations to the governing board regarding strategic quality direction. It should monitor the progress of all initiatives, providing assistance and advisement as necessary to keep initiatives moving along to completion
- **Quality management liaison group (QMLG)**: A QMLG has responsibility for disseminating information about the organization's quality and PI initiatives throughout the middle management of the organization, for educating managers regarding their roles and the roles of their organizational units in quality and PI initiatives, and for developing cross-functional coordination and communication across organizational units in order to accomplish quality

and PI initiatives. In many organizations this type of group is also responsible for maintaining the organization in continuous readiness for accreditation and licensure survey.

The organizational structures and processes that constitute a **quality management** program must be integrated across the entire healthcare organization. To be effective, the organizational unit responsible for quality management must be able to communicate with all areas of the organization and foster interdisciplinary cooperation. Many organizations have actually created a quality management "department" of the organization to help the organization pursue its quality and performance improvement efforts.

The basic responsibilities of the quality management department include

- Helping departments or groups of departments with similar issues to identify potential quality problems
- Assisting determination of the best methods for studying potential problems (for example, survey, chart review, or interview with staff)
- Participating in regular meetings across the organization, as appropriate, and training organization members on quality and performance improvement methodology, tools, and techniques

In addition, the quality management department tracks progress on specific quality studies; distributes study results and recommendations to the appropriate bodies (departments, committees, administration, board of directors or trustees); facilitates implementation of educational or structural changes that flow from the recommendations; and ensures that follow-up studies are performed in a timely manner. Recently, many quality management departments began to assume leadership in the assessing and tracking of organizational compliance with accreditation standards, focus areas, and the Joint Commission's National Patient Safety Goals.

In hospitals and other large healthcare organizations, the board of directors has ultimate responsibility for ensuring the quality of the medical care provided in the organization. In addition, the board is responsible for the organization's fiscal (financial) stability. If the board is to perform its role, it must be provided regular updates on the organization's clinical quality assessment processes and special projects.

Quality management is best implemented as a cross-functional program. Staff training is critical to success, and new employee orientation should include training in quality management. A permanent multidisciplinary committee should be created to coordinate the program and ensure the consistency of clinical quality assessment processes throughout the organization. The committee should include representatives of the medical staff, nursing staff, and infection control team. Depending on the issue under study, representatives from other areas may be consulted or included on a particular assessment. For example, maintenance personnel, safety committee representatives, or departmental supervisors may be included on an issue concerning physical security. In some organizations, specific teams are brought together under the auspices of the quality assessment committee to study a specific issue.

Donabedian's Structural Component of Quality: Ensuring Competent Staff

For many decades, hospitals and other healthcare organizations have had to be concerned with the competence of the staff who provide healthcare services within them. First and most obvious, the members of the medical staff must have been vetted and found to have the appropriate education, experience, and board certifications to practice at the levels of service for which they have applied for privileges. **Privileges** are the formal acknowledgment by the organization that the physician has met the requirements for practice of the organization. The process of reviewing and validating qualifications, granting professional or medical staff membership, and awarding delineated privileges is called the **credentialing process.**

The credentialing process begins with a potential medical staff member submitting an application to the medical staff for membership with a request for clinical privileges of an appropriate type. Some of the categories covered by the application include

- Licensure
- Hospital privileges
- Drug Enforcement Administration registration
- Medical education, including specialty board certification
- Malpractice insurance
- Liability claims history
- National Practitioner Data Bank (NPDB) queries (as required by law)
- Medical board sanctions
- Previous applications for medical staff membership and privileges

In tandem with the medical staff office (a close affiliate of the quality management department), the director of the medical staff department, the chief of service of the medical staff service, or the chief of staff of the entire medical staff begins the review process (depending on the size and complexity of the organization), validating the criteria set out in the application. If everything is found to be in order, a recommendation is made to the credentials committee of the medical staff and then to the board of governance of the entire organization. Please see figure 22.6 for a flowchart of the process.

Initial appointment and awarding of privileges is done for no more than a two-year period. Typically, appointment and designation of clinical privileges are done together. The credentialing process is ongoing. The reappointment and renewal or revision of clinical privileges is completed at least every two years. The reappointment and reappraisal process is continuous within the timeline delineated in the medical staff bylaws.

The reappraisal process includes reviewing objective information collected on each individual who provides patient care services. Data are gathered and maintained on the practice patterns of all healthcare providers. The following may be included in the data:

- Procedures performed and the outcomes
- Pattern of blood and pharmaceutical usage

Figure 22.6.   Flowchart of the credentialing process

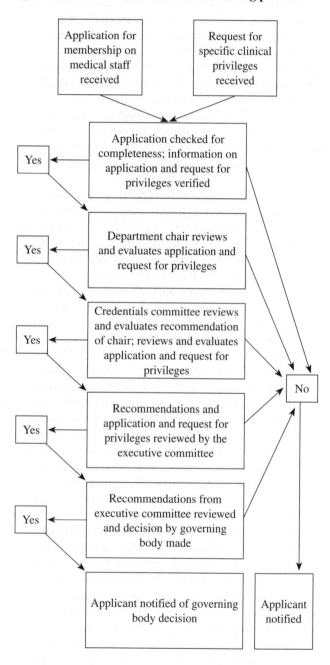

- Requests for tests and procedures
- Length-of-stay patterns
- Morbidity and mortality data
- Appropriateness of clinical practice patterns
- Significant departures from established patterns of clinical practice
- Use of developed criteria for autopsies
- Sentinel event data
- Patient safety data
- Use of consultants

A credentials file is maintained on each member of the medical staff. This information is considered confidential and must be handled in accordance with established policies and procedures contained in the medical staff bylaws and rules and regulations. State and federal peer review and confidentiality legislation should be reviewed.

The initial granting of medical staff membership and privileges, along with any revisions or revocations of clinical privileges, must follow the medical staff bylaws and rules and regulations. All applicants have the right to appeal decisions and to have a fair hearing before a panel of their peers.

Patient Care Review

For many decades, the evaluation of the care provided in a healthcare organization was the almost exclusive purview of the medical staff. Even today, with the kinds of benchmarking and analysis discussed later, much of this review is performed according to the medical staff structure of departments and services. However, today's approach is also expected to be far more multidisciplinary, in recognition of the fact that positive or negative outcomes of patient care are the result of many highly educated personnel doing the right thing to the right patient at the right time. Reviewing the coordination of the care provided by all participants is of ultimate importance. In larger institutions, this coordination of review activities will fall to the quality management department. In smaller ones, department and service chiefs may have to provide the leadership to get it accomplished. Lack of coordinated review can have important negative impacts on accreditation, licensure, and reimbursement outcomes. The following are some of the common types of review undertaken in healthcare organizations today, most having been performed routinely for many years.

Health record review is necessary to ensure that the documentation captured is complete and accurate and reflects the care provided to the patient. At a minimum, the team involved in this improvement process consists of medical staff, nursing, HIM, and administrative services. The review includes health record documentation on both open and closed cases, with the total number of records being reviewed at approximately 5 percent of the overall discharges.

Surgical and procedural review. Data collection systems must be developed and used by healthcare organizations to evaluate all operative procedures. Both invasive and noninvasive procedures should be included in this improvement process. All procedures are a potential risk to the patient, and so the appropriateness of the procedure must be determined. The procedures established that have the greatest risk are reviewed closely as part of a surgical review. Procedural processes and outcomes need to be addressed. The procedural processes to be measured include

- Selection of the appropriate procedure
- Patient preparation for the procedure
- Preprocedure discussion and acquisition of patient or surrogate consent
- Performance of the procedure and patient monitoring
- Postprocedure care
- Postprocedure patient education
- Adherence to all operating room or procedure room procedures such as to avoid wrong side, wrong procedure, or wrong patient mistakes

Medication usage review Medication use is an important method of treatment in healthcare. Because of the growing number of available medications and the potential for adverse effects, such as short-term side effects, interactions of medications, and toxicity, it is essential that the healthcare organization measure the administration and use of medications as part of a medication usage review. Moreover, the healthcare facility should evaluate medication use. Priority is based on:

- Number of patients receiving a medication
- Risk vs. therapeutic value
- Known or suspected problem-prone drugs
- Therapeutic effectiveness

In addition, attention should be given to the following medication processes:

- Ordering or prescribing medications
- Preparing and dispensing medications
- Administrating medications
- Monitoring the effects on patients of medications

Blood and blood component usage review. PI processes should examine the ordering, distribution, handling and dispensing, administration, and monitoring of the effects of blood and blood components. Other considerations include when blood and blood components are ordered but not indicated, when they are indicated but not given, or when they are administered incorrectly. All suspected transfusion reactions of any kind must be thoroughly investigated to be certain that specified procedures were followed.

Mortality review is an important outcome performance measure. Establishing a meaningful evaluation of mortality (death) is essential in the analysis of ongoing outcome and process improvement.

Infection review. The medical staff and the healthcare organization should work together to provide an environment that reduces the risk of infections in both patients and healthcare providers. The healthcare organization should support activities that look for, prevent, and control infections. Information is collected regularly on endemic and epidemic healthcare-associated infections. As appropriate, the healthcare organization must report significant information to both internal groups and public health agencies. The organization also must take the necessary steps to prevent and reduce the risk of infection in visitors to the facility. Monitoring should be ongoing, and the healthcare organization should support a process focused on reducing risks and lowering infection trends.

Nursing staff performance review. Nursing executives and staff must provide the appropriate guidance for all nursing care. Policies and procedures, standards of nursing practice, nursing standards of patient care, and standards to measure, assess, and improve patient outcomes must be defined, documented, available, and used to improve patient care processes. Nurses must work in conjunction with management, the medical staff, and other healthcare providers as part of an organizationwide PI program. Nurse practitioners must undergo credentialing as a licensed independent practitioner similar to that of physicians. RN licenses must be maintained as stipulated by state law for all licensed nursing personnel.

Allied health professional performance review. Similar to the review for nursing staff, other allied health professionals, licensed and unlicensed, must provide evidence of maintenance of credentials and the ability to appropriately follow delineated procedure in their area of expertise in the healthcare organization.

Check Your Understanding 22.3

Instructions: Answer the following questions on a separate piece of paper.

1. The _____ is ultimately responsible for quality improvement activities in an organization.

   A. Quality management department
   B. Quality management council
   C. Top administrative management
   D. Governing body

2. Which of the following is not a component of patient care review?

   A. Blood usage review
   B. Transfusion review
   C. Mortality review
   D. Unbilled discharges review

3. When physicians or other licensed independent practitioners want to be able to admit patients to a healthcare organization they must apply for privileges. This process is called:

   A. Licensure review
   B. Credentialing
   C. Accreditation
   D. None above

Standards of Organizational Quality in Healthcare

A number of private and government entities develop and maintain standards of organizational quality for healthcare. These entities include agencies and departments of the federal government, accreditation organizations, private for-profit organizations, and not-for-profit organizations such as medical societies and organizations dedicated to research on a specific disease or condition. Standards of quality include descriptive statements called by a number of names, including **standards of care,** quality-of-care standards, performance standards, accreditation standards, and practice standards.

A **standard** is a written description of the expected features, characteristics, or outcomes of a healthcare-related service. Standards are generally based on a minimum level of performance. In other words, standards represent the level of performance expected of every healthcare provider and providing organization.

Four types of standards are relevant within the context of clinical quality assessment:

- Clinical practice guidelines and clinical protocols: Detailed step-by-step guides used by healthcare practitioners to make knowledge-based clinical decisions directly related to patient care
- Accreditation standards: Predefined statements of the criteria against which the performance of participating healthcare organizations will be assessed during the voluntary accreditation process
- Government regulations: Detailed descriptions of the compulsory requirements for participation in the federal Medicare and Medicaid programs
- Licensure requirements: Detailed descriptions of the criteria healthcare organizations must fulfill in order to obtain and maintain state licenses to provide specific healthcare services

Clinical Practice Guidelines and Protocols

Standards of clinical quality include both clinical practice guidelines and clinical protocols. According to the Agency for Healthcare Research and Quality, **clinical guidelines** are "systematically developed statements used to assist provider and patient decisions about appropriate healthcare for specific clinical circumstances" (AHRQ 2005). The **Agency for Healthcare Research and Quality (AHRQ)** is an agency within the Department of Health and Human Services (HHS). AHRQ's mission is to improve the quality, safety, efficiency, and effectiveness of healthcare for all Americans. Clinical practice guidelines are developed with the goal of standardizing clinical decision making. As the word *guideline* suggests, clinical practice guidelines are not meant to be inflexible and do not apply in every case. Guidelines are updated periodically to reflect the results of recent research studies. (See figure 22.7.)

In contrast to clinical practice guidelines, clinical protocols are treatment recommendations based on guidelines. They generally describe recommended diagnostic tools and treatment methodologies and must be approved by the medical staff. One example of a clinical protocol is the step-by-step description of the accepted procedure for preparing intravenous solutions at a specific acute-care hospital. Another example is described in figure 22.8.

Case Management

A process used in some hospitals, **case management** is the ongoing review of clinical care to ensure the necessity and effectiveness of the services being provided to the patient.

Figure 22.7. Clinical guideline example

**GUIDELINES FOR SCREENING DIABETES IN PREGNANCY
SAN FRANCISCO COMMUNITY HEALTH NETWORK**

First prenatal visit: Screen and test clients who present with one or more of the following risk factors:

- Obesity (BMI >30, pre-pregnancy weight)
- Diabetes Mellitus in 1st degree relative
- Prior history of
  - Gestational diabetes or glucose intolerance or use of metformin
  - Macrosomia (>4.0 kg or 8lbs 8oz) or larger for gestational age infant (90th percentile)
  - Unexplained stillbirth
  - Malformed infant
- Current glucosuria (100 mg/dl or greater)

24–28 weeks: Screen and test all clients not as yet identified as having gestational diabetes. If initial screening was normal, repeat evaluation.

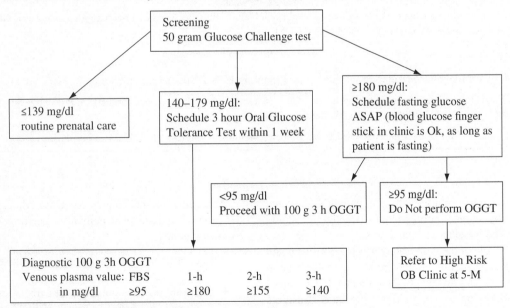

*If two or more values are elevated: treat as gestational diabetes
**If one value is elevated: refer for nutritional counseling. No further testing is necessary. No treatment needed. Re-testing is not necessary if test was done ≥24 weeks.

(continued on next page)

Figure 22.7.   Clinical guideline (*Continued*)

Screening Test for Gestational Diabetes: 50 Gram Oral Glucose Challenge Test (50-g OGCT)

No fasting or dietary restriction required.

Administered during office hours, without respect to time of the day or last meal.

50 grams of glucose, consumed in less than 5 minutes

No smoking

Venous plasma level is drawn one hour from the start of glucose ingestion.

Diagnostic (Confirmatory) Test for Gestational Diabetes:100 Gram Oral Glucose Tolerance Test (100-g OGTT)

a. Pre-test instructions:

   • Fast for at least 8 hours and no more than 14 hours (water is OK)

   • Instruct clients to eat "normally" (without dietary restrictions) for at least 3 days before the test.

b. Fasting venous plasma drawn

c. 100 grams of glucose, consumed in less than 5 minutes

d. No smoking

e. Venous plasma level is drawn at 1, 2, and 3 hours from start of ingestion of the glucose load.

Postpartum: all clients diagnosed with Gestational Diabetes need to be tested for overt Diabetes 6–8 weeks postpartum and annually thereafter with either:

a. 75 gram 2 hour Glucose Tolerance Test (75-g GTT) (preferred test)

   ≥200 mg/dl overt Diabetes*

   140–199 mg/dl Impaired Glucose Tolerance

   <140 mg/dl normoglycemia

b. fasting glucose (if declines the 75-g GTT)

   ≥126 mg/dl overt Diabetes*

   ≥110 < 126 mg/dl Impaired Fasting Glucose

   <100 mg/dl normoglycemia

Patients who are diagnosed with Diabetes need to be referred back to their PCPs!

*In the absence of unequivocal hyperglycemia and acute metabolic decompensation, these criteria should be confirmed by repeat testing on a different day.

Late-to-care patients:

a. <36 weeks: apply same strategy as universal screening at 24–28 weeks.

b. >36 weeks or impending labor regardless of gestational age: obtain fasting glucose (best) >105 mg/dl manage as if GDM, or random glucose (2nd best) >200 mg/dl manage as if GDM.

References:

1. Carr SR. Screening for gestational diabetes mellitus. A perspective in 1998. Diabetes Care. 1998 Aug: 21 Suppl 2:B14–8.

2. Brody SC, Harris R, Lohr K. Screening for gestational diabetes: a summary of the evidence for the U.S. Preventive Services Task Force. Obstet Gynecol. 2003 Feb:101(2):380–92. Review.

3. Kjos SL, Buchanan TA. Current Concepts: Gestational Diabetes Mellitus. N Engl J Med 1999:341:1749–1756.

It is conducted concurrently with the patient's stay and is performed by clinical professionals (usually registered nurses) employed by acute-care hospitals.

The primary role of the case manager is to coordinate and facilitate care. The care-planning process extends beyond the acute-care setting to ensure that the patient receives appropriate follow-up services. Many healthcare insurers and managed care organizations also employ case managers to coordinate medical care and ensure the medical necessity of the services provided to beneficiaries.

According to the Center for Case Management (n.d.), the process of case management is performed to meet the following goals:

- To coordinate multidisciplinary or multisetting patient care
- To ensure positive outcomes of care
- To manage the patient's length of stay in the acute-care facility
- To ensure that the healthcare organization's resources are used efficiently

Figure 22.8.   Example of a clinical protocol

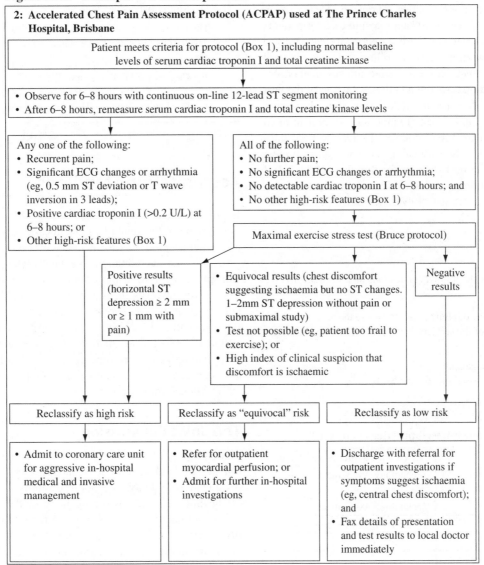

Source: The Prince Charles Hospital, Brisbane.

The need for case management is illustrated by a June 2005 report issued by the Office of Inspector General (OIG). According to the report, which studied patients with three or more stays at an inpatient facility where the admission date for each stay was within one day of the discharge date for the previous stay, 20 percent of the consecutive inpatient stays involved poor-quality care or unnecessary fragmentation of care. The report states that the 20 percent was the result of failure to treat patients in a timely manner, inadequate monitoring and treatment of patients, and inadequate care planning (OIG 2005).

Evidence-Based Practice

The practice of **evidence-based medicine** means integrating decision support systems and best practices in medicine rather than relying on subjective information (AHIMA 2012).

Research is at the root of this clinical approach. It complements the philosophical approach to continually measure performance on a clinical level.

In order to support evidence-based practice in the US the Agency for Healthcare Research and Quality. (AHRQ 2012) has established Evidence-based Practice Centers. EPCs develop evidence reports and technology assessments on relevant topics that are common or significant in the Medicare and Medicaid populations. The Centers review all scientific literature on clinical, behavioral, and organizational and financing topics, then produce evidence reports, as well as technical review and technology assessments. AHRQ's goal is to improve the quality, effectiveness, and appropriateness of healthcare by translating evidence-based research findings. Five-year contracts are awarded to Centers all over the US and Canada. (AHRQ 2012)

Improving quality of care, advancing safety practices, and adopting evidence-based practice complement each other. Introducing a "most beneficial" approach to care for patients allows an opportunity to standardize treatment. Standardized expectations allow more accountability and measurement of outcomes. Evidence-based medicine utilizes methodologies that are based on research and the evaluation of the best external evidence to answer clinical questions. Important recommendations can be made to practitioners to help them determine optimal treatment courses. Is this the best diagnostic tool to use? Is the surgical or medical approach most optimal? Is this the best therapy for this diagnosis? A full discussion of outcomes and effectiveness research is presented in chapter 21. A list of evidence-based practice centers is provided in table 22.2.

Check Your Understanding 22.3

Instructions: Answer the following questions on a separate piece of paper.

1. Ongoing review of clinical care to ensure the necessity and effectiveness of the services being provided to the patient is known as:

   A. Case management
   B. Evidence-based practice
   C. Health care review
   D. Mortality review

2. The most prominent organization involved in the development of patient care standards is:

   A. Health Care Financing Administration
   B. Centers for Medicare and Medicaid Services
   C. Agency for Healthcare Research and Quality
   D. President's Office on Healthcare Quality

Accreditation Standards

In the United States today, many different organizations monitor the quality of healthcare services and offer accreditation programs for healthcare organizations. All the programs base accreditation on a data collection and submission process followed by a comprehensive survey process. The survey involves measurement of a healthcare facility's performance in comparison to pre-established accreditation standards. Participation in accreditation programs is voluntary. Most accreditation standards are provided to participating healthcare organizations in the form of manuals, such as the Joint Commission's Comprehensive Accreditation Manual for Hospitals.

The Joint Commission

Since its beginning in 1952, the Joint Commission has continually evolved to meet the changing needs of healthcare organizations. Today, the Joint Commission is the largest healthcare standards-setting body in the world. It conducts accreditation surveys in more than 17,000 healthcare organizations and programs in the United States, including hospitals and home care organizations and other healthcare organizations that provide long-term care, assisted living, behavioral healthcare, and laboratory and ambulatory care services (Joint Commission 2010, 2).

In the late 1990s, the Joint Commission moved away from traditional quality assessment processes and began emphasizing performance improvement. Today, the Joint Commission's standards give organizations substantial leeway in selecting performance measures and improvement projects. Required since 1998, all hospitals and long-term care facilities must report outcome measures on at least 20 percent of their patients. **Outcome measures** or **core performance measures** document the results of care for individual patients as well as for specific types of patients grouped by diagnostic category. For example, an acute-care hospital's overall rate of postsurgical infection would be considered an outcome or core measure. The core measures must be reported to the Joint Commission via software from vendors that have been approved by the Joint Commission for this purpose.

Table 22.2.   Evidence-based practice centers

Site	EPCs with a Specialized Focus
Blue Cross and Blue Shield Association	Technology Assessments
Duke University	Technology Assessments
ECRI Institute	Technology Assessments
Johns Hopkins University	
McMaster University	
Minnesota Evidence-based Practice Center	
Oregon Evidence-based Practice Center	Evidence Reports for the U.S. Preventive Services Task Force
RTI International–University of CA, San Francisco	
Southern California	
Stanford University–University of CA, San Francisco	
Tufts–New England Medical Center	Technology Assessments
University of Alberta	Technology Assessments
University of Connecticut	
University of Ottawa	
Vanderbilt University	

Source: http://www.ahrq.gov/clinic/ep.

The Joint Commission requires a comprehensive presurvey data collection and submission process that focuses on the following 14 priority areas:

Assessment and care services

Organizational structure

Communication

Orientation and training

Credentialed practitioners

Physical environment

Equipment use

Quality improvement expertise and activity

Infection control

Patient safety

Information management

Rights and ethics

Medication management

Staffing

How an organization uses its selected core measures is evaluated during a Joint Commission on-site accreditation survey. The organization must demonstrate the reliability of the data, conduct credible analysis of the data, and initiate system and process improvements. The data collected are used to help focus the accreditation survey on patient safety and high-quality patient care and to select specific patients to trace during the on-site survey. This approach, known as **tracer methodology,** consists of following (tracing) at the time of the on-site survey a few patients through their entire stay at the hospital in order to identify quality and patient safety issues that might indicate quality problems or patterns of less-than-optimum care. According to the Joint Commission, "tracer methodology is an evaluation method in which surveyors select a patient, resident, or client and use that individual's record as a roadmap to move through an organization to assess and evaluate the organization's compliance with selected standards and the organization's systems of providing care and services" (Joint Commission 2009b). A trace of a surgical patient, for example, might reveal a missing updated history and physical (H&P) on the patient's medical record within 24 hours before surgery. Following this lead, the surveyor might discover that the organization is having an ongoing problem with H&Ps in general, a problem with obtaining the required updated H&P within 24 hours before surgery, or perhaps a problem with just one particular physician.

The use of core measures allows for benchmarking based on processes and outcomes of patient care. Core measures are designed to provide a comprehensive picture of the care provided in a given area. A core measure must

- Demonstrate that it will have a significant impact on the health of specified populations

- Be precisely defined and specify requirements for data collection and for calculation of the core measure value or score
- Consistently identify the events it was designed to identify across healthcare organizations (reliability)
- Measure or capture what it is intended to measure (validity)
- Be interpretable (that is, its results must be easily understood by the users of the data, including accrediting organizations, providers, and consumers)
- Have the ability to be risk-adjusted or stratified (that is, the extent to which differences among population groups can be controlled or taken into account)
- Be assessed for availability and accessibility of the required data elements and the effort and cost of abstracting and collecting data
- Be useful in the accreditation process and support the organization's quality improvement efforts
- Be under the provider's control to influence the processes and outcomes being measured
- Be publicly available

With the introduction of these core performance measures, healthcare facilities are expected to select a performance measurement system that meets the Joint Commission's requirements and to send data to the Joint Commission on a routine basis. A performance measurement system must meet all parameters for data submission as determined by the Joint Commission. (See table 22.3.) Data from similar organizations will be compared and areas for improvement will be identified. If any undesirable patterns or trends are found, further monitoring and evaluation will follow. The performance measurement process can be used internally by hospitals for quality improvement activities and externally to help the Joint Commission focus survey activities. Also, public reporting is possible using the information in the core measure database.

The hospital quality measure sets currently utilized by the Joint Commission and now also by CMS are

- Acute myocardial infarction
- Heart failure
- Pneumonia
- Asthma care for children
- Surgical infection prevention or the Surgical Care Improvement Project

The intent of this joint effort is to reduce data collection requirements put on healthcare organizations. The Joint Commission and CMS have worked together to ensure that these measures are comparable. Data will be calculated in an identical fashion.

Other Measurement Systems

A healthcare organization can measure the quality of the care provided in a variety of ways. Healthcare's complex nature

Table 22.3. Performance measurement systems—ORYX core measure requirements

Attribute 1	Performance Measure Characteristics	Refers to characteristics of the performance measures for use in the ORYX initiative
Attribute 2	Data Collection and Receipt	Refers to the operational characteristics of measurement system
Attribute 3	Data Quality	Refers to the extent to which performance measures correctly identify events they were designed to identify
Attribute 4	Risk Adjustment Stratification	Refers to a process for reducing, removing, or clarifying the information and confounding patient factors that differ among comparison groups
Attribute 5	Technical Reporting Requirements	Refers to requirements related to the transmission of accredited healthcare organization data to the Joint Commission by performance measurement systems

Source: Joint Commission. http://www.jointcommission.org/NR/rdonlyres/64C5EDF0-253A-42CE-9DE5-C8AFE6755267/0/oryx_hap_cm_req.pdf, 2008.

has proved to be challenging, even difficult, to evaluate. Evaluating the care provided to patients continues to evolve and change. Knowledge of current measurement systems being used in today's healthcare environment is necessary if one truly wants to provide the highest-quality healthcare. Six Sigma is a measurement system frequently used in healthcare organization. Refer to chapter 26 and the section of this chapter on recent developments for detailed information on these measurement systems.

Joint Commission Patient Safety Initiative

In 2003 to 2004, the Joint Commission began issuing and scoring healthcare organizations on their compliance with specific **National Patient Safety Goals (NPSGs)**. The National Patient Safety Goals outline for healthcare organizations the areas of organizational practice that most commonly lead to patient injury or other negative outcomes that can be prevented when staff utilize standardized procedures. One Joint Commission safety goal, for example, requires healthcare organizations to eliminate wrong-site, wrong-patient, and wrong-procedure surgery. To accomplish this, organizations must create and use a preoperative verification process, such as a checklist, to confirm the patient's identity and that appropriate documents (for example, medical records, imaging studies) are available. They also must implement a process to mark the surgical site and involve the patient in the marking process.

The Joint Commission's NPSGs (see table 22.4) are central to its mission of ensuring the provision of safe, high-quality care. The Joint Commission reports that more than 90 percent of US hospitals use their standards to help guide and improve healthcare and their annual report *Improving America's Hospitals: A Report on Quality and Safety* has been received with enthusiasm. Many different organizations, providers, and payers have accessed the report, validating the need for increased understanding of how to achieve safer, higher-quality healthcare services. Healthcare organizations are expected to comply with the Joint Commission's

NPSGs in order to be accredited. The Joint Commission's approach to all aspects of improving performance, whether safety or quality, is based on a theme of continual improvement. This approach uses systems redesign and a change in the culture of healthcare organizations as the focus of keeping errors from affecting patient care.

The Joint Commission uses an advisory group to help determine what safety goals are selected. The goals are selected based on the potential impact on patient care. Other factors taken into consideration include cost and practicality of implementation. The Joint Commission's Board of Governors makes the final approval for either deleting or adding goals to the NPSGs. The Joint Commission strongly recommends that healthcare organizations make information about safety and quality readily available. This includes the public, providers, and payers. Private, not-for-profit organizations are also pushing for increased transparency regarding data on the quality and safety of healthcare providers—both organizations and direct care providers. The Joint Commission has made information on quality and safety issues available at its website.

The Joint Commission's patient safety initiative is an integral part of the accreditation process. Commitment to a culture of safety is demonstrated by the number and variety of programs supported by the Joint Commission. The initiatives listed in table 22.5 involve patient safety in one way or another.

The extensive involvement of the Joint Commission in patient safety efforts speaks to a continued focus of providing higher-quality, safer healthcare services.

Sentinel Events

The Joint Commission requires healthcare organizations to conduct in-depth investigations of occurrences that resulted in, or could have resulted in, life-threatening injuries to patients, medical staff, visitors, and employees. The Joint Commission uses the term **sentinel event** for such occurrences. A sentinel event describes an occurrence with

Table 22.4. Joint Commission's 2009 Hospital National Patient Safety Goals

Goal	Goal Name	Suggested Solution
1	Improve the accuracy of patient identification	Use at least 2 identifiers when providing care, treatment, and services
		Eliminate transfusion errors related to patient misidentification
2	Improve the effectiveness of communication among caregivers	Verify by reading back verbal orders, telephone orders, telephone or verbal reports of test results
		Standardize a list of abbreviations, acronyms, symbols, and dose designations *not* to be used
		Improve the timeliness of reporting and receipt of critical test results and values by caregiver
		Implement a standardized way to communicate the hand-off of a patient
		Allow time to ask and respond to questions
3	Improve the safety of using medications	The organization has a list of medications that look and sound alike and updates the list yearly
		Label all medications not already labeled
		Take special precautions with patients who are using anticoagulant therapy
7	Reduce the risk of healthcare associated infections	Comply with WHO or CDC hand hygiene guidelines
		Manage as a sentinel event unanticipated death or major permanent loss of function related to a healthcare associated infection
		Use evidence-based practices to prevent healthcare associated infections due to multidrug resistant organisms (for example, MRSA)
		Use best or evidence-based guidelines to prevent bloodstream infections
		Use best practice for preventing surgical site infections
8	Accurately and completely reconcile medications across the continuum of care	Maintain a reconciled list of all medications taken by the patient and provide this list to all pertinent people including the patient
		Short duration medications are evaluated to make certain they don't react with any other medications
9	Reduce the risk of patient harm resulting from falls	Implement a fall reduction program that identifies all patients at risk for falling and evaluate the program regularly
13	Encourage patients' active involvement in their own care as a patient safety strategy	Identify ways for patient and family to report concerns about safety and encourage them to do so
15	The organization identifies safety risks inherent in its patient population	Patients at risk for suicide are identified
16	Improve recognition and response to changes in a patient's condition	Develop a way for staff to request additional assistance if a patient's condition worsens

Source: Adapted from the Joint Commission's 2009 Hospital National Patient Safety Goals, http://www.jointcommission.org/NR/rdonlyres/40A7233C-C4F7-4680-9861-80CDFD5F62C6/0/09_NPSG_HAP_gp.pdf, 2008.

an undesirable outcome usually occurring only once. The occurrence, however, points to serious issues involved in care processes that must be resolved in order not to suffer the occurrence again. According to the Joint Commission a sentinel event is:

An unexpected occurrence involving death or serious physical or psychological injury, or the risk thereof. Serious injury specifically includes loss of limb or function. The phrase "or the risk thereof" includes any process variation for which a recurrence would carry a significant chance of a serious

adverse outcome, an outcome of such magnitude that each event requires an investigation and response. (Joint Commission 2008)

Examples of sentinel events include medical errors, explosions and fires, and acts of violence. When these occur, the healthcare organization is required to prepare a detailed report of its investigation to explain the root cause of the event so that similar events can be averted in the future. The Joint Commission issues sentinel event alerts when it detects a pattern of similar events reported by the healthcare organizations

Table 22.5.   Joint Commission Safety initiatives and their descriptions

Initiative	Description
Patient-related Standards	Approximately 50 percent of the Joint Commission's standards are related to safety. For example medication use, infection control, transfusions.
Sentinel Event Policy	Identifies events and requires action to prevent recurrence.
Sentinel Event Alert	Newsletter that describes underlying causes of SEs and recommends steps to prevent events.
Sentinel Event Advisory Group	Appointed group of professionals who are experts in safety that advises in the development of the National Patients Safety Goals.
National Patient Safety Goals	Specific goals targeted for improving the safety of patients when receiving healthcare services.
Universal Protocol	Protocol established to prevent wrong-site, wrong-procedure, and wrong-person events.
Office of Quality Monitoring	Receives, evaluates, and tracks complaints and reports of concerns about healthcare organizations.
Patient Safety Research	Works to advance the field of patient safety and adverse event reporting systems.
Patient Safety Resources	A subsidiary that is focused on educating, training, consulting, and publishing information on keeping patients safe.
Speak Up Initiatives	Program that encourages patients to take an active, involved, and informed role in their healthcare.
Quality Check and Quality Reports	Methods for the public and accredited organizations to view performance measure results used in performance improvement initiatives.
Joint Commission International Client Safety	A virtual entity that will utilize a wide variety of experts to help provide safety solutions to healthcare organizations globally.
Legislative Efforts	Lobby for a nonpunitive environment for the reporting of healthcare errors and patient safety.
Patient Safety Coalitions	Involved with a variety of groups with a common interest in patient safety.

Source: Joint Commission. http://www.jointcommission.org, 2008.

it accredits. The Joint Commission uses its sentinel events data as a basis for its National Patient Safety Goals.

Other Voluntary Accreditation Organizations

Other voluntary accreditation organizations include the **National Committee for Quality Assurance (NCQA),** which focuses its accreditation activities on health plans and outpatient provider organizations, and the **Commission on the Accreditation of Rehabilitation Facilities (CARF),** which focuses on long-term rehabilitation and mental health rehabilitation facilities. Both maintain websites where more information regarding them can be found.

Governmental Quality Initiatives

Medicare Conditions of Participation

To participate in the Medicare program, healthcare providers must comply with federal regulations known as the Conditions of Participation. The Conditions of Participation are distributed by the Centers for Medicare and Medicaid Services. CMS administers the Medicare program as well as the federal portion of the Medicaid program. Participation in the

Medicare program is critical to the success of many healthcare organizations because a high percentage of healthcare services are delivered to elderly Medicare beneficiaries.

Health Care Quality Improvement Program

In 1992, CMS and peer review organizations (PROs) working under contract with CMS instituted the **Health Care Quality Improvement Program (HCQIP)**. Originally, the mission of HCQIP was to promote the quality, effectiveness, and efficiency of services to Medicare beneficiaries by strengthening the community of those committed to improving quality. HCQIP was to monitor and improve quality of care; communicate with beneficiaries, healthcare providers, and practitioners; promote informed health choices; and protect beneficiaries from poor care.

Today, HCQIP's approach to improving the health of Medicare beneficiaries involves the analysis of patterns of care to promote changes in the healthcare delivery system.

In 2002, CMS changed the name of the PROs to **quality improvement organizations (QIOs)**. CMS and the QIOs collaborate with practitioners, beneficiaries, providers, plans, and other purchasers of healthcare services to achieve the following goals:

  - Developing quality indicators that are firmly based in science

- Identifying opportunities for healthcare improvements through careful measurement of patterns of care
- Communicating with professional and provider communities about patterns of care
- Intervening to foster quality improvement through system improvements
- Conducting follow-up studies to evaluate success and redirect efforts

HCQIP began work in 1992 with a national quality improvement (QI) project on acute myocardial infarction, the Cooperative Cardiovascular Project. Since then, CMS has expanded its national QI activities and now focuses on six clinical priority areas:

Acute myocardial infarction

Breast cancer

Diabetes

Heart failure

Pneumonia

Stroke

Table 22.6 presents the quality indicators and data sources for each of these clinical topics. CMS selected these priorities because of their importance to public health. In addition, performance in these areas was measurable and there appeared to be a real possibility of improving quality. All are important causes of morbidity and mortality in the US population as a whole and account for large numbers of hospitalizations as well as healthcare expenditures.

CMS's seventh national priority is the reduction of disparities in the healthcare services provided to Medicare beneficiaries. For example, compared to the population overall, African-American Medicare beneficiaries receive fewer preventive services, such as influenza vaccinations. Under CMS's direction, the QIOs are analyzing these disparities in order to implement programs aimed at narrowing the gaps in service.

QIOs use medical peer review, data analysis, and other tools to identify patterns of care and outcomes that need improvement. They then work cooperatively with facilities and individual physicians to improve care. CMS established a comprehensive program in which QIOs use a data-driven approach to monitoring care and outcomes and a shared approach to working with the healthcare community to improve care. In this effort, QIOs also pursue other types of HCQIP projects, such as important state or local issues, care provided in nonacute hospital settings, and managed care.

Table 22.6. Quality indicators: Medicare's Health Care Quality Improvement Program

Clinical Topic	Quality Indicators	Data Sources
Acute myocardial infarction	1. Early administration of aspirin 2. Early administration of beta blocker 3. Timely reperfusion 4. Aspirin at discharge 5. Beta blocker at discharge 6. Angiotensin-converting enzyme inhibitor (ACEI) at discharge for low left ventricular ejection fraction 7. Smoking cessation counseling during hospitalization	Hospital health records for acute myocardial infarction patients
Breast cancer	8. Biennial mammography screening	Medicare claims (bills) for all female beneficiaries
Diabetes	9. Biennial retinal exam by an eye professional 10. Annual hemoglobin (HbA1c) testing 11. Biennial lipid profile	Medicare claims (bills) for all diabetic beneficiaries
Heart failure	12. Appropriate use/nonuse of ACEI at discharge [excluding discharges on angiotensin-II receptor blocker (ARB)]	Hospital health records for heart failure patients
Pneumonia	13. Influenza vaccinations 14. Pneumococcal vaccinations 15. Blood culture before antibiotics are administered 16. Appropriate initial empiric antibiotic selection 17. Initial antibiotic dose within 8 hours of hospital arrival 18. Influenza vaccination or appropriate screening 19. Pneumococcal vaccination or appropriate screening	13–14: Centers for Disease Control and Prevention Behavioral Risk Factor Surveillance System data 15–19: Hospital health records for pneumonia patients
Stroke	20. Discharged on antithrombotic [acute stroke or transient ischemic attack (TIA)] 21. Discharged on warfarin (atrial fibrillation) 22. Avoidance of sublingual nifedipine (acute stroke)	Hospital health records for stroke, TIA, and chronic atrial fibrillation patients

Source: Originally published as part of CMS publication number 10156.

CMS requires QIOs to offer technical assistance and collaboration on QI projects to every Medicare Advantage plan in their state. QIOs can provide clinical and biostatistical expertise. Further, they can design and conduct quality projects, review and analyze project findings, recommend interventions, and provide advice on data collection (CMS 2005).

State and Local Government Regulations and Licensure Requirements

Various agencies and departments of the federal, state, and local governments also review the quality of services provided in healthcare organizations. However, government regulations and licensure requirements are compulsory rather than voluntary and may vary greatly in their requirements from state to state and jurisdiction to jurisdiction.

Every state government has required the licensure of hospitals and other types of healthcare organizations since the early 20th century. Some city and county governments also regulate healthcare facilities that operate within local boundaries. The individual states issue licenses that permit facilities to operate within a defined scope of operation. For example, a long-term care organization would be licensed to perform long-term care services, but not acute-care services.

To maintain its licensed status, each facility must adhere to the state regulations that govern issues related to staffing, physical facilities, services, documentation requirements, and quality of care. Each facility's performance is usually evaluated annually by survey teams from the state department of health. Healthcare facilities that lose their licenses are no longer allowed to operate in the state.

Check Your Understanding 22.5

Instructions: Answer the following questions on a separate piece of paper.

1. QIOs use peer review, data analysis, and other tools to:
    A. Evaluate whether or not a healthcare facility is meeting standards for accreditation and licensing
    B. Calculate reimbursement
    C. Penalize healthcare organizations
    D. Identify areas that need improvement
2. Shared leadership means:
    A. Employees are participants in the performance improvement program
    B. All vice presidents and above are involved in the performance improvement program
    C. Union leadership and administration lead the performance improvement program
    D. Board of directors and organizational leadership are responsible for the performance improvement program
3. The NPSGs score organizations on areas that:
    A. Affect finance stability of the organization
    B. Affect customers
    C. Affect compliance with state law
    D. Commonly lead to patient injury

4. A woman dies in labor and delivery. The Joint Commission would call this type of outcome a(n):
    A. Sentinel event
    B. Potentially compensable event
    C. Incident
    D. Occurrence screens

Instructions: Indicate whether the following statements are true or false.

5. ____ Accreditation standards were developed to standardize clinical decision making.
6. ____ The Conditions of Participation are used to monitor hospitals and other healthcare organizations in becoming licensed by the state.
7. ____ The mission of AHRQ is to improve quality, safety, efficiency, and effectiveness of healthcare for all Americans.

Recent Clinical Quality Management Initiatives

New initiatives and processes that seek to ensure high-quality care and patient safety characterize the beginning of the 21st century. Stemming from the Institute of Medicine (IOM) 1999 and 2001 reports on the quality of healthcare in America, a consensus developed around the need to use information technology as both a methodology and a pathway for managing and improving healthcare quality.

The beginning of the 21st century also has witnessed attempts to link clinical quality to reimbursement for health services. Recent pay-for-performance initiatives by the federal government, the Joint Commission, and private payers are rewarding organizations for quality outcomes. It is hoped that these funds will encourage healthcare providers to invest in technology that will improve patient care and safety.

In recent years, CMS has become an advocate for **pay for performance** within the Medicare program. One of its efforts requires hospitals participating in the Medicare program to collect and report on 10 proven hospital quality measures in three clinical areas to qualify for full inpatient prospective payment. Those that do not report their data on acute myocardial infarction, heart failure, and pneumonia face a 4 percent penalty per case. Medicare expects hospitals to compare their own data to national and regional averages in order to identify areas for quality improvement (see figure 22.9).

Finally, the early part of the 21st century has witnessed new and creative efforts to encourage medical error reporting. Federal legislation enacted in 2005 allows for the voluntary reporting of medical errors, serious adverse events, and their underlying causes. According to then Joint Commission President Dennis O'Leary, the Patient Safety and Quality Improvement Act "was a breakthrough in the blame and punishment culture that has literally held a death grip

Figure 22.9. Ten clinical quality measures

To receive full reimbursement from Medicare under the inpatient prospective payment system (IPPS), hospitals must report data for the following 10 quality measures to CMS:

Acute myocardial infarction

1. Acute myocardial infarction (AMI) patients without aspirin contraindications who received aspirin within 24 hours before or after hospital arrival

2. AMI patients without aspirin contraindications who are prescribed aspirin at hospital discharge

3. AMI patients with left ventricular systolic dysfunction (LVSD) and without angiotensin converting enzyme inhibitor (ACEI) contraindications who are prescribed ACEI at hospital discharge

4. AMI patients without beta blocker contraindications who received a beta blocker within 24 hours after hospital arrival

5. AMI patients without beta blocker contraindications who are prescribed a beta blocker at hospital discharge

Heart failure

6. Heart failure patients with documentation in the hospital record that left ventricular function was assessed before arrival, during hospitalization, or is planned for after discharge

7. Heart failure patients with LVSD and without ACEI contraindications who are prescribed an ACEI at hospital discharge

Pneumonia

8. Pneumonia patients who receive their first dose of antibiotics within four hours after arrival at the hospital

9. Pneumonia patients age 65 and older who were screened for pneumococcal vaccine status and were administered the vaccine prior to discharge, if indicated

10. Pneumonia patients who had an assessment of arterial oxygenation by arterial blood gas measurement or pulse oximetry within 24 hours prior to or after arrival at the hospital

Source: Adapted from CMS 2005.

on healthcare. When caregivers feel safe to report errors, patients will be safer because we can learn from these events and put proven solutions into place" (Glendinning 2005). Subsequent emphasis by the Joint Commission on patient safety issues has resulted in voluminous research and new programs sponsored by the Joint Commission to assist its accreditation customers in improving this all-important area of healthcare organization functioning.

Accountable Care Organizations

Proposed in the Affordable Care Act of 2010, an **accountable care organization (ACO)** is a network of doctors and hospitals that share responsibility for providing care to patients. An ACO would agree to manage all of the healthcare needs of a minimum of 5,000 Medicare beneficiaries for at least three years. Under the proposal, ACOs—teams of doctors, hospitals, and other healthcare providers and suppliers working together—would coordinate and improve care for patients with original Medicare (that is, those who are not in Medicare Advantage private health plans). To share in savings, ACOs would meet quality standards in four key areas:

- Patient/caregiver care experiences
- Patient safety
- Preventive health
- At-risk population/frail elderly health

The intent of the ACO program is to lower healthcare costs while meeting quality and performance standards and focusing on the patient. The proposed rules also include strong protections to ensure patients do not have their care choices limited by an ACO (CMS 2011).

Six Sigma

Benchmarking has long been practiced within the domain of the healthcare system. However, some healthcare organizations have begun to benchmark against other industries and are selecting models that may be adapted to the healthcare industry. For example, many healthcare organizations apply the Six Sigma philosophy to their PI programs. Six Sigma is practiced widely in business sectors outside healthcare, and this philosophy is gaining acceptance in the healthcare industry (Sollecito and Johnson 2013).

Six Sigma uses statistics for measuring variation in a process with the intent of producing error-free results. Sigma refers to the standard deviation used in descriptive statistics to determine how much an event or observation varies from the estimated average of the population sample. For example, a student who scores 130 on an IQ test would be considered to have a higher IQ than 97.5 percent of the population. The average IQ is considered to be 100, and the standard deviation for IQ is 15 points. Thus, a score of 130 is a variation of two standard deviations above the average. Only 2.5 percent of the population is estimated to have scores above two standard deviations.

Six Sigma was chosen as a target statistic because even two or three standard deviations would not be acceptable in certain scenarios. A 2.5 percent error rate for making correct change at a movie theater may be acceptable, but that error rate for airlines avoiding fatal crashes is completely unacceptable, because airlines have hundreds of flights in the air on any given day. Even if there were only 100 flights per day, two to three fatal crashes per day would be devastating to the airline industry, not to mention the population as a whole. Therefore, it is important to keep this PI approach in proper perspective when it is applied to healthcare.

The Six Sigma measure indicates no more than 3.4 errors per 1 million encounters. Consider the challenge of achieving no more than 3.4 errors per 1 million prescriptions, surgeries, or diagnoses. In certain areas, this standard may seem unattainable, and in others, it may not be rigorous enough. However, incorporating Six Sigma into PI requires considerable organizational change.

Actually deploying Six Sigma in healthcare requires the identification of elements of a product line that are "critical to quality," or CTQs. Focus groups or interviews can be used to elicit the CTQs from the customers for the product. Typically in healthcare, the customers will be the patients or consumers and the providers or physicians. All others involved—the corporations, the payers, and the accreditors and licensers—are identified as **stakeholders,** entities with an important interest in the product that do not have consumer relationships to it. Underpinning the CTQs are elements "critical to process" (CTPs). These also can be identified by such techniques as focus groups or interviews and represent those aspects of the living process that make the accomplishment of CTQs possible.

For example, the American Diabetes Association (ADA) and the NCQA have joined together to promote a CTQ (NCQA 2012) "to provide physicians with tools to support the delivery and recognition of diabetes mellitus care" and then to recognize those providers who are able to maintain the CTQ in their practices. The CTPs supporting this CTQ include the first 10 evidence-based measures of the diabetes care rendered seen in Table 22.7. In addition, the program offered by the ADA/NCQA provides a computer application in which the provider can record the findings for each patient on a regular basis. The output of the application is forwarded to the ADA/NCQA also on a regular basis, and when validated by the two associations, the provider is placed on a public recognition list as meeting these evidence-based criteria and thus offering superior care for diabetes mellitus. Patients win as customers. Providers win as customers. The ADA wins as a stakeholder in promoting better diabetes mellitus care. Payers win as stakeholders in identifying providers who use best practices in the management of diabetes mellitus.

Virtuoso Teams

Publications on performance improvement have given much attention to teamwork. A book by Boynton and Fischer (2005) presents cases studying "virtuoso teams" that take a

Table 22.7. Diabetes care CTPs

Diabetes Recognition Measure	Threshold (% of patients in sample)	Weight
HbA1c Control >9.0%	≤15%	15.0
HbA1c Control <7.0%	40%	10.0
Blood Pressure Control ≥140/90 mmHg	≤35%	15.0
Blood Pressure Control <130/80 mmHg	25%	10.0
LDL Control ≥130 mg/dL	≤37%	10.0
LDL Control <100 mg/dL	36%	10.0
Eye Examination	60%	10.0
Foot Examination	80%	5.0
Nephropathy Assessment	80%	5.0
Smoking Status and Cessation Advice or Treatment	80%	10.0
Total Points		**100.0**
Points Needed to Achieve Recognition		**75.0**

different approach to team membership and processes. The authors studied cases in businesses like Ford Motor Company, Cray Computers, IBM, and Microsoft (Boynton and Fischer 2005). Members of virtuoso teams were handpicked for their exceptional expertise in a particular field and given ambitious goals. Rather than selecting team members according to their availability and experience as is done with traditional teams, virtuoso teams focus on providing each team with specialists who have skills to enhance the team. The authors believe this group of handpicked, elite experts "work best when members are forced together in cramped spaces under strict time constraints" (Boynton and Fischer 2005). "When virtuoso teams begin their work, individuals are in and group consensus is out" (Boynton and Fischer 2005). Leaders of these teams encourage collaboration and creative confrontation. Instead of relying on e-mail, phone calls, and occasional meetings, virtuoso teams engage in intense, face-to-face conversations. Where politeness and repression of individual egos is the norm in traditional teams, members of virtuoso teams celebrate individual egos, compete, and create opportunities for solo performances (Boynton and Fischer 2005). Virtuoso teams operate on the assumption that members have a stake in their reputation and are therefore energized to create notable results. Leaders and participants in virtuoso teams will be expected to employ different skills and methods of interaction than they have experienced in previous team participation.

ISO 9000 Certification

If healthcare organizations expand into global entities, they will be required to deal with the same issues that other industries face when doing business outside the United States. **ISO 9000** certification is part of a PI system that is required to conduct business in certain foreign countries. The International Organization for Standardization in Geneva, Switzerland, first published ISO 9000 standards in 1987. Into the 1990s, it was much more prevalent in European countries than in the United States. ISO 9000 sets specification standards for quality management with regard to process management and product control. In the healthcare setting, product control is quality control of patient care activities. Companies that document and demonstrate compliance with ISO 9000 standards can receive certification by independent ISO auditors.

A few hospitals in the United States moved to adopt ISO 9001 standards, an enhancement of the original ISO 9000 standards. A number of hospitals are now accredited by DNV Healthcare, an accreditor incorporating ISO 9001 standards into Medicare certification.

These standards are very similar, as is the survey process, to those of the Joint Commission and incorporate the CMS requirements outlined in its Conditions of Participation. In 2000, ISO made a significant revision to its 9000-level standards, discontinuing its 9002 and 9003 standard sets and refocusing its attention on the 9001 set. This is the current set that is being used for performance improvement purposes in healthcare organizations. The actual requirements for certification begin in the fourth chapter of the standards (with the first three chapters covering a variety of introductory and legalistic subjects):

Chapter 4, section 4.1 sets forth standards for developing, implementing, and improving the quality management system; 4.2 sets forth standards for developing and maintaining quality system documents, manuals, and records.

Chapter 5, section 5.1 sets forth standards for promoting and improving the quality management system; 5.2 sets standards for identifying, meeting, and enhancing customer expectations; 5.3 establishes the organization's quality policy and commitment to continual improvement; 5.4 requires a quality management system plan and objectives; 5.5 and 5.6 control and evaluate the quality management system.

Chapter 6, section 6.1 through 6.4 provides for resources, personnel, infrastructure, and environment to support the quality management system.

Chapter 7 discusses making the quality management system a reality in terms of product and process development, purchasing, and operational activities.

Chapter 8 discusses monitoring and measuring product and process quality and identifying and making necessary quality improvements.

Instructions: Answer the following questions on a separate piece of paper.

1. Quality improvement teams assembled to quickly solve problems that are not excessively complex or interdepartmental can be:
   A. Virtuoso teams
   B. PIP teams
   C. Fast QM teams
   D. None of the above
2. Alternatives to Joint Commission accreditation services can now be sought from:
   A. ISO 9000
   B. Six Sigma processes
   C. CARF
   D. All of the above
3. As part of the Affordable Care Act, healthcare organizations are increasingly expected to meet federal care standards in order to receive reimbursement for care provided. These organizations are termed:
   A. Sentinel organizations
   B. AHRQ-qualified organizations
   C. QIO-qualified organizations
   D. Accountable care organizations

Summary

The pursuit of improvement in the US healthcare system has a long history and is itself based in the history of medicine. Conscious methodologies for this improvement have been put forward since the advent of Medicare, but the greatest focus has been developed over the last 20 years. Benefiting from the theoretical writings of industrial engineers like W. Edwards Deming and John Crosby and from the applications of the theory by many private, governmental, and accreditation entities, healthcare organizations have by and large come to be more adept at pursuing what is now most frequently called performance improvement. Knowledge of it is an important component of the practice of every healthcare professional. All must be able to participate in the common performance improvement cycles. All should be able to design indicators and measures of the important functions of their organizational units. All should be able to apply the common performance improvement tools such as bar graphs, run charts, and affinity diagramming to participate in and assist their PI teams in improving the quality of the care provided by each individual in the organization. Taking these philosophies, tools, and techniques to heart is the only real way that determined and lasting improvement can be effectively accomplished in a healthcare organization today.

References

Agency for Healthcare Research and Quality. 2012. Evidence-based Practice Centers. http://www.ahrq.gov/clinic/epc/

Agency for Healthcare Research and Quality. 2008. CAHPS Hospital Survey. http://www.cahps.ahrq.gov/content/products.

Agency for Healthcare Research and Quality. 2005. Clinical practice guidelines. http://www.ahrq.gov/clinic/cpgarchv.htm.

American Health Information Management Association. 2012. *AHIMA Pocket Glossary for HIM and Technology*. Chicago: AHIMA.

Batalden, P.B., and P.K. Stoltz. 1993. A framework for the continual improvement of health care: Building and applying professional and improvement knowledge to test changes in daily work. *Journal on Quality Improvement* 19(10): 424–447.

Berwick, D.M. 1989. Continuous improvement as an ideal in health care. *New England Journal of Medicine* 320(1): 53–56.

Boynton, A., and B. Fischer. 2005. Virtuoso teams: Lessons from teams that changed their worlds. *Financial Times.*

Centers for Medicare and Medicaid Services. 2011. http://www.cms.gov/Medicare/Medicare-Fee-for-Service-Payment/sharedsavingsprogram/downloads//ACO_QualityMeasures.pdf.

Centers for Medicare and Medicaid Services. 2005. http://www.cms.gov.

Donabedian, A. 1988. The quality of care: How can it be assessed? *Journal of the American Medical Association* 260(12): 1743–1748.

Glendinning, A. 2005. Patient safety gets boost from law easing fear of reporting. *American Medical Association.* http://www.ama-assn.org/amednews/2005/08/15/gvl10815.htm

Imai, M. 1986. *Kaizen: The Key to Japanese Competitive Success.* New York: Random House.

Institute of Medicine. 2001. *Crossing the Quality Chasm: A New Health System for the 21st Century.* Washington, D.C.: National Academies Press.

Institute of Medicine.1999. *To Err Is Human: Building a Safer Health System.* Washington, D.C.: National Academies Press.

Joint Commission. 2010. Inspiring health care excellence. http://www.jointcommission.org/NR/rdonlyres/3602CE1F-E2BB-4FF0-985E-49560E50DE1F/0/InspiringHCexcellenceweb1113.pdf.

Joint Commission. 2009a. *Comprehensive Accreditation Manual for Hospitals.* Oakbrook Terrace, IL: Joint Commission.

Joint Commission. 2009b. Facts about patient safety. http://www.jointcommission.org/PatientSafety.

Joint Commission. 2008. Sentinel Event Alert. http://www.jointcommission.org/SentinelEvents.

Kelly, D.L. 2003. *Applying Quality Management in Healthcare: A Process for Improvement.* Chicago: Health Administration Press.

Meisenheimer, C.G. 1997. *Improving Quality: A Guide to Effective Programs*, 2nd ed. Sudbury, MA: Jones and Bartlett.

National Academy of Engineering and Institute of Medicine. 2005. *Building a Better Delivery System.* Washington, D.C.: National Academies Press.

National Committee for Quality Assurance. 2012. Diabetes Recognition Program. http://www.ncqa.org/tabid/139/Default.aspx.

Office of Inspector General. 2005. Consecutive Medicare inpatient stays. http://www.oig.hhs.gov/oei/reports/oei-03-01-00430.pdf.

Omachonu, V.K. 1999. *Healthcare Performance Improvement.* Norcross, GA: Engineering and Management Press.

Pugh, M.D. 2005. Dashboards and scorecards: Tools for creating alignment. In *The Healthcare Quality Book: Vision, Strategy, and Tools.* Edited by Ransom, S.B., M.S. Joshi, and D.B. Nash. Chicago: Health Administration Press.

Shaw, P., and C. Elliott, 2013. *Performance Improvement in Healthcare: A Programmed Learning Approach.* Chicago: AHIMA.

Sollecito, W.A., and J.K. Johnson. 2013. *McLaughlin and Kaluzny's Continuous Quality Improvement in Health Care*, 4th ed. Burlington, MA: Jones and Bartlett Learning.

Additional Resources

Centers for Medicare and Medicaid Services. 2009. http://www.cms.gov/HospitalQualityInits.

Fried, B., and W. Carpenter. 2006. Understanding and improving team effectiveness in quality improvement. In *Continuous Quality Improvement in Health Care: Theory, Implementation, and Applications*, 3rd ed. Edited by McLaughlin, C.P., and A.D. Kaluzny. Boston: Jones and Bartlett.

Katzenbach, J.R., and D.K. Smith. 1993. *The Wisdom of Teams: Creating the High-Performance Organization.* Boston: Harvard Business School Press.

McClanahan, S., S.T. Goodwin, and F. Houser. 1999. A formula for errors: Good people + bad systems. In *Error Reduction in Health Care: A Systems Approach to Improving Patient Safety.* Edited by P.L. Spath. San Francisco: Jossey-Bass.

McWay, D. 1997. *Legal Aspects of Health Information Management.* Albany, NY: Delmar.

part **VI**

Management of Health Information Services

chapter 23

Managing and Leading During Organization Change

David X. Swenson, PhD

Learning Objectives

- Introduce the management discipline, the evolution of management thought/theories, and the key functions and skills of management
- Describe the functions and roles of a manager
- Describe the relationship between management functions and skills and levels of management
- Identify different approaches to problem solving and decision making
- Describe the emergence and principles of corporate social responsibility

- Describe key practices for effective managerial communication
- Explain the differences between managers and leaders
- Discuss the key ideas of prominent leadership theories
- Recognize that a leadership approach needs to adjust to various situations
- Identify the traits related to leadership effectiveness
- Recognize the stages and impact of organizational change
- Understand how to facilitate a transition in order to minimize stress to people and production

Key Terms

14 principles of management
85/15 rule
Active listening
Administrative management
Adopter group
Autocratic leadership
Balanced scorecard (BSC)
Bureaucracy
Business process reengineering (BPR)
Chain of command
Champion
Change agent
Change driver
Conceptual skills
Consideration
Contingency model of leadership
Controlling

Corporate social responsibility
Critic
Critical path method
Decentralization
Delegation
Democratic leadership
Discipline
Early adopter
Early majority
Emotional intelligence (EI)
Ending
Esprit de corps
Evidence-based management
Exchange relationship
Executive dashboard
Expectancy theory of motivation
Gantt chart

Goal
Great person theory
Groupthink
Hawthorne Effect
Human relations movement
In-group
Initiating structure
Innovator
Interpersonal skills
Inventor
Laggard
Late majority
Leader–member exchange (LMX)
Leader–member relations
Leadership grid
Leading
Least Preferred Coworker (LPC) Scale
Lewin's stages of change
Line authority
Management by objectives (MBO)
Management function
Maslow's Hierarchy of Needs
Mission statement
Neutral zone
New beginnings
Nonprogrammed decision
Normative Decision Model
Operational plan
Operations management
Organization development (OD)
Organizing
Out-group

Path–goal theory
Piece-rate incentive
Planning
Position power
Program evaluation and review technique (PERT)
Programmed decision
Reflective learning cycle
Refreezing
Role theory
Scalar chain
Scientific management
Self-monitoring
Servant Leadership Model
Situational model of leadership
Span of control
Sponsor
Staff authority
Stages of grief
Strategic plan
Tactical plan
Task structure
Technical skills
Theory X and Y
Time and motion studies
Total quality management (TQM)
Trait approach
Unfreezing
Values-based leadership
Vertical dyad linkage
Vertical structure
Vision statement
Worker immaturity–maturity

Introduction

Models for management originally were based on traditional ways of organizing people to accomplish tasks. For thousands of years, these typically involved small family cottage industries, military organizations, or church-directed structures. With the advent of the Industrial Revolution, migration to cities, and specialization of labor, the former methods of management no longer worked effectively. Workers did not necessarily carry on family traditions, could not be commanded to comply with orders, or did not serve out of dedication to some larger corporate value. New ways of thinking about management were needed.

Management theories are not just academic exercises; they are ways of describing how managers think about the way organizations work, which in turn influences their decisions and directs their efforts and behavior. The theories described in this chapter reflect the development of management theories over the decades, as well as newer approaches being developed. Many elements of even the early theories

are still practiced widely. By being able to identify our working theories, we are better able to evaluate how appropriate they are for our settings and how we can revise them to work better.

A key idea in management is the recognition that management theories and practices grow out of the unique constellation of forces or **change drivers** that operate at the time. These large-scale forces consist of demographic, social, political, economic, technical, and more recently, global and informational factors. In a competitive environment, each organization seeks to position itself to succeed against other organizations and does so by the effective and efficient allocation of its resources to respond to these demands.

In this first section of the chapter we summarize some of the key historical and theoretical developments in management, many features of which are still used today in organizations. The functions, skills, and roles of managers are identified, along with trends in management theory related to problem solving. The importance of communication in organizations is emphasized related to the increasing role of information in the healthcare workplace. Finally, leadership of the organization will be examined through the evolution of leadership theories and how transition can be facilitated during organizational change.

Landmarks in Management as a Discipline

Management, as a **discipline,** is a field of study characterized by a knowledge base and perspective that are distinctive from other fields of study. The knowledge base and perspective form a foundation for the discipline's practices. Over time, changing social conditions and growing technological innovations have contributed to the way that the management discipline has evolved and management theories are framed.

Scientific Management

The late 19th and early 20th centuries marked the emergence of scientific management concepts. **Scientific management** was an early effort to apply scientific principles and practices to business processes. The individuals profiled in the following subsections were key players in that development.

Max Weber

Management theory emerged with the onset of the Industrial Revolution in the mid-19th century and initially took the form of scientific management. During this period, Max Weber (1864–1920) began formulating his ideas for the ideal organization. Recognizing the variability in standards that lead to inefficiencies, he proposed that organizations be structured as bureaucracies. This form of organization was typified by clear hierarchies of relationships, rules and regulations to standardize behavior, and using trained specialists for jobs. Consequently, the subjective judgment and favoritism could be eliminated, and planning could be based on the position and task rather person and personal preferences. In the modern marketplace where competitive advantage is maintained through innovation, **bureaucracy** has come more often to refer to slow decision making, unresponsiveness, ignoring the uniqueness of individuals, and rules without reasons.

Frederick Taylor

About the same time that Weber was forming his ideas about bureaucracy, Frederick W. Taylor (1856–1915) discovered that his company and most others had tremendous unused potential. Pay and working conditions were poor, waste and inefficiency were prevalent, and management decision making was unsystematic and not based on research of any sort. Taylor introduced new practices whose success led to his being recognized as the father of scientific management. Although many of his ideas are commonly accepted today,

they were revolutionary at the time. He proposed that organizations observe and study how jobs were performed and then streamline the actions to be more efficient. He conducted time and motion studies in which tasks were subdivided into their most basic movements. Detailed motions were timed to determine the most efficient way of carrying them out. After the "one best way" was found, the best worker match for the job was hired, tools and procedures were standardized, instruction cards were written to guide workers, and breaks were instituted to reduce fatigue. A **piece-rate incentive** system also was developed in which workers received additional pay when they exceeded the standard output level for their task.

Frank and Lillian Gilbreth

In the early 1900s, the Gilbreths were a husband and wife team who developed many of the early ideas of ergonomics and work efficiency. Conducting **time and motion studies** on bricklaying, the Gilbreths divided the process into detailed individual motions they called "therbligs" (Gilbreth nearly spelled backward) to identify unnecessary or inefficient motions. Seeking the single best way to perform the tasks, they reduced the number of motions for bricklaying from 18 to 4.5, which resulted in much higher productivity, less fatigue, and better planning. Lillian was known for her studies on finding innovative ways to design efficient kitchen and home living areas for patients with cardiac-limited conditions.

Henry Gantt

Henry Gantt (1861–1919) worked for Taylor and was known for his promotion of favorable psychological work conditions. He may be best remembered for his development of the **Gantt chart,** which is still used for project management to show how the components of a task are scheduled over time. His chart contributed to development, in the late 1950s, of the **program evaluation and review technique (PERT)** developed by the US Navy and the **critical path method** developed by Dupont. He also contributed his Task and Bonus Plan to management, which provided bonus payment for workers who exceeded their production standards for the day.

Administrative Management

Attempting to compensate for scientific management's exclusion of senior management in the theory, **administrative management** argued that management was a profession and could be learned. The following subsections profile three individuals who played key roles in describing management functions.

Henry Fayol

Henry Fayol's (1841–1925) major contribution includes a description of the key functions of management and 14 principles for organizational design and administration.

Fayol's **management functions** have persisted with some variation into modern organizations and identify key functions that define the manager's role. Fayol's original managerial functions were the following:

- **Planning** consists of examining the future and preparing plans of action to attain goals.
- **Organizing** includes the ways in which the managed system is designed and operated to attain the desired goals. It involves the way that tasks are grouped into departments and resources are distributed to them.
- **Leading** (sometimes also called directing) is the process of influencing the behavior of others. It involves motivating, creating shared culture and values, and communicating with all levels of the organization.
- **Controlling** refers to the monitoring of performance and use of feedback to ensure that efforts are on target toward prescribed goals, making course corrections as necessary.

Fayol also formulated **14 principles of management** to guide managerial activities within the total organization (see figure 23.1). Like his managerial functions, most have been incorporated into modern organizations and are widely

Figure 23.1.   Fayol's fourteen principles

1. *Specialization of labor:* Work allocation and specialization allow concentrated activities, deeper understanding, and better efficiency.

2. *Authority:* The person to whom responsibilities are given has the right to give direction and expect obedience.

3. *Discipline:* The smooth operation of a business requires standards, rules, and values for consistency of action.

4. *Unity of command:* Every employee receives direction and instructions from only one boss.

5. *Unity of direction:* All workers are aligned in their efforts toward a single outcome.

6. *Subordination of individual interests:* Accomplishing shared values and organizational goals take priority over individual agendas.

7. *Remuneration:* Employees should receive fair pay for work.

8. *Centralization:* Decisions are made at the top.

9. *Scalar chain:* Everyone is clearly included in the chain of command and line of authority from top to bottom of the organization.

10. *Order:* People should clearly understand where they fit in the organization, and all people and material have a place.

11. *Equity:* People are treated fairly, and a sense of justice should pervade the organization.

12. *Tenure:* Turnover is undesirable, and loyalty to the organization is sought.

13. *Initiative:* Personal initiative should be encouraged.

14. *Esprit de corps:* Harmony, cohesion, teamwork, and good interpersonal relationships should be encouraged.

accepted today. For example, authority was proposed as the right of an executive to give orders and expect obedience. Unity of command meant that each employee reports to only one boss. The **scalar chain,** or line of authority, ensured that everyone in the organization appears in the **chain of command** and reports to someone. **Esprit de corps** emphasized the work climate in which harmony and cohesion promoted good work.

Chester Barnard

Chester Barnard (1886–1961) elaborated the role of top executives. He proposed that the leader needs information from those below, that the communication system be designed and implemented by the executive, and that the role of middle management be to implement plans and solve problems. In his classic book *Functions of the Executive* in 1938 he emphasized formulating organizational objectives and establishing a system of essential services. His theories of authority and incentives rested on principles of communication: common knowledge and access to communication channels, personal competency, and accuracy in direct communication.

Mary Parker Follett

Another major contributor to the administrative approach was Mary Parker Follett (1868–1933). In contrast to what was often considered a mechanistic view by Taylor, she was interested in broader social ideas and championed the role of relationships in organizations. Although she drew mixed attention in the late 1920s, she foresaw the development of a systems view of business, the role of empowered employees in organizational development, and the use of workgroups to implement solutions. Follett promoted using teamwork and creative group effort, involving people in organizational development, and integrating the organization, which involved many elements of systems theory.

Humanistic Management and the Human Relations Movement

Although the United States has always touted itself as the home of democracy, the equity of power in the workplace has not always existed between workers and management. By the early 1900s, there were growing social pressures to treat workers in a more enlightened manner. Building on Barnard's and Follett's ideas that people should be treated fairly and that effective controls come from individual workers, the stage was set for a shift in management thought stimulated by an experiment at an electric power plant.

The Hawthorne Studies

Between 1927 and 1932 Elton Mayo and others from Harvard University conducted a series of experiments at the Western Electric Hawthorne Works in Chicago. The studies originally were designed to explore how fatigue and monotony affected job productivity and how these might be mitigated by breaks, variable work hours, temperature, humidity, and lighting. Although performance increased when desirable conditions were increased, unexpectedly, performance also improved when these conditions were reduced. The researchers concluded that it was the human factors that made a difference: attention during the study, freedom of participation, and feeling important by being singled out for participation in the project—the so-called **Hawthorne Effect.** Only in later reviews of the study was it also discovered that the participants were motivated by financial incentives. Nonetheless, this popularized study gave strong impetus to the consideration of social factors at work.

Human Resources Management

In the 1950s, the field of psychology in the United States was just coming into its own prominence, as were theories of motivation. Observing that many problems derived from an inability to meet needs, Abraham Maslow (1908–1970) suggested that an understanding of employees' needs might help to explain behavior and provide guidance for managers on how to better motivate workers. His now-famous hierarchy, **Maslow's Hierarchy of Needs,** began with physiological existence needs and progressed through safety, social belongingness, self-esteem, and finally self-actualization or creativity needs. This developmental view of needs meant that to motivate people, lower-order needs should be satisfied before higher-order needs could serve as motivators.

Douglas McGregor

Douglas McGregor (1906–1964) recognized the shift in conceptual models from assumptions that workers were incapable of independent action to beliefs in their potential and high performance. He formulated the contrasting views as **theory X and Y** (1960). Theory X presumed that workers inherently disliked work and would avoid it, had little ambition, and mostly wanted security; therefore, managerial direction and control were necessary. Theory Y took a more enlightened view and assumed that work was as natural as play, that motivation could be both internally and externally driven, and that under the right conditions people would seek responsibility and be creative.

Operations Management

Operations management emerged after World War II as an application of statistical, mathematical, and quantitative methods to decision making in the business setting in order to better understand how products and services could be manufactured and delivered. Such techniques as forecasting, linear programming, break-even analysis, queuing theory, logistics, and more recently data mining emerged from this emphasis on statistical control.

Contemporary Management

Although many aspects of older theories of management are still widely practiced in most organizations, research and practical experience have led to many refinements and new developments in the field. More contemporary approaches to management include management by objectives (MBO), total quality management (TQM), and an emphasis on excellence. Each of these has made a contribution to better understanding how effective management works, but none of them alone has yet succeeded in producing a comprehensive solution for managing organizations.

Management by Objectives
Peter Drucker and Management by Objectives

Often referred to as the guru of management gurus and father of modern management, Peter Drucker (1909–2005) revolutionized the role of strategy by wresting it from the hands of top management and making it everyone's job, helping workers understand how mission, strategy, goals, and performance were related. Because strategy was action oriented, starting in the 1950s, Drucker elaborated on the technique of **management by objectives (MBO),** in which clear target objectives could be stated and measured and could direct behavior (Drucker 1986). Drucker's MBO approach was further developed by his promotion of the ideas that workers should be considered assets rather than liabilities, the corporation is an interpersonal community, and business is customer- centered (Byrne 2005).

Total Quality Management

Total quality management (TQM) purported to overcome the limitations of MBO, criticizing the use of quotas because workers often spent too much time trying to look good or protect themselves by seeking short-term objectives and ignoring long-term and critical outcomes. TQM offered a way to build in high performance by maximizing employee potential and continuous improvement of process. The **85/15 rule** of TQM proposes that 85 percent of problems encountered are the result of faulty systems rather than unproductive employees. W. Edwards Deming proposed his 14 principles for TQM implementation. (See figure 23.2.) The manager's job, then, becomes one of anticipating and removing barriers to high employee performance.

W. Edwards Deming and Quality

From the late 1970s to the mid-1980s, the United States was beset with a series of economic setbacks. Serious recessions, a growing trade deficit, government deregulation, and huge operating losses led to the downsizing of hundreds of thousands of workers. Quality became the focus as a means of increasing competitive position, and much of the idea was derived from W. Edwards Deming (1900–1993), an American

Figure 23.2.   Deming's 14 principles

1. Create a constancy of purpose toward continual improvement of products and services, with the objectives to stay in business, be competitive, and provide jobs.

2. Adopt the new philosophy for a new economic age by correcting superstitious learning, calling for a major change, and looking at the customer rather than competition.

3. Cease dependence on inspection to achieve quality by eliminating emphasis on mass inspection and building quality in from the beginning.

4. Don't award business based on price tag alone, and minimize total costs by developing trusting and loyal long-term relationships with single suppliers.

5. Constantly and continually improve production and service systems and thereby improve quality and decrease costs.

6. Institute training on the job, where barriers to good work are removed and managers provide a setting that promotes worker success.

7. Institute leadership with the aim of revising supervision to better help people, machines, and processes do a better job.

8. Drive out fear so everyone can work effectively toward company goals.

9. Break down barriers between departments so that various departments can work as a team and anticipate problems of production or use of a product or service.

10. Avoid asking for new levels of productivity and zero defects through slogans and targets because most problems of low productivity lie with the system rather than the worker.

11. Replace work standards such as quotas, numerical goals, and MBO with good leadership.

12. Remove barriers that rob people at all levels of their pride of workmanship; shift from numbers to quality.

13. Institute a program of education and self-improvement by emphasizing lifelong learning and employment.

14. Transformation of the workplace occurs through everyone's action.

Source: Deming 1986.

statistician. Deming had initially developed his ideas in the 1940s (Walton 1986), but the American economy was booming at the time and seemed to believe it had found Taylor's "one best way" to do things. Consequently, American industry was inattentive to Deming's ideas about improvement and his statistical control procedures for monitoring quality. However, the Japanese were suffering from an all-but-destroyed economy and were eager to hear new ideas about production. They quickly adopted the concept of total quality management.

Business Process Reengineering

Growing in popularity in the mid-1990s and fostered by Hammer and Champy's book, *Reengineering the Corporation*

(1993), **business process reengineering (BPR)** seeks radical redesign of the organization and its business processes in order to reduce costs, streamline operations, and improve quality of service. Starting with high-level cross-functional team review of mission, strategic goals, and market needs, it proposes significant revision in key business processes. In some ways harkening back to Taylor's "best way," Business Process Reengineering (BPR) attempts to find the best work processes to maximally improve cost, quality, service, and speed. Like TQM it emphasizes ongoing improvement and use of information technology to provide real-time information about customers, competition, and change.

The Search for Excellence

Although elements of most major theories can be found within the practices of successful managers, developments and refinements in thinking have thrived to become part of management history. In 1982, Peters and Waterman published *In Search of Excellence*. Based on a sample of highly successful business firms, they described the management practices that led to their success. Eight characteristics were described that became the rage in management circles for a time, with managers hoping to reproduce in their own organizations what top firms had done (Peters and Waterman 1982) (see figure 23.3). Although the eight practices are very important, a follow-up of the same organizations four years later showed disappointing results. In that short time, 66 percent had fallen from a top position and 19 percent were in a troubled position (Pascale 1990). The fall from excellence appears to be due to those organizations refocusing on their temporary success and not attending sufficiently to the

Figure 23.3.   Characteristics of highly successful firms

1. *A bias for action:* They establish a value for action and implementation rather than overanalyzing and delaying with endless committees.

2. *Close to the customer:* They listen and respond to customers to satisfy their needs.

3. *Autonomy and entrepreneurship:* They empower people and encourage innovation and risk taking.

4. *Productivity through people:* They increase employees' awareness that everyone's contributions lead to shared success.

5. *Hands on, value driven:* Their managers should be visible, involved, and know what is going on.

6. *Stick to the knitting:* They stay with the core business, what they do well, and avoid wide diversification.

7. *Simple form, lean staff:* They have fewer administrative layers and keep the structure simple.

8. *Simultaneous loose–tight properties:* They maintain dedication to core principles but encourage flexibility and experimentation in reaching goals.

Source: Peters and Waterman 1982.

dynamic and strategic processes that were required to keep them there.

Although researchers continue to search for the essential ingredients that will make firms most successful, the lesson from the excellence studies highlights some important principles, including the following:

- Whether you succeed or fail, try to understand what brought that about.
- When you succeed, recognize that the success factors are not static but, rather, are continually changing.
- Do not let past success strategies keep you from discovering new ones for the future.
- What may contribute to the success of one type of organization or competitive setting may not be as useful to other types and settings or at other stages of organizational development.

In summary, the history of management reflects much development in our understanding of how people work and how that work can be more effectively organized. From Taylor's and Fayol's early efforts to create structured work systems to more contemporary views on the importance of integrating human factors with work conditions, management theories continue to evolve (see figure 23.4).

Check Your Understanding 23.1

Instructions: Answer the following questions on a separate piece of paper.

1. What are some of the important management concepts that have persisted over the decades? Why have they persisted?

2. Why have some management ideas been rapidly accepted while others have required years to become popular?

3. Using the example of the Gilbreth time–motion study, identify some complex activity you engage in (such as packing for a trip, dressing in the morning, and so on) and see how you can streamline the sequence to become more efficient.

4. Explore reasons why the top companies identified in Peters and Waterman's *In Search of Excellence* dropped from their top position within a few short years. How might that have been prevented?

Functions and Principles of Management

As mentioned earlier, Fayol identified the key functions of management. Related to these functions are certain categories of skills that are needed to carry them out.

Managerial Functions

As theories of management began to be refined, so too did the formal nature of the manager's role. As organizations increased in diversity, complexity, and size, managers often shifted their expertise from expert knowledge in doing a task to expert knowledge in managing other people. As Mary Parker Follett is reputed to have said, "Management is the art of getting things done through people" (Stoner and Freeman 1989). Specific functions of management came to

Figure 23.4.   Foundations of Management Timeline

Scientific Management	Administrative Management	Humanistic Management	Operations Management	Contemporary Management
1880–1920	**circa 1920s**	**circa 1924**	**1941–present**	
Max Weber: Bureaucracy	Henri Fayol: 4 managament functions and 14 principles	Elton Mayo and Franz Roethlesberger: Hawthorne studies	WWII logistics for troops and materiel	Management by objectives
Frederick Taylor: Best way to perform a job		Abraham Maslow: Hierarchy of Needs	PERT and critical path analysis	Total quality management
Frank and Lillian Gilbreth: Time and motion studies	Chester Barnard: Effectiveness and efficiency, theory of authority, theory of incentives	Douglas McGregor: Theory X and Y	Routing and supply chain management	Business process redesign
Henry Gantt: Gantt chart and project management	Mary Parker Follett: Power sharing, conflict resolution		Scheduling and queuing systems	
			Data mining	

be defined, as did a range of skills and subroles that contribute to successful problem solving.

Planning

Planning is the first step in management and involves determining what should be accomplished and how. Although planning occurs at all levels, top-level or strategic planning is most critical in formulating the mission and providing direction for change. When these strategies are defined, they can be implemented at the lower levels of the organization. High-quality planning and implementation capability provide competitive advantage over those who minimize the importance of planning, as reflected in higher levels of performance such as profits (Hahn and Powers 2010).

Plans are usually organized hierarchically, with a **mission statement** driving the enterprise by defining exactly the purpose of the organization, that is, what business it is in. The mission may also incorporate or be accompanied by a values statement that reflects the social and cultural beliefs an organization wishes to support among its members. For example, the Benedictine Health System acknowledges "hospitality, stewardship, respect and justice" as its core values (Benedictine Health System 2002). A **vision statement** describes the ideal and desired future state toward which an organization is directed, in contrast to the mission statement, which is current and realistic. The **strategic plan** follows from the mission. It is formulated by top management, sets the priorities and positioning of the organization for a time period, and is based on the constellation of internal strengths and weaknesses and external opportunities and threats. These are translated through the lower levels of the organization by middle management, which formulates **tactical plans** for the organization's major divisions. At the lower departmental levels, these finally become **operational plans** that are implemented as daily activities.

Plans are usually expressed in terms of **goals.** Goals are statements of intended outcomes that provide a source of direction and motivation as well as a guideline for performance, decision making, and evaluation. Good goals cover key result areas of the strategy; have the characteristics of being specific, measurable, and challenging, but achievable; and are set for a given period of time.

Organizing

After the goals have been specified, the task changes to deciding how resources can be allocated to achieve them. Traditionally, division of labor has been used to divide work into separate jobs. This specialization allows for development of greater expertise and standardization of tasks and for clear selection and training criteria. However, too narrow or specialized a task, as in assembly-line work, may produce more boredom than productivity. As Bridges predicted in 1994, the emerging economy with downsized and flatter organizations often requires workers to take on multiple roles and, consequently, to have portfolios of skills rather than highly defined job descriptions. Such skill and role portfolios are often found in healthcare, where downsizing and staff shortages occur, resulting in remaining staff assuming a broader range of duties (Apker 2001; Helseth 2007).

Jobs are most often organized by positions, and the positions are arranged hierarchically in the business by an organizational chart. (An example of a typical hospital organizational chart is shown in figure 23.5.) The organizational chart graphically represents the formal structure of an organization, often includes departmental subdivisions, and follows the scalar principle and unity of command discussed earlier. The **vertical structure** of the organization refers to the formal design of positions within departments and divisions, the lines of authority and responsibility, and the allocation of resources to them. Two kinds of authority are found in organizations. **Line authority** is the right of managers to direct the activities of subordinates under their immediate control; **staff authority** is related to the expert knowledge of specialists and involves their advising and recommending courses of action.

Each supervisor has a certain number of people who report to him or her, which is referred to as the span of management or the **span of control.** Although the span of control is often determined by tradition or accident, there are several factors to consider in optimally balancing it. In general, the span is larger when work is routine and homogeneous, workers have similar tasks, rules and guidelines are available, people are well trained and motivated, workers are located together, and task times are short (Meyer 2008). Deciding how a combination of factors leads to a particular span has been facilitated by technology. For example, the Healthcare Management Council (HMC) provides a comprehensive measurement of organizational factors leading to a span of management recommendation. The HMC Span of Control Analysis considers organizational flatness, departmental fragmentation, and layers of management using organizational charts. The HMC report can be used by managers to optimize organizational structure, set staffing and financial targets, and determine needs (HMC 2007).

Related to span is **delegation,** in which managers transfer authority to subordinates to carry out a responsibility. With an increasing focus on customers and rapid response, frontline workers are now trained to make decisions that once were made levels above them. When authority and responsibility move from the organization's top levels to its lower levels where they can be competently exercised, centralized decision making becomes decentralized. Although **decentralization** enables top managers to take on new responsibilities or spend time with other priorities, it places an additional burden on workers.

Directing/Leading

The third managerial function accomplishes goals by influencing behavior and by motivating and inspiring people to high performance. At the turn of the century, an autocratic

Figure 23.5.   Sample hospital organizational chart

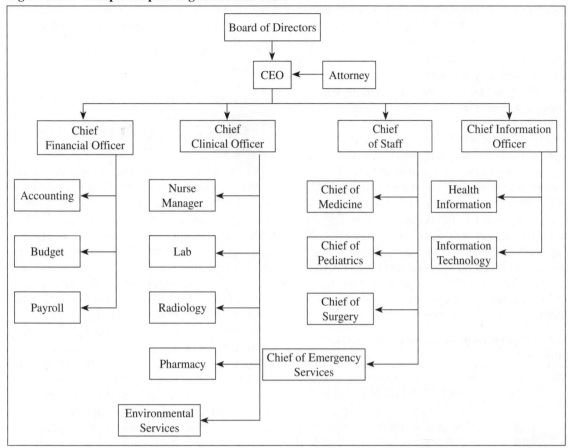

view of leadership was considered to be appropriate, but as humanistic views have prevailed over the decades, leadership has become decentralized and distributed throughout the organization.

Leading is most often accomplished by communicating, directing, and motivating, all intended to influence behavior to perform well. Power, the ability to influence, is central to leadership and derives from several sources, including the following:

- *Authority* or legitimate power comes from the right of the position in the organization to direct the activities of subordinates.
- *Reward power* is based on the leader's ability to withhold or provide rewards for performance.
- *Coercive power* maintains control over punishments.
- *Referent power* exists when the leader possesses personal characteristics that are appealing to the constituency, and the constituency follows out of admiration, charismatic impact, or the desire to be like the leader.
- *Expert power* occurs when the leader has knowledge or expertise that is of value (French and Raven 1959).
- *Information power* is based on the persuasive content of the person's message, apart from personal characteristics (Raven 1983).

Leadership behaviors and most models of leadership fall into two categories: task-oriented behaviors and social or group-oriented behaviors. Task-oriented behaviors are directed toward defining tasks, creating structure and rules, ensuring production, and placing emphasis on quality and speed of output. Social orientation focuses on interpersonal behaviors that develop and maintain harmonious work relationships, encourage morale, reduce stress and conflict, and build worker satisfaction. Several models of leadership, such as the Blake-Mouton Managerial Grid, use these two dimensions and are discussed later in this chapter.

Controlling/Evaluating

The final managerial function refers to the monitoring of performance, determining whether it is on or off course in achieving the goals and making course corrections as needed. Managers are obligated to ensure that progress is made toward achieving goals, although recent trends indicate that employees are empowered to monitor themselves and each other, rather than being monitored from the top. This obviously requires selecting employees who have the maturity and integrity to accept this responsibility, but it corrects for the distortion and delay that can occur in a very hierarchical organization.

Significant breakthroughs have occurred in control with the development of the executive dashboard and balanced scorecard, introduced in 1992 (Kaplan and Norton 1996). The **executive dashboard** is often characterized as a manager's version of a pilot's cockpit dashboard; it contains all the critical information for leading the organization. The dashboard typically contains regularly updated information on key strategic measures such as forecasts, customer satisfaction, billings, profit, and so on.

The **balanced scorecard (BSC)** is an extension of strategic planning in which key performance indicators are measured at all levels of the organization and progress with workers and management receiving ongoing feedback. Categories of feedback usually include financial, customer satisfaction, internal processes (for example, quality, response time), and learning and growth. For example, using the BSC helped University and Hospital Clinics in Holmes County, Mississippi, move much closer to break-even in its revenues, while Harrisburg Medical Center in Illinois reported achieving a consistent 4 percent margin over a four-year period (Rural Health Resource Center 2008).

Figure 23.6.   Management functions by level in the organization

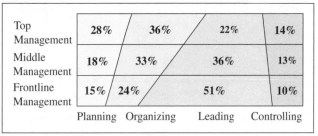

	Planning	Organizing	Leading	Controlling
Top Management	28%	36%	22%	14%
Middle Management	18%	33%	36%	13%
Frontline Management	15%	24%	51%	10%

Levels of Management

The four functions of management vary in emphasis according to the level of management involved (see figure 23.6). In general, as one moves from first-line (supervisory) to middle management to top managers, planning increases, organizing increases, directing decreases, and controlling stays about the same (Jones and George 2006; Mahoney et al. 1965).

Larger organizations often have three levels of management: supervisors, middle managers, and executives and a board of directors. These different levels of management within organizations also have different levels of leadership functions.

Supervisory managers are hands-on managers of daily operations over a unit or division within a department. They ensure that staff meet pre-established standards of performance, policy, and procedures. They often have high technical skills, but may have limited hiring and financial authority.

Middle managers have a broader scope of responsibility than supervisory managers, often overseeing all functions in a department, such as the health information services department, the admission and registration department, and such.

They also are in a position to facilitate the work of positions above and below them, both supervisory and executive. More specifically, their responsibilities often include

- Developing, implementing, and revising the policies and procedures of the organization under direction by the executive level
- Carrying out organizational plans that have been developed at the executive and board level
- Communicating operational information to executives so they can continue ongoing planning.

In a health information services department, middle managers can modify department-level policies and procedures as needed and can analyze information to get at a root cause of a problem and use discretion in dealing with it. They may also track quality of clinical databases, oversee compliance programs, participate on interdisciplinary committees, and conduct risk and quality audits. Middle managers typically report to an executive manager, who could include the chief operating officer (COO), chief information officer (CIO), chief financial officer (CFO), or chief executive officer (CEO).

At the highest level of organization are executive managers and the governing board. Executives are mostly responsible for formulating the strategic plan, ensuring consistency in the direction of the organization with its vision and mission, and allocating assets and resources toward that end. They establish policies and lead the organization toward quality improvement and compliance. In the typical "C-suite" of a large healthcare organization, there is commonly a COO, a CFO, a chief nursing officer (CNO), a CIO, and a chief medical officer (CMO), all of who report to the CEO. The CEO reports directly to the board of directors, also called board of trustees or governing board.

Governing boards are legislated to be responsible for the operation of the entire organization. They are the final authority when it comes to the approval of the strategic plan and mission, vision, ethics, and values statements. A board is usually made up of a chairperson and 10 to 20 board members who represent the interests of the owners of the business (stockholders) or other stakeholders (prominent members of the community and such).

Managerial Skills

The categories of skills required to perform the four management functions are conceptual, interpersonal, and technical skills (Buhler 2007; Katz 1974). As management has become increasingly complex, the requisite skills for carrying out the four managerial functions also vary by level in the organization (see figure 23.7).

Conceptual Skills

The need for **conceptual skills** has increased significantly over the decades. Where it once was important only to have good technical skills, now a successful manager must be

Figure 23.7.   Functional skills by level in the organization

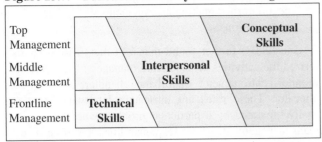

Figure 23.8.   Attributes of emotional intelligence

- Self-awareness: The ability to monitor, notice, and label one's feelings as they occur. This allows one to be more certain about feelings and to identify early vague feelings.
- Self-regulation: The ability to manage one's emotions and impulses. A person with this skill is often viewed as being reflective, comfortable with change and ambiguity, and able to control impulsiveness.
- Motivation: Being highly motivated is essential for focusing attention, mastering situations, showing creativity, and being productive and successful.
- Empathy: The ability to recognize emotions in others. This is important for teamwork as well as for helping adjust one's behavior to the emerging reactions of others.
- Social skills: The ability to handle relationships with others is central to being perceived as popular, effective with others, and having the qualities of a leader.

Source: Adapted from Goleman 1998.

able to understand diverse fields and deal with complex situations. Conceptual skills, especially at the higher levels of the organization, include such competencies as visioning the organization, planning, decision making, problem solving, creativity, and conceptualizing the connections among parts of a complex organizational system, or "systems thinking." Cognitive complexity, or the ability to both see the many parts of a problem and integrate that diversity into a coherent picture, is very important for top managers (Houghton et al. 2009).

Interpersonal Skills

Interpersonal skills involve the ability to work with and through others to accomplish goals. Depending on the nature of the work and the level of interaction needed among individuals, interpersonal skills may or may not be a critical skill for employee success. However, managers, in their interactions with employees and with each other, need to cultivate impeccable interpersonal skills.

Interpersonal competency is based on self-awareness and understanding, and the best managers are those who can articulate both their strengths and weaknesses (Goleman 1998). Yet, self-awareness is not enough, and consistently high performers also demonstrate **self-monitoring** (Riggio and Reichard 2008). Self-monitoring refers to the ability to observe the reactions that one's behavior elicits in others and then adjusting one's behavior to improve the relationship. Other important interpersonal skills include communicating, motivating and influencing, managing conflict, and complementing different ways of interacting.

Emotional intelligence (EI) is currently one of the most widely discussed topics in management and psychology. Advocates of EI believe that awareness and use of feelings complement rational intelligence and experience, and it is the combination of these that is the key to success (see figure 23.8). Studies examining an array of management skills conclude that people management skills are more important to performance than are intellectual abilities (Carmeli and Tishler 2006; Strickland 2000). Other studies support the contention that interpersonal skills are strongly related to overall performance (Sy et al. 2006), successful conflict management (Jordan and Troth 2002), and team performance (Druskat et al. 2005) and that such skills can be enhanced (Meyer et al. 2004).

Technical Skills

Finally, understanding and mastering the technical information, methods, and equipment involved in a discipline constitute the technical skills. Although most important at the employee level of the organization, technical skills are still required for upper management so that there is a comprehensive understanding of the workings of the organization. However, conceptual and interpersonal skills are probably more useful in obtaining promotion in most organizations. This is true because, at higher levels in organizations, these types of skills are used more often and are more important than technical skills. For example, conceptual skills are more useful in the leading and planning function because they involve understanding the systems view of the total organization.

Managerial Activities

The activities of managers and leaders are typically organized around several roles. A role refers to a set of expectations about how a person is to behave from the perspective of oneself, peers, superiors, subordinates, consumers (patients), and others (such as legislators). **Role theory** has been a prominent framework for examining behavior in the field of sociology for decades, and it has been applied in management to clarify the wide range of responsibilities held.

Mintzberg's Role Studies

Henry Mintzberg, Cleghorn Professor of Management at McGill University, completed his dissertation at MIT on the roles of managers. In practice, Mintzberg (1992) found that most chief executives spent less than 10 minutes on any activity and that supervising foremen in industry averaged one activity every 48 seconds. Mintzberg summarized his findings by saying that managers completed a great deal of work at an unrelenting pace, but the activities were characterized by variety, fragmentation, and brevity. Two decades later, the pace for managers has been unrelenting, with information overload and multitasking continuing to pose challenges.

Mintzberg's subsequent research with managers showed that their activities could usually be described by 10 roles organized into three categories (table 23.1):

- *Interpersonal activity* arises from the manager's formal authority in the organization and is supportive of the informational and decisional activities. It includes the roles of figurehead for ceremonial and formal occasions, of leader for motivating and using power, and of liaison to link and network for information and support.
- *Informational activity* includes the roles of monitor of performance information, disseminator of values and information, and spokesperson for the organization with outside groups.
- *Decisional activity* includes the roles of entrepreneur to promote improvement and change, disturbance handler to deal with disruptions, resource allocator

Table 23.1.   Mintzberg's managerial roles

Managerial Activity	Related Roles
Interpersonal	• *Figurehead:* The manager represents the organization and is a symbol for ceremonial, social, legal, and inspirational duties. • *Liaison:* The manager maintains networks of relationships outside his or her organizational unit to gather information and favors. • *Leader:* The manager directs, guides, motivates, and develops subordinates.
Informational	• *Monitor:* The manager oversees internal and external information sources. • *Disseminator:* The manager communicates facts and values to others in the organization. • Spokesperson: The manager communicates with others outside the organization.
Decisional	• *Entrepreneur:* The manager promotes development and planned change in the organization. • *Disturbance handler:* The manager resolves crises and unexpected problems. • *Resource allocator:* The manager uses authority to allocate budget, personnel, equipment, services, and facilities. • *Negotiator:* The manager resolves dilemmas and disputes and determines the use of resources.

for overseeing resources and setting priorities, and negotiator for making arrangements with other organizations.

Guo (2003) further found that 6 of the 10 roles characterized the activities of healthcare managers: leader, liaison, monitor, entrepreneur, disturbance handler, and resource allocator. These roles are intricately intertwined and not easily separated by a particular problem when it comes to team management, where responsibilities are often distributed among team members. However, they provide a realistic portrayal of the wide range of skilled behaviors required of effective managers.

In healthcare, as well as other fields of management, decisions tend to be based more on political and value considerations than on empirical sources. However, with the increased interest in alternative approaches to healthcare (for example, acupuncture, nutrition) and to healthcare delivery in order to reduce errors, decrease costs, improve outcomes of care, and reduce liabilities, an emphasis on **evidence-based management,** or information-based management, is emerging in which more informed decisions are made based on the best clinical and research evidence that proposed practices will work. For example, Australia-based CSIRO works with healthcare organizations to determine factors that influence the use of health information by at-risk segments of a population and also develops performance measures for staff. Their procedures have increased the use of data and information by senior managers in strategic and daily planning. Increasingly, all levels of managers have better information available to support their decision making and performance and the outcomes of the decisions they make.

Check Your Understanding 23.2

Instructions: Answer the following questions on a separate piece of paper.

1. Discuss reasons for the four management functions changing in emphasis over the three levels of management. For example, why would there be less emphasis on the leadership function for top-level managers compared with the strong emphasis for first-line managers?

2. Examine a job description for a position in your field. What is the distribution of conceptual, interpersonal, and technical skills required?

3. Make a list of daily activities engaged in by observing or asking a manager what he or she does. Then, categorize the activities into Mintzberg's 10 managerial roles.

4. Draw an organizational chart of your college, a hospital, or some other organization with which you are familiar. Be sure to designate both line and staff positions.

5. What does quality mean in your work? Identify several tasks you perform, define quality for each task, and consider how you would measure it.

Table 23.2. Paradigm shift in management

Traditional Management Paradigm	New Management Paradigm
Multilevel hierarchical organization	Flatter, distributed organization
Centralized decision making	Decentralized decision making
Status measured by amount of turf controlled	Status measured by success in achieving outcomes
Funding inputs and intentions	Funding outcomes
Face-to-face interaction	Telecommunication and virtual interaction
Homogenous staffing	Workforce diversity
Job description	Skill portfolio
Annual strategic plan	Learning organization
Financial bottom line	Triple bottom line
Efficiency and stability	Ongoing innovation
Mass services	Market segmentation
Work at central office	Work at satellite and home offices

Trends in Management Theory

What we have seen in the several management theories presented in this chapter is that as change drivers have an impact on the marketplace and organizations, organizations must adapt in order to survive and thrive. Management theories become a template for thinking about the structure and processes by which business is conducted. As the marketplace changes, old theories may lose their explanatory power and be replaced with more accurate theories and principles for managing the organization (see table 23.2). At the same time, as managers become accustomed to, and develop expertise with, a certain viewpoint, they may become biased in its use and fail to see exceptions to it. A requisite skill for managers is to know when to use a particular framework and when to change it.

Although Taylor and others at the turn of the 20th century faced a host of changes, the unrelenting pace of change is an even more constant companion to managers today. The successful manager must be able to see patterns of change and prepare others to respond to them.

Problem Solving and Decision Making

Problems are defined as impediments to the attainment of goals. While some managers view problems as negative and something to be avoided, problem solving can also be viewed as an opportunity for managers and organizations to build experience and resilience. Solving problems requires that they be framed or defined in useful and understandable ways. Problem solving involves understanding and resolving the barriers to goal attainment, while decision making refers to making the best choices from among available alternatives.

Steps in Problem Solving

Two primary responsibilities of managers are solving problems and making decisions. In the early years of management practice, these activities were often based on personal preferences and limited experience, with little regard for long-term consequences. Since then, however, formal models of dealing with issues have been developed, and managers are encouraged to proceed systematically through several stages, including

1. Defining the problem and the desired outcome
2. Analyzing and understanding the nature of the problem
3. Generating alternatives
4. Selecting desired alternatives (decision making)
5. Planning and implementing the alternative
6. Evaluating and gathering feedback about the attained outcome

At each step in the problem-solving model, decisions need to be made that lead to the final choice of how to implement a means for solving the problem. Given the changing circumstances of the modern healthcare marketplace, it is unlikely that all the desires of information managers will be available. They will need to make decisions using less than perfect or less than complete information, and under ambiguous or risky circumstances.

Rational versus Administrative Decision Making

In recent years, the importance of rational decision making has become essential in management, and a variety of models have been developed. The Vroom-Yetton (1971) normative decision tree, which is discussed in detail later in this chapter, is an example of a system for responding to key questions, branching to alternatives, and arriving at a conclusion. For more complex decision making where there are several choices and criteria for selection, but the criteria cannot be ordered sequentially as in the Vroom-Yetton model, a decision matrix can be constructed for evaluating and comparing alternatives (see figure 23.9).

Using this method, the decision maker lists the criteria for a good outcome and then rates each possible alternative for the solution to the problem. Each alternative is identified and rated on the extent to which it fulfills the desired outcome criteria. Finally, the criteria weightings are multiplied by the choice ratings and totaled. The alternative with the highest total is considered to provide the best combination of characteristics that meet the most important criteria. This can be a tedious process with very complex problems, and various computer programs and expert systems have been developed to systematically walk the user through the decision process and perform the calculations. An example is a simple expert system software program that prompts the user to answer

Figure 23.9.   Decision matrix

Example—Choosing the Job Offer That Best Meets Your Career Criteria				
Key decision criteria for a good job Criterion 1: Good pay	Rating of the Importance (5 = high)	Rating of extent to which this job meets each criterion (1 = high, 5 = low)		
		Job Choice 1 Rating : Product	Job Choice 2 Rating : Product	Job Choice 3 Rating : Product
	5	3 : 15	4 : 20	2 : 10
Criterion 2: Preferred region of country	2	2 : 4	3 : 6	4 : 8
Criterion 3: Interesting work	4	3 : 12	5 : 20	4 : 16
Additional criteria				
Total ratings for each choice		31	46	34

Step 1: Identify and rate (1–5, 5 high) the importance of the criteria for your desired job.
Step 2: Rate the extent to which each of the job choices meets your criteria (1–5, 5 high).
Step 3: Multiply each rating by the criteria rating.
Step 4: Total the products for all ratings and compare across the choices.
Decision: The higher product total of job choice 2 (in this example, 46) offers greater fit with the applicant's preferred criteria than do choices 1 and 3.

questions about research data and then recommends which statistical procedure to use to analyze it (Van Eck 2004).

Although this classical model of problem solving illustrates what managers should do, the most accurate assessment of a manager's effectiveness is determined by what he or she actually does.

Programmed and Nonprogrammed Decisions

Decisions can be programmed or nonprogrammed. **Programmed decisions** are those in which a problem is so predictable, uniform, and recurring that rules have been developed to standardize or automate the procedure. Such rules enable managers to delegate authority to others to make decisions using predetermined criteria or to develop expert systems in which computers can make decisions. An example of such automation is an inventory system that automatically requests an order for restocking by a supplier when stock reaches a certain level.

Nonprogrammed decisions involve situations that are unpredictable, extremely complex, or ill defined. These situations defy simple decision criteria and usually require careful deliberation, often in consultation with others. Examples of nonprogrammed decisions include those found in market development, strategic management, and new product or service development.

Groupthink: The Hazards of Team Decision Making

Groupthink refers to the tendency of a highly cohesive team to seek consensus. Subsequent research has shown this tendency to be relatively widespread and occurs when a team is very cohesive, there is high external pressure to perform,

and few mechanisms are in place to correct for poor decision making (Janis 1972).

The role of cohesion is an interesting one because most work teams desire to have high cohesion: close familiarity and homogeneity of styles, strong pride in and commitment to the team, and a shared mission and vision (Michalisin et al. 2004). The problem arises when cohesion is so high and pressure to succeed so great that pressure is exerted on members to conform to team processes that can result in poor decisions. Subsequent research (Baron 2005) suggests that some of the antecedents that contribute to groupthink are not as strong as Janis believed; nonetheless, the effects of group conformity on decision making is ubiquitous.

Conditions for the Emergence of Groupthink

Janis (1972) originally proposed eight symptoms of groupthink grouped around three risky tendencies (see figure 23.10).

- *Overconfidence* in the team's prowess can manifest as an illusion of invulnerability that leads team members to be overconfident and take excessive risks. They develop a collective rationalization that is used to discount warnings that would otherwise lead them to reconsider their underlying assumptions.

- *Tunnel vision* restricts the range of factors considered and can lead to a belief in the inherent morality of their cause, thereby allowing decision makers to ignore the ethical consequences of their decisions. Outsiders are often viewed in stereotypical ways in which their threats are minimized.

Figure 23.10.   Symptoms of groupthink

> Team's overestimation of its own power and morality
>
> • *Illusion of invulnerability.* The illusion that they cannot go wrong leads to excessive optimism and risk taking.
>
> • *Unquestioned belief in team's inherent morality.* Members believe their actions are correct, leading them to ignore moral and ethical implications.
>
> Close-mindedness
>
> • *Team rationalization to discount warnings.* Team members collectively minimize indications that would otherwise lead them to reconsider their assumptions and commitments.
>
> • *Stereotypes of the opposition.* Outsiders are viewed as negative, evil, or stupid to justify negotiations or to consider they could counter the team's efforts.
>
> Pressure toward uniformity
>
> • *Self-censorship.* Members tend to minimize and withhold expression of their dissenting views and counterarguments.
>
> • *Illusion of shared unanimity.* Self-censorship and the false belief that silence means consent lead to the shared illusion that everyone agrees with the decision.
>
> • *Pressure to conform.* Members who deviate from team norms by expressing doubts or arguing against the team's position are implicitly and explicitly pressured to conform.
>
> • *Self-appointed "mind guards."* Some members appoint themselves to protect the team from adverse information that might challenge their illusions.

Source: Janis 1972.

• *Team pressures* further contribute to groupthink. Loyal members will disapprove of a member who questions the team and bring sanctions until he or she again conforms. Members also may self-censor when it appears that there is silent consensus, tunnel vision for viewing the problem, and group pressure to conform.

Consequences of Groupthink

The pressures to conform in groupthink often result in the restriction of information and the risk of poor decision making. Such restrictions can limit considerations of objectives, information search, alternative courses of action, examination of the risks of the preferred choice, and reassessment of the preferred choice. Moreover, they can bias the discussion and processing of the problem-solving process and lead to a level of confidence that results in contingency plans being ignored or minimized.

Countermeasures for Groupthink

The conditions that contribute to groupthink are ubiquitous, and it requires deliberate action by the team to minimize their adverse affects. By being aware of the risk of groupthink, alert to the symptoms, and intentionally implementing countermeasures, the team can maintain adequate cohesion

without sacrificing decision quality. Instruments such as the Groupthink Profile (Swenson 2003) enable the team to better assess and discuss the implications of team cohesion, organizational self-correcting processes, pressure on the team, symptoms of groupthink, and countermeasures.

The use of countermeasures is especially important, and they can be internal or external. *Internal procedures* to reduce risk include using brainstorming, revisiting important decisions, monitoring the degree of consensus and disagreement, rotating the devil's advocate's role among members, actively seeking contradictory information, and developing norms to challenge and question each other. In addition, the leader can refrain from stating an opinion that might affect opinions too early, and the team might be divided into subgroups to encourage different conclusions. *External procedures* include discussing decisions with outside experts and non–team members and inviting external observers to provide feedback on meetings, decisions, and team processes. Such procedures increase awareness of group processes and enhance skills at arriving at better decisions.

Instructions: Answer the following questions on a separate sheet of paper.

1. In what ways could you increase the feelings of cohesion for a team? What would be some indications of that cohesion?

2. What are some indications that cohesion has become excessive (for example, signs of groupthink)?

3. What actions might be taken to reduce the risks of groupthink?

Managerial Communication

The exchange of information is central to health information management and one of the most frequently used definitions of *communication*. Although we often take communication for granted, miscommunication poses problems and risks in the healthcare field. It is important for professionals to understand important aspects of communication, including channels and barriers, the challenge of diversity, and ways communication can be improved.

Importance of Communication

Managers get things done through people, and this in turn is accomplished by communicating with them. Communication is the interpersonal process by which information is transferred from one person to another. Nearly everything we do can potentially communicate something to someone, or more economically stated, "You cannot *not* communicate" (Watzlawick et al. 1968).

Face-to-face communication among providers in clinical settings constitutes about 80 percent of interactions, of which about 30 percent are considered interruptions and 10 percent involved two or more concurrent conversations. (Coiera et al 2002). Ineffective communication remains a significant problem in most organizations. This is especially critical in healthcare, where the now famous Institute of Medicine report, *To Err Is Human*, found that insufficient communication among healthcare staff was related to patient care errors (Kohn et al. 2000). It has also been found that lawsuits are less related to negligence and more to poor communication between provider and patient (Liebman and Hyman 2004), and errors in communication were the second most common errors in the recovery room (Kluger and Bullock 2002). For example, a survey of workers who voluntarily quit their organizations found that about 25 percent of their reasons were because they perceived their managers to be poor communicators (Supplee Group 2002). It has also been estimated that as much as 60 percent of time in operational tasks is wasted time, which involves searching for information or working with wrong information (Ameri and Dutta 2005). Similarly, a survey of 839 managers showed that while there was a glut of information available, there was a difference between quality and quantity of communication, and only half of managers believed that leaders spent sufficient time communicating effectively (Holton et al. 2008). The financial consequence of poor communication is an estimated annual loss of $12 billion for hospitals; a 500-bed facility may lose as much as $4 million annually due to inefficient communication (Agarwal et al. 2010).

Formal and Informal Channels

Communication can take place through formal or informal channels. *Formal communication* consists of those intentional messages that are directed to people through their role relationships in the organization and usually through established channels such as e-mail, phone, face-to-face interaction, memo, letter, or other forms of announcement. This kind of communication usually focuses on task accomplishment and related matters. In contrast, *informal communication* may occur across role or department boundaries or organizational levels. It tends to employ face-to-face and social media interactions and focuses on the interpersonal aspects of work, such as rumors and topics outside the immediate scope of the workplace. It is through informal communication that most relationships develop between employees and that influence is exercised.

Barriers to Communication

Complex organizations also have a variety of barriers to the richness or completeness of communication, both structural and interpersonal. *Structural barriers* include the distortion that can occur when a message is passed through several people, each adding or deleting information based on their own perceptions and needs. The increasing use of e-mail in organizations also eliminates the nonverbal cues of voice tone, volume, and inflection, as well as facial cues and gestures that add so much to face-to-face communication. *Interpersonal barriers* include distraction and partial listening, tendency to judge, assumption that we know what others mean, and fear of asking questions. In general, low-richness channels are one-way communication tools such as reports, bulletins, memos, and e-mail, and high-richness channels include telephone and face-to-face interactions.

Practices That Increase the Accuracy of Communications

To communicate effectively, managers must pay just as much attention to how their message is received and interpreted as they do to its content. The following practices can enhance the accuracy and acceptance of communication (Kirvin 2005; Spath 2007):

- Minimize "noise" that can distort the message. Make sure all parties are minimally distracted, can give their undivided attention, and have sufficient time to get their message across.
- Know what outcome you want to communicate through your message and then check to see if you get it.
- Monitor others' nonverbal behaviors for cues that they are following or are confused.
- Vary inflection for attention, but use the lower end of the voice range to communicate assurance, calmness, and confidence in the subject.
- Explain your reasoning to show and lead others to how you have formed your conclusions.
- Consider the effect that different interpersonal styles, cultural backgrounds, and experiences may have on interpretation of the message or how it is delivered.
- Use **active listening** in which you (or the other person) restate in your own words what you have heard the other person say.
- Respond to the feelings, attitudes, and values in the message as well as the content. Show empathy, concern, and compassion, as appropriate.
- Use examples or visual aids to make the message clearer.
- Ask for feedback and listen to it without being judgmental.
- Write clearly and concisely.

When a person models these types of communication skills, through that person's example a norm is established for others to strive for in their communications, as well.

Guidelines for Giving Feedback

Feedback enables people to monitor their own behavior and the reactions of others and to adjust their behavior and communication to be more effective. Feedback enables correction before (or soon after) errors occur and prevents their accumulation. Yet, effective feedback is not just "speaking your mind" to express yourself. If the purpose is to influence behavior, feedback must be used respectfully and strategically. The following characteristics of useful feedback should be kept in mind:

- *Relationship:* Become acquainted and develop a positive working relationship with people before giving feedback.
- *Requested:* People are most receptive when feedback is solicited rather than imposed on them.
- *Confidentiality:* Give feedback in private, especially when it is sensitive.
- *Needs of the recipient:* Effective feedback takes into consideration what the person needs rather than just serving your needs; it should be given to help, not hurt.
- *Practical:* Feedback focuses on what is said or done rather than why; the latter takes us away from a solution focus and toward speculation about motives.
- *Descriptive:* Feedback describes specific behavior and the recipient's reaction rather than judgments. Basing it on direct observation and providing examples can help reduce defensiveness and focus efforts.
- *Manageable amount:* Feedback should be given in a manageable amount; don't give too much feedback or too fast.
- *Balanced:* Provide both positive and negative constructive feedback; start with the positive, then present areas needing improvement, and end with positive.
- *Timing:* Give the feedback as soon after the behavior has occurred as possible; best if done within 24 hours or less.
- *Realistic:* The behavior to be changed should be a behavior the receiver can do something about.
- *Listen and check:* The recipient may be asked to paraphrase what he or she has heard in the feedback to ensure accuracy of perception. Be attentive to the recipient's response to the feedback, and clarify and explain where needed.
- *Climate:* Create an environment in the organization in which the seeking and sharing of feedback is an expectation and a common occurrence.

Most of the management approaches we have focused on to this point have emphasized how to manage and stabilize an organization for effectiveness and efficiency. While this emphasis has been useful in the past, the current changing marketplace is better characterized as "permanent whitewater" (Vaill 1996). On the one hand, managers are tasked with maintaining the organization, and on the other hand, leaders are expected to facilitate change. In this next section of the chapter we examine several theories of leadership, and then explore how organizational change can be facilitated.

Trends in Leadership Theory

The purpose of a theory is to serve as a template for examining some phenomenon, such as leadership. The theory labels important features, then uses them to describe, explain, and help predict what might happen if certain actions were pursued. That leadership makes a difference is undisputed, but exactly how and why it makes a difference is still not well understood, and research reflects an inconsistent picture. For example, leadership has been found to be related to formation of subordinates' values, commitment (Lee 2005), empowerment and team effectiveness (Ozaralli 2003), cohesion, commitment, trust, and motivation (Zhu et al. 2004). Supportive studies have shown that leadership accounts for 15 to 20 percent of the variance in organizational performance (Leadership Trust Foundation 2007), and 98 percent of corporate trainers believe that leadership can have a positive influence on financial stability (Chartered Institute 2005). In contrast, other studies suggest that although leaders shape organizational members' beliefs and behaviors, many external factors that affect the performance of organizations are beyond the influence of leaders (Bass and Avolio 1993). Nonetheless, some generalizations can be made.

Classical Approaches to Leadership Theory

Classical leadership theories tended to focus on the principled and effective use of authority. This emphasis began to change with the many social changes emerging in the early to mid-1900s. Inventions and innovations in manufacturing increased competition, which made managers more open to new ideas. Workers became increasingly better educated and skilled, thereby requiring managers with authoritative styles to adopt more democratic approaches. The workforce also became increasingly diverse, much like today, and this required a broader understanding of different cultures and motivational approaches.

Great Person Theory

The course of human history is marked with the contributions of great people. Such outstanding individuals originally led to the conception of leadership as an inborn ability, sometimes passed down through family, position, or social tradition, as in the cases of royal families in many parts of the world. The problem with the **great person theory** is that some of those who took positions of such greatness were terribly lacking, as in the case of such historical notables as Caligula in ancient Rome, Stalin in Russia, and Kim Jung Il in North Korea. In the United States, there have been people who were leaders in one sphere but who failed in others. General Ulysses S. Grant excelled as a general, which largely got him elected president, a role in which he performed miserably. Jeffrey Skilling, CEO of Enron, while a brilliant consultant and business strategist, was also considered to be unscrupulous, and his illegal manipulation of stocks led to the downfall of Enron, as well as Skilling's 24-year prison sentence.

Trait Approach

The **trait approach** gradually replaced the great person model and proposed that leaders possessed a collection of traits or personal qualities that distinguished them from nonleaders; in other words, they had "the right stuff." During the 1930s and 1940s, hundreds of studies on the trait approach to leadership were conducted, and as many as 18,000 traits were identified (Allport and Odbert 1936). Traits were often grouped into categories related to physical needs, values, intellect, personality, and skill characteristics. Some researchers have organized traits on the three leadership requirements of conceptual, interpersonal, and technical skills. Others add a fourth category—administrative skills—which includes the four managerial functions of planning, organizing, directing, and controlling (Yukl 2006).

Unfortunately, in much of the early research, only a weak relationship was discovered between traits and individuals who would emerge as leaders, and many leaders did not share all the traits in common. During later studies in which traits and skills were correlated with leader effectiveness rather than leader emergence, stronger connections appeared. Some of the more important traits included adaptability, social alertness, ambition, assertiveness, cooperativeness, decisiveness, dominance, energy, stress tolerance, and confidence. Skills included intelligence and conceptual abilities, creativity, tact, verbal fluency, work knowledge, organization, and persuasion (Stogdill 1974). Despite this extensive work, it appears that no single traits are absolutely required for leadership. Having certain traits and skills leads to a greater likelihood that such attributes may be more helpful in some situations and to leader effectiveness in them.

Autocratic versus Democratic Leadership

As Douglas McGregor noted in his formulation of theory X and Y, two types of environments and leaders corresponded to autocratic and democratic behaviors. White and Lippitt (1960), researchers at Iowa State University, conducted studies on democratic and autocratic leaders. They found that groups under **autocratic leadership** performed well as long as they were closely supervised, although levels of member satisfaction were low. In contrast, **democratic leadership** led members to perform well whether the leader was present or absent, and members were more satisfied. This kind of research led to the emphasis on participative management in many organizations. The autocratic–democratic dimension was useful for understanding a range of managerial behavior.

Based on the autocratic–democratic dimension, Tannenbaum and Schmidt (1973) designed a continuum that described seven degrees of leader involvement in a decision (see figure 23.11). At one end (autocratic) of the continuum, the leader makes a decision alone and announces it; at the other end (democratic), the leader encourages his or her subordinates to make their own decisions within prescribed limits. This model reflected a shift from looking at the leader in isolation or in terms of a rigid or permanent style and suggested that a person had available a range of behaviors depending on the situation. But what behaviors made leaders successful?

Check Your Understanding 23.4

Instructions: Complete the following activities on a separate piece of paper.

1. Make two lists of effective and ineffective leaders. What makes them different from each other? Consider their personalities, limitations in skills or adaptability, and changes in the situation, as well as what is required of them.

2. Make a list of your traits and skills. Rank them in order of how effective they would make you as a leader in a given situation. Change the leadership situation and see which

Figure 23.11.   Tannenbaum and Schmidt's leadership continuum

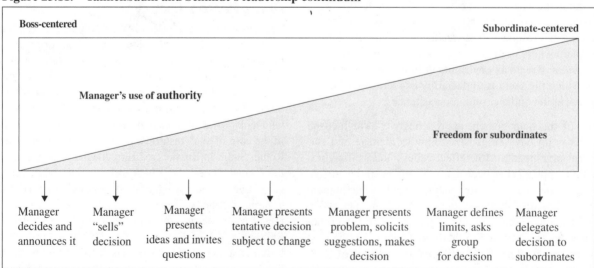

Source: Tannenbaum and Schmidt 1973.

traits and skills might also change to give you an advantage or which ones might unexpectedly become a disadvantage. How could you develop these skills further?

3. Imagine you have been asked to be a consultant to an aspiring political or managerial figure. You are asked to recommend how this person should appear in order to increase his or her chances for election or promotion. What behaviors would you advise for and against? What ethical issues are involved in this type of image building?

4. What can an organization do to reduce the risk of having a flawed leader? Consider hiring practices and the impact of organizational change and crises.

Behavioral Theories of Leadership

While earlier theories focused on what leaders *should* do and what was expected of them, emerging behavioral theories describe what managers *actually* do. The emerging theories clearly emphasize a leader's orientation toward both tasks and people and enabled leaders to describe a variety of styles rather than just the "right" style.

Normative Decision Tree

Using a continuum similar to Tannenbaum and Schmidt's, Victor Vroom and Philip Yetton (1971) developed the **Normative Decision Model** in the early 1970s. They identified a series of intermediate questions and decisions that could be answered yes or no and that would lead to each outcome (see figure 23.12). Crucial aspects of the situation related to the quality of the decision required, the degree of subordinate support for the decision, the amount of information available to leaders and followers, and how well structured or defined the problem was. A decision made exclusively by the leader without member input (autocratic) could create problems in acceptance, just as delegating a decision to a group (democratic) could be costly in time and effort, if unnecessary. The Vroom-Yetton model enables a manager to decide on the level of decision-making involvement (autonomous, consultative, or delegative) to seek out when approaching a decision situation.

Ohio and Michigan Studies

During the 1950s and 1960s, researchers at The Ohio State University examined the behavior of leaders in several hundred studies and reduced them to two categories: **consideration** and **initiating structure** (Shartle 1979). Consideration referred to attention to the interpersonal aspects of work, including respect for subordinates' ideas and feelings, maintaining harmonious work relationships, collaborating in teamwork, and showing concern for the subordinates' welfare. Initiating structure was more task focused and centered on giving direction, setting goals and limits, and planning and scheduling activities. During the same period, researchers at the University of Michigan developed a similar model.

Comparing effective and ineffective managers, they found that a key difference was that the former employee-centered managers focused more on the human needs of their subordinates whereas their less effective job-centered managers emphasized only goal attainment (Likert 1979).

Leadership Grid

Building on the Ohio State and Michigan studies Robert Blake and Jane Srygley Mouton (1976) at the University of Texas identified the same two dimensions: concern for people (consideration) and concern for production (initiating structure). Their **leadership grid** marked off degrees of emphasis toward orientation using a nine-point scale and finally separated the grid into five styles of management based on the combined people and production emphasis. For example, a score of 9,9 (emphasizing both people and production) was called "Team Management." Blake and Mouton considered it the best orientation because it emphasized harmonious cooperation in production to achieve goals. A score of 9,1, an "Authority-Compliance" orientation with an emphasis on production and operational efficiency, afforded little attention to human needs. The 1,9 "Country Club" orientation emphasized group harmony, esprit de corps, and cooperation over production. The 1,1 "Impoverished" orientation reflected inattention toward both relationships and work production. A mix of both dimensions, but less than a team orientation, is the 5,5 "Middle-of-the-Road" approach, which tries to balance the two (see figure 23.13). Although this model has been considered a key theory and it clearly presents a collaborative or team management approach as the ideal, subsequent contingency theories show that there are situations in which other emphases may be as effective.

Contingency and Situational Theories of Leadership

Most of these early theories of leadership have emphasized identifying a cluster of traits or a single style or orientation for leadership. As research in leadership has continued, it has become apparent that successful leadership does not depend on style or skills alone but, rather, on matching a leader's style with the demands or contingencies of a specific situation.

Fiedler's Contingency Model

Fred Fiedler (1967) at the University of Illinois designed his **contingency model of leadership** to compensate for the limitations of the classical and behavioral theories of leadership. Fiedler kept the social-task orientation as the cornerstone of his theory and designed a brief test, the **Least-Preferred Worker (LPC) Scale,** to assess the degree to which a manager was task or relationship oriented.

The second aspect of Fiedler's model was the favorability of the situation in which the leader would operate. Because contingency means "depends on," the favorability or fit of a leader depends on the following three situational factors:

Figure 23.12. Normative decision tree

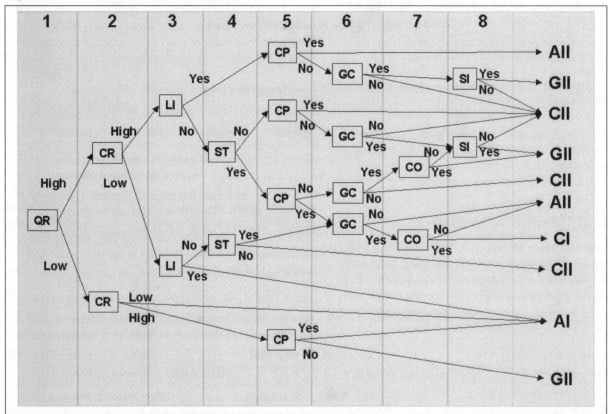

At each step in the process, a question is asked and the response determines the next branch and question. Each node of the tree has a critical criterion for determining the outcome, including

- *Quality requirement (QR):* How important is the technical quality of the decision?
- *Commitment requirement (CR):* How important is subordinate commitment to the decision?
- *Leader's information (LI):* Do you (the leader) have sufficient information to make a high-quality decision on your own?
- *Problem structure (ST):* Is the problem well structured (e.g., defined, clear, organized, lends itself to solution, time limited)?
- *Commitment probability (CP):* If you were to make the decision by yourself, is it reasonably certain that your subordinates would be committed to it?
- *Goal congruence (GC):* Do subordinates share the organizational goals to be attained in solving the problem?
- *Subordinate conflict (CO):* Is conflict among subordinates over preferred solutions likely?
- *Subordinate information (SI):* Do subordinates have sufficient information to make a high-quality decision?

Decision Outcome	Description
Autocratic I (AI)	Leader solves the problem alone using information that is readily available.
Autocratic II (AII)	Leader obtains additional information from group members, then makes decision alone. Group members may or may not be informed.
Consultative I (CI)	Leader shares problem with group members individually and asks for information and evaluation. Group members do not meet collectively, and leader makes decision alone.
Consultative II (CII)	Leader shares problem with group members collectively but makes decision alone.
Group II (GII)	Leader meets with group to discuss situation. Leader focuses and directs discussion but does not impose will. Group makes final decision.

Figure 23.13.   Leadership matrix models

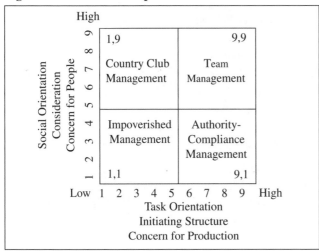

Figure 23.14.   Argyris's worker immaturity–maturity continuum

Assertiveness & initiative	Passivity
Independence	Dependence
Wide behavioral choices	Limited behavioral range
Deep & strong interests	Shallow & casual interests
Past–future perspective	Present-centered perspective
Self-awareness & control	Low self-awareness

Source: Argyris 1957.

- **Leader–member relations,** or "group atmosphere," is much like social orientation and includes the subordinates' acceptance of, and confidence in, the leader as well as the loyalty and commitment they show toward the leader.
- **Task structure** is related to task dimension described by other theories and refers to how clearly and how well defined the task goal, procedures, and possible solutions are.
- **Position power** refers to the authority the leader has to direct others and to use reward and coercive power.

In general, the greater the favorability to the leader, the more the subordinates can be relied on to carry out the task and the fewer challenges to leadership. Situations more favorable to leadership are those in which leader–member relations are positive, task structure is high, and position power is high. Situations in which these factors are reversed are considered unfavorable to leaders because they have less leverage to influence their followers.

Hersey and Blanchard's Situational Model

One of the more popular leadership models used for training, and one that has attempted to integrate other ideas from management, is Hersey and Blanchard's **situational model of leadership** (Hersey et al. 1996). As Dubrin (2004) points out, this is more a model than a theory because it does not explain why things happen but, rather, offers recommendations for behaving differently under various conditions.

To the already widely used task and social dimensions, Hersey and Blanchard added a third: the maturity of the followers. **Worker immaturity–maturity** is a concept borrowed from Chris Argyris, who suggested that job maturity and psychological maturity of subordinates also influence leadership style. Job maturity refers to how much work-related ability, knowledge, experience, and skill a person has; psychological maturity refers to willingness, confidence, commitment, and motivation related to work. Behaviors

associated with maturity include initiative, dependability, perseverance, receptiveness to feedback, goal orientation, and minimal need for supervision. Argyris (1957) suggested that to apply a directive approach with mature workers can result in stifling their maturity and even in forcing them back to lower levels of maturity. Hence, adjusting leadership style to worker maturity is an important consideration (see figure 23.14).

Hersey and Blanchard also adapted the grid format of their predecessors and structured it in a developmental sequence. Borrowing the idea that teams and organizations progress through developmental stages of a life cycle (Edison 2008; Hwang and Park 2007), they suggested that leadership style should be adjusted to the stage of team development. For example, their Situation-1 (S1) involves high-task, but low-social, emphasis, thereby indicating that the leader should focus on task duties such as setting goals, identifying resources and constraints, and so on. As the team moves to Situation-2 (S2), task and social functions of the leader are both involved as members attempt to influence each other and to explore how their styles may conflict with or complement each other. In Situation-3 (S3), members clearly know the task and need little direction, but social interaction around team norms may require intervention and guidance. Finally, Situation-4 (S4) is the stage of high team performance in which both task and relationships require little intervention by the leader. Worker maturity is high, and the leader may be active only in encouraging higher performance and removing barriers to performance.

Path-Goal Theory

A more recent model of leadership, initially introduced by House in 1971 and revised in 1996, is **path–goal theory.** While other theories have focused on the motivation of the leader, this one examines the motives and needs of the subordinates and how the leader can respond to them. This theory was based on the **expectancy theory of motivation,** which proposes that one's degree of effort is influenced by the expectation that the effort will result in the attainment of desired goals and meaningful rewards. Path–goal theory states that a person's ability to perform certain tasks is related to the direction and clarity available that lead to

Figure 23.15.   Path–goal theory

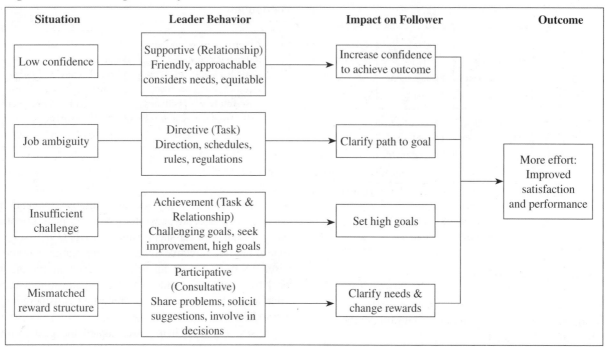

organizational goals. For example, if a worker is unclear about what a task involves and what should be done, performance will be improved when clear instructions are given. The role of leaders, then, is to facilitate the path toward the goal by removing barriers to performance.

Path–goal theory identifies four different situations, each requiring a different facilitative response from leadership (see figure 23.15). When workers lack self-confidence, leaders provide support by being friendly, approachable, concerned about needs, and equitable. This increases the worker's confidence to achieve the work outcome. When the worker has an ambiguous job, the leader is more forthright in providing the worker with direction, schedules, rules, and regulations that clarify the path. When workers do not have sufficient job challenge, the leader uses an achievement approach by setting challenging goals, continually seeking improvement, and expecting high performance. Finally, when the reward is mismatched with worker needs, the leader takes a more consultative or participative role in which workers share work problems, make suggestions, and are included in decision making to ensure more appropriate rewards. All four strategies result in improved task performance and satisfaction—again, the task and social dimensions.

Dyadic Relationship Theory

Some leadership theories are macro theories and attempt to explain leadership across large domains, but there also are micro theories that focus on a specific context for leadership. **Leader–member exchange (LMX)** (Graen and Skandura 1987) and closely related vertical dyad linkage (VDL) represent micro theories that focus on dyadic relationships, or those between two people or between a leader and a small group. More specifically, they explain how **in-group** and **out-group** relationships form with a leader or mentor and how delegation may occur.

VDL was first formulated in 1975 (Dansereau et al. 1975) to describe the single-person mentoring relationships that occur in organizations and was later supplemented by LMX theory, which applied the same idea to the leader's relations with groups. In these situations, leaders look for subordinates with high-performance and leadership potential that distinguishes them from subordinates with less potential. The best predictors of being selected for in-group, in addition to competence, include compatibility of the subordinate with the leader, interpersonal liking for each other, and being extraverted. Once identified, the leader and subordinates form an **exchange relationship,** in which a leader offers greater opportunities and privileges to a subordinate in exchange for loyalty, commitment, and assistance. The leader may delegate special responsibilities, offer interesting and desirable tasks, give opportunities for highly visible or skill-building projects, and provide mentoring.

Those subordinates who form a group around the leader are referred to as the in-group; those subordinates not included form the out-group. Being in the in-group may sound attractive, but it involves performance "beyond the call of duty." In-group members may spend longer hours, take work home or work during off-hours, and take on more difficult tasks compared to members in the out-group. The out-group expects to be treated fairly by the leader, and as long as the exchanges are viewed as fair, there is little or no conflict between the in- and out-groups; they can remain fairly stable over time. However, when the out-group perceives that the in-group is receiving greater privileges for doing the same work as the out-group, the latter can feel resentment, alienation, and hostility and show lower performance. The leader must ensure fair treatment and clear expectations for both groups. In addition, leaders can promote high-quality relationships with all employees by speaking with people personally, using active listening, not imposing the leader's view on issues discussed, and sharing expectations about the job and working relationship. A 2008 study of the theory supported its key hypothesis that when there was variance in employees' perceptions of equity and fairness, this negatively affected job satisfaction and feelings of well-being (Hooper and Martin 2008).

A review of leadership theories by Hogan and Kaiser (2004) shows the relationship among key factors in leader performance. Aspects of the personality of the leader are projected into one's leadership style, the latter of which may have some variance from situation to situation. This style is perceived by and interacts with employee attitudes and team functioning to facilitate the performance of others. This performance is finally expressed in organizational performance and its success or failure.

Values-Based Leadership

The demoralizing impact of corporate scandals, layoffs due to downsizing, and stress, especially in the healthcare industry, has led to the resurgence of a focus on values and ethics in the workplace. Values are core beliefs that guide and motivate attitudes and actions and both form and express an organization's culture. Values make a difference to most people, and ethical leaders tend to promote more trust and loyalty among their employees (Sanford 2006; Verbos et al. 2007).

Role of Values

One of the significant consequences of the organization and its leaders not being perceived as highly ethical is that employees feel less loyalty and commitment and tend to leave the organization. Many organizations find that there are widespread conditions that mitigate employee retention. A 2007 study of 834 people found that 94 percent of workers believed that it is critical or important that the organization they work for is ethical in its practices and management (LRN 2007). The issue of values and ethics is sufficiently important that 84 percent said that they would rather be paid less and work for an ethical organization than paid more for one with unethical practices. However, within the United States, "true loyalty," or the combination of high loyalty and commitment, is only 24 percent. Although two-thirds to three-quarters of employees are often proud of their work, would work above and beyond their requirements, and are highly motivated, they still consider leaving current positions. This discontent is related to questioning the fairness of pay and policy execution, as well as low recognition of achievement and insufficient job performance measures. Less than half of employees feel a sense of caring and concern for them in the organization, perceive that their judgment is trusted, or feel encouraged to be innovative (Walker Information 2001). Clearly, to retain talented people as well as to maintain a competitive position, organizational leadership must reestablish and promote ethical behavior and a culture of strong, consistent, and compatible values.

Many organizations believe that merely sending managers off to training will provide sufficient skill in ethical management. However, for the 75 percent of organizations that provide such training and consulting to their leadership teams at a cost of $15 billion, only about 10 percent actually translate it into behavior change (Hunter 2004). To fully effect change, managers and leaders must implement the values to be developed in an organization into their own behavior.

That ethics is increasingly a high priority and visible issue is shown by the Ethisphere 2008 report on and promotion of the "World's Most Ethical Companies." For this recognition they defined "ethical" performance as proactive engagement in the communities they serve; investment in quality and innovative, sustainable business practices; and efforts made to influence and change the industry and profit fairly. In healthcare, they identified Fresenius Medical Care in Germany and Premier Healthcare in the United States. Becton Dickenson medical devices, Genzyme pharmaceuticals, and AFLAC insurance were other US companies identified with notable ethical practices (Ethisphere 2008). Yet such awards are bittersweet, as the 2011 National Business Ethics Survey shows. The good news is that well-implemented ethics programs dramatically increase reports of misconduct, and in 2011 the percentage of employees who witnessed misconduct at work fell to a new low of 45 percent compared to 49 percent in 2009 and the record high of 55 percent in 2007. The bad news is that "the share of companies with weak ethics cultures climbed to near record levels at 42 percent, up from 35 percent in 2009. The percentage of employees who perceived pressure to compromise standards in order to do their jobs climbed five points to 13 percent, just shy of the all-time high of 14 percent in 2000, and retaliation against employee whistle-blowers rose sharply. More than one in five employees (22 percent) who reported misconduct say they experienced some form of retaliation in return...compared to 12 percent who experienced retaliation in 2007 and 15 percent in 2009" (Ethics Resource Center 2012,12). To remedy these problems in ethical leadership, reinforcement of ethical practices at all levels of management and peer commitments to ethical practices are required so these practices become embedded in the organization's culture.

Servant Leadership

The **values-based leadership** theories are similar to Burns's (1978), transformational leadership as well as other contingency theories such as path–goal leadership in which the leader's role is to empower and facilitate employee satisfaction and productivity. Prominent among values-based approaches is Robert Greenleaf's concept of servant leadership (Greenleaf 1991). Greenleaf was director of management research at AT&T for 38 years, as well as a Quaker with a strong contemplative orientation. To Greenleaf, servant leaders are those who put the needs, interests, and aspirations of others above their own. Larry Spears, CEO of the Greenleaf Center for Servant Leadership, describes it as seeking to "involve others in decision making, be strongly based in ethical and caring behavior, and enhance the personal growth of workers while improving the caring and quality of organizational life" (Spears 1995, 142).

The values-based organization, represented by the **Servant Leadership Model,** promotes 10 essential values (Greenleaf 1991):

- *Listening* intently to clarify the will of the group as well as to hear one's own "inner voice" and seeking to discover what one's body, mind, and spirit are communicating
- *Empathize* with and understand others, assuming their good intentions, even when behaviors must be rejected
- *Healing* as a force for transformation and integration using the subtle communication of valuing the whole
- *Awareness* with courage to persist in recognizing and discussing what may be sensitive issues
- *Persuasion* rather than positional authority to build consensus and make decisions
- *Conceptualization* or vision must be balanced with daily realities
- *Foresight* requires learning lessons from the past, realities of the present, and consequences in the future using intuition
- *Stewardship* in which all stakeholders hold as their goal the greatest good for the larger society
- *Commitment* to the personal, professional, and spiritual growth of people
- *Community building* within the organization to replace what has been lost socially

Although servant leadership does not have strong evidence to support its effectiveness, its popularity has spread worldwide as well as to many of the best companies in the United States. Among the top companies are Southwest Airlines, TDIndustries, Men's Warehouse, Servicemaster, and Toro Company. It has also been explored in healthcare, and an initial study of servant leadership in a hospital setting was conducted in 2009 (Garber et al. 2009). While collaboration across disciplines and levels is necessary in order for servant leadership to work, the study found that nurses were more willing to do so than physicians, and more work on collaboration is recommended.

Check Your Understanding 23.5

Instructions: Complete the following activities on a separate piece of paper.

1. Think of a decision you might be confronted with as a supervisor at work. Use the Vroom-Yetton decision tree to trace how you might choose whether to make the decision yourself, consult with others, or delegate the decision making to someone else.
2. Describe how your approach to leading people should change as they move through the stages of worker maturity. Explain what might happen if your style mismatches what they need at these stages.
3. Make two columns of leadership behaviors related to stereotypes of male and female roles. Make a third column in which you blend the two into an androgynous role. What are the advantages of this intermediate role over the other two?

Diffusion of Innovations

Innovations have occurred throughout history, but little attention was given to exactly how they were adopted until Rogers and Shoemaker (1971) clarified the process in their book, *Communication of Innovations.* Although Rogers and Shoemaker were not the first to develop ideas about diffusion, their presentation of the adopter categories or stakeholders and the diffusion curve came at a time when businesses were eager to understand consumers.

Categories of Adopter Groups

Viewing the organization in much the same way that marketers view market segments, Rogers and Shoemaker identified five **adopter groups** of an innovation that generally fits the normal curve (see figure 23.16):

- **Innovators:** This venturesome group comprises about 2.5 percent of the organization and individuals who are eager to try new ideas. These individuals tend to be more cosmopolitan, to seek out new information in broad networks, and to be willing to take risks.
- **Early adopters:** This respectable group accounts for about 13.5 percent of the organization. The individuals in this group have a high degree of opinion leadership. They are more localized than cosmopolitan and often look to the innovators for advice and information. These are the leaders and respected role models in the organization, and their adoption of an idea or practice does much to initiate change.
- **Early majority:** This group comprises about 34 percent of the organization. Although usually not leaders, the individuals in this group represent the backbone of the organization, are deliberate in thinking about and

Figure 23.16.   Characteristics of innovation stakeholders

2.5%	13.5%	34%	34%	16%
Innovators	**Early Adopters**	**Early Majority**	**Late Majority**	**Laggards**
Cosmopolitan	Localized opinion leader	High interaction	Economic necessity	Past oriented
Networks	Respected role model	Nonleaders "linkers"	Social pressure	Isolated
Risk taking		Deliberate		Suspicious of change

Source: Rogers 1995.

acceptance of an idea, and serve as a natural bridge between early and late adopters.

- **Late majority:** This skeptical group comprises another 34 percent of the organization. The individuals in this group usually adopt innovations only after social or financial pressure to do so.
- **Laggards:** The traditional members of this group are usually the last ones to respond to innovation and make up as much as 16 percent of the organization. The laggards are often characterized as isolated, uninformed, and mistrustful of change and **change agents,** but they may serve a function by keeping the organization from changing too quickly.

When planning a change, each of these groups should be considered as a market segment whose needs must be responded to by leaders. In general, people who are more receptive to innovation are better educated and more literate and have stronger aspirations. In addition, they have higher socioeconomic status, higher occupational prestige, more income, and greater social mobility. Moreover, they are better socially networked, cosmopolitan, diverse in interests, and well integrated into the organization and the community (Rogers 1995).

Diffusion Curve

Each of the adopter categories engages innovation at a different time and a different acceptance rate, as shown by the diffusion of innovation S curve (see figure 23.17). Note that during the early stages of diffusion, there is a shorter period between becoming aware of an innovation and adopting it. Over time, each adopter category becomes aware of the innovation but increasingly takes longer periods to adopt it, which can affect how well an innovation is introduced into the marketplace or how fully it is practiced in the organization. In addition, how quickly an innovation is accepted is based on a number of factors, including whether it offers an advantage relative to its alternative, its compatibility with the potential adopters'

Figure 23.17.   Diffusion S curve

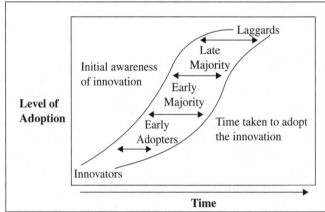

Source: Rogers 1995.

values and lifestyles, how easy it is to understand and use, the degree to which it can be experimented with and the degree to which the results are visible to others (Rogers 1995). These diffusion patterns are relatively consistent for a variety of healthcare innovations, including healthcare technology (Cohen and Hanft 2004), coding technology (Fenton and Gamm 2008), and the intention of students in the health professions to use online courses (Tung and Chang 2008).

Innovator Roles

In the late 1960s and early 1970s, the literature reflected a new interest in the roles of innovators within organizations who become gatekeepers or nodes for the flow of information (Allen and Cohén 1969). Four roles have been identified for the successful implementation of an innovation (Daft and Marcic 1998; Roberts 2007):

- **Inventor** (innovator): The individual who develops a new idea or practice in the organization. However, it is not sufficient to merely originate and understand the new idea. Rather, the idea must be facilitated by several other roles in the organization before it is adopted or brought to market (Daft 2000).

- **Champion:** Someone in the organization who believes in the idea, acknowledges the practical problems of financing and political support, and assists in overcoming barriers.
- **Sponsor:** Usually a high-level manager who approves and protects the idea, expedites testing and approval, and removes barriers within the organization.
- **Critic:** A crucial but sometimes overlooked role. This role is essential in challenging the innovation for shortcomings, presenting strong criteria, and, in essence, providing a reality test for the new idea.

In an innovative environment, all of these roles are important and good examples of how role responsibilities are distributed in an organization.

Change Management

A more global role for practitioners of organizational change is often referred to as the change agent. The change agent is a specialist in organization development and facilitates the change brought about by the innovation. He or she may be internal or external to the organization, as in the case of a consultant specifically hired to assist with the change. **Organization development (OD)** is the process in which an organization reflects on its own processes and consequently revises them for improved performance. Beckhard (1969, 9) has provided a widely accepted definition of OD: "Organization Development is an effort planned, organization-wide, and managed from the top, to increase organization effectiveness and health through planned interventions in the organization's processes, using behavioral-science knowledge."

OD Change Agent Functions

Blake and Mouton (1976) suggested that OD consultants might perform a range of five functions with management:

- *Acceptant function* uses counseling skills to help the manager sort out emotions to gain a more objective perspective of the organization
- *Catalytic function* helps collect and interpret data about the organization
- *Confrontation function* challenges the manager's thinking processes and assumptions
- *Prescriptive function* tells the manager what to do to correct a given situation
- *Theory and principle function* involves helping the client system internalize alternate explanations of what is occurring in the organization

Internal and External Change Agents

Change happens on its own but is usually most desirable when intentionally directed toward the benefit of the organization and its members. The role of the change agent is to facilitate this change process by utilizing reflective learning: drawing attention to important processes, helping people understand what the processes mean, and considering and implementing plans of action. Exactly who performs this role can be critical (Westcott 2005; Weick and Quinn 1995). There are advantages and disadvantages to using change agents from within the organization as well as from outside the organization (see table 23.3).

Advantages and Disadvantages of Using Internal Change Agents

Internal change agents have the clear advantage of being familiar with the organization and its history, subtle dynamics, secrets, and resources. Such people are often well respected, are securely positioned, and have the strong interpersonal relationships to foster change. Moreover, there is an advantage to recognizing the internal expertise of employees, maintaining confidentiality of the process, and using people who are invested in the success of the outcome.

Yet, the strengths of internal change agents can also be weaknesses. Coming from the inside, however reputable they are, their previous relationships with others in the organization could lead to accusations of bias. As a product of the organizational culture, internal change agents may be as blind to certain problems as those they seek to facilitate. Another disadvantage is that they are taken away from their regular duties to conduct the facilitation or perhaps become overextended in trying to handle both responsibilities. Finally, internal change agents may be subject to pressures and sanctions regarding the outcome, whereas an external change agent would have no such obligations.

Advantages and Disadvantages of Using External Change Agents

The external change agent has the advantage of providing a fresh, outside view as well as having the knowledge base to compare performance across organizations. Not having direct connections to the organization, he or she usually feels more comfortable challenging norms and culture, questioning unusual or unfair practices, and generally noting events that others may be reluctant to comment on. Being from the outside, he or she may be seen as having new skills and being more objective, or at least less biased than an internal agent.

The weaknesses of the external agents include not having a history with their client organization that could enhance their awareness of important dynamics. Becoming familiar with the organization takes time, and during a crisis they may move too quickly to conclusions based on limited information. Additionally, external change agents

Table 23.3. Advantages and disadvantages of internal and external change agents

	Internal Change Agent	External Change Agent
Advantages	1. Knows the environment, culture, people, issues, and hidden agendas 2. Develops and keeps expertise and resources internal 3. Creates and maintains norms of organization renewal from within 4. Provides higher security and confidentiality 5. May have trust and respect of others 6. Has strong personal investment in success	1. Provides fresh, outside, objective perspective 2. Is willing to assert, challenge, and question norms 3. May have more legitimacy to insiders by not taking sides 4. Brings skills and techniques not available from within organization 5. Brings diverse organizational experiences to bear; benchmarks comparisons
Disadvantages	1. May be biased; has already taken sides, or may be disliked or mistrusted by some stakeholders 2. May have previous relationships that contribute to subgrouping or fragmentation 3. Takes change agent away from other duties 4. May be enculturated and is "part of the problem" or does not see it 5. Is subject to organizational sanctions and pressures as an employee	1. May or may not be available when needed by the organization; may split time and commitments with other clients 2. Incurs high expense 3. Takes time to become familiar with the system 4. May create codependency or may abandon the system

Source: Weick and Quinn 1995.

may be strongly influenced by the viewpoint of the administrators who contracted with them. External change agents must thoroughly evaluate the relevant people and processes of the organization. Moreover, external agents can be expensive, charging tens to hundreds of thousands of dollars for their consultation. For example, in one hospital system, a consulting group contracted over four years to implement a balanced scorecard system for the fee of about $2.3 million. Finally, a highly charismatic, directive, and successful agent could foster dependency with a client organization, leaving the organization reluctant to learn to manage its own change processes.

Internal versus External Change Agents

When an organization plans to use internal or external change agents, it should consider several questions, including the following:

- How confidential and proprietary is the information involved? Would either type of agent present a disclosure risk?
- Are there conflicts of interest? Is the external agent working with any competitor or internal agent loyal to conflicting parties?
- What level of commitment and availability is required? What is the potential effect of an external agent with many other clients or an internal agent with other work obligations?
- What skills are required for a successful change effort? What constellation of experience and skills do the external and internal agents offer?
- How important is it that stakeholders view the agent as being objective, fair, and neutral? Which type of agent would best be viewed this way?
- To what extent does the culture of the organization require changing? Which type of agent is better positioned to influence the change?

Stages of Change

People and organizations move through stages of change, and as they do, they have different needs and require different skills from the leader.

Lewin's Stages of Change

One of the first models of change was proposed by Kurt Lewin (1951), one of the early behavioral scientists who contributed to the knowledge base of information on group work, leadership, and organization development.

Lewin's model, or **Lewin's stages of change,** identified the initial stage of change as **unfreezing** the status quo, often by presenting the discrepancies between the status quo and the desired goals. Unfreezing often creates a state of cognitive dissonance, which is an uncomfortable awareness of two incompatible perceptions or beliefs, in this case, the discrepancy.

This motivates the person to resolve the dissonance, usually by changing the situation to make the perceptions congruent. This step marks the second stage of change or moving to the new desired state for the organization.

In the final stage of **refreezing,** the new behaviors are reinforced to become as stable and institutionalized as the previous status quo was. Lewin originally conceptualized this three-stage process as one in which the organization would plateau and stabilize for a time before the next change was required. More recent beliefs about organizational change characterize the change process as continuous with little respite for workers, managers, or leaders. The status quo has become one of dealing with continual change, which can be stressful as people learn to let go of past practices and make efforts to learn new ones.

Stages of Grieving

Elizabeth Kubler-Ross (1969) examined the stress of change in her classic study of the **stages of grief** experienced by terminally ill patients and their families. Change in the healthcare system often involves mergers, acquisitions, downsizing, and other transitions that usually involve losses and grief. Her five-stage model has become useful in anticipating and working with people in a dramatic transition, including organizational change (Rogers 2000). As shown in figure 23.18, the five stages of her model are

1. *Shock and denial:* Workers have difficulty believing the proposed transition. They may deny that change is imminent and go about business as usual rather than prepare for the adjustment. News of the change also may stun workers to the extent that they cannot concentrate or work efficiently, and they may isolate themselves.
2. *Anger:* Workers begin to understand the inevitability of the change. They may direct their resentment at the organization or the managers for allowing it to happen. In addition, they may engage in unproductive complaining, organize resistance, or even sabotage operations in attempts to reduce the threat.
3. *Bargaining:* Workers make a final attempt to avoid the change. They may actually try to bargain with managers to delay the change or work intensively to prove their value and reduce the risk of loss.

Figure 23.18.   Kubler-Ross's stages of grief

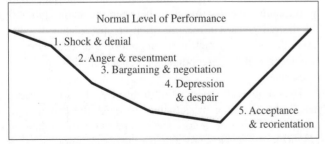

Source: Adapted from Kubler-Ross 1969.

4. *Depression:* Workers may lose their self-esteem and be unresponsive to encouragement.
5. *Acceptance:* Workers begin to redirect their energy toward the new organization.

Resistance to Change

Kurt Lewin is credited with saying, "If you wish to understand something, try changing it." He was referring to the observation that when one attempts to change a system, the mechanisms that maintain it spring to its defense. Change does not come easily to most people, and in organizations, "resistance to change is experienced at almost every step" (DeWine 1994, 281). The first step for leaders who are trying to reduce resistance to change is to understand its source.

Resistance to change occurs for a number of reasons, including self-interest and anxiety about the unknown, different perceptions, suspiciousness, and conservatism. When confronted with change, the first thing most workers want to know is how it will affect them and their jobs. Because the turbulence of the marketplace makes many changes uncertain, workers may not receive satisfactory answers to their questions. Those who have attained expertise and status from their positions now may face new job descriptions or expanded or new duties. For example, many managers in downsized organizations have been reassigned as coaches to newly formed teams. This new role raises questions about their authority, status, and responsibility.

Other workers may resist change simply because they perceive the situation differently and believe the proposed change is unjustified. The result of ongoing change is to make many people uneasy about, and even mistrustful of, any innovation. Some people view all change as just another fad based on the whim of management rather than a survival strategy for the organization. And finally, some people are very conservative in their beliefs, are isolated in their social networks and information, and dislike the inconvenience of change.

Resistance can distract workers from their tasks, preoccupy them with gossiping, and contribute to stress and workplace violence. To confident change leaders, indications of resistance can be viewed as useful information about what stakeholders need before the transition can continue.

Facilitation of Change

The purpose of transition management is to make the potential upheaval and chaos posed by planned changes less disruptive to the people and processes of healthcare. It might be helpful to think of a transition as a series of stages through which people move as they adjust to changes. Each stage has its own set of challenges and tasks to master, the successful completion of which forms the foundation for moving on to the next stage. The role of managers and leaders is to facilitate the movement from stage to stage.

Bridges' Stages of Transition

In recognition of the stresses that change imposes on the organization's employees, Bridges (2004) extended Lewin's three-stage model with recommendations for transition management to ease the struggle. The stages of his model are as follows:

1. The transition process begins with the recognition that the old way of doing things is **ending.** Workers begin to anticipate and experience losses with resulting grief, blame, shock, and fear. They need help in letting go of the way things were. The organization can facilitate the transition by providing reasons for the ending and by indicating what will not change. It is usually best to overcommunicate to ensure that everyone has sufficient information about ongoing developments. Acknowledging losses and accepting grieving also can assist people in the ending stage.

2. The second stage, the **neutral zone,** begins when the old system has been left behind but the new one has not yet been fully accepted. This stage fosters anxiety, uncertainty, and confusion. The organization can facilitate the transition by providing support, encouragement, reassurance, and protection. The employees need to know where they are and where they are going. One creative approach to gaining acceptance of the transition is to have employees generate innovative ideas about how they can move toward the new organization.

3. In the third stage, **new beginnings,** people accept, orient themselves to and engage in the new organization. New goals are created to provide direction, and the workers' relationships with the organization and their jobs are reinvented and integrated. Attitudes and behaviors that support the new beginning are supported by workers and role-modeled by leaders. Retraining, performance feedback, and recognition of new behavior serve to reinforce the transition.

Importance of Reflection

Reflection is the process of examining one's experience. It is an essential skill for developing leadership skills and an important component of team and organization development. However, reflection alone is not sufficient for changing behavior. Reflection involves awareness. Reflective learning, on the other hand, uses awareness to formulate an interpretation of what has been observed, considers what difference can be made by applying what has been learned, and executes the efforts toward change through deliberate action.

Several remarkably similar models of the **reflective learning cycle** have been developed over the years, including those by John Dewey (1938), David Kolb (1970), W. Edwards Deming (1986), and Donald Schon (1983). These models share the following four stages in common (see figure 23.19):

1. *Doing:* At this stage, people are concentrating and working directly on a task. Although most people

Figure 23.19.   Reflective learning process

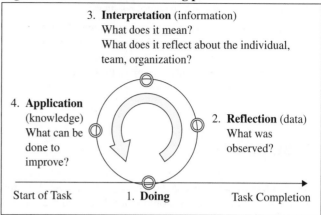

reflect on a task after it is accomplished, this is often too late to make midcourse or more frequent changes. The reflective process should be used often, although too much reflection sometimes is used to avoid task completion.

2. *Reflection:* At this stage, the task is paused and the individual or team members reflect on how they have been working. What do they notice? The raw data become information as reflection progresses to the interpretation stage.

3. *Interpretation:* At this stage, one considers what the information means, what it reflects about the work process, and how various observations might be related.

4. *Application:* The application stage follows as information becomes knowledge and is applied to the work by doing something differently. Finally, the new knowledge is used to return to the action stage.

As the marketplace continues to change, organizations will have to adapt in order to maintain their competitive advantage. Organizational leaders play a key role in helping employees to reduce their resistance to change and to inspire and motivate them to accept it. By understanding leadership theories and the stages and techniques of planned change, and by using the reflective learning cycle, managers will be better prepared to meet the challenge.

Check Your Understanding 23.6

Instructions: Answer the following questions on a separate piece of paper.

1. If you were an OD consultant, what would you tell an executive team about a pending reorganization? What should the executive team expect?

2. If you were informed that your job was being eliminated due to reorganization but that you could reapply for a new position, how would you react? What would you need to cope with the stress?

3. Make a list of reasons that people resist change. For each reason, suggest a way to reduce resistance.

4. Use the reflective learning process to examine a group meeting. What did you notice? What do you think your observations reflected about the group processes? What might you do differently to improve the next meeting?

Summary

As the marketplace has expanded to a global perspective and workplace settings have become more diverse and complex, the discipline of management has likewise evolved. Classical management theories focused on formal authority, hierarchical avenues of communication and accountability, and operational efficiency. Weber's concept of bureaucracy, Taylor's scientific management, and the Gilbreths' and Gantts' operational innovations provided such structure.

As management became professionalized, effective practices and responsibilities became more formal and were incorporated into the administrative model of management. In addition to describing the functions of planning, organizing, leading, and controlling, Fayol formulated 14 principles for management. Prior to emergence of the humanistic approach to management, Bernard emphasized the balance of effectiveness and efficiency. The Hawthorne studies marked the shift from operations and authority to the **human** relations movement and attention to worker motivation. Maslow described a hierarchy of needs that provided managers with a model for targeting efforts to motivate workers, and McGregor recognized the shift from authoritarian to humanistic orientation in his theory X and Y.

As technology and strategy were emphasized in response to international conflicts and competition, management science developed a variety of new tools. Operations management, statistical forecasting, break-even analysis, queuing, modeling, and PERT were used to reemphasize production to balance the renewed emphasis on people.

More contemporary approaches to management have emphasized improved quality of products and services through greater efficiency and increased focus on people. TQM, the Malcolm Baldrige National Quality Award, and the search for best practices have fine-tuned many management and business processes.

Effective management involves not only understanding Fayol's four functions but also understanding and developing conceptual skills for strategy, emotional intelligence or interpersonal skills for working effectively with people, and technical skills for dealing with the specific business field. Moreover, managers must learn to perform multiple roles while working at an unrelenting pace.

Corporate social responsibility has emerged as a strategic focus in recent years, partly due to concerns about inattention to environment and social issues that have been overshadowed by excessive attention solely to finances. It has also helped organizations consider their values and develop guidelines for congruence with those values. Communication errors can be costly in patient safety, liability risk, and staff relationships. Attention to clear communication, such as quality criteria, standards, and staff training, can reduce distortion and error.

Theories of leadership have become more complex over the decades, moving from the simple trait listings of the great person theory to more contingency and complex systems frameworks.

Change management requires strong leadership. Managers traditionally maintain a highly efficient workplace and establish procedures; leaders look to the future and promote change. Both solve problems and make decisions. Recurrent problems lend themselves to clear rules for programmed decisions that can be used routinely; unique, complex, or changing situations require careful thought when nonprogrammed decisions are made. Formal decision making progresses through several stages, including problem definition, problem analysis, generation of alternatives, selection of alternatives, plan implementation, and evaluation and feedback. Although high cohesion and strong organizational culture can be desirable, groupthink can produce riskier decisions and requires review of team norms periodically as well as implementation of countermeasures. Clear communication with consideration of all stakeholders can further reduce distortion and error.

Leadership theories provide a way to examine what is required in a situation to facilitate change through people. Classical approaches to leadership emphasized collections of traits that became unwieldy in practice. However, as society embraced democratic ideals, management began to reflect greater worker participation and involvement in decision making. Vroom and Yetton's normative model of decision making enables managers to decide when to make a decision alone and when to delegate. Studies from The Ohio State University, the University of Michigan, and Blake and Mouton have enabled leadership styles to be described along continua of task and social dimensions. Building on the need for leaders to adjust their styles to meet the unique characteristics of each situation, more recent models have emerged, including Fiedler's leadership contingency model, work done by Hersey and Blanchard, path–goal theory, leader–member exchange, and servant leadership.

Implementing change or innovations goes through different stages in an organization, and each stage has its own group of stakeholders. Plotting actual innovation results in an S-shaped curve with a slow start, rapid development, and a plateau of saturation and adoption. Within the organization, innovations require the key roles of inventor, champion, sponsor, and critic. The change agent spearheads the organization's change efforts, though there are advantages and disadvantages to internal and external change agent roles.

Understanding the stages of change also can relieve resistance to change. The stages of change often parallel the stages of grief identified by Kubler-Ross in her classic study. Similarly, the stages of organizational change can be thought of as an end to the old ways, a neutral time of transition, and new beginnings.

References

Agarwal, R., D.Z. Sands, J.D. Schneider, and D.H. Smaltz, 2010 (July/August). Quantifying the economic impact of communication inefficiencies in US hospitals. *Journal of Healthcare Management* 55(4): 265–282.

Allen, T.J., and S.I. Cohen. 1969. Information flow in two R&D laboratories. *Administrative Science Quarterly* 14(1): 12–19.

Allport, G.W., and H.S. Odbert. 1936. Trait-names: A psycho-lexical study. *Psychological Monographs* (47): 171–220.

Ameri, F., and D. Dutta. 2005. Product lifestyle management: Closing the knowledge loops. *Computer Aided Design and Application* 2(5): 577–590.

Apker, J. 2001. Role development in the managed care era. *Journal of Applied Communication Research* 29(2): 117–136.

Argyris, C. 1957. *Personality and Organization.* New York: Harper & Row.

Baldrige Performance Excellence Program. 2011. 2011–2012 Health care criteria for performance excellence. http://www.nist.gov/baldrige/publications/upload/2011_2012_Health_Care_Criteria.pdf.

Baron, R.S. 2005. So right it's wrong: Groupthink and the ubiquitous nature of polarized group decision making. *Advances in Experimental Social Psychology* 37: 219–252.

Bass, B.M., and B.J. Avolio. 1993. Transformational leadership: A response to critics. In *Leadership Theory and Research: Perspectives and Directions.* Edited by Chemers, M.M., and R. Ayman. San Diego: Academic Press.

Beckhard, R. 1969. *Organization Development: Strategies and Models.* Reading, MA: Addison-Wesley.

Benedictine Health System. 2002. Advancing the BHS ministry through a renewed commitment to mission, values. *BHS System Spirit & Life* 6(3): 1.

Bernard, C. 1938. *The Functions of the Executive.* Cambridge, MA: Harvard University Press.

Blake, R.R., and J.S. Mouton. 1976. *Consultation.* Reading, MA: Addison-Wesley.

Bridges, W. 1994. *Job Shift: How to Prosper in a Workplace without Jobs.* Reading, MA: Addison-Wesley.

Bridges, W. 2004. *Transitions: Making the Most of Change.* New York: Basic Books.

Buhler, P.M. 2007. Managing in the new millennium: Interpersonal skills. *Supervision* 68(7): 20–22.

Burns, J.M. 1978. *Leadership.* New York: Free Press.

Byrne, J.A. 2005 (Nov. 28). The man who invented management. *Business Week*, 97–106.

Carmeli, A., and A. Tishler. 2006. The relative importance of the top management team's managerial skills. *International Journal of Manpower* 27(1): 9–36.

Chartered Institute of Personnel and Development. 2005. Annual survey report, 2005. http://www.cipd.co.uk/NR/rdonlyres/271CD424-507C-4E4A-99B6-1FAD80573E4A/0/traindevtsurvrept05.pdf.

Cohen, A.B., and R.S. Hanft. 2004. *Technology in American Health Care.* Ann Arbor, MI: University of Michigan Press.

Coiera, E.W., Jayasuriya, R.A., Hardy, J., Bannan, A. and Thorpe, M.E.C. (2002). Communication loads on clinical staff in the emergency department. Medical Journal of Australia. 176 (9).

Daft, R.L. 2000. *Management.* Fort Worth, TX: Dryden.

Daft, R.L., and D. Marcic. 1998. *Understanding Management.* Fort Worth, TX: Dryden.

Dansereau, F., G. Graen, and W. Haga. 1975. A vertical dyad linkage approach to leadership within formal organizations: A longitudinal investigation of the role-making process. *Organizational Behavior and Human Performance* 13:46–78.

Deming, W.E. 1986. *Out of the Crisis.* Cambridge: Massachusetts Institute of Technology, Center for Advanced Engineering Study.

Dewey, J. 1938. *Experience and Education.* New York: Collier.

DeWine, S. 1994. *The Consultant's Craft: Improving Organizational Communication.* New York: St. Martin's Press.

Drucker, P. 1986. The appraisal of managerial performance. *Management Decision* 24(4): 67–78.

Druskat, V.U., F. Sala, and G. Mount. 2005. *Linking Emotional Intelligence and Performance at Work.* Maywah, NJ: Lawrence Erlbaum.

Dubrin, A.J. 2004. *Leadership: Research Findings, Practice and Skills.* New York: Houghton Mifflin.

Edison, T. 2008 (May–June). The team development lifecycle. Team dynamics. Defense AT&L. http://www.dau.mil/pubs/dam/2008_05_06/edis_mj08.pdf.

Ethics Business Center. 2012. 2011 National Business Ethics Survey: Workplace ethics in transition. http://www.ethics.org/nbes/files/FinalNBES-web.pdf.

Ethisphere. 2008. 2008 World's most ethical companies. http://ethisphere.com/wme2008.

Fayol, Henri. 1917. *Administration Industrielle et Générale; Prévoyance, Organisation, Commandement, Coordination, Controle.* Paris: H. Dunod et E. Pinat.

Fenton, S.H., and L.D. Gamm. 2008 (Fall). Evaluation and management documentation and coding technology adoption. Perspectives in Health Information Management, Computer Assisted Coding Conference Proceedings. http://library.ahima.org/xpedio/groups/public/documents/ahima/bok1_040477.html.

Fiedler, F.E. 1967. *A Theory of Leadership Effectiveness.* New York: McGraw-Hill.

French, J.R.P., and B. Raven. 1959. The bases of social power. In *Studies in Social Power.* Edited by Cartwright, D. Ann Arbor, MI: Institute for Social Research.

Garber, G., E.A. Madigan, E.R. Click, and J.J. Fitzpatrick. 2009 (July 1). Attitudes toward collaboration and servant leadership among nurses, physicians and residents. *Journal of Interprofessional Care* 23(4): 331–340.

Goleman, D. 1998 (Nov–Dec). What makes a leader? *Harvard Business Review* 74(6): 92–102.

Graen, G., and T.A. Skandura. 1987. Toward a psychology of dyadic organizing. *Research in Organizational Behavior* 9:175–209.

Greenleaf, R.J. 1991. *Servant Leadership.* Mahwah, NJ: Paulist Press.

Guo, K.L. 2003. An assessment tool for developing healthcare management skills and roles. *Journal of Healthcare Management* 48(6): 367–376.

Hahn, W., and T.L. Powers, 2010 (January). Strategic plan quality, implementation capability, and firm performance. *Academy of Strategic Management* 9(1): 63–81.

Hammer, M., and J. Champy. 1993. *Reengineering the Corporation.* New York: Harper.

Healthcare Management Council. 2007. http://hmc-benchmarks.com.

Helseth, C. 2007 (Summer). Recruiting local people to fill health care needs. *The Rural Monitor.* http://www.raconline.org/newsletter/web/summer07.php.

Hersey, P., K.H. Blanchard, and D.E. Johnson. 1996. *Management of Organizational Behavior: Utilizing Human Resources,* 7th ed. Upper Saddle River, NJ: Prentice-Hall.

Hogan, R., and R.B. Kaiser. 2004. What we know about leadership. *Review of General Psychology* 9(2): 169–180.

Holton, V., F. Dents, and J. Rabbetts. 2008. Ashridge Management Index 2008: Meeting the challenges of the 21st century. http://www.ashridge.org.uk/website/IC.nsf/wFARATT/Ashridge%20Management%20Index%202008:%20Meeting%20the%20Challenges%20of%20the%2021st%20Century/$file/MeetingTheChallengesOfThe21stCentury.pdf.

Hooper, D.T., and R. Martin. 2008. Beyond personal leader-member exchange (LMX) quality: The effects of perceived LMX variability on employee reactions. *Leadership Quarterly* 19(1): 20–30.

Houghton, S.M., A.C. Stewart, and P.S. Barr, 2009. Cognitive complexity of the top management team: The impact of team differentiation and integration processes on firm performance. *Current Topics in Management* 14: 95–118.

House, R.J. 1971. A path–goal theory of leader effectiveness. *Administrative Science Leadership Review Quarterly* 16:321–339.

Hunter, J.C. 2004. *The World's Most Powerful Leadership Principle: How to Become a Servant Leader.* New York: Random House.

Hwang, Y.-S. and S.H. Park. 2007. Organizational life cycle as a determinant of strategic alliance tactics: Research propositions. *International Journal of Management* 24(3): 427–435.

Janis, I.L. 1972. *Groupthink: Psychological Studies of Policy Decisions and Fiascos.* Boston: Houghton Mifflin.

Jones, G.R., and J.M. George. 2006. *Contemporary Management,* 4th ed. New York: McGraw-Hill Irwin.

Jordan, P.J., and A. Troth. 2005. Emotional conflict and conflict resolution. *Advances in Developing Human Resources* 4(1): 62–79.

Kaplan, R.S., and D.P. Norton. 1996. *The Balanced Scorecard.* Boston: Harvard Business School Press.

Katz, R.L. 1974. Skills of an effective administrator. *Harvard Business Review* 52: 90–102.

Kirvin, D. 2005 (March 28). Communication skills of the phlebotomist. Advance: For Medical Laboratory Professionals. http://laboratorian.advance web.com/Article/Communications-Skills-of-the-Phlebotomist-32805.aspx.

Kluger, M., and M. Bullock. 2002. Recovery room incidents: A review of 419 reports from the Anaesthetic Incident Monitoring Study (AIMS). *Anaesthesia* 57: 1060–1066.

Kohn, L.T., J.M. Corrigan, and M.S. Donaldson, 2000. *To Err Is Human: Building A Safer Health System.* Washington D.C.: National Academies Press.

Kolb, D.A., and A.L. Frohman. 1970. An organization development approach to consulting. *Sloan Management Review* 12(1): 51–65.

Kubler-Ross, E. 1969. *On Death and Dying.* New York: Simon & Schuster/Touchstone.

Leadership Trust Foundation. 2007. Why leadership? http://www.leadership. org.uk/mainpages.asp?PageID=3.

Lee, J. 2005. The effects of leadership and leader-member exchange on commitment. *Leadership and Organization Development Journal* 26(8): 655–672.

Lewin, K. 1951. *Field Theory in Social Science.* New York: Harper and Brothers.

Liebman, C.B., and C.S. Hyman. 2004. A mediation skills model to manage disclosure of errors and adverse events to patients. *Health Affairs* 23: 22–32.

Likert, R. 1979. From production- and employee-centeredness to systems 1–4. *Journal of Management* 5: 628–641.

LRN. 2007. Ethics study: Employee engagement. http://www.ethics.org/files/u5/LRNEmployeeEngagement.pdf.

Mahoney, T.A., T.H. Jerdee, and S.J. Carroll. 1965. The job(s) of management. *Industrial Relations* 4(2): 97–110.

Meyer, R.M. 2008. Span of management: Concept analysis. *Journal of Advanced Nursing* 63(1): 104-112.

Meyer, B.B., T.B. Fletcher, and S.J. Parker, 2004. Enhancing emotional intelligence in the health care environment: An exploratory study. *Healthcare Manager* 23(3). 225–234.

Michalisin, M.D., S.J. Karau, and C. Tangpong. 2004. Top management team cohesion and superior industry returns: An empirical study of the resource-based view. *Group and Organization Management* 29(1): 125–140.

Mintzberg, H. 1992. The manager's job: Folklore and fact. In *Managing People and Organizations.* Edited by Gabarro, J.J. Boston: Harvard Business School Publications.

Ozaralli, N. 2003. Effects of transformational leadership on empowerment and team effectiveness. *Leadership and Organization Development Journal* 24(6): 16–47.

Pascale, R.T. 1990. *Managing on the Edge*. New York: Simon & Schuster.

Peters, T.J., and R.H. Waterman. 1982. *In Search of Excellence: Lessons from America's Best-Run Companies*. New York: Harper & Row.

Raven, B.H. 1983. Interpersonal influence and social power. In *Social Psychology*. Edited by Raven, B.H., and J.Z. Rubin, 399–444. New York: John Wiley & Sons.

Riggio, R.E., and R.J. Reichard. 2008. The emotional and social intelligences of effective leadership: An emotional and social skill approach. *Journal of Managerial Psychology* 23(2): 169–185.

Roberts, E.B., 2007 (Jan–Feb). Managing invention and innovation. *Research Technology Management*. http://www.iriinc.org/Content/ContentGroups/Research_Technology_Management/Volume_50_2007/Issue_Number_1_January_February_20071/Articles21/MANAGING_INVENTION_AND_INNOVATION.htm.

Rogers, E. 1995. *Diffusion of Innovations,* 4th ed. New York: Free Press.

Rogers, E., and F.F. Shoemaker. 1971. *Communication of Innovations: A Cross-Cultural Approach*. New York: Free Press.

Rogers, K.A. 2000. Transition management as an intervention for survivor syndrome. *Canadian Journal of Leadership Nursing* 13(4).

Rural Health Resource Center. 2008. Balanced Scorecard experiences. http://www.ruralcenter.org/?id=res_bscxp.

Sanford, K. 2006. The ethical leader. *Nursing Administration Quarterly* 30(1): 5–10.

Schon, D.A. 1983. *The Reflective Practitioner*. New York: Basic Books.

Shartle, C.L. 1979. Early years of the Ohio State University leadership studies. *Journal of Management* 5:126–134.

Spath, P. 2007. Spread the word: Communication is the key to effective care. *For the Record* 19(8): 36.

Spears, L. 1995. *Reflections on Leadership: How Robert K. Greenleaf's Theory of Servant Leadership Influenced Today's Top Management Thinkers*. New York: John Wiley & Sons.

Stogdill, R.M. 1974. *Handbook of Leadership: A Guide to Understanding Managerial Work*. Englewood Cliffs, NJ: Prentice-Hall.

Stoner, J.A.F., and R.E. Freeman. 1989. *Management*. Englewood Cliffs, NJ: Prentice-Hall.

Strickland, D. 2000. Emotional intelligence: The most potent factor in the success equation. *Journal of Nursing Administration* 30(3): 112–117.

Supplee Group. 2002 (Jan. 28). Press release: Employees cite poor managers as primary reason for quitting. http://ehstoday.com/news/ehs_imp_35141/.

Swenson, D.X. 2003. The Groupthink Profile. http://www.behaviortrends.com.

Sy, T., S. Tram, and L.A. O'Hara, (2006). Relation of employee and manager emotional intelligence to job satisfaction and performance. *Journal of Vocational Behavior* 68(3): 461–473.

Tannenbaum, T., and W. Schmidt. 1973 (May–June). How to choose a leadership pattern. *Harvard Business Review*. No. 73311. First published in 1958 (March–April) *Harvard Business Review* 36:95–101.

Tung, F.C., and S.C. Chang. 2008. Nursing students' behavior intention to use online courses: A questionnaire survey. *International Journal of Nursing Studies* 45(9): 1299–1309.

Vaill, P.B. 1996. *Learning as a Way of Being*. San Francisco: Jossey-Bass.

Van Eck Computer Consulting. 2004. The decision tree for statistics. http://www.microsiris.com/Statistical%20Decision%20Tree.

Verbos, A.K., J.A. Gerard, P.R. Forshey, C.S. Harding, and J.S. Miller. 2007. The positive ethical organization: Enacting a living code of ethics and ethical organization identity. *Journal of Business Ethics* 76(1): 17–33.

Vroom, V., and P. Yetton. 1971. *Leadership and Decision Making*. Pittsburgh: University of Pittsburgh Press.

Walker Information. 2001. Commitment in the workplace: The 2000 global employee relationship benchmark report. Walker Information Global Network and Hudson Institute. http://www.askemployees.com/why/docs/global.pdf.

Walton, M. 1986. *The Deming Management Method*. New York: Perigee Books.

Watzlawick, P., J.H. Beavin, and D.D. Jackson. 1968. *The Pragmatics of Human Communication*. New York: Norton.

Weick, K.E., and R.E. Quinn. 1995. Organizational change and development. *Annual Review of Psychology* 50:361–386.

Westcott, R.T. 2005. *The Certified Manager of Quality/Organizational Excellence Handbook*. Milwaukee, WI: American Society for Quality.

White, R.K., and R. Lippitt. 1960. *Autocracy and Democracy: An Experimental Inquiry*. New York: Harper.

Yukl, G. 2006. *Leadership in Organizations,* 6th ed. Upper Saddle River, NJ: Prentice-Hall.

Zhu, W., I.K.H. Chew, and W.D. Spangler. 2004. CEO transformational leadership and organizational outcomes: The mediating role of human-capital-enhancing human resource management. *Leadership Quarterly* 16(1): 39–52.

chapter 24

Human Resources Management and Employee Training and Development

Karen R. Patena, MBA, RHIA, and Madonna M. LeBlanc, MA, RHIA

Learning Objectives

- Identify the activities associated with the human resources (HR) management function in an organization
- Associate key federal legislation with each of the human resources management activities
- Develop position descriptions, performance standards, staffing structures, and work schedules for use as tools in human resources management
- Explain how job descriptions are used in employee recruitment and selection
- Identify effective steps for conducting an interview
- Identify alternative staffing trends and discuss their role in workforce retention
- Discuss the roles that employee orientation and communication plans play in the development and retention of staff
- Understand the continuum of employee training and development
- Learn how to develop an orientation program for new employees
- Appreciate the role of staff development in retaining a competent workforce
- Know how to respond to various learning styles and to the needs of adult learners
- Learn how to respond to the needs of a culturally diverse workforce or the needs of employees with disabilities
- Know how to apply appropriate delivery methods to various training needs

- Learn how to prepare and conduct appropriate in-service education programs for various healthcare employees
- Prepare employees for e-HIM roles
- Prepare a training and development plan for a health information management department
- Know how to apply appropriate methods for developing employee potential
- Learn how to assess the needs of current employees for continuing education
- Articulate the benefits of teamwork in an organization, and identify the steps in creating an effective team (team building)
- Identify and differentiate among the four methods of job evaluation
- Describe the relationship among performance standards, performance review, and performance counseling
- Identify the key steps a manager should take in performance counseling and disciplinary action
- Select the appropriate conflict management technique to use in each specific conflict situation
- Explain the process for handling employee complaints and grievances
- Identify the obligations an organization has to maintain the security of employee information and records
- Anticipate the impact of current workforce trends on the organization's human resources management activities

Key Terms

Ability (achievement) test
Accountability
Age Discrimination in Employment
    Act (1967)
Allied Health Reinvestment Act (2005)
Americans with Disabilities Act (ADA) (1990)
Aptitude test
Asynchronous
Audioconferencing
Authority
Avatar
Behavioral description interview
Blended learning
Blog
Civil Rights Act (1991)
Civil Rights Act, Title VII (1964)
Coaching
Communication plan
Compensable factor
Compensation and benefits
Competency
Compressed workweek
Compromise
Computer-based training (CBT)
Conflict management
Constructive confrontation
Continuing education (CE)
Control
Cross-training
Cultural competence
Delegation
Delegation of authority
Disciplinary action
Discrimination
Distance learning
Diversity training
e-HIM
e-learning
Electronic performance support system (EPSS)
Employee handbook
Employee record
Employment contract
Employment-at-will
Empowerment
Equal Employment Opportunity Act (1972)
Equal Pay Act (EPA) (1963)
Ethics training
Exempt employee
Exit interview
Factor comparison method
Fair Labor Standards Act (FLSA) (1938)
Family and Medical Leave Act (FMLA) (1993)
Flex years

Flexible work schedule
Flextime
Grievance
Grievance procedure
Harassment
Hay method of job evaluation
Hiring
Honesty (integrity) test
Incentive pay
In-service education
Interview
Intranet
Job classification method
Job description
Job evaluation
Job ranking
Job rotation
Job sharing
Job specification
Just-in-time training
Labor relations
Labor-Management Relations Act
    (Taft-Hartley Act)
Labor-Management Reporting and Disclosure Act
    (Landrum-Griffin Act)
Layoff
Learning content management system (LCMS)
Learning curve
Learning management system (LMS)
Lecture
M-learning
Massed training
Mental ability (cognitive) test
Mentor
Motivation
Multiuser virtual environment (MUVE)
National Labor Relations Act (Wagner Act)
Needs assessment
Nonexempt employee
Occupational Safety and Health Act (OSHA) (1970)
Offshoring
One-on-one training
On-the-job training
Orientation
Outsourcing
Panel interview
Pay for performance
Performance counseling
Performance review
Performance standard
Point method
Policy
Position (job) description

Pregnancy Discrimination Act (1978)
Procedure
Programmed learning module
Progressive discipline
Promotion
Recruitment
Reference check
Reinforcement
Reliability
Responsibility
Resume
Retention
Reverse mentoring
Role playing
Self-directed learning
Simulation
Socialization
Spaced training
Staffing structure
Structured interview
Succession planning
Synchronous

Task analysis
Team building
Telecommuting
Termination
Testing
360-degree evaluation
Train the trainer
Trainee
Trainer
Training
Training and development model
Uniformed Services Employment and Reemployment
    Rights Act (1994)
Union
Validity
Virtual reality
Web-based training
Wiki
Workers' Adjustment Retraining and
    Notification (WARN) Act
Working conditions

The process of management cannot be practiced or examined meaningfully outside the social, cultural, and ethical contexts in which human organizations of all kinds operate. In modern industrial societies, human resources represent every organization's most valuable asset.

Healthcare organizations are extremely complex. They must operate as effective and efficient businesses in a very tight financial environment. They also must employ a variety of well-educated technical specialists and professional employees to provide or support increasingly sophisticated healthcare services. Contemporary healthcare managers work in a unique environment that is characterized by the need to control costs and, at the same time, meet the needs of healthcare consumers and healthcare workers.

Managers work at many levels within healthcare organizations: as supervisors of functional units, as middle managers of departmental units or service lines, and as executive managers of multiple departmental units or service lines. At each level of management, the practice of managing the human resources within the prescribed scope of authority and responsibility is critical to the manager's success and the success of the entire organization.

Managing human resources (HR) is both an art and a science. Managers can learn much in this arena by partnering with HR management specialists, observing experienced colleagues, reflecting regularly on their own experiences, and continuing to develop their competencies throughout their careers.

As a service industry, healthcare relies on the availability of competent workers. The growth of new technologies, the application of new vocabulary and processes, and the decreasing numbers of employees with adequate skills to respond to the new environment mean that healthcare organizations must frequently assume responsibility for preparing and developing their own labor pool, unless they choose to outsource or use employees overseas. Providing the necessary training to workers is costly in terms of both money and time. Using overseas workers creates its own training needs in areas such as ethics or the English language. Moreover, after the organization has made the investment, it must do what it can to protect its investment by retaining its workforce.

Human resources are the healthcare institution's most valuable asset. Managing employees requires recognizing and meeting the needs of the employees as well as those of the organization. Healthcare organizations must provide employees with the tools for career success and personal achievement if they are to win the long-term commitment of staff.

This chapter is not meant to provide a comprehensive background in human resources management. The purpose of this chapter is to present a general introduction to the subject of managing human resources within the context of health information management (HIM) operations. The chapter begins with a focus on the interrelationship of HIM managers and HR professionals and the roles of the supervisor and middle manager as frontline implementers of the HR policies and practices of healthcare organizations. The chapter then focuses on tools for various HR activities, including recruitment, training and retaining employees in the healthcare organization. It describes the orientation process and different methods for training new employees as well as current employees taking on new job responsibilities. It discusses adult learning strategies, techniques for delivering employee training, including the increasing use of e-learning methods, and ways to enhance job satisfaction. Special training issues, such as diversity, training overseas workers, and preparing for e-HIM roles are addressed. The chapter then continues with a discussion of tools for employee empowerment, compensation and performance reviews, and conflict management.

Role of the Human Resources Department

Payroll and benefits consume the majority of most healthcare organizations' financial resources. Therefore, adequate time and attention must be paid to the management of HR. Effective HR management is also important for reasons beyond financial impact. HR management factors affect the attitudes and morale of healthcare workers and other employees and, therefore, affect their ability to perform their work effectively, as well. Obviously, employee morale becomes extremely important when the work involves caring for patients directly or indirectly, supporting those who provide hands-on care.

Entities such as hospitals, large physician groups, and managed care organizations commonly have a dedicated HR department that acts as a reference and support for managers at all levels. However, every manager must have an understanding of the principles of HR management in order to implement them effectively within the scope of the manager's authority and responsibility. Every manager must also know how to appropriately and effectively work with the organization's HR department.

The HR department is responsible for several types of interrelated activities. Mathis and Jackson (2002) describe HR management as a set of closely related activities focused on contributing to an organization's success by enhancing its productivity, quality, and service. Each of these interrelated activities is shown in figure 24.1 Mathis and Jackson also emphasize the importance of performing HR activities with the organization's unique mission, culture, size, and structure in mind as well as the greater social, political, legal, economic, technological, and cultural environment in which it operates.

Human Resources Planning and Analysis

Human resource planning and analysis ensure the long-term health of the organization's human assets. Internal trends such as the aging of the workforce or the changing nature of the skill mix required to handle the organization's evolving product lines must be addressed. The impact of external trends such as workforce shortages and evolving workforce expectations also must be assessed.

Figure 24.1.   HR management activities

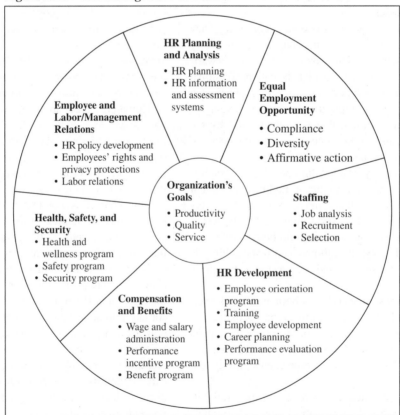

Adapted from Mathis and Jackson 2002, 4.

Equal Employment Opportunity Practices

The HR department takes the lead in ensuring that the various laws and regulations associated with equal employment opportunity (EEO) laws are scrupulously applied in the organization's hiring and promotion practices. Federally enacted EEO legislation includes the **Age Discrimination in Employment Act** of 1967, the **Americans with Disabilities Act (ADA)** of 1990, the **Civil Rights Act, Title VII** (1964) and the **Civil Rights Act** (1991), the **Equal Employment Opportunity Act** of 1972, the **Pregnancy Discrimination Act** of 1978, and the **Uniformed Services Employment and Reemployment Rights Act** of 1994 (Anthony et al. 1996; Buhler 2002). The Equal Employment Opportunity Commission (EEOC) was created by Title VII of the Civil Rights Act of 1964 as the agency responsible for investigating discrimination claims emanating from the Civil Rights Act of 1991.

Discrimination and harassment are two important concepts related to fair employment practices. **Discrimination** refers to practices that result in people being treated differently based solely on their differences. **Harassment** refers to practices that create a hostile work environment. Both are clearly illegal under the EEO laws (Johnson 2004).

Rights of Employees and Employers

Although many of the basic rights of employees are defined in law, others are expectations that may be debated within organizations. For example, **employment-at-will** is a well-established concept: either an employer or an employee can terminate an employment relationship without providing either notice or reason. On the other hand, what are the privacy rights of employees? Can an employer monitor employees' e-mail and voicemail? Organizations are well advised to address the rights of employees and the rights of the employer in an employee handbook to clarify expectations for employees and supervisors. A well-developed employee handbook also improves the organization's legal position should the organization be called on to defend its actions in a court proceeding.

Employment Laws and Regulations Impacting Training

The HR department also helps managers to define staffing needs; develop job descriptions; and recruit, screen, and select staff. After an employee is brought into the organization, the HR department plays a significant role, in partnership with the employee's direct supervisor, by spearheading the employee's immediate orientation to the organization's policies, practices, and procedures. The HR department is also active in addressing the employee's ongoing training and development requirements.

In developing training programs, healthcare organizations must recognize that special accommodations may be required to address the needs of both a culturally diverse workforce and employees with disabilities. Employers need to understand the requirements affecting training that are included under Title VII of the 1964 Civil Rights Act, the 1991 Civil Rights Act, and the ADA. If completion of a training program is part of the selection process for a particular job, the organization must be able to demonstrate that the requirements are valid and do not discriminate against, or have a negative impact on, women, minorities, or disabled individuals. For example, the vocabulary in written documents used for training should match the level required for the job, and training equipment and locations should be accessible to individuals with mobility disabilities.

In order for employers to avoid liability for harassment and discrimination acts of their employees, they must not only implement antidiscrimination policies but also provide training to ensure that employees understand their rights and responsibilities. The courts interpret this as exercising reasonable care to prevent harassment. The training should cover all types of harassment, be provided for all employees shortly after they are hired and periodically thereafter, be of substantial length, and permit the employee to repeat as necessary until competence is demonstrated. Inadequate training exposes employers to potential liability for negligent training if they fail to train adequately and an employee harms a third party.

Occupational Safety and Health Act was established by the federal government to ensure safe working conditions. Among its many requirements is training to reduce unsafe acts. Hospitals are required to train employees in fire safety and other job-related safety measures. The training must be provided in the worker's native language, other than English, if necessary, and the worker must be able to demonstrate proficiency following the training.

The **Allied Health Reinvestment Act (2005)** encourages individuals to seek and complete high-quality allied health education and training by providing funding for their studies. Grants are provided to healthcare organizations for advertising campaigns and for partnerships between healthcare facilities and allied health educational programs. Scholarships may be given to applicants who agree to serve two years in a rural or other medically underserved area with allied health personnel shortages.

The ADA requires employers to provide reasonable accommodations for physical or mental limitations with regard to many employment-related functions, including training. This would require, for example, that accommodations be made to computer-based training to provide accessibility through voice recognition or screen readers, if necessary. The World Wide Web Consortium's Web Accessibility Initiative (2012) publishes information about ADA Compliance for websites. Section 508 of the Rehabilitation Act of 1973 provides accessibility standards for electronic and information technology.

Finally, the Joint Commission requires staff orientation and continuing education to meet requirements of a particular position, and defines several topics for training, including cultural diversity sensitivity.

Compensation and Benefits Program

The organization's **compensation and benefits** program is probably the most prominent activity associated with HR management because it is so directly connected to the employee's pocketbook. This activity involves the establishment of basic definitions of employment and compensation status for the organization (for example, full-time vs. part-time, temporary vs. permanent, independent contractor vs. employee, wage versus salary). The **Fair Labor Standards Act (FLSA)** of 1938 and the **Equal Pay Act (EPA)** of 1963 serve as fundamental legislative mandates in this area.

The HR department also leads the development and administration of the organization's benefits program, job evaluation and classification systems, wage and salary systems, and incentive pay systems.

Social Security, unemployment compensation, and workers' compensation are three benefits organizations are required to offer. Other common benefits offered to employees voluntarily by the organization are health insurance, retirement plans, wellness programs, holidays (time off with pay), vacation time, and employee assistance programs.

The **Family and Medical Leave Act (FMLA)** of 1993 is an example of one legislative initiative that has had a major impact on the benefit programs, as well as on staffing activities (Anthony et al. 1996). Leaves of absence can be granted for a variety of reasons, including personal or family illness, pregnancy, or military service.

Health and Safety Program

The HR department is involved in activities designed to protect the health, safety, and security of the workforce. Healthcare organizations have given substantial attention to safety management since the enactment of the **Occupational Safety and Health Act (OSHA)** of 1970. Its intended purpose is "to assure, so far as possible, every working man or woman in the nation safe and healthful **working conditions** and to preserve our human resources". This act established a national reporting system for accidents and injuries on the job and led to the development of specific safety management programs in most businesses. More recently, health-related hazards associated with the use of technology or chemical substances in the workplace, injuries due to workplace violence, and employee security concerns have begun to receive special attention by HR professionals (Anthony et al. 1996).

Labor Relations

Employee and labor and management relations are established through the day-to-day interactions between employees and their managers. However, the organization's managers and employees often seek leadership and support from the HR department. The HR department sets the stage for developing and sustaining the quality of these critical relationships by establishing and communicating to both managers and employees the contracts, policies, practices, and rules that constitute the organization's expectations of its employees.

HR management activities associated with unions and collective bargaining are referred to as **labor relations.** Labor organizations (**unions**) enter into negotiations with employers on behalf of groups of employees who have elected to join a union. The negotiations relate to compensation and safety and health concerns. In a unionized environment, three laws that came into existence over a period of 25 years (1935–1960) constitute a code of practice for unions and management. HR departments pay strict attention to these three acts (Mathis and Jackson 2002; Anthony et al. 1996):

- **National Labor Relations Act (Wagner Act)**
- **Labor-Management Relations Act (Taft-Hartley Act)**
- **Labor-Management Reporting and Disclosure Act (Landrum-Griffin Act)**

For the manager who oversees a group of employees covered by a union contract, these laws represent the basic rules for their interactions with employees in the areas of pay, benefits, safety, health, and performance evaluation.

Check Your Understanding 24.1

Instructions: Answer the following questions on a separate piece of paper.

1. Indicate whether the following statements are true or false. If the statement is false, explain why it is false.

   A. Internal and external environmental trends are significant factors in HR planning and analysis.
   B. The Fair Labor Standards Act is one piece of the EEO legislation package passed in the early 1960s.
   C. A national system for reporting workplace accidents and injuries was mandated by the Americans with Disabilities Act.
   D. Orientation for new employees and the ongoing training of employees are solely the responsibility of the HR department.
   E. The Fair Labor Standards Act, the Wagner Act, and the Equal Pay Act provide key guidelines for managing union relationships.

2. Discuss two laws that affect training programs, and describe their impact.

Role of the HIM Manager in Human Resources

Because the day-to-day management of the organization's human resources is the responsibility of supervisory, middle, and executive managers, every manager is responsible for the same HR activities as the HR professionals. In an HIM department, for example, the supervisor of coding services would be responsible for the day-to-day management of clinical coding specialists. Managers at all levels can use any of a variety of HR tools and processes to handle these responsibilities efficiently and effectively.

Tools for Human Resources Planning

Several tools may be used to plan and manage staff resources. Position descriptions, for example, outline the work and qualifications needed to perform a job. Performance standards establish the organization's expectations of how well a job must be done and how much work must be accomplished. Routine staff meetings and regular written communications (for example, via departmental websites, bulletin boards, and newsletters) establish a routine process for up-to-date information flow for employees.

Staffing Structure and Work Scheduling

Managers establish **staffing structures** and use work schedules to ensure that there is adequate coverage and staff to complete the required work. Schedules are developed first to provide adequate coverage during the hours the organization or department is open for business.

In hospitals, it is not uncommon to find some part of the HIM department open 24 hours a day, seven days a week. This schedule ensures that HIM staff will be available to provide information for admissions to the hospital and emergency department, support patient discharges and transfers, and handle other HIM functions. In some healthcare organizations, the demand for HIM services outside regular business hours is limited. In such cases, HIM functions can be provided by business office staff, nursing staff, or emergency department staff who have been cross-trained to perform basic HIM tasks.

Another scheduling consideration is space. Space limitations on the number of workstations in the department require that employees work in shifts or on weekends.

In addition, staff preferences need to be considered in creating the work schedule. Balancing the demands of the organization with individual requests for flexible start times makes scheduling an important part of the manager's responsibility. Organizations are commonly establishing **flexible work schedules** to accommodate employee needs to adjust work schedules to lifestyles.

Written policies and procedures that explain the department's staffing requirements and scheduling procedures help the manager to remain fair and objective and help the staff to understand the rules. The amount of personal time off, such as sick leave or vacation, also factors into the development of a staff schedule and the overall assessment of the number of staff positions required.

In addition, most healthcare organizations establish some type of job classification system that combines jobs with similar levels of responsibility and qualifications into job grades that determine salary ranges and benefit packages.

For instance, all supervisory-level managers might be classified into one salary and benefit category, but each would have a unique job description. Job classifications also may determine whether an employee belongs to a union or is a candidate for unionization at the time a union attempts to organize the workforce.

Position Descriptions

A **position (job) description** outlines the work to be performed by a specific employee or group of employees with the same responsibilities. Position descriptions generally consist of three parts: a summary of the position's requirements and purpose, its functions, and the qualifications needed to perform the job. Position descriptions also include the official title of the job.

A **job specification** is a document (or a section of the position description document) that is focused on the knowledge, skills, abilities, and characteristics required of an individual in order to perform the job. These specifications may include the following (Buhler 2002):

- Educational level and professional certifications
- Experience
- General characteristics (team player, good writing skills)
- Specific knowledge (foreign language proficiency, software program proficiency)

Position descriptions, including the job specification, are used during the recruitment process to explain the work to prospective candidates. They also enable managers and HR staff to set appropriate salaries and wages for various positions. Moreover, they may be used to resolve performance problems. For that reason it is essential that position descriptions are written in a criteria-based language directly correlated to the established job functions. The manager can use the position description to clarify the tasks the employee is expected to perform.

Generally, job descriptions are needed and reviewed in the following circumstances:

- When an entirely new kind of work is required
- When a job changes and the old description no longer reflects the work
- When a change in technology or processes dramatically affects the work to be accomplished
- When employee job performances are evaluated, either during probationary periods or annually

Sometimes top performers outgrow their job descriptions. They may find more efficient ways of doing part of their assigned tasks and want more interesting or meaningful work. Some employees request updated job descriptions to support an increase in salary and benefits or a change in title.

When writing new position descriptions, managers may use existing descriptions of other, related jobs or interview staff who are currently performing some of the tasks intended for the new job. They also might ask staff members to keep a record of how they spend their time for a period that reflects a comprehensive cycle of their work. Staff with more repetitive daily activities may only need to record their activities for a week. In contrast, staff with more diverse tasks may need a month to document the scope of their duties.

Performance Standards

In addition to a position description, **performance standards** are often developed for the key functions of the job. These standards indicate the level of acceptable execution for each function. Performance standards are usually set for both quantity and quality and should be as objective and measurable as possible.

Some organizations establish measures that reflect various levels of performance. For example, one measure of a coder's performance might be coding a specified number of charts per day, perhaps no fewer than 20 charts per day. Other organizations might establish several levels of expected performance, such as the following:

30 to 35 charts per day	Outstanding
25 to 29 charts per day	Exceeds expectations
20 to 24 charts per day	Meets expectations
15 to 19 charts per day	Needs improvement
Fewer than 14 charts per day	Unsatisfactory

The following example shows how a quality standard might be used as a performance indicator of coding accuracy:

96% to 100% accuracy	Outstanding
92% to 95% accuracy	Exceeds expectations
89% to 91% accuracy	Meets expectations
84% to 88% accuracy	Needs improvement
Less than 84%	Unsatisfactory

In the preceding example, a definition for coding accuracy might be helpful. For example, accurate coding includes capturing accurate codes and sequencing them appropriately for all diagnoses and procedures that affect reimbursement.

Standards that are measurable and relevant to an employee's overall performance are helpful in setting clear expectations. They also are useful in providing constructive feedback. (See chapter 26 for a full discussion of performance standards and measurement.)

Policies and Procedures

Policies and procedures are critical tools that may be used to ensure consistent quality performance. A **policy** is a statement about what an organization or a department does. For example, a policy might state that patients are allowed to review their health records under certain conditions such as when a clinical professional is present or in the HIM department. Policies should be clearly stated and comprehensive. They must be developed in accordance with applicable laws,

and they must reflect actual practice. And because they may be used as documentation of intended practice in a lawsuit, policies should be developed very carefully.

A **procedure** describes how work is to be done and how policies are to be carried out. Procedures are instructions that ensure high-quality, consistent outcomes for tasks done, especially when more than one person is involved.

One of the benefits of developing a procedure is that time is taken to analyze the best possible method for completing a process. This analysis may begin by developing a flowchart to document workflow, decision points, and the flow required to complete a procedure. (Flowcharting is discussed in further detail in chapter 26.)

After a flowchart is completed, the steps in the process are written down in the order in which they are to be performed. When more than one person is involved in completing a procedure, each person who performs a task is documented. Anyone generally competent to perform a task should be able to complete it after reading a well-written procedure. This usually takes several drafts that have been reviewed by people who actually perform the work. Moreover, it might be useful to ask someone unfamiliar with the job to try to complete the task according to the written procedure.

Writing a procedure also offers a great opportunity to identify ways to streamline the process. Are supplies available and organized in a way that makes work efficient? Would it be faster to complete one type of task for all of the work, or should each job be completed before the next task is begun? The following rules of writing procedures help in creating procedures that are specific and directive:

- Title accurately and state procedure objective clearly: What exactly is the procedure intended to accomplish?
- Number each step.
- Begin each step with an action verb (for example, Open; Confirm; Count).
- Keep sentences short and concise.
- Include only procedures, *not* policy.
- Identify logical beginning and end points (for example, Begin, Finally)
- Consider the audience to determine the level of detail needed to accurately complete each procedure.

For example, a receptionists' initial procedure for the process of logging information requests might include the following steps:

1. Begin by opening all incoming mail daily before 10 a.m.
2. Confirm that the date on the date stamp is accurate and stamp all mail in the upper right-hand corner.
3. Sort requests for medical information into three categories: legal, medical, or insurance.
4. Count the requests in each category, clip or bind the requests for each category together, write the count on a sticky note, and place the note on the top request of each bundle.

5. Finally, forward processed external medical requests for information to the ROI coordinator by 10 a.m. for entering the request details into the ROI module of the department's computerized information system.

This example, although only the first five steps in a full procedure, shows how a detailed procedure would be useful in training a new receptionist or ROI coordinator or in providing instructions to anyone needing to perform this task in the regular employee's absence. It also highlights the fact that the receptionist would need to be trained to identify different types of information requests and the ROI coordinator trained on the ROI module of the department's computerized information system.

Several tools may be used to effectively communicate the purpose, scope, and details of the work done by employees in the organization. The procedure as written should also have any sample forms utilized in the task attached, completed, or filled out to indicate the proper processing (see chapter 26). The manager is responsible for developing and maintaining these tools. However, the manager's role does not end here. Given the tools described so far, he or she is ready to hire, train, and interact with employees.

Tools for Recruitment and Retention

Recruitment is the process of finding, soliciting, and attracting new employees. **Retention** is the ability to keep valuable employees from seeking employment elsewhere.

Staff Recruitment, Selection, and Hiring

Armed with a position description, the manager is ready to begin recruiting candidates for a new or open position. However, the manager should be sure to understand the organization's recruitment and hiring policies and to seek the assistance of the HR department before the vacancy is publicized. This preparation ensures that the organization's legal obligations and policies and procedures are followed throughout the recruitment, selection, and hiring process.

Recruitment

The first thing to consider in recruiting candidates to fill a staff opening is whether to promote someone from inside the organization or to look for candidates outside the organization. The advantage of promoting from within is that the practice often motivates employees to perform well, learn new skills, and work toward advancement. To advertise a vacancy internally, the organization might post it on facility bulletin boards or list it in the organization's newsletter or website. The department manager may announce an opening at a routine staff meeting or use any other communication channels available. Management must communicate an opportunity for promotion to all staff rather than to just the employee who is the most likely candidate. Because employees see widespread posting as a fair practice, it communicates the underlying message that internal candidates are considered first whenever possible.

When the position cannot be filled from within, however, there are several ways to advertise it externally. For example, the organization might run an ad in a newspaper, post the job on Internet recruitment sites, announce the opportunity at professional meetings, contact people who have previously applied or expressed interest in working at the organization, or work through a professional recruiter.

In most cases, the approach used depends on the nature of the open position. For example, the facility might run an ad for a scanning position in a local newspaper, but not in a professional journal. On the other hand, the facility might turn to a professional recruiter when trying to fill a department director or experienced coding position.

As in every industry, job seekers looking for professional-level healthcare positions submit detailed resumes. A **resume** describes the candidate's educational background and work experience and usually includes information on personal and professional achievements. Candidates often submit a cover letter describing the type of position in which they are interested along with the resume. Today, it is common for candidates to submit, and organizations to accept, application letters and resumes through electronic systems.

Most organizations ask every candidate to complete a formal job application. People seeking entry-level positions may be asked to complete an application rather than to submit a resume. In many cases today, completion of applications can be done online.

Selection

When a sufficient pool of applicants has been recruited, the selection process can begin. The goal of the selection process is to identify the candidate most qualified to fill the position.

Testing applicants with reliable and valid instruments designed to objectively assess the applicants' fit for the position and **interviews** are the two basic tools employed in the selection process. **Testing** is commonly conducted during the applicant's first visit to the facility. **Reliability** of a test refers to the consistency with which a test measures an attribute. **Validity** refers to a test's ability to accurately and consistently measure what it purports to measure. Testing practices are under increasing legal scrutiny, which places a special burden on organizations to ensure that tests used are clearly job related. HR professionals are generally familiar with a variety of **ability (achievement) tests, aptitude tests, mental ability (cognitive) tests,** personality tests, and **honesty (integrity) tests** that are suitable for use in the organization (Anthony et al. 1996; Buhler 2002). Many healthcare organizations also perform routine drug testing on candidates for employment in order to create a drug-free work environment.

Mathis and Jackson (2002) agree that the selection interview is generally considered the most important phase of the selection process. They also describe three effective interview formats:

- **Structured interview** uses a set of standardized questions that are asked of all applicants.

- **Behavioral description interview** requires applicants to give specific examples of how they have performed a specific procedure or handled a specific problem in the past.
- **Panel interview** includes a team of people who interview applicants at one time.

Interviewing is one of the most important skills that managers need for selecting new staff. Unfortunately, many managers receive little formal training in interviewing techniques or have little practical experience. Even supervisors and managers with many years of experience sometimes dread the interviewing process. This shortcoming can be overcome through self-education, mentoring by more experienced managers, or instructional sessions with HR professionals in the organization.

Failure to adequately prepare for conducting the interview has consequences that are very serious for the organization and the applicant. Reviewing the position description, reading the applicant's resume and application form, and preparing appropriate and relevant questions are important steps to take before beginning an interview.

The interview itself has four basic purposes:

- Obtain information from the applicant about his or her past work history and future goals
- Give information to the applicant about the organization's mission and goals and the nature of the employment opportunity
- Evaluate the applicant's work experience, attitude, and personality as a potential fit for the organization
- Give the applicant an opportunity to evaluate the organization as a potential fit for his or her current and future employment goals

EEO regulations dictate the types of questions that may be asked during interviews and on job applications. For example, questions pertaining to age, religious affiliation, and marital status should be avoided in most cases. These regulations apply during all activities associated with the interview, including during formal interview sessions and during less formal lunches or dinners or hallway and elevator small talk, when it is very easy to inadvertently lapse into discussions on these topics. Managers should always seek the advice of HR professionals when they are uncertain about which questions to ask.

Healthcare organizations, like other employers, must be certain to conduct careful background checks of potential employees. Managers or HR professionals also check the references of candidates and communicate with the past employers of candidates via telephone or correspondence. **Reference checks** or a background investigation should also be conducted specifically to assess the applicants' fit with the position and to validate the accuracy of information the applicants provide on their resume and applications and during their interviews. According to Mathis and Jackson

(2002, 73), a recent survey of employers revealed that the false information furnished most commonly by candidates for employment dealt with past lengths of employment, salary history, criminal record, and job titles.

Hiring

After all the internal and external interviews, tests, and reference and background checks are complete, the hiring manager usually has enough information to make a **hiring** decision. In some organizations, the manager shares the hiring decision with key department staff, HR staff, and executive staff, depending on the level of the position.

When the details of the job offer have been approved by the HR department, a formal job offer should be made. The HR department should prepare a letter that describes the duties and responsibilities of the position, states the employment start date, and explains the salary and benefits package. In addition, the hiring manager may choose to communicate the offer to the candidate through a personal telephone contact, which is subsequently confirmed by an official letter (Anthony et al. 1996).

Workforce Retention

It is normal to have a certain level of staff turnover. Employees move, retire, or seek other careers. A manager can do little to prevent turnover resulting from changes in the personal lives of employees. However, the actions of managers and the policies of the organization can have an impact, either positive or negative, on staff retention. The following questions should be considered:

- Does the organization support continued education either financially or through flexible work schedules?
- Do employees have opportunities to advance their careers within the organization?
- Are salaries and benefits competitive with similar organizations?
- Do working conditions provide a comfortable and safe environment?

Although individual managers may have limited influence on some of these factors, they must always be aware of the impact that broader organizational HR policies and practices have on employees. Gone unnoticed or left unaddressed, concerns in these areas are often what make employees look for other jobs. For example, employees can become dissatisfied when they feel that they are being treated unfairly or that HR practices are needlessly rigid. In some cases, employees become dissatisfied simply because they do not know the rationale for a particular HR policy or because a concern they have voiced about an unsafe condition in their work area is not acted on by the manager. The challenge to the manager is to anticipate or, at the very least, to find ways to be informed as soon as possible when employees express an HR-related concern.

Turnover and Its Impact

Staff turnover is expensive in terms of both lost productivity and recruitment and training costs. To ensure effective management, turnover should be monitored across time and benchmarked with the rest of the organization and other organizations in the community or geographic area. Routine employee satisfaction surveys can help provide information about how employees feel about their jobs and insights into how the facility might improve working conditions. Conducting routine **exit interviews** with employees who leave the organization is another way to obtain information on how employees feel about their jobs and what issues cause them to leave.

A 1998 study by Aon Consulting identified five factors that influence employee commitment to an organization (Odgers and Keeling 2000, p. 214). They include

- A fearless corporate culture
- Job satisfaction
- Opportunities for personal growth
- Organizational direction
- The company's recognition of employees' need for work–life balance

Many employees leave organizations because of their need for flexibility. As personal lives become more complex, managers must learn to permit their employees more control over their own time if they are to gain their loyalty.

Today's employees have different work expectations than their parents had. They want control of their careers and an employer that rewards them based on their performance. The "traditional" worker felt the employer was responsible for providing a career path and, in return, deserved the employee's long-term commitment to the job. Concerned with job security and stability, yesterday's worker preferred a predictable job, with some opportunity for growth, but desired direction with a small amount of creativity.

The "emerging" worker of the 21st century values growth over predictability, is concerned with opportunities for creativity, and understands that job security must be earned. Personal opportunity for growth, although it requires a job change, is preferred over remaining in a position that is stable but lacks opportunity for advancement.

The costs of hiring and training employees are quite significant. Therefore, organizations should try to minimize turnover by understanding what will retain employees.

Reasons that employees stay in organizations include

- *Culture and work environment:* Employees prefer good communication and friendly workplace relationships.
- *Compensation:* Pay should be fair, based on performance and effort required for the job.
- *Training and development:* There should be opportunities for mentoring and career growth.
- *Role of the supervisor:* A supervisor should demonstrate high performance and good relationships with staff.
- *Growth and earnings potential:* There should be opportunities for new skill development and consequent financial rewards.

Organizations need to support managers to retain employees. Pay should be fair, and job flexibility should be provided. Peer coaches may help employees work through difficulties that may cause them to leave. In addition, screening questions during the hiring process may help identify employees who have a high level of integrity and are less likely to suddenly resign.

Alternative Staffing Structures

One important benefit that can enhance job satisfaction is the ability to balance demands of work and personal life. Alternative staffing structures offer flexibility in hours, location, and job responsibilities as a method to attract and retain employees. Electronic-based health information can be managed in places and at times and by people other than those physically located in the institution. As security and technology advance, new staffing arrangements will present both opportunities and challenges for the health information manager. Alternative staffing structures are also noted in chapter 26 as methods of work design. The use of alternative staffing structures presents challenges and opportunities for orientation, training, and development of employees who do their work in remote locations, in off-peak hours, or as outsourced employees under contract. This will require knowledge of how to manage new legal, technical, and personal issues.

Flextime

Flextime generally refers to the employee's ability to work by varying his or her starting and stopping hours around a core of midshift hours, such as 10 a.m. to 1 p.m. Depending on their position and the institution, employees may have a certain degree of freedom in determining their hours. For example, an employee may be given flexibility to start any time between 6 a.m. and 8 a.m. and leave after having worked seven hours.

Compressed workweeks permit employees to work longer days and three or four days per week rather than the usual five eight-hour days. The advantages of this arrangement include increased productivity due to fewer start-and-stop periods, a reduction in commuting time, and additional days off for personal time. The disadvantages may include fatigue and a greater impact of absenteeism and tardiness.

Another option is **flex years.** With this option, employees may choose (at six-month intervals) the number of hours they work each month for the next year. Flex years are particularly attractive to parents of young children, who can work more hours during the school year and fewer hours during vacation periods, for example. In the HIM department, this may be a good option if an event such as an accreditation survey or the installation of a new computer system necessitates a heavier workload requiring more hours for a short period of time, but fewer hours later.

The advantages of flextime programs include a decrease in tardiness and absenteeism caused by taking time to handle personal matters, more productivity during the hours worked, the ability to adjust hours to the workload, and the opportunity to share limited resources across more employees and hours. Flextime programs also lessen the distinction between employees and supervisors and encourage the delegation of duties. However, such programs can be complex to administer and do not work well in situations where workers depend on the physical presence of others for interactive job responsibilities.

It is important to ensure that the flextime arrangement does not violate provisions of the Fair Labor Standards Act, the Occupational Safety and Health Act (OSHA), or antidiscrimination laws. To avoid problems, the facility's policy should be clear regarding the positions that are eligible for flextime; the work schedule should not be viewed as a reward for only certain employees. In addition, it is important to understand the impact of flextime on benefit plans, which may require employees to work a certain number of hours in a given time period. For example, nonexempt employees may have different regulations than exempt employees regarding overtime pay.

Even with its minor drawbacks, flextime appears to be a viable arrangement and, in most institutions, improves morale, encourages employee responsibility, and results in an overall increase in productivity.

Successful flextime programs have the following conditions in common:

- A person appointed to oversee the program, develop policies and procedures, and resolve differences between supervisors and employees
- A written policy that clearly states the positions that are open to flextime and those that are not
- An orientation program for supervisors when the program is first introduced or as part of a new supervisor's introduction to the organization
- A job function that will benefit from flexibility, for example, one that has high and low workloads at different time periods and one that permits the employee to work independently

Job Sharing

Job sharing is a work arrangement in which two or more people share one full-time job. For example, one employee may work mornings and another afternoons, but it also can mean working different days or weeks. A distinction must be made between job sharing and part-time work. In job sharing, one full-time job is split and all employees sharing the job may perform parts of the same project. Part-time jobs involve employees who work fewer than full-time hours and perform their jobs independently of others.

The main advantage of job sharing is that it enables organizations to attract employees who otherwise may not work because of personal responsibilities. This is an attractive option for parents and employees who want to attend school. The success of job sharing depends on the individuals in the job. They must be mature and cooperative and must want to work toward achieving the objectives of the job. Frequent communication is important regarding the status of projects or unplanned events that may alter the work requirements for a given day.

The disadvantages of job sharing include lack of continuity, particularly when one employee starts a task in the morning and another is responsible for completing it later in the day, and decreased productivity when the employees are not cooperative or fail to communicate well. Job sharing also may cause confusion for other employees or the public who have to interact with several individuals rather than one.

Telecommuting

Computer technology has created a new option for employees who work at home **telecommuting.** HIM departments have seen an increase in the number of coders and medical transcriptionists who choose this option. Telecommuting provides an opportunity for employees who cannot travel from home for reasons such as physical or personal limitations to become employed and helps resolve the problem of shortages of qualified employees in critical job functions. It is an excellent alternative for physically challenged individuals. Individuals who choose this option are employees of the institution and are covered by the same policies and benefits as those who work on-site. The employer usually provides a computer and any networking hardware and software, and the employee is required to submit a detailed time sheet of hours worked.

The advantages of telecommuting include freedom from the time, expense, and physical requirements of commuting; the ability to work flexible hours; increased productivity; lack of distractions from other employees; and an increase in personal time. Telecommuting may be offered as an incentive to retain competent employees when wage increases may not be an option. Moreover, the institution benefits from a reduced need for physical space and improved recruitment.

The disadvantages of telecommuting include employee difficulty in separating work and personal life and feelings of isolation. The "invisible" employee also creates unique challenges for the supervisor. One way to resolve this issue is to have the employee and the manager enter into a telecommuting agreement that defines the expectations of both parties regarding location, hours, equipment, and confidentiality. (See figure 24.2 for a sample agreement.) Suggested items to include in the agreement include work schedule, communication frequency and methods, goals, performance measures, confidentiality requirements, equipment maintenance responsibilities, and environmental safety requirements.

A particular issue for the HIM department is the confidentiality and security of personal health information transmitted over networks as records are sent for coding and dictation is

Figure 24.2.   Sample telecommuting agreement

Telecommuting Agreement

I have read and understand the attached Telecommuting Policy, and agree to the duties, obligations, responsibilities, and conditions for telecommuters described in that document.

I agree that, among other things, I am responsible for establishing specific telecommuting work hours, furnishing and maintaining my remote work space in a safe manner, employing appropriate telecommuting security measures, and protecting company assets, information, trade secrets, and systems.

I understand that telecommuting is voluntary and I may stop telecommuting at any time. I also understand that the company may at any time change any or all of the conditions under which I am permitted to telecommute, or withdraw permission to telecommute.

Note: The following elements are recommended specific to the situation.

1.   Remote work location:

_____

Address of employee residence or work premises

_____

Work phone number, fax number, etc.

_____

Description of work space at remote location

2.   Telecommuting schedule:

_____

On a weekly basis

_____

On a monthly basis

_____

No regular schedule (separate permission for each telecommuting day)

3.   Regular telecommuting work hours:

From _____ to _____

_____

Meal break/other breaks

4.   General description of the activities and functions to be completed by the telecommuter:

5.   Frequency of communication with company (that is, check voice mail, e-mail, etc.):

6.   Productivity requirements or expectations (if applicable):

7.   Company assets to be used at remote work location (description, ID numbers, and value):

8.   Company information systems to be accessed from remote work location (list):

9.   Noncompany services, equipment, software, and data to be used at remote work location (list):

10.   Equipment and services to be provided by the telecommuter (list):

11.   Security measures to be used by the telecommuter and expectations (virus protection and frequency of program updates, use of personal firewalls for computer, shredding company documents, etc.):

12.   Expectations for childcare for infants or young children during work hours:

13.   Obligation to comply with company rules, policies, and procedures while telecommuting:

14.   Other:

This sample form was developed by AHIMA for discussion purposes only. It should not be used without review by your organization's legal counsel to ensure compliance with local and state laws.

Source: Dougherty and Scichilone 2002.

sent for transcription. In addition, the information needs to be secured while in the employee's home, where it can be subject to physical damage or be viewed by the employee's family members or friends. The Health Insurance Portability and Accountability (HIPAA) security standards, in particular, provide specific requirements for remote access, including secure transmission, assurance of data integrity, and authentication methods.

As with flextime, clearly stated policies should be in place regarding who is eligible for telecommuting arrangements and their impact on benefit plans. Workers' compensation issues have not been fully resolved. If an employee trips in the home, for example, is this a workers' compensation injury? The answer appears to center on whether the individual was doing work at the time of the injury. The telecommuting employment option has proven to be valuable in recruiting and retaining satisfied HIM employees.

Outsourcing

In some cases, flexible job arrangements may not be an option for employees. Another solution to the problem of a shortage of qualified staff is **outsourcing.** In this arrangement, the institution contracts with an independent company with expertise in a specific job function. The outside company then assumes full responsibility for performing the function rather than just supplying staff. Thus, the health information manager's responsibility shifts from supervising employees to managing a vendor relationship.

Common functions that are candidates for outsourcing in the HIM department include transcription, release of information, and coding (AHIMA et al. 2006). The outsourcing company may perform the functions either at the institution or partially or completely off-site. Advances in communication and security technology have resulted in many home-based workers being employed by such independent companies.

The advantages of outsourcing to the health information manager include the ability to have work completed efficiently and with high quality while avoiding the problem of staff recruitment and supervision. With the increase in companies providing these services, outsourcing also can mean a reduction in cost because of competitive bidding. The advantages to the employees of outside companies include flextime and telecommuting—the ability to work varying hours, an increase in personal time, and increased morale. The disadvantages for the health information manager include less immediate control over the quantity and quality of the work, the need to know negotiation techniques, and the reliance on the vendor. HIPAA also requires special arrangements regarding security and confidentiality for outsourcing contractors.

Suggestions for successful outsourcing arrangements include

- Seeking assistance from someone skilled in negotiation when developing the contract with the vendor
- Engaging legal counsel to review the language of the contract to ensure that it complies with the HIPAA requirements
- Requiring competitive bidding for each outsourced service at regular intervals
- Establishing expectations and performance standards for contractors
- Monitoring compliance with performance standards
- Performing periodic customer surveys to assess satisfaction with the service

Check Your Understanding 24.2

Instructions: On a separate piece of paper, indicate whether the following statements are true or false. If the statement is false, explain why it is false.

1. To lead effectively, every manager should have an understanding of HR management principles.
2. Position descriptions outline the work that employees are expected to perform.
3. Performance standards are developed to indicate the time frame in which each function of a job must be executed.
4. Procedures are written explanations of how to perform tasks.
5. In healthcare organizations, individuals applying for entry-level positions must submit a resume and a cover letter.
6. The interview process is intended to give the applicant an opportunity to evaluate the organization as a potential fit for his or her current and future employment goals.
7. Staff turnover is expensive in terms of lost productivity and recruitment and training costs.
8. The use of alternative staffing structures makes orientation and training of employees much easier but hurts retention efforts.
9. What is one advantage to the employee of working compressed workweeks? To the department?
10. What is the difference between job sharing and traditional part-time employment?
11. What items should be included in a telecommuting agreement?
12. What two functions does the HIM department commonly outsource?
13. What factors help ensure the success of an outsourcing arrangement?

Tools for Staff Training

New Employee Orientation and Training

One of the key ingredients in employee satisfaction is the feeling of being knowledgeable and competent. This feeling begins with an effective orientation and training program for new employees. Just as the manager prepared for the interview and selection of the new employee, he or she must plan how the new employee will learn about the organization, the department, and the job.

Most large organizations have a formal new employee **orientation** process. This process may involve a one-on-one session with HR, group training with new employees from all over the organization, or some form of computer-based training.

In general, orientation programs in healthcare organizations address the organization's mission and vision, goals, and structure; general employment policies; employee conduct standards; communication processes; and confidentiality policies. Orientation also may include a tour of the facility and cover computer access and responsibilities. When the organization provides this type of orientation, the manager must understand the material covered and feel comfortable answering any questions or directing the new employee to the appropriate resource for follow-up.

The manager must be very patient during the employee's first days and schedule adequate time to spend with the new hire. Everyone learns in different ways and at a different pace. The first days not only establish how the employee will do the job but also contribute to the employee's ongoing relationships with the manager and other staff.

The goal of any institution's training program is to provide employees the skills they need to perform their jobs. Because employees are at different stages in their career development, the training program must be flexible and able to adapt to meet many needs. At any given time, some new employees will need to know basic information about the organization, and long-term employees will want to improve their ability to contribute at higher levels within the organizational structure. Today's workforce needs both technical skills and so-called soft skills, such as **team building** and critical thinking. For example, electronic health records (EHRs) are increasingly becoming an integral part of the healthcare work setting. Thus, whatever the primary task, most employees need to develop skills in using personal computers and related devices.

After employees have been recruited and selected, the first step is to introduce them to the organization and their immediate work setting and functions. New employee orientation includes a group of activities that introduce the employee to the organization's mission, policies, rules, and culture; the department or work group; and the specific job he or she will be performing. In addition to the basic skills needed to do the job, the employee needs to experience a period of **socialization** in which he or she learns the values, behavior patterns, and expectations of the organization.

Needs Assessment

As with all training programs, the orientation must be customized to the particular employee through **needs assessment**. New employees will require a more in-depth orientation than current employees who are starting a different position within the same institution. In a large facility, new employee orientation is usually coordinated by human resources; in a small facility, it may be performed entirely by the employee's supervisor. The orientation may consist of a brief and informal presentation, or it may be a formal program that takes place over several days on a regularly scheduled basis. Formal programs typically begin with presentations by HR and other department heads before the new employee is introduced to his or her immediate supervisor. The supervisor then continues the orientation process within the employee's assigned department.

To develop an orientation program, it is helpful to begin with a **task analysis** to determine the specific skills required for the job. The job description and the job specification are excellent sources for this part of the process. Beyond specific tasks, all new employees need to understand matters common to the institution, such as personnel policies, benefits, and safety regulations. Federal and state governments and accreditation organizations also may require certain subjects to be included in the orientation program.

Requirements

Although the orientation program is typically done at a single point in time, a new employee may not feel completely competent for as long as a year from the date he or she was hired. The program should attempt to make employees feel that they made the right choice in accepting the position. For this to happen, they should feel welcome, comfortable in their new environment, positive about their supervisor, and confident that they are learning the skills they need to do the job. An orientation program should not just be for completing paperwork.

An effective tool used in orienting new workers is the orientation checklist (figure 24.3), which helps the employer know that the employee is receiving the information he or she needs to begin the job and serves as an agenda for presenting the information in a logical manner. Rather than presenting everything the new employee needs to know all at once, it is helpful to spread the orientation over several days.

In addition, it is helpful to present policies and requirements that all employees must know, such as insurance programs, payroll requirements, and personnel policies, in an **employee handbook** given to new employees during the orientation. The handbook provides a handy reference after the immediate orientation period has ended. However, the facility must be careful not to include content that expresses or could imply conditions of an **employment contract.** If the employee views the handbook as a contract, it becomes a legally binding agreement. Employer or employee could be held liable if any conditions set out in the handbook are not strictly followed. Thus, the employee handbook must be viewed as advisory in nature and not as a legal document.

The requirements of an orientation program may be expressed on three levels: organizational, departmental, and individual.

At the *organizational level,* the orientation program provides the information that every employee who works for the company needs to know. This information typically includes

- Background and mission of the organization
- Policies and procedures that apply to all employees, such as confidentiality agreements or infection control procedures
- **Ethics training,** including how to recognize ethical dilemmas and draw upon codes of conduct to resolve problems (see chapter 13 for discussion of ethical issues concerning HIM in detail)

Figure 24.3.   Sample orientation checklist

Orientation Checklist

Supervisor _____ Date _____

Employee _____ Department _____

Before Worker Arrives

(Check off tasks when completed.)

___ 1.   Prepare other employees.

___ 2.   Have desk and supplies ready.

___ 3.   Arrange for luncheon escort.

First Day

___ 1.   Ensure attendance at hospital orientation program.

___ 2.   Review employee handbook and (if applicable) union contract information.

___ 3.   Review benefit information.

___ 4.   Review safety and security regulations, including infection control procedures.

___ 5.   Introduce to immediate associates.

___ 6.   Introduce to the workplace.

___ 7.   Give overview of the job.

___ 8.   Ask whether new employee has any questions.

Second Day

___ 1.   Discuss confidentiality policy.

___ 2.   Give job instructions.

___ 3.   Review compensation.

___ 4.   Explain hours of work.

___ 5.   Discuss attendance requirements.

___ 6.   Explain performance review.

___ 7.   Explain quality and quantity standards.

___ 8.   Encourage employee to ask questions.

___ 9.   Explain where to store work overnight.

Third Day

___ 1.   Explain telephone system, computer system, and fax and copier machines.

___ 2.   Explain reasons for rules and policies.

___ 3.   Explain insurance plans.

___ 4.   Ask whether the new employee has any questions.

Fourth Day

___ 1.   Give employee opportunity to describe how he or she is getting along.

___ 2.   Discuss departmental policies in addition to hospital policies.

___ 3.   Explain hospital continuing education program.

Fifth Day

___ 1.   Describe vacation system.

___ 2.   Explain bulletin board policy.

Sixth Day

___ 1.   Encourage employee to talk to supervisor when necessary.

___ 2.   Administer postorientation assessment.

___ 3.   Give orientation evaluation form to employee to complete.

Orientation Completed _____ (Date)

Signature of Employee _____

Signature of Supervisor _____

Source: Adapted from Keeling and Kallaus 1996, 148.

- Cultural diversity sensitivity and anti-harassment training
- Employee benefits (paid time off, insurance coverage)
- Safety regulations
- Employee orientation handbook
- Tour of the facility

At the *departmental level,* orientation information typically includes

- Departmental policies and procedures
- Introduction to other employees
- Tour of department
- Work hours
- Time sheet requirements
- Training in operation of equipment (for example, photocopying machines or computers)
- Safety regulations specific to the department

At the *individual level,* the new employee learns specific job tasks that, at a minimum, should include

- Specific, measurable objectives for productivity and performance

- An explanation of each job task by the supervisor, followed by a demonstration and an opportunity for the employee to demonstrate the task

The new employee's individual orientation is usually the longest portion of the orientation program.

Components of an Orientation Program

An orientation program should be developed with input from HR, other department heads, and the employee's supervisor. For a typical new employee in the HIM department of an acute-care hospital, the orientation program might follow the schedule shown in figure 24.3. The first portion of the program introduces the employee to the institution and is typically led by the director of education or the director of HR. The employee is given a handbook and any required forms to complete for payroll and insurance. The director of safety and security then introduces safety regulations.

To introduce the employee to the individual job setting as quickly as possible, the general portion of the orientation could be completed within the first half-day. The employee then could meet the immediate supervisor and be matched with a "buddy" to escort him or her to lunch and back to the department. Ideally, the buddy should have the same job as the new employee. On the afternoon of day one, the new worker should be introduced to coworkers, given a tour of the department, and shown his or her workstation. The first day could end with a basic overview explanation of the job's duties, including an opportunity for questions.

The individual portion of the orientation should continue as described in the suggested schedule, with some portion of each day devoted to job training and work rules so that the new employee can gradually understand the requirements of the job and become socialized to the work environment. As the new employee is trained and tested in each important aspect of the job, the supervisor should document his or her demonstrated competency. This documentation will help the organization to comply with the standards of the Joint Commission.

Orientation of Overseas Workers

The demand for health information technicians to fill positions such as transcription, coding, and insurance claims processing exceeds the current US supply. Also, pressure to reduce cost continues to mount on healthcare providers. As with many other industry sectors, US healthcare providers have discovered there are many benefits to be gained as a result of moving some of their work to employees who live overseas (often referred to as **offshoring**). Most frequently these employees are located in India, China, Pakistan, the Philippines, and the United Kingdom, where English is frequently spoken. This has resulted in some unique requirements for training.

In addition to the requirements for orientation of all new employees, orientation training for overseas workers may include English proficiency, American etiquette, and cultural differences. Specific training requirements should be included in a service agreement. For those in the United States supervising the workers, issues of **cultural competence** are essential to be addressed. For example, many Asian countries are much more respectful of the impact of personal lives of employees, which requires breaks for religious practice and other personal obligations.

Quality control is an important issue. Tasks to be performed, acceptable turnaround times, quantity and quality standards, and how the performance measures will be tracked and reported should be spelled out. It is especially important to specify accountability for confidentiality because data are at risk when they are transmitted overseas. HIPAA requirements, including those pertaining to business associate contracts, may be applicable to overseas workers and should be included.

Assessment

After the orientation process, all the participants should be asked for feedback. A form should be developed by HR and completed by the new employee. Figure 24.4 presents an example of a form for evaluating the general portion of the orientation program. Typical questions include the following:

- Was the program relevant to your job and needs?
- What part of the program was most useful to you?
- What part of the program was least useful to you?

In addition, supervisors should be asked to evaluate the effectiveness of the orientation process. For example, they should be asked for feedback on the employee's ability to apply his or her newly acquired job skills and for an assessment of the employee's comfort level with the department.

On-the-Job Training

Preparing staff to carry out the tasks and functions of their particular jobs should be an ongoing effort for both new and experienced employees. A variety of methods are available to employers. Effective training programs begin with a needs assessment and blend an appropriate combination of methods, media, content, and activities into a curriculum that is matched to the specific education, experience, and skill level of the audience.

On-the-job training is a method of teaching an employee to perform a task by actually performing it. Along with teaching basic skills, on-the-job training gives employees and supervisors opportunities to discuss specific problem areas and initiates socialization among the new employees and their coworkers. On-the-job training offers a number of advantages, including its relatively low cost compared to outside training programs and the fact that work is still in progress while the employee is being trained. However, employees may feel burdened if they are held responsible for work they do not accomplish during the training period, and the learning process may be less than optimal if the work setting is disrupted by ongoing distractions and pressures.

Training may be performed by either a supervisor or a coworker with particular expertise. The selection of an appropriate trainer is critical to the success of this method.

Figure 24.4.   Sample orientation evaluation form

Employee Orientation Program Evaluation Form

Date: _____

Job Title: _____

1. Please rate each of the following items to indicate your reaction to the session. If ranking is less than average, please comment on the back of this form.

Item	Poor	Adequate	Average	Good	Excellent

Objective 1: Applicability to your job, responsibilities, and needs

Objective 2: Enough examples and chances to practice so you can apply your new skills at work

Objective 3: Opportunity for discussion with other participants

Objective 4: Length of the program relative to its objectives

2. Which part of the program was of most value to you? Why?

3. Which part of the program was of least value to you? Why?

4a. Please use the following scale to comment on each instructor's ability to lead the program, where 1 = Needs improvement
2 = Adequate   3 = Good   4 = Excellent

Item	Instructor 1	Instructor 2
Organization/preparation of subject matter	1 2 3 4	1 2 3 4
Presentation of subject matter	1 2 3 4	1 2 3 4
Clarity of instructions	1 2 3 4	1 2 3 4
Ability to control time	1 2 3 4	1 2 3 4
Ability to link content to your job functions	1 2 3 4	1 2 3 4
Ability to stimulate productive discussions	1 2 3 4	1 2 3 4
Ability to create a productive learning environment	1 2 3 4	1 2 3 4

4b. Please comment on the instructors' abilities to lead the program:

5. How would you rate your overall reaction to the program?   1 2 3 4

6. How would you rate your level of skill/knowledge:

   a.   Before the program?   1 2 3 4

   b.   After the program?   1 2 3 4

7. Other comments:

Source: O'Connor et al. 2002.

Even though they are very capable at performing the job being taught, some employees may not be effective teachers and may omit vital steps if not motivated to do the teaching.

Requirements of the Job

The training program should begin by reviewing the job description and the job specification. **Job descriptions** and job specifications should include a list of tasks performed for a job; the skills, ability, and knowledge required; and the expected standards of performance for quality and quantity. Next, a performance analysis should be completed to assess the gap between expected performance and the employee's current performance level. In the case of a new employee, this may be verified through a written **competency** assessment. What the employee does not know or cannot do becomes the basis for on-the-job training. The requirements may include any of the following:

- Physical skills (for example, operation of equipment)
- Academic knowledge (for example, medical terminology or English spelling and grammar)
- Knowledge of institutional policies (for example, safety regulations)

● Technical skills, which may include both physical and mental skills (for example, use of computer programs)

Components of On-the-Job Training

On-the-job training offers a variety of delivery options, including

● One-on-one training by a supervisor or an experienced peer
● Job rotation
● Computer-based training
● Coaching or mentoring
● Informal learning during meetings or discussions with supervisors and peers

One-on-one training is the technique used most often. In this type of training, the employee learns by first observing a demonstration and then performing the task. For this type of training to be effective, organizations may offer **train the trainer** workshops in which the **trainer** learns skills in communication and instruction. It is important to select a person to serve as a trainer who is not only competent in the job content, but also able to teach and interact effectively with the **trainee.** One-on-one training by the supervisor gives the supervisor an opportunity to observe how the trainee is doing and to make adjustments to meet the employee's skill level. A trainee who learns quickly can move through the steps at a faster pace; a trainee who learns slowly may need an opportunity for additional practice or a second demonstration.

In **job rotation,** the employee moves from job to job at planned intervals. This method is most useful for supervisory jobs, where the employee needs to learn a variety of tasks performed by several different employees, as well as their interrelationships. In **cross-training,** the employee learns to perform the jobs of many team members. Cross training provides opportunity for competent employees to experience greater task variety in their jobs and affords flexibility in shifting resources for workload or attendance fluctuation. This method is most useful when work teams are involved.

Computer-based training, including **web-based training,** provides an opportunity to supplement job task performance with additional knowledge and simulation. It is effective in situations where repetition aids learning, for example, with medical terminology and tasks that cannot be duplicated entirely in the practice session, such as role playing with different ROI scenarios.

After the trainee has demonstrated the ability to do the job, **coaching** should continue by the supervisor or an expert peer on an ongoing basis. The experienced worker observes or reviews the work of the employee in a nonthreatening manner, offering advice and suggestions for revising techniques to improve productivity and efficient work performance. In a formalized arrangement in which a specific person is assigned to follow up on a regular basis, the coach is referred to as a **mentor.** In this scenario, the mentor meets with the trainee on a regular basis and often gives advice on career growth and development within the organization.

It is estimated that approximately two-thirds of training actually results from informal interactions between the employee and his or her coworkers. Learning occurs even though it is not formally designed or monitored by the organization, for example, during hallway conversations or on lunch breaks when a work topic is discussed and other employees or supervisors offer suggestions or corrections.

On-the-job training methods can be used individually or in combination and should be adapted to each learner. Whatever technique is used, on-the-job training should follow the steps presented in figure 24.5.

Figure 24.5. Steps in on-the-job training

Step 1: Preparation of the learner
    a. Put the learner at ease; relieve the tension.
    b. Explain why he or she is being taught.
    c. Create interest, encourage questions, and find out what the learner already knows about his or her job or other jobs.
    d. Explain the whole job and relate it to some job the worker already knows.
    e. Place the learner as close to the normal working position as possible.
    f. Familiarize the worker with the equipment, materials, tools, and trade terms.

Step 2: Presentation of the operation
    a. Explain quantity and quality requirements.
    b. Go through the job at the normal work pace.
    c. Go through the job at a slow pace several times, explaining each step. Between operations, explain the difficult parts or those in which errors are likely to be made.
    d. Again, go through the job at a slow pace several times; explain the key points.
    e. Have the learner explain the steps as you go through the job at a slow pace.

Step 3: Do a tryout
    a. Have the learner go through the job several times, slowly, explaining each step to you. Correct mistakes and, if necessary, do some of the complicated steps the first few times.
    b. Run the job at the normal pace.
    c. Have the learner do the job, gradually building up skill and speed.
    d. As soon as the learner demonstrates ability to do the job, let the work begin, but don't abandon him or her.

Step 4: Follow-up
    a. Designate to whom the learner should go for help if he or she needs it.
    b. Gradually decrease supervision, checking work from time to time against quality and quantity standards.
    c. Correct faulty work patterns that begin to creep into the work, and do it before they become habits. Show why the learned method is superior.
    d. Compliment good work; encourage the worker until he or she is able to meet the quality/quantity standards.

Source: Dessler 2007.

Training Overseas Workers

Training overseas workers on the job may be performed by a combination of remote web-based training provided from the United States and on-site group or one-on-one training. The trainer may be brought overseas from the United States or based in the country. Areas of training for overseas workers may include workshops to improve proficiency in English writing and verbal communication, medical terminology, and data quality control. Instruction in the technology and equipment related to the job, such as voice recognition technology for transcriptionists or computer-assisted coding, may be provided. For those desiring career advancement, topics such as leadership development and supervision should be added.

Assessment

By its nature, on-the-job training provides an opportunity for immediate assessment of its effectiveness. The trainer can observe the employee's skills as part of the performance try-out and can question the employee on his or her knowledge of policies, procedures, and other academic knowledge that may be required. If the assessment reveals areas of weakness, the training can be adjusted to reinforce knowledge or repeat steps performed incorrectly.

When the employee is working on his or her own, the supervisor should check the quantity and quality of the employee's work against performance standards from time to time. If the employee's performance is below standard, the training can be repeated before bad performance becomes a habit.

Finally, the employee should be encouraged to ask questions both during and after the training and should receive positive and negative feedback as appropriate.

Tools for Staff Development

Staff Development through In-Service Education

The healthcare industry grows and changes constantly. Whether it is a new law passed by the state or the federal government, new reimbursement regulations, updates to ICD or CPT codes, new or revised accreditation standards, or new **e-HIM** roles, change is a permanent factor. Preparing workers for such changes requires continuous training and retraining.

In-service education is the third step in the employee development continuum (table 24.1), which is a continuous process that builds on the basic skills learned through new employee orientation and on-the-job training. In-service education is concerned with teaching employees specific skills and behaviors required to maintain job performance or to retrain workers whose jobs have changed. Although in-service education may include external programs, it is primarily developed and delivered at the work site or through computer-based training.

Needs Assessment

The need for in-service education may be triggered by many events, including

- A restructuring of the department or organization
- Annual updates to coding or reimbursement requirements
- Implementation of electronic health records
- A decline in productivity or morale or an increase in absenteeism
- A new organizational policy or procedure

Table 24.1.   Employee development continuum

Concept	Objectives	Scope of Skill Diversity	Emphasis on Personal/Career Growth	Training Site	Frequency
Orientation training	To introduce staff to the mores, behaviors, and expectations of the organization	Narrow	Narrow	Internal	Single instance
Training	To teach staff specific skills, concepts, or attitudes			Internal	Sporadic
In-service education	To teach staff about skills, facts, attitudes, and behaviors largely through internal programs			Internal	Continuous
Continuing education	To facilitate the efforts of staff members to remain current in the knowledge base of their trade or profession through external programs designed to achieve external standards			External	Continuous
Career development	To expand the capabilities of staff beyond a narrow range of skills toward a more holistically prepared person	Broad	Broad	Internal and external	Continuous

Source: Fottler et al. 1998, 201.

- An external requirement imposed by accreditation or licensing organizations, such as an annual renewal of CPR certification or retraining in infectious disease precautions or safety procedures
- Regulatory changes, such as required by HIPAA or Health Information Technology for Economic and Clinical Health legislation

The amount of in-service education needed varies with the event and the education and experience of the employee. Downsizing or reorganizing organizational structure often causes changes in an individual employee's job responsibilities. Employees may need to learn other job functions within the work group or may even be placed in a new department. This can require a series of formal training sessions, including on-the-job training.

Renewal of training, required by external organizations, may be subject to defined content and duration, often including a test or demonstration of the employee's competence. On the other hand, implementation of a new policy or procedure may simply include distributing the information accompanied by a short meeting.

Decisions need to be made regarding the appropriate format of the in-service education. The following types of questions should be asked:

- Should the instruction be given as **massed training** in a highly concentrated session or as **spaced training** in several shorter sessions?
- Should the task be broken down into parts or be taught as a single unit?
- How will competence be assessed? Is the topic a skill that needs to be demonstrated by the learner, or is it a

level of knowledge that should be tested with a written assessment?

As with other training categories, periodic analysis of actual-vs.-desired job performance will create a list of topics that should be addressed with in-service education.

Requirements

Unlike orientation programs, which are delivered primarily at one point in time, in-service education programs need to be available on an ongoing basis. Depending on the size of the organization, some programs, such as a refresher on the response to the institution's disaster plan, may be offered on a monthly basis. The HR department may coordinate programs on topics that affect the organization as a whole. Programs specific to health information management, such as a coding update, are more likely to be developed by a supervisor or manager in the HIM department.

Finally, some topics serve the needs of more than one department. For example, a program on coding updates may be given by the coding supervisor to employees from the HIM, patient accounting, and physician billing departments. This type of program probably would take place in a more formal setting and require coordination with other department managers.

Examples of in-service education topics and the individuals within the organization who are likely to have responsibility for them are shown in figure 24.6.

Steps in Conducting In-Service Education

Presenting an effective in-service program requires planning. The time frame depends on the complexity of the material and the number of participants but should include enough

Figure 24.6. Examples of responsibility for in-service education

Organization-wide: The human resources department typically assumes responsibility for the following topics and may include staff from other departments in the planning and presentation:
- Fire and safety awareness
- Disaster plan implementation
- Infectious disease/universal precautions
- Diversity training
- Team building
- HIPAA training

Multiple departments: The health information manager may work with managers of several departments to coordinate presentation of the following topics:
- ICD or CPT annual updates
- Medical terminology training
- Use of office productivity software for employee productivity measurement
- Health record documentation

Health information management department: The health information manager may develop in-service training within the department for the following topics:
- Release of information
- Fire, safety, and disaster preparedness
- EHR implementation
- Use of new photocopier

time to prepare materials and publicize the event. Generally, a formal in-service program should follow these steps:

1. *Set objectives.* Is the purpose of the program to teach a new job task to an individual or to improve morale within the department?

2. *Determine the audience.* Is the training intended for one employee or 50 employees? Are the participants from the same department or from several departments?

3. *Determine whether the content should be delivered as a unit or in parts (massed or spaced).* This may be determined by the availability of the employee as well as the topic.

4. *Determine the best method of instruction.* The education and experience of the audience, the time available, and the cost of preparing and delivering the instruction should all be taken into consideration. Is there a qualified expert in-house? Are videotapes or computer-based materials available for rent or purchase? Is space available to train a large group at one time? (See the discussions of adult learning strategies and delivery methods later in this chapter.)

5. *Prepare a budget.* If a specific amount has been allocated, the plan should be compared to the predetermined budget and revised, if necessary. Approval should be obtained if the proposal is a new one. In addition, the proposal should include the costs of photocopying materials, speaker fees, and training resources.

6. *Publicize the program.* Flyers or electronic notices should be posted to announce the program and should include the date, time, location, topic, and a summary of the content. When it is important to know the number of attendees in advance, the notice should include a method for RSVP.

7. *If appropriate, prepare handout materials.* Handouts would include materials to be used for instruction as well as documents to reference following the program. At a minimum, an agenda of the topics and a schedule should be developed.

8. *Practice, practice, practice!* The person presenting the program should be adequately prepared and comfortable with the content. Also, a training room should be scheduled ahead of time, and any needed equipment should be checked to ensure that it is available and in good working order. Anyone planning to use a computer or a projector should know how to operate it.

9. *Use a variety of methods and be alert to your audience.* In addition to the lecture, the presenter should engage the audience through interactive questioning and activities. People learn by doing. Opportunities should be provided from time to time for questions and periodic breaks when the program lasts more than two hours.

10. *Obtain feedback from the audience.* It is important to give the participants an opportunity to document their reactions to the training. To that end, an evaluation form

Figure 24.7.   Sample in-service education evaluation form

In-Service Education Evaluation Form

To help us improve the quality of future programs, please complete the following evaluation of today's session.

Please use the following scale to answer questions 1–5:

1 = Needs improvement   2 = Satisfactory   3 = Excellent

1.   How satisfied were you with the content of the presentation?   1   2   3

2.   How would you rate the organization of the presentation?   1   2   3

3.   How would you rate the effectiveness of visual media used in the presentation?   1   2   3

4.   How would you rate the delivery of the presentation?   1   2   3

5.   How satisfied were you with the following aspects of the program?

    a.   Meeting location   1   2   3

    b.   Parking   1   2   3

    c.   Accessibility   1   2   3

    d.   Registration process   1   2   3

    e.   Meeting room setup/seating   1   2   3

    f.   Handout materials   1   2   3

6.   What is one thing you learned that you did not know prior to attending?

7.   What would you like to have learned more about?

8.   Please provide any additional comments that could improve future programs.

should be created and distributed. A sample in-service education evaluation form is shown in figure 24.7.

Assessment

Because some amount of cost, in terms of both time and resources, is usually involved with in-service training, it is important to determine whether its objectives have been met. Three methods for assessing the impact of in-service education are

- *Completion of an evaluation form at the conclusion of the program:* Immediate feedback provides an assessment of the effectiveness of the delivery methods. Is the employee energized and ready to put the material to use, or was the material overwhelming?
- *Formal or informal feedback from the employee's supervisor:* Within a few days of the program, the supervisor should be contacted to determine whether the learner has applied the new skills and knowledge on the job.
- *Follow-up with the employee at a later time:* Thirty days after the in-service program, the attendees should be asked to validate the value of the program. Are they able to perform their job better? Is there something they feel they did not learn that should have been included? This may be accomplished easily via an e-mail message.

Special Issues for Staff Development

Several issues must be considered in training programs that apply to all levels, from orientation programs to staff development.

Diversity, Sensitivity, and Anti-harassment Training

The September 11, 2001, terrorist attacks had a profound effect on training in the United States. Awareness of the impact of culture on the workforce became an important issue, yet people were afraid to discuss differences for fear of offending others. Organizations found it was important to learn about issues such as the effect of culture on communication and learning styles.

Diversity training attempts to develop sensitivity among employees about the unique challenges facing diverse religious, ethnic, and sexual orientation groups, as well as those with disabilities, and strives to create a more harmonious working environment. It is important to help all employees from diverse backgrounds feel part of the team, respected, committed, and productive and to understand how to respond appropriately to other employees, customers, or patients. The emphasis should be on learning from each other's viewpoints. Training should be provided for the entire organization, with additional specific training for management staff. Figure 24.8 emphasizes the suggested focus of a diversity sensitivity training program.

A training course about ethnic minorities might begin with a review of various cultures from a social studies perspective

Figure 24.8. The four Cs of working with diversity

- Check and test assumptions
- Communicate empathy and respect
- Create a climate of inclusion
- Challenge inappropriate behavior

Source: Bagshaw, M. 2004. Is diversity divisive? A positive training approach. In *Training for Diversity, Industrial and Commercial Training* 36(4): 156, Emerald Group Publishing Limited.

(that is, location of the country, climate, customs, or food preferences). Other topics that might be included later would be cultural norms, such as communication styles (strong eye contact or standing close when conversing), use of first vs. formal names, or tolerance of jokes. Of particular importance to the HIM employee is the perspective of some cultures on the issue of privacy, which may require that permissions be obtained to comply with HIPAA.

A booklet might be prepared about each group that provides knowledge of the culture, communication helps, and tips for nonjudgmental respect. Employees might be advised to read the material and then follow up with a discussion. When the training course has been completed, an employee advisory group might be formed to advise management staff regarding barriers and issues of concern to diverse employees. A calendar with various cultural and religious celebrations might be posted on the company intranet.

For those employees needing training in the English language and American culture, topics might include English reading and writing skills, focusing on general as well as medical terms. Interpersonal skills, customer service, and the US corporate culture also might be helpful training topics.

Employee harassment is prohibited under Title VII of the Civil Rights Act. Anti-harrassment training must cover all types of unlawful harassment based on sex, race, religion, national origin, disability, or sexual orientation. It should be included in new employee orientation and repeated periodically with other training required by accreditation or law. The trainer should be carefully chosen and should be an expert in discrimination laws. The training must be substantial to be effective (that is, the requirement may not be met by simply requiring employees to view a video). Suggested stages for diversity training include

- Anti-harassment and sensitivity training
- Cultural awareness and competence
- Development of multicultural teams
- Full inclusion of minority groups into every level of the organization

Many companies produce materials to help with diversity training, including videotapes, facilitator materials, printed materials, and cases for role playing.

Preparing the HIM Staff for e-HIM

The AHIMA e-HIM initiative seeks to promote the migration from paper to an electronic health information infrastructure, reinvent how institutional and personal health information and records are managed, and deliver measurable cost and quality results from improved information management. The AHIMA e-HIM Task Force (2003) was convened to articulate a vision for the future state of HIM, including roles for HIM professionals and an action plan to achieve the vision.

The task force recommended that HIM professionals continuously transform their knowledge, skills, and abilities to keep pace with the competencies needed for the new roles. Competencies are needed in areas such as data analysis, data integration, privacy and security, methods of encryption and deidentification, clinical vocabulary development and maintenance, and public health surveillance.

In 2011 the American Health Information Management Association (AHIMA) Board of Directors, together with input from AHIMA members and industry experts, announced the new Core Model to describe the roles and functions of current as well as future HIM professionals. The core model focuses on the following five functional areas of health information:

- Data capture, validation, and maintenance
- Data and information analysis, transformation, and decision support
- Information dissemination and liaison
- Health information resource management and innovation
- Information governance and stewardship (AHIMA 2011)

Providing training for these topics should become a focus of the HIM department's training and development plan for all employees.

Working in Teams

Team-building training helps employees learn to work in groups that have the authority to make decisions. Emphasis is on the group rather than individual achievement. Skills are taught that help members diagnose and devise solutions to problems. Exercises such as constructing items within a group encourage creativity. Conflict-resolution training focuses on communication skills needed to resolve gridlock. Facilitators may work with a group, asking group members and leaders to identify problem issues at the beginning of the session. The group then ranks the themes identified, and that becomes the agenda for problem solving. A by-product of team training is improved employee attitudes and satisfaction.

Check Your Understanding 24.3

Instructions: Answer the following questions on a separate piece of paper.

1. What are the purposes of an employee orientation program?
2. What are the three levels of an orientation program? List two items typically included at each level.
3. Who is responsible for conducting employee orientation programs?
4. What are some suggestions for making a new employee feel welcome in the new department?
5. What are two additional topics to be included in orientation training for overseas workers?
6. What are the advantages and disadvantages of on-the-job training?
7. What are two examples of skills that are often included in on-the-job training programs?
8. Which is the most common technique used for on-the-job training? What key factor is essential to the success of this method?
9. When is job rotation a useful training technique?
10. What features characterize the major steps in on-the-job training?
11. What is the purpose of in-service education?
12. List two events that suggest a need for in-service education.
13. What HIM in-service topics might be of interest to other departments? Describe at least one.
14. What printed items should always be distributed at a formal in-service program?
15. What three methods are used to assess the effectiveness of an in-service education program?
16. What is the purpose of AHIMA's e-HIM initiative, and what topics should be included in training programs to develop employees for new roles?
17. What topics should be included in diversity training programs?
18. Describe two skills that are desired as a result of customer service training.

Adult Learning Strategies

Training has been defined as the process of providing individuals with the materials and activities they need to develop the knowledge, skills, abilities, attitudes, and behaviors desired in the workplace. Learning is what occurs in the individual to achieve the changes in behavior, knowledge, attitudes, abilities, and skills that are desired. In the healthcare work environment, learning translates into achieving the goals of the institution, including improved job performance. The objective is for employees to develop effective work habits. To accomplish this objective, it is important to understand how employees learn and the factors that affect the learning environment.

Characteristics of Adult Learners

One of the most difficult tasks faced by employees is achieving balance. Ideally, people shift their time between the demands of work, the demands of home, and their own needs. Everyone wants to accomplish more with fewer and fewer hours. Although a low level of stress is positive, too much can lead to burnout. Therefore, training must be viewed as an integral part of the work environment and not as an add-on requirement. The individuals responsible for training need to understand that time is a very valuable resource.

Because time is scarce, employees need to see relevance in the activities that consume their time. They will be more willing to accept tasks that can be accomplished quickly, provide satisfaction or tangible benefits, and can be completed within short time frames.

Three fundamental concepts in helping adults learn are motivation, reinforcement, and knowledge of results.

Motivation

Motivation is the inner drive to accomplish a task. At different stages in life, adults are motivated by specific needs. Understanding that employees differ in the relative importance of these needs at any given time is important in designing a training program. For example, a newly credentialed health information technician in his early 20s with no dependents may be interested in working long hours. He may demonstrate an eagerness to devote extra hours to training that will advance his career. On the other hand, a young parent may value time to attend his or her children's school activities and want to limit time spent away from home.

Employees will be more motivated when they perceive a need for the training. The trainer should call attention to the important aspects of the job and help employees understand how to perform these tasks efficiently and effectively.

Moreover, employees should see a direct connection between the knowledge learned and the work goal. It is helpful when the trainer explains the reason for performing a task in a certain order and relates policies to objectives. For example, coders may be instructed to review a record in a specific order, beginning with a discharge summary and then lab reports. It is helpful when the trainer explains that the purpose of this process is to ensure appropriate evidence of diagnoses to comply with reimbursement requirements. Work that is interesting and challenging, and provides an opportunity for growth, provides the strongest motivation.

Reinforcement

Reinforcement is a condition following a response that results in an increase in the strength of that response. It is associated with motivation in that the strength of the response is a factor of the perceived value of the reinforcer. For example, the young parent mentioned previously who values time with his or her children may be negatively reinforced by a pay increase given after a training course when the increase requires additional work hours. However, money would serve as a reinforcer for the new health information technician discussed earlier. Reinforcement is most effective when it occurs immediately after a correct response.

Incentive pay systems are a form of positive reinforcement. For example, transcriptionists might be compensated based on the number of lines correctly transcribed rather than on an hourly rate.

Knowledge of Results

Adults like feedback on their performance. It is important to understand the concept of the **learning curve.** When a new task is learned, productivity may decrease while a great deal of material is actually being learned. Later, there is little new learning, but productivity may increase greatly. Either situation can be frustrating, so guidance and feedback are important to help employees understand what they have accomplished. In addition, it is important to explain that the employee may reach a plateau where improvement slows or levels off and that this is normal.

Education of Adult Learners

When an organization wants its workers to improve their work habits, it must demonstrate that it values the effort behind the improvements. The organizational climate must support the continued learning and growth of its employees. Some actions the administration might take to indicate this commitment include

- Providing training during work hours rather than outside the employees' regular work schedules
- Conducting the training off-site to avoid interruptions from day-to-day activities
- Compensating voluntary education with incentives such as bonuses and promotions

Adults will remember and understand material that is relevant and has value to them. Therefore, it is important to present an overall picture along with the objectives they are expected to accomplish. Performance standards should be realistic and attainable. Setting artificially high standards reduces motivation and results in feelings of frustration, anxiety, and stress. Thus, employees should feel challenged, but not overwhelmed.

Consideration should be given to the importance of motivation, reinforcement, and knowledge of results. Setting individual goals that challenge employees and satisfy their particular motivators is the ideal. Training methods that allow for the design of individualized programs, such as computer-based training or print-based programmed learning modules, should be considered. **Programmed learning modules** lead learners through subject material that is presented in short sections, followed immediately by a series of questions that require a written response based on the section just presented. Answers are provided in the module for immediate feedback.

Learning is accomplished best by doing; therefore, it is important to provide as many hands-on activities as possible. In general, people recall 10 percent of what they hear, 20 percent of what they both see and hear, and almost all of what they simultaneously see, hear, and do (Fallon and McConnell 2007, 194). Therefore, the most effective training includes a combination of verbal instruction, demonstration, and hands-on experience. Correct responses should be reinforced immediately. Recognition by the trainer or feedback about achievement may be just as effective as monetary rewards in providing reinforcement.

Adults learn better in small units because their attention span is usually not long. In addition, they want to be in control of the situation and learn at their own pace. Where possible, training should be delivered in a modular fashion over a longer period of time. The employee who learns quickly can move forward whereas the slower learner can devote more time to a specific activity.

Learning Styles

Just as there are many personalities, there are many ways people learn. It would seem appropriate, then, that the greatest amount of learning will take place if the teaching method matches the learning style of the learner. If relevancy, meaning, and emotion are attached to the material taught, the learner will learn. Learners tend to progress only as far as they need to in order to achieve their goal. Therefore, the best time to learn is when it is seen as useful, which has made **just-in-time training** popular.

Although an individual may have a preferred learning style, other approaches may sometimes be used. Learning styles are influenced by factors such as age, maturity, and experience, and they may change over time. In general, active learning is more effective than passive learning. Younger workers prefer concrete, sequential learning, whereas older adults prefer more ambiguity, which permits them to draw on their own experience. Following are various models for categorizing learning styles:

- *Sensory:* The learner may prefer *auditory* (prefers to listen), *visual* (prefers to read), or *kinesthetic* (prefers to practice) learning
- *Personality:* Various personality traits shape our orientation to the world
- *Information processing:* People differ in how they receive and process information
- *Social interaction:* Gender and social context determine learning style
- *Instructional and environmental preference:* Sound, light, structure, and learning relationships affect perceptions

Various teaching techniques may be used to address different learning styles. These include

- Individual tasks (reading, answering questions)
- Working with a partner (exchanging ideas, problem solving)
- Lecture to a group
- Working in groups (role playing, simulations)

When addressing a group with various ages and learning styles, the trainer might offer a project with broad guidelines for group completion. For example, some students might contribute text, some might create graphics, and some might build a database.

Computer technology and the advent of e-learning have offered the ability to deliver content to match a variety of learning styles. Some students may prefer to read text; others may prefer to interact with graphics or solve problems. The material can be delivered in a variety of modes in a cost-efficient manner and at a pace consistent with an individual's learning style.

Additional resources for information about adult learning are the American Society for Training and Development (2008), the association for workplace learning and performance professionals, and Workforce, an organization that provides a variety of human resources tools, including a magazine and an electronic newsletter.

Training Learners with Special Needs

Trainers should be aware of the necessity of addressing issues of diversity and disability when preparing training programs.

Diversity

Content of training programs should be developed in a culturally sensitive manner. For example, speaking in an informal, or offhand, manner may be offensive to some. It also is inappropriate in some cultures to question or challenge an instructor, or communal learning may be more valued than success of the individual. Males may be more used to dominating a discussion; females may need to be encouraged to contribute.

English as Second Language

In addition to considering cultural diversity issues when creating training programs, many healthcare institutions include employees where a language other than English may be primary, either in the United States or overseas. If the number of such employees is significant, thought should be given to obtaining materials written in the primary language. Development in English proficiency in writing or oral communication should be provided if this is needed.

Disabilities

In general, employers are required to make reasonable accommodation for workers with disabilities (Zachary 2004). This may include altering training materials, modifying equipment, and making existing facilities accessible and usable. However, companies are *not* required to train employees on equipment they are not capable of running, or for jobs where using such equipment would cause a drop in productivity.

The US Department of Education (2001) has established minimum requirements for developers of electronic and information technology to ensure accessibility for those with or without disabilities. When designing training programs for use on computer, keep in mind that adjustments may need to be made so that users with disabilities are able to use the program if it requires use of a keyboard and monitor. Some programs may be developed using voice recognition software or screen readers. Web design should be compliant with requirements of the Americans with Disabilities Act. If graphics, audio, or video are to be used, a text alternative should accompany them to be accessible with a screen reader. Options for the user to control animation, flashing or blinking objects, or color contrast should be provided, as well as an option to extend time available on timed responses.

Check Your Understanding 24.4

Instructions: Answer the following questions on a separate piece of paper.

1. What role does motivation play in developing a training program?

2. Give an example of a reinforcer other than a monetary reward.

3. Performance standards should be set higher than may reasonably be accomplished. Explain why you agree or disagree with this statement.

4. What two characteristics of adult learners should be considered when developing training programs?

5. Describe the five models for categorizing learning styles.

6. What adaptations should be made to accommodate diversity and disability issues in training?

Delivery Methods

There are many techniques for delivering training, just as there are many purposes of training. Factors that influence selection of a training method include

- Purpose of the training
- Level of education and experience of the trainees
- Amount of space, equipment, and media available for training
- Number of trainees and their location
- Cost of the method in comparison to desired results
- Need for special accommodation due to disability or cultural differences among the trainees

When the purpose of training is to increase the level of knowledge or to introduce new policies, a different method is appropriate than when the goal is to teach a hands-on skill. Training that requires a lot of room and equipment located near the employees' work area will require a different method than training that needs to be delivered across a distance. Instruction in essential skills or license requirements

Table 24.2. Location and time factors of various training methods

	Same Time	**Different Time**
Same Space	Traditional: Face-to-face meetings Classes	Work station: VCR Computer Interactive video disk
Different Space	Real-time distance learning: Audioconferencing Interactive television (two-way video and two-way audio) Satellite courses (one-way video and two-way audio) Synchronous computer communications	Asynchronous distance learning: Correspondence courses Video-based telecourses Online computer courses (computers and modems) Multimedia on demand (just-in-time)

© 2002 Michigan Virtual University.
Source: Levenburg, N., and H. Major. 1998. Distance learning: implications for higher education in the 21st century. Originally published in *The Technology Source.*
This information is reprinted here with permission of the publisher.

may justify a higher expenditure than instruction that is helpful, but not mandatory.

Table 24.2 presents the time and location requirements for various training delivery methods. Some subjects, such as demonstration of a new fire safety procedure, are best taught to a group of learners at the same time and place, for example, in a traditional classroom setting. Other subjects, such as use of computers, may be taught at a time and place convenient for employees to learn. **Audioconferencing** is a method used to train people located in different offices, but at one time. Each office can be equipped with a speaker and a transmitter, which enables learners to listen and respond to the same material presented by an instructor located at another site.

A recent trend is toward **blended learning,** using several delivery methods and thereby gaining the advantages and reducing the disadvantages of each method alone.

Self-Directed Learning

Self-directed learning allows students to progress at their own pace. It presents material, questions the learner, and provides immediate responses with either positive or negative reinforcement. Providing an employee with the opportunity to control the learning situation is a clear advantage. It is suitable for delivery to one or many employees and is a solution for employees who cannot attend sessions outside work hours because of home or family responsibilities.

Self-directed learning (sometimes called directed reading) was originally delivered via textbooks. Although computers have replaced them in some cases, textbooks still work very well at a relatively low cost. Learners are presented with text and diagrams and then respond to questions. Answers to the questions are provided on another page in the same book for easy checking and feedback. Other advantages to using texts are that they are easily portable and may be supported by other media, such as audiotapes. One disadvantage is that learners may not learn much more than the information in the traditional textbook, and the cost of development may not be paid back unless the book is used several times.

An example of a subject using directed reading is medical terminology. Text and diagrams of a body system are presented, for example, and the learner is asked to label anatomical structures and to answer multiple-choice or fill-in-the-blank questions. An audiotape may be provided to give the pronunciation of the terms introduced in the text.

The same idea can be presented using computer-based training, with the learner interacting with diagrams, text questions, or pronunciation requested via a computer program.

Computer-Based Training

Computer-based training (CBT) is a method designed to provide individual learners with flexible training at their own pace. The students must have access to a computer on which the program is installed. Similar to text-based programmed learning, the explanatory material is presented and followed by a series of questions. The text is accompanied by sounds or drawings to maintain interest and to present the material in a creative way. After each question is answered, there is an immediate response or reinforcement by the computer. In most systems, students can repeat sections of the material until they have mastered it. Students can work on different topics, at varying speeds, and in several languages. The cost of developing CBT courses is higher than classroom instruction or texts, but once developed, the cost of delivery is less because the course can be used multiple times. It is especially useful for content that does not change frequently, such as basic medical terminology or general ROI policies.

CBT is usually delivered via CD-ROM or DVD-ROM. Both provide an excellent way to deliver text, audio, video clips, and animation, and both are particularly useful for providing simulations of work situations. The advantages of DVD-ROM are a large storage capacity and high quality, with full-screen digital video.

The advantages of CBT include lower training costs, reduction in travel or time away from work for workshops, and better learning retention than with traditional classroom teaching. In addition, interactive technology has been demonstrated to reduce learning time by an average of 50 percent.

Electronic Performance Support Systems

Electronic performance support systems (EPSS) are sets of computerized tools and displays that automate training, as well as documentation, and integrate this automation with the computer application. It is true just-in-time training, providing information at the time it is needed. These systems are especially useful for complex jobs with multiple steps. An EPSS prompts the user through a series of questions, similar to a checklist. Training time can be reduced significantly through the use of an EPSS, and quality of work is enhanced. An EPSS is relatively easy to update as policies or requirements change, ensuring that the user has the most up-to-date information available.

Classroom Learning

Classroom learning is still the most popular method of instruction. It enables immediate feedback and can improve communication skills. When the goal is to train a large number of employees on largely factual knowledge within a short period of time, classroom learning may be the best choice. When the intention is to convey information, this method is effective and economical. However, it is not as appropriate for developing problem-solving skills or improving interpersonal competence.

Teaching a class used to mean using the **lecture** method in which the instructor delivers content and the student listens and observes primarily one-way communication. This technique usually involves little active participation by the learner. However, because students learn more by doing, today's classroom instruction usually combines lecture with small group discussion, role playing, student presentations, videotapes, or other means where dialogue is facilitated. Using a combination of methods has proved to be highly effective. Videotape is useful for presenting events or demonstrations not easily accomplished in lectures, such as scenarios on interpersonal communication or conflict resolution or viewing surgical procedures. The class itself may be videotaped and the videotape used to deliver the same material to other shifts or workers unable to attend the class.

Role playing is an activity where learners are presented with a hypothetical situation they may encounter on the job, and they respond by acting out the response. It is useful for tasks such as interviewing, grievance handling, team problem solving, or communication difficulties.

Seminars and Workshops

Seminars or workshops offer training over the course of one or more days and usually consist of several sessions on specific topics related to an overall theme. Some sessions are large, general classes and others are small, "break-out" classes on topics of limited interest. The cost of workshops and seminars, especially when they are held outside the workplace, is usually high because of the costs of materials, room rental, refreshments, and speaker fees. This training is typically conducted by experts on a subject and may be held in-house or offered by professional organizations, public or private colleges, or vocational schools. It is often used to develop new skills or to retrain employees whose jobs have been affected by changes in the organization, external requirements, or new policies or procedures.

Simulations

Simulations are training approaches that utilize devices or programs replicating tasks away from the job site; when computer based they are known as **virtual reality** simulations. A typical simulation provides the learner with a fictional scenario of a problem, and the learner interacts through an interface device and decides what action to take next, as if it were a real experience. These simulations are similar to playing a video game. Learning occurs in two parts. First, the learner is immersed in a true representation of an actual situation, and second, the learner is required to manage several rules and relationships involved in the process. Learning is acquired through understanding the relationships among the complex processes, or learning through exploration. Simulation is helpful for training managers or supervisors.

Distance Learning

Distance learning offers a delivery mode in which the physical classroom, the instructor, and the students are not all present at the same time and in the same location. Distance-learning systems remove barriers associated with location and timing, both individually and simultaneously. This is a particularly important issue for adult learners. In addition, distance learning supports self-directed and individual learning styles.

Methods that support different locations, but same-time delivery, include live audio- or videoconferencing or **synchronous** computer conferencing, where instructors "meet" students at the same time via Internet or intranet delivery. Delivery of courses at both different locations and times is accomplished via **asynchronous** Internet or intranet web-based courses or independent study courses offered through a combination of print-based, video, and computer-based training materials. With asynchronous delivery, instructors and students send messages one way and receive a response later, which is useful when they are in different time zones or have difficulty arranging schedules to meet at the same time.

E-learning

E-learning refers to training courses delivered electronically. Although most often used to designate web-based training, the term also may be used to refer to self-directed computer-based training, video- or audioconferencing, or EPSS. There is increased demand for online training because traditional methods lack the flexibility and broad-based delivery necessary to meet the rising demand for updated skills in many areas of healthcare.

Electronic training is most successful when

- There is a large audience to train
- Employees are geographically dispersed at several sites and work varied schedules
- Just-in-time training is required.
- The purpose is to gain knowledge or learn applications
- There is a blend of solid instructional design, instructor creativity, and proven technology

Advantages of e-learning include flexibility of class time and place, consistency of delivery, reduced time and cost of training, and the ability to reuse and easily maintain content. Drawbacks include technical problems, such as connectivity or availability for large blocks of time, and student issues with motivation or distraction. Trainers may not be available for some time, and therefore a lag may occur between the time a problem arises and the time it can be solved. Figure 24.9 shows a breakdown of frequency of common e-learning delivery methods. As mobile devices increase in use, it is anticipated that the frequency of web-based training will increase. Table 24.3 shows classroom vs. e-learning advantages and disadvantages.

Live Audio- and Video-Based Courses

With audio- or videoconferencing, employees in several locations can learn together via telephone lines or satellite transmission. Audioconferencing enables students to listen to material delivered by a presenter while looking at handout material or books. At selected points in the presentation, the instructor pauses and students interact and share comments or ask questions about the material. The advantage of audioconferencing is its relatively low cost compared to video or computer delivery. Moreover, it eliminates the time and expense of travel to the instruction site. It is useful for

Figure 24.9. E-learning delivery methods

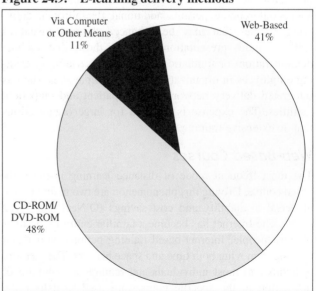

Source: Adapted from Mondy and Noe 2005, 214.

Table 24.3. Classroom vs. E-learning advantages and disadvantages

	Classroom	**Asynchronous Web-Based**	**Synchronous Web-Based**
Advantages	• High-quality delivery • Immediate Q and A	• Just-in-time training • Self-paced learning • Consistency • Training materials easy to update • Flexible time and place • Cost-effective	• High-quality delivery • Immediate Q & A • Rapid, low-cost content
Disadvantages	• Expensive • Training too soon or too late	• Motivation can be difficult • Lack of classroom collaboration • Delay in trainer response	• Higher cost per student than asynchronous • Instructor and students need to be available at same time
Best for:	• Multiple students with similar skills • Training in single location • Interpersonal skills	• Basic training • Students in multiple locations	• Basic training • Students in multiple locations • Highly interactive knowledge sharing
Worst for:	• Students of varying skill levels • Consistency across learner groups	• Observing interpersonal skills/ feedback • Real-time knowledge sharing	• Students of varying skill levels • Observing interpersonal skills/ feedback

Source: Adapted from *Workforce Management Magazine* 2001.

the same kind of purpose as the lecture method, which is to deliver specific content to a large group of people.

Interactive videoconferencing is delivered via satellite, television, or, most recently, computer and offers one- or two-way video together with two-way audio. With one-way video, students receive the image of the instructor and demonstrations and can both see and hear the presenter, but the instructor cannot see the students. Two-way video permits both parties to see each other and to interact. Improved technology is enhancing the quality as well as reducing the cost of this delivery method.

A teleconferencing network usually consists of video and audio recording equipment and a satellite service to broadcast the signal to televisions in a remote location. Videoconferencing permits additional flexibility in delivering courses that may be enhanced through visual as well as audio presentation, such as those that include demonstrations or simulation exercises. It is useful for training employees in organizations with multiple sites, such as integrated delivery networks with inpatient and outpatient facilities. The expense is justified for large organizations that do extensive training.

Web-Based Courses

The most frequent mode of distance learning is the web-based course. Driving this phenomenon are two main factors: universal availability and cost savings (O'Neal and Perez 2006). The Internet has become a familiar entity in the lives of most people. Internet-based training permits on-demand training, removing both time and space barriers. The medium is familiar to most individuals and requires a minimum of instruction in the specific courseware used to deliver the course. This method provides instruction when, where, and at

a pace suited to each learner. The instruction can be delivered in several forms.

Web-based courses can be delivered synchronously, with employees and trainers interacting via chat rooms, whiteboards, or application sharing at a predetermined time with review of materials. This closely mimics a traditional classroom setting. Another option is asynchronous delivery, where students and instructors interact through e-mail or discussion forums. It is not necessary to be online at the same time and is therefore more convenient than synchronous delivery. The discussion board format is the most frequently used, where students post comments and then review and respond at different times. Materials also can be posted for review at the student's convenience.

Software can be distributed simultaneously to students via e-mail. Students can interact with other students and the instructor via a variety of communication tools. The most common form of delivery today is to access courses developed by training organizations or universities via a website. Course authoring tools are now readily available that permit trainers to develop e-learning courses easily and quickly without professional course developers. Most rapid e-learning tools also incorporate search tools, bookmarking, and data tracking. Employees are issued a username and password to access the course. Material can be presented using a variety of methods, including text, audio, or video. Relevant material can be accessed through hypertext links embedded in the website, which students can access with the click of a mouse.

Software for delivering web-based courses is developed as **learning management systems (LMSs)** and **learning content management systems (LCMSs)**. LMSs manage the learning process, tracking grades and access, presenting the content, and collating statistics on use. LCMSs provide a technical framework to develop the content and permit sharing and reusing content. Most courseware used by colleges and universities has both components. Rapid e-learning tools can be linked to learning management systems to facilitate course development.

Intranets are private computer networks that use Internet technologies but are protected with security features and can only be accessed by employees of the organization. Many hospitals use intranets to distribute policies, procedures, and education courses on a variety of topics. Material on CD-ROM can be installed and delivered via intranets for employee self-study, as well as other customized courses for specific employee needs.

The advantages of web-based courses include the availability of the delivery medium (the Internet or intranet), which brings the course to the employee's computer at home or work, and the ability to easily update materials. Multimedia materials, including audio, video, graphics, and animation, provide an interesting way to deliver material and have been shown to result in faster learning and greater retention. They also are well suited to adult learners, meeting their needs for education on their terms of time and location. Although sometimes expensive to develop, the cost of using multimedia materials is usually less compared to the cost of classroom or seminar courses for large numbers of employees.

It is important to remember to start with an understanding of the specific performance goals to be attained with training. Using an authoring tool without good instructional design that is focused on outcomes will likely not achieve success.

Social Networks

The increasing popularity of social networking websites provides another opportunity for e-learning. These sites provide an online community where participants can share information, including file attachments, website bookmarks, or multimedia files. Web logs (**blogs**) provide a web page where users can post text, images, and links to other websites. While blogs originally started as a type of online personal diary, they are now used for a variety of purposes, including communication within organizations, and can be helpful for distributing training materials. **Wikis** are a collection of web pages that together form a collaborative website. A wiki can be modified by its users. Healthcare organizations may use wikis as a tool where trainers or supervisors can post material and employees can respond and discuss questions.

Online, **multiuser virtual environments (MUVEs)**, sometimes called virtual worlds, bring a new dimension to learning. MUVEs are accessed over the Internet and can be used to simulate a work environment. Users create representations of themselves (**avatars**) and interact with other users (Heiphetz and Liverman 2008). Healthcare organizations can use a MUVE in a variety of "soft skills" training exercises

such as interpersonal communication, decision making, and leadership. Individuals can role play to practice skills, try real-world experiences, and learn from their mistakes. Team building scenarios can be developed where avatars, working together as a team, might put together a puzzle or solve a problem. Cultural diversity sensitivity can be explored simulating prohibited inappropriate language and behavior.

MUVEs can also be used for technical training or using new equipment. Group or individual orientation for new hires in a simulation of the actual hospital or HIM department can be provided. This facilitates training of overseas workers and can be completed across different times and locations. Robotic instructors can demonstrate how to use equipment or perform procedures. "Instructors" can be asked to repeat instructions if needed, and can respond with realistic gestures, expressions, and emotion giving positive and negative feedback. Competency exams can be given through asking trainee avatars to perform demonstrations.

Other benefits of using a MUVE include the following:

- Participants can be in multiple locations, with cost savings through avoiding the need to travel to one location for training
- Hands-on, interactive learning results in faster results with higher retention
- Once a simulated environment is created, it can be stored on an organization's intranet and used repeatedly, or it can be easily changed
- The MUVE can be integrated into learning management systems

M-Learning

M-learning, or mobile learning, is an electronic learning mode in which content typically delivered via the Internet to computers can be received via personal digital assistant devices (PDAs), thereby expanding the accessibility to a true anytime, anyplace level. Issues to consider are the type of device (small handheld vs. tablet PC) and type of connectivity. Screens on a tablet PC are larger than on a PDA, permitting more information to be transmitted. Information can be downloaded from a PC to a mobile device and then accessed later away from the organization, or the device can be directly connected to the Internet via wireless connection. As with any form of e-learning, good instructional design is important. M-learning is not appropriate for very long courses with a great deal of material but is appropriate for delivering key points and short updates. It is an effective way to deliver multimedia information to a large number of people quickly. Following review of the material, participants might respond to questions or use social networking tools such as blogs or wikis, providing an interactive learning environment.

Intensive Study Courses

Intensive study courses allow a great deal of material to be compressed into a small time frame. A common example is the weekend college, where students attend 10 to 12 hours per day on Saturday and Sunday. These courses are usually delivered on a college campus or at a hotel setting and require an overnight stay. This training method is suited for teaching special skills that can best be learned in a setting away from day-to-day operations. Examples of courses include cultural awareness, training in teamwork and empowerment, and management development.

A popular exercise is to take the organization's leadership team to an outdoor setting where they learn spirit and cooperation and the need to rely on others in order to overcome physical obstacles. The process builds trust to be transferred back to the work setting.

Check Your Understanding 24.5

Instructions: Answer the following questions on a separate piece of paper.

1. What factors should be considered in selecting a training method?

2. How is computer-based training as a learning method different from self-directed learning with textbooks?

3. When is it appropriate to deliver training in a classroom setting?

4. What training obstacles are reduced with e-learning?

5. How would a healthcare organization use its intranet to deliver training?

6. Describe how social networks and MUVEs can be used for training.

7. What topics are appropriate for intensive study training?

Departmental Employee Training and Development Plan

Every healthcare organization and every HIM department have unique training needs. The level of education and experience of the employees, the tasks they perform, and the resources available will change the focus of training efforts. As table 24.1 shows, employee development is a continuum of concepts. The content, objectives, and frequency of a training program are all dependent on the specific situation that exists in an organization.

Training and Development Model

The following **training and development model** can be applied on various levels and will help an organization's HR department or a health information manager identify and fulfill the training needs of his or her employee group:

1. Perform a needs analysis
2. Set training objectives

3. Design the curriculum
4. Determine the location and method of delivery
5. Pilot the program
6. Implement the program
7. Evaluate the effectiveness of the program
8. Make changes as needed
9. Provide feedback to interested groups

The plan should be approved and supported by upper management. Implementing a training program requires a substantial investment of time, money, and personnel. Developing a curriculum based on a systematic evaluation of needs is a much wiser investment than creating a program around the latest hot topic.

Perform a Needs Analysis

The needs analysis is critical to the design of the plan. This approach typically focuses on three levels: the organization, the specific job tasks, and the individual employee. The outcome of the needs analysis is an understanding of where training is needed in the organization (entry level, remedial, or management development), based on the firm's strategic mission and goals. In addition, a list of the tasks to be learned at each level (based on the job description and the job specification and the specific skills and knowledge required) and an analysis of the deficiencies in knowledge and skills between the desired level and the current level of employees are completed.

This information can be obtained through observation, employee and manager interviews, surveys, tests, and task analysis of the job descriptions and job specifications.

Set Training Objectives

After the needs have been established, specific, measurable training objectives should be set. Objectives specify what the employee should be able to accomplish upon completion of the training program. These are based on the deficiencies that have been identified between the desired and current performance levels. It is important to set objectives before starting the program so that the results can be evaluated following completion of training.

Design the Curriculum

The curriculum is the subject content of the program that will be taught, including the sequence, activities, and materials. A budget needs to be prepared that identifies costs and available resources. Are there individuals within the organization who can develop and teach the program, or is it necessary to purchase an externally prepared program? Do materials such as videotapes or computer-based modules need to be produced? Do printed materials need to be developed and reproduced? Will the program be available over the Internet?

After these decisions are made, the curriculum must be organized into a program that supports adult learning and the stated objectives. All program elements need to be carefully prepared to ensure quality and effectiveness.

Determine the Location and Method of Delivery

Where and when the program should be delivered is an important part of the training plan. When space is available and the instructor and materials are available internally, a classroom setting might be suitable. On the other hand, when employees work over several shifts and days or in remote locations, computer-based CD-ROMs and web-based delivery might permit the employee to more readily achieve the training objectives.

Pilot the Program

It is important to validate the program by introducing it to a test audience. When computer technology is part of the program delivery, all computer programs should be tested to make sure they work with a variety of hardware and web browsers. Following completion of the program by a few employees, feedback should be obtained and the program revised, if necessary.

Implement the Program

The tested program now can be given to the entire audience for which it has been developed. When necessary, train-the-trainer workshops should be conducted for instructors who may not have formal training experience.

Evaluate the Effectiveness of the Program

Two issues should be addressed in evaluating training programs. The first is selecting the method of evaluation; the second is identifying the outcomes that will be measured.

Evaluation is most frequently assessed using a survey (refer to figures 24.4 and 24.7). Opinions obtained immediately after the training, and again after a period of time, are valuable in assessing the effectiveness of the program for both trainees and managers. In addition, pretests and posttests help identify the level of knowledge or skill that has actually been learned.

When possible, an excellent method for evaluating the training program is to conduct a controlled experiment. A control group that receives no training is compared to a group that received training. Data are obtained from both groups before and after training. It is then possible to determine the extent to which the training program caused a change in performance in the training group.

Four outcomes can be measured in evaluating effective training programs:

- *Reaction:* What is the reaction of the trainees immediately after the program? Are they excited about what they learned?
- *Learning:* What have the trainees actually learned? Can they now use a new software program?
- *Behavior:* Have supervisors noticed a change in employee behavior? Has morale improved?
- *Results:* How does the actual level of performance compare with the established objectives? Can the employees assign codes more accurately?

Make Changes as Needed

When the results of the evaluation show less-than-expected results, it is important to determine where changes may be helpful. This may include a change in the materials, the location or time of program delivery, or the subject content. In any case, it is important to adjust. A program that is not meeting the desired objectives is costly.

Provide Feedback to Interested Groups

After tallying the results of the evaluations and making any adjustments that are needed, it is important to provide feedback to the course developers, the managers and supervisors of the involved departments, and the trainees. Communication is vital to maintaining interest in and support for the training program. Feedback demonstrates a desire to respond to the needs of everyone involved in this important activity.

Tools for Effective Communication

Maintaining regular and effective communication with staff is one of the ongoing challenges in managing human resources. Communication is very important because it contributes significantly to the morale of the staff and their ability to contribute to the department's operations as a whole. To address this challenge, a manager should establish a **communication plan** that includes routine and timely opportunities for both verbal and written information sharing within the department or work group. The plan should include, at minimum, the following types of communication:

- Daily personal contact with every employee to maintain a sense of connectedness and, as necessary, to create opportunities for casual discussions of emerging work-related changes or issues
- Web-based or traditional bulletin boards located in an area convenient to staff to publicize official announcements, permissible personal news, written status updates, and written highlights from departmental meetings
- Weekly status meetings with the staff for each functional unit in the department in larger organizations or the entire department in smaller organizations
- Monthly departmental meetings with highlights recorded for posting
- Quarterly performance discussions with individual employees
- Ad hoc verbal or electronic (e-mail) status updates, as appropriate, to alert staff to information of interest from organizational meetings

On a day-to-day basis, when problems emerge that require resolution within the department or when decisions are made that affect the employees in the department, the management team is responsible for establishing a unique communication plan that conforms to the situation. Such a plan identifies the full range of employees affected by the problem or the decision and defines the specific approach that managers will take to engage or inform each person appropriately.

In general, keeping staff well informed is a key factor in developing and sustaining a healthy level of trust in the relationship between employees and managers. Communication plans are simple tools that managers can use to ensure that this critical aspect of their responsibilities is handled with the level of routine and regular attentiveness it requires.

Tools for Employee Empowerment

Creating an environment that encourages and allows employees to use and develop their problem-solving and decision-making competencies is an established HR management practice that has many benefits. For example, it increases the manager's capacity and productivity, improves the quality and timeliness of decision making, enhances employee morale, and contributes to improved employee retention.

Empowerment

Empowerment is the concept of providing employees with the tools and resources to solve problems themselves. In other words, employees obtain power over their work situation by assuming responsibility. Empowered employees have the freedom to contribute ideas and perform their jobs in the best possible way. The idea of empowerment actually began as part of total quality management programs, which many organizations initiated in order to improve the quality of service provided to customers and to increase their competitiveness in the marketplace. A high-quality organization strives to understand and improve work processes in order to prevent problems.

Healthcare organizations that empower their employees believe that all employees can perform—and truly want to perform—to their highest potential when given the proper resources and environment. Because they perform jobs on a regular basis, they are intimately familiar with the steps in the process. What the employees may lack are skills in analysis and problem solving. Training sessions in skills such as data analysis, use of control charts, or flowcharting will help employees to identify problems, develop alternatives, and recommend solutions.

To perform effectively, employees also need to be given responsibility, authority, and the trust to make decisions and act independently within their area of expertise. Figure 24.10 offers suggestions on how managers can empower their employees.

Empowered employees are less likely to complain or feel helpless or frustrated when they cannot resolve a problem on their own. Moreover, they are more likely to feel a sense of accomplishment and to be more receptive to solutions that they develop themselves. In addition, they tend to demonstrate commitment and self-confidence and to produce high-quality work.

Figure 24.10.   How to empower employees

- Get others involved in selecting their work assignments and the methods for accomplishing tasks.
- Create an environment of cooperation, information sharing, discussion, and shared ownership of goals.
- Encourage others to take initiative, make decisions, and use their knowledge.
- When problems arise, find out what others think and let them help design the solutions.
- Stay out of the way; give others the freedom to put their ideas and solutions into practice.
- Maintain high morale and confidence by recognizing successes and encouraging high performance.

Source: Schermerhorn 2005, 328.

One disadvantage that is frequently mentioned by managers is that empowerment involves too much time for meetings and discussion and takes employees away from the "real work." Actually, it is much more efficient to take the time necessary to prevent problems than to solve them after they occur. In the long run, empowered employees work more efficiently and productively.

Indeed, some managers are afraid to share power. They feel that they have worked hard to gain the power they have and are reluctant to give it up. But the manager who empowers others usually increases his or her own power because a high-performing unit reflects the manager's expertise.

An example of empowerment in the HIM department would be to train ROI employees to solve a slow turnaround issue. The employees are probably more aware than the supervisor of problems that prevent them from filling requests for information (missing charts, insufficient fees, and incomplete records). With proper training in brainstorming and flowcharting, as well as a supportive environment, the employees may be able to develop a procedure that can be performed differently to prevent delays.

Delegation

Delegation is the process of distributing work duties and decision making to others. To be effective, delegation should be commensurate with authority and responsibility. A manager must assign **responsibility,** which is an expectation that another person will perform tasks. At the same time, **authority,** or the right to act in ways necessary to carry out assigned tasks, must be granted. An employee cannot be expected to perform a job for which he or she is not given authority to obtain resources. Authority should equal responsibility when work is delegated. Finally, **accountability** must be created, which is the requirement to answer to a supervisor for results. An employee must be empowered to act, given the necessary tools and skills, and held accountable for the quality of his or her work.

Figure 24.11. Ground rules for effective delegation

- Carefully choose the person to whom you delegate.
- Define the responsibility; make the assignment clear.
- Agree on performance objectives and standards.
- Agree on a performance timetable.
- Give authority; allow the other person to act independently.
- Show trust in the other person.
- Provide performance support.
- Give performance feedback.
- Recognize and reinforce progress.
- Help when things go wrong.
- Don't forget *your* accountability for performance results.

Source: Schermerhorn 2005, 264.

Successful delegation includes

- Assigning responsibility
- Granting authority
- Creating accountability

Guidelines for delegating are presented in figure 24.11. As an employee development tool, delegation can provide employees the opportunity to try new tasks previously performed by someone in a higher position and leads to empowerment because employees are given the opportunity to contribute ideas and fully utilize their skills. At the same time, the manager should remain available to provide assistance and support.

Sometimes managers have difficulty delegating because they feel that only they can do the job correctly. In other cases, they feel threatened by the idea that another employee can do their tasks and perhaps do them better. This thinking can lead to poor morale and result in talented employees leaving the organization. In addition, it can lead to managers being overburdened with work that could be done by others and to employees being denied opportunities to learn new skills.

In some situations, employees may be unwilling to accept delegated responsibilities when they feel that they are unqualified to do the tasks or that they are being dumped on. Dumping can involve assigning an employee unpleasant or unpopular work that seems to have little value or asking an employee to take on work in addition to an already demanding workload. This results in resentment or anger. Employees may feel this way when they have a poor working relationship with their supervisor, know that others have refused the same task, or have been taken advantage of in the past.

To avoid these problems, employees should be selected who are either competent to perform the tasks or willing to undergo the necessary training. People are more willing to accept tasks that they understand, have a choice in doing, and recognize value added to the organization and their personal growth. Managers should set checkpoints, monitor how the delegate is doing, and allow the opportunity for questions and feedback.

Delegation is a skill that matches the right employee with the right task. It requires communication, support, and an environment that fosters risk taking. It is essential in order to identify and develop successors and is important if a manager wishes to provide a path for herself to advance in the organization. Effective delegation actually leads to a more efficient and productive department overall and mutually benefits the manager, the employee, and the institution.

Coaching and Mentoring

Both new employees and experienced employees who may be ready for a change can benefit from coaching or mentoring. As discussed earlier in this chapter, coaching is an ongoing process in which an experienced person offers performance advice to a less experienced person. However, coaching goes beyond teaching. A good coach is also a counselor, a resource person, a troubleshooter, and a cheerleader. Coaches deal with improving attitudes, morale, and career development in addition to giving instruction in specific tasks.

Effective coaches are dedicated leaders who display a high level of competence and are able to push or pull employees to their highest level of performance. They are role models who set a good example; show workers what is expected and how to get the job done well; provide praise or constructive feedback, where appropriate; and are ready to help with routine work alongside the employee, if necessary. Department managers are well positioned to share their knowledge and expertise of the job they manage.

Coaching starts with orientation of the new employee and continues throughout his or her time with the organization. The more time the coach spends walking around observing and listening to employees, the more opportunities there will be to support, praise, and offer advice.

Helping employees should be done in a manner that encourages self-sufficiency. For example, when an employee comes forward with a problem, a good coach does not simply give the answer but, rather, asks the employee for suggestions. In other words, the coach's response should be "What do you think?" rather than "Here's what you should do."

Coaches defend and support their employees. They are facilitators who remove obstacles and obtain resources to enable and empower their staffs. It is important to praise performance above and beyond the expected, for example, when the employee completes a task ahead of schedule or offers to help a colleague. It is equally important to praise the worker who consistently meets objectives or improves in an area that was below standard, in other words, for doing what is expected. To be effective, both positive and negative feedback must be timely, specific, and in the right setting (privately or publicly, depending on the circumstance). Good coaches direct negative feedback at the behavior they wish to correct, not at the person.

However, coaching can be done poorly. This happens when criticism is overused or praise is undeserved. In addition, the approach needs to be adjusted to the employee.

Good coaching takes time to allow flexibility and encourage the employee to perform correctly without jumping in too quickly with advice.

Mentoring is a form of coaching. A mentor is a senior employee who works with employees early in their careers, giving them advice on developing skills and career options. Several employees may be assigned as protégés to the mentor, but contact is usually one-on-one. Through the mentoring relationship, employees have an advisor with whom they can solve problems, analyze and learn from mistakes, and celebrate successes. Many organizations have formal mentoring programs where protégés are matched with potential mentors. Other managers voluntarily offer to work with up-and-coming employees.

Mentors share their knowledge of management styles and teach prospective supervisors specific job or interpersonal skills. They may assign challenging projects that allow employees to explore real-life learning experiences while still under the guidance of an experienced teacher.

Mentoring is helpful in teaching diversity tolerance. In **reverse mentoring,** an employee from a minority group will provide mentoring to management staff, sharing his or her day-to-day perspectives and providing cultural awareness to the managers.

Successful mentoring depends on effective interaction between mentor and protégé. Mentors must be chosen who enjoy passing on their experience and knowledge to others.

Promotion

Promotion may be another tool to encourage employee development and commitment. When tied to training programs, it can become a powerful incentive. **Promotion** usually refers to the upward progression of an employee in both job and salary. However, it also can mean a lateral move to a different position with similar job skills or to a change within the same job as a result of completing higher education or credentialing requirements. To attract, retain, and motivate employees, organizations should provide a career development system that promotes from within.

When tied to promotion, career development programs offer an incentive to ambitious employees. Goals can be incorporated into the performance review process. In the HIM department, clerical employees can be encouraged to take classes that would lead to an associate's degree in health information technology or a bachelor's degree in health information administration, making them eligible for certification exams. In addition, employees may be encouraged to enter coding certificate programs and achieve coding certification.

The higher the status of the person in the organization, the more likely it is that promotion will work as a motivator. To improve employee performance, promotion should be awarded based on competence, not on seniority. In some organizations, union contracts emphasize seniority and thus restrict the organizations' ability to use competence as a sole criterion.

Promotion based on performance is usually measured by appraising past performance against standards. However, past performance does not always predict future potential. Some organizations use testing instruments to assess this capability.

Succession planning is a specific type of promotional plan in which senior-level position openings are anticipated and candidates are identified from within the organization. The candidates are given training through formal education, job rotation, and mentoring so that they can eventually assume these positions.

To be effective, promotion criteria should be published in a formal policy and procedure, which usually includes job postings of open positions, so that all employees have the opportunity to apply for consideration. When promotions appear to be given to favored employees, or when the procedure is shrouded in secrecy, promotion ceases to be attractive.

Incentive Programs

Voluntary employee turnover can be disruptive to an organization. Both high and low performers are more likely to leave than are average performers. It is important to try to retain high performers. The usual way to do this is through a **pay for performance** system. In order for these systems to be successful, it is important for the employee to make a connection between pay and performance. Incentive plan effectiveness is affected by differences in employee personalities and values. Each person is motivated by different needs, and none will pursue rewards they do not find valuable. Therefore, an effective incentive program links effort directly to a reward, and the reward must be valued.

Rewards may be in the form of pay or other items, such as vacations, flexible work hours, prizes, or recognition on a plaque or bulletin board, or in a personal note. One reward system allows employees to select a reward from a catalog or website, allowing the employee to select something they value.

Incentives may be given based on the following structures:

- Pay for item completed (lines transcribed, charts coded)
- Pay based on success of a team achieving goals (this encourages collaboration, but high-performing individuals are not recognized)
- Pay based in part on the individual and in part on team performance
- Pay based on a standard rate plus premium if productivity exceeds the standard
- Merit pay given annually as a salary increase

An incentive plan may fail if it appears there is an emphasis on quantity without an associated focus on quality, or if the reward is not valued (such as increased pay given to an employee who would rather have time off). Finally, incentive programs must be accompanied with effective management.

The best incentive programs demonstrate that effort must be instrumental in obtaining the reward. Under the control of the employee, employees should support and value the plan, and employee goals should be SMART—specific, measurable, attainable, relevant, and timely.

Continuing Education

Continuing education (CE) is a requirement of most professionals, including those in HIM. It usually requires a person to complete a certain number of hours of education within a given time period to maintain a credential or license status. Accrediting organizations, such as the Joint Commission, also include CE in their standards. The HIM field is changing rapidly, primarily in the areas of technology, e-HIM, and legal and regulatory requirements. It is important that credentialed professionals remain current in their knowledge of the profession so that they can provide high-quality skills to the organizations for which they work.

CE refers to keeping up with changes in the profession or to improving skills required to perform the same job. It is different from career development, which is geared toward preparing an individual for a new job. Sometimes this line is blurred. In HIM, management development programs may be essential for the current position when one is already a supervisor, for example. On the other hand, preparing a technical employee to assume a new management role would be considered career development. Some organizations have tuition reimbursement policies to encourage career development.

CE programs are most often provided by external organizations, such as AHIMA or its component state associations. Career development, by contrast, usually includes a combination of job rotation through progressively increasing job responsibilities in-house and externally taught formal classes and workshops.

As part of the formal performance appraisal process, CE goals should be set for all employees. A record should be kept in the employee's personnel file that indicates the number of CE hours earned as well as the topic, place, and person who provided the education. Management should support the individual's achievement by providing time off to attend workshops, flexible scheduling for formal classes offered at educational institutions, and financial reimbursement.

CE programs are delivered via many different formats to suit the individual learner. These include classroom as well as computer-based modules or web-based courses that all employees can access, regardless of where they live or their personal or physical limitations. Continued skill development should be an important requirement for all HIM employees.

Team Building

Most people today want to work collaboratively with others, thus, the need for **team building.** The team may consist of people who perform the same function within the same department, for example, a coding team. The team may bring together people who perform different functions within the same department to solve a shared problem or people from across the organization with different expertise to implement a new computer system or to study an issue that would affect the overall organization (for example, improvements in the employee evaluation system).

At their best, teams increase the creativity and improve the quality of problem solving. Often team-based decisions are more widely accepted than managerial decisions because team members enlist support for the decisions from their peers and coworkers. In addition, teams can use their collective energy to produce more work than individuals can. Moreover, teamwork establishes strong relationships among employees. Teamwork also can enrich jobs and provide variety in work assignments. Finally, teams can develop new leaders and expose employees to issues that would not be within the usual scope of their jobs.

One thing that binds team members together is having a common purpose. The purpose for an ongoing work team, for example, might be to ensure cross-training, improve procedures, and monitor quality and productivity. In other cases, teams are created for a specific purpose. Some teams exist for long periods of time because they have an ongoing reason to exist. Other teams function for limited periods of time and disband after their purpose has been fulfilled.

However, having a common purpose is only one element of an effective team. The team also must have an effective leader. This individual must be able to create agendas and organize meetings, lead discussions, and ensure that the work moves forward. The team may either appoint or elect its leader, depending on its purpose and the experience and expertise of its members.

In addition, effective teams set ground rules. For instance, team members might decide that all meetings will start on time, minutes will be recorded, decisions will be reached by consensus, and everyone will participate in discussions. The early establishment of rules can reduce conflict as the team moves forward. Teams work through the same type of decision-making process described earlier in this chapter. However, their strength lies in engaging the collective brainpower of all of their members, and so the team leader should use techniques that effectively engage every member of the team.

Not all teams are effective, and the causes for problems vary. For example, a team without a clear purpose could create a product that does not accomplish the work it was designed to accomplish. A leader who dominates the team could reduce its effectiveness and frustrate its members. Members who do not participate, have insufficient expertise, or are unconcerned with the team's success could cause the team to fail. And members who work outside the team or do not support its decisions can create dissension and reduce support for the outcome.

Managing staff teams is an important aspect of every manager's responsibilities. Careful consideration should be given to developing the team's purpose and composition. Team members need to feel that their work is important and that their contributions make a difference. A well-run team can be an effective and productive force. A poorly run team can waste time and frustrate and demoralize its members.

Delegation of Authority

Managers have specific responsibilities and the authority to act within the scope of those responsibilities. A manager's responsibilities can never be delegated to another person; that is, the manager always remains the one accountable for outcomes in areas within his or her designated scope. However, with appropriate preparation and decision-making guidelines in place, managers can and should delegate the authority to make and act on decisions to employees as individuals or teams. **Delegation of authority** expands the manager's capacity, improves the timeliness of decisions, and develops the competencies of other staff members.

When delegating authority, managers make it possible for staff to succeed by preparing them in advance as follows:

- Explaining exactly what needs to be done
- Describing clear expectations
- Setting clear deadlines
- Granting authority to make relevant decisions
- Ensuring appropriate communication and outcomes reporting
- Providing the resources needed to complete the assigned task

Check Your Understanding 24.6

Instructions: Answer the following questions on a separate piece of paper.

1. What are the steps in a typical training and development plan?

2. What are the three outcomes of a needs analysis?

3. What is the relationship between setting objectives and evaluating a training program?

4. What are three items to consider in designing a training program?

5. What are four outcomes that should be measured in program evaluation?

6. In what three ways can managers empower employees?

7. What two reasons might managers have for not empowering employees?

8. How are the concepts of delegation and empowerment related?

9. What three actions must be done for effective delegation?

10. When might an employee resist accepting delegated responsibilities?

11. What are the basic characteristics of effective coaches?

12. How does mentoring differ from coaching? How is it similar?

13. On what should promotion be based if it is to motivate?

14. Why do incentive programs fail?

15. Why do HIM professionals need continuing education?

Compensation Systems

Employee compensation systems basically serve to reward employees equitably for their service to the organization. Organizations also use compensation systems to enhance employee loyalty and encourage greater productivity.

The FLSA, the EPA, and several of the EEO laws (for example, Title VII of the Civil Rights Act, the Age Discrimination in Employment Act, and the ADA) all have provisions that affect compensation systems. Provisions of the FLSA, for example, cover minimum wage, overtime pay, child labor restrictions, and equal pay for equal work regardless of sex. Federal regulations specify exemptions from some or all of the FLSA provisions for a number of groups of employees (Myers 2011). These groups are referred to as **exempt employees.** Covered groups are referred to as **nonexempt employees.**

Managers who control employee work schedules and process employee timecards at the close of each pay period become quite familiar with the provisions of the FLSA that relate to overtime pay. In general, the FLSA requires that employers pay time and a half for all hours that covered (nonexempt) employees work in excess of 40 per week. Some organizations institute overtime pay for all worked hours in excess of eight hours per day. In calculations of worked hours, the FLSA specifies that rest periods of up to 20 minutes each be counted as worked time, but meal periods of 30 minutes or more are not counted as worked time. Time spent in mandated job-related training is considered worked time, and significant travel time (beyond the usual time required to commute to and from work) associated with a work-related event is counted as worked time. Compensatory time, taken in lieu of overtime pay, may be used when it is part of the organization's compensation plan (Myers 2011).

Because of the complexities and sensitivities associated with compensation issues, HR professionals are a manager's best advisor when questions related to compensation regulations and practices arise.

Compensation Surveys

The HR department routinely consults compensation surveys published by government agencies and professional and trade associations. In some cases, an HR department may choose to conduct an independent survey to obtain data more specific to the organization's needs. Often consultants experienced with survey design and data analysis are employed by the organization to either assist in or do the survey project to ensure a successful outcome from this costly activity. Compensation surveys provide benchmark data that the organization can use to evaluate or establish its compensation system for unique jobs within the organization or for jobs throughout the organization (Myers 2011).

Job Evaluations

Job evaluation projects are undertaken by an organization to determine the relative worth of jobs as a first step toward establishing an equitable internal compensation system. Job evaluation is the process of applying predefined compensable factors to jobs to determine their relative worth (Myers 2011, 691). Myers defines a **compensable factor** as "a characteristic used to compare the worth of jobs" and adds that "the EPA requires employers to consider [several] compensable factors in setting pay for similar work performed by both females and males." These factors include skill, effort, responsibility, and working conditions.

Four job evaluation methods are commonly used:

- **Job ranking** is the simplest and the most subjective method of job evaluation. It involves placing jobs in order from highest to lowest in value to the organization.
- **Job classification method** involves matching a job's written position description with a description of a classification grade. Jobs in the federal government are graded on the basis of this method of job evaluation.
- **Point method** is a commonly used system that places weight (points) on each of the compensable factors in a job. The total points associated with a job establish its relative worth. Jobs that fall within a specific range of points fall into a grade associated with a specific wage or salary.
- **Factor comparison method** is a complex quantitative method that combines elements of both the ranking and point methods. Factor comparison results indicate the degree to which different compensable factors vary by job, making it possible to translate each factor value more easily into a monetary wage (Mathis and Jackson 2002).

In recent years, the **Hay method of job evaluation,** officially known as the Hay Guide Chart-Profile Method of Job Evaluation, has been used extensively. It is adaptable to many types of jobs and organizations and is easy for individuals within organizations to learn to use. The method is essentially a modification of the point method that numerically measures the levels of three major compensable factors—skill, effort, and responsibility—and the working conditions of each job (Myers 2011; Mathis and Jackson 2002).

Performance Management

Most organizations use some form of **performance review** system to evaluate the performance of individual employees. Although performance reviews should be a part of regular communications between managers and employees, formal performance review discussions are routinely held on an annual or biannual basis. The functions of performance reviews include the following:

- Assessment of the employee's performance compared to performance standards or previously set performance goals

- Development of performance goals for the future year
- Development of a plan for professional development

Reviews also may include employee self-assessments. In some organizations, other employees may contribute information to the reviews of colleagues and coworkers. In the case of a supervisory manager, his or her staff may participate in the evaluation. This form of evaluation to which managers, peers, and staff contribute is called a **360-degree evaluation.**

Many organizations' base pay increases on the results of annual performance reviews. Whether or not the evaluation affects salary, the annual review is an opportunity to formally discuss past accomplishments, career development, and expectations for future performance.

Periodic Performance Reviews

Performance management is an ongoing challenge. Information about performance should be collected regularly and shared with employees, whether their jobs involve coding clinical records or directing a department. Good performance results should be shared to encourage and reward ongoing success.

Performance issues are rarely resolved by ignoring them. Understanding the causes of problems and working with employees to resolve them are important management tasks. Actions that can be taken to improve performance include retraining, streamlining responsibilities, reestablishing expectations, and monitoring progress.

Performance Counseling and Disciplinary Action

When actions taken to improve performance are unsuccessful, more formal counseling and even **disciplinary action** may be required. Most organizations have formal processes in place to ensure that all staff are treated fairly and that employment laws are followed. Managers should consult with the HR department to ensure that any disciplinary actions comply with approved procedures.

The steps described in establishing performance standards, hiring and training employees, and conducting routine performance reviews are all necessary before doing **performance counseling** or taking disciplinary action. Moreover, steps to improve performance should be taken in all cases.

Performance counseling usually begins with informal counseling or a verbal warning. No record of these actions is maintained in the employee's file.

The **progressive discipline** process begins with a verbal warning. When a second offense occurs, the process progresses to a written reprimand with formal documentation of the problem and delineation of the steps needed to correct it. Employees may be required to submit a step-by-step action plan to resolve issues and improve their performance. A third offense results in suspension, and a fourth offense generally results in dismissal.

In some environments, disciplinary actions include suspension from employment without pay or demotion to a job with lower expectations and less pay. In some cases, more than one of these actions may be taken. Generally, however, suspension and demotion are less popular than the use of binding performance improvement plans because suspension and demotion create a punitive atmosphere. Such punitive actions also affect the morale of other employees and staff. Empowering employees to create a plan of action places the responsibility for performance improvement in their own hands.

Regardless of the counseling and disciplinary actions mandated by the organization, managers should take some key steps of their own, including

- Discussing performance problems and consequences for poor performance with the employee in a clear and direct manner
- Supporting the employee's efforts to improve performance or resolve performance issues
- Documenting the steps taken to improve performance
- Carefully following the organization's HR policies
- Consulting HR professionals before taking action
- Keeping performance issues confidential
- Following the same process for all employees

Termination and Layoff

One of the most difficult duties of a line manager is delivering the actual notification of **termination** to an employee. The HR department is a vital resource for advising and supporting the manager through this process to ensure that accepted HR practices as established by the organization are adhered to. Buhler (2002) presents these simple, general guidelines:

- State your position and end the discussion
- Be sensitive to appropriate timing for the discussion
- Be prepared with all of the appropriate severance information
- Treat the employee with dignity and respect

Layoffs are essentially unpaid leaves of absence initiated by the employer as a strategy for downsizing staff in response to a change in the organization's status (for example, an unexpected or a seasonal downturn in business volume). In many cases, employees may be called back to work at some future date.

The **Workers' Adjustment Retraining and Notification (WARN) Act** requires that organizations employing more than 100 people give the employees and the community a 60-day notice of its intent to close the business or to lay off 50 or more members of its workforce.

Conflict Management

Sometimes problems arise because of conflicts among employees. It is not unusual for people to disagree. Indeed, sometimes a difference of opinion can increase creativity. However, conflict can also waste time, reduce productivity,

and decrease morale. When taken to the extreme, it can threaten the safety of employees and cause damage to property.

Conflict management focuses on working with the individuals involved to find a mutually acceptable solution. There are three ways to address conflict:

- **Compromise:** In this method, both parties must be willing to lose or give up a piece of their position.
- **Control:** In this method, interaction may be prohibited until the employees' emotions are under control. The manager also may structure their interactions. For example, the manager can set ground rules for communicating or dealing with specific issues. Another form of control is personal counseling. Personal counseling focuses on how people deal with conflict rather than on the cause of specific disagreements.
- **Constructive confrontation:** In this method, both parties meet with an objective third party to explore their perceptions and feelings. The desired outcome is to produce a mutual understanding of the issues and to create a win-win situation.

Grievance Management

Employees have the right to disagree with management and can express their opinions or complaints in a variety of ways. They should be encouraged to bring problems and concerns directly to their manager. When they do not achieve satisfaction at that level, the manager should explain other options to the employee. For example, dissatisfied employees should understand that they can either take their issues to the next management level or discuss them with HR staff.

Organizations establish **grievance procedures** that define the steps an employee can follow to seek resolution of a disagreement they have with management on a job-related issue. A complaint becomes a **grievance** when it has been documented in writing. At that point, the formal grievance procedure is set in motion.

Employees who belong to a union should follow the grievance procedures set by their union. Union contracts usually specify the types of actions employees can take and the time frames for filing grievances. The contracts usually specify time frames for responses and define the formal process for elevating the consideration or resolution of a grievance. Grievances taken to the highest levels will likely have to be resolved through mediation or arbitration.

Each of these steps takes time and can cost money. Therefore, managers should try to avoid grievances by maintaining open and effective communication with their staff.

Maintenance of Employee Records

Official **employee records** must be maintained under the control of the HR department. Any personnel records maintained under the control of the manager must be kept secure at all times.

Federal legislation such as Title VII of the Civil Rights Act of 1964, the Age Discrimination in Employment Act, the Immigration Reform and Control Act, and the FLSA place numerous recordkeeping and reporting requirements on the HR department. The Environmental Protection Agency and the Occupational Safety and Health Administration also have recordkeeping requirements. Myers (2011) outlines several additional recordkeeping obligations, as follows:

- Employers must protect the confidentiality of personnel records and files.
- Employers must protect the health records of employees.
- Employers must avoid intruding into the personal lives of employees, such as their other associations, alcohol use, spending habits, and financial obligations unless there are valid job-related reasons for making such intrusions.
- Employers must prevent the public disclosure of personal information that may be embarrassing to an employee.
- Employers must protect the results of employment-related tests, including written tests used in making selection decisions, and the results of both pre-employment and random drug testing.

Current Human Resources Trends

According to the US Department of Labor (Bureau of Labor Statistics 2011), the following workforce trends in employment are likely to affect the labor market in the United States during the first decade of the 21st century:

- Women constitute a greater proportion of the labor force than in the past, with 59 percent of all US women in the workforce in 2009. In the healthcare industry, women are more than 50 percent of the workforce. Slightly fewer than 73 percent of the women in the workforce have children under the age of 18, and 36 percent of women in the workforce hold college degrees.
- Minority racial and ethnic groups will account for a growing percentage of the overall labor force. Immigrants will expand this growth.
- The average age of the US population will increase, and more workers who retire from full-time jobs will work part-time.
- As a result of these and other shifts, employers in a variety of industries will face shortages of qualified workers.

From this information, it is obvious that employers must be prepared to function with an increasingly diverse workforce in terms of gender, age, health status, race, and ethnicity. In general, the management of an increasingly diverse workforce is receiving considerable attention in the HR literature, and some organizations are initiating diversity training programs. Mathis and Jackson (2002) identify three content areas that are often included in diversity training programs:

- *Legal awareness:* Federal and state laws and regulations on equal employment opportunity and the consequences of violating these laws and regulations
- *Cultural awareness:* Attempts to deal with stereotypes, typically through discussions and exercises
- *Sensitivity training:* Attempts to sensitize people to the differences among them and how their words and behaviors are perceived by others

According to Gillian Flynn (1998), mixed reviews regarding the effectiveness of the diversity training received from both public- and private-sector organizations suggest that either the programs or their implementation is ineffective. There seems to be considerable work still to be done within healthcare organizations and HIM departments to prepare for the anticipated growth in the multicultural profile of HR assets over the coming decade.

The Department of Labor data also indicate that employees will increasingly seek ways to gain more control over their time. The time pressure associated with trying to balance work and personal lives (especially when both parents are working outside the family home) coupled with the time pressure associated with increasingly long commutes appear to be driving this concern to the surface in HR management. Flextime, job sharing, and home-based (telecommuting) staffing options are emerging as viable solutions to the workforce retention issue. Within transcription and coding work units in HIM services, flextime and home-based staffing options are being implemented to address the labor shortages already affecting departmental operations.

Check Your Understanding 24.7

Instructions: On a separate piece of paper, indicate whether the following statements are true or false. If the statement is false, explain why.

1. Employee compensation systems are used to enhance employee loyalty.

2. Minimum wage and overtime policies are impacted by the Taft-Hartley Act.

3. All employees are subject to the provisions of the Fair Labor Standards Act.

4. Trade associations and government agencies are routine sources for compensation benchmark data.

5. The Equal Pay Act requires employers to consider compensable factors when setting pay for similar work performed by both females and males.

6. Job ranking is the most commonly used method for conducting job evaluations.

7. The Hays method is a popular, specialized point method for conducting job evaluations.

8. Formal performance review sessions are routinely done on an annual basis.

9. A 180-degree evaluation involves evaluation feedback from supervisors, peers, and self-assessment.

10. The first step in a progressive disciplinary process is a verbal, undocumented warning.

11. Compromise is a method of conflict resolution with the goal of arriving at a win-win outcome.

12. Grievances taken to the highest levels for resolution will likely be resolved through mediation or arbitration.

13. Organizations are obliged to avoid intrusions into an employee's personal life unless there is a valid job-related reason for doing so.

14. Flextime and home-based staffing alternatives are being employed in health information services to address labor shortage issues.

Summary

Management is key in setting the healthcare organization's direction, establishing its policies, and maximizing its assets. Included among its assets are the people who carry out the organization's mission: the human resources staff. Managers are diffused throughout the organization with different responsibilities assigned at different levels and yet all have important roles to play in creating and maintaining an environment that is prudent in handling its financial resources, focused on providing high-quality services to its customers, and attentive to the basic human needs of its workforce.

Effective management of human resources begins with attention given to the adoption of appropriate policies, procedures, and practices in each of the seven HR activity areas: HR planning and analysis; equal employment opportunity; staffing; HR development; compensation and benefits; health, safety, and security; and employee and labor and management relations. HR professionals working in close partnership with the organization's managers hire and retain qualified employees by following these guidelines and fostering good working relationships between employees and management.

Effective recruitment, selection, and hiring practices involve the consistent use of the tools designed to identify the best-qualified candidates for each position. Once hired, ensuring that employees are well oriented and trained is the critical first step toward a successful long-term outcome. Training and development needs can be viewed on a continuum of five conceptual areas: orientation, training,

in-service education, continuing education, and career development. Each healthcare organization's training program must be able to adapt to the different needs of its employees.

New employees need to be introduced to the rules and culture of the organization, the department, and the specific job duties they will be performing. In-service education builds on basic skills provided during orientation and on-the-job training. It also is used when departments are restructured or when external requirements require employees to update their competency. The techniques used to deliver training should be matched with the purpose of the training, the trainee's level of education and experience, the location, and the budget. Because the training needs of every department are unique, it is important to develop a formal training and development plan. The plan begins with a needs analysis and the establishment of measurable objectives. A curriculum is then designed to meet those needs.

Because training programs require a considerable investment of both time and money, the organization should encourage commitment to long-term employment. An important factor in maintaining job satisfaction is recognition by the company of employee needs for work–life balance. Alternative staffing arrangements permit employees to vary work hours and locations while still satisfying the organization's need for productivity.

Another factor that enhances employee job satisfaction is the opportunity for personal growth. Employees should be empowered with the tools and resources to solve problems themselves. Successful managers delegate effectively. Effective delegation leads to a more efficient and productive department and mutually benefits the manager, the employee, and the institution.

A successful and effective plan for employee training and development requires a substantial investment of time, money, and personnel. It should be approved and supported by upper management and based on a systematic evaluation of needs. Subsequently, maintaining open and meaningful communications with employees, setting realistic performance expectations for employees, engaging employees in ways that give them appropriate control of their work schedule and environment, delegating appropriate levels of decision-making authority, and providing them with opportunities for ongoing staff development all serve to enhance employee morale and increase job satisfaction.

Managing human resources is both a science and an art. As such, it is learned through a combination of study and observation. Published HR management resources are readily available to provide the knowledge foundation associated with this field. In the workplace, HR professionals are available to serve as advisors to managers who want to handle this complex aspect of their management responsibilities knowledgably and artfully.

References

AHIMA Board of Directors. 2011 (September 28). AHIMA report. New view of HIM: Introducing the Core Model.

AHIMA e-HIM Task Force. 2003 (August 15). Vision of the e-HIM future: A report from the AHIMA e-HIM Task Force. Supplement to *Journal of AHIMA.*

American Health Information Management Association, Cumulative Hydrologic Impact Assessment, American Association for Medical Transcription, and Medical Technology and Infrastructure Administration. 2006 (May 4). Joint Position Statement. Regulation of Health Information Processing in an Outsourcing Environment.

American Society for Training and Development. 2008. http://www.astd.org.

Anthony, W.P., P.L. Perrewe, and K.M. Kacmar. 1996. *Strategic Human Resource Management.* Orlando, FL: Harcourt Brace & Company.

Bagshaw, M. 2004. Is diversity divisive? A positive training approach. *Training for Diversity, Industrial and Commercial Training* 36(4). 153–157. http://site.ebrary.com/lib/uic.

Buhler, P. 2002. *Human Resources Management.* Avon, MA: F+W Publications.

Bureau of Labor Statistics. 2011 (March). BLS spotlight on statistics: Women at work. http://www.bls.gov/spotlight/2011/women/pdf/women_bls_spotlight.pdf.

Dessler, G. 2007. *Human Resources Management,* 11th ed. Upper Saddle River, NJ: Pearson Prentice-Hall.

Dougherty, M., and R. Scichilone. 2002. Practice brief: Establishing a telecommuting or home-based employee program. *Journal of AHIMA* 73(7): 72A–72L.

Fallon, L., and C. McConnell. 2007. *Human Resource Management in Healthcare.* Sudbury, MA: Jones and Bartlett.

Flynn, G. 1998. The harsh reality of diversity programs. *Workforce* 12: 26–35.

Fottler, H., S. Hernandez, and C. Joiner, eds. 1998. *Essentials of Human Resource Management in Health Service Organizations.* Albany, NY: Delmar.

Heiphetz, A., and S. Liverman. 2008. Using robotic avatars in Second Life simulations and training. http://www.ahg.com.

Johnson, M. 2004. Harassment and discrimination prevention training: What the law requires. *Labor Law Journal* 55(2): 119–129.

Keeling, B., and N. Kallaus. 1996. *Administrative Office Management,* 11th ed. Cincinnati, OH: South-Western.

Levenburg, N., and H. Major. 1998. Distance learning: Implications for higher education in the 21st century. Originally published in *The Technology Source.* www.technologysource.org/article/distance_learning__implications_for_higher_education_in_the_21st_century.

Mathis, R.L., and J.H. Jackson. 2002. *Human Resource Management: Essential Perspectives,* 2nd ed. Cincinnati: South-Western Publishers.

Mondy, R., and R. Noe. 2005. *Human Resource Management,* 9th ed. Upper Saddle River, NJ: Pearson Prentice-Hall.

Myers, D.W. 2011. *US Master Human Resources Guide.* Chicago: CCH.

O'Connor, B.N., M. Bronner, and C. Delaney. 2002. *Training for Organizations,* 2nd ed. Cincinnati, OH: South-Western.

Odgers, P., and B. Keeling. 2000. *Administrative Office Management,* 12th ed. Cincinnati, OH: South-Western.

O'Neal. H., and R. Perez. 2006. *Web-Based Learning Theory, Research and Practice.* Mahwah, NJ: Lawrence Erlbaum Associates, Inc.

Schermerhorn, J. 2005. *Management,* 8th ed. New York: John Wiley & Sons.

US Department of Education. 2001 (modified 8/31/2007). Requirements for accessible electronic and information technology (E&IT) design. http://www.ed.gov/print/fund/contract/apply/clibrary/software.html.

US Department of Labor. (revised July 2008). Fact Sheet #17A: Exemption for executive, administrative, professional, computer & outside sales employees under the Fair Labor Standards Act (FLSA). http://www.dol.gov/whd/regs/compliance/fairpay/fs17a_overview.pdf.

Workforce Management Magazine. 2001. Pros and cons of training modes. http://www.workforce.com/archive/article/22/13/14.php.

World Wide Web Consortium. 2012. Web Accessibility Initiative. http://www.w3c.org/WAI.

Zachary, M. 2004. Labor law for supervisors: training for the disabled. *Supervision* 65(5): 23–26.

References

chapter 25

Financial Management

Rick Revoir, EdD, MBA, CPA

Learning Objectives

- Read, understand, and use balance sheets and income statements
- Explain the difference between financial accounting and managerial accounting
- Recognize the importance of accounting to nonfinancial managers
- Calculate and identify the components of basic financial ratios

- Explain the importance of internal controls and their role in financial management
- Describe the components of operational and capital budgets
- Discuss the impact of claims processing and reimbursement on financial statements
- Describe the financial management functions of HIM professionals

Key Terms

Accounting
Accounting rate of return (ARR)
Accounts payable
Accounts receivable
Accrue
Acid-test ratio
Activity-based budget
Asset
Balance sheet
Capital budget
Cash
Collateral
Conceptual framework of accounting
Conservatism
Consistency
Contra-account
Corporation
Corrective control
Cost accounting
Credit
Current ratio
Debit

Debt ratio
Debt service
Depreciation
Detective control
Direct cost
Direct method of cost allocation
Disclosure
Double distribution
Entity
Equity
Expense
Favorable variance
Financial Accounting Standards Board (FASB)
Financial data
Financial transaction
Fiscal year
Fixed budget
Fixed cost
Flexible budget
Forecasting
For-profit organization
General ledger

Generally accepted accounting principles (GAAP)
Generally accepted auditing standards (GAAS)
Going concern
Government Accounting Standards Board (GASB)
Historical cost
Income statement
Indirect cost
Interim period
Internal rate of return (IRR)
Invoice
Journal entry
Liability
Liquidity
Long-term asset
Managerial accounting
Matching
Materiality
Mortgage
Net assets
Net income
Net loss
Net present value (NPV)
Not-for-profit organization
Note
Operational budget
Overhead cost
Owner's equity
Partnership

Payback period
Permanent budget variance
Preventive control
Profitability
Profitability index
Public Company Accounting Oversight Board (PCAOB)
Purchase order
Reliability
Request for proposal (RFP)
Return on equity (ROE)
Return on investment (ROI)
Revenue
Revenue Principle
Securities and Exchange Commission (SEC)
Simultaneous equations method
Sole proprietorship
Stable monetary unit
Statement
Statement of cash flow
Statement of retained earnings
Statement of stockholder's equity
Step-down allocation
Temporary budget variance
Unfavorable variance
Variable cost
Variance
Zero-based budget

A physician treats a patient. A hospital admits a woman in labor. A professional association offers continuing education for its members. All of these scenarios are examples of organizations providing services for which they receive compensation. How organizations arrange to provide those services, determine compensation, and handle the flow of funds that these activities both require and generate is guided by financial management.

This chapter focuses on the concepts and tools associated with planning and controlling the financial resources required to operate a department or a work unit. It presents operations, labor, and capital budgeting processes and techniques; reviews organizational and departmental financial performance measures; and explores techniques for improving financial performance at the departmental level. Finally, the chapter acquaints readers with the language of financial and managerial accounting to enhance their understanding of the role of the health information management (HIM) professional as a manager.

Healthcare Financial Management

The process of financial management involves various players within the organization's financial arena. Table 25.1 lists

and describes the roles of the financial personnel who work in hospitals. However, healthcare financial management also involves a number of players outside the financial arena. For example, HIM professionals are involved with reimbursement through the coding function. Record retention and release of information activities help support claims auditing and claims denial appeals. HIM professionals play an important role in documentation improvement activities, including clinical training to support medical necessity. Figure 25.1 illustrates the potential relationship between HIM and the financial personnel in a hospital.

HIM professionals are familiar with **financial data** as one of the components of a health record: the data related to payers and billing. To financial managers, financial data are the individual elements of organizational financial transactions. (The term *financial* refers to money and, as is discussed later, money is the measurement of financial transactions.) A **financial transaction** is the exchange of goods or services for payment or the promise of payment. Financial data are compiled into informational reports for users. The degree of detail that users require depends on their needs and is largely influenced by the relationship of the user to the originator of the transaction.

Financial transactions that originate at the department level require review by that department. For example, the

Table 25.1.   Financial personnel and their roles in a hospital

Position	Typical or Minimum Background	Financial Roles
Board of directors or trustees	Depends on the needs of the facility	Ultimate responsibility for the fiscal integrity of the organization
Chief executive officer (CEO)	Generally, master's-prepared in public administration, hospital administration, or business administration; occasionally, clinical background	Overall responsibility for administration of the organization
Chief financial officer (CFO)	Certified public accountant (CPA) or certified management accountant (CMA)	Overall responsibility for related departments, including patient accounts, internal auditing, and often HIM
Controller or accounting manager	CPA	Oversees accounting and cash disbursement, including payroll
Patient accounts manager	Bachelor's degree	Oversees claims processing

Figure 25.1.   Organization of the nonphysician side of the hospital

pharmacy department will review its drug transactions, and the HIM department will review its purchases of supplies and services. On the administrative level, however, such detail is not usually required. Instead, informative summaries are often more useful. For example, an organization administrator does not usually need to know the number of cases of copier paper purchased in each department. Instead, he or she would look at the total office supply purchases and evaluate whether they were at appropriate and expected levels. Additional detail or explanation would not be required unless the purchases were unusual. The accumulation and reporting of financial data within an organization are accounting functions.

Accounting

Accounting is an activity as well as a profession. Just as there are many HIM roles and functions, so are there diverse accounting roles and functions. The accounting activity involves the collection, recording, and reporting of financial data. Accountants are both the individuals who perform these activities and many of those who use the reported data. Accounting is important because it is the language that organizations use to communicate with each other to effect transactions, determine investment strategies, and evaluate performance.

The **conceptual framework of accounting** underlies all accounting activity and is based on the following ideas:

- The benefits of the financial data should exceed the costs of obtaining them.
- The data must be understandable.
- The data must be useful for decision making. In other words, the data must be relevant, reliable, and comparable.

Although some of these requirements are similar to general data quality concerns, they are discussed specifically with financial data in mind.

Accounting Concepts and Principles

Concepts and principles that define the parameters of accounting activity are briefly discussed here and summarized in figure 25.2.

Concepts

An **entity** is a person or an organization such as a corporation or professional association. A business owner, for example, must not commingle business and personal data. This concept can be very difficult for small business owners who may not understand why business receipts are not the same as personal income. It can be equally difficult for large corporations that own many different companies.

When analysis of an entity's financial data shows that the organization can continue to operate for the foreseeable

Figure 25.2. Basic accounting concepts and principles

Basic Accounting Concepts

- *Entity:* The financial data of different entities are kept separate.
- *Going concern:* Organizations are assumed to continue indefinitely, unless otherwise stated.
- *Stable monetary unit:* Money is the measurement of financial transactions.
- *Time period:* Financial data represent a specified time period.
- *Conservatism:* Resources must not be overstated, and liabilities must not be understated.
- *Materiality:* The financial data collected by an organization are relevant to its goals and objectives.

Basic Accounting Principles

- *Reliability:* Amounts represent the transactions that occurred.
- *Cost:* Transactions are recorded at historical cost.
- *Revenue:* In order to record revenue, it must be earned and measurable.
- *Matching:* Expenses are recorded in the same period as the related revenue.
- *Consistency:* When an accounting rule is followed, all subsequent periods must reflect the same rule.
- *Disclosure:* Financial reports must be accompanied by helpful explanations, when necessary.

---

future, the organization is considered a **going concern.** Assuming that a business is going to continue, projections of future activities can be made based on historical trends and assumptions about future conditions. The concept of going concern also places constraints on the organization to maintain sufficient financial and other resources to ensure future stability and growth.

All of an entity's transactions must be quantified using a standard measurement or **stable monetary unit.** In the United States, financial transactions are recorded in US dollars and cents.

Financial data represent transactions during a specified period of time: hour, day, week, month, quarter, year, and so on. The specific time period depends on the use of the data. The **fiscal year** (also called the financial year) is defined by the tax year. Individuals generally have a tax year that coincides with the calendar year. Organizations, on the other hand, use fiscal years that correspond to their business needs, usually their business cycle, which represents the total activities of the organization. For example, the US government's fiscal year ends September 30.

For financial reporting purposes, a fiscal year is divided into quarters (three-month periods) and months. Because the months generally end on the last calendar day, the quarters can be of slightly different duration. For example, the first quarter of a fiscal year that begins April 1 includes April, May, and June: 91 days. The second quarter of that

Figure 25.3. Impact of days in the month on fiscal quarter and semi-annual reporting (nonleap year)

Month	# of Days	Quarter	# of Days	Half	# of Days
January	31				
February	28				
March	31	Quarter I	90		
April	30				
May	31				
June	30	Quarter II	91	First Half	181
July	31				
August	31				
September	30	Quarter III	92		
October	31				
November	30				
December	31	Quarter IV	92	Second Half	184

same fiscal year includes July, August, and September: 92 days. Figure 25.3 illustrates the extent of the difference in a nonleap year. Over time, it is common to compare similar quarters from year to year, particularly when the business cycle has predictable peaks and valleys.

Not all financial data represent completed transactions within the period represented. Sometimes estimates are involved, or transactions are completed between periods. When amounts are estimated, efforts must be made to ensure that their use does not misrepresent the actual financial transaction. Therefore, financial data must comply with **conservatism** in that they fairly represent the financial results of the period and do not overstate or understate information in a significant (material) way.

Materiality refers to the thresholds below which items are not considered significant for reporting purposes. These thresholds may be a dollar value or a percentage of a dollar value. To a $100,000 professional association with $100,000 in income, $10,000 is a significant (material) amount. To a $100 billion oil company, $10,000 is not material. This issue arises when determining the significance of errors, potential liabilities, and the necessity for disclosures. Items that are considered immaterial individually may, when added to other immaterial items, be of concern on this basis.

Principles

Accounting principles support the quality of financial data. Because they are data, financial data must possess the same data quality characteristics, such as timeliness and validity,

as any other type of data. In financial data, **reliability** refers to whether the data actually represent what occurred and are free of material error both in the current period and over time. Transactions are recorded at their **historical cost** measured at the time of the transaction. For some transactions, such as the purchase of equipment or investment in marketable securities, there may be a change in the actual or perceived value of the underlying asset or liability. In those cases, adjustments or **disclosures** are made when reporting the financial data. The **Revenue Principle** states that earnings as a result of activities and investments may only be recognized when they have been earned, can be measured, and have a reasonable expectation of being collected. For an organization to generate revenue, it must incur expenses, for example, payroll, rent, travel, and raw materials. Whenever possible, expenses are recorded in the same period as the associated revenue, thereby **matching** the expenses and revenues. Some accounting rules include variations. The principle of **consistency** requires that the method not change over the life of the asset. Thus, the financial data are prepared in the same way from one period to the next. In fact, organizations sometimes change their choices. Consistency then requires that financial data be restated to show the effect of the change applied to previous periods. Interestingly, some allowed financial accounting rules differ from tax accounting rules, producing different results. Sometimes the financial data alone do not provide enough information for users of the data to make informed decisions. The impact of a building fire, a potential or ongoing lawsuit, or an expiring collective bargaining agreement cannot be reflected in the financial data when no financial transaction has occurred. Therefore, notes or disclosures that help the user to make informed decisions must accompany all financial reports.

Authorities

Just as clinical data are organized and reported in predetermined formats for ease of communication, financial data also are organized and reported in specific ways. Theoretically, organizations can design their own accounting systems and reporting mechanisms. Internally, this is often the case, as will be seen with budgeting. However, organizations that want to borrow funds or attract investors must follow generally accepted rules that apply to their industry and accounting in general. Five major sources of accounting and reporting rules apply to healthcare organizations: the **Financial Accounting Standards Board (FASB)**, the Securities and Exchange Commission (SEC), the Internal Revenue Service (IRS), the Public Company Accounting Oversight Board (PCAOB), and the Centers for Medicare and Medicaid Services (CMS).

Financial Accounting Standards Board

The FASB is an independent organization that sets accounting standards for businesses in the private sector. Its counterpart, the **Government Accounting Standards Board (GASB)**, sets standards for accounting for government entities. The FASB promulgates the rules by which financial data are compiled, reported, reviewed, and audited. These rules, which include the conceptual framework, are referred to as **generally accepted accounting principles (GAAP)** and **generally accepted auditing standards (GAAS)**.

Securities and Exchange Commission

The **Securities and Exchange Commission (SEC)** is a federal agency that regulates public and some private transactions involving the ownership and debt of organizations. The SEC sets standards regarding reporting financial data, disclosures, timing, marketing, and execution of these transactions. Public transactions take place through an exchange, such as the New York Stock Exchange (NYSE) or the National Association of Securities Dealers Automated Quotation System (NASDAQ). Organizations whose ownership interests (stocks) are traded on these exchanges are called public companies.

Internal Revenue Service

The tax status of an organization influences its administration. The IRS regulates and collects federal taxes. Healthcare organizations fall into one of two major tax categories: for-profit and not-for-profit. The primary differences between for-profit and not-for-profit organizations are related to the level of accountability and the distribution of profits. Within these categories are several legal structures, such as sole

Table 25.2. Common legal structures of nongovernmental organizations

Structure	Description	Healthcare Examples
Sole proprietorship	One owner; all profits are owner's personal income	Solo practitioners
Partnership	Two or more owners; all profits are owners' personal income	Physician group practices
Corporation	One or many owners; profits may be either retained or distributed as dividends. Dividends are income to the owners. May be public or private. "Owners" may be individuals, other organizations, or an interest group.	Hospitals, insurance companies

proprietorship, partnership, and corporation. A summary of legal structures is provided in table 25.2.

Public Company Accounting Oversight Board

Historically, the accounting profession has been largely self-regulated. The FASB and GASB, although technically independent, have strong ties to the profession. Although IRS and SEC standards and regulations constrained the specific representation of financial activities, the accounting profession was free to accomplish its reporting and other activities without government intervention. However, that changed in 2002. The federal government responded to the collapse of ENRON, WorldCom, and others with the Sarbanes-Oxley Act, which restricted the professional services of independent auditors of public companies and, among other things, created the **Public Company Accounting Oversight Board (PCAOB)**. Sarbanes-Oxley had a significant impact on the internal controls, financial reporting, and governance of organizations.

Centers for Medicare and Medicaid Services

Formerly called the Health Care Financing Administration (HCFA), CMS is the federal agency that administers the Medicare program and the federal portion of the Medicaid program. The federal government is the largest single payer of healthcare expenses in the United States. Although CMS does not set accounting rules, it enforces the federal regulations regarding the reimbursement for Medicare and the federal portion of the Medicaid program and sets standards for the documentation and reporting of transactions related to such reimbursement. Since CMS requires significant reporting from participant organizations, its influence on the financial activities and data collection should not be underestimated.

Financial Organization

The way an entity organizes itself depends on its financing, its leadership, and its tax status. The three basic forms of business organization are the sole proprietorship, the partnership, and the corporation. Other organizational entities, such as trusts and variations such as limited liability corporations (LLCs), are beyond the scope of this discussion.

- **Sole proprietorship:** An independent coding consultant who operates from home and has no employees may choose to operate as a sole proprietor. The owner, or proprietor, is the leader of the organization and is responsible for all aspects of the business. Income from the business flows through the owner's individual tax return. If the consultant's business expands, employees or subcontractors can be added without changing the organizational structure. Some physicians are solo practitioners and therefore sole proprietors.
- **Partnership:** Two or more consultants who want to be in business together may choose a partnership structure. Partners share in the responsibility for the business, and income still flows through the individuals' tax returns. Partners do not need to share equally in the financial or other business responsibilities. A partnership agreement details the contractual arrangement. Because a partnership is a separate legal and accounting entity from the individuals, a tax identification number is required for the partnership, and the partnership may be required to file its own tax returns detailing the income allocated to each partner. Partnerships survive as entities only so long as the partners remain together. A change in ownership dissolves the original partnership and a new one must be created.
- **Corporation:** A corporation is a legal entity that exists separately from its owner(s). Corporations pay their own taxes and have their own legal rights and responsibilities. In fact, the owner(s) of the corporation may have nothing to do with its leadership or day-to-day operations. A corporation is typically governed by a board of directors or trustees, and the day-to-day operations are led by one or more administrators who report to the board. The corporation's income after taxes may or may not be distributed in whole or in part to the owner(s). This after-tax distribution is a dividend and is taxable income to the owner(s). This two-tiered taxation, on the corporation and then again on the distributed dividend, is referred to as double taxation and may make this structure less attractive to individuals.

The underlying purpose of the organization drives another consideration in the financial organization of the business. Is the purpose of the business to generate income for the owners, or is there a more altruistic foundation? The answer to this question helps to define the tax status the organization will be able to obtain.

For-Profit Organizations

For-profit organizations may be sole proprietorships, partnerships, or corporations. In this context, profits are the funds remaining after all current obligations have been met, including taxes. Inherently, the underlying goal of for-profit organizations is to increase the wealth of the owners. Increase in wealth can be accomplished through the generation of profits to be distributed to the owners or by increasing the value of the organization so that the owners' investment is more valuable. The leadership of the organization may distribute the profits to the owners or otherwise invest them as they see fit. For-profit organizations may be privately or publicly owned.

Private ownership may be by an individual, a group of individuals, or an organization. Physician practices, urgent care centers, and freestanding ancillary care organizations are often privately owned. The distribution of profits from a privately owned organization is at the discretion of the owners or as defined by contract among owners.

Public ownership means that the ownership interest in the organization may be bought and sold in the financial marketplace. For example, Tenet Healthcare Corporation (THC) is a publicly held organization with hospitals in numerous states. Its stock is traded on the NYSE under the symbol *THC*. A publicly held organization's board of directors determines the distribution of profits. Boards are constrained in these determinations by contractual obligations such as mortgage contracts and preferred stock obligations, stockholder expectations, and strategic organizational goals.

Not-for-Profit Organizations

Not-for-profit organizations are not owned but, instead, are held in trust for the benefit of the communities they serve. Many hospitals fall into this tax category. Other not-for-profit organizations include professional associations such as the American Health Information Management Association (AHIMA), charitable organizations such as the American Red Cross, and educational foundations such as the AHIMA Foundation on Research and Education (FORE) in HIM. The IRS defines numerous types of not-for-profit organizations, some of which are summarized in table 25.3. The two categories of not-for-profit organizations discussed here are 501(c)(6) and 501(c)(3).

501(c)(6)

Most professional associations are organized under 501(c)(6), which gives them some federal tax benefits and the

Table 25.3.   Common not-for-profit tax statuses

Not-for-Profit	Description	Healthcare Examples
501(c)(3)	Largely exempt from taxes, donations to these organizations can be tax deductible. Underlying purpose of the organization must be charitable or educational.	Charities, AHIMA's Foundation on Research and Education (FORE)
501(c)(6)	Partially exempt from taxes. May lobby and sell goods and services. Underlying purpose must benefit the interest group or public.	Professional associations, some hospitals
501(c)(4)	Business leagues	N/A
501(c)(14)	Credit unions	N/A
501(c)(19)	Veterans' organizations	N/A

freedom to engage in some activities unrelated to their organizational purpose. For example, organizations under 501(c)(6) may lobby and sell goods and services but are largely involved in activities that benefit their major interest group, which may be defined as paid membership. Such organizations may be subject to state sales tax, both as purchaser and seller. AHIMA and most of its component state associations are 501(c)(6) organizations.

501(c)(3)

On the other hand, 501(c)(3) organizations are largely exempt from federal taxes but must confine their activities to the public benefit. Donations to 501(c)(3) organizations are generally tax deductible (for the donor) to the extent that no goods or services have been received in return. For that reason, charities are generally 501(c)(3) organizations, and many 501(c)(6) organizations have charitable components that are separately incorporated. For example, AHIMA is a 501(c)(6) organization that has a 501(c)(3) component, FORE. Organizations classified as 501(c)(3) may also be exempt from state sales tax under certain circumstances.

Tax Status Issues

It is important to understand the underlying tax status of an organization because tax status affects the organization's business decisions and long-term strategies. Undistributed profits from a for-profit organization may stay in the business and be available for investment or future distribution. There is no necessity to identify the future use for these funds, although stockholders may ultimately press for distribution when undistributed profits appear excessive. Occasionally, portions of undistributed profits are held in reserve for specific uses.

On the other hand, profits from a not-for-profit organization stay in the business. Because all such profits must be used for the benefit of the community the organization serves, the future use of these profits should be clearly defined. Excessive unrelated business income or high unrestricted reserves (effectively, too much savings) may result in the loss of not-for-profit status. For further information about tax exemptions of organizations, see IRS Publication 557 (IRS 2011).

Sources of Financial Data

Just as a health record is constructed from the data collected, financial records are also composed of data. Health records are built from medical decision making; financial records originate with financial decision making, the smallest component of which is the transaction.

Transactions

Virtually every financial transaction consists of three fundamental steps:

1. Goods or services are provided.
2. A transaction is recorded.
3. Compensation is exchanged.

Each step may require a number of additional steps, depending on the service and the industry. In addition, the steps are not always performed in the same order. Independent contractors that perform hospital coding represent a simple example. The contractor codes the charts, submits an invoice, and receives a check from the hospital. In this case, four specific steps may be needed to support the transaction: keeping a log to track the charts that have been coded, preparing an invoice to bill the hospital, keeping a list of the invoices sent, and checking the invoices off when they are received.

In a hospital, multiple individuals and departments perform services and provide administrative support for financial transactions. Four areas are of particular concern in the context of this discussion: clinical services, patient accounts, health information management, and administration.

Clinical Services

Just as contract coders keep track of the records they have coded, so do clinical, or patient care, services providers keep track of the services they perform. The documents of original entry or source documents enable the healthcare facility to verify that the services were provided and to communicate to supporting departments that a transaction has been initiated. The source document includes two elements: the clinical documentation and the billing documentation.

Clinical documentation is a record of who has seen the patient and why as well as what tests or treatments were performed, in other words, everything clinically relevant that happened to the patient during his or her interaction with the organization.

Along with the recording of clinical documentation is the capture of the associated billing information. Regardless of the reimbursement system (discussed in chapter 16), the organization must capture the billable event in such a way that the financial transaction can be completed. Therefore, when a medication is administered to a patient, the clinical record reflects the medication; dosage; time, date, and route of administration; and the clinical personnel who administered it. At the same time, the charge for the drug must be communicated to patient accounts. This detailed tracking of billable events also supports the cost accounting function, which is discussed later in this chapter.

Patient Accounts

The patient accounts department is responsible for collecting recorded transactions, billing the payer (claim), and ensuring the correct receipt of reimbursement. This department depends on the reliable recording of services. This means that the capture of billing information must be timely and accurate in order to complete the financial transaction efficiently. In addition to the clinical support staff and departments, the patient accounts department relies on the HIM department for coded data.

Health Information Management

The HIM department is responsible for, among other things, identifying and recording the appropriate clinical codes to describe the patient's interaction with the organization. In some cases, this coding drives the reimbursement to the facility; in other cases, it is used to support the billing.

In addition to the coding activity, the HIM department is responsible for aggregating and maintaining the documentation that supports the reimbursement.

Administration

Financial transactions occur throughout the facility. Employees are paid, equipment and supplies are purchased, and departments perform services for each other. The finance department accumulates and analyzes all of the financial data. Ultimately, the entire management team participates in the review and analysis of financial data.

Uses of Financial Data

Financial data are generated virtually everywhere in a healthcare facility. Managerial and supervisory personnel use these data for four key purposes: to track reimbursement, to control costs, to plan future activities, and to forecast results.

Reimbursement

Healthcare facilities are service organizations that derive almost all their income from clinical activities. Therefore,

a key use of financial data is to track reimbursement and ensure that the desired amount of profit is generated. In the current industry environment where payers often dictate the amount of reimbursement, the provider is increasingly unable to control pricing as a method of managing desired profit. Therefore, the cost of providing services has become the controllable factor.

Control

Controlling costs is best done at the departmental level. For example, the chief executive officer (CEO) of a hospital does not shop around for the best price on copier paper, and the chief financial officer (CFO) does not monitor employee productivity in the food services department. Each department is charged with responsibility for ensuring prudent management of financial and other resources. Departments are given this charge through the budget process, which is one of the outcomes of administrative planning.

Planning

Administrative planning reflects the organization's mission. From that mission, goals and objectives are derived that help move the organization toward achieving its mission. Financial data are used to analyze trends, develop budgets, and plan for the future. Planning cannot be accomplished by using historical data alone because the industry changes, sometimes rapidly. Therefore, the administration must forecast future scenarios.

Forecasting

Forecasting is the prediction of future behavior based on historical data as well as environmental scans. It can be as simple as predicting the profits of an organization on the basis of anticipated changes in reimbursement. It also can involve complicated predictions of consumer behavior based on market research and news reports.

Check Your Understanding 25.1

Instructions: Answer the following questions on a separate piece of paper.

1. If an insurance company representative were to contact the HIM department about a claims audit, to which financial personnel should he or she be directed and why?

2. Given that diagnosis-related group (DRG) payments are predetermined, why would a hospital not record revenue on the basis of the working DRG?

3. Big Medical Center earned a lot more revenue than expected this year but does not expect to earn as much next year. To make the financial reports more consistent, a junior accountant suggests that the hospital record some of next year's expenses this year. Would you agree or disagree that this is a good strategy? Why?

4. What influence does CMS have on a hospital's financial management?

5. If a hospital's HIM department has excess coding or transcription staff, can the hospital sell coding or transcription services to other hospitals (based on what has been covered so far in this chapter)? Why or why not?

Basic Financial Accounting

A basic understanding of the mechanics of financial accounting helps department managers to understand the impact of their financial transactions on the overall organization. The system of recording financial transactions is based on balancing the *purpose* of the transactions with their impact on the organization. For example, a facility purchases drugs with the purpose of ensuring that sufficient and appropriate drugs are on hand to treat patients. The purchase of the drugs increases the facility's pharmaceutical inventory. The impact of that purchase is the outlay of cash. After the cash is spent on drugs, it cannot be spent on something else. Recording both the increase in inventory and the outlay of cash enables the organization to understand and communicate information about its activities. Fundamental to this communication is an understanding of the components of financial data and their relationship to each other.

Assets

An **asset** is something that is owned or due to be received. In a transaction, the compensation that has been earned by providing goods or services becomes an asset as soon as it has been earned. Examples of assets include cash, inventory, accounts receivable, buildings, and equipment.

Cash

Cash consists of monetary instruments and those instruments that can be converted into cash quickly. The latter are often referred to as cash equivalents. Included in cash are funds that are maintained in bank accounts. It is important to remember that, for accounting purposes, currency and bank accounts are both considered cash. At the point of sale, such as purchasing lunch in the cafeteria, currency may be tendered. CMS, on the other hand, does not deliver reimbursement to a hospital in truckloads of currency; instead, it wires funds between financial institutions. Nevertheless, both are considered cash to the hospital. Cash is only recorded, and becomes an asset, when it has been received.

Inventory

An organization has inventory if it maintains goods on hand that it intends to sell to a client. Drugs are part of a hospital's pharmaceutical inventory because they are effectively on hand to be sold to patients. It is important to distinguish between goods that are available for sale and goods that are used by the organization in other ways. Photocopy paper is inventory to the office supply store. To the hospital HIM department, it is used for general business purposes and is considered a supply. In this case, the hospital is the client (the consumer of the goods). Because hospitals are primarily service organizations, and the provision of goods is incidental to the services provided, hospitals tend not to have a great deal of inventory other than supplies.

Accounts Receivable

When an organization has delivered goods and/or services, payment for the same is expected. Remember that the second step in a transaction is to record the transaction. Because the revenue has been earned upon delivery or provision of the goods and services, the organization must have some way to keep track of what is owed as a result. **Accounts receivable** then is merely a list of the amounts due from various customers (in this case, patients). Payment on the individual amounts is expected within a specified period. A schedule of those expected amounts is prepared in order to track and follow up on payments that are overdue (late). Figure 25.4 shows one way to prepare a simple aged accounts receivables report. This list also could be sorted by discharge date or payer and the amounts subtotaled.

Building

Many organizations own the buildings in which they reside. These buildings are assets to the organization because they are part of its physical plant, its infrastructure. If an organization leases space for its operations, that space is not considered an asset because the organization does not own it. Buildings are considered **long-term assets** because they are typically owned for many years.

Equipment

Equipment is another long-term asset. Hospitals include CT scanners, computer systems, and vehicles in this category. Each organization decides what items are relevant to this category, depending on industry conventions and materiality. For example, a large hospital would rarely consider a $500 personal computer to be equipment, whereas an independent coding consultant might view it as a significant, long-term investment.

Purchase Price

In acquiring a piece of equipment (and certain other assets), the transaction is recorded at the purchase price. For example, the hospital purchases digital mammography equipment for $200,000. The hospital then would have a $200,000 asset in equipment. However, the equipment gradually wears out from use over time. That $200,000 asset is not worth $200,000 four years after it was purchased.

Figure 25.4.   Aged accounts receivable

A/C #	D/C	SER	0–30 days	31–60 days	61–90 days	91–120 days	>120 days	Total A/R
46153153	04/15/11	ED					149	
46160492	07/06/11	ED				25		
46162518	07/31/11	REC			10			
46162874	08/31/11	REC			30			
46163484	08/07/11	ED					165	
46162580	07/30/11	ED				114		
46125122	06/19/10	OP					16	
46160520	07/06/11	ED				50		
46169245	10/09/11	OP	175					
46165628	09/30/11	REC		266				
46163713	08/12/11	OP			52			
46166048	09/04/11	ED		280				
46161964	07/23/11	OP				94		
46162506	07/30/11	OP				94		
46164953	08/25/11	OP			52			
46169231	10/09/11	ED	25					
46157104	05/30/11	ED					50	
46124652	06/15/10	OBN					84	
46126673	07/09/10	OP					148	
46122161	05/20/10	OP					207	
Total Amounts			**$200**	**$546**	**$144**	**$377**	**$819**	**$2,086**
Total Number of Accounts			**2**	**2**	**4**	**5**	**7**	**20**

Source: Adapted from Schraffenberger 2011, 459.

To provide better information about the financial value of its equipment, the organization provides an estimate of this decrease in value every year. This estimate is called **depreciation.**

Depreciation

Depreciation is an example of a **contra-account.** This estimate of the cumulative decrease in value of an asset actually reduces the cost of the underlying asset. Thus, the mammography equipment purchased for $200,000 may have an accumulated depreciation of $75,000 after two years. At that point, its book value to the organization is $125,000. The cumulative or accumulated depreciation is associated with its underlying assets when the value of those assets is being reported.

Mammograph	$200,000
Accumulated Depreciation	$75,000
Book Value	$125,000

Liabilities

Liabilities are essentially debts. They are amounts that are owed, often due to the acquisition of an asset.

Accounts Payable

Accounts payable is a liability that is created when the organization has received goods or services but has not yet remitted the compensation (that is, paid for the goods/services). Referring to the accounts receivable discussion, the provider of the goods and services records a receivable when payment is not received at the point of the sale. On the other side of that transaction is the organization for which the goods and services were provided. When the recipient of the goods and services does not intend to pay immediately, the amount is recorded by the recipient as an account payable. The recipient also records either the acquisition of an asset or the recognition of an expense (discussed later in this chapter).

Notes Payable

A **note** is a financial obligation that has specific terms of payment in the form of a contract. Effectively, a note is a type of loan. The creation of the note may be associated with the purchase of goods or services, and the material goods may be guaranteed by the value of specific assets (**collateral**). For example, the organization may need $50,000 more than it has on hand in order to purchase a CT scanner. It might take a two-year loan from the bank (or the vendor), using the scanner as collateral. If the organization does not pay the loan back on a timely basis, the lender is entitled by contract to take possession of the scanner.

Mortgage

A **mortgage** is a liability that is created when the organization borrows money and uses a physical asset, such as a building, as collateral.

Equity and Net Assets

All financial accounting is based on an equation that pictures the organization holistically, balancing what is owned against what is owed: assets versus liabilities. **Equity (or owner's equity)** is the arithmetic difference between assets and liabilities. In a not-for-profit environment, the difference between assets and liabilities is referred to as **net assets.** These relationships can be expressed in the following equation:

$$\text{Assets} - \text{liabilities} = \text{net assets (equity)}$$

The purchase of a building illustrates this equation. The purchase of a house typically involves a deposit of cash and an assumption of a mortgage. The building is an asset whose value is, historically, the price that was paid at the time of the purchase. The mortgage is a liability. As mortgage payments are made, the amount of the mortgage owed declines. The deposit of cash is the owner's equity in the building. As mortgage payments are made, the amount of owner's equity in the building increases. For example, Dr. James purchases an office building for $200,000. She makes a down payment (or deposit) of $50,000 and assumes a mortgage of $150,000. As the mortgage is paid over 30 years, the historical value of the house remains the same, the amount of the mortgage decreases, and the owner's equity in the property increases. When the mortgage is completely paid, the owner's equity in the house equals the historical value of the house, as shown here:

	Assets		**Liabilities**		**Equity**
At purchase	$200,000	–	$150,000	=	$ 50,000
After 10 years	$200,000	–	$100,000	=	$100,000
After 20 years	$200,000	–	$ 50,000	=	$150,000
After 30 years	$200,000	–	– 0 –	=	$200,000

Earlier, it was stated that an equation balances what is owned and what is owed. Therefore, another way to look at the accounting equation is

$$\text{Assets} = \text{liabilities} + \text{net assets (equity)}$$

Using the previous mortgage example, the second version of the equation proves useful. At every step in the following

calculation, the equations balance. An increase in assets increases equity. A decrease in assets decreases equity. An increase in assets with an equal increase in liabilities has no impact on equity. Notice that increasing a liability reduces equity in the same manner that decreasing an asset does.

	Assets		**Liabilities**		**Equity**
At purchase	$200,000	=	$150,000	+	$ 50,000
After 10 years	$200,000	=	$100,000	+	$100,000
After 20 years	$200,000	=	$ 50,000	+	$150,000
After 30 years	$200,000	=	– 0 –	+	$200,000

Assets, liabilities, and equity are the components of the balance sheet (discussed later in this chapter). Before that, however, it is important to understand the revenue and expense components of financial information.

Revenue

Revenue consists of earned, known amounts. It is the compensation that has been earned by providing goods and services to the client or patient as well as amounts received or earned from other sources.

Sources of Revenue

Patient services is the main source of revenue for a healthcare facility. Indeed, depending on the nature of the facility, patient services may be its only source of revenue. Examples of nonclinical services include employee food services, donated services, monetary donations, and copy fees.

Categories of Revenue

How an organization describes its revenue depends on industry convention, materiality, and whether the revenue is recurring or unusual. Revenue from any source increases equity. A coding consultant works for a week at a client hospital and earns $1,500. He receives a check from the hospital and deposits it in his bank account. This increases his cash asset by the amount of the deposit: $1,500. The increase in the asset, absent an associated liability, increases equity by the same amount. Most organizations can group their revenue sources into at least two categories: operating and nonoperating.

Operating Revenue

A hospital considers patient services revenue to be operating revenue. Because the hospital is in the business of serving patients, patient services is its main source of revenue and thus falls under the heading of operating revenue. Consider food services. Inpatients must be fed, so food services is a patient service and thus an operating expense. The employee cafeteria also generates revenue, but the revenue it generates is unrelated to patient services. In the HIM department, small revenue streams may be generated through release of information activities or through contracting services out to other facilities. Since the pricing of these activities is generally cost based, it is more appropriately thought of as an offset or quasi-reimbursement of the underlying cost.

Nonoperating Revenue

Another dilemma is investment income. A hospital with a large endowment that generates significant income may want to highlight this investment revenue in a separate category. Investment income is one example of nonoperating income. Other examples include gift shop sales and unrestricted monetary donations.

Expenses

It is unlikely that revenue is generated without any reduction of cash or liability being incurred. The consultant coder in the previous example must purchase coding software, travel from home to the client and back, and engage in continuing education (CE). **Expenses**, then, represent the utilization of resources by the organization in order to generate revenue. The consultant coder uses cash to purchase coding software. The software helps to generate revenue for one year, at which time it expires. Therefore, the price of the software is an expense to the coder.

The simple example that follows illustrates the impact on the accounting equation of the financial transactions discussed thus far.

October Activity					
	Assets	**–**	**Liabilities**	**=**	**Equity**
Beginning balance	$1,500	–	– 0 –	=	$1,500
Purchase codebook	<100>	–		=	<100>
Pay health insurance	<100>	–		=	<100>
Receive payment from client	$1,200	–		=	$1,200
Purchase computer (on credit)	<200>	–	800	=	<1,000>
Receive payment from client	$1,300	–		=	$1,300
Attend CE session	<80>	–		=	<80>
Ending balance	$3,520	–	800	=	$2,720

Purchasing

As previously stated, healthcare organizations typically cannot affect revenue by raising prices. Therefore, they must attempt to control expenses as much as possible. One way to do this is through the purchasing function. Individuals responsible for purchasing activities must adhere to their facility's policies and procedures, which may vary somewhat from the basic descriptions in the following section.

Organization

Organizations handle the purchasing function differently depending on their size and needs. Large organizations tend to maintain a central purchasing and distribution department that is responsible for the acquisition of supplies and equipment.

Significant savings can be obtained by purchasing supplies in bulk and distributing them as needed to departments. Central purchasing also has the benefit of minimizing the space required for storage of items on hand. Central purchasing systems should be designed to minimize the risk of loss due to misappropriation of stored items. The periodic comparison, by counting, of items on hand with the items recorded and the itemized distribution of stored items can assist in this process.

In order to obtain the benefits of purchasing in large quantities, some facilities combine their purchasing efforts. Hospital associations, for example, may offer coordinated purchasing on behalf of multiple facilities. Nevertheless, the control over the use of the items remains with the department.

Maintaining a central purchasing and distribution department results in direct administrative costs to the organization (for example, salary, facility maintenance, and administrative processing). Therefore, the control benefits of centralized purchasing must be weighed against the cost of such operations. Savings also can be obtained by limiting the source of supplies to one or two key vendors who offer discounts to the organization. In this scenario, department managers would order items as needed, but only from approved vendors.

Finally, an organization may choose to allow individual departments to make purchases independently. Although this can result in additional supply and equipment costs, there may be overall savings in not maintaining a central purchasing department. The major disadvantages of independent, or decentralized, purchasing are the need for supply storage space in the ordering department and the allocation of managerial resources to purchasing.

Regardless of the purchasing system used, controls must be in place to ensure the efficient execution of approved transactions. Purchase orders, shipping/receiving documents, and invoices are the key controls over the purchase process.

Purchase Orders

The **purchase order** system ensures that purchases have been properly authorized prior to ordering. Authorization is often tied to dollar limits or the budget process. Purchase orders are numbered sequentially so that all orders can be verified. In a paper environment, a purchase order is a paper form on which all details of the intended purchase are reported. Purchase orders for routine, budgeted items often require only the authorization of a supervisor or manager. For large-dollar items, as specified in the organization's policy and procedure manual, additional authorization may be required. In a computer-based system, there may be no physical form; however, authorization levels are still required.

The purchase order shows that the appropriate individual with the appropriate authorization ordered the specific items. The order is then forwarded to the vendor. The originator of the order keeps a copy, and another copy is sent to the accounts payable department. When there is a central receiving department, that department also should receive a copy of the order. In a computer-based system, access to the orders may suffice.

Shipping/Receiving Documents

Items received from a vendor contain a packing slip, also known as a *shipping/receiving document*. This document lists the quantities and descriptions of the items sent from the vendor, but not usually the price. The recipient of the items must verify that the items received match the ones that were ordered. The verified shipping/receiving document is forwarded to accounts payable.

Invoices

The vendor sends an **invoice** (bill or request for payment) directly to accounts payable. The accounts payable department matches the invoice to the shipping/receiving document and the purchase order on file. When all the documents match, the invoice can be processed and payment scheduled. Invoices generally have terms: for example, payable upon receipt or within 30 days. Some vendors offer discounts for early payment, such as "2/10, net 30," which means that the seller will grant a 2 percent discount for payment within 10 days; otherwise, the full amount is due within 30 days. Other terms may include interest charges for late payment. The facility's accounting department has to balance expected payments (receivables) with obligations (payables). Departments such as HIM often receive invoices directly; it is important to forward all invoices to the accounting department immediately upon receipt and verification so that accounting has the information it needs to make appropriate and timely decisions about payment.

Statements

A **statement** is merely a list of outstanding invoices the vendor has sent but for which no payment has been received. Some companies send statements that include all activity for the period, including payment. The statement is one way the vendor lets the customer know that payments are late. Statements are not payable without supporting documentation. When there is no purchase order, receiving document, and invoice, accounts payable will not remit payment.

Statements received for which there is no underlying documentation should be treated as suspicious. Purchases may have been made without proper authorization. Additionally, there are unscrupulous organizations that send only statements when no transaction has taken place in the hope that

the receiving organization's controls are lax and payment will be made. This is particularly true of certain fraudulent subscriptions and advertising schemes.

Inventory Slips

The purchase of large quantities is supplies inventory and may be recorded as an asset at the time of purchase. Items are then removed from assets and recorded as expenses as they are used. This same system may be used to track pharmacy inventory (by patient rather than department). In a centralized purchasing system, some mechanism must be in place to track the distribution of items to other departments. Frequently paper based, a form is completed requesting items and verifying their receipt. These systems are purely internal because items are on hand. The financial transaction consists of moving the responsibility for the expense of the items from the purchasing department to the requesting department. Table 25.4 shows some common accounts and what they represent.

Recording Transactions

As previously discussed, financial transactions begin with the documents of original entry or source documents. Whether the organization's transactions are recorded on paper or via computer, there must be a way to determine the origination of the transaction. The originating document details the parties involved in the transaction, the amount of the transaction, the type of financial impact involved (revenue or expense, asset or liability), and the individual responsible for the transaction.

Double-Entry Bookkeeping

All financial transactions are recorded with the accounting equation in mind. To simplify the recording of transactions, accountants use special terminology to reflect the maintenance of a balanced equation.

Debits and Credits

Visually, transactions have two sides: left and right. **Debits** are shown on the left; **credits** are shown on the right. Each account has two sides: increase and decrease. In asset accounts, the left-hand debit side represents the natural balance of the account and debits increase the account. Conversely, credits decrease an asset account. Obviously, for the accounting equation to balance, the opposite is true of liability and equity accounts. The right-hand credit side of liability and equity accounts represents the natural balance, and credits increase the accounts. Instead of using minus signs or brackets to represent the increases and decreases, debits and credits provide an additional safeguard against clerical error because every transaction must balance.

Look at the coding consultant example again, using debits and credits.

October Activity								
	Assets		−	Liabilities		=	Equity	
	Debit	Credit		Debit	Credit		Debit	Credit
Beginning balance	$1,500		−	− 0 −		=		$1,500
Purchase codebook		100	−			=	100	
Pay health insurance		100	−			=	100	
Receive payment from client	$1,200		−			=		$1,200
Purchase computer (on credit)		200	−		800	=	1,000	
Receive payment from client	$1,300		−			=		$1,300
Attend CE session		80	−			=	80	

Table 25.4.   Common accounts

Account	Description	Example
Assets		
Cash	Money. Typically, money is represented by several accounts, depending on how the money is stored (for example, in different banks).	Bank account
Inventory	Goods that are available for sale.	Pharmaceuticals
Accounts receivable	Amounts owed the organization for goods and services.	Claims to payers that have not yet been paid
Building	Permanent structures. The land on which they are built is often listed separately.	Office building
Equipment	Represents items that are used to generate revenue or to support the organization during more than one business cycle.	Photocopier CT scanner
Liabilities		
Accounts payable	Amounts the organization owes but has not yet paid.	Supplies purchased on credit
Loans payable	Amounts the organization has borrowed that will be paid over more than one business cycle.	Bank loan
Mortgage payable	Amounts the organization has borrowed to finance the purchase of buildings and equipment.	Building mortgage
Equity		
Capital/stock/fund balance	In a sole proprietorship or partnership, capital is the owner's equity in the organization. In a corporation, stock is the amount invested by owners in the corporation. In a not-for-profit organization, the fund balance is the amount represented by the difference between assets and liabilities.	
Retained earnings/ reserves	In a corporation, retained earnings are profits that have not been distributed. Reserves are amounts that have been designated for a specific purpose.	
Revenue	Temporary account that captures amounts earned by the organization in the current fiscal year.	The difference between revenue and expenses is net income (profits or losses). These accounts are closed at the end of every fiscal year and the net income is moved to retained earnings/reserves.
Expenses	Temporary account that captures amounts disbursed by the organization in the current fiscal year to support the generation of revenue.	

Impact on Individual Accounts

Assets involve multiple accounts as described previously: cash, accounts receivable, and building. Similarly, liabilities have their own accounts. Revenues and expenses fall into the equity section. This system of debits and credits enables us to understand immediately whether a transaction increases or decreases a particular account. Individual accounts increase and decrease in value; however, the overall equation always remains in balance.

Keeping Track of Transactions

Financial transactions are recorded, or posted, to the accounts described earlier according to a system of journal entries.

Journal Entry

Each **journal entry** contains at least one debit and one credit. For every transaction, the sum of the debits must equal the sum of the credits. Ensuring that the debits and credits equal is one aspect of ensuring the accuracy of financial data. Other aspects include posting to the correct accounts and in the correct time period. The following tabulation illustrates the purchase of supplies on credit. The supplies are delivered on February 24, and the supplier's invoice is paid on March 15. Note that no financial transaction is recorded until the supplies are received.

Date	Description	Debit	Credit
2/24	Supplies expense	$300	
	Accounts payable		$300
	Purchase office supplies		
3/15	Accounts payable	$300	
	Cash		$300
	Pay 2/24 office supply invoice		

The accounts payable amount is eliminated when the invoice is paid. It is common business practice to record, or **accrue,** liabilities as they are incurred. This accrual basis of accounting enables organizations to understand their total liabilities continuously and to match expenses with the associated revenue. Some organizations, such as small professional associations and sole proprietorships, only record transactions when the cash is paid or received. This cash basis of accounting is analogous to the way individuals handle their private transactions.

In the preceding tabulation, the supplies expense entry is a debit to increase that account. Expenses are temporary equity accounts that close annually. Revenue increases net income; expenses reduce net income. Therefore, revenue accounts have a natural credit balance and expenses have a natural debit balance.

It should be noted that all the financial accounting examples in this chapter relate to corporate and not-for-profit accounting. Government accounting activity, although a system of debits and credits, is significantly different in some respects. For example, a supply purchase would be recorded (encumbered) at the time the supplies were budgeted and then reduced at the time they were ordered. Government accounting is outside the scope of this discussion.

General Ledger

In a paper-based accounting system, journal entries are recorded chronologically in a general journal and their component debits and credits are posted to the individual accounts. The list of all the individual accounts is referred to as the **general ledger.** In a computer-based environment, only the original journal entry is posted. The computer stores the entries and generates summaries of the individual accounts on request.

The example in figure 25.5 is based on this chapter's original description of a financial transaction. The result of this completed transaction is an increase in cash and an increase in equity (revenue). Note that the amount in accounts receivable is eliminated when the reimbursement is received.

Nonfinancial managers are rarely required to make actual journal entries to record financial transactions. However, they do initiate the transactions and receive reports that detail them. Often the reports only show the department's side of the transaction. For example, a purchase of supplies would appear to the manager on a list of expenses and be added to a summary of all supply expenses on another report. The cash and accounts payable portions of the transaction would not show because they are controlled by the accounting

Figure 25.5.   Example of a financial transaction

Service provided:
Physician sees in the office a new patient, whose chief complaint is an itchy rash.

Transaction recorded:

Clinical record: History and physical/progress note reflect examination of rash and notation that the patient encountered poison ivy while weeding his garden. Over-the-counter (OTC) topical ointment prescribed, and free sample distributed with instructions.

Billing record: Encounter form—office visit code 99201 and ICD-9-CM code 692.6 circled.

Journal entry:

	Debit	Credit
Accounts Receivable—Patient X	60	
Patient Service Revenue		60

Reimbursement received:

Journal entry:

	Debit	Credit
Cash	60	
Accounts Receivable—Patient X		60

department. Another example is the discharged, no final bill (DNFB), which is discussed later in this chapter. The DNFB lists individual patient accounts, which are accounts receivable to the organization. Managerial reporting activity is also discussed later in this chapter.

Financial Statements

At the departmental level, individual financial transactions are reviewed for data quality and compliance with policies and procedures. On an administrative level, the overall impact of transactions is generally of more interest than the individual transactions; therefore, summary reports are prepared. These summaries also are used to communicate with lending institutions, potential investors, and regulatory agencies. A variety of summaries are useful for analyzing an organization's financial activities. The three key reports are the income statement, the statement of retained earnings, and the balance sheet.

Income Statement

The **income statement** summarizes the organization's revenue and expense transactions during the fiscal year. The income statement can be prepared at any point in time and reflects results up to that point. The income statement contains only income and expense accounts and reflects only the activity for the current fiscal year.

The arithmetic difference between total revenue and total expenses is **net income.** When total expenses exceed total revenue, net income is a negative number, or a **net loss.** Net income increases equity; net loss decreases equity.

At the end of the fiscal year, all income statement accounts are closed and the net results are added to, or subtracted from, the appropriate equity account (net asset). For the purposes of periodic reporting, net assets are adjusted in this manner every time this report is prepared. However, at the end of the fiscal year, the income and expense accounts are actually closed so that the new fiscal year begins at zero.

Retained Earnings

The **statement of retained earnings** expresses the change in retained earnings from the beginning of the balance sheet period to the end. Retained earnings are affected, for example, by net income/loss, distribution of stock dividends, and payment of long-term debt. Net income/loss is carried forward from the income statement. When the income statement accounts are closed, the net income/loss is transferred to equity. The "mechanics" of this transaction are to take the balance in each revenue and expense account and record the opposite amount so that all of the income statement accounts have a zero balance. The net dollar amount of the debits and credits is recorded to equity. The statement of changes in retained earnings highlights this transaction. The ending balance in retained earnings is then reported on the balance sheet.

Balance Sheet

The **balance sheet** is a snapshot of the accounting equation at a point in time. Because every financial transaction affects the equation, theoretically, the balance sheet will look different after every transaction. To ensure a meaningful evaluation, the balance sheet is typically reviewed on a periodic basis (monthly, quarterly, semiannually, and annually). It is often compared to balance sheets from previous fiscal years in order to analyze changes in the organization.

The balance sheet lists the major account categories grouped under their equation headings: assets, liabilities, and equity/fund balance. Figure 25.6 shows a set of simple statements, as described earlier. The dollar amount shown next to each account category is the total in each category on the ending date listed at the top of the report. This figure also shows the relationship between the income statement, the statement of retained earnings, and the balance sheet.

Analysis Statements

A number of other types of summary statements are required by users to analyze an organization's financial activity and position. Depending on the organization and its use of the analysis statements, the additional financial statements may be required by GAAP as part of a complete financial summary report. Figure 25.7 shows a two-year comparative balance sheet and three simple examples of statements that help to explain the changes from one year to the next. These statements are included for completeness of discussion and are not statements that HIM professionals generally need to analyze.

Cash Flow

The **statement of cash flow** details the reasons that cash changed from one balance sheet period to another. It shows the analyst whether cash was used to purchase equipment or to pay down debt and whether any unusually large transactions took place.

Stockholder's Equity

The **statement of stockholder's equity** (also called the *statement of net assets*) details the reasons for changes in each of the stockholder's equity accounts, including retained earnings.

Ratio Analysis

After the financial statements have been prepared, they are ready for ratio analysis. Financial analysts can use financial statements, particularly the balance sheet, to determine whether an organization is using its resources similarly to or differently from other organizations in the same industry. In retail sales, analysts compare inventory turnover, that is, how quickly inventory is sold. In any industry, one of the most common reasons to analyze financial statements is to lend money to the organization or to invest in it. Thus, the organization's use of assets compared to its liabilities is extremely important. Changes in an organization's ratios are of particular interest.

Figure 25.6.   Financial statements and relationship between the income statement, net assets, and the balance sheet

Sample Hospital Statement of Revenues and Expenses	12/31/12 (000)
Revenue	
Net patient service revenue	$650
Unrestricted gifts	40
Other	95
Total Revenue	$785
Expenses	
Salaries and wages	$430
Fringe benefits	95
Supplies	175
Total expenses	$700
Income from operations	$ 85
Nonoperating gains	
Unrestricted gifts	$ 15
Excess of revenues over expenses	$100

Sample Hospital Balance Sheet	12/31/12 (000)
Assets	
Cash	$500
Accounts receivable	600
Inventory	400
Building	2,500
Total assets	$4,000
Liabilities	
Accounts payable	600
Mortgage	2,000
Total liabilities	$2,600
Fund Balance	
Restricted funds	400
Unrestricted funds	1,000
Total fund balance	$1,400
Total liabilities and fund balance	$4,000

Sample Hospital Statement of Changes in Unrestricted Fund Balance	2012 (000)
Beginning balance January 1	$ 900
Excess of revenues over expenses	100
Ending balance December 31	$1,000

Ratios, as a comparative tool, are only meaningful within the context of the organization's industry. It is not useful to compare a ratio for a hospital against a ratio for an automobile manufacturer, except to state that one would expect the ratios to be different. Whether an organization's particular ratio is inherently good or bad depends on expected ratios for similar organizations in that industry.

The Healthcare Financial Management Association publishes industry ratio medians annually as a member service. Some state hospital associations also publish ratio information.

Liquidity and Debt Service

A key issue to lenders and investors is the organization's ability to repay its financial obligations. **Liquidity** refers to the ease with which assets can be turned into cash. This is important because payroll, loan payments, and other financial obligations are typically paid in cash. **Debt service** is the extent to which those financial obligations are loans.

Current Ratio

An organization's ability to pay current liabilities with current assets is very important to lenders. Current assets include cash, short-term investments, accounts receivable, and inventory. Current assets implicitly will be (or could be) converted to cash at some point within a year, through collections, sales, or other business activity. Current liabilities include accounts payable and the current portion of loan

Figure 25.7.   Two-year comparative balance sheet with analytical statements

Sample Hospital
Statement of Revenues and Expenses

	12/31/12 (000)	12/31/11 (000)
Revenue		
Net patient service revenue	$650	$500
Unrestricted gifts	40	30
Other	95	70
Total revenue	$785	$600
Expenses		
Salaries and wages	$430	$290
Fringe benefits	95	90
Supplies	175	180
Total expenses	$700	$560
Income from operations	$ 85	$ 40
Nonoperating gains		
Unrestricted gifts	$ 15	$ 10
Excess of revenues over expenses	$100	$ 50

Sample Hospital
Statement of Revenues and Expenses

	2012 (000)	2011 (000)
Beginning balance January 1	$ 900	$850
Excess of revenues over expenses	100	50
Ending balance December 31	$1,000	$900

Sample Hospital
Balance Sheet

	12/31/12 (000)	12/31/11 (000)
Assets		
Cash	$ 500	$ 650
Accounts receivable	600	750
Inventory	400	350
Building	2,500	2,150
Total assets	$4,000	$3,900
Liabilities		
Accounts payable	600	500
Mortgage	2,000	2,100
Total liabilities	$2,600	$2,600
Fund balance		
Restricted funds	400	400
Unrestricted funds	1,000	900
Total fund balance	$1,400	$1,300
Total liabilities and fund balance	$4,000	$3,900

obligations. Again, the term *current* implies that the liability will be discharged within a year. The **current ratio** compares total current assets with total current liabilities:

$$\frac{\text{Total current assets}}{\text{Total current liabilities}}$$

From the balance sheet in figure 25.6, one can take the current assets (cash plus accounts receivable plus inventory) and divide them by the current liabilities (accounts payable) to determine the current ratio:

$$\frac{1,500,000}{600,000} = \frac{15}{6} = 2.5$$

The current ratio indicates that for every dollar of current liability, $2.50 of current assets could be used to discharge the liability, which even common sense tells us is good.

Acid-Test Ratio

Inventory is a current asset because it is presumed that inventory will be sold, or turned over, within one fiscal year. However, inventory can become obsolete very quickly (for example, in the fashion and computer industries). Pharmaceuticals can expire before they are used. For expensive items such as motor vehicles, saleable merchandise may be retained in inventory longer than expected or desirable. Therefore, a stricter measure of an organization's ability to pay current liabilities is needed. The **acid-test ratio** compares current liabilities to the current assets that are truly liquid, that is, able to be turned into cash quickly:

$$\frac{(\text{Cash} + \text{short-term investments} + \text{net current receivables})}{\text{Total current liabilities}}$$

Short-term investments include money market funds, certificates of deposit, and Treasury bills, for example. Using the balance sheet in figure 25.6, the acid-test ratio is:

$$\frac{1,100,000}{600,000} = \frac{1.1}{6.0} = 1.83$$

In this example, the acid-test ratio reveals that for every dollar of current liabilities, $1.83 of current assets could be used immediately or sold quickly to discharge the liabilities.

Debt Ratio

Looking back to the mortgage example, the organization's building asset was purchased using 10 percent cash and 90 percent mortgage. Ninety percent of that asset was financed with debt. Looking at all the liabilities and all the assets together gives the analyst an overall picture of how the assets were acquired. The **debt ratio,** therefore, is total liabilities divided by total assets.

It is important to remember that all ratio analysis is industry specific and varies somewhat depending on the economic environment. Therefore, ratio analysis can be used to compare similar organizations at a specific point in time or the same organization at different points in time. However, a hospital ratio would never be compared with a professional association ratio.

Profitability

The preceding examples illustrate how organizations can evaluate their ability to pay their bills. Another measure of an organization's health is its profitability. **Profitability** refers to an organization's ability to increase in value: how well does it invest its assets? As with other ratios, profitability measures are only meaningful as benchmarks against like organizations or in trending a single organization over time.

Return on Investment

Return on investment (ROI) measures the increase in the value of an asset. In a savings account, this increase is measured as the amount of interest received in a period. The beginning balance in the account is the measurement of the asset. Interest received in the period is the return. Thus,

$$\text{ROI} = \frac{\text{Interest earned in the period}}{\text{Asset value at the beginning of the period}}$$

Return on individual investments can be calculated in this manner. For an entire organization, interest earned is replaced by earnings, usually after taxes. Asset value is replaced by total assets:

$$\text{ROI} = \frac{\text{Earnings (after taxes)}}{\text{Total assets}}$$

Return on Equity

ROI does not tell the whole story because it only indirectly measures the liabilities incurred in order to acquire or generate the asset. Generating sufficient overall profits to ensure ongoing operations, as well as maintaining and upgrading assets, is especially of interest to users of financial information. An organization may use several profitability ratios to gauge overall performance. **Return on equity (ROE)** is an important indicator for determining an organization's efficiency or profitability level. It measures the excess of revenue over expenses (net income) for an accounting period compared to the total net assets (equity).

To illustrate, examine the acquisition of technology to generate income.

Purchase: $100,000 (invest in document imaging system)

Liability: $90,000 (long-term loan from bank)

Net income: $30,000 (after taxes)

$$\text{ROI} = \frac{\$30,000}{\$100,000} = 30\%$$

$$\text{ROE} = \frac{\$30,000}{\$10,000} = 300\%$$

Additional measures of return are discussed later in the section on capital projects.

Check Your Understanding 25.2

Instructions: Answer the following questions on a separate piece of paper.

1. List three assets and three liabilities.

2. Why are revenue and expense accounts part of owner's equity?

3. What inventory does a hospital have?

4. What is the difference between a debit and a credit?

5. Why is knowledge of accounting important to nonfinancial managers?

6. A lender wants to know how quickly a borrower would be able to repay a debt. What is the best ratio to use for this analysis? Why?

Basic Management Accounting

To obtain appropriate compensation for goods and services provided, the organization must understand and measure the resources used to manufacture, acquire, or otherwise produce those goods and services. The measurement of those resources is monetary and is referred to as their cost. In manufacturing and other goods-oriented businesses, sales are compared to the cost of goods sold, which are composed of raw materials and other manufacturing costs. Calculation of the manufacturing cost of goods sold, by-products, salvage, and waste is outside the scope of this discussion. In a service industry, the underlying costs consist largely of human resources, supplies, and the tools of the trade.

Management accounting focuses on the internal communication of accounting and financial data for the purpose of facility-based decision making. Management accountants use the same transaction data that are summarized in a financial statement. They also use a variety of additional data, such as prevailing interest rates and staffing levels, to provide meaningful information required by management.

Describing Costs

Cost accounting is the discipline of identifying and measuring costs and is a unique subset of the accounting profession. However, a general understanding of the terminology helps nonfinancial managers participate in and support the process. There are numerous ways to describe costs, but the most important for purposes of this discussion are included here.

Direct Costs

Direct costs are traceable to a specific good or service provided. To a hospital, the cost of a specific medication can be matched to the specific patient to whom it was administered. Room charges are another example. Similarly, to a consulting firm, the hours that a consultant coder spends coding are directly linked to the services provided to a specific facility.

Indirect Costs

Indirect costs or **overhead costs** are incurred by the organization in the process of providing goods or services; however, they are not specifically attributable to an individual product or service. The costs of providing security services at a hospital or clerical support at the switchboard are indirect costs with respect to patient care. To the consulting firm, the cost of CE for its coding staff is an indirect cost of providing services to a particular client.

The classification of costs as direct or indirect depends on the relationship of the cost to the client, department, product, service, or activity in question. Payroll in the security department is an indirect cost to patient care, but it is a direct cost to the security department. Therefore, the distinction between direct and indirect costs is important in understanding the

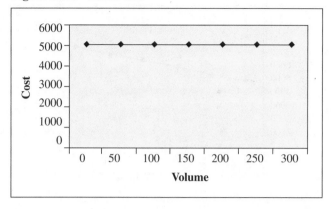

Figure 25.8.   Fixed cost

broader financial impact of activities within the facility. In developing capital projects (discussed later in this chapter) such as the development and implementation of an electronic health record, an understanding of the associated costs (and, conversely, the cost savings) is crucial in making realistic financial estimates and projections.

Fixed Costs

For planning and analysis, it is useful to classify costs as fixed or variable. **Fixed costs** remain the same, despite changes in volume. For example, a manager's base salary does not change, regardless of patient volume or other changes in activity. Mortgage payments also are not dependent on activity. In figure 25.8, the copy machine depreciation expense does not vary, regardless of the number of requests.

Variable Costs

Variable costs are sensitive to volume. Medication is a good example. The more patients are treated, the more medication is used. Paper medical record documentation is another example. The larger the volume of patients, the more paper is used. In figure 25.9, the cost of paper used to print release of information requests rises proportionately with the number of requests.

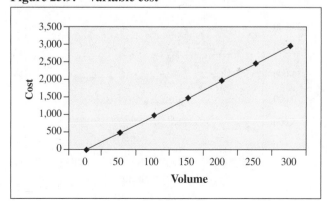

Figure 25.9.   Variable cost

Figure 25.10.   Mixed cost

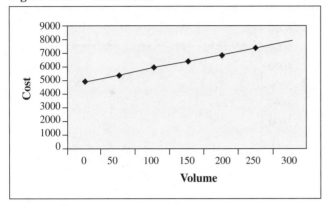

Semi-Fixed Costs

Costs may behave in a combination of fixed and variable ways, and volume is not the only change agent. For example, consider the coding function. Base coding salaries are fixed. Increases in discharges may require a temporary coding consultant. If the consultant charges on a per chart basis, the cost of coding services rises variably with that volume. Similarly, the combination of personnel and paper costs for release of information has a combined mixed variability, as illustrated in figure 25.10.

On the other hand, nursing base salaries are also a fixed cost. However, hospitals do not staff nursing for full capacity. Therefore, increases in census require the use of part-time or per diem nurses, who are added based on established patient-to-nurse ratios. The full cost of nursing services, then, goes up in steps. Figure 25.11 illustrates this type of personnel cost variability, as applied to the copy cost example. (For a detailed discussion of cost classifications, see chapter 14 in Cleverley and Cameron's *Essentials of Health Care Finance* [2012]).

Cost Reports

Prior to implementation of prospective payment systems (PPSs), Medicare reimbursement to hospitals was related

Figure 25.11.   Step mixed cost

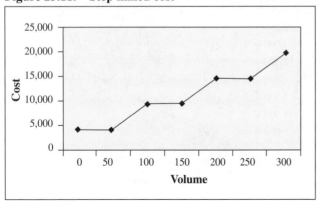

directly to the costs incurred by the facilities. Individual facility cost reports were submitted to Medicare, identifying the direct and indirect costs of providing care to Medicare patients. Direct costs include nursing and radiology; indirect costs include medical records and information systems. Preparation of cost reports requires the definition of products or services, establishment of cost centers, and identification of service units (Dunn 1999, 64–65). The expense of nonrevenue-producing cost centers is allocated to revenue-producing cost centers in order to fully understand the cost of providing services. Although cost reporting is no longer used to directly determine Medicare reimbursement for prospective payment facilities, critical access hospitals are reimbursed 101 percent of eligible Medicare costs. In addition, CMS uses cost reports to help determine facility-specific and regional cost adjustment factors for healthcare PPSs.

Allocation of Overhead

The attribution of indirect or overhead costs to revenue-producing service units illustrates the budget concept that all activities must support the mission of the organization. There are four methods of allocation of overhead:

- **Direct method of cost allocation** distributes the cost of overhead departments solely to the revenue-producing areas. Allocation is based on each revenue-producing area's relative square footage, number of employees, or actual usage of supplies and services. (See figure 25.12.)
- **Step-down allocation** distributes overhead costs once beginning with the area that provides the least amount of nonrevenue-producing services.
- **Double distribution** allocates overhead costs twice, which takes into consideration the fact that some overhead departments provide services to each other.
- **Simultaneous equations method** distributes overhead costs through multiple iterations allowing maximum distribution of interdepartmental costs among overhead departments.

The last three methods of cost allocation listed assume that overhead cost centers (such as housekeeping) perform services for each other as well as for revenue-producing areas. Therefore, overhead costs are distributed among overhead cost centers as well as revenue-producing areas.

Although each of these methods may produce slightly different results, the ultimate goal is to allocate overhead costs appropriately. Appropriate allocation enables the facility to express the full cost of providing services.

Impact of Accounts Receivable on Financial Statements

Accounts receivable represents a current asset. Delays in processing claims cause receivables to age. Aged receivables can negatively affect a facility's ability to

Figure 25.12.   Direct allocation vs. step allocation

| | Nonrevenue-Producing Department | | Revenue-Producing Department | |
	HIM Department	Business Office	Medicine	Laboratory
Direct method:				
Overhead costs before allocation	$360,000	$240,000	$400,000	$250,000
Allocation				
HIM (no. discharges processed)	($360,000)		$340,000	$20,000
Business office (no. labor hours used)		($240,000)	$80,000	$160,000
Total overhead after allocation	$0	$0	$820,000	$430,000
Step method:				
Overhead costs before allocation	$360,000	$240,000	$400,000	$250,000
Allocation				
HIM (no. discharges processed)	($360,000)	$50,000	$300,000	$10,000
Business office (no. labor hours used)		($290,000)	$90,000	$200,000
Total overhead after allocation	$0	$0	$790,000	$460,000

borrow money. Failure to claim and collect receivables affects cash, which in turn negatively affects the facility's ability to discharge its current liabilities, the largest of which is payroll. Therefore, in a facility for which reimbursement is the largest revenue item and payroll is the largest expense, there is a direct relationship between getting paid and paying employees. Thus, the role of HIM becomes a critical component of maintaining the facility's fiscal integrity. Strategies for effectively managing accounts receivable are further discussed in chapter 17.

Internal Controls

In any industry, internal controls must be in place to safeguard assets and to ensure compliance with policies and procedures. Internal controls may be designed to prevent the theft of cash or to ensure that a patient receives the correct medication. The three major categories of internal controls are preventive, detective, and corrective controls.

Preventive

Preventive controls are implemented prior to the activity's taking place because they are designed to stop an error from happening. In financial management, pre-transaction supervisory review and authorization is a preventive control. Computer data-entry validation is another preventive control. Data-entry validation prevents the user from entering "64," for example,

as a day of the month. Preventive controls are sometimes more costly than their effect warrants. In those cases, other types of controls must be put in place to find and correct errors.

Detective

Detective controls are designed to find errors that have already been made. Detective controls tend to be less expensive than preventive controls and can be implemented at many levels. Quantitative record reviews and computer exception reports are examples of detective controls. In accounting, the summing of debits and credits is a detective control because the two sums must always be equal. Footing and cross-footing financial reports are another detective control. (See figure 25.13.)

Corrective

When an error or other problem has been detected, action must be taken to correct the error, solve the problem, or design controls to prevent future errors or problems. The error or problem must be analyzed to determine the cause. When a correction can be made, it is documented and implemented. However, some errors, such as amputation of an incorrect limb, cannot be corrected. In these cases, analysis of the root cause is important so that the error can be prevented in the future. In financial management, very few errors cannot be corrected. Typical errors include posting transactions to an incorrect account, posting transactions that

Figure 25.13.   Footing and cross-footing financial reports

SUMMING OF DEBITS AND CREDITS

Cash $1,345
                Photocopy paper $974
                Toner $362

In this journal entry, the debit ($1,345) does not match the credits ($1,336). This means that an error has been made. Reference back to the original documentation will reveal that the sales tax on the items was not accounted for.

FOOTING AND CROSS-FOOTING

	January	February	March	Year-to-date (Cross-foot)
Payroll	20,000	20,000	20,000	60,000
Benefits	6,000	6,000	6,000	24,000
Office supplies	1,000	1,000	1,000	3,000
Equipment service	400	500	600	500
				87,500?
Monthly Totals	27,400 (Foot)	27,400	27,400	82,200?

The foot is the sum of the columns; the cross-foot is the sum of the rows. Notice that in this example the sums do not match. Footing and cross-footing reports that are supposed to represent arithmetic totals is a very useful detective control, particularly with manually prepared or PC-prepared reports. A simple error in creating a formula in a spreadsheet program can cause an entire report to be wrong.

have not been completed, and posting incorrect amounts. Even financial statement errors can be corrected and the reports redistributed. Problems that cannot always be corrected include theft of assets and failure to invest funds on a timely basis. These problems require analysis and development and implementation of controls for the future.

Corrective controls are designed to fix problems that have been discovered, frequently as a result of detective controls. Many errors and problems occur routinely, such as failing to complete forms, making computation errors, and wrongly posting transactions. Therefore, procedures must be in place to ensure the timely and accurate correction of the error or solution to the problem. In the HIM department, the incomplete chart system is a corrective control. Incomplete charts have been detected, the source of the error identified, and the responsible individual contacted for completion of the chart. In financial management, supervisory review of transactions is typically used to detect errors and problems. The ability to correct errors in journal entries is essential.

Internal controls may be present at every level of the organization. In a service organization, such as a hospital, controls over expenditures are some of the most important responsibilities of individual managers. Two key methods of exerting such controls are through purchasing and analysis of budget variances.

Budgets

Managers must have some understanding of managerial accounting in order to control the financial aspects of their departments' operations. As stated earlier, managers must work within budgets that have been developed based on their organization's goals and objectives. Therefore, it is not sufficient for a manager merely to review for accuracy the financial transactions generated by the department during the period. Rather, the transactions must be compared to the expected or budgeted transactions to ensure that the goals and objectives of both the department and the organization are being met. **Managerial accounting** is the development, implementation, and analysis of systems that track financial transactions for managerial control purposes; it includes both budget and cost analysis systems.

Types of Budgets

In addition to the most familiar budgets, operating and capital budgets (discussed next), organizations develop and monitor other budgets, including financial budgets, cash flow budgets, and incremental budgets. These budgets are the responsibility of the finance department.

The development and monitoring of budgets is guided by the facility's policy and procedures manual and the management styles of the administrative and departmental management team. Therefore, it is extremely important for department managers to understand the facility's budgeting methods, including how administration uses budgets.

At best, a budget is a manager's best guess at the outcomes of future financial transactions. Unexpected events that influence those transactions, such as declining census, increase in interest rates, and staffing changes, create budget variances. Some budgets are specifically designed to take these fluctuations into consideration. A budget can represent virtually any projected set of circumstances. Therefore, there are many different types of budget methodologies. Common methodologies include fixed, flexible, activity-based, and zero-based budgets.

The most common type of budget is a **fixed budget.** Budget amounts are based on expected capacity. Fixed budgets do not change when expected capacity changes. For example, the HIM department would budget outsourced transcription service expense on the basis of the estimated number of discharges and historical need. When the number of discharges materially increases or declines, the outsourced transcription service expense will increase or decrease, thus creating a budget variance.

Flexible budgets are based on projected productivity. In this case, the HIM department would budget outsourced transcription service expense at several levels of discharges. As the actual discharges become known, the budget reflects the estimate at that level of activity. Used primarily in manufacturing, this method of budgeting also is useful for projecting personnel budgets in service areas, such as nursing units, where increased activity has a direct impact on staffing and supplies.

Activity-based budgets are based on activities or projects rather than on departments. Typically used for construction projects, an activity-based budget can be useful for any project that spans multiple budget lines or departments and for projects that span more than one fiscal year. Computer system installation and implementation should be controlled using an activity-based budget.

Different budget methodologies are developed to meet the needs of the organization. Fixed and flexible budgets are characteristic of operating budgets. Activity-based budgets are more often used for capital projects. All three types of budgets can be used by virtually any organization. **Zero-based budgets,** on the other hand, apply to organizations for which each budget cycle poses the opportunity to continue or discontinue services based on the availability of resources. Every department or activity must be justified and prioritized annually in order to effectively allocate the organization's resources. Professional associations and charitable foundations, for example, routinely use zero-based budgeting.

Operational Budgets

The purpose of an operational budget is to allocate and control resources in a manner consistent with the organization's goals and objectives. These goals and objectives are tied to the organization's mission. Each department also should have its own mission, goals, and objectives that identify how it contributes to the organization's overall mission. Every item in the operational budget should have a direct relationship to a departmental goal that supports an organizational goal.

The budget process begins with the board of directors or trustees, which approves the fiscal assumptions for the upcoming year. Those assumptions are quantified and communicated to the department managers, who develop budgets based on those assumptions. Typical assumptions include the desired growth in revenue and targeted cost reductions.

Budget Cycle

The operational budget cycle generally coincides with one fiscal year. The purpose of the **operational budget** is the quantification of the projected results of operations for the coming fiscal year. This process begins three to four months before the end of the current fiscal year. Projected budgets should be collected, compiled, reviewed, and approved prior to the start of the new fiscal year.

Fiscal Period

An organization's budget year coincides with its fiscal year on file with the IRS. Although the actual operational budget generally only applies to one fiscal year, financial managers often project multiple years of budgets with a variety of scenarios in order to test the financial impact of current decision making.

Interim Periods

In a computerized environment, it is relatively easy to generate financial reports as frequently as needed by management. However, monthly budget reporting is most common. Any period that represents less than an entire fiscal year is an **interim period.** Figure 25.14 provides a sample budget report for an HIM department for May. The budgeted amounts for each item are listed next to the actual amounts for the month. As is common, the year-to-date (in this case, January through May) budget and actual amounts also are included. It is useful for budget reports to show the differences between budgeted and actual amounts. Such differences are called variances. Many budget reports also show the percentage variance for each item, based on the budget. Managers may be required to explain variances that exceed a particular dollar value or a specified percentage.

In the budget report shown in figure 25.14, there is a large variance in May's budgeted expense for printer paper. By following that line item across to the year-to-date amount, it is evident that there is no year-to-date variance in the budget. This illustrates a timing difference between the expected expense and the actual expense. The budget may have placed that expense in April even though the actual expense occurred in May. These types of temporary variances are the

Figure 25.14. HIM department budget report for May

Description	May Budget	May Actual	May Variance	YTD Budget	YTD Actual	YTD Variance
Payroll	$25,000	$22,345	$2,655	$125,000	$110,321	$14,679
Fringe benefits	$8,000	$7,360	$640	$40,000	$37,870	$2,130
Contract services	$5,000	$8,000	($3,000)	$25,000	$40,000	($15,000)
Office supplies	$150	$145	$5	$750	$975	($225)
Printer paper	$100	$250	($150)	$500	$500	—
Postage	$95	$97	($2)	$475	$456	$19
Travel	$0	$0	—	$0	$0	—
Continuing education	$0	$0	—	$0	$45	($45)

result of normal business activities, and although they may require explanation, they are usually not of concern.

Budget Components

The components of an operational budget generally follow the format of the income statement and list revenue items and expense items. Every department is different, depending on its unique activities. However, budget reports tend to be uniform throughout the organization. Therefore, line items that do not apply to a particular department are likely to be listed with zero values rather than be omitted.

Revenues

In the HIM department, there is little, if any, revenue. Occasionally, a facility with excess capacity will contract out transcription services. Copy fees are another potential source of revenue; however, because such fees should be cost based, they are probably more appropriately considered a reimbursement (reduction of expenses).

Expenses

The HIM department budget consists primarily of expenses. Expenses may be incurred as a result of financial transactions outside or within the organization. Some departments, such as housekeeping and facilities maintenance, perform services for other facility departments. Therefore, charges from these departments may appear on the budget. Such charges are generally carried forward through the cost allocation process and usually are not estimated by individual managers.

Ordinarily, the single largest expense in a healthcare facility is payroll. This is typical for service organizations. Payroll can be a difficult expense to project because employees have different anniversary dates and different salary increases.

The cost of employee benefits is part of payroll but is often listed separately. Facilities rarely expect department managers to calculate benefits budgets because this is a human resources–controlled line item. The cost of benefits tracks with payroll.

The next largest expense account is often supplies. Clinical supplies are a substantial item on the cardiology or radiology department budget, whereas office supplies might be a large item for HIM.

Cost of goods sold is a manufacturing concept that refers to the underlying cost of making the finished goods. This concept applies to healthcare providers in the sense that there is a cost basis for providing services. For every inpatient treated, there are payroll, utility, office supplies, pharmaceutical, and equipment costs that the facility incurred. Unlike manufacturing, in which the cost of producing items is tracked very closely, healthcare facilities historically have not been good at tracking the underlying costs of providing services to individual patients. The costs of providing care are often analyzed in the aggregate.

Management of the Operating Budget

When the operating budget has been developed and approved, it is the responsibility of the department management to ensure that the budget goals are met. As a general rule, in meeting goals, revenue should meet or exceed budget and expenses should meet or be less than budget. However, because expenses support revenues, an increase in revenues (perhaps due to unexpected volume) may signal an expected increase in expenses, such as variable expenses. This is particularly true when the patient census exceeds expectations. Despite the logical and expected nature of these results, managers are required to investigate and explain differences between budgeted and actual amounts on a regular basis.

Identification of Variances

A **variance** is the arithmetic difference between the budgeted amount and the actual amount of a line item. Variance analysis places accountability for financial transactions on the manager of the department that initiated the transaction.

Variances are often calculated on the monthly budget report. The organization's policies and procedures manual defines unacceptable variances or variances that must be explained. In identifying variances, it is important to recognize whether the variance is favorable or unfavorable and whether it is temporary or permanent.

Timing

The problems identified by variance analysis and the action that must be taken depend largely on whether the variance is temporary or permanent. Temporary variances are generally self-limiting.

Temporary budget variances are not expected to continue in subsequent months. For example, a department may budget for a large purchase of printer paper in May. When that purchase does not actually take place until July, there will be a temporary variance in the May and July monthly report and a temporary variance in the May and June year-to-date numbers. Figure 25.15 illustrates this point. In this example, the HIM department budgeted $260 per month for department supplies, plus an additional $900 in May for printer paper. This created a temporary, favorable variance in expenditures in May and June.

In contrast, **permanent budget variances** do not resolve during the current fiscal year. In the preceding example, a variance still would have existed at the end of December (the close of the fiscal year) if the printer paper had been budgeted in November. The department supplies variance then would be a permanent variance during the current and subsequent fiscal year, unless the subsequent year's budget can include the purchase.

Impact

In addition to identifying whether timing is an issue, the variance analysis is expected to identify whether the variance is favorable of unfavorable. This is often obvious from the budget report but should be stated clearly when discussing the variance.

Favorable variances occur when the actual results are better than budget projections. Actual revenue in excess of budget is a favorable variance. **Unfavorable variances** occur when the actual results are worse than what was budgeted.

Actual expenditure in excess of budget is an unfavorable variance. Note that the terms *favorable* and *unfavorable* refer to the impact on the organization rather than to the magnitude or direction of the variance. Sometimes the terms *negative* and *positive* are used instead. This can be confusing because a negative expense variance is favorable. Therefore, it is extremely important to ensure that the manager understands and correctly uses the language of the organization.

Explanation of Variances

The analysis of budget variances is a financial management control. Administration may review the monthly budget report first and then ask questions of the appropriate manager. In other instances, the department managers are automatically required to respond to certain variances.

In general, the reason for a temporary budget variance is the timing of the transaction. Looking back to the department supplies and printer paper example in figure 25.15, there is a very simple explanation for the temporary variance. In wording the explanation to administration, the department manager should state the following:

- Nature of the variance (favorable or unfavorable, temporary or permanent)
- Exact amount of the variance
- Cause of the variance
- Any ameliorating circumstances or offsetting amounts

Amount

In the analysis of variance, materiality is an issue. Rarely will a manager be required to explain a $5 variance. Clearly, the cost of a manager's time to explain such an insignificant amount far exceeds the benefit of knowing why the variance has occurred. In fact, because budgets are largely estimates, it would be quite odd if the actual amounts always matched the budgeted amounts. Therefore, dollar and percentage limits are set in the organization's policies and procedures manual. Variances that exceed these limits must be explained in detail.

Cause

For the preceding printer paper variance example, the explanation might be something like the following: "In department

Figure 25.15. Examples of budget variances

May Budget Report					
Department supplies	**May Budget**	**May Actual**	**May Variance**	**YTD Budget**	**YTD Actual**	**YTD Variance**
	1,150	250	900	2,150	1,250	900

June Budget Report					
Department supplies	**June Budget**	**June Actual**	**June Variance**	**YTD Budget**	**YTD Actual**	**YTD Variance**
	250	250	0	2,400	1,500	900

July Budget Report					
Department supplies	**July Budget**	**July Actual**	**July Variance**	**YTD Budget**	**YTD Actual**	**YTD Variance**
	250	1,150	− 900	2,650	2,650	0

supplies, the favorable, temporary variance of $900 will resolve in July when the budgeted expenditure for printer paper is processed." For such a temporary variance, no additional explanation is usually necessary.

Temporary variances are not typically of serious concern to administrations. However, permanent variances can be a problem because management of departmental budgets is an important indicator of the competence of department managers.

Whether a variance is temporary or permanent depends on the answers to two questions:

- Are the subsequent transactions that will compensate for the variance likely to occur within the same fiscal year?
- Is it reasonably certain the transactions will occur as predicted?

If the compensating transactions are unlikely to take place during the current fiscal year, the result is a permanent variance in the current budget report. Sometimes the manager may not know when—or if—the transactions will actually take place. For example, the manager may have budgeted $2,000 for attendance at an unspecified CE conference in June. A conflict with the Joint Commission survey prevented the manager from attending the conference, creating a favorable expense variance. As long as the manager believes the amount will be spent appropriately at some time during the fiscal year, the variance is temporary. For example, the manager may be able to attend a conference later in the year. However, if the manager knows that there is no chance of attending a conference and appropriately spending the budgeted amount, the variance should be explained as permanent.

Additional explanation is probably necessary for a permanent variance. An expenditure that must be deferred until the next fiscal year is particularly important. In that case, the explanation might be as follows: "In department supplies, there is a favorable, permanent variance of $900 because a large order of printer paper was planned for this fiscal year but did not occur. This amount is included in next year's budget."

Circumstances

Managers may have the opportunity to utilize favorable variances in one line item to offset unfavorable variances in another line item. For example, unused travel budget may be used for CE. The explanation of these circumstances will generally be carried forward through all remaining variance analyses for the remainder of the fiscal year.

The ability to work with the departmental budget as a whole as opposed to justifying line items is entirely dependent on the administration of the budget process. One typical example of offsetting variances occurs when an employee leaves and cannot be replaced immediately. Several things may happen. The vacancy may cause a favorable variance in payroll expense until the position is filled or an unfavorable

variance in payroll expense if other employees are paid overtime to help fill the vacancy. Both of these variances are permanent. Alternatively, the vacancy may cause a permanent, favorable variance in payroll expense and a permanent, unfavorable variance in consulting expenses when the vacant position is outsourced. In the latter case, the two variances at least partially offset each other, which must be explained in the monthly variance report.

Capital Budget

Unlike the operational budget, which looks primarily at projected income statement activity for the next fiscal year, the **capital budget** looks at long-term investments. Such investments are usually related to improvements in the facility infrastructure, expansion of services, or replacement of existing assets. Capital investments focus on either the appropriateness of an investment (given the facility's investment guidelines) or choosing among different opportunities to invest. The capital budget is the facility's plan for allocating resources over and above the operating budget.

Funding for the capital budget may come from diverse sources. For example, donations or grants may fund a building project or retained earnings or unallocated reserves may fund equipment purchases. Federal and state government funds may be available to offset the cost of capital investments. Regardless of the source of the funds, capital investments are defined by facility policy and selected using financial analysis techniques.

Large-Dollar Purchases

From a departmental perspective, capital budget items are large-dollar purchases, as defined by facility budget policies and procedures. Capital budget items usually have a useful life in excess of one fiscal year, making them long-term assets, and a dollar value in excess of a predetermined amount, often $500 or $1,000. Common HIM department capital budget items include office furniture, photocopying and scanning equipment, and computer equipment. Some organizations maintain a separate capital budget and process for computer-related equipment and software. In addition, in such cases, control over the acquisition of the related long-term assets may rest with the information technology or information systems department.

Acquisitions

The acquisition of long-term assets may be controlled by the purchasing department. The purchasing department may already have a contract with a specific vendor to provide certain types of equipment or furniture. In the absence of an existing contract, it may still be the purchasing department's responsibility to ensure the appropriate acquisition of assets through the **request for proposal (RFP)** process. The RFP process is a preventive control designed to eliminate bias and to ensure competitive pricing in the acquisition of goods and services.

Cost-Benefit Analysis

An old photocopying machine breaks down at least once a week. Repair of the machine takes up to two days and is increasingly expensive. During the downtime, release-of-information clerks must use a machine located two floors below the HIM department and shared by three other departments. It seems obvious to HIM department personnel that a new machine is needed. Including a new machine in the HIM department's capital budget request is certainly warranted. However, funding for a new machine is based on specific, detailed cost justifications and is weighed in comparison to all departments' requests. Facility administration may be forced to choose between a new copier for the HIM department and several new computers for the patient accounts department. All other factors being equal, increased efficiency and productivity in claims processing is likely to be chosen over increased efficiency in release of information.

For this reason, HIM managers should include cost savings calculations in such requests.

Depreciation

As discussed earlier, certain long-term assets, such as equipment and furniture, wear out over time and must be replaced. Such assets contribute to revenue over multiple fiscal periods. Therefore, the cost of these assets is not recorded as an expense at the time of purchase. Rather, the current asset, cash, is exchanged for a long-term asset, equipment. A portion of the historical cost of equipment then is moved from asset into expense each fiscal year and cumulated into the contra-account: accumulated depreciation. Eventually, the cost of equipment has been expensed and equipment account value is zero. The purpose of depreciation is to spread the cost of an asset over its useful life. (See tables 25.5 and 25.6.)

Table 25.5. Sample depreciation methods

Straight Line	The cost of the asset is expensed equally over the expected life of the asset. The estimated sale value of the asset at the end of its useful life is called the residual value and is subtracted from the cost prior to depreciation.	$\dfrac{\text{Cost} - \text{residual value}}{\text{No. of years (useful life)}}$
	Example: Copy machine purchased at a cost of $5,000 Useful life = 4 years Residual value = $200 Annual depreciation $= \dfrac{\$5,000 - \$200}{4} = \$1,200$ per year	
Units of Production	The cost of the asset is expensed over the expected life of the asset, measured in usage. In this case, usage would be the number of copies.	$\dfrac{\text{Cost} - \text{residual value}}{\text{No. of copies (useful life)}}$
	Example: Copy machine purchased at a cost of $5,000 Useful life = 100,000 copies Residual value = $200 Depreciation rate $= \dfrac{\$5,000 - \$200}{100,000} = \$0.048$ (4.8 cents) per copy Annual depreciation = $0.048 times the number of copies actually made	
Accelerated	There are several accelerated depreciation methods, all of which are designed to expense more of the asset's value early in its useful life. One such method is called double declining balance (DDB). DDB expenses the asset at double the straight-line method, based on the book value rather than on the historical cost.	Book value times twice the straight-line rate Straight-line rate $= \dfrac{\text{annual depreciation}}{\text{cost} - \text{residual value}}$
	Example: Copy machine purchased at a cost of $5,000 Useful life = 100,000 copies Residual value = $200 Straight line rate = $1,200/$4,800 = 25% Annual depreciation = Book value times 50%	

Note: These examples of depreciation methods are just a few of the acceptable methods in use today for various purposes. The reader should be aware that there are other methods and that not all methods are acceptable for income tax purposes or for GAAP. Accounting for income taxes is beyond the scope of this discussion.

Table 25.6.   Sample depreciation schedule

Copy machine purchased at a cost of $5,000
Useful life = 100,000 copies
Residual value = $200
Straight-line depreciation (25% of cost minus residual value annually)

	Book Value at Beginning of Year	Depreciation	Accumulated Depreciation	Book Value at End of Year
Year 1	$5,000	$1,200	$1,200	$3,800
Year 2	3,800	1,200	2,400	2,600
Year 3	2,600	1,200	3,600	1,400
Year 4	1,400	1,200	4,800	200
Year 5	200			

Units of Production (4.8 cents per copy annually)

	Book Value at Beginning of Year	Number of Copies Used	Depreciation	Accumulated Depreciation	Book Value at End of Year
Year 1	$5,000	20,000	$ 960	$ 960	$4,040
Year 2	4,040	20,000	960	1,920	3,080
Year 3	3,080	22,000	1,056	2,976	2,024
Year 4	2,024	25,000	1,200	4,176	824
Year 5	824	25,000	624	4,800	200

Notice that in units of production the useful life is based on the number of copies used—not on the time in service. In this example, the copier does not become fully depreciated until year 5. Also, the depreciation cannot exceed the cost less the residual value; therefore, the depreciation in year 5 is only $624.

Double Declining Balance (50% of book value annually)

	Book Value at Beginning of Year	Depreciation	Accumulated Depreciation	Book Value at End of Year
Year 1	$5,000	$2,500	$2,500	$2,500
Year 2	2,500	1,250	3,750	1,250
Year 3	1,250	625	4,375	625
Year 4	625	425	4,800	200
Year 5	200			

Notice that in DDB, the final depreciation entry in year 4 reduces the book value to the residual value (50% of $625 is really $375.50, but we added $49.50 to make the depreciation 425 so that book value drops to $200 at the end of year 4).

Note that the depreciation of long-term assets does not necessarily have a direct relationship to the activity of actually using the asset. It is not unusual to depreciate an asset over five years and then continue to use it for another five. For example, a facility whose equipment is fully depreciated and whose current assets are heavily financed with debt obligations may be unable to reinvest in new equipment. This is another example of how ratio analysis affects lending decisions.

Capital Projects

A facility's ability to invest in capital projects is very important to the continued success of its operations. Because buildings deteriorate, equipment wears out, and new technology is important to healthcare delivery, capital improvements must be implemented. Individual departments request equipment purchases and facility improvements as the needs arise. Facility administration must choose among the suggested projects to optimize use of its resources.

In addition to capital improvements, facilities may make capital investments that improve operational efficiency. Some of these capital investments require broader analysis than the cost of the equipment. Replacing a manual incomplete record tracking system with a computer-based system, for example, involves an analysis of employee time and departmental space allocations as well as the associated equipment and software costs. Medical staff relationship improvement is another factor that is difficult to quantify but should be considered.

Facility administration looks at capital projects differently than it reviews operational activities. Theoretically, operational activities contribute to the generation of revenue for the facility. For example, all hospital activities either provide healthcare services or in some way support departments that provide healthcare services. A hospital may elect to perform its own printing rather than outsource the printing function; however, it is unlikely to provide printing services to the general public. Printing forms supports clinical and administrative services internally; running a printing business does not. Therefore, the justification for operational budget amounts generally rests on the extent to which the underlying activities support the mission of the facility at the projected productivity levels. Capital projects, on the other hand, although still mission supportive, often leverage the facility to higher levels of productivity, increased efficiency, or expansion of services and capacity.

Finally, budgeted capital funds generally must be expended in the time period for which they were approved. Even when allocated, capital budget items may be prioritized and timed so that purchases are made only with administrative approval. Actual funding may not meet anticipated levels, or unforeseen circumstances may change administrative priorities.

For capital budgets, supporting the mission of the facility is not sufficient justification. Capital projects also must satisfy predetermined levels of return on the projected investment.

Cost Justification

All departments in a facility compete for finite facility resources. Therefore, department managers must be familiar with cost justification techniques and with their facility's method of analyzing capital projects. Typical cost justifications are based on increased revenue, increased efficiency, improved customer service, and reduced costs. The analysis of a capital project is based on the estimated ROI, including the weight of the costs versus the benefits to be derived from the project. The specific cost-benefit analysis method used by facility administration depends on the characteristics of the project as well as the preferences of the analyst. When no specific cash inflows are expected, return may be based on depreciation or other cost savings. Sometimes the capital budget includes the allocation of resources for assets whose acquisition will attract or retain valuable personnel or physician relationships. Even in such cases, the acquisition should be analyzed financially, not just politically.

Payback Period

The **payback period** is the time required to recoup the cost of an investment. Mortgage refinancing analysis frequently uses the concept of payback period. Mortgage refinancing is considered when interest rates have dropped. Refinancing may require up-front interest payments, called points, as well

as a variety of administrative costs. In this example, the payback period is the time it takes for the savings in interest to equal the cost of the refinancing.

Payback Period

Investment:	$100,000
Cash in:	$50,000 per year
Payback period:	2 years (100,000/50,000)

The advantage of using a payback period to analyze investments is that it is relatively easy to calculate and understand. For example, a payback period can be used to describe the time it takes for the savings in payroll costs to equal the cost of productivity-enhancing equipment. In the previous photocopy machine example, the payroll costs would be calculated based on downtime incurred when using a copier in another area of the building.

The disadvantage of a payback period is that it ignores the time value of money. Because the funds used for one capital investment could have been invested elsewhere, there is always an inherent opportunity cost of choosing one investment over another. Hence, there is an assumed rate of return against which investments are compared and a benchmark rate of return under which a facility will not consider an investment.

Accounting Rate of Return

Another simple method of capital project analysis is the **accounting rate of return (ARR)**. This method compares the projected annual cash inflows, minus any applicable annual depreciation, divided by the initial investment. Consider the purchase of a CT scanner. Reimbursement from use of the machine is the cash inflow. Depreciation is easily calculated based on the initial investment.

Accounting Rate of Return

Investment:	$100,000
Straight-line depreciation over 5 years:	$20,000 per year
Cash in:	$50,000 per year
ARR:	30 percent [(50,000 − 20,000)/100,000]

Accounting rate of return is another example of a simple method of capital project analysis. However, it also ignores the time value of money. In addition, accounting rate of return is based on an estimate. If the analyst incorrectly projects annual cash inflows, the projected rate of return will be incorrect.

Return on Investment

ROI is most frequently used to analyze marketable securities retrospectively. The increase in market value of the securities divided by the initial investment is the ROI. When an income stream is associated with the investment, the income stream is added to the market value of the securities in calculating return. In comparing the ROI among different securities, the tax implications must be considered. Long-term gains are taxed differently than short-term gains.

Tax-exempt investments result in different returns than taxable investments.

With respect to capital investments, the equation is similar. Divide the controllable operating profits by the controllable net investment. Operating profits are the cash inflow minus the direct costs of operation.

Return on Investment

Investment:	$100,000
Straight-line depreciation over 5 years:	$20,000 per year
Operating costs:	$5,000 per year
Cash in:	$50,000 per year
ROI:	25 percent [(50,000 − 25,000)/100,000]

As with accounting rate of return and payback period, ROI is easy to calculate and understand. Similarly, it does not consider the time value of money.

Net Present Value

To take into consideration the time value of money, the analyst must establish an interest rate at which money could have otherwise been invested. From that implied interest rate and the projected future cash inflows of the investment, the present value of the cash inflows is calculated. Present value is the current dollar amount that must be invested today in order to yield the projected future cash inflows at the implied interest rate. **Net present value (NPV)** is the calculated present value of the future cash inflows compared to the initial investment.

The advantage of using net present value to analyze investments is that it considers the time value of money. When choosing among like investments, net present values can be reliably compared to determine the financial advantages of the investment.

Net Present Value

Investment:	$100,000
Cash in:	$25,000 per year (revenue minus depreciation and operating costs)
Interest rate:	7 percent
NPV:	$2,505 (based on 5 years of service)

As with other analysis tools, analysts may have to estimate the projected cash flows. However, the main disadvantage of net present value is that the interest rate is subjective. Therefore, it is best used to compare multiple investment opportunities rather than to analyze one investment alone. Another disadvantage of using net present value is that it requires some knowledge of mathematics to calculate as well as to accept its validity and understand its relevance. Fortunately, financial calculators and computer spreadsheet programs have made the calculation of net present value relatively simple.

Internal Rate of Return

Internal rate of return (IRR) is the interest rate that makes the net present value calculation equal zero. In other words, it is the interest rate at which the present value of the projected cash inflows equals the initial investment. IRR considers the time value of money. Both individual and multiple investments can be evaluated. As with net present value, knowledge of mathematics is helpful. The main disadvantage is that a project may have multiple IRRs.

Internal Rate of Return

Investment:	$100,000
Cash in:	$25,000 per year (revenue minus depreciation and operating costs)
NPV:	$0 (based on 5 years of service)
Interest rate:	8 percent

Profitability Index

Facilities cannot automatically invest in seemingly profitable projects. For example, a $500,000 radiology equipment investment may have a present value of cash inflows of $1,500,000, for a net present value of $1,000,000. At the same time, a $10,000 pharmacy computer system yields a net present value of $30,000. This seems to be a great investment; however, the facility's capital budget may be limited to $100,000. In this case, a **profitability index** helps the organization prioritize investment opportunities. For each investment, divide the present value of the cash inflows by the present value of the cash outflows. In this example, the pharmacy system has a higher profitability index, illustrated as follows:

Radiology		**Pharmacy**
$1,500,000	Present value of cash inflows	$40,000
$500,000	Present value of cash outflows	$10,000
3	Profitability index	4

Check Your Understanding 25.3

Instructions: Answer the following questions on a separate piece of paper.

1. Compare and contrast financial accounting and managerial accounting.

2. Compare and contrast operational budgets and capital budgets.

3. A not-for-profit organization offers a variety of programs and services. Each functional department in the organization plays some role in delivering all these programs and services. What type of operational budget would be most effective in this environment? Why?

4. Why would an organization choose a fiscal year that does not coincide with the calendar year?

5. The HIM department has a YTD budget for a payroll of $100,000. The actual YTD amount is $98,000. Is this a favorable or an unfavorable variance?

Summary

Management roles in any healthcare facility require some knowledge of accounting and financial management. The ability to read, understand, and interpret pertinent financial reports is a desirable business skill. Because of the close ties between reimbursement and HIM, this basic skill is even more important. Although the financial accounting methodologies of compiling and analyzing financial statements may not be needed routinely, the managerial accounting skills involving budget preparation and analysis are critical. Also important is an awareness of the preventive, detective, and corrective controls that managers must implement to ensure the accuracy of financial data.

Operational budgets are developed annually to allocate resources for the normal functioning of the facility, according to its mission. Operational budgets focus on revenues and expenses. Capital budgets separately identify and analyze long-term asset acquisitions that are designed to maintain and improve the facility's infrastructure, improve operational efficiency, or expand business, for example. Capital budget requests are analyzed for their cost versus benefit as well as return on investment.

Efficient claims processing has a direct impact on the ability of a facility to fund its operations, including paying its bills and meeting payroll obligations. HIM plays a direct role in ensuring efficient claims processing by participating in charge description master review, participating in the analysis and minimization of the AR totals, and ensuring efficient and accurate coding of records.

References

Cleverley, W., and A. Cameron. 2012. *Essentials of Health Care Finance,* 7th ed. Sudbury, MA: Jones and Bartlett.

Dunn, R. 1999. *Finance Principles for the Health Information Manager.* Chicago: AHIMA.

Schraffenberger, L.A., ed. 2011. *Effective Management of Coding Services.* 4th ed. Chicago: AHIMA.

Internal Revenue Service. 2011. Tax Exempt Status for Your Organization. Pub. 557. http://www.irs.gov/pub/irs-pdf/p557.pdf.

chapter 26

Work Design and Process Improvement

Pamela K. Oachs, MA, RHIA

Learning Objectives

- Describe how workflow, space and equipment, aesthetics, and ergonomics factor into the functionality of a work environment
- Identify alternate methods for distributing work assignments and for scheduling staff to ensure adequate staffing to meet the department's or work unit's service requirements
- Explain the role job procedures play to support employees in delivering effective and efficient services
- Develop effective performance standards and provide examples of both qualitative and quantitative standards
- Differentiate the process of standard setting when done through a benchmarking effort versus a work sampling effort
- Identify the steps involved in a work-sampling effort and the tools that can be used with certain steps

- Explain the difference between preventive controls and feedback controls
- Identify potential areas for improvement in departmental or work unit functions through observations and variance analysis, and establish a relevant action plan to address the problem(s) identified
- Differentiate effectiveness, efficiency, and adaptability as goals of process improvement efforts
- Describe the components of a system, how they relate to each other, and how they relate to process improvement
- Explain the purposes of the various continuous quality improvement (CQI) tools and techniques
- Select the appropriate tool(s) for use in different types of performance improvement or process improvement efforts
- Discuss the value of Lean and Six Sigma as process redesign methodologies

Key Terms

Aesthetics
Affinity grouping
Benchmarking
Brainstorming
Business process reengineering (BPR)
Certainty factor
Check sheet
Closed system
Common cause variation
Compressed workweek
Continuous data
Continuous quality improvement (CQI)
Cybernetic system

Cyclical staffing
DMAIC
Employee self-logging
Ergonomics
External customer
Feedback control
Fishbone diagram
Flextime
Float employee
Flow process chart
Flowchart
Force-field analysis
Goal

Hard space
Histogram
Internal customer
Job procedure
Job sharing
Key indicator
Lean
Movement diagram
Multivoting technique
Narrative
Nominal group technique (NGT)
Objective
Offshoring
Open system
Outsourcing
Parallel work division
Pareto chart
PDSA cycle
Performance
Performance measurement
Playscript
Precision factor
Preventive control
Procedure manual
Process redesign
Productivity
Qualitative standard

Quantitative standard
Run chart
Scatter diagram
Serial work division
Service level agreement (SLA)
Shift differential
Shift rotation
Six Sigma
Soft space
Special cause variation
Standard
Statistical process control (SPC) chart
Swimlane diagram
System
Telecommuting
Time ladder
Unit work division
Use case analysis
Volume log
Waste
Work
Work distribution analysis
Work distribution chart
Work measurement
Work sampling
Workflow

Management is commonly defined as getting work done through and with people. It may be thought of as both a science and an art. Management is a science because it is based on theory and principles that have been—and continue to be—tested and explored. It is an art because effective management depends on the use of sound judgment, intuition, communication, and interpersonal skills. Managers engage in specific functions, including planning, organizing, directing, and controlling, to create and facilitate effective work processes so that the desired outcome can be achieved in a cost-efficient manner.

Management of human resources is one of the most challenging and critical functions in a healthcare organization. Whether as a lead staff person, a supervisor, an assistant director, or a health information management (HIM) department director, to a great extent the practitioner's people and performance management skills are key factors impacting that practitioner's ability to successfully achieve organizational goals. Performance management does not occur by accident. Careful consideration of available staff resources and how the staff resources are organized is fundamental to delivering effective and efficient HIM departmental services.

This chapter introduces key concepts, tools, and techniques associated with designing, redesigning, and implementing effective and efficient work processes within an organization. It includes discussion of various methods of work division and work scheduling; management of work procedures; components of the work environment; elements of a performance management program, including methods for establishing performance standards; and various process improvement methodologies to continuously improve or to reengineer workflow, work processes, and staff performance to accommodate changes in service requirements and fiscal limitations.

Functional Work Environment

Considering the fact that the average full-time employee spends more waking hours in the work environment than elsewhere, it would be prudent for management to create a workplace infrastructure and ambiance that evokes comfort and productivity. Whether creating new space or evaluating current space for the telecommuter or on-site employee, developing the work environment involves consideration of these fundamental elements: workflow, space and equipment, aesthetics, and ergonomics.

Departmental Workflow

The **workflow** in a departmental setting is the established path along which tasks are sequentially completed by any number of staff to accomplish a function. Well-designed workflow is critical to achieving optimal efficiency when a function requires the coordinated activity of a group of employees. In a manual process environment, spatial relationships among people who perform tasks and the equipment required to perform them are critical factors in planning efficient workflow. In such situations, creating a layout diagram, sometimes called a **movement diagram** or layout flowchart, helps the manager to visualize the functions and related tasks performed in a defined work area and how they are related. (See figure 26.1.)

Space and Equipment

Workspace design can influence morale, productivity, and job satisfaction. The design of efficient office space involves a number of considerations. For example, in a paper-based health record environment, location of the file room is a primary consideration. If the file room is located on any floor other than ground level, it is important to determine how much weight the suspended floor can support. This is especially critical when planning for additional shelving to store

Figure 26.1. Movement diagram: Inefficient (top) and efficient (bottom)

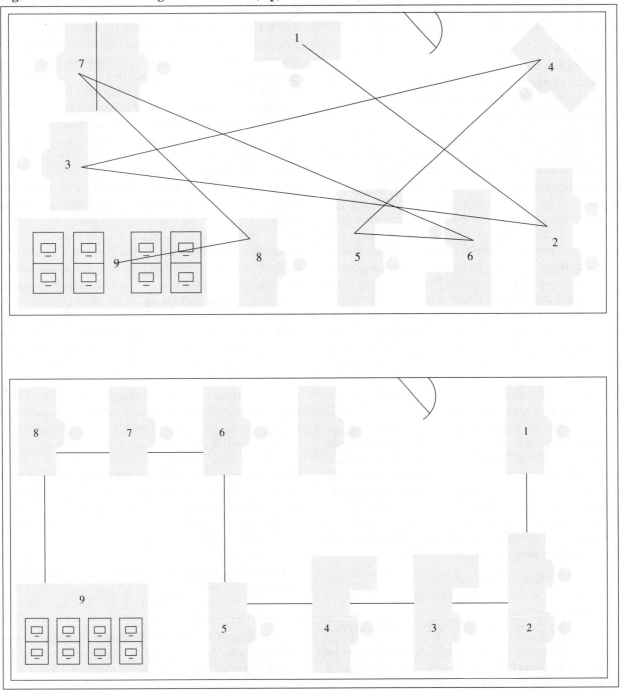

paper medical records. The combined weight of the records and shelving can be extreme, and the floor must be designed to support such weight.

The amount of space designated for the department is the major determining factor in considering office design and equipment specifications. Space is considered a precious and costly commodity in healthcare facilities and must be used efficiently. Designing efficient office space is a highly specialized and intricate process.

Department managers should understand basic facility planning techniques. They also must consider the facility's master plan in developing a plan for the department. This ensures maximum efficiency, consistency, and flexibility. The department plan also should address the department's:

- Physical environment
- Office space utilization
- Telecommuting efforts
- Space planning techniques, guidelines, and standards
- Office furniture and equipment

In an ideal situation, a move into a new space is the reason for engaging in space planning. Reorganization of a department because of changes in workforce numbers resulting from downsizing, increasing telecommuting efforts, or from taking on new functions constitutes a space planning process. Departmental reorganization in response to changes in methods or functions, such as a move to remote coding or transcription or implementation of an electronic health record (EHR), can trigger a call for revised space planning. Sometimes the basic need to improve workflow and the appearance of a department can be a pivotal reason for space planning.

Remodeling existing space, as opposed to designing new space, presents special challenges. There may be space problems that cannot be changed, such as walls and pillars that cannot be moved and inadequate wiring. In addition, employees may resist changes and find it difficult to think creatively. In such instances, managers need to be inventive and creative in their space utilization.

Hard space and soft space are other considerations in designing efficient and effective space utilization. **Hard space** is space that cannot be converted easily to service another function. For example, a file area could have certain structural needs or radiology may require lead walls. **Soft space** is space that is readily expandable or contractible to adjust to changing needs.

Determining how soft and hard space will be utilized is a major component of office space planning. Effective space planning has the following characteristics:

- Keeping costs to a minimum
- Contributing to the quality of the work
- Contributing to employee satisfaction
- Contributing to services provided by the department

Space needs change in the course of time and should be reevaluated periodically to determine whether principles of good space planning are being followed.

Four separate, self-explanatory types of office space are needed:

- Private office space
- General office space
- Service area
- Storage area

Another space consideration is personal space or the area of privacy surrounding an employee. Territoriality is a natural development because employees instinctively control the physical areas where they work.

Aesthetics

Aesthetics of the workplace have the most physiological as well as psychological effects on employees. Aesthetic elements include the lighting of both the office and the workspace, the colors of the walls and furniture, auditory impacts, and atmospheric condition and temperature.

Light should be of sufficient brightness and diffusion for the work situation. Exposures (north, south, east, and west in order of preference) to natural light must be considered when creating new space because natural light is best and easiest on the eyes. Luminance is the quality of light, and lux is a unit of measure. (Candlelight equals 10 lux. A well-lit office equals 500 to 700 lux, whereas the noonday sun produces 160,000 lux.) Desk or task lighting is more physically supportive than overhead florescent lighting alone. Many HIM department functions include computer monitors, and the contrast between the print and the background can influence the employee's comfort level. Typically, a light background with dark print is least taxing on the eyes. Glare from light sources or computer screens can cause discomfort. Display screen fixtures can be used to help reduce glare. In addition, it is important to factor in the age of the staff; people over age 40 have an increased level of discomfort from glare.

Color influences how people feel. For example, dark areas feel brighter or lighter when painted with light colors. Moreover, certain colors evoke a variety of sensations and feelings. Blues are cool, reds are warm, greens evoke luxury, and so on. When choosing color schemes, it is important to consider the area and who will occupy it. Neutral colors can have a calming effect and help avoid the subliminal friction that some primary colors trigger. Also, the finish of the paint should be considered. Matte surfaces absorb more light and reduce glare but are typically not cleanable. On the other hand, gloss surfaces are cleanable, but reflective, and can exacerbate glare.

Music and sound can be incorporated to improve working conditions and relieve both mental and visual fatigue. Certain kinds of music can reduce tension and make employees generally feel better. Sound conditioning and soundproofing are important considerations because a noisy office is seldom efficient. A certain level of routine office background noise is expected and usually is not irritating. However, loud or abrupt sounds can be alarming, distracting, and disruptive.

Planning separate space for noisy work processes, such as copying and printing, is effective because it addresses the source of the noise. Carpeting, window coverings, and partitioning can offer noise control because they absorb significant amounts of sound.

Air conditioning regulates temperature, circulation, and moisture content and determines cleanliness. When considering normal ventilation for the space, at least 2,000 cubic feet per person per hour should be configured to maintain a healthy respiratory atmosphere. Air that is too warm or too cold is equally distracting, and a balance can be difficult to maintain. A range of 68 to 72 degrees Fahrenheit is generally acceptable to most people.

Ergonomics

The word **ergonomics** is derived from the Greek word *ergon,* which means "work," and *nomos,* which means "natural laws of." Developed in the 1950s by a group of scientists and engineers, the discipline of ergonomics has helped redefine the employee workspace with consideration for comfort and safety.

Questions to consider in office layout and design include the following:

- Do staff members assume fixed working postures that remain static for the majority of the workday? For example, do they sit at a keyboard all day?
- Do staff members perform repetitive motions such as filing, typing, stamping, hole punching, and so on?
- Has the psychological stress caused by uncomfortable workstations been taken into consideration?

In effective ergonomic planning, the designer must know the work requirements of the job and the tasks involved. The physical traits of the worker assigned to each workstation also influence ergonomic considerations. For example, height or leg length or back or waist length will determine specific needs. Another consideration is whether an individual or multiple persons share one workstation throughout the workweek. Finally, one must consider what equipment is currently available at the workstation and what equipment must be purchased to create an ergonomically correct work environment.

When the work environment is not ergonomically sound, common cumulative trauma disorders (CTDs) and repetitive strain injuries (RSIs) associated with office personnel can occur, including the following:

- Carpal tunnel syndrome (CTS) is considered an occupational illness rather than an injury because it takes a long time to develop to the point of debilitation. The syndrome causes flexion, with ulnar deviation. Symptoms include tingling, numbness, and pain in the wrist and lower arm.
- Upper back and neck strain is caused by poor posture. Symptoms include tension headaches and muscle pain.
- Eyestrain is caused by incorrect viewing distances and poor illumination. Symptoms include burning, watery eyes and headaches.

Preventive, proactive ergonomic management includes educating staff on how to care for themselves to reduce potential ergonomic injuries or discomfort. A few simple principles help raise employees' awareness of their physical relationship with the work environment. Managers should encourage, if not insist, that staff working at a computer for the majority (more than two-thirds) of a shift take hourly neck, shoulder, and wrist roll breaks, along with stretch routines. In addition, employees should be aware of and be assessed on their use of the 10 basic principles of good sitting posture. (See figure 26.2.). These basic activities can help employees stop the tension cycle and reduce potential long-term problems.

Figure 26.2.   Ten basic principles of good sitting posture

- Feet should rest flat on the floor or footrest.
- A fist-width space should be measurable between the back of the knees and the edge of the seat pan of the chair.
- The hips should be at a 90-degree angle (or slightly greater) in relation to the body. To help ensure this angle, the knees should be at or below hip height.
- The lower back (lumbar region) should be supported.
- Shoulders should be relaxed, not shrugged, slouched, or rolled forward.
- Elbows should rest comfortably at the side or on armrests. When typing, elbows should be at 90-degree angles and preferably supported by an adjustable armrest at an appropriate height.
- Wrists should be maintained in a neutral (straight) position while typing or using any variety of keyboard.
- Head and neck should be in an upright position. To confirm this, the ears should be directly over the shoulders, which are directly over the hips.
- Computer monitors should be positioned directly in front of the worker. The top line of print should be horizontal with the eyes when looking directly forward.
- Ergonomic aids should be used to help maintain comfortable posture. Examples include footrests, wrist rests for keyboard and mouse, antiglare screens for computer monitors, copy stands, and adjustable chair height for those working at a multitask station.

Careful consideration and professional assessment of individual employees' work environment needs will help reduce or eliminate physical barriers to employee comfort and productivity. Preemptive, ergonomically correct practices markedly reduce employee absence and workers' compensation usage due to workplace injury.

Check Your Understanding 26.1

Instructions: Answer the following questions on a separate piece of paper.

1. Name the fundamental elements addressed in good work environment planning.
2. Explain how a movement diagram (or layout flowchart) assists a manager during an office design or redesign effort.
3. Describe what types of impact aesthetic elements, such as lighting, the colors of the walls and furniture, noise, and temperature, have on employees.
4. Identify two simple actions employees can take to help stop the tension cycle and reduce potential long-term physical problems from ergonomic issues at their workstations.

Methods of Organizing Work

Staffing involves the determination of which types of employees are needed, how many of each type are needed, and what kind of work schedule is needed. The types of employees needed depend on the skills, experience, and education required by the specific work that must be done. The number of employees needed depends on the volume of work and the pattern of work division that has been selected for the work setting. Work scheduling is based on when employees are needed to provide the services they are responsible to deliver within the organization.

Work Division Patterns

The type of work division pattern used in a process-oriented department depends in large part on the nature of the work to be performed and the number of employees available to perform it. Three basic types of work division patterns are the following:

- **Serial work division:** The consecutive handling of tasks or products by individuals who perform a specific function in sequence. Often referred to as a production line work division, serial work division tends to create task specialists. This scenario is an example of a serial work division pattern: a receptionist receives a request for release of information (ROI); the request is scanned or entered into the ROI specialist work queue; an ROI specialist validates that the release is authorized, determines where the requested

information can be found, identifies the records that are available electronically, and enters a request to the appropriate staff to retrieve the paper-based medical records that are not available online; the medical record is retrieved and delivered to the ROI specialist, who scans the pages into the electronic system for release; an evening clerk returns the medical record to the file room; and the ROI specialist completes the process by preparing the requested information for release to the requesting party. In this staffing model, each type of employee sequentially handles a step in the total ROI work process.
- **Parallel work division:** The concurrent handling of tasks. Multiple employees do identical types of tasks and basically see the process through from beginning to end. This scenario is an example of a parallel work division pattern: there are three ROI specialists in the department, and each is responsible for receiving requests for release, locating the medical record, identifying the content to be released, and preparing the content for distribution to the requestor. Thus, all three ROI specialists are expected to perform all of the tasks that comprise the release of information work process independent from the others.
- **Unit work division:** Simultaneous assembly in which everyone performs a different specialized task at the same time. The tasks are all related to the same end product but are not dependent on each other. The work is specialized, but the sequence of tasks is not fixed. Unit assembly is rarely used in health information systems (HIS) departments but is a typical work division pattern used in manufacturing. This scenario is an example of a unit work division pattern: one machinist makes metal chair legs, another molds metal chair seats, and another molds metal chair backs. One employee takes four metal chair legs, one metal chair seat, and one metal chair back and assembles them into a complete chair.

Work Distribution Analysis

Work distribution analysis is a process for evaluating the types of work functions being performed in a department, the amount of time given to those functions, who is performing each function, and the way work is distributed among the employees. It is used to determine whether a department's current work assignments and job content are appropriate. Making time to perform this analysis can lead to one or more of the following observations:

- Large amounts of time are being dedicated to functions of minor importance
- Small amounts of time are being dedicated to functions of key importance
- There is too much or too little job function specialization
- There is duplication of efforts or functions

- Some employees are overloaded with work assignments
- Some employees do not have enough work to keep busy
- Staff are performing tasks inappropriate to their positions

Basic work distribution data can be collected in a **work distribution chart** that is initially completed by each employee and includes all responsible task content. (See table 26.1.) Task content should come directly from the employee's current job description. In addition to task content, each employee tracks each task's start time, end time, and volume or productivity within a typical workweek. The results of a work distribution analysis can lead a department to redefine the job descriptions of some employees, redesign the office layout, or establish new or revised procedures for some department functions in order to gain improvements in staff productivity or service quality.

Work Scheduling

After management has determined the appropriate work distribution within a department and makes adjustments accordingly, a work-scheduling system can be developed. Determining the work schedule for departmental staff involves more than simply assigning the correct number of work hours to each employee. Effective scheduling results in the following:

- A core of employees on duty at all times when services must be provided

- A pattern of hours (shifts) to be worked and days off that employees can be reasonably sure will not change except in extreme emergencies
- Fair and just treatment of all employees with regard to hours assigned

Several staffing issues should be considered when devising an effective staff schedule. Answers to the following questions will help determine the department's course of action:

- How is the workweek defined by policy? The workweek is generally established to begin on Sunday, but organizational policy may dictate otherwise.
- What days of the week is the department open? How many and what hours and days are covered?
- What functions must be performed each day and within what time frame?
- How many full-time equivalents (FTEs) are needed to handle the work volume?

HIS departments often are on a standard Monday through Friday, eight-hour-day pattern but also may need evening or weekend coverage to handle specific functions that must be provided 24 hours per day, seven days a week. Uninterrupted work stretches should be no less than two days and no more than seven days. In other words, avoid scheduling staff either every other day or for more than seven days in a row.

Shift Rotation and Shift Differential

Employee schedules may involve **shift rotation** and shift differential when the department has more than the standard Monday through Friday, eight-to-five staffing needs.

Table 26.1. Work distribution chart

Position/ Employee	Supervisor/ J. Johnson		Admissions Clerk/A. Jones		Discharge Clerk/ B. Olson		File Clerk/ R. Smith	
Activity	*Task*	*# of Hours*	*Task*	*# of Hours*	*Task*	*# of Hours*	*Task*	*# of Hours*
Release of information	Post requests; give depositions	2 10	Photocopy/ scan	8	Certify content	15	Retrieve records	10
Analysis	Determine completion	2	Place in queue	3	Tag for incomplete	15	Collect records	9
Filing	Audit file room	2	—	—	Pull for MDs	4	File and retrieve records	20
Administrative overhead	Attend meetings; supervise employees	12 10	Receive visitors; typing	14 14	Generate MD letters	5	—	—
Training	Read literature, etc.	2	Attend software training	1	Attend computer training	1	Attend computer training	1
Totals	40 hours/40 hours		40 hours/40 hours		40 hours/40 hours		40 hours/40 hours	

Table 26.2.   Sample vacation schedule

Employee	Title	Hire Date	Week #	7/1	7/8	7/15	7/22	7/29	8/5	8/12	8/19
Brown	Transcriptionist	2001	1					x			
Dorsey	Transcriptionist	2000	2	x							x
Grunch	Transcriptionist	1999	3		x				x	x	
Glass	Clerk	2000	2			x	x				

Diewell Community Hospital Vacation Policy	
General Employees	**Department Managers/Administrators**
3 years or less = 1 week 4 to 7 years = 2 weeks 8 to 10 years = 3 weeks 11 years and over = 4 weeks	3 years or less = 2 weeks 4 to 7 years = 3 weeks 8 years and over = 4 weeks

Rotation among morning, afternoon, and evening shifts is not the ideal scheduling situation but is often necessary when coverage is needed and personnel have not been specifically hired to work afternoons or evenings on a regular basis. Specific start and end times should be determined for every shift, and at least 12 hours should elapse between the time an individual ends one shift and begins another. Time spent on the more undesirable shifts should not exceed time spent on the preferred shift. For example, a schedule of two weeks of days, one week of afternoons, and one week of evenings is acceptable, but a schedule of one week of days, one week of afternoons, and two weeks of evenings can create problems. In this case, it would be prudent to adopt **cyclical staffing,** which is the rotation of work schedule for a group of employees to allow for a fair distribution of evening and weekend shifts for each person within the group. **Float employees,** staff are cross-trained in a number of departmental functions, can often be utilized to enable this particular type of scheduling.

In situations where weekend coverage is an issue, employees should have at least alternate weekends off. Many employers pay a slightly higher hourly wage to employees who work less desirable shifts (evening, night, weekend). This is referred to as a **shift differential.**

Mandatory activities and the minimal staff needed to cover them should be defined when determining weekend or holiday coverage. All employees should participate in holiday and weekend rotation. Holiday rotations should be posted one year in advance and weekend rotations at least three months in advance. Employees should be required to provide their own holiday or weekend replacements but should not be responsible for providing replacements when their absence is due to illness.

Vacation and Absentee Coverage

To keep productivity optimal, the HIS department manager must plan appropriately for vacation staffing and absentee coverage. Temporary FTEs hired to cover for vacationing employees are most desirable, but not always financially feasible. Moreover, some positions are too complex to be filled with float FTEs. For example, it is unlikely that a temporary assistant director could be hired to fill in for an assistant director on a two-week vacation. In such a case, key tasks that must be attended to must be identified and distributed appropriately among staff who will handle them while the employee is on vacation. Generally staff who are absent for more than a week can add undue stress on the remaining employees and adversely affect department service levels; thus, it would be advisable to hire temporary help when more than one week of absence is expected. See table 26.2.

Alternate Work Schedules

Today's work environment has accepted some work scheduling alternatives to the regular 40-hour workweek; the following are examples:

- **Compressed workweek:** A week in which more hours are combined within fewer days (for example, four 10-hour days, three 12-hour days, seven 10-hour days with seven days off [seven on/seven off], and so on). This type of scheduling has advantages but may present child care issues and psychological or physical fatigue that could reduce efficiency and productivity.
- **Flextime:** Employees choose their arrival and departure times around a fixed core work time. For example, if management feels full coverage is essential between 10 a.m. and 2 p.m., employees could start as early as 5:30 a.m. or end as late as 6:30 p.m. and still provide the department with core coverage.
- **Job sharing:** Divides one job between two part-time employees, each with partial benefits (as they apply). In some organizations, the two employees split full-time benefits (for example, one takes insurance coverage and one takes vacation time). Job sharing may

work well in some cases, but it also can be problematic depending on the compatibility of the two individuals involved. And should one person terminate employment, finding a compatible new job-sharing partner could present a challenge.

In general, the benefits to employers of alternative work schedules include easier staff recruitment and better retention, increased morale, decreased absence and tardiness, and some productivity improvements. For employees, the benefits can include less home stress, reduced commuting time, and a perception of greater autonomy in the workplace. (See chapter 24 for further discussion on alternative work schedules.)

Telecommuting

Under this structure, employees work full- or part-time in their own homes. The first employees in HIS departments to take advantage of **telecommuting** were transcriptionists; they were soon followed by at-home coders. These telecommuters use computers (often provided by the facility) at home to transcribe or code information and then transmit it electronically back to the HIS department. The advantages to this type of work scheduling are that it saves space in the department, reduces long commutes to the workplace, retains parents who prefer to be home, and offers work opportunities to the physically challenged. On the other hand, employers may feel a loss of control when employees telecommute. And some employees in alternative work situations, such as telecommuters, need contact hours with other employees to avoid feeling disconnected from the department. (See chapter 24 for further discussion on managing telecommuters.)

Outsourcing

In some cases, flexible job arrangements may not be an option for employees. Another solution to the problem of a shortage of qualified staff is **outsourcing.** In this arrangement, the organization contracts with an independent company with expertise in a specific job function. The outside company then assumes full responsibility for performing the function rather than just supplying staff. Outsourcing functions (domestic and offshore) provides access to staff as needed, even in a tight labor market; frees up internal resources for other things; eliminates some process or service "headaches"; provides access to the newest technologies quickly; and accelerates change. The disadvantages for the health information manager include less immediate control over the quantity and quality of the work, the need to know negotiation techniques, and the reliance on the vendor. The Health Insurance Portability and Accountability Act (HIPAA) also requires special arrangements regarding security and confidentiality for outsourcing contractors (covered entities). In an outsourced environment, the health information manager's responsibility shifts from supervising employees to managing a vendor relationship.

Common functions that are candidates for outsourcing in the HIM department include transcription, release of information, document imaging, and more recently, coding. The outsourcing company may perform the functions either at the institution or partially or completely off-site. Advances in secure communication have resulted in many remote workers being employed by such independent companies.

When healthcare organizations decide to use outsourcing, a manager is challenged to select the most appropriate vendor to provide the services desired. Specific key factors to consider when selecting a vendor or partner include

- Commitment to quality
- Price
- References and reputation
- Cultural match
- Flexible contract terms
- Value-added capability
- Existing relationship

What leads to success when adopting an outsourcing vendor or contracted service? Senior executive support is a requisite for achieving success in outsourcing. The administration's confidence in the process is essential to creating the seamlessness necessary for continued, smooth functional operation. Administrative support can best be engaged when the manager understands the organization's goals for each outsourcing or contracted service effort being planned. Selecting the right vendor is a definite variable for a successful outsourcing. Good management of the relationship between the healthcare organization and the outsourcing partner includes properly constructed contracts, open communication among partners, and careful attention to personnel issues.

Suggestions for successful outsourcing arrangements include

- Seeking assistance from someone skilled in negotiation when developing the contract with the vendor
- Engaging legal counsel to review the language of the contract to ensure that it complies with HIPAA and other regulatory requirements
- Requiring competitive bidding for each outsourced service at regular intervals
- Establishing quality expectations and performance standards for contractors
- Monitoring compliance with performance standards
- Performing periodic customer surveys to assess satisfaction with the service

Offshoring

Offshoring is a special case of outsourcing, where employees of the company are based overseas, most frequently in India, China, and the United Kingdom. The major benefits are cost savings and availability of a labor pool. Employees in foreign countries are generally paid much less than those in the United States and are extremely productive. There is also less turnover. HIM jobs such as transcription, coding, and insurance claims processing are well suited to these types of workers. Jobs most suitable for offshoring have the following characteristics:

- No face-to-face customer service requirements
- High information content
- High wage differential with workers in the destination country
- Low social networking requirement
- Little management or interaction with others in the organization

Those countries with young populations that speak English are preferred. The country also should have reliable utilities and suitable digital and voice networks.

As in any outsourcing arrangement, quality control and compliance with privacy and security standards are important issues to be addressed in contracts and performance monitoring.

Contracting for Services

When a manager is planning to contract for staffing in a transitional situation in order to meet organizational goals, various types of arrangements can be considered, including

- *Full service:* Contracting for staffing to handle a complete function within the department; for example, cancer registry function
- *Project based:* Contracting for staffing to focus on completion of a specific project
- *Temporary:* Contracting for staffing to cover for a transient event in order to keep productivity in line

Clear definitions of the work or services needed as well as the performance expectations are crucial to a successful contract for services. **Service level agreements (SLAs)** provide this detail in writing, plus price and payment terms, the reporting chain of command, terms for termination of the relationship, and confidentiality expectations of the vendor and vendor staff.

Work Procedures

Management has the responsibility to develop procedures for employees that fully aid them in effectively and efficiently carrying out their job functions. A **job procedure** is a structured, action-oriented list of sequential steps involved in carrying out a specific job or solving a problem.

Rules of Procedure Writing

To be effective, procedure writing requires considerable attention to detail. The following criteria facilitate the development of well-written procedures:

- Display the title of the procedure accurately and clearly.
- Number each step of the procedure for easy reference.

- Begin each activity with an action verb.
- Keep sentences short and concise.
- Include only procedures, not policies. Policy manuals should be maintained as separate documents, though it is appropriate to include references to related policies within the procedure so the employee can easily locate the policy within the policy manual as may be necessary or desired.
- Identify logical beginning and end points to simplify directions.
- Consider the audience and construct the procedure to be of most help to that audience. For example, new staff, temporary staff, or cross-trained staff who performs these procedures only occasionally needs a basic, simplified version to ensure completion of a new or seldom-performed task.

In addition, the written procedure should provide completed samples of forms used during the procedure.

It is considered best practice to have an experienced employee who does the job write (or at least draft) the procedure because he or she knows it best. Supervisory personnel should collect all the written procedures and determine whether they are complete and follow a consistent format. Supervisory personnel are also responsible for ensuring that procedures are reviewed at least annually and updated in a timely way when the procedure is modified.

Procedure Formats

When determining the appropriate format for a procedure, the HIS manager needs to consider the audience as well as the complexity of the task. Several formats can be followed for procedural documentation, including

- **Narrative:** Narrative formats are the most common for procedure writing. The author details the processes of the procedure in a step-by-step description method.
- **Playscript:** This format describes each player in the procedure, the action of the player, and the player's responsibility regarding the process from start to completion of a specific task within the procedure.
- **Flowcharts:** Flowcharts use standard flowcharting symbols provided in software programs such as PowerPoint and VISIO to depict the steps associated with a procedure. Figure 26.3 shows an example of procedure flowcharting applied in the HIS setting.

Sometimes a combination of narrative and flowchart formats is used. However, whatever format is chosen, all procedures should be available to employees at any time.

Procedure Manuals

A **procedure manual** is a compilation of all of the procedures used in a specific unit, department, or organization. Procedure manuals may be kept as hard copies that have been printed and bound together in a book or binder, or they

Figure 26.3.   Loose chart filing flowchart

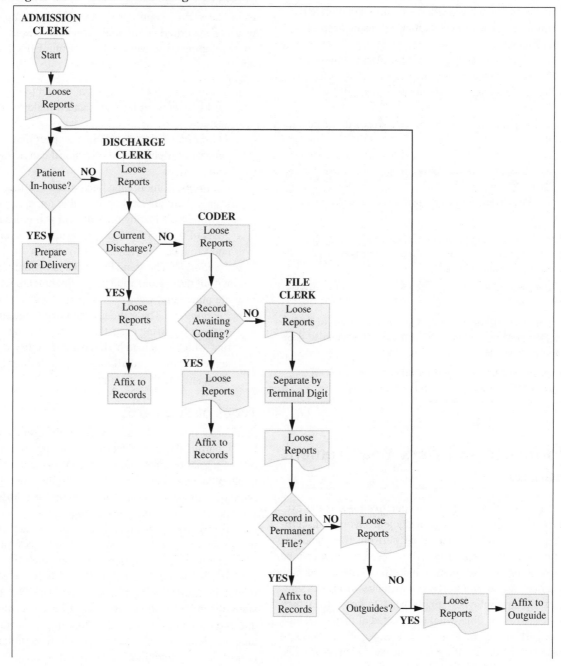

may be maintained on an organization's secure website or intranet. The valuable aspects associated with procedure manuals include

- Promoting teamwork
- Promoting consistency in the work of employees
- Reducing training time
- Establishing guidance on the standards of the work unit
- Explaining what is expected of employees
- Answering employee questions

The manual's content and format are relatively straightforward. Procedure manuals should include the following elements:

- *Title page:* Name of the facility, name of the manual, name of the department, and date
- *Foreword:* Paragraph form, purpose of manual, suggestion for use by employees
- *Table of contents:* List of all procedures in the manual referenced to page number

- *Job procedures:* Step-by-step job procedures and the forms used in each procedure, including completed forms together with explanations to ensure accurate use of forms
- *General rules and regulations:* Information that includes department- or unit-specific details often influenced by state or federal law and regulatory agencies
- *Index:* Alphabetical list of topics covered in the manual (optional)

Check Your Understanding 26.2

Instructions: Answer the following questions on a separate piece of paper.

1. Looking at the sample vacation schedule in table 26.2, identify which weeks the department would be well advised to secure temporary help.
2. List the potential problem areas a work distribution analysis can reveal.
3. Differentiate flextime, job sharing, and the compressed workweek as three unique alternatives to the regular 40-hour staffing schedule.
4. Explain what information is included in a service level agreement (SLA) and why it is needed.

Performance and Work Measurement Standards

Work is the task to be performed; **performance** is the execution of the task. Effective management involves discerning what work is to be done, what performance standards are achievable and appropriate, how performance can be measured in terms of efficiency and effectiveness, and how performance can be monitored for variances from the standards set. Most employees simply want to know for which tasks they are responsible, what is expected of them, and how they are performing relative to that expectation. Through performance standard-setting and measurement processes, managers can confirm the level of success of a work unit or identify opportunities for improvement.

A **standard** may be defined as a performance criterion established by custom or authority for the purpose of assessing factors such as quality, productivity, and performance. Managers are responsible for controlling all of the resources available to them, including men (staff), materials (supplies), machines (equipment), methods (procedures), and money (budget)—often referred to as the five Ms. Thus, managers are expected to set standards for each of these resources and then use them as ways to judge (assess, evaluate) the quality, productivity, and performance of those resources.

Criteria for Setting Effective Standards

To create viable, significant standards, it is important to be aware of the criteria commonly considered as the foundation for developing effective standard setting. Effective standards are

- *Understandable:* The person(s) affected by the standard knows what it means, and it makes sense to him or her.
- *Attainable:* It is reasonable to expect that the person(s) affected by the standard can actually achieve it.
- *Equitable:* If more than one person is affected by the standard, all are held accountable for it.
- *Significant:* Meeting the standard is important to the goals of the work unit or organization; the effort it takes to meet the standard is worth it.
- *Legitimate:* The standard has been formally accepted within the organization and is documented in appropriate places and ways.
- *Economical:* The standard can be met and monitored without incurring costs that are beyond the value of that which is gained by having it. In other words, achieving the standard must be worth the expense associated with achieving it.

Types of Standards

Standards commonly are worded differently at various levels within the organization depending on whether they reflect a goal or an objective. A **goal** is a generalized statement of a unit, departmental, or organizational standard, typically without measurable content. An **objective** is a statement of end result in measurable terms with time and cost limits, as applicable. For example, the HIS department might have a general standard (most commonly called a goal) for its transcription function, such as "to support patient care through accurate and timely transcription of medical reports." The transcription function then might state a standard in objective form to make it more specific and measurable, for example, "to complete routine history and physical, operative, and consultation dictation within eight hours of dictation." Note that this objective is related directly to the timeliness aspect of the preceding goal statement.

Qualitative and Quantitative Standards

Objective-level standards are also commonly characterized in two other ways: as quantitative standards and as qualitative standards.

Qualitative standards specify the level of service quality expected from a function, such as:

- *Accuracy rate:* For example, assignment of diagnostic and procedure codes for inpatient records is at least 98 percent accurate.

- *Error rate:* For example, mistakes in the assignment of diagnostic and procedure codes occur in no more than 2 percent of inpatient records coded.
- *Turnaround time:* For example, dictation must be transcribed within 24 hours.
- *Response time:* For example, requests for information are responded to within seven working days of receipt.

Quantitative standards specify the level of measurable work, or **productivity,** expected for a specific function, such as

- Number of units of work per specified period of time (for example, 70 records per FTE per day)
- Amount of time allotted per unit of work (for example, no more than 15 minutes to code one inpatient record)

Quantity standards (also called productivity standards) and quality standards (also known as service standards) are generally used by managers to monitor individual employee performance and the performance of a functional unit or the department as a whole. To properly communicate performance standards, managers need to make the distinction between quantitative and qualitative standards and identify examples of each for the HIS functions.

Keeping the criteria for effective standards and the difference between qualitative and quantitative standards in mind, it is possible to set about developing standards for any of the resources under the control of management. Several examples of resource management standards are provided here:

- Standards related to men (staff resources)
  - *Qualitative (quality):* Chart deficiency analyst accurately identifies chart completion status in 98 percent of charts analyzed
  - *Quantitative (productivity):* Coders code 25 to 30 inpatient discharges per eight-hour workday
- Standards related to materials (supply resources)
  - *Qualitative (quality):* Monitoring strips must be printed with nonfading permanent ink
  - *Quantitative (productivity):* Each functional work unit in the department maintains no more than one week's volume of consumable supplies on hand
- Standards related to money (budget resources)
  - *Qualitative (quality):* Major expense categories (salaries, supplies, postage, telephone, travel, and maintenance) must remain within plus or minus 3 percent of the budgeted amount monthly.
  - *Quantitative (productivity):* Paid dollars per key statistic (P$PKS) must be less than $2 plus or minus the target P$PKS indicator established for the department.
- Standards related to methods (procedures)
  - *Qualitative (quality):* An employee can complete the entry of a release of information request into

the ROI tracking system with 99 percent accuracy by following the steps outlined in the documented procedure.
  - *Quantitative (productivity):* The steps outlined for completing the entry of a release of information request into the ROI tracking system can be completed in less than one minute per request.
- Standards related to machines (equipment)
  - *Qualitative (quality):* The copier must be functioning properly 99 percent of the time, that is, less than two hours of downtime per month.
  - *Quantitative (productivity):* The document imaging equipment must be able to process 30 to 40 images per minute.

Key Indicators

Key indicators are "live" (versus retrospective) measurement thresholds that alert a department or work unit to its current level of service. Key indicators allow managers to monitor critical service standards on a current basis so they can make timely staffing or process adjustments to ensure that department service performance remains on course. Common key indicators in HIS departments include

- Transcription turnaround time
- Days outstanding in accounts receivable (A/R)
- Release of information turnaround time
- Percentage of incomplete records

The following red flag indicators would certainly move a department manager to take corrective action:

- The number and severity of complaints increase. When the number or severity of complaints increases, the circumstances surrounding the complaints need to be assessed immediately so that corrections to the process or personnel involved can be made.
- Compliance surveys to assess performance on accreditation, legal, or regulatory standards indicate that the organization has failed to comply in one or more areas. When the organization fails to comply with one or more external standards during a survey, the organization needs to correct the variance(s) and return to compliance.

Methods of Communicating Standards

After standards have been created, they must be communicated to staff. All of the given types of standards can be provided to staff in a number of ways, including through

- *Written specifications:* For example, in job descriptions, performance evaluation forms, equipment specification sheets, and forms design guidelines
- *Documented rules, regulations, or policies:* For example, in policy manuals, regulations or accreditation manuals, and employee handbooks

- *Demonstration models:* For example, samples, videos, and computer-based learning modules
- *Verbal confirmations:* For example, in departmental or work unit meetings or individual employee counseling sessions

Methods of Developing Standards

There are several methods that can be employed to develop performance standards in a work unit. Two approaches are commonly used: benchmarking comparable performance and measuring actual performance.

Benchmarking Comparable Performance

Benchmarking is based on researching the performance of similar organizations and programs or gathering data on standards established by national or local sources such as professional associations and standard-setting organizations. Benchmarking has become a more prevalent approach to standard setting in HIS management in the past few years because this type of information is now being published regularly.

To engage in a benchmarking effort, the manager should first select key functions of the department that will be benchmarked (coding service, transcription service, ROI service, and so on). Relating benchmarks to the specific process is critical. Thought must be given to the types of performance measure(s) desired as indicators (for coding, for example, payments remaining in accounts receivable due to uncoded records and payments remaining in accounts receivable due to coding disputes; for transcription, for example, turnaround time [dictation to charting] for consultations, operative reports, history, and physicals).

When the key functional areas have been selected and the types of indicators identified, the research for benchmarks available through published sources (preferably) can begin. Investigation of benchmark standards gathered through this research must also involve a critical assessment of their relevance to the department's specific situation; then the standard can be successfully sold to the rest of the organization. Benchmarking involves the following steps:

1. Identifying peer organizations and departments that have achieved outstanding performance based on some key indicator (for example, 98 percent of health records coded within two days postdischarge)
2. Studying the best practices within the organization that make it possible to achieve that performance level
3. Acting to implement those best practices in one's own organization to achieve a similar performance

Before officially adopting a benchmark standard, a manager should routinely gather performance data in the department to match actual performance against the benchmark and then evaluate factors in department processes that must be changed to eventually move actual performance into the benchmark range.

Measuring Actual Performance

Work measurement is the process of studying the amount of work accomplished and the amount of time it takes to accomplish it. It involves the collection of data relevant to the work, such as the amount of work accomplished per unit of time. Its purpose is to define and monitor productivity.

Work measurement can support a manager in many activities, including

- Setting production standards
- Determining staffing requirements
- Establishing incentive pay systems
- Determining direct costs by function
- Comparing performance to standards
- Identifying activities for process and methods improvement

Gathering the information available through work measurement efforts will be invaluable to the manager in making administrative decisions. But how do managers know which method of work measurement will serve him or her best?

When selecting the work measurement technique that best suits his or her department, the manager should consider the following factors:

- Amount of financial resources available
- Availability of qualified personnel to take part in the study
- Amount of time available to devote to study
- Attitudes of employees toward participation in a study

Work measurement can be accomplished through a variety of techniques, including

- *Analysis of historical (past performance) data:* The analysis of historical data generally uses work volume (direct or estimated) and hours paid from past records to establish the standard. When using historical data, managers are cautioned to keep in mind that volume figures are not adjusted for the level of quality and the number of hours paid is different from the number of hours actually worked.
- *Employee self-logging:* **Employee self-logging** is a form of self-reporting in which the employees simply track their tasks, volume of work units, and hours worked. Employee logging incorporates a **time ladder,** which is a form used by the employee to document the amount of time spent (worked) on various tasks. It can be modified to include the number of units produced per task throughout the day. **Volume logs** are sometimes used in conjunction with a time ladder to obtain information about the volume of work units received

Table 26.3. Sample volume log

Task	Number of Worked Hours	Number of Units
Coding	40 worked hours	120 records
Loose filing	36 worked hours	48 inches
The coding standard calculates at three records per worked hour for this employee (120 records/40 hours) and a filing standard of 1.3 inches per worked hour (48 inches/36 hours). It does not capture any interruptions or unworked time in the eight-hour day but is a simple way to arrive at a ballpark figure.		

and processed in a day by simply keeping track of the number of products produced or activities done. (See table 26.3.)

- *Scientific methods:* The scientific methods of work measurement include time studies and the use of preestablished time/unit standards. For example, time studies use a stopwatch to record and document the time required to accomplish a specified task.
- *Work sampling:* **Work sampling** is a technique of work measurement that involves using statistical probability (determined through random sample observations) to characterize the performance of the department and its work (functional) units.

Each one of the varieties of work measurement techniques offers calculations of employee productivity in either unit/time or time/unit. For example, with the completion of a daily time ladder summary (see table 26.4), a manager can determine simple unit/time productivity statistics by dividing the number of units produced by the number of hours worked. Table 26.4 also contains the type of data needed to calculate weekly activities.

Gathering the information available through any of these work measurement efforts will be invaluable to the manager in making administrative decisions. But how does a manager know which method of work measurement will serve him or her best? The manager should consider the following factors when attempting to select the work measurement method that best suits his or her department:

- Amount of financial resources available
- Availability of qualified personnel to take part in the study
- Amount of time available to devote to study
- Attitudes of employees toward participation in a study

A Focus on Work Sampling

Work sampling is an especially valuable method for developing performance standards. Work-sampling data can help the manager to

- Catalog the activities being performed
- Determine the time devoted to each activity
- Identify inefficiencies
- Set employee performance standards

Work-sampling projects follow an established sequence of steps and use specific tools:

1. Decide which work activities to monitor during the study.
2. Design the form that will be used to record the observations collected during the study. The sample observation

Table 26.4. Sample daily time ladder summary

Unit: <u>Reception</u>   Date: <u>07-04-12</u>
Note: 7.5 worked hours (two 15-minute breaks)

Employee	Code/Task	Total Time (%)	Work Units
Jane	A. Answer phones	3 hr/40%	64
	B. Write requisitions	1.75 hr/23%	92
	C. Personal/setup and such	0.5 hr/7%	NA
	D. Mail handling	2.25 hr/30%	Incoming 80 Outgoing 100
Betty	A. Answer phones	5 hr/66%	100
	B. Write requisitions	0.5 hr/7%	15
	C. Personal/setup and such	0.5/7%	NA
	D. Mail handling	0	NA
	E. Stat record delivery	1.5/20%	10

Table 26.5. Sample observation record form

Activity	Mason Supervisor	Davis Transcriptionists	Perry	Kent	Martin Clerical	Carter	Roth	Evans	Larson Coders	Owens 0.5 FTE	Total
Supervision											
Coding											
Transcription											
Record A&A											
Record retrieval/ filing/transport											
Release of information											
Assisting physicians											
Other clerical											
Idle: gone, rest											
Total observations											

Observation times:

1.   6.
2.   7.
3.   8.   Recorded by: _____
4.   9.
5.   10.   Date: _____

record form shown in table 26.5 captures activities by individuals and by units of function (supervisory, transcription, clerical, and coder).

3. Determine the best size of the study sample by using the precision interval method, a standard formula used to determine sample size. The formula allows for various scenarios of desired **certainty factor** (confidence factor) and **precision factor** (acceptable error) in the study results. The certainty factor is a numerical representation of the confidence the manager has that the results will show the level of acceptable error. The precision factor is the level of tolerable error in the sampling process.

$$\text{Sample size} = 0.25 \times \frac{\text{certainty factor \%}}{\text{precision factor \%}}^2$$

Note that the 0.25 is a fixed (not variable) part of the formula.

If the precision factor is 5 percent, the confidence factor needed is 95 percent. (Note that the precision factor plus the confidence factor equal 100 percent.) For example,

$$25 \times (0.95/0.025)^2 = 0.25 \times (38 \times 38) = 361$$

4. Determine the length of the study and establish appropriate observation times. When the sample size (total number of observations required) has been determined, the number of observations per day can be determined on the basis of the number of days, weeks, or months available to complete the study. The actual time of each observation each day must be determined by using a random observation generator (see figure 26.4) and a random numbers table (see figure 26.5). To create the observation generator, list the period of time the study will take place in a workday (see figure 26.4, from 8 a.m. until 4 p.m., with 10-minute increments) and number each predetermined time increment. Then using a random numbers table (figure 26.5 is a partial table of tables found in any statistics book), randomly select the first number and then a direction to read the numbers (horizontally, vertically, or diagonally). Looking at the first number, refer to the observation generator to find the time of day assigned to that corresponding number. If it does not exist, proceed to the next number until the optimal number to complete the study has been selected. For example, if 500 observations were needed and 50 workdays were allotted to complete the study, 10 observations would need to be made each day of the 50-day study. (See figure 26.6.)

Figure 26.4. Observation generator

Time Block Number	Clock Time	Time Block Number	Clock Time
0	8:00 a.m.	25	12:10 p.m.
1	10	26	20
2	20	27	30
3	30	28	40
4	40	29	50
5	50	30	1:00 p.m.
6	9:00 a.m.	31	10
7	10	32	20
8	20	33	30
9	30	34	40
10	40	35	50
11	50	36	2:00 p.m.
12	10.00 a.m.	37	10
13	10	38	20
14	20	39	30
15	30	40	40
16	40	41	50
17	50	42	3:00 p.m.
18	11:00 a.m.	43	10
19	10	44	20
20	20	45	30
21	30	46	40
22	40	47	50
23	50	48	4:00 p.m.
24	12:00 p.m.	etc.	

Figure 26.5. Random numbers table (partial)

69	18	82	00	97	32	82	53	05	27
90	04	58	54	97	51	98	15	06	54
73	18	95	02	07	47	67	72	62	59
54	01	64	90	04	66	28	13	10	03
75	75	87	64	90	20	97	18	17	49
08	35	86	99	10	78	53	24	27	85
28	30	30	32	64	81	33	31	05	91
53	84	08	62	33	31	59	41	36	28
etc.									

Note: Entry may be made at any point, proceeding horizontally, vertically , or diagonally.

Figure 26.6. Example of a first day's observation times

Observation Times

1.	8:50 a.m.	6.	1:00 p.m.	
2.	9:40 a.m.	7.	1:10 p.m.	
3.	10:20 a.m.	8.	1:20 p.m.	Recorded by:
4.	12:00 noon	9.	2:20 p.m.	Department:
5.	12:40 p.m.	10.	2:30 p.m.	Date:

5. Explain the purpose of the study and how it is conducted to observers and staff. Orientation of observers and personnel is very important because it encourages consistency in data collection among observers and ensures that unbiased and reliable observations are collected on the basis of the observation schedule. At this point in the study, those who will be observed also must be informed of its purpose. It is important that workers perform normally throughout the process. They also should understand that the outcome of the study will be shared with them at the conclusion of the study period.
6. Collect and record observation data at random points. (See table 26.6.)
7. Report the results of the study. (See table 26.7, table 26.8, and table 26.9.)

Check Your Understanding 26.3

Instructions: On a separate piece of paper, indicate whether the following statements are true or false. Then correct any false statement to make it true or explain why it is false.

1. A standard is a criterion established by custom or authority for the purpose of assessing quality, productivity, or performance.

2. Turnaround times are examples of qualitative standards, and error rates are examples of quantitative standards.

3. Work sampling is a work measurement methodology that relies on statistical probability to characterize the performance of the functional work units in a department.

4. Men (staff), money (budget), materials (supplies), machines (equipment), and methods (procedures) are the basic resources under the control of a manager.

Performance Measurement

Performance measurement is the process of comparing the outcomes of an organization, work unit, or employee

Table 26.6.   First day's observations, Cure-All Hospital's HIM department

Activity	Mason Supervisor	Davis	Perry	Kent Transcriptionists	Martin	Carter	Roth	Evans Clerical	Larson	Owens 0.5 FTE Coders	Total
Supervision											2
Coding											0
Transcription											24
Record Analysis											10
Record retrieval/filing/transport											16
Release of information											8
Assisting physicians											8
Other clerical											15
Idle: Gone, rest											10
Total observations	10	10	10	10	10	10	10	10	10	3	93

Table 26.7.   Observation summary, Cure-All Hospital's HIM department

Activity	Previous Observation Days	3/10/xx	Study Total	% Total
Supervision	—	2	90	2.2
Coding	—	0	18	0.4
Transcription	—	24	1,053	25.9
Record Analysis	—	10	540	13.3
Filing/retrieval/transport	—	16	618	15.2
Release of information	—	8	381	9.4
Assisting physicians	—	8	273	6.7
Other clerical	—	15	711	17.5
Idle: Gone, rest	—	10	378	9.4
Total observations	—	93	4,062	100.0

Note: This particular work sampling effort involved a total work sampling of 500 planned observations (10 observations per workday for 50 days). This number of observations gives a ±2.75% precision interval for ≥ 10% activities, a 5.5% accuracy rate, and 94.5% confidence level.

Table 26.8.   Work-sampling results, Cure-All Hospital's HIM department: Actual activity vs. expectations

Activity	Normal Range of Expectations	Department Expectations	Department Actual	Estimated Variation
Supervision	NA	15%	2.2%	−13%
Coding	2–4.5%	3%	0.4%	−2%
Transcription	30–40%	30%	25.9%	−4%
Record Analysis	10–13%	12%	13.3%	+1%
Record retrieval/filing	2–5%	3%	15.2%	+12%
Release of information	6–9%	7%	9.4%	+2%
Assisting physicians	6–10%	8%	6.7%	−1%
Other clerical	8–13%	10%	17.5%	+7%
Idle: Gone, rest	7–14%	12%	9.4%	−3%
Total	NA	100%	100%	NA

Table 26.9. Work sampling results, Cure-All Hospital's HIM department

Activity Area/ Expected %	% of Time	Minutes*	Hours*	Work Volume for Period	Work Units
Supervision/15%	2%	4,560	76	NA	NA
Coding/3%	1%	0.01 × 228,000 or 2,280	0.01 × 3,800 or 38 hours	775	Dx coded
Transcription/30%	26%	0.26 × 228,000 or 59,280	0.26 × 3,800 or 988	150,000	Lines transcribed
Record analysis/12%	13%	29,640	494	2,964	Records analyzed
Record filing, retrieval, and such/3%	15%	34,200	570	11,400	Records pulled/filed
Release of information/7%	9%	20,520	342	1,050	Requests handled
Assisting physicians/8%	7%	15,960	266	NA	NA
Other clerical/10%	18%	41,040	684	NA	NA
Idle: gone, rest/12%	9%	20,520	342	NA	NA
Total	100%	—	—	—	—

Notes:
Working days in the period: 50 days
Current workforce: 9.5 FTE, including the supervisor
Work minutes/day per FTE: 480 minutes (8 hr × 60)

Total study work hours: 3,800 hours (9.5 FTE × 8 × 50)
Total study work minutes: 228,000 minutes (9.5 FTE × 480 × 50) or (3,800 × 60)

*Minutes and hours are calculated based on the percentage of total time represented by each activity area. For example, 2% of 228,000 minutes = 4,560 minutes; 2% of 3,800 hours = 76 hours.

to preestablished performance standards. The results of the performance measurement process generally are expressed as percentages, rates, ratios, averages, and other quantitative assessments. Performance measurement is used to assess quality and productivity in clinical services and in administrative services. Examples of performance measures maintained by acute-care hospitals in clinical services include the rate of nosocomial infection, the percentage of surgical complications, the average length of stay, and the ratio of live births to stillbirths. Examples of performance measures maintained by an administrative service such as the HIS department include transcription lines transcribed and turnaround times per report type, turnaround times for ROI requests, and days in A/R due to uncoded patient discharges.

Performance measurement is a fundamental management activity that supports two of the basic functions of management: controlling and planning. The control function is concerned with ensuring that the work unit or organization is doing what it should be doing in the right way. The planning function is concerned with defining the expectations of performance (standards or objectives), the processes required for achieving those expectations (procedures), and the desired outcomes of performance (goals). The goals, objectives, standards, and processes established during the planning process become the criteria used in the control process to evaluate actual performance.

Performance Controls

In the control process, specific monitors (controls) are established for the purpose of identifying undesirable circumstances occurring in a work process that could lead to an undesirable outcome so appropriate intervention can be introduced into the process.

The characteristics of effective performance controls include the following:

- *Flexibility* refers to the fact that controls must be adaptable to real changes in the requirements of a process. For example, a budget is a control on the use of money. Money budgeted in one category (equipment) may need to be spent in another category (travel) because of a change in a program, a new law or regulation, and so on.
- *Simplicity* refers to the fact that those involved in the process must find the controls understandable and reasonable.
- *Economy* implies that controls should not cost more than they are worth. The time and money spent to implement a control should be in line with the level of risk (loss) involved if the process fails to meet performance expectations. For example, potential loss of a life calls for a significant investment in controls; potential criminal liability calls for significant investment in

controls; while the potential for having to pay for a day of overtime to correct clerical errors calls for a minimal investment in controls.

- *Timeliness* suggests that controls should be implemented so as to detect potential variances within a time frame that allows for corrective action before any adverse effect has occurred. For example, the accuracy of a record number assignment should be confirmed at the time of registration or the coding checked before a bill is transmitted in order to avoid the adverse effects associated with errors that are then transmitted to other areas of the organization or outside the organization (for example, the insurance carrier).
- *Focus on exceptions* demands that controls be targeted at those aspects of a process that are most likely to vary significantly from expectations. For example, a new transcriptionist who is likely to make more errors that could do damage to customer service ratings is generally monitored (controlled) more closely and more frequently than one who is experienced and has performed well for the past year.

There are two general types of controls: preventive (self-correcting) and feedback (non-self-correcting). **Preventive controls** are front-end processes that guide work in such a way that input and process variations are minimized. Simple things such as standard operating procedures, edits on data entered into computer-based systems, and training processes are ways to reduce the potential for error by using preventive controls.

Feedback controls are back-end processes that monitor and measure output and then compare it to expectations and identify variations that then must be analyzed so corrective action plans can be developed and implemented. Processes with feedback controls in place are also called cybernetic processes or systems. Some may be self-regulating (such as thermostatic systems), but most are non-self-regulating, meaning that they require intervention by an oversight agent (a supervisor, a manager, or an auditor) to identify the variance and take action to correct it. A customer survey or routine performance reviews are examples of this type of control.

Variance Analysis

In the context of performance measurement, when variations are identified (that is, actual performance does not meet or significantly exceeds expectations), further analysis is needed. Analysis of the resources involved in the work (people, procedures, supplies, equipment, and money) is conducted to help determine what, if any, changes should be made. Changes may involve activities such as additional staff training, modifications in procedures, adjustments in workflow, revision of policies, or purchases of updated equipment. As a result, the analysis and the changes to address findings may also lead to revisions in performance criteria and expectations.

Assessment of Departmental Performance

When establishing an employee performance assessment program, the steps in the control (evaluation) process include

1. Monitoring and measuring outcomes performance
2. Comparing performance to established goals and standards
3. Evaluating variance and developing action plans
4. Taking appropriate action

Monitoring and Measuring Performance

Monitoring and measuring performance involves taking an aggregate look at performance over a period of time. Options include operating with an employee self-reporting method such as self-logging, using computerized monitoring to audit productivity, manually auditing work samples, or relying on customer feedback to measure performance.

Effective outcomes performance monitoring depends on both employee performance measurement and management execution. The focus of the effort is on service indicators such as turnaround time, cost and revenue reports, and customer feedback. Consider this practical application of department outcomes performance monitoring. Assume that one established expectation of the department is that routine response to an authorized ROI request occurs within five working days of receipt of the request in the department.

The first step in controlling this function would be to set up a data collection and reporting activity to obtain information that can be used to monitor the time it takes the department to respond to a routine ROI. (See table 26.10.)

Next, the department should determine the kinds of controls it wants to establish. The department wants to monitor routine requests, but how are "routine requests" defined? A routine request may be any request that is not stat or emergency (that is, it does not have to be handled within minutes, hours, or some stipulated amount of time under five working days). For example, a subpoena for a record that must be

Table 26.10.   ROI requests

On June 6, 2012, Total Routine ROI Requests in Processing: 130					
Days since Receipt	**6–10 Days**	**11–15 Days**	**16–20 Days**	**>20 Days**	**Summary**
Number of total	12 9%	15 12%	2 2%	1 1%	30 24%
Unable to locate record	0	2	0	1	3 10%
Incomplete record	12	12	2	0	26 87%
Issue with authorization	0	0	0	0	0
Unavailable record	0	1	0	0	1 3%
Other	0	0	0	0	0

Table 26.11. Sample health information services performance report

Indicator	January 2012	February 2012	March 2012	April 2012
Discharge Equivalents	5,000	5,400	5,360	5,500
Labor cost per DCE: <$10.00	$10.00	9.25	9.33	9.90
FTE budgeted at 50	50	50	50	48
Days in analysis at end of month: <2 days	1	2	2	3
Delinquency rate: <50%	35%	40%	43%	45%
Coding: Days in A/R due to uncoded records <5 days	3	5	4	5
Lines transcribed	120,000	130,000	128,000	132,000
Transcription: TAT for H&Ps <24 hours	12	16	18	26
ROI requests received	200	245	300	260
Release of info: TAT <5 days	3	3	6	5
File pull requests	2,000	2,200	2,300	2,500
Retrieval rate: >95%	94%	96%	93%	91%
Loose filing inches received	100 average 25/week	120 average 30/week	80 average 20/week	130 average 32/week
Loose filing inches at end of month: <16	15	20	12	15
Filing: Misfiles <1%	.05%	.08%	.06%	.08%
Resignations: <1%	0	0	0	2/50 = 4%
Education hours	4	16	2	8
Unproductive hours (sick, vacation): <15%	10%	12%	20%	10%

handled within three days or a request for a record needed for an appointment in a clinic the next morning would not be considered a routine request.

The line related to ROI requests in the middle of the performance report shown in table 26.11 indicates the average number of days it took the HIS department to respond to routine ROI requests in January (3), February (3), March (6), and April (5). However, it is important to note that these numbers tell nothing about the routine ROI requests the department received in each of those months that have not yet been responded to.

The average turnaround time number was calculated by dividing the total response days attributed to the volume of routine requests that were responded to within the reporting period by the volume of routine requests responded to. For example, if the department responded to 300 routine requests in the month of May and 100 were responded to in six days, 100 in two days, and 100 in four days, the average turnaround time in May would be four days:

$$\frac{(600 \text{ days} + 200 \text{ days} + 400 \text{ days})}{300 \text{ requests}} = 4 \text{ days (average)}$$

Having the information on a monthly basis to include as part of the regular performance reporting within the department allows the manager to review monthly trends and identify potential focus areas for future process improvement activities.

The underlying data indicate that a considerable number of requests are not responded to within the five-working-days expectation (for example, 100 [or 33 percent] were responded to in six working days). In this case, the direct supervisor of the ROI function would likely want access to data of this nature more often than once a month. For example, a weekly report showing the number of routine requests in the system for five days or more that have not yet been answered would allow the supervisor or ROI clerk to identify problem requests and take corrective actions over the course of the following week.

Comparing Performance to Established Goals and Standards

The next step in monitoring and measuring outcome performance is to compare current performance against established goals (standards). Continuing with the example in the preceding section, when comparing performance against the standard performance indicator of responding to routine ROIs within five days, the data in table 26.11 show an upward trend in March and April.

Evaluating Variance and Developing Action Plans

When comparisons are done, the manager should evaluate any variances and develop an action plan specific to each. For example, in an evaluation of the performance variance in responding to routine ROI requests, the direct supervisor would likely begin to collect data that will provide the following types of information in order to uncover the factors that have triggered the variances:

- How many open ROI requests exist with a date of receipt of more than five working days?
- What is the aging profile of those open ROI requests; that is, how many are six to 10 working days, 10 to 15 working days, 16 to 20 working days, or more than 20 days?
- What are the reasons the requests are still open?
- In what time increments since receipt of the requests has the requesting party been notified of the delay and the reason for the delay?

After the variances have been evaluated, an action plan can be formulated to address areas for performance improvement; for example,

- Establish a procedure to ensure weekly contact with the requestor to determine continuing need for the information and update on the status of the request
- Flag the incomplete record with ROI REQUEST PENDING to ensure that it is routed to ROI immediately when required documentation is complete
- Track the missing record
- Check the status of the unavailable record and contact the current user to obtain the record so that ROI can occur and then (if necessary) the record can be returned to the user.

Taking Appropriate Action

The supervisor, working with the ROI staff, will take the actions put forth in the plan and then continue to monitor the ROI function to determine if the actions taken are effective in resolving the identified performance variance.

Check Your Understanding 26.4

Instructions: Answer the following questions on a separate piece of paper.

1. Define performance measurement and explain why it is a major responsibility of management.

2. Explain the purpose of monitors (or controls) placed on the functions performed in a work unit.

3. Provide examples of the types of changes or actions a manager might take to address performance issues revealed when he or she completes an analysis of performance variances in the department.

Performance Improvement

Clearly, the reason managers set performance standards and routinely measure departmental performance against those standards is to ensure the department is serving its internal and external customers in ways that meet their needs and expectations. A natural outcome of any performance measurement system is the identification of variances from performance expectations and thus the opportunity to engage in performance improvement (PI) activities to bring performance back into line.

The Joint Commission (2011) has standards that specifically require accredited organizations to have PI efforts as an integral aspect of their day-to-day operations, as follows:

- LD.04.04.01   Leaders establish priorities for performance improvement
- LD.04.04.03   New or modified services or processes are well designed
- PI.01.01.01   The hospital collects data to monitor its performance
- PI.02.01.02   The hospital compiles and analyzes data
- PI.03.01.01   The hospital improves performance on an ongoing basis

The Role of Customer Service

All process improvement environments today focus on the customer and work to create a true customer orientation within the work environment by listening and responding to customers, thinking about their needs, and using that information to modify and improve the way our systems work for them.

In the process of customer orientation, management and staff must

- Identify the customers
- Define quality from a customer perspective
- Determine how to judge service
- Obtain regular feedback

Customers are the people, external and internal, who receive and are affected by the work of the organization or department. They have names and needs and are the reason(s) for the collective work of the organization.

Internal customers are located within the organization. They may be anyone within the work unit who is affected by the HIS function. Physicians and clinical staff need high-quality, expedient patient health information in order to deliver high-quality patient care. Administrative staff members are customers of the information harvested from collective databases for use in planning facilities and services. And not least among the department's internal customers are the HIS department staff who work in each of the functional areas and rely on each other in various ways to get their work done.

External customers reside outside the organization. Physicians seen by patients who originated at the facility for care are considered external customers, as are payers who need information so they can reimburse their enrollees in a timely manner. Regulatory agencies look to HIS for data on conditions of accreditation or participation. Vendors assist HIS, with the department's direct input, in making optimal selections of products. Public health agencies look to HIS for information and data on the health status of the community population in order to earmark services the population needs to maintain a healthy existence.

Identification of Performance Improvement Opportunities

In a department that employs performance standards and engages in routine performance measurement, opportunities for performance improvement present themselves as a natural outcome of that effort. Even when a department is lacking a formal performance measurement program, the following common symptoms of performance problems are easily observable by department managers and staff; when observed they present obvious opportunities for performance improvement effort, as well:

- Inaccuracies and errors in work
- Complaints from customers
- Delays in getting things done or lots of interruptions
- Low employee morale or high rates of absenteeism or turnover
- Poor safety records and on-the-job injuries

When inaccuracies and errors are evident in the work products of a group of employees, an investigation of the underlying cause(s) is required and appropriate actions must be taken to address them so the inaccuracies and errors are eliminated.

Customer complaints indicate that performance is not meeting expectations. Managers need to consider each complaint and determine whether it is circumstantial or a signal of something bigger that needs to be investigated and resolved through an improvement effort.

Delays in getting things done or continuous interruptions to a process can warn of roadblocks to success. Delays give time to revisit the current workflow and analyze what might be improved. If transcribed operative reports are not on the patients' charts within the prescribed time, the reason for the delay should be identified and the improvement activity planned to eliminate the delay.

Low employee morale and a high rate of absenteeism or turnover are serious indicators that something needs to be improved. While not always the case, commonly these indicators are a sign that there are training, procedural, or task-related problems that underlie the employees' behavior. High turnover and absenteeism are budget draining and call for an investigation followed by a defined plan of action to avert a continued pattern.

Poor safety records or injuries are indicative of urgent process improvement opportunities. Work-related injuries and accidents are management markers regarding a poorly designed or configured work environment, poor equipment, or poor training. Again, work injuries are a costly burden for both the individual employee and the organization.

Collecting meaningful performance data, being alert, and observing and listening to customers and key staff are all ways to identify improvement opportunities. It is a continuous process that has no tolerance for complacency. Excellence is not an accident; it is an intended outcome that requires a manager's commitment and continuous attention.

Principles of Performance Improvement

The concepts of performance improvement, work improvement, process improvement, and methods improvement are essentially synonymous. They all relate to a management philosophy that is, at its core, systems oriented, meaning it that views the work processes in an organization as being systematic in nature and seeks to constantly improve them by adjusting various components of the system.

A **system** is a set of related elements (components) that are linked together according to a plan in order to meet a specific objective to achieve desired outcomes. Systems come in manual, automated, and hybrid forms. The basic systems model demonstrates that a system is made up of the following components (figure 26.7):

- *Input:* Resources available to system, namely men (staff), money, methods (procedures), machines (equipment), and materials (supplies).
- *Process:* The transformation of the inputs. What is done to or with the inputs that result in something being accomplished?

Figure 26.7.　Basic systems model

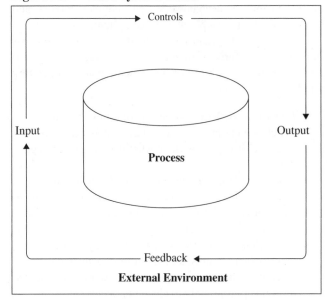

● *Output:* The finished product or the result of the process, such as an educated student, a transcribed report, a coded record, and so on.

● *Controls* and *standards:* The expectations of what the output should be and the mechanisms in place to monitor, track, and observe how well actual performance measures up to expectations.

● *Feedback:* Information that is reported when output is compared to the standards to identify how well actual output met standards (desired output). Feedback sometimes comes in the form of customer complaints, and certainly feedback can and should come in the form of compliments to staff, as well, when performance expectations are met.

● *External environment:* Anything outside the system that affects how the system functions (for example, laws or regulations set by the local, state, or federal government). In HIS departments, examples of external factors that affect its systems include
   — The HIPAA regulations related to patient information confidentiality and security
   — Medicare's Conditions of Participation requirements for patients' medical record content
   — Medicare severity diagnosis-related groups (MS-DRGs) and Present on Admission (POA) regulations that impact coding and reimbursement systems in hospitals
   — A tight labor market, which makes it difficult to hire well-qualified employees for specialized jobs

Systems such as those described here also are called **open systems** because they are affected by what is going on around them and must adjust as the environment changes. They also can be considered **cybernetic systems** because they have standards, controls, and feedback mechanisms built into them. On the other hand, a **closed system** operates in a self-contained environment; that is, it is not affected by outside factors. A mechanical system (engines, motors, and so on) is the best example of a closed system.

The aim of all performance, work, method, or process improvement efforts is to increase the effectiveness, efficiency, or the adaptability of the systems that are operating within an organization.

● *Effectiveness:* How closely the output of a system matches what is expected of it. If a department is effective, it is getting done what it is supposed to get done.

● *Efficiency:* How well the department is using its resources; that is, is the department getting the most bang for its buck, or is it wasting staff time, money, or any other of its resources?

● *Adaptability:* The ease with which the system can adjust when circumstances require it to change to meet new demands or expectations. Adaptable systems respond appropriately to changing needs.

Instructions: On a separate sheet of paper, indicate whether the following sentences are true or false and correct any false statement to make it true or to explain why it is false.

1. The components of an open, cybernetic system are input, process, and output.

2. An efficient process or system is one that uses its resources wisely—does not waste staff, supplies, money, and so on.

3. The Joint Commission requires accredited hospitals to collect data, aggregate it, and analyze it for the purpose of identifying opportunities for change and making improvements in processes.

4. Customers are the government agencies and public health organizations who have established regulations and policies that affect the way the department does its work.

Process Improvement Methodologies

The principle methodologies available to healthcare facilities interested in PI are continuous quality improvement and business process redesign. These approaches have the same goal and use many of the same tools. However, they differ in focus and breadth of improvement effort.

Continuous Quality Improvement

Continuous quality improvement (**CQI**), sometimes still referred to as total quality management (TQM) or service excellence, is a management philosophy that seeks to "involve healthcare personnel in planning and executing a continuous flow of improvements to provide quality healthcare that meets or exceeds expectations" (McLaughlin and Kaluzny 1999, 3). Its focus is on improving the quality of services provided to customers, whether internal (employees) or external (patients, physicians, payers). The approach is to make efforts to meet or exceed customer expectations by conducting small tests of change aimed at improving the quality of services. Of course, not all customer expectations can be met at the same time. In fact, some customers have expectations that conflict with the expectations of other customers. However, the goal is worth pursuing, even when only partly achievable.

CQI casts off the notion of ignoring problems until they become too big to ignore. Rather, it subscribes to the theory of seeking ways to improve the system through the testing of small, incremental changes with the expectation that, over time, the changes will continually improve the quality of care that health facilities provide to their patients (Berwick 1989). To achieve this, CQI relies on the gathering and analysis of data that can be used to make informed decisions.

More than a buzzword in healthcare, CQI is a way of thinking, a way of being, a way of managing, and a way of conducting business. It can be applied to individuals as well as organizations. The expression, "If it ain't broke, don't fix it," is alien to the CQI philosophy. Moreover, CQI does not seek to blame problems on individuals but, instead, suggests that systems or processes may have inherent flaws that contribute to problems.

CQI attempts to involve people in the examination and improvement of existing systems. Several principles are incorporated into the CQI philosophy, including

- *Constancy of variation:* Systems will always produce some normal variation in their output; the manager's job is to reduce the amount of variation as much as possible so that the process can become more stable and produce a more reliable output. Managers should not assume that any variation is a defect but, rather, should monitor and measure data over time to ensure that any variation is, in fact, caused inherently by the system. This type of variation is **common cause variation.** A greater-than-expected variation is a **special cause variation.** Sometimes a change is initiated with the express purpose of producing an improvement effort, in which case it should be encouraged. Other times, changes result in negative outputs and these must be eliminated. An example of variation in HIS departments might be found in the coding and processing of records. A coder may complete 20 records one day but only 18 the next. The variation is not due to the clerk's lack of productivity but perhaps to the size of the records that day. In other words, the change is attributed to common cause variation. A significant drop in coding might indicate that a special cause is in effect. Perhaps the coder was assigned duties that day in addition to coding.

- *Importance of data:* Far too often, decisions for improvement are based on faulty assumptions. CQI recognizes the importance of collecting sufficient data so that informed decisions can be made. Omachonu (1999, 71) states "that the ability to collect, analyze, and use data is a vital component of a successful performance improvement process. Healthcare organizations that do not devote sufficient attention to data collection may be able to speak of only marginal success in their process improvement journey." Individuals planning a CQI effort must take time to develop appropriate data collection methods and instruments (written surveys, direct observation, focus group interviews, reviews of medical records with criteria forms). Appropriate analysis must follow data collection to provide the knowledge on which improvement efforts can be built (White 2002).

- *Vision and support of executive leadership:* CQI gurus such as W. Edwards Deming and Brian Joiner stress that acceptance of the CQI philosophy must funnel down from the top to truly permeate the organization's culture. Executive leadership must communicate a clear vision and mission statement that every employee can understand and share.

- *Focus on customers:* To be successful, the organization must know and understand what its customers need and want. One way to obtain customer feedback is to administer satisfaction surveys on a regular basis. Any needs that are identified should be addressed.

- *Investment in people:* The CQI philosophy assumes that people want to do their jobs well. However, some employees may need training on how they can more adequately serve their customers. Management can empower employees by giving them opportunities to learn and grow and feel more competent in performing their jobs.

- *Importance of teams:* Because CQI seeks to improve processes that may extend beyond the boundaries of individual departments, the people directly involved with the processes must work together. Teams should include individuals with different expertise and from different levels of the organization. Team members should be knowledgeable about portions of the process and be able to contribute to the improvement effort. Having members from different areas on the team brings fresh perspectives and opens communication. A good team also is able to communicate its purpose and activities to other parts of the organization.

Improvement Models

Several models exist for structuring PI. One that is frequently used in hospitals is Hospital Corporation of America's FOCUS-PDCA model. This model includes five steps before initiating its PDCA (plan, do, check, act) cycle. The five initial steps of the FOCUS-PDCA include the following:

1. Find a process to improve
2. Organize a team that knows the process
3. Clarify the current knowledge of the process
4. Understand causes of special variation
5. Select the process improvement

A different, but highly effective, model that can be used for any process targeted for improvement is the Langley, Nolan, and Nolan Foundation for Improvement Model (1994). It is presented here because of its simplicity. The model has two parts. The first part requires an individual or a team to answer three fundamental questions; the second part requires initiation of the PDSA (Plan, Do, Study, and Act) cycle.

The three fundamental questions that must be answered for any improvement project are:

- *What is my aim?* This question forces the responder to determine his or her overall goal.
- *How will I know a change is an improvement?* This question requires the responder to define measures

(preferably quantitative, but also some qualitative) that will indicate progress made toward his or her goal. These measures will enable the individual or team to collect data.

- *What changes have the potential to result in improvement?* This question requires the responder to brainstorm a number of changes that might lead to improvement. He or she must recognize that not all changes do result in improvement.

After changes have been brainstormed, one change deemed to have significant potential for affecting improvement should be tried. This is a small test of change made with one change strategy. If it is successful, other changes may be added. The change strategy is tested using the **PDSA cycle.**

PDSA is a trial and learning cycle. (See figure 26.8.) It is essentially the same as PDCA, both of which are at times referred to as the Deming cycle or the Deming wheel (Six Sigma 2004). The phases of the cycle break down as follows:

1. During the plan phase, preparations are made for implementing the selected change. This is the time to consider who, what, where, when, and how. In addition, this is the time to plan how to collect data that will be used in determining the progress of the implementation. It may be necessary to develop a data collection instrument. Having already determined what the measurements will be, it also may be necessary to collect baseline data before implementing the change. Finally, this phase is the time to decide how often and how long to collect data before the results are analyzed.

2. During the do phase, the change strategy is implemented and data are collected. Perhaps the change strategy and the data collection will go on for two weeks before the analysis. The length of time depends on how frequently data were collected and how long the PDSA cycle is intended to last.

3. During the study phase, the data are analyzed. Is progress being made toward the defined aim? Are there any unanticipated problems? This phase indicates whether a change is an improvement. If it appears to be, the decision will likely be to continue the change strategy. If it is not showing as much improvement as expected, it may be necessary to adjust the change strategy. If it shows no improvement, it may be time to abandon the change strategy and test another one.

4. During the act phase, the knowledge obtained from the PDSA trial and learning cycle is applied, which leads to three possible actions: continue with the current change strategy, adjust it, or try a new one. At this point, a second PDSA cycle is implemented to continue the quest for knowledge about what affects the process and what permits progress. The more knowledge, the greater the likelihood of a successful improvement effort.

Basic PI Tools

A number of tools and techniques are frequently used with PI initiatives (Brassard and Ritter 2010; Johnson and McLaughlin 1999; Cofer and Greeley 1993). Some of them are used to facilitate communication among employees; others are used to assist people in determining the root causes of problems. Some tools show areas of agreement or consensus among team members; others permit the display of data for easier analysis (see chapter 18 for more on data display tools). The following section presents a brief description and discussion of the purpose of tools and techniques commonly used by improvement teams (White 2002).

Work Distribution Chart

A work distribution chart can be helpful in determining the nature of the work being performed in the unit, which employees are performing the activities, and the amount of time spent on each activity. As mentioned earlier, a work distribution chart shows job activities, time spent on them, and the names or titles of the employees who perform them. It can be helpful in determining whether adequate time is available and appropriate for each task and whether employees are overburdened or have time for additional responsibilities. In addition, it can help the manager assess whether the work is organized and distributed appropriately.

Work distribution charts can be formulated in a variety of ways but frequently are tables, with work tasks forming the row headings and a double column of employee names and hours spent on tasks forming the column headings. (Refer to table 26.1.) Data for the work distribution chart come from self-reported activities and hours or parts of hours spent on tasks gathered by employees over a designated period of time. Actual data collection time varies depending on what is needed to get a representative sample of activities and times.

Figure 26.8.   Initiating PDSA cycles to expedite improvement

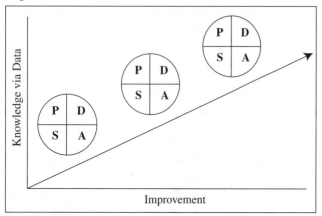

When adequate data have been collected, the manager compiles them, clusters similar job tasks together, and completes the chart.

Movement Diagram

A movement diagram is a visual depiction of the layout of the workspace with all the furniture, equipment, doorways, and so on sketched in. Superimposed on the layout are the movements of either individuals or things (for example, documents, files, and the like). (Refer to figure 26.1.) The movement diagram can be used to evaluate the workflow and to redesign one that is more efficient. An inefficient workflow is depicted in figure 26.1 (top), that is, long distances between connected points in the workflow, crisscrossing paths, and paths that backtrack in the work space. A redesigned movement diagram in figure 26.1 (bottom) depicts a smoother workflow resulting in improved efficiency.

Flow Process Chart

A **flow process chart** is useful in operations analysis. (See figure 26.9.) It charts the flow of work of a material or a task but is limited to the flow of only one unit at a time. Each step of a particular process is shown in chronological order and in great detail (for example, the distance a material moves in each step, the time needed, the quantity moved, and specific notes about the process). Standard symbols are used on the chart to indicate specific processes. An operation is symbolized with a circle, transportation with an arrow, storage with a triangle, inspection with a rectangle, and delay with a figure resembling an uppercase D. When the symbols are connected with a line, the manager can see the actual flow of work.

The flow process chart is an excellent method for indicating time problems with workflow. It can show duplication and inefficiency and also can be useful in verifying procedures or planning a workstation redesign (Liebler et al. 1992). Some flow process charts include two charts in one: a chart showing the current flow of work and a second chart proposing a redesigned workflow.

Brainstorming

Brainstorming is a technique used to generate a large number of creative ideas. It encourages team members to think "outside the box" and offer ideas. There are some variations in using the technique—one can use an unstructured method for brainstorming or a structured method. The unstructured method involves having a free flow of ideas about a situation. The team leader writes down each idea as it is offered so all can see. There should be no evaluative discussion about the worthiness of the idea because we want to do nothing that will inhibit the flow of ideas. Each idea is captured and written for the team to consider at a later point.

Structured brainstorming uses a more formal approach. The team leader asks each person to generate a list of ideas for themselves and then, one by one, the team leader proceeds around the room eliciting a new idea from each member. The process may take several rounds. As team members run out of new ideas, they pass and the next person offers an idea until no one can produce any fresh ideas.

Figure 26.9.   Flow process chart

	PRESENT		PROPOSED		DIFFERENCE		
	NO.	TIME	NO.	TIME	NO.	TIME	
◯ OPERATIONS							Job _____
⇨ TRANSPORTATIONS							Date _____
▢ INSPECTIONS							Man Material
▷ DELAYS							Chartered by _____
▽ STORAGES							
DISTANCE TRAVELED		FT.		FT.		FT.	

DETAILS OF (PRESENT/PROPOSED) METHOD	OPERATION	TRANSPORT	INSPECTION	DELAY	STORAGE	DISTANCE IN FEET	QUANTITY	TIME	ANALYSIS WHY	NOTES	ACTION CHANGE
1	◯	⇨	▢	▷	▽						
2	◯	⇨	▢	▷	▽						
3	◯	⇨	▢	▷	▽						
4	◯	⇨	▢	▷	▽						
5	◯	⇨	▢	▷	▽						
6	◯	⇨	▢	▷	▽						

Brainstorming is highly effective for identifying a number of potential processes that may benefit from improvement efforts and for generating solutions to particular problems. It helps people to begin thinking in new ways and gets them involved in the process. It is an excellent method for facilitating open communication.

Affinity Grouping

Affinity grouping allows the team to organize and group similar ideas together. Ideas that are generated in a brainstorming session may be written on Post-it notes and arranged on a table or posted on a board. Without talking to each other, each team member is asked to walk around the table or board, look at the ideas, and place them in groupings that seem related or connected to each other. Each member is empowered to move the ideas in a way that makes the most sense. As a team member moves the ideas back or places them in other groupings, the other team members consider the merits of the placement and decide if further action is needed. The goal is to have the team eventually feel comfortable with the arrangement. The natural groupings that emerge are then labeled with a category. This tool brings focus to the many ideas generated. (See figure 26.10.)

Nominal Group Technique

Nominal group technique (**NGT**) is a process designed to bring agreement about an issue or an idea that the team considers most important. It produces and permits visualization of team consensus. In NGT, each team member ranks each idea according to its importance. For example, if there were six ideas, the idea that is most important would be given the number 6. The second most important idea would be given the number 5. The least important idea would have the number 1. After each team member has individually ranked the list of ideas, the numbers are totaled. The ideas that are deemed most important are clearly visible to all. Those ideas that people did not think were as important are also made known by their low scores. NGT demonstrates where the team's priorities lie.

Figure 26.10.   Affinity grouping

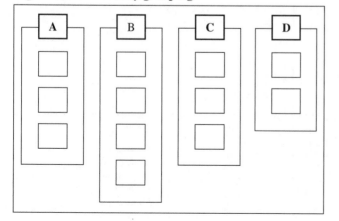

Multivoting Technique

The **multivoting technique** is a variation of NGT and has the same purpose. Rather than ranking each issue or idea, team members are asked to rate the issue using a distribution of points or colorful dots. Weighted multivoting is a variation of this process. For example, a team member may be asked to distribute 25 points among 10 total issues. Thus, one issue of particular importance to him or her may receive 12 points, four others may receive some variation of the remaining 12 points, and five others may receive no points. After the voting, the numbers are added and the team is able to see which issue has emerged as particularly important to its members.

This process also can be done with colored dots. For example, if there are eight items on a chart, each team member may be given four dots to distribute on the four items that are most important to him or her. This method particularly enables team members to see where consensus lies and what issue has been deemed most important by the team as a whole.

Flowchart

Whenever a team examines a process with the intention of making improvements, it must first thoroughly understand the process. Each team member comes to the team with a unique perspective and significant insight about how a portion of the process works. To help all members understand the process, a team will undertake development of a flowchart. (Refer to figure 26.3) This work allows the team to thoroughly understand every step in the process and the sequence of steps. It provides a picture of each decision point and each event that must be completed. It readily points out places where there is redundancy and complex and problematic areas.

Root-Cause Analysis (Fishbone Diagram)

When a team first identifies a problem, it may use a **fishbone diagram,** also known as a cause-and-effect diagram, to help determine the root causes of the problem. (See figure 26.11.) The problem is placed in a box on the right side of the paper. A horizontal line is drawn, somewhat like a backbone, with diagonal bones, like ribs, pointing to the boxes above and below the backbone. Each box contains a category. The categories may be names that represent broad classifications of problem areas (for example, people, methods, equipment, materials, policies and procedures, environment, measurement, and so on). The team determines how many categories it needs to classify all the sources of problems. Usually, there are about four. After constructing the diagram, the team brainstorms possible sources of the problem. These are then placed on horizontal lines extending from the diagonal category line. The brainstorming of root causes continues among team members until all ideas are exhausted. The purpose of this tool is to permit a team to explore, identify, and graphically display all the root causes of a problem.

Figure 26.11.   Fishbone diagram

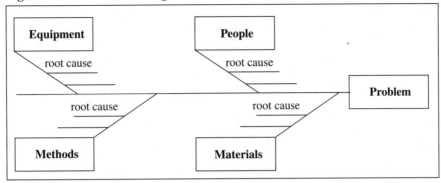

After identifying a number of causes of a problem, a team may decide to begin working to remove one of them. CQI involves continually making efforts to improve processes; certainly removing one cause and then working to remove another cause will eventually improve the process. The question may arise, however, about which cause to remove first. Techniques such as multivoting and NGT, previously discussed, can help bring consensus among the team about what to work on first.

Pareto Chart

When a team decides to use multivoting or NGT to determine consensus among the members about the most important problem to tackle first, each team member places a number or mark next to an item indicating his or her opinion about the item's importance. When the numbers are tallied, the items can be ranked according to importance. This ranking can then be visually displayed in a **Pareto chart** (see figure 26.12). A Pareto chart looks like a bar chart except that the highest-ranking item is listed first, followed by the second highest, down to the lowest-ranked item. Thus, the Pareto chart is a descending bar chart. This visualization of how the problems were ranked allows team members to focus on those few that have the greatest potential for improving the process. The Pareto chart is based on the Pareto principle, which states that 20 percent of the sources of the problem are responsible for 80 percent of the actual problem.

By concentrating on the vital few sources, a large number of actual problems can be eliminated.

Force-Field Analysis

A **force-field analysis** also visually displays data generated through brainstorming. The team leader draws a large *T* formation on a board. (See figure 26.13.) Above the crossbar and on the left side of the T is written the word *drivers,* and above the bar and written on the right side of the T is written the word *barriers.* Team members are then asked to brainstorm and list on the chart under the crossbar the reasons or factors that would contribute to a change for improvement and those reasons or factors that can create barriers. Thus, the force field enables team members to identify factors that support or work against a proposed solution. Often the next step in this activity is to work on ways to either eliminate barriers or reinforce drivers.

Check Sheet

A **check sheet** is a data collection tool permitting the recording and compiling of observations or occurrences. It consists of a simple listing of categories, issues, or observations on the left side of the chart and a place on the right for individuals to record checkmarks next to the item when it is observed or counted (see figure 26.14). After a period of time, the checkmarks are counted and the patterns or trends can be revealed.

A check sheet is a simple tool that allows a clear picture of the facts to emerge. It enables data to be collected. After data are collected, several tools can be used to display the data and help the team more easily analyze them.

Figure 26.12.   Pareto chart

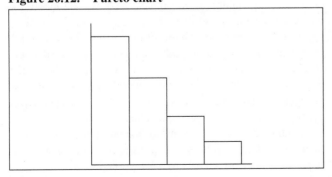

Figure 26.13.   Force-field analysis

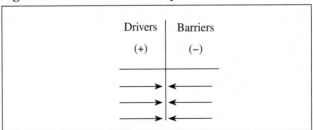

Figure 26.14.   Check sheet

	1	2	Total
A	~~////~/~~	/ / /	8
B	/ / / /	/ / / /	8
C	/ /	/	3

Figure 26.16.   Histogram

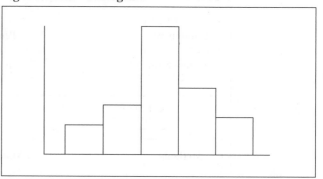

Scatter Diagram

A **scatter diagram** is a data analysis tool used to plot points of two variables suspected of being related to each other in some way. For example, to see whether age and blood pressure are related, one variable (age) would be plotted on one line of the graph, and the other variable (blood pressure) would be plotted on the other line. After several people's blood pressures are plotted along with their ages, a pattern might emerge. If the diagram indicates that blood pressure increases with age, the data could be interpreted as revealing a positive relationship between age and blood pressure. (See figure 26.15.)

In some cases, a negative relationship might exist, such as with the variables "age" and "flexibility" or with the number of hours of training and number of mistakes made. Whenever a scatter diagram indicates that the points are moving together in one direction or another, conclusions can be drawn about the variables' relationship, either positive or negative. In other cases, however, the scatter diagram may indicate no linear relationship between the variables because the points are scattered haphazardly and no pattern emerges. In this case, the conclusion would have to be that the two variables have no apparent relationship.

Histogram

A **histogram** (figure 26.16) is a data analysis tool used to display frequencies of response. It offers a much easier way

to summarize and analyze data than having them displayed in a table of numbers. A histogram displays **continuous data** values that have been grouped into categories. The bars on the histogram reveal how the data are distributed. For example, an HIM administrator may want to show the number of minutes it takes to respond to patient requests for information. Minutes may be categorized into four groupings, for example, 1 to 30 minutes, 31 to 60 minutes, 61 to 90 minutes, and more than 90 minutes. Checkmarks may be recorded indicating the category of minutes taken to respond to the request. After a period of time, the checkmarks are added and the histogram is plotted with the frequencies shown on the vertical axis, or y-axis, and the minute intervals shown on the horizontal axis, or x-axis.

The graph in figure 26.16 indicates the different intervals patients had to wait for their requests to be filled. A histogram can give an excellent idea of how well a process is performing. Thus, it can show how frequently data values occur among the various intervals, how centered or skewed the distribution of data is, and what the likelihood of future occurrences is.

Run Chart

A **run chart** displays data points over a period of time to provide information about performance (see figure 26.17). Measured points of a process are plotted on a graph at regular time intervals to help team members see whether there are substantial changes in the numbers over time. For example, suppose an HIS manager wanted to reduce the number of incomplete records in the HIS department. The manager might first plot on a graph the number of incomplete records each month for the past six months and then enact a change in the processing of records designed to improve the process. Following the improvement effort, data would continue to be collected on the number of incomplete records and would continue to be plotted on the graph. If the run chart shows that the number of incomplete charts has actually decreased, the HIS manager could attribute the decrease to the improvement effort.

A run chart is an excellent tool for providing visual verification of how a process is performing and whether an improvement effort appears to have worked.

Figure 26.15.   Scatter diagram

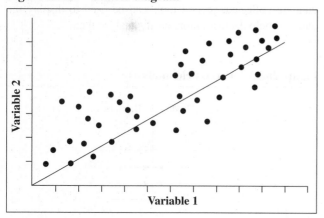

Figure 26.17.   Run chart

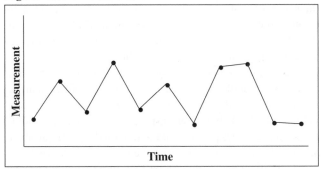

Statistical Process Control Chart

A **statistical process control (SPC) chart** looks like a run chart except that it has a line displayed at the top, called an upper control limit (UCL), and a line displayed at the bottom, called a lower control limit (LCL). (See figure 26.18.) These lines have been statistically calculated from the data generated in the process and represent three units of dispersion above and below the midline (three standard deviations) (Omachonu 1999).

Like the run chart, the SPC chart plots points over time to demonstrate how a process is performing. However, the two control limit lines enable the interpreter to determine whether the process is stable, or predictable, or whether it is out of control. Remembering the constancy of variation principle, it is easy to see the purpose of the SPC chart. The SPC chart indicates whether the variation occurring within the process is a common cause variation or a special cause variation. It indicates whether it is necessary to try and reduce the ordinary variation occurring through common cause or to seek out a special cause of the variation and try to eliminate it.

Business Process Redesign

Used extensively in the mid-1980s and early 1990s, **business process reengineering (BPR)** has met with significant criticism in the healthcare sector because of the fear it has invoked among healthcare workers. As would be expected, reengineering frequently results in the loss of jobs.

Figure 26.18.   Statistical process control chart

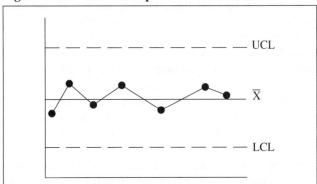

Because salaries and benefits comprise 50 to 60 percent of a healthcare facility's total expenses, a drop in personnel can have a significant impact on reducing expenditures and is often used as an effective strategy in reengineering. Due to negative connotations related to downsizing, restructuring, and outsourcing, the perception of reengineering went from a strategy an organization does to something that is done to the organization. Although the term *reengineering* itself is not always favorable in organizations today, business process redesign is still a focus strategy for rethinking and drastically improving overall performance.

Models and Methodologies

Business process redesign can be undertaken in a variety of ways using a variety of tools; it is built around the foundation of data. The philosophies and methods used to collect, measure, and act on that data are numerous.

Business Process Reengineering

Unlike CQI, which focuses on conducting small tests of change to achieve continuous but incremental improvement over time, BPR focuses on the potential redesign of the entire process to achieve improvement. (See table 26.12 for a comparison of reengineering and quality management.) Reengineering implies making massive changes to the way a facility delivers healthcare services. In *Reengineering the Corporation: A Manifesto for Business Revolution,* Hammer and Champy (1993, 32) defined reengineering as "the fundamental rethinking and radical redesign of business processes to achieve dramatic improvements in critical contemporary measures of performance such as cost, quality, service, and speed."

Philosophy of Reengineering

Business process reengineering has entered the healthcare sector after first being successfully applied in the wider business community. In reengineering, the entire manner and purpose of a work process is questioned. The goal is to

Table 26.12.   Reengineering compared to quality management

Reengineering		Quality Management	
Rethinking and radical redesign	Focus	Incremental improvements	Focus
Rethink	Think outside of the box	Quality planning	Focus on the customer
Redesign	Think both process and outcome	Quality control	Measure and monitor performance
Retool	Use technology to control and define work processes	Quality improvement	Use data, eliminate boundaries, and empower work

achieve the desired process outcome in the most effective and efficient manner possible. Thus, the results expected from reengineering efforts include

- Increased productivity
- Decreased costs
- Improved quality
- Maximized revenue
- More satisfied customers

However, it should be clearly understood that the main focus is on reducing costs (Palmer 1995).

Process of Reengineering

When an organization decides to use reengineering as an improvement strategy, it commits itself to looking at selected processes within the organization in fine detail. Processes are selected for reengineering based on a number of criteria, including

- Frequency and severity of problems created by the process, such as slow turnaround time or excessive waiting time
- Impact on customer satisfaction
- Complex processes involving multiple departments, procedures, and employees
- The feasibility of actually creating improvement (Umiker 1998)

Selecting a process for reengineering raises several questions, including the following:

- What is the intended purpose of the process? Is that purpose being accomplished efficiently?
- Is the process absolutely necessary? Could any redundancies or non-value-added activities be eliminated?
- Which employees are involved in the process, and which ones are actually needed? In other words, what are the minimum qualifications and minimum number of employees needed to do the job?
- Is the process as efficient as it could be, or are there more efficient means for accomplishing the goal?
- Is the process contributing to the efficiency of other processes that may be affected by its results?
- Is there an opportunity to combine processes and to train or use employees to perform more functions than they currently perform?
- Can any steps of the process be eliminated?
- Is outsourcing a feasible and more cost-effective alternative?
- Would new equipment or new technologies improve the process?

Many of the tools and techniques used in systems analysis and CQI also are used in reengineering. In reengineering, it is essential to thoroughly understand how the process contributes to how the organization functions and to determine whether a better method exists. Therefore, observation of processes, customer input, interviews with employees, and the use of cross-functional teams to discuss the current steps of the process are frequently used methods for obtaining data. Data must be collected for a sufficient period of time to actually reflect the effectiveness of the process.

In addition, the data must be analyzed appropriately, and the analysis should include the input of individuals qualified to interpret the findings. Thus, a team composed of individuals involved in various aspects of the process should be permitted access to the data and should give input about alternative strategies. Moreover, the team can investigate the acceptability of new technologies that might allow for greater efficiency. Before new technologies are adopted, however, the team should thoroughly analyze the potential benefits, costs, and feasibility of using them in the organization.

After a reengineered process has emerged, new policies and procedures must be written and distributed to the people involved in the process. In addition, employees should be thoroughly trained in the redesigned process. However, it is important that they be given adequate time to master the process. Managers play an important role in reengineering through their support, encouragement, and commitment to the process.

Factors for Success in Reengineering Efforts

One critical factor for the success of the reengineering effort is the visible and persistent commitment of senior administration. A second critical factor is management's commitment to excellence. Managers must demonstrate a can-do attitude in working through the change. In addition, the fact that change is needed to address an unacceptable problem must be effectively communicated throughout the organization. Having everyone, or almost everyone, acknowledge that a problem exists creates a great deal of buy-in. Employees, including physicians, should be encouraged to overcome any reluctance to participate in the change process due to fears about restructuring. Many healthcare organizations make the mistake of not including their physicians in critical decision making. The likelihood of a successful reengineering effort increases when every stakeholder is involved in the process.

Reengineering takes time. The organization should realize that change cannot be achieved overnight and should avoid trying to change too many processes at one time. Instead, it should focus its efforts on a few processes at a time. A great deal of planning, information gathering, and analysis must occur before an actual redesign can be implemented. When the planning phase has been completed, the organization should revise or develop policies and procedures accordingly and distribute them throughout the organization.

Finally, implementation of the redesigned processes requires patience. Glitches may occur with any new system, but with careful monitoring and persistent adjusting, reengineering can produce significant PI.

Lean

Lean is a management strategy described as a philosophy based on "the continuous pursuit of improving the processes, eliminating all non-value-added activities, and reducing waste within an organization" (Rizzardo and Brooks 2003). Lean is known for its focus on the reduction of waste and is based on the Japanese success story of Toyota. Toyota's steady growth from a small company to one of the largest automobile companies in the world through the use of Lean principles has made Lean a hot topic in management science in the 21st century.

Lean implementation focuses on eliminating waste and creating a smooth workflow. Through analysis of the process versus a prime focus on the end goal, quality problems are exposed and waste reduction occurs naturally as a consequence. The goals of the organization remain the same; the approach toward achieving the goals differs in the Lean methodology. Lean works to eliminate non-value-added work, or waste, brought about by a lack of error detection, confused responsibilities, unnecessary work, disconnects, and workarounds. **Waste** can be defined as anything that does not add value to a product or service from the standpoint of the customer. Lean is about creating a continually improving system that is capable of achieving more while using less.

Lean has been applied in many industries, not just manufacturing. It has been used in healthcare with significant improvements in quality and efficiency. The principles of removing activities that do not add value can be applied anywhere. Value in a hospital setting maybe described as patient comfort, competent caregivers, or patient discharge after achieving the desired outcomes. Anything that helps treat the patient is value-added; everything else is waste. Toyota identified seven areas of waste: delay, overprocessing, inventory, transportation, motion, overproducing, and defects. Zidel (2006) gives examples of how these areas of waste may relate to healthcare. (See table 26.13.) There are a number of Lean tools and techniques used in manufacturing; several have a strong application to the healthcare industry. The following tools are described in Zidel (2006). They seem simple but when intentionally used, can uncover large amounts of waste.

- The 5 Whys: In this technique, simply ask "why" in every situation until you discover the root cause of the problem. Usually this process takes approximately five times before the root cause is identified.
- The 5 Ss: The 5 Ss are sort, straighten, scrub, standardize, and sustain. This method, simply stated, is housekeeping.
  — Sort—Remove everything that is not used or expected to be used
  — Straighten—Organize what is kept, have a place for everything, and keep everything in its place
  — Scrub—Clean the area
  — Standardize—Establish procedures to keep the area organized
  — Sustain—Maintain the gains and avoid backsliding
- Visual Controls: The visual controls tool is used to create a workplace where all that is needed is displayed and immediately available. There are four levels of visual controls:
  — Visual Indicator—Something that just informs, such as a sign on a patient's door with special instructions
  — Visual Signal—An alert or alarm, such as a nurse call light

Table 26.13.   Seven areas of waste related to healthcare

Delay	Waiting for bed assignments, waiting to be discharged, waiting for treatment, waiting for supplies, waiting for approval, waiting for the physician
Over processing	Excessive paperwork, redundant processes, unnecessary tests, multiple bed transfers
Inventory	Lab specimens awaiting analysis, ER patients awaiting a room assignment, patients awaiting diagnostic tests, excess supplies kept on hand, dictation awaiting transcription
Transportation	Transporting lab specimens, transporting patients, transporting medication, transporting supplies or equipment
Motion	Searching for charts, searching for supplies, delivering medications, nurses caring for patients in different areas
Overproducing	Mixing drugs in anticipation of patient needs, creating paperwork packets for an anticipated patient arrival
Defects	Medication errors, wrong-site surgery, improper labeling of specimens, assignment of duplicate medical record numbers

Source: Zidel 2006.

— Visual Control—A mechanism to control behavior, such as a needle box that automatically closes when full to eliminate the risk of overfilling
— Visual Guarantee—A mechanism that allows only a correct response, such as a medication dispensing machine that will not dispense a medication without proper identifiers; a visual guarantee is foolproof

In addition, the following two tools as described by Jones and Mitchell (2006) have applicability in the healthcare setting:

- *Value Stream Mapping:* This is a visual method of documenting both material and information flows of a process. It is a flow diagram that identifies all the value-added and non-value-added activities in the process. This is first developed to analyze the current process and eliminate non-value-added steps; then it is developed again to illustrate the improved, streamlined process. The value stream shows all the actions (both value-added and non-value-added) and related information required to bring a patient through the process from the start to the end of his visit.
- *Pull System:* This is a method of controlling the flow of resources by replacing only what the customer has consumed. Pull systems consist of production based on actual consumption, small volumes, low inventories, management by sight, and better communication. To create value, services must be in line with demand; no less, no more. Delivering services in line with demand means that work, material, and information should be "pulled" toward the task when needed.

Identifying the value streams, mapping and understanding each action in the value stream, and identifying and implementing immediate and future improvements using Lean tools and techniques are all a part of building a culture of continuous improvement in the organization.

Six Sigma

Historically, healthcare has been a follower with regard to quality improvement methods. In the mid-1980s, William Smith, an engineer, developed the concept of **Six Sigma.** Motorola was the first company to adopt the concept and turn itself from a company on the edge of bankruptcy to a highly profitable firm. When Motorola won the coveted Malcolm Baldrige National Quality Award in 1988, the "best-kept secret" was suddenly on the lips of every CEO in the nation (Misra 2008). That best-kept secret, in actuality, is not innovative in the sense that it is new knowledge; actually, it embraces tenets similar to Deming's PDCA. More emphatically, it is a culmination of "old notions" with a technology twist: data informatics. The evidence that gave the old innovation a new visibility is the evidence that the success of the Six Sigma initiative is modeled and measured by data that are collected, cleaned, and considered strategically both in the lines of service and as an outcome. They are data that are, in most cases, already being captured but not leveraged. It was not until 2001 to 2002, however, that healthcare organizations looked seriously at the Six Sigma concept (Lazarus 2003). Healthcare has been slow to adopt this concept because the extensive training involved is expensive, and physician and administrative buy-in is hard to come by. In recent years, however, a number of healthcare organizations have implemented Six Sigma successfully.

Some doubted that Six Sigma could be applied to the healthcare industry because of the human variability of patients. However, the 2000 Institute of Medicine report highlighting the alarming statistic of up to 98,000 deaths linked to medical errors soon resulted in a movement to review statistical data in the healthcare industry with industry eyes. Industry is customer driven and so is healthcare. Industry relies on feedback regarding success and failure in relevant data and so does healthcare. Healthcare leaders became invested in enlisting this philosophy of excellence, reducing costs, lowering lengths of stay, and raising the bar for high-quality healthcare. The healthcare industry leaders who have embraced Six Sigma are quick to share their successes as the industry continues to come to understand the richness of the data that are captured and how to understand their inherent value.

Six Sigma uses a methodology not unique. It uses a scientific methodology that involves the following steps: define, measure, analyze, improve, and control (**DMAIC**). (See figure 26.19.) Each step has substeps that are referred to as "tollgates." The tollgates provide detailed directions on

Figure 26.19.   DMAIC improvement methodology

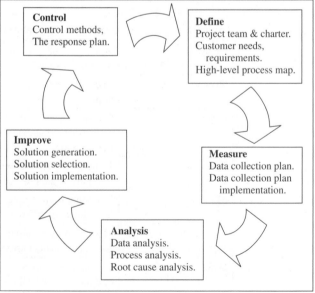

Source: Eckes (2003, 29).

what must be done to complete each step before moving on to the next step (Eckes 2003, 29–65).

Six Sigma uses many of the same tools used by other quality management systems. However, two tools unique to Six Sigma are (1) the critical quality tree (CQT) used in the define stage and (2) the process map used to identify the steps of a current process under review. In addition, Six Sigma uses "soft" tools that do not have a math basis; however, soft tools can be tricky to use because they have a subjective quality to them. Examples of some basic soft tools are a set of ground rules, a team agenda, a parking lot to track ideas not immediately pertinent, and activity or progress reports.

Six Sigma focuses on improving management and clinical processes. Statistical analysis is used to find the most defective part of a process, and rigorous control procedures are used to ensure sustained improvement. The goal of Six Sigma is to control for defects so that a 0.00034 percent defect rate is achieved (Lazarus 2003, 1).

Six Sigma can be used successfully in healthcare. It provides a systematic approach to validate data and focuses on the most meaningful improvements. As in other quality management concepts, the customer defines acceptable performance with the focus on delivery, quality, and cost. This definitely parallels the healthcare mainstays of cost, quality, and access (Lazarus 2003, 1). Successful implementation of Six Sigma in healthcare organizations has produced benefits such as the following:

- Higher productivity
- Fewer errors and adverse effects
- Improved organizational communication
- Improved patient satisfaction
- Better physician satisfaction
- Better nursing satisfaction
- Increased patient flow
- Short patient wait times
- Better use of advanced technologies

Lean Six Sigma

The uses of Lean methods along with Six Sigma techniques have been successful. Despite numerous debates over which process improvement methodology is best, it may be that the two methods work quite well together. Lean provides tools to identify and implement value-added activities designed to streamline processes and improve efficiency as a result of waste reduction. Six Sigma focuses on reducing variation through statistical analysis, validation of data, and measuring improvements. Lean and Six Sigma complement each other with goals aimed toward overall improvement, organizational buy-in, and a culture change that promotes continuous improvement via a structured methodology and identified tools and techniques.

Workflow Analysis and Process Redesign

Whatever the methodology or strategy used, workflow analysis and **process redesign** are necessary components of overall organizational improvement. The study of workflow as "who does what when" has become a critical part of process analysis and design methodologies.

Process and Workflow Theory

The delivery of healthcare is increasingly complex; therefore, the related workflows are also increasingly complex. As the use of technology becomes critical in all aspects of patient care, understanding how the work flows within and between processes is critical. The success of information technology projects is not solely dependent on the technology, but also on the people and the process. A business process can be defined as a collection of interrelated work tasks initiated in response to an event that achieves a specific result for a customer of the process (Sharp and McDermott 2009). A process must remain customer focused; redundancy, delay, and error must be avoided. The goal of workflow analysis is business process redesign.

Workflow analysis should be done any time work involves multiple departments or functions and prior to identifying an IT solution. It is important to ensure all the stakeholders are a part of the analysis, the entire process is considered when making improvements, the business process is accurately identified, and the team does not get stalled in overanalysis of the current process. HIM professionals are well suited for workflow analysis because they can see the big picture of the overall healthcare process, they understand how healthcare professionals work together toward quality patient care, and they understand information flow and the users of the information.

The steps in workflow analysis are described as follows (Sharp and McDermott 2009):

1. Frame the process
2. Understand the current (as-is) process
3. Design the new (to-be) process
4. Develop use case scenarios

Outside of the actual methodology of workflow analysis, related key concepts include understanding the organizational structure and managing change.

An essential, necessary distinction in workflow analysis is the difference between a process and a function. A process, as stated earlier, is a collection of interrelated work tasks done in response to an event that achieves a specific result for a customer. A function is an occupation or a department that focuses on related activities and similar skills. See Table 26.14 for an example distinguishing a process from a function. If a function is identified erroneously as a process for analysis, work methods will be defined for the benefit of the individual function, not to optimize the manner in which work flows through the function and through other areas of the organization as a whole. Focusing on functions and not business process perpetuates the development of functional silos or stovepipes. This should be avoided in process redesign.

Table 26.14.   Process vs. function

Coding Process (Interdepartmental, Multiple Skill Sets)	Coding Function (Intradepartmental, One Skill Set)
Register patient	Go to worklist and select case
Generate clinical documentation about patient assessment and services provided in the course of patient care	Obtain clinical documentation and charges
Enter charges	Review and determine adequacy of information
Process medical record for completeness and accuracy	Apply coding rules and select codes
Generate codes for billing and clinical databases	Enter codes into databases for billing and clinical systems
Analyze remittance advice and denials	

Source: AHIMA 2006.

Once a process is identified, framing that process is crucial in establishing and documenting the process boundaries. This will clarify the scope of the process, what is both within and outside of the scope. Documenting all the pertinent information about the process is called developing the process frame. In the process frame, one must

- Describe the process triggers, steps, results, and stakeholders
- Understand the environment, including the mission, vision, goals, and culture
- State the case for analysis

The purpose of analysis is to understand processes to identify bottlenecks, sources of delay, rework due to errors, role ambiguity, duplication, unnecessary steps, and handoffs. This understanding of the current (as-is) process will lead to a redesigned future (to-be) process that can then be tested through a use case analysis.

Tools and Techniques

As with continuous quality improvement, there are several process mapping tools that can assist with workflow analysis and process redesign. Process mapping shows the activities of the process including the sequence and flow of the work. Tool selection will depend on the level of precision needed and the nature of the process being mapped. Tools may be simple or complex, paper based, automated, or web based. Some of these tools are the same as or similar to the CQI tools.

Workflow Diagram

The workflow diagram is a physical illustration of where there is movement of information. This may also be known as a movement diagram (refer to figure 26.1).

Process Flowchart

The flowchart is a common analysis tool that visually illustrates each step in a process and the sequence of the steps. Flowcharts can be at a high level, defining major steps in the process, or they can be detailed, defining each step including decision points in the process (refer to figure 26.3).

Top-Down Process Map

The top down process map identifies the least number of steps necessary in a process. The main steps are worded broadly and simply, with each step showing only three to four subtasks in more detail (see figure 26.20).

Swimlane Diagram

A **swimlane diagram** shows an entire business process from beginning to end and is especially popular because it

Figure 26.20.   Top-down process maps

Step 1 Plan the Report	Step 2 Organize the Report	Step 3 Write the Report	Step 4 Produce the Report
1.1 Clarify purpose of the report 1.2 Identify elements of the report 1.3 Identify roles 1.4 Decide schedule	2.1 Identify sections of report 2.2 Determine order of topics 2.3 Collect information	3.1 Write report 3.2 Edit for flow and clarity 3.3 Incorporate charts and graphs 3.4 Review and correct	4.1 Lay out text and graphics 4.2 Review and correct layout 4.3 Proofread and correct 4.4 Publish and distribute report

Source: AHIMA 2006.

Figure 26.21.   Sample swimlane diagram

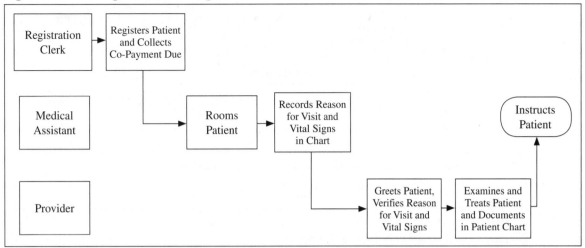

Source: AHIMA 2006.

highlights relevant variables (who, what, and when) while requiring little or no training to use and understand. The swimlane diagram is often used to identify the current (as-is) process as well as to design the new (to-be) process (see figure 26.21).

Process Simulation Software

Process simulation software can show the flow of work, individuals, or movement of information in varying existing or hypothetical situations. This software can show movement in existing situations and can show various alternative designs to help identify the most appropriate workflow.

These tools and techniques assist in analyzing current workflows to focus on facts rather than opinions, to truly understand the existing process, and to document all aspects of the process. Additionally, process maps can bring stakeholders to a common understanding to move forward with process redesign.

Use Case Analysis

A **use case analysis** is a technique to determine how users will interact with a system. It uses the designed future (to-be) process and describes how a user will interact with the system to complete process steps and how the system will behave from the user perspective. The purpose of use case analysis is to bridge the gap between user needs and system functionality. A use case analysis helps identify system requirements, design the user interface, facilitate documentation, create test plans, and develop training and support plans. It is critical to list all use case scenarios that impact each and every user so that no case is overlooked. Priority should go to developing use case scenarios that focus on those areas that have the most

impact on the success of the project such as those that affect workflows of multiple users.

Identifying all potential use cases is valuable to ensure that nothing is overlooked and all users are involved. More value emerges when each use case is not only identified but also described. Basic elements of a use case description are the use case name, a description of the use case, the users of the system for that use case, preconditions that must be in place before the use case can be tested, the normal sequence of steps, the post conditions or results expected, any alternate steps as needed, and any variations or issues known to that particular use case that are important to know. (See example in figure 26.22.)

Check Your Understanding 26.6

Instructions: On a separate piece of paper, indicate whether the following statements are true or false. Then correct any false statement to make it true or explain why it is false.

1. The goal of CQI—to meet or exceed the expectations of all the organization's customers—is generally attainable and achievable.

2. A manager's job with regard to performance improvement is to seek ways to reduce the amount of normal variation that occurs within systems and processes.

3. Obtaining and using actual data to inform managers who need to make decisions is a critically important element of the CQI philosophy.

4. Six Sigma came to the attention of healthcare CEOs in the late 1990s as a completely new and innovative approach to managing quality and cost in healthcare.

5. Lean is particularly focused on the elimination of waste.

Figure 26.22.   Use case description

Use Case Name
Physician orders medication(s) for a patient.

Description
When a physician determines that the patient needs a medication, he or she will complete the ordering process for medication administration.

Actor(s)
Physician; a nurse may also place the medication order (with a separate use case).

Preconditions
• The patient must currently be admitted in the hospital or receiving treatment in the ER. • The physician has active privileges at the facility. • The computerized provider order entry system is functioning properly.

Normal Sequence of Steps
• Physician signs on to the system using a password. • System validates the password and displays the patient search screen. • Physician enters the patient's medical record number. • System verifies the medical record number and displays the patient's electronic medical record. • Physician selects the medication module. • System verifies the user is allowed access to the module and displays the medication module. • Physician selects the medication from drop-down list. • System verifies the medication name. • Physician enters the dosage amount, frequency, method of administration. • System verifies the dosage amount, frequency, method of administration. • Physician submits the medication order by selecting the Submit button.

Postconditions
• The order is submitted to the pharmacy information system. • The pharmacy receives electronic notification of pending order. • A pending order is recorded in the patient's electronic medical record.

Alternative Sequence of Steps
• If the physician does not have the medical record number, he or she may enter the patient's last name and the first name. The system will then provide a list of patient names that the physician may choose from. • An additional free text field may be provided to the physician to record any additional notes or messages in relation to the medication being ordered.

Comments, Issues, and Design Notes
• When searching for a patient's electronic medical record, it may be necessary to also be able to search by patient date of birth. • For the fields of amount, frequency, and method of administration, it may be necessary to create drop-down lists that can be selected from instead of allowing free text. This will allow more control of the data entry and reduce data entry errors.

Used with permission from College of St. Scholastica HIM graduate student D. Parisian. 2008.

Summary

Excellence in management requires the manager to be knowledgeable about the components of systems and work processes; to be aware of the quality and productivity expectations of the customers served by them; and have the ability to define, execute, monitor, and analyze performance based on standards that have been developed through benchmarking and specific types of work measurement methodologies. When variations in performance are identified, they are addressed in a timely way through action plans, which may well include efforts focused on process improvement to achieve greater effectiveness, efficiency, and adaptability of the systems involved.

Continuous quality improvement and business process redesign are two fundamental approaches to improving processes and performance in healthcare organizations. These approaches share many similarities: all are focused on bettering the system to provide high-quality service in a cost-effective manner. They also use similar data-gathering and analysis tools. The differences in the approaches reflect the breadth of change, the duration of the change effort, and the specific focus area for the change. CQI is a test of small changes with the intention of improving services to customers over time. Business process reengineering involves a massive reexamination of processes with the main purpose of reducing costs. In addition, Lean and Six Sigma are commonly being used in healthcare organizations to improve healthcare service delivery.

References

American Health Information Management Association. 2006. *Optimizing Investment in the EHR: Workflow Analysis as the Foundation for Success* [Workshop resource book]. Chicago: AHIMA.

Berwick, D.M.1989. Continuous improvement as an ideal in health care. *New England Journal of Medicine* 320(1): 53–56.

Brassard, M.,and D. Ritter. 2010. *The Memory Jogger II,* 2nd ed. Salem, NH: GOAL/QPC.

Cofer, J.I.,and H.P. Greeley. 1993. *Quality Improvement Techniques for Medical Records.* Marblehead, MA: Opus Communications.

Eckes, G. 2003. *Six Sigma for Everyone.* Hoboken, NJ: John Wiley & Sons.

Hammer, M., and J. Champy. 1993. *Reengineering the Corporation: A Manifesto for Business Revolution.* New York: HarperBusiness.

Institute of Medicine. 2000. *To Err Is Human.* Washington, D.C.: National Academies Press.

Johnson, S.P., and C.P. McLaughlin. 1999. Measurement and statistical approaches in CQI. In *Continuous Quality Improvement in Health Care.* Edited by McLaughlin, C.P., and A.D. Kaluzny. Gaithersburg, MD: Aspen Publishers.

Joint Commission. 2011. *Comprehensive Accreditation Manual.* Oakbrook Terrace, IL: Joint Commission.

Jones, D., and A. Mitchell. 2006. *Lean Thinking for the NHS.* A report commissioned by the NHS. http://www.leanuk.org/downloads/health/lean_thinking_for_the_nhs_leaflet.pdf.

Langley, G.J., K.M. Nolan, and T.W. Nolan. 1994 (June). The foundation of improvement. *Quality Progress* 81–86.

Lazarus, I. 2003 (January. 1). Six Sigma raising the bar. *Managed Healthcare Executive.* http://www.managedhealthcareexecutive .com.mhe/article/articleDetail.jsp?id=43331.

Liebler, J.G., R.E. Levine, and J. Rothman. 1992. *Management Principles for Health Professionals,* 2nd ed. Gaithersburg, MD: Aspen Publishers.

McLaughlin, C.P., and A.D. Kaluzny. 1999. *Continuous Quality Improvement in Health Care: Theory, Implementation and Applications,* 2nd ed. Gaithersburg, MD: Aspen Publishers.

Misra, K.B. 2008. *Handbook of Performability Engineering.* London: Springer.

Omachonu, V.K. 1999. *Healthcare Performance Improvement.* Norcross, GA: Engineering and Management Press.

Palmer, L. 1995. Reengineering healthcare: The future awaits us all. *Journal of AHIMA* 66(2): 32–35.

Parisian, D. 2008. *Use Case Description.* College of St. Scholastica.

Rizzardo, D., and R. Brooks. 2003. Understanding Lean manufacturing. http://www.mtech.umd .edu/MTES/understand_lean.html.

Sharp, A., and P. McDermott. 2009. *Workflow Modeling: Tools for Process Improvement and Application Development,* 2nd ed . Norwood, MA: Arctech House.

Six Sigma. 2004. Deming cycle, PDCA. http://www.isixsigma. com/dictionary/Deming_Cycle,_PDCA-650.htm.

Umiker, W. 1998. *Management Skills for the New Health Care Supervisor,* 3rd ed. Gaithersburg, MD: Aspen Publishers.

White, A. 2002. Performance improvement. In *Health Information Management Technology: An Applied Approach.* Edited by M.L. Johns. Chicago: AHIMA.

Zidel, T.G. 2006 (January/February). Quality toolbox: A Lean toolbox—using Lean principles and techniques in healthcare. *Journal for Healthcare Quality*—web exclusive. http://www .mainenetwork.org/upload_files/Tom%20Zidel%20-%20Lean%20 Toolbox%20-%20JHQ%20JanFeb06.pdf.

chapter 27

Project Management

Patricia B. Seidl, RHIA

Learning Objectives

- Identify how a project differs from an organization's daily operations
- Describe the components of a project
- Discuss reasons for project success versus project failure
- Describe different project team structures
- Understand the responsibilities of the project manager
- Know the project management process and recognize the technical and people skills involved
- Identify the components of a project proposal document
- Understand the steps in planning and organizing a project
- Estimate work, duration, and resource requirements
- Understand how to anticipate and manage project risk
- Know how to track a project's progress and analyze variances
- Describe the types of plan revision
- Understand the concept of project scope management
- Recognize the components of a communication plan

Key Terms

Assumption
Baseline
Change control
Contingency
Critical path
Dependency
Duration
Functional team structure
Gantt chart
Impact factor
Issue log
Matrixed team structure
Predecessor
Probability factor
Project charter
Project component
Project definition
Project definition document
Project deliverable
Project management
Project management life cycle
Project management software
Project manager

Project network
Project office
Project plan
Project schedule
Project scope
Project team
Projectized team structure
Resource
Risk analysis
Risk factor
Scalable
Scheduling engine
Scope creep
Sponsor
Stakeholder
Statement of work
Subproject
Successor
Variance
Work
Work breakdown structure (WBS)
Work product

Although health information management (HIM) professionals practice in many diverse healthcare delivery systems and domains, there is a common responsibility across all lines of business: leading or participating in projects. It is important to understand the concepts and best practices of project management in order to engage fully and effectively as a project team member. Although there are many different types, all projects have similar attributes: their objectives benefit the organization, they all follow the project management process, similar characteristics of the project manager are needed, they all involve a project team, and they all result in some type of outcome.

Projects consist of organizational and behavioral components. Organizational or structural components guide the team toward its end goals. Behavioral components include the concepts of leading, motivating, politics, and interpersonal communication.

This chapter describes the different elements of a project and the different types of projects that healthcare organizations might undertake. It also focuses on how projects are managed and tracked to ensure their success.

The Project

An organization undertakes a project because it has determined the need for some type of change. This need may be the result of a company's strategic agenda, such as implementation of a new software application, or it may be in response to passage of a new government regulation. After the need for the project has been acknowledged, the project enters the project management life cycle or process.

Every project has an identified sponsor. The **sponsor** is the facility employee with the most vested interest in the project's success. It is a good practice to select someone who has responsibility for the organization's departments, divisions, and personnel that will be affected by the project. The project will open up many issues that, in some situations, must be resolved by an authority figure. It is much easier to obtain a decision or consensus when the sponsor already has established control over the areas involved in the project. The sponsor often approves the budget for the project and is ultimately responsible for the project expenditures.

The project also has **stakeholders.** A stakeholder is anyone in the organization who is affected by the project product. Stakeholders include personnel who are on the project team, personnel whose daily work will be changed because of the project's product, and the managers and executives for those departments involved in the project. Each stakeholder has different concerns relative to the project's objectives and goals. The project team wants to produce a high-quality product. Departmental personnel worry about their ability to adapt to the procedures and skills required by the new or changed product. Department managers and executives must support the functional changes that may be needed as a result of the project. Each stakeholder will evaluate the project's success based on these concerns and the expectations they hold for how the project will benefit them.

Definition of a Project

A Guide to the Project Management Body of Knowledge (PMBOK Guide) describes a project as "a temporary endeavor undertaken to create a unique product, service, or result" (PMI 2008, 5). A project has the following characteristics:

- Specific objectives or goals to be achieved
- Defined start and end date
- Defined set of resources assigned to perform the required work
- Specific deliverables or work products
- Defined budget or cost

A project differs from the day-to-day operations of an organization. Operations are concerned with the daily jobs needed to run the business. The personnel involved in the operational aspects of the business perform the same functions on a routine basis. This work does not end. In contrast, a project has a precise, expected result produced by defined resources within a specific time frame.

Project Parameters

A well-defined project has specific objectives. After the project's objectives have been defined, all project activities should be focused on meeting them. The project activities result in project deliverables or **work products.** When the project activities have concluded and the project deliverables have been completed, the project ends.

The process of documenting project parameters is discussed later in this chapter.

Project Components

Lewis (2008) writes that a project's objectives include cost, performance, time, and scope. Cost is the project budget, performance relates to the quality of the project work, time is the schedule, and **project scope** is the magnitude of the work to be done. He illustrates the relationship with the expression "Cost is a function of Performance, Time, and Scope." Should the cost, performance, or schedule variable change, the relationship dictates that the scope will change (Lewis 2008, 127–128). The project manager and the sponsor must acknowledge this relationship and be willing to make the trade-offs that will be needed when the variables change.

When developing the **project plan,** the project manager translates the objectives into three **project components:** scope, resources, and schedule. These components have a strong dependency. If one of the three components changes, then one of the other two parameters must change as well. This is often illustrated as a triangle. (See figure 27.1.)

Figure 27.1.   Illustration of project components

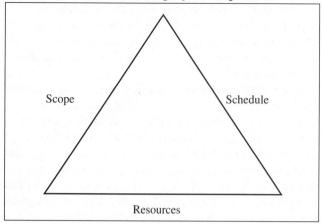

Project resources are not just people. A **resource** is any physical asset needed to complete a task. This includes facilities, equipment, materials, and supplies. Resources also can include individuals from outside organizations, such as suppliers or vendors.

One reason why many projects fail to meet their objectives within the expected time frame and budget is that their scope begins to grow as they progress. For example, new functions or features are added to a software implementation. This is commonly known as **scope creep.** The requestor presents each change as a small revision with low impact on time line or cost. However, several minor changes soon add up to a more significant modification to the original work or cost estimate. The project manager must be diligent to prevent scope creep, which is discussed in detail later in this chapter.

Project Assumptions

Assumptions are scope-limiting parameters. They provide constraints on what is and is not included in the project. For example, if the project is to design a training program, the number of personnel to be trained will need to be defined. This assumption affects the number of copies for any training materials (impacting the cost) and the amount of time it will take to train everyone (impacting the schedule).

Assumptions define answers to unknown questions. For instance, at the beginning of the project, the project manager may not know what personnel will be assigned to the project and thus will not know the skill set that will be available. One assumption might be that a project team member from a particular department on a cross-departmental project is a decision maker. In other words, when the project team meets to design the user interface for a software implementation, the decisions can be made in that meeting and will not be deferred to a person outside the team. If this assumption does not prove to be true, the project manager is faced with a potential delay because the process required for decision making was not accounted for in the project schedule.

Assumptions directly affect the project estimates for the resource and time line requirements. Therefore, it is critical that the project manager obtain agreement from the sponsor and the stakeholders on all assumptions. A lack of buy-in by all the project participants puts the objectives at risk. Many projects immediately start down the path of failure because the assumptions were not addressed adequately at the project start.

Types of Projects

There are many different types of projects. Although they share some attributes, projects can be vastly different in several aspects. Some projects are short term and completed in the span of weeks; other projects take years to complete. One project may involve only a single department; another may require participation across the facilities in an integrated delivery system (IDS).

Following are types of projects in which HIM professionals may be involved:

- Instituting new or revised procedures to address updated privacy and security regulations
- Improving the management of the revenue cycle
- Evaluating the effectiveness of a data governance program
- Instituting a clinical documentation improvement program
- Setting up a Virtual HIM department
- Creating a new employee orientation program
- Implementing a new business procedure or process
- Implementing new technology such as computer-assisted coding

A complex project may comprise several **subprojects.** The subprojects share common milestones and objectives but may be managed by different project managers. Subproject information may be compiled into one report to show information across all associated projects.

Project Risk versus Project Value

Projects are undertaken to specifically incorporate some requirement or business need. Although the organization certainly expects a positive outcome, there are always some risks to the organization as well. One of the project manager's responsibilities is to mitigate risk. However, the organization will need to weigh the cost of potential risks against the perceived value to be gained.

Project risk can take many forms and be of either a technical or psychological nature. For example, implementing a state-of-the-art networking infrastructure may provide leading-edge technology that sets the organization apart from its competitors. However, the availability of personnel who can provide support for new technology may be limited.

Another example would be a project that introduces a significant change to a department employee's responsibilities.

The change positions the employee out of his or her comfort zone. Before the project begins, an employee may be considered an expert in his or her job responsibilities. At the conclusion of the project, the same employee may have new duties and will not have the same proficiency in them. This could cause self-esteem problems. It is not uncommon for employee turnover to occur during a project because of this threat to job security.

Check Your Understanding 27.1

Instructions: Answer the following questions on a separate piece of paper.

1. Why does an organization start a project?

2. What are the similar responsibilities of the project's sponsor and stakeholders? What are examples of different responsibilities?

3. How do projects and organizational processes differ?

4. What is scope creep?

Project Management

The *PMBOK Guide* defines **project management** as "the application of knowledge, skills, tools, and techniques to project activities to meet the project requirements" (PMI 2008, 6). Project management is concerned with completing a project within the expected cost and time line with high-quality results. This is not easy to accomplish and, as a consequence, interest in project management best practices is very high. Many organizations understand the importance of solid project management methodologies and as a result establish project offices to support the organization's project managers. A **project office** is responsible for defining project management procedures, conducting risk analyses on projects, and mentoring project managers.

Overview of Project Management

The discipline of project management has emerged as organizations have come to realize that projects cannot succeed without it. Projects have customarily been deemed successful when they meet their objectives and do not exceed their approved cost and estimated schedule. Lewis (2008) proposes a different definition of project success. He challenges the commonly held belief that a project has failed when it does not meet its cost, performance, time, or scope targets by questioning how these targets were established. The targets may have been unrealistic and therefore impossible to meet. By citing several studies, Lewis concludes that it is how closely the project outcomes align with the perceptions held by the key project personnel that determines project success (105–110). As an example, if a project is completed under budget but ends up solving the wrong problem, is it successful? A project may meet the schedule but have unexpected and undesirable consequences. As Thomas K. Connellan, a speaker, trainer, and business consultant, once said, "There is no point in doing well that which you should not be doing at all."

Kliem (2004) proposes a paradigm shift, noting that project performance has not improved dramatically over the years despite a proliferation of tools, techniques, and expertise. His proposal is to change from a prevailing paradigm that relies too much on the mechanics of project management (for example, creating a project plan) to subjective factors that play a major role in effective leadership. Under this new paradigm, a project is defined as a focused, integrated human endeavor to achieve a specific common purpose. The implications of this new paradigm are illustrated in table 27.1 (Kliem 2004, 29, 47–52).

Project success relies on a balance between project management as a scientific discipline and people-oriented project leadership.

The Project Management Life Cycle

Every project follows a **project management life cycle** regardless of its size or duration. Each process in the life cycle has its own importance. Any one of the processes cannot be eliminated or minimized without endangering the success of the project. As listed in table 27.2, the project management life cycle consists of a number of processes, which are later discussed in detail.

The Project Team

By definition, a project results in an end product through the completion of task activities. The execution of these task activities is the responsibility of the project team. A **project team** is composed of individuals who possess the knowledge and skill set to produce the project deliverables and work products.

The type of project determines the size of the project team and the originating location of the resources. A project that affects only one department will typically have project team members from only that department. A project with organization-wide objectives will have a cross-departmental team, whereas a project for an integrated delivery system (IDS) will include representatives from all the system's facilities.

There are three types of project **team structure: functional, projectized,** and **matrixed** (PMI 2008, 28–32).

Functional Team Structure

In a strictly functional organization, the project is thought to affect only one department. The functional manager may assume responsibility for managing the project. The team members are primarily from the functional department, and the functional manager confers with other functional managers on any issues affecting those departments.

Table 27.1. Implications of the new paradigm

Implication	Prevailing Paradigm	New Paradigm
Results	Best tool or most efficient process becomes an end in itself	Excellence comes from delivering a product or service that achieves a desired result
Interdependence	Places value on defining all the elements of a project in precise detail	Places more value on how to define and improve the relationship of those elements to achieve desired results
Why	Emphasis on determining what must be done, which leads to implementing counterproductive tools, techniques, and methodology	Ask why to determine if a tool, technique, or methodology advances the goal of the project
Responsiveness	When a project deviates from the plan, force feeding tools, techniques, and concepts that don't contribute to the goals of the project	Determine why certain actions must happen. Actions should provide the most leverage to achieve desired results
Qualitative	Relying on quantitative aspects at the expense of people. Uses measures that reflect great efficiencies at the expense of effectiveness.	Recognizes that quantification is not the only driver of a project and that quantification is reflective of qualitative factors such as beliefs and values
Dynamic	Unrealistic emphasis on maintaining control, thereby imposing project management principles and practice instead of adapting them	Projects are seen as dynamic entities. A project and its environment constantly change, and this reality should be accepted
People	People are another resource along with time, money, and equipment	Puts people at the center of the project. It is people who must participate not only in the formulation of plans but also in the implementation of all the tools, techniques, and practices of project management.

Table 27.2. Project management life cycle

Project definition	This process will determine the project objectives, activities, assumptions, high-level cost estimate, and anticipated schedule.
Planning and organization	A detailed project plan is developed that delineates the tasks to be performed, the resources necessary for each task, and the estimated task duration, start, and finish. The project team is assembled.
Tracking and analysis	By tracking project progress and analyzing it against the original plan, the project manager is able to determine when the project is not moving forward as planned.
Project revisions	When the analysis reveals project deviations, the plan may need to be modified in order to still meet the project objectives.
Change control	This is the process of managing change requests to the original project definition.
Communication	This process occurs throughout the project life cycle. Project information is collected from, and disseminated to, all stakeholders.

Projectized Team Structure

The projectized organization has dedicated resources that are involved only in project work. Team members report to the project manager not only on project assignments but also as their direct manager.

Matrixed Team Structure

The matrixed organization maintains the functional organization. Team members report to a functional manager and remain employees of that department. The team members receive their project assignments from the project manager.

In a matrixed organization, assigning the members of the project team can pose a dilemma for the stakeholders and the project manager. Typically, the best people to have on a project team are the ones who most intimately understand the processes and procedures affected by the project. However, these people have operational responsibilities in their respective departments that do not disappear while the project is in progress. Depending on the scope of the project, the time commitment required of the project team can be quite significant.

It is important to define the roles and responsibilities of the project team. In a matrixed organization, the project team members do not report to the project manager in an organizational structure. However, the project manager holds team members accountable for their tasks.

Instructions: On a separate piece of paper, prepare a grid that lists examples of the types of projects an HIM professional may be involved in. For each project list the following:

- The project objectives
- The factors that will be used to measure project success
- The factors that may contribute to project failure
- The members of the project team

The Project Manager

The **project manager** is the individual with responsibility for directing the project activities from initiation through closure. Depending on the size of the project, the project manager may be a dedicated resource or may be performing these duties along with other operational assignments. For example, for a project confined to a single department, an assistant director may be asked to manage the project while the department director takes on the sponsor role. In other situations, one of the team members may be asked to be the project leader while still performing specific task assignments for the project.

In circumstances where the project manager is not fully devoted to the project, it is easy for the project management duties to fall by the wayside, especially because many of these may produce intangible results. (The functions of the project manager are discussed in a subsequent section of this chapter.) The project sponsor must ensure that an adequate percentage of the project manager's time is allocated to these responsibilities.

Competencies and Skills

A project manager must possess both functional and behavioral skills. Some of his or her responsibilities are purely operational, for example, preparing a project plan. However, several skills are required that touch on the human side of projects. All projects result in a change in the organization. Facilitating an organization through the impact of these changes requires attributes that are described as "soft skills."

Project managers are very often in the position of having great responsibility but little authority, because the project team members do not report to them from an organizational perspective. Thus, project managers must get results from the team members through leadership and influence.

Project managers should possess the following skills:

- General management skills of planning, directing, organizing, and prioritizing
- Leadership skills of influencing, motivating, providing vision, and resolving conflict
- Communication skills of being able to interact with all levels of an organization and of being able

to understand different communication styles and mediums
- Facilitation skills, including negotiation, consensus building, and meeting management skills
- Analytical and critical thinking skills, including innovative thinking, problem solving, and decision-making skills

Functions

The project manager performs several functions over the course of the project management life cycle. These functions are described in table 27.3.

The Project Management Process

A project follows a defined process regardless of size, type, or industry. The process is **scalable,** meaning that the depth to which a particular process is performed may vary according to project length, scope, or other parameters. However, to ensure the success of the project, all these processes must be performed to some degree.

Project Definition

Project definition sets the expectation for the what, when, and how of the project. As noted under the project parameters section of this chapter, every project comprises three components: what is to be done (scope), the resources needed to accomplish the objectives, and the amount of time required to complete the project. The project definition process formally documents these variables for the project. This process is important for several reasons. First, it provides all project stakeholders, team members, and other personnel with the same information about the project—what it will accomplish, when it will be done, and what resources it will require. Second, it is used as the basis for understanding when requested changes are out of the project's scope.

Determine Project Scope and Define Project Deliverables

The definition of the project starts with determining its goals. The project's goals or objectives should be measurable. If they are not, it will be impossible for the project manager and the stakeholders to determine whether the project is successful. (Examples of objectives are shown in table 27.4.)

The next step in defining the project is to determine the tangible end results of the project. These are typically called **project deliverables.** The project deliverables indicate when the project activities have been completed. Typical deliverables for a software implementation include

- System requirements
- User interface design document
- Test plans

Table 27.3. Functions of the project manager

Set the project expectations.	As noted earlier, project success is tied to the perception that the project met the objectives. The project manager has responsibility for properly setting the project expectations and continually resetting them as the project progresses.
Create the project plan and recruit the project team.	The project manager generates a project schedule with the estimated work effort. The project team is organized, with each team member understanding his or her roles and responsibilities. The project manager leads team development efforts to form an effective, motivated team. He or she uses interpersonal skills to establish a rapport with team members.
Manage project control.	When the project is under way, the project manager must have a clear understanding of its status. Informal and formal communication methods are used to determine project progress. The project manager maintains the project plan to perform variance analysis. The project manager works with the project team to bring tasks to closure by facilitating decision making and issue resolution. The project manager facilitates the removal of any obstacles that prevent the team from producing the project deliverables.
Recommend plan revisions.	If a plan is not progressing as scheduled, the project manager must determine what actions need to be taken to put the project back on track. He or she gains consensus on the changes from the sponsor and the stakeholders, and monitors any new risks to the plan.
Execute change control.	The project manager institutes a policy and procedure for managing change requests. He or she keeps everyone focused on the end goal.
Prepare, document, and communicate project information.	Project documentation is a key facet of project communication. The project manager creates the communication plan that will be used to determine when, how, and what information is to be gathered and distributed. He or she facilitates the dissemination of information throughout the organization. Although the project team members create much of the documentation through the project deliverables, the project manager is responsible for ensuring that documentation exists and is available.

- Training and procedure manuals
- Production software

Estimate the Project Schedule and Cost

The next step in project definition is to estimate how long the project will take and how much it will cost. At this point in the process, the project may not have been approved, so this information is needed in order for the stakeholders to make an informed decision. This also poses a dilemma for

Table 27.4. Examples of project objectives

Type of Project	Nonmeasurable Objective	Measurable Objective
As part of electronic health record (EHR) implementation, conduct process improvement project for the release of information (ROI) function	Decrease time spent on ROI activities	Improve average release of information turnaround time from 5 days to 3 days
Implementation of EHR system	Decrease required full-time equivalents (FTEs) for file room activities	Decrease file room FTEs from 3 to 1
Institute a home coding program	Improve coder satisfaction	Decrease staff turnover by 20%

the project manager. He or she may not have enough detailed information about the project to make an estimate. (A detailed analysis occurs in the project planning phase.)

In this case, the project manager has a few options. One is to evaluate a past project that is similar in scope and to extract pertinent information from it that can be used in estimating the new project. A second option is to confer with professional colleagues who have experience in the proposed project. If a similar project is unavailable for analysis, a third alternative is for the project manager to use his or her expert judgment and intuition based on other professional experiences. Another opportunity would be available if the project manager were working with a vendor. The vendor would likely have experience in these types of projects and could assist the project manager in formulating estimates.

Prepare the Project Proposal

As stated previously, one of the purposes of the project definition phase is to set project expectations. The project manager now should be ready to record the project objectives, scope, deliverables, expected time line, and anticipated cost in a written document. This document is known by various names. Typical names include **project charter, statement of work,** and **project definition document** or business plan.

The project proposal contains several topics. The following information should be included:

- *Summary:* The summary provides an overview of the project and can provide any relevant background history and reasons why the project is being proposed.
- *Objectives:* The objectives state the project's goals.
- *Project activities:* This section is a high-level description of the major project tasks and maps out how the project will produce the project deliverables.

These activities will be detailed during the project planning phase.

- *Assumptions:* Assumptions provide input on the estimates for the resource and time line requirements. Inclusion of the assumptions in the project definition document sets the stage for their acknowledgment and agreement. Assumptions may or may not prove to be true as the project progresses. The importance of identifying assumptions is that when one does not prove to be true, one of the project components will likely need to be altered.
- *Roles and responsibilities:* This section defines the types of resources needed on the project and delineates who does what. Its concept is not dissimilar to defining a department's organizational structure. The purpose is to ensure that everyone is aware of everyone's duties and the lines of authority. It is a good idea to include a project organizational chart. The project manager usually does not have management authority over the team, so documenting the roles is crucial in understanding how the team will function.
- *Schedule and cost:* Schedule and cost information is provided at a very high level because it will be further refined during the project planning phase. Cost estimates will include those for personnel, equipment, and supplies. If an external company will be providing some project services, this section should indicate whether the engagement is based on time and materials or fixed-fee pricing.
- *Deliverables:* The discussion of deliverables is another component of setting expectations. By documenting the tangible output from the project, everyone will understand when the project tasks are complete. How the deliverables are documented can be specific by including the following types of information for each deliverable:
  — Type (for example, Microsoft Word)
  — Expected length or size
  — Number of copies provided
  — Mode of delivery (for example, via e-mail)

Check Your Understanding 27.3

Instructions: On a separate piece of paper, prepare a project proposal document for one of the projects you listed in Check Your Understanding 27.2. Include the project objectives, deliverables, high-level project activities, assumptions, and roles and responsibilities.

What needs to be considered when estimating the project cost?

Project Planning

After a project has been approved, it moves into the planning phase. The purpose of this phase is to further refine the project work effort, time line, and cost. During the project planning phase, the project manager creates a project plan that details the tasks to be performed, the resources needed to perform each task, the estimated work effort, and the estimated start and finish dates.

The project manager may use **project management software** to aid this process. Also known as a **scheduling engine,** project management software can provide the tools to automate some of the functions the project manager must perform. However, a software tool cannot perform the behavioral roles required of the project manager. Beware of software product literature promising a successful project simply by using it.

Identify Project Activities

When a project is initiated, the project manager is faced with the following question: how do we complete the project objectives and produce the project deliverables? Creating a project plan that lists each activity provides the road map to answer this question. For example, when a person decides to go on a vacation, he or she does not simply go to the airport. First, he or she has to decide where to go and how to get there and then make the appropriate reservations and so on.

A project plan starts with a **work breakdown structure (WBS),** or task list. The WBS is a hierarchical list of steps needed to complete the project. This structure provides levels that are similar to the concept of a book outline. Each level drills down to more detail. The lowest level is the task level, which is the level to which resources are assigned and work effort estimates are made.

A good place to begin in building the WBS is with the deliverables. Every deliverable should have a set of corresponding tasks to produce it. After every deliverable has been covered, the next area to address is the tasks that do not produce deliverables as such. What kind of tasks are they? One such task would be project management. Although project management tasks certainly produce plenty of documentation, the output is not a deliverable for the project itself, meaning that it does not contribute to the project objectives.

When creating the WBS, the project manager is faced with determining the level of task detail to be included. When the task level is not itemized enough, it will be difficult to assess the progress on the task. Having too much detail presents its own problems if the project manager is using project management software because he or she will spend too much time managing the project plan instead of doing the actual project. The level of detail directly correlates to the project manager's ability to control the project. He or she must determine the level of detail that provides this control.

Table 27.5 is an illustration of too much detail in a project plan. The list on the left represents very detailed steps, not tasks. The project plan should not be thought of as a to-do list. The list on the right represents tasks at a more manageable level of detail.

Table 27.5. Illustration of steps versus tasks

Steps	Tasks
Invitations	**Invitations**
Shop for invitations	Select and purchase invitations
Choose invitation	Mail invitations
Purchase invitations	
Address invitations	
Purchase stamps	
Mail invitations	

Construct the Project Network

When all the tasks have been defined, the next step is to determine the **dependency** among tasks. The tasks in the project plan cannot all start at the same time. For example, training on a new software application cannot begin until the training materials have been completed and the system has been thoroughly tested.

The definition of dependencies among the project tasks is the first step in scheduling the project. The purpose of the **project schedule** is to provide information on when the particular tasks can begin and when they are scheduled to end. The overall **project network** is defined through these dependencies.

Figure 27.2 shows an example of a project schedule for a training program project.

There are a few types of dependencies:

- *Finish-to-start:* This means that the first, or **predecessor,** task must finish before the dependent, or **successor,** task can start. Finish-to-start is the most common type of dependency.
- *Start-to-start:* This states that the successor task cannot start until the predecessor task begins. An example of this relationship would be in a software application implementation where outdated hardware must be replaced. The application build cannot begin until the new hardware has been installed.

- *Finish-to-finish:* In this definition, the successor task cannot finish until the predecessor task finishes. An example of this dependency would be completing training materials when the system testing for a software application is complete. The materials cannot be finished until the project manager is assured, via testing, that all modifications to the software have been completed.

Estimate Activity Duration and Work Effort

After the tasks have been defined, the project manager determines who will perform each task (resources), the amount of effort it will take to complete the task (work), and how long it will take to finish the task (duration). **Work** and **duration** are two different values. For example, if Emily is assigned to a task for 24 hours of work effort, how long will it take her to complete the task? It depends on how much of Emily's overall workday she devotes to this particular task. If she spends 100 percent of her day on this task and the assumption is that she is scheduled to work eight hours a day, she can complete the task in three days. If she can only dedicate 50 percent of her time to the task, she will complete the task in six days.

This calculation is shown in table 27.6. If multiple resources can be assigned to the task, the task duration can be reduced.

Estimating the work effort for tasks is difficult and can be time consuming, especially if the organization does not have much experience in the type of project being performed.

It is best to get estimates from the people who will be performing the work. If the team has not been assigned, the functional manager of the area may be called on to provide this information. Either way, the project manager may still encounter unrealistic values because people tend to underestimate the effort in those instances where historical information is unavailable. Some people overcompensate in their estimate if they do have experience in projects, knowing that unforeseen circumstances may arise.

Figure 27.2. Example of a project schedule for a training program

ID	Task Name	Duration
1	**Training Program Assessment**	**3 days**
2	Conduct Needs Assessment	1 day
3	Evaluate Training Methods	1 day
4	Complete Training Program Assessment Document	1 day
5	**Training Program Preparation**	**1 day**
6	Prepare Course Materials	1 day
7	Identify Trainers	1 day
8	Complete List of personnel to be trained	1 day
9	Prepare Training facilities	1 day
10	**Implement Training Program**	**2 days**
11	Prepare Training schedule	1 day
12	Conduct Training Test Runs	1 day
13	Conduct Training	1 day

Table 27.6. Calculation of duration based on work and percentage of day

Situation	Resources	Work	Percentage of Day	Duration
Emily is the only resource assigned to a task and will focus on that task until it is complete.	Emily	40 hours	100%	5 days
Emily is the only resource assigned to a task and can only dedicate half of her time to the task.	Emily	40 hours	50%	10 days
Emily and John are assigned to a task and can share the responsibilities. They will focus on this task until it is complete.	Emily John	20 hours 20 hours	100%	2.5 days
Emily and John are assigned to a task and can share the responsibilities. They can dedicate half of their time to this task.	Emily John	20 hours 20 hours	50% 50%	5 days

And, unfortunately, Parkinson's Law, which says that "Work expands to fill the time," complicates the estimating situation. Typically, if a resource is told that 16 hours of work effort are allocated for a task, he or she will expend all 16 hours.

The assumptions for the project also play a role in defining the estimates. For example, if an assumption is that a software engineer knowledgeable in the applicable software language will be assigned to the project, the work estimates will be lower than if the assumption is that an inexperienced resource will be assigned.

After the work effort values have been determined and the task durations calculated, the project network reflects a more realistic time frame. The project finish date is calculated based on the task dependencies and task durations. Figure 27.3 shows how the project tasks from figure 27.2 are now scheduled.

If a project manager is using project management software, the **critical path** for the project can be determined. The critical path is the series of specific tasks that determine the overall project duration.

The critical path is important for the project manager to understand because any change in the start or finish of one of the tasks on the critical path means the expected project finish date will change. Changes to the critical path can happen in a variety of ways, including the following:

- The duration of a task may change because the work effort or resource availability changes.
- The expected start date for the task changes because the finish date for a predecessor task changes.
- The finish date for a task changes because a resource's availability is changed. Perhaps a person schedules vacation or training for a week or his or her availability for the project changes because he or she is assigned additional duties outside the project.

The project manager also can use the critical path to determine how to shorten the overall project schedule. It is typical for the stakeholders of a project to already have a predetermined expected finish date for the project when it is proposed. It is not uncommon for this date to be earlier than the project finish date calculated by the scheduling engine software. The project manager is faced with the situation of fitting the tasks into this predetermined schedule. The way to do this is to look at the critical path tasks to determine how they could be accomplished sooner.

A project plan for an office move is displayed in figure 27.4. Each task is flagged as to whether or not it is on the critical path. It is easy to see in this illustration that if the start or finish of task 10 (Order office furniture) changes, it will not affect the project end date. However if the dates for task 6 (Finalize lease on office space) changes, there will be an impact on the overall finish date.

Figure 27.3. Example of a project task schedule

Figure 27.4. Example of a project path with a critical path shown

ID	Task Name	Start	Finish	Critical	January	February	March
1	**Office Move**	**Jan 3**	**Mar 8**	**Yes**			
2	**Office Space**	**Jan 3**	**Mar 8**	**Yes**			
3	Identify requirements for new office space	Jan 3	Jan 5	Yes			
4	Identify potential office sites	Jan 6	Jan 12	Yes			
5	Make final decision on office space	Jan 13	Jan 21	Yes			
6	Finalize lease on office space	Jan 24	Jan 27	Yes			
7	Design office space	Jan 28	Mar 1	Yes			
8	Assign office space	Mar 2	Mar 8	Yes			
9	**Office Equipment**	**Jan 24**	**Mar 4**	**No**			
10	Order office furniture	Jan 24	Jan 26	No			
11	Order new office equipment	Mar 2	Mar 4	No			
12	Order phone system	Mar 2	Mar 2	No			
13	**Moving Companies**	**Jan 28**	**Feb 16**	**No**			
14	Select the move day	Jan 28	Jan 28	No			
15	Obtain estimates from moving companies	Jan 31	Feb 15	No			
16	Hire movers	Feb 16	Feb 16	No			

Conduct Risk Analysis

With the project network calculated, the project manager has a plan for the project schedule, work effort, and cost. However, it is a very ideal project; it assumes that all the tasks will occur as scheduled and estimated. For example, as soon as a predecessor task finishes, the successor task begins. It also assumes that the resources will be available on the exact day the task is scheduled to begin. At this point, the project is not accommodating delays such as illness, a delay in hardware acquisition, or the learning curve encountered when using a new technology.

If one thing can be accurately predicted about a project, it is that it will not progress as scheduled. To account for the inevitable changes, the project manager should perform a **risk analysis** and adjust the project schedule, work effort, or cost projections to incorporate any anticipated risk.

To conduct a risk analysis, the project manager first documents the types of risks that may occur. He or she then assigns a probability factor and an impact factor. The **probability factor** indicates the odds of the particular risk occurring. The **impact factor** designates the effect the risk will

have on the project if it does occur. These two factors are then multiplied together to calculate the **risk factor.**

A **contingency** should be put in place for any risk with a high-risk factor. The contingency describes what the project team will do if the risk is realized. For example, to mitigate the risk of losing a key project team member, the project manager would ensure that the project documentation is kept current. The impact of the contingency should be reflected in the project plan. For the example cited, the project manager would make sure that a task is in the project plan for updating project documentation.

An example of a risk analysis can be illustrated by using a situation you may be familiar with—planning a vacation. (See table 27.7.) For this example, the vacation will be to a Caribbean island in October, which happens to be during hurricane season.

As with assumptions, the project manager should obtain consensus from the project team, project sponsor, and stakeholders for the contingency plans. After the initial risk assessment is documented, a synopsis can be included in the project manager's status report. This synopsis could include any changes to the risk factors, realized and unrealized risks, and changes to contingency plans. After the threat of the risk is over, it can be removed from the report.

Table 27.7. Example of risk analysis

Risk Description	Probability Factor Low = 1 Medium = 3 High = 5	Impact Factor Range is 1–10 Low = 1 High = 10	Risk Factor (Probability × Impact)	Contingency
Forget to pack an item	5	3	15	Prepare a packing list
Traffic congestion on the way to the airport	1	10	10	Check road construction hotline and radio traffic reports; allow extra travel time
Rain during the vacation	3	8	24	Plan some indoor activities
Luggage doesn't make it to the destination	1	10	10	Purchase additional baggage insurance
Hurricane strikes the resort	5	10	50	Purchase trip cancellation insurance

Instructions: Prepare a work breakdown structure for the project you initiated in Check Your Understanding 27.3. Include the following for the tasks: task name, predecessor task(s), associated deliverable(s), and a list of the team members who will work on the task. Then answer the following questions on a separate piece of paper.

1. What methods can be used to estimate the work effort for a task?

2. What are some potential risks to the project you selected in Check Your Understanding 27.3? What contingencies can be put in place to mitigate this risk?

Project Implementation

When the project planning is complete, the organization is ready to begin the project. The project manager has prepared the project schedule, identified the work effort requirements, and anticipated potential delays. Before the project begins, he or she will capture a **baseline** of the project schedule and work effort. The baseline is a copy of the original estimates for the project. It is captured so that the progress of the project can be compared to the original plan. This comparison is discussed in further detail later in this chapter.

Hold a Project Kickoff Meeting

It is customary to hold a project kickoff meeting when the project gets under way. This meeting sets the tone for the project and helps everyone understand its importance. A typical agenda for the meeting includes the following items:

- Executive presentation during which the sponsor or key stakeholder presents the background on the project with a particular emphasis on why the organization is embarking on this endeavor
- Project objectives
- Project organization chart
- Team roles and responsibilities
- High-level WBS (approach)
- Project schedule
- Key assumptions and constraints
- Project control and communication plan, including project tracking methodology, meeting schedule, project documentation, change control procedure, and issue tracking plan

Perform Project Tasks and Produce Deliverables

The project team now has responsibility for performing the scheduled tasks and producing the project deliverables. The project manager has responsibility for ensuring that all participants understand what is to be done and when.

At this point in the project, the team may become bogged down in indecisiveness, resistance to change, and bureaucracy. The project manager works with the team, the stakeholders, and the project sponsor to keep the project moving by getting issues resolved and decisions made. The project manager may use various problem-solving and decision-making techniques to facilitate this process. (See chapter 23 for more information on this subject.)

Track Progress and Analyze Variance

When the project is under way, the project manager needs to follow how it is progressing. He or she must be able to provide the following information to the stakeholders and the project team:

- Will the project be completed on time?
- Will the project cost more than planned?
- Will the project objectives be met?

The project manager can answer these questions only by actively tracking the project's progress and analyzing its progress against the original plan.

Project Tracking

The project is tracked through the process of collecting actual progress and remaining effort from the project team members. Each team member should provide information on a periodic basis. The frequency of progress information depends on the duration of the project. For a short project of less than two months in duration, updates may be needed more than once a week. Longer projects may require a weekly progress report. In determining tracking frequency, the project manager should consider the effort of obtaining the information and updating the project plan against the level of information needed to perform the variance analysis and, more importantly, should be able to adequately respond to required plan revisions when a project is in trouble.

Each project team member should report the following information for each task:

- Actual start date or new scheduled start date (when the task was not started on time)
- Percentage of complete or actual work
- Remaining work or expected finish date
- Actual and remaining cost
- Actual finish date (for completed tasks)
- Issues

It is usually difficult to obtain actual progress from the project team members. There are both procedural and psychological reasons for this. With regard to procedural reasons, the project manager has to set up a mechanism for getting the information. This may be a hard-copy report, or it may be automated through project management software. Unfortunately, the process of getting the information can be tedious, and project managers often neglect it to pursue other project management processes they deem to be more important.

With regard to psychological reasons, people are inclined to overestimate their progress. They tend to tell someone what they believe that person wants to hear rather than report true progress. People also may become defensive about their progress, especially in situations where they are behind schedule or over budget. Although some personal accountability may be involved, often the reason for the delay or overrun is not directly within the team member's control. The project manager can set the right tone for the data collection process by letting the team know how the information will be used. Honesty from team members should not result in punitive measures unless an individual has been consistently negligent in his or her project responsibilities. When a project team member is not performing as needed, the project manager needs to address this issue. (Refer to chapter 23 for management strategies that can be used to resolve this situation.)

Variance Analysis and Project Revision

After updating the project schedule with the task progress, the project manager compares the task start date, expected finish date, estimated work effort, estimated cost, and estimated duration to what was originally planned. As stated above, all projects do not progress as originally planned. The project manager must concentrate on those **variances** that are substantially affecting the project's time line, budget, and objectives. For example, a task may start later than planned, but if it is not on the project's critical path, the delay will not affect the project finish date. However, if the task is on the critical path, the project manager must determine how to make up the delay and still complete the project on schedule. A task may have started on time but consume a higher work effort than originally estimated. Unless other tasks in the plan consume less than the original estimate, the overall project will exceed the work estimates and thus the cost estimate.

Figure 27.5 shows a report for the office move project plan that can be used to assess the variances. The work and cost variances are shown directly to the right of the task name.

The right side of the report is known as a **Gantt chart.** The Gantt chart was developed by Henry L. Gantt as a method to illustrate the time needed for each task. On the figure 27.5 report, there are two bars for each task. The top bar shows the start and finish dates as they have been rescheduled based on tracking information. The bottom bar shows the baseline dates. The report shows that due to the fact that task 5 will not finish according to the original schedule, tasks 6 and 7 also will be delayed. These tasks are on the critical path; therefore, the delay must be addressed if the project is to remain on schedule. (Refer to figure 27.4.)

To get the project back on track, the project manager must evaluate the available options. All these options are a variant of the variables that make up the project components: scope, performance, cost, and time line. The project manager needs to clearly document the options and ramifications of each and present the documentation to the project's stakeholders. The sponsor and the stakeholders will make the decision based on what is most important to the success of the project. For example, in a software implementation, it may be more important for the new system to contain all the desired functionality than it is for the implementation to meet the budget. The sponsor may be willing to do this to obtain department satisfaction and compliance with the new system.

Table 27.8 shows the types of plan revisions the project manager may propose and the risks involved in using each option.

Establish Change Control

In addition to proposing project revisions to keep the project on track, the project manager is usually faced with requests for changes to the original project scope. These requests can be the result of any of the following:

- Change in a departmental procedure
- New or revised organizational initiative
- New or revised regulatory requirement
- Desired change in the design of a system function

Figure 27.5. Example of a project plan with information to assess variances

ID	Task Name	Work Variance	Cost Variance	Jan 2	Jan 9	Jan 16	Jan 23	Jan 30
1	**Office Move**	45 hrs	$14,500.00					
2	**Office Space**	10 hrs	$1,000.00					
3	Identify requirements for new office space	0 hrs	$0.00					
4	Identify potential office sites	10 hrs	$1,000.00					
5	Make final decision on office space	0 hrs	$0.00					
6	Finalize lease on office space	0 hrs	$0.00					
7	Design office space	0 hrs	$0.00					
8	Assign office space	0 hrs	$0.00					
9	**Office Equipment**	0 hrs	$10,000.00					
10	Order office furniture	0 hrs	$10,000.00					
11	Order new office equipment	0 hrs	$0.00					
12	Order phone system	0 hrs	$0.00					
13	**Moving Companies**	35 hrs	$3,500.00					
14	Select the move day	0 hrs	$0.00					
15	Obtain estimates from moving companies	35 hrs	$3,500.00					
16	Hire movers	0 hrs	$0.00					

Table 27.8. Potential risks in revising a project plan

Options for Plan Revision	Potential Risks
Decrease the scope of work by removing some of the project requirements. Requirements may be eliminated or deferred to a subsequent project.	Project objectives may be compromised.
Eliminate the nice-to-have features of the project to decrease the scope of work.	Project objectives may be compromised.
Add more resources to get the work done faster.	Project cost may be compromised.
Ask team members to get the work done by putting in extra time.	Project cost may be compromised.
Evaluate the project plan to determine whether some tasks can start sooner. Look for finish-to-start dependencies to determine whether the tasks can overlap.	Quality may suffer when shortcuts are taken to shorten the schedule.

Changes to project scope are inevitable and should not be automatically considered a form of project failure. It is the way project changes are handled that can have a negative impact on the success of the project. The most important factor in scope change is for the stakeholders to understand the impact of the requested change and, if approved, be willing to accept the ramifications the change will have on the project's schedule and cost. In other words, the project manager must be in control of the changes. Just as in plan revision, all changes to the plan will affect the final project outcome in terms of scope, work, time line, or cost. When the project manager, sponsor, and other stakeholders do not acknowledge the impact of the change by approving a corresponding modification to one of the other variables, the quality of the project suffers.

The procedure for **change control** should be established at the beginning of the project in order to set the proper expectations for how scope modifications will be handled. The process should be as follows:

1. The requestor completes a change request form.
2. An impact analysis is performed. Its purpose is to determine the effect the change will have on the project. For example, there may be a positive impact on the relationship to the system's objectives, but the request may increase the work effort.
3. The request is presented to the stakeholders for approval. If the change is approved, the stakeholders have indicated they are willing to accept the ramification on the project time line or cost. In other words, the benefits of the change outweigh the goal to stay within the original project budget.

Communicate Project Information

One of the success factors for a project is good project communication. All involved parties need to be kept apprised of the project's progress, understand any outstanding issues, understand the change control requests, and understand the project politics. Several forms of project communication are used during the project: project status meetings, project status reports, issue logs, and project plans.

Project Status Meetings

A project status meeting is a formal meeting attended by the project team members. Its purpose is to report accomplishments, to review the status of in-progress project tasks, and to discuss issues that are impeding the completion of any tasks.

There are a few cautions for the project manager when conducting the meeting. The first is that project team members may feel pressure to report a rosy picture of the task progress because they are among their peers. A task may be behind schedule to the point that it will most likely delay the overall project schedule, but a team member may be reluctant to report this to avoid being held accountable for the entire project missing its target finish date. Although formal status meetings are important for a project, the informal status reporting from the team members is just as important. The project manager should spend time with team members outside the meeting where the team member may feel that the environment is more conducive to an honest appraisal of the task progress.

The second problem with some status meetings is that participants become bogged down in discussions that cannot be resolved in the meeting. For example, team members may be discussing an issue in terms of what it is instead of actually resolving it. Although everyone must understand all project issues, it is not good use of the status meeting time to discuss the issue unless all the decision makers are in the room. Generally, issues should be handled in separate meetings outside the project status meeting.

Project Status Reports

A project status report is the formal documentation of the project progress. Again, although formal documentation is a required component of the project, the project manager should supplement this reporting with ad hoc conversations with the team members and stakeholders. This informal reporting, sometimes referred to as "walk around" status reporting, can elicit information on the politics, conflicts, personality disputes, and bureaucracy that tend to impede task progress.

The frequency of status reports varies depending on the overall project duration. A short project may require weekly reporting, whereas a long project may require monthly reporting. Whatever frequency is selected, it should support the project manager's ability to react to changes, delays, and issues.

Topics to be included in a status report include

- Objectives for the period
- Accomplishments during the period

- Explanation of any differences
- Objectives for the next period
- Issues

When the task-tracking procedure and the formal status report follow the same frequency schedule (for example, both are completed on a weekly basis), the project manager may choose to collect this information on the same form. The feasibility of this also depends on the method selected for tracking. When task tracking is automated via project management software, the ability to also collect task status information may or may not be supported.

Issue Log

Issues are items that prevent the completion of a project task. Because all projects introduce some type of change, it is inevitable that issues will arise. The purpose of the **issue log** is to document the issues so that the project manager can ensure that they are resolved in a timely manner. The issue log should include

- A description of each issue
- The name of the team member assigned to resolve the issue
- Priority (for example, high, medium, low)
- The date the issue was opened
- Status (open, deferred, or closed)
- The required resolution date
- A descriptive status of the issue
- The resolution date and description of the resolution

After the issue log is established, the team needs to actively work toward resolving the issues. This is where the skills of negotiation, conflict management, and innovative thinking are critical. Consensus among the affected parties is always the best solution in any issue, but in some situations the project sponsor must be called on to end a deadlock.

The issue log also can be used to capture ideas and topics that are not either specifically pertinent to the project or within its scope. These topics are often referred to as "parking lot" items. Placing them on the issue log (with a separate priority or status) is a good time management technique that ensures that the ideas will not be forgotten.

Project Plans

Reports generated from the project plan can provide information on the status of the project tasks. These reports are usually produced for the stakeholders to provide a snapshot of the project. When the project manager is using project management software, it is able to produce a variety of reports, including

- A Gantt chart that visually displays the task start and finish dates along with the percentage of progress completed
- Tasks that are behind schedule
- A task list displaying the critical path tasks
- Tasks exceeding the original work estimate
- Resource reports showing the estimated work for each resource broken down by week or month

An example of a resource report is shown in figure 27.6.

Prepare the Final Report

When the project has been concluded, it is good practice to produce a final project report. The purpose of the report is to

Figure 27.6.   Example of a resource report

ID	Resource Name	Work	Details	January	February	March	April
1	Chief Relocation Officer	30 hrs	Work	30h			
	Identify requirements for new office space	*20 hrs*	Work	20h			
	Make final decision on office space	*5 hrs*	Work	5h			
	Finalize lease on office space	*5 hrs*	Work	5h			
2	Office Manager	257 hrs	Work	64.87h	137.78h	54.35h	
	Identify potential office sites	*20 hrs*	Work	20h			
	Design office space	*100 hrs*	Work	8.7h	86.95h	4.35h	
	Assign office space	*10 hrs*	Work			10h	
	Order office furniture	*30 hrs*	Work	30h			
	Order new office equipment	*30 hrs*	Work			30h	
	Order phone system	*10 hrs*	Work			10h	
	Select the move day	*2 hrs*	Work	2h			
	Obtain estimates from moving companies	*50 hrs*	Work	4.17h	45.83h		
	Hire movers	*5 hrs*	Work		5h		

bring closure to the endeavor by documenting the project's final outcome. The topics to be included in the report include the following:

- List of the project objectives with a description of how each objective was accomplished
- List of the project deliverables
- Final project budget, detailing the comparison of the original estimate to the actual cost
- Final project schedule, detailing the comparison of the original dates to the actual dates

Celebrate Success

Projects can be very stressful to an organization. Therefore, it is important for the stakeholders and the project manager to provide the leadership to motivate team members and departments throughout the project duration. One of the ways this can be accomplished is by emphasizing the project's importance by celebrating accomplishments. For example, several social events might be held during the project to honor key project milestones. The project stakeholder could thank project participants for the effort expended thus far and encourage the same level of commitment for the remaining project activities.

After the project is completed, a more formal celebration may take place. All project contributors should be invited and recognized for their efforts.

Check Your Understanding 27.5

Instructions: Answer the following questions on a separate piece of paper.

1. What project progress information should project team members provide to the project manager?

2. What are some of the barriers to obtaining accurate progress information from team members?

3. What is change control?

4. What are some of the problems with formal project communications methods?

When a project begins, all parties must understand its objectives. The lack of a common vision for what the project will achieve is the first opportunity for the project to fail. All stakeholders must be willing to commit the required resources to the project and to support the procedural changes that will inevitably occur as a result of the project. All project personnel also can contribute to the success of the project by keeping proposed project changes to a minimum.

A project adheres to the project management life cycle. Depending on the size and type of project, each process is scalable. In other words, the extent to which each process is performed may vary, but all processes should be included in every project.

The project manager is in a unique position in situations where a project crosses departmental boundaries. He or she has responsibility for the project success but generally little authority over the members of the project team. The project manager must possess technical, functional, and analytical skills as well as leadership, influential, and motivational abilities.

References

Kliem, R.L. 2004. *Leading High-Performance Projects*. Boca Raton, FL: J. Ross Publishing.

Lewis, J.P. 2008. *Mastering Project Management*. New York: McGraw-Hill.

Project Management Institute. 2008. *A Guide to the Project Management Body of Knowledge*. Newtown Square, PA: PMI.

Summary

The art of project management encompasses a wide variety of responsibilities and skills. Project management does not just involve the creation and maintenance of a project plan. Organizations need to realize that good project management does not just happen. The concepts of project management must be understood and embraced at all levels of the organization. When the organization's executives do not support good project management methodology, the risk of project failure will outweigh any perceived benefits.

chapter 28

Managing Organizational Compliance and Risk

Carol Ann Quinsey, MS, RHIA, CHPS

Learning Objectives

- Identify the required elements of a compliance program
- Describe a corporate integrity agreement
- Discuss regulations addressing identity theft
- Understand the importance of the Office of Inspector General (OIG) Work Plan to organization compliance
- Explain the relationship of accreditation to the Medicare Conditions of Participation

- Articulate a basic understanding of the American Recovery and Reinvestment Act (ARRA)/Health Information Technology for Economic and Clinical Health Act (HITECH) modification to the HIPAA privacy and security rules
- Recognize and understand compliance-related laws such as the Emergency Medical Treatment and Labor Act (EMTALA), the federal anti-kickback law, the Employee Retirement Income Security Act (ERISA), and the Stark laws

Key Terms

Accountable care organization (ACO)
American Recovery and Reinvestment Act (ARRA)
Breach notification
Centers for Medicare and Medicaid Services (CMS)
Compliance
Consolidated Omnibus Budget Reconciliation Act of 1985 (COBRA)
Corporate integrity agreement (CIA)
Emergency Medical Treatment and Active Labor Act (EMTALA)
Emergency preparedness
Employee Retirement Income Security Act (ERISA)
Fair and Accurate Credit Transactions Act of 2003
Federal anti-kickback statute
Generic screening
Health Care Fraud Prevention and Enforcement Action Team (HEAT)

Health information exchange (HIE)
Health Information Technology for Economic and Clinical Health Act (HITECH)
Incident report
Loss prevention
Loss reduction
Meaningful use
Medicaid integrity contractor (MIC)
Medicare administrative contractor (MAC)
Office of Inspector General (OIG) workplan
Potentially compensable event (PCE)
Recovery audit contractor (RAC)
Red Flags Rule
Remediation
Risk management
Root-cause analysis
Safe harbor
Sarbanes-Oxley Act
Sentinel event

Overview of Compliance in the United States

Compliance in the United States in general means to comply with rules, laws, standards, or regulations. Compliance is expected, and noncompliance can have civil or criminal penalties.

Corporate breakdowns, such as the highly publicized scandal with Enron in 2001, highlight the need for stronger compliance and regulations for publicly listed companies. The most significant legislation to arise from this scandal was the **Sarbanes-Oxley Act** in 2002. Sarbanes-Oxley defined significantly higher personal responsibility of top corporate managers for the accuracy of reported financial statements. Although this did not specifically address compliance in healthcare, most healthcare organizations view adherence to similar standards as best practice for their organizations.

The basis for prosecution for healthcare fraud and abuse today is the federal False Claims Act (FCA), signed into law in 1863 by President Abraham Lincoln. The original intent of the legislation was to encourage private citizens to report fraudulent actions taken by the Union Army during the Civil War. The burden of proof for claims arising from this act was on the government, which had to prove that the individual charged with the offense intended to defraud the government.

In 1986 the FCA was amended, removing the requirement that intent to defraud had to be proven. The FCA then became the basis for prosecuting healthcare providers who demonstrated a pattern of coding or charging that resulted in overcharges or submitted false claims for payment to the **Centers for Medicare and Medicaid Services (CMS).** CMS became more concerned about false or fraudulent claims as financial indications are that the Medicare Trust Fund is going bankrupt.

In response to the concerns, since 1997, the United States Office of Inspector General (OIG) has issued annual guidelines for compliance programs for various types of healthcare providers. **OIG Work Plans** are issued at the beginning of each fiscal year and provide for new and ongoing reviews or audits in more than 300 programs administered by the Department of Health and Human Services (HHS). The programs included in the OIG Work Plan reach many venues where healthcare is provided including home care, office and clinic care, hospital, and posthospital care facilities and organizations. The goal of the reviews is to protect the integrity of the programs by detecting and preventing fraud, waste, and abuse; identifying opportunities for improvement in economy, efficiency, and effectiveness; and holding accountable those who do not meet program requirements or who violate federal laws. Healthcare organizations should carefully study the work plan each year to ensure that they are in compliance with specifically targeted areas. In fiscal year 2010, the federal government

won or negotiated approximately $2.5 billion in judgments and settlements. The Medicare Trust Fund received transfers of approximately $2.86 billion during this period, and another $683 million in federal Medicaid money was transferred to the Treasury as a result of audits leading to enforcement activities.

The increasing attention to investigating, preventing, and prosecuting fraud and abuse in healthcare was apparent in 1996 with passage of the Health Insurance Portability and Accountability Act (HIPAA). HIPAA expanded the role of the OIG to include private insurance programs as well as federally funded programs.

Coding Compliance Programs

With concerns about fraud, upcoding, unbundling, and abuse has come the need to ensure that healthcare organizations have rigorous coding compliance programs. Federal and state agencies and insurance companies are vigorously investigating any opportunity to identify and curtail coding practices that lead to overpayment and payment for services not delivered to patients unless they are medically necessary. Implementation of good coding compliance programs will document that sound coding practices are used and routine audit and monitoring activities lead the way to continuous improvement in the quality of documentation and coding.

Typical benefits from a coding compliance program may include improvements in

- Internal controls
- Monitors for coding and documentation
- Education for coders and providers
- Increased and improved communication, productivity, and efficiency
- Ethical practices

Coding compliance programs should address the mission of the department, the code of conduct, policies and procedures, and monitoring and follow-up activities. A typical mission statement might state that coders adhere to ethical coding practices and guidelines adopted by their healthcare organizations as well as following national coding conventions and guidelines. Having coding staff reaffirm in writing their commitment to ethical coding practices on a periodic basis (perhaps during the annual evaluation) is a way to be sure that staff members understand that ethical coding is an ongoing requirement.

Monitors and audits should be conducted on a routine basis according to a schedule. Staff members should be encouraged to participate in the development of the monitoring and audit activities so they understand and support them. Some audits may be conducted on a random basis; some will be focused on particular subject areas. Sources for subjects to monitor can be drawn from the CMS/OIG Work

Plan, data from previous audits, patterns of payer denials at the facility, or procedures where new technology results in changed coding.

Audit processes should clearly document the frequency of the audit, the time period included in the audit, how the records will be selected, how the sample size will be determined, and the objectives of the review. A description of how audit results will be shared should also be included in the design of the audit. Reporting formats should be designed with the recipients in mind, making the information as useful to them as possible. Audits should lead to improvements in quality of coding or documentation.

Documentation of audits, including results of audit and monitoring activities, should be reported as part of the healthcare organization's quality improvement program. When appropriate, planned follow-up activities and reaudit activities should be reported.

Coding compliance programs should be evaluated and improved on a regular basis. Technology and policy changes such as implementation of an electronic health record or computer-assisted coding software may require updates to the compliance plan before the next scheduled review and evaluation of the compliance plan. A practical addition to project plans when implementing new technology or software is a line item calling for review and appropriate updates to the compliance plan (Bowman 2007).

Corporate Compliance Programs

The definition of an effective compliance plan has been elusive. Compliance efforts are meant to establish a culture that promotes prevention, detection, and resolution of conduct that does not conform to federal and state laws; federal, state, and payer healthcare program requirements; and the healthcare organization's ethical and business policies. In order to encourage those who have reason to believe a company is violating a law, rule, or regulation; grossly mismanaging or wasting money; abusing authority; or presenting a substantial danger to health or safety of an individual or the public to come forward, it is critically important that whistleblowers be protected from retaliation. The term *whistleblower* is applied to a person who informs on another or makes public practices that are wrong or corrupt.

Most organizations use the guidance provided by the United States Sentencing Commission in Chapter 8 of the Federal Sentencing Guidelines, which calls for seven required elements in compliance programs. Although the language speaks to hospitals, the guidelines are generally interpreted as applicable to all healthcare settings. The seven required elements are:

1. The development and distribution of written standards of conduct, as well as written policies and procedures, that promote the hospital's commitment to compliance and address specific areas of potential fraud such as claims development and submission processes, code gaming, and financial relationships with physicians and other healthcare professionals;

2. The designation of a chief compliance officer and other appropriate bodies charged with responsibility for operating and monitoring the compliance program and that report directly to the Chief Executive Officer and the governing body;

3. The development and implementation of regular, effective education and training programs for all affected employees;

4. The maintenance of a process, such as a hotline, to receive complaints and the adoption of procedures to protect the anonymity of complainants and to protect whistleblowers from retaliation;

5. The development of a system to respond to allegations of improper or illegal activities and the enforcement of appropriate disciplinary action against employees who have violated internal compliance policies, applicable statutes, and regulations or federal healthcare program requirements;

6. The use of audits and other evaluation techniques to monitor compliance and assist in the reduction of identified problem areas; and

7. The investigation and remediation of identified systemic problems and the development of policies that address the nonemployment or retention of sanctioned individuals. (Compliance360 n.d.)

Compliance programs should guide the healthcare organization's governing body, managers, employees, and providers in management and operation of the facility. They are critical internal controls in the reimbursement and payment areas, which have often been the historical focus of fraud and abuse leading to government regulation, scrutiny, and sanctions.

Every healthcare organization should designate a compliance officer who serves as the focal point for compliance activities. The responsibility for compliance may be the sole duty of the individual or added to other management responsibilities, depending on the organization. For the program to be successful, the compliance officer must have the necessary authority to conduct the program. The compliance officer must also be provided sufficient staff and funding to carry out the duties of the office. Primary responsibilities for the compliance officer include

- Overseeing and monitoring the implementation of the compliance program
- Reporting on compliance activities to the hospital's governing body, chief executive officer (CEO), and others as appropriate (such as the compliance committee, if one is appointed)

- Periodically assessing and revising the compliance plan to reflect changes in the law or policies and procedures
- Coordinating education and training programs to ensure knowledge of the compliance plan and the relationship to other programs such as coding, billing, marketing
- Assisting in financial management, coordinating internal compliance reviews, and monitoring activities of organizational departments
- Investigating and acting on matters related to compliance including any corrective action that results with organizational departments, providers, agents, or contractors
- Developing policies and programs that encourage managers and employees to report suspected fraud and other improprieties without fear of retaliation

Organizations have developed compliance programs usually modeled after the OIG Work Plan. Typically the organization's compliance program is described during new employee orientation, and retraining may be required annually. It addresses organizational values around compliance with laws, rules, and regulations. Corporate compliance presentations usually highlight organizational expectations of employee behaviors that preserve or enhance the image of the organization in the community. There is often discussion of scenarios that could present ethical questions for employees. For example, a common scenario in healthcare is when a vendor invites an employee to lunch or dinner. Even though the decision to do business with that vendor may be outside the influence of that employee, the perception could be that the employee was being rewarded for the vendor's contract with the organization. Even though there are arguments that can legitimately be made that the employee would not be influenced by such an action, it may be against corporate policies for the employee to accept such an invitation. Employees should check their organization's policies before taking any action.

Refreshing awareness of corporate compliance practices and policies on a regular basis is very important if they are to be effective. The most important thing any healthcare organization has is its reputation in the community it serves. Every employee, provider, or agent of that facility needs to take corporate compliance seriously.

Check Your Understanding 28.1

Instructions: Answer the following questions on a separate piece of paper.

1. Describe the required elements of an effective compliance program.

2. Describe the importance of the OIG Work Plan for health information management professionals.

National Influences on Compliance Programs

Accreditation

Many healthcare organizations seek acknowledgment and recognition of the quality of the care they deliver to patients using a voluntary accreditation process. The goals of accreditation processes are generally intended to improve healthcare and safety for the public by evaluating healthcare delivery organizations and encouraging them to provide safe and effective care of high quality and value. Healthcare organizations accredited by companies approved by CMS meet the Medicare Conditions of Participation (CoPs) if CMS deems their surveys equal to or better than the Conditions of Participation. Medicare CoPs are the minimum standards that hospitals must meet in order to be a Medicare or Medicaid provider.

There are alternatives to choose from when seeking accreditation. Since 1965, the best known accrediting body for hospitals and clinics in the United States is the Joint Commission. The Joint Commission is a not-for-profit organization that surveys and accredits healthcare delivery systems, such as medical equipment suppliers, staffing firms, and outpatient clinics. Some states set up their own accrediting processes.

In 2008, CMS approved Det Norske Veritas (DNV) Healthcare Incorporated's National Integrated Accreditation for Healthcare Organizations (NIAHO) accreditation program for hospitals seeking to participate in the federal healthcare programs. DNV's NIAHO program integrates the Medicare CoPs and the International Organization for Standardization's (ISO 9001) quality management system.

CMS regulates all laboratory testing (except research) performed on humans in the United States through the Clinical Laboratory Improvement Amendments (CLIA). In total, CLIA covers approximately 225,000 laboratories. The objective of the CLIA program is to ensure quality laboratory testing.

Accreditation surveys are separate from licensing inspections in most states. In California, however, the Joint Commission participates in a joint survey process with state authorities that leads to both accreditation and licensure.

Conditions of Participation and Conditions for Coverage

CMS developed the Conditions of Participation that healthcare organizations must meet in order to qualify to participate in the Medicare and Medicaid programs. They are health and safety standards designed as the foundation for improving quality of care and protecting the health and safety of patients included in the federal healthcare programs. Rather than conduct surveys of healthcare organizations themselves, CMS may delegate the process of deeming healthcare organizations as meeting or exceeding the standards set forth in the CoPs and Conditions for Coverage (CfCs) to another organization, like the Joint Commission.

CoPs and CfCs have been developed for the following types of healthcare organizations:

- Ambulatory surgical centers (ASCs)
- Comprehensive outpatient rehabilitation facilities (CORFs)
- Critical access hospitals (CAHs)
- End-stage renal disease facilities
- Federally qualified health centers
- Home health agencies
- Hospices
- Hospitals
- Hospital swing beds
- Intermediate care facilities for persons with mental retardation (ICF/MR)
- Organ procurement organizations (OPSs)
- Portable x-ray suppliers
- Programs for all-inclusive care for the elderly (PACE) organizations
- Clinics, rehabilitation agencies, and public health agencies as providers of outpatient physical therapy and speech-language pathology services
- Psychiatric hospitals
- Religious nonmedical healthcare institutions
- Long-term care facilities
- Transplant centers

Accountable Care Organizations

The Medicare **accountable care organization (ACO)** program began in January 2012. ACOs are networks of providers in a geographic area who decide to come together to improve coordination of patient care. The program is voluntary, arising from the Patient Protection and Affordable Care Act of 2010.

The goal for ACO programs is to increase the quality of care to patients and lower the cost of care. Under the program, incentives will be paid to providers who agree to work together to coordinate patient care. The premise is that the better coordinated care an ACO offers, the higher the savings to Medicare, leading to more revenue that partners in the ACO can receive. There are 33 quality standards, based on outcome measures, that ACOs must meet in order to qualify for incentives based on the cost savings they achieve for the Medicare program.

American Recovery and Reinvestment Act

The **American Recovery and Reinvestment Act (ARRA)** is an economic stimulus package enacted in 2009. Although there were a number of objectives for the legislation, the primary objective was to save and create jobs almost immediately. Another objective was to provide investments needed to increase economic efficiency by spurring technological advances in science and health; specifically encouraged was the adoption of electronic health records.

An additional ARRA requirement addresses **breach notification,** which basically entails notifying patients if their protected health information (PHI) has been breached. A breach is defined in the interim final rule at 164.402 as an event that "compromises the security or privacy of PHI which means that it poses a significant risk of financial, reputational, or other harm to the individual" (*Federal Register* 2009). The requirement applies to all healthcare organizations. Rules vary on the number of patients involved and the means of notification, but ARRA specifies that notification be made without unreasonable delay no more than 60 days after the breach becomes known. In addition to notifying the Secretary of HHS and the involved individual(s) whose PHI has been breached when a breach of PHI has occurred, there may be other required notices, such as to Business Associates. If more than 500 patients are involved in a PHI breach, immediate notice to HHS is required, as is public notice in "prominent media outlets" (Nunn 2009b; *Federal Register* 2009). The *Federal Register* does not describe what is meant by "prominent media outlets," stating only that it will differ depending upon the state or jurisdiction affected.

There is some flexibility for breach notification. After investigation, if access is determined to have been unintentional and the employee or other person was acting under the authority of the covered entity or business associate, it may be forgiven. However, there must be evidence that the PHI was reviewed in good faith and the PHI was not further used or disclosed.

Governmental Audits

The federal government has a number of routine audits that are carried out to combat fraud and abuse. Some of the programs have overlapping authority, but each may have different operational requirements, which challenges healthcare organizations to comply. During fiscal year 2010, approximately $2.5 billion was awarded in healthcare fraud judgments and settlements resulting from audit operations.

Some commonly known government auditors in healthcare include the following:

- **Health Care Fraud Prevention and Enforcement Action Team (HEAT),** whose goal is to identify fraud perpetrators and those preying on Medicare and Medicaid beneficiaries
- **Medicare administrative contractors (MACs),** who are charged with performing prepayment reviews to ensure services provided to Medicare beneficiaries are covered and medically necessary
- **Medicaid integrity contractors (MICs),** who review Medicaid claims to determine potential provider waste or abuse, identify overpayments, and provide education to providers on payment integrity and quality-of-care issues

- **Recovery audit contractors (RACs),** who work with a mission of reducing Medicare improper payments through detection and collection of overpayments, the identification of underpayments, and implementation of actions that will prevent future improper payments

When healthcare organizations are notified of an impending audit they should prepare with the following steps:

- Identify who needs to be involved in the audit process
- Ensure that policies and procedures clearly designate roles and responsibilities for the process (including staff who assign codes and process denials, revenue cycle auditors, and those who prepare copies of charts for each request)
- Educate the organization regarding the increase in governmental audit activity and the need for clear and concise documentation
- Develop education specific to each department's role in the revenue cycle and audit process
- Determine the different types of record requests and time frames for response
- Distinguish the various types of appeals to secure each claim

Health Information Technology for Economic and Clinical Health Act

A section within ARRA, the **Health Information Technology for Economic and Clinical Health Act (HITECH)**, provides a combination of incentives and penalties aimed at reducing healthcare costs by automating health records and streamlining health information technology. Definitions of what health information must be safeguarded were expanded, adding new requirements for privacy and security.

A 2006 amendment to the Federal Rules of Civil Procedure (FRCP) expanded electronic access to PHI maintained in electronic health record (EHR) systems. Based on the interim final rule, HITECH will expand the HIPAA requirements for disclosure accounting to include treatment, payment, and operations; reduce the time period that must be documented; and limit what is released from an EHR.

HITECH also mandates that HHS conduct periodic privacy and security audits of HIPAA covered entities and business associates. In June 2011, HHS awarded a $9.2 million contract to KPMG to review audit protocols and audit organizational compliance with the HIPAA privacy and security requirements, conducting potentially 150 audits for covered entities and business associates by December 31, 2012. Site visits will be conducted by three to five auditors with expertise in compliance auditing, HIPAA privacy and security, and information technology (IT) auditing. The visits will include interviews with organizational leaders; physical examination of the facility, operations, and adherence to policies; and observation of compliance with HIPAA regulatory requirements. In advance of the site visits, the auditors will submit a request for documentation to the covered entity. The focus of the audits is prevention and education, though discovery of major violations could lead to enforcement activities.

Covered entities should focus resources on eliminating potential major privacy or security violations. Organizational leaders should certainly review policies and procedures that could lead to noncompliance, ensure that members of the workforce have documented appropriate training, and verify that job-specific protocols and procedures are up to date.

Meaningful Use

Among the many programs in HITECH, some were meant to support and promote adoption and effective use of electronic health records, referred to as EHR incentive programs. The EHR incentive program became known as the "**meaningful use**" program. Under the meaningful use program, Medicare and Medicaid bonuses would be paid to eligible providers who demonstrate meaningful use of their EHRs. There are defined processes for making incentive payments to eligible providers, hospitals, Medicare Advantage contractors, fiscal intermediaries, and carriers.

CMS uses the established definition of *physician*, which includes doctors of medicine, osteopathy, dental surgery, dental medicine, podiatric medicine, optometry, or chiropractic. By law this definition cannot be altered or expanded. Hospital-based providers do not qualify for incentive payment.

Initially voluntary, eligible providers are encouraged to participate in the meaningful use program to improve healthcare quality, safety, and efficiency. However, over time, eligible providers who do not meet the meaningful use requirements will have their Medicare payments reduced.

States will manage the Medicaid incentive program. They are expected to introduce their meaningful use programs on a rolling basis once they receive program approval from CMS.

To encourage early participation in the meaningful use program, the highest incentives were designed to be paid in the first two stages of the program. Knowing that all providers would not be ready to join the program initially, a phased approach was created to extend availability of the highest incentives.

Stage 1 meaningful use criteria were designed to be relatively easy to meet, with subsequent stages increasing in difficulty. Items that were elective in Stage 1 were predicted to become requirements in Stage 2 and beyond. CMS intended that Stage 1 focus on:

- Electronically capturing health information in a structured format, which can then be used to track clinical conditions, and communicating that information for care coordination purposes
- Implementing clinical decision support tools to facilitate disease and medication management
- Using EHRs to engage patients and families
- Reporting clinical quality measures and public health information (AHIMA 2010)

There are substantial financial incentives available to providers to implement EHRs if they document meaningful use of them. The maximum amount eligible providers can receive for documenting meaningful use in 2011 or 2012 is $44,000 per year. Incentive payments will be reduced to $39,000 for providers waiting until 2013 to document meaningful use of their EHRs and further reduced in 2014 to $24,000. No incentive payments will be paid to providers for meaningful use after 2014.

Although incentive payments will not cover the cost of implementing EHRs for eligible providers, it will certainly help to defray some of those costs. CMS will make payment in full if the program requirements are met.

Provisions in Stage 2 requirements give providers who demonstrated meaningful use in 2011 a one-year extension on advancing to Stage 2 criteria, retaining all participants in Stage 1 through 2013. Stage 2 has a uniform start date of 2014. Nearly all Stage 1 core and menu objectives are retained in Stage 2 requirements. Some Stage 1 objectives are combined in Stage 2. The CMS webpage, Medicare and Medicaid Programs; Electronic Health Record Incentive Program—Stage 2, contains all Stage 1 and 2 criteria (CMS 2012).

5010 Code Transaction Implementation

The 5010 healthcare transaction codes are the codes health plans and providers will use for exchanging critical information about eligibility, enrollment, premium payments, referrals, and claims with their business partners. The 5010 electronic code set was mandated by HHS to be implemented by January 1, 2012.

The new code set represents a fivefold increase (approximately 16,000 to more than 65,000 codes) in the codes previously available. Implementation of 5010 is expected to improve transaction uniformity, support pay-for-performance programs, and streamline reimbursement transactions. Launching 5010 also forms the platform for implementing ICD-10 in the United States. Without implementation of 5010, ICD-10 coding cannot be processed by healthcare providers, claims processing entities, and insurance companies.

ICD-10 Implementation

The United States is the last remaining industrialized country in the world to adopt ICD-10. The ability to accurately code diagnoses and procedures has been severely compromised due to the extended period of ICD-9 use. October 1, 2014, marks the proposed date when the United States will implement ICD-10-CM and ICD-10-PCS. Some facilities and providers started work toward implementation as early as 2009. Some vendors, facilities, and providers were late to accept that the implementation date would not be extended and began work considerably later.

ICD-10 implementation requires information technology departments to assess which systems require remediation to accommodate expanded code lengths and alphanumeric makeup. A logical solution to the challenge is to identify systems using ICD-9 codes prior to the implementation date, assuming those systems will use ICD-10 after October 1, 2014. The systems identified should then be evaluated for required changes needed to process ICD-10 codes beginning October 1, 2014, and remediated.

Concerns are significant that there will not be enough trained contract coders from businesses selling coding services available in the pre- and go-live period for ICD-10 to assist with the transition. Therefore, many organizations that rely on contract coding services to assist with coding contracted early in the planning process to ensure that sufficient coding expertise is available when needed. Training resources for both care providers and coders are also of concern to those charged with implementation.

From a compliance perspective, it is imperative that adequate resources be devoted to planning for and carrying out auditing coding compliance after implementation. Implementation plans should include development of a monitoring plan that not only covers coding accuracy but also affirms that provider documentation supports assigned codes. Some organizations plan to conduct provider and coder training well ahead of the implementation date so they can begin coding provider documentation using ICD-10 in advance of the go-live date. This allows feedback to be given to providers when documentation does not support the most accurate ICD-10 coding. Feedback to coders can also be offered so that the transition between ICD-9 and ICD-10 will be smoother.

Corporate Integrity Agreement

A **corporate integrity agreement (CIA)** is a detailed and restrictive agreement imposed on providers by the OIG. CIAs may last for many years and are imposed when serious misconduct (fraud and abuse) is discovered through an audit or self-disclosure. Remediation initiatives, such as training or designation of a compliance officer, are part of the CIA. These initiatives are designed to ensure that fraudulent activities do not occur in the future. **Remediation** activities are intended to offer providers another chance to prove they are worthy of participating in federal healthcare programs.

CIAs outline the obligations an entity agrees to as part of a civil settlement in exchange for the OIG's agreement that it will not seek to exclude the entity from participating in federal healthcare programs. CIAs have common elements but are tailored to address specific facts of the case. CIAs that have been agreed to are available to interested parties on the OIG website.

CIAs generally do not result from unintentional errors or mistakes when those errors are reported appropriately. CIAs are only imposed where there is evidence of intentional fraud.

Emergency Medical Treatment and Active Labor Act

Initially, Congress passed the **Emergency Medical Treatment and Active Labor Act (EMTALA)** in 1986 to stop the practice of refusing to treat people because of inability to pay or insufficient insurance. Patients in this situation were transferred or discharged solely on the basis of the anticipation of high diagnosis or treatment costs from emergency departments. Since passage of the original act, several amendments to EMTALA have been added by Congress and state and local laws have imposed additional requirements on hospitals.

Under EMTALA, hospitals have three obligations:

- Individuals (or their representatives if the patient is unable) requesting emergency care must receive a medical screening examination to determine whether an emergency medical condition exists. Examination cannot be delayed to inquire about payment or insurance, citizenship, or legal status. The process of payment inquiry and billing may only start after the patient has been stabilized and his or her care not compromised.
- Patients with an emergency medical condition must be treated until the condition is resolved or stabilized and the patient is able to care for himself or herself or can otherwise receive continuing care. Patients may not be discharged prior to stabilization if insurance is cancelled or is otherwise discontinued during the course of the patient's stay.
- If the hospital does not have the capability to treat the condition, an appropriate transfer of the patient to a hospital that is capable of delivering the required care must be arranged, including long-term or rehabilitation facilities, if appropriate. Hospitals offering specialized capabilities must accept transfers and may not discharge a patient until the condition is resolved, the patient is able to provide self-care, or the patient is transferred to another facility.

Financial pressures in the years since EMTALA's passage have led to a decrease in the number of emergency departments at the same time there has been an increase in the demand for emergency services. Overcrowding in emergency departments may lead to diversion of ambulances to hospitals further away. In 2007, CMS estimated that 55 percent of emergency care in the United States was uncompensated. Cost control initiatives have limited the extent to which costs for uncompensated care can be shifted to other payers, so many emergency departments are not paid for care they deliver to patients. This confluence of factors makes complying with EMTALA an ongoing concern for healthcare providers.

Employee Retirement Income Security Act

Designed to protect the interests of participants in employee benefit plans, the **Employee Retirement Income Security Act (ERISA)** was enacted in 1974 to establish minimum standards for pension plans in private industry. ERISA includes extensive rules for the federal income tax effects associated with employee benefit plans. Although ERISA does not require employers to provide health insurance to employees or retirees, it regulates the operation of a health plan benefit if an employer chooses to establish one.

Significant amendments to ERISA since 1974 concern the health plan benefit:

- The **Consolidated Omnibus Budget Reconciliation Act of 1985 (COBRA)** provides some employees and beneficiaries the right to continue coverage under an employer-sponsored group health plan for a limited time following certain events that would otherwise result in termination of the coverage (such as loss of employment)
- HIPAA prohibits health plans from refusing coverage for an employee's pre-existing medical condition in some circumstances. It also bars health plans from certain types of discrimination on the basis of health status, genetic information, or disability

Many employers who promised lifetime health coverage for their retirees have chosen to limit or eliminate those benefits. Although ERISA did not promise vesting of health plan benefits in the same way that employees become vested in their pension benefits, some who were promised lifetime benefits have chosen to sue the employer for breach of contract. There have also been challenges to the right of employers to change health plan documents in order to eliminate promised benefits.

Federal Anti-Kickback Statute and Regulatory Safe Harbors

The **federal anti-kickback statute** was enacted in 1972. The main purpose of this statute was to protect patients and federal healthcare programs (such as Medicare and Medicaid) from fraud and abuse by reducing the influence of money on healthcare decisions. The statute basically states that anyone who knowingly and willfully receives or pays anything of value that influences the referral of business of federal healthcare programs may face felony charges. Punishments for violations carry criminal and civil monetary and prison penalties and exclusion from participation in federal healthcare programs.

Although some cases covered under the statute were innocuous or beneficial, some concerns arose. The 1987 Congress authorized the designation of specific **"safe harbors"** for some business or payment arrangements that could be prohibited under the statute but would not be prosecuted. There are currently 13 safe harbors identified:

- Investments in large publicly held healthcare companies
- Investments in small healthcare joint ventures
- Space rental

- Equipment rental
- Personal services and management contracts
- Sales of retiring physicians' practices to other physicians
- Referral services
- Warranties
- Discounts
- Employee compensation
- Group purchasing organizations
- Waivers of Medicare Part A inpatient cost-sharing amounts
- Practices in managed care settings

To be protected in a safe harbor provision, the payment or business arrangement must fit completely within the safe harbor definition. Compliance should be evaluated on a case-by-case basis to be certain that arrangements qualify for this protection.

Stark Law

The Stark laws are related to but not the same as the federal anti-kickback statute. At issue is the practice of physicians referring patients to a medical facility in which the physician has a financial interest, whether ownership or other type of investment. Proponents of the Stark law alleged that there was an inherent conflict of interest given the physician's opportunity to benefit from the referral. Others responded that although problems did exist, they were not widespread or were in areas where a need was demonstrated, such as in a medically underserved area.

"Stark I," effective in January 1992, barred self-referrals to clinical laboratory services under the Medicare program. A number of exceptions were identified to accommodate legitimate business arrangements. "Stark II" resulted from the Omnibus Budget Reconciliation Act of 1993 (OBRA 1993). Stark II expanded the range of health services covered and was extended to include Medicaid as well as Medicare. Amendments were included in the Balanced Budget Act (BBA) of 1995 that repealed the prohibition on compensation arrangements and reduced the list of services subject to the ban.

Identity Theft

In November 2007, the Federal Trade Commission (FTC) and five other federal agencies published what became known as the **Red Flags Rule.** This rule arose from the **Fair and Accurate Credit Transactions Act of 2003,** which requires creditors to develop and implement programs to prevent identity theft. Identity theft may take two forms in healthcare: financial identity theft or medical identify theft.

Financial identity theft occurs when a party steals demographic and financial information about a patient for its own use. This compromises the financial welfare of the person whose identity was stolen.

Medical identity theft occurs when a patient uses another person's name and insurance information to receive healthcare benefits. Most often this is done so a person can receive medical care with an insurance benefit and pay less or nothing for the care he or she receives. The problem with medical identity theft is that it also creates medical information for the person that is inaccurate and could be embarrassing or even life threatening. For example, if Patient A is healthy and without known health problems and Patient B has a sexually transmitted disease (STD) that requires treatment, the health record will document that Patient A received treatment for the STD, which may also have been reported to the local public health authority for follow-up. In this situation the medical information about Patient A is inaccurate and there is no record of Patient B having been treated for anything. In the case where there is a public health issue, Patient B cannot be monitored or followed in any way.

Red Flags Rule enforcement was postponed initially, and ultimately physicians and healthcare organizations may be exempt when the final rule is issued. However, it is important to understand that since healthcare providers may allow deferred payments or bill patients for services provided, most fit the definition of "creditor" under the rule. The FTC has confirmed that if patients are allowed to pay in installments, the provider bills for services, or the provider accepts insurance with the understanding that the patient is ultimately responsible for the bill, the providers are creditors under the law. Therefore, it is prudent to have procedures in place that call out situations where a patient's financial or medical identity could be in question.

A Red Flags Rule program should include activities that

- Identify patterns, practices, or specific actions that indicate the potential of identity theft
- Detect such patterns, practices, or actions
- Provide for an appropriate response to detected red flags
- Ensure that the program is updated periodically to reflect changes in technology, employee and patient behaviors, and theft methodologies

Privacy and Security (HIPAA)

Most healthcare organizations found they needed between 20 and 60 new or revised policies, procedures, forms, or other documents to implement the HIPAA privacy and security rules in 2003 and 2004. Technology, process, and workflow changes since 2004 may have made many of these carefully crafted policies, procedures, or forms out of date.

Training related to privacy and security appropriate to the audience is a major requirement of HIPAA. Current policies and procedures constitute the basis for training and documentation of training for staff, volunteers, clinicians, board members, and such. Training must be ongoing, not a one-time event. Training generally includes three levels:

- Level 1: General training
- Level 2: Job-specific training
- Level 3: Management-specific training.

Core content for HIPAA training should include that federal law

- Defines PHI
- Describes permitted and required uses and disclosures of PHI
- Defines confidentiality
- Describes ramifications of violations for each member of the workforce and the organization
- Requires the workforce to know where to obtain policies and procedures on privacy and security
- Requires reporting, without fear of retaliation, of any suspected breaches of confidentiality

Health Information Exchange

Health information exchange (HIE) among healthcare providers has been slow to gain acceptance and practice. The premise is that a patient's information recorded in the health records of one organization should be reliably available to other providers.

Some healthcare providers believe that a patient's information belongs to the provider rather than the patient and having that PHI gives the provider an advantage. In addition, practical obstacles of ensuring patient privacy and lack of interoperable technology to accomplish HIE have prevailed until recently. With increasing use of EHRs and acceptance of the idea that accurate and timely information in the hands of caregivers will improve the quality of care in communities and increase patient satisfaction, HIE is becoming more of a reality.

There are myriad issues that must be addressed when engaging in HIE. Data integrity, validation of patient identity, and privacy and security considerations must be part of the set-up work. Decisions need to be made about whether or not to require patient consent to the release of PHI, when in the process consent is obtained, what process will be used, and who is authorized to transmit or receive the PHI. See chapter 9 for more detail in HIE.

Check Your Understanding 28.2

Instructions: Answer the following questions on a separate piece of paper.

1. What is the significance of the American Recovery and Reinvestment Act (ARRA) for HIM professionals?

2. Why are HITECH and meaningful use so important in healthcare?

3. Since the Red Flags Rule has not been finalized, why should healthcare providers develop policies and procedures to address it?

Risk Management

Risk management programs are designed to prevent or reduce accidents and injuries in healthcare facilities and organizations. The concept of managing risk has been around for thousands of years, first seen in 400 B.C. in the Code of Hammurabi. Originally these programs focused on injuries to patients from clinicians. Today, a broader goal is to reduce risks to patients, visitors, employees, physicians, or volunteers working in or visiting healthcare facilities for business or personal reasons. Risk management programs seek to identify and prevent **potentially compensable events (PCEs)** and reduce liability from injuries or accidents that occur within the healthcare facility. Risk management programs may be simple or very sophisticated.

Accrediting bodies such as the Joint Commission review risk management programs and activities during accreditation surveys. Insurance carriers for both liability and healthcare require risk management programs to be in place. Federal and state governments require risk management activities aimed at reducing and preventing injuries or accidents in healthcare facilities. Patient safety has become an issue with national visibility. Patients and their families can research and investigate patient safety as they decide whether to be treated in specific facilities or by specific providers. The Internet has put a world of information in the hands of savvy researchers, which is interpreted with varying degrees of skill and accuracy and used by patients or their families for making healthcare decisions.

Policies and procedures specific to the organization are needed to support risk management activities. Organizations that have good policies and procedures for reporting accidents and injuries (or near-accidents and injuries) have the opportunity to correct system problems before a major incident occurs, potentially saving a patient from an accident, injury, or even death. This can save the organization from negative financial impacts and may preserve the reputation of the organization in the community by avoiding legal action and potentially damaging related publicity.

Risk management policies and procedures are the foundation of managing the risk and quality in any organization. Risk management can be very complex. Patient safety, the medical record, and incident reporting (discussed later) are foundational pieces of this process. Complexity is further heightened by the fact that collected information needs to be shared with the quality improvement staff. Clinical and administrative data can be useful in preventing, improving, or identifying areas requiring quality improvement strategies. Collaborative efforts involving risk and quality management personnel will ensure both the safety and quality of patients, staff, and visitors.

Healthcare organizations must fund risk management activities. This can be accomplished by hiring a risk manager who has adequate authority to make changes as necessary, or these duties can be part of the quality and safety areas of the organization. In either case, it is essential that the organization recognize the need to collect and analyze data, make changes, and improve current facility systems and to do so in conjunction with current efforts to improve the quality of care. Another component of a successful risk management program is **loss reduction.** Loss reduction employ techniques used to manage events or claims that have already taken place. Ways to reduce losses incurred include

- Investigating reported incidents or addressing occurrence reports promptly
- Reviewing claims made against the facility
- Managing workers' compensation programs
- Being knowledgeable about alternate dispute resolution processes
- Treating employee injuries on-site
- Implementing back-to-work programs
- Assisting with depositions or other pretrial activities
- Working closely with defense counsel

Another component of a successful risk management program is **loss prevention.** Some of the ways that risk prevention can be attained include

- Educating all employees and medical staff to recognize and properly report all potentially adverse occurrences
- Ensuring that all employees and medical staff are doing their jobs to the best of their ability
- Developing early warning and reporting systems that identify areas of potential adverse effect
- Creating databases to track events and help point out areas where systems can be improved
- Making changes to systems requiring improvement and monitoring these areas to determine success
- Providing employees with appropriate safety training

Incident Reporting

One tool commonly used to conduct risk management activities is incident reporting. Typically, **incident reports** are submitted by anyone who notes situations where injury or harm occurred or could have occurred. Incident reports are confidential and allow analysis of individual incidents to determine whether the incident could have been prevented or resulting harm reduced. Incident reports are not kept in a patient's health record, and complete candor about what happened is necessary if the information is to be useful.

An atmosphere of trust is a critical element in the healthcare organization if incident reporting is to be of value. Employees or clinicians completing incident reports must be confident that information obtained from them will be used to learn what happened, to prevent harm, and to improve patient care. Of equal importance is the reporting of near-misses, such as a dosing error if a medication order is not correctly interpreted by the pharmacy or staff member

dispensing or delivering the medication to the patient, even if no harm results. Near-miss reporting allows the opportunity to proactively evaluate and improve systems, thereby preventing harm to patients or others.

The role of documentation in patient health records is extremely important to carrying out risk management activities. Harmful incidents involving patients should be recorded in a completely factual way in the health record. Near-miss incidents are never recorded in a patient's health record, although an incident report may be filed.

Internal and External Disaster Preparedness Programs

An **emergency preparedness** program addresses disasters and emergency situations both inside and outside the healthcare organization. The September 11, 2001 tragedy involving the World Trade Center and the Pentagon created new challenges for this program. Management plans the response to crisis situations. The organization must have protocols on how patients will be treated, admitted, and discharged. The plan must be developed in cooperation with agencies and organizations within the community. All entities responding to emergency situations must be ready to work together to handle any type of disaster—major fires, floods, and hurricanes have all occurred in the recent past. Natural disasters, such as Hurricane Katrina, have had a devastating impact on patient care for thousands of patients. Health information was lost, destroyed, or otherwise made unavailable for hospitalized and ambulatory patients alike. Additionally, everyone working within organizations—hospitals and provider office practices—must be trained to respond to emergency and disaster situations.

The emergency preparedness plan must address certain areas, for example, how the organization will address the need for backup utilities, communication systems, and radioactive and chemical decontamination and isolation. Personnel must know their roles and responsibilities in a crisis situation. Practice sessions, also called disaster drills, should be held to help personnel react appropriately. Whether the emergency is internal or external to the organization, the appropriate policies and procedures need to be in place and well understood by the organization's personnel to ensure that the response is timely and meaningful.

Routine Monitoring

Another component of risk management programs is reviewing the results of routine monitoring activities. Examples of monitoring activities in successful risk management programs are reviews of incident reports and results of generic screening activities. **Generic screening** reviews are generally carried out using predetermined criteria to review medical records or other information that brings to light opportunities to improve. Examples of generic reviews include checking whether consent forms are completed and signed according to organizational policies; reviewing infection rates (again looking for trends by unit, department, operating room, and such); or evaluating information about patients who returned unexpectedly to the operating room, repeatedly required emergency care, or required readmission to the hospital for the same condition a short time following discharge. Result reviews should look for trends in incidents (by department, specialty, clinician, type of incident, and such). Evidence of regular reviews is required by accrediting bodies and may be used by insurers, surveyors, or investigators when deemed appropriate.

The Joint Commission initiated **sentinel event** reviews in 1998 requiring immediate evaluation in cases when an unexpected incident involves death or serious injury. Immediate evaluation permits changes to be made in a prompt way to prevent serious injury or death to others. Organizations are encouraged (but not required) to report sentinel events to the Joint Commission. A root-cause analysis and an action plan must be completed regardless of whether the event is reported to the Joint Commission. Healthcare organizations reporting a sentinel event can benefit by having an outside, objective third party review their action plan and by obtaining consultation as needed. In addition, the organization should show the public a sincere effort to remedy problems and show improvement.

Root-Cause Analysis

Tools used by quality improvement professionals are commonly being used in risk management activities as well. **Root-cause analysis** is a valuable tool to accurately identify the true cause of incidents or PCEs. The use of root-cause analysis keeps the focus on processes and systems rather than people when evaluating incidents. Once the true cause of an event is understood the organization can focus on remediating systems or processes that allowed the event to occur. Rarely are individual people the true cause of an event. The usual culprits are organizational or clinical processes that cause an untoward event to occur.

Credentialing

The role of credentialing in risk management activities is very important in compliance programs. Providers putting hands on patients or delivering care should be investigated thoroughly to validate that they are who and what they say they are. Today most healthcare organizations require thorough screening, including law enforcement background checks, before anyone can start work in the facility. Clinicians are often brought in to assist or train other clinicians on new surgical procedures. The urgency of these credentialing requests can be overwhelming. However, the organization can be held liable both morally and legally if a PCE occurs and it is determined that administrators knew or should have known that the person was not qualified to do the work he or she was doing at the time the PCE occurred. Having a clearly

defined process for credentialing and following it 100 percent of the time is imperative.

Implications for Health Information Management

The impacts from all the programs swirling in the healthcare landscape at the present time have significant implications for health information management (HIM) professionals. Coordinating disclosure requirements among HITECH, HIPAA, and state regulations is complex. Accounting of disclosures under HITECH in the future could change from the time currently required by HIPAA. Care must be taken to ensure that members of the workforce and vendors involved in disclosing health information are granted appropriate access to clinical patient records. Employees and vendors alike must receive appropriate training to carry out their jobs without increasing the risk of PHI breaches.

Every healthcare provider must define the organization's legal health record. This is an ongoing activity since elements of the health record move from paper to hybrid to electronic format. As technology changes, the definition may also change, and it is imperative that there be clarity about what is released based on a valid request for information.

Ensuring that policies and procedures are current, reflecting both organizational policy and technology, is an onerous job. Ideally, some sort of reference tool or inventory of every policy that exists in the facility and that cross-references each policy to applicable standards is needed. Such an inventory permits documentation of periodic review, validation, and revision when appropriate.

One challenge to HIM professionals in the world of EHRs is that the tight control exercised with paper records is not possible with electronic records. Reviews should be routinely carried out to determine where records are reviewed, used, or released throughout the healthcare system (not just in HIM). Workflows concerning release of information and any gaps identified must be addressed promptly. HIM should play a role in authorizing access to PHI in an EHR.

HIM professionals should also be involved when policies are formulated about the retention and destruction of health information, whether the health information is in paper, hybrid, or electronic records. Policies and procedures for destruction should be rigorously followed for film, hard copy records, disks, and tapes so that PHI cannot be reconstructed.

HIM departments or services should have a compliance plan that ensures the services it provides meet or exceed the federal and state laws, accreditation and professional standards, rules, and regulations. The plan should complement the organization's compliance plan. Should there not be a corporate compliance plan, there should still be one for the HIM department.

Items to consider for inclusion in a departmental compliance plan should reflect the work of the department, such as the:

- Department mission statement
- Employee code of conduct
- Documented training of the workforce on confidentiality, privacy and security, and job-specific responsibilities
- Policy and procedure development and maintenance processes
- Documentation and coding validation policies and procedures
- Release of information policies and procedures
- Analysis and deficiency management policies and procedures
- Customer and service quality evaluation and improvement plans
- Reviewed processes and action plans for regular updates to the plan (Dunn 2001)

The skills required for HIM professionals to carry out compliance activities are part of the core training of our profession. Skills that should be acquired or improved include communication, training and education, conducting assessments and investigations, negotiation of solutions, data analysis, and project and program management. HIM professionals need to have outstanding listening skills, tact and diplomacy, and patience.

Check Your Understanding 28.4

Instructions: Answer the following question on a separate piece of paper.

1. List the items that should be considered for inclusion when developing an HIM department compliance plan.

From initially researching material used for the development of policies and procedures to developing those policies and procedures, ensuring that corporate policies are filtered down to and through department policies and procedures, is the initial challenge. After policies and procedures are created and incorporated into the fabric of the organization, education about them must take place since employees and providers cannot be held accountable if they were not informed about expectations. Then a plan for monitoring and enforcement must be documented and carried out. Prudent organizations will take advantage of the knowledge and skills brought to them by HIM professionals.

References

American Health Information Management Association. 2010 (August). Meaningful Use White Paper Series. Paper no. 2: Meaningful Use—Provider Requirements.

Bowman, S. 2007 *Health Information Management Compliance: Guidelines for Preventing Fraud.* AHIMA. Chicago.

Centers for Medicare and Medicaid Services. 2012 (March 7). Medicare and Medicaid Programs; Electronic Health Record Incentive Program—Stage 2. http://www.gpo.gov/fdsys/pkg/FR-2012-03-07/pdf/2012-4443.pdf.

Compliance360. (n.d.). White Paper: The Seven Elements of an Effective Compliance and Ethics Program.. http://www.compliance360.com/downloads/case/Seven_Elements_of_Effective_Compliance_Programs.pdf.

Department of Health and Human Services and the Department of Justice. 2010. Health Care Fraud and Abuse Control Program Annual Report for Fiscal Year 2010. http://oig.hhs.gov/publications/docs/hcfac/hcfacreport2010.pdf.

Dunn, R.T. 2001 (Winter). Your department compliance plan—Seven easy steps. *Health Information Link* 50(1).

Federal Register. 2009 (August 24). Rules and Regulations. 74(612). Section 164.402.

Nunn S. 2009b (October). Integrating ARRA: Leveraging current compliance efforts to meet the new privacy provisions. *Journal of AHIMA* 80(10):50–51.

Office of the Inspector General. 2012. Corporate Integrity Agreements. http://oig.hhs.gov/faqs/corporate-integrity-agreements-faq.asp.

Summary

Compliance issues are threaded throughout the scope of HIM work. HIM professionals should be involved in every step of the compliance process in a healthcare organization.

chapter 29

Strategic Thinking: Strategic Management and Leading Change

Susan E. McClernon, MHA, FACHE

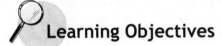

Learning Objectives

- Define and describe strategic management as an essential set of skills for strategic thinking and leading change in health information management (HIM) services
- Explore the attributes and skills that strategic health information managers possess
- Distinguish strategic management from strategic planning and strategic thinking
- Know the steps of the strategic management and strategic thinking processes
- Understand tools and approaches that complement strategic management and thinking
- Describe the benefits of strategic management, and relate these to leadership and management principles and to the change management process

- Appreciate the importance of managing risk in a highly turbulent environment
- Apply theoretical knowledge in the area of a comprehensive environmental assessment
- Identify the concepts of driving force and areas of excellence
- Plan for the future through scenario building, strategic leverage, and innovation
- Describe techniques for considering future HIM and healthcare challenges and identifying strategic options
- Identify examples of innovative strategic management and strategic thinking as applied to HIM practice
- Understand how HIM strategies fit into the broader information system strategies and the overall strategy of the organization

Key Terms

Area of excellence
Balanced scorecard methodology
Coalition building
Critical issue
Driving force
Environmental assessment
Kolb's "Learning Loop"
Mission statement
Operations improvement planning
Paradigm
Process innovation
Scenario

Service innovation
Storytelling
Strategic goal
Strategic management
Strategic objective
Strategic planning
Strategic profile
Strategic thinking
Strategy
Strategy map
SWOT analysis
Vision

Setting strategy is often viewed as the work of senior managers and boards of trustees. Strategy is thought of as being handed down from on high, embodied in slogans, and generally not very relevant to the day-to-day work of most employees in the organization. Sometimes strategy is detailed in a three- to five-year strategic plan that lays out goals and key actions to meet the organization's goals. But strategy is no longer the sole purview of senior managers, planning departments, or consultants. The ability to develop effective strategies is a key attribute and skill of successful managers and leaders at all levels in today's organizations. Employers cite strategic thinking, which includes strategic management and change leadership, as competencies they look for in health information management (HIM) professionals (AHIMA 2004). Managers and directors should be able to lead the development of strategic plans at their department or division level as well as contribute significantly in strategic thinking and planning at an organizational level.

Simply stated, a **strategy** is the art and science of planning and marshalling resources for their most efficient and effective use. An organizational strategy "provides the blueprint by which the end can be attained under conditions of direct combat. This is true whether the 'war' is actual military conflict or market competition" (Luke et al. 2004, 4). Strategy means consciously choosing to be clear about your company's direction in relation to what is happening in a dynamic environment (Olsen 2006, 10). **Strategic management** is a process a leader uses for assessing a changing environment to create a vision of the future; determining how the organization fits into the future environment based on its mission, vision, and knowledge of its strengths, weaknesses, opportunities, and threats; and then setting in motion a strategic plan of action to position the organization accordingly.

Strategic planning is not the same as operations improvement planning. **Strategic planning**

is the formalized roadmap that describes how your company executes the chosen strategy. A plan spells out where an organization is going over the next year or more and how it's going to get there. A strategic plan is a management tool that serves the purpose of helping an organization do a better job, because a plan focuses the energy, resources, and time of everyone in the organization in the same direction. (Olsen 2006, 12)

Operations improvement planning differs as it focuses on improving how existing programs and services are carried out. By definition, it is internally focused and is one part of how to implement strategic thinking.

Management theories about the importance of strategy and how to set strategy are changing. This reconsideration is a reflection of the speed of change in every facet of contemporary life, including healthcare. **Strategic thinking** is

the process of thinking that goes on in the head of the CEO and the key people around him or her that helps them determine the look for the organization at some point in to the

future. Strategic thinking is different from strategic planning and operational planning. In fact, strategic thinking is the framework for the strategic and operational improvement plans. It combines an understanding of a strategic plan and an operational plan which support strategic thinking within an organization. (Robert 1998, 24–25)

This chapter explores the importance of strategic thinking and planning to effective strategic management, describes approaches to making and communicating strategic choices, describes approaches for maximizing organizational learning, and illustrates how HIM professionals can use strategy to shape and effect change in their department and organization.

Skills of Strategic Managers and Strategic Thinkers

The definition of strategy is straightforward, but the skills for setting and executing strategy are far from simple. HIM professionals must take advantage of opportunities to learn and develop skills for strategic management and thinking, including

- Monitoring industry trends in healthcare and information management
- Reflecting on how industry trends can affect existing and new products and services
- Considering how changes in one area can affect others in the organization
- Considering how a strategic course for change is set for their departments and organizations
- Helping others visualize the need for change and recruiting them as partners in moving a change agenda forward
- Implementing and measuring strategic plans effectively
- Questioning the status quo on a continuing basis and leading innovative change
- Being self-reflective and lifelong learners

Strategy is no longer a management domain reserved for senior managers. Today, all managers must develop skills and competencies that enable them to think and act strategically. These skills include sharpening their ability to observe the world around them. Strategic managers watch for changes in the larger environment beyond the healthcare industry, including political, economic, social, and technological changes. Such changes may involve staff attitudes, public policy, ethics, or inventions and innovations within the healthcare industry or externally. Managers must consider how these changes are affecting—or might affect—healthcare and the organizations in which they work. For example, shifts in public attitudes regarding the value placed on personal privacy have implications for health information policies and practices regarding patients who are using online access to or request copies of their personal health records.

Strategic managers develop skills reflecting the implications and opportunities afforded by trends. Whether reading a journal or discussing new ideas with others, strategic managers are always testing new ideas, identifying those that have merit, and discarding those that do not. They are creating links between the trends and the value-adding actions they can take. For example, federal programs to adjust provider reimbursement on the basis of certain quality parameters suggest a need to elevate organizational health information standards for data integrity so that pay-for-performance determinations are accurate and fair.

Effective strategic managers and thinkers are creative in how they make associations among trends, ideas, and new opportunities. These associations are not always direct, as in the examples about privacy and public policy or data quality and pay for performance. Making strategy choices may be the result of drawing lessons from analogous situations. When faced with an unfamiliar problem or opportunity, experienced managers often learn from connecting with colleagues who may have faced similar situations and apply what they have learned from other situations to their current situation (Gavetti and Rivkin 2005, 54–63). For example, faced with a shortage of trained coders, the HIM director institutes a coder training program in partnership with a local community college, modeled after a similar program used to address the shortage of nurses in the community.

Strategic managers also continually look for opportunities to improve on the status quo. They do not accept the old adage, "If it's not broken, don't fix it." They always look for ways to make things better and are willing to take some risks and evaluate new approaches through trial and error. They know that standing still is really moving backward. They understand that no action may be less tolerable than trying something even if it does not fully succeed. For example, the quality of coded data for inpatient services is at 94 percent and the data quality manager thinks that adjusting staff assignments may make better use of staff skills and improve performance.

New managers may lack the confidence to initiate change and may have few analogous experiences to draw on. Still, they should guard against accepting or perpetuating artificial barriers to creativity characterized by common squelchers, such as "We've never done that before," "We have always done it that way," or "That's not my job." Confidence comes from experience, and experience requires asking good questions, action, and thoughtful reflection on what did and did not work.

Finally, strategic managers learn to help their organization contribute to new thinking and new ideas. They know that the best solutions represent the best thinking of all key stakeholders. Thus, strategic managers learn techniques to bring out the best thinking of their staff, superiors, colleagues, and customers for their change agenda. As Drucker (1996, xii) says, "The only definition of a leader is someone who has followers." For example, in pursuit of a goal to decrease the amount of printing of electronic records by physicians,

the health information manager knew that support from nursing and other staff in the patient care units was essential for success. He oversaw implementation of a multifaceted plan to reduce the rate of printing on the units and shared credit with nursing when the print rate began to decline.

The skills of the strategic manager are learned. Learning begins by recognizing the importance of strategy to today's successful managers. For HIM professionals, the learning begins with their professional coursework and directed learning experiences. Skills are learned and subsequently sharpened through work experience, particularly in opportunities to be part of—and to lead—change management projects.

From Strategic Planning to Strategic Management and Thinking

Strategic planning was described in the management literature in the 1960s and the decades that followed. It was a prominent and highly touted organizational function. Strategic planning was developed to prevent organizations from "crisis planning" when they realized that their competitors outpaced them in innovation and they quickly had to develop reactive strategies to keep this from happening again. Early applications were characterized by rigorous and formal analysis of data to deduce a desired future and the steps to achieve it. In large corporations, departments of planners prepared forecasts with the aid of computer analysis. The complex reports were delivered to senior managers, who were largely uninvolved in the process.

These approaches have fallen out of favor for several key reasons. First, forecasting the future, particularly in such rapidly changing times, is difficult. Second, by the time a complex three- to five-year plan is finalized and delivered to senior managers, it is undoubtedly out of date. If customers, employees, and all levels of managers are involved in strategy development, the plan is likely to be seen as relevant and likely to be implemented. Third, for strategic planning and thinking to really be more than an improved operational plan, they need to include innovative strategies that not only help the organization not only redefine the its existing products and services but create new products and services that strategically move the organization forward toward its vision. In order to stay strong and viable as an organization, the HIM professional must understand the organizational vision. He or she must engage the best thinking of everyone in his or her area, look at where the organization is today and where it needs to be in the future, and then find the path to the new vision as a team. When departmental and organizational strategies are updated at least annually, the effort will result in plans that make real organizational change.

No one phrase is the accepted successor for this type of comprehensive strategic planning. In fact, today managers and directors in many organizations are likely to still hear the activity referred to as strategic planning. However, it is important to get beneath the words to understand the process being followed. It may be called strategic planning, but it can embody many of the newer concepts that often are called strategic management and thinking. For example,

- It is framed by organizational vision, mission, and values.
- It takes into account possible future scenarios rather than trying to forecast only one future.
- It is truly the work of management, even when guided by consultants, and has broad input and participation.
- It is action oriented and measured, with a commitment to bringing about change.
- It results in organizational innovation, change, and learning.

Strategic thinking is a way of introducing innovation into decision making and engaging others in the change process. With the rapid changes in HIM practice, this discussion of strategic thinking is not academic. The skills that distinguish a strategic thinker include the following:

- Ability to plan (consensus building) and strategy formation (leadership)
- Flexibility and creativity
- Comfort with uncertainty and risk
- A sense of urgency and vision of how to move change forward positively
- An understanding of how to gain a powerful core of organizational supporters and customers
- An ability to communicate the vision and plans

Strategic management and thinking should be viewed as a component of each of the five functions of management discussed in chapter 23. Every aspect of management involves a strategic management component, as described here.

With organizational learning as a centerpiece, this approach unifies change management, strategy development, and leadership. In all three, managers learn by observing and reflecting on the results of their experiences.

Figure 29.1.   Kolb's "Learning Loop"

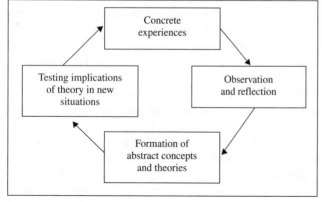

Source: Kolb 1988.

This concept is best depicted in **Kolb's "Learning Loop,"** shown in figure 29.1 (Kolb 1988, 68–88). To undertake deliberate change, individuals reflect on their experiences and become aware of new patterns and trends that they did not previously perceive. They form new ways of looking at the opportunities and the implications of their experiences. They evaluate new theories about what can and should be and then apply these theories and test their implications. They observe and reflect on the results of their experiences, thus beginning the loop again.

Elements of Strategic Thinking and Strategic Management

As shown in figure 29.2, strategic thinking and strategic management are logical processes that comprise a number of steps in strategic planning that may be explicit or implicit. It begins with a current description and an internal assessment of the organization and an assessment of the external environment.

Based on the findings and conclusions from the assessment, a new or updated strategic profile and vision statement of how the organization would like things to be in the future are developed. For example, an updated vision for a managed care health plan might be to have fully engaged patients who are full partners with the health plan in maintaining their health. Obviously, a few key strategies are needed for this vision to be realized, and these must be identified and understood. Strategies are the most important high level, directional goals to pursue to achieve the vision. Once the core strategies are identified, a set of **strategic goals** for each strategy need to be developed that define a series of longer-term action steps of how to achieve each strategy. For example, a strategy for the health plan may be to develop a campaign and personal health record to include patients in focusing on the aspects of self-management, especially those with chronic diseases. Some of the strategic goals might involve a way to develop incentives for patients to engage in wellness activities and use their personal health records (PHRs) and to provide easy access to computer and health literacy education. The next step would be to take each strategic goal and identify the **strategic objectives** or short-term action plans that are needed to accomplish each strategic goal.

Major strategic goals and objectives that are needed to move toward the vision are described. These become more precise than the overall vision and strategy. For example, providing all citizens with access to lifetime electronic PHRs might be a strategy to achieve the vision of empowered and self-managing consumers. The vision and strategy describe where the organization wants to go, and the strategic goals and objectives describe what must be accomplished and how to get there. The strategies are how the organization intends to pursue its vision. The strategic goals

Figure 29.2.   Elements of strategic planning

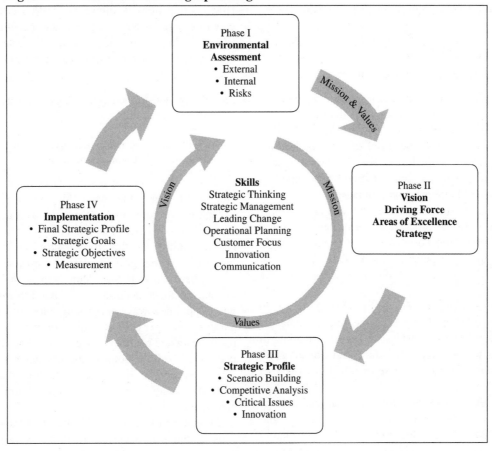

and objectives are the specific action plans needed to imple‑ ment these strategies.

Although depicted as a circular process, overall stra‑ tegic management is never so neat and organized, and the best strategies may emerge from trial and error. But effective strategy will not emerge without a clear idea of where the leader wants to move the organization and a realistic assessment of the issues to overcome. Moreover, strategic management will not happen in isolation. Stakeholders, whether staff, customers, caregivers, patients, or managers, must be engaged in each phase of the process.

Each step involves learning, which in turn enables plans to be improved upon, therefore making subsequent efforts more effective. Thus, experience sharpens and clarifies understanding of the issues, allowing managers to be more precise in setting goals. Strategies and tactics are continu‑ ally modified with experience. Strategic management, like Kolb's "Learning Loop," is a process that leads to orga‑ nizational learning and improvement over time. (Refer to figure 29.1.)

In contrast to traditional strategic planning, where all steps are neatly outlined before implementation is begun, strategic management requires a willingness to learn and change as the leader guides an organization through the process. In a

fast-paced, changing environment, constant review of strat‑ egy, goals, and objectives is required.

Check Your Understanding 29.1

Instructions: On a separate piece of paper, answer the following questions.

1. In two sentences, describe how strategic thinking relates to strategic planning and operational planning.

2. List three skills of a strategic thinker.

Create a Commitment to Change with Vision

The organization's vision sets the broad directional strategy, leaving the details to be worked out. A **vision** is a picture of the desired future state of the organization (Kemp et al. 1993). Kotter (2002, 72) explains that an effective vision statement has the following characteristics:

- Conveys a picture of what the future will look like
- Appeals to the long-term interests of the stakeholders

- Sets forth realistic and achievable goals
- Is clear enough to provide guidance in decision making
- Is flexible so that alternative strategies are possible as conditions change
- Is easy to describe and communicate

An organization may never realize a vision in its entirety. Today's technology may not yet support lifetime PHRs or autocoding of 100 percent of cases, but that does not mean these bold visions should not be sketched. All health information may never be in digital form, but that does not mean this should not be a vision. Visions must be worth pursuing; otherwise, why would others become engaged?

Visions should evoke a sense of excitement and urgency from those closest to the process. If the designers are not getting excited about the possibilities the vision presents, others are not likely to generate excitement. A sense of urgency is essential to overcome the forces that protect the status quo.

According to Kouzes and Posner (1995, 94), "a vision describes a bold and ideal image of the future." It is the catalyst for change. They also state, "if leaders are going to take us to places we've never been before, constituents of all types demand that they have a sense of direction" (Kouzes and Posner 1995, 95).

A vision states the direction for organizational change and helps motivate people to take action. In 2003 and reaffirmed in 2012, the American Health Information Management Association (AHIMA) convened an interdisciplinary panel of experts to craft a vision for the HIM profession in regard to electronic health information management (e-HIM):

> AHIMA proactively promotes the technological advancement of health information systems that enhance the delivery of quality healthcare. (AHIMA 2012)

This vision statement describes features of e-HIM that work in real time to support critical decision making across healthcare and reflects a more diverse field with a critical charge. It has been used to help catalyze the field to embrace e-HIM as a change strategy. The 2012 AHIMA vision articulates new insights about the organization that would secure a strong future for the profession with an even more compelling update.

> AHIMA [is] leading the advancement and ethical use of quality health information to promote health and wellness worldwide. (AHIMA 2012)

Designing a compelling vision requires a solid understanding of the internal and external environment. It also requires the ability to break free of the current paradigm and to think creatively about a new reality for the future. **Paradigm** is broadly defined as a philosophical or theoretical framework within which a discipline formulates its theories and makes generalizations.

The following are examples of vision statements within HIM organizations. A director of HIM services for a health system envisions services that make the fullest use of staff and technology to provide high-quality, cost-effective information to authorized users. He expresses this idealized vision as follows:

> Utilizing state-of-the-art information technology and evidence-based practices,
>
> We will deliver accurate electronic information to support patient care and healthcare operations.

This vision lays out a substantial challenge, yet it provides focus. First, the overarching vision is to be able to deliver all information electronically to all users of HIM services. It acknowledges that technology is only as good as the enabling processes; therefore, it promises use of evidence-based or research-proven practices, practices substantiated by applied research that demonstrates their validity. The vision statement acknowledges that achieving this vision will require new ways of working. First, success will require gaining a deeper understanding of the needs of those in patient care and healthcare operations, who rely on the information and whose collaboration is needed to achieve the vision. Second, it will require effective teamwork among HIM staff, who must become more comfortable with both change and risk taking.

In another example, an HIM consultant for a long-term care system was having difficulty gaining support for her vision of what an EHR could contribute to the residents, staff, and overall organization. She developed the following description of her vision:

> All members of the care team have immediate access to complete and accurate information for each resident. This information recaps care delivered and presents the status of all health, social, ADL, and other resident-specific issues being managed. Information needs to be entered just once and is available for a variety of patient care, quality improvement, and administrative uses. Summary reports are used as the basis for shift change briefings and for periodic care conferences. The information system prompts caregivers to actions that need to be taken and alerts them to changes in status that require special vigilance. Data entered into the system summarizing observations, care given, orders, and activities produce a record of care that meets licensing and other external requirements. The system also automatically accumulates the information needed for care and operations management and for external reporting.

This vision highlights the difficulty many have in creating a brief, compelling vision that doesn't include specific objectives. The vision could be simplified and revised as follows: *All members of the care team will have immediate access to complete and accurate information for each resident to improve patient care, quality, and timeliness.* The vision statement serves as a starting point for creating a more detailed set of specifications and evaluating potential system vendors.

Visions also can be created to more narrowly focused on a particular project. For example, a data quality manager for a multispecialty group practice clinic prepared the following vision statement to help the physicians and coding staff rally around a proposed project to improve the timeliness and accuracy of billing processes through the use of computer-assisted coding tools:

> During each patient visit, the physician will document using a handheld personal digital assistant (PDA). This will assist the practice in achieving 90 percent of visits billed within one business day, 95 percent within three business days, and the balance within five business days.

This vision statement has three major elements. First, it sets an aggressive goal of billing 90 percent of visits on the day of service. To do so, physicians must initiate the process using electronic tools to eliminate time-consuming handling of handwritten information. It also requires physician coding specialists with advanced data quality and compliance management skills.

These vision statements relate to HIM challenges. However, it is important that the HIM vision complements the organization's overall vision and mission. For example, the organization's vision is to be known for its advanced clinical services in cardiac and oncology care. To achieve this vision, the organization is pursuing a strategy of attracting clinical talent with national reputations and expanding clinical research programs. This overall vision and these strategies should be accounted for when crafting the HIM vision and strategies.

Strategic managers must understand the overall organizational goals and take them into account when crafting their own plans. First, they seek ways to support and further the overall goals of the organization through the priorities they set for their areas of responsibility. For example, will the cancer registry program need to be upgraded to support the more sophisticated information needs of a world-class oncology service? As a practical matter, it is hard to sell a plan that is out of step with priorities. Advancing the organization's goals through synergistic efforts is the mark of a successful strategic manager.

Check Your Understanding 29.2

Instructions: On a separate piece of paper, answer the following questions.

1. Based on an expanded understanding of the elements of a vision statement, write a concise, two-sentence vision statement that describes your department's or organization's electronic health record future state in the next three years.

2. Explain how the statement meets the elements of an effective vision statement as outlined by Kotter.

Begin with a Current Profile

The beginning stage in developing a new or updated strategic plan is to develop a good understanding of the organization's current profile. This approach assesses the current mission, vision, and values of the organization or department; completes an internal analysis of the trends within the organization or department; and conducts an external assessment of trends. The final step in completing the current profile is to assess the potential impact of the uncertainties and risks in the internal and external environment on the organization's strategic thinking and plan. Based on all the information and intelligence gathered throughout this profiling process, the strategic thinking tools and techniques described here are then utilized to develop a strategic future profile.

Assess the Current Mission, Vision, and Values

It is important to review the current mission, vision, and values of the organization and department. A **mission statement** is defined as an enduring statement of purpose for an organization that identifies the scope of its operations in services and products and its market terms and reflects its values and priorities (Abrahams 1999, 14). As described earlier, the mission differs from the vision. It is also important to understand the organizational values that are used to describe the basic philosophy, principles, or ideals of the organizational culture and behavioral expectations. Any strategic plan needs to be developed in accordance with the mission, vision, and values of the organization in order to drive change that will be supported by staff and senior leaders.

Understanding Environmental Assessment Trends

Knowledge of the internal and external environment is essential to vision and strategy formulation. An **environmental assessment** is conducted, which is defined as a thorough review of the internal and external conditions in which an organization operates (Jennings 2000, 39). This data-intensive process is the continuous process of gathering and analyzing intelligence about trends that are—or may be—affecting HIM and the healthcare organization and industry. It is both internally focused on the healthcare organization and HIM and externally focused on industry, market, and environmental trends.

Internal Assessment

It is important to fully evaluate and understand the current internal environment of both the department and the organization. This is a critical step to understand the organization's current strategic direction. It is also an opportunity to begin to gain multiple perspectives from key stakeholders on the current state. During this step in the process, differing perspectives that are held by various key stakeholders will emerge. Key themes of consensus will also begin to show.

The current description needs to include a recent **strategic profile** that identifies the existing key services or products of the department or organization, the nature of its customers and users, the nature of its market segments, and the nature of its geographic markets (Robert 1998, 60–61).

Another critical step in the assessment process is to conduct a SWOT (strengths, weaknesses, opportunities, and threats) analysis of the department and organization. A **SWOT analysis** "evaluates the internal organization based on its strengths compared to competitors and regional and societal demands, weaknesses compared to competitors or related to just the internal functions, opportunities for advancing ahead of competitors or serving a patient population not served well currently, and threats from external or internal agents that could stymie the organization's success" (Dunn 2007, 123). This process should involve multiple key stakeholders and will be an opportunity to begin consensus building. At this point in the process, planning assumptions, data analysis, and identification of potential risks and uncertainties should be made.

Internal environmental assessment, as adapted from the work of Bryson (1995, 90–92) includes analysis of

- *Performance indicators:* Budget targets and results, financials, performance and productivity measures, staff and customer feedback
- *Resources:* Budgeted staff, information technology, and educational resources, programs, competencies, and organizational culture
- *Present strategy:* Organization-wide strategy and priorities, information management strategy, information systems plans and priorities, compliance programs, products and services, and business processes

External Assessment

External environmental assessment as adapted from Bryson (1995, 87–89) includes analysis of

- *Forces:* Political, economic, demographic, social, technological, and educational factors that may be impacting the organization
- *Resource constraints:* Healthcare reimbursement systems, patient and customer trends, regulators, and competitors
- *Collaborators:* Current and potential collaborators
- *Trends* in the industry and other related industries or organizations

Other key areas to review and collect information for the external assessment phase of the strategic plan include the following:

- Demographics
- Innovative trends in the industry
- Technology
- Market structure
- Market share
- Market dynamics
- Customers
- Competitors
- Centers of excellence

An HIM manager who focuses exclusively on his or her own area of responsibility, whether managing a department, a service, or a project, will have a difficult time succeeding as a strategic manager. Understanding the environment provides the context for the tough decisions involved in setting direction, designing strategy, and leading change. Some ways to develop access to be better able to gather external assessment information in your environment include

- Taking inventory of sources of internal and external information to identify and fill information gaps
- Building performance measures to gain perspective on trends over time
- Becoming involved in projects and task forces within the organization to interact with a wide range of coworkers
- Developing a personal reading list to follow the thinking of experts in the field
- Reading what futurists are saying about how things will change
- Becoming active in AHIMA and other professional associations and groups
- Building a network of professional colleagues
- Making full use of the information resources that AHIMA and other local, state, and national organizations make available
- Contributing to the professional body of knowledge when developing new HIM practice solutions by presenting at seminars or submitting journal articles

How to Manage Risk and Uncertainty

Analyzing the changing environment and envisioning the future is at the same time an analytic and a highly creative activity. Understanding internal and external trends and forces of risks and uncertainties requires analysis of

- Relationships between trends
- Sequence of events
- Causes and effects
- Priority among items

As a strategic thinker, this is a critical skill that will require the leader to understand that there is risk and uncertainty as an organization begins to predict possible future trends and design strategies that might work based on those different scenarios. It also gives the manager an opportunity to find ways for identifying strategies to avoid some of the possible pitfalls or counteract external or internal forces.

Figure 29.3.   Sources of uncertainty

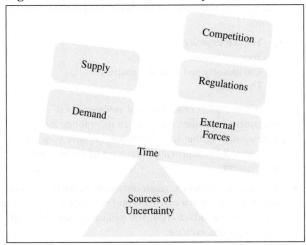

The key risks and uncertainties (see figure 29.3) to review as adapted from Jennings (2000, 7–14) include

- Demand structure—for example, market and industry trends that affect the demand for the service or organization
- Supply structure—for example, access to trained employees, physicians, or supplies needed by the service or organization
- Competitors—for example, information technology, outsourcing, mergers, and acquisitions
- External forces—for example, payers, employers, and customer trends
- Regulation—for example, federal or state government regulatory or legal changes
- Time—for example, when the forces of risk and uncertainty described earlier are predicted to potentially change or not change (immediately, six months, one year, or several years)

Another aspect that is helpful in reviewing the key forces that may bring risk and uncertainty is to understand there are three possible levels of uncertainty to consider about each of the preceding forces. A clear trend is one that is known to be happening with certainty. An "unknown that is knowable" is a force or trend where current facts or information may not be known but it can be researched and become known. A residual uncertainty would be defined as a level of uncertainty that will not be able to be determined as the information will not be knowable during the current time frame, thus assumptions about its level of risk must be made. Based on Jennings (2000, 10–13), part of the strategic process must evaluate each of the identified risks and uncertainties by these three levels. Examples within HIM of these levels are

- Clear trends—moving from a paper medical record to the PHR
- Unknowns that are knowable—consumer preferences of the PHR

- Residual uncertainty—fate of IT companies that make PHRs

When assessing the levels of risk and uncertainty, it is important to understand that elements may be things the leaders won't really be able to totally understand or they may become clearer over time. It is important to decide whether it is important to continue tracking each of the risks or uncertainties or if they pass the "so what?" test. These levels of risk and uncertainty that seem important will be helpful to include in the next phase, which that focuses on tools for strategic thinking, especially the scenario-building exercise.

Tools for Strategic Thinking—Scenario Building

To bring out the best strategic thinking of a team or work group, it is often helpful to use techniques that help participants consider factors from different perspectives. A number of group process techniques such as brainstorming, nominal group technique, and others help unleash each individual's creative talent.

Storytelling is a powerful group process technique. Stories are defined as one way we transmit an organization's truths, insights, and commitments. Using compelling stories is a powerful way to persuade people by uniting an idea with an emotion. In a story, you not only weave a lot of information into the telling but also arouse your listener's emotions and energy. Essentially, a story expresses how and why life changes (McKee 2003). Telling stories about the future suggested by the external and internal assessment of trends has a number of advantages, including the following:

- More people are comfortable with this approach
- Findings can be presented in an understandable and real-world context
- Stories are memorable, making it easier for others to remember essential points
- Stories generate excitement and are fun to develop

One storytelling technique that is used in more sophisticated strategic planning is that of scenarios. The word *scenario* literally means a script of a play or story, or a projected sequence of events. **Scenarios** are "focused descriptions of fundamentally different futures presented in a coherent script-like or narrative fashion" (Schoemaker 1993, 193–213). They are plausible stories about how the future might unfold. They are not meant to predict but, rather, simply to interpret and clarify how environmental trends may play out.

Scenarios are based on analysis and interaction of environmental variables. Environmental assessment, along with risk and uncertainties, are important preparatory steps in scenario development. Based on study of the environment, two to four scenario themes, reflecting alternate possible futures using differing potentials around the key forces or risks and uncertainties described earlier, are developed. Stories or scenarios are constructed that describe how each of these themes might be played out. These scenarios or stories are refined through input and further study until they reflect the planning group's best thinking about what futures might be in store for the organization under various circumstances.

To understand how the clinical coding function might change in the future, an AHIMA task force studied environmental trends and developed four scenarios, each highlighting a slightly different, but plausible, future (Johns 2000, 26–33):

- The first scenario described the impact on coding if a breakthrough technology became available that would automate a great deal of the coding that is now being done manually or with the help of encoders.
- A second scenario described the impact on coding functions if healthcare organizations were strategically committed to using information to improve the quality of care information and hence the organization's strategic positioning.
- A third scenario involved the role of coding in an increasingly regulatory environment in which healthcare spending is ratcheted down and investments in technology are constrained.
- A fourth scenario involved greater consumer involvement in making healthcare decisions and maintaining personal health information.

One can quickly see that all are plausible scenarios. The future of coding will be affected by all these factors, but one or more may have a greater impact than others. Strategic managers would develop plans focused on the key strategic variables that may shape the future vision.

AHIMA also used scenarios to consider how medical transcription would be affected by technology. The steering group for this future project also prepared four likely future scenarios concerning medical transcription practice and a set of strategic actions to ensure that the field is well prepared to adapt regardless of which of the scenarios actually proves true (Fuller and Dennis 2005, 48–51).

The HIM professional should build a portfolio of techniques that a leader can use to bring out the best thinking of others; peruse the business shelves of major bookstores for guidebooks containing exercises and techniques to improve group process; observe techniques used by facilitators to improve how groups work and think together; and keep a notebook or computer file of such techniques and practice them whenever the opportunity arises. Effective strategic managers know how to facilitate groups to help them think and work well together.

Check Your Understanding 29.3

Instructions: Answer the following questions on a separate sheet of paper.

1. List four ways that you, as a leader, do external "environmental scanning" in your everyday life (for example, read the Sunday newspaper, belong to listservs, and so on).

2. Explain how—and how well—you, as a leader, stay in touch with new developments and trends in each of the following sectors:

   - Your community
   - Your healthcare organization
   - The industry and related industries
   - The nation

3. Identify two additional "external environmental assessment" activities that you can incorporate into your professional life that would help you improve your rating in exercise 3 by improving your grasp of the external environment.

4. In groups of four to six, reach consensus on the three most important ways that a new HIM professional can stay current with practice trends in HIM. You will need a flip chart and markers for this exercise.

   In your small group:

   - First, work quietly for five minutes to construct a personal list. Write your best ideas on a piece of paper.
   - Allow each member of the group to contribute one idea. Write each idea on the flip chart. Go around the group until all ideas have been contributed. Do not repeat identical ideas.
   - When all ideas have been contributed, ask the group to rate the importance of each idea using the following scale: 5 points for very important, 3 points for somewhat important, 1 point for minimally important, and 0 points for those suggestions you do not think are at all important.
   - Tally the scores of each rater to produce a total score per idea. Rewrite the ideas in order of the most to least important based on the group's rating scores.

Note: The group process technique used in this exercise is called the *nominal group technique*. Begin your facilitator's notebook with this technique.

Create a Platform for Strategic Innovation

Techniques such as scenario development and environmental assessment are useful in formulating strategy because they include a focus on both the internal and external environments. However, one should not expect to identify exciting new strategies by only looking at the past, looking inward, or looking within the healthcare industry. Take time to look outside the organization and industry; look to the future in formulating innovative strategy. New or innovative services or products come from identifying potential new needs based on determining the possible future scenarios that might occur. Look for innovations that will actually differentiate the organization's services or products from others. "Product or **service innovations** create new market opportunities, and in many industries are the driving force behind growth and profitability. **Process innovations** enable firms to produce existing products or services more efficiently. As such, process and service innovations are one of the main determinants of productivity growth" (Robert 1998, 45–46; emphasis added). It takes understanding the department's and organization's strategic capabilities and anticipating what future needs will come from reviewing and predicting future trends. It takes a willingness to be able to take risks and think strategically. For example, having access to personal health information on the Internet 24 hours a day is an innovation in healthcare. Many of the innovations in healthcare have come from unexpected stress (computerized dictation systems), research and development, and a willingness to test new services or products with the ultimate goal of improving the health of a population. The strategic plan needs to include time for thoughtful development of product, service, and process innovations.

From Vision to Strategy

As defined earlier, a strategy is an action or the set of actions that moves the organization toward its vision. Strategic management is about pursuing a new set of activities or prioritizing ways of carrying out current activities that move the organization toward its vision. It may take the form of new or redesigned programs or services. It may involve implementing new systems, outsourcing certain operations, or merging functions with another organizational entity. It also may entail phasing out an outdated program or adopting new technologies. Finally, it may be aimed at bringing an organization into compliance with new regulations or finding new ways to reduce operating costs.

It is important to remember that strategic management is not the same as operations improvement. Operations improvement is internally focused whereas strategic management seeks to improve the position of the organization in the broader world in which it operates.

To illustrate the thought process involved in moving from vision to strategy, consider the sample shown earlier in figure 29.2 based on the vision statement presented earlier in this chapter to move from a predominantly paper record to a digital record.

Understanding the Driving Force

The most important strategic thinking skill to understand prior to determining strategy is to understand the driving force of the department or organization. **Driving force** is the concept of what a department or an organization uses to determine which products or services to offer, which markets to seek, and which customers to attract (Robert 1998, 63–65). With intentional analysis, it is critical to understand the driving force or strategic drive that propels a department or an organization forward toward its vision.

After the internal and external assessments, decide if that same driving force should continue or if there is a strategic need to change to a different driving force to achieve the organization's vision. According to Robert, every organization is composed of 10 important strategic areas, or driving forces, but only one of these is strategically most important to the company and is the engine that propels, or drives, the company forward to success (Robert 1998, 64–65). For example, AHIMA's driving force is defined as a user or customer class organization that is strategically focusing its business around a describable and specific category of customers—HIM professionals. AHIMA responds by providing a wide variety of services and products that are aimed at this user class. Therefore, it is helpful to keep the key driving force in mind when it determines its future strategies. It becomes the major filter of determining what new strategies or initiatives will continue moving the organization toward its vision.

Defining Areas of Excellence

Once an organization identifies its "driving force," understanding and developing clear **areas of excellence** is another key concept of strategic thinking. This concept refers to a describable skill, competence, or capability that a department or company cultivates to a level of proficiency greater than anything else it does (Robert 1998, 109). To determine a strategic direction, the leader must develop a clear understanding of current key areas of excellence in the organization and what areas of excellence will be needed to achieve the new vision. Over time, the strategy of an organization, like a person, can become stronger and healthier or it can get weaker and sicker. What determines the future success of the strategy are the areas of excellence that a department or an organization deliberately cultivates to keep the strategy strong and healthy (Robert 1998, 109). For an HIM director, understanding special capabilities, such as managing the collection of patient and clinical quality data to improve quality of patient care, can be an important area of excellence. It becomes much easier to make difficult choices involving resources and time allocation if it is clear which strategies and areas of excellence are being pursued.

Strategic Management Implementation

Porter (1996, 61–78) advises that the "essence of strategy is deciding what not to do." He urges managers to view strategy as a series of trade-offs. Major change will impact current activities and may well require their modification or even elimination. No organization has the resources to take on major new programs without considering their impact on current programs. Making trade-offs is difficult for most managers. Letting go of even a marginal program may produce a backlash. However, resources must be reallocated to those programs that will enable the organization to operate at a new level of strategy.

Develop Strategic Findings and Conclusions

After reviewing all of the information from both internal and external assessments, a shared list of findings is developed with the strategic planning team. Based on these findings, the leader should determine if there are further informational needs or data points that will be important for developing a set of strategic findings and conclusions. Strategic findings and conclusions help solidify the new vision, driving force, and areas of excellence and lead to identifying key strategies for achieving the vision. After completing all of the aspects of strategic planning, the leaders will now need to put a strategic "stake in the ground" to move forward.

Defining Key Strategies

The next step in strategic planning is to develop and refine key strategies, aligned with the driving force and areas of excellence, needed to achieve the identified vision. For example, implementing the strategy "Acquire and implement electronic signature software" requires research about areas of excellence within technology vendors that offer software compatible with the clinical data repository.

Building a strategy grounded in a vision provides a context in which one can continually assess whether the organization is on track and if it is making progress. The AHIMA Board of Directors identified six key strategies in its future visioning session that were supported by the e-HIM vision and a deep understanding of the external environment. They were cast as transformative "from–to" statements, reflecting the key changes that AHIMA must lead over the next decade:

- From variable health record content and formats to standardization
- From passive responsiveness to vendors to system-building certification of offerings
- From exclusivity to inclusive membership driven by role, aspirations, and interests
- From academic-only to academic and performance-based certification
- From autonomy and self-sufficiency to working alliance with like-minded bodies
- From traditional leadership to governance adept at advancing change (AHIMA 2005).

It is important to look at the range of strategies being pursued to be clear about priorities, identify opportunities for synergy and integration, and identify strategies that no longer add value. When formulating strategies, question whether the leaders are getting too deeply into how something will be done. Remember that strategy is *what* the organization is going to do; goals and objectives are *how* the organization plans to do it.

Identify Critical Issues

Critical issues are the bridge between the current strategic profile and the future strategic vision and profile of a department or an organization that leadership has deliberately decided to pursue (Robert 1998, 165–168). The strategic direction of the organization has been decided, and this identification of critical issues is the beginning of managing in

the new direction, usually focused on four areas including structure, systems and processes, skills and competencies, and compensation (Robert 1998, 165).

Defining Strategic Goals and Strategic Objectives

The next step in strategic planning is to develop strategic goals and objectives to carry out each identified key strategy. For example, implementing the strategy "Acquire and implement electronic signature software" requires research about technology vendors that offer software compatible with the clinical data repository. It requires budgeting for this technology, securing support for the action plan, issuing an RFP, checking references, connectivity, and so on.

The Role of Strategic Goals

Strategic goals and objectives should not be confused with operational tactics or tactical planning. Often strategic plans are written as operational goals or objectives rather than at a strategic level. A **strategic goal** is defined as a long-term, continuous strategic area that identifies strategic objectives (key activities) that need to be performed to achieve the new organizational vision (Olsen 2006, 37). Strategic goals are needed to describe how to carry out each of the selected key strategies. For example, if the strategy is to have 95 percentile performance on timely billing to payers, the strategic goal might be to reduce the accounts receivable days attributable to coding backlogs, and strategic objectives may include authorizing overtime, hiring contract coders, and redesigning the record completion processes.

The Role of Strategic Objectives

Strategic objectives are more detailed ways to meet a strategic goal and include timelines, resource allocation needs, and assigning responsibility of who will be accountable for implementation. From the example, the strategic objectives would state, in more detail, the person responsible and the action steps of how to authorize more overtime, who and how to hire the contract coders, and who and how the record completion process will be redesigned. For example, for the strategic objective of hiring contract coders, the objective would state who the organization will be contracting with, how many contract coders are needed, the timelines for implementation, and who is responsible for making it happen.

Check Your Understanding 29.4

Instructions: Complete the following steps on a separate piece of paper.

1. Prepare a template for the strategy worksheet shown in figure 29.3 using your PC word-processing or presentation software (Microsoft Word or PowerPoint). Complete the figure using real sources of uncertainty that will impact the vision you outlined in Check Your Understanding 29.2.

2. Select AHIMA's vision statement to identify the organization's driving force and one key area of excellence. Then describe the strategy to achieve that area of excellence in one or two sentences.

3. In the space provided on the form, write at least two strategic goals that would need to be pursued to address the preceding identified strategy.

4. Identify one or more strategic objectives that would need to be implemented to move toward each strategic goal.

Importance of Implementation and Action Plans

In order for any strategic plan to become effective and to ensure a successful implementation plan, detailed strategic goals and objectives must be written and supported by those responsible for the implementation. (See figure 29.4.) This requires having involvement in design and understanding of the rationale for and the outline of detailed responsibilities and expectations required of all leaders and staff in the department or organization. The strategic goals and objectives need to be clearly outlined, with assignments for who will be accountable, timelines, allocation of resources, and measurements that will be used to track success of implementation.

Customer Role in Strategic Thinking

An important part of strategic planning that is often overlooked, yet vital to developing effective strategy, is the role of the customer. Traditional ways of collecting customer information include consumer focus groups, patient advisory boards, and patient surveys. If designed correctly, these tools can be effective in gathering information within the proper context of strategic planning. Unfortunately, the strategic planning process often ignores customers, users, and suppliers or involves them too late to provide effective feedback. In the case of the PHR, it would mean involving patients and their families in the design of the strategies, strategic goals and objectives, and implementation plan for the PHR. During this process, the organization would begin to understand needs and expectations from the customers' perspective. It becomes easier to develop ways to provide a truly innovative product and service. These customers are often readily available, whether it involves using volunteers, staff members, or their family members who are customers of the PHR. Also, physicians and office staff who get calls from patients on a regular basis are well versed in understanding what their customers want and need.

Determine Impact of Competition

Developing ways to understand the department's or organization's competitors is also valuable during the strategic planning process. Innovations or changes are also being planned by the competition. Take time to understand what the organization's key competitor's current and potential strengths and weaknesses are. The organization's strategies should be developed in order to have the most influence on increasing its market share. Once the manager has selected a strategic direction, he or she should take time to evaluate

Figure 29.4.   Detailed implementation plan

	Strategy #1: Transcribed reports currently become part of the EHR through scanning only; content is not in digital form.
Strategic Goal	**Strategic Objectives**	**Implementation Plan**	**Measurements**
A. Physicians are able to review and modify dictated reports online within 3rd quarter of fiscal year.	1. Implement electronic signature software. 2. Design and pilot test a process whereby physicians can authenticate, make changes to, and reassign a transcribed report online. 3. Design a phased plan for implementation of online physician review that is coordinated with the availability of online access to electronic reports.	TIMELINE: RFP—First Quarter Purchased by 2nd Quarter Installed by 3rd Quarter WHO'S RESPONSIBLE: HIM Supervisor and IT Supervisor RESOURCE NEEDS: Capital and Operating budget support, 0.5 FTE Medical Staff HIM Committee	Physicians' dictation achieved: By Q3 = 100% By Q4 = 75% Physician Quality Survey of Dictation System: Score 4.0–5 = 100% Score 3.5–3.99 = 80% Score 3.0–3.49 = 60%
B. Voice recognition converts dictated reports to digital information for storage in the EHR	1. Implement voice recognition in the emergency, cardiac cath, and imaging departments. 2. Upgrade the EHR to accept input from voice recognition in structured reports. 3. Design and pilot test a plan for storing output in the EHR.	TIMELINE: 1st quarter WHO'S RESPONSIBLE: HIM Transcription Manager, Departmental reps from ER, CC, and Imaging RESOURCE NEEDS: Capital and Operating budget	Voice recognition conversion in place: Q1 = 100% Q2 = 75%

and anticipate any impact that competitors, current or future, might have on the strategy.

Support for the Change Program

Sound change strategies and tactics alone do not ensure success. Success depends on great execution, including securing support for the needed organizational change efforts. Healthcare organizations are highly complex with many competing priorities. Gaining approval, even for the best-designed efforts, may be difficult.

An experienced HIM director with support from the IT director tried for three consecutive budget cycles to get funding for a document-imaging program. The request was accompanied by a solid return on investment (ROI) picture in terms of reductions in full-time equivalents, cost of storage, and increased productivity. In year four, the director tied the request not merely to how change would affect the HIM service but also to how it would support improved access to health information, reduce errors caused by illegibility, and improve communication among caregivers. In light of the Joint Commission's patient safety goals, the HIM director enlisted the help of nursing leadership to make the budget case. Nursing spoke to how this solution would improve access to information at the patient care bedside and would help link various electronic documentation systems already in place. The caregivers stressed the need to link the systems to help them do their jobs better. By taking this approach, the document-imaging system was presented to the board of directors by the organization's Patient Safety Council chairperson and was approved by the board without hesitation.

Take a Systems Approach

According to Tichy (1983), "the development of change strategy involves simultaneous attention to three [organizational] systems—technical, political, and cultural." The technical systems are concerned with the business we are in and how we conduct that business (for example, the process we use to manage patient information). Political systems involve the distribution of power and influence in the organization (for example, the authority of the medical staff, the approval and decision-making processes within an organization). Cultural systems are the style and values that define how the organization typically operates.

Major change may throw the organization into chaos as existing systems are deliberately unglued. This is a time of great vulnerability, and managers must be vigilant, watching for and thoughtfully addressing unintended effects that could make it difficult to achieve realignment. Managers must be sensitive to the very real emotional relationships among individuals in a group and how change will affect relationships between individuals and between the manager and others. Times of change

are times of high stress and anxiety. This may play out in a number of ways. For example, in times of great change, employees may be more inclined to look for other employment opportunities as it is threatening and unsettling to go through change. Some turnover in staff may be an acceptable and unavoidable result, but the manager should be attentive and sensitive so that turnover does not derail the ability to carry out the project.

The technical, political, and cultural systems are highly interdependent, and any change will have intended and unintended impact on all three systems. For example, when implementing new technology such as EHRs or other major systems, the focus is often on features and functions of the system. Securing the right champions for the system and understanding how it affects the work and formal and informal interactions of staff are more challenging and important to successful implementation than the features and functions. The successful strategic manager leading wide-scale technology change will be the one who excels at helping people get behind and involved in the change. The manager who focuses only or primarily on installing the hardware and software will not succeed. Managers should not let these challenges keep them from pursuing the strategies their organization needs. However, success will depend on how well change is managed from a systems perspective. The manager must attend to all three identified system aspects throughout the implementation process. He or she also should be aware that implementation is not complete until all three systems are back in a new alignment after the changes are in place.

Create the Structure for Change

Organizational structure is an important element to ensure success of the change process. Once a new vision and strategies are determined, the current structure should be reviewed and focus placed on how to best restructure, if needed, to achieve the new vision. Structure is an organizational function often overlooked and yet important to successful implementation. As strategic goals and objectives are identified, the goals and objectives are assigned to a leader. Another important aspect of consideration regarding structure is where the department is positioned within the structure of the organization. This placement in the structure and strategy is important to understanding how allocation of resources and capital will be made. The importance of structure for accomplishing an organization's strategic goals and objectives should not be underestimated.

Manage the Politics of Change

Organizational change is a political process. Change leadership requires the courage to persevere even in the face of criticism; however, plowing ahead without considering the political implications may be folly. According to

Bryson (1999, 225), managing the politics of change requires "finding ideas (visions, goals, strategies) that people can support and that further their interests . . . and making deals in which something is traded in exchange for that support."

Political savvy entails skill in mediating and shaping conflicts that are inevitable when people are offered real choices with real consequences. Deliberately enlist the support of thought and opinion leaders. Reach out to those who may be most threatened by the proposed change; do not wait for them to come to you. Early engagement may turn potential resisters into supporters. At the very least, it will help change leaders build their arguments and communication plan to address the concerns of those who oppose the change.

Coalition building is one technique for managing the political dimensions of change. Change may threaten to shift the balance of power, and employees or coworkers who feel threatened may react by joining together to increase their own power so as to influence the course of events. Coalitions can be a force for thwarting change, or leaders can use coalition building as a way to build support for change. The example of the manager who gained the support of nursing to move ahead on the document management system project illustrates the power of coalition building.

The first step in building a coalition is to honestly assess subgroups in terms of how they will view the proposed change. Before embarking on a major change, the following questions should be considered carefully:

- Who will be most affected by the change?
- What benefits (for example, power) might these individuals perceive they will lose?
- Are their fears real? If so, what options are available to help overcome their fears?
- Does the change have the potential to create new benefits for these individuals?
- Can a negative reaction be avoided by engaging individuals or groups in the process?
- If the leader is not successful in getting them on board, is their influence likely to be strong enough to derail the change plan?

Even when a leader is not successful in getting resisters on board, he or she will have better information about the strength of their feelings and their resolve to oppose change. At the same time, leaders are always working to diffuse potential resistance and to focus on building support for the change.

Create a Sense of Urgency

Kotter (1995, 59–67) asserts that "by far the biggest mistake people make when trying to change organizations is to plunge ahead without establishing a high enough sense of urgency. Leaders may overestimate the extent to which they can force or drive change on the organization.

To increase the sense of urgency, leaders must remove or minimize the sources of complacency. Some examples of how this might be done include the following:

- Engage employees, customers, and coworkers in a dialogue about change through a series of meetings (participate in the SWOT analysis)
- Convene a project steering committee with representatives from all stakeholder groups
- Identify opinion leaders and secure their support early
- Present believable stories or scenarios that illustrate the potential futures that may occur if action is not taken
- Create new vehicles for communication, such as a project newsletter

Communicate, Communicate, Communicate

Communication is key to engaging others in the vision and change process. DePree (1992, 100) sums it up by saying that "if you're a leader and you are not sick and tired of communicating you probably aren't doing a good enough job".

A benchmarking study of how companies have successfully communicated change showed that communication is critical at three stages of the change process: as it is being planned, throughout implementation, and after it is complete (Powers 1997, 30–33). Effective communication was shown to be critical at each stage, even to the point of releasing partial information when details are incomplete.

At the planning stage, leaders should communicate the need for change and the vision. Remember, if followers do not accept the vision, the rest of the change process is likely to be very rocky. Communicating results, even when they are incomplete, is an important reinforcement. It makes the change real and maintains the necessary momentum.

Communication is most effective if the message is tailored to the recipient. The leader identifies needs and opportunities to customize the organization's message to subgroups that have a particular set of issues. For example, the message to the medical staff will be different from the message to staff in health information services. Before implementing the use of report templates to expedite dictation, the manager may design a tactical plan that details all the elements of the communication plan for each of the constituent groups affected by, or with an interest in, the project.

The communication plan must offer groups the opportunity to "talk back." Kotter reminds us that the "downside of two-way communication is that feedback may suggest that you are on the wrong course and that the vision and plans need to be reformulated. But in the long run, swallowing your pride and reworking the vision and plan is far more productive than heading off in the wrong direction—or in a direction that others won't follow" (Kotter 2002, 100).

Communication comes in two forms—words and actions—and the most effective communication is characterized by deeds. Behavior from important people that is inconsistent with the vision overwhelms other forms of communication (Kotter 2002, 90). Leaders become the symbols for the change. Their motivations may be questioned and their actions scrutinized. Others will watch the leaders' actions for signals of commitment to the course of action and rightly insist on their integrity.

Ethics and integrity must be front and center all the time, but particularly during times of important change. At these times, the political, cultural, and technical systems are out of alignment. There is opportunity for events to take unexpected turns. Leaders' actions are closely scrutinized and their motives may be suspect.

Implementing Strategic Change

Once a vision and strategies are designed, the change management team is in place, and the guiding coalitions are organized, the hard work of implementation begins. Implementation requires all the managerial skills described in chapter 23, including planning, budgeting, monitoring, and producing results.

Create and Communicate Short-Term Wins

Major change takes time. The organization's vision may be compelling and its strategies right on target, but if short-term results cannot be demonstrated, the leaders may lose support and the momentum for change may begin to erode. The best way to sustain change efforts is to sequence the implementation plan through strategic objectives and goals in such a way that short-term successes are clearly demonstrated and celebrated. For example, in implementing a new compliance plan, the data quality manager for a group practice reported statistics to the chiefs of service showing the monthly claims rejection rate. As this rate began to decline, the manager organized special events such as a dessert party and recognition event for office managers and staff at each improvement milestone. These touches garnered attention and maintained momentum for the project.

The implementation plan can be deliberately seeded with a number of short-term objectives and goals that have a high likelihood of success. This tactic enables the implementation team to work together to assess how much effort and how many resources will be required for later phases. It demonstrates that the program of planned change is real and not just talk. Moreover, it strengthens the courage and commitment of the leaders and the guiding coalitions.

New programs can be launched quickly by using techniques such as rapid prototyping, demonstration projects, or pilot tests. The details do not always need to be fully worked out to create visible demonstrations. The leader may not need to secure approval for full implementation, as testing an approach to see its value is often accepted as a pilot.

In test mode, all operational details do not need to be worked out before "going live." The leader need not anticipate all the intricacies up front but should just begin the journey and adjust as he or she is implementing the pilot stage. Prototyping and pilot tests also offer a way to show others how redesigned processes or new technology might work when fully implemented.

Check Your Understanding 29.5

Instructions: Complete the following exercises on a separate sheet of paper.

1. Describe two ways to utilize structure and coalition building to achieve more successful strategy implementation.

2. Describe three ways to communicate to others how the selected strategy could maintain the momentum for achieving the vision.

3. Think back to an experience when you were involved in an organizational or personal change (for example, new computer program implemented at the company where you worked last summer; a committee you were on that was planning an event or a new program). Describe two events or actions that advanced the change agenda (for example, all employees were given a half-day of training and a gift for completing the training course) and two events that impeded it.

Pace and Refine Change Plans

Implementation requires managing interdependent projects at various stages of design, development, and deployment. A difficult implementation challenge is deciding what phases should be advanced first and how fast or slow to move through them. Sequencing and pacing change requires thorough knowledge of the organization and its capacity for change, again considering all organizational components—cultural, political, and technical—and the available financial and managerial resources.

The higher the stakes, the more likely it is that a proposed change will be controversial. If the only viable approach is likely to meet with resistance, more time and effort are needed up front to gain acceptance before the approach is implemented. The importance of two-way communication throughout the process cannot be overemphasized.

The timing of change is critical. Change leaders can cite examples of projects that moved too quickly and projects that moved too slowly. Lawrence sums up this challenge: "I have become convinced that the real art of leadership lies in careful pacing. Pacing means moving simultaneously in a variety of areas and keeping each area progressing so that the combined cadence does not tear the organization apart. I'm positive that nobody gets timing 100 percent right. But the winners do it less wrong" (Lawrence 1998, 291–308).

Implementation is a process of guiding, adjusting, and improving as the plan moves forward. "Invariably, the organizational, strategic and leadership choices made during the earlier phases are only partially informed. As experience and events provide feedback to the organization, adjustments are almost always called for" (Walton 1998, 347–366).

Implementing change is a highly iterative process. Leaders should expect that their plans and tactics will need to be modified as they gain experience. They should create budgets and timetables that permit frequent course corrections.

Maintain Momentum and Stay the Course

Because leading change is a process of learning and adjusting, change leaders must learn to tolerate—and even enjoy—uncertainty. Change sponsors are eager to see their well-crafted strategies take hold and inevitably feel discouraged by a lengthy process. In addition to celebrating short-term wins, other ways to maintain momentum and keep moving include the following:

- Work quickly to resolve the thorny issues.
- Reiterate what will happen if change either does not occur or is watered down by compromise. If possible, focus on the consequences due to external trends.
- Keep focused on the prize. Put every action in context. Regularly revisit the vision, strategies, goals, and objectives to regenerate a sense of purpose. Help others by making the goals as tangible as possible.
- Remember that resistance to change is natural. Do not take it personally.
- Rethink the tactics, sequence, and pace regularly to keep from getting bogged down. If momentum slows, institute actions that will produce short-term gains. Keep moving forward.
- Maintain the sense of urgency. Although it is important to celebrate short-term wins, do not let these celebrations mitigate the sense of urgency the organization has created. Also, do not let intermediate gains be mistaken for the bigger goals.

For maximum and sustained impact, the change being introduced must become part of the fabric of the organization. It must become the way the organization operates, thinks, and behaves. At some point, it must become part of the culture. Even after change is implemented, there often continues to be a tug backward toward the old reality. So strong is the effect of culture, leaders should be on the lookout for signs of slippage and for opportunities to reinforce the value of the new reality. To ensure that change is lasting and to prepare the organization for more change, leaders should

- Quantify the impact, benefits, and value of the changes and use data to identify the direction for future change
- Continue intensive communication on issues facing HIM and the organization

- Integrate change competencies and behaviors into performance appraisal and management development programs
- Approach strategy, change, and organizational development as a continuous process

Measure Your Results

Environmental assessment was shown to be an important prerequisite to launching major change. It is also the way to measure the impact of change and to determine what further change is needed. Any time strategic change is undertaken, the measures by which its success will be judged should be made part of the performance measures data set. Environmental assessment, both internal and external, must become a core competency of the organization and part of its routine work. It need not be an elaborate system, but it should be systematic and ongoing and it must include information on performance, trends, attitudes, and satisfaction.

Once the key strategies are identified, a strategy map is designed that begins with a brief description of the current state and the desired future state. A **strategy map** is a tool that provides a visual representation of an organization's critical strategies and the relationships among them that drive organizational performance toward its vision (Norton et al. 2000, 2, 55). Two sample strategy maps are shown in figures 29.5 and 29.6. Depicting strategies as a road map is a useful way to help others understand the next steps of implementation, which focuses on developing strategic goals and objectives to lead to the needed strategy change.

The **balanced scorecard methodology** is a technique for measuring organizational performance across the following four perspectives (Kaplan and Norton 2004, 31):

- *Customer perspective:* To achieve the vision, how should the organization appear to internal and external customers?
- *Financial perspective:* How must the organization be held financially accountable?
- *Internal process perspective:* To satisfy customers, which operational processes must the organization excel at?
- *Learning and growth perspective:* How will the organization enhance its ability to change and improve?

A strategy map enables examination of the cause-and-effect relationships among the preceding perspectives. Figure 29.6 shows a sample balanced scorecard using these four perspectives based on a strategy map for improving the real and perceived value of HIM services. Refer to figure 29.4 to view a sample detailed implementation plan using the balanced scorecard methodology to demonstrate how a strategy is more clearly defined using a strategic goal, strategic objective, implementation plan, and measurements.

Figure 29.5.   Strategy map: From variable health record content and formats to standardization

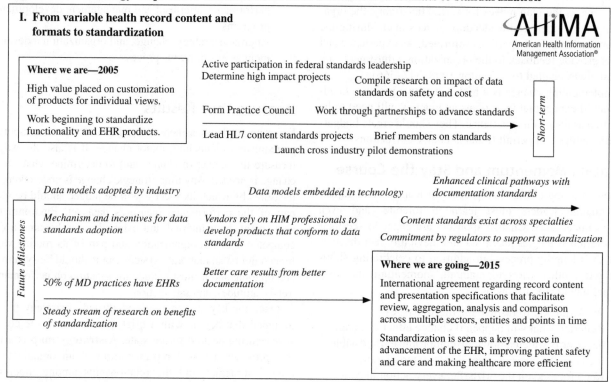

Source: Kloss 2006.

Figure 29.6.   Balanced scorecard with strategy map

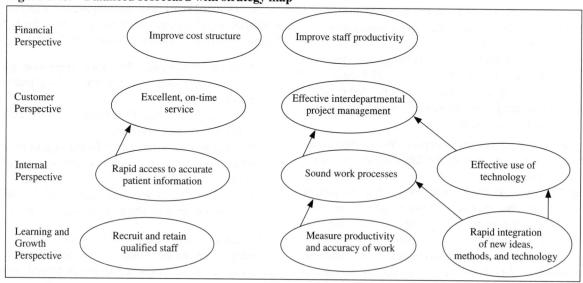

Source: Kloss 2006.

Summary

HIM is a dynamic profession that offers great opportunities to advance and contribute in a variety of important roles. Professional coursework has required that HIM leaders consider the attributes of a professional and the responsibilities of professionalism. In this book, readers have learned about managing systems, resources, and people. This chapter introduces them to the HIM professional as a strategic leader and thinker, a role that probably does not feel comfortable to all managers.

In truth, it will require experience to perfect the skills of strategic management, and it will require a commitment to lifelong learning. One of the first ways to apply the lessons of this chapter is to evaluate options for entry-level positions as an HIM professional.

In the course of interviewing for positions, look closely at the organizational environment to identify evidence that constructive change is valued. What is the organization's strategic focus? Does its culture value idea sharing and innovation? What is the vision for HIM services? What is the political environment, and how are decisions made? Are there any examples of change projects that have been very successful? Have any change projects failed? What lessons were learned from successful or failed projects?

Even seasoned managers are learning and improving their abilities every day. There is no such thing as a master manager who knows it all. What is important is to keep the lessons in mind as one gains experience and grows in confidence as a strategic manager. This chapter has explored the following five lessons (Bryson 1995, 225):

Lesson 1: Leading change is more than a process to be managed; it is a way of thinking and acting.

Managing change is a central strategic challenge for all organizations. The challenge may be even greater in healthcare organizations because their cultures tend to be averse to change and their governance structures and decision-making processes are more complicated than those of the typical business organization. Leading change requires a vision, and it often requires building new organizational capabilities, such as environmental scanning, creative group process, and a more external focus.

Lesson 2: Leading change must be approached as a central and fundamental role of all managers.

The best way to learn how to become more strategic is just to begin. Leading change requires creativity and imagination grounded in good information, managerial competence, and effective decision making. Do not expect to get it exactly right the first time, the second time, or any time. It is better to make mistakes than to take no risks. As lessons are learned, they should be chronicled so that the "learning loop" helps improve future decisions.

Lesson 3: Effective change happens only after others are engaged in a meaningful and personal way and their acceptance is earned.

All change is ultimately about increasing effectiveness. To be successful, a leader must first understand what the customers want and need and how to deliver real value. This requires information and continuous two-way communication about issues, ideas, and trends. Acceptance for change strategies must be earned. Leaders must be politically savvy, learning to communicate the rationale for change, the expected results, and the consequences of no action. They must be sensitive to the fact that it takes time to disseminate a change message and for the message to be assimilated at a personal level. Change projects should move at a deliberate pace, but a pace that takes the needs of others into account.

Lesson 4: Successful organizations will have a bias for action because learning to lead change is a by-product of leading successful change.

A bias for preserving the status quo is strong in most organizations. This must be replaced with a bias for action. Leading change is a learning process, and success increases the sense of possibility and the excitement to tackle the next challenge. Organizations that are on the move are energized, and their employees, coworkers, superiors, and customers feel this energy. Learning to lead change is an essential skill in today's fast-paced world of work.

Lesson 5: There is great opportunity for HIM professionals who understand that leadership, change, and learning are intertwined.

Our society talks a great deal about leadership, change, and learning. What is only now becoming clear is that these concepts are really intertwined. As Beer and colleagues (1993, 217) state, "One cannot contemplate dramatic change occurring within an organization without the exercise of some leadership. And the organization does not change fundamentally without significant reorientation and learning by its leaders and members. Without learning, the attitudes, skills, and behavior needed to formulate and implement a new strategic task will not develop." The goal is to reorient organizations to value strategic thinking that includes innovation and change. This takes time, perseverance, and courage. Nonetheless, this is the goal strategic managers should have for the organizations they are privileged to lead.

References

Abrahams, J. 1999. *The Mission Statement Book*. Berkeley, CA: Ten Speed Press.

American Health Information Management Association. 2012. The vision, mission, and values of the American Health Information Management Association. http://www.ahima.org/about/mission.aspx.

American Health Information Management Association. 2005. AHIMA Strategic Directions. Chicago: AHIMA.

American Health Information Management Association. 2004 (June). Study: Employment of HIM professionals in the U.S.: Current patterns and future prospects. Chicago: AHIMA.

Beer, M., R.A. Eisenstat, et al. 1993. Why change programs don't produce change. In *The Learning Imperative: Managing People for Continuous Innovation.* Edited by R. Howard. Boston: Harvard Business School Press.

Bryson, J.M. 1995. *Strategic Planning for Public and Nonprofit Organizations,* rev. ed. San Francisco: Jossey-Bass.

DePree, M. 1992. *Leadership Jazz.* New York: Dell.

Drucker, P. 1996. Not enough generals were killed. In *The Leader of the Future.* Edited by F. Hesselbein and M. Goldsmith. San Francisco: Jossey-Bass.

Dunn, R.T. 2007. *Haimann's Healthcare Management,* 8th ed. Chicago: Health Administration Press.

Fuller, S.R., and J. Callahan Dennis. 2005. Transcription's future(s): AAMT and AHIMA outline scenarios for the years ahead. *Journal of AHIMA* 76(7): 48–51.

Gavetti, G., and J.W. Rivkin. 2005. How strategists really think: Tapping the power of analogy. *Harvard Business Review* 83(4): 54–63.

Jennings, M.C. 2000. *Health Care Strategy for Uncertain Times.* San Francisco: Jossey-Bass.

Johns, M. 2000. A crystal ball for coding. *Journal of AHIMA* 71(1): 26–33.

Kaplan, R.S., and D.P. Norton. 2004. *Strategy Maps: Converting Intangible Assets into Tangible Outcomes.* Boston: Harvard Business School Press.

Kemp, E., R. Funk, and D. Eadie. 1993. Change in chewable bites: Applying strategic management at EEOC. *Public Administration Review,* 130.

Kloss, L. L. 2006. "Chapter 28: Strategic Management." Health Information Management: Concepts, Principles and Practices. Chicago: AHIMA.

Kolb, D.A. 1988. Integrity, advanced professional development, and learning. In *Executive Integrity.* Edited by S. Srivastra. San Francisco: Jossey-Bass.

Kotter, J.P. 2002. *Heart of Change: Real-Life Stories of How People Change Their Organizations.* Boston: Harvard Business School Press.

Kotter, J.P. 1995. Leading change: why transformation efforts fail. *Harvard Business Review* 73(2): 59–67.

Kouzes, J.M., and B.Z. Posner. 1995. *The Leadership Challenge: How to Keep Getting Extraordinary Things Done in Organizations.* San Francisco: Jossey-Bass.

Lawrence, D.M. 1998. Leading discontinuous change: Ten lessons from the battlefront. In *Navigating Change.* Edited by D.C. Hambrick, D.A. Nadler, and M.L. Tushman. Boston: Harvard Business School Press.

Luke, R.D., S.L. Walstrom, and P.M. Plummey. 2004 *Healthcare Strategy: In Pursuit of Competitive Advantage.* Chicago: Health Administration Press.

McKee, R. 2003 (June). Storytelling that moves people: A conversation with screenwriting coach Robert McKee. *Harvard Business Review* 81(6).

Norton, R., S. Kaplan, and P. David. 2000 (September-October). Having trouble with your strategy? Then map it. *Harvard Business Review* 78. http://hbr.org/2000/09/having-trouble-with-your-strategy-then-map-it/ar/6.

Olsen, E. 2006. *Strategic Planning for Dummies.* Indianapolis: John Wiley & Sons.

Porter, M.E. 1996. What is strategy? *Harvard Business Review* 74(6): 61–78.

Powers, V.J. 1997. Benchmarking study illustrates how best-in-class achieve alignment, communicate change. *Communication World* 14(2): 30–33.

Robert, M. 1998. *Strategy Pure and Simple II.* New York: McGraw-Hill.

Schoemaker, P.J.H. 1993. Multiple scenario development: Its conceptual and behavioral foundation. *Strategic Management Journal* 14: 193–213.

Tichy, N.M. 1983. *Managing Strategic Change: Technical, Political and Cultural Dynamics.* New York: John Wiley & Sons.

Walton, E. 1998. Senior leadership and discontinuous change. In *Navigating Change.* Edited by D.C. Hambrick, D.A. Nadler, and M.L. Tushman. Boston: Harvard Business School Press.

chapter 30

Envisioning the Future of the Health Information Management Profession

Bonnie S. Cassidy, MPA, RHIA, FAHIMA, FHIMSS, 2011 President of AHIMA

Introduction

The first decade of the 21st century has been a turbulent time in the health information management (HIM) profession as the healthcare industry has embarked on some of the greatest transformations in the history of the US healthcare system. The steady stream of change in healthcare and the rapid shift of paradigms challenge and expand the traditional HIM role as the medical record custodian and keeper of clinical information. This necessitates a transformation in the HIM professional. The medical record will cease to be a tangible product or tool as it becomes electronic. Information accuracy and content will continue to be critical; however, clinical information will become intellectual property, organizational capital, and competitive intelligence. Payers, providers, researchers, lawyers, and regulators will require credible information to create knowledge that provides sustainable competitive advantages for their organizations.

These changes have directly impacted health information practice and cannot be done successfully without HIM best practices and leadership. To build best practices and influence policy, the HIM profession is called upon to articulate lessons learned from the implementation of electronic medical records, ICD-10-CM/PCS planning and training, actions taken to achieve meaningful use (MU), computer-assisted coding initiatives, advances in health information exchange, and the introduction of patient-centered care models such as the medical (healthcare) home and accountable care organizations (ACOs).

The HIM profession continues to grow and change, becoming highly visible in the national arena as federal laws have evolved to protect patient privacy, to advance technologies that collect and maintain patient data accurately and securely, to adopt classification systems to increase the quality of data in clinical documentation, and to encourage the use of electronic health records as the primary source for monitoring quality of care. This chapter addresses the role of the American Health Information Management Association (AHIMA) as a thought leadership organization that sets strategy on health information governance and influences current and future initiatives that impact the quality of healthcare data and information. As the healthcare industry transitions to new models of care delivery and meaningful use of health information technologies, the opportunities for the HIM profession are wide-ranging and span healthcare, business, governmental, and many other environments beyond the clinical realm.

The e-HIM Transition

With the widespread adoption of electronic health records and other technology-based information sources and the use of electronically available data for healthcare management measurement purposes, research functions, and governmental initiatives, health informatics and health information technology are being increasingly utilized in HIM practices in the healthcare industry (Cassidy 2011a).

AHIMA has grown to be a thriving association with over 64,000 members, and all HIM professionals now collaborate and learn from each other to strengthen the HIM leadership position in the healthcare industry. AHIMA sought to develop a world-class set of bylaws that strategically align all entities to deliver member value; incorporate association best practices; and comply with the evolution of corporate, federal, and state law. AHIMA has set the course for the 21st century with a renewed focus on governance. The AHIMA Board of Directors sets strategy. In 2011, the AHIMA bylaws were

Figure 30.1.   Key roles of the AHIMA Board of Directors and the AHIMA House of Delegates

Board of Directors	House of delegates
Fiduciary responsibility	Set code of ethics
Strategy development and oversight	Conduct environmental scanning
Authority over governing documents	Vet professional and practice issues, proposed resolutions
Fiscal and financial management	Recommend action to the board

rewritten to reflect the strategic thinking for future generations of HIM professionals. By design, AHIMA has clearly articulated in the bylaws that the Board of Directors governs the association and the House of Delegates governs the HIM profession (Cassidy 2011b). See figure 30.1 for the key roles of the AHIMA Board of Directors and the AHIMA House of Delegates.

As the American healthcare industry moves forward with health information technology (HIT) adoption, providers need the skills and expertise of health information management professionals to support the implementation and achievement of MU of electronic health records. The migration to electronic health records (EHRs) changes the design and operations of traditional HIM departments. These changes add complexity to the management of health information. HIM professionals are now assuming new responsibilities that, in addition to a solid foundation in health data and information systems concepts and principles, require advanced education and experience in leadership and management skills, as well as a solid understanding of the capabilities of information technologies. Roles will continue to evolve, and opportunities await HIM professionals who evaluate and enhance their expertise to keep pace with changing practice.

AHIMA continues to influence policy and position HIM professionals as the qualified experts in EHR clinical content in the industry today. In this transition to e-HIM, HIM professionals serve a broad range of roles in planning, organizing, and managing clinical content, integrity, accessibility, use, and protection. HIM professionals are now project managers who identify work process improvements, employ implementation techniques, and lead efforts to redefine information management practices in healthcare organizations. HIM professionals work at the convergence of people, processes, regulations, organizational structure, standards, and system design.

Given the magnitude of change occurring in the ways health information systems and technology are deployed within organizations, expectations of executives make it clear that the HIM department is responsible for the successful creation of the emerging digital and virtual HIM department

(Cassidy 2011a). HIM professionals are transforming all HIM functions to e-HIM functions. The role of the HIM professional is growing toward being an effective change agent and champion for EHR deployment. With the emergence of electronic systems, the HIM department has a greater capability to be virtual, employing and contracting with off-site staff to create the strongest team possible. HIM professionals are analyzing and visualizing both documented and undocumented intradepartmental and interdepartmental information management functions to understand the current and envision (or establish) the future state of the HIM services within the organization, while ensuring that HIM best practices and standards in such areas as privacy, the legal health record, data quality, and information integrity are consistently maintained.

AHIMA's top 10 tenets for managing the transition from paper to EHRs, shown in figure 30.2, are critical to the successful evolution of managing health information. Transitioning health information services to this virtual environment offers many operational and financial advantages. New HIM roles will be prominent and positioned throughout a healthcare organization: for example, project managers, EHR system managers, and workflow and data analysts. Privacy coordinators, different from privacy officers, will act as directors, creating policy, implementing programs, and directing goals. At the same time, the health information department will continue to serve as the primary location for ensuring the quality of documentation in the patient record, maintaining the organization's legal patient record, responding to authorized requests for release of patient information, and envisioning new and as yet unseen roles that will be necessary to the effective management of health information in the future. Some examples of developing and anticipated new roles are information technology, information workflow designer, data exchange manager, EHR content manager, enterprise master patient index (EMPI) data integrity analyst, corporate record manager, clinical data analyst, and health information exchange (HIE) privacy gatekeeper. See chapter 4 for an expanded discussion of roles and responsibilities. However, every HIM function performed to support the paper health record today will be reengineered. This will challenge HIM directors and managers to not only manage new workflow processes but, for geographically diverse integrated healthcare systems and to enable interoperability, do so remotely. For it to be successful, this transformation to the virtual management of health information requires active engagement of healthcare executives in support of their HIM teams (Cassidy 2011a).

Changing Times: HIM and ICD-10-CM/PCS

How well the healthcare industry implements and executes the strategic and tactical tasks for the ICD-10-CM/PCS, ICD-11, and SNOMED CT transformation will go a long way in determining the future state and success of the HIM profession. HIM involvement with disease classifications

Figure 30.2. Top 10 tenets for transitioning from paper to electronic health records

1. The EHR must be part of an organization's vision and strategic plan. As part of this plan, the organization should have a standard definition for the legal health record.

2. The organization must ensure that adequate leadership, consultation, staff training, equipment, policies and procedures, and funding or other resources are in place to support EHR development.

3. Organizations must establish a legal health record steering committee to guide the organization from a paper to an electronic environment. This group must be empowered to make proactive and constructive changes. Its members should include department managers from health information management; risk, quality, or compliance management; medical staff; nursing; ancillary departments; IT; and the privacy officer.

4. The legal health record steering committee must develop and publish policies and procedures for operating in the paper state, hybrid state, and electronic state and include long-term archive, purge, retention, and destruction guidelines.

5. HIM professionals must participate actively in the development and implementation of the EHR, given the significant operational management effects on workflow within HIM and their role as custodians of the legal health record.

6. There must be a formal process for approving EHR software and hardware to ensure that it can support the organization's operational needs adequately for the paper, hybrid, and electronic medical record.

7. There must be a formal process for managing forms, paper, electronic, hybrid, and system-generated records, including input, output, and versioning of document content and access.

8. There must be a formal process and written guidelines addressing access, confidentiality, security, print control, spoliation mitigation, disclosure, and e-discovery.

9. A complete record inventory of all existing storage and management of paper, hybrid, shadow (duplicate), and electronic records must be maintained by all healthcare organizations.

10. The facility must develop a policy for retention and destruction of medical records, regardless of whether paper, hybrid, or electronic medical records are used.

Source: AHIMA 2010b.

and nomenclatures can be traced back to the early 20th century. The HIM profession has been the recognized expert and leader in data collection, classification, and reporting since Grace Whiting Myers, founder of the association known today as AHIMA, served on the Committee on Uniform Nomenclature, which developed a disease classification system based on etiological groupings. HIM's history is rich with HIM professionals who helped develop the Standard Nomenclature of Disease (SNDO), a forerunner of the widely used clinical terminology SNOMED CT. The medical record professionals working in US hospitals in the mid-20th century were responsible for collecting and reporting disease and procedure information from medical records using SNDO. HIM professionals have an outstanding track record as leaders in employing classification standards consistently, and they will maintain that track record through the processes of change that reflect and support medicine's cutting edge. The United States needs the highest confidence that health information management is ready for this challenge (Cassidy 2011c).

Changing Times: HIM and Patient-Centered Care

Organizations practicing patient-centered care recognize that a patient is an individual to be cared for, not a medical condition to be treated. Patient-centered care is offered in a setting where each patient is viewed as a unique person, with diverse needs. Patients and families are partners and have knowledge and expertise that is essential to their care. Care that is truly patient centered considers patients' cultural traditions, their personal preferences and values, their family situations, and their lifestyles. It makes patients and their loved ones an integral part of the care team who collaborate with healthcare professionals in making clinical decisions. Patient-centered care puts responsibility for important aspects of self-care and monitoring in patients' hands—along with the tools and support they need to carry out that responsibility. Patient-centered care ensures that transitions between providers, departments, and healthcare settings are respectful, coordinated, and efficient. When care is patient centered, unneeded and unwanted services can be reduced.

The new and exciting unique role for HIM is to create HIM governance guidelines and policies for healthcare organizations that address the access to understandable health information and take on the challenge of and responsibility for providing access to that information. Patient-centered care is the core of a high-quality healthcare system and a necessary foundation for safe, effective, efficient, timely, and equitable care.

The Institute of Medicine's 2001 report, *Crossing the Quality Chasm: A New Health System for the 21st Century*, called for healthcare systems that respect patients' values, preferences, and expressed needs; coordinate and integrate care across boundaries of the system; provide the information, communication, and education that people need and want; and guarantee physical comfort, emotional support, and the involvement of family and friends.

HIE, which is the mobilization of healthcare information electronically across organizations within a region, community, or hospital system, is a requirement for achieving the highest standards of quality and continuity of patient care. HIE initiatives today focus on technology, interoperability, standards utilization, and harmonization. With a patient-centered care focus, the HIEs will provide access to the right clinical information to the right person at the right time.

A healthcare organization cannot achieve success in providing patient-centered care without an HIM infrastructure of governance including policies, procedures, guidelines, and protocols that address access to medical information (electronic, paper, or hybrid medical records), personal health records, electronic communications to and from physicians and other providers, and patient education information (Cassidy 2011d).

Employment Outlook for HIM Professionals

The industry today is faced with a major challenge—not enough HIM professionals to help implement and manage health IT. There is a growing need for many HIM professionals in many new roles and functions. Radical change is required to transform a primarily paper-based system to a totally electronic, interoperable healthcare industry. Health IT must enable providers to achieve quality and efficiency in and of the services they provide (Cassidy 2011e).

There exists a dispersion of HIM roles throughout healthcare facilities. HIM professionals still play important roles but are no longer living in a silo or associated with one particular department. HIM professionals are playing key roles in information technology, decision support, identity management, revenue cycle management, risk management, privacy and security, clinical documentation improvement, case management, and many other areas throughout an enterprise. This is a new way of practicing that has positive potential implications for new HIM education models and competition in the job market. One major area of importance is integrity of the HIM certification process and the value that the industry has placed on the AHIMA certifications. All are well recognized in the industry and with that comes an understanding that those credentialed individuals will deliver results. AHIMA's certifications are as follows:

- Registered Health Information Administrator (RHIA)
- Registered Health Information Technician (RHIT)
- Certified Coding Associate (CCA)
- Certified Coding Specialist (CCS)
- Certified Coding Specialist—Physician-based (CCS-P)
- Certified Health Data Analyst (CHDA)

- Certified in Healthcare Privacy and Security (CHPS)
- Certified Documentation Improvement Practitioner (CDIP)

AHIMA leaders have played an active role in initiatives aimed at increasing the much needed healthcare informatics and information management workforce, including the HIT community college and university-based education programs funded by the Office of the National Coordinator for Health Information Technology (ONC). The ONC has identified numerous roles that widen the scope of HIM, requiring expertise throughout an organization. Some of the roles are listed in figure 30.3.

HIM Expertise

HIM professionals are experts in data content standardization and have the necessary skills and competencies to advance improved validation, capture, analysis, and output of information for quality and patient safety initiatives. HIM professionals must lead all efforts on data governance; data standardization; data capture validation and maintenance; and data capture, analysis, and output. MU takes HIM work to the next level. It is what people in the HIM profession have been working toward for all these decades—patient access to data so consumers can be more informed and involved in their own healthcare; improved timeliness, comprehensiveness of health information, accuracy, and reliability of documentation and data; and leveraged use of technology to really improve the quality of care and the efficiency of the care delivery process.

HIM professionals are the ideal candidates to lead organizational HIM initiatives while at the same time playing a pivotal role in the information capturing process and system improvement measures. HIM professionals are able to provide data related to serious adverse events, Present on Admission indicators, and hospital-acquired conditions and are equipped to analyze and interpret these data and participate in the patient safety teams that conduct root-cause analyses and develop action plans for improvement (Cassidy 2011f).

Figure 30.3. ONC-identified roles

- Workflow and information management redesign specialist
- Clinician or practitioner consultant
- Implementation support specialist
- Implementation manager
- Technical and software support
- Trainer
- Public health leader
- Health information exchange specialist
- Privacy and security officer
- Research and development scientist
- Programmer and software engineer

Source: ONC 2011.

As with all professions that must adapt to changes, HIM professionals must continue to learn and HIM professionals are challenged to continuously upgrade their skills and expertise to keep pace and be successful in the new e-HIM practice. Healthcare executives, ever mindful of the need to empower and advance their workforce, should place a high priority on empowering HIM professionals as key leaders in EHR implementation and management (AHIMA 2010a).

Future Roles of HIM Professionals

According to the Bureau of Labor Statistics *2010–2011 Occupational Handbook,* "employment of medical and health services managers is expected to grow 16 percent from 2008 to 2018, faster than the average for all occupations." In addition, only 38 percent of medical and health service managers work in hospitals. Nineteen percent of these positions indicate opportunities in physician offices or nursing or residential care facilities. Additional opportunities are available in home health, government facilities, outpatient facilities, insurance payer groups, and community healthcare facilities.

Strategic thinking and research brought about the development and refinement of the HIM core model, which focuses on the current state and future state of the HIM profession in all areas of education, research, influencing policy, and establishing best practices and standards in HIM. (Refer to chapter 3 for detailed information on the HIM core model). To keep pace, HIM professionals must understand the principles of change management and transition management, and the impact of the EHR on core HIM practices. Some related items include the following items published in the *Journal of AHIMA:*

- "e-HIM Practice Transformation" (AHIMA 2010a)
- "Forces of Change: The Growth of Data Drives Demand for Data Management" (Rollins 2010)
- "Managing the Transition from Paper to EHRs" (AHIMA 2010b)

Health information management roles are evolving with the transformation from paper to electronic health information and medical record management. Some of the HIM functions tied to paper-based systems will disappear. Many HIM functions will be transformed to accommodate electronic systems, and new roles will emerge. This transformation of HIM best practices requires streamlining and standardizing workflow and work processes, implementing new techniques, and redesigning (redefining) information management practices. As HIM professionals are managing health information in the digital world, new challenges and issues arise. For each of these new issues, there are often new process workflows designed that require specialized talent and expertise.

Some of the new roles that have emerged as a result of achieving the MU of EHRs include, but are not limited to, those listed in figure 30.4. HIM professionals are the

Figure 30.4. Roles necessitated by meaningful use (MU) of EHRs

- Identity coordinator or master patient index (MPI) coordinator
- Content management coordinator (working with IT on documentation)
- Electronic health record (EHR) integrity specialist
- Compliance analyst (privacy and documentation audits)
- Applications system analyst
- Regulatory analyst
- Regulatory manager
- Associate director for record design and management
- Physician educator

workforce members most suited to address these needs. They have deep understanding of information management, coding, data integrity, and information workflow.

The HIM core model illustrates new roles including business change manager, EHR system manager, IT training specialist, business process engineer, clinical vocabulary manager, workflow and data analyst, consumer advocate, clinical alerts and reminders manager, clinical research coordinator, privacy coordinator, enterprise application specialist, and many more. The primary roles of the HIM professional in the future state are focused on five main functional areas of health information (AHIMA 2011):

1. Data capture, validation, and maintenance
2. Data and information analysis, transformation, and decision support
3. Information dissemination and liaison
4. Health information resource management and innovation
5. Information governance and stewardship

These five main functional areas of HIM professionals have a common theme of protecting and managing health information. The primary ethical obligation of the HIM professional is to protect the privacy of confidential patient information, which includes oversight of health information systems and health records, the quality of information, and disclosure of information.

Information governance and stewardship are gaining significant attention within the healthcare industry. Data governance is the high-level organizational framework or enterprise-wide infrastructure of accountability and responsibility that define the purpose for collecting data, ownership of data, and intended use of data. One of the critical success factors within the domain of data governance is data stewardship. Data stewardship focuses on the details of data quality management: the processes, workflows, and policies and procedures that support the capture and maintenance of accurate and complete data. A central concept of data stewardship is accountability. The role of data steward should be a formal responsibility within the organization for ensuring appropriate use of data, and with liability for inappropriate use.

Health data stewardship has taken on great practical urgency because of the increase in availability of electronic health data; growing recognition of the value of electronic data in improving healthcare and population health; the acceleration in the use of information and communication technology; and awareness of the potential risks associated with incorrect or inappropriate uses of health data. Health data stewardship supports the benefits to society of using individuals' personal health information to improve understanding of health and healthcare while at the same time respecting individuals' privacy and confidentiality. As such, health data stewardship is a key responsibility of HIM professionals, who strive to ensure the knowledgeable and appropriate use of data derived from individuals' personal health information.

When thinking about the role of an HIM professional serving as the designated data steward of an organization, one must revisit the AHIMA Code of Ethics. The very core values associated with data stewardship are contained in the profession's Code of Ethics. The specific principles within the Code of Ethics most closely aligned with the responsibilities of a data steward are the following:

- Advocate, uphold, and defend the individual's right to privacy and the doctrine of confidentiality in the use and disclosure of information
- Preserve, protect, and secure personal health information in any form or medium and hold in the highest regard health information and other information of a confidential nature obtained in an official capacity, taking into account the applicable statutes and regulations
- Facilitate interdisciplinary collaboration in situations supporting health information practice
- Refuse to participate in or conceal unethical practices or procedures and report such practices

One of the key HIM guiding principles is to facilitate interdisciplinary collaboration in situations supporting health information practice. HIM professionals are the primary drivers of raising awareness to the entire enterprise when it comes to the safeguarding of personal health data and information. HIM professionals fully recognize that data stewardship is not simply a technology solution; it is the term used to define the people, policies, procedures, and technologies necessary to complement the data governance model (Cassidy 2011g).

Vision of the HIM Professional in the C-suite

HIM professionals use technology and data analytics tools to facilitate better patient care delivery, inform policy leaders, and move into the 21st century and beyond.

To meet the needs of various healthcare organizations in their use of emerging technologies HIM professionals need to be involved at an executive level where decisions are made regarding the design, implementation, and use of technology from a systems approach. From an operational perspective this would suggest involvement in the adoption and implementation of systemwide technology; the use of data to improve patient care and reduce cost; and a role as leaders who define future policies and procedures as they relate to the privacy and security of the organization (Cassidy 2011h).

Growing the HIM profession requires a focus on both those who are beginning their education and those already in the workforce. It is important to offer current professionals educational opportunities for growth and development that can lead to decision-making positions within healthcare organizations. As the HIM profession evolves and expertise in information governance is recognized, new career paths that move the current workforce into executive level decision-making positions will be taking place (Cassidy 2011h). There are many possibilities and opportunities for HIM professionals to move into the C-suite, a term used to indicate the "chief" or C-leadership level of an organization, which includes the chief executive officer (CEO), chief information officer (CIO), chief financial officer (CFO), and many other organizational leaders.

The CEO is the guiding force of an organization. CEOs are expected to be more business-centric than to practice in any particular functional area—extensive expertise of HIM, IT, data quality, clinical needs, and workflow processes, as well as leadership ability, are key to CEOs in healthcare-related fields. HIM professionals are particularly well suited to become CIOs, a role that encompasses a perspective of the total organization, an orientation to information processes across the organization, and an understanding of the ways that the organization can effectively use its growing stores of data (Groysberg et al. 2011). HIM professionals who have enterprise-wide responsibility are sometimes referred to as the chief health information officer.

There are many possibilities and opportunities for HIM professionals to advance. The creation of a chief knowledge officer position within the C-suite is one example of a development that would further senior-level positions and advancement opportunities. Another direction for HIM professionals who have expertise in reimbursement is to become a chief revenue cycle officer. Healthcare is in the middle of an information evolution with the convergence of the ICD-10-CM/PCS, the American Reinvestment and Recovery Act (ARRA) and Health Information Technology for Economic and Clinical Health Act (HITECH), and meaningful use EHR initiatives. The explosion of information fuels a vision for care developed by payers and regulators that is predicated on the mitigation of preventable complications, readmissions, and untoward events across the continuum of care. The aggressive transition to the

EHR powered by the MU program will further promote the use of healthcare information. The proliferation and use of health information will intensify even further throughout the industry as information and technology evolve.

Throughout healthcare, industry models for cost reductions, clinical outcomes, pay for performance, competitive advantage, and best practice are the result of improved technology and expanded data assets. As information and technology become richer and more sophisticated, a need will be created within healthcare organizations for a systematic approach to converting data and information into knowledge for strategic value.

The goal of organizations will be to access and use the right information at the right time so the right decisions are made at the right level.

Conclusion

ARRA and HITECH, along with the nation's transition to ICD-10-CM/PCS, have put the spotlight on the HIM profession, and it is up to the HIM professionals, to deliver. Federal, state, and industry initiatives have given HIM professionals a unique opportunity to leverage strengths and demonstrate the ability to deliver value-added services to an organization (Cassidy 2011b). Achieving excellence and MU of electronic health information only comes with a commitment to applying professional HIM principles that guide the development of organizational HIM policy and EHR governance.

HIM professionals are the workforce members most suited to address this need. They have deep understanding of information management, coding, data integrity, and information workflow (Cassidy 2011h).

Healthcare executives and employers in the second decade of the 21st century are counting on HIM professionals to lead the transition to managing health information in an electronic environment; actively involved in information technology (HIT) adoption; creating strategy, managing implementations with new workflows and seeing that the organization demonstrates MU while properly planning for the monumental transition to ICD-10-CM/PCS, and developing policy and practices to govern the capture, maintenance, and use of electronic patient data to meet the needs of a host of authorized healthcare data users.

These are revitalizing times in the history of the health information management profession. It is a time for HIM professionals to come together to promote and advance the values which serve as the foundation of professional practice—a time for HIM professional's voices to be heard (Cassidy 2011b). It is a time for HIM leadership to continue evolving best practices that assure the privacy, security, accuracy and value of health information in the electronic healthcare industry. HIM is uniquely qualified to lead the initiative for successful ICD-10-CM/PCS implementation and establishing strategies for implementing computer-assisted coding.

The new HIM core model focuses on the current and future state of the HIM profession in all areas of education, research, influencing public policy and establishing best practices and standards in HIM (Cassidy 2011i). It is important that HIM professionals continuously improve, make changes, and make significant contributions to support the healthcare system's growing need for high quality healthcare data and information resources. HIM professionals must continue to passionately promote HIM education, best practices, standards, policy, and research and continue to provide services for today while being visionary in setting the bar for the future.

This is the greatest transformation in the history of the healthcare system and cannot be done successfully without leadership (Cassidy 2011j). With electronic health information's widening availability, great advances in medicine are not only possible, they are mandatory for the exchange of healthcare information and affordable quality healthcare worldwide.

References

American Health Information Management Association. 2011. A core model for the HIM future. Chicago: AHIMA. http://library .ahima.org/xpedio/groups/public/documents/ahima/bok1_049283 .pdf.

American Health Information Management Association. 2010a. E-HIM® practice transformation (updated). *Journal of AHIMA* 81(8): 52–55.

American Health Information Management Association. 2010b. Managing the transition from paper to EHRs. *Journal of AHIMA* 81(11).

Cassidy, B.S. 2011a. President's message: Stepping into new e-HIM® roles: The e-HIM® transition changes HIM roles and responsibilities. *Journal of AHIMA* 82(9): 10.

Cassidy, B.S. 2011b. President's message: Leading the e-HIM® transformation. *Journal of AHIMA* 82(1): 10.

Cassidy, B.S. 2011c. President's message: Taking coding to the next level: HIM's long coding history can help transform the industry with ICD-10. *Journal of AHIMA* 82(7): 10.

Cassidy, B.S. 2011d. President's message: Embracing patient-centered care and its roles. *Journal of AHIMA* 82(2): 10.

Cassidy, B.S. 2011e. President's message: Embracing the ICD-10 transition. *Journal of AHIMA* 82(6): 10.

Cassidy, B.S. 2011f. President's message: Taking the lead on meaningful use: Program goals align with HIM expertise and objectives. *Journal of AHIMA* 82(10): 10.

Cassidy, B.S. 2011g. President's message: Data governance—HIM's sweet spot. *Journal of AHIMA* 82(4): 10.

Cassidy, B.S. 2011h. Teaching the future: An educational response to the AHIMA core model. *Journal of AHIMA* 82(10): 34–38.

Cassidy, B.S. 2011i. President's message: A year of progress: Outstanding advancements on 2011 strategic initiatives. *Journal of AHIMA* 82(11): expanded online version.

Cassidy, B.S. 2011j. President's message: Investing in your future: Professional development enables HIM to transition with changing healthcare landscape. *Journal of AHIMA* 82(8): 10.

Groysberg, B., L.K. Kelly, and B. MacDonald. 2011. The new path to the C-suite. *Harvard Business Review* 89(3). http://hbr .org/2011/03/the-new-path-to-the-c-suite/ar/1.

Institute of Medicine. 2001. *Crossing the Quality Chasm: A New Health System for the 21st Century.* Washington, D.C.: National Academies Press.

Office of the National Coordinator for Health Information Technology. 2011. Get the facts about health IT workforce development program. Hyattsville, MD: HHS.

Rollins, G. 2010. Forces of change: The growth of data drives demand for data management. *Journal of AHIMA* 81(10): 28–32.

Glossary

Abbreviated Injury Scale (AIS): A set of numbers used in a trauma registry to indicate the nature and severity of injuries by body system

Ability (achievement) tests: Tests used to assess the skills an individual already possesses

Abstract: Brief summary of the major parts of a research study

Abstracting: 1. The process of extracting information from a document to create a brief summary of a patient's illness, treatment, and outcome   2. The process of extracting elements of data from a source document or database and entering them into an automated system

Accept assignment: A term used to refer to a provider's or a supplier's acceptance of the allowed charges (from a fee schedule) as payment in full for services or materials provided

Acceptance theory of authority: A management theory based on the principle that employees have the freedom to choose whether they will follow managerial directions

Access control: 1. A computer software program designed to prevent unauthorized use of an information resource   2. The process of designing, implementing, and monitoring a system for guaranteeing that only individuals who have a legitimate need are allowed to view or amend specific data sets

Accession number: A number assigned to each case as it is entered in a cancer registry

Accession registry: A list of cases in a cancer registry in the order in which they were entered

Accountable care organization (ACO): An organization of healthcare providers accountable for the quality, cost, and overall care of Medicare beneficiaries who are assigned and enrolled in the traditional fee-for-service program

Accountability: Responsibility for a specific activity

Accounting: 1. The process of collecting, recording, and reporting an organization's financial data   2. A list of all disclosures made of a patient's health information

Accounting rate of return: The projected annual cash inflows, minus any applicable depreciation, divided by the initial investment

Accounts payable (A/P): Records of the payments owed by an organization to other entities

Accounts receivable (A/R): Records of the payments owed to the organization by outside entities such as third-party payers and patients

Accreditation: 1. A voluntary process of institutional or organizational review in which a quasi-independent body created for this purpose periodically evaluates the quality of the entity's work against preestablished written criteria   2. A determination by an accrediting body that an eligible organization, network, program, group, or individual complies with applicable standards

Accreditation Association for Ambulatory Health Care (AAAHC): Association that requires that the history and physical examination, laboratory reports, radiology reports, operative reports, and consultations be signed in a timely manner

Accredited Standards Committee (ASC) X12N: A committee of the American National Standards Institute that develops and maintains standards for the electronic exchange of business transactions, such as 837—Health Care Claim, 835—Health Care Claim Payment/Advice, and others

Accrue: The process of recording known transactions in the appropriate time period before cash payments or receipts are expected or due

Acid-test ratio: A ratio in which the sum of cash plus short-term investments plus net current receivables is divided by total current liabilities

Active listening: The application of effective verbal communications skills as evidenced by the listener's restatement of what the speaker said

Activities of daily living (ADLs): The basic activities of self-care, including grooming, bathing, ambulating, toileting, and eating

Activity-based budget: A budget based on activities or projects rather than on functions or departments

Acute care: Medical care of a limited duration that is provided in an inpatient hospital setting to diagnose and treat an injury or a short-term illness

Acute care prospective payment system (PPS): The reimbursement system for inpatient hospital services provided to

Medicare and Medicaid beneficiaries that is based on the use of diagnosis-related groups as a classification tool

Administrative information: Information used for administrative and healthcare operations purposes such as billing and quality oversight

Administrative information systems: A category of healthcare information systems that supports human resources management, financial management, executive decision support, and other business-related functions

Administrative law: A body of rules and regulations developed by various administrative entities empowered by Congress; falls under the umbrella of public law

Administrative management: A subdivision of classical management theory that emphasizes the total organization rather than the individual worker and delineates the major management functions

Administrative services only (ASO) contract: An agreement between an employer and an insurance organization to administer the employer's self-insured health plan

Adopter groups: Groups of adopters (such as innovators, early adopters, early majority, late majority, and laggards) of an innovation that generally fits the normal curve

Adoption: The decision to purchase, implement, and utilize an information system such as the EHR

Adult learning: Self-directed inquiry aided by the resources of an instructor, colleagues and fellow students, and educational materials

Advance Beneficiary Notice (ABN): A statement signed by the patient when he or she is notified by the provider, prior to a service or procedure being done, that Medicare may not reimburse the provider for the service, wherein the patient indicates that he or she will be responsible for any charges

Advance directive: A legal, written document that describes the patient's preferences regarding future healthcare or stipulates the person authorized to make medical decisions in the event the patient is incapable of communicating his or her preferences

Aesthetics: Elements of the workplace that include the lighting of both the office and the workspace, the colors of the walls and furniture, auditory impacts, and atmospheric condition and temperature

Affinity grouping: A technique for organizing similar ideas together in natural groupings

Age Discrimination in Employment Act (1967): Federal legislation that prohibits employment discrimination against persons between the ages of 40 and 70 and restricts mandatory retirement requirements except where age is a bona fide occupational qualification

Agency for Healthcare Research and Quality (AHRQ): The branch of the US Public Health Service that supports general health research and distributes research findings and treatment guidelines with the goal of improving the quality, appropriateness, and effectiveness of healthcare services

Aggregate data: Data extracted from individual health records and combined to form de-identified information about groups of patients that can be compared and analyzed

Allied health professionals performance review: Similar to the review for nursing staff, other allied health professionals, licensed and unlicensed, must provide evidence of maintenance of credentials and the ability to appropriately follow delineated procedure in their area of expertise in the healthcare organization

Allied Health Reinvestment Act of 2005: Encourages individuals to seek and complete high-quality allied health education and training by providing funding for their studies; grants are provided to healthcare organizations for advertising campaigns and for partnerships between healthcare facilities and allied health educational programs; scholarships may be given to applicants who agree to serve two years in a rural or other medically underserved area with allied health personnel shortages

All-patient diagnosis-related groups (AP-DRGs): A case-mix system developed by 3M and used in a number of state reimbursement systems to classify non-Medicare discharges for reimbursement purposes

All-patient refined diagnosis-related groups (APR-DRGs): An expansion of the inpatient classification system that includes four distinct subclasses (minor, moderate, major, and extreme) based on the severity of the patient's illness

Alternative hypothesis: A hypothesis that states that there is an association between independent and dependent variables

Ambulatory care: Preventive or corrective healthcare services provided on a nonresident basis in a provider's office, clinic setting, or hospital outpatient setting

Ambulatory care center (ACC): A healthcare provider or facility that offers preventive, diagnostic, therapeutic, and rehabilitative services to individuals not classified as inpatients or residents

Ambulatory payment classification (APC) system: The prospective payment system used since 2000 for reimbursement of hospitals for outpatient services provided to Medicare and Medicaid beneficiaries

Ambulatory surgery center or ambulatory surgical center (ASC): Under Medicare, an outpatient surgical facility that has its own national identifier; is a separate entity with respect to its licensure, accreditation, governance, professional supervision, administrative functions, clinical services, recordkeeping, and financial and accounting systems; has as its sole purpose the provision of services in connection with surgical procedures that do not require inpatient hospitalization; and meets the conditions and requirements set forth in the Medicare Conditions of Participation

Ambulatory Surgery Center Prospective Payment System (ASC PPS): The system that resulted from the Medicare Modernization Act (MMA) of 2003 extensively revising the ASC payment system with changes going into effect on January 1, 2008

American Association of Medical Colleges (AAMC): The organization established in 1876 to standardize the curriculum for medical schools in the United States and to promote the licensure of physicians

American College of Healthcare Executives (ACHE): The national professional organization of healthcare administrators that provides certification services for its members and promotes excellence in the field

American College of Radiology and National Electrical Manufacturers Association (ACR-NEMA): Digital Imaging and Communications in Medicine (DICOM) was originally created to permit the interchange of biomedical image waveforms and related information through a cooperative effort between ACR and NEMA

American College of Surgeons (ACS): The scientific and educational association of surgeons formed to improve the quality of surgical care by setting high standards for surgical education and practice

American Health Information Community: Group formed in 2005 for leadership toward a connected system and standards development

American Health Information Management Association (AHIMA): The professional membership organization for managers of health record services and healthcare information systems as well as coding services; provides accreditation, certification, and educational services

American Hospital Association (AHA): The national trade organization that provides education, conducts research, and represents the hospital industry's interests in national legislative matters; membership includes individual healthcare organizations as well as individual healthcare professionals working in specialized areas of hospitals, such as risk management

American Medical Association (AMA): The national professional membership organization for physicians that distributes scientific information to its members and the public, informs members of legislation related to health and medicine, and represents the medical profession's interests in national legislative matters

American Medical Informatics Association (AMIA): The membership organization composed of individuals, institutions, and corporations that develop and use information technologies in healthcare

American National Standards Institute (ANSI): The organization that accredits all US standards development organizations to ensure that they are following due process in promulgating standards

American Nurses Association (ANA): The national professional membership association of nurses that works for the improvement of health standards and the availability of healthcare services, fosters high professional standards for the nursing profession, and advances the economic and general welfare of nurses

American Recovery and Reinvestment Act of 2009 (ARRA): An economic stimulus package enacted by the 111th United States Congress in February 2009; signed into law by President Obama on February 17, 2009; an unprecedented effort to jumpstart the economy, create/save millions of jobs, and put a down payment on addressing long-neglected challenges; an extraordinary response to a crisis unlike any since the Great Depression and includes measures to modernize our nation's infrastructure, enhance energy independence, expand educational opportunities, preserve and improve affordable healthcare, provide tax relief, and protect those in greatest need

American Society for Testing and Materials (ASTM): A national organization whose purpose is to establish standards on materials, products, systems, and services

American Society for Testing and Materials Standard E1384 (ASTM E1384)—Standard Guide for Description of Content and Structure of an Automated Primary Record of Care: A standard that identifies the basic information to be included in electronic health records and requires the information to be organized into categories

Americans with Disabilities Act (ADA) (1990): Federal legislation that makes it illegal to discriminate against individuals with disabilities in employment, public accommodations, public services, transportation, and telecommunications

Analog: Data or information that is not represented in an encoded, computer-readable format

Analysis phase: The first phase of the systems development life cycle during which the scope of the project is defined, project goals are identified, current systems are evaluated, and user needs are identified

Ancillary systems: Electronic systems that generate clinical information (such as laboratory information systems, radiology information systems, pharmacy information systems, and so on)

Ancillary systems applications: *See* **ancillary systems**

Androgynous leadership: Managers who are described as successful more often possessed a combination of stereotypical masculine and feminine qualities

Application programming interface (API): A set of definitions of the ways in which one piece of computer software communicates with another or a programmer makes requests of the operating system or another application; operates outside the realm of the direct user interface

Application service provider (ASP): A third-party service company that delivers, manages, and remotely hosts standardized applications software via a network through an outsourcing contract based on fixed, monthly usage or transaction-based pricing

Application systems analyst: Systems analysts with a clinical background in nursing, medicine, or other health professions, including HIM

Applied artificial intelligence: An area of computer science that deals with algorithms and computer systems that exhibit the characteristics commonly associated with human intelligence

Applied healthcare informatics: Automated information systems applied to healthcare delivery business and workflow processes, including the diagnosis, therapy, and systems of managing health data and information within the healthcare setting

Applied research: A type of research that focuses on the use of scientific theories to improve actual practice, as in medical research applied to the treatment of patients

Appreciative inquiry: Is based on the belief that whatever is needed in organizational renewal already exists somewhere in the organization

Aptitude tests: Tests that assess an individual's general ability to learn a new skill

Architecture: The configuration, structure, and relationships of hardware (the machinery of the computer including input/output devices, storage devices, and so on) in an information system

Area of excellence: A describable skill, competence, or capability that a department or company cultivates to a level of proficiency

Artificial intelligence (AI): High-level information technologies used in developing machines that imitate human qualities such as learning and reasoning

Artificial neural network (ANN): A computational technique based on artificial intelligence and machine learning in which the structure and operation are inspired by the properties and operation of the human brain

Assets: The human, financial, and physical resources of an organization

Association for Healthcare Documentation Integrity (AHDI): Formerly the American Association for Medical Transcription (AAMT), the AHDI has a model curriculum for formal educational programs that includes the study of medical terminology, anatomy and physiology, medical science, operative procedures, instruments, supplies, laboratory values, reference use and research techniques, and English grammar

Association of Clinical Documentation Improvement Specialists (ACDIS): Formed in 2007 as a community in which clinical documentation improvement professionals could communicate resources and strategies to implement successful programs and achieve professional growth

Association rule analysis (rule induction): The process of extracting useful if/then rules from data based on statistical significance; *See* **rule induction**

Assumptions: Undetermined aspects of a project that are considered to be true (for example, assuming that project team members have the right skill set to perform their duties)

ASTM Continuity of Care Record (CCR): Document containing standard content for referrals

Asynchronous: Occurring at different times

Attending Physician Statement (APS) (or COMB-1): The standardized insurance claim form created in 1958 by the Health Insurance Association of America and the American Medical Association

Attributable risk (AR): A measure of the impact of a disease on a population (for example, measuring additional risk of illness as a result of exposure to a risk factor)

Attributes: 1. Data elements within an entity that become the column or field names when the entity relationship diagram is implemented as a relational database   2. Properties or characteristics of concepts

Audioconferencing: A learning technique in which students in different locations can learn together via telephone lines while listening to a presenter and looking at handouts or books

Audit: A review process conducted by healthcare facilities (internally and/or externally) to identify variations from established baselines; *See* **external review**

Audit controls: The mechanisms that record and examine activity in information systems

Audit log: A chronological record of electronic system(s) activities that enables the reconstruction, review, and examination of the sequence of events surrounding or leading to each event and/or transaction from its beginning to end. Includes who performed what event and when it occurred

Audit trail: A chronological set of computerized records that provides evidence of information system activity (log-ins and log-outs, file accesses) used to determine security violations

Auditing: The performance of internal and/or external reviews (audits) to identify variations from established baselines (for example, review of outpatient coding as compared with CMS outpatient coding guidelines)

Authentication: 1. The process of identifying the source of health record entries by attaching a handwritten signature, the author's initials, or an electronic signature   2. Proof of authorship that ensures, as much as possible, that log-ins and messages from a user originate from an authorized source

Authority: The right to make decisions and take actions necessary to carry out assigned tasks

Authorization: The granting of permission to disclose confidential information; as defined in terms of the HIPAA privacy rule, an individual's formal, written permission to use or disclose his or her personally identifiable health information for purposes other than treatment, payment, or healthcare operations

Authorization management: The process of protecting the security and privacy of the confidential data in a database

Autoauthentication: A procedure that allows dictated reports to be considered automatically signed unless the health information management department is notified of needed revisions within a certain time limit

Autocoding: The process of extracting and translating dictated and then transcribed free-text data (or dictated and then computer-generated discrete data) into ICD-9-CM and CPT evaluation and management codes for billing and coding purposes

Autocratic leadership: Iowa State University researchers showed that groups under this leadership performed well as long as they were closely supervised, although levels of member satisfaction were low

Autodialing system: A method used to automatically call and remind patients of upcoming appointments

Automated code assignment: Uses data that have been entered into a computer to automatically assign codes; uses natural language processing (NLP) technology—algorithmic (rules based) or statistical—to read the data contained in a CPR

Automated drug dispensing machines: Machines available that both are secure and make drugs specific to patient orders readily available to nursing staff; these machines are typically filled by pharmacy department staff based on the physician orders.

Automated forms-processing (e-forms) technology: Technology that allows users to electronically enter data into online, digital forms and electronically extract data from online, digital forms for data collection or manipulation

Autonomy: A core ethical principle centered on the individual's right to self-determination that includes respect for the individual; in clinical applications, the patient's right to determine what does or does not happen to him or her in terms of healthcare

Availability: The accessibility for continuous use of data

Avatar: Created representation of oneself by a user of a multiuser virtual environment (MUVE)

Average daily census: The mean number of hospital inpatients present in the hospital each day for a given period of time

Average length of stay (ALOS): The mean length of stay for hospital inpatients discharged during a given period of time

Balance billing: A reimbursement method that allows providers to bill patients for charges in excess of the amount paid by the patients' health plan or other third-party payer (not allowed under Medicare or Medicaid)

Balance sheet: A report that shows the total dollar amounts in accounts, expressed in accounting equation format, at a specific point in time

Balanced Budget Refinement Act (BBRA) of 1999: The amended version of the Balanced Budget Act of 1997 that authorizes implementation of a per-discharge prospective payment system for care provided to Medicare beneficiaries by inpatient rehabilitation facilities

Balanced scorecard (BSC) methodology: A strategic planning tool that identifies performance measures related to strategic goals

Baldrige Award: A congressional award that recognizes excellence in several areas of business

Bar chart: A graphic technique used to display frequency distributions of nominal or ordinal data that fall into categories

Bar code medication administration record (BC-MAR) system: System that uses bar-coding technology for positive patient identification and drug information

Bar-coding technology: A method of encoding data that consists of parallel arrangements of dark elements, referred to as bars, and light elements, referred to as spaces, and interpreting the data for automatic identification and data collection purposes

Baseline: The original estimates for a project's schedule, work, and cost

Basic research: A type of research that focuses on the development and refinement of theories

Beacon Community Program: Provides funding to selected communities to build and strengthen their health information technology infrastructure and exchange capabilities; the program supports these communities at the cutting edge of EHR adoption and health information exchange to push them to a new level of sustainable health care quality and efficiency

Bed count (complement): The number of inpatient beds set up and staffed for use on a given day

Bed count day: A unit of measure that denotes the presence of one inpatient bed (either occupied or vacant) set up and staffed for use in one 24-hour period

Bed turnover rate: The average number of times a bed changes occupants during a given period of time

Behavioral description interview: An interview format that requires applicants to give specific examples of how they have performed a specific procedure or handled a specific problem in the past

Behavioral healthcare: A broad array of psychiatric services provided in acute, long-term, and ambulatory care settings; includes treatment of mental disorders, chemical dependency, mental retardation, and developmental disabilities, as well as cognitive rehabilitation services

Benchmarking: An analysis process based on comparison

Beneficence: A legal term that means promoting good for others or providing services that benefit others, such as releasing health information that will help a patient receive care or will ensure payment for services received

Benefit: Healthcare service for which the healthcare insurance company will pay

Benefits realization: The point in time when the organization believes all end users are trained, the system has gone live, and there has been some period of time to get acclimated and adopt as much of the process changes and functionality as possible

Best of breed: A vendor strategy used when purchasing an EHR that refers to system applications that are considered the best in their class

Best of fit: A vendor strategy used when purchasing an EHR in which all the systems required by the healthcare facility are available from one vendor

Bill hold period: The span of time during which a bill is suspended in the billing system awaiting late charges, diagnosis and procedure codes, insurance verification, or other required information

Bills of Mortality: Documents used in London during the 17th century to identify the most common causes of death

Bioethics: A field of study that applies ethical principles to decisions that affect the lives of humans, such as whether to approve or deny access to health information

Biotechnology: The field devoted to applying the techniques of biochemistry, cellular biology, biophysics, and molecular biology to addressing practical issues related to human beings, agriculture, and the environment

Bit-mapped data: Data made up of pixels displayed on a horizontal and vertical grid or matrix

Bivariate: An adjective meaning the involvement of two variables

Blanket authorization: An authorization for the release of confidential information from a certain point in time and any time thereafter

Blended learning: A training strategy that uses a combination of techniques—such as lecture, web-based training, or programmed text—to appeal to a variety of learning styles and maximize the advantages of each training method

Blogs: Web logs provide a web page where users can post text, images, and links to other websites

Blood and blood component usage review: Evaluation of how blood and blood components are used using Joint Commission guidelines

Blue Cross and Blue Shield (BC/BS): The first prepaid healthcare plans in the United States; Blue Shield plans traditionally cover hospital care and Blue Cross plans cover physicians' services

Blue Cross and Blue Shield Association: The national association of state and local Blue Cross and Blue Shield plans

Blue Cross and Blue Shield Federal Employee Program (FEP): A federal program that offers a fee-for-service plan with preferred provider organizations and a point-of-service product

Board of governors (board of trustees, board of directors): The elected or appointed group of officials who bear ultimate responsibility for the successful operation of a healthcare organization

Body of Knowledge (BoK): The collected resources, knowledge, and expertise within and related to a profession

Bounded rationality: The recognition that decision making is often based on limited time and information about a problem and that many situations are complex and rapidly changing

Boxplot: Tool in the form of a graph that displays five-number data summary

Brainstorming: A group problem-solving technique that involves the spontaneous contribution of ideas from all members of the group

Breach notification: HITECH Act Rule that requires both HIPAA-covered entities and business associates to identify unsecured PHI breaches and notify the involved parties of the breach

Break-even analysis: A financial analysis technique for determining the level of sales at which total revenues equal total costs beyond which revenues become profits

Breast Imaging Reporting and Data System Atlas (BI-RADS): A comprehensive guide providing standardized breast imaging terminology and a report organization, assessment structure, and classification system for mammography, ultrasound, and MRI of the breast

Bridge technology: Technology such as document imaging and/or clinical messaging that provides some, but not all, the benefits of an EHR

Bubble chart: A type of scatter plot with circular symbols used to compare three variables; the area of the circle indicates the value of a third variable

Budget cycle: The complete process of financial planning, operations, and control for a fiscal year; overlaps multiple fiscal years

Buildings: A long-term (fixed) asset account that represents the physical structures owned by the organization

Bundled payments: A period of relatively continuous medical care performed by healthcare professionals in relation to a particular clinical problem or situation

Bureaucracy: A formal organizational structure based on a rigid hierarchy of decision making and inflexible rules and procedures

Business intelligence (BI): The end product or goal of knowledge management

Business process reengineering (BPR): The analysis and design of the workflow within and between organizations

Bylaws/rules and regulations: Operating documents that describe the rules and regulations under which a healthcare organization operates

Capital budget: The allocation of resources for long-term investments and projects

Capitation: A method of healthcare reimbursement in which an insurance carrier prepays a physician, hospital, or other healthcare provider a fixed amount for a given population without regard to the actual number or nature of healthcare services provided to the population

Care map: A proprietary care-planning tool similar to a clinical protocol that outlines the major aspects of treatment on the basis of diagnosis or other characteristics of the patient

Care path: A care-planning tool similar to a clinical practice guideline that has a multidisciplinary focus emphasizing the coordination of clinical services

Career development: The process of growing or progressing within one's profession or occupation

Case definition: A method of determining criteria for cases that should be included in a registry

Case fatality rate: The total number of deaths due to a specific illness during a given time period divided by the total number of cases during the same period

Case finding: A method of identifying patients who have been seen or treated in a healthcare facility for the particular disease or condition of interest to the registry

Case law: *See* **common law**

Case management: 1. The ongoing, concurrent review performed by clinical professionals to ensure the necessity and effectiveness of the clinical services being provided to a patient   2. A process that integrates and coordinates patient care over time and across multiple sites and providers, especially in complex and high-cost cases   3. The process of developing a specific care plan for a patient that serves as a communication tool to improve quality of care and reduce cost

Case manager: 1. A professional nurse who coordinates the daily progress of a patient population by assessing needs, developing goals, individualizing plans of care on an ongoing basis, and evaluating overall progress   2. A medical professional (usually a nurse or a social worker) who reviews cases to determine the necessity of care and to advise providers on payers' utilization restrictions

Case mix: A description of a patient population based on any number of specific characteristics, including age, gender, type of insurance, diagnosis, risk factors, treatment received, and resources used

Case study: A type of nonparticipant observation in which researchers investigate one person, one group, or one institution in depth

Case-control (retrospective) study: A study that investigates the development of disease by amassing volumes of data about factors in the lives of persons with the disease (cases) and persons without the disease

Case-mix group (CMG) relative weights: Factors that account for the variance in cost per discharge and resource utilization among case-mix groups

Case-mix groups (CMGs): The 97 function-related groups into which inpatient rehabilitation facility discharges are classified on the basis of the patient's level of impairment, age, comorbidities, functional ability, and other factors

Case-mix index (CMI): The average relative weight of all cases treated at a given facility or by a given physician, which reflects the resource intensity or clinical severity of a specific group in relation to the other groups in the classification system; calculated by dividing the sum of the weights of diagnosis-related groups for patients discharged during a given period divided by the total number of patients discharged

Cash: The actual money that has been received and is readily available to pay debts; a short-term (current) asset account that represents currency and bank account balances

Categorical data: *See* **scales of measurement**

Categorically needy eligibility: Categories of individuals to whom states must provide coverage under the federal Medicaid program

Causal relationship: A type of relationship in which one factor results in a change in another factor (cause and effect)

Causal-comparative research: A research design that resembles experimental research but lacks random assignment to a group and manipulation of treatment

Cause-specific death rate: The total number of deaths due to a specific illness during a given time period divided by the estimated population for the same time period

Census: The number of inpatients present in a healthcare facility at any given time

Census survey: A survey that collects data from all the members of a population

Center for Drug Evaluation and Research (CDER) Data Standards Manual: A compilation of standardized nomenclature monographs for sharing information regarding manufactured drug dosage forms

Centers for Medicare and Medicaid Services (CMS): The division of the Department of Health and Human Services that is responsible for developing healthcare policy in the United States and for administering the Medicare program and the federal portion of the Medicaid program; called the Health Care Financing Administration (HCFA) prior to 2001

Certainty factor: The defined certainty percentage rate with which an occurrence must present itself to satisfy quality standards

Certification: 1. The process by which a duly authorized body evaluates and recognizes an individual, institution, or educational program as meeting predetermined requirements 2. An evaluation performed to establish the extent to which a particular computer system, network design, or application implementation meets a prespecified set of requirements

Certification Commission for Healthcare Information Technology (CCHIT): A recognized certification body for electronic health records and their networks; a private, non-profit initiative

Certified coding associate (CCA): An AHIMA credential awarded to entry-level coders who have demonstrated skill in classifying medical data by passing a certification examination

Certified coding specialist (CCS): An AHIMA credential awarded to individuals who have demonstrated skill in classifying medical data from patient records, generally in the hospital setting, by passing a certification examination

Certified coding specialist–physician-based (CCS-P): An AHIMA credential awarded to individuals who have demonstrated coding expertise in physician-based settings, such as group practices, by passing a certification examination

Certified in healthcare privacy and security (CHPS): Credential that recognizes advanced competency in designing, implementing, and administering comprehensive privacy and security protection programs in all types of healthcare organizations; requires successful completion of both the CHP and CHS exams (jointly sponsored by AHIMA and HIMSS)

Certified medical transcriptionist (CMT): A certification that is granted upon successful completion of an examination

Certified professional in health information management systems (CPHIMS): Credential (managed jointly by HIMSS, AHA Certification Center, and applied measurement professionals) that certifies knowledge of healthcare information and management systems and understanding of psychometrics (the science of measurement; requires baccalaureate or graduate degree plus associated experience)

Chain of command: A hierarchical reporting structure within an organization

Champion: Someone in the organization who believes in the idea, acknowledges the practical problems of financing and political support, and assists in overcoming barriers

Change agent: A specialist in organizational development who facilitates the change brought about by the innovation

Change control: The process of performing an impact analysis and obtaining approval before modifications to the project scope are made

Change drivers: Forces in the external environment of organizations or industries that force organizations or industries to change the way they operate in order to survive

Change management: Way in which an organization fosters and directs change in conjunction with process improvement

Charge capture: The process of collecting all services, procedures, and supplies provided during patient care

Charge description master (CDM): *See* **chargemaster**

Chargemaster: A financial management form that contains information about the organization's charges for the healthcare services it provides to patients; *See* **charge description master (CDM)**

Charisma: The ability to inspire and motivate people beyond what is expected with exceptionally high levels of commitment

Charity care: Services for which healthcare organizations did not expect payment because they had previously determined the patients' or clients' inability to pay

Chart conversion: An EHR implementation activity in which data from the paper chart are converted into electronic form

Chart reviews: Internal studies and external reviews including billing audits

Chart tracking: A system that identifies the current location of a record or information

Charting by exception: A method of charting only abnormal or unusual findings or deviations from the prescribed plan of care; also known as focus charting

Check sheet: A tool that permits the systematic recording of observations of a particular phenomenon so that trends or patterns can be identified

Chief executive officer (CEO): The senior manager appointed by a governing board to direct an organization's overall long-term strategic management

Chief financial officer (CFO): The senior manager responsible for the fiscal management of an organization

Chief information officer (CIO): The senior manager responsible for the overall management of information resources in an organization

Chief information security officer (CISO): IT leadership role responsible for ensuring that a healthcare organization's information systems are secure and safe from tampering or misuse; role has grown as a direct result of HIPAA security regulations

Chief information technology officer (CITO): IT leadership role that guides an organization's decisions related to technical architecture and evaluates latest technology developments and their applicability or potential use in the organization

Chief knowledge officer (CKO): A position that oversees the entire knowledge acquisition, storage, and dissemination process and that identifies subject matter experts to help capture and organize the organization's knowledge assets

Chief medical informatics officer (CMIO): An emerging position, typically a physician with medical informatics training, that provides physician leadership and direction in the deployment of clinical applications in healthcare organizations

Chief nursing officer (CNO): The senior manager (usually a registered nurse with advanced education and extensive experience) responsible for administering patient care services

Chief operating officer (COO): The role responsible for managing day-to-day activities of an organization

Children's Health Insurance Program (CHIP): The children's healthcare program implemented as part of the Balanced Budget Act of 1997; formerly known as the State Children's Health Insurance Program, or SCHIP

Circuit: The geographic area covered by a US Court of Appeals

Civil law: The branch of law involving court actions among private parties, corporations, government bodies, or other organizations, typically for the recovery of private rights with compensation usually being monetary

Civil Rights Act (1991): The federal legislation that focuses on establishing an employer's responsibility for justifying hiring practices that seem to adversely affect people because of race, color, religion, sex, or national origin

Civil Rights Act, Title VII (1964): The federal legislation that prohibits discrimination in employment on the basis of race, religion, color, sex, or national origin

Civilian Health and Medical Program of the Uniformed Services (CHAMPUS): A federal program providing supplementary civilian-sector hospital and medical services beyond that which is available in military treatment facilities to military dependents, retirees and their dependents, and certain others

Civilian Health and Medical Program–Veterans Administration (CHAMPVA): The federal healthcare benefits program for dependents of veterans rated by the VA as having a total and permanent disability, for survivors of veterans who died from VA-rated service-connected conditions or who were rated permanently and totally disabled at the time of death from a VA-rated service-connected condition, and for survivors of persons who died in the line of duty

Claim: An itemized statement of healthcare services and their costs provided by a hospital, physician office, or other healthcare provider; submitted for reimbursement to the healthcare insurance plan by either the insured party or the provider

Claims data: information required to be reported on a healthcare claim for service reimbursement

Claims processing: The process of accumulating claims for services, submitting claims for reimbursement, and ensuring that claims are satisfied

Claims scrubber software: A type of computer program at a healthcare facility that checks the claim elements for accuracy and agreement before the claims are submitted

Clean claim: A completed insurance claim form that contains all the required information (without any missing information) so that it can be processed and paid promptly

Client/server architecture: A computer architecture in which multiple computers (clients) are connected to other computers (servers) that store and distribute large amounts of shared data

Clinic outpatient: A patient who is admitted to a clinical service of a clinic or hospital for diagnosis or treatment on an ambulatory basis

Clinical analytics: The process of gathering and examining data in order to help gain greater insight about patients

Clinical Care Classification (CCC): Two interrelated taxonomies, the CCC of Nursing Diagnoses and Outcomes and the CCC of Nursing Interventions and Actions, that provide a standardized framework for documenting patient care in hospitals, home health agencies, ambulatory care clinics, and other healthcare settings

Clinical care plans: Care guidelines created by healthcare providers for individual patients for a specified period of time

Clinical communication space: The context and range of electronic and interpersonal information exchanged among staff and patients

Clinical data: Data captured during the process of diagnosis and treatment

Clinical data repository (CDR): A central database that focuses on clinical information

Clinical data specialist: Specialist who concentrates on ensuring accurate and complete coding, validating the information contained in databases for internal and external uses, and providing information for clinical research across the entire integrated healthcare delivery system

Clinical data warehouse (CDW): *See* **data warehouse**

Clinical decision support (CDS): *See* **clinical decision support system**

Clinical decision support system (CDSS): A special subcategory of clinical information systems that is designed to help healthcare providers make knowledge-based clinical decisions

Clinical document architecture (CDA): HL7 electronic exchange model for clinical documents (such as discharge summaries and progress notes)

Clinical Documentation Improvement (CDI): The process an organization undertakes that will improve clinical specificity and documentation that will allow coders to assign more concise disease classification codes

Clinical guidelines/protocols: With clinical care plans and clinical pathways, a predetermined method of performing healthcare for a specific disease or other clinical situation based on clinical evidence that the method provides high-quality, cost-effective healthcare

Clinical informatics: A field of information science concerned with the management of data and information used to support the practice and delivery of patient care through the application of computers and computer technologies

Clinical information system (CIS): A category of a healthcare information system that includes systems that directly support patient care

Clinical messaging: The function of electronically delivering data and automating the workflow around the management of clinical data

Clinical messaging system: Secure messaging systems that are important, pervasive tools included in a broad set of contextual collaboration tools for clinicians

Clinical (or critical) pathways: *See* **clinical practice guidelines**

Clinical practice guidelines: A detailed, step-by-step guide used by healthcare practitioners to make knowledge-based decisions related to patient care and issued by an authoritative organization such as a medical society or government agency

Clinical privileges: The authorization granted by a healthcare organization's governing board to a member of the medical staff that enables the physician to provide patient services in the organization within specific practice limits

Clinical project manager: One who is responsible for managing and frequently participating in defining the scope of work, developing project plans, and maintaining schedules; he or she will finalize the budget, develop plans for minimizing risks, and responsible for implementing improvement processes

Clinical repository: A frequently updated database that provides users with direct access to detailed patient-level data as well as the ability to drill down into historical views of administrative, clinical, and financial data; *See* **data warehouse**

Clinical systems analyst: *See* **systems analyst**

Clinical terminology: A set of standardized terms and their synonyms that record patient findings, circumstances, events, and interventions with sufficient detail to support clinical care, decision support, outcomes research, and quality improvement

Clinical transformation: A comprehensive, ongoing approach to care delivery excellence that offers value while measurably improving quality, enhancing service, and reducing costs through the effective alignment of people, process, and technology

Clinical trial: A controlled research study involving human subjects that is designed to evaluate prospectively the safety and effectiveness of new drugs, tests, devices, or interventions

Clinical value compass: Performance improvement approach that measures the association of quality and value

Clinical workstation: A single point of access that includes a common user interface to view information from disparate applications and to launch applications

Clinical/medical decision support system: A special subcategory of clinical information systems that is designed to help healthcare providers make knowledge-based clinical decisions

Clinician/physician web portals: The media for providing clinician/physician access to the provider organization's multiple sources of data from any network-connected device

Closed records: The records of patients who have been discharged from the hospital or whose treatment has been terminated

Closed systems: Systems that operate in a self-contained environment

Closed-loop medication management: Process wherein patient safety is ensured through proper drug ordering, dispensing, administering, and monitoring of reactions; is a special form of POC documentation

Closed-record review: A review of records after a patient has been discharged from the organization or treatment has been terminated

Cloud computing: The application of virtualization to a variety of computing resources to enable rapid access to computing services via the Internet

Cluster sampling: The process of selecting subjects for a sample from each cluster within a population (for example, a family, school, or community)

CMS-1500: A Medicare claim form used to bill third-party payers for provider services (for example, physician office visits)

Coaching: 1. A training method in which an experienced person gives advice to a less-experienced worker on a formal or informal basis   2. A disciplinary method used as the first step for employees who are not meeting performance expectations

Coalition building: A technique used to manage the political dimensions of change within an organization by building the support of groups for change

Coded data: Data that are translated into a standard nomenclature of classification so that they may be aggregated, analyzed, and compared

Coding: The process of assigning numeric representations to clinical documentation

Coefficient of determination: r^2; the r^2 measures how much of the variation in one variable is explained by the second variable

Cohort study: A study, followed over time, in which a group of subjects is identified as having one or more characteristics in common

Coinsurance: Cost sharing in which the policy or certificate holder pays a preestablished percentage of eligible expenses after the deductible has been met

Collaborative Stage Data Set: A new standardized neoplasm-staging system developed by the American Joint Commission on Cancer

Collateral: The value of specific assets that are used to guarantee the purchase of material goods

College of American Pathologists (CAP): Organization of board-certified pathologists that serves patients, pathologists, and the public by fostering and advocating excellence in the practice of pathology and laboratory medicine

College of Healthcare Information Management Executives (CHIME): A membership association serving chief information officers through professional development and advocacy

Commission on Accreditation of Health Informatics and Information Management Education (CAHIIM): The accrediting organization for educational programs in health informatics and information management

Commission on Accreditation of Rehabilitation Facilities (CARF): A private, not-for-profit organization that develops customer-focused standards for behavioral healthcare and medical rehabilitation programs and accredits such programs on the basis of its standards

Common cause variation: The source of variation in a process that is inherent within the process

Common Formats Version 1.1: The common definitions and reporting formats, specified by AHRQ, that allow healthcare providers to collect and submit standardized information regarding patient safety events; there are two general types, generic and event-specific

Common Framework: A set of tools critical to achieving an interoperable environment that supports modern healthcare practice, including precisely defined and uniform technical standards as well as common policies and methods

Common law: Unwritten law originating from court decisions where no applicable statute exists; *See* **case law**

Common Rule: Federal Policy for the Protection of Human Subjects (45 CFR Part 46 Subpart A) that is a set of regulations regarding research that 18 federal agencies share; these agencies fund research at institutions that provide written assurance to the funding agency that the institutions will comply with the requirements of this policy

Communication plan: A documented approach to identifying the media and schedule for sharing information with affected parties

Community of Practice (CoP): The community for those interested in clinical terminologies and vocabularies

Comorbidity: A medical condition that coexists with the primary cause for hospitalization and affects the patient's treatment and length of stay

Comparative data: Data that are used for benchmarking or other comparisons within or across healthcare organizations

Comparative effectiveness research (CER): Research that generates and synthesizes evidence that compares the benefits and harms of alternative methods to prevent, diagnose, treat, and monitor a clinical condition or to improve the delivery of care

Compensable factor: Characteristic used to compare the worth of jobs (for example, skill, effort, responsibility, and working conditions)

Compensation and benefits: The payment package offered to employees in return for work

Competencies: Demonstrated skills that a worker should perform at a high level

Compliance: 1. The process of establishing an organizational culture that promotes the prevention, detection, and resolution of instances of conduct that do not conform to federal, state, or private payer healthcare program requirements or the healthcare organization's ethical and business policies   2. The act of adhering to official requirements

Compliance officer: Designated individual who monitors the compliance process at a healthcare facility

Compliance program guidance: The information provided by the Office of Inspector General of the Department of Health and Human Services to help healthcare organizations develop internal controls that promote adherence to applicable federal and state guidelines

Complication: A medical condition that arises during an inpatient hospitalization (for example, a postoperative wound infection)

Compressed workweek: A work schedule that permits a full-time job to be completed in less than the standard five days of eight-hour shifts

Compromise: A mutual agreement

Computer output to laser disk (COLD): *See* Computer Output Laser Disk/Enterprise Report Management (COLD/ERM) technology

Computer Output Laser Disk/Enterprise Report Management (COLD/ERM) technology: Technology that electronically stores the documents and distributes them with fax, e-mail, web, and traditional hard-copy print processes

Computer virus: A software program that attacks computer systems and sometimes damages or destroys files

Computer-assisted coding (CAC): The process of extracting and translating dictated and then transcribed free-text data (or dictated and then computer-generated discrete data) into ICD-9-CM and CPT evaluation and management codes for billing and coding purposes

Computer-based training: A type of training that is delivered partially or completely using a computer

Computerized provider order entry (CPOE): Systems that allow physicians to enter medication or other orders and receive clinical advice about drug dosages, contraindications, or other clinical decision support

Concept: A unit of knowledge or thought created by a unique combination of characteristics

Conceptual data model: The highest level of data model, representing the highest level of abstraction, independent of hardware and software

Conceptual framework of accounting: The concept that the benefits of financial data should exceed the cost of obtaining them and that the data must be understandable, relevant, reliable, and comparable

Conceptual skills: One of the three managerial skill categories that includes intellectual tasks and abilities such as planning, deciding, and problem solving

Concurrent analysis: A review of the health record while the patient is still hospitalized or under treatment

Conditions of Participation: The administrative and operational guidelines and regulations under which facilities are allowed to take part in the Medicare and Medicaid programs; published by the Centers for Medicare and Medicaid Services, a federal agency under the Department of Health and Human Services

Confidence interval (CI): A range of values, such that the probability of that range covering the true value of a parameter is a set probability or confidence

Confidence limit: End of the range of a confidence interval, upper and lower, which indicates the reliability of the estimate

Confidentiality: A legal and ethical concept that establishes the healthcare provider's responsibility for protecting health records and other personal and private information from unauthorized use or disclosure

Conflict management: The process of working with individuals to find a mutually acceptable solution to a problem that has arisen between them

Confounding (extraneous, secondary) variable: An event or a factor that is outside a study but occurs concurrently with the study

Consent: A means for residents to convey to healthcare providers their implied or expressed permission to administer care or treatment or to perform surgery or other medical procedures

Consent management: Policies, procedures, and technology that enable active management and enforcement of users' consent directives to control access to their electronic health information and allow care providers to meet patient privacy requirements

Conservatism: The concept that resources must not be overstated and liabilities not understated

Consideration: In an Ohio State University examination of the behavior of leaders in the 1950s and 1960s, referred to attention to the interpersonal aspects of work, including respect for subordinates' ideas and feelings, maintaining harmonious work relationships, collaborating in teamwork, and showing concern with the subordinates' welfare

Consistency: The idea that all time periods must reflect the same accounting

Consolidated health informatics (CHI): The notion of adopting existing health information interoperability standards throughout all federal agencies

Consolidated Health Informatics (CHI) initiative: The effort to achieve CHI through federal agencies spearheaded by the Office of the National Coordinator for Health Information Technology

Consolidated Omnibus Budget Reconciliation Act of 1986 (COBRA): The federal law requiring every hospital that participates in Medicare and has an emergency room to treat any patient in an emergency condition or active labor, whether or not the patient is covered by Medicare and regardless of the patient's ability to pay; COBRA also requires employers to provide continuation benefits to specified workers and families who have been terminated but previously had healthcare insurance benefits

Construct validity: The ability of an instrument to measure hypothetical, nonobservable traits

Constructive confrontation: A method of approaching conflict in which both parties meet with an objective third party to explore perceptions and feelings

Consultant: Employed outside of the healthcare provider arena, he or she works for an external firm or independently; may be responsible for operational assistance with e-HIM conversions, revenue cycle and coding auditing, compliance, privacy and security, or any of the HIM-related functions

Consultation: The response by one healthcare professional to another healthcare professional's request to provide recommendations and opinions regarding the care of a particular patient/resident

Consultation rate: The total number of hospital inpatients receiving consultations for a given period divided by the total number of discharges and deaths for the same period

Consumer Assessment of Healthcare Providers and Systems (CAHPS): A program sponsored and administered by AHRQ, CAHPS has evolved into a source of coordinated survey instruments and reports intended to measure and communicate information on healthcare quality from the consumers' perspective

Consumer health: Providing services that accommodate more knowledgeable patients while helping them to become more informed and to participate as partners in their own healthcare

Consumer informatics: The field of information science concerned with the management of data and information used to support consumers by consumers (the general public) through the application of computers and computer technologies

Content: The substantive or meaningful components of a document or collection of documents

Content analysis: A method of research that provides a systematic and objective analysis of communication effectiveness, such as the analysis performed on tests

Content and records management: *See* **enterprise (or electronic) content and records management**

Content validity: The extent to which an instrument's items represent the content that the instrument is intended to measure

Context: The text that illustrates a concept or the use of a designation

Context-sensitive: Templates that react to the nature of the data being entered and that tailor the template to the specific data entry needs

Contingency: A plan of action to be taken when circumstances affect project performance

Contingency model of leadership: Designed by Fred Fiedler at the University of Illinois to compensate for the limitations of the classical and behavioral theories of leadership; Fiedler kept the social-task orientation as the cornerstone of his theory and designed an innovative test to determine the leader's preferred style

Contingency planning: An administrative security requirement in which applications should be categorized by criticality and backup plans, disaster recovery plans, and emergency mode operations plans developed in accordance with the criticality of the application and its information

Continuing education: A type of training that enables employees to remain current in the knowledge base of their profession

Continuity of care document (CCD): Document that is the result of harmonizing the ASTM International Continuity of Care Record (CCR) standard content for referrals with the HL7 CDA standard for document construction; now widely used in creating PHRs

Continuity of care record (CCR): Documentation of care delivery from one healthcare experience to another

Continuous data: Data that represent measurable quantities but are not restricted to certain specified values

Continuous quality improvement (CQI): 1. A management philosophy that emphasizes the importance of knowing and meeting customer expectations, reducing variation within processes, and relying on data to build knowledge for process improvement 2. A continuous cycle of planning, measuring, and monitoring performance and making knowledge-based improvements

Continuous record review: *See* **open-record review**

Continuous speech input: The quality of speech/voice recognition technology that does not require users to pause between words to allow the computer to distinguish between the beginnings and endings of words

Continuous variables: Discrete variables measured with sufficient precision

Continuum of care: The range of healthcare services provided to patients, from routine ambulatory care to intensive acute care

Contra-account: Any account set up to adjust the historical value of a balance sheet account (for example, cumulative depreciation is a contra-account to an equipment [fixed-asset] account)

Contract law: A branch of law based on common law that deals with written or oral agreements that are enforceable through the legal system

Contract service: An entity that provides certain agreed-upon services for the facility, such as transcription, coding, or copying

Control: One of the four management functions in which performance is monitored in accordance with organizational policies and procedures

Control group: A comparison study group whose members do not undergo the treatment under study

Controlled Substances Act: The legislation that controls the use of narcotics, depressants, stimulants, and hallucinogens

Controlling: The monitoring and maintenance of a project's structure

Convenience sampling: A type of nonrandom sampling in which researchers use any unit at hand

Coordination of benefits (COB) transaction: The electronic transmission of claims and/or payment information from a healthcare provider to a health plan for the purpose of determining relative payment responsibilities

Core data elements/core content: A small set of data elements with standardized definitions often considered to be the core of data collection efforts

Core measure/core measure set: Standardized performance measures developed to improve the safety and quality of healthcare (for example, core measures are used in the Joint Commission's ORYX initiative)

Core performance measures: Measures that are considered tools—standardized metrics—that provide an indication of an organization's performance

Corporate Integrity Agreement (CIA): A compliance program imposed by the government that involves substantial government oversight and outside expert involvement in the organization's compliance activities and is generally required as a condition of settling a fraud and abuse investigation

Corporate social responsibility: A responsibility of an organization that is part of its strategic plan—part of its bottom line—and the core intention is values-based

Corporation: An organization that may have one or many owners in which profits may be held or distributed as dividends (income paid to the owners)

Corrective controls: Internal controls designed to fix problems that have been discovered, frequently as a result of detective controls

Correlation: The existence and degree of relationships among factors

Correlational research: A design of research that determines the existence and degree of relationships among factors

Cost accounting: The specialty branch of accounting that deals with quantifying the resources expended to provide the goods and services offered by the organization to its customers/clients/patients

Cost justification: A rationale developed to support competing requests for limited resources

Cost outlier: Exceptionally high costs associated with inpatient care when compared with other cases in the same diagnosis-related group

Cost outlier adjustment: Additional reimbursement for certain high-cost home care cases based on the loss-sharing ratio of costs in excess of a threshold amount for each home health resource group

Cost report: A report that analyzes the direct and indirect costs of providing care to Medicare patients

Court of Appeals: A branch of the federal court system that has the power to hear appeals on the final judgments of district courts

Coverage error: A systematic (nonrandom) discrepancy between the target population and the sample frame

Covered entity (CE): To make a good faith effort to obtain the patient's written acknowledgment of receipt of the HIPAA Privacy Notice

Covert observation: Observation of participants without their knowledge

CPT® (Current Procedural Terminology): A comprehensive, descriptive list of terms and numeric codes used for reporting diagnostic and therapeutic procedures and other medical services performed by physicians; published and updated annually by the American Medical Association

Credentialing or credentialing process: The process of reviewing and validating the qualifications (degrees, licenses, and other credentials) of physicians and other licensed independent practitioners for granting medical staff membership to provide patient care services

Credits: The amounts on the right side of a journal entry

Criminal law: A branch of law that addresses crimes that are wrongful acts against public health, safety, and welfare, usually punishable by imprisonment and/or fine

Critic: This role is essential in challenging the innovation for shortcomings, presenting strong criteria, and, in essence, providing a reality test for the new idea

Critical issues: The bridge between the current strategic profile and the future strategic vision and profile of a department or an organization that leadership has deliberately decided to pursue

Critical path/critical path method: In project management, the sequence of tasks that determine the project finish date

Cross-sectional study: A biomedical research study in which both the exposure and the disease outcome are determined at the same time in each subject

Cross-training: The training to learn a job other than the employee's primary responsibility

Crosswalk: *See* **data map**

Crude birth rate: The number of live births divided by the population at risk

Crude death rate: The total number of deaths in a given population for a given period of time divided by the estimated population for the same period of time

Cultural competence: Skilled in awareness, understanding, and acceptance of beliefs and values of the people of groups other than one's own

Current Dental Terminology (CDT): A medical code set of dental procedures, maintained and copyrighted by the American Dental Association (ADA), referred to as the Uniform Code on Dental Procedures and Nomenclatures until 1990

Current Procedural Terminology (CPT): Published by the AMA, this codebook has become widely used as a standard for outpatient and ambulatory care procedural coding in contexts related to reimbursement; it is updated every year on January 1

Current ratio: The total current assets divided by total current liabilities

Customer relationship management (CRM): A management system whereby organizational structure and culture and customer information and technology are aligned with business strategy so that all customer interactions can be conducted to the long-term satisfaction of the customer and to the benefit and profit of the organization

Customer service training: Training that focuses on creating a true customer orientation within the work environment

Cybernetic systems: Systems that have standards, controls, and feedback mechanisms built into them

Cyclical staffing: A transitional staffing solution where workers are brought in for specific projects or to cover in busy times

Daily inpatient census: The number of inpatients present at census-taking time each day, plus any inpatients who were both admitted and discharged after the census-taking time the previous day

Dashboard: A launching pad from which one is able to drill down to further detail about a given aspect of the patient's care

Data: The dates, numbers, images, symbols, letters, and words that represent basic facts and observations about people, processes, measurements, and conditions

Data administrator: An emerging role responsible for managing the less technical aspects of data, including data quality and security

Data analytics: Term used to describe a variety of approaches to using data to make business decisions

Data capture: The process of recording healthcare-related data in a health record system or clinical database

Data cleansing: The process of detecting, diagnosing, and editing faulty data

Data confidentiality: The extent to which personal health information is kept private

Data content standards: Standards that make it possible to exchange health information using electronic networks that reach across the country and around the world

Data conversion: The task of moving data from one data structure to another, usually at the time of a new system installation

Data definition language (DDL): A special type of software used to create the tables within a relational database, the most common of which is structured query language

Data dictionary: A descriptive list of the data elements to be collected in an information system or database whose purpose is to ensure consistency of terminology

Data display: A method for presenting or viewing data

Data element: An individual fact or measurement that is the smallest unique subset of a database

Data Elements for Emergency Department Systems (DEEDS): A data set designed to support the uniform collection of information in hospital-based emergency departments

Data exchange standards: Protocols that help ensure that data transmitted from one system to another remain comparable

Data integrity: 1. The extent to which healthcare data are complete, accurate, consistent, and timely 2. A security principle that keeps information from being modified or otherwise corrupted either maliciously or accidentally

Data integrity specialist: One who is responsible for ensuring quality and accuracy of medical information in any form, electronic or hybrid

Data manipulation language (DML): A special type of software used to retrieve, update, and edit data in a relational database, of which the most common is structured query language

Data map: Term that describes the connections, or paths, between classifications and vocabularies; *see* **crosswalk**

Data mart: A well-organized, user-centered, searchable database system that usually draws information from a data warehouse to meet the specific needs of users

Data miners: Those individuals who extract data from a database with the intention of quantifying and filtering them

Data mining: The process of extracting information from a database and then quantifying and filtering discrete, structured data

Data model: A picture or an abstraction of real conditions used to design the definitions of fields and records and their relationships in a database

Data modeling: The process of determining the users' information needs and identifying relationships among the data

Data quality: The reliability and effectiveness of data for its intended uses in operations, decision making, and planning

Data quality management: A managerial process that ensures the integrity (accuracy and completeness) of an organization's data during data collection, application, warehousing, and analysis

Data quality manager/data quality analyst: One who is responsible for data management functions that involve formalized continuous quality improvement activities for data integrity throughout the organization, beginning with the data dictionary and policy development, as well as data quality monitoring and audits

Data quality model: A managerial process that ensures the integrity (accuracy and completeness) of an organization's data during data collection, application, warehousing, and analysis; also called data management model

Data repository: An open-structure database that is not dedicated to the software of any particular vendor or data supplier, in which data from diverse sources are stored so that an integrated, multidisciplinary view of the data can be achieved; also called a central data repository or, when related specifically to healthcare data, a clinical data repository

Data resource manager: A role that ensures that the organization's information systems meet the needs of people who provide and manage patient services

Data security: The process of keeping data safe from unauthorized alteration or destruction

Data set: A list of recommended data elements with uniform definitions that are relevant for a particular use

Data stewardship: The responsibilities and accountabilities associated with managing, collecting, viewing, storing, sharing, disclosing, or otherwise making use of personal health information

Data types: A technical category of data (text, numbers, currency, date, memo, and link data) that a field in a database can contain

Data Use and Reciprocal Support Agreement (DURSA): A trust agreement entered into when exchanging information with other organizations using an agreed upon set of national standards, services, and policies developed in coordination with the Office of the National Coordinator for Health Information Technology

Data warehouse: A database that makes it possible to access data from multiple databases and combine the results into a single query and reporting interface; *See* **clinical repository**

Data warehousing: The acquisition of all the business data and information from potentially multiple, cross-platform sources, such as legacy databases, departmental databases, and online transaction-based databases, and then the warehouse storage of all the data in one consistent format

Database: An organized collection of data, text, references, or pictures in a standardized format, typically stored in a computer system for multiple applications

Database administrator: The individual responsible for the technical aspects of designing and managing databases

Database life cycle (DBLC): A system consisting of several phases that represent the useful life of a database, including initial study, design, implementation, testing and evaluation, operation, and maintenance and evaluation

Database management system (DBMS): Computer software that enables the user to create, modify, delete, and view the data in a database

Data-based DSS: Decision support system that focuses on providing access to the various data sources within the organization through one system

Debit: The amount on the left side of an account entry that represents an increase in an expense or liability account or a decrease in a revenue or asset account

Debt ratio: The total liabilities divided by the total assets

Debt service: The current obligations of an organization to repay loans

Decentralization: The shift of decision-making authority and responsibility to lower levels of the organization

Decision support system (DSS): A computer-based system that gathers data from a variety of sources and assists in providing structure to the data by using various analytical models and visual tools in order to facilitate and improve the ultimate outcome in decision-making tasks associated with nonroutine and nonrepetitive problems

Decision tree: A structured data-mining technique based on a set of rules useful for predicting and classifying information and making decisions

Deductive reasoning: The process of developing conclusions based on generalizations

Deemed status: An official designation indicating that a healthcare facility is in compliance with the Medicare Conditions of Participation; to qualify for deemed status, facilities must be accredited by the Joint Commission or the American Osteopathic Association

Default judgment: A court ruling against a defendant in a lawsuit who fails to answer a summons for a court appearance

Defendant: In civil cases, an individual or entity against whom a civil complaint has been filed; in criminal cases, an individual who has been accused of a crime

Deficiency assignment: Each facility must develop its own procedures for quantitative analysis, and responsibility for completion of the record must be assigned to each responsible provider; the deficiencies, or parts of the record needing completion or signature, are entered into the HIS or on paper worksheets attached to the incomplete, or deficient, health record

Deidentification: The process in which users of secondary data will need to remove identifying data so that data can be used without violating the patient's privacy

Delegation: The process by which managers distribute work to others along with the authority to make decisions and take action

Delegation of authority: The act of assigning responsibility

Delinquent health record: An incomplete record not finished or made complete within the time frame determined by the medical staff of the facility

Democratic leadership: Iowa State University researchers showed that members under this leadership performed well whether the leader was present or absent and members were more satisfied

Demographic data: *See* **demographic information**

Demographic information: Information used to identify an individual, such as name, address, gender, age, and other information linked to a specific person

Denial: When a bill has been returned unpaid for any of several reasons (for example, sending the bill to the wrong insurance company, patient not having current coverage, inaccurate coding, lack of medical necessity, and so on)

Dental informatics: A field of information science concerned with the management of data and information used to support the practice and delivery of dental healthcare through the application of computers and computer technologies

Department of Health and Human Services (HHS): The cabinet-level federal agency that oversees all the health- and human-services–related activities of the federal government and administers federal regulations

Dependency: The relationship between two tasks in a project plan

Dependent variable: A measurable variable in a research study that depends on an independent variable

Depreciation: The allocation of the dollar cost of a capital asset over its expected life

Derived attribute: An attribute whose value is based on the value of other attributes (for example, current date minus date of birth yields the derived attribute age)

Descriptive research: A type of research that determines and reports the current status of topics and subjects

Descriptive statistics: A set of statistical techniques used to describe data such as means, frequency distributions, and standard deviations; statistical information that describes the characteristics of a specific group or a population

Design phase: The second phase of the systems development life cycle during which all options in selecting a new information system are considered

Designated record set: A group of records maintained by or for a covered entity that may include patient medical and billing records; the enrollment, payment, claims adjudication, and cases or medical management record systems maintained by or for a health plan; or information used, in whole or in part, to make patient care–related decisions

Detective control: An internal control designed to find errors that have already been made

Development: The process of growing or progressing in one's level of skill, knowledge, or ability

Diagnosis-related group (DRG): A unit of case-mix classification adopted by the federal government and some other payers as a prospective payment mechanism for hospital inpatients in which diseases are placed into groups because related diseases and treatments tend to consume similar amounts of healthcare resources and incur similar amounts of cost; in the Medicare and Medicaid programs, one of more than 500 diagnostic classifications in which cases demonstrate similar resource consumption and length-of-stay patterns

Diagnostic image data: Bit-mapped images used for medical or diagnostic purposes (for example, chest x-rays or computed tomography scans)

Diffusion S curve: Curve that shows that each of the adopter categories engages innovation at a different time and a different acceptance rate

Digital: 1. A data transmission type based on data that have been binary encoded   2. A term that refers to the data or information represented in an encoded, computer-readable format

Digital dictation: A process in which vocal sounds are converted to bits and stored on computer for random access

Digital Imaging and Communication in Medicine (DICOM): A standard that promotes a digital image communications format and picture archive and communications systems for use with digital images

Digital signature management technology: The practice of validating the identity of an individual sending data through the use of an electronic signature

Direct costs: Resources expended that can be identified as pertaining to specific goods and services (for example, medications pertain to specific patients)

Direct method of cost allocation: A budgeting concept in which the cost of overhead departments is distributed solely to the revenue-producing areas

Direct Project: Launched in March 2010 to offer a simpler, standards-based way for participants to send authenticated, encrypted health information directly to known recipients over the Internet

Disaster recovery plan (DRP): The document that defines the resources, actions, tasks, and data required to manage the businesses recovery process in the event of a business interruption

Discharge analysis: An analysis of the health record at or following discharge

Discharge planning: The process of coordinating the activities related to the release of a patient when inpatient hospital care is no longer needed

Discharge summary: A summary of the resident's stay at the long-term care facility that is used along with the post-discharge plan of care to provide continuity of care for the resident upon discharge from the facility

Discharged, no final bill (DNFB) report: A report that includes all patients who have been discharged from the facility but for whom, for one reason or another, the billing process is not complete

Disciplinary action: Steps taken, such as suspension from employment without pay or demotion to a job with lower expectations and less pay, when actions taken to improve performance are unsuccessful

Discipline: A field of study characterized by a knowledge base and perspective that are different from other fields of study

Disclosure: The act of making information known; in the health information management context, the release of confidential health information about an identifiable person to another person or entity

Discounting: The application of lower rates of payment to multiple surgical procedures performed during the same operative session under the outpatient prospective payment system; the application of adjusted rates of payment by preferred provider organizations

Discrete data: Data that represent separate and distinct values or observations; that is, data that contain only finite numbers and have only specified values

Discrete variables: A dichotomous or nominal variable whose values are placed into categories

Discrimination: The act of treating one entity differently from another

Disease index: A list of diseases and conditions of patients sequenced according to the code numbers of the classification system in use

Disease management: Emphasizes the provider–patient relationship in the development and execution of the plan of care, prevention strategies using evidence-based guidelines to limit complications and exacerbations, and evaluation based on outcomes that support improved overall health

Disease registry: A centralized collection of data used to improve the quality of care and measure the effectiveness of a particular aspect of healthcare delivery

Disposition: For outpatients, the healthcare practitioner's description of the patient's status at discharge (no follow-up planned; follow-up planned or scheduled; referred elsewhere; expired); for inpatients, a core health data element that identifies the circumstances under which the patient left the hospital (discharged alive; discharged to home or self-care; discharged and transferred to another short-term general hospital for inpatient care; discharged and transferred to a skilled nursing facility; discharged and transferred to an intermediate care facility; discharged and transferred to another type of institution for inpatient care or referred for outpatient services to another institution; discharged and transferred to home under care of an organized home health services organization; discharged and transferred to home under care of a home intravenous therapy provider; left against medical advice or discontinued care; expired; status not stated)

Distance learning: A learning delivery mode in which the instructor, the classroom, and the students are not all present in the same location and at the same time

Diversity training: A type of training that facilitates an environment that fosters tolerance and appreciation of individual differences within the organization's workforce and strives to create a more harmonious working environment

DMAIC: Methodology used by Six Sigma that involves the following steps: define, measure, analyze, improve, and control

Do not resuscitate (DNR) order: An order written by the treating physician stating that in the event the patient suffers cardiac or pulmonary arrest, cardiopulmonary resuscitation should not be attempted

Document: Any analog or digital, formatted, and preserved "container" of data or information

Documentation audits: Audits within the EHR that should also look for completeness, timeliness, internal consistency, and other factors that have typically been evaluated in paper documentation

Document image data: Bit-mapped images based on data created and stored on analog paper or photographic film

Document imaging technology: The practice of electronically scanning written or printed paper documents into an optical or electronic system for later retrieval of the document or parts of the document if parts have been indexed

Document management technology: Technology that organizes and assembles, secures, and shares documents, and includes such functions as document version control, check in–check out control, document access control, and text and word searches

Documentation: The methods and activities of collecting, coding, ordering, storing, and retrieving information to fulfill future tasks

Domain: A sphere or field of activity and influence

Double distribution: A budgeting concept in which overhead costs are allocated twice, taking into consideration that some overhead departments provide services to each other

Double-blind study: A type of clinical trial conducted with strict procedures for randomization in which neither researcher nor subject knows whether the subject is in the control group or the experimental group

DRG grouper: A computer program that assigns inpatient cases to diagnosis-related groups and determines the Medicare reimbursement rate

Driving force: The concept of what a department or an organization uses to determine which products or services to offer, which markets to seek, and which customers to attract

Dual core (vendor strategy): A vendor strategy in which one vendor primarily supplies the financial and administrative applications and another vendor primarily supplies the clinical applications

Due diligence: The actions associated with making a good decision, including investigation of legal, technical, human, and financial predictions and ramifications of proposed endeavors with another party

Durable power of attorney (DPOA): A power of attorney that remains in effect even after the principal is incapacitated; some are drafted so that they only take effect when the principal becomes incapacitated

Duration: The amount of time, usually measured in days, for a task to be completed

Early adopters: Account for about 13.5 percent of the organization; the individuals in this group have a high degree of opinion leadership; they are more localized than cosmopolitan and often look to the innovators for advice and information; these are the leaders and respected role models in the organization, and their adoption of an idea or a practice does much to initiate change

Early majority: Comprises about 34 percent of the organization; although usually not leaders, the individuals in this group represent the backbone of the organization, are deliberate in thinking and acceptance of an idea, and serve as a natural bridge between early and late adopters

e-commerce: The use of the Internet and its derived technologies to integrate all aspects of business-to-business and business-to-consumer activities, processes, and communications

e-Discovery: Refers to Amendments to Federal Rules of Civil Procedure and Uniform Rules Relating to Discovery of Electronically Stored Information; wherein audit trails, the source code of the program, metadata, and any other electronic information that is not typically considered the legal health record is subject to a motion for compulsory discovery

e-forms: Electronic forms used to collect specific data for a registry

Edit: A condition that must be satisfied before a computer system can accept data

Effect size: Degree to which the null hypothesis is false as represented by the degree to which the sample results diverge from the null hypothesis; practical (clinical) significance of a study's findings

Effectiveness: The degree to which stated outcomes are attained

Efficiency: The degree to which a minimum of resources is used to obtain outcomes

Effort: The mental and physical exertion required to perform job-related tasks

e-health: The application of e-commerce to the healthcare industry, including electronic data interchange and links among healthcare entities

e-HIM: The application of technology to managing health information

EHR collaborative: A group of healthcare professional and trade associations formed to support Health Level Seven, a healthcare standards development organization, in the development of a functional model for electronic health record systems

Eighty-five/fifteen (85/15) rule: The total quality management assumption that 85 percent of the problems that occur are related to faults in the system rather than to worker performance

e-learning: The use of the Internet and its derived technologies to deliver training and education

Electronic data interchange (EDI): A standard transmission format using strings of data for business information communicated among the computer systems of independent organizations

Electronic document/content management system (EDM): A storage solution based on digital scanning technology in which source documents are scanned to create digital images of the documents that can be stored electronically on optical disks

Electronic health information management: *See* **e-HIM**

Electronic health record (EHR): An electronic record of health-related information on an individual that conforms to nationally recognized standards and that can be created, managed, and consulted by authorized clinicians and staff across more than one healthcare organization

Electronic medical record (EMR): An electronic record of health-related information on an individual that can be created, gathered, managed, and consulted by authorized clinicians and staff within a single healthcare organization

Electronic medication administration record (EMAR): System designed to prevent medication errors by checking a patient's medication information against his or her bar-coded wristband

Electronic performance support system (EPSS): Sets of computerized tools and displays that automate training, documentation, and phone support; that integrate this automation into applications; and that provide support that is faster, cheaper, and more effective than traditional methods

Electronic records management technology: Systems that create and preserve electronic records

Electronic signature: 1. Any representation of a signature in digital form, including an image of a handwritten signature 2. The authentication of a computer entry in a health record made by the individual making the entry

Eligibility verification: Verification that determines if a patient's health plan will provide reimbursement for services to be performed, and sometimes prior-authorization management systems where a health plan requires review and approval of a procedure (or referral) prior to performing the service

Emergency Care Research Institute (ECRI): Group that is currently working with the FDA to produce a map of the Universal Medical Device Nomenclature System to Global Medical Device Nomenclature to coordinate their practices, which may lead to a merger in the near future

Emergency Maternal and Infant Care Program (EMIC): The federal medical program that provides obstetrical and infant care to dependents of active-duty military personnel in the four lowest pay grades

Emergency Medical Treatment and Activity Labor Act (EMTALA): To ensure that emergency patients are made aware of their rights, transfer and acceptance policies and procedures must be delineated to ensure that facilities comply with this act

Emergency outpatient: A patient who is admitted to the emergency department or equivalent service of a hospital for diagnosis and treatment of a condition that requires immediate medical services, dental services, or related healthcare services

Emergency preparedness: A state of readiness to react to an emergency situation

Emotional intelligence (EI): The sensitivity and ability to monitor and revise one's behavior based on the needs of and responses by others

Empiricism: The quality of being based on observed and validated evidence

Employee handbook: Handbook containing policies and requirements that all employees must know, such as insurance programs, payroll requirements, and personnel policies, given to new employees during the orientation

Employee record: The document in which an employee's information relating to job performance and so on is kept

Employee self-logging: A form of self-reporting in which the employees simply track their tasks, volume of work units, and hours worked

Employer-based self-insurance: An umbrella term used to describe health plans that are funded directly by employers to provide coverage for their employees exclusively in which employers establish accounts to cover their employees' medical expenses and retain control over the funds but bear the risk of paying claims greater than their estimates

Employment contract: A legal and binding agreement of terms related to an individual's work, such as hours, pay, or benefits

Employment-at-will: Concept that employees can be fired at any time and for almost any reason based on the idea that employees can quit at any time and for any reason

Empowerment: The condition of having the environment and resources to perform a job independently

Encoder: Specialty software used to facilitate the assignment of diagnostic and procedural codes according to the rules of the coding system

Encounter: The direct personal contact between a patient and a physician or other person who is authorized by state licensure law and, if applicable, by medical staff bylaws to order or furnish healthcare services for the diagnosis or treatment of the patient

Encryption: The process of transforming text into an unintelligible string of characters that can be transmitted via communications media with a high degree of security and then decrypted when it reaches a secure destination

Ending: The transition process begins with the recognition that the old way of doing things is being terminated

Enhancers: Enhancement of a leader's influence can be done by modifying factors such as subordinates not perceiving the leader's expertise, team spirit not related to leadership efforts, subordinates not dependent on the leader, the leader has low power, or workgroups are not cohesive related to leadership

Enterprise information management (EIM): Ensuring the value of information assets, requiring an organizationwide perspective of information management functions; it calls for explicit structures, policies, processes, technology, and controls

Enterprise master patient index (EMPI): An index that provides access to multiple repositories of information from overlapping patient populations that are maintained in separate systems and databases

Enterprise (or electronic) content and records management (ECRM): Systems that enable scanning and indexing of paper documents and other content in digital form; also called *content and records management*

Entity: An individual person, group, or organization

Entity relationship diagram (ERD): A specific type of data modeling used in conceptual data modeling and the logical-level modeling of relational databases

Environmental assessment: A thorough review of the internal and external conditions in which an organization operates

Environmental Protection Agency (EPA) Substance Registry System (SRS): Interoperability standard for chemicals that provides a common basis for identification of chemicals, biological organisms, and other substances listed in EPA regulations and data systems

Epidemiological data: Data used to reveal disease trends within a specific population

Epidemiological studies: Studies that are concerned with finding the causes and effects of diseases and conditions

Episode-of-care (EOC) reimbursement: A category of payments made as lump sums to providers for all healthcare services delivered to a patient for a specific illness and/or over a specified time period; also called bundled payments because they include multiple services and may include multiple providers of care

e-prescribing (e-Rx): A type of ordering application that generates a prescription to be filled by a retail pharmacy that is not exactly equivalent to a medication order that is directed to the clinical pharmacy in a hospital

Equal Employment Opportunity Act (1972): Federal legislation prohibiting discrimination in the workplace based on gender, race, religion, or national origin

Equal Pay Act of 1963 (EPA): The federal legislation that requires equal pay for men and women who perform substantially the same work

Equipment: A long-term (fixed) asset account representing depreciable items owned by the organization that have value over multiple fiscal years (for example, the historical cost of a CT scanner is recorded in an equipment account)

Equity: Securities that are shared in the ownership of the organization

Ergonomics: A discipline of functional design associated with the employee in relationship to his or her work environment, including equipment, workstation, and office furniture adaptation to accommodate the employee's unique physical requirements so as to facilitate efficacy of work functions

Esprit de corps: Enthusiasm among the members of a group supporting the group's existence

Essential Medical Data Set (EMDS): A recommended data set designed to create a health history for an individual patient treated in an emergency service

Established Name for Active Ingredients and FDA Unique Ingredient Identifier (UNII) Codes: Interoperability standard for active ingredients in medications

Ethical agent: An individual who promotes and supports ethical behavior

Ethical decision making: The process of requiring everyone to consider the perspectives of others, even when they do not agree with them

Ethicist: An individual trained in the application of ethical theories and principles to problems that cannot be easily solved because of conflicting values, perspectives, and options for action

Ethics: A field of study that deals with moral principles, theories, and values; in healthcare, a formal decision-making process for dealing with the competing perspectives and obligations of the people who have an interest in a common problem

Ethics training: The act of teaching others about moral principles, theories, and values

Ethnography: A method of observational research that investigates culture in naturalistic settings using both qualitative and quantitative approaches

European Committee for Standardization: A business facilitator in Europe, removing trade barriers for European industry and consumers; through its services it provides a platform for the development of European standards and other technical specifications

Evaluation research: A design of research that examines the effectiveness of policies, programs, or organizations

Evidence: Something that provides proof

Evidence-based management: A management system in which practices based on research evidence will be effective and produce the outcomes they claim

Evidence-based medicine: Healthcare services based on clinical methods that have been thoroughly tested through controlled, peer-reviewed biomedical studies

E-visits: Online provider encounters for which some health plans have started providing reimbursement and that can save patients an office visit and associated costs

Exchange relationship: Relationship in which a leader offers greater opportunities and privileges to a subordinate in exchange for loyalty, commitment, and assistance

Exclusive provider organization (EPO): Hybrid managed care organization that provides benefits to subscribers only when healthcare services are performed by network providers; sponsored by self-insured (self-funded) employers or associations and exhibits characteristics of both health maintenance organizations and preferred provider organizations

Executive dashboard: An information management system providing decision makers with regularly updated information on an organization's key strategic measures

Executive information system (EIS): An information system designed to combine financial and clinical information for use in the management of business affairs of a healthcare organization

Executive manager: A senior manager who oversees a broad functional area or group of departments or services, sets the organization's future direction, and monitors the organization's operations

Exempt employees: Specific groups of employees who are identified as not being covered by some or all of the provisions of the Fair Labor Standards Act

Exit interview: The final meeting an employee has with his or her employer before leaving the organization

Expectancy theory of motivation: Proposes that one's effort will result in the attainment of desired performance goals

Expenses: Amounts that are charged as costs by an organization to the current year's activities of operation

Experimental (study) group: A group of participants in which the exposure status of each participant is determined

and the individuals are followed forward to determine the effects of the exposure

Experimental research: 1. A research design used to establish cause and effect   2. A controlled investigation in which subjects are assigned randomly to groups that experience carefully controlled interventions that are manipulated by the experimenter according to a strict protocol; *See* **experimental study**

Experimental study: *See* **experimental research**

Expert decision support system: A decision support system that uses a set of rules or encoded concepts to construct a reasoning process

Expert system (ES): A type of information system that supports the work of professionals engaged in the development or evaluation of complex activities that require high-level knowledge in a well-defined and usually limited area

Explanation of Benefits (EOB): A statement issued to the insured and the healthcare provider by an insurer to explain the services provided, amounts billed, and payments made by a health plan

Explicit knowledge: Documents, databases, and other types of recorded and documented information

Extended care facility: A healthcare facility licensed by applicable state or local law to offer room and board, skilled nursing by a full-time registered nurse, intermediate care, or a combination of levels on a 24-hour basis over a long period of time

Extensibility: Intention that the vocabulary be extended by users or applications developers

Extensible markup language (XML): A standardized computer language that allows the interchange of data as structured text

External customers: Customers that reside outside the organization

External review (audit): A performance or quality review conducted by a third-party payer or consultant hired for the purpose

External validity: An attribute of a study's design that allows its findings to be applied to other groups

Extranet: A system of connections of private Internet networks outside an organization's firewall that uses Internet technology to enable collaborative applications among enterprises

Facility charge: Allows the capture of an evaluation and management (E/M) charge that represents those resources not included with the CPT code for the clinic environment

Facility-based registry: A registry that includes only cases from a particular type of healthcare facility, such as a hospital or clinic

Factor comparison method: A complex quantitative method of job evaluation that combines elements of both the ranking and point methods

Fair and Accurate Credit Transaction Act (FACTA): Law passed in 2003 that contains provisions and requirements to reduce identity theft

Fair Labor Standards Act of 1938 (FLSA): The federal legislation that sets the minimum wage and overtime payment regulations

Family and Medical Leave Act of 1993 (FMLA): The federal legislation that allows employees time off from work (up to 12 weeks) to care for themselves or their family members with the assurance of an equivalent position upon return to work

Family numbering: A filing system, sometimes used in clinic settings, in which an entire family is assigned one number

Favorable variance: The positive difference between the budgeted amount and the actual amount of a line item, that is, when actual revenue exceeds budget or actual expenses are less than budget

Federal Anti-Kickback Statute: A statute that establishes criminal penalties for individuals and entities that knowingly and willfully offer, pay, solicit, or receive remuneration in order to induce business for which payment may be made under any federal healthcare program

Federal Employees' Compensation Act (FECA): The legislation enacted in 1916 to mandate workers' compensation for civilian federal employees, whose coverage includes lost wages, medical expenses, and survivors' benefits

Federal Register: The daily publication of the US Government Printing Office that reports all changes in regulations and federally mandated standards, including HCPCS and ICD-9-CM codes

Fee schedule: A list of healthcare services and procedures (usually CPT/HCPCS codes) and the charges associated with them developed by a third-party payer to represent the approved payment levels for a given insurance plan; also called table of allowances

Feedback controls: Back-end processes that monitor and measure output, and then compare it to expectations and identify variations that then must be analyzed so corrective action plans can be developed and implemented

Fee-for-service basis: *See* **Traditional fee-for-service (FFS) reimbursement**

Felony: A serious crime such as murder, larceny, rape, or assault for which punishment is usually severe

Fetal autopsy rate: The number of autopsies performed on intermediate and late fetal deaths for a given time period divided by the total number of intermediate and late fetal deaths for the same time period

Fetal death (stillborn): The death of a product of human conception before its complete expulsion or extraction from the mother regardless of the duration of the pregnancy

Fetal death rate: A proportion that compares the number of intermediate or late fetal deaths to the total number of live births and intermediate or late fetal deaths during the same period of time

Financial Accounting Standards Board (FASB): An independent organization that sets accounting standards for businesses in the private sector

Financial and administrative applications: Type of source system (such as Registration-Admission Discharge Transfer [R-ADT], patient accounting, MPI, order communication, and the like) used by hospitals and physicians' offices

Financial data: The data collected for the purpose of managing the assets of a business (for example, a healthcare organization, a product line); in healthcare, data derived from the charge generation documentation associated with the activities of care and then aggregated by specific customer grouping for financial analysis

Financial counselors: Staff dedicated to helping patients and physicians determine sources of reimbursement for healthcare services; counselors are responsible for identifying and verifying the method of payment and debt resolution for services rendered to patients

Financial transaction: The exchange of goods or services for payment or the promise of payment

Firewall: A computer system or a combination of systems that provides a security barrier or supports an access control policy between two networks or between a network and any other traffic outside the network

Fiscal intermediary (FI): An organization that contracts with the Centers for Medicare and Medicaid Services to serve as the financial agent between providers and the federal government in the local administration of Medicare Part B claims

Fiscal year: One business cycle or tax year, which may or may not coincide with the calendar year

Fishbone diagram: A performance improvement tool used to identify or classify the root causes of a problem or condition and to display the root causes graphically

Fixed budget: A type of budget based on expected capacity

Fixed costs: Resources expended that do not vary with the activity of the organization (for example, mortgage expenses do not vary with patient volume)

Flex years: A work arrangement in which employees can choose, at specific intervals, the number of hours they want to work each month over the next year

Flexible budget: A type of budget that is based on multiple levels of projected productivity (actual productivity triggers the levels to be used as the year progresses)

Flexible work schedule: *See* **flextime**

Flextime: A work schedule that gives employees some choice in the pattern of their work hours, usually around a core of midday hours

Float employee: An employee who is not assigned to a particular shift or function and who may fill in as needed in cases of standard employee absence or vacation

Flow process chart: *See* **flowchart**

Flowchart: A graphic tool that uses standard symbols to visually display detailed information, including time and distance, of the sequential flow of work of an individual or a product as it progresses through a process

Focus group: Group of members of the population that are questioned for research purposes

Focused studies: Studies in which a researcher orally questions and conducts discussions with members of a group

Food and Drug Administration (FDA): The federal agency responsible for controlling the sale and use of pharmaceuticals, biological products, medical devices, food, cosmetics, and products that emit radiation, including the licensing of medications for human use

Force-field analysis: A performance improvement tool used to identify specific drivers of, and barriers to, an organizational change so that positive factors can be reinforced and negative factors reduced

Forecasting: To calculate or predict some future event or condition through study and analysis of available pertinent data

Foreign key: A key attribute used to link one entity or table to another

Format: Refers to the organization of information in the health record; there are many possible formats, and most facilities use a combination of formats

For-profit organizations: The tax status assigned to business entities that are owned by one or more individuals or organizations and that earn revenues in excess of expenditures that are subsequently paid out to the owners or stockholders

Foundational applications (for EHR): Applications including those that capture patient and provider demographic and administrative information, maintain and create custom patient lists, maintain problem lists, retain allergy information, manage medication lists, access and view test results during the ordering process, and perform medication reconciliation

Fourteen principles of management: Henri Fayol's key points in the formulation of the administrative approach to management

Fraud and abuse: The intentional and mistaken misrepresentation of reimbursement claims submitted to government-sponsored health programs

Freedom of Information Act (FOIA): The federal law, applicable only to federal agencies, through which individuals can seek access to information without the authorization of the person to whom the information applies

Free-text data: Data that are narrative in nature

Frequency distribution: A table or graph that displays the number of times (frequency) a particular observation occurs

Frequency polygon: A type of line graph that represents a frequency distribution

Functional interoperability: Refers to sending messages between computers with a shared understanding of the structure and format of the message

Functional team structure: In a strictly functional organization, the project is thought to affect only one department, where the functional manager may assume responsibility for managing the project and the team members are primarily from the functional department; the functional manager confers with other functional managers on any issues affecting those departments

Functionality training: Training focused specifically on the capabilities and features of the software; how to navigate through the application, how to enter data into different modules within the application, and such

Fund balance: In a not-for-profit setting, the entity's net assets or resources remaining after subtracting liabilities that are owed; in a for-profit organization, the owner's equity

Gantt chart: A graphic tool used to plot tasks in project management that shows the duration of project tasks and overlapping tasks

General Equivalence Mappings (GEMs): A program created to facilitate the translation between ICD-9-CM and ICD-10-CM/PCS

General ledger: A master list of individual revenue and expense accounts maintained by an organization

Generalizability: The ability to apply research results, data, or observations to groups not originally under study

Generally accepted accounting principles (GAAP): An accepted set of accounting principles and recognized procedures central to financial accounting and reporting

Generally accepted auditing standards (GAAS): The way in which organizations record and report financial transactions so that financial information is consistent between organizations

Generic screening: A risk management technique in which the risk manager reviews the health records of current and discharged hospital inpatients with the goal of identifying potentially compensable events

Geographic information system (GIS): A decision support system that is capable of assembling, storing, manipulating, and displaying geographically referenced data and information

Geographic practice cost index (GPCI): An index developed by the Centers for Medicare and Medicaid Services to measure the differences in resource costs among fee schedule areas compared to the national average in the three components of the relative value unit: physician work, practice expenses, and malpractice coverage

Gesture recognition technology: A method of encoding handwritten, print, or cursive characters and of interpreting the characters as words or the intent of the writer

Global Medical Device Nomenclature (GMDN): A collection of internationally recognized terms used to accurately describe and catalog medical devices, in particular, the products used in the diagnosis, prevention, monitoring, treatment or alleviation of disease or injury in humans

Global payment: A form of reimbursement used for radiological and other procedures that combines the professional and technical components of the procedures and disperses payments as lump sums to be distributed between the physician and the healthcare facility

Global surgery payment: A payment made for surgical procedures that includes the provision of all healthcare services, from the treatment decision through postoperative patient care

Go-live: The final stage that culminates the system implementation; this is the time that the applications are turned on and users are expected to start using the system.

Goal: A specific description of the services or deliverable goods to be provided as the result of a business process

Going concern: An organization that can be assumed to continue indefinitely unless otherwise stated

Government Accounting Standards Board (GASB): The federal agency that sets the accounting standards to be followed by government entities

Granularity: Level of detail

Graphical user interface (GUI): A style of computer interface in which typed commands are replaced by images that represent tasks (for example, small pictures [icons] that represent the tasks, functions, and programs performed by a software program)

Graphics-based decision support system: A decision support system in which the knowledge base consists primarily of graphical data and the user interface exploits the use of graphical display

Great person theory: Outstanding individuals originally led to the conception of leadership as an inborn ability, sometimes passed down through family, position, or social tradition, as in the cases of royal families in many parts of the world

Grievance: A formal, written description of a complaint or disagreement

Grievance procedures: The steps employees may follow to seek resolution of disagreements with management on job-related issues

Gross autopsy rate: The number of inpatient autopsies conducted during a given time period divided by the total number of inpatient deaths for the same time period

Gross death rate: The number of inpatient deaths that occurred during a given time period divided by the total number of inpatient discharges, including deaths, for the same time period

Ground rules: An agreement concerning attendance, time management, participation, communication, decision making, documentation, room arrangements and cleanup, and so forth, that has been developed by PI team members at the initiation of the team's work

Grounded theory: Researchers using this theory to code, categorize, and compare their data; term refers both to the theories generated using this technique and the technique itself

Group health insurance: A prepaid medical plan that covers the healthcare expenses of an organization's full-time employees

Group model health maintenance organization: Type of health plan in which an HMO contracts with an independent multispecialty physician group to provide medical services to members of the plan

Group practice without walls (GPWW): A type of managed care contract that allows physicians to maintain their own offices and share administrative services

Grouper: A computer software program that automatically assigns prospective payment groups on the basis of clinical codes

Groupthink: An implicit form of group consensus in which openness and effective decision making are sacrificed to conformity

Habit: An activity repeated so often that it becomes automatic

Harassment: The act of bothering or annoying someone repeatedly

Hard space: Space that cannot be converted easily to service another function

Hard-coding: The process of attaching a CPT/HCPCS code to a procedure located on the facility's chargemaster so that the code will automatically be included on the patient's bill

Hawthorne effect: A research study that found that novelty, attention, and interpersonal relations have a motivating effect on performance

Hay method of job evaluation: A modification of the point method of job evaluation that numerically measures the levels of three major compensable factors: know-how, problem-solving ability, and accountability

Health Care Fraud Prevention and Enforcement Action Team (HEAT): Group whose goal is to identify fraud perpetrators and those preying on Medicare and Medicaid beneficiaries

Health care provider dimension (HCPD): One of three dimensions of the National Health Information Infrastructure privacy concept that addresses the needs of providers for complete and accurate patient data

Health Care Quality Improvement Program (HCQIP): A quality initiative begun in 1992 by the Health Care Financing Administration and implemented by peer review organizations that uses patterns of care analysis and collaboration with practitioners, beneficiaries, providers, plans, and other purchasers of healthcare services to develop scientifically based quality indicators and to identify and implement opportunities for healthcare improvement

Health information exchange (HIE): The exchange of health information electronically between providers and others with the same level of interoperability, such as labs and pharmacies

Health Information Exchange Challenge Grant Program: Program that awarded an additional $16 million to 10 sites in the spring of 2011, providing funding to innovative use cases for health information exchange that will be scalable and useful in the sustainability of the nationwide health information exchange and interoperability

Health information management (HIM): An allied health profession that is responsible for ensuring the availability, accuracy, and protection of the clinical information that is needed to deliver healthcare services and to make appropriate healthcare-related decisions

Health Information and Management Systems Society (HIMSS): A national membership association that provides leadership in healthcare for the management of technology, information, and change

Health information manager (or director): One who is responsible for the enterprise wide direction of HIM functions

Health Information Security and Privacy Collaboration (HISPC): This project originally included three phases and 34 states and territories in the United States. In the first phase, the 34 teams followed a defined process to assess variances in organization-level business policies and state laws that affect HIE. The second phase focused on identification and proposal of practical solutions while preserving privacy and security requirements in the applicable federal and state laws. In 2008, the third phase, developing detailed plans and implementing solutions, was under way.

Health information resource management: Management that includes responsibility for the health data life cycle and shape management of such across the entire enterprise system

Health information technology (HIT): A term that encompasses the technical roles that process health data and records, such as classification, abstracting, retrieval, and so on

Health Information Technology Expert Panel (HITEP): Formed by the National Quality Forum (NQF) with support from the Agency for Healthcare Research and Quality (AHRQ), the panel was tasked with creating a better link between current quality measurement and EHR reporting capabilities

Health Information Technology for Economic and Clinical Health (HITECH) Act: The part of ARRA that is meant to increase the momentum of developing and implementing the EHR by 2014

Health Information Technology Standards Committee (HITSC): This committee makes recommendations to the National Coordinator on standards, implementation specifications, and certification criteria for the electronic exchange and use of health information for purposes of adoption, consistent with the implementation of the Federal Health IT Strategic Plan and in accordance with policies developed by the HIT Policy Committee

Health Information Technology Standards Panel (HITSP): This organization serves as a cooperative partnership between the public and private sectors for achieving a wide acceptance and usable standards; its specific mission is to enable and support widespread interoperability among healthcare software applications as they interact in a local, regional, and NHIN for the United States

Health Insurance Portability and Accountability Act (HIPAA) of 1996: The federal legislation enacted to provide continuity of health coverage, control fraud and abuse in healthcare, reduce healthcare costs, and guarantee the security and privacy of health information

Health Level Seven (HL7): A standards development organization accredited by the American National Standards Institute that addresses issues at the seventh, or application, level of healthcare systems interconnections

Health maintenance organization (HMO): Entity that combines the provision of healthcare insurance and the delivery of healthcare services, characterized by (1) organized healthcare delivery system to a geographic area, (2) set of basic and supplemental health maintenance and treatment services, (3) voluntarily enrolled members, and (4) predetermined fixed, periodic prepayments for members' coverage

Health management information system (HMIS): An information system whose purpose is to provide reports on routine operations and processing (for example, a pharmacy inventory system, radiological system, or patient-tracking system)

Health record review: A concurrent or ongoing review of health record content performed by caregivers or HIM professionals while the patient is still receiving inpatient services to ensure the quality of the services being provided and the completeness of the documentation being maintained; also called health record analysis

Health Research Extension Act (1985): Federal legislation that established guidelines for the proper care of animals used in biomedical and behavioral research

Health savings accounts: Savings accounts designed to help people save for future medical and retiree health costs on a tax-free basis, part of the 2003 Medicare bill

Health science librarian: A professional librarian who manages a medical library

Health services research: Research conducted on the subject of healthcare delivery that examines organizational structures and systems as well as the effectiveness and efficiency of healthcare services

Health systems agency: An agency that promotes and provides community-based health planning services

Health technology assessment: Evaluation of the utility of health technologies

Health 2.0: Web 2.0 technologies and tools used in the healthcare industry

Healthcare Common Procedure Coding System (HCPCS): A classification system that identifies healthcare procedures, equipment, and supplies for claim submission purposes; the three levels are as follows: I, Current Procedural Terminology codes, developed by the AMA; II, codes for equipment, supplies, and services not covered by Current Procedural Terminology codes as well as modifiers that can be used with all levels of codes, developed by CMS; and III (eliminated December 31, 2003, to comply with HIPAA), local codes developed by regional Medicare Part B carriers and used to report physicians' services and supplies to Medicare for reimbursement

Healthcare Cost and Utilization Project (HCUP): A group of healthcare databases and related software tools developed through collaboration by the federal government, state governments, and industry to create a national information resource for patient-level healthcare data

Healthcare data analytics: The practice of using data to make business decisions in healthcare

Healthcare data organizations (HDOs): Groups that maintain healthcare databases in both the public and private sectors; they may be state owned or privately held; these groups use data to for reporting systems such as hospital discharge data and all-payer claims databases (APCDs)

Healthcare Effectiveness Data and Information Set (HEDIS): Sponsored by the National Committee for Quality Assurance (NCQA), HEDIS is a set of standard performance measures designed to provide purchasers and consumers of healthcare with the information they need for comparing the performance of managed healthcare plans

Healthcare informatics: The field of information science concerned with the management of all aspects of health data and information through the application of computers and computer technologies

Healthcare Information Security and Privacy Collaboration (HISPC): Partnership consisting of a multidisciplinary team of experts and the National Governors Association (NGA) working with approximately 40 states to assess and develop plans to address variations in organization-level business policies and state laws that affect privacy and security practices that may pose challenges to interoperable HIE

Healthcare information standards: Guidelines developed to standardize data throughout the healthcare industry (for example, developing uniform terminologies and vocabularies)

Healthcare Information Technology Standards Panel (HITSP): Private organization formed in 2005; funded by the federal government to address standards harmonization and gaps, especially in light of using a nationwide health information network

Healthcare Integrity and Protection Data Bank (HIPDB): A national database that collects information on cases of healthcare fraud and abuse

Healthcare payer organizations: Organizations that include clearinghouses, the federal and state government, accountable care organizations (ACOs), insurance companies including self-insured organizations, medical billing companies, and medical banking

Healthcare provider: A provider of diagnostic, medical, and surgical care as well as the services or supplies related to the health of an individual and any other person or organization that issues reimbursement claims or is paid for healthcare in the normal course of business

Healthcare provider organizations: Organizations that include, but are not limited to, physician offices, clinics, outpatient facilities, freestanding surgical centers, hospitals, regional health centers, and enterprise wide health systems

Heterogeneity: The state or fact of containing various components

Heuristic thought: Exploratory thinking that helps in solving certain types of problems but offers no guarantees

Hierarchy: An authoritarian organizational structure in which each member is assigned a specific rank that reflects his or her level of decision-making authority within the organization

Hierarchy of needs: Maslow's theory that suggested that human needs are organized hierarchically from basic physiological requirements to creative motivations; *See* **Maslow's hierarchy of needs**

Hill-Burton Act: The federal legislation enacted in 1946 as the Hospital Survey and Construction Act to authorize grants for states to construct new hospitals and, later, to modernize old ones; *See* **Hospital Survey and Construction Act**

Hiring: Engaging the services of an individual in return for compensation

Histocompatibility: The immunologic similarity between an organ donor and a transplant recipient

Histogram: A graphic technique used to display the frequency distribution of continuous data (interval or ratio data) as either numbers or percentages in a series of bars

Historical cost: The resources expended by an organization to acquire an asset

Historical research: A research design used to investigate past events

History: The pertinent information about a patient, including chief complaint, past and present illnesses, family history, social history, and review of body systems

Home Assessment Validation and Entry (HAVEN): A type of data-entry software used to collect Outcome and Assessment Information Set (OASIS) data and then transmit them to state databases; imports and exports data in standard OASIS record format, maintains agency/patient/employee information, enforces data integrity through rigorous edit checks, and provides comprehensive online help

Home health agency (HHA): A program or organization that provides a blend of home-based medical and social services to homebound patients and their families for the purpose of promoting, maintaining, or restoring health or of minimizing the effects of illness, injury, or disability

Home health prospective payment system (HH PPS): The reimbursement system developed by the Centers for Medicare and Medicaid Services to cover home health services provided to Medicare beneficiaries

Home health resource group (HHRG): A classification system with 80 home health episode rates established to support the prospective reimbursement of covered home care and rehabilitation services provided to Medicare beneficiaries during 60-day episodes of care

Home healthcare (HH): The medical and/or personal care provided to individuals and families in their place of residence with the goal of promoting, maintaining, or restoring health or minimizing the effects of disabilities and illnesses, including terminal illnesses

Honesty (integrity) tests: Tests designed to evaluate an individual's honesty using a series of hypothetical questions

Hospice: An interdisciplinary program of palliative care and supportive services that addresses the physical, spiritual, social, and economic needs of terminally ill patients and their families

Hospice care: The medical care provided to persons with life expectancies of six months or less who elect to forgo standard treatment of their illness and to receive only palliative care

Hospital ambulatory care: Hospital-directed preventive, therapeutic, and rehabilitative services provided by physicians and their surrogates to patients who are not hospital inpatients or home care patients

Hospital autopsy: A postmortem (after death) examination performed on the body of a person who has at some time been a hospital patient by a hospital pathologist or a physician of the medical staff who has been delegated the responsibility

Hospital autopsy rate: The total number of autopsies performed by a hospital pathologist for a given time period divided by the number of deaths of hospital patients (inpatients and outpatients) whose bodies were available for autopsy for the same time period

Hospital death rate: The number of inpatient deaths for a given period of time divided by the total number of live discharges and deaths for the same time period

Hospital discharge abstract system: A group of databases compiled from aggregate data on all patients discharged from a hospital

Hospital information system (HIS): The comprehensive database containing all the clinical, administrative, financial, and demographic information about each patient served by a hospital

Hospital inpatient: A patient who is provided with room, board, and continuous general nursing services in an area of an acute-care facility where patients generally stay at least overnight

Hospital inpatient autopsy: A postmortem (after death) examination performed on the body of a patient who died during an inpatient hospitalization by a hospital pathologist or a physician of the medical staff who has been delegated the responsibility

Hospital newborn inpatient: A patient born in the hospital at the beginning of the current inpatient hospitalization

Hospital outpatient: A patient who receives services in one or more of the facilities owned and operated by a hospital

Hospital Survey and Construction Act: *See* **Hill-Burton Act**

Hospital-acquired conditions (HACs): CMS identified eight HACs (not present on admission) as "reasonably preventable," and hospitals will not receive additional payment for cases in which one of the eight selected conditions was not present on admission; the eight originally selected conditions include foreign object retained after surgery, air embolism, blood incompatibility, stage III and IV pressure ulcers, falls and trauma, catheter-associated urinary tract infection, vascular catheter-associated infection, and surgical site infection—mediastinitis after coronary artery bypass graft; additional conditions were added in 2010 and remain in effect: surgical site infections following certain orthopedic procedures and bariatric surgery, manifestations of poor glycemic control, and deep vein thrombosis (DVT)/pulmonary embolism (PE) following certain orthopedic procedures

Hospital-acquired infection rate: The number of hospital-acquired infections for a given time period divided by the total number of inpatient discharges for the same time period

Hospitalization insurance (HI) (Medicare Part A): A federal program that covers the costs associated with inpatient hospitalization as well as other healthcare services provided to Medicare beneficiaries

Human Genome Nomenclature (HUGN): Interoperability standard for exchanging information regarding the role of genes in biomedical research and healthcare

Human Genome Organisation (HUGO): Manages the Human Genome Nomenclature as a confidential database containing more than 16,000 records

Human relations movement: A management philosophy emphasizing the shift from a mechanistic view of workers to concern for their satisfaction at work

Human subjects: Individuals whose physiologic or behavioral characteristics and responses are the object of study in a research program

Human–computer interface: The device used by humans to access and enter data into a computer system, such as a keyboard on a PC, personal digital assistant, voice recognition system, and so on

Hybrid online analytical processing (HOLAP): A data access methodology that is coupled tightly with the architecture of the database management system to allow the user to perform business analyses

Hybrid record: A health record that includes both paper and electronic elements

HyperText Markup Language (HTML): A standardized computer language that allows the electronic transfer of information and communications among many different information systems

Hypothesis: A statement that describes a research question in measurable terms

Hypothesis test: Allows the analyst to determine the likelihood that a hypothesis is true given the data present in the sample with a predetermined acceptable level of making an error

Icarus Paradox: Proposes that successful styles and methods, unrestrained, can become their extreme, or that our strengths can become our weaknesses: Builders become imperialists, pioneers become escapists, salespersons become drifters, and craftspersons become tinkerers

ICD-9-CM (International Classification of Diseases, Ninth Revision, Clinical Modification): A classification system used in the United States to report morbidity and mortality information

ICD-10-CM (International Classification of Diseases, Tenth Revision, Clinical Modification): The coding classification system that will replace ICD-9-CM, Volumes 1 and 2. ICD-10-CM is the United States clinical modification of the World Health Organization's ICD-10. ICD-10-CM has a total of 21 chapters and contains significantly more codes than ICD-9-CM, providing the ability to code with a greater level of specificity

Identifier standards: Recommended methods for assigning unique identifiers to individuals (patients and clinical providers), corporate providers, and healthcare vendors and suppliers

Identity management: In the master patient index, policies and procedures that manage patient identity, such as prohibiting the same record number for duplicate patients or duplicate records for one patient

Impact factor: A factor that designates the effect the risk will have on the project if it does occur

Implementation: Refers to a system having been installed and configured to meet a specific organization's needs; users have begun to be trained and are beginning to use the system

Implementation phase: The third phase of the systems development life cycle during which a comprehensive plan is developed and instituted to ensure that the new information system is effectively implemented within the organization

Implementation plans: Used to manage the literally thousands of tasks the implementation of any given application requires; these are tactical, relatively short-term plans and often are repeated with only slight variation for every application implemented

Imputation: The substitution of values for the missing values

Incentive: Something that stimulates or encourages an individual to work harder

Incentive pay: A system of bonuses and rewards based on employee productivity; often used in transcription areas of healthcare facilities

Incidence: The number of new cases of a specific disease

Incidence rate: A computation that compares the number of new cases of a specific disease for a given time period to the population at risk for the disease during the same time period

Incident: An occurrence in a medical facility that is inconsistent with accepted standards of care

Incident report: A quality/performance management tool used to collect data and information about potentially compensable events (events that may result in death or serious injury)

Incident report review: An analysis of incident reports or an evaluation of descriptions of adverse events

Income statement: A statement that summarizes an organization's revenue and expense accounts using totals accumulated during the fiscal year

Incomplete record processes: Processes including deficiency analysis and chart completion practices

Indemnity plans: Health insurance coverage provided in the form of cash payments to patients or providers

Identifier standards: Recommended methods for assigning unique identifiers to individuals (patients and clinical providers), corporate providers, and healthcare vendors and suppliers

Independent practice organization (IPO) or association (IPA): An open-panel health maintenance organization that provides contract healthcare services to subscribers through independent physicians who treat patients in their own offices; the HMO reimburses the IPA on a capitated basis; the IPA may reimburse the physicians on a fee-for-service or a capitated basis

Independent practitioners: Individuals working as employees of an organization, in private practice, or through a physician group who provide healthcare services without supervision or direction

Independent variable: An antecedent factor that researchers manipulate directly

Index: An organized (usually alphabetical) list of specific data that serves to guide, indicate, or otherwise facilitate reference to the data

Indian Health Service (IHS): The federal agency within the Department of Health and Human Services that is responsible for providing federal healthcare services to American Indians and Alaska Natives

Indirect costs: Resources expended that cannot be identified as pertaining to specific goods and services (for example, electricity is not allocable to a specific patient)

Indirect standardization: Appropriate to use for risk adjustment when the risk variables are categorical and the rate or proportion for the variable of interest is available for the standard or reference group at the level of the risk categories, the expected outcome rate for each risk category is calculated based on the reference group and then weighted by the volume in each risk group at population to be compared to the standard

Individually identifiable health information: Personal information that can be linked to a specific patient, such as age, gender, date of birth, and address

Inductive reasoning: A process of creating conclusions based on a limited number of observations

Infant mortality rate: The number of deaths of individuals under one year of age during a given time period divided by the number of live births reported for the same time period

Infection review: Evaluation of the risk of infection among patients and healthcare providers, looking for, preventing, and controlling the risk

Inference engine: Specialized computer software that tries to match conditions in rules to data elements in a repository (when a match is found, the engine executes the rule, which results in the occurrence of a specified action)

Inferencing: Determining the intended degree of automation in classification; the intention that validation on input be possible

Inferential statistics: A set of statistical techniques that allows researchers to make generalizations about a population's characteristics (parameters) on the basis of a sample's characteristics

Informatics: A field of study that focuses on the use of technology to improve access to, and utilization of, information

Information: Factual data that have been collected, combined, analyzed, interpreted, and converted into a form that can be used for a specific purpose

Information assets: Information that has value for an organization

Information capture: The process of recording representations of human thought, perceptions, or actions in documenting patient care, as well as device-generated information that is gathered and computed about a patient as part of healthcare

Information integrity: The dependability or trustworthiness of information; it concerns more than data quality or data accuracy—it encompasses the entire framework in which information is recorded, processed, and used

Information life cycle: The cycle of gathering, recording, processing, storing, sharing, transmitting, retrieving, and deleting information

Information management: The acquisition, organization, analysis, storage, retrieval, and dissemination of information to support decision-making activities

Information privacy coordinator/privacy officer: Works in collaboration with managers to assess risks to health information security and privacy, monitor organizational privacy compliance issues, and establish policy and procedures to address security risks

Information science: The study of the nature and principles of information

Information system (IS): An automated system that uses computer hardware and software to record, manipulate, store, recover, and disseminate data (that is, a system that receives and processes input and provides output); often used interchangeably with information technology (IT)

Information technology (IT): Computer technology (hardware and software) combined with telecommunications technology (data, image, and voice networks); often used interchangeably with information system (IS)

Information technology (IT) acquisition strategy: Strategy where, as much as possible, all older applications are replaced with new applications from a single vendor, with newer architecture and more clinically oriented approaches

Information technology professional: An individual who works with computer technology in the process of managing health information

Information theory: A branch of applied mathematics and electrical engineering that involves the quantification of information

Informed consent: 1. A legal term referring to a patient's right to make his or her own treatment decisions based on the knowledge of the treatment to be administered or the procedure to be performed 2. An individual's voluntary agreement to participate in research or to undergo a diagnostic, therapeutic, or preventive medical procedure

In-group: Refers to those subordinates who form a group around the leader

Initiating structure: Leaders in this group were more task-focused and centered on giving direction, setting goals and limits, and planning and scheduling activities

Injury Severity Score (ISS): An overall severity measurement maintained in the trauma registry and calculated from the abbreviated injury scores for the three most severe injuries of each patient

Innovators: Comprise about 2.5 percent of the organization and are individuals who are eager to try new ideas; these individuals tend to be more cosmopolitan, to seek out new information in broad networks, and to be willing to take risks

Inpatient: A patient who is provided with room, board, and continuous general nursing services in an area of an acute-care facility where patients generally stay at least overnight

Inpatient admission: An acute-care facility's formal acceptance of a patient who is to be provided with room, board, and continuous nursing service in an area of the facility where patients generally stay at least overnight

Inpatient bed occupancy rate (percentage of occupancy): The total number of inpatient service days for a given time period divided by the total number of inpatient bed count days for the same time period

Inpatient discharge: The termination of hospitalization through the formal release of an inpatient from a hospital

Inpatient hospitalization: The period during an individual's life when he or she is a patient in a single hospital without interruption except by possible intervening leaves of absence

Inpatient psychiatric facility (IPF): A healthcare facility that offers psychiatric medical care on an inpatient basis; CMS established a prospective payment system for reimbursing these types of facilities using the current DRGs for inpatient hospitals

Inpatient rehabilitation facility (IRF): A healthcare facility that specializes in providing services to patients who have suffered a disabling illness or injury in an effort to help them achieve or maintain their optimal level of functioning, self-care, and independence

Inpatient Rehabilitation Validation and Entry (IRVEN): A computerized data-entry system used by inpatient rehabilitation facilities

Inpatient service day (IPSD): A unit of measure equivalent to the services received by one inpatient during one 24-hour period

In-service education: Training that teaches employees specific skills required to maintain or improve performance, usually internal to an organization

Institute for Clinical Systems Improvement (ICSI): A collaboration of healthcare organizations that provides an objective voice dedicated to supporting healthcare quality and helping its members identify and achieve implementation of best practices for their patients

Institute of Electrical and Electronics Engineers (IEEE): A national organization that develops standards for hospital system interface transactions, including links between critical care bedside instruments and clinical information systems

Institute of Electrical and Electronics Engineers (IEEE) 1073: Interoperability standard for electronic data exchange

Institute of Medicine (IOM): A branch of the National Academy of Sciences whose goal is to advance and distribute scientific knowledge with the mission of improving human health

Institutional review board (IRB): An administrative body that provides oversight for the research studies conducted within a healthcare institution

Instrument: A standardized and uniform way to collect data

Insurance certification: The process of determining that the patient has insurance coverage for the treatment that is planned or expected

Insured: A holder of a health insurance policy

Insurer: An organization that pays healthcare expenses on behalf of its enrollees

Integrated delivery network (IDN): *See* **integrated delivery system**

Integrated delivery system (IDS): A system that combines the financial and clinical aspects of healthcare and uses a group of healthcare providers, selected on the basis of quality and cost management criteria, to furnish comprehensive health services across the continuum of care

Integrated health record: A system of health record organization in which all of the paper forms are arranged in strict chronological order and mixed with forms created by different departments

Integrated provider organization (IPO): An organization that manages the delivery of healthcare services provided by hospitals, physicians (employees of the IPO), and other healthcare organizations (for example, nursing facilities)

Integration: The complex task of ensuring that all elements and platforms in an information system communicate and act as a uniform entity; or the combination of two or more benefit plans to prevent duplication of benefit payment

Integrity: The state of being whole or unimpaired

Integrity constraints: Limits placed on the data that may be entered into a database

Intellectual capital: The combined knowledge of an organization's employees with respect to operations, processes, history, and culture

Intelligent character recognition (ICR) technology: A method of encoding handwritten, print, or cursive characters and of interpreting the characters as words or the intent of the writer

Intelligent document recognition (IDR) technology: Technology that automatically recognizes analog items, such as tangible materials or documents, or recognizes characters or symbols from analog items, enabling the identified data to be quickly, accurately, and automatically entered into digital systems

Interface: The zone between different computer systems across which users want to pass information (for example, a computer program written to exchange information between systems or the graphic display of an application program designed to make the program easier to use)

Interface engine: A tool to manage the multiplicity of interfaces and track changes

Interface terminology: Concerned with facilitating clinician documentation within the standardized structure (for example, menus, drop-down boxes) needed for an EHR; provides a limited set of words and phrases in a manner that is consistent with a clinician's thought process used while documenting

Interim period: Any period that represents less than an entire fiscal year

Internal controls: Policies and procedures designed to protect an organization's assets and to reduce the exposure to the risk of loss due to error or malfeasance

Internal customers: Customers located within the organization

Internal rate of return (IRR): An interest rate that makes the net present value calculation equal zero

Internal validity: An attribute of a study's design that contributes to the accuracy of its findings

International Classification for Nursing Practice (ICNP): Unified nursing language system into which existing terminologies can be cross-mapped

International Classification of Diseases (ICD): Used by more than 100 countries worldwide to classify diseases and other health issues; the classification system facilitates the storage and retrieval of diagnostic information and serves as the basis for compiling mortality and morbidity statistics reported by World Health Organization members

International Classification of Diseases, 11th Revision (ICD-11): Edition of ICD that is under way; a significant difference is that it will be designed to include linkages to standardized healthcare terminologies to facilitate processing and use of the data for a variety of purposes such as research

International Classification of Diseases for Oncology, 3rd Revision (ICD-O-3): A classification system used for reporting incidences of malignant disease

International Classification of Diseases, 9th Revision, Clinical Modification (ICD-9-CM): A derivative work of the International Classification of Diseases, 9th Revision, as developed by the World Health Organization; ICD-9-CM is used in the United States only to code and classify diagnoses from inpatient and outpatient records, as well as inpatient procedures

International Classification of Diseases, 10th Revision, Clinical Modification (ICD-10-CM): Modified for the reporting of morbidity data, ICD-10-CM contains a substantial increase in content over ICD-9-CM

International Classification of Diseases, 10th Revision, Procedure Coding System (ICD-10-PCS): A new procedural coding system to replace the Tabular List of Procedures, Volume 3 of ICD-9-CM

International Classification of Primary Care (ICPC-2): Classification used for coding the reasons of encounter, diagnoses, and interventions in an episode-of-care structure

International Classification on Functioning, Disability and Health (ICF): Classification of health and health-related domains that describe body functions and structures, activities, and participation

International Federation of Health Information Management (IFHIM): Organization that supports national associations and health record professionals to improve health records and systems; IFHIM was established in 1968 under the; now known as IFHIM, International Federation of Health Record Organizations, as a forum to bring national organizations together

International Federation of Health Record Organizations (IFHRO): Organization that supports national associations and health record professionals to implement and improve health records and the systems that support them; now known as IFHIM

International Health Terminology Standards Development Organisation (IHTSDO): An international nonprofit organization based in Denmark that distributes SNOMED CT (Systematized Nomenclature of Medicine–Clinical Terminology)

International Medical Informatics Association (IMIA): Worldwide not-for-profit organization that promotes medical informatics in healthcare and biomedical research

International Organization for Standardization (ISO): A nongovernmental global organization established in 1987 that provides more than 17,000 quality standards for nearly every business, technology, and industry sector

Interoperability: The ability, generally by adoption of standards, of systems to work together

Interoperable: Adjective form of interoperability

Interoperate: Verb form of interoperability

Interpersonal skills: One of the three managerial skill categories that includes skills in communicating and relating effectively to others

Interrater reliability: A measure of a research instrument's consistency in data collection when used by different abstractors

Interrogatories: Discovery devices consisting of a set of written questions given to a party, witness, or other person who has information needed in a legal case

Interval data: A type of data that represents observations that can be measured on an evenly distributed scale beginning at a point other than true zero

Interval history: If the history and physical have been completed within the 30 days prior to admission, there must be an updated entry in the medical record that documents an examination for any changes in the patient's condition since the original history and physical examination, and this entry must be included in the record within the first 24 hours of admission

Interval-level data: The intervals between successive values are equal

Interval scale: Situation where the intervals between adjacent scale values are equal with respect to the attributes being measured

Intervention: 1. A clinical manipulation, treatment, or therapy 2. A generic term used by researchers to mean an act of some kind

Interview: A formal meeting, often between a job applicant and a potential employer

Interview guide: A list of written questions to be asked during an interview

Interview survey: A type of research instrument with which the members of the population being studied are asked questions and respond orally

Intranet: A private information network that is similar to the Internet and whose servers are located inside a firewall or security barrier so that the general public cannot gain access to information housed within the network

Intrarater reliability: A measure of a research instrument's reliability in which the same person repeating the test will get reasonably similar findings

Intuition: Unconscious decision making based on extensive experience in similar situations

Inventor: Individual who develops a new idea or practice in the organization

Inventory: Goods on hand and available to sell, presumably within a year (a business cycle)

Investor-owned hospital chain: Group of for-profit healthcare facilities owned by stockholders

Invoice: Bill or request for payment

ISO 9000: An internationally agreed-upon set of generic standards for quality management systems established by the International Standards Organization

Issue log: A form of documentation that describes the questions, concerns, and problems that must be solved in order for a task to be completed

Job classification method: 1. A method of job evaluation that compares a written position description with the written descriptions of various classification grades 2. A method used by the federal government to grade jobs

Job description: A list of a job's duties, reporting relationships, working conditions, and responsibilities

Job evaluation: The process of applying predefined compensable factors to jobs to determine their relative worth

Job procedure: A structured, action-oriented list of sequential steps involved in carrying out a specific job or solving a problem

Job ranking: A method of job evaluation that arranges jobs in a hierarchy on the basis of each job's importance to the organization, with the most important jobs listed at the top of the hierarchy and the least important jobs listed at the bottom

Job rotation: A work design in which workers are shifted periodically among different tasks

Job sharing: A work schedule in which two or more individuals share the tasks of one full-time or one full-time-equivalent position

Job specifications: A list of a job's required education, skills, knowledge, abilities, personal qualifications, and physical requirements

Joint Commission: A private, not-for-profit organization that evaluates and accredits hospitals and other healthcare organizations on the basis of predefined performance standards; formerly the Joint Commission on Accreditation of Healthcare Organizations (JCAHO)

Journal entry: An accounting representation of a financial transaction or transfer of amounts between accounts that contains at least one debit and one credit and in which the dollar value of the debits and the credits is the same

Judge-made law: Unwritten law originating from court decisions where no applicable statute exists; *See* **common law or case law**

Jurisdiction: The power and authority of a court to hear and decide specific types of cases

Justice: The impartial administration of policies or laws that takes into consideration the competing interests and limited resources of the individuals or groups involved

Just-in-time training: Training provided anytime, anyplace, and just when it is needed

Key attributes: Common fields (attributes) within a relational database that are used to link tables to one another

Key indicator: A quantifiable measure used over time to determine whether some structure, process, or outcome in the provision of care to a patient supports high-quality performance measured against best practice criteria

Key performance indicator: Area identified for needed improvement through benchmarking and continuous quality improvement

Knowledge: The information, understanding, and experience that give individuals the power to make informed decisions

Knowledge assets: Assets that are the sources of knowledge for an organization (for example, printed documents; unwritten rules; workflows; customer knowledge; data in databases and spreadsheets; and the human expertise, know-how, and tacit knowledge within the minds of the organization's workforce)

Knowledge base: A database that not only manages raw data but also integrates them with information from various reference works

Knowledge management: 1. The process by which data are acquired and transformed into information through the application of context, which in turn provides understanding   2. A management philosophy that promotes an integrated and collaborative approach to the process of information asset creation, capture, organization, access, and use

Knowledge-based data: The sources of knowledge for an organization (for example, printed documents; unwritten rules; workflows; customer knowledge; data in databases and spreadsheets; and the human expertise, know-how, and tacit knowledge within the minds of the organization's workforce); also called knowledge-based assets

Knowledge-based DSS: Decision support system in which the key element is the knowledge base; often referred to as a rule-based system because the knowledge is stored in the form of rules (for example, the IF, THEN, ELSE format)

Kolb's "Learning Loop": A theory of experiential learning involving four interrelated steps: concrete experiences, observation and reflection, formation of abstract concepts and theories, and testing new implications of theory in new situations

Laboratory information system (LIS): System that, in addition to producing lab results, manages workload balancing, supplies inventories, Medicare medical necessity checking, billing, and public health reporting and generates custom reports for clinical or quality management

Labor relations: Human resources management activities associated with unions and collective bargaining

Labor-Management Relations Act (Taft-Hartley Act): Federal legislation passed in 1947 that imposed certain restrictions on unions while upholding their right to organize and bargain collectively

Labor-Management Reporting and Disclosure Act (Landrum-Griffin Act): Federal legislation passed in 1959 to ensure that union members' interests were properly represented by union leadership; created, among other things, a bill of rights for union members

Laggards: Members of this group are usually the last ones to respond to innovation and make up as much as 16 percent of the organization; they are often characterized as isolated, uninformed, and mistrustful of change and change agents, but they may serve a function by keeping the organization from changing too quickly

Late majority: Skeptical group that comprises another 34 percent of the organization; individuals in this group usually adopt innovations only after social or financial pressure to do so

Layoff: A suspension of work, usually temporary

Leader–member exchange: Micro theory that focuses on dyadic relationships, or those between two people or between a leader and a small group; explains how in-group and out-group relationships form with a leader or mentor, and how delegation may occur

Leader–member relations: Group atmosphere much like social orientation that includes the subordinates' acceptance of, and confidence in, the leader as well as the loyalty and commitment they show toward the leader

Leadership grid: Blake and Mouton's grid that marked off degrees of emphasis toward orientation using a nine-point scale; and finally separated the grid into five styles of management based on the combined people and production emphasis

Leading: One of the four management functions in which people are directed and motivated to achieve goals

Lean: Management strategy known for its focus on the reduction of waste that is based on the Japanese success story of Toyota

Leapfrog Group: Organization that promotes healthcare safety by giving consumers the information they need to make better-informed choices about the hospitals they choose

Learning content management system: Training software development tools that assist with management, sharing, and reuse of course content

Learning curve: The time required to acquire and apply certain skills so that new levels of productivity and performance exceed prelearning levels (productivity often is inversely related to the learning curve)

Learning history: The extensive and relatively long-term process of eliciting stories, experiences, and critical events in the life of the organization and its employees

Learning management system: A software application that assists with managing and tracking learners and learning events and collating data on learner progress

Least preferred coworker (LPC) scale: Presents a series of 16 to 22 bipolar adjectives along an eight-point rating scale; sample items include unfriendly to friendly, uncooperative to cooperative, and hostile to supportive

Lecture: A one-way method of delivering education through speaking in which the teacher delivers the speech and the student listens

Legacy system: A type of computer system that uses older technology but may still perform optimally

Legal health record: The subset of all patient-specific data created or accumulated by a healthcare provider that may be released to third parties in response to legally permissible requests

Length of stay (LOS): The total number of patient days for an inpatient episode, calculated by subtracting the date of admission from the date of discharge

Level of significance: 1. The relative intensity of services given when a physician provides one-on-one services for a patient (such as minimal, brief, limited, or intermediate)   2. The relative intensity of services provided by a healthcare facility (for example, tertiary care); also called level of service

Lewin's stages of change: One of the first models of change proposed by Kurt Lewin (1951), one of the early behavioral scientists who contributed to the knowledge base of information on group work, leadership, and organization development; *see* **refreezing** and **unfreezing**

Lexicon: 1. the vocabulary used in a language or a subject area or by a particular speaker or group of speakers   2. A collection of words or terms and their meanings for a particular domain, used in healthcare for drug terms

Liability: 1. A legal obligation or responsibility that may have financial repercussions if not fulfilled   2. An amount owed by an individual or organization to another individual or organization

Licensure: The legal authority or formal permission from authorities to carry on certain activities that by law or regulation require such permission (applicable to institutions as well as individuals)

Likert scale: An ordinal scaling and summated rating technique for measuring the attitudes of respondents; a measure that records level of agreement or disagreement along a progression of categories, usually five (five-point scale), often administered in the form of a questionnaire

Line authority: The authority to manage subordinates and to have them report back, based on relationships illustrated in an organizational chart

Line graph: A graphic technique used to illustrate the relationship between continuous measurements; consists of a line drawn to connect a series of points on an arithmetic scale; often used to display time trends

Linear programming: An operational management technique that uses mathematical formulas to determine the optimal way to allocate resources for a project

Linkage analysis: A technique used to explore and examine relationships among a large number of variables of different types

Liquidity: The degree to which assets can be quickly and efficiently turned into cash, for example, marketable securities are generally very liquid, the assumption being that they can be sold for their full value in a matter of days, whereas buildings are not very liquid, because they cannot usually be sold quickly

Literature review: A systematic and critical investigation of the important information about a topic; may include books, journal articles, theses, dissertations, periodicals, technical and research reports, proceedings of conferences, audiovisual media, and electronic media

Litigation: A civil lawsuit or contest in court

Local Coverage Determination (LCD): New format for LMRPs, coverage rules, at a fiscal intermediary (FI) or carrier level, that provide information on what diagnoses justify the medical necessity of a test; LCDs vary from state to state

Logical (or conceptual) repository: The compilation of multiple physical repositories

Logical data model: The second level of data model that is drawn according to the type of database to be developed

Logical Observation Identifier Names and Codes (LOINC): A database protocol developed by the Regenstrief Institute for Health Care aimed at standardizing laboratory and clinical codes for use in clinical care, outcomes management, and research

Longitudinal: A type of time frame for research studies during which data are collected from the same participants at multiple points in time

Longitudinal health record: A permanent, coordinated patient record of significant information listed in chronological order and maintained across time, ideally from birth to death

Long-term assets: Assets whose value to the organization extends beyond one fiscal year; for example, buildings, land, and equipment are long-term assets

Long-term care: Healthcare services provided in a nonacute-care setting to chronically ill, aged, disabled, or mentally handicapped individuals

Long-term care hospital (LTCH): A healthcare organization that provides medical, nursing, rehabilitation, and subacute-care services to residents who need continual care

Loss prevention: A risk management strategy that includes developing and revising policies and procedures that are both facility wide and department specific

Loss reduction: A component of a risk management program that encompasses techniques used to manage events or claims that already have taken place

Low-utilization payment adjustment (LUPA): An alternative (reduced) payment made to home health agencies instead of the home health resource group reimbursement rate when a patient receives fewer than four home care visits during a 60-day episode

Machine learning: An area of computer science that studies algorithms and computer programs that improve employee performance on some task by exposure to a training or learning experience

Maintenance and evaluation phase: The fourth and final phase of the systems development life cycle that helps to ensure that adequate technical support staff and resources are available to maintain or support the new system

Major diagnostic category (MDC): Under diagnosis-related groups (DRGs), one of 25 categories based on single or multiple organ systems into which all diseases and disorders relating to that system are classified

Major medical insurance (catastrophic coverage): Prepaid healthcare benefits that include a high limit for most types of medical expenses and usually require a large deductible and sometimes place limits on coverage and charges (for example, room and board)

Malpractice: The improper or negligent treatment of a patient, as by a physician, resulting in injury, damage, or loss

Managed care: 1. Payment method in which the third-party payer has implemented some provisions to control the costs of healthcare while maintaining quality care   2. Systematic merger of clinical, financial, and administrative processes to manage access, cost, and quality of healthcare

Managed care organization (MCO): A type of healthcare organization that delivers medical care and manages all aspects of the care or the payment for care by limiting providers of care, discounting payment to providers of care, and limiting access to care

Management by objectives (MBO): A management approach that defines target objectives for organizing work and comparing performance against those objectives

Management functions: Traditionally, the tasks of planning, organizing, directing, coordinating, and controlling

Management information system (MIS): A computer-based system that provides information to a healthcare organization's managers for use in making decisions that affect a variety of day-to-day activities

Management service organization (MSO): An organization, usually owned by a group of physicians or a hospital, that provides administrative and support services to one or more physician group practices or small hospitals

Managerial accounting: The development, implementation, and analysis of systems that track financial transactions for management control purposes, including both budget systems and cost analysis systems

Many-to-many relationship: The concept (occurring only in a conceptual model) that multiple instances of an entity may be associated with multiple instances of another entity

MAP keys: Each MAP key measures a specific revenue cycle function and provides the purpose for the measurement, the value of the measure, and the specific equation (numerator and denominator) to consistently calculate the measure

Mark sense technology: Technology that detects the presence or absence of hand-marked characters on analog documents; used for processing questionnaires, surveys, and tests, such as filled-in circles by Number 2 pencils on exam forms

Maslow's hierarchy of needs: A theory developed by Abraham Maslow suggesting that a hierarchy of needs might help explain behavior and guide managers on how to motivate employees; *See* **hierarchy of needs**

Massed training: An educational technique that requires learning a large amount of material at one time

Master patient index (MPI): A list or database created and maintained by a healthcare facility to record the name and identification number of every patient who has ever been admitted or treated in the facility

Master planning committee: *See* **steering committee**

Matching: A concept that enables decision makers to look at expenses and revenues in the same period to measure the organization's income performance

Materiality: The significance of a dollar amount based on predetermined criteria

Maternal death rate (hospital based): For a hospital, the total number of maternal deaths directly related to pregnancy for a given time period divided by the total number of obstetrical discharges for the same time period; for a community, the total number of deaths attributed to maternal conditions during a given time period in a specific geographic area divided by the total number of live births for the same time period in the same area

Maternal mortality rate (community based): A rate that measures the deaths associated with pregnancy for a specific community for a specific period of time

Matrixed team structure: The matrixed organization maintains the functional organization. Team members report to a functional manager and remain employees of that department; they receive their project assignments from the project manager

Mean: A measure of central tendency that is determined by calculating the arithmetic average of the observations in a frequency distribution

Meaningful use: A regulation that was issued by the Centers for Medicare and Medicaid Services (CMS) on July 28, 2010, outlining an incentive program for professionals (EPs), eligible hospitals, and critical access hospitals (CAHs) participating in Medicare and Medicaid programs that adopt and successfully demonstrate meaningful use of certified electronic health record (EHR) technology

Measure applications partnership: Performance measures that will be used in public reporting and performance-based payment programs are outlined and described

Measure hierarchy: Used to organize the measure set information

Measures of central tendency: The typical or average numbers that are descriptive of the entire collection of data for a specific population

Median: A measure of central tendency that shows the midpoint of a frequency distribution when the observations have been arranged in order from lowest to highest

Medicaid: An entitlement program that oversees medical assistance for individuals and families with low incomes and limited resources; jointly funded between state and federal governments

Medicaid Integrity Contract (MIC): CMS contracts with eligible entities to review and audit Medicaid claims to identity overpayments and provide education on program integrity issues

Medical care evaluation studies (medical audits): Audits required by the Medicare Conditions of Participation that dictate the use of screening criteria with evaluation by diagnosis and procedure

Medical device: Device used by a physician for a patient who has a condition where a body part does not achieve any of its primary intended purposes such as a heart valve; can be used for life support, such as anesthesia ventilators, as well as for monitoring of patients, such as fetal monitors and other uses such as incubators

Medical foundation: Multipurpose, nonprofit service organization for physicians and other healthcare providers at the local and county level; as managed care organizations, medical foundations have established preferred provider organizations, exclusive provider organizations, and management service organizations, with emphases on freedom of choice and preservation of the physician–patient relationship

Medical identity theft: Committed by family, friends and acquaintances, and strangers who steal someone's identity in order obtain medical care, services, or equipment either because they do not have medical care or their insurance does not cover the needed services

Medical informatics: A field of information science concerned with the management of data and information used to diagnose, treat, cure, and prevent disease through the application of computers and computer technologies

Medical informatics professionals: Individuals who work in the field of medical informatics

Medical Internet: Allows providers of care to electronically exchange data among all electronic health records so that a complete electronic health record can be assembled whenever and wherever a patient presents for care

Medical Literature, Analysis, and Retrieval System Online (MEDLINE): A computerized, online database in the bibliographic Medical Literature Analysis and Retrieval System (MEDLARS) of the National Library of Medicine

Medical necessity: 1. The likelihood that a proposed healthcare service will have a reasonable beneficial effect on the patient's physical condition and quality of life at a specific point in his or her illness or lifetime   2. Healthcare services and supplies that are proven or acknowledged to be effective in the diagnosis, treatment, cure, or relief of a health condition, illness, injury, disease, or its symptoms and to be consistent with the community's accepted standard of care. Under medical necessity, only those services, procedures, and patient care activities warranted by the patient's condition are provided   3. The concept that procedures are only eligible for reimbursement as a covered benefit when they are performed for a specific diagnosis or specified frequency

Medical staff bylaws: A collection of guidelines adopted by a hospital's medical staff to govern its business conduct and the rights and responsibilities of its members

Medical staff classifications: Categories of clinical practice privileges assigned to individual practitioners on the basis of their qualifications

Medical Subject Headings database (MeSH): The National Library of Medicine's (NLM's) controlled vocabulary for indexing journal articles

Medical tourism: The practice of traveling from one country, or city, to another to seek healthcare services

Medical transcription: *See* **transcription**

Medical transcriptionist: A medical language specialist who types or word-processes information dictated by providers

Medically needy option (Medicaid): An option in the Medicaid program that allows states to extend eligibility to persons who would be eligible for Medicaid under one of the mandatory or optional groups but whose income and resources fall above the eligibility level set by their state

Medicare: A federally funded health program established in 1965 to assist with the medical care costs of Americans 65 years of age or older as well as other individuals entitled to Social Security benefits owing to their disabilities

Medicare administrative contractor (MAC): Contracting entities that administer Medicare Part A and Part B as of 2011; MACs replace the carriers and fiscal intermediaries

Medicare Advantage (Medicare Part C): Optional managed care plan for Medicare beneficiaries who are entitled to Part A, enrolled in Part B, and live in an area with a plan; types include health maintenance organization, point-of-service plan, preferred provider organization, and provider-sponsored organization

Medicare carrier: A health plan that processes Part B claims for services by physicians and medical suppliers (for example, the Blue Shield plan in a state)

Medicare fee schedule (MFS): A feature of the resource-based relative value system that includes a complete list of the payments Medicare makes to physicians and other providers

Medicare prospective payment system: The reimbursement system for inpatient hospital services provided to Medicare and Medicaid beneficiaries that is based on the use of diagnosis-related groups as a classification tool

Medicare Provider Analysis and Review (MEDPAR) database system: A database containing information submitted by fiscal intermediaries that is used by the Office of Inspector General to identify suspicious billing and charge practices

Medicare severity diagnosis-related groups (MS-DRGs): The US government's 2007 revision of the DRG system, the MS-DRG system better accounts for severity of illness and resource consumption

Medicare Summary Notice (MSN): A summary sent to the patient from Medicare that summarizes all services provided over a period of time with an explanation of benefits provided

Medication administration records (MARs): The records used to document the date and time each dose and type of medication is administered to a patient

Medication list: An ongoing record of the medications a patient has received in the past and is taking currently; includes names of medications, dosages, amounts dispensed, dispensing instructions, prescription dates, discontinued dates, and the problem for which the medication was prescribed

Medication reconciliation: Checking medications each time a patient transfers to another level of care

Medication usage review: An evaluation of medication use and medication processes

Medigap: A private insurance policy that supplements Medicare coverage

Mental ability (cognitive) tests: Tests that assess the reasoning capabilities of individuals

Mentor: An advisor; an experienced individual who coaches another individual who is at the beginning stages of his or her career

Message format standards: Protocols that help ensure that data transmitted from one system to another remain comparable

Meta-analysis: A specialized form of systematic literature review that involves the statistical analysis of a large collection of results from individual studies for the purpose of integrating the studies' findings

Metadata: Descriptive data that characterize other data to create a clearer understanding of their meaning and to achieve greater reliability and quality of information

Metadata registry: Used to store characteristics of data that are necessary to clearly describe, inventory, analyze, and classify data

Metric: Data that can be measured on some scale; two subtypes are interval and ratio

Microfilming: A photographic process that reduces an original paper document into a small image on film to save storage space

Middle managers: The individuals in an organization who oversee the operation of a broad scope of functions at the departmental level or who oversee defined product or service lines

Migration path: A series of steps required to move from one situation to another

Minimum Data Set 2.0 (MDS): The instrument specified by the Centers for Medicare and Medicaid Services that requires nursing facilities (both Medicare certified and Medicaid certified) to conduct a comprehensive, accurate, standardized, reproducible assessment of each resident's functional capacity

Minimum Data Set 3.0 (MDS): Document created when OBRA required CMS to develop an assessment instrument to standardize the collection of SNF patient data; the MDS is the minimum core of defined and categorized patient assessment data that serves as the basis for documentation and reimbursement in an SNF

Minimum Data Set for Long-Term Care–Version 2.0 (MDS 2.0): A federally mandated standard assessment form that Medicare- and Medicaid-certified nursing facilities must use to collect demographic and clinical data on nursing home residents

Minimum necessary standard: A stipulation of the HIPAA privacy rule that requires healthcare facilities and other covered entities to make reasonable efforts to limit the patient-identifiable information they disclose to the least amount required to accomplish the intended purpose for which the information was requested

Misdemeanor: A crime that is less serious than a felony

Missing values: Variables that do not contain values for some cases

Mission statement: A short description of an organization's or group's general purpose for existing

Mixed methods research: Research that combines quantitative and qualitative techniques within a single study and across related studies

m-learning: Mobile learning; the application of e-learning to mobile computing devices and wireless networks

Mode: A measure of central tendency that consists of the most frequent observation in a frequency distribution

Model: The representation of a theory in a visual format, on a smaller scale, or with objects

Model-based DDS: Decision support system that attempts to include as many different models as can be accommodated to provide the user the greatest flexibility in framing the decision situation

Moral values: A system of principles by which one guides one's life, usually with regard to right or wrong

Morality: A composite of the personal values concerning what is considered right or wrong in a specific cultural group

Morbidity: A diseased state

Morphological: Refers to the study and description of word formation in a language, including inflection, derivation, and compounding

Morphology: In ICD-O-3, this code describes the characteristics of the tumor itself, including cell type and biologic activity

Mortality (attrition): 1. A term referring to the incidence of death in a specific population   2. The loss of subjects during the course of a clinical research study

Mortality review: A review of deaths as part of an analysis of ongoing outcome and performance improvement

Mortgage: A loan that is secured by a long-term asset, usually a building

Motion for summary judgment: A request made by the defendant in a civil case to have the case ruled in his or her favor based on the assertion that the plaintiff has no genuine issue to be tried

Motion (or streaming) video/frame data: A medium for storing, manipulating, and displaying moving images in a format, such as frames, that can be presented on a computer monitor

Motivation: The drive to accomplish a task

Movement diagram: A chart depicting the location of furniture and equipment in a work area and showing the usual flow of individuals or materials as they progress through the work area

Multiaxial: Coding system with more than one axis, such as in the Diagnostic and Statistical Manual of Mental Diseases (DSM)

Multidimensional analysis: Simultaneous analysis of data from multiple dimensions using different data elements

Multidimensional data structure: A structure whereby data are organized according to the dimensions associated with them

Multidimensional database management system (MDDBMS): A database management system specifically designed to handle data organized into a data structure with numerous dimensions

Multidimensional online analytical processing (MOLAP): A data access methodology that is coupled tightly with a multidimensional database management system to allow the user to perform business analyses

Multimedia: The combination of free-text, raster or vector graphics, sound, and motion video/frame data

Multiuser virtual environments (MUVEs): Sometimes called virtual worlds, bring a new dimension to learning as they can be used to simulate a work environment that is accessed over the Internet

Multivariate: A term used in reference to research studies indicating that many variables were involved

Multivoting technique: A decision-making method for determining group consensus on the prioritization of issues or solutions

Narratives: The author details the processes of the procedure in a step-by-step description method

National Alliance for Health Information Technology (NAHIT): A partnership of government and private-sector leaders from various healthcare organizations that worked to use technology to achieve improvements in patient safety, quality of care, and operating performance; founded in 2002 and ceased operations in 2009

National Association for Home Care & Hospice (NAHC): The nation's largest trade association representing the interests and concerns of home care agencies, hospices, and home care aide organizations

National Association for Healthcare Quality (NAHQ): An organization devoted to advancing the profession of healthcare quality improvement through its accreditation program

National CAHPS Benchmarking Database (NCBD): Contains ten years' worth of data from the Health Plan Survey as well as two years of data from the new Hospital Survey; CAHPS is best known for its Health Plan Survey, which is well respected in the healthcare industry for obtaining consumers' perspective of their health plans

National Cancer Institute (NCI) Thesaurus: Interoperability standard that describes anatomical locations for clinical, surgical, pathological, and research purposes

National Cancer Registrars Association (NCRA): An organization of cancer registry professionals that promotes research and education in cancer registry administration and practice

National Center for Health Statistics (NCHS): The federal agency responsible for collecting and disseminating information on health services utilization and the health status of the population in the United States

National Committee for Quality Assurance (NCQA): A private not-for-profit accreditation organization whose mission is to evaluate and report on the quality of managed care organizations in the United States

National Committee on Vital and Health Statistics (NCVHS): A public policy advisory board that recommends policy to the National Center for Health Statistics and other health-related federal programs

National Coverage Determination (NCD): An NCD sets forth the extent to which Medicare will cover specific services, procedures, or technologies on a national basis; Medicare contractors are required to follow NCDs

National conversion factor (CF): A mathematical factor used to convert relative value units into monetary payments for services provided to Medicare beneficiaries

National Correct Coding Initiative (NCCI): A series of code edits on Medicare Part B claims

National Council for Prescription Drug Programs (NCPDP): An organization that develops standards for exchanging prescription and payment information

National Drug Code (NDC) Directory: A list of all drugs manufactured, prepared, propagated, compounded, or processed by a drug establishment registered under the Federal Food, Drug, and Cosmetic Act

National Drug Codes (NDCs): Codes that serve as product identifiers for human drugs, currently limited to prescription drugs and a few selected over-the-counter products

National Health Care Survey: A national public health survey that contains data abstracted manually from a sample of acute-care hospitals or from discharged inpatient records or that are obtained from state or other discharge databases

National health information infrastructure (NHII): An initiative set forth to improve the effectiveness, efficiency, and overall quality of health and healthcare in the United States; a comprehensive knowledge-based network of interoperable systems of clinical, public health, and personal health information that would improve decision making by making health information available when and where it is needed; the set of technologies, standards, applications, systems, values, and laws that support all facets of individual health, healthcare, and public health

National health information network (NHIN): System that links various healthcare information systems together, allowing patients, physicians, healthcare institutions, and other entities nationwide to share clinical information privately and securely

National Hospital and Palliative Care Organization (NHPCO): Organization whose mission is to lead and mobilize social change for improved care at the end of life

National Information Infrastructure–Health Information Network Program (NII-HIN): A national quasi-governmental organization that provides oversight of all healthcare information standards in the United States

National Institute for Standards and Technology (NIST): An agency of the US Department of Commerce, was founded in 1901 as the nation's first federal physical science research laboratory

National Institutes of Health (NIH): Federal agency of the Department of Health and Human Services comprising a number of institutes that carry out research and programs related to certain types of diseases, such as cancer

National Labor Relations Act (Wagner Act): Federal pro-union legislation passed in 1935, later amended by the Taft-Hartley Act

National Library of Medicine (NLM): The world's largest medical library and a branch of the National Institutes of Health

National Patient Safety Goals (NPSGs): The National Patient Safety Goals outline for healthcare organizations the areas of organizational practice that most commonly lead to patient injury or other negative outcomes that can be prevented when staff utilize standardized procedures

National Practitioner Data Bank (NPDB): A data bank established by the federal government through the 1986 Health Care Quality Improvement Act that contains information on professional review actions taken against physicians and other licensed healthcare practitioners, which healthcare organizations are required to check as part of the credentialing process

National provider identifier (NPI): An eight-character alphanumeric identifier used to identify individual healthcare providers for Medicare billing purposes

National Quality Forum: A private, not-for-profit membership organization created to develop and implement a strategy nationwide to improve the measurement and reporting of healthcare quality

National Vaccine Advisory Committee (NVAC): A national advisory group that supports the director of the National Vaccine Program

National Vital Statistics System (NVSS): A federal agency responsible for the collection of official vital statistics for the United States

National health information network (NHIN): Network envisioned by the government whereby health information may be exchanged securely and seamlessly to authorized parties across the country

Natural language processing (NLP): *See* **natural language processing technology**

Natural language processing technology: The extraction of unstructured or structured medical word data, which are then translated into diagnostic or procedural codes for clinical and administrative applications

Naturalism: A philosophy of research that assumes that multiple contextual truths exist and bias is always present

Naturalistic observation: A type of nonparticipant observation in which researchers observe certain behaviors and events as they occur naturally

Needs assessment: A procedure performed to determine what is required, lacking, or desired by an employee, a group, or an organization

Need-to-know principle: The release-of-information principle based on the minimum necessary standard that means that only the information needed by a specific individual to perform a specific task should be released

Negative (inverse) relationship: A relationship in which the effects move in opposite directions

Negligence: A legal term that refers to the result of an action by an individual who does not act the way a reasonably prudent person would act under the same circumstances

Neonatal mortality rate: The number of deaths of infants under 28 days of age during a given time period divided by the total number of births for the same time period

Net assets: The organization's resources remaining after subtracting its liabilities

Net autopsy rate: The ratio of inpatient autopsies compared to inpatient deaths calculated by dividing the total number of inpatient autopsies performed by the hospital pathologist for a given time period by the total number of inpatient deaths minus unautopsied coroners' or medical examiners' cases for the same time period

Net death rate: The total number of inpatient deaths minus the number of deaths that occurred less than 48 hours after admission for a given time period divided by the total number of inpatient discharges minus the number of deaths that occurred less than 48 hours after admission for the same time period

Net income: The difference between total revenues and total expenses

Net loss: The condition when total expenses exceed total revenue

Net present value: A formula used to assess the current value of a project when the monies used were invested in the organization's investment vehicles rather than expended for the project; this value is then compared to the allocation of the monies and the cash inflows of the project, both of which are adjusted to current time

Network administrators: The individuals involved in installing, configuring, managing, monitoring, and maintaining network computer applications and responsible for supporting the network infrastructure and controlling user access

Network model health maintenance program: Program in which participating HMOs contract for services with one or more multispecialty group practices

Network provider: A physician or another healthcare professional who is a member of a managed care network

Neural networks: Nonlinear predictive models that, using a set of data that describe what a person wants to find, detect a pattern to match a particular profile through a training process that involves interactive learning

Neutral zone: Begins when the old system has been left behind but the new one has not yet been fully accepted

Neutralizers: When a leader's behavior becomes abusive or produces adverse effects, but it is not feasible to replace the leader, efforts can be made to neutralize the negative effects; subordinates whose performance is influenced by insightful self-monitoring professional standards, group cohesion and peer feedback, and an objective performance feedback system are less adversely affected

New beginnings: Stage in which people accept, orient themselves, and engage in the new organization

Newborn (NB): An inpatient who was born in a hospital at the beginning of the current inpatient hospitalization

Newborn autopsy rate: The number of autopsies performed on newborns who died during a given time period divided by the total number of newborns who died during the same time period

Newborn death rate: The number of newborns who died divided by the total number of newborns, both alive and dead

Nomenclature: A recognized system of terms used in a science or an art form that follows preestablished naming conventions; a disease nomenclature is a listing of the proper name for each disease entity with its specific code number

Nominal data: *See* **nominal-level data**

Nominal group technique: A group process technique that involves the steps of silent listing, recording each participant's list, discussing, and rank ordering the priority or importance of items

Nominal-level data: Data that fall into groups or categories that are mutually exclusive and with no specific order (for example, patient demographics such as third-party payer, race, and sex)

Nonexempt employees: All groups of employees covered by the provisions of the Fair Labor Standards Act

Nonmaleficence: A legal principle that means "do no harm"

Nonparametric (distribution-free) technique: A type of statistical procedure used for variables that are not normally distributed in a population

Nonparticipant observation: A method of research in which researchers act as neutral observers who do not intentionally interact or affect the actions of the population being observed

Nonparticipating provider: A healthcare provider who did not sign a participation agreement with Medicare and so is not obligated to accept assignment on Medicare claims

Nonprogrammed decision: A decision that involves careful and deliberate thought and discussion because of a unique, complex, or changing situation

Nonrandom sampling: A type of convenience or purposive sampling in which all members of the target population do not have an equal or independent chance of being selected for a research study

Normal distribution: A theoretical family of continuous frequency distributions characterized by a symmetric bell-shaped curve, with an equal mean, median, and mode, at any standard deviation, and with half of the observations above the mean and half below it

Normalization: 1. A formal process applied to relational database design to determine which variables should be grouped together in a table in order to reduce data redundancy across and within the table   2. Conversion of various representational forms to standard expressions so that those that have the same meaning will be recognized by computer software as synonymous in a data search

Normative decision model: Model developed by Victor Vroom and Philip Yetton in the early 1970s; using a continuum similar to Tannenbaum and Schmidt's, they identified a series of intermediate questions and decisions that could be answered yes or no, and that would lead to each outcome

Nosocomial (hospital-acquired) infection: An infection acquired by a patient while receiving care or services in a healthcare organization

Nosology: The branch of medical science that deals with classification systems

Not Elsewhere Classified (NEC): Indicates that you have more information but no place to put it; also means that any additional information will be lost forever if it is assigned the NEC label

Not Otherwise Specified (NOS): Indicates that there is no additional information

Not-for-profit organization: An organization that is not owned by individuals, where profits may be held for a specific purpose or reinvested in the organization for the benefit of the community it serves

Note: A financial obligation that has specific terms of payment in the form of a contract

Notice of Privacy Practices: A statement (mandated by the HIPAA Privacy Rule) issued by a healthcare organization that informs individuals of the uses and disclosures of patient-identifiable health information that may be made by the organization, as well as the individual's rights and the organization's legal duties with respect to that information

Notifiable disease: A disease that must be reported to a government agency so that regular, frequent, and timely information on individual cases can be used to prevent and control future cases of the disease

Null hypothesis: A hypothesis that states there is no association between the independent and dependent variables in a research study

Nursing informatics: The field of information science concerned with the management of data and information used to support the practice and delivery of nursing care through the application of computers and computer technologies

Nursing staff performance review: Policies and procedures, standards of nursing practice, nursing standards of patient care, and standards to measure, assess, and improve patient outcomes must be defined, documented, available, and used to improve patient care processes; nurse practitioners must undergo credentialing as a licensed independent practitioner similar to that of physicians; RN licenses must be maintained as stipulated by state law for all licensed nursing personnel

Object: The basic component in an object-oriented database that includes both data and their relationships within a single structure

Objective: A statement of the end result expected, stated in measurable terms, usually with a time limitation (deadline date) and often with a cost estimate or limitation

Object-oriented database (OODB): A type of database that uses commands that act as small, self-contained instructional units (objects) that may be combined in various ways

Object-oriented database management system (OODBMS): A specific set of software programs used to implement an object-oriented database

Observational research: A method of research in which researchers obtain data by watching research participants rather than by asking questions

Observational study: An epidemiological study in which the exposure and outcome for each individual in the study is observed

Occasion of service: A specified identifiable service involved in the care of a patient that is not an encounter (for example, a lab test ordered during an encounter)

Occupational Safety and Health Act of 1970 (OSHA): The federal legislation that established comprehensive safety and health guidelines for employers

Occurrence/generic screening: A risk management technique in which the risk manager reviews the health records of current and discharged hospital inpatients with the goal of identifying potentially compensable events

Odds ratio: A relative measure of occurrence of an illness; the odds of exposure in a diseased group divided by the odds of exposure in a nondiseased group

Office for Human Research Protections (OHRP): The department within the Department of Health and Human Services that monitors compliance with federal regulations governing the conduct of biomedical research

Office of Management and Budget (OMB): The core mission of OMB is to serve the president of the United States in implementing his vision across the executive branch. OMB is the largest component of the Executive Office of the President. It reports directly to the president and helps a wide range of executive departments and agencies across the federal government to implement the commitments and priorities of the president

Office of Research Integrity (ORI): Organization that provides integrity in biomedical and behavioral research, monitoring incidents of research misconduct and facilitating responsible research conduct through educational, preventive, and regulatory activities

Office of Inspector General (OIG) Workplan: Yearly plan released by the OIG that outlines the focus for reviews and investigations in various healthcare settings

Office of the National Coordinator for Health Information Technology (ONC): Office that provides leadership for the development and implementation of an interoperable health information technology infrastructure nationwide to improve healthcare quality and delivery

Offshoring: Outsourcing jobs to countries overseas, wherein local employees abroad perform jobs that domestic employees previously performed

Omnibus Budget Reconciliation Act (OBRA) of 1989: Federal legislation that mandated important changes in the payment rules for Medicare physicians; specifically, the legislation that requires nursing facilities to conduct regular patient assessments for Medicare and Medicaid beneficiaries

One-sample t-test: Test used to compare a population to a standard value

One-on-one training: Type of training where the employee learns by first observing a demonstration and then performing the task

One-tailed hypothesis: An alternative hypothesis in which the researcher makes a prediction in one direction

One-to-many relationship: A relationship that exists when one instance of an entity is associated with multiple instances of another entity

One-to-one relationship: A relationship that exists when an instance of an entity is associated with only one instance of another entity, and vice versa

Ongoing records review: *See* **open-record review**

Online analytical processing (OLAP): A data access architecture that allows the user to retrieve specific information from a large volume of data

Online analytical processing (OLAP) engine: An optimized query generator that can retrieve the correct information from the warehouse to accommodate what-if queries

Online/real-time analytical processing (OLAP): *See* **online analytical processing**

Online/real-time transaction processing (OLTP): The real-time processing of day-to-day business transactions from a database

On-the-job training: A method of training in which an employee learns necessary skills and processes by performing the functions of his or her position

Open-record review: A review of the health records of patients currently in the hospital or under active treatment; part of the Joint Commission survey process

Open-source technology: Applications whose source (human-readable) code is freely available to anyone who is interested in downloading the code

Open systems: Processes that are affected by what is going on around them and must adjust as the environment changes

Operation index: A list of the operations and surgical procedures performed in a healthcare facility that is sequenced according to the code numbers of the classification system in use

Operational budget: A type of budget that allocates and controls resources to meet an organization's goals and objectives for the fiscal year

Operational definition: Measurable term that comes from the literature and is capable of generating data

Operational plan: The short-term objectives set by an organization to improve its methods of doing business and achieve its planned outcomes

Operationalize: Formulating the question in terms that are capable of generating data and that satisfactorily capture the issues of the question or problem

Operations improvement planning: Focuses on improving how existing programs and services are carried out; is internally focused and is one part of how to implement strategic thinking

Operations management: The application of mathematical and statistical techniques to production and distribution efficiency

Operations research (OR): A scientific discipline primarily begun during World War II that seeks to apply the scientific method and mathematical models to the solution of a variety of management decision problems

Optical character recognition (OCR) technology: A method of encoding text from analog paper into bit-mapped images and translating the images into a form that is computer readable

Optical imaging technology: The process by which information is scanned onto optical disks

Optimization (as related to clinical coding): The process of thoroughly reviewing the health record to identify all procedures performed and services rendered by the physician to ensure accurate and complete coding for optimum reimbursement

Order communications: In hospitals, type of data that may be directed to many of the applications that support CPOE and EMAR and other applications that have been relatively stand-alone applications

Ordinal data: Data with inherent order and with higher numbers usually associated with higher values; also referred to as ordinal-level data

Ordinal-level data: Data in which the order of the numbers is meaningful, not the number itself

Organization: The planned coordination of the activities of more than one person for the achievement of a common purpose or goal

Organization development (OD): The process in which an organization reflects on its own processes and consequently revises them for improved performance

Organizational chart: A graphic representation of an organization's formal structure

Organizational lifeline: A graphic timeline with annual demarcations that show important events in the life of the organization over the years

Organizing: The process of coordinating something, such as activities

Orientation: A set of activities designed to familiarize new employees with their jobs, the organization, and its work culture

Orthographic: Refers to the correctness of spelling or the representation of the sounds of a language by written or printed symbols

ORYX: *See* **ORYX initiative**

ORYX initiative: A Joint Commission initiative that supports the integration of outcomes data and other performance measurement data into the accreditation process; often referred to as ORYX

Outcome indicators: Indicators that measure the actual results of care for patients and populations, including patient and family satisfaction

Outcome measures: The process of systematically tracking a patient's clinical treatment and responses to that treatment, including measures of morbidity and functional status, for the purpose of improving care

Outcomes and Assessment Information Set (OASIS): A standard core assessment data tool developed to measure the outcomes of adult patients receiving home health services under the Medicare and Medicaid programs

Outcomes and effectiveness research (OER): A type of research performed to explain the end results of specific healthcare practices and interventions

Outcomes management: The process of systematically tracking a patient's clinical treatment and responses to that treatment, including measures of morbidity and functional status, for the purpose of improving care

Outcomes research: Research aimed at assessing the quality and effectiveness of healthcare as measured by the attainment of a specified end result or outcome, improved health, lowered morbidity or mortality, and improvement of abnormal states

Out-group: Those subordinates not included in the group formed around the leader

Out-of-pocket expenses: Healthcare costs paid by the insured (for example, deductibles, copayments, and coinsurance) after which the insurer pays a percentage (often 80 or 100 percent) of covered expenses

Outpatient: A patient who receives ambulatory care services in a hospital-based clinic or department

Outpatient code editor (OCE): A software program linked to the Correct Coding Initiative that applies a set of logical rules to determine whether various combinations of codes are correct and appropriately represent the services provided

Outpatient prospective payment system (OPPS): The Medicare prospective payment system used for hospital-based outpatient services and procedures that is predicated on the assignment of ambulatory payment classifications

Outpatient visit: A patient's visit to one or more units located in the ambulatory services area (clinic or physician's office) of an acute-care hospital

Outsourcing: The hiring of an individual or a company external to an organization to perform a function either on-site or off-site

Overhead costs: The expenses associated with supporting but not providing patient care services

Overlap: Occurs when a patient has more than one medical record number assigned across more than one database

Overlay: Occurs when one patient record is overwritten with data from another patient's record

Owner's equity: The value of the investment in an organization by its owners

Packaging: A payment under the Medicare outpatient prospective payment system that includes items such as anesthesia, supplies, certain drugs, and the use of recovery and observation rooms

Panel interview: An interview format in which the applicant is interviewed by several interviewers at the same time

Par level: The accepted, standard inventory level for all supplies and equipment in an organization

Paradigm: A philosophical or theoretical framework within which a discipline formulates its theories and makes generalizations

Parallel work division: A type of concurrent work design in which one employee does several tasks and takes the job from beginning to end

Parametric technique: A type of statistical procedure that is based on the assumption that a variable is normally distributed in a population

Pareto chart: A bar graph that includes bars arranged in order of descending size to show decisions on the prioritization of issues, problems, or solutions

Parsimony: Explanations of phenomena should include the fewest assumptions and conditions

Partial hospitalization: A term that refers to limited patient stays in the hospital setting, typically as part of a transitional program to a less intense level of service; for example, psychiatric and drug and alcohol treatment facilities that offer services to help patients reenter the community, return to work, and resume family responsibilities

Participant observation: A research method in which researchers also participate in the observed actions

Partnership: The business venture of two or more owners for whom the profits represent the owners' personal income

Path–goal theory: States that a person's ability to perform certain tasks is related to the direction and clarity available that lead to organizational goals

Patient information coordinator: Helps consumers manage their personal health information, including personal health histories and release of information; also helps customers understand managed care services and access to health information resources

Patient Medical Record Information (PMRI): Information in which SNOMED CT is part of a core set of terminology

Patient Protection and Affordable Care Act (PPACA): A federal statute that was signed into law on March 23, 2010. Along with the Health Care and Education Reconciliation act of 2010 (signed into law on March 30, 2010), the act is the product of the healthcare reform agenda of the 111th Congress and the Obama administration

Patient registration: Process that provides the organization with the ability to accurately and uniquely identify its patients; it is the first step in the creation of each patient's record within the EHR and initiates the flow of patient information within the EHR

Patient-centered medical home (PCMH): A program to provide comprehensive primary care that partners the physicians with the patient and his or her family to allow better access to healthcare and improved outcomes

Patient-Centered Outcomes Research Institute (PCORI): This group was established to provide evidence that will educate patients and healthcare providers about prevention and treatment care options and the research or comparative evidence that supports these decisions

Patient-identifiable data: Data in the health record that relates to a particular patient identified by name

Patient/member web portals: The media for providing patient/member access to the provider organization's multiple sources of data from any network-connected device

Patient-specific data: *See* **patent-identifiable data**

Pay for performance: The Integrated Healthcare Association initiative in California based on the concept that physician groups would be paid for documented performance

Payback period: A financial method used to evaluate the value of a capital expenditure by calculating the time frame that must pass before inflow of cash from a project equals or exceeds outflow of cash

Payer of last resort (Medicaid): A Medicaid term that means that Medicare pays for the services provided to individuals enrolled in both Medicare and Medicaid until Medicare benefits are exhausted and Medicaid benefits begin

Payment status indicator (PSI): An alphabetic code assigned to CPT/HCPCS codes to indicate whether a service or procedure is to be reimbursed under the Medicare outpatient prospective payment system

PDSA cycle (Plan-do-study-act): A performance improvement model designed specifically for healthcare organizations

Peer review: A service that provides diagnostic and therapeutic services for patients under the age of 14 years

Peer review organization (PRO): Until 2002, a medical organization that performs a professional review of medical necessity, quality, and appropriateness of healthcare services provided to Medicare beneficiaries; now called quality improvement organization (QIO)

Peer-reviewed journal: A type of professional or scientific journal for which content experts evaluate articles prior to publication

Per member per month (PMPM): *See* **per patient per month**

Per patient per month (PPPM): A type of managed care arrangement by which providers are paid a fixed fee in exchange for supplying all of the healthcare services an enrollee needs for a specified period of time (usually one month but sometimes one year)

Performance: Execution of a task

Performance counseling: Guidance provided to an individual in an attempt to improve his or her work performance

Performance improvement (PI): The continuous study and adaptation of a healthcare organization's functions and processes to increase the likelihood of achieving desired outcomes

Performance measure: A quantitative tool used to assess the clinical, financial, and utilization aspects of a healthcare provider's outcomes or processes

Performance measure/measurement system: System designed to improve performance by providing feedback on whether goals have been met

Performance measurement: The process of comparing the outcomes of an organization, work unit, or employee against preestablished performance plans and standards

Performance review: An evaluation of an employee's job performance

Performance standards: The stated expectations for acceptable quality and productivity associated with a job function

Permanence: The notion that terminologies and classifications must be permanent if they are to be useful for longitudinal reporting; concepts may be inactivated but must never be deleted

Permanent budget variance: A financial term the refers to the difference between the budgeted amount and the actual amount of a line item that is not expected to reverse itself during a subsequent period

Persistence: The notion that some vocabularies are intended, at least initially, primarily for a specific study or a specific site; if a vocabulary is intended to be persistent, there should be a means of updating or some kind of change management

Personal digital assistant (PDA): A hand held microcomputer, without a hard drive, that is capable of running applications such as e-mail and providing access to data and information, such as notes, phone lists, schedules, and laboratory results, primarily through a pen device

Personal health dimension (PHD): One of three dimensions of the National Health Information Infrastructure privacy concept that supports individuals in managing their own wellness and healthcare decision making

Personal health record (PHR): An electronic or paper health record maintained and updated by an individual for himself or herself

Peter principle: Principle in which some people are promoted to their level of incompetency

Pharmacy information system (PIS): Ancillary system application in a hospital or physician's office that generates clinical (pharmacological) information

Physical data model: The lowest level of data model with the lowest level of abstraction

Physical data repository: A repository organized into data fields, data records, and data files storing structured, discrete, clinical, administrative, and financial data as well as unstructured, patient free-text, bit-mapped, real audio, streaming video, or vector graphic data

Physician assistant (PA): A healthcare professional licensed to practice medicine with physician supervision

Physician champion: An individual who assists in communicating and educating medical staff in areas such as documentation procedures for accurate billing and appropriate EHR processes

Physician index: A list of patients and their physicians that is usually arranged according to the physician code numbers assigned by the healthcare facility

Physician–hospital organization (PHO): An integrated delivery system formed by hospitals and physicians (usually through managed care contracts) that allows for cooperative activity but permits participants to retain some level of independence

Physiological signal processing systems: Systems that store vector graphic data based on the human body's signals and create output based on the lines plotted between the signals' points

Picture archiving and communication system (PACS): System that digitizes medical images

Pie chart: A graphic technique in which the proportions of a category are displayed as portions of a circle (like pieces of a pie)

Piece-rate incentive: An adjustment of the compensation paid to a worker based on exceeding a certain level of output

Pilot study: A trial run on a smaller scale

Pixel: An abbreviation for the term *picture element,* which is defined by many tiny bits of data or points

Placebo: A medication with no active ingredients

Plaintiff: The group or person who initiates a civil lawsuit

Planning: An examination of the future and preparation of action plans to attain goals; one of the four traditional management functions

Playscript: This format describes each player in the procedure, the action of the player, and the player's responsibility regarding the process from start to completion of a specific task within the procedure

Point method: A method of job evaluation that places weight (points) on each of the compensable factors in a job whereby the total points associated with a job establish its relative worth and jobs that fall within a specific range of points fall into a pay grade with an associated wage

Point-of-care information system: A computer system that captures data at the location (for example, bedside, exam room, or home) where the healthcare service is performed

Point-of-care (POC) patient charting system: Guides the user in the necessary data to collect in the context of the specific patient at the location where the healthcare service is performed

Point-of-care review: *See* **open-record review**

Point-of-service (POS) collection: The collection of the portion of the bill that is likely the responsibility of the patient prior to the provision of service

Point-of-service (POS) plan: A type of managed care plan in which enrollees are encouraged to select healthcare providers from a network of providers under contract with the plan but are also allowed to select providers outside the network and pay a larger share of the cost

Policy: 1. A governing principle that describes how a department or an organization is supposed to handle a specific situation   2. Binding contract issued by a healthcare insurance company to an individual or a group in which the company promises to pay for healthcare to treat illness or injury

Policy development: Includes establishing data security, confidentiality, retention, integrity, and access standards; developing training programs that empower others to carry out the information policies; and advocating for data privacy, confidentiality, and appropriate access

Policyholder: An individual or entity that purchases healthcare insurance coverage

Polyhierarchy: Multiple relationships should exist for every concept

Population: Universe of phenomena, objects, people, or data under investigation from which a sample is taken

Population health dimension (PHD): One of three dimensions of the National Health Information Infrastructure privacy concept that addresses protecting and promoting the health of the community

Population-based registry: A type of registry that includes information from more than one facility in a specific geopolitical area, such as a state or region

Population-based statistics: Statistics based on a defined population rather than on a sample drawn from the same population

Position (job) description: A document that outlines the work responsibilities associated with a job

Position power: Refers to the authority the leader has to direct others and to use reward and coercive power

Positive (direct) relationship: A relationship in which the effect moves in the same direction

Positivism: A philosophy of research that assumes that there is a single truth across time and place and that researchers are able to adopt a neutral, unbiased stance and establish causation; *See* **quantitative approach**

Post–acute care: Care provided to patients who have been released from an acute-care facility to recuperate at home

Postneonatal mortality rate: The number of deaths of persons aged 28 days up to, but not including, one year during a given time period divided by the number of live births for the same time period

Postoperative infection rate: The number of infections that occur in clean surgical cases for a given time period divided by the total number of operations within the same time period

Potentially compensable event (PCE): An event (for example, an injury, an accident, or a medical error) that may result in financial liability for a healthcare organization

Power: The probability of identifying real relationships or differences between groups

Practice guidelines: Protocols of care that guide the clinical care process

Practice management system (PMS): Software designed to help medical practices run more smoothly and efficiently

Precision factor: The definitive tolerable error rate to be considered in calculations of productivity standards

Predecessor: A task that affects the scheduling of a successor task in a dependency relationship

Predictive modeling: A process used to identify patterns that can be used to predict the odds of a particular outcome based on the observed data

Preemption: In law, the principle that a statute at one level supercedes or is applied over the same or similar statute at a lower level (for example, the federal HIPAA privacy provisions trump the same or similar state law with certain exceptions)

Preferred provider organization (PPO): A managed care arrangement based on a contractual agreement between healthcare providers (professional and/or institutional) and employers, insurance carriers, or third-party administrators to provide healthcare services to a defined population of enrollees at established fees that may or may not be a discount from usual and customary or reasonable charges

Pregnancy Discrimination Act (1978): The federal legislation that prohibits discrimination against women affected by pregnancy, childbirth, or related medical conditions by requiring that affected women be treated the same as all other employees for employment-related purposes, including benefits

Premium: Amount of money that a policyholder or certificate holder must periodically pay an insurer in return for healthcare coverage

Present on admission (POA): A condition present at the time the order for inpatient admission occurs; a condition that develops during an outpatient encounter, including the emergency department, observation, or outpatient surgery

Prevalence rate: The proportion of people in a population who have a particular disease at a specific point in time or over a specified period of time

Preventive controls: Internal controls implemented prior to an activity and designed to stop an error from happening

Primary analysis: The analysis of original research data by the researchers who collected them

Primary care manager (PCM): The healthcare provider assigned to a TRICARE enrollee

Primary care physician (PCP): 1. Physician who provides, supervises, and coordinates the healthcare of a member and who manages referrals to other healthcare providers and utilization of healthcare services both inside and outside a managed care plan   2. The physician who makes the initial diagnosis of a patient's medical condition

Primary data source: A record developed by healthcare professionals in the process of providing patient care

Primary key: An explanatory notation that uniquely identifies each row in a database table

Primary source: An original work of a researcher who conducted an investigation

Principal diagnosis: The disease or condition that was present on admission, was the principal reason for admission, and received treatment or evaluation during the hospital stay or visit

Principal investigator: The individual with primary responsibility for the design and conduct of a research project

Principal procedure: The procedure performed for the definitive treatment of a condition (as opposed to a procedure performed for diagnostic or exploratory purposes) or for care of a complication

Prior approval (authorization): Process of obtaining approval from a healthcare insurance company before receiving healthcare services; also called precertification, preauthorization

Priority focus process (PFP): A process used by the Joint Commision to collect, analyze, and create information about a specific organization being accredited in order to customize the accreditation process

Privacy: The quality or state of being hidden from, or undisturbed by, the observation or activities of other persons or freedom from unauthorized intrusion; in healthcare-related contexts, the right of a patient to control disclosure of personal information

Privacy Act of 1974: The legislation that gave individuals some control over information collected about them by the federal government

Privacy Rule: The federal regulations created to implement the privacy requirements of the simplification subtitle of the Health Insurance Portability and Accountability Act of 1996

Privacy standards: Rules, conditions, or requirements developed to ensure the privacy of patient information

Privilege: The professional relationship between patients and specific groups of caregivers that affects the patient's health record and its contents as evidence; the services or procedures, based on training and experience, that an individual physician is qualified to perform; a right granted to a user, program, or process that allows access to certain files or data in a system

Privileging process: The process of evaluating a physician's or other licensed independent practitioner's quality of medical practice and determining the services or procedures he or she is qualified to perform

Probability factor: The probability factor indicates the odds of the particular risk occurring

Problem list: A list of illnesses, injuries, and other factors that affect the health of an individual patient, usually identifying the time of occurrence or identification and resolution

Problem-oriented medical record (POMR): A way of organizing information in a health record in which clinical problems are defined and documented individually; also called problem-oriented health record

Procedure: A document that describes the steps involved in performing a specific function

Procedure manual: A compilation of all of the procedures used in a specific unit, department, or organization

Process and workflow modeling: The process of creating a representation of the actions and information required to perform a function, including decomposition diagrams, dependency diagrams, and data flow diagrams

Process indicators: Indicators that measure the actions by which services are provided, the things people or devices do, from conducting appropriate tests to making a diagnosis to actually carrying out a treatment

Process innovations: Enable firms to produce existing products or services more efficiently

Process measures: Specific measures that enable the assessment of the steps taken in rendering a service; also called process indicators

Process redesign: Change and improvements made that increase efficiency

Productivity: A unit of performance defined by management in quantitative standards

Profession: In HIM, characteristics include professional associations; code of ethics; unique body of knowledge that must be learned through formal education; system of training with entry by examination or other formal prerequisites (certification); professional cohesion; professional literature

Professional component (PC): 1. The portion of a healthcare procedure performed by a physician   2. A term generally used in reference to the elements of radiological procedures performed by a physician

Profitability: Refers to an organization's ability to increase in value; how well it invests its assets

Profitability index: An index used to prioritize investment opportunities, where the present value of the cash inflows is divided by the present value of the cash outflows for each investment and the results are compared

Program evaluation and review technique (PERT) chart: A project management tool that diagrams a project's timelines and tasks as well as their interdependencies

Programmed decisions: An automated decision made by people or computers based on a situation being so stable and recurrent that decision rules can be applied to it

Programmed learning modules: Lead learners through subject material that is presented in short sections, followed immediately by a series of questions that require a written response based on the section just presented; answers are provided in the module for immediate feedback

Programmers: Individuals primarily responsible for writing program codes and developing applications, typically performing the function of systems development and working closely with systems analysts

Programs of All-Inclusive Care for the Elderly (PACE): A state option legislated by the Balanced Budget Act of 1997 that provides an alternative to institutional care for individuals 55 years old or older who require the level of care provided by nursing facilities

Progress notes: The documentation of a patient's care, treatment, and therapeutic response that is entered into the health record by each of the clinical professionals involved in a patient's care, including nurses, physicians, therapists, and social workers

Progressive discipline: A four-step process for shaping employee behavior to conform to the requirements of the employee's job position that begins with a verbal caution and progresses to written reprimand, suspension, and dismissal upon subsequent offenses

Project charter: A document that defines the scope and goals of a specific project

Project components: Related parameters of scope, resources, and scheduling with regard to a project

Project definition: First step in the project management life cycle that sets expectations for the what, when, and how of a project the organization wants to undertake

Project definition document: A document that outlines the objectives, scope, deliverables, expected time line, and anticipated cost of a project; typical names for this document also include project charter, statement of work, or business plan

Project deliverables: The tangible end results of a project

Project management: Project management is concerned with completing a project within the expected cost and timeline with high-quality results

Project management life cycle: The period in which the processes involved in carrying out a project are completed, including project definition, project planning and organization, project tracking and analysis, project revisions, change control, and communication

Project management software: A type of application software that provides the tools to track a project

Project manager: The individual with responsibility for directing the project activities from initiation through closure

Project network: The relationship between tasks in a project that determines the overall finish date

Project office: A support function for project management best practices

Project plan: A plan consisting of a list of the tasks to be performed in a project, a defined order in which they will occur, task start and finish dates, and the resource effort needed to complete each task

Project schedule: The portion of the project plan that deals specifically with task start and finish dates

Project scope: 1. The intention of a project   2. The range of a project's activities or influence

Project team: A collection of individuals assigned to work on a project

Projectized team structure: The projectized organization has dedicated resources that are involved only in project work; team members report to the project manager not only on project assignments but also as their direct manager

Promotion: The act of being raised in position or rank

Proportion: A type of ratio in which the elements included in the numerator also must be included in the denominator

Proportionate mortality ratio (PMR): The total number of deaths due to a specific cause during a given time period divided by the total number of deaths due to all causes

Prosecutor: An attorney who prosecutes a defendant accused for a crime on behalf of a local, state, or federal government

Prospective: In research studies, subjects are followed into the future to examine relationships between variables and later occurrences

Prospective payment system (PPS): A type of reimbursement system that is based on preset payment levels rather than actual charges billed after the service has been provided; specifically, one of several Medicare reimbursement systems based on predetermined payment rates or periods and linked to the anticipated intensity of services delivered as well as the beneficiary's condition

Prospective studies: Studies designed to observe outcomes or events that occur after the identification of a group of subjects to be studied

Protected health information (PHI): Under HIPAA, all individually identifiable information, whether oral or recorded in any form or medium, that is created or received by a healthcare provider or any other entity subject to HIPAA requirements

Protocol: In healthcare, a detailed plan of care for a specific medical condition based on investigative studies; in medical research, a rule or procedure to be followed in a clinical trial; in a computer network, a protocol used to address and ensure delivery of data

Provider portal: System that enables providers to enter orders as if they were in the hospital, based on organizational policy

Public assistance: A monetary subsidy provided to financially needy individuals

Public Company Accounting Oversight Board (PCAOB): A not-for-profit organization that oversees the work of auditors of public companies

Public health: An area of healthcare that deals with the health of populations in geopolitical areas, such as states and counties

Public health service (PHS): Services concerned primarily with the health of entire communities and population groups

Public key infrastructure (PKI): A system of digital certificates and other registration authorities that verify and authenticate the validity of each party involved in a secure transaction

Purchase order: A paper document or electronic screen on which all details of an intended purchase are reported, including authorizations

Purposive sampling: A strategy of qualitative research in which researchers use their expertise to select representative units and unrepresentative units to capture a wide array of perspectives

p-value: The probability of making a Type I error based on a particular set of data

Qualitative analysis: A review of the health record to ensure that standards are met and to determine the adequacy of entries documenting the quality of care

Qualitative approach: *See* **naturalism**

Qualitative standards: Service standards in the context of setting expectations for how well or how soon work or a service will be performed

Quality: The degree or grade of excellence of goods or services, including, in healthcare, meeting expectations for outcomes of care

Quality assurance (QA): A set of activities designed to measure the quality of a service, product, or process with remedial action, as needed, to maintain a desired standard

Quality Data Model (QDM): Also known as Quality Data Set, it clearly defines concepts used in quality measures and clinical care and is intended to enable automation of structured data capture in EHRs, PHRs, and other clinical applications; it provides a grammar to describe clinical concepts in a standardized format so individuals (i.e., providers, researchers, or measure developers) monitoring clinical performance and outcomes can concisely communicate necessary information

Quality gap: The difference between approved standards, criteria, or expectations in any type of process and actual results

Quality improvement (QI): A set of activities that measures the quality of a service or product through systems or process evaluation and then implements revised processes that result in better healthcare outcomes for patients, based on standards of care

Quality improvement organization (QIO): An organization that performs medical peer review of Medicare and Medicaid claims, including review of validity of hospital diagnosis and procedure coding information; completeness, adequacy, and quality of care; and appropriateness of prospective payments for outlier cases and nonemergent use of the emergency room; until 2002, called peer review organization

Quality indicator (QI): A standard against which actual care may be measured to identify a level of performance for that standard

Quality management: Evaluation of the quality of healthcare services and delivery using standards and guidelines developed by various entities, including the government and independent accreditation organizations

Quality management board (QMB): A QMB has responsibility for the PI program across all subunits of the organization and should include membership from top administration, medical staff officers, top clinical operations staff, and top quality management staff

Quality management liaison group (QMLG): A QMLG has responsibility for disseminating information about the organization's quality and PI initiatives throughout the middle management of the organization, for educating managers regarding their roles and the roles of their organizational units in quality and PI initiatives, and for developing cross-functional coordination and communication across organizational units in order to accomplish quality and PI initiatives

Quantitative analysis: A review of the health record to determine its completeness and accuracy

Quantitative approach: *See* **positivism**

Quantitative standards: Measures of productivity in the context of setting expectations for how efficiently or effectively work will be performed

Questionnaire survey: A type of survey in which the members of the population are questioned through the use of electronic or paper forms

Queuing: Involves a process of making the record available to a particular user

Queuing theory: An operations management technique for examining customer flow and designing ideal wait or scheduling times

Radio frequency identification (RFID): An automatic recognition technology that uses a device attached to an object to transmit data to a receiver and does not require direct contact

Radiology information system (RIS): Ancillary system application in a hospital or physician's office that generates clinical (radiological) information

Random sampling: An unbiased selection of subjects that includes methods such as simple random sampling, stratified random sampling, systematic sampling, and cluster sampling

Randomization: The assignment of subjects to experimental or control groups based on chance

Randomized clinical trial (RCT): A special type of clinical trial in which the researchers follow strict rules to randomly assign patients to groups

Range: A measure of variability between the smallest and largest observations in a frequency distribution

Raster image: A digital image or digital data made up of pixels in a horizontal and vertical grid or a matrix instead of lines plotted between a series of points

Rate: A measure used to compare an event over time; a comparison of the number of times an event did happen (numerator) with the number of times an event could have happened (denominator)

Ratio: 1. A calculation found by dividing one quantity by another   2. A general term that can include a number of specific measures such as proportion, percentage, and rate

Ratio analysis: Mathematical computations that compare elements of an organization's financial statements

Ratio data: Data with a defined unit of measure, a real zero point, and with equal intervals between successive values; also called ratio-level data

Ratio-level data: *See* **ratio data**

RAT-STATS: Office of Inspector General (OIG) offers this statistical package, which is free to download and use for both sample size determination and the generation of the random numbers required for sampling

Real audio (or sound) data: The storing, manipulating, and displaying of sound in a computer-readable format

Receiver operating characteristic (ROC) analysis: Used to measure the performance of predictive algorithms (such as in decision support systems), diagnostic tests (such as sputum tests), screening exams (such as mammograms), and other detection technologies

Record locator service (RLS): A key infrastructure component of the Common Framework to support connectivity and interoperability

Recovery audit contractor (RAC): A governmental program whose goal is to identify improper payments made on claims of healthcare services provided to Medicare beneficiaries. Improper payments may be overpayments or underpayments

Recruitment: The process of finding, soliciting, and attracting employees

Red Flags Rule: Federal Trade Commission (FTC)-issued regulations that required certain entities to develop and implement programs to protect consumers from identity theft; the FTC indicated that financial institutions are not the only entities covered: healthcare providers, attorneys, and other businesses are also covered because they provide goods or services and bill after the fact or in installments

Reductionism: Complex processes are reduced to their constituent elements and analyzed by their parts

Redundancy: As data are entered and processed by one server, they are simultaneously being entered and processed by a second server

Redundant array of independent (or inexpensive) disks (RAID): A method of ensuring data security

Reengineering: Fundamental rethinking and radical redesign of business processes to achieve significant performance improvements

Reference check: Contact made with an individual that a prospective employee has listed to provide a favorable account of his or her work performance or personal attributes

Reference data: Information that interacts with the care of the individual or with the healthcare delivery system, such as a formulary, protocol, care plan, clinical alert, or reminder

Reference terminology: A set of concepts and relationships that provide a common consultation point for the comparison and aggregation of data about the entire healthcare process, recorded by multiple individuals, systems, or institutions

Referential integrity: Concept that involves constraints placed on the primary and foreign keys within the database

Referred outpatient: An outpatient who is provided special diagnostic or therapeutic services by a hospital on an ambulatory basis but whose medical care remains the responsibility of the referring physician

Reflective learning cycle: Uses awareness to formulate an interpretation of what has been observed, considers what difference can be made by applying what has been learned, and executes the efforts toward change through deliberate action

Refreezing: Lewin's final stage of change in which the new behaviors are reinforced to become as stable and institutionalized as the previous status quo was

Regional health information network (RHIN): System that links various healthcare information systems in a region together so that patients, healthcare institutions, and other entities can share clinical information

Regional health information organization (RHIO): An organization that manages the local deployment of systems promoting and facilitating the exchange of healthcare data within a national health information network

Registered health information administrator (RHIA): A type of certification granted after completion of an AHIMA-accredited four-year program in health information management and a credentialing examination

Registered health information technician (RHIT): A type of certification granted after completion of an AHIMA-accredited two-year program in health information management and a credentialing examination

Registration data of the admission, discharge, transfer (R-ADT): A type of administrative information system that stores demographic information and performs functionality related to registration, admission, discharge, and transfer of patients within the organization

Registry: A collection of a limited set of information about a patient, often disease specific

Rehabilitation services: Health services provided to assist patients in achieving and maintaining their optimal level of function, self-care, and independence after some type of disability

Reinforcement: The process of increasing the probability of a desired response through reward

Relational database: A type of database that stores data in predefined tables made up of rows and columns

Relational database management system (RDBMS): A database management system in which data are organized and managed as a collection of tables

Relational online analytical processing (ROLAP): A data access methodology that provides users with various drill-down and business analysis capabilities similar to online analytical processing

Relationship: A type of connection between two terms

Relative risk (RR): A ratio that compares the risk of disease between two groups

Relative value unit (RVU): A measurement that represents the value of the work involved in providing a specific professional medical service in relation to the value of the work involved in providing other medical services

Release of information (ROI): The process of disclosing patient-identifiable information from the health record to another party

Reliability: A measure of consistency of data items based on their reproducibility and an estimation of their error of measurement

Religious non-medical health care institutions (RNHCIs): Type of hospital excluded from Medicare's acute-care PPS but still paid on the basis of reasonable cost, subject to payment limits per discharge or under a separate PPS

Remediation: Activities intended to offer providers another chance to prove they are worthy of participating in federal healthcare programs

Remittance advice (RA): An explanation of payments (for example, claim denials) made by third-party payers

Remote connectivity: Ability to access a system from a location other than where the system is based (for example, a hospital or physician's office)

Report generation: The process of analyzing, organizing, and presenting recorded patient information for authentication and inclusion in the patient's healthcare record; the formatting and structuring of captured information

Request for information (RFI): A written communication often sent to a comprehensive list of vendors during the design phase of the systems development life cycle to ask for general product information

Request for production: A discovery device used to compel another party to produce documents and other items or evidence important to a lawsuit

Request for proposal (RFP): A type of business correspondence asking for very specific product and contract information that is often sent to a narrow list of vendors that have been preselected after a review of requests for information during the design phase of the systems development life cycle

Research: An inquiry process aimed at discovering new information about a subject or revising old information

Research and decision support analyst: Ensures the quality of data and information generated through clinical investigations and other research projects

Research data: Data used for the purpose of answering a proposed question or testing a hypothesis

Research design: Structure of a study ensuring that the evidence collected will be relevant and that the evidence will unambiguously and convincingly answer the research question; the design includes a detailed plan that, in a quantitative study, includes controlling variance

Research frame: The overarching structure of the research project

Research method: The particular strategy used by a researcher to collect, analyze, and present data

Research methodology: A set of procedures or strategies used by researchers to collect, analyze, and present data

Resident Assessment Instrument (RAI): A uniform assessment instrument developed by the Centers for Medicare and Medicaid Services to standardize the collection of skilled nursing facility patient data; includes the Minimum Data Set 2.0, triggers, and resident assessment protocols

Resident assessment protocols (RAPs): A summary of a long-term care resident's medical condition and care requirements

Resident Assessment Validation and Entry (RAVEN): A type of data-entry software developed by the Centers for Medicare and Medicaid Services for long-term care facilities and used to collect Minimum Data Set assessments and to transmit data to state databases

Resource Utilization Groups, Version IV (RUG-IV): A case-mix-adjusted classification system based on Minimum Data Set assessments and used by skilled nursing facilities

Resource-based relative value scale (RBRVS): A Medicare reimbursement system implemented in 1992 to compensate physicians according to a fee schedule predicated on weights assigned on the basis of the resources required to provide the services

Resources: The labor, equipment, or materials needed to complete a project

Respect for persons: The principle that all people are presumed to be free and responsible and should be treated accordingly

Respite care: A type of short-term care provided during the day or overnight to individuals in the home or institution to temporarily relieve the family home caregiver

Responsibility: The accountability required as part of a job, such as supervising work performed by others or managing assets or funds

Restitution: The act of returning something to its rightful owner, of making good or giving something equivalent for any loss, damage, or injury

Results management systems: Results retrieval technology that permits viewing of data by type and manipulation of several different types of data

Resume: A document that describes a job candidate's educational background, work experience, and professional achievements

Retail clinics: Clinics located in retail outlets that treat non-life-threatening acute illnesses and offer routine wellness services such as flu shots and sports physicals

Retained earnings: Undistributed profits from a for-profit organization that stay in the business

Retention: 1. The process whereby inactive health records are stored and made available for future use in compliance with state and federal requirements   2. The ability to keep valuable employees from seeking employment elsewhere

Retention schedules: Timetables specifying how long various records are to be maintained according to rules, regulations, standards, and laws

Retrospective: A type of time frame that looks back in time

Retrospective payment system: Type of fee-for-service reimbursement in which providers receive recompense after health services have been rendered; also called retrospective payment method

Retrospective study: A type of research conducted by reviewing records from the past (for example, birth and death certificates and health records) or by obtaining information about past events through surveys or interviews

Return on equity (ROE): A comprehensive measurement of profitability that takes into consideration the organization's net value

Return on investment (ROI): The financial analysis of the extent of value a major purchase will provide

Revenge effects: Unintended and typically negative consequences of a change in technology

Revenue: The charges generated from providing healthcare services; earned and measurable income

Revenue codes: A three- or four-digit number in the chargemaster that totals all items and their charges for printing on the form used for Medicare billing

Revenue cycle: 1. The process of how patient financial and health information moves into, through, and out of the healthcare facility, culminating with the facility receiving reimbursement for services provided   2. The regularly repeating set of events that produces revenue

Revenue cycle management: The supervision of all administrative and clinical functions that contribute to the capture, management, and collection of patient service revenue, with the goals of accelerated cash flow and lowered accounts receivable

Revenue principle: States that earnings as a result of activities and investments may only be recognized when it has been earned, can be measured, and has a reasonable expectation of being collected

Reverse mentoring: The opposite of the usual coaching process where the younger goes to the older instructor

Rip-and-replace: An information technology acquisition strategy in which older technology is replaced with new technology

Risk: 1. The possibility of injury or loss   2. The probable amount of loss foreseen by an insurer in issuing a contract

Risk analysis: An assessment of possible security threats to the organization's data

Risk factor: In conducting a risk analysis, this factor is determined by multiplying the probability factor and the impact factor

Risk management (RM): A comprehensive program of activities intended to minimize the potential for injuries to occur in a facility and to anticipate and respond to ensuing liabilities for those injuries that do occur; the processes in place to identify, evaluate, and control risk, defined as the organization's risk of accidental financial liability

Risk prevention: One component of a successful risk management program

Role playing: A training method in which participants are required to respond to specific problems they may actually encounter in their jobs

Role theory: Thinking that attempts to explain how people adopt specific roles, including leadership roles

Roles and responsibilities: The definition of who does what on a project and the hierarchy for decision making

Root-cause analysis: A technique used in performance improvement initiatives to discover the underlying causes of a problem

Rule induction: *See* **association rule analysis**

Run chart: A type of graph that shows data points collected over time and identifies emerging trends or patterns

RxNorm: A clinical drug nomenclature developed by the Food and Drug Administration, the Department of Veterans Affairs, and HL7 to provide standard names for clinical drugs and administered dose forms

Safe practices: Behaviors undertaken to reduce or prevent adverse effects and medical errors

Sample: A set of units selected for study that represents a population

Sample frame: List of subjects from which the sample is drawn

Sample size: The number of subjects needed in a study to represent a population

Sample size calculation: The qualitative and quantitative procedures to determine an appropriate sample size

Sample survey: A type of survey that collects data from representative members of a population

Sampling: Process of selecting the units to represent the target population

Sarbanes-Oxley Act of 2002: The most significant legislation to arise from the Enron scandal in 2001, the Sarbanes-Oxley act defined significantly higher personal responsibility of top corporate managers for the accuracy of reported financial statements

Satisficing: A decision-making process in which the decision maker accepts a solution to a problem that is satisfactory rather than optimal

Scalable: The depth to which a particular process is performed may vary according to project length, scope, or other parameters

Scalar chain: A theory in the chain of command in which everyone is included and authority and responsibility flow downward from the top of the organization

Scale: Measure with progressive categories, such as size, amount, importance, rank, or agreement

Scales of measurement: A reference standard for data collection and classification

Scanning: The process by which a document is read into an optical imaging system

Scatter chart: *See* **scatter diagram**

Scatter diagram: A graph that visually displays the linear relationships among factors

Scatter plot: A visual representation of data points on an interval or ratio level used to depict relationships between two variables; *See* **scatter diagram**

Scenarios: Stories describing the current and feasible future states of the business environment

Scheduling engine: A specific functionality in project management software that automates the assignment of task start-and-finish dates and, as a result, the expected project finish date

Scientific inquiry: A process that comprises making predictions, collecting and analyzing evidence, testing alternative theories, and choosing the best theory

Scientific management: A principle that states that the best management is a science based on laws and rules and that secures maximum prosperity for both employer and employee

Scope creep: A process in which the scope of a project grows while the project is in process, virtually guaranteeing that it will be over budget and behind schedule

Scope of command: The number and type of employees who report to a specific management position in a defined organizational structure

Scope of work: The time period an organization is under contract to perform as a quality improvement organization

Scorecards: Reports of outcomes measures to help leaders know what they have accomplished

Secondary analysis: A method of research involving analysis of the original work of another person or organization

Secondary data source: Data derived from the primary patient record, such as an index or a database

Secondary release of information: A type of information release in which the initial requester forwards confidential information to others without obtaining required patient authorization

Secondary source: A summary of an original work, such as an encyclopedia

Secure messaging system: A system that eliminates the security concerns that surround e-mail but retains the benefits of proactive, traceable, and personalized messaging

Securities and Exchange Commission (SEC): The federal agency that regulates all public and some private transactions involving the ownership and debt of organizations

Security: 1. The means to control access and protect information from accidental or intentional disclosure to unauthorized persons and from unauthorized alteration, destruction, or loss   2. The physical protection of facilities and equipment from theft, damage, or unauthorized access; collectively, the policies, procedures, and safeguards designed to protect the confidentiality of information, maintain the integrity and availability of information systems, and control access to the content of these systems

Security standards: Statements that describe the processes and procedures meant to ensure that patient-identifiable health information remains confidential and protected from unauthorized disclosure, alteration, and destruction

Selection: The act or process of choosing

Self-directed learning: An instructional method that allows students to control their learning and progress at their own pace

Self-efficacy: Confidence in one's personal capabilities to do a job

Self-monitoring: The act of observing the reactions of others to one's behavior and making the necessary behavioral adjustments to improve the reactions of others in the future

Semantic clinical drug (SCD): Standardized names created in RxNorm for every clinical drug; consists of components and a dose form

Semantic Clinical Drug (SCD) of RxNorm: *See* **semantic clinical drug**

Semantic differential scale: A measure that records a group's perception of a product, an organization, or a program through bipolar adjectives on a seven-point continuum, resulting in a profile

Semantic interoperability: Mutual understanding of the meaning of data exchanged between information systems

Semantics: The meaning of a word or term; sometimes refers to comparable meaning, usually achieved through a standard vocabulary

Semistructured question: A type of question that begins with a structured question and follows with an unstructured question to clarify

Sensitivity: Ability to detect a characteristic when the characteristic exists; *see* **specificity**

Sentinel event: According to the Joint Commission, an unexpected occurrence involving death or serious physical or psychological injury, or the risk thereof

Serial numbering system: A type of health record identification and filing system in which patients are assigned a different but unique numerical identifier for every admission

Serial work division: A system of work organization where each task is performed by one person in sequence

Serial-unit numbering system: A health record identification system in which patient numbers are assigned in a serial manner but records are brought forward and filed under the last number assigned

Servant leadership model: Model for a values-based organization that promotes 10 essential values: listening, empathy, healing, awareness, persuasion, conceptualization, foresight, stewardship, commitment, and community building

Service innovations: Changes that create new market opportunities and in many industries are the driving force behind growth and profitability

Service level agreement (SLA): A contract between a customer and a service provider that records the common understanding about service priorities, responsibilities, guarantees, and other terms, especially related to availability, serviceability, performance, operation, or other attributes of the service, like billing and penalties in the case of violation of the SLA

Service quality: Level specified by qualitative standards that is expected from a function

Severity indexing: 1. The process of using clinical evidence to identify the level of resource consumption   2. A method for determining degrees of illness

Shift differential: An increased wage paid to employees who work less desirable shifts, such as evenings, nights, or weekends

Shift rotation: The assignment of employees to different periods of service to provide coverage, as needed

Simon's decision-making model: A model proposing that the decision-making process moves through three phases: intelligence, design, and choice

Simple linear regression (SLR): A type of statistical inference that not only measures the strength of the relationship between two variables but also estimates a functional relationship between them; SLR may be used when one of the two variables of interest is dependent on the other

Simple random sampling: The process of selecting units from a population so that each one has exactly the same chance of being included in the sample

Simulation: A training technique for experimenting with a real-world situation by means of a computerized model that represents the actual situation

Simulation and inventory modeling: The key components of a plan that are computer simulated for testing and experimentation so that optimal operational procedures can be found

Simulation observation: A type of nonparticipant observation in which researchers stage events rather than allowing them to happen naturally

Simultaneous equations method: A budgeting concept that distributes overhead costs through multiple iterations, allowing maximum distribution of interdepartmental costs among overhead departments

Single-blinded study: A study design in which (typically) the investigator, but not the subject, knows the identity of the treatment and control groups

Situational model of leadership: Hersey and Blanchard's model that is more a model than a theory because it does not explain why things happen but, rather, offers recommendations for behaving differently under various conditions

Six Sigma: Disciplined and data-driven methodology for getting rid of defects in any process

Skill: The ability, education, experience, and training required to perform a job task

Skilled nursing facility (SNF): A long-term care facility with an organized professional staff and permanent facilities (including inpatient beds) that provides continuous nursing and other health-related, psychosocial, and personal services to patients who are not in an acute phase of illness but who primarily require continued care on an inpatient basis

Skilled nursing facility prospective payment system (SNF PPS): A per-diem reimbursement system implemented in July 1998 for costs (routine, ancillary, and capital) associated with covered skilled nursing facility services furnished to Medicare Part A beneficiaries

SMART goals: Stands for goals that are specific, measurable, attainable, realistic, and timely

Smart peripherals: Medical instruments that have information processing components including medication dispensing devices, robotics, smart infusion pumps, and vital signs monitoring equipment

Snowflake schema: A modification of the star schema in a relational database in which the dimension tables are further divided to reduce data redundancy

Social Security Act 1935: The federal legislation that originally established the Social Security program as well as unemployment compensation and support for mothers and children; amended in 1965 to create the Medicare and Medicaid programs

Social Security number (SSN): A unique numerical identifier assigned to every US citizen

Socialization: The process of influencing the behavior and attitudes of a new employee to adapt positively to the work environment

Soft space: Space that is readily expandable or contractible to adjust to changing needs

Software as a Service (SaaS): Software that is provided through an outsourcing contract

Software engineers: Positions that combine aspects of systems analysis and programming; they analyze users' needs and design, test, and develop software to meet those needs

Sole proprietorship: A venture with one owner in which all profits are considered the owner's personal income

Source systems: An information system that operates independently of a CPR system but provides data to it

Source-oriented health record: A system of health record organization in which information is arranged according to the patient care department that provided the care

Spaced training: The process of learning a task in sections separated by time

Span of control: The number of subordinates reporting to a supervisor

Special cause variation: An unusual source of variation that occurs outside a process but affects it

Specialty clinical applications: Systems for intensive care, perioperative or surgical services, cardiology, oncology, emergency medicine, labor and delivery, infection control, and others; many of these specialty clinical applications have been less mainstream, in that they are less widely used and frequently not able to be integrated as well with financial and administrative data or other ancillary systems

Specificity: Ability to detect the absence of a characteristic when the characteristic is absent; *See* **sensitivity**

Speech recognition technology: Technology that translates speech to text

Spoliation: The intentional destruction, mutilation, alteration, or concealment of evidence

Sponsor: A person or an entity that initiates a clinical investigation of a drug (usually the drug manufacturer or research institution that developed the drug) by distributing it to investigators for clinical trials; a person in an organization who supports, protects, and promotes an idea within the organization; the company position with the ultimate responsibility for a project's success

Stable monetary unit: The currency used as the measurement of financial transactions

Staff authority: The lines of reporting in the organizational chart in which the position advises or makes recommendations

Staff model health maintenance organization: A type of HMO that employs physicians to provide healthcare services to subscribers

Staffing structure: The arrangement of staff positions within an organization

Stages of grief: Elizabeth Kubler-Ross' examination of the stress of change experienced by terminally ill patients; the five stages of grief are shock and denial, anger, bargaining, depression, and acceptance

Staging system: A method used in cancer registers to identify specific and separate different stages or aspects of the disease

Stakeholder: An individual within the company who has an interest in, or is affected by, the results of a project

Standard: 1. A scientifically based statement of expected behavior against which structures, processes, and outcomes can be measured   2. A model or example established by authority, custom, or general consent or a rule established by an authority as a measure of quantity, weight, extent, value, or quality

Standard deviation: A measure of variability that describes the deviation from the mean of a frequency distribution in the original units of measurement; the square root of the variance

Standard of care: An established set of clinical decisions and actions taken by clinicians and other representatives of healthcare organizations in accordance with state and federal laws, regulations, and guidelines; codes of ethics published by professional associations or societies; regulations for accreditation published by accreditation agencies; usual and common practice of equivalent clinicians or organizations in a geographical regions

Standardized mortality ratio: Observed mortality rate divided by the expected mortality rate

Standards and Interoperability (S&I) Framework: According to this initiative's charter, the exchange of clinical summaries is hampered by ambiguous common definitions of what data elements must at a minimum be exchanged, how they must be encoded, and how those common semantic elements map to MU-specified formats; an outcome of the initiative is a clinical information model (CIM) consisting of unambiguous, clinically relevant definitions of the core data elements that should be included in care transitions

Standards development organization (SDO): A private or government agency involved in the development of healthcare informatics standards at a national or international level

Star schema: A visual method of expressing a multidimensional data structure in a relational database

State Health Information Exchange Cooperative Agreement Program: A grant program that supports states or state-designated entities (SDEs) in establishing health information exchange (HIE) services among healthcare providers and hospitals in their regions

State workers' compensation insurance funds: Funds that provide a stable source of insurance coverage for work-related illnesses and injuries and serve to protect employers from underwriting uncertainties by making it possible to have continuing availability of workers' compensation coverage

Statement: A list of unpaid invoices; sometimes a cumulative list of all transactions between purchaser and vendor during a specific time period

Statement of cash flows: A statement detailing the reasons why cash amounts changed from one balance sheet period to another

Statement of retained earnings: A statement expressing the change in retained earnings from the beginning of the balance sheet period to the end

Statement of stockholder's equity: A statement detailing the reasons for changes in each stockholder's equity accounts

Statement of work: A document that defines the scope and goals of a specific project

Statistical process control chart: A type of run chart that includes both upper and lower control limits and indicates whether a process is stable or unstable

Statute of limitations: A specific time frame allowed by a statute or law for bringing litigation

Statutory law: Written law established by federal and state legislatures

Steerage: Occurs when an insurer provides financial incentive or discounted rates to a facility to obtain a flow of patients they would not otherwise receive

Steering committee: An interdisciplinary oversight committee set up to guide and manage the strategic planning process

Stem and leaf plots: Visual displays that organize data to show their shape and distribution, using two columns with the stem in the left-hand column and all leaves associated with that stem in the right-hand column; the "leaf" is the ones digit of the number, and the other digits form the "stem"

Step-down allocation: A budgeting concept in which overhead costs are distributed once, beginning with the area that provides the least amount of non-revenue-producing services

Stewardship: The responsible management of something entrusted to one's care

Stop order: An order given that calls for the discontinuation of medications unless the physician gives a specific order to continue the medication; this method prevents patients from receiving drugs for a longer period of time than is necessary

Storage area network (SAN): Storage devices organized into a network so that they can be accessible from any server in the network

Storage management: The process of determining on what type of media to store data, how rapidly data must be accessible, arranging for replication of storage for backup and disaster recovery, and where storage systems should be maintained

Storytelling: A group process technique in which group members create stories describing the plausible future state of the business environment

Straight numeric filing system: Records are filed in numerical order according to the number assigned

Strategic goal: An observable and measurable end result having one or more objectives to be achieved within a more or less fixed time frame

Strategic IS planning: A process for setting IS priorities within an organization; the process of identifying and prioritizing IS needs based on the organization's strategic goals with the intent of ensuring that all IS technology initiatives are integrated and aligned with the organization's overall strategic plan

Strategic management: The art and science of formulating, implementing, and evaluating cross-functional decisions that enable an organization to achieve its objectives

Strategic objectives: Detailed ways to meet a strategic goal that include timelines, resource allocation needs, and assigning responsibility of who will be accountable for implementation

Strategic plan: A broad organization wide plan by which the facility accomplishes its strategic goals

Strategic planning: A disciplined effort to produce fundamental decisions that shape and guide what an organization is, what it does, and why it does it

Strategic profile: Identifies the current existing key services or products, the nature of its customers and users, the nature of its market segments, and the nature of its geographic markets

Strategic thinking: The framework for the strategic and operational improvement plans; it combines an understanding of a strategic plan and an operational plan, which support strategic thinking within an organization

Strategy: A course of action designed to produce a desired (business) outcome

Strategy map: A visual representation of the cause-and-effect relationships among the components of an organization's strategy

Stratified random sampling: The process of selecting the same percentages of subjects for a study sample as they exist in the subgroups (strata) of the population

Strengths, weaknesses, opportunities, and threats (SWOT) analysis: A strategic planning method used to evaluate the strengths, weaknesses, opportunities, and threats involved in a project or in a business venture

Structure: A term from Donabedian's model of quality assessment that assesses an organization's ability to provide services in terms of both the physical building and equipment and the people providing the healthcare services

Structure and content standards: Common data elements and definitions of the data elements to be included in an electronic patient record

Structure indicators: Indicators that measure the attributes of the setting, such as number and qualifications of the staff, adequacy of equipment and facilities, and adequacy of organizational policies and procedures

Structure measures: Indicators that measure the attributes of the healthcare setting (for example, adequacy of equipment and supplies)

Structured analysis: A pattern identification analysis performed for a specific task

Structured (closed-ended) question: A type of question that limits possible responses

Structured data: Binary, computer-readable data

Structured decision: A decision made by following a formula or a step-by-step process

Structured interview: An interview format that uses a set of standardized questions that are asked of all applicants

Structured Product Labeling (SPL): Used by LOINC, which was adopted as a federal health information interoperability standard for the electronic exchange of laboratory test orders and drug label section headers

Structured query language (SQL): A fourth-generation computer language that includes both DDL and DML components and is used to create and manipulate relational databases

Subacute care: A type of step-down care provided after a patient is released from an acute-care hospital (including nursing homes and other facilities that provide medical care, but not surgical or emergency care)

Subprojects: Smaller components of a larger project

Substitutes: The characteristics of subordinates to the leader that can provide substitutes to the leader's lack of skill; subordinates can have high ability, good experience, expert knowledge, and training—all of which tend to replace the expertise of the absent leader

Succession planning: A specific type of promotional plan in which senior-level position openings are anticipated and candidates are identified from within the organization; the candidates are given training through formal education, job rotation, and mentoring so that they can eventually assume these positions

Successor: A task in a dependency relationship between two tasks that is dependent on the predecessor task

Supervised learning: Any learning technique that has as its purpose to classify or predict attributes of objects or individuals

Supervisory managers: Managers who oversee small (two- to 10-person) functional workgroups or teams and often perform hands-on functions in addition to supervisory functions

Supplemental medical insurance (SMI) (Medicare Part B): A voluntary medical insurance program that helps pay for physicians' services, medical services, and supplies not covered by Medicare Part A

Surgical operation: One or more surgical procedures performed at one time for one patient via a common approach or for a common purpose

Surgical procedure: Any single, separate, systematic process upon or within the body that can be complete in itself; is normally performed by a physician, dentist, or other licensed practitioner; can be performed either with or without instruments; and is performed to restore disunited or deficient parts, remove diseased or injured tissues, extract foreign matter, assist in obstetrical delivery, or aid in diagnosis

Surgical review: Evaluation of operative and other procedures, invasive and noninvasive, using Joint Commission guidelines

Survey: A method of self-report research in which the individuals themselves are the source of the data

Survey feedback: The results of the survey are presented to decision makers as feedback, with the intention that any discrepancies between what they believe and what is actually occurring in the organization will prompt corrective action

Sustainability: Refers generally to the ability to maintain certain resources or processes indefinitely, and more specifically to meet present needs without compromising ability to meet the needs of future generations

Swimlane diagram: Diagram that shows an entire business process from beginning to end and is especially popular because it highlights relevant variables (who, what, and when) simply while requiring little or no training to use and understand

Synchronous: Occurring at the same time

Synergy: The combination of efforts produces more than acting alone

Syntactic: Refers to the formal properties of language

Syntax: A term that refers to the comparable structure or format of data, usually as they are being transmitted from one system to another

System: A set of related and highly interdependent components that are operating for a particular purpose

System build (or configuration): The creation of data dictionaries, tables, decision support rules, templates for data entry, screen layouts, and reports used in a system

System catalog: An integrated data dictionary (which is a component of a database management system) that generally contains information on data tables and relationships in addition to data definitions

Systematic literature review: Methodical approach to literature review that reduces the possibility of bias; characterized by explicit search criteria to identify literature, inclusion, and exclusion criteria to select articles

and information sources, and evaluation against consistent methodological standards

Systematic sampling: The process of selecting a sample of subjects for a study by drawing every nth unit on a list

Systematized Nomenclature of Dentistry (SNODENT): A clinical vocabulary developed by the American Dental Association (ADA) for data representation of clinical dentistry content

Systematized Nomenclature of Medicine (SNOMED): A comprehensive clinical vocabulary developed by the College of American Pathologists that is the most promising set of clinical terms available for a controlled vocabulary for healthcare

Systematized Nomenclature of Medicine Clinical Terminology (SNOMED CT): A comprehensive, controlled clinical vocabulary developed by the College of American Pathologists

Systematized Nomenclature of Medicine Reference Terminology (SNOMED RT): A concept-based terminology consisting of more than 110,000 concepts with linkages to more than 180,000 terms with unique computer-readable codes

Systems analyst: An individual who investigates, analyzes, designs, develops, installs, evaluates, and maintains an organization's healthcare information systems; is typically involved in all aspects of the systems development life cycle; and serves as a liaison among end users and programmers, database administrators, and other technical personnel

Systems development life cycle (SDLC): A model used to represent the ongoing process of developing (or purchasing) information systems

Systems theory: A reaction against reductionism; proponents of this theory believe that important information is lost by too specific a focus and thus emphasize the interconnections, organization, and wholeness of these constituents rather than their inspection in isolation

Tacit knowledge: The actions, experiences, ideals, values, and emotions of an individual that tend to be highly personal and difficult to communicate (for example, corporate culture, organizational politics, and professional experience)

Tactical plan: A strategic plan at the level of divisions and departments

Target population: A large group of individuals who are the focus of a study

Task: The steps to be performed in order to complete a project or part of a project

Task analysis: A procedure for determining the specific duties and skills required of a job

Task structure: Refers to how clearly and how well defined the task goal, procedures, and possible solutions are

Tax Equity and Fiscal Responsibility Act of 1982 (TEFRA): The federal legislation that modified Medicare's retrospective reimbursement system for inpatient hospital stays by requiring implementation of diagnosis-related groups and the acute-care prospective payment system

Taxonomy: The principles of a classification system, such as data classification, and the study of the general principles of scientific classification

Team building: The process of organizing and acquainting a team, and building skills for dealing with later team processes

Technical component (TC): The portion of radiological and other procedures that is facility based or nonphysician based (for example, radiology films, equipment, overhead, endoscopic suites, and so on)

Technical Interoperability: The interoperability achieved through application of message format standards

Technical skills: One of the three managerial skill categories, related to knowledge of the technical aspects of the business

Telecommuting: A work arrangement (often used by coding and transcription personnel) in which at least a portion of the employee's work hours is spent outside the office (usually in the home) and the work is transmitted back to the employer via electronic means; *See* **telestaffing**

Telehealth: A telecommunications system that links healthcare organizations and patients from diverse geographic locations and transmits text and images for (medical) consultation and treatment; also called telemedicine

Telestaffing: *See* **telecommuting**

Temporary Assistance for Needy Families (TANF): A federal program that provides states with grants to be spent on time-limited cash assistance for low-income families, generally limiting a family's lifetime cash welfare benefits to a maximum of five years and permitting states to impose other requirements

Temporary budget variance: The difference between the budgeted and actual amounts of a line item that is expected to reverse itself in a subsequent period; the timing difference between the budget and the actual event

Temporary privileges: Privileges granted for a limited time period to a licensed, independent practitioner on the basis of recommendations made by the appropriate clinical department or the president of the medical staff

Ten characteristics of data quality: Characteristics of a data quality model by AHIMA: accuracy, accessibility, comprehensiveness, consistency, currency, definition, granularity, precision, relevancy, and timeliness

Ten-step monitoring and evaluation process: The systematic and ongoing collection, organization, and evaluation of data related to indicator development promoted by the Joint Commission in the mid-1980s

Terminal-digit filing system: A system of health record identification and filing in which the last digit or group of digits (terminal digits) in the health record number determines file placement

Termination: The act of ending something (for example, a job)

Terminology: A set of terms representing the system of concepts of a particular subject field; a clinical terminology provides the proper use of clinical words as names or symbols

Test statistics: A set of statistical techniques that examines the psychometric properties of measurement instruments

Testing: The act of performing an examination or evaluation

Text mining: The process of extracting and then quantifying and filtering free-text data

Theory: A systematic organization of knowledge that predicts or explains the behavior or events

Theory X and Y: A management theory developed by McGregor that describes pessimistic and optimistic assumptions about people and their work potential

360-degree evaluation: A method of performance evaluation in which the supervisors, peers, and other staff who interact with the employee contribute information

Time and motion studies: Studies in which complex tasks are broken down into their component motions to determine inefficiencies and to develop improvements

Time ladder: A form used by employees to document time spent on various tasks

Time period: A specific span of dates to which data apply

Topography: Code that describes the site of origin of the neoplasm and uses the same three- and four-character categories as in the neoplasm section of the second chapter of ICD-10

Tort: An action brought when one party believes that another party caused harm through wrongful conduct and seeks compensation for that harm

Total length of stay (discharge days): The sum of the days of stay of any group of inpatients discharged during a specific period of time

Total quality management (TQM): A management philosophy that includes all activities in which the needs of the customer and the organization are satisfied in the most efficient manner by using employee potentials and continuous improvement

Tracer methodology: A process the Joint Commission surveyors use during the on-site survey to analyze an organization's systems, with particular attention to identified priority focus areas, by following individual patients through the organization's healthcare process in the sequence experienced by the patients; an evaluation that follows (traces) the hospital experiences of specific patients to assess the quality of patient care; part of the new Joint Commission survey processes

Traditional fee-for-service (FFS) reimbursement: A reimbursement method involving third-party payers who compensate providers after the healthcare services have been delivered; payment is based on specific services provided to subscribers

Train the trainer: A method of training certain individuals who, in turn, will be responsible for training others on a task or skill

Trainee: A person who is learning a task or skill

Trainer: A person who gives instruction on a task or skill

Training: A set of activities and materials that provide the opportunity to acquire job-related skills, knowledge, and abilities

Training and development model: A nine-step plan designed to help the health information manager or human resources department identify the training needs of an employee group

Trait approach: Proposes that leaders possess a collection of traits or personal qualities that distinguishes them from nonleaders

Transaction standards: Standards that support the uniform format and sequence of data during transmission from one healthcare entity to another

Transactional leadership: Refers to the role of the manager who strives to create an efficient workplace by balancing task accomplishment with interpersonal satisfaction

Transactional system: A computer-based information system that keeps track of an organization's business transactions through inputs (for example, transaction data such as admissions, discharges, and transfers in a hospital) and outputs (for example, census reports and bills); also called transaction-processing system

Transcription: The process of deciphering and typing medical dictation

Transformation: Mappings to other vocabularies; identifying what mappings are supported for the intended purpose

Transformational leadership: Leaders promote innovation and organizational change

Translational research: Type of research that converts new knowledge, mechanisms, and techniques generated by advances in basic science research into new approaches for prevention, diagnosis, and treatment of disease

Transparency: Refers to the degree to which patients included in secondary data sets are aware of their inclusion

Traumatic injury: A wound or an injury included in a trauma registry

Treatment: The manipulation, intervention, or therapy; a broad term used by researchers to generically mean some act, such as a physical conditioning program, a computer training program, a particular laboratory medium, or the timing of prophylactic medications

Triangulation: The use of multiple sources or perspectives to investigate the same phenomenon

TRICARE: The federal healthcare program that provides coverage for the dependents of armed forces personnel and for retirees receiving care outside military treatment facilities in which the federal government pays a percentage of the cost; formerly known as Civilian Health and Medical Program of the Uniformed Services

TRICARE Extra: A cost-effective preferred provider network TRICARE option in which costs for healthcare are lower than for the standard TRICARE program because a physician or medical specialist is selected from a network of civilian healthcare professionals who participate in TRICARE Extra

TRICARE Prime: A TRICARE program that provides the most comprehensive healthcare benefits at the lowest cost of the three TRICARE options, in which military treatment facilities serve as the principal source of healthcare and a primary care manager is assigned to each enrollee

TRICARE Prime Remote: A program that provides active-duty service members in the United States with a specialized version of TRICARE Prime while they are assigned to duty stations in areas not served by the traditional military healthcare system

TRICARE Senior Prime: A managed care demonstration TRICARE program designed to better serve the medical needs of military retirees, dependents, and survivors who are 65 years old or older

TRICARE Standard: A TRICARE program that allows eligible beneficiaries to choose any physician or healthcare provider, which permits the most flexibility but may be the most expensive

Trier of fact: The judge or jury hearing a civil or criminal trial

Triple bottom line: This expanded criteria (beyond the financial bottom line) includes the sustainability of environmental and social performance of the organization as well, or people, planet, and profit

Two-tailed hypothesis: A type of alternative hypothesis in which the researcher makes no prediction about the direction of the results

Type I error: A type of error in which the researcher erroneously rejects the null hypothesis when it is true

Type II error: A type of error in which the researcher erroneously fails to reject the null hypothesis when it is false

UB-04 (Uniform Bill-04): The single standardized Medicare form for standardized uniform billing, implemented in 2007 for hospital inpatients and outpatients; this form is also used by the major third-party payers and most hospitals

Unallocated reserves: Monies that have not been assigned a specific use

Unbundling: The practice of using multiple codes to bill for the various individual steps in a single procedure rather than using a single code that includes all of the steps of the comprehensive procedure

Unfavorable variance: The negative difference between the budgeted amount and the actual amount of a line item, where actual revenue is less than budget or where actual expenses exceed budget

Unfreezing: In Lewin's stages of change, the initial stage of change is unfreezing the status quo, often by presenting the discrepancies between the status quo and the desired goals; often creates a state of cognitive dissonance, which is an uncomfortable awareness of two incompatible perceptions or beliefs, in this case, the discrepancy; *See* **Lewin's stages of change** and **refreezing**

Unified Medical Language System (UMLS): A program initiated by the National Library of Medicine to build an intelligent, automated system that can understand biomedical concepts, words, and expressions and their interrelationships

Unified Medical Language System (UMLS) Metathesaurus: A list containing information on biomedical concepts and terms from more than 100 healthcare vocabularies and classifications, administrative health data, bibliographic and full-text databases, and expert systems

Unified Medical Language System (UMLS) Semantic Network: A categorization of all UMDNS concepts in the UMLS Metathesaurus

Unified Medical Language System (UMLS) SPECIALIST Lexicon: An English-language lexicon containing biomedical terms

Unified modeling language (UML): A common data-modeling notation used in conjunction with object-oriented database design

Uniform Ambulatory Care Data Set (UACDS): A data set developed by the National Committee on Vital and Health Statistics consisting of a minimum set of patient/client-specific data elements to be collected in ambulatory care settings

Uniform Hospital Discharge Data Set (UHDDS): A core set of data elements adopted by the US Department of Health, Education, and Welfare in 1974 that are collected by hospitals on all discharges and all discharge abstract systems

Uniformed Services Employment and Reemployment Rights Act (1994): Federal legislation that prohibits discrimination against individuals because of their service in the Armed Forces Reserves, National Guard, or other uniformed services

Union: A collective bargaining unit that represents groups of employees and is authorized to negotiate with employers on the employees' behalf in matters related to compensation, health, and safety

Unique identification number: A combination of numbers or alphanumeric characters assigned to a particular patient

Unique identifier: A type of information that refers to only one individual or organization

Unique physician identification number (UPIN): A unique numerical identifier created by the Health Care Financing Administration (now called the Centers for Medicare and Medicaid Services) for use by physicians who bill for services provided to Medicare patients

Unit numbering system: A health record identification system in which the patient receives a unique medical record number at the time of the first encounter that is used for all subsequent encounters

Unit work division: A method of work organization where each task is performed by one person at the same time that another person is doing a task, but one does not have to wait for the other

Unity of command: A human resources principle that assumes that each employee reports to only one specific management position

Univariate: A term referring to the involvement of one variable

Universal chart order: A system in which the health record is maintained in the same format while the patient is in the facility and after discharge

Universal Medical Device Nomenclature System (UMDNS): A standard international nomenclature and computer coding system for medical devices, developed by ECRI

Universal protocol: A written checklist developed by the Joint Commission to prevent errors that can occur when physicians perform the wrong procedure, for example

Unstructured data: Nonbinary, human-readable data

Unstructured decision: A decision that is made without following a prescribed method, formula, or pattern

Unstructured (open-ended) question: A type of question that allows free-form responses

Unsupervised learning: Any learning technique that has as its purpose to group or cluster items, objects, or individuals

Upcoding: The practice of assigning diagnostic or procedural codes that represent higher payment rates than the codes that actually reflect the services provided to patients

Usability: The overall ability of a user to capture and retrieve data efficiently and effectively

Use: Sharing, employing, applying, utilizing, examining, or analyzing individually identifiable health information *within* an entity that maintains such information

Use case: A technique that develops scenarios based on how users will use information to assist in developing information systems that support the information requirements

Use case analysis: A technique to determine how users will interact with a system; it uses the designed future (to-be) process and describes how a user will interact with the system to complete process steps and how the system will behave from the user perspective

User-centered design: A concept that involves the user throughout the entire design and development process; involving the user throughout the entire process enables the developers to make sure the users' needs are met; in healthcare, it translates to patient-centered, caregiver-centered, support staff–centered, employee-centered, and the like

Usual, customary, and reasonable (UCR) charges: Method of evaluating providers' fees in which the third-party payer pays for fees that are "usual" in that provider's practice, "customary" in the community, and "reasonable" for the situation

Utilization management: 1. The planned, systematic review of the patients in a healthcare facility against care criteria for admission, continued stay, and discharge   2. A collection of systems and processes to ensure that facilities and resources, both human and nonhuman, are used maximally and are consistent with patient care needs

Utilization review (UR): The process of determining whether the medical care provided to a specific patient is necessary according to preestablished objective screening criteria at time frames specified in the organization's utilization management plan

Utilization Review Act: The federal legislation that requires hospitals to conduct continued-stay reviews for Medicare and Medicaid patients

Validity: 1. The extent to which data correspond to the actual state of affairs or that an instrument measures what it purports to measure   2. A term referring to a test's ability to accurately and consistently measure what it purports to measure

Values-based leadership: Theory similar to other contingency theories such as path–goal leadership; *See* **path–goal theory**

Value-based purchasing (VBP): CMS incentive plan that links payments more directly to the quality of care provided, rewards providers for delivering high-quality and efficient clinical care; it incorporates clinical process-of-care measures as well as measures from the Hospital Consumer Assessment of Healthcare Providers and Systems (HCAHPS) survey on how patients view their care experiences

Values statement: A short description that communicates an organization's social and cultural belief system

Variability: The dispersion of a set of measures around the population mean

Variable: A factor

Variable costs: Resources expended that vary with the activity of the organization, for example, medication expenses vary with patient volume

Variance: A measure of variability that gives the average of the squared deviations from the mean; in financial management, the difference between the budgeted amount and the actual amount of a line item; in project management, the difference between the original project plan and current estimates

Variance analysis: An assessment of a department's financial transactions to identify differences between the budget amount and the actual amount of a line item

Vector graphic (or signal tracing) data: Digital data that have been captured as points and are connected by lines (a series of point coordinates) or areas (shapes bounded by lines)

Vendor neutral: Classifications and terminologies must be neutral so that they can be readily used as national standards by all vendors without conferring a competitive advantage to any one of them

Vendor system: A computer system developed by a commercial company not affiliated with the healthcare organization

Verification service: An outside service that provides a primary source check on information that a physician makes available on an application to the medical staff

Vertical dyad linkage: Formulated in 1975 to describe the single-person mentoring relationships that occur in organizations and was later supplemented by leader–member relations theory that applied the same idea to the leader's relations with groups

Vertical structure: The levels and relationships among positions in an organizational hierarchy

Virtual reality (VR): An artificial form of reality experienced through sensory stimuli and in which the participant's actions partly affect what happens

Virtualization: The emulation of one or more computers within a software platform that enables one physical computer to share resources across other computers

Vision: A picture of the desired future that sets a direction and rationale for change

Vision statement: A short description of an organization's ideal future state

Vital statistics: Data related to births, deaths, marriages, and fetal deaths

Vocabulary: A list or collection of clinical words or phrases and their meanings

Vocabulary standard: A common definition for medical terms to encourage consistent descriptions of an individual's condition in the health record

Voice recognition technology: A method of encoding speech signals that do not require speaker pauses (but uses pauses when they are present) and of interpreting at least some of the signals' content as words or the intent of the speaker

Volume logs: Forms used (sometimes in conjunction with time ladders) to obtain information about the volume of work units received and processed in a day

Voluntary Disclosure Program: A program unveiled in 1998 by the OIG that encourages healthcare providers to voluntarily report fraudulent conduct affecting Medicare, Medicaid, and other federal healthcare programs

Vulnerable subject: A person with limited mental or other capacity who is unable to freely volunteer in a study

Waste: Anything that does not add value to a product or service from the standpoint of the customer

Web browser–based (or web native) architectures: Systems and applications written in one or more web programming languages; also called web browser–based systems

Web content management systems: Systems in which information placed in a website can be labeled and tracked so that it can be easily located, modified, and reused

Web portal: A website entryway through which to access, find, and deliver information

Web services: an open, standardized way of integrating disparate, web browser–based and other applications

Web services architecture: A way of integrating web-based applications using open standards over an Internet protocol backbone; it allows organizations to share data across different system platforms behind a firewall without being tied to one operating system or programming language

Web 2.0: The second generation of Internet-based services that emphasizes online collaboration and sharing among users; some of these applications and technologies include blogs, social networks, content communities, wikis, and podcasts

Web 3.0: Technologists are beginning to discuss the concept of Web/Health 3.0, and while the definitions vary widely, it will likely focus on expanding the participatory and collaborative nature of social networks that defined Web 2.0 to include more real-time video and 3D elements; other commentators argue that Web 3.0 will adopt semantic web standards, thereby allowing computers to read and generate content similar to humans.

Web-based systems and applications: Systems and applications that use Internet technology

Web-based training: Instruction via the Internet that enables learners to work when, where, and at a pace suited to them and offers interaction with other students and the instructor via the listserv

Webmasters/web developers: Individuals who support web applications and the healthcare organization's intranet and Internet operations

Wiki: A collection of web pages that together form a collaborative website

Wireless on wheels (WOWs): Notebook computers mounted on carts that can be moved through the facility by users

Wireless technology: A type of technology that uses wireless networks and wireless devices to access and transmit data in real time

Work: The effort, usually described in hours, needed to complete a task

Work breakdown structure: A hierarchical structure that decomposes project activities into levels of detail

Work distribution analysis: An analysis used to determine whether a department's current work assignments and job content are appropriate

Work distribution chart: A matrix that depicts the work being done in a particular workgroup in terms of specific tasks and activities, time spent on tasks, and the employees performing the tasks

Work division: The way in which tasks are handled within an organization

Work measurement: The process of studying the amount of work accomplished and how long it takes to accomplish work in order to define and monitor productivity

Work products: Documents produced during the completion of a task that may be a component of, or contribute to, a project deliverable

Work sampling: A work measurement technique that uses random sample measurements to characterize the performance of the whole

Worker immaturity–maturity: Concept borrowed from Chris Argyris, who suggested that job and psychological maturity also influence leadership style; job maturity refers to how much work-related ability, knowledge, experience, and skill a person has; psychological maturity refers to willingness, confidence, commitment, and motivation related to work

Workers' Adjustment and Retraining Notification (WARN) Act: Federal legislation that requires employers to give employees a 60-day notice in advance of covered plant closings and covered mass layoffs

Workers' compensation: The medical and income insurance coverage for certain employees in unusually hazardous jobs

Workflow: Any work process that must be handled by more than one person

Workflow technology: Technology that automatically routes electronic documents into electronic in-baskets of its department clerks or supervisors for disposition decisions

Working conditions: The environment in which work is performed (surroundings) and the physical dangers or risks involved in performing the job (hazards)

World Health Organization (WHO): Responsible for maintaining the International Classification of Diseases (ICD)

World Organization of National Colleges, Academies, and Academic Associations of General Practitioners/Family Physicians (WONCA): Developed the International Classification of Primary Care (ICPC-2), a coding terminology for the classification of primary care

XML: *See* **Extensible markup language**

X12N: Referring to standards adopted for electronic data interchange

Zero-based budget: Types of budgets in which each budget cycle poses the opportunity to continue or discontinue services based on available resources so that every department or activity must be justified and prioritized annually to effectively allocate resources

A

AAAHC (Accreditation Association for Ambulatory Health Care), 253

AALL (American Association of Labor Legislation), 413

AAMC (American Association of Medical Colleges), 9–10

AAMRL (American Association of Medical Record Librarians) Code of Ethics, 344, 345t

Abbreviated injury scale (AIS), 372

Ability (achievement) tests, 725

ABN. See Advance Beneficiary Notice of Noncoverage

Absentee coverage, 802

Abstract, 592

Abstracting, 287, 382

Abstracting of data. See Data abstraction

ACA. See Patient Protection and Affordable Care Act

Acceptance (contract law), 308

Accept assignment, 449

Access controls, 133

Accession number, 371

Accession registries, 371

Accountability, 165t, 750–751

Accountable Care Organizations (ACOs), 43, 526
and ACA, 17–18
compliance programs, 855
defined, 43
EHM reporting and analytics, 128–129
ethical issues, 344
and quality improvement, 677
as setting for HIM professionals, 59

Accounting, 764–769
authorities, 766–767
basic financial accounting, 770–780
basic management accounting, 781–783
concepts and principles, 764–766, 764t
equity and net assets, 772
expenses, 773–774
financial organization, 767–768
managerial accounting, 781–783
ratio analysis, 777–780
recording transactions, 774–777
revenue, 772–773
sources of financial data, 768–769
uses of financial data, 769

Accounting rate of return, 791

Accounts payable, 771

Accounts receivable
accounting definition, 770, 771t
claims processing, 445
impact on financial statements, 782–783

Accounts receivable days (A/R), 471

Accreditation
beginning of modern process, 11
compliance programs, 854
of healthcare facilities, 38
legal issues, 309–310
legal record retention requirements, 275
and quality management, 670–674

Accreditation Association for Ambulatory Health Care (AAAHC), 253

Accreditation organizations/agencies, 195, 309–310. See also specific organizations and programs, e.g.: The Joint Commission

Accreditation standards, 670–674

Accreditation Standards Committee X12 (ASC X12), 132–133, 206

Accrual, 776

ACCs (ambulatory care centers), 29

ACDIS (Association of Clinical Documentation Improvement Specialists), 69

ACHE (American College of Healthcare Executives), 21

Acid-test ratio, 780

ACOs. See Accountable Care Organizations

ACP (American College of Physicians), 11

Acquisition of long-term assets, 788

ACR-NEMA (American College of Radiology and the National Electrical Manufacturers Association), 207

ACS (American College of Surgeons), 11, 239–240

Action plans, 877

Active listening, 698

Active problem list, 203t

Activities of daily living (ADLs), 379

Activity-based budgets, 785

Actor (in use case), 230

Acute care, 22, 485

Acute care facilities, 484

Acute care prospective payment system (PPS), 431–433

ADA. See Americans with Disabilities Act

ADLs (activities of daily living), 379

Administrative applications, 123

Administrative decision making, 695–696

Administrative information, 243–244

Administrative law, 301–302

Administrative management, 685–686, 686t, 689t

Administrative planning, 769

Administrative services only (ASO) contracts, 417

Administrative statistical data, 485–491

Administrative support services, 28

Administrative system (legal), 300

Adopter groups, 706–707, 707t

Adoption information, 358

Adoption of EHR system, 119

Adult day-care services, 32

Adult learning, 719–720
education of adult learners, 741–742
learning with special needs, 742–743
strategies for, 740–743

Advance Beneficiary Notice of Noncoverage (ABN), 449, 450t

Advance directives, 244

Advance Notice of Proposed Rulemaking (ANPRM), 610

Adverse event(s). See Sentinel events

Adverse event reports, 613

Aesthetics of the workplace, 798–799

Affinity grouping, 822, 822t

Affordable Care Act. See Patient Protection and Affordable Care Act

AGA (American Gastroenterological Association), 376

Against medical advice (AMA), 253

AGA Registry, 376

Age Discrimination in Employment Act (1967), 721

Agency for Healthcare Policy and Research (AHCPR), 16, 629

Agency for Healthcare Research and Quality (AHRQ)
Common Formats Version 1.1, 202
and current outcomes movement, 629–631
health services research databases, 381
QDM, 201
and QI, 667, 669

Aggregate data, 194, 368
Agreement (contract law), 307–308
AHA (American Hospital Association), 11, 20–21
AHCPR. *See* Agency for Healthcare Policy and Research
AHDI (Association for Healthcare Documentation Integrity), 261
AHIC (American Health Information Community), 223
AHIMA. *See* American Health Information Management Association
AHIMA Clinical Terminology and Vocabulary Community of Practice (CoP), 407
AHIMA Code of Professional Ethics, 69
AHIMA Core Model. *See* Core Model of HIM practice
AHIMA Council for Excellence in Education (CEE), 51
AHIMA Curriculum Competencies and Knowledge Clusters-Health Information Management Baccalaureate Degree, 74–80
AHLTA (Armed Forces Health Longitudinal Technology Application), 401
AHRQ. *See* Agency for Healthcare Research and Quality
AIS (abbreviated injury scale), 372
Alert fatigue, 126
Allied health (AMA definition), 11–12
Allied health professionals performance review, 666
Allied health professions, 11–12
Allied Health Reinvestment Act (2005), 721
All patient diagnosis-related groups (AP-DRGs), 433
All patient refined diagnosis-related groups (APR-DRGs), 433
ALOS. *See* Average length of stay
Alphabetic patient identifier, 270
Alternative hypothesis, 571
AMA. *See* American Medical Association
AMA (against medical advice), 253
Ambulance fee schedule, 438
Ambulatory care, 28–30, 253
Ambulatory care centers (ACCs), 29
Ambulatory payment classification (APC) system, 435–437
Ambulatory Surgery Center Prospective Payment System (ASC PPS), 437
Ambulatory surgery centers (ASCs), 30, 253, 437, 498
American Association of Labor Legislation (AALL), 413
American Association of Medical Colleges (AAMC), 9–10
American Association of Medical Record Librarians (AAMRL) Code of Ethics, 344, 345*t*

American College of Healthcare Executives (ACHE), 21
American College of Nurse-Midwives, 10
American College of Physicians (ACP), 11
American College of Radiology and the National Electrical Manufacturers Association (ACR-NEMA), 207
American College of Surgeons (ACS), 11, 239–240
American Gastroenterological Association (AGA), 376
American Health Benefit Exchanges, 17
American Health Information Community (AHIC), 223
American Health Information Management Association (AHIMA)
 CDI toolkit, 470
 certification and employment outlook for HIM professionals, 888
 certification management, 62–63
 code of ethics, 70–71, 344, 347*t*–348*t*
 continuing education requirements, 67–68
 curriculum competencies and knowledge clusters-Health Information Management Baccalaureate Degree, 74–80
 data quality best practices, 180
 data quality model, 175, 176*t*–179*t*
 e-Discovery, 325, 326
 e-HIM transition, 885–886
 legacy of previous organizations, 5
 and LHR, 143
 mission, 69
 origins and mission, 21–22
 PHR definition, 98
 professional cohesion, 71
 record destruction recommendations, 279
 role of, 3
 roles of Board of Directors/House of Delegates, 886*t*
 10 characteristics of data quality, 175, 180, 181*t*–183*t*
 top 10 tenets for managing transition from paper to EHRs, 886, 887*t*
American Hospital Association (AHA), 11, 20–21
American Indians. *See* Indian Health Service
American Medical Association (AMA)
 CPT, 393–394
 and Joint Commission, 11
 origins and mission, 20
 standardization of nursing practice, 10
American Medical Informatics Association (AMIA), 69
American Medical Record Association (AMRA) bylaws/code of ethics, 345*t*–346*t*

American National Standards Institute (ANSI), 210, 224
American National Standards Institute (ANSI) ASC X12N, 206
American Nurses Association (ANA), 10, 21
American Osteopathic Association (AOA) Hospital Accreditation Program, 38, 309–310
American Psychiatric Association (APA), 394–395
American Recovery and Reinvestment Act (ARRA), 17. *See also* Patient Protection and Affordable Care Act
 compliance programs, 855
 disclosure rule changes, 312–313
 ethical issues, 344
 grant-funded programs, 66
 HITECH act, 310
 and information technology, 3
 and meaningful use, 17
American Recovery and Reinvestment Act/ Health Information Technology for Economic and Clinical Health Act (ARRA/HITECH)
 enforcement and penalties for disclosure violations, 322–324
 HIPAA security provisions, 314
 patient access rights, 314, 315
 use/disclosure without patient authorization, 322
 use/disclosure with patient authorization, 317, 318
American Society for Testing and Materials (ASTM), 99, 205, 405
Americans with Disabilities Act (ADA), 721, 743
AMIA (American Medical Informatics Association), 69
AMRA (American Medical Record Association) bylaws/code of ethics, 345*t*–346*t*
ANA (American Nurses Association), 10, 21
Analog photographic films, 84
Analysis phase of SDLC, 105
Analysis statements, 777, 779*t*
Ancillary materials, 275
Ancillary services, 249–250
Ancillary systems (clinical department applications), 123–124
Anesthesia, 19
Anonymity, in research, 596
ANPRM (Advance Notice of Proposed Rulemaking), 610
ANSI. *See* American National Standards Institute
Anti-harassment training, 739
AOA (American Osteopathic Association) Hospital Accreditation Program, 38, 309–310

APA (American Psychiatric Association), 394–395
APC (ambulatory payment classification) system, 435–437
AP-DRGs (all patient diagnosis-related groups), 433
APIs (Application programming interfaces), 221
Application programming interfaces (APIs), 221
Application service provider (ASP), 140
Application systems analysts, 110
Applied healthcare informatics, 83
Applied research, 548
APR-DRGs (all patient refined diagnosis-related groups), 433
Aptitude tests, 725
AR (Attributable risk), 626
Areas of excellence, 875
Argyris, Chris, 703
Armed Forces Health Longitudinal Technology Application (AHLTA), 401
ARRA. *See* American Recovery and Reinvestment Act
ARRA/HITECH. *See* American Recovery and Reinvestment Act/Health Information Technology for Economic and Clinical Health Act
Article (defined), 592
ASC PPS (Ambulatory Surgery Center Prospective Payment System), 437
ASCs. *See* Ambulatory surgery centers
ASC X12. *See* Accreditation Standards Committee X12 (ASC X12)
ASO (administrative services only) contracts, 417
ASP (Application service provider), 140
Assault, 305
Assessment
   of in-service education, 738*t,* 739
   of on-the-job training, 736
   of orientation program, 733, 734*t*
Assets, 770–771, 775*t*
Associate degrees in HIM, 65
Association for Healthcare Documentation Integrity (AHDI), 261
Association of Clinical Documentation Improvement Specialists (ACDIS), 69
Association of Record Librarians of North America, 5
Assumptions
   in projects, 837
   work duration estimates, 843–844
ASTM. *See* American Society for Testing and Materials
ASTM International, 203
ASTM Standard E1384-07, 205
ASTM Standard E2087-00, 405
Asynchronous web-based learning, 745

ATCBs (Authorized Testing and Certification Bodies), 224
ATLAS.ti software, 589
Attributable risk (AR), 626
Attributes, 185
Audioconferencing, 743, 745–746
Audiologists, 12
Auditing/audits (continuing education), 68
Auditing/audits (performance)
   coding and corporate compliance, 455, 455*t*
   compliance programs, 855–856
   revenue cycle management, 472
Audit logs, 134
Audit trails, 101
Authentication
   digital signature management technology, 87
   of health record entries, 264–265
   and transcription, 258
   two-factor, 134
Authority, 750–751
Authorization, 461
Authorization forms, 244
Authorization management, 188
Authorized Testing and Certification Bodies (ATCBs), 224
Autoauthentication, 264–265
Autocoding, 86
Autocratic leadership, 700, 700*t*
Autodialing systems, 376
Automated code assignment, 444
Automated drug dispensing machine, 127
Automated forms-processing (e-forms) technology, 87, 125
Automatic recognition technologies, 88–89
Automatic time limits (medications), 248
Autonomy, 342
Autopsy rates, 493–496
Availability
   EHR supporting infrastructure, 134
   GAARP principles, 165*t*
Avatars, 747
Average daily census, 487, 487*t*
Average length of stay (ALOS), 22–23, 440, 490, 490*t*

B

Bacteria, 19
Balance billing, 449
Balanced Budget Act of 1997 (BBA), 435
Balanced Budget Refinement Act (BBRA) of 1999, 439
Balanced scorecard (BSC), 692, 881, 882*t*
Balance sheet, 777
Bar charts, 510–511, 510*t,* 511*t*
Bar code medication administration record (BC-MAR) system, 120, 126
Bar coding technology, 88, 268

Barnard, Chester, 686
Baseline, 846
Basic research, 548
Battery, 305
Baylor University Hospital (Dallas, Texas), 415
BBA (Balanced Budget Act of 1997), 435
BBRA (Balanced Budget Refinement Act) of 1999, 439
BC/BS. *See* Blue Cross and Blue Shield
BC-MAR (bar code medication administration record) system, 120, 126
Beacon Community Program, 221
Bed capacity (term), 23
Bed count, 488
Bed count days, 488
Bed turnover rate, 488–489, 489*t*
Behavioral description interviews, 726
Behavioral healthcare, 32, 138, 253
Behavioral theories of leadership, 701–702
Belmont Report: Ethical Principles and Guidelines for the Protection of Human Subjects of Research, 609
Benchmarking
   of comparable performance, 808
   in quality management, 653
   revenue cycle management, 473*t*
   revenue cycle performance measurement, 526
   Six Sigma and, 677–678
Beneficence, 342, 609
Benefits, of EHR systems, 139
Benefits realization, 150
Best of breed, 147
Best of fit, 147
Best practices in health record documentation, 180
Beta (probability), 572
Bias, in survey response, 583
Biddle v. Warren General Hospital, 318
Bierstock, Sam, 118
Bill hold, 465
Billing. *See* Reimbursement
Billing software, 287
Bills of Mortality, 194
Bioethics, 343
Biologics Control Act (1902), 14
Biomedical research, 607–647
   comparative data use in outcomes research, 631, 634
   conflicts of interest, 611–612
   defined, 608
   ethical treatment of human subjects, 608–610
   informed consent, 613–617
   outcomes and effectiveness research, 626–634
   oversight, 620
   privacy considerations, 618–620

protection of human subjects, 610–611
risk assessment, 625
role of HIM professional, 618–626
types of studies, 622–625
vulnerable subjects, 616–618
Biometrics technology, 100
Biotechnology, 20, 43–44
Birth defects registries, 373
Birth rates, 502–504, 503t
Bit-mapped data, 84
Bivariate correlation coefficient, 586
Blake, Robert, 701
Blanchard, K. H., 703
Blanket authorization, 354
Blended learning, 743
Blogs, 747
Blood/blood component usage review,
665–666
Blue Cross and Blue Shield (BC/BS), 21,
38, 415, 417–418
Blue Cross and Blue Shield Federal
Employee Program (FEP), 417–418
Blumenthal, David, 117–118
Board of directors (BOD), 25, 663
Board of trustees (BOT), 663
BOD. See Board of directors
Body of Knowledge (BoK)
defined, 61
and HIM profession, 61–62, 597–598,
598t
and literature review, 555
BOT (board of trustees), 663
Box and whisker plots, 585, 586t
Boxplots, 515, 516t
BPM (business process management), 87
BPR. See Business process reengineering
Brainstorming, 821–822
Breach notification, 855
Breach of the duty of care, 304
Breach of warranty, 307
Break the glass, 134
Bridges's stages of transition, 711
Bridge technology, 124
BSC. See Balanced scorecard
Bubble charts, 514–515, 514t, 515t
Budgets, 784–792
Buildings, 770
Bundled payments, 430
Bureaucracy, 685
Bush, George W., and administration
EHRs, 115
HSAs, 41
Medicare Prescription Drug Improve-
ment and Modernization Act, 421
ONC, 223
Business intelligence, 164
Business process management (BPM), 87
Business process reengineering (BPR), 688,
825–829
Bylaws, 240, 267

C

CA (Certification authority), 100
CAA (Care Area Assessment), 199
CAC. See Computer-assisted coding
CAHIIM. See Commission on Accreditation
of Health Informatics and Information
Management Education
CAHPS (Consumer Assessment of Health-
care Providers and Systems), 654, 656
Canadian Institute for Health Information,
407
Canadian Medical Association, 11
Cancer registries, 370–372, 371t
Cancer Registry Management, 70
Capital budgets, 788–790
Capital projects, 790–792
Capitation, 430
Care Area Assessment (CAA), 199
Career development, 753
Care paths, 249
CARF (Commission on the Accreditation of
Rehabilitation Facilities), 674
Caring Connections, 244
Carnegie Foundation for the Advancement of
Teaching, 9, 11
Carpal tunnel syndrome (CTS), 799
Case-control (retrospective) studies, 561,
623, 623t, 624t
Case definition, 370
Case fatality rate, 504, 505t
Case finding, 370
Case law, 300–301, 327–328
Case management
defined, 464
nurses and, 26
and QI, 667–669
and revenue cycle management, 464
Case managers, 249
Case mix, 496
Case-mix group (CMG), 439
Case-mix group (CMG) relative weight, 439
Case mix index (CMI), 433, 470, 496–497,
497t
Case-mix statistical data, 496–497, 497t
Case studies, 565
Cash, 770
Cash flow, 777
Cash payment insurance plans, 38
Cassidy, Bonnie, 50
Categorical data, 587
Categorically needy eligibility groups
(Medicaid), 422
Causal-comparative research, 561
Causal relationship, 560
Cause-specific death rate, 504, 504t, 505t
CBACs (context-based access controls), 133
CBT (computer-based training), 735, 744
CCAs (Certified Coding Associates), 62, 66
CCC. See Clinical Care Classification

CCDs. See Continuity of care documents
CCHIIM. See Commission on Certification
for Health Informatics and Informa-
tion Management
CCHIT (Certification Commission for
Healthcare Information Technology),
133, 172
CCMC (Committee on the Cost of Medical
Care), 414
CCRs. See Continuity of care records
CCs (complications or comorbidities), 432
CCSPs (Certified Coding Specialists-
Physician-Based), 62, 66
CCSs (Certified Coding Specialists), 66
CDA. See Clinical document architecture
CDC. See Centers for Disease Control and
Prevention
CDC EZ-Text software, 589
CDI. See Clinical documentation
improvement
CDIP (Clinical Documentation
Improvement Professional), 67
CDM. See Charge Description Master
CDRs (clinical data repositories), 84–85,
131
CDS systems. See Clinical decision support
systems
CDT (Current Dental Terminology), 396
CDW (clinical data warehouse), 131
CE. See Continuing education
CEE. See AHIMA Council for Excellence
in Education (CEE)
Census data, 486–487, 487t
Census surveys, 562
Center for Health Information Management
(CHIM), 69
Center for Medicare and Medicaid
Innovation, 18
Centers for Disease Control and Prevention
(CDC)
DEEDS 1.0, 199–201
immunization registry standards, 376
NEDSS, 379
NPCR, 372
Centers for Medicare and Medicaid
Services (CMS)
and CAHPS, 656
certification for Medicare participation,
37
compliance programs, 854–855
and false claims, 852
and federal accounting regulations,
766–767
hospital coding guidelines, 466–467
ICD-9-CM, 390
and meaningful use, 35
"meaningful use" reimbursements, 83
OASIS, 199
origins of, 414

Council on Recertification of Nurse Anesthetists, 10
Course correction, 150
Court of Appeals, 302
Court system, 302
Coverage error, 578
Covered entities (CEs)
and disclosure, 314
enforcement and penalties for disclosure violations, 323
and PHR software, 99
use/disclosure without patient authorization, 320, 321
Cover letters, 725
Covert observation, 566
CPHIMS (certified professional in health information management systems), 70
CPHQ (Certified Professional in Healthcare Quality), 70
CPOE system. *See* Computerized provider order entry system
CPR (computer-based patient record). *See* Electronic health records
CPT. *See* Current Procedural Terminology
CQI. *See* Continuous quality improvement
Credentialing
accessibility and confidentiality of files pertaining to, 331
administrative databases for, 377
by CAHIIM, 22
revocation and restoration, 68
and risk management, 862
Credentialing process, 330, 664, 664*t*
Credits, 774, 775*t*
CRI (CHAMPUS Reform Initiative), 424
Criminal law, 303
Criminal negligence, 304
Critic (innovator role), 708
Critical issues, identifying, 876
Critical path, 685, 844, 845*t*
Critical pathways (CareMaps), 97
Critical to process (CTP), 678, 678*t*
Critical to quality (CTQ), 678
Crosby, Philip B., 651*t*
Cross-footing, 783, 784*t*
Cross-sectional studies, 562, 622–623, 623*t*
Cross-training, 735
Crosswalks, 185
Crude birth rate, 503, 503*t*
Crude death rate, 504, 505*t*
Cryptography, 99–100
CSAs (component state associations), 69
CSTE (Council of State and Territorial Epidemiologists), 506
C-suite, 890–891
CT (computerized tomography), 19
CTDs (cumulative trauma disorders), 799
CTP (Critical to process), 678, 678*t*
CTQ (Critical to quality), 678

CTR (certified cancer registrar), 372
CTR (Certified Tumor Registrar), 70
CTS (Carpal tunnel syndrome), 799
Cultural competence, 733
Cultural systems, 878
Cumulative trauma disorders (CTDs), 799
Current Dental Terminology (CDT), 396
Current outcomes movement, 628–631, 631–*t*633*t*
Current Procedural Terminology (CPT), 393–394, 436, 449, 451
Current ratio, 778–779
Curriculum design, for employee training, 748
Customer(s)
identifying, 660
role in strategic thinking, 877–878
Customer focus, 654, 655*t*
Customer service, 816–817
Cybernetic systems, 818
Cyclical staffing, 802

D

Daily inpatient census, 486, 487*t*
Darling v. Charleston Community Memorial Hospital, 329–330
Dashboards, 541, 654, 692
Data, 169–192
AHIMA data quality model, 175–180, 176*t*–179*t*
analysis, transformation, and decision support, 53–54
analyzing, 585–589
capture, validation, and maintenance of, 51–52, 52*t*
capture of, 172
clinical (*See* Clinical data)
collection procedures, 580–583, 581*t*, 582*t*
current initiatives for capture, maintenance, and quality, 183–185
defined, 170, 194
discrete *vs.* continuous, 483
gathering, 578–584
information as an organizational resource, 170–171, 170*t*
information *vs.*, 170
integrity/security safeguards, 187–188
and knowledge management, 171–172
maintenance, 172
path to knowledge from, 171, 171*t*
and PI, 658
preparing for analysis, 584–585
quality, 173
quality standards, 173–183
scales of measurement, 482
secondary uses, 189
various sources/uses of tools for capture, maintenance, and quality, 188–191

Data abstraction, 149, 262–263
Data administrators. *See* Database administrators
Data analytics, 525. *See also* Healthcare data analytics
Data availability. *See* Availability
Database(s), 367–385
for analysis of health information, 368
clinical trials databases, 380–381
data for performance measurement, 382
health information exchange, 381
health services research databases, 381
national, state, and county public health databases, 378–380
National Library of Medicine, 381
national/state administrative databases, 377–378
vital statistics, 380
Database administrators (DBAs)/data administrators (DAs), 110, 151, 188
Database management system (DBMS) data dictionaries, 185–187, 186*t*
Data capture, 172, 183–185, 184*t*
Data cleansing, 585
Data collection, 382
Data confidentiality, 383
Data conversion, 149, 289–290
Data dictionaries
AHIMA definition, 185
Common Formats Version 1.1, 202, 202*t*
defined, 172
development, 187
organization-wide, 186–187
as tool in controlling data quality, 185–187, 186*t*
for uniformity, 383
Data elements, 194, 207–208
Data Elements for Emergency Department Systems (DEEDS) 1.0, 199–201
Data exchange standard, 132
Data gathering, 4
Data governance. *See* Information governance (IG)
Data integrity, 134, 161, 162*t*, 187–188
Data maintenance, 172, 183–185, 184*t*
Data maps, 185
Data marts, 93–94
Data mining, 86, 539, 569
Data privacy, 384
Data quality, 173
AHIMA model, 175–180, 176*t*–179*t*
current initiatives for, 183–185, 184*t*
data dictionaries for, 185–187, 186*t*
requirements for information systems, 180, 181*t*–183*t*
in secondary databases, 382–383
Data quality management, 129–131, 130*t*, 144, 175*t*
Data quality model, 175–180, 176*t*–179*t*
Data quality monitoring, 108

P4P programs, 526, 676
patient's rights statement, 244
retention schedules, 275
Centers for Medicare and Medicaid Services (CMS) Meaningful Use Incentive Payment Program. *See also* Meaningful Use
compliance programs, 856
and EHRs, 286
and security auditing, 294
Centralized model, 221
Central tendency, measures of, 517–519, 532
CEO. *See* Chief executive officer
CER (comparative effectiveness research), 560
Certainty factor, 810
Certificate of death, 501*t*
Certificate of live birth, 500*t*
Certificate programs, 66
Certification
AHIMA, 71
of healthcare facilities, 37
for HIM professional, 62–63
trauma registrars, 373
Certification authority (CA), 100
Certification Commission for Healthcare Information Technology (CCHIT), 133, 172
Certification maintenance, 67
Certified cancer registrar (CTR), 372
Certified Coding Associates (CCAs), 62, 66
Certified Coding Specialists (CCSs), 66
Certified Coding Specialists-Physician-Based (CCSPs), 62, 66
Certified Healthcare Privacy and Security (CHPS), 62, 67
Certified Health Data Analyst (CHDA), 67
Certified medical transcriptionists (CMTs), 259, 261
Certified Professional in Healthcare Quality (CPHQ), 70
Certified professional in health information management systems (CPHIMS), 70
Certified Tumor Registrar (CTR), 70
CEs. *See* Covered entities
CEUs (continuing education units), 67
CF (National conversion factor), 434
CFO. *See* Chief financial officer
Chain of command, 686
Champion (innovator role), 708
CHAMPUS (Civilian Health and Medical Program of the Uniformed Services), 39, 424
CHAMPUS Reform Initiative (CRI), 424
CHAMPVA (Civilian Health and Medical Program-Veterans Administration), 424–425
Champy, J., 688, 825

Change, organizational. *See* Organizational change, managing/leading during
Change, stages of, 709–710
Change agents, 707–709
Change control, 148, 847–848
Change drivers, 684
Change leadership
implementing strategic change, 880–882
and information management, 166
support for the change program, 878–880
Change management, 708–709
Charge capture, 123, 465–467
Charge Description Master (Chargemaster; CDM), 449–451, 451*t*, 452*t*, 462–469, 467*t*, 468*t*
Charitable services, 415
Charity care, 461
Chart conversion, 149
Charting by exception, 249
Chart reviews, 286–287
Charts and graphs (for statistical data presentation), 510–515. *See also specific types, e.g.:* Bar charts
Chart tracking, 123, 266
CHDA (Certified Health Data Analyst), 67
CHDR (Consolidated Health Data Repository), 406
Check sheets, 823, 824*t*
CHI (Consolidated Health Informatics), 400
Chief executive officer (CEO), 26, 171, 890
Chief financial officer (CFO), 26, 890
Chief information officer (CIO), 26, 109, 144, 890
Chief information security officer (CISO), 109
Chief information technology officer (CITO), 109
Chief knowledge officer, 56
Chief medical informatics officer (CMIO), 109, 141, 151
Chief nursing officer (CNO), 26
Chief operating officer (COO), 26
Children, as vulnerable research subjects, 617
CHIM (Center for Health Information Management), 69
CHIME (College of Healthcare Information Management Executives), 69
CHPS (Certified Healthcare Privacy and Security), 62, 67
CIA (Corporate Integrity Agreement), 857
CIO. *See* Chief information officer
Circuit courts (US Courts of Appeals), 302
CIs. *See* Confidence intervals
C-I-SAID (Code-A-Text Integrated System for the Analysis of Interviews and Dialogues), 589
CISO (chief information security officer), 109

CISs (clinical information systems), 90
Citizens Memorial Healthcare (CMH), 150–151
CITO (chief information technology officer), 109
Civil False Claims Act, 452
Civilian Health and Medical Program of the Uniformed Services (CHAMPUS), 39, 424
Civilian Health and Medical Program-Veterans Administration (CHAMPVA), 424–425
Civil law, 302–304
Civil Rights Act (1964), 721
Civil Rights Act (1991), 721
Civil War, 19
Claims, 413
Claims data, 122–123, 377
Claims processing, 445–448, 471
Claims scrubbing software, 287, 465
Classical leadership theories, 699–700
Classroom learning, for employee training, 744, 746*t*
Clean claims, 471
Clinical analytics, 129, 164
Clinical Care Classification (CCC), 400, 401*t*
Clinical care plans, 97
Clinical case studies, 565
Clinical classifications/terminologies, 387–407
AHIMA Clinical Terminology and Vocabulary CoP, 407
ASTM Standard E2087-00, 405
CCC, 400
CDT, 396
CPT, 393–394
current systems of classification/nomenclature, 389–397
development of classification systems/terminologies, 388–389
DSM, 394–395
HCPCS, 394
healthcare terminologies, 397–407
HL7 Vocabulary Workgroup, 407
ICD, 390–393
ICPC-2, 395
LOINC, 399–400
mapping initiatives, 407
MEDCIN, 401
MeSH, 406
NDCs, 396–397
NLM, 405
RxNorm, 400–401
SNOMED CT, 397–399
UMLS, 405–406
UMLS Metathesaurus, 406
UMLS Semantic Network, 406
UMLS SPECIALIST Lexicon, 406

Clinical coding. *See* Coding
Clinical data, 244–251, 490–496
Clinical data analysts, 151
Clinical data repositories (CDRs), 84–85, 131
Clinical data warehouse (CDW), 131
Clinical decisions, 93–95, 241
Clinical decision support (CDS) systems
  and e-discovery, 132
  and EHR, 127–128
  and EHR data entry, 118
  information management for, 163
Clinical document architecture (CDA), 135, 203, 206, 213
Clinical documentation, 469–470
Clinical documentation analysis. *See* Qualitative analysis
Clinical documentation improvement (CDI), 52, 69, 189, 470
Clinical Documentation Improvement Professional (CDIP), 67
Clinical documentation improvement (CDI) programs, 442, 443*t*
Clinical documentation improvement (CDI) specialist, 52
Clinical guidelines, 667–*t*668*t*
Clinical information, 308–309
Clinical information systems (CISs), 90
Clinical knowledge bases, 124–125
Clinical laboratory services, 27
Clinical laboratory technicians, 11–12
Clinical management, 94
Clinical messaging, 124
Clinical messaging systems, 90
Clinical nutritionists, 12
Clinical observations, 248–251
Clinical practice guidelines, 97, 667
Clinical privileges, 26
Clinical protocols, 667, 669*t*
Clinical quality management, 649–680
  accreditation standards, 670–674
  continuous performance improvement principles, 656–659
  formal performance improvement activities, 659–662
  governmental quality initiatives, 674–676
  managing quality and performance improvement, 662–666
  performance measurement and quality improvement, 650–656
  quality masters, 651*t*
  recent initiatives, 676–679
  reengineering *vs.*, 825*t*
  standards of organizational quality in healthcare, 666–670
Clinical resumes. *See* Discharge summaries
Clinical services, accounting for, 768–769
Clinical statistical data, 490–496
Clinical summary, 203
Clinical support services, 28

Clinical systems analysts, 110
Clinical terminology, 389
Clinical transformation, 119
Clinical trials, 380–381, 608, 624–625, 625*t*
Clinical trials databases, 380–381
Clinical vocabularies, 85
Clinical workstations, 91
Clinicians/physicians
  EHR system adoption, 140–142
  HIM professionals' role in EHRs, 144
  web portals, 91
Clinic outpatient, 498
Clinton, Bill, and administration, 13
Closed-loop medication management, 125
Closed record(s), 265
Closed-record review, 265
Closed systems, 818
Cloud computing, 105, 132
Cluster sampling, 578, 578*t*
CMG. *See* Case-mix group
CMH (Citizens Memorial Healthcare), 150–151
CMI. *See* Case mix index
CMIO. *See* Chief medical informatics officer
CMS. *See* Centers for Medicare and Medicaid Services
CMS-1500, 445
CMTs (certified medical transcriptionists), 259, 261
CNO (chief nursing officer), 26
Coaching, 735, 751–752
Coalition building, 879
COBRA (Consolidated Omnibus Budget Reconciliation Act), 16, 858
COB (coordination of benefits) transaction, 445
Code-A-Text Integrated System for the Analysis of Interviews and Dialogues (C-I-SAID), 589
Code on Dental Procedures and Nomenclature, 396
Code sets, 207–208
Codes of conduct, 454
Codes of ethics, 70–71, 344–348, 345*t*–348*t*
Coding
  application of technology to, 444–445
  CDI programs and, 442, 443*t*
  compliance programs, 852–853
  and corporate compliance, 452–456
  elements of coding quality, 442
  ethical issues, 356
  quality assessment, 442, 443
  and revenue cycle management, 470
Coding programs, 66
Coding workflows, 287
Codman, Ernest, 11
Coefficient of determination, 537
Cognitive work analysis, 563
Cohort studies, 623–624

Coinsurance, 415
COLD (computer output to laser disk), 124, 250
COLD/ERM (computer output to laser disk/ enterprise report management), 87
Collaborative Stage Data Set, 371
College of Healthcare Information Management Executives (CHIME), 69
Colleges and universities, as setting for HIM professionals, 59
Commission on Accreditation of Health Informatics and Information Management Education (CAHIIM), 21–22, 62–63, 65
Commission on Certification for Health Informatics and Information Management (CCHIIM), 62–63
Commission on the Accreditation of Rehabilitation Facilities (CARF), 674
Committee on the Cost of Medical Care (CCMC), 414
Common cause variation, 657, 819
Common Formats Version 1.1, 202
Common Framework, 223–224
Common law, 300–301
Common Rule, 596, 609–610
Communication
  and change process, 879–880
  managerial, 697–699
  and performance improvement, 658–659
Communication plan, 749
Community-based ambulatory care services, 29
Community-based death rates, 505*t*
Community hospitals, 8, 32
Community of Practice (CoP), 407
Co-morbidities, 432. *See also* Complications or comorbidities (CCs)
Comparative effectiveness research (CER), 560
Compensable factors, 755
Compensation and benefits, 722, 754
Compensation surveys, 754
Compensation systems, 754
Competency assessment, 734
Competition, determining impact of, 877–878
Completeness, 383
Compliance, 852–860, 862–863
  bill/claim accuracy and, 413
  coding compliance programs, 852–853
  corporate compliance programs, 853–854
  defined, 852
  GAARP principles, 165*t*
  HIM definition, 60
  implications for HIM, 862–863
  national influences on compliance programs, 854–860

overview, 852
  and physical examinations, 246
Compliance officer, 58
Compliance program guidance, 453
Complications (term), 432
Complications or comorbidities (CCs), 432
Component state associations (CSAs), 69
Compressed workweek, 727, 802
Compromise, 756
Computer-assisted coding (CAC), 52, 86, 444–445
Computer-based training (CBT), 735, 744
Computerized provider order entry (CPOE) system, 247
  EHR and medication management, 126
  EHR future issues, 151
  EHR migration, 120
  EHR practice, 115
  EHR system adoption by physicians, 141
Computerized tomography (CT), 19
Computer output to laser disk (COLD), 124, 250
Computer output to laser disk/enterprise report management (COLD/ERM), 87
Computer viruses, 384
Concepts, 398
Conceptual framework of accounting, 764
Conceptual skills, 692–693, 693*t*
Concurrent analysis, 263
Concurrent review, 331
Conditions for Coverage (CfC), 854–855
Conditions of Participation
  accreditation, 309–310
  behavioral healthcare record requirements, 253
  compliance programs, 854–855
  health record content, 309
  health record standards, 240
  Medicare/Medicaid reimbursement, 37
  privacy, 310–311
  quality initiatives, 674
Confidence intervals (CIs)
  defined, 527
  for mean, 533–534
  in research, 573
  sampling and, 528–530, 529*t*
Confidence limit, 573
Confidentiality
  EHR supporting infrastructure, 134
  ethical issues, 343
  in research, 596–597
Confidentiality of Alcohol and Drug Abuse Patient Records (42CFR part 2), 311
Conflict management, 756
Conflicts of interest, in biomedical research, 611–612, 614*t*–615*t*
Confounding variable, 559
Connecting for Common Health Framework (Markle Foundation), 222

Connellan, Thomas K., 838
Consent(s), 244. *See also* Informed consent
Consent management, 137
Consent to treatment, 244
Consent to use, 244
Conservatism (accounting), 765
Consideration (leadership theory), 701
Consistency (accounting), 765
Consolidated billing, 435
Consolidated Health Data Repository (CHDR), 406
Consolidated Health Informatics (CHI), 400
Consolidated Omnibus Budget Reconciliation Act (COBRA), 16, 858
Constant comparative method, 587–588
Constitutional law, 300
Constructive confrontation, 756
Construct validity, 575
Consultation(s), 249
Consultation rates, 496, 496*t*
Consumer Assessment of Healthcare Providers and Systems (CAHPS), 654, 656
Consumer-driven healthcare, 40–41
Consumer Operated and Oriented Plan (CO-OP), 17
Consumer organizations, 60
Content analysis, 588
Content and records management, 162–163, 163*t*
Content validity, 575
Context, 405
Context-based access controls (CBACs), 133
Context representation, 405
Contingency, 845
Contingency model of leadership, 701, 703
Contingency planning, 132, 292, 293*t*–294*t*
Continuing education (CE), 67–68, 71, 753
Continuing education units (CEUs), 67
Continuity of care documents (CCDs), 135, 203, 207, 219, 226
Continuity of care records (CCRs), 207
  EHR connectivity, 135
  and HIE, 224–225
  patient clinical summary core data set, 203, 203*t*
  XML for, 212–213
Continuous data, 532–534, 587, 824
Continuous quality improvement (CQI), 35–36, 650, 656–659, 818–825
Continuous record review, 265
Continuous speech input, 85
Continuous variables, 483, 532–534
Continuum of care, 31
Contra-account, 771
Contracting for services, 804
Contract law, 307–308
Contract management, 463

Contract services, 260
Control
  and conflict management, 756
  of costs, 769
  as management function, 686, 69[1]
Control group, 561
Controlled Substances Act, 310
Controls, in case-control studies, 623
Convenience sampling, 578
COO (chief operating officer), 26
CO-OP (Consumer Operated and Orient[ed] Plan), 17
Coordination of benefits (COB) transacti[on], 445
COP. *See* Conditions of Participation
Core data elements, 198
Core measures, 201
Core Model of HIM practice, 5, 50–51, 72
  data capture, validation, and maintenance, 51–52, 52*t*, 189, 190*t*–191*t*
  data/information analysis, transformation, and decision support, 53–54
  and e-HIM, 740
  functional components with practice roles, 51–58
  and future roles of HIM professionals, 889–891
  health information resource management and innovation, 55–56, 56*t*–57*t*
  information dissemination and liaison, 54, 55*t*
  information governance and stewardship, 57–58, 58*t*, 60*t*–61*t*
Core performance measures, 670–671
Core values, 690
Corporate compliance, 452–456, 454*t*, 853–854
Corporate Integrity Agreement (CIA), 857
Corporate social responsibility, 712
Corporation (accounting concept), 766, 766*t*, 767
Corrective controls, 783–784
Correlation, 536–537, 537*t*
Correlational research, 559
Cortez, Hernando, 9
Cost accounting, 781–782
Cost-benefit analysis, 106, 789
Cost controls, 42, 769
Cost outlier(s), 433
Cost outlier adjustment, 438
Cost reports, 782–783
Costs
  and EHR selection criteria, 147–148
  EHR system challenges, 139
  in managerial accounting, 781–782
Council of State and Territorial Epidemiologists (CSTE), 506
Council on Certification of Nurse Anesthetists, 10

Data repositories
   clinical (*See* Clinical data repositories)
   and data warehousing, 93–94
   and DSSs, 94
   EHR supporting infrastructure, 131
Data security, 383–384
   defined, 383
   EHR system challenges, 140
   ethical issues, 343
   and HIM professionals' role in EHRs, 144
   safeguards for insuring, 187–188
   supporting technologies for, 99–101
Data sets, 188–189, 195. *See also specific types of data sets, e.g.:* Minimum Data Set
Data stewardship, 143
Data type, 84
Data Use and Reciprocal Support Agreement (DURSA), 219, 228
Data warehouses, 93–94
DBAs. *See* Database administrators
DBMS (database management system) database dictionaries, 185–187, 186*t*
Death. *See* Mortality
Debits, 774, 775*t*
Debt ratio, 780
Debt service, 778
Decentralization, 690
Decision making, 695–697
Decision matrix, 695, 696*t*
Decision support systems (DSSs), 94–95, 171. *See also* Clinical decision support systems
Decision tree, 695, 696
Declaration of Helsinki, 608–609
Deductibles, 415
Deductive reasoning, 549
DEEDS (Data Elements for Emergency Department Systems) 1.0, 199–201
Deemed status, 38
Defamation of character, 305–306
Default judgment, 303
Defendant(s), 302–303
Defense, U.S. Department of, 401
Defenses in response to lawsuit, 307
Deficiency assignment, 264
Deidentification, 384
Delegation, 690, 704, 750–751, 751*t*
Delegation of authority, 754
Delinquent health records, 266
Deliverables. *See* Project deliverables
Deming, W. Edwards, 651*t*, 687–688, 688*t*, 819
Democratic leadership, 700, 700*t*
Demographic data/information
   defined, 243
   in health records, 243–244
   legal issues, 308–309

in registries, 371
use/disclosure without patient authorization, 321–322
Denial management, 471–472
Denials, 471–472
Department of Health and Human Services (HHS). *See* Health and Human Services, U.S. Department of
Dependencies, 121, 843
Dependent variables, 560
Depreciation, 771, 789–790, 789*t*
Descriptive research, 559
Descriptive (summary) statistics, 517–520, 585, 586*t*
   defined, 527
   inferential statistics *vs.,* 527–532
   for rates and proportions, 534–535
Designated record set (DRS), 314, 334
Design phase of SDLC, 105–106
Destruction of health records, 276, 278–279
Detective controls, 783, 784*t*
Det Norwke Veritas (DNV), 854
Diabetes registries, 373–374
Diagnosis-related groups (DRGs), 16, 196, 431
Diagnostic and Statistical Manual of Mental Disorders, 394–395
Diagnostic and therapeutic services, 27–29
Diagnostic image data, 84
Diagnostic imaging technicians, 12
Diagnostic imaging technologies, 87
Diagnostic orders, 247–248
Diagnostic services, 27
DICOM. *See* Digital Imaging and Communications in Medicine
Dietetics, 12
Diffusion S-curve, 707, 707*t*
Digital dictation, 258–259
Digital image data, 84
Digital Imaging and Communications in Medicine (DICOM), 132–133, 207, 398
Digital signature management technology, 87
Direct costs, 781
Directing, 690–691
Direct method of cost allocation, 782, 783*t*
Direct patient care (treatment), 319
Direct Project, 219
Direct (positive) relationship, 559
Disabilities, 742–743
Disaster recovery plan, 292
Discharge analysis, 263. *See also* Quantitative analysis
Discharged, no final bill (DNFB), 470
Discharge orders, 248
Discharge planning, 251, 430
Discharge summaries, 251
Disciplinary action, 755–756

Discipline, 685
Disclosure (health information)
   defined, 313
   legal issues, 312–324
   with patient authorization, 316–318
   patient rights, 314–315
   penalties for violating rules, 322
   types requiring opportunity to agree or object, 316
   without patient authorization, 318–322
Disclosures (accounting), 765
Discounting, 437
Discovery. *See* e-Discovery
Discrete data, 84, 586
Discrete reportable transcription (DRT), 124
Discrete variables, 483
Discrimination, 721
Disease index, 369
Disease registries, 370. *See also* Registries
Disposition (information life cycle stage), 165*t*
Disposition of health records, 274–275
Disproportionate Share Hospital (DSH), 433
Distance learning, 745
Diversity, 742
Diversity training, 739, 739*t*
DKB (drug knowledge database), 118
DMAIC, 828–829, 828*t*
DME (durable medical equipment), 419, 438
DNFB (discharged, no final bill), 470
DNR (do not resuscitate) order, 248
DNV (Det Norwke Veritas), 854
Document, 86
Documentation
   AHIMA definition, 173–175
   clinical (*See* Clinical documentation)
   Ethical issues, 353
   monitoring quality after EHR implementation, 293
   MRI principles, 173–175, 174*t*–175*t*
Documentation audits, 130, 130*t*
Document authentication, 87
Document image data, 84–85
Document imaging technology
   acceptable/unacceptable forms for record retention, 278
   for ED/CM system, 86
   and EHRs, 288, 289*t*
   as part of retention program, 277–278
Document management technology, 86–87
Domains
   for certificate programs, 66
   of HIM graduate programs, 65
Donabedian, A., 664
Do not resuscitate (DNR) order, 248
Double-blind studies, 561, 624–625
Double distribution, 782

Double-entry bookkeeping, 774–776
DRG grouper, 432
DRGs. *See* Diagnosis-related groups
Driving force, 875
DRS (designated record set), 314, 334
DRT (discrete reportable transcription), 124
Drucker, Peter, 687
Drug knowledge database (DKB), 118
DSH (Disproportionate Share Hospital), 433
DSSs. *See* Clinical decision support systems; Decision support systems
Dual core, 147
Due diligence, 147
Durable medical equipment (DME), 419, 438
Durable power of attorney, 244
Duration, 843–844, 844*t*
DURSA (Data Use and Reciprocal Support Agreement), 219, 228
Duty of care, 304
Dyadic relationship theory, 704–705

E
Early adopters, 706
Early majority, 706–707
EBM. *See* Evidence-based medicine
e-commerce, 91
ECRM (enterprise/electronic content and record management), 124
ED/CM (electronic document/content management) system, 86–88
EDI (electronic data interchange), 90–91, 205–206
e-Discovery, 132, 325–326
Edits, in databases, 383
EDM (electronic document management) system, 120, 278–279
EDSS (Electronic Disease Surveillance System), 379
Education
  for AHIMA members, 71
  Core Model of HIM practice, 51
  health records and, 241
Education, U.S. Department of, 742–743
Educational reform, 9–10
Effect size, 570, 573
e-forms, 87, 125
e-health, 91
e-HIM
  ethical issues, 360
  health information resource management and innovation, 56
  preparing HIM staff for, 739–740
  staff development tools, 736
  transition, 50
e-HIM practice transformation, 4–5
EHR. *See* Electronic health records
EHR extensions model, 98

EHR incentive programs. *See* Centers for Medicare and Medicaid Services (CMS) Meaningful Use Incentive Payment Program; Meaningful Use (MU)
EHRs. *See* Electronic health records
EHR-System Functional Model, 117, 143
EHs (eligible hospitals), 220–221
EI (emotional intelligence), 693, 693*t*
Eight characteristics of highly successful firms, 688, 688*t*
Eighty-five/fifteen (85/15) rule, 687
EIM. *See* Enterprise information management
EISs (executive information systems), 95
Elderly, 44–45
e-learning, 745, 745*t*, 746*t*
Electronically stored information (ESI), 326
Electronic data interchange (EDI), 90–91, 205–206
Electronic Disease Surveillance System (EDSS), 379
Electronic document/content management (ED/CM) system, 86–88
Electronic document management (EDM) system, 120, 278–279
Electronic forms and templates, 290–291
Electronic health records (EHRs). *See also* Meaningful Use
  abstracting, 287
  application in practice, 281–296
  and ARRA, 17
  billing, 287
  CCHIT criteria, 172
  certification, 224, 224*t*
  chart reviews, 286–287
  clinical data repositories, 84–85, 85*t*
  and clinical decision support, 127–128
  coding, 287
  conceptual framework, 113–152
  core clinical applications, 125–129
  data conversion, 289–290
  data quality management, 129–131, 130*t*
  document imaging, 288, 289*t*
  electronic form and template design/management, 290–291
  EMRs *vs.*, 116–117
  ethical issues, 344
  evolution, 115–121
  file room activities, 284–285
  functionality and technology, 122–137
  functionality training, 290
  future directions, 150–152
  healthcare data analytics, 526
  health information resource management and innovation, 56
  HIM professionals' role, 143–145
  incomplete record process, 285
  IOM definition, 115–116
  legal health record maintenance, 282, 282*t*, 283*t*

  legal issues, 142–143
  LHR liability issues, 333–335
  liability issues, 332
  litigation issues, 325–326
  maintenance issues, 292–296
  meaningful use, 17
  migration path, 119–121, 120*t*
  MPI maintenance, 283–284
  NAHIT definition, 116
  and patient/member web portals, 91
  patient registration, 283, 284
  in practice, 115
  release of information, 285–286
  reporting and analytics, 128–129
  and RHIAs, 65
  as secondary data source, 583
  source systems, 122–124
  staffing during implementation, 291
  structural changes in HIM department after implementation, 291–292
  supporting infrastructure, 131–135
  system challenges, 138–145
  system implementation, 116–118
  system planning/acquisition, 145–150
  systems to provide connectivity, 135
  terms, 116–117
  transcription, 287–288
  transition to, 4–5, 119
  in various healthcare institutions, 137–138
  workflow analysis, 290
  workflow training, 290
Electronic health record (EHR) systems, 98
  acquisition strategies, 146–148, 146*t*
  clinician adoption, 140–142
  cost-benefit, return on investment, and financing, 139–140
  ethical issues, 360–361
  executive commitment, 140
  migration path, 119–121, 120*t*
  organizational goals, 145
  planning and acquisition, 145–150, 146*t*
  source systems, 122–124
  system implementation, 116–118, 117*t*, 148–150
  systems to support access to clinical information, 124–125
  technical components, 122*t*
  vendor selection, 146–148
Electronic medical records (EMRs)
  EHRs *vs.*, 116–117
  NAHIT definition, 116
Electronic medication administration records (eMARs), 126
Electronic patient records (EPRs). *See* Electronic health records
Electronic performance support system (EPSS), 744
Electronic records management technology, 87

Electronic signature, 264
Eligibility verification, 122–123
Eligible hospitals (EHs), 220–221
Eligible professionals (EPs), 220–221
e-mail, 252
eMARs. *See* Electronic medication administration records
Emergency and trauma care, 29
    DEEDS 1.0, 199–201
    in health record, 252–253
    use/disclosure without patient authorization, 321
Emergency Maternal and Infant Care (EMIC) Program, 424
Emergency medical technicians (EMTs), 12
Emergency Medical Treatment and Active Labor Act (EMTALA), 253, 327, 858
Emergency outpatients, 498
Emergency preparedness programs, 861
EMIC (Emergency Maternal and Infant Care) Program, 424
Emotional intelligence (EI), 693, 693t
Empiricism, 548
EMPIs. *See* Enterprise master patient indexes
Employee(s). *See* Staff
Employee handbook, 731
Employee immaturity-maturity, 703, 703t
Employee records, 756–757
Employee Retirement Income Security Act (ERISA), 858
Employee self-logging, 808–809
Employees' rights, 721
Employee training and development. *See* Training and development
Employer-based self-insurance, 417
Employers' rights, 721
Employment-at-will, 721
Employment contracts, 731
Employment laws, 721, 728
Employment outlook for HIM professionals, 888–891
    in the C-suite, 890–891
    future roles of HIM professionals, 889–891, 889t
    HIM expertise, 888–889
Empowerment, 750–754, 750t
EMRs. *See* Electronic medical records
EMTALA. *See* Emergency Medical Treatment and Active Labor Act
EMTs (emergency medical technicians), 12
Encoders, 123, 444
Encounter(s), 498
Encryption (term), 384
Encryption technology, 99–100
Ending (transition stage), 711
End-of-life decisions, 357
English as a second language, 742
Enhancements, 150
Enron, 699, 766

Enterprise Content and Record Management, 767
Enterprise (or electronic) content and record management (ECRM), 124
Enterprise information management (EIM)
    access, security, and confidentiality, 160–161, 160t
    components, 159–164, 160t
    content/records management, 162–163, 163t
    goals, 160t
    information analysis/use, 163–164, 164t
    information design/capture, 161–162, 162t
    and information governance, 159
    information integrity/quality, 161, 162t
    potential benefits of, 159
    scope, 158
Enterprise master patient indexes (EMPIs), 89–90, 123, 171, 271, 294–295. *See also* Master patient indexes (MPIs)
Entity (accounting), 764
Environmental assessment, 871–874
    defined, 871
    external assessment, 872
    internal assessment, 871–872
    strategic IS planning, 103–104
Environmental Protection Agency (EPA) Substance Registry System (SRS), 402t, 404t
EOB. *See* Explanation of Benefits
EOC (episode-of-care) reimbursement, 430–431
EPA (Environmental Protection Agency) Substance Registry System, 402t, 404t
Epidemics, 9
Epidemiological studies, 622
Epi-Info (software), 588
Episode-of-care (EOC) reimbursement, 430–431
EPOs (exclusive provider organizations), 428
e-prescribing (e-Rx), 125, 126
EPs (eligible professionals), 220–221
EPSS (electronic performance support system), 744
Equal Employment Opportunity Act (1972), 721
Equal Pay Act (EPA) (1963), 722
Equal Pay Act (1963), 722
Equity, 772, 775t
Ergonomics, 799–800, 799t
ERISA (Employee Retirement Income Security Act), 858
Error reduction, 139
Errors, 698
ESI (electronically stored information), 326
Esprit de corps, 686
Ethical agent, 342
Ethical decision making, 343

Ethical issues, 341–362
    decision making, 343, 355, 355t
    documentation and privacy, 353
    ethical foundations in HIM, 343–350
    important problems, 356–361
    medical identity theft, 351–353
    moral values and ethical competencies, 342–343
    privacy, confidentiality, and security, 343–344
    professional code of ethics, 344–348, 345t–348t
    professional values/obligations, 346–350
    responsibilities of HIM professional, 350–351
    and ROI, 353–354
    theory into practice, 342
    treatment of human subjects, 608
Ethical Standards for Clinical Documentation Improvement (CDI) Professionals, 353
Ethicists, 343
Ethics (term), 343
Ethics training, 731
Ethnography, 566
Evaluating (management function), 691–692
Evaluation research, 559–560
Evidence, 302
Evidence-based management, 694
Evidence-based medicine (EBM)
    defined, 44, 669
    and EHR data entry, 118
    and QI, 669–670, 670t
e-visits, 135
Exchange relationship, 704
Exclusive provider organizations (EPOs), 428
Executive commitment to EHR systems, 140
Executive dashboards, 692
Executive information systems (EISs), 95
Executive managers, 692
Exempt employees, 754
Exit interviews, 727
Expectancy theory of motivation, 703
Expedited research, 612
Expedited review procedure, 613
Expenses
    in accounting, 773–774, 773t
    in budgets, 786
Experiment(s), 566–567
Experimental (study) group, 561
Experimental research, 560–561, 566–569
Experimental studies, 566–567, 568t, 622
Explanation of Benefits (EOB), 123, 445–446, 472
Explicit knowledge, 171
Express warranty, 307
Extended care facilities, 15

Extensible Markup Language (XML)
and CDA, 135
and COLD/ERM, 87
for data sharing, 212–213
EHR supporting infrastructure, 133
Level Seven electronic transaction
standards, 206–207
and web services, 92
External assessment, 872
External change agents, 708–709, 709*t*
External customers, 654, 816–817
External environmental assessment
(strategic IS planning), 103–104
External reviews (audits), 455
External validity, 574
Extraneous variable, 559
Extranets, 91–92

F

Facial image recognition, 100
Facility-based long-term care. *See* Skilled
nursing facilities (SNFs)
Facility-based registries, 370
Facility-based statistics, 484
Facility charge, 466
Factor comparison method, 755
Fair and Accurate Credit Transaction Act of
2003, 859
Fair Labor Standards Act (FLSA), 722, 754
False imprisonment, 305
Family and Medical Leave Act (FMLA),
722
Family numbering, 270
FASB (Financial Accounting Standards
Board), 766
Favorable variances, 787
Fayol, Henry, 685–686, 686*t*
FCA (Federal False Claims Act), 852
FDA. *See* Food and Drug Administration
FECA (Federal Employees' Compensation
Act), 425
Federal Anti-Kickback Statute, 858–859
Federal court system, 302
Federal Employees' Compensation Act
(FECA), 425
Federal False Claims Act (FCA), 852
Federal Food, Drug, and Cosmetic Act, 310
Federal laws, 13–17. *See also specific laws*
Federal Policy for the Protection of Human
Subjects, 596
Federal Register, 301–302
Federal Rules of Civil Procedure (FRCP)
and compliance programs, 856
e-Discovery, 325
and EHRs, 142
LHR liability issues, 333
Federal Sentencing Guidelines, 853
Federal Trade Commission (FTC), 335–336
Federated model, 221

Federation of State Medical Boards of the
United States, 10
Feedback
and employee training plans, 749
managerial, 698–699
Feedback controls, 814
Fee-for-service plans, 421
Fee-for-service reimbursement, 40,
414–415, 417, 429–430
Fee schedules, 430, 448–451
Feigenbaum, Armand F., 651*t*
Felonies, 303
FEP (Blue Cross and Blue Shield Federal
Employee Program), 418
Fetal autopsy rates, 494, 495*t*
Fetal death (stillborn), 492, 492*t*, 502*t*
Fiedler, Fred, 701, 703
Field experiments, 561
File room activity, 284–285
Filing equipment, 274
Filing systems, 270–272
Financial Accounting Standards Board
(FASB), 766
Financial counselors, 461–462
Financial data, 762
Financial management, 761–793
accounting, 764–769
basic financial accounting, 770–780
budgets, 784–792
internal controls, 783–784
overview, 762–764, 763*t*
Financial statements, 777–779, 778*t*,
782–783
Financial transaction, 762, 764
Fingerprint matching, 100
Firewalls, 90, 100–101
Fiscal year, 764–765, 765*t*, 785
Fishbone diagrams, 822–823, 825*t*
501(c)(3) organizations, 768, 768*t*
501(c)(6) organizations, 767–768, 768*t*
5010 healthcare transaction codes, 857
Fixed budgets, 785
Fixed costs, 781, 781*t*
Flexible budgets, 785
Flexible work schedules, 723
Flexner, Abraham, 9
Flextime, 727–728, 802
Flex years, 727
Float employees, 802
Flowcharts, 804, 805*t*, 822, 830
Flow process charts, 821, 821*t*
FLSA (Fair Labor Standards Act), 722, 754
FMLA (Family and Medical Leave Act),
722
Focus charting. *See* Charting by exception
Focused studies, 562
Focus groups, 562, 563
FOCUS-PDCA model, 819–820
FOIA (Freedom of Information Act), 310

Follett, Mary Parker, 686, 689
Food and Drug Administration (FDA)
clinical decision support and EHR, 128
clinical trials, 624–625
implant registries, 374
NDCs, 396–397
protection of human subjects in research,
610
Food and Drug Administration Moderniza-
tion Act (1977), 380
Footing (financial control), 783, 784*t*
Force-field analysis, 823, 823*t*
Forecasting, 769
Formal communication, 698
Format (term), 255
For-profit healthcare organizations, 25, 767
For-profit hospitals, 8
Fourteen principles of management
Deming's, 688
Fayol's, 686
Franklin, Benjamin, 9
Franklin Health Assurance Company of
Massachusetts, 415
Fraud, 306, 452
FRCP. *See* Federal Rules of Civil Procedure
Freedom of Information Act (FOIA), 310
Freestanding ambulatory care centers
(ACCs), 29
Freestanding ambulatory surgery centers, 30
Free-text data, 84
Frequency distribution, 512, 517
Frequency polygons, 513, 513*t*
Freud, Sigmund, 565
FTC (Federal Trade Commission), 335–336
Function, 830*t*
Functional interoperability, 397
Functionality training, 290
Functional relationships, 27
Functional team structure, 838
Future of HIM profession, 885–891
e-HIM transition, 885–888
employment outlook for HIM profession-
als, 888–891
HIM and ICD-10-CMP/PCS, 886–887
HIM and patient-centered care, 887–888

G

GAAP (Generally accepted accounting
principles), 766
GAAS (Generally accepted auditing stan-
dards), 766
Gantt, Henry, 685
Gantt chart, 685, 845*t*, 847, 847*t*
GARP (Generally Accepted Recordkeeping
Principles), 165–166, 165*t*–166*t*
GASB (Government Accounting Standards
Board), 766
GDP (gross domestic product), 8
GEMs (General Equivalence Mappings),

392

General acute care hospitals, 25

General Equivalence Mappings (GEMs), 392

Generalizability, 559

General ledger, 776–777, 776t

Generally accepted accounting principles (GAAP), 766

Generally accepted auditing standards (GAAS), 766

Generally Accepted Recordkeeping Principles (GARP), 165–166, 165t–166t

Generic screening, 861–862

Genetic information, 357

Genetic Information Nondiscrimination Act (GINA), 357

Geographic information systems (GISs), 95

Geographic practice cost indices (GPCIs), 434–435, 434t

Gesture recognition technologies, 89

Gilbreth, Frank and Lillian, 685

GINA (Genetic Information Nondiscrimination Act), 357

GISs (geographic information systems), 95

Gleick, James, 158

Globalization (web content management systems), 92

Global payment, 430–431

Global surgery payments, 431

Goals, 658, 690, 806

Going concern, 764

Go-live, 149

Good Samaritan rules, 307

Governance and stewardship of health information. See Information governance (IG)

Governing boards, 692

Government Accounting Standards Board (GASB), 766

Government-owned hospitals, 25

Government right of access to health records, 326–327, 356–357

Government-sponsored healthcare plans, 418–425

GPCIs (geographic practice cost indices), 434–435, 434t

G-Power, 530

GPWWs (group practices without walls), 428

Graduate degrees in HIM, 65

Grant, Ulysses S., 699

Granularity, 180, 389

Graunt, John, 194

Great Depression, 13–14

Great person theory, 699

Great Society programs, 13

Greenleaf, Robert, 706

Grief, stages of, 710, 710t

Grievance(s), 756

Grievance management, 756

Grievance procedures, 756

Griswold v. Connecticut, 310

Gross autopsy rates, 493–494, 494t

Gross death rate, 490, 490t

Gross domestic product (GDP), 8

Gross negligence, 304

Grounded theory, 587–588

Ground rules, for PI, 660

Group health insurance, 415

Group model HMOs, 427

Group practices without walls (GPWWs), 428

Groupthink, 696–697, 697t

H

HACs (hospital-acquired conditions), 433–434

Hammer, M., 688, 825

Harassment, 721

Hard-coding, 452t

Hard space, 798

Harmonization, 212

HAVEN (Home Assessment Validation and Entry), 438

Hawthorne effect, 686–687

Hay method of job evaluation, 755

HCAHPS (Hospital Consumer Assessment of Healthcare Providers and Systems), 634

HCFA (Healthcare Financing Administration), 16, 414. *See also* Centers for Medicare and Medicaid Services

HCI (human-computer interface), 133

HCOs (Healthcare organizations), 17

HCPCS. *See* Healthcare Common Procedure Coding System

HCQIP (Health Care Quality Improvement Program), 674–675, 675t

HCUP. *See* Healthcare Cost and Utilization Project

HDOs (Healthcare Data Organizations), 59

Health 2.0, 99

Health and Human Services, U.S. Department of

healthcare informatics standards, 195

HIT PRO, 67

Indian Health Service, 39

Medicare/Medicaid, 414

mission, 18

National Strategy for Quality Improvement in Healthcare, 184–185, 184t

and NHIN, 218–219

OIG workplans, 852

protection of human subjects in research, 609, 610

and public health, 30

vulnerable subject rules, 616–618

Health and safety programs, 722

Health breach notification, 135

Healthcare Common Procedure Coding System (HCPCS), 394, 394t, 434t

chargemaster management, 449, 451

Medicare SNF PPS, 435

Healthcare Cost and Utilization Project (HCUP), 381, 631–t633t

Healthcare data analytics, 525–543

analytics in practice, 539–541

analyzing continuous variables, 532–534

analyzing rates/proportions, 534–536

analyzing relationships between two variables, 536–538

correlation, 536–537

data mining, 539

defined, 525

descriptive statistics for rates and proportions, 534–535

descriptive *vs.* inferential statistics, 527–530

HIM professional opportunities, 541–543

impact of sampling, 528–530, 528–t529t

inferential statistics for continuous data, 532–534

inferential statistics for rates and proportions, 535–536

measures of central tendency, 532

measures of spread, 532

predictive modeling, 539–540

real-time analytics, 541

risk-adjusted quality indicators, 540–541, 541t

simple linear regression, 537–538, 537–t538t

tools for sampling and design, 530–532, 530t

Healthcare data life cycle, 157–167

Healthcare Data Organizations (HDOs), 59

Healthcare data sets, 188–189

Healthcare delivery system, U.S., 7–45

ambulatory care, 28–30

biomedical and technological advances, 18–20

cost/quality controls, 42

forces affecting hospitals, 34–36

future issues, 43–45

healthcare providers/settings, 22–32

history of Western medicine, 8–11

hospital organization/operation, 22–28

integrated delivery systems, 33–34

licensure, certification, and accreditation of healthcare facilities, 37

long-term care, 30–32

modern healthcare delivery, 13–20

professionalism of the allied health professions, 11–12

professional/trade associations, 20–22

reimbursement of healthcare expenditures, 38–42

Healthcare directives. *See* Advance directives
Healthcare Effectiveness Data and Information Set (HEDIS), 200–201
healthcare environment, modern, 3–4
Healthcare financial management. *See* Financial management
Healthcare Financial Management Association (HFMA), 473, 474t, 526
Healthcare Financing Administration (HCFA), 16, 414. *See also* Centers for Medicare and Medicaid Services
Health Care Fraud Prevention & Enforcement Action Team (HEAT), 855
Healthcare informatics, 83
Healthcare informatics standards, 193–214
   common formats for reporting patient safety events, 202
   data collection/reporting standards, 195–201
   defined, 204–205
   development, coordination, testing, harmonization, 208–212
   evolving/emerging standards, 212–213
   and HIE, 222–223
   inadequacy of current data sets for, 195
   patient clinical summary, 203
   standards to support interoperability and connectivity, 203–208
Healthcare Information and Management Systems Society (HIMSS), 69–70, 117, 290
Healthcare Integrity and Protection Data Bank (HIPDB), 17, 377–378
Healthcare operations, 319–322
Healthcare organizations (HCOs), 17
Healthcare payer organizations, 59
Healthcare provider, 413
Healthcare provider organizations, 59
Healthcare Quality Improvement Act (1986), 16, 42
Health Care Quality Improvement Program (HCQIP), 674–675, 675t
Healthcare reform, 13, 413–415
Healthcare reform bill. *See* American Recovery and Reinvestment Act
Healthcare statistics, 481–523
   ambulatory care statistical data, 498–506
   common statistical measures used in healthcare, 484–485
   descriptive statistics, 517–520
   how to analyze information, 522
   measurement, 482–483
   normal distribution, 521
   presentation of statistical data, 508–517
   statistical data used in healthcare facilities, 485–498
Healthcare supplier organizations, 59
Healthcare terminologies, 389, 389t, 397–407

Health data, 51–52, 52t
Health data stewardship, 889–890
Health informatics and information management (HIIM), 158
Health information exchange (HIE), 217–233
   AHIC, 223–224
   ARRA, 17
   CCD, 207
   compliance programs, 860
   conceptual framework, 218–220
   consumer empowerment, 228–229
   and databases, 381
   defined, 34, 218
   early adopters and private sector contributors, 221–222
   EHR certification, 224
   and EHR connectivity, 136–137, 136t
   federal support for standards development, 222–223
   and future of HIM, 888
   information dissemination and liaison, 54
   meaningful use, 219–221
   NHIN, 218
   patient identity management, 229
   security and privacy, 224, 229
   standards development, 224–226
   strategic goals/objectives, 224, 227t
   timeline of key developments, 220t
   trial implementations, 226, 228
   use case scenarios, 229–233
   use of CCR/CCD for summaries, 224–226
   for various healthcare institutions, 228
Health Information Exchange Challenge Grant Program, 221
Health information exchange organization (HIEO), 136–137, 137t
Health information management (HIM)
   current status of, 4–5
   electronic (*See* e-HIM practice transformation)
Health information management (HIM) department
   compliance program, 454–456
   and EHM transition, 291–292
   financial documentation functions, 769
   and revenue cycle management, 470
   and risk manager, 336
Health information management (HIM) manager, 722–730
Health information management (HIM) profession/professionals, 49–72, 74–80
   academic education and professional certification, 62–68
   AHIMA curriculum competencies and knowledge clusters-Health Information Management Baccalaureate Degree, 74–80
   as allied health profession, 12

body of knowledge, 61–62
certification, 71
clinical support services, 28
code of ethics, 70–71
current status of, 3–5
defined, 50
and e-Discovery, 325–326
ethical responsibilities, 350–351
functional components with practice roles, 51–58
healthcare data analytics opportunities, 541–543
ongoing education, 71
professional associations, 69–70 (*See also specific associations*)
professional cohesion, 71
professional core model, 50–51
professional literature, 71
records storage and retrieval, 273–274
role in biomedical research, 618–626
role in data capture, validation, and maintenance, 189, 190t–191t
role in EHRs, 143–145
role in maintaining health records, 266
role of, 3, 63t–64t
roles in HIM technology services, 110–111
settings of practice, 59–61
transcription management, 260
Health information resource management, 55–56, 56t–57t
Health Information Security and Privacy Collaboration (HISPC), 224, 228–229
Health Information Technology Expert Panel (HITEP), 201
Health Information Technology for Economic and Clinical Health (HITECH) Act
   and ARRA, 17, 310
   and compliance programs, 856
   disclosure rule changes, 312–313
   EHR meaningful use incentives, 115, 856
   EHR supporting infrastructure, 133, 134
   enforcement and penalties for disclosure violations, 322–324
   HIE development, 221
   HIPAA security provisions, 314
   and information technology, 3
   "meaningful use" reimbursements, 83
   patient access rights, 314, 315
   use/disclosure without patient authorization, 322
   use/disclosure with patient authorization, 317, 318
Health Information Technology Standards Committee (HITSC), 195
Health Information Technology Standards Panel (HITSP), 225, 225t–226t

Health insurance, 13, 415–416. *See also* Prepaid healthcare
  BC/BS plans, 417–418
  and behavioral healthcare, 32
  commercial insurance, 417
  coverage status (1990-2010), 416*t*
  evolution of reimbursement, 38
  and HSAs, 41
  national, 13–14
  public/private coverage in U.S., 39–40
Health Insurance Portability and Accountability Act (HIPAA), 17
  and ACA, 18
  Administrative Simplification, 310
  biometrics technology, 100
  case law since passage of, 327–328
  CDT, 396
  and CISOs, 109
  coding and corporate compliance, 453
  compliance programs, 858–860
  consent in research, 620*t*–621*t*
  and consent to use health record information, 244
  and e-discovery, 132
  EHR supporting infrastructure, 133
  encryption requirements, 229
  ethical issues, 344
  health record use notification, 241–242
  HIM professionals' role in EHRs, 144
  and HIPDB, 377–378
  impact on EHR adoption, 151
  invasion of privacy, 306
  and medical identity theft, 351–352
  OIG expansion, 852
  and PHR software, 98–99
  preemption provisions, 313
  Privacy Rule (*See* Privacy Rule)
  privacy standards, 208
  and RCM, 123
  and release of information, 285
  security auditing after EHR implementation, 294
  and telecommuting, 729
  unique identification numbers, 205
  use/disclosure without patient authorization, 318–320
Health Insurance Prospective Payment System Codes (HIPPS), 438
Health Level Seven (HL7)
  CDA, 203
  and CDA, 135
  and DEEDS 1.0, 200
  EHR-System Functional Model, 117, 117*t*
  electronic transaction standards, 206
  and LHR, 143
  and PHR software, 99
Health Level Seven (HL7) Vocabulary Workgroup, 407

Health maintenance organization (HMO), 40, 421, 427–428
Health Maintenance Organization Assistance Act (1973), 427
Health plan(s), 137–138
Health Plan Employer Data and Information Set (HEDIS), 427
Health Planning and Resources Development Act (1974), 15–16
Health Professions Education Amendment (1991), 11
Health record(s)
  abstracting, 262–263
  administrative/demographic information, 243–244
  authentication, 264–265
  clinical data, 244–251
  completion policies/procedures, 265
  conclusions at termination of care, 251–252
  content management, 258–262
  content of, 243–254
  defined, 241
  documentation and maintenance standards, 239–240
  electronic forms management, 268–269
  evolution of, 239–242
  filing systems, 270–272
  format of paper-based/hybrid, 255–258
  functions, 241
  historical overview, 239
  incomplete record control, 263
  legal aspects of form/content, 308–311
  legal aspects of ownership/control, 312–324
  legal aspects of retention, 310–312
  in litigation, 324–326
  management of incomplete records, 266–267
  modern, 241–242
  qualitative analysis, 265–266
  quantitative analysis, 263–264
  responsibility for quality documentation, 242–243, 242*t*
  specialized content, 252–254
  template design/management, 267–269
Health record review process, 665
Health Research Extension Act (1985), 620
Health savings accounts (HSAs), 41
Health services research (HSR), 381, 560, 608
Health summary, 118
Health systems agency (HSA), 15–16
Health technology assessment, 560
Healthy People 2010, 375
HEAT (Health Care Fraud Prevention & Enforcement Action Team), 855
HEDIS (Health Plan Employer Data and Information Set), 427

HEDIS (Healthcare Effectiveness Data and Information Set), 200–201
Hersey, P., 703
Heterogeneity, 579
HFMA. *See* Healthcare Financial Management Association
HHAs (home health agencies), 419
HH PPS (home health prospective payment system), 438
HHRGs (home health resource groups), 438, 438*t*
HHS. *See* Health and Human Services, U.S. Department of
HI. *See* Hospitalization insurance (HI) (Medicare Part A)
HIE. *See* Health information exchange
HIEO (health information exchange organization), 136–137, 137*t*
Hierarchy of needs, 712
High-deductible insurance plans, 41
HIIM (Health informatics and information management), 158
Hill-Burton Act (Hospital Survey and Construction Act), 14, 414
HIM. *See* Health information management
HIM Education, 51
HIM Professional Core Model. *See* Core Model of HIM practice
HIMSS. *See* Healthcare Information and Management Systems Society
HIMSS Analytics™ EMR Adoption Model[SM], 117, 117*t*, 151
HINNs (Hospital-Issued Notices of Noncoverage), 464
HIPAA. *See* Health Insurance Portability and Accountability Act
HIPDB (Healthcare Integrity and Protection Data Bank), 17, 377–378
Hippocrates, 650
HIPPS (Health Insurance Prospective Payment System Codes), 438
Hiring of staff, 726
HISPC (Health Information Security and Privacy Collaboration), 224, 228–229
Histocompatibility, 375
Histograms, 513, 513*t*, 824, 824*t*
Historical cost, 765
Historical research, 558
History (medical history), 240, 245, 246*t*–247*t*
HITECH Act. *See* Health Information Technology for Economic and Clinical Health Act
HITEP (Health Information Technology Expert Panel), 201
HIT PRO, 67
HITSC (Health Information Technology Standards Committee), 195

HITSP (Health Information Technology Standards Panel), 225, 225t–226t
HL7. *See* Health Level Seven
HMO. *See* Health maintenance organization
HMO Act (1973), 40
Home Assessment Validation and Entry (HAVEN), 438
Home health agencies (HHAs), 419
Home healthcare, 30, 421
Home health prospective payment system (HH PPS), 438
Home health resource groups (HHRGs), 438, 438t
Home health services, 253–254
Honesty (integrity) tests, 725
Hospice, 419
Hospice care, 31, 254
Hospital-acquired conditions (HACs), 433–434
Hospital-acquired (nosocomial) infection rates, 495, 495t
Hospital ambulatory care, 498
Hospital autopsy, 493
Hospital autopsy rates, 493–496, 494–t496t
Hospital-based mortality rates, 493t
Hospital Consumer Assessment of Healthcare Providers and Systems (HCAHPS), 634
Hospital death rate, 490, 493t
Hospital discharge abstract systems, 195
Hospital infection rates, 495–496
Hospital inpatient(s), 486
Hospital inpatient autopsy, 493
Hospital Inpatient Quality Reporting, 36
Hospital-Issued Notices of Noncoverage (HINNs), 464
Hospitalization insurance (HI) (Medicare Part A), 418. *See also* Medicare Part A
Hospital newborn inpatient, 486
Hospital outpatient(s), 486, 498
Hospitals
  contemporary forces affecting, 34–36
  decline in charitable services, 415
  early American, 9
  growth and decline in numbers, 1873-present, 14–15
  modern organization/operation, 22–28
  standardization of care, 11
  type of ownership and size (1975 *vs.* 2005), 23t–24t
Hospital Survey and Construction Act (Hill-Burton Act), 14, 414
House, R. J., 703
HSA (health systems agency), 15–16
HSAs (health savings accounts), 41
HSR. *See* Health services research
HTML (HyperText Markup Language), 87
Human-computer interface (HCI), 133
Humanistic management, 686–687, 689t

Human relations movement, 686–687, 712
Human resources management, 687, 717–758
  activities, 720t
  adult learning strategies, 740–743
  current trends, 757
  departmental employee training and development plan, 748–755
  maintenance of employee records, 756–757
  performance management, 755–756
  role of HIM manager, 722–730
  role of HR department, 720–722, 720t
  tools for staff development, 736–740
  tools for staff training, 730–736
  training and development, 730–758
  training methods, 743–748, 743t
Human services agencies, 138
Human subjects
  ethical issues, 608–611
  IRB definition, 611
  management of handling problems, 613
Hurricane Katrina, 861
Hybrid health records
  abstracting of data, 262–263
  content and structure, 237–280
  creation and identification, 269–272
  defined, 243
  destruction and transfer, 276–279
  and EHR migration, 120
  format, 255–258
  legal issues, 142–143
  retention and disposition, 274–275
  storage and retrieval, 273–274
  strengths and weaknesses, 257
Hybrid model, 221
HyperText Markup Language (HTML), 87
Hypotheses, 549, 571, 571t
Hypothesis test, 527

I

IAM (information asset management), 159
ICD (International Classification of Diseases), 369, 390
ICD-9-CM. *See* International Classification of Diseases, 9th Revision, Clinical Modification
ICD-10-CM. *See* International Classification of Diseases, 10th Revision, Clinical Modification
ICD-10-PCS. *See* International Classification of Diseases, 10th Revision, Procedure Coding System
ICF (International Classification on Functioning, Disability, and Health), 393, 394t
ICPC-2 (International Classification of Primary Care), 395, 395t
ICR (Intelligent character recognition)

technology, 89
Identifier standards, 205
Identity management, 90, 137
Identity-matching algorithms, 137
Identity theft. *See* Medical identity theft
IDNs (integrated delivery networks), 33–34, 89–90
IDR (intelligent document recognition) technology, 89
IDSs (integrated delivery systems), 33–34, 428
IEEE 802.11 wireless standard, 96
IEEE (Institute of Electrical and Electronics Engineers) 1073, 207
IFHIM (International Federation of Health Information Management), 70
IG. *See* Information governance
IHS. *See* Indian Health Service
IHTSDO (International Health Terminology Standards Development Organisation), 398
IM. *See* Information management
Imaging of documents. *See* Document imaging technology
IMIA (International Medical Informatics Association), 70
Immaturity-maturity of workers, 703, 703t
Immunization registries, 375–376
Impact factor, 845
Implant registries, 374
Implementation of EHR system, 119, 148–150
  benefits realization, 150
  chart conversion, 149
  data conversion, 148
  end user training, 148–149
  go-live, 149
  hardware/software installation, 148
  implementation plans, 121, 877, 877t
  initial planning/super user training, 148
  migration plans, 121
  roll-out, 149
  system configuration, 148
  system testing, 148
Implementation phase of SDLC, 106–107, 108t
Implied warranty, 307
Imputation, 584–585
Incentive pay, 262, 741
Incentive programs, 752–753
Incidence, 370, 625
Incidence rate, 506, 506t, 625
Incident(s). *See* Sentinel events
Incident reports, 335, 861
Income statements, 777
Incomplete health records
  control, 263
  incomplete record process, 285
  management, 266–267
Incomplete record process, 285

Indemnity plans, 415
Independent practice associations (IPAs), 427
Independent variables, 560
Index (term), 369
Indexing, 277–278
Indian Health Service (IHS), 39, 310, 425
Indirect costs, 781
Indirect standardization, 540
Individually identifiable health information, 310
Inductive reasoning, 549
Infant mortality rates, 503*t*, 504
Infection review, 666
Inference engine, 127
Inferential statistics, 520, 586
    for continuous data, 532–534
    defined, 527
    descriptive statistics *vs.*, 527–532
    for rates and proportions, 535–536, 535*t*
Inflation, 40–42
Informal communication, 698
Informatics. *See* Healthcare informatics
Informatics standards. *See* Healthcare informatics standards
Information
    analysis, transformation, and decision support, 53–54
    as an organizational resource, 170–171, 170*t*
    data *vs.*, 170
    defined, 158, 194
    first use in scientific context, 158
Information asset management (IAM), 159
Information content, 161
Information design and capture (EIM function), 161–162, 162*t*
Information dissemination and liaison, 54, 55*t*
Information governance (IG), 57–58, 58*t*, 60*t*–61*t*, 164–166
    defined, 164
    and EIM, 159
    and future roles of HIM professionals, 889–890
    potential benefits of, 159
    principles for, 165–166, 165*t*–167*t*
Information integrity. *See* Data integrity
Information life cycle, 158–159
Information management (IM), 157–167
    contemporary concepts of, 158
    and EIM, 163–164
    and informatics, 83
    as organization-wide function, 158–159
    as priority for healthcare institutions, 3–4
Information science, 83, 158
Information security, 99–101
Information systems (ISs)
    data quality requirements for, 180,

181*t*–183*t*
    development life cycle, 105–108 (*See also* Systems development life cycle)
    strategic planning, 102
Information technology (IT), 33
Information technology departments, 144
Information theory, 158
Informed consent, 244, 613–617, 614*t*–615*t*, 637–647
In-group, 704–705
Initiating structure, 701
Injury severity score (ISS), 372
Innovations, diffusion of, 706–708
Innovators (adopter group), 706–708
Inpatient(s), 197
Inpatient admission, 486
Inpatient bed occupancy rate (percentage of occupancy), 488, 488*t*, 489*t*
Inpatient census data, 486–487, 487*t*
Inpatient discharge, 486
Inpatient hospitalization, 486
Inpatient psychiatric facilities (IPFs), 440–441, 441*t*
Inpatient psychiatric facilities prospective payment system (IPF PPS), 440–441, 441*t*
Inpatient rehabilitation facility (IRF), 439, 439*t*
Inpatient rehabilitation facility prospective payment systems (IRF PPSs), 439
Inpatient Rehabilitation Validation and Entry (IRVEN) system, 439
Inpatient service day (IPSD), 486–487
In Search of Excellence (Peters and Waterman), 688–689
In-service education, 736–739
    assessment, 738*t*, 739
    needs assessment, 736–737
    requirements, 737, 737*t*
    steps in conducting, 737–738
Institute for Safe Medication Practices (ISMP), 118
Institute of Electrical and Electronics Engineers (IEEE) 1073, 207
Institute of Medicine (IOM), 115–116
Institutional Assurances of Compliance, 610
Institutional review boards (IRBs)
    conflict of interest controls, 611–612
    defined, 580
    protection of human subjects in research, 610–611
    retention of activity documentation, 613
    role in biomedical research, 618
    submission procedures, 612–613, 614*t*–615*t*
Instrument (data collection), 575–578, 575*t*
Insurance. *See* Health insurance
Insurance verification, 460–461
Insured (policyholder), 415

Insurer, 415
Integrated delivery networks (IDNs), 33–34, 89–90
Integrated delivery systems (IDSs), 33–34, 428
Integrated health record, 257
Integrated provider organizations (IPOs), 428
Integration, 132
Integrity
    of data (*See* Data integrity)
    EHR supporting infrastructure, 134
    GAARP principles, 165*t*
Integrity constraints, 187
Intelligent character recognition (ICR) technology, 89
Intelligent document recognition (IDR) technology, 89
Intensive study courses, 747–748
Intentional torts, 305–306
Interface, 132
Interface engines, 133
Interface terminology, 398
Interim periods, 785–786, 786*t*
Internal assessment, 871–872
Internal auditing, 455. *See also* Auditing/audits (performance)
Internal change agents, 708, 709, 709*t*
Internal controls, 783–784
Internal customers, 654, 816
Internal environmental assessment (strategic IS planning), 103–104
Internal rate of return (IRR), 139, 792
Internal Revenue Service (IRS), 766
Internal standards, 240
Internal validity, 574, 574*t*
International Classification of Diseases (ICD), 369, 390
International Classification of Diseases, 9th Revision, Clinical Modification (ICD-9-CM), 390
    certificate programs, 66
    coded data, 66, 189
    limitations of, 630
    Medicare acute care PPS, 431
International Classification of Diseases, 10th Revision, Clinical Modification (ICD-10-CM), 390–392, 391*t*
    and e-HIM transformation, 886–887
    Field Testing Project, 391–392
    implementation, 857
    and NVSS, 499–500
International Classification of Diseases, 10th Revision, Procedure Coding System (ICD-10-PCS), 392, 392*t*, 393*t*, 886–887
International Classification of Diseases, 11th Revision (ICD-11), 390
International Classification of Diseases for

Oncology, 3rd Revision (ICD-O-3), 392–393
International Classification of Primary Care (ICPC-2), 395, 395t
International Classification on Functioning, Disability, and Health (ICF), 393, 394t
International Federation of Health Information Management (IFHIM), 70
International Health Terminology Standards Development Organisation (IHTSDO), 398
International Medical Informatics Association (IMIA), 70
International Organization for Standardization (ISO), 206, 678–679
International Society for Disease Surveillance (ISDS), 200
Internet surveys, 581
Interoperability
    common terminologies and, 397
    defined, 116
    and HIE, 222
    and web services, 92
    and wireless technology, 96
Interpersonal barriers to communication, 698
Interpersonal skills, 693, 693t
Interrater reliability, 383, 575
Interrogatories, 303
Interval history, 245
Interval-level data, 483, 527t, 587
Interventions (in experiments), 560–561
Interview(s), 725–726
Interview guide, 563
Interview surveys, 562–563
Intranets, 91–92, 747
Intraoperative anesthesia records, 250
Intrarater reliability, 575
Invasion of privacy, 306
Inventor (innovator role), 707–708
Inventory, 770
Inventory slips, 774
Inverse (negative) relationship, 559
Investor-owned hospital chains, 40
Invoices, 774
IOM (Institute of Medicine), 115–116
IPAs (independent practice associations), 427
IPF PPS. See Inpatient psychiatric facilities prospective payment system
IPFs. See Inpatient psychiatric facilities
IPOs (integrated provider organizations), 428
IPSD (inpatient service day), 486–487
IRBs. See Institutional review boards
IRF (inpatient rehabilitation facility), 439, 439t
IRF PPSs (inpatient rehabilitation facility prospective payment systems), 439
IRR (internal rate of return), 139, 792

IRS (Internal Revenue Service), 766
IRVEN (Inpatient Rehabilitation Validation and Entry) system, 439
ISDS (International Society for Disease Surveillance), 200
ISMP (Institute for Safe Medication Practices), 118
ISO (International Organization for Standardization), 206, 678–679
ISO 9000 certification, 678–679
ISs. See Information systems
ISS (injury severity score), 372
Issue logs, 849
IT (information technology), 33

J
JCAHO. See Joint Commission
Job classification method, 723, 755
Job descriptions, 723–724, 734
Job evaluations, 754–755
Job procedures, 804
Job ranking, 755
Job rotation, 735
Job sharing, 728, 802–803
Job specification, 723–724
Johnson, Lyndon, 13
Joiner, Brian, 651t, 819
Joint Commission (on Accreditation of Healthcare Organizations)
    accreditation and quality management, 670–671, 672t
    accreditation by, 38, 309–310
    compliance programs, 854
    credentialing files, 331
    deemed status, 38
    delinquent records policy, 266
    healthcare organizations surveyed by, 11
    health record standards, 239–240
    HIM professionals' role in EHRs, 144
    human subject requirements, 613, 617t
    information governance standards, 166
    origins and mission, 21
    ORYX initiative, 201
    outcomes research, 631
    patient safety initiative, 672, 673–t674t
    performance improvement (See Performance improvement)
    PI standards, 816
    sentinel event policy, 672–674
Journal entries, 776, 776t
Journal of the American Health Information Management Association (Journal of AHIMA), 71, 592
Journals, 592–595, 594t, 595t
Judge-made law, 300–301
Judicial system, 300
Juran, Joseph M., 651t
Jurisdiction, 302

Justice
    in biomedical research, 609
    in HIM, 342
Just-in-time training, 742

K
Key indicators, 807
Key performance indicators (KPIs), 473, 474t, 541
Kinyoun, Joseph, 14
Knowledge, 171t
Knowledge-based CDS systems, 127
Knowledge management, 171–172, 172t
Kolb's "Learning Loop," 868, 868t
KPIs. See Key performance indicators
Kubler-Ross, Elizabeth, 710, 710t

L
Labor and delivery records, 252
Laboratory information systems (LISs), 123–124
Labor-Management Relations Act (Taft-Hartley Act), 722
Labor-Management Reporting and Disclosure Act (Landrum-Griffin Act), 722
Labor relations, 722
Laggards (adopter group), 707
Languages, 389t
Late majority, 707
Lateral relationships, 27
Lau, Francis, 171
Law v. Zuckerman, 327
Layoffs, 756
LCDs (Local Coverage Determinations), 462
LCMSs (learning content management systems), 746–747
LCTH PPS (long-term care hospital prospective payment system), 439–440
Leader-member exchange (LMX), 704
Leader-member relations, 703
Leadership, during organizational change. See Organizational change, managing/leading during
Leadership grid, 701, 703t
Leading, as managerial function, 686, 690–691
Lean philosophy, 827
Lean Six Sigma, 829
Learning content management systems (LCMSs), 746–747
Learning curve, 741
"Learning Loop" (Kolb), 868, 868t
Learning management systems (LMSs), 746–747
Learning styles, 742
Least Preferred Coworker (LPC) scale, 701
Lecture method (training), 744
Legacy systems, 147

Legal admissibility of health records, 132
Legal EHR-System Functional Profile, 143
Legal health record (LHR)
    AHIMA and, 143
    AHIMA definition, 282
    definitions and liability issues, 332–335
    maintenance of, 282, 282t, 283t
    matrix, 282t
    sample template, 283t
Legal issues, 299–336
    actions encountered in healthcare,
        304–308
    case law since HIPAA, 327–328
    court system, 302
    defense in response to lawsuit, 307
    elements of US legal system, 300
    form and content of health record,
        308–311
    health records and, 241–242
    legal aspects of health information man-
        agement, 308–324
    legal process, 302–304
    medical staff appointments, privileges,
        and peer review, 329–332
    ownership and control of health record,
        312–324
    record retention requirements, 275
    release of information process/function,
        328–329
    retention of health record, 310–312
    sources of law, 300–302
    torts, 304–308
    uses of health records in litigation,
        324–327
    various liability issues, 332–336
Length of stay (LOS), 483, 489–491, 490t,
    491t
Level of significance, 572
Lewin, Kurt, 709–711
Lewin's stages of change, 709–710
Lexicon, 389
LHR. See Legal health record
Liabilities, 771–772, 775t
Liability, 307
Liable/not liable, 303
Libel, 305
Licensed practical nurses (LPNs), 10
Licensed vocational nurses (LVNs), 10
Licensure, 37, 240, 309
Licensure agencies, 309
Likert scale, 577
Lincoln, Abraham, 852
Line authority, 690
Line graphs, 511–512, 512t
Line relationships, 27
Linked Birth and Infant Death Data Set, 380
Liquidity, 778
LISREL (software), 588
LISs (laboratory information systems),
    123–124
Lister, Joseph, 19
Literature, professional, 71
Literature review, 551–557
    defined, 551
    development of, 555–557, 556t
    meanings of, 551t
    process, 552–555
    purpose, 551–552
    retrieval of information, 555
    search techniques, 554–555
    sources of information, 552–554, 552–
        t553t
Litigation, 324–327
Living wills. See Advance directives
LMSs (learning management systems),
    746–747
LMX (leader-member exchange), 704
Local Coverage Determinations (LCDs),
    462
Local government regulations/licensure,
    676
Logical Observation Identifiers Names and
    Codes (LOINC), 125, 399–400, 400t
LOINC. See Logical Observation Identifiers
    Names and Codes
London Bills of Mortality, 194
Longitudinal health record, 242
Longitudinal studies, 562
Long-term acute care hospitals (LTACHs),
    31
Long-term and post-acute care (LTPAC),
    138
Long-term assets, 770, 788
Long-term care
    facility-based (See Skilled nursing facili-
        ties (SNFs))
    health record requirements, 254
    settings and providers, 30–32
    uniform data for, 198–199
Long-term care hospital prospective pay-
    ment system (LCTH PPS), 439–440
Long-term care hospitals (LTCHs), 432,
    439–440
LOS. See Length of stay
Loss reduction, 861
Low-utilization payment adjustments (LU-
    PAs), 438
LPC (Least Preferred Coworker) scale, 701
LPNs (licensed practical nurses), 10
LTACHs (long-term acute care hospitals),
    31
LTCHs (long-term care hospitals), 432,
    439–440
LTPAC (long-term and post-acute care), 138
LUPAs (low-utilization payment adjust-
    ments), 438
LVNs (licensed vocational nurses), 10

M

MACs (Medicare Administrative Contrac-
    tors), 445–446, 855
Maintenance, of EHR system, 150
Maintenance and evaluation phase of
    SDLC, 107–108
Major diagnostic categories (MDCs), 432
Major medical insurance (catastrophic
    coverage), 38, 415
Malfeasance, 304
Malpractice, 44, 304, 377
Malpractice insurance, 44
Managed care, 35, 414, 425–428. See also
    specific plans, e.g.: Health mainte-
    nance organizations
    defined, 426
    development and growth, 40
    ethical issues, 357
    federal legislation, 426t
Managed care organizations (MCOs), 40
Managed fee-for-service reimbursement,
    430
Management, as a discipline
    communication, 697–699
    functions and principles, 689–694
    landmarks in, 685–689, 689t
    leadership theory trends, 699–706
    trends in management theory, 695–697,
        695t
Management by objectives (MBO), 687
Management during organizational change.
    See Organizational change, managing/
    leading during
Management functions, 686
Management information systems (MISs),
    95
Management of healthcare IS resources,
    109–110, 109t
Management service organizations (MSOs),
    428
Managerial accounting, 781–783
    cost reports, 782–783
    defined, 784
    describing costs, 781–782
Managerial decisions
    ethical issues, 361
    supporting technologies for, 93–95
Manuscript, 592
MAP (Measure, Apply, Perform) indicators,
    526
MAP keys, 473, 475t
Mappings, 407
MAPs (measure applications partnerships),
    185
Markle Foundation, 222
Mark sense technology, 89
MARs (medication administration records),
    249
Martin, Franklin H., 11

Martinez, Ricardo, 327
Maslow, Abraham, 687
Maslow's Hierarchy of Needs, 687
Massachusetts General Hospital, 9
Massed training, 737
Master patient indexes (MPIs), 89–90, 170, 170t, 271–272, 369. *See also* Enterprise master patient indexes (EMPIs)
  and disaster recovery, 292, 293t–294t
  and HIE, 230
  maintenance, 283–284
  monitoring after EHR implementation, 294–295
Master planning or steering committee, 104
Master population indexes. *See* Master patient indexes (MPIs)
Master's degree, 65
Matching (accounting), 765
Materiality, 765
Maternal death rate (hospital based), 492–493, 493t, 504–505, 505t
Maternal mortality rate (community-based), 504–505, 505t
Matrixed team structure, 839
Maturity Model, 165–166
Mayo, Elton, 686
MBO (management by objectives), 687
McGregor, Douglas, 687
MCOs (managed care organizations), 40
MDCs (major diagnostic categories), 432
MDIS (medical director of information systems), 141
MDS. *See* Minimum Data Set
Mead, Margaret, 548
Mean (frequency distribution), 518–519, 518t
  confidence interval for, 533–534
  finding, 532
Meaningful Use (MU), 35
  CCR/CCD standards, 135
  CMS reimbursements for, 83
  compliance programs, 856–857
  and EHR adoption, 152
  and EHRs, 115, 285–286
  and EHR supporting infrastructure, 133
  and future roles of HIM professionals, 889, 889t
  health records and, 241
  and HIE, 219–221
  and security auditing, 294
Measure applications partnerships (MAPs), 185
Measures of central tendency, 517–519
Measures of variability, 519–520
MEDCIN, 401, 401t
Media, outdated, 279
Median (frequency distribution), 519, 532
Medicaid, 422–423
  and ACA, 18

changes in reimbursement system in 1990s, 3–4
coverage and financing, 39
creation of program, 13, 15, 39
eligibility criteria, 422
enactment of, 414
government right of access to health records, 326–327
and managed care, 40
Medicare and, 423, 423t
OPPS, 435–437, 436t
as secondary data source, 584
services, 422–423
Medicaid Integrity Contractors (MICs), 855
Medical devices, 20
Medical director of information systems (MDIS), 141
Medical foundations, 428
Medical history. *See* History
Medical identity theft, 335–336, 351–353, 859
Medical informatics, 109
Medical Internet, 218
Medical Literature, Analysis, and Retrieval System Online (MEDLINE), 381
Medically needy option (Medicaid), 422
Medical necessity, 462
Medical Records Institute (MRI), 173–175, 174t–175t
Medical staff. *See also specific staff positions, e.g.:* Physicians
  duty to use reasonable care in granting appointments, 329–330
  role in maintaining health records, 266
Medical staff bylaws, 26
Medical staff classifications, 26
Medical Subject Headings database (MeSH), 406
Medical tourism, 45
Medical transcription, 258
Medicare
  and ACA, 17, 18
  acute care PPS, 431–433
  ASCs, 437
  changes in reimbursement system in 1990s, 3–4
  Conditions of Participation (*See* Conditions of Participation)
  coverage and financing, 39
  creation of program, 13, 15, 39
  and current outcomes movement, 628
  enactment of, 414
  government right of access to health records, 326–327
  HCQIP, 674–675, 675t
  health record standards, 240
  and home healthcare, 30
  and managed care, 40
  and Medicaid, 423, 423t
  OPPS, 435–437, 436t

  origins of, 418
  patient's rights statement, 244
  SNF PPS, 435
  structure of program, 418–422
  Value-Based Purchasing, 36
Medicare Administrative Contractors (MACs), 445–446, 855
Medicare Advantage, 418, 421
Medicare Conditions of Participation (COP). *See* Conditions of Participation
Medicare fee schedule (MFS), 434
Medicare Part A, 39, 418–419, 419t, 421
Medicare Part B, 39, 419–421, 420t
Medicare Part D, 35, 39, 418
Medicare Prescription Drug Improvement and Modernization Act, 421
Medicare prospective payment systems, 431–433
Medicare Provider Analysis and Review (MEDPAR), 377
Medicare severity diagnosis-related groups (MS-DRGs)
  case-mix index, 496–497, 497t
  IPF PPS, 440–441, 441t
  Medicare acute care PPS, 431–433
Medicare severity long-term care diagnosis-related groups (MS-LTC-DRGs), 440, 440t
Medicare Summary Notice (MSN), 445, 446–t447t
Medication administration records (MARs), 249
Medication list, 126–127
Medication management, 125–127
Medication reconciliation, 127
Medication usage review, 665
Medicomp Systems, 401
Medigap, 421–422
MEDLINE (Medical Literature, Analysis, and Retrieval System Online), 381
MEDPAR (Medicare Provider Analysis and Review), 377
MedWatch, 374
Mental ability (cognitive) tests, 725
Mental distress, intentional/reckless infliction of, 306
Mental health. *See* Behavioral healthcare
Mental Health Parity Act (MHPA), 17
Mentally disabled, as vulnerable research subjects, 617
Mentor/mentoring, 735, 752
MeSH (Medical Subject Headings database), 406
Message format standards, 133
Meta-analysis, 569–570
Metadata, 94, 143, 213, 325
Metadata registries, 210
Metric data, 587
MFS (Medicare fee schedule), 434

MHPA (Mental Health Parity Act), 17
Microfilming, 274–277
MICs (Medicaid Integrity Contractors), 855
Middle managers, 692
Migration path, 119
Migration path for EHR system, 119–121, 120*t*
Minimum Data Set (MDS), 254
Minimum Data Set (MDS) Version 3.0, 199, 435
Minimum necessary standards, 133
Mintzberg, Henry, 693–694, 694*t*
Misdemeanors, 303
Misfeasance, 304
MISs (management information systems), 95
Missing values, 584–585
Mission statements, 690, 871
Mixed costs, 782, 782*t*
Mixed methods research, 549
M-learning, 747
Mode (frequency distribution), 519, 519*t*, 532
Model (term), 547
Morality, 608
Moral values, 342
Morbidity, 388
Morbidity rates, 485, 506
Morphological information, 406
Morphology code, 393
Mortality, 388, 574
Mortality (death) rates, 485, 504–505, 504*t*, 505*t*
Mortality review, 666
Mortgages, 772
Motion or streaming video/frame data, 85
Motions for summary judgment, 303
Motivation, 741
Motivation theory, 687
Motorola, 828
Mouton, Jane Srygley, 701
Movement diagrams, 797, 797*t*, 821, 830, 831*t*
MPIs. *See* Master patient indexes
MRI. *See* Medical Records Institute
MS-DRGS. *See* Medicare severity diagnosis-related groups
MS-LTC-DRGs. *See* Medicare severity long-term care diagnosis-related groups
MSN (Medicare Summary Notice), 445, 446–*t*447*t*
MSOs (management service organizations), 428
MU. *See* Meaningful Use
Multiaxial coding system, 395
Multihospital systems, 8
Multimedia systems, 85
Multiuser virtual environments (MUVEs), 747

Multivariate correlational methods, 586
Multivoting technique, 822
Myers, Grace Whiting, 343, 887

N

NAHC (National Association for Home Care & Hospice), 253–254
NAHIT (National Alliance for Health Information Technology), 116–117
NAHQ (National Association for Healthcare Quality), 70
Narratives, 804
National Alliance for Health Information Technology (NAHIT), 116–117
National Ambulatory Medical Care Survey, 378
National Association for Healthcare Quality (NAHQ), 70
National Association for Home Care & Hospice (NAHC), 253–254
National CAHPS Benchmarking Database (NCBD), 654, 656
National Cancer Registrars Association (NCRA), 70
National Center for Health Statistics (NCHS), 195, 378, 380, 390
National Center for Injury Prevention and Control (NCIPC), 199–201
National Committee for Quality Assurance (NCQA), 200–201, 427, 631, 674
National Committee on Vital and Health Statistics (NCVHS), 195, 218, 222–223
National conversion factor (CF), 434
National Correct Coding Initiative (NCCI), 447–448
National Council for Prescription Drug Programs (NCPDP), 126, 207
National Coverage Determinations (NCDs), 462
National Drug Codes (NDCs), 126–127, 396–397, 396–*t*397*t*
National Health Care Survey, 378–380, 379*t*
National health information infrastructure (NHII), 222–223, 344
National Health Information Network (NHIN), 351
National health insurance, 13–14, 413–415
National Home and Hospice Care Survey, 379
National Hospice and Palliative Care Organization (NHPCO), 254
National Hospital Care Survey (NHCS), 379–380
National Hospital Discharge Survey, 378
National Institute for Standards and Technology (NIST), 195, 210, 212
National Institutes of Health (NIH), 14, 18–19

National Integrated Accreditation for Healthcare Organizations (NIAHO), 854
National Labor Relations Act (Wagner Act), 722
National Library of Medicine (NLM), 381, 400, 405
National Notifiable Diseases Surveillance System, 506, 507*t*
National patient safety goals (NPSGs), 672, 673–*t*674*t*
National Practitioner Data Bank (NPDB), 16, 377
  credentialing process, 330
  establishment of, 42
National Program of Cancer Registries (NPCR), 370, 372
National Provider Identifier (NPI), 205
National Provider Identifier (NPI) Registry, 376
National Quality Forum (NQF), 201
National Quality Strategy, 634
National Strategy for Quality Improvement in Healthcare, 184–185, 184*t*, 634
National Vaccine Advisory Committee (NVAC), 375
National Vital Statistics System (NVSS), 499–500, 500–*t*503*t*, 503
National Voluntary Hospital Reporting Initiative, 526
Nationwide Health Information Network (NHIN), 137, 137*tt*
  design of, 223–224
  and EHR connectivity, 137
  federal support activities, 222–223
  trial implementations, 226, 228
Nationwide Health Information Network Exchange (NHIN Exchange), 218–219, 219*t*
Native Americans. *See* Indian Health Service
Natural experiments, 561
Naturalism, 548
Naturalistic studies, 565
Natural language processing (NLP), 86, 124, 444
NBs (Newborns), 487
NCBD (National CAHPS Benchmarking Database), 654, 656
NCCI (National Correct Coding Initiative), 447–448
NCDs (National Coverage Determinations), 462
NCHS. *See* National Center for Health Statistics
NCIPC. *See* National Center for Injury Prevention and Control
NCPDP (National Council for Prescription Drug Programs), 126, 207

NCQA. *See* National Committee for Quality Assurance

NCRA (National Cancer Registrars Association), 70

NCVHS. *See* National Committee on Vital and Health Statistics

NDCs. *See* National Drug Codes

Nebraska Registry Partnership (NRP), 376

NEC (Not Elsewhere Classified), 405

Needs analysis, 748

Needs assessment, 731, 736–737

Need-to-know principle, 353–354

Negative (inverse) relationship, 559

Negligence, 304–307

Negligent torts, 304–305

Neonatal care, 252

Neonatal mortality rate, 503, 503*t*

Net assets, 772

Net autopsy rates, 494, 494*t*

Net death rate, 492, 492*t*

Net income, 777

Net loss, 777

Net present value, 792

Network administrators, 110

Network model HMOs, 427

Network providers, 428

Neural networks, 89

Neutral zone, 711

New beginnings (transition stage), 711

Newborn autopsy rates, 494, 494*t*

Newborn death rate, 492, 492*t*

Newborns (NBs), 487

New Deal, 13

New England Hospital for Women and Children, 10

New York Hospital, 9

NFs (nursing facilities). *See* Skilled nursing facilities

NGT (nominal group technique), 822

NHCS (National Hospital Care Survey), 379–380

NHII (national health information infrastructure), 222–223, 344

NHIN (National Health Information Network), 351

NHPCO (National Hospice and Palliative Care Organization), 254

NHQI (Nursing Home Quality Initiative), 37

NIAHO (National Integrated Accreditation for Healthcare Organizations), 854

Nightingale, Florence, 626

NIH (National Institutes of Health), 14, 18–19

NIST (National Institute for Standards and Technology), 195, 210, 212

NLM. *See* National Library of Medicine

NLP. *See* Natural language processing

Nomenclatures, 207–208, 388, 389*t*

Nominal group technique (NGT), 822

Nominal-level data, 482, 527*t*, 587

Nonclinical information. *See* Administrative information

Nonexempt employees, 728, 754

Nonfeasance, 304

Nonmaleficence, 342

Non-operating revenue, 773

Nonparametric (distribution-free) techniques, 587

Nonparticipant observation, 564–565

Nonparticipating providers (NonPARs), 449

Nonprogrammed decisions, 696

Nonrandom sampling, 578–579

Normal distribution, 521, 521*t*

Normative Decision Model/Tree, 695, 696, 701, 702*t*

NOS (Not Otherwise Specified), 405

Nosocomial infection. *See* Hospital-acquired infection

Not Elsewhere Classified (NEC), 405

Notes (accounting), 771–772

Notes payable, 771–772

Not-for-profit healthcare organizations, 25, 767–768, 768*t*

Notice of Privacy Practices, 244, 314

Notice of Proposed Rulemaking (NPRM), 610

Notifiable disease, 506

Not Otherwise Specified (NOS), 405

NPCR (National Program of Cancer Registries), 370, 372

NPDB. *See* National Practitioner Data Bank

NPI (National Provider Identifier), 205

NPRM (Notice of Proposed Rulemaking), 610

NPSGs. *See* National patient safety goals

NQF (National Quality Forum), 201

NRP (Nebraska Registry Partnership), 376

Nuclear medicine services, 27

Null hypothesis, 571

Numeric patient identifier, 270

Nuremburg Code, 608–609

Nurses/nursing staff
  and direct patient care, 26–27
  EHR system adoption, 142
  performance review, 666
  standardization of practice, 10

Nursing facilities (NFs). *See* Skilled nursing facilities

Nursing Home Quality Initiative (NHQI), 37

Nursing homes. *See* Skilled nursing facilities (SNFs)

Nursing research, 400

Nursing services, 249

NVAC (National Vaccine Advisory Committee), 375

NVivo software, 589

NVSS. *See* National Vital Statistics System

O

OASIS (Outcomes and Assessment Information Set), 199, 438

Obama, Barack, 336

Objectives, 806

Object-oriented databases, 94

OBRA. *See* Omnibus Budget Reconciliation Act

Observational research, 564

Observational studies, 622

Obstetrical care, 252

Occasion of service, 498

Occupational Safety and Health Act (OSHA), 721, 722

Occupational Safety and Health Administration (OSHA), 275

Occupational therapists (OTs), 12, 27

Occupational therapy services, 27

OCE (outpatient code editor), 448

OCR. *See* Office for Civil Rights

OC/RR (order communication/results reporting), 123

OCR (optical character recognition) technology, 88–89

OD (organization development), 708

Odds ratio, 625–626

ODPHP (Office of Disease Prevention and Health Promotion), 30

OER. *See* Outcomes and effectiveness research

Offer (contract law), 307–308

Office for Civil Rights (OCR), 312–313, 322, 324

Office for Human Research Protections (OHRP), 610

Office of Disease Prevention and Health Promotion (ODPHP), 30

Office of Management and Budget (OMB), 610

Office of Research Integrity (ORI), 620–621

Office of the Inspector General (OIG), 452–454

Office of the Inspector General (OIG) workplans, 852, 854

Office of the National Coordinator for Health Information Technology (ONC), 17
  Core Model of HIM practice standards, 50–51
  and EHRs' effect, 117–118
  establishment of, 83, 223
  future roles of HIM professionals, 888
  healthcare informatics standards, 195, 204–205
  and NHIN, 223–224
  standards harmonization, 212

Office of Workers' Compensation Programs (OWCP), 425

Offshoring, 733, 803–804
OHRP (Office for Human Research Protections), 610
OIG. *See* Office of the Inspector General
OLAP (online/real-time analytical processing), 94, 131
OLTP (online/real-time transaction processing), 94, 131
OMB (Office of Management and Budget), 610
Omnibus Budget Reconciliation Act (1986), 16, 431
Omnibus Budget Reconciliation Act (1989), 16
Omnibus Budget Reconciliation Act (1990), 16
ONC. *See* Office of the National Coordinator for Health Information Technology
Oncology. *See* Cancer
One-on-one training, 735
One sample T-test, 532–533, 533*t*
One-tailed hypothesis, 571
Ongoing record review, 265
Online/real-time analytical processing (OLAP), 94, 131
Online/real-time transaction processing (OLTP), 94, 131
On-the-job training
    assessment of, 736
    components, 735, 735*t*
    defined, 733
    and job description, 734
    of overseas workers, 736
Open-record review, 248, 265
Open source technology, 92
Open systems, 818
Operating revenue, 772–773
Operational budgets, 785–788
Operational definitions, 571
Operationalize (term), 550
Operational management, health records and, 241
Operational plans, 690
Operation index, 369
Operations improvement planning, 866
Operations management, 94, 687, 689*t*
Operative reports, 250
OPOs (Organ Procurement Organizations), 251, 321
OPPS (Outpatient Prospective Payment System), 435–437, 436*t*
Optical character recognition (OCR) technology, 88–89
Optical imaging technology. *See* Document imaging technology
Optimization of EHR system, 119
Opting in/opting out, 229
Order communication/results reporting (OC/RR), 123

Ordinal-level data, 483, 527*t*, 587
Ordinary negligence, 304
Organizational change, managing/leading during
    diffusion of innovations, 706–708
    facilitation of change, 710–711
    functions and principles of management, 689–694
    landmarks in management as a discipline, 685–689
    leadership theory trends, 699–706
    management of change, 708–709
    management theory trends, 695–697, 695*t*
    managerial communication, 697–699
    resistance to change, 710
    stages of change, 709–710
Organizational chart, 690, 691*t*
Organization development (OD), 708
Organized healthcare delivery, 8
Organizing, 686, 690, 691*t*
Organ Procurement Organizations (OPOs), 251, 321
Organ transplantation records, 250–251
ORI (Office of Research Integrity), 620–621
Orientation, new employee, 730–733
    assessment of program, 733, 734*t*
    checklist for, 731, 732*t*
    of overseas workers, 733
    program components, 733
Orthographic information, 406
ORYX initiative, 21, 201, 672*t*
OSHA (Occupational Safety and Health Act), 721, 722
OSHA (Occupational Safety and Health Administration), 275
OTs (occupational therapists), 12, 27
Outcome indicators, 653
Outcome measures, 670
Outcomes and Assessment Information Set (OASIS), 199, 438
Outcomes and effectiveness research (OER), 626–634
    current outcomes movement, 628–631
    measures used in, 627–628, 628*t*
    research strategies, 627, 627*t*
Outcomes management, 94
Outcomes research, 559–560
Outdated media, 279
Out-group, 704–705
Out-of-pocket expenses, 415, 421–422
Outpatient (term), 197, 498
Outpatient care, 253
Outpatient code editor (OCE), 448
Outpatient Prospective Payment System (OPPS), 435–437, 436*t*
Outpatient statistics, 498
Outpatient surgical services, 29
Outpatient visit, 498

Outsourcing, 260–261, 730, 803
Overhead costs, 781, 782
Overlap, 272
Overlay, 272
Overseas workers, orientation/training for, 733, 736
Overtime, reduction of, 139
OWCP (Office of Workers' Compensation Programs), 425
Owner's equity, 772
Ownership of the health record, 312

P

PACE (Programs of All-Inclusive Care for the Elderly), 423
Pacing, of change plans, 880–881
Packaging, 437
PACS. *See* Picture archiving and communications systems
PAI (patient assessment instrument), 439
Palliative care, 254
Panel interviews, 726
Paper-based health records
    abstracting of data, 262–263
    content and structure, 237–280
    creation and identification, 269–272
    destruction and transfer, 276–279
    filing and storage equipment, 274
    format, 255–258
    legal issues, 142–143
    retention and disposition, 274–275
    storage and retrieval, 273–274
    strengths and weaknesses, 257
Paradigm, 547, 870
Paradigm shift, 695*t*, 838, 839*t*
Parallel work division, 800
Parametric techniques, 587
Pareto chart, 823, 823*t*
Parkinson's Law, 844
Parsimony, 574
Partial hospitalization, 420
Participant observation, 565
Partnership, 766, 766*t*, 767
PAs (physician assistants), 10
Pasteur, Louis, 19
Path-goal theory, 703–704, 704*t*
Pathology reports, 250
Patient accounts department, 769
Patient assessment instrument (PAI), 439
Patient care review, 665–666
Patient-centered care, 887–888
Patient-centered medical homes (PCMHs), 43, 129, 183
Patient-Centered Outcomes Research Institute (PCORI), 631–634
Patient clinical summary, 203
Patient financial services (PFS) systems, 122–123
Patient-focused care, 36

Patient-identifiable data, 196, 368
Patient identity management (PIM), 229
Patient medical record information (PMRI), 152, 398
Patient/member web portals, 91, 135, 252, 286
Patient Protection and Affordable Care Act (ACA or PPACA), 17, 416
  data capture/maintenance/quality initiatives, 183–184
  healthcare reform, 13
  and PCORI, 631, 634
  potential impact, 43
  Value-Based Purchasing, 36
Patient registration, 283, 284
Patient Safety and Quality Improvement Act, 202
Patient's rights, 314–315
Patient's rights statement, 244
Payback period, 139, 791
Payer of last resort (Medicaid), 423
Pay for performance (P4P) programs, 526, 676, 677t, 752
Payment posting, 471
Payment purposes, 319
Payment status indicators (PSIs), 436
PC (professional component), 430
PCAOB (Public Company Accounting Oversight Board), 766
PCM (primary care manager), 424
PCMHs. See Patient-centered medical homes
PCORI (Patient-Centered Outcomes Research Institute), 631–634
PCP (primary care physician), 428
PDAs (personal digital assistants), 96, 747
PDP (prescription drug plan), 35
PDSA cycle, 820, 820t
Pearson's Correlation Coefficient, 536–537, 537t
Peer review, 35, 554
Peer-reviewed (refereed) journal, 554
Peer Review Improvement Act (1982), 16
Peer review organizations (PROs), 16, 674. See also Quality improvement organizations
Pennsylvania Hospital, 9
Percentage of occupancy. See Inpatient bed occupancy rate
Performance, 650, 806
Performance controls, 813–814
Performance counseling, 755–756
Performance improvement (PI), 650–653, 652t, 816–818. See also Continuous quality improvement (CQI)
  contemporary approach, 653
  customer focus, 654, 655t
  defined, 650, 652
  formal activities, 659–661, 659–t660t, 662t

fundamental principles, 656–659
managing, 662–666
organizational components, 662–663
process improvement methodologies, 818–832
Performance management, 755–756
Performance measure, 652
Performance measurement, 811, 813–816
  assessment of departmental performance, 814–816
  performance controls, 813–814
  and quality improvement, 650–656
  variance analysis, 814
Performance review, 755
Performance standards, 724, 806–813
  criteria for, 806
  methods of communicating standards, 807–808
  methods of developing standards, 808–813
  types of standards, 806–807
Period data, 512
Permanence, 403
Permanent budget variances, 787
Per member per month (PMPM), 430
Per patient per month (PPPM), 430
Personal digital assistants (PDAs), 96, 747
Personal health records (PHRs), 98–99, 252
  AHIMA definition, 98
  EHR connectivity, 136
  EHR data entry, 118
  medical identity theft, 352
  setting for HIM professionals, 60
Personal Responsibility and Work Opportunity Reconciliation Act of 1996 (PRWORA), 15, 422
Perspectives in Health Information Management (PHIM), 71, 592
PERT (program evaluation and review technique), 685
PERUSE (perceived usability), 133
Peters, T. J., 688
PFS (Patient financial services) systems, 122–123
Pharma, 20
Pharmaceuticals, 40
Pharmacy information systems, 123
PHI. See Protected health information
PHIN (Public Health Information Network), 379
PHOs (physician-hospital organizations), 428
PHRs. See Personal health records
PHS (Public Health Service), 30, 620
PHSS (public health syndromic surveillance), 200
Physical examination, 245–246
Physical safety, 332
Physical therapists (PTs), 12
Physical therapy services, 27–28

Physician(s), 140–142, 141t. See also Clinicians/physicians
Physician assistants (PAs), 10
Physician champions, 141
Physician-hospital organizations (PHOs), 428
Physician index, 369–370
Physician notification, 267
Physician Quality Reporting System (PQRS), 129
Physiological signal processing systems, 95–96
PI. See Performance improvement
Picture archiving and communications systems (PACS), 87, 124, 207, 249
Piece-rate incentive, 685
Pie charts, 510–511, 511t
Pilot studies, 580–581
PIM (patient identity management), 229
Pixel, 84
PKI (Public key infrastructure) encryption, 100, 229
Placebo, 561
Plaintiff, 302
Planning
  financial data for, 769
  as management function, 686, 690
Planning organizations, 59
Playscripts, 804
PMPM (per member per month), 430
PMR. See Proportionate mortality ratio
PMRI (patient medical record information), 152, 398
PMSs (practice management systems), 123
POA (present on admission), 433
POC. See Point-of-care entries
Point data, 512
Point method, 755
Point-of-care information systems, 96
Point-of-care patient charting/documentation, 125, 128–129
Point-of-care review, 265
Point-of-service collection, 461–462
Point-of-service (POS) plans, 418, 428
Policies
  and Core Model of HIM practice, 50
  and EHR system implementation, 118–119
  and human resource management, 724
Policyholders, 415
Political systems, 878
Politics of change, 878–879
Polyhierarchy, 404
POMR. See Problem-oriented medical record
Population, 561
Population-based registries, 370
Population-based statistics, 502–506
Population management (plan members), 94

Position (job) descriptions. *See* Job descriptions
Position power, 703
Positive (direct) relationship, 559
Positivism, 548
POS (point-of-service) plans, 418, 428
Post-acute care, 31
Post-anesthesia evaluation, 250
Poster sessions, 591
Postgraduate education, 10
Postneonatal mortality rate, 503–504, 503*t*
Postoperative infection rates, 495–496, 496*t*
Posture, ergonomics and, 799, 799*t*
Potentially compensable events, 860. *See also* Sentinel events
Power (management), 690–691
Power (probability), 572
PowerPoint, 592, 592*t*
PPACA. *See* Patient Protection and Affordable Care Act
PPNs (preferred provider networks), 424
PPOs. *See* Preferred provider organizations
PPPM (per patient per month), 430
PPSs. *See* Prospective payment systems
PQRS (Physician Quality Reporting System), 129
Practice management systems (PMSs), 123
Pre-anesthesia evaluation, 250
Pre-authorization, 461
Pre-certification, 461
Precision factor, 810
Predecessor, 843
Predetermination, 461
Predictive modeling, 129, 539–540
Preemption, 313
Preferred provider networks (PPNs), 424
Preferred provider organizations (PPOs), 418, 421, 428
Pregnancy, termination of, 503*t*
Pregnancy Discrimination Act (1978), 721
Pregnant women, as vulnerable research subjects, 617
Premiums, 417
Prenatal care summary, 252
Prepaid healthcare, 13, 415–416. *See also* Health insurance
Preponderance of the evidence, 303
Prescription drug plan (PDP), 35
Present on admission (POA), 433
Prevalence, 625
Prevalence rate, 506, 506*t*, 625
Preventive controls, 783, 814
Primary analysis, 569
Primary care manager (PCM), 424
Primary care physician (PCP), 428
Primary data source, 368
Primary source, 553
Principal diagnoses, 251, 432
Principal investigator, 616
Principal procedure, 432

Prior approval, 461
Prior authorization, 461
Prisoners, as vulnerable research subjects, 618
Privacy
    biomedical research, 618–620
    EHR supporting infrastructure, 133
    ethical issues, 343, 353
    HIM professionals' role in EHRs, 144
    invasion of, 306
    statutory/regulatory law, 310–311
Privacy Act of 1974, 310
Privacy Rule, 300
    biomedical research applications, 618–620, 619*t*–621*t*
    deidentification, 384
    disclosure, 313, 316
    and disclosure, 313–314, 316
    enforcement and penalties for disclosure violations, 322
    ethical issues, 343–344
    use/disclosure definitions, 313
    use/disclosure without patient authorization, 319–322
    use/disclosure with patient authorization, 316–318
Privacy standards, 208
Private fee-for-service plans, 421
Private insurance plans, 417
Private medical practices, 29
Privilege(s)
    and defamation defense, 306
    defined, 664
    in litigation, 326
    waiver of, 326
Privileging process, 330–331
Probability factor, 845
Problem (research question), 549–550, 550*t*
Problem list, 295–296
Problem-oriented medical record (POMR), 249, 255–257
Problem solving, 695
Procedural review, 665
Procedure(s)
    and human resource management, 724–725
    rules for writing, 804
    work, 804
Procedure manuals, 804–805
Process, function *vs.*, 830*t*
Process, in quality improvement, 661
Process improvement. *See also* Work design and process improvement
    business process reengineering, 825–829
    CQI, 818–825
    methodologies, 818–832
    workflow analysis and process redesign, 829–832
Process indicators, 653
Process innovations, 875

Process redesign, 829–832
Process simulation software, 831
Productivity, 807
Products liability, 307
Profession, defined, 68
Professional cohesion, 71
Professional component (PC), 430
Professional literature, 71
Professional standards review organization (PSRO) program, 16
Professional/trade associations, 20–22. *See also specific organizations*
Profitability, 780
Profitability index, 792
Program evaluation and review technique (PERT), 685
Programmed decisions, 696
Programmed learning modules, 741
Programmers, 110
Programs of All-Inclusive Care for the Elderly (PACE), 423
Progressive discipline, 755–756
Progress notes, 248–249
Project, 836
Project charter, 841
Project components, 836–837, 837*t*
Project definition, 840–842, 841*t*
Project definition document, 841
Project deliverables, 840–842, 846
Projectized team structure, 839
Project management, 835–850
    defined, 838
    EHR systems, 145–146
    implementation phase, 846–849
    overview, 838–839
    planning phase, 842–845
    process of, 840–850
    and the project, 836–838
    project definition, 840–842, 841*t*
    project manager, 840
Project management life cycle, 838, 839*t*
Project management software, 842
Project managers, 840
    for EHR systems, 145–146
    functions, 840, 841*t*
    for implementation of new IS, 106–107
Project networks, 843
Project office, 838
Project plans, 146, 836–837, 842, 843*t*, 849
Project proposals, 841–842
Project revisions, 847, 848*t*
Project risk, 837–838
Project schedules, 843, 843*t*
Project scope, 836, 837
Project teams, 838–839
Project value, project risk *vs.*, 837–838
Promotion, 752
Property/valuables list, 244
Proportionate mortality ratio (PMR), 504, 505*t*

Proportions (statistics), 484, 484*t*, 534–536
Proprietary hospitals, 25
PROs. *See* Peer review organizations
Prosecutors, 303
Prospective Payment Act (1982), 16
Prospective payment systems (PPSs)
    and ambulatory care, 197
    and current outcomes movement, 628
    origins of, 414
    quality measures, 676, 677*t*
    reimbursement, 429
Prospective research studies, 562, 624, 624*t*
Protected health information (PHI)
    biomedical research applications,
      618–620, 619*t*–621*t*
    breach notification, 855
    and compliance programs, 856
    consent to use, 244
    disclosure, 313, 316
    EHR supporting infrastructure, 134
    HIPAA encryption requirements, 229
    patient access rights, 314
    use/disclosure without patient authoriza-
      tion, 318–321
Protection, 165*t*
Protocols
    and automated clinical care plans, 97
    for clinical trials, 624–625
    defined, 380
    and QI, 667
    and sample size, 579
    and web services, 93*t*
Providence Health and Services case, 328
Provider portals, 135
Provider-sponsored information manage-
    ment, 98
PRWORA (Personal Responsibility and
    Work Opportunity Reconciliation Act
    of 1996), 15, 422
PSIs (payment status indicators), 436
PSRO (Professional standards review orga-
    nization) program, 16
Psychiatric healthcare. *See* Behavioral
    healthcare
Psychiatric hospitals, 24–25
Psychopharmacology, 32
PTs (physical therapists), 12
Public assistance, 414
Publication of research, 592–595, 593*t*–595*t*
Public Company Accounting Oversight
    Board (PCAOB), 766
Public health, 378
Public health databases, 378–380
Public Health Information Network (PHIN),
    379
Public Health Service (PHS), 30, 620
Public Health Services syphilis study,
    609–610, 609*t*
Public health statistics, 499–506

Public health syndromic surveillance
    (PHSS), 200
Public hospitals, 416
Public key infrastructure (PKI) encryption,
    100, 229
Public Law 89-97 (1965), 15, 39
Public Law 98-21 (1983), 16
Pull system, 828
Purchase orders, 773–774
Purchasing, 773
Purposive sampling, 578–579
p-value, 528, 572

Q
QDM (Quality Data Model), 201, 201*t*
QI. *See* Quality improvement
QIOs (quality improvement organizations),
    16, 674–676
QIs. *See* Quality indicators
QMB (quality management board), 663
QMLG (quality management liaison group),
    663
Qualitative analysis, 265–266
Qualitative approach, 548, 548*t*
Qualitative data analysis, 587–588
Qualitative standards, 806–807
Quality controls
    and coding, 442, 443
    ethical issues, 356–357
    and healthcare reengineering, 35–36
    health records and, 241
    and NPDB, 42
    and overseas employees, 733
Quality Data Model (QDM), 201, 201*t*
Quality improvement (QI), 35
    confidentiality of activities, 331–332
    managing, 662–666
    patient care review, 665–666
    revenue cycle management, 473–475,
      473–*t*475*t*
    and ROI, 328–329
    staff selection, 664–665
Quality improvement organizations (QIOs),
    16, 674–676
Quality indicators (QIs), 653, 675, 675*t*
    current outcomes movement, 629–631,
      629–*t*630*t*
    risk-adjusted, 540–541, 541*t*
Quality management. *See* Clinical quality
    management
Quality management board (QMB), 663
Quality management liaison group
    (QMLG), 663
Quality management programs, 663–664
Quality outcomes, 356–357
Quantitative analysis, 263–264
Quantitative approach, 548, 548*t*
Quantitative data analysis, 585–587, 586*t*,
    588–589

Quantitative standards, 806–807
Quasi-experimental studies, 568*t*, 569
Questionnaire surveys, 562–564
Queuing, 278

R
RA (remittance advice), 445, 448*t*
RACs (Recovery Audit Contractors), 856
Radiation therapy services, 27
Radio frequency identification (RFID), 89,
    126
Radiology information systems (RISs),
    123–124
Radiology services, 27
RAI (Resident Assessment Instrument), 199
Randomization, 561
Randomized clinical trials (RCTs), 570,
    624–625
Random sampling, 561, 578, 578*t*
Range, 520, 532
Raster image, 84
Rates (statistical measure), 484–485, 484*t*,
    485*t*, 534–536
Ratio(s), 484, 484*t*
Ratio analysis, 777–780
Ratio-level data, 483, 527*t*, 587
Rational decision making, 695
RAT-STATS, 530–532, 530*t*
RAVEN (Resident Assessment Validation
    and Entry), 435
RBACs (role-based access controls), 133,
    228
RBRVS. *See* Resource-based relative value
    scale
RCM. *See* Revenue cycle management
RCTs (randomized clinical trials), 570,
    624–625
RDs (registered dietitians), 12, 28
Real audio data, 85
Real-time analytics, 541
Real zero point, 483
Receiver operating characteristic (ROC)
    analysis, 573
Record locator service (RLS), 137, 221, 222
Recovery Audit Contractors (RACs), 856
Recruitment, 725
Red Flag Rule, 335–336, 351, 859
Redisclosure, 312
Redundancy, 132
Reengineering, 35–36, 825*t*
Reengineering the Corporation (Hammer
    and Champy), 688
Reference checks, 726
Reference terminology, 397
Referential integrity, 187
Referred outpatient, 498
Reflective learning cycle, 711, 711*t*
Refreezing, 710

Regional health information organizations (RHIOs), 221, 222, 224, 229–230
Registered dietitians (RDs), 12, 28
Registered Health Information Administrators (RHIAs), 12, 62–63, 65, 67
Registered health information technicians (RHITs), 12, 67
Registered nurses (RNs), 10
Registration (revenue cycle management), 460, 461t
Registries, 125, 370–376. *See also specific registries, e.g.:* Cancer registries
Regulatory agencies, 309. *See also specific regulatory agencies, e.g.:* Food and Drug Administration
Regulatory law, 310–311
Regulatory system, 300
Rehabilitation care, 254
Rehabilitation hospitals, 24
Rehabilitation services, 28
Reimbursement, 411–456
  ambulance fees, 438
  ASCs, 437
  BC/BS plans, 417–418
  claims processing, 445–448
  coding and, 442–445
  coding and corporate compliance, 452–456
  coding and technology, 447
  commercial insurance, 417
  EOC, 430–431
  fee-for-service, 429–430
  government-sponsored healthcare plans, 418–425
  of healthcare expenditures, 38–42
  health records and, 241
  HH PPS, 438
  HHRGs, 438, 438t
  history of healthcare reimbursement in the U.S., 413–416
  hospital-acquired conditions, 433–434
  IRF PPS, 439
  managed care, 425–428
  Medicare/Medicaid OPPS, 435–437
  Medicare Prospective Payment System, 431–433
  Medicare SNF PPS, 435
  present on admission indicator reporting, 433
  RBRVS system, 434–435
  reimbursement methodologies, 429–441
  reimbursement support processes, 448–452
  reimbursement systems, 417–428
  uses of financial data, 769
Reinforcement, 741
Reisner v. Regents of University of California, 319
Relationships, in SNOMED CT, 398
Relative risk (RR), 625

Relative value units (RVUs), 434, 434t
Release of information (ROI)
  assessment of departmental performance, 814–816, 814t, 815t
  and EHRs, 285–286
  ethical issues, 353–354
  and HIE, 222
  process and function, 328–329
Reliability
  of accounting, 765–766
  of data in secondary databases, 383
  of research, 575
  of staff selection tests, 725
Religious Non-Medical Health Care Institutions (RNHCIs), 432
Remediation, 857
Remittance advice (RA), 445, 448t
Request for information (RFI), 106
Request for production, 303
Request for proposal (RFP), 106, 147, 788
Research. *See also* Biomedical research
  analyzing the data, 585–589
  and Core Model of HIM practice, 51
  defined, 570
  defining the research question, 549–550
  design determination, 557–562, 558t, 570t
  disseminating, 590–595, 591t
  ethical issues, 358, 358t–359t, 360
  evaluation of findings, 598–600, 598t, 600t
  gathering the data, 578–584
  health records and, 241
  instrument selection, 575–578
  IRB definition, 611
  literature review, 551–557
  method determination, 558t, 562–570
  methodology, 548–549
  preparing data for analysis, 584–585
  presenting results, 589–590, 590t, 592t
  publication, 592–595, 593–t595t
  theories and models, 547
  use/disclosure without patient authorization, 321
Research design, 557–562, 558t, 570t
Research frame, 547–549
Research institutions, 60
Research methodology, 548–549
Research methods, 545–601
  data access and confidentiality, 596–597
  research and the practitioner, 597–600
  research frame, 547–549
  research methodology and, 548
  research process, 549–595
  selection of, 574
Resident Assessment Instrument (RAI), 199
Resident Assessment Validation and Entry (RAVEN), 435
Residential care facilities, 31
Residential treatment centers, 32

Resource-based relative value scale (RBRVS), 434–435, 434t
Resource report, 849, 849t
Resources, in projects, 837
Resource Utilization Groups (RUG), 199
Resource Utilization Groups, Version IV (RUG-IV), 435
Respect for persons, 609
Respiratory therapists (RTs), 12
Respiratory therapy, 28
Respite care, 419
Response rate (surveys), 581, 581t
Responsibility, 750–751
Restitution, 302
Restoration of credentials, 68
Results management systems, 125
Resumes, 725
Retail clinics, 29
Retained earnings, statement of, 777
Retained object radiopaque, 202t
Retention
  ancillary materials, 275
  defined, 274
  development of program for, 276–279
  of IRB activity documentation, 613
  legal issues, 310–312
  of workforce, 726
Retention period, 278
Retention program development, 276–279
Retention schedules, 165t, 275
Retinal scanning, 100
Retrieval of health records, 273–274
Retrospective payment system, 429
Retrospective research design, 561
Retrospective review, 331–332
Retrospective (case-control) studies, 561, 623, 623t, 624t
Retrospective time frame, 561–562
Return on equity (ROE), 780
Return on investment (ROI), 108, 139–140, 780, 791–792
Revenue(s), 772–773, 786
Revenue audit/recovery, 472
Revenue codes, 449, 452t
Revenue cycle, 460, 526
Revenue cycle management (RCM), 122–123, 459–475
  back end process, 471–472
  front end process, 460–463, 461t
  middle process, 464–471
  strategies for success, 473–475
Revenue management, 94
Revenue Principle, 765
Reverse mentoring, 752
Revocation of credentials, 68
RFI (request for information), 106
RFID (radio frequency identification), 89, 126
RFP. *See* Request for proposal

RHIAs. *See* Registered Health Information Administrators

RHIOs. *See* Regional health information organizations

RHITs (registered health information technicians), 12, 67

Rights, patient's. *See* Patient's rights

Rip-and-replace, 147

Risk-adjusted quality indicators, 540–541, 541*t*

Risk analysis, 845, 845*t*

Risk assessment, in biomedical research, 625

Risk factor, 845

Risk management, 860–863, 872–873, 873*t*

Risk manager, 336

Risk prevention, 861

Risk Standardized Mortality Rate (RSMR), 540

RISs (radiology information systems), 123–124

RLS. *See* Record locator service

RM. *See* Risk management

RNHCIs (Religious Non-Medical Health Care Institutions), 432

RNs (registered nurses), 10

ROC (receiver operating characteristic) analysis, 573

ROE (return on equity), 780

Roentgen, Wilhelm, 19

Rogers, E., 706–707

ROI. *See* Release of information; Return on investment

Role-based access controls (RBACs), 133, 228

Role playing, 744

Role theory, 693–694, 694*t*

Roll-out, 149

Roosevelt, Franlkin D., and administration, 13, 14

Roosevelt, Theodore, and administration, 425

Root-cause analysis, 822–823, 823*t*, 862

Roper, William, 628

Rounding of statistical information, 485

RR (relative risk), 625

RSMR (Risk Standardized Mortality Rate), 540

RTs (respiratory therapists), 12

RUG (Resource Utilization Groups), 199

Run charts, 824, 825*t*

RVUs (relative value units), 434, 434*t*

RxNorm, 126–127, 400–401

S

Safe harbor (Federal Anti-Kickback Statute), 858–859

Safe Medical Devices Act of 1990, 374

Safety, physical, 332

Sample, target population and, 578

Sample frame, 578

Sample size
  adequacy of, 579–580
  calculation, 579–580, 580*t*
  defined, 579

Sample surveys, 562

Sampling
  impact on analytics, 528–530, 528–*t*529*t*
  methods, 578

Sarbanes-Oxley Act, 766, 852

SAs (surgeon assistants), 10

SAS (Statistical Analysis System) software, 589

Scalable process, 840

Scalar chain, 686

Scales (research), 577–578, 577*t*

Scales of measurement, 482

Scanned health records, 257

Scanning, 277

Scatter charts/diagrams, 513–514, 514*t*, 824, 824*t*

Scenarios, 873–874

Scheduling engine, 842

Scheduling of work, 801–804

SCHIP (State Children's Health Insurance Program), 424

Scientific inquiry, 548

Scientific management, 685, 689*t*

Scope creep, 837

Scorecards, 654

SCRIPT standard, 126, 207

SDLC. *See* Systems development life cycle

SDOs. *See* Standards development organizations

SEC (Securities and Exchange Commission), 766

Secondary analysis, 569–570

Secondary data
  birth defects registries, 373
  cancer registries, 370–372
  diabetes registries, 373–374
  facility-specific indexes, 369–370
  immunization registries, 375–376
  implant registries, 374
  primary data *vs.*, 368–369
  purposes/users of, 368–369
  registries, 370–376
  sources of, 583–584
  transplant registries, 374–375
  trauma registries, 372–373
  trends in collection of, 384–385

Secondary databases, 382–385

Secondary data sources, 368–369

Secondary data uses, 189

Secondary records, 367–385

Secondary release of information, 354

Secondary source (research literature), 553

Secondary Uses and Reuses of Healthcare Data: Taxonomy for Policy Formulation and Planning, 204

Secondary variables, 559

Secure messaging systems, 90

Securities and Exchange Commission (SEC), 766

Security, 343. *See also* Data security

Security audit program, 294

Security risk analysis, 134, 134*t*

Security standards, 208

Self-directed learning, 743–744

Self-monitoring, 693

Semantic differential scale, 577, 577*t*

Semantic interoperability, 397

Semantics, 133

Semi-fixed costs, 782, 782*t*

Seminars, for employee training, 744–745

Semistructured questions, 576

Sensitive health information, ethical issues related to, 357–358

Sensitivity, in research, 573

Sensitivity training (staff development), 739

Sensmeier, Joyce, 33

Sentinel events, 672–674, 862

September 11, 2001, terrorist attacks, 861

Serial numbering system, 270

Serial-unit numbering system, 270

Serial work division, 800

Servant Leadership Model, 705–706

Service innovations, 874–875

Service level agreements, 804

Service quality, 806–807

Shared data record, 98

Shewhart, Walter A., 651*t*

Shift differentials, 801–802

Shift rotations, 801–802

Shipping/receiving documents, 774

Shoemaker, F. F., 706–707

SHOP (Small Business Health Options Program) Exchanges, 17

Signal tracing data. *See* Vector graphic (signal tracing) data

Signatures, 248

Significance, in research, 571–574, 572*t*

Simple linear regression (SLR), 537–538, 537–*t*538*t*

Simple random sampling, 578, 578*t*

Simulation observation, 565

Simulations, for employee training, 745

Simultaneous equations method, 782

Single-blind studies, 624–625

Situational model of leadership, 703

Six Sigma, 677–678, 828–829

Skewness, 521

Skilled nursing care, 30, 421

Skilled nursing facilities (SNFs), 30, 31, 418–419

Skilled nursing facility prospective payment system (SNF PPS), 435

Skilling, Jeffrey, 699
Slander, 305
SLR (simple linear regression), 537–538, 537–*t*538*t*
Small Business Health Options Program (SHOP) Exchanges, 17
SMART (specific, measurable, attainable, relevant, timely) goals, 120–121, 753
Smart peripherals, 124
SMI (supplemental medical insurance), 418. *See also* Medicare Part B
Smith, William, 828
SNDO (Standard Nomenclature of Disease), 887
SNF PPS (skilled nursing facility prospective payment system), 435
SNFs. *See* Skilled nursing facilities
SNOMED CT. *See* Systematized Nomenclature of Medicine-Clinical Terminology
SNOMED RT. *See* Systematized Nomenclature of Medicine-Reference Terminology
SOAP (subjective, objective, assessment, plan), 256, 257
Socialization, 731
"Socialized medicine," 13
Social media, 252
Social networks, 747
Social Security, 13
Social Security Act (1935), 14
Social Security Act Amendments (1965), 37, 39, 414
Soft space, 798
Software as a service (SaaS), 132, 140
Software engineers, 110
Software packages, for data analysis, 588–589
Sole proprietorship, 766, 766*t*, 767
Solomon four-group method, 567
Source-oriented health record, 255, 255*t*–256*t*
Source systems, 122–123, 122*t*
Space, in functional work environment, 797–798
Spaced training, 737
Span of control, 690
SPC (Statistical process control) chart, 825, 825*t*
Spears, Larry, 706
Specialcause variation, 657, 658, 819
Special consent. *See* Informed consent
Special needs plans, 421
Specialty clinical applications, 124
Specialty hospitals, 25
Specificity, 573
Speech-language pathologists, 12
Speech recognition technology, 85–86, 445
SPL (Structured Product Labeling), 207, 400

Spoliation, 325
Sponsors
  clinical trials, 625
  innovator role, 708
  project, 836
Spreadsheets and statistical packages, 516
SPSS (Statistical Package for Social Sciences) software, 589
SRS (Environmental Protection Agency Substance Registry System), 402*t*, 404*t*
Stable monetary unit, 764
Staff, HIM
  development issues, 738–739
  development tools, 736–740
  duty to use reasonable care in appointments of, 329–330
  recruitment, selection, and hiring, 725–726
  selection of, 725–726
  training tools, 730–736
Staff, medical. *See* Medical staff
Staff authority, 690
Staff development
  special issues, 738–739
  tools for, 736–740, 736*t*
Staffing
  alternate structures for, 727–730
  during EHR implementation, 291
  structures, 723
Staff model HMOs, 427–428
Stages of change, 709–710
Stages of grief, 710, 710*t*
Stages of transition, 711
Staging systems, 371
Stakeholders, 678, 836
Standard(s)
  and Core Model of HIM practice, 50–51
  defined, 208, 666, 806
  of organizational quality, 666
Standard deviation, 520
  measure of spread, 532
  in normal distribution, 521
  Six Sigma and, 677–678
Standardization
  of healthcare data, 195–196
  of hospital care, 11
  of medical practice, 9–10
  of nursing practice, 10
Standardized mortality ratio, 541
Standard Nomenclature of Disease (SNDO), 887
Standard of care
  defined, 304
  incidents, 335
  and physical safety of premises, 332
  and QI, 666
Standard report of fetal death, 502*t*
Standards and Interoperability (S&I) Framework, 203, 204

Standards coordination, 210–212
Standards development organizations (SDOs), 208–211, 209*t*–210*t*. *See also specific organizations, e.g.:* American National Standards Institute
Standards harmonization, 212
Standards of Ethical Coding, 454
Standards testing, 210–212
Standards value chain, 208, 211*t*
Stare decisis, 301
Stark Law, 859
State Children's Health Insurance Program (SCHIP), 424
State court system(s), 302
State Health Information Exchange Cooperative Agreement Program, 221
State licensure, 37, 676
Statement(s) (accounting), 774, 777–779
Statement of cash flow, 777
Statement of retained earnings, 777
Statement of stockholder's equity, 777
Statement of work, 841
State workers' compensation insurance funds, 425
STATISTICA (software), 588
Statistical Analysis System (SAS) software, 589
Statistical Package for Social Sciences (SPSS) software, 589
Statistical process control (SPC) chart, 825, 825*t*
Statistical software packages, 588–589
Statistics. *See* Healthcare statistics
Statutory (legislative) law, 301, 310–311
Steerage, 463
Stem and leaf plots, 515, 515*t*
Step-down allocation, 782, 783*t*
Steps, tasks *vs.,* 843*t*
Sterilization, 19
Stewardship, 57–58, 58*t*, 60*t*–61*t*. *See also* Information governance (IG)
  defined, 165
  and future roles of HIM professionals, 889–890
  and information governance standards, 165–166
Stockholder's equity, statement of, 777
Stop order, 248
Storage area networks, 131–132
Storage equipment, 274
Storage management, 131
Storage of records, 273–274. *See also* Retention
Storytelling, 873
Straight numeric filing system, 270
Strategic change, implementing, 880–882
Strategic goals, 868, 876
Strategic HIT planning, 102
Strategic innovation, 874–875

Strategic IS planning, 102, 104
  gaining approval for plan, 104
  generic approach, 102, 103*t*
  identifying needs and prioritizing
    projects, 104
  master planning or steering committee,
    104
  reviewing the plan/assessing
    environment, 103–104
Strategic management
  assessment of current mission, vision,
    and values, 871
  beginning state, 871
  creating a platform for strategic
    innovation, 874–875
  customer role in strategic thinking,
    877–878
  defined, 866
  elements of strategic management/
    thinking, 868–871, 869*t*
  identification of critical issues, 876
  implementation of strategy, 875
  implementing strategic change, 880–882
  skills of strategic managers/strategic
    thinkers, 866–868
  from strategic planning to strategic
    management/thinking, 866–868
  support for the change program, 878–880
  understanding environmental assessment
    trends,
    871–874
  from vision to strategy, 875–876
Strategic objectives, 868, 876
Strategic planning
  defined, 866
  elements of, 869*t*
  path to strategic management/thinking,
    866–868, 868*t*
Strategic plans, 690
Strategic profile, 872
Strategic thinking
  customer role in, 877–878
  defined, 866
  path from strategic planning to, 866–868,
    868*t*
  skills of, 866–868
  skills of strategic managers/strategic
    thinkers, 866–868
Strategy (term), 866, 868
Strategy map, 881, 882*t*
Stratified random sampling, 578, 578*t*
Strict liability, 307
Structural barriers to communication, 698
Structure and content standards, 205
Structured data, 84, 118
Structured data input, 444–445
Structured interviews, 725
Structured Product Labeling (SPL), 207,
    400
Structured (closed-ended) questions, 576

Structure indicators, 653
Subprojects, 837
Succession planning, 752
Successor, 843
Sudden unexpected infant death (SUID)
    registry, 376
SUID (Sudden unexpected infant death)
    registry, 376
Supervisory managers, 692
Supplemental medical insurance (SMI),
    418. *See also* Medicare Part B
Supporting technologies, 81–111
  for capture of different types of data and
    formats, 84–88
  current/emerging information technolo-
    gies in healthcare, 84
  for diagnosis, treatment, care of patients,
    95–99
  for efficient access to/flow of data and
    information, 88–92
  HIM professional roles in health infor-
    mation technology services, 110–111
  informatics, 83
  for managerial/clinical decision making,
    93–95
  for security of data/information, 99–101
Support staff for IT, 107–108
Surgeon assistants (SAs), 10
Surgery, 29
Surgical operation (term), 496
Surgical procedure (term), 496
Surgical review, 665
Surgical service reports, 250
Surveys, 562–564
Swimlane diagram, 831–832, 831*t*
SWOT (Strength, Weaknesses, Opportuni-
    ties, and Threats) analysis, 872
Symmetric (single-key) encryption, 100
Synchronous computer conferencing, 745
Syntactic information, 406
Syntax, 133
Syphilis (Tuskegee study), 609–610
System (term), 817
Systematic literature review, 557
Systematic sampling, 578, 578*t*
Systematized Nomenclature of Medicine-
    Clinical Terminology (SNOMED CT),
    397–399, 398–*t*399*t*, 886–887
Systematized Nomenclature of Medicine-
    Reference Terminology (SNOMED
    RT), 398–399
System build, 148
System catalogs, 185. *See also* Database
    management system (DBMS) data
    dictionaries
System crashes, 132
Systems, continuous performance improve-
    ment and, 657, 817–818, 817*t*
Systems analysts, 110

Systems approach to change strategy, 878
Systems development, 81–111
  demand for healthcare information sys-
    tems in today's environment, 101–104
  HIM professional roles in health infor-
    mation technology services, 110–111
  life cycle, 105–108
  management of healthcare information
    system resources, 109–110
Systems development life cycle (SDLC),
    105–108
  analysis phase, 105
  design phase, 105–106
  implementation phase, 106–107, 108*t*
  maintenance and evaluation phase,
    107–108

T

Tables (for statistical data presentation),
    508–509, 509*t*
Tablet (computer), 747
Tacit knowledge, 171
Tactical Committee on Medical Care, 414
Tactical plans, 690
TANF (Temporary Assistance for Needy
    Families), 422
Tarasoff v. Board of Regents, 319
Target population, 562, 578, 587
Task analysis, 731
Tasks, steps *vs.,* 843*t*
Task structure, 703
Tax Equity and Fiscal Responsibility Act
    (TEFRA), 16, 431
Tax status of healthcare organizations, 768
Taylor, Frederick W., 685
TC (technical component), 430
TCO (total costs of ownership), 139
Team-based PI process, 660, 660*t*, 662*t*
Team building, 731, 740, 753
Technical component (TC), 430
Technical interoperability, 133
Technical skills, 693, 693*t*
Technical staff for IS, 109–110
Technical systems, 878
TEFRA (Tax Equity and Fiscal Responsibil-
    ity Act), 16, 431
Telecommuting, 728–730, 729*t*, 803
Teleconferencing, 746. *See also* Audiocon-
    ferencing; Videoconferencing
Telehealth, 44–45, 97–98, 136
Telemedicine, 97–98
Telepathology, 97–98
Telephone surveys, 563
Teleradiology, 97–98
Telestaffing, 261
Telesurgery, 98
Temporary Assistance for Needy Families
    (TANF), 422
Temporary budget variances, 787

10 characteristics of data quality, 175, 180, 181*t*–183*t*
Terminal-digit filing system, 270–271, 270*t*, 271*t*
Termination of employee, 756
Termination of pregnancy, 503*t*
Terminology(ies), healthcare, 389, 389*t*, 397–407
Testing
  healthcare informatics standards, 210–212
  during implementation of EHR system, 148
  of new ISs, 106–107, 148
  for staff selection, 725
Test statistics, 586
Text mining, 86
Theory, in research, 547, 548*t*
Theory X and Y, 687
Therapeutic orders, 247–248
Therapeutic services, 27–28
Third-party compliance organizations, 60
Third-party payers
  evolution of reimbursement, 38
  and home healthcare growth, 30
  and revenue cycle management, 465
Thoughtflow, 118
3M Health Information Systems, 392
360-degree evaluation, 755
Time and motion studies, 685
Time frame, 561–562
Time ladders, 808, 809*t*
Timeliness, 383
Title VII (Civil Rights Act of 1964), 721
Title XVIII, 39
Title XIX, 39, 422
Top-down process map, 830, 830*t*
Topography code, 393
Torts, 304–308
Total costs of ownership (TCO), 139
Total length of stay (discharge days), 489–491
Total quality management (TQM), 35–36, 650, 687, 818. *See also* Continuous quality improvement (CQI)
Toyota, 827
TQM. *See* Total quality management
Tracer methodology, 671
Trainee, 735
Training and development, 730–758
  adult learning strategies, 740–743
  departmental employee training and development plan, 748–755
  employment laws and, 721
  maintenance of employee records, 756–757
  model for identifying/fulfilling needs, 748–749
  orientation, 730–733
  performance management, 755–756

  tools for, 730–736
  tools for staff development, 736–740
  tools for staff training, 730–736
  training methods, 743–748, 743*t*
Training for new ISs, 106–107
  and EHRs, 290
  implementation of EHR system, 148–149
"Training the trainer," 735
Trait approach (leadership theory), 700
Transactions and Code Sets Rule, 310
Transaction standards, 206
Transcription, 258–262
  components of system, 258
  and EHRs, 287–288
  equipment planning/selection, 259
  evaluation of effectiveness/efficiency, 262
  of health record content, 258
  incentive programs, 262
  internal *vs.* outsourcing, 260–261
  management issues, 260–262
  productivity management, 261–262
  staffing, 261–262
  voice recognition technology, 262
Transfer of health records, 276
Translational research, 548
Transparency, 165*t*, 384–385
Transplant registries, 374–375
Trauma care. *See* Emergency and trauma care
Trauma registries, 372–373
Traumatic injury, 372
Treatments (in experiments), 560–561
Triangulation, 564
TRICARE, 39, 424
TRICARE Extra, 424
TRICARE Prime, 424
TRICARE Prime Remote, 424
TRICARE Senior Prime, 424
TRICARE Standard, 424
Trier of fact, 303
Truman, Harry, 13, 414
Turnover (employee), 727
Tuskegee syphilis study, 609–610
Two-factor authentication, 134
Two-tailed hypothesis, 571
Type I error, 527, 528, 572, 572*t*
Type II error, 572, 572*t*

U

UACDS. *See* Uniform Ambulatory Care Data Set
UB-04, 445, 452*t*
UCLA Health System case, 328
UCR (usual, customary, and reasonable) charges, 429
UHDDS. *See* Uniform Hospital Discharge Data Set

UMLS. *See* Unified Medical Language System
Unbundling, 453
Uncertainty management, 872–873, 873*t*
Undergraduate degrees in HIM, 62–63, 65
Unfavorable variances, 787
Unfreezing, 710
Unified Medical Language System (UMLS), 210, 381, 405–406
Unified Medical Language System (UMLS) Metathesaurus, 406
Unified Medical Language System (UMLS) Semantic Network, 406
Unified Medical Language System (UMLS) SPECIALIST Lexicon, 406
Uniform Ambulatory Care Data Set (UACDS), 197–198, 198*t*
Uniformed Services Employment and Re-employment Rights Act (1994), 721
Uniform Hospital Discharge Data Set (UHDDS), 196, 196*t*–197*t*, 378
Uniform Rules Relating to the Discovery of Electronically Stored Information, 142
Uninsured Americans, 8
Unions, 722
Unique identification numbers, 205
Unique identifier, 243–244, 269–270
United Kingdom National Health Services, 166, 166*t*
United Network of Organ Sharing (UNOS), 250–251
United States Health Information Knowledgebase (USHIK), 210–212
United States v. Gibson, 327
Unit numbering system, 270
Unit work division, 800
Unity of command, 686
Univariate statistical techniques, 585
Universal chart order, 263–264
Universities, as setting for HIM professionals, 59
UNOS (United Network of Organ Sharing), 250–251
Unstructured data, 85, 118
Unstructured (open-ended) questions, 576
Upcoding, 453
Upgrades, 150
UR. *See* Utilization review
Urgency, creating a sense of, 879
Usability, 133
Use, 313. *See also* Disclosure
Use case, 229–230, 231*t*–233*t*
Use case analysis, 831, 832*t*
USHIK (United States Health Information Knowledgebase), 210–212
US Standard Report of Induced Termination of Pregnancy, 503*t*
Usual, customary, and reasonable (UCR) charges, 429

Utilization controls, 430
Utilization management, 464
Utilization review (UR), 15, 16, 464
Utilization Review Act (1977), 16

V

VA (Veterans Administration), 39, 136
Vacations, 802, 802*t*
Vaccines, 19
Validity
  of data in secondary databases, 382–383
  in research plans, 574–575
  of testing, 725
Valo, Carolyn, 56
Value-Based Purchasing, 36
Values-based leadership, 705–706
Value statements, 690
Value Stream Mapping, 828
Variability, 517, 519–520
Variable costs, 781, 781*t*
Variables
  analyzing relationships between two, 536–538
  in correlational research, 559
Variance(s)
  in budgets, 786–788, 787*t*
  of frequency distribution, 520, 520*t*
  measure of spread, 532
  project implementation, 847, 847*t*
Variance analysis, 814–816, 847
Variation, continuous performance improvement and, 657–658, 677–678
VDL (vertical dyad linkage), 704–705
Vector graphic (signal tracing) data, 85
Vendor neutrality, 405
Vendor selection, 146–148
Versioning, 92
Vertical dyad linkage (VDL), 704–705
Vertical structure, 690
Veterans Administration (VA), 39, 136
Veterans Affairs, U.S. Department of, 399
Veterans Health Administration (VHA), 310
Veterans Integrated Service Networks (VISNs), 39
VHA (Veterans Health Administration), 310
Videoconferencing, 745–746
Video data, 85
Virtualization, 132
Virtual reality, 745
Virtuoso teams, 678
Vision, 869–871
Vision 2016: A blueprint for Quality Education in Health Information Management (white paper), 62, 72
Vision statements, 690, 870–871
VISNs (Veterans Integrated Service Networks), 39
Vital statistics, 380, 499

Vocabulary
  defined, 389
  EHR supporting infrastructure, 133
  for speech recognition software, 85
Vocabulary standards, 207–208
Voice recognition technology, 262, 288
Volume logs, 808–809, 809*t*
Voluntary agencies, 30
Voluntary Disclosure Program, 453
Voluntary hospitals, 25
Vroom, Victor, 701
Vroom-Yettom normative decision tree, 695, 696, 701, 702*t*
Vulnerable populations, 358, 358*t*–359*t*, 360
Vulnerable subjects, 616–618

W

Wagner National Health Act (1939), 414
Waiver of privilege, 326
WARN (Workers' Adjustment Retraining and Notification) Act, 756
Waste, 827, 827*t*
Waterman, R. H.., 688
WBS (work breakdown structure), 842
Web 2.0, 99
Web 3.0, 99
Web-based courses, 746–747
Web-based training, 735
Web content management systems, 92
Weber, Max, 685
Webmasters/web developers, 110
Web portals, 91, 135
Web services, 92, 93*t*
Web services architecture (WSA), 133, 140
Welfare reform, 15, 422
Western medicine, history of, 8–11
Whistleblower, 853
WHO (World Health Organization), 70, 390
Wikis, 747
Wireless technology, 96
Women, in labor force, 757
WONCA (World Organization of National Colleges, Academies, and Academic Associations of General Practitioners/ Family Physicians), 395
Work, 806, 843–844, 844*t*
Work breakdown structure (WBS), 842
Work design and process improvement, 795–833
  functional work environment, 796–800
  methods of organizing work, 800–806
  performance and work measurement standards, 806–813
  performance improvement, 816–818
  performance measurement, 811, 813–816
  process improvement methodologies, 818–832

Work distribution analysis, 800–801, 801*t*
Work distribution charts, 801, 801*t*, 820–821
Work environment, 796–800
Worker immaturity-maturity, 703, 703*t*
Workers. *See* Employee *entries;* Staff *entries*
Workers' Adjustment Retraining and Notification (WARN) Act, 756
Workers' compensation, 39, 425
Workflow, 141*t*, 796–797, 797*t*
Workflow analysis, 290, 829–832
Workflow and process management, 118
Workflow diagram, 830, 831*t*
Workflow re-evaluation, 293
Workflow technology, 87
Workflow training, 290
Workforce retention, 726
Working conditions, 722
Work measurement, 808–809
Work plan (OIG), 454
Work procedures, 804
Work products, 836
Work sampling, 809–813, 810–*t*813*t*
Work schedules, flexible, 723
Work scheduling, 801–804
Workshops, for employee training, 744–745
Workstation on wheels (WOW), 126
WorldCom, 766
World Health Organization (WHO), 70, 390
World Organization of National Colleges, Academies, and Academic Associations of General Practitioners/Family Physicians (WONCA), 395
WOW (workstation on wheels), 126
WSA (Web services architecture), 133, 140

X

XML. *See* Extensible Markup Language
X-rays, 19

Y

Yetton, Philip, 701

Z

Zero-based budgets, 785
Zhou, Huping, 328

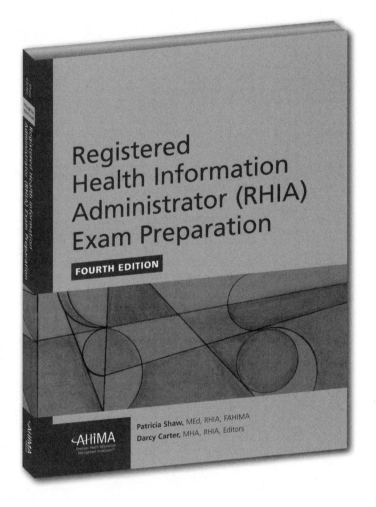